REFERENCE

THE

Oxford
American
Thesaurus
of
Current
English

REFERENCE

THE

Oxford American Thesaurus of Current English

Edited by

Christine A. Lindberg

New York   Oxford
Oxford University Press
1999

Oxford University Press

New York   Oxford

Athens   Auckland   Bangkok   Bogota   Bombay
Buenos Aires   Calcutta   Cape Town   Dar es Salaam
Delhi   Florence   Hong Kong   Istanbul   Karachi
Kuala Lumpur   Madras   Madrid   Melbourne
Mexico City   Nairobi   Paris   Singapore
Taipei   Tokyo   Toronto   Warsaw

and associated companies in
Berlin   Ibadan

Library of Congress Cataloging-in-Publication Data

The Oxford American thesaurus of current English / edited by Christine
A. Lindberg.
   p.   cm.
   "First British edition published in 1997 as The concise Oxford
thesaurus, based on the Oxford paperback thesaurus (1995), edited by
Betty Kirkpatrick"—T.p. verso.
   ISBN 0-19-513375-7 (acid-free paper)
   1. English language—Synonyms and antonyms.   I. Lindberg,
Christine A., 1954–   .   II. Oxford paperback thesaurus.
PE1591.089   1999
423'.1—dc21   99-31092
                                                                CIP

3   5   7   9   8   6   4   2
Printed in the United States of America
on acid-free paper

Contents

Project Staff

Editor:	Christine A. Lindberg
Project Editors:	Deborah Argosy, Laurie H. Ongley
Contributing Editor:	Sue Ellen Thompson
Editorial Assistant:	Karen Fisher
Proofreaders:	Adrienne Makowski, Ruth Handlin Manley, Julie Marsh
Data Entry:	Kimberly Roberts
Editor in Chief:	Frank R. Abate
Managing Editor:	Elizabeth J. Jewell

Guide to
The Oxford American Thesaurus of Current English

HEADWORDS

The text of *The Oxford American Thesaurus of Current English* is organized under headwords, which are printed in bold type. The headwords are listed in strict alphabetical order.

Many English words have two or more acceptable spellings; in this book, the one used is the one regarded as being the most common. Occasionally, two spellings share nearly equal usage; in such cases, the headwords include both forms. For example:

> **cagey, cagy** *adjective* guarded, secretive, non-committal, cautious, chary, wary, careful, shrewd, wily . . . .

PARTS OF SPEECH

A headword is always followed by its part of speech. When a word has two or more different parts of speech, it is listed more than once with separate entries for each. For example:

> **obscure** *adjective* **1** *obscure references* unclear, indeterminate, opaque . . . .

> **obscure** *verb* **1** *obscure the main issue* confuse, blur, muddle . . . .

Not all parts of speech of a word are necessarily included as headwords. For example, many words that function as adjectives can also function as adverbs. In such cases, the adverbial senses are included only when they have useful sets of synonyms.

HOMOGRAPHS

Certain words have the same spelling but different meanings and different etymologies (origins). Such words, known as homographs, are treated as separate headwords, even when they have the same part of speech. For the purposes of cross-referencing, homograph numbers are included in order to distinguish identical headwords with the same part of speech. For example:

> **bank**[1] *noun* **1** *a grassy bank* slope, rise, incline . . . .

> **bank**[2] *verb* *bank an aircraft* tilt, slope, slant . . . .

> **bank**[3] *noun* **1** *borrow from the bank* financial institution; commercial bank, ...

If two or more headwords are identical in spelling but have different parts of speech, homograph numbers are not used. This does not necessarily imply that these entries share the same etymology.

ENTRIES

Each entry contains a list of words that are synonyms of the headword: i.e., the words can be used in place of the headword in most (although not all) contexts. When a word has more than one meaning, the different senses of the word are numbered. In many instances, example phrases (in italic type) indicate the particular sense and illustrate the use of the word. In some cases, two or more examples are given; these are separated by a vertical bar (|). For example:

> **contribute** *verb* **1** *contribute money/time to the charity* | *happy to contribute* give, donate, hand out, ...

Note that a slash (/) is used to separate alternative words in order to save space. The slash applies only to the two words it separates; thus "contribute time/money" can be read as "contribute time" and "contribute money".

SUBENTRIES
Verb phrases are included as subentries (in bold type) under a main entry. For example:

> **chance** *verb* **1** *it chanced that they arrived last* happen, occur, take place, come about, ... **2** *have to chance it* risk, hazard, gamble, ... **chance on/upon** *chance upon an old friend* | *chanced on the answer* come across, meet, stumble on, come upon, encounter; *inf.* bump into, run into.

GROUPS WITHIN SENSES
In general, the synonyms in an entry are separated by commas. However, there are cases in which the words fall naturally into two or more distinct groups, which are separated by semicolons. There are various reasons for subdividing a sense in this way:

Grammatical Differences
Within a given sense, some synonyms may function differently from others. For example:

> **acclaim** *noun* . . . . praise, commendation, approval, approbation, homage, tribute, extolment, laudation; cheers, congratulations, plaudits, bouquets.

In the **acclaim** entry, the semicolon separates the singular nouns from the plural nouns. There are other grammatical reasons for subdividing synonym groups; for instance, a headword may function as both a transitive verb (taking a direct object) and an intransitive verb (without an object), whereas some of the synonyms may be only intransitive or only transitive.

Relationship of Meanings
Within a given sense, there sometimes are synonyms whose meanings share a relationship that sets them apart from the other synonyms in that sense. For example:

> **age** *verb* mature, ripen, grow up, come of age; grow old, decline, wither, fade, become obsolete.

> **bag** *noun* receptacle; handbag, pocketbook, purse, shoulder bag; case, suitcase, grip, flight bag, ...

In the entry for **age**, a semicolon is used to separate the "maturing" senses of *age* from the "growing old" senses. In the **bag** entry, semicolons separate the general synonym "receptacle" from the specific synonyms, which themselves are separated into categories of bags.

Restricted Usage
Some synonyms are separated into labeled groups of restricted usage. Such groups are always set off by semicolons. For example:

> **acquit** *verb* . . . . vindicate, liberate, free, deliver; *fml.* exculpate.

> **work** *noun* . . . . effort, exertion, labor, toil, sweat,

> drudgery, trouble, industry; *lit.* travail; *inf.*
> grind, elbow grease.

the usage labels used in this thesaurus are abbreviated as follows:

derog.	derogatory
fml.	formal
inf.	informal
lit.	literal
Med.	Medicine
TM	trademark

CROSS-REFERENCES

A cross-reference to a main entry is indicated by small capitals and is preceded by "*See*". Where necessary, the part of speech and sense number are also given. For example:

> **abasement** *noun* humiliation, belittlement, low-
> ering, ... *See* ABASE.

> **alternate** *adjective* **1** *alternate weeks* every other,
> every second. . . . . *See* ALTERNATIVE *adjective* 1.

A cross-reference to a subentry follows the same format but also includes the main entry (given in parentheses). For example:

> **discount** *verb* . . . . **4** *discount the products* mark
> down, reduce, put on sale.
> ***Antonyms:*** NOTE; INCREASE; mark up (*see* MARK).

ANTONYMS

Many entries contain a list of antonyms (opposites). For example:

> **dally** *verb* . . . .
> ***Antonyms:*** HURRY; HASTEN.

Note that antonyms in small capitals are cross-references.

THE
Oxford
American
Thesaurus
of
Current
English

A

abandon *verb* 1 *abandon one's family* desert, leave, forsake, depart from, leave behind, cast aside, jilt; *inf.* run out on. 2 *abandon ship* leave, depart from, go away from, vacate, withdraw from, quit. 3 *abandon hope* give up, renounce, relinquish, dispense with, forgo, desist from, forswear. 4 *abandon a country to the enemy* yield, surrender, give up, cede, relinquish, abdicate, deliver up, resign. 5 *abandon smoking* stop, give up, cease, drop, forgo, desist from, dispense with. **abandon to** *abandon oneself to despair* give way to, give up to, yield to, indulge in, lose to/in.
Antonyms: KEEP; RETAIN; CONTINUE.

abandon *noun behave with reckless abandon* recklessness, lack of restraint/inhibition, unrestraint, carelessness, wildness, impulse, impetuosity, immoderation, wantonness.

abandoned *adjective* 1 *an abandoned child* deserted, forsaken, cast aside. See ABANDON *verb* 1. 2 *an abandoned ship* vacated, evacuated, deserted, unoccupied, empty, unused. See ABANDON *verb* 2. 3 *abandoned behavior* reckless, unrestrained, uninhibited, impetuous, wild, careless, wanton. 4 *an abandoned young man* dissipated, debauched, profligate, dissolute, immoral, corrupt, depraved, reprobate, wild, unrestrained, reckless, wanton.

abase *verb abase oneself before the judge | abase one's servants* humiliate, humble, belittle, lower, degrade, disparage, debase, demean, discredit, mortify, bring low, demote, reduce.

abasement *noun* humiliation, belittlement, lowering, degradation, disparagement, debasement, mortification, demotion, reduction. See ABASE.

abashed *adjective* embarrassed, ashamed, shamefaced, mortified, humiliated; taken aback, disconcerted, nonplussed, discomfited, perturbed, confounded, dismayed, dumbfounded.

abate *verb* 1 *the storm/pain abated* die down, lessen, ease, subside, let up, decrease, diminish, moderate, decline, fade, slacken, wane, ebb, alleviate, attenuate. 2 *trying to abate the pain* ease, lessen, decrease, diminish, moderate, soothe, relieve, dull, blunt, alleviate, mitigate, allay, assuage, palliate, appease, attenuate. 3 *attempts to abate the noise levels* decrease, reduce, lessen, lower, diminish.
Antonyms: INCREASE; INTENSIFY.

abatement *noun* 1 *the abatement of the wind* lessening, moderation, decrease, decline, ebb, alleviation, attenuation. See ABATE 1. 2 *the abatement of the pain* easing, decrease, moderation, relief, mitigation, assuagement, palliation, appeasement, attenuation. See ABATE 2. 3 *the abatement of noise levels* decrease, reduction, lowering. See ABATE 3.

abbey *noun* religious house; monastery, priory, cloister, friary, convent, nunnery.

abbreviate *verb* shorten, reduce, cut, cut short/down, contract, condense, compress, abridge, truncate, clip, crop, shrink, constrict, summarize, abstract, synopsize.
Antonyms: LENGTHEN; EXPAND; ELONGATE.

abbreviation *noun* 1 *the abbreviation of his name* shortening, reduction, cutting, contraction, condensation, compression, abridgment. See ABBREVIATE. 2 *the postal abbreviation for Florida is FL* shortened form, contraction, abridgment.

abdicate *verb* 1 *the king abdicated due to illness* resign, stand down, retire, quit. 2 *abdicate the throne* give up, renounce, resign from, relinquish, abjure, cede; *Law* disclaim. 3 *abdicate all responsibility* give up, renounce, relinquish, abjure, repudiate, reject, disown, waive, yield, forgo, refuse, abandon, surrender, cast aside, drop, turn one's back on, wash one's hands of.

abdication *noun abdication of responsibility* renunciation, relinquishment, abjuration, repudiation, rejection, waiving, refusal, abandonment, surrender. See ABDICATE 3. **abdication from** *abdication from the throne* giving up of, renunciation of, resignation from, relinquishment of, abjuration of, ceding of.

abdomen *noun* stomach, belly, intestines; *inf.* tummy, insides, guts, pot, paunch, bread basket.

abdominal *adjective* gastric, intestinal, visceral, ventral.

abduct *verb* kidnap, carry off, run away/off with, make off with, seize, hold as hostage, hold for ransom; *inf.* snatch.

aberrant *adjective* deviant, deviating, divergent, anomalous, abnormal, irregular, atypical, freakish.

aberration *noun* 1 *a statistical aberration* deviation, divergence, anomaly, abnormality, irregularity, variation, freak. 2 *in a moment of aberration* abnormality, irregularity, eccentricity, deviation, straying, aberrancy. 3 *suffering from a mental aberration* disorder, disease, irregularity, instability, derangement, vagary.

abet *verb* assist, aid, help, support, back, second,

encourage, promote, cooperate with, connive at, endorse, sanction, succor.

abeyance *noun the decision was in abeyance* a state of suspension/dormancy/latency, suspension, suspense, remission; *inf.* cold storage.

abhor *verb* detest, loathe, hate, abominate, feel aversion to, shrink/recoil from, dislike. *Antonyms:* LOVE; ADMIRE; delight in (*see* DELIGHT).

abhorrent *adjective* detestable, loathsome, hated, abominable, repellent, repugnant, repulsive, revolting, disgusting, distasteful, horrible, horrid, heinous, obnoxious, odious, offensive; *inf.* yucky.

abide *verb* **1** *abide by the rules* keep to, comply with, observe, follow, obey, agree to, hold to, conform to, adhere to, stick to, stand by. **2** *I cannot abide them or their habits* stand, tolerate, bear, put up with, endure, stomach, suffer, accept, brook.

abiding *adjective* lasting, everlasting, eternal, unending, continuing, durable, constant, permanent, stable, enduring, persisting, unchanging, steadfast, immutable. *Antonyms:* SHORT-LIVED; EPHEMERAL; TRANSITORY.

ability *noun* **1** *a person of outstanding ability* talent, competence, competency, proficiency, skill, expertise, expertness, adeptness, aptitude, dexterity, adroitness, qualification, cleverness, flair, gift, knack, savoir faire; *inf.* knowhow. **2** *the ability to cope* capacity, capability, potential, potentiality, power, aptness, facility, faculty, propensity. *Antonyms:* INABILITY; INCAPACITY.

abject *adjective* **1** *abject poverty* wretched, miserable, hopeless, pathetic, pitiable, piteous, stark. **2** *an abject coward* base, low, vile, worthless, contemptible, debased, degraded, despicable, ignominious, mean. **3** *an abject apology* obsequious, groveling, servile, cringing, sniveling, ingratiating, sycophantic, submissive.

abjure *verb* **1** *abjure a claim* give up, renounce, relinquish, retract, abandon, deny, abdicate, disclaim, disavow, forswear, renege on. **2** *abjure worldly pleasures* give up, renounce, relinquish, abandon, forswear, forgo, forsake, abstain from, refrain from, reject, repudiate, eschew.

ablaze *adjective* **1** *the house was ablaze* on fire, burning, blazing, alight, flaming; *lit.* afire, aflame. **2** *the house was ablaze with lights* lit up, alight, gleaming, glowing, aglow, illuminated, brilliant, radiant, shimmering, sparkling, flashing, incandescent. **3** *ablaze with excitement/anger* passionate, aroused, excited, stimulated, animated, impassioned, ardent, fervent, frenzied.

able *adjective* *an able student* competent, capable, talented, skillful, skilled, clever, intelligent, accomplished, gifted, proficient, apt, fit, expert, adept, efficient, effective, qualified, adroit.

Antonyms: INCOMPETENT; INCAPABLE; INEPT.

able-bodied *adjective* healthy, in good health, fit, robust, strong, sound, sturdy, vigorous, hardy, hale and hearty, muscular, strapping, tough, powerful, mighty, rugged, burly, stalwart, staunch; in good shape, in tip-top condition. *Antonyms:* INFIRM; FRAIL; FEEBLE.

ablution *noun* *perform one's ablutions* washing, cleansing, bathing, showering, scrubbing, purification; wash, bath, shower; *fml.* lavage.

abnegation *noun* renunciation, self-denial, self-sacrifice, resignation, abstinence, temperance; relinquishment, abdication.

abnormal *adjective* unusual, strange, odd, peculiar, uncommon, curious, queer, weird, eccentric, extraordinary, unexpected, exceptional, irregular, unnatural, erratic, singular, atypical, nontypical, anomalous, deviant, deviating, divergent, aberrant; *inf.* oddball, off the wall, wacko. *Antonyms:* NORMAL; REGULAR; TYPICAL.

abnormality *noun* **1** *the abnormality of their behavior* unusualness, strangeness, oddness, eccentricity, unexpectedness, irregularity, singularity, atypicality, anomalousness, deviation, divergence, aberrance, aberration. **2** *X rays showing a physical abnormality* irregularity, malformation, deformity, anomaly, flaw, deviation, aberration.

abode *noun* *welcome to my humble abode* home, house, place of residence/habitation, dwelling place, domicile, dwelling, habitat; accommodations, habitation; quarters; *inf.* pad.

abolish *verb* do away with, put an end to, end, stop, terminate, eliminate, eradicate, exterminate, destroy, annihilate, stamp out, obliterate, wipe out, extinguish, quash, expunge, extirpate, annul, cancel, invalidate, nullify, void, rescind, repeal, revoke, vitiate, abrogate; *inf.* ax. *Antonyms:* KEEP; RETAIN; MAINTAIN.

abolition *noun* ending, termination, elimination, extermination, destruction, annihilation, obliteration, extirpation, annulment, cancellation, nullification, invalidation, rescindment, repeal, revocation, vitiation, abrogation.

abominable *adjective* hateful, loathsome, detestable, odious, obnoxious, base, despicable, contemptible, damnable, cursed, disgusting, revolting, repellent, repulsive, offensive, repugnant, abhorrent, reprehensible, foul, vile, wretched, horrible, nasty, disagreeable, unpleasant, execrable; *inf.* yucky, god-awful.

abominate *verb* detest, loathe, hate, abhor, dislike, feel aversion/revulsion to, shudder at, recoil from.

abomination *noun* **1** *regard with abomination* detestation, loathing, hatred, aversion, antipathy, repulsion, abhorrence, repugnance, disgust, distaste, dislike; *fml.* odium. **2** *the building is an abomination* atrocity, disgrace, horror, obscenity, curse, anathema.

aboriginal *adjective* indigenous, native, original,

earliest, first, ancient, primitive, primeval, primordial.

abort verb **1** *abort a pregnancy/fetus* terminate. **2** *the expectant mother aborted* miscarry, have a miscarriage. **3** *abort a space mission* call off, halt, stop, end, terminate, arrest, nullify; *inf.* ax. **4** *the space mission aborted* come to a halt, end, terminate, fail.

abortion noun **1** *she had an abortion* feticide. **2** *the mission was an abortion* failure, nonsuccess, fiasco, misadventure, disappointment, defeat.

abortive adjective *an abortive attempt/plan* failed, unsuccessful, nonsuccessful, vain, futile, useless, worthless, ineffective, ineffectual, fruitless, unproductive, unavailing.
Antonyms: SUCCESSFUL; PRODUCTIVE; FRUITFUL.

abound verb *weeds abound around here* be plentiful, proliferate, superabound, thrive, flourish.
abound with/in *a river abounding with/in fish* be full of, overflow with, teem with, be packed/crowded/thronged/jammed with, be alive with, swarm with; *inf.* be crawling/lousy with.

about preposition **1** *talk about it* with reference to, referring to, with regard to, regarding, concerning, with respect to, respecting, relating to, on, touching on, dealing with, with relevance to, connected with; *inf.* re. **2** *somewhere about here* near, nearby, close to, adjacent to, beside, around. **3** *about ten o'clock* approximately, roughly, nearly, in the neighborhood of. **4** *dancing about the maypole* around, round, encircling, surrounding. **5** *traveling about the world* around, round, throughout, over, all over, in all parts of, through. **6** *when you're about it* occupied with, concerned with, busy with. **about to** *they're about to die* going to, ready to, preparing to, soon to, intending to.

about adverb **1** *running and jumping about* around, here and there, to and fro, from place to place, hither and thither. **2** *it costs about $10* approximately, roughly, nearly, in the neighborhood/region of. **3** *she's somewhere about* around, near, nearby, about the place, in the vicinity, hereabouts. **4** *turn the ship about* in the reverse/opposite direction, into reverse, backward. **5** *a lot of flu about* around, in circulation, going on, in existence, current, prevailing, prevalent, happening, in the air. **6** *just about enough* nearly, almost, not quite, scarcely, barely.

above preposition **1** *above the horizon* over, higher than, on top of; atop. **2** *the rank above captain* over, higher than, superior to. **3** *a temperature above the average* over, higher than, greater than, more than, exceeding, in excess of, over and above, surpassing. **4** *above suspicion* beyond, not subject/liable/open to. **5** *prize honor above life* in preference to, more than, rather than, before, in favor of. **6** *above the bridge* upstream from, northward of, north from.

above adverb **1** *on the shelf above* overhead, on/at the top, on/at a higher place, high up; *fml.*

on high. **2** *as stated above* earlier, previously, before, formerly.

above adjective *the above reference* aforementioned, aforesaid, preceding, earlier, foregoing, previous, prior.

aboveboard adverb/adjective *the deal was made aboveboard | an aboveboard discussion* honest, fair, open, frank, straight, overt, candid, forthright, unconcealed, unequivocal.

abrasion noun **1** *skin abrasions* graze, scrape, scratch, sore, ulcer, chafe. **2** *the abrasion of the rock* erosion, wearing down/away, corrosion, chafing, rubbing, scraping, excoriation.

abrasive adjective **1** *an abrasive substance* erosive, eroding, corrosive, chafing, rubbing, coarse, harsh. **2** *an abrasive manner* caustic, cutting, grating, biting, rough, harsh, irritating, sharp, nasty.

abreast adverb *running abreast* side by side, alongside, level, beside each other, shoulder to shoulder. **abreast of** *keeping abreast of the news/changes* up-to-date with, up with, in touch with, familiar/acquainted with, informed/knowledgeable about, conversant with.

abridge verb shorten, cut down, condense, contract, compress, abbreviate, reduce, decrease, diminish, curtail, truncate, lessen, trim, summarize, abstract, epitomize, synopsize, digest.

abridgment noun **1** *prepare an abridgment of the report* summary, synopsis, précis, abstract, outline, résumé, shortening, digest. **2** *the abridgment of a novel* shortening, cutting, condensation, contraction, reduction, summarization. *See* ABRIDGE.

abroad adverb **1** *go abroad for the summer* overseas, out of the country, to/in foreign parts, to/in a foreign country/land, beyond the seas, across the ocean. **2** *spreading the rumor abroad* about, widely, far and wide, everywhere, publicly, extensively, at large, forth.

abrogation noun repeal, annulment, cancellation, countermanding, reversal, withdrawal, revocation, retraction, abolition, ending, quashing, scrapping, invalidation, nullification, voiding, repudiation.

abrupt adjective **1** *an abrupt ending* sudden, quick, hurried, hasty, swift, rapid, headlong, instantaneous, surprising, unexpected, unanticipated, unforeseen. **2** *an abrupt manner* curt, blunt, brusque, short, terse, brisk, crisp, gruff, snappish, unceremonious, rough, rude. **3** *an abrupt slope* steep, sheer, precipitous, sudden, sharp. **4** *an abrupt style of writing* jerky, uneven, irregular, disconnected, discontinuous, broken, rough, inelegant.
Antonyms: GRADUAL; UNHURRIED; SMOOTH.

abscess noun ulcer, ulceration, boil, pustule, carbuncle, pimple.

abscond verb *abscond with the stolen goods* run away, bolt, clear out, flee, make off, escape, take flight, fly, decamp, disappear, slip/steal/

sneak away, take to one's heels, make a quick getaway, beat a hasty retreat, run for it; *inf.* cut and run, skedaddle, skip, beat it.

absence *noun* **1** *the teacher noted their absence* nonattendance, nonappearance, truancy, absenteeism. **2** *in the absence of proof* lack, want, nonexistence, unavailability, deficiency, omission, default, need, privation.
Antonyms: PRESENCE; ATTENDANCE.

absent *adjective* **1** *absent overseas | absent from school* away, off, out, gone, missing, truant, lacking, unavailable, nonexistent, nonattendant. **2** *an absent expression* absentminded, distracted, preoccupied, daydreaming, dreaming, faraway, blank, empty, vacant, inattentive, vague, absorbed.

absentminded *adjective* *an absentminded professor* distracted, preoccupied, absorbed, abstracted, inattentive, forgetful, oblivious.

absolute *adjective* **1** *absolute trust* complete, total, utter, out and out, outright, perfect, entire, undivided, unqualified, unadulterated, unalloyed, downright, undiluted, solid, consummate, unmitigated. **2** *the absolute truth* certain, positive, definite, unquestionable, undoubted, unequivocal, decisive, unconditional, categorical, conclusive, confirmed, infallible. **3** *an absolute standard* fixed, independent, nonrelative, nonvariable, rigid, established, set, definite. **4** *absolute power* unlimited, unrestricted, unrestrained, unbounded, boundless, infinite, ultimate, total, supreme, unconditional, full, utter, sovereign, omnipotent. **5** *absolute monarch* despotic, dictatorial, autocratic, tyrannical, authoritarian, arbitrary, autonomous, sovereign.
Antonyms: QUALIFIED; CONDITIONAL; LIMITED.

absolutely *adverb* **1** *absolutely correct* completely, totally, utterly, perfectly, entirely, wholly, fully, thoroughly. **2** *absolutely the worst driver* certainly, positively, definitely, unquestionably, undoubtedly, without a doubt, unequivocally, unconditionally, conclusively, unreservedly. **3** *absolutely pouring down* positively, actually, in actual fact, really, in truth. **4** *ruling absolutely* despotically, dictatorially, autocratically, tyrannically, autonomously, arbitrarily, unrestrictedly, totally, supremely, unconditionally, utterly, omnipotently.

absolutely *interjection* *Are you going? Absolutely!* certainly, yes, indeed, of course, positively, naturally, without doubt, unquestionably.

absolution *noun* forgiveness, pardoning, exoneration, freedom, liberation, deliverance, remission, dispensation, condoning, vindication, exculpation; pardon, acquittal, reprieve, discharge, amnesty, release, delivery.

absolve *verb* **1** *absolve them from blame* acquit, exonerate, discharge, release, free, deliver, liberate, let off, clear, exempt, exculpate. **2** *absolve repentant sinners* forgive, pardon, excuse,

reprieve, give amnesty to, give dispensation/indulgence to, clear, set free, vindicate.
Antonyms: BLAME; CHARGE; CONDEMN.

absolve
acquit, exempt, exonerate, forgive, pardon, vindicate

To varying degrees, all of these words mean to free from guilt or blame, and some are most frequently heard in a legal or political context. **Absolve** is the most general term, meaning to set free or release—not only from guilt or blame, but from a duty or obligation (*absolved from her promise to serve on the committee*) or from the penalties for their violation. **Pardon** is usually associated with the actions of a government or military official (*President Gerald Ford pardoned Richard Nixon following his resignation in the wake of the Watergate scandal*) and specifically refers to a release from prosecution or punishment. It is usually a legal official who decides to **acquit**, or release someone from a specific and formal accusation of wrongdoing (*the court acquitted the accused due to lack of evidence*). **Exonerate** suggests relief (its origin suggests the lifting of a burden), often in a moral sense, from a definite charge so that not even the suspicion of wrongdoing remains (*completely exonerated from the accusation of cheating*). A person who is **vindicated** is also off the hook, usually due to the examination of evidence (*she vindicated herself by producing the missing documents*). **Exempt** has less to do with guilt and punishment and more to do with duty and obligation (*exempt from paying taxes*). To **forgive**, however, is the most magnanimous act of all: It implies not only giving up on the idea that an offense should be punished, but also relinquishing any feelings of resentment or vengefulness (*To err is human; to forgive divine*).

absorb *verb* **1** *absorb liquid* soak up, suck up, draw up/in, take up/in, blot up, mop, sponge up, sop up. **2** *absorb food* consume, devour, eat up, swallow, assimilate, digest, ingest. **3** *absorb smaller companies* take in, incorporate, assimilate, appropriate, co-opt; *derog.* swallow up. **4** *absorb them | absorb their attention* occupy, engage, preoccupy, captivate, engross, monopolize, rivet.

absorbed *adjective* **absorbed by/in** *absorbed in a book* occupied with, taken up with/by, engaged in, preoccupied with, engrossed in, immersed in, captivated by, riveted by.

absorbent *adjective* porous, spongy, spongelike, permeable, pervious, penetrable, assimilative, receptive, soaking, blotting.

absorbing *adjective* *an absorbing book* fascinating, gripping, interesting, captivating, engrossing, riveting, spellbinding, intriguing.
Antonyms: BORING; UNINTERESTING; DULL.

absorption *noun* **1** *absorption of liquid* soaking up, sucking up. *See* ABSORB 1. **2** *absorption of* *food* consumption, devouring, assimilation, ingestion. *See* ABSORB 2. **3** *absorption of small companies* incorporation, assimilation, appropriation, co-opting; *inf.* swallowing up.

abstain *verb* **1** *abstain from voting/pleasure* refrain, decline, forbear, desist, hold back, keep from, refuse, renounce, avoid, shun, eschew. **2** *most voted but I abstained* decline/refuse to vote. **3** *I used to drink, but I now abstain* teetotal, be teetotal, be/stay sober, refrain, take the pledge; *inf.* be on the wagon.

Antonyms: join in (*see* JOIN); VOTE; INDULGE.

abstemious *adjective* moderate, temperate, abstinent, self-denying, austere, sober, self-restrained, ascetic, puritanical, nonindulgent, self-abnegating.

abstention *noun* abstaining, refraining, forbearing, desistance, refusal, renunciation, self-control, self-denial.

abstinence *noun* **1** *practice total abstinence* teetotalism, temperance, sobriety. *See* ABSTAIN 3. **2** *abstinence from pleasure* refraining, forbearing, desistance, renunciation. *See* ABSTAIN 1.

---

abstinence
abnegation, abstemiousness, continence, forbearance, moderation, temperance

Abstinence implies voluntary self-denial and is usually associated with the non-indulgence of an appetite (*total abstinence from cigarettes and alcohol*). **Abstemiousness** is the quality or habit of being abstinent; an abstemious person would be one who is moderate when it comes to eating and drinking. **Continence, temperance,** and **moderation** all imply various forms of self-restraint or self-denial: *moderation* is the avoidance of extremes or excesses (*he drank in moderation*); *temperance* is habitual moderation, or even total abstinence, particularly with regard to alcohol (*the 19th century temperance movement*); and *continence* (in this regard) refers to self-restraint with regard to sexual activity. **Forbearance** is self-control, the patient endurance that characterizes deliberately holding back from action or response. **Abnegation** is the rejection or renunciation of something that is generally held in high esteem (*abnegation of the Christian Church*), although it can also mean to refuse or deny oneself a particular right, claim, or convenience (*abnegation of worldly goods*).

---

abstract *adjective* **1** *beauty is abstract* theoretical, conceptual, notional, intellectual, metaphysical, philosophical. **2** *abstract art* nonrepresentational, nonrealistic, unrealistic. **3** *abstract theories of cosmology* complex, abstruse, recondite, obscure, deep.

Antonyms: ACTUAL; CONCRETE.

abstract *noun* *an abstract of/from a scientific paper* summary, synopsis, précis, résumé, outline, abridgment, condensation, digest.

abstract *verb* **1** *abstract metal from ore* extract, remove, take out/away, separate, detach, draw away, isolate. **2** *abstract goods from the store* steal, rob, thieve, appropriate, make off with, filch, purloin; *inf.* pinch, lift. **3** *abstract a book* abridge, summarize, condense, compress, shorten, cut down, abbreviate, contract, synopsize.

abstracted *adjective* **1** *an abstracted expression* absentminded, distracted, preoccupied, faraway, inattentive, thoughtful, pensive, musing, absorbed, woolgathering, absent. **2** *an abstracted book* abridged, summarized, condensed, compressed, abbreviated. *See* ABSTRACT *verb* 3.

abstraction *noun* **1** *the abstraction of metal from ore* extraction, removal, separation, detachment, isolation. **2** *lost in abstraction* absentmindedness, distraction, preoccupation, daydreaming, inattentiveness, thoughtfulness, absorption. *See* ABSTRACTED 1. **3** *facts rather than an abstraction* concept, generality, generalization, idea, theory, hypothesis, supposition, notion, presumption.

abstruse *adjective* obscure, deep, profound, complex, hidden, esoteric, mysterious, incomprehensible, unfathomable, inscrutable, enigmatic, perplexing, puzzling, recondite, arcane, nebulous.

absurd *adjective* ridiculous, foolish, silly, idiotic, stupid, nonsensical, senseless, inane, crazy, ludicrous, funny, laughable, comical, preposterous, farcical, harebrained, asinine; *inf.* daft.

---

absurd
foolish, ludicrous, preposterous, ridiculous, unreasonable

We call something **absurd** when it is utterly inconsistent with what common sense or experience tells us (*she found herself in the absurd position of having to defend the intelligence of a cockroach*). **Ludicrous** applies to whatever is so incongruous that it provokes laughter or scorn (*a ludicrous suggestion that he might escape unnoticed if he dressed up as a woman*), and **ridiculous** implies that ridicule or mockery is the only appropriate response (*she tried to look younger, but succeeded only in making herself look ridiculous*). **Foolish** behavior shows a lack of intelligence or good judgment (*it was foolish to keep that much money under a mattress*), while **unreasonable** behavior implies that the person has intentionally acted contrary to good sense (*his response was totally unreasonable in view of the fact that he'd asked for their honest opinion*). **Preposterous** should be reserved for those acts or situations that are glaringly absurd or ludicrous. For example, it might be *unreasonable* to judge an entire nation on the basis of one tourist's experience and *foolish* to turn down an opportunity to visit that country on those grounds alone, but it would be *preposterous* to suggest that everyone who comes to the United States will be robbed at gunpoint.

absurdity *noun* **1** *the absurdity of the situation* ridiculousness, foolishness, silliness, idiocy, stupidity, inanity, folly, incongruity, irrationality, ludicrousness, funniness, comedy, humor, joke, farce. *See* ABSURD. **2** *talking absurdities* nonsense, foolishness, rubbish, gibberish, drivel, balderdash; *inf.* bunk.

abundance *noun* plenty, plentifulness, profusion, copiousness, amplitude, affluence, lavishness, bountifulness; *inf.* heaps, lots, stacks, loads, tons, oodles.
Antonyms: LACK; SCARCITY.

abundant *adjective* plentiful, large, great, huge, ample, well-supplied, well-provided, profuse, copious, lavish, bountiful, teeming, overflowing; *inf.* galore.

abuse *verb* **1** *abuse power/alcohol* misuse, misapply, misemploy, mishandle, exploit. **2** *abuse children* mistreat, maltreat, ill-use, ill-treat, manhandle, injure, hurt, harm, beat, damage, wrong, oppress, torture. **3** *abusing trespassers* insult, swear at, curse, scold, rebuke, upbraid, reprove, castigate, revile, vilify, slander.

abuse *noun* **1** *the abuse of power* | *alcohol abuse* misuse, misapplication, misemployment, mishandling, exploitation. **2** *child abuse* mistreatment, maltreatment, ill-use, ill-treatment, manhandling, injury, hurt, harm, beating, damage, oppression, torture. **3** *guilty of political abuse* corruption, wrongdoing, wrong, misconduct, misdeeds, offense, crime, fault, sin. **4** *torrents of abuse* swearing, cursing, scolding, rebuke, upbraiding, reproval, invective, castigation, revilement, vilification, vituperation, defamation, slander; insults, curses, expletives, swearwords.

abusive *adjective* *abusive remarks* | *becoming abusive* insulting, rude, blasphemous, offensive, vulgar, vituperative, reproachful, reproving, derisive, scornful, castigating, slanderous, defamatory, calumniating.

abut *verb* adjoin, border, verge on, join, touch, meet, impinge on.

abutting *adjective* adjacent, next to, neighboring, adjoining, contiguous, bordering, verging, joining, touching, meeting.

abysmal *adjective* *abysmal ignorance/poverty* extreme, utter, complete, thorough, profound, deep, endless, immeasurable, boundless, incalculable, unfathomable, bottomless.

abyss *noun* **1** *a yawning abyss* chasm, gorge, cavity, void, pit, bottomless pit, hole, gulf, depth, ravine, canyon, crevasse. **2** *the abyss of despair* chasm, void, bottomless pit, hell, hellhole; depths.

academic *adjective* **1** *academic considerations* educational, scholastic, instructional, pedagogical. **2** *of an academic turn of mind* scholarly, studious, literary, well-read, intellectual, erudite, learned, cultured, bookish, highbrow, pedantic, professorial, cerebral; *inf.* brainy. **3**

an academic rather than a practical solution theoretical, hypothetical, abstract, conjectural, notional, impractical, unrealistic, speculative, ivory-towerish.

academic *noun* scholar, lecturer, teacher, tutor, professor, fellow, pedant, pedagogue; *inf.* bookworm, egghead.

accede *verb* **accede to 1** *accede to the request* agree to, consent to, accept, assent to, acquiesce to, endorse, comply with, go along with, concur with, grant, yield to. **2** *accede to the throne* succeed to, assume, attain, come to, inherit.

accelerate *verb* **1** *the car accelerated* speed up, go faster, pick up speed; *inf.* open up. **2** *the process accelerated* speed up, go faster, hasten, hurry, quicken, advance rapidly. **3** *accelerate the process* speed up, hasten, quicken, expedite, step up, advance, forward, further, spur on, facilitate, precipitate, stimulate.
Antonyms: DECELERATE; slow down (*see* SLOW); DELAY.

acceleration *noun* **1** *the acceleration of the car* increased speed, speeding up; *inf.* opening up. **2** *the acceleration of the process* speeding up, hastening, quickening, expedition, stepping up, advancement, forwarding, facilitation, precipitation, stimulation.

accent *noun* **1** *a British accent* pronunciation, intonation, enunciation, articulation, inflection, tone, modulation, utterance. **2** *the accent on the first syllable* stress, emphasis, accentuation, force, beat, prominence; primary stress, secondary stress. **3** *the accent on comfort* emphasis, stress, prominence, importance, accentuation, priority, underlining, underscoring. **4** *an acute accent* | *an accent on the e* accent mark, mark, diacritic, diacritical (mark), sign; circumflex, acute accent, grave accent, cedilla, umlaut, tilde.

accent *verb* **1** *accent the first syllable* stress, put/lay the stress on, emphasize, put/lay the emphasis on, put the force on, accentuate. **2** *accent the advantages* accentuate, emphasize, highlight, underline, draw attention to. *See* ACCENTUATE 1.

accentuate *verb* **1** *the black dress accentuated her paleness* emphasize, stress, highlight, underline, draw attention to, give prominence to, heighten, point up, underscore, accent. **2** *accentuate the pulse of the music* stress, put the stress/emphasis on, emphasize, accent.

accept *verb* **1** *accept the award* receive, take, take receipt of, get, gain, obtain, acquire, come by. **2** *accept the decision* accede to, agree to, consent to, acquiesce in, concur with, endorse, comply with, go along with, defer to, put up with, recognize, acknowledge, cooperate with, adopt, admit. **3** *accept the responsibility/project* take on, undertake, assume, bear, tackle, be responsible for. **4** *accept their story* | *accept what they say* believe, trust, credit, be convinced of, have faith in, count/rely on. **5** *never accepted as one of the family* welcome, receive, receive

favorably, embrace, offer friendship to, integrate. **6** *accept the invitation* say yes to, reply in the affirmative, comply with.
Antonyms: REFUSE; REJECT; DENY.

acceptable *adjective* **1** *an acceptable present* welcome, agreeable, delightful, pleasing, desirable, satisfying, gratifying. **2** *a standard of work not acceptable* satisfactory, good enough, adequate, passable, admissible, tolerable. **3** *an acceptable risk* allowable, tolerable, admissible, bearable, supportable.
Antonyms: UNACCEPTABLE; unsatisfactory; UNDESIRABLE.

acceptance *noun* **1** *the acceptance of an award* receipt, receiving, taking, obtaining, acquiring. *See* ACCEPT 1. **2** *the acceptance of a decision* accedence, accession, acquiescence, endorsement, recognition, acknowledgment, adoption, admission. *See* ACCEPT 2. **3** *the acceptance of responsibility* undertaking, assumption, tackling, adoption. *See* ACCEPT 3. **4** *acceptance as one of the family* welcome, welcoming, favorable reception, embracing, integration, approval, adoption. **5** *acceptances to an invitation* yes, affirmative reply, affirmation, confirmation, ratification. **acceptance of** *the acceptance of their story | acceptance of what they said* belief in, trust in, faith in, reliance on. *See* ACCEPT 4.

accepted *adjective* **1** *an accepted opinion* approved, recognized, sanctioned, authorized, received, allowable, acceptable. **2** *the accepted manner of behaving* usual, customary, normal, expected, standard, conventional, recognized, acknowledged, established, traditional, confirmed.

access *noun* **1** *a building with a rear access | access to the building* entry, entrance, way in, means of entry/entrance; admittance, admission; approachability, accessibility; approach, means of approach; gateway, driveway, road, path, avenue, passage. **2** *access to the prison/prisoner | access to secret information* admission, admittance, entrée, right of entry, permission/opportunity to enter/reach/use; accessibility, attainability.

access *verb* *access the data/information* gain access to, retrieve, gain, acquire.

accessibility *noun* **1** *the accessibility of sources of entertainment* attainability, reachability, availability, approachability, achievability. **2** *accessibility of the manager to the staff* approachability, availability, informality, friendliness, agreeableness, congeniality, affability, cordiality. **3** *accessibility of information* comprehensibility, intelligibility, penetrability. *See* ACCESSIBLE 3.

accessible *noun* **1** *an accessible source of entertainment* attainable, reachable, available, approachable, obtainable, achievable. **2** *accessible to the staff* approachable (by), available, easygoing, informal, friendly, pleasant, agreeable, obliging, congenial, affable, cordial. **3**

accessible information understandable, comprehensible, intelligible, penetrable, fathomable.
Antonyms: INACCESSIBLE; UNAPPROACHABLE.

accession *noun* *museum collection enhanced by recent accessions* addition, increase, augmentation, increment, gain, enlargement, expansion, extension. **accession to 1** *accession to the throne/title* succession to, inheritance of, attainment of. **2** *accession to the request/treaty* agreement to, consent to, acceptance of, acquiescence to.

accessory *noun* **1** *his accessories in the raid* accomplice, associate, confederate, abettor, helper, assistant, partner. **2** *bicycle accessories* attachment, extra, addition, adjunct, appendage, supplement. **3** *accessories matching her outfit* adornment, trimming, ornament, ornamentation, embellishment, trappings; handbag, shoes, gloves, hat, belt, ribbon; jewelry.

accessory *adjective* *an accessory part/factor* additional, extra, supplementary, contributory, subsidiary, ancillary, auxiliary, secondary, assisting.

accident *noun* **1** *an accident at work | an industrial accident* mishap, casualty, misfortune, misadventure, injury, disaster, tragedy, blow, catastrophe, calamity. **2** *the police were called to an accident* crash, collision; *inf.* pile-up. **3** *met by accident* chance, mere chance, fate, twist of fate, fortune, good fortune, luck, good luck, fortuity, hazard; *inf.* fluke.

accidental *adjective* **1** *accidental death | an accidental meeting* chance, occurring by chance/accident, unintentional, unintended, inadvertent, unexpected, unforeseen, unlooked-for, fortuitous, unanticipated, unplanned, uncalculated, unpremeditated, unwitting, adventitious. **2** *an accidental consideration* nonessential, inessential, incidental, extraneous, extrinsic, supplementary, subsidiary, subordinate, secondary, accessory, irrelevant.
Antonyms: INTENTIONAL; CALCULATED.

---

accidental
adventitious, casual, contingent, fortuitous, incidental

Things don't always go as planned, but there are many ways to describe the role that chance plays. **Accidental** applies to events that occur entirely by chance (*an accidental encounter with the candidate outside the men's room*); but it is so strongly influenced by the noun accident that it carries connotations of undesirable or possibly disastrous results (*an accidental miscalculation of the distance he had to jump*). A **casual** act or event is one that is random or unpremeditated (*a casual conversation with her son's teacher in the grocery store*), in which the role that chance plays is not always clear. Something that is **incidental** may or may not involve chance; it typically refers to what is secondary or non-essential (*incidental expenses in the budget*) or what occurs without design or regularity (*incidental lighting throughout the garden*). **Adventitious** also implies the lack of an essential relationship, referring to something that is a mere random occurrence (*adventitious circumstances that led to victory*). In contrast, **contingent** points to something that is entirely dependent on an uncertain event for its existence or occurrence (*travel plans that are contingent upon the weather*). **Fortuitous** refers to chance events of a fortunate nature; it is about as far as one can get from *accidental* (*a fortuitous meeting with the candidate outside the men's room just before the press conference*).

accidentally adverb *killed/met accidentally* by accident, by chance, unintentionally, inadvertently, without design, unexpectedly, adventitiously, unwittingly; *inf.* by a fluke. *See* ACCIDENTAL 1.

acclaim verb **1** *acclaim his victory* applaud, cheer, celebrate, salute, welcome, approve, honor, praise, commend, hail, extol, laud, eulogize, exalt. **2** *acclaim her queen* declare, announce, proclaim, hail.

acclaim noun *returning to the acclaim of the crowd* applause, ovation, praise, commendation, approval, approbation, homage, tribute, extolment, laudation; cheers, congratulations, plaudits, bouquets.

acclamation noun **1** *acknowledge the acclamations of the crowd* applause, ovation, praise, salutation, welcome, homage, tribute, approval; cheers, congratulations, plaudits. *See* ACCLAIM noun. **2** *the acclamation of her as queen* declaration, announcement, proclamation, hailing. **3** *elected by acclamation* shouting, calling out, oral vote, nonballot; shouts.

acclimatization noun *acclimatization to the heat | acclimatization to new conditions* adjustment, adaptation, habituation, accommodation, familiarization, inurement, naturalization, acclimation, acculturation.

acclimatize verb *acclimatize to tropical conditions* acclimate, adjust, adapt, accustom, get used, accommodate, accustom/habituate oneself, become seasoned, familiarize oneself, become inured, become naturalized.

accommodate verb **1** *we can accommodate four people* put up, house, cater for, board, lodge, provide shelter for, shelter, harbor, billet. **2** *accommodate oneself to new circumstances | accommodate our plans to suit yours* adapt, adjust, modify, reconcile, fit, harmonize, conform. **3** *accommodate you with a loan* provide, supply, furnish, serve, grant. **4** *accommodate them whenever possible* help, assist, aid, lend a hand to, oblige, meet the needs/wants of, do a favor for, indulge.

accommodating adjective *an accommodating person/attitude* obliging, cooperative, helpful, adaptable, pliable, compliant, complaisant, considerate, unselfish, willing, polite, kindly, hospitable, kind, friendly, agreeable.

accommodation noun **1** *the accommodation to new circumstances | accommodation of our plans to suit yours* adaptation, adjustment, modification, reconciliation, fitting, harmonization. **2** *the accommodation of the firm with a loan* provision, supply, supplying, furnishing, serving. **3** *recipients of our accommodation* help, assistance, aid, obliging, indulgence.

accommodations plural noun *provide accommodations for four | do you have accommodations?* housing, lodging, board, shelter; place of residence, house, billet; rooms, quarters; *inf.* digs.

accompaniment noun **1** *the accompaniment of speech with/by gestures* coexistence, coincidence, concurrence, supplement. **2** *a musical accompaniment* backup, support, background, obbligato. **3** *salad as an accompaniment* supplement, addition, adjunct, appendage, complement.

accompany verb **1** *accompany her to the dance* escort, go with, go along with, keep company, squire, usher, conduct, convoy, chaperon. **2** *vegetables accompanying the meat | gestures accompany his speech* go with, go along with, go together with, coexist/occur/coincide with, supplement. **3** *accompany them on the piano* play a musical accompaniment with, play with/for, back up, support.

accomplice noun confederate, accessory, collaborator, abettor, associate, partner, ally, assistant, helper, aider, henchman, right hand, right-hand man, fellow conspirator, partner in crime, friend; *inf.* sidekick.

accomplish verb **1** *accomplish an aim* achieve, carry out, fulfill, perform, attain, realize, succeed in, bring off, bring about, effect, execute, effectuate. **2** *accomplish a task* finish, complete, carry through, do, perform, conclude, effect, execute, consummate.
Antonyms: FAIL; give up (*see* GIVE).

accomplished adjective **1** *an accomplished player* skilled, skillful, expert, gifted, talented, proficient, adept, masterly, polished, practiced, capable, able, competent, experienced, professional, deft, consummate. **2** *an accomplished aim* achieved, fulfilled, realized. *See* ACCOMPLISH 1. **3** *an accomplished task* finished, completed, executed. *See* ACCOMPLISH 2.

accomplishment noun **1** *a woman of accomplishment | proud of her social accomplishments* talent, ability, skill, gift, attainment, achievement, capability, proficiency. **2** *the army's proud accomplishments* achievement, act, deed, exploit, performance, attainment, feat, coup, triumph. **3** *the accomplishment of aims* achievement, fulfillment, attainment, realization, success, effecting, execution. *See* ACCOMPLISH 1. **4** *the accomplishment of tasks* finishing, comple-

accord verb 1 *his statement does not accord with hers* agree, concur, fit, correspond, match, conform, harmonize, be in tune. 2 *accord them permission | accord a welcome* give, grant, confer, bestow, tender, offer, present, award, vouchsafe, concede.
Antonyms: DISAGREE; CONTRAST; WITHHOLD.

accord noun *accord between former enemies | in accord with our plans* agreement, harmony, rapport, unison, concord, amity, sympathy, unanimity, accordance. **of one's own accord** *leaving of their own accord* of one's own free will, of one's own volition, voluntarily, willingly, freely, unforced. **with one accord** unanimously, in complete agreement, with one mind, of one voice, unitedly, concertedly.

accordance noun 1 *the accordance of permission | the accordance of a welcome* granting, conferring, bestowal, tendering. *See* ACCORD verb 2. 2 *accordance between opponents* accord, agreement, harmony, concord, rapport. *See* ACCORD noun. 3 *acting in accordance with their wishes* agreement, conformity, compliance.

according adverb **according to** 1 *according to the manager* as stated/maintained by, as claimed by, on the authority of, on the report of. 2 *acting according to their principles* in accordance with, in agreement with, in line with, in keeping with, in compliance with, in harmony with, in conformity with, in obedience to, following, after. 3 *salary according to experience* in proportion to, commensurate with, in relation to.

accordingly adverb 1 *you know the truth and must act accordingly* appropriately, correspondingly, suitably, properly, fitly, consistently. 2 *they could not pay the rent and accordingly left* as a result, consequently, therefore, so, thus, as a consequence, in consequence, hence, ergo.

accost verb 1 *the reporter accosted him in the hallway* address, speak to, confront, approach; greet, hail, salute. 2 *accosted by a prostitute* solicit, importune.

account noun 1 *a full account of the accident* statement, report, description, record, narration, narrative, story, recital, explanation, tale, chronicle, history, relation, version. 2 *pay their accounts on time* bill, invoice; charges, debts. 3 *accounts with several banks* bank account; deposit account, savings account. 4 *the firm's accounts are in good order* ledger, balance sheet, financial statement; books. 5 *a person/matter of no account* importance, consequence, significance. **on account of** because of, owing to, on (the) grounds of. **on no account** not under any circumstances, under no circumstances, certainly not, absolutely not, not in any event.

account verb *they are accounted guilty | account her to be guilty* consider, regard, reckon, believe, think, look upon, view as, judge, count, deem. **account for** 1 *they must account for the delay* explain, explain away, give reasons for, show

grounds for, justify, elucidate. 2 *oil accounts for most of their exports* be responsible for, make up, supply, provide, give.

accountability noun 1 *the accountability of the police for their actions* responsibility, answerability, liability. 2 *their accountability to the manager* responsibility, answerability. 3 *the accountability of his actions* explicability, comprehensibility, intelligibility.

accountable adjective 1 *accountable for one's actions* responsible, answerable, liable, chargeable. 2 *accountable to the manager* responsible, answerable. 3 *his actions are not accountable* explicable, explainable, understandable, comprehensible, intelligible.

accouterments plural noun equipment, gear, tackle, paraphernalia, apparatus, adornment, ornamentation; trappings, appurtenances, furnishings, appointments, fittings; *inf.* things, bits and pieces.

accredit verb 1 *accredited with the invention* credit with, have ascribed/attributed to, receive the credit for. 2 *accredited to Shakespeare* ascribe, attribute.

accredited adjective 1 *our accredited representative* official, authorized, legal, appointed, approved, recognized, certified, sanctioned. 2 *accredited theories* accepted, recognized, believed, endorsed, orthodox. 3 *an accredited day-care center* certified, attested, licensed.

accrue verb 1 *bank interest accrued* accumulate, build/mount up, amass, collect, gather, grow, increase, augment. 2 *medical advances accrued from the new technology* arise, follow, ensue, result/emanate from.

accumulate verb 1 *dust accumulated over the weeks* gather, pile/build up, collect, amass, increase, augment, accrue. 2 *accumulate money/books* amass, gather, collect, stockpile, pile/heap up, store, hoard.

accumulation noun 1 *an accumulation of rubbish/money* stockpile, pile, heap, mass, collection, buildup, gathering, stock, store, hoard, stack, cumulation, accrual, aggregation. 2 *the accumulation of piles of dust | the accumulation of his collection of coins* gathering, collection, amassing, building up, stockpiling, accrual.

accuracy noun 1 *the accuracy of the statistics* correctness, precision, exactness, rightness, validity. 2 *the accuracy of the description | say with any accuracy* correctness, exactness, closeness, faithfulness, truth, truthfulness, authenticity, factuality, veracity. 3 *the accuracy of the aim* precision, carefulness, meticulousness.

accurate adjective 1 *accurate statistics* correct, precise, exact, right, errorless, without error, valid. 2 *an accurate description* correct, exact, close, faithful, true, truthful, authentic, factual, literal, veracious, strict. 3 *take accurate aim* precise, careful, meticulous, painstaking.
Antonyms: INACCURATE; INEXACT.

accursed adjective **1** *that accursed noise | those accursed loan sharks* hateful, detestable, despicable, horrible, foul, abominable, odious, obnoxious. **2** *the witch and her accursed victims under a curse,* cursed, curse-laden, bewitched, bedeviled, damned, doomed, ill-fated, wretched.

accusation noun *deny the accusation* charge, allegation, attribution, incrimination, imputation, denouncement, indictment, arraignment, impeachment, citation, inculpation, blame.

accuse verb **accuse of 1** *accused of murder* charge with, indict for, arraign for, impeach for, summon with/for, cite for, inculpate for. **2** *accuse her of tearing the curtain* blame for, lay the blame on (someone) for, hold responsible/accountable/answerable for, impute blame to (someone) for.
Antonyms: ABSOLVE; EXONERATE; DEFEND.

accustom verb **accustom to** *accustom herself to the new situation* adapt to, adjust to, acclimatize to, get used to, make familiar/acquainted with, habituate to.

accustomed adjective *his accustomed style* usual, normal, customary, habitual, regular, routine, ordinary, fixed, set, typical, established, common, general. **accustomed to** *accustomed to public speaking | accustomed to the situation* used to, familiar/acquainted with, adapted to, adjusted to, habituated to, inured to.

ace noun *a tennis ace* expert, champion, master, star, winner, genius, virtuoso, adept; *inf.* whiz, pro.

ace adjective *an ace player* expert, champion, brilliant, great, superb, outstanding, excellent, first-rate, fine, skillful, adept; *inf.* crack, A-1, tip-top, hotshot.

acerbic adjective **1** *an acerbic wit/tone* harsh, sarcastic, sharp, biting, stinging, caustic, trenchant, bitter, astringent, vitriolic, virulent, mordant. **2** *an acerbic taste* sour, tart, bitter, acid, sharp, acrid, acidulous, pungent.

ache noun **1** *an ache in my back* pain, dull pain, soreness; pang, throb, twinge, smarting, gnawing, stabbing, spasm; suffering. **2** *an ache in my heart* suffering, sorrow, misery, distress, grief, anguish, affliction, woe, mourning. **3** *feel an ache for old times* longing, yearning, craving, desire, hunger, hungering, pining, hankering.

ache verb **1** *my head aches* hurt, be sore, be painful, be in pain, pain; throb, pound, twinge, smart. **2** *my heart aches* grieve, be sorrowful, be distressed, be in distress, be miserable, mourn, agonize, suffer. **ache for** *she aches for sunshine* long for, yearn for, crave, desire, hunger for, pine for.

achieve verb **1** *achieve success* attain, reach, arrive at, gain, earn, realize, win, acquire, obtain, procure, get, wrest. **2** *achieve all the tasks begun* complete, finish, accomplish, carry through,

fulfill, execute, conclude, perform, effect, consummate.

achievement noun **1** *the achievement of success/objectives* attainment, gaining, realization, acquiral, procurement. *See* ACHIEVE 1. **2** *the achievement of tasks begun* completion, finishing, accomplishment, fulfillment, execution, conclusion, consummation. **3** *proud of their child's achievement* accomplishment, feat, performance, act, action, deed, effort, exploit.

acid adjective **1** *an acid taste/fruit* sour, tart, bitter, sharp, biting, acrid, pungent, acerbic, vinegary, vinegarish, acetic, acetous, acidulous. **2** *an acid wit/reply* acerbic, sarcastic, sharp, caustic, trenchant, vitriolic, mordant. *See* ACERBIC 1.

acknowledge verb **1** *acknowledge the need for reform* admit, grant, allow, recognize, accept, subscribe to, approve, agree to, acquiesce in, concede. **2** *acknowledge him with a wave* greet, salute, address, hail, recognize, notice. **3** *acknowledge a letter* answer, reply to, respond to, react to. **4** *acknowledge help* show appreciation for/of, express gratitude for, give thanks for, thank.

acknowledged adjective *the acknowledged leader* admitted, recognized, accepted, approved, accredited, declared, avowed.

acknowledgment noun **1** *the acknowledgment of the need for reform* admission, granting, recognition, acceptance, approval, agreement, acquiescence. **2** *the acknowledgment of his presence with a wave* greeting, saluting, recognition, notice. **3** *the acknowledgment of a letter | gave an acknowledgment* answering, answer, reply, response, reaction. **4** *the/an acknowledgment of help* expression of appreciation/gratitude, thanks.

acme noun peak, pinnacle, zenith, climax, culmination, height, high point, crown, summit, optimum, apex.
Antonyms: NADIR; BOTTOM.

acolyte noun assistant, helper, attendant, follower.

acquaint verb *acquaint oneself/you with the facts* familiarize, make familiar/conversant, make known to, make aware of, advise of, inform, apprise of, enlighten, let know.

acquaintance noun **1** *an acquaintance, not a close friend* associate, colleague, contact. **2** *our acquaintance with them* association, relationship, contact, social contact, fellowship, companionship. **3** *have some acquaintance with his poetry* familiarity, knowledge, awareness, understanding, cognizance.

acquainted adjective **acquainted with 1** *acquainted with his poems* familiar with, conversant with, well versed in, knowledgeable in, cognizant of/in, apprised of, instructed in. **2** *acquainted with the mayor* known to, on friendly terms with, friendly with, on a sociable footing with.

acquiesce verb consent, agree, accept, concur, approve, assent, allow, comply, conform, concede, go along with, bow to, yield.

acquiescence noun consent, agreement, acceptance, concurrence, approval, assent, compliance, conforming, conceding, concession, yielding.

acquiescent adjective **1** their response was acquiescent rather than disapproving consenting, concurrent, compliant, concessionary. See ACQUIESCE. **2** an acquiescent personality/attitude submissive, servile, subservient, obsequious, ingratiating, self-effacing; inf. bootlicking.

acquire verb obtain, come by, get, receive, gain, procure, earn, win, secure, take possession of, gather, collect, pick up, achieve, attain, appropriate, amass.

acquirement noun **1** acquirements are as important as natural talent attainment, achievement, accomplishment, skill, qualification. **2** the acquirement of money acquisition, obtaining, procurement, collecting, collection, achievement, attainment, appropriation. See ACQUIRE.

acquisition noun **1** the library's/museum's recent acquisitions gain, purchase, buy, possession, accession, addition; accretion, property. **2** the acquisition of money obtaining, procurement, collecting, collection, attainment, appropriation.

acquisitive adjective greedy, grasping, covetous, avaricious, predatory, avid, rapacious, mercenary.

acquisitiveness noun greed, covetousness, avarice, avidity, rapaciousness, rapacity.

acquit verb acquit the murder suspect clear (of charges), absolve, exonerate, discharge, release, vindicate, liberate, free, deliver; fml. exculpate. **acquit oneself** they acquitted themselves well/badly perform, act, behave, conduct oneself, comport oneself, bear oneself.
Antonyms: CONVICT; find guilty; BLAME.

acquittal noun the acquittal of the accused clearing, absolution, exoneration, discharge, release, vindication, liberation, deliverance; fml. exculpation.

acrid adjective **1** an acrid taste/smell pungent, sharp, sour, bitter, tart, harsh, acid, stinging, burning, irritating, vinegary, acerbic, acetic. **2** an acrid wit/remark acerbic, sarcastic, sharp, stinging, caustic, astringent, trenchant, vitriolic, virulent.

acrimonious adjective an acrimonious attitude/remark bitter, caustic, cutting, sarcastic, harsh, sharp, acid, acerbic, virulent, trenchant, stringent, spiteful, crabbed, vitriolic, venomous, irascible.

acrimony noun bitterness, sarcasm, harshness, sharpness, acidity, acerbity, virulence, trenchancy, stringency, spitefulness, crabbedness, irascibility.

acrobatics plural noun **1** acrobatics in the circus ring gymnastics, gymnastic feats/skills. **2** mental acrobatics agility, skill, quick thinking.

act noun **1** a daring/shameful act | acts of bravery/cowardice deed, action, feat, performance, undertaking, operation, execution, exploit, enterprise, achievement, accomplishment. **2** acts of Congress bill, law, decree, statute, edict, dictum, enactment, resolution, ruling, judgment, ordinance, measure. **3** an act of a play division, part, section, segment. **4** a music hall act performance, turn, routine, show, sketch, skit. **5** putting on an act | it's just an act pretense, sham, fake, make-believe, show, feigning, affectation, counterfeit, front, posture, pose.

act verb **1** you must act now | act wisely take action, do, move, be active, perform, function, react, behave, be employed, be busy. **2** the painkiller will act soon work, take effect, operate, function, be efficacious. **3** she's acting in a Shakespeare play perform, play, play a part, be an actor/actress, turn, be one of the cast; inf. tread the boards. **4** he's acting the part of Lear perform, play, portray, enact, represent, characterize, personify, stage. **5** he's not ill but just acting pretend, fake, feign, pose. **act for** act for his sick father represent, stand/fill in for, cover/substitute for, replace, take the place of, act in place of. **act on/upon 1** alcohol acts on the brain affect, have an effect on, influence, alter, change, modify, transform. **2** act on official instructions act in accordance with, follow, obey, comply with, take heed/notice of, heed, conform to. **act up** my car/child is acting up misbehave, give/cause trouble, malfunction.

acting noun **1** she wants to go in for acting the theater, drama, the performing arts, dramatics, stagecraft, theatricals, performing, portraying. **2** acting now will save trouble taking action, moving, functioning, reacting. See ACT verb 1. **3** the quick acting of the pills action, working, taking effect. See ACT verb 2. **4** the acting of the part of Lear performance, playing, portrayal, enacting. See ACT verb 4. **5** his acting is sometimes taken as real illness pretending, pretense, faking, feigning, play-acting, posturing.

acting adjective an acting head of the department deputy, substitute, temporary, interim, provisional, pro tem, pro tempore; inf. fill-in.

action noun **1** their prompt action saved lives act, deed, move, effort, operation, performance, undertaking, maneuver, endeavor, exertion, exploit. **2** time for action | put ideas into action acting, activity, doing, movement, motion, operating, operation, work, working, functioning, performance, effort, exertion. **3** men of action activity, energy, vitality, vigor, forcefulness, spirit, liveliness, vim; inf. get-up-and-go. **4** the action of acid on metal effect, influence, power, result, consequence. **5** the action of the play is set in Spain activity; events, happenings, incidents, episodes. **6** a piece of the action | miss the action activity, excitement, bustle; happenings, incidents; inf. goings-on. **7** soldiers seeing action overseas conflict, combat, warfare, fighting, battle. **8** the military action at Gettysburg battle, fighting, engagement, clash, encounter, skirmish, affray. **9** raise an *action* lawsuit, case, prosecution, litigation; legal proceedings.

actions *plural noun a man is judged by his actions, not his beliefs* behavior, conduct, activity, comportment, deportment; ways.

activate *verb* **1** *activate the alarm system* switch on, turn on, start, set going, trigger (off), set in motion, energize. **2** *activated by envy* actuate, motivate, stimulate, move, drive, rouse, prompt. *See* ACTUATE.

active *adjective* **1** *an active member of the team | an active volcano* working, functioning, operating, operative, in action, in operation, in force, effective. **2** *active people | old people leading active lives* mobile, energetic, vigorous, vital, sprightly, lively, spry, busy, bustling, occupied, involved; *inf.* on the go/move. **3** *the active ingredients* effective, effectual, operational, powerful, potent, nonpassive, noninert.
Antonyms: INACTIVE; DORMANT; INERT.

activity *noun* **1** *markets are places of great activity* business, bustle, hustle and bustle, liveliness, movement, life, stir, animation, commotion, flurry, tumult; *inf.* comings and goings. **2** *schoolwork and outside activities* interest, hobby, pastime, pursuit, occupation, venture, undertaking, enterprise, project, scheme. **3** *return to activity after being ill* functioning, mobility, effectiveness, vigor, strength, potency.

actor, actress *noun* performer, player, dramatic artist, thespian; stage performer/player, play actor, film actor, film star, starlet, leading man/woman, trouper, tragedian.

actual *adjective her actual words | the actual cost* real, true, factual, genuine, authentic, verified, confirmed, veritable, existing.

actually *adverb* **1** *he's actually brilliant, though quiet | actually, he's very clever* really, in fact, in point of fact, as a matter of fact, in reality, indeed, truly, in truth. **2** *she was actually expected to lie* literally, even, in reality.

actuate *verb people actuated by greed* motivate, stimulate, move, drive, rouse, arouse, prompt, influence, impel, incite, spur on, urge, goad, animate, excite, kindle, awaken, activate.

acumen *noun showing business acumen* astuteness, shrewdness, sharpness, cleverness, smartness, judgment, discernment, wisdom, perspicacity, ingenuity, insight, sagacity.

acute *adjective* **1** *an acute sense of hearing* sharp, keen, penetrating, discerning, sensitive, incisive. **2** *an acute mind/analysis* astute, shrewd, sharp, clever, smart, discerning, perceptive, perspicacious, penetrating, incisive, piercing, discriminating, sagacious, judicious. **3** *an acute shortage of food* severe, critical, crucial, grave, serious, urgent, pressing, vital, dangerous, precarious. **4** *an acute pain* sharp, shooting, piercing, keen, penetrating, stabbing, intense, excruciating, fierce, racking; *fml.* exquisite. **5** *an acute illness* intense, severe, short and sharp, short-lasting.
Antonyms: DULL; CHRONIC.

acutely *adverb acutely conscious of his poverty* very, markedly, extremely, intensely, deeply, profoundly, keenly, sharply, painfully.

adage *noun as the old adage has it* saying, maxim, axiom, proverb, aphorism, saw, dictum, precept, truism, platitude; *fml.* apothegm.

adamant *adjective* resolute, determined, firm, immovable, unshakable, uncompromising, unrelenting, unyielding, unbending, inflexible, obdurate, inexorable, intransigent.

adapt *verb* **1** *adapt a dress/novel | adapt one's way of life* adjust, tailor, convert, change, alter, modify, transform, remodel, reshape. **2** *you must adapt to the new environment* adjust, conform, acclimatize, accommodate, familiarize oneself with, habituate oneself.

adaptable *adjective* **1** *an adaptable design | an adaptable way of life* adjustable, convertible, alterable, modifiable, variable, versatile. **2** *you must try to be adaptable* adjustable, flexible, pliant, compliant, malleable, versatile, resilient, easygoing, conformable.

adaptation *noun* **1** *the adaptation of a dress/novel* adjustment, tailoring, converting, alteration, changing, modification, remodeling, reshaping. *See* ADAPT 1. **2** *the adaptation to a new environment* adjustment, conformity, acclimatization, accommodation, familiarization, habituation.

add *verb* **1** *he added an extra sentence* include, put on/in, attach, append, affix; *fml.* adjoin. **2** *add all the numbers* add up, add together, total, count, count up, compute; *inf.* tot up. **3** *"That's fine," he added* go on to say, state further; *inf.* tack on. **add to** *this added to their pain* increase, magnify, amplify, augment, intensify, aggravate, exacerbate. **add up 1** *add up the column of figures* add, add together, total, count, count up, compute; *inf.* tot up. **2** *it doesn't add up* make sense, be/seem reasonable, be/seem plausible; *inf.* ring true, hold water, stand to reason. **add up to 1** *it adds up to $100* amount to, come to, total. **2** *it all adds up to a disaster* amount to, constitute, comprise, signify; *inf.* spell, spell out.
Antonyms: DEDUCT; REMOVE; SUBTRACT.

addendum *noun* addition, appendix, codicil, postscript, appendage, supplement, adjunct.

addict *noun* **1** *a drug/heroin addict* abuser, user; *inf.* junkie, head, fiend. **2** *a football addict* fan, enthusiast, devotee, follower, adherent; *inf.* buff, freak, nut.

addicted *adjective* **addicted to 1** *addicted to drugs* dependent on; *inf.* hooked on. **2** *addicted to football* devoted to, obsessed with, dedicated to; *inf.* hooked on.

addiction *noun* dependency, craving, devotion, obsession, dedication, enslavement, habit.

addition *noun* **1** *the addition of an extra sentence* inclusion, adding on, attachment, appendage. *See* ADD 1. **2** *the addition of a row of figures | check my addition* adding up, counting, totaling, computation, calculation. **3** *an addition to the family/library* increase, increment, extension, augmentation, gain, supplement, appendage. **in addition** *in addition, you may take three books | in addition to Jane* additionally, besides, as well, as well as.

additional *adjective additional help* extra, supplementary, further, more, other, over and above, fresh, supplemental.

additionally *adverb additionally he gave money* in addition, also, as well, besides, moreover, further, to boot.

additive *noun additives to food | chemical additives* supplement, addition, add-on; preservative.

address *noun* **1** *the address on the envelope* inscription, label, superscription; directions. **2** *moved to a new address* house, home, location, place, residence, abode, domicile, dwelling, situation; whereabouts. **3** *an address to the crowd* speech, lecture, talk, dissertation, discourse, oration, sermon, harangue, diatribe.

address *verb* **1** *address an envelope* direct, label, inscribe, superscribe. **2** *address the audience* talk to, speak to, give a talk to, make a speech to, lecture, give a discourse/dissertation/oration to, preach to, declaim to, harangue; *inf.* spout to. **3** *address someone across the street* greet, speak to, hail, salute. **4** *how to address the mayor* name, call, speak to, write, describe, designate; *fml.* denominate. **5** *address any remarks to the manager* direct, send, communicate, convey, forward, remit. **6** *address the golf ball* take aim at, aim at, face. **address oneself to** apply oneself to, attend to, direct one's attention to, turn to, get down to, devote oneself to, take up, engage in, undertake, concentrate on.

adduce *verb* cite, put forward, mention, point out, quote, name, instance, present, offer, advance, propose, proffer.

adept *adjective adept at games | adept at growing roses* expert, clever, proficient, skillful, accomplished, brilliant, talented, first-rate, masterly; *inf.* top-notch, A-1.

adequacy *noun* **1** *dispute the adequacy of their working conditions* sufficiency, ampleness, reasonableness. **2** *work noted for its adequacy rather than its excellence* passableness, tolerableness, acceptability, mediocrity, indifference. **3** *not disputing his adequacy* capability, competence, suitability, ability, qualifications, fitness.

adequate *adjective* **1** *adequate grounds for divorce | an adequate salary* sufficient, enough, ample, reasonable, satisfactory, requisite. **2** *your work is adequate but not good* passable, tolerable, acceptable, fair, middle-of-the-road, mediocre, unexceptional, indifferent, average, so-so, minimal; *inf.* nothing to write home about, no great shakes. **adequate to** *he did not feel adequate to the task* up to, equal to, capable of (doing/performing), competent for, suited to, suitable for, able to (do/perform), qualified for, fit for.

Antonym: INADEQUATE; INSUFFICIENT.

adhere *verb* **adhere to 1** *sticky tape adhering to the wall* stick to, stick fast to, cling to, hold fast to, cohere to, be fixed to, be pasted/glued to. **2** *adhering to their principles* stick to, hold to, abide by, comply with, stand by, be faithful to, follow, obey, fulfill. **3** *adhere to the Democratic Party* be attached to, support, give support to, be connected with, be affiliated to, be a member of, follow.

adherent *noun* **1** *an adherent of communism* supporter, follower, upholder, advocate, disciple, votary, partisan, sectary, member; *inf.* hanger-on. **2** *an adherent of the theater* fan, admirer, follower, enthusiast, devotee, lover, addict, aficionado; *inf.* buff, freak, fiend.

adherent *adjective an adherent surface* sticky, sticking, adhering, clinging, viscous, adhesive. *See* ADHESIVE *adjective.*

adhesive *adjective an adhesive substance* sticky, sticking, adhering, adherent, clinging, tacky, gluey, gummy, cohesive, viscous, viscid, glutinous; *fml.* mucilaginous.

adhesive *noun* glue, fixative, gum, paste, cement; *fml.* mucilage.

adieu *interjection/noun* goodbye, farewell. *See* GOODBYE.

adjacent *adjective* adjoining, neighboring, next door, abutting, close, near, bordering, alongside, contiguous, proximate, attached, touching, conjoining.

adjoining *adjective an adjoining house* neighboring, next door, adjacent, abutting, bordering, connected, connecting, contiguous, interconnecting, attached. *See* ADJACENT.

adjourn *verb* **1** *adjourn our meeting* break off, discontinue, interrupt, suspend, dissolve, postpone, put off, defer, delay, shelve. **2** *the court adjourns for lunch* break, break off, discontinue, pause, take a recess. **3** *we adjourned to the judge's chambers* withdraw, retire, retreat; *fml.* repair.

adjournment *noun* **1** *the adjournment of our meeting* breaking-off, discontinuation, interruption, suspension, postponement, deferment, deferral, delay, shelving. **2** *the court's adjournment* breaking-off, break, discontinuation, pause, recess. **3** *our adjournment to the judge's chambers* withdrawing, retirement, retreat; *fml.* repairing.

adjudicate *verb* **1** *adjudicate at a musical competition* judge, arbitrate, referee, umpire. **2** *adjudicate a claim* judge, decide on, settle, determine, pronounce on, give a ruling on.

adjudication *noun* **1** *the adjudication at a*

competition judging, arbitration, refereeing, umpiring. **2** *the judge's adjudication* judgment, decision, pronouncement, ruling, settlement, determination, finding, verdict.

adjunct noun *a mere adjunct to the rest of the equipment* extra, addition, attachment, accessory, appendage, add-on, addendum, appurtenance, supplement.

adjust verb **1** *I cannot adjust to the new situation* adapt, become accustomed, get used (to), accommodate, acclimatize, reconcile oneself, habituate oneself, assimilate. **2** *adjust the decor* adapt, rearrange, alter, modify, change, remodel. **3** *adjust the setting* regulate, modify, fix, repair, rectify, put in working order, set to rights, tune.

adjustable adjective **1** *adjustable seat belts* alterable, adaptable, modifiable, movable. **2** *adjustable attitude* adaptable, accommodating, amenable, obliging, flexible, malleable, pliable, pliant, tractable.

adjustment noun **1** *the adjustment to a new situation* adaptation, accustoming, accommodation, acclimatization, reconciliation, habituation, assimilation. **2** *the adjustment of the decor* adaptation, alteration, modification. See ADJUST 2. **3** *the adjustment of the setting* regulating, modifying, modification, fixing, repair. See ADJUST 3. **4** *make a small adjustment* adaptation, alteration, change, modification, rearrangement.

ad lib verb *the speaker cannot ad lib* extemporize, improvise, speak off the cuff, make an impromptu speech, speak impromptu.

ad lib adjective *an ad lib speech* off the cuff, impromptu, on the spot, extempore, improvised, unrehearsed, extemporaneous.

ad lib adverb *speak ad lib* off the cuff, impromptu, extempore, without preparation, without rehearsal, extemporaneously; *inf.* off the top of one's head.

administer verb **1** *administer the firm's financial affairs* manage, direct, control, conduct, run, govern, operate, superintend, supervise, oversee, preside over. **2** *administer justice/comfort* dispense, hand out, discharge, allot, deal, distribute, mete out, disburse, bestow, provide. **3** *administer a remedy/medicine* apply, give, dispense, provide, treat with.

administration noun **1** *he's in business/hospital administration* management, direction, control, conduct, execution, government, operation, supervision. **2** *the Nixon administration* government, regime, term of office; ministry. **3** *the administration of justice* dispensation, discharge, allotment, dealing, distribution, disbursement, bestowal. **4** *the administration of a remedy* application, dispensation, provision. See ADMINISTER 3.

administrative adjective *in an administrative role* managerial, management, directorial, executive, organizational, controlling, governmental, supervisory, regulatory.

administrator noun manager, director, executive, controller, head, chief, superintendent, supervisor.

admirable adjective **1** *admirable conduct in the circumstances* worthy, commendable, praiseworthy, laudable, good, estimable, honorable. **2** *an admirable musical performance* excellent, superb, brilliant, first-rate, first-class, supreme, great, fine, masterly, marvelous.

admiration noun **1** *filled with admiration for his courage* approval, regard, high regard, respect, approbation, appreciation, praise, esteem, veneration. **2** *she was the admiration of the whole village* object of admiration, pride, pride and joy, wonder, delight, marvel, sensation.

admire verb **1** *admire his courage* approve of, respect, think highly of, appreciate, applaud, praise, hold in high regard/esteem, venerate. **2** *she admired her hat* approve of, like, express admiration for, compliment, sing the praises of, be taken with. **3** *he admired her from afar* adore, love, be enamored of, idolize; *inf.* carry a torch for.
Antonyms: DISAPPROVE; DESPISE.

admirer noun **1** *an admirer of modern art* enthusiast, fan, devotee, aficionado, supporter, adherent, follower, disciple, votary; *inf.* buff, freak. **2** *they teased her about her admirer* suitor, wooer, beau, sweetheart, lover, boyfriend, girlfriend.

admissible adjective *admissible evidence/behavior* allowable, allowed, permissible, permitted, acceptable, passable, justifiable, tolerable.

admission noun **1** *admission to the university | admission to the private party* admittance, entry, right of entry, entrance, access, entrée; *fml.* ingress. **2** *admission is $3* entrance fee, entry charge, ticket, cover charge. **3** *an admission of guilt/failure* acknowledgment, confession, revelation, disclosure, divulgence, expression, declaration, utterance, avowal.

admit verb **1** *one ticket admits two people | the window admits little light* let in, allow/permit entry to, give access to. **2** *they admitted their guilt | admitting that they were wrong* acknowledge, confess, reveal, make known, disclose, divulge, declare, avow. **3** *admit that you may be right* concede, accept, grant, acknowledge, agree, allow, concur.
Antonyms: EXCLUDE; PROHIBIT; DENY.

admittance noun *no admittance to the private party* entry, right of entry, entrance, access. See ADMISSION 1.

admonish verb **1** *admonish the boys for smoking* reprimand, rebuke, scold, reprove, upbraid, chide, censure, berate. **2** *she admonished us to seek help* advise, urge, caution, warn, counsel, exhort.

admonition noun **1** *deliver an admonition to the culprits* reprimand, rebuke, scolding. See ADMONISH 1. **2** *gave them an admonition to seek help*

piece of advice, warning, exhortation; advice.
See ADMONISH 2.

admonitory *adjective* **1** *admonitory remarks to the culprits* admonishing, reprimanding, rebuking, reproving, reproachful. *See* ADMONISH 1. **2** *admonitory suggestions to seek help* admonishing, advisory, cautioning, cautionary, exhortative. *See* ADMONISH 2.

ado *noun* *we set off without further ado* fuss, trouble, bother, commotion, upset, agitation, hubbub, confusion, disturbance, flurry, to-do; *inf.* fuss and feathers.

adolescence *noun* *have acne during adolescence* teenage years, teens, youth, pubescence.

adolescent *adjective* **1** *adolescent problems* teenage, youthful, pubescent. **2** *despite her age she has an adolescent sense of humor* immature, juvenile, childish, puerile.

adolescent *noun* teenager, youngster, young person, youth.

adopt *verb* **1** *adopt a child* take as one's own child, be adoptive parents to, take in, take care of. **2** *adopt Eastern customs* assume, take on, take over, affect, embrace, espouse, appropriate. **3** *adopt a candidate* select, choose, vote for. **4** *adopt the new measures* approve, endorse, accept, ratify, sanction, support, back.

adoption *noun* **1** *the adoption of a child* adopting, taking as one's own, taking in. *See* ADOPT 1. **2** *the adoption of Asian customs* assumption, taking on, affecting, affectation, espousal, appropriation. **3** *the adoption of the candidate* selection, choosing, choice, voting for. **4** *the adoption of the new measures* approval, endorsement, acceptance, ratification, sanctioning, support, backing.

adorable *adjective* lovable, appealing, charming, sweet, enchanting, captivating, dear, darling, delightful, attractive, winsome, winning, fetching.

adoration *noun* **1** *the adoration of their children* love, loving, doting, devotion, idolization, worship. **2** *the adoration of God* worship, glorification, praising, praise, homage, exaltation, magnification, extolment, veneration. **3** *their adoration of travel* love, liking, enjoyment, great liking/enjoyment, relishing. *See* ADORE 3.

adore *verb* **1** *adore their children* love, be devoted to, dote on, cherish, hold dear, idolize, worship. **2** *let us adore God* worship, glorify, praise, revere, reverence, exalt, magnify, laud, extol, esteem, venerate. **3** *they adore ice cream* like, love, be fond of, enjoy, delight in, take pleasure in, relish.

Antonyms: HATE; LOATHE; DETEST.

adorn *verb* *flowers adorn the room* decorate, embellish, add ornament to, ornament, trim, enhance, beautify, enrich, bedeck, deck, array, grace, emblazon.

adornment *noun* **1** *the adornment of the Christmas tree* decorating, decoration, embellishment, ornamentation, trimming, arraying, enhancement, beautification, enrichment. **2**

simply dressed with no adornment ornamentation, ornament, embellishment, decoration; frills, accessories, trimmings.

adrift *adjective* **1** *a boat adrift on the sea* drifting, unmoored, unanchored. **2** *young people adrift in city streets* aimless, purposeless, without purpose/goal, directionless, unsettled, rootless. **3** *our plans have gone badly adrift* wrong, awry, amiss, astray, off course.

adroit *adjective* **1** *his adroit handling of the boat* | *adroit at tennis* skillful, skilled, expert, adept, dexterous, deft, clever, able, capable, competent, masterly, proficient. **2** *an adroit politician* skillful, expert, adept, clever, quick-thinking, quick-witted, cunning, artful, resourceful, astute, shrewd.

Antonyms: CLUMSY; INEPT.

adroitness *noun* **1** *her adroitness at sailing* skill, skillfulness, expertise, adeptness, dexterity, deftness, cleverness, ability, capability, competence, proficiency. **2** *his political adroitness* skill, skillfulness, expertise, adeptness, cleverness, quick-wittedness, cunning, artfulness, resourcefulness, astuteness, shrewdness.

adulation *noun* *adulation of movie stars* worship, hero-worship, idolization, adoration, glorification, praising, praise, flattery; blandishments.

adult *adjective* **1** *an adult female/tree* mature, grown-up, fully grown, full-grown, fully developed; *fml.* of age. **2** *adult magazines/videos* sexually explicit, obscene, pornographic; *inf.* full-frontal.

adulterate *verb* *adulterate the water/brandy* make impure, debase, degrade, spoil, contaminate, taint, doctor, water down, weaken, bastardize; *fml.* vitiate.

advance *verb* **1** *the army advanced* go/come/move forward, proceed, go ahead, move along, press on, push forward, make progress, make headway, forge ahead, gain ground. **2** *advance the date of publication* | *advance our lunch appointment* bring/put forward, make earlier. **3** *advance his promotion* | *advance the building schedule* speed up, accelerate, step up, hasten, expedite, hurry, quicken, forward. **4** *advance his chances of promotion* further, forward, help, assist, facilitate, promote, boost, improve, benefit, foster. **5** *her career advanced rapidly* go forward, go ahead, progress, develop, improve, thrive, flourish. **6** *advance a suggestion/theory* put forward, suggest, propose, submit, recommend, present, introduce, offer, proffer. **7** *the company advanced him $500 pay* lend, supply on credit. **8** *prices are advancing rapidly* rise, increase, go up, mount. **9** *war advanced prices* raise, increase, put up, inflate; *inf.* jack up, hike up.

Antonyms: RETREAT; POSTPONE; IMPEDE.

advance *noun* **1** *the advance of the army* going/coming/moving forward, movement forward, progress, headway. *See* ADVANCE *verb* 1. **2** *the* *advance of civilization* progress, development, advancement, movement forward, headway, improvement, betterment, furtherance. **3** *recent medical advances* development, discovery, breakthrough, finding, invention. **4** *an advance in the price of oil* rise, increase, markup. **5** *they paid me an advance of $500* down payment, deposit, retainer. **in advance** beforehand, ahead of time, earlier, previously.

advance *adjective* **1** *the advance party* sent ahead, leading, first. **2** *given advance warning* early, previous, prior, beforehand.

advanced *adjective* **1** *advanced technology* progressive, forward, highly developed, modern, ultramodern, avant-garde, ahead of the times. **2** *advanced studies* higher-level.

advancement *noun* **1** *furthering the advancement of knowledge* progress, development, improvement, furtherance. *See* ADVANCE *noun* 2, 3. **2** *the job offers advancement* promotion, improvement, progress, betterment, growth, rise, preferment.

advances *plural noun* *make friendly advances* approaches, overtures, moves, proposals, propositions.

advantage *noun* **1** *its main advantage is size* benefit, asset, good point, boon, blessing. **2** *he had an advantage over her | the advantage of age* benefit, superiority, dominance, ascendancy, supremacy, power, mastery, upper hand, trump card. **3** *little advantage in going | not to one's advantage* benefit, profit, gain, good.
Antonyms: DISADVANTAGE; HANDICAP; DETRIMENT.

advantageous *adjective* **1** *in an advantageous position* favorable, superior, dominant, powerful. **2** *advantageous to your career* beneficial, of benefit, helpful, of assistance, useful, valuable, of service, profitable.

advent *noun* *the advent of war | advent of modern techniques* arrival, coming, appearance, approach, occurrence.
Antonyms: DEPARTURE; DISAPPEARANCE.

adventitious *adjective* *an adventitious encounter* accidental, unexpected, unplanned, chance, fortuitous, casual.

adventure *noun* **1** *a spirit of adventure | a life full of adventure* risk, hazard, danger, peril, gamble, gambling, uncertainty, precariousness. **2** *tales of the sailor's adventures* exploit, deed, feat, experience, incident.

adventurous *adjective* **1** *adventurous explorers* daring, daredevil, bold, intrepid, audacious; *fml.* adventuresome, venturesome. **2** *an adventurous life* risky, dangerous, perilous, hazardous, precarious.

adversary *noun* opponent, opposer, antagonist, rival, enemy, foe, fellow contestant/competitor.

adverse *adjective* **1** *adverse circumstances | adverse weather conditions* unfavorable, unlucky, disadvantageous, inauspicious, unpropitious, unfortunate, untoward. **2** *adverse criticism* hostile, unfriendly, unfavorable, antagonistic, negative, opposing, inimical, antipathetic. **3** *adverse to health* harmful, dangerous, injurious, detrimental, disadvantageous, hurtful.
Antonyms: FAVORABLE; AUSPICIOUS; BENEFICIAL.

adversity *noun* **1** *face adversity with courage* misfortune, ill luck, bad luck, trouble, hardship, distress, disaster, suffering, affliction, sorrow, misery, tribulation, woe; hard times. **2** *many adversities in their lives* misfortune, mishap, accident, shock, reverse, setback, disaster, catastrophe, tragedy, calamity, trial.

advertise *verb* **1** *advertise details of a meeting* make known/public, publicize, give publicity to, announce, broadcast, proclaim, call attention to. **2** *advertise a product* promote, publicize, give publicity to, call attention to, display, tout, promulgate; *inf.* push, plug.

advertisement *noun* **1** *put an advertisement in the paper* notice, announcement; *inf.* ad; display ad, want ad, classified ad. **2** *a television advertisement | an advertisement for soap* promotion, commercial, blurb; *inf.* ad, plug. **3** *the advertisement of products* advertising, promotion, publicizing, touting; *inf.* plugging, pushing.

advice *noun* **1** *give advice to young people* guidance, counseling, counsel, help; recommendations, suggestions, hints, tips, ideas, opinions, views. **2** *an advice sent from the bank* notification, communication, information; data.

advisability *noun* desirability, wisdom, soundness, prudence, appropriateness, fitness, suitability, aptness, judiciousness, expediency.

advisable *adjective* desirable, best, wisest, sensible, sound, prudent, proper, appropriate, suitable, fitting, apt, judicious, recommended, suggested, expedient, politic.

advise *verb* **1** *cannot advise you on your affairs* give guidance to, guide, counsel, give counsel to, give recommendations to, offer suggestions/opinions to, give hints/tips to, instruct. **2** *advise you of the facts* inform, notify, give notice to, apprise, acquaint with, warn. **3** *advise caution* suggest, recommend, urge.

adviser, advisor *noun* counselor, mentor, guide, consultant, confidant, confidante, coach, teacher, tutor, therapist.

advisory *adjective* advising, consultative, counseling, recommendatory, assisting.

advocacy *noun* *advocacy of political freedom* advising, recommending, support (for), backing, arguing/argument (for), promotion. *See* ADVOCATE *verb*.

advocate *verb* *advocate reducing expenditure* recommend, advise, favor, support, uphold, back, subscribe to, champion, speak for, campaign on behalf of, argue/plead/press for, urge, promote.

advocate *noun* **1** *an advocate of political freedom* supporter, upholder, backer, champion, spokesman, spokeswoman, spokesperson, speaker, campaigner, pleader, promoter, proponent, exponent, apostle, apologist. **2** *the defendant's advocate* counsel, lawyer, attorney.

aegis *noun* protection, guardianship, support, patronage, sponsorship, safeguarding, defense, championship, aid, guaranty; auspices.

aeon *noun* See EON.

affability *noun* friendliness, amiability, geniality, congeniality, cordiality, pleasantness, agreeableness, good-humoredness, kindliness, courtesy, civility, approachability, sociability.

affable *adjective* friendly, amiable, genial, congenial, cordial, pleasant, agreeable, easygoing, good-humored, good-natured, kindly, courteous, civil, approachable, sociable.

affair *noun* **1** *that's my own affair* concern, business, matter, responsibility. **2** *forget the sad affair* event, happening, occurrence, incident, episode, circumstance, adventure, case. **3** *an informal affair* party, function, reception, gathering; *inf.* get-together, do. **4** *an affair with a married man* love affair, relationship, romance, liaison, affair of the heart, intrigue, amour.

affairs *plural noun* *commercial/foreign affairs* concerns, matters, activities, transactions, undertakings, ventures, business.

affect[1] *verb* **1** *it affected his health | affected our attitude* have an effect on, influence, act on, work on, have an impact on, change, alter, transform. **2** *the disease affected his lungs* attack, strike at, infect, take hold of. **3** *the experience deeply affected us* move, touch, upset, disturb, trouble, perturb, agitate, stir, tug at the heartstrings.

affect[2] *verb* **1** *affect long words | affect bright clothes* assume, put on, adopt, like, have a liking for, espouse. **2** *affect a foreign accent | affect ignorance* pretend, feign, fake, simulate.

affectation *noun* **1** *tired of his affectation | without affectation* pretense, pretension, pretentiousness, affectedness, artificiality, insincerity, posturing. **2** *his affectations annoy me* airs, pretensions; posing, posturing. **3** *an affectation of interest* façade, show, appearance, false display, pretense, feigning, simulation.

affected[1] *adjective* influenced, altered, changed. See AFFECT[1].

affected[2] *adjective* **1** *an affected style of writing* pretentious, artificial, unnatural, assumed, high-flown, ostentatious, contrived, studied, pompous, mannered. **2** *an affected politeness* put on, pretended, feigned, fake, counterfeit, sham, simulated.

Antonyms: NATURAL; UNPRETENTIOUS; GENUINE.

affecting *adjective* *an affecting scene* moving, touching, poignant, upsetting, pathetic, heartrending. See AFFECT[1] 3.

affection *noun* *affection for her sister* love, liking, fondness, warmth, devotion, caring, attachment, friendship, amity; warm feelings.

affectionate *adjective* *an affectionate wife/hug* loving, fond, devoted, caring, tender, doting, friendly. See AFFECTION.

affianced *adjective* engaged, betrothed, contracted, pledged.

affiliate *verb* **affiliate with** *the college is affiliated with the university* associate with, unite with, combine with, join with, ally with, amalgamate with, coalesce into, form a federation/confederation with, annex to, merge with, incorporate into.

affiliation *noun* **1** *the affiliation of the college with the university* uniting, combining, allying, amalgamation. See AFFILIATE. **2** *affiliations between clubs* connection, link, bond, tie, relationship; communication.

affinity *noun* **1** *the human's affinity with the ape* likeness, similarity, resemblance, correspondence, analogy, similitude. **2** *have an affinity for each other* liking, fondness, attraction, inclination, rapport, sympathy, partiality, penchant, predilection. **3** *the witness's affinity with the accused* relationship, connection.

affirm *verb* state, assert, declare, aver, proclaim, pronounce, swear, attest.

affirmation *noun* statement, assertion, declaration, averment, proclamation, pronouncement, swearing, attestation.

affirmative *adjective* assenting, consenting, agreeing, concurring, corroborative, favorable, approving, positive.

Antonyms: dissenting; NEGATIVE.

affix *verb* **1** *affix a stamp to the envelope* attach, stick, fasten, fix, tack, glue, paste. **2** *affix a signature to a document* append, add, add on, attach.

afflict *verb* trouble, burden, distress, beset, harass, oppress, torment, plague, rack, smite.

affliction *noun* **1** *bearing affliction bravely* trouble, distress, pain, misery, suffering, wretchedness, hardship, misfortune, sorrow, torment, tribulation, woe. **2** *the afflictions of the old* trouble, disorder, disease, pain, suffering, trial, hardship, ordeal, scourge, plague, woe.

affluence *noun* wealth, prosperity, opulence, fortune, richness; riches, resources. See AFFLUENT.

affluent *adjective* rich, wealthy, prosperous, opulent, well off, moneyed, well-to-do, comfortable; *inf.* well-heeled, in the money, loaded.

afford *verb* **1** *cannot afford a new dress* pay for, meet the expense of, spare the price of. **2** *cannot afford the loss of staff* bear, sustain, stand. **3** *the tree affords shade* provide, supply, offer, give, impart, bestow, furnish, yield. **4** *the orchard affords a large crop* yield, produce, bear, supply, give.

affray *noun* fight, brawl, battle, quarrel, set-to, fracas, altercation, disturbance, commotion, breach of the peace, melee, scrap, clash, scuffle, tussle; *inf.* free-for-all.

affront *noun* *sexist remarks are an affront* insult, offense, indignity, slight, snub, aspersion, provocation, injury, outrage; *inf.* slap in the face.

affront *verb he was affronted by her behavior* insult, offend, outrage, provoke, slight, hurt.

afoot *adjective/adverb trouble afoot | evil plans afoot* around, about, going on, abroad, circulating, current, stirring; *lit.* astir.

aforesaid *adjective* aforementioned, forenamed, previously described, foregoing, preceding, earlier, previous.

afraid *adjective* **1** *noises made them afraid* frightened, scared, nervous, apprehensive, fearful, terrified, alarmed (at), intimidated (by), terror-stricken. **2** *I'm afraid I can't help* sorry, regretful, apologetic, unhappy.

afresh *adverb* anew, again, over again, once again, once more.

after *preposition* **1** *leave after lunch* following, subsequent to, at the close/end of, later than. **2** *shut the door after you* behind, following, in the rear of. **3** *B comes after A* following, next to, nearest to, below. **4** *run after the thief | be after a job* in pursuit of, in search of, in quest of. **5** *after the way he acted, she hates him* following, because of, as a result of, in view of, owing to, on account of. **6** *after all that, she still loves him* despite, in spite of, regardless of, notwithstanding. **7** *inquire after her health* about, concerning, regarding, with reference to. **8** *named after his grandfather* with the name of, the same as, in remembrance/honor of, as a tribute to, for. **9** *a painting after Rubens* in the style of, in the manner of, in imitation of, on the model of, following the pattern of.

after *adverb* **1** *the week after* later, following, afterward, subsequently, thereafter. **2** *following on after* behind, in the rear, at the back. *Antonyms:* PREVIOUSLY; BEFORE.

after *adjective* *in after years* later, succeeding, subsequent, following.

afterlife *noun* life after death, the hereafter, afterworld.

aftermath *noun* aftereffects, effects, consequences, results; end result, outcome, upshot, issue, end.

afterward *adverb afterward they left* later, subsequently, then, thereupon, after, next.

again *adverb* **1** *start again* once more, afresh, anew, a second time, another time. **2** *again there is the question of money* moreover, besides, also, furthermore, further. **3** *he might come, and again he might not* on the other hand, on the contrary, conversely. **4** *half as much again* in addition, over and above, also, too. **again and again** often, frequently, repeatedly, over and over, time and time again, continually, persistently.

against *preposition* **1** *people against the movement* opposed to, in opposition to, hostile to, at odds with, in disagreement with, versus, at cross-purposes with. **2** *rowing against the tide* in opposition to, counter to, resisting. **3** *leaning against the fence* touching, in contact with, close up to, up against, abutting. **4** *silhouetted against a black background* in contrast to. **5** *saving against a rainy day* in preparation for, in anticipation of, in expectation of, as provision for. **6** *his age is against him* disadvantageous to, unfavorable to, damaging to, detrimental to, prejudicial to. **7** *the exchange rate against the dollar* in exchange for, in return for, in compensation for.

age *noun* **1** *what age is the tree?* number of years, lifetime, duration, stage of life, generation; years. **2** *wisdom comes with age | age can bring infirmity* maturity, seniority, elderliness, oldness, old age; advancing years, declining years; *fml.* senescence. **3** *the Elizabethan/nuclear age* era, epoch, period, time.

age *verb* mature, ripen, grow up, come of age; grow old, decline, wither, fade, become obsolete.

aged *adjective* old, elderly, superannuated; *fml.* senescent; *inf.* as old as the hills.

agency *noun* **1** *advertising agency* business, organization, company, firm, office, bureau, concern. **2** *brought together through the agency of friends* mediation, intervention, intercession; activity, action, influence.

agenda *noun* program, schedule, timetable, plan, list, scheme.

agent *noun* **1** *an insurance agent* representative, negotiator, emissary, envoy, factor, go-between; *inf.* rep. **2** *an enemy agent* spy, secret agent; *inf.* mole. **3** *a cleansing agent* factor, cause, instrument, vehicle, means, power, force.

ages *plural noun we waited for ages* a long time, an eternity, an eon; hours, days, months, years, eons, hours/days/months on end.agglomeration

agglomeration *noun* collection, accumulation, mass, cluster, lump, clump, pile, heap, aggregate, miscellany, jumble, hodgepodge.

aggravate *verb* **1** *aggravate the situation/pain* worsen, make worse, exacerbate, inflame, intensify, increase, heighten, magnify. **2** *aggravate the teacher* annoy, irritate, anger, exasperate, provoke, irk, vex, get on one's nerves, rub the wrong way; *inf.* needle. *Antonyms:* ALLEVIATE; IMPROVE; CALM; MOLLIFY.

aggravation *noun* **1** *the aggravation of the situation/pain* worsening, exacerbation, intensification, increase, magnification. **2** *the aggravation of the teacher* annoyance, irritation, angering, exasperation, provocation, vexation; *inf.* needling. **3** *just one more aggravation* irritant, nuisance, pest, grievance, thorn in the flesh; *inf.* headache.

aggregate *noun* **1** *the aggregate of goals* total, sum total, whole amount, totality, entirety, summation, gross. **2** *an aggregate of minerals* collection, accumulation, mass, cluster, clump, lump, pile, heap, concentration, assemblage, mixture, combination, agglomeration.

aggregate *adjective* **1** *the aggregate score* total, combined, whole, added. **2** *aggregate rock* composite, compound, combined, massed, clustered.

aggression *noun* **1** *an act of aggression* attack, assault, injury, encroachment, offense, invasion, infringement. **2** *a bloody aggression* attack, assault, onslaught, foray, raid, sortie, offensive, invasion.

aggressive *adjective* **1** *an aggressive person* quarrelsome, argumentative, belligerent, pugnacious, militant, warring. **2** *an aggressive act* hostile, belligerent, warring, combative, bellicose, invasive, intrusive. **3** *an aggressive salesman* | *aggressive sales promotion* assertive, forceful, insistent, vigorous, energetic, dynamic, bold, enterprising, zealous; *inf.* pushy.
Antonyms: PEACEABLE; FRIENDLY; RETIRING.

aggressor *noun* attacker, assaulter, invader, assailant, provoker, instigator, initiator.

aggrieved *adjective* **1** *aggrieved at her treatment* resentful, angry, distressed, disturbed, piqued; *inf.* peeved. **2** *the aggrieved party* wronged, injured, abused, harmed, mistreated, ill-used.

aghast *adjective* horrified, appalled, astounded, amazed, thunderstruck, stunned, shocked, flabbergasted, awestruck; *inf.* floored.

agile *adjective* **1** *an agile body* active, nimble, spry, lithe, fit, supple, sprightly, in good condition, lively, quick-moving, limber. **2** *an agile mind* active, nimble, alert, sharp, acute, clever, quick-witted.
Antonyms: INACTIVE; STIFF.

agility *noun* **1** *the agility of their bodies* activeness, nimbleness, litheness, fitness, suppleness. *See* AGILE 1. **2** *the agility of her mind* activeness, nimbleness, alertness. *See* AGILE 2.

agitate *verb* **1** *she was agitated by the delay* upset, work up, perturb, fluster, ruffle, disconcert, disquiet, flurry, trouble, worry. **2** *agitate the mixture* stir, whisk, beat, churn, shake, toss. **3** *rebels agitating the crowd* stir up, rouse, arouse, disturb, perturb, excite, inflame, incite, foment.

agitation *noun* **1** *the agitation caused by delays* upset, perturbation, fluster, disconcertment, disquiet, flurry, trouble, worry. **2** *the agitation of the mixture* stirring, whisking, beating, shaking, tossing, churning. **3** *the rebels' agitation of the crowd* stirring up, rousing, arousal, disturbance, perturbation, exciting, inflammation, inciting, incitement, fomenting, fomentation.

agitator *noun* troublemaker, instigator, agent provocateur, inciter, rabble-rouser, provoker, fomenter, firebrand, revolutionary, demagogue.

agnostic *noun* skeptic, unbeliever, disbeliever, doubter, questioner, doubting Thomas.

ago *adverb* in the past, in time gone by, since, formerly.

agog *adverb* eager, excited, impatient, in suspense, keen, curious, expectant, enthralled, enthusiastic, avid.

agonizing *adjective* excruciating, harrowing, racking, painful, acute, searing, insufferable, piercing, unendurable, torturous, tormenting; *lit.* exquisite.

agony *noun* suffering, pain, hurt, distress, torture, torment, anguish, misery, woe; pangs, throes.

agree *verb* agree on *we agreed on a time* settle on, arrange, arrive at, decide on. agree to *agree to your proposals* consent to, accept, approve, acquiesce in, assent to, concede to, allow, admit, grant. agree with **1** *agree with you* | *agree with your proposals* concur with, be of the same mind/opinion with, comply with, see eye to eye with. **2** *the statements do not agree with each other* match, correspond to, conform to, coincide with, fit, harmonize with. **3** *the warm climate agrees with me* suit, be good for.
Antonyms: DISAGREE; REJECT; DIFFER.

agreement *noun* **1** *we are in total agreement* accord, assent, concurrence, harmony, accordance, unity, concord. **2** *sign a business/international agreement* contract, compact, treaty, covenant, pact, bargain, settlement, proposal; *inf.* deal; *fml.* concordat. **3** *the agreement of the statements* matching, similarity, accordance, correspondence, conformity, coincidence, harmony.

agriculture *noun* farming, husbandry; animal husbandry, cultivation, tillage, horticulture; agribusiness, agronomics, agronomy.

aground *adverb/adjective* beached, grounded, foundered, ashore, stuck, shipwrecked, on the ground/bottom.

ahead *adverb* **1** *they went ahead* in the front, at the head, in the lead, in the vanguard. **2** *the way ahead* forward, onward, on. ahead of **1** *straight ahead of us* in front of, toward the front of, before. **2** *ahead of time* in advance of, before, earlier than. **3** *he's ahead of us in algebra* further (on) than, more advanced than, superior to, outdistancing.
Antonyms: BEHIND; AFTER.

aid *verb* **1** *aid us in our effort* | *aid our effort* help, assist, support, lend a hand, succor, sustain, second. **2** *aid recovery/sleep* help, speed up, hasten, facilitate, expedite, encourage, promote.
Antonyms: HINDER; IMPEDE; DISCOURAGE.

aid *noun* **1** *give aid to a motorist* help, assistance, support, a helping hand, succor, encouragement. **2** *foreign aid* contribution, subsidy, gift, donation.
Antonym: HINDRANCE; OBSTRUCTION.

aide *noun* aide-de-camp; assistant, helper, help; associate, collaborator; *inf.* right arm, girl/man Friday.

ailing *adjective* ill, unwell, sick, sickly, poorly, weak, indisposed, under the weather.

ailment *noun* illness, disease, disorder, sickness, complaint, infection.

aim *verb* **1** *aim a gun* point, direct, take aim, train, sight, focus, position. **2** *aim to increase profits* plan, intend, resolve, propose, purpose, design. **aim at/for** *aim at/for a scholarship* set one's sights on, try for, strive for, work toward, be after, seek, aspire to.

aim *noun* **1** *the aim of a gun* pointing, directing, training; line of sight. *See* AIM *verb* 1. **2** *our aim is to win* goal, ambition, objective, object, end, target, intention, plan, purpose, aspiration, resolve, proposal, design, desire, wish.

aimless *adjective* **1** *an aimless life* purposeless, pointless, goalless, futile, undirected, objectless. **2** *aimless young people* goalless, unambitious, purposeless, undirected, drifting, wandering.
Antonyms: PURPOSEFUL; DETERMINED.

air *noun* **1** *the birds of the air* | *propelled through the air* atmosphere, sky, heavens, aerospace. **2** *let's get some air* | *feel the air on our faces* breeze, breath of air, gust/movement of wind, zephyr, draft. **3** *an air of peace* impression, appearance, look, atmosphere, mood, quality, ambience, aura, manner, bearing, character, feeling, flavor, effect, tone. **4** *playing an old air* tune, melody, song, theme, strain.

air *verb* **1** *air the room/clothes* ventilate, aerate, freshen. **2** *air one's views/objections* make public, publicize, express, voice, publish, vent, disseminate, circulate, communicate, broadcast, reveal, proclaim, divulge.

airily *adverb* *greeted us airily* lightly, lightheartedly, breezily, flippantly, gaily, blithely, jauntily, nonchalantly, cheerfully.

airing *noun* **1** *the airing of the room/clothes* ventilating, ventilation, aerating, freshening. **2** *the airing of one's views* publicizing, expression, voicing, publishing, venting, dissemination, circulation, communication, revelation, broadcast, broadcasting, proclamation, divulgence.

airless *adjective* stuffy, close, stifling, suffocating, unventilated, sultry, muggy, oppressive.

airs *plural noun* affectedness, posing, posturing; affectations, pretensions.

airtight *adjective* **1** *an airtight container* closed, sealed, hermetically sealed, shut tight, impermeable. **2** *an airtight alibi* indisputable, incontrovertible, incontestable, irrefutable, unassailable.

airy *adjective* **1** *an airy day* breezy, windy, gusty. **2** *a light and airy office* well-ventilated, spacious, open. **3** *an airy being* delicate, insubstantial, ethereal, flimsy, wispy, incorporeal, vaporous. **4** *an airy promise/reply* lighthearted, breezy, flippant, blithe, gay, jaunty, nonchalant, insubstantial, cheerful.

aisle *noun* gangway, passageway, passage, corridor, path, lane, alley.

ajar *adjective/adverb* half open, slightly open, unfastened, unsecured, unlatched.

akin *adjective* **akin to** *akin to sailing/murder* related to, allied with, connected with, similar to, corresponding to.

alacrity *noun* readiness, promptness, willingness, eagerness, enthusiasm, haste, swiftness.

alarm *noun* **1** *have/hear a burglar/fire alarm* warning sound/device, alarm signal, alarm bell, danger/distress signal, siren, alert. **2** *rumors causing alarm* fear, fright, terror, apprehension, panic, trepidation, nervousness, anxiety, unease, distress, consternation, disquiet, perturbation.

alarm *verb* **1** *crowds alarm her* frighten, scare, terrify, panic, startle, unnerve, distress, intimidate. **2** *saw the fire and alarmed the neighborhood* warn, alert, arouse, signal.

alarming *adjective* frightening, disturbing, terrifying, startling, shocking, distressing, dismaying, perturbing.

alarmist *noun* scaremonger, voice of doom, doomster, doom merchant.

alcohol *noun* strong drink, liquor, intoxicating liquor; spirits; *inf.* booze, firewater, hooch, rotgut, hard stuff.

alcoholic *adjective* *alcoholic drinks* intoxicating, inebriating, strong, hard.

alcoholic *noun* *a confirmed alcoholic* alcohol addict, dipsomaniac, hard/heavy drinker, drunk, drunkard, tippler, sot, toper, inebriate, imbiber; *inf.* boozer, lush, alky, tosspot, wino.

alcove *noun* niche, recess, nook, opening, bay, hollow, cavity, corner.

alert *adjective* *an alert mind/youngster* wide awake, sharp, bright, quick, keen, perceptive; *inf.* on the ball, on one's toes. **alert to** *you must always be alert to danger* wide awake to, on the lookout for, aware of, heedful of, watchful of, attentive to, vigilant of, observant of, circumspect to, wary of, on one's guard for; *fml.* on the qui vive for.
Antonyms: SLOW; INATTENTIVE; OBLIVIOUS.

alias *adverb* also known as, also called, otherwise known as, otherwise; *inf.* a.k.a.

alias *noun* assumed name, false name, pseudonym, stage name, nom de plume, sobriquet; *fml.* nom de guerre.

alibi *noun* defense, plea, justification, explanation, reason, vindication, excuse, pretext.

alien *adjective* **1** *an alien culture* foreign, overseas, nonnative, unnaturalized. **2** *an alien environment* strange, unfamiliar, unknown, outlandish, remote, exotic. **3** *behavior alien to his principles* opposed, conflicting, contrary, adverse, incompatible, unacceptable, repugnant, hostile, antagonistic, inimical.

alien *noun* **1** *aliens deported in wartime* foreigner, outsider, stranger. **2** *aliens from Mars* extraterrestrial, *inf.* E.T., little green man.

alienate *verb* **1** *alienate his daughter from her mother* estrange, set against, turn away, make hostile, sever, divorce, separate, cut off, divide. **2** *alienate property* transfer, convey.

alienation *verb* **1** *alienation of his daughter* estrangement, severance, divorce, separation, cutting off. *See* ALIENATE 1. **2** *alienation of property* transfer, conveyance.

alight *adjective* **1** *the fire was still alight* on fire, ablaze, burning, lighted, lit, blazing, flaming, ignited. **2** *faces alight with joy* lit up, shining, bright, brilliant, illuminated.

alight *verb* **1** *alight from the bus* get off, dismount, disembark, descend. **2** *birds alighting on branches* land, come down, come to rest, touch down, settle, perch.
Antonyms: get on (*see* GET); BOARD; fly off.

align *verb* **1** *align the books on the shelves* line up, arrange, arrange in line, put in order, straighten. **2** *align with a political party* affiliate, ally, associate, join, cooperate, side, sympathize, agree.

alignment *noun* **1** *the alignment of the books* lining up, arrangement in line, straightening. **2** *the alignment with a political party* affiliation, alliance, association, siding, sympathy. *See* ALIGN 2.

alike *adjective* *the sisters are so alike* like, similar, the same, indistinguishable, resembling, identical, interchangeable, corresponding, comparable.

alike *adverb* *think alike* similarly, the same, just the same, in the same way, identically, in like manner.

alimony *noun* maintenance, support, keep, sustenance, livelihood.

alive *adjective* **1** *at least the captives are alive* living, live, breathing; *inf.* in the land of the living, alive and kicking; *fml.* animate. **2** *interest/debate is still very much alive* active, continuing, going on, existing, extant, prevalent, functioning, in the air/wind, in existence, in operation; *fml.* existent. **3** *seeming very much alive today* full of life, lively, active, energetic, alert, animated, vivacious, vigorous, spry, sprightly, vital, zestful, spirited. **4** *alive to the possibilities* alert to, awake to, aware/cognizant of. **5** *alive with vermin/crowds* overflowing, teeming, crowded, packed, bristling, swarming, thronged, bustling; *inf.* crawling, hopping.
Antonyms: DEAD; EXTINCT; INACTIVE.

---

alive
animate, animated, living, vital
Dead is dead, but one can be **alive** to varying degrees The broadest of these terms describing what has life or shows signs of having it, *alive* can refer to what barely exists (*he was unconscious but still alive when they found him*) as well as to what is bursting with (literal or figurative) life (*her face was alive with excitement and anticipation*). **Living**, on the other hand, is more limited in scope and implies the condition of not being dead (*at 92, she was the oldest living member of the family*) or a state of continued existence or activity (*America's greatest living historian*). **Animate** has fewer connotations than *living* or *alive*; though rare, it is used to distin-

guish living organisms as opposed to dead ones (*one of the few animate creatures after the devastating explosion*). **Animated**, on the other hand, is used to describe inanimate things to which life or the appearance of life has been given (*an animated cartoon*), or things that are vigorous and lively (*an animated debate on the death penalty*). Anything that is essential to life is **vital** (*vital functions; vital organs*), but it can also be used to describe the energy, activity, and alertness of living things (*an aging but vital member of the historical society*).

---

all *adjective* **1** *all suggestions are welcome* each, each one of, every, every one of, every single. **2** *he worked all summer* | *buy all the wood* the whole of, every bit of, the complete, the entire, the totality of. **3** *in all earnestness* complete, entire, total, full, utter, greatest, perfect.

all *noun* **1** *all died* everyone, everybody, every/each person; *inf.* the whole lot. **2** *all were thrown away* everything, each thing; *inf.* the whole lot; lock, stock, and barrel. **3** *take all of it* everything, the whole/total amount, the entirety, the sum total, the aggregate.

all *adverb* *dressed all in black* completely, entirely, totally, wholly, altogether, fully, utterly.

allay *verb* *allay suffering/fears* lessen, diminish, reduce, relieve, calm, lull, alleviate, assuage, appease, quell, check, mitigate.

allegation *noun* claim, charge, accusation, professing, declaration, statement, assertion, averment, avowal, deposition, plea, affirmation.

allege *verb* claim, profess, declare, state, assert, aver, avow, affirm.

alleged *adjective* supposed, so-called, claimed, professed, declared, stated, designated.

allegiance *noun* loyalty, obedience, fidelity, faithfulness, duty, devotion, constancy, adherence, homage; *fml.* fealty.

allegorical *adjective* symbolic, metaphorical, figurative, emblematic, parabolic.

allegory *noun* **1** *Orwell's Animal Farm is an allegory* parable, fable. **2** *illustrate by allegory* symbolism, symbol, metaphor, analogy.

allergic *adjective* **1** *allergic to cow's milk* hypersensitive, sensitive, susceptible. **2** *allergic to work* averse, opposed, loath, hostile, antagonistic, disinclined.

allergy *noun* **1** *an allergy to cow's milk* hypersensitivity, sensitivity, susceptibility. **2** *an allergy to work* aversion, antipathy, opposition, hostility, antagonism, dislike.

alleviate *verb* *alleviate pain/poverty* reduce, lessen, diminish, relieve, ease, allay, abate, mitigate, assuage, palliate.

---

alleviate
abate, allay, assuage, mitigate, relieve, temper
To **alleviate** is to make something easier to endure (*alleviate the pain following surgery*); **allay**

is often used interchangeably, but it also means to put to rest, to quiet or calm (*to allay their suspicions*). **Assuage** and *allay* both suggest the calming or satisfying of a desire or appetite, but *assuage* implies a more complete or permanent satisfaction (*we allay our hunger by nibbling hors d'oeuvres, but a huge dinner assuages our appetite*). To **relieve** implies reducing the misery or discomfort to the point where something is bearable (*relieve the monotony of the cross-country bus trip*) and **mitigate**, which comes from a Latin word meaning to soften, usually means to lessen in force or intensity (*mitigate the storm's impact*). **Abate** suggests a progressive lessening in degree or intensity (*her fever was abating*). To **temper** is to soften or moderate (*to temper justice with mercy*), but it can also mean the exact opposite: to harden or toughen something (*tempering steel; a body tempered by lifting weights*).

alley *noun* alleyway, lane, passage, passageway, path, pathway, corridor, backstreet.

alliance *noun* **1** *form an alliance* | *working in alliance with the French* union, association, coalition, league, confederation, federation, partnership, affiliation. **2** *the alliance between physics and math* affinity, association, relationship.

allied *adjective a union of allied industries* associated, related, connected, linked, kindred.

allocate *verb* allot, assign, distribute, give out, share/mete/parcel out, dispense, apportion.

allocation *noun* **1** *spend our allocation for the year* allowance, quota, share, ration, portion, lot. **2** *the allocation of resources* allotment, assignment, distribution, giving out, apportionment. *See* ALLOCATE.

allot *verb* **1** *we allotted money for expenses* set aside, designate, earmark, assign, appropriate. **2** *allot portions to everyone* allocate, distribute, give out, dispense, apportion. *See* ALLOCATE.

allotment *noun* **1** *the allotment of money for expenses* setting aside, appropriation. *See* ALLOT 1. **2** *the allotment of portions* allocation, distribution, dispensing, apportionment. *See* ALLOT 2. **3** *your allotment for the year* allocation, allowance, quota. *See* ALLOCATION 1.

all-out *adjective* thorough, thoroughgoing, complete, total, exhaustive, vigorous, determined.

allow *verb* **1** *allow them to enter* permit, give permission to, let, authorize, sanction; *inf.* give the go-ahead to, give the green light to. **2** *allow $50 for expenses* allocate, allot, grant, give, assign, remit, spare. **3** *I allow that you won* admit, acknowledge, concede, grant, own, confess, agree. **allow for** *allow for wastage* plan for, take into consideration/account, make provision for, provide for.

Antonyms: PREVENT; FORBID; DENY.

allowable *adjective allowable expenses* permis-

sible, admissible, authorized, sanctioned, justifiable, legitimate, lawful, legal; *inf.* legit.

allowance *noun* **1** *father gives her an allowance* remittance, payment, subsidy, grant, contribution. **2** *our book allowance* allocation, quota, share, ration, portion. **3** *tax/business allowances* rebate, discount, deduction, reduction, concession. **make allowances for** **1** *make allowances for his youth* take into consideration/account, bear in mind, have regard to. **2** *make allowances for him* make excuses for, excuse, forgive, pardon.

alloy *noun* compound, mixture, amalgam, blend, combination, admixture, composite.

all right *adjective* **1** *the children are all right* safe, safe and sound, secure, unharmed, uninjured, well, fine; *inf.* OK, okay. **2** *the coffee's all right?* satisfactory, acceptable, adequate, fine, passable; *inf.* OK, okay.

all right *adverb* **1** *reached home all right* safely; *inf.* OK, okay. **2** *worked out all right* satisfactorily, acceptably, fine; *inf.* OK, okay.

all right *interjection all right! I'll go* yes, very well; *inf.* OK, okay.

allude *verb* **allude to** refer to, mention, touch upon, mention in passing, make an allusion to, cite.

allure *verb* attract, fascinate, entice, seduce, charm, enchant, bewitch, beguile, captivate, tempt, lure.

alluring *adjective* attractive, fascinating, charming, enchanting, captivating.

allusion *noun* reference, citation, mention, hint, intimation, suggestion.

ally *noun* confederate, partner, associate, accomplice, colleague, friend, helper, accessory, abettor.

Antonyms: ENEMY; OPPONENT; ADVERSARY.

ally *verb allied with France* unite, join, join forces, band together, go into partnership, combine, go into league, affiliate, form an alliance.

almanac *noun* yearbook, calendar, register, annual, annals.

almighty *adjective* **1** *Almighty God* all-powerful, omnipotent, supreme, most high. **2** *an almighty crisis* terrible, awful, dreadful, great, extreme.

almost *adverb* nearly, close to, just about, not quite, all but, not far from, approximately, practically, as good as, virtually, approaching, verging on, bordering on.

alone *adjective/adverb* **1** *be alone in the house* by oneself, solitary, unaccompanied, unattended, unescorted, companionless. **2** *succeed alone* by oneself, single-handed, single-handedly, unassisted, unaided. **3** *left (all) alone* solitary, lonely, deserted, abandoned, forsaken, forlorn, desolate, isolated. **4** *house standing alone* by itself, separate, detached, apart, unconnected. **5** *in his field the professor stands alone* unique, unparalleled, unequaled, unsurpassed, matchless, peerless. **6** *you alone can help* only, solely, just, exclusively, no one else but, nothing but.

along *preposition* **1** *walk along the corridor/road* throughout the length of, from one end of to the other, through. **2** *grew along the fence* beside, by the side of, alongside, close by, on the edge of. **3** *somewhere along the way* in the course of, during, in the middle of.

along *adverb* **1** *move along* on, onward, ahead, forward. **2** *bring a friend along* in accompaniment, in company, as a partner. **along with** *poverty along with illness* together with, in addition to, plus, coupled with, accompanying, accompanied by.

aloof *adverb* *stand aloof* at a distance, apart, separately, distanced, at arm's length.

aloof *adjective* *she's rather aloof* distant, detached, unresponsive, remote, unapproachable, standoffish, indifferent, unsympathetic, unsociable, unfriendly, cold, chilly.

aloud *adverb* out loud, audibly, clearly, distinctly, plainly, intelligibly.

already *adverb* **1** *known already* by this time, by now, before, before now, previously. **2** *young children reading already* as early as this, as soon as this, so soon, so early.

also *adverb* **1** *come along also* too, as well, besides, in addition, additionally, on top of that, to boot. **2** *also, he's ill* besides, furthermore, moreover, in addition, too, and, plus.

alter *verb* change, make different, adjust, adapt, modify, convert, reshape, remodel, vary, transform, transfigure, diversify, metamorphose.

alteration *noun* change, adjustment, adaptation, modification, conversion, variation, revision, amendment, transformation, transfiguration, metamorphosis.

altercation *noun* quarrel, argument, fight, squabble, fracas; *inf.* set-to.

alternate *adjective* **1** *alternate weeks* every other, every second. **2** *alternate joy and sadness* in rotation, rotating, occurring in turns, interchanging, following in sequence, sequential. **3** *take an alternate route* alternative, different. *See* ALTERNATIVE *adjective* 1.

alternate *verb* *rain and sun alternated | rain alternated with sunshine* take turns, rotate, interchange, oscillate.

alternative *adjective* **1** *an alternative route* another, other, second, different. **2** *alternative medicine* nonstandard, unconventional, nonconventional.

alternative *noun* **1** *no alternative but to go* choice, option. **2** *have the alternative of going* choice, option, preference, election, substitute.

alternatively *adverb* *alternatively, you can stay* on the other hand, otherwise, instead, if not, or, as an alternative.

although *conjunction* though, even though, even if, even supposing, despite the fact that, while, whilst, albeit, notwithstanding the fact that.

altitude *noun* height, elevation; tallness, loftiness.

altogether *adverb* **1** *not altogether happy* completely, thoroughly, totally, entirely, absolutely, fully, utterly, perfectly, quite. **2** *altogether the day was fine* on the whole, all things considered, all in all, by and large, in general, in the main. **3** *nine of us altogether* in all, all told, *in toto*, taken together, in sum.
Antonyms: PARTIALLY; RELATIVELY.

altruistic *adjective* unselfish, self-sacrificing, selfless, nonegotistical, public-spirited, philanthropic, humanitarian, benevolent, charitable, openhanded.
Antonym: SELFISH.

always *adverb* **1** *he always comes early* every time, on every occasion, consistently, invariably, without exception, regularly, repeatedly, unfailingly. **2** *she's always complaining* continually, constantly, forever, repeatedly, perpetually, incessantly, eternally. **3** *you can always go by bus* whatever the circumstances, no matter what, in any event, in any case, come what may. **4** *he will love her always* forever, forever and ever, evermore, eternally, ever, everlastingly, endlessly.
Antonyms: SELDOM; NEVER; TEMPORARILY.

amalgamate *verb* combine, merge, unite, integrate, fuse, blend, mingle, intermingle, mix, intermix, incorporate; *lit.* commingle.

amass *verb* collect, gather, accumulate, pile/heap up, hoard, store up, assemble, garner; *inf.* stash away.

amateur *noun* nonprofessional, dilettante, layman, tyro, dabbler.
Antonyms: PROFESSIONAL; EXPERT.

amateurish *adjective* unprofessional, unskillful, inexperienced, inexpert, incompetent, clumsy, crude, bungling.

amaze *verb* astonish, astound, surprise, dumbfound, flabbergast, daze, shock, stun, startle, bewilder, stupefy; *inf.* bowl over, strike dumb.

amazement *noun* astonishment, surprise, shock, bewilderment, stupefaction, wonder. *See* AMAZE.

ambassador *noun* diplomat, consul, envoy, emissary, legate, attaché, plenipotentiary, representative, deputy.

ambiguity *noun* **1** *the ambiguity of his remark* equivocacy, ambivalence, two-edgedness. **2** *the ambiguity of his meaning* doubtfulness, obscurity, unclearness, vagueness, uncertainty, abstruseness. *See* AMBIGUOUS 2. **3** *full of ambiguities* equivocation, double-talk, obscurity, doubt, uncertainty, puzzle, enigma, paradox.

ambiguous *adjective* **1** *we misunderstood because his remark was ambiguous* equivocal, ambivalent, two-edged. **2** *his meaning was ambiguous* cryptic, obscure, doubtful, dubious, unclear, vague, uncertain, indefinite, abstruse, puzzling, perplexing, enigmatic, paradoxical.
Antonyms: CLEAR; UNEQUIVOCAL; DEFINITE.

ambition *noun* **1** *full of ambition to succeed* desire, aspiration, drive, striving, force, enterprise, eagerness, zeal, longing, yearning, hankering;

inf. get-up-and-go, oomph. **2** *her ambition is to be boss* goal, aim, objective, purpose, intent, desire, wish, design, end, dream, hope.

ambitious *adjective* **1** *an ambitious man* aspiring, forceful, enterprising, zealous, purposeful, assertive, designing; *inf.* pushy. **2** *an ambitious task* challenging, demanding, exacting, formidable, arduous, difficult, bold.
Antonyms: AIMLESS; APATHETIC; EASY.

ambivalent *adjective an ambivalent attitude* equivocal, uncertain, doubtful, indecisive, inconclusive, irresolute, unresolved, hesitating, fluctuating, vacillating, mixed, opposing, conflicting, clashing.
Antonyms: UNEQUIVOCAL; CERTAIN; CONCLUSIVE.

amble *verb* stroll, saunter, dawdle, wander, ramble; *inf.* mosey along.

ambush *noun* **1** *wait in ambush* hiding, concealment, cover, shelter. **2** *lay an ambush* trap, snare, pitfall, lure.

ambush *verb ambush the soldiers* waylay, lay a trap for, lie in wait for, trap, entrap, ensnare, decoy.

amenable *adjective* **1** *find her amenable to suggestion* tractable, agreeable, responsive, pliant, flexible, persuadable, adaptable, acquiescent, manageable, susceptible. **2** *amenable to the law* accountable, answerable, subject, liable, responsible.
Antonyms: INFLEXIBLE; OBSTINATE.

amend *verb* **1** *amend a text* revise, alter, correct, modify, change, adjust. **2** *amend the situation* improve, remedy, ameliorate, better, fix, set right, repair, enhance.

amendment *noun* **1** *the amendment of the text* revision, alteration, correction, modification, adjustment. **2** *the amendment of the situation* improvement, remedying, amelioration, betterment, fixing. *See* AMEND 2. **3** *amendments to the bylaws* alteration, addendum, addition, adjunct, attachment, appendage.

amends *plural noun make amends for the mistake* compensation, recompense, reparation.

amenity *noun* **1** *amenities provided by the hotel* facility, service, convenience, resource, advantage. **2** *the amenity of his surroundings* pleasantness, agreeableness, pleasurableness, enjoyableness, niceness.

amiable *adjective* friendly, pleasant, agreeable, pleasing, charming, delightful, good-natured, sociable, genial, congenial.
Antonyms: UNFRIENDLY; DISAGREEABLE.

amicable *adjective an amicable settlement* friendly, good-natured, civil, harmonious, cordial, nonhostile, peaceful.
Antonyms: UNFRIENDLY; HOSTILE.

amid *preposition* in the midst of, amidst, in the middle/course of, among, amongst, in the thick of.

amiss *adjective something was amiss* | *flowers wouldn't seem amiss* wrong, awry, faulty, out of order, defective, unsatisfactory, incorrect, inappropriate.

ammunition *noun* **1** *running out of ammunition for the guns* projectiles; bullets, cartridges, shells, shot, slugs, grenades, gunpowder, powder, bombs, missiles. **2** *his speech ran out of ammunition* information, data, input; pointers, points, arguments, advantages.

amnesty *noun* general pardon, pardon, pardoning, reprieve; absolution, forgiveness, dispensation, indulgence.

amok *adverb* frenziedly, in a frenzy, berserk, wildly, uncontrollably, maniacally, crazily, insanely, violently, destructively.

among, amongst *preposition* **1** *live among trees/friends* in the midst of, amid, amidst, in the middle of, surrounded by, in the thick of. **2** *divide it among you* between, to each of. **3** *among us was a doctor* included in, out of, in the group of, in the number of, in the company of. **4** *decide among yourselves* by the joint action of, by all of, by the whole of, with one another, together, mutually, reciprocally.

amorous *adjective* loving, passionate, sexual, lustful, erotic, amatory.

amorphous *adjective* formless, unformed, shapeless, unshaped, structureless, unstructured, indeterminate, ill-organized, vague, nebulous; *fml.* inchoate.

amount *noun* **1** *a large amount of money/fog/experience* quantity, measure, mass, volume, bulk, expanse, extent. **2** *calculated the (full) amount* total, grand/sum total, aggregate; *inf.* whole kit and caboodle, whole shebang.

amount *verb* **amount to** **1** *the bill amounted to $50* add up to, total, come to, run to. **2** *their silence amounts to a confession* equal, add up to, be equivalent to, correspond to, approximate to. **3** *he never amounted to anything* become, grow/develop/mature into, progress/advance to.

ample *adjective* **1** *ample food to live on* enough, sufficient, adequate, plenty (of), more than enough, enough and to spare. **2** *an ample supply of wine* plentiful, abundant, copious, lavish, generous, liberal, profuse, bountiful, plenteous. **3** *of ample proportions* | *an ample bed* large, big, substantial, extensive, wide, spacious, roomy, capacious, commodious.
Antonyms: INSUFFICIENT; SCANTY; MEAGER.

amplify *verb* **1** *amplify the sound/signal* increase, boost, magnify, intensify, heighten, augment, supplement. **2** *amplify your statement* expand, enlarge on, elaborate on, add to, develop, flesh out, go into detail about, expound on, explicate.
Antonyms: REDUCE; CONDENSE.

amputate *verb* cut off, sever, remove, excise, lop, lop off, dismember.

amuse *verb* **1** *the clowns amused them* entertain, gladden, cheer, please, charm, delight, divert, beguile, enliven, regale with. **2** *amuse yourselves when I'm out* occupy, interest, entertain, divert, absorb, engross.

Antonyms: BORE; DEPRESS.

amusement *noun* **1** *smiling with amusement* mirth, laughter, fun, merriment, gaiety, hilarity, enjoyment, pleasure, delight. **2** *provide a range of amusements* entertainment, diversion, interest, recreation, sport, pastime, hobby. **3** *the amusement of the children* entertaining, entertainment, diverting. *See* AMUSE 1.

amusing *adjective* *an amusing tale/storyteller* humorous, funny, comical, witty, entertaining, hilarious, facetious, droll, jocular.
Antonyms: BORING; TEDIOUS; SOLEMN.

analogous *adjective* similar, parallel, comparable, like, corresponding, related, kindred, matching, equivalent.

analogy *noun* similarity, parallel, correspondence, likeness, resemblance, correlation, relation, equivalence, similitude.

analysis *noun* **1** *carry out analysis of the sample/structure* breakdown, dissection, fractionation, decomposition, assay, examination; *fml.* anatomization. **2** *the analysis of the debate* study, examination, investigation, inquiry, dissection, review, evaluation, interpretation.

analytical, analytic *adjective* *an analytical mind/approach* investigative, inquiring, dissecting, inquisitive, searching, critical, interpretative, diagnostic.

analyze *verb* **1** *analyze the sample/structure* break down, dissect, separate out, fractionate, assay, decompose, examine; *fml.* anatomize. **2** *analyze the results of the debate* study, examine, investigate, inquire into, dissect, review, evaluate, interpret.

anarchic *adjective* lawless, ungoverned.

anarchist *noun* revolutionist, revolutionary, nihilist, rebel, insurgent, terrorist.

anarchy *noun* **1** *state of anarchy in the country* absence of government, nihilism, lawlessness, misgovernment, misrule, revolution. **2** *anarchy in the classroom* riot, disorder, chaos, rebellion, mutiny, tumult, mayhem, insurrection, disorganization.
Antonyms: LAW; ORDER; GOVERNMENT.

anathema *noun* **1** *racism is anathema to them* abomination, abhorrence, aversion, bane, bugbear, bête noir. **2** *following an anathema of the Church* excommunication, damnation, proscription, denunciation, curse, ban, malediction.

anatomy *noun* **1** *the anatomy of dogs* structure, makeup, composition, framework. **2** *undertake the anatomy of the animal/plant* dissection, cutting up, division, dismemberment, vivisection. **3** *the anatomy of crime* analysis, examination, study, investigation, scrutiny, research, inquiry.

ancestor *noun* forebear, progenitor, forerunner, precursor, prototype.
Antonym: DESCENDANTS; SUCCESSOR.

ancestral *adjective* *ancestral home* inherited, hereditary, lineal.

ancestry *noun* **1** *of noble ancestry* lineage, descent, extraction, parentage, origin, derivation, genealogy, pedigree, blood, stock. **2** *research into one's ancestry* ancestors, antecedents, forefathers, forebears, progenitors; family tree.

anchor *noun* **1** *a ship's anchor* mooring, kedge, kedge anchor, grapnel. **2** *mother was the family's anchor* mainstay, support, protection; stability, security.

anchor *verb* **1** *anchor the boat* secure by anchor, secure, fasten, moor. **2** *anchor the bush to a trellis* fasten, attach, connect, bind, affix.

ancient *adjective* **1** *in ancient times* earliest, early, of longago, primeval, prehistoric, primordial. **2** *an ancient custom* age-old, time-worn, antique, long-lived, very old. **3** *positively ancient ideas* antiquated, old-fashioned, out of date, outmoded, archaic, bygone, obsolete, passé, superannuated, atavistic.
Antonyms: RECENT; MODERN; NEW.

ancillary *adjective* auxiliary, secondary, subsidiary, subordinate, accessory, contributory, supplementary, additional, extra, attendant.

and *conjunction* along with, with, together with, as well as, also, in addition to, including, plus.

anecdote *noun* story, tale, narrative, yarn, sketch, reminiscence.

anemic *adjective* **1** *anemic and frail* weak, pale, wan, colorless, pallid, ashen; *inf.* bloodless. **2** *an anemic effort/group* weak, feeble, powerless, impotent, ineffective, ineffectual, enervated.

anesthetic *noun* *give an anesthetic to the patient* narcotic, opiate, soporific, stupefacient, painkiller, sedative, analgesic; general anesthetic, local anesthetic.

anesthetic *adjective* *an anesthetic substance/effect* numbing, deadening, dulling, narcotic, opiate, soporific, stupefacient, painkilling, sedative, analgesic.

anew *adverb* again, afresh, once more, once again, over again.

angel *noun* **1** *heavenly angels* messenger of god, heavenly messenger; archangel, seraph, cherub. **2** *thanks! you're an angel* darling, dear, gem, saint, paragon. **3** *a play staged with an angel's help* backer, supporter, benefactor, promoter.

angelic *adjective* **1** *angelic beings* seraphic, cherubic, celestial, heavenly, ethereal; *fml.* empyrean. **2** *an angelic child* virtuous, innocent, pure, good, saintly, beautiful, adorable.

anger *noun* *shout in anger* annoyance, rage, fury, indignation, temper, wrath, exasperation, irritation, vexation, ire, ill humor, irritability, outrage, pique, spleen; *lit.* choler.

anger *verb* *it angered him* annoy, infuriate, enrage, exasperate, irritate, incense, madden, vex, outrage, provoke, nettle, rile, pique, gall.
Antonyms: PACIFY; PLACATE.

angle[1] *noun* **1** *a right angle | the angle of the walls* intersection, inclination; projection, corner, bend, fork, nook, niche, recess, elbow. **2** *take an angle on a news story* slant, spin, approach, viewpoint, standpoint, point of view, position, opinion.

angle² *verb* **1** *angle the rearview mirror* slant, tilt, slope, turn. **2** *angle a news item* slant, skew, distort.

angle³ *verb angle by the riverside* fish, cast, go fishing. **angle for** *angle for a compliment* seek, solicit, scheme for, aim for, fish for; *inf.* be after.

angry *adjective* annoyed, furious, infuriated, indignant, enraged, irate, wrathful, exasperated, irritated, irascible, heated, incensed, maddened, ill-humored, hot-tempered, outraged, vexed, provoked; *inf.* mad, hot under the collar; *fml.* choleric.
Antonyms: CALM; PLEASED.

angst *noun* anxiety, fear, apprehension, foreboding, disquiet.

anguish *noun* agony, suffering, torture, torment, pain, distress, misery, sorrow, grief, woe; pangs, throes.

angular *adjective* **1** *an angular shape* sharp-cornered, pointed, V-shaped, Y-shaped, forked, bifurcate. **2** *an angular physique* bony, gaunt, rawboned, rangy, scrawny, spare, skinny, lean.

animal *noun* **1** *plants and animals* beast, creature, brute. **2** *the man was an animal* beast, brute, monster, barbarian, savage, fiend; *inf.* swine.

animal *adjective* **1** *animal as opposed to plant characteristics* animalistic, zooid, zooidal. **2** *animal passions* carnal, sensual, fleshly, bodily, physical, brutish, bestial.

animate *verb* **1** *a smile animated her face* | *music animated the group* give life to, enliven, liven up, cheer up, gladden, vitalize; *inf.* pep up. **2** *fresh hope animated them* encourage, hearten, inspire, excite, fire, rouse, stir, stimulate, incite, energize.

animate *adjective something animate* living, alive, live, breathing.

animated *adjective* **1** *an animated discussion* lively, energetic, active, vigorous, excited, enthusiastic, spirited, fiery, passionate, dynamic, forceful, vital, fervent, vivacious, buoyant. **2** *an animated cartoon* moving.
Antonyms: APATHETIC; INACTIVE; SLUGGISH.

animation *noun the animation of the discussion* liveliness, energy, vigor, excitement, enthusiasm, fieriness, dynamism, passion, forcefulness, vitality, fervor, vivacity, buoyancy, verve, zest, sparkle; *inf.* zing.

annals *plural noun* archives, chronicles, records, accounts; register, history.

annex *verb* **1** *annex a garage to the house* add, attach, join, connect, append, adjoin, affix. **2** *annex a smaller country* take over, occupy, seize, conquer, appropriate, expropriate.

annex *noun a school annex* supplementary/additional building, extension, wing, ell.

annihilate *verb* destroy, wipe out, exterminate, decimate, eliminate, liquidate, abolish, obliterate, eradicate, extinguish, erase.
Antonyms: CREATE; BUILD; ESTABLISH.

annotate *verb annotate a text* gloss, comment on, add notes/footnotes to, explain, interpret, elucidate, explicate.

annotation *noun* **1** *annotations in the margin* note, comment, gloss, commentary, footnote, explanation, interpretation, observation, elucidation, explication. **2** *the annotation of the text* glossing, commenting on, explaining, explanation. *See* ANNOTATE.

announce *verb* **1** *announce the results* make known/public, give out, declare, intimate, proclaim, report, disclose, reveal, divulge, publicize, broadcast, publish, advertise, promulgate. **2** *announce a guest* give the name of, name, herald, usher in. **3** *cigar smoke announcing his approach* signal, indicate, signify, give notice of, warn, foretell, herald, betoken, augur, portend, harbinger.

---

announce
blazon, publish, proclaim, declare, promulgate
When you **announce** something, you communicate it in a formal and public manner, often for the first time (*to announce the arrival of the guest of honor*). But just how you go about announcing something depends on what you're trying to convey. If you want to make sure no one misses your message, use **blazon** (*signs along the highway blazoned the local farmers' complaints*). If you plan to make your views known to the general public through the medium of writing, use **publish** (*to publish a story on drunk driving in the local newspaper*). Use **proclaim** if you have something of great importance that you want to announce very formally and officially (*proclaim a national day of mourning*). Although **declare** also implies a very formal announcement (*declare war*), it can refer to any clear and explicit statement (*declare one's love*). **Promulgate** is usually associated with the communication of a creed, doctrine, or law (*promulgate the views of the Democratic Party*).

---

announcement *noun* **1** *the announcement of the results* declaration, intimation, proclamation, report, disclosure. *See* ANNOUNCE 1. **2** *make an announcement* | *give out an announcement* statement, report, intimation, bulletin, communiqué, message; information.

announcer *noun* commentator, presenter, newscaster, broadcaster, reporter, anchor, master of ceremonies, emcee, herald.

annoy *verb* **1** *their behavior annoyed her* irritate, exasperate, vex, ruffle, rile, irk, provoke, displease, anger, madden, rub one the wrong way, get on one's nerves; *inf.* get to, bug. **2** *don't annoy her when she's reading* bother, disturb, pester, worry, harass, trouble, plague, harry.

annoyance *noun* **1** *to our annoyance* irritation, exasperation, displeasure, anger, vexation, ire.

2 *an annoyance to work late* nuisance, pest, bother, trial, irritant; *inf.* pain, pain in the neck, hassle.

annual *adjective* **1** *annual report* yearly, once a year. **2** *annual subscription* year-long.

annually *adverb* **1** *payable annually* yearly, by the year, once a year, per annum. **2** *visit annually* once a year, every year, each year.

annul *verb* nullify, declare null and void, quash, cancel, invalidate, rescind, revoke, repeal, abrogate, void, negate.

anoint *verb* **1** *anoint the body* oil, apply ointment; spread over, smear, rub, embrocate. **2** *anoint the new priest* consecrate, sanctify, bless, ordain, hallow.

anomalous *adjective* abnormal, atypical, irregular, deviant, deviating, aberrant, exceptional, rare, unusual, eccentric, odd, bizarre, peculiar, inconsistent.
Antonyms: NORMAL; REGULAR.

anomaly *noun* abnormality, irregularity, deviation, aberration, departure, rarity, eccentricity, oddity, peculiarity, inconsistency.

anon *adverb* soon, shortly, presently, in a short time, in a little while, by and by, before long, ere long.

anonymous *adjective* *an anonymous donor* unnamed, nameless, unidentified, unknown, unspecified, undesignated, unacknowledged, uncredited, unsigned, incognito.

another *adjective* **1** *another chance* second, further, additional. **2** *it was another girl, not Jane* different, some other, not the same.

answer *noun* **1** *receive an answer* reply, response, acknowledgment, rejoinder, retort, riposte; *inf.* comeback. **2** *the answer to the clue* solution, explanation, resolution. **3** *his answer to the charge* defense, plea, refutation, rebuttal, vindication. **4** *his answer was to leave the room* reaction, response.
Antonyms: QUESTION; QUERY; PUZZLE.

answer *verb* **1** *answer a question/letter* reply to, respond to, acknowledge, come back to, make a rejoinder, retort, riposte. **2** *answer the bell/phone* respond to, react to. **3** *answer our requirements* meet, satisfy, fulfill, fill, measure up to, serve. **4** *answer for her crimes* pay, suffer, be punished, make amends, make reparation, atone. **5** *cannot answer for my sister* vouch for, be responsible for, be accountable for, be liable for, take the blame for; *inf.* take the rap for. **answer back** talk back, be impertinent, contradict, argue with, disagree with. **answer to 1** *answer to the description* fit, match, correspond to, be similar to, conform to, correlate to. **2** *answers to the name of Dave* respond to, reply to, recognize, acknowledge.

answerable *adjective* *answerable to the manager* | *answerable for your safety* responsible, accountable, liable.

antagonism *noun* hostility, opposition, animosity, antipathy, enmity, rivalry, competition, dissension, friction, conflict.

antagonist *noun* adversary, enemy, foe, opponent, rival, competitor, contender.

antagonistic *adjective* hostile, ill-disposed, opposed, dissenting, adverse, antipathetic, inimical, at odds with.
Antonyms: FRIENDLY; SYMPATHETIC.

antagonize *verb* arouse hostility/enmity in, alienate, put against, estrange; *fml.* disaffect.

antecedents *plural noun* **1** *inherited from his antecedents* ancestors, forefathers, forebears, predecessors. **2** *check his antecedents* record, history, past, background.

antedate *verb* **1** *antedate a check* backdate, predate, assign to an earlier date. **2** *antedate the Civil War* precede, predate, come/go before, anticipate.

antediluvian *adjective* **1** *in antediluvian times* prehistoric, primeval, primordial; *inf.* before the flood. **2** *antediluvian attitudes* antiquated, old-fashioned, outmoded, out-of-date, archaic, obsolete.

anteroom *noun* outer room, waiting room, reception area, vestibule, lobby, foyer; *fml.* antechamber.

anthem *noun* **1** *church anthems* hymn, psalm, song of praise, chorale, chant, canticle. **2** *a national anthem* song of praise, paean, state song.

anthology *noun* collection, compendium, treasury, compilation, miscellany, selection; *lit.* garland; *fml.* collectanea, ana, analects.

anticipate *verb* **1** *anticipate trouble* | *anticipate that trouble will occur* expect, foresee, predict, forecast; count on, look for, prepare for, await, contemplate. **2** *anticipating her birthday with pleasure* look forward to, await, look toward. **3** *anticipate his chess move* forestall, intercept, prevent, nullify; *inf.* beat one to it, beat to the draw on. **4** *anticipate the invention of radio* antedate, predate, come/go before, be earlier than.

anticipation *noun* **1** *in anticipation of success/war* expectation, prediction, preparation, awaiting, contemplation. **2** *full of anticipation before the party* expectancy, hope, hopefulness.

anticlimax *noun* letdown, disappointment, comedown; disillusionment.

antics *plural noun* pranks, capers, larks, tricks, romps, frolics; horseplay.

antidote *noun* **1** *an antidote to poison* antitoxin, countermeasure. **2** *an antidote to sadness* cure, remedy, corrective, countermeasure, counteragent.

antipathy *noun* aversion, hostility, dislike, enmity, opposition, antagonism, animosity, hatred, abhorrence, loathing, repugnance, animus.
Antonyms: LIKING; FRIENDSHIP; RAPPORT.

antiquated *adjective* *antiquated attitudes* out of date, old-fashioned, outmoded, passé, archaic, obsolete, antediluvian.

antique *adjective* **1** *antique furniture* antiquarian, old, vintage. **2** *antique customs* age-old, timeworn, early, earliest, prehistoric, primeval, primordial. **3** *antique attitudes* old-fashioned. *See* ANTIQUATED.

antique *noun the chair's an antique* heirloom, relic, curio, collectible, collector's item.

antiseptic *adjective* **1** *an antiseptic substance* disinfectant, germicidal, bactericidal. **2** *an antiseptic surface* sterile, germ-free, uncontaminated, unpolluted, aseptic, sanitary, hygienic. **3** *antiseptic surroundings* clinical, characterless, undistinguished, unexciting.

antiseptic *noun swab with antiseptic* disinfectant, germicide, bactericide.

antisocial *adjective* **1** *littering is antisocial* disruptive, disorderly, lawless, rebellious, asocial. **2** *feeling antisocial* unsociable, uncommunicative, reserved, unfriendly, withdrawn, retiring.

antithesis *noun* **1** *wrong is the antithesis of right* opposite, converse, reverse, inverse, other extreme. **2** *an attitude the antithesis of mine* opposite, contrast, contrariety, inverse, reversal.

anxiety *noun* **1** *anxiety about the future* worry, concern, uneasiness, apprehension, disquiet, nervousness, tenseness, misgiving, angst. **2** *full of anxiety to win* eagerness, desire, longing, yearning, avidity.

anxious *adjective* **1** *anxious about the future | anxious about her health* worried, concerned, uneasy, apprehensive, fearful, nervous, disturbed, tense. **2** *anxious to please* eager, keen, longing, yearning, avid.

Antonyms: CAREFREE; UNCONCERNED; NONCHALANT.

any *adjective* **1** *did you get any books/meat?* some, some of (the). **2** *any book will do* any one, whatever, whichever; *inf.* any old.

any *pronoun* **1** *there were many celebrities, but I did not recognize any* anyone, anybody, somebody, someone. **2** *don't give him any* even one, even the smallest amount.

any *adverb is your father any better?* at all, in the least, to any extent, to some extent, somewhat, in any degree.

anyhow *adverb* **1** *go anyhow you like* in any way, anyway, in any manner, by any means. **2** *anyhow, you must go* in any case, in any event, no matter what. **3** *lying around anyhow* haphazardly, carelessly, heedlessly, negligently.

apart *adverb* **1** *with feet apart* separate, separately, separated, at a distance. **2** *a person/house standing apart* to one side, aside, to the side, separately, alone, by oneself/itself, distant, isolated. **3** *a couple living apart* separate, separately, separated, divorced, not together. **4** *blow/break apart* to pieces, in pieces, to bits, asunder. **apart from** *no one apart from him* except, but, other than, aside from, excluding, not counting, save.

apartment *noun* living quarters, quarters, rooms, suite, flat; apartment building; *inf.* pad, digs.

apathetic *adjective* uninterested, unmoved, unconcerned, unfeeling, unemotional, emotionless, unresponsive, indifferent, impassive, passive, listless, lethargic, languid, phlegmatic, torpid.

apathy *noun* lack of interest/concern/feeling/emotion, unconcern, unresponsiveness, indifference, impassivity, passivity, dispassion, dispassionateness, listlessness, lethargy, languor, torpor.

Antonyms: ENTHUSIASM; EMOTION; PASSION.

ape *verb* imitate, mimic, copy, echo, mock, parody, parrot.

aperture *noun* opening, gap, hole, orifice, window, crack, slit, space, chink, fissure, perforation, breach, eye, interstice.

apex *noun* top, summit, peak, pinnacle, tip, crest, vertex, acme, zenith, apogee.

aphrodisiac *noun* love potion, philter, stimulant, stimulative.

apiece *adverb* each, for/from/to each, respectively, individually, separately.

aplomb *noun* poise, assurance, self-confidence, self-assurance, calmness, composure, collectedness, equanimity, levelheadedness, sangfroid.

apocryphal *adjective* **1** *apocryphal evidence* unverified, unauthenticated, unsubstantiated, spurious, debatable, questionable, dubious, doubtful. **2** *apocryphal tales of his sexual prowess* mythical, fictitious, legendary, false, untrue, phony.

apologetic *adjective* sorry, regretful, contrite, remorseful, penitent, repentant, rueful.

Antonyms: UNREPENTANT; IMPENITENT.

apologize *verb* say one is sorry, make an apology, express regret, ask forgiveness, ask for pardon, beg pardon; *inf.* eat humble pie.

apology *noun* **1** *deliver an apology* expression of regret; regrets. **2** *present my apologies for my absence* excuses. **3** *an/the apology for their beliefs* defense, vindication, justification, argument, apologia; plea, excuse. **apology for** *an apology for a man/meal* travesty of, poor excuse for, excuse for, mockery of, caricature of, imitation of, substitute for, makeshift, stopgap.

apostle *noun* **1** *Christian apostles* missionary, evangelical, evangelist, preacher, teacher, reformer, spreader of the faith/word; *fml.* proselytizer. **2** *an apostle of acupuncture* advocate, supporter, crusader, campaigner, proponent, propagandist, pioneer.

appall *verb* shock, dismay, horrify, outrage, astound, alarm.

appalling *adjective* shocking, horrifying, frightful, outrageous, terrible, awful, dreadful, ghastly, hideous, harrowing, dire.

apparatus *noun* **1** *laboratory/gymnastic apparatus* equipment, gear, tackle, mechanism, outfit, plant; appliance, machine, device, contraption; instruments, tools. **2** *the apparatus of government* structure, system, organization, network, setup, hierarchy.

apparel *noun* clothing, dress, attire, outfit, wear,

costume, garb, habit; clothes, garments, robes, vestments; *inf.* gear, togs.

apparent *adjective* **1** *problems apparent from the start* clear, plain, obvious, evident, discernible, perceivable, perceptible, manifest, patent. **2** *apparent calmness* seeming, ostensible, outward, superficial, specious, quasi.

apparently *adverb* *apparently he's ill* seemingly, it seems that, it appears that, on the face of it.

apparition *noun* **1** *frightened of the apparition* ghost, specter, phantom, spirit; *inf.* spook. **2** *the sudden apparition of the black figure* appearance, manifestation, materialization, emergence, visitation.

appeal *noun* **1** *an appeal for help* request, call, plea, entreaty, petition, supplication, solicitation, imploration. **2** *attorney asking for an appeal* reconsideration, reexamination, review, another opinion. **3** *hold little appeal* attraction, attractiveness, allure, charm, interest, fascination, temptation, enticement.

appeal *verb* **appeal for** *appeal for money* ask for, request, put in a plea for, entreat, beg/beseech/plead for, implore, solicit, petition for. **appeal to 1** *appeal to a higher court* apply for an appeal, seek reconsideration/reexamination/review/another opinion from. **2** *appeals to her* attract, charm, interest, engage, fascinate, tempt, entice, allure, invite.

appear *verb* **1** *a messenger/solution appeared* come into view/sight, emerge, come forth, arrive, turn/show/crop up, materialize, surface, loom. **2** *he may appear in time to start the meeting* attend, be present, turn up; *inf.* show up, show. **3** *she appeared sad* seem, look, have the appearance/air of being, give the impression of being. **4** *the new line of spring fashions finally appeared | has his new book appeared?* come into being/existence, come out, become available, come on the market, be published/produced. **5** *she appears nightly* perform, play, act, take part, be on stage, come on.
Antonyms: DISAPPEAR; VANISH.

appearance *noun* **1** *the appearance of the messenger/solution* coming into view, emergence, arrival, advent, materialization, surfacing, looming. *See* APPEAR 1. **2** *his weekly appearance at meetings* attendance, presence, turning up. *See* APPEAR 2. **3** *having an appearance of sadness* look, air, expression, impression, manner, demeanor, bearing, aspect; *lit.* mien. **4** *poor but giving the appearance of being rich* semblance, guise, show, pretense, image, outward appearance, front, impression.

appease *verb* **1** *appease the enemy with gifts* placate, pacify, make peace with, conciliate, calm, tranquilize, soothe, quiet down, mollify, soften, propitiate. **2** *appease one's appetite/curiosity* satisfy, assuage, take the edge off, blunt, relieve, quench, diminish.

appeasement *noun* **1** *policy of appeasement* conciliation, placation, concession, acquiescence, acceding, peace offering, accommodation, propitiation. **2** *the appeasement of the enemy* placating, pacification, conciliation, calming. *See* APPEASE 1. **3** *the appeasement of one's appetite* satisfying, assuagement. *See* APPEASE 2.

append *verb* *append one's signature | append a clause* add, attach, affix, adjoin.

appendage *noun* **1** *an appendage to a will/family* addition, attachment, adjunct, addendum, appurtenance, accessory. **2** *an animal's appendage* extremity, protuberance, projection, member, limb, tail.

appendix *noun* *appendix to a book* supplement, addendum, postscript, addition, extension, adjunct, codicil.

appertain *verb* **appertain to** belong to, relate to, be connected with, be part of, be relevant to, have relevance to, have to do with, be pertinent to, have reference to, have a bearing upon.

appetite *noun* **1** *an appetite for food* hunger, taste, palate, desire, relish. **2** *an appetite for adventure* hunger, thirst, need, liking, inclination, passion, longing, craving, yearning, hankering, zest, gusto, propensity, proclivity.

appetizer *noun* starter, hors d'oeuvre, antipasto, canapé.

appetizing *adjective* **1** *an appetizing dish* mouthwatering, tasty, succulent, delicious, palatable. **2** *an appetizing prospect* tempting, inviting, enticing, appealing, alluring.

applaud *verb* **1** *the audience applauded* clap, cheer, whistle, give a standing ovation to, ask for an encore, put one's hands together; *inf.* give someone a big hand. **2** *applaud their courage* praise, express admiration/approval for, admire, compliment on, commend, acclaim, extol, laud.
Antonyms: HISS; CONDEMN; CENSURE.

applause *noun* **1** *the applause of the audience* clapping, handclapping, cheering, whistling, standing ovation; cheers, whistles, encores, bravos, curtain calls. **2** *won the applause of the neighborhood* praise, admiration, approval, approbation, commendation, acclaim, acclamation, extolment, laudation; compliments, accolades, plaudits.

appliance *noun* **1** *an electrical appliance* device, gadget, convenience, apparatus, implement, machine, instrument, tool, mechanism. **2** *the appliance of force* application, use. *See* APPLICATION 1.

applicable *adjective* **1** *rules applicable to everyone* relevant, appropriate, pertinent, apposite, apropos. **2** *an applicable remedy* fitting, suitable, useful.
Antonyms: INAPPLICABLE; IRRELEVANT.

applicant *noun* candidate, interviewee, competitor, inquirer, claimant, suppliant, supplicant, petitioner, suitor, postulant.

application *noun* **1** *the application of force* use, exercise, administration, employment, putting into operation/practice, practice. **2** *a remark* *having no application to the case* relevance, bearing, significance, pertinence, aptness, appositeness, germaneness. **3** *the application of ointment* putting on, rubbing in. *See* APPLY 3. **4** *students with application* industry, diligence, attentiveness, effort, hard work, assiduity, commitment, dedication, perseverance, persistence, sedulousness. **5** *an application for a job* | *application for a tax rebate* request, claim, appeal, petition, entreaty, suit, solicitation, requisition, demand. **6** *a healing application* ointment, lotion, cream, rub, emollient, balm, poultice, unguent.

apply *verb* **1** *apply force/tact* | *apply the brakes* use, put to use, employ, utilize, administer, exercise, put into practice, bring into effect/play, bring to bear. **2** *the remark did not apply to the situation* be relevant/significant/pertinent, be apt/apposite/germane, have a bearing on. **3** *apply ointment* put on, rub in, cover with, spread, smear. **apply for** *apply for a job* | *apply for tax relief* make out/put in an application for, put in for, try for, inquire after, request, claim, seek, appeal for, petition for, make an entreaty for, solicit. **apply oneself** be industrious/diligent/assiduous, study, work hard, make an effort, pay attention, be attentive, commit/devote oneself, persevere, persist, put one's shoulder to the wheel; *inf.* buckle down.

appoint *verb* **1** *appoint him manager* name, designate, nominate, select, choose, elect, install as. **2** *appoint a time* set, fix, arrange, choose, establish, settle, determine, assign, designate, allot.

appointment *noun* **1** *cancel an appointment* meeting, engagement, date, interview, arrangement, rendezvous, assignation; *lit.* tryst. **2** *his new appointment as manager* job, post, position, situation, place, office, station. **3** *the appointment of him as boss* naming, nomination, selection. *See* APPOINT 1. **4** *the appointment of a time* setting, arrangement, establishment. *See* APPOINT 2.

apportion *verb* allocate, distribute, share, divide (out), hand/deal out, ration/mete/dole out, allot, dispense, assign.

apposite *adjective* appropriate, suitable, fitting, apt, relevant, to the point, pertinent, applicable, germane.

appraisal *noun* **1** *make an appraisal of the house* valuation, pricing, survey. **2** *an appraisal of their ability* assessment, evaluation, summing-up, estimation, estimate, judgment, sizing-up.

appraise *verb* **1** *appraise the property* value, survey, price, set a price on. **2** *appraise his ability* assess, evaluate, sum up, estimate, gauge, judge, review; *inf.* size up.

appreciable *adjective* *an appreciable amount* considerable, substantial, significant, sizable, visible, goodly.

appreciate *verb* **1** *appreciate your help* be appre-
ciative of, be thankful/grateful for, give thanks for, be indebted/beholden for. **2** *appreciate good staff/wine* value, hold in high regard, hold in esteem, prize, cherish, treasure, rate highly, respect, think highly of, think much of. **3** *appreciate the importance of* recognize, acknowledge, realize, know, be aware of, be conscious/cognizant of, understand, comprehend, perceive, discern. **4** *the house appreciated in value* increase, gain, grow, rise, mount, inflate, escalate.

Antonyms: DISPARAGE; IGNORE; DEPRECIATE.

appreciation *noun* **1** *express his appreciation for their help* gratitude, gratefulness, thankfulness, indebtedness, obligation. **2** *the appreciation of good staff/wine* valuing, esteem, regard, prizing, respect. *See* APPRECIATE 2. **3** *the appreciation of its importance* recognition, acknowledgment, realization, knowledge, awareness, consciousness, cognizance, comprehension, perception, discernment. **4** *the appreciation of housing values* increase, rise, growth, gain, improvement, inflation, escalation. **5** *an appreciation of the poetry* review, critique, criticism, critical analysis, notice, commentary; praise, acclamation.

appreciative *adjective* **1** *your help has made me most appreciative* grateful, thankful, indebted, obliged, beholden. **2** *an appreciative audience* enthusiastic, responsive, supportive, encouraging, sympathetic, sensitive.

apprehend *verb* **1** *apprehend the criminal* arrest, catch, seize, capture, take prisoner, take into custody, haul in, detain; *inf.* collar, nab, nail, run in, bust. **2** *apprehend the significance* understand, grasp, realize, recognize, appreciate, comprehend, discern, perceive; *inf.* get the picture.

apprehension *noun* **1** *full of apprehension about the interview/future* anxiety, dread, alarm, worry, uneasiness, unease, nervousness, fear, misgiving, disquiet, concern, trepidation, perturbation, foreboding, presentiment, angst; nerves; *inf.* butterflies in the stomach, the willies, the heebie-jeebies. **2** *the apprehension of criminals* arrest, seizure, capture, detention; *inf.* collaring, nabbing, nailing. *See* APPREHEND 1. **3** *the apprehension of problems* understanding, realization, recognition, appreciation, comprehension, discernment, perception.

apprehensive *adjective* anxious, alarmed, worried, uneasy, nervous, frightened, fearful, mistrustful, concerned. *See* APPREHENSION 1.

apprentice *noun* trainee, learner, beginner, probationer, pupil, student, cub, greenhorn, tyro, novice, neophyte; *inf.* rookie.

apprise *verb* inform, notify, tell, let know; *inf.* clue in, fill in.

approach *verb* **1** *someone's approaching the house* come/go/draw near/nearer, come/go/draw close/closer, move/edge near/nearer, draw nigh, catch up, gain on, near, advance, push forward, reach, arrive. **2** *don't approach* *strangers in the street* talk/speak to, make conversation with, engage in conversation with, greet, address, salute, hail. **3** *approach them for a contribution* apply/appeal to, broach the matter to, make advances/overtures to, make a proposal to, sound out, proposition, solicit. **4** *approach the problem with care* set about, tackle, begin, start, commence, embark on, make a start on, undertake. **5** *a price approaching $600* come near/close to, approximate, be comparable/similar to, compare with.

Antonyms: LEAVE; AVOID.

approach *noun* **1** *the approach of footsteps* coming near/nearer, nearing, advance, advent, arrival. *See* APPROACH *verb* 1. **2** *the approach to the estate* driveway, drive, access road, road, avenue, street, passageway. **3** *make an approach to* | *make approaches* application, appeal, proposal, proposition; advances, overtures. **4** *the merest approach to a smile* approximation, likeness, semblance. **5** *a new approach to teaching* method, procedure, technique, style, way, manner, mode, modus operandi; means.

appropriate *adjective an appropriate time/remark* suitable, fitting, befitting, proper, seemly, right, apt, relevant, pertinent, apposite, applicable, congruous, opportune, felicitous, germane; *fml.* appurtenant.

Antonyms: INAPPROPRIATE; UNSUITABLE; IRRELEVANT.

appropriate *verb* **1** *appropriate a country/house* take possession of, take over, seize, commandeer, expropriate, annex, arrogate. **2** *appropriate money for education* set apart/aside, assign, allot, allocate, earmark, devote, apportion. **3** *appropriate company money* embezzle, misappropriate, steal, pilfer, filch, pocket, purloin; *inf.* pinch, swipe; *fml.* peculate.

approval *noun* **1** *look on with approval* favor, liking, approbation, acceptance, admiration, appreciation, regard, esteem, respect, commendation, applause, acclaim, acclamation, praise. **2** *give approval to the minutes/application* acceptance, agreement, consent, assent, sanction, endorsement, blessing, permission, leave, confirmation, ratification, authorization, mandate, license, validation, acquiescence, concurrence; *inf.* the go-ahead, the green light, the OK. **on approval** on trial, under probation.

approve *verb approve the minutes/application* accept, pass, agree to, sanction, consent/assent to, ratify, authorize, validate, accede to, acquiesce in, concur in, warrant; *inf.* give the go-ahead to, give the OK to, give the green light to, buy. **approve of** *approve of their behavior* think well of, like, look on with favor, give one's blessing to, be pleased with, admire, hold in regard/esteem, commend, favor, applaud, acclaim, praise.

Antonyms: CONDEMN; DISAPPROVE; REJECT.

approve
certify, commend, endorse, ratify, sanction

There are a number of ways to show your support for something. The most general way is to **approve** it, a term that covers everything from simple, technical agreement (*to approve the plan*) to enthusiastic support (*she was quick to approve her son's decision to marry*). **Endorse** implies a more public and official expression of support and is used primarily in reference to things that require promotion or publicity (*endorse a political candidate*), while **commend** is to make a formal and usually public statement of approval or congratulation (*he was commended for his heroism*). **Sanction, certify,** and **ratify** imply that approval is not only official but that it makes something legal. To *sanction* is not only to *approve* but to authorize (*school authorities would not sanction the wearing of hats in class*), while *certify* implies conformity with certain standards (*certified to teach in the State of New York*). *Ratify* is usually confined to only the most official and authoritative settings. For example, an employer might *sanction* the idea of hiring a woman to perform a job that only men have performed in the past, and the woman in question might have to *certify* that she possesses the necessary training and qualifications. But to *ratify* a constitutional amendment granting equal rights to women requires a lengthy set of legislative procedures.

approximate *adjective* **1** *the approximate price* rough, estimated, near, close, inexact. **2** *your approximate neighbor* adjacent, next-door, next, neighboring, near, nearby, close by, adjoining, contiguous.

approximate *verb approximating (to) the truth* be close/near to, come close/near to, approach, border on, verge on, resemble, be similar to.

approximately *adverb approximately 40 miles* roughly, about, just about, around, circa, or so, more or less, in the neighborhood of, in the region of, nearly, not far off, close to, near to, almost.

approximation *noun* **1** *200 is an approximation* guess, estimate, estimation, conjecture, rough calculation, rough idea; guesswork; *inf.* guesstimate. **2** *an approximation to the truth* semblance, similarity, likeness, correspondence. *See* APPROXIMATE *verb.*

appurtenances *plural noun* appendages, accouterments, accessories, belongings, trappings; equipment, paraphernalia, *inf.* stuff.

apropos *adjective the remark was extremely apropos* appropriate, pertinent, relevant, apposite, apt, applicable, germane. **apropos of** *apropos of that remark* concerning, with reference to, with regard/respect to, regarding, respecting, on the subject of, re.

apropos *adverb* **1** *talked apropos* appropriately,

pertinently. **2** *apropos, we're not going* by the way, incidentally.

apt *adjective* **1** *an apt remark* suitable, fitting, appropriate, applicable, apposite, felicitous, apropos. **2** *apt to get angry* inclined, given, likely, liable, disposed, prone, ready, subject. **3** *an apt student* quick to learn, quick, bright, sharp, clever, smart, intelligent, able, gifted, talented, adept, competent, astute.
Antonyms: INAPPROPRIATE; UNLIKELY; SLOW.

aptitude *noun an aptitude for drawing* talent, gift, flair, bent, skill, knack; ability, proficiency, quickness, competence, capability, potential, capacity, faculty.

aptness *noun* **1** *the aptness of the remark* suitability, appropriateness, applicability. *See* APT 1. **2** *the aptness of the student* quickness, brightness, sharpness, cleverness, intelligence. *See* APT 3.

aquatic *adjective aquatic plants/sports* water, sea, river, marine, maritime, fluvial.

aqueduct *noun* channel, conduit, race, watercourse, waterway, bridge.

arable *adjective* plowable, tillable, tilled, cultivated, cultivable, cultivatable, farmable; fertile, productive, fruitful, fecund.

arbiter *noun* **1** *an arbiter of fashion* authority, judge, determiner, controller, director, governor, master, expert, pundit. **2** *the arbiter in the case* adjudicator. *See* ARBITRATOR.

arbitrary *adjective* **1** *a completely arbitrary decision* discretionary, discretional, personal, subjective, random, chance, whimsical, capricious, erratic, inconsistent, unreasoned, unreasonable, unsupported, irrational. **2** *an arbitrary ruler* despotic, tyrannical, tyrannous, absolute, autocratic, dictatorial, imperious, domineering, high-handed.
Antonyms: OBJECTIVE; RATIONAL; REASONED.

arbitrate *verb* adjudicate, judge, referee, umpire, adjudge, sit in judgment, pass judgment, settle, decide, determine.

arbitration *noun* adjudication, judgment, settlement, decision, determination.

arbitrator *noun* adjudicator, judge, referee, umpire, arbiter.

arbor *noun* bower, alcove, grotto, recess.

arc *noun* curve, bow, arch, bend, crescent, half-moon, semicircle, circular section/line; curvature.

arcade *noun* gallery, colonnade, cloister, piazza, portico, shopping mall.

arcane *adjective* secret, mysterious, hidden, concealed, recondite, covert, enigmatic, inscrutable, abstruse, esoteric, cryptic, occult.

arch *noun* **1** *a bridge with three arches* archway, vault, span. **2** *the arch of the rainbow* arc, bow, curve, semicircle; curvature, convexity.

arch *verb the cat arched its back* curve, bow, bend, arc; *fml.* embow.

arch *adjective an arch smile* playful, mischievous,

roguish, saucy, artful, sly, knowing, frolicsome.

arch- *prefix archbishop | archenemy* chief, foremost, principal, leading, main, prime, primary, first, top, highest, greatest, preeminent.

archaic *adjective* old, obsolete, out of date, old-fashioned, outmoded, bygone, passé, antiquated, antique; *inf.* old hat.
Antonyms: NEW; MODERN; UP-TO-DATE.

arched *adjective* curved, vaulted, domed; *fml.* embowed.

archer *noun* bowman, toxophilite; Sagittarius, Orion.

archetype *noun* prototype, original, pattern, model, standard, exemplar, mold, paradigm, ideal.

architect *noun* **1** *the architect of the house* designer, planner, building consultant, draftsman. **2** *the architect of the scheme* author, engineer, creator, originator, planner, deviser, instigator, founder, inventor, contriver, prime mover.

architecture *noun* **1** *studying architecture* design, planning, building, construction. **2** *colonial architecture* construction, style, design, structure, framework.

archives *plural noun* **1** *study the firm's archives* records, annals, chronicles, papers, documents, registers, rolls; history, documentation. **2** *the archives are situated in the basement* records office, registry, museum, repository.

arctic *adjective* **1** *arctic regions* polar, far northern, northern; *fml.* boreal. **2** *arctic conditions* freezing, frigid, frozen, icy, glacial, frosty, chilly, cold; *fml.* gelid.

ardent *adjective* passionate, avid, impassioned, fervent, fervid, zealous, eager, earnest, enthusiastic, emotional, vehement, intense, fierce, fiery, profound, consuming.

ardor *noun* passion, avidity, fervor, zeal, eagerness, enthusiasm, earnestness, emotion, emotionalism, vehemence, intensity, fierceness, fire, fieriness, profundity.

arduous *adjective* taxing, difficult, hard, onerous, heavy, laborious, burdensome, exhausting, wearying, fatiguing, tiring, strenuous, grueling, punishing, vigorous, tough, formidable, Herculean.
Antonyms: EASY; EFFORTLESS.

area *noun* **1** *the area around the city* region, district, zone, sector, territory, tract, stretch, quarter, locality, neighborhood, domain, realm, sphere. **2** *the area of the room | the area of my knowledge* extent, size, expanse, scope, compass, range; measurements. **3** *specializing in the area of finance* field, sphere, discipline, realm, department, sector, province, domain, territory.

arena *noun* **1** *circus/boxing arena* grounds, field, stadium, ballpark, ring, stage, platform, amphitheater, coliseum; *inf.* park, bowl. **2** *the political arena* area/field of conflict, sphere of action/activity, battleground, battlefield, area, scene, sphere, realm, province, territory, domain, sector, theater.

argue *verb* **1** *the children are always arguing* disagree, quarrel, squabble, bicker, fight, dispute, feud. **2** *argue that they are right* assert, declare, maintain, insist, hold, claim, contend. **3** *argue the point/case* debate, dispute, discuss, controvert. **4** *argue him out of going* | *argue him into going* persuade, convince, prevail upon. **5** *the essay argued much research* point to, indicate, demonstrate, show, suggest, imply, exhibit, denote, be evidence of, display, evince.

argument *noun* **1** *the couple had an argument* disagreement, quarrel, squabble, fight, difference of opinion, dispute, clash, altercation, controversy, feud; *inf.* tiff, falling out. **2** *stick to the argument that they are right* assertion, declaration, claim, plea, contention. **3** *the argument against capital punishment* line of reasoning, reasoning, logic, case, defense, evidence, argumentation, polemic; reasons, grounds. **4** *the argument of the biography* theme, topic, subject matter, gist, outline, plot, story line, summary, synopsis, abstract, précis.

argumentative *adjective* quarrelsome, belligerent, disputatious, contentious, combative, litigious, dissentient.

arid *adjective* **1** *arid areas* dry, dried up, desert, waterless, moistureless, parched, baked, scorched, dehydrated, desiccated, barren. **2** *arid surroundings/discussion* uninspiring, unstimulating, dull, dreary, drab, dry, colorless, flat, boring, uninteresting, monotonous, lifeless, tedious, vapid, jejune.
Antonyms: WET; FERTILE; INTERESTING.

arise *verb* **1** *a difficulty arose* appear, come to light, make an appearance, crop/turn up, spring up, emerge, occur, ensue, set in, come into being/existence, begin. **2** *accidents arising from carelessness* result, be caused (by), proceed, follow, stem, originate, emanate, ensue. **3** *arise and go* rise, stand up, get to one's feet, get up. **4** *birds arising* rise, ascend, go up, mount, climb, fly, soar.

aristocracy *noun* nobility, peerage, gentry, upper class, privileged/ruling class, elite, high society; *inf.* upper crust, blue bloods; *lit.* haut monde.

aristocrat *noun* noble, nobleman, noblewoman, lord, lady, peer, peeress, patrician, Brahmin; *inf.* blue blood.

aristocratic *adjective* **1** *an aristocratic family* noble, titled, blue-blooded, high-born, upper-class, patrician, elite. **2** *aristocratic bearing/manners* well-bred, dignified, courtly, refined, elegant, stylish, gracious, fine, polite, haughty, proud.
Antonyms: PLEBEIAN; VULGAR.

arm *noun* **1** *arms and legs* limb, upper limb, forelimb, member, appendage. **2** *arm of the sea* inlet, estuary, channel, branch, strait, sound. **3** *an arm of the civil service* branch, offshoot, section, department, division, sector, detach-ment, extension. **4** *the arm of the law* power, force, authority, strength, might, potency.

arm *verb* **1** *arm with guns/information* provide, supply, equip, furnish, issue. **2** *arm oneself against criticism* prepare, forearm, make ready, brace, steel, fortify, gird one's loins.

armada *noun* fleet, flotilla, navy, squadron.

armaments *plural noun* arms, weapons, firearms, munitions; weaponry, ordnance, matériel.

armistice *noun* truce, ceasefire, peace, suspension of hostilities.

armor *noun* armor plate, protective covering, covering, protection, sheathing, mail, chain mail.

armory *noun* arms depot, ordnance depot, arsenal, magazine, ammunition dump.

arms *plural noun* **1** *carrying arms* weapons, firearms, guns, armaments; weaponry. **2** *the family arms* heraldic device, coat of arms, emblem, crest, insignia, escutcheon, shield, blazonry.

army *noun* **1** *the invading army* armed/military force, land force, soldiery, infantry; troops, soldiers, land forces; military. **2** *an army of tourists* horde, pack, host, multitude, mob, crowd, swarm, throng, array.

aroma *noun* smell, scent, odor, bouquet, fragrance, perfume, redolence.

aromatic *adjective* fragrant, sweet-smelling, scented, perfumed, balmy, piquant, spicy, savory, pungent, odoriferous.

around *preposition* **1** *around the tree* on all sides of, on every side of, circling, encircling, surrounding, encompassing. **2** *thrown around the room* about, here and there, all over, everywhere, in all parts of. **3** *around 9 o'clock* | *around three miles* about, approximately, roughly, close to, near to, nearly, circa. **4** *turn around* in the opposite direction, in reverse, backward, to the rear.

around *adverb* **1** *litter scattered around* about, here and there, all over, everywhere, in all directions, throughout. **2** *can't see anyone around* nearby, near, close by, close, at hand, at close range.

arouse *verb* **1** *arouse them at dawn* rouse, awaken, waken, wake, wake up. **2** *arouse panic* cause, induce, stir up, inspire, call forth, kindle, provoke, foster, whip up, sow the seeds of. **3** *arouse the crowd* rouse, incite, excite, provoke, goad, prompt, spur on, urge, encourage, egg on, animate, inflame, build a fire under. **4** *arouse sexually* excite, stimulate; *inf.* turn on.

arraign *verb* *arraign the assembled crowd* criticize, censure, find fault with, upbraid, reproach, rebuke, reprove, take to task. **arraign for** *arraign for murder* accuse of, charge with, lay charges against for, indict for, impeach.

arrange *verb* **1** *arrange the books/flowers* put in order, order, set out, group, sort, organize, tidy, position, dispose, marshal, range, align,

line up, rank, file, classify, categorize, array, systematize. **2** *arrange to meet* | *arrange an appointment* settle on, decide, determine, agree, come to an agreement, settle on, come to terms about, plan, schedule, devise, contrive. **3** *arrange for her to be met* make preparations, prepare, plan, organize. **4** *music arranged for the piano* score, adapt, orchestrate, harmonize.
Antonyms: DISARRANGE; DISTURB; CANCEL.

arrangement *noun* **1** *the arrangement of books/flowers* order, ordering, grouping, organization, positioning, system, disposition, marshalling, ranging, alignment, filing, classification, categorization, array. **2** *make an arrangement* | *make arrangements* preparation, plan, provision; agreement, contract, compact. **3** *a musical arrangement* score, adaptation, orchestration, instrumentation, harmonization.

arrant *adjective* utter, downright, outright, absolute, out and out, rank, thorough, thoroughgoing, through and through, total, unmitigated, blatant, barefaced.

array *noun* **1** *an array of bottles/facts* collection, arrangement, assembling, assemblage, lineup, formation, ordering, disposition, muster, amassing, show, display, agglomeration, aggregation. **2** *in silken array* attire, apparel, clothing, dress, garb, finery; garments.

array *verb* **1** *the books/troops are arrayed* assemble, arrange, draw up, group, order, line up, place, position, dispose, muster, amass, agglomerate, aggregate. **2** *they were arrayed in silk* attire, clothe, dress, fit out, garb, deck, robe, apparel, accouter.

arrears *plural noun* **1** *pay the arrears* outstanding payment, debt, balance, deficit. **2** *arrears of work* backlog, accumulation, pile-up. **in arrears** behind, behindhand, late, overdue, in the red, in default, in debt.

arrest *verb* **1** *arrest the thief* apprehend, take into custody, take prisoner, detain, seize, capture, catch, lay hold of, haul in; *inf.* run in, nab, pinch, collar, bust, nail, pick up. **2** *arrest the spread of disease* stop, halt, end, bring to a standstill, check, block, hinder, delay, interrupt, prevent, obstruct, inhibit, slow down, retard, nip in the bud, stay. **3** *arrest their attention* attract, capture, catch, catch hold of, grip, engage, absorb, occupy, rivet, engross.

arrest *noun* **1** *the arrest of the thieves* apprehension, taking into custody, detention, seizure, capture; *inf.* running in. *See* ARREST *verb* 1. **2** *the arrest of the disease* stopping, stoppage, halt, ending, end, check, blocking, hindrance, delay, interruption, prevention, obstruction, retardation. *See* ARREST *verb* 2.

arresting *adjective* *an arresting face* striking, impressive, remarkable, extraordinary, unusual, noticeable, outstanding, conspicuous, stunning.

arrival *noun* **1** *the arrival of the guest/winter* coming, advent, appearance, entrance, entry, occurrence, approach. **2** *several recent arrivals* newcomer, visitor, visitant, guest, immigrant.

arrive *verb* **1** *the guests/winter arrived* come, appear, put in an appearance, come on the scene, enter, get here/there, happen, occur, present itself, turn/show up; *inf.* blow in. **2** *the actor has really arrived* succeed, make good, reach the top, prosper, flourish, get ahead, become famous, achieve recognition; *inf.* make it, make the grade, get somewhere.
Antonyms: DEPART; LEAVE.

arrogance *noun* haughtiness, pride, self-importance, conceit, egotism, snobbishness, snobbery, pomposity, superciliousness, high-handedness, condescension, disdain, imperiousness, lordliness, presumption, pretentiousness, swagger, bluster, bumptiousness, insolence; *inf.* uppitiness.

arrogant *adjective* haughty, proud, self-important, conceited, egotistic, snobbish, pompous, supercilious, overbearing, overweening, high-handed, condescending, disdainful, imperious, lordly, presumptuous, pretentious, swaggering, blustering, bumptious, insolent; *inf.* stuck-up, uppity, high and mighty.
Antonyms: MODEST; DIFFIDENT.

arrogate *verb* appropriate, assume, expropriate, seize, avail oneself of, commandeer.

arrow *noun* **1** *bow and arrow* shaft, bolt, dart. **2** *follow the arrows* pointer, indicator, marker.

arsenal *noun* **1** *weapons in the arsenal* arms depot, magazine, armory, ammunition dump, ordnance depot, repository. **2** *an arsenal of sharp remarks* store, supply, stock, stockpile, storehouse.

arson *noun* incendiarism, pyromania.

art *noun* **1** *studying art* painting, drawing, design; visual arts. **2** *the art of writing/conversation* skill, craft, aptitude, talent, flair, gift, knack, facility; artistry, mastery, dexterity, expertness, skillfulness, adroitness, cleverness, ingenuity, virtuosity. **3** *use art to win* artfulness, cunning, deceit, deception, wiliness, slyness, craft, craftiness, guile, trickery, duplicity, artifice; wiles.

artery *noun* **1** *a blocked artery* blood vessel. **2** *crowded urban arteries* main road, throughway, highway, freeway, expressway, motorway.

artful *adjective* cunning, deceitful, wily, sly, crafty, duplicitous, scheming, designing, shrewd, politic, ingenious.

article *noun* **1** *three black articles* object, thing, item, commodity; *inf.* thingamajig, thingamabob, what-d'ya-call-it, watchamacallit. **2** *an article in the newspaper* item, piece, story, feature, report, account, write-up. **3** *an article in a legal document* | *articles of faith* clause, section, point, paragraph, division, part, passage.

articulate *adjective* **1** *an articulate speaker* eloquent, fluent, well-spoken, communicative, coherent, lucid, expressive, silver-tongued,

vocal. **2** *an articulate speech* eloquent, clear, fluent, intelligible, comprehensible, understandable, lucid, coherent. **3** *articulate limbs* articulated, jointed, segmented.
Antonyms: INARTICULATE; HESITANT; UNINTELLIGIBLE.

articulate *verb* **1** *articulate words/ideas* enunciate, pronounce, voice, say, utter, express, vocalize. **2** *articulated parts* joint, hinge, connect, link, couple.

artifice *noun* **1** *an artifice to mislead* trick, stratagem, ruse, dodge, subterfuge, machination, maneuver, tactic, device, contrivance. **2** *win by using artifice* trickery, strategy, cunning, deceit, deception, craftiness, artfulness, wiliness, slyness, duplicity, guile, chicanery.

artificial *adjective* **1** *artificial silk/flowers* manmade, manufactured, synthetic, imitation, simulated, pseudo, ersatz, plastic, mock, sham, fake, bogus, counterfeit; *inf.* phony. **2** *an artificial smile* feigned, false, affected, unnatural, assumed, pretended, insincere, contrived, forced, labored, strained, hollow, spurious, meretricious; *inf.* phony.
Antonyms: NATURAL; GENUINE; SINCERE.

artisan *noun* craftsman, craftswoman, skilled worker, journeyman, artificer, technician.

artist *noun* **1** *the artist's exhibition* painter, drawer, sculptor, old master. **2** *furniture carved by an artist* craftsman, craftswoman, expert, adept, genius, past master, maestro.

artistic *adjective* **1** *an artistic person* creative, talented, gifted, accomplished, imaginative, sensitive, cultivated. **2** *an artistic flower arrangement* decorative, beautiful, attractive, lovely, tasteful, graceful, stylish, elegant, exquisite, aesthetic, ornamental. **3** *the artistic temperament* temperamental, unconventional, bohemian, nonconformist.

artistry *noun* art, skill, ability, talent, genius, brilliance, expertness, flair, gift, creativity, proficiency, virtuosity, craftsmanship, workmanship.

artless *adjective* *an artless smile/remark* natural, simple, innocent, childlike, naïve, ingenuous, guileless, sincere, frank, unpretentious.

as *conjunction* **1** *she came as we were leaving* just as, at the same time that, during the time that, at the time that, while, when. **2** *I must go home as it's late* since, because, seeing that, considering that, on account of. **3** *old as he is, he's healthy* although, though, even if. **4** *do as I say* in the manner that, in the way that. **5** *they live as their ancestors did* in the same manner that, in the same way that; *inf.* like. **6** *the well-paid, as doctors and lawyers* such as, for instance, for example, namely, viz; *inf.* like. **7** *as you know, he's dead* a fact which, that which. **as for/to** on the subject of, as regards, with reference to, with regard to, with respect to. **as it were** so to speak, in a manner of speaking, in a way. **as yet** until now, up to/till now, up to the present time.

as *preposition* **1** *dressed as a policeman* in the guise

of, with the appearance of, in the character of, so as to appear to be. **2** *as their employer, I must sack them* in the role of, being, acting as, functioning as.

ascend *verb* climb, go/move up, mount, scale, rise, levitate, fly up, soar, slope upward.

ascendancy, ascendency *noun* dominance, domination, control, power, authority, mastery, rule, command, supremacy, sway, sovereignty, the upper hand.

ascendant, ascendent *adjective* ascending, rising, going up, climbing, mounting, on the way up, on the rise, growing, increasing, flourishing, on the up and up, up-and-coming.

ascertain *verb* find out, get to know, ferret out, establish, discover, learn, determine, settle, identify, decide, verify, make certain, confirm; *inf.* pin down.

ascetic *noun* recluse, hermit, solitary, anchorite, self-denier, abstainer, celibate, nun, monk, dervish, yogi.

ascetic *adjective* *an ascetic way of life* self-denying, abstinent, abstemious, self-disciplined, austere, frugal, rigorous, strict, moderate, temperate, celibate, spartan, puritanical.

ascribe *verb* attribute, assign, accredit, credit, give credit to, put/set down to, chalk up to, impute, charge with, lay on, blame.

ashamed *adjective* **1** *ashamed of his conduct* humiliated, conscience-stricken, sorry, mortified, abashed, crestfallen, shamefaced, remorseful, discomfited, embarrassed, distressed, sheepish, red-faced, blushing, with one's tail between one's legs. **2** *ashamed to say* reluctant, unwilling, hesitant, restrained.
Antonyms: PROUD; SHAMELESS; PLEASED.

ashen *adjective* pale, pale-faced, pallid, wan, gray, gray-faced, white, colorless, anemic, washed out, bleached, ghostly, deathlike, leaden.

ashes *plural noun* **1** *ashes in the grate* cinders, embers; residue. **2** *the city was left in ashes* rubble, ruin; ruins. **3** *bury her ashes* remains, cremains.

ashore *adverb* to/on the shore, on land, on dry land, on the beach, shoreward, landward.

aside *adverb* **1** *stand aside* to/on one side, to the side, alongside, apart, away, separately, detached, in isolation. **2** *joking aside* apart, notwithstanding.

aside *noun* *make an aside* whispered/confidential remark, casual remark.

asinine *adjective* stupid, silly, idiotic, foolish, brainless, nonsensical, senseless, halfwitted, fatuous, inane, imbecilic, moronic; *inf.* daft, dopey, balmy, batty, nutty, dumb, gormless.

ask *verb* **1** *ask her why | ask her about it* inquire, question, put a question to, query, interrogate, quiz, cross-examine, catechize; *inf.* grill, pump, give the third degree to. **2** *asked a favor | ask the boss for a raise* request, demand,

appeal to, apply to, petition, call upon, entreat, beg, implore, beseech, plead, supplicate. **3** *ask them to dine* invite, bid, summon.
Antonyms: ANSWER; REPLY.

askance *adverb* **1** *look askance at her neighbor* sideways, indirectly, obliquely, out of the corner of one's eye. **2** *look askance at their antics* disapprovingly, mistrustfully, suspiciously, with distrust/doubt.

askew *adverb/adjective* to one side, sideways, at an oblique angle, awry, out of line.

asleep *adjective/adverb* **1** *asleep in bed* sleeping, fast asleep, sound asleep, in a deep sleep, slumbering, napping, catnapping, dozing, resting, reposing, dormant, comatose; *inf.* snoozing, dead to the world, out like a light; *lit.* in the arms of Morpheus. **2** *my leg's asleep* numb, without feeling, deadened, benumbed.
Antonym: awake.

aspect *noun* **1** *look at every aspect of the problem* feature, facet, side, angle, slant, viewpoint, standpoint, light. **2** *a man with a fierce aspect* appearance, look, expression, air, countenance, demeanor, bearing; features; *fml.* mien. **3** *the southern aspect of the house* direction, situation, position, location, exposure, outlook. **4** *affording a pleasant aspect* outlook, view, scene, prospect.

asperity *noun* harshness, sharpness, roughness, severity, acerbity, bitterness, acrimony, sourness, astringency, virulence, sarcasm, irritability, irascibility, churlishness, crabbedness, peevishness, crossness.

aspersions *plural noun* *resent your aspersions | cast aspersions* disparaging/denigrating/malicious remarks, defamatory/slanderous remarks; disparagement, deprecation, denigration, defamation, slander.

asphyxiate *verb* choke, suffocate, smother, stifle, throttle, strangle, strangulate.

aspiration *noun* *aspirations to succeed* desire, longing, yearning, hankering, wish, ambition, hope, aim, objective, goal, object, dream, eagerness, enthusiasm.

aspire *verb* desire, long to/for, yearn to/for, hanker after, be ambitious for, hope to/for, wish to/for, dream of, hunger for, aim to/for, seek, pursue.

aspiring *adjective* *an aspiring leader* would-be, expectant, hopeful, ambitious, enterprising, optimistic, eager, striving, wishful.

ass *noun* **1** *riding on an ass* jackass, donkey, burro. **2** *a silly ass* fool, idiot, dolt, ninny, imbecile, nincompoop, blockhead, numskull, halfwit, dunce, simpleton, jackass; *inf.* twit, twerp, chump, nerd, nitwit, dimwit, fathead.

assail *verb* **1** *assail the enemy with blows | a mind assailed by doubts* attack, assault, set about, lay into, beset, fall/set upon, accost, mug, charge; *inf.* jump. **2** *assailed with angry words/insults* bombard, berate, belabor, lash, abuse, criticize, harangue, revile, lambaste, fulminate against; *inf.* sail into, tear into.

assailant *noun* attacker, mugger, aggressor, assaulter, accoster, assailer.

assassin *noun* murderer, killer, slayer, executioner, liquidator; *inf.* hit man, contract man.

assassinate *verb* murder, kill, slay, execute, liquidate, eliminate; *inf.* hit.

assault *noun* **1** *lead an army assault* attack, onslaught, onset, charge, offensive, act of aggression, storming. **2** *found guilty of assault* violent act, physical/verbal attack; molesting, molestation, threat, threatening.

assault *verb* **1** *assault the enemy forces* attack, make an onslaught/onset on, charge, undertake an offensive against, storm. **2** *assault a policeman* attack, strike, hit; *inf.* lay into. **3** *assault a pedestrian* attack, mug, molest, rape.

assay *verb* **1** *assay metals* test, check, analyze, assess, evaluate, appraise, examine, inspect, investigate, scrutinize, probe. **2** *assay a reply* attempt, venture, try.

assay *noun* *metal assays* test, trial, check, analysis, assessment, evaluation, appraisal, examination, investigation, inspection, probe.

assemblage *noun* *an assemblage of old vases* collection, accumulation, conglomeration, cluster, medley, jumble.

assemble *verb* **1** *assemble the children/books/evidence* get together, bring/put together, gather, collect, round up, marshal, muster, summon, congregate, accumulate, amass, rally, convoke. **2** *the crowd assembled* gather, collect, come together, foregather, meet, congregate, convene, flock together. **3** *assemble the parts of the airplane* put together, piece/fit together, build, fabricate, construct, erect, manufacture, set up, connect, join.
Antonyms: DISPERSE; DEMOLISH.

assembly *noun* **1** *talking to a crowded assembly* gathering, meeting, group, body of people, crowd, throng, congregation, convention. **2** *the assembly of furniture/cars* putting/fitting together, building, fabrication, construction, erection, manufacture.

assent *noun* *give one's assent* agreement, concurrence, acceptance, approval, consent, acquiescence, compliance, approbation, permission, sanction, accord, accordance, accession.
Antonyms: DISSENT; REFUSAL.

assert *verb* **1** *assert that she is innocent* declare, state, announce, maintain, pronounce, proclaim, contend, aver, swear, avow, attest, affirm, allege, claim, postulate. **2** *assert one's rights* uphold, press/push for, insist upon, stand up for, defend, vindicate. **assert oneself** behave confidently, make one's presence felt, exert one's influence.

assertive *adjective* *an assertive personality* positive, confident, self-assured, dogmatic, aggressive, self-assertive, strong-willed, forceful, dominant, domineering; *inf.* pushy.
Antonyms: RETIRING; BASHFUL; TIMID.

assess *verb* **1** *assess the quality/value* evaluate, judge, gauge, rate, estimate, appraise, determine, weigh up, compute. **2** *assess taxation contributions* fix, evaluate, levy, impose, demand, rate.

assessment *noun* **1** *continuous assessment | the assessment of quality* evaluation, judgment, gauging, rating, estimation, appraisal. *See* ASSESS 1. **2** *tax assessment* evaluation, levy, charge, rate, toll, tariff, demand, fee.

asset *noun make the most of one's assets | an asset to the school* advantage, benefit, blessing, strong point, strength, boon, aid, help.
Antonyms: LIABILITY; HANDICAP.

assets *plural noun* property, estate, capital, wealth, money; resources, reserves, securities, holdings, possessions, effects, goods, valuables, belongings, chattels.

assiduous *adjective* diligent, industrious, hard-working, studious, persevering, persistent, laborious, unflagging, indefatigable, zealous, sedulous.

assign *verb* **1** *assign duties to all* allocate, allot, distribute, give out, dispense, apportion, consign. **2** *assign him to the post* appoint, select, install, designate, nominate, name, delegate, commission. **3** *assign Thursdays for trips* fix, appoint, decide on, determine, set aside/apart, stipulate, appropriate. **4** *assign her behavior to jealousy* ascribe, put down, attribute, accredit, chalk up. **5** *assign her property* transfer, convey, consign.

assignation *noun lovers making an assignation* rendezvous, tryst, date, appointment, meeting.

assignment *noun* **1** *carry out an assignment* task, job, duty, commission, charge, mission, responsibility, obligation. **2** *the assignment of duties* allocation, allotment, dispensation, apportionment, consignment. **3** *his assignment to the post* appointment, selection, installation, nomination. *See* ASSIGN 2. **4** *its assignment to jealousy* ascribing. *See* ASSIGN 4. **5** *the assignment of property* transfer, conveyance, consignment.

assimilate *verb* **1** *assimilate food/facts | assimilate people into a group* absorb, take in, incorporate, digest, ingest. **2** *assimilate your way of life to theirs* adapt, adjust, accustom, acclimatize, accommodate, become like/similar, blend in, fit, homogenize.

assist *verb* **1** *assist the old lady | assist the police | I'm here to assist* help, aid, lend a hand, succor, support, cooperate/collaborate with, abet, work with, play a part. **2** *he was only assisting his mentor* be the assistant/subordinate to, help out, support, back, second. **3** *assist the factory's smooth operation* make easier, facilitate, expedite.
Antonyms: HINDER; IMPEDE.

assistance *noun* help, aid, succor, support, reinforcement, cooperation, collaboration; a helping hand.

assistant *noun* **1** *her assistant is in charge* subordinate, deputy, auxiliary, second in command; *inf.* right-hand man/woman, man/girl Friday, henchman. **2** *an assistant in the project* helper, colleague, associate, partner, confederate, accomplice, collaborator, accessory, abettor. **3** *an assistant in a department store* sales assistant, clerk, salesclerk, salesperson, saleswoman, salesman, cashier.

associate *verb* **1** *associate wine with France* link, connect, relate, think of together, couple. **2** *they associate with criminals* mix, keep company, mingle, socialize, hobnob, fraternize; *inf.* run around, hang out, pal around. **3** *their clubs are associated* combine, join, connect, attach, affiliate, band together, ally, syndicate, incorporate, conjoin.

assorted *adjective* mixed, varied, variegated, miscellaneous, diverse, diversified, motley, sundry, heterogeneous.
Antonyms: HOMOGENEOUS; SIMILAR; IDENTICAL.

assortment *noun* mixture, variety, miscellany, selection, medley, mélange, diversity, jumble, mishmash, hodgepodge, potpourri.

assuage *verb* **1** *assuage the pain* relieve, ease, alleviate, soothe, mitigate, lessen, allay, moderate, diminish, calm, palliate, abate, lull, temper, mollify. **2** *assuage their hunger/thirst* appease, satisfy, relieve, slake, quench, dull, blunt, allay, pacify, take the edge off.
Antonyms: AGGRAVATE; INTENSIFY.

assume *verb* **1** *assume he's coming* suppose, take for granted, presuppose, presume, imagine, think, believe, fancy, expect, accept, suspect, surmise, understand, gather, guess. **2** *assume a thorough knowledge* feign, pretend, simulate, put on. **3** *assume an air of authority | assume massive proportions* adopt, take on, acquire, come to have. **4** *assume a position of responsibility* undertake, enter upon, begin, set about, take on/up, embark on, take upon oneself, accept, shoulder. **5** *the invaders assumed power* seize, take, take over, appropriate, usurp, preempt, commandeer.

assumed *adjective an assumed name* false, fictitious, fake, feigned, pretended, made-up, bogus, sham, spurious, make-believe, counterfeit, pseudo; *inf.* phony.

assumption *noun* **1** *on the assumption that you're right* supposition, presupposition, presumption, premise, belief, expectation, conjecture, surmise, guess, theory, hypothesis, suspicion, postulation. **2** *the assumption of a thorough knowledge* feigning, pretending, simulation. *See* ASSUME 2. **3** *the assumption of an air of authority* adoption, taking on. *See* ASSUME 3. **4** *the assumption of a position of responsibility* undertaking, entering upon, setting about, embarkation on. *See* ASSUME 4. **5** *the invaders' assumption of power* seizure, appropriation, usurping. *See* ASSUME 5. **6** *amazed at his assumption* arrogance, presumption, conceit, impertinence.

assurance noun **1** *shows remarkable assurance for her age* self-assurance, self-confidence, confidence, self-reliance, nerve, poise, positiveness. **2** *you have my assurance that I'll be there* word of honor, word, guarantee, promise, pledge, vow, oath, affirmation. **3** *no assurance of her success* certainty, guarantee. *See* ASSURE 3.

assure verb **1** *I assure you that he's wrong* declare to, affirm to, give one's word to, guarantee, promise, swear to, certify to, pledge to, vow to, attest to. **2** *they assured him of their ability* convince, persuade, reassure, prove to. **3** *success is assured* ensure, make certain, make sure, secure, guarantee, seal, clinch, confirm.

assured adjective **1** *an assured manner* self-assured, self-confident, confident, self-reliant, poised, positive. **2** *an assured market* certain, sure, guaranteed, secure, reliable, dependable.

astonish verb amaze, astound, dumbfound, stagger, surprise, stun, take aback, confound, take one's breath away; *inf.* flabbergast, floor.

astonishing adjective amazing, astounding, staggering, surprising, breathtaking, striking, impressive, bewildering, stunning.

astonishment noun *he failed to conceal his astonishment* surprise, amazement, wonder, disbelief; shock, numbness, bewilderment, confusion.

astound verb amaze, astonish, dumbfound, stagger, surprise. *See* ASTONISH.

astounding adjective amazing, astonishing, staggering, surprising. *See* ASTONISHING.

astray adverb/adjective **1** *go astray in the fog* off course, off the right track, adrift; lost. **2** *led astray by wicked men* into wrongdoing, into error/sin, to the bad.

astringent adjective **1** *an astringent lotion* contracting, constricting, constrictive, constringent, styptic. **2** *astringent criticism/conditions* severe, stern, harsh, rough, stringent, acerbic, austere, caustic, mordant, trenchant.

astronaut noun spaceman, spacewoman, cosmonaut, space traveler.

astute adjective shrewd, sharp, acute, quick, quick-witted, clever, cunning, artful, ingenious, perceptive, discerning, crafty, wily, calculating, perspicacious, sagacious.
Antonyms: STUPID; DULL.

asunder adverb into pieces, to pieces, to bits, apart.

asylum noun **1** *seek an asylum in the church* | *political asylum* refuge, sanctuary, shelter, safety, safekeeping, protection; haven, retreat, harbor, port in a storm. **2** *shut away in an asylum* mental hospital, psychiatric hospital, institution; *derog.* madhouse, nuthouse, loony bin, funny farm.

asymmetrical adjective disproportionate, misproportioned, irregular, uneven, distorted, malformed, formless.

atavism noun reversion, throwback; recurrence, reappearance, resurgence.

atheism noun disbelief, nonbelief, unbelief, heresy, godlessness, skepticism, irreligion, heathenism, freethinking, apostasy, nihilism.

atheist noun nonbeliever, disbeliever, unbeliever, heretic, skeptic, heathen, freethinker, nihilist, infidel.

athlete noun sportsman, sportswoman, runner, player; gymnast, competitor, contestant; *inf.* jock, fitness freak.

athletic adjective **1** *an athletic person* | *of an athletic build* muscular, powerful, robust, able-bodied, sturdy, strong, strapping, vigorous, hardy, stalwart, well-built, brawny, thickset, Herculean. **2** *an athletic event* sports, sporting.

athletics plural noun sporting events, sports, games, matches, contests.

atmosphere noun **1** *the city's polluted atmosphere* air, aerosphere, aerospace, sky, heavens. **2** *a friendly/unfriendly atmosphere* environment, milieu, medium, background, setting, air, ambience, aura, climate, mood, feeling, character, tone, tenor, spirit, quality, flavor; surroundings.

atom noun iota, jot, bit, whit, particle, scrap, shred, trace, speck, spot, dot, crumb, fragment, grain, morsel, mite.

atone verb make amends/reparation, compensate, pay the penalty, pay for, recompense, expiate, do penance.

atonement noun reparation, compensation, recompense, redress, indemnity, restitution, expiation, penance, redemption.

atrocious adjective **1** *atrocious crimes* brutal, barbaric, barbarous, savage, vicious, wicked, cruel, ruthless, merciless, villainous, murderous, heinous, nefarious, monstrous, inhuman, infernal, fiendish, diabolical, flagrant, outrageous. **2** *atrocious weather* very bad, unpleasant, appalling, dreadful, terrible, shocking.

atrocity noun **1** *atrocities committed in wartime* act of brutality/barbarity/savagery, crime, offense, injury; brutality, cruelty, barbarity. **2** *the atrocity of war* abomination, enormity, outrage, horror, evil, monstrosity, violation.

atrophy verb waste, waste away, wither, shrivel up, shrink, dry up, decay, wilt, decline, deteriorate, degenerate.

attach verb **1** *attach a label to the briefcase* fasten, fix, affix, join, connect, couple, link, secure, tie, stick, adhere, pin, hitch, bond, add, append, annex, subjoin. **2** *attach no significance to it* ascribe, assign, attribute, accredit, apply, put, place, lay. **3** *the state attaching criminals' property* seize, confiscate, appropriate; *Law* distrain. **4** *he is attached to the military unit* assign, second, allot, allocate, detail, appoint. **attach to** *attach oneself to a group* affiliate with, join, join forces with, associate/combine with, ally/unite with, latch on to.
Antonyms: DETACH; SEPARATE.

attached adjective *is she attached?* married, engaged, having a partner, spoken for; *inf.* going steady. **attached to** *she is attached to her father* be fond of, full of regard for, devoted to.

attachment *noun* **1** *an electric drill and attachments* supplementary part, accessory, extension, fitting, extra, adjunct, addition, appurtenance, appendage, accouterment. **2** *the cable attachment is loose* junction, connector, coupling, fastening, link, clamp. **3** *the attachment of a label* fastening, fixing, affixing. *See* ATTACH 1. **4** *my/the attachment of others to the group* affiliation, joining, uniting, union, allying, alliance, association. **5** *the attachment of criminals' property* seizure, confiscation, appropriation. **attachment to** *a strong attachment to one's aunt* fondness of/for, love for, liking for, affection for, devotion to, loyalty to/toward, tenderness for, bond to/with, affinity for.

attack *verb* **1** *attack the enemy | let us attack* assault, set/fall upon, strike at, rush, storm, charge, pounce upon, beset, besiege, beleaguer; strike, begin hostilities; *inf.* lay into, let one have it. **2** *an article attacking the writer* criticize, censure, berate, reprove, rebuke, impugn, harangue, find fault with, blame, revile, fulminate against, vilify; *inf.* knock, slam. **3** *attack a pile of work* set about, get/go to work on, get started on, undertake, embark on. **4** *a disease attacking the nervous system* affect, have an effect on, infect.
Antonyms: DEFEND; PROTECT; PRAISE.

---

attack
assail, assault, beset, besiege, bombard, charge, molest, storm

There is no shortage of fighting words. **Attack** is the most general verb, meaning to set upon someone or something in a violent, forceful, or aggressive way (*the rebels attacked at dawn*); but it can also be used figuratively (*attack the government's policy*). **Assault** implies a greater degree of violence or viciousness and the infliction of more damage. As part of the legal term assault and battery, it suggests an attempt or threat to injure someone physically. **Molest** is another word meaning to *attack* and is used today almost exclusively of sexual molestation (*she had been molested as a child*). **Charge** and **storm** are primarily military words, both suggesting a forceful assault on a fixed position. To *charge* is to make a violent onslaught (*the infantry charged the enemy camp*) and is often used as a command (*Charge! the general cried*). To *storm* means to take by force, with all the momentum and fury of a storm (*after days of planning, the soldiers stormed the castle*), but there is often the suggestion of a last-ditch, all-out effort to end a long siege or avoid defeat. To **assail** is to attack with repeated thrusts or blows, implying that victory depends not so much on force as on persistence. To **bombard** is to assail continuously with bombs or shells (*they bombarded the city without mercy for days*).

Besiege means to surround with an armed force (*to besiege the capital city*). When used figuratively, its meaning comes close to that of *assail*, but with an emphasis on being hemmed in and enclosed rather than punished repeatedly (*besieged with fears*). **Beset** also means to attack on all sides (*beset by enemies*), but it is also used frequently in other contexts to mean set or placed upon (*a bracelet beset with diamonds*).

---

attack *noun* **1** *an attack on the enemy* assault, onslaught, offensive, onset, strike, storming, charge, foray, rush, incursion, inroad. **2** *launch an attack on his writing* criticism, censure, berating, rebuke, reproval, impugnment, blame, revilement, vilification. **3** *mount an attack on a pile of work* start, beginning, commencement, undertaking, onslaught. **4** *an asthmatic attack | had another of his attacks* fit, bout, seizure, spasm, convulsion, paroxysm, stroke.
Antonym: DEFENSE.

attacker *noun* assailant, aggressor, assaulter, striker, mugger.

attain *verb* achieve, accomplish, obtain, gain, procure, secure, get, grasp, win, earn, acquire, reach, arrive at, realize, fulfill, succeed in, bring off, be successful.

attainable *adjective* achievable, obtainable, accessible, within reach, at hand, reachable, winnable, realizable, practicable, feasible, possible, potential, conceivable, imaginable.

attainment *noun* **1** *the attainment of his goal* achievement, accomplishment, gaining, procurement, acquirement, acquisition, realization, fulfillment, completion, consummation, success. **2** *musical attainment* accomplishment, ability, art, skill, proficiency, mastery, talent, gift, capability, competence.

attempt *verb* **1** *attempt to explain* try, strive, aim, venture, endeavor, seek, undertake, set out, do one's best, take it upon oneself, essay; *inf.* give it a whirl. **2** *attempt an escape* try, venture, undertake, tackle, have a go/shot at, essay; *inf.* have a crack at.

attempt *noun* effort, try, endeavor, venture, trial, experiment, essay; *inf.* crack, go, shot.

attend *verb* **1** *attend a meeting | can you attend?* be present, be at, be here/there, appear, put in an appearance, turn up, visit, frequent, haunt; *inf.* show up, show. **2** *attend the sick* look after, take care of, care for, tend, nurse, mind, minister to. **3** *the president attended by top aides* accompany, escort, guard; chaperon, squire, convoy. **attend to** *attend to this matter/customer* deal/cope with, see to, handle, take care of, give one's attention to, take charge of. **attend with** *a plan attended with problems* accompanied by, be associated/connected with, go hand in hand with, occur/coexist with, result/arise from, be a consequence of.

attendance *noun* **1** *attendance is not compulsory* presence, attending, appearance, being there; *inf.* showing up, showing. **2** *attendances vary* number present, turnout, crowd, audience, house, gate. **in attendance** present, giving assistance, supervising, monitoring, on guard.

attendant *noun* **1** *parking attendant* assistant, helper, auxiliary, steward, waiter, servant, menial. **2** *the queen and her attendants* companion, escort, aide, guard, custodian, guide, usher.

attendant *adjective* *attendant circumstances* accompanying, concomitant, related, accessory, resultant, consequent.

attention *noun* **1** *wandering attention | give more attention to the problem* concentration, attentiveness, intentness, notice, observation, heed, heedfulness, regard, contemplation, deliberation, scrutiny; thought, thinking, studying. **2** *attract their attention* notice, awareness, observation, consciousness, heed, recognition, regard. **3** *for the personal attention of the manager* consideration, action, notice, investigation. **4** *medical attention* care, treatment, ministration, therapy. **5** *appreciate his attentions* civility, politeness, courtesy, respect, gallantry, urbanity, deference; compliments.

attentive *adjective* **1** *keen and attentive* alert, aware, awake, watchful, wide awake, observant, noticing, concentrating, heeding, heedful, mindful, vigilant, on guard; *inf.* all ears; *fml.* on the qui vive. **2** *an attentive host* considerate, thoughtful, kind, polite, courteous, gracious, conscientious, civil, obliging, accommodating, gallant, chivalrous.
Antonyms: INATTENTIVE; HEEDLESS; DISCOURTEOUS.

attenuated *adjective* **1** *attenuated limbs | attenuated lengths of silk* thin, slender, threadlike, thinned down, stretched out, drawn out. **2** *attenuated force* weakened, reduced, lessened, decreased, diminished, impaired, enervated.

attest *verb* *witnesses attest his account* affirm, aver, asseverate, confirm, testify to, vouch for, bear witness to, bear out, endorse, back up, support, corroborate, verify, authenticate. **attest to** *footsteps attested to his presence* prove, give proof of, provide evidence of, evidence, demonstrate, evince, display, exhibit, show, manifest, substantiate, confirm, verify, vouch for.

attic *noun* loft, garret, mansard.

attire *noun* *evening attire* clothing, dress, wear, outfit, apparel, garb, ensemble, costume, array, habit, wardrobe; clothes, garments, habiliments, accouterments; *inf.* gear, togs, threads, glad rags.

attire *verb* *attired in silk* dress, clothe, dress up, garb, robe, array, deck out, costume; *inf.* doll up.

attitude *noun* **1** *one's attitude toward marriage* point of view, viewpoint, opinion, frame of mind, outlook, perspective, reaction, stance, position, approach; thoughts, ideas. **2** *bodies adopting different attitudes* position, stance, pose, stand; bearing, deportment, carriage.

attract *verb* **1** *magnets attract iron filings* draw, pull, magnetize. **2** *attracted by beauty | moths attracted to light* allure, entice, tempt, interest, fascinate, charm, engage, enchant, captivate, bewitch, seduce, inveigle.

attraction *noun* **1** *magnetic attraction* pull, draw, magnetism. **2** *the attraction of foreign travel* appeal, attractiveness, allure, pull, draw, enticement, temptation, inducement, interest, charm, fascination, glamour, enchantment, captivation, seduction; *inf.* come-on. **3** *one of the city attractions* interest, feature, entertainment, activity, diversion.

attractive *adjective* **1** *an attractive proposal* appealing, agreeable, pleasing, inviting, tempting, interesting. **2** *an attractive woman/man* good-looking, striking, beautiful, handsome, pretty, stunning, gorgeous, prepossessing, fetching, comely, captivating, charming, fascinating, interesting, appealing, enchanting, alluring.
Antonyms: UNINVITING; UGLY; unattractive.

attribute *noun* **1** *kindness is one their attributes* quality, feature, characteristic, property, mark, trait, distinction, idiosyncrasy. **2** *the throne is an attribute of a king* symbol, indicator, mark, sign, trade mark, status symbol.

attribute *verb* *success attributed to hard work* ascribe, assign, accredit, put down, chalk up.

attrition *noun* **1** *the smoothing of rock by attrition* abrasion, friction, rubbing, chafing, corroding, corrosion, erosion, eating away, grinding, scraping, wearing away, excoriation, detrition. **2** *defeat the enemy by a war of attrition* wearing down, weakening, debilitation, enfeebling, enervation, sapping, attenuation.

attune *verb* *attune an instrument* tune, regulate, modulate, harmonize. **attune to** *not yet attuned to the situation | attuned to their ideas* accustom to, adjust to, adapt to, familiarize with, acclimatize to, assimilate to, tailor to, be fitted to, be in tune/harmony/accord with.

auburn *adjective* reddish-brown, Titian, Titian red, chestnut-colored, chestnut, copper-colored, copper, rust-colored, russet.

audacious *adjective* **1** *an audacious scheme/traveler* bold, daring, fearless, intrepid, brave, courageous, valiant, adventurous, plucky, daredevil, reckless; *inf.* gutsy, spunky. **2** *an audacious youth/remark* impudent, impertinent, insolent, presumptuous, forward, rude, brazen, shameless, saucy, defiant.

audacity *noun* **1** *the audacity of the scheme/man* boldness, daring, fearlessness, intrepidity, bravery, courage, valor, pluck, recklessness; *inf.* guts, spunk. **2** *the child had the audacity to swear* impudence, impertinence, insolence, presumption, forwardness, rudeness, brazenness, shamelessness, defiance.

audible *adjective* heard, hearable, clear, distinct, perceptible, discernible.
Antonyms: INAUDIBLE; FAINT; INDISTINCT.

audience *noun* 1 *a concert/TV audience* listeners, spectators, viewers, onlookers; assembly, gathering, crowd, assemblage, house, turnout, congregation, gallery. 2 *publications aimed at a wide audience* public, market, following; fans, devotees, aficionados. 3 *an audience with the pope* interview, meeting, hearing, consultation, discussion, reception.

audit *noun an audit of the firm's accounts* inspection, examination, scrutiny, investigation, review, check.

audit *verb audit the books* inspect, examine, go over/through, scrutinize, investigate, review, check.

augment *verb* 1 *augment one's income | augment the audience* increase, make larger/bigger/greater, boost, build up, enlarge, add to, expand, extend, amplify, raise, enhance, heighten, multiply, magnify, elevate, swell, inflate, escalate, intensify. 2 *his fortune augmented* increase, grow, build up, enlarge, expand, extend, rise, multiply, swell, inflate, escalate.
Antonyms: DECREASE; DIMINISH.

augur *verb* be a sign of, foretell, forecast, predict, prophesy, bode, foreshadow, promise, presage, portend, herald, betoken.

augur *noun* seer, soothsayer, prophet, oracle.

august *adjective* dignified, solemn, majestic, stately, magnificent, noble, regal, imposing, impressive, exalted, lofty, grand, high-ranking, illustrious, distinguished, awe-inspiring.

aura *noun* ambience, atmosphere, air, quality, mood, character, spirit, feeling, tone, suggestion, emanation; *inf.* vibrations; *inf.* vibes.

auspices *plural noun under the auspices of* patronage, guidance, influence, responsibility, control, protection.

auspicious *adjective* propitious, favorable, promising, bright, optimistic, hopeful, encouraging, opportune, timely, lucky, fortunate, providential, felicitous, rosy.

austere *adjective* 1 *an austere manner* harsh, stern, severe, strict, unfeeling, hard, rigorous, stringent, grim, cold, distant, formal, stiff, aloof, forbidding, grave, solemn, serious, unsmiling, unyielding, unbending, unrelenting, inflexible. 2 *monks leading an austere life* strict, self-denying, self-abnegating, ascetic, Spartan, abstemious, abstinent, moral, upright, celibate, chaste, puritanical. 3 *decorated in an austere style* plain, simple, severe, unadorned, unornamented, unembellished, stark, subdued, somber.
Antonyms: GENIAL; IMMODERATE; ELABORATE.

authentic *adjective* 1 *an authentic painting* genuine, true, bona fide, rightful, legitimate, lawful, legal, valid; *inf.* the real McCoy, kosher. 2 *an authentic statement* reliable, dependable,

trustworthy, true, truthful, honest, faithful, credible; *inf.* straight from the horse's mouth.
Antonyms: FAKE; COUNTERFEIT; UNRELIABLE.

authenticate *verb* 1 *authenticate an agreement* validate, ratify, confirm, certify, seal, endorse, guarantee, warrant, underwrite. 2 *authenticate the work as being Shakespeare's* verify, substantiate, support, prove, evidence.

authenticity *noun* 1 *the authenticity of the painting* genuineness, rightfulness, legitimacy, legality, validity. 2 *the authenticity of the statement* reliability, dependability, trustworthiness, truth, honesty, faithfulness, credibility.

author *noun* 1 *the author of the book/article* writer, composer; novelist, dramatist, playwright, screenwriter, poet, essayist, biographer, librettist, lyricist, songwriter, journalist, columnist, reporter. 2 *the author of their misfortune* cause, creator, originator, initiator, founder, planner, prime mover, designer.

authoritarian *noun the new headmaster is an authoritarian* disciplinarian, autocrat, despot, dictator, tyrant, absolutist.

authoritarian *adjective an authoritarian approach* disciplinarian, harsh, strict, autocratic, despotic, dictatorial, tyrannical, domineering, dogmatic, imperious, absolute, draconian.

authoritative *adjective* 1 *an authoritative biography* official, approved, authorized, sanctioned, validated, authentic, genuine. 2 *authoritative information* sound, dependable, reliable, trustworthy, authentic, valid, certified, attested, definitive, factual, accurate, scholarly. 3 *an authoritative manner* self-assured, confident, assertive, imposing, masterful, dogmatic, peremptory, arrogant, commanding, dominating, domineering, imperious, overbearing, authoritarian.

authorities *plural noun* administration, the establishment, government, officialdom, management, legislation, the police, bureaucracy, red tape; the powers that be.

authority *noun* 1 *have the authority to decide | a person of/in authority* authorization, right, power, might, sanction, influence, force, control, charge, prerogative, jurisdiction, rule, command, dominion, sovereignty, ascendancy, supremacy; *inf.* say-so. 2 *he is an authority on ecology* expert, specialist, professional, master, scholar, pundit; *inf.* walking encyclopedia. 3 *quoting authorities used* source, reference, documentation, bibliography, citation, quotation, quote, excerpt, passage. 4 *have his authority to act* permission, authorization, sanction, license, warrant; *inf.* say-so. 5 *have on their authority that they were there* testimony, evidence, witness, attestation, sworn statement, declaration, word, avowal, deposition, profession.

authorize *verb* 1 *authorize them to represent us* give authority to, commission, empower, entitle, enable, accredit, license, certify, validate. **2** *authorize the sale* give authority/permission for, permit, allow, approve, give one's assent to, agree to, sanction, ratify, warrant, countenance, accede to; *inf.* give the green light to, give the go-ahead for.

autobiography *noun* memoirs; life story, diary, journal, personal account.

autocratic *adjective* despotic, dictatorial, tyrannical, domineering, imperious, omnipotent, all-powerful, absolute, draconian, oppressive, high-handed; *inf.* bossy.

autograph *noun get an actor's autograph* signature, inscription, mark, cross, X.

autograph *verb autograph a program* sign, attach one's signature to, initial, countersign, mark, put one's cross/X on.

automatic *adjective* **1** *an automatic washing machine* automated, mechanized, mechanical, push-button, robotic, self-activating, self-regulating, self-directing, self-propelling. **2** *an automatic reaction* instinctive, spontaneous, involuntary, unconscious, reflex, natural, mechanical. **3** *promotion is automatic* inevitable, routine, certain, assured, unavoidable, necessary.

autonomy *noun the people fought for autonomy* | *the region gained autonomy* independence, self-determination, autarchy; self-sufficiency, individualism.

available *adjective tickets are still available* unoccupied, free, untaken, vacant, usable, employable, ready; accessible, obtainable, at hand, convenient.

avarice *noun she turned to crime because of avarice* greed, acquisitiveness, covetousness, materialism; selfishness, self-interest, meanness, miserliness.

average *noun she calculated the average* mean, median, midpoint, center; norm, standard, yardstick, rule.

average *adjective* **1** *the team played an average game* | *the house was an average size* ordinary, normal, typical, everyday; common, widespread, prevalent. **2** *she wrote average essays* | *his ability was no better than average* mediocre, moderate, unexceptional; second-rate, banal; pedestrian.
Antonyms: OUTSTANDING; EXCEPTIONAL.

aversion *noun* **aversion to** *she had an aversion to spiders* | *his aversion to work became a problem* dislike of, distaste for, hatred of/for, repugnance of; avoidance of, evasion, shunning of.
Antonyms: LIKING; INCLINATION.

avid *adjective she was an avid reader* | *he was an avid fan* keen, eager, enthusiastic, partial to, fond of, fervent, zealous, passionate about; *inf.* crazy about, mad about.
Antonyms: APATHETIC; INDIFFERENT.

avoid *verb he tried to avoid paying taxes* | *he avoided her in the street* shun, keep away from, eschew, steer clear of; evade, hide from, elude, shirk, dodge; abstain from, refrain from, hold back from.
Antonyms: CONFRONT; FACE.

aware *adjective the watchmen were always aware* awake, watchful, vigilant, alert, cautious, paying attention. **aware of** *he was aware of the problem* | *she was aware of hostility* conscious of, informed of, familiar with, sensitive to; *inf.* clued in on, in the know about.
Antonyms: UNAWARE; IGNORANT; OBLIVIOUS.

awe *noun she gazed in awe* | *they were filled with awe* amazement, wonder, astonishment, stupefaction; reverence, honor, veneration; dread, fear.

awful *adjective* **1** *she had an awful cough* | *his new coat looked awful* nasty, unpleasant, distressing, troublesome, horrible; serious, severe; ugly, unattractive, foul, disgusting. **2** *the awful power of the gods* awe-inspiring, awesome, venerable, demanding respect, admirable, impressive, authoritative, daunting.

awkward *adjective* **1** *the appointment was at an awkward time* inconvenient, difficult, problematic; unhelpful, annoying, obstructive, vexatious, perverse. **2** *the gymnast had been an awkward child* clumsy, ungainly, inelegant, inept, gauche; lumbering, out of proportion, unwieldy.
Antonyms: CONVENIENT; ADROIT.

awry *adjective the storm left the fence awry* lopsided, uneven, unequal, asymmetrical, askew, crooked.

B

babble *verb* **1** *babbling away unintelligibly* jabber, chatter, mutter, mumble, prate, drivel, cackle; *inf.* run on. **2** *he babbled the secret* blab, blurt out, reveal, divulge, let slip. **3** *the stream babbled quietly* murmur, whisper, gurgle.

babble *noun* *the babble of voices* jabbering, gibberish, chatter, muttering, mumbling, clamor.

babe *noun* **1** *a newborn babe* baby, infant, child. **2** *just a babe in the world of business* innocent, ingenue, babe in arms, greenhorn, novice, tyro, beginner.

babel *noun* commotion, clamor, babble, hubbub, tumult, uproar, din.

baby *noun* **1** *holding a tiny baby* infant, newborn, child, babe, tiny tot. **2** *the baby of the team* junior, youngest, subordinate.

baby *verb* *baby the children | baby his wife* pamper, spoil, indulge, pet, humor, coddle, mollycoddle, overindulge, spoonfeed.

baby *adjective* *baby carrots* miniature, mini, diminutive, dwarf, tiny, minute, small, little, wee, midget.

babyish *adjective* childish, immature, infantile, juvenile, puerile, adolescent, jejune, pathetic, inane, namby-pamby.

back *noun* **1** *hurt one's back* spine, backbone, spinal column; posterior; *Med.* dorsum. **2** *the back of the building* rear, rear end, far end, end, reverse, reverse side, other side; hind part, posterior, tail end, backside, hindquarters, stern. **behind one's back** secretly, deceitfully, slyly, sneakily, surreptitiously, covertly.
Antonym: FRONT.

back *adjective* **1** *back garden/shed/teeth* rear, hind, end, hindmost, posterior. **2** *back copies* past, previous, earlier, former, bygone, expired, elapsed, obsolete.
Antonyms: FRONT; FOREMOST; FUTURE.

back *adverb* **1** *without looking back* backward, behind, to the rear, rearward. **2** *a few days back* earlier, previously, before, since, ago, heretofore. **3** *standing back from the road* to the rear, at a distance, remote from.

back *verb* **1** *back the proposal/candidate* support, endorse, approve, favor, advocate, help, assist, aid, promote, uphold, champion, encourage, second, abet. **2** *back the theatrical venture* sponsor, finance, subsidize, underwrite, subscribe to. **3** *back her statement* support, confirm, corroborate, substantiate, endorse, second, bolster, reinforce, stand by, side with, vouch for, attest to, sanction. **4** *back a horse/runner* bet on, place a bet on, gamble on. **5** *the car backed*

out go/move backward, reverse. **back away** withdraw, retire, retreat, fall back, recede, turn tail. **back down** yield, submit, surrender, give in, climb down, concede, concede defeat, backtrack, back-pedal, retract. **back out** go back on, withdraw from, cancel, renege on, abandon, retreat from, get cold feet, recant; *inf.* chicken out of. **back up** support, confirm. *See* BACK *verb* 3.
Antonyms: OPPOSE; HINDER; DENY.

backbiting *noun* slander, libel, defamation, abuse, scandalmongering, disparagement, denigration, detraction, malice, spite, spitefulness, cattiness, vilification, vituperation, calumny; slurs, aspersions; *inf.* bitching, knocking, mudslinging, bad-mouthing.

backbone *noun* **1** *an injured backbone* spine, spinal/vertebral column. **2** *the backbone of the organization* framework, mainstay, support, basis, foundation, structure. **3** *lacking backbone* strength of character, firmness, determination, resolve, resolution, steadfastness, character, courage, grit, nerve, mettle, pluck, fortitude, tenacity, stamina, willpower.

backer *noun* **1** *the theater's backers* sponsor, patron, financier, benefactor, subsidizer, underwriter, well-wisher; *inf.* angel. **2** *backers of the plan/candidate* supporter, advocate, promoter, upholder, champion, seconder, abettor.

backfire *verb* **1** *the engine backfired* explode, detonate, discharge. **2** *the plan backfired* miscarry, rebound, recoil, boomerang, fail, disappoint; *inf.* flop.

background *noun* **1** *in the background of the painting* distance, rear, horizon. **2** *models posing against a white background* setting, backcloth, backdrop, scene, stage. **3** *check the employee's background* upbringing, rearing, education, history, environment, class, culture, experience; family circumstances, circumstances, qualifications, credentials. **4** *the political background* conditions, circumstances, environment, milieu, framework; factors, influences.
Antonyms: FOREGROUND; FRONT.

backhanded *adjective* indirect, oblique, ambiguous, equivocal, double-edged, two-edged, sarcastic, ironic, sardonic.

backing *noun* **1** *have the school's backing* support, approval, commendation, help, assistance, aid, helping hand, encouragement, cooperation, championship, promotion, advocacy, endorsement. **2** *set up with the* *backing of private donations* sponsorship, financing; finance, grant, subsidy; funds. **3** *the backing of the bank* security, surety, collateral, assurance, insurance, guarantee, warranty. **4** *musical backing* accompaniment, backup, harmony, obbligato.

backlash *noun* reaction, counteraction, repercussion, recoil, kickback, rebound, boomerang, retroaction, retaliation.

backlog *noun* accumulation, stockpile, heap, excess, hoard, stock, supply; arrears, reserves; *inf.* mountain.

backpedal *verb* retract, take back, withdraw, retreat, reverse, backtrack, back up, back down, renege, do an about face.

backslide *verb* relapse, lapse, regress, retrogress, revert, fall back, slip/fall from grace, stray, go astray, leave the straight and narrow, degenerate, deteriorate, turn one's back.

backslider *noun* recidivist, turncoat, relapser, renegade, deserter, regressor, apostate; *inf.* fallen angel.

backward *adjective* **1** *a backward look/somersault* rearward, toward the back/rear, reverse. **2** *a backward area* slow, behind, behindhand, underdeveloped, undeveloped, retarded, unprogressive, dull, sluggish, subnormal, unsophisticated. **3** *rather backward in a crowd* bashful, shy, retiring, diffident, hesitant, shrinking, timid, demure, reluctant.
Antonyms: FORWARD; ADVANCED; BOLD.

backward, backwards *adverb* **1** *look backward* rearward, toward the back/rear, behind. **2** *running backward* in reverse. **3** *a country going/moving backward* in reverse, worse, retrogressively, retrogradely.

backwash *noun* **1** *backwash of a ship* wash, backflow, wake, path, churning, disturbance. **2** *the backwash of the war* aftermath, result, effect; repercussions, reverberations, consequences, aftereffects.

backwoods *plural noun* wilderness, no man's land; country, rural area; *inf.* middle of nowhere, the wilds, the sticks.

bacteria *plural noun* germs, microorganisms, microbes, parasites, bacilli.

bad *adjective* **1** *bad workmanship* | *a bad driver* poor, unsatisfactory, inadequate, deficient, imperfect, defective, inferior, substandard, faulty, unacceptable, useless, worthless, inept, ineffectual; *inf.* lousy, crummy. **2** *smoking is a bad habit* | *it's bad for you* harmful, hurtful, damaging, dangerous, injurious, detrimental, destructive, ruinous, deleterious, unhealthy, unwholesome, poisonous. **3** *a bad man* | *leading a bad life* immoral, wicked, wrong, evil, sinful, corrupt, base, reprobate, depraved, dishonest, dishonorable, crooked. **4** *a bad child* naughty, mischievous, disobedient, unruly, wayward, refractory. **5** *bad weather* | *having a bad time* disagreeable, unpleasant, unwelcome,

uncomfortable, nasty, terrible, dreadful, adverse, grim, gloomy, unfortunate, unfavorable, unlucky, distressing. **6** *a bad time for house-buying* adverse, difficult, unfavorable, unfortunate, unsuitable, inappropriate, inapt. **7** *a bad mistake/accident* serious, severe, grave, disastrous, terrible, critical, acute. **8** *bad eggs* | *meat going bad* rotten, decayed, moldy, putrid, tainted, spoiled, contaminated, putrescent, putrefacient. **9** *an invalid feeling bad* ill, unwell, sick, poorly, indisposed, ailing, weak, feeble, diseased; *inf.* under the weather, below par. **10** *feeling bad about their actions* sorry, apologetic, regretful, conscience-stricken, contrite, remorseful, guilty, penitent, rueful, sad, upset. **11** *a bad check* worthless, invalid, counterfeit, false, spurious, fraudulent, fake; *inf.* bogus, phony. **not bad** all right, quite good, passable, tolerable, fair, average, moderate; *inf.* OK, okay, so-so.
Antonyms: GOOD; BENEFICIAL; VIRTUOUS; PLEASANT.

badge *noun* **1** *a badge on a uniform* crest, emblem, insignia, device, shield, escutcheon, brand. **2** *showing the badge of servility* mark, sign, symbol, indication, indicator, signal, characteristic, trademark.

badger *verb* pester, harass, plague, torment, bother, provoke, hound, nag, goad, bully, importune, harry; *inf.* bug, hassle.

badinage *noun* banter, repartee, wordplay, raillery, drollery; *inf.* joshing, kidding, ribbing, ragging.

badly *adverb* **1** *do the job badly* poorly, wrongly, incorrectly, unsatisfactorily, inadequately, imperfectly, defectively, faultily, ineptly, inefficiently, shoddily, carelessly, ineffectually. **2** *work out badly* unsuccessfully, unfortunately, unhappily, unluckily, unfavorably. **3** *badly hurt/defeated* greatly, deeply, severely, seriously, extremely, intensely, exceedingly, gravely, acutely. **4** *behave badly* naughtily, wrongly, immorally, wickedly, improperly, evilly, criminally. **5** *want something badly* very much, greatly, exceedingly, extremely, enormously, tremendously, considerably.
Antonym: WELL.

baffle *verb* **1** *baffled by the problem* puzzle, perplex, mystify, nonplus, stump, flummox, confound, dumbfound, bamboozle, bewilder, confuse, amaze, stagger, stun. **2** *baffle their plans* thwart, frustrate, foil, check, block, hinder, obstruct, bar, prevent, deflect, divert.

bag *noun* receptacle; handbag, pocketbook, purse, shoulder bag; case, suitcase, grip, flight bag, satchel, duffel bag; briefcase, attaché case; backpack, rucksack, haversack.

bag *verb* **1** *bag three pheasants* catch, capture, shoot, kill, trap, snare, land. **2** *the pants bagged* sag, hang loosely. **bag out** *it was so windy, our jackets bagged out* bulge, swell, balloon, fill out, inflate.

baggage *noun* luggage, gear, equipment, pack;

belongings, things, suitcases, bags, effects, paraphernalia, trappings, accouterments.

baggy *adjective* loose, slack, roomy, oversize, oversized, shapeless, ill-fitting, sagging; bulging, ballooning, floppy.

bail *noun pay the prisoner's bail* surety, security, bond, guarantee, warranty, pledge, collateral.

bail *verb* **bail out 1** *bail them out of their financial difficulties* | *we came to bail you out* help, assist, aid, rescue, relieve, give/lend a helping hand to. **2** *they bailed out before the crash* escape, get out, withdraw, retreat, beat a retreat, quit.

bait *noun* **1** *used as bait for the trap/fish* lure, decoy; troll, plug, fly, chum. **2** *low prices as bait for the consumer* attraction, lure, incentive, snare, temptation; allurement, enticement, incitement, inducement.

bait *verb* torment, persecute, badger, plague, harry, harass, hound, provoke, tease, annoy, irritate; *inf.* hassle, needle, give a hard time to.

bake *verb* **1** *bake the bread/dish* cook. **2** *earth baked by the sun* scorch, burn, sear, parch, dry, desiccate, fire.

balance *noun* **1** *weigh it on the balance* scale, scales, weighing machine. **2** *maintain the balance of international power* equilibrium, evenness, symmetry, parity, equity, equipoise, correspondence, uniformity, equivalence. **3** *I tripped and lost my balance* steadiness, stability. **4** *people of ability and balance* composure, poise, equanimity, aplomb, stability, assurance, confidence, self-possession, coolness, levelheadedness, sang-froid. **5** *her practicality acts as a balance to his genius* counterbalance, countercheck, counterweight, stabilizer, compensation, recompense, ballast. **6** *pay the balance of the account* | *collect the balance of the order* remainder, rest, residue, difference, surplus, excess. **in the balance** uncertain, at a turning point, critical, at a crisis. **on balance** taking everything into consideration, considering everything, all in all.
Antonyms: DIFFERENCE; INSTABILITY; UNCERTAINTY.

balance *verb* **1** *balancing the book on her head* steady, stabilize, poise. **2** *the weights must balance each other* | *advantages balancing disadvantages* counterbalance, counterweigh, counteract, offset, equalize, neutralize, compensate for, make up for, counterpoise. **3** *the profit and loss columns must balance* | *leisure and work time must balance* correspond, match, be level/parallel. **4** *balance the advantages and disadvantages* weigh, compare, evaluate, consider, deliberate, assess, appraise, estimate, review.

balcony *noun* **1** *the balcony of a villa* veranda, terrace, portico. **2** *the balcony of a theater* gallery, upper circle.

bald *adjective* **1** *a bald head* | *man* hairless, baldheaded, depilated. **2** *a bald landscape* barren, treeless, bare, uncovered, stark, exposed, bleak, unsheltered. **3** *a concise bald statement* blunt, direct, forthright, straight, straightforward, downright, outright, plain, simple, unadorned, unvarnished, unembellished, stark, severe, austere.
Antonyms: HAIRY; FERTILE; embellished.

balderdash *noun* nonsense, rubbish, twaddle, drivel, foolishness, gibberish, bunkum, claptrap; *inf.* bunk, hot air, bilge, poppycock, rot, bullshit, crap.

bale *noun* bundle, truss, pack, parcel, load.

baleful *adjective* threatening, menacing, evil, wicked, malevolent, malignant, sinister, venomous, harmful, injurious, dangerous, deadly, noxious, pernicious.

balk *verb* *balk their advance* hinder, prevent, impede, obstruct, thwart, foil, check, stop, halt, bar, block, forestall, frustrate, baffle. **balk at** *balk at the high fence* refuse, hesitate over, draw back from, flinch/recoil/shrink/shy from, evade, dodge, resist, eschew.
Antonyms: ACCEPT; ASSIST.

ball[1] *noun* **1** *a rubber ball* | *a ball of wool* sphere, globe, orb, globule, spheroid. **2** *shot a ball from the cannon* projectile; shot, grapeshot, bullet, pellet, slug.

ball[2] *noun* **1** *invited to the ball* dance, formal dance, social gathering; *inf.* prom, hop. **2** *they had a ball* great time; fun.

ballad *noun* folk song, song, lay, ditty.

ballast *noun* stabilizer, weight, counterweight; packing, filling.

balloon *noun* *travel in a balloon* hot-air balloon, airship, dirigible, Zeppelin, blimp.

balloon *verb skirts ballooning* swell out, puff out, fill out, billow, blow up, inflate.

ballot *noun* vote, poll, election, referendum, plebiscite; voting, polling.

ballyhoo *noun* **1** *disturbed by the ballyhoo from the party* fuss, commotion, to-do, hullabaloo, racket. **2** *a lot of ballyhoo about the new movie* publicity, propaganda, promotion, buildup; *inf.* hype.

balm *noun* **1** *apply balm to the burns* ointment, lotion, cream, salve, emollient, embrocation, liniment, unguent. **2** *balm for a troubled mind* remedy, curative, cure, restorative, palliative, solace, consolation, comfort.

balmy *adjective* **1** *balmy breezes* mild, gentle, temperate, calm, tranquil, soothing, soft, fragrant, scented, perfumed. **2** *a balmy idea* | *you're balmy* mad, foolish, stupid, idiotic, insane, silly, odd, queer, eccentric, peculiar, weird; *inf.* crazy, daft, batty, nutty, loony, loopy, crackpot, goofy, out to lunch.
Antonyms: SANE; SENSIBLE.

bamboozle *verb* **1** *bamboozled by their actions* puzzle, perplex, mystify, baffle, stump, bewilder, confuse, confound. **2** *bamboozle them into agreeing* trick, cheat, deceive, delude, hoodwink, mislead, hoax, fool, dupe, defraud, swindle; *inf.* gull, con.

ban *verb ban smoking* prohibit, forbid, veto,

disallow, bar, debar, outlaw, proscribe, suppress, interdict, reject, restrict, banish.
Antonyms: ALLOW; SANCTION.

ban *noun impose a ban on smoking* prohibition, veto, bar, embargo, boycott, proscription, interdict, interdiction, suppression, stoppage, restriction, taboo; censorship, banishment.
Antonyms: PERMISSION; SANCTION.

banal *adjective* hackneyed, trite, clichéd, commonplace, platitudinous, humdrum, stock, stereotyped, pedestrian, unoriginal, unimaginative, stale, uninspired, prosaic, dull, everyday, ordinary, tired, inane, fatuous, jejune; *inf.* old hat.
Antonyms: ORIGINAL; IMAGINATIVE; FRESH.

banality *noun* **1** *the banality of his remarks* triteness, platitudinousness, pedestrianism, lack of originality, unimaginativeness, staleness, prosaicness, dullness, ordinariness, fatuity. *See* BANAL. **2** *talking in banalities* cliché, trite phrase, platitude, truism, bromide, triviality.

band¹ *noun* **1** *iron/rubber band* bond, binding, cord, strap, tie, connection, link, chain, thong, fetter, manacle, shackle, ligature, ring, hoop. **2** *a band round the waist/hair* belt, cord, braid, sash, girdle, ribbon, fillet, cincture; waistband, headband, hatband, wristband, sweatband. **3** *a band of white on the black* strip, stripe, streak, line, bar, striation.

band² *noun* **1** *a band of robbers* group, troop, company, gang, mob, pack, bunch, body, gathering, crowd, horde, throng, assembly, assemblage, association, society, club, clique, set, coterie. **2** *a singer with the band | a brass/jazz band* musical group, group, pop group, combo, ensemble, orchestra.

band³ *verb band together* join, group, unite, merge, combine, team up, gather, ally, affiliate, associate, federate, consolidate.

bandage *noun* dressing, gauze, compress; *Trademark* Band-Aid.

bandage *verb* bind, bind up, dress, cover, plaster.

bandit *noun* robber, brigand, outlaw, desperado, hijacker, plunderer, marauder, gangster, criminal, crook, thief, gunman, highwayman, pirate, racketeer.

bandy *adjective having bandy legs* bandy-legged, bowed, bowlegged, curved, crooked, bent, misshapen.

bandy *verb* **1** *bandy words* exchange, swap, trade, interchange, barter, reciprocate. **2** *bandy rumors about* circulate, spread, pass, toss about, disseminate.

bane *noun* ruin, death, ruination, destruction, scourge, torment, plague, affliction, calamity, despair, misery, woe, trouble, nuisance, trial, burden, blight, curse, nightmare, bête noir.

bang *noun* **1** *a loud bang* explosive noise, report, burst, boom, clash, clang, peal, clap, pop, slam, thud, thump. **2** *a bang on the head* blow, bump,

hit, slap, punch, knock, stroke, smack, whack, rap, cuff, box, buffet; *inf.* wallop, bash, sock.

bang *verb* **1** *bang the table | banged her nose* hit, strike, beat, thump, hammer, knock, rap, pound, thud, pummel, whack; *inf.* bash. **2** *bang the door* slam, crash. **3** *the fireworks banged* explode, burst, blow up, detonate, pop, resound, echo.

bang *adverb* **1** *fell bang on the floor | bang went her hopes* noisily, violently, suddenly, abruptly. **2** *bang in the middle* precisely, right, exactly, absolutely, directly; *inf.* slap-bang, smack.

bangle *noun* bracelet, wristlet, anklet, armlet.

banish *verb* **1** *banish from the country* exile, deport, expel, eject, drive away, expatriate, cast out, outlaw, transport, oust, evict, throw out, exclude, proscribe, excommunicate. **2** *banished from her presence | banish fear* dismiss, drive/send away, dispel, oust, cast/shut out, get rid of, ban, bar, exclude, eliminate, dislodge.
Antonyms: ADMIT; ACCEPT; WELCOME.

banishment *noun* exile, deportation, expulsion, expatriation, transportation, proscription. *See* BANISH 1.

banisters *plural noun* handrail, railing, rail, balustrade; balusters.

bank¹ *noun* **1** *a grassy bank* slope, rise, incline, gradient, mound, hillock, knoll. **2** *a river/canal bank* edge, side, shore, brink, margin, embankment.

bank² *verb bank an aircraft* tilt, slope, slant, incline, pitch. **bank up 1** *bank up the leaves | snow banked up* pile/heap up, stack up, gather, accumulate. **2** *bank up the fire/flames* damp down, stifle.

bank³ *noun* **1** *borrow from the bank* financial institution; commercial bank, merchant bank, savings bank. **2** *empty the child's bank* piggy bank, cashbox, safe, strongbox, coffer. **3** *a bank of information | blood bank* store, reserve, accumulation, stock, stockpile, reservoir, supply, fund, hoard, storehouse, repository, depository.

bank⁴ *verb* **1** *bank the money* deposit, save, save up, keep, lay by, put aside, put by for a rainy day; *inf.* salt away, stash away. **2** *bank with the local bank* deal, do business, have an account, invest. **bank on/upon** rely on, count on, depend on, lean on, trust, believe in, have/place confidence in, pin one's hopes on.

bank⁵ *noun a bank of switches* row, line, tier, array, group, series, chain, course, progression, rank, succession.

bankrupt *adjective bankrupt businessmen/businesses* insolvent, failed, ruined, penurious, impecunious, financially embarrassed, distressed, in the red; *inf.* on the rocks, broke, hard up. **bankrupt of** *bankrupt of funds/ideas* lacking, in need of, deficient in, wanting, without, deprived of, bereft of, exhausted of, depleted of.
Antonym: SOLVENT.

bankrupt *verb* ruin, beggar, cripple, impoverish; *inf.* bust.

bankruptcy *noun* insolvency, liquidation, indebtedness, failure, ruin, ruination, disaster, penury; straitened circumstances.

banner *noun* **1** *the ship's banner | hung banners in the stadium* flag, standard, pennant, pennon; colors; sign. **2** *the banner on the paper's front page* banner line, headline, streamer, screamer.

banner *adjective a banner year for apples* excellent, red-letter, outstanding, notable, exceptional, leading.

banquet *noun* dinner, dinner party, feast, meal, party, repast, treat, revel.

banter *noun indulge in lighthearted banter* repartee, badinage, teasing, joking, jesting, jocularity, raillery, wordplay, mockery, ridicule; *inf.* kidding, ribbing, joshing.

banter *verb bantering not insulting* tease, joke, jest, mock, ridicule, make fun of, twit; *inf.* kid, rib, rag, josh.

baptism *noun* **1** *the baptism of the child* christening, naming, immersion, sprinkling; *fml.* aspersing. **2** *survive his baptism as a teacher* debut, initiation, introduction, inauguration, launch, beginning, commencement, rite of passage.

baptize *verb* **1** *baptize a baby* christen, name, immerse, sprinkle. **2** *baptize as a teacher* initiate, introduce, inaugurate, launch.

bar *noun* **1** *an iron bar | a window bar* rod, pole, stake, stick, shaft, rail, spar, crosspiece. **2** *a bar of soap/gold* block, brick, cake, wedge, lump. **3** *no bar to promotion* obstacle, barrier. *See* BARRIER 2. **4** *bar of light* band, strip, line, belt, streak, stripe. **5** *a ship stuck on a bar* sandbar, shoal, shallow, reef, sandbank, ridge, ledge, shelf. **6** *drinking in a bar* tavern, saloon, pub, lounge. **7** *snack bar* counter, luncheonette, lunchroom.

bar *verb* **1** *bar the door* bolt, lock, fasten, padlock, secure, latch. **2** *barred from entering | barred from the competition* debar, prohibit, preclude, forbid, ban, exclude, keep out, block, impede; obstruct, hinder, restrain, check, stop, defer. *Antonyms:* UNLOCK; ADMIT; ACCEPT.

bar *preposition bar a few* except, excepting, except for, with the exception of, apart from, besides, other than, excluding, barring, omitting, leaving out.

barb *noun* **1** *a barb in one's finger* thorn, needle, spike, prickle, bristle, prong, point. **2** *the barbs of his rival* insult, sneer, gibe, affront; scoffing, scorn, sarcasm; *inf.* dig.

barbarian *noun* **1** *knights defeating the barbarians* savage, brute, wild man/woman, troglodyte, monster. **2** *a classroom full of barbarians* ruffian, lout, vandal, hooligan, boor, ignoramus, philistine, yahoo.

barbarian *adjective* **1** *barbarian tribes* savage, uncivilized, primitive, brutish, wild, heathen. **2** *barbarian football fans* loutish, hooligan, boorish, uncivilized, wild, rough, coarse, gross, uncouth, vulgar, philistine.

barbaric *adjective* **1** *barbaric tribes* savage, unciv-
ilized, primitive. *See* BARBARIAN adjective 1. **2** *barbaric customs* brutal, savage, cruel, vicious, fierce, ferocious, bestial, barbarous, murderous, inhuman, ruthless, remorseless.

barbarism *noun* **1** *the barbarism of ancient tribes* savagery, uncivilizedness, primitiveness, brutishness, heathenism. **2** *the barbarism of the punishment* brutality, savagery, cruelty, barbarity. *See* BARBARITY 1. **3** *a speech full of barbarisms* misuse, misusage, misapplication, corruption; error, slip.

barbarity *noun* **1** *the barbarity of the punishment* brutality, savagery, cruelty, viciousness, bestiality, inhumanity, ruthlessness. **2** *barbarities committed* atrocity, brutality, outrage, enormity.

barbarous *adjective* **1** *barbarous tribes* savage, uncivilized, barbarian. *See* BARBARIAN adjective 1. **2** *barbarous punishment* brutal, savage, cruel, barbaric. *See* BARBARIC adjective 2. **3** *barbarous tastes* unrefined, unsophisticated, uncultivated, uncultured, ignorant, vulgar, crude, uncouth, coarse.

barbecue *noun hold a barbecue* cookout, picnic, outdoor meal.

barbecue *verb barbecue the steaks* grill, charcoal-broil, charcoal, broil, cook.

bare *adjective* **1** *sunbathing bare | a bare chest* naked, stark naked, nude, uncovered, exposed, unclothed, undressed, unclad, stripped, denuded. **2** *a bare room* empty, vacant, unfurnished, unadorned, uncovered, stark, austere, unembellished. **3** *a bare landscape* bleak, unsheltered, unprotected, unshielded, desolate, barren, treeless, without vegetation. **4** *the bare facts* simple, plain, bald, basic, essential, straightforward, stark, unvarnished, unembellished, cold, hard, sheer, literal. **5** *the bare minimum* mere, basic, meager, scanty, inadequate. **bare of** *a cupboard bare of food* without, lacking, devoid of, wanting, destitute of. *Antonyms:* clothed; embellished.

bare *verb bared his soul | saw his strength when he bared his arms* reveal, uncover, expose, lay bare, unveil, disclose, show, divulge, unmask, bring to light.

barefaced *adjective* blatant, flagrant, glaring, arrant, shameless, brazen, bold, impudent, insolent, audacious, brash, open, undisguised, unconcealed, transparent, patent, manifest, palpable.

barely *adverb* hardly, scarcely, only just, just, by the skin of one's teeth. *Antonym:* FULLY.

bargain *noun* **1** *make a bargain* agreement, contract, pact, transaction, deal, treaty, negotiation, arrangement, compact, covenant, concordat, understanding, pledge, promise, engagement. **2** *get a bargain* discount, reduction, good buy, sales article; *inf.* steal, giveaway. **in/into the bargain** *in/into the bargain it rained* moreover, besides, also, over and above that, additionally, as well.

bargain *verb buyer and seller were bargaining* haggle, barter, deal, trade, traffic. **bargain for** *more than we bargained for* expect, anticipate, be prepared for, allow for, take into account/consideration, foresee, look for, contemplate, imagine. **bargain on** *bargaining on victory* rely on, depend on, count on, bank on, hope for, plan on, expect, anticipate.

barge *noun* canal boat, flatboat, flat-bottomed boat, lighter, houseboat.

barge *verb* **barge in** *barge in during prayers* burst in, break in, intrude, interrupt; *inf.* butt in, horn in. **barge into** *people barging into each other* bump into, crash into, collide with, plow into, smash into.

bark[1] *noun the bark of a tree/shrub* covering, cortex, husk, coating, casing, crust, skin; hide, rind, shell, hull, sheath.

bark[2] *verb* **bark one's shin** scrape, skin, abrade, rub, excoriate, strip, flay, shave.

bark[3] *verb* **1** *the dog barked* howl, woof, yelp, yap, bay, growl, snarl. **2** *the teacher barked at the students* shout, yell, bawl, thunder, scream, screech, shriek, snap, snarl, bluster.

barn *noun* outbuilding, shed, shelter; stables.

baron *noun* **1** *the king and the barons* noble, nobleman, aristocrat, peer, lord. **2** *oil barons* tycoon, magnate, executive, industrialist, financier, captain of industry.

baroque *adjective* ornate, elaborate, decorated, embellished, flamboyant, ostentatious, extravagant, showy; fussy, florid, convoluted; rococo, grotesque.

barracks *plural noun* billet, garrison, camp, encampment, fort, cantonment, caserne; quarters.

barrage *noun* **1** *soldiers killed by the enemy's barrage* gunfire, bombardment, shelling, battery, cannonade, volley, broadside, salvo, fusillade, wall/curtain of fire. **2** *a barrage of criticism* deluge, stream, storm, torrent, onslaught, flood, avalanche, hail, burst, mass, abundance, superabundance, plethora, profusion.

barrel *noun* cask, keg, butt, vat, tun, tub, tank, hogshead.

barren *adjective* **1** *a barren woman* infertile, sterile, childless. **2** *barren land* infertile, unproductive, uncultivable, unfruitful, arid, desert, waste, desolate. **3** *barren discussion | barren way of life* uninteresting, boring, dull, uninspiring, stale, prosaic, futile, worthless, useless, valueless, unrewarding, purposeless, vapid, lackluster. **Antonyms:** FERTILE; FRUITFUL; PRODUCTIVE.

barricade *noun barricades keeping back the crowd* barrier, obstacle, blockade, bar, fence, obstruction, roadblock, bulwark, stockade, rampart, palisade.

barricade *verb barricade the door/house* block,

blockade, obstruct, bar, shut off/in, fence in, defend, fortify.

barrier *noun* **1** *the barrier in the parking lot* barricade, bar, fence, railing, obstacle, blockade, roadblock. **2** *a barrier to success | the language barrier* obstacle, hindrance, impediment, drawback, check, hurdle, restriction, stumbling block, handicap, difficulty, restraint.

barter *noun an economy based on barter* trading, exchange, swapping, bargaining, haggling, trafficking.

barter *verb* **1** *barter his horse for food* trade, trade off, exchange, swap. **2** *bartered for a better price* bargain, haggle.

base *noun* **1** *the base of a column* foundation, support, prop, stay, stand, pedestal, rest, bottom, bed, foot, substructure, plinth. **2** *paints with an oil base* basis, core, essence, component, essential, fundamental, root, heart, principal, source, origin. **3** *mountaineers setting up a base* headquarters, center, camp, site, station, settlement, post, starting point. **Antonyms:** TOP; APEX.

base *verb* **1** *based on historical facts* found, build, construct, form, establish, ground, rest, root, fasten, hinge, derive. **2** *based in Chicago* locate, station, situate, post, place, install.

base *adjective* **1** *base motives* low, mean, sordid, bad, wrong, immoral, dishonorable, evil, wicked, nefarious, debased, sinful, unprincipled, dissolute, disreputable, reprobate, corrupt, depraved, vile, shameful, disgraceful, scandalous, infamous, ignoble, vulgar, foul, despicable, contemptible. **2** *base servitude* menial, subservient, servile, lowly, mean, low, slavish, groveling, sniveling, cowering, wretched, downtrodden, obsequious, sycophantic. **3** *base coin* debased, alloyed, impure, adulterated, spurious, counterfeit. **4** *base metal* inferior, nonprecious. **Antonyms:** GOOD; ADMIRABLE; LOFTY.

baseless *adjective* groundless, unfounded, unsupported, unsubstantiated, uncorroborated, unconfirmed, unjustifiable, unjustified.

basement *noun* cellar; crypt, vault.

bashful *adjective* shy, reserved, diffident, retiring, modest, self-conscious, coy, demure, reticent, self-effacing, hesitant, shrinking, backward, timid, timorous, abashed, blushing, embarrassed, shamefaced, sheepish. **Antonyms:** BOLD; confident; FORWARD.

bashfulness *noun* shyness, reserve, modesty, self-consciousness, coyness, demureness, reticence, self-effacement, hesitancy, timidity, timorousness, embarrassment. *See* BASHFUL.

basic *adjective* **1** *basic principles* fundamental, elementary, rudimentary, primary, radical, key, central, essential, vital, necessary, indispensable, intrinsic, underlying. **2** *basic salary* bottom, lowest-level, lowest, starting, ground, without commission. **3** *pretty basic accommodations* plain, simple, spartan, sparse, stark, unadorned, without frills, no-frills.

basically *adverb* fundamentally, at heart, intrinsically, essentially, inherently, primarily, firstly, radically, mostly, for the most part, in the main, in substance.

basics *plural noun* fundamentals, (bare) essentials, facts, hard facts, rudiments, principles, practicalities, realities, ABCs; *inf.* nitty-gritty, brass tacks, nuts and bolts.

basin *noun* 1 *carry water in a basin* container, receptacle, vessel; bowl, dish, pan. 2 *the river basin* bed, channel.

basis *noun* 1 *no scientific basis for the statement* support, foundation, base, footing, reasoning; grounds. 2 *the statement will form the basis of the discussion* starting point, premise, fundamental point/principle, principal constituent, main ingredient; groundwork, core, essence. 3 *on a part-time basis* footing, procedure, condition, status, position.

bask *verb* 1 *bask in the sunshine* lie, laze, lounge, relax, loll, sunbathe, sun/warm oneself. 2 *bask in their admiration* luxuriate, revel, wallow, enjoy, delight, take pleasure, rejoice, relish, savor, indulge oneself.

basket *noun* container, receptacle; hamper, creel, pannier.

bass *adjective* deep, deep-pitched, deep-toned, low, low-pitched, low-toned, resonant, sonorous.

bastard *noun* 1 *born a bastard* illegitimate child, love child. 2 *a rotten bastard* scoundrel, cad, blackguard, villain, rascal.

bastard *adjective* 1 *bastard child* illegitimate. 2 *a bastard language* adulterated, impure, hybrid, alloyed, inferior, imperfect, spurious, counterfeit, artificial, sham, false, fake.

bastardize *verb* *bastardize the language* debase, degrade, devalue, depreciate, corrupt, adulterate, defile, contaminate.

bastion *noun* 1 *the bastion of a fort* projection, bulwark, rampart, parapet. 2 *storm the enemy bastion* fort, fortress, citadel, keep, stronghold, garrison. 3 *the last bastion of freedom* protection, protector, defense, defender, support, supporter, prop, mainstay, stronghold.

batch *noun* group, quantity, lot, bunch, accumulation, mass, cluster, set, collection, assemblage, pack, crowd, aggregate, conglomeration.

bath *noun* 1 *a warm bath* soak, dip, shower. 2 *install a bath* bathtub, tub, whirlpool, sauna, steam bath.

bathe *verb* 1 *bathe every day* have/take a bath, wash, soak, shower. 2 *bathe the wound* clean, cleanse, wash, soak, steep, immerse, wet, moisten, rinse, suffuse. 3 *bathe in the sea* swim, take a dip. 4 *bathed in sunlight* envelope, suffuse.

bathing suit *noun* swimsuit, swimming trunks, trunks, bikini, swimwear.

bathos *noun* anticlimax, letdown; sentimentality, mawkishness.

bathroom *noun* toilet, men's/ladies' room, facilities, lavatory, washroom; *inf.* john.

baton *noun* stick, bar, wand, rod, staff, club, truncheon, mace.

battalion *noun* 1 *military battalions* unit; troops, forces; garrison, division, regiment, brigade, squadron, company, platoon, section, detachment, contingent, legion. 2 *battalions of protesters* crowd, mob, throng, horde, multitude, herd, host.

batten[1] *noun* *a wooden batten* board, strip, bar, bolt, clamp.

batten[2] *verb* *batten down the hatches* fasten, fix, secure.

batten[3] *verb* *batten on the poor* thrive/flourish/prosper/fatten/increase at the expense of, be a parasite on.

batter *verb* 1 *battering their prisoners* hit, strike, beat, bash, assault, wallop, thump, thrash, lash, pound, deliver/rain blows on, pummel, buffet, abuse; *inf.* whack. 2 *countries battered by war* damage, injure, hurt, harm, bruise, wound, crush, shatter, smash, destroy, demolish, ruin, impair, mar, spoil.

battered *adjective* *battered children* beaten, assaulted, thrashed, abused. *See* BATTER 1.

battery *noun* 1 *a battery of tests* series, sequence, set, cycle, chain, string, progression, succession. 2 *convicted of assault and battery* attack, mugging, grievous bodily harm, beating, striking, thumping, thrashing, bashing; aggression. 3 *the military battery* artillery, cannonry; guns, cannons.

battle *noun* 1 *battle between enemy forces* war, armed conflict, conflict, fight, clash, contest, struggle, skirmish, engagement, encounter, confrontation, collision, meeting, campaign, crusade, tussle, scuffle, scrap, melee; fighting, warfare, combat, action; hostilities. *See also table at* WAR. 2 *a battle of wills* clash, conflict, contest, competition, tournament, struggle, disagreement, argument, dispute, controversy, debate; dissension, altercation, strife.

Antonyms: TRUCE; PEACE.

battle *verb* 1 *battling against the elements* | *battle for fair wages* fight, struggle, strive, combat, contend, war, feud. 2 *battle one's way through the crowd* fight, struggle, labor, push. 3 *neighbors constantly battling* fight, war, feud, argue, quarrel, disagree, bicker, wrangle, cross swords, lock horns.

battle-ax *noun* *not the battle-ax we thought she was* harridan, martinet, termagant, virago, shrew, fury.

battle cry *noun* 1 *the battle cry of the invaders* war cry, rallying call. 2 *the battle cry of the women's movement* slogan, motto, watchword, catchword, catchphrase, shibboleth.

battlefield *noun* battleground, front, battlefront, battle lines, field of operations, field of battle, combat zone, theater/arena of war, war zone.

battlement *noun* parapet, rampart, balustrade, wall, bulwark; fortification, breastwork, crenellation, outwork.

battleship *noun* warship, man-of-war, ship of the line, cruiser, battle cruiser, capital ship, dreadnought.

batty *adjective* mad, foolish, stupid, idiotic, insane, silly, odd, queer, eccentric; *inf.* crazy, daft, bats, bonkers, nutty, nuts, loony, off one's rocker, around/round the bend, out to lunch.

bauble *noun* trinket, knickknack, trifle, ornament, toy, plaything, gewgaw, gimcrack, bagatelle.

bawd *noun* prostitute, whore, streetwalker; *inf.* hooker.

bawdy *adjective* pornographic, obscene, vulgar, indecent, blue, racy, titillating, crude, coarse, rude, gross, ribald, lewd, dirty, filthy, smutty, off-color, naughty, suggestive, indelicate, unseemly, indecorous, salacious, erotic, prurient, lascivious, licentious, risqué, scatological; *inf.* raunchy.
Antonyms: DECENT; SEEMLY; CLEAN.

bawl *verb* **1** *a child bawling* cry, sob, weep, wail, blubber, snivel, squall. **2** *he bawled a reply* shout, call/cry out, yell, roar, bellow, screech, scream, howl, whoop, vociferate; *inf.* holler.
bawl out *bawled me out for being late* rebuke, chastise, yell at, scold.

bay¹ *noun ships moored in the bay* cove, inlet, indentation, natural harbor, gulf, basin, sound, arm.

bay² *noun a table in the bay* alcove, recess, niche, opening, nook.

bay³ *noun the bay of the hounds* baying, howl, howling, bark, cry, ululation. *See* BAY⁴ *verb.*

bay⁴ *verb hounds baying* howl, bark, yelp, cry, growl, bellow, roar, clamor, ululate.

bayonet *noun* blade, knife, dagger, poniard.

bazaar *noun* **1** *a Turkish bazaar* market, marketplace, mart, exchange. **2** *the church bazaar* fête, fair, sale.

be *verb* **1** *will there be many people at the party?* exist, live, be alive, have life/being, breathe. **2** *the lamp is on the table | Mary is at the farm* be situated, be located, dwell, reside. **3** *the concert is tomorrow* take place, occur, come about, come to pass, arise, crop up, transpire. **4** *she has been there all her life* remain, stay, last, continue, survive, endure, persist, prevail, obtain. **5** *he was at church* attend, be present, be at.

beach *noun sunbathing at/on the beach* seaside, coast; seashore, shore, water's edge, coastline, sands, sand, strand.

beachcomber *noun* **1** *beachcombers collecting wood* scavenger, forager, gatherer, collector, accumulator. **2** *beachcombers and other homeless* tramp, vagrant, hobo, wanderer, scrounger; *inf.* bum.

beached *adjective* aground, ashore, grounded, high and dry, marooned, stranded, wrecked, abandoned.

beacon *noun* signal fire/light, bonfire, smoke signal, flare, beam, rocket, signal, danger signal; lighthouse, watchtower.

bead *noun* **1** *glass beads* ball, pellet, pill, globule, spheroid, oval. **2** *beads of sweat* drop, droplet, bubble, blob, dot, glob, dewdrop, teardrop.

beads *plural noun* **1** *wearing beads and earrings* string of beads, necklace, pendant, choker. **2** *saying one's beads* rosary, chaplet.

beak *noun* **1** *a bird's beak* bill, nib, mandible; *dial.* neb. **2** *the man's large beak* nose, snout, proboscis. **3** *a ship's beak* prow, bow, bowsprit, stem, rostrum, ram.

beam *noun* **1** *the roof beams* board, timber, plank, joist, rafter, girder, spar, support, lath. **2** *a beam of light* ray, shaft, stream, streak, flash, gleam, glow, glimmer, glint; radiation, emission. **3** *a beam of happiness* smile, grin.

beam *verb* **1** *light beamed from the window* emit, radiate, shine. **2** *beam radio/television programs* broadcast, transmit, direct, aim. **3** *beaming from ear to ear* smile, grin.

bear *verb* **1** *bear gifts* carry, bring, transport, move, convey, take, fetch, haul; *inf.* tote. **2** *bear tales* spread, transmit, carry. **3** *bear a signature/ inscription* carry, display, exhibit, show, be marked with. **4** *bear a crop* yield, produce, give forth, give, provide, supply, generate. **5** *bear a son* give birth to, breed, bring forth, beget, engender. **6** *bear the cost* carry, sustain, support, shoulder, uphold. **7** *cannot bear his attitude | can't bear the thought* stand, endorse, tolerate, put up with, abide, stomach, permit, allow, admit, brook. **8** *much pain to bear* suffer, endure, undergo, tolerate, put up with, experience, go through, support, weather. **9** *bear a grudge | bear evil thoughts* have, hold, harbor, possess, entertain, cherish. **10** *bear left* veer, curve, go, move, turn, fork, diverge, deviate, bend. **bear out** *bear out the facts* confirm, corroborate, substantiate, endorse, vindicate, give credence to, support, ratify, warrant, uphold, justify, prove, authenticate, verify. **bear up** *bearing up against disaster* cope, persevere, carry on, manage, endure, withstand, grin and bear. **bear with** *bear with us during the delay* tolerate, put up with, endure, make allowances for, be patient with, show forbearance toward.
Antonyms: ABANDON; give up (*see* GIVE).

bearable *adjective* endurable, tolerable, supportable, sufferable, sustainable, admissible, passable, manageable.
Antonyms: UNBEARABLE; INTOLERABLE; INSUFFERABLE.

beard *noun a man with a beard* facial hair, whiskers, bristle, stubble, five o'clock shadow; full beard, goatee, Vandyke, sideburns, muttonchops.

beard *verb beard the opposition* brave, confront, face, challenge, come face-to-face with, oppose, defy, stand up against, dare.

bearded *adjective* unshaven, whiskered, bewhiskered, stubbly, bristly, hairy, hirsute, bushy, shaggy.

bearer *noun* **1** *a luggage bearer* carrier, porter, conveyor, transporter. **2** *a bearer of good news* messenger, agent, runner, courier. **3** *pay the bearer of the check* payee, consignee, beneficiary.

bearing *noun* **1** *having a distinguished bearing* deportment, posture, carriage, gait. **2** *her bearing throughout the trial* attitude, behavior, manner, demeanor, air, aspect, mien. **3** *the bearing of a ship* course, direction. **4** *have a bearing on the case* relevance, pertinence, connection. **5** *lose one's bearings* orientation, location, position, situation, whereabouts, track, way.

beast *noun* **1** *a beast of the jungle* animal, creature, brute; mammal, quadruped. **2** *a cruel beast to his family* brute, monster, savage, swine, pig, ogre, fiend, sadist, barbarian.

beastly *adjective* **1** *a beastly apparition* beastlike, bestial, animal, animal-like, brutal. **2** *a beastly cold* awful, terrible, horrible, rotten, nasty, foul, unpleasant, disagreeable, vile.

beat *verb* **1** *beat the drum* bang, hit, strike, pound. **2** *he would never beat the dog/child* hit, strike, batter, thump, wallop, hammer, punch, knock, thrash, pound, pummel, slap, smack, flay, whip, lash, chastise, thwack, cuff, bruise, buffet, box, cudgel, club, maul, pelt, drub; *inf.* belt, bash, whack, clout, slug, tan, bop, lay into, knock about, rough up. **3** *their hearts beating* throb, pound, thump, pulsate, pulse, palpitate, vibrate, tremble. **4** *the bird's wings beat* flap, flutter, quiver, tremble, vibrate. **5** *beat the eggs* mix, blend, whip, whisk, stir. **6** *waves beating against/on the shore* strike, dash, break against, lap, wash. **7** *beating metal into rods* hammer, forge, form, shape, work, stamp, fashion, model. **8** *beat a path* tread, tramp, trample, wear, track, groove. **9** *beat the opposition* defeat, conquer, vanquish, trounce, rout, overpower, overcome, overwhelm, overthrow, subdue, quash; *inf.* lick. **10** *beat the record* outdo, surpass, exceed, eclipse, transcend, top, outstrip. **beat up** assault, attack, mug, batter, thrash; *inf.* knock about/around, work over, clobber, rough up.

beat *noun* **1** *the beat of the drum | three beats given to the carpet* bang, banging, stroke, striking, blow, hit, punch, pound, pummel, slap, smack, thwack. **2** *the beat of his heart* throb, throbbing, pounding, pulsating, pulsing, beating, thumping, palpitating, vibrating, vibration. **3** *musical/metrical beat* rhythm, stress, meter, time, measure, accent, cadence. **4** *policeman's beat* round, circuit, course, route, way, path, orbit.

beat *adjective* *I'm just beat after the hike* exhausted, tired, worn out, fatigued, wearied, spent.

beaten *adjective* **1** *the beaten contestant/army* defeated, vanquished, trounced, routed, overcome, overwhelmed, overpowered, bested, quashed; *inf.* licked. **2** *beaten metal* hammered,

forged, formed, shaped, worked. *See* BEAT *verb* 7. **3** *beaten paths* trodden, well-trodden, much-trodden, well-used, much-traveled, trampled, worn, well-worn. **4** *the beaten eggs/cake batter* mixed, blended, whipped, whisked, stirred, frothy, foamy.

Antonyms: VICTORIOUS; SUCCESSFUL.

beatific *adjective* **1** *a beatific existence* blessed, blissful, heavenly, celestial, paradisiacal. **2** *children with beatific smiles* rapturous, joyful, ecstatic, blissful, happy, glad.

beating *noun* **1** *the savage beating of the prisoners* hitting, striking, battering, thrashing; corporal punishment, chastisement; *inf.* belting, bashing, pasting. *See* BEAT *verb* 2. **2** *recovering from their beating by the opposition* defeat, conquest, vanquishing, trouncing, overthrow, downfall. *See* BEAT *verb* 9. **3** *the beating of their hearts* throb, pulsating, pulse, pulsing, palpitating. *See* BEAT *noun* 2. **4** *the beating of the waves* striking, dashing, breaking. *See* BEAT *verb* 6.

beatitude *noun* blessedness, bliss, ecstasy, exaltation, supreme happiness, divine rapture, sainthood.

beau *noun* **1** *his sister's beau* boyfriend, sweetheart, lover, fiancé, partner, significant other, escort, admirer, suitor, follower; *lit.* swain. **2** *beaux of the eighteenth century* dandy, fop, coxcomb, gallant, cavalier, popinjay.

beautiful *adjective* ravishing, gorgeous, stunning, alluring, lovely, attractive, pretty, handsome, good-looking, pleasing, comely, charming, delightful, glamorous, appealing, fair, fine, becoming, seemly, winsome, graceful, elegant, exquisite.

Antonyms: UGLY; HIDEOUS.

beautify *verb* **1** *beautify the surroundings* adorn, embellish, enhance, decorate, ornament, garnish, gild, smarten, prettify, glamorize. **2** *beautify oneself* apply makeup/cosmetics, prettify, glamorize, primp, preen; *inf.* do/doll oneself up.

beauty *noun* **1** *the beauty of the women/surroundings* loveliness, attractiveness, prettiness, handsomeness, allure, allurement, charm, glamour, grace, artistry, symmetry; *fml.* pulchritude. *See* BEAUTIFUL. **2** *the sisters were all great beauties* belle, charmer, enchantress, seductress, femme fatale, Venus, goddess; *inf.* good-looker, lovely, stunner, knockout, dish. **3** *the beauty of the scheme* attraction, good thing, advantage, benefit, asset, strong point, boon, blessing.

becalmed *adjective* motionless, at a halt, still, at a standstill, stranded, stuck, marooned.

because *conjunction* *he left because he was ill* since, as, in view of the fact that, owing to the fact that, seeing that. **because of** *leaving because of ill health* on account of, as a result of, owing to, by reason of, as a consequence of, thanks to, by virtue of.

beckon verb **1** *beckon to the waiter* signal, gesture, make a gesture, gesticulate, motion, wave, nod, call, summon, bid. **2** *the sea beckons him* draw, pull, call, invite, attract, tempt, entice, allure, coax, persuade, induce.

become verb **1** *she became rich* | *become a scientist* come to be, turn out to be, grow, grow into, mature into, evolve into, pass into, change into, turn into, alter into, transform into, be transformed into, be converted into, metamorphose into. **2** *the dress becomes her* suit, flatter, look good on, set off, enhance, embellish, ornament, grace. **3** *it ill becomes you to behave like that* befit, behoove, suit, be suitable/fitting to. **4** *what became of him?* happen to, befall, be the fate/lot of.

becoming adjective **1** *a becoming hat* flattering, comely, attractive, lovely, pretty, handsome, stylish, elegant, chic, tasteful. **2** *hardly becoming behavior* suitable, fitting, appropriate, apt, proper, right, decent, seemly, worthy, decorous, graceful. **3** *behavior becoming to a teacher* befitting, suitable for, appropriate to, in keeping with, compatible with, consistent with, congruous with.
Antonyms: UNBECOMING; INAPPROPRIATE; IMPROPER.

bed noun **1** *she liked to sleep in her own bed* divan, bunk, cot, berth, couch, hammock, litter, stretcher, double bed, single bed, four-poster, bunk bed, water bed, crib, cradle, bassinet; *inf.* sack. **2** *a flower bed* plot, area, lot, patch, space, border, strip, row. **3** *a bed of concrete* base, basis, foundation, bottom, support, substructure, substratum; groundwork. **go to bed 1** retire, go to sleep; *inf.* turn in, hit the sack/hay. **2** have sex, make love.

bed verb **1** *stones bedded in concrete* embed, set, fix into, insert, inlay, implant, bury, base, establish, found. **2** *desiring to bed her* go to bed with, have sex with, sleep with, spend the night with. **3** *bed out the pansies* plant, set in beds/soil. **bed down 1** *bed down in the shed* go to bed/sleep, retire, settle down, have a nap; *inf.* turn in, hit the sack/hay. **2** *bed the children down* put to bed, tuck in, settle down, say goodnight to.

bedclothes plural noun bedding, bedcovers, covers; blankets, duvets, quilts, eiderdowns, sheets, bed linen, linen.

bedeck verb deck, decorate, adorn, ornament, trim, festoon, array, embellish, garnish.

bedevil verb afflict, torment, beset, plague, harass, distress, trouble, worry, frustrate, annoy, vex, irritate, irk, pester, torture.

bedlam noun uproar, pandemonium, commotion, confusion, furor, hubbub, clamor, disorder, chaos, turmoil, tumult, noise, disarray; *inf.* madhouse.

bedraggled adjective muddy, muddied, wet, dirty, messy, sodden, soaking, soaking wet, soaked, drenched, saturated, dripping, soggy, splashed, soiled, stained, disheveled, disordered, untidy, unkempt.

bedridden adjective confined to bed, housebound; *inf.* laid up, flat on one's back.

bedrock noun **1** *the bedrock beneath the soil* substratum, foundation, rock bed. **2** *the finances are at bedrock* lowest point/level, rock bottom, nadir. **3** *the bedrock of their beliefs* | *get down to bedrock* basis, core, nitty-gritty; basics, fundamentals, essentials.

beef noun **1** *more noted for his beef than his brain* brawn, muscle, muscularity, heftiness, burliness, bulk, physique, strength, powerfulness, robustness. *See* BEEFY 1. **2** *tired of the beef about the traffic* complaint, grumbling, grumble, criticism, objection, protestation, grievance; *inf.* griping, gripe, grousing, nitpicking.

beefy adjective **1** *beefy wrestler* brawny, muscular, hefty, burly, hulking, strapping, thickset, solid, strong, powerful, heavy, robust, sturdy, stocky. **2** *a beefy youngster* heavy, solid, fat, chubby, plump, overweight, stout, buxom, obese, fleshy, podgy, rotund, portly, corpulent, paunchy, dumpy.
Antonyms: SCRAWNY; PUNY.

beer noun ale, stout, lager, malt liquor, porter; *inf.* brew, suds.

beetling adjective *beetling brows/cliffs* overhanging, projecting, protruding, sticking/jutting out.

befall verb happen, occur, take place, chance, crop up, arise, come about, come to pass, transpire, materialize, ensue, follow, result, fall, supervene.

befitting adjective fitting, fit, suitable, appropriate, apt, proper, right, seemly, decorous.

before adverb **1** *we've met before* previously, earlier, formerly, hitherto, in the past. **2** *they went on before* ahead, in front, in advance, in the lead.

before preposition **1** *before lunch* | *before the war* | *before going out* prior to, previous to, earlier than. **2** *B comes before C* in front of, ahead of, in advance of. **3** *said before witnesses* in the presence of, in the sight of. **4** *death before dishonor* in preference to, rather/sooner than.
Antonyms: AFTER; BEHIND.

beforehand adverb before, before now, earlier, previously, in advance, in readiness, ahead of time, already, sooner.

befriend verb make friends with, make a friend of, look after, protect, keep an eye on, help, assist, aid, support, back, stand by, side with, encourage, sustain, uphold, succor, advise.

befuddled adjective **1** *befuddled from the anesthetic* confused, dazed, groggy, muddled, bewildered, stunned, numbed; *inf.* woozy. **2** *befuddled drunks* drunk, drunken, intoxicated, inebriated, stupefied, muddled, dazed, bewildered; *inf.* blotto, bombed, out of it, blitzed, smashed, wasted, wrecked, zonked.

beg verb **1** *beg in order to live* ask for money, solicit money, seek charity/alms, cadge, scrounge; *inf.* sponge, bum, mooch. **2** *beg for* *money/mercy* ask for, request, seek, look for, desire, crave, solicit, plead for, beseech, entreat, importune, plead with.

beg
beseech, entreat, implore, importune, petition, plead, solicit

How badly do you want something? You can **beg** for it, which implies a humble and earnest approach. If you **entreat**, you're trying to get what you want by ingratiating yourself (*she entreated her mother to help her prepare for the exam*). To **plead** involves more urgency (*he pleaded with the judge to spare his life*) and is usually associated with the legal system (*she was advised to plead guilty*). **Beseech** also suggests urgency, as well as an emotional appeal (*he beseeched her to tell the truth*). **Implore** is still stronger, suggesting desperation or great distress (*the look in his mother's eyes implored him to have mercy*). If you really want to get your way, you can **importune**, which means to *beg* not only urgently but persistently and to risk making a pest of yourself (*he importuned her daily to accept his invitation*). **Petition** suggests an appeal to authority (*to petition the government to repeal an unjust law*), while **solicit** suggests petitioning in a courteous, formal way (*soliciting financial support for the school carnival*).

beget verb **1** *fathers begetting able sons* father, sire, procreate, generate, engender, spawn. **2** *differing opinion begetting strife* cause, give rise to, bring, bring about, create, produce, result in, occasion, effect, bring to pass, engender.

beggar noun *accosted by a beggar* tramp, vagrant, mendicant, cadger, vagabond, pauper, down-and-out, derelict; *inf.* scrounger, sponger, bum, moocher, bag lady, hobo.

beggar verb *a nation beggared by war* impoverish, make poor, reduce to poverty, bankrupt, pauperize.

beggarly adjective **1** *a beggarly wage* inadequate, meager, paltry, slight, miserly, pitiful, pathetic, stingy, niggardly, ungenerous, contemptible, despicable. **2** *beggarly accommodations* miserable, wretched, mean, base, vile, foul, sordid, shabby, shoddy, despicable. **3** *beggarly creatures* poor, poverty-stricken, impoverished, needy, penniless, destitute, indigent, impecunious.

begin verb **1** *begin work* start, commence, set about, embark on, initiate, set in motion, institute, inaugurate. **2** *begin now!* start, commence, go ahead, get going; *inf.* fire away, kick off, get the show on the road, get to it, start the ball rolling, take the plunge. **3** *trouble began immediately* start, commence, arise, come into existence/being, happen, occur, spring up, crop up, emerge, dawn, appear, originate. **4** *rain began to fall* start, commence.
Antonyms: FINISH; END; STOP.

beginner noun novice, trainee, learner, apprentice, student, pupil, recruit, raw recruit, tyro,

fledgling, neophyte, initiate, novitiate, tenderfoot; *inf.* greenhorn, rookie.
Antonyms: EXPERT; VETERAN.

beginning noun **1** *from the beginning of time | beginning of the match* start, starting point, commencement, onset, outset, dawn, birth, inception, conception, emergence, rise; *inf.* kickoff. **2** *the beginning of the book* start, commencement, first part, opening, prelude, preface, introduction. **3** *philosophy has its beginnings in religion* origin, source, starting point, fountainhead, spring, mainspring, embryo, germ; roots, seeds.

begrudge verb **1** *begrudge him his success* grudge, envy, resent, hold against, be jealous of. **2** *begrudge the time spent* grudge, resent, give unwillingly, be dissatisfied with.

beguile verb **1** *beguiled by her beauty* charm, attract, delight, please, enchant, bewitch, seduce. **2** *the comedian beguiling the audience* entertain, amuse, occupy, absorb, engage, distract, divert, engross. **3** *beguile the hours* pass, while away, spend.

beguiling adjective *a beguiling smile* charming, attractive, delightful, pleasing, enchanting, bewitching, seductive.

behalf noun **on behalf of 1** *acting on behalf of his client* for, representing, as a representative of, in the interests of, in the name of, in place of. **2** *collecting on behalf of the blind* in the interests of, for, for the benefit/good/sake of, to the advantage of, on account of, in support of.

behave verb **1** *they behaved well/badly* act, perform, conduct oneself, acquit oneself, comport oneself. **2** *she behaves like a dictator | the engine behaved badly/well* act, perform, function, operate. **behave oneself** *the children must behave themselves* act correctly/properly, conduct oneself well, act in a polite way, show good manners, mind one's manners.

behavior noun **1** *criticize his opponent's behavior* conduct, way of acting, response, comportment, deportment, bearing; actions, manners, ways. **2** *the erratic behavior of the machine | study the behavior of bees* action, performance, functioning, operation, reaction, response; actions, reactions, responses.

behead verb decapitate, guillotine, decollate.

behest noun order, command, decree, edict, rule, ruling, directive, direction, instruction, request, requirement, charge, bidding, wish, dictate, injunction, mandate, precept.

behind preposition **1** *behind the woodshed* at the back of, at the rear of, beyond, on the further side of, on the other side of, in back of. **2** *running behind us* after, at the back of, to the rear of, following, in the wake of, close upon, hard on the heels of. **3** *behind the others in English* less advanced than, slower than, weaker than, inferior to. **4** *behind schedule* later than, after. **5** *he's behind the trouble* at the back of, at the bottom of, responsible for, causing, the cause/source of, giving rise to, instigating, initiating, urging. **6** *we're behind you all the way* backing, supporting, for, on the side of, in agreement with, financing.

behind *adverb* **1** *with the dog running behind* after, at the back, in the rear, in the wake. **2** *look behind to/toward the back/rear*, over one's shoulder. **3** *stay/leave behind* afterward, remaining after departure. **4** *we're behind so don't stop* behindhand, behind schedule, late, slow. **5** *behind in payments* behindhand, in arrears, overdue, in debt.
Antonyms: in front (*see* FRONT); AHEAD.

behindhand *adverb* **1** *behindhand in paying* late, slow, dilatory, tardy, remiss. **2** *too behindhand for modern times* out of date, old-fashioned, behind the times/time, backward.

behold *verb* look at, see, observe, view, watch, survey, gaze at, stare at, scan, witness, regard, contemplate, inspect, take note of, mark, consider, pay heed to.

behold *interjection* look!, see!, lo!, *ecce!*, voila!

beholden *adjective* indebted, under obligation, obligated, bound, owing, thankful, grateful.

behoove *verb* **1** *it behooves him to take over his father's business* be incumbent on, be necessary for, be essential for, be expected of, be advisable for, be sensible for, be wise for. **2** *it ill behooves him to have an affair with his brother's fiancée* be fitting, befit, be suitable, be seemly, be proper, be decorous.

beige *adjective* fawn, mushroom, neutral, buff, sand, oatmeal, ecru, coffee.

being *noun* **1** *the purpose of our being* existence, living, life, animation, actuality, life blood, vital force, entity. **2** *shocked to the depths of her being* spirit, soul, nature, essence, substance, entity. **3** *a sentient being* creature, person, human being, human, individual, mortal, living thing, man, woman, animal.
Antonyms: NOTHINGNESS; OBLIVION.

belabor *verb* **1** *belabor the prisoner with blows* beat, hit, strike, batter, attack, flog, thrash, whip, lambaste, bombard, pelt. **2** *belabor the actor* criticize, attack, berate, censure, castigate, lay into, flay. **3** *belabor the point* overelaborate, discuss at length, go through with a fine-tooth comb.

belated *adjective* late, overdue, behindhand, behind time, delayed, tardy, unpunctual.

belch *verb* **1** burp, eruct, eructate. **2** *factory chimneys belching smoke* give out, give off, pour out, discharge, emit, issue, vent, gush, eject, disgorge, spew out, vomit, cough up.

beleaguered *adjective* **1** *a beleaguered city* besieged, under siege, surrounded, blockaded, encircled, hemmed in, under attack. **2** *a movie star beleaguered by fans* besieged, badgered, harassed, bothered, beset, pestered, plagued, tormented, vexed, set upon, persecuted.

belie *verb* **1** *her smile belied her anger* contradict, deny, disprove, refute, gainsay, confute. **2** *the official report belies the enormity of the disaster* misrepresent, falsify, distort, conceal, disguise. **3** *her performance belied our faith in her* fail to justify, be at odds with, do not live up to.

belief *noun* **1** *it is my belief that she is dead* opinion, feeling, impression, view, viewpoint, conviction, judgment, thinking, way of thinking, theory, notion. **2** *no belief in his powers* faith, credence, freedom from doubt, trust, reliance, confidence. **3** *Christian/political beliefs* doctrine, teaching, creed, dogma, ideology, principles, tenet, canon, credence, credo.
Antonyms: DISBELIEF; DOUBT; SKEPTICISM.

believable *adjective* credible, plausible, likely, creditable, probable, possible, acceptable, within the bounds of possibility, conceivable, imaginable.
Antonyms: UNBELIEVABLE; INCREDIBLE.

---

believable
cogent, convincing, credible, creditable, plausible, valid

Believable is the most general of these terms, used to describe anything we accept as true, even in the absence of absolute proof (*a believable story about why she was late*). **Credible** also means worthy of belief or confidence and is often used interchangeably with *believable*, but it goes one step further: a *credible* excuse is one that is supported by known facts. **Creditable**, often confused with *credible*, at one time meant worthy of belief but nowadays is used to mean respectable or decent, deserving of honor, reputation, or esteem (*leading a creditable life*). Something that is **convincing** is *believable* because it overcomes doubts or opposition (*a convincing performance*), while something that is **plausible** may appear to be convincing or believable on the surface, but may not be so upon closer examination. **Valid** means legally sound, just, or authoritative; a *valid* criticism seldom provokes opposition. **Cogent**, on the other hand, means having the power to convince; a *cogent* argument is believable because of its clear, forceful, or incisive presentation.

---

believe *verb* **1** *I don't believe you* consider honest/true, be convinced by, trust. **2** *don't believe his story* regard/accept as true, accept, credit, be convinced by, trust; *inf.* swallow, fall for, buy. **3** *I believe he's retired* | *believed the earth to be flat* think, be of the opinion that, understand, suppose, assume, presume, surmise, reckon, guess, postulate/theorize that. **believe in 1** *believe in God/ghosts* be convinced/sure/persuaded of the existence of. **2** *believe in alternative medicine* have faith in, trust, be convinced/persuaded by, set store by, value, swear by.
Antonyms: DISBELIEVE; DOUBT.

believer *noun* follower, adherent, supporter, disciple, upholder.

belittle verb disparage, decry, deprecate, undervalue, underrate, underestimate, minimize, make light of, slight, detract from, downgrade, play down, depreciate, derogate, scoff at, sneer at.

Antonyms: PRAISE; EXAGGERATE; MAGNIFY.

belligerent adjective **1** in a belligerent mood | a belligerent patient quarreling with everyone aggressive, antagonistic, militant, pugnacious, quarrelsome, argumentative, disputatious, combative, quick-tempered, hot-tempered, irascible. **2** belligerent nations at war, warring, battling, contending, militant, martial, warlike, warmongering.

Antonyms: FRIENDLY; PEACEABLE; PEACEFUL.

bellow verb roar, shout, bawl, yell, shriek, howl, scream, screech, call, cry out, whoop, ululate; inf. holler.

belly noun **1** a stabbing pain in the belly stomach, abdomen, paunch; intestines, innards; inf. tummy, insides, guts, pot, bread basket, potbelly, beer belly. **2** the belly of the planes underside, underpart, underbelly.

belly verb the sail bellied out swell, billow, bulge, fill out, balloon out, bag.

belong verb **1** where does this book belong? have a place/home, be classified, be categorized. **2** they do not belong here fit in, be suited to, have a rightful place, be part of; inf. go, click. **belong to 1** the house belongs to them be owned by, be the property of, be under the ownership of, be held by, be at the disposal of. **2** she belongs to the sailing club/it belongs to the cat family be a member of, be affiliated to/with, be allied to, be associated with, be connected to, be included in, be an adherent of. **3** this lid belongs to that box be part of, be an adjunct of, attach to, go with, relate to, be relevant to.

belongings plural noun possessions, personal-possessions/effects, effects, goods, accouterments, appurtenances; property, paraphernalia; inf. gear, things, stuff, junk.

beloved adjective **1** my beloved children dear, dearest, darling, adored, much loved, precious, cherished, sweet, treasured, prized, worshiped, idolized. **2** beloved of everyone loved, liked, adored, admired, respected, valued, esteemed, revered.

beloved noun married her beloved sweetheart, fiancé, fiancée, boyfriend, girlfriend, love, lover, betrothed; fml. paramour, inamorato, inamorata.

below adverb **1** we could see it down below further/lower down, in/to a lower position, underneath, beneath, downstairs. **2** for further details see below further on, at a later point/place.

below preposition **1** skirts below the knee | the valley below the village further down than, lower than, under, underneath. **2** prices/temperatures below average less/lower than. **3** ranking below him lower than, inferior to, subordinate to. **4** that remark was below you beneath, unworthy of, undignified for, degrading to, not befitting, unsuitable for, inappropriate for.

Antonyms: ABOVE; OVER.

belt noun **1** wearing a leather belt girdle, sash, cummerbund, waistband, band. **2** mechanics mending the machine's belt band, conveyor belt, fan belt. **3** America's corn belt zone, region, area, district, tract, stretch, extent. **4** a belt of white in the black strip, band, stripe, bar, line, stria. **5** a belt across the ear blow, punch, smack, bang, thump; inf. clout, bash, wallop.

belt verb **1** with her waist belted encircle, gird, encompass, bind, tie, fasten. **2** belt prisoners on their backs strap, flog, whip, lash, cane, thrash, scourge, flail. **3** belt the heckler with fists strike, hit, beat, punch, smack, thrash, thump, bang, batter, pound, pummel; inf. bash, sock.

bemoan verb lament, mourn, deplore, regret, grieve for/over, express sorrow for, sorrow for, bewail, sigh over, weep over, repent, rue.

bemused adjective a bemused look | bemused by the events confused, bewildered, puzzled, perplexed, dazed, stunned, muddled, overwhelmed, disconcerted, discomfited, astonished, astounded, stupefied, preoccupied, absentminded, engrossed.

bench noun **1** pupils sitting on a bench seat, pew, settle. **2** carpenters at the bench workbench, worktable, table, counter. **3** appear before the bench court, bar, courtroom, tribunal. **4** a member of the bench judges, magistrates; judiciary.

benchmark noun standard, point of reference, gauge, criterion, test, norm, guideline, specification, model, pattern, touchstone, yardstick.

bend verb **1** bend the iron bar | bend the little finger make crooked/curved, curve, crook, flex, twist, bow, arch, warp, contort. **2** the road bends to the right curve, turn, twist, swerve, veer, incline, diverge, deviate, deflect, coil, spiral, loop. **3** bend down over the sink stoop, crouch, lean down/over, bow, hunch. **4** bend them to our will mold, shape, direct, force, influence, compel, persuade, subdue, sway, subjugate. **5** bend our minds to the task direct, point, aim, turn, train, steer, set.

Antonym: STRAIGHTEN.

bend noun curve, turn, corner, twist, angle, arc, swerve, incline, divergence, crook, deviation, deflection, coiling, spiral, loop, hook; dogleg, hairpin turn, zigzag.

beneath adverb to a world beneath below, underneath, in/to a lower place.

Antonyms: ABOVE; OVER.

beneath preposition **1** sank beneath the waves below, under, underneath, lower than. **2** people beneath her socially below, lower than, inferior to, secondary to, subservient to. **3** beneath him to behave like that below, unworthy of, undignified for, unbefitting, unbecoming.

benediction *noun* **1** *say a benediction* blessing, prayer, invocation; grace, thanksgiving; *lit.* orison. **2** *a state of benediction* blessedness, grace, beatitude, bliss, favor.

benefactor *noun* helper, patron, backer, sponsor, supporter, promoter, contributor, subscriber, subsidizer, donor, philanthropist, sympathizer, well-wisher; *inf.* angel, friend.

beneficial *adjective* advantageous, favorable, propitious, promising, helpful, accommodating, obliging, useful, serviceable, valuable, profitable, rewarding, gainful.
Antonyms: DISADVANTAGEOUS; DETRIMENTAL.

beneficiary *noun* heir, inheritor, recipient, receiver, legatee, payee, assignee.

benefit *noun* **1** *for the benefit of all* advantage, good, gain, profit, help, aid, assistance, interest, welfare, well-being, betterment, asset, avail, use, service. **2** *enjoy the benefits of modern medicine* advantage, blessing, boon; good, usefulness; perquisites, perks, fringe benefits. **3** *living on government benefits* social security, disability, unemployment (insurance), workers'/workmen's compensation, welfare; *inf.* workers'/workmen's comp.
Antonyms: DISADVANTAGE; DETRIMENT.

benefit *verb* **1** *discoveries benefiting society* do good to, be of service to, profit, serve, be of advantage to, help, aid, assist, contribute to, better, improve, advance, further. **2** *criminals benefiting from their deeds* profit, gain, reap benefits, make money; *inf.* cash in, make a killing.
Antonyms: DAMAGE; INJURE.

benevolence *noun* kindness, kindheartedness, goodness, generosity, charity, altruism, goodwill, humanity, compassion, humanitarianism, philanthropism.

benevolent *adjective* **1** *a benevolent attitude to others* kind, kindly, kindhearted, friendly, amiable, benign, generous, magnanimous, warmhearted, considerate, thoughtful, well-meaning, altruistic, humane, compassionate, caring, sympathetic, obliging, helpful, humanitarian, philanthropic, bountiful, liberal, bounteous, beneficent. **2** *a benevolent institution* charitable, nonprofit.
Antonyms: MALEVOLENT; UNKIND; UNSYMPATHETIC.

benighted *adjective* ignorant, unenlightened, backward, uncivilized, uncultured, uneducated, illiterate, crude.

benign *adjective* **1** *with a benign smile/attitude* kind, kindly, friendly, amiable, genial, gracious, cordial, generous, benevolent, gentle, sympathetic, obliging, accommodating, liberal. **2** *a benign climate* healthy, health-giving, wholesome, salubrious, temperate, pleasant, mild, balmy, agreeable, refreshing. **3** *in benign circumstances* favorable, advantageous, beneficial, propitious, auspicious, lucky, opportune, providential, encouraging, conducive, helpful,

benevolent. **4** *a benign tumor* nonmalignant, harmless, innocent, curable, remediable, treatable.
Antonyms: UNFRIENDLY; HOSTILE; UNFAVORABLE; MALIGNANT.

bent *adjective* **1** *a bent iron rod* curved, crooked, twisted, bowed, angled, warped, contorted. **2** *bent backs* bowed, arched, curved, stooped, hunched. **bent on** *bent on winning* determined to, set on, insistent on, resolved to, fixed on, inclined to, disposed to, predisposed to.
Antonyms: STRAIGHT; UPRIGHT.

bent *noun* *an artistic bent* | *a bent for design* inclination, predisposition, disposition, leaning, tendency, penchant, bias, predilection, proclivity, propensity, talent, gift, flair, ability, knack, aptitude, facility, skill, capability, capacity, forte, genius.

bequeath *verb* **1** *bequeath her estate to her son* leave, will, cede, endow on, bestow on, consign, commit, entrust, grant, transfer. **2** *ideas bequeathed by previous inventors* hand down, pass down/on, impart, transmit.

bequest *noun* **1** *receive a bequest of $10,000* legacy, inheritance, endowment, estate, heritage, bestowal, bequeathal, gift, settlement. **2** *the bequest of her collection to the museum* bequeathing, leaving, willing. *See* BEQUEATH 1.

berate *verb* scold, rebuke, reprimand, chide, reprove, upbraid, castigate, censure, criticize, rail at, harangue, lambaste, fulminate against, vituperate, read the riot act to; *inf.* tell off, give a dressing-down to, bawl out.

bereave *verb* *an accident bereaved him of his wife* deprive, dispossess, rob, divest, strip.

bereavement *noun* **1** *sympathize with her in her bereavement* loss, deprivation, dispossession. *See* BEREAVE. **2** *a series of family bereavements* death, loss, passing, demise.

bereft *adjective* **bereft of** deprived of, robbed of, cut off from, parted from, devoid of, wanting, lacking, minus.

berserk *adjective* frenzied, mad, insane, crazed, crazy, hysterical, maniacal, manic, raving, wild, enraged, raging, uncontrollable, amok, unrestrainable; *inf.* out of one's mind, hyper, ape.

berth *noun* **1** *book a berth in the train/ship* bed, bunk, sleeping accommodations, billet, hammock, cot. **2** *ships at their berths* anchorage, mooring, docking site. **3** *a well-paid berth* job, post, position, situation, place; employment, appointment, living. **give a wide berth to** *we gave a wide berth to the rowdies in the bar* avoid, keep a careful distance from, stay away from.

berth *verb* **1** *berth the ship* moor, dock, anchor, land, tie up. **2** *the ship berthed at dawn* moor, dock, drop anchor, land. **3** *the yacht berths four* provide beds for, sleep, accommodate, put up, house, shelter, lodge.

beseech *verb* beg, implore, entreat, ask, plead with, pray, petition, call upon, appeal to, supplicate, invoke, adjure, crave.

beset *verb* **1** *beset with fears* | *beset by anxieties* attack, harass, assail, worry, plague, bother, trouble, perplex, torment, pester, hound, nag, bedevil, harry. **2** *beset by enemy forces* surround, besiege, encircle, enclose, encompass, hem in, shut/fence in.

besetting *adjective* *his besetting sins* habitual, persistent, inveterate, prevalent, troublesome, harassing, assailing.

beside *preposition* **1** *walking beside him* alongside, by/at the side of, abreast of, next to, with, by, adjacent to, close to, near, nearby, neighboring, next door to. **2** *beside her work, his is poor* compared with, in comparison with, next to, against, contrasted with, in contrast to/with. **beside oneself** berserk, frenzied, in a frenzy, mad, frantic, demented, insane, crazed, crazy, deranged, unbalanced, distraught, hysterical, uncontrolled, unrestrained, unhinged, out of one's mind. **beside the point** irrelevant, not applicable, immaterial.

besides *adverb* *besides, it's too late* also, in addition, additionally, moreover, furthermore, further, as well, too, what's more.

besides *preposition* *three besides him* apart from, in addition to, aside from, over and above, other than, not counting, excluding, not including, without.

besiege *verb* **1** *the castle was besieged by the enemy* lay siege to, beleaguer, blockade, surround, encircle, encompass. **2** *movie stars besieged by reporters* surround, enclose, encircle, beleaguer, beset, shut in, hem in, fence in, hedge in. **3** *besieged with doubts* harass, assail, worry, plague, beset. *See* BESET 1.

besmirch *verb* *besmirch the firm's reputation* sully, slander, defame, tarnish, smear, stain, taint, damage.

besotted *adjective* **1** *besotted with his secretary* infatuated with, doting on, smitten, bewitched by, spellbound by, hypnotized by. **2** *besotted with drink* befuddled, drunk, intoxicated, stupefied, confused, muddled, dazed, bewildered; *inf.* blotto, bombed, out of it, smashed, zonked. *See* BEFUDDLED.

bespatter *verb* spatter, splatter, splash, muddy, dirty, smear, besmirch, sully.

bespeak *verb* *actions bespeaking a kind heart* give evidence of, indicate, demonstrate, exhibit, show, display, evince, manifest, reveal, betray, testify to, bear witness to.

best *adjective* **1** *the best player* foremost, finest, leading, top, chief, principal, highest, worthiest, supreme, superlative, unsurpassed, unexcelled, excellent, first-class, first-rate, outstanding, preeminent; *inf.* ace. **2** *the best way to get there* | *the best solution* right, correct, most fitting, most suitable, most desirable, apt, advantageous. **Antonym:** WORST.

best *adverb* **1** *he played best* in the best way, superlatively, unsurpassedly, excellently, outstandingly. **2** *he likes tennis best* to the highest/

greatest degree, greatly, extremely. **3** *her behavior is best ignored* most sensibly, most wisely, most suitably, most fittingly, most advantageously.

best *noun* **1** *only the best may enter* finest, first class, top, cream, pick, flower, choice, elite. **2** *do your best* utmost, hardest, best endeavor; *inf.* damnedest. **3** *at his best in the morning* peak, prime, top form, height, apex. **4** *dressed in her best* best clothes, finery, finest clothes; *inf.* Sunday best, best bib and tucker. **5** *give him my best* best wishes, regards, kindest regards, greetings, love.

best *verb* *best the opposition* defeat, beat, conquer, get the better of, trounce, thrash, triumph over, get the upper hand of, prevail over, outdo, outclass, surpass, outwit, outsmart, worst; *inf.* lick, make mincemeat of.

bestial *adjective* **1** *bestial treatment of prisoners* brutish, savage, brutal, inhuman, beastly, barbarous, barbaric, abominable, atrocious, cruel, primitive, wild, heathen. **2** *bestial sexual practices* depraved, vile, sordid, degenerate, degraded, gross, carnal, lustful, lecherous, prurient, lascivious, lewd, crude. **3** *bestial shapes* beastlike, animal.

bestow *verb* give, present, confer on, grant, donate, endow with, hand over, allot, assign, consign, apportion, distribute, bequeath, impart, accord, award, honor with, entrust with, commit.

bet *verb* **1** *bet $100 that he wins* wager, gamble, stake, pledge, risk, venture, hazard, chance. **2** *he never bets* gamble, wager, speculate. **3** *you can bet they've gone* be certain/sure, state confidently, predict.

bet *noun* **1** *enter into a bet* wager, gamble, speculation, venture, game of chance, lottery, sweepstake. **2** *place a bet of $100* wager, stake, ante, pledge. **3** *my bet is that they'll go* prediction, forecast, opinion, belief, feeling, view, theory. **4** *they're/that's our best bet* choice, option, alternative, selection, possibility, course of action.

bête noire *noun* anathema, aversion, bugbear, abomination.

betoken *verb* **1** *her blank expression betokened indifference* indicate, denote, signify, suggest, evidence, typify, represent, show, demonstrate, manifest, bespeak. **2** *clouds betokening a storm* augur, forebode, bode, portend, presage, foreshadow, prophesy, prognosticate, promise.

betray *verb* **1** *betray one's friends* inform on/against, be disloyal/unfaithful to, treat treacherously, break faith with, break one's promise to; *inf.* tell on, double-cross, stab in the back, sell down the river, sell out, blow the whistle on, squeal on. **2** *betray a secret* | *a smile betraying his feelings* reveal, disclose, divulge, give away, let slip, blurt out, blab, lay bare, bring to light, uncover, expose, exhibit, manifest, unmask. **3** *betrayed his wife for another woman* abandon, desert, forsake, walk out on, jilt; *inf.* leave flat.

Antonyms: stand by (*see* STAND); CONCEAL.

betrayal *noun* **1** *the betrayal of his friends* informing on/against, being disloyal to, breaking faith with; *inf.* double-crossing. See BETRAY 1. **2** *the betrayal of a secret* | *betrayal of his feelings* revelation, disclosure, divulgence, giving away. *See* BETRAY 2. **3** *the betrayal of his wife* abandonment, desertion, forsaking. *See* BETRAY 3. **4** *appalled by their betrayal* act of betrayal, breach of faith, bad faith, disloyalty, perfidy, treachery, duplicity, double-dealing, subversion, sedition, treason; *inf.* double-crossing, backstabbing, whistleblowing.

betroth *verb* engage, affiance, pledge, promise, contract, covenant; *lit.* espouse.

betrothal *noun* engagement, marriage contract, pledge, promise, compact, covenant; *lit.* espousal.

better *adjective* **1** *the better players* finer, of higher quality, greater, superior, worthier, fitter. **2** *a better course of action* more fitting, more suitable, more appropriate, more desirable, more advantageous, more useful, more valuable. **3** *feeling better* | *I am better* healthier, fitter, less ill, stronger, well, cured, recovered, recovering, progressing, improving; *inf.* mending, on the mend.

better *adverb* **1** *he plays better now* in a better way, in a superior/finer way. **2** *I understand him better* more, to a greater degree. **3** *her advice is better ignored* more sensibly, more wisely, more suitably, more fittingly, more advantageously.

better *verb* **1** *better the conditions of the poor* make better, raise, improve, ameliorate, advance, amend, rectify, relieve, reform, enhance, enrich. **2** *better the previous record* improve on, beat, surpass, exceed, top, outstrip, outdo, go one better than.

Antonym: WORSEN.

betterment *noun* improvement, amelioration, furtherance, reform, enhancement, enrichment.

between *preposition* **1** *standing between them* | *sharing things between them* in the middle of, amid, amidst, in the midst of, among. **2** *somewhere between the two cities* on the course connecting, in the space separating. **3** *the bond between mother and baby* connecting, linking, joining, uniting, allying. **4** *the difference between them* separating, distinguishing, differentiating, discriminating.

bevel *noun* slope, slant, oblique, tilt, angle, cant, bezel.

beverage *noun* drink, potation, potable; refreshment, liquid, liquor; *inf.* libation.

bevy *noun* **1** *a bevy of quail/birds* flock, covey, flight, group. **2** *a bevy of noisy spectators* collection, gathering, assembly, array, galaxy, group, band, troupe, cluster; *inf.* bunch, gaggle.

bewail *verb* mourn, lament, grieve over, sorrow for/over, express woe/sorrow for, cry/weep over, bemoan, regret, repent, rue, pine for.

beware *verb* *you must beware* | *beware of thieves* be careful/wary, be cautious, be on one's guard, take heed, watch out, look out, watch/look out for, be on the lookout/alert for.

Antonym: IGNORE.

bewilder *verb* confuse, mix up, muddle, puzzle, perplex, baffle, mystify, nonplus, disconcert, confound, bemuse, daze, stupefy, befuddle, obfuscate; *inf.* stump, bamboozle.

bewildered *adjective* confused, muddled, puzzled, perplexed, nonplussed, uncertain, speechless, startled, taken aback, all at sea, thrown off balance. *See* BEWILDER.

bewitch *verb* **1** *the wizard bewitched the prince* put a spell on, cast a spell over, enchant, entrance, curse; *inf.* hex. **2** *he was bewitched by her beauty* charm, enchant, beguile, captivate, entrance, fascinate, delight, allure, enrapture, spellbind, hypnotize, mesmerize, transfix.

bewitched *adjective* charmed, enchanted, beguiled, captivated, entranced, fascinated, enraptured, spellbound, hypnotized, mesmerized.

beyond *preposition* **1** *beyond the mountains* on the farther/far side of, on the other side of, further on than, past, after, over, behind. **2** *beyond midnight* | *beyond retirement age* after, past, later than, on the other side of. **3** *beyond our understanding* | *beyond repair* outside the reach/range of, outside the limitations of, beyond the power/capacity of, surpassing. **4** *inflation beyond 10 percent* above, more than, greater than, exceeding, in excess of, over and above. **5** *notice nothing beyond his beard* other than, apart from, except.

beyond *adverb* *what lies beyond* | *the mountains beyond* yonder, further on, far off, far away, at a distance, afar.

Antonyms: NEAR; CLOSE.

bias *noun* **1** *cut on the bias* slant, cross, diagonal, skew, angle, oblique, slope. **2** *have a bias in favor of/against socialism* | *have a musical bias* tendency, inclination, leaning, bent, partiality, penchant, predisposition, propensity, proclivity, proneness, predilection, prejudice, bigotry, intolerance, narrow-mindedness, one-sidedness.

Antonyms: OBJECTIVITY; FAIRNESS; IMPARTIALITY.

---

bias
bigotry, intolerance, narrow-mindedness, parochialism, partiality, prejudice, provincialism
Bias is a predisposition either for or against something; one can have a *bias* against police officers or a *bias* for French food and wines. Partiality, on the other hand, is a favorable *bias* (*the partiality of parents for their own children; the partiality of Americans for fast food*), while

prejudice implies a preconceived and usually negative judgment or opinion (*a decision motivated by racial prejudice*). **Bigotry** is an even stronger term, referring to an intense dislike and often violent hatred for the members of a particular race, religion, or ethnic group. **Narrow-mindedness** also points to rigidly preconceived ideas, but implies that they are the result of lack of education or understanding, rather than outright hostility (*her parents' narrow-mindedness prevented her from meeting any boys her age*). **Parochialism** is another term meaning excessive narrowness of mind (from *parochial*, pertaining to a parish or parishes; that is, concerned mainly about local issues), while **provincialism** is narrow-mindedness that results from lack of exposure to cultural or intellectual activity, characteristic of a province or non-urban area. **Intolerance** is a broad term used to describe the inability to put up with almost anything (*parents' intolerance of their children's misbehavior*).

bias *verb* **1** *bias the judges* prejudice, influence, sway, predispose. **2** *bias their decision* prejudice, influence, sway, distort, bend, twist, warp, weight, predispose.

biased *adjective a biased attitude* prejudiced, partial, one-sided, influenced, slanted, weighted, swayed, distorted, predisposed.
Antonyms: UNBIASED; IMPARTIAL; FAIR.

Bible *noun* **1** *Christians studying the Bible* (Holy) Scriptures, the Good Book. **2** *the gardener's bible* authority, handbook, manual, guide, textbook, primer.

bibliography *noun* book list, list, catalog.

bicker *verb* wrangle, quarrel, argue, squabble, fight, have a disagreement, disagree, dispute, spar; *inf.* scrap.

bicycle *noun* bike, cycle; tandem, unicycle, tricycle, racer, mountain bike.

bid *verb* **1** *bid $100 for the vase* offer, tender, proffer, propose, submit, put forward, advance. **2** *they bade him go* command, order, instruct, ask, tell, call for, direct, demand, enjoin, charge, summon, require, invite. **3** *bid them farewell* wish, greet, tell, call, say.

bid *noun* **1** *put in a bid of $3,000* offer, proposition, proffer, proposal, submission, tender, advance, ante, price, sum, amount. **2** *a bid for power* attempt, effort.

bidding *noun* **1** *he left at his father's bidding* command, order, instruction, injunction, direction, demand, mandate, charge, summons, request, call, behest, invitation. **2** *present at the bidding* auction; making of bids, tendering; offers, tenders, proposals.

big *adjective* **1** *a big garden/car* large, sizable, great, huge, enormous, immense, vast, massive, extensive, substantial, spacious, colossal, gigantic, mammoth, prodigious. **2** *a big man* large, tall, bulky, burly, hulking, huge, enormous, muscular, beefy, brawny, strapping,

thickset, heavy, solid, corpulent, fat, obese, stout, gargantuan, elephantine. **3** *a big boy now* | *a big sister* grown-up, adult, grown, mature, elder. **4** *a big decision/moment* important, significant, serious, momentous, salient, weighty, paramount. **5** *a big figure in the movement* important, influential, powerful, prominent, outstanding, leading, well-known, principal, foremost, noteworthy, notable, eminent, distinguished. **6** *big ideas/talk* arrogant, pretentious, ambitious, inflated, pompous, proud, haughty, conceited, boastful, bragging, bombastic. **7** *a big heart* | *it was big of her to forgive us* generous, kindly, kindhearted, benevolent, magnanimous, unselfish, altruistic, philanthropic, beneficent, humane.
Antonyms: SMALL; LITTLE; MINOR.

bigot *noun* fanatic, zealot, sectarian, dogmatist, chauvinist, jingoist, racist, sexist.

bigoted *adjective* prejudiced, intolerant, fanatical, narrow-minded, illiberal, biased, partial, one-sided, dogmatic, warped, twisted, jaundiced, chauvinistic, jingoistic, racist, sexist.
Antonyms: TOLERANT; LIBERAL.

bigotry *noun* prejudice, intolerance, fanaticism, narrow-mindedness, bias, partiality, dogmatism, discrimination, unfairness, injustice, chauvinism, jingoism, racism, sexism, provincialism. *See* BIGOTED.

bigwig *noun* VIP, dignitary, notable, notability, personage, celebrity; *inf.* somebody, heavyweight, big shot, big gun, big cheese, top brass.

bilge *noun* *don't talk bilge* rubbish, nonsense, drivel, gibberish, balderdash, bunkum, hogwash, twaddle; *inf.* rot.

bilious *adjective* **1** *feeling bilious* out of sorts, queasy, nauseated, sick. **2** *of a bilious temperament* bad-tempered, ill-tempered, short-tempered, ill-humored, cross, irritable, crotchety, grumpy, peevish, edgy, touchy, crabby, cantankerous, testy, nasty; *inf.* grouchy.

bilk *verb* swindle, cheat, defraud, exploit, fleece, deceive, trick, bamboozle, rook, gull; *inf.* con, do.

bill[1] *noun* **1** *a bill for damages* | *a restaurant bill* account, invoice, statement, list of charges, reckoning, tally, score; check; *inf.* tab. **2** *post no bills* | *distribute bills* poster, advertisement, flyer, notice, announcement, leaflet, circular, handout, handbill, brochure, placard, bulletin; *inf.* ad. **3** *top of the bill* program, playbill, list, listing, agenda, card, schedule, timetable, syllabus, roster, calendar, catalog, inventory. **4** *a congressional bill* proposal, measure, projected/proposed law, piece of legislation.

bill[2] *verb* **1** *bill them for the goods* invoice, send an invoice to, charge, debit, send a statement to. **2** *billed as the year's best musical* advertise, announce, post, give notice of, put up in lights.

bill[3] *noun* *a bird's bill* beak; *dial.* neb.

billet *noun* **1** *billets for soldiers* quarters, living quarters, barracks, rooms; accommodations, lodging, housing, cantonment. **2** *an easy, well-paid billet* job, post, situation, position, office, appointment, commission, assignment; employment.

billet *verb* *billet the soldiers in the town* accommodate, put up, house, quarter, station, shelter.

billow *noun* wave, surge, swell, tide, rush, deluge, flood, breaker, roller.

billow *verb* puff up, swell, fill out, balloon, belly, surge, roll.

billowy *adjective* wavelike, swelling, surging, undulating, rolling, tossing, rising, rising and falling, ebbing and flowing.

bin *noun* container, receptacle, box, can, crate.

bind *verb* **1** *bind the twigs together* | *with their legs bound* tie, tie up, fasten, secure, attach, rope, strap, truss, lash, tether, fetter, chain, hitch, wrap. **2** *bind the wound* bandage, dress, tape, wrap, cover, swathe. **3** *bind the surfaces together* stick, glue, cement, paste. **4** *bind the seams with gold* edge, trim, hem, border, finish. **5** *bound to answer/secrecy* compel, obligate, oblige, constrain, force, impel, engage, require, prescribe. **6** *bound by family ties* constrain, restrain, restrict, hamper, hinder, inhibit, yoke.
Antonyms: LOOSEN; SEPARATE.

bind *noun* *in a bind over what to do* quandary, dilemma, predicament, difficulty, spot, tight spot.

binding *adjective* *the agreement is binding* irrevocable, unalterable, compulsory, obligatory, imperative, mandatory, necessary, conclusive.

binge *noun* spree, orgy, drinking bout, fling; *inf.* bender, jag.

biography *noun* life history, life, life story, memoir, profile, account; *inf.* bio.

bird *noun* songbird, songster, warbler, fowl, fledgling, feathered friend.

birth *noun* **1** *present at the child's birth* childbirth, delivery, parturition, nativity. **2** *the birth of jazz* origin, beginnings, start, source, emergence, commencement, fountainhead, genesis. **3** *of noble birth* origin, descent, ancestry, lineage, line, extraction, derivation, family, parentage, house, blood, breeding, genealogy, pedigree, heritage, patrimony, stock, race, strain, background.
Antonyms: DEATH; DEMISE.

birthmark *noun* blemish, discoloration, nevus, strawberry, mole.

birthright *noun* right, due, privilege, heritage, patrimony, legacy.

bisect *verb* cut in half, halve, cut/divide/split in two, split down the middle, cleave, separate into two, bifurcate, dichotomize.

bisexual *adjective* hermaphrodite, hermaphroditic, androgynous, epicene; *Tech.* monoclinous; *inf.* AC/DC, swinging both ways, switch-hitting, bi.

bisexual *noun* hermaphrodite, androgyne; *inf.* switch-hitter, bi.

bit[1] *noun* **1** *bits of bread/paper/debris* small piece, piece, section, part, segment, chunk, lump, hunk, portion, particle, fragment, atom, flake, sliver, chip, crumb, grain, speck, scrap, shred, trace, morsel, iota, jot, whit, modicum, shard, hint, tinge, suggestion. **2** *see you in a bit* little, little while, short time, moment, minute, second, instant, short spell, short period, flash, blink of an eye; *inf.* jiffy, two shakes of a lamb's tail.

bit[2] *noun* *a horse's bit* restraint, check, curb, brake, snaffle.

bitch *noun* **1** shrew, vixen, virago, harpy, she-devil. **2** *this job's a real bitch* problem, difficulty, predicament, dilemma.

bitch *verb* *stop your incessant bitching* complain, grumble, moan, carp, grouse, whine; *inf.* gripe, beef, bellyache. **bitch about** *always bitching about the boss* slander, decry, disparage, malign; *fml.* calumniate.

bitchy *adjective* nasty, mean, spiteful, malicious, catty, vindictive, rancorous, venomous, snide, shrewish, cruel, backbiting.

bite *verb* **1** *bite one's nails* chew, nibble at, gnaw at. **2** *dogs biting people* sink one's teeth into, nip, snap at, tear at, wound. **3** *insects biting them* sting, prick, wound. **4** *biting on his pipe* clamp, grip, hold on to. **5** *measures beginning to bite* take effect, work, have results. **6** *fish biting* | *new clients not biting* take the bait, be lured, be enticed, be tempted, be allured. **7** *what's biting you?* annoy, irritate, bother, displease, peeve, provoke, vex; *inf.* bug, get at, needle. **bite into 1** *bite into the food* eat, masticate, chew, munch, crunch, nibble. **2** *acids biting into the metal* eat into, corrode, burn, eat away at, erode, dissolve, wear away.

bite *noun* **1** *the dog gave her a playful bite* nip, snap. **2** *suffering from insect bites* sting, prick, puncture, wound, lesion, itch, smarting. **3** *a bite of the apple/food* mouthful, piece, morsel, bit. **4** *have a bite to eat* snack, refreshment. **5** *the sauce had a bite to it* sharpness, spiciness, piquancy, pungency, edge; *inf.* kick, punch.

biting *adjective* **1** *biting winds* sharp, freezing, cold, bitterly cold, harsh, nipping, stinging, piercing, penetrating. **2** *biting words* sharp, bitter, cutting, caustic, sarcastic, scathing, trenchant, mordant, stinging, withering, incisive, acid.

bitter *adjective* **1** *a bitter substance* acid, pungent, acrid, tart, sour, biting, harsh, unsweetened, vinegary, acetous, acerbic. **2** *a bitter old woman* | *feeling bitter* resentful, embittered, rancorous, acrimonious, piqued, ill-disposed, indignant, sullen, crabbed, sour, morose, begrudging, petulant, peevish. **3** *from bitter experience* | *bitter memories* painful, distressing, distressful, harrowing, heartbreaking, heart-rending, agonizing, unhappy, sad, poignant, grievous, tragic, galling, vexatious. **4** *bitter*

north winds biting, sharp, intensely cold, freezing, harsh, stinging, piercing, penetrating, fierce. **5** *bitter quarrels/controversy* virulent, acrimonious, hostile, antagonistic, spiteful, vicious, rancorous, vindictive, malicious, malevolent, venomous.
Antonyms: SWEET; PLEASANT; HAPPY.

bitterness *noun* **1** *the bitterness of the medicine* acidity, pungency, acridity, tartness, sourness, vinegariness, acerbity. *See* BITTER 1. **2** *the bitterness of the old woman* resentment, resentfulness, embitteredness, rancor, animosity, acrimony, grudge, sullenness, sourness. *See* BITTER 2. **3** *the bitterness of the experience/memories* pain, painfulness, distress, agony, unhappiness, sadness, poignancy, tragedy. *See* BITTER 3. **4** *the bitterness of the wind* sharpness, harshness, coldness, intensity, penetration. *See* BITTER 4. **5** *the bitterness of the quarrel/controversy* acrimony, hostility, antagonism, spitefulness, rancor, malice, malevolence, venom. *See* BITTER 5.

bizarre *adjective* strange, weird, peculiar, odd, unusual, uncommon, curious, abnormal, extraordinary, queer, freakish, offbeat, outlandish, unconventional, fantastic, *outré*, eccentric, grotesque, ludicrous, comical, ridiculous, droll, deviant, aberrant; *inf.* oddball, wacky, way-out, off-the-wall.
Antonyms: ORDINARY; NORMAL.

blab *verb* **1** *blab a secret* blurt out, let slip, reveal, disclose, divulge, tell. **2** *they won't know unless he's blabbed* tell, inform, report, let the cat out of the bag, tattle; *inf.* squeal, sing. **3** *blabbing away on the phone* gossip, chat, chatter, blabber.

black *adjective* **1** *black horses* dark, pitch-black, pitch-dark, pitch, jet-black, jet, ebony, raven, sable, inky, coal-black, dusky, swarthy, blackish. **2** *the black race* African-American, Negro, Negroid, colored, dark-skinned. **3** *black nights/skies* dark, starless, moonless, unlit, unlighted, unilluminated, gloomy, dusky, dim, overcast, crepuscular. **4** *children with black hands | black corners* dirty, grubby, filthy, grimy, unclean, muddy, sooty, soiled, stained, dingy. **5** *black news | a black day* sad, melancholy, depressing, dismal, distressing, gloomy, hopeless, somber, doleful, mournful, lugubrious, funereal, pessimistic, ominous, foreboding. **6** *the crowd in a black mood* angry, threatening, menacing, hostile, furious, aggressive, belligerent, resentful, sullen. **7** *a black deed | black hearts* evil, wicked, sinful, bad, vile, villainous, criminal, iniquitous, nefarious, heinous, foul, ignoble, base, corrupt, depraved, devilish, diabolic. **8** *black humor* cynical, sick, macabre.
Antonyms: WHITE; CLEAR; LIGHT; CHEERFUL.

black *noun* **in the black** solvent, without debt. **in black and white 1** *wish to see the proposals in black and white* in print, written down, clearly/plainly/explicitly defined. **2** *see everything in black* *and white* in absolute terms, unequivocally, categorically, uncomprisingly.

blackball *verb* vote against, blacklist, debar, bar, ban, exclude, shut out, expel, drum out, oust, cashier, ostracize, reject, repudiate, boycott, snub, shun, give the cold shoulder to.

blacken *verb* **1** *smoke blackening the walls* make black, darken, make dirty/sooty/smoky, besmudge. **2** *the sky blackened* grow/become black, darken, grow dim. **3** *they blackened his character* defame, speak ill/evil of, slander, libel, denigrate, disparage, slur, sully, decry, run down, vilify, malign, defile, impugn, smear, besmirch, tarnish, taint, stain, dishonor, drag through the mud, calumniate, traduce.

blackguard *noun* scoundrel, rogue, villain, wretch, cad, rascal, devil, miscreant; *inf.* jerk, rat, creep, louse, bounder, swine; *derog.* bastard; *inf.* scumbag.

blacklist *verb* debar, bar, ban, exclude, shut out, preclude, reject, repudiate, boycott, proscribe, blackball. *See* BLACKBALL.

blackmail *noun* *get the money by blackmail* extortion, exaction, extraction, intimidation, bribery, wresting, wringing, milking, bleeding, bloodsucking.

blackmail *verb* **1** *blackmail large sums of money from them* extort, exact, extract, bribe, wrest, force. *See* BLACKMAIL *noun*. **2** *blackmail people into paying* hold to ransom, threaten, coerce, force, compel.

blackout *noun* **1** *suffer a blackout* loss of consciousness, fainting, coma, passing-out, swoon; *Med.* syncope. **2** *using candles during the blackout* power outage. **3** *information blackout* cutoff, suppression, withholding, noncommunication, censorship.

blame *verb* **1** *blame him for the accident* hold responsible/accountable, condemn, assign fault/liability/guilt. **2** *they're always blaming the child* find fault with, criticize, censure, reprimand, reproach, reprove, upbraid, scold, chide, berate, take to task. **blame on** *blame the accident on him* ascribe to, attribute to, lay at the door of; *inf.* pin on, stick on.
Antonyms: FORGIVE; ABSOLVE; PRAISE.

blame *noun* **1** *put the blame for the accident on him* responsibility, guilt, accountability, liability, onus, culpability, fault; *inf.* rap. **2** *incur much blame for his behavior* censure, criticism, incrimination, accusation, condemnation, reprimanding, reproach, recrimination, reproof, castigation, complaint, indictment, berating. *See* BLAME *verb* 2.
Antonyms: INNOCENCE; ABSOLUTION; PRAISE.

blameless *adjective* innocent, not to blame, guiltless, above reproach/suspicion, in the clear, without fault, virtuous, moral, upright, irreproachable, unimpeachable, unoffending, sinless.

Antonyms: GUILTY; BLAMEWORTHY.

blameworthy *adjective* to blame, guilty, at fault, culpable, offending, wrong, erring, condemnable.

Antonyms: INNOCENT; BLAMELESS; PRAISEWORTHY.

blanch *verb* **1** *blanch in fear* go/become pale, pale, whiten, go white, become pallid. **2** *illness had blanched her skin* made pale, whiten, made pallid, bleach, wash out. **3** *blanch the almonds/peppers* scald, boil.

bland *adjective* **1** *bland food* tasteless, flavorless, mild, insipid. **2** *a bland speech* dull, middle-of-the-road, mediocre, nondescript, humdrum, boring, uninteresting, monotonous, unexciting, tedious, uninspiring, weak, vapid. **3** *a bland manner* suave, urbane, smooth, affable, amiable, agreeable, gentle, gracious, courteous, congenial, unemotional, undemonstrative. **4** *bland breezes* mild, soft, calm, temperate, balmy, soothing, benign, mollifying.

Antonyms: SPICY; INTERESTING; STIMULATING.

blandishments *plural noun* flattery, cajolery, coaxing, wheedling, praise, fawning, ingratiating, inveiglement; compliments, soft words; *inf.* sweet talk, soft soap.

blank *adjective* **1** *a blank sheet of paper* void, empty, unfilled, unmarked, unwritten, clear, bare, clean, plain, spotless, white, vacant. **2** *a blank expression* expressionless, empty, vacant, deadpan, impassive, poker-faced, vacuous, lifeless, uninterested, emotionless, indifferent, uncomprehending. **3** *he looked blank | my mind went blank* uncomprehending, without ideas, at a loss, confused, puzzled, perplexed, bewildered, disconcerted, nonplussed, muddled, dumbfounded; *inf.* floored. **4** *a blank refusal* outright, absolute, unqualified, utter, complete, thorough.

Antonyms: FULL; EXPRESSIVE.

blank *noun* empty space, space, gap, emptiness, void, vacuum, vacancy, vacuity, nothingness.

blanket *noun* **1** *cover with a warm blanket* cover, covering, coverlet, bedcover, spread, afghan; *inf.* throw. **2** *a blanket of snow/mist* covering, mass, layer, coat, coating, film, sheet, carpet, veneer, overlay, cloak, mantle, envelope, wrapping.

blanket *adjective* *a blanket agreement* across the board, overall, inclusive, all-inclusive, comprehensive, general, wide-ranging, sweeping.

blanket *verb* *snow blanketing the earth | mist blanketing the hills* cover, overlay, coat, carpet, conceal, hide, mask, cloud, cloak, veil, shroud, envelop, surround. **blanket out** *the storm blanketed out the broadcast | hecklers blanketing out his speech* obscure, suppress, extinguish, stifle, smother.

blankness *noun* **1** *blankness of the paper/walls* voidness, emptiness, bareness, whiteness. *See* BLANK *adjective* 1. **2** *the blankness of her expression* expressionlessness, vacancy, lifelessness,

emotionlessness, indifference, abstraction. *See* BLANK *adjective* 2. **3** *the blankness of her mind* lack of ideas, obliviousness, no recollection, lack of comprehension, confusion, perplexity, bewilderment. *See* BLANK *adjective* 3. **4** *the blankness of the refusal* outrightness, absoluteness, lack of qualification. *See* BLANK *adjective* 4.

blare *verb* **1** *car horns blaring* sound loudly, trumpet, blast, clamor, boom, roar, bellow, resound, honk, toot, peal, clang, screech. **2** *radios blaring out music* utter loudly, blast, boom, screech.

blasé *adjective* indifferent, apathetic, uninterested, unexcited, nonchalant, uncaring, unmoved, emotionless, phlegmatic, lukewarm, unconcerned, offhand, bored, weary, world-weary, jaded, surfeited, glutted, cloyed, satiated.

Antonyms: ENTHUSIASTIC; EXCITED; RESPONSIVE.

blaspheme *verb* **1** *told to stop blaspheming* swear, curse, utter profanities; *inf.* cuss. **2** *blaspheming Christ* profane, desecrate, revile, abuse.

blasphemous *adjective* profane, sacrilegious, irreligious, irreverent, impious, ungodly, godless, unholy.

blasphemy *noun* **1** *guilty of blasphemy* profanity, sacrilege, irreligiousness, irreverence, impiety, impiousness, profaneness, ungodliness, unholiness, desecration, execration. **2** *utter blasphemies* cursing, swearing, execration; curses, oaths, profanities.

blast *noun* **1** *a sudden blast of cold air* gust, rush, draft, blow, gale, squall, storm. **2** *heard a blast | a sudden blast of noise* blare, blaring, trumpeting, clamor, bellowing, boom, roar, clang, screech, wail, toot, honk, peal. **3** *people killed by the blast* explosion, detonation, discharge, blow-up, blowing-up, eruption. **4** *receive a blast from the teacher* outburst, attack, reprimand, rebuke, criticism, castigation, reproof.

blast *verb* **1** *car horns blasting away | blast the car horn* sound loudly, trumpet, blare, boom, roar. *See* BLARE 1. **2** *radios blasting out rock music* blare, boom, screech. **3** *blast the building to bits* blow, demolish, shatter, explode, break up. **4** *frost blasted the plants* blight, kill, destroy, wither, shrivel. **5** *poverty blasting their hopes* kill, destroy, crush, dash, blight, wreck, ruin, spoil, mar, annihilate, disappoint, frustrate. **6** *blasting the pupils for being late* attack, reprimand, rebuke, criticize, upbraid, berate, castigate, reprove, rail at, flay. **7** *guns blasting* shoot, fire, blaze away, discharge. **blast off** *the rocket blasted off successfully* be launched, take off, lift off.

blatant *adjective* flagrant, glaring, obtrusive, obvious, overt, manifest, conspicuous, prominent, pronounced, bare-faced, naked, sheer, outright, out-and-out, unmitigated, brazen, shameless.

Antonyms: INCONSPICUOUS; SUBTLE.

blaze *noun* **1** *the house was destroyed in the blaze* fire, conflagration, holocaust; flames. **2** *a sudden blaze of light* beam, flash, flare, glare, streak, glitter; brightness, radiance, brilliance. **3** *left in a blaze of anger* outburst, burst, eruption, flare-up, explosion, outbreak, storm, torrent, blast, rush.

blaze *verb* **1** *the logs blazed* burn, be ablaze, flame, burst into flames, catch fire. **2** *lights blazed in the street* shine, beam, flash, flare, glare, glitter. **3** *she blazed with fury* flare up, blow up, explode, seethe, fume, boil, smolder; *inf.* see red, work oneself up, get steamed up.

blazon *verb blazoned all over the newspapers* publicize, proclaim, broadcast, advertise, publish, make known, trumpet.

bleach *verb* **1** *the sun bleaching her hair/the carpet* make white/whiter, make pale/paler, lighten, blanch, fade, wash out. **2** *bones bleaching in the desert* grow white/whiter, grow pale/paler, lighten, blanch, fade.

bleached *adjective* lightened, blanched, faded, washed-out, stone-washed.

bleak *adjective* **1** *a bleak landscape* bare, barren, desolate, exposed, unsheltered, open, windswept, windy, chilly, cold, waste, arid, desert. **2** *bleak surroundings/prospects* dreary, dismal, dark, gloomy, drab, somber, wretched, depressing, grim, miserable, cheerless, joyless, uninviting, discouraging, disheartening, unpromising, hopeless.
Antonyms: SHELTERED; COZY; CHEERFUL.

bleary *adjective* **1** *bleary eyes* blurred, blurry, tired, watery. **2** *bleary view* indistinct, dim, unclear, hazy, foggy, fogged, fuzzy, clouded, misty, murky.

bleed *verb* **1** *the wounded/wounds were bleeding badly* shed/lose blood, emit blood. **2** *doctors formerly bled patients* draw blood from, remove/take blood from; *fml.* phlebotomize. **3** *sap bleeding from a cut in the trunk* flow, run, ooze, seep, exude, trickle, weep, gush, spurt. **4** *bleeding money from the old man* extort, extract, squeeze, fleece, milk. **5** *bleeding their resources* drain, exhaust, sap, deplete, reduce. **6** *hearts are bleeding for them* ache, grieve, mourn, sorrow, suffer, agonize, anguish, sympathize, feel.

blemish *noun* **1** *a blemish on the fruit/skin* mark, blotch, spot, patch, bruise, scar, speck, speckle, imperfection, discoloration, disfigurement, birthmark, nevus, pimple; *inf.* zit. **2** *a character blemish* defect, flaw, blot, taint, stain, smirch, dishonor, disgrace.
Antonyms: IMPROVEMENT; ENHANCEMENT.

blemish *verb* **1** *frost blemishing the fruit | her blemished skin* damage, mar, spoil, flaw, mark, spot, speckle, blotch, disfigure, discolor, deface. **2** *blemishing his reputation* sully, tarnish, blot, taint, stain, besmirch, injure, damage, impair, flaw.

blend *verb* **1** *blend the ingredients* mix, combine, intermix, admix, mingle, commingle, amalgamate, coalesce, unite, merge, compound, alloy, fuse, synthesize, homogenize. **2** *colors blending with each other* harmonize, go with, go well with, complement, fit, suit.

blend *noun a blend of colors* mixture, mix, combination, admixture, mingling, commingling, amalgamation, amalgam, uniting, union, merging, compound, alloy, fusion, composite, concoction, synthesis, homogenization.

bless *verb* **1** *bless the altar* consecrate, sanctify, hallow, dedicate. **2** *bless God's name* glorify, praise, laud, exalt, magnify, extol. **3** *the priest blessed the children* ask God's favor/protection for, give a benediction for, invoke happiness on. **4** *I bless the day I met her | bless you for helping* give thanks for/to, thank. **5** *they were blessed with good looks | blessed with three children* endow, bestow, favor, provide, grace. **6** *the committee blessed the enterprise* sanction, approve, give approval for, be in favor of, endorse, support, give consent, smile upon.
Antonyms: CURSE; DAMN; BLIGHT.

blessed *adjective* **1** *a blessed place* consecrated, sanctified, hallowed, sacred, holy, divine, venerated, revered, beatified; glorified, exalted. **2** *blessed with talent* fortunate, lucky, favored, endowed. **3** *blessed days of peace* happy, joyful, joyous, blissful, glad, cheerful, blithe, contented.

blessing *noun* **1** *utter a blessing* benediction, dedication, thanksgiving, consecration, invocation, commendation; grace. **2** *give the plan his blessing* approval, approbation, sanction, endorsement, support, backing, permission, leave, consent, assent, concurrence; good wishes. **3** *have the blessing of good health | what a blessing you're here* advantage, benefit, help, boon, godsend, favor, gift; luck, good fortune, gain, profit, bounty.
Antonyms: CURSE; DISADVANTAGE; BLIGHT.

blight *noun* **1** *plants killed by blight* disease, canker, infestation, pestilence, fungus, mildew. **2** *the blight that destroyed the city* affliction, plague, scourge, bane, woe, curse, misfortune, calamity, trouble, tribulation, evil, corruption, pollution, contamination.
Antonyms: BLESSING; FAVOR.

blight *verb* **1** *trees blighted by frost* kill, destroy, wither, shrivel, blast, mildew. **2** *hopes blighted by war* kill, destroy, crush, dash, blast, wreck, ruin. See BLAST verb 5.

blind *adjective* **1** *guide dogs for blind people* unsighted, sightless, visually impaired, visionless, unseeing, stone-blind; *inf.* visually challenged. **2** *he must be blind not to know she loves him* imperceptive, slow, slow-witted, dim-witted, obtuse, dense, thick. **3** *blind loyalty* unreasoned, uncritical, unthinking, mindless, injudicious, undiscerning, indiscriminate, prejudiced, biased. **4** *in a blind rage* rash, impetuous, hasty, reckless, uncontrolled, uncontrollable, unrestrained, wild, frantic, violent, furious, irrational. **5** *a blind entrance* concealed, hidden, obscured, out of sight. **6** *a blind alley* dead-end, without exit, exitless, blocked, closed,

barred, impassable. **blind to** *blind to danger* unmindful of, careless of, heedless of, oblivious to, inattentive to, indifferent to, neglectful of, unaware of, unconscious of, unobservant of, ignorant of, insensitive to.
Antonyms: SIGHTED; PERCEPTIVE; MINDFUL.

blind *verb* **1** *blinded in the accident* make blind, deprive of sight/vision, render unsighted/sightless, put one's eyes out. **2** *blinding the driver* obscure/block (one's) vision, get in (one's) line of vision, dazzle. **3** *blinded by love* deprive of judgment/reason/sense, deceive, delude, beguile, hoodwink.

blind *noun* **1** *a window blind* screen, shade, curtain, shutter; venetian blind. **2** *the duck hunters' blind* camouflage, screen, façade, cover.

blindly *adverb* **1** *feeling his way blindly* without sight, sightlessly, unseeingly. **2** *rushing on blindly* unmindfully, carelessly, heedlessly, rashly, impetuously, recklessly, uncontrolledly, wildly, frantically, irrationally. *See* BLIND *adjective* 4. **3** *loving him blindly* uncritically, injudiciously, undiscerningly, indiscriminately. *See* BLIND *adjective* 3.

blink *verb* **1** *eyes blinking in the light* flutter, flicker, wink, bat, nictitate, nictate. **2** *people blinking in the sunlight* wink, peer, squint, screw up the eyes. **3** *city lights blinking* flicker, twinkle, waver, wink, glimmer, glitter, sparkle, shimmer, scintillate, flash, gleam, shine. **4** *the police blinked at the governor's traffic violation* turn a blind eye to, take no notice of, disregard, overlook, ignore, condone.

bliss *noun* **1** *the bliss of being in love* ecstasy, joy, elation, rapture, euphoria, happiness, delight, gladness, pleasure, heaven, paradise, seventh heaven, Utopia; halcyon days. **2** *in a state of bliss* blessedness, rapture, heavenly joy, divine happiness, beatitude.
Antonyms: MISERY; HELL.

blister *noun* **1** *blisters on the skin caused by burns* pustule, pimple, boil, cyst, abscess, carbuncle, ulcer. **2** *blisters on the painted surface* bubble, swelling, bulge, protuberance.

blistering *adjective* **1** *at blistering speed | in blistering heat* extreme, very great, greatest, intense, maximum, utmost. **2** *blistering criticism* scathing, fierce, severe, savage, sharp, biting, harsh, sarcastic, caustic, searing, mordant, trenchant.

blithe *adjective* **1** *in a blithe mood* happy, cheerful, cheery, lighthearted, jolly, merry, gay, joyful, carefree, buoyant, jaunty, animated, sprightly, vivacious, spirited, frisky, gladsome, mirthful. **2** *with a blithe disregard for others* casual, indifferent, careless, thoughtless, nonchalant, uncaring, unconcerned, heedless, untroubled, cool, blasé.
Antonyms: SAD; THOUGHTFUL.

blitz *noun* **1** *the blitz on London* bombardment, attack, assault, raid, offensive, onslaught, strike, blitzkrieg. **2** *a cleaning blitz* attack, onslaught, all-out effort, endeavor.

blizzard *noun* snowstorm, snow squall, snowfall, winter storm, blast, gale.

bloat *verb* swell, puff up/out, blow up, distend, inflate, balloon, enlarge, expand, dilate.

blob *noun* **1** *a blob of ink/whipped cream* globule, glob, drop, droplet, bead, ball, bubble, pellet, pill; dollop, lump, smidgen; *inf.* smidge. **2** *a blob of paint* spot, dab, splash, daub, blotch, blot, smudge, smear, mark.

bloc *noun* alliance, coalition, union, federation, league, ring, group, syndicate, combine, entente, party, wing, faction, cabal, clique, coterie.

block *noun* **1** *block of chocolate/soap* bar, cake, brick, chunk, hunk, lump, cube, ingot, wedge, mass, piece, wad. **2** *building a new science block* building, complex. **3** *block of seats/shares* group, batch, band, cluster, set, section, quantity. **4** *a block in the pipe* blockage, obstruction, stoppage. **5** *a block to progress* obstacle, bar, barrier, impediment, hindrance, deterrent, check, hurdle, stumbling block, drawback, hitch.

block *verb* **1** *block the pipe* clog, stop up, choke, plug, close, obstruct. **2** *block progress* hinder, obstruct, impede, halt, stop, bar, check, arrest, deter, thwart, frustrate, stand in the way of. **3** *block hats* shape, mold, form, fashion.
Antonyms: CLEAR; FACILITATE.

blockade *noun* **1** *blockade of the city* siege, beleaguerment, investment, encirclement. **2** *a blockade at the border | a blockade to progress* barrier, barricade, obstacle, obstruction, block, hindrance, impediment, check, deterrent, hurdle, stoppage.

blockage *noun* **1** *a blockage in the pipes* obstruction, stoppage, block, occlusion, impediment. **2** *the blockage of the pipes* obstructing, blocking, stopping up, occluding.

blockhead *noun* dunce, numskull, dolt, fool, simpleton, oaf, ass, dullard, idiot, ignoramus, bonehead, nincompoop; *inf.* chump, dingbat.

blond, blonde *adjective* fair, fair-haired, golden-haired, flaxen, tow-headed; fair-skinned, fair-complexioned, light, light-colored.

blood *noun* **1** *a blood disease | blood was flowing* lifeblood, vital fluid, whole blood; *lit.* ichor. *See also table at* VEIN. **2** *of noble blood* ancestry, lineage, line, family, birth, extraction, descent, origin, genealogy, heritage, stock, race, pedigree, kinship, consanguinity. **3** *own flesh and blood* relations, kin, kindred; relationship, kinship. **4** *of hot blood* temperament, disposition, nature, humor, temper, spirit, feeling.

blood-curdling *adjective* spine-chilling, chilling, terrifying, hair-raising, horrifying, horrific, horrendous, frightening, fearful, appalling, scary.

bloodless *adjective* **1** *looking bloodless since the surgery* anemic, pale, wan, colorless, pallid, ashen, chalky, pasty, sallow, sickly, peaked, ghostlike, white as a sheet. **2** *a bloodless young man* listless, languid, feeble, sluggish, lifeless, apathetic, spiritless, passionless, phlegmatic, torpid, lackadaisical.

bloodshed *noun* killing, slaughter, slaying, carnage, butchery, massacre, murder, blood-letting, blood bath, gore, pogrom, decimation.

bloodthirsty *adjective* murderous, homicidal, savage, vicious, ruthless, barbarous, barbaric, brutal, bloody, sadistic, slaughterous, warlike, bellicose; *fml.* sanguinary.

bloody *adjective* **1** *a bloody nose* bleeding. **2** *a bloody cloth* blood-stained, blood-soaked, blood-marked, blood-spattered; *fml.* sanguinary. **3** *bloody actions/thoughts* bloodthirsty, murderous, homicidal, savage, vicious, slaughterous; *fml.* sanguinary. *See* BLOODTHIRSTY.

bloom *noun* **1** *perfect blooms* flower, blossom, floweret; flowering, blossoming, efflorescence. **2** *beauty losing its bloom* freshness, glow, luster, sheen, radiance, flush, perfection, blush. **full bloom** *the full bloom of youth* prime, perfection, heyday, vigor, flourishing, strength.

bloom *verb* **1** *plants blooming* flower, blossom, be in flower/blossom, come into flower/blossom, open, open out, bud, burgeon. **2** *they've bloomed since moving to the country* flourish, thrive, be in good health, get on well, prosper, succeed, progress.

Antonyms: WITHER; FADE; FAIL.

blossom *noun* *apple blossom* blooms, flowers, flowerets; blossoming, efflorescence.

blossom *verb* **1** *trees blossoming* be in flower, flower, bloom, burgeon. **2** *she blossomed in her new environment | the friendship blossomed* bloom, flourish, thrive, get on well, prosper, succeed, progress, develop, grow, mature.

blot *noun* **1** *blots of ink/grease* spot, blotch, smudge, patch, dot, mark, speck, smear. **2** *a blot on his character* stain, blemish, taint, flaw, fault, defect, tarnishing, imperfection, disgrace.

blot *verb* **1** *paper blotted with ink-spots* spot, blotch, smudge, dot, mark, speckle, smear, bespatter. **2** *the event blotted his reputation* stain, sully, tarnish, taint, besmirch, blacken. **blot out 1** *blot out the typist's mistake* erase, obliterate, delete, rub out. **2** *a tree blotting out the view* hide, conceal, obscure, obliterate, darken, dim, shadow. **3** *time blotting out memories* wipe out, erase, efface, obliterate, expunge, destroy, exterminate. **blot up** *blot up the grease* soak up, absorb, dry up, dry out, take up.

blotch *noun* **1** *a blotch of ink* smudge, dot, spot, speck, blot, stain, smear. **2** *a blotch on the skin* patch, blemish, mark, spot, eruption, birthmark, nevus.

blow[1] *verb* **1** *the wind was blowing* in motion, puff, flurry, bluster, blast. **2** *hair blowing in the breeze* move, wave, flap, flutter, waft, stream, drift, whirl, undulate. **3** *wind blowing the leaves/boats* move, toss, sweep, whisk, drive,

buffet, whirl, transport, convey. **4** *blow cigarette smoke* breathe out, puff out, exhale, emit, expel. **5** *he was blowing a bit* breathe hard, puff, pant, wheeze, gasp, huff and puff. **6** *blow the trumpet* sound, play, toot, blare, blast. **7** *blow $100 on a meal* squander, fritter away, spend freely. **8** *blow one's chances* spoil, ruin, bungle, make a mess of, muff; *inf.* botch, screw up. **blow out 1** *blow out the candle* put out, extinguish, snuff, douse. **2** *the walls suddenly blew out* break open, burst, explode, blow up, shatter, rupture, crack. **blow over** *their anger had blown over by morning* pass away, pass, die down, be forgotten, sink into oblivion, come to an end, disappear, vanish, cease, subside, settle down, terminate. **blow up 1** *the bombed building blew up* explode, burst open, break open, shatter, rupture. **2** *the bomb blew up* explode, go off, detonate, erupt. **3** *blow up the building* bomb, detonate, explode, blast. **4** *blow up the tire/stomach* inflate, pump up, fill up, swell, enlarge, distend, expand, puff up, balloon. **5** *blow up the story* exaggerate, overstate, embroider, color, magnify, heighten, expand on. **6** *he blew up at the news* lose one's temper, become angry/enraged/furious, go into a rage/fury, erupt, go wild, rage; *inf.* hit the roof, go off the deep end, fly off the handle.

blow[2] *noun* *a blow on the trumpet* blast, blare, toot, sound.

blow[3] *noun* **1** *a blow on the head* hit, knock, bang, punch, thump, smack, whack, thwack, buffet, stroke, rap; *inf.* bash, belt, clout, sock, wallop, battering, bat. **2** *her death was a blow* shock, upset, calamity, catastrophe, disaster, misfortune, setback, disappointment, jolt, reversal.

blowout *noun* **1** *the car veered due to a blowout* puncture, bursting, burst tire; *inf.* flat. **2** *a birthday blowout* party, feast, celebration, binge, spree; *inf.* bash, shindig.

blowzy *adjective* **1** *a blowzy young woman* disheveled, slovenly, tousled, unkempt, untidy, sloppy, slipshod, messy, bedraggled. **2** *a blowzy drunk* coarse-looking, florid, ruddy-complexioned, red-faced.

bludgeon *noun* *beaten with a bludgeon* club, cudgel, stick, truncheon, heavy weapon.

bludgeon *verb* **1** *bludgeoned to death* club, cudgel, strike, hit, beat, beat up; *inf.* clobber. **2** *bludgeoned into agreeing* coerce, force, compel, browbeat, dragoon, bulldoze, bully, railroad, steamroll, steamroller, pressure; *inf.* strong-arm.

blue *adjective* **1** *a blue dress | blue walls* azure, sky-blue, powder-blue, deep blue, royal blue, sapphire, ultramarine, navy blue, navy, indigo, cyan, cobalt, cerulean. **2** *feeling blue* depressed, gloomy, dejected, despondent, low, downcast, downhearted, unhappy, sad, melancholy, glum, morose, dismal; *inf.* down in the dumps. **3** *blue jokes* obscene, indecent, dirty, coarse, vulgar, bawdy, lewd, risqué, improper, smutty, offensive; *inf.* naughty.

blueprint *noun* plan, design, prototype, draft, outline, sketch, pattern, layout, representation.

blues *plural noun a case of the blues* depression, gloominess, gloom, dejection, despondency, downheartedness, unhappiness, sadness, melancholy, glumness, moroseness, dismalness; low spirits, doldrums; *inf.* dumps.

bluff[1] *verb* **1** *he's only bluffing* pretend, fake, feign, put on, lie. **2** *he's bluffing you* deceive, delude, mislead, trick, hoodwink, hoax, take in, humbug, bamboozle; *inf.* put one over on.

bluff[2] *noun it's just a bluff* deception, deceit, pretense, sham, subterfuge, fake, show, false show, idle boast, feint, delusion, hoax, fraud.

bluff[3] *adjective* **1** *a bluff manner* frank, open, candid, outspoken, blunt, direct, plainspoken, straightforward, downright, hearty. **2** *a bluff slope* steep, sheer, vertical, precipitous, abrupt, sudden, perpendicular.

Antonyms: DIPLOMATIC; EVASIVE.

bluff[4] *noun* cliff, headland, ridge, promontory, peak, crag, bank, slope, height, escarpment, scarp.

blunder *noun* mistake, error, inaccuracy, fault, slip, oversight, *faux pas*, gaffe; *inf.* slipup, booboo.

blunder *verb* **1** *management blundered badly* make a mistake, err; *inf.* slip up, screw up, blow it. **2** *blundering about in the dark* stumble, flounder, lurch, stagger, falter. **3** *blunder the situation* mismanage, botch, bungle, make a mess of.

blunt *adjective* **1** *a blunt knife/blade* not sharp, unsharpened, dull, dulled, edgeless. **2** *a blunt remark/manner/person* frank, candid, outspoken, plainspoken, straightforward, direct, bluff, to the point, brusque, abrupt, curt, short; *inf.* upfront.

Antonyms: SHARP; KEEN; SUBTLE.

blunt *verb* **1** *blunt the blade* dull, make less sharp, make blunt/dull. **2** *blunt the appetite/enthusiasm* dull, take the edge off, deaden, dampen, numb, weaken, impair, appease.

blur *verb* **1** *blurring the view* make indistinct, make vague, obscure, dim, bedim, make hazy, befog, fog, cloud, becloud, mask, veil. **2** *blur the windshield* smear, besmear, smudge, spot, blotch, besmirch. **3** *blur one's judgment/memory* dull, numb, make dim, make less sharp, deaden.

blur *noun* **1** *just a blur on the landscape* | *a blur in my memory* something hazy/indistinct/vague, haze; haziness, indistinctness, obscureness, obscurity, dimness, fogginess, cloudiness. **2** *a blur on the windshield* smear, smudge, spot, blotch.

blurred *adjective* hazy, indistinct, faint, fuzzy,

blurry, misty, foggy, unclear, vague, lacking definition, out of focus, nebulous.

Antonyms: CLEAR; DISTINCT; SHARP.

blurt *verb* **blurt out** call out, cry out, utter suddenly, exclaim, ejaculate, blab, disclose, divulge, reveal, let slip, babble, let the cat out of the bag; *inf.* spill the beans, spout.

blush *verb* *blushing in embarrassment* redden, go pink/red, turn red/crimson/scarlet, flush, be red-faced, burn up.

blush *noun the blush of their cheeks* flush; reddening, color, rosiness, pinkness, ruddiness.

bluster *verb* **1** *wind blustering* blow fiercely, blast, gust, storm, roar. **2** *bullies blustering* rant, bully, domineer, harangue, threaten, boast, brag, swagger, throw one's weight about, be overbearing, lord it.

bluster *noun* **1** *the bluster of the wind* noise, roar, tumult, blasting, gusting, storming. **2** *the bullies' bluster* ranting, bravado, domineering, bombast, boasting, bragging, swaggering, braggadocio; empty threats.

blustery *adjective* stormy, gusty, gusting, windy, squally, wild, tempestuous.

board *noun* **1** *a wooden board* plank, beam, panel, slat, length of timber, piece of wood. **2** *pay for one's board* food, sustenance; meals, daily meals, provisions, victuals; *inf.* grub, nosh. **3** *the board met to discuss policy* committee, council, panel, directorate, advisory group, panel of trustees.

board *verb* **1** *they board with her* lodge, live, room, be quartered, be housed. **2** *she boards three people* take in, put up, accommodate, house, feed. **3** *board the plane/train/bus* get on, enter, go/get on board, go/get aboard, embark.

board up *board up the windows* cover up/over, close up, shut up, seal.

boast *verb* **1** *always boasting about his achievements* brag, crow, exaggerate, overstate, swagger, blow one's own trumpet, sing one's own praises, congratulate oneself, pat oneself on the back; *inf.* talk big, blow hard. **2** *the town boasts two museums* possess, have, own, enjoy, pride oneself/itself on.

Antonyms: DEPRECATE; BELITTLE.

boast *noun* **1** *his boast is that he's best* brag, overstatement, self-praise, bluster; bragging, crowing, blustering. See BOAST *verb* 1. **2** *the building is the boast of the town* pride, pride and joy, treasure, gem, pearl, valued object, source of satisfaction.

boastful *adjective* bragging, crowing, swaggering, cocky, conceited, arrogant, vain, egotistical, overbearing, blustering, overweening; *fml.* vainglorious; *inf.* swanky, big-headed, swellheaded.

Antonyms: MODEST; UNASSUMING.

boat *noun* vessel, craft; yacht, dinghy, sloop, sailboat, motorboat, speedboat, rowboat, punt, canoe, kayak.

bob[1] *verb* **1** *bobbing in the water* move up and

down, float, bounce, quiver, wobble. **2** *bobbed* **bob ~ bold**

her head nod, jerk, twitch, duck.

bob[2] *verb* *bobbed her hair* cut short, dock.bode
bode *verb* augur, presage, portend, betoken, foretell, prophesy, predict, forebode, foreshadow, indicate, signify, purport.
bodily *adjective* *bodily functions/injuries* physical, corporeal, corporal, carnal, fleshly.
bodily *adverb* **1** *the audience rising bodily* as a body/group/mass, in a mass, as a whole, together, as one, collectively, en masse. **2** *threw him bodily into the river* wholly, completely, entirely, totally.
body *noun* **1** *well-formed bodies* frame, form, figure, shape, build, physique, framework, skeleton, trunk, torso. **2** *a body in the morgue* dead body, corpse, cadaver, carcass; remains; *inf.* stiff. **3** *more bodies than the room could hold* person, individual, being, human being, human, creature, mortal. **4** *the body of the plane* main part, principal part, hub, core. **5** *a body of water* mass, expanse, extent, aggregate. **6** *the body of political opinion* majority, preponderance, bulk, mass. **7** *the ruling body* group, party, band, association, company, confederation, bloc, congress, corporation, society. **8** *material with little body* substance, firmness, solidity, density, shape, structure.

body
cadaver, carcass, corpse, cremains, remains

The problem of what to call the human **body** after it has departed this life is a delicate one. Although a *body* can be either dead or alive, human or animal, a **corpse** is most definitely a dead human body and a **carcass** is the body of a dead animal. The issue has been confused, of course, by the figurative use of *carcass* as a term of contempt (*Get your carcass out of bed and come down here!*). While *carcass* is often used humorously, there's nothing funny about *corpse*, a no-nonsense term for a lifeless physical body (*the battlefield was littered with corpses*). A funeral director is likely to prefer the term **remains**, which is a euphemism for the body of the deceased (*he had his wife's remains shipped home for burial*), or **cremains**, if the body has been cremated. A medical student, on the other hand, is much more likely to use the term **cadaver**, which is a corpse that is dissected in a laboratory for scientific study.

bog *noun* marsh, marshland, swamp, mire, quagmire, morass, slough, fen.
bogged *verb* **bogged down** stuck, impeded, obstructed, halted, stopped, delayed, stalled, slowed down; trapped, entangled, ensnared.
bogeyman *noun* *children imagining a bogeyman* monster, evil spirit, ghost, apparition, specter, phantom, goblin, hobgoblin; *inf.* spook.
boggle *verb* **1** *boggled at paying so much* hesitate, flinch, waver, falter at. **2** *they boggled at the sight* be surprised, take fright, start, be startled, be astounded/staggered, shy. **3** *the sight boggled*

my mind startle, astound, astonish, amaze, overwhelm, shock, bowl over; *inf.* flabbergast.
bogus *adjective* fraudulent, counterfeit, fake, spurious, false, forged, sham, artificial, mock, make-believe, quasi, pseudo; *inf.* phony.
Antonyms: GENUINE; AUTHENTIC.
bohemian *adjective* *a bohemian lifestyle* unconventional, unorthodox, nonconformist, offbeat, avant-garde, original, eccentric, alternative, artistic; *inf.* arty, way-out, off-the-wall, oddball.
Antonyms: CONVENTIONAL; CONSERVATIVE.
bohemian *noun* *bohemians of the 1960s* unconventional person, nonconformist, hippie, beatnik, dropout.
boil *verb* **1** *the soup is boiling* bubble, simmer, cook, seethe, heat, stew. **2** *boil the soup* bring to a boil, simmer, cook, heat. **3** *the sea was boiling* seethe, bubble, churn, froth, foam, fizz, effervesce. **4** *the teacher boiled with impatience* be/made angry/furious/indignant, rage, fume, seethe, rant, rave, storm, fulminate, bluster, explode, flare up; *inf.* blow one's top, fly off the handle, go off the deep end, hit the roof, go up the wall, blow a fuse.
boil *noun* carbuncle, furuncle, abscess, pustule, pimple.boiling
boiling *adjective* **1** *boiling hot | boiling weather* very hot, scorching, roasting, baking, blistering, sweltering, searing, torrid. **2** *she was boiling at his insults* furious, angry, incensed, fuming, in a rage, raging, enraged, infuriated, seething, indignant, irate, angry; *inf.* mad. *See* BOIL *verb* 4.
boisterous *adjective* **1** *boisterous children/parties* lively, active, bouncy, frisky, exuberant, spirited, noisy, loud, rowdy, unruly, wild, unrestrained, romping, rollicking, disorderly, rambunctious. **2** *boisterous winds* blustery, gusting, gusty, breezy, stormy, squally, rough, turbulent, raging, wild.
Antonyms: CALM; QUIET.
bold *adjective* **1** *a bold explorer | bold deeds* daring, intrepid, audacious, courageous, brave, valiant, fearless, gallant, heroic, adventurous, enterprising, confident, undaunted, valorous. **2** *a bold young woman* brazen, shameless, forward, brash, impudent, audacious, saucy, pert, immodest, unabashed; *inf.* brassy. **3** *bold colors* striking, vivid, bright, eye-catching, conspicuous, distinct, pronounced, prominent, well-marked, showy, flashy.
Antonyms: TIMID; RETIRING; PALE.

bold
aggressive, audacious, bumptious, brazen, intrepid, presumptuous

Is walking up to an attractive stranger and asking him or her to have dinner with you tonight a **bold** move or merely an **aggressive** one? Both words suggest assertive, confident behavior that is a little on the shameless side, but *bold* has a wider range of application. It can suggest self-confidence that borders on impudence (*to be so bold as to call the president by his first name*), but it can also be used to describe a daring temperament that is either courageous or defiant (*a bold investigator who would not give up*). *Aggressive* behavior, on the other hand, usually falls within a narrower range, somewhere between menacing (*aggressive attacks on innocent villagers*) and just plain pushy (*an aggressive salesperson*). **Brazen** implies a defiant lack of modesty (*a brazen stare*), and **presumptuous** goes even further, suggesting overconfidence to the point of causing offense (*a presumptuous request for money*). **Bumptious** behavior can also be offensive, but it is usually associated with the kind of cockiness that can't be helped (*a bumptious young upstart*). An **audacious** individual is bold to the point of recklessness (*an audacious explorer*), which brings it very close in meaning to **intrepid**, suggesting fearlessness in the face of the unknown (*the intrepid settlers of the Great Plains*).

---

bolster *noun laid his head on the bolster* pillow, cushion, pad, support.

bolster *verb bolster morale/bolster up the economy* strengthen, reinforce, support, boost, give a boost to, prop up, buoy up, shore up, hold up, maintain, buttress, aid, assist, help, revitalize, invigorate.

bolt *noun* 1 *window bolts* bar, catch, latch, lock, fastener, hasp. 2 *nuts and bolts* rivet, pin, peg. 3 *bolt of lightning* flash, shaft, streak, burst, discharge, flare. 4 *escape in one bolt | make a bolt for it* dash, dart, run, sprint, rush, bound, spring, leap, jump.

bolt *verb* 1 *bolt the door* bar, lock, fasten, latch. 2 *bolt the pieces together* rivet, pin, clamp, fasten, batten. 3 *they bolted from the room* dash, dart, run, sprint, hurtle, rush, bound, hurry, flee, fly, spring, leap, abscond, escape, make a break/run for it; *inf.* tear from. 4 *bolting his food* gulp, gobble, devour, wolf, guzzle.

bolt *adverb* **bolt upright** straight up, very straight, rigid, stiff, completely upright.

bomb *noun* 1 *dropped a bomb on the target* explosive, incendiary device, incendiary, blockbuster; grenade, shell, missile, torpedo, projectile, trajectile, letter bomb, nuclear bomb. 2 *the movie was a bomb* flop, failure, fiasco; *inf.* washout, turkey.

bomb *verb* 1 *bombed the target* bombard, blow up; shell, torpedo, blitz, strafe, cannonade. 2 *the movie bombed at the box office* flop, fail, fall flat, founder; *inf.* go up in smoke, go belly up.

bombard *verb* 1 *bombard military establishments* bomb, shell, torpedo, pound, blitz, strafe, pepper, cannonade, fusillade, fire at, attack, assault, raid. 2 *bombard with questions* assail, attack, besiege, beset, bother, subject to, hound, belabor.

bombardment *noun* 1 *the bombardment of London* bombing, shelling, strafing, torpedoing, blitz, blitzkrieg, air raid, strafe, cannonade, fusillade, attack, assault. 2 *the bombardment of the movie star with photographers* assailing, attack, besieging, barraging. *See* BOMBARD 2.

bombast *noun* pomposity, ranting, rant, bluster, turgidity, verbosity, pretentiousness, affectedness, ostentation, grandiloquence, rodomontade.

bona fide *adjective* genuine, authentic, real, true, actual, sterling, sound, legal, legitimate.

bonanza *noun* windfall, godsend, stroke/run of luck, boon, bonus.

bond *noun* 1 *the bond/bonds of friendship* tie, link, binding, connection, attachment, union, ligature, nexus. 2 *sign a bond* agreement, contract, pact, transaction, bargain, deal, covenant, compact, pledge, promise, treaty, concordat. **bonds** *freed from his bonds* chains, fetters, shackles, manacles.

bond *verb* *bond the pieces of metal together* join, connect, fasten, stick, unite, attach, bind; glue, gum, fuse, weld.

bondage *noun* slavery, enslavement, captivity, servitude, serfdom, oppression.

bonus *noun* 1 *the pleasant environment was a bonus* extra, plus, gain, benefit, boon, perquisite, dividend, premium. 2 *a Christmas bonus* gratuity, tip, gift, perk, honorarium, reward, bounty, commission.
Antonyms: DISADVANTAGE; PENALTY.

bony *adjective* *a bony frame* angular, rawboned, gaunt, scraggy, scrawny, skinny, thin, emaciated, skeletal, cadaverous.

book *noun* 1 *read/publish a book* volume, tome, work, publication, title, opus, treatise, manual. 2 *the exercise/rent book* booklet, pad, loose-leaf notebook, notebook, ledger, log.

book *verb* 1 *book a room | book the seats/speaker* reserve, make reservations for, arrange in advance, engage, charter. 2 *book the meeting* arrange, program, schedule, line up.

bookish *adjective* studious, scholarly, academic, literary, intellectual, brainy, highbrow, erudite, learned, pedantic, pedagogic.

books *plural noun* *checking the books* accounts, records.

boom *verb* 1 *guns booming in the distance* resound, sound loudly, explode, bang, blast, blare, roar, bellow, rumble, reverberate, thunder. 2 *the teacher boomed* roar, bellow, shout, thunder. 3 *the housing market booming* burgeon, flourish, thrive, prosper, progress, do well, succeed, grow, develop, expand, increase, swell, intensify, mushroom.

boom *noun* 1 *the boom of the guns* resounding, loud noise, explosion, banging, bang, blasting, blast, blare, roaring, roar, bellow, rumble, reverberation, thundering, thunder. 2 *the boom in low-income housing* increase, upturn, up-

surge, upswing, advance, growth, spurt, progress, development, expansion, improvement, boost, success.
Antonyms: DECLINE; SLUMP.

boomerang *verb* rebound, come back, spring back, return, recoil, reverse, ricochet, backfire.

boon *noun* benefit, advantage, gain, plus, bonus, good thing, blessing, godsend, windfall, perk, perquisite.
Antonyms: DISADVANTAGE; CURSE.

boon *adjective a boon companion* close, intimate, favorite, special, best, inseparable; jovial, convivial, congenial.

boor *noun* lout, oaf, philistine, vulgarian, yahoo, barbarian; *inf.* clodhopper, clod, peasant.

boorish *adjective* rough, rude, coarse, ill-bred, ill-mannered, uncouth, churlish, gruff, uncivilized, unsophisticated, unrefined, crude, vulgar, gross, brutish, bearish, barbaric.
Antonyms: REFINED; CULTIVATED; SOPHISTICATED.

boost *verb* **1** *boost him up the tree* lift, raise, hoist, push, thrust, shove, heave, elevate, help, assist. **2** *boost morale* raise, increase, improve, encourage, heighten, help, promote, foster, inspire, uplift. **3** *boost sales* increase, expand, raise, add to, improve, amplify, enlarge, inflate, promote, advance, develop, further, foster, facilitate, help, assist; *inf.* jack up, hike up. **4** *boost their products* promote, advertise, publicize, praise, write up; *inf.* plug, give a plug to.
Antonyms: DECREASE; HINDER.

boost *noun* **1** *give him a boost into the tree* lift up, push, thrust, shove, heave. **2** *give a boost to morale* uplift, shot in the arm; encouragement, help, inspiration, stimulus. **3** *a boost in sales* increase, expansion, rise, improvement, advance. *See* BOOST *verb* 3.

boot *verb boot the ball* kick, punt. **boot out** *boot him out* throw out, kick out, dismiss, sack, expel, eject, oust. **boot up** *boot up the computer* load, prepare, make ready.

booth *noun* **1** *selling magazines/tickets at a booth* stall, stand, kiosk. **2** *telephone booth* cubicle, compartment, enclosure.

bootless *adjective bootless attempts* futile, vain, unsuccessful, useless, ineffective, ineffectual, abortive, unproductive, fruitless, unavailing.

booty *noun* spoil, loot, plunder, pillage, prize, haul; spoils, profits, pickings, takings, winnings; *inf.* swag, boodle, the goods.

bordello *noun* brothel, house of ill repute, bawdy house, whorehouse.

border *noun* **1** *the border of the lake/lawn* edge, verge, perimeter, boundary, margin, brink, skirt; fringes, bounds, limits, confines. **2** *passport checks at the border* frontier, boundary, divide.

---

border

brim, brink, edge, margin, rim, verge

A **border** is the part of a surface that is nearest to its boundary (*a rug with a flowered border*)—although it may also refer to the boundary line

itself (*the border between Vermont and New Hampshire*). A **margin** is a *border* of a definite width that is usually distinct in appearance from what it encloses; but unlike *border*, it usually refers to the blankness or emptiness that surrounds something (*the margin on a printed page*). While *border* and *margin* usually refer to something that is circumscribed, **edge** may refer to only a part of the perimeter (*the edge of the lawn*) or the line where two planes or surfaces converge (*the edge of the table*). *Edge* can also connote sharpness (*the edge of a knife*) and can be used metaphorically to suggest tension, harshness, or keenness (*there was an edge in her voice; take the edge off their nervousness*). **Verge** may also be used metaphorically to describe the extreme limit of something (*on the verge of a nervous breakdown*), but in a more literal sense, it sometimes is used of the line or narrow space that marks the limit or termination of something (*the verge of a desert or forest*). **Brink** denotes the edge of something very steep or an abrupt division between land and water (*the brink of the river*), or metaphorically the very final limit before an abrupt change (*on the brink of disaster*). **Rim** and **brim** apply only to things that are circular or curving. But while *rim* describes the edge or lip of a rounded or cylindrical shape (*the rim of a glass*), *brim* refers to the inner side of the rim when the container is completely full (*a cup filled to the brim with steaming coffee*). However, when one speaks of the *brim* of a hat, it comes closer to the meaning of *margin* or *border*.

---

border *verb* **1** *woods bordering the fields* edge, skirt, bound. *See* BORDER *noun* 1. **2** *Portugal borders Spain* | *his garden borders (on) mine* adjoin, abut (on), be adjacent to, be next to, neighbor, touch, join, connect. **3** *border the skirt with lace* edge, fringe, hem, trim, bind, decorate. **border on** *his reply is bordering on rudeness* | *bordering on the obscene* verge on, approximate to, approach, come close to, near/similar to, resemble.

bore[1] *verb bore into the wood* | *bore a hole* pierce, perforate, puncture, penetrate, drill, tap, tunnel, burrow, mine, dig out, gouge out, sink.

bore[2] *noun* **1** *sink a bore to find oil* borehole, hole, shaft, tunnel. **2** *the bore of a rifle* caliber, diameter, gauge.

bore[3] *verb the talk/speaker bored her* weary, be tedious to, tire, fatigue, send to sleep, exhaust, wear out; bore to tears, bore to death, bore out of one's mind.
Antonyms: INTEREST; AMUSE; ENTERTAIN.

bore[4] *noun* tiresome person/thing, tedious person/thing, nuisance, bother, pest; *inf.* drag, pain, pain in the neck.

boredom *noun* tedium, tediousness, dullness, monotony, flatness, sameness, humdrum,

dreariness, weariness, apathy, languor, ennui, world-weariness, malaise.
Antonyms: INTEREST; AMUSEMENT; ENTERTAINMENT.

boring *adjective* tedious, dull, monotonous, humdrum, repetitious, unvaried, uninteresting, unexciting, flat, dry as dust, weary, wearisome, tiring, tiresome.
Antonyms: INTERESTING; AMUSING; ENTERTAINING.

borrow *verb* **1** *borrow some money* ask for the loan of, receive/take as a loan, use/have temporarily; *inf.* cadge, mooch, scrounge, sponge, beg, bum. **2** *borrow another writer's plots* appropriate, commandeer, use as one's own, copy, plagiarize, pirate, take, adopt, purloin, steal, grab, filch, pinch, help oneself to; abstract, imitate, simulate. **3** *English borrowing words from French* adopt, appropriate, take in, take over, acquire, embrace.
Antonyms: LEND; LOAN.

bosom *noun* **1** *woman with a large bosom* breasts, bust, chest; *inf.* boobs, tits, knockers. **2** *bosom of the family/Church* heart, center, core, midst, circle, protection, shelter, aegis. **3** *nurturing warm feelings in their bosoms* heart, soul, being; emotions, affections.

bosom *adjective* *bosom friends/companions* close, intimate, boon, confidential, dear, inseparable, faithful, thick as thieves.

boss *noun the boss of the factory* head, chief, manager, director, chief executive, administrator, leader, superintendent, supervisor, foreman, overseer, employer, master, owner; *inf.* honcho, bossman, top dog.

boss *verb.* **boss around** *he's always bossing his brothers around* order about/around, give orders/commands to, bully, push around, domineer, dominate, ride roughshod over, control; throw one's weight about.

bossy *adjective* domineering, dominating, overbearing, dictatorial, authoritarian, despotic, imperious, high-handed, autocratic.

botch *verb* *botch (up) the situation/repair* bungle, make a mess of, spoil, mar, muff, mismanage, mangle, fumble; *inf.* mess up, foul up, screw up, blow, louse up.

both *adjective/pronoun* *both boys | both are here* the two, the two together.

bother *verb* **1** *don't bother your father* disturb, trouble, worry, pester, harass, annoy, upset, irritate, vex, inconvenience, provoke, plague, torment, nag, molest; *inf.* hassle, give someone a hard time, get in someone's hair. **2** *don't bother yourself with that | don't bother* concern oneself, occupy/busy oneself, take the time, make the effort, trouble oneself, go to the/any trouble, inconvenience oneself, worry oneself. **3** *it bothers me that I lost it* upset, trouble, worry, concern, distress, perturb, disconcert.

bother *noun* **1** *don't go to any bother* trouble, effort, inconvenience, exertion, strain; pains. **2** *what a bother we've missed it* nuisance, pest, annoyance, irritation, inconvenience, difficulty, problem, vexation.

bottle *noun* *a bottle of wine* container; flask, carafe, decanter, pitcher, flagon, demijohn, magnum. **the bottle** *fond of the bottle* alcoholic drink, alcohol, drink, liquor; *inf.* booze.

bottle *verb* **bottle up** *bottle up your feelings* keep back, suppress, restrain, keep in check, curb, contain, shut in, conceal.

bottleneck *noun* constriction, narrowing, obstruction, congestion, block, blockage, jam, traffic jam, gridlock, holdup.

bottom *noun* **1** *the bottom of the hill/pile* foot, lowest part/point, base. **2** *the bottom of the pillar* base, foundation, basis, support, pedestal, substructure, substratum, groundwork, underpinning. **3** *the bottom of the car* underside, lower side, underneath, undersurface, belly. **4** *the bottom of the sea* floor, bed, depths. **5** *the bottom of the class* lowest level/position, least important/successful part, least honorable/valuable part. **6** *sitting on his bottom* hindquarters, buttocks; rear end, rear, seat, tail, posterior, rump; *inf.* backside, behind, derrière, butt, ass. **7** *his jealousy was at the bottom of it* origin, cause, root, source, starting point, core, center, heart, base. **8** *get to the bottom of it* basis, foundation, reality, essence, nitty-gritty, substance; essentials.
Antonyms: TOP; APEX; SURFACE.

bottom *adjective* *on the bottom shelf* lowest, last, undermost, ground.
Antonyms: TOP; UPPER; highest.

bottomless *adjective* **1** *bottomless pit* deep, immeasurable, fathomless, unfathomable, unfathomed. **2** *bottomless reserves of energy* boundless, inexhaustible, infinite, unlimited, immeasurable, endless, limitless.

bough *noun* branch, limb, twig.

boulder *noun* rock, stone.

boulevard *noun* avenue, drive, road, thoroughfare, promenade.

bounce *verb* **1** *the ball bounced* rebound, spring back, bob, recoil, ricochet. **2** *children bouncing about* leap, bound, jump, spring, bob, skip, prance, romp, caper, hurtle. **3** *bounce the troublemakers* throw out, eject, remove, expel, oust, get rid of, evict; *inf.* kick out, boot out.

bounce *noun* **1** *ball/material not having much bounce* spring, springiness, rebound, recoil, resilience, elasticity, give. **2** *losing bounce over the years* vitality, vigor, energy, vivacity, liveliness, life, animation, spiritedness, spirit, dynamism; *inf.* go, get-up-and-go, pep, oomph, pizzazz, zing, zip. **3** *with a run and a bounce* leap, bound, jump, spring, bob, skip.

bouncing *adjective* *a bouncing baby* robust, strong, vigorous, healthy, thriving, flourishing.

bound[1] *adjective* **1** *the bound prisoners* tied, tied up, secured, roped, tethered, fettered. *See* BIND *verb* 1. **2** *the bound pages* fastened, secured, fixed. **3** *she's bound to win* certain, sure, very likely, destined, predestined, fated. **4** *doctors*

bound by their professional code obligated, obliged, duty-bound, constrained, pledged to, committed to, beholden to, compelled, required. **bound up in** *bound up in their own affairs* occupied with, busy with, preoccupied with, engrossed in, obsessed with. **bound up with** *a future bound up with hers* connected with, tied up with, allied to, attached to, dependent on.

bound² *verb bound over the fence | bound into the room* leap, jump, spring, bounce, hop, vault, hurdle, skip, bob, dance, prance, romp, caper, frolic, gambol.

bound³ *noun reach in a single bound* leap, jump, spring, bounce, hop, vault, hurdle; skip, bob, dance, prance, romp, caper, frolic, gambol.

bound⁴ *verb* **1** *views bounded by prejudice* limit, confine, restrict, cramp, straiten, restrain, demarcate, delimit, circumscribe, define. **2** *estates bounded by walls* enclose, surround, wall in, encircle, hem in, circumscribe. **3** *Germany is bounded on the west by France* border, adjoin, abut.

boundary *noun* **1** *the boundary between the countries* border, frontier, partition, dividing/bounding line. **2** *the boundary of the forest* bounds, border, periphery, perimeter; confines, limits, extremities, margins, edges. *See* BOUNDS 2. **3** *the boundary between sentiment and sentimentality* dividing line, borderline, demarcation line. **4** *pushing back the boundaries of knowledge* bounds, limits, outer limits, confines, extremities, barriers.

boundless *adjective* limitless, without limit, unlimited, illimitable, unbounded, endless, unending, never-ending, without end, inexhaustible, infinite, interminable, unceasing, everlasting, untold, immeasurable, measureless, incalculable, immense, vast, great. *Antonyms:* LIMITED; RESTRICTED.

bounds *plural noun* **1** *within the bounds of possibility* limits, boundaries, confines, restrictions, limitations, demarcations. **2** *within the bounds of the estate* boundaries, borders, confines, limits, extremities, margins, edges, fringes, marches; periphery, perimeter, precinct, pale.

bountiful *adjective* **1** *a bountiful hostess* generous, magnanimous, liberal, kind, giving, open-handed, unstinting, unsparing, munificent, benevolent, beneficent, philanthropic. **2** *a bountiful supply of food* ample, abundant, bumper, superabundant, plentiful, copious, lavish, prolific, profuse, bounteous, luxuriant, plenteous. *Antonyms:* MEAN; INHOSPITABLE; MEAGER.

bounty *noun a bounty for finding the treasure* reward, recompense, remuneration, gratuity, tip, premium, bonus.

bouquet *noun* **1** *the bride carrying a bouquet* bunch/spray of flowers, spray, posy, wreath, garland, nosegay, boutonnière, chaplet, corsage. **2** *the wine's bouquet* aroma, smell, fragrance, perfume, scent, redolence, savor, odor;

odoriferousness. **3** *bouquets from the management* compliment, commendation, tribute, eulogy; praise; congratulations.

bourgeois *adjective* **1** *the bourgeois classes* middle-class, conventional, conservative, propertied. **2** *bourgeois values* materialistic, capitalistic, money-oriented. **3** *bourgeois way of life* conventional, ordinary, uncultured, philistine, uncreative, unimaginative.

bout *noun* **1** *bouts of inactivity* spell, period, time, stretch, stint, turn, fit, run, session, round, season. **2** *a bout of flu* attack, fit, spell, paroxysm. **3** *defeated in the last bout* match, contest, round, competition, encounter, fight, struggle, set-to.

bovine *adjective* **1** *bovine creatures* cowlike, cattle-like. **2** *bovine people hating activity* lifeless, sluggish, stolid, inanimate, phlegmatic, torpid. **3** *too bovine to grasp the facts* dull, stupid, thick, dense, slow, dimwitted, dull-witted, doltish.

bow¹ *verb* **1** *bow to the queen* incline the head/body, make obeisance, nod, curtsy, genuflect, bend the knee, salaam, prostrate oneself. **2** *age had bowed his back* bend, stoop, curve, arch, crook. **3** *bow to the inevitable* give in, give way, yield, submit, surrender, succumb, capitulate, defer, acquiesce, kowtow. **4** *bowing them into the restaurant* usher, conduct, show, guide, direct, escort. **bow out** leave, resign, retire, withdraw, step down, give up, get out, quit, pull out, back out.

bow² *noun make a bow to the queen* inclination of the head/body, obeisance, nod, curtsy, salaam; genuflection, prostration.

bow³ *noun the bow of a ship* prow, front, fore-part, fore end, stem, head.

bowdlerize *verb* expurgate, censor, sanitize, blue-pencil; *inf.* clean up.

bowel *noun* intestine, small intestine, large intestine, colon.

bowels *plural noun* **1** *an infection affecting the bowels* intestines, entrails, guts; *inf.* insides, innards; *fml.* viscera. **2** *the bowels of the earth/machine* interior, inside, core, belly, cavity; depths; *inf.* innards.

bower *noun a bower in the garden* arbor, shady place, leafy shelter, recess, alcove, grotto.

bowl *noun* **1** *a bowl of fruit* dish, basin, vessel, container. **2** *the bowl of a tobacco pipe* hollow part, hollow, depression. **3** *dust bowl* hollow, crater, hole, depression, valley.

bowl *verb bowl a strike* roll, throw, spin, send, deliver. **bowl over** **1** *bowled over by her beauty/news* overwhelm, astound, amaze, astonish, dumbfound, stagger, flabbergast, stun, surprise; *inf.* floor. **2** *bowl over the store display* knock down, bring down.

box¹ *noun* **1** *a box of cigars/crackers | a box shipped from Hawaii* container, receptacle, crate, case, carton, pack, package, chest, trunk, bin, casket. **2** *a theater/jury box* compartment, cubicle, enclosure.

box[2] *verb* *box the dishes carefully* package, pack, wrap, bundle up. **box in/up** enclose, shut in, hem in, fence in, confine, restrain, constrain, cage in, coop up.

box[3] *noun* *give him a box on the ears* thump, cuff, slap, punch. *See* BOX[2] *verb* 2.

box[4] *verb* **1** *he boxes professionally* fight, spar, grapple. **2** *box him on the ears* strike, hit, thump, cuff, slap, punch, knock, wallop, batter, pummel, thwack, buffet; *inf.* belt, sock, clout, whack, slug, slam, whop.

boxer *noun* fighter, pugilist, prizefighter, sparring partner.

boy *noun* *men and boys* youth, lad, youngster, young person, kid, junior, stripling, whippersnapper.

boy *interjection* *boy, what a great book* wow, gosh, gee, god, Lord, holy cow, jeepers, goodness.

boycott *verb* **1** *boycott their company* | *the party* stay away from, ostracize, spurn, avoid, eschew, shun, reject, blackball, blacklist. **2** *boycott their goods* ban, bar, blacklist, embargo, place an embargo on, prohibit, debar, outlaw, proscribe, stop buying.
Antonyms: WELCOME; SUPPORT; PROMOTE.

boyfriend *noun* sweetheart, young man, lover, man, suitor, beau, admirer; *inf.* steady, date.

boyish *adjective* youthful, young, childlike, immature, adolescent, juvenile, childish, callow, green, puerile.

brace *noun* **1** *holding the pieces of metal in a brace* clamp, vice, fastener, coupling. **2** *the wall's brace* support, prop, beam, strut, stay, truss, reinforcement, buttress, shoring-up, stanchion. **3** *a brace of pheasants* two, couple, pair, duo. **4** *printing braces* bracket, parenthesis.

brace *verb* **1** *beams firmly braced* support, strengthen, reinforce, fortify, shore up, prop up, hold up, buttress. **2** *braced his foot against the wall* steady, secure, stabilize, make fast. **3** *brace oneself for the results* prepare, steady, strengthen, fortify, tense.

bracelet *noun* bangle, band, wristlet, circlet, anklet.

bracing *adjective* invigorating, refreshing, stimulating, energizing, exhilarating, reviving, fortifying, strengthening, restorative, tonic, vitalizing, rousing, healthful, health-giving, fresh, brisk, crisp, cool.
Antonyms: TIRING; TAXING.

bracket *noun* **1** *a wall bracket* support, prop, buttress. **2** *put the words in brackets* parenthesis, brace. **3** *in a different social/financial bracket* group, grouping, category, categorization, grade, grading, classification, class, set, section, division, order.

brackish *adjective* slightly salty/briny, saline, bitter, impure, undrinkable, unsavory.

brag *verb* boast, crow, show off, bluster, blow one's own trumpet, sing one's own praises, pat

oneself on the back; *inf.* talk big, blow hard, lay it on thick.

braggart *noun* boaster, brag, show-off, trumpeter, braggadocio; *inf.* blowhard, bigmouth, bag of wind, windbag, loudmouth, gasbag, bullshitter.

braid *verb* **1** *braid the thread/hair* weave, interweave, plait, entwine, twine, intertwine, interlace, twist, wind. **2** *braid the jacket* trim, decorate, edge, fringe.

braid *noun* **1** *trim it with braid* cord, thread, tape, twine, yarn, edging, rickrack. **2** *hair in braids* plait, pigtail.

brain *noun* **1** *studying the brain* cerebral matter; *fml.* encephalon. **2** *have a good brain* mind, intellect, brainpower, intelligence, wit, head; power of reasoning; *inf.* gray matter. **3** *one of the brains of our group* genius, intellectual, intellect, thinker, mind, scholar, mastermind, sage, pundit; *inf.* highbrow, egghead, Einstein.

brains *plural noun* *not to have the brains to do it* intellect, intelligence, wit, head, sense, cleverness, brightness, understanding, shrewdness, sagacity, acumen, capacity, capability; *inf.* savvy.

brainwashing *noun* indoctrination, inculcation, persuasion, conditioning, infixation.

brainy *adjective* clever, intelligent, bright, brilliant, smart, gifted.
Antonyms: STUPID; DULL.

brake *noun* *a brake on spending/enthusiasm* curb, check, damper, restraint, constraint, rein, control.

brake *verb* *brake as you approach the intersection* reduce speed, slow, slow down, decelerate, put on the brakes, hit the brake/brakes.

branch *noun* **1** *the branch of a tree* bough, limb, stem, twig, shoot, sprig, arm. **2** *the branch of the deer's antlers* offshoot, prong. **3** *the local branch of the bank* division, subdivision, section, subsection, department, part, wing, office. **4** *branches of the stream* subdivision, subsidiary, tributary, feeder.

branch *verb* *the road branches before the village* | *the road branched off* fork, divide, subdivide, furcate, bifurcate, divaricate; separate, diverge. **branch off** *they branched off from the highway/topic* diverge, deviate, depart, turn aside, shoot off. **branch out** *the firm must branch out into new areas* extend, spread out, widen, broaden, diversify, open up, expand, enlarge, multiply.

brand *noun* **1** *a brand of canned soup* make, kind, type, sort, variety, line, label, trade name, trademark, registered trademark. **2** *her particular brand of humor* kind, type, sort, variety, style, stamp, cast. **3** *recognize the cow by its brand* identifying mark, identification, tag, marker, earmark. **4** *a brand on him for life* stigma, stain, blot, taint, slur.

brand *verb* **1** *identifying marks branded on cattle* burn, burn in, scorch, sear, stamp, mark. **2** *unhappy experiences branded on his mind* stamp, imprint, print, engrave, impress, fix. **3** *brand-ed as a thief* stigmatize, mark, disgrace, discredit, denounce, besmirch, taint.

brandish *verb* wave, flourish, wield, raise, swing, shake, wag, display, flaunt, show off.

brash *adjective* **1** *a loud, brash young man* bold, self-confident, self-assertive, audacious, aggressive, brazen, forward, cocky, impudent, insolent, impertinent, rude. **2** *brash actions* hasty, rash, impetuous, impulsive, reckless, precipitate, careless, heedless, incautious. **3** *brash colors* loud, showy, garish, gaudy, ostentatious, vulgar, tasteless, tawdry.
Antonyms: RESERVED; CAUTIOUS; QUIET.

brassy *adjective* **1** *a brassy teenager* loud, brazen, shameless, forward, bold, self-assertive, brash, pert, impudent, insolent, flashy, vulgar, showy, garish; *inf.* pushy. **2** *brassy music* blaring, loud, noisy, thundering, deafening, harsh, raucous, dissonant, cacophonous, jangling, grating, jarring, strident, piercing, shrill.

brat *noun* imp, rascal, little devil, urchin, minx, whippersnapper, spoiled brat.

bravado *noun* show of courage/confidence, swagger, swaggering, boldness, audacity, blustering, boasting, boastfulness, bragging, bombast, swashbuckling; *lit.* braggadocio.

brave *adjective* **1** *brave soldiers* courageous, valiant, intrepid, fearless, plucky, game, gallant, heroic, bold, daring, audacious, resolute, undaunted, dauntless, lionhearted, valorous; *inf.* gutsy, spunky. **2** *a brave show* splendid, spectacular, fine, grand, handsome, ostentatious, showy.
Antonyms: COWARDLY; FEARFUL; TIMID.

brave *noun* *Cherokee braves* warrior, soldier, fighter, fighting man.

brave *verb* *brave the weather* face, stand up to, endure, put up with, bear, suffer, withstand, defy, challenge, confront. **brave it** *don't worry, I'll brave it* bell the cat, beard the lion in his den, bite the bullet.

bravery *noun* courage, courageousness, valor, intrepidity, fearlessness, pluck, pluckiness, gameness, gallantry, heroism, boldness, daring, audacity, resolution, fortitude, grit, mettle, spirit, dauntlessness; *inf.* guts, spunk.

bravo *interjection* well done, take a bow, encore.

brawl *noun* *a brawl in the tavern* fight, affray, fracas, wrangle, melee, rumpus, scuffle, altercation, squabble, clash, quarrel, argument, disagreement, free-for-all, tussle, brouhaha, commotion, uproar, donnybrook; fisticuffs; *inf.* scrap, ruckus.

brawl *verb* *brawling in the street* fight, wrangle, wrestle, scuffle, tussle, clash, battle, quarrel, argue; *inf.* scrap.

brawn *noun* brawniness, muscle, muscular strength, muscularity, burliness, heftiness, huskiness, physical strength, physique, robustness, might; *inf.* beefiness, beef.

brawny *adjective* muscular, burly, hefty, powerfully built, strong, robust, sturdy, powerful, strapping, husky, bulky, stalwart, mighty, sinewy, well-knit.
Antonyms: SCRAWNY; PUNY; WEAK.

bray *verb* whinny, neigh, hee-haw.

brazen *adjective* *a brazen young man* bold, audacious, defiant, forward, brash, presumptuous, impudent, insolent, impertinent, brassy, pert, saucy, shameless, immodest, unashamed, unabashed; *inf.* pushy.
Antonyms: RESERVED; MODEST; SHY.

brazen *verb* **brazen it out** be defiant, be unrepentant, be impenitent, be unashamed, be unabashed, stand one's ground, show a bold front, put on a bold face.

breach *noun* **1** *a breach in the seawall* break, rupture, split, crack, fissure, fracture, rent, rift, cleft, opening, gap, hole, aperture, chasm, gulf. **2** *a breach of the agreement | a breach of confidence* breaking, contravention, violation, infringement, transgression, neglect, infraction. **3** *a breach in diplomatic relations | a breach between the two families* breaking-off, estrangement, separation, severance, parting, parting of the ways, division, rift, schism, disunion, alienation, disaffection, variance, difference, dissension, falling-out, quarrel, discord.

breach *verb* **1** *breach the enemy defenses* break/burst through, rupture, split, make a gap in, open up. **2** *breach the contract/law* break, contravene, violate, infringe, defy, disobey, flaunt, transgress against, infract.

bread *noun* **1** *serve bread with the soup | loaves of bread* white bread, brown bread, rye bread, whole-wheat bread, whole-grain bread, unleavened bread, soda bread, sourdough bread, French bread, French stick, baguette, pita bread, bun, croissant, brioche, bagel. **2** *our daily bread* food, nourishment, sustenance, subsistence, fare, nutriment, diet; provisions, victuals. **3** *spend the bread* money, cash, finance; funds; *inf.* dough, cabbage, loot.

breadth *noun* **1** *the breadth of the room* width, broadness, wideness, thickness, span, spread. **2** *the breadth of her knowledge | the breadth of support* extent, extensiveness, scope, range, scale, degree, compass, spread, sweep, comprehensiveness, vastness, expanse, magnitude, measure, volume, immensity; dimensions. **3** *breadth of spirit* liberality, liberalness, broad-mindedness, open-mindedness, freedom, latitude, magnanimity.

break *verb* **1** *break the cup/rope | broke his arm* smash, shatter, crack, fracture, split, burst, fragment, splinter, shiver, crash, snap, rend, tear, divide, sever, separate, part, demolish, disintegrate. **2** *the cup/rope/arm broke* smash, shatter, crack, fracture, split, burst, fragment, splinter, crash, snap, tear, sever, separate. **3** *the machine broke* become damaged, cease to operate/work/function, become unusable; *inf.* go kaput. **4** *the skin is not broken* pierce, puncture, perforate, penetrate, open up. **5** *break the law* contravene, violate, infringe, breach, commit a breach of, defy, disobey, flaunt, transgress against; *fml.* infract. **6** *break for lunch* take a break, stop, pause, discontinue, rest; *inf.* knock off, take five. **7** *break one's concentration/journey/sleep* interrupt, suspend, discontinue, cut, disturb, interfere with. **8** *break his resolve | it broke her morale* overcome, crush, overpower, overwhelm, subdue, defeat, cow, suppress, extinguish, weaken, impair, undermine, dispirit, demoralize, incapacitate, cripple, enfeeble. **9** *he broke under questioning* be overcome, crack, collapse, give in, yield, cave in, crumple, go to pieces. **10** *the recession/scandal broke him* ruin, crush, bring to one's knees, humble, degrade, reduce to nothing, bankrupt, make bankrupt. **11** *break the news gently* tell, announce, impart, reveal, divulge, disclose, let out, make public, proclaim. **12** *break the record* beat, surpass, outdo, better, exceed, outstrip, top; *inf.* cap. **13** *break the code* decipher, decode, unravel, solve, figure out. **14** *the day/storm/scandal broke* begin, come into being, come forth, emerge, erupt, burst out, appear, occur. **15** *the weather broke* change, alter, vary, shift, metamorphose. **16** *break one's fall* cushion, soften, lessen, diminish, moderate. **17** *waves breaking against the seawall* crash, hurl, dash. **break away** *the prisoner broke away* run away, make a break for it, flee, make off, escape, decamp; *inf.* make a run for it, run for it, leg it. **break away from** *break away from the main political party* break with, detach oneself from, secede from, separate from, part company with, leave, form a splinter group from. **break down 1** *the car broke down* stop working, cease to function, seize up, fail; *inf.* conk out, go kaput. **2** *the talks broke down | law and order broke down* fail, collapse, come to nothing, founder, fall through, disintegrate; *inf.* fizzle out. **3** *he broke down and cried* lose control, collapse, cave in, crumble, be overcome, go to pieces, disintegrate, come apart at the seams; *inf.* lose one's cool, crack up. **4** *break down the resistance* overcome, crush, overpower, overwhelm, subdue, defeat, cow, suppress. *See* BREAK *verb* 8. **5** *break down the figures in the budget* separate/divide out, segregate, analyze, dissect, categorize, classify, itemize. **break in 1** *break in hurriedly* burst in, barge in, push one's way in. **2** *he broke in with his own comments* interrupt, butt in, intervene, cut in, intrude, interfere, put one's oar in. **3** *he broke in last night* break and enter, commit burglary, burgle, rob. **4** *break in the horse | break in the new recruits* train, tame, condition, prepare, initiate, show the ropes to. **5** *break in new shoes* begin to wear/use, become/get used/accustomed to. **break into 1** *break into the conversation* interrupt, butt into, intervene in. **2** *break into a gallop/song* begin

suddenly, commence, launch into, burst into, give way to. **3** *break into his savings* begin to use, use part of, open and use. **4** *break into the room hurriedly* burst/barge into, push one's way into. **5** *break into the house* burgle, rob. **break off 1** *break off a branch* pull off, snap off, detach, separate, sever. **2** *the handle broke off* come off, snap off, become detached, become separated/severed. **3** *break off diplomatic relations | broke off their engagement* end, bring to an end, terminate, stop, cease, finish, discontinue, call a halt to, suspend, desist from. **break out 1** *war/fighting broke out* start/commence/occur suddenly, erupt, burst out, set in, arise. **2** *it's time she broke out and made her own decisions* become free/liberated, become emancipated, unshackle/unfetter oneself. **3** *break out in a rash* erupt, burst out. **4** *"Wait!" he broke out* exclaim, call out, cry, shout, utter, yell. **break out of** *break out of prison* escape from, make one's escape from, break loose of/from, burst out of, get free of/from, free oneself of/from, flee from, abscond from, bolt from. **break up 1** *the meeting broke up at midnight | school breaks up tomorrow* adjourn, end, come to an end, stop, discontinue, terminate. **2** *the crowd broke up* disperse, scatter, disband, part, separate, go their separate ways, part company. **3** *the police broke up the crowd* disperse, scatter, disband, separate, put to rout, send off. **4** *the couple have broken up* separate, part, divorce, split up, dissolve a marriage/relationship, come to a parting of the ways. **5** *jealousy broke up their marriage* bring to an end, end, terminate, bring to a halt, kill, destroy. **6** *breaking up at his jokes* laugh, burst out laughing, giggle, chuckle, chortle, guffaw, double up, split one's sides, hold one's sides; *inf.* in stitches.

Antonyms: REPAIR; MEND; JOIN; ABIDE; OBEY.

break *noun* **1** *a break in the seawall* crack, hole, gap, opening, gash, chink, fracture, split, fissure, tear, rent, rupture, rift, chasm, cleft. **2** *a break for lunch* interval, stop, pause, halt, rest, respite, lull, interlude, intermission, recess; coffee break; *inf.* breather, breathing spell, letup, time out, down time. **3** *a weekend break* vacation, time off, recess. **4** *a break in their education* interruption, discontinuation, suspension, hiatus. **5** *a break in the weather* change, alteration, variation. **6** *a break in diplomatic relations* rift, breach, split, rupture, discontinuation, schism, chasm, alienation, disaffection. **7** *although losing, we got a break* lucky break, stroke of luck, advantage, gain, opportunity, chance, opening.

breakable *adjective* fragile, frangible, frail, delicate, flimsy, insubstantial, brittle, crumbly, friable, destructible, gimcrack, jerry-built.

breakdown *noun* **1** *the car's/machine's breakdown* stopping, stoppage, seizing up, failure, malfunctioning; *inf.* conking out. *See* BREAK *verb*: break down 1. **2** *the breakdown of the talks* failure, collapse, foundering, falling through; *inf.*

fizzling out. *See* BREAK *verb*: break down 2. **3** *suffer a breakdown* collapse, nervous breakdown, loss of control, going to pieces, disintegration, caving in; *inf.* crack-up. *See* BREAK *verb*: break down 3. **4** *a breakdown of the figures* separation, division, segregation, itemization, analysis, dissection, categorization, classification.

breaker *noun swimmers riding the breakers to shore* wave, roller, swell, whitecap.

break-in *noun break-ins in the neighborhood* breaking and entering, housebreaking, burglary, forced/unlawful entry; robbery, theft. *See* BREAK *verb*: break in 3.

breakneck *adjective* fast, rapid, speedy, swift, reckless, dangerous.

breakthrough *noun a breakthrough in cancer research* advance, step forward, leap, quantum leap, discovery, find, development, improvement; progress.

breakup *noun the breakup of their marriage/partnership* end, termination, cessation, dissolution, disintegration, splitting up, breakdown, failure, collapse, foundering. *See* BREAK *verb*: break up 4, 5.

breakwater *noun* seawall, jetty, embankment, barrier.

breast *noun* **1** *a woman's breasts* bust, bosom, chest, front; *inf.* boob, tit, knocker. **2** *warm feelings in their breasts* heart, soul, being, core, seat of the emotions/affections; feelings.

breath *noun* **1** *take a deep breath | is pained by each breath* gulp of air, inhalation, inspiration, exhalation, expiration, pant, gasp, wheeze; breathing, respiration. **2** *no breath left in him* breath of life, life, life force, animation, vital force. **3** *hardly a breath of air* breeze, puff, gust, waft, zephyr. **4** *a breath of spring* hint, suggestion, whiff, undertone, trace, touch, whisper, suspicion. **5** *stop for breath* break, interval, pause, lull, rest, respite, breathing space; *inf.* breather. **6** *all over in a breath* moment, instant, minute, second.

breathe *verb* **1** *she breathed deeply* respire, inhale, inspire, exhale, expire, puff, pant, gasp, wheeze, gulp. **2** *as long as he breathes* be alive, live, have life. **3** *breathe new life/courage into them* infuse, instill, inject, impart, transfuse. **4** *breathe a message of love* whisper, murmur, sigh, say, utter, voice, articulate, express. **5** *her whole appearance breathed defiance* express, suggest, indicate, manifest, intimate, betoken, augur. **6** *the wind breathing through the trees* blow, whisper, murmur, sigh.

breather *noun* **1** *let's take a breather from work* break, interval, stop, pause, halt, rest, respite, lull, breathing space, recess. *See* BREAK *noun* 2. **2** *I'm going out for a breather* breath of air, bit of fresh air.

breathless *adjective* **1** *find myself breathless when climbing stairs* out of breath, wheezing, panting, puffing, gasping, choking, gulping, winded. **2** *breathless with excitement* agog, all agog,

avid, eager, excited, on edge, on tenterhooks, in suspense, open-mouthed, anxious.

breathtaking *adjective* spectacular, impressive, magnificent, awesome, awe-inspiring, astounding, astonishing, amazing, thrilling, stunning, exciting.

breed *verb* **1** *lions breeding in captivity* reproduce, procreate, multiply, give birth, bring forth young, beget, propagate. **2** *breed horses* raise, rear, nurture. **3** *born and bred in the town* bring up, rear, raise, develop, educate, train, nurture. **4** *breed disease/discontent* cause, bring about, give rise to, create, produce, generate, arouse, stir up, induce, originate, occasion, make for.

breed *noun* **1** *a breed of cows* family, variety, type, kind, class, strain, stock, line. **2** *of European breed* stock, race, lineage, extraction, pedigree. **3** *a new breed of doctor* kind, type, variety, class, brand, strain.

breeding *noun* **1** *the season for breeding* reproducing, reproduction, generation, multiplying, propagation. *See* BREED *verb* 1. **2** *the breeding of horses/plants* raising, rearing, nurturing. **3** *a lady by breeding* upbringing, rearing, education, training, nurture. **4** *people of breeding* refinement, cultivation, culture, polish, civility, gentility, courtesy; manners.

breeze *noun* gentle wind, breath of wind, puff of air, zephyr, gust, flurry, waft, current of air, draft; sea breeze, land breeze, onshore breeze, offshore breeze.

breeze *verb the family breezed in | leaves breezing along the surface of the water* stroll, sally, sail, sweep, glide, drift, flit.

breezy *adjective* **1** *a breezy day* windy, blustery, gusty, squally, airy. **2** *a breezy manner/individual* jaunty, cheerful, cheery, lighthearted, carefree, blithe, free and easy, easygoing, casual, airy, sprightly, lively, spirited, buoyant, sparkling, animated, vivacious, frisky, sunny; *inf.* bright-eyed and bushy-tailed.

brevity *noun* **1** *the brevity of the report* shortness, briefness, conciseness, succinctness, compactness, terseness, economy of language, pithiness, crispness, concision, condensation, pointedness, curtness, compendiousness. **2** *the brevity of summer | the brevity of his life* shortness, briefness, transitoriness, transience, impermanence, ephemerality.
Antonyms: VERBOSITY; LENGTH.

brew *verb* **1** *brew beer* make, ferment. **2** *brew tea* infuse, steep, prepare. **3** *the tea is brewing* steep. **4** *trouble is brewing* gather, gather force, form, loom, threaten, impend. **5** *brewing something evil* plot, scheme, hatch, plan, devise, invent, concoct, stir up, foment; *inf.* cook up.

brew *noun favorite brew | home brew* drink, beverage, liquor, ale, beer, tea; infusion, preparation; witches' brew.

bribe *noun give the mayor a bribe to get the contract* inducement, enticement, lure, subornation, carrot; *inf.* graft, hush money, protection money, boodle, kickback, payola.

bribe *verb* *bribe the mayor to get the contract* buy off, corrupt, give an inducement to, suborn; *inf.* grease/oil the palm of, get at, pay off.

bric-à-brac *noun* knickknacks, trinkets, collectibles, gewgaws, baubles, curios, ornaments.

bridal *adjective* nuptial, marital, matrimonial, connubial, conjugal.

bride *noun* wife; newlywed, honeymooner, blushing bride; war bride.

bridge *noun* **1** *a bridge over the river* arch, span, overpass, viaduct. **2** *a bridge between the two families* bond, link, tie, connection, cord, binding.

bridge *verb* **1** *bridge the river* span, cross, cross over, go over, pass over, traverse, extend across, reach across, arch over. **2** *bridge our differences* overcome, reconcile, bridge the gap between.

Antonyms: DIVIDE; SEPARATE.

bridle *noun* **1** *a horse's bridle* halter. **2** *put a bridle on your temper* curb, check, restraint, control.

bridle *verb* **1** *bridle your tongue/anger* curb, restrain, hold back, keep control of, keep in check, put a check on, check, govern, master, subdue. **2** *she bridled at his insults* bristle, get angry, become indignant, rear up, draw oneself up, feel one's hackles rise.

brief *adjective* **1** *a brief report* short, concise, succinct, to the point, compact, terse, economic, pithy, crisp, condensed, compressed, pointed, curt, thumbnail, epigrammatic, sparing, compendious. **2** *brief summer days* | *a brief life* short, short-lived, fleeting, momentary, passing, fading, transitory, transient, temporary, impermanent, ephemeral, evanescent. **3** *a brief skirt* short, scanty, skimpy. **4** *the boss was rather brief with him* short, abrupt, curt, sharp, brusque, blunt.

Antonyms: LONG; LENGTHY; LONG-DRAWN-OUT.

brief *noun* **1** *a brief of the proceedings* outline, summary, abstract, résumé, synopsis, précis, sketch, digest, epitome. **2** *the attorney's brief* argument, case, proof, defense, evidence, demonstration.

brief *verb* *brief the delegates* instruct, inform, give instructions/information/directions to, direct, guide, advise, prepare, prime; *inf.* give someone the rundown/low-down, fill in.

briefing *noun* **1** *at a briefing to discuss the situation* conference, meeting, discussion, forum, seminar, symposium. **2** *recruits being given their briefing* information, guidance, preparation, data, intelligence; instructions, directions; *inf.* rundown, low-down.

briefly *adverb* **1** *he spoke briefly* concisely, succinctly, to the point, tersely, economically, sparingly. **2** *briefly, I want to say goodbye* in

brief, concisely, succinctly, in a few words, in a nutshell. **3** *living briefly* fleetingly, momentarily, transitorily, transiently, temporarily, ephemerally.

brigade *noun* *fire brigade* | *the brigade of workers* group, band, team, squad, party, association, body, contingent, crew, force, outfit, section, organization.

brigand *noun* robber, bandit, outlaw, ruffian, desperado, plunderer, marauder, gangster, criminal, highwayman, pirate, freebooter.

bright *adjective* **1** *a bright light* shining, brilliant, vivid, intense, blazing, dazzling, beaming, sparkling, flashing, glittering, scintillating, gleaming, glowing, twinkling, glistening, shimmering; illuminated, luminous, lustrous, radiant, effulgent, incandescent, phosphorescent. **2** *a bright day* clear, cloudless, unclouded, fair, sunny, pleasant, clement. **3** *bright colors* vivid, brilliant, intense, glowing, bold, rich. **4** *bright children/minds* clever, intelligent, sharp, quick-witted, quick, smart, brainy, brilliant, astute, acute, ingenious, inventive, resourceful, proficient, accomplished. **5** *a bright smile/personality* happy, genial, cheerful, jolly, joyful, gay, merry, lighthearted, vivacious, lively, buoyant. **6** *a bright future* promising, optimistic, hopeful, favorable, propitious, auspicious, providential, encouraging, lucky, fortunate, good, excellent, golden.

Antonyms: DULL; DARK; STUPID.

---

bright
brilliant, effulgent, luminous, lustrous, radiant, refulgent, resplendent, shining

Looking for just the right word to capture the quality of the light on a moonlit night or a summer day? All of these adjectives describe an intense, steady light emanating (or appearing to emanate) from a source. **Bright** is the most general term, applied to something that gives forth, reflects, or is filled with light (*a bright and sunny day*; *a bright star*). **Brilliant** light is even more intense or dazzling (*the brilliant diamond on her finger*), and **resplendent** is a slightly more formal, even poetic, way of describing a striking brilliance (*the sky was resplendent with stars*). Poets also prefer adjectives like **effulgent** and **refulgent**, both of which can be applied to an intense, pervading light, sometimes from an unseen source (*her effulgent loveliness*); but *refulgent* specifically refers to reflected light (*a chandelier of refulgent crystal pendants*). **Radiant** is used to describe the power of giving off light, either literally or metaphorically (*a radiant June day*; *the bride's radiant face*); it describes a steady, warm light that is emitted in all directions. Like *radiant*, **luminous** suggests sending forth light, but light of the glow-in-the-dark variety (*the luminous face of the alarm clock*). While diamonds are known for being *brilliant*, fabrics like satin and surfaces like polished wood, which reflect light and take on a gloss or sheen, are often called **lustrous**. If none of these words captures the exact quality of the light you're trying to describe, you can always join the masses and use **shining**, a word that has been overworked to the point of cliché (*my knight in shining armor*).

brighten verb **1** *lights brightening the room* make bright/brighter, light up, lighten, illuminate, illumine, irradiate. **2** *her mood brightening* cheer up, perk up. **3** *brightening her day/mood* cheer up, gladden, enliven, buoy up, animate; *inf.* buck up, pep up.

brilliance noun **1** *the brilliance of the lights* brightness, vividness, intensity, blaze, beam, dazzle, sparkle, flash, glitter, luminosity, luster, radiance, effulgence, resplendence. **2** *the brilliance of the spectacle* magnificence, splendor, splendidness, grandeur, glamour, pomp, luster, resplendence, illustriousness, éclat.

brilliant adjective **1** *a brilliant light* bright, shining, vivid, intense, blinding, radiant, beaming, gleaming, dazzling, luminous, lustrous, scintillating, resplendent, effulgent, coruscating. **2** *brilliant children* bright, clever, intelligent, smart, brainy, intellectual, gifted, talented, accomplished, educated, scholarly, learned, erudite, cerebral, precocious. **3** *a brilliant course of action* clever, intelligent, smart, astute, masterly, resourceful, inventive, discerning. **4** *a brilliant display* magnificent, splendid, superb, impressive, remarkable, exceptional, glorious, illustrious.
Antonyms: DIM; STUPID.

brim noun **1** *the brim of the cup | full to the brim* rim, lip, brink, edge. **2** *the brim of the hat/cap* projecting edge, visor, shield, shade.

brim verb *the cup was brimming | eyes brimming with tears* full, filled up, filled to the top, full to capacity, overflow, run/well over.

bring verb **1** *bring books/water | bringing the group of children* come conveying/carrying, carry, bear, take, fetch, convey, transport, deliver, lead, guide, conduct, usher, escort. **2** *war brought hardship* cause, create, produce, result in, wreak, effect, contribute to, engender, occasion. **3** *bring a legal action* put forward, prefer, propose, initiate, institute. **4** *his job brings good wages* make, fetch, yield, net, gross, return, produce, command. **bring about 1** *bring about reforms* cause to happen/occur, cause, create, produce, give rise to, achieve, result in, effect, occasion, bring to pass, effectuate. **2** *bring a ship about* turn, turn around, reverse, reverse the direction of. **bring down 1** *bring down prices* cause to fall, lower, reduce, cut. **2** *bring down the government* cause to fall, overthrow, pull down, lay low. **3** *the bad news brought her down* depress, sadden, cast down, make desolate, weigh down. **bring forward** *bring forward points for discussion* raise, put forward, propose, suggest, bring to/put on the table. **bring in 1** *his son/job brings in $3000* earn, yield,

gross, net, return, realize. **2** *bring in a new bill* introduce, launch, inaugurate, initiate, institute, usher in. **bring off** *bring off the attempt* pull off, carry off, achieve, succeed in, accomplish, bring about, carry out, execute, perform, discharge, complete. **bring up 1** *bring up the children* rear, raise, train, educate, care for, nurture, foster, develop. **2** *bring up the subject* raise, broach, introduce, mention, allude to, touch upon, propose, submit.

brink noun **1** *the brink of the cliff/lake* edge, verge, margin, rim, extremity, limit, border, boundary, fringe, skirt. **2** *on the brink of disaster* verge, edge, threshold, point.

brisk adjective **1** *at a brisk pace* quick, rapid, fast, swift, speedy, energetic, lively, vigorous, agile, nimble, spry, sprightly, spirited. **2** *brisk weather* bracing, crisp, keen, biting, invigorating, refreshing, exhilarating, energizing; *inf.* nippy. **3** *a brisk manner | brisk speech* no-nonsense, brusque, abrupt, sharp, curt, crisp, snappy. **4** *business was brisk* rapid, busy, bustling, active, hectic.
Antonyms: SLUGGISH; QUIET.

bristle noun **1** *shave off his bristles* hair, stubble; whiskers. **2** *a wild boar's bristles | the bristles on the chestnut burr* prickle, spine, quill, thorn, barb.

bristle verb **1** *the dog's hair bristled* stiffen, rise, stand up, stand on end. **2** *she bristled at the insults* bridle, get angry/infuriated, become indignant, be irritated/defensive, rear up, draw oneself up. **3** *the place bristled with tourists* swarm, teem, crawl; *inf.* be thick, be alive.

bristly adjective hairy, stubbly, unshaven, whiskered, whiskery, bewhiskered, bearded, rough; prickly, thorny, spiny, barbed.

brittle adjective **1** *a brittle substance* breakable, splintery, shatterable, hard, crisp, fragile, frail, delicate, frangible. **2** *a brittle laugh* harsh, hard, sharp, strident, grating, rasping. **3** *a brittle relationship* frail, fragile, weak, unstable.

broach verb *broach the subject* introduce, bring up, raise, mention, open, put forward, propound, propose, suggest, submit.

broad adjective **1** *a broad street* wide, large. **2** *broad plains* extensive, vast, spacious, expansive, sweeping, boundless. **3** *offers a broad range of subjects* wide, wide-ranging, broad-ranging, general, comprehensive, inclusive, encyclopedic, all-embracing, universal, unlimited. **4** *the broad outline of the plan* general, nonspecific, unspecific, vague, loose. **5** *a broad hint* clear, obvious, direct, plain, explicit, straightforward, clear-cut, unmistakable, undisguised, unconcealed. **6** *broad daylight* full, complete, total, clear, open. **7** *a woman of broad views* broad-minded, liberal, open-minded, tolerant, unprejudiced, unbiased, fair, just, freethinking, progressive. **8** *somewhat broad humor* coarse, vulgar, gross, unrefined, indelicate, indecent, improper, blue. *Antonyms:* NARROW; LIMITED; DETAILED.

broadcast *verb* 1 *broadcast a program* transmit, relay, beam, send out, put on the air, radio, televise, telecast. 2 *broadcast the news of his downfall* make public, announce, report, publicize, publish, advertise, proclaim, air, spread, circulate, pass around, disseminate, promulgate, blazon. 3 *broadcast seed* scatter, sow, disperse, strew.

broadcast *noun appeared on a last night's broadcast* program, radio/television show, show, transmission, telecast.

broaden *verb* 1 *broaden the road* make broader, widen, make wider. 2 *his shoulders broadened* become broader, widen, become wider, fill out. 3 *broaden his knowledge/experience/horizons* widen, expand, enlarge, extend, increase, augment, supplement, add to, amplify, fill out, develop, open up, swell.

broad-minded *adjective* open-minded, liberal, tolerant, forbearing, indulgent, impartial, unprejudiced, unbiased, unbigoted, undogmatic, catholic, flexible, dispassionate, just, fair, progressive, free-thinking.

broadside *noun* 1 *fire a broadside at the enemy ship* volley, salvo, cannonade, barrage. 2 *receive broadsides from the press* attack, criticism, censure, assault, onslaught, abuse, battering, harangue, diatribe.

brochure *noun* booklet, leaflet, pamphlet, folder, handbill, handout, circular, notice, advertisement, flyer.

broil *verb* 1 *broil meat* grill, barbecue, cook. 2 *broil in the hot sun* be hot, be roasting, be burning, be boiling.

broiling *adjective a broiling day* hot, scorching, roasting, blistering, boiling/burning/blistering hot.

broke *adjective* penniless, moneyless, bankrupt, insolvent, poverty-stricken, impoverished, impecunious, penurious, indigent, destitute, ruined, without a penny to one's name, stonebroke, flat broke; *inf.* cleaned out, strapped for cash, bust.

broken *adjective* 1 *a broken cup* smashed, shattered, cracked, fractured, split, burst, fragmented, splintered, shivered, crushed, snapped, rent, torn, separated, severed, destroyed, demolished, disintegrated. 2 *the machine is broken* damaged, faulty, defective, out of order/commission, nonfunctioning, inoperative, imperfect; kaput, bust, busted. 3 *broken skin* pierced, punctured, perforated. 4 *broken laws* contravened, violated, infringed, disobeyed, disregarded, ignored, flaunted, transgressed, infracted. 5 *a broken sleep/journey | a broken chain of thought* interrupted, disturbed, disconnected, disrupted, discontinuous, fragmentary, incomplete, intermittent, spas-

modic, erratic. 6 *a broken man/army* beaten, defeated, vanquished, overpowered, overwhelmed, subdued, crushed, humbled, dishonored, ruined, crippled, demoralized, dispirited, discouraged. 7 *broken businesses* ruined, crushed, bankrupt, bankrupted, humbled. 8 *broken English* halting, hesitating, disjointed, faltering, stumbling, stammering, imperfect.

broken-down *adjective* 1 *a broken-down machine* broken, damaged, faulty, defective, out of order/commission, nonfunctioning, inoperative; *inf.* on the blink, kaput, bust, busted. 2 *a broken-down old shack* dilapidated, in disrepair, ramshackle.

brokenhearted *adjective* heartbroken, griefstricken, desolate, despairing, devastated, inconsolable, prostrated, miserable, overwhelmed, wretched, sorrowing, mourning, forlorn, woeful, bowed down, crestfallen.

broker *noun* agent, negotiator, middleman, intermediary, factor, dealer, broker-dealer, stockbroker, insurance broker.

bronze *adjective* bronze-colored, rust, henna, copper-colored, copper, reddish-brown, chestnut, metallic brown, rust-colored.

brooch *noun* pin, clip, breastpin, tiepin.

brood *noun* 1 *the hen and her brood* young, offspring, progeny, family, hatch, clutch, nest, litter. 2 *Mrs. Smith and her brood* children, offspring, family; youngsters; *inf.* kids.

brood *verb* 1 *brood over/about the problem* worry, fret, agonize, think, ponder, meditate, muse, mull, dwell (on/upon), ruminate. 2 *hens brooding* sit on/hatch/incubate eggs, cover young.

brook *noun a mountain brook* stream, streamlet, creek, rivulet, rill, brooklet, runnel.

brook *verb brook no delay* tolerate, stand, bear, allow.

brothel *noun* bordello, house of ill repute, bawdy house, whorehouse.

brother *noun* 1 *she has two brothers* sibling, blood-brother; kinsman; *inf.* sib, bro. 2 *brothers in crime* associate, colleague, companion, partner, comrade; *inf.* pal, chum. 3 *brothers praying* cleric, monk, friar.

brotherhood *noun* 1 *ties of brotherhood* brotherliness, fraternalism, kinship. 2 *feelings of brotherhood* comradeship, fellowship, companionship, camaraderie, friendship, *esprit de corps*. 3 *a brotherhood of merchants* association, alliance, society, union, league, guild, coalition, affiliation, consortium, fraternity, club, lodge, clique, coterie.

brotherly *adjective* 1 *siblings ignoring brotherly ties* fraternal. 2 *the Bible tells us to practice brotherly love* friendly, affectionate, amicable, kind, kindly, cordial, sympathetic, benevolent, neighborly, philanthropic, charitable, altruistic.

brow *noun* 1 *furrowing her brow* forehead, temple. 2 *plucking her brows* eyebrows. 3 *the brow*

browbeat *verb* bully, force, coerce, compel, badger, dragoon, intimidate, tyrannize, hector, terrorize; *inf.* bulldoze.

brown *adjective* **1** *of a brown color | brown hair/ horses* dark brown, chocolate, cocoa, umber, reddish-brown, auburn, copper, copper-colored, bronze, henna, mahogany, walnut, rust, brick, terra-cotta, puce, yellowish-brown, tan, tawny, ginger, cinnamon, hazel, gold, light brown, fawn, beige, ecru; brunette; bay, chestnut, sorrel, roan. **2** *brown bodies on the beach* tanned, sunburned, sunburnt, browned, bronze, bronzed.

brown *verb brown the meat* sear, seal, fry, grill, sauté.

browse *verb* **1** *not reading in detail, just browsing* scan, skim, glance/look through, thumb/leaf/ flip through. **2** *not buying anything, just browsing* look around, have a look, window-shop. **3** *cows browsing* graze, feed, eat, nibble, pasture.

bruise *verb* **1** *bruise the skin* make black and blue, discolor, blacken, mark, blemish, contuse, injure, hurt. **2** *bruise the fruit* damage, mark, discolor, spoil, blemish. **3** *her feelings are easily bruised* hurt, upset, offend, insult, wound, displease, peeve, vex, distress.

bruise *noun a bruise on her face* black-and-blue mark, skin discoloration, blackening, mark, blemish, contusion, injury, swelling.

brunette *adjective* dark, dark-haired, brown-haired, black-haired.

brunt *noun bear the brunt of it* full force, force, impact, shock, burden, thrust, violence, pressure, strain, stress; repercussions, consequences.

brush *noun* **1** *sweep/clean/paint with a brush* broom, besom, whisk, whisk broom, hairbrush, clothes brush, scrub/scrubbing brush, toothbrush, paintbrush. **2** *with a brush of his arm* touch, stroke; *inf.* swipe. **3** *a brush with the law/enemy* encounter, clash, conflict, confrontation, skirmish, tussle, fight, battle, engagement; *inf.* scrap, set-to. **4** *lost in the brush* brushwood, undergrowth, underwood, scrub, thicket, copse; bushes.

brush *verb* **1** *brush the crumbs off the table | brush one's clothes/teeth* sweep, groom, clean, buff. **2** *lips brushing her cheek* touch, caress, kiss, glance, contact, stroke, sweep, scrape. **brush aside** *brush aside his objections* put aside, sweep aside, dismiss, shrug off, disregard, ignore, think no more of, forget about, have no time for. **brush off** *brush him off* cold-shoulder, give the cold shoulder to, rebuff, snub, dismiss, ignore, spurn, slight, disregard, reject, repudiate, refuse, disown, deny, scorn, disdain. **brush up/brush up on** *brush up his manners/brush up on his French* revise, read up on, polish up, go over, study, refresh one's memory of, relearn; *inf.* bone up.

brusque *adjective* abrupt, curt, blunt, short, sharp, terse, caustic, gruff, bluff, hasty, outspoken, plainspoken, discourteous, impolite, rude, churlish.
Antonyms: POLITE; COURTEOUS.

---

brusque
bluff, blunt, curt, gruff, surly

Brusque, which comes from an Italian word meaning rude, describes an abruptness of speech or manner that is not necessarily meant to be rude (*a brusque handshake; a brusque reply*). **Curt** is more deliberately unfriendly, suggesting brevity and coldness of manner (*a curt dismissal*). There's nothing wrong with being **blunt,** although it implies an honesty and directness that can border on tactlessness (*a blunt reply to his question about where the money went*). Someone who is **bluff** is usually more likable, possessing a frank, hearty manner that may be a little too outspoken but is seldom offensive (*a bluff man who rarely minced words*). Exhibiting **gruff** or **surly** behavior will not win friends, since both words suggest bad temper if not rudeness. But *gruff* is used to describe a rough or grouchy disposition and, like *bluff*, is applied more often to a man. Anyone who has had to deal with an overworked store clerk while shopping during the holidays knows the meaning of *surly*, which is worse than *gruff*. It describes not only a sour disposition but an outright hostility toward people, and it can apply to someone of either sex (*that surly woman at the customer service desk*).

---

brutal *adjective* **1** *a brutal attack/murderer* savage, cruel, bloodthirsty, vicious, ruthless, callous, heartless, merciless, pitiless, remorseless, uncivilized, inhuman, barbarous. **2** *brutal instincts* bestial, brutish, beastly, animal, coarse, carnal, sensual.
Antonyms: GENTLE; HUMANE; CIVILIZED.

brute *noun* **1** *the howling brutes of the jungle* beast, wild beast, wild animal, animal, creature. **2** *a murderous brute* beast, monster, animal, swine, savage, sadist, barbarian, devil, fiend, ogre. **3** *more rudeness from that brute of a neighbor* lout, oaf, boor, churl, dolt.

bubble *noun* **1** *blowing soap bubbles | bubbles in champagne* globule, glob, bead, blister, drop, droplet, vesicle, air cavity. **2** *misled by the real-estate bubble* illusion, delusion, fantasy, dream, chimera.

bubble *verb* **1** *champagne bubbling* fizz, effervesce, sparkle, foam, froth, spume. **2** *stew bubbling on the stove* boil, simmer, seethe, percolate. **3** *bubble with happiness* overflow, brim over, be filled.

bubbly *adjective* **1** *bubbly soda | bubbly detergent* fizzy, effervescent, carbonated, sparkling, foamy, frothy, sudsy. **2** *a bubbly personality* bubbling, vivacious, effervescent, sparkling, animated, ebullient, scintillating, bouncy, buoyant, excited, elated, lively, merry, happy.

buccaneer *noun* pirate, corsair, sea rover, free-booter, Viking.

buck *verb* **buck up** *buck up, don't be sad* cheer up, perk up, take heart; *inf.* shake it off.

bucket *noun* pail, scuttle, can.

buckle *noun* **1** *the belt buckle* clasp, clip, catch, fastener, fastening, hasp. **2** *a buckle in the floorboards* kink, warp, curve, distortion, wrinkle, bulge.

buckle *verb* **1** *buckling his belt* fasten, hook, secure, clasp, catch, clip. **2** *the floorboards buckled* become warped, become twisted, become curved, become distorted, become contorted, develop a kink/wrinkle/fold, bulge, crumple, cave in.

bucolic *adjective* rural, rustic, pastoral, country, agricultural.

bud *noun* *buds on the branches* shoot, sprout, flowerlet, floret.

bud *verb* *flowers/trees were budding* sprout, send out shoots, form/develop buds, germinate, burgeon.

budding *adjective* promising, potential, developing, beginning, fledgling, growing, burgeoning, incipient, embryonic.

budge *verb* **1** *the car won't budge* move, shift, stir, go, proceed. **2** *I can't budge the car* move, shift, get going. **3** *he's obstinate so he won't budge* change one's mind, give way, give in, yield, acquiesce. **4** *you won't budge him as he's determined* influence, sway, convince, persuade, bend.

budget *noun* **1** *draw up a budget for the year* financial plan/estimate/statement/blueprint. **2** *be over budget for the term* allowance, allocation, allotment, quota, ration.

budget *verb* **1** *budget her money/time* plan, schedule, allocate, ration, apportion. **2** *budget for a new car | we can budget $5000* plan, allow, save, set aside money, set aside.

buff *adjective* **buff-colored** *buff-colored envelopes* beige, straw-colored, sandy-colored, yellowish, yellowish-brown.

buff *verb* *buff one's nails | buff metal* polish, burnish, rub up, rub, smooth, polish, shine.

buff *noun* **1** *a theater buff* fan, enthusiast, devotee, aficionado, addict, admirer, expert; *inf.* freak. **2** *gloves made from yellow buff* ox leather, leather, tanned hide. **in the buff** naked, nude, bare, in the raw, buck naked, *au naturel*, undressed; *inf.* in one's birthday suit.

buffer *noun* cushion, bulwark, guard, safeguard, shield, screen, intermediary.

buffet[1] *noun* **1** *a wedding buffet* smorgasbord; *inf.* spread. **2** *buying a buffet for the dining room* sideboard, cabinet, china cabinet/cupboard.

buffet[2] *noun* **1** *a buffet on the head* blow, slap, smack, bang, box, cuff, thump, wallop, clout,

whack, thwack, battering, knock, rap, poke, jab. **2** *the buffets of life* shock, jolt, jar.

buffet[3] *verb* **1** *winds buffeting the trees* batter, beat/knock against, strike, hit, bang, push against. **2** *the fighter buffeted his opponent* slap, smack, thump, wallop, clout, whack, thwack, cuff.

buffoon *noun* **1** *the buffoons in Shakespeare's plays* fool, clown, jester, comic, comedian, wit, wag, merry andrew, droll. **2** *he's just a buffoon* fool, dolt, idiot, nincompoop; *inf.* chump, numskull, dope, twit, nitwit, halfwit.

bug *noun* **1** *bitten by bugs* insect, beetle, fly, flea, mite; *inf.* creepy-crawly. **2** *an illness caused by a bug | he's caught a bug* bacterium, germ, virus, microorganism; infection. **3** *he's caught the dancing bug* craze, fad, mania, obsession, passion, fixation. **4** *get rid of all the bugs in the machine* fault, flaw, defect, imperfection, failing, error, obstruction; *inf.* glitch, gremlin. **5** *place a bug in the phone* listening device, wiretap, tap.

bug *verb* **1** *they've bugged his phone* tap, wiretap. **2** *bugging his conversation* tap, listen in on, eavesdrop on. **3** *he really bugs me* annoy, irritate, exasperate, anger, irk, vex, infuriate, inflame, provoke, try one's patience, get one's hackles up; *inf.* get one's back up, get on one's nerves, get in one's hair, be a thorn in one's flesh.

bugbear *noun* bane, anathema, abomination, pet hate, hate, nightmare, horror, dread, bête noire; goblin, bogeyman, hobgoblin.

build *verb* **1** *build a house/road/car* construct, erect, put up, assemble, set up, raise, make, manufacture, fabricate, form. **2** *hopes built on false premises* found, base, establish. **3** *build a business from nothing | build a new career* establish, found, set up, originate, institute, start, begin, inaugurate, initiate, develop. **build up 1** *build up a business* establish, develop, expand. *See* BUILD *verb* 3. **2** *build up her morale* boost, strengthen, increase. **3** *build up the product* advertise, promote, publicize; *inf.* plug, hype. **4** *important to build up his strength* develop, increase, improve, strengthen, augment, intensify, escalate. **5** *the wind is building up* strengthen, get stronger, increase, intensify, escalate. *Antonyms:* DEMOLISH; DISMANTLE; DESTROY.

build *noun* *of a heavy build* body, frame, physique, figure, form, structure, shape.

building *noun* **1** *putting up new buildings* structure, construction, edifice, erection. **2** *the building of new houses* construction, erection, putting up, raising.

buildup *noun* **1** *the buildup of resources* expansion, increase, growth, enlargement, escalation, development, accumulation. **2** *the buildup of paperwork/traffic* accumulation, stockpile, accretion, mass, heap, store, stack, pile. **3** *tired of the play's/product's buildup* promotion, publicity, advertising; *inf.* hype, plugging, plug, ballyhoo.

built-in *adjective* **1** *built-in bookcases* integral, integrated, incorporated. **2** *built-in disadvan-*

tages in-built, inherent, intrinsic, incorporated, inseparable, included, essential, implicit.

bulge noun **1** *a bulge in her pocket | body bulges* swelling, bump, lump, protuberance, protrusion, prominence, projection. **2** *a population bulge* boost, increase, rise, surge, intensification, augmentation.

bulge verb *with pockets/stomach bulging* swell, swell out, puff up/out, stick out, bag, balloon, balloon up/out, project, protrude, jut out, distend, expand, dilate, enlarge, bloat.

---

bulge
project, protrude, protuberate

While all of these verbs mean to extend outward, beyond the normal line or surface of something, it is almost impossible not to associate the word **bulge** with the human body (*a stomach that bulges over a waistband, muscles that bulge beneath a shirt*). *Bulge* suggests a swelling out that is quite noticeable or even abnormal, and that may be the result of internal pressure, although a brick wall can *bulge*, as can a bicep muscle. **Protuberate** is a less common word meaning to swell or stick out, but it does not necessarily imply that anything is abnormal or radically wrong (*he was so thin that his knees protuberated*). To **protrude** is to thrust forth in an unexpected way or to stick out in a way that is abnormal or disfiguring (*her eyes protruded from her skull*). **Project** is the least upsetting of all these words, probably because it is used less often with reference to the human body. Anything that juts out abruptly beyond the rest of a surface is said to *project* (*the balcony projected from the south side of the house*).

---

bulk noun **1** *the sheer bulk of the packages/work* size, volume, bulkiness, quantity, weight, extent, mass, substance, magnitude, massiveness, hugeness, largeness, bigness, ampleness, amplitude; dimensions. **2** *the bulk of the applicants are women* majority, greater part/number, preponderance, major/main/better part, mass, body, lion's share.

bulky adjective **1** *bulky bags of trash* large, big, substantial, huge, enormous, massive, vast, immense, voluminous, colossal, hulking, heavy, weighty, ponderous. **2** *Mr. Smith's bulky body* stout, thickset, plump, fat, chubby, portly, tubby, obese. **3** *bulky items of furniture* awkward-shaped, awkward, unwieldy, cumbersome, unmanageable.
Antonyms: SMALL; SLIM; MANAGEABLE.

bulldoze verb **1** *bulldoze the area/buildings* demolish, flatten, level, raze. **2** *bulldoze his way through | bulldoze a path through the crowds* force, push, drive, shove, propel. **3** *they bulldozed him into going* bully, browbeat, coerce, intimidate, cow, bludgeon, dragoon, steamroll, steamroller, railroad; *inf.* strong-arm.

bullet noun pellet, ball, slug, shot, missile, projectile. **bullets** ammunition *inf.* ammo, lead.

bulletin noun **1** *a television bulletin* news report, report, statement, announcement, news flash, flash, account, message, communication, communiqué, dispatch, notification. **2** *an inhouse bulletin* newspaper, newsletter, pamphlet, leaflet, broadsheet; listings.

bullish adjective **1** *bullish stock market* rising, advancing, up, improving, confident. **2** *feeling very bullish about the future* optimistic, hopeful, confident, positive, assured, cheerful, sanguine.

bully noun *the school bully* browbeater, intimidator, coercer, oppressor, persecutor, tyrant, tormentor, tough, ruffian, thug, hooligan, rowdy; *inf.* hood.

bully verb *bully the younger children* browbeat, intimidate, coerce, oppress, domineer, persecute, cow, tyrannize, pressurize, pressure, bulldoze; *inf.* push, strong-arm.

bulwark noun **1** *the fort's bulwarks | a bulwark against flooding* rampart, fortification, buttress, bastion, embankment, breastwork, redoubt; wall, dam. **2** *a bulwark of classical education* support, mainstay, defense, guard, safeguard; defender, protector.

bum noun **1** *a bum begging for money* tramp, vagrant, beggar, derelict, mendicant; bag lady, hobo. **2** *just a lazy bum* loafer, idler, good-for-nothing, ne'er-do-well, scrounger.

bum verb *bum money from him* borrow, scrounge, sponge; *inf.* mooch. **bum around** *just bumming around | bum around with his friends* loaf, lounge, idle, laze, wander; *inf.* hang out.

bum adjective **1** *a bum stereo | gave me a bum deal* useless, worthless, inferior, unsatisfactory, low-grade, poor, bad. **2** *a bum leg* lame, game, bad.

bumble verb **1** *the speaker was bumbling* ramble, babble, mumble, mutter, stumble. **2** *bumbling through the dark woods* stumble, lurch, blunder, muddle, flounder.

bumbling adjective *a bumbling idiot* clumsy, blundering, awkward, bungling, incompetent, inept, inefficient, stumbling, lumbering, foolish.

bump verb **1** *the bus bumped the car* hit, bang, strike, knock, crash into, collide with; *inf.* slam. **2** *bump his head on the bar* hit, bang, strike, knock, hurt, injure, damage. **3** *the wagon bumping along the road* bounce, jolt, jerk, rattle, shake, jounce. **4** *bumped from their seats* displace, supplant, dismiss, remove, eject, oust. **bump into 1** *the cars bumped into each other* collide with, crash/smash into, run into. **2** *we bumped into old friends* run into, come/run across, meet by chance, meet, meet up with, encounter, chance/happen upon. **bump off** *bump off his enemy* kill, murder, do away with, assassinate, eliminate, liquidate.

bump noun **1** *hear a bump* thud, thump, bang,

crash. **2** *land with a bump* jolt, crash, smash, bang, thud, thump, knock, rap, impact. **3** *he has a bump on his head* lump, swelling, injury, contusion, nodule, node, tumescence, intumescence, protuberance. **4** *a bump in the road* | *a strange fruit covered with bumps* bulge, hump, lump, knob, knot, protuberance.

bumper *adjective a bumper crop* large, big, abundant, huge, massive, bountiful, exceptional, unusual, excellent; *inf.* whopping.

bumpkin *noun* country bumpkin, yokel, clodhopper, oaf, boor, lout, peasant, rustic; *inf.* hillbilly, hick, hayseed, rube.

bumptious *adjective* self-important, conceited, arrogant, self-assertive, full of oneself, overbearing, puffed up, self-opinionated, cocky, presumptuous, pompous, forward; *inf.* pushy.

bumpy *adjective* **1** *a bumpy road* uneven, rough, potholed, rutted, pitted, lumpy, knobby. **2** *a bumpy flight* choppy, jolting, jolty, jerky, jarring, bouncy, rough.
Antonyms: EVEN; SMOOTH.

bunch *noun* **1** *a bunch of flowers* bouquet, spray, posy, sheaf, nosegay, corsage. **2** *a bunch of keys/bananas* cluster, assemblage, collection. **3** *a bunch of papers* batch, pile, stack, heap, bundle, mass, quantity, accumulation, agglomeration. **4** *a bunch of people* group, collection, gathering, band, gang, cluster, party, crowd, flock, swarm, troop, mob, multitude.

bunch *verb the crowd bunched together* cluster, huddle, gather, group, bundle, pack, herd, crowd, flock, mass, cram. **bunch up** *bunching up the cloth* gather, fold, pleat.

bundle *noun* **1** *a bundle of papers* collection, batch, pile, stack, heap, bunch, mass, quantity, accumulation, agglomeration. **2** *send off bundles of mail/clothes* package, pack, bale, parcel, packet. **3** *a bundle of sticks* bunch, bale, truss, faggot.

bundle *verb* **1** *bundle the clothes into a bag* | *bundle them up* tie, tie up, tie together, package, wrap, bind, fasten together, bale, truss. **2** *bundle people inside/outside* | *bundled them off the road* hurry, hustle, rush, push, shove, thrust, throw. **3** *bundle children up in warm clothes* clothe, wrap, cover.

bungle *verb* botch, muff, spoil, make a mess of, mess up, mishandle, mismanage, fudge, mar, ruin; *inf.* louse up, screw up, foul up.

bungling *adjective* clumsy, incompetent, inept, unskillful, inexpert, blundering, maladroit; *inf.* ham-handed.

bunk[1] *noun* bed, berth, bunk bed.

bunk[2] *noun* nonsense, bunkum. *See* BUNKUM

bunkum *noun* nonsense, rubbish, balderdash, twaddle, claptrap, humbug, tomfoolery; *inf.* rot, poppycock, baloney, piffle, bilge, bosh, hogwash, hooey; *vulg.* bullshit.

buoy *noun* **1** *a harbor buoy* marker, navigation mark, guide, beacon, signal. **2** *the buoy kept him* *afloat* lifebuoy, lifebelt, life jacket, life preserver; *inf.* Mae West.

buoy *verb* **buoy up** **1** *buoying up the bereaved woman* cheer, cheer up, hearten, encourage, support, sustain; *inf.* keep afloat. **2** *buoying up her spirits* cheer up, raise, boost, uplift, lift, give a lift to.

buoyancy *noun* **1** *the buoyancy of the boat/water* floatability, lightness, levity, lifting effect, lift. **2** *the buoyancy of her mood/personality* cheerfulness, cheeriness, lightheartedness, carefreeness, joy, vivacity, animation, liveliness, high spirits, verve, sparkle, sprightliness, spiritedness, blitheness, jauntiness, breeziness, pep, happiness, merriment; *inf.* zing, zip.

buoyant *adjective* **1** *a buoyant substance* floatable, floating, afloat, light. **2** *a buoyant mood/personality* cheerful, cheery, lighthearted, bouncy, carefree, joyful, vivacious, animated, lively, high-spirited, sparkling, sprightly, blithe, jaunty, breezy, happy, merry; *inf.* peppy, zingy, zippy.
Antonyms: LEADEN; DEPRESSED.

burden *noun* **1** *the donkey's burden* load, cargo, weight, freight. **2** *the burden of parenthood* responsibility, onus, charge, duty, obligation, tax, trouble, care, worry, anxiety, tribulation, difficulty, strain, stress, weight, encumbrance, millstone, albatross; trials, tribulations.

burden *verb* **1** *donkeys were burdened with heavy loads* load, lade, weight, charge, weigh down, encumber, hamper. **2** *burdened with great sorrow* oppress, trouble, worry, distress, bother, afflict, torment, strain, stress, tax, overwhelm.

bureau *noun* **1** *a travel bureau* agency, office, service. **2** *a government bureau* department, division, branch. **3** *polish the bureau* dresser, chest of drawers, highboy.

bureaucracy *noun* **1** *rule by bureaucracy* civil service, central administration, directorate; government officials. **2** *cut through the bureaucracy to get a passport* red tape, officialdom; formalities, rules and regulations.

bureaucrat *noun* administrator, official, officeholder, civil servant, public servant.

bureaucratic *adjective* official, administrative, governmental, red-tape, by-the-book, rigid, inflexible.

burgeon *verb* **1** *flowers burgeoning* bud, sprout, put forth shoots, shoot, germinate. **2** *a population burgeoning* grow, develop, flourish, thrive, mushroom, proliferate, snowball, increase, multiply, expand, escalate.

burglar *noun* housebreaker, cat burglar, thief, sneak thief, robber, crook, pilferer, filcher, picklock; *inf.* second-story man.

burglary *noun* **1** *arrested for burglary* housebreaking, breaking and entering, breaking in, forced entry, theft, robbery, larceny, pilfering, filching. **2** *suffered a burglary* break-in, theft, robbery.

burial *noun* **1** *the burial of the body* burying, interment, entombment, inhumation, sepulture. **2** *present at the burial* funeral, sepulture; obsequies, exequies. **burial ground** burial place, cemetery, graveyard, churchyard; *inf.* potter's field.

burlesque *noun* parody, caricature, travesty, farce, mockery, imitation, satire, lampoon; *inf.* send-up, takeoff, spoof.

burly *adjective* thickset, brawny, powerfully built, well-built, muscular, strapping, big, hulking, hefty, beefy, bulky, sturdy, stocky, stout.
Antonyms: SCRAWNY; PUNY; SLIGHT.

burn *verb* **1** *watching the house burn* be on fire, be afire, be ablaze, blaze, go up, smoke, flame, be aflame, flare, flash, flicker, glow. **2** *he burned the papers* set on fire, set alight, ignite, put a match to, light, kindle, incinerate, reduce to ashes. **3** *burn the shirt with the iron | burn the toast* scorch, singe, sear, char. **4** *her forehead burned with fever* be hot, be warm, feel hot, be feverish, be fevered; *inf.* be on fire. **5** *his throat burned with pain* smart, sting, tingle, be sore, hurt, throb. **6** *liquid burning his throat* sting, bite, prickle, irritate, pain, hurt. **7** *burn with excitement/passion* be aroused, be emotional, simmer, smolder, seethe. **8** *he was burning to get the prize* long, yearn, desire, hunger after, lust, itch, pant, wish, want. **9** *burn energy* use, use up, consume, expend, eat up, exhaust.

---

burn

cauterize, char, scald, scorch, sear, singe

If you're not an experienced cook, you're likely to **burn** your vegetables, **char** your meat, and, if you put your face too close to the stove, you might even **singe** your eyebrows. All of these verbs mean to injure or bring about a change in something by exposing it to fire or intense heat. *Burn*, which is the most comprehensive term, can mean to change only slightly (*she burned her face by staying out in the sun*) or to destroy completely (*the factory was burned to the ground*). To *char* is to reduce a substance to carbon or charcoal (*the beams in the ceiling were charred by the fire*). Like *char*, **singe** and **scorch** mean to burn only partially or superficially (*scorched the blouse while ironing it*; singe the chicken before cooking it). *Singeing* is often done deliberately to remove the hair, bristles, or feathers from the carcass of an animal or bird. **Scald** refers specifically to burning with, or as if with, a hot liquid or steam (*the cook scalded herself when she spilled the boiling water*); it can also mean to parboil or heat to a temperature just below boiling (*scald the milk to make the sauce*). **Sear** is also a term used in cooking, where it means to brown the outside of a piece of meat by subjecting it briefly to intense heat to seal in the juices. When it's human flesh that's being seared in surgery, the correct verb is **cauterize**, which means to burn for healing purposes (*the doctor cauterized the wound to ward off infection*).

burning *adjective* **1** *a burning house* blazing, aflaming, flaring, raging, ignited, glowing, flickering, smoldering, scorching. **2** *the burning meat* scorching, singeing, searing, charring. **3** *a burning forehead/day* hot, warm; *inf.* scorching, roasting, boiling, baking. **4** *a burning sensation* smarting, stinging, biting, prickling, irritating, caustic, searing, corroding, corrosive, painful. **5** *a burning desire* intense, fervent, fervid, ardent, passionate, eager. **6** *the burning issues of the day* important, crucial, significant, urgent, pressing, compelling, critical, vital, essential, acute, pivotal, climacteric.

burnish *verb* polish, shine, brighten, rub, buff, buff up, smooth.

burp *verb* belch, eruct, eructate.

burrow *noun* *rabbit burrows* tunnel, hole, hollow, excavation, lair, den, retreat.

burrow *verb* **1** *burrowing holes* dig, tunnel, excavate, hollow out, gouge out, scoop out. **2** *burrow one's way out* dig, tunnel. **3** *burrowing under the blankets* go under, hide, shelter, conceal oneself.

burst *verb* **1** *the pipe has burst* split, split open, break open, rupture, crack, fracture, fragment, shatter, shiver, fly open. **2** *the cold weather burst the pipes* split, break open, tear apart, rupture, crack, fracture, fragment, shatter, shiver, rend asunder. **3** *the grenade burst* blow up, explode, detonate, fulminate. **4** *the water burst through the dam* break out, burst forth, pour forth, gush out, surge out, rush out. **5** *he burst into/from the room* barge, push/shove one's way. **6** *burst into tears/laughter* break out, erupt. **burst out 1** *"coward!" she burst out* exclaim, cry out, call out, shout, yell. **2** *burst out crying* begin/start suddenly.

bury *verb* **1** *bury the corpse* inter, lay to rest, consign to the grave, entomb, inhume, sepulcher. **2** *bury her head in her hands* conceal, hide, put out of sight, submerge, sink, secrete, enshroud. **3** *bury the nail in the wood* drive in, embed, implant, sink, submerge. **4** *bury yourself in your work | be buried in a book* absorb oneself, immerse oneself, engross oneself, engage oneself, interest oneself.
Antonyms: EXHUME; UNEARTH; EXPOSE.

bush *noun* **1** *plant bushes in the garden* shrub, woody plant. **2** *lost in the Australian bush* brush, scrub land, scrub, the wild; backwoods. **bushes** *birds taking cover in the bushes* thicket, undergrowth, shrubbery.

bushy *adjective* thick, shaggy, fuzzy, fluffy, luxuriant, unruly, rough.

business *noun* **1** *what business is he in?* occupation, line, profession, career, trade, work, employment, job, pursuit, vocation, métier. **2** *do business with the French* trade, trading, commerce, trafficking, buying and selling, merchandizing, bargaining; dealings, transactions, proceedings. **3** *running her own business* firm, company, concern, enterprise, organization, corporation, establishment, store, shop, venture, industry. **4** *that's none of your business* concern, affair, responsibility, duty, function, task, assignment, obligation, problem. **5** *the main business of the meeting* matter, subject, topic, point of discussion, theme, issue, question, problem, thesis. **6** *it was a peculiar business* affair, matter, thing, case, set of circumstances, issue.

businesslike *adjective* **1** *businesslike behavior* professional, efficient, methodical, systematic, orderly, organized, well-ordered, practical, pragmatic, thorough, painstaking, meticulous, correct. **2** *the businesslike performance of the play* workaday, routine, prosaic, down-to-earth, conventional, unimaginative.

bust *noun* **1** *a woman with a large bust* chest, breasts, bosom, torso; *inf.* boobs, tits, knockers. **2** *a bust of Julius Caesar* sculptured/carved head and shoulders, head and shoulders.

bust *verb* **1** *they busted the machine* break, fracture, burst, rupture, crack. **2** *the crash will bust him* bankrupt, ruin, impoverish, pauperize, break. **3** *the police busted him* arrest, capture, catch, seize; *inf.* collar, nab.

bust *adjective* **go bust** become bankrupt, fail, be ruined, become insolvent.

bustle *verb* *bustle about* | *bustle to and fro* hurry, rush, dash, scuttle, scurry, hasten, scamper, scramble, flutter, fuss; *inf.* tear.

bustle *noun* *the bustle of the crowd* activity, flurry, stir, briskness, commotion, tumult, excitement, agitation, fuss; *inf.* to-do.

bustling *adjective* *a bustling crowd of theatergoers* active, full of activity, energetic, lively, busy, brisk, animated.

busy *adjective* **1** *the doctor's busy* occupied, engaged, working, at work, on duty, in a meeting, otherwise engaged. **2** *busy wrapping the gifts* occupied in, engaged in, employed in, involved in, absorbed in, engrossed in, preoccupied with, working at, laboring at, toiling at, slaving at. **3** *a busy day* active, energetic, strenuous, full, hectic, exacting, bustling. **4** *busy as bees* active, energetic, industrious, lively, tireless, restless; *inf.* on the go. **5** *busy patterns* ornate, overelaborate, overdetailed, overdecorated, cluttered, fussy.

Antonyms: UNOCCUPIED; INACTIVE; QUIET; IDLE.

---

busy
assiduous, diligent, engaged, industrious, sedulous

There are varying degrees of busyness. **Busy** implies actively and attentively involved in work or a pastime (*too busy to come to the phone*). It can also be used to describe intensive activity of any kind (*a busy intersection; a busy day*). Someone who is **engaged** is also *busy*, but in a more focused way (*engaged in compiling a dic-*

tionary). **Diligent** is used to describe earnest and constant effort, and it often connotes enjoyment of or dedication to what one is doing (*diligent efforts to rescue injured animals*). To be **industrious** is to be more focused still, often with a definite goal in mind (*an industrious employee working for a promotion*). **Sedulous** also applies to goal-oriented activity, but it suggests more close care and perseverance than *industrious* does (*a sedulous investigation of the accident*). The award for concentrated effort goes to the person who is **assiduous**, which suggests painstaking preoccupation with a specific task (*an assiduous student is the one most likely to win his or her teacher's favor*).

---

busy *verb* *busy himself in the garden* occupy, engage, employ, absorb, immerse, engross, involve, interest.

busybody *noun* meddler, interferer, snooper, snoop, mischief-maker, troublemaker, gossip, scandalmonger, muckraker.

but *conjunction* **1** *she's ill, but she's going* nevertheless, yet, still, however. **2** *he went, but she did not* on the other hand, on the contrary. **3** *cannot choose but to do it* other than, otherwise than, except.

but *preposition* *everyone but him* except, with the exception of, excepting, other than, excluding, bar, barring, save. **but for** *but for the rain he would have gone* without, except for, barring, notwithstanding.

but *adverb* *we can but try* only, just, simply, merely.

butch *adjective* mannish, masculine.

butcher *noun* *the butcher responsible for these killings* slaughterer, murderer, mass murderer, slayer, killer, serial killer, homicide, homicidal maniac, bloodshedder.

butcher *verb* **1** *butchering cattle* slaughter, cut up, carve up, slice up, prepare, dress. **2** *butchering the enemy* slaughter, slay, massacre, murder, kill, put to death, exterminate, liquidate, assassinate, put to the sword, cut down, destroy. **3** *butcher the piano concerto* | *butcher the sewing project* botch, make a botch/mess of, wreck, ruin, spoil, bungle; *inf.* louse up, screw up, foul up.

butchery *noun* *tribes noted for their butchery* | *the butchery of the enemy* slaughter, massacre, slaying, murdering, murder, mass murdering, homicide, bloodshedding.

butt[1] *noun* **1** *the butt of a gun* handle, shaft, hilt, haft. **2** *the butt of a cigarette* stub, end, remnant; *inf.* roach. **3** *sitting on his butt* bottom, buttocks.

butt[2] *noun* *the butt of his jokes* scapegoat, dupe, target, victim, laughingstock, object, subject.

butt[3] *noun* *a butt of wine* barrel, cask.

butt[4] *verb* **1** *the ram butted her with his horns* push, thrust, shove, ram, bump, buffet, prod, poke, jab, knock, bunt. **2** *his land butts mine* abut, join, meet, conjoin. **butt into** *butt into a conver-*

sation | *butt into a private matter* interrupt, intrude/interfere in, put one's oar into; *inf.* stick one's nose into.

buttocks *noun* bottom, posterior, rump; hindquarters; *inf.* behind, backside, butt, can, ass.

button *noun* **1** *buttons on the sweater* fastener, stud, link. **2** *the button on the radio* knob, switch.

buttonhole *verb* *buttonholed by a reporter* accost, waylay, take aside, importune, detain, grab, catch, talk at.

buttress *noun* **1** *a stone buttress* prop, support, abutment, strut, reinforcement, stanchion, pier. **2** *a buttress to the family* mainstay, upholder, sustainer, cornerstone, pillar.

buttress *verb* *buttress the economy* | *buttress your argument* strengthen, reinforce, prop up, support, shore up, underpin, brace, uphold, defend, back up.

buxom *adjective* plump, large-bosomed, big-bosomed, full-bosomed, shapely; *inf.* busty.

buy *verb* **1** *buy a house* purchase, make a purchase of, pay for, invest in, procure. **2** *he bought his way in* bribe, suborn, corrupt; *inf.* fix, rig. *Antonym:* SELL.

buy *noun* *a good buy* purchase, acquisition, deal, bargain.

buzz *noun* **1** *the buzz of the bees* buzzing, hum, humming, murmur, drone, whir, whirring, hiss, sibilation, whisper. **2** *the buzz of the telephone/machines* ring, ringing, purr, purring. **3** *the buzz is he's gone* rumor, gossip, talk, scuttlebutt, news, report, whisper, scandal, hearsay, word around town/here, word going around.

buzz *verb* **1** *bees buzzing* hum, murmur, drone, whir, hiss, whisper, sibilate. **2** *telephone/machines buzzing* ring, reverberate, purr. **3** *tongues buzzing* gossip, chatter, tattle, spread

rumors. **4** *people buzzing about* bustle, rush, dash, hurry.

buzzing *adjective* *a place buzzing with excitement* active, busy, bustling, alive, energetic, on the move.

by *preposition* **1** *the house by the school* next to, beside, alongside, near, close to. **2** *enter by the side door* | *come by the quiet roads* through, along, over, by way of, via. **3** *go by the building* past, in front of. **4** *be there by midday* no later than, at, before. **5** *arrested by the police* | *contact him by telephone* through the agency/means/instrumentality of, under the aegis of, through. **6** *meet by chance* through, because of, as a result of.

bygone *adjective* past, departed, dead, former, one-time, previous, forgotten, lost, of old, olden, ancient, antiquated, of yore, obsolete, extinct, out of date, outmoded, passé

bylaw, byelaw *noun* local regulation, rule, regulation, statute.

bypass *noun* *the bypass avoids the city* detour, circuitous route, roundabout way, alternative route.

bypass *verb* **1** *bypass the city* make a detour around, go around, pass around. **2** *bypass the difficulties* get around, circumvent, find a way around, avoid, evade. **3** *bypass the salesperson and go to the manager* ignore, pass over, miss out, circumvent, avoid, go over the head of.

bystander *noun* onlooker, looker-on, observer, eyewitness, witness, spectator, watcher, viewer, beholder, gaper, passerby; *inf.* rubberneck.

byword *noun* *old bywords dying out* proverb, maxim, adage, aphorism, apothegm. **byword for** *a byword for reliability* slogan for, catchword for, motto for/of, example of, personification of, embodiment of.

C

cab *noun* **1** *order a cab* taxi, taxicab, hackney carriage, hackney, *inf.* hack. **2** *the driver's cab* cabin, compartment, quarters, cubicle.

cabal *noun* **1** *a political plot laid by a cabal* clique, faction, coterie, league, confederacy, band, gang, party, set, ring, junta, junto. **2** *the cabal was discovered in time* intrigue, conspiracy, plot, scheme, plan, design.

cabaret *noun* **1** *watching the hotel's cabaret* entertainment, show, floorshow. **2** *employed as a singer in a cabaret* nightclub, club, nightspot, disco, discotheque.

cabbage *noun* **1** *cabbage and carrot salad* green cabbage, white cabbage, red cabbage, winter cabbage, savoy, Chinese cabbage, bok choy. **2** *their little business enterprise has brought in a lot of cabbage* money; *inf.* dough, bread, loot.

cabin *noun* **1** *a cabin by the lake* log cabin, hut, chalet, cottage, shack, shanty, shed. **2** *a first-class cabin in the ship* stateroom, room, sleeping quarters, berth, compartment. **3** *an aircraft's cabin* compartment, passenger space.

cabinet *noun* **1** *a china cabinet | a filing cabinet* cupboard, chest, locker, dresser, closet, chiffonier, case, container. **2** *a member of the president's cabinet* advisers, council, committee, board, administration.

cable *noun* **1** *tied with cable* rope, cord, wire, line, cordage. **2** *send a cable* cablegram, telegram, telegraph, wire.

cable *verb* *cable the news* telegraph, wire, radio.

cache *noun* **1** *hide the treasure in a cache* hiding place, hide-out, secret place, hole. **2** *find the cache of jewels* hoard, store, collection, fund, supply, hidden treasure, treasure, loot; *inf.* stash.

cachet *noun* prestige, distinction, stature, eminence, respect, admiration, approbation, approval, seal of approval, stamp of approval.

cackle *verb* **1** *hens cackling* cluck, clack, squawk. **2** *the audience cackling at his jokes* chuckle, chortle, laugh, giggle, titter, snigger, tee-hee. **3** *people cackling at the bus stop* chatter, jabber, prattle, babble, gibber, blather, blab; *inf.* spout away.

cacophony *noun* discord, dissonance, discordance, jarring, stridency, grating, rasping, caterwauling.

cad *noun* scoundrel, rat, rogue, rascal, double-crosser; *inf.* bounder, heel.

cadaver *noun* corpse, dead body, remains, carcass; *inf.* stiff.

cadaverous *adjective* corpselike, deathlike, gaunt, haggard, drawn, emaciated, skeletal, thin, hollow-eyed, ashen, pale, wan, ghostly.

cadence *noun* **1** *musical/metrical cadence | the cadence of the music* rhythm, beat, pulse, rhythmical flow/pattern, measure, meter, tempo, swing, lilt, cadency. **2** *the cadence of her speech* intonation, inflection, accent, modulation.

café *noun* coffee shop, snack bar, tearoom, restaurant, cafeteria, bar, bistro; *inf.* greasy spoon.

cafeteria *noun* self-service restaurant, canteen.

cage *noun* *cages in the zoo* enclosure, pen, corral, pound, lockup, coop; birdcage, aviary.

cage *verb* *cage the animals* confine, shut in, impound, pen, corral, lock up, incarcerate, imprison, coop, coop up. **cage in** *don't cage him in* confine, hem in, restrict, restrain.

cagey, cagy *adjective* guarded, secretive, noncommittal, cautious, chary, wary, careful, shrewd, wily.
Antonyms: GUILELESS; STRAIGHTFORWARD.

cajole *verb* wheedle, coax, beguile, flatter, seduce, lure, entice, tempt, inveigle, maneuver, humor; *inf.* sweet-talk, soft-soap, butter up.

cake *noun* **1** *cakes from the bakery* cupcake, sponge cake, angel food cake, chocolate cake, layer cake, fruitcake, cheesecake, gingerbread, shortcake, bun, pastry. **2** *a cake of soap* block, bar, slab, lump, mass, cube, loaf, chunk.

cake *verb* **1** *blood caking on the wound* solidify, harden, thicken, dry, bake, coagulate, consolidate, ossify. **2** *boots caked with mud* cover, coat, encrust, plaster.

calamitous *adjective* disastrous, catastrophic, cataclysmic, devastating, ruinous, dire, tragic, fatal, wretched, woeful.

calamity *noun* disaster, catastrophe, tragedy, misfortune, cataclysm, devastation, scourge, misadventure, mischance, mishap, ruin, tribulation, woe.

calculate *verb* **1** *calculate the sum* work out, compute, estimate, count up, figure out, evaluate, enumerate, determine, gauge. **2** *she calculated her chances* estimate, gauge, judge, measure, weigh, reckon, rate. **3** *the proposal was calculated to appeal to the investors* design, plan, aim, intend. **4** *we calculated on their early arrival* rely, depend, count, bank.

calculated *adjective* *a calculated crime/risk* considered, planned, premeditated, deliberate, intentional, intended, purposeful.
Antonyms: UNINTENTIONAL; SPONTANEOUS.

calculating *adjective* *a calculating young woman/killer* scheming, designing, contriving, devious,

Antonyms: INGENUOUS; GUILELESS.

calculation noun **1** *by their calculations it will cost $3000* computation, estimation, estimate, reckoning, figuring, forecast, gauging, judgment. See CALCULATE 1, 2. **2** *the calculation is wrong* result, answer. **3** *she got the job by sheer calculation* scheming, designing, contriving, deviousness, shrewdness, manipulation, slyness, craft, expedience, circumspection, deliberation.

caliber noun **1** *the caliber of a gun* bore, diameter. **2** *statesmen of his caliber* quality, worth, distinction, stature, excellence, merit, ability, talent, capability, competence, capacity, endowments, gifts, strengths, scope.

call verb **1** *call out in pain* cry, cry out, shout, exclaim, yell, scream, shriek, roar. **2** *call him in the morning* awaken, waken, arouse, rouse. **3** *call her tomorrow* call up, phone, telephone, give one a ring; *inf.* give one a buzz. **4** *call at the house* pay a call, pay a visit, pay a brief visit, stop by; *inf.* drop in, pop in. **5** *call a meeting* call together, convene, summon, order, convoke, assemble, announce, declare, proclaim, decree. **6** *call a doctor/taxi* send for, ask for, summon, contact, order, bid, fetch. **7** *they called the baby Jane | the flowers are called primulas* name, christen, designate, dub, entitle, denominate, describe as, label, term. **8** *I call it disgraceful* consider, think, regard, judge, estimate. **9** *called to the bar | he was called to the church* appoint, elect, ordain. **call for 1** *this calls for a celebration | rudeness is not called for* need, require, be grounds for, justify, necessitate, demand, entail. **2** *call for the packages* collect, pick up, fetch, go for. **call off 1** *call off the dogs* order off, order away, stop, hold back, check, rein in. **2** *call off the date* cancel, postpone, countermand, rescind, revoke. **call on/upon 1** *call on his aunt* visit, pay a visit to, go and see; *inf.* look up, look in on, drop in on. **2** *call on/upon them to help* appeal to, ask, request, entreat, urge, supplicate, invoke. **call up 1** *call her up tomorrow* call, telephone, phone. See CALL verb 3. **2** *it calls up painful memories* recall, bring/call to mind, summon up, evoke. **3** *call up all the young men* enlist, recruit, sign up; draft.

call noun **1** *a call of pain* cry, shout, exclamation, yell, scream, shriek, roar. **2** *the calls of the bird* cry, song, chirp, chirping, tweet. **3** *have a prearranged call* signal, hail, whoop. **4** *give her a call tomorrow* telephone call, ring; *inf.* buzz. **5** *paid her a call* visit, brief visit. **6** *first call for the plane | a call for unity* summons, invitation, request, plea, bidding, order, command, appeal, notice. **7** *there's no call to be rude* need, occasion, reason, cause, justification, grounds, excuse. **8** *there's no call for expensive wine here* demand, request, requirement, need, want, requisition. **9** *the call of the wild* attraction, lure, allurement, fascination, appeal, bewitchment.

call girl noun prostitute, whore, harlot, street walker, courtesan, woman of ill repute, fallen woman, loose woman, scarlet woman, woman of the night, *fille de joie*; *inf.* hooker, hustler.

calling noun vocation, occupation, career, profession, business, work, employment, job, trade, craft, line, line of work, pursuit, *métier*, walk of life, province, field.

callous adjective **1** *a callous jail warden* hard, hardened, tough, harsh, cold, insensitive, unfeeling, cold-hearted, hard-hearted, heartless, hard-bitten, cruel, obdurate, inured, uncaring, unsympathetic, unresponsive, indifferent, soulless. **2** *callous skin* hard, hardened, thickened, leathery.

Antonyms: KIND; COMPASSIONATE.

callow adjective immature, inexperienced, uninitiated, naïve, unsophisticated, innocent, undeveloped, adolescent.

Antonyms: EXPERIENCED; SOPHISTICATED.

calm adjective **1** *a calm day* still, windless, mild, tranquil, balmy, halcyon, quiet, peaceful, pacific, undisturbed, restful. **2** *a calm sea* still, smooth, motionless, placid, waveless, unagitated, storm-free. **3** *be/remain calm during the trouble* composed, collected, cool, controlled, cool-headed, self-controlled, self-possessed, quiet, tranquil, unruffled, relaxed, serene, unexcited, unexcitable, unflappable, undisturbed, unagitated, imperturbable, unemotional, unmoved, equable, stoical; *inf.* together.

Antonyms: STORMY; EXCITED; FRANTIC.

---

calm
halcyon, peaceful, placid, serene, tranquil

We usually speak of the weather or the sea as **calm**, meaning free from disturbance or storm. When applied to people and their feelings or moods, *calm* implies an unruffled state, often under disturbing conditions (*to remain calm in the face of disaster*). **Halcyon** is another adjective associated with the weather (*the halcyon days of summer*); it comes from the name of a mythical bird, usually identified with the kingfisher, that builds its nest on the sea and possesses a magical power to calm the winds and waves. **Peaceful** also suggests a lack of turbulence or disorder, although it is usually applied to situations, scenes, and activities rather than to people (*a peaceful gathering of protesters; a peaceful resolution to their problems*). **Serene, tranquil,** and **placid** are more often used to describe human states of being. *Serene* suggests a lofty and undisturbed calmness (*he died with a serene look on his face*), while *tranquil* implies an intrinsic calmness (*they led a tranquil life in the country*). **Placid** usually refers to a prevailing tendency and is sometimes used disparagingly to suggest a lack of responsiveness or a dull complacency (*with her placid disposition, she seldom got involved in family arguments*).

calm *noun* **1** *the calm before the storm* | *disturbing the day's calm* stillness, tranquillity, serenity, quietness, quietude, peace, peacefulness, harmony, restfulness, repose. **2** *nothing disturbs her calm* composure, coolness, self-control, tranquillity, serenity, equanimity, unflappability, imperturbability, equability, poise, sangfroid; *inf.* cool.
Antonyms: TURMOIL; UPHEAVAL.

calm *verb* **1** *try to calm the child* | *calm her fears* soothe, quieten, pacify, hush, lull, tranquilize, mollify, appease, allay, alleviate, assuage. **2** *the wind eventually calmed* quieten, still, settle, settle down, die down. **calm down** quieten; relax, settle.
Antonyms: AGITATE; STIR.

calumny *noun* slander, calumniation, defamation, libel, misrepresentation, false accusation, denigration, vilification, aspersions, mudslinging, backbiting, detraction, disparagement, deprecation, evil-speaking, insult, abuse, vituperation, obloquy, revilement, smear campaign.

camaraderie *noun* comradeship, companionship, brotherliness, fellowship, friendship, closeness, affinity, sociability.

camouflage *noun the soldiers' khaki uniforms were a camouflage* | *the polar bear's coat is a camouflage* disguise, protective coloring, mask, screen, cloak, cover, cover-up, false front, front, façade, masquerade, blind, concealment, subterfuge.

camouflage *verb camouflaged in white against the snow* disguise, hide, conceal, mask, screen, veil, cloak, cover, cover up, obscure.

camp[1] *noun* **1** *soldier's/Scout camp* encampment, camping ground, campsite, tents, bivouac, cantonment. **2** *the right-wing camp* faction, party, group, clique, coterie, set, sect, cabal.

camp[2] *verb we camped in a field* pitch tents, pitch camp, set up camp, encamp, tent. **camp out 1** *we camped out in that field* sleep out, camp. **2** *we're camping out here till the house is decorated* live simply; *inf.* rough it, slum it.

camp[3] *verb* **camp it up** overdo it, overact, behave theatrically, posture, behave affectedly, ham it up, lay it on, spread it on thick.

camp[4] *adjective* **1** *camp mannerisms* effeminate, affected, artificial, posturing, mannered, studied; homosexual, gay; *inf.* campy. **2** *camp humor* exaggerated, theatrical, flamboyant, overdone, extravagant, overdrawn, artificial; *inf.* over the top, camped up.

campaign *noun* **1** *Grant's Vicksburg Campaign* war, battle, expedition, offensive, attack, crusade. **2** *an advertising campaign* | *a campaign against litter* course of action, operation, promotion, strategy, set of tactics, drive, push, crusade, movement, maneuver, battle plan.

campaign *verb campaigning for civil rights* fight, battle, work, push, crusade, strive, struggle, agitate.

can *noun* **1** *a can of beans* tin can, container, receptacle. **2** *threw him in the can for ninety days* jail, prison, lockup, penitentiary; *inf.* pen, cooler, slammer, clink, hoosegow. **3** *went to the can between classes* toilet, lavatory; *inf.* john, lav. **4** *shouldn't sit around on your can all day* buttocks, rump, rear, rear end; *inf.* butt, ass. **can of worms** problem, hornet's nest, complication.

can *verb* **1** *can fruit* preserve, bottle. **2** *they canned him for his poor attendance* dismiss, fire, let go, oust, lay off.

canal *noun* **1** *barges on the canal* channel, race, watercourse, waterway. **2** *the alimentary canal* tube, duct, conduit, pipe.

cancel *verb* **1** *cancel a vacation/date* call off, stop, discontinue, give up, withdraw from, countermand, revoke, rescind. **2** *cancel an order* annul, declare void, declare null and void, nullify, quash, invalidate, set aside, retract, negate, revoke, rescind, repudiate, abrogate, repeal, abolish. **3** *cancel that last paragraph* delete, cross out, erase, strike out, rub out, blot out, expunge, eliminate, obliterate, eradicate, efface. **4** *his friendliness cancels out her hostility* counterbalance, balance, offset, compensate, make up for, counteract, neutralize, redeem.
Antonym: CONFIRM.

cancer *noun* **1** *cancer of the breast* tumor, malignant tumor, malignancy, growth, malignant growth; *Med.* carcinoma, sarcoma, melanoma, metastasis. **2** *a cancer in our society* canker, blight, evil, corruption, sickness, disease, pestilence, scourge, plague.

candid *adjective* **1** *she's always candid* | *candid remarks* frank, open, honest, truthful, sincere, forthright, direct, plainspoken, outspoken, blunt, unequivocal, bluff, brusque; *inf.* straight from the shoulder. **2** *candid camera shots* unposed, spontaneous, impromptu, extemporary, uncontrived, informal, unstudied.
Antonyms: SECRETIVE; GUARDED; EQUIVOCAL.

candidate *noun* **1** *two candidates for the post* | *congressional candidates* applicant, job applicant, office seeker, contender, nominee, contestant, aspirant, possibility; *inf.* runner. **2** *candidates for the final exams* entrant, examinee.

candle *noun* taper.

candor *noun* frankness, openness, honesty, truthfulness, sincerity, forthrightness, directness, plainspokenness, outspokenness, unequivocalness, bluntness, bluffness, brusqueness.

candy *noun* sweet, sweets, confectionery, confection, toffee, chocolate, fudge, caramel, bonbon, bonbons.

cane *noun* **1** *a walking cane* | *canes supporting plants* stick, staff, rod, stave; walking stick,

stem, stalk, shoot, reed.

cane *verb cane the mutineers* beat, strike, hit, flog, thrash, lash, strap, scourge; *inf.* tan one's hide.

canker *noun* **1** *a canker in the dog's ear* ulcer, ulceration, sore, running sore, lesion, blister, abscess. **2** *tree canker* fungus disease, blight, plant rot. **3** *a canker in society* cancer, blight, evil, corruption, rot, sickness, scourge. *See* CANCER 2.

cannibal *noun* man-eater, people-eater; savage, barbarian, wild man; *fml.* anthropophagite.

cannon *noun* gun, field gun, mounted gun; *inf.* big gun.

cannonade *noun* barrage, bombardment, shelling, battery, pounding, attack, salvo, volley, broadside.

canny *adjective* **1** *canny with the accounts* | *a canny response* careful, cautious, prudent, thrifty. **2** *a canny businesswoman* shrewd, sharp, astute, discerning, penetrating, perspicacious, clever, sensible, wise, judicious, sagacious, circumspect.
Antonyms: CARELESS; FOOLISH.

canon[1] *noun* **1** *the canons of good taste* rule, ruling, principle, standard, criterion, test, measure, yardstick, benchmark, pattern, model, exemplar, precept, norm, formula, convention. **2** *a Church canon* law, rule, regulation, statute, decree, edict, dictate. **3** *a canon of saints* | *the canon of Shakespeare's plays* official list, list, catalog, enumeration, litany, roll.

canon[2] *noun* prebendary. *See* ECCLESIASTIC *noun.*

canopy *noun* awning, shade, sunshade, cover, covering, tarpaulin.

cant[1] *noun* **1** *thieves' cant* slang, jargon, patter, lingo, terminology, argot. **2** *religious cant* hypocrisy, insincerity, sanctimony, sanctimoniousness, humbug, lip service, pretense.

cant[2] *noun the table is on a cant* slant, slope, tilt, angle, inclination.

cant[3] *verb the boat began to cant* tilt, tip, slope, slant, lean, incline, angle, overturn.

cantankerous *adjective* bad-tempered, short-tempered, ill-natured, crabby, surly, irascible, irritable, grumpy, brusque, curt, abrupt, difficult, disagreeable, quarrelsome, touchy, perverse, testy, peevish, crusty, choleric, captious; *inf.* grouchy, crotchety, cranky.

canter *noun* amble, saunter, trot, jog, lope, gallop.

canvass *verb* **1** *canvassing during the general election* solicit votes, seek votes, campaign, electioneer, drum up support, persuade, convince. **2** *canvassing people's views* | *canvass buying habits* investigate, find out about, inquire into, look into, examine, scrutinize, explore, study, analyze, evaluate, survey, scan, poll. **3** *canvass an idea/suggestion/theory* discuss, debate, air, ventilate, argue, dispute.

canyon *noun* ravine, gully, valley, gorge, chasm, gulf, abyss.

cap *noun* **1** *doffing his cap* hat, bonnet, headgear; *inf.* baseball cap, bathing cap, skullcap, nightcap, stocking cap. *See* HAT. **2** *replace the cap on the bottle* top, lid, stopper, cork, plug. **3** *the cap of a wave* | *mountain caps* top, crest, peak, summit, apex, pinnacle.

cap *verb* **1** *mountains capped with snow* cover, top, crown, overlie, overspread, coat, blanket. **2** *cap the high-jump record* beat, better, surpass, excel, outshine, transcend, eclipse, overshadow, outdo, outstrip, exceed. **3** *cap the price* limit, set a limit to, restrict, keep within bounds, curb.

capability *noun* **1** *have the capability to do well* | *the capability of winning* ability, capacity, potential, aptitude, faculty, facility, power, competence, efficiency, effectiveness, proficiency, accomplishment, talent, adeptness, skill, skillfulness, experience, cleverness, intelligence, smartness. *See* CAPABLE. **2** *offer capabilities* talent, gifts, skill, aptitude, flair, knack, forte, strong point.

capable *adjective a very capable young woman* able, competent, adequate, efficient, effective, proficient, accomplished, talented, gifted, adept, skillful, masterly, experienced, practiced, qualified, clever, intelligent, smart.

capable of **1** *capable of murder/lying* having the inclination/temperament to do, having a tendency/propensity to do, tending to, inclined to, predisposed to, prone to, liable to, likely to do. **2** *capable of improvement* needing, in need of, requiring, wanting, susceptible to, admitting of, receptive of.
Antonyms: INCAPABLE; INCOMPETENT.

capacious *adjective* roomy, commodious, spacious, ample, large, voluminous, sizable, substantial, vast, immense.
Antonyms: CRAMPED; NARROW; SMALL.

capacity *noun* **1** *the capacity to seat twenty* space, room, size, largeness, ampleness, amplitude, scope, magnitude, dimensions, proportions, extent. **2** *have the capacity to do the job* ability, capability, aptitude, potential, faculty, facility, power, competence, competency, proficiency, accomplishment, cleverness, intelligence, brains, head. *See* CAPABILITY. **3** *in his capacity as a teacher* position, post, job, office, function, role, appointment.

cape[1] *noun wearing a black cape* cloak, mantle, shawl, wrap, poncho, pelisse.

cape[2] *noun drowned off the cape* headland, head, point, promontory, neck, peninsula.

caper *verb goats/children capering about* frolic, frisk, romp, skip, gambol, cavort, prance, dance, leap, hop, jump, bound, spring, bounce.

caper *noun* **1** *the energetic capers of the children/ goats* frolics, frisking, romping, skipping, gambols, gamboling, cavorting, prancing, dancing, leap. *See* CAPER *verb.* **2** *tired of their mischievous capers* prank, trick, practical joke, antic, lark, jest, jesting, high jinks, mischief, escapade, stunt, game, sport, fun; *inf.* shenanigan.

capital *adjective* **1** *our capital concern* principal, chief, main, major, prime, paramount, foremost, predominant, overruling, leading, cardinal, central, key. **2** *make a capital error* grave, vital, important, serious, crucial, fatal. **3** *a capital show | a capital piece of work* splendid, excellent, first-rate, first-class, superb, fine, outstanding; *inf.* super, top-notch.

capital *noun* **1** *Juneau is the capital of Alaska* first city, seat of government, center of administration. **2** *write in capitals* capital letter, uppercase letter, uncial, uncial letter; *inf.* cap. **3** *enough capital to buy the firm* money, finance, finances, funds, cash, hard cash, wherewithal, means, assets, liquid assets, wealth, resources, reserves, principal.

capitalism *noun* free enterprise, private enterprise, private ownership, privatized industries, *laissez-faire.*

capitalist *noun* financier, investor, banker, tycoon, moneyman; wealthy/rich person, plutocrat, nabob.

capitalize *verb capitalize the firm* finance, back, provide backing for, fund, sponsor. **capitalize on** *capitalize on her rival's mistakes* take advantage of, put to advantage, profit from, cash in on, make the most of, exploit.

capitulate *verb* surrender, yield, submit, give in, give up, come to terms, succumb, accede, back down, cave in, relent, acquiesce; *inf.* throw in the towel.

caprice *noun* whim, whimsy, vagary, fancy, notion, fad, freak, humor, impulse, quirk; changeableness, fickleness, volatility, inconstancy.

capricious *adjective* changeable, unpredictable, fickle, variable, inconstant, unstable, mercurial, volatile, impulsive, erratic, fanciful, faddish, freakish, irregular, fitful, whimsical, wayward, quirky. *Antonyms:* STABLE; CONSISTENT; CONSTANT.

capsize *verb* overturn, turn over, upset, upend, knock over, tip over, invert, keel over.

capsule *noun* **1** *pain-relieving capsules* pill, tablet, lozenge. **2** *plant capsules* seed case, pod, pericarp. **3** *space capsule* craft, probe; detachable compartment, section.

captain *noun* **1** *the captain of the ship* commander, master, skipper; *inf.* old man. **2** *team captain* leader, head, skipper. **3** *captains of industry* chief, head, leader, boss, principal; *inf.* honcho.

caption *noun* heading, title, wording, head, legend, inscription.

captious *adjective* carping, criticizing, critical, faultfinding, quibbling; *inf.* nitpicking.

captivate *verb* charm, delight, enchant, bewitch, fascinate, beguile, enthrall, entrance, enrapture, attract, allure, lure, win, infatuate, se-

duce, ravish, ensnare, dazzle, hypnotize, mesmerize.

captive *noun take captives | captives clamoring for freedom* prisoner, prisoner of war, hostage, slave, bondsman, convict, jailbird, detainee; *inf.* con.

captive *adjective captive animals* imprisoned, incarcerated, locked up, caged, interned, confined, penned up, detained, restrained; in captivity, in bondage.

captivity *noun* imprisonment, custody, detention, confinement, internment, incarceration, restraint, constraint, committal, bondage, slavery, servitude, enslavement, subjection. *Antonyms:* FREEDOM; LIBERTY.

capture *verb* catch, arrest, apprehend, take prisoner, take captive, take into custody, seize, take, lay hold of, trap; *inf.* nab, collar, pinch, nail, bag. *Antonyms:* FREE; LIBERATE.

capture *noun* **1** *involved in the criminal's capture* arrest, apprehension, imprisonment, seizure, trapping; *inf.* nabbing, collaring, pinching. *See* CAPTURE *verb.* **2** *the captures of war* prize, trophy, gain; booty, pickings, pillage.

car *noun* **1** *renting a car* vehicle, motor vehicle, automobile, motorcar; sedan, station wagon, hatchback, coupé, sports car, racing car, stock car, police car, patrol car; *inf.* wheels, heap, crate, jalopy, limo, auto. *See also table at* VEHICLE. **2** *railroad car* carriage, coach; dining car, sleeping car, Pullman; cable car.

carafe *noun* flask, decanter, jug, pitcher, flagon.

caravan *noun* **1** *a gypsy caravan* wagon, covered cart, cart. **2** *caravan of pilgrims in the desert* convoy, troop, band, company, group, cavalcade, procession.

carcass *noun* **1** *vultures searching for carcasses* corpse, dead body, body; remains; *Med.* cadaver; *inf.* stiff. **2** *move your carcass* body, person, self, oneself. **3** *the carcass of the building* frame, framework, skeleton, shell, hulk.

card *noun* **1** *send a card to her* postcard, greeting card, Christmas card, birthday card, get well card, sympathy card. **2** *here's my card* identification; business card, calling card, ID card, identification card. **3** *draw a card* playing card, tarot card. **cards** *I brought the cards | played cards all night* pack of cards; card game. **in the cards** *an election's in the cards* likely, possible, probable; most likely, certain.

cardinal *adjective* **1** *cardinal sins/errors* main, chief, capital, principal, important, greatest, highest, vital, key, central, major, essential, foremost, leading, prime, paramount, preeminent, fundamental, basic, primary. **2** *painted cardinal* red, scarlet, crimson, vermilion.

cardinal *noun cardinals in Rome* cardinal bishop, cardinal priest, high priest, archpriest. *See* ECCLESIASTIC *noun.*

care *noun* **1** *wished he could be free from care* worry, anxiety, trouble, disquiet, unease, distress, sorrow, anguish, grief, sadness, affliction, woe,

hardship, tribulation, responsibility, stress, pressure, strain; burdens. **2** *no care for others* concern, regard, attention, interest, solicitude, looking after, sympathy. **3** *arrange the flowers with care* carefulness, attention, thought, regard, heed, forethought, mindfulness, conscientiousness, painstakingness, pains, accuracy, precision, meticulousness, punctiliousness, fastidiousness. **4** *cross the road with care* attention, caution, heedfulness, alertness, watchfulness, vigilance, wariness, awareness, circumspection, prudence. **5** *in the care of her uncle | in the care of the local authority* charge, protection, custody, keeping, safekeeping, control, management, supervision; guardianship, wardship.
Antonyms: HAPPINESS; NEGLECT; carelessness; INATTENTION.

care *verb she cared about her work | he didn't care what happened* be concerned, be interested, interest oneself, have regard, worry, trouble, bother, mind; *inf.* give a damn, give a hoot, give a rap. **care for 1** *he cares for his wife deeply* love, be fond of, be in love with, cherish, hold dear, treasure. **2** *I don't care for her* like, be fond of, find congenial. **3** *would you care for some tea?* wish, want, desire, fancy, hanker after, long for; *inf.* have a yen for. **4** *care for the children* take care of, look after, mind, watch, tend, attend to, minister to, foster, nurse, provide for.

career *noun* **1** *choose a career* occupation, profession, vocation, calling, employment, job, métier. **2** *watch the career of the political party* course, progress, progression, procedure, passage, path. **3** *stop the horse in mid-career* rush, onrush, run, race, bolt, dash, gallop, impetus.

carefree *adjective* lighthearted, happy-go-lucky, cheerful, cheery, happy, merry, jolly, buoyant, breezy, easygoing, jaunty, frisky, blithe, airy, nonchalant, unworried, untroubled, insouciant; *inf.* upbeat.
Antonyms: ANXIOUS; WORRIED; MISERABLE.

careful *adjective* **1** *be careful crossing the road* cautious, heedful, alert, aware, attentive, watchful, vigilant, wary, on guard, chary, circumspect, prudent, mindful. **2** *be careful of your reputation* mindful, heedful, protective; *be careful about what you say* solicitous, thoughtful, attentive, concerned. **3** *a careful worker* attentive, conscientious, painstaking, meticulous, accurate, precise, scrupulous, punctilious, fastidious. **4** *a careful housekeeper | careful with her money* canny, cautious, thrifty, economical, economic.
Antonyms: CARELESS; INATTENTIVE; EXTRAVAGANT.

careless *adjective* **1** *a careless driver* inattentive, thoughtless, unthinking, forgetful, absentminded, negligent, remiss, irresponsible, slapdash, slipshod, lax, slack; *inf.* sloppy. **2** *a careless piece of work* hasty, cursory, perfunctory, inaccurate, disorganized, slapdash, slipshod; *inf.* sloppy. **3** *a careless remark* unthinking, thoughtless, insensitive, indiscreet, unguard-

ed. **4** *careless of her appearance* negligent, remiss, slapdash, slipshod, untidy, slovenly, slatternly; *inf.* sloppy, messy. **5** *careless rapture* carefree, lighthearted, happy-go-lucky, cheerful, merry, buoyant, blithe, nonchalant. See CAREFREE. **6** *careless elegance* unstudied, artless, casual, nonchalant, informal.
Antonyms: CAREFUL; METICULOUS.

caress *noun a loving caress* touch, stroke, fondle, fondling, pat, embrace, cuddle, hug, nuzzle, kiss.

caress *verb caress her* cuddle, fondle, pet, pat, embrace, hug, nuzzle, kiss; *caress her throat* kiss, touch/stroke lovingly.

caretaker *noun* superintendent, janitor, warden, porter, custodian, keeper, watchman, steward, curator.

cargo *noun* freight, freightage, load, lading, haul, consignment, contents, goods, merchandise, baggage; shipment, shipload, boatload, truckload.

caricature *noun* cartoon, parody, burlesque, mimicry, travesty, distortion, satire, farce, lampoon; *inf.* send-up, takeoff, spoof.

---

caricature
burlesque, lampoon, mimicry, parody, travesty
Skilled writers and artists who want to poke fun at someone or something have a number of weapons at their disposal. An artist might come up with a **caricature**, which is a drawing or written piece that exaggerates its subject's distinguishing features or peculiarities (*the cartoonist's caricature of the presidential candidate*). A **parody** is similar to a caricature in purpose, but is used of written work, or performances that ridicule an author or performer's work by imitating its language and style for comic effect (*a parody of the scene between Romeo and Juliet*). While a *parody* concentrates on distorting the content of the original work, a **travesty** retains the subject matter but imitates the style in a grotesque or absurd way (*their version of the Greek tragedy was a travesty*). A **lampoon** is a strongly satirical piece of writing that attacks or ridicules an individual or an institution; it is more commonly used as a verb (*to lampoon the government in a local newspaper*). While a *caricature*, a *parody*, and a *travesty* must have an original to imitate, a **burlesque** can be an independent creation or composition; it is a comic or satiric imitation, often a theatrical one, that treats a serious subject lightly or a trivial subject with mock seriousness (*the play was a burlesque of Homer's great epic*). **Mimicry** is something you don't have to be an artist, a writer, or an actor to be good at. Anyone who successfully imitates another person's speech or gestures is a good mimic or impressionist, whether the intent is playful or mocking (*he showed an early talent for*

mimicry; entertaining his parents with imitations of their friends).

caricature verb parody, mimic, mock, ridicule, distort, satirize, lampoon, burlesque; *inf.* send up, take off.

carnage noun slaughter, wholesale slaughter, butchery, massacre, mass murder, mass destruction, indiscriminate bloodshed; blood bath, holocaust, pogrom; *inf.* shambles.

carnal adjective sexual, sensual, fleshly, erotic, lustful, lascivious, libidinous, lecherous, lewd, prurient, salacious, coarse, gross, lubricious.

carnival noun **1** *we are looking forward to the carnival* fiesta, festival, fête, gala, jamboree, holiday; revelry, merrymaking, festivity, celebration; Mardi Gras. **2** *the carnival has moved to another town* fair, sideshows, circus.

carol noun Christmas song, hymn, canticle; *inf.* noel.

carol verb *children caroling loudly* sing carols, go caroling, sing, warble, trill, chant.

carouse verb go on a spree, go on a binge, binge, party, paint the town red, overindulge, live it up, go on a bender.

carp verb complain, faultfind, find fault, criticize, cavil, pick on, quibble, censure, reproach, nag; *inf.* nitpick.
Antonyms: APPLAUD; PRAISE.

carpenter noun joiner, cabinetmaker, woodworker.

carpet noun **1** *the living room carpet* floor covering, wall-to-wall carpeting, runner, rug. **2** *a carpet of leaves* covering, layer, expanse.

carriage noun **1** *carriages of former times* coach, cab; coach-and-four, stagecoach, hackney, hansom, gig, chaise, phaeton, surrey. **2** *an elegant carriage* posture, bearing, stance, deportment, comportment, attitude, manner, presence, air, guise, demeanor, mien, behavior, conduct. **3** *free carriage* transport, transportation, freight, freightage, conveyance, delivery, carrying.

carry verb **1** *carry a parcel* transport, convey, transfer, move, take, bring, bear, lug, haul, shift, fetch; conduct, pass on, transmit, relay. **2** *carry the weight of the column | carry responsibilities* support, sustain, bear, shoulder. **3** *carry the day/victory/motion* win, capture, gain, secure, effect, accomplish. **4** *a store carrying a brand* sell, stock, offer, have for sale, retail. **5** *carrying the latest news* communicate, give, release, publish, broadcast. **6** *carry the audience/crowd* influence, affect, have an effect on, motivate, stimulate, urge, spur on, impel, drive. **7** *carrying themselves well* bear oneself, hold oneself, comport oneself, deport oneself, conduct oneself. **carry on 1** *carry on talking* go on, continue, keep, keep on, persist in, maintain, persevere in. **2** *carry on a business* run, operate, conduct, manage, administer, transact. **3**

he's carrying on with his secretary have an affair, commit adultery; *inf.* fool around. **4** *children carrying on* cause a fuss/commotion; cry, create a scene. **carry out 1** *carry out a promise/threat* fulfill, carry through, achieve, implement, realize, execute, effect, discharge. **2** *carry out an experiment/inquiry* conduct, perform, implement, execute.

cart noun *collect the raked leaves in a cart* handcart, wheelbarrow, pushcart.

cart verb **1** *cart away the trash* transport, convey, haul, transfer, move, shift. **2** *carting the luggage* lug, tote, carry.

carton noun box, package, cardboard box, container, case.

cartoon noun **1** *children's cartoons* comic strip; animated movie; animation. **2** *a political cartoon* caricature, parody, lampoon, satire, burlesque; *inf.* takeoff, send-up, spoof.

cartridge noun case, container, cylinder, capsule, cassette, magazine.

carve verb **1** *carve a figure out of stone* sculpt, sculpture, cut, chisel, hew, whittle, chip, form, shape, fashion, mold. **2** *carve initials on a tree* engrave, etch, notch, cut in, incise. **3** *carve meat* slice, cut up. **carve up** *carve up the territory* divide, partition, parcel out, apportion, dole out, subdivide, split up, separate out.

cascade noun waterfall, falls, fountain, shower, cataract, torrent, flood, deluge, outpouring, avalanche.

cascade verb tumble, descend, pour, gush, surge, spill, overflow.

case^1 noun **1** *a cigarette case* container, box, receptacle, holder, canister. **2** *a case of wine* crate, box, carton; coffer, casket. **3** *bullet case | tape case* casing, covering, sheath, sheathing, wrapper, wrapping, cover, envelope, housing, jacket, capsule, folder. **4** *display case* cabinet, cupboard.

case^2 noun **1** *as has been the case previously stated* position, situation, circumstances, instance, occurrence, happening, occasion, conditions, plight, predicament, event, contingency, phenomenon. **2** *a case of cheating* instance, occurrence, occasion, example, illustration, specimen. **3** *the case comes up next week* lawsuit, suit, action, trial, proceedings, legal proceedings, legal process, legal cause, legal dispute. **4** *his case was that he was elsewhere* statement, plea, claim, alibi, postulation, explanation, exposition, thesis, testing, presentation. **5** *terminal cases* patient, sick person, invalid, sufferer, victim.

cash noun **1** *no cash with me* money, ready money, coinage, notes, bank notes, currency; *fml.* specie, legal tender. **2** *he has no cash of any kind* money, finance, wherewithal, resources, funds, capital, investment capital; *inf.* dough, bread, cabbage.

cash verb *cash the check/bills* exchange, change, turn into cash/money.

cashier noun bank clerk, bank teller, teller,

banker, treasurer, bursar, purser, accountant, controller, comptroller, money man.

cashier *verb* dismiss, discharge, expel, drum out, throw out, cast out, discard, get rid of; *inf.* sack, give the boot to, boot out.

casino *noun* gambling club, gaming club, gambling house, gambling den.

cask *noun* barrel, keg, tun, vat, vessel, hogshead.

casket *noun* 1 *funeral casket* coffin, pall, sarcophagus; *inf.* box. 2 *a jewel casket* box, case, container, receptacle, chest, coffer.

cast *verb* 1 *cast a stone in the lake* throw, toss, fling, pitch, hurl, sling, heave, shy, lob, launch, let fly. 2 *cast their skins/coats* shed, discard, slough off, peel off, throw off, get rid of, let fall, let drop. 3 *cast a glance* shoot, direct, turn, throw, send out. 4 *cast a soft light | cast a shadow* emit, give off, send out, shed, radiate, diffuse, spread out; form, create. 5 *cast doubt* throw, bestow, impart, confer, give, grant. 6 *cast one's vote* register, record, enter, vote. 7 *cast bronze | cast figures in bronze* shape, fashion, form, mold, model, sculpt. 8 *cast actors for the play* choose, select, pick, name, assign, appoint, allot. 9 *cast a fortune* predict, forecast, foretell, foresee, prophesy.

cast *noun* 1 *the cast of the dice* throw, toss, fling, pitch, hurl, lob. *See* CAST *verb* 1. 2 *cast of features/mind* sort, kind, style, type, stamp, nature. 3 *plaster cast* figure, shape, mold, form. 4 *a cast in her eye* squint, twist, defect.

caste *noun* *a member of the upper caste* class, social class, order, social order, grade, grading, station, place, standing, position, status.

castigate *verb* punish, discipline, chastise, rebuke, reproach, scold, reprimand, censure, reprove, upbraid, berate, chide, admonish, criticize, chasten, take to task, dress down, give a dressing-down to, rake over the coals.

castle *noun* stronghold, fortress, keep, hold, citadel, palace, chateau.

casual *adjective* 1 *a casual meeting* chance, accidental, unintentional, unexpected, unforeseen, unanticipated, fortuitous, serendipitous. 2 *a casual remark* offhand, random, impromptu, spontaneous, unpremeditated, unthinking. 3 *casual work* part-time, temporary, irregular. 4 *a casual read* cursory, perfunctory, superficial, desultory, hasty, hurried. 5 *a casual attitude* indifferent, apathetic, uncaring, uninterested, unconcerned, lackadaisical, blasé, nonchalant, lukewarm, insouciant. 6 *casual clothes* informal, not formal, unceremonious, relaxed, leisure; *inf.* sporty. 7 *a casual acquaintance* slight, superficial, shallow.

Antonyms: INTENTIONAL; THOROUGH; FORMAL.

casualties *plural noun* *the casualties of the last war* dead, fatalities, losses, dead and wounded, wounded, injured, missing in action, missing.

casualty *noun* 1 *a war casualty* fatality, dead/wounded/injured person, victim. 2 *the firm was a casualty of the recession* victim, sufferer, loser, loss.

cat *noun* 1 *a cat by the fire* feline, domestic cat; *inf.* pussy, pussy cat, puss; tabby, tomcat, tom, tortoiseshell, Siamese, Burmese, kitten, mouser, alley cat. 2 *the cats of Africa* big cat; lion, tiger, leopard, lynx.

catacombs *plural noun* underground tunnels/labyrinth/maze, tomb, underground cemetery, underground burial ground.

catalog *noun* *a catalog of library books* list, record, register, inventory, directory, index, roll, table, calendar, classification, guide, brochure.

catalog *verb* list, classify, categorize, index, make an inventory of, inventory, record, register, file, alphabetize.

catapult *verb* *he was catapulted to fame/success* launch/propel rapidly, hurtle, shoot, fling.

cataract *noun* 1 *cataracts falling from the rocks* cascade, waterfall, falls, rapids, torrent, downpour. 2 *eye surgeons operate on cataracts* opacity, opaqueness.

catastrophe *noun* disaster, calamity, tragedy, blow, adversity, trouble, trials, mishap, misfortune, mischance, misadventure, failure, reverses, affliction, distress.

catcall *noun* whistle, boo, hiss, jeer; *inf.* raspberry, Bronx cheer.

catch *verb* 1 *catch the ball* grasp, snatch, grab, seize, grip, clutch, clench, pluck, receive, acquire, come into the possession of, intercept. 2 *catch the prisoner* capture, seize, take captive, apprehend, take, arrest, lay hold of, trap, snare; *inf.* nab, collar. 3 *catch what he said* understand, follow, grasp, comprehend, make out, take in, fathom, discern, perceive, apprehend; *inf.* get the drift of, get the hang of. 4 *catch him unawares* surprise, discover, come across, startle, detect. 5 *catch pneumonia* contract, get, become infected with, develop, succumb to, suffer from; *inf.* come down with. 6 *catch his attention/fancy* capture, attract, draw, captivate, bewitch. 7 *catch a likeness* capture, reproduce, represent, photograph, draw, paint.

catch on 1 *sports catching on* become popular, become fashionable, come into fashion/vogue; *inf.* become trendy, become all the rage. 2 *eventually catch on to his intentions* see through, find out, fathom, grasp, understand, comprehend, see the light about; *inf.* figure out, get the picture about.

Antonyms: DROP; RELEASE; LOSE.

catch *noun* 1 *the catch of the door/suitcase* bolt, lock, fastener, fastening, clasp, hasp, hook, clip, latch. 2 *what's the catch?* snag, disadvantage, drawback, stumbling block, hitch, fly in the ointment, trap, trick, snare; *inf.* catch-22. 3 *sell the catch at the fish market* bag, haul, net, take, yield. 4 *he/she is quite a catch* eligible man/woman/person, marriage prospect, suitable husband/wife/spouse.

catching *adjective* 1 *is the disease catching?* contagious, infectious, communicable, transmittable, transmissible. **2** *a catching manner* attractive, appealing, winning, captivating, charming, fetching, taking, fascinating, enchanting, bewitching, alluring.

catchword *noun* slogan, motto, password, watchword, byword, shibboleth, formula, refrain, saying.

catchy *adjective* memorable, popular, appealing, captivating, haunting, melodious, singable.

catechize *verb* interrogate, cross-examine, question, quiz, examine, grill, pump, give the third degree to, put through the third degree.

categorical *adjective* unqualified, unconditional, unequivocal, explicit, unambiguous, unreserved, absolute, direct, downright, emphatic, positive, express, conclusive.

Antonyms: QUALIFIED; EQUIVOCAL; TENTATIVE.

categorize *verb* classify, class, group, grade, order, arrange, sort, rank, break down, catalog, list, tabulate.

category *noun* class, classification, group, grouping, head, heading, list, listing, designation, type, sort, kind, variety, grade, grading, order, rank, status, division, section, department.

cater *verb* *cater for large parties* provide food, feed, provision. **cater to** *cater to their every need* provide, furnish, supply, purvey.

caterwauling *noun* howl, howling, screech, screeching, shriek, shrieking, scream, screaming.

catharsis *noun* purging, purgation, purification, cleansing, depuration, release, emotional release; *Tech.* abreaction.

cathartic *adjective* purgative, purifying, cleansing, release-bringing.

catholic *adjective* **1** *of catholic interest* general, universal, widespread, global, worldwide, all-encompassing, all-embracing, all-inclusive, comprehensive. **2** *catholic tastes/views* wide, broad, broad-based, eclectic, liberal, open-minded, tolerant, unbigoted, unsectarian, ecumenical.

Antonyms: LIMITED; NARROW.

cattle *plural noun* bovines, steer, oxen; stock, livestock.

catty *adjective* *catty remark* spiteful, malicious, venomous, malevolent, nasty, ill-natured, mean.

caucus *noun* **1** *attend a Senate caucus* assembly, meeting, gathering, session, conference, convention, conclave. **2** *a local party caucus* group, party, bloc, faction, cabal, clique, coterie.

cause *noun* **1** *the cause of the fire* | *the cause of her misfortune* origin, root, source, beginning, genesis, occasion, mainspring, originator, author, creator, producer, agent, prime mover, maker. **2** *no cause for alarm* reason, grounds, justification, call, basis, motive, motivation. **3** *devoted to the cause of human rights* principle, ideal, belief, conviction, tenet, object, aim, objective, purpose, *raison d'être*. **4** *plead his cause* case, point of view, contention.

Antonyms: EFFECT; RESULT.

cause *verb* *cause trouble* | *cause the explosion* be the cause of, make happen, bring about, give rise to, begin, create, produce, originate, occasion, generate, effect, engender, lead to, result in, precipitate, provoke.

caustic *adjective* **1** *caustic chemical substances* corrosive, corroding, mordant, burning, acrid, destructive. **2** *a caustic wit* sarcastic, cutting, biting, mordant, stinging, sharp, scathing, trenchant, virulent, acrimonious, astringent.

cauterize *verb* burn, sear, singe, disinfect, sterilize.

caution *noun* **1** *proceed with caution* alertness, care, carefulness, attention, wariness, attentiveness, heed, heedfulness, watchfulness, vigilance, guardedness, circumspection, discretion, forethought, prudence, mindfulness. **2** *her uncle's a caution* comic, comedian, wit, humorist, wag, clown, joker, jester.

caution *verb* **1** *caution against driving fast* | *caution not to go* warn, advise, counsel, urge, admonish. **2** *cautioned by the judge* give/deliver a warning to, admonish, warn, give an injunction to.

cautious *adjective* careful, wary, watchful, shrewd, prudent, circumspect, discreet, guarded, chary, alert, heedful, attentive, vigilant, mindful; *inf.* cagey.

Antonyms: INCAUTIOUS; CARELESS; RECKLESS.

cavalcade *noun* procession, parade, march, column, troop, file, train, caravan, cortège, retinue.

cavalier *noun* **1** *foot soldiers and cavaliers* horseman, horse soldier, mounted soldier, equestrian, knight. **2** *cavaliers at the ball* escort, beau, gallant, gentleman, courtier.

cavalier *adjective* *a cavalier attitude toward his colleagues* offhand, condescending, haughty, arrogant, lofty, lordly, disdainful, supercilious, patronizing, scornful, contemptuous, discourteous, insolent.

cavalry *noun* **1** *infantry and cavalry* mounted troops, horse soldiers, horsemen, horse, troopers; light cavalry, heavy cavalry, dragoons, lancers. **2** *the cavalry arrived just as we were going bankrupt* timely/fortuitous help, help, aid.

cave *noun* cavern, grotto, hollow, cavity, underground chamber, tunnel, cellar, dugout, den.

caveat *noun* warning, caution, admonition, monition; *inf.* red flag.

caveman *noun* *cavemen and their stone tools* primitive man, prehistoric man, primordial man, Stone Age man, paleolithic man, Neanderthal man.

caveman *adjective* *women resenting caveman tactics* primitive, uncivilized, crude, brutal, savage; masterful, domineering, autocratic.

cavern *noun* large cave, cave, grotto, hollow. *See* 95 CAVE.

cavernous *adjective* *cavernous depths/eyes* large, huge, deep, hollow, sunken, yawning, unfathomable, dark.

cavil *verb* carp, find fault, quibble, complain, criticize, censure, object, make objections; *inf.* nitpick.

cavity *noun* hole, hollow, crater, pit, orifice, aperture, gap, dent.

cease *verb* 1 *cease working* stop, discontinue, desist, desist from, end, finish, leave off, quit, conclude, terminate, suspend, bring to a halt, bring to an end, break off. 2 *the rain ceased* stop, halt, finish, come to a stop, come to an end, let up, die away, abate, terminate. *Antonyms:* START; BEGIN; COMMENCE.

cease *adverb* **without cease** continuously, incessantly, unendingly, unremittingly, without cessation/stopping/letup, without a pause/break, on and on. *See* CESSATION.

ceaseless *adjective* incessant, unceasing, unending, endless, never-ending, interminable, nonstop, constant, continuous, continual, uninterrupted, eternal, perpetual, unremitting, persistent.

cede *verb* yield, surrender, concede; abdicate, resign, hand over; relinquish, renounce, forsake, abandon, make over, turn over, transfer, deliver up, grant, give, bequeath. *Antonyms:* RETAIN; KEEP.

ceiling *noun* 1 *the ceiling of the building* overhead, upper side, roof. 2 *a ceiling on prices* limit, upper limit, maximum, summit, pinnacle.

celebrate *verb* 1 *celebrate their anniversary* commemorate, observe, honor, mark, keep, drink to, toast. 2 *celebrate after the exams* rejoice, enjoy oneself, party, paint the town; *inf.* go on a spree, go out on the town, whoop it up. 3 *celebrate his achievement* proclaim, make known, herald, announce, publicize, broadcast, advertise. 4 *a poem celebrating the joys of love* praise, laud, extol, glorify, exalt, eulogize, reverence. 5 *celebrate a religious ceremony* perform, solemnize, ceremonialize.

celebrated *adjective* famous, famed, notable, noted, renowned, well-known, popular, prominent, distinguished, great, eminent, preeminent, outstanding, illustrious, acclaimed, revered, glorious, legendary, lionized. *Antonyms:* UNKNOWN; OBSCURE; UNSUNG.

celebration *noun* 1 *the celebration of his birthday* | *anniversary celebrations* commemoration, observance, honoring, keeping, remembrance. 2 *having a celebration* party, carousal, festival, fête, carnival, gala; festivity, merrymaking, revelry; *inf.* spree, binge, bash. 3 *celebration of a religious ceremony* performance, solemnization.

celebrity *noun* 1 *celebrities at a charity ball* VIP, famous person, dignitary, big name, name, personality, star, superstar, lion, notable, luminary, personage; *inf.* bigwig, big shot, big wheel. 2 *his celebrity spread far* fame, renown,

notability, popularity, reputation, honor, prominence, prestige, distinction, eminence, preeminence, glory, illustriousness, stardom. *Antonyms:* NONENTITY; OBSCURITY.

celestial *adjective* 1 *celestial beings* heavenly, divine, godly, godlike, ethereal, sublime, paradisiacal, elysian, spiritual, immortal, angelic, seraphic, cherubic. 2 *celestial bodies/navigation* heavenly, astronomical, extraterrestrial, stellar, of the sky/heavens.

celibacy *noun* chastity, singleness, abstinence, self-denial, self-restraint, continence, abnegation, asceticism, virginity, bachelorhood, spinsterhood, monkhood, nunhood, monasticism; *inf.* single blessedness. *Antonyms:* MARRIAGE; PROMISCUITY.

cell *noun* 1 *a prison/monastic cell* cubicle, room, apartment, compartment, chamber, stall, enclosure, dungeon, lockup. 2 *honeycomb cells* compartment, cavity, hole. 3 *a political cell* faction, caucus, nucleus, clique, coterie, group, party, unit.

cement *noun* adhesive, bonding, binder, glue, superglue, gum, paste.

cement *verb* bind, bond, stick, join, unite, attach, cohere, combine, affix, glue, gum, paste, solder, weld.

cemetery *noun* graveyard, burial ground, burial place, churchyard.

censor *verb* *censor letters* | *censor the play* cut, delete, delete from, make cuts/changes to, blue-pencil, expurgate, bowdlerize.

censor *noun* *the movie censor* examiner, inspector, expurgator, bowdlerizer.

censorious *adjective* faultfinding, critical, disapproving, condemnatory, reproachful, censuring.

censure *verb* *censure him for his behavior* criticize, condemn, blame, castigate, denounce, disapprove of, berate, upbraid, reprove, reproach, rebuke, reprimand, scold, chide, reprehend. *Antonyms:* PRAISE; APPROVE; COMMEND.

censure *noun* *open to public censure* | *a vote of censure* criticism, condemnation, blame, castigation, denunciation, disapproval, berating, upbraiding, reproval, reproof, reproach, rebuke, reprimand, scolding, chiding, reprehension.

center *noun* *the center of the town* middle, middle point, midpoint, nucleus, heart, core, hub, focus, focal point. *Antonyms:* EDGE; PERIPHERY; OUTSKIRTS.

center *verb* *her interests center on basketball* concentrate, focus, pivot, converge, close in.

central *adjective* 1 *a central position* middle, mid, median, mean. 2 *central Chicago* middle, mid, inner, interior. 3 *a central issue* main, chief, principal, foremost, fundamental, basic, key, essential, primary, pivotal, focal, core, cardinal.

Antonyms: OUTER; SUBORDINATE; MINOR.

centralize *verb centralize the administration* concentrate, center, concenter, consolidate, amalgamate, condense, compact, unify, incorporate, streamline, focus, rationalize.

ceramics *plural noun* pottery, earthenware, clay pots, crocks.

cereal *noun* 1 *farmers growing cereals* grain; corn, wheat, rye, oats, barley. 2 *she ate her cereal* cornflakes, oatmeal, raisin bran, shredded wheat, muesli.

ceremonial *adjective ceremonial occasion/dress* formal, ritual, ritualistic, stately, solemn, dignified, celebratory, sacramental, liturgical.

ceremonial *noun the ceremonial of coronations* ceremony, rite, ritual, formality, custom, solemnity, sacrament, liturgy.

ceremonious *adjective* 1 *a ceremonious occasion* ceremonial, formal, ritual. *See* CEREMONIAL *adjective*. 2 *behave in a ceremonious manner* formal, punctilious, precise, scrupulous, stately, courtly, courteous, civil, deferential, stiff, rigid, affected; *inf.* just-so.

ceremony *noun* 1 *a wedding ceremony* rite, service, formality, observance, function, custom, sacrament, show. *See* CEREMONIAL *noun*. 2 *conducted with ceremony* formalities, niceties, pomp, protocol, decorum, etiquette, propriety, conventionality, attention to detail; *inf.* fuss.

certain *adjective* 1 *I'm certain he's guilty* sure, positive, confident, convinced, assured, unwavering, unshaken, secure, satisfied, persuaded. 2 *her success/failure is certain* sure, assured, destined, fated, inevitable, reliable, inescapable, bound to happen, inexorable; *inf.* in the bag. 3 *it is certain that he will go* sure, definite, unquestionable, beyond question, indubitable, undeniable, irrefutable, incontrovertible, incontestable, obvious, evident, plain, clear, conclusive. 4 *no certain cure* | *a certain sign* sure, definite, assured, unfailing, unquestionable, undisputed, dependable, reliable, trustworthy, sound, foolproof; *inf.* sure-fire. 5 *there is no certain date yet* definite, decided, settled, fixed, established, determined. 6 *a certain lady/place that will remain anonymous* particular, specific, individual, special, especial, precise. 7 *to a certain extent* indeterminate, moderate, minimum.

Antonyms: UNCERTAIN; UNSURE; INDEFINITE.

certainly *adverb* 1 *he will certainly die* surely, definitely, assuredly, undoubtedly, undeniably, obviously, plainly, clearly. *See* CERTAIN 3. 2 *certainly, he'll be there* yes, of course, by all means.

certainty *noun* 1 *I cannot say with certainty* sureness, assuredness, positiveness, confidence, conviction, reliability, validity, conclusiveness, authoritativeness, truth, fact, factualness. 2 *it's a certainty that they will lose* inevitability, indubitability, inescapability, fact; *inf.* sure

thing, cinch. 3 *that horse is a certainty* certain winner, certain happening; *inf.* sure-fire winner, cinch.

Antonyms: UNCERTAINTY; DOUBT.

certificate *noun* certification, document, authorization, credentials, testimonial, warrant, license, voucher, diploma.

certify *verb* 1 *a document certifying their marriage* testify to, attest, corroborate, substantiate, verify, confirm, endorse, validate, vouch for, guarantee, authenticate, document, bear witness to, ratify, warrant; *certified dead* verified as, confirmed as, officially declared. 2 *she has been certified to teach* give a certificate/diploma, recognize, accredit, license, authorize, qualify.

cessation *noun* end, termination, finish, conclusion, pause, break, respite, letup; ceasing, stopping, halting, ending, finishing.

chafe *verb* 1 *his neck chafed by his shirt* rub, abrade, graze, excoriate, scrape, scratch, rasp. 2 *fabric chafed by the rock* wear, wear away/down, wear out, wear to shreds, fray, tatter, erode. 3 *the passengers were chafed by the delay* annoy, anger, irritate, exasperate, infuriate, enrage, incense, inflame, provoke, vex, worry, peeve, irk, ruffle. 4 *passengers chafing at the delay* be impatient, be angry/annoyed/irritated/exasperated, fret, fume.

chaff *noun* 1 *chaff from the grain* husks, hulls, pods, shells, cases, casing. 2 *chaff for the cattle* straw, hay, fodder, silage. 3 *throw away the chaff* | *separate the chaff from the wheat* rubbish, refuse, waste, garbage, trash, dregs, remains, debris, junk, dross, detritus. 4 *the chaff of her classmates* | *the chaff of the comedian* banter, bantering, joking, jesting, badinage, raillery, teasing, joshing, humor, wit, repartee; *inf.* kidding, ragging, wisecracking, ribbing.

chaff *verb chaffing his sister* banter, tease, josh; *inf.* kid, rag, rib.

chagrin *noun feeling chagrin at their treatment* annoyance, anger, irritation, vexation, displeasure, worry, dissatisfaction, resentment, rankling, smarting, discomposure, discomfiture, disquiet, fretfulness, embarrassment, mortification, humiliation, shame.

chagrin *verb chagrined by their treatment* annoy, anger, enrage, irritate, vex, displease, worry, peeve, irk, chafe, fret, dissatisfy, discompose, discomfit, disquiet, embarrass, mortify, humiliate, shame. *See* CHAGRIN *noun*.

chain *noun* 1 *a chain of events* series, succession, string, sequence, train, progression, course, set, cycle, line, row, concatenation. 2 *a chain of stores* group; firm, company.

chain *verb chain the dog to the wall* fasten, secure, tie, bind, tether, shackle, fetter, manacle, hitch, moor, handcuff, confine, restrain, trammel, gird, imprison.

chains *plural noun prisoners in chains* bonds, fetters, shackles, manacles, trammels.

chair *noun* 1 *tables and chairs* seat; armchair, easy chair, rocking chair, wing chair, swivel chair, wheelchair, stool, bench, pew, stall, throne. **2** *a university chair* professorship, professorate, headship. **3** *elected chair of the society* chairperson, chairman, chairwoman, president, spokesperson, spokesman, spokeswoman, MC, master/mistress of ceremonies. **the chair** *sent to the chair* the electric chair; electrocution, execution; *inf.* the hot seat.

chair *verb chair the meeting* preside over, lead, direct, manage, control, oversee, supervise.

chalk *verb* **chalk up 1** *chalk it up to experience* put down, ascribe, attribute, accredit, impute, charge. **2** *chalk up the score* record, register, enter, mark, log, score.

chalky *adjective* white, pale, wan, pallid, ashen, pasty, waxen, blanched, bleached, colorless.

challenge *noun* **1** *accept a sporting challenge* summons, call, invitation, bidding. **2** *a new challenge in his life* difficult task/venture, hazard, risk, obstacle. **challenge to** *a challenge to tradition* | *a challenge to the government* questioning of, interrogation of, stand against, countercharge, ultimatum against; opposition to, defiance of, confrontation with.

challenge *verb* **1** *challenge someone to a competition* dare, summon, invite, bid, throw down the gauntlet to. **2** *challenge their authority* question, call into question, dispute, protest against, take exception to, object to, disagree with, demur against, be a dissenter of. **3** *the job really challenges him* test, tax, stimulate, arouse, inspire, excite, spur on.

chamber *noun* **1** *the judge's chambers* room, apartment, compartment, cubicle, hall. **2** *the princess retiring to her chamber* room, bedroom, bedchamber, boudoir. **3** *the chambers in the caves/heart* compartment, cavity, hollow, cell. **4** *the upper chamber of the government* legislative body, legislature, assembly, council, house.

champion *noun* **1** *the champion of the competition* winner, title-holder, victor, conqueror, hero. **2** *the champion of the cause* defender, protector, upholder, supporter, advocate, backer, patron; *inf.* angel. **3** *champions returning from their conquests* knight, paladin, hero, warrior.

champion *verb* *champion the cause* defend, protect, uphold, support, stand up for, fight for, speak for, advocate, back, promote, espouse.

chance *noun* **1** *meet by chance* accident, coincidence, fortuity, serendipity, fate, destiny, fortune, luck, providence. **2** *a good chance that he'll win* prospect, possibility, probability, likelihood, likeliness, conceivability, odds. **3** *to get a second chance* opportunity, opening, occasion, turn, time; *inf.* shot. **4** *take a chance and run* risk, gamble, hazard, venture, speculation, long shot. *Antonyms:* DESIGN; CERTAINTY.

chance *verb* **1** *it chanced that they arrived last* happen, occur, take place, come about, come to pass, befall, turn up, crop up. **2** *have to chance it* risk, hazard, gamble, venture, specu-

late, take a chance that, try one's luck, take a leap in the dark. **chance on/upon** *chance upon an old friend* | *chanced on the answer* come across, meet, stumble on, come upon, encounter; *inf.* bump into, run into.

chance *adjective* *a chance meeting/discovery* accidental, unexpected, unanticipated, unforeseen, unforeseeable, unlooked-for, unintended, unintentional, unpremeditated, unplanned, fortuitous, serendipitous.

chancy *adjective* risky, uncertain, hazardous, speculative, perilous, dangerous; *inf.* dicey, iffy.

change *verb* **1** *change one's attitude/plans* alter, modify, transform, convert, vary, remodel, recast, restyle, reconstruct, reorder, reorganize, metamorphose, transmute, permutate, permute. **2** *she's changed* | *the world's changed* alter, be transformed, move on, evolve, metamorphose, fluctuate, diversify; *inf.* do an aboutface, do a U-turn. **3** *change jobs/sides* | *change a pair of pants* exchange, interchange, substitute, switch, replace, trade, barter; *inf.* swap. *Antonyms:* RETAIN; STAY.

change *noun* **1** *a change in attitude/plan* difference, alteration, modification, transformation, conversion, variation, remodeling, reconstruction, reorganization, transition, innovation, metamorphosis, transfiguration, vicissitude, transmutation, mutation, permutation; *inf.* about-turn, U-turn. *See* CHANGE *verb* 1. **2** *a change of jobs* exchange, interchange, substitution, switch, trade, bartering; *inf.* swap. **3** *he's tired and needs a change* diversion, variation, variety; *inf.* break. **4** *have no change* coins, coinage, cash, silver, petty cash. *Antonyms:* ENDURANCE; STABILITY.

changeable *adjective* **1** *of changeable moods* | *changeable weather* changing, variable, varying, changeful, chameleonlike, chameleonic, protean, shifting, vacillating, volatile, mercurial, capricious, fluctuating, fluctuant, fluid, kaleidoscopic, fitful, wavering, unstable, unsteady, unsettled, irregular, erratic, unreliable, inconstant, fickle, mutable, unpredictable, manyfaceted, checkered, vicissitudinous. **2** *changeable structures/laws* alterable, modifiable, convertible, mutable, permutable. *Antonyms:* UNCHANGEABLE; CONSTANT; INVARIABLE.

channel *noun* **1** *the channel connecting the seas* passage, sea passage, strait, neck, narrows, waterway, watercourse, fiord. **2** *the channel of the canal* bed, floor, bottom, depths. **3** *rainwater running through the channels* gutter, groove, furrow, conduit, duct, culvert, ditch. **4** *new channels for their energy* course, way, direction, path, route, approach. **5** *channels of communication* means, medium, agency, vehicle, route.

channel *verb* **1** *grooves channeling the rock* furrow, groove, flute, hollow out, cut. **2**

channeling water/energies transmit, convey, transport, conduct, direct, guide.

chant noun *a religious chant* | *a victory chant* song, singing, chorus, melody, ditty, carol, psalm.

chant verb **1** *chant the liturgy* sing, recite, intone, cantillate. **2** *football fans chanting* shout, sing, chorus, carol.

chaos noun disorder, confusion, pandemonium, bedlam, tumult, upset, upheaval, disorganization, uproar, disruption, disarray, anarchy, lawlessness, riot.
Antonyms: ORDER; TRANQUILLITY.

chaotic adjective in chaos, disordered, confused, tumultuous, upset, disorganized, jumbled, topsy-turvy, askew, awry, disrupted, in disarray, anarchic, lawless, orderless.
Antonyms: ORDERLY; ordered.

chap verb *wind having chapped her hands* roughen, make raw, crack, make sore, redden, chafe.

chaperon, chaperone noun *the young lady's chaperon* companion, duenna, escort.

chaperon, chaperone verb *chaperoning the girls to/at the ball* accompany, escort, attend, watch over, take care of, keep an eye on, protect, guard, safeguard.

chapter noun **1** *the next chapter in the book* division, section, part, portion, episode. **2** *a tragic chapter in the club's history* period, time, phase, stage, episode. **3** *chapter of the cathedral* council, assembly, convocation, convention, synod. **4** *a chapter of the society* branch, section, division, wing, offshoot, lodge.

char verb *char the paper* scorch, singe, sear, toast, carbonize, cauterize.

character noun **1** *her character's changed* | *the character of the town has altered* personality, nature, disposition, temperament, temper; essential quality, ethos, individuality, complexion, constitution, makeup, cast, attributes, bent, genius. **2** *a person of character* moral strength/fiber, strength, honor, integrity, rectitude, uprightness, fortitude, backbone. **3** *damage his character* reputation, name, standing, position, status. **4** *he's one of our local characters* eccentric, oddity, original, individual; *inf.* oddball, queer fish, card. **5** *they're all friendly characters* person, individual, human being, fellow; *inf.* guy, sort, type, customer. **6** *characters in Austen's novels* persona, person, portrayal, representation, role, part. **7** *in bold characters* | *Chinese characters* letter, sign, mark, symbol, type, cipher, hieroglyph, figure, device, rune, logo, emblem.

characteristic noun *one of her appealing/annoying characteristics* quality, essential quality, attribute, feature, trait, property, mannerism, mark, trade mark, idiosyncrasy, peculiarity, quirk.

characteristic adjective *their characteristic modesty* typical, distinguishing, distinctive, particular, special, individual, specific, peculiar, idiosyncratic, singular, representative, symbolic, symptomatic, diagnostic.
Antonyms: uncharacteristic; untypical; UNUSUAL.

characterize verb **1** *the landscape is characterized by hills and rivers* typify, distinguish, identify, specify, signalize, indicate, denote, designate, mark, stamp, brand, label. **2** *the playwright characterizing the heroine as hysterical* portray, depict, present, represent, describe.

charade noun pretense, travesty, fake, farce, parody, pantomime.

charge verb **1** *what do you charge for a room?* ask in payment, ask, fix a charge/price, expect, impose, levy. **2** *charge it to my account* debit, put down to, bill. **3** *charge the murder suspect* accuse, indict, arraign, impeach, impute, blame, incriminate. **4** *charge the enemy* attack, storm, assault, rush, open fire on, fall on; *inf.* lay into, tear into. **5** *charged with the guardianship of the child* entrust, tax, weigh, weigh down, load, burden, encumber, hamper, saddle. **6** *charge a vessel/gun* fill, fill up, load, load up, pack, plug. **7** *charged with emotion* fill, load, imbue, suffuse, pervade, permeate, infuse, instill.
Antonyms: ABSOLVE; ACQUIT.

charge noun **1** *what is the charge for a room?* cost, price, fee, amount, rate, payment, expense, expenditure, outlay, dues, levy, toll. **2** *murder charge* accusation, allegation, indictment, arraignment, impeachment, citation, imputation, blame, incrimination. **3** *the charge of the cavalry* attack, storming, assault, onrush, onslaught, onset, sortie, incursion. **4** *have charge of the children* responsibility, care, custody, guardianship, trust, protection, safekeeping, surveillance. **5** *your charge is to drive the car* duty, task, job, responsibility, office, obligation, assignment, business, burden. **6** *pay for his charge's education* ward, protégé, dependent, minor. **7** *the judge's charge to the jury* instruction, direction, order, command, dictate, injunction, exhortation, mandate.

charitable adjective **1** *be charitable toward the poor* philanthropic, giving, benevolent, generous, liberal, open-handed, kind, magnanimous, beneficent, bountiful, bounteous, munificent, big-hearted, humane. **2** *a charitable interpretation of the situation* generous, liberal, tolerant, broad-minded, understanding, sympathetic, compassionate, lenient, indulgent, forgiving, kindly, favorable, gracious.
Antonyms: UNCHARITABLE; UNKIND.

charity noun **1** *relying on charity for survival* financial assistance, donations, contributions, handouts, gifts, funding, endowments, financial relief, philanthropy, benefaction. **2** *behave with charity toward fellow human beings* goodwill, compassion, humanity, humanitarianism, kindliness, love, sympathy, tolerance, indulgence, altruism, thoughtfulness, generosity, liberality, benevolence.

charlatan noun quack, sham, fraud, fake, impostor, confidence trickster, confidence man, pretender, cheat, deceiver, swindler; inf. con man, phony.

charm noun **1** the charm of the resort/hostess attractiveness, attraction, appeal, allure, allurement, fascination, captivation, pleasingness, desirability, engagingness, delightfulness. **2** captivated by her charms attractiveness, appeal, allure, beauty, wiles, blandishments. **3** the sorcerer's charm spell, magic formula, magic word, abracadabra; sorcery, magic. **4** the charms on her bracelet trinket, ornament, bauble, souvenir. **5** wear/carry a lucky charm good-luck charm, token, amulet, talisman, fetish.

charm verb charmed by the little girl | charmed by the music delight, please, attract, win, win over, captivate, allure, lure, draw, fascinate, bewitch, beguile, enchant, enrapture, enamor, seduce, cajole, hypnotize, mesmerize. **Antonyms:** REPEL; ALIENATE.

charming adjective delightful, pleasing, pleasant, appealing, attractive, winning, fetching, taking, captivating, winsome, engaging, lovely, agreeable, alluring, fascinating, bewitching, beguiling, enchanting, delectable, irresistible, seductive. **Antonyms:** DISGUSTING; REPULSIVE.

chart noun plot it out on a chart graph, table, map, diagram, plan, blueprint, guide, scheme, tabulation.

chart verb **1** chart the results tabulate, map, map out, plot, graph, delineate, diagram, sketch, chart a course of, draft. **2** chart their progress follow, record, register, note.

charter noun **1** privileges granted by royal charter authority, authorization, sanction, warrant, document, covenant, deed, bond, permit, prerogative, privilege, right. **2** the charter of the United Nations constitution, code, canon, body of laws; principles, rules, laws. **3** the charter of a boat hiring, leasing, renting, engaging. **4** have a charter to run a ferry permit, license, warrant, concession, franchise, indenture.

chary adjective cautious, wary, leery, careful, circumspect, watchful, distrustful, apprehensive. **Antonyms:** HEEDLESS; TRUSTFUL; unwary.

chase verb dogs chasing rabbits | police chasing after burglars give chase to, pursue, run after, follow, hunt, hound, track, trail, tail. **chase away** chase away the intruder/blues put to flight, drive away, send away, send packing.

chase noun take part in the chase pursuit, hunt, trail; hunting.

chasm noun **1** a landscape full of chasms gorge, abyss, canyon, ravine, pit, crater, crevasse, hole, hollow, opening, gap, fissure, crevice, cleft, rift, rent. **2** a chasm between their points of view schism, breach, gulf, rift; separation, alienation.

chassis noun framework, frame, skeleton, substructure.

chaste adjective **1** a chaste young woman | nuns leading a chaste life virgin, virginal, vestal, celibate, abstinent, self-restrained, unmarried. **2** chaste conduct/speech virtuous, good, innocent, pure, decent, moral, decorous, modest, wholesome, righteous, upright, uncorrupted, incorrupt, uncontaminated, undefiled, unsullied. **3** a chaste style simple, plain, unadorned, unembellished, unaffected, unpretentious, austere, restrained. **Antonyms:** PROMISCUOUS; IMMORAL.

chasten verb **1** chastened by the experience subdue, restrain, tame, curb, check, humble, cow, tone down. **2** chasten the pupils discipline, punish, penalize, castigate, scold, upbraid, reprimand, reprove, chide, take to task, rake over the coals.

chastise verb **1** mutineers chastising their harsh captain punish, discipline, castigate, beat, thrash, smack, flog, whip, strap, cane, lash, scourge; inf. wallop, thump, tan one's hide. **2** the staff were chastised for arriving late scold, upbraid, reprimand, reprove, chide, take to task, haul over the coals, chasten, castigate. **Antonyms:** PRAISE; REWARD.

chastity noun **1** nuns taking vows of chastity chasteness, virginity, celibacy, abstinence, self-restraint, self-denial, continence, singleness, unmarried state; virtue, immaculateness. **2** chastity of conduct/speech virtue, goodness, innocence, purity, decency, morality, decorum, modesty, wholesomeness, righteousness. See CHASTE 2. **3** chastity of style simplicity, plainness, unpretentiousness, austerity. See CHASTE 3. **Antonyms:** PROMISCUITY; IMMORALITY.

chat verb chat with her colleagues talk, gossip, chatter, have a conversation, converse, prattle, jabber, prate; inf. have a confab, jaw, chew the fat with, rap.

chat noun have a chat with talk, gossip, conversation, chatter, heart-to-heart, tête-à-tête; inf. confab.

chatter verb children chattering in groups chat, gossip, jabber, prattle, babble. See CHAT verb.

chatter noun tired of the children's/local chatter talk, gossip, chit-chat, jabber, prattling, babbling, chin-wagging. See CHAT noun.

chatterbox noun gossiper, jabberer, babbler; inf. windbag.

chatty adjective **1** a chatty person talkative, gossipy, gossiping, garrulous, loquacious, voluble, glib, effusive, gushing. **2** a chatty style informal, conversational, colloquial, gossipy, familiar, friendly, lively. **Antonyms:** TACITURN; FORMAL.

chauvinism noun jingoism, partisanship, excessive loyalty, prejudice, bias.

cheap adjective **1** cheap prices/housing inexpensive, low-priced, low-cost, economical, reasonable, moderately priced, bargain, economy, sale, reduced, marked-down, slashed,

discounted; *inf.* bargain-basement. **2** *cheap and gaudy jewelry* poor-quality, inferior, shoddy, common, trashy, tawdry, paltry, worthless, second-rate, gimcrack; *inf.* tacky. **3** *a cheap joke* despicable, contemptible, low, base, unpleasant, mean, sordid, vulgar. **4** *he felt so cheap after what he had done* ashamed, shameful, embarrassed, humiliated, mortified, debased, degraded, abashed, discomfited, disconcerted. **5** *he's too cheap to buy a raffle ticket* mean, stingy, parsimonious, tight-fisted, niggardly, money-grubbing, penny-pinching, frugal, sparing.
Antonyms: EXPENSIVE; HIGH-CLASS; ADMIRABLE.

cheapen *verb* **1** *cheapen the cost of travel* lower, reduce, cut, mark down, slash, discount, depreciate. **2** *cheapening herself by working in that club* degrade, debase, demean, devalue, lower, belittle, denigrate, discredit, depreciate, derogate.

cheat *verb* **1** *cheat his partner* | *cheated into giving him money* deceive, trick, swindle, defraud, dupe, hoodwink, double-cross, gull; exploit, take advantage of, victimize; *inf.* con, bamboozle, finagle, bilk; rip off, fleece, take for a ride. **2** *cheat the bad weather* | *cheat death* avoid, elude, evade, dodge, escape, steer clear of, shun, eschew. **3** *husbands and wives cheating* be unfaithful, commit adultery; *inf.* two-time.

cheat *noun* **1** *a cheat at card games* | *a cheat for a business partner* cheater, swindler, fraud, confidence man/woman, trickster, deceiver, double-crosser, crook, rogue, shark, charlatan; *inf.* con man. **2** *win by a cheat* swindle, fraud, deception, deceit, trick, trickery, imposture, artifice; *inf.* con.

check *verb* **1** *luggage checked at the airport* | *checking the roof for holes* examine, inspect, look at, look over, scrutinize, test, monitor, investigate, probe, study; *inf.* give the once-over to. **2** *check that the door's locked* confirm, make sure, verify, corroborate, validate, substantiate. **3** *check the disease* | *runaway horse* stop, arrest, halt, bring to a standstill, slow down, brake, bar, obstruct, impede, block, retard, curb, delay. **4** *check one's laughter/tears* restrain, suppress, repress, contain, control, bridle, inhibit; *inf.* nip in the bud. **5** *their stories don't check* correspond, agree, tally, dovetail, harmonize. **check up on** *check up on his background* investigate, examine, inspect, research, scrutinize, probe, inquire into.
Antonyms: NEGLECT; IGNORE; START; RELEASE.

check *noun* **1** *a luggage check* examination, inspection, scrutiny, scrutinization, test, monitoring, investigation, probe, inquiry, study; *inf.* once-over. **2** *make a check that you have everything* confirmation, verification, corroboration. *See* CHECK *verb* 2. **3** *a check in the production rate* stop, stopping, stoppage, arrest, halt, slowing-down, braking, obstruction, retarda-

tion, delay. *See* CHECK *verb* 3. **4** *act as a check to the riot/celebration* restraint, constraint, control, deterrent, hindrance, impediment, obstruction, inhibition, limitation, curb. **5** *the customer asked for his check* bill, account, invoice, reckoning, tally; *inf.* tab.

checkered *adjective* *a checkered career* mixed, varied, diverse, diversified, eventful; full of ups and downs.

checkmate *noun* *the checkmate of the chess player's king* | *the checkmate of enemy forces* defeat, beating, overthrow, rout, conquest, vanquishment, trouncing, drubbing.

checkmate *verb* *checkmate his king* | *checkmate the opposing army* defeat, beat, overthrow, rout, vanquish, trounce, give a drubbing to.

checkup *noun* *a checkup from the doctor* | *giving the car a checkup* examination, inspection, appraisal, assessment, analysis, scrutinization, scrutiny, exploration, probe.

cheek *noun* **1** jowl, chop, gill. **2** *have the cheek to appear* impudence, audacity, temerity, brazenness, effrontery, nerve, impertinence, insolence; *inf.* gall.

cheeky *adjective* impudent, audacious, impertinent, insolent, forward, pert, disrespectful, fresh, insulting; *inf.* saucy, sassy.

cheep *verb* chirp, chirrup, twitter, tweet, warble, trill, chatter.

cheer *verb* **1** *crowds cheering the president* hail, acclaim, hurrah, hurray, applaud, shout at, clap for. **2** *his arrival cheered her* raise the spirits of, brighten, buoy up, perk up, enliven, animate, elate, exhilarate, hearten, uplift, give a lift to, gladden, encourage, incite, stimulate, arouse, comfort, solace, console, inspirit; *inf.* buck up. **cheer up 1** *his arrival cheered her up* raise the spirits of. *See* CHEER *verb* 2. **2** *she cheered up on his arrival* brighten, perk up, liven up, rally; *inf.* buck up.
Antonyms: DERIDE; DISCOURAGE; SADDEN.

cheer *noun* **1** *the cheers of the crowd* acclaim, acclamation, hurrah, hurray, applause, ovation, plaudit, hailing, shout, shouting, clapping. **2** *Christmas is a time of cheer* cheerfulness, gladness, happiness, merriment, mirth, gaiety, joy, pleasure, blitheness, jubilation, high spirits, animation, buoyancy, lightheartedness, glee, optimism, hopefulness, merrymaking, rejoicing, revelry, festivity. **3** *tables laden with Christmas cheer* fare, food, provisions, foodstuffs, drink; *inf.* eats.

cheerful *adjective* **1** *a cheerful mood/disposition* happy, bright, merry, glad, gladsome, gay, sunny, joyful, jolly, blithe, animated, buoyant, lighthearted, sparkling, gleeful, carefree, happy-go-lucky, breezy, cheery, sprightly, jaunty, smiling, laughing, bright-eyed and bushy-tailed, optimistic, hopeful, positive; in good spirits; *inf.* peppy, chipper. **2** *a cheerful room/color* bright, sunny, cheering, pleasant, agreeable, friendly, happy. **3** *his cheerful acceptance of the situation* willing, obliging, cooper-

ative, compliant, complying, acquiescent, agreeing, assenting.
Antonyms: SAD; CHEERLESS; DULL; UNWILLING.

cheerless *adjective* gloomy, dreary, miserable, dull, depressing, dismal, bleak, drab, grim, austere, desolate, dark, dingy, somber, uninviting, comfortless, forlorn.
Antonyms: CHEERFUL; HAPPY; BRIGHT.

cheers *interjection* here's to you, good luck, here's to your health, *skol, prosit; inf.* here's mud in your eye, bottoms up, down the hatch.

cheery *adjective* cheerful, happy, merry, glad; in good spirits. *See* CHEERFUL 1.

chef *noun* cook, cordon bleu cook, baker, pastry chef, sous chef.

cherish *verb* **1** *cherish his loved one* care for, treasure, prize, hold dear, love, dote on, adore, idolize, revere, indulge. **2** *cherish the plants/orphans* care for, look after, tend, protect, preserve, shelter, support, nurture, foster. **3** *cherish hopes* have, entertain, harbor, cling to, foster, nurture.
Antonyms: ABANDON; NEGLECT.

cherub *noun* **1** *heavenly cherub* angel, seraph. **2** *cherubs in the baby contest* baby, babe, infant, innocent child, pretty child, lovable child, well-behaved child.

chest *noun* **1** *injured her chest* thorax, breast, sternum. **2** *pack his belongings in chests* box, crate, case, trunk, container, coffer, casket.

chew *verb* *chew one's food* masticate, munch, champ, crunch, bite, gnaw, grind. **chew over** meditate on, ruminate on, mull over, consider, weigh up, ponder on, deliberate upon, reflect upon, muse upon, cogitate about.

chic *adjective* stylish, fashionable, smart, elegant, modish, voguish; *inf.* trendy, dressy, snazzy.
Antonyms: UNFASHIONABLE; INELEGANT.

chicanery *noun* misleading talk, fraud, fraudulence, deception, deceitfulness, duplicity, guile, cheating, duping, hoodwinking, dishonesty, subterfuge, craftiness, wiles, sophistry.

chide *verb* scold, upbraid, rebuke, reprimand, reproach, admonish, lecture, call to account, take to task, berate, castigate; *inf.* give adressing-down to.
Antonyms: PRAISE; LAUD; EXTOL.

chief *noun* **1** *the chief of the tribe/village* head, headman, leader, chieftain, ruler, overlord, lord and master, commander, sachem. **2** *the chief of the firm* head, principal, leader, director, chairman, chairperson, chief executive, manager, superintendent, master, foreman; *inf.* boss, bossman, gaffer, kingpin, top dog, big cheese, Mr. Big.

chief *adjective* **1** *chief priest* supreme, head, foremost, principal, highest, leading, grand, superior, premier, directing, governing. **2** *the chief point* main, principal, most important, uppermost, primary, prime, cardinal, central, key, vital, essential, predominant, preeminent.
Antonyms: MINOR; SUBORDINATE.

chiefly *adverb* mainly, in the main, principally,

primarily, predominantly, especially, particularly, essentially, mostly, for the most part, on the whole, above all.

child *noun* **1** *two adults and a child* youngster, young person, young one, little one, boy, girl, baby, babe, infant, toddler, tot, tiny tot, adolescent, youth, juvenile, minor; *derog.* brat; *inf.* kid, nipper, shaver. **2** *parents and their children* offspring, progeny, issue; descendant, scion; son, daughter.

childbirth *noun* labor, parturition, delivery, accouchement; *archaic* confinement, lying-in, travail.

childhood *noun* youth, infancy, babyhood, preteens, minority, immaturity; boyhood, girlhood.

childish *adjective* **1** *the childish behavior of the adults* immature, infantile, juvenile, puerile, silly, foolish, irresponsible, jejune. **2** *childish laughter* children's, childlike, youthful; boyish, girlish.
Antonyms: ADULT; MATURE.

childlike *adjective* **1** *childlike activities* children's, youthful. **2** *childlike reactions/innocence* ingenuous, innocent, artless, guileless, simple, naïve, trusting, trustful, credulous, gullible.

chill *noun* **1** *a chill in the air* chilliness, coldness, coolness, iciness, crispness, rawness, sharpness, nip, bite, frigidity, gelidity. **2** *catch a chill* cold, flu, influenza, respiratory infection, virus. **3** *a chill in her manner* chilliness, coldness, coolness, aloofness, distance, unresponsiveness, lack of sympathy, frigidity, lack of welcome, hostility, unfriendliness. **4** *cast a chill over the proceedings* dread, fear, gloom, cloud, depression, damper.
Antonyms: WARMTH; HEAT.

chill *adjective* **1** *a chill wind* chilly, cold, cool, icy, raw, biting. *See* CHILLY 1. **2** *a chill manner* chilly, cold, cool, aloof, distant, frigid, unresponsive, hostile. *See* CHILLY 3.
Antonyms: WARM; HOT.

chill *verb* **1** *chilled by the wind* made cold, made colder, cool down. **2** *chill food* make colder, cool down, freeze, refrigerate. **3** *chill the enthusiasm/spirit of the party* lessen, reduce, dampen, depress, dispirit, discourage, dishearten.

chilly *adjective* **1** *a chilly breeze* cold, cool, icy, crisp, brisk, fresh, raw, sharp, biting, penetrating, freezing, frigid, chill; *inf.* nippy. **2** *feeling chilly* cold, cool, freezing, frozen to the bone/marrow, shivery. **3** *a chilly manner* cold, cool, aloof, distant, unresponsive, unsympathetic, frigid, unwelcoming, hostile, unfriendly.
Antonyms: WARM; PASSIONATE.

chime *verb* **1** *bells chiming* ring, peal, toll, sound, ding, dong, clang, boom, tinkle, resound, reverberate. **2** *chime the bells* ring, peal, toll, strike, sound. **3** *bells/clock chiming 6 o'clock* indicate, mark, show. **chime in 1** *just chime in when* *we get to the chorus* harmonize, sing along, join in; *inf.* jump in. **2** *he's always chiming in when we're talking* interrupt, cut in, interpose; *inf.* butt in; jump in.

chimes *plural noun* bells, carillon, wind chimes.

china *noun* **1** *ornaments made of china* porcelain, faience, ceramics, pottery. **2** *set out the best china* dishes, tableware, dinner/tea service.

chink *noun* crack, fissure, crevice, cleft, cut, rift, split, slit, gap, opening, aperture, cavity, cranny.

chip *noun* **1** *chips on the sawmill's floor* shaving, paring, shard, flake, shred, sliver, splinter, fragment, snippet, scrap. **2** *the cup with a chip in it* nick, crack, notch, flaw. **3** *gambling chips* counter, token, disk.

chip *verb* **1** *chip a glass* nick, crack, damage. **2** *the paint chips easily* break off, crack, fragment, crumble. **3** *chipping away at a chunk of wood* whittle, chisel, hew. **chip in 1** *he's always chipping in with his suggestions* interrupt, cut in, interpose; *inf.* chime in, butt in. **2** *chip in to buy a present* | *chip in some money* contribute, make a contribution, subscribe, donate, make a donation, pay.

chirp *verb* chirrup, cheep, twitter, tweet, warble, trill, chatter.

chitchat *noun* chat, chatting, small talk, idle gossip, gossip, chatter.

chivalrous *adjective* **1** *behaving in a chivalrous way toward women* gallant, gentlemanly, courteous, gracious, mannerly, well-mannered, polite, thoughtful, protective, courtly. **2** *chivalrous followers of King Arthur* knightly, courtly, bold, courageous, brave, valiant, heroic, daring, intrepid, honorable, high-minded, just, fair, loyal, constant, true, gallant, magnanimous, protective.

Antonyms: RUDE; BOORISH; UNMANNERLY; COWARDLY.

chivalry *noun* **1** *his chivalry toward women* gallantry, gentlemanliness, courtesy, courteousness, graciousness, mannerliness, politeness, thoughtfulness, protectiveness, courtliness. **2** *chivalry at medieval courts* knightly code, knighthood, knight errantry; courtly manners. **3** *the chivalry of King Arthur's followers* knightliness, courtliness, boldness, courage, bravery, valor, heroism, daring, intrepidity, honor, high-mindedness, integrity, justice, justness, fairness, loyalty, constancy, trueness, truthfulness, magnanimity, protectiveness.

choice *noun* **1** *the choice of candidates* choosing, selection, picking, option, preference, election, adoption. **2** *no choice but to resign* alternative, option, possibility, solution, answer, way out. **3** *a wide choice of candy* selection, range, variety, supply, store, array, display. **4** *he was considered the right choice* selection, appointment, appointee, nominee, candidate.

choice *adjective* **1** *choice fruit* best, select, supe-

rior, first-class, first-rate, excellent, prime, prize, special, rare, exclusive. **2** *a few choice phrases* well-chosen, select, handpicked, appropriate, apposite, apt.

choke *verb* **1** *choked to death* strangle, strangulate, throttle. **2** *smoke choking him* asphyxiate, suffocate, smother, stifle, overpower. **3** *he choked on a fish bone* gag, gasp, retch, struggle for air, asphyxiate, suffocate. **4** *the storm drains are choked with leaves* clog, block, obstruct, occlude, plug, dam up, congest. **choke back** *choke back her tears* check, restrain, contain, suppress, control, repress, curb, bridle.

choose *verb* **1** *choose a book/career* select, pick, pick out, handpick, take, opt for, settle on, decide on, fix on, single out, adopt, designate, elect, espouse. **2** *do as you choose* prefer, like, wish, want, desire, fancy, favor.

Antonyms: REJECT; DECLINE.

choosy *adjective* fussy, finicky, persnickety, fastidious, particular, exacting, discriminating.

chop *verb* *chop meat/vegetables* chop up, cut up, cube, dice, fragment, crumble. **chop down** *chop down the trees* cut down, fell, hew, bring down, hack down, saw down. **chop off** *chop off branches* cut off, lop, sever, hack off, saw off.

choppy *adjective* rough, bumpy, turbulent, blustery, stormy, tempestuous.

chore *noun* task, job, duty, errand, burden, routine; work, domestic work.

chortle *verb* chuckle, cackle, guffaw, laugh uproariously, roar/shake with laughter, split one's sides, be convulsed.

chorus *noun* **1** *singing in the school chorus* choir, ensemble, choral group; choristers, singers, vocalists. **2** *joined the show as a member of the chorus* dance troupe/company, corps de ballet. **3** *the chorus of the song* refrain, strain, response. **in chorus** *give a reply in chorus* in unison, in concert, in harmony.

christen *verb* **1** *christen a child in church* baptize, give a name to, name, sprinkle, immerse. **2** *she was christened Sara* name, call, dub, style, term, designate, denominate. **3** *christen the new glasses* begin using, break in.

Christianity *noun.* See also table at ECCLESIASTIC.

chronic *adjective* **1** *a chronic illness* persistent, long-lasting, long-standing, constant, continual, continuous, incessant, lingering, unabating, deep-rooted, deep-seated, ingrained. **2** *a chronic liar* inveterate, confirmed, habitual, hardened.

Antonyms: ACUTE; TEMPORARY; MILD.

chronicle *noun* *a chronicle of historical events* register, record, annals, calendar, diary, journal, log, account, archive, history, story.

chronicle *verb* *chronicle events* record, put on record, set down, document, register, report, enter, note, relate, tell about.

chronological *adjective* sequential, consecutive, progressive, serial, ordered, historical; in order of time, in sequence.

chubby *adjective* plump, tubby, rotund, stout,

paunchy.

Antonyms: SKINNY; SLENDER.

chuck verb 1 *chuck it in the bucket* toss, fling, throw, cast, pitch, hurl, shy, heave, sling, let fly. 2 *chuck his job/girlfriend* abandon, give up, relinquish, quit, forsake; *inf.* drop.

chuckle verb laugh quietly, laugh to oneself, chortle, giggle, titter, cackle.

chum noun friend, bosom friend, companion, comrade, crony, alter ego; *inf.* pal, buddy.

chunk noun lump, hunk, block, slab, mass, square, wedge, dollop, piece, portion, part.

church noun place of worship, the house of God, the Lord's house; cathedral, minster, chapel, temple, tabernacle, mosque, synagogue.

churlish adjective boorish, oafish, loutish, ill-mannered, unmannerly, rude, impolite, discourteous, uncivil, surly, sullen, ill-tempered, curt, brusque, rough.

Antonyms: MANNERLY; POLITE.

churn verb 1 *churn milk into butter* beat, whip up, agitate. 2 *churning the peaceful waters* agitate, disturb, stir up, shake up. 3 *water churning under the rocks* seethe, foam, froth, boil, swirl, toss, convulse.

cigarette noun *inf.* smoke, butt, cancer stick, coffin nail.

cinder noun ash, ember, charcoal.

cinema noun films, pictures, movies, motion pictures; *inf.* big screen, silver screen.

cipher noun 1 *written in cipher* code, secret writing; coded message, cryptograph. 2 *a row of ciphers* zero, nil. 3 *Arabic ciphers* number, numeral, figure, digit, integer, character, symbol, sign.

circle noun 1 *draw a circle* ring, disk, loop, circumference, ball, globe, sphere, orb. 2 *move in different circles* area of activity, field of interest, scene, sphere, domain, province, realm, range, region, circuit, orbit, compass. 3 *her circle of friends* group, set, company, crowd, ring, coterie, clique, assembly, fellowship, class.

circle verb 1 *vultures circling above* move round, rotate, revolve, circulate, wheel, whirl, gyrate, pivot, swivel. 2 *circle the estate* surround, encircle, ring, enclose, envelop, hedge in, hem in, gird, belt, circumscribe; *circle the world* go around, orbit, circumnavigate.

circuit noun 1 *run a circuit of the track* lap, turn, beat, ambit, cycle, loop, compass, circumference. 2 *the circuit of the estate/field* border, boundary, bounding line, bounds, compass, limits, circumference. 3 *the judge's circuit* tour, journey, trip, excursion.

circuitous adjective roundabout, winding, meandering, tortuous, twisting, rambling, indirect, maze-like, labyrinthine.

circular adjective round, ring-shaped, annular, spherical, spheroid, globular.

circulate verb 1 *circulate the news* spread, spread around, disseminate, propagate, distribute, transmit, give out, issue, make known, make

public, broadcast, publicize, advertise, publish, promulgate, pronounce. 2 *blood/air circulating* flow, move round, go round, rotate, revolve, whirl, gyrate.

circumference noun perimeter, periphery, border, boundary, bounds, limits, confines, outline, circuit, compass, extremity, edge, rim, verge, fringe, skirt.

circumlocution noun periphrasis, tautology, redundancy, convolution, discursiveness, circuitousness, verbosity, wordiness, prolixity, long-windedness, gobbledygook.

circumscribe verb 1 *circumscribe the area that will be the park* enclose, encircle, bound, encompass, gird, circumvent; define, delineate, outline, demarcate, delimit, mark off. 2 *activities circumscribed by poverty* restrict, limit, curb, confine, restrain, trammel, hamper.

---

circumscribe

encircle, enclose, encompass, envelop, surround
Strictly speaking, to **circumscribe** is to draw a line around something to mark its limits or boundary (*a square circumscribed by a circle*). Beyond the realm of geometry, however, it suggests something that is hemmed in on all sides (*a lake circumscribed by mountains*). **Encompass** is used when something is set within a circle or within limits (*a road that encompassed the grounds of the estate; a view that encompassed the harbor*). **Surround** is a less formal word for *circumscribe*, but it can also refer to an undesirable, threatening, or dangerous situation (*surrounded by angry demonstrators; surrounded by skyscrapers*). **Encircle** is similar to *surround* in meaning, but it suggests a tight or quite circular clustering around a central object (*a bowl of fruit encircled by flowers*) or a deliberate attempt to surround someone or something for a definite reason (*to encircle the enemy camp*). **Envelop** is the right word if something is surrounded to the point where it can barely be seen (*a lonely figure enveloped in fog*) or if it is surrounded by layers or folds of an amorphous material (*enveloped in soft cotton to prevent breakage*). **Enclose** is very similar to *envelop*, but it suggests that something has been especially designed to fit around something else for protection or containment (*a ship model enclosed in a glass case*).

---

circumspect adjective wary, cautious, careful, chary, watchful, alert, attentive, guarded, canny, vigilant, observant, suspicious, apprehensive, leery, prudent, judicious, politic, discerning, sagacious.

circumstances plural noun 1 *I know nothing of the circumstances | in the circumstances* situation, state of affairs, conditions, set of conditions, position, event, occurrence, background. 2 *living in poor circumstances* state, situation, conditions, times, financial position, plight, predicament, lot, fortune, means, resources, lifestyle, station.

circumstantial *adjective* **1** *circumstantial evidence* based on circumstances, indirect, incidental, evidential, deduced, presumed, inferential, conjectural. **2** *a circumstantial account* detailed, precise, particular, exact, accurate, minute, explicit, pointed, to the point.

citadel *noun* fortress, fort, fortification, stronghold, keep, castle, tower, bastion.

citation *noun* **1** *citations from famous authors* quotation, quote, extract, excerpt, reference, illustration, allusion, passage, source. **2** *a citation for heroism* commendation, award, honor, mention. **3** *a citation from the courts* summons, subpoena, arraignment.

cite *verb* **1** *cite the statistics as evidence* | *cite extracts from the poem* quote, mention, name, enumerate, evidence, refer to, allude to, exemplify, excerpt, extract. **2** *cite him for his heroism* commend, recommend, pay tribute to, mention. **3** *cited by the courts* summon, subpoena, arraign, serve with a writ.

citizen *noun* resident, inhabitant, dweller, denizen, townsman, townswoman, taxpayer, voter, constituent, subject.

city *noun* conurbation, metropolitan area, metropolis, municipality, town; *inf.* concrete jungle.

civic *adjective* municipal, public, community, local, civil, communal, urban, metropolitan.

civil *adjective* **1** *civil war* interior, internal, domestic, at home. **2** *civil responsibilities* civic, municipal, public, community, local. *See* CIVIC. **3** *civil government/rulers* civilian, lay, nonmilitary, nonreligious, secular. **4** *a civil young man* | *in a civil manner* polite, courteous, well-mannered, mannerly, well-bred, gentlemanly, ladylike, refined, urbane, polished, cultured, cultivated, civilized, cordial, genial, pleasant, affable, amiable.
Antonyms: MILITARY; RELIGIOUS; RUDE; UNCIVIL.

civilian *noun civilians called up* ordinary citizen, private citizen, nonmilitary person/personnel, layperson.

civilian *adjective a civilian guard* civil, lay, nonmilitary. *See* CIVILIAN *noun*.

civility *noun* **1** *treat even his opponents with civility* courtesy, courteousness, politeness, good manners, mannerliness, graciousness, cordiality, geniality, pleasantness, affability, amiability, urbanity, gallantry. **2** *exchange civilities* polite act, courtesy; etiquette, protocol, propriety, decorum.

civilization *noun* **1** *a threat to modern civilization* development, advancement, progress, enlightenment, culture, cultivation, edification, refinement, sophistication. **2** *ancient civilizations* society, community, nation, country, people, way of life. **3** *the civilization of the tribes* civi-

lizing, enlightenment, socialization, humanizing, edification, education, improvement. *See* CIVILIZE.

civilize *verb* enlighten, socialize, humanize, edify, cultivate, educate, instruct, improve, culture, refine, polish, sophisticate.

civilized *adjective* **1** *civilized tribes* developed, modern, socialized, educated. *See* CIVILIZE. **2** *she's very civilized but he's a boor* cultured, cultivated, sophisticated, educated, enlightened, urbane.
Antonyms: UNCIVILIZED; BARBAROUS; UNSOPHISTICATED.

clad *adjective clad in wool* | *warmly clad* clothed, dressed, attired, covered.

claim *verb* **1** *claim the prize* lay claim to, ask as one's right, establish rights to, ask for, demand, request, requisition, require. **2** *claim that he's innocent* profess, maintain, assert, declare, protest, avow, aver, allege, postulate, affirm, hold. **3** *the fire claimed lives* take, cause, result in, involve.

claim *noun* **1** *a claim for damages* demand, request, application, petition, call. **2** *put forward his claim to the crown* right, rights, title, prerogative, privilege, heritage, inheritance, legacy. **3** *dispute his claims of innocence* profession, assertion, declaration, protestation, avowal, allegation, postulation, affirmation.

claimant *noun* applicant, candidate, petitioner, supplicant, suppliant, suitor, postulant, pretender, plaintiff.

clairvoyance *noun* second sight, psychic powers, ESP, extrasensory perception, telepathy, sixth sense.

clamber *verb* scramble, climb, scale, ascend, mount, shin, shinny, scrabble, claw one's way.

clammy *adjective* moist, damp, humid, sweaty, sticky.

clamor *noun* **1** *the clamor of children's voices* uproar, noise, din, racket, shout, shouting, yelling, blaring, commotion, brouhaha, hubbub, hullabaloo, outcry, vociferation. **2** *answer their clamors for more money* demand, call, petition, request, urging, protest, complaint, insistence, exigency.
Antonyms: QUIET; SERENITY.

clamp *noun held tightly in a clamp* vice, press, brace, clasp, fastener, hasp.

clamp *verb* **1** *a pipe clamped between his teeth* grip, hold, fix, clench, press, squeeze, secure, make fast, brace. **2** *clamp a curfew on the city* impose, inflict, lay on, set, charge, burden. **clamp down on** *clamp down on spending/crime* limit, restrain, restrict, confine, hold in check, crack down on, be severe with, suppress, prevent.

clampdown *noun a clampdown on spending/crime* limitation, restraint, restriction, holding in check, crackdown, severe treatment, suppression, prevention.

clan *noun* **1** *the Scottish clans* family, house, tribe, line. **2** *tired of the clan of socialites* set, circle, crowd, in-crowd, gang, band, group, faction, clique, coterie, fraternity, brotherhood, community, society. **3** *our clan gathers for every holiday* family, kin, kinfolk, group of relatives, kith and kin.

clandestine *adjective* secret, undercover, surreptitious, cloak-and-dagger, back-alley, furtive, concealed, hidden, underhand.
Antonyms: OPEN; ABOVEBOARD.

clang *noun the clang of the bell | the clang of two gates closing* ringing, ring, resounding, reverberation, clank, clash, clangor, bong, chime, toll, clink, clunk, jangle.

clang *verb bells clanging | gates clanging shut* ring, resound, reverberate, clank, clash, bong, clink, chime, toll, peal.

clank *noun the clank of chains* metallic sound, clang, clangor, clink, clunk, jangle.

clank *verb chains clanking* clang, clink, clunk, jangle.

clannish *adjective* cliquish, insular, exclusive, narrow, parochial, provincial.

clap *verb* **1** *clap one's hands* strike/slap together. **2** *the audience clapping* applaud, cheer, acclaim; show one's appreciation, put one's hands together.

claptrap *noun* nonsense, drivel, rubbish, humbug, insincerity; *inf.* bunk.

clarify *verb* **1** *clarify the situation* make clear, clear up, resolve, make plain, explain, elucidate, illuminate, throw light on, make simple, simplify. **2** *clarify butter* purify, refine.
Antonyms: CONFUSE; MUDDY.

---

clarify

construe, elucidate, explain, explicate, interpret

When a biology teacher gets up in front of a class and tries to **explain** how two brown-eyed parents can produce a blue-eyed child, the purpose is to make an entire process or sequence of events understandable. In a less formal sense, to *explain* is to make a verbal attempt to justify certain actions or to make them understood (*she tried to explain why she was so late*). That same teacher might **clarify** a particular exam question that almost everyone in the class got wrong—a word that means to make an earlier event, situation, or statement clear. **Elucidate** is a more formal word meaning to *clarify*, but where the root of the latter refers to clearness, the root of the former refers to light; to *elucidate* is to shed light on something through explanation, illustration, etc. (*the principal's comments were an attempt to elucidate the school's policy on cheating*). A teacher who **explicates** something discusses a complex subject in a point-by-point manner (*to explicate a poem*). If a personal judgment is inserted in making such an explication, the correct word is **interpret** (*to interpret a poem's symbolic meanings*). To **construe** is to make a careful interpretation of something, especially where the meaning is ambiguous. For example, when a class misbehaves in front of a visitor, the teacher is likely

to *construe* that behavior as an attempt to cause embarrassment or ridicule.

---

clarity *noun* **1** *the clarity of his prose* clearness, lucidity, lucidness, plainness, simplicity, intelligibility, comprehensibility, obviousness, explicitness, unambiguity, precision. **2** *the clarity of the water* clearness, transparency, limpidity, translucence, pellucidity, glassiness.
Antonyms: OBSCURITY; DARKNESS.

clash *verb* **1** *clash the cymbals* strike, bang, clang, crash, clatter, clank, clink, rattle, jangle. **2** *the two sides clashed* be in conflict, war, fight, contend, do battle, come to blows, feud, grapple, wrangle, quarrel, cross swords, lock horns. **3** *the appointments clash* coincide, occur simultaneously, conflict. **4** *the colors clash* be discordant, do not match, lack harmony, jar, be incompatible; *inf.* scream.
Antonyms: AGREE; HARMONIZE.

clash *noun* **1** *the clash of cymbals* striking, bang, clang, crash, clatter, clank. *See* CLASH *verb* 1. **2** *the clash of the opposing sides* conflict, collision, confrontation, brush, warring, fighting, contending, feud, grappling, wrangling, quarreling. **3** *the clash of the dates* coincidence, co-occurrence, concurrence, conflict. **4** *the clash of the colors* discordance, discord, lack of harmony, incompatibility, jarring.
Antonyms: HARMONY; ACCORD.

clasp *noun* **1** *the clasp of the necklace* catch, fastener, fastening, clip; hook, hook and eye, snap fastener, buckle, hasp. **2** *wearing a diamond clasp* pin, brooch. **3** *engage in a loving clasp* embrace, hug, cuddle, hold, grip, grasp.

class *noun* **1** *middle classes | professional class* social order, social division, stratum, rank, level, status, sphere, grade, group, grouping, set, classification, caste. **2** *in the highest class | degrees divided into three classes* category, classification, division, section, group, set, grade. **3** *a class of objects* category, group, set, kind, sort, type, collection, denomination, order, species, genre, genus. **4** *what class is the student in?* study group, school group, seminar, tutorial. **5** *a player of class | a woman of class* quality, excellence, distinction, stylishness, elegance, chic.

class *verb books classed as textbooks* classify, categorize, group, grade, arrange, order, sort, codify, file, index, pigeonhole.

classic *adjective* **1** *a classic performance* first-rate, first-class, excellent, brilliant, finest, outstanding, exemplary, masterly, consummate. **2** *a classic case/example* typical, standard, model, guiding, archetypal, stock, true-to-form, paradigmatic, prototypical. **3** *classic styles* simple, traditional, timeless, ageless, long-lasting, enduring, abiding, undying, time-honored, long-standing, long-established.

classic *noun* **1** *reading the classics* great work, established work, standard work, masterpiece. **2**

the match was a classic masterpiece, excellent example. *See* CLASSIC *adjective* 1.

classical *adjective* 1 *a classical scholar* | *classical architecture* Greek, Grecian, Hellenic, Attic, Greco-Roman, Roman, Latin. 2 *classical music* orchestral, symphonic. 3 *a classical style of design* simple, plain, restrained, pure, understated, harmonious, well-proportioned, balanced, symmetrical, elegant, aesthetic.

classification *noun the classification of books/ blood* classifying, categorizing, categorization, grouping, grading, arrangement, codifying, codification, taxonomy. *See* CLASSIFY.

classify *verb classify books/blood* categorize, class, group, grade, arrange, order, sort, type, rank, rate, designate, codify, catalog, tabulate, file, index, assign, pigeonhole, brand.

clatter *verb* rattle, clang, clank, clunk, bang.

clause *noun clause 9 of the document* section, paragraph, article, note, item, point, passage, part, heading, condition, provision, proviso, stipulation.

claw *noun a cat's/bird's/lobster's claws* nail, talon, pincer, nipper, chela.

claw *verb claw his face* scratch, tear, lacerate, scrape, graze, rip, dig into, maul.

clay *noun* 1 *clay used for pottery* slip, kaolin, adobe, loam. 2 *buried beneath the clay* earth, ground, soil, sod.

clean *adjective* 1 *clean hands/clothes* unsoiled, spotless, unstained, unspotted, unsullied, unblemished, immaculate, speckless, hygienic, sanitary, washed, cleansed, laundered, scrubbed. 2 *clean air* pure, clear, natural, unpolluted, unadulterated, uncontaminated, untainted, unmixed. 3 *living clean lives* good, upright, honorable, respectable, virtuous, righteous, moral, reputable, upstanding, exemplary, innocent, guiltless, pure, decent, chaste, undefiled. 4 *a clean piece of paper* unused, unmarked, blank, vacant, void. 5 *the clean lines of the airplane* streamlined, smooth, well-defined, definite, clean-cut, regular, symmetrical, simple, elegant, graceful, uncluttered, trim, shapely. 6 *a clean break to the marriage* complete, thorough, total, entire, conclusive, decisive, final. 7 *found to be clean after investigation* innocent, guiltless, guilt-free, crime-free.

Antonyms: DIRTY; FILTHY; IMMORAL.

clean *adverb a bullet clean through his shoulder* | *go clean out of my mind* completely, entirely, totally, fully, wholly, thoroughly, altogether, quite, utterly, absolutely.

clean *verb* 1 *clean one's hands/walls* wash, cleanse, wipe, sponge, scrub, scour, swab. 2 *clean one's clothes* dry-clean, launder. 3 *clean the room* tidy, pick up; vacuum, dust, mop, sweep; *inf.* do.

Antonyms: DIRTY; SOIL; MESS.

cleanse *verb* 1 *cleanse the wound* clean, make clean, clean up, wash, bathe, rinse, disinfect. 2 *cleanse of his sins* purify, purge, absolve.

clear *adjective* 1 *a clear day* | *clear weather* bright, cloudless, unclouded, fair, fine, light, undimmed, sunny, sunshiny. 2 *clear water/ glass* transparent, limpid, translucent, crystalline, diaphanous, see-through. 3 *it was clear that he was guilty* obvious, evident, plain, apparent, sure, definite, unmistakable, manifest, indisputable, patent, incontrovertible, irrefutable, palpable, beyond doubt, beyond question. 4 *a clear account of the incident* understandable, comprehensible, intelligible, plain, explicit, lucid, coherent, distinct. 5 *a clear thinker* astute, keen, sharp, quick, perceptive, discerning, perspicacious, penetrating. 6 *a clear road/view* open, empty, free, unobstructed, unimpeded, unhindered, unlimited. 7 *a clear conscience* untroubled, undisturbed, peaceful, at peace, tranquil, serene, calm, innocent, guiltless, guilt-free, clean, sinless, stainless. 8 *four clear days* whole, full, entire, complete, total.

Antonyms: CLOUDY; OPAQUE; VAGUE; AMBIGUOUS.

clear *adverb* 1 *hear him loud and clear* clearly, distinctly, plainly, audibly. 2 *got clear away* completely, entirely, thoroughly, fully, wholly, clear. *See* CLEAR *adjective* 8. **clear of** *stand clear of the door* away from, at a distance from, apart from, out of contact with.

clear *verb* 1 *the weather cleared* clear up, brighten, lighten, break. 2 *clear the plates* remove, take away, tidy up/away. 3 *clear the drains* unblock, unclog, unstop. 4 *clear the room of objects* empty, vacate, evacuate, void, free, rid. 5 *clear the accused of charges* absolve, acquit, discharge, let go, exonerate, vindicate, excuse, pardon. 6 *clear the fence* jump, vault, leap, hop, pass over. 7 *clear $500* net, make a profit of, realize a profit of, gain, earn, make, acquire, secure, bring, reap. 8 *clear goods* | *the ship was cleared* authorize, sanction, pass, approve, give consent to, permit/allow to pass, give one's seal of approval to; *inf.* give the go-ahead to, give the green light to. **clear out** 1 *clear out the cupboard* empty, evacuate, tidy, tidy up. 2 *clear out the trash* get rid of, throw out, throw away, eject, eliminate. 3 *boys told to clear out* go away, get out, leave, depart, take oneself off, make oneself scarce, withdraw, retire, decamp. **clear up** 1 *clear up the mystery/problem* solve, resolve, straighten out, find an answer to, unravel, untangle, explain, elucidate; *inf.* crack. 2 *the weather cleared up* improve, brighten. *See* CLEAR *verb* 1.

clearance *noun* 1 *slum clearance* clearing, removal, evacuation, eviction, emptying, depopulation, unpeopling, withdrawal, decanting. 2 *the clearance under the bridge* clearing, space, gap, allowance, margin, headroom, leeway, room to spare. 3 *get clearance for their plans* authorization, consent, permission, sanction, go-ahead, leave, endorsement; *inf.* green light.

clear-cut *adjective clear-cut proposals* definite,

specific, precise, explicit, unambiguous, unequivocal.

clearly adverb *clearly he's ill | clearly a mistake* obviously, undoubtedly, without doubt, indubitably, plainly, undeniably, decidedly, surely, certainly, incontrovertibly, irrefutably, incontestably, patently.

cleave[1] *verb* **1** *cleave the logs* split, split open, open, crack, lay open, divide, hew, hack, chop/slice up, sever, rend, rive. **2** *cleave a path* make, cut, plow, drive, bulldoze.

cleave[2] *verb* **cleave to** cling to, stick to, hold to, stand by, abide by, adhere to, be loyal/faithful to.

cleaver *noun* knife, chopper, hatchet, axe; butcher knife.

cleft *noun* split, crack, gap, fissure, crevice, rift, break, fracture.

clemency *noun* **1** *treat the prisoners with clemency* mercy, leniency, compassion, humanity, pity, sympathy, kindness, magnanimity, fairness, temperance, moderation, indulgence. **2** *the clemency of the weather* mildness, balminess, warmness.

clench *verb* **1** *clench the teeth* close, shut, seal, fasten. **2** *clench the table edge* grip, grasp, clutch, hold, seize.

clergy *noun* clergymen, churchmen, priests, clerics, ecclesiastics; ministry, priesthood, the cloth, first estate.

clergyman, clergywoman *noun* churchman, churchwoman, man/woman of the cloth, man/woman of God, cleric, ecclesiastic, divine; vicar, parson, pastor, priest, father, padre, reverend, rector, rabbi, chaplain.

clerical *adjective* **1** *a clerical post in the office | clerical duties* secretarial, office, writing, typing, filing, bookkeeping. **2** *clerical clothes* ecclesiastical, churchly, priestly, pastoral, sacerdotal, apostolic, canonical.

clever *adjective* **1** *both stupid and clever people* intelligent, bright, sharp-witted, quick-witted, talented, gifted, smart, capable, able, competent, apt, knowledgeable, educated, sagacious; *inf.* brainy. **2** *a clever move* shrewd, astute, adroit, canny, cunning, ingenious, artful, wily, inventive. **3** *clever with their hands* dexterous, skillful, adroit, nimble, deft, handy.
Antonyms: DULL; STUPID; AWKWARD.

cliché *noun* hackneyed phrase, platitude, banality, truism, saw, maxim, bromide; *inf.* old chestnut.

click *noun* *the click of the key in the lock* clink, clack, chink, snap, tick.

click *verb* **1** *the key clicked in the lock* clink, clack, chink, snap, tick. **2** *I see it's suddenly clicked* become clear, fall into place, come home to one, make sense. **3** *the two girls clicked immediately* get on, take to each other, hit it off, be compatible, be on the same wavelength, feel a rapport. **4** *the new toys clicked with the children* make a hit, prove popular, be successful, be a success, succeed, go down well.

client *noun* customer, patron, regular, habitué, buyer, purchaser, shopper, consumer, user; patient.

clientele *noun* clients, customers, patrons, regulars; patronage, following, trade, business, market. *See* CLIENT.

cliff *noun* precipice, rock face, face, crag, bluff, escarpment, scarp, overhang, promontory, tor.

climate *noun* **1** *temperate climate* weather pattern, weather conditions, weather, temperature. **2** *visit various climates* clime, country, place, region, area, zone. **3** *the political climate* atmosphere, mood, temper, spirit, feeling, feel, ambience, aura, ethos.

climax *noun* **1** *the climax of her campaign/career* culmination, height, peak, pinnacle, high point, summit, top, highlight, acme, zenith, apex, apogee, crowning point. **2** *reach climax* sexual climax, orgasm.
Antonyms: NADIR; ANTICLIMAX.

climax *verb* **1** *the campaign climaxed in victory* culminate, peak, come to a head, result, end. **2** *climax together* have an orgasm; *inf.* come.

climb *verb* **1** *climb up the ladder | climb to the top* go, ascend, mount, scale, clamber. **2** *prices/temperatures are climbing* goup, rise, increase, shoot up, soar. **3** *the road climbs steeply* slope upward, incline, bank. **4** *climbing toward the presidency* make progress, get ahead, advance, work one's way up, make strides. **climb down** *climb down the ladder/tree* go down, descend.
Antonym: DESCEND.

clinch *verb* **1** *clinch the deal* settle, secure, seal, set the seal on, complete, confirm, conclude, assure, cap, close, wind up; *inf.* sew up. **2** *clinch a nail* fasten, make fast, secure, fix, clamp, bolt, rivet, pinion. **3** *boxers/lovers clinching* hug, embrace, cuddle, squeeze, clutch, grasp, grapple.

cling *verb* *the surfaces clung together* stick, adhere, hold, grip, clasp, clutch. **cling to 1** *cling to the rope | clung to his friend* hold on to, hang on to, clutch, grip, grasp, clasp, cleave to, attach to, embrace. **2** *cling to one's beliefs* stick to, hold to, stand by, abide by, adhere to, be loyal/faithful to, remain true to, remain attached to; *inf.* stick with.

clinic *noun* medical center, health center, infirmary; sick bay, first-aid station.

clinical *adjective* **1** *a clinical attitude to others' problems* objective, dispassionate, detached, uninvolved, cold, unsympathetic, unfeeling. **2** *clinical designs* plain, simple, unadorned, unornamented, stark, austere, severe, spartan.

clip[1] *verb* **1** *clip hair/hedges* cut, cut short, crop, snip, trim, shear, prune. **2** *clip him across the jaw* hit, strike, box, cuff, smack, wallop, thump, punch, knock; *inf.* clout, whack. **3** *the train was clipping along* speed, go fast, race, gallop, rush, dash, zoom, whip, go like lightning.

clip[2] *noun* **1** *my hair needs a clip* cut, trim, shortening, shear, shearing, pruning. **2** *a clip across* *the jaw* cuff, smack, wallop; *inf.* clout. *See* CLIP[1] verb 2. **3** *going at a clip* fast rate, swift pace. **4** *a clip from a movie/newspaper* clipping, cutting, extract, excerpt, snippet, fragment.

clip[3] verb *clip the papers together* staple, fasten, fix, attach, hold.

clip[4] noun *a paper clip* | *snaps together with clips* fastener, coupler, clasp.

clique noun coterie, circle, crowd, in-crowd, set, gang, group, clan, faction, pack, band, ring, fraternity, society, mob.

cloak noun **1** *wearing a black cloak* cape, mantle, wrap, shawl, pelisse, coat. **2** *a cloak of darkness/ secrecy* cover, screen, blind, mask, mantle, veil, shroud, shield, front, camouflage, pretext.

cloak verb *meetings cloaked in secrecy* hide, conceal, cover,cover up, screen, mask, veil, shroud, shield, cloud, camouflage, obscure, disguise.

Antonym: REVEAL; EXPOSE.

clock noun timekeeper, timepiece, timer; chronometer, chronograph.

clock verb **1** *clock the race* time, record the time. **2** *she clocked a record time* register, record, achieve, attain.

clog noun sabot, wooden shoe, wooden-soled shoe.

clog verb **1** *leaves clogging the drains* clog up, block, obstruct, dam, congest, jam, occlude; stop up, dam up. **2** *clogging the system with red tape* obstruct, hinder, impede, hamper, shackle, burden.

cloister noun **1** *ecclesiastics in a cloister* convent, nunnery, monastery, abbey, priory, friary. **2** *walking in the cloisters* covered walk, walkway, corridor, aisle, arcade, gallery, piazza.

cloistered adjective *leading cloistered lives* secluded, sheltered, sequestered, shielded, shut-off, withdrawn, confined, restricted, insulated, reclusive, hermitic.

close[1] verb **1** *close the door* shut, slam, fasten, secure, lock, bolt, bar, latch, padlock. **2** *close the bottle/opening* stop up, plug, seal, clog, choke, obstruct, occlude. **3** *close the meeting* bring to an end, end, conclude, finish, terminate, wind up, adjourn, discontinue. **4** *he closed by praying* come to an end, end, conclude, finish, cease, wind up, adjourn. **5** *close the bargain* complete, conclude, settle, clinch, seal, establish, fix. **6** *the gap closed* narrow, lessen, grow smaller, dwindle, reduce. **7** *his arms closed around her* | *the boxers closed* come together, join, connect, come into contact, unite, clutch one another, grip, clench, grapple, couple.

Antonyms: OPEN; CLEAR; START.

close[2] noun *at the close of day/play* end, finish, conclusion, termination, cessation, completion, culmination, finale, wind-up.

close[3] adjective **1** *our two houses are close* near, adjacent, in close proximity, adjoining, neighboring, abutting; *birthdays close together* near,

occurring/falling near. **2** *a close resemblance* | *close in appearance* near, similar, like, alike, comparable, parallel, corresponding, akin. **3** *a close friend* intimate, dear, bosom, close-knit, inseparable, loving, devoted, attached, confidential; *inf.* chummy. **4** *close formation* dense, condensed, compact, crowded, packed, solid, tight, cramped, congested, crushed, squeezed. **5** *a close game* evenly matched, well-matched, hard-fought, sharply contested, neck-and-neck, nose-to-nose; *inf.* fifty-fifty. **6** *a close description* accurate, true, faithful, literal, exact, precise, conscientious. **7** *pay close attention* | *on close examination* careful, concentrated, attentive, assiduous, alert, vigilant, intent, dogged, painstaking, detailed, minute, intense, keen, thorough, rigorous, searching. **8** *under close arrest* strict, stringent, rigorous, thorough, tight. **9** *close weather* humid, muggy, airless, stuffy, heavy, oppressive, stifling, suffocating, musty, unventilated. **10** *he's very close about his affairs* quiet, reticent, uncommunicative, reserved, private, unforthcoming, secretive, evasive. **11** *close with his money* mean, miserly, stingy, niggardly, parsimonious, penny-pinching, tight-fisted, tight.

Antonyms: FAR; DISTANT; REMOTE; FRESH.

closet noun *a clothes closet* cupboard, wardrobe, cabinet, locker, storage room.

closet adjective *a closet homosexual/socialist* secret, unrevealed, undisclosed, hidden, concealed, furtive.

closure noun closing down, shutting down, winding up, cessation of operations, cessation, termination, finish, conclusion.

clot noun *a clot of blood* glob, lump, gob, clump, mass, obstruction, thrombus.

clot verb *blood clotting* coagulate, set, congeal, jell, thicken, cake, curdle.

cloth noun *silk cloth* fabric, material, stuff; textiles, dry goods, soft goods.

clothe verb **1** *clothed in pure wool* dress, attire, rig, rig out, turn out, apparel, fit out, outfit, robe, garb, array, deck out, drape; *inf.* doll up. **2** *hills clothed in clouds* cover, wrap, cloak, envelop, swathe.

Antonyms: UNDRESS; UNCOVER.

clothes plural noun *put away one's clothes* | *wearing expensive clothes* garments, articles of clothing/dress; clothing, attire, outfits. *See* CLOTHING.

clothing noun clothes, garments; dress, attire, apparel, outfit, costume, garb, ensemble, vestments, raiment; *inf.* gear, togs, get-up.

cloud noun **1** *clouds in the sky* rain cloud, storm cloud, thundercloud, billow; cirrus, cumulus, altostratus, altocumulus, cumulonimbus; haze, cloudbank, mackerel sky. **2** *a cloud of smoke* pall, shroud, mantle, cloak, screen, cover. **3** *a cloud on their happiness* shadow, threat; gloom, darkness. **4** *a cloud of insects* swarm, flock, mass, multitude, host, horde, throng.

cloudy *adjective* **1** *a cloudy sky* overcast, hazy, dark, gray, somber, leaden, heavy, gloomy, dim, lowering, sunless, starless. **2** *cloudy recollections* blurred, vague, indistinct, hazy, indefinite, nebulous, obscure, confused, muddled. **3** *cloudy liquids* opaque, nontransparent, murky, muddy, milky, emulsified, opalescent, turbid.
Antonyms: BRIGHT; CLEAR.

clout *verb clout the punching bag* hit, strike, smack, slap, cuff, box, thump, wallop; *inf.* whack, clobber, sock.

clout *noun* **1** *give him a clout* smack, slap, thump. *See* CLOUT *verb*. **2** *because of your clout in the firm* influence, power, pull, weight, authority, prestige, standing.

clown *noun* **1** *circus clowns* jester, fool, buffoon, zany, harlequin. **2** *he's sedate but his brother's a real clown* joker, comedian, comic, humorist, funnyman, wag, wit, prankster. **3** *the clown who crashed into my car* fool, idiot, dolt, nitwit, halfwit; *inf.* jerk, dope.

clown *verb clown around* | *clowning for the kids* fool, act foolishly, jest, joke; *inf.* cut up.

cloy *verb* satiate, pall, surfeit, dull, sicken, nauseate.

cloying *adjective* sickly sweet, sugary, saccharine, sickening, nauseating.

club *noun* **1** *hit him with a club* cudgel, bludgeon, stick, staff, truncheon, bat, baton, blackjack. **2** *a swimming/bridge club* society, group, association, organization, circle, set, clique, coterie, affiliation, league, union, federation, company, fraternity, brotherhood, sorority.

club *verb* hit, strike, beat, batter, bash, cudgel, bludgeon, truncheon; *inf.* clout, clobber.

clue *noun* hint, indication, sign, evidence, information, intimation, pointer, guide, lead, tip, tip-off, inkling.

clump *noun* **1** *a clump of trees* group, cluster, bunch, collection, assembly, assemblage. **2** *clump of earth* | *clump of blood cells* mass, lump, clod, glob, agglutination.

clump *verb* **1** *houses clumped together* group, cluster, bunch, collect, assemble, congregate, mass, lump, bundle, pack. **2** *clump around in heavy boots* clomp, stamp, stump, stomp, thump, thud, bang, tramp, lumber, plod, trudge, stumble.

clumsy *adjective* **1** *clumsy and always breaking things* awkward, uncoordinated, ungainly, blundering, bungling, bumbling, inept, maladroit, inexpert, unhandy, unskillful, like a bull in a china shop; *inf.* ham-handed, butter-fingered. **2** *a clumsy piece of furniture* awkward, unwieldy, hulking, heavy, solid, unmaneuverable. **3** *a clumsy apology* awkward, gauche, graceless, tactless, unpolished, crude, uncouth, crass.
Antonyms: ADROIT; GRACEFUL.

cluster *noun* **1** *a cluster of berries/flowers* bunch, clump, collection, knot, group; *Tech.* raceme, panicle. **2** *cluster of people* gathering, group,

collection, bunch, band, company, knot, body, assemblage, congregation.

cluster *verb people clustering around the church* gather, collect, assemble, congregate, group, come together, flock together.

clutch *verb* **1** *clutching her purse* grip, grasp, clasp, cling to, hang on to, clench. **2** *clutch at the branch* reach for, snatch at, grab, make a grab for, seize, catch at, claw at.

clutch *noun a clutch of eggs* set, setting, hatch, hatching, nest, incubation.

clutches *plural noun fall into the clutches of the cult leaders* hands, power, control, hold, grip, grasp, claws, tyranny, possession, keeping, custody.

clutter *noun clean up your clutter* | *can't work in all this clutter* mess, muddle, disorder, chaos, disarray, state of confusion/untidiness; heap, litter; *inf.* junk, stuff.

clutter *verb papers cluttering up the room* litter, make untidy, make a mess of, mess up, be strewn about, be scattered about.

coach¹ *noun* **1** *travel by express coach* bus, omnibus. **2** *horses pulling a coach* stagecoach, carriage, gig, surrey.

coach² *noun tennis coach* instructor, trainer, teacher, tutor, mentor.

coach³ *verb coach the team* | *coach tennis* instruct, train, teach, tutor, drill, put one through one's paces.

coagulate *verb* congeal, clot, gel, thicken, curdle.

coalesce *verb* unite, join together, combine, merge, amalgamate, integrate, affiliate, blend, fuse; *lit.* commingle.

coalition *noun* union, alliance, affiliation, league, association, federation, confederacy, bloc, compact, amalgamation, merger, conjunction, combination, fusion.

coarse *adjective* **1** *coarse material* rough, bristly, scratchy, prickly, hairy, shaggy. **2** *coarse features* heavy, rough, rugged, craggy, unrefined. **3** *coarse flour* crude, unrefined, unprocessed, unpurified. **4** *coarse behavior/manners* rude, ill-mannered, uncivil, rough, boorish, loutish, churlish, uncouth, crass. **5** *coarse humor* bawdy, earthy, blue, ribald, vulgar, smutty, obscene, indelicate, indecent, offensive, lewd, pornographic, prurient; *inf.* raunchy.
Antonyms: FINE; REFINED; DECENT.

coarsen *verb* roughen, thicken, toughen, harden, harshen.

coast *noun a rugged coast* coastline, shore, seashore, shoreline, seacoast, beach, strand, seaboard, water's edge.

coast *verb bicycles coasting downhill* | *coasting through life* freewheel, cruise, taxi, drift, glide, sail.

coat *noun* **1** *a winter coat* overcoat, topcoat, jacket; trench coat, parka, mackintosh, raincoat, fur coat, fur. **2** *animals' coats* fur, hair, wool; fleece, hide, pelt, skin. **3** *a coat of paint* layer, covering, overlay, coating. **4** *a coat of dust* coating, layer, film. *See* COATING.

coating *noun* covering, layer, film, coat, dusting, blanket, sheet, glaze, skin, veneer, finish, lamination, patina, membrane.

coax *verb* wheedle, cajole, talk into, beguile, flatter, inveigle, entice, induce, persuade, prevail upon, win over; *inf.* sweet-talk, soft-soap.

cock *noun* rooster, chanticleer.

cock *verb* **1** *cocking the pistol* prepare to fire, pull/pull back the hammer of. **2** *cocked his hat* tilt, tip, slant, incline.

cocky *adjective* arrogant, conceited, egotistical, swellheaded, vain, cocksure, swaggering, brash.

coddle *verb* pamper, mollycoddle, indulge, spoil, baby, humor.

code *noun* **1** *a message in code* cipher, secret writing; coded message, cryptograph. **2** *code of honor* ethics, morals, principles, maxims; morality, convention, etiquette, custom. **3** *building code* | *legal code* laws, rules, regulations, system, canon.

coerce *verb* compel, force, pressure, pressurize, drive, impel, constrain, oblige; *inf.* twist one's arm, lean on, put the screws on, strong-arm.

coffer *noun* strongbox, moneybox, money chest, safe, chest, casket, box.

coffin *noun* casket, box, sarcophagus.

cogent *adjective* convincing, forceful, forcible, effective, conclusive, persuasive, compelling, powerful, strong, potent, weighty, influential, authoritative, telling.
Antonyms: WEAK; unconvincing; INEFFECTIVE.

cogitate *verb* think, ponder, contemplate, consider, give consideration to, deliberate, meditate, reflect, mull over, muse, ruminate.

cognate *adjective* **1** *cognate words* related, kindred, akin, allied, consanguine. **2** *cognate sciences* allied, affiliated, associated, similar, alike, connected, corresponding, correlated, analogous.

cognition *noun* perception, discernment, understanding, awareness, comprehension, apprehension, enlightenment, insight, intelligence, reason.

cognizant *adjective* aware, conscious, knowing, alive to, sensible of, familiar with, acquainted with, conversant with; *inf.* wise to.

cohabit *verb* live together, cohabitate; *inf.* shack up.

coherent *adjective* *a coherent argument* logical, rational, reasoned, lucid, articulate, systematic, orderly, organized, consistent, comprehensible, intelligible.
Antonyms: INCOHERENT; MUDDLED.

cohort *noun* troop, brigade, legion, squad, squadron, column, group, company, body, band.

coil *verb* wind, spiral, loop, curl, twist, twine, entwine, snake, wreathe, convolute.

coin *noun* **1** *need a coin for the machine* | *gold coins* token, piece; dime, nickel, quarter, penny, half dollar. **2** *pay in coin* coins, coinage, change, specie, silver, copper, gold.

coin *verb* *coin a word* invent, create, make up, devise, conceive, originate, think up, dream up, formulate, fabricate.

coincide *verb* **1** *dates coinciding* be concurrent, occur simultaneously, happen together, coexist, concur, synchronize. **2** *stories coinciding* accord, agree, correspond, concur, match, square, tally, harmonize.

coincidence *noun* **1** *arrive together by coincidence* accident, chance, a fluke, luck, fortuity, serendipity. **2** *the coincidence of events/stories* coinciding. *See* COINCIDE.

coincidental *adjective* **1** *a coincidental meeting* accidental, chance, unplanned, unintentional, casual, lucky, fortuitous, serendipitous; *inf.* fluky. **2** *coincidental concerts* simultaneous, concurrent, synchronous, coexistent.

cold *adjective* **1** *a cold day* chilly, chill, cool, freezing, bitter, raw, icy, frigid, wintry, frosty, arctic, inclement, sunless, windy, glacial, polar; *inf.* nippy. **2** *feeling cold* chilly, chilled, cool, freezing, frozen, frozen stiff, frozen/chilled to the bone/marrow, shivery, numbed, benumbed. **3** *a cold person/attitude* frigid, unresponsive, unfeeling, unemotional, phlegmatic, unexcitable, passionless, spiritless, unmoved, indifferent, lukewarm, apathetic, dispassionate, aloof, distant, reserved, remote, standoffish, insensitive, unsympathetic, uncaring, heartless, callous, cold-hearted, unfriendly, inhospitable. **4** *the story is cold* dead, gone, extinguished, finished, defunct.
Antonyms: HOT; WARM; PASSIONATE.

cold-blooded *adjective* savage, inhuman, barbarous, barbaric, heartless, ruthless, pitiless, merciless.

collaborate *verb* **1** *collaborate on a book* cooperate, work together/jointly, join forces, join, unite, combine. **2** *collaborate with the enemy* conspire, fraternize, collude.

collaborator *noun* **1** *his collaborator on the book* coworker, associate, colleague, partner, confederate. **2** *collaborators executed* conspirator, fraternizer, traitor, quisling, turncoat, colluder.

collapse *verb* **1** *the roof collapsed* fall in, cave in, give way, come apart, fall to pieces, crumple. **2** *the onlooker collapsed* faint, pass out, lose consciousness, fall unconscious, keel over, fall prostrate, swoon. **3** *the business/talks collapsed* break down, fall through, fail, disintegrate, fold, founder, fall flat, miscarry, come to nothing; *inf.* flop. **4** *collapse in/into tears* break down, go to pieces; *inf.* crack up.

collapse *noun* **1** *the collapse of the roof* cave-in, giving way. *See* COLLAPSE *verb* 1. **2** *the collapse of the onlooker* fainting, faint, passing out, loss of consciousness, swooning, swoon. *See* COLLAPSE *verb* 2. **3** *the collapse of the talks/firm* breakdown, failure, disintegration, unsuccessfulness, foundering; *inf.* flop. *See* COLLAPSE *verb* 3. **4** *suffer a collapse* breakdown, nervous breakdown, attack, seizure, prostration; *inf.* crack-up.

collar *noun* *the shirt collar* neckband; ruff, wimple.

collar *verb* *collar the thief* catch, seize, grab, capture, arrest, apprehend; *inf.* nab.

collate *verb* *collate pages/information* arrange, put in order, order, sort, categorize.

collateral *noun* *collateral for a bank loan* security, surety, guarantee, pledge.

colleague *noun* associate, partner, teammate, workmate, fellow worker, coworker, collaborator, confederate, comrade.

collect *verb* **1** *collect all sorts of stuff* gather, accumulate, assemble, amass, pile up, stockpile, save, store, hoard, heap up, aggregate. **2** *a crowd collected* gather, assemble, congregate, converge, cluster, flock together, mass, convene, rally. **3** *collect money for a present* gather, solicit, raise, secure, obtain, acquire. **4** *collect one's wits/strength* get together, muster, summon, assemble, rally.
Antonyms: DISPERSE; DISTRIBUTE.

collected *adjective* *calm and collected* cool, calm, serene, poised, controlled, composed, unperturbed, unruffled, unshaken.
Antonyms: EXCITED; HYSTERICAL.

collection *noun* **1** *a collection of junk* accumulation, pile, stockpile, store, supply, stock, hoard, heap, mass, aggregation. **2** *a collection of people* gathering, assembly, assemblage, crowd, body, group, cluster, company, number, throng, congregation, flock, convocation. **3** *a collection of stamps* set, series, array, assortment. **4** *a collection of essays* anthology, corpus, compilation, ana, miscellanea; collected works, analects, analecta. **5** *the amount of the collection for the present* subscription, donation, contribution, gift, alms. **6** *the church collection* offering, offertory, tithe.

collective *adjective* *collective action* joint, united, combined, shared, common, concerted, cooperative, corporate, collaborative, cumulative, aggregate.

college *noun* **1** *she went to college | the college of her choice* school, educational establishment/institution; technical college, community college, university. **2** *the college of thespians | the electoral college* association, fellowship, society, academy, union.

collide *verb* **1** *cars colliding* crash, crash head on, come into collision, smash, bump, bang. **2** *views collide* conflict, be in conflict, clash, differ, disagree, be at variance.

collision *noun* **1** *a highway collision* crash, accident, smash, pile-up, impact. **2** *a collision of views* conflict, clash, difference, disagreement, variance, opposition. **3** *take part in a military collision* confrontation, encounter, skirmish.

colloquial *adjective* conversational, informal, everyday, casual, familiar, chatty, idiomatic, vernacular.

collusion *noun* connivance, complicity, secret understanding, collaboration, intrigue, plotting; *inf.* cahoots.

colonize *verb* settle, people, populate, pioneer, open up, found.

colonnade *noun* portico, arcade, covered walk, cloisters.

colony *noun* **1** *the king visited the colony* settlement, territory, province, dominion, protectorate, dependency, possession, satellite state. **2** *the Chinese colony in San Francisco* community, section, ghetto, district, quarter. **3** *a nudist colony* community, group, association, commune, settlement.

color *noun* **1** *a red color* hue, shade, tint, tone, tinge. **2** *add color to her cheeks* pinkness, rosiness, redness, ruddiness, blush, flush, glow, bloom. **3** *nations of different colors* skin color, skin coloring, skin tone, complexion, coloring, pigmentation. **4** *add color to the description* vividness, life, animation, richness. **5** *under the color of friendship* outward appearance, false show, guise, show, front, façade, cloak, mask, semblance, pretense, pretext.

color *verb* **1** *color the walls/fabric yellow* tint, paint, dye, stain, tinge. **2** *she colored with embarrassment* blush, flush, redden, go red, burn. **3** *attitude colored by childhood experiences* influence, affect, prejudice, distort, slant, taint, pervert, warp. **4** *color the account* exaggerate, overstate, overdraw, embroider, varnish, misrepresent, falsify, disguise, garble.

colorful *adjective* **1** bright-colored, intense, deep-colored, bright, brilliant, vivid, rich, vibrant, multicolored, many-colored, motley, variegated, psychedelic; *inf.* jazzy. **2** *a colorful description* vivid, graphic, interesting, lively, animated, rich.
Antonyms: COLORLESS; DRAB; DULL.

colorless *adjective* **1** *colorless fabric* uncolored, achromatic, achromic, white, bleached, faded. **2** *colorless city people* pale, wan, anemic, washed-out, ashen, sickly. **3** *colorless accounts* uninteresting, dull, boring, tame, lifeless, dreary, lackluster, characterless, insipid, vapid, vacuous.

colors *plural noun* **1** *raised the colors* flag, standard, banner, ensign. **2** *a club's colors* badge, uniform, insignia, ribbon, rosette. **3** *finally saw true colors* nature, character, identity, aspect.

colossal *adjective* **1** *a colossal building* huge, gigantic, immense, enormous, massive, vast, gargantuan, mammoth, prodigious, mountainous, elephantine. **2** *a colossal task* huge, enormous, immense, prodigious, Herculean, monumental, titanic.
Antonyms: TINY; MICROSCOPIC.

column *noun* **1** *marble columns* pillar, support, upright, post, shaft; pilaster, obelisk. **2** *a*

column of people line, file, row, rank, string, procession, train, progression, cavalcade. **3** *a newspaper column* article, piece, item; editorial, leader, gossip column.

coma *noun* unconsciousness, insensibility, stupor, oblivion, blackout, torpor, trance, sopor.

comatose *adjective* **1** *comatose after the accident* in a coma, unconscious, insensible, out cold, blacked-out, torpid, insentient. **2** *feeling comatose after the night shift* drowsy, sleepy, sluggish, lethargic, somnolent, torpid.

comb *noun* **1** *a brush and comb* hair comb, fine-tooth comb, currycomb. **2** *a fowl's comb* coxcomb, crest, tuft, plume.

comb *verb* **1** *comb one's hair* groom, untangle, curry, arrange. **2** *comb wool* dress, card, tease, hackle, heckle. **3** *comb the area for clues* search, scour, ransack, go over with a fine-tooth comb, rake, hunt, sift, rummage.

combat *noun* *engage in mortal combat* battle, fight, conflict, clash, skirmish, encounter, engagement, single combat, hand-to-hand combat; fighting, hostilities.

combat *verb* **1** *combat with the enemy* fight, do battle, wage war, clash, enter into conflict, take up arms (against), grapple; *combat the enemy* fight with/against. **2** *combat disease* fight, battle against, oppose, strive against, make a stand against, resist, withstand, defy.

combatant *noun* **1** *several combatants injured* fighter, fighting man/woman, soldier, serviceman, servicewoman, warrior, battler, contender. **2** *the combatants in the dispute* adversary, antagonist, contender, opponent, enemy, foe, rival.

combatant *adjective* *combatant forces/parties* combating, fighting, warring, battling, opposing, conflicting, clashing, contending, belligerent.

combative *adjective* pugnacious, belligerent, aggressive, militant, bellicose, warlike, quarrelsome, argumentative, contentious, antagonistic, truculent.

combination *noun* **1** *in combination with the other forces* cooperation, association, union, alliance, partnership, coalition, league, consortium, syndication, federation. **2** *a combination of guilt and grief* mixture, mix, blend, amalgam, amalgamation, compound, alloy, composite.

combine *verb* **1** *combine to finish their work* join forces, get together, unite, team up, cooperate, associate, ally, pool resources, amalgamate, merge, integrate. **2** *combine their efforts* join, put together, unite, pool, merge, integrate, fuse, marry, unify, synthesize. **3** *combine the ingredients* mix, blend, admix, amalgamate, bind, bond, compound, alloy, homogenize.
Antonyms: SEPARATE; PART.

combustible *adjective* inflammable, flammable, incendiary, explosive, conflagratory.
Antonym: INCOMBUSTIBLE.

combustion *noun* burning, firing, fire, kindling, igniting, ignition.

come *verb* **1** *they came last night* arrive, appear, put in an appearance, turnup, enter, materialize; *inf.* show up, blow in. **2** *Easter came in March* occur, fall, takeplace, happen, transpire, come about, come to pass. **3** *the dress comes to her ankles* reach, extend, stretch. **4** *the car comes in red* be available, be made, be produced, be offered. **5** *come the fool* act, play, play the part of, behave like, imitate. **6** *come during intercourse* climax, achieve orgasm. **come about** happen, occur, take place, arise, come to pass, transpire, result, befall. **come across 1** *come across an old friend* | *come across an interesting fact* meet, encounter, run into, run across, chance upon, stumble upon, happen upon, light upon, hit upon, find, discover, unearth; *inf.* bump into. **2** *his message/sadness came across* be communicated, be understood, be clear, be perceived. **come across with** *come across with the money/information* give, hand over, deliver, produce, pay up; *inf.* come up with, fork over, cough up. **come along 1** *students/patients coming along well* progress, make progress, develop, improve, show improvement, make headway, get better, pick up, rally, recover, mend. **2** *come along there!* hurry, hurry up, make haste, speed up; *inf.* get a move on, move it, step on it, make it snappy. **come apart** break up, fall to pieces, disintegrate, come unstuck, crumble, separate, split, tear. **come around 1** *coming around annually* occur, take place, happen. **2** *come around after fainting* come to, regain consciousness, revive, wake up, recover. **3** *come around in the evening* come round, visit, call; *inf.* drop in, drop by, stop by, pop in. **come around to** *come around to one's way of thinking* be converted to, be persuaded by, give way to, yield to. **come by** get, obtain, acquire, procure, get possession of, get/lay hold of, get one's hands on, secure, win. **come clean** make a clean breast of it, own up, confess, admit to one's actions/crimes/sins. **come down** *the report came down against punishment* | *they came down in favor of an increase* decide, reach a decision, recommend, choose, opt. **come down on** rebuke, reprimand, reproach, criticize, berate; *inf.* jump on. **come down to** amount to, boil down to, end up as, result in. **come down with** fall ill with, become sick with, catch, contract, fall victim to, be stricken with. **come forward** *helpers coming forward* step forward, volunteer, offer one's services. **come into** *come into money* inherit, be left, be willed, acquire, obtain. **come off** *the attempt did not come off* succeed, be successful, be accomplished, work out, transpire, occur, happen, take place. **come out 1** *the newspaper comes out daily* be published, appear, be in print. **2** *the full story came out* become known, become common knowledge, be revealed, be divulged, be disclosed, be publicized, be released. **3** *flowers coming out* come into bloom, flower, appear. **4** *come out all right* end, finish, conclude, terminate. **5** *debutantes coming out* enter society, be presented, debut. **6** *a gay athlete reluctant to come out* declare oneself a homosexual; *inf.* come out of the closet.

come out with 1 *coming out with a new movie/novel* release, bring out, circulate, publish, make public. **2** *come out with a surprise confession* reveal, utter, say, speak, let out, blurt out.

come through 1 *come through the war* get through, survive, outlast, outlive. **2** *we have come through* get through, survive, remain alive, live on, endure. **come to 1** *come to us* approach, advance, near, draw near to, reach; move/travel toward, bear down on, close in on. **2** *the bill comes to $5* total, add up to, amount to. **3** *come to after fainting* come around, regain consciousness, awaken. *See* COME AROUND 2 (above). **come up** *something came up* arise, occur, happen, crop up, turn up, spring up. **come up to 1** *she came up to his shoulder* come to, reach, extend to. **2** *come up to their standards* reach, measure up to, match up to, compare with, bear comparison with, hold a candle to. **come up with** *come up with a plan* suggest, propose, submit, put forward, present, advance, put up, offer.

Antonyms: GO; LEAVE.

comeback *noun* **1** *the actor making a comeback* return, rally, resurgence, recovery, revival, rebound. **2** *making witty comebacks* retort, reply, rejoinder, response, answer, retaliation, riposte.

comedian *noun* **1** *television comedian* comic, stand-up comic, funny man, funny woman, comedienne, comedy actor/actress, humorist. **2** *her uncle's a real comedian* comic, joker, wit, wag, jester, clown; *inf.* card, laugh.

comedown *noun* loss of status, loss of face, demotion, downgrading, degradation, humiliation, deflation, decline, reversal, anticlimax.

comedy *noun* **1** *theaters staging both comedy and tragedy* light entertainment, humorous play, farce, musical comedy, situation comedy, comedy of errors, burlesque, pantomime, slapstick, satire, vaudeville, comic opera; *inf.* sitcom. **2** *the comedy of the situation* humor, fun, funniness, wit, wittiness, hilarity, levity, facetiousness.

Antonyms: TRAGEDY; GRAVITY.

comely *adjective* **1** *a comely young woman* attractive, good-looking, pretty, beautiful, beauteous, handsome, lovely, fair, fetching, appealing, charming, winsome, pleasing, engaging. **2** *not comely behavior* fit, fitting, suitable, proper, seemly, decent, decorous.

Antonyms: UGLY; IMPROPER.

come-on *noun* inducement, lure, enticement, allurement, temptation, tantalization.

comeuppance *noun* deserved fate, just deserts, deserts, due reward, retribution, punishment, recompense, requital.

comfort *noun* **1** *live in comfort* freedom from hardship, serenity, repose, tranquillity, contentment, content, well-being, coziness, plenty, sufficiency, luxury, opulence. **2** *bring comfort to the bereaved* consolation, solace, condolence, sympathy, commiseration, help, support, succor, relief, easement, alleviation, cheer, gladdening. **3** *a comfort to her parents* solace, consolation, help, aid, support.

Antonyms: DISCOMFORT; GRIEF; AGGRAVATION.

comfort *verb* **1** *comfort the bereaved* bring comfort to, console, solace, give condolences to, give sympathy to, help, support, succor, reassure, soothe, assuage, cheer, gladden. **2** *comforted by the fire* ease, soothe, refresh, revive, hearten, cheer, invigorate, strengthen.

Antonyms: DISTRESS; DEPRESS.

comfortable *adjective* **1** *a comfortable room* homey, cozy, snug. **2** *comfortable clothes/shoes* well-fitting, loose-fitting, roomy. **3** *a comfortable lifestyle* pleasant, adequate, free from hardship, well-off, well-to-do, affluent, luxurious, opulent. **4** *feeling comfortable* at ease, at one's ease, relaxed, serene, tranquil, contented, cozy.

Antonyms: UNCOMFORTABLE; TIGHT; TENSE.

comforting *adjective* consoling, consolatory, soothing, easing, cheering, reassuring, encouraging, assuaging.

comic *adjective* funny, humorous, amusing, entertaining, diverting, droll, jocular, joking, facetious, comical, witty, farcical, hilarious, zany, sidesplitting, priceless, waggish, whimsical.

Antonyms: SERIOUS; GRAVE.

comic *noun* **1** *worked as a comic* stand-up comic, comedian, funny man/woman, humorist. *See* COMEDIAN 1. **2** *he's a real comic* comedian, joker, wag. *See* COMEDIAN 2. **comics** *reading the comics* comic strips, comic books; *inf.* funnies.

comical *adjective* **1** *a comical performance* comic, funny, humorous, amusing. *See* COMIC *adjective*. **2** *a comical hat* absurd, ridiculous, silly, laughable, ludicrous.

coming *noun* *the coming of Christ/summer* advent, approach, nearing, arrival, appearance, accession.

coming *adjective* **1** *the coming appearance | the coming storm* approaching, advancing, forthcoming, nearing, imminent, impending, close at hand, in store, in the wind. **2** *the coming actor* promising, aspiring.

command *verb* **1** *command you to go* order, give orders to, direct, charge, instruct, bid, enjoin, adjure, summon, prescribe, require. **2** *he commands the unit* be in command of, have charge of, control, have control of, rule, govern, direct, preside over, head, lead, manage, supervise, superintend.

command *noun* **1** *follow the commands* order, decree, dictate, edict, instruction, directive, direction, bidding, injunction, behest, mandate, fiat, precept, commandment, enjoining. *See*

COMMAND *verb* 1. **2** *under the command of the French* charge, control, authority, power, mastery, ascendancy, government, direction, management, administration, supervision, dominion, sway, domination.

commandeer *verb* seize, take possession of, requisition, expropriate, appropriate, sequestrate, sequester, hijack.

commander *noun* **1** *the commander of the expedition* leader, head, director, chief, boss; *inf.* top dog, kingpin, big cheese. **2** *naval commander* officer, captain. **3** *army commander* commander-in-chief, C in C, commanding officer, CO.

commanding *adjective* **1** *a commanding position/ lead* controlling, directing, dominating, dominant, superior, advantageous. **2** *a commanding manner/personality* authoritative, autocratic, masterful, assertive, peremptory, imposing, impressive, august.

commemorate *verb* celebrate, pay tribute to, pay homage to, remember, honor, salute, mark, memorialize.

commemorative *adjective* memorial, celebratory, celebrative, remembering, honoring, saluting, in honor of, in memory of, in remembrance of, in tribute to.

commence *verb* **1** *ready to commence* begin, start, make a beginning/start, go ahead, be off, embark, set sail, set the ball rolling, get something off the ground; *inf.* get the show on the road. **2** *commence the proceedings* begin, start, open, enter/embark upon, inaugurate, initiate, originate.
Antonyms: FINISH; END; CONCLUDE.

commend *verb* **1** *commend his work* praise, applaud, speak highly of, approve, acclaim, extol, laud, eulogize. **2** *commend action* recommend, approve, endorse, advocate. **3** *commend her to your care* entrust, trust, deliver, commit, hand over, give, consign, assign.
Antonyms: CRITICIZE; DISAPPROVE.

commendable *adjective* praiseworthy, admirable, laudable, estimable, meritorious, creditable, reputable, worthy, deserving.
Antonyms: DEPLORABLE; LAMENTABLE.

commendation *noun* **1** *receive the judge's commendation* praise, applause, high opinion, acclaim, acclamation, approval, approbation, good opinion, credit, eulogies, extolment, laudation, encomium, panegyric. **2** *the commendation of his soul to God* entrusting, trusting, committal. *See* COMMEND 3.
Antonyms: condemnation; CENSURE.

commensurate *adjective* **1** *a commensurate amount of water to wine* equivalent, equal, corresponding, comparable, proportionate, proportional, commensurable. **2** *a salary commensurate with experience* in accordance with, according to, proportionate to, appropriate to, consistent with, corresponding to.

comment *verb* **1** *he commented unfavorably on her actions* remark, speak, make remarks, make a comment on, express an opinion on, say something about. **2** *"Good," he commented* say, remark, state, observe, interpose. **3** *comment on the text* write notes, annotate, explain, interpret, elucidate, clarify, shed light on.

comment *noun* **1** *pass comments on her appearance | arouse comment* remark, opinion, observation, view, statement, criticism. **2** *textual comment* annotation, note, footnote, gloss, marginalia, explanation, interpretation, elucidation, exposition.

commentary *noun* **1** *a television commentary* narration, description, account, review, analysis. **2** *textual commentary* annotation, notes, interpretation, analysis, exegesis, critique. *See* COMMENT *noun* 2.

commentator *noun* **1** *television commentator* reporter, commenter, broadcaster, narrator, correspondent; newscaster, sportscaster. **2** *text commentator* annotator, interpreter, critic. **3** *commentator on society* commenter. *See* COMMENT *verb* 1, WRITER.

commerce *noun* **1** *work in commerce* business, trade, buying and selling, merchandising, dealing, financial transaction, marketing, traffic. **2** *everyday (social) commerce* social relations, socializing, communication, dealings, traffic, intercourse.

commercial *adjective* **1** *commercial training* business, trade, marketing, merchandising, sales, mercantile. **2** *not a commercial proposition* profitable, profit-making, business. **3** *town becoming too commercial* profit-oriented, mercenary, money-oriented, mercantile, materialistic.

commission *noun* **1** *get a commission on the sale* percentage, brokerage, share, fee, compensation; *inf.* cut. **2** *given the commission of designing the building* task, employment, piece of work, work, duty, charge, mission, responsibility. **3** *receive the commission to be official representative* authority, sanction, warrant, license. **4** *set up a commission of inquiry* committee, board, board of commissioners, council, advisory body, delegation. **5** *the commission of a crime | sin of commission* committing, committal, execution, perpetration, performance.

commission *verb* **1** *commission an artist to paint a portrait* employ, engage, contract, appoint, book, authorize. **2** *commission a portrait* order, put in an order for, place an order for, contract for, pay for, authorize. **3** *commission the representatives* authorize, empower, accredit, sanction, invest.

commit *verb* **1** *commit a crime | commit suicide* perform, carry out, execute, enact, perpetrate, effect, do. **2** *commit to one's care* entrust, trust, deliver, hand over, give, consign, assign. **3** *commit oneself to take part* pledge, promise, engage, bind, covenant, obligate, dedicate. **4** *commit the thief* imprison, jail, confine, lock up, put into custody, put away. **5** *commit the suicidal woman* hospitalize, institutionalize, confine.

commitment *noun* **1** *have too many commitments* undertaking, obligation, responsibility, duty, liability, tie, task, engagement. **2** *have no commitment to the job* dedication, devotion, loyalty, allegiance, adherence. **3** *make a commitment to go* pledge, promise, vow, assurance, covenant.

commodious *adjective* roomy, spacious, capacious, large, extensive, ample.

commodity *noun* thing, item, article, product, article of merchandise.

common *adjective* **1** *the common people* ordinary, average, normal, typical, unexceptional, run-of-the-mill, plain, simple. **2** *a common style of writing* ordinary, unexceptional, undistinguished, run-of-the-mill, workaday, commonplace, mediocre, pedestrian, hackneyed, trite, humdrum. **3** *a common occurrence* usual, ordinary, everyday, daily, regular, frequent, customary, habitual, routine, standard, repeated, recurrent, commonplace, run-of-the-mill. **4** *a common response* usual, ordinary, familiar, routine, stock, standard, conventional, traditional. **5** *a common belief* widespread, general, universal, popular, accepted, prevalent, prevailing. **6** *for the common good* communal, collective, community, public, popular. **7** *a common young woman* low, vulgar, coarse, uncouth, inferior, plebeian.
Antonyms: UNCOMMON; SPECIAL; RARE.

commonplace *adjective* **1** *a commonplace novel/ youngster* ordinary, unexceptional, undistinguished, mediocre, pedestrian, dull, uninteresting, humdrum, hackneyed, trite. **2** *air travel is now commonplace* | *commonplace events* common, usual, ordinary, routine. *See* COMMON 3.
Antonyms: UNUSUAL; EXTRAORDINARY.

common sense *noun* good sense, sense, practicality, judgment, native wit/intelligence, levelheadedness, prudence, discernment, astuteness, shrewdness, judiciousness, wisdom; *inf.* horse sense, gumption.

commotion *noun* disturbance, racket, uproar, rumpus, tumult, clamor, riot, hubbub, hullabaloo, brouhaha, furor, disorder, confusion, upheaval, disruption, agitation, excitement, fuss, disquiet, ferment, to-do, bustle, hustle and bustle.

communal *adjective* common, collective, shared, joint, general, public, community, cooperative, communalist.
Antonyms: INDIVIDUAL; EXCLUSIVE.

commune *verb* **1** *commune with close friends* converse, talk, communicate, speak, have a tête-à-tête, confer, confide. **2** *commune with nature* feel in close touch, feel at one, empathize, identify.

commune *noun* collective, cooperative, co-op, community, kibbutz.

communicable *adjective* infectious, contagious, catching, transmittable, transmissible, transferable.

communicate *verb* **1** *communicate information* transmit, pass on, transfer, impart, convey, relay, spread, disseminate, make known, publish, broadcast, announce, report, divulge, disclose, unfold, proclaim. **2** *not to communicate with him* be in touch, be in contact, have dealings, interface. **3** *you must be able to communicate* get one's ideas/message across, interface, be articulate, be fluent, be eloquent. **4** *communicate a disease* transmit, pass on, transfer, spread.

communication *noun* **1** *communication is difficult* information transmission/transfer, transmission, dissemination, contact, getting in touch, radio/telephone link, connection, interface, social intercourse. **2** *received the communication* message, letter, report, statement, dispatch, news, information, data, intelligence, word.

communications *noun* **1** *all communications under enemy control* links, channels, routes, passages. **2** *studying communications* electronic communication, telecommunications, data communications, information technology, IT.

communicative *adjective* *not a very communicative person* expansive, forthcoming, talkative, loquacious, voluble, chatty, conversational, informative, frank, open, candid.
Antonyms: UNCOMMUNICATIVE; TACITURN; RESERVED.

communion *noun* **1** *a strange communion between each other* | *communion with nature* rapport, empathy, sympathy, accord, affinity, fellowship, togetherness, harmony, closeness, agreement, sharing, concord, unity, fusion, communication. **2** *Holy Communion* Eucharist.

communiqué *noun* official communication, bulletin, dispatch, report, news flash, announcement.

communism *noun* state ownership, collectivism, Sovietism, Bolshevism, Marxism, Leninism.

community *noun* **1** *move to a new community* locality, district, neighborhood. **2** *the community condemned her* residents, inhabitants; population, populace. **3** *work for the community* society, public, general public, body politic, nation, state. **4** *the Jewish community in New York* group, section, body, company, set, ghetto. **5** *religious community* brotherhood, sisterhood, association. **6** *community of interests* similarity, likeness, agreement, affinity. **7** *community of property* shared possession, joint liability, common ownership, joint participation.

commute *verb* **1** *commute from the suburbs* travel to and from, travel back and forth, shuttle. **2** *commute a sentence/penalty* lessen, reduce, shorten, curtail, mitigate, modify. **3** *commute an annuity to a lump sum* exchange, change, interchange, substitute, trade, barter, switch.

commuter *noun* daily traveler.

compact *adjective* **1** *a compact parcel* dense, packed close, pressed together, close, firm, solid, compressed, condensed. **2** *a compact car/machine* small, economy-sized. **3** *a compact style* concise, succinct, terse, brief, condensed, pithy, to the point, epigrammatic, compendious.
Antonyms: LOOSE; LARGE; LENGTHY; RAMBLING.

compact *verb* *compact the sand* pack down, press down, compress, press together, condense, tamp.

compact *noun* *the two sides signed the compact* contract, agreement, covenant, pact, indenture, bond, treaty, alliance, bargain, deal, transaction, settlement, entente.

companion *noun* **1** *with an unknown companion* | *the girl and her companions* partner, escort, consort, friend, crony, comrade, colleague, associate, ally, confederate; *inf.* buddy, pal. **2** *the princess and her companion* attendant, aide, chaperon, duenna, squire. **3** *the companion of this bookend/volume* fellow, mate, twin, match, counterpart, complement. **4** *the Reader's Companion* guide, handbook, manual, reference book.

companionship *noun* friendship, fellowship, company, society, togetherness, social intercourse, comradeship, camaraderie, association, brotherhood, sisterhood, intimacy, rapport.

company *noun* **1** *enjoy their company* companionship, friendship, fellowship. *See* COMPANIONSHIP. **2** *address the company* assembly, assemblage, gathering, meeting, audience, group, crowd, throng, congregation, convention. **3** *a company of actors/artisans* group, band, party, body, association, society, fellowship, troupe, collection, circle, league, crew, guild. **4** *a retail company* business, firm, concern, corporation, house, establishment, conglomerate; *inf.* outfit. **5** *a company of soldiers* subdivision, unit, detachment. **6** *expecting company* guest(s), visitor(s), caller(s).

comparable *adjective* *comparable pay for comparable work* equivalent, commensurable, corresponding, proportional, proportionate, similar, like, parallel, analogous, related.
comparable to *his acting is not comparable to his father's* as good as, equal to, on a par with, in the same class/league as/with, on a level with.
Antonyms: DISSIMILAR; UNLIKE.

comparative *adjective* *living in comparative affluence* relative, in/by comparison, qualified, modified.

compare *verb* **1** *compare the two styles* contrast, juxtapose, weigh/balance/measure the differences between, collate, differentiate. **2** *the is-*land *has been compared to heaven* liken, equate, analogize. **compare with** *his work does not compare with Hardy's* bear comparison to, be comparable to, be the equal to, be on a par with, be in the same class with, compete with, match, approach, come up to, hold a candle to. *See* COMPARABLE, COMPARABLE TO.

comparison *noun* **1** *make a comparison* contrast, juxtaposition, collation, differentiation. *See* COMPARE 1. **2** *no comparison between their works* comparability, analogy, resemblance, likeness, similarity, correlation.

compartment *noun* **1** *luggage/bomb compartment* section, part, partition, bay, chamber, niche. **2** *compartments of one's life* part, section, division, department, area. **3** *train compartment* car, coach.

compass *noun* *within the compass of his power* scope, range, area, extent, reach, span, stretch, limits, bounds, field, sphere, zone, circumference.

compassion *noun* pity, tender-heartedness, softheartedness, tenderness, gentleness, mercy, leniency, understanding, sympathy, concern, consideration, humanity, kindness, kindheartedness, charity, benevolence.

compassionate *adjective* softhearted, tender, gentle, merciful, lenient, understanding, sympathetic, pitying, humanitarian, humane, kindly, kindhearted, charitable, benevolent.
Antonyms: CRUEL; UNKIND; UNSYMPATHETIC.

compatible *adjective* **1** *couples not compatible* well-suited, suited, like-minded, of the same mind, in agreement, in tune, in harmony, reconcilable, having affinity/rapport, accordant. **2** *views not compatible with actions* consistent, in keeping, reconcilable, consonant, congruous, congruent.
Antonyms: INCOMPATIBLE; INCONSISTENT.

compatriot *noun* fellow countryman, fellow countrywoman, countryman, countrywoman, fellow citizen.

compel *verb* **1** *compel them to leave* force, make, coerce, drive, pressure, pressurize, dragoon, constrain, impel, oblige, necessitate, urge; *inf.* bulldoze, railroad, twist one's arm, strong-arm, put the screws on. **2** *compel obedience* force, enforce, exact, insist upon, necessitate, extort.

---

compel
coerce, constrain, force, necessitate, oblige

A parent faced with a rebellious teenager may try to **compel** him to do his homework by threatening to take away his allowance. *Compel* commonly implies the exercise of authority, the exertion of great effort, or the impossibility of doing anything else (*compelled to graduate from high school by her eagerness to leave home*). It typically requires a personal object, although it is possible to *compel* a reaction or response (*she compels admiration*). **Force** is a little stronger, suggesting the exertion of power, energy, or physical strength to accomplish something or to subdue resistance (*his mother forced him to confess that he'd broken the basement window*). **Coerce** can imply the use of force, but often stops short of using it (*she was coerced into obedience by the threat of losing her telephone privileges*). **Constrain** means *compel*, but by means of restriction, confinement, or limitation (*constrained from dating by his parents' strictness*). **Necessitate** and **oblige** make an action necessary by imposing certain conditions that demand a response (*Her mother's illness obliged her to be more cooperative; it also necessitated giving up her social life*).

---

compelling *adjective* **1** *a compelling story* fascinating, gripping, enthralling, irresistible, hypnotic, mesmeric. **2** *compelling reasons* cogent, convincing, forceful, powerful, weighty, telling, conclusive, irrefutable.
Antonyms: BORING; WEAK.

compensate *verb* **1** *compensate for his evil deed* make amends, make restitution, make reparation, make up for, atone, expiate. **2** *compensate her for her loss* recompense, repay, reimburse, requite, indemnify. **compensate for** *the cargo compensating for the lightness of the boat* counterbalance, counterpoise, counteract, balance, cancel out, neutralize, nullify.

compensation *noun* **1** *receive compensation for her loss* recompense, repayment, reimbursement, requital, indemnification, indemnity, damages. **2** *make compensation for his deed* amends, restitution, redress, atonement, expiation.

compete *verb* **1** *compete in the race* | *have decided to compete* take part, enter, participate, be a contestant; *inf.* throw one's hat in the ring, be in the running. **2** *compete against/with his brother* contend, vie, strive, struggle, fight, pit oneself (against).

competence *noun* **1** *the competence of the player* capability, ability, capacity, proficiency, adeptness, expertise, skill. **2** *the competence of the answer* adequacy, appropriateness, suitability, pertinence, appositeness. **3** *competence to plead* fitness, qualification.

competent *adjective* **1** *a very competent player* capable, able, proficient, qualified, efficient, adept, accomplished, skillful. **2** *a competent answer* adequate, appropriate, suitable, pertinent, apposite. **3** *not competent to plead* fit, fitted, qualified.
Antonyms: INCOMPETENT; INEPT.

competition *noun* **1** *a chess competition* contest, match, game, tournament, event, meet, quiz. **2** *the competition between opponents* rivalry, vying, contest, opposition, struggle, contention, strife. **3** *the competition is poor* | *went to meet my competition* field, opposition; challengers, opponents, rivals.

competitive *adjective* **1** *a very competitive young man* competition-oriented, ambitious, combative, aggressive. **2** *a competitive industry* aggressive, dog-eat-dog, cutthroat.

competitor *noun* **1** *competitors in the race* contestant, contender, challenger, participant, candidate, entrant. **2** *his business competitors* rival, opponent, adversary, antagonist; opposition.
Antonyms: ALLY; COLLEAGUE.

compilation *noun* *a compilation of short stories* collection, anthology, album, corpus, ana.

compile *verb* gather, collect, accumulate, amass, assemble, put together, collate, marshal, organize, systematize, anthologize.

complacent *adjective* smug, self-satisfied, pleased with oneself, satisfied, contented, self-contented, pleased, gratified, placid, serene, bovine, self-righteous.
Antonyms: DISSATISFIED; DISCONTENTED.

complain *verb* **1** *complain about the service* lodge a complaint, criticize, find fault, carp, make a fuss; *inf.* kick up a fuss. **2** *always complaining* grumble, grouse, gripe, moan, grouch, whine, lament, bewail; *inf.* bellyache, beef, bitch.

complaint *noun* **1** *manager attending to complaints* criticism, grievance, charge, accusation, protest, remonstrance, statement of dissatisfaction; faultfinding; *Law* plaint. **2** *always full of complaint* grumbling, grousing. *See* COMPLAIN 2. **3** *a painful complaint* illness, disease, ailment, disorder, sickness, affliction, malady.

complement *noun* **1** *the perfect complement to the food* companion, addition, supplement, accessory, final/finishing touch. **2** *the school's full complement* amount, allowance, total, aggregate, load, capacity, quota.

complement *verb* *wine complementing the food* complete, round/set off, add to, go well with, be the perfect companion/addition to, add the final/finishing touch to, supplement.

complementary *adjective* complemental, completing, finishing, perfecting, culminative, consummative.

complete *adjective* **1** *the complete collection* entire, whole, full, total, intact, unbroken, undivided, uncut, unshortened, unabridged, plenary. **2** *the task is complete* completed, finished, ended, concluded, accomplished, finalized. **3** *a complete fool* absolute, out-and-out, thoroughgoing, thorough, utter, total, perfect, consummate, unqualified, dyed-in-the-wool.
Antonyms: INCOMPLETE; PARTIAL.

complete *verb* **1** *complete the task* finish, end, conclude, finalize, realize, accomplish, achieve, fulfill, execute, effect, discharge, settle, clinch, do; *inf.* wrap up, polish off. **2** *complete the outfit* finish off, round off, make perfect, perfect, crown, cap, add the final/finishing touch to.
Antonyms: BEGIN; COMMENCE.

completely *adverb* *completely exhausted* totally,

utterly, absolutely, thoroughly, quite, wholly, altogether.

completion *noun* finish, ending, conclusion, close, finalization, realization, accomplishment, achievement, fulfillment, execution, consummation.

complex *adjective* 1 *a complex subject* complicated, difficult, involved, intricate, convoluted, knotty, perplexing, puzzling, cryptic, enigmatic. 2 *a complex structure* composite, compound, compounded, multiple, manifold, multiplex, heterogeneous.
Antonyms: SIMPLE; EASY; ELEMENTARY.

complex *noun* 1 *building complex* | *complex of regulations* structure, scheme, composite, conglomerate, aggregation, network, system, organization, synthesis. 2 *a complex about her nose* obsession, phobia, fixation, preoccupation, idée fixe.

complexion *noun* 1 *ruddy complexion* skin, skin color, skin coloring, skin tone, coloring, pigmentation. 2 *put a new complexion on it* aspect, appearance, guise, look, angle. 3 *his brother is of a different complexion* character, nature, disposition, cast, stamp.

complexity *noun* *the complexities of the situation* complication, difficulty, intricacy, convolution, problem, puzzle, enigma, ramification, entanglement.

compliance *noun* *noted for his compliance* yielding, submissiveness, submission, deference, passivity, subservience, servility. **compliance with** *compliance with the law* obedience to, observance of, abiding by, conforming to, acquiescence to, agreement with/to, accordance with.

complicate *verb* make difficult, make involved/intricate, confuse, muddle, jumble, snarl up, entangle.

complicated *adjective* difficult, involved, intricate, complex, convoluted, perplexing, puzzling, enigmatic, cryptic, entangled, Byzantine.
Antonyms: EASY; SIMPLE; STRAIGHTFORWARD.

complication *noun* 1 *meet complications* difficulty, problem, drawback, snag, obstacle, aggravation. 2 *a great deal of complication* difficulty, intricacy, complexity, confusion, muddle.

complicity *noun* collusion, conspiracy, collaboration, connivance, abetment.

compliment *noun* *receive a compliment* flattering remark/comment, bouquet. **compliments** praise, tribute, homage, admiration, flattery, commendation, laudation, eulogy.
Antonyms: INSULT; CRITICISM.

compliment *verb* congratulate, felicitate, speak highly of, praise, sing the praises of, pay tribute/homage to, salute, admire, flatter, commend, honor, acclaim, laud, eulogize.
Antonyms: INSULT; CRITICIZE; CONDEMN.

complimentary *adjective* 1 *complimentary re-* marks congratulatory, admiring, appreciative, approving, flattering, commendatory, laudatory, eulogizing, panegyrical. 2 *complimentary tickets* free of charge, given free, gratis; *inf.* on the house.

compliments *plural noun* *the compliments of the season* greetings, good wishes, regards, respects, salutations.

comply *verb* **comply with** *comply with the ruling* obey, observe, abide by, adhere to, conform to, acquiesce to, assent to, consent to, accord with, agree with, follow, respect, yield, submit.
Antonyms: IGNORE; DISOBEY; DISAGREE.

component *noun* part, piece, section, constituent, element, unit, module, item.

component *adjective* constituent, composing, integral, sectional, fractional.

compose *verb* 1 *compose a poem* write, make up, create, think up, devise, concoct, invent, compile, contrive, formulate, fashion, produce. 2 *compose one's dress/plans* put together, arrange, put in order, align, organize, assemble, collate, systematize. 3 *peoples composing a nation* make up, form, constitute, comprise. 4 *compose oneself* calm, calm down, quiet, collect, control, soothe, still, tranquilize, quell, pacify, assuage.

composed *adjective* *feeling composed* | *a composed manner* calm, cool, collected, cool and collected, serene, tranquil, relaxed, poised, at ease, unruffled, self-controlled, untroubled, undisturbed, unperturbed, unworried, confident, self-possessed, levelheaded; *inf.* together.
Antonyms: EXCITED; OVERWROUGHT.

composite *adjective* *a composite structure* compound, complex, conglomerate, combined, blended, mixed, synthesized.

composite *noun* *a composite of various elements* compound, amalgam, blend, mixture, complex, combination, fusion, conglomerate, synthesis.

composition *noun* 1 *the composition of the soil* structure, constitution, makeup, conformation, configuration, organization, arrangement, layout, character. 2 *an adhesive composition* compound, amalgam, blend, mixture, mix, admixture. *See* COMPOUND *noun*. 3 *the composition of a poem* writing, making-up, creation, concoction, invention, compilation. *See* COMPOSE 1. 4 *a brilliant composition* work of art, creation, literary/musical/artistic work, poem, novel, opus, arrangement, symphony, picture. 5 *students writing a composition* essay, theme, piece of writing. 6 *admire the painting's composition* arrangement, proportions, harmony, balance, symmetry.

compost *noun* fertilizer, manure, humus, mulch.

composure *noun* aplomb, poise, self-possession, presence of mind, sang-froid, equanimity, equilibrium, self-control, self-command, calm, calmness, coolness, collectedness, serenity, tranquillity, imperturbability, inexcitability, placidity.

compound *noun a chemical/verbal compound* amalgam, blend, mixture, admixture, complex, combination, fusion, alloy, conglomerate, synthesis, medley, hybrid.

compound *adjective a compound substance* composite, complex, conglomerate, blended, not simple, fused. *See* COMPOUND *noun*.
Antonym: SIMPLE.

compound *verb* **1** *compound the two ideas/substances* mix, blend, combine, put together, amalgamate, unite, coalesce, alloy, fuse, mingle, intermingle, synthesize. **2** *compound the problem/fear compounded with poverty* worsen, make worse, add to, augment, exacerbate, magnify, aggravate, intensify, heighten.

comprehend *verb* **1** *comprehend the facts* understand, grasp, take in, assimilate, fathom, perceive, discern, apprehend. **2** *cannot comprehend how he won* understand, conceive, imagine. *See* FATHOM 2.
Antonyms: MISUNDERSTAND; EXCLUDE.

comprehensible *adjective* intelligible, understandable, graspable, fathomable, discernible, conceivable, plain, clear, explicit, coherent, lucid.

comprehension *noun beyond one's comprehension* understanding, grasp, perception, ken, discernment, conception.

comprehensive *adjective* inclusive, all-inclusive, all-embracing, complete, full, encyclopedic, exhaustive, thorough, extensive, broad, widespread, far-reaching, blanket, universal, catholic.
Antonyms: PARTIAL 1; LIMITED.

compress *verb* **1** *compress the pile of sand* pack down, press down, press together, squeeze together, squash, crush, condense, compact, cram, tamp, constrict. **2** *compress the text* abbreviate, shorten, abridge, contract, reduce.
Antonyms: EXPAND; SPREAD.

comprise *verb* **1** *a board comprising only men* consist of, contain, include, be composed of, take in, embrace, encompass. **2** *children comprising the audience* make up, form, constitute, compose.

compromise *verb* **1** *compromise on the wording* come to terms, come to an understanding, make a deal, make concessions, find a happy medium, find the middle ground, strike a balance, meet halfway, give and take, take part in a trade-off. **2** *compromise him | compromise his reputation* discredit, dishonor, bring shame to, bring into disrepute, shame, embarrass, endanger, jeopardize, imperil. **3** *compromise his chances* prejudice, damage, injure, endanger, weaken.

compromise *noun reach a compromise* understanding, deal, happy medium, middle course, balance, trade-off, settlement by concession; set of terms; middle ground, give and take, adjustment.

compulsion *noun* **1** *under no compulsion to go* obligation, force, duress, constraint, coercion, pressure, oppression, enforcement. **2** *feel a compulsion to travel* urge, need, desire, motivation, necessity, preoccupation, obsession.

compulsive *adjective* **1** *compulsive viewing* fascinating, gripping, irresistible, compelling. *See* COMPELLING 1. **2** *a compulsive desire to wash* obsessive, uncontrollable, irresistible, compelling, driving, overwhelming, urgent, besetting. **3** *compulsive eating* addictive, obsessional, obsessive, uncontrollable, out of control, ungovernable. **4** *a compulsive gambler/drinker* addicted, addictive, obsessive, obsessional, dependent; *inf.* hooked.

compulsory *adjective* obligatory, mandatory, required, binding, forced, necessary, essential, de rigueur.
Antonyms: OPTIONAL; elective.

compunction *noun* remorse, regret, pangs of conscience, guilt, contrition, contriteness, penitence, repentance; scruples.

compute *verb* calculate, reckon, count, add up, total, figure out, work out, enumerate, sum, tally, cast up, measure, rate.

comrade *noun* companion, friend, colleague, partner, associate, coworker, fellow worker, mate, teammate, ally, confederate, compatriot; *inf.* pal, buddy.

con *verb conned us into investing* swindle, deceive, cheat, hoodwink, mislead, delude, bamboozle.

con *noun* confidence trick, swindle, deception, fraud, cheating; racket; con man, confidence man, swindler, deceiver, cheater; *inf.* rip-off, scam, gyp.

concave *adjective* curved in, hollow, hollowed out, depressed, sunken, indented, scooped-out.

conceal *verb* **1** *conceal her face | conceal the letter* hide, cover, keep out of sight, keep hidden, screen, obscure, disguise, camouflage, mask, secrete, shelter, bury, tuck away. **2** *conceal his identity* hide, keep secret, keep dark, hush up, cover up, dissemble; *inf.* keep the lid on.
Antonyms: REVEAL; EXPOSE.

concealed *adjective a concealed entrance* hidden, obscured, unseen, invisible, screened, secreted, tucked away.

concealment *noun a place of concealment* hiding, hideaway, hide-out, retreat; secrecy, privacy, sheltering, secretion, camouflage.

concede *verb* **1** *concede defeat* acknowledge, admit, accept, own, allow, grant, accede, confess, recognize. **2** *concede some territory/goals* give up, yield, surrender, relinquish, cede, hand over.
Antonyms: DENY; DISPUTE; RETAIN.

conceit *noun* **1** *the winner full of conceit* pride, arrogance, vanity, self-admiration, self-love, self-importance, self-adulation, narcissism, self-satisfaction, egotism, complacency, boasting, swagger, vain glory. **2** *exchanging clever conceits* witticism, quip, *bon mot*, pleasantry, epigram. **3** *a mind occupied with conceits* fancy idea, notion, whim; fantasy, imagination, whimsy, vagary.

Antonyms: MODESTY; HUMILITY; self-effacement.

conceited *adjective* proud, arrogant, vain, self-important, cocky, haughty, supercilious, overweening, narcissistic, immodest, egotistical, puffed up, self-satisfied, complacent, boastful, swaggering, vainglorious; *inf.* bigheaded, swellheaded, stuck-up.

Antonyms: HUMBLE; MODEST.

conceivable *adjective* *not conceivable that he would lose* credible, believable, imaginable, thinkable, possible, understandable, comprehensible.

conceive *verb* **1** *women unable to conceive* become pregnant, become impregnated, become fertilized. **2** *conceive the idea* | *conceive a plan* think up, draw up, form, formulate, produce, develop, project, devise, contrive, conjure up, envisage. **3** *cannot conceive that/how he lost* imagine, think, believe, realize, appreciate, suppose, understand, comprehend, perceive, grasp, apprehend, envisage, visualize, fancy.

concentrate *verb* **1** *concentrate one's attention/efforts on* focus, center, converge, centralize, consolidate, bring to bear, congregate, cluster. **2** *troops concentrating on the border* | *concentrate the troops* collect, gather, congregate, accumulate, amass, cluster, rally, huddle. **3** *concentrate the liquid* condense, boil down, reduce, compress, distill. **concentrate on** *concentrate on one's studies* be absorbed in, focus attention on, be engrossed in, give one's attention/mind to, put one's mind to, think about closely, consider closely, rack one's brains about/over.

Antonyms: DIFFUSE; DISPERSE; DISSIPATE.

concentrated *adjective* *a concentrated effort* intensive, intense, consolidated, rigorous, vigorous; *inf.* all-out.

concentration *noun* **1** *lose one's concentration* close attention, absorption, application, engrossment, single-mindedness, heed. **2** *the concentration of one's attention/efforts* focusing, centralization, consolidation. *See* CONCENTRATE 1. **3** *the concentration of troops* collection, gathering, congregation. *See* CONCENTRATE 3.

concept *noun* idea, notion, abstraction, conceptualization, conception, hypothesis, theory, image, view.

conception *noun* **1** *when conception took place* conceiving, fertilization, impregnation, fecundation, inception of pregnancy. **2** *in at the conception of the project* inception, beginning, origination, origin, birth, initiation, formation, launching, invention, outset. **3** *a brilliant conception* plan, design, invention, creation, project, scheme, proposal. **4** *the conception of quantum mechanics* idea, abstraction, concept.

See CONCEPT. **5** *no conception of how to behave* idea, notion, perception, appreciation, understanding, clue, inkling, impression, picture.

concern *verb* **1** *affairs that concern you* be the business of, affect, be relevant to, involve, apply to, pertain to, have a bearing on, bear on, be of interest to, touch. **2** *a report concerning cancer* be about, deal with, be connected with, relate to, have to do with, appertain to. **3** *you should not concern yourself (in/with)* interest/involve oneself (in), be interested/involved (in), take/have a hand (in), busy oneself (with), devote one's time (to), be busy (with). **4** *their behavior concerned us* worry, disturb, trouble, bother, perturb, make anxious, cause disquiet to, distress.

concern *noun* **1** *none of your concern* business, affair, interest, matter of interest, involvement, responsibility, charge, duty, job, task, occupation, mission, department, field, subject, discipline. **2** *news of concern to all of us* interest, importance, relevance, bearing, applicability. **3** *parents full of concern* worry, disturbance, anxiety, disquiet, perturbation, distress, apprehension. **4** *parents demonstrating their concern* care, caringness, solicitude, attentiveness, attention, consideration, regard. **5** *start a publishing concern* business, firm, company, enterprise, organization, corporation, establishment, house.

Antonyms: disinterest; INDIFFERENCE.

concerned *adjective* **1** *concerned parties* interested, involved, implicated. **2** *concerned citizens going to the police* worried, disturbed, anxious, upset, uneasy, troubled, perturbed, distressed, bothered, apprehensive. **3** *concerned parents* caring, attentive, solicitous, responsible, considerate.

Antonyms: DISINTERESTED; INDIFFERENT.

concerning *preposition* about, on the subject of, relating to, relevant to, regarding, as regards, with regard to, with reference to, referring to, with respect to, respecting, as to, touching on, in the matter of, re, apropos of.

concert *noun* **1** *a hall designed for concerts* musical entertainment, show, performance. **2** *no concert in their actions* agreement, accordance, accord, unanimity, harmony, concord, concordance, unity, unison, consensus. **in concert** *act in concert* together, jointly, in combination, cooperatively, in cooperation, in collaboration, in league, in unison, shoulder to shoulder, side by side, concertedly.

concerted *adjective* *a concerted effort* jointly planned, combined, cooperative, joint, coordinated, united, collaborative, synchronized, interactive, synergetic.

Antonym: SEPARATE.

concession *noun* **1** *the concession of defeat* acknowledgement, admission, acceptance, allowance, recognition. **2** *the concession of territory* yielding, surrender, relinquishment, ceding, giving up, handing over. **3** *make con-*

cessions | *as a concession to their youth* allowance, adjustment, modification, compromise, indulgence, exception. **4** *price concessions* reduction, cut, discount, decrease. **5** *grant the concession* franchise, license, permit, warrant, authorization.

conciliate *verb* placate, appease, pacify, propitiate, mollify, assuage, calm down, soothe, humor, reconcile, disarm, win over, restore harmony to.

conciliatory *adjective* appeasing, pacifying, pacificatory, propitiative, mollifying, assuaging, disarming, reconciliatory, peacemaking; *fml.* irenic.

concise *adjective* succinct, compact, terse, brief, short, condensed, compressed, crisp, pithy, to the point, epigrammatic, compendious, summary, synoptic.
Antonyms: LENGTHY; DISCURSIVE; WORDY.

conclave *noun* private meeting, secret meeting, conference, council, parley, session, assembly, congress, gathering, forgathering, congregation.

conclude *verb* **1** *the meeting concluded at 9 o'clock* end, finish, close, come/draw to an end, halt, cease, terminate, discontinue; *inf.* wind up. **2** *we concluded the meeting* end, finish, close, bring to an end. **3** *conclude an agreement* negotiate, come to terms on, reach terms on, bring about, pull off, clinch, work out, accomplish, fix, effect, establish, engineer, settle, decide, determine, resolve. **4** *conclude that he had won* come to the conclusion, deduce, infer, decide, gather, reckon, judge, assume, presume, suppose, conjecture, surmise.
Antonyms: START; COMMENCE; EXTEND.

conclusion *noun* **1** *the conclusion of the meeting* end, finish, close, halting, cessation, termination, discontinuance; *inf.* wind-up. **2** *the conclusion of the agreement* negotiation, clinching, accomplishment, establishment, settling, resolution. *See* CONCLUDE 3. **3** *a predictable conclusion* outcome, result, upshot, issue, culmination, consequence. **4** *reach the conclusion that he was guilty* deduction, inference, decision, opinion, judgment, verdict, conviction, assumption, presumption. **in conclusion** in closing, to sum up, finally, lastly, in winding up.
Antonyms: BEGINNING; OPENING; commencement; START.

conclusive *adjective* decisive, clinching, definitive, definite, final, ultimate, categorical, incontestable, irrefutable, convincing, cogent.

concoct *verb* **1** *concoct a meal/stew* prepare, put together, make, cook, muster, mix, blend, brew; *inf.* rustle up. **2** *concoct an excuse* devise, invent, make up, think up, dream up, fabricate, form, formulate, hatch, plot, forge, scheme, design, fashion; *inf.* cook up.

concoction *noun* **1** *a tasty concoction* preparation, mixture, blend, combination, brew, creation. **2** *don't believe that concoction* invention, fabrication, plot, scheme, designing.

concomitant *adjective* attendant, accompanying, associated, belonging, linked, affiliated, accessory, auxiliary.

concord *noun* agreement, harmony, accord, unity, oneness, consensus.
Antonyms: DISAGREEMENT; DISCORD.

concrete *adjective* **1** *concrete evidence* actual, real, factual, definite, genuine, substantial, material, tangible, unimaginary, specific. **2** *a concrete substance* solid, solidified, firm, consolidated, compact, dense, condensed, compressed, coalesced, petrified, calcified.
Antonyms: ABSTRACT; UNREAL.

concubine *noun* mistress, paramour, kept woman, courtesan.

concur *verb* **1** *they concur on/over the verdict* agree, be in accord, accord, be in harmony, acquiesce, assent, be in assent, be of the same mind, be in concord. **2** *the two events concurred* coincide, happen/occur together, be simultaneous, coexist, synchronize. **3** *they concurred in the attempt* cooperate, combine, unite, collaborate, join forces, act together, work together, pool resources.
Antonym: DISAGREE.

concurrent *adjective* **1** *concurrent sentences* simultaneous, parallel, coexisting, coexistent, coincident, contemporaneous, synchronous, side-by-side. **2** *concurrent lines* converging, convergent, meeting, joining, uniting, intersecting. **3** *concurrent attitudes* agreeing, in agreement, in accord, in harmony, harmonious, assenting, in assent, of the same mind, like-minded, as one, at one, in rapport, compatible, consentient. **4** *concurrent action* cooperative, combined, united, joint, collaborative.

concussion *noun* **1** *suffer (a) concussion in the accident* brain injury, unconsciousness, loss of consciousness. **2** *damage caused by concussion* jarring, jar, jolting, jolt, shaking, shock, blow, bump, impact, clash, collision.

condemn *verb* **1** *condemn all violence | condemn him for his action* censure, denounce, deprecate, disapprove of, criticize, berate, upbraid, reprove, reproach, blame, reprehend, reprobate. **2** *condemn him to death* sentence, pass sentence on, convict. **3** *condemn the building* declare unfit, forbid the use of, proscribe, ban, bar. **4** *his action condemned him* declare guilty, prove one's guilt, accuse, incriminate, indict, inculpate, implicate. **5** *condemned to misery/poverty* doom, damn, force, compel, coerce, impel.
Antonyms: PRAISE; ACQUIT.

condemnatory *adjective* condemning, censuring, censorious, denunciatory, deprecatory, disapproving, critical, reproving, vituperative, reproachful.

condensation *noun* **1** *the condensation of the sauce* concentration, concentrating, boiling down, reduction. *See* CONDENSE 1. **2** *the condensation of steam* liquefaction, liquidization, deliquescence, precipitation, distillation. **3** *the condensation of the report* shortening, abridgment, abbreviation, cutting, summarization. See CONDENSE 3. **4** *read the condensation* abridgment, summary, précis, digest, abstract, synopsis.

condense *verb* **1** *condense the sauce by boiling* concentrate, thicken, boil down, reduce, solidify, coagulate. **2** *steam condensing on the mirror* liquefy, liquidize, deliquesce, precipitate. **3** *condense the report* shorten, abridge, abbreviate, cut, compress, contract, compact, curtail, summarize, epitomize, encapsulate.
Antonyms: DILUTE; LENGTHEN; EXPAND.

condescend *verb* **1** *condescend to speak to him* lower oneself, deign, stoop, descend, unbend, humble/demean oneself, vouchsafe; *inf.* come down from one's high horse. **2** *condescend to younger people* treat condescendingly, patronize, talk down to, look down one's nose at.

condescending *adjective* patronizing, disdainful, supercilious, superior, snobbish, lofty, lordly; *inf.* snooty, snotty, uppity.

condition *noun* **1** *the human condition | the condition of slavery* state, state of existence, circumstance, situation, predicament. **2** *in a miserable condition* state, state of affairs, circumstance, situation, position, plight, predicament, quandary. **3** *athletes in good/poor condition* shape, form, order, fitness, physical fitness, health, state of health, fettle, kilter, trim, working order. **4** *a condition of the job* qualification, requirement, necessity, essential, demand, prerequisite, stipulation; terms. **5** *the conditions of the agreement | make certain conditions* restriction, rule, provision, proviso, contingency, stipulation, prerequisite, limitation, modification; term, limit. **6** *a heart condition* disease, disorder, illness, complaint, problem, ailment, weakness, infirmity, malady. **7** *people of various conditions* social position, class, rank, status, station, stratum, grade, order, footing, caste, estate.

condition *verb* **1** *lotions conditioning the skin/leather* make healthy, improve, tone, tone up, prepare, make ready. **2** *cats conditioned to live in city apartments* train, teach, educate, coach, tutor, accustom, adapt, habituate, inure. **3** *childhood experiences conditioning later responses* influence, affect, govern, determine.

conditional *adjective* **1** *an offer conditional on references* dependent on, contingent on, subject to, based upon. **2** *given a conditional offer* qualified, having conditions, with reservations, restrictive, provisional, provisory, stipulatory.
Antonyms: UNCONDITIONAL; ABSOLUTE.

conditioned *adjective* *a conditioned response* learned, trained, taught, habituated.

conditions *plural noun* *live in pleasant conditions* circumstances, surroundings, environment, situation, milieu, way of life.

condolence *noun* commiseration, sympathy, fellow feeling, compassion, feeling, pity, solace, comfort.

condom *noun* contraceptive, prophylactic, sheath; *inf.* rubber.

condone *verb* overlook, disregard, let pass, turn a blind eye to, wink at, excuse, pardon, forgive, make allowances for, forget.
Antonyms: CONDEMN; PUNISH.

conducive *adjective* *hardly conducive to study* contributing, contributory, helpful, instrumental, useful, favorable, advantageous.

conduct *noun* **1** *guilty of evil conduct* behavior, way of behaving, comportment, bearing, deportment; actions, ways, habits, practices, manners. **2** *the conduct of the war* direction, running, management, administration, organization, control, guidance, supervision, leadership.

conduct *verb* **1** *conduct oneself well/badly* behave, act, comport, deport, acquit. **2** *conduct the proceedings* direct, run, be in charge of, manage, administer, organize, handle, be in control of, control, govern, regulate, supervise, lead, preside over. **3** *conduct us to our seats* show, guide, lead, escort, accompany, take.

conduit *noun* duct, pipe, tube, channel, canal, trough, passageway.

confectionery *noun* candy, sweets, chocolates, bonbons.

confederacy *noun* alliance, federation, partnership, union, collaboration, association, league, coalition.

confederate *noun* *the villain had his confederates* accomplice, abettor, accessory, ally, associate, collaborator, colleague, partner.

confederate *adjective* *the confederate states* federal, federated, allied, in alliance, associated, united, combined, amalgamated.

confer *verb* **1** *confer a title/favor* bestow, present, grant, award, give, give out, hand out, accord. **2** *confer with her colleagues* have discussions, discuss, talk, consult, converse, exchange views, discourse, parley.

conference *noun* **1** *attend a conference* meeting, congress, convention, seminar, symposium, colloquium, forum, convocation. **2** *be in conference* discussion, consultation, conversation, deliberation, debate, communication, dialogue.

confess *verb* **1** *confess her guilt* admit, acknowledge, make a clean breast of, own up to, declare, make known, disclose, reveal, divulge, blurt out, expose. **2** *criminals forced to confess* own up, admit guilt, plead guilty, accept blame/responsibility, make a clean breast of it; *inf.* tell all, spill the beans, get something off one's chest. **3** *I must confess I don't know* admit, acknowledge, concede, grant, allow, own, say, declare, affirm, profess, assert.
Antonyms: CONCEAL; DENY.

confession *noun* *listening to their confession* admission, owning-up, disclosure, revelation, divulgence, exposure, acknowledgment, avowal.

confidant, confidante noun close friend, friend, crony, intimate, familiar, alter ego, second self; *inf.* chum, pal, mate, buddy, bosom buddy.

confide verb **1** *confide a secret to | confide that he was ill* disclose, reveal, divulge, impart, tell, intimate, confess, admit. **2** *confide in a friend* open one's heart to, unburden oneself to, tell one's all to. **3** *confide a task* entrust, consign, hand over, make over, turn over, give over, commit, commend, assign.

confidence noun **1** *candidates full of confidence* self-confidence, self-assurance, assurance, self-reliance, self-possession, aplomb, poise, nerve, firmness, courage, boldness, mettle, fortitude. **2** *have no confidence in them* trust, reliance, faith, dependence, belief, credence. **3** *exchange confidences* secret, private affair, confidentiality, intimacy.
Antonyms: DOUBT; UNCERTAINTY; DISTRUST.

confidential adjective **1** *confidential information* secret, private, classified, nonpublic, off-the-record, restricted, personal, intimate, privy; *inf.* hush-hush. **2** *a confidential friend* close, bosom, dear, intimate, familiar, trusted, trustworthy, trusty, faithful, reliable, dependable.

confidentially adverb *told confidentially* in confidence, in secret, in private, privately, between ourselves, behind closed doors, *sub rosa*.

confine verb **1** *birds confined in a cage* enclose, shutup, shut, cage, keep, coop up, pen, box up, lock up, imprison, intern, hold captive,incarcerate, impound. **2** *remarks confined to the discussion | confined tobed* restrict, limit.
Antonyms: RELEASE; FREE.

confinement noun *keep in confinement* custody, imprisonment, detention, captivity, internment, incarceration.

confirm verb **1** *evidence confirming her statement | a letter confirming a booking* bear out, verify, corroborate, prove, endorse, validate, authenticate, substantiate, give credence to, evidence. **2** *confirm that he would appear* reassert, assert, give assurance, assure, affirm, pledge, promise, guarantee. **3** *confirm his appointment* ratify, endorse, approve, sanction, underwrite, authorize, warrant, accredit. **4** *confirm my doubts* strengthen, make firmer, reinforce, fortify.
Antonyms: DENY; CONTRADICT.

confirmation noun **1** *confirmation of her statement/booking* verification, corroboration, proof, evidence, endorsement, validation, authentication, substantiation. **2** *confirmation of the appointment* ratification, endorsement, approval, sanction, authorization, accreditation.

confirmed adjective *a confirmed bachelor* long-established, established, dyed-in-the-wool, habitual, inveterate, through-and-through, seasoned, inured, settled, set, fixed, rooted.

confiscate verb seize, impound, take possession of, appropriate, commandeer, expropriate, sequestrate, sequester, arrogate.

conflagration noun blaze, raging fire, inferno, wall of flames, holocaust.

conflict noun **1** *the military conflict* battle, fight, war, warfare, clash, engagement, encounter, hostilities, contest, combat, collision, struggle, strife, tussle, scuffle, fracas, scrap; *inf.* set-to. **2** *bitter conflict between the families* disagreement, dissension, hostility, feud, discord, friction, strife, antagonism, antipathy, ill will, bad blood, contention. **3** *the conflict between love and duty* clash, variance, divided loyalties, opposition, friction, schism.
Antonyms: HARMONY; AGREEMENT; PEACE.

conflict verb **1** *their opinions conflict* clash, differ, disagree, be at variance, be in opposition, be at odds, be incompatible, collide. **2** *conflict for victory* contend, contest, fight, combat, struggle, strive.

conflicting adjective *conflicting opinions/statements* clashing, differing, disagreeing, contradictory, contrary, opposing, incompatible, inconsistent, discordant, paradoxical, at odds, at variance.

conform verb *refuse to conform* follow convention, be conventional, comply, obey the rules, adapt, adjust, follow the crowd, run with the pack, go with the flow. **conform to** *conform to accepted standards* comply with, fall in with, follow, obey, adapt to, accommodate to, adjust to, observe, yield to. **conform with** *conform with my idea of an actor* fit, match, agree with, correspond to, square with, accord with, harmonize with.
Antonyms: REBEL; CONTRADICT; DIFFER.

conformation noun **1** *a rocky conformation* structure, form, shape, formation, framework, build, configuration. **2** *conformation to accepted standards* compliance, adjustment, adaptation, accommodation.

conformist noun conventionalist, traditionalist, conservative; *inf.* yes-man, stick-in-the-mud, square.

conformity noun **1** *noted for their conformity* conventionality, traditionalism, orthodoxy. *See* CONFORM 1. **2** *their conformity to accepted standards* compliance, obedience, observance, adaptation, adjustment, accommodation. **3** *having a certain conformity* likeness, similarity, resemblance, correspondence, agreement, harmony, accord, affinity, compatibility, congruity, consonance.

confound verb **1** *confounded at the news* dumbfound, astound, amaze, astonish, stun, flabbergast, surprise, startle, disconcert, perplex, puzzle, mystify, baffle, nonplus, confuse, bewilder, dismay. **2** *confound the enemy* thwart, frustrate, foil; *inf.* short-circuit. **3** *confound the argument* refute, contradict, demolish, annihilate, explode.

confront verb **1** *confronting the enemy* face, face up to, stand up to, resist, defy, oppose,

challenge, attack, assault, accost, waylay. **2** *confront one's problems* face, tackle, come to grips with, meet head on. **3** *confront them with the proof* bring face to face, show, present. **4** *the problems confronting us* face, be in one's way, threat, trouble, harass, annoy, molest.
Antonyms: AVOID; DODGE.

confrontation *noun a confrontation with the government* conflict, clash, contest, collision, encounter; *inf.* set-to, showdown.

confuse *verb* **1** *confused by all the questions* bewilder, bemuse, perplex, baffle, puzzle, confound, mystify, nonplus, befog. **2** *confuse the issue* muddle, mix up, throw into disorder, disorder, disarrange, tangle up; *inf.* snarl up. **3** *confuse the twins with each other* mistake, mixup.
Antonyms: ENLIGHTEN; CLARIFY; DIFFERENTIATE.

confused *adjective* **1** *a confused recollection* unclear, blurred, indistinct, hazy, foggy, obscure. **2** *a confused mess* muddled, jumbled, untidy, disordered, disorderly, disarranged, out of order, chaotic, disorganized, upset, topsyturvy. **3** *a confused old woman* muddled, addled, befuddled, bewildered, dazed, disoriented, disorientated, at sea, unbalanced, unhinged, demented; *inf.* discombobulated.
Antonyms: CLEAR; ORDERLY; PERCEPTIVE.

confusing *adjective confusing instructions* unclear, puzzling, baffling, complicated, difficult, ambiguous, misleading, inconsistent.

confusion *noun* **1** *people in a state of confusion* bewilderment, perplexity, bafflement, puzzlement, mystification, disorientation, befuddlement. **2** *the room in a state of confusion* untidiness, disorder, chaos, shambles, disorderliness, disarrangement, disorganization. **3** *frightened by the confusion at the airport* disorganization, bustle, commotion, upheaval, turmoil.
Antonyms: ENLIGHTENMENT; ORDER; ORGANIZATION.

congeal *verb* solidify, harden, coagulate, thicken, set, concentrate, cake.

congenial *adjective* **1** *a congenial companion* genial, agreeable, friendly, pleasant, kindly, pleasing, amiable, nice, companionable, good-natured, sympathetic, compatible, like-minded, kindred. **2** *congenial work/places* agreeable, pleasant, pleasing, nice, suitable, well-suited, fit, favorable.
Antonyms: UNFRIENDLY; DISAGREEABLE; UNPLEASANT.

congenital *adjective* **1** *a congenital disease* inborn, inbred, innate, inherent, constitutional, inherited, hereditary. **2** *a congenital liar | congenital dishonesty* inveterate, dyed-in-the-wool, out-and-out, thoroughgoing, thorough, utter, complete, established, rooted, ingrained, fixed, settled, set.

congested *adjective* **1** *congested roads* crowded, overcrowded, packed, jammed, blocked, ob-

structed, overflowing, teeming. **2** *congested lungs/noses* blocked, clogged, choked, plugged, stopped up, gorged.

congestion *noun* **1** *congestion on the roads* overcrowding, crowding, obstruction, jam, bottleneck. **2** *congestion of the lungs* blocking, clogging, choking, plugging.

conglomerate *noun* **1** *an international conglomerate* corporation, multinational, merger, joint concern, firm, company, trust, cartel. **2** *a rocky conglomerate* aggregate, agglomerate.

conglomerate *adjective a conglomerate mass* aggregate, agglomerate, amassed, gathered, clustered, combined.

congratulate *verb* wish joy to, felicitate, compliment, offer good wishes to.

congratulations *plural noun* felicitations, compliments, good wishes, best wishes, greetings.

congregate *verb* gather, assemble, group, flock together, convene, meet, amass, crowd, cluster, throng, rendezvous.
Antonyms: DISPERSE; SCATTER.

congregation *noun* **1** *a congregation of people* gathering, assembly, group, flock, convention, meeting, crowd, conference, congress, mass, throng, conclave, convocation. **2** *the minister's congregation* flock, parishioners, parish.

congress *noun* **1** *attend an international congress* assembly, meeting, gathering, conference, convention, convocation, council, synod. **2** *served in (the) congress* legislative assembly, legislature, parliament; senate, house of representatives.

conic, conical *adjective* cone-shaped, pyramid-shaped, pyramidal, tapered, tapering, pointed, funnel-shaped, infundibular.

conjecture *verb conjecture about the future* guess, surmise, speculate, infer, imagine, fancy, suspect, assume, suppose, believe, think, presume, presuppose, theorize, hypothesize.

conjecture *noun just a conjecture | open to conjecture* guess, guesstimate, inference, fancy, notion, suspicion, presumption, presupposition, theory, hypothesis; guessing, surmise, surmising, imagination, speculation, theorizing.

conjugal *adjective* connubial, matrimonial, nuptial, marital, married, wedded, spousal, bridal.

conjunction *noun* **1** *the conjunction of workers* association, union, uniting, affiliation, cooperation, combination, collaboration, coaction, alliance, federation. **2** *the conjunction of events* coincidence, co-occurrence, simultaneousness, coexistence, contemporaneousness, concomitance.

conjure *verb conjure rabbits from a hat* summon, call up, invoke, rouse, raise up. **conjure up** *conjure up memories* recall, bring/call to mind, call up, evoke, re-create.

connect *verb* **1** *connect the hose to the faucet* join, attach, fasten, affix, couple, clamp, secure, rivet, fuse, solder, weld. **2** *a road connecting the towns* join, link, unite, bridge. **connect with 1**

houses connecting with each other adjoin, abut, touch, neighbor, lie next to, border, be adjacent to, impinge upon. **2** *she connects him with sadness* associate with, link with/to, relate to, identify with, equate with.
Antonyms: DISCONNECT; SEVER; SEPARATE.

connection *noun* **1** *the connection has come loose* attachment, fastening, coupling, clamp, clasp, joint. **2** *the connection between the events* link, relationship, relation, relatedness, association, bond, tie-in, correspondence, parallel, analogy. **3** *in connection with this | in that connection* context, reference, frame of reference, relation. **4** *get a job through a connection* contact, friend, acquaintance, ally, associate, sponsor.

connive *verb connive with others in the plot* conspire, collaborate, collude, be in collusion, intrigue, plot, scheme, be a party to, be an accessory to.

conniving *adjective a conniving scoundrel* scheming, colluding, nasty, unprincipled.

connoisseur *noun* gourmet, epicure, aesthete, expert, authority, specialist, pundit, cognoscenti (pl.), devotee, aficionado, appreciator, fan, savant; *inf.* buff.

connotation *noun* undertone, undermeaning, nuance, hint, intimation, suggestion, implication, allusion, insinuation, reference.

conquer *verb* **1** *conquer the enemy* defeat, beat, overpower, overthrow, vanquish, subdue, rout, trounce, subjugate, triumph over, crush, quell. **2** *conquer the territory* seize, take possession of, occupy, invade, annex, appropriate, overrun, win. **3** *conquer one's fears* overcome, get the better of, vanquish, master, surmount, rise above, prevail over.
Antonyms: SURRENDER; YIELD.

conqueror *noun* victor, winner, vanquisher, defeater, subjugator, champion, hero, lord, master, conquistador.

conquest *noun* **1** *the conquest of/over the enemy* conquering, victory, defeat, beating, overpowering, overthrow, vanquishment, rout, trouncing, subjugation, triumph, mastery, crushing, discomfiture. **2** *the conquest of the territory* seizing, possession, occupation, invasion, annexation, appropriation, overrunning, subjection. **3** *the conquest of the young ladies* captivation, enchantment, bewitching, seduction, enticement, enthrallment. **4** *yet another of her conquests* captive, catch, acquisition, prize, admirer, fan, adherent, follower, supporter, worshiper; *inf.* pushover.

conscience *noun* sense of right and wrong, moral sense, still small voice; morals, scruples, principles, ethics.

conscience-stricken *adjective* contrite, penitent, repentant, remorseful, sorry, regretful, guilty, guilt-ridden, troubled, ashamed.

conscientious *adjective* **1** *a conscientious person* diligent, careful, attentive, thorough, meticulous, punctilious, painstaking, hard-working,

dedicated. **2** *a conscientious piece of work* careful, thorough, meticulous, precise, accurate, detailed.
Antonyms: CARELESS; INATTENTIVE; LAX; SLAPDASH.

conscious *adjective* **1** *a conscious attempt at humor* deliberate, calculated, premeditated, on purpose, reasoned, knowing, studied, willed, volitional. **2** *in a conscious state* awake, aware, sentient, responsive, alert. **conscious of** *conscious of the problem* aware of, awake to, alert to, cognizant of; wise to.
Antonyms: UNCONSCIOUS; UNAWARE.

consciousness *noun* **1** *regain consciousness* wakefulness, awakeness, awareness, sentience, responsiveness, alertness. **2** *lack of consciousness of the situation* awareness, realization, cognizance, perception, apprehension, recognition.

conscript *verb conscript recruits* enlist, recruit, call up, mobilize, levy.

consecrate *verb* **1** *consecrate the building* sanctify, bless, make holy, hallow, dedicate to God. **2** *a life consecrated to religion* dedicate, devote, pledge, commit, vow, set apart.

consecutive *adjective* successive, succeeding, following, in sequence, sequential, serial, in turn, progressive, step-by-step, continuous, uninterrupted, unbroken, chronological, seriate.

consensus *noun* agreement, consent, common consent, unanimity, harmony, concord, unity, concurrence.

consent *verb* **consent to** *consent to their proposals* agree to, accept, approve, go along with, acquiesce in/to, accede to, concede to, yield to, give in to, submit to, comply with, abide by, concur with, conform to.
Antonyms: DISSENT; DISAGREE; REFUSE.

consent *noun give their consent* agreement, assent, acceptance, approval, permission, sanction, acquiescence, compliance, concurrence; *inf.* go-ahead, OK, green light.
Antonyms: REFUSAL; DISSENT.

consequence *noun* **1** *the consequence of the decision* result, effect, upshot, outcome, issue, event, end, aftermath, repercussion, reverberation. **2** *a matter of consequence* importance, note, significance, import, moment, weight, substance, portent. **3** *a person of consequence* importance, note, distinction, standing, status, prominence, prestige, eminence, repute, mark, esteem, rank.
Antonyms: CAUSE; IMPETUS.

consequent *adjective* resulting, resultant, ensuing, following, subsequent, successive, sequential.

consequently *adverb* as a result, therefore, thus, hence, subsequently, accordingly, *ergo.*

conservation *noun* preservation, protection, safeguarding, safekeeping, guarding, saving, care, charge, custody, husbandry, supervision, upkeep, maintenance.

conservative adjective 1 *politically conservative* right-wing, reactionary, traditionalist. 2 *a conservative hairstyle* conventional, traditional, reactionary, orthodox, cautious, prudent, careful, moderate, middle-of-the-road, temperate, stable, unchanging, old-fashioned, unprogressive, sober. 3 *a conservative attitude to the environment* conserving, preservative, protective, saving.
Antonyms: RADICAL; PROGRESSIVE.

conservatory noun 1 *plants in the conservatory* greenhouse, hothouse. 2 *studying at the conservatory* conservatoire, music school, drama school, academy/institute of music/drama.

conserve verb preserve, save, keep, protect, take care of, hoard, store up, husband, use sparingly, reserve, nurse.
Antonyms: SQUANDER; WASTE.

consider verb 1 *consider your application* think about, weigh up, give thought to, examine, study, mull over, ponder, contemplate, deliberate over, cogitate about, chew over, meditate over, ruminate over, turn over in one's mind. 2 *consider the feelings of others* take into consideration, take into account, make allowances for, respect, bear in mind, have regard to, reckon with, remember. 3 *consider you suitable* think, believe, regard as, deem, hold to be, judge, rate. 4 *consider the horizon* contemplate, look at, observe, regard, survey, view, scrutinize, scan, examine, inspect.
Antonyms: IGNORE; NEGLECT; DISREGARD.

considerable adjective 1 *a considerable amount* sizable, substantial, appreciable, goodly, tolerable, fair, reasonable, tidy, ample, plentiful, abundant, marked, noticeable, comfortable, decent, great, large, lavish. 2 *in considerable pain* much, a lot of, a great deal of, great, a fair amount of. 3 *a considerable artist* distinguished, noteworthy, noted, important, significant, influential, illustrious, renowned.
Antonyms: LITTLE; NEGLIGIBLE; PALTRY; INSIGNIFICANT.

considerably adverb *considerably older* much, very much, a great deal, significantly, substantially, markedly, appreciably.

considerate adjective thoughtful, attentive, concerned, solicitous, mindful, heedful, kind, kindly, unselfish, compassionate, sympathetic, patient, charitable, generous, obliging, accommodating.
Antonyms: THOUGHTLESS; SELFISH.

consideration noun 1 *give consideration to the proposal* thought, attention, heed, notice, regard, deliberation, discussion, reflection, contemplation, cogitation, rumination, examination, inspection, scrutiny, analysis, review. 2 *show consideration to their parents* thoughtfulness, attentiveness, concern, solicitousness,

solicitude, mindfulness, kindness, kindliness, unselfishness, compassion, sympathy, patience, charity, generosity, benevolence, friendliness. 3 *money a major consideration* issue, factor, point, concern, item, detail, aspect. 4 *for a small consideration* payment, fee, remuneration, compensation, recompense, emolument, perquisite. 5 *take age into consideration* account, reckoning, allowance.

considering preposition 1 *considering her age* taking into consideration, giving consideration to, bearing in mind, keeping in mind, in view of, in (the) light of. 2 *she's very well, considering* all things considered, considering everything, all in all.

consign verb 1 *consign her to his care* hand over, give over, deliver, assign, entrust, commend, remit, bequeath. 2 *consign to the junk pile* | *consign to misery* dismiss, assign, deliver, commit; reduce, dispossess. 3 *consign the package by air* send, dispatch, transmit, convey, mail.

consignment noun 1 *consignment to his care* handing over, assignment, entrusting, commendation. See CONSIGN 1. 2 *the consignment of parcels by air* sending, dispatch, conveyance. See CONSIGN 3. 3 *a consignment of coal* delivery, batch, load, shipment.

consist verb 1 *consist of flour and water* be composed of, be made up of, be formed of, comprise, contain, include, incorporate, embody, involve. 2 *her beauty consisting in her fine features* lie, reside, have its existence/being, be contained.

consistency noun 1 *mix to the right consistency* degree of thickness, degree of density, thickness, density, firmness, solidity, viscosity, cohesion. 2 *attitudes lacking consistency* steadiness, dependability, constancy, uniformity, lack of change, lack of deviation.

consistent adjective 1 *consistent attitudes* steady, dependable, constant, uniform, unchanging, undeviating, true to type. 2 *testimony consistent with the facts* | *behavior consistent with politeness* compatible, congruous, agreeing, accordant, consonant.
Antonyms: INCONSISTENT; IRREGULAR; INCOMPATIBLE.

consolation noun 1 *words of consolation* comfort, solace, sympathy, compassion, pity, commiseration, relief, help, support, cheer, encouragement, soothing, easement, succor, assuagement, alleviation. 2 *the baby is a consolation to her* comfort, solace, help, support.

console verb *console the loser* comfort, solace, sympathize with, express sympathy to, pity, commiserate with, help, cheer, encourage, ease, alleviate, assuage.
Antonyms: DISTRESS; UPSET.

consolidate verb 1 *consolidate his position* make stronger, strengthen, make secure, secure, make stable, stabilize, reinforce, fortify, cement. 2 *consolidate the territories* | *firms consol-*

idating combine, unite, merge, amalgamate, join, affiliate, fuse, federate. **3** *time for the business to consolidate* become stronger, become more secure, stabilize, strengthen one's position.

consonant adjective *behavior consonant with status* | *consonant to wealth* compatible, consistent, in accordance, in harmony, suitable, suited, appropriate.

consort noun *the queen and her consort* spouse, partner, companion, escort; husband, wife.

consort verb *consort with criminals* associate, keep company, hang around, go around, mix, spend time, fraternize, have dealings.

conspicuous adjective **1** *conspicuous changes* easily seen, clear, visible, obvious, evident, apparent, noticeable, observable, recognizable, discernible, perceptible, distinguishable, manifest, vivid. **2** *conspicuous colors* | *conspicuous modern buildings* striking, glaring, obtrusive, blatant, flagrant, showy, garish, bold, ostentatious. **3** *conspicuous members of the community* distinguished, outstanding, prominent, eminent, well-known, notable, famous, renowned, celebrated, illustrious.
Antonyms: INCONSPICUOUS; UNOBTRUSIVE; OBSCURE.

conspiracy noun **1** *a conspiracy to overthrow the government* plot, scheme, stratagem, plan, machination, cabal; *inf.* frame-up. **2** *guilty of conspiracy* plotting, collusion, intrigue, connivance, collaboration, machination, treason.

conspirator noun conspirer, plotter, schemer, intriguer, colluder, collaborator, confederate, cabalist, traitor.

conspire verb **1** *conspire against the leader* form a conspiracy, plot, hatch a plot, scheme, intrigue, collude, collaborate, cabal, machinate; *inf.* be in cahoots with. **2** *events conspire against us* act together, work together, combine, join, unite, join forces, cooperate, coact, gang up (on).

constancy noun **1** *her lover's constancy* faithfulness, fidelity, devotion, loyalty, staunchness, dependability, adherence. **2** *constancy of purpose* firmness, steadfastness, steadiness, resolution, resoluteness, fixedness, determination, perseverance, tenacity, application, doggedness. **3** *constancy of temperature* uniformity, evenness, regularity, stability, steadiness, invariableness, unchangingness, immutability.

constant adjective **1** *at a constant speed/temperature* uniform, even, regular, stable, steady, fixed, invariable, unvarying, unchanging, immutable. **2** *a constant stream of people* continuous, unbroken, uninterrupted. **3** *constant chattering* continual, never-ending, endless, unending, nonstop, incessant, unceasing, ceaseless, perpetual, persistent, interminable, unremitting, sustained, relentless, unrelenting. **4** *a constant lover* faithful, devoted, loyal, staunch, dependable, true, trustworthy, trusty. **5** *constant in his purpose* firm, steadfast,

steady, resolute, determined, persevering, tenacious, dogged, unwavering, unflagging, unshaken.
Antonyms: INCONSTANT; VARIABLE; FICKLE.

constantly adverb always, all the time, continually, continuously, endlessly, nonstop, incessantly, ceaselessly, perpetually, persistently, interminably, relentlessly.

consternation noun surprise, amazement, astonishment, dismay, bewilderment, perturbation, mystification, confusion, anxiety, distress, alarm, panic, fear, fright, dread, horror, trepidation, shock, terror, awe.

constituent adjective *constituent parts* component, integral, elemental, basic, essential.

constituent noun **1** *analyze the constituents* component, component part, part, ingredient, element, integral part, unit, piece, fragment. **2** *talking to his constituents* voter, elector.

constitute verb **1** *the countries that constitute the alliance* form, make up, compose, comprise. **2** *his suggestion constitutes a warning* be tantamount to, be the equivalent of, be, be regarded as, act as. **3** *constitute a committee* appoint, inaugurate, formally establish, authorize, commission, charter, induct, invest, empower, ordain.

constitution noun **1** *the Constitution of the United States* | *the society's constitution* body of law, system of laws/rules, code, charter, canon; laws, rules, fundamental principles. **2** *the constitution of the committees varies* composition, makeup, structure, organization. **3** *people having a strong constitution* state of health, health, physique, physical condition, physical strength. **4** *people of a nervous constitution* disposition, temperament, temper, nature, character, mood.

constitutional adjective **1** *a constitutional body* constituted, legal, lawful, legitimate, authorized, statutory, chartered, vested. **2** *a constitutional weakness* inherent, inbred, intrinsic, congenital, organic, inborn, innate.

constitutional noun *go for a constitutional* walk, stroll, saunter; *inf.* breath of fresh air.

constrain verb **1** *feel constrained to cooperate* force, compel, coerce, drive, impel, oblige, press, pressure, pressurize, urge, railroad, hustle. **2** *research constrained by lack of resources* hold back, restrict, hinder, impede, hamper, limit, curb, check, restrain. **3** *constrain political opponents* restrain, restrict, curb, confine, chain, shut in, lock up, imprison, incarcerate.

constrained adjective *a constrained manner* forced, uneasy, unnatural, inhibited, reserved, reticent, guarded.

constraint noun **1** *act under constraint* force, compulsion, coercion, obligation, pressure, impulsion. **2** *no constraints on their activities* restriction, hindrance, impediment, hampering, limitation, curb, check, restraint, damper. **3** *subject political opponents to constraint* restraint, restriction, confinement, imprisonment, incarceration. *See* CONSTRAIN 3. **4** *constraint of manner* forcedness, uneasiness, unnaturalness, inhibition, reservedness, reticence, guardedness, repression.

constrict *verb* **1** *a medication that constricts the blood vessels* narrow, make smaller, tighten, compress, contract, squeeze, strangle, strangulate. **2** *constrict the flow of traffic* impede, obstruct, hinder, hamper, limit, restrict, check, curb, inhibit.

construct *verb* **1** *construct a housing project* | *construct a bridge* build, erect, put up, set up, raise, elevate, establish, assemble, manufacture, fabricate, make. **2** *construct a plan/theory* form, formulate, put together, create, devise, design, invent, compose, fashion, mold, model, shape, frame, forge, engineer, fabricate, manufacture.
Antonyms: DESTROY; DEMOLISH.

construction *noun* **1** *a bridge under construction* building, erection, elevation, establishment, assembly, manufacture, fabrication. *See* CONSTRUCT 1. **2** *an impressive construction* structure, building, edifice, assembly, framework. **3** *the construction of a sentence* composition, formation, structure. **4** *put a different construction on her words* interpretation, reading, meaning, explanation, inference, explication.

constructive *adjective* *constructive suggestions* useful, helpful, productive, practical, positive, valuable.
Antonyms: DESTRUCTIVE; NEGATIVE.

consul *noun* attaché, consul general; consulate, consulship.

consult *verb* **1** *consult an expert* ask, seek advice/information from, call in, turn to, take counsel from. **2** *consult a reference book* look up in, check (in), refer to, turn to. **3** *consult with his colleagues* confer, discuss, talk, talk over, exchange views, deliberate, parley, powwow, palaver; *inf.* talk turkey. **4** *consult her feelings before acting* consider, take into consideration/account, have regard to, respect, have an eye to.

consultant *noun* *we called in a consultant* adviser, expert, authority, specialist.

consultation *noun* **1** *have a consultation with one's adviser* meeting, talk, discussion, interview, session, audience, tête-à-tête, parley, powwow. **2** *international consultations* conference, convention, symposium, forum, session, seminar.

consume *verb* **1** *consume dinner/lemonade* eat, eat up, drink, drink up, devour, ingest, swallow, gobble, gobble up, guzzle, snack on; *inf.* tuck into, scoff, down, put away, polish off, graze on. **2** *consumed by a desire* absorb, preoccupy, engross, eat up, devour, obsess, grip, monopolize, enthrall. **3** *buildings consumed by*

fire destroy, demolish, lay waste, wipe out, annihilate, devastate, raze, gut, ravage. **4** *cars consuming too much gasoline* use, use up, utilize, expend, deplete, exhaust, waste, squander, drain, dissipate, fritter away.

consumer *noun* user, buyer, purchaser, customer, shopper, client, patron.

consuming *adjective* *a consuming passion* absorbing, compelling, preoccupying, engrossing, devouring, obsessive, gripping, overwhelming.

consummate *adjective* complete, total, utter, absolute, perfect, superb, supreme, superior, ultimate, accomplished, expert, proficient, skillful, skilled, masterly, talented, gifted, polished, practiced.

consummate *verb* *consummate his life's work* put the finishing touch to, perfect, complete, finish, accomplish, achieve, execute, carry out, perform, end, conclude, effectuate, crown, cap, set the seal on.

consumption *noun* **1** *unfit for human consumption* eating, drinking, devouring, ingestion. *See* CONSUME 1. **2** *consumption by fire* destruction, demolition, annihilation, devastation, razing, gutting, ravaging. **3** *the consumption of fuel* using, using up, utilization, expending, expenditure, depletion, exhaustion, waste, draining, dissipation.

contact *noun* **1** *following contact with chemicals* | *on contact with an infected person* touch, touching, proximity, exposure, contiguity, junction, union, tangency. **2** *be in contact with* touch, communication, connection, correspondence, association. **3** *get a job through contacts* connection, acquaintance.

contact *verb* *contact the head office* get/be in touch with, get hold/ahold of, communicate with, be in communication with; write to, write, notify, phone, call, speak to, reach.

contagious *adjective* catching, communicable, transmittable, transmissible, transferable, spreadable, infectious, epidemic, pandemic.

contain *verb* **1** *the cabin contained four people* hold, have capacity for, carry, accommodate, seat. **2** *the committee contains six members* include, comprise, embrace, take in, incorporate, involve. **3** *could not contain themselves* | *contain your laughter* keep back, hold in, restrain, control, keep under control, keep in check, suppress, repress, curb, stifle.

container *noun* receptacle, vessel, holder, repository.

contaminate *verb* make impure, pollute, adulterate, defile, debase, corrupt, taint, infect, foul, spoil, soil, sully, tarnish, stain, befoul, vitiate, radioactivate.

contemplate *verb* **1** *contemplate the portrait* look at, view, regard, examine, inspect, observe, survey, scrutinize, scan, stare at, gaze at, eye. **2** *contemplate the future* think about, meditate over, consider, ponder, reflect over, mull over, muse on, dwell on, deliberate over, cogitate over, ruminate over, turn over in one's mind. **3** *he is contemplating going* think about, give thought to, consider, have in mind/view, envisage, intend, plan, propose, aim at, foresee.

contemplation noun **1** *his contemplation of the painting* viewing, examination, inspection, observation, survey, scrutiny, scanning, gazing at, eyeing, regard. **2** *contemplation of the future* meditation, consideration, pondering, reflection, rumination, deliberation, cogitation. *See* CONTEMPLATE 2. **3** *lost in contemplation* thought, meditation, reflection; *inf.* brown study.

contemplative adjective *a contemplative mood/look* thoughtful, pensive, reflective, meditative, musing, ruminative, introspective, intent, rapt, deep/lost in thought; *inf.* in a brown study.

contemporary adjective **1** *Shakespeare and his contemporary writers* contemporaneous, coexisting, coexistent, concurrent, synchronous. **2** *contemporary fashion* modern, present-day, present, current, present-time, up-to-date, up-to-the-minute, fashionable, latest, recent, ultramodern, newfangled, à la mode; *inf.* with it. *Antonyms:* OLD-FASHIONED; OUT OF DATE.

contemporary noun *Shakespeare and his contemporaries* peer, compeer, fellow.

contempt noun **1** *feel/show contempt for the bully* scorn, disdain, disrespect, condescension, derision, mockery, disgust, loathing, abhorrence. **2** *fined for contempt of court* disregard, disrespect, slighting, neglect. *Antonyms:* ADMIRATION; RESPECT.

contemptible adjective *contemptible behavior* despicable, detestable, ignominious, lamentable, pitiful, low, mean, shameful, abject, unworthy, worthless, base, vile, shabby, cheap, sordid, degenerate. *Antonyms:* ADMIRABLE; HONORABLE.

contemptuous adjective *with a contemptuous shrug* scornful, disdainful, disrespectful, insulting, insolent, derisory, derisive, mocking, sneering, jeering, condescending, supercilious, arrogant, high and mighty.

contend verb **1** *armies contending with each other* | *the contending teams* compete, oppose, challenge, vie, contest, clash, strive, struggle, tussle, grapple, wrestle, scuffle, skirmish, battle, combat, fight, war, wage war, join battle, cross swords. **2** *contend that he's mad* state, declare, assert, maintain, hold, claim, profess, allege, affirm, aver, pronounce. **contend with** *contending with problems* cope with, face, grapple with, take on, pit oneself against.

content[1] noun **1** *the content of the mixture* component parts/elements. *See* CONTENTS 1. **2** *the essay content is good, the style poor* subject matter, subject, material, substance, matter, theme, ideas, gist. **3** *foods with a low sodium content* amount, proportion, quantity. **4** *the barrel's content* volume, capacity, size.

content[2] adjective *content with life* contented, satisfied, pleased, happy, cheerful, glad, gratified, fulfilled, at ease, at peace, comfortable, serene, tranquil, unworried, untroubled, complacent. *Antonyms:* DISCONTENTED; DISSATISFIED; UNHAPPY.

content[3] noun *See* CONTENTMENT.

content[4] verb **1** *content oneself with a little* make content, satisfy, be pleased/happy/glad, be fulfilled, be gratified. **2** *music will content the child* pacify, placate, soothe, appease, mollify.

contented adjective content, satisfied, pleased. *See* CONTENT[2] adjective.

contention noun **1** *two groups in contention for the title* competition, contest, rivalry, opposition, striving, struggle, tussle, grappling, combat, battle, fighting, war. *See* CONTEND 1. **2** *much contention between the families* argument, disagreement, quarreling, dispute, discord, feuding, hostility, enmity, strife, dissension. **3** *it was her contention that she won* argument, assertion, declaration, affirmation, allegation, claim, stand, position, opinion, view, belief, thesis.

contentious adjective **1** *contentious people* argumentative, quarrelsome, bickering, wrangling, disputatious, captious, factious, litigious, competitive, combative, pugnacious, cross, perverse, querulous. **2** *a contentious subject* controversial, disputable, debatable, controvertible.

contentment noun content, contentedness, satisfaction, pleasure, happiness, cheerfulness, gladness, gratification, fulfillment, ease, comfort, peace, equanimity, serenity, tranquillity, repletion, complacency.

contents plural noun **1** *the contents of the mixture/box* constituents, components, ingredients, elements, items; content, load; *inf.* guts. **2** *the contents of the book* text, subject matter, theme; sections, divisions, chapters.

contest noun **1** *take part in a sport/dancing contest* competition, match, game, event, tournament, meet, trial. **2** *a leadership contest* struggle, conflict, battle, fight, combat, tussle, skirmish.

contest verb **1** *contest the decision* challenge, question, call into question, oppose, doubt, dispute, object to, litigate. **2** *contest the point* argue, debate, dispute, quarrel over, be in contention about.

contestant noun competitor, entrant, candidate, participant, player, contender, rival, opponent, adversary, antagonist, aspirant.

context noun **1** *in the present financial context* circumstances, conditions; situation, state of affairs, background, environment. **2** *take a statement out of its context* text, frame of reference, contextual relationship, subject, theme, topic.

contiguous adjective touching, in contact, meeting, joining, connecting, abutting, bordering, neighboring, adjacent, near, nearby, close.

continent *adjective* **1** *continent in one's drinking habits* self-restrained, abstemious, abstinent, sober, austere, ascetic, self-denying. **2** *sexually continent* chaste, celibate, pure, virtuous, self-restrained, virgin, virginal.

contingency *noun* chance event, event, eventuality, incident, happening, occurrence, juncture, accident, chance, possibility, fortuity, emergency, uncertainty.

contingent *adjective* *contingent effects* chance, incidental, accidental, possible, fortuitous, uncertain, random, haphazard. **contingent on/upon** *help contingent upon resources* conditional on, dependent on, subject to, hinging on, controlled by.

contingent *noun* *an advance contingent* detachment, group, party, body, division, section, company, complement, mission; *inf.* bunch, gang.

continual *adjective* **1** *continual complaints* frequent, repeated, constant, regular, persistent, habitual, recurrent, repetitive, oft-repeated. **2** *continual noise* continuous, perpetual, endless, constant, interminable. *See* CONTINUOUS.

Antonyms: INTERMITTENT; IRREGULAR.

continually *adverb* *continually interrupted* frequently, repeatedly, constantly, regularly, habitually, recurrently.

continuance *noun* continuation, persistence, staying power, endurance, survival, protraction.

continuation *noun* **1** *support the continuation of the search* continuance, carrying on, extension, furtherance, prolongation, perpetuation, continuity, progression. **2** *suggest a continuation in the morning* resumption, renewal, recommencement. **3** *the continuation of the story* sequel, postscript, addition, supplement, appendix. **4** *the road is a continuation of Main Street* extension, prolongation.

continue *verb* **1** *the desert continues for miles* go on, extend, keep on, carry on, maintain course, drag on. **2** *the firm may continue* go on, carry on, last, remain, stay, endure, survive, live on, persist, subsist, abide. **3** *continue the session as long as possible* maintain, sustain, retain, prolong, protract, perpetuate, preserve. **4** *continue trying* go on, carry on, keep on, keep at, not stop, persist in, persevere in, prolong, pursue; *inf.* stick with/at. **5** *continue the search after a break* resume, renew, recommence, start again, carry on with, return to, take up. **6** *continue after lunch* go on, carry on, resume, recommence, proceed, pick up where one has left off.

Antonyms: STOP; DISCONTINUE; give up (*see* GIVE).

continuity *noun* **1** *ensure continuity of supplies* continuousness, uninterruptedness, flow, regular flow, progression. **2** *lack of continuity in the prose* cohesion, coherence, connection, interrelatedness, linkage, sequence.

continuous *adjective* *a continuous supply* | *continuous noise* uninterrupted, unbroken, consecutive, constant, without stopping, nonstop, perpetual, ceaseless, incessant, unceasing, unremitting, endless, everlasting, interminable, undivided.

Antonyms: INTERMITTENT; SPORADIC.

contort *verb* twist, wrench/bend out of shape, warp, deform, misshape.

contour *noun* outline, silhouette, profile, figure, shape, form; lines, curves.

contraband *noun* *accused of contraband* smuggling, illegal traffic, trafficking, black marketing, black marketeering, bootlegging, drug trafficking.

contraband *adjective* *contraband goods* illegal, illicit, unlawful, prohibited, banned, proscribed, taboo, interdicted, smuggled, black-market, bootleg, bootlegged.

contraceptive *noun* oral contraceptive, birth-control pill, the pill, the morning-after pill, diaphragm, IUD, intrauterine device, coil, loop, condom, sheath, prophylactic; *inf.* rubber.

contract *noun* agreement, compact, covenant, pact, settlement, arrangement, understanding, transaction, bargain, deal, treaty, concordat, convention, bond, commitment, entente.

contract *verb* **1** *metals contracting* get smaller, become smaller, become shorter, shrink, reduce, shrivel. **2** *contracting metals* make smaller, make shorter, shrink. **3** *blood vessels contracting* | *muscles contracting* become narrower, narrow, tighten, become tighter, tense, draw in. **4** *contract your muscles* make narrower, narrow, constrict, tighten, make tighter, tense, draw in. **5** *contract a word/text* shorten, abbreviate, abridge, lessen, compress, condense, curtail, concentrate, summarize, synopsize. **6** *contract (with) them to do the work* arrange, agree, reach an arrangement, establish, come to terms, negotiate, bargain, strike a bargain, close/clinch a deal, close, engage, settle, covenant. **7** *contract a disease* catch, get, come down with, develop, become infected with, be afflicted with. **8** *contract a debt* incur, acquire, fall into.

Antonyms: EXPAND; distend; LENGTHEN.

contraction *noun* **1** *the contraction of metals* getting smaller, shrinking. *See* CONTRACT *verb* 1, 2. **2** *the contraction of blood vessels* | *muscle contraction* narrowing, tightening, constricting, tensing. **3** *pregnant women experiencing contractions* muscle-tightening/-tensing, cramps. **4** *"isn't" is a contraction* shortened form, short form, shortening, elision, abridgment, abbreviation.

contradict *verb* **1** *contradict his father* say the opposite of, oppose, challenge, counter, be at variance with. **2** *contradict his father's statement* say the opposite of, oppose, deny, challenge, dispute, counter, refute, rebut, be at variance with, controvert, impugn, confute. **3** *the two sets of facts contradict each other* be at variance with, disagree with, be in conflict with, clash

with, contravene, run counter to, be inconsistent with, dissent from, negate.
Antonyms: AGREE; CONFIRM; VERIFY.

contradiction *noun* **1** *the contradiction of his statement* denial, disputing, countering, refuting, rebuttal, controverting, impugning, confutation. **2** *the contradiction between the two statements* variance, variation, disagreement, conflict, clash, inconsistency, dissension, contravention, negation.

contradictory *adjective* **1** *hold a contradictory view* opposing, opposite, dissenting, contrary, dissident; at variance, at odds. **2** *contradictory statements* contradicting, disagreeing, conflicting, clashing, contrasting, incompatible, irreconcilable, inconsistent, incongruous, contravening, negating, antithetical.

contraption *noun* device, machine, mechanism, gadget, contrivance, apparatus, invention, appliance; *inf.* thingamajig, thingamabob, whatsit, doodad, gizmo.

contrary *adjective* **1** *holding contrary views* opposite, opposing, contradictory, clashing, conflicting, contrasting, incompatible, irreconcilable, inconsistent, incongruous, antithetical. **2** *a contrary young woman* willful, obstinate, stubborn, headstrong, pigheaded, unaccommodating, intractable, recalcitrant, intransigent, refractory, cantankerous.
Antonyms: COMPATIBLE; ACCOMMODATING.

contrary *noun the contrary is true* opposite, antithesis, reverse, contrariety. **on the contrary** quite the opposite, just the reverse, not at all, conversely, in contrast.

contrary *adverb* **contrary to** against, in opposition to, not in accord with.

contrast *noun* **1** *a marked contrast between them* difference, dissimilarity, distinction, disparity, dissimilitude, differentiation, distinguishment. **2** *he is a complete contrast to his brother* opposite, antithesis. **3** *fair by contrast with his sister* comparison, differentiation, distinguishment.
Antonyms: SIMILARITY; SAMENESS.

contrast *verb* **1** *contrast the two writers* compare, juxtapose, set side by side, distinguish, differentiate, discriminate. **2** *theories and actions contrast sharply* form a contrast, contradict, be at variance, be contrary, diverge, differ.

contravene *verb* **1** *contravene a law* disobey, break, infringe, violate, transgress. **2** *evidence contravening the theory* contradict, be in conflict with, be in opposition to, clash with, be at variance with, run counter to, refute, rebut.

contretemps *noun* mishap, misadventure, unfortunate occurrence, accident, awkward moment.

contribute *verb* **1** *contribute money/time to the charity | happy to contribute* give, donate, hand out, present, grant, endow, bestow, accord, confer, provide, supply, furnish; *inf.* chip in, pitch in. **2** *contributing articles to magazines* supply, provide. **3** *sensible eating contributing to*

good health be conducive to, lead to, be instrumental in, have a hand in, bear a part in, add to, help, promote, advance.

contribution *noun* **1** *contributions to the fund* donation, gift, offering, present, grant, bestowal, allowance, subsidy, endowment. **2** *the paper accepts contributions* article, piece, story, item. **3** *appreciated your contribution during the discussion* input, participation; *inf.* two cents' worth.

contributor *noun* **1** *the charity's contributors* giver, donor, patron, supporter, backer, benefactor, subsidizer. **2** *newspaper contributors* correspondent, journalist, reporter, columnist, writer, critic, reviewer, freelance writer, freelance, freelancer.

contrite *adjective* penitent, repentant, remorseful, regretful, sorry, chastened, conscience-stricken, guilt-ridden, in sackcloth and ashes, wearing a hair shirt.

contrivance *noun* **1** *a contrivance for plowing* device, invention, gadget, contraption, appliance, apparatus, implement, tool, machine, mechanism, equipment, gear, tackle. **2** *fooled by a clever contrivance* stratagem, scheme, ruse, trick, plot, plan, dodge, intrigue, machination, expedient, fabrication, artifice. **3** *have to admire the contrivance of the schemer* inventiveness, ingenuity, creativity, originality.

contrive *verb* **1** *contrive a brilliant scheme* devise, concoct, engineer, invent, originate, create, construct, design, plan, work out, think/dream up, plot, fabricate. **2** *contrive to win* manage, find a way, engineer, maneuver, plot, plan, intrigue, scheme.

contrived *adjective* unnatural, artificial, forced, strained, labored, overdone, elaborate, planned, invented, nonspontaneous.

control *verb* **1** *control the organization* be in control of, be in charge of, head, manage, direct, preside over, conduct, be in authority over, command, rule, govern, lead, supervise, superintend, oversee, dominate, master, reign over, be in the driver's seat of, be in the saddle of; *inf.* be the boss of. **2** *control prices | control the fire* keep in check, restrain, curb, contain, hold back, restrict, limit, regulate, constrain, subdue, bridle. **3** *control the traffic/machine* regulate, guide, monitor, steer, pilot.

control *noun* **1** *have control over the organization* charge, management, authority, power, command, direction, rule, government, jurisdiction, supervision, superintendence, guidance, dominance, mastery, reign, supremacy. **2** *get control of oneself* self-control, self-restraint, restraint, hold, check, curb, constraint. **3** *arms control | import controls* limitation, restriction, regulation, restraint, check, curb. **4** *used as an experimental control* standard of comparison, standard, check. **5** *mission control* headquarters, base, center of operations, command post.

controls *plural noun* **1** *import controls* means of limitation/restriction. *See* CONTROL *noun* 3. **2** *the machine's controls* instruments, levers, switches, dials, knobs; control panel, console, dashboard.

controversial *adjective* open to discussion/question, disputed, disputable, debatable, under discussion, at issue, contentious, contended, controvertible.

controversy *noun* dispute, argument, debate, disagreement, dissension, contention, altercation, wrangle, wrangling, quarreling, squabbling, bickering, polemic.
Antonyms: ACCORD; HARMONY.

contumely *noun* insult, scorn, derision, abuse, insolence, rudeness, churlishness, discourtesy.

contusion *noun* bruise, discoloration, blemish, injury, bump, lump.

conundrum *noun* **1** *children solving conundrums* riddle, puzzle, word game; *inf.* brainteaser. **2** *a conundrum for the politicians* puzzle, problem, difficult question, enigma, mystery.

convalescence *noun* recovery, recuperation, improvement, getting better, rehabilitation, return to health, mending, restoration.

convene *verb* **1** *convene a meeting* call, call together, summon, convoke, round up, rally. **2** *the meeting convened* assemble, gather, collect, congregate, meet, muster.

convenience *noun* **1** *books arranged alphabetically for convenience* accessibility, handiness, availability. **2** *the convenience of the time* suitability, appropriateness, fitness, fittingness, favorableness, favorability, advantageousness, opportuneness, propitiousness, timeliness, expedience, usefulness, utility, serviceability. **3** *do it at your convenience* suitable opportunity, leisure, freedom, spare moment, spare time, free time. **4** *for the convenience of all* service, use, benefit, advantage, accommodation, enjoyment, satisfaction, comfort, ease. **5** *few conveniences in the kitchen* gadget, labor-saving device, appliance, device, appurtenance, amenity, facility.

convenient *adjective* **1** *stores convenient to the highway* accessible, handy, at hand, close at hand, within reach, nearby, just around the corner, at one's fingertips, available. **2** *choose a convenient time/setting* suitable, suited, appropriate, fit, fitting, favorable, advantageous, opportune, timely, well-timed, expedient, useful, serviceable.
Antonyms: INCONVENIENT; INACCESSIBLE; UNSUITABLE.

convent *noun* nunnery, religious community, priory; mother house; convent school.

convention *noun* **1** *a medical/political convention* conference, congress, gathering, meeting, assembly, convocation, council of delegates/representatives, synod, conclave. **2** *follow convention* | *obey the conventions* conventionality, etiquette, formality, protocol, propriety, code, custom, tradition, usage, practice. **3** *draw up a convention between countries* agreement, contract, pact, treaty, bargain, deal, compact, concordat.

conventional *adjective* **1** *conventional behavior/attitudes* accepted, expected, customary, usual, standard, regular, normal, ordinary, correct, decorous, proper, orthodox, traditional, prevailing, prevalent, conformist, conservative, formal, ritual; *inf.* square, straight, straitlaced. **2** *conventional works of art* run-of-the-mill, commonplace, common, ordinary, everyday, common garden variety, prosaic, routine, stereotyped, pedestrian, hackneyed, unoriginal, clichéd, trite, platitudinous, bourgeois.
Antonyms: UNCONVENTIONAL; UNORTHODOX; ORIGINAL.

converge *verb* **1** *lines/opinions converging* meet, intersect, join, merge, unite, come together, become one, coincide, concur. **2** *crowds converging on the stage* approach, move toward, come closer to, close in on, center on, focus on.
Antonyms: DIVIDE; SEPARATE; DIVERGE.

conversant *adjective* acquainted with, familiar with, knowledgeable about, well-versed in, informed about, well-informed about, apprised of, *au fait* with, experienced in, proficient in, practiced in, skilled in; *inf.* (well) up on.

conversation *noun* **1** *deep in conversation* talk, discussion, chat, dialogue, discourse, communication, conference, gossip, colloquy, intercourse. **2** *having a conversation* talk, discussion, chat, dialogue, exchange, gossip, powwow, tête-à-tête; *inf.* confab, rap session.

---

conversation
chat, colloquy, communion, dialogue, parley, tête-à-tête

It is nearly impossible for most people to get through a day without having a **conversation** with someone, even if it's only a **chat** with the mailman. Although *conversation* can and does take place in all sorts of contexts, both formal and informal, the word usually implies a relaxed, casual exchange. A *chat* is the least formal of all conversations, whether it's a father talking to his son about girls or two women having a **tête-à-tête** (French for head to head, meaning a confidential conversation) about their wayward husbands. Men, of course, often complain that women don't understand the meaning of **dialogue**, which is a two-way conversation that may involve opposing points of view. Argument is even more likely to play a role in a **parley**, which formally is a discussion between enemies regarding the terms of a truce. A **colloquy** is the most formal of all conversations (*a colloquy on nuclear disarmament*); it can also be used to jocularly describe a guarded exchange (*a brief colloquy with the arresting officer*). **Communion** is a form of conversation as well—one that may take place on such a profound level that no words are necessary (*communion with nature*).conversational

converse[1] *verb converse with others* talk, speak, discuss, chat, have a talk/discussion, communicate.

converse[2] *noun the converse is true* opposite, contrary, reverse, antithesis, obverse, other side of the coin; *inf.* flip side.

converse[3] *adjective converse views* opposite, opposing, contrary, reverse, counter, antithetical, obverse.

conversion *noun* **1** *the conversion of liquid to gas* change, transformation, metamorphosis, transfiguration, transmutation; *inf.* transmogrification. **2** *the conversion of the building* alteration, adaptation, modification, reshaping, refashioning, remodeling, remaking, reconstruction, rebuilding. **3** *religious conversion* reformation, regeneration, proselytization. **4** *the conversion of yards to meters | conversion of pounds to dollars* change, turning, exchange, substitution, switch.

convert *verb* **1** *convert liquid to gas* change, transform, metamorphose, transfigure, transmute; *inf.* transmogrify. **2** *the sofa converts to a bed* change (into), make (into), adapt, transform (into). **3** *convert the building* alter, adapt, modify, reshape, refashion, remodel, restyle, remake, reconstruct, rebuild, reorganize. **4** *convert the heathens* reform, regenerate, convince, cause to change beliefs, bring to God, baptize, proselytize, cause to be reborn. **5** *convert yards to meters | convert pounds to dollars* change, turn into; exchange for, substitute by, switch from.

convey *verb* **1** *convey the goods* transport, carry, bring, fetch, bear, move, shift, transfer, cart, lug. **2** *pipes conveying water* conduct, transmit, channel, guide. **3** *convey information | convey the idea* transmit, pass on, hand on, send, dispatch, communicate, make known, impart, relate, announce, tell, reveal, disclose. **4** *convey property* give the rights to, transfer, transmit, grant, cede, devolve, lease, bequeath, will; *Law* demise.

conveyance *noun* **1** *by public conveyance* transport, transportation, carriage, transfer, transference, transmission, movement, haulage, portage, cartage, shipment, freightage. **2** *the conveyance broke down* transport, vehicle; car, bus, coach, van, truck. **3** *the conveyance of information* transmission, passing on, communication, imparting. *See* CONVEY 3. **4** *conveyance of property* transfer, granting, ceding, cession. *See* CONVEY 4.

convict *verb convict him of the crime* declare/find/pronounce/judge guilty, sentence, condemn.

convict *noun ex-convicts getting jobs* prisoner, criminal, offender, lawbreaker, felon; *inf.* crook, con, jailbird.

conviction *noun* **1** *she has previous convictions* declaration/pronouncement of guilt, sentence, judgment, condemnation. **2** *she spoke with conviction* confidence, assurance, belief, certainty, certitude, persuasion, firmness, trust, earnestness. **3** *my conviction is that he is dead* belief, opinion, view, thought, idea, persuasion. **4** *a person of conviction* principle, belief, faith, creed.

convince *verb* **1** *she convinced me that I was wrong* make one certain, prove to, satisfy, assure, reassure. **2** *convince him to vote for them* persuade, prevail upon, sway, bring around, win over.

convincing *adjective* **1** *a convincing argument* cogent, powerful, persuasive, plausible, incontrovertible, conclusive. **2** *a convincing person* persuasive, plausible, credible. **3** *a convincing victory* impressive, decisive, conclusive.

convivial *adjective* genial, cordial, sociable, friendly, affable, amiable, congenial, agreeable, jolly, cheerful.
Antonyms: UNFRIENDLY; UNSOCIABLE.

convocation *noun* assembly, gathering, meeting, congregation, conference, convention, congress, conclave, synod.

convolution *noun* **1** *carvings with curves and convolutions* twist, turn, coil, spiral, curl, twirl, kink, curlicue, whorl. **2** *the convolutions of the plot* complication, complexity, involvement, entanglement.

convoy *noun* **1** *the convoy set off* group, company, assemblage, line, fleet, cortege, caravan. **2** *a fleet/company under convoy* escort, protection, guard, bodyguard, defense, shield, guidance.

convoy *verb* **1** *convoy a company of ships* escort, accompany, attend, protect, guard, defend, guide, shepherd, flank. **2** *convoy the children home* escort, accompany, go along with, attend, chaperon.

convulse *verb* **1** *audiences convulsed with laughter* shake, churn up, discompose, unsettle. **2** *a city convulsed with rioting* shake, agitate, disturb, upset, disorder, unsettle, wrack.

convulsion *noun* **1** *the child went into convulsions* fit, seizure, paroxysm, spasm, contractions, attack. **2** *political convulsions in the city* turmoil, tumult, commotion, upheaval, agitation, disturbance, disruption, unrest, upset, disorder, chaos. **3** *have the audience in convulsions* uncontrollable laughter, fit of laughter, paroxysm.

cook *verb* **1** *cook a dish/meal* prepare, put together, improvise; bake, roast, grill, stew, steam, braise, sauté, fry, deep-fry. **2** *cook the books* falsify, forge, alter. **3** *what's cooking?* happen, occur, take place. **cook up** concoct, make up, put together, devise, invent, create, contrive, fabricate, prepare, improvise, plot, plan, scheme.

cool *adjective* **1** *a cool drink | cool weather* fresh, refreshing, coldish, chilly, chilled, chilling, nippy, unheated, sunless, windy, breezy, drafty. **2** *keep cool in an emergency* calm,

composed, collected, self-possessed, self-controlled, levelheaded, unexcited, unperturbed, unmoved, unruffled, unemotional, relaxed, placid, quiet, serene; *inf.* together. **3** *a cool young woman* aloof, distant, reserved, standoffish, unfriendly, offhand, unwelcoming, uncommunicative, chilly, impassive, undemonstrative, unresponsive, unenthusiastic, indifferent, unconcerned, uninterested. **4** *the cool way she stole* bold, audacious, brazen, presumptuous, overconfident, impudent, insolent, impertinent, forward, shameless. **5** *the cool method of the killer* calculated, premeditated, planned, deliberate, intentional, purposeful; dispassionate, cold, cold-blooded. **6** *thinks she's really cool* sophisticated, suave, stylish, urbane, cosmopolitan, elegant; *inf.* streetwise, in. **7** *what a cool idea* great, superb, excellent, very good, splendid; *inf.* awesome, far-out.
Antonyms: WARM; EXCITED; PASSIONATE.

cool *verb* **1** *cool the milk* cool down, make cold/colder, chill, refrigerate, freeze. **2** *the metal/milk cooled* cool down, become cold/colder, lose heat. **3** *cool his passion* lessen, abate, moderate, temper, diminish, reduce, dampen, quiet, soothe, assuage, allay, mollify, settle. **4** *his passion cooled* cool off, lessen, abate, moderate, diminish.
Antonyms: WARM; INTENSIFY.

cool *noun* **1** *lose one's cool* self-control, control, calmness, composure, poise, self-possession, self-discipline. **2** *the cool of the evening* coolness, freshness, crispness, coldness, chill.

coop *noun* *chicken coop* cage, pen, enclosure, hutch, pound, lockup.

coop *verb* **coop up** *chickens cooped up | feeling cooped up during the winter* cage, cage/pen in, confine, enclose, hem in, shut/lock up, imprison.

cooperate *verb* **1** *cooperate in the venture* work together, act/pull together, join forces, unite, act jointly, combine, collaborate, pool resources, conspire, connive, concur, coordinate, coact. **2** *he'll be released if he cooperates* be of assistance, assist, help, lend a hand, contribute, aid, abet, participate, go along; *inf.* pitch in, play ball.

cooperation *noun* **1** *the cooperation between the departments* combined effort, working together, joint action, unity, collaboration, connivance, concurrence, coordination, teamwork, give and take, synergy. **2** *thank you for your cooperation* assistance, help, aid, contribution, helping hand, participation, support, backing, good offices.

cooperative *adjective* **1** *a cooperative venture* joint, united, shared, unified, combined, concerted, collected, coordinated, collaborative, coactive. **2** *the public's being cooperative* of assistance, assisting, helpful, helping, obliging, accommodating, aiding, contributing, participating, responsive.

coordinate *verb* **1** *coordinate the effort* arrange, organize, order, integrate, synchronize, correlate, harmonize, systematize. **2** *coordinating for the common good* cooperate, unite, combine, collaborate, coact, interrelate.

cope *verb* *single parents unable to cope* manage, succeed, survive, carry on, get through, get on, get along, get by, subsist, make the grade, come through, hold one's own; *inf.* make out. **cope with** *cope with the situation* handle, deal with, treat, weather, contend with, take care of, dispose of, grapple with, wrestle with, struggle with, tussle with.

copious *adjective* abundant, superabundant, plentiful, ample, profuse, full, extensive, generous, lavish, rich, liberal, bounteous, bountiful, exuberant, luxuriant, overflowing, abounding.
Antonyms: SCARCE; SPARSE; PALTRY.

copse *noun* thicket, grove, brush.

copy *noun* **1** *a copy of the document* transcript, facsimile, duplicate, duplication, carbon, carbon copy, photocopy; *Trademark* Xerox, Photostat. **2** *a clever copy of the vase* imitation, reproduction, replica, replication, likeness, counterfeit, forgery, fake, sham. **3** *three copies of the book* specimen, example, sample, issue.

copy *verb* **1** *copy the document* duplicate, photocopy, Xerox, Photostat, transcribe. **2** *copy the vase/painting* reproduce, replicate, forge, counterfeit. **3** *copy his style* imitate, mimic, emulate, follow, echo, mirror, simulate, ape, parrot.

cord *noun* **1** string, rope, twine, cable, line, ligature. **2** *cords of friendship* bond, link, tie, connection.

cordial *adjective* **1** *a cordial welcome* friendly, warm, genial, affable, amiable, pleasant, gracious, warmhearted, good-natured, welcoming, sincere, affectionate, hearty, wholehearted, heartfelt. **2** *cordial dislike* intense, acute, strong, fierce, keen, wholehearted, heartfelt.
Antonyms: UNFRIENDLY; INSINCERE.

cordon *noun* **1** *a police/military cordon* barrier, line, chain, ring; picket line. **2** *wearing a cordon indicating rank* braid, cord, ribbon, sash, decoration.

cordon *verb* **cordon off** *cordon off the area* close off, fence off, shut off, separate off, isolate, enclose, encircle, surround, picket.

core *noun* center, heart, nucleus, nub, kernel, crux, heart of the matter, essence, quintessence, substance, gist, pith; *inf.* nitty-gritty.

cork *noun* stopper, stop, plug.

corn *noun* **1** *served corn with dinner* sweet corn, corn on the cob, maize, Indian corn. **2** corniness, schmaltz, sentimentality. *See* CORNY.

corner *noun* **1** *the corner of the road* angle, bend, curve, crook, turn. **2** *the corner where the roads meet* angle, projecting angle, intersection, junction, fork, convergence, juncture. **3** *hidden in secret corners* nook, cranny, niche, recess, crevice, cavity, hole, secret place, hideaway, hide-out. **4** *in a remote corner of Maine* part, region, area, district, section, quarter; *inf.* neck of the woods. **5** *in a difficult corner* predicament, plight, tight spot; *inf.* pickle. **6** *gain a corner of the property market* control, position of control, dominance, monopoly.

corner *verb* **1** *corner the enemy* drive into a corner, run to earth, block off, trap, bring to bay. **2** *corner the market* gain control/dominance of, control, dominate, monopolize; *inf.* hog.

corny *adjective* banal, trite, hackneyed, stale, commonplace, stereotyped, platitudinous, inane, fatuous, jejune, sentimental, mawkish, weak, feeble; *inf.* old hat.

corollary *noun* consequence, result, upshot, conclusion.

coronation *noun* crowning, enthronement, enthroning, accession to the throne, investiture, anointing, inauguration.

coronet *noun* crown, circlet, garland, wreath, chaplet.

corporal *adjective* bodily, fleshly, physical, corporeal, material, carnal.

corporate *adjective* **1** *review corporate finances* company, organization, business. **2** *for the corporate good* combined, joint, united, communal, collective, shared, pooled, merged, allied, collaborative.

corporation *noun* **1** *a business corporation* company, firm, trust, partnership, combine, conglomerate. **2** *municipal corporation* council, town council, municipal authorities, civic authorities.

corps *noun* **1** *an army corps* unit, division, detachment, company, troop, contingent, squad, squadron. **2** *diplomatic/press corps* group, body, band, team, party, contingent, troupe, gang, pack, crew.

corpse *noun* dead body, body, cadaver, carcass, skeleton; remains; *inf.* stiff.

corpulent *adjective* fat, obese, plump, portly, stout, tubby, chubby, pudgy, overweight, beefy, thickset, heavy, heavyset, burly, bulky, well-padded, fleshy, rotund, roly-poly.

correct *adjective* **1** *the correct answer* right, accurate, true, actual, exact, precise, unerring, close, faithful, strict, faultless, flawless; *inf.* OK, okay, on the mark, on the beam. **2** *correct behavior* proper, suitable, fit, fitting, befitting, appropriate, apt, seemly, conventional, approved, accepted, standard, usual, customary; *inf.* OK, okay.
Antonyms: INCORRECT; WRONG; IMPROPER.

correct *verb* **1** *correct the spelling errors* make/set right, rectify, right, amend, emend, remedy, redress, cure, improve, better, ameliorate, repair. **2** *correct an exam paper* indicate errors in, show mistakes in, point out faults in. **3** *correct a defect* rectify, counteract, offset, counterbalance, compensate for, make up for, neutralize. **4** *correct an instrument* adjust, regulate, fix, set, standardize, normalize, make conform. **5** *correct the children* scold, rebuke, chide, reprimand, reprove, admonish, lecture, berate, discipline, punish, chastise.

correction *noun* **1** *the correction of the text* amendment, emendation, rectifying, rectification, improvement, modification, alteration, amelioration, repair. **2** *a house of correction* punishment, discipline, chastisement, castigation, admonition, reproof, reformation.

corrective *adjective* **1** *corrective surgery* remedial, therapeutic, restorative, curative, reparatory, reparative, rehabilitative. **2** *corrective training* punitive, disciplinarian, penal, castigatory, castigative, reformatory.

correctly *adverb* **1** *answer correctly* right, rightly, accurately, unerringly, precisely, faultlessly. **2** *dressed correctly* properly, suitably, fittingly, appropriately, aptly.

correlate *verb* **1** *subjects correlating with each other* correspond, tie in, equate, interact, relate, agree, coordinate. **2** *correlate the facts* bring together, compare, show a connection/relationship/association/correspondence, connect.

correlation *noun* correspondence, equivalence, reciprocity, mutual relationship, interrelationship, interdependence, interaction, mutuality, connection, relationship.

correspond *verb* **1** *accounts not corresponding* agree, be in agreement, accord, concur, coincide, conform, match, fit together, square, tally, dovetail, correlate. **2** *Congress corresponds to Parliament* be analogous, be similar, be comparable, be equivalent, be akin. **3** *correspond with a friend* | *we've corresponded for years* exchange letters, write, communicate, keep in touch/contact.
Antonyms: DIFFER; VARY.

correspondence *noun* **1** *lack of correspondence between the accounts* agreement, accordance, accord, concurrence, coincidence, conformity, harmony, matching. **2** *the correspondence between/of Congress and Parliament* analogy, similarity, resemblance, comparability, correlation, relation. **3** *a backlog of correspondence* mail, communication; letters, notes, E-mail, messages. **4** *enter into correspondence* letter-writing, writing, written communication.

correspondent *noun* **1** *her brothers are regular correspondents* letter writer, pen pal, communicator. **2** *newspaper correspondent* reporter, journalist, contributor, newspaperman, newspaperwoman; special correspondent, foreign correspondent; *inf.* stringer.

correspondent *adjective* *correspondent forms of legislature* analogous, similar, like, comparable, parallel, equivalent, akin, kindred.

corridor *noun* passage, passageway, aisle; hallway.

corroborate *verb* confirm, verify, bear out,

authenticate, validate, certify, endorse, ratify, substantiate, back up, uphold, support, attest to, sustain, evidence.
Antonyms: DISPROVE; CONTRADICT.

corrode verb **1** *pipes corroded by rust* eat away, wear away, erode, gnaw, abrade, destroy, consume, rust, oxidize, oxidate. **2** *the metal has corroded* wear away, waste away, rust, disintegrate, crumble, fragment, be destroyed.

corrosive adjective *acid is corrosive* corroding, eroding, erosive, abrasive, biting, caustic, acrid, mordant, consumptive, destructive.

corrugated adjective furrowed, grooved, ridged, fluted, channeled, folded, crinkled, puckered, creased, wrinkled, crumpled, striate.

corrupt adjective **1** *corrupt officials* dishonest, bribable, crooked, fraudulent, dishonorable, unscrupulous, untrustworthy, venal; *inf.* bent, shady. **2** *a corrupt young man* | *corrupt acts* immoral, depraved, wicked, evil, sinful, degenerate, reprobate, perverted, dissolute, debauched, decadent, abandoned, lascivious, lewd, lecherous. **3** *a corrupt society/atmosphere* rotten, polluted, putrid, decayed, putrescent, tainted, infected, contaminated. **4** *a corrupt substance* adulterated, impure, alloyed, contaminated, tainted.
Antonyms: HONEST; ETHICAL; MORAL; PURE.

corrupt verb **1** *corrupt the new official* bribe, suborn, buy, buy off, induce, lure, entice; *inf.* pay off, grease the palm of. **2** *corrupt the young boy* deprave, pervert, warp, make degenerate, debauch. **3** *corrupt the atmosphere* make rotten, pollute, putrefy, taint, infect, contaminate, blight, mar. **4** *corrupt the substance* adulterate, alloy, contaminate, taint, defile, debase. **5** *corrupt the text* alter, tamper with, falsify, doctor.
Antonyms: PURIFY; SANCTIFY.

corruption noun **1** *officials involved in corruption* bribery, bribing, subornation, extortion, dishonesty, crookedness, fraud, fraudulence, unscrupulousness, shadiness, profiteering, criminality, villainy, venality; *inf.* graft. **2** *found guilty of moral corruption* immorality, depravity, vice, wickedness, evil, sin, iniquity, turpitude, degeneracy, perversion, dissolution, debauchery, decadence, lasciviousness, lewdness, lechery, impurity. **3** *corruption of the atmosphere* pollution, contamination. *See* CORRUPT verb 3. **4** *corruption of the substance* adulteration, debasement. *See* CORRUPT verb 4. **5** *text corruptions* alteration, falsification.

corset noun girdle, foundation garment, foundation, corselet.

cortege noun **1** *a funeral cortege* procession, column, file, line, parade, cavalcade. **2** *the bride and her cortege* retinue, entourage, train; attendants.

cosmetic noun *apply cosmetics* beauty product, beauty aid. *See* MAKEUP 1.

cosmetic adjective **1** *a cosmetic product* beauty, beautifying. **2** *a purely cosmetic improvement* superficial, surface, touching-up. **3** *cosmetic surgery* beautifying, improving, nonessential, nonmedical.

cosmic adjective **1** *cosmic laws* universal, worldwide. **2** *cosmic rays/dust* in/from space, occurring in space. **3** *disasters of cosmic proportion* vast, huge, immense, enormous, immeasurable, measureless, infinite, limitless.

cosmonaut noun astronaut, spaceman, spacewoman.

cosmopolitan adjective **1** *a cosmopolitan city/cosmopolitan influences* international, multiethnic, universal, global, worldwide. **2** *a cosmopolitan attitude* liberal, broad-minded, unprejudiced, sophisticated, urbane, worldly, worldly-wise, well-traveled, jet-setting, globe-trotting, unprovincial, cultivated, cultured.
Antonyms: PROVINCIAL; PAROCHIAL; UNSOPHISTICATED.

cost verb **1** *the book costs $30* be priced at, sell for, be valued at, fetch, come to, amount to; *inf.* set one back. **2** *tragedy costing lives* | *work costing effort* involve, result in, lead to, involve the loss/expense/sacrifice of, necessitate. **3** *it cost them dearly* do a disservice to, harm, hurt, injure, damage.

cost noun **1** *the cost of the house* | *what's the cost?* price, asking price, selling price, charge, amount, value, valuation, quotation, rate, worth, payment, expenditure, expense, outlay; *inf.* damage. **2** *the cost in lives* | *work done at great cost* sacrifice, expense, loss, penalty, suffering, harm, hurt, injury, damage, deprivation, detriment.

costly adjective **1** *a costly house* expensive, high-cost, high-priced, valuable, exorbitant, extortionate, extravagant; *inf.* steep. **2** *a costly victory* sacrificial, catastrophic, disastrous, ruinous, damaging, harmful, deleterious.
Antonyms: CHEAP; INEXPENSIVE.

costs plural noun expenses, outgoings; expenditure, money spent.

costume noun **1** *dressed in national costume* style of dress, dress, fashion, clothing, attire, apparel, garb, ensemble, outfit, uniform, livery, habit; clothes, garments, robes; *inf.* get-up, gear, togs. **2** *a woman in a green costume* suit, outfit, ensemble.

coterie noun clique, set, crowd, circle, gang, club, community, league, alliance, faction, cabal.

cottage noun *a cottage by the lake* small house, cabin, chalet, hut, bungalow, shack.

couch noun *a couch and matching chairs* sofa, settee; ottoman, *chaise longue*, chesterfield, davenport, divan, day bed, love seat.

couch verb *couched in loving terms* express, phrase, word, say, state, utter, set forth, frame, style.

cough verb *cough noisily* hack, hawk, clear one's throat, bark.

cough noun *coughs and sneezes* hacking, hawking, bark; *inf.* frog/tickle in one's throat.

council noun **1** *the town council | the governor's council* local authority, governing body, cabinet, parliament, ministry; advisory body, board, board of directors, committee, assembly, panel, trustees, synod, diet, convocation. **2** *the council of committee members* conference, conclave, assembly, convocation; meeting, gathering.

counsel noun **1** *seek expert counsel* advice, guidance, direction, recommendation, information; opinion, suggestion, warning, admonition, caution. **2** *hold counsel with a friend* consultation, discussion, conference, deliberation, dialogue. **3** *counsel handling his case* lawyer, attorney, advocate.

counsel verb *counsel him against going* advise, give guidance/direction, guide, direct, recommend, give one's opinion/suggestions, warn, admonish, caution.

counselor noun adviser, guidance counselor, director, mentor, confidant, guide.

count verb **1** *count the numbers* add up, total, sum up, calculate, compute, enumerate, tally. **2** *count the people* keep a count of, count off, enumerate, keep a tally of. **3** *counting everyone* include, take into account/consideration, number among, embrace, embody. **4** *count himself lucky* consider, think, regard, look upon, hold, judge, rate, deem, esteem. **5** *his presence does not count* matter, enter into consideration, be of account, be of consequence, have effect, signify, carry weight, weigh, mean anything, amount to anything, make a difference, rate; *inf.* carry (any) weight/clout. **count on** rely on, depend on, lean on, bank on, trust, believe in, put/pin one's faith in, swear by, take for granted. **count out** exclude, disregard, leave out, ignore, except, pass over, neglect.

count noun **1** *after the ballot count* counting, enumeration, calculation, computation, tally, tallying, poll. **2** *know the calorie count* total number, total, sum/grand total, amount, full amount, aggregate, whole, tally, reckoning.

countenance noun **1** *angry countenance* face, features, facial expression, expression, look, appearance, aspect, air, complexion, visage, physiognomy; *lit.* mien. **2** *not give countenance to the plan* support, backing, encouragement, endorsement, assistance, aid, approval, sanction, approbation, favor, acceptance, adoption, advocacy. **3** *lose countenance* composure, calmness, coolness, poise, self-possession, self-control, levelheadedness, coolheadedness, equanimity, equilibrium; *inf.* one's cool.

countenance verb **1** *cannot countenance such behavior* tolerate, approve, put up with, permit, allow, endure, brook; *inf.* stand for. **2** *countenance him in his project* encourage, support, back, help, aid, assist, champion, abet, take the side of, sanction, condone, endorse, warrant.

counter noun **1** *drinks on the counter* counter-top, bar, work surface, table, checkout. **2** *game counters* token, disk, chip, piece, man, marker.

counter adverb **counter to** *run counter to expectation* against, in opposition to, contrary to, at variance with, in defiance of, against the tide of, contrarily to, contrariwise to, conversely to.

counter adjective **counter to** *an outcome counter to our expectations* opposing, opposed to, opposite to, contrary to, adverse to, conflicting with, contradictory to, contrasting, obverse to.

counter verb *counter the attack* oppose, resist, rebut, combat, dispute, argue against, hit back at, contradict, retaliate, ward off.

counteract verb **1** *counteract the attack* act against, act counter to, hinder, oppose, thwart, frustrate, foil, impede, check, restrain, resist, withstand, defeat. **2** *counteract the effects* counterbalance, offset, neutralize, annul, negate, invalidate, countervail, counterpoise.

counterbalance verb balance, equalize, compensate for, make up for, neutralize, offset, set off, undo, countervail, counterpoise.

counterfeit adjective *counterfeit money* fake, faked, copied, forged, imitation, feigned, simulated, fraudulent, sham, spurious, bogus, ersatz; *inf.* phony, pseudo.
Antonyms: GENUINE; AUTHENTIC.

counterfeit noun *not the original, a counterfeit* fake, copy, forgery, reproduction, imitation, fraud, sham; *inf.* phony.

counterfeit verb *a crime to counterfeit money* fake, copy, reproduce, imitate, simulate, feign, falsify, sham.

countermand verb cancel, annul, revoke, rescind, reverse, repeal, retract, abrogate, quash, override, invalidate.

counterpart noun equivalent, equal, opposite number, parallel, complement, match, twin, mate, fellow, analog, correlative, copy, duplicate.

countless adjective innumerable, incalculable, immeasurable, endless, limitless, without end/limit, boundless, infinite, inexhaustible, untold, legion, myriad, no end to.

country noun **1** *countries at war* nation, state, sovereign state, kingdom, realm, people, community, commonwealth. **2** *love for one's country* native land, homeland, fatherland, motherland, mother country, land of one's birth; one's roots. **3** *driving through rough country* terrain, land, territory; region, area, district, part, neighborhood; parts; *inf.* neck of the woods. **4** *the will of the country* people, nation, public, population, populace, community, citizenry; inhabitants, residents, citizens, electors, voters. **5** *live in the country, not the city* countryside, rural area/district, farmland, great outdoors; *derog.* backwoods, sticks, wilds, wilderness, middle of nowhere; *inf.* boondocks, boonies.

country *adjective* rural, agrarian, agricultural, rustic, provincial, pastoral, Arcadian, bucolic; *lit.* sylvan.

countryman, countrywoman *noun meet a fellow countryman abroad* compatriot, fellow citizen.

countryside *noun* **1** *surrounded by beautiful countryside* landscape, scenery; scene, panorama, view, prospect, vista. **2** *living in the countryside* country, rural area/district, farmland. *See* COUNTRY *noun* 5.

county *noun the southern counties | the County of Los Angeles* administrative division/unit; *Louisiana* parish; *Alaska* borough.

coup *noun* **1** *pull off the coup of getting the governor to attend* successful action/act, feat, masterstroke, deed, accomplishment, stroke, stroke of genius, maneuver, stratagem, stunt, *tour de force*. **2** *a coup planned by the military* overthrow, seizure of power, *coup d'état*, violent change, revolt, revolution, rebellion, mutiny, insurgence.

couple *noun an established couple* pair, duo, twosome, dyad; partners, lovers, husband and wife, cohabitees. **a couple of 1** *a couple of drinks* two, two or three, a few, a small number of. **2** *a couple of men* two, a pair.

couple *verb* **1** *couple the joints* join, fasten, attach, connect, unite, hitch together, fuse, weld, bind, buckle, clasp, conjoin, marry. **2** *their names coupled together* join, link, associate, connect, ally. **3** *lovers coupling* copulate, have sex/intercourse, have sexual relations, make love, fornicate.

coupon *noun* **1** *give a coupon to the cashier* stub, voucher, ticket, slip, certificate. **2** *fill in the coupon* form, entry/application form.

courage *noun* bravery, valor, gallantry, heroism, fearlessness, pluck, nerve, intrepidity, lionheartedness, stoutheartedness, boldness, daring, audacity, dauntlessness, mettle, fortitude, firmness, resolution, tenacity, determination; *inf.* spunk, guts, grit, moxie.
Antonyms: cowardice, FEAR.

---

courage
fortitude, guts, nerve, pluck, resolution, tenacity

Courage is what makes someone capable of facing extreme danger and difficulty without retreating (*the courage to confront the enemy head-on*). It implies not only bravery and a dauntless spirit but the ability to endure in times of adversity (*a mother's courage in the face of her loss*). Someone who has **guts**, a slang word indicating an admirable display of courage when it really counts (*having the guts to stand up to one's boss*), might also be described as having intestinal fortitude, a clich&eacu that is more formal and means the same thing. **Fortitude** is the most formal of any of these words; it suggests firmness or strength of mind rather than

physical bravery (*the fortitude to stand up for his beliefs*). **Resolution** also implies firmness of mind rather than fearlessness, but the emphasis is on the determination to achieve a goal in spite of opposition or interference (*a woman of strong resolution, not easily held back by her male superiors*). **Tenacity** goes one step beyond *resolution*, adding stubborn persistence and unwillingness to acknowledge defeat (*the tenacity of a bulldog*). **Nerve** and **pluck** are informal words. *Pluck* connotes high spirits, conviction, and eagerness (*the pluck to volunteer her time even after she'd been laid off*), while *nerve* is the cool, unflappable daring with which someone takes a calculated risk (*the nerve to take over the controls and land the plane safely*). *Nerve* can also refer to brashness or even rudeness in social situations (*She had the nerve to go to his house without calling first*).

---

courageous *adjective* brave, valiant, valorous, gallant, heroic, fearless, intrepid, lionhearted, plucky, bold, daring, audacious, dauntless, firm, resolute, tenacious, determined, indomitable.
Antonyms: COWARDLY; TIMID.

courier *noun send the letter/information by courier* messenger, special messenger, letter carrier, mail carrier, bearer, runner, conveyor, envoy, emissary, harbinger, herald.

course *noun* **1** *the course of history* progression, progress, advance, advancement, rise, march, furtherance, proceeding, development, unfolding, flow, movement, continuity, sequence, order, succession. **2** *go a bit off course* route, way, track, direction, tack, path, line, lane, road, passage, channel, trail, trajectory, orbit, circuit, ambit. **3** *pursue a different course (of action)* method, way, line (of action), process, procedure, manner, mode of behavior/conduct, plan, system, policy, program, regimen. **4** *in the course of an hour* duration, passing, passage, lapse, period, term, span, spell, sweep. **5** *taking an English course* course of study, set of lectures, curriculum, program, schedule; classes, lectures, studies. **6** *a course of treatment* sequence, series, system, regimen. **7** *a waterlogged course* racecourse, track, circuit, ground. **in due course** in time, at the appropriate time, in the course of time, when the time is ripe, sooner or later, in the end, eventually. **of course** naturally, obviously, certainly, definitely, undoubtedly, without a doubt, indubitably.

course *verb* **1** *blood coursing* flow, move, run, rush, surge, gush, race, hurry, speed, charge, dash. **2** *coursing small game* hunt, pursue, chase, follow, run after, track.

court *noun* **1** *appear in court | appear before the court* court of law, bench, bar, court of justice, justiciary, tribunal. **2** *the queen's court* royal household, retinue, entourage, train, suite, cortege; attendants. **3** *situated near the queen's* *court* royal residence, palace, castle, manor, hall, chateau. **4** *monarch holding court* assembly, reception. **5** *paying court to the young lady* attention, homage, deference, suit, wooing, courtship; respects. **6** *walking in the campus court* courtyard, quadrangle, square, cloister, atrium, esplanade, patio, piazza, plaza; *inf.* quad. **7** *tennis court* playing area/enclosure, game area/enclosure, arena.

court *verb* **1** *he's courting her sister* pay court to, woo, pursue, chase, run after, set one's cap for, pay suit to. **2** *the couple are courting* go out, go out together, go with each other, go steady, date, keep company. **3** *court the manager* curry favor with, try to win over, pander to, fawn over; *inf.* soft-soap, butter up. **4** *court fame* seek, solicit, ask for, crave. **5** *court disaster* invite, risk, provoke, lead to, cause, bring on, elicit.

courteous *adjective* polite, well-mannered, mannerly, civil, chivalrous, gallant, gracious, kind, considerate, pleasant, tactful, diplomatic, politic, cordial, genial, affable, respectful, deferential, well-bred, polished, refined, civilized, urbane.
Antonyms: DISCOURTEOUS; RUDE.

courtesan *noun* prostitute, harlot, whore, woman of ill repute, streetwalker, call girl, lady of the evening.

courtesy *noun* **1** *have the courtesy to wait* politeness, civility, courteousness, chivalry, gallantry, gallantness, good breeding, gentility, graciousness, kindness, consideration, tact, cordiality, respect, respectfulness, deference, decorum, refinement, urbanity, courtliness, elegance; good manners, manners. **2** *your tickets are by courtesy of the management* kindness, generosity, benevolence, indulgence, favor, consideration, consent, permission.
Antonyms: rudeness; INCIVILITY.

courtier *noun* attendant, follower; lady-in-waiting, page, squire.

courtly *adjective* polite, well-mannered, civil, courteous, chivalrous, gallant, gentlemanly, ladylike, aristocratic, well-bred, dignified, decorous, formal, ceremonious, stately, proper, polished, refined, cultivated, urbane, elegant, suave, debonair.

courtship *noun* **1** *his courtship of her* courting, wooing, pursuit, suit. *See* COURT *verb* 1. **2** *married after a long (period of) courtship* romance, going steady, dating, keeping company.

courtyard *noun* quadrangle, square, cloister, esplanade, court. *See* COURT *noun* 6.

cove *noun* *a sandy cove* bay, inlet, creek, sound, anchorage.

covenant *noun* *sign a covenant* contract, guarantee, agreement, bond, deed, warrant, pledge, promise, indenture, trust, commitment, compact, bargain, pact, arrangement, deal, treaty, concordat, convention.

cover *verb* **1** *a pile of earth covering potatoes* place over, place under cover, protect, shield, shelter, conceal, hide, house, secrete, bury. **2** *snow covering the fields* overlay, overspread, blanket, carpet, overlie, extend over, coat, layer, pave, submerge. **3** *girls covered in silk* clothe, attire, outfit, garb, robe, wrap, accouter, sheathe. **4** *cover all the entrances* protect, defend, guard, shield, safeguard. **5** *cover several issues* include, deal with, contain, take in, comprise, involve, provide for, embrace, embody, incorporate, subsume, refer to, consider, examine, review, survey, take stock of. **6** *journalists covering the trial* report (on), write up, describe, tell of, give an account of, give details of, investigate. **7** *money to cover expenses* be enough for, offset, balance, counterbalance, compensate for, make up for. **8** *cover against fire* insure, provide for, indemnify, protect. **9** *cover 30 miles* | *cover the ground rapidly* travel, travel/pass over, traverse, cross, range/tramp over. **cover for 1** *doctors covering for each other* relieve, act/double/substitute for, take over for/from, replace, stand/fill in for. **2** *the thief's sister covering for him* give an alibi, provide an alibi, shield, protect. **cover up 1** *trying to cover up the mistake/scandal* conceal, hide, keep secret, hush up, keep dark, suppress, stonewall; *inf.* whitewash. **2** *cover up the potatoes* cover, place under cover, protect, shield, shelter. *See* COVER *verb* 1. **3** *cover yourself up* put on more clothes, dress, wrap up.
Antonyms: UNCOVER; EXPOSE; EXCLUDE.

cover *noun* **1** *take cover from the storm* covering, protection, shield, shelter, concealment, housing, refuge, sanctuary, haven, hiding place. **2** *the cover for the pot/box* lid, top, cap, covering. **3** *a cover of dust/snow* covering, layer, coat, coating, film, blanket, overlay, carpet, mantle, canopy, crust. **4** *the business is a cover for spying* cover-up, disguise, front, camouflage, pretense, façade, pretext, false front, screen, smokescreen, mask, cloak, veil, window dressing. **5** *the artillery providing cover for the infantry* protection, defense, guard, shield. **6** *provide (a) cover for the doctor* relief, replacement, stand-in, substitute. **7** *the cover of the book* jacket, dust jacket. **8** *under plain cover* envelope, wrapper, package; wrapping, packaging. **9** *protecting the cover for wildlife* undergrowth, woods, shrubbery, thicket, copse.

coverage *noun* **1** *news coverage* reporting, reportage; reports, accounts, articles, pieces, stories. **2** *a policy giving coverage against fire* insurance, protection, compensation, indemnification, indemnity.

covering *noun* **1** *provide covering for the children* cover, protection, shelter, housing. *See* COVER *noun* 1. **2** *a covering of dust/snow* layer, coat, coating, film, blanket, carpet. *See* COVER *noun* 3. **3** *the boiler covering* casing, case, sheath, sheathing, jacket, housing.

covering *adjective a covering letter* cover, accompanying, explanatory, introductory.

coverlet *noun* bedspread, bedcover, comforter.

covers *noun pull up the covers* bedclothes, sheets, blankets; bedcovers, quilts, comforters, duvets, bedspreads.covert

covert *adjective* secret, concealed, hidden, surreptitious, furtive, stealthy, private, underground.
Antonyms: OVERT; OPEN.

covet *verb* desire, want, wish for, long/yearn for, crave, hanker/lust after, thirst for, hunger after, set one's heart on, aspire to, aim after.

covetous *adjective* **covetous of** *covetous of her sister's house* desirous of, wanting, craving, yearning/longing for, greedy for, envious of. *See* COVET.

cow *noun* bovine, heifer; Guernsey, Jersey, Holstein. **cows** cattle.

cow *verb teachers cowing the students* intimidate, overawe, awe, daunt, dismay, subdue, scare, frighten, petrify, terrorize, unnerve, browbeat, bully, domineer, bulldoze.

coward *noun* poltroon, craven, dastard, recreant, renegade; *inf.* chicken, scaredy-cat, yellowbelly, sissy, big baby.

cowardly *adjective* lily-livered, faint-hearted, chickenhearted, craven, base, spineless, timorous, timid, fearful, shrinking, pusillanimous, dastardly, afraid of one's (own) shadow; *inf.* chicken, yellow, weak-kneed, gutless, yellow-bellied.
Antonyms: BRAVE; COURAGEOUS.

cowboy *noun* cowhand, cowman, cattleman, cowherd, herd, herdsman, drover, stockman, rancher, ranchero; *inf.* cowpuncher, cowpoke, broncobuster; gaucho.

cower *verb* cringe, shrink, flinch, draw back, recoil, crouch, wince, blench, quail, quake, tremble, quiver, grovel.

coy *adjective* arch, coquettish, flirtatious, kittenish, skittish, shy, modest, bashful, reticent, diffident, retiring, backward, self-effacing, shrinking, withdrawn, timid, demure, prudish, unconfident, lacking confidence, unsure.
Antonyms: BOLD; BRAZEN; IMPUDENT.

cozen *verb* cheat, deceive, beguile, trick, dupe, double-cross, swindle, take advantage of, defraud, fleece, hoodwink.

cozy *adjective* snug, comfortable, warm, homelike, homey, sheltered, secure, safe, at ease; *inf.* comfy, snug as a bug.
Antonym: UNCOMFORTABLE.

crabbed *adjective* **1** *a crabbed old man* crabby, cross, bad-tempered, surly, grouchy, discontented. *See* CRABBY. **2** *crabbed handwriting* cramped, squeezed, scribbled, labored, illegible, unreadable, indecipherable, hieroglyphical.

crabby *adjective* crabbed, bad-tempered, ill-tempered, ill-natured, ill-humored, cross, cantankerous, crotchety, irritable, touchy, testy, grouchy, snappy, prickly, crusty, peevish, churlish, surly, sour, morose, acrimonious, captious.

crack *verb* **1** *crack the cup* chip, fracture, fragment, break, split, splinter, snap, cleave. **2** *the rifle cracked* ring out, go bang, pop, snap, crackle, boom, explode, detonate. **3** *crack his head on a beam* hit, bang, bump, strike, knock, smack, whack, thump; *inf.* wallop, clout, clip. **4** *crack under questioning* give way, break down, collapse, go to pieces, lose control, yield, succumb, founder; *inf.* fall/come apart at the seams. **5** *crack the problem* solve, work out, get the answer to, find the solution to, fathom, decipher. **crack open** *crack open a bottle/case of wine* open, uncork, drink. **crack up** break down, have a breakdown, collapse, go to pieces, lose control, go out of one's mind, go mad; *inf.* fall/come apart at the seams, go crazy, freak out.

crack *noun* **1** *a crack in the cup/wall* chip, fracture, break, split, crevice, fissure, chink, gap, cavity, breach, rift, rupture, cleft, slit, cranny, interstice. **2** *the crack of the gun* bang, report, pop, snap, crackle, boom, explosion, detonation. **3** *get a crack on the head* blow, hit, bang, bump, strike, knock, smack, whack, thump; *inf.* wallop, clout, clip. **4** *another crack at the competition* attempt, try, shot, opportunity; *inf.* go, stab. **5** *laugh at his cracks* joke, funny remark, quip, witticism, wisecrack, gag, jibe, satirical remark, insult; *inf.* dig.

crack *adjective a crack tennis-player* | *crack shot* expert, first-rate, first-class, excellent, brilliant, elite, choice, superior; *inf.* ace, A1.

cracked *adjective* **1** *cracked cups/walls* chipped, fractured, broken, split, splintered, damaged, defective, flawed, imperfect, crazed. **2** *he seems a bit cracked* mad, insane, out of one's mind, touched, crazed, crackbrained; *inf.* crazy, nuts, nutty, bats, batty, off one's head/nut, around/round the bend, loony, off the mark.

crackle *verb* crack, crepitate, decrepitate, snap.

cradle *noun* **1** *babies sleeping in cradles* crib, bassinet, bed, cot. **2** *the cradle of democracy* birthplace, fount, fountainhead, source, place of origin, wellspring, beginning, breeding place, nursery; origins, beginnings.

cradle *verb cradle the baby* | *cradle his head in her arms* hold, rock, nestle, shelter, support.

craft *noun* **1** *admire the artist's craft* skill, skillfulness, expertise, expertness, ability, mastery, artistry, art, technique, workmanship, aptitude, dexterity, talent, flair, knack, cleverness, genius; *inf.* know-how. **2** *use craft to get his way* craftiness, cunning, artfulness, artifice, scheming, guile, subterfuge, stratagem, slyness, wiliness, shrewdness, trickery, duplicity, deceit; wiles, ruses. **3** *take up a new craft* occupation, trade, vocation, calling, pursuit, business, line, work, employment. **4** *pilot a craft* vessel, ship, boat, aircraft, plane, spacecraft.

craftsman, craftswoman noun master, expert, skilled worker, dedicated/meticulous worker, artist, artificer, artisan, technician, maker, smith, wright.

craftsmanship noun workmanship, technique, artistry, expertise, skill, mastery.

crafty adjective cunning, artful, scheming, designing, calculating, wily, sly, devious, guileful, tricky, shrewd, astute, canny, sharp, duplicitous, deceitful, subtle, insidious, treacherous, crooked, fraudulent, underhand, underhanded.
Antonyms: NAÏVE; HONEST; INGENUOUS.

crag noun cliff, bluff, escarpment, scarp, ridge, peak, pinnacle, tor.

cram verb 1 cram clothes into the suitcase stuff, push, shove, force, pack in, ram down, press, squeeze, jam, crush, compress, compact, condense. 2 cram the baskets | a bus crammed with people stuff, overfill, fill, fill up, fill to overflowing, stuff to the gills, fill to the brim, overcrowd. 3 cram for exams study, revise, grind, grind away.

cramp verb cramp one's progress/style restrict, limit, hamper, hinder, impede, hamstring, constrain, check, arrest, bridle, handicap, inhibit, thwart, stymie, obstruct, restrain, confine, shackle, encumber, clog.

cramp noun the cramp in my leg muscular contraction, muscle spasm, pang, twinge, pain, shooting pain, ache, crick, stiffness.

cramped adjective 1 cramped accommodations narrow, small, restricted, limited, confined, uncomfortable, closed in, hemmed in, tight, crowded, overfull, packed, squeezed, jammed in, congested. 2 cramped handwriting close, tightly packed, small, squeezed, crabbed, illegible, unreadable, indecipherable.

crane noun derrick, winch, hoist, davit, windlass, tackle.

cranium noun skull, head, crown; inf. noodle, nut, noggin.

crank noun turned the crank lever, arm, bar, shaft, spindle, crankshaft.

crank verb 1 crank the engine start, turn over, get going. 2 crank up production speed up, accelerate, hasten, hurry up, increase, improve.

cranky adjective 1 a cranky old man | a cranky diet eccentric, unconventional, odd, peculiar, queer, strange, bizarre, idiosyncratic, quirky, freakish, freaky, obsessive, fanatical; inf. funny, wacky. 2 a cranky teacher bad-tempered, cross, crabby.
Antonym: GOOD-NATURED.

cranny noun chink, crack, crevice, slit, split, fissure, rift, cleft, opening, gap, cavity, hole, nook, interstice.

crash verb 1 the sea crashed against the rocks | the glass crashed on the floor smash, batter, dash, shatter, break, disintegrate, shiver, splinter, fracture, fragment. 2 the cymbals crashed clash, clang, clank, clatter, bang, smash, boom, thunder, explode. 3 the trees crashed to the ground fall, topple, tumble, pitch, plunge, hurtle, lurch. 4 crash the car smash, wreck. 5 the business crashed collapse, fail, fold, fold up, go under, smash, founder, be ruined, cave in; inf. go broke/bust, come a cropper. 6 crash the party gatecrash, come uninvited to, intrude, sneak/slip into, invade; inf. horn in on. **crash into** the car crashed into the van bump/run/drive/bang into, collide with, hit, hurtle/smash/plow into.

crash noun 1 the crash of dishes/cymbals clash, clank, clang, clatter, bang, smash, clangor, racket, din, boom, thunder, explosion. 2 involved in a crash accident, smash, smash-up, collision, pile-up. 3 lost money in the crash collapse, failure, bankruptcy, fold, smash, fall, ruin, ruination, downfall, depression, debacle.

crash adjective a crash course/diet intensive, concentrated, telescoped, rapid, urgent.

crass adjective 1 don't be so crass stupid, insensitive, blundering, dense, thick, doltish, oafish, boorish, asinine, coarse, gross, vulgar, crude, rude, uncouth, unsophisticated, unrefined. 2 crass ignorance gross, utter, downright, out-and-out, very great, complete, blatant, glaring, undisguised, naked.

crate noun box, case, packing case, chest, container, receptacle.

crater noun hole, hollow, depression, dip, cavity, chasm.

crave verb 1 crave a chocolate bar long/yearn for, desire, want, wish for, hanker after, need, require, hunger/thirst for, be dying for, cry out for, lust after, pant for, be panting for, pine/sigh for; inf. fancy, have a yen for. 2 crave pardon ask for, plead/beg for, seek, entreat, beseech, implore, petition, pray for, solicit/sue for, supplicate.

craven adjective cowardly, chickenhearted, lily-livered, faint-hearted, timorous, fearful, base, timid, pusillanimous, dastardly, recreant, poltroon; inf. chicken, yellow.

craving noun longing, yearning, desire, hankering, need, urge, hunger, thirst, lust, appetite, addiction; inf. yen.

crawl verb creep, go on all fours, move on hands and knees, inch, drag/pull oneself along, drag, slither, squirm, wriggle, writhe, worm one's way, advance slowly/stealthily, sneak.

craze noun fad, vogue, trend, fashion, enthusiasm, passion, infatuation, obsession, mania, fixation, fancy, novelty, whim, fascination, preoccupation, rage; inf. thing, the latest.

crazed adjective insane, mad, wild, unbalanced, crazy. See CRAZY 1.

crazy adjective 1 a crazy person crazed, of unsound mind, insane, mad, mad as a hatter, mad as a March hare, lunatic, idiotic, wild, unbalanced, demented, deranged, berserk, unhinged, touched, maniacal, delirious, out of one's mind/head; inf. cracked, daft, bats, batty,

loony, loopy, screwy, flaky, nuts, nutty, nutty as a fruit cake, cuckoo, bonkers, mental, not all there, out to lunch, off one's nut/rocker, around/round the bend/twist. **2** *a crazy idea* absurd, idiotic, stupid, silly, ridiculous, foolish, peculiar, odd, strange, queer, weird, eccentric, bizarre, fantastic, outrageous, wild, fatuous, inane, puerile, impracticable, senseless, unworkable, foolhardy, unrealistic, unwise, imprudent, ill-conceived, preposterous; *inf.* screwy, screwball, harebrained, cockeyed, half-baked. **crazy about** *crazy about opera* enthusiastic about, mad about, wild about, avid about, keen about, infatuated with, passionate about, smitten with/by, fanatical about, devoted to, fond/enamored of, zealous about/for, fervent, fervid about, excited about; *inf.* nuts about/on, gone on.
Antonyms: SANE; LUCID; RATIONAL.

creak *verb* squeak, screech, squeal, groan, grate, grind, jar, rasp, scrape, scratch.

cream *noun* **1** *beauty/antiseptic cream* lotion, emulsion, emollient, paste; cosmetic, ointment, salve, unguent, liniment. **2** *the cream of the college* best/choice part, flower, elite, pick, prime, quintessence, *crème de la crème*.

cream *adjective* *a cream dress* cream-colored, off-white, whitish, yellowish-white, buff.

crease *noun* **1** *a crease in the paper/pants leg* ridge, furrow, groove, corrugation, fold, line, pleat, tuck. **2** *facial creases* wrinkle, line, crinkle, pucker; crow's foot.

crease *verb* **1** *the dress was creased during the trip* crumple, wrinkle, crinkle, rumple, pucker. **2** *crease the paper/pants leg* put a crease/fold in, corrugate, pleat, tuck.

create *verb* **1** *create a new generation* bring into being/existence, give birth/life to, procreate, father, sire, beget, spawn. **2** *create a new environment* generate, originate, invent, initiate, engender, produce, design, devise, make, frame, fabricate, build, construct, erect, develop, shape, form, mold, forge, concoct, hatch. **3** *create a good impression* produce, make, result in, cause, be the cause of, bring about, give rise to, lead to. **4** *create a new system of government* invest, appoint, install, make, establish, found, institute, constitute, inaugurate, set up.
Antonyms: DEMOLISH; DESTROY.

creation *noun* **1** *the creation of a new generation* birth, procreation, fathering, begetting, genesis, spawning. *See* CREATE 1. **2** *the creation of a new environment* generation, origination, invention, initiation, inception, design, devising, formation, production, fabrication, building, shaping, hatching. *See* CREATE 2. **3** *everything in creation* the world, the living/natural world, the universe, the cosmos, nature, life; all living things. **4** *the creation of a new system of government* investing, investiture, appointment, in-

stallation, establishment, foundation, institution, inauguration. **5** *the poet's creation* work, work of art, achievement, production, opus, invention, handiwork, masterpiece, *pièce de résistance*, *magnum opus*. **6** *Paris creations* fashion, design, dress; clothes.

creative *adjective* inventive, imaginative, original, artistic, inspired, visionary, talented, gifted, resourceful, ingenious, clever, productive, fertile.

---

creative
inventive, original, resourceful, imaginative, ingenious

Everyone likes to think that he or she is **creative**, which is used to describe the active, exploratory minds possessed by artists, writers, and inventors (*a creative approach to problem-solving*). Today, however, *creative* has become an advertising buzzword (*creative cooking, creative hair-styling*) that simply means new or different. **Original** is more specific and limited in scope. Someone who is *original* comes up with things that no one else has thought of (*an original approach to constructing a doghouse*), or thinks in an independent and creative way (*a highly original filmmaker*). **Imaginative** implies having an active and creative imagination, which often means that the person visualizes things quite differently than the way they appear in the real world (*imaginative illustrations for a children's book*). The practical side of *imaginative* is **inventive**; the *inventive* person figures out how to make things work (*an inventive solution to the problem of getting a wheelchair into a van*). But where an *inventive* mind tends to comes up with solutions to problems it has posed for itself, a **resourceful** mind deals successfully with externally imposed problems or limitations (*A resourceful child can amuse herself with simple wooden blocks*). Someone who is **ingenious** is both *inventive* and *resourceful*, with a dose of cleverness thrown in (*the ingenious idea of using recycled plastic to create a warm, fleece-like fabric*).

---

creator *noun* **1** *praise their Creator* God, the Almighty. *See* GOD. **2** *the creator of the series* author, inventor, originator, initiator, maker, designer, producer, architect, prime mover, begetter, generator.

creature *noun* **1** *all God's creatures* living thing/entity, being. **2** *the creatures of the forest* animal, beast; *inf.* critter. **3** *beautiful/poor creatures* person, human being, human, individual, character, fellow, soul, mortal; *inf.* body.

credence *noun* *place no credence in his statement* belief, faith, trust, confidence, reliance.

credentials *plural noun* testimonial, proof of identity/qualifications, certificate, diploma, document, warrant, license, permit, card, voucher, passport, letter of introduction/recommendation, missive, deed, title; references; attestation, documentation.

credibility *noun* **1** *the credibility of the story* plausibility, tenability. *See* CREDIBLE 1. **2** *the government lacking credibility* acceptability, faith, trust, trustworthiness, reliability, dependability, integrity.

credible *adjective* **1** *a scarcely credible story* believable, conceivable, imaginable, plausible, tenable. **2** *the more credible party* acceptable, trustworthy, reliable, dependable.
Antonyms: INCREDIBLE; UNBELIEVABLE; UNTRUSTWORTHY.

credit *verb* *he couldn't credit it* believe, accept, put confidence in, trust, have faith in, rely on, depend on; *inf.* fall for, swallow, buy. **credit with** *credit him with the discovery* ascribe to, attribute to, assign to, accredit with, give credit to, chalk up to, put down to, impute to.
Antonym: DISBELIEVE; DISCREDIT.

credit *noun* **1** *receive credit for his performance* praise, acclaim, approval, commendation, acknowledgment, tribute, kudos, glory, recognition, regard, esteem, respect, merit, veneration, laudation; thanks. **2** *he gained credit in the city* name, reputation, repute, character, prestige, influence, standing, status, regard, esteem, estimation, acceptability, credibility; *inf.* clout. **3** *a credit to the town* source of honor/pride, feather in the cap, asset, boast, glory, flower, gem. **4** *the story gaining credit* belief, believability, credence, faith, trust, reliability, reliance, confidence. **5** *his credit is good* financial standing/status, solvency. **on credit** *buy on credit* in installments, by deferred payment, on account.

creditable *adjective* praiseworthy, commendable, laudable, meritorious, admirable, exemplary, worthy, up to the mark, respectable, reputable, estimable, honorable, deserving.

credulity *noun* credulousness, gullibility, gullibleness, naïveté, naïveness, blind faith, greenness. *See* CREDULOUS.

credulous *adjective* overtrusting, overtrustful, gullible, naïve, green, dupable, deceivable, unsuspicious, unskeptical, uncritical; *inf.* wet behind the ears.
Antonyms: INCREDULOUS; SKEPTICAL.

creed *noun* set of principles, system/statement of beliefs, profession of faith, teaching, doctrine, canon, dogma, tenet, catechism; beliefs, principles, rules, articles of faith, maxims.

creek *noun* **1** *the creek dried up in July* stream, brook, rivulet, small river, channel; *inf.* crick. **2** *sailed into the creek for shelter* inlet, bay, cove.

creep *verb* **1** *creeping along the ground* crawl, go on all fours, move on hands and knees, inch, slither, squirm, wriggle, writhe, worm one's way, insinuate. **2** *creep up on them* move stealthily, steal, sneak, tiptoe, approach unnoticed, slink, skulk. **3** *employees went creeping to the boss* grovel, kowtow, bow and scrape, fawn, cower, cringe, *inf.* suck up to.

creep *noun* *hate the little creep* bore; *inf.* dweeb, nerd, jerk.

creeper *noun* trailing plant, trailer, climbing plant, climber, rambler.

creeps *plural noun* *gave me the creeps* feeling of horror/fear/terror/disgust/repulsion/revulsion; *inf.* heebie-jeebies.

creepy *adjective* *a creepy movie* hair-raising, horrifying, horrific, horrible, frightening, terrifying, awful, disturbing, eerie, sinister, weird, nightmarish, macabre, menacing, ominous, threatening, disgusting, repellent, repulsive, revolting; *inf.* scary.

crescent *noun* *shaped like a crescent* half moon, new moon, old moon; *Tech.* meniscus.

crest *noun* **1** *a cock's crest* | *the helmet crest* cockscomb, comb, tuft, plume, topknot, tassel, mane, panache; *Tech.* caruncle. **2** *the crest of the hill* summit, top, pinnacle, peak, crown, apex, ridge; heights. **3** *the club crest* regalia, insignia, badge, emblem, device, coat of arms; *Heraldry.* bearing, charge.

crestfallen *adjective* downcast, dejected, depressed, glum, downhearted, disheartened, discouraged, dispirited, despondent, disappointed, disconsolate, in the doldrums, down in the dumps.

crevice *noun* fissure, cleft, chink, crack, cranny, split, rift, slit, gash, rent, fracture, opening, gap, hole, interstice.

crew *noun* **1** *the crew prepared to sail* hands, sailors, seamen, mariners, ship's company, ship's complement. **2** *the camera crew* team, company, party, working party, gang, squad, force, corps, posse. **3** *that peculiar crew over there* crowd, lot, gang, mob, pack, horde, multitude, troop, swarm, herd, band, group, bunch, set.

crib *noun* **1** *a baby's crib* cradle, bassinet, bed. **2** *a crib of animal fodder* stall, manger, bin, box, rack, bunker, container.

crick *noun* **1** *a crick in my neck* pain, cramp, twinge, spasm, pang; stiffness. **2** *caught crayfish in the crick* creek, stream, brook, rivulet, small river, channel.

crier *noun* town crier, announcer, proclaimer, herald.

crime *noun* **1** *convicted of the crime* offense, unlawful/illegal act, misdemeanor, misdeed, wrong, felony, violation, transgression, trespass, fault, injury; *Law* malfeasance, tort. **2** *a crime against humanity* sin, immoral act, evil, evil action, wrong, wrongdoing, vice, iniquity. **3** *crime is on the increase* lawbreaking, delinquency, wrongdoing, villainy, malefaction, illegality, misconduct, lawlessness, felony, corruption, wickedness, evil; *Law* malfeasance.

criminal *adjective* **1** *a criminal act* unlawful, illegal, lawbreaking, illicit, lawless, felonious, indictable, delinquent, culpable, wrong, villainous, corrupt, evil, wicked, iniquitous, nefarious; *Law* malfeasant; *inf.* crooked, bent.

2 *a criminal waste of resources* deplorable, scandalous, preposterous, shameful, reprehensible, senseless, foolish, ridiculous, sinful, immoral.
Antonyms: LAWFUL; LAW-ABIDING; COMMENDABLE.

criminal *noun* lawbreaker, offender, wrongdoer, felon, delinquent, miscreant, malefactor, culprit, villain, gangster, bandit, transgressor, sinner, trespasser; *Law* malfeasant; *inf.* crook, con.

crimp *verb* **1** *crimp cloth/paper* flute, ruffle, pleat, corrugate, furrow, groove, ridge, crease, wrinkle, crinkle, crumple, pucker, gather, smock. **2** *crimp hair* wave, curl, frizz.

cringe *verb* **1** *cringe in fear* cower, shrink, draw back, quail, flinch, recoil, start, shy, blench, dodge, duck, crouch, wince, tremble, quiver, shake. **2** *cringe to the boss* kowtow, grovel; *inf.* crawl, creep.

crinkly *adjective* wrinkled, wrinkly, crinkled, crumpled, creased, crimped, corrugated, fluted, furrowed, ridged, gathered, puckered, smocked.

cripple *verb* **1** *the accident crippled him* make lame, disable, incapacitate, debilitate, impair, damage, hamstring, maim, weaken, enfeeble, paralyze. **2** *businesses crippled by the recession* damage, injure, ruin, destroy, weaken, impair, hamstring, hamper, impede, cramp, spoil, bring to a standstill, paralyze, enfeeble, vitiate.

crippled *adjective* lame, disabled, incapacitated, physically impaired/handicapped, deformed, housebound, bedridden; *inf.* laid up.

crisis *noun* **1** *the crisis of the fever* | *reaching a crisis* turning point, critical/decisive point, crux, climax, culmination, height, moment of truth, zero hour, Rubicon; *inf.* crunch. **2** *a financial crisis* emergency, disaster, catastrophe, calamity, extremity, predicament, plight, mess, trouble, difficulty, dilemma, quandary, exigency; dire straits; *inf.* fix, pickle, scrape.

crisp *adjective* **1** *crisp toast* brittle, crispy, crumbly, crunchy, breakable. **2** *crisp lettuce* firm, fresh, unwilted, unwithered. **3** *crisp weather* brisk, bracing, fresh, refreshing, invigorating, dry, cool, chilly. **4** *a crisp account* brief, terse, succinct, concise, short, incisive, clear, pithy. **5** *a crisp manner* brisk, vigorous, decisive, brusque, curt, abrupt. **6** *a crisp appearance* clean-cut, neat, smart, spruce, trim, well-groomed; *inf.* snappy.
Antonyms: SOFT; FLACCID; WORDY.

criterion *noun* measure, gauge, scale, yardstick, standard, norm, benchmark, touchstone, barometer, model, exemplar, classic example, rule, law, principle, canon.

critic *noun* **1** *theater critics* reviewer, commentator, pundit, arbiter, evaluator, analyst, judge, expounder. **2** *answer his critics* faultfinder, attacker, censurer, detractor, backbiter, reviler, vilifier; *inf.* nitpicker.

critical *adjective* **1** *a critical point in history* crucial, deciding, decisive, climacteric, pivotal, important, momentous, high-priority, serious, vital, urgent, pressing, compelling, essential, exigent. **2** *in a critical condition* dangerous, grave, serious, risky, perilous, hazardous, touch-and-go, uncertain, precarious; *inf.* chancy. **3** *a critical attitude* faultfinding, captious, censorious, carping, quibbling, disapproving, disparaging, judgmental, hypercritical, overcritical; *inf.* nitpicking. **4** *a critical essay* evaluative, analytic, interpretative, expository, commentative, explanatory, explicative, elucidative, annotative.
Antonyms: UNIMPORTANT; SAFE; COMPLIMENTARY.

criticism *noun* **1** *actions receiving criticism* faultfinding, censure, reproof, condemnation, disapproval, disparagement, captiousness, carping; *inf.* nitpicking, flak, bad press, bad notices, knocking, panning, slamming. **2** *studying literary criticism* evaluation, comment, commentary, assessment, appreciation, appraisal, analysis, interpretation, explanation, explication, elucidation, annotation. **3** *read the criticism* review, notice, commentary, evaluation, critique, analysis, appraisal; *inf.* write-up.

criticize *verb* *criticize his behavior* | *stop criticizing me* find fault with, censure, denounce, blame, condemn, pick holes in, disapprove of, disparage, carp at, cavil at, excoriate; *inf.* nitpick, hand out brickbats, give flak to, knock, pan, slam.

critique *noun* evaluation, analysis, assessment, appraisal; textual examination, commentary, critical essay, review.

croak *verb* **1** *"who's there?" he croaked* speak/utter hoarsely/huskily/throatily/harshly, rasp, speak thickly, squawk, caw, grunt, wheeze. **2** *always croaking about something* grumble, complain, moan, grouse, whine, mutter, murmur. **3** *when the crook croaked* die, pass away, perish, expire; *inf.* kick the bucket.

crock[1] *noun* *a crock of jam* earthenware pot, pot, jar, vessel, container, pitcher, jug, ewer.

crock[2] *noun* *what a crock his story is* lie, exaggeration, piece/bunch of nonsense; *inf.* piece/bunch of garbage/hooey/crap/bull.

crockery *noun* dishes, earthenware, pottery, china, stoneware, porcelain.

crony *noun* friend, companion, chum, comrade, associate, confederate; *inf.* pal, buddy.

crook *noun* **1** *crooks imprisoned* criminal, villain, rogue, lawbreaker, thief, robber, swindler, cheat, racketeer; *inf.* shark, con man. **2** *the crook of one's arm* | *crook of the river* bend, curve, curvature, angle, bow.

crook *verb* *crook one's finger* bend, curve, angle, flex, hook, bow.

crooked *adjective* **1** *a crooked branch/road* bent, curved, twisted, contorted, warped, irregular, angled, bowed, hooked, flexed, winding, twisting, zigzag, meandering, deviating, sinuous, tortuous, serpentine. **2** *a crooked back* deformed, misshapen, out of shape, disfigured, crippled. **3** *the picture's crooked* not straight, tilted, at an angle, angled, slanted, aslant, slanting, sloping, askew, awry, to one side, off-center, lopsided, uneven, unsymmetrical, asymmetric. **4** *a crooked politician/deal* criminal, dishonest, corrupt, dishonorable, unscrupulous, unprincipled, fraudulent, illegal, unlawful, nefarious, crafty, deceitful, shifty, underhand, underhanded, questionable, dubious; *inf.* shady.

Antonyms: STRAIGHT; HONEST.

croon *verb* hum, sing softly, warble.

crop *noun* **1** *the apple crop* year's growth, harvest, yield, produce, vintage, gathering, reaping, gleaning, garnering, garner; fruits. **2** *the year's crop of students* batch, lot, collection, assortment, selection, supply. **3** *a bird's crop* craw, gullet, maw, throat.

crop *verb crop the dog's tail/hair* cut, cut short, clip, trim, snip, shear, lop, curtail, reduce, prune. **crop up** *something cropped up* happen, occur, arise, turn up, spring up, emerge, appear, come to pass.

cross *noun* **1** *the sign of the cross* crucifix, rood. **2** *a cross to bear* trouble, worry, burden, trial, disaster; tribulation, affliction, misfortune, adversity, misery, woe, pain, suffering, calamity, catastrophe. **3** *a cross between two breeds/types* crossbreed, hybrid, hybridization, mixture, amalgam, blend, combination, mongrel, cur.

cross *verb* **1** *the bridge crossing the river* go across, span, extend/stretch across, pass over, bridge, ford. **2** *cross the road* go/travel across, cut across, traverse. **3** *the roads/lines crossed there* intersect, meet, join, converge, crisscross, interweave, intertwine, zigzag. **4** *hates being crossed* oppose, resist, thwart, frustrate, foil, obstruct, impede, hinder, hamper, block, check, deny, contradict. **5** *cross two species* crossbreed, interbreed, cross-fertilize, cross-pollinate, intercross, hybridize, mix, intermix, blend. **cross out** *cross out his name* delete, strike out, bluepencil, cancel, eliminate, obliterate.

cross *adjective* **1** *she was cross at/with the children* angry, annoyed, irritated, in a bad mood, peeved, vexed, upset, piqued, out of humor. **2** *a cross old woman* irritable, short-tempered, bad-tempered, ill-humored, surly, churlish, disagreeable, irascible, touchy, snappy, snappish, impatient, peevish, petulant, fractious, crotchety, grouchy, grumpy, querulous, cantankerous, testy, captious, splenetic, waspish. **3** *cross purposes* contrary, opposing, opposite, adverse, unfavorable.

Antonyms: PLEASED; GOOD-HUMORED; AGREEABLE.

cross-examine *verb* cross-question, question, interrogate, quiz, pump, catechize; *inf.* grill.

crossing *noun a crash at the crossing* junction, crossroads, intersection; crosswalk.

crotchety *adjective* crabbed, bad-tempered, ill-natured, ill-humored, cross, crabby, awkward, difficult, grumpy, grouchy, disagreeable, irri-

table, irascible, churlish, surly, touchy, testy, fractious, crusty, cantankerous, curmudgeonly.

crouch *verb* squat, bend, bend down, hunker, stoop, hunch over, cower, cringe.

crow *verb the winners were crowing over/about their victory* boast, brag, trumpet, gloat, show off, swagger, bluster, strut; *inf.* blow one's own horn.

crowd *noun* **1** *a crowd of people* throng, horde, mob, rabble, large number, mass, multitude, host, army, herd, flock, drove, swarm, troupe, pack, flood, collection, company, gathering, assembly, assemblage, array, congregation, convention, concourse. **2** *he always follows the crowd and doesn't think for himself* majority, multitude, common people, populace, general public, mob, rank and file, hoi polloi, proletariat; riff-raff; masses. **3** *the late-night crowd* group, set, lot, gang, bunch, circle, fraternity, clique, coterie. **4** *the hit show played to a capacity crowd* gate, house, turnout, audience, attendance; spectators, listeners, viewers.

crowd *verb* **1** *crowd around the teacher* gather, cluster, congregate, flock, swarm, throng, huddle, concentrate. **2** *people crowding into the hall* push, push one's way, shove, thrust forward, elbow, squeeze, pile, pack. **3** *tourists crowding the streets | streets crowded with tourists* throng, pack, fill, overfill, congest. **4** *crowd people into the trains* pack, squeeze, cram, jam, stuff, pile. **5** *don't crowd him with your endless questions* pressure, pressurize, harass, badger, pester, hound, nag, torment, plague; *inf.* hassle.

crowded *adjective crowded streets/buses* full, overfull, busy, overflowing, packed, jam-packed, crushed, cramped, congested, teeming, swarming, thronged, populous, mobbed; *inf.* full to bursting.

crown *noun* **1** *the king's crown* diadem, coronet, coronal, tiara, chaplet, circlet, wreath. **2** *the champion winning the crown* laurel wreath, victor's garland, prize, trophy; honor, distinction, glory, kudos; laurels. **3** *the power of the Crown* monarchy, monarch, sovereignty, sovereign, ruler, king, queen, emperor, empress, royalty; *inf.* royals. **4** *the crown of the hill* top, crest, summit, apex, head, tip, pinnacle. **5** *the crown of his achievements* climax, height, culmination, pinnacle, zenith, acme, ultimate, flower.

crown *verb* **1** *crown the queen* invest, inaugurate, induct, install. **2** *crown his career* cap, round off, be the culmination/climax of, put the finishing touch/touches to, consummate, top off, complete, perfect, conclude. **3** *the steeple crowning the church* top, surmount, overtop. **4** *he crowned his attacker* hit over the head, strike, cuff, punch, buffet; *inf.* wallop, bash.

crucial *adjective* **1** *a crucial moment in the talks* decisive, critical, determining, pivotal, central, testing, trying, searching. **2** *the matter is of crucial importance* very important, high-priority, essential, momentous, vital, urgent, pressing, compelling.

---

crucial
acute, critical, deciding, pressing, urgent

In any emergency or crisis situation, there is usually a turning point. Such an event is called **critical** if it determines the outcome of a situation (*a critical point in the nuclear disarmament negotiations*; *a critical election for the Democratic Party*). **Crucial** can also refer to a turning point, but it emphasizes the necessity of something happening before a result can be achieved (*the battle was crucial to their victory*), while *critical* suggests more of a balance between positive and negative outcomes (*a critical debate on foreign policy*). **Acute** describes the intensification of a situation that is rapidly approaching a climax (*an acute shortage of O-negative blood*), while **deciding** refers to something that forces a certain outcome (*a deciding factor in his recovery*). **Pressing** and **urgent** are milder words. A situation that is *pressing* may be chronic rather than *acute* (*a pressing need for changes in the political system*), while an *urgent* situation may be approaching a crisis without reference to a specific turning point (*an urgent meeting between the two presidents*). While *urgent* expresses more intensity than *pressing*, neither adjective conveys the same sense of intensity as *crucial*, *critical*, or *acute*.

crucify *verb* **1** *crucify the wrongdoers* nail to a cross, execute/put to death on a cross. **2** *bullies crucifying the new students* persecute, torment, distress, harrow, torture. **3** *his play was crucified by the critics* tear apart, tear to pieces/shreds, criticize, attack, lampoon; *inf.* pan.

crude *adjective* **1** *crude oil/flour* raw, unrefined, natural, coarse, unprocessed, unmilled, unpolished. **2** *a crude sculpture/dwelling* rudimentary, primitive, rough, rough-and-ready, rough-hewn, makeshift, unfinished, unpolished, unformed, undeveloped, rude. **3** *a crude sense of humor* coarse, vulgar, rude, uncouth, indelicate, earthy, indecent, dirty, bawdy, smutty, obscene, offensive, lewd, ribald, boorish, crass, tasteless; *inf.* blue, raunchy. *Antonyms:* REFINED; SOPHISTICATED; DELICATE.

cruel *adjective* **1** *a cruel dictator/action* savage, brutal, inhuman, barbaric, barbarous, bloodthirsty, vicious, ferocious, fierce, evil, fiendish, callous, cold-blooded, sadistic, ruthless, merciless, pitiless, unrelenting, remorseless, unfeeling, heartless, inhumane, severe, harsh, stern, stony-hearted, hard-hearted. **2** *a cruel stroke of fate* unkind, painful, distressing, harrowing, harsh, grim, heartless. *Antonyms:* KIND; MERCIFUL; COMPASSIONATE.

cruelty *noun* **1** *the cruelty of the dictator* | *cruelty of his actions* savageness, savagery, brutality, inhumanity, barbarism, barbarousness, viciousness, ferocity, fierceness, evil, fiendishness, callousness, sadism, ruthlessness, pitilessness, relentlessness, severity, harshness, inclemency. *See* CRUEL 1. **2** *the cruelty of the blow* unkindness, painfulness, harshness, grimness, heartlessness; pain, resulting distress. *Antonyms:* COMPASSION; KINDNESS.

cruise *verb* **1** *ships cruising* sail, voyage, journey. **2** *cars cruising along coast,* travel steadily, drift.

cruise *noun* go on a cruise sea/boat trip, voyage, sail.

crumb *noun* bit, fragment, morsel, particle, grain, atom, speck, scrap, shred, sliver, snippet, mite.

crumble *verb* **1** *crumble the crackers* break up, crush, pulverize, pound, grind, powder, granulate, fragment. **2** *the empire was crumbling* disintegrate, fall to pieces, fall apart, collapse, break down/up, tumble down, decay, deteriorate, degenerate, fall into decay, go to rack and ruin, decompose, rot, rot away, molder, perish, vanish, fade away, come to dust.

crumple *verb* **1** *crumple the dress* crush, crease, rumple, wrinkle, crinkle. **2** *the child's face crumpled* pucker, screw up. **3** *resistance crumpling* collapse, fail, cave in, fall apart, give way, go to pieces, topple, shrivel. *Antonyms:* IRON; STRAIGHTEN; SURVIVE.

crunch *verb* **1** *crunching carrots* chew noisily, bite, munch, champ, chomp, gnaw, masticate. **2** *crunch the snow* crush, grind, pulverize, pound, smash. **3** *crunch through the snow* move noisily, sound noisy/harsh.

crunch *noun* **1** *carpooling during the fuel crunch* shortage, (period of) reduction, deficit, deficiency, scarcity, shortfall, lack. **2** *came through in the crunch* crux, crisis, critical point, test, moment of truth/decision.

crusade *noun* **1** *soldiers on a crusade* military campaign, holy war. **2** *a crusade against smoking* campaign, drive, push, struggle, cause, movement.

crusade *verb* *crusading for more resources* campaign, fight, work, do battle, take up arms, take up a cause.

crusader *noun* campaigner, fighter, battler, champion, advocate, reformer.

crush *verb* **1** *crush the grapes* squash, squeeze, mash, press, press down, compress, bruise. **2** *crush the material* crease, crumple, rumple, wrinkle, crinkle. **3** *crush the stones* break up, smash, shatter, pound, pulverize, grind, crumble, crunch. **4** *crush the rebellion* | *crush their opponents* put down, quell, quash, suppress, subdue, overcome, overwhelm, overpower, stamp out, defeat, conquer, vanquish, extinguish. **5** *crushed by his criticism* mortify, humiliate, abash, quash, shame, chagrin; *inf.* put down. **6** *crush her in his arms* embrace, enfold, hug, squeeze, hold/press tight, clutch.

crush *noun* crush on *a crush on the teacher* infat-

crust *noun* **1** *the crust of the bread/pie* outside, casing, shell, husk. **2** *a crust of hard snow/skin* covering, cover, coating, caking, topping, layer, film, skin, blanket, mantle, incrustation, concretion, scab.

crusty *adjective* **1** *crusty pastry* crisp, crispy, brittle, hard, well-baked, well-done. **2** *a crusty old man | a crusty manner* brusque, surly, curt, gruff, cross, crabbed, crabby, grouchy, bad-tempered, short-tempered, irritable, irascible, ill-humored, ill-natured, snappish, touchy, testy, snarling, cantankerous, choleric, splenetic, captious.

cry *verb* **1** *babies crying* shed tears, weep, sob, wail, snivel, blubber, whimper, whine, bawl, howl. **2** *he cried out her name | cried in terror* call out, exclaim, yell, scream, screech, bawl, shout, bellow, howl. **cry down** *cry down his achievement* decry, run down, disparage, belittle, denigrate.

Antonyms: LAUGH; WHISPER.

cry *noun* *cry of terror/pain* call, exclamation, scream, screech, yell, shout, bellow, howl. **cries** *the baby's cries* weeping, sobbing, sniveling, blubbering, wailing, lamenting, lamentation; sobs, wails, howls.

crypt *noun* tomb, vault, burial chamber, sepulcher.

cub *noun* **1** *a bear and her cubs* young, offspring, whelp. **2** *newspaper cubs* trainee, learner, recruit, tenderfoot, youngster; *inf.* greenhorn.

cubbyhole *noun* *put the document in his cubbyhole* pigeonhole, compartment, slot, recess, niche; *inf.* cubby.

cube *noun* six-sided body/shape, hexahedron; block, brick, chunk, hunk.

cube *verb* *cube the potatoes* dice, cut up, cut into cubes, chop.

cuddle *verb* **1** *cuddling his wife* hug, embrace, enfold, clasp. **2** *cuddling by the fire* embrace, pet, fondle; *inf.* neck, smooch. **3** *cuddle (up) in bed* snuggle, nestle, curl up.

cuddly *adjective* cuddlesome, huggable, warm, soft.

cudgel *noun* *hit with a cudgel* club, bludgeon, stick, baton, truncheon, bat, blackjack.

cudgel *verb* *the attacker cudgeled his victim* bludgeon, club, beat/strike with a stick, truncheon.

cue *noun* **1** *"away" is your cue* catchword, keyword, prompt, prompt-word, prompting, reminder. **2** *your cue to begin* signal, sign, indication, hint, suggestion, intimation.

cuff *verb* *cuff him on the head* slap, strike, hit, buffet. **off the cuff** impromptu, ad lib, extempore, extemporaneous, extemporaneously, off the top of one's head, unrehearsed, improvised, offhand, on the spur of the moment, spontaneous, spontaneously.

cuisine *noun* cooking, cookery, *cordon bleu.*

cul-de-sac *noun* blind alley, dead end.

culminate *verb* come to a climax, peak, reach a

pinnacle, come to a crescendo, come to an end, end, close, finish, conclude, terminate, come to a head; *inf.* wind up.

culmination *noun* high point, height, top, summit, climax, peak, pinnacle, crest, crown, crowning touch, zenith, acme, apex, high noon, consummation, completion, close, finish, conclusion, termination.

culpable *adjective* at fault, in the wrong, guilty, answerable, blameworthy, blamable, to blame, censurable, reproachable, reprovable, reprehensible, sinful.

Antonyms: BLAMELESS; INNOCENT.

culprit *noun* person responsible, guilty party, wrongdoer, evildoer, lawbreaker, criminal, miscreant, delinquent, reprobate, transgressor, felon, sinner, malefactor; *inf.* baddie, bad guy.

cult *noun* **1** *belong to a secretive cult* sect, religion, church, denomination, body, affiliation, faith, belief, persuasion, following, party, school, faction, clique. **2** *the rap music cult* craze, fashion, fad; admiration, devotion, obsession, homage, worship, reverence, veneration, idolization.

cultivate *verb* **1** *cultivate the fields* till, farm, work, plow, dig, prepare, fertilize. **2** *cultivate a crop* plant, raise, tend, bring on, produce. **3** *cultivate the mind* culture, educate, train, civilize, enlighten, enrich, improve, better, develop, refine, polish, ameliorate, elevate. **4** *cultivate people* seek the friendship/company of, run after, make advances to, ingratiate oneself with, curry favor with, woo, court, associate/consort with; *inf.* butter up, suck up to. **5** *cultivate a friendship* pursue, devote oneself to, foster, promote, advance, further, forward, encourage, support, back, aid, help, assist, abet.

cultivated *adjective* *a cultivated young woman* cultured, educated, civilized, enlightened, refined, polished, sophisticated, discerning, discriminating, urbane.

cultural *adjective* **1** *cultural interests* artistic, educational, educative, enlightening, enriching, broadening, developmental, edifying, civilizing, elevating. **2** *cultural differences* lifestyle, ethnic, folk, racial.

culture *noun* **1** *a woman of culture* cultivation, education, enlightenment, accomplishment, edification, erudition, refinement, polish, sophistication, urbanity, discernment, discrimination, good taste, taste, breeding, politeness, gentility, *savoir faire.* **2** *seek culture* the arts, works of art, intellectual achievements; intellectual achievement, intellectual activity. **3** *belong to a different culture* civilization, way of life, lifestyle; customs, habits, ways, mores. **4** *silkworm culture* cultivation, farming, agriculture, husbandry, agronomy.

cultured *adjective* cultivated, artistic, educated,

enlightened, learned, knowledgeable, intellectual, highbrow, scholarly, well-informed, well-read, erudite, accomplished, well-versed, refined, genteel, polished, sophisticated, urbane.
Antonyms: IGNORANT; UNREFINED; UNSOPHISTICATED.

culvert *noun* channel, conduit, drain, gutter, watercourse.

cumbersome *adjective* 1 *cumbersome packages* awkward, unwieldy, bulky, weighty, heavy, hefty, clumsy, unmanageable, burdensome, inconvenient. 2 *cumbersome procedures* slow, slow-moving, inefficient, unwieldy.
Antonyms: MANAGEABLE; CONVENIENT; EFFICIENT.

cumulative *adjective* accumulative, increasing, growing, enlarging, swelling, accruing, snowballing, collective, aggregate, amassed.

cunning *adjective* 1 *a cunning thief* crafty, devious, deceitful, wily, sly, shifty, artful, foxy, tricky, guileful, shrewd, astute, sharp, knowing, subtle, Machiavellian. 2 *a cunning device/artist* clever, ingenious, resourceful, inventive, imaginative, skillful, deft, adroit, subtle, dexterous.
Antonyms: HONEST; GUILELESS; INGENUOUS.

cunning *noun* 1 *the cunning of the thief* craftiness, deviousness, deceitfulness, deceit, wiliness, slyness, artfulness, foxiness, trickery, trickiness, guile, shrewdness, astuteness, sharpness, subtlety. 2 *admire the cunning of the process/artist* cleverness, ingenuity, resourcefulness, inventiveness, imaginativeness, skill, skillfulness, deftness, adroitness, subtlety, finesse, dexterity, ability, capability.
Antonyms: openness; SIMPLICITY.

cup *noun* 1 *cups and saucers* teacup, coffee cup, mug, demitasse. 2 *win the cup* trophy, award, prize. 3 *two cups of sugar* cupful, measuring cup.

cupboard *noun* cabinet, locker, closet, storeroom, pantry.

Cupid/cupid *noun* 1 *a statue of Cupid* god of love, Eros. 2 *acting cupid* matchmaker, marriage broker.

cupidity *noun* greed, avarice, avariciousness, acquisitiveness, covetousness, rapacity, rapaciousness, voracity, voraciousness, desire, avidity.

cur *noun* 1 *bitten by a cur* dog, mongrel; *inf.* mutt. 2 *married to a nasty cur* scoundrel, cad, blackguard, ne'er do well, villain; *inf.* rat, creep, louse.

curative *adjective* curing, healing, therapeutic, medicinal, remedial, restorative.

curator *noun* keeper, custodian, conservator, guardian, caretaker, steward.

curb *verb* curb one's anger restrain, check, keep in check, control, constrain, contain, hold back, bite back, repress, suppress, moderate, dampen, put a brake on, impede, retard, subdue, bridle.

curb *noun* curbs on expenditure restraint, check, control, constraint, deterrent, curtailment, limitation, limit, damper, brake, rein, suppressant, hindrance, retardant.

curdle *verb* turn, turn sour, congeal, coagulate, clot, solidify, thicken, condense.

cure *noun* a cure for this ailment remedy, curative, medicine, cure-all, panacea, restorative, corrective, antidote, nostrum; treatment, therapy, healing, alleviation.

cure *verb* 1 *cure the patient* heal, restore, restore to health, make well/better, rehabilitate, treat. 2 *cure the disease* heal, remedy, doctor, put/set right, fix, repair. 3 *cure meat* preserve, smoke, salt, dry, pickle.

curio *noun* trinket, knickknack, doodad, keepsake, *objet d'art*; rarity.

curiosity *noun* 1 *curiosity about what is happening* inquisitiveness, spirit of inquiry, interest, investigativeness, researching, querying, asking questions, questioning, prying, snooping; *inf.* nosiness. 2 *he is a curiosity* eccentric, individual, oddity, character, card, freak, original; *inf.* weirdo, oddball. 3 *looking at the curiosities of the East* novelty, oddity, phenomenon, rarity, wonder, marvel, sight, spectacle.

curious *adjective* 1 *curious to know the facts* inquisitive, inquiring, interested, investigating, searching, researching, querying, questioning, interrogative, puzzled, burning with curiosity. 2 *curious about others' affairs* inquisitive, prying, snooping, meddling, meddlesome, interfering, intrusive; *inf.* nosy, snoopy. 3 *a curious site* strange, unusual, rare, odd, peculiar, out of the ordinary, unexpected, extraordinary, remarkable, singular, novel, queer, bizarre, unconventional, unorthodox, phenomenal, weird, freakish, marvelous, wonderful, prodigious, exotic, mysterious, puzzling, quaint, unique; *inf.* far out.
Antonyms: UNINTERESTED; INDIFFERENT; ORDINARY.

curl *verb* 1 *the smoke curled upward* spiral, coil, twist, twist and turn, wind, curve, bend, loop, twirl, wreathe, meander, snake, corkscrew. 2 *the heat curled the leaves (up)* bend, twist, curve, coil, crisp. 3 *curl the hair* crimp, crinkle, kink, frizz, coil, wave.

curl *noun* 1 *put curls in one's hair* kink, ringlet, coil, wave, curlicue, corkscrew. 2 *curls of smoke* spiral, coil, twist, whorl, helix.

curly *adjective* 1 *curly hair* curling, curled, crimped, crinkly, kinked, wavy, waved, frizzy, permed, fuzzy, corkscrew. 2 *a curly pattern* spiraled, spiraling, coiling, coiled, curving, winding, corkscrew. *See* CURL *verb* 1.

currency *noun* 1 *foreign currency* money, medium of exchange, legal tender, cash, coinage, coin, specie, paper money; coins, bank notes, notes, bills. *See* MONEY 1. 2 *story gaining currency* prevalence, acceptance, popularity, vogue, circulation, communication, transmission, dissemination, publicity, exposure.

current adjective **1** *current fashions* present, present-day, contemporary, ongoing, extant, existing, popular, modern, fashionable, in fashion/vogue, up-to-date, up-to-the-minute; *inf.* trendy, now, in. **2** *ideas no longer current* prevalent, prevailing, accepted, in circulation, circulating, going around, making the rounds, talked of, common, general, popular, widespread, rife, on everyone's lips.
Antonyms: OUT OF DATE; OBSOLETE.

current noun **1** *current of air* steady flow, draft, updraft, downdraft, wind, thermal. **2** *swimmers swept away by the current* | *a strong current* steady flow, stream, tide, channel. **3** *disturb the even current of their life* course, flow, progress, progression, tide. **4** *currents of opinion* trend, drift, tendency, tenor.

curse noun **1** *a voodoo curse* malediction, evil eye, execration, imprecation, anathema, damnation, excommunication; *inf.* jinx. **2** *angrily uttering curses* oath, swearword, expletive, profanity, obscenity; swearing, blasphemy, bad/foul language; *inf.* cussword. **3** *the curse of poverty* evil, affliction, burden, cross, bane, misfortune, misery, trouble, blight, harm, disaster, calamity, ordeal, tribulation, scourge, plague, torment.
Antonyms: BENEDICTION; BLESSING.

curse verb **1** *the sorcerer cursed them* put a curse on, accurse, put the evil eye on, execrate, imprecate, anathematize, damn, excommunicate; *inf.* put a jinx on, jinx. **2** *curse at the policeman* utter oaths, swear, use bad/foul language, blaspheme, take God's/the Lord's name in vain, be foul-mouthed; *inf.* cuss. **3** *poverty cursed his childhood* blight, afflict, trouble, beset, harm, burden, plague, torment, destroy, ruin, scourge.

cursed adjective **1** *that cursed table/neighbor* accursed, annoying, confounded, unpleasant, hateful, detestable, odious, loathsome, foul, damnable, abominable, vile, pestilential, infernal, devilish, fiendish, infamous, nefarious, pernicious. **2** *believed they were a cursed people* accursed, under a curse, curse-laden, doomed, ill-fated, damned, execrated, anathematized; *inf.* jinxed. *See* CURSE verb 1.

cursory adjective hasty, rapid, hurried, quick, superficial, perfunctory, desultory, ephemeral, fleeting, passing, transient.
Antonyms: THOROUGH; LEISURELY.

curt adjective terse, abrupt, brusque, blunt, short-spoken, short, snappy, snappish, sharp, crisp, tart, gruff, offhand, summary, rude, impolite, unceremonious, ungracious, uncivil, brief, concise, succinct, compact, pithy.
Antonyms: POLITE; SUAVE; VERBOSE.

curtail verb reduce, cut short, cut, cut down/back, decrease, lessen, diminish, retrench, slim down, tighten up, pare down, trim, dock, lop, truncate, shorten, abridge, abbreviate, contract, compress, shrink.
Antonyms: INCREASE; LENGTHEN; EXPAND.

curtain noun **1** *hang curtains* drape, drapery, window hanging; screen, blind. **2** *a curtain of secrecy* screen, cover, shield, cloak, veil.

curtsy, curtsey verb drop a curtsy, bob, bow, genuflect, salaam.

curve noun arc, bend, arch, turn, bow, loop, hook, half moon, crescent; winding, camber, curvature.

curve verb bend, arc, arch, bow, turn, inflect, swerve, twist, wind, hook, loop, spiral, coil.

curved adjective bent, arched, rounded, bowed, twisted, crooked, humped, sinuous. *See* CURVE verb.

cushion noun *resting on a cushion* pillow, throw pillow, bolster, pad; hassock, mat, beanbag.

cushion verb **1** *cushioning her head* pillow, bolster, cradle, support, prop up. **2** *cushion the blow* soften, lessen, diminish, mitigate, allay, deaden, muffle, stifle. **3** *cushion the child from reality* protect, shield, buttress.

custody noun **1** *in the custody of his mother* | *having custody of the children* guardianship, wardship, trusteeship, charge, care, keeping, keep, safekeeping, protection, guidance, supervision, superintendence, surveillance, control, tutelage, aegis; auspices. **2** *suspects in custody* imprisonment, detention, confinement, incarceration, restraint, constraint, duress.

custom noun **1** *it was their custom to leave early* habit, practice, routine, way, wont, policy, rule. **2** *local customs* practice, convention, ritual, procedure, ceremony, form, formality, usage, observance, way, fashion, mode, style.

customarily adverb as a rule, usually, generally, in the ordinary way, ordinarily, normally, commonly, habitually, routinely, traditionally.

customary adjective *customary to tip* | *her customary practice* accustomed, usual, regular, common, habitual, traditional, routine, fixed, set, established, everyday, familiar, confirmed, normal, ordinary, favorite, popular, stock, well-worn.
Antonyms: UNUSUAL; EXCEPTIONAL; RARE.

customer noun patron, client, buyer, purchaser, shopper, consumer; clientele; *inf.* regular.

customs plural noun import taxes; duty, toll, levy, tariff.

cut verb **1** *cut his finger/throat* gash, slash, lacerate, slit, nick, notch, pierce, penetrate, wound, lance, incise, score. **2** *cut the logs/meat* cut up, chop, sever, divide, cleave, carve, slice. **3** *cut a key/gem* shape, fashion, form, mold, chisel, carve, sculpt, sculpture, chip away, whittle. **4** *cut a design* carve, engrave, incise, score. **5** *cut their hair* | *cut the hedge/grass* trim, clip, snip, crop, prune, dock, shear, shave, pare, mow. **6** *cut some flowers* detach, gather, harvest, reap. **7** *cut expenditures* reduce, curtail, curb, retrench, cut back/down on, decrease, lessen, lower, diminish, contract, ease up on, prune, slash, slim down, slenderize, economize on. **8**

cut the text shorten, abridge, condense, abbreviate, contract, compact, summarize, epitomize. **9** *cut the unsuitable parts* delete, editout, blue-pencil, excise. **10** *his behavior cut me* hurt, offend, wound, distress, grieve, pain, sting, trouble, discomfort. **11** *his old friend cut him* shun, ignore, snub, spurn, give the cold-shoulder to, look right through, turn one's back on, slight, scorn, insult. **12** *the lines cut here* intersect, bisect, cross. **13** *cut the engine* | *the engine suddenly cut* stop, come to a stop, halt, turn off, switch off, stop working, malfunction. **14** *cut a record/tape* record, make a recording on, put on disk/tape, make a tape of, tape-record. **cut across** *cut across national prejudices* transcend, go beyond, rise above. **cut back (on)** *cut back on expenditure* economize, reduce. See CUT *verb* 7. **cut down (on)** **1** *cut down a tree* fell, saw down, hew, chop/hack down. **2** *cut down on expenditures* economize, reduce. See CUT *verb* 7. **3** *cut down in his prime* kill, slay, slaughter, massacre, mow down, dispatch. **cut in** *"Wait," he cut in* | *cut in on a conversation* interrupt, interpose, break in, intervene, intrude; *inf.* butt in. **cut off** **1** *cut off supplies/communication* break off, disconnect, interrupt, suspend, bring to an end, discontinue, halt, stop, intercept, obstruct, hinder, thwart. **2** *cut off from the town by snow* isolate, separate, sever. **3** *cut off without a penny* disinherit, disown, renounce. **4** *cut off in his prime* kill. See CUT DOWN 3 (above). **cut out** **1** *cut out the bad part* remove, delete, excise, extract. **2** *cut out eating chocolate* give up, refrain from, stop, cease. **3** *cut out the middleman* leave out, omit, eliminate, exclude, do away with. **4** *cut out the competition* oust, supplant, displace, supersede. **5** *the engine cut out* stop, stop working. See CUT *verb* 13. **6** *not cut out for teaching* suit, equip/design for. **cut short** *cut short a vacation* interrupt, break off, leave unfinished, truncate, abort, bring to an untimely end. **cut up** *verb* **1** *cut up the meat* slice, carve, chop, dice, mince, grind, divide up. **2** *cut up in a street fight* slash, knife, stab, lacerate, wound, injure. **3** *the teacher really cut up his essay/friend* criticize, ridicule, find fault with, tear to pieces/shreds, take apart, give a hard time to; *inf.* pan, knock.

cut *noun* **1** *a cut on his finger* gash, slash, laceration, incision, slit. **2** *a cut of meat* section, piece. **3** *go for a cut at the hairdresser* trim, clip, crop. **4** *a cut in expenditure/salary* cutback, decrease, reduction, lessening, curtailment, retrenchment, contraction. **5** *cut of her jacket* fashion, style. **6** *power cut* loss, temporary interruption. **7** *I want my cut* share, portion, proportion.

cut-rate *adjective* reduced, cheap, bargain.

cutthroat *noun* *set upon by cutthroats* thug, killer, murderer, assassin, butcher, liquidator, slayer, executioner; *inf.* hit man.

cutthroat *adjective* **1** *a cutthroat attack* murderous, death-dealing, homicidal, savage, violent, bloody, bloodthirsty, fierce, ferocious, barbarous, cruel. **2** *a cutthroat business* ruthless, merciless, pitiless, unfeeling, relentless, dog-eat-dog, fiercely competitive.

cutting *adjective* **1** *a cutting wind* biting, bitter, piercing, raw, keen, penetrating, stinging, sharp, chill, chilling, icy. **2** *a cutting remark* hurtful, wounding, caustic, acid, barbed, acrimonious, trenchant, mordant, scathing, acerbic, sarcastic, sardonic, spiteful, vicious, malicious.

cutting *noun* **1** *take cuttings from the plants* root, stem, slip, scion.

cycle *noun* **1** *occur in cycles* recurrent period, rotation, round, revolution. **2** *compare the completed cycles* series, sequence, succession, run. **3** *travel by cycle* bicycle, bike, tandem, tricycle, monocycle.

cyclone *noun* windstorm, storm, gale, squall, hurricane, whirlwind, tornado, typhoon.

cynic *noun* pessimist, skeptic, scoffer, doubter, doubting Thomas, misanthrope.

cynical *adjective* pessimistic, skeptical, scoffing, doubting, unbelieving, disbelieving, distrustful, suspicious, misanthropic, critical, sardonic.

Antonyms: OPTIMISTIC; CREDULOUS; TRUSTFUL.

cynicism *noun* pessimism, skepticism, scoffing, doubt, unbelief, disbelief, distrust, suspicion, misanthropy, criticism, sardonicism.

D

dab verb *dab one's eyes* | *dab paint on* pat, press, touch, blot, smudge, besmear, bedaub.

dab noun **1** *give one's eyes a quick dab* pat, press, touch, blot, smudge. **2** *add a dab of paint/butter* touch, bit, speck, spot, trace, drop, dash, tinge, suggestion, hint, modicum.

dabble verb *dabble one's fingers/feet in water* | *dabble the wall with paint* dip, splash, paddle, wet, moisten, dampen, sprinkle, spray, spatter, slosh. **dabble in** *dabble in politics* toy with, dip into, scratch the surface of, flirt with, tinker with, trifle with, play with, fiddle with, dally with, have a smattering of.

dabbler noun *a dabbler in art* dilettante, amateur, nonprofessional, layman, laywoman, tinkerer, putterer, trifler, dallier.

daft adjective **1** *a daft idea* silly, absurd, stupid, foolish, idiotic, insane, crazy, mad, lunatic, nonsensical, senseless, fatuous, ridiculous, ludicrous, asinine, witless; *inf.* dopey, cracked. **2** *he's too daft to understand* simple, simpleminded, feebleminded, slow-witted, dim-witted, dull-witted, touched, deranged, unhinged, demented, out of one's mind, insane, mad; *inf.* not all there, not quite right, crazy, mental, nuts, nutty, dopey, crackers, cracked, balmy, batty, cuckoo, bonkers.
Antonyms: SENSIBLE; INTELLIGENT.

dagger noun stiletto, dirk, bayonet, knife, blade.

daily adjective **1** *a daily newspaper* of/occurring each day, everyday, diurnal, quotidian, circadian. **2** *a daily occurrence* everyday, day-to-day, routine, ordinary, common, commonplace, usual, regular, habitual, customary.

daily adverb *visit her daily* every day, once a day, day after day, day by day, per diem.

dainty adjective **1** *dainty china figures* | *dainty little girls* petite, neat, delicate, exquisite, refined, tasteful, fine, elegant, graceful, trim, pretty. **2** *a dainty morsel* tasty, delicious, appetizing, choice, delectable, palatable, flavorsome, savory, toothsome, luscious, juicy, succulent. **3** *a dainty eater* particular, discriminating, fastidious, fussy, choosy, finicky, refined, nice, scrupulous, meticulous.
Antonyms: CLUMSY; NASTY; UNCOUTH.

dais noun platform, stage, stand, podium, pulpit.

dale noun valley, vale, glen, dell.

dally verb **1** *dallying on the way home* dawdle, delay, loiter, linger, tarry, waste/kill time, take one's time, while away time; *inf.* dilly-dally. **2** *dally with his affections* | *dally with an idea* trifle, toy, flirt, tinker; *inf.* fool.

Antonyms: HURRY; HASTEN.

dam noun *a river dam* barricade, barrier, barrage, wall, embankment, obstruction, hindrance.

damage verb *damage one's property/reputation* do damage to, harm, injure, hurt, impair, abuse, spoil, mar, deface, defile, vandalize, wreck, destroy, ruin, play havoc with, devastate, do mischief to, tamper with, mutilate.
Antonyms: REPAIR; IMPROVE.

damage noun **1** *damage to one's property/reputation* harm, injury, hurt, impairment, abuse, defilement, defacement, detriment, vandalism, destruction, ruin, havoc, devastation, mischief, outrage, accident, loss, suffering. **2** *what's the damage?* cost, expense, charge, bill, account, total.

damages plural noun *receive damages from the court* compensation, indemnity, reparation, reimbursement, restitution, satisfaction.

dame noun peeress, baroness, noblewoman, lady, dowager, aristocrat, *grande dame.*

damn verb **1** *damned for his blasphemy* curse, doom, execrate, imprecate, excommunicate, anathematize, proscribe, interdict. **2** *damned by his neighbors* condemn, censure, criticize, castigate, denounce, berate, reprimand, reprove, abuse, inveigh against, excoriate. **3** *a play damned by the critics* criticize, attack, flay; *inf.* pan, slam, knock, blast, take to pieces, take apart.
Antonyms: BLESS; ACCLAIM; PRAISE.

damn noun *not be worth a damn* | *I don't give a damn* jot, whit, iota, hoot, two hoots; *inf.* darn, tinker's damn.

damn interjection *inf.* darn, rats, doggone it, shoot.

damnable adjective **1** *damnable cruelty* accursed, cursed, diabolical, fiendish, infernal, abominable, atrocious, execrable, base, wicked, heinous, vile, despicable, detestable, hateful, horrible, hideous, obnoxious, revolting, repulsive, foul, repugnant. **2** *damnable weather* nasty, unpleasant, disagreeable, foul, objectionable.

damnation noun **1** *suffer damnation* sending to hell, eternal punishment, perdition, doom. **2** *the damnation of/by the priest* curse, execration, imprecation, excommunication, anathema, anathematization, proscription, interdict. **3** *the damnation of his neighbors* condemnation, censure, criticism, castigation, denunciation. *See* DAMN verb 3. **4** *the damnation of the play* criticism, attacking. *See* DAMN verb 3.

damned adjective **1** *damned souls* cursed,

accursed, doomed, lost, condemned, execrated, excommunicated, anathematized. *See* DAMN *verb* 1. **2** *this damned machine/weather* annoying, confounded, uncooperative, nasty, hateful, detestable, odious.

damning *adjective damning evidence* incriminating, condemnatory, condemning, damnatory, implicating, implicatory, accusatorial.

damp *adjective* **1** *damp clothes/grass* wettish, moist, dank, soggy, dewy. **2** *a damp day* | *damp weather* wettish, rainy, drizzly, humid, clammy, muggy, misty, foggy, vaporous.
Antonyms: DRY; ARID.

damp *noun See* DAMPNESS.

damp *verb* **1** *damp the clothes See* DAMPEN 1. **2** *damp their enthusiasm See* DAMPEN 2. **3** *damp the fire* | *damp down the furnace* bank, smother, stifle, extinguish.

dampen *verb* **1** *dampen the clothes/atmosphere* wet, moisten, damp, humidify, vaporize. **2** *dampen their enthusiasm* damp, discourage, dull, dispirit, depress, dash, cool, chill, check, curb, restrain, stifle, inhibit, deter, lessen, limit, diminish, allay, put a damper on, throw cold water on.

damper *noun act as a damper on our enthusiasm* discouragement, depression, chill, pall, gloom, cloud, check, curb, obstacle, hindrance, impediment, restraint, deterrent; *inf.* wet blanket.

dampness *noun* **1** *dampness in the house* damp, wetness, moisture, dankness. **2** *the dampness of the weather* damp, wetness, raininess, drizzliness, dankness, humidity, clamminess, mugginess; wet, mist, fog, vapor, rain, drizzle.

damsel *noun* young woman, girl, young lady, maid, maiden, lass.

dance *verb* **1** *dance in the dancehall* | *dance with her* move/sway to music, execute dance steps, twirl, pirouette; *inf.* shake a leg, hoof it, cut the rug, trip the light fantastic. **2** *children dancing about* caper, skip, prance, hop, frolic, gambol, jump, jig, romp, bounce, whirl, spin.

dance *noun* **1** *go to a dance* ball; *inf.* hop. **2** *learn/perform a dance* | *study dance* dancing; ballroom dance, folk dance, tap dance, modern dance; ballet, eurythmics.

dandy *noun* fop, popinjay, beau, blade, man about town, sharp dresser.

danger *noun* **1** *an element of danger* risk, peril, hazard, jeopardy, endangerment, imperilment, precariousness, insecurity, instability. **2** *a danger to society* menace, threat, peril, risk.
Antonyms: SAFETY; SECURITY.

dangerous *adjective* **1** *involved in a dangerous venture* risky, perilous, hazardous, chancy, precarious, uncertain, insecure, unsound, unsafe, exposed, defenseless; *inf.* hairy. **2** *a dangerous outlaw/omen* menacing, threatening, alarming, ominous, nasty, ugly, treacherous.
Antonyms: SAFE; HARMLESS.

dangle *verb* **1** *keys dangling from her waist* hang, hang down, swing, sway, trail, droop. **2** *dangle the keys* swing, sway, wave, brandish, flourish, flaunt. **3** *he dangled the temptation of a trip to Hawaii* hold out, entice someone with, lure someone with, tempt someone with. **dangle after** *he is always dangling after her* follow, follow on the heels of, hang around, attach oneself to.

dangling *adjective* hanging, drooping, swinging, swaying, trailing, unconnected, disconnected, loose.

dank *adjective* damp, wet, moist, humid, clammy, chilly.

dapper *adjective* **1** *a dapper man dressed in black* smartly dressed, smart, well-groomed, well-turned-out, neat, trim, spruce, stylish, chic; *inf.* natty. **2** *dapper for his age* active, agile, spry, sprightly, nimble, lively, brisk.

dapple *verb dapple with paint* | *sunlight dappling the leaves* dot, spot, fleck, bespeckle, mottle.

dappled *adjective dappled leaves* | *a dappled horse* spotted, marked, mottled, flecked, blotched, blotchy, variegated, parti-colored, pied, piebald, brindled, pinto.

dare *verb* **1** *dare to go* have the courage, take the risk, be brave enough, have the nerve, risk, hazard, venture. **2** *dare him to go* challenge, provoke, goad, taunt. **3** *dare his father's anger* | *dared the rapids* defy, brave, face, meet, meet head on, confront, stand up to.

dare *noun accept his dare* challenge, provocation, goad, taunt, ultimatum.

daredevil *adjective a daredevil attitude* | *daredevil actions* daring, adventurous, bold, audacious, courageous, intrepid, fearless, undaunted, dauntless, rash, heedless, madcap, harebrained, foolhardy, impetuous, imprudent, incautious, desperate.

daredevil *noun daredevils on the racing circuit* adventurer, desperado, stunt man, madcap, exhibitionist; *inf.* show-off.

daring *adjective a daring person/plan* bold, adventurous, brave, courageous, valiant, audacious, intrepid, fearless, undaunted, dauntless, unshrinking, rash, reckless, madcap, foolhardy, wild, daredevil, desperate.
Antonyms: COWARDLY; CAUTIOUS.

daring *noun the daring of the explorers* boldness, adventurousness, bravery, courage, courageousness, valor, audacity, nerve, pluck, grit, intrepidity, fearlessness, rashness, recklessness, temerity, foolhardiness, wildness, desperation; *inf.* guts, spunk.

dark *adjective* **1** *a dark night* black, pitch-black, pitch-dark, inky, jet-black, unlit, unlighted, ill-lighted, poorly lit, dim, dingy, indistinct, shadowy, shady, murky, foggy, misty, cloudy, overcast, sunless. **2** *dark of hair* dark-haired, brunette, dark brown, jet-black, sable, ebony. **3** *dark of skin*, dark-skinned, swarthy, sallow, olive-skinned, dusky, black, ebony. **4** *dark thoughts* dismal, gloomy, somber, cheerless,

bleak, joyless, drab, dreary, depressed, dejected, melancholy, grim, grave, funereal, morose, mournful, doleful. **5** *in a dark mood* angry, moody, brooding, sullen, dour, glum, morose, sulky, frowning, scowling, glowering, forbidding, threatening, ominous. **6** *dark deeds* evil, wicked, sinful, villainous, iniquitous, vile, base, foul, horrible, atrocious, abominable, nefarious, barbaric, barbarous, sinister, damnable, fiendish, infernal, satanic, hellish. **7** *the dark ages* unenlightened, ignorant, uneducated, unschooled, uncultivated, uncultured. **8** *a dark meaning* abstruse, recondite, arcane, profound, deep, incomprehensible, obscure, unfathomable, puzzling, enigmatic, cryptic, complicated, complex, difficult, intricate. **9** *a dark secret | keep it dark* concealed, hidden, veiled, secret, mysterious, mystic, esoteric, occult.
Antonyms: LIGHT; FAIR; CHEERFUL.

dark *noun* **1** *sitting in the dark* darkness, blackness, absence of light, gloom, gloominess, dimness, murk, murkiness, shadowiness, shade. **2** *when dark comes/falls* night, nighttime, nightfall, dead of night, evening, twilight. **3** *in the dark about his motives* a state of ignorance/unenlightenment.

darken *verb* **1** *the sky darkened* grow dark/darker, blacken, cloud over, dim, grow dim. **2** *darken the room* make dark/darker, make dim, shade. **3** *darken one's skin* make dark/darker, tan, blacken, black, make opaque. **4** *his mood/face darkened* blacken, grow angry/annoyed, grow/become gloomy, become depressed/dispirited, grow troubled, sadden.
Antonyms: LIGHTEN; BRIGHTEN.

darkness *noun* **1** *the darkness of the room | darkness fell* dark, blackness, gloom, dimness, murk, shadowiness; twilight, nightfall. *See* DARK *noun* 1, 2. **2** *the darkness of the early Middle Ages* ignorance, lack of knowledge, unenlightenment. **3** *the darkness of her secret* mystery, concealment, secrecy, obscurity, veiledness.
Antonyms: LIGHT; ENLIGHTENMENT.

darling *noun* **1** *goodbye, darling* dear, dearest, dear one, love, sweetheart, beloved, sweet, honey. **2** *the child's a little darling* charmer, pet, sweetheart, honey; *inf.* sweetie. **3** *the darling of the press* favorite, pet, apple of one's eye, toast; *inf.* fair-haired boy.

darling *adjective* **1** *his darling wife* dear, dearest, loved, beloved, adored, cherished, treasured, precious, prized, valued. **2** *a darling little girl* adorable, sweet, lovely, attractive, charming, winsome, enchanting, engaging, captivating, bewitching, alluring; *inf.* cute.

darn *verb* *darn socks* mend, repair, sew up, stitch, patch.

darn *interjection* *See* DAMN *interjection.*

dart *noun* **1** *throwing a poisoned dart* arrow, barb. **2** *make a sudden dart* dash, rush, run, bolt, bound, spring, leap, start.

dart *verb* **1** *dart into the bushes* dash, rush, bolt,

fly, flash, sprint, tear, run, bound, shoot, spring, leap, start; *inf.* scoot. **2** *dart an angry look* throw, cast, shoot, send, fling, toss, flash, hurl, sling, propel, project.

dash *noun* **1** *make a dash for freedom* rush, bolt, run, race, flight, dart, sprint, sortie, spurt; *inf.* scoot. **2** *a dash of water on his face* splash, sprinkle, spattering. **3** *a dash of salt* little, bit, drop, pinch, sprinkling, grain, touch, trace, tinge, smack, suspicion, suggestion. **4** *carry it off with dash* style, élan, verve, vigor, spirit, vivacity, liveliness, flair, panache, flourish; *inf.* pizzazz.

dash *verb* **1** *dash into the road* rush, hurry, hasten, bolt, run, race, fly, dart, sprint, tear, speed; *inf.* scoot. **2** *waves dashing against the shore* strike, beat, break, crash, smash, batter, splinter, shatter. **3** *dash the plate to the floor* smash, crash, throw, hurl, fling, slam, sling, cast, pitch, catapult. **4** *dash her hopes* shatter, destroy, ruin, blight, spoil, frustrate, thwart, check. **5** *spirits dashed by the misfortune* depress, dispirit, deject, cast down, lower, sadden, dishearten, discourage, daunt, abash, dampen.

dashing *adjective* **1** *a dashing young officer* debonair, stylish, spirited, lively, buoyant, energetic, animated, dynamic, gallant, bold, daring, plucky, dazzling, swashbuckling; *inf.* peppy. **2** *dashing uniforms* smart, jaunty, sporty, stylish, elegant, fashionable, chic, dazzling, showy, flamboyant.

dastardly *adjective* cowardly, craven, fearful, faint-hearted; despicable; *inf.* yellow.

data *plural noun* basic facts, facts, figures, statistics, details; information, material, input.

date *noun* **1** *on a certain date* day, point in time. **2** *artifacts from a previous date* time, age, period, era, century, decade, year, stage. **3** *we have a lunch date* appointment, engagement, meeting, rendezvous, assignation, tryst. **4** *who is his date?* partner, escort, girlfriend, boyfriend, beau; *inf.* steady. **to date** so far, as of now, up to now, up to the present, up to this point.

date *verb* **1** *the vase dates from the seventeenth century* originate in, come from, belong to, exist from, bear the date of. **2** *can you date this table?* assign a date to, put a date to, determine the date of, fix the period of. **3** *he's dating the girl next door* go out/around with, go with, take out; *inf.* go steady with.

dated *adjective* *dated fashions* out of date, outdated, old-fashioned, outmoded, antiquated, passé; *inf.* old hat.
Antonyms: FASHIONABLE; UP-TO-DATE.

daub *verb* **1** *daub paint on* smear, plaster, smudge, spatter, splatter, slap, slop. **2** *daub the walls with paint* smear, besmear, bedaub, plaster, spatter, splatter, cover, coat, deface.

daub *noun* *a daub of paint* smear, smudge, blot, spot, patch, blotch, splotch.

daunt *verb* intimidate, frighten, scare, alarm, overawe, dismay, disconcert, unnerve, take aback, abash, cow, discourage, dishearten, dispirit, deter, put off.

Antonyms: ENCOURAGE; HEARTEN.

dawdle verb go/walk slowly, move at a snail's pace, loiter, take one's time, dally, linger, delay, lag/trail behind, kill/waste time, fritter time away, idle; *inf.* dilly-dally.

Antonyms: HURRY; HASTEN.

dawn noun **1** *get up at dawn* daybreak, break of day, sunrise, first light, early morning, crack of dawn, sunup; *lit.* aurora. **2** *the dawn of civilization* dawning, beginning, birth, start, rise, emergence, commencement, origin, inception, genesis, outset, onset, advent, appearance, arrival, unfolding, development.

Antonyms: DUSK; END.

dawn verb **1** *day dawned* begin, break, lighten, brighten, gleam. **2** *civilization dawning* begin, be born, come into being/existence, start, rise, emerge, commence, originate, appear, arrive, unfold, develop. **dawn on** *the truth suddenly dawned on them* occur to one, strike, hit, register with, cross/enter one's mind, come into one's head, come to mind, pass through one's mind, flash across one's mind.

day noun **1** *when day dawns* daytime, daylight, daylight hours, broad daylight. **2** *work all day* twenty-four hours, full day, working day, solar day. **3** *in this modern day* period, time, age, era, epoch, generation. **4** *the steam train has had its day* prime, heyday, full flowering, useful/productive lifetime, peak, zenith, ascendancy. **5** *set a day* date, set time, time, particular day, appointed day. **day after day** *raining day after day* continuously, relentlessly, persistently, without respite, continually, ceaselessly, regularly. **day by day** *grow bigger day by day* daily, gradually, steadily, progressively.

daybreak noun dawn, break of day, sunrise, first light. *See* DAWN noun 1.

daydream noun **1** *lost in a daydream* reverie, woolgathering, musing, imagining, fantasy, vision, fancy, hallucination. **2** *their daydream never materialized* dream, pipedream, figment of the imagination; wishful thinking; fond hopes, wishes, castles in the air.

daydream verb dream, muse, be lost in thought, stare into space, indulge in woolgathering, fantasize, indulge in fancy, hallucinate; *inf.* space.

daylight noun **1** *look at the colors in daylight* light of day, natural light, sunlight. **2** *children coming home in daylight* daytime, daylight hours; broad daylight. **3** *wake at daylight* dawn, daybreak, break of day, sunrise. *See* DAWN noun 1. **see daylight** **1** *after being confused she finally saw daylight* understand, comprehend, see the light, fathom, discern; *inf.* get the idea, catch on, get the hang of it, get the picture. **2** *his project never saw daylight* be completed/accomplished, see light of day, come to public attention.

days *plural noun days of wine and roses* | *in the days of Julius Caesar* period, time, age, era, epoch, generation.

daze verb **1** *dazed by the blow* stun, stupefy, shock, confuse, bewilder, befuddle, muddle, addle, numb, benumb, paralyze. **2** *dazed by the news* stun, shock, amaze, astonish, astound, dumbfound, stagger, startle, surprise, dismay, disconcert, take aback, bewilder, perplex, nonplus; *inf.* flabbergast, floor, take one's breath away.

daze noun *in a daze* stupor, state of shock, trance-like state, confused state; confusion, bewilderment, distraction, numbness.

dazzle verb **1** *dazzled by the car's headlights* blind temporarily, deprive of sight, bedazzle, daze, overpower. **2** *dazzled by her beauty/wit* overpower, overwhelm, overawe, awe, stagger, fascinate, hypnotize, strike dumb, dumbfound, strike, impress, amaze, astonish; *inf.* bowl over, take one's breath away.

dazzle noun **1** *overcome by the dazzle of the lights* brightness, brilliance, gleam, flash. **2** *fascinated by the dazzle of the circus* brilliance, splendor, magnificence, glitter, sparkle, glory; *inf.* razzle-dazzle, razzmatazz, pizzazz.

dead adjective **1** *the dead man/flower* deceased, late, defunct, departed, lifeless, extinct, perished, gone, no more, passed on/away. **2** *dead matter* inanimate, lifeless, without life, exanimate. **3** *a dead issue/language* obsolete, outmoded, outdated, extinct, lapsed, passed, passé, discontinued, disused, fallen into disuse, stagnant, inactive, invalid, ineffective, inoperative, not working, barren, sterile. **4** *dead to my pleas* unresponsive, insensitive, indifferent, apathetic, dispassionate, unsympathetic, emotionless, unemotional, unfeeling, lukewarm, cold, frigid, wooden, inert. **5** *dead fingers* numb, numbed, benumbed, unfeeling, paralyzed. **6** *dead eyes* emotionless, glazed, glassy, spiritless, impassive. **7** *dead desire* extinguished, finished, terminated, quenched, quashed, quelled, suppressed, smothered, stifled. **8** *a dead place to live* | *a dead time of day* dull, boring, uninteresting, tedious, tiresome, wearisome, uneventful, humdrum, flat, stale, insipid, vapid. **9** *a dead loss* complete, absolute, total, entire, outright, utter, downright, out-and-out, thorough, unqualified, unmitigated. **10** *come to a dead halt* abrupt, sudden, quick, rapid, swift, hurried, instantaneous, unexpected, unforeseen. **11** *a dead shot* accurate, exact, precise, unerring, unfailing, sure, correct, direct. **12** *feeling dead* tired, tired out, exhausted, worn out, fatigued, spent; *inf.* dead beat, played out, pooped.

Antonyms: LIVE; ALIVE; LIVING; LIVELY.

dead adverb *dead right/serious/tired* completely, absolutely, totally, entirely, exactly, utterly, thoroughly, categorically, without qualification.

deaden verb **1** *deaden the pain* | *deaden the effects* of the blow blunt, dull, muffle, weaken, diminish, reduce, subdue, suppress, moderate, soothe, assuage, abate, mitigate, alleviate, smother, stifle, damp, damp down, numb. **2** *deaden the sound* dull, muffle, reduce, moderate, stifle, damp down, mute. **3** *emotions deadened by grief* render/make insensitive, desensitize, numb, benumb, anesthetize, impair, incapacitate, paralyze.

deadlock noun **1** *the talks ended in deadlock* stalemate, impasse, standstill, halt, stop, stoppage, cessation, standoff. **2** *the game ended in deadlock* tie, draw, dead heat.

deadly adjective **1** *deadly poisons* fatal, lethal, mortal, death-dealing, dangerous, destructive, harmful, pernicious, noxious, malignant, venomous, toxic, poisonous, virulent. **2** *deadly enemies* mortal, hated, hostile, murderous, fierce, implacable, remorseless, unrelenting, grim, savage; *inf.* at each other's throats. **3** *deadly seriousness* intense, great, marked, extreme, excessive, immoderate, inordinate. **4** *deadly paleness* deathlike, deathly, ashen, ghostly, white, pallid, wan, pale, ghastly. **5** *a deadly aim* precise, accurate, unerring, unfailing, sure, true, on target, on the mark. **6** *a deadly speaker/speech* boring, dull, tedious, uninteresting, dry, monotonous, wearisome, humdrum, lackluster.

deadly adverb completely, absolutely. *See* DEAD adverb.

deaf adjective unhearing, hard of hearing, stone deaf. **deaf to** *deaf to their pleas* unmoved by, indifferent to, oblivious to, heedless of, unconcerned with, unmindful of.
Antonyms: HEEDFUL; ATTENTIVE.

deafen verb *the noise deafened us* make temporarily deaf, deprive of hearing, impair one's hearing, burst one's eardrums.

deafening adjective very loud, earsplitting, earpiercing, overpowering, overwhelming, booming, thunderous, resounding, reverberating, ringing, dinning.

deal verb **1** *deal with a problem* attend to, see to, take care of, cope with, handle, manage, sort out, tackle, take measures. **2** *the book deals with skin problems* be about, have to do with, concern, concern itself with, discuss, consider, treat of. **3** *deal honorably with the prisoners* act, behave, conduct oneself. **4** *deal in stocks and bonds* trade, traffic, do business, buy and sell, be concerned/engaged, negotiate, bargain. **5** *deal cards* distribute, give out, share out, divide out, hand out, dole out, mete out, allocate, dispense, allot, assign, apportion, bestow. **6** *deal a blow* deliver, administer, give, direct, aim.

deal noun **1** *a deal of trouble | a great deal of money | feel a good deal better* amount, quantity, degree. **2** *finalize the deal* arrangement, transaction, agreement, negotiation, bargain, contract, pact, understanding, compact, concordat. **3** *be given a fair deal* treatment, handling, usage, procedure.

dealer noun **1** *a dealer in used cars* trader, salesman, saleswoman, salesperson, tradesman, merchant, marketer, retailer, wholesaler, vendor, trafficker, peddler. **2** *a dealer in the stock market* agent, broker.

dealing noun *a business noted for fair dealing* business methods/practices, actions; treatment, policy, behavior, conduct.

dealings plural noun *have dealings with the firm* business, trade, commerce, trafficking, truck; transactions, relations, negotiations.

dean noun faculty head, head of department, university official, provost.

dear adjective **1** *his dear wife | dear friends* beloved, loved, darling, adored, cherished, close, intimate, esteemed, respected. **2** *her dearest possessions/possessions dear to him* precious, treasured, valued, prized, cherished, favorite, favored. **3** *what a dear child* sweet, darling, endearing, lovable, attractive, winning, enchanting, winsome, angelic. **4** *the car was too dear for me* expensive, costly, highly priced, high-priced, overpriced, exorbitant, valuable; *inf.* pricey, steep.
Antonyms: WORTHLESS; DISAGREEABLE; CHEAP.

dear noun **1** *goodbye, my dear* love, beloved, darling, loved one, sweetheart, sweet, honey, pet, precious, treasure. **2** *his mother's a dear* lovable person, darling, sweetheart, pet, angel.

dearly adverb **1** *loving her dearly* very much, greatly, deeply, extremely, profoundly. **2** *pay dearly for mistakes* at great cost, at a heavy cost, at a high price, much, with great loss/damage.

dearth noun lack, scarcity, scarceness, want, deficiency, shortage, shortness, insufficiency, paucity, sparseness, meagerness, scantiness, rareness, exiguity.
Antonyms: ABUNDANCE; SURFEIT.

death noun **1** *death by drowning* dying, demise, end, passing, passing away, passing on, loss of life, expiration, departure from life, eternal rest; *inf.* curtains. *See* DIE 1. **2** *the death of his hopes* end, finish, termination, cessation, ruin, ruination, extinction, destruction, extermination, eradication, annihilation, obliteration, extirpation. **3** *death came in the night* angel of death, grim reaper. **4** *their deaths on his conscience | horrified by the death on the battlefield* killing, slaying, murder, slaughter, fatality; bloodshed, massacre, carnage.
Antonyms: LIFE; BIRTH.

deathless adjective immortal, undying, everlasting, eternal, unfading, perpetual, imperishable, timeless, memorable.

debacle noun fiasco, failure, downfall, collapse, disintegration, disaster, catastrophe, tumult, turmoil, havoc, ruin, ruination, devastation, defeat, rout, overthrow.

debar verb **1** *debarred from the club* shut out, exclude, bar, keep out, preclude. **2** *debarred from*

voting exclude, bar, prevent, prohibit, forbid, proscribe, disallow, veto.
Antonyms: ADMIT; ALLOW.

debase verb **1** *debase the sport* | *debase oneself* degrade, devalue, demean, drag down, disgrace, dishonor, shame, bring shame to, discredit, lower/reduce the status of, cheapen, humble, humiliate. **2** *debase the mixture* alloy, adulterate, depreciate, dilute, contaminate, pollute, taint, corrupt, bastardize, vitiate.

debatable adjective arguable, disputable, questionable, open to question, controversial, contentious, doubtful, open to doubt, dubious, uncertain, unsure, unsettled, undecided, borderline, moot.

debate noun **1** *a formal debate* | *open to debate* discussion, argument, dispute, disputation, difference of opinion, wrangle, altercation, controversy, contention, war of words, polemic. **2** *after some debate with himself* consideration, deliberation, reflection, contemplation, musing, meditation, cogitation.

debate verb **1** *debate the issue* | *wish to debate no further* discuss, argue, argue the pros and cons of, dispute, wrangle, bandy words, contend, contest, altercate, controvert; *inf.* kick around. **2** *he debated in his mind* consider, think over, deliberate, reflect, contemplate, muse, meditate, cogitate.

debauched adjective dissipated, dissolute, degenerate, corrupt, immoral, abandoned, profligate, intemperate, licentious, promiscuous, wanton.

debauchery noun dissipation, dissoluteness, degeneracy, corruption, immorality, profligacy, intemperance, licentiousness, promiscuity, wantonness, rakishness, libertinism, perversion.

debilitate verb *debilitated by his illness* weaken, make feeble, enfeeble, enervate, incapacitate, cripple, impair, sap, undermine, exhaust, wear out, prostrate, devitalize.

debility noun weakness, feebleness, frailty, infirmity, enfeeblement, enervation, incapacity, impairment, lack of energy, exhaustion, fatigue, lack of vitality, sickliness, decrepitude, malaise.

debonair adjective **1** *a debonair young man* suave, urbane, self-assured, elegant, refined, well-bred, genteel, smart, dashing, dapper, charming, courteous, mannerly, gallant, chivalrous; *inf.* smooth. **2** *debonair young people* carefree, jaunty, lighthearted, cheerful, cheery, merry, vivacious, buoyant, breezy, sprightly.

debris noun rubble, wreckage, detritus, rubbish, litter; remains, ruins, fragments.

debt noun **1** *pay my debts* money owed, bill, balance due, account, score, tally; dues, arrears, debits. **2** *acknowledge his debt to his family* indebtedness, obligation, liability. **3** *customers in debt* | *got himself into debt* a state of

owing money, indebtedness; arrears; *inf.* the red.

debunk verb cut down to size, deflate, puncture, expose, show up, show in one's/its true light, mock, ridicule.

debut noun first appearance, first performance, first time, premiere, beginning, introduction, launching, coming-out, entrance.
Antonyms: FAREWELL; swansong; END; FINISH.

decadence noun **1** *the decadence of the empire* decay, degeneration, deterioration, decline, wane, ebb, debasement, degradation, retrogression. **2** *the decadence of the wealthy set* dissipation, dissoluteness, moral decay, debauchery, degeneracy, immorality, self-indulgence, licentiousness, hedonism, epicureanism, corruption, depravity.

decadent adjective **1** *a decadent empire* decaying, degenerating, deteriorating, declining, waning, ebbing, debased, degraded, falling off, on the wane. **2** *decadent behavior/people* dissipated, dissolute, debauched, degenerate, immoral, self-indulgent, licentious, hedonistic, epicurean, corrupt, depraved.
Antonyms: PROSPEROUS; MORAL; VIRTUOUS.

decamp verb **1** *the manager decamped with the firm's profits* make off, run off/away, flee, take off, abscond, escape, cut and run; *inf.* skedaddle, hightail it, hotfoot it, vamoose, skip. **2** *the soldiers decamped* break camp, move on.

decant verb pour out, draw off, drain, tap.

decapitate verb behead, execute, guillotine, put on the block.

decay verb **1** *food/material decaying* rot, go bad, decompose, putrefy, spoil, perish, corrode. **2** *an empire decaying* degenerate, deteriorate, decline, fail, wane, ebb, dwindle, crumble, disintegrate, fall to pieces, sink, collapse, molder, shrivel, wither, die, waste/wear away, atrophy.
Antonyms: THRIVE; FLOURISH; PROSPER.

decay noun **1** *the decay of the food/material* rotting, going bad, decomposition, putrefaction, putrescence, putridity, spoilage, perishing, corrosion. **2** *spot the decay in the food/teeth/flesh* rot, decomposition; caries, gangrene. **3** *the decay of the empire* degeneration, deterioration, decline, failure, waning, ebb, crumbling, disintegration, collapse, withering, death, atrophy. See DECAY verb 2.

decease verb *he deceased before his wife* die, pass away/on, expire, perish, meet one's death.

deceased adjective *his deceased wife* late, dead, departed, defunct, lost, expired. See DEAD adjective 1.

deceit noun **1** *practice deceit* deceitfulness, deception, duplicity, double-dealing, fraud, fraudulence, cheating, trickery, duping, chicanery, underhandedness, cunning, craftiness, craft, wiliness, guile, pretense, artifice, treachery; *inf.* hanky-panky. **2** *win by a deceit* deception, trick, stratagem, ruse, dodge, subterfuge, fraud, cheat, swindle, sham, impos-

ture, hoax, pretense, fake, misrepresentation, wile, artifice, Trojan horse.
Antonyms: HONESTY; CANDOR; SINCERITY.

deceitful adjective **1** *don't believe that deceitful child* lying, untruthful, dishonest, mendacious, insincere, false, untrustworthy, two-faced, underhand, underhanded, crafty, cunning, sly, guileful, hypocritical, perfidious. **2** *deceitful practices* deceptive, duplicitous, misleading, double-dealing, fraudulent, cheating, underhand, underhanded, crooked, counterfeit, sham, bogus, dissembling, treacherous, perfidious, illusory, spurious, specious; *inf.* sneaky, tricky.
Antonyms: HONEST; OPEN; SINCERE.

deceive verb **1** *his friendliness deceived us* take in, mislead, delude, fool, pull the wool over one's eyes, misguide, lead on, trick, hoodwink, hoax, dupe, swindle, outwit, bamboozle, seduce, ensnare, entrap, beguile, double-cross, cozen, gull; *inf.* con, pull a fast one on, pull one's leg, take one for a ride. **2** *he's deceiving his wife* be unfaithful to, betray; *inf.* two-time, cheat on.

decelerate verb slow down, reduce speed, ease up, brake, put the brakes on.

decency noun propriety, decorum, seemliness, modesty, good taste, respectability, purity, correctness, good form, etiquette, delicacy, dignity, appropriateness, fitness, suitability.

decent adjective **1** *a scarcely decent exhibition* decorous, seemly, modest, proper, nice, tasteful, polite, respectable, pure, correct, dignified, delicate, appropriate, fitting, fit, suitable, becoming. **2** *decent kind of person* obliging, helpful, accommodating, generous, kind, thoughtful, courteous, civil, honest, honorable, trustworthy, dependable, worthy, respectable, upright. **3** *earning quite a decent salary* acceptable, adequate, sufficient, ample, average, competent.
Antonyms: INDECENT; UNSUITABLE; DISHONEST.

deception noun **1** *practice deception* deceit, deceitfulness, double-dealing, duplicity, fraud, fraudulence, cheating, chicanery, trickery, underhandedness, cunning, pretense, artifice. *See* DECEIT 1. **2** *win by a deception* trick, stratagem, ruse, dodge, subterfuge, fraud, cheat, swindle, sham, pretense. *See* DECEIT 2.
Antonyms: HONESTY; openness.

deceptive adjective **1** *appearances can be deceptive* deceiving, misleading, false, illusory, delusive, fallacious, ambiguous, specious, spurious, mock, pseudo. **2** *deceptive practices* deceitful, duplicitous, fraudulent, cheating, underhand, underhanded, cunning, crafty, crooked, counterfeit, sham, bogus; *inf.* sneaky, tricky.
Antonyms: AUTHENTIC; TRUE; HONEST.

decide verb **1** *to decide to go | I cannot decide* come to a decision, reach/make a decision, make up one's mind, resolve, come to a conclusion, commit oneself, choose. **2** *that decided the matter* settle, resolve, bring to a conclusion, determine, workout, clinch; *inf.* sew up. **3** *the judge* will decide the case | *the judge decided for/against the defense* judge, adjudge, adjudicate, arbitrate, umpire, referee; make a judgment on, pass/pronounce judgment, give a verdict, make a ruling.
Antonyms: HESITATE; WAVER.

decided adjective **1** *a decided difference between them* distinct, clear, clear-cut, definite, certain, marked, pronounced, obvious, express, unmistakable, absolute, emphatic, categorical, unambiguous, undeniable, unequivocal, indisputable, undisputed, unquestionable. **2** *he's quite decided | a decided effort* determined, resolute, firm, strong-minded, dogged, purposeful, unhesitating, unwavering, unswerving, unfaltering, incisive, forceful, emphatic. **3** *the matter was decided* settled, resolved, concluded, determined, brought to a conclusion, clinched; *inf.* sewn up.
Antonyms: DOUBTFUL; INDECISIVE.

decidedly adverb *decidedly unwell* distinctly, clearly, definitely, certainly, positively, markedly, unmistakably, absolutely, downright, undeniably, unquestionably. *See* DECIDED 1.

deciding adjective **1** *the deciding factor* crucial, critical, decisive, determining, conclusive, most influential, significant, chief, principal, prime. **2** *the deciding vote* casting, determining, conclusive.

decipher verb **1** *decipher the coded message* decode, translate, interpret, construe, solve, work out, figure out, unravel, unfold, reveal; *inf.* crack. **2** *cannot decipher her handwriting* make out, read, understand, comprehend, deduce.

decision noun **1** *come to a decision* resolution, conclusion, determination, settling, settlement. **2** *the judge announced his decision* judgment, ruling, pronouncement, verdict, adjudgment, adjudication, arbitration; findings. **3** *a man of decision* decisiveness, determination, resolution, resoluteness, resolve, firmness, strong-mindedness, doggedness, strength of mind/will, firmness of purpose, purpose, purposefulness.

decisive adjective **1** *a decisive person* determined, resolute, firm, dogged, purposeful, unhesitating, unwavering, unswerving, unfaltering, incisive, forceful, emphatic. **2** *a decisive factor* deciding, determining, determinate, definitive, conclusive, final, settling, critical, crucial, momentous, emphatic, absolute, categorical, significant, influential, important, definite, positive.
Antonyms: HESITANT; INDECISIVE; IRRESOLUTE; INSIGNIFICANT.

deck verb *deck the rooms for Christmas* decorate, adorn, ornament, trim, embellish, garnish, festoon, beautify, prettify, enhance, grace, enrich.
deck out *people all decked out in their Sunday best* dress up, clothe, attire, array, outfit.

declaim verb **1** *ministers declaiming from the pulpit* make a speech, speak, hold forth, lecture, harangue, rant, rail, pronounce, sermonize, speechify, spout, make an oration, orate; *inf.* sound off, spiel. **2** *declaiming against taxes* speak out, protest, rail, inveigh.

declamation noun *a passionate declamation* speech, address, oration, lecture, delivery, sermon, discourse, recitation, harangue, tirade.

declamatory adjective *declamatory style* rhetorical, oratorical, theatrical, high-flown, bombastic, pompous, pretentious.

declaration noun **1** *the declaration of his interests* | *declaration of war* announcement, statement, proclamation, notification, pronouncement, publishing, broadcasting, promulgation, edict, manifesto. **2** *his declaration that he was innocent* statement, assertion, maintaining, insistence, protestation, averment, affirmation, contention, profession, claim, allegation, avowal, swearing. **3** *his behavior is a declaration of his innocence* acknowledgment, revelation, disclosure, manifestation, confirmation, proof, testimony, validation, certification, attestation.

declare verb **1** *declare one's interests* | *declare war* announce, make known, proclaim, pronounce, publish, broadcast, promulgate, trumpet, blazon. **2** *he declared that he was innocent* state, assert, maintain, aver, affirm, contend, profess, claim, allege, avow, swear. **3** *his behavior declared his innocence* show, make known, reveal, disclose, manifest, confirm, prove, testify to, validate, certify, attest.
Antonyms: DENY; SUPPRESS; CONCEAL.

decline verb **1** *decline an invitation* | *we must decline* | *decline to comment* turn down, give the thumbs down to, rebuff, repudiate, forgo; refuse, say no, send one's regrets. **2** *his influence declined* get less, lessen, decrease, diminish, wane, dwindle, fade, ebb, fall/taper off, abate, flag. **3** *the empire is declining* | *his strength is declining* deteriorate, degenerate, decay, fail, fall, wither, weaken, fade away, wane, ebb, sink. **4** *the terrain declines here* descend, slope/slant down, dip, sink.
Antonyms: ACCEPT; FLOURISH; INCREASE.

decline noun **1** *the decline of his influence/strength* lessening, decrease, downturn, downswing, diminishing, diminution, waning, dwindling, fading, ebb, falling off, abatement, flagging, slump, plunge, nosedive. **2** *the decline of the empire* deterioration, degeneration, decay, failure, fall, withering, enfeeblement, wane, ebb, atrophy. *See* DECLINE verb 3. **3** *hikers sighting a decline* slope, declivity, dip.
Antonyms: GROWTH; IMPROVEMENT.

decompose verb **1** *corpses decomposing* decay, rot, go bad, putrefy, fester. **2** *the structure gradually decomposing* break up, fall apart, disintegrate, crumble. **3** *decompose the chemical substance* separate, break up/down, divide, disintegrate, dissect, analyze, atomize, dissolve.

decomposition noun **1** *the decomposition of the corpses* decay, rot, rotting, putrefaction, putrescence, putridity. **2** *the decomposition of the structure* disintegration, crumbling. *See* DECOMPOSE 2. **3** *the decomposition of the substance* separation, breakup, breakdown, division, disintegration, dissection, analysis, atomization, dissolution.

decor noun decoration, furnishing, furbishing, color scheme, ornamentation.

decorate verb **1** *decorate the Christmas tree* adorn, ornament, trim, embellish, garnish, festoon, garland, beautify, prettify, enhance, grace, enrich. **2** *decorate the house* paint, wallpaper, paper, renovate, refurbish, furbish; *inf.* do up, spruce up. **3** *decorated him for bravery* cite, honor, confer an award on, give a medal to, pin a medal on.

decoration noun **1** *the decoration of the tree* adornment, ornamentation, trimming, embellishment, garnishing, beautification, prettification, enhancement. *See* DECORATE 1. **2** *admire the decoration* furnishing, color scheme. *See* DECOR. **3** *buy tree decorations* ornament, trinket, bauble, knickknack, doodad, gewgaw; trimming, tinsel. **4** *a dress with many decorations* trimming, frill, folderol, frippery, flourish, scroll, arabesque, curlicue. **5** *a decoration for bravery* award, medal, badge, star, ribbon, laurel, wreath; colors, insignia.

decorative adjective *decorative features* ornamental, fancy, adorning, embellishing, garnishing, beautifying, prettifying, enhancing, nonfunctional.

decorous adjective **1** *decorous behavior* proper, seemly, decent, becoming, befitting, tasteful, in good taste, correct, appropriate, suitable, fitting, apt, apposite, polite, well-mannered, mannerly, well-behaved, genteel, refined, well-bred, dignified, respectable. **2** *decorous young ladies* modest, demure, reserved, sedate, staid.
Antonyms: INDECOROUS; UNSEEMLY; IMMODEST.

decorum noun **1** *behave with decorum* decorousness, propriety, properness, seemliness, decency, good taste, correctness, appropriateness, politeness, courtesy, refinement, breeding, deportment, dignity, respectability. **2** *observe decorum* etiquette, protocol, punctilio, customary behavior, good form, politeness, politesse, conformity; *inf.* the thing to do.

decoy noun *a wooden duck as a decoy* | *an undercover cop acting as a decoy* lure, bait, enticement, inducement, temptation, attraction, allurement, ensnarement, entrapment, snare, trap, pitfall.

decrease verb **1** *numbers/volume decreasing* lessen, grow less, diminish, reduce, drop, fall off, decline, dwindle, contract, shrink. **2** *decrease the numbers/amount* lessen, make fewer/less, lower, reduce, cut down/back, cut down/

back on, curtail, contract, diminish. **3** *the wind/storm decreased* die down, abate, subside, let up, slacken, ebb, wane, taper off, peter out. **Antonym:** INCREASE.

decrease *noun* **1** *the decrease in numbers/amount* lessening, lowering, reduction, drop, decline, falling off, downturn, cutback, curtailment, diminution, contraction, shrinkage. **2** *the decrease in the wind/storm* dying down, abatement, subsidence, letting up, letup, slackening, ebb, wane. **Antonym:** INCREASE.

decree *noun* **1** *the emperor's decree* edict, order, law, statute, act, ordinance, regulation, rule, injunction, enactment, command, mandate, proclamation, dictum, precept, manifesto. **2** *the judge's decree* ruling, verdict, judgment, decision; findings.

decree *verb the judge decreed it | fate decreed it* ordain, rule, order, command, dictate, lay down, prescribe, pronounce, proclaim, enact, adjudge, enjoin, direct, decide, determine.

decrepit *adjective* **1** *decrepit old men* feeble, enfeebled, infirm, weak, weakened, weakly, frail, wasted, debilitated, disabled, incapacitated, crippled, doddering, tottering, aged, old, elderly, senile, effete, emasculated. **2** *decrepit old furniture/houses* dilapidated, rickety, broken-down, tumbledown, ramshackle, rundown, worn-out, battered, decayed, deteriorated, antiquated, the worse for wear, on its last legs. **Antonyms:** STRONG; FIT.

decry *verb* disparage, deprecate, belittle, cry down, discredit, depreciate, devalue, play down, derogate, detract, diminish, minimize, underestimate, underrate, undervalue, criticize, carp at, cavil at, censure, blame, condemn, denounce, run down, rail against, rap; *inf.* knock, do a hatchet job on. **Antonyms:** PRAISE; OVERRATE.

dedicate *verb* **1** *dedicate her life to the poor* devote, give, give over, commit, pledge, surrender. **2** *dedicate the book to him* inscribe, address, name, assign, offer. **3** *dedicate a church* devote to God, bless, make holy, consecrate, sanctify, hallow.

dedicated *adjective a dedicated teacher* devoted, committed, wholehearted, single-minded, enthusiastic, zealous, sworn, pledged. **Antonyms:** INDIFFERENT; APATHETIC.

dedication *noun* **1** *work with dedication* devotion, devotedness, commitment, wholeheartedness, single-mindedness, enthusiasm, zeal. **2** *her dedication to the poor* devotion, commitment, allegiance, loyalty, faithfulness, adherence. **3** *the dedication in the book* inscription, address, message. **4** *the dedication of the church* blessing, consecration, sanctification, hallowing.

deduce *verb* conclude, come to the conclusion, infer, reason, gather, glean, come to understand, understand, assume, presume.

deduct *verb* subtract, take away, take off, withdraw, abstract, remove, discount; *inf.* knock off. **Antonym:** ADD.

deduction *noun* **1** *the detectives' sound deduction* conclusion, inference, reasoning, assumption, presumption, corollary; results, findings. **2** *the deduction of tax* subtraction, taking off, withdrawal, removal. *See* DEDUCT.

deed *noun* **1** *brave deeds* act, action, feat, exploit, performance, achievement, accomplishment, undertaking, enterprise. **2** *in deed but not in name* fact, reality, truth. **3** *legal deeds* signed document, contract, legal agreement, indenture, instrument; title deed, deed of covenant.

deem *verb* think, believe, consider, judge, feel, imagine, conceive, regard, see, hold, estimate, calculate, suppose, reckon, account.

deep *adjective* **1** *a deep hole/wound* extending far down/in, cavernous, yawning, profound, bottomless, immeasurable, fathomless, unfathomable. **2** *a deep voice* low, low-pitched, full-toned, bass, rich, powerful, resonant, sonorous, rumbling, booming, resounding. **3** *a deep red color* dark, intense, vivid, rich, strong. **4** *deep distrust* profound, extreme, intense, very great, great, grave, deep-seated, deep-rooted. **5** *a deep thinker/person* clever, intellectual, learned, wise, sagacious, sage, discerning, penetrating, perspicacious. **6** *deep affection* intense, heartfelt, deep-felt, fervent, ardent, impassioned, deep-seated, deep-rooted. **7** *a deep plot* cunning, crafty, artful, shrewd, astute, devious, scheming, designing, insidious, wily, ingenious. **8** *a deep mystery/secret* obscure, unclear, abstruse, mysterious, hidden, secret, unfathomable, recondite, esoteric, enigmatic, arcane. **9** *deep in thought* absorbed, engrossed, preoccupied, rapt, immersed, lost, intent, engaged. **Antonyms:** HIGH; SHALLOW; LIGHT; SUPERFICIAL.

deep *adverb* **1** *dig deep* far down, far in. **2** *deep into the wood/night* far, long, late.

deep *noun* **1** *ships wrecked on the deep* sea, ocean, main; high seas; *inf.* the briny. **2** *in the deep of the night* deepness, middle, midst, midpoint, central point.

deepen *verb* **1** *his distress/love deepened* grow, increase, intensify. **2** *deepen the hole* dig out, excavate, scoop out, hollow out. **3** *deepen his distress/love* increase, add to, intensify, magnify, strengthen, heighten, reinforce.

deeply *adverb* **1** *deeply impressed/hurt* very, greatly, extremely, profoundly, intensely, keenly, acutely. **2** *feel his death deeply* acutely, keenly, intensely, sharply, with feeling, feelingly, passionately, with distress.

deface *verb deface the book/wall with writing* spoil, disfigure, mar, blemish, deform, ruin, sully, tarnish, damage, vandalize, injure. **Antonyms:** BEAUTIFY; DECORATE.

de facto *adjective a de facto ruler* actual, existing, existent, real.

defamation *noun* slander, libel, character assassination, aspersion, calumny, smear campaign, backbiting, vilification, traducement, defilement, obloquy, contumely, malicious gossip, scandal, abuse, malediction, disparagement, denigration, detraction, derogation; smear, slur, insult; *inf.* mudslinging.

defamatory *adjective* slanderous, libelous, calumnious, calumniatory, slurring, backbiting, vilifying, traducing, defiling, contumelious, malicious, abusive, injurious, maledictory, maledictive, disparaging, denigratory, detracting, derogatory, insulting; *inf.* mudslinging.

defame *verb* slander, libel, cast aspersions on, asperse, blacken the name/character of, malign, smear, run down, speak evil of, backbite, vilify, traduce, besmirch, defile, stigmatize, disparage, denigrate, discredit, decry, insult; *inf.* do a hatchet job on, sling/throw mud at, drag through the mud; bad-mouth.

default *noun* **1** *debtors guilty of default* nonpayment, failure to pay, nonremittance; *inf.* welshing/welching, bilking. **2** *lose the game by default | in default of evidence* absence, failure to appear, nonappearance, omission, lack, want, deficiency, neglect, negligence, delinquency, dereliction.

defaulter *noun* **1** *defaulters ordered to pay* nonpayer, debt-dodger; *inf.* welsher/welcher, bilker. **2** *several defaulters in the competition* nonappearer, absentee.

defeat *verb* **1** *defeat their team/army* beat, conquer, win a victory over, get the better of, vanquish, rout, trounce, thrash, overcome, overpower, overthrow, overwhelm, crush, quash, quell, subjugate, subdue, repulse; *inf.* wipe the floor with, clobber, zap. **2** *your attitude defeats me | the problem defeats me* baffle, puzzle, perplex, confound, frustrate. **3** *defeat your own purpose* hinder, prevent, ruin, thwart, frustrate, foil, balk, hamper, obstruct, impede, discomfit; *inf.* put the kibosh on, nip in the bud. **4** *the motion was defeated* reject, overthrow, throw out, outvote.
Antonyms: LOSE; SURRENDER; ADVANCE.

defeat *noun* **1** *suffer defeat by the enemy* conquest, vanquishment, rout, beating, trouncing, thrashing, debacle, reverse, overpowering, overthrow, subjugation. *See* DEFEAT *verb* 1. **2** *the defeat of their plans* downfall, breakdown, collapse, failure, ruin, abortion, miscarriage; undoing, reverse, disappointment, setback, discomfiture, rejection, overthrow.
Antonyms: victory; SUCCESS; TRIUMPH.

defeatist *noun* quitter, yielder, pessimist, prophet of doom.

defecate *verb* pass/discharge/excrete feces, have a bowel movement, void excrement, have di-

arrhea; *inf.* do number two, have a BM, poop, do a poop; *vulg.* crap.

defect *noun* **1** *a defect in the machine/writing* fault, flaw, imperfection, deficiency, weakness, weakspot/point, shortcoming, failing, snag, kink, deformity, blemish, crack, break, tear, scratch, spot, mistake, error; *inf.* bug. **2** *defects in the educational system* deficiency, shortage, shortfall, inadequacy, insufficiency, shortcoming, lack, want, omission, weakness, failing, fault, flaw, absence.
Antonyms: PERFECTION; flawlessness.

defect *verb* **1** *soldiers defected | party members defecting* go over to the enemy, desert, turn traitor, change sides/allegiances, desert one's side/cause, shift ground, break faith, apostatize. **2** *defect from one's country/party* desert, abandon, forsake, renounce, repudiate, secede from, rebel against, revolt against; *inf.* rat on.
Antonyms: JOIN; SUPPORT.

defection *noun* *soldiers guilty of defection* desertion, treason, betrayal, changing sides/allegiances, disloyalty, rebellion, mutiny, perfidy, apostasy, secession, dereliction.

defective *adjective* **1** *a defective machine* faulty, flawed, imperfect, weak, deficient, deformed, incomplete, malfunctioning, in disrepair, cracked, torn, scratched. **2** *defective in character* lacking, wanting, deficient, inadequate, insufficient, short, low, scant. **3** *mentally defective* having learning difficulties, impaired, retarded, abnormal, subnormal.
Antonyms: PERFECT; INTACT; NORMAL.

defector *noun* deserter, turncoat, traitor, renegade, apostate, recreant; *inf.* rat, Benedict Arnold.

defend *verb* **1** *defend the city* protect, guard, safeguard, watch over, keep from harm, preserve, secure, shield, shelter, screen, fortify, garrison, fight for. **2** *defend one's ideas* vindicate, justify, argue/speak for, speak on behalf of, give an apologia for, make a case for, plead for, explain, give reasons for, give the rationale behind, exonerate. **3** *the newspaper defended its journalist* support, back, stand by, stand/stick up for, argue for, champion, endorse, uphold, sustain, bolster.
Antonyms: ATTACK; CRITICIZE.

defendant *noun* accused, prisoner at the bar, appellant, litigant, respondent.

defender *noun* **1** *defenders of the city* protector, guard, bodyguard, guardian, preserver, keeper. **2** *defenders of the faith* supporter, backer, champion, upholder, endorser, sustainer, bolsterer.

defense *noun* **1** *built as a defense against the enemy* protection, shield, safeguard, guard, security, cover, shelter, screen, fortification, resistance, deterrent. **2** *build defenses against the enemy* barricade, fortification, rampart, bulwark, buttress, fortress, keep, bastion. **3** *money spent on defense* military measures/resources, armaments, weapons. **4** *published a defense of his* *ideas* vindication, justification, apologia, apology, argument, plea, explanation, explication, excuse, extenuation, exoneration. **5** *the accused gave his defense* denial, rebuttal, plea, pleading, testimony, declaration, case, excuse, alibi.

defenseless *adjective* **1** *defenseless old people* helpless, vulnerable, weak, powerless, impotent. **2** *defenseless cities* undefended, unprotected, unguarded, unfortified, unarmed, vulnerable, open to attack, wide open, exposed, endangered.

defensible *adjective* **1** *a defensible position/attitude* defendable, justifiable, arguable, tenable, valid, maintainable, sustainable, plausible, permissible, excusable, pardonable, vindicable. **2** *defensible terrain* invulnerable, impregnable, impenetrable, secure, safe, unattackable, unassailable, fortified.

defensive *adjective* **1** *defensive enemy tactics* defending, protecting, protective, safeguarding, shielding, watchful, averting, withstanding, opposing. *See* DEFEND 1. **2** *his defensive attitude* self-defensive, oversensitive, thin-skinned; *inf.* uptight.

defer[1] *verb* *defer the meeting* postpone, put off, adjourn, delay, hold over, shelve, put on ice, pigeonhole, suspend, table, stay, hold in abeyance, prorogue.

defer[2] *verb* *defer to the expert* | *defer to your superior knowledge* yield, submit, bow, give way, give in, surrender, accede, capitulate, acquiesce.

deference *noun* **1** *showing deference for the old* respect, regard, consideration, attentiveness, attention, thoughtfulness, esteem, courteousness, courtesy, politeness, civility, dutifulness, reverence, veneration, homage. **2** *his deference to the expert* yielding, submission, surrender, capitulation, accession, acquiescence, complaisance, obeisance.
Antonyms: DISRESPECT; DISCOURTESY.

deferential *adjective* **1** *a deferential regard for the old* respectful, considerate, thoughtful, attentive, courteous, polite, civil, reverent, reverential, dutiful, regardful. **2** *a deferential attitude to the experts* respectful, reverential, yielding, submissive, acquiescent, compliant, complaisant, tractable, obsequious, obeisant.

deferment *noun* **1** *the deferment of the meeting* postponement, deferral, putting off, adjournment, delay, shelving, suspension, tabling. **2** *be granted a deferment* postponement, respite, stay, moratorium, reprieve.

defiance *noun* **1** *treat the enemy with defiance* resistance, opposition, confrontation, noncompliance, disobedience, recalcitrance, rebelliousness, insubordination, contempt, disregard, scorn, insolence, contumacy. **2** *a spirit of defiance* challenge, provocation, daring, boldness, audacity, bravado, aggression, truculence; *lit.* derring-do.
Antonyms: SUBMISSION; OBEDIENCE.

defiant *adjective* **1** *defiant opposition* resistant, non-

compliant, disobedient, recalcitrant, rebellious, insubordinate, mutinous, refractory, contemptuous, scornful, indifferent, insolent. **2** *with a defiant air* challenging, provocative, bold, audacious, aggressive, truculent.
Antonyms: SUBMISSIVE; yielding.

deficiency *noun* **1** *vitamin deficiency* lack, want, shortage, dearth, insufficiency, inadequacy, scarcity, deficit, scantiness, paucity, absence. **2** *a deficiency in the system* defect, fault, flaw, imperfection, weakness, weak point/spot, failing, shortcoming, snag.

deficient *adjective* **1** *deficient in vitamins* lacking, wanting, short of, low on, defective. **2** *deficient quantities* insufficient, inadequate, scanty, meager, skimpy, sketchy, exiguous. **3** *a deficient system* defective, faulty, flawed, imperfect, incomplete.

deficit *noun* **1** *the deficit is $100* shortfall, deficiency, shortage. **2** *we created a deficit* loss, minus amount; indebtedness, debt.
Antonyms: SURPLUS; SURFEIT.

defile *verb* **1** *streets defiled by filth* pollute, foul, befoul, dirty, soil. **2** *defile young minds* corrupt, contaminate, taint, infect, tarnish, sully, pervert, vitiate. **3** *defile reputations* defame, sully, blacken, cast aspersions on, cast a slur on, denigrate, besmirch, stigmatize. **4** *defile the altar* desecrate, profane, treat sacrilegiously, make impure, contaminate, vitiate. **5** *defile young girls* ravish, rape, deflower, violate.
Antonym: PURIFY.

definable *adjective* determinable, ascertainable, fixable, fixed, definite, clear-cut, precise, exact, specific.

define *verb* **1** *define one's terms* give the meaning of, state precisely, spell out, describe, explain, expound, interpret, elucidate, clarify. **2** *define one's position* describe, determine, set out, outline, detail, specify, designate. **3** *define the boundary* mark out, fix, establish, settle, demarcate, bound, delimit, delineate, circumscribe. **4** *a tree defined against the light* outline, delineate, silhouette.

definite *adjective* **1** *definite plans* specific, particular, precise, exact, defined, well-defined, clear, clear-cut, explicit, express, determined, fixed, established, confirmed. **2** *it's definite that he's going* certain, sure, positive, guaranteed, settled, decided, assured, conclusive, final. **3** *definite boundaries* fixed, marked, demarcated, delimited, circumscribed.
Antonyms: INDEFINITE; UNCERTAIN; INDETERMINATE.

definitely *adverb* *definitely the best applicant* certainly, surely, for sure, without doubt/question, beyond any doubt, undoubtedly, indubitably, positively, absolutely, undeniably, unmistakably, plainly, clearly, obviously, categorically, decidedly, unequivocally, easily, far and away, without fail.

definition noun 1 *the definition of one's terms* meaning, statement of meaning, description, explanation, exposition, expounding, interpretation, elucidation, clarification. 2 *the definition of the boundaries* marking out, fixing, settling, establishment, determination, demarcation, bounding, delimiting, delimitation, delineation, circumscribing. 3 *the definition of the image* precision, sharpness, distinctness, clearness, clarity, contrast, visibility, focus.

definitive adjective 1 *the definitive answer* conclusive, final, ultimate, decisive, unconditional, unqualified, absolute, categorical. 2 *the definitive edition* authoritative, most reliable, most complete, exhaustive.

deflate verb 1 *deflate the air mattress* let down, collapse, flatten, void, puncture. 2 *the air mattress deflated* collapse, empty of air, shrink, contract, flatten. 3 *deflate the pompous man* squash, humble, humiliate, mortify, chasten, subdue, dispirit; *inf.* put down, debunk. 4 *deflate a currency* | *deflate the economy* devalue, depreciate, depress, diminish, reduce.
Antonyms: INFLATE; blow up (*see* BLOW).

deflect verb 1 *cause the bullet to deflect* turn aside/away, turn, alter course, change course/direction, diverge, deviate, veer, swerve, slew, drift, bend, twist, curve, shy, ricochet, glance off, divaricate. 2 *deflect the projectile* | *deflect him from his purpose* turn aside/away, turn, divert, switch, avert, sidetrack.

deflection noun deviation, divergence, diversion, declination, aberration, divarication; turn, veer, swerve, drift, bend, curve.

deform verb 1 *bodies deformed by the fire* disfigure, deface, misshape, mar, ruin, spoil, damage, maim, injure, cripple, mutilate, mangle. 2 *deform the pieces of metal* misshape, distort, contort, buckle, twist, warp, malform, gnarl.

deformed adjective 1 *deformed bodies* misshapen, malformed, distorted, contorted, twisted, crooked, curved, gnarled, crippled, maimed, humpbacked, hunchbacked, disfigured, ugly, unsightly, damaged, marred, mutilated, mangled. 2 *deformed minds* twisted, warped, perverted, corrupted, depraved, vile, gross.

deformity noun 1 *deformity of the body* malformation, misshapenness, misproportion, disfigurement, imperfection, abnormality, irregularity, defacement, distortion, crookedness, ugliness, unsightliness; defect, flaw. 2 *deformity of minds* warpedness, perversion, corruption, depravity, vileness, grossness.

defraud verb cheat, swindle, rob, fleece, sting, dupe, rook, bilk, trick, fool, take in, hoodwink, mislead, delude, deceive, beguile, outwit; *lit.* cozen; *inf.* gyp, con, rip off, take for a ride, pull a fast one on, put one over on.

deft adjective dexterous, adroit, handy, nimble, nimble-fingered, agile, skillful, skilled, proficient, adept, able, clever, expert, experienced.
Antonyms: CLUMSY; AWKWARD; MALADROIT.

defunct adjective 1 *defunct ancestors* dead, deceased, departed, extinct, gone. 2 *defunct practices/organizations* obsolete, expired, nonexistent, inoperative, invalid, nonfunctioning, bygone, outmoded, old-fashioned, *passé.*
Antonyms: ALIVE; EXTANT.

defy verb 1 *defied their parents* disobey, disregard, ignore, slight, flout, fly in the face of, thumb one's nose at, spurn, scoff at, deride, scorn. 2 *defy the enemy forces* resist, withstand, brave, stand up to, confront, face, meet head-on, square up to, beard, defeat, repulse, repel, thwart, frustrate, foil. 3 *I defy you to stay* challenge, dare, throw down the gauntlet to.
Antonyms: OBEY; SURRENDER.

degeneracy noun corruption, decadence, immorality, depravity, dissoluteness, debauchery, profligacy, wickedness, vileness, sinfulness, baseness, turpitude.

degenerate adjective *degenerate function/person* degenerated, deteriorated, debased, declined, degraded, corrupt, decadent, immoral, depraved, dissolute, debauched, abandoned, profligate, wicked, vile, sinful, vice-ridden, disreputable, despicable, base, sordid, low, mean, ignoble.

degenerate verb deteriorate, decline, worsen, decay, rot, fail, fall off, sink, slip, slide, go downhill, regress, retrogress, lapse; *inf.* go to pot, go to the dogs, hit the skids.
Antonym: IMPROVE.

degenerate noun pervert, deviant, deviate, fiend, wretch.

degeneration noun deterioration, debasement, degradation, regression, retrogression; decay, decline, descent, drop, sinking, slide, lapse. *See* DEGENERATE *verb.*

degradation noun 1 *the degradation of his family* debasement, discrediting, demeaning, deprecation, shaming, disgracing, dishonoring, humiliation, mortification. *See* DEGRADE 1. 2 *the degradation of the officers* downgrading, demotion, reduction to the ranks, deposition. *See* DEGRADE 2. 3 *witnessing a scene of degradation* degeneracy, corruption, decadence, immorality, depravity, dissolution, debauchery, vice, wickedness, sordidity, squalor.

degrade verb 1 *his family degraded by his behavior* debase, discredit, cheapen, belittle, demean, deprecate, deflate, devalue, lower, reduce, shame, disgrace, dishonor, humble, humiliate, mortify, abase, vitiate. 2 *officers degraded* downgrade, demote, reduce/lower in rank, reduce to the ranks, strip of rank, cashier, depose, remove from office, unseat, dethrone; *inf.* kick upstairs, drum out. 3 *degraded by her immoral associates* debase, corrupt, pervert, defile, sully, debauch.
Antonyms: DIGNIFY; UPGRADE; PROMOTE; IMPROVE.

degraded adjective *a morally degraded crowd*

degenerate, debased, corrupt, decadent, immoral, depraved, dissolute, debauched, abandoned, profligate, despicable, sordid. *See* DEGENERATE *adjective.*

degrading *adjective* a *degrading experience* debasing, discrediting, cheapening, belittling, demeaning, lowering, shaming, shameful, humiliating, mortifying, disgraceful, dishonorable, undignified; *inf.* infra dig.

degree *noun* **1** *reach a high degree of competence* | *third-degree burns* stage, level, grade, step, gradation, rung, point, mark, measure, notch, limit. **2** *to a marked degree* extent, measure, magnitude, level, amount, quality, intensity, strength, proportion, ratio. **3** *people of higher degree* rank, class, standing, status, station, position, grade, level, order, condition, estate. **by degrees** gradually, slowly, by stages, step by step, little by little, bit by bit, inch by inch.

dehydrate *verb* **1** *they dehydrated the vegetables* | *heat was dehydrating the walkers* dry, dry up/out, sun-dry, desiccate, parch, sear. **2** *plants/bodies dehydrating* dry up, lose water, become thirsty.

deify *verb* idolize, exalt, aggrandize, worship, adore, venerate, revere, pay homage to.

deign *verb* condescend, stoop, lower oneself, think/see fit, deem worthy, consent.

deity *noun* God, god, goddess, divine being, celestial being, supreme being, divinity; godhead. *See* GOD.

dejected *adjective* depressed, dispirited, discouraged, disheartened, downhearted, crestfallen, cast down, downcast, down, disappointed, unhappy, sad, miserable, blue, wretched, despondent, woebegone, forlorn, sorrowful, disconsolate, doleful, glum, gloomy, melancholy, morose, low in spirits, low-spirited, long-faced; *inf.* down in the mouth/dumps.
Antonyms: CHEERFUL; LIGHTHEARTED; HAPPY.

dejection *noun* depression, downheartedness, dispiritedness, discouragement, disappointment, unhappiness, sadness, misery, wretchedness, despondency, sorrowfulness, sorrow, disconsolateness, disconsolation, dolefulness, glumness, gloom, melancholy, despair; low spirits, blues; *inf.* the dumps.

delay *verb* **1** *delay our meeting* postpone, put off, adjourn, defer, hold over, shelve, suspend, table, stay, hold in abeyance, put on hold, put on ice, put on the back burner. **2** *visitors delayed by the traffic* hold up/back, detain, slow up, set back, hinder, obstruct, hamper, impede, bog down, check, hold in check, restrain, halt, stop, arrest. **3** *hurry, don't delay!* linger, loiter, hold back, dawdle, dally, dilly-dally, lag/fall behind, not keep pace, procrastinate, stall, tarry.
Antonyms: ADVANCE; ACCELERATE.

delay *noun* **1** *the delay to the meeting* postponement, adjournment, deferment, suspension, tabling, stay. *See* DELAY *verb* 1. **2** *holiday traffic delays* holdup, wait, setback, detainment, detention, hindrance, obstruction, impediment, check, stoppage, halt, interruption. **3** *the delay between trains* wait, waiting period, interval, lull, interlude, intermission. **4** *her delay made us late* lingering, loitering, dawdling, dallying, dilly-dallying, lagging/falling behind, procrastination, stalling, tarrying.

delectable *adjective* **1** *delectable food* delicious, appetizing, inviting, tasty, savory, enjoyable, luscious, palatable, flavorful, flavorsome, toothsome; *inf.* scrumptious, yummy, ambrosial. **2** *delectable manner/appearance* delightful, charming, enchanting, adorable, captivating, winning, engaging, winsome, dainty, attractive, pleasing, agreeable, ravishing, exciting, titillating.
Antonyms: REVOLTING; NASTY.

delectation *noun* for *your delectation* delight, pleasure, enjoyment, entertainment, amusement, diversion, happiness, gratification, satisfaction, excitement, relish, titillation.

delegate *noun* our *country's/conference delegate* representative, deputy, agent, spokesman, spokeswoman, spokesperson, ambassador, envoy, legate, messenger, go-between, proxy, emissary, commissary.

delegate *verb* **1** *delegate tasks* pass on, hand over, transfer, give, commit, entrust, assign, relegate, consign. **2** *delegate him leader* appoint, designate, nominate, name, authorize, deputize, commission, mandate, empower, choose, select, elect, ordain.

delegation *noun* **1** *our country's delegation* deputation, legation, contingent, mission, commission, embassy; delegates, envoys. **2** *the delegation of tasks* transference, committal, entrustment, assignment, relegation, consignment. *See* DELEGATE *verb* 1. **3** *his delegation as leader* appointment, designation, nomination, authorization, commissioning, selection, election.

delete *verb* cross/strike out, rub out, cut out, erase, cancel, blue-pencil, edit out, remove, take out, expunge, eradicate, obliterate, efface, wipe/blot out; *inf.* scratch, kill.
Antonyms: ADD; INSERT.

deleterious *adjective* harmful, injurious, hurtful, damaging, destructive, ruinous, bad, disadvantageous, noxious.
Antonyms: HEALTHY; HELPFUL; BENEFICIAL.

deliberate *adjective* **1** *a deliberate act* intentional, planned, considered, calculated, designed, studied, studious, painstaking, conscious, purposeful, willful, premeditated, preplanned, prearranged, preconceived, predetermined, aforethought. **2** *slow deliberate speech/steps* careful, unhurried, cautious, thoughtful, steady, regular, measured, unwavering, unhesitating, unfaltering, determined, resolute, ponderous, laborious.
Antonyms: ACCIDENTAL; UNINTENTIONAL; HASTY.

deliberate verb 1 *looking out of the window deliberating* think, ponder, muse, meditate, reflect, cogitate, ruminate, brood, excogitate. 2 *deliberate the advantages* think over, consider, ponder, reflect on, mull over, review, weigh up, evaluate. 3 *deliberate with colleagues* discuss, debate, confer, consult.

deliberately adverb 1 *deliberately hurt her* intentionally, on purpose, purposefully, by design, knowingly, wittingly, consciously, premeditatedly, calculatedly, in cold blood. *See* DELIBERATE adjective 1. 2 *speak/walk very deliberately* carefully, unhurriedly, cautiously, steadily, measuredly, unwaveringly, unhesitatingly, determinedly, ponderously. *See* DELIBERATE adjective 2.

deliberation noun 1 *after his deliberation* thinking, thought, consideration, pondering, musing, mulling, meditation, reflection, cogitation, rumination, brooding, weighing up, excogitation. *See* DELIBERATE verb 1, 2. 2 *after deliberation with colleagues* discussion, debate, consultation, conferring, conference. 3 *speak with deliberation* care, carefulness, no hurry, caution, thoughtfulness, steadiness, determination, resoluteness, laboriousness. *See* DELIBERATE adjective 2.

delicacy noun 1 *the delicacy of the china/material* fineness, exquisiteness, fragility, slenderness, slightness, elegance, gracefulness, grace, daintiness, flimsiness, silkiness. *See* DELICATE 1. 2 *the delicacy of his health/wife* frailty, fragility, weakness, debilitation; sickliness, infirmity, poor/ill health. 3 *delicacy of the colors* paleness, mutedness, subtlety, softness, understatement. 4 *delicacy of the situation* difficulty, trickiness, sensitivity, ticklishness, precariousness. 5 *handle the matter with delicacy* care, consideration, sensitivity, sensibility, tact, discretion, finesse, diplomacy, politeness. 6 *the delicacy of her palate* discrimination, discernment, refinement, perceptiveness, criticalness, fastidiousness. *See* DELICATE 6. 7 *the delicacy of the mechanism* sensitivity, precision, accuracy, exactness. 8 *delicacy of touch* deftness, skill, expertise. 9 *buying some delicacies* gourmet food, tidbit, treat, appetizer.

delicate adjective 1 *delicate china/material* fine, exquisite, fragile, slender, slight, elegant, graceful, dainty, flimsy, silky, gauzy, gossamer, wispy. 2 *his wife is delicate* frail, sickly, weak, debilitated, infirm, ailing, in poor health, unwell. 3 *delicate colors* pastel, pale, muted, subtle, soft, subdued, understated, faint. 4 *a delicate matter/situation* difficult, tricky, sensitive, ticklish, critical, precarious, touchy; *inf.* sticky, dicey. 5 *require delicate handling* careful, considerate, sensitive, tactful, discreet, diplomatic, politic, kid-glove. 6 *a delicate palate* discriminating, discerning, refined, perceptive, critical, fastidious, finicky, persnickety, squea-

mish. 7 *a delicate mechanism* sensitive, precise, accurate, exact. 8 *a delicate touch* deft, skilled, skillful, expert. 9 *delicate food* choice, delicious. *See* DELICACY 9.

Antonyms: COARSE; ROBUST; STRONG; ROUGH.

delicious adjective 1 *delicious food* tasty, appetizing, mouthwatering, delectable, choice, savory, flavorsome, flavorful, luscious, palatable, toothsome, ambrosial, ambrosian; *inf.* scrumptious, yummy. 2 *a delicious evening* delightful, enchanting, exquisite, enjoyable, pleasurable, entertaining, amusing, diverting, pleasant, agreeable, charming, nice.

Antonyms: REVOLTING; DISGUSTING; NASTY.

delight noun *filled with delight* pleasure, joy, happiness, gladness, gratification, bliss, rapture, ecstasy, elation, jubilation, excitement, entertainment, amusement; transports.

Antonyms: REVULSION; DISGUST.

delight verb 1 *delighted by the news* please, gladden, cheer, gratify, thrill, excite, transport, enchant, captivate, entrance, charm, entertain, amuse, divert; *inf.* send. 2 *delight in reading* take/find pleasure, indulge, glory.

Antonyms: DISMAY; DISPLEASE; DISGUST.

delighted adjective pleased, joyful, happy, glad, gratified, overjoyed, blissful, enraptured, ecstatic, jubilant, thrilled, transported, excited, enchanted, captivated, entranced, charmed, entertained, amused, diverted; *inf.* sent.

delightful adjective *a delightful occasion/woman* pleasant, pleasing, agreeable, enjoyable, amusing, entertaining, diverting, pleasurable, pleasure-giving, gratifying, delectable, joyful, exciting, thrilling, rapturous, enchanting; captivating, fascinating, entrancing, ravishing, charming, attractive, beautiful, pretty, engaging, winning.

Antonyms: UNPLEASANT; DISAGREEABLE.

delineate verb 1 *delineate her features* trace, draw the lines of, outline, draw, sketch, draft, block in, contour. 2 *delineate the statistics* make a diagram of, make a chart of, chart, map, map out, diagram. 3 *delineate his achievements* describe, define, set forth, outline, depict, portray.

delinquency noun 1 *juvenile delinquency* wrongdoing, misdemeanor, misconduct, misbehavior, mischievousness, transgression; offense, misdeed, crime. 2 *the soldier's delinquency* negligence, remissness, dereliction, omission, failure.

delinquent noun *damage done by delinquents* offender, wrongdoer, culprit, lawbreaker, criminal, hooligan, vandal, ruffian, hoodlum, miscreant, malefactor, transgressor; juvenile delinquent, young offender.

delinquent adjective 1 *delinquent young people* mischievous, culpable, transgressing, offending, criminal. 2 *delinquent policemen* negligent, neglectful, remiss, careless, slack, derelict.

delirious adjective 1 *delirious patients* raving, incoherent, babbling, light-headed, irrational, deranged, demented, unhinged, mad, insane, crazy, out of one's mind. **2** *delirious at the good news* ecstatic, euphoric, beside oneself, carried away, transported, hysterical, frenzied, wild with excitement, distracted, frantic, out of one's wits, feverish.

Antonyms: RATIONAL; COHERENT; DEPRESSED.

delirium *noun* **1** *affected by delirium* temporary madness/insanity, irrationality, incoherence, light-headedness, raving, babbling. **2** *happy delirium* ecstasy, euphoria, hysteria, frenzy, wild emotion, wildness, excitement, distraction, feverishness, fever, passion.

deliver *verb* **1** *deliver the mail/groceries* distribute, carry, bring, take, transport, convey, send, dispatch, remit. **2** *deliver the prisoners to the enemy* hand over, turn over, transfer, commit, grant, make over, give up, yield, surrender, relinquish, cede, resign. **3** *deliver them from enemies* set free, free, liberate, release, save, rescue, set loose, loose, extricate, discharge, ransom, emancipate, redeem. **4** *deliver a speech/sigh* utter, give voice to, voice, speak, give, give forth, express, pronounce, enunciate, proclaim, announce, declare, read, recite, broadcast, promulgate. **5** *deliver a blow* | *deliver a shot at* direct, aim, give, deal, administer, launch, inflict, throw, strike, hurl, pitch, discharge. **6** *deliver better sales figures* come up with, achieve, attain, provide, supply.

Antonyms: COLLECT; RECEIVE.

deliverance *noun* **1** *deliverance from prison/evil* liberation, release, rescue, escape, discharge, ransom, emancipation, salvation, redemption, manumission. **2** *deliverances from the pulpit* pronouncement, declaration, announcement, proclamation, report, lecture, sermon, speech.

delivery *noun* **1** *delivery is extra* distribution, carriage, transporting, transport, conveyance, dispatch. **2** *receive a delivery* consignment, load, batch. **3** *admire his clear delivery* manner of speaking, enunciation, articulation, intonation, elocution, utterance, presentation. **4** *a mother having a difficult delivery* labor, childbirth, parturition. **5** *delivery from the enemy* deliverance, liberation, release, rescue, escape. *See* DELIVERANCE 1. **6** *the delivery of a blow/ball* directing, aiming, launching, throwing, pitching. *See* DELIVER 5.

delude *verb* mislead, deceive, fool, take in, trick, dupe, cheat, hoodwink, beguile, outwit, misguide, lead on, bamboozle, defraud, swindle, double-cross; *lit.* cozen; *inf.* con, pull a fast one on, lead up the garden path, take for a ride, put one over on, two-time.

deluge *noun* **1** *houses swept away by the deluge* flood, spate, inundation, overflowing, flash flood, cataclysm. **2** *caught in the deluge without an umbrella* downpour, torrent, torrential rain, cloudburst. **3** *a deluge of correspondence* flood, rush, spate, torrent, avalanche, barrage, outpouring.

deluge *verb* **1** *towns deluged with polluted water* flood, inundate, swamp, engulf, submerge, drown, soak, drench, douse. **2** *deluged by correspondence* inundate, flood, overrun, overwhelm, engulf, swamp, overload.

delusion *noun* **1** *delusions of grandeur* false impression, false belief, misconception, misapprehension, misunderstanding, misbelief, mistake, self-deception, deception, error, fallacy, illusion, fancy, phantasm, fool's paradise. **2** *victims of their own delusion* deluding, misleading, deception, fooling, tricking, duping. *See* DELUDE.

deluxe *adjective* luxurious, sumptuous, palatial, opulent, lavish, grand, rich, superior, exclusive, choice, select, elegant, splendid, costly, expensive; *inf.* plush, upscale, upmarket.

Antonyms: BASIC; PLAIN; POOR.

delve *verb* **delve into1** *delve into one's pockets/cupboards* search, rummage through, ransack, dig into, ferret around in, hunt through. **2** *delve into local history* research, investigate, look into, examine, probe (into), dig into, hunt through.

demagogue *noun* political agitator, agitator, soapbox orator, rabble-rouser, firebrand, haranguer, troublemaker.

demand *verb* **1** *workers demanding a raise* ask/call for, request, press for, insist on, urge, clamor for, make a claim for, lay claim to, claim. **2** *"What's that?" he demanded* ask, inquire, question, interrogate, challenge. **3** *work demanding care* require, need, necessitate, call for, take, involve, want, cry out for. **4** *parents demanding obedience* | *demand payment* expect, insist on, exact, impose, order, requisition.

demand *noun* **1** *give in to their demands* request, entreaty, claim, requisition; insistence, pressure, clamor. **2** *answer his demand* inquiry, question, interrogation, challenge. **3** *the demands of the job* requirement, need, necessity, want, claim, imposition, exigency. **in demand** requested, required, sought-after, popular, in vogue, fashionable; *inf.* trendy.

demanding *adjective* **1** *demanding children* nagging, harassing, clamorous, importunate, insistent, imperious. **2** *demanding jobs* challenging, taxing, exacting, exigent, tough, hard, difficult, tiring, wearing, exhausting.

Antonyms: EASYGOING; EASY; EFFORTLESS.

demarcation *noun* **1** *drew a line of demarcation* boundary, border, limit, bound, margin, frontier. **2** *the demarcation between the two jobs* separation, division, distinction, differentiation, delimitation, marking off, definition.

demean *verb* lower, degrade, debase, devalue, demote, humble, abase, belittle, deprecate.

demeanor *noun* behavior, conduct, bearing, air, appearance, mien, deportment, carriage, comportment.

demented *adjective* insane, mad, crazy, crazed, deranged, of unsound mind, out of one's mind, unhinged, unbalanced, touched, *non compos*

mentis, maniacal, manic, frenzied, distraught, foolish, idiotic, crackbrained, lunatic; *inf.* daft, balmy, loopy, batty, dippy, wacky.
Antonyms: SANE; RATIONAL.

dementia *noun* madness; senile dementia, Alzheimer's disease, Alzheimer's.

demise *noun* death, passing, expiration, end, termination, cessation.
Antonyms: BIRTH; START.

democracy *noun* representative government, constitutional government, popular government, self-government; republic, commonwealth.

democratic *adjective* of the people, representative, popular, popularist, egalitarian, republican, self-governing, autonomous.

demolish *verb* **1** *demolish the building* knock down, pull/tear down, bring down, flatten, raze, level, bulldoze, dismantle, break up, pulverize. **2** *demolish the argument* | *demolish his self-confidence* destroy, put an end to, ruin, wreck, undo. **3** *demolish the opposition* defeat, conquer, vanquish, overthrow, overturn, quell, quash, suppress, destroy, annihilate, wipe out, finish off. **4** *demolish a plate of cookies* eat up, consume, devour, gobble up, put away.
Antonyms: BUILD; CONSTRUCT; CREATE.

demolition *noun* **1** *the demolition of the buildings* knocking down, pulling down, flattening, razing, leveling, bulldozing. *See* DEMOLISH 1. **2** *the demolition of the argument* destruction, ruin, ruination, wrecking, undoing. **3** *demolition of the opposition* defeat, conquest, vanquishing, overthrow, destruction, annihilation. *See* DEMOLISH 3.

demon *noun* **1** *the demons from hell* devil, evil/malignant spirit, fiend. **2** *the dictator's a demon* devil, fiend, brute, monster, savage, beast, barbarian, villain. **3** *the demon of creativity* genius, guardian/ministering angel. **4** *he's a real demon for work* man/woman of action, hard worker, powerhouse, human dynamo, workaholic; *inf.* whiz kid, eager beaver, busy bee. **5** *a demon at sailing* master, wizard, addict, fanatic; *inf.* ace, whiz.
Antonym: ANGEL.

demonic, demoniac, demoniacal *adjective* **1** *demonicspirits* diabolic, diabolical, devilish, fiendish, satanic, hellish, infernal, evil, wicked, Mephistophelean. **2** *demonic eyes/laughter* like one possessed, maniacal, manic, mad, crazed, frenzied, frantic, feverish, frenetic, hectic, furious, hysterical.

demonstrable *adjective* provable, verifiable, attestable, confirmable, evincible.

demonstrate *verb* **1** *demonstrate the proof of the proposition* show, indicate, determine, prove, validate, confirm, verify, establish. **2** *blushes demonstrating embarrassment* show, indicate, display, exhibit, express, manifest, evince, ev-

idence. **3** *demonstrate putting on a bandage* show, illustrate, give an idea of, teach (about), describe, explain (about), expound on. **4** *demonstrate against nuclear weapons* protest, march, parade, rally, sit in, picket.

demonstration *noun* **1** *demonstration of the proof of the proposition* indication, substantiation, confirmation, affirmation, verification, validation. *See* DEMONSTRATE 1. **2** *a demonstration of his embarrassment* indication, expression, manifestation, evincement; evidence. **3** *a demonstration of putting on a bandage* illustration, description, explanation, exposition. **4** *a demonstration of the new product* exposition, presentation, exhibition; *inf.* expo. **5** *take part in a student demonstration* protest, protest march, march, parade, rally, mass rally/lobby, sit-in, picket.

demonstrative *adjective* **1** *a demonstrative person/reaction* emotional, unreserved, unrestrained, expressive, open, effusive, expansive, gushing, nonreticent, affectionate, loving, warm. **2** *demonstrative of their skill* indicative, illustrative, evincive, expository. **3** *demonstrative evidence* conclusive, convincing, telling, material, incontrovertible, irrefutable.
Antonyms: UNDEMONSTRATIVE; UNEMOTIONAL; RESERVED.

demoralize *verb* **1** *workers demoralized by the setbacks* discourage, dishearten, cast down, dispirit, deject, depress, daunt, crush, sap, shake, undermine, devitalize, cripple, paralyze, weaken, enervate. **2** *brutes demoralizing the young* corrupt, deprave, debauch, pervert, debase, contaminate, defile, vitiate.
Antonyms: ENCOURAGE; HEARTEN.

demote *verb* downgrade, lower/reduce in rank, relegate, degrade, declass, strip of rank, reduce to the ranks, humble; *inf.* kick upstairs.
Antonyms: PROMOTE; UPGRADE.

demur *verb* raise objections, object, take exception, express reluctance/reservations/doubts, be unwilling, protest, lodge a protest, dispute, refuse, dissent, balk at, hesitate, cavil.

demur *noun* go without demur objection, protest, dispute, dissent, reluctance, reservation, unwillingness; doubts, qualms, misgivings.

demure *adjective* **1** *demure young girls* modest, unassuming, decorous, meek, reserved, quiet, shy, bashful, retiring, diffident, reticent, timid, timorous, shrinking, serious, grave, sedate, staid. **2** *demure young ladies* overmodest, coy, prim, priggish, prissy, prudish, goody-goody, straitlaced, puritanical.
Antonyms: BRAZEN; SHAMELESS.

den *noun* **1** *the fox's den* lair, hole, hollow, shelter, hide-out. **2** *thieves retreating to their den* | *den of iniquity* place of crime/vice, site, haunt; *inf.* dive, joint. **3** *writing in his den* study, retreat, sanctum, *sanctum sanctorum*, sanctuary, hideaway.

denial *noun* **1** *a denial of the statement* contradiction, repudiation, disclaimer, retraction,

abjuration, disaffirmation; negation, dissent. **2** *the denial of the request* refusal, rejection, dismissal, rebuff, repulse, declination, veto, turndown; *inf.* thumbs down. **3** *denial of one's own citizenship* renunciation, renouncement, disowning, repudiation, disavowal.
Antonyms: CONFESSION; ACCEPTANCE.

denigrate *verb* disparage, belittle, diminish, deprecate, detract from, decry, blacken one's character, defame, slander, libel, cast aspersions on, malign, vilify, calumniate, besmirch, run down, abuse, revile; bad-mouth.
Antonyms: EXTOL; LAUD; ACCLAIM.

denizen *noun* inhabitant, habitant, dweller, resident, occupier, occupant.

denomination *noun* **1** *religious denominations* creed, faith, religious belief, church, sect, religious group, persuasion, communion, order, fraternity, brotherhood, sisterhood, school. **2** *coins/weights of various denominations* value, unit, grade, size. **3** *creatures under various denominations* classification, class, category, grouping, group, type. **4** *things going under various denominations* name, title, term, designation, appellation, epithet, style, label, tag; *inf.* handle, moniker.

denote *verb* **1** *a smile denoting delight | the color yellow denoting happiness* indicate, be a sign/mark of, signify, betoken, symbolize, represent, stand for, typify. **2** *the word bankruptcy denotes financial ruin* mean, convey, designate, suggest, bring to mind, intimate, refer to, allude to, imply, connote.

denouement *noun* **1** *miss the denouement of the plan* resolution, solution, clarification, unraveling, final/last act, finale. **2** *the denouement of the argument* outcome, upshot, result, culmination, climax.

denounce *verb* **1** *denounce the council's policies* condemn, criticize, attack, censure, castigate, decry, rail/inveigh/fulminate against, declaim against, arraign, denunciate, revile. **2** *denounce his partner* accuse, inform against, incriminate, implicate, inculpate, charge, file charges, indict, impeach, take to court.

dense *adjective* **1** *a dense forest/crowd* close-packed, tightly packed, crowded, thickset, closely set, jammed together, crammed, compressed, compacted. **2** *a dense liquid/substance* of high density, heavy, concentrated, condensed. **3** *dense fog/smoke* thick, concentrated, opaque, impenetrable. **4** *too dense to understand* stupid, thick, slow-witted, slow, dull-witted, blockish, obtuse; *inf.* dim.
Antonyms: SPARSE; THIN; LIGHT; CLEVER.

deny *verb* **1** *deny the charge/statement* declare untrue, contradict, negate, nullify, dissent from, disagree with, repudiate, refute, controvert, disclaim, retract, take back, back-pedal, abjure, disaffirm, gainsay. **2** *deny the request* refuse, reject, turn down, dismiss, repulse, decline, veto; *inf.* give the thumbs down to, give the red light to. **3** *to deny one's citizenship* re-

nounce, disown, turn one's back on, repudiate, discard, disavow.
Antonyms: ADMIT; ACCEPT.

deodorant *noun* **1** *body deodorant* antiperspirant. **2** *room deodorants* air freshener, deodorizer, fumigant; *inf.* odor eater.

depart *verb* **1** *they departed at noon* leave, go, go away/off, take one's leave, take oneself off, withdraw, set off/out, start out, get going, get under way, quit, make an exit, exit, break camp, decamp, retreat, retire; *inf.* make tracks, shove off, split, cut out, vamoose, hightail it. **2** *depart from the norm* deviate, diverge, differ, vary, digress, veer, branch off, fork, swerve, turn aside.
Antonyms: ARRIVE; STAY.

departed *adjective* *departed loved ones* dead, deceased, late, gone, passed away/on, expired.

department *noun* **1** *the accounting department* section, division, subdivision, unit, branch, segment, compartment, office, bureau, agency. **2** *that's the cook's department* area, area of responsibility, responsibility, area of interest, specialty, line, province, sphere, sphere of activity, domain, realm, jurisdiction, authority, function.

departure *noun* **1** *the hour of their departure* leaving, leave-taking, going, going away/off, withdrawal, setting off/out, starting out, exit, exodus, decamping, retreat. *See* DEPART 1. **2** *a departure from the norm* deviation, divergence, variation, digression, veering, branching off, swerving. *See* DEPART 2. **3** *the export market is a new departure for the firm* change of direction, change, difference of emphasis, shift, innovation, branching out, novelty.
Antonyms: ARRIVAL; RETURN.

depend *verb* **1** *success depends on hard work | it depends on how he proceeds* be dependent on, turn/hinge on, hang on, rest on, be contingent upon, be subject to, be controlled/determined by, be based on, revolve around, be influenced by, be resultant from, be subordinate to. **2** *depend on him for help* rely on, place reliance on, count/bank on, lean on, cling to, reckon/calculate on, trust in, put one's faith in, have confidence in, swear by, be sure of, be supported/sustained by.

dependable *adjective* reliable, trustworthy, faithful, responsible, steady, stable, sure, unfailing, true, steadfast.
Antonyms: UNRELIABLE; UNTRUSTWORTHY.

dependence *noun* **1** *pity the children's dependence* helplessness, weakness, defenselessness, vulnerability, exposure. **2** *alcohol dependence* addiction, overuse, reliance, dependency; abuse.

dependence on/upon 1 *the venture's dependence on hard work* reliance on, turning on, hinging on, bearing on, relevancy to/with, relationship to, connection to/with, interconnection to/with, interdependence on. *See* DEPEND 1. **2** *their* *dependence on their mother* reliance on, trust in, faith in, confidence in. *See* DEPEND 2.

dependency *noun* **1** *his dependency on his mother* dependence, reliance. *See* DEPEND 2. **2** *the children's utter dependency* dependence, helplessness, defenselessness. *See* DEPENDENCE 3. **3** *alcohol dependency* dependence, addiction, overuse, reliance. **4** *formerly a dependency of the United States* colony, protectorate, province, fief. **5** *a dependency of the parent firm* subsidiary, adjunct, appendage, auxiliary, subject, attachment.

dependent *adjective* **1** *dependent on circumstances* depending on, conditional on, contingent on, determined by, subject to. **2** *dependent children* reliant, helpless, weak, defenseless, vulnerable, immature. **3** *dependent countries* subsidiary, subject, subservient. **dependent on/upon** *dependent on their mother* relying on, reliant on, counting on, leaning on, supported by, sustained by. *See* DEPEND 2.
Antonym: INDEPENDENT.

dependent *noun* minor, child, charge, protégé; minion, parasite, hanger-on, henchman.

depict *verb* **1** *a painting depicting him sitting* portray, represent, draw, paint, sketch, illustrate, delineate, outline, reproduce, render, limn, chart, map out. **2** *an account depicting his faults* describe, set forth/out, outline, sketch, detail, relate, narrate, recount, record, chronicle.

deplete *verb* exhaust, use up, consume, expend, spend, drain, empty, milk, evacuate, bankrupt, impoverish, reduce, decrease, diminish, lessen, lower, attenuate.
Antonyms: AUGMENT; INCREASE.

depletion *noun* exhaustion, using up, consumption, expenditure, draining, emptying, reduction, decrease, dwindling, diminution, lessening, lowering, attenuation.

deplorable *adjective* **1** *deplorable behavior* disgraceful, shameful, dishonorable, blameworthy, disreputable, scandalous, reprehensible, despicable, abominable, base, sordid, vile, contemptible. **2** *in deplorable circumstances* lamentable, regrettable, unfortunate, wretched, dire, miserable, pitiable, pathetic, unhappy, sad, tragic, disastrous, distressing, grievous, calamitous.
Antonyms: HONORABLE; ADMIRABLE; FORTUNATE.

deplore *verb* **1** *deplore his dreadful behavior* be scandalized/shocked by, be offended by, disapprove of, condemn, censure, deprecate, denounce, decry, abhor. **2** *deplore the passing of steam trains* regret, lament, mourn, rue, bemoan, grieve/sorrow over, bewail, pine for, shed tears for, weep over.

deploy *verb* **1** *deploy troops* arrange, position, dispose, spread out, extend, redistribute, station. **2** *deploy new arguments* use, utilize, set out/up, bring into play, have recourse to.

deport *verb* **1** *deport the refugees* banish, expel,

exile, evict, transport, oust, expatriate, extradite. **2** *deport oneself badly* behave, conduct oneself, act, acquit oneself, comport oneself, bear/carry/hold oneself.

deportation *noun* *the deportation of refugees* banishment, expulsion, exile, eviction, ousting, transportation, extradition, expatriation.

deportment *noun* **1** *have lessons in deportment* carriage, bearing, posture, comportment, stance, attitude, demeanor, mien, air, appearance, aspect, style, manner. **2** *complain about the child's deportment* behavior, conduct, etiquette; manners, actions.

depose *verb* *depose the leader/king* remove from office, remove, unseat, dethrone, oust, displace, dismiss, discharge, cashier, strip of rank, demote; *inf.* sack, fire, give the boot to.

deposit *verb* **1** *deposit the package on the floor* put, lay, set, set/put/lay down, drop, let fall. **2** *rivers depositing mud* let settle, set down, precipitate, dump. **3** *deposit money/jewels in the safe* bank, entrust, consign, save, store, hoard, stow, put away, lay in, squirrel away.

deposit *noun* **1** *leaving a chemical deposit* precipitation, sediment, sublimate, accumulation, deposition; dregs, lees; silt, alluvium. **2** *coal/iron deposits* bed, vein, lode, layer. **3** *put a deposit on the goods* down/part payment, installment, security, retainer.

deposition *noun* **1** *the deposition of the leader* removal, unseating, dethronement, ousting, displacement, dismissal, discharge, demotion. *See* DEPOSE 1. **2** *the witnesses' depositions* testimony, evidence, sworn statement/declaration, affidavit, attestation, affirmation.

depository *noun* repository, store, storehouse, warehouse, depot, reservoir, safe deposit, bank.

depot *noun* **1** *buses/trains returning to the depot* terminal, terminus; bus/railroad station, garage. **2** *stored in the depot* storehouse, warehouse, repository, depository, magazine, cache, arsenal.

deprave *verb* corrupt, debauch, lead astray, pervert, seduce, debase, degrade, make degenerate, defile, pollute, contaminate, vitiate, brutalize, abuse.

depraved *adjective* corrupt, corrupted, immoral, unprincipled, reprobate, debauched, dissolute, abandoned, perverted, degenerate, profligate, debased, degraded, wicked, sinful, vile, base, iniquitous, criminal, vicious, brutal, lewd, licentious, lascivious, lecherous, prurient, obscene, indecent, libertine.
Antonyms: UPRIGHT; VIRTUOUS; PURE.

---

depraved
corrupt, debased, degenerate, perverted, vile
There are many terms to describe the dark side of human nature. Someone who preys on young children would be considered **depraved**, a term that means totally immoral and implies a warped character or a twisted mind (*a de-*

praved man who stole money from his own mother and eventually murdered her). While *depraved* suggests an absolute condition, **degenerate** is a relative term that implies deterioration from a mental, moral, or physical standard (*her degenerate habits eventually led to her arrest for possession of drugs*). **Corrupt** also suggests a deterioration or loss of soundness, particularly through a destructive or contaminating influence. But unlike *depraved*, which usually applies to the lower end of the human spectrum, people in high positions are often referred to as *corrupt* (*a corrupt politician from a prominent family*). To say that someone or something is **debased** suggests a lowering in quality, value, dignity, or character (*debased by having to spend time in prison*). **Perverted** and **vile** are the strongest of these words describing lack of moral character. *Perverted* suggests a distortion of someone or something from what is right, natural, or true; in a moral sense, it means to use one's appetites or natural desires for other ends than those which are considered normal or natural (*a perverted individual who never should have been left alone with young children*). Most people find criminals who prey on either very old or very young victims to be **vile**, a more general term for whatever is loathsome, repulsive, or utterly despicable (*a vile killer who deserved the maximum sentence*).

depravity *noun* corruption, corruptness, corruptedness, immorality, debauchery, dissoluteness, abandonment, perversion, degradation, degeneracy, lechery, profligacy, contamination, vitiation, wickedness, sinfulness, vileness, baseness, iniquity, criminality, viciousness, brutality, brutishness, lewdness, licentiousness, lasciviousness, prurience, obscenity, indecency.

deprecate *verb* **1** *deprecate the committee's actions* disapprove of, criticize, deplore, frown upon, censure, condemn, protest against, inveigh/rail against, denounce; *inf.* knock. **2** *deprecate his achievement* belittle, disparage, denigrate, decry, discredit, deflate, diminish, depreciate. See DEPRECIATE 3.
Antonyms: PRAISE; EXTOL; EMPHASIZE.

deprecatory *adjective* **1** *make deprecatory remarks about the opposition* disapproving, critical, protesting, condemnatory, reproachful, upbraiding, castigatory, admonishing, denunciatory. See DEPRECATE 1. **2** *give a deprecatory smile at his mistake* apologetic, regretful, sorry, remorseful, contrite, penitent, repentant, rueful, compunctious, propitiatory. **3** *a deprecatory account of their achievement* belittling, disparaging, denigratory, derogatory, discrediting, deflating, diminishing, disdainful, derisive, snide, sneering, mocking, jibing.

depreciate *verb* **1** *the furniture has depreciated* decrease in value, lose value, decline in price. **2** *depreciate the value | depreciate the furniture*

devalue, reduce, lower in value/price, mark down, cheapen, cut, slash. **3** *depreciate efforts to help* belittle, disparage, denigrate, decry, deprecate, make light of, discredit, underrate, undervalue, underestimate, deflate, detract from, derogate, diminish, minimize, run down, disdain, ridicule, deride, sneer at, mock, defame, traduce.
Antonyms: APPRECIATE; PRAISE; OVERRATE.

depreciation *noun* **1** *the depreciation of the furniture* devaluation, decrease/lowering/reduction in value, cheapening, markdown. See DEPRECIATE 1, 2. **2** *the depreciation of their efforts* belittlement, disparagement, denigration, deprecation, discrediting, underrating, undervaluing. See DEPRECIATE 3.

depredation *noun the depredation of the town by the army/storm* plundering, pillaging, ravaging, despoliation, devastation, laying waste.

depress *verb* **1** *news that depressed her* make sad/unhappy, sadden, deject, cast down, make gloomy/despondent, dispirit, dishearten, discourage, dampen the spirits of, daunt, desolate, make desolate, weigh down, oppress. **2** *depress economic activity* slow down/up, weaken, lower, reduce, sap, enervate, debilitate, devitalize, impair, enfeeble, exhaust, drain. **3** *depress prices* reduce, lower, cut, cheapen, put/keep down, slash, depreciate, devalue, diminish, downgrade. **4** *depress the lever* push down, press down, lower.
Antonyms: CHEER; ENCOURAGE; RAISE.

depressant *noun* sedative, tranquilizer, sleeping pill, soporific, opiate, hypnotic; *inf.* downer.

depressed *adjective* **1** *depressed at the news* sad, saddened, unhappy, gloomy, blue, glum, dejected, downhearted, cast down, downcast, down, crestfallen, despondent, dispirited, low, low in spirits, low-spirited, melancholy, disheartened, discouraged, fed up, daunted, desolate, moody, morose, pessimistic, weighed down, oppressed; *inf.* down in the dumps. **2** *a depressed section of land* sunken, hollow, concave, indented, dented, pushed in, recessed, set back. **3** *a depressed economy* weak, weakened, slow, enervated, debilitated, devitalized, impaired. See DEPRESS 2. **4** *depressed prices* reduced, lowered, cut, cheapened, slashed, devalued, marked-down, discounted. **5** *a depressed area* poverty-stricken, poor, destitute, disadvantaged, deprived, needy, distressed, rundown, down-at-the-heels.
Antonyms: CHEERFUL; STRONG; PROSPEROUS.

depressing *adjective depressing news* saddening, sad, unhappy, gloomy, dismal, bleak, black, somber, grave, dreary, melancholy, dispiriting, disheartening, dejecting, discouraging, daunting, distressing, painful, heartbreaking.

depression *noun* **1** *patients suffering from depression* clinical depression, endogenous depression, reactive depression, melancholia. **2**

bad news caused her depression sadness, unhappiness, despair, gloom, glumness, dejection, downheartedness, despondency, dispiritedness, melancholy, discouragement, desolation, dolefulness, moodiness, moroseness, pessimism, hopelessness; low spirits, blues; *inf.* the dumps. **3** *a depression in the landscape* hollow, indentation, dent, cavity, concavity, dip, valley, pit, hole, bowl, sink, sinkhole, excavation. **4** *an economic depression* slump, recession, decline, slowdown, standstill; paralysis, inactivity, stagnation; hard/bad times.

deprivation *verb* **1** *the deprivation of their rights* withholding, denial, withdrawal, removal, dispossession, taking away, stripping, expropriation, seizure, confiscation, robbing, appropriation, divestment, divestiture, wresting. **2** *areas of social deprivation* poverty, hardship, privation, destitution, disadvantage, need, neediness, want, distress, detriment.

deprive *verb* *deprive them of their rights* dispossess, strip, expropriate, divest, wrest, rob.

deprived *adjective the deprived section of the community* poor, destitute, disadvantaged, needy, in need, in want, lacking, distressed, forlorn. *Antonyms:* FORTUNATE; WEALTHY.

depth *noun* **1** *measure the depth of the hole* deepness, distance downward/inward, drop, vertical extent, profundity. **2** *a person/thinker of depth* deepness, profoundness, profundity, wisdom, understanding, sagacity, discernment, insight, awareness, intuition, penetration, astuteness, acumen, shrewdness, acuity. **3** *an essay/issue of great depth* deepness, gravity, seriousness, weight, importance, moment, solemnity, complexity, intricacy, obtuseness, abstruseness, obscurity, reconditeness. **4** *the depth of the color* deepness, intensity, richness, darkness, vividness, strength, brilliance. **5** *investigating the depths of the cave/sea* deepest part, remotest area, bottom, floor, bed, abyss, back, pit; bowels. **in depth** *investigate in depth* thoroughly, extensively, comprehensively, intensively. *Antonyms:* HEIGHT; shallowness; TRIVIALITY.

deputation *noun* **1** *a deputation representing the homeless* delegation, legation, commission, embassy, committee; delegates, envoys, deputies. **2** *the deputation of new officers* appointment, designation, nomination, commission, assignment, installation, investiture, induction, ordination.

depute *verb* **1** *depute a representative* appoint, designate, nominate, commission, assign, install, invest, ordain. **2** *depute authority* delegate, transfer, assign, pass on, consign.

deputy *noun act as the chairman's deputy* substitute, stand-in, representative, second in command, assistant, surrogate, proxy, delegate, agent, spokesperson, ambassador, lieutenant,

legate, commissioner, envoy, go-between, mediator, vice president.

deputy *adjective a deputy manager* assistant, substitute, stand-in, representative, surrogate, proxy, subordinate.

deranged *adjective* mentally deranged, disturbed, unbalanced, unhinged, touched, insane, mad, crazy, crazed, demented, irrational, of unsound mind, *non compos mentis*, berserk, frenzied; *inf.* cracked, bonkers, nuts, balmy, bats, batty, dippy, cuckoo, screwy, off one's trolley/rocker, out to lunch. *Antonyms:* SANE; RATIONAL.

derelict *adjective* **1** *derelict factories/ships* abandoned, forsaken, deserted, discarded, rejected, cast off, relinquished, ownerless. **2** *living in derelict properties* dilapidated, ramshackle, tumbledown, rundown, broken-down, in disrepair, crumbling, falling to pieces, rickety, neglected. **3** *derelict officers* negligent, neglectful, remiss, lax, careless, sloppy, slipshod, slack, irresponsible, delinquent.

derelict *noun derelicts begging in the street* vagrant, tramp, beggar, bum, hobo, outcast, pariah, ne'er-do-well, good-for-nothing, wastrel.

dereliction *noun* **1** *the dereliction of the factories/ships* abandonment, forsaking, desertion, rejection, relinquishment, renunciation. *See* DERELICT *adjective* 1. **2** *accused of dereliction* negligence, neglect, neglectfulness, remissness, laxity, carelessness, sloppiness, slackness, irresponsibility, nonperformance, delinquency.

deride *verb* mock, ridicule, jeer at, scoff at, sneer at, make fun of, poke fun at, laugh at, scorn, pooh-pooh, lampoon, satirize, taunt, insult, torment, rag, tease, chaff, disdain, disparage, denigrate, slight, detract from, vilify; *fml.* contemn.

derision *noun* mockery, ridicule, jeering, scoffing, sneering, scorn, contempt, taunting, ragging, teasing, raillery, disdain, disrespect, disparagement, denigration, vilification; jeers, sneers, taunts, insults; satire, lampoon. *See* DERIDE.

derisive *adjective derisive shouts* mocking, ridiculing, jeering, scoffing, scornful, contemptuous, taunting, insulting, satirical, sarcastic, disdainful, disparaging, denigratory, derisory.

derisory *adjective* **1** *a derisory wage increase* laughable, ludicrous, ridiculous, insulting, contemptible, preposterous, outrageous, inadequate, tiny, minimal. **2** *derisory shouts* derisive, mocking, ridiculing, jeering, scoffing, scornful, contemptuous, taunting. *See* DERISIVE.

derivation *noun* **1** *the derivation of the word/custom* origin, source, root, etymology, fountainhead, wellspring, origination, beginning, foundation, basis, cause; ancestry, descent, genealogy, development, evolution. *See* DERIVE 1. **2** *undertake the derivation of the custom* tracing, tracing back. **3** *the derivation of satisfaction* *from work* deriving, acquisition, extraction. *See* DERIVE 4. **4** *the derivation of facts* deriving, collecting, collection, gathering, gleaning, winnowing, drawing out, eliciting, eduction, deduction, inference.

derivative *adjective* **1** *derivative conclusions* derived, collected, elicited, educed, deduced, inferred. *See* DERIVE 5. **2** *derivative research* imitative, unoriginal, uninventive, noninnovative, copied, plagiaristic, plagiarized, secondhand, secondary, rehashed, warmed-up, thinly disguised.

Antonyms: ORIGINAL; INVENTIVE; innovative.

derivative *noun* **1** *a derivative of coal* spin-off, by-product, offshoot. **2** *a word and its derivatives* derived word, descendant.

derive *verb* **1** *derive from a Latin word* originate in, have one's/its origins in, have as a source, stem from, descend from, spring from, arise in. **2** *derive a word* trace back, follow back, etymologize. **3** *happiness deriving from marriage* originate, stem, proceed, flow, emanate, issue. **4** *derive satisfaction* acquire, obtain, get, gain, procure, extract. **5** *derive sufficient facts* collect, gather, glean, winnow, draw out, elicit, educe, deduce, infer.

derogate *verb* **1** *derogate their achievement/character* disparage, denigrate, belittle, diminish, deprecate, depreciate, downplay, detract from, deflate, decry, discredit, downgrade, defame, vilify. **2** *derogate from old standards* deviate, degenerate, deteriorate, decline, worsen, retrogress, retrograde.

derogatory *adjective a derogatory remark* disparaging, denigratory, belittling, diminishing, slighting, deprecatory, depreciatory, depreciative, detracting, deflating, discrediting, dishonoring, unfavorable, disapproving, uncomplimentary, unflattering, insulting, offensive, damaging, injurious, defamatory, vilifying.

Antonyms: COMPLIMENTARY; FLATTERING; LAUDATORY.

descend *verb* **1** *descend the hill/stairs* go down, come down, move down, climb down, pass down. **2** *the balloon descended* go down, come down, drop, fall, sink, subside, plummet, plunge, tumble, slump. **3** *descend from the train* get down, get off, alight, dismount, disembark; detrain, deplane. **4** *the hill descended to the valley* go down, slope, incline, dip, slant. **5** *will not descend to talk to servants* condescend, stoop, lower/abase oneself. **6** *descend in quality/values* degenerate, deteriorate, decline, sink, go downhill; *inf.* go to pot, go to the dogs. **7** *enemies/visitors descending on us* attack, assault, assail, pounce, raid, swoop, charge, come in force, arrive in hordes. **8** *a family descended from John Adams* be a descendant of, derive/originate from, issue/spring from. **9** *houses descending from father to son* be handed/passed down, pass by heredity, be transferred by inheritance.

Antonyms: ASCEND; CLIMB.

descendants *plural noun* offspring, progeny, issue, family; scions.

descent *noun* **1** *the descent of the hill* going down, coming down. *See* DESCEND 1. **2** *the descent of the balloon* going down, drop, fall, sinking, subsiding, plummeting, plunge. *See* DESCEND 2. **3** *the descent from the train* getting down/off, alighting. *See* DESCEND 3. **4** *walk down the descent* slope, incline, dip, drop, gradient, declivity, declination, slant. **5** *descent in quality/values* degeneracy, deterioration, decline, debasement, degradation, sinking, decadence. *See* DESCEND 6. **6** *the descent of enemies/visitors* attack, assault, assailing, raid, charge, onslaught, incursion, foray, sortie. **7** *of German descent* ancestry, parentage, lineage, extraction, genealogy, heredity, succession, stock, line, pedigree, blood, strain; origins.

describe *verb* **1** *describe the incident* give a description/account of, give details of, detail, tell, narrate, put into words, express, recount, relate, report, set out, chronicle, define, explain, elucidate, illustrate. **2** *he was described as brilliant* designate, pronounce, style, label, characterize, portray, depict. **3** *describe a circle* draw, delineate, mark out, outline, trace, sketch.

description *noun* **1** *give a description of the incident* account, detailed statement, report, setting out, chronicle, narration, recounting, relation, commentary, explanation, elucidation, illustration; details. **2** *the description of him as dishonest* designation, pronouncement, styling, labeling, characterization, portrayal, depiction. **3** *the description of a circle* drawing, delineation, outline, tracing. *See* DESCRIBE 3. **4** *vegetables of every description* kind, sort, variety, type, brand, breed, category, class, designation, genre, ilk, mold.

descriptive *adjective* detailed, explanatory, elucidatory, graphic, vivid, striking, expressive, illustrative, pictorial, depictive, picturesque, circumstantial.

descry *verb* catch sight of, see, make out, notice, discern, perceive, observe, detect, distinguish.

desecrate *verb* violate, defile, profane, treat sacrilegiously, blaspheme, pollute, contaminate, infect, befoul, debase, degrade, dishonor, vitiate.

desert *verb* **1** *desert one's wife/post* abandon, forsake, give up, cast off, leave, turn one's back on, leave high and dry, leave in the lurch, throw over, betray, jilt, strand, leave stranded, maroon, neglect, shun, relinquish, renounce; *inf.* walk/run out on. **2** *the soldier has deserted* abscond, defect, run away, make off, decamp, flee, fly, bolt, turn tail, go AWOL, depart, quit, escape. **3** *desert a cause* abandon, forsake, turn one's back on, relinquish, renounce, betray, renege, apostatize.

Antonyms: MAINTAIN; STAY; stand by (*see* STAND).

desert *noun* **1** *lost in the African desert* wasteland, waste, wilderness, barrenness, solitude; wilds. **2** *living in a cultural desert* uninteresting place/period, unproductive place/period, wasteland.

desert *adjective* **1** *African desert regions* arid, dry, moistureless, parched, scorched, dried up, burnt, hot, burning, torrid. **2** *Arctic desert region* desolate, barren, bare, wild, empty, uninhabited, solitary, lonely, uncultivable, uncultivatable, infertile, unproductive, sterile, uncultivated, untilled.

deserted *adjective* **1** *a deserted wife* abandoned, forsaken, cast off, betrayed, jilted, stranded, marooned, neglected, shunned, relinquished, renounced, forlorn, bereft. **2** *deserted buildings* abandoned, forsaken, neglected, empty, vacant, uninhabited, unoccupied, untenanted, tenantless, unfrequented, secluded, isolated, desolate, lonely, solitary, godforsaken. **Antonyms:** CROWDED; POPULOUS.

deserter *noun* **1** *army deserters* absconder, defector, runaway, fugitive, truant, escapee, derelict. **2** *deserters from the cause* defector, renegade, turncoat, traitor, betrayer, apostate, derelict; *inf.* rat.

desertion *noun* **1** *the desertion of his wife* | *sued for desertion* abandonment, forsaking, betrayal, relinquishment, renunciation. **2** *desertion from the army* | *disciplined for desertion* absconding, defection, decamping, flight, truancy, going AWOL, departure, escape, dereliction. **3** *desertion from/of the cause* defection, betrayal, apostasy.

deserve *verb* merit, be worthy of, warrant, rate, justify, earn, be entitled to, have a right to, have a claim on, be qualified for.

deserved *adjective* well-earned, merited, warranted, justified, justifiable, earned, rightful, due, right, just, fair, fitting, appropriate, suitable, proper, reasonable.

deserving *adjective* worthy, meritorious, commendable, praiseworthy, laudable, admirable, estimable, creditable, virtuous, righteous, upright, good.

design *verb* **1** *architects designing the structure* plan, draw, draw plans of, sketch, outline, map out, plot, block out, delineate, draft, depict. **2** *designing clothes* | *designing schemes in his head* create, invent, originate, think up, conceive, fashion, fabricate, hatch, innovate; *inf.* dream up. **3** *words designed to hurt* | *a course designed for beginners* intend, aim, devise, contrive, plan, tailor, mean, destine.

design *noun* **1** *the design was left in the office* plan, blueprint, drawing, sketch, outline, map, plot, diagram, delineation, draft, depiction, scheme, model. **2** *admire the fabric designs* pattern, motif, style, arrangement, composition, makeup, constitution, configuration, organization, construction, shape, figure. **3** *a clever design to defeat the enemy* plan, enterprise, undertaking, scheme, plot, intrigue, expedient, stratagem, device, artifice. **4** *with the design of entering* intention, aim, purpose, plan, objective, goal, end, target, point, hope, desire, wish, dream, aspiration, ambition.

designate *verb* **1** *a new atomic particle designated "quark"* call, name, entitle, term, christen, dub, style, label, denominate, nickname. **2** *designated ambassador* appoint, nominate, depute, delegate, select, choose, elect, assign, allot, ordain, induct. **3** *designate the place* | *at designated times* state, appoint, specify, define, stipulate, particularize, earmark, set aside, pinpoint. **4** *arrows designating direction* show, indicate, point out, mark, denote.

designation *noun* **1** *going under the designation of financial consultant* title, name, label, appellation, epithet, tag, style, denomination, nickname, sobriquet, cognomen; *inf.* moniker. **2** *opposing his designation as ambassador* appointment, nomination, selection, election, induction. *See* DESIGNATE 2. **3** *the designation of place and time* specification, defining, stipulation, earmarking. *See* DESIGNATE 3. **4** *the designation of direction by arrows* indication, marking, denotement, denoting. *See* DESIGNATE 4.

designer *noun* **1** *designer of bridges/buildings/fabrics* creator, inventor, deviser, fashioner, originator, author, producer, architect, artificer. **2** *dress designer* couturier, fashion designer, creator, fashioner.

designing *adjective* scheming, plotting, intriguing, conspiring, conniving, calculating, Machiavellian, cunning, crafty, artful, wily, devious, shrewd, astute, sharp, insidious, treacherous, sly, underhand, deceitful, tricky; *inf.* crooked.

desirability *noun* **1** *the desirability of the property* attractiveness, allure, appeal, popularity, eligibility, agreeableness, excellence, worth. *See* DESIRABLE 1. **2** *the desirability of no one's knowing* preferableness, advisability, advantageousness, advantage, benefit, merit, value, profit, expedience. **3** *the desirability of the young woman* sexual attractiveness/attraction, attractiveness, seductiveness, allurement, eroticism, fascination; *inf.* sexiness.

desirable *adjective* **1** *a desirable job* attractive, sought-after, in demand, popular, covetable, enviable, eligible, agreeable, appealing, pleasant, admirable, worthwhile, profitable, good, excellent. **2** *it is desirable that no one knows* preferable, advisable, recommendable, advantageous, beneficial, expedient, in everyone's interests. **3** *a desirable young woman* sexually attractive, attractive, seductive, alluring, erotic, fetching, fascinating, beguiling; *inf.* sexy. **Antonyms:** UNDESIRABLE; INADVISABLE; UGLY.

desire *verb* **1** *desire happiness* wish for, want, long/yearn for, crave, set one's heart on, hanker after, have a fancy for, fancy, be bent on, covet, aspire to; *inf.* have a yen for. **2** *desire to go* wish, want, long, crave, have a fancy. **3** *desire his/her body* lust after, burn for; *inf.* lech after, have the hots for. **4** *desire a cup of tea* request, ask for, want.

desire *noun* **1** *express a desire to go* | *her desire for success* wish, want, fancy, inclination, preference; wanting, longing, yearning, craving, eagerness, enthusiasm, hankering, predilection, aspiration, proclivity, predisposition. **2** *overcome by desire* sexual attraction, lust, lustfulness, sexual appetite, passion, carnal passion, concupiscence, libido, sensuality, sexuality, lasciviousness, lechery, salaciousness, libidinousness, prurience; *inf.* the hots.

desired *adjective* **1** *fitted to the desired length* required, necessary, proper, right, correct, exact, accurate, precise, specific, particular, appropriate, fitting, suitable, preferred, expected, express. **2** *the desired prize* wished for, longed for, yearned for, craved, coveted. *See* DESIRE *verb* 1.

desirous *adjective* *desirous to win* desiring, keen, avid, eager, ambitious, hoping, aspiring, anxious, willing, wishing, ready. **desirous of** *desirous of success* desiring, wishing (for), wishful of, hopeful of, avid/eager/anxious for, craving, ambitious for.
Antonyms: averse; LOATH.

desist *verb* *they've been asked to desist* | *desist from laughing* stop, cease, discontinue, abstain, give up, forbear/refrain from, break/leave off.
Antonyms: CONTINUE; PERSIST.

desolate *adjective* **1** *desolate plains* bare, barren, bleak, dismal, desert, waste, wild. **2** *desolate farms* deserted, uninhabited, unoccupied, depopulated, forsaken, abandoned, unpeopled, untenanted, unfrequented, unvisited, solitary, lonely, isolated. **3** *desolate at the news* sad, unhappy, miserable, brokenhearted, wretched, downcast, cast down, dejected, downhearted, melancholy, gloomy, despondent, depressed, disconsolate, forlorn, cheerless, distressed, grieving, bereft.
Antonyms: FERTILE; POPULOUS; JOYFUL.

desolation *noun* **1** *the desolation of the war-torn city* destruction, laying waste, ruin, ruination, devastation, despoliation, havoc, ravaging. **2** *the desolation of the landscape* bareness, barrenness, bleakness, dismalness, wildness, isolation, solitude, solitariness, loneliness, remoteness; wasteland, wilderness, desert. **3** *her desolation at the news* sadness, unhappiness, misery, brokenheartedness, wretchedness, dejection, downheartedness, depression, melancholy, gloom, despondency, distress, grief.

despair *noun* **1** *unemployed and full of despair* hopelessness, dejection, depression, desperation, disheartenment, discouragement, despondency, disconsolateness, defeatism, pessimism, resignedness, melancholy, gloom, melancholia, misery, wretchedness, distress,

anguish. **2** *the boy is the despair of the teacher* hopeless case, bane, burden, bother, scourge.
Antonyms: HOPE; JOY.

despair *verb* lose hope, give up hope, give up, lose heart, be discouraged, be despondent, be pessimistic, resign oneself, throw in the towel.

despairing *adjective* hopeless, dejected, depressed, desperate, suicidal, disheartened, discouraged, despondent, disconsolate, inconsolable, defeatist, pessimistic, resigned, melancholy, gloomy, downcast, forlorn, miserable, wretched, distressed, brokenhearted, heartbroken, grief-stricken, sorrowing, anguished.

desperado *noun* criminal, lawbreaker, gangster, terrorist, outlaw, bandit, gunman, thug, ruffian, hooligan, villain, hoodlum, mugger.

desperate *adjective* **1** *a desperate criminal* reckless, rash, hasty, impetuous, foolhardy, audacious, daring, bold, madcap, wild, violent, frantic, mad, frenzied, lawless. **2** *a desperate act* reckless, rash, foolhardy, risky, hazardous, daring, precipitate, harebrained, wild, imprudent, incautious, injudicious, indiscreet, ill-conceived. **3** *in desperate need* urgent, pressing, compelling, acute, critical, crucial, drastic, serious, grave, dire, extreme, great. **4** *desperate for money* in great need of, urgently requiring, in want of, lacking. **5** *the desperate state of the country* grave, very bad, appalling, outrageous, intolerable, deplorable, lamentable. **6** *trying to help desperate people* despairing, hopeless, wretched. *See* DESPAIRING. **7** *desperate measures* last-ditch, last-resort, do-or-die.

desperately *adverb* *desperately ill/poor* seriously, gravely, severely, extremely, critically, acutely, dangerously, perilously.

desperation *noun* **1** *the desperation of the act* recklessness, rashness, impetuosity, foolhardiness, riskiness, audacity, boldness, wildness, imprudence, injudiciousness, violence, frenziedness, lawlessness. *See* DESPERATE 1, 2. **2** *the desperation of their state* urgency, criticalness, crucialness, seriousness, gravity, direness, extremity. **3** *the desperation of the homeless* hopelessness, despair, dejection, depression, despondency, disconsolateness, forlornness, melancholy, gloom, misery, wretchedness, distress, anguish, sorrow, pain. *See* DESPAIR *noun* 1.

despicable *adjective* contemptible, beyond contempt, reprehensible, vile, base, low, mean, scurvy, abominable, loathsome, hateful, detestable, odious, disreputable, infamous, villainous, ignoble, disgusting, sordid, distasteful, shameful, degrading, ignominious, cheap, shabby, miserable, wretched, sorry.
Antonyms: ADMIRABLE; NOBLE.

despise *verb* scorn, look down on, spurn, shun, disdain, slight, undervalue, deride, scoff/jeer at, sneer at, mock, revile, hate, detest, loathe, abhor, abominate, execrate; *fml.* contemn.

despise

abhor, contemn, detest, disdain, loathe, scorn

It's one thing to dislike someone; it's quite another to **despise** or **detest** the person. Both are strong words, used to describe extreme dislike or hatred. *Detest* is probably the purest expression of hatred (*she detested the woman who had raised her, and longed to find her own mother*), while *despise* suggests looking down with great contempt and regarding the person as mean, petty, weak, or worthless (*he despised men whose only concern was their own safety*). **Disdain** carries even stronger connotations of superiority, often combined with self-righteousness (*to disdain anyone lacking a college education*). **Scorn** is a stronger word for *disdain*, and it implies an attitude of not only contempt but of haughty rejection or refusal (*to scorn the woman he'd once loved*). To **loathe** something is to feel utter disgust toward it (*he grew to loathe peanut butter and jelly sandwiches*) and to **abhor** it is to feel a profound, shuddering, repugnance (*she abhorred the very idea of asking her husband for the money*). **Contemn** is a more literary word meaning to treat with disdain, scorn, or contempt.

---

despite *preposition* in spite of, notwithstanding, regardless of, in defiance of, in the face of.

despoil *verb* **1** *despoil the country* plunder, pillage, rob, ravage, harry, maraud, ravish, rape, depredate, raid, forage, ransack, loot, sack, rifle, devastate, lay waste, wreak havoc on, vandalize, destroy, ruin, wreck. **2** *despoil the museum of its treasures* rob, dispossess, strip, deprive, denude, divest.

despondency *noun* hopelessness, disheartenment, discouragement, disconsolateness, dispiritedness, downheartedness, despair, defeatism, melancholy, gloom, melancholia, misery, wretchedness, distress, sorrow, sadness; low spirits, doldrums, blues.

despondent *adjective* hopeless, downcast, cast down, down, low, disheartened, discouraged, disconsolate, low-spirited, dispirited, downhearted, in despair, despairing, defeatist, blue, melancholy, gloomy, glum, morose, doleful, woebegone, miserable, wretched, distressed, sorrowful, sad.
Antonyms: HOPEFUL; CHEERFUL; HAPPY.

despot *noun* absolute ruler, autocrat, dictator, tyrant, oppressor, monocrat.

despotic *adjective* absolute, autocratic, dictatorial, tyrannical, oppressive, totalitarian, domineering, imperious, arrogant, high-handed, authoritarian, arbitrary, unconstitutional.

despotism *noun* absolutism, autocracy, dictatorship, tyranny, oppression, totalitarianism, monocracy, autarchy.

destination *noun* *Vermont was our destination* journey's end, landing place, point of disem-barkation, terminus, end of the line, end, station, stop, stopping place, port of call.

destined *adjective* **1** *a plane destined for Chicago* bound for, en route for, heading for/toward, directed/routed to, scheduled for. **2** *destined for the state* designed, intended, meant, set, set apart, designated, appointed, allotted. **3** *destined to die young* fated, ordained, preordained, foreordained, predestined, predetermined, doomed, foredoomed, certain, sure, bound, written in the cards.

destiny *noun* **1** *couldn't escape his destiny* fate, fortune, lot, portion, cup, due, future, doom. **2** *destiny drew them together* fate, divine decree, predestination, luck, fortune, chance, karma, kismet; the stars.

destitute *adjective* **1** *destitute refugees* poverty-stricken, indigent, impoverished, penurious, impecunious, penniless, insolvent, beggarly, down-and-out, poor, needy, hard up, badly off, on the breadline, hard-pressed, distressed, pauperized; *inf.* up against it. **2** *destitute of ideas* devoid of, without, bereft of, deficient in, lacking, wanting, deprived of, empty, drained.
Antonyms: PROSPEROUS; WEALTHY; RICH.

destitution *noun* **1** *the destitution of the refugees* dire poverty, poverty, indigence, penury, insolvency, privation, financial distress, pauperdom; impoverishment, impecuniousness, neediness. **2** *destitution of ideas* deficiency, dearth, lack, want, need, scarcity, meagerness, deprivation.

destroy *verb* **1** *destroy the bridge* demolish, knock down, pull down, tear down, level, raze, fell, dismantle, wreck, smash, shatter, crash, blow up, blow to bits, explode, annihilate, wipe out, bomb, torpedo. **2** *destroy the countryside* ruin, spoil, devastate, lay waste, ravage, wreak havoc on, ransack. **3** *destroy their confidence* terminate, quash, quell, crush, stifle, subdue, squash, extinguish, extirpate. **4** *destroy the herd/tribe* kill, kill off, slaughter, put to sleep, exterminate; slay, murder, assassinate, wipe out, massacre, liquidate, decimate. **5** *destroy the enemy/opponents* defeat, beat, conquer, vanquish, trounce, rout, drub; *inf.* lick, thrash.
Antonyms: BUILD; CONSTRUCT; CREATE.

---

destroy

annihilate, demolish, eradicate, exterminate, extirpate, raze

If you're interested in getting rid of something, you've got a number of options at your disposal. **Destroy** is a general term covering any force that wrecks, ruins, kills, etc. (*to destroy an ant hill by pouring boiling water on it*). If it's a building, you'll want to **demolish** or **raze**, two words that are generally applied only to very large things. *Raze* is used almost exclusively with structures; it means to bring something down to the level of the ground (*they razed the apartment building to make way for the new hospital*). **Demolish** implies pulling or smashing something to pieces; when used with regard to buildings, it conjures up a vision of complete wreckage and often a heap of rubble (*their new house was demolished by the first hurricane of the season*). But unlike *raze*, demolish can also be applied to non-material things (*to demolish the theory with a few simple experiments*). If you **eradicate** something, you eliminate it completely, literally, pull it out by the roots (*to eradicate smallpox with a vaccine*) and prevent its reappearance. **Extirpate**, like *eradicate*, implies the utter destruction of something (*the species was extirpated from the park by the flooding*). If you're dealing with cockroaches, you'll probably want to **exterminate** them, which means to wipe out or kill in great numbers. Or better yet, you'll want to **annihilate** them, which is the most extreme word in this group and literally means to reduce to nothingness.

destruction *noun* **1** *the destruction of the building* demolition, knocking down, pulling down, tearing down, leveling, razing, dismantling, wrecking, smashing, blowing up, wiping out, annihilation. *See* DESTROY 1. **2** *the destruction of the countryside* ruination, spoiling, devastation, laying waste, desolation, ransacking, ravaging; ruin, havoc. **3** *the destruction of their confidence* termination, quashing, quelling, crushing, stifling, subduing, squashing, extinguishing, extirpation, extinction. **4** *the destruction of the herd/tribe* killing, slaughter, slaying, murder, assassination, massacre. *See* DESTROY 4. **5** *the destruction of the enemy/opponents* defeat, beating, conquest, vanquishing, trouncing, rout. *See* DESTROY 5.
Antonyms: CONSTRUCTION; CREATION.

destructive *adjective* **1** *destructive winds/wars* ruinous, devastating, disastrous, catastrophic, calamitous, cataclysmic, ravaging, fatal, deadly, dangerous, lethal, damaging, pernicious, noxious, injurious, harmful, detrimental, deleterious, disadvantageous. **2** *destructive children* damaging, injurious, harmful, hurtful, mischievous, pernicious. **3** *destructive comments/ criticism* nonconstructive, negative, unfavorable, adverse, antagonistic, hostile, unfriendly, contrary, discrediting, invalidating, derogatory, denigrating, disparaging, disapproving, discouraging, undermining.

desultory *adjective* halfhearted, haphazard, random, aimless, rambling, erratic, irregular, unmethodical, unsystematic, chaotic, inconsistent, inconstant, fitful, capricious.
Antonyms: THOROUGH; METHODICAL; SYSTEMATIC.

detach *verb* **1** *detach the collar* unfasten, disconnect, unhitch, remove, separate, uncouple, loosen, free, sever, tear off, disengage, disjoin, disunite. **2** *detach oneself from the group* separate, move off, dissociate, segregate, isolate, cut off, disconnect, divide.
Antonyms: ATTACH; JOIN.

detached *adjective* **1** *a detached garage* standing alone, separate, unconnected, not attached. **2** *a detached collar* unfastened, disconnected, unhitched, separate, loosened, free, severed. *See* DETACH 1. **3** *observing in a detached way* dispassionate, aloof, indifferent, unconcerned, reserved, unemotional, impersonal, cool, remote. **4** *detached commentators* objective, disinterested, unbiased, unprejudiced, impartial, nonpartisan, neutral, fair.
Antonyms: PASSIONATE; BIASED; INVOLVED.

detachment *noun* **1** *the detachment of the collar* unfastening, disconnection, unhitching, separation, uncoupling, loosening, severing, disengagement, disuniting. *See* DETACH 1. **2** *look on with detachment* dispassionateness, dispassion, aloofness, indifference, unconcern, lack of concern/emotion, reserve, coolness, remoteness. **3** *the detachment of the panel* objectivity, disinterest, lack of bias/prejudice, impartiality, nonpartisanship, neutrality, fairness. **4** *a detachment of soldiers* separate/specialized unit, task force, detail, patrol.

detail *noun* **1** *to the smallest detail* item, particular, fact, point, factor, element, circumstance, aspect, feature, respect, attribute, part, unit, component, member, accessory. **2** *don't bother with such a detail* unimportant point, insignificant item, trivial fact. **3** *the detail of soldiers for kitchen duty* assignment, allotment, delegating, deputing. **4** *pass a detail of soldiers* detachment, task force, patrol. *See* DETACHMENT 4. **details** *fill in the details* particulars, fine points, niceties, minutiae, trivia. **in detail** point by point, item by item, comprehensively, fully, thoroughly, exhaustively, blow by blow.

detail *verb* **1** *detail the arrangements* specify, set forth, set out, list, enumerate, tabulate, catalog, spell out, delineate, relate, recount, narrate, recite, rehearse, describe, cite, point out, indicate, portray, depict, itemize, particularize, individualize. **2** *detail personnel for duty* appoint, assign, allocate, delegate, select, choose, name, nominate, elect, charge, commission, send.

detailed *adjective* **1** *a detailed bill/description* itemized, particularized, full, comprehensive, thorough, exhaustive, all-inclusive, circumstantial, precise, exact, specific, particular, meticulous. **2** *a detailed picture/story* complex, involved, elaborate, complicated, intricate, convoluted, entangled.

detain *verb* **1** *detained by business* hold/keep back, hold up, delay, keep, slow up/down, hinder, impede, check, retard, inhibit, stay. **2** *detain the accused* put/keep in custody, confine, imprison, lock up, incarcerate, impound, intern, restrain, hold.

detect *verb* **1** *detect hostility/smoke* notice, note, discern, perceive, make out, observe, spot, become aware of, recognize, distinguish, identify, catch, decry, sense, see, smell. **2** *accountants* *detected the error* discover, find out, turn up, uncover, bring to light, expose, unearth, reveal, unmask, unveil.

detection *noun* **1** *the detection of hostility/smoke* noticing, discernment, perception, observation, awareness, recognition, distinguishing, identification. *See* DETECT 1. **2** *the early detection of the crime* discovery, uncovering, exposure, exposé, revelation, unmasking. *See* DETECT 2.

detective *noun* investigator; private investigator, FBI agent, police officer; *inf.* sleuth, tec, dick, private eye, private dick, tail, shadow, cop, gumshoe, G-man.

detention *noun* **1** *unavoidable detention at work* holdup, delay, slowing up, hindrance, impediment, check, retardation. *See* DETAIN 1. **2** *kept in/under detention* | *boys with a detention after school* custody, confinement, imprisonment, incarceration, internment, restraint, detainment, duress, quarantine, arrest; punishment.

deter *verb* put off, prevent, stop, discourage, dissuade, talk out of, check, restrain, caution, frighten, intimidate, daunt, scare off, warn against, hold back, prohibit, hinder, impede, obstruct, block, inhibit.
Antonyms: ENCOURAGE; PERSUADE.

detergent *noun* cleaner, cleanser; soap powder/flakes.

deteriorate *verb* **1** *moral values deteriorating* get worse, worsen, decline, degenerate, sink, slip, go downhill, slide, lapse, fail, fall, drop, ebb, wane, retrograde, retrogress, slump, depreciate; *inf.* go to pot, go to hell, go to the dogs. **2** *deteriorate their moral values* corrupt, debase, defile, impair. **3** *buildings/food deteriorating* disintegrate, become dilapidated, decline, degenerate, crumble, fall apart, fall to pieces, fall down, break up, decay, decompose, go bad.
Antonyms: IMPROVE; ameliorate.

deterioration *noun* **1** *the deterioration of morals* worsening, decline, degeneration, lapse, failure, downturn, ebb, waning, retrogression, slump, depreciation; corruption, debasement, defilement, contamination, pollution, vitiation, tainting, corrosion, impairment. *See* DETERIORATE 1,2. **2** *the deterioration of buildings/food* disintegration, dilapidation, decline, degeneration, crumbling, falling apart, erosion, decay, decomposition. *See* DETERIORATE 3.

determination *noun* **1** *behave with determination* firmness, firmness of purpose, resoluteness, steadfastness, tenacity, single-mindedness, resolve, drive, push, thrust, fortitude, dedication, backbone, stamina, mettle, strong will, persistence, perseverance, conviction, doggedness, stubbornness, obduracy, intransigence. **2** *the committee's determination* | *the legal determination* decision, conclusion, judgment, verdict, opinion, decree, solution, result, arbitration, settlement, diagnosis, prognosis.

determine *verb* **1** *determine the place of meeting* | *determine who should go* settle, fix, decide, agree on, establish, judge, arbitrate, decree, ordain. **2** *determine the argument* settle, decide, resolve, conclude, end, terminate, finish. **3** *determine the room dimensions* find out, discover, learn, establish, calculate, work out, ascertain, check, verify, certify. **4** *determine to go alone* make up one's mind, decide, resolve, choose, elect. **5** *conditions determining the nature of the soil* affect, influence, act/work on, condition, regulate, decide, control, direct, rule, dictate, govern, form, shape, modify.

determined *adjective* **1** *a determined person/attitude* firm, resolute, steadfast, tenacious, purposeful, single-minded, dedicated, strong-willed, mettlesome, plucky, persistent, persevering, dogged, unflinching, unwavering, stubborn, obdurate, intransigent, indomitable, inflexible. **2** *asked him to stay, but he was determined to go* | *determined on going* bent, intent, set.
Antonyms: IRRESOLUTE; HESITANT.

determining *adjective* *determining factors* deciding, conclusive, settling, decisive, definitive, crucial, critical, pivotal, important, essential.

deterrent *noun* curb, disincentive, discouragement, check, restraint, obstacle, hindrance, impediment, obstruction, block, barrier, inhibition.
Antonyms: INCITEMENT; INCENTIVE.

detest *verb* loathe, abhor, hate, despise, abominate, execrate, feel aversion/hostility/animosity toward, feel disgust/distaste for, recoil/shrink from, feel repugnance toward.
Antonyms: LOVE; ADORE.

detestable *adjective* loathsome, abhorrent, hateful, odious, despicable, contemptible, abominable, reprehensible, execrable, distasteful, disgusting, repugnant; *inf.* beastly.

detonate *verb* **1** *the bomb detonated* explode, go off, blow up, burst apart; bang, blast, boom. **2** *detonate the bomb* explode, set off, discharge, ignite, kindle, light, spark.

detour *noun* indirect course, roundabout/circuitous route, scenic/tourist route, diversion, digression, deviation, bypass, byway, bypath.

detract *verb* *detract his attention* distract, divert, turn away, deflect, avert, shift. **detract from** *their conduct detracts from their achievement* take away from, diminish, reduce, lessen, lower, devalue, devaluate, depreciate.
Antonym: INCREASE; ENHANCE; AUGMENT.

detractor *noun* *criticism from her detractors* belittler, disparager, denigrator, deprecator, deflater, defamer, vilifier, backbiter, carper, caviler, scandalmonger, muckraker.

detriment *noun* injury, harm, damage, impairment, hurt, loss, disadvantage, disservice, ill, wrong, mischief.
Antonyms: BENEFIT; GOOD.

detrimental *adjective* injurious, harmful, damaging, hurtful, deleterious, destructive, pernicious, disadvantageous, adverse, unfavorable, inimical, prejudicial.

Antonyms: ADVANTAGEOUS; BENEFICIAL; FAVORABLE.

detritus *noun* debris, rubble, rubbish; remains, fragments, shards, ruins; flotsam and jetsam, grit, gravel, sand, powder, dust.

devastate *verb* **1** *fire devastated the warehouse* lay waste, leave desolate, destroy, ruin, demolish, wreck, raze, level, annihilate, ravage, ransack, sack, despoil, spoil. **2** *devastated by the news* overcome, overwhelm, shock, traumatize, take aback, confound, bewilder, nonplus, disconcert, discompose, discomfit, perturb, chagrin; *inf.* floor.

devastating *adjective* **1** *devastating storms/criticism* destructive, ruinous, wrecking, deleterious, harmful, savage, annihilative. **2** *devastating news* overwhelming, shocking, traumatic, confounding, bewildering, disconcerting. *See* DEVASTATE 2. **3** *looking devastating in evening dress* stunning, glamorous, dazzling, ravishing, gorgeous, beautiful, lovely; *inf.* out of this world. **4** *devastating wit* effective, incisive, cutting, keen, mordant, biting, trenchant, satirical, sardonic, sarcastic, withering, savage.

devastation *noun* **1** *a scene of devastation* desolation, destruction, waste, ruin, wreckage. **2** *the devastation of war* laying waste, destruction, demolition, razing, annihilation. *See* DEVASTATE 1. **3** *her complete devastation* shock, traumatization, bewilderment, discomposure, discomfiture, perturbation. *See* DEVASTATE 2.

develop *verb* **1** *cities developing rapidly* grow, evolve, mature, expand, enlarge, spread, advance, progress, prosper, flourish, make headway. **2** *children developing into adults* grow, mature, turn. **3** *develop a plan* begin, commence, start, set in motion, originate, invent, form, establish, institute, fashion, generate. **4** *develop a new breed of pig/rose* generate, breed, propagate, rear, cultivate. **5** *develop a cough* begin to have, acquire, contract, pick up. **6** *develop a theme* elaborate (on), unfold, work out, enlarge on, expand (on), broaden, amplify, add to, augment, magnify, supplement, reinforce. **7** *an argument developed* begin, start, come about, follow, happen, result, ensue, breakout.

Antonyms: DETERIORATE; DEGENERATE.

development *noun* **1** *the development of cities* growth, evolution, maturing, expansion, spread, progress, headway. *See* DEVELOP 1. **2** *the development of a plan* originating, invention, forming, establishment, institution, generation. **3** *the development of a new breed* generation, breeding, propagation, rearing, cultivation. **4** *the development of themes* elaboration, unfolding, enlarging, expansion, augmentation. *See* DEVELOP 6. **5** *new developments in the affair* event, turn of events, occurrence, happening, circumstance, incident, situation, issue, outcome, upshot. **6** *a housing develop-*

ment complex, estate, structure, conglomeration.

deviant *adjective* *deviant behavior* deviating, aberrant, divergent, digressive, abnormal, irregular, nonstandard, anomalous, odd, freakish, peculiar, curious, queer, bizarre, eccentric, idiosyncratic, unorthodox, offbeat, wayward, perverse, devious, warped, twisted, perverted; *inf.* bent, kinky, quirky.

Antonyms: NORMAL; REGULAR; ORTHODOX.

deviant *noun* nonconformist, misfit, freak, rare bird, odd sort, pervert; *inf.* oddball, weirdo, dingbat, queer bird.

deviate *verb* diverge, turn aside, step aside, depart from, digress, deflect, differ, vary, change, veer, swerve, bend, drift, stray, tack.

deviation *noun* *deviation from the norm* divergence, turning aside, departure, digression, deflection, difference, variation, alteration, veering, straying, fluctuation, aberration, abnormality, irregularity, anomaly, inconsistency, discrepancy, variableness, oddness, freakishness; change, shift, veer, swerve, bend, drift.

device *noun* **1** *a handy device* appliance, gadget, implement, utensil, tool, piece of equipment/apparatus, apparatus, instrument, machine, contrivance, contraption, invention; *inf.* gizmo. **2** *win by a cunning device* design, plan, plot, scheme, ploy, project, stratagem, trick, artifice, ruse, dodge, stunt, gambit, shift, subterfuge, blind, maneuver, expedient, machination, strategy, improvisation, intrigue, conspiracy, fraud, wile, deception, imposture, sleight, humbug. **3** *the club device* emblem, symbol, insignia, crest, coat of arms, seal, badge, token, motif, design, mark, figure, motto, slogan, legend, logo, colophon, trademark.

devil *noun* **1** *the Devil defeated by God* Satan, Lucifer, Prince of Darkness, the Evil One, the Archfiend, Beelzebub, the Tempter, Lord of the Flies, *inf.* Old Nick. **2** *tempted by devils* demon, fiend, evil spirit. **3** *the master was a devil* brute, savage, beast, monster, ogre, demon, fiend, terror, barbarian, blackguard, rogue, thug, scoundrel, villain, bully, knave. **4** *the child's a little devil* imp, scamp, rascal, rogue, mischief-maker, troublemaker. **5** *feel pity for the poor devils* wretch, unfortunate, beggar, creature, thing, sad case.

devilish *adjective* **1** *devilish practices* diabolic, diabolical, demonic, demoniacal, fiendish, satanic, infernal, hellish. **2** *a devilish creature* wicked, evil, abominable, atrocious, detestable, villainous, sinister, accursed, damnable.

devil-may-care *adjective* careless, reckless, heedless, rash, audacious, wanton, impetuous, impulsive, jaunty, swaggering, nonchalant, happy-go-lucky, easygoing, casual, flippant, indifferent, unconcerned, cavalier, insouciant.

devilry, deviltry noun **1** *enemy leaders full of devilry* evil, wickedness, vice, iniquity, sin, malevolence, maliciousness, malice, viciousness, nefariousness, cruelty, savagery, villainy. **2** *the devilry of the children* devilment, mischief-making, troublemaking, roguery, impishness; mischief; *inf.* monkey business. **3** *dealing in devilry* black magic, sorcery, witchcraft, black art, diabolism.

devious adjective **1** *a devious merchant* underhand, underhanded, cunning, crafty, sly, wily, artful, guileful, scheming, designing, calculating, dishonest, deceitful, double-dealing, treacherous, misleading, subtle, insidious, surreptitious, furtive, secretive; *inf.* crooked. **2** *go by a devious route* indirect, roundabout, deviating, circuitous, tortuous, rambling, wandering, erratic, digressive, excursive.
Antonyms: HONEST; CANDID; DIRECT.

devise verb concoct, contrive, work out, plan, form, formulate, plot, scheme, project, invent, originate, create, compose, construct, frame, think/dream up, conceive, imagine, fabricate, hatch, put together, arrange, prepare, order.

devoid adjective *devoid of water/people/interest* lacking, wanting, without, deficient in, empty/vacant of, void/bare/barren of, bereft/denuded of, free from.

devolve verb **1** *power devolved to the regions* pass, hand over, transfer, delegate, consign, entrust. **2** *property devolving to a cousin* hand down, pass, transfer, convey; *Law* alienate. **3** *the argument devolves on a belief in God* depend, be dependent, rely, turn, hinge.

devote verb assign, allot, allocate, set aside, set apart, reserve, commit, apply, consign, pledge, give, offer, dedicate, surrender.

devoted adjective **1** *a devoted follower* loyal, faithful, true, true blue, staunch, steadfast, constant, committed, dedicated, devout, fond, loving, admiring, affectionate, caring, attentive, warm, ardent. **2** *time devoted to the children | time devoted to reading* assigned, allotted, set aside, dedicated. *See* DEVOTE. **3** *buildings devoted to God* dedicated, consecrated, blessed, sanctified, hallowed.
Antonyms: DISLOYAL; UNFAITHFUL; INDIFFERENT.

devotee noun enthusiast, fan, admirer, addict, follower, adherent, disciple, supporter, champion, advocate, votary, fanatic, zealot; *inf.* buff, freak.

devotion noun **1** *the devotion of his followers* loyalty, faithfulness, fidelity, trueness, staunchness, steadfastness, constancy, commitment, adherence, allegiance, dedication, devoutness, fondness, love, admiration, affection, attentiveness, care, caring, warmness, closeness. **2** *churchgoers full of devotion* devoutness, piety, religiousness, spirituality, godliness, holiness, sanctity, saintliness. **3** *look at her husband with devotion* ardor, idolization, love, fondness, affection, infatuation, passion, fervor, admiration, eagerness, yearning.
Antonyms: DISLOYALTY; INDIFFERENCE; HATRED.

devotions plural noun *morning devotions* religious worship, worship, religious observance; prayers, vespers, matins; prayer meeting, church service.

devour verb **1** *devour the feast* eat greedily/hungrily, eat up, consume, swallow up, gulp down, gobble up, bolt, wolf down, guzzle, stuff down, cram in, gorge oneself on, feast on; *inf.* tuck into, pack away, dispatch, polish off, stuff one's face with, pig out on. **2** *flames devouring the house* consume, engulf, envelop, destroy, devastate, lay waste, demolish, wipe out, ruin, wreck, annihilate. **3** *hobbies devouring time/money* consume, use up, cost, spend, waste. **4** *children devouring books* be absorbed in, be engrossed in, take in, drink in/up, feast on, revel in, delight in, enjoy, relish, appreciate. **5** *devoured by anxiety/jealousy* consume, swallow up, engulf, swamp, overcome, overwhelm.

devout adjective **1** *a devout Christian* pious, religious, reverent, churchgoing, godly, saintly, holy, prayerful, orthodox, pure, righteous. **2** *devout hope* sincere, genuine, deep, profound, heartfelt, earnest, fervent, fervid, intense, ardent, vehement, passionate, zealous.
Antonyms: IMPIOUS; IRREVERENT; INSINCERE.

dexterity noun **1** *craftsmen showing dexterity* manual dexterity, deftness, adroitness, nimbleness of fingers, nimbleness, agility, skillfulness, skill, knack, adeptness, handiness, facility, proficiency, expertise, talent, artistry, craft, mastery, finesse, effortlessness, felicity. **2** *crisis management requires dexterity* mental dexterity/agility, cleverness, shrewdness, smartness, astuteness, cunning, craft, sagacity, sharp-wittedness, acuteness, ingenuity, resourcefulness, inventiveness.

dexterous adjective **1** *dexterous craftsmen* deft, adroit, nimble, agile, skillful, skilled, adept, handy, proficient, expert, talented, accomplished, artistic. *See* DEXTERITY 1. **2** *a dexterous businessman* clever, shrewd, smart, astute, cunning, crafty, wily, artful, sagacious, sharp-witted, acute, ingenious, resourceful, inventive.
Antonyms: CLUMSY; AWKWARD; INEPT.

diabolic, diabolical adjective **1** *diabolic forces* devilish, fiendish, demonic, demoniacal, satanic, infernal, hellish. **2** *a diabolic slave master* fiendish, wicked, evil, sinful, savage, brutish, monstrous, barbaric, cruel, malevolent, malicious, black-hearted, nasty, abominable, hateful, damnable. **3** *a diabolic task* difficult, complicated, complex, tricky, nasty, unpleasant, dreadful, vile.

diadem noun crown, coronet, tiara, circlet, headband, wreath, chaplet, fillet.

diagnose verb *diagnose measles* identify, determine, distinguish, recognize, detect, pinpoint, pronounce.

diagnosis noun **1** *a diagnosis of measles* identification, recognition, detection, pinpointing. *See* DIAGNOSE. **2** *tests confirming the doctor's diagnosis* opinion, pronouncement, judgment, conclusion, interpretation.

diagonal *adjective* crossing, crossways, crosswise, slanting, slanted, sloping, oblique, angled, cornerways, cornerwise.

diagonally *adverb* crossways, crosswise, on the cross, on the slant, aslant, obliquely, at an angle, on the bias, cornerways, cornerwise.

diagram *noun* line drawing, drawing, sketch, draft, illustration, picture, representation, outline, delineation.

dial *verb* *dial the number* telephone, phone, call.

dialect *noun* regional language, variety of language, vernacular, patois, nonstandard language; regionalism, localism, provincialism; *inf.* local lingo.

---

dialect
argot, cant, jargon, lingo, slang, vernacular

When a New York City cab driver calls out the window, "Hey, wassa madda wichoo?" he is using the **vernacular**, which is the authentic, natural pattern of speech among those belonging to a certain community. In some areas of London, on the other hand, one might hear the Cockney **dialect**, which is a form or variety of a language that is confined to a specific group or locality; it has its own pronunciation, usage, and vocabulary, and may persist for generations or even centuries (*he spoke in the dialect of the Appalachian backwoodsman*). A teenager who tells his parents to "Chill out" is using **slang**, which is a very informal language that includes substitute vocabulary (wheels for *car*, rug for *toupee*), grammatical distortions, and other departures from formal or polite usage. **Argot** refers to the slang of a group that feels threatened by the hostility of society as a whole; it traditionally refers to the slang used by criminals and thieves, although it may refer to any peculiar language that a clique or other closely knit group uses to communicate with each other. At one time **cant** was a synonym for *argot*, but now it usually refers to pompous, inflated language or the hackneyed use of words and phrases by members of a particular class or profession (*the cant of the fashion industry*). In contrast to *cant*, which can at least be understood, **jargon** is nearly impossible for the average person to decipher. This term refers to the technical or highly specialized language used by members of an occupational or professional group (*medical jargon , the jargon of the theater*). If you are frustrated because you can't understand the language used by a particular class or group, you're apt to refer to their way of talking as **lingo**, which is a term for any language that is not readily understood (*she tried to reason with the cab driver, but she couldn't understand his lingo*).

dialectic *noun* discussion, debate, dialogue, disputation, argument, argumentation, contention, polemic, war of words, reasoning.

dialectic *adjective* dialectical, logical, analytical, disputatious, argumentative, contentious, polemic, rational, rationalistic.

dialogue *noun* **1** *the dialogue between friends | dialogue between the two sides* conversation, talk, tête-à-tête, chat, chitchat, gossip, communication, debate, argument, exchange of views, discourse, discussion, conference, converse, colloquy, interlocution, duologue, confabulation, parley, palaver; *inf.* powwow, confab, rap session. **2** *the dialogue of the novel/play* conversation, spoken part, script; lines.

diameter *noun* breadth, width, thickness, caliber.

diametrical *adjective* *diametrical differences/opposition* direct, absolute, complete, exact, extreme, diametrically opposite, opposite, contrasting, conflicting, contrary, counter, antithetical, antipodal.

diaphanous *adjective* sheer, fine, delicate, light, thin, silken, chiffony, gossamer, gauzy, cobwebby, translucent, transparent, see-through. *Antonyms:* THICK; COARSE; OPAQUE.

diarrhea *noun* loose bowels, looseness of the bowels; *inf.* the runs, the trots, Montezuma's revenge.

diary *noun* **1** *noted the meeting in her diary* appointment/engagement book, personal organizer. **2** *kept a diary of her vacation* day-by-day account, daily record, journal, chronicle, log, logbook, history, annals.

diatribe *noun* tirade, harangue, verbal onslaught, stream of abuse, denunciation, philippic, reproof, reprimand, rebuke, upbraiding; invective, vituperation, abuse, castigation, criticism, stricture; *inf.* tongue-lashing, knocking.

dicey *adjective* uncertain, risky, chancy, difficult, tricky, dangerous, ticklish; *inf.* hairy.

dictate *verb* **1** *dictate the letter* read out/out loud, read aloud, speak, say, utter, recite. **2** *dictate terms* prescribe, lay down, impose, set down, order, command, decree, ordain, direct, pronounce, enjoin, promulgate. **3** *always dictating to others* give orders, order about, lay down the law, impose one's will, boss about, domineer; *inf.* call the shots, throw one's weight around.

dictate *noun* **1** *at the commander's dictate* order, command, decree, edict, ordinance, dictum, direction, bidding, charge, behest, pronouncement, mandate, requirement, enjoining, injunction, ultimatum, promulgation. **2** *the dictates of conscience* code, guiding principle, law, rule, precept, dictum, axiom, maxim.

dictator *noun* absolute ruler, despot, autocrat, tyrant, oppressor.

dictatorial *adjective* **1** *dictatorial government* absolute, unlimited, unrestricted, arbitrary, omnipotent, all-powerful, autocratic, totalitarian,

authoritarian, despotic, tyrannical, autarchic. **2** *dictatorial bosses* tyrannical, despotic, oppressive, iron-handed, imperious, overbearing, domineering, peremptory, high-handed, authoritarian, dogmatic, high and mighty; *inf.* bossy.
Antonyms: DEMOCRATIC; LIBERAL; LIMITED; SUBMISSIVE.

dictatorship *noun* **1** *living in dictatorships* autarchy, totalitarian state, absolute monarchy, reign of terror. **2** *revolting against dictatorship* absolute rule, despotism, autocracy, tyranny, authoritarianism, totalitarianism, absolutism.

diction *noun* **1** *learn diction through elocution lessons* enunciation, articulation, elocution, pronunciation, speech, intonation, inflection, delivery, fluency, rhetoric. **2** *impressed by the writer's diction* style, language, phraseology, phrasing, wording, usage, vocabulary, terminology, expression, idiom.

dictionary *noun* glossary, lexicon, wordbook, vocabulary list.

dictum *noun* **1** *the chairman's dictum* utterance, pronouncement, direction, injunction, assertion, statement, dictate, command, order, decree, edict. **2** *as the dictum has it* saying, maxim, axiom, proverb, adage, aphorism, saw, truism, platitude, cliché.

didactic *adjective* *didactic prose* instructive, instructional, educational, educative, informative, informational, edifying, preceptive, pedagogic, pedantic, moralistic.

die *verb* **1** *she died last night* pass away, pass on, lose one's life, depart this life, expire, decease, breathe one's last, meet one's end, lay down one's life, be no more, perish, go to one's last resting place; *inf.* give up the ghost, kick the bucket, push up the daisies, bite the dust, snuff it, croak, turn up one's toes, cash in one's chips. **2** *hope died* come to an end, end, vanish, disappear, pass, fade, fall away, dwindle, melt away, dissolve, subside, decline, sink, lapse, ebb, wane, wilt, wither, evanesce. **3** *the engine died* stop, halt, fail, break down, peter out, fizzle out, run down, fade away, lose power. **4** *thought I would die laughing* collapse with, be overcome with, be overwhelmed/overpowered by, succumb to. **5** *she's dying for water* | *dying to see you* be eager, be desperate, long.
Antonyms: LIVE; EXIST; START.

diehard *adjective* ultraconservative, conservative, reactionary, dyed in the wool, intransigent, inflexible, immovable, unchanging, uncompromising, unyielding, indomitable, adamant, rigid.

diet[1] *noun* **1** *eat a healthy diet* selection of food, food and drink, food, fare; foodstuffs, provisions, victuals, comestibles, edibles, viands, rations; nourishment, nutriment, sustenance, aliment. **2** *go on a diet* dietary regimen/regime,

abstinence, period of fasting, fast; restricted diet, crash diet.

diet[2] *verb* *dieting to lose several pounds* follow a diet, be on a diet, eat sparingly/selectively, abstain, fast, reduce, lose weight.
Antonyms: OVERINDULGE; GUZZLE.

diet[3] *noun* **1** *elected to the diet* legislative assembly, congress, parliament, council, senate, synod. **2** *attend an international diet* conference, convention, assembly, convocation, conclave, session.

differ *verb* **1** *tastes differ* be different, be unlike, be dissimilar, be distinguishable, vary, diverge. **2** *parties agreeing to differ* disagree, fail to agree, dissent, be at variance, be in dispute/opposition, oppose, take issue, conflict, clash, quarrel, argue, wrangle, quibble, squabble, altercate. **differ from** *results differing from the norm* vary from, diverge from, deviate from, depart from, run counter to, contravene, contradict, contrast with.
Antonyms: AGREE; COINCIDE.

difference *noun* **1** *the difference between/in their lifestyles* dissimilarity, unlikeness, dissimilitude, contrast, distinction, distinctness, differentiation, variance, variation, divergence, deviation, contrariety, antithesis, contradiction, contradistinction, nonconformity, disparity, imbalance, incongruity. **2** *spot the difference* distinction, peculiarity, oddity, idiosyncrasy, singularity, eccentricity, individuality. **3** *the two had a difference* difference of opinion, disagreement, dispute, disputation, argument, debate, misunderstanding, quarrel, row, wrangle, set-to, tiff, altercation, contretemps, clash, controversy, feud, vendetta. **4** *pay the difference* balance, remainder, rest, residue, residuum, excess.
Antonyms: SIMILARITY; LIKENESS; AFFINITY.

different *adjective* **1** *our lifestyles are different* | *tastes different from ours* unlike, dissimilar, nonidentical, contrasting, diverse, divergent, deviating, disparate, incompatible, inconsistent, opposed, at variance, at odds, clashing, conflicting, discrepant. **2** *looking completely different from last year* changed, altered, modified, transformed, metamorphosed. **3** *a different dress every day* separate, other, not the same, nonidentical, distinct, individual, discrete. **4** *different people have commented* | *available in different colors* various, several, many, numerous, some, sundry, certain, assorted, varied, miscellaneous, diverse, manifold, multifarious, motley, variegated. **5** *looking for something different* unusual, out of the ordinary, uncommon, distinctive, rare, unique, novel, special, singular, remarkable, extraordinary, noteworthy, unconventional, atypical, odd, strange, bizarre; *inf.* something else.
Antonyms: SIMILAR; ALIKE; SAME; ORDINARY.

differential *adjective* *differential treatment/rates* distinctive, distinguishing, discriminating, discriminatory, different.

differential noun *maintain salary differentials* distinction, discrimination, difference; amount of difference, disparity, discrepancy.

differentiate verb **1** *differentiate between grades | can you differentiate the twins?* distinguish, discriminate, make a distinction, contrast, see/discern a difference; tell apart, set apart, separate, mark off. **2** *the yellow beak differentiates the male bird* make different, distinguish, set apart, contrast, identify. **3** *in time the species differentiated* modify, alter, change, become different, transform, adapt.

difficult adjective **1** *digging in this soil is difficult* hard, strenuous, arduous, laborious, demanding, formidable, tough, onerous, burdensome, exhausting, tiring, wearisome, backbreaking, painful, oppressive; *inf.* no picnic. **2** *a difficult problem* hard, complicated, complex, involved, intricate, puzzling, problematic, baffling, perplexing, knotty, thorny, ticklish, delicate, obscure, abstract, abstruse, recondite, enigmatic, profound, deep. **3** *a difficult child* troublesome, tiresome, demanding, unmanageable, intractable, perverse, recalcitrant, obstreperous, refractory, fractious, unaccommodating, uncooperative, uncompliant, unamenable. **4** *difficult people to choose presents for* hard to please/satisfy, fussy, particular, fastidious, perfectionist, critical, hypercritical, finicky. **5** *arrive at a difficult time* inconvenient, ill-timed, disadvantageous, unfavorable. **6** *go through difficult times* hard, straitened, hard-pressed, bad, tough, grim, dark.
Antonyms: EASY; SIMPLE; ACCOMMODATING.

difficulty noun **1** *dig with difficulty* difficultness, hardness, strenuousness, arduousness, laboriousness, toughness, struggling, awkwardness; labor, strain, struggle. **2** *the difficulty of the problem* difficultness, hardness, complicatedness, complexity, intricacy, perplexity, knottiness, delicacy, obscurity, abstruseness. **3** *encounter a difficulty* complication, problem, snag, hitch, hindrance, obstacle, pitfall, hurdle, impediment, obstruction, barrier. **4** *raise difficulties* protest, objection, complaint, gripe, demur, cavil. **5** *in difficulty | in financial difficulties* predicament, quandary, dilemma, plight, distress, embarrassment, trouble, hot/deep water; straits; *inf.* fix, jam, spot, scrape. **6** *the difficulty of the times* hardship, trial, tribulation, ordeal, exigency.
Antonym: EASE.

diffidence noun shyness, bashfulness, modesty, sheepishness, timidity, timidness, timorousness, apprehension, reserve, hesitancy, reluctance, constraint, doubt, insecurity, distrust, suspicion, unobtrusiveness, self-effacement, humility, meekness.

diffident adjective shy, bashful, modest, sheepish, unconfident, unassertive, timid, timorous, apprehensive, fearful, shrinking, reserved, withdrawn, hesitant, reluctant, doubtful, unsure,

insecure, distrustful, suspicious, unobtrusive, self-effacing, unassuming, humble, meek.
Antonyms: BOLD; ASSERTIVE.

diffuse adjective **1** *diffuse light* diffused, spread out, scattered, dispersed, not concentrated. **2** *a diffuse style* verbose, wordy, prolix, longwinded, copious, profuse, discursive, rambling, wandering, meandering, digressive, circuitous, roundabout, circumlocutory, waffling, loose, vague.
Antonyms: CONCENTRATED; CONCISE; SUCCINCT.

diffuse verb spread around, send out, scatter, disperse, disseminate, dissipate, dispel, distribute, dispense, circulate, propagate, broadcast, promulgate, effuse.

diffusion noun **1** *the diffusion of light/knowledge* scattering, spreading, dispersal, dissemination, dispelling, distribution, dispensation, circulation, propagation, broadcasting, promulgation, effusion. **2** *writers given to diffusion* diffuseness, verbosity, verbiage, wordiness, prolixity, long-windedness, loquaciousness, loquacity, profuseness, discursiveness, rambling, wandering, digressiveness, circuitousness, circumlocution, waffling.

dig verb **1** *enjoy digging | dig the earth* break up soil/ground; work, break up, loosen up, turn over, spade, delve, till, cultivate, harrow, plow. **2** *dig a tunnel/hole* dig out, excavate, quarry, hollow out, scoop out, gouge, tunnel, burrow, mine, channel. **3** *dig someone in the ribs* poke, prod, jab, thrust, drive, push, punch. **4** *dig into the history* delve, search, probe, investigate, research. **5** *dig potatoes* unearth, dig up. **6** *dig the music* like, love, enjoy, appreciate. **7** *I dig what you're saying* understand, comprehend, follow, grasp, make out; *inf.* get. **dig up 1** *dig up the corpse* exhume, bring to the surface, unearth. **2** *dig up new information* unearth, uncover, root out, extricate, bring to light, come up with, expose, discover, find, come across.

dig noun **1** *a dig in the ribs* poke, prod, jab, thrust, push, punch. **2** *tired of digs at/about his baldness* cutting remark, gibe, jeer, taunt, sneer, insult, slur, quip, insinuation; *inf.* wisecrack, crack.

digest verb **1** *digest food* assimilate, absorb, break down, dissolve, macerate. **2** *digest the facts* assimilate, absorb, take in, understand, comprehend, grasp, master, consider, think about, contemplate, mull over, weigh up, reflect on, ponder, meditate on, study. **3** *digest the information* shorten, reduce, condense, abridge, compress, compact, summarize, précis.

digest noun *a digest of the week's news* summary, synopsis, abstract, précis, résumé, outline, abridgment, epitome, review, compendium.

digestion noun **1** *digestion of food* assimilation, absorption, breaking down, dissolution, maceration. **2** *digestion of facts* assimilation, absorption, understanding, comprehension, mastery, consideration, contemplation. *See* DIGEST *verb* 2.

dignified *adjective* stately, noble, solemn, grave, formal, decorous, reserved, ceremonious, courtly, majestic, august, lofty, exalted, regal, lordly, imposing, impressive, grand.

dignify *verb* add dignity/distinction to, distinguish, honor, grace, adorn, exalt, enhance, ennoble, glorify, elevate, make lofty, aggrandize, upgrade.

dignitary *noun* public figure, notable, notability, worthy, personage, luminary, VIP, pillar of society, leading light, celebrity, big name, somebody, star, lion; *inf.* bigwig, top brass, big gun, big shot, big wheel, celeb.

dignity *noun* **1** *the dignity of the occasion* stateliness, nobleness, nobility, solemnity, gravity, formality, decorum, propriety, reserve, ceremoniousness, courtliness, majesty, augustness, loftiness, exaltedness, regalness, regality, lordliness, impressiveness, grandeur. **2** *the dignity of work* worthiness, honorability, nobility, excellence, respectability; worth, merit, virtue. **3** *achieve dignity in social affairs* high rank, high standing, high station, status, elevation, eminence, honor, glory, greatness, importance. **4** *conscious of their dignity* pride, self-esteem, self-conceit, self-regard, self-importance, self-respect.
Antonyms: INFORMALITY; DISHONOR; DEGRADATION.

digress *verb* get off the subject, stray from the point, deviate/deflect from the topic, go off at a tangent, diverge, turn aside, depart, drift, ramble, wander, meander.

digression *noun* **1** *his usual digression from the subject* straying, deviation, divergence, diversion, departure, drifting, rambling. *See* DIGRESS. **2** *an essay full of digressions* aside, deviation, deflection, detour, excursion, excursus, apostrophe, incidental remark.

dilapidated *adjective* rundown, broken-down, tumbledown, ramshackle, in ruins, ruined, falling to pieces, falling apart, in disrepair, shabby, battered, rickety, shaky, crumbling, decayed, decaying, decrepit, worn-out, neglected, uncared-for.

dilate *verb* **1** *her pupils dilated* enlarge, widen, expand. **2** *dilate on the subject* expand, expound, expatiate, elaborate.
Antonyms: NARROW; CONTRACT.

dilatory *adjective* slow, tardy, sluggish, snail-like, lazy, slack, indolent, delaying, dallying, dilly-dallying, loitering, lingering, dawdling, tarrying, procrastinating, postponing, deferring, putting off, tabling, shelving, temporizing, stalling, time-wasting.
Antonyms: FAST; PROMPT.

dilemma *noun* difficult choice, devil and the deep blue sea, Catch-22, vicious circle, quandary, predicament, plight, difficulty, tight corner/spot, problem, puzzle, mess, muddle; trouble, perplexity, confusion, embarrassment.

dilettante *noun* **1** *plays tennis well for a dilettante* dabbler, trifler, dallier, amateur, nonprofessional. **2** *dilettantes always at the art gallery* art lover, lover of the arts, connoisseur, aesthete.

diligence *noun* assiduity, assiduousness, application, concentration, industriousness, conscientiousness, attentiveness, heedfulness, constancy, intentness, earnestness, perseverance, sedulousness, persistence, tenacity, pertinacity, doggedness, laboriousness; care, attention, industry.

diligent *adjective* assiduous, industrious, conscientious, hardworking, painstaking, meticulous, thorough, careful, attentive, heedful, intent, earnest, studious, constant, persevering, sedulous, persistent, tenacious, zealous, active, busy, untiring, tireless, indefatigable, dogged, plodding, slogging, laborious.
Antonyms: LAZY; CARELESS; INDIFFERENT.

dilly-dally *verb* dally, dawdle, loiter, linger, take one's time, delay, waste time, tarry, hover, kill time, trifle, procrastinate, dither, hesitate, falter, vacillate, waver, shilly-shally, hem and haw, fluctuate.

dilute *verb* **1** *dilute the solution* make weaker, weaken, make thinner, thin out, water down, cut, adulterate. **2** *dilute the colorful details | dilute standards* make weaker, weaken, attenuate, reduce, diminish, decrease, lessen, mitigate, temper.
Antonyms: CONCENTRATE; THICKEN; INTENSIFY.

dim *adjective* **1** *a dim light* faint, weak, feeble, pale, dull, dingy, lusterless, muted. **2** *dim skies* dark, darkish, gray, overcast, leaden, gloomy, somber, dusky, lowering, cloudy, hazy, misty, foggy, crepuscular, tenebrous. **3** *dim corridors* dark, darkened, gloomy, badly lit, poorly lit, dingy, dismal. **4** *a dim shape* vague, ill-defined, indistinct, unclear, shadowy, blurred, blurry, fuzzy, imperceptible, nebulous, obscured, bleared, bleary, obfuscated. **5** *a dim recollection* vague, indistinct, hazy, confused, blurred, shadowy, imperfect, obscure, remote. **6** *rather dim people* stupid, thick, dense, slow-witted, slow, dull, doltish, limited, obtuse; *inf.* dumb, slow on the uptake. **7** *prospects are rather dim* gloomy, somber, unpromising, unfavorable, discouraging, disheartening, depressing, dispiriting.
Antonyms: BRIGHT; DISTINCT; CLEVER.

dim *verb* **1** *dim the stage lights* turn down, lower. **2** *the light dimmed* grow dim, fade, grow faint/feeble, dull, pale, blur. **3** *the skies dimmed* grow dark, darken, cloud over, grow leaden. *See* DIM *adjective* 2. **4** *memories/recollections dimming* grow dim, fade, blur, become blurred/confused.
Antonym: BRIGHTEN.

dimension *noun* **1** *of huge dimension | the dimensions of the tank* measured extent, extent;

length, width, breadth, depth, area, size, volume, capacity, bulk; proportions. **2** *add another dimension to entertainment* aspect, side, feature, facet, element. **dimensions** *underestimate the dimensions of the problem* size, extent, scope, measure, scale, range, magnitude, greatness, importance.

diminish *verb* **1** *their power/strength diminished* lessen, grow less, decrease, reduce, shrink, contract, abate, grow weak/weaker. **2** *time diminished their power/strength* lessen, lower, decrease, reduce, curtail, cut, contract, narrow, constrict, truncate, retrench. **3** *the storm/empire diminished* subside, ebb, recede, wane, dwindle, slacken, die/fall away, fade, decline, die/peter out. **4** *try to diminish him* | *diminish his reputation* belittle, disparage, denigrate, depreciate, deprecate, derogate, devalue, demean, detract from, cheapen, defame, vilify. **Antonyms:** INCREASE; GROW; BOOST.

diminution *noun* **1** lessening, lowering, decrease, reduction, contraction, abatement, weakening, curtailment, cut, cutback, constriction, truncating, retrenchment. *See* DIMINISH 1, 2. **2** *the diminution of the storm/empire* subsidence, ebb, receding, recession, wane, slackening, dying away, failing, decline. *See* DIMINISH 3.

diminutive *adjective* small, little, tiny, petite, slight, elfin, minute, miniature, mini, small-scale, compact, microscopic, midget, undersized, dwarfish, pygmy, Lilliputian; *inf.* wee, baby. **Antonyms:** ENORMOUS; GIGANTIC.

din *noun* loud noise, uproar, row, racket, commotion, hullabaloo, hubbub, tumult, clangor, outcry, brouhaha, crash, clatter, clash, shouting, yelling; clamor, noise, pandemonium, bedlam, babel. **Antonyms:** SILENCE; HUSH.

dine *verb* *we dine at eight* have dinner/supper, eat, sup, feed, feast, banquet. *See* DINNER. **dine on** *dine on game* eat, consume, feed on.

dingy *adjective* dark, dull, dim, gloomy, drab, dismal, dreary, cheerless, dusky, somber, murky, hazy, smoggy, smoky, sooty, dirty, discolored, grimy, soiled, faded, shabby, worn, seedy, run-down, tacky. **Antonyms:** BRIGHT; well-lit; CLEAN.

dinky *adjective* *stopped at a dinky restaurant* small, shabby, unimpressive, unimportant, trifling.

dinner *noun* *come to dinner* | *the firm's annual dinner* evening meal, supper, main meal, lunch, repast, refection; feast, banquet; *inf.* spread, blowout.

dinosaur *noun. See also table at* FOSSIL.

dint *noun* **by dint of** by means of, by (the) force/power of, by use of, by virtue of.

dip *verb* **1** *dip the garment in dye* immerse, submerge, plunge, duck, dunk, lower, sink, souse, douse, soak, drench, steep, bathe, rinse. **2** *the sun dipping behind the horizon* sink, set, go/drop down, descend, fade, disappear, subside. **3** *profits dipping* fall, go down, drop, drop/fall off, decrease, decline, slump. **4** *the road dips* slope down, slope, descend, go down, fall, sink, decline, slant down, droop, sag. **5** *dip water* scoop up, scoop, spoon, ladle. **dip into 1** *dip into a book* skim, browse, look through, glance at, run through. **2** *dip into art* dabble in, scratch the surface of, play at, sample. **3** *dip into one's purse* | *dip into the barrel* reach into, put one's hand into, go into. **4** *dip into one's savings* draw on, take out of, use/spend part of. **Antonyms:** RISE; ASCEND.

dip *noun* **1** *give the garment/sheep a dip* immersion, plunge, ducking, dunking, sousing, dousing, soaking, drenching. *See* DIP *verb* 1. **2** *take a dip* swim, dive, plunge. **3** *a dip in profits* fall, falling-off, drop, dropping-off, decrease, decline, lowering, slump. **4** *a dip in the terrain* slope, incline, decline, slant, descent, hollow, concavity, depression, basin.

diplomacy *noun* **1** *ministers skilled in diplomacy* statesmanship, statecraft, international relations/politics; negotiations. **2** *treating her parents' objections with diplomacy* tactfulness, subtlety, discretion, judiciousness, prudence, delicacy, sensitivity, finesse, savoir faire, politeness, cleverness, artfulness, cunning, tact, care, skill.

diplomat *noun* **1** *an international meeting of diplomats* ambassador, foreign minister, envoy, emissary, legate, consul, attaché. **2** *the diplomat of the firm* tactful person, conciliator, reconciler, peacemaker, mediator, negotiator, tactician, arbitrator, intermediary, moderator, go-between, middleman, public relations officer.

diplomatic *adjective* **1** *a diplomatic post* ambassadorial, consular, foreign office. **2** *diplomatic handling* | *a diplomatic young woman* tactful, subtle, discreet, judicious, prudent, careful, delicate, sensitive, polite, politic, clever, skillful, artful. **Antonyms:** INDISCREET; TACTLESS.

dire *adjective* **1** *in dire straits* | *dire poverty* terrible, dreadful, appalling, frightful, awful, horrible, atrocious, grim, cruel, grievous, disastrous, ruinous, miserable, wretched, woeful, calamitous, catastrophic, cataclysmic, distressing, harrowing, alarming, unspeakable, shocking, outrageous. **2** *dire warnings* ominous, sinister, portentous, gloomy, gloom-and-doom, grim, dreadful, dismal, unpropitious, inauspicious, unfavorable, pessimistic. **3** *in dire need of money* urgent, desperate, drastic, pressing, crying, vital, grave, critical, crucial, extreme, compelling, exigent. **Antonyms:** WONDERFUL; DELIGHTFUL.

direct *verb* **1** *direct the operation* administer, manage, be in charge/control/command of, lead, run, command, control, govern, conduct, handle, preside over, rule, supervise, superintend, oversee, guide, mastermind, regulate, orchestrate, engineer, dispose, dominate, domineer; *inf.* be the boss of, run the show, call the shots. **2** *directed to work late* command, order, give orders to, instruct, charge, bid, dictate, adjure, enjoin. **3** *direct them to the station* give directions to, show/point/indicate the way, guide, steer, lead, conduct, accompany, usher, escort, navigate, pilot. **4** *direct the correspondence* address, label, superscribe, post, send, mail. **direct at** *remarks directed at parents* aim at, address to, intend/mean for, destine for, focus on, point/level at, train at, turn on, fix on.

direct *adjective* **1** *a direct road* straight, undeviating, unswerving, uncircuitous, shortest. **2** *a direct train/journey* straight through, through, nonstop, unbroken, uninterrupted. **3** *a direct approach* immediate, firsthand, personal, face-to-face, head-on, noninterventional. **4** *a direct statement/manner* frank, blunt, straightforward, straight, straight to the point, explicit, clear, plain, unequivocal, unambiguous, honest, candid, open, sincere, plainspoken, outspoken, forthright, downright, point blank, matter-of-fact, categorical. **5** *the direct opposite* exact, absolute, complete, downright, thorough, diametrical. **6** *a direct quotation* exact, precise, word for word, verbatim, accurate, correct.
Antonyms: INDIRECT; EVASIVE; AMBIGUOUS.

direction *noun* **1** *the/his direction of the project* administration, management, government, supervision, superintendence, regulation, orchestration; control, command, conduct, handling, running, overseeing, masterminding, disposal; leadership, guidance. *See* DIRECT *verb* 1. **2** *ignore the teacher's direction* command, order, instruction, bidding, charge, dictate, enjoinment, prescription. **3** *which direction did they take?* way, route, course, path, track, road, line, run, bearing, orientation. **4** *the direction of their policy/statement* drift, aim, tack, scope, bent, bias, tendency, current, trend, tenor, inclination, leaning, proclivity, orientation.

directions *plural noun* instructions, guidelines, rules, regulations, recommendations, indications; guidance, briefing; plan.

directive *noun* direction, command, order, instruction, charge, bidding, injunction, ruling, regulation, dictate, decree, edict, notice, ordinance, enjoinment, prescription, mandate, fiat.

directly *adverb* **1** *travel directly* straight, in a straight line, as the crow flies, by the shortest route, without deviation. **2** *leave directly* immediately, at once, instantly, right/straight away, now, instantaneously, without delay/hesitation, quickly, speedily, promptly, soon, as soon as possible, shortly, in a little while; *inf.* pronto. **3** *speak directly* frankly, bluntly, straightforwardly, explicitly, clearly, plainly,

unequivocally, unambiguously, sincerely, truthfully, outspokenly, forthrightly, pointblank, matter-of-factly, categorically, without prevarication. **4** *talk directly to the manager* at first hand, firsthand, personally, face to face, head on. **5** *it's directly opposite* exactly, immediately, diametrically.

director *noun* administrator, controller, manager, executive, chairman, chairwoman, chairperson, chair, head, chief, principal, leader, governor, president, superintendent, supervisor, overseer, organizer, producer; *inf.* boss, kingpin, top dog, honcho.

dirge *noun* elegy, lament, funeral song/chant, burial hymn, dead march, requiem, keen, threnody.

dirt *noun* **1** *clean the dirt from the room* grime, dust, soot, smut, muck, mud, filth, mire, sludge, slime, ooze, waste, dross, pollution; smudge, stain, tarnish; *inf.* crud, yuck, grunge. **2** *piles of dirt by the roadside* earth, soil, loam, clay, silt. **3** *disapprove of the dirt in modern novels* obscenity, indecency, smut, sordidness, coarseness, bawdiness, ribaldry, salaciousness, lewdness, pornography; *inf.* sleaze, sleaziness. *See* DIRTY *adjective* 2. **4** *spreading dirt about the neighbors* scandal, gossip, talk, rumor, slander, libel; revelations.

dirty *adjective* **1** *dirty rooms/clothes* unclean, soiled, grimy, begrimed, grubby, messy, dusty, sooty, mucky, muddy, filthy, bedraggled, slimy, polluted, sullied, foul, stained, spotted, smudged, tarnished, defiled, nasty; *inf.* cruddy, yucky, grungy. **2** *dirty jokes* blue, obscene, indecent, vulgar, smutty, coarse, bawdy, suggestive, ribald, salacious, risqué, prurient, lewd, lascivious, licentious, pornographic, off color; *inf.* sleazy. **3** *a dirty cheat* nasty, unpleasant, mean, base, low, vile, contemptible, despicable, cowardly, ignominious, sordid, beggarly, squalid. **4** *a dirty trick | dirty play* unsporting, unfair, dishonorable, unscrupulous, dishonest, crooked, illegal, deceitful, fraudulent, double-dealing, corrupt, treacherous. **5** *give a dirty look* full of dislike/hate, malevolent, smoldering, resentful, bitter, angry, indignant, annoyed, peeved, offended. **6** *dirty weather* unpleasant, nasty, foul, stormy, squally, gusty, rainy, misty, gloomy, murky, overcast. **7** *a dirty shade of white* dingy, dull, muddy, dark, cloudy, not clear/pure. **8** *a dirty rumor* nasty, unkind, scandalous, defamatory, slanderous, libelous.
Antonyms: CLEAN; HONORABLE; PLEASANT.

dirty *verb* *don't dirty your clothes* soil, stain, muddy, begrime, blacken, mess up, spatter, smudge, smear, spot, splash, spoil, sully, pollute, foul, defile, besmirch.

disability *noun* **1** *suffering from a physical disability* impairment, disablement, infirmity, defect, handicap, disorder, affliction, ailment, complaint, illness, malady. **2** *physical disability prevented him going* incapacity, infirmity, unfitness, weakness, powerlessness, impotence,

disable verb 1 *the accident disabled him* incapacitate, impair, damage, put out of action, debilitate, indispose, weaken, enfeeble, make unfit, render infirm, cripple, lame, handicap, immobilize, hamstring, paralyze, prostrate. 2 *disable the machinery* render inoperative, make ineffective, paralyze, make harmless.

disabled adjective incapacitated, impaired, handicapped, debilitated, unfit, out of action, infirm, weak, weakened, enfeebled, crippled, lame, immobilized, bedridden, paralyzed.

disabuse verb undeceive, set right/straight, open the eyes of, wake someone up.

disadvantage noun 1 *the advantages and disadvantages of the situation* drawback, snag, downside, weak spot/point, weakness, flaw, defect, fault, handicap, trouble, liability, nuisance, hindrance, obstacle, impediment; *inf.* minus, fly in the ointment. 2 *people suffering from financial disadvantage* deprivation, privation, hardship, lack, burden. 3 *to their disadvantage* disservice, detriment, prejudice, harm, damage; loss, injury, hurt, mischief.
Antonyms: ADVANTAGE; BENEFIT; GAIN.

disadvantaged adjective deprived, in need, in want, in distress, poor, poverty-stricken, discriminated against.

disadvantageous adjective unfavorable, adverse, unfortunate, unlucky, hapless, detrimental, prejudicial, deleterious, harmful, damaging, injurious, hurtful, destructive, inconvenient, inopportune, ill-timed, inexpedient, inadvisable.

disaffected adjective alienated, estranged, unfriendly, disunited; dissatisfied, disgruntled, discontented, disloyal, rebellious, mutinous, seditious, up in arms, hostile, antagonistic.

disagree verb 1 *the two sides disagreed* differ, fail to agree, dissent, stand opposed, be in dispute/contention, be at variance/odds, diverge, disaccord. 2 *the stories disagreed* differ, be dissimilar, be unlike, be different, vary, conflict, clash, contrast, diverge, not correspond, not accord, be discordant. 3 *children constantly disagreeing* quarrel, argue, bicker, wrangle, squabble, spar, dispute, debate, take issue with, altercate; *inf.* fall out, have words. **disagree with** *food disagreeing with him* be incompatible with, make ill/unwell, cause discomfort/distress, be injurious to.

disagreeable adjective 1 *a disagreeable experience* unpleasant, displeasing, nasty, horrible, dreadful, hateful, detestable, abominable, odious, objectionable, offensive, obnoxious, repugnant, repulsive, repellent, revolting, disgusting, distasteful, nauseating, unsavory, unpalatable. 2 *a disagreeable old man* bad-tempered, ill-natured, unfriendly, unpleasant, difficult, nasty, cross, irritable, rude, surly, discourteous, impolite, churlish, peevish, brusque, abrupt, disobliging, contrary.

disagreement noun 1 *the disagreement of the two sides* lack of agreement, difference of opinion, dissent, dispute, variance, contention, disaccord, discord. 2 *the disagreement of/between the accounts* difference, dissimilarity, unlikeness, variation, variance, discrepancy, disparity, dissimilitude, incompatibility, incongruity, contradiction, conflict, clash, contrast, divergence, deviation, contravention, nonconformity, diversity. 3 *the disagreement between the children* quarrel, argument, wrangle, squabble, altercation, dispute, debate, disputation, discord, strife, conflict, war of words; bickering, sparring, contention, dissension, disharmony; *inf.* falling out.

disallow verb reject, say no to, refuse, dismiss, rebuff, repel, repulse, repudiate, ban, bar, debar, forbid, prohibit, veto, embargo, proscribe, negative, cancel, disclaim, disown, abjure, disavow.

disappear verb 1 *the sun disappearing below the horizon* pass from sight, cease to be visible, vanish from sight, vanish, be lost to view/sight, recede, recede from view, fade, fade/melt away, withdraw, depart, retire, go, pass, flee, retreat, ebb, wane, dematerialize, evanesce, evaporate; *inf.* vamoose. 2 *customs/railroads that have disappeared* die out, die, cease to be/exist, be no more, come to an end, end, vanish, pass away, expire, perish, become extinct, fade away, leave no trace, pass into oblivion.
Antonyms: APPEAR; EMERGE.

disappearance noun 1 *the disappearance of the sun* passing from sight, vanishing, receding from view, fading, melting away, withdrawal, departure, exit, retiral, passing, retreat, ebb, wane, eclipse, dematerialization, evanescence, evaporation. *See* DISAPPEAR 1. 2 *the disappearance of the customs/steam trains* dying out, death, vanishing, passing away, perishing, eclipse, extinction.

disappoint verb 1 *sorry to disappoint you* | *the news disappointed him* let down, fail, dishearten, depress, dispirit, upset, sadden, dash the hopes of, chagrin, dismay, disgruntle, disenchant, disillusion, dissatisfy, vex. 2 *disappoint their plans* thwart, frustrate, foil, defeat, baffle, hinder, obstruct, hamper, impede, interfere with.
Antonyms: CHEER; DELIGHT; FULFILL.

disappointed adjective 1 *disappointed children* upset, saddened, let down, disheartened, downhearted, cast down, downcast, depressed, dispirited, despondent, distressed, chagrined, disgruntled, disenchanted, disillusioned, discontented, dissatisfied, vexed. 2 *disappointed plans* thwarted, frustrated, foiled, defeated, failed, baffled. *See* DISAPPOINT 2.

disappointing adjective 1 *disappointing news* upsetting, saddening, disagreeable, disheartening, discouraging, depressing, dispiriting, distressing, disenchanting, dissatisfying, disconcerting, vexing. See DISAPPOINT 1. **2** *a disappointing effort* unsatisfactory, inadequate, insufficient, unworthy, inferior, second-rate, pathetic, lame.

disappointment noun **1** *hide one's disappointment* sadness, regret, depression, dispiritedness, despondency, distress, chagrin, disgruntlement, displeasure, disenchantment, disillusionment, discontent, dissatisfaction, vexation. **2** *the disappointment of their plans* thwarting, frustration, foiling; defeat, failure, nonsuccess, ill-success, unfulfillment. **3** *the event was a disappointment* letdown, failure, fiasco, setback, blow, misfortune, disaster; *inf.* washout.

disapproval noun disapprobation, disfavor, displeasure, dislike, dissatisfaction, criticism, censure, blame, condemnation, denunciation, objection, exception, reproach, rebuke, reproof, remonstration, disparagement, deprecation.

disapprove verb **1** *disapprove of their behavior* have/express a poor opinion of, dislike, find unacceptable, be against, be dissatisfied/displeased with, deplore, criticize, frown on, take a dim view of, look askance at, censure, blame, condemn, denounce, object to, take exception to, reproach, rebuke, reprove, remonstrate against, disparage, deprecate; *inf.* look down one's nose at. **2** *disapprove the plans* turn down, reject, veto, disallow, set aside; *inf.* give the thumbs down to.

disarm verb **1** *disarm the terrorists/nation* unarm, deprive of arms, demilitarize, demobilize, render defenseless, make powerless. **2** *the country is disarming* lay down arms, demilitarize; *lit.* turn swords into plowshares. **3** *disarmed by his smile* charm, win over, persuade, convert, mollify, appease, placate, conciliate, propitiate.

disarmament noun demilitarization, demobilization, arms reduction, weapons control, arms limitation; nuclear disarmament.

disarming adjective *a disarming smile* charming, winning, persuasive, irresistible, conciliatory. See DISARM 3.

disarrange verb bring/throw into disorder, order, make disorderly, disorder, untidy, make untidy, mess up, displace, disorganize, disturb, confuse, jumble, mix up, muddle, turn upside-down, upset, unsettle, throw into disarray, derange, discompose, scatter, shake up, dishevel, tousle, rumple; *inf.* turn topsy-turvy, muss up.

disarray noun **1** *troops in disarray* disorder, confusion, upset; disorderliness, disorganization, discomposure, unsettledness, disunity, indiscipline, unruliness. **2** *rooms/clothes in disarray* disorder, untidiness, confusion, chaos, dishevelment; mess, muddle, clutter, jumble, mix-up, tangle; shambles.

disaster noun **1** *natural disasters* catastrophe, calamity, cataclysm, tragedy, act of God, accident, mishap, misadventure, mischance, stroke of ill-luck, setback, reverse/reversal of fortune, reversal, heavy blow, shock, buffet; adversity, trouble, misfortune, ruin, ruination. **2** *the play was a disaster* failure, fiasco; *inf.* flop, bomb, dud, washout.
Antonyms: BLESSING; GODSEND; SUCCESS.

disastrous adjective *disastrous events* catastrophic, calamitous, cataclysmic, tragic, adverse, devastating, ravaging, dire, terrible, shocking, appalling, dreadful, black, harmful, injurious, detrimental, ruinous, unfortunate, unlucky, hapless, ill-fated, ill-starred.

disavowal noun denial, contradiction, disclaimer, repudiation, renunciation, disowning, rejection.

disband verb **1** *the group disbanded* break up, disperse, dissolve, separate, go separate ways. **2** *disband the group* break up, dissolve, disperse, dismiss, demobilize.

disbelief noun unbelief, lack of belief, skepticism, incredulity, nonconviction, doubt, discredit, distrust, mistrust, questioning, agnosticism, atheism, nihilism.
Antonyms: BELIEF; TRUST; CERTAINTY.

disbelieve verb not believe, not credit, give no credence to, be incredulous, be unconvinced, discredit, discount, not accept, reject, repudiate, distrust, mistrust, question, challenge, scoff at.

disbeliever noun unbeliever, skeptic, doubter, doubting Thomas, questioner, challenger, scoffer, agnostic, atheist, nihilist.

disburse verb pay out, lay out, spend, expend; *inf.* fork out, shell out, dish out.

discard verb throw away/out, get rid of, dispose of, toss out, jettison, scrap, dispense with, cast aside, reject, repudiate, abandon, relinquish, forsake, drop, have done with, shed; *inf.* dump, ditch.
Antonyms: KEEP; RETAIN.

discern verb see, notice, observe, perceive, make out, distinguish, detect, descry, recognize, determine, differentiate.
Antonyms: OVERLOOK; MISS.

discernible adjective visible, noticeable, observable, perceptible, perceivable, distinguishable, detectable, recognizable, apparent, obvious, clear, manifest, conspicuous, patent.

discerning adjective discriminating, astute, shrewd, ingenious, clever, intelligent, perceptive, sharp, quick, perspicacious, penetrating, critical, percipient, judicious, sensitive, subtle, prudent, sound, wise, aware, knowing, sagacious, sapient.

discharge verb **1** *discharge the prisoner* set free, free, let go, release, liberate, acquit, clear, absolve, pardon, exonerate, reprieve, exculpate, emancipate, manumit. **2** *discharge from employment* dismiss, remove, get rid of, discard, eject, oust, expel, cashier, deprive of office; *inf.*

sack, fire, ax, send packing, give the ax/sack/ boot to, boot out. **3** *discharge a weapon* fire, shoot, let/set off, explode, detonate. **4** *discharge pus/fumes* exude, ooze, excrete, give off, leak, dispense, emit, send out, send/pour forth, eject, release, gush, void. **5** *discharge a duty* carry out, perform, do, accomplish, achieve, fulfill, execute, observe, abide by. **6** *discharge a load* unload, disburden, remove, unburden, off-load, relieve. **7** *discharge a debt/obligation* pay, settle, clear, honor, meet, liquidate, satisfy; *inf.* square.
Antonyms: IMPRISON; ENGAGE; NEGLECT.

discharge *noun* **1** *prisoners receiving a discharge* release, liberation, acquittal, clearance, absolution, pardon, exoneration, reprieve, exculpation, manumission. **2** *hear about his discharge from the firm* dismissal, removal, ejection, ousting, expulsion, cashiering, *inf.* firing, axing, sacking. *See* DISCHARGE *verb* 2. **3** *the/a discharge from a weapon* discharging, firing, shooting, explosion, detonation, blast, burst, pop, report, volley, salvo, fusillade. **4** *the discharge of pus/fumes* exuding, oozing, excretion, emission, ejection, release, emptying, voiding, voidance. **5** *exuding a watery discharge* excretion, exudate, emission, flow, secretion, ooze, suppuration, pus, seepage. **6** *discharge of one's duty* carrying out, performing, doing, accomplishment, achievement, fulfillment, execution, observance; performance. **7** *the discharge of a debt* payment, settlement, clearance, honoring, meeting. *See* DISCHARGE *verb* 7.

disciple *noun* apostle, follower, pupil, student, believer, adherent, devotee, votary, upholder, supporter, advocate, proponent, satellite, partisan.

disciplinarian *noun* martinet, authoritarian, taskmaster, tyrant, despot.

discipline *noun* **1** *school discipline | yoga is a useful discipline* training, drilling, exercise, regimen, routine, method; instruction, coaching, teaching, indoctrination, inculcation, systematization. **2** *discipline required for the exercise* control, self-control, self-restraint, strictness, orderliness, regulation, direction, government, restriction, limitation; restraint, check, curb. **3** *students in need of discipline* punishment, chastisement, castigation, correction; penalty, reprimand, rebuke, reproof. **4** *literature and other disciplines* field of study, field, branch of knowledge, course of study, course, area, subject, specialist subject, speciality, specialty.

discipline *verb* **1** *discipline the troops* train, drill, break in, exercise, instruct, coach, teach, educate, tutor, prepare, ground, indoctrinate, inculcate, inure, toughen. **2** *discipline oneself* control, restrain, regulate, govern, restrict, limit, check, curb. **3** *discipline the children* punish, chastise, castigate, correct, penalize, reprimand, rebuke, reprove.

disclaim *verb* deny, renounce, repudiate, reject,

refuse, decline, disown, cast off, discard, abandon, wash one's hands of, turn one's back on, abjure, forswear, disavow, disaffirm.

disclaimer *noun* denial, renunciation, repudiation, rejection, abjuration, disavowal, disaffirmation.

disclose *verb* **1** *disclose confidential details* make known, reveal, divulge, tell, impart, communicate, make public, broadcast, publish, release, unveil, leak, let slip, blurt out, blab, admit, confess, avow; *inf.* spill the beans about, let the cat out of the bag about, blow the lid off, squeal about. **2** *disclose the contents of the box* reveal, show, exhibit, expose, uncover, lay bare, unveil, bring to light.
Antonyms: CONCEAL; HIDE.

disclosure *noun* **1** *make disclosures of secret ceremonies* revelation, divulgence, exposé, communication, leak, admission, confession, avowal. **2** *the disclosure of vice by the newspaper* revealing, revelation, bringing to light, divulging, divulgence, broadcasting, publishing, uncovering, laying bare, unveiling; release, announcement, declaration, exposure.

discolor *verb* stain, soil, mark, streak, spot, tarnish, fade, bleach, wash out.

discoloration *noun* stain, soiling, mark, streak, spot, blotch, tarnishing; blemish, flaw.

discomfit *verb* **1** *discomfited by personal questions* embarrass, disconcert, make uncomfortable, take aback, nonplus, abash, confuse, ruffle, fluster, upset, disturb, perturb, discompose, discomfort; *inf.* faze, rattle, discombobulate. **2** *discomfit the enemy's plans* thwart, frustrate, foil, obstruct, hinder, hamper, check, upset.

discomfiture *noun* *the discomfiture of the interviewee* embarrassment, disconcertment, uneasiness, unease, confusion, discomposure. *See* DISCOMFIT 1.

discomfort *noun* **1** *experience some discomfort in the injured leg* ache, pain, soreness, twinge, hurt, irritation, pang, throb, smart, malaise. **2** *lead the life of discomfort* lack of comfort/ease, trouble, unpleasantness, hardship, distress. **3** *blushing with discomfort* embarrassment, anxiety, disconcertment, unease, uneasiness, discomfiture, discomposure, disquietude. **4** *the discomforts of travel* inconvenience, difficulty, trouble, bother, nuisance, vexation, drawback, disadvantage, problem, trial, tribulation.

discomfort *verb* *discomforted by the hostile audience* make uncomfortable/uneasy, embarrass, disconcert, upset, ruffle, discompose, discomfit.

discomposure *noun* agitation, fluster, flurry, restlessness, nervousness, perturbation, disturbance, anxiety, uneasiness, unease, disquiet, disquietude, embarrassment, disconcertment, confusion, discomfiture, discomfort.

disconcert *verb* **1** *disconcerted by the silence in the room* unsettle, shake, disturb, perturb, daunt, take aback, abash, nonplus, confuse, bewilder, fluster, ruffle, upset, agitate, worry, embarrass, discomfit, discompose, perplex, confound, distract, throw off balance, put off one's stroke; *inf.* throw, faze, rattle. **2** *disconcerting their plans* thwart, frustrate, foil, obstruct, hinder, hamper, upset, undo.

disconcerting *adjective a disconcerting habit of grinning* unsettling, disturbing, perturbing, daunting, confusing, bewildering, upsetting, worrying, alarming, embarrassing, discomfiting, perplexing, bothering, bothersome, distracting, dismaying, awkward.

disconnect *verb* **1** *disconnect the electrical supply* undo, cut off, sever, uncouple, disengage, detach, unhook, unhitch, unlink, disjoin, disunite. **2** *cannot disconnect the two philosophies* separate, sever, divide, part, split up, dissociate, disentangle. **3** *our telephone conversation got disconnected* discontinue, interrupt, suspend, halt, stop.
Antonyms: CONNECT; ENGAGE; TIE; BIND.

disconnected *adjective* **1** *disconnected ideas* unconnected, separate, separated, unattached, dissociated. **2** *disconnected speech* disjointed, garbled, confused, jumbled, mixed-up, incoherent, unintelligible, rambling, wandering, disordered, illogical, irrational, uncoordinated.

disconsolate *adjective* sad, unhappy, miserable, despondent, wretched, heartbroken, forlorn, grief-stricken, inconsolable, woebegone, dejected, low, low-spirited, dispirited, down, depressed, downcast, gloomy, melancholy, blue; *inf.* down in the mouth/dumps.
Antonyms: HAPPY; JOYFUL.

discontent *noun* discontentment, dissatisfaction, restlessness, impatience, fretfulness, displeasure, unhappiness, misery, wretchedness, envy, regret, umbrage, disaffection, disquiet, vexation, exasperation, irritation, chagrin, pique.

discontented *adjective* dissatisfied, fed up, restless, impatient, fretful, complaining, displeased, disgruntled, querulous, unhappy, miserable, wretched, envious, regretful, disaffected, exasperated, irritated, chagrined, annoyed, peeved, piqued; *vulg.* pissed off.
Antonyms: CONTENT; satisfied; PLEASED.

discontinue *verb* **1** *discontinue the service* stop, end, put an end/stop to, finish, bring to a halt, terminate, cease, abandon, give up, break off, cancel, drop, refrain from, quit, suspend, interrupt; *inf.* cut out. **2** *the road/conversation discontinued* stop, come to a stop/halt, terminate, leave off, pause.
Antonyms: BEGIN; START.

discontinued *adjective a discontinued line/product* no longer available/produced, abandoned, given up, ended, finished, terminated, halted.

discord *noun* **1** *bitter discord between the leaders*

disagreement, difference of opinion, dissension, dispute, argument, conflict, friction, contention, strife, opposition, hostility, wrangling, clashing, quarreling, falling-out, war, division, incompatibility, variance, disunity, rupture. **2** *the discord of the instruments* lack of harmony, disharmony, dissonance, cacophony, harshness, jarring, jangling, din, racket.
Antonyms: ACCORD; CONCORD; HARMONY.

discordant *adjective* **1** *discordant attitudes* disagreeing, differing, contradictory, contrary, dissenting, disputatious, conflicting, at variance, at odds, contentious, opposing, hostile, clashing, divergent, incompatible, incongruous. **2** *discordant sounds* inharmonious, harsh, strident, shrill, grating, jarring, jangling, dissonant, cacophonous.
Antonyms: COMPATIBLE; HARMONIOUS; DULCET.

discount *verb* **1** *discount what he says* disregard, ignore, pass over, overlook, pay no attention to, take no notice of, brush off, gloss over. **2** *discount $5 from the price* deduct, take off, rebate; *inf.* knock off. **3** *discount the regular price* reduce, lower, lessen; *inf.* knock down. **4** *discount the products* mark down, reduce, put on sale.
Antonyms: NOTE; INCREASE; mark up (*see* MARK).

discount *noun* **1** *a big discount on the order* markdown, deduction, price cut, cut, rebate, concession. **2** *goods at a discount* lower price, cut price, concessionary price, reduction.

discourage *verb* **1** *he was discouraged by lack of success* dishearten, dispirit, deject, cast down, depress, demoralize, disappoint, daunt, put off, intimidate, cow, unnerve. **2** *discourage them from applying* put off, dissuade, deter, talk out of, advise against, urge against, caution against, restrain, inhibit, divert from, sidetrack from. **3** *discourage the idea* oppose, disapprove of, repress, deprecate, put a damper on, throw cold water on. **4** *a preparation discouraging mildew* prevent, check, curb, hinder, obstruct, suppress, inhibit.
Antonyms: ENCOURAGE; PERSUADE.

discouraged *adjective discouraged job hunters* disheartened, dispirited, dejected, cast down, downcast, depressed, demoralized, disappointed, daunted, put off, crestfallen, glum; *inf.* down in the mouth/dumps. *See* DISCOURAGE 1.

discouragement *noun* **1** *experience discouragement* dispiritedness, downheartedness, dejection, depression, demoralization, disappointment, despondency, hopelessness, lack of confidence, pessimism, despair, gloom, melancholy; low spirits. **2** *ideas meeting with discouragement* opposition, disapproval, repression, deprecation. **3** *tired of discouragements to progress* deterrent, hindrance, obstacle, impediment, barrier, curb, check, damper, restraint, constraint, restriction, disincentive, setback, rebuff; *inf.* put-down.

discouraging *adjective discouraging news* disheartening, dispiriting, depressing, demoralizing, disappointing, gloomy, unfavorable, unpropitious, inauspicious.

discourse *noun* **1** *engage in discourse* conversation, talk, dialogue, communication, discussion, conference, colloquy, converse, verbal exchange, chat, chitchat, confabulation; *inf.* confab. **2** *a discourse on art* address, speech, lecture, oration, sermon, homily, essay, treatise, dissertation, paper, study.

discourse *verb* **1** *discourse with colleagues* converse, talk, discuss, debate, confer, speak, chat; *inf.* have a confab, chew the fat, rap. **2** *discourse on morals* give an address/talk, deliver a speech/lecture, lecture, sermonize, preach, hold forth, write at length; *inf.* spout.

discourteous *adjective* rude, impolite, uncivil, ill-mannered, bad-mannered, unmannerly, curt, abrupt, brusque, short, gruff, boorish, churlish, ungracious, ungentlemanly, unladylike, ill-bred, uncouth, disrespectful, ungallant, insolent, impertinent, impudent.

discourtesy *noun* rudeness, impoliteness, lack of civility, incivility, ill-manneredness, unmannerliness, curtness, abruptness, brusqueness, ungraciousness, ill-breeding, uncouthness, disrespect, disrespectfulness, insolence. *See* DISCOURTEOUS.

discover *verb* **1** *discover a new place to ski | discover new talent* find, come across/upon, stumble upon, chance upon, light upon, locate, bring to light, uncover, unearth, turn up; *inf.* dig up. **2** *discover that he was lying* find out, come to know, learn, realize, detect, determine, ascertain, recognize, see, spot, notice, perceive, reveal, disclose; *inf.* get wise to the fact. **3** *discover a new drug* invent, originate, devise, pioneer, design, contrive, conceive of. **4** *discover America* found, explore, pioneer. **Antonyms:** CONCEAL; HIDE.

discoverer *noun* **1** *the discoverer of a mountain pass* founder, explorer, pioneer. **2** *the discoverer of penicillin* inventor, originator, pioneer, deviser, designer, initiator.

discovery *noun* **1** *the discovery of a quiet village | new talent* finding, locating, location, uncovering. *See* DISCOVER 1. **2** *the discovery that they lied* finding out, learning, realization, detection, determination, recognition, revelation, disclosure. *See* DISCOVER 2. **3** *discovery of new drugs* invention, origination, devising, pioneering, introduction. **4** *recent discoveries* find, invention, breakthrough, innovation, lucky strike, bonanza; findings. **5** *a voyage of discovery* exploration, pioneering, research.

discredit *verb* **1** *discredit their rivals* detract from, bring into disrepute, defame, slur, slander, cast aspersions on, vilify, disparage, deprecate, denigrate, devalue, devaluate, degrade, belittle, decry, dishonor, disgrace, censure. **2** *evidence to discredit the research* disprove, invalidate, refute, dispute, challenge, destroy the credibility of, shake one's faith in, reject, deny.

3 *the jury discredited the witness* disbelieve, give no credence to, discount, doubt, distrust, mistrust.

discredit *noun* **1** *bring discredit on the neighborhood* disrepute, ill repute, infamy, disgrace, dishonor, shame, humiliation, ignominy, stigma, harm, damage, censure, blame, reproach, scandal, odium. **2** *regard the story with discredit* disbelief, lack of credence, incredulity, question, doubt, distrust, mistrust, skepticism, suspicion.

discredited *adjective* brought into disrepute, disproved, invalidated, refuted, rejected, discarded, denied, exploded, debunked.

discreet *adjective* careful, cautious, prudent, judicious, circumspect, wary, guarded, chary, tactful, reserved, diplomatic, considerate, politic, strategic, wise, sensible, sagacious. **Antonyms:** INDISCREET; RASH; TACTLESS.

discrepancy *noun* inconsistency, variance, variation, disparity, deviation, divergence, incongruity, difference, disagreement, dissimilarity, contrariety, conflict, discordance, gap.

discrete *adjective* separate, distinct, individual, detached, unattached, disconnected, discontinuous.

discretion *noun* **1** *act with discretion* care, carefulness, caution, prudence, judiciousness, judgment, circumspection, wariness, guardedness, chariness, tactfulness, tact, reserve, diplomacy, consideration, strategy, discrimination, wisdom, sense, good sense, discernment, sagacity, acumen, forethought, maturity. **2** *at the discretion of the manager* choice, option, volition, will, preference, inclination, pleasure, liking, wish, desire, predilection, election, disposition, mind.

discretionary *adjective* optional, elective, open, open to choice, nonmandatory, unrestricted, voluntary, volitional.

discriminate *verb* **1** *discriminate between right and wrong* distinguish, make/draw a distinction, differentiate, tell the difference, make a difference, discern; separate, separate the men from the boys, separate the wheat from the chaff, segregate. **2** *discriminate against women | discriminate in favor of Protestants* show prejudice against/toward, be biased against/toward, treat differently, treat as inferior/superior, disfavor/favor, be intolerant/overtolerant toward.

discriminating *adjective* **1** *a discriminating concertgoer* discerning, perceptive, astute, shrewd, selective, particular, fastidious, critical, keen, tasteful, refined, sensitive, cultivated, cultured, artistic, aesthetic. **2** *discriminating rules* distinguishing, differentiating, prejudiced. *See* DISCRIMINATORY 1.

discrimination *noun* **1** *wine lovers of discrimination* discernment, perception, penetration, perspicacity, acumen, astuteness, shrewdness, selectivity, fastidiousness, judgment, keenness, taste, refinement, sensitivity, insight, subtlety, cultivation, culture, artistry, aestheticism. **2** *guilty of discrimination* prejudice, bias, unfairness, inequity, intolerance, bigotry, narrow-mindedness, favoritism, segregation; positive discrimination.

discriminatory *adjective discriminatory employment rules* prejudiced, prejudicial, biased, preferential, unfair, unjust, inequitable, weighted, one-sided, partisan.

discursive *adjective* digressive, rambling, wandering, meandering, diffuse, episodic, circuitous, verbose, long-winded, wordy, circumlocutory.
Antonyms: CONCISE; BRIEF.

discuss *verb discuss the problem with colleagues* talk over, talk/chat about, converse about, confer about, debate, exchange views on/about, deliberate, consider, go into, thrash out, examine, review, study, scrutinize, analyze, weigh up, sift, ventilate, argue, dispute; *inf.* kick around.

discussion *noun* talk, conversation, dialogue, chat, conference, debate, discourse, exchange of views, symposium, seminar, consultation, deliberation, parley, examination, review, study, scrutiny, analysis, ventilation, argument, dispute; *inf.* confab.

disdain *noun look with disdain on their jokes* scorn, scornfulness, contempt, contemptuousness, derision, sneering, deprecation, disparagement, denigration, arrogance, super ciliousness, haughtiness, hauteur, snobbishness, aloofness, indifference, dislike, abhorrence.
Antonyms: ADMIRATION; RESPECT.

disdain *verb disdain offers of help* scorn, show-contempt for, spurn, reject, refuse, rebuff, disregard, sneer at, deride, belittle, undervalue, slight, despise, look down on; *inf.* pooh-pooh, look down one's nose at.
Antonyms: ADMIRE; RESPECT.

disdainful *adjective* scornful, contemptuous, sneering, derisive, slighting, disparaging, arrogant, proud, supercilious, haughty, superior, lordly, pompous, snobbish, insolent, aloof, indifferent; *inf.* high and mighty, hoity-toity.

disease *noun* illness, sickness; disorder, complaint, malady, ailment, affliction, condition, indisposition, infirmity, disability, abnormality; infection, contagion, pestilence, plague, canker, blight.
Antonym: HEALTH.

diseased *adjective* unhealthy, ill, ailing, sick, sickly, unwell, unsound, unwholesome, infirm, infected, abnormal, blighted, rotten, cankerous.

disembark *verb* land, arrive, get off, step off, alight, go ashore, dismount, deplane, detrain; *inf.* pile out.

disembodied *adjective* bodiless, incorporeal, discarnate, immaterial, intangible, insubstan-

tial, impalpable, spiritual, ghostly, spectral, phantom.

disembowel *verb* eviscerate, exenterate, gut, draw.

disenchanted *adjective* disillusioned, disabused, undeceived, set straight, disappointed, let down, blasé, cynical, soured, jaundiced, sick, out of love, indifferent.

disenchantment *noun* disillusion, cynicism; disillusionment, disappointment, rude awakening.

disengage *verb disengage the clutch | disengage oneself from an embrace* release, loosen, loose, unfasten, detach, separate, disjoin, disunite, uncouple, undo, unhook, unloose, unhitch, unclasp, untie, free, set free, liberate, disentangle, disentwine, extricate.

disentangle *verb* **1** *disentangle the knotted yarn* unravel, straighten, unwind, untwist, undo, unknot, untie, unsnarl, unkink, smooth out, comb, card. **2** *disentangle oneself* extricate, disentwine, release, loosen, detach, unfasten, unclasp, free, set free, liberate, disconnect.

disfavor *noun* **1** *look upon with disfavor* lack of favor, disapproval, disapprobation, dislike, displeasure, dissatisfaction, disregard, low opinion, low esteem. **2** *fall into disfavor* disapproval, unpopularity, discredit, disrepute, ill repute, ignominy, disgrace, shame. **3** *do someone a disfavor* disservice, bad turn, ill deed, discourtesy.

disfigure *verb* deface, deform, mutilate, blemish, flaw, scar, make ugly, uglify, spoil, mar, damage, injure, maim, vandalize, ruin.
Antonyms: ADORN; ENHANCE.

disfigurement *noun* **1** *the disfigurement of the landscape* defacement, mutilation, scarring, spoiling, uglification, damaging, vandalizing, ruin. *See* DISFIGURE. **2** *an obvious disfigurement* blemish, flaw, blotch, imperfection, defect, scar, deformity, malformation, injury.

disgorge *verb* **1** *volcanoes disgorging lava | disgorging phlegm* spit out, spew out, belch, discharge, spout, vomit, regurgitate, throw up, eject, emit, expel, empty. **2** *disgorging their hold on the territory* give up, surrender, yield, cede, relinquish, hand over, renounce, resign, abandon.

disgrace *noun* **1** *the disgrace of being inprison* shame, humiliation, dishonor, scandal, degradation, ignominy, infamy, discredit, debasement, vitiation. **2** *be indisgrace | brought him disgrace* disfavor, discredit, disrepute, loss of-face, disrespect, disapproval, disapprobation, disesteem, contempt. **3** *his behavior was a disgrace* blot, stain, blemish, black mark, scandal, smear, smirch, stigma, slur, dishonor, aspersion, defamation.
Antonyms: RESPECT; APPROVAL.

disgrace *verb* **1** *disgrace the family* bring disgrace to, bring shame upon, shame, humiliate, bring dishonor to, dishonor, discredit, degrade, debase, sully, besmirch, taint, stain, slur, stigma-

tize, brand, drag through the mud. **2** *the soldier was publicly disgraced* discredit, reproach, censure, blame, dishonor, disfavor, humiliate, mortify, disparage, demean, denigrate, belittle.
Antonyms: HONOR; ESTEEM; FAVOR.

disgraceful *adjective* **1** *disgraceful behavior by the minister* scandalous, shocking, outrageous, shameful, shameless, dishonorable, disreputable, degrading, ignominious, blameworthy, culpable, contemptible, despicable, reprehensible, improper, unseemly, unworthy. **2** *your work is disgraceful* very bad, appalling, dreadful, terrible, shocking, intolerable, unworthy.

disgruntled *adjective* discontented, dissatisfied, displeased, unhappy, disappointed, annoyed, exasperated, vexed, irritated, peeved, put out, resentful, sulky, sullen, petulant, grumpy, churlish, testy; *inf.* ticked off, fed up.

disguise *verb* **1** *disguised as a policeman* camouflage, dress up, be under cover, be incognito, cover up, conceal, hide, mask, screen, shroud, veil, cloak. **2** *disguise the truth* cover up, misrepresent, falsify, give a false picture of, fake, fudge, feign, dissemble, gloss over, varnish.
Antonyms: REVEAL; DISPLAY.

disgust *verb* **1** *the slimy food disgusted me* sicken, nauseate, turn one's stomach, revolt, repel, cause aversion; *inf.* turn off. **2** *her behavior disgusted me* offend, outrage, shock, appall, scandalize, displease, dissatisfy, annoy, anger.

disgust *noun* **1** *look with disgust at the food* revulsion, repugnance, repulsion, aversion, nausea, distaste, abhorrence, loathing, detestation. **2** *disgust at her behavior* offense, outrage, shock, disapproval, displeasure, dissatisfaction, annoyance, anger.
Antonyms: PLEASURE; ADMIRATION; APPROVAL.

disgusting *adjective* **1** *disgusting odor* sickening, nauseating, nauseous, revolting, repellent, unpalatable, foul, nasty, unappetizing, distasteful, abhorrent, loathsome, detestable, obnoxious, odious; *inf.* gross. **2** *disgusting behavior* offensive, objectionable, outrageous, shocking, shameless, shameful, appalling, scandalous, vulgar, gross, vile, displeasing, annoying.
Antonyms: ATTRACTIVE; appealing.

dish *noun* **1** *food served on dishes* container, receptacle, bowl, plate, platter, salver. **2** *prepare a new dish* food, fare, recipe, menu item, *plat du jour*. **3** *television set hooked up to a dish* dish antenna, satellite dish, microwave dish.

dish *verb* **dish it out** *the drill sergeant can really dish it out* criticize, lambaste, spew insults, rebuke, berate, rake (one) over the coals. **dish out** distribute, hand out, deal out, allocate, dole out, mete out. **dish up** **1** *dish up the potatoes* serve, serve up, spoon, ladle, scoop. **2** *dish up the old material in a new form* present, offer, produce, prepare.

dishearten *verb* discourage, cast down, dispirit, make dispirited/dejected, depress, crush,

make crestfallen/downhearted, dash, dampen, put a damper on, daunt, disappoint, deter, sadden, weigh down.

disheveled *adjective* untidy, tousled, rumpled, bedraggled, disordered, disarranged, messy, in a mess, unkempt, uncombed, slovenly, slatternly, blowzy, frowzy; *inf.* mussed.
Antonyms: TIDY; NEAT.

dishonest *adjective* fraudulent, cheating, untrustworthy, false, untruthful, dishonorable, unscrupulous, unprincipled, corrupt, swindling, deceitful, deceiving, deceptive, lying, crafty, cunning, designing, mendacious, double-dealing, underhand, underhanded, treacherous, perfidious, unfair, unjust, disreputable, rascally, roguish, knavish; *inf.* crooked, shady, bent.
Antonyms: HONEST; UPRIGHT.

dishonesty *noun* fraud, fraudulence, cheating, chicanery, untrustworthiness, falseness, falsity, falsehood, untruthfulness, dishonor, unscrupulousness, corruption, criminality, sharp practice, deceit, deception, duplicity, lying, craft, cunning, trickery, wiliness, guile, double-dealing, underhandedness, treachery, perfidy, graft, unfairness, unjustness, improbity, rascality, knavishness; *inf.* crookedness, shadiness.

dishonor *noun* **1** *bring dishonor to the regiment* disgrace, shame, humiliation, scandal, discredit, degradation, ignominy, infamy, disrepute, ill repute, loss of face, disfavor, debasement, abasement, odium. **2** *do him a dishonor* indignity, insult, affront, offense, abuse, outrage, slight, discourtesy. **3** *a dishonor to his profession* disgrace, blot, blemish, stigma. See DISGRACE *noun* 3.

dishonor *verb* **1** *dishonor the flag* disgrace, bring dishonor/shame to, shame, humiliate, discredit, degrade, debase, sully, stain, stigmatize. See DISGRACE *verb* 1. **2** *dishonor their hosts* insult, affront, abuse, slight, offend. **3** *dishonor the captives* rape, violate, ravish, defile, seduce, deflower.

dishonorable *adjective* **1** *a dishonorable act* disgraceful, shameful, shameless, shaming, disreputable, degrading, debasing, ignominious, ignoble, blameworthy, contemptible, despicable, reprehensible, base. **2** *a dishonorable man* unprincipled, blackguardly, unscrupulous, corrupt, untrustworthy, treacherous, perfidious, traitorous, disreputable, discreditable; *inf.* shady.

disillusion *verb* disabuse, disenchant, open the eyes of, shatter the illusions of, undeceive, set straight, enlighten, disappoint, make sadder and wiser.

disincentive *noun* discouragement, deterrent, damper, dissuasion, impediment, hindrance.

disinclination *noun* reluctance, lack of enthusiasm, hesitancy, hesitance, unwillingness, loathness, aversion, dislike, distaste, objection, demur, resistance, opposition, recalcitrance.

disinclined *adjective* reluctant, unenthusiastic, not in the mood, hesitant, unwilling, loath, averse, antipathetic, resistant, opposed, recalcitrant.

disinfect *verb* sterilize, sanitize, clean, cleanse, purify, fumigate, decontaminate.

disinfectant *noun* antiseptic, bactericide, germicide, sterilizer, sanitizer, cleansing agent, cleanser, fumigant, decontaminant.

disingenuous *adjective* insincere, feigned, deceitful, underhand, underhanded, duplicitous, double-dealing, two-faced, false, lying, untruthful, artful, cunning, crafty, wily, sly, shifty, scheming, calculating, designing, insidious.

disinherit *verb* cut off, cut off without a penny, dispossess, oust, disown, repudiate, renounce.

disintegrate *verb* fall apart, fall to pieces, break up, break apart, shatter, splinter, crumble, decompose, decay, rot, molder, erode, dissolve, go to wrack and ruin.

disinterested *adjective* **1** *disinterested judges* unbiased, unprejudiced, impartial, detached, objective, uninvolved, dispassionate, impersonal, open-minded, neutral, outside, fair, just, equitable, evenhanded, unselfish. **2** *disinterested in the lecture* uninterested, unconcerned, uninvolved, unresponsive, indifferent, bored, apathetic, blasé.
Antonyms: BIASED; PARTIAL; INTERESTED.

disjointed *noun* **1** *a disjointed talk* incoherent, unconnected, disconnected, without unity, ununified, discontinuous, rambling, wandering, disorganized, confused, disordered, fitful, spasmodic, aimless, directionless. **2** *disjointed limbs* dislocated, displaced, dismembered, disconnected, severed, separated, disarticulated, torn apart, disunited.

dislike *verb* have no liking for, have an aversion to, regard with distaste/animosity, feel hostility toward, be unable to tolerate/stomach, hold in disfavor, disfavor, have no taste for, object to, hate, detest, loathe, abominate, abhor, despise, scorn, shun, have a grudge against.

dislike *noun* aversion, disapproval, disapprobation, distaste, animosity, hostility, antipathy, antagonism, disinclination, disfavor, disesteem, hate, detestation, loathing, disgust, repugnance, enmity, abhorrence.

dislocate *verb* **1** *dislocate a bone* put out of joint, put out of place, displace, disjoint, disconnect, disengage. **2** *dislocate our plans* disrupt, disturb, throw into disorder/disarray/confusion, confuse, disorganize, mess up, disorder, disarrange, turn topsy-turvy.

dislodge *verb* remove, displace, force out, oust, eject, evict, unseat.

disloyal *adjective* unfaithful, faithless, false, falsehearted, untrue, inconstant, untrustworthy, treacherous, perfidious, traitorous, disaffect-ed, subversive, seditious, unpatriotic, renegade, apostate, dissident, two-faced, double-dealing, deceitful.

disloyalty *noun* unfaithfulness, infidelity, faithlessness, breach of trust, breaking of faith, falseness, false-heartedness, falsity, inconstancy, untrustworthiness, treachery, perfidy, treason, disaffection, subversion, sedition, apostasy, dissidence, double-dealing.

dismal *adjective* **1** *children looking dismal* gloomy, sad, unhappy, miserable, wretched, despondent, disconsolate, sorrowful, solemn, blue, melancholy, morose, woebegone, forlorn, lugubrious. **2** *dismal surroundings* gloomy, dreary, bleak, drab, dull, dark, dingy, cheerless, desolate, depressing, grim, funereal, comfortless, inhospitable, uninviting. **3** *a dismal piece of work* bad, poor, inept, bungling, disgraceful.
Antonyms: CHEERFUL; BRIGHT.

dismantle *verb* take apart, take to pieces, disassemble, pull apart, tear down, demolish, fell, destroy.
Antonym: ASSEMBLE.

dismay *verb* **1** *dismayed by the arrival of the police* disconcert, take aback, startle, surprise, shock, disturb, perturb, upset, jolt, unsettle, unnerve, alarm, frighten, scare. **2** *dismayed by their failure* discourage, put off, dishearten, dispirit, cast down, depress, disappoint, daunt, abash.
Antonyms: ENCOURAGE; HEARTEN.

dismiss *verb* **1** *dismissed from the firm for theft* give notice to, discharge, expel, cashier, remove, oust, eject, lay off; *inf.* sack, give the sack to, fire, give one one's marching orders, send packing, give the boot/heave-ho to, boot out. **2** *dismiss an assembly/army* disband, disperse, dissolve, discharge, send away, let go, release, free. **3** *dismiss foolish thoughts* put away, banish, think no more of, put out of one's mind, set/lay aside, abandon, have done with, reject, drop, disregard, repudiate, spurn; *inf.* pooh-pooh.
Antonyms: ENGAGE; RETAIN.

dismissal *noun* **1** *his dismissal from the firm* notice, discharge, expulsion, removal, ejection; *inf.* sacking, firing. See DISMISS 1. **2** *the dismissal of the assembly* disbandment, dispersal, dissolution, discharge, permission to go/depart/leave, release.

disobedience *noun* insubordination, unruliness, waywardness, rebellion, defiance, mutiny, revolt, recalcitrance, delinquency, noncompliance, infraction, perversity, naughtiness, mischievousness, mischief. See DISOBEDIENT.

disobedient *adjective* insubordinate, unruly, wayward, undisciplined, rebellious, defiant, mutinous, recalcitrant, intractable, willful, refractory, disorderly, delinquent, noncompliant, perverse, naughty, mischievous, contrary.

disobey *verb* defy, not comply with, disregard,

flout, contravene, infringe, overstep, resist, rebel against, fly in the face of, transgress, violate.

disobliging *adjective* unhelpful, uncooperative, unaccommodating, unfriendly, unsympathetic, discourteous, uncivil.

disorder *noun* **1** *tidy up the disorder* untidiness, mess, chaos, muddle, clutter, jumble, confusion, disorderliness, disarray, disorganization; *inf.* shambles. **2** *police quelling the disorder* disturbance, disruption, tumult, riot, breach of the peace, fracas, rumpus, brouhaha, melee, unrest. **3** *a disorder of the kidneys* disease, ailment, complaint, affliction, malady, sickness, illness.
Antonyms: neatness; ORGANIZATION; ORDER.

disorderly *adjective* **1** *disorderly rooms* untidy, messy, chaotic, cluttered, jumbled, muddled, out of order, out of place, in disarray, disorganized, confused, deranged, upside-down, at sixes and sevens, unsystematic, irregular. **2** *disorderly crowds* unruly, boisterous, rough, rowdy, disobedient, undisciplined, lawless, wild, unmanageable, uncontrollable, ungovernable, refractory, rebellious, mutinous, turbulent, tumultuous, rioting.

disorganized *adjective* **1** *disorganized piles of books* disorderly, chaotic, jumbled, muddled, out of order, in disarray, confused, haphazard, random, unsystematic, irregular. **2** *a disorganized person* unorganized, unmethodical, unsystematic, haphazard, muddled, careless; *inf.* hit-or-miss.

disown *verb* repudiate, renounce, reject, cast off, abandon, forsake, turn one's back on, disclaim, deny, disallow, abnegate, disavow, disinherit.

disparage *verb* **1** *disparage their efforts* belittle, slight, decry, depreciate, devalue, devaluate, downgrade, demean, detract from, discredit, deprecate, denigrate, derogate, deflate, minimize, undervalue, underestimate, underrate, make light of, play down, disdain, dismiss, ridicule, deride, mock, scorn, lampoon. **2** *disparage their competitors* defame, run down, slander, libel, malign, speak ill/evil of, cast aspersions on, impugn, calumniate, vilify, traduce; *inf.* do a hatchet job on, bad-mouth, trash.
Antonyms: PRAISE; OVERRATE.

disparity *noun* discrepancy, inequality, unevenness, inconsistency, imbalance, incongruity, difference, dissimilarity, contrast, gap.

dispassionate *adjective* **1** *a dispassionate attitude to suffering* unemotional, emotionless, unmoved, unexcited, unexcitable, unflappable, unperturbed, nonchalant, unruffled, cool, collected, cool and collected, calm, composed, self-possessed, levelheaded, self-controlled, temperate, sober, placid, equable, tranquil, serene; *inf.* laid-back, together. **2** *dispassionate judges* detached, impartial, objective, disinterested, indifferent, uninvolved, impersonal, unbiased, unprejudiced, neutral, fair, just, equitable, evenhanded, square dealing, open-minded.

dispatch *verb* **1** *dispatch a letter* send, send off, post, mail, forward, transmit, consign, remit, convey. **2** *dispatch the meeting in an hour* | *dispatch the task* finish, dispose of, conclude, settle, discharge, execute, perform, expedite, push through, accelerate, hasten, speed up, hurry on; *inf.* make short work of. **3** *a flurry of bullets dispatched the terrorists* kill, put to death, slay, do to death, put an end to, finish off, take the life of, slaughter, murder, assassinate, execute; *inf.* bump off, do in, knock off, eliminate, erase.

dispatch *noun* **1** *carried out with dispatch* promptness, promptitude, speed, alacrity, quickness, haste, hurry, swiftness, rapidity, expedition, expeditiousness. **2** *military dispatches* | *a journalist's dispatch* communication, communiqué, bulletin, report, account, document, missive, letter, epistle, message, item, piece, article, news, instruction.
Antonyms: slowness; hesitancy.

dispel *verb* drive away, drive off, chase away, banish, rout, expel, disperse, scatter, dissipate, disseminate, dismiss, eliminate, allay.

dispensable *adjective* expendable, disposable, unnecessary, unessential, nonessential, needless, superfluous, uncalled-for.
Antonyms: INDISPENSABLE; ESSENTIAL.

dispensation *noun* **1** *dispensation of supplies* distribution, handing out, dealing out, dividing out, division, allocation, allotment, apportionment, assignment, bestowal, conferment, supplying, disbursement. *See* DISPENSE 1. **2** *receive a dispensation of food* quota, portion, share, part, award. **3** *the dispensation of justice* administration, discharge, execution, implementation, application, enforcement, effectuation, operation, direction. **4** *given dispensation from a duty* | *given a dispensation from attending* exemption, immunity, exception, indulgence; release, relief, reprieve, remission, relaxation, absolution; *inf.* letting off.

dispense *verb* **1** *dispense supplies* distribute, hand out, deal out, dole out, share out, divide out, parcel out, allocate, allot, apportion, assign, bestow, confer, supply, disburse. **2** *dispense justice* administer, discharge, carry out, execute, implement, apply, enforce, effectuate, operate, direct. **3** *dispense medicines* make up, prepare, mix, supply. **4** *dispense him from eating fish on Fridays* grant a dispensation to, exempt, excuse, except, release, relieve, reprieve, absolve; *inf.* let off. **dispense with 1** *dispense with the formalities* waive, do without, omit, forgo, give up, relinquish, renounce, ignore, disregard, pass over, brush aside. **2** *dispense with their services* do away with, get rid of, dispose of, abolish, revoke, rescind, cancel, shake off, manage without.

disperse verb **1** *the crowd dispersed* break up, disband, separate, go separate ways, scatter, dissolve, leave, vanish, melt away. **2** *the wind dispersed the clouds* break up, scatter, dissipate, dispel, drive away, banish, dissolve. **3** *disperse seeds* scatter, scatter to the winds, disseminate, distribute, sow, sprinkle, spread, diffuse, strew, bestrew. **4** *disperse information* put into circulation, circulate, broadcast, publish, publicize, spread, diffuse.
Antonyms: GATHER; ASSEMBLE; COLLECT.

dispirit verb dishearten, discourage, cast down, make dejected, depress, crush, dash, dampen the spirits of, daunt, disappoint, deter, sadden; *inf.* throw cold water on.

displace verb **1** *displace the furniture* | *displace the remnants of the tribe* put out of place/order, disarrange, move, shift, relocate, transpose, derange, disorder, throw into disorder, dislocate; transfer, resettle, unsettle; disturb. **2** *displace from office* remove, dismiss, discharge, depose, dislodge, eject, expel, force out, discard, cashier; *inf.* sack, fire. **3** *displaced the aging chairman* replace, take the place of, take over from, supplant, oust, supersede, succeed; *inf.* crowd out.

displaced adjective **displaced person** refugee, DP, exile, émigré, fugitive.

display verb **1** *display the goods* put on show, show, exhibit, put on view, expose to view, present, unveil, set forth, arrange, dispose, array, demonstrate, advertise, publicize. **2** *display their military power* show off, flaunt, parade, flourish, boast, vaunt; *inf.* flash. **3** *display emotion* show, evince, manifest, betray, show evidence of, reveal, disclose.
Antonyms: CONCEAL; HIDE.

display noun **1** *put on a display of sculpture* show, exhibition, exhibit, presentation, demonstration, spectacle, array. **2** *military display* show, spectacle, parade, pageant; pomp, flourish, ostentation. **3** *the display of emotion* showing, evincement, manifestation, betrayal, evidence, revelation, disclosure.

displease verb dissatisfy, put out, annoy, irritate, anger, irk, vex, provoke, offend, pique, peeve, gall, nettle, incense, exasperate, upset, perturb, disturb, discompose, disgust; *inf.* aggravate.

displeasure noun dissatisfaction, discontentment, disgruntlement, disfavor, disapproval, disapprobation, distaste, annoyance, irritation, anger, ire, wrath, pique, chagrin, offense, rancor, indignation, exasperation, perturbation, disturbance, disgust.

disposable adjective **1** *disposable plates* throwaway, nonreturnable, paper, plastic, biodegradable. **2** *disposable assets* available, usable, accessible, obtainable.

disposal noun **1** *the disposal of trash* throwing away, clearance, discarding, ejection, scrapping, destruction; *inf.* dumping. **2** *the disposal of the business matters* settlement, determination, deciding, finishing up, conclusion. **3** *the disposal of his estate* distribution, allotment, allocation, transfer, transference, assignation, making over, conveyance, bestowal, gift, bequest, sale. **4** *the disposal of the troops* arrangement, ordering, positioning, placement, lining-up, setting-up, organization, marshaling, grouping. See DISPOSE 1. **5** *at one's disposal* power, authority, control, direction, discretion, responsibility, management, government, determination, regulation.

dispose verb **1** *troops disposed in rows* arrange, order, place, put, position, array, range, line up, set up, organize, marshal, group, rank, categorize, systematize, adjust, fix, regulate. **2** *behavior not disposing me to believe him* incline, make willing, predispose, make, move, prompt, lead, induce, tempt, actuate, motivate, bias, influence, condition, direct. **dispose of 1** *dispose of the trash* get rid of, throw away/out, clear out, discard, eject, unload, scrap, destroy; *inf.* dump. **2** *dispose of the business* deal with, settle, determine, decide, finish, conclude, end. **3** *dispose of his estate* distribute, give out, allot, allocate, assign, part with, transfer, make over, give away, bestow, sell, auction. **4** *dispose of his enemy* kill, do away with, put to death, slay, murder, slaughter; *inf.* bump off, knock off. **5** *rapidly disposed of the food* consume, eat up, devour, finish off, put away; *inf.* polish off.
Antonyms: KEEP; RETAIN.

disposed adjective **1** *disposed to help them* inclined, willing, of a mind to, in the mood to, ready, prepared. **2** *disposed to black moods* inclined, given, prone, liable, apt.

disposition noun **1** *people of a calm disposition* nature, character, temperament, humor, make-up, constitution, spirit, temper, mood. **2** *a disposition to/for moodiness* inclination, tendency, proneness, propensity, leaning, proclivity, bias, bent, predilection, weakness, habit, readiness. **3** *the disposition of the troops* disposal, arrangement, ordering, positioning, placement, lining-up, setting-up, organization, marshaling, grouping. **4** *disposition of property* disposal, distribution, allocation, transfer, transference, bestowal. See DISPOSAL 3. **5** *have at one's disposition* disposal, power, authority, control, direction, management. See DISPOSAL 5.

dispossess verb **1** *dispossess them of their property* deprive, divest, strip, bereave. **2** *dispossess the tenants* dislodge, oust, eject, drive out, evict, turn out, dismiss.

disproportionate adjective *clothes disproportionate to his height* | *a reaction disproportionate to the danger* out of proportion, not in proportion, not commensurate, unbalanced, uneven, unequal, irregular, relatively too large/long/much, relatively too small/short/little, excessive, unreasonable.

disprove *verb* prove false, invalidate, refute, negate, rebut, confute, deny, contradict, controvert, discredit, expose.

disputable *adjective* debatable, open to discussion, arguable, contestable, controvertible, moot, open to question, questionable, doubtful.

disputation *noun a disputation ensued | open to disputation* debate, dispute; argumentation, altercation, dissension; polemics.

disputatious *adjective* disputative, argumentative, contentious, captious, quarrelsome, litigious, polemical.

dispute *verb* **1** *dispute with colleagues | dispute over what to do* debate, discuss, argue, disagree, have an altercation, altercate, clash, quarrel, wrangle, bicker, squabble. **2** *dispute his right to go* question, call into question, challenge, contest, deny, doubt, contradict, object to, oppose, controvert, impugn, gainsay.
Antonyms: AGREE; CONFIRM.

dispute *noun* **1** *open to dispute* debate, discussion, argument, controversy, contention, disagreement, altercation, dissension, conflict, friction, strife, discord, litigation. **2** *have a dispute over boundaries* argument, row, altercation, clash, quarrel, wrangle, squabble, feud, disturbance, fracas, brawl.
Antonyms: AGREEMENT; ACCORD.

disqualify *verb disqualify the runner* declare ineligible, rule out, preclude, debar, reject, prohibit, disentitle.

disquiet *noun* disquietude, inquietude, uneasiness, unease, unrest, anxiety, anxiousness, angst, nervousness, agitation, perturbation, upset, worry, concern, distress, trouble, alarm, fear, fretfulness, restlessness, dread, foreboding.

disquiet *verb* make uneasy/anxious/nervous, agitate, perturb, upset, disturb, unsettle, discompose, ruffle, worry, concern, distress, trouble, bother, alarm, frighten, make fretful/restless, vex.

disregard *verb* **1** *disregard the consequences* ignore, take no notice/account of, pay no attention/heed to, discount, set aside, neglect, forget, never mind, overlook, turn a blind eye to, pass over, gloss over, brush aside, laugh off, make light of; *inf.* play down. **2** *disregard the neighbors | disregard their achievement* slight, disparage, denigrate, disdain, despise, shun, cold shoulder, insult, affront; *inf.* turn one's nose up at.

disregard *noun* **1** *treat danger with disregard* lack of notice/attention/heed, inattention, heedlessness, carelessness, neglect, negligence, indifference. **2** *treat staff/achievements with disregard* scorn, contempt, disparagement, denigration, disdain, disrespect, disesteem.

disrepair *noun* dilapidation, deterioration, decay, collapse, shabbiness, ruin, ruination, decrepitude.

disreputable *adjective* **1** *disreputable dealer* of bad reputation, infamous, dishonorable, dishonest, unprincipled, villainous, notorious, ignominious, corrupt, unworthy, base, low, mean, questionable, unsavory, unscrupulous, rascally, contemptible, reprehensible, despicable, discreditable, disgraceful, shameful, shocking, outrageous, scandalous; *inf.* crooked, shady. **2** *of disreputable appearance* shabby, slovenly, down-at-the-heels, seedy, dilapidated, threadbare, untidy, disheveled, bedraggled; *inf.* scruffy.

disrepute *noun fall into disrepute* bad reputation, lack of respectability, notoriety, discredit, ill repute, unpopularity, disfavor, ill favor, disesteem, disgrace, shame, dishonor, infamy, ignominy, degradation, odium.

disrespect *noun* lack of respect, discourtesy, lack of civility, incivility, impoliteness, unmannerliness, rudeness, ungraciousness, irreverence, lack of consideration, disregard, insolence, impudence, scorn, contempt; ill manners.

disrespectful *adjective* discourteous, uncivil, impolite, unmannerly, ill-mannered, rude, irreverent, inconsiderate, insolent, impudent, impertinent, scornful, contemptuous, insulting.
Antonyms: respectful; COURTEOUS.

disrupt *verb disrupt the meeting/traffic/on-line service* throw into disorder/disarray, disorder, disorganize, cause confusion/turmoil in, disarrange, disturb, upset; interrupt, suspend, discontinue, interfere with, obstruct, impede, hamper; *inf.* throw a monkey wrench in/into (the works of).

disruption *noun the disruption of meetings/traffic/services* disorderliness, disorder, disorganization, confusion, turmoil, disarrangement, disarray, disturbance, upset; interruption, suspension, discontinuation, stoppage, interference, obstruction, impeding, hampering.

disruptive *adjective disruptive children* troublemaking, troublesome, divisive, unruly, disorderly, undisciplined, upsetting, disturbing, distracting, noisy.

dissatisfaction *noun* discontent, discontentment, disapproval, disapprobation, disappointment, frustration, unhappiness, regret, chagrin, dismay, vexation, annoyance, irritation, anger, exasperation, resentment, disquiet, restlessness, malaise.

dissatisfied *adjective* discontented, displeased, disgruntled, disapproving, unsatisfied, disappointed, unfulfilled, frustrated, unhappy, regretful, vexed, angry, resentful, restless. *See* DISSATISFACTION.

dissect *verb* **1** *dissect and examine the tissue* cut up, cut/lay open, dismember, vivisect. **2** *dissect the information* analyze, break down, examine, study, inspect, scrutinize, probe, explore, investigate.

dissection noun **1** *dissection in the laboratory* cutting up, cutting open, dismemberment; vivisection, autopsy, postmortem, zootomy. **2** *the dissection of the information* analysis, breakdown, examination, study, inspection, scrutinization, probing, exploration, investigation.

disseminate verb *disseminate ideas/seeds* spread, circulate, broadcast, publish, publicize, proclaim, promulgate, propagate, dissipate, scatter, distribute, disperse, diffuse.

dissension noun disagreement, difference of opinion, dispute, argument, dissent, nonconformity, variance, conflict, friction, strife, discord, contention, quarreling, wrangling, bickering.

dissent verb **dissent from** **1** *dissent from official policy* express disagreement with, disagree with, differ from, be at variance with, decline/refuse to support, not ratify, protest against, object to, dispute. **2** *dissent from established practice* reject, repudiate, renounce, abjure, secede from, apostatize.
Antonyms: ASSENT; ACCEPT.

dissenter noun dissident, objector, protester, protestant, disputant, rebel, revolutionary, nonconformist, apostate, sectarian, heretic.

dissentient adjective dissenting, dissident, disagreeing, differing, protesting, objecting, opposing, nonconformist, noncompliant, apostate, schismatic, unorthodox, heterodox.

dissertation noun treatise, thesis, discourse, essay, critique, exposition, disquisition.

disservice noun bad/ill turn, dirty trick, disfavor, unkindness, injury, harm, hurt, damage, wrong, injustice; *inf.* kick in the teeth.

dissident adjective *dissident opinions in the organizations* dissentient, dissenting, disagreeing, differing, nonconformist, apostate, schismatic, heterodox. *See* DISSENTIENT.

dissident noun *expelling dissidents from the party* dissenter, rebel, objector, protester, nonconformist, apostate, heretic. *See* DISSENTER.

dissimilar adjective unlike, unalike, different, varying, variant, disparate, unrelated, divergent, deviating, diverse, various, contrasting, mismatched, distinct.

dissimilarity noun difference, unlikeness, dissimilitude, variance, disparity, unrelatedness, discrepancy, divergence, deviation, diversity, variation, nonuniformity, contrast, distinction, incomparability.

dissipate verb **1** *dissipate one's fears* disperse, scatter, drive away, dispel, dissolve. **2** *the crowd dissipated* break up, disperse, scatter, dissolve, disappear, vanish, melt away, melt into thin air, evaporate. **3** *dissipate their resources* squander, fritter, misspend, lavish, waste, exhaust, drain, deplete, spend, expend, burn up, use up, consume, run through.
Antonyms: ASSEMBLE; CONSERVE.

dissipated adjective **1** *a dissipated young man* dis-

solute, debauched, intemperate, profligate, abandoned, rakish, licentious, promiscuous, drunken, self-indulgent, wild, unrestrained, wanton, depraved, degenerate, corrupt. **2** *dissipated resources* squandered, frittered away, wasted, exhausted, depleted, consumed. *See* DISSIPATE 3.

dissociate verb **1** *dissociate his actions from his theories* separate, set apart, segregate, isolate, detach, disconnect, sever, divorce. **2** *dissociate the teams* disband, break up, dissolve, disperse, scatter, dismiss. **dissociate oneself from** sever connections with, break off relations with, withdraw from, part company with, quit, take one's leave of.

dissolute adjective debauched, dissipated, intemperate, profligate, abandoned, rakish, licentious, promiscuous, drunken, self-indulgent, wild, unrestrained, wanton, depraved, degenerate, corrupt.

dissolution noun **1** *the dissolution of salt in water* dissolving, liquefaction, melting, deliquescence. **2** *the dissolution of the compound* breaking up, separation, resolution, decomposition, disintegration. **3** *the dissolution of the Roman empire* breaking up, disintegration, decay, collapse, death, demise, extinction, destruction, ruin, overthrow. **4** *the dissolution of hopes* disappearance, vanishing, evaporation, dwindling, dispersal, dissipation, evanescence. *See* DISSOLVE 3. **5** *the dissolution of the partnership/marriage* end, ending, finish, termination, conclusion, breakup, discontinuation, winding-up, disbanding, suspension. **6** *the dissolution of the societies/crowds* disbandment, separation, dispersal, scattering. *See* DISSOLVE 5. **7** *the dissolution of the idle rich* debauchery, dissipation, intemperance, profligacy, abandonment, licentiousness, promiscuity, drunkenness, self-indulgence, wildness, lack of restraint, depravity, degeneracy, corruption.

dissolve verb **1** *salt dissolves in water* go into solution, liquefy, melt, deliquesce. **2** *dissolve the salt in water* liquefy, melt, form into a solution. **3** *his hopes dissolved* disappear, vanish, melt away, evaporate, dwindle, disperse, dissipate, disintegrate, crumble, decompose, perish, die, evanesce. **4** *dissolve a partnership/society* bring to an end, end, terminate, break up, discontinue, wind up, disband, dismiss, suspend, ruin. **5** *the societies/crowds dissolved* break up, split up, disband, separate, sever, disunite, disjoin, disperse, scatter, go their separate ways. **6** *dissolve in tears/mirth* break into, collapse into, be overcome with.

dissonance noun **1** *the dissonance of the music* discordance, inharmoniousness, unmelodiousness, cacophony, harshness, stridency, grating, jarring, jangle. **2** *the dissonance between their actions and theories* disagreement, difference, dissimilarity, variance, inconsistency, disparity, discrepancy, incongruity. **3** *the dissonance between the families* discord, disagreement, difference of opinion, dissension, quarreling, feuding.

dissuade *verb* persuade/advise against, persuade/advise/urge not to, put off, stop; talk out of, discourage/deter from, divert, turn aside from, disincline from.

distance *noun* **1** *the distance between the fields* space, interval, span, gap, separation, stretch, extent; length, width, depth. **2** *the distance of the farm from the highway* remoteness, farness. **3** *upset by her colleague's distance* aloofness, reserve, remoteness, reticence, coolness, coldness, frigidity, stiffness, formality, restraint, unresponsiveness. *See* DISTANT 6. **in the distance** far away, far off, on the horizon, afar, yonder.

distance *verb* **1** *distance oneself from the organization* place far off, set apart, separate, dissociate, remove. **2** *distance the rest of the runners* outdistance, outstrip, outrun, leave behind, pass, outdo, surpass.

distant *adjective* **1** *a distant place* far, faraway, far off, remote, out of the way, outlying, abroad, far-flung. **2** *a distant time* far-off, long ago. **3** *three miles distant from each other* away, off, apart, separated, dispersed, scattered. **4** *a distant relative/likeness* not close, remote, indirect, slight. **5** *a distant memory* vague, faint, indistinct, obscure, uncertain. **6** *a distant smile* aloof, reserved, remote, uncommunicative, unapproachable, standoffish, withdrawn, reticent, restrained, cool, cold, frigid, stiff, formal, ceremonious, unresponsive, unfriendly, haughty, condescending.
Antonyms: NEAR; RECENT; FRIENDLY; approachable.

distaste *noun* dislike, displeasure, disfavor, disinclination, dissatisfaction, aversion, disgust, revulsion, repugnance, antipathy, loathing, detestation, horror.

distasteful *adjective* **1** *distasteful behavior* unpleasant, disagreeable, displeasing, undesirable, uninviting, objectionable, offensive, obnoxious, unsavory, disgusting, revolting, repugnant, abhorrent, loathsome, detestable. **2** *distasteful food* unpalatable, unsavory, unappetizing, disgusting, sickening, nauseating, nauseous.

distended *adjective* enlarged, swollen, puffed-up, puffy, inflated, ballooning, bloated, dilated, stretched, expanded, extended.

distill *verb* **1** *distill fresh water from seawater* vaporize/evaporate and condense, sublime, sublimate, fractionate. **2** *distill the essence from a plant* extract, press out, squeeze out, express, draw out. **3** *distill the chemical* separate, concentrate, purify, refine, rectify. **4** *distilling beads of liquid* exude, give out, sweat, drip, leak, dribble.

distillation *noun* essence, extract, spirit, quintessence, elixir, decoction.

distinct *adjective* **1** *a distinct resemblance* clear, clear-cut, well-defined, sharp, marked, decided, definite, unmistakable, recognizable, obvious, plain, plain as day, evident, apparent, manifest, patent, palpable, unambiguous, unequivocal. **2** *two distinct jobs* separate, individual, different, unconnected, unassociated, detached, discrete, dissimilar, unlike, disparate.
Antonyms: INDISTINCT; INDEFINITE; VAGUE.

distinction *noun* **1** *make the distinction between right and wrong* differentiation, contradistinction, discrimination, division, separation, dividing line, contrast. **2** *fail to notice the identifying distinctions* difference, dissimilarity, dissimilitude, contrast, differential, subtlety, nicety, nuance. **3** *the distinctions of wealth and rank* feature, characteristic, mark, individuality, peculiarity. **4** *pass the exam with distinction* honor, credit, excellence, merit. **5** *people of distinction* note, consequence, importance, account, significance, greatness, prestige, prominence, eminence, repute, reputation, renown, fame, mark, celebrity, honor, merit, worth, excellence, glory, name, rank, quality, superiority.

distinctive *adjective* distinguishing, characteristic, typical, individual, particular, peculiar, special, different, uncommon, unusual, remarkable, singular, extraordinary, noteworthy, original, idiosyncratic.
Antonyms: ORDINARY; RUN-OF-THE-MILL.

distinctly *adverb* **1** *distinctly annoyed* clearly, markedly, decidedly, definitely, unmistakably, obviously, plainly, evidently, apparently, manifestly, patently, palpably. **2** *speak distinctly* clearly, plainly, intelligibly, precisely.

distinguish *verb* **1** *distinguish one color from another* tell apart, differentiate, discriminate, determine; tell the difference between, decide between. **2** *his hair distinguishes him from the others* make distinctive, set apart, separate, single out, mark off, characterize, individualize, designate, categorize, classify. **3** *distinguish a black shape* make out, see, discern, perceive, observe, notice, detect, recognize, identify, pick out. **4** *distinguish himself in battle* make famous, bring fame/honor to, bestow honor on, ennoble, dignify, glorify, win acclaim for, lionize, immortalize.

---

distinguish
descry, differentiate, discern, discriminate

What we **discern** we see apart from all other objects (*to discern the lighthouse beaming on the far shore*). **Descry** puts even more emphasis on the distant or unclear nature of what we're seeing (*the lookout was barely able to descry a man approaching in the dusk*). To **discriminate** is to perceive the differences between or among things that are very similar; it may suggest that some aesthetic evaluation is involved (*to discriminate between two painters' styles*). **Distinguish** requires making even finer distinctions among things that resemble each other even more closely (*unable to distinguish the shadowy figures moving through the forest*). *Distinguish* can also mean recognizing by some special mark or outward sign (*the sheriff could be distinguished by his silver badge*). **Differentiate**, on the other hand, suggests the ability to perceive differences between things that are easily confused. In contrast to *distinguish*, *differentiate* suggests subtle differences that must be compared in some detail (*the color of her dress was difficult to differentiate from the color of the chair in which she was seated; it took a sharp eye to distinguish where her skirt ended and the upholstery began*) If you have trouble *differentiating* among these closely related verbs, you're not alone.

distinguishable *adjective no distinguishable difference* clear, plainly seen, obvious, evident, marked, well-defined, conspicuous, noticeable, discernible, perceptible, recognizable, manifest.

distinguished *adjective a distinguished scientist* famous, famed, eminent, renowned, prominent, well-known, noted, notable, esteemed, acclaimed, illustrious, celebrated, respected, legendary.
Antonyms: UNKNOWN; OBSCURE.

distinguishing *adjective a distinguishing mark* distinctive, differentiating, discriminating, determining, individualistic, peculiar, singular, characteristic, typical.

distort *verb* **1** *distort the metal* | *distort their features* twist, warp, contort, bend, buckle, deform, misshape, disfigure, mangle, wrench, wring, wrest. **2** *distort the facts* misrepresent, pervert, twist, falsify, garble, slant, bias, color, tamper with, alter, change, torture.

distortion *noun* **1** *a distortion in the metal* twist, warp, contortion, bend, buckle, curvature, deformation, deformity, malformation, gnarl, knot; crookedness. **2** *a distortion of the truth* misrepresentation, perversion, twisting, falsification, garbling, coloring, alteration; slant, bias, change.

distract *verb* **1** *distract them from work* deflect, divert, sidetrack, turn aside, draw away. **2** *distract the children* amuse, entertain, divert, beguile, absorb, engage, occupy. **3** *bright lights distracting her* confuse, bewilder, perplex, puzzle, disturb, fluster, agitate, disconcert, discompose, confound, annoy, trouble, harass, worry, torment; *inf.* hassle. **4** *grief distracting her* make frantic, drive/make mad, madden, drive insane, make crazy, derange, throw into a frenzy.
Antonyms: FOCUS; CONCENTRATE.

distracted *adjective* **1** *rushing around in a distracted way* confused, bewildered, bemused, perplexed, agitated, flustered, troubled, harassed, worried; *inf.* hassled. *See* DISTRACT 3. **2**

distracted women mourning their sons griefstricken, distraught, frantic, frenzied, raving, wild, hysterical, overwrought, mad, maddened, insane, crazed, deranged, out of one's mind.

distraction *noun* **1** *distraction from their work* diversion, interruption, disturbance, interference, obstruction. **2** *distractions for the children* amusement, entertainment, diversion, pastime, recreation, hobby, game, occupation. **3** *a look of distraction amid the crowds* confusion, bewilderment, befuddlement, perplexity, disturbance, agitation, perturbation, harassment. *See* DISTRACT 3. **4** *pity the distraction of the widow* frenzy, hysteria, mental distress, madness, insanity, craziness, mania, derangement, delirium.

distress *noun* **1** *the lost child's distress* anguish, suffering, pain, agony, ache, affliction, torment, torture, misery, wretchedness, discomfort, heartache, heartbreak, sorrow, grief, woe, sadness, desolation, trouble, worry, anxiety, perturbation, uneasiness, angst; tribulations, cries, wails. **2** *old people in distress* hardship, adversity, misfortune, trouble, calamity, need, want, poverty, lack, privation, destitution, indigence, impoverishment, penury; difficulties, dire straits.
Antonyms: TRANQUILLITY; SERENITY.

distress *verb* **1** *the news distressed her* cause anguish/suffering, pain, upset, make miserable/wretched, grieve, sadden, trouble, worry, bother, arouse anxiety in, perturb, disturb, vex, harrow, torment. **2** *distress the furniture* dent, scratch, antique, simulate age/wear in.
Antonyms: PLEASE; GLADDEN.

distressing *adjective* *distressing news/sights* disturbing, worrying, upsetting, affecting, painful, sad, heartbreaking.

distribute *verb* **1** *distribute rations to the crowd* give out, hand out, allocate, allot, issue, dispense, administer, apportion, assign, deal out, share out, divide out, dole out, measure out, mete out, parcel out, dispose. **2** *distribute advertising leaflets* circulate, pass out/around, hand out, deliver, convey, transmit. **3** *distribute seeds evenly* disseminate, disperse, diffuse, scatter, spread, strew, sow. **4** *luggage distributed by size* place, position, arrange, organize, dispose, group, class, classify, categorize, file, assort, compart, locate.

distribution *noun* **1** *distribution of rations* giving out, allocation, allotment, dispensation, administering, assignment, dealing out, division. *See* DISTRIBUTE 1. **2** *distribution of seeds* dissemination, dispersal, diffusion, scattering. *See* DISTRIBUTE 3. **3** *the distribution of luggage by size* placement, position, arrangement, organization, disposition, grouping, classification, assortment, location. *See* DISTRIBUTE 4. **4** *in charge of sales and distribution* handling, delivery, transport, transportation, conveyance, mailing. **5** *an abnormal statistical distribution*

district noun 1 *live in a pleasant district* area, region, place, locality, neighborhood, quarter, sector, vicinity, territory, domain. 2 *an administrative district* administrative division, county, ward, parish, community, constituency, department, canton.

distrust verb mistrust, be suspicious of, be wary/chary of, be skeptical of, have doubts about, doubt, have misgivings about, wonder about, question, suspect, disbelieve, discredit; *inf.* be leery of.
Antonym: TRUST.

distrust noun mistrust, lack of trust, no confidence, lack of faith, suspicion, wariness, chariness, skepticism, doubt, doubtfulness, dubiety, misgiving, questioning, qualms, disbelief, unbelief, incredulity, incredulousness, discredit; *inf.* leeriness.

disturb verb 1 *disturb them while they are working* interrupt, butt in on, distract, bother, trouble, pester, intrude on, interfere with, hinder, plague, harass, molest; *inf.* hassle. 2 *disturb papers on a desk* disarrange, muddle, disorganize, disorder, confuse, throw into disorder/confusion, derange, unsettle. 3 *the news disturbed them* concern, perturb, trouble, worry, upset, agitate, fluster, discomfit, disconcert, alarm, frighten, startle, dismay, distress, discompose, unsettle, ruffle, shake, confuse, bewilder, perplex, confound, excite. 4 *disturb the water* agitate, churn up, convulse, roil. 5 *don't disturb yourself* inconvenience, put out, put to trouble.
Antonyms: CALM; EASE.

disturbance noun 1 *resent the disturbance to their work* interruption, distraction, intrusion, interference, hindrance, harassment. *See* DISTURB 1. 2 *the disturbance of papers* disarrangement, muddling, disorganization, confusing; muddle, disorder, confusion. 3 *causing emotional disturbance* concern, perturbation, trouble, worry, upset, agitation, discomfiture, alarm, distress, bewilderment. *See* DISTURB 3. 4 *the disturbance of the water* agitation, churning. *See* DISTURB 4. 5 *police called to a disturbance* uproar, commotion, row, rumpus, hullabaloo, tumult, turmoil, fracas, affray, brawl, riot; *inf.* ruckus.

disturbed adjective *emotionally disturbed* upset, troubled, unbalanced, disordered, maladjusted, neurotic, psychotic; *inf.* screwed up.

disturbing adjective *disturbing news* perturbing, troubling, worrying, upsetting, agitating, disconcerting, alarming, disquieting, startling, dismaying, frightening, distressing, unsettling, bewildering. *See* DISTURB 3.

disuse noun nonuse, nonemployment, lack of use, neglect, abandonment, cessation, discontinuance, obsolescence.

disused adjective unused, neglected, abandoned, discontinued, obsolete.

ditch noun trench, channel, watercourse, dike, canal, drain, gutter, gully, moat, furrow, rut.

ditch verb 1 *be engaged in digging and ditching* dig, trench, excavate, gouge, hollow out, drain. 2 *ditch the plan* abandon, throw out, discard, drop, scrap, jettison, get rid of, dispose of; *inf.* dump. 3 *ditch the police* evade, escape, elude, shake off, defeat, frustrate, balk.

diurnal adjective 1 *a diurnal occurrence* daily, occurring every day, daytime, circadian. 2 *a diurnal flower/animal* of the day, daytime, nonnocturnal.

divan noun sofa, couch, settee, *chaise longue*, davenport, ottoman, day bed.

dive verb 1 *dive from the springboard* plunge/descend into water, go/jump into water, plummet, jump, leap, bound, spring, nosedive, fall, descend, submerge, drop, swoop, dip, bellyflop. 2 *dive out of sight* move quickly, leap, jump, lunge, rush, dart, dash, duck, dodge.

dive noun 1 *a dive from the springboard* plunge, plummet, jump, leap, spring, nosedive, fall, drop, swoop, bellyflop. 2 *a quick dive under the bed* leap, jump, lunge, rush, dart, dash, duck, dodge. 3 *drinking in dives* sleazy bar/nightclub/saloon; *inf.* joint, dump.

diverge verb 1 *the roads diverged* separate, divide, subdivide, split, part, disunite, fork, branch off, radiate, spread out, bifurcate, divaricate. 2 *opinions diverge* differ, disagree, be at variance/odds, conflict, clash. 3 *diverge from the norm* deviate, digress, depart, veer, stray, drift, turn aside, wander.
Antonyms: JOIN; CONVERGE; AGREE; STAY.

divergence noun 1 *the divergence of the roads* separation, dividing, parting, forking, branching, bifurcation; fork, division. *See* DIVERGE 1. 2 *divergence of opinions* difference, disagreement, variance, varying, conflict. *See* DIVERGE 2. 3 *divergence from the norm* deviation, digression, departure, straying, deflection.

divergent adjective 1 *divergent opinions* differing, different, diverse, disagreeing, in disagreement, varying, conflicting, clashing, dissenting. 2 *divergent statistical results* deviating, digressing, abnormal, aberrant.
Antonyms: SIMILAR; NORMAL.

divers adjective several, numerous, many, some; sundry, various, different, manifold.

diverse adjective various, miscellaneous, assorted, mixed, diversified, variegated, varied, varying, heterogeneous, different, differing, distinct, unlike, dissimilar, distinctive, contrasting, conflicting.
Antonyms: IDENTICAL; SIMILAR; LIKE.

diversify verb 1 *diversify the range* vary, bring variety to, variegate, modify, assort, mix, alter, change, transform. 2 *firms must diversify* extend operations/products, expand, spread.

diversion noun 1 *the diversion of the stream* redirection, turning aside, deflection, digression, deviation, divergence. **2** *take the diversion* alternative route, detour. **3** *diversions provided for the children* amusement, entertainment, pastime, distraction, recreation, fun, relaxation, game, play, sport, hobby, pleasure, delight, enjoyment, beguilement, enchantment. *Antonym:* ROUTINE.

diversity *noun* *diversity of opinion* diverseness, variety, miscellany, assortment, mixture, range, medley, multiplicity, variegation, heterogeneity, diversification, difference, unlikeness, dissimilarity, distinctiveness, dissimilitude, contrast, conflict.

divert *verb* **1** *divert the stream* turnaside, deflect, draw away, avert, switch/change the course of, redirect. **2** *divert him from his work* distract, detract, sidetrack, leadaway, turn aside, deflect. **3** *clowns diverted the children*amuse, entertain, distract, delight, give pleasure to, beguile, enchant,interest, occupy, absorb, engross, recreate. *Antonyms:* BORE; WEARY.

diverting *adjective* amusing, entertaining, humorous, fun, enjoyable, pleasurable, recreational, beguiling, interesting, absorbing.

divest *verb* **1** *divest himself of his clothes* | *trees divested of their leaves* unclothe, undress, disrobe, strip, denude. **2** *divest them of power/property* deprive, strip, dispossess, relieve, bereave.

divide *verb* **1** *divide the apple in two* | *divide one group from another* cut up, sever, split, shear, bisect, halve, quarter, cleave, rend, sunder, rive; separate, part, segregate, partition, detach, disconnect, disjoin. **2** *the road divides here* diverge, branch, fork, split in two, divaricate. **3** *divide the food* share, allocate, allot, apportion, portion out, distribute, dispense, deal out, hand out, dole out, measure out, parcel out, *inf.* divvy (up/out). **4** *politics divided them* estrange, alienate, break up, separate, spilt up, disunite, disaffect, set/pit against one another, cause disagreement between, sow dissension between, set at variance/odds, come between. **5** *divide into types* classify, sort, arrange, order, group, grade, rank, categorize, dispose, separate, segregate. *Antonyms:* JOIN; UNITE; COMBINE.

dividend *noun* **1** *dividends paid to shareholders* share, portion, gain, surplus; *inf.* cut, divvy. **2** *dividends brought by hard work* bonus, extra, plus, benefit, fringe benefit, perquisite; *inf.* perk.

divine *adjective* **1** *a divine being* godly, godlike, heavenly, celestial, holy, angelic, seraphic, spiritual, saintly. **2** *divine worship* religious, holy, sacred, sanctified, consecrated, spiritual. **3** *divine music* supernatural, superhuman, mystical, exalted, beatific, blissful, ethereal, transcendental, transcendent. **4** *looking divine* | *a divine evening* lovely, beautiful, charming, perfect, excellent, superlative, wonderful, glorious, marvelous, admirable; *inf.* super, stunning. *Antonyms:* MORTAL; HELLISH; MUNDANE; UGLY.

divine
consecrated, hallowed, holy, sacred
Holy is the only one of these words associated with religion and worship that may be applied directly to the Supreme Being. Something that is *holy* is regarded with the highest reverence because of its connection with God or a god (*Christmas is a holy day in the Christian calendar*). Something that is **sacred**, on the other hand, is set apart as *holy* or is dedicated to some exalted purpose (*sacred music*) but may derive its holiness from a human source rather than from God (*a sacred oath between brothers*). In its strictest sense, **divine** means associated with or derived from God (*the divine right of kings*), but it has also been used to describe anything that is admirable or treasured (*her wedding dress was divine*). **Hallowed** and **consecrated** refer to what has been made sacred or holy, with *hallowed* connoting intrinsic holiness (*they walked on hallowed ground*) and *consecrated* meaning blessed by a formal rite or formally dedicated to some religious use (*the old building had been consecrated as a church*).

divine *noun* theologian, clergyman, churchman, churchwoman, cleric, ecclesiastic, minister, priest, pastor, parson, reverend.

divine *verb* **1** *divine their plans* | *divine that they are going* guess, surmise, conjecture, speculate, suspect, suppose, assume, presume, deduce, infer, theorize, hypothesize. **2** *divine their need* intuit, discern, perceive, understand, grasp, apprehend, comprehend. **3** *divine the future* foretell, predict, foresee, forecast, presage, augur, portend, prognosticate, forebode. **4** *divine for water* dowse.

divinity *noun* **1** *the theological study of divinity* divine nature, divineness, deity, godhead, godliness, holiness, sanctity. **2** *worship the divinity* deity, god, goddess, genius, spirit, guardian, angel.

division *noun* **1** *the division of the apple/groups* dividing, cutting up, severance, splitting, bisection, cleaving; parting, separation, segregation, partitioning, disconnection, detachment. *See* DIVIDE 1. **2** *the division of rations* sharing, allocation, allotment, apportionment, distribution. *See* DIVIDE 3. **3** *cross the division* dividing line, divide, boundary, boundary line, border, partition, line of demarcation. **4** *divisions of equal size* section, part, portion, piece, bit, segment, slice, fragment, chunk, component, share; compartment, category, class, group, grade, family. **5** *divisions of the firm* branch, department, section, sector, arm. **6** *a bitter division between the families* disagreement, difference of opinion, feud, breach, rupture, split; dissension, conflict, discord, variance, disunion, estrangement, alienation.

divisive *adjective* alienating, estranging, disruptive, troublemaking, troublesome, detrimental, damaging, injurious, pernicious, discordant, inharmonious.

divorce *noun* **1** *marriage ended in divorce* dissolution, disunion, breakup, split-up, annulment, official separation, separation, severance, breach, rupture. **2** *the divorce between their theories and their actions* separation, severance, division, split, partition.

divorce *verb* **1** *the couple divorced* annul/dissolve a marriage, split up, break up, separate, part. **2** *she divorced him | she (got) divorced last year* end a marriage with/to, have/get a marriage annulled/dissolved. **3** *their views are divorced from reality* separate, disconnect, divide, dissociate, detach, disunite, sever, disjoin, split.
Antonyms: MARRY; CONNECT; JOIN.

divulge *verb* disclose, reveal, make known, tell, impart, communicate, publish, broadcast, proclaim, promulgate, declare, utter, expose, uncover, bring into the open, let slip, leak, let the cat out of the bag about, confess, betray; *inf.* spill the beans about.
Antonyms: CONCEAL; HIDE.

dizzy *adjective* **1** *get dizzy on top of the ladder* lightheaded, faint, vertiginous, weak at/in the knees, shaky, wobbly, off-balance, reeling, staggering; *inf.* woozy. **2** *feeling dizzy at the amount of information* dazed, bewildered, confused, muddled, bemused, befuddled, puzzled, perplexed; *inf.* woozy. **3** *dizzy young girls* giddy, scatterbrained, featherbrained, flighty, foolish, silly, light-headed, fickle, capricious, inconstant.

do *verb* **1** *do as you know you should* act, behave, conduct oneself, comport oneself. **2** *do the job* perform, carry out, undertake, discharge, execute, accomplish, implement, achieve, complete, finish, conclude, bring about, effect, effectuate, realize, produce, engineer. **3** *this amount will do* be enough, be sufficient, be adequate, suffice, be satisfactory, be of use, fill/fit the bill, answer/serve the purpose, meet the needs, pass muster, measure up. **4** *do the meals* make, prepare, get ready, fix, produce, see to, arrange, organize, be responsible for, be in charge of, look after, take on. **5** *do a large picture* create, make, produce, originate, form, fashion, design, fabricate, manufacture. **6** *they're doing three plays* put on, perform, act, present, produce, give. **7** *do me a favor* render, afford, give, bestow, grant, pay. **8** *can't do this math problem* solve, resolve, work out, figure out, decipher. **9** *what does he do?* work at, be employed at, have as a job/profession/occupation, earn a living at. **10** *how are you doing?* get on/along, progress, fare, make out, manage, continue. **11** *the play was done in Russian* translate, put, render, adapt, transform. **12** *the car was doing 90 mph* travel at, go/proceed at, be driven at. **13** *we did 50 miles* travel, journey, cover, traverse. **14** *they're doing the museums*

today sightsee, look at, visit, tour. **do away with 1** *do away with the penalty* abolish, get rid of, discard, remove, discontinue, eliminate, repeal, revoke, rescind, cancel, annul, nullify. **2** *do away with his enemy* kill, put to death, slay, murder, slaughter, liquidate, assassinate, execute, dispatch; *inf.* do in, bump off, knock off, eliminate. **do in 1** *do in his enemy* kill, put to death, slay, murder, assassinate; *inf.* do away with, bump off. **2** *do in his business* ruin, reduce to nothing, wreck, destroy, smash, crush, wreak havoc on. **3** *the walk did me in* tire out, exhaust, wear out, fatigue, weary. **do out of** prevent from having, deprive of, swindle/cheat/trick out of; *inf.* con out of. **do without** forgo, dispense with, abstain from, give up, refrain from, eschew.

do *noun* party, function, affair, occasion, fête, soirée; *inf.* bash, blowout.

docile *adjective* manageable, controllable, tractable, malleable, amenable, accommodating, compliant, pliant, obedient, biddable, dutiful, submissive, yielding, ductile.
Antonyms: DISOBEDIENT; WILLFUL; INTRACTABLE.

dock *noun* *tie up at the dock* pier, quay, wharf, jetty, marina, waterfront.

dock *verb* **1** *dock the dogs' tails* cut, cut short, shorten, crop, lop, truncate. **2** *dock money from wages* deduct, subtract, remove, take off. **3** *dock their wages* reduce, decrease, lessen, diminish.

docket *noun* *the bailiff announced today's docket* court list/agenda, agenda, roster, schedule, slate, program.

doctor *noun* medical practitioner, physician, surgeon, medical man/woman/person; general practitioner, GP; medicine man, healer, shaman; *inf.* doc, sawbones, quack; witch doctor.

doctor *verb* **1** *doctor the patients* treat, prescribe for, attend to, minister to, care for, cure, heal. **2** *doctor the machinery* patch up, repair, fix, mend, botch. **3** *doctor the drinks* adulterate, contaminate, dilute, water down, weaken, mix, cut, lace; *inf.* spike. **4** *doctor the evidence* tamper with, interfere with, alter, change, falsify, disguise, fudge, pervert, misrepresent.

doctrinaire *adjective* **1** *doctrinaire teachers* dogmatic, authoritarian, rigid, inflexible, insistent, domineering, opinionated, intolerant, biased, prejudiced, fanatical. **2** *doctrinaire schemes* impractical, unpragmatic, unrealistic, theoretical, hypothetical, ideological, speculative, visionary.

doctrine *noun* creed, credo, dogma, belief, conviction, teaching, tenet, principle, precept, maxim; articles of faith, canons.

document *noun* *business documents* official paper, legal paper, paper, form, certificate, record, report, deed, voucher, instrument, charter; paperwork, documentation.

document verb **1** *document their statement* prove, back up, support, give weight to, corroborate, substantiate, authenticate, verify, validate, certify. **2** *the war was well documented in the press | his marriage is not documented* report, record, detail, tabulate, chart, register, cite, instance.

documentary adjective **1** *documentary evidence* documented, recorded, registered, tabulated, charted, written. **2** *a documentary film* factual, nonfictional, real-life, true to life, realistic.

dodder verb totter, teeter, stagger, shuffle, falter, shake, tremble, quiver.

doddering adjective tottering, staggering, shuffling, faltering, shaky, unsteady, trembling, trembly, quivering, infirm, decrepit, aged, in one's dotage, senile.

dodge verb **1** *dodge behind the door* dart, duck, dive, swerve, sidestep, veer, jump away, move aside. **2** *dodge the police* evade, elude, escape, fend off, avoid, stay/steer clear of, deceive, trick; *inf.* give the slip to. **3** *dodge awkward questions* evade, get out of, parry, fend off, fudge. **4** *dodge hard work* avoid, evade, shirk, shun, stay/steer clear of.

dodge noun **1** *a dodge to the right* dart, duck, dive, swerve, jump. **2** *a dodge to avoid work | a tax dodge* ruse, ploy, scheme, stratagem, subterfuge, trick, wile, deception, maneuver, device, machination, contrivance, artifice, expedient.

doer noun **1** *the doer of the deed* performer, executor, accomplisher. **2** *doers rather than thinkers* worker, organizer, achiever, high achiever, activist, hustler, entrepreneur; *inf.* busy bee, live wire, go-getter, whiz kid, powerhouse, wheeler-dealer.

doff verb **1** *doff their hats* raise, lift, remove, take off, tip. **2** *doff their clothes* take off, remove, shed, strip off, throw off, cast off.

dog noun **1** *cats and dogs* canine, hound, mongrel, cur; bitch, sire; pup, puppy, whelp; *inf.* doggy, doggie, pooch, mutt. **2** *he's a dirty dog* scoundrel, blackguard, beast, cad, rogue, villain, cur, knave, heel, bastard. **3** *a lucky dog* person, fellow; *inf.* guy.

dog verb *dogged by ill luck* pursue, follow, track, trail, shadow, hound, plague, trouble, haunt; *inf* tail.

dogged adjective determined, resolute, obstinate, stubborn, tenacious, relentless, intent, single-minded, unshakable, unflagging, indefatigable, tireless, unfaltering, unwavering, persistent, persevering, pertinacious, unyielding, obdurate, firm, steadfast, steady, staunch. **Antonyms:** HESITANT; HALFHEARTED.

doggedness noun determination, resolution, obstinacy, stubbornness, tenacity, relentlessness, single-mindedness, tirelessness, persistence, perseverance, endurance, steadfastness, steadiness. *See* DOGGED.

dogma noun **1** *Christian dogma* creed, credo,

code of belief, conviction, teaching; belief, tenet, principle, precept, maxim; articles of faith, canons. **2** *tired of political dogma* unquestioned belief, unchallengeable conviction, arrogant conviction.

dogmatic adjective **1** *dogmatic religious tenets* doctrinal, doctrinaire, canonical, authoritative, *ex cathedra*. **2** *dogmatic statement/manner* assertive, insistent, emphatic, categorical, downright, authoritarian, opinionated, peremptory, domineering, imperious, arrogant, overbearing, dictatorial, intolerant, biased, prejudiced; *inf.* pushy.

doing noun **1** *the doing of the deed* performance, carrying out, discharging, execution, accomplishment, implementation, achievement, effectuation, realization. **2** *famous for brave doings* deed, act, action, feat, exploit, work, enterprise, achievement; handiwork. **3** *take a lot of doing* effort, activity, exertion, work, application, struggle.

doldrums plural noun **1** *a fit of the doldrums* downheartedness, dejection, depression, melancholy, gloom, inertia, apathy, listlessness, malaise, boredom, tedium, ennui; blues, low spirits. **2** *a business in the doldrums* inactivity, inertia, flatness, stagnation, dullness, sluggishness, torpor.

dole verb **dole out** deal out, allocate, allot, apportion, share (out), mete out, distribute, divide up, dispense, hand out, give out, issue, assign, administer.

doleful adjective mournful, sorrowful, sad, dejected, disconsolate, depressed, gloomy, melancholy, blue, miserable, wretched; *inf.* down in the mouth/dumps. **Antonyms:** CHEERFUL; JOYFUL; HAPPY.

doll noun figure, figurine, model, puppet, marionette, toy, plaything; *inf.* dolly.

dolor noun sorrow, grief, sadness, heartache, anguish, misery, distress, suffering.

dolt noun blockhead, dunderhead, thickhead, numskull, nitwit, dunce, fool, idiot, ass, simpleton, nincompoop, ignoramus, dullard; *inf.* dope, chump, clod, boob, jerk, dimwit, nerd, airhead.

domain noun **1** *the king's domain* realm, kingdom, empire, dominion, estate. *See* DOMINION 2. **2** *working in the scientific domain* area, field, region, province, sphere, section, discipline.

dome noun cupola, rotunda; hemisphere.

domestic adjective **1** *an unhappy domestic life | domestic water supply* home, family, household, domiciliary, residential, private. **2** *preferring domestic people* domesticated, housewifely, stay-at-home, home-loving. **3** *a domestic animal* domesticated, tame, pet, house-trained, housebroken, trained, not wild. **4** *domestic markets* home, internal, not foreign, not export. **5** *domestic plants* native, indigenous, homegrown, home-bred, aboriginal. **Antonyms:** PUBLIC; WILD; FOREIGN.

domestic noun *employ a domestic* domestic help,

help, maid, domestic servant, servant, au pair, hired help.

domesticate *verb* **1** *domesticate an animal* tame, house-train, housebreak, train, break in, gentle. **2** *domesticate a foreign tree* naturalize, acclimatize, habituate, accustom, familiarize, assimilate.

domesticated *adjective* **1** *domesticated animals* tame, tamed, pet, house-trained, housebroken. **2** *domesticated plants* naturalized, acclimatized, habituated. **3** *domesticated people* domestic, housewifely. *See* DOMESTIC *adjective* 2.

domicile *noun* home, house, residence, residency, dwelling, dwelling place, abode, habitation, lodging, accommodation.

domicile *verb* *they are domiciled in Switzerland* establish, settle, make one's home, take up one's abode, ensconce oneself.

dominant *adjective* **1** *the dominant member of the committee* ruling, governing, controlling, commanding, ascendant, presiding, supreme, authoritative, most influential, superior, most assertive, domineering. **2** *the dominant issue* predominant, most important, chief, main, principal, leading, primary, paramount, preeminent, outstanding, prominent, prevailing. **Antonyms:** SUBMISSIVE; SUBSERVIENT.

dominate *verb* **1** *dominate the council* | *mother dominated in our house* rule, govern, control, exercise control over, command, direct, preside over, have ascendancy/mastery over, master, domineer, tyrannize, intimidate, have the upper hand over, ride roughshod over; have under one's thumb, be in the driver's seat, be in the saddle, wear the pants; *inf.* boss, call the shots. **2** *hostility/silence dominated* predominate, be paramount, be preeminent, prevail, be conspicuous, be most obvious, be most important. **3** *the hill dominates the town* overlook, tower above, stand over, project/jut over, hang/loom over, bestride.

domination *noun* *under foreign domination* rule, government, control, command, direction, authority, power, mastery, supremacy, sway, tyranny, intimidation, oppression, dictatorship.

domineer *verb* browbeat, bully, intimidate, hector, lord it over, tyrannize, be overbearing, ride roughshod over, trample on, have under one's thumb, rule with an iron hand, rule with a rod of iron, bend to one's will, subjugate; *inf.* boss around/about.

domineering *adjective* overbearing, imperious, authoritarian, high-handed, autocratic, peremptory, arrogant, haughty, dictatorial, masterful, forceful, coercive, tyrannical, despotic, oppressive, subjugating, iron-fisted, iron-handed; *inf.* bossy, pushy. **Antonyms:** MEEK; SERVILE.

dominion *noun* **1** *have dominion over smaller states* supremacy, ascendancy, sway, mastery, rule, government, sovereignty, jurisdiction, control, command, direction, authority, power, domination, the upper hand, suzerainty. **2** *the king's dominions* realm, kingdom, empire, domain, country, province, territory, region, estate.

don *verb* put on, slip on, slip into, get into, pull on, dress/clothe oneself in. **Antonym:** DOFF.

donate *verb* give, contribute, make a contribution of, subscribe, make a gift of, gift, present, pledge, put oneself down for, bestow; *inf.* chip in, kick in.

donation *noun* contribution, subscription, gift, present, grant, offering, gratuity; alms; charity, benefaction, largesse.

done *adjective* **1** *the job is done* accomplished, complete, completed, executed, perfected, finished, ended, concluded, terminated, realized, consummated. **2** *the meat is done* cooked, ready. **3** *feeling done after a long day* worn out, exhausted, tired out, weary; *inf.* done in. **4** *such behavior is not done* acceptable, proper, seemly, decorous, conventional, de rigueur. **be/have done with** be finished/through with, have no further dealings with, be no longer involved with/in, end relations with, give up, wash one's hands of. **done for** finished, ruined, destroyed, broken, wrecked, undone, dashed, dead, doomed, lost, defeated, beaten, foiled, frustrated, thwarted; *inf.* washed-up. **done in** worn out, exhausted, tired out, weary, fatigued, played out, on one's last legs; *inf.* done, dog-tired, all in, dead beat, bushed, pooped, worn to a frazzle.

done *interjection* *you're offering $10? Done!* agreed, settled, that's a deal, accepted, right; *inf.* OK, you're on.

donkey *noun* **1** *fed hay to the donkey* ass, mule, jackass, burro, jack, jenny, hinny. **2** *a silly donkey* fool, ass, idiot, nincompoop, nitwit, blockhead, dolt; *inf.* dope, chump, nerd.

donor *noun* giver, contributor, donator, grantor, benefactor, benefactress, supporter, backer, philanthropist; *inf.* angel.

doom *noun* **1** *companies/people facing doom* grim/terrible fate, ruin, ruination, rack and ruin, downfall, destruction, catastrophe, disaster, extinction, annihilation, death, termination, quietus. **2** *the prisoner hearing his doom* condemnation, guilty verdict, sentence, judgment, pronouncement, decree, damnation. **3** *predicting doom* the Last Judgment, Judgment Day, doomsday, Armageddon, end of the world.

doom *verb* **1** *children doomed to be poor* fate, destine, predestine, ordain, preordain, foreordain, consign, condemn. **2** *prisoners doomed to die* condemn, sentence, judge, pronounce, decree, damn.

doomed *adjective* *doomed plans/lovers* ill-fated, star-crossed, foredoomed, unlucky, damned, bedeviled, ruined, crushed.

door *noun* **1** *wooden doors* doorway, portal, entrance, entry, exit, barrier; front door, back door, side door, cupboard door, sliding door, revolving door, trapdoor. **2** *doors to academic success* entrance, entry, access, opening, entrée, gateway, way, path, road, ingress. **out of doors** outside, outdoors, out, in/into the open air, alfresco.

dope *noun* **1** *smuggling dope* drugs, narcotics. *See* DRUG *noun* 2. **2** *a stupid dope* dolt, blockhead, dunderhead, thickhead, dunce, fool, idiot, nincompoop, nitwit; *inf.* chump, dimwit, nerd. **3** *what's the latest dope?* information, inside information, story, news; facts, data, details; *inf.* info, poop, word, low-down.

dope *verb* **1** *the patient is heavily doped* drug, administer drugs/narcotics/opiates to, knock out, anesthetize, stupefy, sedate, narcotize. **2** *dope his drink* add drugs/narcotics/opiates to, doctor; *inf.* spike.

dormant *adjective* sleeping, asleep, slumbering, inactive, inert, latent, fallow, quiescent, inoperative, hibernating, comatose, stagnant, sluggish, lethargic, torpid, passive, motionless, immobile.

Antonyms: awake; ACTIVE.

dose *noun* *a dose of cough syrup* amount, quantity, measure, portion, draft.

dot *noun* spot, speck, fleck, point, mark, dab, particle, atom, iota, jot, mote, mite; period, decimal point. **on the dot** *3 o'clock on the dot* | *arrive on the dot* exactly, precisely, to the minute, on time, punctually, promptly; *inf.* on the button.

dot *verb* **1** *dotted with stains/ships* spot, fleck, bespeckle, mark, dab, stud, bestud, stipple, pock, freckle, sprinkle, scatter, pepper. **2** *dot the letters* mark with a dot, add a dot to, punctuate.

dotage *noun* senility, old age, second childhood, decrepitude, infirmity, feebleness; declining years.

dote *verb* **dote on/upon** *she dotes on her grandchildren* idolize, adore, hold dear, love dearly, treasure, prize, make much of, lavish affection on, indulge, spoil, pamper.

doting *adjective* adoring, devoted, loving, fond, indulgent, pampering.

double *adjective* **1** *double yellow lines* duplicate, twin, paired, in pairs, dual, coupled, twofold, binal, binate. **2** *a double portion* doubled, twice as much/many as usual, twofold, large. **3** *a double thickness* doubled, twofold, folded, folded in two, two-ply. **4** *a double meaning* dual, ambiguous, double-edged, two-edged, ambivalent, equivocal. **5** *a double life* dual, deceitful, false, dishonest, hypocritical, insincere, double-dealing, two-faced, treacherous, perfidious, Janus-faced.

Antonym: SINGLE.

double *adverb* **1** *seeing double* two together, two

at a time, in twos, by twos, two by two. **2** *pay double* twice, twice over, twice the amount.

double *verb* **1** *double the amount* multiply by two, increase twofold, enlarge, magnify. **2** *double as a bed and sofa* have/serve a dual purpose, have a dual role. **3** *he doubled for the main part* | *she doubles in the musical* be an understudy/substitute, understudy; act two roles/parts. **4** *double the paper* fold, bend over.

double *noun* *the double of his cousin* | *the double of the other picture* look-alike, twin, clone, doppelgänger, duplicate, replica, copy, facsimile, counterpart, match, mate, fellow; *inf.* spitting image, dead ringer, ringer. **on the double** at full speed, as fast as possible, very quickly, rapidly, briskly, with haste, in double time, posthaste, right away, immediately, without delay, straight away; *inf.* p.d.q. (= pretty damn/darn quick).

double-cross *verb* betray, cheat, defraud, trick, hoodwink, mislead, deceive, swindle; *inf.* two-time, take for a ride.

double-dealing *noun* duplicity, treachery, betrayal, double-crossing, bad faith, perfidy, breach of trust, fraud, fraudulence, underhandedness, cheating, dishonesty, untrustworthiness, mendacity, deception, trickery, deceit, two-facedness, hypocrisy; *inf.* crookedness.

double entendre *noun* ambiguity, double meaning, suggested meaning, innuendo, play on words, wordplay, pun.

doubt *verb* **1** *doubt his motives* have/entertain doubts about, be suspicious of, harbor suspicions about, suspect, distrust, mistrust, lack confidence in, have misgivings about, feel uneasy/apprehensive about, call in question, query, question. **2** *doubt that it is genuine* have doubts, be dubious, hesitate to believe, feel uncertain, be undecided, lack conviction, query, question, challenge.

Antonyms: TRUST; BELIEVE.

doubt *noun* **1** *have doubts about his motives* distrust, mistrust, lack of confidence/faith, skepticism, uneasiness, apprehension; reservations, misgivings, suspicions, qualms. **2** *express doubt that it is genuine* dubiousness, lack of certainty, uncertainty, indecision, lack of conviction, incredulity; queries, questions. **3** *full of doubts/doubt about his faith* uncertainty, indecision, hesitation; hesitancy, wavering, vacillation, irresolution, lack of conviction. **in doubt** *the issue is still in doubt* | *he is in doubt about it* doubtful, uncertain, undecided, unsettled, unresolved, confused, open to question, ambiguous, problematic; in a quandary/dilemma. **no doubt** *no doubt he will win* doubtless, certainly, of course, surely, assuredly, admittedly, probably, it is likely that.

Antonyms: TRUST; CONFIDENCE; CERTAINTY.

doubter *noun* skeptic, questioner, disbeliever, doubting Thomas, unbeliever, agnostic, scoffer, dissenter, pessimist.

doubtful *adjective* **1** *it is doubtful that he will come* in doubt, uncertain, unsure, unconfirmed, unsettled, improbable, unlikely. **2** *doubtful of/about his motives* suspicious, distrustful, mistrustful, skeptical, having reservations/misgivings, apprehensive, uneasy, questioning, unsure, incredulous. **3** *its genuineness is doubtful* uncertain, dubious, open to question, questionable, debatable, disputable, not definite, inconclusive, unresolved, unconfirmed, unsettled. **4** *the meaning of the word is doubtful* dubious, unclear, ambiguous, equivocal, obscure, vague, nebulous. **5** *doubtful about his religious convictions* uncertain, indecisive, hesitating, irresolute, wavering, vacillating. **6** *spending time with doubtful people* dubious, questionable, suspicious, suspect, under suspicion, unreliable, potentially disreputable.
Antonyms: CERTAIN; SURE; CLEAR.

---

doubtful
ambiguous, dubious, enigmatic, equivocal, problematic, questionable

If you are **doubtful** about the outcome of a situation, you might be understandably **dubious** about getting involved in it. While all of these adjectives express suspicion, indecision, or a lack of clarity, *doubtful* carries such strong connotations of uncertainty that the thing being described is as good as worthless, unsound, invalid, unlikely, or doomed to fail (*it was doubtful that the plane could land safely*). *Dubious* is not quite as strong, suggesting suspicion, mistrust, or hesitation (*a dubious reputation*). It can also mean inclined to doubt or full of hesitation. If you're *doubtful* about the outcome of a particular situation, it means that you are fairly certain it will not turn out well. If you're *dubious*, on the other hand, it means that you're wavering or hesitating in your opinion. **Questionable** may merely imply the existence of doubt (*a questionable excuse*), but like *dubious*, it also has connotations of dishonesty and immorality (*a place where questionable activities were going on*). **Problematic**, in contrast to both *dubious* and *questionable*, is free from any suggestion of moral judgment or suspicion. It is applied to things that are genuinely uncertain, and to outcomes that are as likely to be positive as negative (*getting everyone in the family to agree could be problematic*). **Ambiguous** and **equivocal** refer to lack of clarity. But while *ambiguous* can refer to either an intentional or unintentional lack of clarity (*her ambiguous replies to our questions*), *equivocal* suggests an intentional wish to remain unclear (*his equivocal responses indicated that he wasn't keen to cooperate*). It can also mean capable of different interpretations (*an equivocal statement that could be taken to mean opposite things*). Something that is **enigmatic** is likely to be intentionally unclear as well (*an enigmatic statement designed to provoke controversy*), although

enigmatic can also mean perplexing or mysterious.

---

doubtless *adverb* undoubtedly, without doubt, no doubt, of course, certainly, truly, assuredly, surely, positively, beyond a doubt, unquestionably, indisputably, clearly, obviously, very probably, very/most likely, presumably.

dour *adjective* unsmiling, sullen, morose, sour, gruff, churlish, uncommunicative, unfriendly, forbidding, grim, stern, severe, austere, harsh, dismal, dreary, gloomy.
Antonyms: CHEERFUL; FRIENDLY; SOCIABLE.

douse, dowse *verb* **1** *douse the walls with soapy water* drench, saturate, soak, souse, flood, deluge, wet, splash, hose down. **2** *douse the clothes in the tub* plunge, immerse, submerge, dip, dunk. **3** *douse the light/candle* extinguish, put out, blow out, quench, snuff.

dovetail *verb* **1** *dovetail the pieces of wood* join, unite, fit, fit together, link, interlock, splice, mortise, tenon. **2** *our plans dovetailed with theirs* fit in, go together, coincide, go hand in glove, fall in, correspond, concur, agree, accord, harmonize.

dowdy *adjective* *dowdy clothes/people* frumpish, frumpy, drab, dull, old-fashioned, unfashionable, inelegant, shabby, untidy, dingy, frowzy; *inf.* tacky.
Antonyms: CHIC; FASHIONABLE.

down[1] *adverb* **1** *the elevator going down* downward, to a lower point/part, to a low point, in a lower place/position. **2** *fall down* downward, to the ground, to the floor, below, beneath.

down[2] *preposition* **1** *walk down the street* to a lower part of, along, through. **2** *cut the apple down the middle* through, throughout, straight/right through.

down[3] *adjective* **1** *feeling down* downcast, downhearted, dejected, depressed, sad, unhappy, miserable, wretched, low, blue, gloomy, melancholy; *inf.* down in the mouth/dumps. **2** *the computer is down* not working, nonfunctioning, inoperative, out of order. **3** *stock prices are down* lower, reduced, of lower/less value. **4** *the water level is down* lower, less, reduced. **down on** *wish I hadn't been do down on school* against, prejudiced against, set against, antagonistic to/toward, hostile to/toward, negative toward/about.

down[4] *verb* **1** *down three of the enemy* knock/throw/bring down, floor, fell, tackle, trip up, overthrow, defeat, conquer, subdue. **2** *down three glassfuls* drink, gulp down, swallow; *inf.* put away, chug (down), chug-a-lug, swill.

down[5] *noun* *he has his ups and downs* fit/period of depression, unpleasant time, bad time, hard time, low point, nadir, reversal, setback, comedown.

down[6] *noun* fluff, fuzz, bloom, soft feathers, eiderdown, goose down, fine hair.

down-at-the-heels *adjective* shabby, shabbily dressed, poorly dressed, out-at-the-elbows, seedy, rundown, slovenly, slipshod.

downbeat *adjective* **1** *bored and downbeat* down, downcast, low, depressed, dejected, miserable, gloomy, pessimistic. **2** *too many downbeat stories in the news* depressing, sad, gloomy, disheartening, dreary, dispiriting, bleak.

downcast *adjective* *downcast at the news* disheartened, dispirited, downhearted, dejected, depressed, discouraged, daunted, dismayed, disappointed, disconsolate, crestfallen, despondent, sad, unhappy, miserable, wretched, down, low, blue, gloomy, glum, melancholy, sorrowful, doleful, mournful.
Antonyms: CHEERFUL; upbeat.

downfall *noun* **1** *the downfall of the leader* loss of power/prestige/wealth, fall, collapse, undoing, ruin, ruination, crash, destruction, debasement, degradation, disgrace, overthrow, defeat. **2** *soaked in a downfall* heavy rain/snow. *See* DOWNPOUR.
Antonyms: RISE; SUCCESS.

downgrade *verb* **1** *downgrade the officers* demote, reduce in rank, remove from office, degrade, humble, debase; *inf.* take down a peg or two. **2** *downgrade their achievement* disparage, denigrate, detract from, run down, decry, belittle, make light of, minimize, defame; *inf.* bad-mouth.
Antonyms: UPGRADE; overplay.

downhearted *adjective* disheartened, dispirited, downcast, dejected, depressed, discouraged, daunted, dismayed, disappointed, disconsolate, crestfallen, despondent. *See* DOWNCAST.

downpour *noun* rainstorm, snowstorm, deluge, torrential/pouring rain, cloudburst, downfall; torrents of rain.

downright *adjective* **1** *a downright lie* complete, total, absolute, out and out, outright, utter, sheer, thorough, thoroughgoing, categorical, unmitigated, unqualified, unconditional, positive, simple, wholesale, all out, arrant, rank. **2** *a very downright person* frank, forthright, straightforward, open, candid, plainspoken, matter-of-fact, outspoken, blunt, brusque.

downright *adverb* *downright rude* completely, totally, absolutely, utterly, thoroughly, profoundly, categorically, positively.

down-to-earth *adjective* practical, sensible, realistic, matter-of-fact, no-nonsense, hardheaded, sane, mundane, unromantic, unidealistic.
Antonyms: ROMANTIC; IDEALISTIC; DREAMY.

downtrodden *adjective* oppressed, burdened, weighed down, overwhelmed, tyrannized, ground down, helpless, powerless, prostrate, poor, miserable, wretched, distressed.

downward *adjective* going down, moving down, descending, sliding down, earthbound.

dowry *noun* dower, marriage portion/settlement; endowment, gift.

doze *verb* sleep lightly, nap, take a nap, catnap, slumber, take a siesta; *inf.* nod off, drift off, snooze, have a snooze, catch forty winks, get some shut-eye, catch/grab some Z's.

drab *adjective* **1** *drab clothes/surroundings* dull, dull-colored, colorless, mousy, gray, grayish, dingy, dreary, dismal, cheerless, gloomy, somber, depressing. **2** *a drab talk* uninteresting, boring, tedious, dry, dreary, lifeless, lackluster, uninspired.
Antonyms: BRIGHT; GAUDY; CHEERFUL; INTERESTING.

draft *noun* **1** *a draft of the speech* preliminary version, rough sketch, outline, plan, skeleton, abstract. **2** *a draft of the new building* plan, sketch, drawing, line drawing, diagram, blueprint, delineation. **3** *a bank draft* money order, check, bill of exchange. **4** *discontinued the draft during peacetime* conscription, call-up, selective service.

draft *verb* **1** *draft a proposal* outline, plan, draw (up), frame, sketch (out), design, delineate. **2** *drafted by/into the army* recruit, conscript, call up, induct.

drag *verb* **1** *drag the body from the sea* haul, pull, draw, tug, yank, trail, tow, lug. **2** *time dragged* go/move slowly, creep/limp along, crawl, go at a snail's pace. **3** *the movie dragged | his lecture dragged (on)* go on too long, go on and on, become tedious. **drag out** *drag out the lecture* protract, prolong, draw out, spin out, stretch out, lengthen, extend.

drag *noun* *the assignment/job is a drag* nuisance, source of annoyance, pest, trouble, bother, bore; *inf.* pain in the neck.

dragoon *verb* *dragoon them into helping* force, coerce, compel, drive, impel, constrain, browbeat, bully, tyrannize; *inf.* strong-arm, put the screws on.

drain *verb* **1** *drain the water from the tank* draw off, extract, withdraw, remove, pump off, milk, bleed, tap, filter. **2** *drain the tank* empty, void, evacuate. **3** *the liquid drained (away)* flow out, ooze, trickle, seep out, leak, discharge, exude, effuse. **4** *legal costs draining resources* use up, exhaust, deplete, consume, expend, empty, sap, strain, tax, bleed. **5** *drain a drink* drink up, finish, gulp down, swallow, quaff; *inf.* down.

drain *noun* **1** *a sewage drain* channel, conduit, culvert, duct, gutter, sewer, trench, ditch, dike, pipe, outlet. **2** *a drain on resources* exhaustion, depletion, consumption, expenditure, outflow, sapping, strain, tax.

drama *noun* **1** *studying drama* dramatic art, stagecraft, theater, acting, dramatics. **2** *a Chekhov drama* play, show; stage play, screenplay, radio play, television play, stage show, theatrical work, theatrical piece. **3** *the drama at the police station* exciting/emotional scene, thrilling/tense/sensational spectacle, excitement, crisis; dramatics, theatrics, histrionics.

dramatic *adjective* **1** *dramatic art* theatrical, stage, thespian. **2** *dramatic scenes in court* exciting, sensational, spectacular, startling, unexpected, thrilling, tense, suspenseful, electrifying, stirring, affecting. **3** *a dramatic view/description* striking, impressive, vivid, spectacular, breathtaking, moving, affecting, emotive, graphic, effective, powerful. **4** *a dramatic gesture* theatrical, artificial, exaggerated, overdone, stagy, histrionic.

dramatist *noun* playwright, scriptwriter, screenwriter, tragedy writer, comedy writer, dramaturgist, dramaturge.

dramatize *verb* **1** *dramatize the novel* turn/adapt into a play, make a screenplay/stage play of, put into dramatic form. **2** *dramatize the incident* exaggerate, make a drama/performance of, overdo, overstate; *inf.* lay it on thick, ham it up.

drape *verb* **1** *drape the walls in tapestry* cover, envelope, blanket, overlay, cloak, veil, shroud, decorate, adorn, array, deck, festoon. **2** *drape a shawl around her* hang, arrange, let fall in folds. **3** *drape an arm on the chair* hang, let fall, place loosely, lean, dangle, droop.

draperies, drapes *plural noun* *pulled the draperies closed* curtains, window treatment, valance.

drastic *adjective* extreme, severe, desperate, dire, radical, harsh, sharp, forceful, rigorous, draconian.

Antonyms: MILD; MODERATE.

draw *verb* **1** *draw a chair up | draw the table away* pull, haul, tow, trail, tug, yank. **2** *draw alongside | drew to a close* move, go, come, proceed, approach. **3** *draw a sword/gun* pull out, take out, bring out, extract, withdraw, produce, unsheathe. **4** *draw the curtains* shut, close, pull together. **5** *draw attention | draw large crowds* attract, allure, lure, entice, invite, engage, interest, win, catch the eye of, capture, captivate, fascinate, tempt, seduce. **6** *draw a breath* breathe in, inhale, suck in, inspire, respire. **7** *draw a salary* take, take in, receive, be in receipt of, get, procure, obtain, earn. **8** *draw a conclusion* deduce, infer, conclude, derive, gather, glean. **9** *draw liquid* drain, siphon off, pump off, tap, milk, bleed, filtrate. **10** *draw lots/straws* choose, pick, select, opt for, make a choice of, decide on, single out. **11** *draw a house | she loved to draw in the garden* make a drawing of, sketch, make a picture/diagram of, portray, depict, delineate, represent, trace, map out, mark out, chart, paint, design; make drawings/pictures. **draw on** *draw on experience* make use of, use, have recourse to, exploit, employ, rely on. **draw out** *draw out a gun* pull out. *See* DRAW *verb* 3. **2** *draw out the talk* prolong, protract, extend, lengthen, stretch out, drag out, spin out, make go on and on. **3** *draw the child out* induce to talk, persuade to speak, put at ease. **draw up 1** *draw up a document | draw up a set of rules* compose, formulate, frame, write out, put in writing, put down on paper, draft, prepare. **2** *troops drawn up for battle* arrange, put into position, order, marshal, range, rank.

draw *noun* **1** *the draw of the circus* attraction, lure, allure, pull, enticement, magnetism. **2** *the match ended in a draw* tie, dead heat, stalemate.

drawback *noun* disadvantage, snag, catch, problem, difficulty, trouble, flaw, stumbling block, hitch, handicap, hindrance, obstacle, impediment, hurdle, obstruction, barrier, curb, check, discouragement, deterrent, damper, inconvenience, nuisance, detriment, fault, weak spot, weakness, imperfection, defect; *inf.* fly in the ointment.

Antonyms: ADVANTAGE; BENEFIT.

drawing[1] *noun* sketch, picture, illustration, representation, portrayal, delineation, depiction, composition, study, diagram, outline.

drawing[2] *noun* *there will be a drawing at the dance* raffle, sweepstake, lottery.

drawl *noun* slow speech, drawn-out speech, twang, drone.

drawn *adjective* *pale and drawn* pinched, haggard, hollow-cheeked, strained, tense, taut, stressed, fraught, fatigued, tired, worn, drained, wan, sapped.

dread *verb* *dread the bully's arrival* fear, be afraid of, be terrified by, worry about, be anxious about, have forebodings about, tremble/shudder about, cringe/shrink from, quail/cower/flinch from; *inf.* have cold feet about, be in a blue funk about.

dread *noun* fear, fearfulness, fright, alarm, terror, apprehension, trepidation, horror, anxiety, concern, foreboding, dismay, perturbation, trembling, shuddering, flinching; *inf.* blue funk, heebie-jeebies. *See* DREAD *verb.*

dread, dreaded *adjective* *the dread disease* dreaded, feared, frightening, alarming, terrifying, frightful, terrible, horrible, dreadful, awful, dire, awesome.

dreadful *adjective* **1** *a dreadful sight/accident* terrible, frightful, horrible, grim, awful, dire, frightening, terrifying, alarming, distressing, shocking, appalling, harrowing, ghastly, fearful, hideous, horrendous, gruesome, tragic, calamitous, grievous. **2** *a dreadful man to deal with | dreadful weather* nasty, unpleasant, disagreeable, frightful, shocking, very bad, distasteful, repugnant, odious. **3** *a dreadful waste of time* shocking, outrageous, inordinate, great, tremendous.

Antonyms: PLEASANT; AGREEABLE.

dream *noun* **1** *saw his mother in a dream* dream sequence, nightmare; vision, fantasy, hallucination. **2** *his dream to become rich* ambition, aspiration, goal, design, plan, aim, hope, yearning, desire, wish, notion, daydream, fantasy; castles in the air. **3** *the bride was a dream* beauty, vision of loveliness, vision, delight, pleasure to behold, joy, marvel. **4** *go around in a dream* daydream, reverie, state of unreality, trance, daze, fog, stupor.

dream *verb* **1** *dream at night* have dreams/

nightmares. **2** *he thought he saw a ghost but he was dreaming* hallucinate, have a vision, imagine things, fantasize. **3** *she was dreaming instead of working* daydream, be in a trance/reverie, be lost in thought, muse, be preoccupied. **4** *not dream of upsetting them | never dream that they would go* think, consider, visualize, conceive, suppose. **dream up** *dream up new schemes* conjure up, think up, invent, concoct, devise, create, hatch, fabricate; *inf.* cook up.

dreamer *noun* daydreamer, visionary, fantasist, fantasizer, romantic, romancer, idealist, impractical/unrealistic person, theorizer, Utopian, Don Quixote.

dreamland *noun* **1** *existing only in dreamland* land of make-believe, never-never land, fairyland, world of fantasy. **2** *children in dreamland* sleep, slumber, land of Nod.

dreamy *adjective* **1** *a dreamy person* visionary, fanciful, fantasizing, romantic, idealistic, impractical, unrealistic, theorizing, daydreaming, quixotic. **2** *in a dreamy mood* daydreaming, thoughtful, lost in thought, pensive, speculative, preoccupied, absentminded, in a brown study, with one's head in the clouds. **3** *a dreamy recollection of the events* dreamlike, vague, dim, hazy, shadowy, misty, faint, indistinct, unclear. **4** *dreamy music* romantic, relaxing, soothing, calming, lulling, gentle, tranquil, peaceful. **5** *a dreamy young man | a dreamy dress* wonderful, marvelous, terrific, fabulous, gorgeous, heavenly; *inf.* to die for. **Antonyms:** PRACTICAL; DOWN-TO-EARTH.

dreary *adjective* **1** *a dreary day* gloomy, dismal, bleak, somber, dull, dark, overcast, depressing. **2** *lead a dreary life* dull, drab, uninteresting, flat, dry, colorless, lifeless, tedious, wearisome, boring, humdrum, routine, monotonous, uneventful, run-of-the-mill, prosaic, commonplace, unvaried, repetitive. **3** *in a dreary frame of mind* gloomy, glum, sad, miserable, wretched, downcast, dejected, depressed, despondent, doleful, mournful, melancholic. **Antonyms:** BRIGHT; INTERESTING; CHEERFUL.

dregs *plural noun* **1** *the dregs of the wine* sediment, deposit, residue, precipitate, sublimate, scum, debris, dross, detritus, refuse, draff; lees, grounds. **2** *the dregs of society* scum, riff-raff, rabble, refuse; down-and-outs, good-for-nothings, outcasts, deadbeats, tramps, vagrants.

drench *verb* soak, saturate, permeate, drown, inundate, flood, steep, douse, souse, wet, slosh.

dress *noun* **1** *wearing a black dress* gown, garment, robe. **2** *with her dress in disarray* clothes, garments; clothing, attire, apparel, costume, outfit, ensemble, garb; *inf.* gear, get-up, togs, duds. **3** *birds/trees in their winter dress* covering, outer covering, plumage, feathers, pelt.

dress *verb* **1** *she was dressed in black* clothe, attire, garb, fit out, turn out, array, apparel, robe.

2 *she dressed quickly* put on clothes, don clothes, slip into clothes. **3** *dress for dinner* change, wear formal clothes, put on evening dress. **4** *dress poultry* prepare, get ready, clean; stuff. **5** *dress a wound* cover, bandage, bind up, put a plaster on. **6** *dress troops* line up, put in line, align, straighten, arrange, put into order, dispose, set out. **dress down** reprimand, scold, upbraid, rebuke, reprove, berate, castigate, rake over the coals; *inf.* tell off. **dress up 1** *dress up for the occasion* dress formally/smartly, wear evening dress; *inf.* doll oneself up, dress to the nines, put on one's glad rags. **2** *dress the child up* dress smartly; *inf.* doll up. **3** *dress up the plain garment | dress the room up* decorate, adorn, ornament, trim, embellish, beautify, prettify. **4** *dress up as Santa Claus* put on a costume, put on a disguise, disguise oneself, wear a disguise. **Antonyms:** UNDRESS; STRIP.

dressing *noun* **1** *a dressing for the salad* relish, sauce, condiment. **2** *put a dressing on the wound* covering, bandage, gauze.

dressmaker *noun* couturier, tailor, modiste, seamstress.

dribble *verb* **1** *water dribbling from the tap* drip, trickle, fall in drops, drop, leak, ooze, exude, seep. **2** *the baby's dribbling* drool, slaver, slobber.

dribble *noun* *a dribble of water* trickle, drip, small stream.

drift *verb* **1** *boats/leaves drifting along* be carried along/away, be borne, be wafted, float, go with the current, coast. **2** *people drifting about* wander aimlessly, wander, roam, rove, meander, coast, stray. **3** *snow drifting* pile up, bank up, accumulate, gather, form heaps, amass.

drift *noun* **1** *a drift to the right* movement, deviation, digression, variation. **2** *the drift of his argument* gist, essence, meaning, substance, core, significance, import, purport, tenor, vein, implication, direction, course, tendency, trend. **3** *a snow drift* pile, heap, bank, mound, mass, accumulation.

drill *verb* **1** *drill the new recruits* train, instruct, coach, teach, ground, inculcate, discipline, exercise, rehearse, put one through one's paces. **2** *drill the wood* bore/make a hole in, bore, pierce, puncture, penetrate, perforate.

drill *noun* **1** *military drill* training, instruction, coaching, teaching, grounding, indoctrination. See DRILL *verb* 1. **2** *early morning drill* exercises, physical exercises; strict training, workout. **3** *not to know the drill* procedure, routine, practice. **4** *an electric drill* boring/drilling tool.

drink *verb* **1** *drink the water* swallow, gulp down, drain, quaff, imbibe, partake of, swill, guzzle, sip; *inf.* swig. **2** *her husband drinks* take alcohol, be a serious/hard drinker, tipple, indulge, be an alcoholic; *inf.* hit the bottle, bend one's elbow, booze. **drink in** be absorbed/rapt/lost in, be fascinated by, pay close attention to. **drink**

drink *noun* **1** *food and drink | water is the commonest drink* beverage, drinkable/potable liquid, liquid refreshment; thirst-quencher. **2** *no drink at the dance* alcoholic/strong drink, alcohol, liquor, intoxicating liquor; spirits; *inf.* booze, hard stuff, hooch. **3** *take a drink from the cup* swallow, gulp, sip, swill; *inf.* swig, slug. **4** *a drink of water* cup, glass, mug, container.

drinkable *adjective* fit to drink, potable.

drinker *noun* social drinker, heavy/hard drinker, serious drinker, alcoholic, problem drinker, alcohol abuser, drunk, drunkard, dipsomaniac, tippler, toper, sot, inebriate, imbiber; *inf.* boozer, soak, lush, wino, alky, elbow-bender.

drip *verb* *water/blood/coffee is dripping* drop, dribble, trickle, splash, sprinkle, plop, leak, ooze, exude, filter, percolate.

drip *noun* **1** *paint drips* drop, dribble, trickle, splash, plop, leak. **2** *a boring drip* ineffective person, weakling, ninny, milksop; *inf.* nerd, dweeb.

drive *verb* **1** *drive a car* operate, steer, handle, guide, direct, manage. **2** *we drove here* come/ go/travel by car; *inf.* travel on wheels. **3** *he drove us here* chauffeur, run, give one a lift. **4** *drive cattle to the barn* move, get going, urge, press, push, impel, propel, herd, round up. **5** *driven to steal/despair* force, compel, constrain, impel, oblige, coerce, make, pressure, goad, spur, prod. **6** *drove himself too hard* work, overwork, tax, overtax, overburden. **7** *drive the stake into the ground* hammer, ram, bang, sink, plunge, thrust, stab. **drive at** *what are you driving at?* mean, suggest, imply, infer, hint at, refer to, allude to, intimate, indicate, have in mind; *inf.* get at.

drive *noun* **1** *go for a drive* run, trip, jaunt, outing, journey, excursion, tour, turn; *inf.* spin, joyride. **2** *the tree-lined drive* driveway, road, roadway, avenue. **3** *a sales drive* effort, push, campaign, publicity campaign, crusade, surge. **4** *a young man with drive* energy, vigor, verve, ambition, push, enterprise, motivation, initiative, action, aggressiveness; *inf.* get-up-and-go, zip, pizzazz, punch.

drivel *noun* **1** *speaking drivel* nonsense, twaddle, gibberish, balderdash, rubbish, mumbo-jumbo; *inf.* rot, poppycock, garbage, tripe, bunk, hogwash, crap. **2** *wipe away the drivel* saliva, drool, drooling, dribble, slaver, slobber.

drivel *verb* **1** *drivel about the rules* talk nonsense, babble, ramble, gibber, blather. **2** *babies driveling* drool, slaver, slobber, dribble.

driver *verb* **1** *passengers paying the driver | drivers of heavy vehicles* chauffeur, taxi driver, cab driver; operator; (train) engineer, bus driver, truck driver. **2** *drivers charged with drunk driving* motorist, operator.

drizzle *noun* *a drizzle falling* fine rain, sprinkle of rain, sprinkling, light shower.

droll *adjective* funny, humorous, amusing, comic, comical, clownish, farcical, zany, laughable, ridiculous, ludicrous, risible, jocular, facetious, waggish, witty, whimsical, entertaining, diverting.

drone[1] *verb* **1** *aircraft droning overhead* make a humming noise, hum, buzz, whir, vibrate, murmur, purr, whisper, sigh. **2** *drone on about cutting costs* go on and on, speak monotonously/boringly, talk interminably, intone.

drone[2] *noun* *the drone of aircraft* hum, buzz, whir, whirring, vibration, purr, whispering, sigh.

drone[3] *noun* *the workers and the drones in the firm* idler, loafer, layabout, lounger, do-nothing, sluggard, parasite, leech; *inf.* lazybones, scrounger, sponger.

droop *verb* **1** *flowers drooping* hang, hang down, bend, bow, stoop, sag, sink, slump, fall down, drop. **2** *drooping after the news | spirits drooping* be despondent, lose heart, give up hope, become dispirited/dejected, flag, fade, languish, falter, weaken, wilt, shrivel, wither, decline, diminish, deteriorate.

drop *noun* **1** *a drop of water* droplet, globule, bead, bubble, blob, spheroid, oval. **2** *add just a drop* little, bit, dash, spot, dribble, splash, sprinkle, trickle, taste, trace, pinch, dab, speck, particle, modicum; *inf.* smidgen, smidge, tad. **3** *a drop in prices* decline, decrease, reduction, cut, cutback, lowering, falling-off, downturn, depreciation, devaluation, slump. **4** *the path ended in a sudden drop* descent, incline, declivity, slope, plunge; abyss, chasm, precipice, cliff.

drop *verb* **1** *water dropping from the trees* fall in drops, fall, drip, dribble, trickle, plop, leak. **2** *the plane dropped out of the sky* drop down, fall, descend, plunge, plummet, dive, tumble. **3** *she dropped the package/ball* let fall/go, fail to hold. **4** *the girl dropped from exhaustion* fall/sink down, collapse, faint, swoon, drop/fall dead. **5** *prices dropped* fall, decrease, lessen, diminish, depreciate, go into decline, dwindle, sink, slacken off, plunge, plummet. **6** *drop singing lessons* give up, discontinue, end, stop, cease, terminate, finish with, withdraw/retire from, quit, abandon, forgo, relinquish, dispense with. **7** *drop his girlfriend* desert, abandon, forsake, leave, throw over, jilt, discard, reject, repudiate, renounce, disown; *inf.* ditch, chuck, run out on, leave flat. **8** *drop half the workforce* dismiss, discharge, let go; *inf.* sack, fire, boot out. **9** *drops the second syllable in "mathematics"* omit, leave out, eliminate, elide, contract, slur. **drop off** *sales have dropped off* drop, fall, decrease, decline, plummet. See DROP *verb* 5. **2** *drop the goods/passengers off* deliver, deposit, set down, unload, leave. **3** *people dropping off* fall asleep, doze, doze off, have a nap, catnap, drowse; *inf.* nod off, snooze, take forty winks, get some shut-eye. **drop out (of)** *students dropping out of college | dropped out after one month* give up,

abandon, renounce, leave, quit, forsake, back out (of), withdraw (from), renege (on), turn one's back (on).
Antonyms: LIFT; RISE; take up (*see* TAKE); RETAIN.

drought *noun* dry spell/period, lack of rain.

drove *noun* **1** *a drove of cattle/sheep* herd, flock, pack. **2** *droves of people going shopping* crowd, horde, swarm, multitude, mob, throng, host, collection, gathering, assembly, company, herd.

drown *verb* **1** *the cornfields were drowned when the dam burst* flood, submerge, immerse, inundate, deluge, swamp, engulf, drench. **2** *outside noise drowning her speech* drown out, make inaudible, muffle, be louder than, deaden, stifle, overpower, overwhelm, overcome, engulf, swallow up. **3** *drowning his grief in work* suppress, deaden, stifle, quash, quench, extinguish, obliterate, wipe out, get rid of.

drowsy *adjective* **1** *feeling drowsy* sleepy, half asleep, tired, weary, heavy-eyed, yawning, lethargic, sluggish, somnolent, dazed, drugged; *inf.* dopey. **2** *drowsy weather* sleepy, sleep-inducing, soporific, lulling, soothing, dreamy, somniferous.
Antonyms: ALERT; LIVELY.

drubbing *noun* beating, thrashing, walloping, thumping, battering, trouncing, whipping, flogging, pounding, pummeling, bludgeoning; *inf.* hammering, licking, clobbering, working-over.

drudge *noun* *drudges working in the kitchen* menial, servant, slave, laborer, worker, toiler.

drudge *verb* toil, labor, slave, plod on, grind/slog away, keep one's nose to the grindstone.

drudgery *noun* menial/hard work, toiling, toil, labor, hard labor, slavery, plodding; chores; *inf.* grind.

drug *noun* **1** *a new cancer drug* medical drug, medicine, medication, medicament, remedy, cure, cure-all, panacea, physic. **2** *addicted to drugs* addictive drug, narcotic; opiate; *inf.* dope.

drug *verb* *drug the patient before the operation* | *drug the captive* anesthetize, give an anesthetic to, knock out, make/render unconscious, make/render insensible, stupefy, befuddle; *inf.* dope (up).

drugged *adjective* anesthetized, knocked out, comatose, stupefied, insensible, befuddled; *inf.* doped, stoned, dopey, on a trip, spaced out, zonked, high, high as a kite, turned on, flying, charged up.

drum *verb* **1** *drum on the table* | *drum one's fingers* tap, beat, rap, knock, strike. **2** *drum information into the students* drive home, instill, hammer, inculcate. **drum out** *drum out of the club/regiment* expel from, dismiss/discharge from, throw out, oust from. **drum up** *drum up business/support* gather, collect, round up, summon, ob-

tain, get, attract, canvass, solicit, petition, bid for.

drunk *adjective* *left the bar too drunk to drive* drunken, blind drunk, dead drunk, intoxicated, inebriated, inebriate, under the influence, tipsy, soused; *inf.* tight, tiddly, woozy, pie-eyed, three sheets to the wind, under the table, out of it, legless, plastered, smashed, sloshed, stoned, well-oiled, blotto, blitzed, lit up, stewed, pickled, tanked up, bombed.
Antonym: SOBER.

drunk

blotto, drunken, inebriated, intoxicated, tight, tipsy
Anyone who is obviously or legally under the influence of alcohol is said to be **drunk**. **Drunken** means the same thing, but only *drunk* should be used predicatively, that is, after a linking verb (*she was drunk*) while *drunken* is more often used to modify a noun (*a drunken sailor*) and, in some cases, to imply habitual drinking to excess. *Drunken* is also used to modify nouns that do not refer to a person (*a drunken celebration*). To say **intoxicated** or **inebriated** is a more formal and less offensive way of calling someone *drunk*, with *intoxicated* implying that the individual is only slightly drunk, and *inebriated* implying drunkenness to the point of excitement or exhilaration (*the streets were filled with inebriated revelers*). **Tight** and **tipsy** are two of the more common slang expressions (there are literally hundreds more) meaning *drunk*. Like *intoxicated*, *tipsy* implies that someone is only slightly drunk, while *tight* implies obvious drunkenness but without any loss of muscular coordination. An elderly woman who has had one sherry too many might be described as *tipsy*, but someone who has been drinking all evening and is still able to stand up and give a speech might be described as *tight*. Either condition is preferable to being **blotto**, a word that means drunk to the point of incomprehensibility or unconsciousness.

drunk *noun* drunkard, inebriate, heavy/hard drinker, sot, toper, tippler, alcoholic, dipsomaniac, serious/problem drinker; *inf.* boozer, lush, alky, wino, elbow-bender.

drunken *adjective* **1** *drunken partygoers* drunk, intoxicated, inebriated. *See* DRUNK *adjective*. **2** *a drunken party* debauched, dissipated, riotous, carousing, reveling, intemperate, bacchanalian.

drunkenness *noun* intoxication, inebriation, inebriety, insobriety, tipsiness, intemperance, overindulging, debauchery, hard drinking, serious drinking, alcoholism, alcohol abuse, dipsomania.

dry *adjective* **1** *dry ground/regions* arid, dried up/out, parched, scorched, dehydrated, desiccated, waterless, unwatered, moistureless, rainless, torrid, thirsty, droughty, barren, unproductive, sterile. **2** *dry leaves* withered, shriveled, wilted, dehydrated, desiccated, wizened, sapless, juiceless. **3** *dry cheese* dried out, hard, hardened, stale. **4** *a dry talk* dull, uninteresting, boring, tedious, tiresome, wearisome, dreary, monotonous, flat, unimaginative, commonplace, prosaic, run-of-the-mill, humdrum, vapid. **5** *a dry wit* subtle, low-key, deadpan, laconic, sly, sharp, ironic, sarcastic, satirical, cynical, droll, waggish. **6** *a dry response/greeting* unemotional, indifferent, cool, cold, aloof, remote, impersonal. **7** *a dry county* prohibitionist, teetotal, teetotaling, alcohol-free.

Antonyms: WET; FRESH; INTERESTING.

---

dry
arid, dehydrated, desiccated, parched, sere

Almost anything lacking in moisture (in relative terms)—whether it's a piece of bread, the basement of a house, or the state of Arizona—may be described as **dry**, a word that also connotes a lack of life or spirit (*a dry lecture on cell division*). **Arid**, on the other hand, applies to places or things that have been deprived of moisture and are therefore extremely or abnormally *dry* (*one side of the island was arid*); it is most commonly used to describe a desertlike region or climate that is lifeless or barren. **Desiccated** is used as a technical term for something from which moisture has been removed, and in general use it suggests lifelessness, although it is applied very often to people who have lost their vitality (*a desiccated old woman who never left her house*) or to animal and vegetable products that have been completely deprived of their vital juices (*desiccated oranges hanging limply from the tree*). **Dehydrated** is very close in meaning to *desiccated* and is often the preferred adjective when describing foods from which the moisture has been extracted (*they lived on dehydrated fruit*). *Dehydrated* may also refer to an unwanted loss of moisture (*the virus had left him seriously dehydrated*), as may the less formal term **parched**, which refers to an undesirable or uncomfortable lack of water in either a human being or a place (*parched with thirst; the parched landscape*). **Sere** is associated primarily with places and means *dry* or *arid* (*a harsh, sere land where few inhabitants could survive*).

---

dry *verb* **1** *the sun drying the earth* make dry, dry out/up, parch, scorch, dehydrate, desiccate, dehumidify, sear. **2** *the sun drying the leaves* dry up, wither, shrivel, wilt, dehydrate, desiccate, wizen, mummify. **3** *dry meat* dehydrate, desiccate, preserve, cure. **4** *dry the wet patch* dry off, mop up, blot up, towel, drain. **dry up 1** *dry up the ground* parch, scorch, dehydrate. *See* DRY *verb* 1. **2** *dry up leaves/skin* wither, shrivel, wizen, mummify. *See* DRY *verb* 2. **3** *inspiration dried up* fail, become unproductive, grow barren/sterile, cease to yield. **4** *actors drying up* |

she dried up at the sight stop speaking/talking, forget one's lines/words, shut up.

dual *adjective* double, twofold, duplicate, duplex, binary, twin, matched, paired, coupled.

dub *verb* **1** *dubbed the greatest jazz singer* call, name, christen, designate, term, entitle, style, label, denominate, nominate, tag, nickname. **2** *queen dubbing a courtier* knight, confer/bestow a knighthood on, invest with a knighthood.

dubiety *noun* doubtfulness, uncertainty, lack of certainty, unsureness, hesitancy, dubiosity, incertitude; doubt.

dubious *adjective* **1** *dubious about going* doubtful, uncertain, unsure, hesitant, undecided, wavering, vacillating, irresolute, on the horns of a dilemma, skeptical, suspicious; *inf.* iffy. **2** *the outcome is dubious* doubtful, undecided, unsure, unsettled, undetermined, indefinite, unresolved, up in the air, open, equivocal, debatable, questionable. **3** *give a dubious reply* equivocal, ambiguous, indeterminate, indefinite, unclear, vague, imprecise, hazy, puzzling, enigmatic, cryptic. **4** *a dubious character* questionable, suspicious, suspect, under suspicion, untrustworthy, unreliable, undependable; *inf.* shady, fishy.

Antonyms: CERTAIN; SURE; DEFINITE.

duck *verb* **1** *duck behind the wall* bend, bow down, bob down, stoop, crouch, squat, hunch down, hunker down. **2** *duck one's head* bow, lower, drop. **3** *duck him in the pond* immerse, submerge, plunge, dip, souse, douse, dunk. **4** *duck the police/work* dodge, evade, sidestep, avoid, steer clear of, elude, escape, shirk, shun.

duct *noun* pipe, tube, conduit, channel, passage, canal, culvert.

ductile *adjective* **1** *a ductile substance* pliable, pliant, flexible, plastic, malleable, tensile. **2** *ductile people* pliable, malleable, compliant, tractable, manipulable, docile, accommodating, cooperative, gullible.

dud *noun* *the lightbulb/project is a dud* failure, flop; *inf.* washout, lemon, loser.

dud *adjective* *a dud lightbulb/project* defective, broken, not working, not functioning, inoperative, ineffectual, failed, worthless; *inf.* busted, kaput.

dudgeon *noun* **in high dudgeon** angry, annoyed, furious, in a temper, indignant, enraged, fuming, vexed, offended, resentful; *inf.* peeved.

due *adjective* **1** *money/thanks due (to) them* owing, owed, payable, payable now, receivable immediately, outstanding. **2** *recognition due (to) a hero* deserved by, merited by, earned by, justified by, appropriate to, fit for, fitting to, suitable for, right for. **3** *treat with due respect* proper, right and proper, correct, rightful, fitting, appropriate, apt, adequate, sufficient, enough, ample, satisfactory, requisite, apposite. **4** *the essay is due tomorrow* scheduled, expected, required, awaited, anticipated. **due to** *due to* *uncertainty* attributable to, ascribed to, ascribable to, caused by, assignable to, because of, owing to.

due *adverb due north* directly, straight, without deviating, undeviatingly, dead, exactly.

due *noun receive only his due* rightful treatment; rights, just deserts, deserts; *inf.* comeuppance.

duel *noun* **1** *challenge his rival to a duel* affair of honor; single combat. **2** *engage in a duel of wits* contest, competition, struggle, clash, battle, fight, encounter, engagement.

dues *plural noun pay one's dues to the club* fee, membership fee, subscription, charge, levy; charges.

dulcet *adjective* sweet, melodious, musical, lyrical, silver-toned, euphonious, pleasant, agreeable, soothing, mellow.

dull *adjective* **1** *dull of wit* dull-witted, slow, slow-witted, unintelligent, stupid, dense, doltish, stolid, vacuous; *inf.* dim, dim-witted, thick, dumb, birdbrained. **2** *a dull reaction to others' pain* insensitive, unfeeling, unemotional, indifferent, unsympathetic, unresponsive, apathetic, blank, uncaring, passionless, callous. **3** *feeling dull in the winter* inactive, inert, slow, slow-moving, sleepy, drowsy, idle, sluggish, stagnant, lethargic, listless, languid, heavy, apathetic, torpid, phlegmatic, vegetative. **4** *trade is dull* slow, slack, sluggish, stagnant, depressed. **5** *a dull speech* dull as dishwater, uninteresting, boring, tedious, tiresome, wearisome, dry, monotonous, flat, bland, unimaginative, commonplace, prosaic, run-of-the-mill, humdrum, uneventful, vapid. **6** *dull weather* overcast, cloudy, gloomy, dark, dim, dismal, dreary, bleak, somber, leaden, murky, sunless. **7** *dull colors* drab, dreary, somber, dark, subdued, muted, toned-down, lackluster, lusterless, colorless, faded, washed-out. **8** *a dull sound* muffled, muted, indistinct, feeble. **9** *a dull edge* blunt, blunted, not sharp, unkeen, unsharpened, dulled, edgeless.
Antonyms: CLEVER; ACTIVE; INTERESTING; BRIGHT.

dull *verb* **1** *dull the appetite | dulled their grief* take the edge off, blunt, lessen, decrease, diminish, reduce, deaden, mute, tone down, allay, ease, soothe, assuage, alleviate, palliate. **2** *drugs dulling the senses* numb, benumb, stupefy, drug, sedate, tranquilize. **3** *time dulling the colors* fade, bleach, wash out. **4** *the sky dulled by clouds* darken, dim, bedim, obscure. **5** *spirits dulled by the bad news* dispirit, dishearten, depress, deject, sadden, discourage, cast down, dampen, put a damper on, cast a pall over.

duly *adverb* **1** *suggestions duly noted* in due manner, properly, correctly, rightly, fittingly, appropriately. **2** *spring duly arrived* in due time, at the proper/right time, on time, punctually.

dumb *adjective* **1** *struck dumb at the sight* speechless, wordless, silent, mute, at a loss for words, voiceless, soundless, inarticulate, taciturn, un-

communicative, tongue-tied; *inf.* mum. **2** *dumb people and clever people* stupid, dull, dull-witted, slow, slow-witted, unintelligent, dense, foolish, doltish; *inf.* dim, dim-witted, thick.
Antonyms: INTELLIGENT; BRIGHT; QUICK.

dumbfound *verb* astound, astonish, amaze, startle, surprise, stun, take aback, stagger, overwhelm, confound, shock, confuse, bewilder, baffle, nonplus, perplex, disconcert; *inf.* flabbergast, throw, shake, throw for a loop.

dummy *noun* **1** *a tailor's/ventriloquist's dummy* lifelike model, mannequin, manikin, figure, lay figure. **2** *not a real book/shoe, just a dummy* representation, reproduction, sample, copy, imitation, counterfeit, sham, substitute. **3** *that dummy can't do anything* idiot, fool, dolt, dunce, blockhead, numskull, oaf, nincompoop, ninny, ass, dullard; *inf.* clod, nitwit, dimwit, dope, chump, bonehead, jerk, airhead, schmuck.

dump *verb* **1** *dump the goods on the floor* place, put, put down, lay down, deposit, drop, let fall, throw down, fling down. **2** *dump the unwanted goods* dispose of, get rid of, throw away/out, scrap, jettison. **3** *the tanker dumped its load* discharge, empty out, pour out, tip out, unload, jettison. **4** *dump his wife* abandon, desert, leave, leave in the lurch, forsake, walk out on.

dump *noun* **1** *take the debris to the dump* refuse/rubbish dump, rubbish heap, junkyard, scrapyard; transfer station. **2** *what a dump!* hovel, shack, slum, shanty, pigsty; *inf.* hole, joint.

dumps *plural noun* **in the dumps** depressed, dejected, gloomy, despondent, downcast, disconsolate, melancholic; *inf.* blue.

dun *verb dun people for payment* press, importune, pressurize, solicit, plague, pester, nag, beset.

dunce *noun* dolt, blockhead, dunderhead, thickhead, numskull, nincompoop, ninny, simpleton, halfwit, idiot, moron, ass, ignoramus, dullard; *inf.* dimwit, dummy, bonehead, deadhead.

dungeon *noun* underground cell, cell, lockup, black hole, oubliette; keep.

duplicate *adjective a duplicate set of keys* identical, twin, matching, matched, paired, corresponding, twofold.

duplicate *noun* **1** *a duplicate of the chair* copy, replica, facsimile, reproduction, exact/close likeness, twin, double, clone, match, mate, fellow, counterpart; *inf.* look-alike, spitting image, ringer, dead ringer. **2** *make a duplicate of the document* copy, carbon copy, carbon, photocopy, facsimile, fax; *Trademark* Photostat, Xerox, Xerox copy.

duplicate *verb* **1** *duplicate the documents* copy, make a carbon/facsimile of, photocopy, fax, reproduce, make a replica of, replicate, clone; *Trademark* Photostat, Xerox. **2** *duplicate the task* repeat, do over again, perform again, replicate.

duplicity noun deceitfulness, double-dealing, trickery, guile, chicanery, artifice, dishonesty, knavery, two-facedness.

Antonyms: HONESTY; CANDOR.

durable adjective **1** *durable affection* lasting, long-lasting, enduring, persisting, persistent, abiding, continuing, constant, stable, fast, firm, fixed, permanent, unfading, changeless, unchanging, invariable, dependable, reliable. **2** *durable clothing/goods* long-lasting, hard-wearing, strong, sturdy, sound, tough, resistant, substantial, imperishable.

Antonyms: EPHEMERAL; FLIMSY.

duress noun **1** *sent away under duress* force, compulsion, coercion, pressure, pressurization, constraint, arm-twisting, enforcement, exaction. **2** *prisoners of war kept in duress* imprisonment, confinement, incarceration, detention, custody, captivity, restraint, constraint, bondage.

during conjunction throughout, through, throughout the time of, for the time of, in, within.

dusk noun twilight, evening, sunset, sundown, nightfall; *dial.* eventide.

dusky adjective **1** *dusky complexion* dark, dark-skinned, dark-colored, olive-skinned, swarthy. **2** *dusky light* shadowy, dim, dark, darkish, gloomy, murky, cloudy, misty, hazy, foggy, tenebrous.

dust noun **1** *dust on the furniture* dirt, soot. **2** *kneel in the dust* ground, earth, soil, dirt, clay. **3** *kick up a dust* fuss, commotion, disturbance, uproar, fracas, rumpus, racket.

dust verb **1** *dust the furniture* wipe, brush, clean, mop. **2** *dust with powdered sugar* sprinkle, dredge, sift, scatter, powder, spray, cover, spread, strew.

dusty adjective **1** *a dusty room* dust-covered, dust-filled, undusted, dirty, grubby, grimy, unclean, sooty. **2** *a dusty substance* powdery, chalky, crumbly, friable. **3** *a dusty pink* grayish, muted, dull, pale.

dutiful adjective respectful, filial, deferential, reverent, reverential, conscientious, devoted, considerate, thoughtful, obedient, compliant, pliant, docile, submissive.

Antonyms: DISRESPECTFUL; REMISS.

duty noun **1** *a sense of duty to one's country/parents* responsibility, obligation, obedience, allegiance, loyalty, faithfulness, fidelity, respect, deference, reverence, homage. **2** *share the duties* task, job, chore, assignment, commission, mission, function, office, charge, part, role, requirement, responsibility, obligation; work, burden, onus. **3** *pay duty* tax, levy, tariff, excise, toll, fee, impost; customs, dues. **off duty** not working, at leisure, on vacation, off, free. **on duty** at work, working, busy, occupied, engaged, tied up; *inf.* on the job.

dwarf verb **1** *dwarfed by the effects of a drug* stunt, arrest/check growth, atrophy. **2** *a novelist dwarfing his contemporaries* tower above/over, overshadow, stand head and shoulders over, dominate. **3** *their efforts dwarfing his* overshadow, diminish, minimize.

dwell verb *dwell in the suburbs* reside, live, be domiciled, lodge, stay, abide. **dwell on/upon** *dwell on details/complaints* spend time on, linger over, harp on, discuss at length, expatiate on, elaborate on, expound on, keep talking/writing about, be preoccupied with/by, be obsessed with/by.

dwelling noun dwelling place, residence, home, house, abode, domicile, establishment.

dwindle verb **1** *savings/hope dwindling* become/grow less, become/grow smaller, decrease, lessen, diminish, shrink, contract, fade, wane. **2** *the Roman empire dwindling* decline, fail, sink, ebb, wane, degenerate, deteriorate, decay, wither, rot, disappear, vanish, die out; *inf.* peter out.

Antonyms: INCREASE; GROW; FLOURISH.

dye noun **1** *dip the dress in a dye* colorant, coloring agent, coloring, pigment, tint, stain, wash. **2** *of a green dye* color, shade, hue, tint.

dye verb *dye a dress* color, tint.

dyed-in-the-wool adjective entrenched, inveterate, established, deep-rooted, confirmed, complete, absolute, through and through, utter, thoroughgoing.

dying adjective **1** *a dying woman* terminally ill, breathing one's last, on one's deathbed, passing away, sinking fast, expiring, moribund, *in extremis*; *inf.* in the jaws of death, having one foot in the grave, on one's/its last legs, at death's door. **2** *dying customs* passing, fading, vanishing, failing, ebbing, waning. **3** *dying words* final, last.

dynamic adjective energetic, active, lively, alive, spirited, vital, vigorous, strong, forceful, powerful, potent, effective, effectual, high-powered, magnetic, aggressive, go-ahead, driving, electric; *inf.* go-getting, zippy, peppy.

Antonyms: LISTLESS; LACKADAISICAL.

dynasty noun line, succession, house, regime, rule, reign, dominion, empire; sovereignty, ascendancy, government, authority, administration, jurisdiction.

E

each *adjective* *each student received a book* every, every single.

each *pronoun* *each was nastier than the other* each one, every one, each and every one, one and all.

each *adverb* *a dollar each* apiece, per person, per capita, to each, for/from each, individually.

eager *adjective* **1** *eager students* keen, enthusiastic, impatient, avid, fervent, earnest, diligent, zealous, passionate, wholehearted, ambitious, enterprising; *inf.* bright-eyed and bushy-tailed. **2** *eager to learn* | *eager for news* agog, anxious, intent, longing, yearning, itching, wishing, desirous, hopeful, thirsty, hungry, greedy; *inf.* hot.
Antonyms: INDIFFERENT; UNINTERESTED; APATHETIC.

---

eager

ardent, avid, enthusiastic, fervent, keen, zealous
You've heard of the eager beaver? Anyone who has a strong interest or an impatient desire to pursue or become involved in something is called **eager** (*eager to get started*; *an eager learner*). Someone who is especially *eager* might be called **avid**, a word that implies greed or insatiable desire (*an avid golfer, he was never at home on weekends*). **Ardent** combines eagerness with intense feelings of passion or devotion (*an ardent lover*; *an ardent theatergoer*), while **fervent** suggests an eagerness that is ready, at least figuratively, to boil over (*their fervent pleas could not be ignored*). Anyone who is deeply interested in something or who shows a spirited readiness to act is called **keen** (*he was keen on bicycling*), while **zealous** implies the kind of eagerness that pushes all other considerations aside (*a zealous environmentalist*). **Enthusiastic** may connote participation rather than expectation: One can be *eager* to take a trip to Switzerland, an *ardent* student of Swiss history, and an *avid* outdoorsperson who is *keen* on hiking, but one is usually called *enthusiastic* about a trip to Switzerland when it is under way or is over; *enthusiastic* also very often applies to someone who outwardly and forcefully expresses eagerness.

---

eagerness *noun* keenness, enthusiasm, impatience, avidity, fervor, earnestness, diligence, zeal, passion, wholeheartedness, desire, longing, yearning, wishing, itch, hope, thirst, hunger, greed, ambition, enterprise. *See* EAGER.

ear *noun* **1** *an infection of the ear* inner ear, middle ear, external ear, outer ear. **2** *have the ear of the president* attention, attentiveness, notice, heed, regard, consideration. **3** *an ear for a good song/musical* appreciation, discrimination, perception, musical taste.

early *adverb* **1** *get up and set off early* early in the day, in the early morning, at dawn, at the crack/break of dawn, at daybreak. **2** *guests should not arrive early* ahead of time, too soon, beforehand, before the usual/appointed time, prematurely. **3** *you should arrive early for the interview* in good time, before the appointed time, ahead of schedule.

early *adjective* **1** *an early crop/birth* advanced, premature, untimely. **2** *an early reply* prompt, without delay, quick, speedy, rapid, fast, expeditious, timely. **3** *early man/settlements* primitive, primeval, primordial, prehistoric.
Antonyms: LATE; BELATED; OVERDUE.

earmark *verb* *earmark the money for a vacation* set/lay aside, keep back, allocate, reserve, designate, label, tag.

earn *verb* **1** *earn a good salary* make, get, receive, obtain, draw, clear, collect, bring in, take home, pull in, pocket, gross, net. **2** *earn their admiration* gain, win, rate, merit, attain, achieve, secure, obtain, deserve, be entitled to, be worthy of, have a right to, warrant.

earnest *adjective* **1** *an earnest young man* serious, solemn, grave, intense, staid, studious, thoughtful, committed, dedicated, assiduous, keen, diligent, zealous, steady, hard-working. **2** *her earnest request/hope* sincere, fervent, fervid, ardent, passionate, warm, intense, heartfelt, wholehearted, profound, enthusiastic, zealous, urgent.
Antonyms: FRIVOLOUS; FLIPPANT; INSINCERE.

earnest *noun* in earnest **1** *he was in earnest about the punishment* serious, not joking, unsmiling, sincere. **2** *they set to work in earnest* zealously, ardently, fervently, fervidly, passionately, wholeheartedly, with dedication/commitment, determinedly, resolutely.

earnings *plural noun* income, salary, wage, pay, take-home pay, gross/net pay, remuneration, emolument, fee, stipend, honorarium, revenue, yield, profit, gain, return; wages.

earth *noun* **1** *earth, moon, and stars* globe, world, planet, sphere, orb. **2** *dig up the earth* soil, loam, clay, dirt, sod, clod, turf, ground. **3** *between the earth and the sky* ground, dry ground, land.

earthenware *noun* pottery, crockery, stoneware; pots, crocks.

earthly *adjective* **1** *earthly beings* terrestrial, telluric, tellurian. **2** *earthly joys* worldly, temporal, secular, mortal, human, mundane, material, nonspiritual, materialistic, carnal, fleshly, physical, corporeal, gross, sensual, base, sordid, vile, profane. **3** *no earthly chance* feasible, possible, conceivable, imaginable, likely.
Antonyms: HEAVENLY; SPIRITUAL.

earthy *adjective* **1** *earthy smell* soil-like, dirtlike. **2** *earthy peasants/pleasures* down-to-earth, unsophisticated, unrefined, simple, plain, unpretentious, natural, uninhibited, rough, robust. **3** *an earthy sense of humor* bawdy, crude, coarse, rough, ribald, blue, indecent, indecorous, obscene.

ease *noun* **1** *succeed with ease* no difficulty, no trouble/bother, facility, facileness, simplicity, effortlessness, deftness, adroitness, dexterity, proficiency, mastery. **2** *his ease of manner* naturalness, casualness, informality, unceremoniousness, lack of reserve/constraint, relaxedness, amiability, affability, unconcern, composure, aplomb, nonchalance, insouciance, urbanity, suaveness. **3** *ease of mind* peace, peacefulness, calmness, tranquillity, composure, serenity, repose, restfulness, quiet, contentment, security, comfort. **4** *a life of ease* comfort, contentment, content, enjoyment, affluence, wealth, prosperity, prosperousness, luxury, opulence; bed of roses.
Antonyms: DIFFICULTY; TROUBLE.

ease *verb* **1** *ease the pain* mitigate, lessen, reduce, lighten, diminish, moderate, abate, ameliorate, relieve, assuage, allay, soothe, soften, palliate, mollify, appease. **2** *the storm/pain eased* lessen, grow less, moderate, abate, diminish, grow quiet, slacken off. **3** *ease her mind* comfort, give solace to, solace, console, soothe, calm, quieten, pacify. **4** *ease his promotion* make easy/easier, facilitate, expedite, speed up, assist, help, aid, advance, further, forward, smooth/clear the way for, simplify. **5** *ease it into position* guide, maneuver, inch, edge, steer, slide, slip, squeeze.
Antonyms: AGGRAVATE; INCREASE; HINDER.

easy *adjective* **1** *an easy task* not difficult, simple, effortless, uncomplicated, straightforward, undemanding, painless, trouble-free, facile, idiot-proof. **2** *an easy prey* compliant, exploitable, susceptible, accommodating, obliging, amenable, docile, gullible, manageable, maneuverable, tractable, pliant, yielding, trusting, acquiescent. **3** *an easy manner* natural, casual, informal, unceremonious, unreserved, unconstrained, unforced, easygoing, amiable, affable, unconcerned, composed, carefree, nonchalant, insouciant, urbane, suave; *inf.* laid-back. **4** *an easy mind* at ease, trouble-free, untroubled, unworried, at peace, calm, tranquil, composed, serene, quiet, contented, secure, relaxed, comfortable. **5** *go at an easy pace* even, steady, regular, comfortable, moderate, unexacting, undemanding, leisured, unhurried.
Antonyms: DIFFICULT; DEMANDING; FORMAL; UNEASY.

easygoing *adjective* even-tempered, placid, happy-go-lucky, serene, relaxed, carefree, nonchalant, insouciant, tolerant, undemanding, amiable, patient, understanding, imperturbable; *inf.* laid-back, together.
Antonyms: INTOLERANT; TENSE.

eat *verb* **1** *eat chocolate* consume, devour, swallow, chew, munch, gulp down, bolt, wolf, ingest; *inf.* put away, scoff (up/down). **2** *eat out | eat in the evening* have a meal, take food, feed, partake of food; breakfast, lunch, dine; *inf.* snack, graze. **3** *eat away material/rock* erode, corrode, wear, gnaw away, crumble, dissolve, waste away, rot, decay, destroy.

eavesdrop *verb* listen in, snoop, spy; monitor, tap, wiretap, overhear; *inf.* bug.

ebb *verb* **1** *the tide ebbed* go out, flow back, retreat, draw back, fall back, fall away, recede, abate, subside, retrocede. **2** *its popularity ebbed* decline, die/fade away, die out, lessen, wane, decrease, diminish, flag, dwindle, peter out, sink, weaken, deteriorate, decay, degenerate.

ebb *noun* **1** *the ebb of the tide* going out, flowing back, retreat, retreating, drawing back, receding, abating, subsiding, retrocession. **2** *the ebb of popularity* decline, dying/fading away, lessening, waning, decrease, flagging, diminution, dwindling, petering out, sinking, deterioration, decay, degeneration.

ebony *adjective* black, jet black, pitch black, coal black, black as night/pitch/hell, sable, inky, sooty.

ebullience *noun* exuberance, effervescence, buoyancy, exhilaration, elation, euphoria, high-spiritedness, jubilation, animation, sparkle, vivacity, enthusiasm, zest, irrepressibility; high spirits.

ebullient *adjective* exuberant, effervescent, buoyant, exhilarated, elated, euphoric, high-spirited, in high spirits, jubilant, animated, sparkling, vivacious, enthusiastic, irrepressible.

eccentric *adjective* odd, queer, strange, peculiar, weird, bizarre, outlandish, freakish, uncommon, irregular, abnormal, aberrant, anomalous, nonconformist, unconventional, singular, idiosyncratic, capricious, whimsical, quirky; *inf.* way-out, offbeat, nutty, screwy.
Antonyms: ORDINARY; CONVENTIONAL.

eccentric *noun* oddity, freak, character, case; *inf.* oddball, weirdo, nut, screwball.

eccentricity *noun* oddness, queerness, strangeness, weirdness, bizarreness, freakishness, unconventionality; peculiarity, irregularity, abnormality, anomaly, foible, idiosyncrasy, caprice, whimsy, quirk. *See* ECCENTRIC *adjective.*

ecclesiastic *noun* clergyman, minister, parson,

priest, vicar, chaplain, padre, churchman, churchwoman, man/woman of the cloth, preacher, reverend, cleric, holy man/woman, abbé, divine, theologian. *See also table at* PRIEST.

ecclesiastic *adjective* church, churchly, religious, spiritual, nonsecular, nontemporal, pastoral, priestly, ministerial, holy, divine, clerical, sacerdotal; *inf.* churchy.

echelon *noun* level, grade, rank, step, rung, tier, degree.

echo *noun* **1** *the cave's echo* | *the echo of her call* reverberation, reverberating, resounding, ringing, repeating. **2** *the son an echo of his father* copy, imitation, reproduction, clone, duplicate, repeat, reflection, mirror image, parallel, parody. **3** *echoes of Picasso* suggestion, hint, trace, allusion, memory, reminder, remembrance, evocation, intimation; overtones, reminiscences.

echo *verb* **1** *echo around the room* reverberate, resound, reflect, ring, repeat. **2** *echo a statement* | *echo the main theme* copy, imitate, reproduce, repeat, reiterate, parrot, reflect, mirror, parallel, parody.

eclectic *adjective* **1** *eclectic interests* wide-ranging, broad, broad-based, comprehensive, general, varied, diverse, diversified, catholic, liberal, all-embracing, nonexclusive, many-sided, multifaceted, multifarious. **2** *eclectic philosophy* selective, selecting, choosing, picking and choosing.

eclipse *verb* **1** *eclipse the sun* blot out, block, cover, obscure, conceal, cast a shadow over, darken, shade, veil, shroud. **2** *eclipse his rival/success* outshine, overshadow, dwarf, put in the shade, surpass, excel, exceed, outstrip, transcend, outrival.

eclipse *noun* **1** *the eclipse of the sun* blotting out, blocking, covering, obscuring, concealing, veiling, shrouding, occultation. *See* ECLIPSE *verb* 1. **2** *the eclipse of the empire* decline, fall, failure, deterioration, degeneration, weakening, ebb, waning. **3** *the eclipse of his rival/success* outshining, overshadowing, dwarfing, surpassing, excelling, outstripping, transcending. *See* ECLIPSE *verb* 2.

economic *adjective* **1** *the government's economic policy* financial, monetary, budgetary, fiscal, commercial, trade, mercantile. **2** *an economic venture* profitable, profit-making, moneymaking, remunerative, viable, cost-effective, productive, solvent. **3** *an economic vacation* economical, cheap. *See* ECONOMICAL 2.

economical *adjective* **1** *economical with resources* | *economical with the salt* economizing, thrifty, sparing, careful, prudent, frugal, scrimping, mean, niggardly, stingy, parsimonious, conservationist; *inf.* penny-pinching. **2** *an economical vacation* cheap, inexpensive, reasonable, low-cost, low-price, low-budget, budget.

Antonyms: EXTRAVAGANT; WASTEFUL; EXPENSIVE.

---

economical
frugal, miserly, parsimonious, provident, sparing, thrifty

If you don't like to spend money unnecessarily, you may simply be **economical**, which means that you manage your finances wisely and avoid any unnecessary expenses. If you're **thrifty**, you're both industrious and clever in managing your resources (*a thrifty shopper who never leaves home without her coupons*). **Frugal**, on the other hand, means that you tend to be sparing with money—sometimes getting a little carried away in your efforts—by avoiding any form of luxury or lavishness (*too frugal to take a taxi, even at night*). If you're **sparing**, you exercise such restraint in your spending that you sometimes deprive yourself (*sparing to the point where she allowed herself only one new item of clothing a season*). If you're **provident**, however, you're focused on providing for the future (*never one to be provident, she spent her allowance the day she received it*). **Miserly** and **parsimonious** are both used to describe frugality in its most extreme form. But while being *frugal* might be considered a virtue, being *parsimonious* is usually considered to be a fault or even a vice (*they could have been generous with their wealth, but they chose to lead a parsimonious life*). And no one wants to be called *miserly*, which implies being stingy out of greed rather than need (*so miserly that he reveled in his riches while those around him were starving*).

---

economize *verb* *we must economize because we are short of money* cut back, retrench, budget, cut expenditure, be economical, besparing/frugal, reduce/decrease waste/wastage, save, scrimp, scrimp and save; *inf.* cut corners, tighten one's belt, pinch pennies.

Antonym: SQUANDER.

economy *noun* **1** *the national economy* wealth, resources; financial state, financial management. **2** *practice economy* | *use with economy* thriftiness, sparingness, carefulness, prudence, frugalness, scrimping, meanness, niggardliness, stinginess, parsimony, parsimoniousness; thrift, care, restraint, frugality, husbandry, conservation; *inf.* penny-pinching.

ecstasy *noun* bliss, rapture, elation, euphoria, joy, joyousness, jubilation, exultation, cloud nine, seventh heaven; rhapsodies.

Antonyms: MISERY; ANGUISH; TORMENT.

ecstatic *adjective* blissful, enraptured, rapturous, joyful, joyous, overjoyed, jumping for joy, jubilant, exultant, elated, rhapsodic, delirious with happiness/delight, on cloud nine, in seventh heaven.

Antonyms: MISERABLE; DEPRESSED.

eddy *noun* whirlpool, vortex, maelstrom, swirling, swirl, countercurrent, counterflow.

eddy *verb* swirl, swirl around, whirl.

edge *noun* **1** *the edge of the lake/plate* border, side,

boundary, rim, margin, fringe, outer limit, extremity, verge, brink, lip, contour, perimeter, periphery, parameter, ambit. **2** *a voice with an edge* sting, bite; sharpness, severity, pointedness, acerbity, causticity, acidity, acrimony, virulence, trenchancy, pungency. **3** *have the edge on her* advantage, upper hand, lead, head start, dominance, superiority. **on edge** edgy, nervous, tense, uneasy. See EDGY.
Antonyms: CENTER; MIDDLE.

edge *verb* **1** *edge the blade* put an edge on, sharpen, hone, whet, strop, file. **2** *edge with lace* trim, bind, hem, border, fringe. **3** *edge one's way through the crowd* inch, ease, elbow, worm, work, sidle, sidestep, gravitate. **4** *edge forward* inch, sidle, creep, steal.

edgy *adjective* on edge, nervous, tense, ill at ease, anxious, on tenterhooks, keyed up, restive, apprehensive, uneasy, irritable, irascible, touchy, tetchy; *inf.* nervy, twitchy, uptight, wired.
Antonyms: TRANQUIL; CALM; relaxed.

edible *adjective* fit/good to eat, consumable, digestible, palatable, comestible.
Antonym: INEDIBLE.

edict *noun* decree, order, command, law, rule, ruling, regulation, act, enactment, statute, injunction, mandate, manifesto, proclamation, pronouncement, ordinance, dictate, dictum, fiat, ukase.

edification *noun* instruction, education, tuition, teaching, schooling, tutoring, coaching, guidance, enlightenment, improvement, uplifting, elevation.

edifice *noun* building, structure, construction, erection; *inf.* pile.

edify *verb* instruct, educate, teach, school, tutor, coach, guide, inform, enlighten, improve, uplift, elevate.

edit *verb* **1** *edit her book* copyedit, revise, correct, emend, polish, check, modify, rewrite, rephrase, prepare/adapt/assemble for publication, redact; *inf.* clean up. **2** *he edits the paper* be the editor of, run, direct, be in charge of, be chief of, head, head up.

edition *noun* **1** *Sunday edition of the paper* issue, number, printing, version. **2** *a first edition of the book* printing, impression, publication, issue.

educate *verb* instruct, teach, school, tutor, coach, train, drill, prime, inform, indoctrinate, inculcate, enlighten, edify, cultivate, develop, improve, prepare, rear, nurture, foster.

educated *adjective* *educated people* literate, schooled, well-read, informed, knowledgeable, enlightened, lettered, erudite, cultivated, cultured, refined; *inf.* highbrow.
Antonyms: ILLITERATE; IGNORANT.

education *noun* **1** *the education of the children* schooling, teaching, instruction, tuition, coaching, training, tutelage, drilling, disciplining, priming, informing, indoctrination, inculcation, enlightenment, edification, culti-

vation, development, improvement, preparation, rearing, nurturing, fostering. **2** *people of education* literacy, schooling, scholarship, knowledge, enlightenment, cultivation, culture, refinement; letters.

educational *adjective* **1** *an educational establishment* academic, learning, teaching, pedagogic. **2** *the film is educational* instructive, informative, enlightening, edifying, improving, didactic.

educator *noun* educationalist, teacher, schoolteacher, schoolmaster, schoolmistress, lecturer, tutor, coach, academic, pedagogue.

eerie *adjective* uncanny, unearthly, ghostly, spectral, mysterious, strange, unnatural, frightening, fearful, scaring, chilling, spine-chilling, blood-curdling; *inf.* spooky, scary, creepy.

efface *verb* **1** *efface the graffiti/memory* remove, rub out, blot out, wipe out, blank out, obliterate, erase, delete, eradicate, expunge, eliminate, excise, annihilate, extirpate. **2** *efface oneself | be self-effacing* make inconspicuous, withdraw, keep out of the limelight, regard/treat as unimportant, be modest/diffident/retiring.

effect *noun* **1** *the effect of the changes* result, net result, outcome, upshot, consequence, conclusion, aftermath, issue; results, fruits. **2** *the law/plan goes into effect tomorrow* force, enforcement, operation, implementation, execution, action. **3** *speak to great effect | act with great effect* effectiveness, success, influence, efficacy, effectuality, weight, power, cogency. See EFFECTIVENESS. **4** *or words to that effect* sense, meaning, drift, tenor, significance, import, purport, essence. **in effect** effectively, actually, really, in actual fact, in reality, in truth, to all intents and purposes, for all practical purposes, essentially, in essence, virtually. **take effect 1** *rules taking effect from tomorrow* come into being/force/operation, begin, become operative, become valid, become law. **2** *medicine taking effect* be effective, work, produce results, have the desired effect.
Antonym: CAUSE.

effect *verb* *effect a plan* effectuate, bring about, carry out, cause, make, produce, create, give rise to, perform, achieve, accomplish, complete, fulfill, implement, execute, actuate, initiate.

effective *adjective* **1** *effective administration* successful, productive, competent, capable, able, efficient, efficacious, effectual, useful, adequate, active, energetic. **2** *effective lighting* striking, impressive, exciting, attractive. **3** *effective arguments* powerful, forceful, forcible, cogent, compelling, potent, telling, persuasive, convincing, moving. **4** *rules become effective tomorrow* valid, in force, in operation, operative, active, effectual.
Antonyms: INEFFECTIVE; INCOMPETENT; WEAK.

effective
effectual, efficacious, efficient

All of these adjectives mean producing or capable of producing a result, but they are not interchangeable. Use **effective** when you want to describe something that produces a definite effect or result (*an effective speaker who was able to rally the crowd's support*) and **efficacious** when it produces the desired effect or result (*an efficacious remedy that cured her almost immediately*). If something produces the desired effect or result in a decisive manner, use **effectual** (*an effectual recommendation that got him the job*), an adjective that is often employed when looking back after an event is over (*an effectual strategy that finally turned the tide in their favor*). Reserve the use of **efficient** for when you want to imply skill and economy of energy in producing the desired result (*so efficient in her management of the company that layoffs were not necessary*). When applied to people, *efficient* means capable or competent (*an efficient homemaker*) and places less emphasis on the achievement of results and more on the skills involved.

effectiveness *noun* **1** *the effectiveness of the administration* success, productiveness, competence, competency, capability, ability, efficiency, efficacy, effectuality, effectualness, usefulness, adequacy. *See* EFFECTIVE 1. **2** *the effectiveness of the argument* power, force, forcefulness, cogency, potency, persuasion, persuasiveness. *See* EFFECTIVE 3.

effects *plural noun* belongings, (personal) possessions, goods, trappings, accouterments, paraphernalia; property, luggage, baggage, bag and baggage, gear, equipment, tackle; *inf.* things, stuff.

effectual *adjective* **1** *effectual actions/measures* effective, successful, efficacious, productive, efficient, powerful, potent, capable, competent, useful, functional, forcible. **2** *effectual documents* valid, legal, binding, lawful, in force, sound, licit.

effectuate *verb* effect, bring about, cause, make, produce, achieve, accomplish, implement, execute, actuate. *See* EFFECT *verb*.

effeminate *adjective* womanish, unmanly, effete, milksoppish; *inf.* wimpish, pansy-like, sissy. **Antonyms:** VIRILE; MANLY.

effervesce *verb* **1** *wine effervescing* sparkle, bubble, fizz, froth, foam, ferment. **2** *effervescing over his success* sparkle, be animated, be lively, be jubilant, be exuberant. *See* EFFERVESCENT 2.

effervescence *noun* **1** *the effervescence of the wine/water* bubbliness, sparkle, carbonation, fizziness, frothiness, foam, fermentation. **2** *the effervescence of the happy young people* vivacity, animation, liveliness, buoyancy, exuberance, exhilaration, ebullience, jubilation, sparkle, bubbliness, merriment, irrepressibility.

effervescent *adjective* **1** *effervescent wine* sparkling, carbonated, bubbly, bubbling, fizzy, fizzing, frothy, foamy, fermenting. **2** *effervescent partygoers* vivacious, animated, lively, buoyant, exuberant, exhilarated, ebullient, jubilant, sparkling, bubbly, merry, irrepressible.

effete *adjective* **1** *effete civilization* weakened, worn out, exhausted, finished, burnt out, played out, drained, spent, enfeebled, enervated, powerless. **2** *effete young men* effeminate, womanish, unmanly, milksoppish; *inf.* pansy-like, sissy, wimpish.

efficacious *adjective* effective, successful, efficient, effectual, productive, useful, competent, adequate, capable, able, potent, powerful.

efficacy *noun* effectiveness, success, successfulness, efficiency, effectuality, productiveness, usefulness, potency. *See* EFFICACIOUS.

efficiency *noun* **1** *admire her efficiency* capability, ability, competence, competency, effectiveness, productivity, skill, expertise, proficiency, adeptness, deftness, mastery, organization. *See* EFFICIENT 1. **2** *the efficiency of the office* organization, well-orderedness, streamlinedness. *See* EFFICIENT 2.

efficient *adjective* **1** *an efficient person* capable, able, competent, effective, productive, skillful, expert, proficient, adept, deft, organized, workmanlike, businesslike. **2** *an efficient office* organized, well-organized, well-run, well-ordered, streamlined, laborsaving. **Antonyms:** INEFFICIENT; INEPT; DISORGANIZED.

effigy *noun* likeness, image, model, dummy, representation, guy, carving, statue, bust.

effluent *noun* **1** *factory effluent* waste, waste stream, sewage, pollutant, pollution, effluvium. **2** *the effluent of the dirty water* discharge, outflow, emission, emanation, exhalation.

effort *noun* **1** *put effort into it* exertion, force, power, energy, work, muscle, application, labor, striving, endeavor, toil, struggle, strain, stress; *lit.* travail; *inf.* elbow grease. **2** *win at the third effort* attempt, try, endeavor; *inf.* shot, go, crack, stab. **3** *admire his artistic efforts* achievement, accomplishment, attainment, result, creation, production, opus, feat, deed.

effortless *adjective* easy, simple, uncomplicated, undemanding, unexacting, painless, trouble-free, facile. **Antonyms:** DIFFICULT; DEMANDING.

effrontery *noun* impertinence, insolence, boldness, audacity, arrogance, impudence, cheek, audacity, temerity, presumption, gall, brashness; *inf.* nerve, brass.

effulgent *adjective* shining, bright, brilliant, dazzling, blazing, glowing, radiant, luminous, lustrous, incandescent, fluorescent, vivid, splendid.

effusion *noun* **1** *effusion of blood* gush, stream, outpouring, outflow, discharge, issue, efflux, spilling, shedding, voidance. **2** *amazed at her passionate effusion* outburst, outpouring, stream of words, flow of speech, utterance, wordiness, speech, address, talk; words, writings.

effusive *adjective* gushing, unrestrained, unreserved, extravagant, fulsome, demonstrative, lavish, enthusiastic, rhapsodic, lyrical, exuberant, ebullient, expansive, wordy, verbose, longwinded, profuse.

egg *verb* **egg on** encourage, urge, push, drive, goad, spur on, prod, prompt, excite, exhort.

egghead *noun* intellectual, academic, scholar, brain, genius, bookworm, pedagogue, pedant; *inf.* highbrow, Einstein, know-it-all, walking encyclopedia.

ego *noun* self, the self, oneself, identity; self-importance, self-esteem, self-conceit, self-image, self-confidence.

egoism *noun* self-interest, self-centeredness, selfishness, egocentricity, egomania, egotism, looking out for number one, self-seeking, self-absorption, self-love, narcissism, vanity, conceit, pride, self-esteem, self-importance. *Antonyms:* self-effacement; humbleness.

---

egoism
conceit, egotism, narcissism, solipsism, vanity

Is the handsome, arrogant, successful politician who thinks the world revolves around him an egoist or an egotist? **Egotism** is a negative term that combines extreme self-preoccupation with a tendency to show off or attract attention, while **egoism** is a more neutral term for those who are preoccupied with their own needs and interests but do not necessarily consider themselves superior (*the egoism of teenagers is well-documented*). There is nothing neutral about **conceit**, which carries strong connotations of superiority and a failure to see oneself realistically (*he was so rich and powerful that conceit came easily*). **Vanity,** on the other hand, is not based so much on feelings of superiority as it is on a love for oneself and a craving for the admiration of others (*his vanity drove him to cosmetic surgery*). **Narcissism** and **solipsism** were once considered technical terms drawn from psychology and philosophy, respectively, but nowadays they are also in the general language. *Narcissism* means self-love and preoccupation with one's physical or mental attributes (*the beautiful young actress had a reputation for narcissism*), while *solipsism* refers to someone who is completely wrapped up in his or her own concerns (*the solipsism of the theoretical mathematician*).

---

egoist *noun* self-seeker, egocentric, egomaniac, egotist, narcissist.

egoistic *adjective* self-centered, selfish, egocentric, egotistic, self-seeking, self-absorbed, self-obsessed, self-loving, narcissistic, vain, conceited, proud, self-important.

egotism *noun* self-admiration, self-love, egomania, egocentricity, egoism, narcissism, self-conceit, conceit, vanity, pride, arrogance, self-esteem, self-importance, self-glorification, superiority, self-praise, boastfulness, bragging, braggadocio; *inf.* blowing one's own trumpet.

egotist *noun* self-admirer, egomaniac, egocentric, egoist, boaster, bragger; *inf.* blowhard, bighead.

egotistic *adjective* self-admiring, egocentric, egoistic, narcissistic, conceited, vain, proud, arrogant, self-important, superior, boastful, bragging.

egregious *adjective* glaring, flagrant, blatant, gross, outrageous, monstrous, rank, enormous, shocking, scandalous, appalling, heinous, intolerable, infamous, notorious, grievous, arrant.

egress *noun* **1** *seek a means of egress* exit, way out, door/gate out, escape route, outlet, vent. **2** *the egress of the crowd* leaving, departure, exit, withdrawal, exodus, issue, emergence, flowing out, escape, emanation.

ejaculate *verb* **1** *ejaculate fluid/semen* emit, eject, discharge, release, expel, spurt (out). **2** *men unable to ejaculate* emit/discharge semen, climax, have an orgasm, orgasm; *inf.* come. **3** *ejaculate a cry* utter, call out, voice, vocalize. **4** *"Watch out!" he ejaculated* cry out, call out, exclaim, shout out, blurt out, yell.

ejaculation *noun* **1** *the ejaculation of fluid/semen* emission, ejection, discharge, release. *See* EJACULATE 1. **2** *his premature ejaculation* emission/discharge of semen, climax, orgasm. **3** *they heard an ejaculation* cry, call, exclamation, shout, yell, utterance.

eject *verb* **1** *eject sewage/smoke/semen* emit, discharge, exude, excrete, expel, cast out, release, spew out, disgorge, spout, vomit, ejaculate. **2** *he was ejected from the plane/vehicle* propel, thrust out, throw out, expel. **3** *eject the intruder from the building* | *eject him from his house* | *ejected from the country* throw out, turn out, put out, cast out, remove, evict, expel, oust, put out in the street, dispossess, banish, deport, exile; *inf.* kick out, boot out, bounce. **4** *eject her from a senior post* sack, dismiss, discharge, oust, dislodge, get rid of, send packing; *inf.* fire, axe, hand someone his/her pink slip, kick out, boot out, give the boot to.

---

eject
dismiss, evict, expel, oust

Want to get rid of someone? You can **eject** him or her, which means to throw or cast out (*he was ejected from the meeting room*). If you hope the person never comes back, use **expel**, a verb that suggests driving someone out of a country, an organization, etc., for all time (*to be expelled from school*); it can also imply the use of voluntary force (*to expel air from the lungs*). If you exercise force or the power of law to get rid of someone or something, **oust** is the correct verb (*ousted after less than two years in office*). If as a property owner you are turning someone out of a house or a place of business, you'll want to **evict** the person (*she was evicted for not paying the rent*). **Dismiss** is by far the mildest of these terms, suggesting that you are rejecting or refusing to consider someone or something (*to dismiss a legal case*). It is also commonly used of loss of employment (*dismissed from his job for excessive tardiness*).

ejection *noun* **1** *ejection of sewage/smoke/semen* emission, discharge, exudation, excretion, expulsion, ejaculation, release. *See* EJECT 1. **2** *his ejection from the plane* propulsion, expulsion. *See* EJECT 2. **3** *ejection from the building/house/country* throwing out, removal, eviction, expulsion, ousting, dispossessing, banishment, deportation, exile. *See* EJECT 3. **4** *her ejection from a senior post* sacking, dismissal, discharge, ousting; *inf.* firing, axing, heave-ho. *See* EJECT 4.

eke *verb* **eke out** **1** *eke out a living* scrape for/out, scratch for/out, scrimp for. **2** *you must eke out the butter ration* be economical with, economize on, be frugal/sparing with; *inf.* go easy on/with.

elaborate *adjective* **1** *elaborate plans* complicated, detailed, complex, involved, intricate, studied, painstaking, careful. **2** *elaborate patterns* detailed, complex, ornate, fancy, showy, ostentatious, extravagant.
Antonyms: SIMPLE; PLAIN.

elaborate *verb* **1** *elaborate on a plan* expand on, enlarge on, amplify, flesh out, add flesh to, add detail to, expatiate on. **2** *elaborate the plan* develop, work out, improve, refine, polish, perfect, embellish, enhance, ornament, embroider.
Antonyms: SIMPLIFY; streamline.

élan *noun* style, flair, flourish, dash, verve, panache, spirit, vivacity, vitality, zest, *esprit; inf.* oomph, pizzazz.

elapse *verb* pass, go by, go on, slip away, slip by, roll by, slide by, steal by.

elastic *adjective* **1** *elastic material* stretchy, stretchable, springy, flexible, pliant, pliable, supple, yielding, rubbery, plastic, rebounding, recoiling, resilient. **2** *elastic plans/attitudes* flexible, adaptable, fluid, adjustable, accommodating, variable, yielding; *inf.* easy.
Antonyms: RIGID; INFLEXIBLE.

elasticity *noun* **1** *elasticity of the fiber* stretchiness, springiness, flexibility, pliancy, suppleness, rubberiness, plasticity, resilience; *inf.* give. **2** *elasticity of plans/attitude* flexibility, adaptability, adjustability, fluidity, variability.

elated *adjective* *elated at the news | an elated smile* overjoyed, ecstatic, blissful, joyful, jubilant, euphoric, exultant, rhapsodic, exhilarated, ebullient, delighted, cheered, excited, animated, roused, gleeful, in seventh heaven. *See* ECSTATIC.
Antonyms: MISERABLE; DEJECTED.

elation *noun* ecstasy, bliss, euphoria, rapture, joy, jubilation, exhilaration, rhapsody, ebullience, delight, glee, excitement, animation.

elbow *noun* *elbow of the pipe* bend, joint, turning, corner, right angle, crook.

elbow *verb* *elbow out of the way | elbow one's way through the crowd* push, jostle, nudge, shoulder, knock, bump, crowd, bulldoze.

elbowroom *noun* space, room, room to maneuver, breathing space, scope, freedom, latitude, leeway.

elder *adjective* older, senior, first-born.

elderly *adjective* aging, aged, old, oldish, advanced in years, gray-haired, ancient, superannuated, past one's prime; *inf.* over the hill, long in the tooth.
Antonyms: YOUNG; YOUTHFUL.

elderly *plural noun* **the elderly** older people, senior citizens, seniors, golden agers.
Antonyms: YOUNG; YOUTH.

elect *verb* *elect a senator | elect a team captain* vote for, cast one's vote for, choose by ballot, choose, pick, select, appoint, opt for, decide on, designate, determine.

elect *plural noun* **the elect** the chosen, the selected, the preferred, the appointed, the designated, the elite.

election *noun* **1** *vote in an election* ballot, poll; general election, local election. **2** *the election of the senator | the election for team captain* voting, choosing, picking, selection, choice, appointment; vote, ballot. *See* ELECT *verb.*

elector *noun* voter, member of the electorate, constituent, selector, chooser.

electric *adjective* **1** *electric power* generated by electricity, galvanic, voltaic. **2** *electric can openers* electrically operated/powered, battery-operated, electrically charged. **3** *an electric moment | the effect was electric* tense, charged, exciting, dynamic, thrilling, startling, stimulating, rousing, stirring, moving, jolting, shocking, galvanizing.

electrify *verb* excite, thrill, startle, shock, arouse, rouse, move, stimulate, stir, animate, fire, charge, invigorate, jolt, galvanize.

elegance *noun* style, gracefulness, grace, taste, tastefulness, fashion, culture, beauty, charm, polish, refinement, exquisiteness, finesse, discernment, dignity, distinction, propriety, luxury, sumptuousness, opulence, *haute couture.*

elegant *adjective* stylish, graceful, tasteful, artistic, fashionable, cultured, beautiful, lovely, charming, exquisite, polished, cultivated, refined, aesthetic, suave, debonair, modish, dignified, luxurious, sumptuous, opulent.
Antonyms: INELEGANT; UNFASHIONABLE; GAUCHE.

elegiac *adjective* funereal, lamenting, doleful, mournful, dirgelike, melancholic, plaintive, sad, nostalgic, valedictory.

elegy *noun* funeral poem/song, lament, dirge, plaint, requiem.

element *noun* **1** *an element of truth | a stable el-*

ement of the group basis, ingredient, factor, feature, detail, trace, component, constituent, part, section, portion, piece, segment, member, unit, module, subdivision. **2** *in his natural element* environment, habitat, medium, milieu, sphere, field, domain, realm, circle, resort, haunt.

elemental *adjective* **1** *elemental truth* basic, fundamental, rudimentary, embryonic, primitive, radical, essential, elementary. **2** *elemental influences* natural, atmospheric, meteorological, environmental.

elementary *adjective* **1** *elementary puzzle* easy, simple, straightforward, uncomplicated, rudimentary, facile, simplistic. **2** *elementary mathematics* basic, fundamental, rudimentary, primary, preparatory, introductory.
Antonyms: COMPLICATED; ADVANCED; SENIOR.

elements *plural noun* **1** *exposed to the elements* weather, climate, atmospheric conditions/forces, environment; *lit.* clime. **2** *the elements of good manners* basics, essentials, principles, foundations, fundamentals, rudiments.

elephantine *adjective* huge, massive, enormous, immense, hulking, bulky, mammoth, gargantuan, heavy, weighty, ponderous, lumbering, clumsy, laborious.

elevate *verb* **1** *elevate the load* raise, lift, hoist, hike up, raise up/aloft. **2** *elevate to management* promote, give promotion, upgrade, improve the position/status of, advance, give advancement, exalt, prefer, aggrandize; *inf.* kick upstairs. **3** *elevate her spirits* | *she felt elevated* cheer, gladden, brighten, perk up, give a lift/boost to, lighten; cheer up, animate, exhilarate, elate, boost, buoy up, uplift.
Antonyms: LOWER; DEMOTE; DEPRESS.

elevated *adjective* **1** *elevated banners* raised, lifted up, hoisted, high up, aloft, upraised, uplifted. **2** *an elevated position* high, higher, high/higher up, great, grand, lofty, dignified, noble, exalted, magnificent, sublime, inflated, pompous, bombastic. **3** *elevated spirits/state* cheerful, cheered up, glad, joyful, happy, overjoyed, gleeful, excited, animated, elated, exhilarated, in high spirits, blithe. **4** *elevated literary style* lofty, exalted, inflated, pompous, bombastic.

elevation *noun* **1** *elevation of the building* height, altitude, tallness. **2** *the elevation behind the town* height, rise, raised/rising ground, hill, mountain, hillock, mound, mount, eminence; *fml.* acclivity. **3** *elevation to the board* promotion, upgrading, advancement, preferment, aggrandizement, step up the ladder. **4** *elevation of thought* grandeur, greatness, nobility, magnificence, loftiness, majesty, grandioseness, sublimity.

elf *noun* fairy, pixie, sprite, dwarf, gnome, goblin, hobgoblin, imp, brownie, leprechaun, puck, troll, banshee.

elfin *adjective* **1** *elfin features/child* elflike, elfish, elvish, pixie-like, puckish, small, little, tiny,

dainty, diminutive, wee, pint-sized, Lilliputian. **2** *elfin mischief* mischievous, impish, puckish, playful, arch.

elicit *verb* obtain, bring out, draw out, extract, extort, exact, wrest, evoke, derive, call forth, educe.

elite *noun* **1** *the elite among the students* best, pick, cream, *crème de la crème*, elect, meritocracy. **2** *the elite of society* aristocracy, nobility, gentry, establishment, high society, jet set, beautiful people, upper crust.
Antonyms: RIFF-RAFF; RABBLE.

elixir *noun* **1** *an elixir for all ills* panacea, cure-all, universal remedy, wonder drug, magic bullet, nostrum. **2** *elixir of eucalyptus* extract, essence, concentrate, quintessence, pith, mixture, solution, potion, tincture.

elliptical *adjective* **1** *an elliptical shape* oval, egg-shaped, ovate, ovoid. **2** *an elliptical style of writing* terse, concise, succinct, compact, economic. **3** *elliptical prose/speech* abstruse, cryptic, ambiguous, obscure, recondite.

elocution *noun* diction, speech, enunciation, articulation, voice production, pronunciation, phrasing, delivery, utterance, speech-making, public speaking, oratory, declamation.

elongate *verb* lengthen, stretch out, make longer, extend, draw out, prolong, protract.

elope *verb* run off/away together, run off/away with a lover, run away to marry, slip away, sneak off, steal away; escape, make one's escape, flee, abscond.

eloquence *noun* **1** *the eloquence of the speaker/argument/speech* expressiveness, articulacy, articulateness, fluency, facility, diction, enunciation, command of language, power of speech, oratory, rhetoric, persuasiveness, forcefulness; *inf.* gift of (the) gab. **2** *the eloquence of the glance* expressiveness, significance, meaningfulness, suggestiveness, revelation, pregnancy.

eloquent *adjective* **1** *an eloquent speaker/argument/speech* expressive, well-spoken, articulate, fluent, graceful, silver-tongued, smooth-tongued, well-expressed, vivid, effective, graphic, pithy, persuasive, glib, forceful. **2** *an eloquent look* expressive, significant, meaningful, suggestive, revealing, telling, pregnant.
Antonyms: INARTICULATE; TONGUE-TIED.

elsewhere *adverb* somewhere else, in/to another place, in/to a different place, not here, not present, absent, away, abroad, hence.

elucidate *verb* *please elucidate!* | *elucidate the meaning* explain; make clear/plain, interpret, illuminate, throw light on, comment on, annotate, gloss, spell out; *fml.* explicate.

elucidation *noun* explanation, clarification, interpretation, illumination, comment, commentary, annotation, gloss, explication, exposition.

elude *verb* *the fox eluded the hunter* avoid, get away from, dodge, evade, escape, lose, duck, shake off, give the slip to, throw off the scent, flee, circumvent; *inf.* ditch.

elusive *adjective* **1** *an elusive person* difficult to catch/find, evasive, slippery, shifty, cagey. **2** *an elusive perfume* indefinable, subtle, unanalyzable, intangible, impalpable, fleeting, transient, transitory, fugitive. **3** *an elusive answer* ambiguous, baffling, puzzling, misleading, evasive, equivocal, deceitful, deceptive, fallacious, fraudulent, elusory.

Elysium *noun* heaven, paradise, eternity, kingdom come.

emaciated *adjective* wasted, gaunt, skeletal, anorexic, scrawny, cadaverous, shriveled, shrunken, withered, haggard, drawn, pinched, wizened, attenuated, atrophied.

emaciation *noun* gauntness, scrawniness, cadaverousness, haggardness. *See* EMACIATED.

emanate *verb* **1** *desire emanating from jealousy* arise, originate, stem, derive, emerge, proceed, come forth, issue. **2** *emanating fumes* give off, give out, send out, send forth, discharge, emit, exhale, radiate.

emanation *noun* **1** *emanation of hostility from rivalry* arising, origination, derivation, emergence. **2** *a foul-smelling emanation* discharge, emission, effluent, exhalation, radiation, effusion, efflux.

emancipate *verb* **1** *emancipate slaves* free, set free, liberate, release, let loose, deliver, discharge, unchain, unfetter, unshackle, untie, unyoke, manumit. **2** *emancipate women* allow to vote, give voting rights to, enfranchise; free from restriction/restraint.

emancipation *noun emancipation of slaves* setting free, liberation, release, deliverance, discharge, unfettering, unshackling, manumission; freedom, liberty. *See* EMANCIPATE 1.

emasculate *verb* **1** *emasculate a bull* castrate, neuter, geld, spay, desex, unman. **2** *emasculate the power of the state* weaken, debilitate, make feeble/feebler, enfeeble, enervate, impoverish.

embalm *verb* **1** *embalm a corpse* preserve, treat, anoint, mummify, lay out. **2** *embalm memories* remember, keep in mind, look back on, reminisce about, cherish, treasure, conserve, store, consecrate, immortalize, enshrine. **3** *flowers embalming the air* perfume, make fragrant, scent, aromatize.

embargo *noun* ban, bar, prohibition, stoppage, interdict, proscription; restriction, restraint, blockage, check, barrier, impediment, obstruction, hindrance.

embargo *verb* ban, bar, prohibit, stop, interdict, debar, proscribe; restrict, restrain, block, check, impede, obstruct, hinder.

embark *verb passengers embarking* board ship, enplane, go on board, go aboard; set sail, put to sea, weigh anchor, take off. **embark on** *embark on an adventure* begin, start, commence, undertake, enter on, go into, take up, venture

into, launch into, turn one's hand to, engage in, institute, initiate; *inf.* have a go at.

Antonyms: DISEMBARK; LAND; END.

embarrass *verb* make uncomfortable/awkward, make self-conscious, upset, disconcert, discomfit, discompose, confuse, fluster, agitate, nonplus, distress, chagrin, shame, humiliate, abash, mortify.

embarrassed *adjective* uncomfortable, awkward, self-conscious, disconcerted, upset, discomfited, discomposed, confused, flustered, agitated, nonplussed, distressed, chagrined, shamed, humiliated, abashed, mortified; *inf.* with egg on one's face.

embarrassing *adjective* **1** *embarrassing remark* disconcerting, discomfiting, discomposing, upsetting, confusing, flustering, agitating, distressing, shaming, humiliating, mortifying. **2** *embarrassing moment* awkward, compromising, tricky.

embarrassment *noun* **1** *overcome with embarrassment* discomfort, awkwardness, self-consciousness, bashfulness, discomfiture, discomposure, confusion, agitation, distress, chagrin, shame, humiliation, mortification. **2** *financial embarrassment* difficulty, predicament, plight, mess, dilemma, entanglement, imbroglio; *inf.* bind, pickle, fix, scrape, quandary. **3** *embarrassment of riches* excess, surplus, abundance, overabundance, profusion, glut, surfeit, superfluity, avalanche, deluge.

embassy *noun* **1** *the British embassy* consulate, legation, ministry. **2** *sent our embassy to China* envoy, representative, legate; delegation.

embed *verb* imbed, insert, implant, plant, set/fix in, root, drive in, hammer in, ram in, sink.

embellish *verb embellish a ceiling* | *embellish the truth* decorate, adorn, ornament, dress, dress up, beautify, enhance, trim, garnish, gild, varnish, embroider, enrich, deck, bedeck, festoon, emblazon, bespangle, elaborate, exaggerate.

embellishment *noun the embellishment of a ceiling/story* decoration, ornamentation, adornment, beautification, enhancement, trimming, garnishing, gilding, varnishing, embroidery, enrichment, bedecking, festooning, emblazoning, elaboration, exaggeration.

embezzle *verb* steal, rob, thieve, pilfer, appropriate, misappropriate, purloin, filch, abstract, put one's hand in the till, dip into the till/funds, peculate, defalcate; *inf.* rip off.

embezzlement *noun* thieving, stealing, robbing, fraud, larceny, pilfering, appropriation, misappropriation, purloining, filching, abstraction, peculation, defalcation; theft, robbery, misuse of funds; *inf.* ripping off.

embitter *verb* **1** *embittered by her divorce* make bitter, make resentful, sour, anger, disillusion, poison, disaffect, envenom. **2** *embitter the situation* aggravate, worsen, exacerbate, exaggerate.

emblazon *verb* **1** *emblazoning a shield* decorate,

adorn, ornament, embellish, illuminate, color, paint. **2** *emblazoned on the screen* proclaim, publicize, publish, trumpet, glorify, extol, praise, laud.

emblem *noun* crest, badge, symbol, device, representation, token, image, figure, mark, sign; insignia.

---

emblem
attribute, image, sign, symbol, token, type

When it comes to representing or embodying the invisible or intangible, you can't beat a **symbol**. It applies to anything that serves as an outward sign of something immaterial or spiritual (*the cross as a symbol of salvation*; *the crown as a symbol of monarchy*), although the association between the symbol and what it represents does not have to be based on tradition or convention and may, in fact, be quite arbitrary (*the annual gathering at the cemetery became a symbol of the family's long and tragic history*). An **emblem** is a visual symbol or pictorial device that represents the character or history of a family, a nation, or an office (*the eagle is an emblem of the United States*). It is very close in meaning to **attribute**, which is an object that is conventionally associated with either an individual, a group, or an abstraction (*the spiked wheel as an attribute of St. Catherine*; *the scales as an attribute of Justice*). An **image** is also a visual representation or embodiment, but in a much broader sense (*veins popping, he was the image of the angry father*). **Sign** is often used in place of *symbol* to refer to a simple representation of an agreed-upon meaning (*the upraised fist as a sign of victory*; *the white flag as a sign of surrender*), but a *symbol* usually embodies a wider range of meanings, while a *sign* can be any object, event, or gesture from which information can be deduced (*her faltering voice was a sign of her nervousness*). A **token**, on the other hand, is something offered as a symbol or reminder (*he gave her his class ring as a token of his devotion*) and a **type**, particularly in a religious context, is a symbol or representation of something not present (*Jerusalem as the type of heaven*; *the paschal lamb as the type of Christ*).

---

embodiment *noun* **1** *the embodiment of new design features in the car* incorporation, combination, bringing together, collecting, inclusion, consolidation, assimilation, integration, organization, systemization. *See* EMBODY 1. **2** *he is the embodiment of good manners* personification, representation, incarnation, incorporation, symbol, symbolization, typification, exemplification, example, exemplar, realization, manifestation, expression.

embody *verb* **1** *a vehicle embodying technological advances* incorporate, combine, bring together, comprise, collect, include, contain, constitute, take in, consolidate, encompass, assimilate, integrate, concentrate, organize, systematize. **2** *he embodies good manners* per-

sonify, represent, symbolize, stand for, typify, exemplify, incorporate, realize, manifest, express, incarnate.

embolden *verb* give courage to, make brave/braver, encourage, hearten, strengthen, rouse, stir, stimulate, cheer, fire, inflame, animate, invigorate, vitalize, inspirit.

embrace *verb* **1** *embrace his wife* take/hold in one's arms, hold, hug, cuddle, clasp, squeeze, clutch, seize, grab, nuzzle, enfold, enclasp, encircle; *inf.* neck with. **2** *embrace the new philosophy* welcome, accept, receive enthusiastically/wholeheartedly, take up, adopt; *fml.* espouse. **3** *embrace the whole area* cover, include, take in, deal with, involve, take into account, contain, comprise, incorporate, encompass, embody, subsume, comprehend, enfold.
Antonyms: REJECT; EXCLUDE.

embrace *noun* hug, bear hug, cuddle, squeeze, clasp, hold, clutch, clinch, nuzzle.

embroider *verb* **1** *embroider a design/tablecloth* sew, decorate with needlework. **2** *embroider the story/truth* touch up, dress up, embellish, elaborate, color, enlarge on, exaggerate, paint, gild, invent, fabricate.

embroidery *noun* **1** *thread for embroidery* needlework, needlepoint, sewing, tatting; tapestry, sampler. **2** *embroidery of the story/truth* touching up, dressing up, embellishment, adornment, ornamentation, elaboration, coloring, exaggeration, gilding; invention, fabrication, tall story, fish story.

embryonic *adjective* just beginning, early, undeveloped, unformed, rudimentary, immature, incipient, primary, elementary, seminal, germinal, inchoate.

emend *verb* edit, correct, revise, alter, rewrite, rectify, improve, polish, refine, expurgate, censor, bowdlerize, redact.

emendation *noun* editing, correction, revision, alteration, rewriting, rectification, improving, improvement, polishing, refinement, expurgation, censoring, bowdlerization, redaction.

emerge *verb* **1** *emerge from a building* | *emerge from a state of depression* come out, come into view, appear, come up, become visible, surface, spring up, crop up, materialize, arise, proceed, issue, come forth, emanate. **2** *facts emerging* become known, become common knowledge, come out, come to light, get around, become apparent, transpire, come to the fore.
Antonyms: ENTER; DISAPPEAR; FADE.

emergence *noun* **1** *his emergence from the building* coming out, appearance, arrival, arising, surfacing, springing up, materializing, materialization, issue, emanation. **2** *emergence of the facts* becoming known, coming to light, disclosure, exposure, unfolding, publication, publicizing, publishing, broadcasting.

emergency *noun supplies for an emergency* urgent

situation, crisis, danger, accident, difficulty, plight, predicament, quandary, dilemma, crunch, scrape, extremity, exigency, necessity; unforeseen circumstances, dire/desperate straits; *inf.* pickle.

emergency *adjective emergency situation/exit/supplies* urgent; reserve, backup, substitute, alternative, spare, extra.

emergent *adjective* emerging, developing, beginning, coming out, budding, arising, dawning, embryonic.

emigrate *verb* move abroad, leave one's country, migrate, relocate, resettle, defect, trek.

emigration *noun* moving abroad, migration, departure, relocation, resettling, expatriation, exodus, defection, trekking.

eminence *noun* **1** *eminence of the statesman* importance, greatness, prestige, reputation, fame, distinction, renown, preeminence, celebrity, prominence, illustriousness, notability, rank, standing, station, note, dignity. **2** *church built on an eminence* elevation, rise, rising/raised ground, height.

eminent *adjective* important, great, distinguished, well-known, celebrated, famous, renowned, noted, prominent, esteemed, noteworthy, preeminent, superior, outstanding, high-ranking, exalted, revered, elevated, august, paramount.
Antonyms: UNIMPORTANT; UNKNOWN.

eminently *adverb eminently suitable* very, well, greatly, highly, exceedingly, extremely, exceptionally, remarkably, singularly, outstandingly, strikingly, notably, prominently, surpassingly.

emissary *noun* ambassador, envoy, agent, delegate, representative, deputy, go-between, attaché, legate, courier, herald, scout, spy.

emission *noun* **1** *the emission of fumes/light* discharge, outpouring, issue, oozing, leaking, excretion, secretion, ejection, emanation, radiation, exhalation, exudation, effusion, ejaculation, disgorgement, issuance. **2** *a deafening emission* utterance, declaration, expression, pronouncement, vocalization.

emit *verb* **1** *emit fumes/light* discharge, pour out, give out/off, issue, send forth, throw out, ooze, leak, excrete, secrete, eject, emanate, radiate, exhale, ejaculate, exude. **2** *emit a terrified scream* utter, express, voice, pronounce, declare, articulate, vocalize.

emolument *noun* payment, pay, salary, income, fee, stipend, revenue, return, profit, gain, reward, compensation, recompense, honorarium; wages, earnings, fees, profits, proceeds.

emotion *noun* feeling, sentiment, passion, reaction, response, sensation; warmth, ardor, fervor, vehemence, joy, sorrow, pity, fear, horror.

---

emotion
affect, feeling, passion, sentiment

A **feeling** can be almost any subjective reaction or state—pleasant or unpleasant, strong or mild, positive or negative—that is characterized by an emotional response (*a feeling of insecurity*; *a feeling of pleasure*). An **emotion** is a very intense feeling, which often involves a physical as well as a mental response and implies outward expression or agitation (*to be overcome with emotion*) **Passion** suggests a powerful or overwhelming emotion, with connotations of sexual love (*their passion remained undiminished after 30 years of marriage*) or intense anger (*a passion for revenge*). There is more intellect and less feeling in **sentiment**, which is often applied to an emotion inspired by an idea (*political sentiments*; *antiwar sentiments*). *Sentiment* also suggests a refined or slightly artificial feeling (*a speech marked by sentiment rather than passion*). **Affect** is a formal psychological term that refers to an observed emotional state (*heavily sedated, he spoke without affect*).

---

emotional *adjective* **1** *emotional person* feeling, passionate, hot-blooded, warm, responsive, demonstrative, tender, loving, sentimental, ardent, fervent, sensitive, excitable, temperamental, melodramatic. **2** *an emotional farewell* moving, touching, affecting, poignant, emotive, pathetic, tear-jerking, heart-rending, soul-stirring, impassioned.
Antonyms: UNEMOTIONAL; APATHETIC; COLD.

emotionless *adjective emotionless person/response/stave* unemotional, unfeeling, undemonstrative, cold, cold-blooded, impassive, indifferent, detached, remote, imperturbable, frigid, phlegmatic, glacial, blank, toneless.

emotive *adjective an emotive issue* sensitive, delicate, controversial, touchy, awkward.

empathize *verb* identify with, be in tune with, be on the same wavelength as, talk the same language as; sympathize, understand.

emperor *noun* ruler, sovereign, monarch, king; czar, kaiser, sultan, khan.

emphasis *noun* **1** *putting the emphasis on the first syllable* stress, accent, accentuation, weight. **2** *putting the emphasis on talent* importance, stress, attention, priority, weight, urgency, force, accent, accentuation, insistence, significance, prominence, underlining, intensity, import, mark, power, moment, preeminence, underscoring.

emphasize *verb* **1** *emphasize the first word* put the stress/accent/force on, stress, accentuate. **2** *emphasize the problems* put/lay stress on, give an emphasis to, stress, accent, accentuate, underline, call attention to, highlight, give prominence to, point up, spotlight, play up, feature, intensify, strengthen, heighten, deepen, underscore.
Antonyms: UNDERSTATE; play down (*see* PLAY); MINIMIZE.

emphatic *adjective* **1** *emphatic improvement* marked, pronounced, decided, positive, defi-

nite, distinctive, unmistakable, important, significant, strong, striking, powerful, resounding, telling, momentous. **2** *he was emphatic | an emphatic denial* definite, decided, certain, determined, absolute, direct, forceful, forcible, earnest, energetic, vigorous, categorical, unequivocal.
Antonyms: INSIGNIFICANT; HESITANT; TENTATIVE.

empire *noun* kingdom, realm, domain, territory, jurisdiction, province, commonwealth; sovereignty, dominion.

empirical, empiric *adjective* practical, observed, pragmatic, seen, experimental, experiential, heuristic.

employ *verb* **1** *employ three people* hire, have in employment, engage, take on, take into employment, sign up, put on the payroll, enroll, commission, enlist, retain, indenture, apprentice. **2** *employed in polishing the floor* occupy, engage, keep busy. **3** *employs all his waking hours in reading* occupy, take up, use up, put to use, make use of, fill, spend. **4** *employ cunning* use, apply, make use of, exercise, exert, utilize, ply, bring to bear.

employed *adjective* **1** *no longer employed* having work, working, in employment, in a job. **2** *employed in gazing out of the window* occupied, busy, engaged, preoccupied.
Antonyms: UNEMPLOYED; JOBLESS; UNOCCUPIED.

employee *noun* worker, blue-collar worker, white-collar worker, workman, member of staff, wage-earner, hand, hired hand, assistant, laborer, hireling.
Antonyms: EMPLOYER; BOSS.

employer *noun* boss, manager, owner, proprietor, patron, contractor, director, head man/woman, top man/woman; firm (of employment), organization.
Antonyms: EMPLOYEE; hireling; UNDERLING.

employment *noun* **1** *the employment of new staff* hiring, hire, engagement, taking on, signing up, enrollment, commissioning, enlisting, apprenticing. **2** *employment as a teacher* job, work, business, line, occupation, profession, trade, calling, vocation, craft, métier, employ, service, pursuit. **3** *employment of resources/cunning* use, application, exercise, utilization, exertion.

emporium *noun* store, shop, bazaar, marketplace, market, fair, mart, mall, shopping center.

empower *verb* **1** *empowered to arrest you* authorize, license, certify, accredit, qualify, sanction, warrant, commission, delegate. **2** *resources empowering him to act* allow, enable, give power/means/strength to, equip.

emptiness *noun* **1** *an emptiness in her life* vacuum, void, hollowness. **2** *the emptiness of the place/house/page* vacantness, hollowness, voidness, desolation, bareness, barrenness, lack of contents/adornment, blankness, clearness. **3** *the emptiness of the threats/gestures* meaninglessness, futility, ineffectiveness, ineffectuality, uselessness, worthlessness, fruitlessness, in-

substantiality, idleness. **4** *the emptiness of her existence* aimlessness, purposelessness, meaninglessness, worthlessness, hollowness, barrenness, senselessness, silliness, banality, frivolity, inanity, triviality. **5** *the emptiness of the expression/stare* blankness, expressionlessness, vacantness, vacuousness, unintelligence.

empty *adjective* **1** *empty bowl/house/page* containing nothing, without contents, unfilled, vacant, hollow, void, unoccupied, uninhabited, desolate, bare, unadorned, barren, blank, clear. **2** *empty threats/gestures* meaningless, futile, ineffective, ineffectual, useless, worthless, idle, insubstantial, fruitless. **3** *empty existence* aimless, purposeless, meaningless, hollow, barren, senseless, unsatisfactory, silly, banal, inane, frivolous, trivial, worthless, valueless, profitless. **4** *empty expression/stare* blank, expressionless, vacant, unintelligent, deadpan, vacuous, absent. **5** *thirsty and empty* hungry, starving, famished, ravenous, unfed.
Antonyms: FULL; OCCUPIED; MEANINGFUL; WORTHWHILE.

empty *verb* **1** *empty the room/truck* make vacant, vacate, clear, evacuate, void, unload, unburden. **2** *empty the liquid* drain, pour out, exhaust, use up, deplete, sap. **3** *the room emptied* clear, become vacant/empty. **4** *the liquid emptied* flow out, pour out, drain, discharge, issue, emit, exude, ooze.

empty-headed *adjective* stupid, silly, brainless, harebrained, scatterbrained, featherbrained, giddy, flighty, frivolous, dizzy, vacuous; *inf.* airheaded, dopey, batty.

enable *verb* **1** *enable you to vote* allow, permit, authorize, entitle, qualify, fit, license, sanction, warrant, accredit, validate, commission, delegate, legalize, empower. **2** *enable you to cross the river* allow, permit, give the means/resources to, equip, prepare, facilitate, capacitate.

enact *verb* **1** *enact Hamlet | enact the role of Hamlet* act, act out, play, perform, stage, appear as, portray, depict, represent, impersonate, personify; *fml.* personate. **2** *a bill enacted by Congress* legislate, rule, make law, pass, approve, ratify, sanction; order, decree, ordain, pronounce.

enactment *noun* **1** *the enactment of scene 3 | enactments of King Lear* acting, playing, performing, staging, performance, appearance, portrayal, depiction, representation, personification; *fml.* personation. **2** *the enactment of the new law* passing, legislating, approval, ratification, sanction; decreeing, ordaining. **3** *enactments of Congress* law, bill, act, statute, measure, regulation; order, decree, edict, motion, proclamation, command, commandment, pronouncement, ordinance, dictate, ratification; legislation.

enamored *adjective* in love, loving, infatuated,

captivated, charmed, enchanted, fascinated, bewitched, enthralled, entranced, enraptured; *inf.* smitten, mad, crazy, nuts, wild.

encampment *noun* camp, military camp, bivouac, campsite, camping ground.

encapsulate *verb* 1 *encapsulate the views of the committee* sum up, summarize, condense, abridge, compress, digest, epitomize. 2 *encapsulate all the main points* include, contain, embrace, capture.

enchant *verb* bewitch, make spellbound, fascinate, charm, captivate, entrance, enthrall, beguile, hypnotize, mesmerize, enrapture, delight, enamor.

enchanter *noun* wizard, witch, enchantress, sorcerer, warlock, necromancer, magician, spellbinder, conjuror, hypnotist, mesmerist, witch doctor, medicine man, soothsayer, seer.

enchanting *adjective* bewitching, charming, delightful, attractive, appealing, captivating, irresistible, fascinating, engaging, endearing, entrancing, alluring, winsome, ravishing.

enchantment *noun* 1 *witches with powers of enchantment* magic, witchcraft, sorcery, wizardry, necromancy, hypnotism, mesmerism, charm. 2 *a time of enchantment* bliss, ecstasy, heaven, rapture, joy. 3 *the enchantment of the view/dancing* charm, delight, attractiveness, appeal, captivation, irresistibility, fascination, entrancement, allure, allurement, glamour.

enchantress *noun* witch, sorceress, fairy, fairy godmother, siren, Circe. *See* ENCHANTER.

encircle *verb* 1 *enemy troops encircling the town* surround, enclose, circle, ring, encompass, circumscribe. 2 *trees encircling the lake* close in, shut in, fence in, wall in, hem in, confine.

enclose *verb* 1 *enclosing the garden* surround, circle, ring, close in, shut in, fence/wall/hedge in, hem in, confine, encompass, encircle, circumscribe, encase; *fml.* gird. 2 *enclose a check* include, send with, put in, insert.

enclosure *noun* 1 *spectators/cattle in the enclosure* special/assigned area, arena; compound, ring, yard, pen, pound, fold, paddock, stockade, sty, corral, court. 2 *the enclosure of a check* inclusion, insertion. 3 *an enclosure with the letter* insertion, thing enclosed.

encompass *verb* 1 *encompass the castle* surround, enclose, ring, encircle, close in, shut in, fence/wall/hedge in, hem in, confine. 2 *encompassing all disciplines* include, cover, embrace, take in, contain, envelop, deal with, comprise, incorporate, embody.

encore *noun* *play/take an encore* repeat, repeat/extra performance, replay; curtain call.

encounter *verb* 1 *encounter an old friend* meet, meet by chance, run into, run across, come upon, stumble across, chance/happen upon; *inf.* bump into. 2 *encounter problems* be faced with, confront, contend with, tussle with. 3 *encounter the enemy* accost, confront; fight, do

battle with, clash with, come into conflict with, engage with, struggle with, contend with, combat, skirmish with, tussle with.

encounter *noun* 1 *an encounter with an old friend* meeting, chance meeting. *See* ENCOUNTER *verb* 1. 2 *an encounter with the enemy* fight, battle, clash, conflict, contest, dispute, combat, collision, confrontation, engagement, skirmish, scuffle, tussle, brawl; *inf.* run-in, set-to, brush.

encourage *verb* 1 *encourage the losers* cheer, rally, stimulate, motivate, inspire, stir, incite, animate, hearten, invigorate, embolden, inspirit; *inf.* buck up. 2 *encourage him to try again* urge, persuade, egg on, prompt, influence, exhort, sway, spur, goad. 3 *feared that legalizing gambling would encourage crime* help, assist, aid, support, back, advocate, abet, boost, favor, promote, further, advance, forward, foster, strengthen.

Antonyms: DISCOURAGE; DISSUADE; HINDER.

---

encourage
embolden, foster, hearten, inspire, instigate, stimulate

To **encourage** is to give active help or to raise confidence to the point where one dares to do what is difficult (*encouraged by her teacher, she set her sights on attending Harvard*). **Embolden** also entails giving confidence or boldness, but it implies overcoming reluctance or shyness (*success as a public speaker emboldened her to enter politics*). To **hearten** is to put heart into or to renew someone's spirit (*heartened by the news of his recovery*), and to **inspire** is to infuse with confidence, resolution, or enthusiasm (*inspired by her mother's example, she started exercising regularly*). To **foster** is to encourage by nurturing or extending aid (*to foster the growth of small businesses by offering low-interest loans*); in some contexts, *foster* suggests an unwise or controversial kind of help (*to foster rebellion among local farmers*). **Instigate** also implies that what is being encouraged is not necessarily desirable (*to instigate a fight*), while **stimulate** is a more neutral term meaning to rouse to action or effort (*to stimulate the growth of crops; to stimulate an interest in literature*).

---

encouragement *noun* 1 *the encouragement of the losers* rallying, stimulation, motivation, inspiration, incitement, animation, heartening, invigorating, emboldening, inspiriting. 2 *encouragement to go ahead* urging, persuasion, egging on, prompting, exhortation; spur, goad. 3 *encouragement of exports* help, assistance, support, promotion, furtherance, advocacy, backing, boosting, favoring, furthering, advancing, forwarding, fostering, strengthening.

encroach *verb* trespass, intrude, invade, infringe, impinge, infiltrate, overrun, usurp, appropriate, tread on someone's toes; *inf.* muscle in on, invade someone's space.

encroachment *noun* trespassing, intrusion, invasion, infringement, impinging, infiltration, incursion, overrunning, usurping, appropriation.

encumber *verb* **1** *injury encumbered his efforts | encumbered with two small children* hinder, hamper, obstruct, impede, inconvenience, handicap, retard, check, cramp, constrain, restrain. **2** *a room encumbered with old furniture* block up, fill up, stuff, clog, congest. **3** *encumbered with taxes* burden, load, weigh down, tax, overtax, saddle, trammel, stress, strain.

encumbrance *noun* **1** *the encumbrance of heavy luggage* hindrance, hampering, obstruction, impediment, inconvenience, handicap, restraint, constraint. **2** *the encumbrance of a room with old furniture* blocking up, filling, stuffing, clogging, congestion. **3** *debts are an encumbrance* burden, weight, load, responsibility, obligation, stress, strain, tax, onus, trammel.

encyclopedic *adjective* comprehensive, complete, wide-ranging, all-inclusive, thorough, exhaustive, all-embracing, universal, all-encompassing, vast, compendious.

end *noun* **1** *the end of the table | the north end* edge, border, boundary, extremity, limit, margin, furthermost part, point, tip, extent. **2** *the end of the affair/novel* ending, finish, close, conclusion, termination, completion, resolution, climax, finale, culmination, denouement, epilogue; *inf.* wind-up. **3** *the end of a pencil* remnant, remainder, fragment, vestige; leftovers. **4** *her end in life* aim, goal, purpose, intention, intent, objective, object, design, motive, aspiration, *raison d'être*. **5** *the commercial end of the business* side, section, area, field, part, share, portion, segment; responsibility, burden, load. **6** *a peaceful/sad end* death, dying, demise, doom, extinction, annihilation, extermination; ruin, ruination, destruction, dissolution; death-blow, *coup de grâce*, finishing stroke; curtains. **7** *the end was that he got the promotion* result, consequence, outcome, upshot, issue.

Antonyms: BEGINNING; START; BIRTH.

end *verb* **1** *the show/book ended* come to an end, finish, close, stop, cease, conclude, terminate, discontinue, break off, fade away, peter out. **2** *to end a relationship/book* bring to an end, finish, close, stop, cease, conclude, terminate, break off, discontinue, complete, dissolve, resolve; *inf.* wind up. **3** *end his life/hopes* put an end to, destroy, annihilate, extinguish.

Antonyms: BEGIN; START.

endanger *verb* *endangering the species* threaten, put in danger, expose to danger, put at risk, expose, risk, jeopardize, imperil, hazard, compromise.

Antonyms: SECURE; PROTECT.

endearing *adjective* charming, attractive, adorable, lovable, sweet, engaging, winning, captivating, enchanting, winsome.

endearment *noun* **1** *affectionate endearments* sweet talk, sweet nothings, soft words, blandishments. **2** *words of endearment* love, affection, fondness, liking, attachment.

endeavor *verb* *endeavor to win* try, attempt, strive, work at, try one's hand at, do one's best, venture, aspire, undertake, struggle, labor, essay; *inf.* have a go/shot/stab at.

endeavor *noun* *make an endeavor to win | his best endeavor* try, attempt, trial, effort, striving, venture, undertaking, aspiration, enterprise, struggle, laboring, essay; *inf.* go, crack, shot, stab.

ending *noun* end, finish, close, conclusion, stopping, cessation, termination, expiration, resolution, completion.

Antonyms: BEGINNING; START.

endless *adjective* **1** *endless patience* unending, without end, unlimited, infinite, limitless, boundless, continual, constant, unfading, everlasting, unceasing, interminable, incessant, measureless, untold, incalculable. **2** *an endless loop* continuous, uninterrupted, unbroken, whole, entire, never-ending. **3** *endless talk/traveling* nonstop, interminable, monotonous, unremitting, boring.

Antonyms: FINITE; LIMITED; TRANSIENT.

endorse *verb* **1** *endorse a check* countersign, sign, autograph, underwrite, superscribe, validate. **2** *endorse the course of action* approve, support, back, favor, recommend, advocate, champion, subscribe to, uphold, authorize, ratify, sanction, warrant, affirm, confirm, vouch for, corroborate.

endorsement *noun* **1** *the endorsement on the document/check | endorsement of the signature* countersignature, autograph, underwriting, validation. **2** *the endorsement of their actions* approval, support, backing, recommendation, advocacy, championship, authorization, ratification, warrant, affirmation, corroboration. *See* ENDORSE 2.

endow *verb* **1** *endow with talent* provide, give, present, gift, confer, bestow, enrich, supply, furnish, award, invest. **2** *endow a foundation | endow a hospital wing* bequeath money for, bestow, will, donate money for, leave money for, make over to, settle on; pay for, finance, fund.

Antonym: DIVEST.

endowment *noun* **1** *offer an endowment to the school* gift, present, bestowal, grant, donation, award, proffering, bequeathing, settlement, legacy, provision; largesse, finance, funding, revenue, income. **2** *natural endowments* ability, gift, talent, flair, aptitude, genius, attribute, power, strength, capability, capacity, facility, faculty, qualification, characteristic, quality, feature.

endurance *noun* **1** *endurance of his love* lasting power, durability, stability, permanence, continuance, continuity, changelessness, immutability, longevity, everlastingness, immortality. **2** *beyond endurance* toleration, sufferance, fortitude, forbearance, perseverance, acceptance, patience, resignation. **3** *sports that are tests of endurance* stamina, staying power, fortitude, perseverance, tenacity; *inf.* guts.

endure *verb* **1** *love endures* last, live on, continue, persist, remain, stay, hold on, survive, wear well; *lit.* abide, bide, tarry. **2** *endure the difficult situation | can't endure the new manager* put up with, stand, bear, tolerate, suffer, abide, submit to, countenance, brook; *inf.* stomach, swallow. **3** *endure poverty/pain* experience, undergo, go through, meet, encounter; bear, tolerate, cope with, suffer, brave, withstand, sustain, weather.
Antonyms: DIE; FADE.

enduring *adjective* lasting, long-lasting, durable, permanent, stable, steady, steadfast, imperishable, continuing, remaining, persisting, prevailing, abiding, eternal, immortal, perennial, unwavering, unfaltering.
Antonyms: SHORT-LIVED; TRANSIENT.

enemy *noun* foe, opponent, rival, adversary, antagonist, hostile party; opposition, competition.
Antonyms: ALLY; FRIEND.

energetic *adjective* **1** *energetic exercises/person* active, lively, vigorous, strenuous, brisk, dynamic, spirited, animated, vital, vibrant, sprightly, tireless, indefatigable, peppy, zippy; bright-eyed and bushy-tailed. **2** *energetic approach* forceful, forcible, determined, emphatic, aggressive, high-powered, driving, effective, effectual, powerful, potent.
Antonyms: LAZY; INACTIVE; WEAK.

energize *verb* **1** *energize him to get up* activate, stimulate, arouse, rouse, motivate, stir, goad, spur on, prompt. **2** *music might energize the party* enliven, liven up, animate, invigorate, pep up, electrify, vitalize. **3** *energize the device* activate, start up, switch on, turn on, get going.

energy *noun* vigor, strength, stamina, forcefulness, power, might, potency, drive, push, exertion; enterprise, enthusiasm, animation, life, liveliness, pep, vivacity, vitality, spirit, spiritedness, fire, zest, verve, dash, élan, sparkle, buoyancy, effervescence, exuberance, ardor, zeal, passion; *inf.* vim, zip, zing.
Antonyms: LETHARGY; WEAKNESS.

enervate *verb* weaken, make feeble, exhaust, tire, fatigue, wear out, strain, wash out, debilitate, enfeeble, sap, incapacitate, devitalize, prostrate.
Antonym: INVIGORATE.

enfold *verb* **1** *mist enfolded the valley* enclose, envelop, encircle, shroud. **2** *enfolded in his arms* clasp, embrace, hug, hold, wrap.

enforce *verb* **1** *enforce the law* apply, carry out, administer, implement, bring to bear, impose, discharge, fulfill, execute, prosecute, put through. **2** *enforce silence* force, compel, insist on, require, necessitate, oblige, urge, exact, coerce, pressure, pressurize, dragoon, bulldoze, constrain, extort.

enforced *adjective* *enforced silence* forced, compelled, required, prescribed, imposed, necessitated, obliged, urged, exacted, coerced, pressured, pressurized, dragooned, bulldozed, constrained, extorted; unwilling, involuntary, unwarranted.
Antonyms: VOLUNTARY; OPTIONAL.

enforcement *noun* **1** *enforcement of the law* application, carrying out, administering, implementation, imposition, discharge, fulfillment, execution, prosecution. **2** *enforcement of silence* coercement, exactment, coercing, exacting, requiring, pressurizing, dragooning, bulldozing.

enfranchise *verb* *enfranchise women* give the vote to, give voting rights to, give/grant suffrage to; give/grant franchise to; naturalize, give citizenship to.

engage *verb* **1** *engage a housekeeper* employ, hire, take on, appoint, put on the payroll, enlist, enroll, commission. **2** *engage a boat/room* rent, hire, book, reserve, charter, lease, prearrange, bespeak. **3** *engage one's interest | engaged in a book* occupy, fill, employ, hold, grip, secure; preoccupy, absorb, engross. **4** *engage one's attention/affection* catch, attract, draw, gain, win, capture, captivate, arrest. **5** *engage in a project | engage in many sports* enter into, become involved in, undertake, occupy oneself with, embark on, set about, take part in, join in, participate in, partake in/of, launch into, throw oneself into, tackle **6** *engage in a contract | engage to marry* contract, promise, agree, guarantee, undertake, pledge, oblige, obligate, vouch, vow, commit oneself, bind oneself, covenant. **7** *engaging at dawn | engage in battle* join battle, do battle with, fight with, wage war with, attack, enter into combat, clash with, encounter, take on, set to, skirmish with, grapple with, wrest with, take the field. **8** *engage the gears* fit together, join together, join, interconnect, mesh, intermesh.
Antonyms: DISMISS; DISCHARGE; give up (*see* GIVE).

engaged *adjective* **1** *the manager is engaged* busy, occupied, in conference, unavailable; *inf.* tied up. **2** *the conference room is engaged* occupied, in use, unavailable, reserved, booked. **3** *engaged couples* betrothed, affianced, espoused; *inf.* spoken for.
Antonyms: FREE; UNOCCUPIED; UNATTACHED.

engagement *noun* **1** *her engagement as housekeeper* employment, appointment, work, job, post, situation, hire, business, stint. **2** *the engagement of a boat/room* rent, hire, booking, reservation, charter, lease, prearrangement. **3** *enter into a contractual engagement* contract, agreement, bond, pact, compact, promise, obligation, stipulation. **4** *they broke off their engagement* betrothal, marriage pledge. **5** *total* *engagement in the subject* absorption, preoccupation. **6** *a previous engagement* appointment, date, commitment, arrangement, meeting, interview, assignation, rendezvous, tryst. **7** *an engagement at sea* fight, battle, clash, conflict, struggle, attack, assault, confrontation, encounter, offensive; warfare, action, combat, strife; hostilities.

engaging *adjective* attractive, charming, appealing, pleasing, pleasant, agreeable, delightful, likable, lovable, sweet, winning, taking, captivating, fetching, enchanting, winsome, fascinating.
Antonyms: BORING; REPELLENT.

engender *verb* **1** *engender feelings of hostility* | *engender hostility* cause, produce, create, give rise to, bring about, lead to, arouse, rouse, excite, provoke, incite, induce, instigate, generate, hatch, effect, occasion, effectuate, foment. **2** *engender sons* give birth to, father, breed, create, conceive, procreate, reproduce, bring forth, propagate, spawn, sire, beget.

engine *noun* **1** *the engine of the car* motor, mechanism, machine, power source, turbine, dynamo, generator; internal combustion engine. **2** *engines of war* instrument, implement, device, appliance; machinery, apparatus, means.

engineer *noun* **1** *the engineer who designed the bridge* civil engineer, electrical engineer, mechanical engineer, aeronautical engineer, chemical engineer; planner, designer, builder, architect; inventor, originator, deviser, contriver. **2** *railroad engineer* operator, controller, handler, director, driver.

engineer *verb* bring about, cause, plan, plot, scheme, contrive, devise, maneuver, manipulate, orchestrate, mastermind, originate, manage, control, superintend, direct, conduct, handle, concoct.

engrave *verb* **1** *engrave the silver cup* | *engrave her initials* carve, etch, inscribe, cut, chisel, imprint, impress, print, mark. **2** *word's engraved on/in/into my heart* fix, set, imprint, stamp, brand, impress, embed, ingrain, lodge.

engraving *noun* **1** *the engraving of the stone* carving, etching, sculpting, inscribing, inscription, cutting, chiseling, lithography, photoengraving. **2** *we bought three engravings* carving, etching, print, lithograph, impression, block, plate, cut, woodcut.

engross *verb* **1** *engross in the work* occupy, preoccupy, absorb, engage, rivet, grip, hold, interest, catch, captivate, arrest, immerse, involve, envelop, engulf, fixate. **2** *engross the market* corner, monopolize, capture, sew up. **3** *engross a legal document* reproduce, copy, type; rewrite/reproduce in larger form.

engrossed *adjective* *looking completely engrossed* preoccupied, absorbed, engaged, riveted, gripped, caught up, captivated, immersed, intent, rapt, involved, enveloped, engulfed.

engrossing *adjective* *an engrossing article* absorbing, riveting, gripping, captivating, arresting, interesting, fascinating, intriguing, compelling, enthralling.

engulf *verb* consume, overwhelm, flood, deluge, swamp, swallow up, submerge, bury, immerse, inundate, envelop, encompass.

enhance *verb* **1** *enhance her beauty/reputation* add to, increase, heighten, stress, emphasize, strengthen, improve, augment, boost, intensify, reinforce, magnify, amplify, enrich, complement. **2** *enhance property prices* raise, lift, increase, escalate, elevate, augment, swell, aggrandize; *inf.* jack up, hike.

enhancement *noun* **1** *enhancement of beauty* heightening, emphasis, stress, strengthening, augmenting, intensification, reinforcement, magnification, amplification, enrichment. **2** *enhancement of property prices* rise, increase, increment, escalation, elevation, augmentation, swelling, aggrandizement; *inf.* jacking-up, hike.

enigma *noun* mystery, puzzle, riddle, conundrum, paradox, problem, quandary, dilemma, labyrinth, maze; *inf.* poser, teaser, brainteaser.

enigmatic *adjective* mysterious, puzzling, baffling, obscure, perplexing, mystifying, cryptic, unfathomable, incomprehensible, inexplicable, inscrutable, Sphinxlike, recondite, esoteric, arcane, secret; ambiguous, equivocal, paradoxical, doubtful.

enjoin *verb* **1** *enjoin people to stay indoors* direct, order, command, urge, bid, demand, instruct, decree, ordain, warn, require, call upon, charge, advise, counsel. **2** *enjoin after-hours clubs* ban, bar, prohibit, forbid, disallow, embargo, interdict, place an injunction on, proscribe, preclude, obstruct, restrain.

enjoy *verb* **1** *enjoy music* like, love, be entertained/amused by, find/take pleasure in, delight in, appreciate, rejoice in, relish, revel in, savor, luxuriate in; *inf.* fancy. **2** *enjoy good health/facilities* | *enjoy a good standard of living* have, possess, own, benefit from, have the benefit/advantage/use of, avail oneself of, be blessed/favored with. **enjoy oneself** have fun, have a good time, have the time of one's life, party; *inf.* have a ball, let one's hair down.
Antonyms: DISLIKE; HATE.

enjoyable *adjective* entertaining, amusing, delightful, nice, pleasant, lovely, fine, good, great, agreeable, pleasurable, delicious, delectable, diverting, satisfying, gratifying.
Antonyms: UNPLEASANT; DISAGREEABLE; HATEFUL.

enjoyment *noun* **1** *find enjoyment in reading* | *eat with enjoyment* amusement, entertainment, diversion, recreation, pleasure, delight, happiness, gladness, joy, fun, gaiety, jollity, satisfaction, gratification, delectation, zeal, relish, gusto. **2** *the enjoyment of good health/facilities* possession, use, ownership, benefit, advantage, blessing.

enlarge *verb* **1** *enlarge the living area* make

larger/bigger, expand, extend, add to, stretch, amplify, augment, supplement, magnify, multiply; widen, broaden, lengthen, elongate, deepen, thicken. **2** *his spleen is enlarged* distend, dilate, swell, blow up, inflate, bloat, bulge. **3** *enlarge a photograph* make larger/bigger, blow up. **4** *enlarge on the topic* elaborate, expound.
Antonyms: REDUCE; DIMINISH; LESSEN.

enlargement *noun* **1** *enlargement of the living area* increase, expansion, extension, magnification, amplification, augmentation, supplementation, supplement, multiplication, broadening, lengthening, elongation, deepening, thickening. **2** *enlargement of the spleen* distension, dilation, swelling, bloating; bulge, protrusion. **3** *photographic enlargement* magnification, blow-up, large print.

enlighten *verb* inform, make aware, instruct, teach, educate, tutor, indoctrinate, illuminate, apprise, edify, civilize, cultivate, counsel, advise.
Antonyms: CONFUSE; MUDDLE.

enlightened *adjective* informed, aware, educated, knowledgeable, learned, wise, literate, intellectual, tutored, indoctrinated, illuminated, apprised; civilized, refined, cultured, cultivated, sophisticated, liberal, open-minded, broad-minded.
Antonyms: IGNORANT; ILLITERATE; NARROW-MINDED.

enlightenment *noun* awareness, understanding, insight, education, learning, knowledge, erudition, wisdom, instruction, teaching, indoctrination, illumination, edification, awakening; culture, refinement, cultivation, civilization, sophistication, liberalism, open-mindedness, broad-mindedness.

enlist *verb* **1** *enlist soldiers/staff | enlist her help* enroll, sign up, recruit, hire, employ, register, take on, engage, obtain, procure, secure, gather, muster. **2** *enlist in the army/venture* join, join up, enroll/register in, sign on/up for, enter into, volunteer for.

enliven *verb* brighten up, cheer up, wake up, give a lift/boost to, buoy up, hearten, gladden, excite, stimulate, rouse, refresh, exhilarate, invigorate, revitalize, vitalize, light a fire under; *inf.* perk up, spice up, jazz up.

enmity *noun* hostility, ill will, hate, hatred, antagonism, antipathy, aversion, animosity, bitterness, spite, malice, venom, rancor, malevolence, animus.
Antonyms: FRIENDSHIP; LOVE; GOODWILL.

en masse *adverb* as a group, in a body, as one, as a whole, in a mass.

ennoble *verb* *ennobled by grief | ennobling the author* make noble/great, dignify, exalt, elevate, raise, enhance, magnify, aggrandize, honor, glorify, lionize.

ennui *noun* boredom, tedium, listlessness,

lethargy, lassitude, languor, sluggishness, dissatisfaction, melancholy.

enormity *noun* **1** *the enormity of the crime/act/suggestion* outrageousness, wickedness, evilness, vileness, monstrousness, hideousness, dreadfulness, heinousness, atrocity, cruelty, brutality, depravity, nefariousness. **2** *condemn the war as an enormity* outrage, horror, evil, crime, atrocity, abomination, violation, villainy, transgression, disgrace.

enormous *adjective* huge, immense, massive, vast, gigantic, colossal, astronomic, mammoth, mountainous, gargantuan, prodigious, tremendous, stupendous, excessive, titanic, Herculean, Brobdingnagian; *inf.* jumbo.
Antonyms: MINUTE; TINY.

enormously *adverb* *enormously wealthy* to a very large/great extent, tremendously, markedly, hugely, massively.

enormousness *noun* *enormousness of the dinosaur bones* hugeness, massiveness, vastness, immenseness, magnitude, greatness, largeness.

enough *adjective* *enough food/time* sufficient, adequate, ample, abundant.
Antonyms: INSUFFICIENT; INADEQUATE.

enough *noun* *we've had enough* sufficient/adequate amount, sufficiency, adequacy, ample supply, abundance, amplitude; plenty, full measure; *inf.* plenitude.

enough *adverb* *not warm enough | paints well enough* sufficiently, adequately, amply, satisfactorily, passably, tolerably, reasonably, fairly.

enquire *verb.* *See* INQUIRE.

enquiry *noun.* *See* INQUIRY.

enrage *verb* annoy, anger, infuriate, irritate, madden, exasperate, provoke, incense, irk, agitate, inflame, incite, make one's hackles rise, make one's blood boil; *inf.* get one's back/dander up.
Antonyms: PACIFY; APPEASE.

enraged *adjective* angry, angered, furious, annoyed, irate, livid, raging, fuming, irritated, maddened, exasperated, incensed, provoked, irked, agitated, inflamed; *inf.* mad, wild, wound-up.

enrapture *verb* delight, thrill, charm, captivate, fascinate, enchant, bewitch, entrance, enthrall, beguile, transport, ravish; *inf.* blow one's mind, turn on.

enrich *verb* **1** *a nation enriched by oil* make rich/richer, feather the nest of. **2** *enrich the soil | enrich one's quality of life* make richer, improve, enhance, add to, augment, supplement, upgrade, refine, polish, ameliorate, aggrandize.

enroll *verb* **1** *enroll three new students* register, sign on/up, take on, enlist, recruit, enter, engage, admit, accept. **2** *he enrolled for military service | enrolling for a new course* sign on, volunteer, register, matriculate. **3** *enroll the statistics* record, enter, put down, note.

enrollment *noun* **1** *the enrollment of students/sol-*

diers registration, signing on/up, joining up, enlisting, recruitment, engagement, admission, acceptance. **2** *the enrollment of statistics* record, register, list, note, catalog.

en route *adverb* on the way, in transit, along/on the road.

ensconce *verb* settle, install, establish, nestle, curl up, snuggle up.

ensemble *noun* **1** *the parts forming a pleasing ensemble* whole, whole thing, collection, set, combination, accumulation, sum, total, totality, entirety, assemblage, aggregate, composite; *inf.* whole kit and caboodle. **2** *a green ensemble* outfit, costume, suit; *inf.* get-up. **3** *a jazz ensemble* group, band, company, troupe, cast, chorus, association; trio, quartet, quintet.

enshrine *verb* **1** *enshrine the saint's relic* sanctify, dedicate, consecrate, hallow, deify, exalt. **2** *enshrine it in his heart* preserve, cherish, revere, hold sacred, treasure, venerate, immortalize.

enshroud *verb* shroud, cloak, cloud, veil, enfold, enwrap, cover, obscure, bury, conceal, hide, pall, mask.

ensign *noun* **1** *ensign of the ship* flag, banner, standard, pennant, streamer. **2** *ensign of the family* badge, shield, crest, escutcheon; coat of arms, armorial bearings.

ensnare *verb* catch, capture, trap, net, snare, entangle, embroil, enmesh, entrap.

ensue *verb* follow, come next/after, result, occur, happen, turn up, arise, come to pass, transpire, befall, proceed, succeed, issue, derive, stem, supervene.

ensure *verb* **1** *ensure success* | *ensure that he will win* make certain, make sure, guarantee, secure, effect, warrant, certify, confirm. **2** *ensure his inheritance* make safe, protect, guard, safeguard, secure.

entail *verb* *entails hard work* involve, require, call for, necessitate, demand, impose; cause, bring about, produce, result in, lead to, give rise to, occasion.

entangle *verb* **1** *entangle the power lines* tangle, twist, ravel, knot, intertwine, snarl up. **2** *entangle in a net* catch, trap, snare, ensnare, entrap, enmesh. **3** *entangled business affairs* complicate, confuse, muddle, mix up. **4** *entangle them in his affairs* involve, implicate, embroil, incriminate, inculpate.

Antonyms: DISENTANGLE; UNRAVEL; RELEASE.

entanglement *noun* **1** *the entanglement of his business affairs* complication, involvement, confusion, muddle, tangle, mix-up, mess. **2** *his entanglement with his secretary* affair, liaison, amour, intrigue.

enter *verb* **1** *enter a room* | *a river entering the sea* | *a bullet entering the chest* come in/into, go in/into, pass into, move into, flow into, penetrate, pierce, puncture. **2** *enter the army* | *enter the teaching profession* become a member of, join, enroll in, enlist in, sign up for, take up, become connected/associated with, commit oneself to. **3** *enter a competition* | *entered school* take part in, become a competitor in, participate in, put one's name down for, go in for, obtain/gain entrance to. **4** *enter the date of birth* record, register, put down, set/take down, note, mark down, catalog, document, list, log, file, index. **5** *enter a protest* put forward, offer, present, proffer, submit, register, tender. **6** *enter another term of office* | *enter into negotiations* begin, start, commence, embark on, engage in, undertake, venture on. **7** *enter into details/conversation* become involved with/in, concern oneself with, participate in, engage in, join in.

Antonyms: LEAVE; DEPART; WITHDRAW.

enterprise *noun* **1** *the building campaign is a challenging enterprise* venture, undertaking, project, operation, endeavor, effort, task, plan, scheme, campaign. **2** *a young person with enterprise* resourcefulness, resource, initiative, drive, gumption, imagination, imaginativeness, spirit, spiritedness, enthusiasm, zest, dash, ambition, energy, vigor, vitality, boldness, daring, spirit of adventure, audacity, courage, intrepidity; *inf.* get-up-and-go, go, push, oomph, zip, vim. **3** *a thriving enterprise* | *private enterprise* business, industry, firm, commercial concern/operation, corporation, establishment, house.

enterprising *adjective* resourceful, go-ahead, entrepreneurial, imaginative, spirited, enthusiastic, eager, keen, zealous, ambitious, energetic, active, vigorous, vital, bold, daring, adventurous, audacious, courageous, intrepid; *inf.* peppy, pushy, up-and-coming.

Antonyms: UNIMAGINATIVE; unadventurous.

entertain *verb* **1** *entertain the guests with music* amuse, divert, delight, please, charm, cheer, beguile, interest, engage, occupy. **2** *entertain at home* play host/hostess, have/receive guests, provide hospitality, have company, have/hold/throw a party, keep open house, have a dinner party. **3** *entertain colleagues at home* play host/hostess to, show hospitality to, invite to a meal/party, wine and dine, treat, welcome, fête. **4** *entertain evil intentions* harbor, nurture, foster, cherish, hold, have, possess, hide, conceal. **5** *entertain the idea/proposal* consider, give consideration to, take into consideration, give some thought to, think about/over, contemplate, weigh (up), ponder, muse over, cogitate, bear in mind, heed, pay attention to.

Antonyms: BORE; DEPRESS; REJECT.

entertainer *noun* performer, artiste, actor, actress, comedian, comedienne, singer, dancer, comic, impressionist, mime, acrobat, magician.

entertaining *adjective* *an entertaining recital/comic* amusing, diverting, recreational, delightful, pleasurable, pleasing, charming, enchanting, beguiling, engaging, interesting, funny, humorous, witty, comical, hilarious.

Antonyms: BORING; UNINTERESTING.

entertainment noun **1** *play the piano for entertainment* amusement, fun, enjoyment, diversion, recreation, distraction; pastime, hobby, leisure activity/pursuit, sport. **2** *a one-woman entertainment* show, performance, concert, play, cabaret, presentation, spectacle, pageant.

enthrall verb **1** *enthralled by the performance* hold spellbound, captivate, enchant, beguile, entrance, fascinate, bewitch, grip, rivet, charm, delight, enrapture, transport, carry away, intrigue, mesmerize, hypnotize. **2** *conquerors enthralling the villagers* enslave, subjugate, subdue, vanquish, conquer.

enthralling adjective spellbinding, captivating, enchanting, fascinating, bewitching, gripping, riveting, charming, delightful, intriguing, mesmerizing, hypnotic.

enthuse verb **1** *enthuse about astronomy* be enthusiastic, rave, praise to the skies, gush, wax lyrical, bubble over, effervesce; *inf.* get all worked up. **2** *her excitement enthused the others* make enthusiastic. *See* ENTHUSIASTIC.

enthusiasm noun **1** *greet with enthusiasm* eagerness, keenness, ardor, fervor, warmth, passion, zeal, zest, vehemence, fire, excitement, exuberance, ebullience, avidity, wholeheartedness, commitment, devotion, devotedness, fanaticism, earnestness. **2** *stamp collecting is one of her enthusiasms* hobby, pastime, interest, recreation, passion, fad, craze, mania.

Antonyms: INDIFFERENCE; APATHY.

enthusiast noun fan, supporter, follower, devotee, lover, admirer, fanatic, zealot, aficionado; *inf.* buff, freak.

enthusiastic adjective eager, keen, ardent, fervent, warm, passionate, zealous, vehement, excited, exuberant, ebullient, spirited, avid, hearty, wholehearted, committed, devoted, fanatical, earnest.

Antonyms: APATHETIC; UNINTERESTED; INDIFFERENT.

entice verb lure, tempt, seduce, inveigle, lead astray/on, beguile, coax, cajole, wheedle, decoy, bait.

enticement noun **1** *enticements such as high salaries* lure, temptation, allure, attraction, bait, decoy; *inf.* come-on. **2** *the enticement of the child* luring, tempting, seduction, inveiglement, beguilement, coaxing, cajoling, decoying.

entire adjective **1** *one's entire life* whole, complete, total, full, continuous, unbroken. **2** *not an entire success* absolute, total, outright, unqualified, thorough, unreserved, unmitigated, unmodified, unrestricted. **3** *surprised to find an entire vase in the rubble* sound, intact, undamaged, unmarked, unharmed, perfect, unbroken, unimpaired, unblemished, unflawed, unspoiled, unmutilated.

Antonyms: PARTIAL; INCOMPLETE; QUALIFIED.

entirely adverb **1** *not entirely correct* absolutely, completely, totally, fully, wholly, altogether, utterly, in every respect, unreservedly, without reservation, without exception, thoroughly, perfectly. **2** *entirely yours* only, solely, exclusively.

Antonyms: PARTLY; PARTIALLY; SLIGHTLY.

entirety noun **1** *the population in its entirety* totality, wholeness, completeness, fullness, unity, undividedness. **2** *the entirety of the firm's income* sum, total, aggregate.

entitle verb **1** *entitle you to claim the estate* give the right to, qualify, make eligible, authorize, sanction, allow, permit, enable, empower, warrant, accredit, enfranchise, capacitate. **2** *they entitled the song "Gray Skies"* call, name, give the title of.

entity noun **1** *a living entity* body, being, person, creature, individual, organism, object, article, thing, real thing, substance, quantity, existence. **2** *the organization's very entity* being, inner being, existence, life, substance, essence, essential nature, quintessence.

entourage noun **1** retinue, escort, attendant, company, cortege, train, suite, bodyguard; attendants, companions, members of court, followers, camp followers, associates; *inf.* groupies. **2** *a pleasant entourage* surroundings, environs, circumstances; environment, milieu, element, ambience.

entrails plural noun intestines, internal organs, bowels, vital organs, viscera; *inf.* guts, insides, innards.

entrance verb **1** *they entranced us with their dancing/beauty* hold spellbound, captivate, enchant, bewitch, beguile, enthrall, enrapture, ravish, charm, delight. **2** *entranced by a wizard* put under a spell, put in a trance, bewitch, hypnotize, mesmerize.

entrance noun **1** *the entrance to the building* way in, entry, means of entry/access, access, approach, door, doorway, gate, gateway, drive, driveway, passageway, gangway, entrance hall, foyer, lobby, porch, portal, threshold. **2** *the entrance of the gladiators* | *the hero making an entrance* coming/going in, entry, appearance, arrival, introduction, ingress. **3** *refused entrance to the club* entry, admission, admittance, permission to enter, right of entry, access, ingress, entrée.

Antonyms: EXIT; DEPARTURE.

entrant noun **1** *entrants to the club* new member, beginner, newcomer, freshman, new arrival, trainee, novice, initiate, neophyte, proselyte, cub, greenhorn; *inf.* rookie. **2** *the entrants for javelin throwing* competitor, contestant, participant, player, candidate, applicant, rival, opponent.

entrap verb **1** *entrap his prey* trap, snare, catch, net, enmesh, bag. **2** *entrap him into marriage* lure, trick, inveigle, seduce, lead on, entice, bait, decoy.

entreat verb beg, implore, beseech, plead with,

appeal to, petition, solicit, pray, crave, exhort, enjoin, importune, supplicate.

entreaty *noun* appeal, plea, beseeching, pleading, petition, solicitation, prayer, importuning, supplication, suit. *See* ENTREAT.

entrée *noun entrée to high society* entry, entrance, means of entry, access, admission, admittance, right of entry, permission to enter.

entrench *verb the army entrenched across the river* install, settle, establish, ensconce, lodge, set, root, plant, embed, anchor, seat; *inf.* dig in. **entrench on/upon** *entrench on their neighbor's territory* encroach on/upon, trespass on/upon, infringe on/upon, impinge on/upon, intrude on/upon, infiltrate, invade, interlope.

entrenched *adjective entrenched political bias* deep-seated, deep-rooted, rooted, set firm, well-established, fixed, firm, ingrained, unshakable, irremovable, indelible, dyed-in-the-wool.

entrepreneur *noun* businessman, businesswoman, business person, business owner, risktaker, enterpriser.

entrust *verb* **1** *entrust his children to her* give custody of, hand over, commit, assign, consign, deliver. **2** *entrusted with the task | entrust the responsibility to him* give into the charge/care/custody of, charge, invest, commit; turn over, hand over, consign, delegate, commend; put into the hands of.

entry *noun* **1** *the main entry to the building* way in, entrance, means of access, access, approach, door, doorway, gate, gateway, drive, driveway, passageway, gangway, entrance hall, foyer, lobby, porch, portal, threshold. **2** *the entry of the soldiers/actors* coming/going in, entrance, appearance, arrival, introduction, ingress. **3** *refuse entry to the protesters* entrance, admission, admittance, permission to enter, access. *See* ENTRANCE *noun* 3. **4** *an entry in the accountant's ledger | an entry in his diary* item, line item, statement, listing, record, note, jotting, memo, account, description. **5** *fifty entries in the competition* entrant, competitor, contestant, participant, player, candidate. *See* ENTRANT 2. **6** *you can submit four entries* attempt, try, effort, turn, submission; entry form.

Antonyms: EXIT; DEPARTURE.

entwine *verb* wind around, twist around, intertwine, interlink, interlace, interweave, twine, link, lace, braid, plait, knit, criss-cross, entangle.

enumerate *verb* **1** *enumerate the qualities required* list, itemize, specify, spell out, name, give, cite, detail, recite, quote, relate, recount. **2** *enumerate the sums of money involved* count, calculate, add up, total, compute, tally, sum up, reckon, number.

enunciate *verb* **1** *enunciate her words with clarity* pronounce, articulate, sound, speak, say, utter, voice, vocalize, enounce. **2** *enunciate his controversial opinions* give voice to, express,

utter, state, declare, pronounce, assert, affirm, put forward, propound, proclaim, promulgate, publish, broadcast.

envelop *verb the coat/fog enveloped him* enfold, cover, wrap, enwrap, cloak, blanket, surround, engulf, encircle, encompass, conceal, hide, obscure.

envelope *noun put the letter in an envelope* wrapping, wrap, cover, covering, casing, case, jacket, shell, sheath.

enviable *adjective* desirable, worth having, covetable, tempting, excellent, fortunate, lucky, favored.

envious *adjective* jealous, covetous, desirous, green with envy, green, green-eyed, grudging, begrudging, resentful, jaundiced.

environment *noun* surroundings, conditions, circumstances; habitat, territory, domain, milieu, medium, element, situation, location, locale, background, setting, scene, context, ambience, atmosphere, mood.

environmentalist *noun* conservationist, preservationist, ecologist, green.

environs *plural noun Detroit and its environs* surrounding area, neighborhood, vicinity, locality; precincts, outskirts, suburbs.

envisage *verb* **1** *envisage the future/consequences* foresee, predict, imagine, visualize, picture, anticipate, envision. **2** *cannot envisage failure* imagine, contemplate, conceive of, think of, visualize, accept.

envoy *noun* **1** *envoys living in the embassy* legate, consul, attaché, chargé d'affaires, plenipotentiary. **2** *the president's envoy* emissary, accredited messenger, courier, representative, intermediary, delegate, deputy, agent, mediator, go-between.

envy *noun* **1** *envy of her beautiful hair | envy of his rich neighbor* enviousness, covetousness, jealousy, desire; resentment, resentfulness, discontent, spite. **2** *it was the envy of the town* object/source of envy.

envy *verb envy him his large house* be envious of, be jealous of, be covetous of, covet, begrudge, grudge.

eon *noun* age, long time/period, ages, eternity.

ephemeral *adjective* fleeting, short-lived, transitory, momentary, transient, brief, short, temporary, passing, impermanent, evanescent.

epic *noun epics by Homer | direct an epic* long poem, heroic poem, saga, history, legend; long movie/motion picture/film, long story.

epic *adjective* **1** *an epic poem* heroic, grand, long. **2** *of epic proportions | an epic journey* very great, very large, huge, very long, grand, extraordinary, ambitious.

epicene *adjective* **1** *epicene individuals/hairstyles* bisexual, hermaphrodite, hermaphroditic, androgynous; unisex, unisexual. **2** *epicene creatures* neuter, sexless, asexual. **3** *epicene men* effeminate, womanish, unmanly, effete, weak.

epicure noun 1 *a restaurant guide for epicures* gourmet, bon vivant, gastronome, connoisseur. 2 *epicures interested only in sensual pleasures* hedonist, sensualist, voluptuary, libertine, glutton, gourmand.

epicurean adjective 1 *epicurean banqueters* sensualist, pleasure-seeking, hedonistic, self-indulgent, libertine, gluttonous, gourmandizing. 2 *epicurean attitude to food* gourmet, gastronomic.

epidemic noun 1 *many people died in the epidemic* widespread illness/disease, outbreak, plague, scourge. 2 *an epidemic of burglaries* outbreak, wave, upsurge, upswing, upturn, increase, growth, rise, mushrooming.

epidemic adjective *reaching epidemic proportions* rife, rampant, wide-ranging, extensive, widespread, sweeping, prevalent, predominant.

epigram noun 1 *puns and epigrams* witticism, quip, bon mot, pun, double entendre. 2 *proverbs and epigrams* saying, proverb, maxim, adage, axiom, aphorism, saw; words of wisdom.

epigrammatic adjective succinct, concise, terse, compact, crisp, short, brief, tight, pointed, to the point, witty, pithy, sharp.

epilogue noun conclusion; concluding speech, swan song, postscript, PS, afterword, coda, codicil, appendix, postlude.

episode noun 1 *the second episode of the story* installment, part, section, chapter, passage, scene. 2 *an episode in his life* incident, occurrence, event, happening, experience, adventure, occasion, matter, affair, business, interlude, circumstance.

episodic adjective intermittent, irregular, sporadic, occasional, rambling, disconnected, digressive, discursive, wandering, anecdotal, picaresque.

epistle noun letter, missive, communication, correspondence, message, bulletin, note, line.

epitaph noun inscription, commemoration, elegy.

epithet noun 1 *"blessed" was an epithet often applied to her* | *his epithet was "the Iron Horse"* description, descriptive word/expression/phrase, appellation, designation, label, tag; nickname, name, pet name, title. 2 *shouting epithets at the policeman* term of abuse, oath, curse, swearword, obscenity, expletive, four-letter word.

epitome noun 1 *the epitome of politeness* personification, embodiment, essence, quintessence, archetype, representation, model, typification, type, example, exemplar, prototype. 2 *an epitome of his written works* summary, précis, résumé, outline, synopsis, abstract, digest, abridgment, abbreviation, condensation, compendium.

epitomize verb 1 *epitomize the spirit of the age* personify, embody, exemplify, typify, represent, be representative of, symbolize, illustrate,

incarnate. 2 *epitomize his works* summarize, make a résumé/outline of, abridge, condense, shorten, reduce.

epoch noun era, age, period, time, date.

equable adjective 1 *an equable disposition* even-tempered, easygoing, calm, composed, collected, cool, calm and collected, serene, tranquil, placid, levelheaded, imperturbable, unexcitable, unflappable, unruffled; inf. unfazed. 2 *equable temperatures* uniform, even, constant, steady, stable, regular, unvarying, consistent, unchanging. 3 *an equable climate* uniform, moderate, nonextreme.

Antonyms: TEMPERAMENTAL; EXCITABLE; UNEVEN; EXTREME.

equal adjective 1 *of equal height* the same, one and the same, identical, alike, like, comparable, commensurate. 2 *a sum equal to the previous sum* the same as, identical to, equivalent to, commensurate with, proportionate to, tantamount to, on a par with. 3 *an equal contest* even, evenly matched, evenly balanced, balanced, level, evenly proportioned; inf. fifty-fifty, neck and neck. 4 *receive equal treatment* the same, identical, like, uniform, unbiased, impartial, nonpartisan, fair, just, evenhanded, egalitarian. 5 *keep it at an equal temperature* even, constant, uniform, steady, stable, level, unchanging, unvarying, unfluctuating. **equal to** *equal to the task* capable of, fit for, up to, strong/good enough for, adequate for, sufficient for, suitable for, suited to/for, ready for.

Antonyms: UNEQUAL; DIFFERENT; UNEVEN.

equal noun *treat their staff as equals* | *they are equals in strength* equivalent, peer, compeer, co-equal, mate, twin, alter ego, counterpart, match, parallel.

equal verb 1 *four plus five equals nine* be equal to, be equivalent to, come to, amount to, add up to, make, total, correspond to. 2 *she equals him in strength* be equal/even/level with, be equivalent to, match, parallel, correspond to, come up to, measure up to, equate with, be tantamount to, vie with, rival, emulate. 3 *equal the previous record* match, be level with, reach, parallel, come up to, measure up to, achieve.

equality noun sameness, identicalness, identity, equitability, parity, likeness, similarity, uniformity, evenness, levelness, balance, correspondence, parallelism, comparability, fairness, justness, impartiality, egalitarianism, equal opportunity.

Antonyms: INEQUALITY; DIFFERENCE; unevenness.

equalize verb 1 *equalize the score* make equal, make even, even up, make level, level up, balance, square, match. 2 *equalize the irregularities* level, level off, smooth, even off, balance, make uniform, regularize.

equanimity noun composure, presence of mind, self-possession, self-control, levelheadedness, even-temperedness, equilibrium, poise, aplomb, sang-froid, calmness, calm, coolness, coolheadedness, serenity, placidity, tranquillity, imperturbability, unexcitability; *inf.* cool, unflappability.

equate *verb* **1** *equate disagreement with disloyalty* regard as the same, regard as identical, liken, compare, associate, think of together, connect, link, ally. **2** *the two sides of the accounts do not equate* be equal, be alike, balance, correspond, agree, be commensurate, square, tally, compare, match, be equivalent, be parallel.

equation *noun* equality, equalization, likeness, identity, balance, balancing, correspondence, equivalence, agreement, comparison, matching, equating, paralleling.

equatorial *adjective* tropical, torrid, sultry, humid, steamy, sweltering, junglelike.

equestrian *adjective* *an equestrian event/statue* on horseback, mounted, in the saddle.

equestrian *noun* horseman, horsewoman, rider; mounted soldier, mounted policeman, cavalryman, cowboy, cowgirl.

equilibrium *noun* **1** *a state of equilibrium between the physical forces* balance, stability, steadiness, evenness, symmetry, equipoise, counterpoise. **2** *lost her equilibrium and began to shout* equanimity, composure, calmness, coolness, sangfroid, tranquillity, collectedness, serenity, poise, self-possession, imperturbability, steadiness, stability; *inf.* cool, unflappability.

equip *verb* *equipped for the sea crossing* | *not equipped for academic life* fit out, rig out, prepare, supply, stock, arm, array, attire, dress, outfit; suit, endow.

equipment *noun* gear, tools, tackle, stuff, apparatus, baggage, luggage, outfit, furniture, matériel; things, supplies, paraphernalia, accouterments, furnishings; *inf.* bag of tricks.

equipoise *noun* **1** *physical forces in equipoise* equilibrium, balance, stability, steadiness. *See* EQUILIBRIUM **1**. **2** *scales using an equipoise* counterweight, counterbalance, counterpoise, ballast, stabilizer; compensation.

equitable *adjective* fair, fair-minded, just, evenhanded, right, rightful, proper, reasonable, honest, impartial, unbiased, unprejudiced, nondiscriminatory, disinterested, dispassionate, open-minded.

Antonyms: INEQUITABLE; UNFAIR; UNJUST.

equity *noun* equitableness, fairness, fair-mindedness, fair play, justness, justice, evenhandedness, rightness, rightfulness, rectitude, righteousness, properness, reasonableness, honesty, integrity, uprightness, impartiality, lack of discrimination/bias/prejudice, disinterest, disinterestedness, open-mindedness.

equivalence *noun* equalness, equality, sameness, identicalness, identity, similarity, likeness, comparability, interchangeability, correspondence, commensurateness. *See* EQUIVALENT *noun.*

equivalent *adjective* *a job with equivalent status* equal, the same, much the same, identical, sim-

ilar, like, alike, interchangeable, comparable, corresponding, correspondent, commensurate, matching, on a par, tantamount, synonymous.

Antonyms: DIFFERENT; DISSIMILAR.

equivalent *noun* *an ambassador or his equivalent* equal, counterpart, parallel, alternative, match, double, twin, peer.

equivocal *adjective* **1** *an equivocal reply* ambiguous, ambivalent, two-edged, indefinite, vague, obscure, unclear, uncertain, hazy, indeterminate, roundabout, oblique, circuitous, misleading, evasive, duplicitous, paradoxical. **2** *equivocal character* doubtful, dubious, questionable, suspicious, suspect.

Antonyms: UNEQUIVOCAL; DEFINITE.

equivocate *verb* prevaricate, evade/dodge the issue, beat around/about the bush, sit on the fence, hedge, hedge one's bets, quibble, fence, parry questions, fudge the issue, vacillate, shilly-shally, hesitate, hem and haw; *inf.* pussyfoot around.

equivocation *noun* prevarication, evasion, dodging, hedging, quibbling, quibble, fencing, parrying, fudging, vacillation, shilly-shallying, hesitation, hemming and hawing, shuffling, qualification; *inf.* pussyfooting.

era *noun* age, epoch, eon, period, time, generation, stage, cycle, season; times, days. *See also table at* AGE.

eradicate *verb* get rid of, root out, uproot, remove, extirpate, wipe out, weed out, eliminate, do away with, abolish, stamp out, annihilate, extinguish, excise, erase, obliterate, efface, expunge, destroy, kill.

eradication *noun* removal, extirpation, elimination, abolition, annihilation, extinguishing, excision, erasure, obliteration, effacement, expunging, expunction, destruction, killing.

erase *verb* remove, rub out, wipe out, wipe off, blot out, scrape off, obliterate, efface, expunge, excise, cross out, strike out, delete, cancel, blue-pencil.

erect *verb* **1** *erect a building* build, construct, put up, assemble, put together. **2** *erect a flagpole* put up, raise, elevate, mount. **3** *erect a tent* put up, set up, set upright, assemble. **4** *erect a theory/institution* establish, form, set up, found, institute, initiate, create, organize.

Antonyms: DEMOLISH; DISMANTLE; DESTROY.

erect *adjective* **1** *stand erect* | *erect rows of soldiers* upright, straight, vertical. **2** *erect flagpoles* raised, elevated. **3** *an erect penis* hard, rigid, stiff, firm.

Antonyms: BENT; HORIZONTAL; FLACCID.

erection *noun* **1** *the erection of the building* building, construction, putting up, assembly. *See* ERECT *verb* **1**. **2** *the erection of a flagpole* raising, elevation. *See* ERECT *verb* **2**. **3** *the erection of a theory/institution* establishment, formation, setting up, foundation, institution, initiation, creation, organization. **4** *an ugly brick erection* building, structure, edifice, construction.

erode *verb wind eroded the rocks | envy eroded the friendship* wear, wear away/down, eat, eat away at, corrode, abrade, gnaw, gnaw away at, grind down, excoriate, consume, devour, spoil, disintegrate, deteriorate, destroy.

erosion *noun* wearing away, corrosion, abrasion, excoriation, consumption, disintegration, deterioration, attrition, destruction.

erotic *adjective* titillating, sexually stimulating/exciting/arousing, erogenous, aphrodisiac, seductive, sensual, carnal, amatory, salacious, suggestive, pornographic; *inf.* sexy, steamy.

err *verb* **1** *err in thinking them guilty* be in error, be wrong, be incorrect, be inaccurate, make a mistake, be mistaken, make a blunder, blunder, misjudge, miscalculate, misunderstand, misapprehend, misconstrue, get things/it wrong, bark up the wrong tree, be wide of the mark; *inf.* slip up, make a booboo. **2** *to err is human* do wrong, go wrong, go astray, sin, behave badly, misbehave, transgress, trespass, fall from grace, lapse, degenerate.

errand *noun* message, task, job, commission, chore, assignment, undertaking, charge, mission.

errant *adjective* **1** *errant knights of old* itinerant, peripatetic, roaming, roving, wandering, journeying, traveling, nomadic. **2** *errant schoolboys* erring, mischievous, badly behaved, misbehaving, lawless, criminal, delinquent, sinning, offending, transgressing, aberrant, deviant.

erratic *adjective* **1** *erratic conduct* inconsistent, variable, varying, irregular, unstable, unreliable, unpredictable, capricious, whimsical, fitful, wayward, abnormal, eccentric, aberrant, deviant. **2** *steer an erratic course* wandering, meandering, wavering, directionless.
Antonyms: CONSISTENT; PREDICTABLE.

erring *adjective* errant, mischievous, badly behaved, misbehaving, lawless, criminal, delinquent, sinning. *See* ERRANT 2.

erroneous *adjective* wrong, incorrect, inaccurate, inexact, untrue, false, mistaken, fallacious, unfounded, without foundation, spurious, invalid, faulty, flawed, unsound, specious.
Antonyms: RIGHT; CORRECT.

error *noun* **1** *detect an error in the arithmetic | errors in his report* mistake, inaccuracy, miscalculation, blunder, fault, flaw, oversight, misprint, erratum, misinterpretation, misreading, fallacy, misconception, delusion; *inf.* slipup, booboo, boner. **2** *done in error* mistake, erroneousness, oversight, misjudgment, miscalculation, misconception. **3** *see the error of his ways* wrongdoing, mischief, mischievousness, misbehavior, misconduct, lawlessness, criminality, delinquency, sin, sinfulness, evil, evildoing.

ersatz *adjective* artificial, imitation, fake, simulated, synthetic, substitute, man-made, plas-

tic, sham, counterfeit, pretended, pretend, bogus, spurious; *inf.* phony, pseudo.

erudite *adjective* learned, educated, well-read, well-educated, scholarly, intellectual, knowledgeable, literate, lettered, cultivated, cultured; *inf.* brainy, highbrow.
Antonyms: ILLITERATE; IGNORANT.

erudition *noun* learning, scholarship, education, intellect, knowledge, literacy, cultivation, culture; letters.

erupt *verb* **1** *lava erupted from the volcano | the volcano erupted* belch/pour forth, gush, vent, spew, boil over; become active, flare up, eject/vent material, eruct, eructate. **2** *violence erupted* break out, flare up, blow up, burst forth, explode, go off. **3** *spots erupted on her face* break out, flare up, appear suddenly, burst forth, make an appearance, pop up, emerge, become visible.

eruption *noun* **1** *an eruption of violence | volcanic eruptions* outbreak, outburst, flare-up, explosion, flaring, venting. **2** *a skin eruption* outbreak, rash, inflammation.

escalate *verb* **1** *the war effort escalated | the war escalated* grow/develop rapidly, mushroom, increase, be increased, be stepped up, heighten, intensify, accelerate, be extended, be enlarged, be magnified, be amplified. **2** *prices will escalate* go up, mount, soar, climb, spiral; *inf.* be jacked/hiked up, go through the roof/ceiling.
Antonyms: DECREASE; DIMINISH; LESSEN.

escapade *noun* adventure, act of recklessness, stunt, prank, trick, caper, romp, frolic, fling, spree; antics; *inf.* lark, fooling around, shenanigans.

escape *verb* **1** *the prisoners escaped* make one's escape, get away, run away, run off, break out, break free, make a break for it, flee, make one's getaway, bolt, abscond, decamp, fly, slip away, steal away; *inf.* vamoose, skedaddle, hightail it, fly the coop, take a powder. **2** *escape punishment* avoid, evade, dodge, elude, sidestep, circumvent, shake off, give the slip to, keep out of the way of, shun, steer clear of, shirk; *inf.* duck. **3** *gas escaping* leak, seep, pour out/forth, gush, spurt, issue, flow, discharge, emanate, drain.

escape *noun* **1** *the escape from jail | an escape route* running away, breakout, flight, getaway, bolting, absconding, decamping, fleeing. *See* ESCAPE *verb* 1. **2** *an escape from punishment/death* avoidance, evasion, dodging, eluding, elusion, circumvention; *inf.* ducking. *See* ESCAPE *verb* 2. **3** *an escape of gas* leak, leakage, seepage, gush, spurt, issue, flow, discharge, outflow, outpouring, emanation, efflux. **4** *write as a means of escape* escapism, fantasy, fantasizing, woolgathering, nonrealism, getting away from it all.

escapism *noun* escape, fantasy, fantasizing, dreaming, daydreaming, woolgathering, wishful thinking.

eschew *verb* avoid, abstain from, give up, refrain from, forgo, shun, renounce, forswear, swear off, abjure, steer clear of, have nothing to do with, give a wide berth to, shy away from.

escort noun 1 *the bridal party and its escort | the ship's escort* entourage, retinue, train, cortège, attendant company, protection, bodyguard, defense, convoy, contingent; attendant, guide, chaperon, guard, protector, safeguard, defender. 2 *her escort for the evening | an escort agency* partner, companion, beau, attendant, gigolo, call girl, prostitute; *inf.* date.

escort verb 1 *escort the bridal party | escort the ship/ambulance* accompany, guide, conduct, lead, usher, shepherd, guard, protect, safeguard, defend, convoy. *See* ESCORT noun 1. 2 *escort her to the dance* accompany, take out, go out with.

esoteric adjective abstruse, obscure, cryptic, recondite, arcane, abstract, inscrutable, mysterious, hidden, secret, private, mystic, magical, occult, cabalistic.

especial adjective 1 *people of especial talent* special, exceptional, extraordinary, out of the ordinary, uncommon, unusual, outstanding, striking, remarkable, marked, notable, noteworthy, signal, superior, eminent, distinguished. 2 *her own especial brand of charm* special, individual, particular, distinctive, peculiar, personal, own, unique, singular, exclusive, specific, private.

especially adverb 1 *especially talented* exceptionally, extraordinarily, uncommonly, unusually, outstandingly, strikingly, remarkably, markedly, notably, signally, eminently. 2 *especially in the summer* particularly, above all, mainly, chiefly, principally. 3 *bought especially for you* specially, specifically, with someone in mind, exclusively, expressly, particularly, uniquely.

espionage noun spying, intelligence, undercover work, surveillance, infiltration, reconnaissance, counterespionage, counterintelligence.

espousal noun *the espousal of Christianity/socialism* embracing, adoption, taking up, support, backing, championship, promotion, advocacy, defense. *See* ESPOUSE.

espouse verb *espouse Christian/socialist principles* embrace, adopt, take up, take to one's heart, side with, be on the side of, support, back, champion, promote, advocate, defend, stand up for.

espy verb catch sight of, glimpse, spot, see, notice, observe, make out, spy, sight, discern, behold, perceive, descry.

essay noun 1 *write an essay* composition, dissertation, paper, article, thesis, discourse, treatise, tract; *inf.* piece. 2 *make a final essay* attempt, try, effort, endeavor, venture, undertaking; *inf.* shot, go, crack, stab.

essay verb *essay the higher ascent* attempt, make an attempt at, try, try one's hand at, venture, undertake, take on; *inf.* have a shot/go/crack/stab at.

essence noun 1 *the essence of truth* essential part/

constituent, fundamental nature/quality, innermost being/entity, quintessence, substance, sum and substance, nature, crux, heart, soul, life, lifeblood, kernel, marrow, pith, quiddity, *esse*, reality, actuality. 2 *essence of peppermint* extract, concentrate, concentration, distillate, tincture, elixir, abstraction; scent, perfume. **in essence** basically, fundamentally, to all intents and purposes, essentially, in effect, substantially, in the main, at heart, virtually. **of the essence** essential, necessary, indispensable, vital, crucial, of the greatest/utmost importance.

essential adjective 1 *cost-cutting is essential* necessary, indispensable, vital, crucial, requisite, important, needed. 2 *the essential theme of the play* basic, fundamental, inherent, intrinsic, innate, elemental, characteristic, indigenous, principal, cardinal. 3 *the essential gentleman* absolute, complete, perfect, ideal, quintessential. *Antonyms:* NONESSENTIAL; DISPENSABLE; SECONDARY.

essential noun *experience is an essential* necessity, prerequisite, requisite, basic, fundamental, *sine qua non*, rudiment; *inf.* must.

establish verb 1 *establish a new firm/colony* set up, form, found, institute, start, begin, bring into being, create, inaugurate, organize, build, construct, install, plant. 2 *establish his guilt | establish that he is guilty* prove, show to be true, show, demonstrate, attest to, certify, confirm, verify, evidence, substantiate, corroborate, validate, authenticate, ratify. *Antonyms:* DEMOLISH; DESTROY; DISPROVE.

established adjective accepted, official, conventional, traditional, proven, settled, fixed, entrenched, dyed-in-the-wool, inveterate.

establishment noun 1 *the establishment of the firm/colony* setting up, formation, founding, foundation, inception, creation, inauguration, organization, building, construction, installation. *See* ESTABLISH 1. 2 *a gentleman's establishment* residence, house, household, home, dwelling, abode, domicile, estate. 3 *clients patronizing his establishment* firm, business, place of business, company, store, shop, office, factory, emporium, concern, organization, enterprise, corporation. **the Establishment** the authorities, the powers that be, the system, government, bureaucracy, officialdom; *inf.* Big Brother.

estate noun 1 *a large country estate* property, piece of land, landholding, manor, domain; lands. 2 *his estate amounted to $300,000* assets, resources, effects, possessions, belongings; wealth, fortune, property. 3 *the press is called "the fourth estate"* social/political group, level, order, stratum, grade, class, rank, standing, status, caste. 4 *the estate of matrimony* state, condition, situation, circumstance, lot, position.

esteem noun *hold in high esteem* estimation, good opinion, regard, respect, admiration, honor, reverence, deference, veneration, appreciation, approval, approbation, favor, credit.
Antonyms: SCORN; CONTEMPT.

esteem verb **1** *highly esteemed by the community* regard, respect, value, admire, honor, look up to, think highly of, revere, venerate, appreciate, approve of, favor, like, love, cherish, prize, treasure. **2** *esteem it a favor* consider, regard as, think, deem, hold, view as, judge, adjudge, rate, reckon, account, believe; *lit.* opine.
Antonyms: DISDAIN; SCORN.

---

esteem
admire, appreciate, prize, regard, respect

If you're a classical music aficionado, you might **appreciate** a good symphony orchestra, **admire** someone who plays the oboe, and **esteem** the works of Beethoven above all other classical composers. All three of these verbs are concerned with recognizing the worth of something, but in order to *appreciate* it, you have to understand it well enough to judge it critically. If you *admire* something, you appreciate its superiority (*to admire a pianist's performance*), while *esteem* goes one step further, implying that your admiration is of the highest degree (*a musician esteemed throughout the music world*). You **prize** what you value highly or cherish, especially if it is a possession (*she prized her Stradivarius violin*), while **regard** is a more neutral term meaning to look at or to have a certain mental view of something, either favorable or unfavorable (*to regard him as a great musician; to regard her as a ruthless competitor*). To **respect** is to have a deferential regard for someone or something because of its worth or value (*to respect the conductor's interpretation of the music*).

---

estimate verb **1** *estimate the cost* make an estimate, calculate roughly/approximately, work out, assess, compute, gauge, reckon, evaluate, judge, appraise, guess; *inf.* guesstimate. **2** *I estimate him to be honest* consider, believe, think, regard as, judge, rate, view as, reckon, guess, conjecture, surmise; *lit.* opine.

estimate noun **1** *the plumber's estimate* estimated price/cost/value, price, costing, valuation, evaluation, assessment, appraisal. **2** *make an estimate of the cost* estimation, approximate/rough calculation, educated/informed guess, rough guess; *inf.* guesstimate.

estimation noun **1** *in my estimation he is the better candidate* opinion, judgment, consideration, mind, thinking, way of thinking, view, point of view, viewpoint, conviction, feeling, deduction, conclusion. **2** *go down in one's estimation* esteem, good opinion, favorable opinion, regard, respect, admiration, deference,

reverence, veneration, appreciation, approval, approbation, favor.

estrange verb *circumstances estranged the couple* | *he was estranged* alienate, drive apart, set apart, part, separate, divorce, sever, disunite, cause antagonism between, set against, set at odds, disaffect.

estrangement noun alienation, parting, separation, divorce, breakup, split, breach, severance, disunity, division, hostility, antagonism, antipathy, embitteredness, disaffection.

estuary noun inlet, river mouth, cove, bay, creek, arm of the sea.

et cetera adverb and so on, and so forth, and the rest, and/or the like, and/or more of the same, et al., etc.; *inf.* and what have you.

etch verb engrave, carve, cut, furrow, burn into, eat into, imprint, impress, stamp, inscribe, ingrain.

etching noun engraving, carving, cut, print, imprint, impression, stamp, inscription.

eternal adjective **1** *life eternal* everlasting, without end, endless, never-ending, immortal, infinite, enduring, deathless, permanent, immutable, indestructible, imperishable. **2** *stop that eternal racket* | *those eternal questions* endless, never-ending, without end, ceaseless, incessant, nonstop, constant, continuous, continual, unbroken, without respite, interminable, unremitting, relentless, persistent, perpetual.
Antonyms: TRANSIENT; INTERMITTENT.

---

eternal
endless, everlasting, interminable, never-ending, unending

There are some things in life that seem to exist beyond the boundaries of time. **Endless** is the most informal and has the broadest scope of all these adjectives. It can mean without end in time (*an endless argument*) or space (*the endless universe*), and it implies never stopping, or going on continuously as if in a circle (*to consult an endless succession of doctors*). **Unending** is a less formal word used to describe something that endures or has no end, and it can be used either in an approving sense (*unending devotion*) or a disapproving one (*unending conflict*). **Never-ending** is a more emphatic term than *unending*; it, too, can be used in either a positive or a negative sense (*a never-ending delight; a never-ending source of embarrassment*). In contrast, **interminable** is almost always used in a disapproving or negative sense for something that lasts a long time (*interminable delays in construction*). **Everlasting** refers to something that will continue to exist once it is created, while **eternal** implies that it has always existed and will continue to exist in the future. In Christian theology, for example, believers in the *eternal* God look forward to *everlasting* life.

---

eternally adverb **1** *eternally grateful* everlastingly, forever, for always, evermore, for all time, till the end of time, world without end. **2** *eternally on the phone* constantly, continuously, morning noon and night, day and night, perpetually, incessantly, unceasingly, interminably, persistently.

eternity noun **1** *believe in eternity* immortality, everlasting life, afterlife, the hereafter, world without end, world hereafter, next world, heaven, paradise, nirvana. **2** *on the phone for an eternity* long time, age, seemingly forever, the duration; ages, ages and ages.

ethereal adjective **1** *ethereal beauty/fabric* delicate, fairylike, fragile, exquisite, dainty, fine, gossamer, gossamerlike, gossamery, wispy, diaphanous, insubstantial, airy, shadowy, subtle, tenuous. **2** *ethereal regions/music* heavenly, celestial, unearthly, otherworldly, paradisiacal, Elysian, sublime, divine.
Antonyms: SUBSTANTIAL; SOLID; EARTHLY.

ethical adjective moral, honorable, upright, righteous, good, virtuous, high-minded, decent, principled, honest, just, fair, right, correct, proper, fitting, seemly, decorous.
Antonyms: UNETHICAL; IMMORAL; UNPRINCIPLED.

ethics plural noun moral code, morality; morals, moral principles, moral values, principles, rules of conduct, standards, virtues, dictates of conscience.

ethnic adjective racial, cultural, national, tribal, native, indigenous, aboriginal, traditional, folk.

ethos noun spirit, character, tenor, flavor, disposition, rationale, code, morality, moral code; attitudes, beliefs, principles, standards, ethics.

etiolated adjective blanched, bleached, whitened, white, colorless, pale, chalky, chalk-white, faded, washed-out, wan, ghostly.

etiquette noun rules of conduct/behavior, good manners, manners; code of behavior/conduct, code of practice, proper/good conduct, accepted behavior, protocol, good form, form, courtesy, politeness, civility, propriety, decorum, convention, custom, usage, politesse.

eugenics plural noun racial improvement, controlled/selective breeding, planned evolution.

eulogize verb praise highly, praise to the skies, sing the praises of, wax lyrical about, extol, laud, acclaim, pay tribute to, applaud, magnify, exalt, glorify, commend, compliment, pay compliments to; *inf.* rave about.

eulogy noun praise, accolade, extolment, lauding, acclamation, acclaim, paean, panegyric, tribute, applause, magnification, exaltation, glorification, encomium, commendation; praises, plaudits, compliments; *inf.* raving. *See* EULOGIZE.
Antonyms: CRITICISM; CENSURE.

euphemism noun understatement, softening, substitute, polite term, politeness, genteelism.

euphemistic adjective understated, softened, indirect, vague, inoffensive, polite, genteel.

euphonious adjective harmonious, melodious, melodic, musical, pleasant-sounding, sweet-sounding, mellow, mellifluous, tuneful, dulcet, lyrical, rhythmical, symphonious.

euphoria noun elation, joy, joyousness, jubilation, ecstasy, rapture, bliss, exhilaration, exaltation, glee, excitement, buoyancy, intoxication, merriment; high spirits.

euphoric adjective elated, joyful, jubilant, ecstatic, enraptured, rapturous, blissful, exhilarated, exalted, high-spirited, gleeful, excited, buoyant, intoxicated, merry, on cloud nine, in seventh heaven; *inf.* on a high.

euthanasia noun mercy killing, merciful release, quietus.

evacuate verb **1** *people evacuated the flooded town* leave, vacate, abandon, move out of, quit, withdraw from, retreat from, flee, depart from, go away from, retire from, decamp from, desert, forsake; *inf.* pull out of. **2** *firemen evacuated the room* empty, make empty, clear. **3** *evacuate waste matter | evacuate the bowels* excrete, expel, eject, discharge, eliminate, void, purge, empty out, drain, defecate.

evacuation noun **1** *the people's evacuation of the town* leaving, vacating, abandonment, withdrawal, retreat, exodus, departure, flight, desertion, forsaking. *See* EVACUATE 1. **2** *evacuation of waste products | bodily evacuations* excretion, expulsion, ejection, discharge, elimination, voiding, voidance, purging, emptying, draining, defecation; bowel movement/motion, stool, excrement, urination, urine; feces.

evade verb **1** *evade the enemy | evade one's share of the work* avoid, dodge, escape from, elude, sidestep, circumvent, shake off, give the slip to, keep out of the way of, keep one's distance from, steer clear of, shun, shirk; *inf.* duck. **2** *evade the question/issue* avoid, quibble about, be equivocal/evasive about, dodge, hedge, fence, fend off, parry, skirt around, fudge, not give a straight answer to; *inf.* duck, cop out of.
Antonyms: FACE; CONFRONT.

evaluate verb assess, put a value/price on, appraise, size up, weigh up, gauge, judge, rate, rank, estimate, calculate, reckon, measure, determine.

evaluation noun assessment, appraisal, assay, weighing up, gauging, ranking, estimation, reckoning. *See* EVALUATE.

evanesce verb vanish, vanish into thin air, fade, disappear, evaporate, melt away, peter out, disperse, dissolve.

evanescent adjective **1** *evanescent summer days* vanishing, fading, evaporating. *See* EVANESCE. **2** *evanescent youth* ephemeral, fleeting, short-lived, transitory, transient, fugitive, momentary, temporary, brief.

evangelical adjective **1** *evangelical beliefs* according to the Gospel, scriptural, biblical, canonical, textual, orthodox. **2** *evangelical spirit* evangelistic, missionary. *See* EVANGELISTIC.

evangelist noun missionary, preacher, revivalist,

reformer, converter, crusader, propagandist, proselytizer.

evangelistic *adjective* missionary, preaching, revivalist, reforming, crusading, propagandist, evangelical, proselytizing.

evangelize *verb* spread the faith/word, act as a missionary, preach, reform, convert, crusade, campaign, spread propaganda, proselytize.

evaporate *verb* **1** *water evaporates in heat* become vapor, vaporize. **2** *the hot sun evaporated the puddles* vaporize, dry, dry up, dry out, remove moisture from, dehydrate, desiccate, sear, parch. **3** *the vision evaporated* vanish, fade, disappear, melt away, dissolve, disperse, dissipate, dematerialize, evanesce.

evaporation *noun* **1** *the evaporation of water* vaporizing. **2** *the evaporation of political support* vanishing, fading, disappearance, dispersal, evanescence. *See* EVAPORATE 3.

evasion *noun* **1** *the evasion of the enemy* | *evasion of one's share of the work* avoidance, dodging, escape, eluding, elusion, sidestepping, circumvention, shunning, shirking; *inf.* ducking. *See* EVADE 1. **2** *skilled at evasion* subterfuge, deception, trickery, cunning, prevarication, quibbling, equivocation, dodging, hedging, fencing, parrying, skirting around, fudging; *inf.* ducking.

evasive *adjective* **1** *evasive tactics* avoiding, dodging, escaping, eluding, sidestepping, shunning, shirking. *See* EVADE 1. **2** *evasive replies* equivocal, indirect, roundabout, circuitous, oblique, cunning, artful, casuistic; *inf.* cagey. **Antonyms:** FRANK; DIRECT.

eve *noun* **1** *on the eve of the election* evening before, night before, day before, period before. **2** *a summer eve* evening, night.

even *adjective* **1** *an even surface* level, flat, plane, smooth, uniform, flush, true. **2** *an even temperature/color/rhythm* uniform, constant, steady, stable, consistent, unvarying, unchanging, unwavering, unfluctuating, regular. **3** *even amounts* | *even chances of success* equal, the same, much the same, identical, like, alike, similar, to the same degree, comparable, commensurate, corresponding, parallel, on a par, on an equal footing, evenly matched; *inf.* even steven. **4** *the players/scores are even* all square, drawn, tied (up), neck and neck; *inf.* even steven. **5** *of an even disposition* even-tempered, equable, placid, serene, well-balanced, composed, calm, tranquil, cool, unperturbable, unexcitable, unruffled, unflappable, peaceful. **get even** have/take one's revenge, be revenged, revenge oneself, even the score, settle accounts, get one's own back, give as good as one gets, return tit for tat, pay someone back, reciprocate. **get even with** have/take one's revenge on, be revenged on, revenge oneself on, get one's own back on one, repay. **Antonyms:** UNEVEN; BUMPY; UNEQUAL; VARIABLE.

even *adverb* **1** *even colder* yet, still, more so, all the more, all the greater, to a greater extent. **2** *even a kid can do it* | *even the teacher laughed* unexpectedly, paradoxically, surprisingly. **3** *she was attractive, even beautiful* indeed, to be sure, you could say, possibly, more precisely, veritably. **even as** *even as we speak* at the very time/moment that, just as, as, exactly when, while, whilst, during the time that. **even so** *even so I shall attend* nevertheless, nonetheless, all the same, despite that, in spite of the fact, be that as it may, still, yet, notwithstanding. **not even** *I could not even get up* not at all, not quite, so much as, hardly, barely, scarcely, no more than.

even *verb* **1** *even out the bumps/imperfections* smooth, level, flatten, make flush, plane. **2** *even up the differences in wages* make equal, make the same, make uniform, make comparable, balance up, standardize, regularize, equalize.

evenhanded *adjective* fair, just, impartial, unbiased, unprejudiced, nonpartisan, nondiscriminatory, disinterested, dispassionate, equitable.

evening *noun* **1** *go out in the evening* late afternoon, night, close of day, twilight, dusk, nightfall, sunset, sundown; *lit.* eve, even, eventide. **2** *the evening of her life* | *the evening of the Renaissance* close, end, declining years, last/latter part, epilogue. **Antonyms:** DAWN; sunup.

event *noun* **1** *sudden death is a sad event* | *the garden party was a successful event* occasion, affair, business, matter, happening, occurrence, episode, experience, circumstance, fact, eventuality, phenomenon. **2** *track events* | *the javelin event* competition, contest, game, tournament, round, bout, race. **3** *in the event he won* end, conclusion, outcome, result, upshot, consequence, issue, termination, effect, aftermath. **in any event** at any rate, in any case, anyhow, anyway, whatever happens, come what may, regardless, regardless of what happens.

eventful *adjective* busy, event-filled, action-packed, full, lively, active, important, noteworthy, memorable, notable, remarkable, outstanding, fateful, momentous, significant, crucial, critical, historic, consequential, decisive. **Antonyms:** UNEVENTFUL; DULL; INSIGNIFICANT.

eventual *adjective* final, end, closing, concluding, last, ultimate, later, resulting, ensuing, consequent, subsequent.

eventuality *noun* event, occurrence, happening, case, contingency, chance, likelihood, possibility, probability.

eventually *adverb* in the end, at the end of the day, ultimately, in the long run, finally, when all is said and done, one day, some day, sooner or later, sometime.

eventuate *verb* **1** *the election eventuated in a change of leadership* end in, result in, have as a result/consequence. **2** *after the war famine eventuated* be the result, be a consequence, follow, ensue, come about, happen, occur, take place.

ever *adverb* **1** *'twas ever thus* always, at all times, forever, eternally, everlastingly, until the end of time; *inf.* until the cows come home. **2** *will he ever go?* at any point, at any time, on any occasion, in any circumstances. **3** *grew ever larger | ever present | ever changing* always, at all times, constantly, continually, endlessly, unendingly, everlastingly, incessantly, unceasingly, perpetually, repeatedly, habitually, recurrently, unremittingly. **4** *when will she ever learn?* at all, in any way, on earth. **5** *as beautiful as ever* up till now, until now, before. **ever so** *ever so easy* very, to the greatest extent/degree, very much so.

everlasting *adjective* **1** *everlasting life* without end, never-ending, endless, eternal, perpetual, undying, immortal, deathless, indestructible, abiding, enduring, infinite, boundless, timeless. **2** *their everlasting complaints* endless, interminable, never-ending, nonstop, incessant, ceaseless, constant, continual, continuous, unremitting, relentless, uninterrupted, recurrent, monotonous, tedious, wearisome, tiresome, boring.
Antonyms: TRANSIENT; OCCASIONAL.

evermore *adverb* forever, always, for always, for all time, until the end of time, until death, until death do us part, endlessly, without end, ceaselessly, unceasingly, constantly.

every *adjective* **1** *every house/child* each, every single. **2** *there is every chance of recovery* as much/great/likely as possible, all possible, all probable.

everyday *adjective* **1** *an everyday occurrence* daily, diurnal, circadian. **2** *everyday wear* ordinary, common, usual, regular, customary, habitual, accustomed, familiar, frequent, routine, run-of-the-mill, stock, conventional, plain, workaday, mundane, unimaginative, prosaic, dull.
Antonyms: UNUSUAL; EXTRAORDINARY.

everyone *pronoun* everybody, each one, every person, each person, each and every one, all, one and all, all and sundry, the whole world, every mother's son; every Tom, Dick, and Harry.

everything *pronoun* each thing, each item/article, every single thing, all, the lot, the whole lot, the entirety, the total, the aggregate; *inf.* the whole kit and caboodle, the whole shooting match, the whole shebang, everything but the kitchen sink.

everywhere *adverb* all around, all over, in all places, in every place/spot/part, in each place, far and wide, near and far, high and low, throughout the land, the world over, ubiquitously.

evict *verb* turn out, put out, throw out, throw out on the streets, throw out on one's ear, eject, expel, oust, remove, dispossess, dislodge, drum out, show the door to; *inf.* chuck out,

kick out, boot out, heave out, give the heave-ho to, bounce, give the bum's rush to.

eviction *noun* ejection, expulsion, removal, dispossession, clearance. *See* EVICT.

evidence *noun* **1** *produce evidence of guilt* proof, confirmation, verification, substantiation, corroboration, affirmation, authentication, support; grounds. **2** *give evidence in court* testimony, sworn statement, attestation, deposition, declaration, allegation, affidavit. **3** *evidence of a struggle* sign, indication, mark, manifestation, token; signs. **in evidence** *with police very much in evidence* noticeable, conspicuous, visible, on view, on display.

evidence *verb* *blushes evidencing guilt* indicate, show, be evidence of, reveal, display, exhibit, manifest, denote, evince, signify, testify to.

evident *adjective* obvious, clear, apparent, plain, plain as daylight, plain as the nose on your face, unmistakable, noticeable, conspicuous, perceptible, visible, discernible, transparent, manifest, patent, palpable, tangible, indisputable, undoubted, incontrovertible, incontestable.
Antonyms: OBSCURE; DUBIOUS.

evidently *adjective* **1** *evidently he disagrees* it seems, it would seem, it appears, apparently, seemingly, so it seems, as far as one can tell/judge, from all appearances, outwardly, ostensibly. **2** *quite evidently furious* obviously, clearly, plainly, unmistakably, perceptibly, indisputably, undoubtedly, without question. *See* EVIDENT.

evil *adjective* **1** *evil deeds* wicked, bad, wrong, morally wrong, immoral, sinful, vile, base, corrupt, iniquitous, depraved, heinous, villainous, nefarious, reprobate, sinister, atrocious, vicious, malicious, malevolent, demonic, devilish, diabolic. **2** *evil influence* bad, harmful, hurtful, injurious, destructive, detrimental, deleterious, mischievous, pernicious, malignant, venomous, noxious. **3** *evil weather/temper* unpleasant, nasty, disagreeable, horrible, foul, vile. **4** *fall on evil times* unlucky, unfortunate, unfavorable, adverse, unhappy, disastrous, catastrophic, ruinous, calamitous, unpropitious, inauspicious, dire, woeful.
Antonyms: VIRTUOUS; GOOD; PLEASANT.

evil *noun* **1** *more evil in the world than good* wickedness, bad, badness, wrong, wrongdoing, sin, sinfulness, immorality, vice, iniquity, vileness, baseness, corruption, depravity, villainy, atrocity, malevolence, devilishness. *See* EVIL *adjective* 1. **2** *the evils of war* harm, pain, hurt, misery, sorrow, suffering, disaster, misfortune, catastrophe, ruin, calamity, affliction, woe; ills.
Antonyms: VIRTUE; GOODNESS; BENEFIT.

evince *verb* indicate, show, reveal, display, exhibit, make clear/plain, manifest, demonstrate, signify, evidence.

evocative *adjective* reminiscent, suggestive, reawakening, rekindling.

evoke *verb* **1** *evoke a response* cause, bring about, bring forth, induce, arouse, excite, awaken, give rise to, stir up, kindle, stimulate, elicit, educe. **2** *evoke memories/spirits* summon, summon up, call forth, conjure up, invoke, raise, recall.

evolution *noun* evolvement, development, unfolding, unrolling, growth, progress, progression, working out, expansion; natural selection, Darwinism. *See* EVOLVE 1.

evolve *verb* **1** *the subject evolved* develop, unfold, unroll, grow, progress, open out, work out, mature, expand, elaborate, disclose. **2** *gases were evolved* emit, yield, give off.

exacerbate *verb* aggravate, make worse, worsen, intensify, add fuel to the fire, put salt on the wound.

exact *adjective* **1** *an exact description* precise, accurate, correct, unerring, faithful, close, true, just, veracious, literal, strict, errorless; *inf.* on the mark. **2** *an exact person* precise, careful, meticulous, painstaking, methodical, punctilious, conscientious, rigorous, scrupulous, exacting.
Antonyms: INEXACT; INACCURATE; CARELESS.

exact *verb* **1** *exact obedience* demand, require, insist on, compel, command, call for, impose, request. **2** *exact a ransom* demand, extort, extract, force, wring, wrest, squeeze; *inf.* bleed.

exacting *adjective* **1** *an exacting task* demanding, difficult, hard, arduous, tough, laborious, tiring, taxing, troublesome, stringent, onerous. **2** *an exacting person* demanding, strict, stern, firm, rigorous, harsh, rigid, unyielding, unsparing, imperious.

exactly *adverb* **1** *exactly right* | *exactly as I expected* precisely, absolutely, just, quite, in every respect. **2** *work the prices out exactly* precisely, accurately, correctly, without error. **3** *repeat my words exactly* word for word, literally, to the letter, closely, faithfully. **not exactly** *not exactly pleased to see us* not at all, by no means, not by any means, in no way, certainly not; not really.

exactly *interjection* precisely, just so, quite so, quite, indeed, absolutely, truly, certainly, definitely, assuredly, undoubtedly.

exactness *noun* **1** *the exactness of thedescription* precision, accuracy, accurateness, correctness, veracity. *See* EXACT *adjective* 1. **2** *the exactness of our teacher* precision, care, meticulousness, punctiliousness, conscientiousness, rigor. *See* EXACT *adjective* 2.
Antonyms: INACCURACY; NEGLIGENCE.

exaggerate *verb* **1** *exaggerate the difficulties* | *exaggerate how difficult it was* overstate, overemphasize, overstress, overestimate, overvalue, magnify, amplify, aggrandize. **2** *he's not that tall—you're exaggerating* overstate, embellish,

amplify, embroider, add color, overelaborate, overdraw, make a mountain out of a molehill, hyperbolize; *inf.* lay it on thick.
Antonyms: UNDERSTATE; play down (*see* PLAY); MINIMIZE.

exaggerated *adjective* **1** *an exaggerated account* overstated, overemphasized, extravagant, inflated, highly colored, excessive, hyperbolic; *inf.* tall. **2** *an exaggerated frown* | *exaggerated makeup* overdone, extravagant, theatrical.

exaggeration *noun* **1** *say without exaggeration* overstatement, overemphasis, magnification, amplification, embroidery, embellishment, extravagance, excessiveness, excess, pretentiousness, hyperbole. **2** *the exaggeration of their ability* overstatement, overestimation, overvaluation, aggrandizement.

exalt *verb* **1** *exalt to the highest rank* elevate, promote, raise, advance, upgrade, ennoble, aggrandize. **2** *exalt the composer* praise, extol, glorify, acclaim, pay homage/tribute to, laud, reverence, worship, revere, lionize, magnify. **3** *exalt one's spirits* excite, stimulate, animate, enliven, exhilarate, uplift, elevate, inspire.

exaltation *noun* **1** *exaltation to high rank* promotion, advancement, raising, ennoblement, aggrandizement; rise, elevation. **2** *the exaltation of royalty* high rank, eminence, grandeur, dignity, honor, loftiness, prestige, fame. **3** *greet with exaltation* praise, extolment, glorification, acclamation, applause, homage, tribute, reverence, worship; plaudits. **4** *exaltation of the spirits* stimulation, animation, exhilaration, elevation, inspiration. **5** *full of exaltation* elation, exultation, joy, rapture, rhapsody, ecstasy, bliss, happiness, delight.

exalted *adjective* **1** *from his exalted position in the firm* high, high-ranking, lofty, grand, eminent, prestigious, elevated, august. **2** *exalted aims* high-minded, lofty, elevated, noble, intellectual, ideal, sublime, inflated, pretentious. **3** *in an exalted mood* elated, exultant, jubilant, joyful, triumphant, rapturous, rhapsodic, ecstatic, blissful.

exam *noun* *an English exam* examination, test, set of questions/exercises; paper, oral; *inf.* midterm, final.

examination *noun* **1** *the examination of the facts* study, inspection, scrutiny, investigation, analysis, review, research, observation, exploration, consideration, appraisal. *See* EXAMINE 1. **2** *the physical examination of a patient* checkup, inspection, assessment, observation, scrutiny. **3** *examination of witnesses* questioning, interrogation, cross-examination, cross-questioning, third degree. *See* EXAMINE 3. **4** *completed the examination* exam, test. *See* EXAM.

examine *verb* **1** *examine the facts* look at, look into, study, inspect, survey, scrutinize, investigate, analyze, review, scan, observe, research, sift, explore, probe, check out, consider, appraise, weigh, weigh up. **2** *examine a patient* look at, inspect, check over, give a checkup to, assess, observe, scrutinize. **3** *examine the candidates/witnesses* put/address questions to, question, test, quiz, interrogate, cross-examine, cross-question, give the third degree to; *inf.* grill, pump.

example *noun* **1** *an example of cave painting* sample, specimen, instance, representative case, case in point, illustration. **2** *follow someone else's example* model, pattern, precedent, paradigm, standard, criterion. **3** *the hero is an example to everyone* model, ideal, pattern, standard, paradigm, paragon. **4** *punished him as an example to other prisoners* warning, caution, lesson, admonition. **for example** for instance, e.g., to give an example/instance, by way of illustration, as an illustration, to illustrate.

exasperate *verb exasperate the teacher* anger, annoy, infuriate, irritate, incense, madden, enrage, provoke, irk, vex, gall, pique, try the patience of, get on the nerves of, make one's blood boil; *inf.* bug, needle, get to, rile.

exasperation *noun show exasperation at their behavior* anger, annoyance, fury, irritation, rage, vexation, pique. *See* EXASPERATE.

excavate *verb* **1** *excavate a trench* dig, dig out, hollow out, scoop out, gouge, cut out, quarry, mine. **2** *excavate an ancient city/vase* unearth, dig up, uncover, bring to the surface, reveal, disinter, exhume.

excavation *noun* **1** *the excavation of the site* digging, hollowing, quarrying. *See* EXCAVATE 1. **2** *mining/archaeological excavations* hole, hollow, cavity, pit, crater, cutting, trench, trough; burrow, quarry, mine, colliery.

exceed *verb* **1** *if the price exceeds $10* be greater/more than, go beyond, pass, top. **2** *her abilities far exceed his* be greater than, surpass, be superior to, better, pass, beat, outdo, outstrip, outshine, transcend, top, cap, overshadow, eclipse. **3** *exceed the speed limit | exceed one's responsibility* go beyond, go over, do more than, overstep.

exceedingly *adverb* extremely, exceptionally, extraordinarily, tremendously, enormously, vastly, greatly, highly, hugely, supremely, inordinately, surpassingly, superlatively, especially, unusually, very.

excel *verb* **1** *excel at tennis* be preeminent/outstanding, be skillful/talented, be proficient, shine, be a master, wear the crown. **2** *her cousin excels her in sports* be better than, be superior to, surpass, outshine, eclipse, overshadow, outdo, outrival, outclass, outstrip, top, pass, transcend.

excellence *noun* merit, eminence, preeminence, distinction, greatness, fineness, quality, superiority, supremacy, transcendence, value, worth, skill.
Antonym: INFERIORITY.

excellent *adjective* very good, of high quality, of a high standard, first-rate, first-class, great, fine, distinguished, superior, superb, outstanding, marvelous, brilliant, noted, notable,

eminent, preeminent, supreme, superlative, admirable, worthy, sterling, prime, select; *inf.* A-1, aces, top-notch, tip-top.
Antonyms: POOR; INFERIOR.

except *preposition except you | except for me* with the exception of, excepting, excluding, leaving out, but, besides, barring, bar, other than, omitting, with the omission/exclusion of, exclusive of, saving, save.

except *verb I except present company* exclude, leave out, omit, rule out, pass over, bar.

exception *noun* **1** *with the exception of you* exclusion, omission, noninclusion. *See* EXCEPT *verb*. **2** *the case being an exception* special case, departure, deviation, anomaly, irregularity, inconsistency, quirk, peculiarity, oddity, freak.
take exception object, be offended, take offense, raise an objection, resent, take umbrage, disagree.

exceptionable *adjective rude and exceptionable behavior* objectionable, offensive, disagreeable, obnoxious, repugnant. *See* OBJECTIONABLE.

exceptional *adjective* **1** *this noise is exceptional* unusual, uncommon, abnormal, out of the ordinary, atypical, rare, odd, anomalous, singular, peculiar, inconsistent, deviant, divergent, aberrant. **2** *a person of exceptional ability* unusually good, excellent, extraordinary, remarkable, outstanding, special, especial, phenomenal, prodigious.
Antonyms: USUAL; NORMAL; AVERAGE.

excerpt *noun* extract, citation, quotation, quote, passage, selection, part, section, fragment, piece, portion.

excess *noun* **1** *an excess of fat/enthusiasm* surplus, surfeit, overabundance, superabundance, superfluity, plethora, glut, overkill, oversufficiency; too much, more than enough, enough and to spare. **2** *throw out the excess* remainder, residue, overload, overflow; leftovers. **3** *a life of excess* immoderation, lack of restraint, overindulgence, prodigality, intemperance, debauchery, dissipation, dissoluteness.
Antonyms: DEARTH; SHORTAGE; MODERATION.

excess *adjective excess baggage/food* extra, additional, too much, surplus, superfluous, spare, redundant.

excessive *adjective* too much, to too great a degree, superfluous, immoderate, extravagant, lavish, superabundant, unreasonable, undue, uncalled-for, extreme, inordinate, unwarranted, unnecessary, needless, disproportionate, exorbitant, enormous, outrageous, intemperate, unconscionable.

excessively *adverb* to too great a degree, unduly, immoderately, unreasonably. *See* EXCESSIVE.

exchange *verb exchange compliments* trade, swap, barter, interchange, reciprocate, bandy.

exchange *noun* **1** *the exchange of information* interchange, trade, trade-off, swapping, barter, giving and taking, bandying, traffic, reciprocity, tit for tat; dealings. **2** *the floor of the exchange* stock exchange, stock market, market.

excise *verb* **1** *surgeons excised the spleen* cut out, cut off, remove, eradicate, extirpate; *Tech.* resect. **2** *excise the offending passage* remove, delete, cut out, cut, cross/strike out, erase, blue-pencil, expunge, eliminate, expurgate, bowdlerize.

excise *noun* duty, tariff, toll, levy; customs.

excitable *adjective* temperamental, emotional, highly strung, nervous, edgy, mercurial, volatile, tempestuous, hot-tempered, quick-tempered, hot-headed, passionate, fiery, irascible, testy, moody, choleric.

excite *verb* **1** *excite the children too much* stimulate, rouse, arouse, animate, move, thrill, inflame, titillate; *inf.* turn on, wind up. **2** *excite feelings of love* cause, bring about, rouse, arouse, awaken, incite, provoke, stimulate, kindle, evoke, stir up, elicit. **3** *excite a rebellion* cause, incite, bring about, stir up, instigate, foment.

excited *adjective* *excited children* stimulated, aroused, animated, thrilled, agitated, over-wrought, feverish, wild; *inf.* high, wound up, turned on. *See* EXCITE 1.
Antonyms: INDIFFERENT; APATHETIC.

excitement *noun* **1** *jumping up and down with excitement* agitation, animation, emotion, anticipation, exhilaration, elation, enthusiasm, feverishness, ferment, tumult. **2** *one of the excitements of travel* adventure, thrill, pleasure, stimulation; *inf.* kick. **3** *the excitement of feelings* arousal, awakening, stimulation, evocation, kindling. *See* EXCITE 2.

exciting *adjective* *an exciting event* thrilling, stirring, stimulating, exhilarating, intoxicating, rousing, electrifying, invigorating, moving, inspiring, titillating, provocative, sensational; *inf.* sexy.
Antonyms: BORING; UNINTERESTING; FLAT.

exclaim *verb* call, cry, call/cry out, shout, yell, roar, bellow, shriek, ejaculate, utter, proclaim; *fml.* vociferate.

exclamation *noun* call, cry, shout, yell, roar, bellow, shriek, ejaculation, interjection, utterance; expletive.

exclude *verb* **1** *exclude women from membership* debar, bar, keep out, shut out, prohibit, forbid, prevent, disallow, refuse, ban, blackball, veto, stand in the way of, proscribe, interdict. **2** *exclude the possibility* eliminate, rule out, preclude, count out, reject, set aside, except, repudiate, omit, pass over, leave out, ignore. **3** *the price excludes drinks* be exclusive of, not include, not be inclusive of, omit, leave out. **4** *exclude from a building* throw out, turn out, eject, remove, evict, expel, oust, ban; *inf.* bounce, kick/boot out.
Antonyms: INCLUDE; ACCEPT; ADMIT.

exclusion *noun* **1** *the exclusion of women* debarment, barring, keeping out, prevention, refusal, proscription. *See* EXCLUDE 1. **2** *the exclusion of robbery as a motive* elimination, ruling out, precluding, rejection, omission. *See* EXCLUDE 2. **3** *the exclusion of meals from the price* noninclusion, omission, leaving out. **4** *the exclusion of drunks* throwing out, ejection, removal, eviction, expulsion. *See* EXCLUDE 4.

exclusive *adjective* **1** *an exclusive club* select, selective, choice, restrictive, restricted, closed, private, limited, discriminating, cliquish, clannish, snobbish, fashionable, chic, elegant, luxurious, high-class, aristocratic; *inf.* posh, ritzy, classy, up-scale. **2** *my exclusive attention* complete, undivided, full, absolute, entire, whole, total, all of, unshared. **3** *the exclusive means of travel* sole, only, unique, individual, single. **4** *exclusive of drinks* not including, excluding, leaving out, omitting, excepting, with the exception of, except for, not counting, barring. **5** *mutually exclusive* incompatible, inimical, antithetical.
Antonyms: OPEN; PARTIAL; INCLUSIVE.

excommunicate *verb* exclude, expel, cast out, banish, eject, remove, bar, debar, proscribe, interdict, repudiate; *fml.* anathematize, unchurch.

excoriate *verb* **1** *excoriate skin* abrade, scrape, scratch, strip, peel, skin, decorticate. **2** *excoriate the wrongdoers* denounce, censure, condemn, criticize, blame, accuse, berate, upbraid, rebuke, reprimand, reprove, scold, chide, read someone the riot act, chastise, castigate, inveigh/rail against, abuse, attack, revile, vilify; *inf.* lambaste, bawl out, tear into, give someone what for.

excrement *noun* waste matter, ordure, dung, manure; excreta, feces, stools, droppings.

excrescence *noun* **1** *excrescence on the body/tree* growth, lump, swelling, protuberance, outgrowth, eruption; cancer, boil, carbuncle, pustule. **2** *excrescence on the landscape* something ugly, eyesore, monstrosity, disfigurement; *inf.* sight.

excrete *verb* *excrete feces/urine* pass, void, discharge, eject, evacuate, expel, eliminate, exude, emit, egest; defecate, urinate.

excruciating *adjective* *an excruciating pain* agonizing, racking, torturous, insufferable, unbearable, severe, intense, extreme, harrowing, searing, piercing, acute; *fml.* exquisite.

excursion *noun* **1** *an excursion to the mountains* | *a shopping excursion* trip, day trip, expedition, jaunt, outing, journey, tour. **2** *an excursion from the main topic* digression, deviation, detour, wandering, rambling.

excusable *adjective* forgivable, pardonable, defensible, justifiable, understandable, condonable, venial.
Antonyms: INEXCUSABLE; UNFORGIVABLE.

excuse *verb* **1** *excuse the wrongdoer* forgive, pardon, exonerate, absolve, acquit, make al-

lowances for, bear with, tolerate, indulge; *fml.* exculpate. **2** *excuse their behavior* forgive, pardon, condone, justify, defend, vindicate, mitigate, explain. **3** *excuse them from heavy work* let off, exempt, spare, absolve, release, relieve, free, liberate.
Antonyms: PUNISH; CONDEMN; OBLIGE.

excuse *noun* **1** *their excuse for being late* defense, justification, reason, explanation, apology, vindication, mitigation; grounds, mitigating circumstances. **2** *his illness was just an excuse for his absence* pretext, ostensible reason, pretense, front, cover-up, subterfuge, fabrication, evasion, escape; *inf.* cop-out. **poor excuse for/of** *a poor excuse for a man/car* travesty of, poor specimen of, pitiful example of, mockery of, poor substitute for.

execrable *adjective* abominable, abhorrent, loathsome, odious, heinous, hateful, detestable, despicable, foul, vile, deplorable, invidious, atrocious, offensive, disgusting, repulsive, obnoxious, nauseous, damnable.

execrate *verb* **1** *execrate violence* abhor, abominate, loathe, hate, detest, despise, deplore, be repelled by, have an aversion to, feel hostility to, not be able to stand. **2** *execrate and blaspheme* curse, swear at, revile, imprecate, inveigh, fulminate, vituperate, condemn, damn, censure, denounce, excoriate.

execute *verb* **1** *execute a murderer* put to death, carry out a sentence of death, kill; hang, send to the gallows, behead, guillotine, decapitate, electrocute, send to the electric chair, send to the chair, shoot, put before a firing squad, send to the gas chamber, give a lethal injection to, crucify, stone to death; *inf.* string up, fry. **2** *execute a plan of action* carry out, accomplish, perform, implement, effect, bring off, achieve, complete, fulfill, enact, enforce, put into effect, do, discharge, prosecute, engineer, administer, attain, realize, render. **3** *execute a dance | execute a piece of music* perform, present, stage, render.

execution *noun* **1** *the execution of a murderer* putting to death, capital punishment; death sentence. See EXECUTE 1. **2** *the execution of a plan* carrying out, accomplishment, performance, implementation, effecting, bringing off, achievement, completion, fulfillment, enactment, enforcement, discharge, prosecution, engineering, administering, attainment, realization, rendering. **3** *execution of a piece of music | her superb execution of the dance* performance, presentation, staging, rendition, delivery, technique, style, mode.

executioner *noun* **1** *public executioner* hangman, headsman, member of the firing squad. **2** *the executioner of a rival gang member* assassin, killer, murderer; *inf.* hit man.

executive *noun* administrator, official, director, leader, manager, VIP; *inf.* boss, bigwig, big wheel, honcho.

executive *adjective* *executive powers* administra-

tive, decision-making, directing, controlling, managerial; lawmaking.

exegesis *noun* *exegesis of a scriptural text* explanation, explication, interpretation, exposition, elucidation, clarification, annotation.

exemplar *noun* **1** *an exemplar of morality* model, ideal, standard of perfection/excellence, epitome, paradigm, paragon, pattern, criterion, benchmark. **2** *an exemplar of birds of prey* example, specimen, exemplification, type, illustration, prototype, instance.

exemplary *adjective* **1** *exhibiting exemplary behavior* ideal, model, perfect, excellent, admirable, commendable, faultless, laudable, praiseworthy, meritorious, honorable. **2** *exemplary jail sentences* warning, cautionary, admonitory, monitory, example-setting, lesson-teaching. **3** *exemplary member of the species* typical, representative, illustrative, characteristic, epitomic.

exemplify *verb* **1** *exemplify Impressionist painting* typify, epitomize, represent, personify, embody, illustrate. **2** *exemplify the talk with slides* illustrate, give an example/instance of, demonstrate, instance, depict.

exempt *verb* *exempt from taxation* free from, release from, make an exception of/for, exclude from, excuse from, let off, give/grant immunity from, absolve/except from, liberate from, spare, exonerate from, relieve of, discharge from, dismiss from; *inf.* let off.
Antonyms: LIABLE; SUBJECT.

exempt *adjective* *declared exempt from taxation* free from, excused from, immune to, not subject/liable to, absolved/excepted from, spared, released from, discharged from, dismissed from.

exemption *noun* *be granted exemption from military service* immunity, indemnity, dispensation, freedom, exclusion, release, absolution, exception, exoneration, relief, discharge, special treatment, privilege, favoritism.

exercise *noun* **1** *physical exercise* activity, exertion, effort, action, work, movement, training, physical training, drill, drilling, discipline; workout, warm-up, limbering-up; gymnastics, sports, aerobics, calisthenics. **2** *the exercise of patience* employment, use, application, utilization, implementation, practice, operation, exertion, discharge, accomplishment. **3** *an algebra exercise* problem, task, piece of work; practice.

exercise *verb* **1** *exercise in order to lose weight* do exercises, work out, train, exert oneself, drill. See EXERCISE *noun* 1. **2** *exercise patience* employ, use, make use of, utilize, apply, implement, practice, exert.

exert *verb* **1** *exert pressure* exercise, employ, use, make use of, utilize, apply, wield, bring into play, bring to bear, set in motion, expend, spend. **2** *exert yourself and you will be able to do it* apply oneself, put oneself out, make an effort, spare no effort, try hard, do one's best, give one's all, strive, endeavor, struggle, labor, toil, strain, work, push, drive, go all out; *inf.* put one's back into it.

exertion *noun* **1** *physical exertion* effort, exercise, work, struggle, strain, stress, endeavor, toil, labor, action, industry, assiduity; pains. **2** *the exertion of pressure* exercise, employment, use, utilization, expenditure, application.

exhaust *verb* **1** *the climb exhausted them* tire, tire out, wear out, fatigue, drain, weary, sap, enervate, tax, overtax, debilitate, prostrate, enfeeble, disable; *inf.* take it out of, poop out, fag out, knock out, burn out. **2** *exhaust the supply of fuel* use up, consume, finish, deplete, expend, spend, run through, dissipate, waste, squander, fritter away; *inf.* blow. **3** *exhaust a well of its water* empty, drain, void, evacuate, deplete. **4** *exhaust the subject* say all there is to say about, treat in detail, treat thoroughly, develop completely, expound in detail about, study in great detail, research completely, go over with a fine-toothed comb.
Antonyms: INVIGORATE; REPLENISH.

exhausted *adjective* **1** *cold and exhausted* tired out, worn out, fatigued, weary, sapped, enervated, weak, faint, debilitated, prostrate, enfeebled, spent; *inf.* all in, done in, dead beat, dead tired, dog-tired, ready to drop, dead on one's feet, burnt out, played out, pooped, pooped out, fagged out, wasted. **2** *exhausted supplies* used up, at an end, consumed, finished, depleted. *See* EXHAUST 2. **3** *an exhausted well* empty, drained, depleted, dry, void.

exhausting *adjective* tiring, fatiguing, wearying, wearing, grueling, punishing, strenuous, arduous, backbreaking, taxing, laborious, enervating, sapping, debilitating. *See* EXHAUST 1.

exhaustion *noun* **1** *fail to go on because of exhaustion* fatigue, great tiredness, weakness, debility, collapse, weariness, faintness, prostration, enervation, lassitude. **2** *the exhaustion of resources* using up, consumption, depletion, dissipation. *See* EXHAUST 2.

exhaustive *adjective* all-inclusive, comprehensive, intensive, all-out, in-depth, total, all-embracing, encyclopedic, thorough, complete, full, thoroughgoing, extensive, profound, far-reaching, sweeping.
Antonyms: PERFUNCTORY; SKETCHY.

exhibit *verb* **1** *exhibit products* put on display/show/view, display, show, demonstrate, set out/forth, present, model, expose, air, unveil, array, flaunt, parade. **2** *exhibit signs of sadness* show, express, indicate, reveal, display, demonstrate, make clear/plain, betray, give away, disclose, manifest, evince, evidence.
Antonyms: CONCEAL; HIDE.

exhibit *noun* *a furniture exhibit* display, show, showing, demonstration, presentation, exhibition, viewing.

exhibition *noun* **1** *a book exhibition* display, show, fair, demonstration, presentation, exhibit, exposition, spectacle. *See* EXHIBIT *verb* 1. **2** *an exhibition of bad temper* display, show, expression, indication, revelation, demonstration, betrayal, disclosure, manifestation.

exhilarate *verb* make happy/cheerful, cheer up, enliven, elate, gladden, delight, brighten, excite, thrill, animate, invigorate, lift, stimulate, raise the spirits of, revitalize, exalt, inspirit; *inf.* perk/pep up.

exhilaration *noun* elation, joy, happiness, gladness, delight, excitement, gaiety, merriment, mirth, hilarity, glee, animation, vivacity, invigoration, stimulation, revitalization, exaltation; high spirits.

exhort *verb* urge, persuade, press, encourage, sway, prompt, advise, counsel, incite, goad, stimulate, push, beseech, entreat, bid, enjoin, admonish, warn.

exhortation *noun* urging, persuasion, pressing, insistence, encouragement, swaying, prompting, advice, recommendation, counseling, incitement, goading, pushing, beseeching; entreaty, enjoinder, admonition, warning, instruction, injunction, lecture, harangue.

exhume *verb* *exhume a corpse* | *exhume old memories* dig up, unearth, disinter, disentomb, unbury, resurrect.

exigency *noun* **1** *a situation of exigency* urgency, emergency, crisis, criticalness, necessity, imperativeness, stress, extremity, difficulty, trouble, pressure. **2** *the exigencies of war* need, demand, requirement, necessity, want, essential, requisite.

exiguous *adjective* scant, scanty, meager, sparse, bare, slim, slight, slender, paltry, skimpy, negligible, mere, trifling, diminutive.

exile *verb* *be exiled from one's native country* banish, expatriate, deport, expel, drive out, eject, oust, proscribe, outlaw, bar, ban, ostracize, uproot, separate, excommunicate.

exile *noun* **1** *sent into exile* banishment, expatriation, deportation, expulsion; uprooting, separation. *See* EXILE *verb*. **2** *exiles from their homeland* expatriate, deportee, displaced person, refugee, outlaw, outcast, pariah.

exist *verb* **1** *doubting that ghosts exist* be, have being, have existence, live, have life, be living, subsist, breathe, draw breath, be extant, be viable. **2** *cannot exist in a cold climate* live, survive, subsist, occur, remain, continue, last, endure, prevail. **3** *enough money barely to exist on* survive, live, stay alive, eke out a living, subsist.
Antonyms: DIE; FADE.

existence *noun* **1** *come into existence* | *the existence of ghosts* being, existing, actuality, reality, fact, living. **2** *a poverty-stricken existence* way of life, lifestyle, manner of living/survival, mode of being.

existent *adjective* existing, in existence, living, extant, surviving, remaining, abiding, enduring, prevailing, present, current.

exit noun **1** *theater exit* door, gate, door out, passage out, outlet, egress. **2** *his exit from politics* departure, leaving, withdrawal, retirement, going, retreat, leave-taking, flight, exodus, farewell, adieu.
Antonyms: ENTRANCE; ENTRY; ARRIVAL.

exodus noun mass departure, flight, withdrawal, exit, leaving, escape, fleeing, evacuation, migration, emigration, retreat, retirement, hegira.

exonerate verb **1** *exonerate from any responsibility* absolve, acquit, clear, discharge, vindicate, exculpate, declare innocent, dismiss, let off, excuse, pardon, justify. **2** *exonerate from duty* excuse, exempt, except, release, relieve, free, let off, liberate, discharge.
Antonyms: CHARGE; IMPLICATE; INCRIMINATE.

exoneration noun **1** *exoneration from responsibility* acquittal, absolution, discharge, vindication, exculpation, dismissal, excusing, pardon, amnesty, justification. **2** *exoneration from duty* excusing, exemption, release, liberation, freedom, discharge, indemnity, immunity, dispensation.

exorbitant adjective **1** excessive, extortionate, extreme, unreasonable, immoderate, inordinate, outrageous, preposterous, monstrous, unwarranted, undue, unconscionable.
Antonyms: CHEAP; MODERATE.

exorcise verb **1** *exorcise the evil spirit* drive out, cast out, expel. **2** *exorcise a place of evil spirits* deliver, free, purify, rid, disenchant.

exorcism noun **1** *exorcism of evil spirits* driving out, casting out, expulsion. **2** *exorcism of a place of evil spirits* deliverance, freeing, purification, ridding, disenchantment.

exotic adjective **1** *exotic fruits* foreign, nonnative, tropical, imported, introduced, novel, alien, external, extraneous, extrinsic. **2** *exotic clothing* striking, outrageous, colorful, extraordinary, extravagant, sensational, unusual, remarkable, astonishing, strange, outlandish, bizarre, peculiar, impressive, glamorous, fascinating, mysterious, curious, different, unfamiliar. **3** *exotic dancing* erotic, go-go, striptease, titillating, risqué, sexy.

expand verb **1** *metals expand when heated | the company is expanding* become/grow larger, enlarge, increase, increase in size/scope, swell, inflate, magnify, amplify, distend, lengthen, stretch, extend, multiply. **2** *expand the territory/business* make larger/greater/bigger, increase, magnify, amplify, add to, extend, multiply. **3** *petals expanding in the sunshine | faces expanding in smiles* open out, spread out, unfold, unfurl, unroll, unravel. **4** *expand one's account of the accident* elaborate on, add detail to, amplify, embellish, enlarge on, flesh out, develop, expound.
Antonyms: CONTRACT; CONDENSE.

expanse noun *an expanse of green/water* area, stretch, region, tract, breadth, extent, sweep, space, plain, field, extension, vastness.

expansion noun **1** *expansion of metals/business* enlargement, increase, magnification, amplification, stretching, distension, protraction, extension, multiplication. **2** *flowers expanding in the sun* opening out, unfolding, unfurling, unrolling, unraveling. **3** *an expansion of one's account* elaboration, amplification, embellishment, fleshing out, development, expounding.

expansive adjective **1** *the expansive qualities of metal when heated* expandable, expanding, extendable, extending; extensive, wide. **2** *on an expansive scale* extensive, wide-ranging, broad, wide, widespread, all-embracing, comprehensive, thorough, universal.

expatiate verb *expatiate on the plans* expand on, enlarge on, elaborate on, amplify, embellish, expound, go into detail about, discourse on, dwell on, dissertate on.

expatriate noun *expatriates working abroad* emigrant, émigré, exile, displaced person, refugee, outcast.

expatriate adjective emigrant, living abroad, exiled, banished, cast out, deported.

expect verb **1** *don't expect that he will come* think, believe, assume, suppose, imagine, presume, conjecture, calculate, surmise, reckon. **2** *expect a letter | expect a large crowd* anticipate, await, envisage, look for, look forward to, watch for, hope for, contemplate, bargain for, have in prospect, predict, forecast. **3** *teachers expect your complete attention* insist on, require, demand, exact, count on, call for, rely on, look for, wish, want, hope for.

expectancy noun **1** *in a state of excited expectancy* anticipation, expectation, eagerness, hope, waiting, suspense, conjecture, anxiety. **2** *life expectancy* prospect, outlook, likelihood, probability.

expectant adjective **1** *children's expectant faces* anticipating, anticipatory, expecting, awaiting, eager, hopeful, in suspense, ready, watchful, anxious, on tenterhooks. **2** *expectant mothers* pregnant, expecting, expecting a child; *inf.* in a family way.

expectation noun **1** *in expectation of the arrival of Christmas* anticipation, expectancy, readiness, hope. See EXPECTANCY 1. **2** *an expectation that she will win* assumption, belief, supposition, presumption, assurance, conjecture, surmise, reckoning, calculation; confidence.

expectations plural noun *future expectations* prospects, hopes; outlook, speculation, good fortune.

expecting adjective pregnant, expectant. See EXPECTANT 2.

expediency, expedience noun *interested only in the expediency of the plan, not in moral principles* convenience, advantageousness, advantage, usefulness, benefit, profitability, profit, gain, gainfulness, practicality, utilitarianism, utility, pragmatism, desirability, suitability, advisability, appropriateness, aptness, fitness, effectiveness, helpfulness, judiciousness, timeliness, opportunism, propitiousness.

expedient *adjective expedient to tell a white lie | an expedient rather than moral course of action* convenient, advantageous, useful, beneficial, profitable, gainful, practical, pragmatic, desirable, suitable, advisable, appropriate, apt, fit, effective, helpful, politic, judicious, timely, opportune, propitious.

expedient *noun an expedient to achieve an end* means, measure, method, resource, scheme, plan, plot, stratagem, maneuver, machination, agency, trick, ruse, artifice, device, tool, contrivance, invention, shift, stopgap.

expedite *verb* **1** *expedite the procedure of obtaining permission* accelerate, speed up, hurry, hasten, step up, precipitate, quicken, urge on, forward, advance, facilitate, further, promote, press. **2** *expedite the task* finish/accomplish/achieve quickly, dispatch; *inf.* dash off, make short work of.
Antonyms: DECELERATE; OBSTRUCT; HINDER.

expedition *noun* **1** *an expedition to find the source of the river* organized journey/voyage, undertaking, enterprise, mission, project, quest, exploration, safari, trek. **2** *a shopping expedition* trip, excursion, outing, journey, jaunt. **3** *three members of the expedition died* group, team, party, company, crew, band, troop, crowd. **4** *carry out orders with maximum expedition* speed, haste, promptness, swiftness, alacrity, quickness, rapidity, velocity, celerity, readiness, dispatch.

expeditious *adjective an expeditious response* speedy, immediate, instant, prompt, swift, quick, rapid, fast, punctual, ready, brisk, nimble, hasty, summary.

expel *verb* **1** *expel them from the country* banish, exile, evict, oust, drive out, throw out, cast out, deport, proscribe, outlaw; *inf.* kick/boot out, give the bum's rush to, send packing. **2** *expel someone from a club* bar, ban, debar, blackball, throw out, drum out, oust, reject, dismiss, ostracize. **3** *expel cooking smells* discharge, eject, eliminate, excrete, evacuate, belch, void, spew out.
Antonyms: ADMIT; WELCOME.

expend *verb* **1** *expend time and money on luxuries* spend, lay out, pay out, disburse, lavish, squander, waste, fritter, dissipate; *inf.* fork out, shell out, dish out. **2** *expend all one's ammunition/energy* use up, consume, exhaust, deplete, drain, sap, empty, finish off.

expendable *adjective workers considered expendable* dispensable, able/likely to be sacrificed, replaceable, nonessential, inessential, unimportant.

expenditure *noun* **1** *limit expenditure and save money* spending, outlay; outgoings, costs, expenses, payments. **2** *the expenditure of money on*

defense spending, outlay, disbursement, lavishing, squandering. *See* EXPEND 1. **3** *the expenditure of one's ammunition* using up, consumption, exhaustion, depletion, draining, sapping.
Antonyms: INCOME; CONSERVATION.

expense *noun* **1** *the expense of private schooling* cost, price, charge, outlay, fee, amount, rate, figure, quotation. **2** *the expense of time, energy, and money* spending, outlay, laying out, paying out, disbursement, lavishing, squandering. *See* EXPEND 1. **3** *victory at the expense of lives* cost, sacrifice.

expensive *adjective expensive clothes/tastes* costly, high-priced, exorbitant, overpriced, lavish, extravagant; *inf.* steep.
Antonyms: CHEAP; ECONOMICAL.

experience *noun* **1** *a frightening/wonderful experience* event, incident, occurrence, happening, affair, episode, adventure, encounter, circumstance, case, test, trial, ordeal. **2** *experience more valuable than a college degree* skill, practical knowledge, practice, training, learning, understanding, wisdom, maturity; *inf.* knowhow. **experience of** *experience of teaching | experience of prison life* involvement in, practice of, participation in, contact with, familiarity with, acquaintance with, exposure to, observation of.
Antonyms: INEXPERIENCE; NAÏVETÉ.

experience *verb experience hardship | experience great happiness* have experience of, undergo, encounter, meet, feel, know, become familiar with, come into contact with, face, participate in, live/go through, sustain, suffer.

experienced *adjective* **1** *experienced workers* having experience, practiced, accomplished, skillful, proficient, seasoned, trained, expert, adept, competent, capable, hnowledgeable, qualified, well-versed, professional, mature, master, veteran. **2** *an experienced woman, not an innocent girl* worldly-wise, sophisticated, knowing, mature, worldly, initiated; *inf.* having been around.
Antonyms: NOVICE; untrained; NAÏVE.

experiment *noun* **1** *medical experiments with rats* test, investigation, trial, trial run, tryout, examination, observation, inquiry, questioning, pilot study, demonstration, venture. **2** *results obtained by experiment* research, experimentation, observation, trial and error, tryout, analysis, testing.

experiment *verb experiment on animals | experiment with new methods* conduct experiments, carry out trials/tests, conduct research; test, investigate, examine, explore, observe.

experimental *adjective experimental basis/stage* trial, test, trial and error, exploratory, empirical, investigational, observational, pilot, tentative, speculative, preliminary, probationary, at the trial stage, under review, under the microscope, on the drawing board.

expert *noun an expert on ancient Rome | experts at playing golf* authority, past master, specialist, professional, adept, pundit, maestro, virtuoso, wizard, connoisseur; *inf.* old hand, ace, buff, pro.

expert *adjective an expert tennis player* skillful, experienced, practiced, qualified, knowledgeable, specialist, professional, proficient, adept, master, masterly, brilliant, accomplished, able, deft, dexterous, adroit, apt, capable, competent, clever, well-versed, *au fait; inf.* ace, crack, top-notch.

Antonyms: INEXPERT; AMATEUR.

expertise *noun* skill, skillfulness, mastery, proficiency, knowledge, command, professionalism, deftness, dexterity, facility, ability, knack, capability, competence, cleverness; *inf.* know-how.

expiate *verb expiate his wrongdoing* atone for, make amends for, make up for, do penance for, pay for, redress, make redress/reparation for, make recompense for.

expiation *noun* atonement, redemption, penance, redress, reparation, recompense; amends.

expiration *noun the expiration of the contract* finish, end, termination, conclusion, discontinuation, cessation, lapse, expiration, invalidity.

expire *verb* **1** *your license has expired | your contract expires in May* be no longer valid, run out, finish, end, come to an end, terminate, conclude, discontinue, stop, cease, lapse. **2** *the patient expired at midnight* die, pass away/on, decease, depart this life, perish, breathe one's last, meet one's Maker, give up the ghost, go to the great beyond, cross the great divide; *inf.* kick the bucket.

explain *verb* **1** *explain the procedure* give an explanation of, describe, define, make clear/plain/intelligible, spell out, interpret, unfold, clarify, throw light on, clear up, decipher, decode, elucidate, expound, explicate, delineate, demonstrate, teach, illustrate, expose, resolve, solve. **2** *explain their actions* give an explanation for, account for, give a reason/justification for, justify, give an excuse/alibi for, defend, vindicate, mitigate.

explanation *noun* **1** *the explanation of the procedure* description, definition, interpretation, clarification, deciphering, decoding, elucidation, expounding, explication, demonstration, illustration, exposure, resolution, solution. **2** *an explanation of their motives* account, justification, reason, excuse, defense, vindication, mitigation, apologia.

explanatory *adjective* by way of explanation, descriptive, illustrative, interpretive, demonstrative, illuminative, elucidative, elucidatory, explicative, expository.

expletive *noun* swearword, oath, curse, obscenity, epithet, exclamation; *inf.* dirty word, four-letter word, cussword.

explicable *adjective* explainable, accountable, definable, understandable, interpretable, intelligible, ascertainable, resolvable, soluble.

explicate *verb* **1** *explicate a literary text* explain, explain in detail, make explicit, clarify, make plain/clear, spell out, interpret, elucidate, illuminate, expound, unfold, untangle, put into plain English. **2** *explicate an idea* develop, evolve, work out, construct, formulate, devise, build, concoct, assemble.

explicit *adjective* **1** *explicit instructions* clearly expressed, easily understandable, detailed, clear, crystal-clear, direct, plain, obvious, precise, exact, straightforward, definite, distinct, categorical, specific, positive, unequivocal, unambiguous. **2** *explicit criticism | explicit sexual description* outspoken, unrestrained, unreserved, uninhibited, open, candid, frank, forthright, direct, plainspoken, point-blank, full-frontal, no holds barred.

Antonyms: VAGUE; IMPLICIT; INDIRECT.

explode *verb* **1** *the fireworks/boiler exploded* blow up, detonate, burst, fly apart, fly into pieces, go off, erupt; *inf.* go bang. **2** *explode the fireworks* detonate, set off, let off, fire off. **3** *explode in anger* give vent to, blow up, rage, rant and rave, storm; *inf.* fly off the handle, hit the roof, blow one's cool/top, blow a fuse, flip one's lid, freak out. **4** *explode a myth* disprove, invalidate, refute, repudiate, discredit, debunk, belie. **5** *world population exploding* increase suddenly/rapidly/dramatically, mushroom, escalate, burgeon, rocket, accelerate, heighten.

exploit *noun* feat, deed, adventure, stunt, achievement, accomplishment, attainment.

exploit *verb* **1** *exploit natural resources* make use of, put to use, utilize, use, use to good advantage, turn/put to good use, turn to account, profit from/by, capitalize on; *inf.* cash in on, milk. **2** *exploit the workers | exploit his good nature* make use of, take advantage of, abuse, impose upon, play upon, misuse; *inf.* walk all over, walk over, take for a ride.

exploration *noun* **1** *the exploration of space | a voyage of exploration* investigation, study, survey, research, inspection, probe, examination, scrutiny, observation, search, inquiry, analysis. **2** *conduct an exploration into the interior of the continent* expedition, trip, tour, survey, reconnaissance; travels.

exploratory *adjective* investigative, probing, fact-finding, analytic, experimental, trial, searching.

explore *verb* **1** *explore the Antarctic* travel, traverse, tour, range over, survey, take a look at, inspect, scout, reconnoiter, prospect. **2** *explore several possible solutions* investigate, look into, inquire into, consider, examine, research, survey, scrutinize, study, review, take stock of.

explorer *noun* traveler, discoverer, tourer, surveyor, scout, reconnoiterer, prospector.

explosion *noun* **1** *a loud explosion* bang, blast, boom, rumble, crash, crack, report, thunder, roll, clap, detonation, discharge, eruption. **2**

an explosion of anger outburst, flare-up, fit, outbreak, paroxysm, eruption. **3** *an explosion of population* sudden/rapid/dramatic increase, mushrooming, escalation, burgeoning, rocketing, acceleration, heightening.

explosive *adjective* **1** *explosive substance* inflammable, volatile, eruptive, unstable. **2** *explosive temperament* fiery, angry, touchy, stormy, violent, vehement, volatile, volcanic. **3** *an explosive situation* tense, charged, critical, serious, inflammable, volcanic, dangerous, perilous, hazardous, ugly.

exponent *noun* **1** *an exponent of traditional teaching methods* advocate, supporter, upholder, backer, defender, champion, spokesperson, promoter, propagandist, proponent. **2** *an exponent lecturing on modern art* interpreter, commentator, expounder, explainer, expositor, elucidator, illustrator, demonstrator. **3** *a famous exponent of mime* practitioner, performer, player, interpreter, presenter. **4** *the finest extant exponent of cave painting* example, illustration, specimen, sample, type, exemplar, instance, model, representation.

export *verb* **1** *export goods* sell overseas/abroad, market overseas/abroad, send overseas/abroad. **2** *export ideas* transmit, spread.

Antonym: IMPORT.

expose *verb* **1** *expose the skin to sunlight* uncover, lay bare, bare, leave unprotected, strip, reveal, denude. **2** *expose to danger/abuse* lay open to, leave unprotected from, put at risk of, put in jeopardy of, make vulnerable to, make subject to, subject to; endanger, risk, hazard. **3** *expose one's ignorance* reveal, uncover, show, display, make obvious, exhibit, disclose, manifest, unveil. **4** *expose a crime/criminal* bring to light, disclose, uncover, reveal, make known, let out, divulge, unearth, unmask, detect, betray, smoke out; *inf.* spill the beans on, blow the whistle on. **5** *expose to new ideas* bring into contact with, introduce to, present with, make familiar/conversant/acquainted with, familiarize/acquaint with, make aware of. **expose oneself** display/reveal/show the genitalia; *inf.* flash.

Antonyms: COVER; PROTECT; CONCEAL.

exposé *noun* exposure, disclosure, investigative report, uncovering, revelation, divulgence.

exposed *adjective* *an exposed hillside* open, unprotected, without shelter/protection, unsheltered, open to the elements/weather.

exposition *noun* **1** *the exposition of modern educational theories* explanation, interpretation, description, elucidation, explication, illustration; *fml.* exegesis. **2** *give an exposition on how to start a business* explanation, account, description, commentary, study, treatise, discourse, dissertation, critique. **3** *an art exposition* exhibition, fair, display, show, presentation, demonstration; *inf.* expo, demo.

expository *adjective* *an expository statement of the theory* explanatory, interpretative, descriptive, elucidatory, explicatory, explicative, illustrative; *fml.* exegetic.

expostulate *verb* *expostulate with an opponent* remonstrate with, argue with, reason with, make a protest to, raise an objection with.

exposure *noun* **1** *the exposure of the skin to sunlight* uncovering, baring, stripping, revelation, denudation. **2** *exposure to danger/abuse* subjection/submission to, laying open to. *See* EXPOSE 2. **3** *exposure of one's ignorance* revelation, uncovering, showing, display, exhibition, disclosure, manifestation, unveiling. **4** *exposure of a crime/criminal* disclosure, uncovering, revelation, divulgence, denunciation, unmasking, detection, betrayal. *See* EXPOSE 4. **5** *exposure to new ideas* contact with, introduction/presentation to. *See* EXPOSE 5. **6** *resent the exposure given to the affair* publicity, publicizing, advertising, broadcasting, airing. **7** *a sunny exposure* position, setting, location, aspect, view, outlook, frontage.

expound *verb* **1** *expound one's views on education* explain, detail, spell out, set forth, describe, discuss. **2** *expound (on) the Scriptures* interpret, explain, give a commentary on, annotate, illustrate, explicate.

express *verb* **1** *express one's feelings in a speech* put into words, state, voice, give voice to, enunciate, communicate, utter, pronounce, articulate, verbalize, give vent to, word, proclaim, assert, point out, speak, say. **2** *express appreciation with a gift* show, indicate, demonstrate, convey, communicate, intimate, denote, exhibit, illustrate, manifest, make manifest, reveal, evince, evidence, symbolize, embody. **3** *express juice from fruit* press out, squeeze, extract, force out. **express oneself** communicate one's thoughts/opinions/views, put thoughts into words, speak one's mind, say one's piece.

express *adjective* **1** *express service* rapid, swift, fast, quick, speedy, prompt, high-speed, brisk, expeditious, direct, nonstop. **2** *express instructions* explicit, clear, plain, distinct, unambiguous, precise, specific, well-defined, unmistakable, unequivocal, pointed, exact, outright. **3** *done with the express purpose of embarrassing them* particular, sole, purposeful, special, especial, specific, singular.

expression *noun* **1** *public expression of grievances* statement, voicing, uttering, utterance, pronouncement, articulation, verbalization, venting, wording, proclamation, assertion. **2** *send flowers as an expression of appreciation* indication, demonstration, show, conveyance, communication, intimation, exhibition, illustration, manifestation, revelation, embodiment. **3** *a particularly apt expression* word, phrase, term, choice of words, wording, language, phrasing, phraseology; speech, diction, idiom, style, delivery, intonation, execution; *fml.*

locution. **4** *a sad expression on her face* look, appearance, air, countenance, aspect; *fml.* mien. **5** *playing the piano with expression* feeling, emotion, passion, intensity, poignancy, artistry, depth, spirit, vividness, ardor, power, force, imagination.

expressionless *adjective* **1** *expressionless reading of poetry* dull, dry, boring, wooden, undemonstrative, apathetic, unimpassioned, weak, devoid of feeling/emotion. **2** *a totally expressionless face* blank, deadpan; *inf.* poker-faced, inscrutable, emotionless, vacuous.

expressive *adjective* **1** *an expressive face/gesture* full of emotion/feeling, indicating emotion/feeling, emotional, eloquent, telling, demonstrative, suggestive, vivid. **2** *an expressive piece of music* emotional, eloquent, passionate, intense, poignant, moving, striking, evocative, sympathetic, artistic, vivid, graphic, ardent, powerful, imaginative. **3** *expressive of their contempt* showing, indicative, demonstrating, demonstrative, suggesting, revealing, underlining.
Antonyms: EXPRESSIONLESS; INEXPRESSIVE; UNEMOTIONAL.

expressly *adverb* **1** *expressly forbidden* absolutely, explicitly, clearly, plainly, distinctly, precisely, specifically, unequivocally. **2** *laws expressly made to stop vandalism* purposefully, particularly, solely, specially, especially, specifically, singularly.

expropriate *verb* seize, take away, take over, take, appropriate, take possession of, misappropriate, requisition, commandeer, impound, confiscate, usurp, assume.

expulsion *noun* **1** *expulsion from school* removal, eviction, ejection, banishment, debarment, dismissal, discharge; *inf.* sacking. **2** *the expulsion of waste materials* ejection, discharge, elimination, excretion, voiding, voidance, evacuation.

expunge *verb* erase, remove, rub out, wipe out, cross out, strike out, delete, eradicate, cancel, blot out, efface, destroy, obliterate, annul, extinguish, abolish, annihilate.

expurgate *verb* bowdlerize, censor, blue-pencil, clean up, purge, purify.

exquisite *adjective* **1** *exquisite skin/grace* beautiful, lovely, delicate, fragile, elegant, fine, subtle, ethereal. **2** *exquisite taste* discriminating, discerning, sensitive, selective, refined, cultivated, cultured, appreciative, educated, fastidious, impeccable, polished, consummate. **3** *exquisite pain* intense, acute, keen, piercing, sharp, excruciating, poignant.

extant *adjective* still existing, in existence, living, alive, surviving, remaining, undestroyed, subsisting, present, existent.
Antonyms: EXTINCT; DEAD.

extemporaneous, extemporary *adjective* *an extemporaneous vote of thanks* extempore, impromptu, spontaneous, ad lib, improvised, unrehearsed, unplanned, unprepared, un-

premeditated; *inf.* off the cuff; *fml.* improvisatory.

extemporaneous
impromptu, improvised, impulsive, offhand, spontaneous, unpremeditated
If you're the kind of person who acts first and thinks about it later, your friends are likely to describe you as **spontaneous**, which means that you behave in a very natural way, without prompting or premeditation (*a spontaneous embrace*; *a spontaneous burst of applause*). Or they may call you **impulsive**, which has somewhat less positive connotations, suggesting someone who is governed by his or her own moods and whims without regard for others. Although *impulsive* behavior may be admirable (*his impulsive generosity prompted him to empty his pockets*), it is just as likely to be ugly or disruptive (*impulsive buying*; *an impulsive temper*). **Offhand** also has negative overtones, implying behavior that is spontaneous to the point of being cavalier or brusque (*her offhand remarks offended them*). **Unpremeditated** is a more formal term, often used in a legal context to describe an impulsive crime committed without forethought (*unpremeditated murder*). In the world of public speaking, an **extemporaneous** speech is one that is delivered without referring to a written text, although the speaker may have been aware that he or she would be called upon to speak, while an **impromptu** speech is one that the speaker was not expecting to give. **Improvised** is often used in the context of a musical or theatrical performance, suggesting a basic structure within which the performers are free to play in a spontaneous manner (*by its very nature, jazz is improvised*). But it has broader applications as well; in fact, anything that is devised on the spur of the moment may be described as *improvised*.

extempore *adjective* *an extempore speech* impromptu, spontaneous, ad lib, improvised, unrehearsed, unplanned, unprepared, extemporaneous; *inf.* off the cuff, off the top of one's head.

extempore *adverb* *he spoke extempore* ad lib, spontaneously, extemporaneously; *inf.* off the cuff.

extemporize *verb* improvise, ad lib, play it by ear, think on one's feet. *See* EXTEMPORE *adjective.*

extend *verb* **1** *extend the territory/ladder* expand, increase, enlarge; lengthen, widen, broaden, stretch, stretch out, draw out, elongate. **2** *extend the scope of the law* widen, increase, add to, expand, broaden, enlarge, augment, amplify, supplement, enhance, develop. **3** *extend the period of credit* prolong, increase, lengthen, stretch out, protract, drag out. **4** *extend one's arms* stretch out, reach out, spread out, straighten out, unroll, unfurl. **5** *extend a*

welcome offer, give, grant, proffer, present, confer, hold out, advance, impart, put forth, reach out. **6** *the road extends for many miles* continue, stretch, stretch out, carry on, run on, last, unroll, unfurl, unfold, range.
Antonyms: DECREASE; CONTRACT; NARROW; CURTAIL.

extended *adjective* **1** *extended contract | extended hours* longer lasting, prolonged, increased, lengthened, elongated, protracted. **2** *met them with extended arms* stretched out, outstretched, spread out, unrolled, unfurled, unfolded.

extension *noun* **1** *the extension of the territory/ladder* expansion, increase, enlargement; elongation. *See* EXTEND 1. **2** *the extension of a period of credit* prolongation, increase, lengthening, protraction. *See* EXTEND 3. **3** *an extension to the house/collection* annex, wing; addition, add-on, adjunct, addendum, augmentation, supplement, appendage. **4** *ask for an extension to complete an essay* more/extra time, increased time, additional time, a longer period.

extensive *adjective* **1** *extensive grounds around the house* large, large-scale, sizable, substantial, spacious, considerable, capacious, commodious, vast, immense. **2** *an extensive knowledge of the subject* comprehensive, thorough, complete, broad, wide, wide-ranging, all-inclusive, all-embracing, universal, boundless, catholic.
Antonyms: SMALL; LIMITED.

extent *noun* **1** *the full extent of the track/park* length, area, expanse, stretch, range, scope. **2** *the extent of her knowledge* coverage, breadth, range, scope, degree, comprehensiveness, thoroughness, all-inclusiveness, completeness.

extenuating *adjective* *extenuating circumstances* mitigating, palliating, palliative, justifying, moderating, qualifying.

exterior *noun* *the exterior of the building* outside, outside surface, outer/external surface, outward appearance/aspect, façade, covering, shell.
Antonyms: INTERIOR; INSIDE.

exterior *adjective* *the exterior layer* outer, outside, outermost, outward, external, surface, superficial.
Antonyms: INNER; INSIDE.

exterminate *verb* kill, destroy, eradicate, annihilate, eliminate, abolish, extirpate; *inf.* bump off.

external *adjective* **1** *an external wall* outer, outside, outward, exterior, surface, superficial, extraneous, extrinsic. **2** *external affairs* foreign, international, alien, overseas, outside.
Antonyms: INTERNAL; INNER; INSIDE.

extinct *adjective* **1** *an extinct species* died-out, defunct, no longer existing, vanished, wiped-out, gone, lost. **2** *an extinct volcano/fire* inactive, no longer active; extinguished, burnt out, quenched, put out, doused. **3** *extinct beliefs/*

passions dead, defunct, ended, terminated, obsolete, outmoded, out of date, antiquated.
Antonyms: EXTANT; ALIVE.

extinction *noun* dying out, death, vanishing, extinguishing, quenching, ending, termination.
See EXTINCT.

extinguish *verb* **1** *extinguish the light/fire* put out, blow out, quench, smother, douse, snuff out, stifle, choke. **2** *extinguish passion* destroy, kill, end, remove, annihilate, wipe out, eliminate, abolish, eradicate, erase, expunge, exterminate, extirpate, obscure, suppress.
Antonyms: LIGHT; KINDLE.

extol *verb* praise, praise highly, praise to the skies, sing the praises of, applaud, acclaim, pay tribute to, laud, eulogize about, exalt, commend, congratulate, celebrate, compliment, glorify, magnify.
Antonyms: CONDEMN; CRITICIZE.

extort *verb* *extort money | extort a confession* extract, force, exact, coerce, wring, wrest, squeeze, milk, obtain by blackmail; *inf.* put the screws to/on to obtain.

extortion *noun* *obtain money by extortion* force, coercion, compulsion, exaction, oppression, blackmail. *See* EXTORT.

extortionate *adjective* **1** *extortionate prices* exorbitant, excessive, outrageous, preposterous, immoderate, unreasonable, inordinate, inflated, sky-high. **2** *extortionate methods* exacting, grasping, bloodsucking, avaricious, rapacious, usurious, harsh, severe, rigorous, hard, oppressive.

extortionist, extortioner *noun* blackmailer, bloodsucker, exacter.

extra *adjective* **1** *extra money required* more, additional, further, supplementary, supplemental, added, auxiliary, ancillary, subsidiary, other, accessory. **2** *we always have extra food* spare, surplus, leftover, excess, superfluous, redundant, reserve, unused.

extra *adverb* **1** *try extra hard* especially, exceptionally, extremely, unusually, particularly, extraordinarily, uncommonly, remarkably; *inf.* with all the stops out. **2** *charge shipping and handling extra* in addition, as well, besides, over and above, on top, to boot.

extra *noun* **1** *an optional extra* addition, supplement, adjunct, addendum. **2** *movie extras* extra person/actor, supernumerary, walk-on.
Antonyms: NECESSITY; ESSENTIAL.

extract *verb* **1** *extract a tooth* draw out, pull out, remove, take out, pluck out, wrench out, tear out, uproot, withdraw, extirpate. **2** *extract money* extort, force, exact, elicit, coerce, wrest, wring, squeeze. **3** *extract juice* squeeze, press, express, distill, separate, take out. **4** *extract a section from a chapter* abstract, select, choose, reproduce, copy, quote, cite, cull. **5** *extract a principle* deduce, educe, derive, elicit, develop.

extract *noun* **1** *vanilla extract* concentrate, essence, distillate, juice, solution, decoction. **2** *extracts from newspapers* excerpt, passage, abstract, citation, selection, quotation, cutting, clipping, fragment.

extraction noun **1** *the extraction of a tooth* removal, drawing out, pulling out, uprooting, extirpation. *See* EXTRACT *verb* 1. **2** *extraction of money* extortion, exacting, wresting. *See* EXTRACT *verb* 2. **3** *extraction of juice* squeezing, expressing, distillation, separation. **4** *Irish by extraction* descent, ancestry, parentage, lineage, blood, derivation, origin, race.

extradite verb *extradite a criminal* deport, expel, banish, exile, outlaw.

extradition noun deportation, expulsion, banishment, exile, outlawing.

extraneous adjective **1** *extraneous forces* external, outside, exterior, extrinsic, alien, foreign. **2** *extraneous material* irrelevant, immaterial, inapplicable, inapt, inappropriate, inapposite, unrelated, unconnected, off the subject, peripheral, beside the point, wide of the mark, not pertinent, not germane.

extraordinary adjective **1** *extraordinary talent* exceptional, unusual, uncommon, rare, unique, singular, signal, peculiar, unprecedented, outstanding, striking, remarkable, phenomenal, marvelous, wonderful; *inf.* fabulous. **2** *how extraordinary that we met* amazing, surprising, strange, unusual, remarkable, astounding, curious. **3** *an extraordinary color combination* odd, weird, strange, curious, bizarre, unconventional.

Antonyms: ORDINARY; COMMONPLACE.

extravagance noun **1** *extravagance leading to debt* spendthrift behavior/ways, squandering, overspending, profligacy, prodigality, wastefulness, lavishness, recklessness, excess. **2** *the extravagance of his compliments* excessiveness, exaggeration, exaggeratedness, unreservedness, outrageousness, immoderation, preposterousness, absurdity, irrationality, recklessness, wildness; excess, overkill, lack of restraint/reserve. **3** *extravagance of the prices/clothes* exorbitance, excessiveness, expensiveness, unreasonableness, immoderation; costliness; *inf.* steepness.

extravagant adjective **1** *extravagant way of life* spendthrift, squandering, thriftless, profligate, prodigal, improvident, wasteful, lavish, reckless, imprudent, excessive. **2** *extravagant compliments* excessive, exaggerated, unrestrained, unreserved, outrageous, immoderate, preposterous, absurd, irrational, reckless, wild. **3** *extravagant prices/clothes* exorbitant, excessive, extortionate, unreasonable, immoderate, inordinate; expensive, costly, overpriced; *inf.* steep.

Antonyms: THRIFTY; RESTRAINED; CHEAP.

extravaganza noun spectacle, pageant, spectacular/impressive show/display.

extreme adjective **1** *in extreme danger | extreme cold* utmost, uttermost, maximum, supreme, greatest, great, acute, intense, severe, highest, high, ultimate, exceptional, extraordinary. **2**

extreme punitive measures harsh, severe, draconian, stringent, stern, strict, drastic, unrelenting, relentless, unbending, unyielding, uncompromising, unmitigated, radical, overzealous. **3** *a person of extreme views | an extreme radical* immoderate, intemperate, fanatical, exaggerated, excessive, overzealous, outrageous, inordinate, unreasonable. **4** *on the extreme edge | in the extreme south* outermost, farthest, most remote, remotest, most distant, outlying, far-off, faraway, ultimate, last, endmost, final, terminal.

Antonyms: MODERATE; MILD; NEAR.

extreme noun **1** *the extremes of heat/wrath* highest/greatest degree, maximum, height, ultimate, zenith, pinnacle, climax, acme, apex. **2** *the extremes of bliss and despair* opposite, pole, contrary, counter, contradiction, antonym. **in the extreme** *generous in the extreme* extremely, exceedingly, exceptionally, excessively, extravagantly, inordinately.

extremely adverb very, exceedingly, exceptionally, intensely, greatly, acutely, utterly, excessively, inordinately, extraordinarily, markedly, uncommonly, severely; *inf.* awfully, terribly.

extremist noun radical, fanatic, zealot, die-hard, ultra.

extremity noun **1** *the extremities of the territory* limit, outer limit, farthest point, end, boundary, bound, border, frontier, edge, margin, termination, periphery, verge, brink, horizon. **2** *frostbite of the extremities* limb, appendage, digit; arm, leg, hand, foot, finger, toe. **3** *the extremity of the heat* the greatest/highest degree, extreme, maximum degree, intensity, acuteness, excess, zenith, pinnacle, top, acme, apex; *fml.* apogee. **4** *help the poor in their extremity* hardship, adversity, trouble, misfortune, plight, destitution, indigence, exigency; crisis, emergency, setback; dire straits, hard times.

extricate verb *extricate oneself/someone from a difficult situation* extract, free, release, disentangle, get out, remove, withdraw, let loose, detach, disengage, liberate, rescue, save, disencumber, deliver; *inf.* get off the hook.

extrinsic adjective **1** *extrinsic influence* extraneous, external, exterior, outside, outward, alien, foreign, not intrinsic. **2** *extrinsic information* extraneous, irrelevant, immaterial, inapplicable, inapt, inappropriate, inapposite, unrelated, unconnected, off the subject, peripheral, beside the point, wide of the mark, not pertinent, not germane.

extrovert, extroverted adjective outgoing, outwardly directed, sociable, socializing, social, friendly, people-oriented, lively, cheerful, effervescent, exuberant.

Antonyms: INTROVERTED; INTROSPECTIVE.

extrovert noun outgoing person, socializer, mixer, mingler, life of the party.

extrude verb **1** *extrude glue from a tube* force out, thrust out, press out, squeeze out, eject, expel. **2** *a branch extruding from the tree* protrude, project, jut out, stick out, poke out, extend, hang out.

exuberant *adjective* **1** *exuberant with joy at winning* elated, animated, exhilarated, lively, high-spirited, spirited, buoyant, cheerful, sparkling, full of life, effervescent, vivacious, excited, ebullient, exultant, enthusiastic, irrepressible, energetic, vigorous, zestful; *inf.* bouncy, upbeat. **2** *exuberant expressions of thanks* effusive, lavish, fulsome, exaggerated, unreserved, unrestrained, unlimited, wholehearted, generous, excessive, superfluous, prodigal. **3** *exuberant foliage* profuse, luxuriant, lush, thriving, abundant, superabundant, prolific, teeming, lavish, copious, rich, plentiful, abounding, overflowing, rank.

Antonyms: DEPRESSED; RESTRAINED; MEAGER.

exude *verb* **1** *sweat exuding through the pores* ooze, seep, filter, filtrate, leak, discharge, trickle, drip, issue. **2** *exuding beads of sweat* ooze, secrete, excrete, discharge, emit, issue, emanate, give out, pour out, gush, jet. **3** *exuding confidence* ooze, give out, give forth, send out, issue, emit, emanate, display.

exult *verb* **1** *exult at/in his sister's success* rejoice, be overjoyed, be joyful, be jubilant, be elated, be delighted, be ecstatic, jump for joy, revel, be in ecstasy, be on cloud nine, be in seventh heaven. **2** *exulting over their opponents* triumph, gloat, crow.

exultant *adjective* exulting, rejoicing, overjoyed, joyful, jubilant, elated, triumphant, delighted, ecstatic, gleeful, enraptured, transported.

exultation *noun* rejoicing, joy, jubilation, elation, exhilaration, delight, ecstasy, glee, rapture, triumph, glory.

eye *noun* **1** *injury to the eye* organ of sight, eyeball; *inf.* peeper; *lit.* orb. **2** *have a sharp eye* eyesight, vision, sight, observation; powers of observation. **3** *an eye for art* appreciation, perception, discernment, discrimination, taste, judgment, recognition, awareness, sensitivity. **4** *keep an eye on | under her mother's eagle eye* watch, observance, lookout; observation, surveillance, vigilance, view, notice. **5** *to my eye/in my eyes they are guilty* estimation, opinion, view, point of view, judgment, belief, viewpoint, mind. **6** *eye of the needle* hole, aperture, perforation, eyelet. **7** *the eye of a daisy* center, middle, heart, kernel, hub. **see eye to eye** agree, be in agreement/accord, concur, be on the same wavelength, get along. **up to one's eyes** fully occupied, very busy, engrossed, engaged, overwhelmed, inundated, caught up, wrapped up; *inf.* up to here.

eye *verb* **1** *eye with longing* look at, gaze at, stare at, contemplate, study, survey, view, inspect, scrutinize, scan, glance at, regard, behold; *inf.* eyeball. **2** *eye the girls* ogle, leer at, make eyes at; *inf.* give the eye to.

eye-catching *adjective* striking, arresting, spectacular, captivating, attractive, showy.

eyeful *noun* **1** *get an eyeful of that* look, good look, stare, gaze, view; *inf.* gander, load. **2** *the model is quite an eyeful* vision, dream, beauty, dazzler; *inf.* stunner, good-looker, knockout, sight for sore eyes.

eyesight *noun* sight, vision, range of vision, observation, perception.

eyesore *noun* blemish, blot, scar, blight, disfigurement, defacement, defect, monstrosity, carbuncle, atrocity, disgrace, ugliness; *inf.* sight.

eyewitness *noun* witness, observer, onlooker, bystander, spectator, watcher, viewer, beholder, passerby; *inf.* rubberneck.

F

fable *noun* **1** *a fable about a fox* tale, fairy tale, moral tale, parable. **2** *heroes in Norse fables* story, legend, myth, traditional story, saga, epic, lay. **3** *children telling fables* lie, untruth, falsehood, white lie, fib, piece of fiction, fabrication, invention, story, fairy tale/story, cock-and-bull story, figment of the imagination, fantasy; *inf.* tall story, yarn.

fabric *noun* **1** *made of a silky fabric* cloth, material, textile, stuff, web. **2** *the fabric of the building | the fabric of society* framework, frame, structure, makeup, constitution, essence.

fabricate *verb* **1** *fabricate the furniture from components* assemble, construct, build, erect, put together, make, form, frame, fashion, shape, manufacture, produce. **2** *fabricate a reason for lateness* make up, invent, think up, concoct, hatch, trump up, devise, formulate. **3** *fabricate a document* forge, falsify, fake, counterfeit.

fabulous *adjective* **1** *of fabulous wealth* incredible, unbelievable, inconceivable, unimaginable, astounding, amazing, astonishing, breathtaking, prodigious, phenomenal, remarkable, extraordinary, tremendous; *inf.* legendary. **2** *a fabulous time at the party* marvelous, wonderful, great, superb, spectacular; *inf.* fab, fantastic, super, super-duper, out of this world. **3** *fabulous creatures* mythical, imaginary, legendary, fantastical, fictitious, fictional, made-up, invented, unreal, hypothetical, apocryphal.

façade *noun* **1** *the façade of the building* front, frontage, face, exterior, outside. **2** *a façade of friendliness* show, appearance, guise, semblance, mask, veneer, masquerade, camouflage, pretense, illusion.

face *noun* **1** *a beautiful face* countenance, visage, physiognomy; features; *inf.* mug, kisser. **2** *with a furious face* expression, look, air, demeanor, aspect. **3** *what a face! | make a face* scowl, grimace, frown, pout, moue. **4** *the face of the building* front, frontage, façade. *See* FAÇADE 1. **5** *face of a diamond* facet, side, plane, surface. **6** *the face of the countryside* outward appearance, appearance, aspect, air. **7** *put a brave/bold face on it* appearance, façade, display, show, exterior, guise, mask, veneer, camouflage, pretense. **8** *lose face* prestige, standing, status, dignity, honor, respect, image. **9** *have the face to turn up* audacity, effrontery, impudence, impertinence, cheek, boldness, presumption, temerity; *inf.* nerve, gall. **face to face** facing, confronting, opposing, conflicting; *inf.* eyeball to eyeball. **on the face of it** from appearances, to all appearances, so it appears/seems, so it would appear/seem, apparently, seemingly.

face *verb* **1** *buildings facing the sea* look toward, look onto, overlook, be opposite to. **2** *the problems facing us* confront, present itself, meet, be in the way of, stand in the way of. **3** *face rejection/reality* encounter, meet, come across, be confronted by, come up against, experience; face up to, come to terms with, accept, confront, meet head-on, cope with, deal with, come to grips with. **4** *face criticism/danger* encounter, meet, face out, meet head-on, confront, dare, brave, defy, oppose, resist, withstand. **5** *face the collar of the coat* put a facing on, cover, line. **6** *face stone* dress, finish, polish, smooth, level, coat, cover, surface, clad, veneer. **face up to** face, come to terms with, accept, confront, cope with. *See* FACE *verb* 4.
Antonyms: EVADE; DODGE.

facet *noun* **1** *one facet of the problem* aspect, angle, side, slant, feature, characteristic, factor, element, point, part, phase. **2** *facet of a gem* side, plane, surface, face.

facetious *adjective* jocular, flippant, playful, frivolous, lighthearted, nonserious, funny, amusing, humorous, comical, comic, joking, jesting, witty, droll, whimsical, tongue-in-cheek, waggish, jocose.
Antonyms: SERIOUS; GRAVE.

facile *adjective* *facile tasks* easy, simple, uncomplicated, unchallenging.

facilitate *verb* make easy/easier, ease, make smooth/smoother, smooth, smooth the path of, assist, help, aid, expedite, speed up, accelerate, forward, advance, promote, further, encourage.
Antonyms: HINDER; OBSTRUCT.

facilities *plural noun* rest room, toilet, lavatory, men's room, ladies' room, convenience; *inf.* john, can, head.

facility *noun* **1** *perform the task with facility* ease, effortlessness, smoothness, absence/lack of difficulty. **2** *facility of expression* ease, smoothness, fluency, eloquence, articulateness, slickness, glibness. **3** *a facility for wood carving* skill, skillfulness, dexterity, adroitness, adeptness, deftness, aptitude, ability, gift, talent, expertise, expertness, knack, proficiency, bent, readiness. **4** *a research facility | excellent facilities for a conference* establishment, structure, building, buildings, complex, system, plant; resource; equipment.

facing *noun* **1** *the facing of a jacket* lining,

interfacing, reinforcement. **2** *the facing of the building* façade, front, surface, fronting, false front, coating, covering, cladding, veneer, protective/decorative layer, overlay, stucco, revetment.

facsimile *noun* copy, replica, reproduction, duplicate, carbon, carbon copy, photocopy, transcript, reprint, clone, image; fax; *Trademark* Xerox, Photostat.

fact *noun* **1** *fact, not rumor* actuality, reality, certainty, factuality, certitude; truth, naked truth, gospel. **2** *do not omit a single fact* detail, particular, point, item, piece of information/data, factor, feature, element, component, circumstance, specific. *See* FACTS. **3** *charged with being an accessory after the fact* happening, occurrence, incident, event, act, deed. **in fact** *in fact he's gone already* actually, in point of fact, indeed, in truth, in reality.

Antonyms: UNTRUTH; FALSEHOOD; FICTION.

faction *noun* **1** *the younger faction | a more radical faction* sector, section, group, side, party, band, set, ring, division, contingent, lobby, camp, bloc, clique, coalition, confederacy, coterie, caucus, cabal, junta, splinter group, pressure group, minority (group); *inf.* gang, crew. **2** *a club full of faction* infighting, dissension, discord, strife, contention, conflict, friction, argument, difference of opinion, disagreement, controversy, quarreling, division, divisiveness, clashing, disharmony, disunity, variance, rupture, tumult, turbulence, upheaval, dissidence, rebellion, insurrection, sedition, mutiny, schism.

factious *adjective* dissenting, contentious, discordant, conflicting, argumentative, disagreeing, disputatious, quarreling, quarrelsome, divisive, clashing, warring, at variance, at loggerheads, at odds, disharmonious, tumultuous, turbulent, dissident, rebellious, insurrectionary, seditious, mutinous, schismatic, sectarian, partisan.

factor *noun* element, part, component, ingredient, constituent, point, detail, item, facet, aspect, feature, characteristic, consideration, influence, circumstance, thing, determinant.

factory *noun* manufacturing building/complex, plant; works; workshop, mill, foundry.

factotum *noun* handyman, jack-of-all-trades, man Friday, girl Friday; servant.

facts *plural noun* *the police just want the facts* information, whole story; details, data; *inf.* info, low-down, poop, word, score, dope.

factual *adjective* *a factual account* fact-based, realistic, real, true to life, circumstantial, true, truthful, accurate, authentic, genuine, sure, veritable, exact, precise, strict, honest, faithful, literal, matter-of-fact, verbatim, word for word, unbiased, objective, unprejudiced, unvarnished, unadorned, unadulterated, unexaggerated.

Antonyms: UNTRUE; FICTITIOUS; UNREAL.

faculties *plural noun* *old people in possession of all their faculties* powers, capabilities, senses, wits; reason, intelligence.

faculty *noun* **1** *the faculty of speech* power, capability, capacity, attribute, property. **2** *a faculty for learning languages* aptitude, ability, facility, flair, gift, talent, bent, knack, disposition, proficiency, readiness, skill, dexterity, adroitness. **3** *the faculty approved the decision to extend the school year* teaching staff, teachers, professors. **4** *the Church conferring the faculty to conduct marriage services* authorization, license, power, right, prerogative, privilege, permission, sanction.

fad *noun* craze, mania, rage, enthusiasm, fancy, passing fancy, whim, vogue, fashion, trend, mode.

fade *verb* **1** *the curtains/color faded* lose color, become pale/paler, grow pale, pale, become bleached, become washed out, dull, dim, grow dull/dim, lose luster. **2** *time had faded the colors* pale, bleach, whiten, wash out, dull, discolor, decolorize, dim. **3** *flowers fading* wither, wilt, die, droop, shrivel, decay. **4** *light/hope fading* grow less, dim, die away, dwindle, grow faint, fail, wane, disappear, vanish, die, decline, dissolve, peter out, melt away, evanesce. **5** *the Roman empire was fading* die out, diminish, decline, fail, deteriorate, degenerate. *See* FAIL *verb* 9.

Antonyms: THRIVE; INCREASE.

fail *verb* **1** *their attempt failed* not succeed, be unsuccessful, lack success, fall through, fall flat, break down, abort, miscarry, be defeated, suffer defeat, be in vain, be frustrated, collapse, founder, misfire, meet with disaster, come to grief, come to nothing/naught, fizzle out, miss the mark, run aground, go astray; *inf.* flop, come a cropper, bite the dust. **2** *fail the exam | failed twice* not pass, be unsuccessful, be found wanting/deficient/defective, not make the grade, not pass muster, be rejected; *inf.* flunk. **3** *fail to understand/attend* be unable; neglect, forget. **4** *fail them in their hour of need* let down, neglect, desert, forsake, abandon, disappoint. **5** *the crops failed* be insufficient, be inadequate, be deficient, be wanting, be lacking, fall short. **6** *the light/hope failing* fade, grow less, dim, die away, dwindle, wane, disappear, vanish, peter out, dissolve. *See* FADE 4. **7** *the engine failed* break down, stop working, cease to function; *inf.* conk out. **8** *the old man is failing* grow weak/weaker, become feeble, lose strength, flag, become ill, sink. **9** *her health failed* decline, go into decline, fade, diminish, dwindle, wane, ebb, deteriorate, sink, collapse, pass, decay, crumble, degenerate. **10** *his business failed* collapse, crash, smash, go under, go to the wall, go bankrupt, become insolvent, go into receivership, cease trading, be closed, close down; *inf.* fold, flop, go bust/broke.

Antonyms: SUCCEED; INCREASE; THRIVE.

fail *noun* failure, nonsuccess. *See* FAILURE 1. **without fail** for certain, certainly, with certainty, definitely, whatever happens.

failing *noun* *tardiness is his failing* fault, shortcoming, weakness, weak spot, imperfection, defect, flaw, blemish, frailty, foible, drawback. *Antonyms:* STRENGTH; FORTE; ASSET.

failure *noun* **1** *the failure of their attempt* nonsuccess, lack of success, nonfulfillment, abortion, miscarriage, defeat, frustration, collapse, foundering, misfiring, coming to nothing, fizzling out. *See* FAIL *verb* 1. **2** *their plan was a failure* vain attempt, abortion, defeat, fiasco, debacle, botch, blunder; *inf.* flop, washout. **3** *he sees himself as a failure since losing his job* incompetent, loser, nonachiever, ne'er-do-well, disappointment; *inf.* flop, dud, washout. **4** *failure to attend | failure in the line of duty* omission, neglect; negligence, remissness, nonobservance, nonperformance, dereliction, delinquency. **5** *the failure of the crops* insufficiency, inadequacy, deficiency, lack, dearth, scarcity, shortfall. **6** *the failure of the light* fading, lessening, dimming, waning, vanishing. *See* FAIL *verb* 6. **7** *the failure of the engine* breaking down, nonfunction; *inf.* conking out. **8** *the failure of his health* failing, decline, fading, dwindling, waning, sinking, deterioration, collapse, breakdown, loss, decay, crumbling, degeneration. **9** *the failure of his business* collapse, crashing, going under, bankruptcy, ruin, ruination; *inf.* folding, flop. *Antonyms:* SUCCESS; TRIUMPH.

faint *adjective* **1** *a faint mark | faint traces* indistinct, unclear, dim, obscure, pale, faded, bleached. **2** *a faint noise* indistinct, scarcely audible/perceptible, vague, low, soft, muted, muffled, stifled, subdued, weak, feeble, whispered. **3** *a faint chance of success* slight, small, remote, vague, minimal. **4** *a faint response | faint praise* weak, feeble, unenthusiastic, half-hearted, low-key. **5** *feeling faint* giddy, dizzy, light-headed, weak-headed, weak; *inf.* woozy. *Antonyms:* CLEAR; LOUD; GREAT; STRONG.

faint *verb* *faint from loss of blood* lose consciousness, black out, pass out, collapse; *inf.* keel over, conk out; *lit.* swoon.

faint *noun* *fall over in a faint* loss of consciousness, blackout, collapse; *lit.* swoon; *Med.* syncope.

faint-hearted *adjective* timid, timorous, fearful, spiritless, weak, cowardly, unmanly, lily-livered; *inf.* chickenhearted, yellow.

faintly *adverb* **1** *not faintly amusing* slightly, remotely, vaguely, somewhat, a little, in the least. **2** *call faintly* indistinctly, softly, weakly, feebly, in a whisper, in subdued tones.

fair *adjective* **1** *a fair trial* just, impartial, unbiased, unprejudiced, objective, evenhanded, dispassionate, disinterested, detached, equitable, aboveboard, lawful, legal, legitimate, proper, square; *inf.* on the level. **2** *a fair person* fair-minded, just, impartial, unbiased, unprej-

udiced, open-minded, honest, upright, honorable, trustworthy, aboveboard. **3** *fair weather* fine, dry, bright, clear, sunny, cloudless, unclouded. **4** *fair winds* favorable, advantageous, helpful, beneficial. **5** *fair hair* blond/blonde, yellow, flaxen, light brown, strawberry blond, fair-haired, light-haired, flaxen-haired, tow-headed. **6** *fair skin* pale, light-colored, white, cream-colored, creamy, peaches and cream, chalky. **7** *fair maidens* beautiful, pretty, lovely, attractive, good-looking, comely; *lit.* beauteous. **8** *a fair number of people | a fair chance of winning* reasonable, passable, tolerable, satisfactory, respectable, decent, all right, pretty good, not bad, moderate, so-so, average, fair-to-middling, ample, adequate, sufficient. *Antonyms:* UNFAIR; DARK; UGLY.

fair *noun* *a job/agricultural fair* exhibition, display, show, exhibit, exposition; *inf.* expo.

fairly *adverb* **1** *treated fairly* justly, equitably, impartially, without prejudice, objectively, evenhandedly, properly, lawfully, legally, legitimately. **2** *fairly good* quite, reasonably, passably, tolerably, satisfactorily, moderately, rather, somewhat, adequately; *inf.* pretty. **3** *children fairly shrieking with laughter* positively, really, absolutely, decidedly, veritably.

fair-minded *adjective* fair, just, impartial, unprejudiced, open-minded, honest, honorable. *See* FAIR *adjective* 2.

fairness *noun* **1** *treat everyone with fairness* justness, impartiality, objectivity, evenhandedness, disinterest, equitability, equity, legality, properness. *See* FAIR *adjective* 1. **2** *the fairness of the judge* fair-mindedness, justness, impartiality, open-mindedness, honesty, integrity, probity, rectitude, trustworthiness. *See* FAIR *adjective* 2. **3** *the fairness of the maidens* beauty, prettiness, loveliness, attractiveness, comeliness.

fairy *noun* pixie, elf, sprite, imp, brownie, leprechaun, dwarf, gnome, goblin, hobgoblin.

fairy tale *noun* **1** *read the child a fairy tale* fairy story, folk tale, fable, legend, romance. **2** *the child's telling fairy tales* lie, white lie, untruth, tall story, fairy story, fabrication, invention, piece of fiction; *inf.* cock-and-bull story.

faith *noun* **1** *have faith in the cure/doctor* trust, belief, confidence, conviction, credence, credit, reliance, dependence, optimism, hopefulness. **2** *of what faith are they?* religion, church, persuasion, belief, creed, teaching, dogma, doctrine, sect, denomination. **3** *keep/break faith* loyalty, allegiance, faithfulness, fidelity, fealty, constancy, devotion, obedience, commitment. *Antonyms:* DISBELIEF; DISTRUST; DISLOYALTY.

faithful *adjective* **1** *faithful followers* loyal, constant, devoted, dependable, reliable, true, true-blue, trusty, trustworthy, staunch, unswerving, unwavering, steadfast, obedient, dutiful, dedicated, committed. **2** *a faithful copy*

accurate, true, exact, precise, close, strict, without error, unerring, just so.
Antonyms: DISLOYAL; UNFAITHFUL; TREACHEROUS; IMPRECISE.

faithful noun **the faithful** believers, loyal members, adherents, followers, communicants; congregation, brethren.

faithfulness noun **1** *the faithfulness of the followers* fidelity, loyalty, constancy, devotion, dependability, reliability, trustworthiness, staunchness, steadfastness, obedience, duty, dedication, commitment, allegiance, adherence, fealty. **2** *the faithfulness of the description* accuracy, truth, exactness, precision, closeness, strictness, justness.

faithless adjective **1** *faithless followers* unfaithful, disloyal, false, false-hearted, untrue, untrustworthy, traitorous, treacherous, perfidious, inconstant, fickle, unreliable, undependable, deceitful, two-faced. **2** *the missionary appealed to the faithless crowd* unbelieving, disbelieving, doubting, skeptical, agnostic, atheistic, irreligious.

faithlessness noun unfaithfulness, infidelity, disloyalty, falseness, false-heartedness, betrayal, untrustworthiness, traitorousness, treachery, perfidy, inconstancy, fickleness, unreliability, undependability, deceit, deceitfulness, two-facedness.

fake adjective **1** *a fake driver's license* counterfeit, forged, sham, imitation, fraudulent, false, bogus, spurious, pseudo; *inf.* phony. **2** *fake furs/pearls* sham, imitation, artificial, synthetic, mock, simulated, reproduction, ersatz. **3** *a fake accent* affected, put-on, assumed, feigned, pseudo, insincere; *inf.* phony.
Antonyms: GENUINE; AUTHENTIC; SINCERE.

fake noun **1** *the document is a fake* counterfeit, forgery, copy, sham, imitation, fraud, reproduction, hoax; *inf.* phony. **2** *the doctor is a fake* charlatan, impostor, mountebank, quack; *inf.* phony.

fall verb **1** *leaves/rain falling* come/go down, descend, drop, drop down, sink, gravitate, cascade, plop, plummet. **2** *the child fell* fall down, fall over, trip, trip over, stumble, slip, slide, tumble, topple over, keel over, go head over heels, collapse, fall in a heap, take a spill. **3** *ground falling* fall away, slope, slope down, incline/slant downward. **4** *water levels falling* sink, sink lower, subside, recede, abate, settle. **5** *demand/prices fell* fall off, drop off, go down, decline, decrease, grow less, diminish, dwindle, depreciate, plummet, slump. **6** *empires falling* die, fade, fail, decline, deteriorate, flag, wane, ebb, degenerate, go downhill; *inf.* go to the dogs. **7** *soldiers falling in war* die, be killed/slain, be a casualty/fatality, be lost, drop dead, perish, meet one's end. **8** *towns falling to the enemy* | *fall to temptation* surrender, yield, submit, give in, give up, give way, capitulate, suc-

cumb, resign oneself; be overthrown by, be taken by, be defeated by, be conquered by, lose one's position to, pass into the hands of. **9** *Christmas falls on a Saturday* | *darkness fell* take place, occur, happen, come about, come to pass. **10** *it so fell that she died* occur, happen, come about, come to pass, befall, chance, arise, result. **11** *the horse fell lame* | *she fell asleep* | *falling in love* become, grow, pass into. **12** *God punishing angels for falling* sin, do wrong, transgress, err, go astray, yield to temptation, commit an offense, lapse, fall from grace, backslide, trespass. **fall apart 1** *the table/system fell apart* fall to pieces, disintegrate, break up, crumble, dissolve. **2** *her leaving made him fall apart* fall/go to pieces, fall apart at the seams, have a (nervous) breakdown, collapse, crumble; *inf.* lose it. **fall back** retreat, withdraw, draw back, retire. **fall back on** resort to, call upon, call into play/action, call/press into service, have recourse to, make use of, use, employ, rely on, depend on. **fall behind 1** *fall behind in the race* be/get left behind, fall/drop back, lose one's place, lag, trail, not keep up. **2** *fall behind with the rent* get into arrears/debt, not keep up with. **fall down 1** *the child fell down* fall, fall over, trip. *See* FALL *verb* 2. **2** *fall down on the task* fail, be unsuccessful, not succeed, not make the grade, not come up to expectations, fall short, disappoint. **fall for 1** *fall for his friend's sister* fall in love with, become infatuated with, desire, be attracted/smitten by, lose one's heart to; *inf.* fancy. **2** *fall for an old trick* be taken in by, be fooled/deceived/duped by, accept; *inf.* swallow. **fall in** *the roof fell in* cave in, collapse, sink inward, come down about one's ears, crash in, crumble. **fall in with 1** *fall in with bad company* meet, encounter, get involved with, take up with. **2** *fall in with their plans* agree to/with, accept, assent to, concur with, go along with, support, back, give one's backing to, cooperate with. **fall off** *demand fell off* drop off, go down, decrease, decline, slump, deteriorate. *See* FALL *verb* 5. **fall out** *husband and wife falling out* quarrel, argue, squabble, fight, bicker, have a difference of opinion, differ, have a disagreement, disagree, clash, wrangle, get into conflict, get into a dispute. **fall short (of)** *the charity appeal fell short* | *fall short of perfection* be deficient, be/prove inadequate, disappoint; fail to meet/reach, fail to live up to, miss. **fall through** come to nothing, fail, fail to happen, miscarry, abort, go awry; *inf.* fizzle out.
Antonyms: RISE; THRIVE; SURVIVE.

fall noun **1** *the child had a fall* trip, tumble, spill, stumble, slipping, slip, slide, topple, nosedive, collapse. **2** *a fall in demand/prices* drop, dropping off, decline, decrease, cut, lessening, lowering, dip, diminishing, dwindling, reduction, depreciation, plummeting, slump, deterioration. **3** *the fall of the Roman empire* death, demise, downfall, ruin, collapse, failure, decline, deterioration, wane, ebb, degeneration, destruction, overthrow. **4** *the fall of the city to the enemy* surrender, yielding, submission, giving in, capitulation, succumbing, resignation, defeat. **5** *the fall of the land* slope, downward slope/slant/incline, declivity, descent, downgrade. **6** *the fall of Lucifer* sin, wrongdoing, transgression, error, yielding to temptation, offense, lapse, fall from grace, backsliding; original sin, the Fall.

fallacious *adjective* false, erroneous, untrue, wrong, incorrect, faulty, flawed, inaccurate, inexact, imprecise, mistaken, misleading, fictitious, spurious, counterfeit, deceptive, fraudulent, delusive, delusory, illusory, sophistic; *inf.* bogus, phony.
Antonyms: TRUE; CORRECT; AUTHENTIC.

fallacy *noun* mistaken belief, misbelief, misconception, false notion, misapprehension, misjudgment, miscalculation, error, mistake, untruth, inconsistency, illusion, delusion, deceit, deception, sophism; sophistry.

fallen *adjective* **1** *fallen women* immoral, loose, shamed, disgraced, dishonored, ruined, sinful, unchaste. **2** *fallen soldiers* dead, killed, slain, lost, perished, slaughtered.

fallible *adjective* liable/prone/open to error, error-prone, erring, errant, imperfect, flawed, frail, weak, mortal.
Antonyms: INFALLIBLE; PERFECT.

fallow *adjective fallow land | fields/ideas lying fallow* uncultivated, unplowed, untilled, unplanted, unsown, unseeded, unused, undeveloped, dormant, resting, inactive, idle, inert, empty, neglected, barren, unproductive.

false *adjective* **1** *a false interpretation/account* untrue, incorrect, wrong, erroneous, faulty, invalid, unfounded; untruthful, fictitious, concocted, fabricated, invented, inaccurate, inexact, imprecise, flawed, unreal, counterfeit, forged, fraudulent, spurious, misleading. **2** *a false friend* false-hearted, unfaithful, faithless, treacherous, disloyal, traitorous, perfidious, two-faced, double-dealing, untrustworthy, untrue, deceitful, deceiving, deceptive, dishonorable, dishonest, duplicitous, hypocritical, unreliable, unsound, untruthful, lying, mendacious. **3** *false furs/pearls* fake, artificial, imitation, synthetic, simulated, sham, mock, bogus, ersatz, spurious, counterfeit, feigned, forged, make-believe, pseudo; *inf.* phony.
Antonyms: TRUE; LOYAL; FAITHFUL; GENUINE.

falsehood *noun* **1** *telling falsehoods* lie, fib, untruth, false statement, falsification, perjury, fabrication, invention, piece of fiction, fiction, story, fairy story/tale, exaggeration. **2** *guilty of falsehood* deceit, deception, deceitfulness, two-facedness, double-dealing, prevarication, equivocation, mendacity, untruthfulness, perjury, perfidy, treachery, treason.
Antonyms: TRUTH; verity.

falsetto *noun* high voice, high-pitched tone, squeak, squeal.

falsify *verb* **1** *falsify a document* alter, counter-feit, forge, fake, doctor, tamper with, distort, adulterate, pervert. **2** *falsify their statement* disprove, show to be false, prove unsound, refute, confute, rebut, contradict, oppose; misrepresent, garble, misstate, misquote.

falter *verb* **1** *falter before proceeding* hesitate, waver, oscillate, fluctuate, delay, vacillate, be undecided, blow hot and cold, shilly-shally, hem and haw, drag one's feet, sit on the fence. **2** *falter over her words* stammer, stutter, stumble, speak haltingly.

fame *noun* renown, celebrity, eminence, notability, note, distinction, mark, prominence, esteem, importance, greatness, account, preeminence, glory, honor, illustriousness, stardom, reputation, repute; notoriety, infamy.
Antonyms: OBSCURITY; DISGRACE; DISREPUTE.

familiar *adjective* **1** *familiar face/task/excuse* well-known, known, recognized, customary, accustomed, common, everyday, ordinary, commonplace, frequent, habitual, usual, repeated, routine, stock, mundane, run-of-the-mill, conventional, household. **2** *a familiar atmosphere* informal, casual, relaxed, comfortable, easy, free, free and easy, at ease, at home, friendly, unceremonious, unrestrained, unconstrained, unreserved, open, natural, simple. **3** *familiar acquaintances* close, intimate, dear, near, confidential, bosom, friendly, neighborly, sociable, amicable; *inf.* pally, chummy, buddy-buddy, thick as thieves. **4** *object to him being familiar with the staff* overfamiliar, presumptuous, disrespectful, forward, bold, impudent, impertinent, intrusive; *inf.* pushy. **familiar with** *familiar with the system* acquainted with, conversant with, versed in, with knowledge of, knowledgeable about, instructed in, *au fait* with, at home with, no stranger to.
Antonyms: UNFAMILIAR; STRANGE; FORMAL.

familiarity *noun* **1** *the familiarity of the atmosphere* informality, casualness, ease, comfortableness, friendliness, lack of ceremony/restraint/reserve, naturalness, simplicity. *See* FAMILIAR 2. **2** *the familiarity of their relationship* closeness, intimacy, nearness, friendliness. *See* FAMILIAR 3. **3** *object to his familiarity* overfamiliarity, presumption, presumptuousness, disrespect, forwardness, boldness, impudence, impertinence, intrusiveness; liberties. **familiarity with** *his familiarity with the technique* acquaintance with, knowledge of, grasp of, mastery of, understanding of, comprehension of, experience of, skill with.

familiarize *verb* *a scientific journal familiarizing new research* make known, bring to notice, bring to public attention, make familiar. **familiarize with** *familiarize the students with the system* make familiar with, make conversant with, acquaint with, accustom to, habituate to, instruct in, coach in, train in, teach in, school in, prime in, indoctrinate in, initiate into.

family *noun* **1** *two families living together* parent/parents and child/children, household, clan, tribe; nuclear family, extended family. **2** *she wants a family* children, offspring, little ones, progeny, descendants, issue, scions; brood; *inf.* kids. **3** *the man had no family* relatives, relations, people, kin, next of kin, kinsfolk, kinsmen, one's own flesh and blood, folk. **4** *of a noble family* ancestry, extraction, parentage, birth, pedigree, genealogy, background, family tree, descent, lineage, line, bloodline, blood, race, strain, stock, breed; dynasty, house; forebears, forefathers, antecedents, roots. **5** *a family of plants* class, genus, species, kind, type, group, taxonomic group.

famine *noun* **1** *famine striking the village* scarcity of food, food shortage. **2** *water famine* scarcity, lack, dearth, want, deficiency, shortage, insufficiency, paucity, drought. **3** *dying of famine* starvation, hunger, food deprivation, lack of food.

famished *adjective* starving, starving to death, starved, ravenous, hungry, undernourished.

famous *adjective* well-known, renowned, celebrated, famed, prominent, noted, notable, great, eminent, preeminent, distinguished, esteemed, respected, venerable, illustrious, acclaimed, honored, exalted, glorious, remarkable, signal, popular, legendary, lionized, much-publicized. **Antonyms:** UNKNOWN; OBSCURE.

fan¹ *noun* *install a fan* air conditioner, air cooler, ventilator, blower, aerator.

fan² *verb* **1** *fan the atmosphere | fanning her face* cool, ventilate, air, aerate, blow, freshen, refresh. **2** *fan the flames/passion* intensify, increase, arouse, excite, agitate, ignite, kindle, stimulate, stir up, work up, whip up, incite, instigate, provoke. **fan out** *people/flags fanning out* spread, spread out, open out, open up, unfurl, unfold, outspread, stretch out.

fan³ *noun* admirer, lover, enthusiast, devotee, addict, aficionado, zealot, follower, disciple, adherent, supporter, backer, champion, votary; *inf.* buff, fiend, freak, nut, groupie.

fanatic *noun* *a religious fanatic* zealot, extremist, radical, activist, militant, sectarian, bigot, partisan, devotee, addict, enthusiast, visionary.

fanatical *adjective* **1** *a fanatical religious sect* extremist, extreme, zealous, radical, activist, militant, sectarian, bigoted, dogmatic, prejudiced, intolerant, narrow-minded, partisan, rabid. **2** *a fanatical moviegoer* enthusiastic, eager, fervent, passionate, overenthusiastic, obsessive, immoderate, frenzied, frenetic; *inf.* wild, gung-ho.

fanciful *adjective* **1** *fanciful notions/beings* imaginary, fancied, fantastic, romantic, mythical, fabulous, legendary, unreal, illusory, visionary, made-up, make-believe, fairy-tale, extravagant. **2** *a fanciful child* imaginative, inventive,

impractical, whimsical, capricious, visionary, chimerical. **3** *fanciful decoration* imaginative, creative, curious, extravagant, fantastic, bizarre, strange, eccentric.

fancy *noun* **1** *a child subject to fancy* caprice, whimsy, sudden impulse, vagary, eccentricity, peculiarity; whim, quirk, notion, kink. **2** *have a fancy for ice cream* desire, urge, wish, want, yearning, longing, inclination, bent, hankering, impulse; fondness, liking, love, partiality, preference, predilection, taste, penchant; *inf.* yen, itch. **3** *the poet's fancy* imagination, imaginative power, creativity, conception; images, mental images, visualizations. **4** *I have a fancy it will rain* idea, vague idea, guess, thought, notion, supposition, opinion.

fancy *verb* **1** *we fancy it will rain* have an idea, guess, think, think it likely/conceivable, believe, suppose, surmise, suspect, conjecture, reckon. **2** *he fancies a drink* would like, wish for, want, desire, long for, yearn for, crave, have a yearning/craving for, hanker after; *inf.* have a yen for. **3** *he fancies the new girl* find attractive, be attracted to, be captivated/infatuated by, take to, desire, lust after, burn for; *inf.* have taken a shine to, have a crush on, be wild/mad about, go for.

fancy *adjective* **1** *fancy decorations* ornate, elaborate, ornamented, ornamental, decorated, decorative, adorned, embellished, intricate, lavish, ostentatious, showy, luxurious, sumptuous, baroque, rococo; *inf.* jazzy, ritzy, snazzy, posh, classy. **2** *fancy notions* fanciful, imaginary, fantastic, romantic, make-believe, farfetched, illusory, delusive, extravagant, flighty, whimsical, capricious, chimerical; *inf.* far-out.

fanfare *noun* **1** *the queen greeted by a fanfare* flourish, trumpet call, blast of trumpets, fanfaronade. **2** *the new store opened with much fanfare* show, showiness, display, ostentation, commotion, fuss, publicity, sensationalism, ballyhoo; *inf.* to-do, hype.

fantastic *adjective* **1** *fantastic notions* fanciful, imaginary, romantic, unreal, illusory, make-believe, irrational, extravagant, wild, mad, absurd, incredible, strange, eccentric, whimsical, capricious. **2** *fantastic shapes* strange, weird, queer, peculiar, outlandish, eccentric, bizarre, grotesque, freakish, whimsical, fanciful, quaint, imaginative, exotic, unreal, extravagant, elaborate, ornate, intricate, rococo, baroque, phantasmagoric. **3** *a fantastic amount of work* tremendous, enormous, huge, very great, terrific, impressive, overwhelming. **4** *the movie was fantastic* marvelous, wonderful, sensational, superb, excellent, brilliant, great, first-class, top-notch; *inf.* cool, awesome. **Antonyms:** REAL; ORDINARY; POOR.

fantasy *noun* **1** *novels full of fantasy* fancy, imagination, creativity, invention, originality, vision, myth, romance. **2** *indulge in fantasy* fancy, speculation, daydreaming, reverie; flight of fancy, fanciful notion, dream, daydream, pipedream. **3** *seeing fantasies* apparition, phantom, specter, ghost, figment of the imagination, hallucination, vision, illusion, mirage.

far *adverb* **1** *it's not far to the house | far away | far into the night* a long way, a great distance, any great distance, a good way, afar. **2** *far the best | far too soon* to a great extent/degree, very much, much, by much, by a great amount, considerably, by a long way, markedly, immeasurably, decidedly, by far. **by far, by far and away** to a great extent/degree, very much, much, by a great amount/deal, considerably, immeasurably, decidedly, markedly, positively, easily, beyond a/the shadow of a doubt. **far and wide** *search far and wide* everywhere, in all places, extensively, widely, broadly, worldwide; here, there, and everywhere. **far out** *her clothes/ideas are far out* weird, bizarre, outlandish, unorthodox, unconventional, radical, extreme, esoteric; *inf.* way out, kinky. **go far** *the young man will go far* get on, get on in the world, be successful, succeed, make one's way in the world, make headway/progress, gain advancement, make a name for oneself, climb the ladder of success, rise in the world, set the world on fire; *inf.* go places. **so far** *the play's OK so far* up till/to now, until now, up to this point, to date.

far *adjective* *visit far places* faraway, far-off, distant, remote, out of the way, far-flung, far-removed, outlying, inaccessible, back of beyond, godforsaken.
Antonyms: NEAR; NEIGHBORING.

farce *noun* **1** *starring in a bedroom farce* slapstick, slapstick comedy, burlesque, burlesque show/routine, satire, parody, travesty, buffoonery, absurdity, ridiculousness. **2** *the interviews were just a farce* mockery, absurdity, sham, pretense, joke.

farcical *adjective* **1** *a farcical situation* ridiculous, ludicrous, absurd, laughable, risible, preposterous, facetious, silly, foolish, nonsensical, asinine. **2** *a farcical play* comic, slapstick, humorous, amusing.

fare *noun* **1** *how much is the air fare?* ticket price, price, cost, charge, fee. **2** *pick up three fares* passenger, traveler, fare payer. **3** *serving plain fare* food, menu, diet, table, nourishment, nutriment; meals, eatables, rations, provisions, commons, victuals, viands; *inf.* eats, nosh.

fare *verb* **1** *how did you fare?* get on, proceed, get along, progress, make out, do, manage, succeed, prosper. **2** *it fared badly with him* turn out, go, happen, proceed, progress.

farewell *interjection* goodbye, so long, adieu, ciao, adios, *auf Wiedersehen, au revoir; inf.* see you, see you later, toodle-oo.

farewell *noun* *farewells are sad* goodbye, adieu, leave-taking, parting, send-off, departure, departing, going away.

far-fetched *adjective* improbable, unlikely, remote, implausible, incredible, scarcely credi-

ble, unbelievable, difficult to believe, dubious, doubtful, unconvincing, strained, labored, strange, fantastic, fanciful, unrealistic; *inf.* hard to swallow/take.

farm *noun* farmland, land; homestead, grange, plantation, ranch.

farm *verb* **1** *farm the land* cultivate, bring under cultivation, till, work, plow, plant. **2** *her husband farms* be a farmer, practice farming, cultivate/till/work the land, raise/rear livestock, do agricultural work, raise crops/vegetables. **farm out** *farm out his work/workers/franchise* contract out, subcontract, delegate, assign to others; rent, rent out, lease, let.

farmer *noun* agriculturalist, agronomist, rancher.

farming *noun* agriculture, agronomy, husbandry, tilling, tillage, cultivation, agribusiness.

farsighted *adjective* **1** *the eye doctor said he was farsighted* longsighted, hyperopic, hypermetropic. **2** *farsighted in his choice* having foresight, prudent, prescient, discerning, judicious, shrewd, provident, politic, canny, cautious, careful, watchful, wise, sagacious.

farther *adjective* *the farther boat is almost out of sight* more distant/advanced. See FURTHER *adjective* 2.

farther *adverb* *she stopped and would come no farther* to a more advanced point. See FURTHER *adverb* 2.

farthest *adjective* most distant. See FURTHEST.

fascinate *verb* captivate, enchant, beguile, bewitch, enthrall, infatuate, enrapture, entrance, hold spellbound, transfix, rivet, mesmerize, hypnotize, allure, lure, tempt, entice, draw, tantalize, charm, attract, intrigue, delight, absorb, engross.
Antonyms: BORE; REPEL; turn off (*see* TURN).

fascinating *adjective* captivating, enchanting, beguiling, bewitching, enthralling, ravishing, entrancing, compelling, spellbinding, riveting, gripping, alluring, tempting, enticing, irresistible, seductive, charming, attractive, intriguing, delightful, absorbing.
Antonyms: BORING; DULL.

fascination *noun* captivation, enchantment, allure, lure, allurement, attraction, attractiveness, appeal, charm, magnetism, pull, draw, spell, sorcery, magic, glamour.

fashion *noun* **1** *the fashion in clothes/behavior* current/latest style, style, vogue, trend, latest thing, mode, craze, rage, fad, convention, custom, practice. **2** *she works in fashion* clothes, clothes industry, clothes design, couture; *inf.* rag trade. **3** *people of fashion* fashionable society, high society, society, social elite, the beautiful people, beau monde; *inf.* jet set. **4** *working in an untidy fashion* manner, way, style, method, mode, system, approach. **5** *they built a boat of some fashion* kind, type, sort, make, design, description. **after a fashion** *he put the tent up after a fashion* somehow or other, somehow, in a way, in a rough way, in an approximate manner, to a certain extent, in a manner of speaking.

fashion *verb* *fashion a boat out of logs* make, construct, build, manufacture, create, devise, shape, form, mold, forge.

fashionable *adjective* **1** *fashionable clothes* in fashion, stylish, up-to-date, up-to-the-minute, modern, voguish, in vogue, modish, popular, all the rage, trendsetting, latest, smart, chic, elegant, natty; *inf.* trendy, with it, ritzy. **2** *fashionable areas/restaurants* high-class; *inf.* classy, swank.

Antonyms: UNFASHIONABLE; OLD-FASHIONED; DATED.

fast *adjective* **1** *at a fast pace* quick, rapid, swift, speedy, brisk, fleet-footed, hasty, hurried, accelerated, express, flying. **2** *remain fast friends* loyal, devoted, faithful, firm, steadfast, staunch, constant, lasting, unchanging, unwavering, enduring. **3** *held fast by a rope* fastened, closed, shut, secured, secure, firmly fixed. **4** *fast women* promiscuous, licentious, dissolute, loose, wanton. **5** *lead fast lives* wild, dissipated, dissolute, debauched, promiscuous, intemperate, immoderate, rakish, unrestrained, reckless, profligate, self-indulgent, extravagant.

Antonyms: SLOW; DISLOYAL; VIRTUOUS.

fast *adverb* **1** *run fast* quickly, rapidly, swiftly, speedily, briskly, hastily, with all haste, in haste, hurriedly, in a hurry, post-haste, expeditiously, with dispatch, like the wind, like a shot/flash, hell-bent, hell-bent for leather, like a bat out of hell; *inf.* lickety-split. **2** *stuck fast* firmly, tightly, securely, immovably, fixedly. **3** *fast asleep* sound, deeply, completely. **4** *live fast* wildly, dissipatedly, intemperately, rakishly, recklessly. *See* FAST *adjective* 5.

fast *verb* *fasting during Lent* abstain from food, refrain from eating, deny oneself food, go without food, go hungry, eat nothing, starve oneself, go on hunger strike.

Antonyms: EAT; FEAST.

fasten *verb* **1** *fasten a brooch to the dress* attach, fix, affix, clip, pin, tack. **2** *fasten the door* bolt, lock, secure, make secure/fast, chain, seal. **3** *fasten the links of the chain* join, connect, couple, unite, link. **4** *fasten the goat to the tree* attach, tie, bind, tether, hitch, anchor. **5** *fasten his gaze on her* direct, aim, point, focus, fix, rivet, concentrate, zero in. **6** *the dress fastens at the back* become closed, close; button, zip. **7** *the lions fastening on their prey* take hold of, seize, catch/grab hold of, grab, snatch.

Antonyms: UNFASTEN; OPEN; UNLOCK.

fastidious *adjective* hard to please, critical, overcritical, hypercritical, fussy, finicky, overparticular; *inf.* choosy, picky, persnickety.

Antonyms: EASYGOING; SLOPPY.

fat *adjective* **1** *fat people* plump, stout, overweight, obese, heavy, large, solid, corpulent, chubby, tubby, portly, rotund, pudgy, flabby, gross, potbellied, paunchy; *inf.* beefy, roly-poly, elephantine. **2** *fat substances* fatty, greasy, oily, oleaginous, adipose, unctuous, sebaceous. **3** *fat land* fertile, productive, fruitful, rich, lush, flourishing, thriving. **4** *a fat part in a play* substantial, large, sizable, major, important, significant, considerable. **5** *a fat income* large, substantial, profitable, remunerative, lucrative. **6** *a fat book* thick, big, substantial, broad, extended. **7** *fat chance* very little, not much, minimal, hardly any.

Antonyms: THIN; LEAN; MINOR.

fat *noun* **1** *too much fat in the meat* fatty tissue, fat cells, adipose tissue. **2** *he'll have to get rid of his fat* excessive weight, fatness, plumpness, stoutness, obesity, chubbiness, tubbiness, flabbiness, corpulence, bulk; *inf.* flab, blubber, beef. *See* FAT *adjective* 1. **3** *add fat to the pan* oil, cooking oil, animal/vegetable fat; lard, suet, butter, margarine, oleomargarine; *inf.* oleo.

fatal *adjective* **1** *a fatal blow/illness* causing death, mortal, deadly, lethal, death-dealing, killing, terminal, final, incurable. **2** *fatal to our plans* ruinous, destructive, disastrous, catastrophic, calamitous, cataclysmic. **3** *the fatal moment* fateful, critical, crucial, decisive, determining, pivotal, momentous, important.

Antonyms: HARMLESS; BENEFICIAL.

fatalism *noun* stoicism, resignation, passive acceptance, acceptance; predeterminism, predestinarianism, necessitarianism.

fatality *noun* **1** *three fatalities in the accident* dead person, death, casualty, mortality, loss; dead. **2** *the fatality of the blow* deadliness, lethalness. **3** *a road noted for its fatalities* fatal accident, disaster, catastrophe.

fate *noun* **1** *fate meant them to meet* destiny, providence, God's will, kismet, predestination, predetermination, chance, one's lot in life; the stars. **2** *courts deciding our fate* future; outcome, upshot, end. **3** *met his fate in battle* death, end, destruction, ruin, doom, catastrophe, downfall, disaster, collapse, defeat.

fated *adjective* *a fated meeting* | *fated to meet* predestined, preordained, foreordained, destined, inevitable, inescapable, sure, ineluctable, doomed.

fateful *adjective* **1** *a fateful meeting* critical, crucial, decisive, determining, pivotal, momentous, important, fated. **2** *a fateful course of action* disastrous, ruinous, destructive, fatal, lethal, deadly.

father *noun* **1** male parent, begetter, paterfamilias, patriarch; adoptive father, stepfather; *inf.* dad, daddy, pop, pops, poppa, pa, old man. **2** *investigate the history of his fathers* forefather, ancestor, forebear, progenitor, primogenitor, predecessor, forerunner, precursor. **3** *the father of modern history* founder, originator, initiator, prime mover, architect, inventor, creator, maker, author. **4** *the city fathers* leader, elder, patriarch, senator. **5** *God bless you, Father* priest, pastor, padre, parson, clergyman, abbé.

father verb **1** *he fathered three sons* sire, beget, procreate, engender, bring into being, give life to. **2** *father the project* found, establish, institute, originate, initiate, invent, create, generate, conceive.

fatherland noun native land/country, native soil, homeland, home, mother country, motherland, land of one's birth/fathers, the old country.

fatherly adjective paternal, kindly, kind, affectionate, tender, caring, benevolent, sympathetic, understanding, indulgent, protective, supportive, patriarchal.

fathom verb **1** *fathom the depth of the water* sound, plumb, measure, estimate, gauge, probe. **2** *fathom their motives* understand, comprehend, grasp, perceive, penetrate, divine, search out, get to the bottom of, ferret out.

fatigue verb *it fatigues him to walk* tire, tire out, overtire, make weary, weary, exhaust, wear out, drain, prostrate, enervate; *inf.* take it out of, do in, poop out.

fatigue noun *suffering from fatigue* tiredness, overtiredness, weariness, exhaustion, prostration, lassitude, debility, enervation, lethargy, listlessness.
Antonyms: ENERGY; VIGOR.

fatness noun plumpness, stoutness, obesity, heaviness, largeness, corpulence, portliness, chubbiness, tubbiness, rotundity, pudginess, flabbiness, grossness; *inf.* beefiness.

fatten verb **1** *fatten the cattle for market* make fat/fatter, feed, build up, overfeed, bloat. **2** *children fattening up on good food* grow fat/fatter, get fat, put on weight, gain weight, get heavier, thicken, widen, broaden, expand, spread out. **3** *fatten the land* feed, fertilize, nourish, nurture, enrich.

fatty adjective fat, greasy, oily, oleaginous, adipose, unctuous, sebaceous.

fatuous adjective silly, foolish, stupid, inane, pointless, senseless, nonsensical, childish, puerile, idiotic, brainless, mindless, vacuous, asinine, moronic, witless, ridiculous, ludicrous, laughable, risible.

fault noun **1** *a fault in the material* defect, flaw, imperfection, blemish, snag. **2** *a fault in her character* defect, flaw, failing, shortcoming, weakness, weak point, infirmity, lack, deficiency. **3** *a fault in the calculation* error, mistake, inaccuracy, blunder, oversight; *inf.* slipup, booboo. **4** *blame one child for another's faults* misdeed, wrongdoing, offense, misdemeanor, misconduct, sin, vice, lapse, indiscretion, peccadillo, transgression, trespass. **5** *whose fault was the accident?* culpability, blameworthiness, responsibility, accountability, answerability. **at fault** *which driver was at fault?* to blame, blameworthy, blamable, in the wrong, culpable, responsible, accountable, answerable. **to a fault** *generous to a fault* excessively, unduly, in the extreme, immoderately, out of all proportion, overmuch, needlessly, overly.
Antonyms: MERIT; STRENGTH; ASSET.

---

fault

blemish, defect, failing, flaw, foible, shortcoming
No one is perfect. But when it comes to cataloguing your own imperfections, it's best to start with your **foibles**—the slight weaknesses or eccentricities for which you will be most quickly forgiven. You also have a good chance of being forgiven for your **shortcomings**, which are not necessarily damaging to others (*his tendency to procrastinate was a shortcoming that was readily overlooked*). **Failing** suggests a more severe shortcoming, usually with more serious consequences (*chronic tardiness was one of her failings*) , but a *failing* can also be a weakness of character that you're not responsible for and perhaps not even aware of (*pride is a common failing among those who have met with great success early in life*). **Fault** also implies failure—but not necessarily a serious failure—to reach moral perfection (*his major fault was his outspokenness*). While *fault* usually indicates something inherent in your nature rather than external to it, a **flaw** can be either superficial (*a flaw in his otherwise immaculate appearance*) or profound (*a personality flaw that made her impossible to work with*), and it can refer to things as well as people (*a flaw in the table's finish*). A **blemish** is usually a physical flaw (*a facial blemish*), although it can be anything that disfigures or mars the perfection or someone or something (*a blemish on her otherwise spotless academic record*). You can get rid of a blemish and even overcome your shortcomings, but a **defect** is a flaw so serious that you may never be able to get rid of it (*a defect in his hearing*).

---

fault verb **1** *cannot fault his behavior* find fault with, criticize, complain about, quibble about, find lacking, censure, impugn, pick holes in. **2** *the judge failed to fault him* hold responsible/accountable/blameworthy/culpable, hold to blame, call to account.

faultfinding noun criticism, carping, complaining, captiousness, caviling, quibbling, niggling, hairsplitting; *inf.* nitpicking.

faultfinding adjective critical, overcritical, hypercritical, censorious, carping, captious, caviling, quibbling, niggling, hairsplitting; *inf.* nitpicking.

faultless adjective **1** *a faultless piece of work* without fault, perfect, flawless, without blemish, unblemished, impeccable, accurate, correct, exemplary, model. **2** *the wife of the prisoner was faultless* innocent, without guilt, guiltless, blameless, above reproach, irreproachable, sinless, pure, unsullied.

Antonyms: IMPERFECT; GUILTY.

faulty adjective **1** a faulty lock broken, not working, malfunctioning, out of order, damaged, defective, unsound; inf. on the blink, kaput. **2** faulty reasoning defective, flawed, unsound, wrong, inaccurate, incorrect, erroneous, imprecise, fallacious, impaired, weak, invalid.

Antonyms: PERFECT; WORKING; CORRECT.

faux pas noun blunder, gaffe, mistake, slipup, indiscretion, impropriety, lapse of etiquette, peccadillo; inf. booboo.

favor noun **1** do me a favor good turn, service, kind act, good deed, kindness, courtesy, benefit. **2** look on him with favor approval, approbation, esteem, goodwill, kindness, benevolence, friendliness. **3** owe his job to favor rather than merit favoritism, bias, partiality, prejudice, partisanship. **4** enjoy the favor of the queen patronage, backing, support, aid, assistance. **5** give party favors trinket, toy, treat; noisemaker; balloon. **in favor of** in favor of capital punishment on the side of, for, pro, giving support/backing to, right behind; all for.

Antonyms: DISFAVOR; DISAPPROVAL; DISSERVICE.

favor verb **1** he favors returning advocate, approve of, recommend, support, back, endorse, sanction. **2** the young man favored blondes prefer, go in for, go for, choose, opt for, select, pick, single out, fancy, like, incline toward. **3** the father favors his son show favoritism toward, have a bias toward, treat with partiality, indulge, pamper, spoil. **4** the wind favored the other team be to the advantage of, be advantageous to, benefit, help, assist, aid, advance, abet. **5** favor us with a smile oblige, serve, accommodate, satisfy, please.

Antonyms: OPPOSE; DISLIKE; HINDER.

favorable adjective **1** a favorable report good, approving, commendatory, praising, well-disposed, enthusiastic. **2** the circumstances are favorable in one's favor, advantageous, beneficial, on one's side, helpful, good, hopeful, promising, fair, auspicious, propitious, opportune, timely, encouraging, conducive, convenient, suitable, fit, appropriate. **3** a favorable reply affirmative, in the affirmative, positive, encouraging. **4** make a favorable impression good, pleasing, agreeable, successful, positive.

Antonyms: UNFAVORABLE; CRITICAL; DISADVANTAGEOUS.

favorite adjective my favorite book best-loved, most-liked, pet, favored, dearest, preferred, chosen, choice, treasured, ideal.

favorite noun **1** the daughter is the father's favorite preference, first choice, choice, pick, pet, beloved, darling, idol, god, goddess, jewel, jewel in the crown; blue-eyed boy, apple of one's eye, teacher's pet. **2** the favorite won expected/probable winner, front runner.

Antonyms: BÊTE NOIRE; AVERSION.

favoritism noun guilty of favoritism bias, partiality, prejudice, unfair preference, partisanship, one-sidedness, nepotism, inequality, unfairness, inequity.

fawn adjective fawn sweater yellowish-brown, grayish-brown, buff, beige, neutral.

fawn verb fawn on fawning on the boss kowtow to, bow and scrape to, grovel before, be obsequious/servile to, curry favor with, ingratiate oneself with, lick the boots of; inf. butter up.

fawning adjective obsequious, servile, sycophantic, slavish, bowing and scraping, groveling, abject, crawling, creeping, cringing, prostrate, flattering, ingratiating; inf. bootlicking.

fear noun **1** filled with fear at the danger fright, fearfulness, terror, alarm, panic, trepidation, apprehensiveness, dread, nervousness, fear and trembling, timidity, disquiet, trembling, quaking, quivering, consternation, dismay; shivers, butterflies, tremors. **2** all her fears were removed phobia, aversion, dread, bugbear, nightmare, horror, terror. **3** express fear that he would die anxiety, worry, unease, uneasiness, apprehension, nervousness, agitation, concern, disquiet, disquietude, foreboding, misgiving, doubt, suspicion, angst. **4** fear of the Lord awe, wonder, amazement, reverence, veneration. **5** there is little fear of her leaving likelihood, probability, possibility, chance, prospect.

fear verb **1** they fear their father be afraid/fearful/apprehensive of, be scared of, dread, live in fear/dread of. **2** she fears spiders be afraid of, dread, have a horror/dread of, have a phobia about, shudder at. **3** they fear God stand in awe of, revere, reverence, venerate. **4** I fear that you may be right be afraid, suspect, have a suspicion, expect, anticipate, foresee, have a foreboding. **fear for** I fear for her health worry about, feel anxious/concerned about, have anxieties/qualms about, feel disquiet for. **fear to** fear to go out be too afraid/scared/apprehensive to, dare not, hesitate to.

fearful adjective **1** fearful of making a noise | footsteps made them fearful afraid, frightened, scared, terrified, alarmed, apprehensive, uneasy, nervous, tense, nervy, panicky, timid, timorous, faint-hearted, diffident, intimidated, hesitant, disquieted, trembling, quaking, quivering, shrinking, cowering, cowardly, pusillanimous; inf. jittery, jumpy. **2** a fearful accident terrible, dreadful, appalling, frightful, ghastly, horrific, horrible, horrendous, shocking, awful, atrocious, hideous, monstrous, dire, grim, unspeakable, gruesome, distressing, harrowing, alarming. **3** a fearful cold/mess terrible, appalling, very bad, extremely bad, very great. **4** a fearful vision of an angel awesome, awe-inspiring, imposing, impressive.

Antonyms: INTREPID; BOLD.

fearfully adverb **1** crawl forward fearfully apprehensively, in fear and trembling, uneasily, nervously, timidly, timorously, diffidently, hesitantly, with one's heart in one's mouth. **2** *she's fearfully polite* extremely, exceedingly, remarkably; *inf.* tremendously, awfully, terribly, frightfully.

fearless *adjective* unafraid, brave, courageous, valiant, intrepid, valorous, gallant, plucky, lionhearted, stouthearted, heroic, bold, daring, confident, audacious, indomitable, undaunted, unflinching, unshrinking; *inf.* game, gutsy, spunky.
Antonyms: COWARDLY; CRAVEN.

fearsome *adjective a fearsome sight* frightening, alarming, unnerving, daunting, horrifying, horrendous, dismaying, awe-inspiring, awesome.

feasibility *noun* practicability, possibility, workability, viability, suitability, expedience. *See* FEASIBLE.

feasible *adjective* practicable, possible, likely, workable, doable, achievable, attainable, accomplishable, realizable, reasonable, viable, realistic, within reason, useful, suitable, expedient.
Antonyms: IMPRACTICAL; IMPOSSIBLE.

feast *noun* **1** banquet, lavish meal/dinner, repast; orgy; revels, festivities; *inf.* blowout, spread, bash. **2** *the feast of St. Stephen* celebration, festival, religious festival, feast day, saint's day, holy day, holiday, fête, festivity. **3** *a feast for the eyes* pleasure, gratification, delight, treat, joy.
Antonyms: FAST; FAMINE.

feast *verb feast the visiting dignitaries* throw a feast for, hold a banquet for, wine and dine, regale, entertain, treat. **feast on** *feast on a holiday dinner* wine and dine, gorge oneself on, eat one's fill of, partake of, indulge in, overindulge in, gormandize, stuff one's face with, stuff oneself with. **feast one's eyes (on)** gaze/look (upon) with great joy/delight/pleasure.

feat *noun* deed, act, action, exploit, performance, accomplishment, achievement, attainment, move, stunt.

feather *noun a bird's feather* plume, quill, pinion. **feathers** *the bird's feathers* plumage, down; crest, tuft.

feathery *adjective* **1** *feathery chicks* feathered, downy, fluffy, fleecy, plumed, plumy. **2** *feathery material* light, featherlike, light as a feather, gossamer, gossamerlike, wispy, unsubstantial, ethereal.

feature *noun* **1** *one feature of life in the country* aspect, characteristic, facet, side, point, attribute, quality, property, trait, mark, hallmark, trademark, peculiarity, idiosyncrasy. **2** *the tractor pull is a popular feature of the fair* special attraction, attraction, highlight, focal point, focus, draw. **3** *read the features in the magazine section* main item/article, article, piece, item, report, story, column.

feature *verb* **1** *the festival features a new opera* present, give prominence to, promote, star, spot-

light, highlight, emphasize, play up, accentuate. **2** *do women feature in his life?* have prominence, play a part, have a place.

features *plural noun* face, countenance, visage, physiognomy; *inf.* mug, kisser.

feces *plural noun* excrement, bodily waste, waste matter, dung, manure; excreta, stools, droppings.

fecund *adjective* fruitful, productive, fertile, potent, prolific, proliferating, propagative.

federal *adjective federal statutes* national, civil, nationwide, governmental.

federation *noun* confederation, confederacy, federacy, league, alliance, coalition, union, syndicate, association, amalgamation, combination, combine, entente, society, fraternity.

fee *noun* charge, price, cost, payment, remuneration, emolument.

feeble *adjective* **1** *grow feeble with age* weak, weakly, weakened, frail, infirm, delicate, slight, sickly, puny, failing, ailing, helpless, powerless, debilitated, decrepit, doddering, tottering, enervated, enfeebled, effete. **2** *a feeble attempt at humor* ineffective, ineffectual, unsuccessful, inadequate, unconvincing, futile, poor, weak, tame, paltry, slight. **3** *he's too feeble to stand up to his boss* weak, ineffective, ineffectual, inefficient, incompetent, inadequate, indecisive, wishy-washy. **4** *a feeble light/voice* dim, indistinct, faint, unclear, vague, inaudible.
Antonyms: STRONG; ROBUST; EFFECTIVE; FORCEFUL.

feebleminded *adjective he must be feebleminded to believe that* stupid, idiotic, foolish, halfwitted, slow on the uptake; *inf.* boneheaded, dumb, soft in the head, out to lunch.

feed *verb* **1** *feed the baby* give food/nourishment to, nurture; suckle, breast-feed, bottle-feed. **2** *feed the family/guests* give food to, nourish, sustain, cater for, provide for, wine and dine. **3** *the baby is feeding* eat, take nourishment, partake of food, consume, devour food. **4** *cattle feeding* graze, browse. **5** *feed on grass* live on, exist on, subsist on. **6** *feed his self-esteem* gratify, bolster up, strengthen, augment, add to, encourage, minister to, add fuel to. **7** *feed information to the troops* supply, provide, give, furnish.

feed *noun* **1** *cattle feed* food, fodder, provender, forage, pasturage, silage. **2** *have a good feed* feast, meal, dinner, repast, banquet; *inf.* spread.

feel *verb* **1** *feel her face* touch, stroke, caress, fondle, finger, thumb; handle, manipulate; paw, maul. **2** *feel the ship's motion* be aware/conscious of, notice, observe, perceive, be sensible of, have a sensation of. **3** *feel pain* experience, know, have, undergo, go through, bear, endure, suffer. **4** *feel one's way* grope, fumble, poke, explore. **5** *feel the temperature of the water* sense, try, try out, test, sound out. **6** *he feels* *that he should go* think, believe, consider it right, consider, be of the opinion, hold, judge, deem. **7** *I feel that he's hiding something* have a feeling, sense, get the impression, feel in one's bones, have a hunch, have a funny feeling, just know. **8** *the air feels damp* seem, appear, strike one as. **feel for** *feel for the poor* sympathize with, be sorry for, pity, feel sympathy/compassion for, be moved by, weep for, grieve for, one's heart bleeds for, commiserate with, empathize with. **feel like** *feel like a vacation* would like, want, wish, desire, fancy, feel in need of; *inf.* have a yen for.

feel *noun* **1** *you can tell by feel* touch, sense of touch, tactile sense. **2** *the material has a nice feel* texture, surface, finish. **3** *I don't like the feel of the place* atmosphere, ambience, aura, mood, air, impression; *inf.* vibrations, vibes. **4** *have a feel for that kind of work* knack, aptitude, flair, talent, gift, art, faculty.

feeler *noun* **1** *the creature's feeler* antenna, tentacle, whisker. **2** *put out feelers to get people's opinions* probe, trial balloon, tentative proposal/suggestion, advance, leak; overtures.

feeling *noun* **1** *tell what it is by feeling* feel, touch, sense of touch, tactile sense. **2** *a feeling of pain* awareness, consciousness, sensation, sense, perception. **3** *I had a feeling that you would be there* idea, vague idea, funny feeling, impression, suspicion, sneaking suspicion, notion, inkling, hunch, apprehension, presentiment, premonition, foreboding. **4** *look at him with feeling* emotion, affection, fondness, warmth, love, sentiment, passion, ardor, fervor, intensity, heat, fire, vehemence. **5** *show feeling for others* sympathy, pity, compassion, understanding, concern, sensitivity, condolence, tender-heartedness, grief, commiseration, empathy. **6** *my feeling is that he will go* instinct, opinion, intuition, impression, point of view, thought, way of thinking, theory, hunch. **7** *a feeling of neglect about the place* feel, atmosphere, ambience, aura, mood, air, impression; *inf.* vibrations, vibes.

feeling *adjective* **1** *a feeling person* sensitive, warm, tender, caring, soft-hearted, sympathetic, compassionate, responsive, sentient, sensible, emotional, demonstrative. **2** *a feeling letter* emotional, passionate, impassioned, ardent, intense, fervent, fervid.

feelings *plural noun* *hurt their feelings* | *strong feelings* sensibilities, sensitivities, self-esteem, ego; emotions, passions, sentiments.

feign *verb* **1** *feign sleep* fake, simulate, sham, affect, give the appearance of. **2** *he's only feigning* pretend, fake, make believe, sham, put it on, act, play-act, malinger.

felicitations *plural noun* congratulations, good wishes, best wishes, blessings, greetings, salutations, compliments.

felicitous *adjective* **1** *a felicitous expression* apt,

well-chosen, well-expressed, well-put, fitting, suitable, appropriate, apposite, pertinent, germane, to the point. **2** *a felicitous event* happy, joyful, harmonious, fortunate, lucky, successful, prosperous.

feline *adjective* catlike, leonine, graceful, sinuous, slinky, sensual, stealthy.

fell *verb* **1** *fell a tree/building* cut down, hew, level, raze, raze to the ground, demolish, knock down. **2** *fell him with one blow* knock down/over, strike down, flatten, ground, floor, prostrate, overthrow, kill.

fellow *noun* *that fellow over there* man, male, boy, person, individual; *inf.* chap, guy, character, customer.

fellowship *noun* **1** *join the club for fellowship* companionship, companionability, sociability, comradeship, fraternization, camaraderie, friendship, amiability, amity, affability, geniality, kindliness, cordiality, intimacy, social intercourse; *inf.* chumminess. **2** *the church fellowship* association, society, club, league, union, guild, affiliation, order, fraternity, brotherhood, sorority, amalgamation, consortium, corporation.

female *noun* *a rest room for females only* woman, lady, girl; *inf.* chick, dame, lass.

female *adjective* feminine, womanly, womanlike, ladylike.

Antonyms: MALE; VIRILE.

feminine *adjective* **1** *a very feminine young woman* delicate, gentle, tender, graceful, womanly, ladylike, girlish, refined, modest. **2** *a feminine manner* effeminate, womanish, effete, unmanly, unmasculine, weak; *inf.* sissy, sissyish, limp-wristed.

Antonyms: MASCULINE; MANNISH; MANLY.

fence *noun* **1** *a fence around the field/town* enclosure, barrier, railing, rail, wall, hedge; barricade, rampart, stockade, palisade. **2** *stolen goods sold to a fence* receiver, dealer. **on the fence** uncommitted, uncertain, undecided, vacillating, irresolute, neutral, impartial.

fence *verb* **1** *fence the garden* | *fence off the field* enclose, surround, circumscribe, encircle, encompass. **2** *he fences as a hobby* go/do fencing, engage in swordplay/swordsmanship. **3** *fence when asked questions* hedge, be evasive, beat around/about the bush, dodge the issue, prevaricate, equivocate, fudge the issue, shilly-shally, vacillate. **fence in** *fence in the cows* shut in, confine, pen, separate off, secure, imprison.

fend *verb* **fend off** *fend off their blows* | *fend off questions* ward off, keep off, turn aside, stave off, divert, deflect, avert, defend oneself against, guard against. **fend for oneself** provide/shift for oneself, take care of oneself, get by.

ferment *noun* **1** *add a ferment to the mix* fermenting substance, fermentation agent, yeast, mold, bacteria, leaven, leavening. **2** *children in a ferment of excitement* stir, fever, furor, frenzy, brouhaha, confusion, fuss, stew, hubbub, racket, imbroglio; tumult, commotion, uproar, turmoil, agitation, disruption, turbulence.

ferment *verb* 1 *beer/yeast mixtures fermenting* undergo fermentation, foam, froth, bubble, effervesce, seethe, boil, rise, work. 2 *ferment the beer/yeast mixture* subject to fermentation, cause to effervesce. 3 *his words fermenting the crowd* excite, agitate, inflame, incite. 4 *ferment trouble* cause, incite, excite, provoke, arouse, stir up, foment. 5 *the crowd fermenting with excitement* seethe, smolder, boil, be agitated.

ferocious *adjective* 1 *a ferocious animal* fierce, savage, wild, feral, untamed, predatory, rapacious. 2 *ferocious troops* fierce, savage, ruthless, brutal, brutish, cruel, pitiless, merciless, vicious, violent, inexorable, barbarous, barbaric, inhuman, bloodthirsty, murderous. 3 *ferocious heat* fierce, very great, intense, extreme, acute.
Antonyms: TAME; GENTLE; MILD.

ferret *verb.* **ferret in/through** *ferreting in/through her handbag* rummage in/through, search about (in), rifle through, forage around (in), sift through. **ferret out** *ferret out the facts* search out, unearth, discover, disclose, elicit, bring to light, get at, run to earth, track down, dig up, root out, hunt out, drive out, fish out, nose out, sniff out, smell out.

ferry *noun the ferry runs hourly* ferryboat, shuttle; packet boat, packet.

ferry *verb* 1 *the boat ferries across every day* go back and forth, come and go, run, shuttle. 2 *ferry the passengers across the water* carry, transport, convey, run, ship, shuttle, chauffeur.

fertile *adjective* 1 *fertile soil* fruitful, productive, fecund, rich. 2 *reach the age of being fertile* potent, virile, child-producing, fecund, reproductive, propagative. 3 *fertile imaginations* inventive, resourceful, original, ingenious, creative, visionary, constructive, productive.
Antonyms: INFERTILE; BARREN.

---

fertile
fecund, fruitful, prolific

A **fertile** woman is one who has the power to produce offspring, just as *fertile* soil produces crops and a *fertile* imagination produces ideas. This adjective pertains to anything in which seeds (or thoughts) can take root and grow. A woman with ten children might be described as **fecund**, which means that she is not only capable of producing many offspring but has actually done it. A woman can be *fertile*, in other words, without necessarily being *fecund*. **Fruitful**, whose meaning is very close to that of *fecund* when used to describe plants and may replace *fertile* in reference to soil or land, pertains specifically to something that promotes fertility or fecundity (*a fruitful downpour*). It can also apply in a broader sense to anything that bears or promotes results (*a fruitful idea; a fruitful discussion*). While it's one thing to call a woman with a large family *fe-*

cund, **prolific** is more usually applied to animals or plants in the literal sense of fertility, and suggests reproducing in great quantity or with rapidity. Figuratively, prolific is often used of highly productive creative efforts (a prolific author with 40 titles published).

---

fertilize *verb* 1 *fertilize the soil* add fertilizer to, feed, enrich, mulch, compost, dress, top-dress. 2 *fertilize the egg/cow* impregnate, inseminate, fecundate, make pregnant. 3 *fertilize the plant* pollinate, make fruitful, fructify.

fertilizer *noun* plant food, manure, dung, compost, dressing, top dressing; bonemeal, guano.

fervent *adjective* passionate, ardent, impassioned, intense, vehement, heartfelt, fervid, emotional, emotive, warm, devout, sincere, eager, earnest, zealous, enthusiastic, excited, animated, spirited.
Antonyms: APATHETIC; COLD; UNEMOTIONAL.

fervid *adjective* fervent, passionate, ardent, impassioned, intense. *See* FERVOR.

fervor *noun* fervency, passion, ardor, impassionedness, intensity, vehemence, fervidness, emotion, warmth, devoutness, sincerity, eagerness, earnestness, zeal, enthusiasm, excitement, animation, spirit.
Antonyms: APATHY; INDIFFERENCE.

fester *verb* 1 *a wound festering* suppurate, matter, come to a head, gather, maturate, run, discharge. 2 *animal corpses festering* rot, decay, go bad, go off, decompose, disintegrate. 3 *resentment festering in their minds* rankle, chafe, gnaw, cause bitterness/resentment/vexation.

festival *noun* 1 *a church festival* saint's day, holy day, feast day, holiday, anniversary, commemoration, rite, ritual, day of observance. 2 *take part in the town's annual festival* fair, gala, fête, carnival; celebrations, festivities.

festive *adjective festive occasions* joyous, joyful, happy, jolly, merry, gay, jovial, lighthearted, cheerful, cheery, jubilant, convivial, good-time, gleeful, mirthful, uproarious, rollicking, backslapping, celebratory, gala, holiday, carnival, sportive, festal.

festivity *noun* 1 *the festivity of the occasion* joyfulness, jollity, merriment, pleasure, amusement, gaiety, cheerfulness, jubilance, conviviality, cheeriness, gleefulness, glee, mirthfulness, mirth, revelry, sportiveness. 2 *enjoy the festivities* festive event, celebration, festival, entertainment, party, jollification, revelry, carousal, sport; fun and games, celebrations, festive proceedings.

festoon *noun a festoon of flowers* garland, wreath, chaplet, lei, swag.

festoon *verb* be *festooned with flowers* garland, wreathe, hang, drape, decorate, adorn, ornament, array, deck, bedeck, swathe, beribbon.

fetch *verb* 1 *fetch the milk/doctor* go and get, get, go for, bring, carry, deliver, convey, transport, escort, conduct, lead, usher in. **2** *the vase fetched $40* sell for, go for, bring in, realize, yield, earn, cost.

fetching *adjective* attractive, charming, enchanting, sweet, winsome, taking, captivating, fascinating, alluring.

fête *noun* gala, fair, garden party, festival, celebration.

fetish *noun* **1** *a foot/leather fetish* fixation, sexual fixation, compulsion, obsession, mania, *idée fixe; inf.* thing. **2** *carry a fetish* talisman, charm, amulet.

fetter *verb* **1** *fetter the prisoners* chain, chain up, shackle, bind, tie, tie up, hobble. **2** *fettered by petty restrictions* restrict, hinder, impede, obstruct, constrain, confine, restrain.

fetters *plural noun* chains, shackles, bond, irons, manacles, trammels; restraint, tether, check.

fettle *noun* condition, shape, form, state, order, way; *inf.* kilter.

fetus *noun* embryo, fertilized egg, unborn baby.

feud *noun* **1** *a state of feud between the families* vendetta, rivalry, hostility, enmity, conflict, strife, discord, bad blood, animosity, antagonism, unfriendliness, grudge, estrangement, schism. **2** *start a feud* vendetta, quarrel, conflict, argument, bickering, falling-out.

fever *noun* **1** *the child's fever subsided* feverishness; *inf.* temperature, temp. **2** *in a fever of excitement* ferment, frenzy, furor; turmoil, agitation, excitement, restlessness, unrest, passion, intensity.

feverish *adjective* **1** *the child is feverish* fevered, febrile, burning, hot. **2** *look feverish* flushed, red-faced, red. **3** *feverish excitement* frenzied, frenetic, agitated, excited, restless, nervous, worked up, overwrought, frantic, distracted, flustered, impatient; *inf.* in a tizzy.

few *adjective* **1** *few people were there* not many, hardly any, scarcely any, one or two, a handful of, a sprinkling of; *inf.* a couple of. **2** *very few buses* few and far between, infrequent, sporadic, irregular. **3** *opportunities are few* scarce, rare, negligible, scant, hard to find.
Antonyms: MANY; FREQUENT; PLENTIFUL.

few *noun* *a few were there* a small number, one or two, a handful, a sprinkling.

fiancé, fiancée *noun* husband-to-be, wife-to-be, bride-to-be, future husband/wife, prospective husband/wife, prospective spouse, betrothed; *inf.* intended.

fiasco *noun* failure, disaster, catastrophe, mess, ruination, debacle; *inf.* flop, washout.

fib *noun* *tell a fib* lie, white lie, untruth, falsehood, fabrication, piece of fiction, fiction, fairy story/tale, tall tale; *inf.* whopper.

fiber *noun* **1** *the fibers of the carpet* thread, strand, tendril, filament, fibril. **2** *made of a coarse fiber* material, substance, cloth, stuff. **3** *a person of a different fiber* character, nature, makeup, spirit, disposition, temperament. *See* MORAL FIBER.

fickle *adjective* capricious, changeable, variable, unpredictable, volatile, mercurial, inconstant, unstable, vacillating, unsteady, unfaithful, faithless, irresolute, flighty, giddy, erratic, fitful, irregular, mutable.
Antonyms: CONSTANT; STABLE.

fickleness *noun* capriciousness, unpredictableness, volatility, inconstancy, instability, vacillation, unfaithfulness, fitfulness, mutability. *See* FICKLE.

fiction *noun* **1** *a work of fiction* storytelling, romance, fable, fantasy, legend. **2** *his fiction about what happened is almost believable* piece of fiction, fabrication, invention, concoction, lie, fib, untruth, falsehood, fairy tale/story, tall story, improvisation, prevarication; *inf.* cock-and-bull story, whopper, fish story.
Antonyms: FACT; TRUTH.

---

fiction
deception, fable, fabrication, falsehood, figment

If a young child tells you there is a dinosaur under his bed, you might assume that his story is a **fiction**, but it is probably a **figment**. A *fiction* is a story that is invented either to entertain or to deceive (*her excuse was ingenious, but it was pure fiction*), while *figment* suggests the operation of fancy or imagination (*a figment of his imagination*). If a child hides his sandwich under the sofa cushions and tells you that a dinosaur ate it, this would be a **fabrication**, which is a story that is intended to deceive. Unlike a *figment*, which is mostly imagined, a *fabrication* is a false but thoughtfully constructed story in which some truth is often interwoven (*the city's safety record was a fabrication designed to lure tourists downtown*). A **falsehood** is basically a lie—a statement or story that one knows to be false but tells with intent to deceive (*a deliberate falsehood about where the money had come from*). A **deception**, on the other hand, is an act that deceives but not always intentionally (*a foolish deception designed to prevent her parents from worrying*). A **fable** is a fictitious story that deals with events or situations that are clearly fantastic, impossible, or incredible. It often gives animals or inanimate objects the power to speak and conveys a lesson of practical wisdom, as in *Aesop's Fables*.

---

fictional *adjective* *a fictional character* fictitious, made up, invented, imaginary, unreal, nonexistent.
Antonyms: REAL; ACTUAL.

fictitious *adjective* **1** *a fictitious character* made up, imaginary. *See* FICTIONAL. **2** *a fictitious address* false, untrue, bogus, sham, counterfeit, fake, fabricated. **3** *a fictitious name* false, assumed, invented, made up, concocted, spurious, improvised. **4** *his account is fictitious* made up, untrue, false, imagined, imaginary, apocryphal.
Antonyms: FACTUAL; REAL; GENUINE.

fiddle *noun play the fiddle* violin, viola, cello, double bass, *inf.* bass fiddle.

fiddle *verb* **1** *stop fiddling with your pencil* fidget, play, fuss, toy, mess about, fool around; waste time, act aimlessly. **2** *he's fiddling with the engine* tinker, tamper, interfere; *inf.* monkey around.

fidelity *noun* **1** *his fidelity to his wife/country* faithfulness, loyalty, devotedness, devotion, allegiance, commitment, constancy, dependability, true-heartedness, trustworthiness, reliability, staunchness, obedience. **2** *the fidelity of the copy* accuracy, exactness, exactitude, precision, preciseness, strictness, closeness, faithfulness, correspondence, conformity, authenticity.
Antonyms: DISLOYALTY; TREACHERY; PERFIDY.

fidget *verb* **1** *children fidgeting* move restlessly, wriggle, squirm, twitch, jiggle; *inf.* have ants in one's pants. **2** *fidget with one's pencil* fiddle, play, fuss. *See* FIDDLE *verb* 1.

fidgety *adjective* restless, restive, on edge, jumpy, uneasy, nervous, nervy, twitchy; *inf.* jittery, like a cat on a hot tin roof.

field *noun* **1** *cows in the field* pasture, meadow; grassland; *lit.* lea, greensward. **2** *specializing in the field of electronics* area, area of activity, sphere, regime, discipline, province, department, line, speciality, métier. **3** *in his field of vision* range, scope, purview; limits, confines. **4** *the field for the race/job is high quality* applicants, candidates, entrants, competitors, runners, possibles, possibilities; competition.

field *verb* **1** *field the ball* catch, stop, retrieve, return, throw back. **2** *field questions deftly* deal with, handle, cope with, answer, respond/react to, reply to.

fiend *noun* **1** *fiends of hell* devil, demon, evil spirit. **2** *the slave driver was a fiend* brute, savage, beast, barbarian, monster, ogre, sadist, blackguard. **3** *a drug fiend* addict, abuser, user.

fiendish *adjective* **1** *a fiendish stepfather* wicked, cruel, brutal, brutish, savage, barbaric, barbarous, inhuman, murderous, vicious, bloodthirsty, ferocious, ruthless, heartless, pitiless, merciless, black-hearted, unfeeling, malevolent, malicious, villainous, odious, base, malignant, devilish, diabolical, hellish, demonic, satanic, ungodly. **2** *a fiendish plan* cunning, clever, ingenious. **3** *a fiendish problem* difficult, complex, complicated, intricate.

fierce *adjective* **1** *a fierce animal/enemy* ferocious, savage, wild, vicious, feral, untamed, bloodthirsty, dangerous, cruel, brutal, murderous, slaughterous, menacing, threatening, terrible, grim. **2** *a fierce love* intense, ardent, passionate, impassioned, fervent, fervid, fiery, uncontrolled. **3** *a fierce wind* violent, strong, stormy, blustery, gusty, boisterous, tempestuous, raging, furious, turbulent, tumultuous, cyclonic, typhonic. **4** *suffer from fierce headaches* very bad, severe, intense, grave, awful, dreadful. **5**

fierce competition competitive, keen, intense, strong, relentless, cutthroat.
Antonyms: TAME; GENTLE; MILD.

fight *verb* **1** *the armies fought* battle, do battle, give battle, war, wage war, go to war, make war, attack, mount an attack, take up arms, combat, engage, meet, come to blows, exchange blows, close, clash, skirmish, struggle, contend, grapple, wrestle, scuffle, tussle, collide, spar, joust, tilt. **2** *the two men fought* come to blows, exchange blows, attack/assault each other, hit/punch each other, box, brawl; *inf.* scrap. **3** *the two families have been fighting for years* feud, quarrel, argue, bicker, squabble, wrangle, dispute, be at odds, disagree, battle, altercate; *inf.* fall out. **4** *we fought the council's decision* contest, take a stand against, oppose, dispute, object to, withstand, resist, defy, strive/struggle against, take issue with. **5** *fight a battle* wage, carry on, conduct, engage in, wage, prosecute. **fight back 1** *children told to fight back* defend oneself, put up a fight, retaliate, counterattack, give tit for tat. **2** *fight back the tears* suppress, repress, check, curb, restrain, contain, bottle up. **fight off** ward off, beat off, stave off, repel, repulse, hold at bay, resist.

fight *noun* **1** *the army lost the last fight* battle, engagement, action, clash, conflict, combat, contest, encounter, skirmish, scuffle, tussle, brush, exchange. **2** *a fight outside the bar* brawl, affray, fracas, melee, sparring match, exchange, free-for-all, struggle, disturbance; fisticuffs; *inf.* set-to, scrap. **3** *the two families have had a fight* quarrel, disagreement, difference of opinion, dispute, argument, altercation, feud. **4** *lose all the fight in him* spirit, will to win, gameness, pluck, aggression, belligerence, militancy, resistance, power to resist.

fighter *noun* **1** *the military fighters* fighting man/woman, soldier, warrior. **2** *place bets on the younger fighter* boxer, pugilist, wrestler; prizefighter; *inf.* bruiser. **3** *fighters for the title* contestant, contender, competitor, rival.

figurative *adjective* nonliteral, metaphorical, allegorical, representative, emblematic, symbolic.

figure *noun* **1** *add up a column of figures* number, whole number, numeral, digit, integer, cipher, numerical symbol. **2** *be unable to put a figure on the work involved* cost, price, amount, value, total, sum, aggregate. **3** *figures unrecognizable in the mist* shape, form, outline, silhouette. **4** *have a well-developed figure* body, physique, build, frame, torso; proportions; *inf.* vital statistics, chassis. **5** *see figure 20* diagram, illustration, picture, drawing, sketch, chart, plan, map. **6** *artists good at drawing figures* human representation, likeness, image of a person. **7** *the lily is a figure of purity* symbol, emblem, sign, representative. **8** *the figures on the wood* pattern, design, motif, device, depiction. **9** *one of* *the figures of the town council* dignitary, notable, notability, personage, somebody, worthy, celebrity, leader, force, personality, presence, character; *inf.* big shot, bigwig.

figure *verb* **1** *figure a total* calculate, work out, compute, tally, reckon. **2** *she figures in his autobiography* appear, feature, be featured/mentioned, be referred to, play a part/role, be conspicuous. **3** *we figure that they'll go* think, consider, conclude. **4** *that figures* be likely/probable, be understandable, make sense. **figure out 1** *figure out the cost* work out, calculate, compute, reckon, assess. **2** *figure out why they came* understand, comprehend, work out, make out, fathom, see, reason, imagine, decipher, resolve; *inf.* make heads or tails of.

figurehead *noun* **1** *the king is just a figurehead* titular head, nominal leader, token, mouthpiece, puppet. **2** *figurehead on the ship's prow* carving, bust, sculpture, image, statue.

figures *plural noun* *good at figures* arithmetic, counting; calculations, statistics.

filament *noun* fiber, fibril, thread, strand, string, tendril, wire, cable, cord.

filch *verb* steal, thieve, pilfer, rob, take, purloin, abstract, misappropriate, embezzle, shoplift; *inf.* walk off with, swipe, lift.

file[1] *noun* **1** *put documents/data in a file* folder, box, portfolio, document case, filing cabinet; card file, computer file, data file. **2** *get out your file* dossier, folder, information; documents, records, data, particulars, case notes. **3** *a file of people* line, column, row, string, chain, queue.

file[2] *verb* **1** *file the information* categorize, classify, organize, put in place, put in order, pigeonhole, put on record, record, enter, store. **2** *file for divorce* apply, put in, register, sign up. **3** *people filing in* walk/march in a line, march, parade, troop, pass in formation.

file[3] *verb* *file one's nails* smooth, shape, buff, rub, rub down, polish, burnish, furbish, refine, scrape, abrade, rasp, sandpaper, pumice.

filigree *noun* wirework, fretwork, fret, latticework, lattice, grillwork, scrollwork.

fill *verb* **1** *fill the cup* | *the pond slowly filled* make/become full, fill up, fill to the brim, fill to overflowing. **2** *people filled the room* occupy all of, crowd, overcrowd, congest, cram, pervade. **3** *fill the shelves* stock, pack, load, supply, furnish, provide, replenish, restock, refill. **4** *fill the children* feed fully, satisfy, stuff, cram, satiate, sate, surfeit, glut. **5** *perfume/hostility filled the air* pervade, spread throughout, permeate, suffuse, imbue, charge, saturate. **6** *fill the hole* stop, stop up, block up, plug (up), seal, close, clog. **7** *he filled the post of manager* occupy, hold, take up. **8** *fill the order/commission* carry out, execute, perform, complete, fulfill. **fill in 1** *fill in the blanks* complete, answer, fill out. **2** *fill in for the manager* substitute, stand in, take over. **3** *fill me in on the events* inform, advise, tell, notify,

acquaint, apprise, update; *inf.* put wise, bring up to speed. **fill out 1** *the children have filled out* grow fatter, become plumper/rounder. **2** *fill out the story* round out, expand. **3** *fill out the form* complete, reply to.

Antonyms: EMPTY; VACATE.

fill *noun* *one's fill eat one's fill* | *have had one's fill of her* all one wants, as much as one can take, enough, more than enough, plenty, ample, sufficient.

film *noun* **1** *a film of dust* layer, coat, coating, covering, cover, dusting, sheet, blanket, skin, tissue, membrane. **2** *see the mountain through a film* haze, mist, cloud, blur, veil; murkiness. **3** *see a recent film* movie, motion picture, picture; *inf.* video, flick.

film *verb* **1** *film the wedding* photograph, record on film, take pictures of, shoot, make a film of, videotape. **2** *her eyes filmed (over)* become blurred, blur, cloud over, mist over, dull, blear.

filmy *adjective* diaphanous, transparent, see-through, translucent, sheer, gauzelike, gauzy, gossamer, gossamery, cobwebby, delicate, fine, light, thin, airy, floaty, fragile, flimsy, unsubstantial.

filter *noun* *pipe the water through a filter* strainer, purifier, cleaner, gauze, netting, cheesecloth.

filter *verb* **1** *filter the liquid* strain, sieve, sift, filtrate; clarify, purify, clear, refine. **2** *light filtering through* trickle, ooze, seep, leak, dribble, percolate, flow out, drain, exude, escape, leach.

filth *noun* **1** *the floors covered in filth* | *the filth of the house* dirt, muck, grime, mud, mire, sludge, slime, squalor, foul matter, excrement, dung, manure, sewage, rubbish, refuse, garbage, trash, pollution, contamination, defilement, decay, putrefaction, putrescence; filthiness, uncleanness, foulness, nastiness; *inf.* crud. **2** *objecting to filth in magazines* pornography, obscenity, indecency, smut, corruption, vulgarity, vileness; *inf.* porn, hard porn, raunchiness.

filthy *adjective* **1** *filthy water* dirty, mucky, muddy, murky, slimy, squalid, unclean, foul, nasty, feculent, polluted, contaminated, rotten, decaying, smelly, fetid, putrid. **2** *filthy faces/clothes* unwashed, unclean, dirty, dirt-encrusted, grubby, muddy, mucky, black, blackened. **3** *a filthy liar* low-down, despicable, contemptible, base, mean, vile, nasty, sordid. **4** *filthy magazines* pornographic, obscene, indecent, smutty, corrupt, coarse, bawdy, vulgar, lewd, licentious, vile, depraved, foul, dirty, impure; *inf.* blue, raunchy.

Antonyms: SPOTLESS; CLEAN; PURE.

final *adjective* **1** *the final act* last, closing, concluding, finishing, end, ending, terminating, terminal, ultimate, eventual, endmost. **2** *their decision is final* absolute, conclusive, irrevocable, unalterable, irrefutable, incontrovertible, indisputable, unappealable, decisive, definitive, definite, settled, determinate.

Antonyms: FIRST; INTRODUCTORY.

finale *noun* end, finish, close, conclusion, climax, culmination, denouement, last act, final scene, final curtain, epilogue; *inf.* wind-up.

finality *noun* conclusiveness, decisiveness, definiteness, definitiveness, completeness, absoluteness, irrevocableness, irrefutability, inevitability, unavoidableness.

finalize *verb* complete, conclude, settle, decide, agree on, work out, tie up, wrap up, put the finishing touches to; *inf.* sew up, clinch.

finally *adverb* **1** *we finally won* in the end, at last, at long last, ultimately, eventually, at the last minute, at the very last minute, at length, in the long run, when all was said and done. **2** *"finally, I declare the meeting over"* to conclude, in conclusion, lastly. **3** *they have separated finally* absolutely, conclusively, irrevocably, decisively, definitively, definitely, for ever, for good, for all time, once and for all, permanently, inexorably.

finance *noun* **1** *she works in finance* financial affairs, money matters, pecuniary/fiscal matters, economics; money management, commerce, business, investment, banking, accounting. **2** *finances are low* funds, assets, resources; money, capital, cash, wealth, wherewithal, revenue, stock; financial condition/state.

finance *verb* pay for, fund, back, subsidize, underwrite, capitalize, guarantee, provide capital/security for, furnish credit for.

financial *adjective* money, monetary, pecuniary, fiscal, economic, budgetary.

---

financial
fiscal, monetary, pecuniary

What's the difference between a **financial** crisis and a **fiscal** one? It all depends on who's having trouble with money and the scale of the difficulties. *Financial* usually applies to money matters involving large sums or transactions of considerable importance (*the auction was a financial success*). *Fiscal* refers specifically to the financial affairs of a government, organization, or corporation (*the end of the company's fiscal year*), while **pecuniary** refers to money matters of a more personal or practical nature and is preferred to *financial* when money is being discussed on a smaller scale (*pecuniary motives, pecuniary assistance, pecuniary difficulties*). Of all these words, **monetary** refers most directly to money as such and is often used when discussing the coinage, distribution, and circulation of money (*the European monetary system; the monetary unit of a country*).

---

find *verb* **1** *find a gold watch* come across, chance upon, light upon, happen upon, stumble on. **2** *find a cure/answer/hotel* discover, come up with, hit upon, turn up, bring to light, uncover, unearth, ferret out, locate, lay one's hands on, encounter. **3** *we found the missing glove* get back, recover, retrieve, regain, repossess, recoup. **4** *find the money* | *find happiness* get, obtain, acquire, procure, gain, earn, achieve, at-

tain, win. **5** *find it pays to be honest* | *found that everyone had gone* discover, become aware, realize, learn, conclude, detect, observe, notice, note, perceive. **6** *find the cheese too strong* consider, regard as, think, judge, deem, gauge, rate. **7** *the arrow found its mark* reach, attain, arrive at, gain, achieve. **find out 1** *we found out they were lying* discover, become aware that, realize, learn. *See* FIND *verb* 5. **2** *find out the truth* discover, detect, bring to light, reveal, expose, unearth, disclose, unmask, ferret out, lay bare. *Antonyms:* LOSE; MISLAY.

find *noun the vase is quite a find* asset, acquisition, lucky discovery, catch, bargain, good buy, godsend, boon, windfall.

finding *noun the finding of the committee* | *the findings of the court* decision, verdict, conclusion, pronouncement, judgment, decree, order, recommendation.

fine *adjective* **1** *that's fine with me* all right, satisfactory, acceptable, agreeable, convenient, suitable, good; *inf.* OK. **2** *I'm fine, thanks* all right, in good health, quite well; *inf.* OK. **3** *a fine painting/performance/wine* excellent, first-class, first-rate, great, exceptional, outstanding, admirable, quality, superior, splendid, magnificent, beautiful, exquisite, choice, select, prime, supreme, rare; *inf.* A-1, splendiferous, top-notch. **4** *a fine day* fair, dry, bright, clear, cloudless, sunny, balmy, clement. **5** *fine china/bones* fragile, delicate, frail, dainty, slight. **6** *fine material* sheer, light, lightweight, chiffony, diaphanous, filmy, gossamer, gossamery, gauzelike, gauzy, cobwebby, transparent, translucent, airy, ethereal, thin, flimsy. **7** *a fine sand/powder* fine-grained, powdery, powdered, ground, crushed, pulverized. **8** *fine clothes* expensive, elegant, stylish, smart, chic, fashionable, modish, high-fashion, lavish. **9** *fine gold* refined, pure, solid, unadulterated, unalloyed, unpolluted, one hundred percent. **10** *a fine distinction* subtle, fine-drawn, tenuous, hairsplitting, precise, minute, elusive, abstruse. **11** *a fine taste in art* discriminating, discerning, tasteful, fastidious, critical, sensitive, refined, intelligent. **12** *a fine mind* keen, acute, sharp, quick, perspicacious, clever, intelligent, brilliant, finely honed/tuned. **13** *a fine young man/woman* good-looking, attractive, handsome, lovely, pretty, striking. *Antonyms:* POOR; DULL; COARSE.

fine *noun get a fine for illegal parking* penalty, financial penalty, punishment, forfeit, forfeiture; damages.

fine *verb fine for stealing* impose a fine on, exact a penalty, penalize, punish by fining.

finery *noun* Sunday best, adornment, splendor, showiness, gaudiness; elaborate/best clothes, trappings, decorations; *inf.* glad rags, best gear, best bib and tucker.

finesse *noun* **1** *handle the problem with finesse*

tact, discretion, diplomacy, delicacy, refinement, grace, elegance, sophistication, subtlety, polish, savoir faire, skill, expertise, wisdom, worldly wisdom, craft; tactfulness, adroitness, adeptness, skillfulness, cleverness, artfulness. **2** *win by a clever finesse* trick, stratagem, ruse, maneuver, scheme, artifice, machination, bluff, wile; *inf.* dodge.

finger *verb finger the fruit/material* touch, feel, handle, toy with, play with, fiddle with, stroke, caress, maul, meddle with; *inf.* paw.

finicky *adjective* fussy, overparticular, fastidious, persnickety, hard to please, overcritical, difficult; *inf.* picky, choosy.

finish *verb* **1** *finish the task* complete, accomplish, execute, discharge, carry out, deal with, do, get done, fulfill, achieve, attain, end, conclude, close, bring to a conclusion/end/close, finalize, stop, cease, terminate, round off, put the finishing touches to; *inf.* wind up, wrap up, sew up, polish off, knock off. **2** *finish working* stop, cease, discontinue, give up, have done with, suspend. **3** *finish the milk* | *finish up/off the food* use, use up, consume, eat, devour, drink, exhaust, empty, deplete, drain, expend, dispatch, dispose of. **4** *the job finished her* | *finish off the enemy* overcome, defeat, overpower, conquer, overwhelm, get the better of, best, worst, rout, bring down, put an end to, do away with, dispose of, get rid of, destroy, annihilate, kill, exterminate, liquidate, drive to the wall; *inf.* wipe out, do in. **5** *finish her education* perfect, polish, refine, put the final/finishing touches to, crown. **6** *finish the surface of the table/vase* put a finish on, varnish, lacquer, stain, coat, veneer, wax, gild, glaze, give a shine to, polish, burnish, smooth off.
Antonyms: START; BEGIN.

finish *noun* **1** *at the finish of the task/race* completion, accomplishment, execution, fulfillment, achievement, consummation, end, conclusion, close, closing, cessation, final act, finale, denouement; last stages; *inf.* winding up. **2** *the finish of the enemy* defeat, overpowering, destruction, rout, bringing down, end, annihilation, death, extermination, liquidation, ruination; *inf.* ruin, curtains. **3** *people of finish* cultivation, culture, refinement, polish, style, sophistication, suaveness, urbanity, education. **4** *a table/material with a beautiful finish* surface, texture, grain, veneer, coating, lacquer, glaze, luster, gloss, polish, shine, patina, smoothness.

finished *adjective* **1** *finished tasks* completed, accomplished, executed, over and done with, over, in the past; *inf.* wrapped up, sewn up. *See* FINISH *verb* 1. **2** *the finished carton of milk* empty, drained, used up, exhausted, spent. **3** *a finished performance* accomplished, expert, proficient, masterly, polished, impeccable, classic, consummate, flawless, skillful, skilled, dexterous, adroit, professional, talented, gifted, ele-

gant, graceful. **4** *finished hopes* | *the business was finished* at an end, gone, gone to the wall, over with, doomed, lost, ruined, bankrupt, wrecked; *inf.* washed up.

finite *adjective* not infinite, bounded, limited, subject to limitations, restricted, delimited, demarcated, terminable.

fire *noun* **1** *killed in a fire* blaze, conflagration, inferno, holocaust; flames. **2** *hit by enemy fire* gunfire, sniping, flak, bombardment, shelling; volley, barrage, fusillade, salvo. **3** *people of fire* energy, spirit, life, liveliness, animation, vigor, verve, vivacity, sparkle, scintillation, dash, vim, gusto, élan, enthusiasm, fervor, eagerness, impetuosity, force, potency, driving power, vehemence, ardor, passion, intensity, zeal; *inf.* pep. **4** *writings with fire* passion, ardor, intensity, inspiration, imagination, creativity, inventiveness, flair. **on fire 1** *houses on fire* burning, ablaze, blazing, aflame, in flames, flaming, alight, fiery. **2** *on fire with passion* passionate, ardent, fervent, intense, excited, eager, enthusiastic.

fire *verb* **1** *fire the haystacks* set fire to, set on fire, set alight, set ablaze, put a match to, light, ignite, kindle. **2** *fire the guns* shoot, let off, discharge, trigger, set off. **3** *fire a missile* launch, hurl, discharge, eject. **4** *fire the explosives* explode, detonate, touch off. **5** *they fired him with enthusiasm* arouse, rouse, stir up, excite, enliven, inflame, put/breathe life into, animate, inspire, motivate, stimulate, incite, galvanize, electrify, impassion. **6** *fire the assistant* dismiss, discharge, give someone his/her marching orders, get rid of, show someone the door, oust, depose, cashier; *inf.* sack, ax.

firebrand *noun* troublemaker, agitator, rabble-rouser, demagogue.

fireproof *adjective* nonflammable, noninflammable, incombustible, unburnable, flame-resistant, flame-retardant, flameproof, fire-resistant.

fireworks *plural noun* **1** *a fireworks display on Independence Day* pyrotechnics; firecrackers, bottle rockets, sparklers, starbursts. **2** *there were fireworks when she heard the news* tantrums, hysterics, paroxysms, pyrotechnics; outburst, fit, frenzy, uproar.

firm *adjective* **1** *a firm surface* hard, hardened, stiff, rigid, inflexible, inelastic, unyielding, resistant, solid, solidified, compacted, compressed, condensed, dense, close-grained, congealed, frozen, set, jelled. **2** *the poles were firm in the ground* fixed, fast, secure, secured, stable, set, established, tight, immovable, irremovable, unshakable, stationary, motionless, taut, anchored, rooted, embedded; riveted, braced, cemented, nailed, tied. **3** *firm plans* fixed, settled, decided, definite, established, unalterable, unchangeable. **4** *a firm handshake* strong, vigorous, sturdy. **5** *a firm friendship* constant, unchanging, enduring, abiding, durable, deep-rooted, long-standing, long-

lasting, steady, stable, staunch. **6** *firm about not going* resolute, determined, decided, resolved, unfaltering, unwavering, unflinching, unswerving, unyielding, unbending, inflexible, obdurate, obstinate, stubborn, hard-line, strict, intransigent, unmalleable.
Antonyms: SOFT; FLABBY; UNSTABLE; INDEFINITE.

firm *noun a manufacturing firm* company, business, concern, house, establishment, organization, corporation, conglomerate, partnership, cooperative; *inf.* outfit.

firmament *noun* sky, heaven, blue sky, the blue, vault of heaven, vault, celestial sphere; heavens, skies.

firmness *noun* **1** *the firmness of the surface* hardness, stiffness, rigidity, inflexibility, inelasticity, resistance, solidity. *See* FIRM *adjective* 1. **2** *the firmness of the handshake* strength, vigor, sturdiness. **3** *the firmness of the friendship* constancy, endurance, durability, steadiness, stability, staunchness. *See* FIRM *adjective* 5. **4** *the firmness of the refusal/teacher* resolution, determination, resolve, strength of purpose, obduracy, inflexibility, stubbornness, strictness, intransigence. *See* FIRM *adjective* 6.

first *adjective* **1** *the first stages of life on earth* earliest, initial, opening, introductory, original, premier, primitive, primeval, primordial, pristine. **2** *first principles* primary, beginning, basic, fundamental, key, rudimentary, cardinal. **3** *the first people in the land* leading, foremost, principal, highest, ruling, chief, head, main, major, greatest, preeminent, supreme.
Antonyms: LAST; SUBSIDIARY; LOWLY.

first *adverb* **1** *first he said hello* at first, to begin with, at the beginning/start, at the outset, initially. **2** *first we must wash our hands* before anything/all else, first and foremost. **3** *first, I don't want it, second . . .* in the first place, firstly. **4** *I'd die first* sooner, rather, in preference, more willingly.

first *noun from the first* beginning, very beginning, start, outset, commencement; *inf.* the word go.

firsthand *adverb/adjective learn firsthand* direct, directly, from the original source, straight from the horse's mouth.

first-rate *adjective* first-class, second to none, top, premier, superlative, prime, excellent, superb, outstanding, exceptional, tip-top, admirable; *inf.* top-notch, ace, A-1, crack.

fiscal *adjective* financial, economic, monetary, money, pecuniary, capital.

fish *verb* **1** *boys fishing in the stream* go fishing, angle, cast. **2** *fish for keys* look, search, hunt, grope, delve, cast about. **fish out** pull out, haul out, extricate, extract, retrieve, produce.

fisherman *noun* angler, trawler, fly-fisherman.

fishy *adjective* **1** *a fishy smell* fishlike, piscatorial, piscine. **2** *something fishy about it* questionable, dubious, doubtful, suspect, suspicious, odd, queer, peculiar, strange, not quite right; *inf.* funny, shady, not kosher.

fission *noun* splitting, parting, division, cleaving, rupture, breaking, severance, disjuncture.

fissure *noun* opening, crack, crevice, cleft, chink, cranny, groove, slit, gash, gap, hole, breach, break, fracture, fault, rift, rupture, split, rent, interstice.

fit *adjective* **1** *feeling fit* well, healthy, in good health, in shape, in good shape, in good trim, in trim, in good condition, strong, robust, hale and hearty, sturdy, hardy, stalwart, vigorous. **2** *fit to drive* able, capable, competent, adequate, good enough, satisfactory, ready, prepared, qualified, trained, equipped, eligible, worthy; *inf.* up to scratch. **3** *a fit occasion | fit behavior* fitting, proper, due, seemly, decorous, decent, right, correct, apt, appropriate, suitable, convenient, apposite, relevant, pertinent.
Antonyms: UNHEALTHY; UNFIT; INAPPROPRIATE.

fit *verb* **1** *the shoes don't fit* be the right/correct size, be big/small enough, be the right shape. **2** *facts fitting our theory* agree with, be in agreement with, concur with, correspond with, match, dovetail with, tally with, suit, go with, be congruent with, conform to, be consonant with. **3** *fit the parts together* join, connect, put together. **4** *fit the carpet* put in place/position, position, lay, fix, insert, arrange, adjust, shape. **5** *fit your expenditure to your income* adjust, adapt, modify, alter, regulate, accommodate. **6** *the training will fit him for many jobs* make suitable, qualify, prepare, make ready, prime, condition, train. **7** *fit the kitchen with units* fit out, equip, provide, supply, furnish. **fit in** belong to, match, square with; accord, agree, concur, conform. **fit out** *fit out the army* equip, provide, supply, furnish, outfit.

fit *noun* **1** *an epileptic fit* convulsion, spasm, paroxysm, seizure, attack. **2** *a fit of coughing* attack, bout, spell. **3** *a fit of the giggles* bout, burst, outburst, outbreak. **4** *she'll have a fit* fit of temper, tantrum, outburst of anger/rage. **by fits and starts** on and off, off and on, spasmodically, intermittently, sporadically, erratically, irregularly, interruptedly, fitfully.

fitful *adjective fitful sleep* broken, disturbed, irregular, uneven, intermittent, sporadic, spasmodic, disconnected, unsteady, variable.

fitness *noun* **1** *improve your fitness* physical fitness, health, good health, condition, shape, good condition/shape, strength, robustness, sturdiness, vigor. **2** *his fitness to drive* ability, capability, competency, preparedness, qualification, eligibility, worthiness. *See* FIT *adjective* 2. **3** *the fitness of the occasion* properness, propriety, seemliness, correctness, aptness, suitability, convenience, relevance, pertinence. *See* FIT *adjective* 3.

fitted *adjective not fitted to the life* suited, suitable, right, equipped, cut out for.

fitting *adjective a fitting occasion | not fitting to go* *early* fit, proper, due, right, suitable, appropriate. See FIT *adjective* 3.

fitting *noun* **1** *an electrical fitting* part, piece, component, attachment, accessory. **2** *kitchen fittings* furnishings, units, fixtures, appointments, accouterments, appurtenances; furniture, equipment.

fix *verb* **1** *fix the shelf to the wall* fasten, secure, make fast, attach, connect, join, couple; stick, glue, cement, pin, nail, screw, bolt, clamp, bind, tie, pinion. **2** *fix the post in the ground* plant, implant, install, anchor, embed, establish, position, station, situate. **3** *fix a date/price* decide on, settle, set, agree on, arrive at, arrange, determine, establish, define, name, specify. **4** *fix the car* repair, mend, see to, patch up, put right, put to rights, restore, remedy, rectify, adjust. **5** *fix her gaze on them* direct, focus, level at, rivet. **6** *fix the color/dye* make fast, set, make permanent. **7** *has the glue fixed?* set, solidify, congeal, harden, stiffen. **8** *fix one's hair* arrange, put in order, adjust, dress. **9** *fix something to eat* prepare, make, make ready, put together, cook. **10** *I'll fix him for that* get even with, revenge oneself on, get one's revenge on, wreak vengeance on, take retribution on, give someone his/her just deserts, punish, deal with; *inf.* get back at, pay someone back, cook someone's goose. **11** *fix the outcome of the race* rig, manipulate, maneuver, arrange fraudulently; *inf.* fiddle with. **12** *fix the judges* bribe, influence, influence unduly. **fix up 1** *fix up a meeting* fix, arrange, organize, plan, agree on, settle on, decide on. **2** *fix you up a room* | *fix you up with a bed* provide, supply, furnish, accommodate.
Antonyms: BREAK; CANCEL; CHANGE.

fix *noun* *in a bit of a fix* predicament, plight, quandary, dilemma, difficulty, spot of trouble, bit of bother, muddle, mess, corner, ticklish/tricky situation, tight spot; *inf.* pickle, jam, hole, spot, scrape, bind.

fixation *noun* obsession, preoccupation, complex, compulsion, mania, *idée fixe*, phobia; *inf.* hang-up, thing.

fixture *noun* **1** *kitchen fixtures* appliance, attachment. **2** *he became a fixture at the local bar* regular, habitué, regular customer, frequenter, (daily) patron.

fizz *verb* **1** *wine fizzing* bubble, effervesce, sparkle, froth, foam. **2** *the solution fizzing* hiss, sputter, fizzle, sibilate.

fizzle *verb* **fizzle out** peter out, come to nothing, fall through, come to grief, end in failure, fail, miscarry, abort, collapse; *inf.* flop, fold.

fizzy *adjective* bubbly, bubbling, sparkling, effervescent, carbonated, gassy.

flabbergast *verb* astound, amaze, dumbfound, strike dumb, render speechless, stun, stagger, confound, daze, overcome, overwhelm, nonplus, disconcert; *inf.* bowl over.

flabby *adjective* flaccid, unfirm, out of tone, drooping, pendulous, limp; *inf.* out of shape.
Antonyms: FIRM; TAUT; STRONG.

flaccid *adjective* flabby, unfirm, drooping, limp. See FLABBY.
Antonyms: FIRM; TAUT; STRONG.

flag[1] *noun* standard, ensign, banner, pennant, burgee, streamer; bunting; colors.

flag[2] *verb* *flag the places on the map* indicate, mark, mark out, label, tab. **flag down** *the police flagged him down* wave down, signal to stop, signal, hail, gesture/motion to stop.

flag[3] *verb* **1** *I'm flagging from the heat* tire, become fatigued, grow tired/weary, weaken, grow weak, lose one's strength. **2** *his strength/interest is flagging* fade, fail, decline, wane, ebb, diminish, decrease, taper off.

flagon *noun* bottle, decanter, carafe, flask, jug.

flagrant *adjective* glaring, obvious, blatant, egregious, outrageous, scandalous, shocking, disgraceful, shameless, dreadful, terrible, gross; notorious, heinous, atrocious, monstrous, wicked, iniquitous, villainous.
Antonyms: UNOBTRUSIVE; SLIGHT.

flagstone *noun* paving stone, stone block/slab, slab.

flail *verb* **1** *with arms flailing* swing wildly, wave helplessly, thrash about, move erratically. **2** *flail the corn/enemy* thresh, thrash, beat, strike, batter, drub.

flair *noun* **1** *have a flair for languages* natural ability, ability, aptitude, capability, facility, skill, talent, gift, knack, bent, feel, genius. **2** *all the women of the family had flair* style, panache, elegance, dash, élan, taste, good taste, discernment, discrimination.

flake *noun* *a flake of paint/snow* chip, shaving, peeling, scale, sliver, wafer, fragment, bit, particle.

flake *verb* *paint/skin flaking* chip, peel, peel off, scale off, blister; *Tech.* exfoliate.

flamboyant *adjective* **1** *flamboyant gestures* extravagant, theatrical, showy, ostentatious, dashing, swashbuckling. **2** *flamboyant clothes/colors* colorful, brilliantly colored, bright, exciting, dazzling, glamorous, splendid, resplendent, showy, gaudy, flashy. **3** *flamboyant architecture* elaborate, ornate, fancy, baroque, rococo, arabesque.
Antonyms: NATURAL; DULL; SIMPLE.

flame *noun* **1** *flames burst from the ashes* fire, blaze, conflagration. **2** *burn with a flame* brilliant light, brightness, glow, gleam. **3** *flame is a bright color* red, reddish-orange. **4** *the flame of love* passion, passionateness, warmth, ardor, fervor, fire, excitement, intensity, keenness, eagerness, enthusiasm. **5** *an old flame* boyfriend, girlfriend, sweetheart, lover, partner, beloved, beau.

flame *verb* **1** *the wood flamed* burn, blaze, burst into flame, catch fire. **2** *the light flamed* glow, shine, flash, beam, glare, sparkle.

flameproof *adjective* nonflammable, noninflammable, flame-resistant, fire-resistant, incombustible, fireproof.

flaming *adjective* **1** *a flaming bonfire* blazing, ablaze, burning, on fire, afire, in flames, aflame, ignited, fiery, red-hot, raging, glowing. **2** *a flaming mood* furious, enraged, fuming, incensed, infuriated, mad, angry, raging, wrathful; *inf.* livid. **3** *flaming colors* bright, brilliant, vivid, flamboyant, red, reddish-orange, scarlet. **4** *a flaming idiot* utter, absolute, damned, damnable.

flank *noun* **1** *the animal's flank* side, haunch, loin, quarter, thigh. **2** *the flank of the enemy/mountain* side, wing.

flank *verb* *lawns flank the house* be situated along, border, edge, bound, fringe, skirt.

flap *verb* move up and down, flutter, sway, beat, thresh, thrash, wave, agitate, vibrate, wag, waggle, shake, swing, oscillate, flail.

flap *noun* **1** *the flap of wings* flutter, beat, fluttering, beating, waving, shaking, flailing. *See* FLAP *verb.* **2** *a flap of material* fold, overlap, overhang, covering, tab, apron.

flare *verb* **1** *the fire flared* flare up, blaze, flame, burn unsteadily. **2** *lights flared on the shore* flash, gleam, glow, sparkle, glitter, flicker. **3** *his nostrils flared* spread outward, broaden, widen, widen at the bottom, splay. **flare up 1** *the fire flared up* blaze, burn violently. *See* FLARE *verb* 1. **2** *trouble/disease flared up* broke out, burst out, recur. **3** *the two women flared up* lose one's temper, lose control, become blazing mad, explode, boil over, boil over with rage, go berserk, throw a tantrum; *inf.* blow one's top, fly off the handle, lose one's cool.

flare *noun* **1** *burn with a flare* unsteady flame, blaze, burst, flash, flicker, glimmer, shimmer, dazzle, glare, gleam. **2** *flares for ships* signal, distress signal, rocket, light. **3** *a skirt with a flare* gradual widening, outward spread.

flash *verb* **1** *lights flashed* light up, shine out, flare, blaze, glare, beam, gleam, glint, sparkle, flicker, shimmer, twinkle, glimmer, glisten, scintillate, coruscate. **2** *the runners/cars/time flashed past* dart, dash, tear, shoot, zoom, streak, fly, rush, bolt, race, bound, speed; *inf.* scoot. **3** *flash her new ring* show off, flaunt, flourish, display, exhibit.

flash *noun* **1** *a flash of light* blaze, burst, glare, flare, shaft, ray, streak, gleam, glint, sparkle, flicker, shimmer, twinkle, glimmer. *See* FLASH *verb* 1. **2** *he came in a flash* instant, moment, second, split second, minute, trice, twinkling, twinkling of an eye, twinkle, wink of an eye, two shakes, two shakes of a lamb's tail; *inf.* jiffy, bat of an eye. **3** *a flash of enthusiasm/wit* sudden show, outburst, burst, outbreak, brief display/exhibition.

flashy *adjective* *flashy clothes/cars* ostentatious, showy, in bad/poor taste, tasteless, pretentious, cheap, cheap and nasty, tawdry, garish, loud, flamboyant, gaudy; *inf.* tacky, snazzy, jazzy, glitzy, ritzy.

flask *noun* bottle, flagon, decanter, carafe.

flat *adjective* **1** *a flat surface* level, horizontal, leveled, even, smooth, unbroken, plane. **2** *lying flat on the ground* stretched out, spread-eagle, prone, supine, prostrate, recumbent. **3** *a flat dish* shallow, not deep. **4** *a flat tire* deflated, collapsed, blown out, burst, punctured, ruptured. **5** *a flat denial* outright, direct, out-and-out, downright, straight, plain, explicit, absolute, definite, positive, firm, final, conclusive, complete, utter, categorical, unqualified, unconditional, unquestionable, unequivocal. **6** *in a flat voice* | *flat jokes* monotonous, boring, dull, tedious, uninteresting, lifeless, lackluster, dead, vapid, bland, insipid, prosaic. **7** *feeling rather flat* depressed, dejected, dispirited, low, down, without energy, enervated. **8** *the market is flat* slow, inactive, sluggish, slack, not busy. **flat-out** *a flat-out lie* downright, absolute, out-and-out.
Antonyms: UNEVEN; VERTICAL; EXCITING.

flat *adverb* *she told him flat that she was going* outright, directly, straight, plainly, explicitly, absolutely, definitely, conclusively, categorically. *See* FLAT *adjective* 5. **flat out 1** *asked flat out for a raise* directly, bluntly, openly; *inf.* without batting an eye. **2** *the boat passed us flat out* at full speed, all out, as fast as possible, post-haste, at full tilt, full steam ahead; *inf.* hell-bent for leather.

flatten *verb* **1** *flatten the surface* make flat, level, level out/off, make even, even out, smooth, smooth out/off, plane. **2** *the crowd flattened the grass* compress, trample, press down, crush, squash, compact. **3** *flatten the old buildings* demolish, tear down, knock down, raze, raze to the ground. **4** *flatten his opponent* knock down, knock to the ground, floor, knock off one's feet, fell, prostrate. **5** *even sarcasm fails to flatten him* crush, quash, squash, deflate, snub, humiliate; *inf.* put down.

flatter *verb* **1** *salesmen flattering the customers* | *he flattered her by buying her painting* compliment, praise, sing the praises of, praise to excess, praise to the skies, eulogize, puff up, blandish, fawn upon, cajole, humor; *inf.* sweet-talk, soft-soap, butter up, lay it on thick to/for, play up to. **2** *that dress flatters her coloring* suit, become, set off, show to advantage, enhance; *inf.* do something for.

flattering *adjective* **1** *flattering words* complimentary, fulsome, adulatory, praising, blandishing, laudatory, ingratiating, cajoling; *inf.* sweet-talking, soft-soaping. **2** *a flattering dress* becoming, enhancing.
Antonyms: UNFLATTERING; CONDEMNATORY; UNBECOMING.

flattery *noun* praise, adulation, overpraise, false praise, eulogy, puffery, fawning, cajolery; compliments, blandishments; *inf.* sweet talk, soft soap, buttering-up.

flatulence *noun* wind, gas, intestinal gas; belching; *inf.* farting.

flaunt *verb* show off, parade, display ostentatiously, exhibit, draw attention to, make a show of, wave, dangle, brandish.

flavor *noun* **1** *dislike the flavor of the herb* taste, savor, tang, relish. **2** *add some flavor to the sauce* flavoring, seasoning, tastiness, tang, relish, piquancy, spiciness, zest; *inf.* zing. **3** *capture the flavor of the poem/place* spirit, essence, soul, nature, character, quality, feel, feeling, ambience, tone, style, stamp, property.

flavor *verb* **1** *flavor the stew* add flavor/flavoring to, season, add seasoning/herbs/spices to, spice, add piquancy to. **2** *flavor the punch with cinnamon* season, lace, imbue, infuse.

flavoring *noun* **1** *add flavoring to the stew* flavor, seasoning. *See* FLAVOR *noun* 2. **2** *vanilla flavoring* essence, extract, tincture.

flaw *noun* **1** *a flaw in his character* fault, defect, imperfection, blemish, failing, foible, shortcoming, weakness, weak spot. **2** *a flaw in the china/material* fault, defect, crack, chip, fracture, break, crevice, fissure, rent, split, tear.

Antonyms: ASSET; STRENGTH.

flawless *adjective* **1** *a flawless performance* faultless, perfect, impeccable. **2** *a flawless complexion* perfect, blemish-free, unflawed, unimpaired, unmarred. **3** *a flawless piece of china* perfect, whole, intact, sound, unbroken, undamaged.

Antonyms: IMPERFECT; DEFECTIVE.

fleck *noun* *a fleck of white in the black cloth* spot, mark, speck, speckle, freckle.

fleck *verb* *black material flecked with white* spot, mark, speckle, dot, sprinkle, spatter, stipple, mottle, streak, freckle.

flee *verb* **1** *she fled from the blaze* | *the burglar fled when disturbed* run, run away, run off, bolt, rush, speed, take flight, take to flight, make off, fly, abscond, retreat, beat a retreat, beat a hasty retreat, depart hastily/abruptly, make a quick exit, run for it, make a run for it, take off, take to one's heels, decamp, escape, make one's escape/getaway, do a disappearing act, vanish; *inf.* cut and run, make oneself scarce, beat it, skedaddle, split, scram. **2** *they fled the country* run away from, leave hastily/abruptly, fly, escape from; *inf.* skip.

fleece *noun* *a sheep's fleece* wool, coat.

fleece *verb* **1** *fleece the sheep* shear, clip. **2** *a con man fleeced the old lady of her savings* swindle, defraud, cheat, rob, strip, bilk, overcharge; *inf.* con, take for a ride, rip off, sting, bleed, take to the cleaners, soak.

fleecy *adjective* woolly, downy, fluffy, shaggy, soft, smooth; fleecelike, lanate.

fleet *noun* *the fleet set sail* flotilla, naval force, navy, convoy, squadron, armada; *lit.* argosy.

fleet *adjective* swift, fast, rapid, quick, speedy, expeditious, nimble, fleet of foot, nimble-footed, swift-footed, like the wind.

fleeting *adjective* rapid, swift, brief, short-lived, short, momentary, transient, transitory, ephemeral, fugitive, evanescent, fugacious, vanishing, flying, passing, flitting, here today and gone tomorrow, temporary, impermanent.

Antonyms: PERMANENT; ENDURING.

fleetness *noun* swiftness, fastness, rapidity, quickness, speed, speediness, velocity, celerity, nimbleness, nimble-footedness, swift-footedness.

flesh *noun* **1** *flesh and bones* muscle, tissue, muscle tissue, brawn. **2** *carry too much flesh* fat; fatness, obesity, corpulence. **3** *not much flesh in the essay* substance, pith, matter, body. **4** *the spirit is willing but the flesh is weak* | *the pleasure of the flesh* body, human body, human nature, physical nature, physicality, corporeality, carnality, animality, sensuality, sensualism. **5** *all flesh would perish in such conditions* mankind, man, humankind, people, human race/species, humanity, *Homo sapiens*; animate life, the living; human beings, living creatures. **flesh and blood** *ignored their own flesh and blood* family, kin, kinfolk, kinsfolk; relatives, relations, blood relations; *inf.* folk. **in the flesh** *saw the actor in the flesh* in person, before one's eyes, in front of one, in one's presence.

flesh *verb* **flesh out 1** *the children have fleshed out a bit* put on weight, grow fatter, fatten up. **2** *flesh out the material* fill out, expand, make more substantial, add substance/detail to.

flex *verb* **1** *flex one's muscles* contract, tighten, make taught. **2** *flex one's arm* bend, curve, crook, angle.

flexible *adjective* **1** *flexible materials* bendable, pliant, pliable, elastic, springy, plastic, moldable. **2** *flexible young bodies* supple, agile, limber, lithe, lissome, double-jointed. **3** *my arrangements are flexible* adaptable, adjustable, open-ended, open, open to change, changeable, variable. **4** *the young man is too flexible* tractable, malleable, compliant, manageable, amenable, biddable, docile, submissive, yielding.

Antonyms: RIGID; STIFF; INFLEXIBLE; SET.

---

flexible
elastic, limber, pliable, pliant, resilient, supple

If you can bend over and touch your toes, you are **flexible**. But a dancer or gymnast is **limber**, an adjective that specifically applies to a body that has been brought into condition through training (*to stay limber, she did yoga every day*). *Flexible* applies to whatever can be bent without breaking, whether or not it returns to its original shape (*a flexible plastic hose; a flexible electrical conduit*); it does not necessarily refer, as *limber* does, to the human body. Unlike *flexible*, **resilient** implies the ability to spring back into shape after being bent or compressed, or to recover one's health or spirits quickly (*so young and resilient that she was back at work in a week*). **Elastic** is usually applied to substances or materials that are easy to stretch or expand and that quickly recover their shape or size (*pants with an elastic waist*), while **supple** is applied to whatever is easily bent, twisted, or folded without breaking or cracking (*a soft, supple leather*). When applied to the human body, *supple* suggests the ability to move effortlessly. **Pliant** and **pliable** may used to describe either people or things that are easily bent or manipulated. *Pliant* suggests a tendency to bend without force or pressure from the outside, while *pliable* suggests the use of force or submission to another's will. A *pliant* person is merely adaptable, but a *pliable* person is easy to influence and eager to please.

flick *verb* **1** *flick the horse with a whip* strike, hit, rap, tap, touch. **2** *flick (on) the switch* click, flip, tap. **3** *cows' tails flicking* swish, wag, waggle. **flick through** skim (through), flip over, glance over/through, browse through, thumb through, skip over.

flicker *verb* **1** *lights flickering* twinkle, sparkle, blink, flash, shimmer, glitter, glimmer, glint, flare. **2** *with eyelids flickering* flutter, quiver, vibrate, bat, open and shut.

flight[1] *noun* **1** *watching the flight of the eagle* flying, soaring, mounting. **2** *a flight of geese/birds* flying group, flock; skein, bevy, covey; migration. **3** *a flight of bees* swarm, cloud. **4** *a history of flight* aviation, flying, air transport, aerial navigation; aeronautics. **5** *have a good flight* airline trip, journey, shuttle; *inf.* plane trip. **6** *climb two flights* flight of stairs, staircase, set of steps/stairs.

flight[2] *noun* *the flight of the beaten army* fleeing, running away, absconding, retreat, departure, hasty departure, exit, exodus, decamping, escape, getaway, disappearance, vanishing. *See* FLEE. **put to flight** chase, chase off, drive off, scare off, rout, scatter, scatter to the four winds, disperse, stampede. **take flight** flee, run away, bolt, make off, fly, abscond, beat a hasty retreat, take off, decamp.

flighty *adjective* frivolous, giddy, scatterbrained, harebrained, fickle, changeable, inconstant, unsteady, whimsical, capricious, skittish.

flimsy *adjective* **1** *a flimsy box* insubstantial, unsubstantial, slight, makeshift, jerry-built, gimcrack, rickety, ramshackle, shaky, fragile, frail. **2** *made of a flimsy material* thin, light, lightweight, delicate, sheer, filmy, diaphanous, transparent, translucent, see-through, gossamer, gauzy. **3** *a flimsy excuse* feeble, weak, poor, inadequate, thin, transparent, unconvincing, implausible, unsatisfactory, paltry, trifling, trivial, shallow.

Antonyms: STURDY; THICK; SOLID.

flinch *verb* *did not flinch at the loud noise* draw back, pull back, start back, recoil, withdraw, shrink back, shy away, cringe, cower, crouch, quail, wince, blench. **flinch from** *flinch from his duty* shrink from, shy away from, shirk away from, swerve from, dodge, avoid, duck, balk at.

fling *verb* *fling the clothes in the river* throw, toss, hurl, cast, pitch, sling, heave, fire, shy, launch, propel, catapult, send flying, let fly; *inf.* lob, chuck.

fling *noun* **1** *with one fling of the javelin* throw, toss, hurl, cast, pitch, shot, heave; *inf.* lob, chuck. *See* FLING *verb*. **2** *have a last fling before marriage* binge, spree, good time, bit of fun, night on the town. **3** *have a fling at winning the match* try, attempt, go, shot, stab, venture; *inf.* crack, whirl.

flip *verb* **1** *flip a coin* flick, toss, throw, pitch, cast, spin, twist. **2** *flip a switch* flick, click, tap. **flip through** skim (through), glance over/through, browse through, thumb through, skip over.

flippant *adjective* *a flippant remark* frivolous, superficial, shallow, glib, thoughtless, carefree, irresponsible, insouciant, offhand, disrespectful, impertinent, impudent, irreverent, saucy; *inf.* flip.

Antonyms: SERIOUS; RESPONSIBLE.

flirt *verb* **flirt with 1** *she's always flirting with the boys* toy with, trifle with, make eyes at, ogle, lead on; philander with, dally with. **2** *flirt with the idea of going* toy with, trifle with, play with, entertain, consider, give thought to, dabble in.

flirt *noun* *the new employee is a flirt* coquette, tease, vamp, heartbreaker, trifler, philanderer.

flirtatious *adjective* coquettish, provocative, teasing, amorous, philandering, dallying.

float *verb* **1** *things light enough to float on water* stay afloat, be buoyant, be buoyed up. **2** *craft floating along* bob, glide, sail, drift. **3** *not working, just floating about* move aimlessly, drift, wander, meander; *inf.* bum (around).

Antonyms: SINK; SUBMERGE.

floating *adjective* **1** *floating substances* buoyant, buoyed up, nonsubmerged, afloat; suspended, drifting. **2** *floating craft* bobbing, gliding, sailing, drifting. **3** *floating voters* uncommitted, unattached, fluctuating, variable. **4** *a floating population* not fixed, moving, unsettled, wandering, migratory. **5** *floating currencies* fluctuating, variable, not fixed.

flock *verb* collect, gather, foregather, come together, assemble, group, bunch, congregate, converge, crowd, herd, troop, throng, swarm, mill, huddle.

flock *noun* **1** *a flock of sheep* fold, drove, herd. **2** *a flock of birds/geese* flight, bevy, skein, gaggle. **3** *a flock of people* crowd, gathering, assembly, company, collection, congregation, group, throng, mass, host, multitude, troop, herd, convoy.

flog *verb* whip, horsewhip, lash, flay, flagellate, birch, scourge, belt, cane, strap, thrash, beat, whack, wallop, chastise, trounce; *inf.* lambaste, tan the hide of.

flood *noun* **1** *houses damaged in the flood* deluge, inundation, torrent, spate, overflow, flash flood. **2** *a flood of rain* downpour, torrent, cloudburst. **3** *a flood of mail* profusion, overabundance, superabundance, plethora, superfluity, glut; *inf.* tons, heaps. **4** *a flood of tears* outpouring, rush, stream, flow.

flood *verb* **1** *rivers flooding* overflow, break the banks, brim over, swell, surge, pour forth. **2** *flood the town* inundate, deluge, pour over, immerse, submerge, swamp, drown, engulf. **3** *mail flooding in* | *relief flooded through her* pour, flow, surge. **4** *flood the market with fruit* overfill, oversupply, saturate, glut, overwhelm.

floor *noun* *on the second floor* story, level, tier, deck.

floor *verb* **1** *floor him with one blow* knock down, ground, fell, prostrate. **2** *this problem/attitude floors me* defeat, beat, baffle, stump, perplex, puzzle, nonplus, confound, dumbfound, confuse, discomfit, disconcert; *inf.* throw.

flop *verb* **1** *flop into a chair* collapse, slump, drop, fall, tumble. **2** *the old man's head flopped to the side* dangle, droop, sag, hang limply. **3** *the play flopped* fail, fall flat, founder, close, be unsuccessful, be a disaster, miss the mark, go over/down like a lead balloon; *inf.* bomb.

Antonyms: SUCCEED; FLOURISH.

flop *noun* *the play was a flop* failure, fiasco, loser, disaster, debacle; *inf.* no-go, washout, dud, lemon, bomb, bust.

floral *adjective* *a floral dress* flower-patterned, flowery.

florid *adjective* **1** *a florid complexion* ruddy, red-faced, red, reddish, high-colored, flushed, blushing, rubicund. **2** *florid decorations* ornate, flamboyant, overelaborate, embellished, busy, baroque. **3** *florid prose* high-flown, flowery, verbose, overelaborate, grandiloquent, purple. *See* FLOWERY 2.

Antonyms: PALE; PLAIN.

flotsam *noun* *flotsam floating on the surface* wreckage, cargo, floating remains. **flotsam and jetsam 1** *clear up the flotsam and jetsam in the yard* rubbish, trash, junk, odds and ends, debris, detritus. **2** *looked upon them as little more than flotsam and jetsam* vagrants, (the) penniless, derelicts; riff-raff, (the) dregs of society.

flounder *verb* **1** *floundering about in the mud/dark* thrash, struggle, stumble, blunder, fumble, grope. **2** *he's floundering when it comes to math* struggle, find difficulties, be confused, be in the dark, be out of one's element. **3** *flounder his way through the speech* stumble, falter, blunder, muddle, bungle.

flourish *verb* **1** *flourish the sword/prize* brandish, wave, twirl, wield, swing, hold aloft, display, exhibit, flaunt, parade, vaunt; *inf.* show off. **2** *the plants are flourishing* thrive, grow, grow/do

well, develop, burgeon, bloom, blossom, bear fruit, burst forth. **3** *we are all flourishing* be well, be in good health, be strong, be vigorous, bloom, thrive, get on/ahead, get on well, prosper, be successful, succeed, make progress/headway; *inf.* be in the pink, be fine and dandy, go great guns.

Antonyms: FAIL; WITHER; DECLINE.

flout *verb* *flout convention* | *flout the rules* defy, scorn, disdain, show contempt for, spurn, scoff at, mock, laugh at, deride, ridicule, sneer at, jeer at, gibe at, insult, poke fun at, make a fool of.

Antonyms: OBEY; OBSERVE.

flow *verb* **1** *blood/rivers flowing* move, go along, course, run, circulate, proceed, glide, stream, ripple, swirl, surge, sweep, roll, rush, whirl, drift, slide, trickle, gurgle, babble. **2** *blood flowing from the wound* gush, stream, well, spurt, spout, squirt, spew, jet, spill, leak, seep, ooze, drip. **3** *springs flowing from the mountains* | *ideas flowing from her pen* arise, issue, spring, originate, derive, emanate, emerge, pour, proceed. **flow with** *the lands flowed with milk and honey* overflow with, be abundant in, abound in, teem with, be rich in, be full of.

flow *noun* **1** *the flow of the water* course, current, drift, stream, spate, tide. **2** *stem the flow of blood* gush, stream, welling, spurting, spouting, outpouring, outflow. *See* FLOW *noun* 2. **3** *a flow of words/complaints* flood, deluge, outpouring, outflow, abundance, superabundance, plethora, excess, effusion, succession, train.

flower *noun* **1** *pick/plant several flowers* bloom, blossom, floweret, floret; annual, perennial. **2** *in the flower of their youth* prime, peak, zenith, acme, height, heyday, springtime; salad days. **3** *the flower of the nation died in battle* finest, best, pick, choice, elite, cream, crème de la crème.

flowery *adjective* **1** *flowery patterns* floral, flower-covered, flower-patterned. **2** *flowery language* high-flown, ornate, fancy, elaborate, overelaborate, highly figurative, verbose, grandiloquent, purple, rhetorical, bombastic.

flowing *adjective* **1** *flowing streams* coursing, gliding, rippling, swirling, drifting, trickling. *See* FLOW *verb* 1. **2** *flowing prose* fluent, free-flowing, effortless, smooth, unbroken, uninterrupted, continuous, graceful, elegant. **3** *flowing hair* loose, hanging loose/free, unconfined.

fluctuate *verb* **1** *prices fluctuating* rise and fall, go up and down, seesaw, yo-yo, be unstable, be unsteady, vary, shift, change, alter, swing, oscillate, undulate, ebb and flow. **2** *she fluctuates between going and not going* waver, vacillate, hesitate, change one's mind, alternate, veer, shilly-shally, hem and haw, teeter, totter, seesaw, yo-yo, blow hot and cold.

fluctuation *noun* **1** *fluctuation in prices/results* rise and fall, rising and falling, seesawing, instability, unsteadiness, variation, shift, change, alteration, swing, oscillation, undulation, ebb and flow. **2** *the fluctuation of her opinion* wavering, vacillation, hesitation, alternation, shilly-shallying, inconstancy, fickleness. *See* FLUCTUATE 2.

flue *noun* duct, passage, channel, shaft, air passage, airway, vent.

fluency *noun* **1** *fluency as a speaker* articulacy, articulateness, eloquence, volubility. **2** *the fluency of the prose* smoothness, flowingness, fluidity, gracefulness, effortlessness, naturalness. *See* FLUENT 2. **3** *her fluency in German* command, facility, articulacy.

fluent *adjective* **1** *a fluent speaker* articulate, eloquent, smooth-spoken, silver-tongued, voluble. **2** *fluent prose* smooth, flowing, fluid, easy, graceful, effortless, natural, elegant, smooth-sounding, mellifluous, euphonious. **3** *fluent in French* having a command of, articulate in.

Antonyms: HESITANT; INARTICULATE.

fluff *noun* **1** *picking bits of fluff off the blankets* down, fuzz, lint; dust, dustball, fuzzball. **2** *the fluff of the chicks* down, downiness, fuzz, soft fur. **3** *not notice the actor's fluff* mistake, error, bungle, forgetfulness; *inf.* foul-up, screw-up. **4** *the movie was nothing but fluff* drivel, piffle, meaninglessness, frivolousness, superficiality.

fluff *verb* **1** *actors fluffing their lines* forget, deliver badly, bungle, muddle up, make a mess of; *inf.* mess up, foul up, screw up. **2** *the outfielder fluffing a catch* miss, bungle. **fluff up** *fluffing up the pillows* make fluffy, puff up/out, shake out, plump, aerate.

fluffy *adjective* **1** *a fluffy blanket* soft, downy, cottony, puffy, airy. **2** *fluffy biscuits* light, airy, flaky. **3** *a fluffy personality | a movie of fluffy substance* frivolous, superficial, meaningless, thin, insubstantial, nonintellectual.

fluid *noun* flowing substance; liquid, gas, solution.

fluid *adjective* **1** *a fluid substance moving along the pipe* gaseous, gassy, liquid, liquefied, melted, molten, uncongealed, running, flowing. **2** *a fluid prose style | a fluid movement* fluent, smooth, smooth-flowing, flowing, graceful, elegant, effortless, easy, natural. **3** *our plans are fluid* flexible, open to change, adaptable, adjustable, not fixed, not settled, variable, mutable. **4** *the situation is fluid* subject/likely to change, unstable, unsteady, ever-shifting, fluctuating, mobile, mercurial.

Antonyms: SOLID; FIRM; STILTED.

fluke *noun* *win by a fluke* lucky stroke, stroke of luck, stroke of good fortune, piece of good luck, lucky chance/shot/break.

flunk *verb* **1** *almost flunked the exam* fail, fail to pass, be unsuccessful (in), be/prove inadequate (in). **2** *the teacher flunked him* fail, choose not to pass, judge unsuccessful; reject, *inf.* give thumbs down to.

flunky *noun* **1** *the queen and her flunkies* manservant, footman, valet, liveried servant, lackey, page. **2** *the politician and his flunkies* lackey,

toady, minion, yes-man, sycophant, hanger-on, camp follower, puppet; *inf.* bootlicker.

flurry *noun* **1** *a flurry of snow/rain* squall, gust, shower. **2** *a sudden flurry of activity* burst, spurt, outbreak, spell, bout. **3** *the hostess in a flurry of excitement* fluster, fuss, bustle, whirl, stir, ferment, hubbub, commotion, hustle, flap, tumult, hurry, pother, agitation, disturbance, furor, excitement, perturbation; *inf.* to-do.

flush *verb* **1** *she flushed with embarrassment* blush, turn red, go red/rosy, redden, crimson, color, burn up, flame up, glow, suffuse with color. **2** *flush the water main* wash out, rinse (out), clean, cleanse. **3** *flush away the waste* eject, expel.

flush *noun* **1** *embarrassed flushes* blush. *See* FLUSH *verb* 1. **2** *the first flush of youth* bloom, glow, freshness, radiance, vigor.

flushed *adjective* **1** *flushed faces* blushing, red, reddened, crimson, ruddy, rosy, rubicund, burning, fiery, flaming, glowing, feverish. **2** *flushed with success* elated, delighted, thrilled, exhilarated, excited, worked up, animated, aroused, inflamed, impassioned, intoxicated; *inf.* high.

fluster *verb* *unexpected guests fluster her* make nervous, agitate, ruffle, unsettle, upset, bother, put on edge, discompose, panic, perturb, disconcert, confuse, throw off balance, confound, nonplus; *inf.* hassle, rattle, faze, throw into a tizzy.

fluster *noun* *unexpected guests putting her into a fluster | causing fluster* nervous state, state of agitation, flurry, bustle, flutter, panic, upset; discomposure, agitation, perturbation, confusion, turmoil, commotion; *inf.* dither, state, tizzy.

flutter *verb* **1** *a bird fluttering its wings* flap, beat, quiver, agitate, vibrate, ruffle. **2** *flutter one's eyelashes* flicker, bat. **3** *butterflies fluttering in the air* flit, hover, flitter. **4** *flags fluttering in the breeze* flap, wave, flop, ripple, quiver, shiver, tremble. **5** *with hearts fluttering* beat rapidly, pulsate, palpitate.

flutter *noun* **1** *the flutter of the birds' wings* flapping, beating, quivering. *See* FLUTTER *verb* 1. **2** *the flutter of her eyelashes* flickering, batting. **3** *the flutter of the flags* flapping, waving, flopping, rippling. *See* FLUTTER *verb* 4. **4** *in a flutter at the unexpected news* fluster, flurry, bustle, panic; *inf.* dither, state, tizzy. *See* FLUSTER *noun.*

fly *verb* **1** *birds flying overhead* flutter, flit, hover, soar, wing, wing its way, take wing, take to the air, mount. **2** *flying to Paris* go by airplane, travel/go by air; *inf.* jet. **3** *fly the plane* pilot, operate, control, maneuver. **4** *ships flying the American flag* display, show, wave. **5** *flags flying* flap, wave, flutter, toss. **6** *time flew past* go quickly, pass swiftly, slip past, race, rush/tear past. **7** *the runners flew by* race, dash, shoot, rush, tear, bolt, zoom, scoot, dart, speed, hasten, hurry, scamper, career, go like the wind; *inf.* be off like a shot. **8** *watched their beaten opponents fly* flee, run, run away, bolt, take flight, make off, abscond, beat a retreat, run for it, take to one's heels, decamp, make one's escape; *inf.* cut and run, skedaddle. *See* FLEE.

flying *adjective* **1** *flying creatures* airborne, fluttering, flitting, hovering, soaring, winging. **2** *a flying visit* brief, short, short-lived, hurried, hasty, rushed, fleeting, transitory, transient. **3** *her flying footsteps* fast, rapid, swift, quick, speedy, fleet; *lit.* winged.

foal *noun* young horse, colt, filly, pony.

foam *noun* froth, bubbles, fizz, effervescence, head, spume, lather, suds.

foam *verb* froth, froth up, cream, bubble, fizz, effervesce, spume, lather.

focus *noun* **1** *the focus of attention/activity* focal point, center, central point, center of attention, core, hub, pivot, magnet, cynosure. **2** *the focus of the light* focal point, point of convergence.

focus *verb* **1** *focus the camera on her* turn, converge, bring into focus, bring to a focus. **2** *focus our attention on budgets* concentrate, fix, bring to bear, center, pinpoint, rivet; *inf.* zero/zoom in on.

foe *noun* enemy, opponent, adversary, rival, antagonist, combatant.

fog *noun* **1** *fog decreasing visibility* mist, mistiness, smog, murk, murkiness, haze; *inf.* pea soup. **2** *go around in a mental fog* haze, daze, stupor, trance; bewilderment, confusion, perplexity, bafflement, vagueness, stupefaction, disorientation.

fog *verb* **1** *windshields fogging over/up* mist over, become misty, cloud over, steam up. **2** *alcohol fogging their minds/judgment* befuddle, becloud, bedim, bewilder, confuse, muddle, perplex, baffle, blind, darken, obscure, daze, stupefy, obfuscate.

foggy *adjective* **1** *a foggy day* misty, smoggy, dark, dim, gray, overcast, murky, hazy, gloomy; *inf.* soupy. **2** *have only a foggy recollection of the event* vague, indistinct, dim, hazy, shadowy, cloudy, clouded, dark, obscure, unclear, befuddled, confused, bewildered, muddled, dazed, stupefied.

foible *noun* weakness, weak point, failing, shortcoming, flaw, blemish, defect, frailty, infirmity, quirk, idiosyncrasy.
Antonyms: STRENGTH; ASSET.

foil *noun* *his shyness was a foil for his wife's lively manner* contrast, striking difference, antithesis, complement.

foil *verb* *foil the attempt* thwart, frustrate, put a stop to, stop, baffle, defeat, check, checkmate, circumvent, counter, disappoint, impede, obstruct, hamper, hinder, cripple, nip in the bud; *inf.* mess up, screw up.

foist *verb* **1** *foist his ideas on/upon everyone | foist the vase off as antique* force, impose, thrust, unload; palm, pass. **2** *foist an illegal clause into the document* sneak, insinuate, interpolate, insert, introduce, stick, squeeze, edge.

fold[1] *noun* **1** *a fold for the sheep* enclosure, pen, sheepfold. **2** *welcome them into the fold of the church* congregation, assembly, body, church membership, brethren; parishioners, churchgoers; *inf.* flock.

fold[2] *noun* **1** *a fold in the cloth/paper* folded portion, double thickness, overlap, layer, pleat, turn, gather, crease, knife pleat; dog-ear. **2** *a fold in the skin* wrinkle, pucker, furrow, crinkle; crow's foot.

fold[3] *verb* **1** *fold the paper* double, double over, double up, crease, turn under, turn up, bend, overlap, tuck, gather, pleat, crimp, crumple, dog-ear. **2** *fold her in his arms* enfold, wrap, wrap up, enclose, envelop, clasp, embrace, hug, squeeze. **3** *the firm folded* fail, collapse, go out of business, close, shut down, go bankrupt, crash; *inf.* go bust, go under, flop.

folder *noun* file, binder, portfolio, envelope.

foliage *noun* leaves; leafage, greenery, vegetation.

folk *noun* **1** *country folk* people, citizenry, populace, population, general public, public, race, clan, tribe, ethnic group. **2** *has she no folk of her own?* relatives, relations, family, kinsfolk, kinsmen, kin, kindred, flesh and blood.

folklore *noun* legend, myth, mythology, lore, oral history, tradition, folk tradition; legends, fables, myths, old wives' tales.

follow *verb* **1** *children following after each other* go behind/after, come behind/after, walk behind, tread on the heels of. **2** *he followed his father as mayor* come after, succeed, replace, take the place of, step into the shoes of, supersede, supplant. **3** *he objects to his sister following him everywhere* come/go after, go with, escort, accompany, trail; *inf.* tag. **4** *dogs following rabbits | detectives following criminals* chase, pursue, run after, trail, shadow, hunt, stalk, track, dog, hound, course; *inf.* tail. **5** *follow the rules | follow etiquette* obey, observe, comply with, conform to, heed, pay attention to, note, have regard to, mind, be guided by, accept, yield to. **6** *his conclusion follows from your theory | the conclusion follows logically* result, arise, develop, ensue, emanate, issue, proceed, spring, flow, supervene. **7** *cannot follow your argument* understand, comprehend, take in, grasp, fathom, get, catch on to, appreciate, keep up with, see; *inf.* latch on to. **8** *he followed the poetic style of Dickinson | he follows Dickinson* copy, imitate, emulate, take as a pattern/example; pattern oneself on, adopt the style of, style oneself on. **9** *he follows science fiction* be a follower of, be a fan/admirer/devotee of, be devoted to, be interested in, cultivate an interest in, be a supporter of, support, keep abreast of, keep up to date with. **follow through (on)** *follow through (on) a project* continue to the end, complete, bring to completion, bring to a finish, see something

Antonyms: LEAD; PRECEDE; FLOUT.

follower *noun* **1** *the gang leader and his followers* companion, escort, attendant, henchman, minion, lackey, toady; servant, page, squire; *inf.* hanger-on, sidekick. **2** *Picasso and his followers* imitator, emulator, copier; *inf.* copycat. **3** *followers of Christ* apostle, disciple, adherent, supporter, believer, worshiper, votary, student, pupil. **4** *followers of the Yankees* supporter, enthusiast, fan, admirer, devotee; *inf.* groupie, camp follower, rooter.

following *adjective* **1** *the following day* next, ensuing, succeeding, subsequent, successive. **2** *will the following people leave* about to be mentioned/specified. **3** *there was a quarrel and a following fight* resulting, ensuing, consequent, consequential.

Antonyms: PRECEDING; FOREGOING.

following *noun the new ideas/leaders have quite a following | brought their following with them* body of support, backing, clientele, public, audience, circle, coterie, retinue, train; supporters, backers, admirers, fans, adherents, devotees, advocates, patrons.

folly *noun* foolishness, absurdity, absurdness, stupidity, silliness, nonsense, nonsensicalness, senselessness, illogicality, inanity, madness, craziness, idiocy, imbecility, lunacy, ridiculousness, ludicrousness, fatuousness, fatuity, rashness, recklessness, imprudence, indiscretion, irrationality; *inf.* daftness.

Antonyms: WISDOM; SENSE.

foment *verb* instigate, incite, provoke, agitate, excite, stir up, arouse, encourage, urge, actuate, initiate.

fond *adjective* **1** *his fond wife* adoring, devoted, loving, affectionate, caring, warm, tender, amorous, doting, indulgent, overindulgent, overfond; uxorious. **2** *fond hopes of success* deep, cherished, heartfelt. **fond of** *fond of music* having a liking/love for, having a taste/fancy for, partial to, keen on, attached to, in love with, enamored of, having a soft spot for, addicted to; *inf.* hooked on.

Antonyms: HOSTILE; INDIFFERENT.

fondle *verb* caress, stroke, touch, pat, pet, cuddle, hug, nuzzle.

fondness *noun* **1** *look upon his brother with fondness* affection, love, warmth, tenderness, kindness, devotion, care, attachment, excessive devotion. **2** *have a fondness for chocolate* liking, love, taste, partiality, preference, weakness, soft spot, penchant, predilection, fancy, susceptibility.

Antonyms: HATRED; DISLIKE.

food *noun* **1** *give food to the children* nourishment, sustenance, nutriment, subsistence, aliment, fare, diet, menu, table, bread, daily bread, board, provender, cooking, cuisine; foodstuffs, refreshments, edibles, meals, provisions, rations, stores, viands, victuals/vittles, commons, comestibles; solids; *inf.* eats, eatables, nosh, grub, chow. **2** *food for the cattle* fodder, feed, provender, forage. **3** *food for thought* stimulus, mental nourishment, something to think about.

fool *noun* **1** *don't try to explain—he's a fool* idiot, ass, nitwit, halfwit, numskull, nincompoop, ninny, blockhead, dunce, dunderhead, dolt, ignoramus, dullard, illiterate, moron, simpleton, jackass, loon; *inf.* dope, clod, chump, bonehead, fathead, birdbrain, twit, twerp, nerd, airhead. **2** *she always makes him look like a fool | make a fool of him* dupe, butt, laughingstock, pushover, easy mark; *inf.* stooge, sucker, sap, fall guy. **3** *the fools of Shakespeare's day* jester, clown, buffoon, comic, jokester, zany, merry andrew, harlequin.

fool *verb* **1** *they certainly fooled the teacher* deceive, trick, play a trick on, hoax, make a fool of, dupe, take in, mislead, hoodwink, bluff, delude, beguile, bamboozle, cozen, gull; *inf.* con, kid, put one over on. **2** *we thought he was dead but he was only fooling* pretend, make believe, feign, put on an act, act, fake, counterfeit; *inf.* kid. **fool around 1** *the boys are always fooling around* play the fool, jest, joke, play tricks, clown, caper, cavort. **2** *fool around with the controls* fiddle, play, fiddle/play around, toy, trifle, meddle, tamper, mess, interfere, monkey, monkey around. **3** *fool around with someone else's wife* have an affair, philander, flirt, commit adultery.

foolery *noun* fooling, clowning, tomfoolery, hoaxing, horseplay, mischief, buffoonery, silliness; antics, capers, practical jokes, pranks, shenanigans.

foolhardy *adjective* reckless, rash, daredevil, devil-may-care, impulsive, hotheaded, impetuous, madcap, heedless, precipitate, daring, bold, adventurous, venturous, venturesome, incautious, imprudent, irresponsible, injudicious, desperate.

foolish *adjective* **1** *a foolish plan/idea* silly, absurd, senseless, nonsensical, unintelligent, inane, pointless, fatuous, ridiculous, laughable, derisible, risible, imprudent, incautious, irresponsible, injudicious, indiscreet, unwise, unreasonable, ill-advised, ill-considered, impolitic; *inf.* damfool, damfoolish, crackbrained, nutty, for the birds. **2** *a foolish fellow* stupid, silly, idiotic, simple, unintelligent, halfwitted, brainless, doltish, dull, dull-witted, dense, ignorant, illiterate, moronic, witless, weak-minded, mad, crazy; *inf.* dumb, dopey, daft, balmy, batty, dippy, cuckoo, screwy, wacky.

Antonyms: SENSIBLE; WISE; SOUND.

foolishness *noun* **1** *the foolishness of their actions* folly, stupidity, silliness, imprudence, lack of caution/foresight, indiscretion, irresponsibility, foolhardiness, senselessness, absurdity, inanity, madness, craziness, lunacy. **2** *talking foolishness* nonsense, rubbish, bunkum, gobbledygook, humbug, balderdash, claptrap, hogwash, rigmarole; *inf.* rot, bunk, poppycock, piffle, hooey, garbage, crap.

foolproof *adjective* infallible, never-failing, unfailing, certain, sure, guaranteed, safe, dependable, trustworthy.

foot *noun* **1** *an animal's foot* paw, hoof, pad. **2** *the foot of the structure* base, bottom, foundation, substructure, understructure. **3** *the foot of the road* bottom, end, edge, boundary, extremity, limit, border.

footing *noun* **1** *lose one's footing* foothold, secure position, grip, toehold, support. **2** *his business was on a secure footing* basis, foundation, groundwork, establishment. **3** *on a friendly footing* relationship, standing, state, condition, position, basis, foundation; relations, terms.

footstep *noun* **1** *hear her footsteps* footfall, step, tread. **2** *see footsteps in the snow* footprint, trace, track.

fop *noun* dandy, coxcomb, popinjay, beau.

forage *noun* **1** *forage for cattle* fodder, feed, food, foodstuff, provender, herbage, pasturage. **2** *an enemy forage into the castle* raid, foray, assault, invasion, incursion, plundering, ravaging, looting.

forage *verb* **1** *forage about for food | forage for her keys* search, look around, hunt, rummage around, scour; *inf.* scrounge around. **2** *the enemy forces foraged the village* raid, assault, invade, plunder, ravage, loot.

forbear *verb* refrain from, abstain from, desist from, keep from, restrain oneself from, hold back from, resist the temptation to, stop oneself from, withhold from, eschew, avoid, shun, decline, cease, give up, leave off, break off.

forbearance *noun* **1** *teachers showing great forbearance* tolerance, toleration, patience, resignation, endurance, long-suffering, self-control, restraint, leniency, clemency, moderation, temperance, indulgence. **2** *his forbearance from speaking* refraining, abstinence, desisting, resistance, withholding, avoidance. *See* FORBEAR.

forbid *verb* *the hospital forbids smoking* prohibit, ban, bar, debar, outlaw, veto, proscribe, disallow, interdict, preclude, exclude, rule out, stop, declare taboo. *Antonyms:* ALLOW; AUTHORIZE; PERMIT.

forbidden *adjective* *forbidden territory* prohibited, out of bounds, banned, debarred, outlawed, vetoed, proscribed, interdicted, taboo, verboten.

forbidding *adjective* **1** *a forbidding manner* stern, harsh, grim, hard, tough, hostile, unfriendly, disagreeable, nasty, mean, abhorrent, repellent. **2** *a forbidding landscape* frightening, threatening, ominous, menacing, sinister, daunting, foreboding.

force *noun* **1** *requiring a lot of force* strength, power, potency, vigor, energy, might, muscle, stamina, effort, exertion, impact, pressure, life, vitality, stimulus, dynamism; *inf.* punch. **2** *use force to persuade them* compulsion, coercion, duress, pressure, pressurization, constraint, enforcement, violence; *inf.* arm twisting. **3** *arguments with force* persuasiveness, cogency, validity, weight, effectiveness, efficacy, efficaciousness, influence, power, strength, vehemence, significance; *inf.* bite, punch. **4** *from force of habit* agency, effect, influence. **5** *speaking with great force* vehemence, intensity, vigor, drive, fierceness, feeling, passion, vividness. **6** *a task force/a military force* body of people, corps, detachment, unit, squad, squadron, battalion, division, patrol, regiment, army. **in force 1** *rules no longer in force* in operation, operative, valid, on the statute book, current, effective, binding. **2** *the fans were out in force* in full strength, in great numbers, in great quantities, in hordes.

force *verb* **1** *force them to go* exert/use force on, compel, coerce, make, use duress on, bring pressure to bear on, pressurize, pressure, constrain, impel, drive, oblige, necessitate, urge by force; *inf.* put the squeeze/bite on, use strong-arm tactics on. **2** *force the door/safe* force open, break open, burst open, blast, prize open, crack. **3** *the wind forced them back* drive, propel, push, thrust, shove, press. **4** *force a confession from them* wrest, extract, wring, extort, drag.

forced *adjective* **1** *a forced confession* enforced, compulsory, compelled, obligatory, mandatory, involuntary, unwilling. **2** *a forced laugh* strained, unnatural, artificial, false, feigned, overdone, affected, contrived, stilted, labored, wooden, self-conscious.

forceful *adjective* *forceful speakers/arguments* vigorous, powerful, potent, strong, weighty, dynamic, energetic, assertive, effective, cogent, telling, persuasive, convincing, compelling, moving, impressive, valid. *Antonyms:* WEAK; FEEBLE.

forcible *adjective* **1** *forcible entry* by force, using force, forced, violent. **2** *forcible conscription* compulsory, obligatory, imposed, required, binding. **3** *forcible arguments* forceful, vigorous, powerful, potent. *See* FORCEFUL.

forcibly *adverb* **1** *thrown out forcibly* compulsorily, under compulsion, by force, under coercion, against one's will, under protest. **2** *speak forcibly* forcefully, vigorously, powerfully, potently, dynamically, energetically, assertively, effectively, cogently, tellingly, persuasively, convincingly, movingly, impressively.

forebear *noun* forefather, ancestor, forerunner, progenitor, primogenitor, predecessor, father.

forebode *verb* augur, presage, portend, foreshadow, foreshow, foretoken, betoken, prefigure, presignify, signify, mean, indicate, point to, foretell, forecast, predict, prophesy, forewarn, warn of, prognosticate.

foreboding noun **1** *a foreboding that the car would crash* presentiment, premonition, intuition, sixth sense, feeling, vague feeling, misgiving, suspicion, anxiety, apprehension, apprehensiveness, fear, dread. **2** *listening to the forebodings of the soothsayer* augury, prophecy, prediction, presage, prognostication, forecast, warning, omen, portent, sign, foretoken, token.

forecast verb *he forecast that they would be late* predict, foretell, foresee, prophesy, forewarn, prognosticate, augur, divine, guess, hazard a guess, conjecture, speculate, estimate, calculate.

forecast noun *his forecast proved wrong* prediction, prophecy, forewarning, prognostication, augury, guess, conjecture, speculation, prognosis, projection; *inf.* guesstimate.

forefather noun forebear, ancestor, forerunner. *See* FOREBEAR.

forefront noun **1** *in the forefront of my mind* front, forward/foremost position, fore, foreground. **2** *in the forefront of the party* lead, leading position, head, position of prominence, van, vanguard, spearhead. **Antonyms:** BACK; BACKGROUND.

forego[1] verb go before, precede, predate, antedate.

forego[2] *See* FORGO, FOREGO.

foregoing adjective preceding, precedent, prior, previous, former, above, aforesaid, aforementioned, antecedent, anterior.

foregone adjective **1** *in foregone days* past, former, earlier, previous, prior. **2** *foregone conclusions* predetermined, predecided, preordained, predestined, fixed, cut-and-dried, inevitable.

foreground noun **1** *in the foreground of the picture* front, fore, forefront. **2** *in the foreground* forefront, lead, position of prominence, vanguard. *See* FOREFRONT 2.

foreign adjective **1** *from foreign parts* overseas, alien, distant, remote. **2** *foreign objects* strange, unfamiliar, unknown, exotic, outlandish, odd, peculiar, curious. **3** *matters foreign to the discussion* irrelevant, not pertinent, unrelated, unconnected, inappropriate, inapposite, extraneous, extrinsic, outside. **Antonyms:** HOME; NATIVE; FAMILIAR; RELEVANT.

foreigner noun nonnative, alien, immigrant, newcomer, stranger, outsider.

foreman noun overseer, supervisor, manager, superintendent; *inf.* boss.

foremost adjective leading, principal, premier, prime, top, first, primary, front, advanced, paramount, chief, main, most important, supreme, highest, preeminent.

forerunner noun predecessor, precursor, ancestor, antecedent, forefather, herald, harbinger, usher, advance guard.

foresee verb foreknow, anticipate, envisage, predict, foretell, forecast, prophesy, divine, prognosticate, forebode, augur.

foreshadow verb forebode, bode, presage, augur, portend, omen, foretoken, betoken, foreshow, indicate, signify, mean, point to, suggest, signal, prefigure, promise.

foresight noun forethought, discernment, farsightedness, circumspection, prudence, presence of mind, judiciousness, discrimination, perspicacity, care, caution, precaution, readiness, preparedness, anticipation, provision, prescience.

forest noun woods, wood, woodland, tree plantation, plantation; trees.

forestall verb preempt, intercept, anticipate, be beforehand, get ahead of, thwart, frustrate, stave off, ward off, fend off, avert, prevent, hinder, impede, obstruct, sidetrack.

forestry noun forest management, forest planting, tree growing, arboriculture, silviculture, dendrology.

foretell verb **1** *she foretold his death* predict, forecast, foresee, prophesy, forewarn, prognosticate, augur, divine. **2** *the first match foretold the final result* forebode, augur, presage, portend, foreshadow, foreshow, foretoken, betoken, prefigure, point to, indicate.

forethought noun foresight, farsightedness, circumspection, prudence, judiciousness, care, precaution, anticipation, provision. *See* FORESIGHT.

forever adverb **1** *loving each other forever* always, ever, evermore, for all time, till the end of time, till the cows come home, till hell freezes over, till doomsday, eternally, undyingly, perpetually, in perpetuity; *inf.* for keeps, for good. **2** *he's forever playing loud music* all the time, incessantly, continually, constantly, perpetually, endlessly, unremittingly, interminably, everlastingly.

forewarn verb prewarn, warn, give advance/fair warning to, put on one's guard, tip off, put on the qui vive, alert, caution, advise, apprise, precaution, premonish.

foreword noun introduction, preface, preamble, preliminary/front matter, prologue.

forfeit noun *pay/suffer a forfeit as a punishment* forfeiture, fine, penalty; damages; loss, relinquishment.

forfeit verb *had to forfeit their prize winnings* relinquish, hand over, give up, surrender, renounce, be stripped/deprived of.

forge[1] verb **1** *blacksmiths forging horseshoes* hammer out, beat into shape, shape, form, fashion, mold, found, cast, make, manufacture, frame, construct, create. **2** *forge an excuse* invent, make up, devise, coin, fabricate, put together. **3** *forge handwriting/checks* copy, copy fraudulently, imitate, fake, falsify, counterfeit.

forge[2] verb **forge on** *soldiers forging on* advance steadily/gradually, press on, push on, plod along. **forge ahead** *forge ahead with our plans* advance rapidly, progress quickly, make swift progress, increase speed.

forger *noun* counterfeiter, falsifier, faker, copyist, coiner.

forgery *noun* **1** *accused of forgery of signatures/coins* fraudulent copying/imitation, falsification, faking, counterfeiting, coining. **2** *the vase is a forgery* fake, counterfeit, sham, fraud, imitation, reproduction; *inf.* phony.

forget *verb* **1** *forget her phone number* fail to remember/recall, fail to think of, let slip; *inf.* draw a blank on. **2** *it's best to forget unhappy times* | *will never forget* cease to remember, put out of one's mind, disregard, ignore, let bygones be bygones. **3** *I forgot my gloves* leave behind, go/come without, overlook, miss. **forget oneself** misbehave, behave improperly.

Antonyms: REMEMBER; RECOLLECT.

forgetful *adjective* **1** *growing forgetful* apt to forget, absentminded, amnesic, amnesiac, abstracted, vague. **2** *forgetful of one's duties* neglectful, negligent, heedless, careless, unmindful, inattentive, oblivious, lax, remiss, disregardful.

forgetfulness *noun* **1** *suffering from forgetfulness* absentmindedness, amnesia, poor memory, lapse of memory, abstraction, vagueness, woolgathering. **2** *guilty of forgetfulness of their duty* negligence, heedlessness, carelessness, inattention, obliviousness, laxness, remissness, disregard.

forgive *verb* pardon, excuse, exonerate, absolve, acquit, let off, let bygones be bygones, bear no malice, harbor no grudge, bury the hatchet; *inf.* let someone off the hook.

Antonyms: BLAME; CONDEMN; CONVICT.

forgiveness *noun* pardon, amnesty, exoneration, absolution, acquittal, remission, absence of malice/grudges, mercy.

forgiving *adjective* *a forgiving nature* lenient, merciful, compassionate, magnanimous, humane, clement, mild, softhearted, forbearing, tolerant, placable.

forgo, forego *verb* do/go without, waive, renounce, relinquish, sacrifice, forswear, surrender, abjure, abandon, cede, yield, abstain from, refrain from, eschew.

forgotten *adjective* unremembered, out of mind, beyond/past recall/recollection, consigned to oblivion, obliterated, blotted out, buried, left behind, bygone, past, gone, lost, irrecoverable.

fork *verb* *our road forks (to the) left* | *the road forks* branch, branch off, diverge, bifurcate, divaricate, divide, split, separate, go in different directions, go separate ways.

forked *adjective* branching, branched, diverging, bifurcate, divaricate, Y-shaped, V-shaped, pronged, divided, split, separated.

forlorn *adjective* **1** *looking forlorn* unhappy, sad, miserable, wretched, pathetic, woebegone, lonely, disconsolate, desolate, cheerless, pitiable, pitiful, uncared-for. **2** *a forlorn farmhouse* abandoned, forsaken, deserted, forgotten, neglected. **3** *a forlorn attempt* hopeless, desperate, despairing, in despair.

Antonyms: HAPPY; HOPEFUL.

form *verb* **1** *form shapes* make, fashion, shape, model, mold, forge, found, construct, build, assemble, put together, set up, erect, create, produce, concoct, devise. **2** *form plans* formulate, devise, think up, plan, draw up, frame, forge, hatch, develop, organize; *inf.* dream up. **3** *form an alliance* set up, bring about, devise, establish, found, organize, institute, inaugurate. **4** *shapes began to form* take shape, materialize, appear, show up, become visible, come into being/existence. **5** *form bad habits* acquire, develop, get, pick up, contract, grow into; *inf.* get into. **6** *form the children into lines* arrange, draw up, line up, assemble, organize, order, rank. **7** *these books form the complete series* make, make up, comprise, constitute, compose. **8** *this plank will form the bridge* constitute, serve as, be a component/element/part of. **9** *forming young children's minds* develop, train, teach, instruct, educate, school, drill, discipline.

form *noun* **1** *observe the form of the crystals* shape, configuration, formation, conformation, structure, construction, arrangement, disposition, outward form/appearance, exterior. **2** *of a well-built form* body, physique, figure, shape, build, frame, anatomy, silhouette, contour. **3** *help came to the farmers in the form of rain* shape, appearance, manifestation, semblance, guise, character, description. **4** *a form of punishment* type, kind, sort, variety, species, genus, genre, stamp. **5** *admire the form of the painting* | *his literary work lacks form* structure, framework, format, organization, planning, order, orderliness, symmetry, proportion. **6** *put the mixture into a form* mold, cast, shape, matrix, pattern. **7** *the form of the athletes matters most* fitness, condition, good condition, health, shape, trim, fettle. **8** *not good form to yawn* manners; behavior, conduct, etiquette, convention, protocol. **9** *convention has followed the same form for years* manner, method, mode, style, system, formula, set formula, procedure, correct/usual way, convention, custom, ritual, protocol, etiquette; rules. **10** *fill in the forms* document, application form, application, sheet of paper, paper.

formal *adjective* **1** *formal documents/procedures* official, set, fixed, conventional, standard, regular, customary, approved, prescribed, pro forma, legal, lawful, ceremonial, ritual. **2** *a formal dinner* ceremonial, ceremonious, ritualistic, elaborate. **3** *a very formal person* | *have a formal manner* reserved, aloof, remote, correct, proper, conventional, precise, exact, punctilious, stiff, unbending, inflexible, standoffish, prim, stuffy, straitlaced. **4** *a formal garden* symmetrical, regular, orderly, arranged, methodical.

formal
ceremonial, ceremonious, pompous, proper, punctilious

Formal suggests a suit-and-tie approach to certain situations—reserved, conventional, obeying all the rules (*an engraved invitation to a formal dinner requiring black tie or evening gown*). **Proper**, in this regard, implies scrupulously correct behavior that observes rules of etiquette (*the proper way to serve a guest; the proper spoon for dessert*). **Punctilious** behavior observes all the proper formalities (a *punctilio* is a detail or fine point), but may verge on the annoying (*her punctilious attention to the correct placement of silverware made setting the table an ordeal*). Someone (usually a man) who likes to show off just how *formal* and *proper* he can be runs the risk of becoming the most dreaded dinner guest of all: the **pompous** ass. *Pompous* individuals may derive more than the normal amount of pleasure from participating in **ceremonial** acts or events, which are those performed according to set rules, but **ceremonious** suggests a less negative and more ritualized approach to formality (*the Japanese woman could not have been more ceremonious than when she was carrying out the ceremonial serving of tea*).

formality *noun* **1** *dislike the formality of the occasion* conventionality, ceremoniousness, ritual, red tape, decorum, etiquette, protocol. **2** *obey the formalities* rule, convention, custom, matter of form, official procedure, formal gesture; form, punctilio.

formation *noun* **1** *planes flying in formation* configuration, format, structure, organization, order, arrangement, pattern, design, disposition, grouping, layout. **2** *the formation of the new buildings is nearly complete* manufacture, making, construction, building, erecting, fashioning, shaping. *See* FORM *verb* 1. **3** *the formation of a new government* setting up, establishment, founding, institution, creation, inauguration. **4** *dislike the formation of the committee* composition, makeup, constitution, organization. **5** *the formation of the national character* genesis, development, evolution, emergence.

formative *adjective* **1** *in a child's formative years* developing, developmental, growing, moldable, malleable, impressionable, susceptible, educable, teachable. **2** *a formative influence on the child* forming, shaping, molding, determinative, influential.

former *adjective* **1** *the former ruler* ex-, previous, prior, preceding, precedent, foregoing, earlier, one-time, erstwhile, antecedent, late, sometime. **2** *in former times* earlier, past, long past, bygone, long ago, long departed, long gone, old, ancient, of yore. **3** *the former person* first-mentioned, first.

formerly *adverb* previously, at an earlier time, in earlier times, at one time, once, once upon a time, in times past, heretofore.

formidable *adjective* **1** *of a formidable appearance* intimidating, redoubtable, daunting, alarming, frightening, terrifying, petrifying, horrifying, dreadful, awesome, fearsome, menacing, threatening, dangerous; *inf.* scary. **2** *a formidable task* arduous, onerous, difficult, tough, colossal, mammoth, challenging, overwhelming, staggering, huge, tremendous; *inf.* mind-boggling, mind-blowing. **3** *a formidable opponent* strong, powerful, mighty, impressive, terrific, tremendous, great, redoubtable, indomitable, invincible.
Antonyms: PLEASANT; EASY; WEAK.

formula *noun* **1** *a legal/mathematical formula* formulary, established form of words, set of words/symbols, set expression, code. **2** *the formula for his special sauce* recipe, list of ingredients; contents, ingredients; prescription. **3** *the formula for writing a successful novel* recipe, prescription, rubric, blueprint, method, procedure, convention, ritual, modus operandi; principles, rules, precepts.

formulate *verb* **1** *formulate one's thoughts in plain English* express/state clearly, define, articulate, set down, frame, give form to, specify, particularize, itemize, detail, designate, systematize, indicate. **2** *formulate our plans* draw up, work out, map out, plan, prepare, compose, devise, think up, conceive, create, invent, originate, coin, design.

fornication *noun* premarital/extramarital sex; sexual intercourse, sex, coitus, copulation.

forsake *verb* **1** *forsake his wife and children* desert, abandon, leave, leave in the lurch, quit, throw over, jilt, cast off, discard, repudiate, reject, disown; *inf.* leave flat, give someone the air. **2** *forsake her life of luxury* give up, renounce, relinquish, forgo, turn one's back on, repudiate, have done with, discard, set aside.
Antonyms: KEEP; RETAIN.

forsaken *adjective* **1** *forsaken wives* deserted, abandoned, cast-off, discarded, jilted, rejected. **2** *what a forsaken place* godforsaken, remote, isolated, marooned, lonely, solitary, deserted, derelict, desolate, dreary, forlorn.

forswear *verb* *forswear drinking* give up, renounce, abjure, reject, relinquish, forgo, quit, do without; *inf.* cut out.

fort *noun* fortress, stronghold, citadel, garrison, castle, tower, keep, turret, fortification, redoubt, battlement.

forte *noun* strong point, strength, métier, specialty, talent, skill, gift, bent; *inf.* bag, thing.

forth *adverb* **1** *from that day forth* onward, onwards, forward, forwards. **2** *go forth from the tent | sent him forth into the world* out, outside, away, off, away from home, abroad.

forthcoming *adjective* **1** *forthcoming events*

future, coming, approaching, expected, prospective, imminent, impending. **2** *no reply was forthcoming* made available, available, ready, at hand, accessible, obtainable, at one's disposal; *inf.* on tap. **3** *the children are not very forthcoming* communicative, informative, talkative, expansive, voluble, chatty, conversational, loquacious, open, unreserved.
Antonyms: PAST; RETICENT.

forthright *adjective a forthright person* direct, frank, candid, blunt, outspoken, plainspeaking, plainspoken, straightforward, open, honest.
Antonyms: SECRETIVE; RETICENT; DISHONEST.

forthwith *adverb* right away, immediately, at once, instantly, this instant, directly, straightaway, without delay, quickly.

fortification *noun* **1** *the fortification of the walls* strengthening, reinforcement, bracing. **2** *soldiers manning the fortifications* battlement, rampart, bastion, bulwark, parapet, blockhouse, barricade, buttress, stronghold, palisade, stockade, outwork.

fortify *verb* **1** *fortify the town* build defenses around, garrison, embattle, guard, cover, protect, secure. **2** *fortify the walls* strengthen, reinforce, shore up, brace, buttress. **3** *fortify himself with a drink* strengthen, invigorate, energize, revive, embolden, give courage to, encourage, cheer, hearten, buoy up, reassure, make confident, brace, sustain. **4** *fortify wine* add spirits/alcohol to. **5** *fortify food* add vitamins/minerals to.

fortitude *noun* strength, strength of mind, moral strength, firmness of purpose, backbone, grit, mettle, courage, nerve, pluck, bravery, fearlessness, valor, intrepidity, stoutheartedness, endurance, patience, forbearance, tenacity, pertinacity, perseverance, resolution, resoluteness, determination.

fortress *noun* fort, stronghold, citadel. *See* FORT.

fortuitous *adjective* chance, unexpected, unanticipated, unforeseen, serendipitous, casual, haphazard, random, accidental, unintentional, unplanned, unpremeditated, incidental; lucky, fortunate, felicitous; *inf.* fluky.

fortunate *adjective* **1** *a fortunate person* lucky, in luck, favored, blessed, born with a silver spoon in one's mouth, born under a lucky star, having a charmed life, happy, felicitous, prosperous, well-off, successful, flourishing; *inf.* sitting pretty. **2** *in a fortunate position* advantageous, favorable, helpful, providential, auspicious, propitious, promising, encouraging, opportune, felicitous, profitable, fortuitous, timely, well-timed, convenient.

fortune *noun* **1** *a merchant of great fortune* wealth, treasure, affluence, opulence, opulency, prosperity, substance, property; riches, assets, means, possessions, estates. **2** *the ring cost a fortune* huge amount, mint, king's ransom; *inf.*

packet, bundle, bomb, pile. **3** *by good fortune he won* chance, mere chance, accident, coincidence, contingency, happy chance, fortuity, serendipity, luck, providence. **4** *tell one's fortune* destiny, fate, lot, cup, portion, kismet; stars. **5** *fortune smiled on him* Lady Luck, Dame Fortune, fate.

fortunes *plural noun the fortunes of youth* state of affairs, condition, position; circumstances.

fortune-teller *noun* seer, soothsayer, prophet, prophetess, augur, diviner, sibyl, oracle, clairvoyant, psychic, prognosticator; astrologer, palm reader, phrenologist; *inf.* stargazer.

forum *noun* **1** *a forum for discussion about the new road* meeting, assembly, symposium, round-table conference, debate, discussion place, discussion medium. **2** *awarded damages by the forum* court, tribunal. **3** *Caesar and Brutus meeting in the forum* public meeting place, public square, marketplace.

forward *adjective* **1** *a forward movement* moving forward/ahead, onward, advancing, progressing, progressive. **2** *the plants are forward this year* | *forward for her age* advanced, well-advanced, early, premature, precocious. **3** *the forward force* front, at the front/fore, fore, frontal, foremost, head, leading, advance. **4** *a forward young woman* bold, brash, brazen, audacious, presumptuous, presuming, assuming, familiar, overfamiliar, overassertive, overconfident, overweening, aggressive, pert, impudent, impertinent, insolent, unabashed; *inf.* pushy, cocky, fresh. **5** *forward planning* future, for the future, prospective.
Antonyms: BACKWARD; LATE; SHY.

forward *adverb* **1** *move forward* toward the front, frontward, onward, on, ahead, forth. **2** *step forward for the prize* out, forth, into view, into the open, into public notice, into prominence. **3** *from today forward* on, onward, hence.

forward *verb* **1** *forward the letter/package* send on, send, pass on, dispatch, transmit, post, mail, ship, freight, deliver. **2** *his help forwarded our plans* advance, further, speed up, hasten, hurry along, expedite, accelerate, step up, aid, assist, help, foster, encourage, promote, favor, support, back, give backing to.

forward-looking *adjective* progressive, modern, enterprising, reforming, radical, liberal.

forwardness *noun the forwardness of the young woman* boldness, brashness, brazenness, audacity, presumption, overfamiliarity, overconfidence, aggressiveness, pertness, impudence, impertinence, cheek, cheekiness, insolence; *inf.* pushiness, cockiness.

forwards *adverb* toward the front, frontward. *See* FORWARD *adverb* 1.

fossil *noun* remains, petrified remains; surviving trace/impression, remnant, relic. *See also table at* DINOSAUR.

foster *verb* **1** *foster freedom of thought* encourage, promote, further, stimulate, boost, advance, forward, cultivate, foment, help, aid, assist, support, uphold, back, give backing to, facilitate. **2** *foster a child* bring up, rear, raise, care for, take care of, mother, parent. **3** *foster hopes of being rich* cherish, harbor, entertain, nurse, nourish, nurture, hold, sustain.

foul *adjective* **1** *that drink looks foul* disgusting, revolting, repulsive, nauseating, sickening, loathsome, abominable, odious, offensive, nasty. **2** *that cheese smells foul* foul-smelling, evil-smelling, ill-smelling, stinking, fetid, rank, mephitic. **3** *foul water* contaminated, polluted, adulterated, infected, tainted, defiled, impure, filthy, dirty, unclean. **4** *foul carcasses* rotten, rotting, decayed, decomposed, putrid, putrescent, putrefactive, carious. **5** *use foul language* foul-mouthed, blasphemous, profane, obscene, vulgar, gross, coarse, filthy, dirty, indecent, indelicate, suggestive, smutty, blue, off-color, low, lewd, ribald, salacious, scatological, offensive, abusive. **6** *he's a foul creature* horrible, detestable, abhorrent, loathsome, hateful, despicable, contemptible, abominable, offensive, odious, disgusting, revolting, dishonorable, disgraceful, base, low, mean, sordid, vile, wicked, vicious, heinous, execrable, iniquitous, nefarious, notorious, infamous, scandalous, egregious. **7** *foul play by their competitors* unfair, unjust, dishonorable, dishonest, underhand, underhanded, unsportsmanlike, unsporting, unscrupulous, unprincipled, immoral, crooked, fraudulent, dirty; *inf.* shady. **8** *foul clothes* dirty, filthy, unwashed, soiled, grimy, grubby, stained, dirt-encrusted, muddied. **9** *foul weather* nasty, disagreeable, bad, rough, wild, stormy, rainy, wet, blustery, foggy, murky, gloomy.

Antonyms: ATTRACTIVE; FRAGRANT; PURE; FAIR.

foul *noun the referee ruled it a foul* violation, infraction, breach, illegality.

foul *verb* dirty, soil, stain, blacken, muddy, splash, spatter, smear, besmear, besmirch, defile, pollute, contaminate, taint, sully. **foul up 1** *foul up the fishing line* snarl, entangle, twist, tangle, muddle. **2** *fouled up our plans* ruin, spoil, bungle, mismanage, mishandle, botch (up), mess up, make a mess of; *inf.* blow, screw up, louse up.

found *verb* **1** *found a new company* establish, set up, institute, originate, initiate, bring into being, create, start, inaugurate, constitute, endow, organize, develop. **2** *found the building* lay the foundations of, build, construct, erect, put up, elevate. **3** *his story was founded on rumors and lies* base, ground, construct, build, rest.

foundation *noun* **1** *the foundation of the building* base, bottom, bedrock, substructure, substratum, understructure, underpinning. **2** *lay the foundations of mathematics* basis, groundwork; principles, fundamentals, rudiments. **3** *the foundation of the company* founding, establishing, setting up, institution, initiation, inauguration, constitution, endowment. *See* FOUND 1.

4 *set up an educational foundation* endowed institution, institution.

founder *noun* builder, constructor, maker, establisher, institutor, initiator, beginner, inventor, discoverer, framer, designer, architect, creator, author, originator, organizer, developer, generator, prime mover, father, patriarch.

founder *verb* **1** *ships foundered* sink, submerge, go to the bottom, go down, be lost at sea, capsize, run aground, be swamped; *inf.* go to Davy Jones's locker. **2** *plans foundered* fail, not succeed, fall through, break down, go wrong/awry, misfire, come to grief/nothing, miscarry, abort, flounder, collapse; *inf.* come a cropper. **3** *the horse foundered* stumble, trip, stagger, lurch, fall, topple, sprawl, go lame, collapse.

foundling *noun* abandoned infant, orphan, waif, stray, outcast.

fountain *noun* **1** *fountains built in the square* water fountain, jet, spray, spout, spurt, well, fount. **2** *fountains welling up from the mountain* spring, stream, source, well, fountainhead. **3** *the fountain of knowledge* fount, fountainhead, source, rise, well-spring, well, beginning, commencement, origin, cause, birth, genesis, root, mainspring, derivation, inception, inspiration.

fowl *noun* bird; chicken, hen, cock, rooster, bantam, duck, turkey, goose; poultry.

foyer *noun* entrance hall, reception area, hall, vestibule, lobby, anteroom, antechamber.

fracas *noun* disturbance, quarrel, altercation, fight, brawl, affray, row, rumpus, scuffle, tussle, skirmish, free-for-all, brouhaha, melee, donnybrook, riot, uproar, commotion; trouble, tumult, turmoil, pandemonium.

fraction *noun* **1** *a fraction of the population* part, subdivision. **2** *cost a fraction of what you paid* | *move a fraction closer* small part, tiny piece, minute amount, bit, mite, scrap, trifle.

fractious *adjective* **1** *fractious children* cross, irritable, fretful, bad-tempered, crabbed, peevish, petulant, ill-humored, ill-natured, querulous, testy, snappish, touchy, irascible, sulky, sullen, morose. **2** *the fractious element on the committee* unruly, rebellious, insubordinate, stubborn, obstinate, contrary, refractory, recalcitrant, unmanageable, intractable.

fracture *noun* **1** *the fracture of a bone* breaking, breakage, splitting, cleavage, rupture. **2** *a fracture in the bone* break, breakage, crack, split. **3** *a fracture in the rock* split, crack, fissure, cleft, rift, slit, rent, chink, crevice, gap, opening, aperture.

fracture *verb the bone/material fractured* break, crack, split, splinter, rupture.

fragile *adjective* easily broken, breakable, brittle, frangible, smashable, splintery, flimsy, frail, insubstantial, delicate, dainty, fine.

Antonyms: DURABLE; TOUGH; STRONG.

fragment *noun* **1** *fragments of glass from the bowl* piece, part, particle, chip, chink, shard, sliver, splinter, smithereen. **2** *a fragment of cloth* scrap, bit, snip, snippet, wisp, tatter. **3** *find the fragments of a book* remnant, remainder, fraction; remains, shreds.

---

fragment
fraction, part, piece, portion, section, segment

The whole is equal to the sum of its **parts**—*part* being a general term for any of the components of a whole. But how did the whole come apart? **Fragment** suggests that breakage has occurred (*fragments of pottery*) and often refers to a brittle substance such as glass or pottery. **Segment** suggests that the whole has been separated along natural or pre-existing lines of division (*a segment of an orange*), and **section** suggests a substantial and clearly separate *part* that fits closely with other parts to form the whole (*a section of a bookcase*). **Fraction** usually suggests a less substantial but still clearly delineated *part*(*a fraction of her income*), and a **portion** is a *part* that has been allotted or assigned to someone (*her portion of the program*). Finally, the very frequently used **piece** is any *part* that is separate from the whole.

---

fragmentary, fragmental *adjective fragmentary evidence* incomplete, disconnected, disjointed, broken, discontinuous, uneven, piecemeal, incoherent, sketchy, unsystematic.

fragrance *noun* **1** *the fragrance of the roses* scent, perfume, bouquet, aroma, smell, sweet smell, redolence, balm, balminess. **2** *a bottle of fragrance* scent, perfume, toilet water; cologne, eau de cologne.

fragrant *adjective fragrant flowers* scented, perfumed, aromatic, sweet-smelling, redolent, balmy, odorous, odoriferous.
Antonyms: SMELLY; FOUL.

frail *adjective* **1** *frail china* fragile, easily broken, breakable, frangible, delicate. *See* FRAGILE 1. **2** *frail old ladies* infirm, weak, delicate, slight, slender, puny, unsound, ill, ailing, unwell, sickly. **3** *frail creatures* weak, easily led/tempted, susceptible, impressionable, vulnerable, fallible.
Antonyms: TOUGH; ROBUST; STRONG.

frailty *noun* **1** *the frailty of the china* fragility, brittleness, frangibility, flimsiness, insubstantiality, delicacy, daintiness, fineness. **2** *the frailty of the old* infirmness, infirmity, weakness, delicacy, slightness, puniness, illness. *See* FRAIL 2. **3** *the frailty of human nature* weakness, susceptibility, impressionability, vulnerability, fallibility. **4** *excuse their frailties* foible, weakness, weak point, flaw, blemish, defect, failing, fault, shortcoming, deficiency, peccadillo.

frame *noun* **1** *built on a frame of steel* framework, substructure, structure, shell, casing, support, skeleton, scaffolding, foundation, body, chassis. **2** *the man had a huge frame* body, physique, build, figure, shape, size, skeleton, carcass. **3**

a picture frame mount, mounting, setting. **4** *alter the frame of society* order, organization, scheme, system, plan, fabric, form, constitution. **5** *a sad frame of mind* state, condition; mood, humor, temper, spirit, attitude.

frame *verb* **1** *frame the structure* assemble, put together, put/set up, build, construct, erect, elevate, make, fabricate, manufacture, fashion, mold, shape, forge. **2** *frame a policy* put together, formulate, draw up, plan, draft, map/plot/sketch out, shape, compose, form, devise, create, establish, conceive, think up, hatch; *inf.* dream up, cook up. **3** *frame a picture | hair framing his face* enclose, encase, surround. **4** *to frame a colleague* incriminate, fabricate charges/evidence against; *inf.* set up.

frame-up *noun* false charge, trumped-up charge, plot, conspiracy, collusion; *inf.* put-up job, set-up.

framework *noun* **1** *the framework of the building* frame, substructure, shell, skeleton. *See* FRAME *noun* 1. **2** *the framework of society* frame, order, organization, scheme, system, plan, fabric, form, constitution.

franchise *noun* **1** *women given the franchise* right to vote, the vote, suffrage, enfranchisement. **2** *grant him a fast-food franchise | the corporation was given a franchise* warrant, warranty, charter, license; permission, leave, consent, privilege, prerogative.

frank *adjective* **1** *a frank person/reply* candid, direct, forthright, plain, plainspoken, straight, straight from the shoulder, downright, explicit, outspoken, blunt, bluff, open, sincere, honest, truthful, undissembling, guileless, artless. **2** *show frank admiration* open, obvious, transparent, patent, manifest, undisguised, unconcealed, unmistakable, evident, noticeable, visible.
Antonyms: RETICENT; EVASIVE; INSINCERE.

frankly *adverb* **1** *frankly, I think he is lying* to be frank/honest, candidly, honestly, truthfully. *See* FRANK *adjective* 1. **2** *he spoke frankly* candidly, directly, plainly, explicitly, bluntly, openly, honestly, truthfully.

frantic *adjective* panic-stricken, panic-struck, panicky, beside oneself, at one's wits' end, frenzied, wild, hysterical, frenetic, berserk, distraught, overwrought, worked up, distracted, agitated, distressed, out of control, uncontrolled, unhinged, mad, crazed, out of one's mind, maniacal; *inf.* fraught.

fraternity *noun* **1** *a strong bond of fraternity in the family* brotherhood, kinship. **2** *join a university fraternity* club, society, association, guild, set, circle.

fraternize *verb* associate, mix, go around with, keep company with, hobnob with, socialize, mingle, consort; *inf.* hang around/out with.

fraud *noun* **1** *found guilty of fraud* fraudulence, cheating, swindling, trickery, deceit, double-dealing, duplicity, treachery, chicanery, skullduggery, imposture, embezzlement, crookedness; *inf.* monkey business. **2** *perpetrate a fraud* ruse, trick, hoax, deception, subterfuge, stratagem, wile, artifice, swindle; *inf.* con, rip-off. **3** *the man is a fraud* impostor, fake, sham, cheat, cheater, swindler, double-dealer, trickster, pretender, charlatan; *inf.* phony, quack, con man. **4** *the vase/check is a fraud* fake, sham, counterfeit, forgery; *inf.* phony.

fraudulent *adjective* dishonest, cheating, swindling, criminal, deceitful, double-dealing, duplicitous, dishonorable, unscrupulous; *inf.* crooked, shady.

fraught *adjective the fraught young mother* anxious, overwrought, distraught, worked up, distracted, agitated, distressed. **fraught with** *fraught with danger* full of, filled with, teeming with, attended by, accompanied by.

fray *verb* **1** *the cloth is fraying* unravel, wear, wear thin, wear out/away, become threadbare, become tattered/ragged. **2** *tempers/nerves were frayed by the experience* strain, tax, overtax, irritate, put on edge, make edgy/tense.

freak *noun* **1** *that animal is a freak* freak of nature, aberration, abnormality, irregularity, oddity, monster, monstrosity, malformation, mutant, rara avis. **2** *the neighbors think he's a bit of a freak* oddity, peculiar person; *inf.* queer fish, oddball, weirdo, way-out person, nutcase, nut. **3** *they are sci-fi freaks* enthusiast, fan, fanatic, addict, aficionado, devotee; *inf.* buff, fiend, nut. **4** *the storm was a freak* anomaly, unusual occurrence, peculiar turn of events, quirk, quirk/twist of fate; chance; *inf.* fluke.

freak *adjective a freak storm* abnormal, unusual, atypical, aberrant, exceptional, unaccountable, unpredictable, unforeseeable, bizarre, queer, odd, unparalleled; *inf.* fluky.

free *adjective* **1** *a free booklet* free of charge, for nothing, complimentary, gratis, without charge, at no cost; *inf.* for free, on the house. **2** *he is free today* unoccupied, available, not at work, not busy, not tied up, idle, at leisure, with time on one's hands, with time to spare. **3** *is this seat free?* empty, vacant, available, spare, unoccupied, untaken, uninhabited, tenantless. **4** *a free nation* independent, self-governing, self-governed, self-ruling, self-directing, sovereign, autonomous, democratic, emancipated, enfranchised, manumitted. **5** *the animals are free* at liberty, at large, loose, on the loose, unconfined, unbound, untied, unchained, unshackled, unfettered, unrestrained, wild. **6** *free to choose* able, allowed, permitted, unrestricted. **7** *a free flow of water | is the road ahead free?* unobstructed, unimpeded, unhampered, clear, unblocked. **8** *the free end of the rope* not fixed, unattached, unfastened, loose. **9** *free with their money* generous, lavish, liberal, openhanded, unstinting, giving, munificent, bountiful, bounteous, charitable, extravagant, prodigal. **10** *a free manner* free and easy, easygoing, natural, open, frank, relaxed, casual, informal, unceremonious, unforced, sponta-

neous, uninhibited, artless, ingenuous; *inf.* laid-back. **free and easy** easygoing, natural, relaxed, casual, informal, tolerant. *See* FREE *adjective* 10. **free of** *free of responsibilities* without, devoid of, lacking in, exempt from, not liable to, safe from, immune to, unaffected by, clear of, unencumbered by, relieved of, released from, rid of; *inf.* sans.

Antonyms: OCCUPIED; BUSY; DEPENDENT; CAPTIVE.

free *verb* **1** *free the prisoners/animals* set free, release, let go, set at liberty, liberate, set/let/turn loose, untie, unchain, unfetter, unshackle, unmanacle, uncage, unleash, deliver. **2** *free the accident victims from the car* get free, rescue, release, get loose, extricate, disentangle, disengage, disencumber. **3** *freed from paying tax* exempt, make exempt, except, excuse, relieve.

freedom *noun* **1** *colonies seeking their freedom* independence, self-government, sovereignty, autonomy, democracy, emancipation, manumission, enfranchisement, home rule. **2** *prisoners enjoying their freedom* liberty, release, deliverance, nonconfinement. **3** *freedom from tax* exemption, immunity, impunity. **4** *freedom of speech* right, privilege, prerogative. **5** *freedom to move around | freedom to operate* scope, latitude, elbow room, wide margin, flexibility, facility, free rein, license. **6** *admire her freedom of manner* naturalness, openness, lack of reserve/inhibition, casualness, informality, lack of ceremony, spontaneity, artlessness, ingenuousness.

Antonyms: DEPENDENCE; CAPTIVITY.

freely *adverb* **1** *speaking freely, I do not like them* frankly, openly, candidly, plainly, bluntly, unreservedly, without constraint. **2** *prisoners not allowed to speak freely* of one's own volition/accord, voluntarily, of one's own free will.

freeze *verb* **1** *the lake has frozen* ice over/up, glaciate, solidify, harden. **2** *freeze to death | I'm freezing* get chilled, get chilled to the bone/marrow, go numb with cold, turn blue with cold, shiver, shiver with cold. **3** *freeze the vegetables* deep-freeze. **4** *he froze as he saw the gun* stop dead, stop in one's tracks, stop, stand still, go rigid, become motionless. **5** *freeze prices* fix, hold, peg, suspend.

freezing *adjective* **1** *freezing winds* bitterly cold, chill, chilling, frosty, glacial, arctic, wintry, raw, biting, piercing, penetrating, cutting, stinging, numbing, Siberian. **2** *freezing children/toes* chilled through, chilled to the bone/marrow, numb with cold, frostbitten.

freight *noun* **1** *a separate shipping charge for the freight* transportation, conveyance, freightage, carriage, portage, haulage. **2** *unload the freight* cargo, load, lading, consignment, merchandise; goods.

frenzied *adjective* frantic, frenetic, panic-stricken, panic-struck, beside oneself, at one's wits' end, wild, hysterical, distraught, distracted, overwrought, agitated, mad, crazed, out of one's mind, maniacal; *inf.* fraught.

frenzy *noun* **1** *go into a frenzy at the news* mental derangement, madness, mania, insanity, wild excitement, wildness, hysteria, distraction, agitation; fit. **2** *a frenzy of activity* bout, outburst, fit.

frequency *noun* **1** *the frequency of accidents on that road* frequentness, recurrence, repetition, persistence. **2** *infant mortality has decreased in frequency* rate of occurrence, rate of repetition, commonness.

frequent *adjective* **1** *frequent accidents* occurring often, recurrent, repeated, persistent, continuing, many, numerous, quite a few/lot, several. **2** *a frequent caller* regular, habitual, customary, common, usual, familiar, everyday, continual, constant, incessant.
Antonyms: INFREQUENT; FEW; RARE.

frequent *verb* visit, visit often, go to regularly/repeatedly, attend, attend frequently, haunt, patronize; *inf.* hang out at.

frequenter *noun* regular visitor, regular customer, regular, habitué.

frequently *adverb* often, very often, many times, many a time, again and again, over and over again, on several occasions, repeatedly, recurrently, habitually, continually, constantly.

fresh *adjective* **1** *is the fruit fresh?* garden-fresh, newly harvested, crisp, unwilted, unfaded, not stale. **2** *fresh fruit, not canned* raw, natural, unprocessed, unpreserved, undried, uncured, crude. **3** *fresh ideas* new, brand-new, recent, latest, up-to-date, modern, modernistic, ultramodern, newfangled, different, innovative, original, novel, unusual, unconventional, unorthodox. **4** *feeling fresh and alive* energetic, vigorous, invigorated, vital, lively, vibrant, spry, sprightly, bright, alert, bouncing, refreshed, rested, restored, revived, like a new person, fresh as a daisy; *inf.* full of vim/beans, raring to go, bright-eyed and bushy-tailed, chipper. **5** *a fresh complexion* healthy-looking, healthy, clear, bright, youthful-looking, wholesome, glowing, fair, rosy, pink, reddish, ruddy. **6** *curtains looking fresh* bright, clean, spick-and-span, unfaded. **7** *fresh supplies* more, other, additional, further, extra, supplementary, auxiliary. **8** *a fresh morning | fresh air* bright, clear, cool, crispy, crisp, sparkling; pure, unpolluted, clean, refreshing. **9** *fresh winds* cool, chilly, brisk, bracing, invigorating. **10** *fresh recruits* young, youthful, new, newly arrived, untrained, inexperienced, untried, raw, callow, green, immature, artless, ingenuous, naïve; *inf.* wet behind the ears. **11** *a fresh young man* familiar, overfamiliar, presumptuous, forward, bold, audacious, brazen, impudent, impertinent, insolent, disrespectful; *inf.* cocky.
Antonyms: STALE; TIRED; DULL.

freshen *verb* **1** *a walk will freshen you | the swim*

freshened her up refresh, rouse, stimulate, revitalize, restore, revive, liven up. **2** *freshen the room* air, ventilate, deodorize, purify. **3** *freshen a drink* top up, refill. **freshen up** *I must freshen up* wash, wash up, wash oneself, tidy oneself, tidy/spruce oneself up.

fret *verb* be distressed, be upset, feel unhappy, be anxious, worry, agonize, anguish, pine, brood, mope, fuss, make a fuss, complain, grumble, whine; *inf.* feel peeved.

fretful *adjective* distressed, upset, miserable, cross, crabbed, fractious, peevish, petulant, out of sorts, irritable, bad-tempered, ill-natured, edgy, irascible, grumpy, crotchety, touchy, captious, testy, querulous, complaining, grumbling, whining, cranky.

friction *noun* **1** *ropes worn by friction* rubbing, abrading, abrasion, attrition, chafing, gnawing, grating, rasping, scraping, excoriation. **2** *cause friction in the family* dissension, dissent, disagreement, discord, strife, conflict, clashing, contention, dispute, disputation, arguing, argument, quarreling, bickering, squabbling, wrangling, fighting, hostility, rivalry, animosity, antagonism, resentment, bad feeling, ill feeling, bad blood, disharmony.

friend *noun* **1** *on vacation with friends* companion, crony, comrade, playmate, soul mate, intimate, confidante, confidant, familiar, alter ego, ally, associate; *inf.* pal, chum, buddy. **2** *friends of the local theater* patron, backer, supporter, benefactor, well-wisher; *inf.* angel.
Antonyms: ENEMY; FOE.

friendless *adjective* companionless, alone, all alone, by oneself, lone, lonely, lonesome, with no one to turn to, solitary, with no ties, unattached, single, forlorn, unpopular, unbefriended.

friendliness *noun* affability, amiability, warmth, geniality, affection, companionability, cordiality, conviviality, sociability, comradeship, neighborliness, approachability, communicativeness, good-naturedness, amenability, benevolence.

friendly *adjective* **1** *a friendly person* affable, amiable, warm, genial, agreeable, affectionate, companionable, cordial, convivial, sociable, hospitable, comradely, neighborly, outgoing, approachable, accessible, communicative, open, unreserved, easygoing, good-natured, kindly, benign, amenable, well-disposed, sympathetic, benevolent; *inf.* chummy, buddy-buddy. **2** *on friendly terms* amicable, congenial, cordial, close, intimate, familiar, peaceable, peaceful, conciliatory, nonhostile. **3** *a friendly wind swept the boat to the shore* helpful, favorable, advantageous, benevolent, well-disposed.
Antonyms: UNFRIENDLY; UNSOCIABLE; HOSTILE.

friendship *noun* **1** *their friendship lasted years* companionship, friendly/close relationship, intimacy, amity, mutual affection, affinity, rapport, mutual understanding, harmony, comradeship, fellowship, attachment, alliance; cordial relations. **2** *she always shows friendship to new people* friendliness, affability, amiability, warmth, geniality, cordiality, neighborliness, good-naturedness, kindliness.

fright noun **1** *start back in fright* fear, fear and trembling, terror, alarm, horror, dread, fearfulness, apprehension, trepidation, consternation, dismay, perturbation, disquiet, panic, nervousness, jitteriness. **2** *give them a fright* scare, shock; shivers; *inf.* jitters, the heebie-jeebies. **3** *woke up looking a fright* ugly/horrible/grotesque sight, eyesore; *inf.* mess, sight.

frighten verb scare, alarm, startle, terrify, terrorize, petrify, give a shock to, shock, appall, panic, throw into panic, unnerve, intimidate, cow, daunt, dismay, make one's blood run cold; *inf.* scare the living daylights out of, scare stiff, scare out of one's wits, make one's hair stand on end, make one's hair curl, make someone jump out of his/her skin, spook.
Antonyms: REASSURE; COMFORT; ENCOURAGE.

frightful adjective **1** *the corpse was a frightful sight* dreadful, terrible, horrible, horrid, hideous, ghastly, grisly, gruesome, macabre, grim, dire, abhorrent, revolting, repulsive, loathsome, odious, fearful, fearsome, terrifying, alarming, shocking, harrowing, appalling, daunting, unnerving. **2** *a frightful woman* unpleasant, disagreeable, dreadful, horrible, terrible, awful, appalling, ghastly, insufferable, unbearable, annoying, irritating. **3** *have a frightful cold* very bad, terrible, dreadful, awful, ghastly, nasty.

frigid adjective **1** *frigid conditions* very cold, bitterly cold, bitter, freezing, frozen, icy, frosty, chilly, wintry, arctic, glacial, Siberian, polar. **2** *a frigid look/welcome* cold, icy, austere, distant, aloof, remote, unapproachable, forbidding, stiff, formal, unbending, cool, unfeeling, unemotional, unfriendly, hostile, unenthusiastic.

frill noun flounce, ruffle, ruff, gather, tuck, fringe.

frills plural noun *a plain meal with no frills* ornamentation, decoration, embellishment, fanciness, ostentation, fuss; trimmings, folderols, affectations, extras, additions, superfluities; *inf.* jazz, flash.

fringe noun **1** *a skirt with a fringe* border, trimming, frill, edging; tassels. **2** *on the fringe of the forest* | *the fringe of society* outer edge, edge, borderline, perimeter, periphery, margin, rim; limits, borders, outskirts, verges.

fringe adjective *fringe theater* experimental, unconventional, unorthodox.

fringe verb **1** *fringe a skirt* trim, edge. **2** *trees fringe the lake* edge, border, skirt, surround, enclose.

frisk verb **1** *lambs frisking about* frolic, gambol, cavort, caper, skip, dance, leap, romp, trip, prance, hop, jump, bounce, rollick. **2** *frisked at the airport* search, examine, check, inspect, *inf.* shake down.

frisky adjective lively, bouncy, active, frolicsome,

coltish, playful, romping, rollicking, spirited, in high spirits, high-spirited, exuberant, joyful.

fritter verb **fritter away 1** *fritter away money* squander, waste, overspend, misspend, spend like water, dissipate, run through, go through. **2** *fritter away time* waste, squander, misuse, idle away, while away.

frivolity noun **1** *the serious student needs a little frivolity* lightheartedness, levity, gaiety, fun, silliness, foolishness. **2** *the frivolity of the girls* frivolousness, giddiness, flightiness, dizziness, flippancy, silliness, zaniness, empty-headedness. *See* FRIVOLOUS 1. **3** *the frivolity of the remark* frivolousness, flippancy, superficiality, shallowness. *See* FRIVOLOUS 2.

frivolous adjective **1** *frivolous young girls* lacking seriousness, nonserious, lacking in sense, senseless, flippant, giddy, flighty, dizzy, silly, foolish, facetious, zany, lighthearted, merry, superficial, shallow, empty-headed, featherbrained; *inf.* flip. **2** *a frivolous remark* nonserious, flippant, ill-considered, superficial, shallow, inane, facetious; *inf.* flip. **3** *frivolous clothes* impractical, flimsy, frothy. **4** *frivolous details* trivial, trifling, minor, petty, insignificant, unimportant, paltry, niggling, peripheral.

frolic verb frisk, gambol, cavort, caper, skip. *See* FRISK 1.

frolic noun **1** *enjoy a frolic in the garden* game, romp, lark, antic, caper, escapade, prank, revel, spree. **2** *the children's frolic* fun, fun and games, gaiety, merriment, mirth, amusement, laughter, jollity; *inf.* skylarking, high jinks.

front noun **1** *toward the front of the building* fore, forepart, foremost part, forefront, foreground, anterior. **2** *paint the front of the building* frontage, face, facing, façade. **3** *at the front in the battle* front line, vanguard, van, first line, firing line. **4** *at the front of the ticket line* beginning, head, top, lead. **5** *put on a brave front* look, appearance, face, exterior, air, manner, expression, show, countenance, demeanor, bearing, mien, aspect. **6** *the pawnshop is a front for his drug dealing* cover, cover-up, blind, façade, disguise, pretext, mask. **in front (of) 1** *the runners in front* in the lead, to the fore, ahead, in the van, in advance. **2** *in front of her in the ticket line* ahead of, before, preceding.
Antonyms: BACK; REAR.

front adjective *the front runners* first, foremost, leading, lead.

front verb *the house fronts on the lake* face toward, look out on, overlook, lie opposite to.

frontier noun border, boundary, bound, limit, edge, rim.

frost noun **1** *frost on the trees* ice crystals, frozen dew, frosting over, white frost, hoarfrost, rime; *inf.* (the work of) Jack Frost. **2** *frost in her greeting* coldness, coolness, iciness, frigidity, hostility, unfriendliness.

frosty adjective **1** *a frosty morning* freezing,

frozen, rimy, frigid, glacial, arctic, icy, wintry, bitterly cold, bitter, cold; *inf.* nippy. **2** *a frosty welcome* cold, cool, icy, glacial, frigid, unfriendly, unwelcoming, unenthusiastic.

froth *noun a froth on the liquid* foam, spume, fizz, effervescence, scum, lather; head; bubbles, suds.

froth *verb beer frothing in the glass | soap suds frothing* foam, spume, cream, bubble, fizz, effervesce, lather.

frothy *adjective* **1** *frothy lemonade* foaming, foamy, foamlike, spumy, bubbling, bubbly, fizzy, effervescent, sparkling. **2** *a frothy novel* light, lightweight, insubstantial, lacking substance, trivial, trifling, petty, paltry, insignificant, worthless, trite, hackneyed.

frown *verb* **1** *frowning at each other* scowl, glower, glare, look daggers at; *inf.* give a dirty look to. **2** *frowning in thought* knit one's brows. **3** *the club frowned at/on sloppy clothes* disapprove of, show/indicate disapproval of, view with dislike/disfavor, dislike, discourage, look askance at, not take kindly to, not think much of, take a dim view of.

frozen *adjective* **1** *frozen ground* ice-covered, icy, icebound, frosted, hard, hard as iron. **2** *frozen conditions* frosty, icy, bitterly cold, glacial, frigid, arctic, Siberian, polar. **3** *children are frozen* freezing, very cold, chilled, chilled to the bone/marrow, numb with cold, shivering; frostbitten; *inf.* frozen to death.

frugal *adjective* **1** *a frugal old man* thrifty, sparing, economical, saving, careful, prudent, provident, unwasteful, abstemious, scrimping, niggardly, penny-pinching, miserly, parsimonious, stingy. **2** *a frugal amount of food* meager, scanty, paltry, insufficient.
Antonyms: EXTRAVAGANT; SPENDTHRIFT; LAVISH.

fruitful *adjective* **1** *fruitful trees* fruit-bearing, fruiting. **2** *a fruitful family* fertile, fecund, potent, progenitive. **3** *fruitful discussions* useful, worthwhile, productive, well-spent, profitable, advantageous, beneficial, rewarding, gainful, successful, effective.
Antonyms: BARREN; FUTILE; FRUITLESS.

fruition *noun* fulfillment, realization, materialization, actualization, achievement, attainment, success, completion, consummation, perfection, maturity, maturation, ripening.

fruitless *adjective* futile, vain, in vain, useless, abortive, to no avail, worthless, pointless, to no effect, idle, ineffectual, ineffective, inefficacious, unproductive, unrewarding, profitless, unsuccessful, unavailing.
Antonyms: PRODUCTIVE; PROFITABLE; FRUITFUL.

fruits *plural noun the fruits of our labors* results, consequences, effects, advantages; outcome, upshot, benefit, profit, reward.

frustrate *verb* **1** *frustrate their attempts* defeat, thwart, check, block, counter, foil, balk, disappoint, forestall, baffle, stymie, stop, spoil, cripple, nullify, obstruct, impede, hamper, hinder, circumvent. **2** *lack of success frustrated him* discourage, dishearten, dispirit, depress, dissatisfy, make discontented, anger, annoy, vex, irk, irritate, embitter.
Antonyms: FACILITATE; ENCOURAGE.

frustration *noun* **1** *the frustration of their plans* defeat, lack of success, nonsuccess, nonfulfillment, thwarting, foiling, balking, forestalling, hampering, circumvention. See FRUSTRATE 1. **2** *full of frustration at their failure* dissatisfaction, disappointment, discontentment, anger, annoyance, irritation, vexation, resentment, bitterness.

fuddy-duddy *noun* old fogy, museum piece, conservative; *inf.* stick-in-the-mud, square, stuffed shirt.

fudge *verb* **1** *fudge the issue* evade, dodge, skirt, avoid. **2** *fudge the accounts/books* falsify, fake; *inf.* cook. **3** *fudge his way through the speech* equivocate, hedge, hem and haw, shuffle.

fuel *noun* **1** *fuel for the furnace/car* heat/power source; coal, wood, oil, gasoline, gas, diesel oil, kerosene. **2** *need fuel before the race* nourishment, food, sustenance, fodder. **3** *his answer was fuel to her anger* incitement, provocation, goading, stimulus, incentive, encouragement, ammunition.

fuel *verb* **1** *fuel the steam engine* supply with fuel, fire, stoke up, charge, power. **2** *fuel her anger* fan, inflame, incite, provoke, goad, stimulate, encourage.

fugitive *noun* escapee, runaway, deserter, refugee.

fugitive *adjective* **1** *a fugitive prisoner* escaping, runaway, fleeing, deserting; *inf.* AWOL, on the run. **2** *fugitive happiness* transient, transitory, fleeting, ephemeral, evanescent, elusive, momentary, short-lived, short, brief, passing, impermanent.

fulfill *verb* **1** *fulfill his task* carry out, accomplish, achieve, execute, perform, discharge, implement, complete, bring to completion, finish, conclude, effect, effectuate, perfect. **2** *fulfill his desire* satisfy, realize, attain, consummate. **3** *fulfill the job requirements* fill, answer, meet, obey, comply with, satisfy, conform to, observe.
Antonyms: FAIL; NEGLECT.

fulfilled *adjective she doesn't feel fulfilled* satisfied, content, happy.

full *adjective* **1** *the cup is full* filled, filled up, filled to the brim, brimful, brimming, filled to capacity. **2** *the theater was full* crowded, packed, crammed, chock-full; *inf.* jam-packed, wall-to-wall. **3** *the seats/rooms are full* occupied, taken, in use. **4** *full supermarket shelves* filled, loaded, well-stocked. **5** *dinner guests feeling full* replete, satisfied, sated, gorged, glutted, cloyed. **6** *a full list of names* complete, entire, whole, comprehensive, thorough, exhaustive, detailed, all-inclusive, all-encompassing, extensive, unabridged. **7** *a full program of events | give full*

details abundant, plentiful, copious, ample, sufficient, broad-ranging, satisfying, complete. **8** *a full figure* well-rounded, rounded, plump, buxom, shapely, curvaceous, voluptuous; *inf.* busty. **9** *a full skirt* loose-fitting, baggy, voluminous, capacious. **10** *a full voice* rich, deep, resonant, loud, strong. **full of** *full of energy/smiles/mistakes* filled with, abounding in, replete with; *inf.* loaded with.
Antonyms: EMPTY; INCOMPLETE; LIMITED.

full *noun* **in full** *give me the account in full* in its entirety, in total, *in toto*, without omission/abridgment. **to the full** *live life to the full* fully, thoroughly, completely, to the utmost, to capacity.

full *adverb hit him full in the face* directly, right, straight, squarely; *inf.* smack-dab.

full-fledged *adjective* mature, fully developed, complete; qualified, fully ranked, experienced, proficient, trained; official.

full-grown *adjective* fully grown, mature, adult, grown-up, of age, fully developed, fully fledged, in full bloom, ripe, in one's prime.

fullness *noun* **1** *the fullness of the list* completeness, comprehensiveness, thoroughness, exhaustiveness, extensiveness. *See* FULL *adjective* 6. **2** *the fullness of her figure* roundedness, plumpness, buxomness. *See* FULL *adjective* 8. **3** *the fullness of his voice* richness, resonance, loudness, strength. **4** *the doctors detected a fullness in her stomach* swelling, enlargement, distension, dilation, tumescence. **in the fullness of time** in due course, when the time is ripe, eventually.

full-scale *adjective* **1** *a full-scale search/reorganization* thorough, comprehensive, extensive, exhaustive, all-out, all-encompassing, all-inclusive, thoroughgoing, wide-ranging, sweeping, major, in-depth. **2** *a full-scale drawing* full-size, unreduced.

fully *adverb* **1** *fully covered by the insurance* completely, entirely, wholly, totally, thoroughly, in all respects, utterly. **2** *fully staffed* completely, amply, sufficiently, satisfactorily, enough. **3** *he's fully 80 years old* quite, at least, without exaggeration.

fulminate *verb* **1** *fulminate against the government* protest against, rail against, denounce, decry, disparage, condemn, criticize, censure, arraign. **2** *chemicals fulminating* explode, detonate, blow up.

fulmination *noun his fulmination against the government* denunciation, violent protest, railing, decrying, condemnation, invective, tirade, diatribe.

fulsome *adjective fulsome compliments* excessive, extravagant, overdone, immoderate, inordinate, overappreciative, insincere, ingratiating, fawning, sycophantic, adulatory, cloying, nauseating, sickening, saccharine, unctuous; *inf.* smarmy.

fumble *verb* **1** *fumble for his keys* grope, feel about/around, fish (around), search blindly. **2** *fumble around in the dark* feel/grope one's way, stumble, blunder, flounder. **3** *fumble her speech* bungle, botch, mismanage, mishandle, muff, spoil; *inf.* make a mess/hash of, fluff, screw up, foul up, flub. **4** *fumble a ball* fail to catch, miss, drop, mishandle, misfield, bobble.

fume *verb* be enraged, seethe, boil, be livid, rage, rant and rave, be furious, be incensed, flare up; *inf.* be up in arms, get hot under the collar, fly off the handle, be at boiling point, foam at the mouth, get all steamed up, raise the roof, flip one's lid, blow one's top.

fumes *plural noun* **1** *fumes from the exhaust* vapor, gas, smoke, exhalation, exhaust, pollution. **2** *the gasoline fumes sickened her* smell, stink, reek, stench.

fumigate *verb* disinfect, purify, sterilize, sanitize, sanitate, cleanse, clean out.

fun *noun* **1** *what do you do for fun?* amusement, entertainment, relaxation, recreation, enjoyment, pleasure, diversion, distraction, play, good time, merrymaking; *inf.* living it up. **2** *she's full of fun* merriment, gaiety, mirth, laughter, hilarity, glee, gladness, cheerfulness, joy; zest; high spirits. **3** *it was just a bit of fun* joking, jest, teasing, banter, badinage. **fun and games** play, playfulness, horseplay, clowning/fooling around, tomfoolery, buffoonery. **in fun** jokingly, as a joke, in jest, to tease, teasingly, for a laugh. **make fun of** ridicule, rag, deride, mock, scoff at, sneer at, taunt, jeer at, parody, lampoon; *inf.* rib, send up, take off.
Antonyms: WORK; MISERY.

fun *adjective* **1** *a fun time* amusing, entertaining, enjoyable, diverting, pleasurable. **2** *a fun person* amusing, witty, entertaining, lively, convivial.

function *noun* **1** *his function in the firm* role, capacity, responsibility, duty, task, chore, job, post, situation, office, occupation, employment, business, charge, concern, province, part, activity, operation, line, mission, *raison d'être*; *inf.* thing, bag. **2** *what is that machine's function?* use, purpose, task. **3** *invited to a function* social event/occasion, affair, gathering, reception, party; *inf.* do.

function *verb is the machine functioning?* work, go, run, be in working/running order, operate. **function as** *she functions as mayor | the sofa functions as a bed* serve as, act as, perform, operate as, officiate as, do (the) duty of, have/do the job of, play the role of, act the part of.

functional *adjective* **1** *functional clothes* practical, useful, serviceable, utilitarian, utility, working, workaday. **2** *is the machine functional?* working, in working order, going, running, operative, in operation, in commission.

functionary *noun* official, officeholder, public servant, civil servant, bureaucrat.

fund *noun* **1** *the church preservation fund* reserve, pool, collection, kitty, endowment, foundation, grant, investment, capital; savings. **2** *a fund of knowledge* stock, store, accumulation, mass, mine, reservoir, supply, storehouse, treasury, treasure-house, hoard, repository.

fund verb *fund the project* finance, back, pay for, capitalize, provide finance/capital for, subsidize, stake, endow, support, float.

fundamental adjective *fundamental principles* basic, basal, foundational, rudimentary, elemental, underlying, primary, cardinal, initial, original, prime, first, principal, chief, key, central, structural, organic, constitutional, inherent, intrinsic, vital, essential, important, indispensable, necessary.

fundamentally adjective *fundamentally he is an honest man* basically, at heart, deep down, essentially, intrinsically.

fundamentals plural noun *get down to fundamentals* basics, first/basic principles, essentials, rudiments; crux, crux of the matter, sine qua non; *inf.* nuts and bolts, nitty-gritty.

funds plural noun *totally out of funds* money, ready money, cash, hard cash, capital, the wherewithal; means, assets, resources, savings; *inf.* dough, bread, the ready.

funeral noun burial, burying, interment, inhumation, entombment, cremation; funeral rites.

funereal adjective **1** *funereal colors* black, dark, drab. **2** *a funereal atmosphere* | *wearing a funereal expression* gloomy, dismal, dreary, depressing, somber, grave, solemn, sad, melancholy, lugubrious.

fungus noun parasite, saprophyte; mushroom, toadstool, mold, mildew, rust.

funny adjective **1** *a funny story/situation* amusing, comic, comical, humorous, hilarious, entertaining, diverting, laughable, hysterical, riotous, sidesplitting, droll, absurd, rich, ridiculous, ludicrous, risible, farcical, silly, slapstick. **2** *he can be very funny* amusing, humorous, entertaining, droll, witty, waggish, jocular. **3** *what a funny hat* strange, peculiar, odd, queer, weird, bizarre, curious. **4** *he's a funny character* strange, peculiar, odd, mysterious, suspicious, dubious; *inf.* shady.

Antonyms: SERIOUS; SAD; NORMAL.

furious adjective **1** *furious parents* enraged, raging, infuriated, fuming, boiling, incensed, inflamed, frenzied, very angry, indignant, mad, raving mad, maddened, wrathful, beside oneself, in high dudgeon; *inf.* livid, hot under the collar, up in arms, foaming at the mouth. **2** *a furious storm/struggle* violent, fierce, wild, intense, vehement, unrestrained, tumultuous, turbulent, tempestuous, stormy, boisterous.

furnish verb **1** *furnish a room* provide with furniture, fit out, outfit. **2** *furnish you with what you require* supply, equip, provide, provision, give, grant, present, offer, bestow on, endow.

furniture noun furnishings, effects; tables and chairs; *inf.* stuff, things.

furor noun **1** *a furor when they found out* commotion, uproar, disturbance, hullabaloo, turmoil, tempest, tumult, brouhaha, stir, excitement, to-do, outburst, outcry. **2** *in a furor* rage, madness, frenzy, fit.

furrow noun **1** groove, trench, channel, rut, trough, hollow, ditch, seam. **2** *furrows on her brow/skin* crease, line, wrinkle, corrugation, crinkle, crow's foot.

further adjective **1** *further supplies* additional, more, extra, supplementary, other, new, fresh. **2** *the further boat is almost out of sight* more distant/advanced/remote, remoter, further away/off, farther.

further adverb **1** *and further, there's a chance of rain* furthermore, moreover, what's more, also. *See* FURTHERMORE. **2** *she stopped and would come no further* to a more advanced point, more forward/onward, farther.

further verb *further our plans* advance, forward, facilitate, aid, assist, help, lend a hand to, abet, expedite, hasten, speed up, push, give a push to, promote, back, contribute to, encourage, foster, champion.

furtherance noun **1** *furtherance in the firm* advancement, promotion, elevation, preferment; *inf.* step-up. **2** *the furtherance of our plans* furthering, advancement, forwarding, facilitating, aiding, assisting, pushing, promotion, backing. *See* FURTHER verb.

furthermore adverb moreover, what's more, also, besides, additionally, as well, further, to boot, on top of that, over and above that, by the same token.

furthest adjective furthest away, farthest, furthermost, most distant, most remote, outermost, outmost, extreme, uttermost, ultimate.

furtive adjective secret, secretive, stealthy, surreptitious, sneaky, sneaking, skulking, slinking, clandestine, hidden, covert, cloaked, conspiratorial, sly, underhand, underhanded, under the table, wily.

Antonyms: OPEN; ABOVEBOARD.

fury noun **1** *the fury of the parents* great anger, rage, ire, wrath, madness, passion, frenzy, furor. **2** *the fury of the storm* fierceness, ferocity, violence, turbulence, tempestuousness, severity, intensity, vehemence, force, great force, power, potency. **3** *she is a real fury* virago, hellcat, termagant, spitfire, vixen, shrew, hag.

fuse verb **1** *fuse the ingredients* combine, amalgamate, put together, unite, blend, intermix, intermingle, merge, meld, coalesce, compound, agglutinate, join, integrate, weld, solder. **2** *fuse the solid* melt, melt down, smelt, dissolve, liquefy.

Antonyms: SEPARATE; DISCONNECT.

fuss noun **1** *the fuss over the preparations* fluster, flurry, bustle, to-do, ado, agitation, excitement, bother, stir, commotion, confusion, tumult, uproar, upset, worry, overanxiety; *inf.* tempest in a teacup, much ado about nothing, flap, tizzy, stew. **2** *a fuss in the bar last night* row, altercation, squabble, argument, quarrel, dis-

fuss about the service complaint, objection.

fuss *verb* **1** *tell the organizers to stop fussing* | *fuss over details* bustle, bustle about, dash about, rush about, tear around, buzz around; worry, be agitated/worried, make a big thing out of nothing, make a mountain out of a molehill; *inf.* get worked up over nothing, be in a tizzy, be in a stew. **2** *fuss about the service* kick up a fuss, make a fuss, complain, raise an objection; *inf.* grouse, gripe. **3** *the baby is fussing* be upset, fret, cry, be cross.

fussy *adjective* particular, overparticular, finicky, persnickety, fastidious, hard to please, difficult, exacting, demanding, discriminating, selective, dainty; *inf.* choosy, picky, nitpicking.

futile *adjective* **1** *a futile search* vain, in vain, to no avail, unavailing, useless, ineffectual, ineffective, inefficacious, unsuccessful, fruitless, abortive, unproductive, impotent, barren, unprofitable, hollow. **2** *a futile statement* trivial, unimportant, petty, trifling, valueless, worthless, inconsequential, idle.
Antonyms: USEFUL; FRUITFUL; SIGNIFICANT.

futility *noun* **1** *the futility of the search* uselessness, ineffectiveness, fruitlessness, abortiveness. *See* FUTILE 1. **2** *the futility of the statement* triviality, unimportance, pettiness, worthlessness. *See* FUTILE 2.

future *noun* **1** *things might improve in the future* time to come, time ahead, hereafter; coming times. **2** *no future in the firm* prospects, expectations; anticipation, outlook, likely success/advancement/improvement.

fuzzy *adjective* **1** *fuzzy hair* | *a fuzzy peach* frizzy, downy, down-covered, woolly, linty. **2** *everything's gone all fuzzy* out of focus, unfocused, blurred, blurry, bleary, misty, indistinct, unclear, distorted, ill-defined, indefinite. **3** *fuzzy recollection* confused, muddled, fuddled, befuddled, foggy, misty, shadowy, blurred.

G

gad *verb* *he's always gadding about* gallivant, roam, wander, travel around, rove, ramble, run around, range, flit about, meander, stray; *inf.* traipse.

gadabout *noun* gallivanter, rambler, rover, wanderer, traveler, nomad, globe-trotter.

gadget *noun* appliance, apparatus, instrument, implement, tool, contrivance, device, mechanism, invention, thing; *inf.* contraption, widget, gizmo.

gaffe *noun* mistake, blunder, slip, indiscretion, faux pas; *inf.* blooper, goof, boner, booboo.

gag *noun* *his gags amused her* joke, jest, witticism, quip, funny remark, hoax, prank; *inf.* wisecrack, crack.

gag *verb* **1** *gag his mouth* put a gag on, stop up, block, plug, clog, stifle, smother, muffle. **2** *the press have been gagged* silence, muzzle, curb, check, restrain, suppress, repress. **3** *he gagged when he saw the corpse* choke, retch, gasp, struggle for breath, convulse, almost vomit.

gaiety *noun* **1** *the gaiety of the children* gayness, cheerfulness, lightheartedness, merriment, glee, blitheness, gladness, happiness, high spirits, good spirits, delight, pleasure, joy, joyfulness, joyousness, exuberance, elation, mirth, joviality, liveliness, vivacity, animation, effervescence, buoyancy, sprightliness, exultation, *joie de vivre.* **2** *join in the gaiety of the fair* fun, festivity, merrymaking, revelry, revels, celebration. **3** *the gaiety of the dresses* colorfulness, brightness, brilliance, sparkle, glitter, gaudiness, showiness, show, garishness.

Antonyms: GLOOM; MISERY.

gain *verb* **1** *gain an advantage* obtain, get, acquire, procure, secure, attain, build up, achieve, arrive at, come to have, win, capture, net, pick up, reap, gather. **2** *gain experience/weight* get more of, increase in, add on. **3** *gain awage* earn, bring in, make, get, clear, gross, net, realize, produce. **gain on 1** *the police were gaining on the escaped prisoner* catch up with, catch up on, narrow the gap between, get nearer to, close in on, overtake, come up to, approach. **2** *the escaped prisoner was gaining on the police* widen the gap between, get further ahead of, leave behind, draw away from, outdistance, do better than. **gain time** stall, procrastinate, delay, use delaying tactics, temporize.

Antonyms: LOSE; FORFEIT.

gain *noun* **1** *his gain from the deal was negligible* profit, earnings, income, advantage, benefit, reward, emolument, yield, return, winnings, proceeds, dividend, interest. **2** *a gain in experience/weight* more of, increase, augmentation, addition, rise, increment, accretion, accumulation. **3** *their gain against the enemy* advance, advancement, progress, forward movement, headway, improvement, step forward. **4** *show off his latest gains* acquisition, acquirement, achievement.

Antonyms: LOSS; DECREASE.

gainful *adjective* profitable, remunerative, paying, financially rewarding, rewarding, lucrative, moneymaking, productive, beneficial, advantageous, worthwhile, useful.

gainsay *verb* *there's no gainsaying his honesty* deny, dispute, disagree with, disbelieve, contradict, contravene, challenge, oppose, controvert, disaffirm.

gait *noun* walk, step, stride, pace, tread, manner of walking, bearing, carriage.

gala *noun* festival, fête, festivities, carnival, pageant, jamboree, party, celebration.

gala *adjective* *a gala occasion* festive, celebratory, merry, gay, joyous, joyful, jovial, entertaining, spectacular, showy, ceremonial, ceremonious.

galaxy *noun* *a galaxy of stars* dazzling assemblage, host, brilliant gathering, illustrious group.

gale *noun* **1** *lost at sea in a gale* storm, tempest, squall, hurricane, tornado, cyclone, typhoon, mistral, sirocco. **2** *gales of laughter* outburst, peal, ring, shriek, shout, roar, scream, howl, fit, eruption.

gall[1] *noun* **1** *have the gall to answer back* impudence, insolence, impertinence, nerve, audacity, brashness, effrontery, temerity; *inf.* brass, chutzpah. **2** *words full of gall* bitterness, resentment, rancor, acrimony, malice, spite, venom, malevolence, virulence, sourness, acerbity, asperity, animosity, antipathy, hostility, enmity, bad blood, ill feeling, animus, bile, spleen.

gall[2] *noun* **1** *a gall on the horse's skin* sore, abrasion, scrape, scratch, graze, canker, ulceration. **2** *they are a gall to him* source of vexation/irritation/annoyance, vexation, irritation, irritant, annoyance, pest, nuisance, provocation, bother, torment, plague; *inf.* botheration, aggravation.

gall[3] *verb* **1** *gall the skin* abrade, chafe, rub, rub raw, scrape, graze, skin, scratch, excoriate, rasp, bark. **2** *her attitude galls him* vex, irritate, infuriate, irk, annoy, rub the wrong way, provoke, exasperate, rile, nettle, bother, ruffle, pester, torment, harass, rankle, embitter; *inf.* aggravate, peeve.

gallant *adjective* **1** *gallant soldiers* brave, courageous, valiant, valorous, bold, plucky, daring, fearless, intrepid, manly, manful, dashing, heroic, heroical, lionhearted, stouthearted, doughty, mettlesome, great-spirited, honorable, noble. **2** *gallant to the ladies* chivalrous, gentlemanly, courtly, courteous, mannerly, polite, attentive, gracious, considerate, thoughtful, obliging, deferential. **3** *a gallant ship* fine, great, dignified, stately, noble, splendid, elegant, magnificent, majestic, imposing, glorious, regal, august.
Antonyms: COWARDLY; DISCOURTEOUS; RUDE.

gallant *noun* man about town, man of fashion, man of the world, ladies' man, lady-killer, dandy, fop; beau, suitor, wooer, admirer, lover, boyfriend, paramour.

gallantry *noun* **1** *the gallantry of the troops* bravery, braveness, courage, courageousness, valor, boldness, pluck, daring, fearlessness, intrepidity, manliness, heroism, doughtiness. *See* GALLANT *adjective* 1. **2** *the gallantry of the gentlemen* chivalry, chivalrousness, gentlemanliness, courtliness, courteousness, politeness, mannerliness, attentiveness, graciousness, consideration, thoughtfulness.

galling *adjective* *a galling experience* vexing, vexatious, irritating, infuriating, irksome, annoying, provoking, exasperating, troublesome, bothering, harassing, rankling, embittering, bitter. *See* GALL² *verb* 2.

gallivant *verb* gad about, roam, wander, travel around, rove, ramble. *See* GAD.

gallop *verb* **1** *the horse galloped* go/run at full speed, canter, lope, run. **2** *the children galloped home* race, rush, dash, tear, sprint, bolt, fly, run, shoot, dart, hurry, hasten, speed, career, scamper, scurry, zoom.

gallows *noun* gibbet, scaffold.

galore *adverb* *have books/food/friends galore* in abundance, in profusion, in great quantity, in plenty, aplenty, in huge numbers, to spare, everywhere, all over the place.

galvanize *verb* *galvanize them into action* electrify, shock, startle, jolt, stir, excite, rouse, arouse, awaken, spur, prod, urge, stimulate, give a stimulus to, invigorate, fire, animate, vitalize, energize, exhilarate, thrill, inspire.

gambit *noun* stratagem, maneuver, machination, move, play, ruse, trick, ploy, artifice.

gamble *verb* **1** *he loves to gamble* bet, wager, place a bet, lay a wager/bet, game, try one's luck; *inf.* play the ponies. **2** *he gambled when he invested in that firm* take a chance, take a risk, leave things to chance, speculate, venture, buy a pig in a poke; *inf.* stick one's neck out, go out on a limb. **gamble on** *gamble on his parents' being absent* act in the hope that, trust that, chance that, take a chance that, bank on.

gamble *noun* risk, hazard, chance, lottery, speculation, venture, uncertainty, pig in a poke.

gambol *verb* frolic, frisk, cavort, caper, skip, dance, leap, romp, trip, prance, hop, jump, spring, bounce, rollick.

game *noun* **1** *children playing a game* pastime, diversion, entertainment, amusement, recreation, play, sport, distraction. **2** *we were only playing a game on him* joke, practical joke, prank, jest, trick, hoax. **3** *there's a game tomorrow* match, contest, tournament, meeting, sports/sporting event, athletic event, round, bout. **4** *he's in the oil game* business, line, occupation, trade, profession, industry, enterprise, activity, calling. **5** *what's his game?* scheme, trick, plot, ploy, stratagem, strategy, cunning plan, tactics, artifice, device, maneuver. **6** *they went shooting game* wild animals, wild fowl, quarry, prey, big game. **make game of** make fun of, make a fool of, poke fun at, ridicule, deride, make a laughingstock (out) of, mock, scoff at, jeer at, make sport of, make the butt of one's jokes, taunt; *inf.* rib, rag. **play the game** play by the rules, play fair, be a good sport.

game *verb* gamble, bet, wager. *See* GAMBLE *verb* 1.

game *adjective* **1** *who's game enough to knock at her door?* plucky, brave, courageous, valiant, unafraid, fearless, gallant, bold, intrepid, stouthearted, lionhearted, dauntless, undaunted, daring, dashing, spirited, unflinching. **2** *I'm game to go if you are* willing, favorably inclined, desirous, eager, interested, enthusiastic, ready, prepared, disposed.

gamut *noun* entire range, whole spectrum, complete scale, complete sequence, whole series, full sweep, full compass, entire scope, entire area.

gang *noun* **1** *a gang of people gathered* group, band, crowd, company, gathering, pack, horde, mob, herd. **2** *the young man and his gang* clique, circle, social set, coterie, lot, ring, club; fraternity, sorority; *inf.* crew. **3** *gang of workers* crew, squad, team, troop, shift, detachment, posse, troupe.

gangling, gangly *adjective* *gangling lad of sixteen* lanky, rangy, spindly, spindling, loosely built, loosely jointed, stringy, skinny, angular, awkward, awkwardly tall.

gangster *noun* gang member, racketeer, bandit, brigand, robber, ruffian, thug, hoodlum, tough, desperado, Mafioso, terrorist; *inf.* crook, mobster, hood.

gap *noun* **1** *a gap in the wall* opening, cavity, hole, aperture, space, breach, orifice, break, fracture, rift, rent, fissure, cleft, chink, crack, crevice, cranny, divide, discontinuity, interstice. **2** *gaps in the program* pause, intermission, interval, interlude, break, recess. **3** *gaps in his account* omission, blank, hole, void. **4** *the gap between the old and the young* breach, difference, divergence, disparity.

gape *verb* **1** *gaping at the procession* stare, stare in wonder, gaze, ogle; *inf.* gawk, rubberneck. **2** *the chasm gaped before them* open wide, become open wide, open up, yawn, part, crack, split.

garb *noun* **1** *admire the fine garb* clothes, clothing, garments, dress, attire, apparel, costume, outfit, wear, habit, uniform, array, habiliment, vestments, livery, trappings; *inf.* gear, get-up, togs, duds. **2** *dressed in the garb of a soldier* clothes, attire, uniform, style, fashion, look. **3** *wearing the garb of sanity* outward appearance, appearance, guise, outward form, exterior, aspect, semblance, look.

garb *verb* *garbed in black* clothe, dress, attire, array, robe, cover, outfit.

garbage *noun* **1** *put the garbage out* trash, waste, rubbish, refuse, debris, litter, junk, discarded matter; swill, detritus; scraps, leftovers, remains, slops. **2** *talking a lot of garbage* nonsense, rubbish, twaddle, drivel, foolishness, balderdash; *inf.* hogwash, poppycock, rot, crap, baloney, piffle.

garble *verb* *garbled the message* mix up, get mixed up, jumble, confuse, change around, distort, twist, twist around, warp, slant, mutilate, tamper with, doctor, falsify, pervert, corrupt, adulterate, misstate, misquote, misreport, misrender, misrepresent, mistranslate, misinterpret, misunderstand.

gargantuan *adjective* extremely big/large, gigantic, giant, enormous, monstrous, huge, colossal, vast, immense, tremendous, massive, hulking, towering, mammoth, prodigious, elephantine, mountainous, monumental, titanic; *inf.* jumbo, humongous, whopping.

garish *adjective* *garish colors* | *wearing a garish shirt* flashy, loud, showy, gaudy, glaring, flaunting, bold-colored, glittering, tinselly, brassy, tawdry, raffish, tasteless, in bad taste, vulgar, cheap, flashy.

Antonyms: DRAB; SOBER; TASTEFUL.

garland *noun* *wear a garland of flowers* wreath, festoon, lei, laurel, laurels, coronet, crown, circlet, chaplet, fillet, headband.

garland *verb* *garland in flowers* wreathe, festoon, adorn, decorate, deck, crown.

garment *noun* **1** *wearing a white garment* piece of clothing, article of clothing, item of dress, cover, covering. **2** *wearing strange garments* clothes, clothing, dress, attire, apparel, costume, outfit, garb. *See* GARB *noun* 1.

garner *verb* *squirrels garnering nuts* gather, collect, accumulate, heap, pile up, amass, assemble, stack up, store, lay by, put/stow away, hoard, stockpile, deposit, husband, reserve, save, preserve, save for a rainy day.

garnish *verb* *garnish the dish with parsley* decorate, adorn, trim, ornament, embellish, deck, deck out, bedeck, festoon, enhance, grace, beautify, prettify, set off, add the finishing touch to.

garnish *noun* *a parsley garnish for the meat* decoration, adornment, trim, trimming, ornament, ornamentation, embellishment, enhancement, beautification, finishing touch.

garret *noun* attic, loft, mansard.

garrison *noun* **1** *the garrison arrived at the fort* armed force, military detachment/unit, platoon, brigade, squadron; troops, militia, soldiers. **2** *the garrison was under siege* fort, fortress, fortification, stronghold, blockhouse, citadel, camp, encampment, command post, base, station; barracks.

garrison *verb* **1** *the town was garrisoned by the allied forces* defend, guard, protect, preserve, fortify, man, occupy, supply with troops. **2** *troops garrisoned in the town* station, post, put on duty, assign, position, billet; send in.

garrulity *noun* **1** *the garrulity of the man* garrulousness, talkativeness, chattiness, loquacity, gift of the gab, volubility, verbosity, prating, long-windedness, prattling; *inf.* mouthiness, gabbiness. *See* GARRULOUS 1. **2** *the garrulity of the account* wordiness, long-windedness, verbosity, prolixity, diffuseness.

garrulous *adjective* **1** *a garrulous old man* talkative, chatty, chattering, gossiping, loquacious, voluble, verbose, long-winded, babbling, prattling, prating, blathering, jabbering, gushing, effusive; *inf.* mouthy, gabby. **2** *a garrulous account* long-winded, wordy, verbose, rambling, prolix, diffuse.

Antonyms: TACITURN; RETICENT.

gash *noun* *a gash in his hand* cut, slash, wound, tear, laceration, gouge, incision, slit, split, nick, cleft.

gash *verb* *gash his hand* cut, slash, wound, tear, lacerate, gouge, incise, slit, split, rend, nick, cleave.

gasp *verb* *gasping as he climbed the hill* pant, puff, blow, catch one's breath, draw in one's breath, gulp, choke, fight for breath, wheeze, huff and puff.

gasp *noun* (sudden/short) breath/inhalation, pant, puff, gulp, choke.

gastric *adjective* stomach, abdominal, intestinal.

gate *noun* **1** *build a gate* barrier, door, portal. **2** *crowds blocking the gates to the stadium* gateway, doorway, access, entrance, exit, egress, opening, passage.

gather *verb* **1** *people gathered in the church* come together, collect, assemble, congregate, meet, group, cluster together, crowd, mass, flock together, convene, converge. **2** *gather the children* call together, summon, get together, assemble, collect, congregate, convene, round up, muster, marshal. **3** *gather cans of food* | *gather the facts* get/put together, collect, accumulate, amass, assemble, garner, store, stockpile, heap up, pile up, stack up, hoard; *inf.* stash away. **4** *the event gathered a huge audience* attract, draw, draw together/in, pull, pull in, collect, pick up. **5** *we gather that he is dead* understand, be given to understand, believe, be led to believe, hear,

learn, infer, draw the inference, deduce, conclude, come to the conclusion, assume, surmise. **6** *gather to one's bosom* embrace, clasp, enfold, hold, hug, cuddle. **7** *gather the harvest* harvest, collect, pick, pluck, cull, garner, crop, reap, glean. **8** *gather in strength/force* increase, grow, rise, build, expand, enlarge, swell, extend, wax, intensify, deepen, heighten, thicken. **9** *gather the waist of the dress* ruffle, shirr, pleat, pucker, tuck, fold.
Antonyms: SCATTER; DISPERSE; SEPARATE.

---

gather
assemble, collect, congregate, convene, marshal, muster

Gather is the most general of these terms meaning to come or bring together. It implies bringing widely scattered things or people to one place but with no particular arrangement (*to gather shells at the beach; to gather the family in the living room*). **Collect**, on the other hand, implies both selectivity (*to collect evidence for the trial*) and organization (*to collect butterflies as a hobby*). To *gather* one's thoughts means to bring them together because they have been previously scattered; to *collect* one's thoughts is to organize them. **Assemble** pertains to objects or people who are brought together for a purpose (*to assemble data for a report; to assemble Congress so that legislation will be passed*), while **congregate** may be more spontaneous, done as a free choice (*people congregated in front of the palace, hoping to catch a glimpse of the queen*). **Convene** is a formal word meaning to *assemble* or meet in a body (*to convene an international conference on the subject of global warming*) **Marshal** and **muster** are usually thought of as military terms. *Muster* implies bringing together the parts or units of a force (*troops mustered for inspection*), and *marshal* suggests a very orderly and purposeful arrangement (*to marshal the allied forces along the battle front*).

---

gathering *noun* **1** *a gathering of people* assembly, assemblage, collection, company, congregation, group, party, band, knot, crowd, flock, throng, mass, mob, horde, meeting, meet, convention, conclave, rally, turnout, congress, convocation, concourse, muster; *inf.* get-together. **2** *his gathering of coins* collection, accumulation, assemblage, aggregation, aggregate, mass, store, stock, stockpile, heap, pile, cluster, agglomeration, conglomeration, concentration. **3** *the gathering of shells/facts* collecting, accumulation, assembly, assembling, garnering. *See* GATHER 3.

gauche *adjective* *a gauche manner/person/remark* awkward, clumsy, gawky, ungainly, bumbling, lumbering, maladroit, socially inept, lacking in social graces, inelegant, graceless, unpolished, unsophisticated, uncultured, uncultivated.
Antonyms: SOPHISTICATED; ELEGANT; ADROIT.

gaudy *adjective* *wearing a very gaudy shirt* bold-colored, garish, loud, glaring, bright, brilliant, flashy, showy, ostentatious, tawdry, raffish, tasteless, in bad taste, vulgar, cheap.
Antonyms: DRAB; SOBER; TASTEFUL.

gauge *verb* **1** *gauge the thickness of the metal* measure, calculate, compute, determine, count, weigh, check, ascertain. **2** *you must gauge his aptitude* evaluate, appraise, assess, place a value on, estimate, guess, judge, adjudge, rate, reckon, determine; *inf.* guesstimate.

gauge *noun* **1** *find a gauge of his abilities* measure, basis, standard, guide, guideline, touchstone, yardstick, benchmark, criterion, rule, norm, example, model, pattern, exemplar, sample, test, indicator. **2** *the gauge of a barrel/gun/wire/railroad* extent, degree, scope, area, size, measure, capacity, magnitude, depth, height, width, thickness, span, bore.

gaunt *adjective* **1** *illness had left her gaunt* haggard, drawn, cadaverous, skeletal, emaciated, skin and bones, skinny, spindly, stalky, spare, bony, angular, lank, lean, rawboned, pinched, hollow-cheeked, starved-looking, scrawny, scraggy, shriveled, wasted, withered; *inf.* looking like death warmed over. **2** *gaunt landscape* bleak, barren, bare, desolate, dreary, dismal, forlorn, grim, stern, harsh, forbidding.
Antonyms: OBESE; FAT; LUSH.

gawk *verb* stare, gape, gaze, ogle; *inf.* rubberneck.

gawky *adjective* *a shy, gawky teenager* ungainly, ungraceful, uncoordinated, lanky, clumsy, lumbering, blundering, maladroit, oafish, loutish, doltish, clodhopping.
Antonyms: GRACEFUL; ADROIT.

gay *adjective* **1** *feeling gay* merry, jolly, lighthearted, cheerful, mirthful, jovial, glad, happy, bright, in good spirits, in high spirits, joyful, elated, exuberant, animated, lively, sprightly, vivacious, buoyant, effervescent, playful, frolicsome. **2** *have a gay time* merry, festive, amusing, enjoyable, entertaining, convivial, hilarious. **3** *gay colors* bright, brightly colored, vivid, brilliant, many-colored, multicolored, flamboyant, gaudy. **4** *gay men/women* homosexual, lesbian; *derog. inf.* queer, limp-wristed, butch.
Antonyms: GLOOMY; DULL; DRAB.

gay *noun* homosexual, lesbian; *derog. inf.* queer, homo, dyke, fag.

gaze *verb* stare, look fixedly, gape, stand agog, watch in wonder, ogle, eye, take a good look, contemplate; *inf.* gawk, rubberneck, give the once-over.

gaze *noun* *fix his gaze on her* stare, fixed look, intent look, gape.

gazette *noun* newspaper, journal, periodical, paper, newsletter; *inf.* rag.

gear *noun* **1** *the car's gear* gearwheel, cog, cogwheel. **2** *the steering gear of a boat* gears, mechanism, machinery, works. **3** *the workman's gear* equipment, apparatus, tools, implements, tackle, appliances, contrivances, utensils, supplies, accouterments, trappings, accessories, paraphernalia; *inf.* stuff. **4** *wearing modern gear* clothes, clothing, garments, dress, attire, apparel, garb, outfit, wear, costume, array, vestments; *inf.* get-up, togs, duds. **5** *their daughter and all her gear* belongings, things, luggage, baggage, effects, paraphernalia, accouterments, personal possessions, trappings; *inf.* stuff.

gelatinous *adjective* jellylike, glutinous, viscid, viscous, gummy, sticky, gluey, mucilaginous, slimy; *inf.* gooey.

geld *verb* castrate, neuter, emasculate, asexualize.

gelid *adjective* freezing, frozen, icy, ice-cold, arctic, glacial, polar, frosty, wintry, snowy, bitterly cold, chilly, Siberian.

gem *noun* **1** *a ring set with gems* jewel, precious stone, semiprecious stone, stone. **2** *the gem of his collection of books* jewel, jewel in the crown, pick, flower, cream, crème de la crème, prize, treasure, pearl, masterpiece.

genealogy *noun* pedigree, family tree, ancestry, line, lineage, descent, parentage, birth, derivation, extraction, family, dynasty, house, race, strain, stock, breed, bloodline, heritage, history, roots.

general *adjective* **1** *the general practice is to apply in writing* usual, customary, common, ordinary, normal, standard, regular, typical, conventional, everyday, habitual, run-of-the-mill. **2** *in general use | the general feeling* common, extensive, widespread, broad, wide, accepted, prevalent, prevailing, universal, popular, public, generic. **3** *a general tax hike/rule* across-the-board, blanket, universal, sweeping, broad, broad-ranging, comprehensive, all-inclusive, encyclopedic, indiscriminate, catholic. **4** *a general store | his general knowledge* mixed, assorted, miscellaneous, variegated, diversified, composite, heterogeneous. **5** *a general account* nondetailed, undetailed, broad, loose, approximate, nonspecific, unspecific, vague, ill-defined, indefinite, inexact, imprecise, rough. **6** *a general view* panoramic, sweeping, extended, bird's-eye.

Antonyms: UNUSUAL; SPECIFIC; DETAILED.

generality *noun* **1** *talking in generalities* generalization, general statement, general principle, nonspecific statement, loose/vague statement, indefinite statement, sweeping statement. **2** *a situation not conforming to the generality* general principle/rule/law. **3** *the generality of people are kind* majority, greater part, bulk, mass, body. **4** *the generality of its use* commonness, widespread nature, broadness, prevalence, universality, popularity. **5** *the generality of the rule* universality, broadness, comprehensiveness, all-inclusiveness, catholicity. *See* GENERAL 3. **6** *the generality of the statement* lack of detail, broadness, looseness, approximation, lack of

specification, vagueness, indefiniteness, inexactitude, imprecision, roughness.

generally *adverb* **1** *it generally rains there in the spring* in general, usually, as a rule, normally, ordinarily, almost always, customarily, habitually, typically, regularly, for the most part, mainly, by and large, on average, on the whole, in most cases. **2** *not generally known* commonly, widely, extensively, comprehensively, universally. **3** *speaking generally* in a general sense, without detail, loosely, approximately, broadly, in nonspecific terms. *See* GENERAL 5. **4** *they are generally liked* mostly, for the most part, mainly, in the main, largely, chiefly, predominantly, on the whole.

Antonyms: unusually; PARTICULARLY; RARELY.

generate *verb* **1** *generate electricity* bring into being, cause to exist, produce. **2** *generating children* beget, procreate, engender, sire, father, breed, spawn, produce, propagate. **3** *generate an argument* cause, give rise to, create, produce, initiate, originate, occasion, sow the seeds of, arouse, whip up, propagate.

generation *noun* **1** *the generation of the human race* begetting, procreation, engendering, genesis, reproduction, siring, propagation. **2** *the generation of ideas* causing, creation, production, initiation, origination, inception, occasioning, propagation. **3** *people of the same generation* age, age group, peer group. **4** *a generation ago* life span, lifetime; *inf.* couple of decades. **5** *generations ago* age, era, epoch, times, days.

generic *adjective* **1** *the generic name for beer, wines, and liquors is "alcohol"* nonspecific, general, common, collective, inclusive, all-inclusive, all-encompassing, comprehensive, blanket, sweeping, universal. **2** *brand-name goods rather than generic goods* nonproprietary, nonexclusive, nontrademarked, nonregistered.

generosity *noun* **1** *the generosity of our host* liberalness, liberality, kindness, magnanimity, benevolence, beneficence, bounteousness, bounty, munificence, hospitality, charitableness, charity, openhandedness, lavishness. **2** *the generosity of his spirit* nobility, nobleness, magnanimity, loftiness, high-mindedness, honorableness, honor, goodness, unselfishness, altruism.

generous *adjective* **1** *generous with money | a generous host* liberal, kind, magnanimous, benevolent, beneficent, bountiful, bounteous, munificent, hospitable, charitable, openhanded, lavish, ungrudging, unstinting. **2** *a generous spirit* noble, magnanimous, lofty, high-minded, honorable, good, unselfish, altruistic, unprejudiced, disinterested. **3** *a generous supply of caviar* liberal, abundant, plentiful, lavish, ample, copious, rich, superabundant, overflowing.

Antonyms: STINGY; SELFISH; MEAGER.

genesis *noun* beginning, commencement, start, outset, birth, origin, source, root, creation,

genial *adjective* *genial person/manner/smile* amiable, affable, good-humored, good-natured, warm, warm-natured, pleasant, agreeable, cordial, well-disposed, amenable, cheerful, cheery, friendly, congenial, amicable, sociable, convivial, kind, kindly, benign, happy, sunny, jovial, easygoing, sympathetic.
Antonyms: UNFRIENDLY; UNKIND; MOROSE.

geniality *noun* amiability, affability, good humor, warmth, pleasantness, agreeableness, cordiality, cheerfulness, cheeriness, friendliness, congeniality, amicableness, sociability, conviviality, kindness, happiness, joviality.

genius *noun* **1** *the boy is a genius* brilliant person, virtuoso, prodigy, master, mastermind, maestro, gifted child, intellectual, intellect, expert; *inf.* brains, mental giant, Einstein. **2** *a person of genius* brilliance, great intelligence/intellect, remarkable cleverness, brains, fine mind, creative power. **3** *a genius for carpentry/cooking* gift, talent, flair, bent, knack, aptitude, forte, faculty, ability, capability, capacity, endowment, propensity, inclination.
Antonyms: DOLT; DUNCE; STUPIDITY.

genre *noun* genus, species, kind, sort, type, variety, style.

genteel *adjective* **1** *living in genteel surroundings* well-born, aristocratic, noble, blue-blooded, patrician, well-bred, respectable, refined, ladylike, gentlemanly. **2** *genteel behavior* polite, well-mannered, mannerly, courteous, civil, decorous, gracious, courtly, polished, cultivated, stylish, elegant. **3** *the king's servants were very genteel* overpolite, mannered, with affected manners, affected, exaggeratedly well-mannered, ultrarefined.
Antonyms: PLEBEIAN; RUDE; COARSE.

gentility *noun* **1** *proud of her gentility* nobility, noble birth, blue blood, good breeding, respectability, refinement, ladylikeness, gentlemanliness. **2** *the gentility of their behavior* politeness, good manners, mannerliness, courteousness, civility, decorum, propriety, graciousness, courtliness, polish, cultivation, stylishness, elegance. **3** *the gentility of the royal court* overpoliteness, affectation, ultrarefinement.

gentle *adjective* **1** *a gentle person* kind, kindly, tender, benign, humane, lenient, merciful, clement, compassionate, tender-hearted, sweet-tempered, placid, serene, mild, soft, quiet, still, tranquil, peaceful, pacific, reposeful, meek, dovelike. **2** *a gentle wind* mild, moderate, light, temperate, balmy, soft, zephyrlike. **3** *her gentle touches* soft, light, smooth, soothing. **4** *a gentle animal* tame, placid, docile, manageable, tractable, meek, easily handled, trained, schooled, broken. **5** *a gentle slope* gradual, slight, easy, imperceptible. **6** *of gentle birth* genteel, aristocratic, noble, well-born, well-bred, blue-blooded, patrician, upper-

class, high-born, respectable, refined, cultured, elegant, polished, polite, ladylike, gentlemanly.
Antonyms: CRUEL; HARSH; ROUGH; FIERCE.

gentlemanly *adjective* gentlemanlike, well-mannered, mannerly, well-bred, well-behaved, civil, courteous, polite, chivalrous, considerate, obliging, accommodating, honorable, gallant, noble, cultivated, cultured, civilized, polished, refined, suave, urbane.

genuine *adjective* **1** *a genuine diamond* real, authentic, true, pure, actual, bona fide, veritable, sound, sterling, legitimate, lawful, legal, valid, original, unadulterated, unalloyed; *inf.* the real McCoy, honest-to-goodness, kosher. **2** *she's a very genuine person* sincere, truthful, honest, frank, candid, open, undeceitful, natural, unaffected, artless, ingenuous; *inf.* up-front.
Antonyms: FAKE; BOGUS; INSINCERE.

genuine
actual, authentic, bona fide, legitimate, veritable
A car salesperson might claim that the seats of that pricey sedan you're considering are made from **genuine** leather, a word that applies to anything that is really what it is claimed or represented to be. If you're in the market for a Model T Ford, however, you'll want to make sure that the car is **authentic**, which emphasizes formal proof or documentation that an object is what it is claimed to be. Use **bona fide** when sincerity is involved (*a bona fide offer*), and **legitimate** when you mean lawful or in accordance with established rules, principles, and standards (*a legitimate business*). **Veritable** implies correspondence with the truth but not necessarily a literal or strict correspondence with reality (*a veritable supermarket for car-buyers*). How will it feel to drive that Mercedes out of the showroom? You won't know until you're the **actual** owner of the car—a word that means existing in fact rather than in the imagination.

genus *noun* subdivision, subfamily; kind, sort, type, variety, class, category, genre.

germ *noun* **1** *illness caused by a germ* microbe, microorganism, bacillus, bacterium, virus; *inf.* bug. **2** *the germ of an idea* beginning, start, commencement, inception, seed, embryo, bud, root, rudiment, origin, source, fountain, fountainhead.

germane *adjective* relevant, pertinent, material, applicable, related, connected, akin, allied, analogous, apropos, apposite, appropriate, apt, fitting, suited, felicitous, proper, to the point, to the purpose.

germinate *verb* **1** *plants germinating* sprout, burgeon, bud, develop, grow, shoot, shoot up, spring up, swell, vegetate. **2** *an idea germinating in his mind* originate, grow, begin, start, commence, take root, develop.

gestation *noun* development, incubation, maturation, ripening, pregnancy.

gesticulate *verb* gesture, make a sign, sign, signal, motion, wave, indicate.

gesture *noun* **1** *make a gesture for them to sit down* sign, signal, motion, motioning, wave, indication, gesticulation. **2** *a political/friendly gesture* action, deed, act.

gesture *verb* gesticulate, make a sign, signal, motion, wave, indicate.

get *verb* **1** *I get a new book | where did you get that hat from?* acquire, obtain, come by, come into possession of, procure, secure, buy, purchase. **2** *get a letter from her father* receive, be sent, be given. **3** *go and get that book | she got her hat from the hall* go for, fetch, bring, collect, carry, transport, convey. **4** *get what you want* gain, acquire, achieve, attain, reach, win, find; *inf.* bag. **5** *get $400 per week* earn, be paid, bring in, make, clear, gross, net, pocket; *inf.* pull in, take home. **6** *the police got the thief* capture, seize, grab, lay hold of, grasp, collar, take captive, arrest, apprehend, take, trap, entrap; *inf.* nab, bag. **7** *get flu/measles* catch, become infected by, contract, be smitten by, come down with, be afflicted by. **8** *try to get him on the phone/radio* telephone, call, phone, ring, radio, reach, communicate with, contact, get in touch with. **9** *I didn't get what he said* hear, catch, take in, perceive. **10** *don't you get what he means?* understand, grasp, comprehend, see, fathom, follow, make head or tail of; *inf.* catch on to, get the hang of. **11** *we got home/there early* arrive, reach, come; *inf.* make it. **12** *we got her to go* persuade, induce, coax, wheedle into, talk into, prevail upon, influence, sway, convince, win over. **13** *get to see the new movie* manage, succeed, arrange, contrive. **14** *get fat/wet/old* become, grow, come to be, turn, turn into, wax. **15** *get a meal* prepare, make preparations for, get ready, cook; *inf.* fix. **16** *that music gets me* affect, have an effect on, move, touch, stir, arouse, stimulate, excite, grip, impress, leave an impression on; *inf.* send, turn on. **17** *I'll get him for that* avenge oneself on, take vengeance on, get even with, pay someone back, give tit for tat to, settle the score with, demand an eye for an eye and a tooth for a tooth with; *inf.* get back at. **18** *you've really got me there with that brainteaser* baffle, puzzle, stump, mystify, confound, nonplus. **get across** *get across the message* communicate, make understood/clear, impart, convey, transmit. **get ahead** *young man getting ahead* make good, do well, succeed, be successful, progress, advance, prosper, flourish, rise in the world; *inf.* go places, get somewhere. **get along 1** *I don't get along with his mother* get on, be on friendly terms, be friendly, be in harmony, be compatible, agree, see eye to eye; *inf.* hit it off. **2** *how are you getting along?* get on, fare, manage, cope; *inf.* get by, make out. **get**

around 1 *get around his objections* circumvent, bypass, outmaneuver, outwit; *inf.* outsmart. **2** *get around his father* persuade, induce, prevail upon, talk around, wheedle, coax, win over, convert, sway. **3** *she certainly gets around* travel, visit, circulate, socialize. **get at** *what are you getting at?* suggest, hint, imply, intend, lead up to, mean. **get away** *the prisoners got away* escape, make good one's escape, flee, break free, break out, decamp, depart. **get back 1** *get back at dawn* return, come home, come back, arrive home, arrive back. **2** *get back her lost gloves* recover, retrieve, regain, repossess, recoup. **3** *get back at his torturer* take vengeance on, avenge oneself on, get even with, get. *See* GET 17. **get by** *get by on little money* cope, manage, subsist, survive, exist, fare, get along, contrive to get along, make both ends meet, keep the wolf from the door; *inf.* keep one's head above water, make out. **get off** *get off the bus* alight from, climb off, dismount from, leave; descend from, disembark, exit. **get on 1** *get on the bus* board, climb on; mount, ascend, embark. **2** *how are you getting on?* get along, fare, manage, cope; *inf.* get by, makeout. **3** *husband and wife do not get on* get along, be on friendly terms, be in harmony. *See* GET ALONG 1 (above). **get out 1** *let's get out now* leave, depart, go away, be off, withdraw; *inf.* vamoose, clear out. **2** *prisoners getting out* escape, break free, break out, free oneself, extricate oneself, abscond, decamp. **3** *the news has got out* be made public, become known, be revealed, be publicized, be disclosed, leak, be leaked, spread, circulate. **get out of** *get out of digging the garden* avoid, dodge, evade, escape, shirk. **get over 1** *get over the flu* recover from, recuperate from, get better after, pull through, survive. **2** *get over a love affair* forget, think no more of, write off, come around from. **3** *get over one's fear of dogs* overcome, master, get the better of, shake off, defeat. **get to** *her nagging is beginning to get to me* irritate, get on someone's nerves, annoy, vex, provoke, anger, exasperate, infuriate, rile, rub someone the wrong way, upset, bother, nettle; *inf.* bug, get someone's goat. **get together 1** *get together the evidence* collect, gather, assemble, accumulate, compile, amass. **2** *we must get together soon* meet, meet up, have a meeting, see each other, socialize, congregate.

---

get

acquire, attain, gain, obtain, procure, secure

Get is a very broad term meaning to come into possession of. You can *get* something by fetching it (*get some groceries*), by receiving it (*get a birthday gift*), by earning it (*get interest on a bank loan*), or by any of a dozen other familiar means. It is such a common, over-used word that many writers try to substitute **obtain** for it whenever possible, perhaps because it sounds less colloquial. But it can also sound pretentious (*all employees were required to obtain an an-*

nual physical exam) and should be reserved for contexts where the emphasis is on seeking something out (*to obtain blood samples*). **Acquire** often suggests a continued, sustained, or cumulative acquisition (*to acquire poise as one matures*), but it can also hint at deviousness (*to acquire the keys to the safe*). Use **procure** if you want to emphasize the effort involved in bringing something to pass (*procure a mediated divorce settlement*) or if you want to imply maneuvering to possess something (*procure a reserved parking space*). But beware: *Procure* is so often used to describe the act of obtaining partners to gratify the lust of others (*to procure a prostitute*) that it has acquired somewhat unsavory overtones. **Gain** also implies effort, usually in *getting* something advantageous or profitable (*gain entry, gain victory*). In a similar vein, **secure** underscores the difficulty involved in bringing something to pass and the desire to place it beyond danger (*secure a permanent peace; secure a lifeline*). **Attain** should be reserved for achieving a high goal or desirable result (*If she attains the summit of Mt. Everest, she will secure for herself a place in mountaineering history*).

getaway *noun* escape, flight, breakout, break, decampment.

get-together *noun* meeting, party, social gathering, gathering; *inf.* do, bash.

get-up *noun* outfit, clothes, clothing, dress, garb, apparel, garments.

get-up-and-go *noun* go, energy, vigor, vitality, vim, enthusiasm, eagerness, drive, push, initiative, ambition; *inf.* bounce.

ghastly *adjective* **1** *a ghastly murder/accident* terrible, horrible, frightful, dreadful, awful, horrid, horrendous, hideous, shocking, grim, grisly, gruesome, gory, terrifying, frightening. **2** *feel ghastly* ill, unwell, sick; *inf.* awful, terrible, dreadful. **3** *feels ghastly about losing her temper* bad, ashamed, shameful; *inf.* awful, terrible, dreadful. **4** *a ghastly mistake* very bad, serious, grave, critical, unforgivable; *inf.* awful, terrible, dreadful. **5** *what a ghastly man* odious, loathsome, nasty, foul, contemptible, low, mean, base; *inf.* horrible, dreadful, abominable, appalling. **6** *her ghastly appearance* deathlike, deathly pale, pale, pallid, wan, ashen, colorless, white, white as a sheet, haggard, drawn, ghostlike, ghostly, spectral, cadaverous.
Antonyms: PLEASANT; CHARMING; HEALTHY.

ghost *noun* **1** *haunted by a ghost* specter, apparition, phantom, spirit, phantasm; *inf.* spook. **2** *the ghost of a smile* suggestion, hint, trace, glimmer, semblance, shadow, impression, faint appearance.

ghostly *adjective* *a ghostly figure* ghostlike, spectral, phantomlike, phantom, phantasmal, phantasmic, unearthly, supernatural, otherworldly, insubstantial, illusory, shadowy, eerie, weird, uncanny; *inf.* spooky.

giant *noun* *giants in legend* colossus, Titan, Goliath, behemoth, leviathan; superhuman. *See also table at* MONSTER.

giant *adjective* *a giant insect* gigantic, enormous, colossal, huge, immense, vast, mammoth, monumental, monstrous, gargantuan, titanic, elephantine, prodigious, stupendous, very large; *inf.* jumbo, humongous, industrial-size.

gibberish *noun* meaningless talk, babble, jabbering, nonsense, rubbish, twaddle, drivel, balderdash, mumbo jumbo, blather, doubletalk, prattle; *inf.* poppycock, gobbledygook, rot, piffle.

gibe, jibe *verb* *the students gibed at the politician* jeer, mock, sneer at, scoff at, taunt, scorn, deride, ridicule, hold up to ridicule, laugh at, poke fun at, make fun of, tease, twit; *inf.* rib, rag.

gibe, jibe *noun* *the gibes of the crowd* taunt, sneer, jeer; mocking, sneering, scoffing, taunt, scorn, derision, ridicule, teasing, sarcasm; *inf.* dig.

giddy *adjective* **1** *get giddy climbing ladders* dizzy, light-headed, faint, reeling, unsteady; *inf.* woozy. **2** *a giddy girl* flighty, silly, frivolous, skittish, irresponsible, flippant, whimsical, capricious, featherbrained, scatterbrained, fickle, erratic, changeable, inconstant, irresolute, mercurial, volatile, unsteady, unstable, unbalanced, impulsive, reckless, wild, careless, thoughtless, heedless, carefree, insouciant.

gift *noun* **1** *receive a birthday/going-away gift* | *gift shop/certificate* present, offering, bounty, largesse, donation, contribution, boon, grant, bonus, gratuity, benefaction, bequest, legacy, inheritance, endowment. **2** *the gift of a car* giving, presentation, bestowal, conferment, donation, contribution, grant, endowment. **3** *a gift for foreign languages* talent, flair, aptitude, facility, knack, bent, turn, aptness, ability, faculty, capacity, capability, attribute, skill, expertise, genius; mind for.

gifted *adjective* *gifted child* | *gifted at singing/dancing* talented, brilliant, intelligent, clever, bright, smart, sharp, ingenious, able, accomplished, capable, masterly, skilled, adroit, proficient, expert.
Antonyms: STUPID; UNSKILLED; INEPT.

gigantic *adjective* giant, enormous, colossal, huge, immense, vast, mammoth, gargantuan. *See* GIANT *adjective*.
Antonyms: DIMINUTIVE; TINY.

giggle *verb* titter, snigger, snicker, chuckle, chortle, laugh, cackle; *inf.* tee-hee, ha-ha.

gigolo *noun* *a gigolo who hangs around rich women* male prostitute, ladies' man, lady-killer; *inf.* toy boy.

gild *verb* **1** *gild the tabletop* make golden/gilt, inlay with gold, cover with gold, paint/lacquer gold. **2** *gild the lily* adorn, decorate, embellish, ornament, bedeck, deck, garnish, array, enrich, enhance, brighten up, dress up, prettify, beautify, grace. **3** *gild the truth* dress up, embroider, sugar-coat, window-dress, camouflage, disguise.

gimcrack *adjective* shoddy, cheap, tawdry, flimsy, poorly/badly made, jerry-built; *inf.* tacky, tatty.

gimmick *noun* publicity device, contrivance, eye-catching novelty, stunt, scheme, trick, dodge, ploy, stratagem.

gingerly *adverb* cautiously, with caution, warily, charily, cannily, carefully, attentively, heedfully, vigilantly, watchfully, guardedly, prudently, circumspectly, judiciously, suspiciously, hesitantly, reluctantly, timidly, timorously.

gird *verb* **1** *gird on his sword* belt, bind, fasten. **2** *trees girded the lake* surround, circle, encircle, ring, enclose, encompass, compass, confine, hem in, pen, enfold, engird, girdle. **3** *gird oneself for battle* prepare, make ready, get ready, ready, brace, fortify, steel, buttress.

girdle *noun* **1** *wearing a red girdle around the dress* sash, belt, cummerbund, band, obi. **2** *a light-support girdle* corset, corselet, foundation garment; *Med.* truss.

girdle *verb* *trees girdling the lake* surround, circle, encircle, ring, enclose, encompass, gird. *See* GIRD 2.

girl *noun* **1** *a teenage girl | he has a boy and a girl* female child, daughter, miss, lass, young woman, young lady, young unmarried woman; *derog. inf.* babe, chick. **2** *he and his girl* girlfriend, sweetheart, fiancée, lover, ladylove, mistress, inamorata.

girth *noun* circumference, size, bulk, measure, perimeter.

gist *noun* substance, essence, quintessence, drift, sense, general sense, significance, idea, import, core, nucleus, nub, kernel, pith, marrow, burden, crux, important point.

give *verb* **1** *gave him the book | give a donation to the hospital* hand, present, donate, bestow, contribute, confer, hand over, turn over, award, grant, accord, leave, will, bequeath, make over, entrust, consign, vouchsafe. **2** *give the impression* show, display, demonstrate, set forth, indicate, manifest, evidence. **3** *give them time* allow, permit, grant, accord, offer. **4** *give a reprimand* administer, deliver, deal. **5** *give advice* provide, supply, furnish, proffer, offer. **6** *give no trouble* cause, be a source of, make, create. **7** *give news of the battle* impart, communicate, announce, transmit, convey, transfer, send, purvey. **8** *land giving a good crop | giving good results* produce, yield, afford, result in. **9** *the car gave a jolt* perform, execute, make, do. **10** *give a shout/yell* let out, utter, issue, emit. **11** *give his life for his country* give up, sacrifice, relinquish, devote. **12** *gave his seat to the new senator* surrender, concede, yield, give up, cede. **13** *she gave me to believe* lead, make, cause, force. **14** *the chair gave* give way, collapse, break,

break down, fall apart, come apart; bend, buckle. **give away 1** *give away secrets* reveal, disclose, divulge, let slip, leak, let out, expose, uncover. **2** *give his friend away* betray, inform on; *inf.* rat on, blow the whistle on. **give in** give up, surrender, admit/concede defeat, concede, yield, capitulate, submit, comply, succumb, quit, retreat; *inf.* throw in the towel. **give off** emit, send out, give out, pour out, throw out, discharge, exude, exhale, release, vent, produce. **give out 1** *give out fumes* give off, emit, send out, discharge, exude, release, vent, produce. **2** *give out the prizes* distribute, allocate, allot, mete out, hand out, disperse, apportion, dole out, assign; *inf.* dish out. **3** *give out that he is leaving* announce, declare, make known, communicate, impart, broadcast, publish, disseminate. **4** *supplies were giving out* run out, be used up, be consumed, be exhausted, be depleted, come to an end, fail. **give up 1** *give up smoking* stop, cease, quit, desist from, leave off, swear off, renounce, forswear, abandon, discontinue; *inf.* cut out. **2** *give up in the face of the enemy* give in, surrender, admit/concede defeat, yield, capitulate, succumb, quit, retreat; *inf.* throw in the towel. **3** *she's just given up* despair, lose heart, abandon hope, give up hope.

Antonyms: ACCEPT; RECEIVE; TAKE.

---

give
afford, award, bestow, confer, donate, grant
You **give** a birthday present, **grant** a favor, **bestow** charity, and **confer** an honor. While all of these verbs mean to convey something or transfer it from one's own possession to that of another, the circumstances surrounding that transfer dictate which word is the best one. *Give* is the most general, meaning to pass over, deliver, or transmit something (*give him encouragement*). *Grant* implies that a request or desire has been expressed, and that the receiver is dependent on the giver's discretion (*grant permission for the trip*). **Award** suggests that the giver is in some sense a judge, and that the thing given is deserved (*award a scholarship*), while *bestow* implies that something is given as a gift and may imply condescension on the part of the giver (*bestow a large sum of money on a needy charity*). To *confer* is to give an honor, a privilege, or a favor; it implies that the giver is a superior (*confer a knighthood; confer a college degree*). **Donate** implies that the giving is to a public cause or charity (*donate a painting to the local art museum*), and to **afford** is to give or bestow as a natural consequence (the window afforded a fine view of the mountains).

---

giver *noun* donor, donator, contributor, granter, grantor, benefactor, backer, fairy godmother; *inf.* angel.

glacial *adjective* *glacial conditions* freezing, frozen, icy, ice-cold, icy-cold, frigid, bitterly cold, wintry, arctic, polar, Siberian.

glad *adjective* **1** *glad you're here* happy, pleased, pleased as Punch, well-pleased, delighted, gratified, thrilled, overjoyed, elated, satisfied, contented, grateful; *inf.* tickled pink. **2** *glad to help* willing, more than willing, eager, ready, prepared, happy, pleased, delighted. **3** *hear the glad news* happy, joyful, delightful, welcome, cheering, cheerful, pleasing, gratifying. **4** *the children's glad laughter* merry, gay, jolly, cheerful, cheery, joyful, joyous, gleeful, mirthful, happy, animated.
Antonyms: UNHAPPY; SAD; RELUCTANT.

gladden *verb* make happy, delight, cheer, cheer up, hearten, brighten up, raise the spirits of, please, elate, buoy up, give a lift to; *inf.* buck up.

gladly *adverb* *I'll gladly help* with pleasure, happily, willingly, cheerfully, eagerly, ungrudgingly.

glamorous *adjective* **1** *a glamorous woman* alluring, dazzling, glittering, well-dressed, smart, elegant, beautiful, lovely, attractive, charming, fascinating, exciting, beguiling, bewitching, enchanting, entrancing, irresistible, tantalizing; *inf.* glitzy, ritzy. **2** *a glamorous career* exciting, fascinating, stimulating, thrilling, high-profile, dazzling, glossy, glittering; *inf.* ritzy, glitzy.
Antonyms: DOWDY; DULL; BORING.

glamour *noun* **1** *women with glamour* beauty, loveliness, attractiveness, allure, attraction, elegance, charm, fascination; *inf.* glitz, pizzazz. *See* GLAMOROUS 1. **2** *the glamour of foreign travel* allure, attraction, charm, fascination, excitement, enchantment, captivation, magic, spell.

glance *verb* **1** *glance at the stranger* look quickly/briefly, take a quick look, cast a brief look, look hurriedly, glimpse, peek, peep; *inf.* sneak a look. **2** *glance through the paper* skim, leaf, flip, thumb, scan. **3** *lights glancing on water* flash, gleam, glitter, glisten, glint, glimmer, shimmer, flicker, sparkle, twinkle, reflect. **4** *the arrow glanced off the tree* ricochet, rebound, be deflected; bounce. **5** *the car glanced the wall* graze, skim, touch, brush. **glance at/over** *glance at/over the subject of money* touch upon, mention in passing, give a mention to, mention, refer to, allude to, make an allusion to, skim over.
Antonyms: STUDY; SCRUTINIZE.

glance *noun* **1** *take a glance at* brief look, quick look, rapid look, glimpse, peek, peep; *inf.* gander, once-over. **2** *the glance of the sun on the water* flash, gleam, glitter, glittering, glint, glimmer, shimmer, flicker, sparkle, twinkle, reflection.

glare *verb* **1** *glaring at the trespassers* stare angrily, glower, scowl, frown, look threateningly/menacingly at, give someone dirty looks, look daggers. **2** *lights glaring* blaze, flare, flame, beam, dazzle.

glare *noun* **1** *give a glare at his enemy* angry stare, glower, scowl, frown, threatening/menacing look, dirty look. **2** *the glare of lights* blaze, flare, flame, harsh beam, dazzle.

glaring *adjective* **1** *glaring lights* blazing, dazzling. *See* GLARE *verb* 2. **2** *a glaring error* conspicuous, obvious, overt, manifest, patent, visible, unconcealed, flagrant, blatant, egregious, outrageous, gross.
Antonyms: DIM; INCONSPICUOUS.

glass *noun* **1** *a glass of water* tumbler, goblet, wineglass, chalice; beaker. **2** *held up his glass to see the details* magnifying glass; monocle.

glasses *plural noun* *put on his glasses* eyeglasses, spectacles, bifocals, sunglasses, lorgnette, pince-nez; field glasses, binoculars, opera glasses.

glassy *adjective* **1** *a glassy surface on the table* glasslike, shiny, glossy, highly polished, smooth. **2** *the sea is glassy* glasslike, mirrorlike, smooth, clear, crystal-clear, transparent, translucent, limpid. **3** *the pavement is glassy* slippery, icy, ice-covered. **4** *a glassy stare* expressionless, glazed, blank, empty, vacant, vacuous, deadpan, fixed, unmoving, motionless, lifeless.

glaze *verb* **1** *glaze china* enamel, lacquer, varnish, coat, polish, burnish, gloss. **2** *glaze the cake/ham* coat, cover, ice, frost. **glaze over** *his eyes glazed over* become glassy, grow expressionless, go blank, be motionless. *See* GLASSY 4.

glaze *noun* **1** *add a glaze to the china* enamel, lacquer, gloss, luster, finish. *See* GLAZE *verb* 1. **2** *put a glaze on the cake/ham* coating, icing, frosting.

gleam *noun* **1** *a gleam of light* beam, flash, glow, shaft, ray, flare, glint. *See* GLEAM *verb*. **2** *the gleam of the polished brass* glow, luster, gloss, shine, sheen, brightness, brilliance, flash. **3** *a gleam of hope* glimmer, flicker, ray, trace, suggestion, hint, inkling, grain.

gleam *verb* *lights gleaming* shine, radiate, flash, glow, flare, glint, glisten, glitter, beam, shimmer, glimmer, glance, sparkle, twinkle, scintillate.

glee *noun* merriment, gaiety, mirth, mirthfulness, delight, joy, joyfulness, joyousness, gladness, happiness, pleasure, jollity, hilarity, jocularity, joviality, exhilaration, high spirits, blitheness, cheerfulness, exaltation, elation, exuberance, verve, liveliness, triumph.

gleeful *adjective* merry, gay, delighted, mirthful, joyful, overjoyed, joyous, glad, happy, pleased, jolly, jovial, exhilarated, high-spirited, blithe, cheerful, elated, exuberant, triumphant.

glib *adjective* slick, smooth, smooth-talking, smooth-spoken, fast-talking, plausible, fluent, suave; talkative, voluble, loquacious, unctuous; *inf.* sweet-talking, having the gift of gab.
Antonyms: TONGUE-TIED; INARTICULATE.

glide *verb* *skaters/ships gliding along* slide, move smoothly, slip, skim, sail, skate, float, drift, flow, coast. **glide by** *time glided by* pass (by), slip by/away, elapse, steal away, roll on.

glimmer *noun* **1** *a glimmer of light* gleam, flash, flicker, glint, shimmer, blink, twinkle, sparkle, glow, ray. **2** *a glimmer of hope* gleam, flicker, ray, trace. See GLEAM *noun* 3.

glimmer *verb lights glimmering* gleam, flash, flicker, shimmer, blink, twinkle, sparkle, glow.

glimpse *noun* glance, brief look, quick look, peek, peep. See GLANCE *noun* 1.

glimpse *verb* catch a glimpse of, catch sight of, spot, spy, espy.

glint *verb diamonds glinting* shine, sparkle, flash, twinkle, glitter, glimmer, blink, wink, shimmer, glisten, dazzle, gleam, scintillate.

glint *noun the glint of diamonds* sparkle, flash, twinkle, glitter, glimmer, blink, gleam. See GLINT *verb*.

glisten *verb face glistened with tears/sweat* shine, shimmer, sparkle, twinkle, flicker, blink, wink, glint, glance, gleam, flash, scintillate.

glitter *verb stars glittering* sparkle, twinkle, flicker, blink, wink, shimmer, glimmer, glint, gleam, flash, scintillate, coruscate.

glitter *noun* **1** *the glitter of stars* sparkle, twinkle, flicker, blink, winking. See GLITTER *verb*. **2** *the glitter of show business* showiness, flashiness, ostentation, glamour, pageantry, fanfare, splendor; *inf.* razzle-dazzle, glitz, ritziness, pizzazz.

gloat *verb* relish, take pleasure in, delight in, revel in, rejoice in, glory in, exult in, triumph over, crow about; *inf.* rub it in.

global *adjective* **1** *global recession* worldwide, world, universal, international, planetary. **2** *a global rule* general, comprehensive, all-inclusive, all-encompassing, all-out, encyclopedic, exhaustive, thorough, total, across-the-board, with no exceptions.

globe *noun* **1** *everywhere in the globe* world, universe, earth, planet. **2** *in the shape of a globe* sphere, spheroid, orb, ball.

globule *noun* bead, ball, drop, droplet, pearl, particle.

gloom *noun* **1** *the gloom of the night/room* gloominess, dimness, darkness, dark, blackness, murkiness, murk, shadowiness, shadow, shade, shadiness, cloud, cloudiness, dullness, obscurity, dusk, twilight. **2** *a state of gloom* low spirits, melancholy, sadness, unhappiness, sorrow, grief, woe, despondency, misery, dejection, downheartedness, dispiritedness, glumness, desolation, depression, the blues, despair, pessimism, hopelessness.

Antonyms: LIGHT; GAIETY; CHEER.

gloomy *adjective* **1** *a gloomy day* dark, cloudy, overcast, sunless, dull, dim, shadowy, dismal, dreary. **2** *a gloomy room* dark, black, unlit, murky, shadowy, somber, dingy, dismal, dreary. **3** *gloomy news* bad, black, sad, saddening, distressing, somber, melancholy, depressing, dispiriting, disheartening, disappointing,

cheerless, comfortless, pessimistic, hopeless. **4** *feeling gloomy* in low spirits, melancholy, sad, unhappy, sorrowful, woebegone, despondent, disconsolate, miserable, dejected, downcast, downhearted, dispirited, glum, desolate, depressed, blue, despairing, pessimistic, morose; *inf.* down in the mouth.

Antonyms: BRIGHT; HAPPY; CHEERFUL.

glorify *verb* **1** *glorify God* worship, adore, exalt, extol, pay homage to, pay tribute to, honor, revere, reverence, venerate. **2** *wars glorified the position of the king* add luster to, aggrandize, ennoble, exalt, elevate, raise, lift up, magnify, add dignity to, dignify, augment, increase, advance, boost, promote. **3** *glorify the conqueror* praise, sing/sound the praises of, extol, laud, eulogize, magnify, acclaim, applaud, cheer, hail, celebrate, lionize.

glorious *adjective* **1** *our glorious history* illustrious, noble, celebrated, famous, famed, renowned, distinguished, honored, eminent, excellent, magnificent, majestic, splendid, supreme, sublime, triumphant, victorious. **2** *a glorious day* beautiful, bright, brilliant, sunny, perfect. **3** *have a glorious time* splendid, marvelous, wonderful, delightful, enjoyable, pleasurable, excellent, fine; *inf.* terrific, great, fab.

Antonyms: UNKNOWN; DULL; MISERABLE.

glory *noun* **1** *to the glory of God* worship, adoration, exaltation, extolment, honor, reverence, veneration, thanksgiving. **2** *win glory in battle* renown, fame, prestige, honor, distinction, illustriousness, acclaim, credit, accolade, recognition, laudation, extolment; *inf.* kudos. **3** *the glory of Versailles* splendor, resplendence, magnificence, grandeur, majesty, pomp, pageantry, beauty.

Antonyms: BLASPHEMY; SHAME; DISGRACE; ugliness.

glory *verb* **glory in** *glory in their success* exult in, rejoice in, take pleasure in, take pride in, be proud of, delight in, revel in, triumph over, boast about, crow about, gloat about.

gloss[1] *noun* **1** *the gloss on the furniture* shine, sheen, luster, gleam, brightness, brilliance, sparkle, shimmer, polish, burnish. **2** *a gloss of respectability* façade, front, camouflage, disguise, mask, false appearance, semblance, show, deceptive show, veneer, surface.

gloss[2] *verb* **1** *gloss the furniture* make glossy, shine, give a shine to, polish, burnish. **2** *gloss the china* glaze, varnish, lacquer, enamel. **gloss over** *gloss over the truth* deal rapidly with, evade, avoid, smooth over, conceal, hide, cover up, camouflage, disguise, mask, veil, draw/pull a veil over, whitewash.

gloss[3] *noun* *add glosses to the text* explanation, explication, interpretation, elucidation, annotation, commentary, comment, note, footnote, translation.

gloss[4] *verb* *gloss the text* give an explanation/ explication of, explain, interpret, elucidate, annotate, add a commentary to, comment on, add notes/footnotes to, translate, construe.

glossy *adjective* **1** *glossy furniture* shining, shiny, glassy, gleaming, bright, brilliant, sparkling, shimmering, polished, burnished, glazed. **2** *glossy hair* shining, gleaming, sleek, smooth, silky, silken.
Antonyms: DULL; LUSTERLESS.

glow *noun* **1** *the glow from the light* subdued light, gleam, glimmer, incandescence, luminosity, phosphorescence. **2** *the glow of the garden flowers* brightness, vividness, brilliance, colorfulness, richness, radiance, splendor. **3** *the glow of her complexion* blush, flush, rosiness, pinkness, redness, crimson, scarlet, reddening, bloom. **4** *induce a warm glow* warmth, happiness, contentment, satisfaction. **5** *the glow of his love* passion, ardor, fervor, vehemence, intensity, earnestness, impetuosity.

glow *verb* **1** *the light glowed* shed a glow, gleam, glimmer, shine. **2** *the fire glowed* burn without flames, smolder. **3** *she glowed with pleasure* blush, flush, redden, color. **4** *glow with pride* radiate, thrill, tingle.

glower *verb* *glower at his enemy* scowl, stare angrily, glare, frown, give someone dirty looks, look daggers.
Antonyms: SMILE; GRIN.

glower *noun* *give a glower* scowl, angry stare, glare, frown, dirty look.

glowing *adjective* **1** *glowing coals* aglow, smoldering, incandescent, candescent, luminous, phosphorescent. **2** *a glowing complexion* rosy, pink, reddish, red, ruddy, florid. **3** *glowing colors* bright, vivid, brilliant, colorful, rich, radiant. **4** *a glowing report* complimentary, highly favorable, enthusiastic, ecstatic, rhapsodic, eulogistic, laudatory, acclamatory, adulatory; *inf.* rave.

glue *noun* adhesive, fixative, gum, paste, cement, mucilage, epoxy resin.

glue *verb* stick, gum, paste, affix, fix, cement.

glum *adjective* in low spirits, gloomy, melancholy, sad, despondent, miserable, dejected, downcast, downhearted, dispirited, depressed; *inf.* down in the mouth. *See* GLOOMY 4.
Antonyms: CHEERFUL; MERRY.

---

glum
doleful, dour, lugubrious, melancholy, saturnine, sullen

All happy people are alike, to paraphrase Tolstoy, but each unhappy person is unhappy in his or her own way. A **sullen** person is gloomy, untalkative, and ill-humored by nature; a **glum** person is usually silent because of low spirits or depressing circumstances (*to be glum in the face of a plummeting stock market*). **Melancholy** suggests a more or less chronic sadness (*her melancholy was the result of an unhappy childhood*), while a person who is **saturnine** has a forbiddingly gloomy and taciturn nature (*his request was met with a saturnine and scornful silence*). **Dour** refers to a grim and bitter outlook or disposition (*a dour old woman who never smiled*), and **doleful** implies a mournful sadness (*the child's doleful expression as his parents left*). Someone or something described as **lugubrious** is mournful or gloomy in an affected or exaggerated way (*lugubrious songs about lost love*).

---

glut *noun* *a glut of apples* surplus, excess, surfeit, superfluity, overabundance, superabundance, oversupply, overprofusion, saturation.
Antonyms: DEARTH; SCARCITY.

glut *verb* **1** *glut the market* saturate, supersaturate, overload, oversupply, flood, inundate, deluge. **2** *glutted ourselves at dinner* cram full, stuff, gorge, satiate, overfeed, fill up. **3** *glut the passage* clog, choke up, obstruct, stop up, dam up.

glutinous *adjective* gluelike, sticky, gummy, adhesive, viscid, mucilaginous, viscous, pasty, tacky, mucous.

glutton *noun* gourmand, gormandizer, overeater, gorger, gobbler, guzzler; *inf.* hog, pig, greedy pig.

gluttonous *adjective* greedy, gormandizing, insatiable, voracious; *inf.* piggish, hoggish.

gluttony *noun* greed, greediness, gourmandism, gormandizing, insatiability, voraciousness, voracity; *inf.* piggishness, hoggishness.

gnarled *adjective* **1** *a gnarled tree* knotty, knotted, lumpy, bumpy, nodular, knurled, rough, twisted, crooked, distorted, contorted. **2** *gnarled hands* knotty, lumpy, knurled, rough, twisted, arthritic, leathery, wrinkled, rugged, weatherbeaten. **3** *a gnarled disposition* cantankerous, crabbed, crabby, crotchety, grumpy, snappish, peevish, disagreeable; *inf.* grouchy, cranky.

gnash *verb* grind, strike together, grit, rasp, grate.

gnaw *verb* *dogs gnawing the bone* chew, munch, crunch, masticate, bite. **gnaw at** *worry gnawing at her* prey on someone's mind, nag, torment, plague, harry, harass, fret, distress, trouble, worry. **gnaw away** *rust gnawing away (at) the metal* erode, corrode, wear away, wear down, eat away, fret, consume, devour.

go *verb* **1** *go forward/backward/up* move, proceed, progress, pass, walk, travel, journey, repair. **2** *time to go* go away, leave, depart, withdraw, set off, set out, decamp; *inf.* beat it, scram. **3** *does the machine go?* work, be in working order, function, operate, be operative, run, perform. **4** *go pale/peculiar/bad* become, grow, get, come to be, wax. **5** *go bang/"moo"* | *the bell went* make/emit a sound, sound, sound out, resound. **6** *this road goes all the way to the sea* extend, stretch, reach, spread, give access, lead. **7** *where does this book go?* belong, have a place, fit in, be located, be situated, be found, lie, stand. **8** *her headache has gone* stop, cease, disappear, vanish, be no more, fade away, melt away. **9** *all my money has gone* be finished, be spent, be used up, be exhausted, be consumed. **10** *the elderly patient has gone* die, be dead, pass away, decease, expire, perish; *inf.* give up the ghost, kick the bucket. **11** *these clothes will have to go* be discarded, be thrown away, be disposed of. **12** *some of the staff will have to go* be dismissed, be laid off; *inf.* be fired, be axed, get the ax. **13** *the money will go to charity* be assigned, be allotted, be applied, be devoted, be awarded, be granted/given, be ceded. **14** *how did your interview go?* turn out, work out, fare, progress, develop, result, end, end up, eventuate. **15** *the carpet and curtains don't go* go together, go with each other, match, harmonize, blend, suit each other, be suited, complement each other, be in accord, accord, be compatible. **16** *this goes to prove his theory* serve, contribute, help, incline, tend. **17** *the bridge went* break, give way, collapse, fall down, cave in, crumble, disintegrate, fall to pieces. **go about** *how do you go about buying a house?* set about, begin, approach, tackle, undertake. **go ahead** *work is going ahead* go, progress, make progress, proceed, advance. **go along with 1** *we went along with our neighbors* go with, accompany, escort. **2** *I'll go along with your plans* comply with, cooperate with, acquiesce in, follow, agree with, assent to, concur with. **go around** *a rumor going around* circulate, pass around; be passed around, be spread, be broadcast. **go back on** *go back on one's word* renege on, repudiate, retract. **go by 1** *as time goes by* pass, pass by, elapse, move on, proceed, flow, lapse, slip away, tick away, fly. **2** *go by the rules* follow, obey, observe, be guided by, take as a guide, heed. **go down 1** *the ship went down in a storm* sink, be submerged, founder, go under. **2** *prices are going down* decrease, drop, fall, become lower, be reduced, decline, plummet. **3** *the champion went down in the first round* be beaten, be defeated, suffer defeat, lose, fail, collapse. **4** *his name will go down in history* be commemorated, be remembered, be recalled, be immortalized. **go far** *a young man bound to go far* do well, do well for oneself, be successful, succeed, make progress, get on, get on in the world, get ahead, make a name for oneself, advance oneself, set the world on fire. **go for 1** *go for the newspapers* go and get, fetch. **2** *the dog went for him* attack, assault, assail, launch oneself at, set upon, spring at/upon, rush at. **3** *he doesn't go for quiet women* be attracted to, be fond of, admire, favor, like, prefer, choose, hold with. **go in for** *go in for tennis* engage in, take part in, participate in, practice, pursue, take up, espouse, adopt, embrace. **go into 1** *go into everything wholeheartedly* participate in, take part in, undertake, enter. **2** *the police are going into the evidence thoroughly* investigate, research, inquire into, look into, examine, study, review, check,

scrutinize, analyze, delve into, dig into, pursue, probe. **go off 1** *the bomb went off* explode, detonate, blow up, burst, erupt; *inf.* go bang. **2** *we went off at dawn* leave, go away, depart, set out, set off, decamp, move out. **go on 1** *how long did the talk go on?* last, continue, proceed, endure, persist, stay, remain, happen, occur. **2** *she did go on too long* ramble on, talk on and on, carry on talking, chatter, prattle. **go out 1** *he has gone out of the office* leave, exit, depart from. **2** *the lights/passion went out* be extinguished, be turned off, be doused, be quenched, fade, die out. **3** *a boy and girl going out* go with each other, go together, see each other, court; *inf.* go steady, date. **go over** *go over the accounts* read over, look over, inspect, examine, study, scan, run over; *inf.* give the once-over. **go through 1** *go through torture* undergo, be subjected to, suffer, experience, bear, stand, tolerate, endure, weather, brook, brave. **2** *go through money* spend, use up, run through, consume, exhaust. **3** *go through someone's pockets* look through, search, hunt through, check, inspect, examine; *inf.* frisk. **go together 1** *the carpets and curtains do not go together* go, match, harmonize, blend, suit each other. *See* GO *verb* 15. **2** *they have been going together for months* go out, go out together, go with each other, see each other, court, keep company; *inf.* go steady, date. **go under 1** *the ship went under in a storm* go down, sink, be submerged, founder. **2** *the firm has gone under* fail, founder, go bankrupt, go into receivership, go to the wall; *inf.* go bust, fold, flop. **go with 1** *we'll go with you* go along with, accompany, escort. **2** *the carpets do not go with the curtains* match, complement, harmonize/blend, accord with. **3** *his sister is going with her brother* go out with, see; *inf.* go steady with, date. **4** *his behavior does not go with his theories* fit, fit in with, conform to, comply with, be in line with. **go without 1** *go without chocolate* do without, abstain from, deny oneself, be denied, lack, want. **2** *she went without to feed her children* be in need, be in want.

go *noun* **1** *have a go at hang gliding* try, attempt, effort, bid, essay, endeavor; *inf.* shot, stab, crack, whirl, whack. **2** *people with a lot of go* energy, vigor, dynamism, force, verve, vim, vitality, spirit, animation, vivacity, drive, push, determination, enterprise; *inf.* get-up-and-go, pep, oomph.

goad *noun* **1** *a goad to spur cattle* spiked stick, stick, spike, prod, staff, crook, pole, rod. **2** *a goad to action* stimulus, incentive, incitement, instigation, inducement, stimulation, impetus, motivation, pressure, spur, prick, jolt, poke.

go-ahead *noun* *get the go-ahead for the scheme* permission, assent, consent, authorization, sanction, leave, warranty, confirmation; *inf.* green light, OK, okay, thumbs up.

goal *noun* *the goals of the organization* aim, objective, object, end, purpose, target, ambition, design, intention, intent, aspiration, ideal.

goat *noun* **1** *conned into being their goat* scapegoat, victim; *inf.* fall guy. **2** *he's nothing but an old goat* lecher, lascivious man; *inf.* lech, dirty old man.

gobble *verb* gulp, swallow hurriedly, wolf (down), bolt, guzzle, devour, stuff down, gluttonize, gormandize; *inf.* scarf up, shovel in/down.

gobbledygook *noun* jargon, obscure language, unintelligible language, pretentious language, verbosity, prolixity, verbiage, circumlocution, periphrasis; *inf.* gibberish.

go-between *noun* intermediary, mediator, middleman, medium, agent, broker, dealer, factor, liaison, contact, contact person; pander, panderer.

goblet *noun* wine glass, chalice, cup.

goblin *noun* hobgoblin, gnome, dwarf, imp, elf, sprite.

God *noun* God Almighty, the Almighty, the Godhead, the Supreme/Divine Being, the Deity, the Holy One, God the Father, Our Father, the Creator, Our Maker, the Lord, Jehovah, Allah.

god *noun* **1** *tribal gods* deity, divine being, divinity, spirit. **2** *false gods* idol, graven image, icon, golden calf.

godforsaken *adjective* *a godforsaken place* desolate, dismal, dreary, bleak, wretched, miserable, gloomy, deserted, abandoned, forlorn, neglected, remote, backward.

godless *adjective* **1** *professing to be godless* atheistic, agnostic, skeptical, faithless. **2** *missionaries perceiving the tribesmen as godless* heathen, pagan, ungodly, impious, irreligious, unrighteous, unprincipled, sinful, wicked, evil, depraved.

godlike *adjective* **1** *godlike forgiveness* godly, divine, celestial, heavenly, sacred, holy, saintly. **2** *a godlike beauty* divine, deific, deiform, transcendent, superhuman.

godly *adjective* God-fearing, devout, pious, religious, pietistic, believing, righteous, moral, virtuous, good, holy, saintly.

godsend *noun* boon, blessing, benediction, stroke of luck, bit/piece of good fortune, windfall, bonanza.

goings-on *plural noun* *strange goings-on at the bank* misconduct, misbehavior, conduct, behavior, mischief, pranks; *inf.* funny business, monkey business, hanky-panky.

gold *noun* **1** *gold is more precious than silver* gold pieces, gold nugget, bullion, gold ingot, gold bar. **2** *misers counting their gold* money, wealth, treasure, fortune, riches.

golden *adjective* **1** *golden hair* gold-colored, blond, blonde, yellow, yellowish, fair, flaxen, tow-colored, bright, gleaming, resplendent, brilliant, shining. **2** *a golden future* successful, prosperous, flourishing, thriving, rosy, bright, brilliant, rich. **3** *golden memories* happy, joyful, delightful, glorious, precious, treasured. **4** *golden opportunities* fine, superb, excellent, favorable, opportune, promising, rosy, advantageous, profitable, fortunate, providential, auspicious, propitious. **5** *the golden boy of the track team* talented, gifted, special, favorite, favored, cherished, beloved, pet, acclaimed, applauded, praised, lauded.
Antonyms: DARK; UNFAVORABLE.

good *adjective* **1** *a good person* virtuous, moral, ethical, honest, right-minded, right-thinking, righteous, honorable, upright, high-minded, noble, worthy, admirable, estimable, exemplary. **2** *a good child* well-behaved, obedient, well-mannered, manageable, tractable. **3** *that's good* satisfactory, acceptable, good enough, passable, tolerable, adequate, fine, excellent; *inf.* great, OK, okay, hunky-dory. **4** *a good thing to do* right, correct, proper, fitting, suitable, appropriate, decorous, seemly. **5** *a good driver* competent, capable, able, accomplished, efficient, skillful, adept, proficient, dexterous, expert, excellent, first-class, first-rate; *inf.* A-1, tip-top, top-notch. **6** *good brakes/friends* reliable, dependable, trustworthy. **7** *in good condition* fine, healthy, sound, robust, strong, vigorous. **8** *a good party* enjoyable, pleasant, agreeable, pleasing, pleasurable, amusing, cheerful, convivial, congenial, sociable, satisfying, gratifying, to one's liking. **9** *good of you to come* kind, kindly, kindhearted, good-hearted, friendly, obliging, well-disposed, charitable, gracious, sympathetic, benevolent, benign, altruistic. **10** *come at a good time* convenient, fitting, suitable, favorable, advantageous, fortunate, lucky, propitious, auspicious. **11** *broccoli is good for you* wholesome, health-giving, healthful, nutritional, beneficial, salubrious, salutary. **12** *is this cheese still good?* fit to eat, eatable, edible, untainted, fresh. **13** *the food here is good* delicious, tasty, appetizing; *inf.* scrumptious, yummy. **14** *a good reason for going* valid, genuine, authentic, legitimate, sound, bona fide. **15** *wait a good hour* full, entire, whole, complete, solid, not less than. **16** *a good number came* considerable, substantial, goodly, sizable, large, sufficient, ample; *inf.* tidy. **17** *good friends* close, intimate, bosom, fast, dear, valued, treasured. **18** *wear her good clothes* best, finest, newest, nicest, smartest, special, party, Sunday. **19** *good weather* fine, fair, mild, clear, bright, cloudless, sunshiny, sunny, calm, balmy, tranquil, clement, halcyon. **make good 1** *make good the damage* compensate for, make recompense for, make amends for, make restitution for, pay for, reimburse for. **2** *make good a promise* fulfill, carry out, effect, discharge, live up to. **3** *make good a statement* substantiate, back up, demonstrate the truth of, confirm, prove, validate, authenticate. **4** *he made good in America* be successful, succeed, do well, get ahead, reach the top, set the world on fire.

Antonyms: BAD; INADEQUATE; POOR.

good *noun* **1** *for your own good* benefit, advantage, behalf, gain, profit, interest, well-being, welfare, usefulness, avail, service. **2** *tell good from bad* virtue, goodness, morality, ethics, righteousness, rightness, rectitude, honor, honesty, uprightness, integrity, probity, worth, merit. **for good** for always, for ever, permanently, never to return.

good *interjection* fine, very well, all right; *inf.* okay, OK, okeydoke, okeydokey.

goodbye *interjection* farewell, au revoir, adieu; *inf.* bye, cheers, see you later, see you, toodle-oo, so long, ciao; *inf.* bye-bye, ta-ta.

good-for-nothing *adjective* useless, of no use, no-good, lazy, idle, slothful, feckless.

good-for-nothing *noun* ne'er-do-well, wastrel, black sheep, layabout, idler, loafer, sluggard.

good-humored *adjective* amiable, affable, easygoing, genial, cheerful, cheery, happy, pleasant, good-tempered.

good-looking *adjective* attractive, handsome, pretty, lovely, beautiful, personable, comely, fair.

goodly *adjective* *a goodly amount* considerable, substantial, sizable, significant, large, great, ample, sufficient; *inf.* tidy.

good-natured *adjective* kind, kindly, kindhearted, warmhearted, generous, benevolent, charitable, friendly, helpful, accommodating, amiable, tolerant.

goodness *noun* **1** *the goodness of the saint* virtue, virtuousness, morality, righteousness, rectitude, honor, honesty, uprightness, integrity, probity, nobility, worthiness, merit. **2** *she had the goodness to stay* kindness, kindliness, kindheartedness, warmheartedness, generosity, obligingness, benevolence, beneficence, friendliness, goodwill, compassion, graciousness, charitableness, unselfishness. **3** *the goodness in the food* nourishment, nutritional value, nutrition, wholesomeness. *See* GOOD *adjective* 11.

Antonyms: badness; MEANNESS; HARM.

---

goodness
morality, probity, rectitude, virtue

Of all these words denoting moral excellence, **goodness** is the broadest in meaning. It describes an excellence so well established that it is thought of as inherent or innate and is associated with kindness, generosity, helpfulness, and sincerity (*she has more goodness in her little finger than most people have in their whole body*). **Morality**, on the other hand, is moral excellence based on a code of ethical conduct or religious teaching (*his behavior was kept in line by fear of punishment rather than morality*). Although it is often used as a synonym for *goodness*, **virtue** suggests moral excellence that is acquired rather than innate and that is con-

sciously or steadfastly maintained, often in spite of temptations or evil influences (*her virtue was as unassailable as her noble character*). **Rectitude** is used to describe strict adherence to the rules of just or right behavior and carries strong connotations of sternness and self-discipline (*he had a reputation for rectitude and insisted on absolute truthfulness*). **Probity** describes an honesty or integrity that has been tried and proved (*as mayor, she displayed a probity that was rare in a politician*).

---

goods *plural noun* belongings, possessions, property, effects, gear, things, paraphernalia, chattels, appurtenances, trappings, accouterments; *inf.* stuff.

goodwill *noun* *full of goodwill* friendliness, friendship, kindness, kindliness, benevolence, compassion, amity.

Antonyms: ILL WILL; HOSTILITY; ENMITY.

gorge *noun* *the stream at the foot of the gorge* chasm, canyon, ravine, abyss, defile, pass, cleft, crevice, rift, fissure.

gorge *verb* *gorge the food* bolt, gobble, guzzle, gulp down, wolf (down), devour, stuff down, gormandize; *inf.* shovel in. **gorge on** *gorge (oneself) on ice cream* stuff with, cram with, fill with, fill up on, glut with, satiate with, surfeit with, overeat.

gorgeous *adjective* **1** *a gorgeous sight* magnificent, splendid, superb, grand, resplendent, stately, impressive, imposing, sumptuous, luxurious, elegant, opulent, dazzling, brilliant, glittering, breathtaking. **2** *we had a gorgeous time* wonderful, marvelous, first-rate, delightful, enjoyable, entertaining, excellent; *inf.* glorious, terrific. **3** *a gorgeous blonde* attractive, beautiful, lovely, good-looking, sexy; *inf.* stunning.

Antonyms: DULL; MISERABLE; UGLY.

gory *adjective* **1** *a gory film* bloody, bloodthirsty, violent, murderous, brutal, savage, horror-filled, horrific; *inf.* blood-and-guts. **2** *a gory garment* bloody, blood-stained, blood-soaked.

gospel *noun* **1** *studying the Gospel* Christian doctrine, Christ's teaching, New Testament, good news, writings of the evangelists. **2** *believing in the gospel of hard work* principle, tenet, doctrine, ethic, belief, creed, credo.

gossamer *noun* cobweb, spider's web, silky substance, gauze, tissue, chiffon, thistledown.

gossamer *adjective* *a scarf of gossamer material* cobwebby, silky, gauzy, chiffony, feathery, light, fine, delicate, frail, flimsy, insubstantial, airy, diaphanous, sheer, transparent, see-through, translucent.

gossip *noun* **1** *have you heard the gossip about her?* rumors, scandal, idle talk, hearsay, smear campaign; *inf.* mudslinging, dirt, low-down. **2** *he's just a gossip* gossipmonger, scandalmonger, busybody, blabbermouth, tattletale.

gossip *verb* spread gossip/rumors, circulate rumors, spread stories; talk, blab, tattle.

govern verb **1** *govern the country* rule, reign over, be in power over, exercise control over, hold sway over, preside over, administer, lead, be in charge of, control, command, direct, order, guide, manage, conduct, oversee, supervise, superintend, steer, pilot. **2** *govern one's passions* control, restrain, keep in check, check, curb, hold back, keep back, bridle, rein in, subdue, constrain, contain, arrest. **3** *the weather will govern our decision* determine, decide, sway, rule, influence, have an influence on, be a factor in.

government noun **1** *the country's government is weak* administration, regime, congress, parliament, ministry, council, executive, (the) powers that be. *See also table at* POLITICS. **2** *their government of the country has been criticized* rule, administration, leadership, command, direction, control, guidance, management, conduct, supervision, superintendence. **3** *the government of one's emotions* control, restraint, checking, curbing, bridling, constraint, discipline.

gown noun dress, evening gown, ball gown.

grab verb **1** *grab his collar* grasp, clutch, grip, clasp, lay hold of, catch hold of, take hold of, fasten upon. **2** *grab the money from him* seize, snatch, pluck, snap up, appropriate, capture; *inf.* bag, nab.

grab noun clutch, grasp, firm hold; hug, embrace. **up for grabs** available, accessible, obtainable, to be had, up for sale, for the taking.

grace noun **1** *the grace of the ballerina* gracefulness, suppleness, fluidity of movement, smoothness, ease, elegance, agility; *inf.* poetry in motion. **2** *admire the grace of the women* elegance, refinement, finesse, culture, cultivation, polish, suaveness, good taste, taste, tastefulness, charm, attractiveness, beauty, loveliness, comeliness. **3** *have the grace to apologize* manners, mannerliness, courtesy, courteousness, decency, consideration, tact, tactfulness, breeding, decorum, propriety, etiquette. **4** *fall from grace* favor, goodwill, preferment. **5** *built the new wing by the grace of our benefactors* goodwill, generosity, kindness, kindliness, benefaction, beneficence, indulgence. **6** *beg for grace from the jury* mercy, mercifulness, compassion, pardon, reprieve, forgiveness, leniency, lenity, clemency, indulgence, charity, quarter. **7** *ask for a year's grace* delay, postponement, deferment, deferral. **8** *say grace* blessing, benediction, thanks, thanksgiving, prayer.

grace verb **1** *paintings gracing the room* adorn, decorate, ornament, embellish, enhance, beautify, prettify, set off, deck, enrich, garnish. **2** *grace the gathering with his presence* dignify, distinguish, add distinction to, honor, favor, glorify, elevate.

graceful adjective **1** *graceful ballerinas* supple, fluid, flowing, smooth, easy, elegant, agile, nimble. **2** *graceful women* elegant, refined, cultured, cultivated, polished, suave, having good taste, charming, appealing, attractive, beautiful, lovely, comely.
Antonyms: INELEGANT; UNGAINLY.

gracious adjective **1** *a gracious lady* kind, kindly, kindhearted, warmhearted, benevolent, friendly, amiable, affable, pleasant, cordial, courteous, considerate, polite, civil, chivalrous, well-mannered, charitable, indulgent, obliging, accommodating, beneficent, benign. **2** *a gracious room* | *gracious way of life* elegant, tasteful, comfortable, luxurious. **3** *gracious God* merciful, compassionate, gentle, mild, lenient, humane, clement.
Antonyms: DISCOURTEOUS; ungracious; INELEGANT; CRUEL.

grade noun **1** *what grade did he reach?* degree of proficiency/quality/merit, level, stage, echelon, rank, standing, station, position, order, class. **2** *all belonging to the same grade* category, class, classification, type, brand. **3** *progress one grade at a time* stage, step, rung, notch. **4** *a steep grade* gradient, slope, incline, hill, rise, bank, acclivity, declivity. **make the grade** pass, pass muster, measure up, measure up to expectation, come up to standard, come up to scratch/snuff, succeed, be successful, come through with flying colors, win through, qualify, get through.

grade verb *grade the vegetables* classify, class, categorize, sort, group, order, brand, size, rank, evaluate, rate, value, range, graduate.

gradient noun slope, incline, hill, rise, rising ground, bank, acclivity, declivity, grade.

gradual adjective **1** *a gradual improvement* step-by-step, degree-by-degree, progressive, successive, continuous, systematic, regular, steady, even, moderate, slow, measured, unhurried. **2** *a gradual slope* gentle, not steep, moderate.
Antonyms: SUDDEN; ABRUPT.

gradually adverb *gradually improve* bit by bit, little by little, by degrees, step by step, inch by inch, piece by piece, drop by drop, slowly, progressively, successively, continuously, constantly, regularly, at a regular pace, steadily, evenly, moderately.

graduate verb **1** *graduated last summer* take an academic degree, receive one's degree/diploma, become a graduate. **2** *graduate a scale* mark off, measure off, divide into degrees, grade, calibrate. **3** *graduate to a more senior post* move up, progress, advance, gain promotion, be promoted.

graft[1] noun **1** *a plant graft* shoot, bud, scion, slip, new growth, sprout, splice. **2** *a skin graft* transplant, implantation, implant.

graft[2] verb **1** *graft a shoot on to a stock* insert, affix, slip, join. **2** *graft skin* transplant, implant.

graft[3] noun *get ahead in business by graft* bribery, illegal means, unlawful practices, underhand/

underhanded means, payola; *inf.* palm-greasing.

grain *noun* **1** *farmers growing grain* cereal, cereal crops; corn, wheat, barley, rye, oats. **2** *a grain of wheat* kernel, seed, grist. **3** *grains of sand* particle, granule, bit, piece, scrap, crumb, fragment, morsel, mote, speck, mite, molecule, atom. **4** *not a grain of truth in it* iota, trace, hint, suggestion, suspicion, scintilla. **5** *the grain of the wood/cloth* texture, surface, fabric, weave, nap, fiber, pattern. **6** *a man of a different grain* disposition, character, nature, make-up, humor, temperament, temper, inclination.

grand *adjective* **1** *grand houses* impressive, magnificent, imposing, splendid, striking, superb, palatial, stately, large, monumental, majestic. **2** *a grand feast* splendid, luxurious, sumptuous, lavish, magnificent, glorious, opulent, princely. **3** *in the company of grand people* great, noble, aristocratic, distinguished, august, illustrious, eminent, esteemed, elevated, exalted, celebrated, preeminent, prominent, leading, notable, renowned, famous. **4** *make a grand gesture* ostentatious, showy, pretentious, lordly, ambitious, imperious. **5** *the grand total* complete, comprehensive, total, all-inclusive, inclusive, exhaustive, final. **6** *the grand hall/master* principal, main, chief, leading, head, supreme. **7** *have a grand time* very good, excellent, wonderful, marvelous, splendid, first-class, first-rate, outstanding, fine, enjoyable, admirable; *inf.* superb, terrific, great, super, smashing.
Antonyms: INFERIOR; unimpressive; LOWLY.

grandeur *noun* **1** *the grandeur of the houses* impressiveness, magnificence, splendor, splendidness, superbness, stateliness, largeness, majesty. **2** *the grandeur of the feast* splendor, luxuriousness, luxury, sumptuousness, lavishness, magnificence, opulence. **3** *the grandeur of the ruling classes* greatness, nobility, illustriousness, eminence, elevation, exaltation, prominence, preeminence, renown, fame.

grandfather *noun* **1** *a little girl playing with her grandfather inf.* granddad, grandpa; *inf.* grampa, gramps, grandaddy, granddaddy. **2** *writing the history of their grandfathers* forefather, ancestor, forebear, progenitor, father.

grandiloquent *adjective* *grandiloquent speech/writing* pompous, pretentious, ostentatious, high-flown, wordy, bombastic, magniloquent, euphuistic, periphrastic.

grandiose *adjective* **1** *grandiose plans* ambitious, overambitious, extravagant, high-flown, high-sounding, pompous, pretentious, flamboyant. **2** *grandiose buildings* grand, impressive, magnificent, imposing, splendid, striking, superb, stately, majestic.
Antonyms: MODEST; HUMBLE.

grandmother *noun inf.* grandma; *inf.* gramma, gram, grammy, grammie, granny, gran.

grant *verb* **1** *grant them an interview* agree/consent/assent/accede to give, give one's assent to, permit, allow, accord. **2** *grant them an award* bestow on, confer on, give to, impart to, award with, present with, donate to, contribute to, provide with, endow with, furnish with, supply with, allocate to, allot to, assign to. **3** *I grant you that you may be right* admit to, acknowledge to, concede to, go along with, yield to. **4** *grant property to his heirs* transfer, convey, transmit, pass on, hand over, assign, bequeath.

grant *noun* *a grant for studying* award, endowment, donation, contribution, allowance, subsidy, allocation, allotment, gift, present.

granule *noun* grain, particle, crumb, fragment, bit, scrap, mite, molecule, atom, iota, jot.

graph *noun* grid, chart, diagram, histogram, bar chart.

graphic *adjective* **1** *a graphic description of the events* vivid, striking, expressive, descriptive, illustrative, lively, forcible, detailed, well-defined, well-delineated, well-drawn, telling, effective, cogent, clear, lucid, explicit. **2** *a graphic representation* diagrammatic, presentational, pictorial, illustrative, drawn, delineative.
Antonyms: VAGUE; FUZZY.

---

graphic
pictorial, picturesque, vivid

A photograph of a car accident on the front page of a newspaper might be described as **graphic**, while a photograph of a mountain village would be called **picturesque**. Both adjectives are used to describe things that have visual impact or that produce a strong, clear impression, but **graphic** means having the power to evoke a strikingly lifelike representation, whether it is in pictures or in words (*the driving instructor gave them a graphic description of what happens in a 50-mph head-on collision*). **Vivid** is a more general term suggesting something that is felt, seen, heard, or apprehended with a sense of intense reality (*the vivid colors of the landscape; a vivid memory of the horrors of war*). Something that is **pictorial** aims to present a vivid picture (*a pictorial writing style*), while **picturesque** usually applies to scenes, pictures, etc. that are visually striking because they are panoramic, quaint, or unusual (*from a distance the village looked picturesque, but up close it was seen to be rundown*).

---

grapple *verb* *grapple (with) the enemy* wrestle, fight, struggle, tussle, clash, close, engage, combat, battle, brawl. **grapple with** *grapple with a problem* tackle, face, cope with, deal with, confront, address oneself to, attack, get down to, come to grips with.

grasp *verb* **1** *grasp his hand* grip, clutch, clasp, hold, clench, latch on to, take/lay hold of, catch, seize, grab, snatch. **2** *grasp the point* understand, comprehend, follow, see, take in, realize, perceive, apprehend; *inf.* get, get the picture, get the drift, catch on.

grasp *noun* **1** *take a firm grasp of the rail* grip, hold, clutch, clasp, clench. **2** *beyond the grasp of her enemy* clutches, power, control, command, mastery, dominion, rule. **3** *well within your grasp* capacity, reach, scope, limits, range, compass. **4** *have a good grasp of the subject* understanding, comprehension, perception, apprehension, awareness, grip, realization, knowledge, ken, mastery.

grate *verb* **1** *grate cheese/onions* shred, rub into pieces, pulverize, mince, grind, granulate. **2** *the knife grated against the metal surface* rasp, scrape, jar, scratch, grind, creak, rub. **grate on** *his voice/behavior grates on me* irritate, set someone's teeth on edge, rub someone the wrong way, irk, annoy, vex, gall, nettle, peeve, rankle with, anger, rile, exasperate, chafe; get on someone's nerves, aggravate.

grateful *adjective* **1** *grateful to you* thankful, filled with gratitude, indebted, obliged, obligated, under obligation, beholden. **2** *a grateful letter* thankful, appreciative. **3** *a grateful rest* pleasant, agreeable, pleasing, pleasurable, satisfying, gratifying, cheering, refreshing, welcome, acceptable, nice.
Antonyms: UNGRATEFUL; unappreciative.

gratify *verb* **1** *their appreciation gratified her* please, give pleasure to, make happy, make content, delight, make someone feel good, gladden, satisfy, warm the cockles of the heart, thrill. **2** *gratify their desires* fulfill, indulge, humor, comply with, pander to, cater to, pacify, appease, give in to.

grating *adjective* **1** *a grating noise* rasping, scraping, jarring, scratching, grinding, creaking. **2** *a grating voice* harsh, raucous, strident, screeching, piercing, shrill, squawking, squawky, squeaky, discordant, hoarse, croaky. **3** *a grating personality* irritating, jarring, annoying, vexatious, irksome, galling, exasperating, offensive, disagreeable, unpleasant.

gratis *adverb* free of charge, free, without charge, for nothing, at no cost, without paying, without payment, on the house, freely, gratuitously; *inf.* for free.

gratitude *noun* gratefulness, thankfulness, thanks, thanksgiving, appreciation, indebtedness, recognition, acknowledgment, sense of obligation.
Antonyms: INGRATITUDE; thanklessness.

gratuitous *adjective* **1** *gratuitous work* free, gratis, complimentary, voluntary, unpaid, unrewarded, unasked-for, free of charge, without charge, for nothing, at no cost, without payment, on the house; *inf.* for free. **2** *gratuitous insults/violence* unjustified, unprovoked, groundless, ungrounded, causeless, without cause, without reason, unfounded, baseless, uncalled-for, unwarranted, unmerited, needless, unnecessary, superfluous.

gratuity *noun* tip, perquisite, fringe benefit, bonus, gift, present, donation, reward, recompense, largesse; *inf.* perk.

grave *noun* burying place, burial ground, tomb, sepulcher, vault, burial chamber, mausoleum, crypt, last/final resting place.

grave *adjective* **1** *a grave expression/mood* solemn, earnest, serious, sober, somber, severe, unsmiling, long-faced, stone-faced, grim-faced, grim, gloomy, preoccupied, thoughtful, pensive, subdued, muted, quiet, sedate, dignified, staid, dour. **2** *grave matters* serious, important, all-important, significant, momentous, weighty, urgent, pressing, of great consequence, vital, crucial, critical, acute, pivotal, life-and-death, exigent, perilous, hazardous, dangerous, threatening, menacing.
Antonyms: CAREFREE; FRIVOLOUS; TRIVIAL.

graveyard *noun* cemetery, burial ground, churchyard, memorial park; *inf.* boneyard, potter's field.

gravitate *verb* **1** *gravitate to the bottom of the sea* sink, fall, drop, descend, precipitate, be precipitated, settle. **2** *gravitate toward the attractive girl* move toward, head toward, be drawn to, be pulled toward, be attracted to, drift toward, lean toward, incline toward.

gravity *noun* **1** *the gravity of her expression/mood* solemnity, earnestness, seriousness, sobriety, somberness, severity, grimness, thoughtfulness, pensiveness, sedateness, dignity, staidness, dourness. *See* GRAVE *adjective* 1. **2** *the gravity of the situation* seriousness, importance, significance, momentousness, moment, weightiness, consequence, vitalness, crucialness, criticalness, acuteness, exigence, perilousness, peril, hazard, danger. *See* GRAVE *adjective* 2.

graze[1] *verb* *sheep grazing* feed, browse, ruminate.

graze[2] *verb* **1** *the car grazed the wall* brush, brush against, touch, touch lightly, rub lightly, shave, glance off, skim, kiss. **2** *graze his knee* scrape, abrade, skin, scratch, chafe, bark, bruise, contuse.

graze[3] *noun* *he has a graze on his knee* scrape, abrasion, scratch, bruise, contusion.

gray *adjective* **1** *a gray dress* grayish, silver-gray, silvery; pearl-gray, pearly, gunmetal gray, battleship gray, smoke-colored. **2** *complexion looking gray* ashen, wan, pale, pallid, colorless, bloodless, anemic. **3** *a gray day* cloudy, overcast, dull, dark, sunless, gloomy, dim, dreary, dismal, drab, cheerless, depressing, misty, foggy, murky. **4** *gray people* characterless, colorless, dull, uninteresting, neutral, anonymous. **5** *a gray area* doubtful, unclear, uncertain, indistinct, mixed. **6** *the gray vote* gray-haired, elderly, old, aged, ancient, venerable.

greasy *adjective* **1** *greasy food* fatty, fat, oily, buttery, adipose, sebaceous. **2** *greasy roads* slippery, slippy, slimy. **3** *a greasy fellow* unctuous, oily, slimy, smooth-tongued, smooth, glib, suave, slick, fawning, ingratiating, groveling, sycophantic, toadying, flattering, gushing; *inf.* smarmy.

great *adjective* **1** *a great expanse of forest* large, big, extensive, vast, immense, unlimited, boundless, spacious, huge, enormous, gigantic, colossal, mammoth, monstrous, prodigious, tremendous, stupendous. **2** *describe in great detail* considerable, substantial, pronounced, exceptional, inordinate, sizable. **3** *the great cities of the world* major, main, most important, leading, chief, principal, capital, paramount, primary. **4** *a great occasion* grand, impressive, magnificent, imposing, splendid, majestic, glorious, sumptuous. **5** *the great people of the land* prominent, eminent, preeminent, distinguished, august, illustrious, celebrated, noted, notable, noteworthy, famous, famed, renowned, leading, top, high, high-ranking, noble. **6** *a great thinker* gifted, talented, outstanding, remarkable, exceptional, first-rate, incomparable. **7** *a great tennis player* expert, skillful, skilled, able, masterly, adept, adroit, proficient, good; *inf.* crack, ace, A-1. **8** *a great moviegoer* enthusiastic, eager, keen, zealous, devoted, active. **9** *we had a great time* enjoyable, excellent, marvelous, wonderful, first-class, first-rate, admirable, fine, very good; *inf.* terrific, tremendous, fantastic, fabulous, fab. **10** *he's a great fool* absolute, utter, out-and-out, downright, thoroughgoing, total, complete, perfect, positive, arrant, unmitigated, unqualified, consummate, egregious.
Antonyms: SMALL; UNIMPORTANT; ORDINARY.

greatly *adverb* *greatly admired/superior* very much, much, by a considerable amount, considerably, to a great extent, extremely, exceedingly, enormously, vastly, immensely, tremendously, hugely, markedly, mightily, remarkably, abundantly.

greatness *noun* **1** *the greatness of the forest* largeness, bigness, boundlessness, extensiveness, vastness, immensity, hugeness, enormity, spaciousness, prodigiousness, magnitude, size, bulk, mass, length. **2** *the greatness of the occasion* grandness, grandeur, impressiveness, magnificence, pomp, splendor, gloriousness, sumptuousness, majesty. **3** *the greatness of the leaders* eminence, distinction, luster, illustriousness, celebrity, noteworthiness, fame, renown, nobility. **4** *admire the greatness of the players* talent, expertness, expertise, skill, skillfulness, adeptness, proficiency.

greed, greediness *noun* **1** *the greed of the miser* avarice, acquisitiveness, graspingness, rapacity, covetousness, cupidity, miserliness, tightfistedness, parsimony. **2** *greed for knowledge* avidity, eagerness, desire, hunger, craving, longing, enthusiasm, impatience.

greedy *adjective* **1** *a greedy miser* avaricious, acquisitive, grasping, rapacious, grabbing, cov-
etous, hoarding, miserly, niggardly, tightfisted, close-fisted, parsimonious; *inf.* money-grubbing. **2** *greedy for knowledge* avid, eager, hungry, desirous, craving, longing, enthusiastic, anxious, impatient.
Antonyms: GENEROUS; ALTRUISTIC; APATHETIC.

---

greedy
acquisitive, avaricious, covetous, gluttonous, rapacious
The desire for money and the things it can buy is often associated with Americans. But not all Americans are **greedy**, which implies an insatiable desire to possess or acquire something, beyond what one needs or deserves (*greedy for profits*). Someone who is *greedy* for food might be called **gluttonous**, which emphasizes consumption as well as desire (*a gluttonous appetite for sweets*), but *greedy* is a derogatory term only when the object of longing is itself evil or when it cannot be possessed without harm to oneself or others (*a reporter greedy for information*). A *greedy* child may grow up to be an **avaricious** adult, which implies a fanatical greediness for money or other valuables. **Rapacious** is an even stronger term, with an emphasis on taking things by force (*so rapacious in his desire for land that he forced dozens of families from their homes*). **Acquisitive**, on the other hand, is a more neutral word suggesting a willingness to exert effort in acquiring things (*an acquisitive woman who filled her house with antiques and artwork*), and not necessarily material things (*a probing, acquisitive mind*). **Covetous**, in contrast to *acquisitive*, implies an intense desire for something as opposed to the act of acquiring or possessing it. It is often associated with the Ten Commandments (*Thou shalt not covet thy neighbor's wife*) and suggests a longing for something that rightfully belongs to another.

---

green *adjective* **1** *green clothes* greenish; sea-green, aquamarine, aqua, olive-green, pea-green, emerald-green, sage-green, chartreuse. **2** *green land* verdant, grass-covered, grassy, leafy. **3** *green plums* unripe, not ripe, immature. **4** *green wood* unseasoned, not aged, unfinished, pliable, supple. **5** *green tobacco/tea/bacon* raw, fresh, undried, unfermented, unsmoked. **6** *a green apprentice* inexperienced, untrained, inexpert, unqualified, ignorant, unversed, new, raw, immature, simple, unsophisticated, unpolished, naïve, innocent, ingenuous, callow, credulous, gullible, wet behind the ears. **7** *feel green on seeing his friend's new bike* envious, jealous, covetous, grudging, resentful. **8** *look/go green* greenish, pale, wan, pallid, ashen, ill, sick, sickly, unhealthy, nauseous. **9** *green issues | Green politicians* environmentalist, conservationist, preservationist; environmentally sound/friendly, ecologically sound.

green *noun* *a picnic on the green* village/town green, common, grassy area, grass, lawn.

green light *noun* *give the plans the green light* permission, approval, assent, consent, authorization, sanction, leave, warranty, confirmation, blessing; *inf.* OK, okay, go-ahead, thumbs up.

greens *plural noun eat up your greens* vegetables, leafy vegetables; *inf.* veggies.

greet *verb* **1** *greet his neighbor in the street* say hello to, address, salute, hail, nod to, wave to, raise one's hat to, acknowledge the presence of, accost. **2** *the hostess greeted the guests at the door* receive, meet, welcome.

greeting *noun* **1** *return his neighbor's greeting* hello, salute, salutation, address, nod, wave, acknowledgment. **2** *receive a birthday greeting* message, tidings.

greetings *plural noun send birthday greetings* good wishes, best wishes, regards, kind regards, congratulations, compliments, respects.

gregarious *adjective* sociable, social, company-loving, companionable, convivial, outgoing, friendly, affable, cordial, hospitable.
Antonyms: UNSOCIABLE; RESERVED.

grey *See* GRAY.grief

grief *noun grief at his death* sorrow, mourning, mournfulness, bereavement, lamentation, misery, sadness, anguish, pain, distress, agony, affliction, suffering, heartache, heartbreak, brokenheartedness, heaviness of heart, trouble, woe, tribulation, trial, desolation, despondency, dejection, despair, remorse, regret. **come to grief** fail, miscarry, meet with failure, meet with disaster; *inf.* come a cropper.
Antonyms: JOY; DELIGHT; CELEBRATION.

grievance *noun* **1** *answer the workers' grievances* complaint, charge, protest, moan, ax to grind, bone to pick; *lit.* plaint; *inf.* grouse, gripe, beef. **2** *workers claiming a grievance* wrong, injustice, unjust act, unfairness, injury, damage, hardship, offense, affront, insult.

grieve *verb* **1** *the widow is still grieving | grieving for/over/about his dead wife* mourn, lament, be sorrowful, sorrow, be sad, weep and wail, cry, sob, suffer, ache, be in anguish, be distressed, eat one's heart out; bewail, bemoan. **2** *his behavior grieved her* hurt, wound, pain, sadden, break someone's heart, upset, distress, cause suffering to, crush. **3** *grieve the loss of her dog* bewail, bemoan, regret, rue, deplore, take to heart.
Antonyms: REJOICE; CHEER.

grievous *adjective* **1** *a grievous injury* painful, agonizing, hurtful, afflicting, wounding, damaging, injurious, severe, sharp, acute. **2** *grievous news* calamitous, disastrous, distressing, sorrowful, mournful, sad, crushing. **3** *grievous sins/crimes* heinous, flagrant, glaring, outrageous, shocking, appalling, atrocious, gross, dire, iniquitous, nefarious, grave, deplorable, shameful, lamentable, dreadful, egregious. **4** *a grievous sound* grief-stricken, anguished, agonized, mournful, sorrowful, tragic, pitiful, heart-rending.

grim *adjective* **1** *giving a grim look* stern, forbidding, formidable, fierce, ferocious, threatening, menacing, harsh, somber, cross, churlish, crabbed, morose, surly, sour, ill-tempered, implacable, cruel, ruthless, merciless. **2** *grim determination* resolute, determined, firm, decided, obstinate, adamant, unyielding, unwavering, unfaltering, unshakable, obdurate, inflexible, unrelenting, relentless. **3** *a grim sight/accident* dreadful, dire, ghastly, horrible, horrendous, horrid, terrible, awful, appalling, frightful, shocking, unspeakable, harrowing, grisly, gruesome, hideous, macabre.
Antonyms: GENTLE; AMIABLE; PLEASANT.

grimace *verb grimace behind her back* make a face, make faces, scowl, frown, mouth, sneer, pout.

grimace *noun make a grimace* scowl, frown, sneer, face, wry face, distorted expression, pout, mouth, moue.

grime *noun* dirt, smut, soot, dust, mud, filth; *inf.* muck, grunge, yuck, crud.

grimy *adjective* begrimed, dirty, dirt-encrusted, grubby, soiled, stained, smutty, sooty, dusty, muddy, muddied, filthy; *inf.* mucky, grungy, yucky, cruddy.

grin *verb she grinned at him | grin like a Cheshire cat* smile broadly, smile/grin from ear to ear.
Antonyms: FROWN; GLOWER.

grind *verb* **1** *grind coffee beans/nuts* crush, pound, pulverize, mill, powder, granulate, grate, crumble, mash, smash. **2** *grind knives* sharpen, file, whet, smooth, polish, sand. **3** *grind one's teeth* gnash, grit, grate, scrape, rasp. **4** *grind away at the task* labor, toil, slog, slave, drudge, plod, sweat; *inf.* plug. **grind down** *grind down the poor* oppress, persecute, tyrannize, afflict, maltreat, ill-treat, scourge, torture, torment, molest, harass, harry.

grind *noun he regards his job as a grind* drudgery, chore, slog, travail, toil, hard work, labor, slavery, forced labor, exertion; *inf.* drag, sweat.

grip *noun* **1** *lose his grip of the railing* hold, grasp, clutch, clasp, clench. **2** *have a firm grip* handgrip, handshake, handclasp, clasp. **3** *have her in a grip* hold, hug, embrace; *inf.* clinch. **4** *have a grip of the problem* grasp, understanding, comprehension, perception, awareness, apprehension. *See* GRASP *noun* 4. **5** *in the grip of an addiction | the tyrant's grip* clutches, control, domination, dominion, command, power, mastery, influence, hold, possession, rule. **6** *pack a grip* bag, carryall, overnight bag, travel bag, duffel bag, valise. **come to grips with** *come to grips with his opponent/problem* face, face up to, meet head on, confront, encounter, deal with, cope with, handle, tackle, grasp, undertake, take on, grapple with, contend with.

grip *verb* **1** *grip the railing* grasp, clutch, clasp, clench, hold, grasp/take/lay hold of, latch on to, grab, seize, catch, catch at. **2** *the actor/speech gripped the audience* absorb, engross, rivet, spellbind, hold spellbound, entrance, fascinate, enthrall, hold, catch, compel, mesmerize.

gripe verb *griping about money* complain, grumble, moan, groan, protest, whine; *inf.* grouse, bellyache, beef, bitch, grouch.

gripe noun *listen to their gripes* complaint, complaining, grumble, grumbling, moan, groan, moaning and groaning, grievance, objection, protest, whine, whining; *inf.* grouse, grousing, bellyaching, beefing, beef, bitching, grouching.

gripping adjective *a gripping story* riveting, spellbinding, compelling, absorbing, engrossing, entrancing, fascinating, enthralling, thrilling, exciting.

grisly adjective *a grisly sight/story* gruesome, ghastly, frightful, horrid, horrifying, horrible, horrendous, grim, awful, dreadful, terrible, fearful, hideous, disgusting, repulsive, repugnant, revolting, repellent, macabre, spine-chilling, sickening, shocking, appalling, abominable, loathsome, abhorrent, odious.
Antonyms: PLEASANT; ATTRACTIVE.

grit noun **1** *boots tracking grit into the carpet* granules, sand, abrasive particles, gravel, pebbles, dust, dirt. **2** *he has no grit* pluck, mettle, mettlesomeness, backbone, spirit, strength of character, nerve, gameness, courage, bravery, valor, fortitude, stamina, toughness, hardiness, determination, resolution, doggedness, tenacity, perseverance, endurance; *inf.* gumption, guts, spunk.

grit verb *grit one's teeth* grate, grind, gnash, scrape, rasp; clamp, clench.

gritty adjective **1** *a gritty substance* sandy, grainy, granular, gravelly, pebbly, powdery, dusty. **2** *a gritty fighter* plucky, mettlesome, spirited, game, courageous, brave, hardy, tough, determined, resolute, dogged, tenacious, enduring; *inf.* gutsy, spunky.

groan noun **1** *a groan of pain* moan, cry, sigh, murmur, whimper. **2** *sick of your groans* complaint, grumble, whine, whining, objection, protest, grievance, moan; *inf.* grouse, gripe, beefing, bellyaching, bitching. **3** *the groan of the gate* creak, grating, squeak, screech.

groan verb **1** *groan in pain* moan, cry, call out, sigh, murmur, whimper. **2** *groaning about working conditions* complain, grumble, whine, object, moan, lament; *inf.* grouse, gripe, beef, bellyache, bitch. **3** *the gate groaned* creak, grate, squeak, screech.

groggy adjective *dazed, stunned, stupefied, in a stupor, dizzy, faint, befuddled, muddled, confused, bewildered, punch-drunk, shaky, staggering, reeling, unsteady, wobbly; *inf.* woozy.

groom noun **1** *the groom brushing the horse* stableboy, stablegirl, stableman, stablewoman. **2** *her groom was late* bridegroom, husband-to-be, newly married man, newlywed.

groom verb **1** *groom one's hair* | *groom oneself* arrange, fix, adjust, do, dress, put in order, tidy, make tidy, brush, comb, smooth, spruce up, smarten up, preen, primp, freshen up. **2** *groom the horses* curry, brush, rub, rub down, clean. **3** *groom the students for college* train, coach, prepare, prime, make ready, ready, instruct, tutor, drill, teach, educate, school.

groove noun **1** *a groove in the ground* furrow, channel, trench, trough, canal, gouge, hollow, indentation, rut, gutter, cutting, cut, score, rabbet. **2** *the same old groove* rut, routine, habit, treadmill; *inf.* daily grind.

grope verb **1** *grope around in the dark* feel, fumble, move blindly. **2** *grope for one's keys* fumble, fish, search, hunt, look, feel.

gross adjective **1** *gross in size* obese, massive, immense, huge, colossal, corpulent, overweight, bloated, bulky, hulking, fat, big, large, cumbersome, unwieldy. **2** *gross jokes* coarse, crude, vulgar, obscene, rude, ribald, lewd, bawdy, dirty, filthy, earthy, smutty, blue, risqué, indecent, indelicate, improper, impure, unseemly, offensive, sensual, sexual, pornographic. **3** *her brother is gross* boorish, loutish, oafish, coarse, crass, vulgar, ignorant, unrefined, unsophisticated, uncultured, uncultivated, undiscriminating, tasteless, insensitive, unfeeling, imperceptive, callous. **4** *a gross error* flagrant, blatant, glaring, outrageous, shocking, serious, egregious, manifest, obvious, plain, apparent. **5** *gross income* total, whole, entire, aggregate, before deductions, before taxes.
Antonyms: SLENDER; PURE; REFINED; NET.

gross verb *he grosses $50,000 per year* earn, make, bring in, take (in); *inf.* rake in.

grotesque adjective **1** *a grotesque costume/sight* bizarre, weird, outlandish, freakish, strange, odd, peculiar, unnatural, fantastic, fanciful, whimsical, ridiculous, ludicrous, absurd, incongruous, preposterous, extravagant. **2** *a grotesque shape* misshapen, distorted, twisted, deformed, malformed, misproportioned.

ground noun **1** *fall to the ground* earth, terra firma, floor; *inf.* deck. **2** *the ground is wet* earth, soil, dirt, land, terrain, clay, loam, turf, sod. *See* GROUNDS.

ground verb *ground his suspicions on her behavior* base, found, establish, set, settle. **ground in** *a calculus course for those grounded in algebra* teach, instruct in, coach in, tutor in, train in, drill in, educate in, school in, prepare in, initiate in, familiarize with, acquaint with, inform in/about.

groundless adjective *groundless fears* without basis, baseless, without foundation, unfounded, unsupported, imaginary, illusory, false, unsubstantiated, unwarranted, unjustified, unjustifiable, uncalled-for, unprovoked, without cause/reason/justification, unreasonable, irrational, illogical, empty, idle, chimerical.

grounds plural noun **1** *take a walk around the grounds* surroundings, land, property, estate, acres, tract of land, lawns, gardens, park, area, domain, holding, territory. **2** *best grounds we've played in this season* stadium, field, arena, ballpark, park. **3** *grounds for concern* reason, cause, basis, base, foundation, call, justification, rationale, argument, premise, occasion, factor, excuse, pretext, motive, inducement. **4** *coffee grounds* dregs, lees, deposit, sediment, precipitate, settlings, grouts.

groundwork *noun* foundation, base, basis, cornerstone, footing, underpinning, fundamentals, basics, ABCs, elements, essentials, preliminaries, preparations, spadework.

group *noun* **1** *divide the books into groups* category, classification, class, set, lot, batch, family, species, genus, bracket. **2** *a group of people* band, company, party, body, gathering, congregation, assembly, collection, cluster, crowd, flock, pack, troop, gang, batch; *inf.* bunch. **3** *belong to the radical group on the committee* clique, coterie, faction, circle, set. **4** *she joined a sewing group* society, association, league, guild, circle, club, work party. **5** *a group of trees* clump, cluster.

group *verb* **1** *group students according to ability* classify, class, categorize, sort, grade, rank, bracket. **2** *group the children for a photograph* assemble, collect, gather together, arrange, organize, marshal, line up. **3** *the police grouped around the prisoner* collect, gather, assemble, cluster. **4** *they grouped (together) to form a club* get together, band together, associate, consort.

grouse *verb* grouse *about the weather* complain, grumble, moan, groan, protest; *inf.* gripe, bellyache, beef, bitch, grouch.

grovel *verb* abase oneself, humble oneself, kowtow, bow and scrape, kneel before, fall on one's knees, prostrate oneself, fawn, fawn upon, curry favor, curry favor with, flatter; *inf.* crawl, butter someone up, be all over someone, suck up to, lick someone's boots, bootlick, throw oneself at someone's feet.

grow *verb* **1** *the child/pile grew* get taller, get bigger, get larger, stretch, heighten, lengthen, enlarge, extend, expand, spread, thicken, widen, fill out, swell, increase, multiply. **2** *the plants are growing* shoot up, spring up, develop, sprout, burgeon, bud, germinate, flourish, thrive. **3** *her fear grows from her insecurity* arise, originate, stem, spring, issue. **4** *the business is growing* flourish, thrive, prosper, succeed, progress, make progress, make headway, advance, improve, expand. **5** *grow prettier* become, come to be, get to be, get, turn, wax. **6** *grow corn* cultivate, produce, farm, propagate, raise.

Antonyms: SHRINK; DECREASE; FAIL.

growl *verb* snarl, howl, yelp, bark.

grown-up *noun* adult, grown man, man, grown woman, woman, mature man, mature woman.

grown-up *adjective* adult, mature, of age, fully grown, full-grown, fully developed.

growth *noun* **1** *the growth in population* | *the*

growth of the town augmentation, increase, proliferation, multiplication, enlargement, expansion, extension, development, evolution, aggrandizement, magnification, amplification, growing, deepening, heightening, widening, thickening, broadening, swelling. **2** *the growth of the plants* development, maturation, germination, shooting up, springing up, burgeoning, sprouting, blooming, vegetation. **3** *the growth of the industry* expansion, rise, progress, success, advance, advancement, improvement, headway. **4** *find a growth on her body* tumor, lump, excrescence, intumescence, tumefaction.

Antonyms: DECREASE; DECLINE; FAILURE.

grub *verb* **1** *grub through the old papers* search, hunt, rummage, probe, root around. **2** *grub away at the task* grind, labor, toil, drudge, slog, slave, plod, sweat; *inf.* plug. **grub out** *grub out information* search out, ferret out, root out, uncover, unearth. **grub up** *grub up plants/shrubbery* dig up, unearth, disinter, root out, uproot, root up, pull out, tear out. grub

grub *noun* **1** *grubs developing* larva, caterpillar, maggot. **2** *cheap grub* food, meals, sustenance, victuals, rations; *inf.* eats, nosh.

grubby *adjective* dirty, unwashed, grimy, filthy, messy, soiled, smutty, scruffy, shabby, untidy, unkempt, slovenly, squalid; *inf.* grungy, cruddy.

Antonyms: CLEAN; SPOTLESS.

grudge *noun* resentment, spite, malice, bitterness, ill-will, pique, umbrage, grievance, hard feelings, rancor, malevolence, venom, hate, hatred, dislike, aversion, animosity, antipathy, antagonism, enmity.

grudge *verb* **1** *grudge her a piece of the cake* begrudge, give unwillingly, give reluctantly, give stintingly. **2** *grudge her her success* resent, mind, begrudge, envy, be jealous of.

grueling *adjective* *a grueling five-hour walk* exhausting, tiring, fatiguing, wearying, taxing, demanding, trying, arduous, laborious, backbreaking, strenuous, punishing, crushing, draining, difficult, hard, harsh, severe, stiff, grinding, brutal, relentless, unsparing, inexorable.

gruesome *adjective* *gruesome details of the murder* | *gruesome sight* grisly, ghastly, frightful, horrid, horrible, horrifying, horrendous, awful, grim, dreadful, terrible, fearful, hideous, disgusting, repulsive, repugnant, revolting, repellent, macabre, spine-chilling, sickening, shocking, appalling, abominable, loathsome, abhorrent, odious.

gruff *adjective* **1** *a gruff voice* hoarse, harsh, rough, throaty, husky, croaking, rasping, low, thick, guttural. **2** *a gruff old man* surly, churlish, brusque, curt, blunt, abrupt, grumpy, crotchety, crabby, crabbed, cross, bad-tempered, ill-natured, crusty, bearish, sullen,

sour, uncivil, rude, unmannerly, impolite, discourteous, ungracious; *inf.* grouchy.
Antonyms: SOFT; COURTEOUS; GRACIOUS.

grumble *verb* **1** *always grumbling about the weather* complain, moan, groan, protest, object, find fault with, carp, whine; *inf.* grouse, gripe, bellyache, beef, bitch, grouch. **2** *stomach was grumbling* rumble, gurgle, murmur, growl, mutter, roar.

grumble *noun* **1** *listen to their grumbles* complaint, moan, groan, protest, grievance, objection, whine; *inf.* grouse, gripe, bellyaching, beefing, beef, bitching, grouching. **2** *the grumble of his stomach* rumble, gurgle, murmur, growl, muttering, roar.

grumpy *adjective* bad-tempered, surly, churlish, crotchety, crabby, crusty, bearish, ill-natured; *inf.* grouchy.

guarantee *noun* **1** *get a guarantee that the goods are perfect* warranty, warrant, contract, covenant, bond, guaranty. **2** *give his guarantee that he will return* pledge, promise, assurance, word, word of honor, oath, bond. **3** *the house acts as a guarantee for a loan* collateral, security, surety, earnest, guaranty. **4** *her father is the guarantee of the loan* guarantor, warrantor, underwriter, voucher, sponsor, supporter, backer; *Law* bondsman.

guarantee *verb* **1** *guarantee a loan* put up collateral for, give earnest money for, provide surety for, provide security for, underwrite, sponsor, vouch for, support, back. **2** *I guarantee that I shall return* promise, pledge, give a pledge, give an assurance, give assurances, give one's word, swear, swear to the fact.

guarantor *noun* guarantee, warrantor, underwriter. *See* GUARANTEE *noun* 4.

guard *verb* **1** *guard the town* stand guard over, protect, watch over, cover, patrol, police, defend, shield, safeguard, preserve, save, conserve, secure, screen, shelter. **2** *guard the prisoners* keep under guard, keep under surveillance, keep watch over, mind, supervise, restrain. **guard against** *guard against losing your bag | guard against thieves* beware of, keep watch against, be alert/watchful of, take care against, keep an eye out for, be on the alert against/for, be on the qui vive against/for, be on the lookout against/for; *inf.* keep one's eyes peeled for.

guard *noun* **1** *volunteer as guards* protector, defender, guardian, guarder, bodyguard, custodian, sentinel, sentry, watchman, night watchman, scout, lookout, watch, picket. **2** *prison guards* jailer, keeper; *inf.* screw. **3** *act as a guard for the truckload of supplies* escort, convoy, patrol. **4** *soldiers on guard* watch, close watch, watchfulness, vigilance, caution, attention, care, wariness. **5** *a guard for a machine* safety guard, safety device, safeguard, protective device, shield, screen, fence, fender, bumper,

buffer, cushion, pad. **off one's guard, off guard** *the question/enemy caught him off his guard* unprepared, unready, unalert, unwatchful, napping, with one's defenses down. **on one's guard** *keep on your guard* on the alert, vigilant, wary, watchful, cautious, careful, heedful, circumspect, on the lookout, on the qui vive, prepared, ready.

guarded *adjective* *a guarded reply* careful, cautious, circumspect, wary, chary, reluctant, noncommittal, reticent, restrained, reserved, discreet, prudent; *inf.* cagey.

guardian *noun* *the guardian of the castle | guardians of public morals* guard, protector, defender, preserver, champion, custodian, warden, keeper, curator, caretaker, steward, trustee.

guerrilla *noun* freedom fighter, underground fighter, terrorist, member of the resistance, partisan, irregular soldier, irregular.

guess *verb* **1** *guess the weight* make a guess at, conjecture, surmise, estimate, reckon, fathom, hypothesize, postulate, predict, speculate; *inf.* guesstimate. **2** *I guess that you're right* conjecture, surmise, reckon, hazard a guess, suppose, believe, think, imagine, judge, consider, feel, suspect, dare say, fancy, deem.

guess *noun* *my guess was wrong* conjecture, surmise, estimate, guesswork, hypothesis, theory, reckoning, judgment, supposition, feeling, assumption, inference, prediction, speculation, notion; *inf.* guesstimate.

guesswork *noun* guessing, conjecture, surmise, estimate, supposition, hypothesis, theory, presupposition, assumption, presumption, prediction, suspicion, speculation; *inf.* guesstimate.

guest *noun* **1** *the hostess welcoming guests* visitor, caller, company. **2** *a guest in the hotel* boarder, lodger, roomer, patron, customer.
Antonyms: HOST; LANDLADY, LANDLORD.

guidance *noun* **1** *under the guidance of the president/teacher* direction, leadership, auspices, management, control, handling, conduct, government, charge, rule, teaching, instruction. **2** *career guidance* counseling, counsel, advice, direction, recommendation, suggestion, tip, hint, pointer, intelligence, information, instruction.

guide *verb* **1** *guide them to their seats* lead, lead the way to, conduct, show, usher, shepherd, direct, show the way to, pilot, steer, escort, accompany, convoy, attend. **2** *guide the firm through its problems* control, direct, steer, manage, command, be in charge of, govern, rule, preside over, superintend, supervise, handle, regulate, manipulate, maneuver. **3** *guide the young graduates* give counseling to, counsel, give advice to, advise, give direction to, make recommendations to, make suggestions to, give someone tips/hints/pointers to, inform, give information/intelligence to, instruct.

guide *noun* **1** *a tourist guide* leader, conductor,

director, courier, pilot, usher, escort, attendant, convoy, chaperon. **2** *act as a career guide* counselor, adviser, mentor, confidant, tutor, teacher, guru, therapist. **3** *the lighthouse was the captain's guide* marker, indicator, pointer, mark, landmark, guiding light, sign, signal, beacon, lodestar, signpost, key, clue. **4** *use that essay as a guide* model, pattern, example, exemplar, standard, criterion, touchstone, measure, benchmark, yardstick, gauge, norm, archetype, prototype, paradigm, ideal, precedent, guiding principle. **5** *read a guide to Paris* guidebook, tourist guide, travelogue, directory, handbook, manual, instructions, key, catalog.

guideline *noun* guiding principle, criterion, measure, standard, gauge, yardstick, benchmark, touchstone, rule, regulation.

guild *noun* association, society, club, union, league, federation, organization, company, fellowship, order, lodge, brotherhood, fraternity, sisterhood, sorority, alliance, combine, corporation, consortium, syndicate, trust.

guile *noun* cunning, duplicity, craftiness, craft, artfulness, art, artifice, wiliness, wiles, foxiness, slyness, deception, deceit, underhandedness, double-dealing, trickery, trickiness, treachery, chicanery, skullduggery, fraud.
Antonyms: HONESTY; CANDOR.

guileless *adjective* ingenuous, artless, open, sincere, genuine, naïve, simple, innocent, unsophisticated, unworldly, trustful, trusting, honorable, frank, candid.

guilt *noun* **1** *prove/admitted his guilt* guiltiness, culpability, blame, blameworthiness, censurableness, wrongdoing, wrong, wrongfulness, criminality, unlawfulness, misconduct, delinquency, sin, sinfulness, iniquity. **2** *haunted by guilt* guiltiness, feelings of guilt, guilty conscience, bad conscience, remorse, regret, contrition, contriteness, repentance, penitence, compunction, conscience, self-accusation, self-reproach, self-condemnation, shame, disgrace, dishonor, stigma.
Antonyms: INNOCENCE; shamelessness.

guiltless *adjective* free from guilt, innocent, blameless, free from blame, unblamable, uncensurable, unimpeachable, inculpable, irreproachable, above reproach, clear, pure, sinless, faultless, spotless, stainless, immaculate, unsullied, uncorrupted, undefiled, untainted, unblemished, untarnished, impeccable.

guilty *adjective* **1** *found guilty of the crime* to blame, blameworthy, blamable, culpable, at fault, responsible, censurable, criminal, convicted; reproachable, condemnable, erring, errant, wrong, delinquent, offending, sinful, wicked, evil, unlawful, illegal, illicit, reprehensible, felonious, iniquitous. **2** *feel guilty* conscience-stricken, remorseful, ashamed, shamefaced, regretful, contrite, compunctious, repentant, penitent, rueful, sheepish.
Antonyms: INNOCENT; BLAMELESS; UNREPENTANT.

guise *noun* **1** *in the guise of a witch* external appearance, likeness, costume, clothes, outfit, dress, habit, style. **2** *under the guise of friendship* pretense, disguise, show, external appearance, outward form, screen, cover, blind.

gulf *noun* **1** *ships sailing into the gulf* bay, cove, inlet, bight, creek. **2** *a gulf opened up by an earthquake* chasm, abyss, hollow, pit, hole, opening, rift, cleft, fissure, split, crevice, gully, canyon, gorge, ravine. **3** *a gulf has developed between husband and wife* chasm, abyss, rift, split, wide difference, area of difference, division, gap, separation.

gullet *noun* esophagus, throat, pharynx, crop, craw.

gullible *adjective* credulous, trustful, overtrustful, easily deceived, easily taken in, unsuspecting, unsuspicious, ingenuous, naïve, innocent, simple, inexperienced, green, foolish, silly, wet behind the ears.
Antonyms: CYNICAL; SUSPICIOUS.

---

gullible
callow, credulous, ingenuous, naïve, trusting, unsophisticated

Some people will believe anything. Those who are truly **gullible** are the easiest to deceive, which is why they so often make fools of themselves. Those who are merely **credulous** might be a little too quick to believe something, but they usually aren't stupid enough to act on it. **Trusting** suggests the same willingness to believe (*a trusting child*), but it isn't necessarily a bad way to be (*a person so trusting he completely disarmed his enemies*). No one likes to be called **naïve** because it implies a lack of street smarts (*she's so naïve she'd accept a ride from a stranger*), but when applied to things other than people, it can describe a simplicity and absence of artificiality that is quite charming (*the naïve style in which 19th century American portraits were often painted*). Most people would rather be thought of as **ingenuous**, meaning straightforward and sincere (*an ingenuous confession of the truth*), because it implies the simplicity of a child without the negative overtones. **Callow**, however, comes down a little more heavily on the side of immaturity and almost always goes hand-in-hand with youth. Whether young or old, someone who is **unsophisticated** suffers because of lack of experience.

---

gully *noun* ravine, canyon, gorge, valley, gulf, chasm, abyss, gulch. *See* GULF 2.

gulp *verb* **1** *gulp a drink* swallow, quaff, swill; *inf.* swig, knock back. **2** *gulp one's food* bolt, wolf (down), gobble, guzzle, devour. **gulp back** *gulp back the tears* fight back, suppress, stifle, smother, choke back, strangle.

gulp *noun* *take a gulp of the water* swallow, mouthful, draft; *inf.* swig, slurp.

gum noun *stick the pages together with gum* glue, adhesive, fixative, paste, cement, mucilage, resin, epoxy resin.

gum verb *gum the pieces together* stick, glue, paste, affix, cement. **gum up 1** *gum up the mechanism* clog, choke up, stop up, obstruct. **2** *gum up the works* obstruct, impede, hinder, interfere with, bring to a halt.

gumption noun *hasn't got much gumption* initiative, resourcefulness, enterprise, cleverness, astuteness, shrewdness, acumen, common sense, wit, mother wit, discernment, sagacity, native ability, spirit, forcefulness, backbone, pluck, mettle, nerve, courage; *inf.* get-up-and-go, grit, spunk, savvy, horse sense.

gun noun firearm, pistol, revolver, automatic, repeater, six-shooter, handgun, side arm, rifle, shotgun, sawn-off shotgun, musket, flintlock, blunderbuss, field gun, cannon, mortar, machine gun, howitzer, Gatling gun; *inf.* gat, piece, rod, heater, Saturday-night special.

gunman noun holdup man, armed robber, sniper, gunfighter, shootist, gangster, terrorist, assassin, murderer, liquidator, bandit; *inf.* gunslinger, hitman, hired gun, hood, mobster.

gurgle verb **1** *water gurgling* bubble, ripple, murmur, babble, burble, tinkle, lap, splash. **2** *babies gurgling* burble, babble, chuckle, laugh.

gurgle noun **1** *the gurgle of water* bubbling, ripple, babble, tinkle. *See* GURGLE verb 1. **2** *the gurgle of babies* burbling, babbling, chuckle, laughing, laughter.

guru noun teacher, spiritual teacher, tutor, sage, swami, maharishi, guiding light, mentor, leader, master, authority.

gush verb **1** *water gushing from the pipe* stream, rush forth, spout, spurt, surge, jet, well out, pour forth, burst forth, cascade, flood, flow, run, issue, emanate. **2** *she gushed about the beautiful room* be effusive, effuse, overenthuse, enthuse, wax enthusiastic, wax lyrical, effervesce, bubble over, get carried away, fuss, babble, prattle, jabber, blather, chatter, make too much, overstate the case.

gush noun *a gush of water* stream, outpouring, spurt, jet, spout, burst, rush, surge, cascade, flood, torrent, spate, freshet.

gust noun **1** *a gust of wind blew the hat away* blast, flurry, puff, blow, rush, squall, breeze, gale. **2** *a gust of laughter/temper* outburst, burst, out-

break, eruption, explosion, gale, fit, paroxysm, storm, surge.

gust verb *wind gusting* blast, blow, puff, rush, squall.

gusto noun *perform/eat with gusto* relish, zest, enthusiasm, zeal, fervor, verve, enjoyment, delight, exhilaration, pleasure, appreciation, liking, fondness, appetite, savor, taste.
Antonyms: APATHY; INDIFFERENCE; DISTASTE.

gut noun **1** *a sore gut* stomach, belly, abdomen, bowels, colon; *inf.* insides, innards; *Med.* solar plexus. **2** *remove the guts from the animal* intestines, entrails, vital organs, vital parts, viscera; *inf.* insides, innards.

gut verb **1** *gut the fish/rabbit* eviscerate, disembowel, draw, dress, clean. **2** *thieves/fire gutted the empty house* ransack, strip, empty, plunder, loot, rob, rifle, ravage, sack, clear out, destroy, devastate, lay waste (to).

gut adjective *a gut reaction* instinctive, intuitive, involuntary, spontaneous, unthinking, natural, basic, emotional, heartfelt, deep-seated.

guts plural noun courage, bravery, valor, backbone, nerve, fortitude, pluck, mettle, mettlesomeness, gameness, spirit, boldness, audacity, daring, hardiness, toughness, forcefulness, stamina, willpower, tenacity; *inf.* grit, gumption, spunk.

gutter noun *water running in the gutter* drain, sewer, sluice, culvert, conduit, pipe, duct, channel, trough, trench, ditch, furrow.

guttersnipe noun street urchin, ragamuffin, waif, gamin.

guttural adjective *guttural voice/accent* throaty, husky, gruff, gravelly, croaking, harsh, rasping, deep, low, rough, thick.

guy noun man, male, fellow, person; *inf.* dude.

guzzle verb **1** *guzzle food | stop guzzling!* gulp, gobble, bolt, wolf (down), devour; cram oneself, stuff oneself, gormandize; *inf.* scarf up, put away. **2** *guzzle beer* gulp down, swallow greedily, quaff, swill; *inf.* chug, chug-a-lug.

gypsy noun traveler, migrant, rover, roamer, wanderer, rambler; *derog.* transient, vagrant, vagabond.

gyrate verb rotate, revolve, wheel around, turn around, circle, whirl, pirouette, twirl, swirl, spin, swivel.

gyration noun rotation, circumrotation, revolution, wheeling, turning around, circling, convolution, circumconvolution, whirling, pirouetting, twirling, swirling, spinning, swiveling.

H

habit noun 1 *it was his habit to go for a morning walk* custom, practice, procedure, wont, way, routine, matter of course, style, pattern, convention, policy, mode, rule. 2 *smoking is a bad habit* addiction, dependence, weakness, fixation, obsession. 3 *a riding habit* costume, dress, garb, attire, apparel, clothes, clothing, garments, livery, uniform; *inf.* gear, togs, duds. **habit of** *he had a habit of staring* tendency for, propensity for, predisposition for, proclivity for, penchant for, inclination for, custom of, practice of, quirk of.

habitable *adjective* inhabitable, fit to live/reside in, fit to occupy, tenantable.

habitat noun 1 *the animal's natural habitat* environment, natural environment, natural setting/background/element, home, abode. 2 *the habitat of students* home, abode, residence, residency, dwelling, dwelling place, habitation, location, address; *inf.* digs.

habitation noun 1 *fit for habitation* occupancy, occupation, tenancy, residence, residency, living, dwelling, housing, inhabitance, inhabitancy, inhabitation, lodging, billeting, quartering. 2 *settled into a new habitation* home, house, residence, residency, dwelling, dwelling place, abode, domicile, lodging, quarters, living quarters, rooms, apartment, flat, accommodation, housing, roof over one's head; *inf.* pad, digs.

habitual *adjective* 1 *taking his habitual route/place* customary, accustomed, regular, usual, normal, set, fixed, established, routine, wonted, common, ordinary, familiar, traditional. 2 *their habitual grumbling* persistent, constant, continual, recurrent, repeated, perpetual, nonstop, continuous, frequent. 3 *a habitual smoker* by habit, confirmed, addicted, chronic, inveterate, hardened, ingrained. **Antonyms:** UNACCUSTOMED; INFREQUENT; OCCASIONAL.

habituate *verb* **habituate to** *habituate oneself to a hot climate* accustom to, make used to, adapt to, acclimatize to, condition to, break in to, inure to, harden to, familiarize with, make familiar with.

habitué noun frequenter, frequent visitor, regular visitor, regular customer, regular patron/client, constant visitor, familiar face.

hack *verb* 1 *hack one's way through the jungle* cut, hew, slash, clear. 2 *you really hacked (up) the roast* gash, cut, chop, mangle, butcher, mutilate, lacerate. 3 *children hacking away with*

bronchitis cough, rasp; *inf.* bark. **hack down** *hack down the tree* cut down, chop down, fell, hew, saw down.

hack noun 1 *drives a hack* taxi, taxicab, cab. 2 *expected real writers, not these hacks* drudge, factotum, plodder; scribbler.

hack *adjective* *using hack phrases* banal, trite, overused, tired, worn-out, stale, stereotyped. *See* HACKNEYED.

hackle noun **make someone's hackles rise** anger, annoy, enrage, vex; *inf.* make someone see red, get someone's dander up, rile.

hackneyed *adjective* *using hackneyed phrases* hack, banal, trite, overused, overworked, tired, worn-out, time-worn, stale, stereotyped, clichéd, platitudinous, unoriginal, unimaginative, commonplace, common, pedestrian, prosaic, run-of-the-mill, stock, conventional; *inf.* played-out, corny, old-hat. **Antonyms:** FRESH; ORIGINAL.

hag noun crone, witch, gorgon, harridan, fury, hellcat, harpy, shrew, virago, vixen, termagant; *inf.* battleax, old bat.

haggard *adjective* drawn, gaunt, hollow-eyed, hollow-cheeked, pinched, ghastly, ghostlike, deathlike, wan, pallid, cadaverous, peaked, drained, careworn, emaciated, wasted, thin. **Antonyms:** SLEEK; PLUMP; HALE.

haggle *verb* 1 *haggle over the price* bargain, drive a hard bargain, argue, dicker. 2 *children haggling* squabble, bicker, quarrel, argue, dispute.

hail¹ *verb* 1 *hail a friend* salute, greet, say hello to, nod to, wave to, smile at, lift one's hat to, acknowledge. 2 *hail a taxi* signal, make a sign to, flag, flag down, wave down, call, shout to. 3 *hail the king* acclaim, applaud, cheer, praise, sound the praises of, laud, extol, pay tribute to, pay homage to, exalt, glorify. 4 *I hail from Philadelphia* come from, be a native of, be born in, originate in, have one's roots in.

hail² noun give a hail call, cry, shout, signal, greeting, salutation, salute, hello, acknowledgment.

hail³ noun 1 *hail falling* hailstones, sleet, frozen rain. 2 *a hail of bullets/protest* shower, rain, storm, volley, barrage, bombardment, pelting.

hail⁴ *verb* **hail down on** *insults/mortar fragments hailed down on him* shower, rain down on/upon, pelt, pepper, batter, bombard; beat down upon.

hair noun 1 *brushed her hair* head of hair, locks, tresses; *inf.* mane, mop. 2 *animal's hair* coat, fur, pelt, hide, wool, fleece, mane. **by a hair, by a hair's breadth** by the narrowest of margins, by a narrow margin, by the skin of one's teeth, by a split second; *inf.* by a whisker. **let one's hair down** throw off one's inhibitions, relax, be informal; *inf.* hang loose, let it all hang out, chill out. **split hairs** quibble, argue over nothing, niggle, cavil; *inf.* nitpick.

hair-raising *adjective* bloodcurdling, spine-chilling, spine-tingling, terrifying, exciting, horrifying, frightening, alarming, shocking, petrifying, thrilling; *inf.* scary, creepy.

hairy *adjective* hair-covered, hirsute, woolly, shaggy, bushy, furry, fleecy, fuzzy, bearded, unshaven, bewhiskered, stubbly; *Tech.* pilose, pileous.

halcyon *adjective* **1** *halcyon weather* mild, calm, still, tranquil, quiet, serene, pleasant, moderate, temperate, gentle, placid, peaceful, windless, stormless. **2** *halcyon days of youth* carefree, happy, blissful, golden, joyful, joyous, contented, flourishing, thriving, prosperous.

hale *adjective* healthy, in good health, well, fit, bursting with good health, flourishing, blooming, in excellent shape, in fine fettle, strong, robust, vigorous, hardy, sturdy, hearty, full of vim, able-bodied, lusty; *inf.* in the pink, fit as a fiddle, in tip-top condition.

half *noun* *take a half* equal part/portion/section/division, fifty percent; hemisphere, semisphere. **by half** *too smart by half* excessively, far, to too great an extent, by an excessive amount, considerably, very much. **by halves** *See* HALVES.

half *adjective* **1** *a half pint* halved, divided in two, in two equal parts, bisected; hemispherical. **2** *half measures | a half smile* partial, incomplete, limited, moderate, slight, inadequate, insufficient.

half *adverb* **1** *half-cooked | she half smiled* partly, partially, in part, part, incompletely, inadequately, insufficiently, slightly, barely. **2** *half inclined to agree* nearly, very nearly, to a certain extent, to a considerable extent, all but, almost. **not half** *not half good enough | not half bad* not at all, not in any way, not nearly.

half-baked *adjective* **1** *half-baked plans* ill-conceived, poorly planned, unplanned, not thought through, premature, undeveloped, unformed, ill-judged, shortsighted, injudicious, impractical; *inf.* crackpot. **2** *a half-baked young man* foolish, senseless, ignorant, inexperienced, immature, callow, green; *inf.* wet behind the ears.

halfhearted *adjective* *plan received a halfhearted welcome* lukewarm, unenthusiastic, apathetic, indifferent, uninterested, unconcerned, cool, listless, lackluster, dispassionate, unemotional, cursory, perfunctory, superficial, passive, neutral.

halfway *adverb* **1** *go halfway* midway, to/in the middle, to/at the midpoint. **2** *halfway finished* almost, nearly, just about, in part, partly, part, to a certain degree/extent, in some measure.

meet someone halfway reach a compromise with, come to terms with, strike a balance with, find a happy medium with, establish a middle ground with, give and take with; *inf.* go fifty-fifty with.

halfway *adjective* *the halfway point* midway, equidistant, mid, middle, intermediate, central, mean, medial, median.

halfwit *noun* simpleton, idiot, dolt, blockhead, dunderhead, dullard, dunce, fool, numskull; *inf.* nitwit, moron, dimwit, imbecile, crackpot, nut.

halfwitted *adjective* simpleminded, feebleminded, simple, stupid, idiotic, doltish, dull-witted, foolish, silly, half-baked; *inf.* dimwitted, crazy, moronic, balmy, batty, nutty, crackpot.

hall *noun* **1** *concerts held in the main hall* auditorium, assembly room, chamber; assembly hall, conference hall, concert hall, church hall, town hall. **2** *hostesses greeting their guests in the hall* entrance hall, vestibule, hallway, entry, lobby, foyer, passageway, passage.

hallmark *noun* **1** *the hallmark on the silver cup* assay mark, stamp of authenticity, authentication seal, endorsement of authentication. **2** *good craftsmanship is his hallmark* mark, trademark, stamp, sign, sure sign, telltale sign, badge, device, symbol, indicator, indication, index.

hallucinate *verb* *certain drugs can make you hallucinate* have/experience hallucinations, see visions, have a vision, fantasize, imagine things, dream, be delirious; *inf.* see things, trip.

hallucination *noun* *this drug causes hallucinations* illusion, figment of the imagination, imagining, vision, mirage, false conception, fantasy, apparition, dream, delirium, phantasmagoria.

halo *noun* nimbus, aureole, aureola, aura, ring of light, crown of light, radiance, corona.

halt[1] *verb* **1** *halt at the traffic lights* come to a halt, stop, come to a stop, come to a standstill, pull up, draw up, wait. **2** *halt for the day* stop, finish, cease, break off, call it a day, desist, discontinue, rest; *inf.* knock off. **3** *work has halted* stop, finish, cease, come to an end, be at an end, draw to a close, run its course. **4** *halt progress* bring to a halt/stop, arrest, check, block, curb, stem, terminate, end, put an end to, put a stop to, bring an end to, crush, nip in the bud, frustrate, balk, obstruct, impede, hold back.

Antonyms: GO; BEGIN; FURTHER.

halt[2] *noun* **1** *a halt in the work* stop, stopping, stoppage, cessation, close, end, desistance, discontinuation, discontinuance, standstill, pause, interval, interlude, intermission, break, hiatus, rest, respite, breathing space, time out; *inf.* breather. **2** *come/draw/grind to a halt* stop, standstill.

halt[3] *verb* **1** *keep halting when speaking* falter, hesitate, stammer, stutter, stumble, flounder, fumble for words. **2** *halting between going and staying* hesitate, waver, vacillate, dither, be un-

sure, be undecided, be in doubt, have qualms/
misgivings.

halter *noun* bridle, harness.

halting *adjective* 1 *walk with a halting gait* limping, hobbling, stumbling, unsteady, awkward. 2 *speak in halting tones* faltering, hesitating, stammering, stuttering, stumbling, labored.

halve *verb* *halved the orange with a knife* | *try to halve imports* cut in half, divide into two equal parts, divide in two, divide equally, split in two, sever in two, share equally, dichotomize, reduce by fifty percent.

halves *plural noun* **by halves** *do something by halves* inadequately, insufficiently, incompletely, imperfectly, skimpily; halfheartedly.

hammer *noun* claw hammer, sledgehammer, tack hammer, ball-peen hammer, mallet, gavel.

hammer *verb* 1 *hammer (out) a horseshoe* | *hammer it on the anvil* beat, shape, form, mold, forge, fashion, make, fabricate. 2 *hammering the punching bag* beat, batter, pound, pummel, hit, strike, slap, cudgel, bludgeon, club; *inf.* wallop, clobber. 3 *hammer the opposition* trounce, defeat utterly, inflict heavy damage on, bring someone to their knees, beat, thrash, worst, drub, give a drubbing to; *inf.* murder, clobber. 4 *hammer facts into their heads* drum, drive, drub. **hammer away at** *hammer away at the problem* persevere at, persist at; work at, pound away at, keep (on) attacking, plod away at, grind away at; *inf.* stick to/with, plug away at. **hammer out** *hammer out a solution* | *still hammering out the details* thrash out, work out, resolve, form a resolution about, sort out, settle, negotiate, bring about, bring to a satisfactory conclusion, bring to a finish, come to a decision on, complete, accomplish, produce, carry through, effect.

hamper *verb* *hamper progress* hinder, obstruct, impede, hold back, inhibit, retard, slow down, hold up, restrain, block, check, frustrate, balk, thwart, foil, curb, interfere with, cramp, restrict, bridle, handicap, stymie, hamstring, shackle, fetter, encumber, cumber, trammel; *inf.* throw a monkey wrench in the works.
Antonyms: AID; EXPEDITE; FACILITATE.

hamper *noun* laundry hamper, laundry basket, basket; picnic hamper, picnic basket.

hamstring *verb* 1 *hamstring the athlete* cripple, injure, disable, hock. 2 *hamstring the opposition's plans* frustrate, thwart, balk, foil, check, curb, hamper, ruin, prevent, stop.

hand *noun* 1 *large hands* palm, fist; *inf.* paw, mitt, duke. 2 *the hand of a clock dial* pointer, indicator, needle. 3 *give me a hand* helping hand, help, assistance, aid, support, succor, relief. 4 *hired a number of hands* worker, workman, work person, employee, operative, hired hand, hired man, hired person, hired help, laborer, artisan, crewman. 5 *have a neat hand* writing, handwriting, penmanship, script, calligraphy. 6 *try your hand at baking* ability, skill, art, artistry,

craftsmanship. 7 *give a big hand to the singer* applause, round of applause, clapping of hands, clap, ovation. **at hand** 1 *help is at hand* readily available, available, at one's disposal, handy, ready, within reach, accessible, close, close at hand, near, nearby; *inf.* on tap. 2 *your big moment is at hand* close at hand, imminent, approaching, coming, about to happen, impending. **by hand** *make it by hand* manually, with one's hands, using one's hands; *inf.* from scratch. **from hand to mouth** *live from hand to mouth* in poverty, meagerly, scantily, skimpily, precariously, uncertainly, insecurely, improvidently; *inf.* on the breadline. **hand in glove** *working hand in glove with the enemy* in partnership, in league, in close association, in collusion; *inf.* in cahoots. **hand in hand** 1 *walking hand in hand* holding hands, clasping hands, with hands clasped. 2 *working hand in hand* together, closely, side by side, in close association, in partnership, conjointly, concurrently. **in hand** 1 *the matter is in hand* receiving attention, being dealt with, under control, under way. 2 *have money in hand* ready, available, available for use, in reserve, put by. **try one's hand** try, make an attempt, attempt, essay; *inf.* have/take a shot, have a go.

hand *verb* *hand the book to her* give, pass, pass over, hand over, deliver, present. **hand down** *hand down the family jewels* pass down, pass on, give, transfer, transmit, bequeath, will. **hand out** *hand out food supplies* distribute, give out, pass out, deal out, dole out, mete out, dispense, apportion, disseminate, disburse; *inf.* dish out. **hand over** *hand over the money* give, give up, pass, pass over, present, turn over, deliver, surrender, yield, release; *inf.* fork out/over.

handbag *noun* purse, bag, shoulder bag, clutch, clutch purse, pocketbook, evening bag; flight bag, travel bag; *inf.* tote bag.

handbill *noun* circular, flyer, advertisement, notice, pamphlet, leaflet, brochure, bulletin; *inf.* junk mail.

handbook *noun* guide, guidebook, travel guide, tourist guide, manual, owner's manual, instruction manual, instructions, directory.

handcuff *verb* put handcuffs on, manacle, fetter, shackle.

handcuffs *plural noun* manacles, fetters, shackles; *inf.* cuffs, bracelets.

handful *noun* 1 *not too many people, just a handful* few, small number, small amount, small quantity, sprinkling. 2 *the child is a handful* nuisance, pest, bother, irritant, source of annoyance; *inf.* pain, pain in the neck.

handicap *noun* 1 *born with a handicap* physical/mental disability, physical/mental disadvantage, physical/mental abnormality, impairment. 2 *her poverty was a handicap* disadvantage, impediment, hindrance, obstruction, obstacle, encumbrance, check, block, curb,

trammel, barrier, stumbling block, constraint, restriction, limitation, drawback, shortcoming.
Antonyms: ADVANTAGE; BENEFIT.

handicap *verb handicapped by his slight build* put at a disadvantage, disadvantage, impede, hinder, impair, hamper, obstruct, check, block, encumber, curb, trammel, bridle, hold back, constrain, restrict, limit.

handicraft, handcraft *noun* craft, handiwork, craftsmanship, workmanship, artisanship, art, skill.

handiwork *noun* **1** *admire the handiwork at the crafts exhibition* handicraft, craft, craftsmanship. *See* HANDICRAFT, HANDCRAFT. **2** *this is the handiwork of a maniac* action, achievement, work, doing, creation, design, product, production, result.

handle *noun held the handle of the tool/sword* shaft, grip, handgrip, hilt, haft, knob, stock.

handle *verb* **1** *handle the goods* touch, feel, finger, hold, grasp, grip, pick up, caress, stroke, fondle, poke, maul; *inf.* paw. **2** *handle difficult problems/people* cope with, deal with, treat, manage, control. **3** *handle their business affairs* be in charge of, control, manage, administer, direct, guide, conduct, supervise, take care of. **4** *handle a car* drive, steer, operate, maneuver. **5** *the newspaper handled the story well* deal with, treat, discuss. **6** *dealers handling grain* deal in, traffic in, trade in, market, sell, stock, carry.

handout *noun* **1** *beggars waiting for handouts* alms, charity, gifts of food/money/clothes. **2** *read the handout* press release, circular, flyer, advertising leaflet, brochure, pamphlet, bulletin, notice, literature. **3** *accept handouts from the reps* sample, free sample; *inf.* freebie.

handpicked *adjective handpicked team of negotiators* select, specially selected, elite, choice, specially chosen, elect.

hands *plural noun in the hands of the enemy* possession, keeping, clutches, grasp, charge, care, power, authority, command, management, control, custody, guardianship, supervision, disposal, jurisdiction. **hands down** *win hands down* easily, with no trouble, effortlessly, without effort; *inf.* no sweat.

handsome *adjective* **1** *a handsome man* good-looking, attractive; *inf.* gorgeous, easy on the eyes, foxy, todie for. **2** *a handsome woman* good-looking, attractive, personable, elegant, fine, well-formed, well-proportioned, stately, dignified. **3** *a handsome gift* generous, magnanimous, liberal, lavish, bounteous, considerable, sizable, large, ample, abundant, plentiful.
Antonyms: UGLY; PLAIN; MEAGER.

handwriting *noun* writing, hand, penmanship, script, calligraphy; *inf.* scrawl, scribble.

handy *adjective* **1** *is the book handy?* at hand, available, within reach, accessible, near, nearby, close, at one's fingertips, convenient; *inf.* on tap. **2** *a handy instrument* useful, helpful, practicable, practical, serviceable, functional, expedient, easy-to-use, neat, convenient. **3** *a handy person* dexterous, deft, nimble-fingered, adroit, adept, proficient, skillful, skilled, expert, clever/good with one's hands.
Antonyms: INCONVENIENT; USELESS; INEPT.

hang *verb* **1** *mobiles hanging from the ceiling* hang down, be suspended, dangle, swing, sway, be pendent. **2** *hang the picture* suspend, put up, put on a hook. **3** *hang the convicted killer* send to the gallows, put the noose on, send to the gibbet, gibbet, execute; lynch; *inf.* string up. **4** *hang wallpaper* stick on, attach, fix, fasten on, append, paste, glue, cement. **5** *walls hung with tapestries* decorate, adorn, ornament, deck, drape, cover, furnish. **6** *hawks hanging in the air* hover, float, be poised, flutter, flit, drift, remain static. **hang around/about 1** *hang around, he won't be long* hold on, wait, wait a minute, linger, loiter, tarry, dally, waste time; *inf.* hang on. **2** *hang around bars* frequent, be a regular visitor to, be a regular client of, haunt; *inf.* hang out in. **3** *hang around with thugs* associate, keep company; *inf.* hang out. **hang back** hold back, stay back, stay in the background, be reluctant, hesitate, demur, recoil, shrink back. **hang down** *with her skirt hanging down* droop, trail, sag. **hang fire** *they're hanging fire until prices rise* delay, hang back, hold back, procrastinate, stall. **hang on 1** *everything hangs on the budget* depend, be dependent on, turn on, hinge on, rest on, be conditional on, be contingent upon, be determined by, be conditioned by. **2** *hang on his every word* listen closely to, be very attentive to, concentrate hard on, be rapt by, give ear to; be all ears for. **3** *hang on till things improve* hold out, hold on, persevere, persist, go on, carry on, continue, remain, endure. **4** *hang on, I'll get him* hold on, wait, wait a minute, stop, stay, remain, hold the line. **hang on to** *hang on to her mother's hand* hold, hold fast to, cling to, cling on to, grip, clutch, grasp, cleave to. **hang over 1** *trees hanging over* lean over, bend over, bend downward, bend forward, bow, droop. **2** *the threat of layoffs is hanging over them* loom over, be imminent for, impend for, menace, threaten, approach, draw near to; *inf.* be just around the corner for.

hang *noun* **get the hang of** get the knack of, acquire the technique of, catch on, grasp, comprehend, understand.

hangdog *adjective looked at him with a hangdog expression* shamefaced, ashamed, embarrassed, guilty-looking, sheepish, abashed, abject, cowed, cringing, downcast, crestfallen, browbeaten, defeated, intimidated, wretched.

hanger-on *noun* follower, henchman, adherent, appendage, dependent, parasite, minion, lackey, vassal, flunky, camp follower, sycophant, fawner, sponger, leech; *inf.* groupie, freeloader.

hangover *noun* aftereffects, effects of alcohol, crapulence, crapulousness; *inf.* morning after, morning-after feeling.

hang-up *noun* **1** *a hang-up about/with misspelled words* preoccupation, fixation, obsession, bee in one's bonnet, *idée fixe; inf.* thing. **2** *she has a hang-up about/with math* mental block, psychological block, block, inhibition, difficulty, problem; *inf.* thing.

hank *noun hanks of colored wool* skein, coil, loop, twist, length, roll, piece.

hanker *verb* **hanker after/for** *hanker after/for a trip abroad* long for, have a longing for, yearn for, crave, desire, hunger for, thirst for, be bent on, covet, want, wish for, set one's heart on, pine for, be itching for, lust after; *inf.* be dying for, have a yen for.

hankering *noun* longing, yearning, craving, desire, hunger, thirst, want, wish, urge, itch, lust; *inf.* yen.

haphazard *adjective* unplanned, random, unsystematic, unorganized, unmethodical, orderless, aimless, indiscriminate, undirected, irregular, slapdash, thrown together, careless, casual, hit-or-miss.
Antonyms: METHODICAL; SYSTEMATIC.

hapless *adjective the hapless child began to cry* unlucky, luckless, out of luck, unfortunate, ill-starred, forlorn, wretched, woebegone, unhappy; *inf.* down on one's luck.

happen *verb the accident happened at dawn* take place, occur, come about, come to pass, present itself, arise, materialize, appear, come into being, chance, arrive, transpire, crop up, develop, supervene, eventuate; *inf.* come off. **happen to 1** *what happened to her?* become of, befall. **2** *I happened to meet her* chance to, have the good/bad fortune to, be someone's fortune/misfortune to. **happen upon** *happen upon hidden treasure* chance upon, stumble on, discover unexpectedly, find, meet by chance, encounter.

---

happen
befall, chance, occur, transpire

When things **happen**, they come to pass either for a reason or by chance (*it happened the day after school started; she happened upon the scene of the accident*), but the verb is more frequently associated with **chance** (*it happened to be raining when we got there*). **Occur** can also refer either to something that comes to pass either accidentally or as planned, but it should only be used interchangeably with **happen** when the subject is a definite or actual event (*the tragedy occurred last winter*). Unlike *happen, occur* also carries the implication of something that presents itself to sight or mind (*it never occurred to me that he was lying*). **Transpire** is a more formal (and some would say undesirable) word meaning to *happen* or *occur,* and it conveys the sense that something has leaked out or become known (*he told her exactly what had transpired while she was away*).

While things that *happen, occur,* or *transpire* can be either positive or negative, when something **befalls** it is usually unpleasant (*he had no inkling of the disaster that would befall him when he got home*).

---

happening *noun* occurrence, event, incident, occasion, affair, circumstance, action, case, phenomenon, eventuality, episode, experience, adventure, scene, proceedings, chance.

happily *adverb* **1** *I shall happily go* with pleasure, gladly, delightedly, willingly, freely, contentedly, enthusiastically, with all one's heart and soul. **2** *children playing happily* cheerfully, merrily, gaily, lightheartedly, joyfully, blithely. *See* HAPPY 1. **3** *happily, it turned out all right* luckily, fortunately, as luck would have it, providentially.

happiness *noun* cheerfulness, cheeriness, merriness, gaiety, good spirits, high spirits, lightheartedness, joy, joyfulness, joviality, glee, blitheness, carefreeness, enjoyment, gladness, delight, exuberance, elation, ecstasy, bliss, blissfulness, euphoria.

happy *adjective* **1** *happy children* cheerful, cheery, merry, gay, in good spirits, in high spirits, lighthearted, joyful, joyous, jovial, gleeful, buoyant, blithe, blithesome, carefree, untroubled, smiling, glad, delighted, exuberant, elated, ecstatic, blissful, euphoric, overjoyed, thrilled, in seventh heaven, floating/walking on air; *inf.* on cloud nine, on top of the world. **2** *happy to see you* glad, pleased, delighted, contented, satisfied, gratified, thrilled. **3** *by a happy chance* lucky, fortunate, favorable, advantageous, beneficial, helpful, opportune, timely, convenient, propitious, auspicious. **4** *a happy choice* apt, appropriate, fitting, fit, good, right, proper, seemly.
Antonyms: SAD; displeased; UNFORTUNATE.

happy-go-lucky *adjective he's always so happy-go-lucky | has such a happy-go-lucky manner* carefree, lighthearted, devil-may-care, blithe, free and easy, easygoing, nonchalant, casual, untroubled, unworried, unconcerned, insouciant, heedless, irresponsible, improvident.

harangue *noun* lecture, tirade, diatribe, speech, talk, sermon, exhortation, declamation, oration, address, homily; *inf.* spiel.

harass *verb* **1** *children harassing their mother* bother, pester, annoy, exasperate, worry, fret, disturb, agitate, provoke, badger, hound, torment, plague, persecute, harry, tease, bait, nag, molest, bedevil; *inf.* hassle, give someone a hard time, drive someone up the wall. **2** *troops harassing the enemy* harry, attack repeatedly, raid, beleaguer, press hard, oppress.

harassed *adjective harassed parents* distraught, under pressure, stressed, under stress, strained, worried, careworn, troubled, vexed, agitated, fretting; *inf.* hassled.

harbinger *noun* herald, forerunner, precursor, usher, announcer, sign, portent, omen, augury.

harbor *noun* **1** *ships in the harbor* port, anchorage, haven, dock, marina. **2** *a harbor for refugees* place of safety, refuge, shelter, haven, sanctuary, retreat, asylum, sanctum, covert.

harbor *verb* **1** *harbor criminals* give shelter to, shelter, house, lodge, put up, take in, billet, provide refuge for, shield, protect, conceal, hide, secrete. **2** *harbor resentment* nurture, maintain, hold on to, cherish, cling to, retain, entertain, brood over.

hard *adjective* **1** *hard ground* firm, solid, solidified, compact, compacted, condensed, close-packed, compressed, dense, rigid, stiff, unyielding, resistant, unmalleable, inflexible, unpliable, tough, strong, stony, rocklike. **2** *hard physical work* arduous, strenuous, heavy, tiring, fatiguing, exhausting, backbreaking, laborious, rigorous, exacting, formidable, tough, difficult, uphill, toilsome, Herculean. **3** *a hard problem* difficult, complicated, complex, involved, intricate, puzzling, perplexing, baffling, knotty, thorny, bewildering, enigmatic, insoluble, insolvable, unfathomable, incomprehensible. **4** *a hard master* harsh, hardhearted, severe, stern, cold, cold-hearted, unfeeling, unsympathetic, grim, ruthless, oppressive, tyrannical, pitiless, merciless, unrelenting, unsparing, lacking compassion, callous, cruel, vicious, implacable, obdurate, unyielding, unjust, unfair. **5** *hard living conditions* difficult, grim, harsh, unpleasant, disagreeable, uncomfortable, intolerable, unendurable, unbearable, insupportable, distressing, painful, disastrous, calamitous. **6** *a hard blow/knock* forceful, violent, heavy, strong, powerful, sharp, fierce, harsh. **7** *a hard worker* hardworking, energetic, industrious, diligent, assiduous, conscientious, sedulous, keen, enthusiastic, zealous, earnest, persevering, persistent, unflagging, untiring, indefatigable. **8** *hard words* | *no hard feelings* angry, acrimonious, bitter, antagonistic, hostile, resentful, rancorous. **9** *the hard facts* actual, definite, undeniable, indisputable, verifiable, plain, cold, bare, bold, harsh, unvarnished, unembellished. **10** *hard liquor* alcoholic, strong, potent. **11** *hard drugs* potent, hard-core, addictive, habit-forming, harmful, noxious, injurious. *Antonyms:* SOFT; EASY; GENTLE.

---

hard
arduous, difficult, laborious, trying
For the student who doesn't read well, homework is **hard** work, which means that it demands great physical or mental effort. An English assignment to write an essay might be particularly **difficult**, meaning that it not only requires effort but skill. Where *hard* suggests toil, *difficult* emphasizes complexity (*a difficult math problem*). Memorizing long lists of vocabulary words would be **laborious**, which is even more restrictive than *hard* and suggests prolonged, wearisome toil with no suggestion of the skill required and no reference to the complexity of the task. Reading *War and Peace*, however, would be an **arduous** task, because it would require a persistent effort over a long period of time. A school assignment may be *difficult*, but is usually not *arduous*; that is, it may require skill rather than perseverance. It may also be *arduous* without being particularly *difficult*, as when a student is asked to write I will not throw spitballs five hundred times. A student who is new to a school may find it especially **trying**, which implies that it taxes the individual's patience, skill, or capabilities.

---

hard *adverb* **1** *push hard* strenuously, energetically, powerfully, heavily, with all one's might, with might and main, heartily, vigorously, with vigor, forcefully, with force, forcibly, with great effort, fiercely, intensely. **2** *work hard* energetically, industriously, diligently, assiduously, conscientiously, enthusiastically, sedulously, with application, earnestly, with perseverance, persistently, indefatigably; *inf.* like a slave. **3** *our victory was hard won* with difficulty, with effort, laboriously, after a struggle, painfully. **4** *her death hit him hard* badly, intensely, violently, forcefully, harshly, distressingly, painfully, agonizingly. **5** *it was raining hard* heavily, steadily; *inf.* cats and dogs, buckets. **6** *look hard at* keenly, sharply, carefully, closely, painstakingly. **7** *they followed hard on his heels* close, near. **hard by** *living hard by the highway* right by, beside, near, near to, nearby, close to, close by, not far from, a step away from, within a stone's throw of. **hard up** poor, short of money/cash, in financial difficulties, penniless, impoverished, destitute, impecunious, bankrupt, in the red, without means of support; *inf.* broke, stone-broke, cleaned out, bust, busted, strapped.

hard-and-fast *adjective* *hard-and-fast rules* binding, set, strict, stringent, inflexible, rigorous, immutable, unalterable, uncompromising, incontestable, incontrovertible.

hardbitten *adjective* *hardbitten journalists* hardened, case-hardened, hardened, inured, toughened by experience, tough, cynical, down-to-earth.

hard-boiled *adjective* cynical, unsentimental, lacking sentiment, tough, down-to-earth, world-weary.

hard-core *adjective* **1** *hard-core socialists* diehard, dyed-in-the-wool, staunch, steadfast, dedicated, intransigent, uncompromising, obstinate, stubborn, extreme. **2** *hard-core pornography* explicit, blatant, obscene; *inf.* full-frontal, raw.

harden *verb* **1** *the cement hardened* become hard, solidify, set, stiffen, bake, anneal, cake, freeze, congeal, clot, coagulate. *See* HARD *adjective* 1. **2** *harden one's heart* toughen, make insensitive/unfeeling, deaden, numb, benumb. **3** *life had hardened him* case-harden, make tough, toughen, make unfeeling, brutalize, make callous. **4** *harden to cold* accustom, habituate, acclimatize, inure. **5** *harden one's defenses* strengthen, fortify, reinforce, buttress, brace, gird.

hardened *adjective a hardened criminal* habitual, accustomed, chronic, inured, seasoned, inveterate, incorrigible, irredeemable, reprobate, impenitent, unregenerate, shameless.

hardheaded *adjective hardheaded businessmen* shrewd, astute, sharp, sharp-witted, tough, unsentimental, hardbitten, practical, pragmatic, realistic, levelheaded, coolheaded, sensible, rational, with one's feet on the ground.

hard-hearted *adjective mother could be so hard-hearted* hard, heartless, unfeeling, unsympathetic, uncompassionate, lacking compassion, without sentiment, cold, cold-hearted, uncaring, unconcerned, indifferent, unmoved, unkind, cruel, callous, inhuman, merciless, pitiless, stony-hearted, stony. *See* HARD *adjective* 4.

hard-hitting *adjective a hard-hitting report* tough, uncompromising, unsparing, strongly worded, vigorous, pulling no punches, critical, straight-talking, blunt, frank.

hardiness *noun the hardiness of the children* healthiness, strength, robustness, sturdiness, toughness, ruggedness, vigor. *See* HARDY 1.

hard-line *adjective hard-line members of the party* extreme, tough, uncompromising, inflexible, unyielding, intransigent, not giving an inch.

hardly *adverb hardly able to walk | can hardly see | hardly alive* scarcely, barely, only just, just, almost not, with difficulty, with effort.

hard-pressed *adjective* **1** *the retreating army was hard-pressed* closely pursued, hotly pursued, harried, hounded, under attack, in a tight corner. **2** *hard-pressed workers* overloaded, overburdened, overworked, overtaxed, under pressure, harassed, in difficulties, with one's back to the wall; *inf.* pushed, up against it.

hardship *noun suffer great hardship* adversity, deprivation, privation, want, need, destitution, poverty, austerity, desolation, misfortune, distress, suffering, affliction, pain, misery, wretchedness, tribulation, trials, trials and tribulation, burdens, calamity, catastrophe, disaster, ruin, ruination, oppression, persecution, torment, torture, travail.

Antonyms: PROSPERITY; EASE; COMFORT.

hardwearing *adjective hardwearing shoes/carpet* durable, strong, tough, stout, rugged, made to last, resilient, well-made.

hardworking *adjective* diligent, industrious, conscientious, assiduous, sedulous, energetic, keen, enthusiastic, zealous, busy, with one's shoulder to the wheel.

Antonyms: LAZY; IDLE.

hardy *adjective* **1** *hardy children* healthy, fit, strong, robust, sturdy, tough, rugged, vigorous, lusty, stalwart, hale and hearty, fit as a fiddle, in fine fettle, in good kilter, in good condition. **2** *hardy men defying death* brave, courageous, valiant, bold, valorous, intrepid, fearless, heroic, stouthearted, daring, plucky, mettlesome.

Antonyms: DELICATE; WEAK; COWARDLY.

harebrained *adjective* **1** *a harebrained scheme* foolish, foolhardy, rash, reckless, madcap, wild, ridiculous, half-baked, ill-thought-out, ill-conceived; *inf.* crackpot. **2** *a harebrained young girl* foolish, silly, empty-headed, scatterbrained, featherbrained, brainless, giddy, dizzy, whimsical, capricious, flighty; *inf.* halfwitted.

hark *verb hark! the birds are singing* harken, listen, pay attention, pay heed, give ear. **hark back to** *hark back to subjects previously discussed* go back to, turn back to, look back at/to/on/upon, think back on, revert to, regress to, retrovert to, remember, recall, recollect.

harlequin *noun dressed as a harlequin* jester, fool, buffoon, zany.

harlequin *adjective a harlequin pattern* checkered, variegated, varicolored, particolored, multicolored, many-colored, motley.

harlot *noun* whore, prostitute, call girl, streetwalker, loose woman, fallen woman, lady of the evening, madam, procuress; *inf.* tramp, hooker.

harm *noun* **1** *inflict harm* hurt, injury, pain, suffering, trauma, adversity, disservice, abuse, damage, mischief, detriment, defacement, defilement, impairment, destruction, loss, ruin, havoc. **2** *full of harm* badness, evil, wrongdoing, wrong, wickedness, vice, iniquity, sin, sinfulness, immorality, nefariousness.

Antonyms: GOOD; BENEFIT.

harm *verb harm the child/building | try not to harm their relationship* hurt, injure, wound, inflict pain/suffering/trauma on, abuse, maltreat, illtreat, ill-use, molest, do violence to, damage, do mischief to, deface, defile, impair, spoil, mar, blemish, destroy.

harmful *adjective* **1** *harmful effects* hurtful, injurious, wounding, abusive, detrimental, deleterious, disadvantageous, destructive, dangerous, pernicious, noxious, baneful, toxic. **2** *a harmful influence* bad, evil, malign, wicked, corrupting, subversive.

Antonyms: HARMLESS; BENEFICIAL; GOOD.

harmless *adjective* **1** *a harmless substance* innocuous, innoxious, safe, nondangerous, nontoxic, nonirritant, mild. **2** *a harmless old man* innocuous, inoffensive, unoffending, innocent, blameless, gentle.

harmonious *adjective* **1** *a harmonious musical piece* melodious, tuneful, musical, harmonizing, sweet-sounding, mellifluous, dulcet, euphonious, symphonious, rhythmic, consonant. **2** *a harmonious atmosphere/relationship*

peaceful, peaceable, friendly, amicable, cordial, amiable, agreeable, congenial, united, in harmony, in rapport, in tune, attuned, in accord, compatible, sympathetic. **3** *a harmonious collection of colors/buildings* compatible, congruous, coordinated, concordant, well-matched, matching.
Antonyms: DISCORDANT; HOSTILE; INCONGRUOUS.

harmonize *verb* **1** *the colors harmonize well* be harmonious, go together, fit together, be compatible, blend, mix well, be congruous, be consonant, be well-coordinated, match. **2** *their stories/thoughts harmonize* be in accord, agree, be in assent, correspond, coincide, tally, be in unison, be congruent, be of one mind. **3** *harmonize relations | time for our nations to harmonize* restore harmony to, settle differences, reconcile, patch up, make peaceful, negotiate peace between, heal the breach, pour oil on troubled waters.

harmony *noun* **1** *working in harmony* agreement, assent, accord, accordance, concordance, concurrence, cooperation, unanimity, unity, unison, oneness, amity, amicability, goodwill, affinity, rapport, sympathy, like-mindedness, friendship, fellowship, comradeship, peace, peacefulness. **2** *the harmony of the colors* compatibility, congruity, consonance, concord, coordination, blending, balance, symmetry, suitability. **3** *enjoy the harmony at the concert* tunefulness, melodiousness, mellifluousness, euphony, euphoniousness.
Antonyms: DISAGREEMENT; INCONGRUITY; DISSONANCE.

harness *noun* *horse's harness* tackle, tack, equipment, gear, accouterment, trappings, yoke, bridle. **in harness** working, at work, employed, in action, active, busy.

harness *verb* **1** *harness the horses* put in harness, saddle, yoke, bridle, hitch up, couple. **2** *harness the sun's rays | must harness her energies* control, utilize, put to use, render useful, make productive, apply, exploit, channel, mobilize, capitalize on.

harp *noun* *playing the harp* lyre; jew's harp, Celtic harp. **harp on** *harp on his untidiness* dwell on, persist in talking about, repeat complaints about, nag about, press/labor/belabor the point about; *inf.* go on and on about.

harridan *noun* shrew, harpy, virago, termagant, vixen, scold, nag, fishwife, witch, hellcat, spitfire, fury, hag, gorgon; *inf.* old bag, battleax.

harrowing *adjective* *harrowing cries/sight/experience* distressing, agonizing, excruciating, traumatic, heartbreaking, heart-rending, painful, racking, afflicting, chilling, disturbing, vexing, alarming, perturbing, unnerving, horrifying, terrifying.

harry *verb* **1** *invaders harrying the villagers* plunder, rob, raid, sack, pillage, devastate, ravage, despoil, lay waste to. **2** *children harrying their*

mother harass, annoy, bother, pester, disturb, worry, badger, plague, vex, torment, tease, molest, persecute, bedevil; *inf.* hassle, drive someone up the wall.

harsh *adjective* **1** *a harsh noise* grating, jarring, grinding, rasping, strident, jangling, raucous, ear-piercing, discordant, dissonant, unharmonious. **2** *a harsh voice* rough, coarse, guttural, hoarse, croaking, raucous, strident, gravelly, gruff. **3** *harsh colors* gaudy, garish, glaring, bold, loud, flashy, showy, crass, crude, vulgar. **4** *harsh conditions/countryside* grim, severe, desolate, stark, austere, barren, rough, bleak, bitter, wild, inhospitable, comfortless, spartan. **5** *a harsh winter* severe, hard, bitter, bitterly cold, freezing, arctic, Siberian. **6** *a harsh reply* abrupt, brusque, blunt, curt, gruff, short, surly, concise, impolite, discourteous, uncivil, ungracious. **7** *a harsh ruler* cruel, brutal, savage, barbarous, hard-hearted, despotic, tyrannical, ruthless, uncompassionate, unfeeling, merciless, pitiless, relentless, unrelenting, inhuman. **8** *harsh rules/measure* stern, severe, grim, stringent, austere, uncompromising, inflexible, punitive, draconian.
Antonyms: MELLIFLUOUS; SOFT; GENTLE; LENIENT.

harum-scarum *adjective* reckless, rash, wild, impetuous, daredevil, madcap, harebrained, foolhardy, thoughtless, careless, heedless, frivolous.

harvest *noun* **1** *celebrate the end of the harvest* harvesttime, harvesting, reaping, ingathering. **2** *a good harvest of wheat/apples* crop, yield, vintage. **3** *the squirrels have a harvest of nuts* store, supply, stock, stockpile, hoard, cache, accumulation. **4** *the harvest of hard work* product, fruits, return, effect, result, consequence.

harvest *verb* **1** *harvest the crop* gather in, gather, reap, glean, pick, pluck, collect. **2** *squirrels harvesting nuts* collect, amass, accumulate, hoard, garner. **3** *harvest benefits from his experience* acquire, gain, obtain, get, derive, procure, secure, net.

hash[1] *noun* **make a hash of** make a mess of, botch, bungle, mishandle, mismanage, muddle up, mix up; *inf.* screw up.

hash[2] *noun* hashish, marijuana, cannabis, hemp; *inf.* grass, pot, weed.

hassle *noun* **1** *tired of all the hassle* inconvenience, trouble, bother, annoyance, nuisance, trials and tribulation, harassment, badgering, difficulty, problem, struggle. **2** *a hassle at the bar last night* fight, quarrel, squabble, argument, disagreement, dispute, altercation, tussle.

hassle *verb* *stop hassling him* annoy, badger, harass, hound, pester, bother, trouble, worry, torment, plague; *inf.* give someone a hard time.

haste *noun* **1** *fulfill the order with haste* speed, swiftness, rapidity, rapidness, quickness, fastness, alacrity, promptness, dispatch, expeditiousness, expedition, celerity, fleetness, briskness, immediateness, urgency. **2** *haste causes*

carelessness hastiness, hurriedness, hurry, rushing, hustling, impetuosity, recklessness, rashness, foolhardiness, impulsiveness, heedlessness, carelessness.
Antonyms: DELAY; CARE.

hasten *verb* **1** *you must hasten to get there on time* make haste, hurry, hurry up, go fast, move faster, go quickly, dash, rush, speed up, run, race, sprint, fly, tear along, bolt, scurry, scamper, scuttle; *inf.* get a move on, step on it, hotfoot it, hightail it. **2** *hasten the growth/work* speed up, accelerate, hurry on, quicken, advance, push forward, urge on, facilitate, precipitate, aid, assist, help, boost, increase, step up.
Antonyms: SLOW; DAWDLE; DECELERATE; DELAY.

hasty *adjective* **1** *with hasty steps* swift, rapid, quick, fast, speedy, hurried, hurrying, running, prompt, expeditious, fleet, brisk, urgent. **2** *a hasty visit/glance* quick, short, rapid, brief, rushed, short-lived, fleeting, transitory, cursory, perfunctory, superficial, slight. **3** *a hasty decision* hurried, rushed, impetuous, reckless, rash, foolhardy, precipitate, impulsive, headlong, ill-conceived, heedless, thoughtless, careless. **4** *a hasty temper/nature* hot-headed, quick-tempered, irascible, irritable, impatient, fiery, excitable, volatile, choleric, snappish, snappy, brusque.
Antonyms: SLOW; LEISURELY; CAUTIOUS.

hat *noun* cap, bonnet, beret, tam-o'-shanter, hard hat, bowler, top hat, deerstalker, Homburg, Stetson, straw hat, boater, panama, toque, cloche, pillbox, helmet, turban, fez, skullcap, yarmulke.

hatch *verb* **1** *hatch eggs* incubate, brood, sit on, cover. **2** *hatch chicks* bring forth. **3** *hatch a scheme* devise, concoct, contrive, plan, scheme, design, invent, formulate, originate, conceive, dream up, think up; *inf.* cook up.

hatchet *noun* ax, tomahawk.

hate *verb* **1** *hate his rival/job* loathe, detest, abhor, dislike, abominate, despise, have an aversion to, feel hostile toward, be unable to abide/bear/stand, view with dislike, be sick of, be tired of, shudder at the thought of, be repelled by, recoil from. **2** *I hate to upset her* be reluctant, be loath, be unwilling, feel disinclined, be sorry, dislike, not have the heart.
Antonyms: LOVE; LIKE; RELISH.

hate *noun. See* HATRED.

hateful *adjective* loathsome, detestable, abhorrent, abominable, despicable, odious, revolting, repugnant, repellent, disgusting, obnoxious, offensive, insufferable, horrible, unpleasant, nasty, disagreeable, foul, vile, heinous.
Antonyms: ADMIRABLE; LOVABLE.

hatred *noun* hate, loathing, detestation, abhorrence, dislike, abomination, aversion, hostility, ill will, enmity, animosity, antagonism, antipathy, revulsion, repugnance, odium, rancor.

haughty *adjective she is so haughty | had a haughty*

expression proud, arrogant, conceited, self-important, egotistical, vain, swellheaded, overweening, overbearing, presumptuous, supercilious, condescending, lofty, patronizing, snobbish, scornful, imperious, lordly, high-handed; *inf.* on one's high horse, snooty, high and mighty, stuck-up, hoity-toity, uppity.
Antonyms: MODEST; HUMBLE.

haul *verb* **1** *haul it out of the water* drag, draw, pull, tug, heave, trail, lug, tow, take in tow. **2** *hauling lumber to Albany* transport, convey, move, cart, carry, convoy, ship.

haunt *verb* **1** *ghosts haunting the castle* walk, roam, visit; *inf.* spook. **2** *haunt bars* frequent, be a regular client of, visit regularly, spend all one's time in; *inf.* hang out in, hang around/about. **3** *thoughts of guilt haunted him* obsess, prey on the mind of, prey on, torment, plague, beset, harry, disturb, trouble, worry, oppress, burden, weigh on, recur to, come back to, stay with.

haunt *noun the local bar was one of his haunts* stamping ground, frequented place, favorite spot, resort, rendezvous, meeting place; *inf.* hangout.

haunting *adjective* **1** *haunting music* evocative, poignant, atmospheric, wistful, disturbing, nostalgic. **2** *haunting memories* persistent, recurring, recurrent, indelible, unforgettable.

have *verb* **1** *we have two cars* own, possess, keep, keep for one's use, use, hold, retain, occupy. **2** *we had three cups of tea* get, be given, receive, accept, obtain, acquire, procure, secure, gain. **3** *the apartment has five rooms* contain, include, comprise, embrace, embody, incorporate. **4** *she had a lot of trouble with him* experience, undergo, go through, encounter, meet, find, be subjected to, submit to, suffer from, endure, tolerate, put up with. **5** *have a good time* experience, enjoy. **6** *have doubts/misgivings* feel, entertain, have/keep/bear in mind, harbor, foster, nurse, cherish. **7** *have the impudence to answer back* show, display, exhibit, demonstrate, manifest, express. **8** *they had her do all their work* make, cause to, require to, force to, coerce to, induce to, prevail upon to, talk into, persuade to. **9** *I'll have the technician repair the telephone* ask to, request that, bid to, tell to, order to, command to, direct to, enjoin to. **10** *she won't have such behavior* permit, allow, put up with, tolerate, stand, brook, support, endure, abide. **11** *she had a baby daughter* give birth to, bear, deliver, be delivered of, bring into the world, bring forth, beget. **12** *they certainly had you* fool, trick, take in, dupe, outwit, deceive, cheat, swindle. **13** *he boasted that he had had all the women there* have sexual intercourse with, have sex with, make love to/with, copulate with; *inf.* bed, lay. **have had it 1** *he won't win now, he's had it* have no chance, have no chance of success, have no hope, be finished, be out, be defeated, have lost. **2** *you've had it when your mother finds you* be about to be punished, be going to be chastised, be in for a scolding; *inf.* be in for it. **have on 1** *she had on a blue dress* wear, be wearing, be dressed in, be clothed in. **2** *I have something on today* have planned, have arranged, be committed to, have on the agenda. **3** *have someone on* tease, joke with, play a joke on, trick, play a trick on, pull someone's leg; *inf.* kid. **4** *the police have something on him* have information about, have evidence against, know something bad/incriminating about. **have to** *have to clean the floor* must, have got to, be bound to, be obliged to, be under an obligation to, be forced to, be compelled to.

haven *noun* **1** *ships entering a haven* harbor, port, anchorage, moorage, dock, cove, bay. **2** *refugees seeking a safe haven* refuge, shelter, sanctuary, asylum, retreat, sanctum, sanctum sanctorum, covert.

haversack *noun* knapsack, rucksack, backpack, satchel, kit bag.

havoc *noun* **1** *forest fires causing/wreaking havoc* devastation, destruction, damage, ruination, ruin, rack and ruin, waste, wreckage, desolation, extermination, disaster, catastrophe, cataclysm. **2** *the havoc in the room after the party* chaos, disorder, confusion, disruption, disorganization, mayhem; *inf.* shambles.

hawk *verb* peddle, sell, market, vend, tout.

hay *noun* straw, pasturage, fodder, forage, feed. **make hay while the sun shines** make the most of an opportunity, capitalize on an advantageous situation, exploit an opportune occasion, strike while the iron is hot, *carpe diem*, seize the day.

haywire *adjective* **go haywire** go wrong, go out of control, become disorganized, cease to function properly.

hazard *noun* danger, peril, risk, jeopardy, threat, menace.

hazard *verb* **1** *hazard a guess* venture, put forward, proffer, offer, submit, advance, volunteer. **2** *hazard his life* risk, put at risk, endanger, expose to danger, imperil, put in jeopardy, jeopardize.

hazardous *adjective* **1** *a hazardous journey* dangerous, danger-filled, risky, perilous, fraught with danger/risk/peril, precarious, unsafe, insecure, threatening, menacing; *inf.* dicey, hairy. **2** *a hazardous venture* open to chance, chancy, risky, uncertain, unpredictable, precarious, speculative.

Antonyms: SAFE; SURE.

haze *noun* **1** *a haze covered the town* mist, film of mist, mistiness, fog, cloud, cloudiness, smog, vapor. **2** *her mind is in a state of haze* vagueness, confusion, befuddlement, bewilderment, obscurity, dimness, indistinctness.

hazy *adjective* **1** *a hazy day* misty, foggy, cloudy, smoggy, overcast. **2** *hazy memories* vague, indefinite, blurred, fuzzy, faint, confused, muddled, unclear, obscure, dim, indistinct, ill-defined.

Antonyms: CLEAR; DISTINCT.

head *noun* **1** *hurt his head* skull, cranium; *inf.* pate, nut, noodle, noggin, bean. **2** *he has a good head* | *use your head* mind, intellect, intelligence, brain, brains, mentality, wit, wits, wisdom, sense, reasoning, rationality, understanding; *inf.* gray matter. **3** *a head for business* mind, brain, aptitude, ability, capacity, flair, talent, faculty. **4** *the head of the organization/team/school/nation* leader, chief, commander, director, chairman, chair, chairperson, manager, superintendent, controller, administrator, supervisor, captain, principal, governor, president, premier, prime minister. **5** *(at) the head of the firm* top, command, control, controls, charge, leadership, directorship. **6** *at the head of the hill* top, summit, peak, crest, crown, tip, brow, apex, vertex. **7** *at the head of the line* front, fore, forefront, van, vanguard. **8** *matters coming to a head* climax, culmination, crisis, critical point, turning point, crossroads. **9** *at the head of the stream* origin, source, fountainhead, fount, wellhead, wellspring, headwater. **10** *a head on the beer* froth, foam, lather, suds. **11** *standing on the head looking out to sea* headland, promontory, point, cape. **12** *the material is listed under various heads* heading, category, class, classification. See HEADING 1. **13** *rushed to the head to be sick* toilet, lavatory, bathroom; latrine; *inf.* john, can. **go to one's head 1** *the wine has gone to my head* make someone intoxicated, intoxicate someone, make someone dizzy, make someone's head spin; *inf.* make someone woozy. **2** *their praise went to her head* make someone conceited/arrogant/boastful, puff someone up. **head first 1** *fall head first down the stairs* on one's head, head foremost, headlong, head on, diving, plunging. **2** *rush into things head first* without thinking, rashly, recklessly, precipitately, carelessly, heedlessly. See HEADLONG 2. **head over heels** *head over heels in love* utterly, completely, thoroughly, fully, wholeheartedly, intensely, passionately, fervently, fervidly, uncontrollably; *inf.* madly. **keep one's head** *keep one's head in a crisis* keep calm, keep cool, remain unruffled, maintain one's equilibrium, keep control of oneself; *inf.* keep one's cool. **lose one's head** panic, lose control of oneself, lose control of the situation, get flustered/confused, get angry, get excited, get hysterical; *inf.* lose one's cool, blow one's top, freak out, fly off the handle.

head *adjective* the head gardener/teacher/priest chief, leading, main, principal, first, prime, premier, foremost, topmost, supreme, cardinal.

head *verb* **1** *head the expedition* be at the head/front of, lead, be the leader of, lead the way for, go/be first for/in, precede. **2** *head the firm* be at the head of, be in charge of, be in command of, command, be in control of, control, run, lead, be the leader of, manage, direct, administer, supervise, rule, govern, guide. **3** *a tower headed by a spire* crown, top, surmount, cap, tip. **4** *head for town* make for, go to, go in the direction of, direct one's steps toward, point oneself toward, aim for, set out for, start out for, go/turn toward, steer toward, make a beeline for. **head off 1** *head off the charging bull* divert, deflect, turn aside, intercept, stop in midcourse, block off, cut off. **2** *head off disaster* ward off, fend off, forestall, avert, prevent, parry, check, stop.

headache *noun* **1** *she is susceptible to headaches* sore head, pain in the head, migraine. **2** *her nephew is nothing but a headache to her* nuisance, bother, pest, trouble, vexation, bane, bugbear, worry, inconvenience; *inf.* pain, pain in the neck.

heading *noun* **1** *materials listed under various headings* head, category, class, classification, subject, topic, division, section, branch, department. **2** *put the headings on the illustrations/articles* title, caption, headline, name, rubric, banner headline.

headlong *adverb* **1** *fall headlong into the bushes* head first, on one's head, head foremost, head on, diving, plunging. **2** *rush headlong into a decision* hastily, in haste, hurriedly, impetuously, impulsively, unrestrainedly, impatiently, without thinking, rashly, recklessly, wildly, prematurely, precipitately, carelessly, heedlessly.

head-on *adjective* **1** *a head-on collision* direct, front-to-front. **2** *a head-on confrontation* direct, directly opposing/opposite, straight-on, face-to-face; *inf.* eyeball-to-eyeball, full-frontal.

headquarters *plural noun* HQ, main office, head office, main branch, center of operations, home base, command post.

headstone *noun* gravestone, tombstone, stone, monument, memorial.

headstrong *adjective* stubborn, stubborn as a mule, obstinate, obdurate, mulish, inflexible, intransigent, intractable, pigheaded, unyielding, self-willed, refractory, recalcitrant, ungovernable, wayward, contrary, willful, perverse, unruly, wild, reckless, heedless, rash.

headway *noun* **make headway** make progress, make way, progress, advance, get ahead, get on, proceed, develop, gain ground, go forward by leaps and bounds, make strides.

heady *adjective* **1** *a heady drink* intoxicating, inebriating, inebriant, potent, strong. **2** *she was heady with success* exhilarated, excited, overjoyed, thrilled, overwhelmed, euphoric, ecstatic; *inf.* in seventh heaven, on cloud nine. **3** *the heady days of youth* exhilarating, exciting, stimulating, rousing, arousing, invigorating, thrilling, galvanizing, electrifying. **4** *a heady person/action* impetuous, rash, reckless, wild, foolhardy, thoughtless, heedless, imprudent, incautious, impulsive, precipitate.

heal *verb* **1** *heal the wound* cure, make well, make better, remedy, treat, mend, restore, regenerate. **2** *the skin began to heal* get better, get well, be cured, mend, be on the mend, be restored, improve, show improvement. **3** *heal the breach* conciliate, reconcile, patch up, settle, set right, put right, make good, harmonize. **4** *heal the sorrow* alleviate, appease, mitigate, ameliorate, assuage, allay, palliate, soften.

health *noun* **1** *full of health* healthiness, fitness, well-being, good condition, good trim, good shape, fine fettle, soundness, robustness, strength, vigor, salubrity. **2** *his health is not good* state of health, constitution, physical state, physical health, physical shape, condition, form, tone.

healthy *adjective* **1** *a healthy young man* in good health, fit, physically fit, in good condition/trim/shape, in fine fettle, in fine/top form, robust, strong, vigorous, hardy, flourishing, hale and hearty, hale, hearty, bursting with health; *inf.* in the pink. **2** *a healthy climate* health-giving, salubrious, invigorating, bracing, stimulating, refreshing, tonic. **3** *a healthy diet* health-giving, healthful, good for one, nutritious, nourishing, wholesome, beneficial.
Antonyms: UNHEALTHY; ILL.

heap *noun* *a heap of rubbish* pile, stack, mass, mound, mountain, stockpile, accumulation, collection, lot, assemblage, aggregation, agglomeration, conglomeration, hoard, store, stock, supply. **heaps, a heap 1** *a heap of trouble* a lot, lots, a great deal, an abundance, plenty, a superabundance; *inf.* loads, tons. **2** *lost a heap of money | earn heaps of money* a lot, lots, a great deal, an abundance, considerable quantities, huge quantities, plenty, a mint; *inf.* oodles, loads, tons.

heap *verb* **heap on** *heap praise/insults on him* bestow on, confer on, shower on, give to, grant to, assign to, load on. **heap up** *heap up leaves/money* pile up, stack, stack up, amass, stockpile, mound, mound up, accumulate, collect, assemble, hoard, store, store up, stock up, set aside, lay by.

hear *verb* **1** *he does not hear* have the sense of hearing, perceive sound, have the faculty of hearing, have the auditory faculty. **2** *I didn't hear what he said* catch, take in, overhear; *inf.* get. **3** *we heard that he was dead | how did you hear of his appointment?* be informed, be told, be made aware, receive information, find out, discover, learn, gather, pick up, be given to understand, hear tell, get wind. **4** *the judge heard the case* try, judge, pass judgment on, adjudicate, examine, investigate, inquire into, consider.

hearing *noun* **1** *his hearing is poor* power of hearing, faculty/sense of hearing, ability to hear, aural faculty, auditory perception. **2** *give someone a hearing* chance to speak, opportunity to express one's point of view, opportunity to be heard, chance to put one's side of the story, interview, audience. **3** *they were within hearing* earshot, hearing distance/range, reach, carrying range, range of one's voice, auditory range. **4** *present at the hearing* inquiry, trial, inquest, investigation, inquisition, review, examination.

hearsay *noun according to (the) hearsay, he is a thief* rumor, gossip, idle talk, mere talk, talk of the town, word of mouth; *inf.* buzz, grapevine.

heart *noun* **1** *his heart isn't right* cardiac organ, circulatory organ; *inf.* ticker. **2** *love her with all his heart* passion, love, affection, emotions, feelings. **3** *he has no heart* tender feelings, tenderness, warm emotions, compassion, sympathy, empathy, responsiveness to others, humanity, fellow feeling, concern for others, pathos, goodwill, humanitarianism, benevolence, kindness, kindliness, brotherly love. **4** *I don't have the heart to tell him the truth | heroes with great heart* courage, bravery, valor, intrepidity, fearlessness, heroism, stoutheartedness, boldness, pluck, mettle, backbone, nerve, fortitude, purpose, resolution, determination; *inf.* guts, spunk, gumption. **5** *the heart of the matter/universe* center, central part, core, nucleus, middle, kernel, essential part, hub, quintessence, essence, crux, marrow, pith, substance, sum and substance. **after one's own heart** *a person after my own heart* of the kind that one likes, to one's liking, attractive to one, favored by one, desirable. **at heart** *at heart he is a kind man* basically, fundamentally, in essence, essentially, intrinsically, innately, in reality, really, in fact, actually, truly, in truth. **by heart** *learn by heart* by rote, word for word, pat, by memory. **do one's heart good** do someone good, give someone pleasure, please, gladden, make happy, cheer, delight, gratify, satisfy. **eat one's heart out** *jilted lovers eating their hearts out* sorrow, grieve, mourn, ache, suffer, agonize, pine, mope, fret, regret, brood, repine, be filled with envy. **from the bottom of one's heart** *apologize from the bottom of my heart* with all one's heart, profoundly, deeply, sincerely, devoutly, heartily, fervently, passionately. **have a change of heart** *they had a change of heart about moving* change one's mind, change one's tune, rethink. **have a heart** *have a heart and let them off* be kind, be merciful, be lenient, be compassionate, be sympathetic, be considerate. **have one's heart set on** *the little girl had her heart set on the doll* long for, yearn for, desire, be desirous of, wish for, want badly, crave. **heart and soul** *devote oneself heart and soul to the project* enthusiastically, eagerly, zealously, wholeheartedly, gladly, with open arms, thoroughly, completely, entirely, absolutely. **lose one's heart to** *she lost her heart to a soldier* fall in love with, fall for, take a liking/fancy to, become

infatuated with. **take heart** *take heart from the fact that you did better than many others* cheer up, brighten up, be heartened, be encouraged, be comforted, perk up, revive, derive comfort/satisfaction from; *inf.* buck up. **with one's heart in one's mouth** *she looked into the dark space with her heart in her mouth* in fear, fearfully, with apprehension, apprehensively, with fear and trembling, with alarm, with trepidation, with bated breath.

heartache *noun* sorrow, grief, sadness, anguish, pain, hurt, agony, suffering, misery, wretchedness, despair, desolation, despondency, woe; *lit.* dolor.

heartbreaking *adjective* *heartbreaking cries/tale* heart-rending, sad, pitiful, poignant, tragic, painful, agonizing, distressing, affecting, grievous, bitter, cruel, harsh, harrowing, tear-jerking, excruciating.

heartbroken *adjective* brokenhearted, heartsick, miserable, sorrowful, sad, anguished, suffering, grieving, grieved, dejected, dispirited, disheartened, downcast, disconsolate, crestfallen, disappointed, crushed, desolate, despondent, in low spirits.

heartburn *noun* dyspepsia, indigestion; *Med.* pyrosis.

hearten *verb* cheer, cheer up, raise the spirits of, invigorate, revitalize, energize, animate, revivify, exhilarate, uplift, elate, comfort, encourage, buoy up, pep up; *inf.* buck up, give a shot in the arm to.
Antonyms: DISCOURAGE; DEPRESS; DISHEARTEN.

heartfelt *adjective* *sends his heartfelt sympathy* deeply felt, deep, profound, wholehearted, sincere, honest, devout, genuine, unfeigned, earnest, ardent, fervent, passionate, kindly, warm, cordial, enthusiastic, eager.

heartily *adverb* **1** *thanked/welcomed them heartily* warmly, cordially, feelingly, from the bottom of one's heart, deeply, profoundly, wholeheartedly, sincerely, genuinely, unfeignedly. **2** *eat heartily* with eagerness, eagerly, with enthusiasm, enthusiastically, zealously, earnestly, vigorously, energetically, resolutely. **3** *dislike him heartily | am heartily sick of this weather* very much, completely, totally, absolutely, thoroughly.

heartless *adjective* unfeeling, unsympathetic, uncompassionate, unkind, uncaring, unmoved, untouched, cold, cold-hearted, cold-blooded, hard-hearted, cruel, harsh, stern, hard, brutal, merciless, pitiless, ruthless.
Antonyms: COMPASSIONATE; KIND; MERCIFUL.

heart-rending *adjective* heartbreaking, sad, pitiful, painful, distressing, affecting, harrowing, tear-jerking. *See* HEARTBREAKING.

heartsick *adjective* sick at heart, heavy-hearted, dejected, downcast, dispirited, depressed, despondent, disappointed; *lit.* heartsore.

heart-to-heart *adjective* *a-heart-to-heart talk* intimate, personal, unreserved, candid, frank, open.

heart-to-heart *noun have a heart-to-heart* tête-à-tête, intimate talk, cozy chat.

heartwarming *adjective* **1** *a heartwarming story* touching, moving, affecting, warming, cheering, cheerful, gladdening, encouraging, uplifting. **2** *a heartwarming job* gratifying, satisfying, rewarding, pleasing.

hearty *adjective* **1** *a hearty welcome* enthusiastic, eager, warmhearted, warm, cordial, jovial, friendly, affable, unreserved, uninhibited, ebullient, exuberant, effusive. **2** *a hearty dislike* wholehearted, complete, total, absolute, thorough, genuine, unfeigned. **3** *a hearty young/old man* strong, robust, hardy, vigorous, stalwart, healthy, sound, sturdy, active, energetic, hale, hale and hearty. **4** *a hearty meal* substantial, solid, abundant, ample, sizable, filling, nutritious, nourishing.
Antonyms: COOL; SLIGHT; WEAK.

heat *noun* **1** *the heat melted the ice* hotness, warmth, warmness, torridness. **2** *the heat of summer* hotness, warmth, sultriness, torridness, torridity, swelter, heatwave, hot spell; *inf.* dog days. **3** *the heat of the child frightened her* high temperature, fever, feverishness, febrility. **4** *got caught up in the heat of his speech* warmth, passion, vehemence, intensity, ardor, fervor, fervency, fervidness, zeal, eagerness, enthusiasm, animation, earnestness, excitement, agitation.
Antonyms: COLD; APATHY.

heat *verb* **heat up 1** *heat up the milk* warm, warm up, make hot, make warm, reheat, cook. **2** *the day heated up* grow hot, grow warm, become hotter/warmer, get hotter/warmer. **3** *the argument heated up* grow passionate/vehement/fierce/angry. *See* HEATED 1.

heated *adjective* **1** *a heated argument* passionate, vehement, fierce, angry, furious, stormy, tempestuous, frenzied, raging, intense, impassioned, violent. **2** *both parties were rather heated* excited, roused, animated, inflamed, angry, furious, enraged.

heathen *noun* **1** *missionaries converting heathens* unbeliever, infidel, pagan, idolater/idolatress, atheist, disbeliever, agnostic, skeptic, heretic. **2** *lands invaded by heathens* barbarian, savage.

heathen *adjective* **1** *converting a heathen tribe* heathenish, infidel, pagan, godless, irreligious, idolatrous, atheistic, agnostic, heretical. **2** *invaded by heathen tribes* barbarian, barbarous, savage, uncivilized, brutish.

heave *verb* **1** *heaving heavy weights* lift, haul, pull, tug, raise, hoist, upheave. **2** *heave the hammer in the games* throw, cast, toss, fling, hurl, let fly, pitch, send; *inf.* sling, chuck. **3** *heave a sigh* give, utter, let out, pant, gasp, blow, puff, breathe, sigh, sob. **4** *people heaving as the ship sailed* vomit, be sick, spew, retch, gag; *inf.* throw up.

heaven *noun* **1** *departed souls abiding in heaven* Kingdom of God, paradise, next life, life to come, next world, the hereafter, Zion, nirvana, Valhalla, Elysium, Elysian Fields, empyrean, happy hunting ground. **2** *she was in heaven when she heard the news* ecstasy, bliss, sheer bliss, rapture, supreme happiness, supreme joy, perfect contentment, seventh heaven, paradise, Eden, Utopia, dreamland. **3** *the heavens opened* sky, skies, firmament, ether, empyrean, aerosphere, vault of heaven; *inf.* (wild) blue yonder.

heavenly *adjective* **1** *heavenly concerns* cosmic, extraterrestrial, unearthly, extramundane, not of this world, otherworldly, celestial, paradisiacal, empyrean, empyreal, Elysian. **2** *heavenly beings* celestial, divine, angelic, seraphic, cherubic, blessed, blest, beatific, beatified, holy, godlike, immortal, superhuman, paradisiacal. **3** *a heavenly party* delightful, pleasurable, enjoyable, marvelous, gratifying, wonderful, blissful, rapturous, sublime; *inf.* glorious, divine. **4** *a heavenly dress* beautiful, exquisite, perfect, superb, ravishing, alluring, enchanting, entrancing, ideal; *inf.* divine.
Antonyms: HELLISH; DREADFUL; UGLY.

heavily *adverb* **1** *walking heavily* with difficulty, slowly, laboriously, painfully, awkwardly, clumsily, ponderously. **2** *heavily defeated* utterly, completely, thoroughly, absolutely, decisively, roundly, soundly. **3** *drink heavily* excessively, to too great an extent, to a great extent, too much, very much, a great deal, copiously. **4** *ground heavily packed* compactly, densely, closely, hard, thick, thickly.

heavy *adjective* **1** *a heavy log/load* weighty, bulky, hefty, big, large, substantial, massive, enormous, mighty, colossal, ponderous, unwieldy, cumbersome, burdensome, awkward, unmanageable. **2** *a heavy responsibility* onerous, burdensome, difficult, oppressive, unbearable, intolerable. **3** *a heavy task* hard, difficult, arduous, laborious, demanding, exacting, irksome, troublesome, trying. **4** *a heavy blow* hard, forceful, strong, severe, grievous, harsh, intense, sharp, stinging, penetrating, overwhelming. **5** *a heavy man* large, bulky, hulking, stout, overweight, fat, obese, corpulent, portly, tubby, paunchy, lumbering. **6** *a heavy mist* dense, thick, solid. **7** *heavy ground* difficult, muddy, sticky, considerable, boggy, clayey, clogged. **8** *heavy traffic/losses/crop* very much/great, large, considerable, considerable quantities of, abundant, copious, profuse, superabundant, huge numbers of. **9** *heavy fighting* severe, intense, serious, grave. **10** *heavy newspaper headlines* serious, grave, deep, somber, profound. **11** *heavy reading* difficult, dull, tedious, boring, uninteresting, dry, wearisome, dry as dust. **12** *feeling heavy after dinner* sleepy, drowsy, sluggish, inactive, indolent, inept, idle, apathetic, listless, torpid. **13** *heavy of heart* sad, sorrowful, downcast, dejected, disconsolate, disheartened, despondent,

downhearted, depressed, crestfallen, disappointed, grieving, gloomy, melancholy. **14** *heavy with child* burdened, encumbered, weighted down, laden, loaded, oppressed. **15** *heavy seas/waves* rough, wild, stormy, tempestuous, turbulent, squally, boisterous, violent. **16** *heavy day/skies* cloudy, overcast, gray, dark, dull, gloomy, dreary, leaden. **17** *heavy pastries* filling, indigestible, dense; sickening. **heavy on (the)** *heavy on the decorations/butter* using a lot of, using too much, overusing, extravagant with, lavish with.
Antonyms: LIGHT; SLIGHT; HAPPY.

---

heavy
burdensome, cumbersome, massive, ponderous, weighty

Trying to move a refrigerator out of a third-floor apartment is difficult because it is **cumbersome**, which means that it is so heavy and bulky that it becomes unwieldy or awkward to handle. Cartons filled with books, on the other hand, are merely **heavy**, which implies greater density and compactness than the average load. A huge oak dining table might be described as **massive**, which stresses largeness and solidity rather than weight, while something that is **ponderous** is too large or too *massive* to move, or to be moved quickly (*a ponderous printing press*). Most of these terms can be used figuratively as well. *Heavy*, for example, connotes a pressing down on the mind, spirits, or senses (*heavy with fatigue; a heavy heart*) and *ponderous* implies a dull and labored quality (*a novel too ponderous to read*). **Burdensome**, which refers to something that is not only *heavy* but must be carried or supported, is even more likely to be used in an abstract way to describe something that is difficult but can, with effort, be managed (*a burdensome task*). Both a package and a problem may be described as **weighty**, meaning actually (as opposed to relatively) heavy; but it is more commonly used to mean very important or momentous (*weighty matters to discuss*).

---

heavy-handed *adjective* **1** *heavy-handed and always breaking things* clumsy, awkward, maladroit, bungling, blundering, unhandy, inept, unskillful, inexpert, graceless, ungraceful, like a bull in a china shop; *inf.* ham-handed, ham-fisted. **2** *too heavy-handed to deal with the bereaved* insensitive, tactless, thoughtless, inept. **3** *a heavy-handed father* harsh, hard, stern, severe, oppressive, domineering, overbearing, tyrannical, despotic, autocratic, ruthless, merciless.

heckle *verb* shout down, shout at, interrupt, disrupt, jeer, taunt, badger, bait, harass, give trouble to, pester; *inf.* give someone a hard time.

hectic *adjective a hectic day/life* very busy, very active, frantic, frenetic, frenzied, bustling, flus-

tering, flurried, fast and furious, turbulent, tumultuous, confused, exciting, excited, wild.
Antonyms: QUIET; CALM; LEISURELY.

hedge *noun* **1** *planted a hedge* row of bushes/shrubs, hedgerow; natural fence, barrier, screen, protection, windbreak. **2** *a hedge against inflation* safeguard, guard, protection, shield, cover, insurance.

hedge *verb* **1** *she hedged when questioned* equivocate, prevaricate, be vague/ambivalent, be noncommittal, dodge the question/issue, sidestep the issue, hem and haw, beat around/about the bush, pussyfoot around, temporize, quibble; *inf.* duck the question. **2** *hedge yourself against inflation* safeguard, guard, protect, cover, shield, insure. **hedge in 1** *the trees hedge in the garden* surround, enclose, encircle, circle, border, edge, skirt. **2** *hedged in by petty restrictions* hem in, confine, restrict, limit, hinder, obstruct, impede.

heed *noun pay no heed* heedfulness, attention, attentiveness, notice, note, regard, mindfulness, mind, respect, consideration, thought, care, caution, watchfulness, wariness, chariness.

heed *verb heed what they say* pay heed to, be heedful of, pay attention to, attend to, take notice of, take note of, notice, note, pay regard to, bear in mind, be mindful of, mind, mark, consider, take into account/consideration, be guided by, follow, obey, adhere to, observe, take to heart, be on guard for, be alert to, be cautious of, watch out for.

heedful *adjective* attentive, careful, mindful, cautious, prudent, circumspect, wary, chary, observant, watchful, vigilant, alert, on guard, on the alert, on one's toes, on the qui vive.

heedless *adjective* unheeding, inattentive, careless, incautious, unmindful, disregardful, regardless, unnoticing, unthinking, thoughtless, improvident, unwary, oblivious, unobservant, unwatchful, unvigilant, negligent, neglectful, rash, reckless, foolhardy, precipitate.
Antonyms: HEEDFUL; ATTENTIVE; MINDFUL.

heel *noun* **1** *the heel of a shoe* heelpiece, wedge, stiletto, stiletto heel, platform heel. **2** *the heel of the loaf* crust, end, remnant, remainder, tail-end, stump, butt, rump. **3** *he's an utter heel* scoundrel, cad, blackguard; *inf.* rat, swine, bounder. **Achilles' heel** weak spot/point, weakness, vulnerable spot, failing, shortcoming. **down at (the) heel(s)** shabby, shabbily dressed, poorly dressed, out at the elbows, seedy, run-down, slovenly, slipshod. **take to one's heels** run away, run off, take flight, flee, escape; *inf.* skedaddle, hightail it, hotfoot it, split, vamoose.

heel *verb ships heeling* cant, tilt, list, tip, lean, lean over, keel over, incline, careen.

heft *noun a thin boy self-conscious about his lack of heft* heaviness, weight, mass; *inf.* meat.

heft *verb heft the load* lift, lift up, raise, raise up, hoist, hike up, heave, throw up, boost, boost up.

hefty *adjective* **1** *hefty young man* heavy, bulky, hulking, big, large, stout, massive, huge, muscular, brawny, strapping, solidly built, powerfully built, sturdy, rugged, stalwart, beefy. **2** *a hefty blow* hard, forceful, heavy, powerful, vigorous, mighty. **3** *a hefty load* heavy, weighty, big, large, massive, tremendous, immense, bulky, awkward, unwieldy, cumbersome, ponderous. **4** *a hefty price/bill* substantial, sizable, expensive, huge, colossal, overpriced.
Antonyms: SLIGHT; LIGHT; SMALL.

height *noun* **1** *measure the height* highness, altitude, loftiness, elevation, distance/extent upward. **2** *six feet in height* tallness, highness, stature. **3** *on the height overlooking the valley* top, mountaintop, hilltop, summit, crest, crown, pinnacle, peak, apex, vertex, apogee. **4** *at the height of his powers* culmination, crowning point, high point, peak, zenith, climax, consummation, perfection, apex. **5** *the height of fashion/rudeness* utmost degree, uttermost, ultimate, acme, *ne plus ultra*, very limit, limit, extremity, maximum, ceiling.

heighten *verb* **1** *heighten the ceiling* make higher, raise, lift, elevate. **2** *heighten their status* magnify, ennoble, exalt, enhance. **3** *heighten the tension* make greater, intensify, raise, increase, add to, augment, build up, boost, strengthen, amplify, magnify, aggravate, enhance, improve.

heights *plural noun afraid of heights* | *the heights above the town* high ground, high places, rising ground, hill, mountain, cliff, precipice, summit. *See* HEIGHT 3.

heinous *adjective heinous crimes/criminal* atrocious, abominable, abhorrent, odious, detestable, loathsome, hateful, execrable, wicked, monstrous, horrible, ghastly, shocking, flagrant, contemptible, reprehensible, despicable.

heir, heiress *noun* beneficiary, legatee, inheritor, inheritress, inheritrix, successor, next in line, scion.

helix *noun* spiral, screw, corkscrew, whorl, twist, coil, loop, volute, curl, curlicue.

hell *noun* **1** *wicked spirits in hell* infernal regions, inferno, hellfire, eternal fire, fire and brimstone, nether world, lower world, abode of evil spirits, abode of the damned, perdition, abyss, bottomless pit, Hades. **2** *it was hell in the battle* purgatory, torment, torture, misery, suffering, affliction, anguish, agony, ordeal, wretchedness, nightmare, woe, tribulation, trials and tribulations. **3** *get hell from the teacher* upbraiding, scolding, castigation, vituperation, reprimand, censure, criticism, disapprobation; *inf.* what for. **hell for leather** as fast/quickly/rapidly/speedily/swiftly as possible, very fast/quickly/rapidly/speedily/swiftly, hurriedly, pell-mell, post-haste, at the double, helter-skelter, headlong, full tilt; *inf.* like a bat out of hell. **raise hell 1** *partygoers raising hell* party, carouse, revel, make a noise, cause a disturbance, cause a commotion, be loud and noisy, raise the roof, raise Cain. **2** *his father raised hell* be very angry, be furious, be enraged, protest, expostulate, complain, object, remonstrate, raise the roof, raise Cain.

hellish *adjective* **1** *hellish spirits* diabolical, demonic, demoniac, demoniacal, devilish, fiendish, satanic, infernal. **2** *a hellish slavemaster* brutal, brutish, barbarous, barbaric, savage, murderous, bloodthirsty, cruel, wicked, inhuman, ferocious, vicious, ruthless, relentless, detestable, abominable, accursed, execrable, nefarious. **3** *a hellish day* unpleasant, nasty, disagreeable; *inf.* horrible, horrid, awful.

hellish *adverb hellish cold/expensive* very, to a great extent, extremely, excessively; *inf.* awfully, jolly, ever so.

helm *noun the captain of the ship at the helm* wheel, tiller, rudder, steering gear, automatic pilot. **at the helm** *the executive at the helm of the firm* in charge, in command, in control, directing, in authority, in the seat of authority, at the wheel, in the driving seat, in the saddle.

help *verb* **1** *help the old lady* assist, aid, lend a helping hand to, lend a hand to, guide, be of service to, be useful to, succor, befriend. **2** *help the charity* assist, aid, contribute to, support, back, promote, boost, give a boost to, uphold. **3** *help the pain/situation* soothe, relieve, ameliorate, alleviate, mitigate, assuage, remedy, cure, heal, improve, ease, facilitate, restore. **4** *can I help you?* serve, be of assistance/help to, give help to. **cannot help** *he cannot help it/snoring* be unable to prevent/stop/cease/halt/avoid/abstain from/refrain from/keep from/forbear from/break the habit of. **help oneself to** *he helped himself to my books* take, appropriate, take possession of, commandeer, steal, make free with; *inf.* pinch, walk off with.

help *noun* **1** *give the old lady some help* assistance, aid, helping hand, service, use, guidance, benefit, advantage, avail, support, backing, succor. **2** *no help for the condition* relief, amelioration, alleviation, mitigation, assuagement, remedy, cure, healing, improvement, ease, restorative, corrective, balm, salve. **3** *ask the help for assistance* helper, assistant, employee, worker, hired help, maid, servant.

helper *noun* **1** *recruited helpers for the rummage sale* assistant, worker, volunteer. **2** *the chief and his helper* assistant, subsidiary, aide, adjutant, deputy, second, second-in-command, auxiliary, right-hand man/woman, henchman, girl/man Friday; *inf.* sidekick. **3** *the author and his helpers* colleague, associate, co-worker, helpmate, partner, ally, collaborator.

helpful *adjective* **1** *a helpful suggestion* useful, of use, of service, beneficial, advantageous, valuable, profitable, instrumental, constructive, practical, productive. **2** *helpful people*

supportive, friendly, kind, obliging, accommodating, cooperative, sympathetic, considerate, caring, neighborly, charitable, benevolent.
Antonyms: USELESS; FUTILE.

helping *noun* *a second helping of potatoes* serving, portion, ration, piece, plateful, bowlful, spoonful.

helpless *adjective* **1** *a helpless invalid* weak, feeble, disabled, impotent, incapable, infirm, debilitated, powerless, dependent, unfit, invalid, bedridden, paralyzed; *inf.* laid-up. **2** *troops left helpless in the wilderness* defenseless, unprotected, vulnerable, exposed, abandoned, forlorn, destitute, desolate.
Antonyms: FIT; CAPABLE.

helpmate *noun* associate, partner, companion, helper.

helter-skelter *adverb* *run helter-skelter* hastily, hurriedly, as fast/quickly/rapidly/speedily as possible, pell-mell, headlong, rashly, recklessly, precipitately, impetuously, impulsively, carelessly, heedlessly, wildly.

hem *noun* *the decorative hem on a skirt* border, edge, edging, trim, trimming, fringe, frill, flounce, valance.

hem *verb* **1** *hem the dress* put a hem on, bind, edge, trim, fringe. **2** *trees hemming the lake* border, edge, skirt, surround, encircle, circle, enclose, encompass. **hem in** *feel hemmed in by trees/restrictions* close in, shut in, hedge in, pen in, keep within bounds, confine, constrain, restrain, restrict, limit, trap.

hence *adverb* *hence my decision not to go* therefore, thus, on that account, because of that, for this reason, consequently, ergo.

henceforth *adverb* *henceforth you will arrive on time* from now on, from this day/time on, from this day forth/forward, hereafter, in future, in the future, hence, henceforward, hereinafter, subsequently, in time to come, after this.

henchman *noun* assistant, aide, supporter, follower, right-hand man/woman, girl/man Friday, adjutant, subordinate, underling, lackey, flunky, toady, hired killer/assassin; *inf.* sidekick, hit man, hatchet man, hood.

henpecked *adjective* *henpecked husbands* bullied, dominated, browbeaten, nagged, subjugated, led by the nose, without a mind of one's own, cringing, cowering, meek, timid, docile; *inf.* under the thumb.

herald *noun* **1** *the Roman emperor awaited news from his herald* messenger, crier, announcer, bearer of tidings, courier. **2** *a herald of things to come* forerunner, precursor, harbinger, usher, sign, omen, portent, indication, augury.

herald *verb* **1** *companies heralding their new products* announce, make public, make known, proclaim, broadcast, publicize, advertise, promote, promulgate, trumpet, beat the drum about. **2** *prototypes heralding major new inventions* usher in, pave the way for, show in, precede, be the forerunner/precursor of, portend, indicate, augur, presage, promise, foreshadow, forebode, foretoken.

Herculean *adjective* *a Herculean task* arduous, laborious, backbreaking, onerous, strenuous, difficult, hard, tough, formidable, huge, massive, uphill.

herd *noun* **1** *a herd of cattle* drove, collection, assemblage, flock, pack, cluster. **2** *flocks tended by a herd* shepherd, cowherd, cattle-man, cowman, herdsman, herder, drover. **3** *a herd of people* crowd, horde, multitude, mob, mass, host, throng, swarm, press. **4** *ignore the tastes of the herd* masses, mob, populace, rabble, riff-raff, hoi polloi, peasants; *inf.* great unwashed.

herd *verb* **1** *herd the sheep into the pens* drive, round up, shepherd, guide, lead, force, urge, goad. **2** *people herding (together) in the hall* assemble, gather, collect, congregate, flock, rally, muster, huddle, get together. **3** *shepherds herding the sheep* look after, take care of, watch, stand guard over, guard, tend.

here *adverb* **1** *bring it here* | *he died here* to/at/in this place/spot/location, hither, to here. **2** *here I must pause* now, at this point, at this point in time, at this time, at this juncture.

hereafter *adverb* *hereafter to be called the author* after this, from now on, hence. See HENCEFORTH.

hereafter *noun* *the hereafter* *believe in the hereafter* life after death, the afterlife, life to come, the afterworld, the next world, the beyond, eternity, immortality, heaven, paradise.

hereditary *adjective* **1** *hereditary characteristics* genetic, congenital, innate, inborn, inherent, inbred, family, transmissible, transferable. **2** *hereditary property* inherited, handed down, obtained by inheritance, bequeathed, willed, transferred, transmitted, family, ancestral.

heredity *noun* *this disorder is the result of heredity* genetics, genetic makeup, genes, congenital characteristics/traits.

heresy *noun* apostasy, dissent, dissension, dissidence, unbelief, skepticism, agnosticism, atheism, nonconformity, unorthodoxy, separatism, sectarianism, freethinking, heterodoxy, revisionism, idolatry, paganism.

heretic *noun* apostate, dissenter, dissident, unbeliever, skeptic, agnostic, atheist, nonconformist, separatist, sectarian, freethinker, renegade, revisionist, idolater, pagan, heathen.

heretical *adjective* *heretical beliefs/views* dissident, skeptical, agnostic, atheistical, nonconformist, separatist, sectarian, freethinking, heterodox, unorthodox, renegade, revisionist, idolatrous, pagan.

heritage *noun* **1** *proud of his country's heritage* history, tradition, background. **2** *proud of his family heritage* ancestry, lineage, descent, extraction, family, dynasty, bloodline, heredity, birth. **3** *receive a heritage from his father* inheritance, legacy, bequest, endowment, estate, patrimony, portion, birthright, lot.

hermit noun recluse, solitary, anchorite/ anchoress, eremite, ascetic.

hermitage noun retreat, refuge, haven, shelter, sanctuary, sanctum, sanctum sanctorum, asylum, hideaway.

hero noun 1 *the hero of the battle/hour* champion, conquering hero, victor, conqueror, brave man, man of courage, great man, man of the hour, celebrity, lion, cavalier, paragon, shining example, exemplar, paladin, knight. 2 *the teacher was the girl's hero* idol, ideal, ideal man/woman, popular figure; *inf.* heartthrob. 3 *the hero of the opera* principal male character/role, lead actor, leading man, male lead, male star/superstar, male protagonist.
Antonyms: COWARD; VILLAIN.

heroic adjective 1 *heroic soldier/deeds* brave, courageous, valiant, valorous, intrepid, fearless, gallant, stouthearted, lionhearted, bold, daring, undaunted, dauntless, doughty, manly, virile, chivalrous. 2 *read tales of heroic characters/myths* classic, classical, Homeric, mythological, legendary, fabulous. 3 *heroic language* epic, epical, Homeric, grandiloquent, high-flown, high-sounding, extravagant, grandiose, bombastic, rhetorical, pretentious, elevated.
Antonyms: COWARDLY; TIMID; SIMPLE.

heroine noun 1 *declared a heroine for saving the child* brave woman, woman of courage, great woman, woman of the hour, celebrity, paragon, shining example. 2 *the heroine of the opera* principal female character/role, lead actress, leading lady, female lead, female star/superstar, prima donna, diva, female protagonist.

heroism noun bravery, courage, courageousness, valor, valiance, intrepidity, fearlessness, gallantry, stouteartedness, lionheartedness, boldness, daring, dauntlessness, doughtiness, manliness, virility, mettle, spirit, fortitude, chivalry.

hero worship noun idolization, putting on a pedestal, adulation, worship, adoration, glorification, exaltation, idealization, admiration, high esteem, veneration.

hesitancy noun 1 *hesitancy when making decisions* uncertainty, unsureness, doubt, doubtfulness, skepticism, irresolution, indecision, indecisiveness, vacillation, oscillation, shilly-shallying, stalling. 2 *show hesitancy about interfering* reluctance, unwillingness, disinclination, scruples, misgivings, qualms.

hesitant adjective 1 *hesitant when making decisions* hesitating, uncertain, unsure, doubtful, dubious, skeptical, irresolute, indecisive, vacillating, wavering, oscillating, shilly-shallying, hanging back, stalling, delaying, disinclined, unwilling, halfhearted, lacking confidence, diffident, timid, shy. 2 *hesitant about giving advice* reluctant, unwilling, disinclined, diffident, having scruples/misgivings/qualms.
Antonyms: DETERMINED; FIRM; confident.

hesitate verb 1 *always hesitate before making a decision* pause, delay, hang back, wait, be uncertain, be unsure, be doubtful, be indecisive, vacillate, oscillate, waver, shilly-shally, dally, stall, temporize; *inf.* dilly-dally. 2 *she hesitates to interfere | just speak up, don't hesitate* be reluctant, be unwilling, be disinclined, shrink (from), hang back (from), think twice (about), balk (at), have misgivings/qualms (about), be diffident (about). 3 *he hesitates a lot when giving a speech* stammer, stumble, stutter, falter, hem and haw, fumble for words, be halting, halt.

hesitation noun 1 *they never acted without some hesitation* pause, delay, hanging back, waiting, waiting period, uncertainty, unsureness, doubt, doubtfulness, dubiousness, skepticism, irresolution, indecisiveness, vacillation, wavering, oscillation, shilly-shallying, stalling, temporizing; *inf.* dilly-dallying. 2 *feel some hesitation about interfering* reluctance, unwillingness, disinclination, scruples, misgivings, qualms. 3 *distracted by his hesitation when speaking* stammering, stumbling, stuttering, faltering, hemming and hawing, fumbling for words.

hew verb *hew a piece of wood into a figure* carve, sculpt, sculpture, shape, fashion, form, model, whittle, chip, chisel, rough-hew. **hew down** *hew down a tree* chop, chop down, hack, hack down, ax, cut/saw down, fell. **hew off** *hew off branches* lop, cut off, chop off, sever, trim, prune.

heyday noun prime, prime of life, bloom, full flowering, flowering, peak, peak of perfection, pinnacle, culmination, crowning point, salad days.

hiatus noun 1 *a hiatus in the manuscript* gap, break, lacuna, blank, discontinuity, interruption. 2 *an anatomical hiatus* opening, aperture, cavity, hole, fissure, cleft, breach. 3 *a hiatus in the program* interval, intermission, pause, lull, rest, break, suspension, abeyance.

hibernate verb sleep, winter, overwinter, winter over, lie dormant, be idle, lie low, stagnate, vegetate; *inf.* hole up.

hidden adjective 1 *hidden treasure* concealed, unrevealed, secret, unseen, out of sight, not visible, not in view, covered, masked, shrouded. 2 *a hidden meaning/motive* secret, concealed, obscure, indistinct, indefinite, unclear, vague, cryptic, mysterious, covert, under wraps, abstruse, arcane, recondite, clandestine, ulterior, unfathomable, inexplicable, occult, mystical.

hide verb 1 *prisoners hiding from the police* go into hiding, conceal oneself, take cover, find a hiding place, lie low, keep out of sight, secrete oneself, go underground, cover one's tracks; *inf.* hole up. 2 *hide the jewels* secrete, conceal, put in a hiding place, store away, stow away, stash, lock up. 3 *clouds hiding the sun* obscure, cloud, darken, block, eclipse, obstruct. 4 *hide one's* *motives* keep secret, conceal, keep dark, withhold, suppress, hush up, mask, veil, shroud, camouflage, disguise; *inf.* keep mum, keep under one's hat.

Antonyms: REVEAL; DISCLOSE.

hide *noun an animal's hide* skin, pelt, coat, fur, fleece.

hideaway *noun* hiding place, den, lair, retreat, shelter, refuge, hermitage, cache; *inf.* hide-out.

hidebound *adjective hidebound officials/ideas* narrow-minded, narrow, intolerant, conventional, fixed in one's views, set in one's opinions/ways, intractable, uncompromising, rigid, prejudiced, bigoted, conservative, ultraconservative, reactionary, orthodox, fundamentalist, straitlaced.

hideous *adjective* 1 *a hideous sight* ugly, unsightly, grotesque, monstrous, repulsive, repellent, revolting, gruesome, disgusting, grim, ghastly, macabre. 2 *a hideous crime* horrible, horrific, horrendous, horrifying, frightful, shocking, dreadful, outrageous, monstrous, appalling, terrible, terrifying, heinous, abominable, foul, vile, odious, loathsome, contemptible, execrable.

Antonyms: BEAUTIFUL; PLEASANT.

hide-out *noun* hiding place, hideaway, retreat, shelter. *See* HIDEAWAY.

hie *verb* hurry, hasten, go quickly, speed, rush, run, dash, scamper, scuttle, dart, tear.

hierarchy *noun* ranking, grading, social order, class system, pecking order.

hieroglyphics *plural noun* code, cipher, cryptogram, cryptograph, shorthand; *inf.* scribble, scrawl.

high *adjective* 1 *a high building* tall, lofty, elevated, soaring, towering, steep. 2 *a high official* high-ranking, leading, top, ruling, powerful, important, principal, chief, main, prominent, eminent, influential, distinguished, notable, exalted, illustrious. 3 *high ideals* high-minded, noble, virtuous, moral, lofty. 4 *a high wind* intense, extreme, strong, forceful, vigorous, powerful, potent, sharp, violent. 5 *high prices* dear, top, excessive, stiff, inflated, exorbitant, extortionate, high-priced, expensive, costly; *inf.* steep. 6 *a high lifestyle* high-living, extravagant, luxurious, lavish, rich, grand, prodigal. 7 *have a high opinion of them* good, favorable, approving, admiring, flattering. 8 *feeling high before the holidays* overexcited, excited, boisterous, in high spirits, high-spirited, ebullient, bouncy, elated, ecstatic, euphoric, exhilarated, joyful, merry, happy, cheerful, jolly; *inf.* high as a kite. 9 *high on drugs* drugged, intoxicated, inebriated, delirious, hallucinating; *inf.* stoned, turned on, tripping, hyped up, freaked out, spaced out. 10 *high voice/notes* high-pitched, acute, high-frequency, soprano, treble, piping, shrill, sharp-toned, piercing, penetrating. **high and dry** *ships/people left high and*

dry stranded, marooned, abandoned, helpless, destitute, bereft. **high and mighty** *high and mighty people looking down on the poor* haughty, arrogant, self-important, proud, conceited, egotistic, overweening, overbearing, snobbish, condescending, disdainful, supercilious, imperious; *inf.* stuck-up, uppity, highfalutin. **in high dudgeon** in indignation, indignant, in anger, angrily, angry, with resentment, resentful, offended, vexed, in a huff; *inf.* peeved.

Antonyms: LOW; LOWLY; DEEP.

high *adverb flying high in the sky* high up, far up, way up, at a great height, at altitude, aloft. **high and low** *look high and low* everywhere, all over, far and near, far and wide, in every nook and cranny, extensively, exhaustively.

high *noun* 1 *profits/temperatures reached a new high* high level, height, record, record level, peak, summit, top, zenith, apex. 2 *he's on a drug high* intoxication, delirium, ecstasy, euphoria; *inf.* trip.

highborn *adjective* noble, of noble birth, wellborn, aristocratic, patrician, blue-blooded.

highbrow *noun* intellectual, scholar, savant, mastermind, genius; *inf.* egghead, brain, bookworm.

highbrow *adjective highbrow person/music/pursuits* intellectual, scholarly, bookish, cultured, cultivated, educated, sophisticated; *inf.* brainy.

high-class *adjective* superior, luxurious, deluxe, select, choice, elite, top-flight, first-rate, elegant, posh, upper-class, upscale, upmarket; *inf.* tip-top, A-1, super, super-duper, classy.

highfalutin *adjective* pompous, pretentious, affected, supercilious, condescending, grandiose, lofty, bombastic; *inf.* swanky.

high-flown *adjective uses very high-flown language* high-sounding, bombastic, grandiloquent, overdone, overdrawn, ornate, exaggerated, elaborate, extravagant, flowery, florid, pretentious, overblown.

high-handed *adjective high-handed person/manner* arbitrary, autocratic, dictatorial, despotic, tyrannical, domineering, oppressive, peremptory, imperious, overbearing, arrogant, haughty, lordly; *inf.* bossy.

highland *noun* plateau, tableland, ridge, heights, hill, hilly country, mountain, mountainous region, uplands.

highlight *noun this is the highlight of the day/show/tour* outstanding feature, main feature, feature, high point, high spot, best part, climax, peak, memorable part, focal point, focus, center of interest, cynosure.

highlight *verb a program highlighting famine* give prominence to, call attention to, bring to the fore, focus attention on, feature, place emphasis on, give emphasis to, emphasize, accentuate, accent, stress, underline, spotlight, bring home, point up.

highly *adverb* 1 *highly entertaining/inflammable* very, very much, to a great extent, greatly, extremely, decidedly, certainly, exceptionally, tremendously, vastly, immensely, eminently, supremely, extraordinarily. **2** *speak highly of* approvingly, favorably, well, warmly, appreciatively, admiringly, with approbation, enthusiastically.

high-minded *adjective high-minded intellectuals/ ideals* noble-minded, moral, virtuous, ethical, upright, righteous, principled, honorable, good, fair, pure, lofty, elevated.

high-powered *adjective high-powered executives* dynamic, aggressive, assertive, energetic, driving, ambitious, effective, enterprising, vigorous, forceful; *inf.* go-getting.

high-pressure *adjective high-pressure salesmen | used high-pressure sales techniques* aggressive, insistent, persistent, intensive, forceful, high-powered, importunate, bludgeoning, coercive, compelling, persuasive, not taking no for an answer; *inf.* pushy.

high-priced *adjective* expensive, costly, exorbitant, extortionate, excessive, stiff; *inf.* pricey, steep.

high-sounding *adjective high-sounding language/ phrases* high-flown, bombastic, grandiloquent, elaborate, pretentious. *See* HIGH-FLOWN.

high-spirited *adjective* spirited, lively, full of life, animated, vibrant, vital, dynamic, active, energetic, full of vim, vigorous, boisterous, bouncy, frolicsome, effervescent, buoyant, cheerful, exuberant, ebullient, exhilarated, vivacious, joyful, full of fun.

high spirits *plural noun* liveliness, animation, vitality, dynamism, boisterousness, bounciness, cheerfulness, exuberance, vivacity, joy, joie de vivre. *See* HIGH-SPIRITED.

high-strung *adjective high-strung artist/racehorse* nervous, nervy, easily upset/agitated, on edge, edgy, excitable, tense, taut, stressed, temperamental, neurotic, irritable, overwrought, restless, wound up.

hijack *verb* commandeer, seize, expropriate, take over, skyjack.

hike *verb hike over the hills* walk, march, tramp, trek, trudge, plod, ramble, wander, backpack; *inf.* hoof it. **hike up 1** *he hiked up his pants/load* hitch up, pull up, jack up, lift, raise. **2** *they've hiked up the prices* raise, increase, add to; *inf.* jack up.

hike *noun go on a hike* walk, march, tramp, trek, ramble, trudge.

hilarious *adjective* **1** *a hilarious play/story* very funny, extremely amusing, humorous, entertaining, comical, uproarious, sidesplitting. **2** *a hilarious party* amusing, entertaining, uproarious, merry, jolly, mirthful, animated, vivacious, sparkling, exuberant, boisterous, noisy, rowdy.

Antonyms: SAD; SERIOUS.

hilarity *noun the joke provoked great hilarity* amusement, comedy, mirth, laughter, merriment, levity, glee, high spirits.

hill *noun* **1** *the hills behind the town* elevation, heights, high land, hillock, hilltop, knoll, hum-

mock, mound, rising ground, tor, mount, ridge. **2** *cars going slowly up the hill* slope, rise, incline, gradient, acclivity. **3** *a hill of garbage* mountain, heap, pile, mound, stack, drift.

hillock *noun* knoll, knob, hummock.

hilt *noun* handle, haft, handgrip, grip, shaft, hold. **to the hilt** *back the leader to the hilt* completely, fully, wholly, entirely, totally, to the maximum extent, all the way.

hind *adjective horse's hind legs* rear, back, hinder, posterior, caudal.

hinder *verb hinder their efforts/progress* hamper, impede, hold back, interfere with, delay, hold up, slow down, retard, obstruct, inhibit, handicap, hamstring, block, interrupt, check, trammel, forestall, curb, balk, thwart, frustrate, foil, baffle, stymie, stop, bring to a halt, arrest, abort, defer, prevent, debar.

Antonyms: AID; FACILITATE; EXPEDITE.

---

hinder
encumber, hamper, impede, obstruct, prevent

If you're about to set off on a cross-country trip by car and wake up to find that a foot of snow has fallen overnight, it would be correct to say that the weather has **hindered** you. But if you're trying to drive through a snowstorm and are forced to creep along at a snail's pace behind a snowplow, it would be correct to say you were **impeded**. To **hinder** is to delay or hold something back, especially something that is under way or is about to start (*she entered college but was hindered by poor study habits*); it connotes a thwarting of progress, either deliberate or accidental. **Impede**, on the other hand, means to slow the progress of someone or something by a deliberate act; it implies that the obstacles are more serious and suggests that movement or progress is so slow that it is painful or frustrating (*the shoes were so tight they impeded his circulation*). Both **hamper** and **encumber** involve hindering by outside forces. To *hamper* is to impede by placing restraints on someone or something so as to make action difficult (*hampered by family responsibilities*), while **encumber** means to hinder by the placing of a burden (*encumbered with several heavy suitcases*). To **obstruct** is to place obstacles in the way, often bringing progress or movement to a complete halt (*obstruct traffic; obstruct justice*). **Prevent** suggests precautionary or restraining measures (*the police prevented him from entering the burning building*) and is also used to describe a nonhuman agency or cause that hinders something (*the snow prevented us from leaving that day*).

hindmost *adjective hindmost car in the train* last, furthest behind, furthest back, rearmost, rear, nearest the rear, endmost, most remote.

hindrance *noun prove a hindrance to their plans* impediment, obstacle, interference, obstruction, handicap, block, restraint, interruption,

check, bar, barrier, drawback, snag, difficulty, stumbling block, encumbrance, curb, stoppage, trammel, deterrent, prevention, debarment.
Antonyms: AID; HELP; ADVANTAGE.

hinge *verb* *hinge on* *plans hinge on finance* depend on, turn on, be contingent on, hang on, pivot on, revolve around, rest on, center on.

hint *noun* 1 *give a hint that he was leaving* inkling, clue, suggestion, innuendo, tip-off, insinuation, implication, indication, mention, allusion, intimation, whisper, a word to the wise. 2 *write gardening hints* tip, pointer, advice, help, suggestion; *inf.* wrinkle. 3 *just a hint of garlic* suspicion, suggestion, trace, touch, dash, soupçon, speck, sprinkling, tinge, whiff, breath, taste, scent.

hint *verb* *he hinted that he was leaving* give a clue, suggest, give someone a tip-off, insinuate, imply, indicate, mention, allude to the fact, make an allusion, intimate, let it be known, signal, make a reference to the fact, refer to the fact.

hippie *noun* beatnik, flower person/child, bohemian; *inf.* longhair, dropout.

hire *verb* appoint, sign on, take on, engage, employ, secure the services of, enlist.

hiss *noun* 1 *the hiss of the snake/kettle* hissing, sibilation, sibilance, buzz, whistle, wheeze. 2 *the hisses of the audience* boo, jeer, shout of derision, catcall, hoot, whistle, clamor, scoffing; *inf.* raspberry.

hiss *verb* 1 *snake/kettle was hissing* sibilate, buzz, whistle, wheeze. 2 *the audience is hissing* boo, jeer, shout one's disapproval, deride, catcall, utter catcalls, hoot, scoff at, scorn, mock, taunt, decry, ridicule, revile.

historian *noun* chronicler, annalist, archivist, recorder, historiographer, paleographer, biographer, antiquarian.

historic *adjective* *historic event/house* famous, famed, notable, celebrated, renowned, momentous, significant, important, consequential, red-letter, memorable, remarkable, outstanding, extraordinary.

historical *adjective* 1 *a historical rather than a legendary account* factual, recorded, documented, chronicled, archival, authentic, actual, attested, verified, confirmed. 2 *in historical times* old, past, former, prior, bygone, ancient; *lit.* of yore.

history *noun* 1 *the history of the times* annals, chronicles, records, public records, account, study, story, tale, saga, narrative, recital, reports, memoirs, biography, autobiography. 2 *what is the young man's history?* life story, background, antecedents, experiences, adventures, fortunes. 3 *that is history now* the past, former times, bygone days, yesterday, the old days, the good old days, days of old, time gone by, antiquity; *lit.* days of yore, olden days/times, yesteryear.

hit *verb* 1 *hit him in anger* strike, slap, smack, buffet, punch, box, cuff, beat, thump, batter, pound, pummel, thrash, hammer, bang, knock, swat; *inf.* whack, wallop, bash, belt, clout, clip, clobber, sock, swipe. 2 *the car hit the truck* run into, bang into, smash into, crash into, knock into, bump into, collide with, meet head-on. 3 *her death really hit him* affect, have an effect on, make an impression on, influence, make an impact on, leave a mark on, impinge on, move, touch, overwhelm, devastate, damage, hurt. 4 *hit the right tone in his speech* | *hit the bull's-eye* achieve, accomplish, reach, attain, arrive at, gain, secure, touch, strike. **hit home** *his remarks hit home* have the intended effect, reach the target, strike home, hit the mark. **hit it off** *the children hit it off right away* get on well, be/get on good terms, become friends, take to each other, warm to each other, find things in common; *inf.* be on the same wavelength. **hit on/upon** *hit on the solution* stumble on, chance on, light on, come upon, blunder on, discover, uncover, arrive at, think of, come up with. **hit out at** *hit out at his enemies* lash out at, attack, assail, strike out at, rail against, inveigh against, denounce, revile, condemn, castigate, censure, vilify.

hit *noun* blow, slap, smack, punch, beating, thump, thumping, battering; *inf.* whack, wallop, bashing, belting, clout, clobbering, swipe.

hitch *verb* 1 *hitch the trailer to the car* fasten, connect, attach, join, couple, unite, tie, tether, bind, harness, yoke. 2 *hitching up their skirts/socks* pull up, hike up, jerk up; *inf.* yank up. 3 *hitching along the highway* hitchhike, hitch a ride, thumb a ride.

hitch *noun* *what's the hitch?* hindrance, holdup, delay, impediment, obstacle, obstruction, barrier, stoppage, stumbling block, block, check, snag, catch, difficulty, problem, trouble.

hither *adverb* *he came hither* here, to here, over here, to this place, near, nearer, close, closer.

hitherto *adverb* *hitherto he was unemployed* until now, up until now, till now, up to now, so far, previously, thus far, heretofore, before, beforehand.

hit-or-miss *adjective* *a hit-or-miss attempt/method* haphazard, random, aimless, undirected, disorganized, indiscriminate, careless, casual, offhand, cursory, perfunctory.

hoar *noun* hoarfrost, frost, rime, rime frost; *inf.* Jack Frost.

hoard *noun* *a hoard of food/money* store, stockpile, supply, reserve, reservoir, fund, cache, accumulation, heap, pile, mass, aggregation, conglomeration, treasure house, treasure trove; *inf.* stash.

hoard *verb* *hoard food/money* store, store up, stock up, stockpile, put by, put away, lay by, lay in, set aside, pile up, stack up, stow away, husband, save, buy up, accumulate, amass, heap up, collect, gather, garner, squirrel away; *inf.* stash away.

hoarder *noun* collector, saver, miser, niggard, squirrel.

hoarse *adjective a hoarse voice* croaking, croaky, throaty, harsh, rough, gruff, husky, gravelly, grating, rasping, guttural, raucous, discordant, cracked.

Antonyms: MELLOW; SMOOTH; SOFT.

hoary *adjective* 1 *hoary hair/head* gray, gray-haired, white, white-haired, silvery, silvery-haired, grizzled, grizzly. 2 *hoary gentleman* old, elderly, aged, at an advanced age, venerable, time-honored. 3 *hoary jokes* old, antiquated, ancient, antique, old as the hills, hackneyed, trite.

hoax *noun the magazine article was a hoax* practical joke, joke, jest, prank, trick, ruse, deception, fraud, imposture, cheat, swindle; *inf.* con, fast one, spoof, scam.

hoax *verb those who paid to see the ape-boy were hoaxed* play a practical joke on, play a joke/jest on, play a prank on, trick, fool, deceive, bluff, hoodwink, delude, dupe, take in, cheat, swindle, defraud, pull the wool over someone's eyes, gull; *inf.* con, pull a fast one on, take someone for a ride, put one over on someone, spoof; *lit.* cozen.

hobble *verb* walk with difficulty, limp, walk with a limp, walk lamely, walk haltingly, falter, move unsteadily, shuffle, totter, stagger, reel.

hobby *noun* leisure activity, leisure pursuit, leisure interest, pastime, diversion, recreation, relaxation, divertissement, sideline, entertainment, amusement, sport, game.

hobgoblin *noun* goblin, imp, elf, gnome, dwarf, bogeyman, evil spirit.

hobnob *verb hobnobbing with journalists* fraternize, associate, socialize, mingle, mix, keep company, go around, consort; *inf.* hang around, hang out.

hocus-pocus *noun* 1 *accuse the salesman of hocus-pocus* trickery, chicanery, deception, deceit, artifice, stratagem, sleight of hand, legerdemain, ruse, hoax, sham, delusion, pretense, imposture. 2 *the hocus-pocus spoken by the magician* spell, mumbo-jumbo, abracadabra, magic words, magic formula, incantation, chant, invocation, charm.

hodgepodge *noun* mixture, jumble, mishmash, miscellany, medley, mélange, mess, clutter, odds and ends, potpourri, olio, olla podrida.

hog *noun* 1 *farmer raising hogs* pig, boar, swine, porker, grunter. 2 *hogs at the table* glutton, gourmand, gormandizer, wolf, big eater; *inf.* pig.

hogwash *noun talking hogwash* nonsense, rubbish, gibberish, twaddle, drivel, balderdash, humbug, bunkum, trash; *inf.* gobbledygook, piffle, bunk, bosh, tosh, bilge, tripe, rot, tommyrot, crap, hooey.

hoi polloi *noun* the common people, the populace, the masses, the many, the proletariat, the peasants, the commons, the commonality, the lower orders, the third estate, the rabble, the riff-raff, the herd, the common herd, the mob; *inf.* the great unwashed.

hoist *verb hoist the load on to the truck* lift, raise, upraise, heave, jack up, hike up, elevate, erect.

hoist *noun need a hoist for the heavy load* crane, winch, tackle, capstan, pulley, jack, elevator, lift.

hold *verb* 1 *hold his hand* hold on to, clasp, clutch, grasp, grip, seize, clench, cling to; *lit.* cleave to. 2 *hold his sweetheart in his arms* embrace, hug, enfold, clasp, cradle, fondle. 3 *hold the relevant documents* have, possess, own, retain, keep. 4 *hold pleasant memories* cherish, harbor, treasure, retain. 5 *will it hold his weight?* bear, carry, take, support, hold up, keep up, sustain, prop up, buttress, brace, suspend. 6 *police are holding the suspect* detain, confine, hold in custody, impound, constrain, keep under constraint, lock up, imprison, put behind bars, incarcerate. 7 *you cannot hold him from going* hold back, restrain, impede, check, bar, curb, stop, retard, delay, prevent. 8 *hold the interest of the audience* keep, maintain, occupy, engage, involve, absorb, engross, immerse, monopolize, arrest, catch, spellbind, fascinate, rivet. 9 *he holds a well-paid post* hold down, be in, occupy, fill, maintain, continue in, enjoy, boast. 10 *the bottle holds one quart | the hall holds 400 people* contain, have a capacity for, accommodate, take, comprise. 11 *we hold that he is guilty* maintain, think, believe, consider, regard, deem, judge, assume, presume, reckon, suppose, esteem. 12 *will the good weather hold?* go on, carry on, remain, continue, stay, persist, last, endure, keep up, persevere. 13 *the old rule still holds* hold good, stand, apply, be in force, be in operation, operate, remain valid, remain, exist, be the case. 14 *hold you responsible* make, think, consider, regard as, view, treat as. 15 *hold a meeting* call, convene, assemble, conduct, run, preside over, officiate at. **hold back** 1 *hold back a laugh* keep back, suppress, repress, stifle, smother. 2 *hold back progress* prevent, impede, obstruct, hinder, check, curb, inhibit, restrain, control. 3 *hold back from hitting him* keep, desist, forbear, stop oneself, restrain oneself. 4 *hold back information* withhold, not disclose, suppress, refuse to disclose. **hold down** 1 *hold down the people* oppress, repress, tyrannize, dominate. 2 *hold down prices* keep low, keep down, keep at a low level. 3 *hold down a job* hold, be in, occupy, fill, maintain, continue in. **hold forth** 1 *hold forth about politics* speak at length, speak, talk, declaim, discourse, lecture, harangue, preach, orate, speechify, sermonize; *inf.* spout, spiel. 2 *hold forth the hand of friendship* hold out, extend, present, proffer, offer. **hold off** 1 *the storm held off* not occur, not happen, be delayed. 2 *hold off the attack* keep off, keep at bay, fend off, stave off, ward off, repel, repulse,

rebuff. **3** *hold off making a decision* delay, postpone, put off, defer, keep from, refrain from, avoid. **hold on** *if the survivors can hold on* survive, last, carry on, keep going, continue; *inf.* hang on. **hold on to 1** *hold on to his hand* clasp, clutch, grasp. *See* HOLD *verb* 1 **2** *hold on to the house* keep, keep/retain possession of, retain ownership of, not sell/give away, keep for oneself. **hold one's own 1** *they held their own in the battle* stand firm, stand fast, stand one's ground, maintain one's position, stay put, not be defeated. **2** *the patient is holding his own* survive, be still alive, not lose strength, do well. **hold out 1** *hold out the hand of friendship* extend, proffer, offer, present, hold forth. **2** *as long as supplies hold out* last, continue, remain. **hold out against** *hold out against the attack* stand fast against, stand firm against, resist, withstand, endure, carry on against, persist against, persevere against, fight to the end against, fight to the last man against; *inf.* hang on against. **hold over** *hold the matter over until the next meeting* put off, postpone, defer, delay, adjourn, suspend, waive. **hold up 1** *hold up progress* delay, hinder, impede, obstruct, retard, slow, slow down, set back, stop, bring to a halt, prevent. **2** *hold up his weight* hold, bear, carry, support, sustain. *See* HOLD *verb* 5. **3** *hold up the flag* | *she held up her father as an example* display, exhibit, show, put on show, present, flaunt, brandish. **4** *hold up a bank/train* | *they held up the tourists* rob, commit armed robbery on, hold to ransom, waylay, mug; *inf.* stick up. **5** *will his story hold up?* survive investigation, be convincing, bear examination, be verifiable, be provable, hold water. **hold with** *he doesn't hold with modern education trends* approve of, agree with, be in favor of, support, give support to, subscribe to, countenance, take kindly to.
Antonyms: give up (*see* GIVE); hand over (*see* HAND); RELEASE.

hold *noun* **1** *keep a firm hold of the child's hand* grasp, grip, clutch, clasp. **2** *lose his hold on the cliff* foothold, footing, toehold, anchorage, leverage. **3** *the government tightened its hold on the country* grip, power, control, dominion, authority, ascendancy. **4** *he has a hold over the younger boy* influence, mastery, dominance, sway; *inf.* pull, clout. **5** *put it on hold* pause, delay, postponement, deferment.

holder *noun* **1** *ticket holder* | *the present holder of the title* owner, possessor, bearer, proprietor, keeper, custodian, purchaser, incumbent, occupant. **2** *pencil holder* container, case, casing, receptacle, stand, cover, covering, housing, sheath.

holdup *noun* **1** *a holdup on the highway* delay, wait, stoppage, obstruction, bottleneck, traffic jam, hitch, snag, setback, trouble, problem. **2** *a bank holdup* robbery, theft, burglary, mugging; *inf.* stick-up.

hole *noun* **1** *a hole in the wall/material* opening, aperture, orifice, gap, space, breach, break, fissure, crack, rift, puncture, perforation, cut, incision, split, gash, rent, slit, vent, notch. **2** *a hole in the ground* excavation, pit, crater, shaft, mine, dugout, cave, cavern, pothole, cavity, chamber, hollow, scoop, pocket, depression, dent, dint, dip. **3** *an animal's hole* burrow, lair, den, covert, nest, retreat, shelter, recess. **4** *they took us to a real hole for dinner* slum, hovel; *inf.* dump, dive, joint. **5** *the captives were thrown into the hole* dungeon, prison, cell. **6** *spot the hole in their argument* flaw, fault, defect, loophole, inconsistency, discrepancy, error, fallacy. **7** *they are in a financial hole* predicament, mess, plight, difficulty, trouble, corner, tight corner, spot, tight spot, quandary, dilemma, muddle, tangle, imbroglio; *inf.* fix, jam, scrape, pickle, hot water. **pick holes in** find fault with, criticize, pull to pieces, run down, cavil at, carp at, disparage, denigrate.

hole *verb rocks holed the ship* make a hole in, puncture, perforate, pierce, spike, stab, lacerate, gash, split, rent. **hole up 1** *the animals have holed up for the winter* hibernate, retire, go to sleep, lie dormant. **2** *the thieves have holed up somewhere* hide, hide out, lie low, conceal oneself, go underground.

holiday *noun* saint's day, feast day, holy day, day of observance, celebration, anniversary; *inf.* day off.

holier-than-thou *adjective* sanctimonious, self-righteous, unctuous, pietistic, pietistical, religiose, priggish, smug, self-satisfied; *inf.* goody-goody.

holiness *noun* sanctity, sanctitude, saintliness, sacredness, divineness, divinity, godliness, blessedness, spirituality, religiousness, piety, righteousness, goodness, virtue, virtuousness, purity.

hollow *adjective* **1** *a hollow vessel* empty, unfilled, vacant, void, not solid, hollowed out. **2** *hollow cheeks/marks* sunken, deep-set, dented, indented, depressed, concave, caved-in, incurvate, cavernous. **3** *a hollow sound* muffled, muted, low, dull, deep, rumbling, flat, toneless, dead, sepulchral. **4** *a hollow victory/triumph* valueless, worthless, useless, of no use, of no avail, unavailing, empty, fruitless, profitless, unprofitable, pointless, meaningless, insignificant, specious, pyrrhic. **5** *hollow compliments/condolences* insincere, hypocritical, feigned, artificial, false, dissembling, deceitful, sham, counterfeit, spurious, untrue, unsound, flimsy, faithless, treacherous, two-faced. **6** *feeling hollow* empty, hungry, famished, starving, starved, half-starved, ravenous.
Antonyms: SOLID; FULL; MEANINGFUL.

hollow *noun* **1** *hollows in the ground* depression, indentation, concavity, dent, dint, dip, dimple, hole, crater, cavern, pit, cavity, well, trough, basin, cup, bowl, niche, nook, cranny, recess. **2** *picnic in the hollow* valley, dell, dale, glen, gorge, ravine.

hollow *verb* **hollow out** *riverbanks hollowed out by water* scoop out, gouge out, dig out, excavate, furrow, groove, channel, indent, dent.

holocaust *noun* fire, inferno, conflagration, destruction, devastation, demolition, ravaging, annihilation; massacre, mass murder, carnage, slaughter, butchery, extermination, genocide, ethnic cleansing.

holy *adjective* **1** *a holy person* God-fearing, godly, pious, pietistic, devout, spiritual, religious, righteous, good, virtuous, moral, saintly, saintlike, sinless. **2** *a holy place* blessed, blest, sanctified, consecrated, hallowed, sacred, sacrosanct, dedicated, venerated, divine, religious. **Antonyms:** SACRILEGIOUS; IMPIOUS.

home *noun* **1** *where is his home?* house, abode, domicile, residence, dwelling, dwelling place, habitation. **2** *live a long way from one's home* home town, birthplace, homeland, native land, fatherland, motherland, mother country, country of origin. **3** *she comes from a good home* family, family background, family circle, household. **4** *agents advertising homes* house, apartment, condominium, bungalow, cottage; *inf.* condo, digs, pad. **5** *couldn't bear to put her mother in a home* residential home, institution, shelter, refuge, hostel, hospice, retirement home, nursing home, rest home, convalescent home/hospital, children's home; *inf.* old folk's home. **6** *the home of the buffalo | ancient tribes had their home here* abode, habitat, natural habitat, environment, natural element, natural territory, original habitation, home ground, stamping ground, haunt, domain. **at home** *is Jane at home?* in, present, available. **at home in** *at home in the academic world* familiar with, used to, comfortable in, at ease in, relaxed in, in one's element in, on familiar territory in, on home ground in. **at home with** *at home with computers* familiar with, proficient in, conversant with, skilled in, competent at, well-versed in; *inf.* up on. **bring home** *the program brought home the tragedy of famine | bring home to her the risk she is taking* drive home, make someone aware of, make someone conscious of, emphasize, stress, impress upon someone, underline, highlight. **nothing to write home about** nothing important, nothing worth mentioning, nothing to comment on, nothing out of the ordinary.

home *adjective* **1** *home issues, as opposed to international* domestic, internal, interior, local, national, native. **2** *home produce* homegrown, homemade, homespun.

home *verb* **home in on** *home in on the main issue* aim at, focus on, focus attention on, concentrate on, pinpoint, zero in on, zoom in on.

homeland *noun* native land, country of origin, fatherland, motherland, mother country.

homeless *adjective* down-and-out, destitute, derelict, dispossessed, on the streets, without a roof over one's head, vagrant.

homelike *adjective* homely, homey, comfortable, cozy, snug, cheerful, welcoming, friendly, con-

genial, hospitable, informal, relaxed, intimate, downhome, homestyle; *inf.* comfy.

homely *adjective* **1** *a homely girl* plain, plain-featured, plain-looking, unattractive, ugly; *inf.* not much to look at, short on looks. **2** *homely atmosphere/place* homelike, comfortable, cozy, snug, welcoming, informal, relaxed. *See* HOMELIKE. **3** *a homely but friendly place* plain, simple, modest, unsophisticated, natural, everyday, ordinary, unaffected, unassuming, unpretentious. **Antonyms:** ELEGANT; GRAND; ELABORATE; BEAUTIFUL.

homeowner *noun* householder, resident, occupant, occupier, tenant.

homespun *adjective* *homespun advice/philosophy* plain, simple, homely, modest, natural, artless, unsophisticated, unpolished, unrefined, inelegant, coarse, rough, rude, rustic.

homicidal *adjective* *homicidal maniac | has homicidal tendencies* murderous, death-dealing, mortal, deadly, lethal, violent, maniacal, berserk.

homicide *noun* **1** *found guilty of homicide* murder, manslaughter, killing, slaying, slaughter, assassination, patricide, matricide, fratricide, infanticide. **2** *a convicted homicide* murderer, killer, slayer, assassin, patricide, matricide, fratricide, infanticide; *inf.* hit man.

homily *noun* *gave a short homily on forgiveness* sermon, preaching, lecture, discourse, lesson, talk, speech, address, oration.

homogeneous *adjective* **1** *consisting of homogeneous parts* identical, alike, all alike, of the same kind, all the same, the same, all one, all of a piece, uniform, unvaried, unvarying, consistent. **2** *homogeneous substances* similar, kindred, akin, comparable, analogous, corresponding, parallel, correlative, cognate. **Antonyms:** DIFFERENT; DISSIMILAR; heterogeneous.

homogenize *verb* make uniform, combine, coalesce, fuse, merge, blend, emulsify.

homogenous *adjective. See* HOMOGENEOUS.

homosexual *adjective* **1** *homosexual men/organization* gay, homoerotic, homophile; *inf. derog.* queer. **2** *homosexual women/organization* gay, lesbian, homoerotic, homophile; *inf. derog.* butch.

homosexual *noun* **1** *he's a homosexual* gay, homophile; *inf. derog.* queer, queen, faggot, fag. **2** *she's a homosexual* gay, lesbian, homophile; *inf. derog.* butch, dyke.

honest *adjective* **1** *honest people* upright, honorable, moral, ethical, principled, righteous, right-minded, virtuous, good, worthy, decent, law-abiding, high-minded, upstanding, just, fair, incorruptible, truthful, true, veracious, trustworthy, trusty, reliable, conscientious, scrupulous, reputable, dependable, loyal, faithful. **2** *an honest reply* truthful, sincere,

candid, frank, direct, forthright, straightforward, open, genuine, plain-speaking, matter-of-fact, outspoken, blunt, undisguised, unfeigned, unequivocal. **3** *an honest mistake* real, true, genuine, authentic, actual, aboveboard, bona fide, proper, straight, fair and square; *inf.* on the level, honest-to-goodness. **4** *an honest judgment* fair, just, equitable, evenhanded, impartial, objective, balanced, unprejudiced, disinterested, unbiased.
Antonyms: DISHONEST; INSINCERE; UNFAIR.

honestly adverb **1** *earn his living honestly* fairly, by fair means, by just means, lawfully, legally, legitimately, honorably, decently, ethically, morally, without corruption; *inf.* on the level. **2** *honestly, I tell you he's not going* | *she told me honestly that she was leaving* to be honest, speaking truthfully, truthfully, speaking frankly, in all sincerity, candidly, frankly, openly, plainly, in plain language, to someone's face, straight out; *inf.* straight up, Scouts' honor.

honesty noun **1** *honesty is its own reward* uprightness, honorableness, honor, integrity, morals, morality, ethics, principle, high principles, righteousness, rectitude, virtue, goodness, probity, worthiness, justness, fairness, incorruptibility, truthfulness, truth, veracity, trustworthiness, reliability, conscientiousness, reputability, loyalty, faithfulness, fidelity. **2** *the honesty of his reply* truthfulness, truth, sincerity, candor, frankness, forthrightness, openness, genuineness, bluntness. *See* HONEST 2. **3** *the honesty of his judgment* fairness, justness, justice, equitability, evenhandedness, impartiality, objectiveness, lack of prejudice, lack of bias, balance.

honor noun **1** *a man of honor* honesty, uprightness, integrity, ethics, morals, high principles, righteousness, rectitude, virtue, goodness, decency, probity, worthiness, worth, fairness, justness, justice, truthfulness, trustworthiness, reliability, dependability, faithfulness, fidelity. **2** *the honor of winning the battle* fame, renown, glory, prestige, illustriousness, noble reputation, esteem, distinction, notability, credit. **3** *his honor is at stake* reputation, good name, name. **4** *protecting a lady's honor* chastity, virginity, virtue, purity, innocence, modesty. **5** *treat the hero with honor* acclaim, acclamation, applause, accolades, tributes, homage, praise, compliments, lauding, eulogy, paeans, adoration, reverence, veneration, adulation, exaltation, glorification. **6** *it was an honor to serve him* privilege, source of pleasure/pride/satisfaction, pleasure, joy.
Antonyms: DISHONOR; DISGRACE; condemnation.

---

honor

deference, homage, obeisance, reverence
The Ten Commandments instruct us to **Honor** thy father and mother. But what does *honor*

entail? While all of these nouns describe the respect or esteem that one shows to another, *honor* implies acknowledgment of a person's right to such respect (*honor one's ancestors; honor the dead*). **Homage** is honor with praise or tributes added, and it connotes a more worshipful attitude (*pay homage to the king*). **Reverence** combines profound respect with love or devotion (*he treated his wife with reverence*), while **deference** suggests courteous regard for a superior, often by yielding to the person's status or wishes (*show deference to one's elders*). **Obeisance** is a show of honor or reverence by an act or gesture of submission or humility, such as a bow or a curtsy (*the schoolchildren were instructed to pay obeisance when the Queen arrived*).

---

honor verb **1** *all his pupils honor him* hold in honor, have a high regard for, hold in esteem, esteem, respect, admire, defer to, reverence, revere, venerate, worship, idolize, value, prize. **2** *the crowd honored the victor* acclaim, applaud, give accolades to, pay homage to, pay tribute to, lionize, praise, cheer, compliment, laud, eulogize. **3** *honor the agreement/guarantee* fulfill, discharge, carry out, observe, keep, be true to, be faithful to, live up to. **4** *honor the check* cash, pay out money for, clear, accept, take, pass.

honorable adjective **1** *honorable men* honest, upright, ethical, moral, principled, righteous, high-principled, upstanding, right-minded, virtuous, good, decent, worthy, fair, just, true, truthful, trustworthy, trusty, reliable, dependable, faithful. **2** *an honorable victory* famous, renowned, glorious, prestigious, distinguished, esteemed, notable, noted, great, eminent, noble, illustrious, creditable. **3** *an honorable member of the community* worthy, respected, respectable, reputable, decent, venerable.

honors plural noun *honors given to the victor* rewards, awards, prizes, decorations, commendations, recognition, titles, distinctions, laurels.

honorarium noun remuneration, recompense, fee, salary, pay, emolument, reward.

honorary adjective *made an honorary member* nominal, in name/title only, titular, unofficial, ex officio, complimentary, unpaid.

hood[1] noun head covering, cowl, head scarf.

hood[2] noun *See* HOODLUM.

hood[3] noun *See* NEIGHBORHOOD.

hoodlum noun **1** *hoodlums vandalizing telephone booths* ruffian, hooligan, thug, rowdy, delinquent, vandal, mugger; *inf.* tough, rough, hood. **2** *hoodlums killing policemen* gangster, mobster, gunman, murderer, assassin, terrorist; *inf.* hit man, hatchet man; hood.

hoodwink verb deceive, delude, dupe, outwit, fool, trick, get the better of, cheat, take in, hoax, mislead, defraud, swindle, gull, pull the

hook *noun* **1** *hang your coat on the hook* peg. **2** *the hook of the dress is broken* hook and eye, fastener, catch, clasp, clip, link. **3** *a hook in the river* crook, angle, loop, curve, bend, bow, arc, dogleg, horseshoe bend, oxbow, hairpin turn. **by hook or by crook** by any means whatsoever, by any means, by fair means or foul, no matter how, somehow or other, somehow, in one way or another. **hook, line, and sinker** *believe the story hook, line, and sinker* completely, entirely, thoroughly, wholly, totally, utterly, through and through. **off the hook 1** *her evidence got him off the hook* acquitted, cleared of the charge, exonerated, in the clear, let off, vindicated. **2** *I found a ride to the airport—you're off the hook* under no obligation, uncommitted, not bound, free.

hook *verb* **1** *hook the dress/necklace* fasten, secure, fix, close the clasp. **2** *finally hooked a marriage partner* snare, ensnare, trap, entrap.

hooked *adjective* **1** *a hooked nose* hook-shaped, hooklike, aquiline, curved, bent, bowed, angular. **2** *cigarettes have had him hooked for years* dependent, addicted. **hooked on** *they're hooked on drugs/television/gambling* addicted to, devoted to, given to.

hooligan *noun* ruffian, thug, rowdy, delinquent, vandal, mugger, hoodlum; *inf.* tough, rough.

hoop *noun* ring, band, circle, circlet, loop, wheel, girdle.

hoot *noun* **1** *the owl's hoot* call, screech, whoop, cry. **2** *the hoots of the audience* boo, hiss, jeer, catcall, yell, shout of derision, whistle; *inf.* raspberry, Bronx cheer. **3** *the woman/story is a hoot* somebody/something very funny; *inf.* scream, laugh, card, caution.

hoot *verb* **1** *the owls hooted* call, screech, whoop, cry. **2** *the audience hooted at the comedian* boo, hiss, jeer, deride, mock, taunt, decry, ridicule, condemn, shout, yell.

hop *verb* *frogs hopping* jump, leap, bound, spring, vault, bounce, skip, caper, dance, frisk.

hop *noun* **1** *get there in one hop* jump, leap, bound, spring, vault, bounce, skip. **2** *it's just a short hop from here* short flight/trip/journey, quick trip. **3** *a hop in the school gym* dance, party, social.

hope *noun* *full of hope that we shall win | becoming a doctor was her greatest hope* hopefulness, expectation, expectancy, anticipation, desire, longing, wish, wishing, craving, yearning, aspiration, ambition, dream, belief, assurance, assumption, confidence, conviction, faith, trust, optimism.
Antonyms: DESPAIR; PESSIMISM.

hope *verb* *hope to win | hope for a victory* be hopeful of, expect, anticipate, look forward to, await, contemplate, foresee, desire, long, wish, crave, yearn, aspire, be ambitious, dream, believe, feel assured, assume, have confidence, be convinced, rely on, count on, trust in.

hopeful *adjective* **1** *hopeful candidates | hopeful of winning* full of hope, expectant, anticipating, anticipative, looking forward to, optimistic, confident, assured, buoyant, sanguine. **2** *hopeful news/signs* promising, encouraging, heartening, gladdening, optimistic, reassuring, auspicious, favorable, propitious, cheerful, bright, pleasant, rosy.
Antonyms: HOPELESS; PESSIMISTIC; DISCOURAGING.

hopefully *adverb* **1** *traveling hopefully* with hope, full of hope, expectantly, with anticipation, optimistically, confidently, with assurance, buoyantly, sanguinely. **2** *hopefully he will win* it is to be hoped that, with luck, all being well, if all goes well, if everything turns out all right, probably, conceivably, feasibly.

hopeless *adjective* **1** *feeling hopeless* without hope, despairing, in despair, desperate, pessimistic, defeatist, dejected, downhearted, despondent, demoralized, disconsolate, downcast, wretched, woebegone, forlorn, suicidal. **2** *a hopeless case* beyond hope, despaired of, lost, beyond remedy, irremediable, beyond recovery, past cure, incurable, beyond repair, irreparable, irreversible, serious, grave, fatal, deadly. **3** *a hopeless task/situation* impossible, impracticable, futile, useless, vain, pointless, worthless, forlorn, no-win, unattainable, unachievable. **4** *she's hopeless at math* poor, incompetent, ineffective, ineffectual, inadequate, inferior; *inf.* no good, useless.
Antonyms: HOPEFUL; OPTIMISTIC; ACCOMPLISHED.

horde *noun* *a horde of people/penguins on the beach* crowd, mob, throng, mass, large group, multitude, host, army, pack, gang, troop, drove, crew, band, flock, swarm, gathering, assemblage.

horizon *noun* **1** *disappearing over the horizon* skyline, range of vision, field of view, view, vista. **2** *broaden the child's horizon* scope, range of experience, area of knowledge, perspective, perception, prospect, outlook, compass, sphere, purview.

horizontal *adjective* flat, flat as a pancake, plumb, level, supine, prone, flush.
Antonyms: VERTICAL; ERECT.

horrendous *adjective* **1** *a horrendous sight* dreadful, awful, horrid. *See* HORRIBLE 1. **2** *a horrendous child* nasty, disagreeable, unpleasant. *See* HORRIBLE 2.

horrible *adjective* **1** *a horrible sight/accident* dreadful, awful, horrid, terrible, horrifying, terrifying, frightful, fearful, horrendous, shocking, appalling, hideous, grim, ghastly, harrowing, gruesome, disgusting, revolting, repulsive, loathsome, abhorrent, detestable, hateful, abominable. **2** *horrible child/weather/food/picture/mess* nasty, disagreeable, unpleasant, mean, unkind, obnoxious, odious; *inf.*

horrid, awful, dreadful, terrible, beastly, ghastly, frightful, fearful, horrendous, shocking, appalling, hideous, revolting, abominable. *Antonyms:* PLEASANT; AGREEABLE.

horrid *adjective* **1** *a horrid sight* dreadful, awful, horrifying, terrible, frightful, hideous, grim, ghastly, revolting, abhorrent, abominable. *See* HORRIBLE 1. **2** *a horrid child* horrible, nasty, disagreeable, unpleasant, mean, unkind, obnoxious. *See* HORRIBLE 2.

horrify *verb* **1** *the apparition horrified the children* terrify, terrorize, intimidate, frighten, frighten out of one's wits, alarm, scare, scare to death, startle, panic, throw into a panic, make someone's blood run cold; *inf.* make someone's hair stand on end, make someone's hair curl, scare stiff, scare the living daylights out of. **2** *his attitude horrifies me* shock, appall, outrage, scandalize, disgust, revolt, repel, nauseate, sicken, offend, dismay; *inf.* turn off.

horror *noun* **1** *full of horror at the sight of the ghost* terror, fear, fear and trembling, fearfulness, fright, alarm, dread, awe, panic, trepidation, apprehensiveness, uneasiness, nervousness, dismay, consternation. **2** *view his attitude with horror* abhorrence, abomination, loathing, hate, detestation, repulsion, revulsion, disgust, distaste, aversion, hostility, antipathy, animosity.

horse *noun* mount, steed, pony, racehorse, draft horse, packhorse, bay, sorrel, pinto, piebald; Arabian, Clydesdale, palomino; foal, colt, stallion, mare; *inf.* nag, dobbin, filly. *See also table at* HARNESS.

horseman, horsewoman *noun* rider, equestrian, horse soldier, cavalier, dragoon, jockey; cavalryman, cowboy/cowgirl.

horseplay *noun* clowning, fooling, fooling around, tomfoolery, buffoonery, pranks, practical jokes, antics, capers, high jinks, rough-and-tumble, romping; *inf.* roughhousing, shenanigans, monkey business.

horse sense *noun* common sense, sense one is born with, mother wit, judgment, soundness of judgment, practicality; *inf.* gumption, savvy.

horticulture *noun* cultivation of gardens, gardening, floriculture, arboriculture.

hosanna *noun* shout of praise, alleluia, song of praise, paean, laudation, glorification, hurrah, cheer.

hose *noun* **1** *a rubber hose* tube, tubing, pipe, siphon, conduit, channel, outlet. **2** *wearing red hose* socks, stockings, tights, hosiery.

hosiery *noun* hose, socks, stockings, tights, knee socks, ankle socks, leggings.

hospitable *adjective* welcoming, sociable, convivial, generous, liberal, bountiful, openhanded, congenial, friendly, neighborly, warm, warmhearted, cordial, kind, kindly, kindhearted, amicable, well-disposed, amenable, helpful.

Antonyms: INHOSPITABLE; UNFRIENDLY.

hospital *noun* medical center, clinic, infirmary, sanatorium.

hospitality *noun* hospitableness, welcome, sociability, conviviality, generosity, liberality, bountifulness, openhandedness, friendliness, neighborliness, warmth, warmheartedness, cordiality, kindness, kindheartedness, amicability, amenability, helpfulness.

host[1] *noun* **1** *the host of the ski lodge* proprietor, proprietress, landlord, landlady, manager, innkeeper, hotelkeeper, hotelier. **2** *the host greeting his guests* party-giver, entertainer. **3** *the host of the radio/TV show* presenter, master of ceremonies, MC, anchorman, anchorwoman; *inf.* emcee.

Antonyms: GUEST; attendee.

host[2] *verb* **1** *host a party* be the host/hostess of, give. **2** *host a radio/TV show* present, introduce; *inf.* emcee.

host[3] *noun* *a host of people gathered for the march* multitude, crowd, throng, horde, mob, army, legion, herd, pack, flock, swarm, troop, band, mass, assemblage, assembly, array, myriad.

hostage *noun* pawn, security, surety, pledge, captive, prisoner.

hostile *adjective* **1** *hostile to the idea* antagonistic, opposed, averse, opposite, ill-disposed, against, inimical; *inf.* anti. **2** *hostile weather conditions* adverse, unfavorable, unpropitious, disadvantageous, inauspicious. **3** *a hostile crowd* belligerent, bellicose, aggressive, warlike, warring, militant, antagonistic, unfriendly, unkind, unsympathetic, malevolent, malicious, spiteful, wrathful, angry.

Antonyms: FRIENDLY; FAVORABLE; PEACEFUL.

---

hostile
adverse, bellicose, belligerent, inimical

Few people have trouble recognizing hostility when confronted with it. Someone who is **hostile** displays an attitude of intense ill will and acts like an enemy (*the audience grew hostile after waiting an hour for the show to start*). Both **bellicose** and **belligerent** imply a readiness or eagerness to fight, but the former is used to describe a state of mind or temper (*after drinking all night, he was in a bellicose mood*), while the latter is normally used to describe someone who is actively engaged in hostilities (*the belligerent brothers were at it again*). While *hostile* and *belligerent* usually apply to people, **adverse** and **inimical** are used describe tendencies or influences. *Inimical* means having an antagonistic tendency (*remarks that were inimical to everything she believed in*), and *adverse* means turned toward something in opposition (*an adverse wind; under adverse circumstances*). Unlike *hostile, adverse* and *inimical* need not connote the involvement of human feeling.

---

hostilities *plural noun* war, warfare, fighting, conflict, militancy, strife, action, battles.

hostility *noun* **1** *their hostility to the idea* antagonism, opposition, aversion, animosity, ill will, enmity, inimicalness. **2** *the hostility of the crowd* belligerence, bellicosity, aggression, warlikeness, militancy, antagonism, unfriendliness, unkindness, malevolence, malice, spite, wrath, anger.

hot *adjective* **1** *hot food straight from the oven* heated, very warm, boiling, boiling hot, piping, piping hot, scalding, red-hot, sizzling, steaming, scorching, roasting, searing. **2** *a hot day* very warm, boiling hot, boiling, blazing hot, sweltering, parching, scorching, roasting, searing, blistering, baking, ovenlike, torrid, sultry. **3** *the curry is very hot* peppery, spicy, pungent, piquant, fiery, sharp, biting. **4** *the child is hot* feverish, fevered, febrile, flushed, red. **5** *hot on/ about the idea of free speech* ardent, eager, enthusiastic, keen, fervent, fervid, zealous, vehement, passionate, animated, excited. **6** *hot with anger* inflamed, furious, infuriated, seething, raging, fuming, wrathful, angry, indignant. **7** *hot young lovers* passionate, impassioned. *See* HOT-BLOODED. **8** *a hot temper/argument* heated, violent, furious, fierce, ferocious, stormy, tempestuous, savage. **9** *hot from the presses/warehouses* new, fresh, recent, late, brand-new, just out, just released, just issued. **10** *these cameras are hot this year* popular, in vogue, in demand, sought-after, well-liked, well-loved. **11** *hot on their heels* close, following closely, near. **12** *hot goods* stolen, illegally obtained, smuggled, wanted. **hot air** empty talk, nonsense, bombast, verbiage, wind, blather, claptrap; *inf.* gas, bunkum, guff.
Antonyms: COLD; MILD.

hotbed *noun* *the place is a hotbed of vice/crime* breeding ground, seedbed, nursery, cradle, nest, womb.

hot-blooded *adjective* **1** *hot-blooded young lovers* hot, passionate, impassioned, ardent, sensual, sex-hungry, lustful, libidinous; *inf.* horny. **2** *hot-blooded people quarreling* excitable, temperamental, fiery, spirited, impulsive, rash, wild, quixotic.

hotel *noun* inn, hostelry, motel, boardinghouse, guesthouse.

hotfoot *verb* **hotfoot it** *hotfoot it to the airport* hurry, rush, hasten, make haste, dash, make a dash; *inf.* get cracking, hightail it, step on it.

hotheaded *adjective* fiery, hasty, excitable, hot-tempered, short-tempered, quick-tempered, volatile, rash, impetuous, impulsive, reckless, foolhardy, wild, unruly.

hothouse *noun* greenhouse, conservatory.

hothouse *adjective* *hothouse children* overprotected, pampered, coddled, overindulged, spoiled, spoonfed, sheltered, shielded, delicate, frail, fragile, sensitive, dainty.

hound *noun* **1** *she breeds hounds* bloodhound, foxhound, wolfhound, greyhound, dog, hunting dog. **2** *he's a mean hound* scoundrel, cad, blackguard, rascal, rogue, villain, miscreant, knave, scalawag; *inf.* bounder.

hound *verb* **1** *police hounding the criminal* chase, give chase to, pursue, follow, hunt, hunt down, stalk, track, trail, follow on the heels of, shadow; *inf.* tail. **2** *hound him to do as they wished* nag, bully, browbeat, pester, harass, harry, keep after, urge, badger, goad, prod, provoke, impel, force, pressure, pressurize.

house *noun* **1** *new development of 200 houses* | *his house is over there* abode, residence, domicile, home, habitation; condominium, cottage; *inf.* condo. **2** *how many are in the house?* household, family, family circle, home, ménage. **3** *descended from a royal house* family, clan, family tree, line, lineage, dynasty, ancestry, ancestors, kindred, blood, race, strain, tribe. **4** *a publishing house* firm, business, company, concern, corporation, enterprise, organization; *inf.* outfit. **5** *the House of Representatives* legislative body, legislative assembly, congress, parliament, chamber. **6** *a large house for the event* audience, gathering, assembly, congregation, listeners, spectators. **on the house** free, for nothing, gratis, without payment.

house *verb* **1** *the building houses 20 people* accommodate, lodge, put up, take in, have room for, have space/capacity for, sleep, shelter, harbor. **2** *the box houses the machinery* cover, sheathe, protect, shelter, guard, contain, keep.

household *noun* *how many are in the household?* family, family circle, house, home, ménage.

household *adjective* *household articles/bleach* domestic, family, ordinary, everyday, common, usual, run-of-the-mill.

housekeeping *noun* household management, home economics, housecraft, domestic science, housewifery.

housing *noun* **1** *a shortage of housing* accommodations, houses, dwellings, homes, shelter, habitations. **2** *housing for machinery* case, casing, cover, covering, sheath, container, enclosure, jacket, capsule, holder.

hovel *noun* shack, shanty, hut; *inf.* dump, hole.

hover *verb* **1** *kites hovering in the air* be suspended, hang, fly, flutter, float, drift, be wafted. **2** *hovering between going and staying* waver, vacillate, fluctuate, oscillate, alternate, seesaw. **hover by/around/near** *students hovering by the grade-posting board* linger around/by/near, hang around/about, wait near, stay near.

however *adverb* *however, you will have to go* nevertheless, be that as it may, nonetheless, notwithstanding, anyway, anyhow, regardless, despite that, still, yet, just the same, though.

however *conjunction* *however he approached the problem* whatever way, regardless of how.

howl *verb* **1** *dogs howling* bay, yowl, yelp. **2** *children howling* yell, wail, bawl, scream, shriek, bellow, roar, shout, caterwaul, yelp, cry, weep, ululate; *inf.* holler. **3** *howling at the clown's antics* laugh loudly, roar with laughter, split one's sides.

howl noun **1** *the howls of the dogs* bay, yowl, yelp. **2** *children's howls* yell, wail, bawl, bellow, roar, caterwauling, crying. See HOWL verb 2.

hub noun **1** *the hub of a wheel* pivot, axis, nave. **2** *the hub of the firm* center, center of activity, middle, core, heart, nerve center, focus, focal point.

huddle verb *huddle into the hall* crowd, press, throng, flock, pack, cram, herd, squeeze, bunch up, cluster, gather, congregate. **huddle up** *huddle up under her coat* curl up, snuggle (up), cuddle (up), nestle.

huddle noun **1** *a huddle of people* crowd, throng, pack, cluster, gathering. **2** *people going into a huddle* conference, discussion, consultation, meeting, powwow; *inf.* confab.

hue[1] noun **1** *a blue hue* color, tone, shade, tint, tinge, dye. **2** *political opinions of every hue* complexion, cast, aspect, light.

hue[2] noun **hue and cry** outcry, uproar, commotion, racket, clamor, furor, brouhaha, hullabaloo, much ado. See HULLABALOO.

huff noun **in a huff** in a bad mood, sulky, having a sulk, peeved; *inf.* miffed.

hug verb **1** *hug his wife* embrace, cuddle, take in one's arms, hold close, enfold in one's arms, clasp/press to one's bosom, squeeze. **2** *hug the shore* keep close to, stay near to, follow closely, follow the course of. **3** *hug his memories* cling to, hold onto, cherish, harbor, nurse, keep close.

hug noun *give the child a hug* embrace, cuddle, squeeze, hold, clasp, bear hug; *inf.* clinch.

huge adjective enormous, immense, great, massive, colossal, vast, prodigious, gigantic, giant, gargantuan, mammoth, monumental, monstrous, elephantine, extensive, bulky, mountainous, titanic, Herculean; *inf.* jumbo.
Antonyms: TINY; DIMINUTIVE.

hulk noun **1** *the hulk of a ship* wreck, shipwreck, ruin, shell, skeleton, hull, frame. **2** *a clumsy hulk* oaf, lout; *inf.* bull in a china shop, lummox, klutz.

hulking adjective cumbersome, unwieldy, bulky, weighty, massive, ponderous; clumsy, awkward, ungainly, lumbering, loutish.

hull noun **1** *the hull of a ship* body, framework, frame, skeleton, structure, casing, covering. **2** *the hull of the fruit* rind, skin, peel, shell, husk, pod, shuck, capsule, integument, pericarp.

hull verb *hull the fruit* peel, pare, skin, trim, shell, husk, shuck.

hullabaloo noun uproar, commotion, roar, racket, din, noise, clamor, disturbance, hubbub, outcry, furor, brouhaha, hue and cry, pandemonium, tumult, turmoil, fuss, to-do, much ado, bedlam, babel; *inf.* ruckus.

hum verb **1** *bees/machines humming* drone, murmur, vibrate, throb, thrum, buzz, whir, purr. **2** *humming a tune* sing, croon, whisper, mumble. **3** *things are humming* be busy, be active, bustle, move quickly, vibrate, pulsate, buzz.

hum noun *the hum of bees/machines* drone, murmur, vibration, throb, thrum, buzz, whir, purr.

human adjective **1** *a human creature* anthropoid, mortal. **2** *human frailty/weaknesses* mortal, physical, bodily, fleshly, carnal, corporal. **3** *a very human person* kind, kindly, considerate, understanding, sympathetic, compassionate, approachable, accessible, humane. See HUMANE. **4** *they're only human* mortal, flesh and blood, fallible, weak, frail, vulnerable, erring.
Antonyms: ANIMAL; SPIRITUAL; INHUMAN.

human noun *animals and humans* human being, mortal, member of the human race, individual, living soul, soul; man, woman, child; *inf.* body.

humane adjective *a humane ruler | humane to animals* kind, kindly, kindhearted, good, good-natured, compassionate, considerate, understanding, sympathetic, forgiving, merciful, lenient, forbearing, gentle, tender, mild, clement, benign, benevolent, charitable, generous, magnanimous, approachable, accessible.
Antonyms: CRUEL; BRUTAL; INHUMANE.

humanitarian adjective **1** *humanitarian enemy soldiers* humane, kind, good, compassionate, sympathetic, merciful, lenient, gentle, magnanimous. See HUMANE. **2** *interested in humanitarian issues* philanthropic, altruistic, welfare, charitable.

humanitarian noun philanthropist, altruist, benefactor, good Samaritan, social reformer, do-gooder.

humanities plural noun liberal arts, literature, literae humaniores; classics, classical studies, classical languages, classical literature.

humanity noun **1** *the cultural history of humanity* humankind, the human race, the human species, mankind, man, people, humans, human beings, mortals, *Homo sapiens.* **2** *err because of their humanity* humanness, human nature, mortality, flesh and blood. **3** *monks noted for their humanity* kindness, kindheartedness, goodness, good-heartedness, benevolence, compassion, sympathy, understanding, pity, mercy, mercifulness, gentleness, tenderness, leniency, tolerance, goodwill, brotherly love, fellow-feeling, generosity, magnanimity, charity, philanthropy.

humble adjective **1** *brilliant but humble* modest, unassuming, self-effacing, unassertive, unpretentious, unostentatious, meek. **2** *born of humble people* plain, common, ordinary, simple, poor, of low birth, low-born, of low rank, low-ranking, low, lowly, inferior, plebeian, proletarian, base, mean, unrefined, vulgar, unimportant, insignificant, inconsequential, undistinguished, ignoble. **3** *hate his humble attitude to the boss* servile, submissive, obsequious, subservient, deferential, slavish, sycophantic.

humble *verb* **1** *humble them by his criticism* humiliate, mortify, shame. *See* HUMILIATE. **2** *feel humbled in the presence of the great man* belittle, demean, deflate, depreciate, disparage. **3** *humble the enemy* crush, trounce, rout, break, conquer, vanquish, defeat, utterly overwhelm, smash, bring to one's knees.

---

humble
abase, debase, degrade, demean, humiliate
While all of these verbs mean to lower in one's own estimation or in the eyes of others, there are subtle distinctions among them. **Humble** and **humiliate** sound similar, but *humiliate* emphasizes shame and the loss of self-respect and usually takes place in public (*humiliated by her tearful outburst*), while *humble* is a milder term implying a lowering of one's pride or rank (*to humble the arrogant professor by pointing out his mistake*). **Abase** suggests groveling or a sense of inferiority and is usually used reflexively (*got down on his knees and abased himself before the king*), while **demean** is more likely to imply a loss of dignity or social standing (*refused to demean herself by marrying a common laborer*). When used to describe things, **debase** means a deterioration in the quality or value of something (*a currency debased by the country's political turmoil*), but in reference to people it connotes a weakening of moral standards or character (*debased himself by accepting bribes*). **Degrade** is even stronger, suggesting the destruction of a person's character through degenerate or shameful behavior (*degraded by long association with criminals*).

---

humbug *noun* **1** *taken in by the humbug* hoax, trick, trickery, cheat, cheating, bluff, ruse, wile, stratagem, fraud, swindle, deceit, deception, imposture, pretense, sham, delusion; *inf.* con. **2** *the salesman's a humbug* charlatan, imposter, fake, sham, fraud, cheat, trickster, swindler, quack, deceiver; *inf.* con man, phony. **3** *he talks a lot of humbug* nonsense, rubbish, balderdash, twaddle, bunkum; *inf.* rot, bunk, baloney, hogwash, crap.

humdrum *adjective* *humdrum life/routine* commonplace, run-of-the-mill, routine, unvaried, unvarying, ordinary, everyday, mundane, uneventful, monotonous, repetitious, dull, uninteresting, banal, boring, tedious, tiresome, wearisome.
Antonyms: REMARKABLE; EXCITING.

humid *adjective* *humid atmosphere/day* muggy, sticky, steamy, clammy, close, sultry, damp, moist, dank, wet, wettish, soggy, misty.
Antonyms: DRY; ARID.

humidity *noun* humidness, mugginess, stickiness, steaminess, clamminess, closeness, sultriness, dampness, damp, moistness, dankness, moisture, wetness, sogginess.

humiliate *verb* mortify, humble, shame, bring low, put to shame, make ashamed, disgrace, embarrass, discomfit, chasten, subdue, abash, abase, debase, degrade, crush, make someone eat humble pie, take down a peg or two; *inf.* put down; make someone eat crow.

humiliation *noun* mortification, humbling, loss of pride, shame, disgrace, loss of face, dishonor, indignity, discredit, ignoring, embarrassment, discomfiture, affront, abasement, debasement, degradation, submission, humble pie; *inf.* put-down.

humility *noun* **1** *the winner showed humility* lack of pride, humbleness, modesty, modestness, meekness, self-effacement, unpretentiousness, unobtrusiveness, diffidence. **2** *dislike his humility toward the boss* servility, submissiveness, obsequiousness, subservience, deference, sycophancy.
Antonyms: ARROGANCE; PRIDE.

humorist *noun* comic writer, writer of comedy, cartoonist, caricaturist, comic, comedian, comedienne, joker, jokester, clown, jester, wag, wit, funny man.

humor *noun* **1** *not to see the humor of the situation* funny side, funniness, comic side, comical aspect, comedy, laughableness, facetiousness, farcicalness, farce, jocularity, hilarity, ludicrousness, absurdness, absurdity, drollness. **2** *entertain them with his humor* comedy, jokes, joking, jests, jesting, gags, wit, wittiness, witticisms, waggishness, pleasantries, buffoonery; *inf.* wisecracks. **3** *what humor is she in today?* mood, temper, temperament, frame of mind, state of mind, disposition, spirits.
Antonyms: GRAVITY; SOLEMNITY.

humor *verb* **1** *humor the child* indulge, pamper, spoil, coddle, mollycoddle, mollify, soothe, placate, gratify, satisfy, pander to, go along with, accommodate. **2** *humor their idiosyncrasies* adapt to, make provision for, give in to, yield to, go along with, acquiesce in, indulge, pander to, tolerate, permit, allow, suffer.

humorous *adjective* **1** *a humorous story* funny, comic, comical, witty, jocular, amusing, laughable, hilarious, sidesplitting, rib-tickling, facetious, farcical, ridiculous, ludicrous, absurd, droll. **2** *a humorous person* funny, amusing, entertaining, witty, jocular, facetious, waggish, whimsical.
Antonyms: SERIOUS; SOLEMN.

hump *noun* *a hump on his back* | *hump in the tree* protuberance, protrusion, projection, bulge, swelling, lump, bump, knob, hunch, mass, nodule, node, intumescence, tumefaction. **over the hump** *we were doing badly but we're over the hump* over the worst part, over the worst of it, out of the woods, in the clear, on the road to recovery, getting better, on the way up, making progress.

hump *verb* **1** *stop humping your back* hunch, arch, curve, crook, curl up. **2** *hump the luggage to the train* lug, heave, carry, lift, shoulder, hoist.

hunch noun **1** *a hunch on his back* hump, protrusion, bulge. *See* HUMP *noun.* **2** *have a hunch that she will win* feeling, presentiment, premonition, intuition, sixth sense, suspicion, inkling, impression, idea.

hunch verb *hunching his back* hump, arch, curve, crook, curl up. **hunch up** *working at his desk, all hunched up* crouch over, stoop over, bend over, huddle over.

hunger noun **1** *suffering from hunger* hungriness, need for food, lack of food, emptiness, ravenousness, starvation, famine, voracity; greed, greediness. **2** *a hunger for knowledge/travel* craving, longing, yearning, desire, want, need, thirst, appetite, pining, itch, lust, hankering; *inf.* yen.

hunger verb *hunger for food* be hungry, feel hunger, be ravenous, be famished, be starving. **hunger for/after** *hungering for/after knowledge* crave, have a craving for, long for, yearn for, have a yearning for, desire, want, need, thirst for, have an appetite for, pine for, lust after, itch for, hanker after; *inf.* have a yen for.

hungry adjective *hungry children* | *the people are hungry* in need of food, empty, hollow, ravenous, famished, famishing, starving, starved, half-starved; greedy, voracious; *inf.* peckish. **hungry for** *hungry for knowledge* craving, in need/want of, eager/keen for, desirous of, covetous of, longing/yearning/pining/thirsting/itching for.
Antonyms: FULL; satiated.

hunk noun **1** *a hunk of cheese* large piece, block, chunk, lump, mass, slab, wedge, square, dollop, portion. **2** *the movie star is a hunk* he-man, muscle man, Adonis.

hunt verb **1** *hunt deer/criminals* chase, give chase, pursue, stalk, track, trail, follow, shadow, hunt down, hound; *inf.* tail. **2** *hunt for her keys* search, look, look high and low, forage, fish, rummage.

hunt noun **1** *the hunt for deer/criminals* chase, pursuit, course, coursing, stalking, tracking, trailing, shadowing; *inf.* tailing. **2** *the hunt for her keys* search, quest, rummage; foraging, ransacking.

hurdle noun **1** *runners clearing hurdles* fence, railing, rail, wall, hedge, bar, barrier, barricade. **2** *a hurdle in the way of their plans* barrier, obstacle, hindrance, impediment, obstruction, stumbling block, snag, complication, difficulty, handicap.

hurl verb *hurl stones/insults* throw, fling, pitch, cast, toss, heave, fire, launch, let fly, propel, project, dart, catapult; *inf.* sling, chuck.

hurly-burly noun commotion, hubbub, bustle, tumult, turmoil, turbulence, pandemonium, bedlam, furor, uproar, upheaval, disorder, confusion, chaos, unrest, agitation, disruption, trouble.

hurricane noun typhoon, tropical storm, gale, tempest, whirlwind.

hurried adjective **1** *with hurried steps* quick, fast, swift, rapid, speedy, hasty, breakneck, posthaste. **2** *a hurried glance* hasty, quick, swift, rapid, rushed, cursory, superficial, perfunctory, offhand, passing, fleeting, transitory.
Antonyms: SLOW; LEISURELY; THOROUGH.

hurry verb *hurry or we'll be late* hurry up, move quickly, be quick, make haste, hasten, speed, speed up, lose no time, press on, push on, run, dash, rush, go hell for leather; *inf.* get a move on, step on it, get cracking, shake a leg, fly, race, scurry, scamper, go like a bat out of hell, hightail it, hotfoot it. **hurry on** *hurry them on* speed up, quicken, hasten, accelerate, expedite, urge on, drive on, push on, goad, prod, hustle.
Antonyms: DAWDLE; DELAY.

hurry noun **1** *surprised at the hurry of the crowd* speed, quickness, fastness, swiftness, rapidity, haste, celerity, expedition, dispatch, promptitude. **2** *what's all the hurry?* haste, urgency, rush, flurry, bustle, hubbub, turmoil, agitation, confusion, commotion.

hurt verb **1** *my foot hurts* be sore, be painful, cause pain, ache, smart, nip, sting, throb, tingle, burn. **2** *he has hurt his leg* injure, cause injury to, wound, cause pain to, bruise, cut, scratch, lacerate, maim, mutilate, damage, disable, incapacitate, debilitate, impair. **3** *his cruel words hurt her* upset, sadden, cause sorrow, cause suffering, grieve, wound, distress, pain, cut to the quick, sting, cause anguish, offend, give offense, discompose. **4** *that will not have hurt his reputation* harm, damage, spoil, mar, blight, blemish, impair.
Antonyms: HEAL; CHEER; SOOTHE; IMPROVE.

hurt noun **1** *the hurt in his hand was acute* pain, soreness, ache, smarting, stinging, throbbing, suffering, pangs, discomfort. **2** *a hurt on his leg* sore, wound, injury, bruise, cut, scratch, laceration. **3** *the hurt he caused her* upset, sadness, sorrow, suffering, grief, distress, pain, misery, anguish, affliction. **4** *the hurt caused to his reputation* harm, damage, injury, detriment, blight, loss, disadvantage, mischief.

hurt adjective **1** *a hurt leg* wounded, injured, bruised, cut, lacerated, sore, painful, aching, smarting, throbbing. *See* HURT *verb* 1, 2. **2** *a hurt child/expression* upset, sad, sorrowful, grieving, grief-stricken, aggrieved, distressed, anguished, offended, piqued. *See* HURT *verb* 3.

hurtful adjective **1** *hurtful remarks* upsetting, wounding, injurious, distressing, unkind, nasty, mean, malicious, spiteful, cutting, cruel, mischievous, offensive. **2** *actions hurtful to his career* harmful, damaging, injurious, detrimental, disadvantageous, deleterious, destructive, prejudicial, ruinous, inimical.

husband noun spouse, consort, partner, groom, bridegroom; *inf.* hubby, old man, the other half; *dial.* man.

husband verb *husband resources* conserve, preserve, save, save for a rainy day, put aside, put by, reserve, store, hoard, use sparingly, use economically, manage thriftily, budget.

husbandry noun **1** *men engaged in husbandry* farming, agriculture, farm management, land management, agronomy, agronomics, agribusiness, cultivation, tillage; animal husbandry. **2** *practice husbandry with the available resources* budgeting, economy, good housekeeping, careful management, thrift, frugality, sparingness, saving.

hush verb **1** *hush the children* silence, shush; *inf.* shut up. **2** *they suddenly hushed* fall silent, become silent; *inf.* pipe down, shut up. **3** *hush their fears* still, quieten, calm, soothe, allay, assuage, pacify, mollify, compose. **hush up** *hush up the scandal* suppress, conceal, cover up, keep secret, keep dark, smother, stifle, squash.

hush noun *a hush fell over the room* quiet, quietness, silence, stillness, still, soundlessness, peacefulness, peace, calm, tranquillity.

hush-hush adjective *hush-hush information* top secret, secret, confidential, classified, restricted.

husk noun hull, shell, covering, pod, shuck, rind, skin, peel, integument, pericarp.

husky adjective **1** *a husky voice* throaty, gruff, deep, gravelly, hoarse, coarse, croaking, croaky, rough, thick, guttural, harsh, rasping. **2** *a husky young man* brawny, well-built, strapping, muscular, big and strong, rugged, burly, sturdy, powerfully built, thickset; *inf.* beefy.

hussy noun minx, seductress, trollop, slut, loose woman; *inf.* vamp, tramp, bimbo, floozy.

hustle verb **1** *hustle them out of the way* push, shove, thrust, crowd, jostle, elbow, nudge, shoulder. **2** *hustle them into making a decision* force, coerce, impel, pressure, badger, pester, prompt, urge, goad, prod, spur, propel, egg on. **3** *have to hustle to get there on time* hurry, be quick, hasten, make haste, move quickly, dash, rush, fly; *inf.* get a move on, step on it.

hustle noun *tired of the hustle of life* activity, hurry, rushing, haste, flurry, bustle, hubbub, tumult, fuss.

hut noun shed, lean-to, shack, cabin, shanty, hovel.

hybrid noun crossbreed, cross, mixed-breed, half-blood, mixture, conglomerate, composite, compound, amalgam; *derog.* half-breed.

hygiene noun cleanliness, personal hygiene, personal cleanliness, public health, environmental health, sanitation, sanitary measures.

hygienic adjective *kitchens must be hygienic* sanitary, clean, germ-free, disinfected, sterilized, aseptic, sterile, unpolluted, uncontaminated, healthy, pure.
Antonyms: DIRTY; FILTHY; INSANITARY.

hymn noun psalm, anthem, carol, religious song,

paean, song of praise, chant, plainsong, spiritual.

hype noun *a lot of hype for the new movie* publicity, promotion, advertising, ballyhoo; *inf.* plugging.

hyperbole noun exaggeration, overstatement, excess, overkill.

hypercritical adjective overcritical, captious, faultfinding, overexacting, hairsplitting, niggling, quibbling, pedantic; *inf.* nitpicking.

hypnosis noun hypnotic suggestion, autosuggestion, mesmerism.

hypnotic adjective *hypnotic drugs/effect* mesmerizing, sleep-inducing, sleep-producing, soporific, somniferous, somnific, numbing, sedative, stupefactive.

hypnotize verb **1** *hypnotize the patient* put under, put out, send into a trance, mesmerize, put to sleep. **2** *they were hypnotized by her beauty* fascinate, bewitch, entrance, beguile, spellbind, magnetize.

hypocrisy noun sanctimoniousness, sanctimony, pietism, false goodness, insincerity, falseness, falsity, deceptiveness, deceit, deceitfulness, deception, dishonesty, duplicity, imposture, two-facedness, double-dealing, pretense, speciousness; *inf.* phoniness.
Antonyms: HONESTY; SINCERITY.

hypocrite noun pharisee, deceiver, impostor, pretender, charlatan, mountebank; *inf.* quack, phony.

hypocritical adjective sanctimonious, pietistic, unctuous, insincere, false, fraudulent, deceitful, deceptive, dishonest, untruthful, lying, duplicitous, two-faced, double-dealing, untrustworthy, perfidious, specious, spurious; *inf.* phony.

hypothesis noun **1** *a working hypothesis* theorem, thesis, proposition, theory, postulate, axiom, premise. **2** *impossible to deduce anything from his hypothesis* supposition, assumption, presumption, conjecture, speculation.

hypothetical adjective *to take a hypothetical case* supposed, assumed, presumed, theoretical, conjectured, imagined, speculative, academic.

hysteria noun hysterics, loss of control, frenzy, outburst/fit of agitation, panic attack, loss of reason, fit of madness, delirium.

hysterical adjective **1** *hysterical at the news of his death* frenzied, in a frenzy, frantic, out of control, berserk, beside oneself, distracted, distraught, overwrought, agitated, in a panic, mad, crazed, delirious, out of one's mind/wits, raving. **2** *hysterical play/game* very funny, wildly amusing, hilarious, uproarious, sidesplitting, comical, farcical, screamingly funny.
Antonyms: CALM; COMPOSED; SERIOUS.

I

ice *noun* **1** *ships encountering ice* frozen water; frost, rime, icicle, iceberg, glacier. **2** *ice in a drink* ice cubes, crushed ice; *inf.* rocks. **3** *you could feel the ice in her greeting* coldness, coolness, frigidity, stiffness, aloofness, distance, unresponsiveness, reserve, reticence, constraint, restraint. **on ice** *our project is on ice for the moment* in abeyance, in reserve, awaiting attention, pending.

ice *verb* **1** *ice the drinks* add ice to, cool, chill, refrigerate. **2** *ice the cake* cover with icing, frost, add frosting to, glaze. **ice over** *the lake has iced over* freeze, freeze over, harden, solidify.

icing *noun* *icing on the birthday cake* frosting, glaze; butter icing.

icon *noun* image, idol, likeness, representation, figure, statue.

icy *adjective* **1** *icy winds/weather* freezing, frigid, chill, chilly, chilling, frosty, biting, bitter, raw, arctic, glacial, Siberian, polar, gelid. **2** *icy roads* frozen over, ice-bound, frosty, rimy, glassy, like a sheet of glass, slippery. **3** *an icy welcome* cold, cool, frigid, frosty, stiff, aloof, distant, unfriendly, unwelcoming, unresponsive, uncommunicative, reserved, reticent, constrained, restrained.
Antonyms: BOILING; HOT; WARM.

idea *noun* **1** *the idea of death scares her* concept, conception, conceptualization, perception, thought, image, abstraction, notion. **2** *tell him your ideas on the subject* thought, theory, view, viewpoint, opinion, feeling, outlook, belief, judgment, conclusion. **3** *I had an idea that he was dead* thought, understanding, belief, impression, feeling, notion, suspicion, fancy, inkling. **4** *could you give me some idea of the cost?* estimation, approximation, guess, surmise; *inf.* guesstimate. **5** *our idea is to open a new store* plan, design, scheme, aim, intention, objective, object, purpose, end, goal, target. **6** *she's not my idea of a good mother* notion, vision, archetype, ideal example, exemplar, pattern.

---

idea
concept, conception, impression, notion, thought
If you have an **idea** it might refer to something perceived through the senses (*I had no idea it was so cold out*), to something visualized (*the idea of a joyous family outing*), or to something that is the product of the imagination (*a great idea for raising money*). *Idea* is a comprehensive word that applies to almost any aspect of mental activity. A **thought**, on the other hand, is an

idea that is the result of meditation, reasoning, or some other intellectual activity (*she hadn't given much thought to the possibility of losing*). A **notion** is a vague or capricious idea, often without any sound basis (*he had a notion that he could get there by hitchhiking*). A widely held idea of what something is or should be is a **concept** (*the concept of loyalty was beyond him*), while a **conception** is a concept that is held by an individual or small group and that is often colored by imagination and feeling (*her conception of marriage as a romantic ideal*). An idea that is triggered by something external is an **impression**, a word that suggests a half-formed mental picture or superficial view (*he made a good impression; she had the impression that everything would be taken care of*).

---

ideal *noun* standard of perfection/excellence, epitome, peak of perfection, paragon, nonpareil; archetype, prototype, model, pattern, exemplar, example, paradigm, criterion, yardstick.

ideal *adjective* **1** *ideal beauty* perfect, consummate, supreme, absolute, complete, flawless, exemplary, classic, archetypal, model, quintessential. **2** *confusing ideal and concrete matters* abstract, conceptual, intellectual, mental, philosophical, theoretical, hypothetical. **3** *she dreams of an ideal world* unattainable, Utopian, unreal, impracticable, ivory-towered, imaginary, romantic, visionary, fanciful.

idealist *noun* **1** *an idealist who does not accept second-best* perfectionist. **2** *idealist dreaming of a perfect world* Utopian, visionary, romanticist.

idealistic *adjective* Utopian, perfectionist, visionary, romantic, quixotic, unrealistic, impracticable, castle-building.
Antonyms: PRACTICAL; REALISTIC; DOWN-TO-EARTH.

ideally *adverb* *ideally, everyone should have enough to live on* in a perfect world, in a Utopia, all things being equal, theoretically, hypothetically, in theory.

ideals *plural noun* *a man of high ideals* principles, standards, moral values; morals, morality, ethics, code of ethics.

identical *adjective* **1** *that is the identical dress that she wore last night* same, very same, one and the same, selfsame. **2** *they have identical personalities* alike, like, very much the same, indistinguishable, corresponding, matching, twin.
Antonyms: DIFFERENT; UNLIKE.

identification noun **1** *witnesses helping in the identification of the criminal* recognition, singling out, spotting, pinpointing, naming; *inf.* fingering. See IDENTIFY 1. **2** *the identification of the best method* establishment, finding out, ascertainment, diagnosis, selection, choice. **3** *show the doorman his identification* ID card, ID, badge, letter of introduction; papers, credentials. **4** *her identification with her fellow patient* empathy, rapport, bond of sympathy, sympathy.

identify verb **1** *identify the criminal* recognize, single out, pick out, spot, point out, pinpoint, discern, distinguish, name; *inf.* put the finger on, finger. **2** *identify the problem* establish, find out, ascertain, diagnose, select, choose. **3** *I identify her with my youth* associate, connect, think of in connection. **identify with** *she identifies with all struggling artists* empathize with, sympathize with, relate to, respond to.

identity noun **1** *the identity of the criminal has not been established* name, specification. **2** *felt that he lost his identity on emigrating* personality, self, selfhood, ego, individuality, distinctiveness, singularity, uniqueness, differentness. **3** *a case of mistaken identity* identification, recognition, naming. **4** *the identity of their interests* identicalness, sameness, selfsameness, indistinguishability, interchangeability, likeness, alikeness, similarity, closeness, accordance.

ideology noun doctrine, creed, credo, teaching, dogma, theory, thesis; tenets, beliefs, opinions.

idiocy noun **1** *the idiocy of their actions* stupidity, stupidness, foolishness, senselessness, inanity, absurdity, fatuity, fatuousness, asininity, lack of intelligence, lunacy, craziness, insanity; *inf.* dumbness, daftness. **2** *tired of your idiocy* stupid actions, inane remarks; foolish talk, absurdity.
Antonyms: WISDOM; SENSE.

idiom noun **1** *unable to think of a clever idiom* turn of phrase, fixed expression, phrase, expression, locution. **2** *adopt the modern idiom* language, mode of expression, phraseology, style of speech, speech, talk, usage, parlance, vernacular, jargon, patois; *inf.* lingo.

idiosyncrasy noun peculiarity, individual/personal trait, singularity, oddity, eccentricity, mannerism, quirk, habit, characteristic, speciality, quality, feature.

idiot noun *the idiots stole the car* blockhead, nitwit, dunderhead, dolt, dunce, halfwit, fool, ass, boob, nincompoop, ninny, ignoramus, cretin, moron; *inf.* numskull, dimwit.

idiotic adjective *an idiotic idea/action* stupid, foolish, senseless, inane, absurd, fatuous, asinine, unintelligent, halfwitted, harebrained, lunatic, crazy, insane, moronic; *inf.* dumb, daft.

idle adjective **1** *an idle fellow* lazy, indolent, slothful, shiftless, sluggish, loafing, do-nothing, dronish. **2** *machines lying idle* not in operation, not operating, inoperative, not working, inactive, out of action, unused, not in use, moth-

balled. **3** *the building workers are idle just now* not working, unemployed, out of work, jobless, out of a job, redundant; *inf.* on the dole. **4** *pass away the idle hours* unoccupied, empty, vacant, unfilled. **5** *idle rumors* groundless, without grounds, baseless, foundationless, lacking foundation. **6** *idle remarks* unimportant, trivial, trifling, shallow, foolish, insignificant, superficial, without depth, inane, fatuous, senseless, meaningless, purposeless, unnecessary. **7** *idle threats* useless, in vain, vain, worthless, futile, ineffective, ineffectual, inefficacious, unproductive, fruitless, pointless, meaningless. **8** *idle pleasures* frivolous, trivial, trifling, shallow, insubstantial, worthless, nugatory.
Antonyms: INDUSTRIOUS; ACTIVE; BUSY; MEANINGFUL.

idle verb **1** *idle away the hours* while, laze, loaf, lounge, loiter, dawdle, dally, fritter, putter, waste. **2** *stop idling and work* do nothing, sit back and do nothing, laze, loaf, be inactive, mark time, shirk, slack, vegetate; *inf.* take it easy, rest on one's oars.

idol noun **1** *pagans worshiping idols* icon, god, false god, effigy, image, graven image, fetish, likeness. **2** *the singer is the idol of teenagers* hero, heroine, favorite, darling, beloved, pet, apple of one's eye, blue-eyed boy/girl, star, superstar; *inf.* pinup.

idolatrous adjective **1** *idolatrous tribes of old* idol-worshiping, icon-worshiping, pagan, heathen, heretical. **2** *idolatrous fans of the singer* hero-worshiping, idolizing, worshiping, worshipful, adulatory, adoring, reverential.

idolatry noun **1** *religion based on idolatry* idolism, idolization, idolatrism, idol-worship, fetishism, icon-worship, paganism, heathenism. **2** *the fans responded to her with pure idolatry* idolization, idolizing, doting, worshiping, hero-worshiping, adulation, adoring, adoration, blind adoration, admiration, lionization, lionizing, reverence, glorification.

idolize verb **1** *idolize false gods* worship, bow down before, glorify, exalt, revere, deify. **2** *idolize the singer* hero-worship, worship, adulate, adore, love, look up to, admire, dote upon, lionize, reverence, revere, venerate.

idyll noun **1** *poets writing idylls* pastoral, eclogue, rural poem. **2** *enjoying an idyll* wonderful/perfect/romantic time, moment of bliss, paradise, heaven on earth.

if conjunction **1** *if you go, he will go* on condition that, provided, providing, supposing, assuming, on the assumption that, allowing that. **2** *I don't know if he will come* whether, whether or not. **3** *a boring if well-paid job* although, even though, however, yet.

if noun *the situation is full of ifs* doubt, uncertainty, hesitation, condition, stipulation.

iffy adjective **1** *the situation is a bit iffy* doubtful, uncertain, unsure, undecided, unsettled, indeterminate, unresolved; *inf.* up in the air. **2** *I'm a bit iffy about going* doubtful, dubious, unsure, uncertain, undecided, hesitant, tentative.

ignite *verb* **1** *ignite the fire* light, set fire to, set on fire, set alight, fire, kindle, inflame, touch off; *inf.* set/put a match to. **2** *the fire ignited* catch/take fire, catch, burst into flames, burn up, burn, flame up, kindle.
Antonyms: EXTINGUISH; DOUSE, DOWSE.

ignominious *adjective* **1** *an ignominious defeat* shameful, dishonorable, disgraceful, humiliating, mortifying, discreditable, disreputable, undignified, infamous, ignoble, inglorious, scandalous, abject, sorry, base. **2** *his ignominious behavior* contemptible, despicable, offensive, revolting, wicked, vile, base, low.
Antonyms: HONORABLE; GLORIOUS; ADMIRABLE.

ignominy *noun* **1** *the ignominy of defeat* shame, dishonor, disgrace, humiliation, mortification, discredit, stigma, disrepute, infamy, ignobleness, scandal, opprobrium, abjectness. **2** *behave with ignominy* contemptibleness, dishonor, wickedness, baseness, vileness, dishonesty, treachery.
Antonyms: HONOR; GLORY.

ignorance *noun* **1** *ignorance of the law* unawareness, unfamiliarity, unconsciousness, lack of enlightenment, lack of knowledge/information, inexperience, greenness, innocence. **2** *appalled at the ignorance of the pupils* lack of education/knowledge, illiteracy, lack of intelligence, unintelligence, stupidity, thickness, denseness, unenlightenment, benightedness.
Antonyms: KNOWLEDGE; EDUCATION; ENLIGHTENMENT.

ignorant *adjective* **1** *ignorant of legal procedure* unaware of, unfamiliar with, unconversant with, unacquainted with, unconscious of, uninformed about, unenlightened about, inexperienced in, blind to, uninitiated in, unschooled in, naïve about, innocent about; *inf.* in the dark about. **2** *ignorant pupils* unscholarly, uneducated, untaught, unschooled, untutored, untrained, illiterate, unlettered, unlearned, unread, uninformed, unknowledgeable, unintelligent, stupid, unenlightened, benighted; *inf.* thick, dense, dumb. **3** *ill-mannered, ignorant louts* rude, crude, coarse, vulgar, gross, insensitive.

---

ignorant
illiterate, uneducated, uninformed, unlearned, unlettered, untutored

Someone who knows nothing about growing things might be called **ignorant** by a farmer who never went to high school but has spent his life in the fields. Although all of these adjectives refer to a lack of knowledge, *ignorant* refers to a lack of knowledge in general (*a foolish, ignorant person*) or to a lack of knowledge of some particular subject (*ignorant of the fine points of financial management*). A professor of art history might refer to someone who doesn't know how to look at a painting as **uneducated** or **untutored**, both of which refer to a lack of formal education in schools (*she was very bright but basically uneducated, and completely untutored in the fine arts*). Someone who cannot read or write is **illiterate**, a term that may also denote a failure to display civility or cultivated behavior (*the professor routinely referred to his students as illiterate louts*). Someone who is **unlettered** lacks a knowledge of fine literature (*a scientist who was highly trained but unlettered*); it also implies being able to read and write, but with no skill in either of these areas. **Unlearned** is similar to *ignorant* in that it refers to a lack of learning in general or in a specific subject (*an unlearned man who managed to become a millionaire*), but it does not carry the same negative connotations. **Uninformed** refers to a lack of definite information or data. For example, one can be highly intelligent and well educated but still *uninformed* about the latest developments in earthquake prediction.

---

ignore *verb* **1** *ignore their nasty remarks* disregard, pay no attention/heed to, take no notice of, brush aside, pass over, shrug off, push aside, shut one's eyes to, be oblivious to, turn a blind eye to, turn a deaf ear to. **2** *ignore her former friend* slight, spurn, cold-shoulder, look right through, look past, turn one's back on; *inf.* give someone the brush-off, pass up. **3** *just ignore the first question* set aside, pay no attention to, take no account of, omit, leave out, overlook, neglect; *inf.* skip.

ill *adjective* **1** *the patient has been ill for some time* | *feeling rather ill* not well, unwell, ailing, poorly, sick, sickly, on the sick list, infirm, off-color, afflicted, indisposed, out of sorts, diseased, bedridden, weak, feeble; *inf.* under the weather, laid up, queasy. **2** *the ill feeling/will in the firm* hostile, antagonistic, acrimonious, belligerent, bellicose, unfriendly, unkind, spiteful, rancorous, resentful, malicious, malevolent, bitter. **3** *his ill temper* fractious, irritable, irascible, cross, cantankerous, crabbed, surly, snappish, gruff, sullen. **4** *an ill wind* | *suffering ill luck* adverse, unfavorable, unadvantageous, unlucky, unfortunate, unpropitious, inauspicious, unpromising, ominous, infelicitous. **5** *the ill effects of the medicine/accident* harmful, detrimental, deleterious, hurtful, damaging, pernicious, destructive, ruinous. **6** *a person of ill repute* bad, infamous, low, wicked, nefarious, vile, evil, foul, sinful, iniquitous, sinister, corrupt, depraved, degenerate. **7** *ill manners* rude, unmannerly, impolite, objectionable, boorish. **8** *ill management* unsatisfactory, unacceptable, inadequate, deficient, faulty, poor, unskillful, inexpert. **ill at ease** *adjective* uncomfortable, uneasy, awkward, embarrassed, self-

conscious, out of place, strange, unsure, uncertain, unsettled, hesitant, faltering, restless, unrelaxed, disquieted, unquiet, disturbed, discomfited, troubled, anxious, on edge, edgy, nervous, tense, on tenterhooks, apprehensive, distrustful; *inf.* on pins and needles.
Antonyms: HEALTHY; WELL; FRIENDLY; FAVORABLE.

ill noun **1** *she meant him no ill* harm, hurt, injury, mischief, pain, trouble, unpleasantness, misfortune. **2** *the ills of life* pain, misfortune, suffering, misery, woe, affliction, damage, disaster, tribulation; troubles, problems, trials. **3** *bodily ills* illness, ill/poor health; ailment, disorder, complaint, sickness, disease, malady, infirmity, indisposition, infection, contagion.

ill adverb **1** *speak ill of them* badly, unfavorably, with disfavor, with disapproval, with hostility, hostilely, unkindly, maliciously, spitefully. **2** *it went ill with them* badly, hard, adversely, unsuccessfully, unfortunately, unluckily, inauspiciously. **3** *we could ill afford it* barely, scarcely, hardly, with difficulty. **4** *ill-adapted to country life* badly, poorly, insufficiently, inadequately, unsatisfactorily, faultily.

ill-advised adjective unwise, ill-considered, imprudent, incautious, injudicious, ill-judged, impolitic, misguided, foolish, foolhardy, rash, hasty, shortsighted, uncircumspect, thoughtless, careless, reckless.
Antonyms: WISE; SENSIBLE.

ill-bred adjective ill-mannered, bad-mannered, unmannerly, rude, impolite, discourteous, uncivil, ungentlemanly, unladylike, boorish, churlish, loutish, vulgar, coarse, crass, uncouth, crude, unrefined, uncivilized, ungallant, indelicate, indecorous, unseemly.

ill-defined adjective indistinct, unclear, blurred, fuzzy, vague, nebulous, shadowy, dim.

ill-disposed adjective hostile, opposing, opposed, antagonistic, unfriendly, unsympathetic, averse, contrary, antipathetic, inimical; *inf.* down on.

illegal adjective unlawful, illegitimate, illicit, lawless, criminal, actionable, felonious, unlicensed, unauthorized, unsanctioned, unwarranted, unofficial, outlawed, forbidden, banned, barred, prohibited, interdicted, proscribed, contraband, black-market, under the counter, bootleg.
Antonyms: LEGAL; LAWFUL.

illegible adjective unreadable, hard to read, indecipherable, unintelligible, scrawled, scribbled, hieroglyphic, squiggly, crabbed, faint, obscure; *inf.* clear as mud.
Antonyms: LEGIBLE; READABLE.

illegitimate adjective **1** *illegitimate use of property* illegal, unlawful, illicit, lawless, criminal, unlicensed, unauthorized, unsanctioned. *See* ILLEGAL. **2** *an illegitimate child* natural, love, born out of wedlock, fatherless, bastard. **3** *an illegitimate deduction* illogical, wrongly inferred/deduced, unsound, spurious, incorrect, invalid. **4** *illegitimate language usage* irregular,

nonstandard, substandard, ungrammatical, dialectal, colloquial, informal.
Antonyms: LAWFUL; LEGAL; LEGITIMATE.

ill-fated adjective unlucky, luckless, unfortunate, hapless, unhappy, doomed, blighted, star-crossed, ill-starred, ill-omened.

ill-favored adjective plain, ugly, ugly looking, hideous, unsightly, unlovely, unattractive, homely.

ill feeling noun ill will, bad blood, hostility, enmity, hatred, no love lost, antipathy, aversion, dislike, antagonism, acrimony, animus, indignation, anger, wrath, unfriendliness, unkindness, spite, spitefulness, rancor, grudge, resentment, bitterness, dissatisfaction, malice, malevolence, belligerence, bellicosity; hard feelings.
Antonyms: FRIENDSHIP; GOODWILL.

ill-founded adjective baseless, groundless, without foundation, foundationless, unjustified, unsupported, unsubstantiated, unproven, unverified, unauthenticated, unreliable.

ill humor noun ill temper, bad temper, temper, bad mood, huff, pet, fit of pique, rage; moodiness, irritability, irascibility, peevishness, crossness, crabbedness, testiness.

illicit adjective illegal, unlawful, illegitimate, lawless, criminal, unlicensed, unauthorized, unsanctioned, unofficial, outlawed, banned, forbidden, prohibited. *See* ILLEGAL.
Antonyms: LICIT; LEGAL; LAWFUL.

illiteracy noun illiterateness, inability to read; lack of education, ignorance, unenlightenment; *lit.* nescience.

illiterate adjective unable to read; uneducated, untaught, unschooled, untutored, uninstructed, unlearned, unlettered, ignorant; *lit.* nescient.

ill-judged adjective ill-advised, ill-considered, unwise, imprudent, injudicious, misguided, foolish, foolhardy, rash, hasty, shortsighted. *See* ILL-ADVISED.

ill-mannered adjective unmannerly, mannerless, rude, impolite, discourteous, uncivil, insolent, impertinent, badly behaved, ill-behaved, boorish, loutish, oafish, uncouth, coarse, gross, ill-bred.

ill-natured adjective ill-tempered, bad-tempered, ill-humored, moody, irritable, irascible, surly, peevish, petulant, cross, crabbed, testy, grouchy, disagreeable, perverse, mean, nasty, disobliging, spiteful, malicious.

illness noun ailment, sickness, disorder, complaint, malady, disease, affliction, attack, disability, indisposition, infection, contagion; ill health, poor health.
Antonyms: HEALTH; FITNESS.

illogical adjective unsound, unreasonable, unreasoned, irrational, faulty, spurious, fallacious, fallible, unproved, untenable, specious, unscientific, sophistic, casuistic, inconclusive, inconsistent, incorrect, invalid, wrong, absurd, preposterous, meaningless, senseless.

ill-starred *adjective* ill-fated, unlucky, unfortunate, doomed. *See* ILL-FATED.

ill-tempered *adjective* ill-humored, cross, bad-tempered, irritable, irascible, peevish, crabbed, choleric, cantankerous, grumpy, grouchy, crusty, splenetic.

ill-timed *adjective* inopportune, inconvenient, awkward, inappropriate, untimely, mistimed, badly timed, unwelcome, unfavorable, unfortunate, inept.
Antonyms: OPPORTUNE; TIMELY.

ill-treat *verb* treat badly, abuse, harm, injure, damage, handle roughly, mishandle, ill-use, maltreat, misuse; *inf.* knock about.
Antonyms: PAMPER; COSSET; SPOIL.

illuminate *verb* **1** *lights illuminating the hall* light, light up, throw/cast light upon, brighten, shine on, irradiate; *lit.* illumine. **2** *illuminate the problem* clarify, make clear, clear up, shed/cast light on, elucidate, explain, make explicit, explicate, expound. **3** *illuminate a manuscript* adorn, decorate, ornament, embellish, enhance, illustrate.
Antonyms: DARKEN; CONFUSE.

illuminating *adjective* *an illuminating talk* instructive, informative, enlightening, explanatory, revealing, helpful.

illumination *noun* **1** *the illumination of the hall* lighting, lighting up, brightening, irradiation. *See* ILLUMINATE 1. **2** *see the illumination in the dark* light, beam/ray/shaft of light, radiance, gleam, glitter, effulgence; lights. **3** *the illumination of the problem* clarification, elucidation, explanation, explication. *See* ILLUMINATE 2. **4** *the speech provided us with further illumination* enlightenment, understanding, awareness, insight, learning, education, instruction, information, knowledge, revelation.

illusion *noun* **1** *create the illusion of depth* false/deceptive appearance, deception, faulty perception, misperception. **2** *under the illusion that he was her first love* delusion, misapprehension, misconception, deception, false/mistaken impression, fallacy, error, misjudgment, fancy. **3** *see an illusion* hallucination, figment of the imagination, phantom, specter, mirage, phantasm, fantasy, will-o'-the-wisp, ignis fatuus.
Antonyms: REALITY; TRUTH.

illusive, illusory *adjective* deceptive, delusory, delusional, delusive, illusionary, false, fallacious, mistaken, erroneous, misleading, untrue, specious, unreal, imagined, imaginary, fancied, nonexistent, fanciful, chimerical, notional, dreamlike.

illustrate *verb* **1** *illustrate the story* add pictures/drawings/sketches to, provide artwork for, adorn, decorate, ornament, embellish. **2** *illustrate his point* exemplify, demonstrate, point up, show, instance, make plain/clear, clarify, bring home, emphasize, interpret.

illustration *noun* **1** *the illustration in the child's book* picture, drawing, sketch, plate, figure; artwork, adornment, decoration, ornamentation, embellishment. **2** *interesting illustrations explaining his theory* example, typical case, case in point, instance, specimen, sample, exemplar, analogy. **3** *appreciate the illustration of his theory* exemplification, demonstration, pointing up, showing, instancing, clarification, emphasis, interpretation.

illustrative *adjective* exemplifying, explanatory, elucidative, explicative, expository, interpretative, interpretive.

illustrious *adjective* renowned, famous, famed, well-known, celebrated, acclaimed, noted, notable, distinguished, esteemed, honored, prominent, preeminent, splendid, brilliant, remarkable, great, noble, glorious, exalted, venerable.
Antonyms: UNKNOWN; OBSCURE.

ill will *noun* ill feeling, bad blood, hostility, enmity, hatred, antipathy, antagonism, acrimony, animus, unfriendliness, spite, rancor, resentment, malice; hard feelings.

image *noun* **1** *images of the saints* likeness, representation, resemblance, effigy, figure, figurine, doll, statue, statuette, sculpture, bust, idol, icon, fetish, graven image, painting, picture, portrait. **2** *the image formed by the camera/telescope* reproduction, optical representation, reflection; picture, facsimile, photograph, snapshot, photo. **3** *an image of what the new country would be like* mental picture/representation, vision, concept, conception, idea, perception, impression, fancy, thought. **4** *he is the image of his father* double, living image, replica, clone, copy, reproduction, counterpart, similitude, doppelgänger; *inf.* spitting image, chip off the old block, ringer, dead ringer. **5** *politicians trying to improve their images* public impression/perception/conception. **6** *he is the image of goodness* emblem, symbol, archetype, perfect example, embodiment, incarnation. **7** *the use of images in poetry* figure of speech, conceit, figurative expression.

imaginable *adjective* thinkable, conceivable, supposable, believable, credible, comprehensible, possible, within the bounds of possibility, probable, likely, plausible, feasible.

imaginary *adjective* fanciful, fancied, fantastic, unreal, nonexistent, illusory, illusive, visionary, dreamy, dreamlike, shadowy, unsubstantial, chimerical, figmental, notional, assumed, supposed, suppositious, fictitious, fictional, legendary, mythical, mythological, made-up, invented, hallucinatory, phantasmal, phantasmic, spectral, ghostly, ideal, idealistic, Utopian, romantic.
Antonyms: REAL; ACTUAL.

imagination *noun* **1** *the poem shows imagination* |

handling the project needs imagination imaginative faculty, creative power, creativity, vision, inspiration, fancifulness, insight, inventiveness, originality, invention, innovation, resourcefulness, ingenuity, enterprise, cleverness, wit. **2** *I thought I saw her but it was only my imagination* mental image, illusion, fancy, figment of the imagination, vision, dream, chimera, shadow, phantom, conceptualization, unreality.

imaginative *adjective an imaginative writer/cook/ planner* creative, visionary, inspired, fanciful, inventive, original, innovative, resourceful, ingenious, enterprising, clever, whimsical.
Antonyms: UNIMAGINATIVE; RUN-OF-THE-MILL; PEDESTRIAN.

imagine *verb* **1** *he imagines a bright future for himself* picture, see in the mind's eye, visualize, envisage, envision, conjure up, dream about, dream up, fantasize about, conceptualize, think up, conceive, think of, plan, project, scheme. **2** *I imagine he will be late* assume, presume, suppose, think, believe, be of the opinion that, take it, gather, fancy, judge, deem, infer, deduce, conjecture, surmise, guess, reckon, suspect, realize.

imbecile *noun* fool, idiot, dolt, halfwit, nitwit, dunce, dunderhead, dullard, simpleton; *inf.* dimwit, dope.

imbecilic *adjective* stupid, foolish, idiotic, doltish, halfwitted, witless, dull; silly, senseless, absurd, crazy, mad, fatuous, inane, asinine; *inf.* dim-witted, dopey.

imbed *verb See* EMBED *verb.*

imbibe *verb* **1** *imbibe some water* drink, quaff, swallow, consume; *inf.* swig, knock back. **2** *he doesn't imbibe any more* drink, drink alcohol, take strong drink. **3** *imbibe the fresh air* drink in, breathe in, inhale. **4** *imbibe ideas* assimilate, absorb, take in, digest, learn, acquire, gain, pick up. **5** *imbibe moisture* absorb, soak up, blot up, sop up, suck up, draw up, take up.

imbroglio *noun* **1** *the heads of state met to prevent an international imbroglio* complicated situation, complication, complexity, problem, difficulty, trouble, entanglement, confusion, muddle, mess, quandary. **2** *an imbroglio of papers* confused heap, jumble, muddle, mess. **3** *people involved in an imbroglio in the bar* disagreement, conflict, altercation, argument, quarrel, fight, commotion, disturbance, turmoil, fracas.

imbue *verb* *he imbues his sermons with topicality* fill, impregnate, inject, inculcate, instill, ingrain, inspire, permeate, charge.

imitate *verb* **1** *imitate the language of Shakespeare | imitate his elder brother in everything* copy, emulate, take as a model/pattern, follow the example of, follow as an example, take after, follow, follow suit, take a page from someone's book, tread in the steps of, walk in the footsteps of, echo. **2** *comics imitating celebrities | imitate a dog* mimic, ape, imper-

sonate, do an impression of, parody, mock, caricature, burlesque, travesty; *inf.* send up, take off, spoof, do, make like. **3** *the stage set imitated a city street* look like, simulate, echo, mirror. **4** *imitate the portrait* copy, reproduce, replicate, duplicate, counterfeit, forge, fake.

---

imitate
ape, copy, impersonate, mimic, mock

A young girl might **imitate** her mother by answering the phone in exactly the same tone of voice, while a teenager who deliberately *imitates* the way her mother talks for the purpose of irritating her would more accurately be said to **mimic** her. *Imitate* implies following something as an example or model (*he imitated the playing style of his music teacher*), while *mimic* suggests imitating someone's mannerisms for fun or ridicule (*they liked to mimic the teacher's southern drawl*). To **copy** is to imitate or reproduce something as closely as possible (*he copied the style of dress and speech used by the other gang members*). When someone assumes another person's appearance or mannerisms, sometimes for the purpose of perpetrating a fraud, he or she is said to **impersonate** (*arrested for impersonating a police officer; a comedian well known for impersonating political figures*). **Ape** and **mock** both imply an unflattering imitation. Someone who mimics in a contemptuous way is said to **ape** (*he entertained everyone in the office by aping the boss's phone conversations with his wife*), while someone who imitates with the intention of belittling or irritating is said to *mock* (*the students openly mocked their teacher's attempt to have a serious discussion about sex*).

---

imitation *noun* **1** *the house was built in imitation of Frank Lloyd Wright* emulation, resemblance. *See* IMITATE 1. **2** *the comic's imitations of celebrities* mimicking, mimicry, aping, impersonation, impression, parody, mocking, mockery, caricature, burlesque, travesty; *inf.* send-up, take-off, spoof. **3** *a bad imitation of the portrait* copy, reproduction, counterfeit, forgery, fake.

imitation *adjective* *imitation leather/antiques* artificial, synthetic, simulated, man-made, ersatz, mock, sham, fake, reproduction, repro; *inf.* pseudo, phony.
Antonyms: REAL; GENUINE.

imitative *adjective* **1** *an imitative style | a style imitative of Steinbeck* in imitation of, copying, copied, emulating, emulated, derivative, unoriginal, mimicking, mimetic, echoic, parrotlike, plagiarized, secondhand; *inf.* copycat. **2** *an imitative word* onomatopoeic, echoic.

imitator *noun* copier, copyist, emulator, follower, mimic, echo, impersonator, epigone, plagiarist, counterfeiter, forger, ape, parrot.

immaculate *adjective* **1** *immaculate white sheets | immaculate rooms* clean, spotless, unsoiled, unstained, snowy-white, whiter than white,

speckless, spick-and-span, neat, neat as a pin, spruce, trim. **2** *of immaculate character* flawless, faultless, stainless, unblemished, spotless, pure, perfect, above reproach, innocent, virtuous, incorrupt, guiltless, sinless, unsullied, undefiled, untarnished, uncontaminated, unpolluted.
Antonyms: FILTHY; DIRTY; blemished; tarnished.

immaterial *adjective* **1** *it's immaterial what he thinks* unimportant, inconsequential, of no matter, of little account, irrelevant, insignificant, trivial, petty, slight, inappreciable. **2** *as immaterial as ghosts* not material, incorporeal, bodiless, unembodied, disembodied, discarnate, intangible, impalpable, ethereal, unsubstantial, airy, aerial, spiritual, ghostly, transcendental, unearthly, supernatural.
Antonyms: IMPORTANT; SIGNIFICANT; TANGIBLE.

immature *adjective* **1** *immature fruit/plans* unripe, undeveloped, unformed, imperfect, unfinished, incomplete, half-grown, crude, raw, green, unmellowed, unfledged, untimely. **2** *an immature young man* adolescent, childish, babyish, infantile, juvenile, puerile, jejune, callow, inexperienced, green, unsophisticated; *inf.* wet behind the ears.
Antonyms: RIPE; MATURE.

immaturity *noun* **1** *the immaturity of the fruit/plans* unripeness, imperfection, lack of completion, crudeness, crudity, rawness, greenness. *See* IMMATURE 1. **2** *the immaturity of the young men* adolescence, childishness, babyishness, infantileness, juvenility, puerility, lack of experience, inexperience. *See* IMMATURE 2 .

immeasurable *adjective* not measurable, measureless, limitless, boundless, unbounded, illimitable, infinite, incalculable, unfathomable, fathomless, undeterminable, indeterminate, inestimable, extensive, vast, innumerable, countless, numberless, endless, never-ending, interminable, inexhaustible, bottomless.

immediate *adjective* **1** *an immediate reaction* instant, instantaneous, on the spot, prompt, swift, speedy, sudden, abrupt. **2** *his immediate neighbor* near, nearest, next, next door, close, closest, adjacent, adjoining, abutting, contiguous, proximate. **3** *the immediate cause of his failure* direct, primary. **4** *in the immediate past* recent. **5** *our immediate plans* present, current, existing, existent, actual, extant, urgent, pressing. **6** *get immediate experience* direct, firsthand, hands on, in service, in the field, on the job.

immediately *adverb* **1** *he went away immediately* right away, right now, straight away, at once, instantly, instantaneously, now, this/that very second/minute, this/that instant, directly, promptly, forthwith, without delay, without hesitation, unhesitatingly, post-haste, *tout de suite*; *inf.* before you can/could say Jack Robinson, in the wink/twinkling of an eye, lickety-

split, pronto. **2** *he was immediately behind us* right, directly, closely, at close quarters. **3** *I heard the news immediately from the victim* directly, firsthand, at first hand, without intermediary.

immemorial *adjective* ancient, age-old, timeless, dateless, archaic, of yore, rooted in the past, long-standing, time-honored, ancestral, traditional.

immense *adjective* huge, vast, massive, enormous, gigantic, colossal, giant, great, very large, extensive, infinite, immeasurable, illimitable, monumental, tremendous, prodigious, elephantine, monstrous, titanic; *inf.* mega.
Antonyms: TINY; MINUTE.

immerse *verb* **1** *immerse the cloth in the dye* submerge, plunge, dip, dunk, duck, sink, douse, souse, soak, drench, imbue, saturate. **2** *immerse the Christian converts* baptize, christen, purify, lustrate. **3** *immerse oneself in one's work* absorb, engross, occupy, engage, preoccupy, involve, engulf; *inf.* lose.

immigrant *noun* nonnative, settler, incomer, newcomer, new arrival, migrant, naturalized citizen, expatriate.

imminent *adjective* impending, at hand, fast-approaching, close, near, approaching, coming, forthcoming, on the way, about to happen, upon us, in the offing, on the horizon, in the air, brewing, threatening, menacing, looming.
Antonyms: DISTANT; REMOTE.

immobile *adjective* immobilized, without moving, unmoving, motionless, unable to move, immovable, still, static, at rest, stationary, at a standstill, stock-still, dormant, rooted, fixed to the spot, rigid, frozen, stiff, riveted, like a statue, as if turned to stone, immotile, immotive.

immobilize *verb* bring to a standstill/halt, halt, stop, put out of action, render inactive, inactivate, paralyze, make inoperative, freeze, transfix, disable, cripple.

immoderate *adjective* excessive, extreme, intemperate, lavish, undue, inordinate, extravagant, unreasonable, unjustified, unwarranted, uncontrolled, uncalled-for, outrageous, egregious, unrestrained, unrestricted, unlimited, unbridled, uncurbed, self-indulgent, overindulgent, prodigal, profligate, wanton, dissipative.

immoderation *noun* excess, excessiveness, intemperateness, inordinateness, lavishness, lack of restraint, self-indulgence, overindulgence, profligacy, wantonness, dissipation. *See* IMMODERATE.

immodest *adjective* forward, bold, brazen, impudent, unblushing, shameless, wanton, indecorous, improper, indecent; *inf.* fresh, cheeky.

immoral *adjective* bad, wrong, unprincipled, dishonest, unethical, wicked, evil, sinful, impure, iniquitous, corrupt, depraved, vile, base, degenerate, debauched, abandoned, dissolute, villainous, nefarious, miscreant, reprobate, perverted, indecent, lewd, licentious, pornographic, unchaste, of easy virtue, bawdy.

immorality *noun* badness, wrongdoing, dishonesty, unethicalness, wickedness, evil, impurity, sinfulness, sin, iniquity, corruption, depravity, vileness, vice, turpitude, degeneracy, debauchery, dissolution, perversion, indecency, lewdness, licentiousness, bawdiness. *See* IMMORAL.

immortal *adjective* **1** *immortal beings/love* never dying, undying, deathless, eternal, ever-living, everlasting, never-ending, endless, imperishable, perdurable, timeless, indestructible, unfading, undecaying, perennial, evergreen, perpetual, lasting, enduring, constant, abiding, immutable, indissoluble; *lit.* sempiternal. **2** *immortal poets* famous, celebrated, remembered, commemorated, honored, lauded, glorified.
Antonyms: MORTAL; EPHEMERAL; TRANSITORY.

immortal *noun* **1** *mythological immortals* god, goddess, Olympian. **2** *the immortals of poetry* great, hero, genius, celebrity.

immortality *noun* **1** *gods blessed with immortality* eternal life, deathlessness, everlastingness, endlessness, imperishability, timelessness, unfadingness, evergreenness, perpetuality, constancy. *See* IMMORTAL *adjective* 1. **2** *the immortality of the poet* fame, renown, repute, celebrity, commemoration, honor, glory.

immortalize *verb* commemorate, memorialize, eternalize, eternize, perpetuate, exalt, laud, glorify.

immovable *adjective* **1** *immovable concrete pillars* set firm/fast, fast, firm, fixed, secure, stable, rooted, riveted, moored, anchored, stuck, jammed, stiff, unbudgeable. **2** *the spectators stood immovable* motionless, unmoving, stationary, still, stock-still, at a standstill, dead still, statuelike. **3** *the court was immovable in its ruling* adamant, firm, steadfast, unwavering, unswerving, resolute, determined, tenacious, stubborn, dogged, obdurate, inflexible, unyielding, unbending, uncompromising, unshakable, inexorable.

immune *adjective* not subject to, not liable to, protected from, safe from, unsusceptible to, secure against, exempt from, clear of, free from, freed from, absolved from, released from, excused from, relieved of, spared from, excepted from, exempted from, unaffected by, resistant to, protected from/against, proof against; *inf.* let off.
Antonyms: LIABLE; SUSCEPTIBLE; PRONE.

immunity *noun* *diplomatic immunity* indemnity, privilege, prerogative, special treatment, right, charter, liberty, license, permission. **immunity from 1** *immunity from the disease* nonsusceptibility to, resistance to, protection from, immunization/inoculation against. **2** *immunity from tax* | *the priest's immunity from testifying* nonliability for, exemption from, exception

from, freedom from, release from, indemnity from, dispensation from, absolution from, exoneration from, excusal from.

immunize *verb* inoculate, vaccinate, protect, shield, safeguard; *inf.* give a jab to.

imp *noun* **1** *devils and imps* little devil, demon, hobgoblin, goblin, elf, sprite, puck, gnome, dwarf. **2** *the child's a little imp* scamp, rogue, rascal, minx, mischief-maker, troublemaker, prankster, brat, gamin, urchin.

impact *noun* **1** *the impact of the two cars* collision, contact, crash, striking, clash, bumping, banging; jolt, thump, whack, thwack, slam, smack, slap. **2** *the impact of his talk* influence, effect, impression; results, consequences, repercussions. **3** *he took the full impact of the blow* force, full force, shock, brunt, impetus, pressure.

impair *verb* weaken, lessen, decrease, reduce, blunt, diminish, deteriorate, enfeeble, debilitate, enervate, damage, mar, spoil, injure, harm, hinder, disable, cripple, impede, undermine, vitiate.
Antonyms: IMPROVE; ENHANCE.

impale *verb* transfix, pierce, stab, prick, stick, spear, spike, run through, disembowel.

impalpable *adjective* **1** *if there is a lump in the abdomen, it is impalpable* intangible, imperceptible to the touch. **2** *find his conclusions impalpable* abstruse, obscure, unclear, indiscernible, tenuous, esoteric, recondite.

impart *verb* **1** *impart the good news* pass on, convey, communicate, transmit, relate, tell, make known, report, disclose, reveal, divulge, proclaim, broadcast. **2** *his age imparts wisdom to his words* bestow, confer, give, grant, lend, accord, afford, assign, offer, yield, contribute, dispense.

impartial *adjective* unbiased, unprejudiced, disinterested, detached, objective, neutral, equitable, evenhanded, fair, fair-minded, just, open-minded, without favoritism, free from discrimination, nonpartisan, with no ax to grind, without fear or favor.

impartiality *noun* lack of bias/prejudice, disinterest, detachment, objectivity, neutrality, evenhandedness, fairness, justness, openmindedness. *See* IMPARTIAL.

impassable *adjective* **1** *impassable roads* unnavigable, untraversable, impenetrable, closed, blocked, obstructed, pathless, trackless. **2** *impassable obstacles* insurmountable, insuperable, unconquerable.

impasse *noun* deadlock, dead end, stalemate, checkmate, standstill, full/dead stop, standoff.

impassioned *adjective* passionate, amorous, ardent, fervent, fervid, vehement, intense, violent, fiery, burning, inflamed, emotional, emotive, zealous, eager, enthusiastic, animated, excited, aroused, feverish, frantic.

impatience *noun* **1** *wait with impatience for the*

doors to open restlessness, restiveness, impetuosity, eagerness, avidity, excitability, anxiety, agitation, nervousness, edginess, fretfulness, jitteriness, fluster, disquiet, disquietude. **2** *answer with impatience* abruptness, brusqueness, shortness, curtness, irascibility, irritability, testiness, snappiness, querulousness, peevishness, intolerance.

impatient *adjective* **1** *an impatient crowd* restless, restive, impetuous, eager, excitable, anxious, agitated, nervous, edgy. **2** *an impatient answer* abrupt, brusque, terse, short, short-tempered, quick-tempered, curt, irritated, angry, testy, snappy, querulous, peevish, intolerant. **3** *impatient to see her boyfriend* anxious, eager, keen, avid, desirous, yearning, longing.

impeach *verb* **1** *impeach the president for high crimes* charge, accuse, bring a case/charge against, indict, inculpate, implicate, blame, censure, hold accountable, denounce, arraign. **2** *they impeached his honor* challenge, question, call into question, cast doubt on, impugn, attack, assail, revile, discredit, deprecate, cast slurs/aspersions on, malign, slander.

impeccable *adjective* **1** *impeccable behavior* | *speak impeccable French* perfect, faultless, flawless, unblemished, exemplary, correct, exact, precise, ideal. **2** *an impeccable young woman* virtuous, innocent, chaste, pure, pure as the driven snow, sinless, upright, irreproachable, unimpeachable, blameless, above suspicion, incorrupt.
Antonyms: IMPERFECT; SINFUL.

impecunious *adjective* penniless, insolvent, poor, poor as a church mouse, without a penny, without a sou, hard up, impoverished, poverty-stricken, destitute, unable to make ends meet, needy, indigent, penurious; *inf.* broke, flat-broke, stone-broke, strapped for cash, cleaned out.
Antonyms: WEALTHY; AFFLUENT.

impede *verb* hinder, obstruct, hamper, handicap, block, check, bar, curb, hold back, hold up, delay, interfere with, disrupt, retard, slow, slow down, brake, restrain, thwart, frustrate, balk, stop; *inf.* throw a monkey wrench in the works.
Antonyms: ASSIST; ADVANCE; FACILITATE.

impediment *noun* **1** *an impediment to our plans* hindrance, obstruction, obstacle, handicap, block, stumbling block, check, encumbrance, bar, barrier, curb, brake, restraint, drawback, difficulty, snag, setback. **2** *she has an impediment so has to speak slowly* stammer, stutter, speech defect, hesitancy, faltering.

impedimenta *plural noun* equipment, gear, baggage, luggage; effects, possessions, belongings, goods, movables, trappings, accouterments, odds and ends, things; *inf.* stuff.

impel *verb* **1** *impel him to go* urge, press, exhort, force, oblige, constrain, necessitate, require,

demand, make, apply pressure to, pressure, pressurize, spur, prod, goad, incite, prompt, persuade, inspire. **2** *impel the vehicle* actuate, set in motion, get going, get moving, propel.

impending *adjective* imminent, at hand, approaching, coming, forthcoming, close, near, nearing, on the way, about to happen, upon us, in the offing, on the horizon, in the air/wind, brewing, looming, threatening, menacing.

impenetrable *adjective* **1** *impenetrable containers* impervious, impermeable, solid, dense, thick, hard, closed, sealed, hermetically sealed, resistant, waterproof, puncture-proof, tight, unpierceable. **2** *impenetrable forests* impassable, unpassable, inaccessible, thick, dense, overgrown, jungly, pathless, trackless, untrodden. **3** *impenetrable jargon* incomprehensible, unintelligible, indiscernible, baffling, puzzling, abstruse, obscure, hidden, inexplicable, unfathomable, recondite, inscrutable, enigmatic. **4** *impenetrable ignorance* stupid, senseless, prejudiced, obtuse, gross, bigoted, biased, narrow-minded.

impenitent *adjective* unrepentant, unrepenting, uncontrite, remorseless, obdurate, unfeeling, uncaring, abandoned.

imperative *adjective* **1** *it is imperative that you stay* important, vital, essential, of the essence, crucial, critical, necessary, indispensable, required, mandatory, obligatory, exigent, pressing, urgent. **2** *an imperative tone of voice* imperious, authoritative, peremptory, commanding, lordly, masterful, autocratic, dictatorial, domineering, overbearing, magisterial.
Antonyms: UNIMPORTANT; OPTIONAL; SUBMISSIVE.

imperceptible *adjective* unnoticeable, unobtrusive, unapparent, slight, small, gradual, subtle, faint, fine, inappreciable, inconsequential, tiny, minute, minuscule, microscopic, infinitesimal, undetectable, indistinguishable, indiscernible, invisible, indistinct, unclear, obscure, vague, indefinite, shadowy, inaudible, muffled, impalpable.
Antonyms: OBVIOUS; NOTICEABLE.

imperceptibly *adverb* unnoticeably, unobtrusively, unseen, gradually, slowly, subtly, inappreciably, undetectably, infinitesimally, little by little, bit by bit.

imperfect *adjective* **1** *imperfect goods sold cheaply* faulty, flawed, defective, blemished, damaged, impaired, broken. **2** *an imperfect set of books* incomplete, not whole/entire, deficient, broken, partial. **3** *imperfect knowledge of the subject* deficient, inadequate, insufficient, lacking, rudimentary, limited, patchy, sketchy. **4** *imperfect plants* undeveloped, immature, premature.

imperfection *noun* **1** *an imperfection in the finish* fault, flaw, defect, deformity, blemish; crack, break, scratch, cut, tear, stain, spot. **2** *the imperfection of the set* incompleteness, deficiency, partialness. **3** *an imperfection in his character* failing, flaw, foible, deficiency, weakness, weak point, shortcoming, fallibility, frailty, infirmity, peccadillo.

imperial *adjective* **1** *his/her imperial majesty* royal, sovereign, regal, monarchal, kingly, queenly, princely, majestic, imperatorial. **2** *he walks with an imperial air about him* majestic, magnificent, grand, great, lofty, imposing, august, stately, splendid, glorious, exalted. **3** *the imperial ruler of the region* supreme, absolute, dominant, predominant, paramount, chief. **4** *very imperial in her manner* commanding, lordly, masterful, authoritative, imperious, peremptory, domineering. *See* IMPERIOUS.

imperil *verb* endanger, expose to danger, put in danger/jeopardy, put at risk, risk, jeopardize, hazard, gamble with, take a chance with.

imperious *adjective* peremptory, overbearing, overweening, domineering, high-handed, assertive, authoritative, commanding, lordly, masterful, dictatorial.

impermanent *adjective* not permanent, nonpermanent, temporary, transient, transitory, passing, fleeting, momentary, short-lived, ephemeral, evanescent, volatile.

impersonal *adjective* **1** *an impersonal assessment of the candidates* detached, objective, disinterested, dispassionate, neutral, unbiased, unprejudiced, unswayed, fair, equitable, evenhanded. **2** *an impersonal manner* cold, cool, frigid, aloof, formal, stiff, rigid, wooden, starchy, stilted, stuffy, matter-of-fact, businesslike, bureaucratic.

Antonyms: BIASED; FRIENDLY; WARM.

impersonate *verb* imitate, mimic, personate, mock, ape, parody, caricature, burlesque, masquerade as, pose as, pass oneself off as; *inf.* take off, do.

impersonation *noun* imitation, mimicry, impression, personation, mockery, parody, caricature, burlesque, travesty; *inf.* take-off.

impertinence *noun* **1** *the impertinence of the young woman* insolence, impudence, cheek, rudeness, impoliteness, unmannerliness, lack of civility, discourtesy, boldness, brazenness, audacity, effrontery, presumptuousness, brashness; *inf.* nerve, lip, gall. *See* IMPERTINENT 1. **2** *impertinence of the information* irrelevance, inapplicability, inappositeness, unrelatedness. *See* IMPERTINENT 2.

impertinent *adjective* **1** *an impertinent youth/act* insolent, impudent, cheeky, rude, impolite, unmannerly, ill-mannered, uncivil, coarse, crude, uncouth, discourteous, disrespectful, bold, brazen, audacious, presumptuous, forward, pert, brash, shameless; *inf.* fresh, flip. **2** *this document is impertinent to the case* irrelevant, inapplicable, inapposite, immaterial, unrelated, unconnected, not germane; beside the point.

Antonyms: MANNERLY; POLITE; PERTINENT.

impertinent
impudent, insolent, intrusive, meddlesome, obtrusive

All of these adjectives mean exceeding the bounds of propriety; the easiest way to distinguish **impertinent** from the others is to think of its root: *impertinent* behavior is not pertinent—in other words, it is inappropriate or out of place. The *impertinent* individual has a tendency to be rude or presumptuous toward those who are entitled to deference or respect (*it was an impertinent question to ask a woman who had just lost her husband*). The **intrusive** person is unduly curious about other people's affairs (*her constant questions about the state of their marriage were intrusive and unwelcome*), while **obtrusive** implies objectionable actions rather than an objectionable disposition. The *obtrusive* person has a tendency to thrust himself or herself into a position where he or she is conspicuous and apt to do more harm than good (*they tried to keep him out of the meeting because his presence would be obtrusive*). To be **meddlesome** is to have a prying or inquisitive nature and a tendency to interfere in an annoying way in other people's affairs (*a meddlesome neighbor*). **Impudent** and **insolent** are much stronger words for inappropriate behavior. Young people are often accused of being *impudent*, which means to be *impertinent* in a bold and shameless way (*an impudent young man who had a lot to learn about tact*). Anyone who is guilty of insulting and contemptuously arrogant behavior might be called *insolent* (*he was so insolent to the arresting officer that he was handcuffed*).

imperturbable *adjective* self-possessed, composed, collected, calm, cool, calm and collected, tranquil, serene, inexcitable, unflappable, even-tempered, easygoing, unperturbed, at ease, unruffled, untroubled, undismayed, unmoved, nonchalant.

Antonyms: NERVOUS; EDGY; EXCITABLE.

impervious *adjective* *impervious containers* impenetrable, impermeable, sealed, hermetically sealed. *See* IMPENETRABLE 1. **impervious to** *impervious to arguments* unmoved by, unaffected by, proof against, immune to, invulnerable to, unreceptive to, untouched by, unswayable by, closed to.

impetuous *adjective* **1** *an impetuous action* hasty, precipitate, headlong, impulsive, spontaneous, impromptu, spur-of-the-moment, unthinking, unplanned, unthought out, reckless, ill-conceived, ill-considered, unreasoned, rash, foolhardy, heedless. **2** *an impetuous person* impulsive, hasty, spontaneous, eager, enthusiastic, impatient, excitable, ardent, passionate, zealous, headstrong, rash, reckless, foolhardy, wild, uncontrolled. **3** *an impetuous wind* violent, forceful, powerful, vigorous,

vehement, raging, rampant, unrestrained, uncontrolled, unbridled.
Antonyms: CAUTIOUS; WARY.

impetus *noun* **1** *the car lost impetus on the steep slope* momentum, propulsion, impelling force, continuing motion, energy, force, power. **2** *the student needs some impetus to start studying* stimulus, instigation, actuation, moving force, motivation, incentive, inducement, inspiration, encouragement, influence, push, urging, pressing, spur, goading, goad.

impiety *noun* **1** *the impiety of the nonbelievers* godlessness, ungodliness, unholiness, irreligion, sinfulness, unrighteousness, sacrilege, irreverence, disrespect, profaneness, scoffing, derision, apostasy, atheism, agnosticism, paganism, heathenism. **2** *appalled at their impieties* sin, vice, wrongdoing, evildoing, transgression, desecration, profanity, blasphemy.

impinge *verb* **impinge on 1** *impinge on other people's rights* encroach on, infringe (on/upon), intrude on, invade, trespass on, obtrude into, make inroads into, violate, usurp. **2** *impinge on her consciousness* affect, have an effect/bearing on, impress, touch, exert influence on, bear upon. **3** *the rain impinging on the roof* strike, hit, dash/crash/smash against, collide with.

impious *adjective* godless, ungodly, unholy, irreligious, sinful, unrighteous, sacrilegious, profane, blasphemous, irreverent, disrespectful, apostatic, atheistic, agnostic, pagan, heathen.

impish *adjective* **1** *impish little boys* mischievous, mischief-making, full of mischief, rascally, roguish, prankish, unruly, troublemaking, devilish, sportive. **2** *an impish smile* elfin, pixieish, puckish, mischievous, roguish.

implacable *adjective* unappeasable, unpacifiable, not to be appeased/pacified, unmollifiable, rancorous, grudge-holding, unforgiving, inexorable, adamant, intractable, unyielding, rigid, inflexible, uncompromising, unrelenting, relentless, ruthless, unsympathetic, remorseless, merciless, pitiless, heartless, cruel, hard.

implant *verb* **1** *implant radical ideas in her head* inculcate, instill, insinuate, inject, inseminate, sow, infuse, introduce. **2** *implant the posts in the ground* embed, fix firmly, fix, place, plant, root, set. **3** *implant silicone under the skin* insert, place, put in place. **4** *implant skin tissue from a different part of the body* graft, engraft.

implausible *adjective* not likely, unlikely, improbable, hard to believe, incredible, unbelievable, unimaginable, inconceivable, debatable, questionable, doubtful.

implement *noun* **1** *garden/kitchen implements* tool, utensil, appliance, instrument, device, apparatus, contrivance, gadget; *inf.* gizmo. **2** *use her faith as an implement of peace* agent, medium, channel, expedient; means.

implement *verb* *implement their instructions* ful-

fill, carry out, execute, perform, discharge, accomplish, achieve, realize, put into effect/action, bring about, effect, enforce.
Antonyms: IMPEDE; NEGLECT.

implementation *noun* *the implementation of their instructions* fulfillment, execution, discharge, accomplishment, realization, effecting, enforcement. *See* IMPLEMENT *verb.*

implicate *verb* **1** *try to implicate his friend when he was accused* incriminate, compromise, inculpate, accuse, charge, blame, impeach, involve, entangle. **2** *he was not implicated in the events* involve, concern, include, associate, connect, embroil, entangle; be a part of, tie up with.
Antonyms: ABSOLVE; DISSOCIATE.

implication *noun* **1** *resent the implication that he was lying* suggestion, inference, insinuation, innuendo, hint, allusion, reference, assumption, presumption. **2** *the implication of his friend in the charge* incrimination, inculpation, blame. *See* IMPLICATE 1. **3** *their implication in the events* involvement, concern, association, connection, entanglement. *See* IMPLICATE 2.

implicit *adjective* **1** *there was implicit criticism in his voice* implied, indirect, inferred, deducible, unspoken, unexpressed, undeclared, unstated, tacit, understood, hinted, suggested. **2** *implicit in the argument was a lack of confidence in management* implied, inherent, latent, taken for granted. **3** *have implicit trust in the doctor* absolute, complete, entire, total, wholehearted, perfect, sheer, utter, unqualified, unconditional, unreserved, positive, unshaken, unshakable, unhesitating, unquestioning, firm, steadfast, constant.
Antonyms: DIRECT; EXPLICIT; OBVIOUS; LIMITED.

implicitly *adverb* *trust the doctor implicitly* absolutely, completely, totally, wholeheartedly, utterly, unconditionally, unreservedly, without reservation, positively, unhesitatingly, unquestioningly, firmly. *See* IMPLICIT 3.

implied *adjective* *their implied criticism* implicit, indirect, inferred, deducible, unspoken, unexpressed, tacit, hinted, suggested. *See* IMPLICIT 1.

implore *verb* *implored her to come* | *implore forgiveness* appeal to, beg, entreat, plead with, beseech, pray, ask, request, solicit, supplicate, importune, press; crave, plead for, appeal for.

imply *verb* **1** *he implied that all was not well* insinuate, say indirectly, hint, suggest, infer, intimate, give to understand, signal, indicate. **2** *being a civil servant implies discretion* involve, entail, presuppose, presume, assume. **3** *war implies bloodshed* signify, mean, indicate, denote, connote, betoken, point to.

impolite *adjective* unmannerly, ill-mannered, bad-mannered, rude, discourteous, uncivil, ill-bred, ungentlemanly, unladylike, ungracious, ungallant, disrespectful, inconsiderate, boorish, churlish, loutish, rough, crude, unrefined, indelicate, indecorous, insolent, impudent, impertinent.

impolitic *adjective* injudicious, ill-judged, undiplomatic, unwise, imprudent, ill-advised, misguided, ill-considered, shortsighted, uncircumspect, indiscreet, incautious, maladroit, inexpedient, untimely.

import *noun* **1** *exports and imports* imported commodity/service, foreign commodity, non-domestic commodity. **2** *did you get the import of what he said?* gist, drift, sense, essence, meaning, purport, message, thrust, implication, pith, core, sum and substance. **3** *persons of import in the town* importance, significance, consequence, moment, magnitude, substance, weight.

importance *noun* **1** *the importance of the talks* significance, momentousness, seriousness, graveness, urgency, gravity, weightiness, value. *See* IMPORTANT 1. **2** *people of importance* prominence, eminence, preeminence, note, notability, noteworthiness, influence, power, high rank, status, prestige, standing, mark.

important *adjective* **1** *important talks* of import, consequential, significant, of great import/consequence, far-reaching, critical, crucial, pivotal, momentous, of great moment, serious, grave, urgent, substantial, weighty, valuable. **2** *the important points to remember* significant, salient, chief, main, principal, major. **3** *it is important to the project that he is there* of concern, of interest, relevant, of value, valuable, necessary, essential. **4** *the important people in the town* prominent, eminent, preeminent, leading, foremost, outstanding, distinguished, esteemed, notable, noteworthy, of note, of import, influential, of influence, powerful, power-wielding, high-ranking, high-level, top-level, prestigious.

Antonyms: UNIMPORTANT; INSIGNIFICANT; MINOR.

importunate *adjective* persistent, insistent, pertinacious, dogged, earnest, unremitting, continuous, pressing, urgent, demanding, exigent, exacting, clamorous, entreating, solicitous, suppliant, imploratory, imprecatory.

importune *verb* **1** *importune him for money* beg, beseech, entreat, implore, plead with, appeal to, call upon, supplicate, solicit, petition, harass, beset, press, dun. **2** *importune men in the street* solicit, make sexual advances toward.

impose *verb* **1** *impose a tax* enforce, apply, exact, levy, charge, put on, lay on, set, establish, fix, decree, ordain, institute, introduce, promulgate; require, demand, dictate; *inf.* saddle with. **2** *impose her views on the group* force, foist, inflict, thrust, obtrude. **3** *impose fake antiques on the public* palm off, foist, pass off. **impose on** *not wishing to impose on your good nature* take advantage of, abuse, exploit, play on, be a burden on. **impose oneself** *impose herself on the company* force/foist/thrust oneself, intrude, break in, obtrude, interlope, trespass; *inf.* gatecrash, crash, butt in, horn in.

imposing *adjective* impressive, striking, splendid, grand, majestic, august, lofty, stately, dignified.

Antonyms: MODEST; unimposing.

imposition *noun* **1** *the imposition of new taxes* enforcement, application, exacting, levying, fixing, decreeing, institution. *See* IMPOSE 1. **2** *new impositions on taxpayers* tax, levy, charge, tariff, toll, tithe. **3** *unfair impositions on the poor* burden, load, charge, onus, encumbrance. **4** *the imposition of her values on the company* intrusion, obtrusion, interlopement, trespassing; *inf.* gatecrashing, butting in, horning in.

impossible *adjective* **1** *an impossible task* not possible, beyond the bounds of possibility, out of the question, unthinkable, unimaginable, inconceivable, beyond the realm of reason, impracticable, unattainable, unachievable, unobtainable, beyond one, hopeless. **2** *an impossible story* unbelievable, incredible, absurd, ludicrous, ridiculous, preposterous, outlandish, outrageous. **3** *an impossible child* unmanageable, intractable, recalcitrant, wayward, objectionable, intolerable, unbearable. **4** *life became impossible for the homeless* unbearable, intolerable, unendurable, hopeless.

Antonyms: POSSIBLE; PLAUSIBLE; TOLERABLE.

impostor, imposter *noun* masquerader, pretender, deceiver, fake, fraud, sham, charlatan, quack, mountebank, hoodwinker, bluffer, trickster, deluder, duper, cheat, cheater, swindler, defrauder, exploiter, confidence man/woman, rogue; *inf.* phony, con man, con artist.

imposture *noun* misrepresentation, pretense, deceit, fraudulence, deception, fraud, charlatanry, quackery, trickery, duping, cheating, swindling.

impotence *noun* powerlessness, lack of power, helplessness, inability, incapability, incapacity, incompetence; weakness, feebleness, exhaustion, enervation, debilitation; ineffectiveness, ineffectualness, inefficiency, inadequacy, uselessness, futility, unsuccessfulness.

impotent *adjective* powerless, helpless, unable, incapable, incapacitated, incompetent; enfeebled, weak, feeble, frail, worn out, exhausted, spent, enervated, debilitated, prostrate, crippled, paralyzed, infirm; ineffective, ineffectual, inefficient, inadequate, inept, useless, worthless, vain, futile, unavailing, unsuccessful, profitless.

Antonyms: POWERFUL; STRONG; EFFECTIVE.

impound *verb* **1** *impound stray animals* shut up/in, pen up/in, fence in, coop up, hem in, tie up, cage, enclose, confine, imprison, incarcerate, immure. **2** *impound legal documents* appropriate, take possession of, seize, commandeer, expropriate; *Law* distrain.

impoverished *adjective* **1** *impoverished homeless people* poverty-stricken, destitute, penurious, beggared, indigent, impecunious, penniless,

poor, needy, in distressed/reduced/straitened circumstances, down-and-out, bankrupt, insolvent, ruined; *inf.* broke, flat-broke, stonebroke. **2** *impoverished soil* exhausted, depleted, diminished, weakened, drained, used up, spent, played out. **3** *impoverished region/landscape* barren, bare, arid, desolate, empty, dead, waste, denuded.
Antonyms: WEALTHY; AFFLUENT.

impracticable *adjective an impracticable plan* not feasible, impossible, out of the question, unworkable, unachievable, unattainable, unrealizable, unsuitable.
Antonyms: POSSIBLE; FEASIBLE.

impractical *adjective* **1** *an impractical solution* unworkable, useless, ineffective, ineffectual, inefficacious, unrealistic, impossible, nonviable, inoperable, inoperative, unserviceable. **2** *his work is too impractical for a civil engineer* theoretical, abstract, academic, speculative. **3** *an impractical young woman* unrealistic, unbusinesslike, idealistic, romantic, starry-eyed, visionary, quixotic.
Antonyms: PRACTICAL; FEASIBLE; REALISTIC.

imprecation *noun* **1** *under an imprecation* curse, malediction, execration. **2** *embarrassed by his imprecations* swearing, cursing, blaspheming, blasphemy, foul language.

imprecise *adjective* **1** *an imprecise estimate of the cost* inexact, approximate, estimated, rough, inaccurate, incorrect. **2** *an imprecise account of the incident* vague, loose, indefinite, inexplicit, hazy, blurred, indistinct, woolly, confused, ambiguous, equivocal.

impregnable *adjective* **1** *an impregnable castle* impenetrable, unattackable, unassailable, inviolable, secure, strong, stout, invulnerable, invincible, unconquerable, unbeatable, indestructible. **2** *an impregnable argument* irrefutable, indisputable, incontestable, unquestionable, flawless, faultless.

impregnate *verb* **1** *impregnate the cloth with dye* permeate, suffuse, imbue, penetrate, pervade, fill, infuse, soak, steep, saturate, drench, inundate. **2** *impregnate the woman* make pregnant, inseminate; *inf.* put in the family way; *vulg.* knock up. **3** *impregnate the ovum* fertilize, fecundate.

impresario *noun* organizer, manager, producer; director, conductor, maestro, precentor, ballet master.

impress *verb* **1** *impress the crowd with his speech* make an impression/impact on, move, sway, bend, influence, affect, affect deeply, stir, rouse, excite, inspire, galvanize; *inf.* grab. **2** *impress upon them the need for immediate action* emphasize, stress, bring home, establish, fix deeply, instill, inculcate, urge. **3** *impress one's name on a metal strip* stamp, imprint, print, mark, engrave, emboss. **4** *she's always trying to impress her friends* make an impression on, draw attention to oneself to, show off to, show off in front of.

impression *noun* **1** *make an impression on the crowd* effect, influence, sway, impact, hold, power, control. **2** *the impression where his head lay* | *the impression made by the ring* mark, indentation, dent, hollow, outline, stamp, stamping, imprint, impress. **3** *I have the impression that he is bored* feeling, vague feeling, sense, sensation, awareness, perception, notion, idea, thought, belief, opinion, conviction, fancy, suspicion, inkling, intuition, hunch; *inf.* funny feeling. **4** *his impression of the politician* impersonation, imitation, mimicry, parody, caricature, burlesque, travesty; *inf.* send-up, take-off.

impressionable *adjective* susceptible, suggestible, persuadable, receptive, responsive, sensitive, open, gullible, ingenuous, pliable, malleable, moldable.

impressive *adjective* **1** *an impressive building* imposing, magnificent, splendid. **2** *an impressive musical performance* moving, affecting, touching, stirring, rousing, exciting, powerful, inspiring.
Antonyms: ORDINARY; unexciting.

imprint *noun the imprint of his feet* impression, print, mark, indentation, stamp, sign.

imprint *verb* **1** *imprint a seal on wax* stamp, print, impress, mark, engrave, emboss. **2** *imprint the details on his mind* fix, establish, stamp, impress, etch.

imprison *verb* put in prison, send to prison, jail, lock up, take into custody, put under lock and key, put away, incarcerate, intern, confine, detain, constrain, immure; *inf.* send up, send up the river.
Antonyms: FREE; LIBERATE; RELEASE.

imprisonment *noun* custody, incarceration, internment, confinement, detention, duress.

improbable *adjective* unlikely, highly unlikely, doubtful, dubious, questionable, implausible, far-fetched, unconvincing, unbelievable, incredible, ridiculous.

impromptu *adjective an impromptu speech* ad lib, unrehearsed, unprepared, extempore, extemporized, extemporaneous, spontaneous, improvised, unscripted, unstudied, unpremeditated; *inf.* off the cuff.

impromptu *adverb she spoke impromptu* ad lib, without preparation/rehearsal, extempore, spontaneously, on the spur of the moment; *inf.* off the cuff, off the top of one's head.

improper *adjective* **1** *improper behavior* unseemly, indecorous, unbecoming, unfitting, unladylike, ungentlemanly, impolite, indiscreet, injudicious. **2** *an improper remark* indecent, risqué, off-color, indelicate, suggestive, blue, smutty, obscene, lewd, pornographic. **3** *draw an improper inference* inaccurate, incorrect, wrong, erroneous, false. **4** *an improper tool for the job* inappropriate, unsuitable, unsuited, unfitting, inapt, inapplicable, incongruous.

impropriety noun **1** *guilty of impropriety* incorrectness, indecorum, indecorousness, unseemliness, indiscretion, bad taste, immodesty, indecency. **2** *appalled at her improprieties* improper act, improper remark. *See* IMPROPER 1, 2.

improve verb **1** *try to improve conditions* make better, better, ameliorate, amend, mend, reform, rehabilitate, set/put right, correct, rectify, help, advance, upgrade, revamp, modernize; *inf.* give a face-lift to, gentrify. **2** *things are improving* get/grow better, make headway, advance, come along, develop, progress, make progress, pick up, rally, perk up; *inf.* look up, take a turn for the better, get a new lease on life. **3** *she was ill but she's improving now* recover, get better/well, recuperate, convalesce, gain strength; *inf.* be on the mend, turn the corner. **improve on** *can you improve on your offer* increase, make larger, raise; *inf.* jack up.
Antonyms: WORSEN; DETERIORATE; IMPAIR; REDUCE.

improvement noun **1** *the improvement of conditions* betterment, amelioration, reform, rehabilitation, rectifying, rectification, advance, upgrading; *inf.* face-lift, gentrification. *See* IMPROVE 1. **2** *there has been an improvement in the economy* betterment, change for the better, advance, development, rally, recovery, upswing, comeback; progress, growth.

improvident adjective **1** *improvident people left penniless in old age* thriftless, unthrifty, spendthrift, wasteful, prodigal, extravagant, squandering, unfrugal, uneconomical, shiftless. **2** *improvident troops* incautious, unobservant, unwatchful, unwary, unvigilant, unalert, heedless, careless, inattentive; *inf.* asleep on the job, asleep at the wheel.
Antonyms: THRIFTY; CAUTIOUS.

improvise verb **1** *if you haven't prepared anything, you will have to improvise* ad lib, extemporize, make it up as you go along; *inf.* speak off the cuff, play it by ear. **2** *we will have to improvise a shelter* throw/put together, devise, contrive, concoct, rig, jury-rig.

improvised adjective **1** *improvised entertainment* impromptu, ad lib, unrehearsed, extempore, spontaneous; *inf.* off the cuff. *See* IMPROMPTU adjective. **2** *an improvised shelter* thrown together, makeshift, devised, rigged, jury-rigged.

imprudent adjective indiscreet, ill-considered, thoughtless, unthinking, incautious, unwary, improvident, irresponsible, foolish, injudicious, ill-judged, unwise, ill-advised, impolitic, careless, hasty, overhasty, rash, reckless, heedless, foolhardy.

impudence noun impertinence, insolence, cheek, boldness, effrontery, audacity, brazenness, pertness, sauciness, presumption, bumptiousness, rudeness, shamelessness; bad/ill manners; *inf.* nerve, gall, lip. *See* IMPUDENT.

impudent adjective impertinent, insolent, cheeky, bold, audacious, brazen, brazen-faced, pert, saucy, presumptuous, forward, bumptious, impolite, rude, disrespectful, ill-bred, ill-mannered, bad-mannered, unmannerly, shameless, immodest; *inf.* fresh, cocky.
Antonyms: POLITE; respectful; MODEST.

impugn verb *impugn his motives* challenge, call into question, question, dispute, query, cast aspersions on, look askance at, attack, assail, berate, criticize, denounce, censure.

impulse noun **1** *the impulse driving the machine* impetus, propulsion, impulsion, momentum, force, thrust, push, surge. **2** *the literary impulse* stimulus, inspiration, stimulation, incitement, incentive, inducement, motivation, urge. **3** *buy the coat on impulse | an impulse to buy* sudden desire/fancy, (the) spur of the moment, notion, whim, caprice. **4** *suppress one's sexual impulse* drive, urge, instinct, appetite, proclivity.

impulsive adjective **1** *an impulsive action* hasty, impromptu, snap, spontaneous, extemporaneous, sudden, quick, precipitate, impetuous, ill-considered, unplanned, unpremeditated, thoughtless, rash, reckless. **2** *an impulsive person* hasty, spontaneous, impetuous, instinctive, intuitive, passionate, emotional, rash, reckless, madcap, devil-may-care, foolhardy.
Antonyms: DELIBERATE; PREMEDITATED; CAUTIOUS.

impunity noun exemption/freedom from punishment/retribution/harm, immunity, indemnity, excusal, nonliability, license, dispensation, pardon, reprieve, stay of execution.

impure adjective **1** *impure chemicals* adulterated, alloyed, mixed, admixed, combined, blended, debased. **2** *impure water* contaminated, polluted, tainted, infected, foul, dirty, filthy, unclean, feculent, sullied, defiled, unwholesome, poisoned. **3** *impure persons* unchaste, unvirginal, immoral, loose, promiscuous, wanton, immodest, shameless, corrupt, dissolute, depraved, licentious, lascivious, prurient, lustful, lecherous, lewd. **4** *impure thoughts* lewd, lustful, lecherous, obscene, dirty, indecent, ribald, risqué, smutty, pornographic, improper, crude, vulgar, coarse, gross.

impurity noun **1** *the impurity of the chemical* adulteration, admixture, debasement. *See* IMPURE 1. **2** *the impurity of the water* contamination, pollution, foulness, filthiness, unwholesomeness. *See* IMPURE 2. **3** *impurities in the chemicals/water* foreign body, contaminant, pollutant, adulterant; dross, dirt, filth, grime, scum. **4** *regretted the impurity of their past* unchasteness, unchastity, immorality, looseness, promiscuity, wantonness, immodesty, lasciviousness, lust, lechery, lewdness. *See* IMPURE 3. **5** *the impurity of their thoughts* lewdness, lustfulness, obscenity, ribaldry, smut, smuttiness, impropriety, crudity, vulgarity. *See* IMPURE 4.

impute verb **impute to** *impute the crime to him* ascribe to, attribute to, assign to, credit (with), accredit to; connect with, associate with, lay at the door of.

in *adjective short skirts were once in* fashionable, in fashion, in vogue, voguish, stylish, in style; *inf.* trendy, all the rage. **in with** *she seems to be in with the teacher* in favor with, favored by, liked by; *inf.* in the good graces of.

in *noun* **ins and outs** *the ins and outs of the situation* intricacies, particulars, facts, details, features, characteristics, traits, particularities, peculiarities, idiosyncrasies.

inability *noun* incapability, incapableness, incapacity, incompetence, ineptitude, inaptitude, unfitness, ineffectiveness, powerlessness, uselessness, inefficacy, ineligibility, unqualifiedness.

inaccessible *adjective houses inaccessible in the winter | an inaccessible control switch* unreachable, out of reach, beyond reach, unapproachable, impenetrable, unattainable, out of the way, remote, godforsaken.

inaccuracy *noun* **1** *the inaccuracy of the results* incorrectness, erroneousness, wrongness, mistakenness, fallaciousness, faultiness, inexactness, inexactitude, imprecision. **2** *the accounts were full of inaccuracies* error, mistake, miscalculation, erratum, corrigendum, slip, fault, blunder, defect; *inf.* slipup, booboo. **3** *a document full of inaccuracies* error, mistake, slip, slip of the pen, printer's error, literal; *inf.* typo.

inaccurate *adjective* **1** *your calculation is inaccurate* incorrect, wrong, erroneous, faulty, inexact, imprecise. **2** *the report is inaccurate* incorrect, wrong, erroneous, fallacious, false, not true, not right, imperfect, flawed, defective, unsound, unreliable, wide of the mark; *inf.* full of holes.

inactive *adjective* **1** *he hates to be inactive but he has to stay in bed* immobile, motionless, inert, stationary. **2** *all the machines lying inactive* idle, inoperative, nonfunctioning, not working, out of service, unused, out of use, not in use, unoccupied, unemployed, inert, mothballed. **3** *a former athlete now completely inactive* idle, inert, slow, sluggish, indolent, lazy, lifeless, slothful, lethargic, stagnant, vegetating, dilatory, torpid. **4** *an inactive volcano* dormant, quiescent, latent, passive.

inadequacy *noun* **1** *the inadequacy of the food supply* inadequateness, insufficiency, dearth, deficiency, meagerness, scantness, scarcity, paucity. *See* INADEQUATE 1. **2** *war brought food inadequacies* shortage, deficit, lack, dearth, scarcity. **3** *the inadequacy of the present staff* incompetence, incapability, unfitness, ineffectiveness, ineffectuality, inefficiency, inefficacy, inexpertness, lack of skill/proficiency, inaptness, ineptness. **4** *show up his inadequacies as a manager* shortcoming, fault, failing, flaw, defect, imperfection, weakness, foible.

inadequate *adjective* **1** *inadequate food supplies* insufficient, not enough, too little, too few, lacking, found wanting, deficient, short, in short supply, meager, scanty, scant, niggardly, scarce, sparse, skimpy, sketchy, incomplete. **2** *an inadequate teacher* incompetent, incapable, not able, unfit, ineffective, ineffectual, inefficient, inefficacious, unskillful, inexpert, unproficient, inapt, inept; *inf.* not up to scratch/snuff.

Antonyms: ADEQUATE; SUFFICIENT; COMPETENT.

inadmissible *adjective inadmissible evidence* not allowable, unallowable, prohibited, precluded, unacceptable, improper, inappropriate, inapposite, irrelevant, immaterial, impertinent, not germane, beside the point.

inadvertent *adjective* **1** *an inadvertent omission* accidental, unintentional, chance, unpremeditated, unplanned, uncalculated, unconscious, unwitting, involuntary. **2** *an inadvertent driver* inattentive, careless, negligent, thoughtless, heedless, unheeding, unmindful, unobservant.

Antonyms: DELIBERATE; INTENTIONAL; CAREFUL.

inadvisable *adjective* ill-advised, unwise, injudicious, ill-judged, imprudent, impolitic, inexpedient, foolish.

inalienable *adjective inalienable rights* untransferable, unforfeitable, inherent, unchallengeable, inviolable, sacrosanct.

inane *adjective* silly, foolish, stupid, idiotic, absurd, ridiculous, ludicrous, fatuous, trifling, frivolous, senseless, nonsensical, unintelligent, mindless, puerile, asinine, futile, worthless, vacuous, vapid; *inf.* daft.

inanimate *adjective* **1** *inanimate objects* lifeless, without life, exanimate, dead, inert, insentient, insensate, extinct, defunct. **2** *inanimate people* spiritless, apathetic, lazy, inactive, phlegmatic, listless, lethargic, sluggish, torpid.

inapplicable *adjective rules inapplicable to the situation* irrelevant, immaterial, not germane, inapposite, not pertinent, impertinent, inappropriate, unrelated, unconnected, beside the point.

inapposite *adjective* irrelevant, immaterial, not germane, not pertinent, impertinent, inapplicable. *See* INAPPLICABLE.

inappreciable *adjective* imperceptible, microscopic, infinitesimal, miniscule, minute, tiny, slight, small, insignificant, negligible, petty, trivial, trifling, paltry; *inf.* piddling.

inappropriate *adjective* **1** *inappropriate behavior* unsuitable, unfitting, unseemly, unbecoming, indecorous, improper, ungentlemanly, unladylike, ungenteel. **2** *inappropriate dress* unsuitable, inapposite, incongruous, out of place/keeping. **3** *it would be inappropriate to comment* unsuitable, inexpedient, inadvisable, injudicious, infelicitous, untimely.

inapt *adjective* **1** *an inapt remark* inappropriate, unsuitable, unsuited, unfitting, out of place, inapposite, inapplicable, not pertinent, impertinent, not germane, incongruous, out of keeping, unrelated, unconnected. **2** *an inapt plumber* inept, incompetent, unadept, incapable, unskillful, inexpert, clumsy, awkward, maladroit, undexterous, heavy-handed.

inarticulate *adjective* **1** *inarticulate cries/sounds* unintelligible, incomprehensible, incoherent, unclear, indistinct, blurred, muffled, mumbled, muttered. **2** *inarticulate speakers* noneloquent, uneloquent, poorly spoken, nonfluent, faltering, hesitating, halting, stumbling, stuttering, stammering. **3** *inarticulate emotion* unspoken, unuttered, unexpressed, unvoiced, wordless, silent, mute, dumb, speechless, voiceless, soundless, taciturn, tongue-tied.

inattention *noun* **1** *students guilty of inattention* inattentiveness, distraction, preoccupation, absentmindedness, daydreaming, reverie, woolgathering, mental wandering, lack of concentration/application, staring into space. **2** *inattention to duty* neglect, negligence, remissness, forgetfulness, carelessness, thoughtlessness, heedlessness, disregard, indifference, unconcern, inconsideration.

inattentive *adjective* **1** *inattentive students* distracted, preoccupied, absentminded, daydreaming, woolgathering, lost in thought, off in a world of one's own, lacking concentration/application, with one's head in the clouds; *inf.* miles away. **2** *inattentive to duty* | *inattentive guards* neglectful, negligent, remiss, forgetful, careless, thoughtless, heedless, disregarding, indifferent, unconcerned, inconsiderate.

inaudible *adjective* not heard, hard to hear, hard to make out, indistinct, imperceptible, out of earshot, faint, muted, soft, low, muffled, stifled, dull, whispered, muttered, murmured, mumbled.

inaugural *adjective* first, initial, introductory, opening, maiden, dedicatory.

inaugurate *verb* **1** *inaugurate the conference proceedings* initiate, begin, start, commence, launch, start off, set in motion, get going, get under way, raise the curtain on, get off the ground. **2** *inaugurate the new president* install, instate, induct, invest, ordain. **3** *inaugurate the new building* open, open officially, dedicate. **4** *transistors inaugurated the age of electronics* introduce, usher in, launch; initiate, instigate; pave the way for, make possible.
Antonyms: TERMINATE; wind up (*see* WIND).

inauspicious *adjective* unpropitious, unpromising, unlucky, unfortunate, infelicitous, unhappy, unfavorable, ill-omened, ominous, ill-fated, ill-starred, untoward, untimely.

inborn *adjective* innate, inherent, inherited, congenital, hereditary, in the family, in the blood/genes, inbred, connate, ingrained, constitutional, structural.

inbred *adjective* inherent, innate, ingrained, deep-seated.

incalculable *adjective* **1** *the distance/number is incalculable* immeasurable, measureless, inestimable, uncountable, incomputable, not to be reckoned, endless, without end, infinite, boundless, limitless, fathomless, bottomless, innumerable, countless, without number, numberless, multitudinous, enormous, immense, vast. **2** *an incalculable risk* unpredictable, indeterminable, unforeseeable.

incandescent *adjective* white-hot, intensely hot, red-hot, bright, brilliant, dazzling, shining, gleaming, glowing, aglow.

incantation *noun* chant, chanting, invocation, conjuration, spell, magic formula/word; abracadabra, open sesame.

incapable *adjective* *tired of employing incapable people* lacking ability, incompetent, ineffective, ineffectual, inefficacious, inadequate, unfit, unqualified, inept, inapt, unable, useless, feeble; *inf.* not up to scratch/snuff. **incapable of 1** *incapable of doing good* unable to, not capable of, lacking experience to, lacking the ability to. **2** *problems incapable of solution* not open to, impervious to, resistant to, not susceptible to.

incapacitated *adjective* *incapacitated and unable to play football* disabled, debilitated, unfit, immobilized, crippled, indisposed; *inf.* laid up, out of action.
Antonyms: FIT; ABLE.

incapacity *noun* **1** *his incapacity to do a job well* inability, incapability, incompetence, incompetency, inadequacy, unfitness, ineffectiveness, ineffectuality, inefficiency, powerlessness, impotence. **2** *legal incapacity* lack of entitlement, lack of legal ability, inability, disqualification.

incarcerate *verb* imprison, jail, put in prison/jail, throw in prison/jail, lock up, put under lock and key, intern, impound, take captive, put into detention, detain, confine, shut away, shut in, coop up, immure, restrain, restrict; *inf.* send up, send up the river.

incarceration *noun* imprisonment, internment, captivity, detention, bondage, confinement, restraint.

incarnate *adjective* **1** *the devil incarnate* in bodily/human form, in the flesh, made manifest, embodied, corporeal, fleshly. **2** *tactlessness incarnate* embodied, personified, typified.

incarnation *noun* **1** *in another incarnation* life, bodily form, manifestation, embodiment. **2** *she is the incarnation of motherliness* embodiment, personification, exemplification, type, avatar.

incautious *adjective* **1** *incautious guards not spotting the enemy* unwary, unchary, unwatchful, unvigilant, unalert, off-guard, inattentive, unobservant, inadvertent; *inf.* asleep on the job, asleep at the wheel. **2** *incautious of him to trust her* unwise, imprudent, ill-advised, ill-judged, injudicious, uncircumspect, improvident, thoughtless, careless, impetuous, hasty, precipitate, rash, reckless, foolhardy.

incendiary *adjective* **1** *an incendiary bomb*

combustible, flammable, fire-producing. **2** *an incendiary speech* inflammatory, incensing, inciting, instigating, arousing, stirring, provocative, rabble-rousing, seditious, subversive.

incendiary *noun* **1** *buildings deliberately set on fire by incendiaries* arsonist, fire-setter, pyromaniac; *inf.* firebug. **2** *crowds driven to rioting by incendiaries* demagogue, agitator, agent provocateur, rabble-rouser, instigator, inciter, insurgent, firebrand, revolutionary.

incense *verb* anger, enrage, infuriate, exasperate, irritate, madden, provoke, rile, inflame, agitate, nettle, vex, irk, get one's hackles up; *inf.* make one's blood boil, make one see red, ruffle one's feathers, get one's dander up.

incense *noun* *sweet-smelling incense* perfume, fragrance, scent, aroma, bouquet, redolence, balm.

incentive *noun* inducement, incitement, stimulus, stimulant, impetus, encouragement, motivation, inspiration, impulse, goad, spur, lure, bait; *inf.* carrot.
Antonyms: DETERRENT; DISCOURAGEMENT.

inception *noun* beginning, commencement, start, starting point, outset, opening, debut, inauguration, initiation, institution, birth, dawn, origin, rise; *inf.* kickoff.

incessant *adjective* ceaseless, unceasing, nonstop, endless, unending, never-ending, everlasting, eternal, constant, continual, perpetual, continuous, uninterrupted, unbroken, ongoing, unremitting, persistent, recurrent.
Antonyms: INTERMITTENT; interrupted.

incidence *noun* rate, frequency, prevalence, occurrence, amount, degree, extent.

incident *noun* **1** *unhappy incidents in her life* event, happening, occurrence, episode, adventure, experience, proceeding, occasion, circumstance, fact, matter. **2** *the police were called to an incident in the bar* disturbance, commotion, scene, fracas, contretemps, skirmish, clash, conflict, confrontation.

incidental *adjective* **1** *her part in the event was incidental* accidental, by chance, chance, fortuitous, random. **2** *incidental expenses* minor, trivial, trifling, petty, small, meager. **incidental to** *travel incidental to her job* related to, connected with, associated with, accompanying, attendant to, concomitant to, contingent to/on, by way of. **incidental upon** *her social engagements are incidental upon her job* ancillary to, subordinate to, subsidiary to, secondary to.
Antonyms: DELIBERATE; ESSENTIAL; MAJOR.

incidentally *adverb* **1** *incidentally, I'm leaving tomorrow* by the way, by the by, in passing, speaking of which, while we're on the subject, apropos. **2** *she helped quite incidentally* accidentally, by chance, fortuitously, by a fluke, as luck would have it.

incinerate *verb* burn, burn up, reduce to ashes, carbonize, cremate.

incipient *adjective* beginning, commencing, starting, inceptive, initial, inchoative, original, inaugural, nascent, newborn, embryonic, embryonal, germinal, rudimentary, developing.
Antonyms: FINAL; MATURE.

incise *verb* **1** *incise the skin* cut, cut into, make an incision in, slit, slit open, gash, slash, notch, nick, furrow. **2** *incise the stone* engrave, etch, sculpt, sculpture, carve.

incision *noun* cut, opening, slit, gash, slash, notch, nick.

incisive *adjective* **1** *an incisive mind* keen, acute, sharp, penetrating, astute, shrewd, perspicacious, clever, smart, quick. **2** *an incisive remark* caustic, acid, sharp, biting, cutting, stinging, tart, trenchant, mordant, sarcastic, sardonic.
Antonyms: VAGUE; DULL; MILD.

incite *verb* **1** *incite a rebellion* instigate, provoke, foment, whip up, stir up, prompt. **2** *incite them to rebel* egg on, encourage, urge, goad, spur on, prod, stimulate, drive on, excite, arouse, agitate, inflame, stir up, provoke.
Antonyms: DISCOURAGE; DETER.

---
incite
arouse, exhort, foment, instigate, provoke
The best way to start a riot is to **incite** one, which means to urge or stimulate to action, either in a favorable or an unfavorable sense. If you **instigate** an action, however, it implies that you are responsible for initiating it and that the purpose is probably a negative or evil one (*the man who instigated the assassination plot*). **Foment** suggests agitation or incitement over an extended period of time (*foment a discussion; foment the rebellion that leads to war*). An instigator, in other words, is someone who initiates the idea, while a fomenter is someone who keeps it alive. You can **provoke** a riot in the same way that you instigate one, but the emphasis here is on spontaneity rather than on conscious design (*her statement provoked an outcry from animal rights activists*). To **arouse** is to awaken a feeling or elicit a response (*my presence in the junkyard aroused suspicion*), or to open people's eyes to a situation (*we attempted to arouse public awareness*). But once you've aroused people, you may have to **exhort** them, meaning to urge or persuade them, by appealing to their sympathy or conscience, to take constructive action.

---

incitement *noun* *incitement to action* encouragement, urging, goading, spurring, prodding, stimulation, agitation, provocation, instigation; spur, impetus.

incivility *noun* bad/ill manners; unmannerliness, impoliteness, discourtesy, discourteousness, rudeness, disrespect, boorishness.

inclement *adjective* **1** *inclement weather* rough, stormy, squally, blustery, severe, bitter, raw, foul, nasty, harsh. **2** *inclement judges* harsh, unmerciful, pitiless, unpitying, ruthless, re-

morseless, hard-hearted, hard, cruel, inexorable, unrelenting, callous, severe, rigorous, draconian.
Antonyms: FINE; MILD.

inclination *noun* **1** *he has an inclination to overeat | an inclination toward overeating* tendency, leaning, propensity, proclivity, proneness, liableness, disposition, predisposition, subjectability, weakness. **2** *an inclination for blondes* penchant, predilection, predisposition, partiality, preference, affinity, attraction, fancy, liking, fondness, affection, love. **3** *an inclination of the head* bow, bowing, bend, bending, nod, lowering, stooping. **4** *an inclination in the terrain* incline, slope, slant, gradient, bank, ramp, lift, tilt, acclivity, rise, ascent, declivity, descent, drop, dip, sag, cant, bevel, angle.
Antonyms: AVERSION; DISLIKE; DISINCLINATION.

incline *verb* **1** *the land inclines toward the shore* curve, bend, slope, slant, bank, cant, bevel, tilt, lean, tip, list, deviate. **2** *that inclines me to believe you | I'm inclined to believe you* predispose, dispose, influence, bias, prejudice, sway, make willing, persuade, bend. **3** *the door is inclined to bang* have a tendency, be liable/likely. **4** *incline the head* bow, bend, nod, lower, stoop, cast down. **incline to/toward** *he inclines toward the left in politics* tend to/toward, lean to/toward, swing to/toward, veer to/toward, have a preference/penchant for, be attracted to, have an affinity for.

include *verb* **1** *the group includes representatives from all countries* contain, hold, take in, admit, incorporate, embrace, encompass, comprise, embody, comprehend, subsume. **2** *remember to include them on the invitation list* allow for, add, insert, put in, enter, introduce, count in, take account of, build in, number, incorporate.
Antonyms: EXCLUDE; OMIT.

including *preposition* *everyone is going, including me* counting, inclusive of.

inclusion *noun* *the inclusion of new material* addition, insertion, incorporation, introduction.

inclusive *adjective* **1** *an inclusive price* comprehensive, all-embracing, with everything included, *in toto.* **2** *from Monday to Friday inclusive* including the limits stated, encompassed. **inclusive of** *the total inclusive of sales tax* including, taking into account/consideration, counting, taking account/cognizance of.

incognito *adjective/adverb* under an assumed name, with one's identity concealed, in disguise, disguised, in masquerade, camouflaged, unrecognized, unidentified, sailing under false colors.

incognizant *adjective* unaware, unconscious, ignorant, unknowing, unsuspecting, unknowledgeable, unenlightened.

incoherent *adjective* *incoherent speech* unconnected, disconnected, disjointed, disordered, confused, mixed-up, muddled, jumbled, scrambled, rambling, wandering, discursive,

illogical, unintelligible, inarticulate, mumbled, muttered, stuttered, stammered.

incombustible *adjective* noncombustible, not flammable, nonflammable, flameproof, fireproof, flame-retardant, flame-resistant, unburnable, unignitable.
Antonyms: flammable; inflammable.

income *noun* salary, pay, remuneration, revenue; earnings, wages, receipts, takings, profits, gains, proceeds, means.

incoming *adjective* **1** *the incoming tide/train* coming, coming in, approaching, entering, arriving. **2** *the incoming president* new, succeeding.
Antonyms: OUTGOING; departing.

incomparable *adjective* beyond compare, inimitable, unequaled, without equal, matchless, nonpareil, paramount, unrivaled, peerless, unparalleled, unsurpassed, transcendent, superior, superlative, supreme.

incomparably *adverb* beyond compare, by far, far and away, easily, immeasurably.

incompatible *adjective* **1** *he and his wife are incompatible* inharmonious, unsuited, mismatched, uncongenial, incongruous, like day and night, uncomplementary, conflicting, antagonistic, antipathetic, dissentient, disagreeing, discordant, like oil and water. **2** *incompatible colors* inharmonious, discordant, clashing, jarring, uncomplementary. **incompatible with** *views incompatible with his behavior* differing from, contrary to, at odds with, inconsistent with, in opposition to, diametrically opposed to. *See* INCONGRUOUS WITH (INCONGRUOUS).
Antonyms: COMPATIBLE; HARMONIOUS; CONSISTENT.

incompetent *adjective* **1** *incompetent to do the task* unable, incapable, unfitted, unfit, unsuitable, unqualified, inapt, inept, inefficient, ineffectual, ineffective, inadequate, deficient, insufficient, useless. **2** *an incompetent performance* unskillful, inexpert, inept, bungling, botched, awkward, maladroit, clumsy, gauche, floundering.

incomplete *adjective* **1** *an incomplete task* unfinished, unaccomplished, partial, undone, unexecuted, unperformed, undeveloped. **2** *an incomplete set of books* deficient, lacking, wanting, defective, imperfect, not entire, not total, broken. **3** *an incomplete text* deficient, shortened, curtailed, abridged, expurgated, bowdlerized.

incomprehensible *adjective* **1** *incomprehensible writing* illegible, unintelligible, indecipherable, unreadable. **2** *an incomprehensible theory* unintelligible, inapprehensible, too difficult, too hard, complicated, complex, involved, intricate; *inf.* over one's head, tough. **3** *his motives are incomprehensible* beyond comprehension, unfathomable, impenetrable, profound, deep, inexplicable, puzzling, enigmatic, mysterious, abstruse, recondite.

inconceivable adjective unimaginable, unthinkable, incomprehensible, incredible, unbelievable, implausible, impossible, out of the question, preposterous, ridiculous, ludicrous.

inconclusive adjective indefinite, indecisive, indeterminate, undetermined, still open to question, open to doubt, vague, unestablished, unsettled, ambiguous; inf. up in the air.

incongruity noun incompatibility, inconsistency, inappropriateness, unsuitability, inaptness, inharmoniousness, discordancy, disparity, discrepancy.

incongruous adjective modern furniture seeming incongruous in the old-fashioned setting out of place/keeping, strange, odd, absurd, unsuitable, inappropriate, incompatible, inharmonious, discordant, clashing, jarring. **incongruous with** behavior incongruous with his principles incompatible with, inconsistent with, out of keeping/place with, differing from, contrary to, inappropriate to, unsuited to, at odds with, in opposition to, diametrically opposed to, conflicting with, irreconcilable with.
Antonyms: APPROPRIATE; CONSISTENT; SUITABLE.

inconsequential adjective his influence is inconsequential insignificant, negligible, inappreciable, unimportant, of minor importance, of little/no account, trivial, trifling, petty; inf. piddling.

inconsiderable adjective not an inconsiderable sum of money insignificant, negligible, trifling, petty, small, slight, niggling, minor, inappreciable; inf. piddling.

inconsiderate adjective thoughtless, unthinking, unthoughtful, uncaring, heedless, unmindful, regardless, undiscerning, insensitive, unsolicitous, tactless, uncharitable, unkind, unbenevolent, ungracious, selfish, self-centered, egotistic.

inconsistent adjective inconsistent character/actions inconstant, unstable, unsteady, changeable, variable, erratic, irregular, unpredictable, capricious, fickle, whimsical, mercurial, volatile. **inconsistent with** actions inconsistent with his politics incompatible with, out of keeping with, out of place with, differing from, contrary to, at odds with, at variance with, in opposition to, conflicting with, in conflict with, irreconcilable with, discordant with, discrepant with.

inconsolable adjective grief-stricken, brokenhearted, heartbroken, sick at heart, bowed down, miserable, wretched, woebegone, disconsolate, desolate, despairing, forlorn, unhappy, sad, upset.

inconspicuous adjective **1** an inconspicuous house unnoticeable, unobtrusive, indistinct, ordinary, plain, run-of-the-mill, unremarkable, undistinguished, unostentatious, unimposing, hidden, camouflaged. **2** try to be as inconspicuous as possible unnoticeable, unob-

trusive, insignificant, quiet, retiring, in the background; inf. low-key.

inconstant adjective **1** inconstant quantities not constant, changeable, variable, mutable, unstable, unsteady, unsettled, unfixed. **2** inconstant friends changeable, fickle, capricious, volatile, mercurial, faithless, unfaithful.

incontestable adjective indisputable, incontrovertible, undeniable, irrefutable, unquestionable, beyond dispute/question/doubt, indubitable, unshakable, beyond a shadow of a doubt, conclusive, decisive, definite, established, sure, certain, positive.

incontinent adjective **1** incontinent desires unrestrained, unbridled, unchecked, uncurbed, ungoverned, uncontrolled, uncontrollable. **2** incontinent young men licentious, lascivious, lustful, lecherous, lewd, libidinous, promiscuous, debauched, dissolute, dissipated, loose, degenerate, wanton. **3** incontinent following surgery lacking bladder/bowel control.

incontrovertible adjective incontestable, indisputable, undeniable, irrefutable, unquestionable, beyond question/doubt, indubitable, conclusive, decisive, positive. See INCONTESTABLE.

inconvenience noun **1** not wishing to cause you any inconvenience trouble, bother, disruption, disturbance, vexation, worry, annoyance, disadvantage, difficulty, embarrassment. **2** their arrival was an inconvenience trouble, bother, source of disruption/vexation/annoyance, nuisance, burden, hindrance; inf. pain, drag, bore. **3** the inconvenience of the furniture awkwardness, unwieldiness, cumbersomeness, unhandiness.

inconvenience verb disturb, bother, trouble, worry, disrupt, put out, impose upon, burden, distract, annoy.

inconvenient adjective **1** call at an inconvenient time awkward, unsuitable, inappropriate, inopportune, inexpedient, disadvantageous, disturbing, troublesome, bothersome, tiresome, vexatious, annoying, embarrassing, ill-timed, untimely, unseasonable. **2** an inconvenient size of luggage awkward, unwieldy, cumbersome, unmanageable, unhandy, difficult.

incorporate verb **1** incorporate the various ingredients to form a whole merge, coalesce, fuse, blend, mix, amalgamate, combine, unite, integrate, unify, compact. **2** the document incorporates all our thoughts embody, include, comprise, embrace, absorb, subsume, assimilate.

incorrect adjective **1** incorrect answers not right, wrong, inaccurate, erroneous, wide of the mark. **2** an incorrect account of what happened not right, inaccurate, mistaken, faulty, inexact, untrue, fallacious, nonfactual, flawed; inf. full of holes. **3** incorrect behavior improper, lacking in propriety, unbecoming, unseemly, indecorous, unsuitable, inappropriate, unladylike, ungentlemanly.

incorrigible adjective an incorrigible criminal

hardened, incurable, inveterate, unreformable, irreformable, unreformative, irredeemable, hopeless, beyond hope/redemption, impenitent, uncontrite, unrepentant.

incorruptible *adjective* **1** *incorruptible members of society* virtuous, upright, high-principled, honorable, honest, moral, ethical, trustworthy, straight, unbribable, untemptable. **2** *incorruptible materials* imperishable, indestructible, nonbiodegradable, not decaying, indissoluble, indissolvable, everlasting.

increase *verb* **1** *demand has increased* grow, grow greater/larger/bigger, expand, extend, multiply, intensify, heighten, mount, escalate, snowball, mushroom, swell, wax. **2** *increase the demand* add to, boost, enhance, build up, augment, enlarge, expand, extend, spread, heighten, raise, intensify, strengthen, magnify, proliferate, inflate; *inf.* step up.
Antonyms: DECREASE; REDUCE.

increase *noun the increase in size/demand* growth, rise, enlargement, expansion, extension, increment, addition, development, intensification, heightening, escalation, snowballing, mushrooming, boost, augmentation, strengthening, magnification, inflation; *inf.* stepping-up, step-up. *See* INCREASE *verb.*

increasingly *adverb he is increasingly annoying* more and more, progressively.

incredible *adjective* **1** *find his story incredible* unbelievable, hard to believe, beyond belief, far-fetched, inconceivable, unimaginable, unthinkable, impossible, implausible, highly unlikely, quite improbable, absurd, preposterous, questionable, dubious, doubtful, fictitious, mythical. **2** *an incredible athletic performance* extraordinary, supreme, great, wonderful, marvelous, tremendous, prodigious, astounding, amazing, astonishing, awe-inspiring, awesome, superhuman; *inf.* fabulous, fantastic.

incredulity *noun view his story with incredulity* incredulousness, disbelief, unbelief, skepticism, distrust, mistrust, doubt, dubiousness, dubiety, suspicion.

incredulous *adjective incredulous listeners to his tale* disbelieving, unbelieving, skeptical, cynical, distrusting, distrustful, mistrusting, mistrustful, doubtful, doubting, dubious, unconvinced, suspicious.

increment *noun* **1** *an increment in salary* increase, gain, addition, augmentation, supplement, addendum, adjunct, accretion, accrual, accruement, profit. **2** *appalled by the increment in quantities/prices* enlargement, expansion, extension, escalation, mushrooming; *inf.* step-up. *See* INCREASE *noun.*

incriminate *verb* charge, accuse, indict, impeach, arraign, blame, implicate, inculpate, involve, inform against, blacken the name of, stigmatize; *inf.* finger, point the finger at, stick/pin the blame on, rat on.

inculcate *verb* **inculcate in/upon** *discipline was inculcated in the recruits* instill upon, implant into, fix upon/into, ingrain into, infuse into, imbue upon/into, impress upon, imprint upon/on, indoctrinate into, teach to, hammer into, din into.

inculpate *verb* charge, accuse, indict, impeach, arraign, incriminate, blame. *See* INCRIMINATE.

incumbent *adjective* **incumbent on/upon** *incumbent on you to be present* binding on, obligatory for, mandatory for/that, necessary for/that, compulsory for/that, expected of.

incumbent *noun the incumbent of the office* officeholder, official, functionary, occupier.

incur *verb incur his wrath | incurred huge debts* bring upon oneself, expose oneself to, lay oneself open to, provoke, be liable/subject to, contract, meet with, experience.

incurable *adjective* **1** *an incurable illness* beyond cure, cureless, unhealable, terminal, fatal, untreatable, inoperable, irremediable. **2** *an incurable romantic* inveterate, dyed-in-the-wool, incorrigible, hopeless, beyond hope.

incursion *noun the enemy's midnight incursion* raid, foray, sortie, attack, assault, onslaught, invasion, onset, sally.

indebted *adjective indebted to you for your help* in (someone's) debt, beholden, under an obligation, obliged, obligated, grateful, thankful, appreciative.

indecency *noun* **1** *the indecency of the remark* suggestiveness, indelicacy, improperness, impurity, risquéness, ribaldry, bawdiness, foulness, vulgarity, grossness, crudity, dirtiness, smuttiness, smut, coarseness, obscenity, blueness, lewdness. **2** *the indecency of the abrupt departure* impropriety, unseemliness, indecorum, indecorousness, unsuitableness, inappropriateness, bad taste, tastelessness, unacceptability, offensiveness.

indecent *adjective* **1** *an indecent suggestion/joke* suggestive, indelicate, improper, impure, risqué, off-color, ribald, bawdy, foul, vulgar, gross, crude, dirty, smutty, coarse, obscene, blue, lewd, lascivious, licentious, salacious, pornographic, scatological; *inf.* raunchy. **2** *marry with indecent haste after the funeral* improper, unseemly, indecorous, unbecoming, unsuitable, inappropriate, unfitting, unbefitting, in bad taste, tasteless, unacceptable, offensive, outrageous.
Antonyms: CLEAN; INOFFENSIVE; PROPER; SEEMLY.

indecipherable *adjective* illegible, unreadable, unclear, indistinct, unintelligible, cramped, crabbed.

indecision *noun his indecision lost him the job* indecisiveness, irresolution, irresoluteness, vacillation, fluctuation, hesitancy, hesitation, tentativeness, ambivalence, doubt, uncertainty, shilly-shallying. *See* INDECISIVE 1.

indecisive *adjective* **1** *an indecisive person* irresolute, vacillating, wavering, fluctuating, hesitant, tentative, faltering, ambivalent, doubtful, in two minds, shilly-shallying, undecided, indefinite, uncertain, unresolved, undetermined, sitting on the fence; *inf.* blowing hot and cold. **2** *an indecisive ballot* inconclusive, open, indeterminate, undecided, unsettled, indefinite, unclear; *inf.* up in the air.

indecorous *adjective* unbecoming, unseemly, improper, unsuitable, inappropriate, impolite, unladylike, ungentlemanly, in bad taste, illbred, ill-mannered, crude.

indecorum *noun* unbecomingness, unseemliness, impropriety, improperness, unsuitability, inappropriateness, impoliteness, bad taste, crudeness. *See* INDECOROUS.

indeed *adverb* **1** *he is indeed her brother* in fact, in point of fact, in truth, truly, actually, really, in reality, certainly, surely, for sure, to be sure, positively, absolutely, doubtlessly, undoubtedly, without doubt, undeniably, veritably. **2** *indeed I shall come | very pleased indeed* yes, certainly, emphatically.

indefatigable *adjective* *indefatigable workers* tireless, untiring, never-tiring, unwearied, unflagging, persistent, tenacious, dogged, assiduous, industrious, indomitable, relentless, unremitting.

indefensible *adjective* **1** *indefensible behavior* inexcusable, unjustifiable, unpardonable, unforgivable, inexpiable. **2** *an indefensible theory* untenable, unarguable, insupportable, unmaintainable, unwarrantable, flawed, faulty, specious, implausible. **3** *indefensible buildings* defenseless, vulnerable, exposed, pregnable, unfortified, unguarded, unprotected, unshielded, unarmed.

indefinable *adjective* *an indefinable atmosphere in the room* indescribable, inexpressible, nameless, obscure, unanalyzable.

indefinite *adjective* **1** *the venue for the meeting is as yet indefinite* undecided, unfixed, undetermined, unsettled, inconclusive, undefined, unknown, uncertain, unspecific, inexplicit, unexplicit, imprecise, inexact, vague, doubtful. **2** *an indefinite shape in the distance* illdefined, indistinct, blurred, fuzzy, hazy, dim, vague, obscure. **3** *an indefinite answer* vague, unclear, imprecise, inexact, ambiguous, ambivalent, equivocal, confused, evasive, abstruse. **4** *she's a bit indefinite about whether she's going or not* undecided, indecisive, irresolute, vacillating, wavering, hesitant, tentative, uncertain. *See* INDECISIVE 1. **5** *an indefinite number/amount* indeterminate, unspecified, unlimited, limitless, infinite, immeasurable, boundless.

indefinitely *adverb* *suspended indefinitely* for an unspecified time/period, for an unlimited time/period, without a fixed limit, sine die.

indelible *adjective* *indelible marks/memories* inerasable, ineradicable, unobliterable, ineffaceable, indestructible, permanent, lasting, abiding, constant, durable, ingrained, engrained, persistent, enduring, inextirpable, unfading, imperishable.

indelicate *adjective* **1** *indelicate manners/behavior* vulgar, coarse, rough, unrefined, uncultivated, tasteless, unmannerly, unseemly, unbecoming, indecorous, immodest, boorish, churlish, loutish, offensive. **2** *indelicate jokes* indecent, impure, risqué, ribald, bawdy, vulgar, gross, crude, dirty, smutty, obscene, blue, lewd. *See* INDECENT 1.

indemnify *verb* **1** *indemnify them for their loss* reimburse, compensate, make restitution/amends to, recompense, repay, pay, pay back, remunerate. **2** *indemnify passengers against travel risks* insure, underwrite, guarantee, protect, secure, make secure, give security to, endorse.

indemnity *noun* **1** *receive indemnity for losses sustained* reimbursement, compensation, restitution, reparation, redress, requital, atonement, payment, repayment, remuneration, recompense; amends. **2** *take out indemnity against lost luggage* insurance, assurance, protection, security, endorsement; guarantee, safeguard. **3** *receive diplomatic indemnity for his crimes* legal exemption, immunity, diplomatic immunity, privilege, prerogative, impunity.

indent *verb* **1** *the sea had indented the coastline* notch, nick, make notches/nicks in, scallop, serrate, pink. **2** *indent the line* move right, move further from the margin/edge.

indent *noun* notch; dent, impression. *See* INDENTATION.

indentation *noun* indent, notch, cut, nick, groove, furrow, gouge, score; recess, niche, concavity, hollow, impression, depression, dimple, cranny.

indenture *noun* contract, written agreement, compact, covenant, certificate, deed, document, lease, warranty, bond, written commitment.

independence *noun* **1** *states seeking independence* self-government, self-rule, home rule, self-legislation, self-determination, sovereignty, autonomy, nonalignment, freedom, separation, autarchy. **2** *financial independence* self-sufficiency, self-reliance. **3** *independence of spirit* individualism, boldness, liberation, unconstraint, unrestraint, lack of constraint/restraint.

independent *adjective* **1** *an independent state* self-governing, self-ruling, self-legislating, free, self-determining, sovereign, autonomous, autonomic, absolute, nonaligned, autarchic. **2** *two independent units make up the desk* separate, individual, free-standing, self-contained. **3** *the two firms are quite independent of/from each other* separate, unconnected, unrelated, unattached, distinct, individual. **4** *independent people not requiring financial help* self-sufficient, self-supporting, self-reliant; *inf.* standing on one's own feet. **5** *an independent spirit* free-thinking, individualistic, unconventional, bold, liberated, unconstrained, unrestrained, unfettered, untrammeled.

Antonyms: DEPENDENT; SUBSERVIENT.

indescribable *adjective* undescribable, inexpressible, undefinable, beyond words/description, surpassing description, incommunicable, ineffable, unutterable, incredible, extraordinary, remarkable, prodigious.

indestructible *adjective* durable, enduring, unbreakable, infrangible, imperishable, inextinguishable, undecaying, perennial, deathless, undying, immortal, endless, everlasting.

indeterminate *adjective* **1** *an indeterminate number of people are expected* undetermined, unfixed, indefinite, unspecified, unstipulated, unknown, uncertain, unpredictable, uncounted, uncalculated. **2** *an indeterminate reply* vague, hazy, unclear, obscure, ambiguous, ambivalent, equivocal, inconclusive, inexact, imprecise, inexplicit, ill-defined.

index *noun* **1** *an index to the information* guide, key, directory, catalog; table of contents, thumb index, card index. **2** *his untidy appearance was a good index of his character* mark, token, sign, symptom, indication, clue, hint. **3** *the index on the compass* pointer, indicator, needle, hand. **index finger** forefinger, first finger; *inf.* pointing finger, pointer.

indicate *verb* **1** *his lack of concentration indicates his distress* point to, show, evince, manifest, reveal, be a sign/symptom of, be symptomatic of, mark, signal, denote, bespeak, betoken, connote, suggest, imply. **2** *he indicated the right direction* point to/out, designate, specify. **3** *he indicated his displeasure* show, demonstrate, exhibit, display, manifest, evince, express, make known, tell, state, reveal, disclose, register, record.

indication *noun* **1** *his tiredness is an indication of his overwork* sign, symptom, mark, manifestation, signal, omen, augury, portent, warning, hint. **2** *the indication of the right direction* pointing out, designation, specification. **3** *he frowned as an indication of his displeasure* show, demonstration, exhibition, display, manifestation, evincement, revelation, disclosure, register, record.

indicative *adjective his behavior is indicative of his attitude* indicatory, demonstrative, suggestive, symptomatic, typical, characteristic, symbolic, emblematic. *See* INDICATE 1.

indicator *noun* **1** *the indicator on the dial* pointer, needle, marker, index. **2** *a temperature indicator* gauge, meter, display. **3** *an economic indicator* index, guide, mark, sign, signal, signpost, symbol.

indict *verb* accuse, charge, arraign, impeach, prosecute, bring to trial, put on trial, cite, summons, incriminate, inculpate.

indictment *noun* accusation, charge, arraignment, impeachment, prosecution, citation, summons, incrimination, inculpation.

indifference *noun* **1** *the indifference of the spectators* apathy, lack of concern, unconcernedness, heedlessness, disregard, lack of interest, aloofness, detachment, coldness, coolness, impassivity, lack of passion/emotion/feeling. *See* INDIFFERENT 1. **2** *the indifference of the players* mediocrity, adequacy, averageness, ordinariness, lack of distinction. *See* INDIFFERENT 2. **3** *the indifference of the issues* unimportance, insignificance, inconsequence, triviality, slightness, pettiness, irrelevance. *See* INDIFFERENT 3. **4** *the indifference of the judges* impartiality, disinterest, lack/absence of bias, nonpartisanship, neutrality, objectivity, dispassionateness, dispassion, detachment, justness, justice, equitability, fairness, fair-mindedness, evenhandedness.

indifferent *adjective* **1** *totally indifferent spectators* | *indifferent to their suffering victims* apathetic, unconcerned, careless, heedless, regardless, uncaring, uninterested, unimpressed, aloof, detached, distant, cold, cool, impassive, dispassionate, unresponsive, passionless, unemotional, emotionless, unmoved, unexcited, unfeeling, unsympathetic, uncompassionate, callous. **2** *an indifferent player* mediocre, middling, moderate, medium, fair, not bad, passable, adequate, barely adequate, average, ordinary, commonplace, undistinguished, uninspired; *inf.* OK, okay, so-so. **3** *an indifferent issue* unimportant, insignificant, inconsequential, of no importance/consequence, minor, trivial, trifling, slight, of no matter, petty, irrelevant, immaterial. **4** *an indifferent judge* impartial, disinterested, unbiased, nondiscriminatory, neutral, unprejudiced, nonpartisan, uninvolved, objective, dispassionate, detached, just, equitable, evenhanded, fair, fair-minded.

Antonyms: ENTHUSIASTIC; BRILLIANT; BIASED.

indigenous *adjective* native, original, local, endemic, aboriginal.

indigent *adjective* poverty-stricken, impoverished, penniless, penurious, impecunious, poor, destitute, in want, in need, needy, in distress, in financial/dire straits, down-and-out; *inf.* broke, stone-broke, hard up, strapped for cash.

Antonyms: WEALTHY; AFFLUENT.

indigestion *noun* dyspepsia, hyperacidity, acidity, heartburn, pyrosis; upset stomach, stomach ache; *inf.* tummy ache.

indignant *adjective* angry, angered, irate, incensed, furious, infuriated, annoyed, wrathful, enraged, exasperated, heated, riled, in a temper, in high dudgeon, provoked, piqued, disgruntled, in a huff; *inf.* fuming, livid, aggravated, mad, seeing red, up in arms, peeved, huffy, miffed.

indignation noun anger, fury, rage, wrath, exasperation, pique, disgruntlement, umbrage, offense, resentment, ire. See INDIGNANT.

indignity noun affront, insult, abuse, mistreatment, injury, offense, outrage, slight, snub; humiliation, aspersion, disrespect, discourtesy, dishonor, obloquy; inf. slap in the face.

indirect adjective 1 an indirect route roundabout, circuitous, deviant, divergent, wandering, meandering, winding, curving, tortuous, zigzag. 2 an indirect way of giving the news oblique, discursive, digressive, long-drawn-out, rambling, circumlocutory, periphrastic, allusive. 3 an indirect insult backhanded, left-handed, devious, insidious, deceitful, underhand, surreptitious; inf. sneaky. 4 an indirect result of the talks incidental, accidental, unintended, secondary, subordinate, ancillary, collateral, contingent.

indirectly adverb 1 hear the information indirectly secondhand, in a roundabout way. 2 tell them the news indirectly by implication, obliquely, circumlocutorily, periphrastically.

indiscernible adjective 1 an indiscernible difference in attitude imperceptible, imperceivable, unnoticeable, unapparent, hidden, indistinguishable, inappreciable, impalpable, subtle, minute, minuscule, microscopic. 2 indiscernible to the naked eye invisible, imperceivable, undetectable, indistinct, indefinite, obscure, shadowy, unclear, dim.

indiscreet adjective 1 an indiscreet course of action | an indiscreet remark unwise, imprudent, injudicious, impolitic, ill-advised, ill-thought-out, ill-considered, ill-judged, ill-gauged, foolish, incautious, careless, unwary, hasty, rash, reckless, impulsive, precipitate, foolhardy, tactless, untactful, insensitive, undiplomatic. 2 indiscreet behavior immodest, indelicate, indecorous, unseemly, indecent, shameless, brazen, bold.

indiscretion noun 1 guilty of indiscretion imprudence, injudiciousness, foolishness, folly, lack of caution, carelessness, hastiness, rashness, tactlessness, lack of diplomacy. See INDISCREET 1. 2 embarrassed by her indiscretions gaffe, faux pas, breach of etiquette, slip, blunder, lapse, mistake, error; inf. slipup. 3 the indiscretion of her behavior immodesty, indelicacy, indecorum, indecorousness, unseemliness, indecency, shamelessness, brazenness, boldness.

indiscriminate adjective 1 indiscriminate reading habits | indiscriminate choice of clothes undiscriminating, unselective, unparticular, uncritical, undifferentiating, aimless, careless, haphazard, random, unsystematic, unmethodical, broad-based, wholesale, general, sweeping; inf. hit-or-miss. 2 an indiscriminate collection of furniture jumbled, mixed, haphazard, motley, miscellaneous, diverse, varied, mongrel, confused, chaotic, thrown together; inf. higgledy-piggledy.

Antonyms: SELECTIVE; SYSTEMATIC.

indispensable adjective essential, of the essence, vital, crucial, imperative, key, necessary, requisite, required, needed, needful, important, of the utmost importance, urgent, pressing, high-priority, fundamental. **Antonyms:** DISPENSABLE; SUPERFLUOUS; NONESSENTIAL.

indisposed adjective 1 indisposed and so unable to be present ill, unwell, sick, ailing, confined to bed, incapacitated; inf. on the sick list, under the weather, poorly, out of sorts/commission, laid up. 2 indisposed to believe him unwilling, disinclined, reluctant, hesitant, loath, averse, not in favor of.

indisposition noun absent owing to indisposition illness, sickness, ill health; ailment, complaint, disorder, malady, disease. **indisposition to/toward** his indisposition toward modernizing the factory unwillingness to (be), disinclination to (be), reluctance to (be), hesitation to (be), hesitancy to (be), loathness of/for, aversion to, dislike of/for, distaste of/for.

indisputable adjective incontestable, incontrovertible, undeniable, irrefutable, unquestionable, indubitable, beyond dispute/question/doubt, beyond the shadow of a doubt, unassailable, certain, sure, positive, definite, absolute, final, conclusive.

indistinct adjective 1 indistinct figures in the distance blurred, fuzzy, out of focus, bleary, hazy, misty, shadowy, dim, obscure, indefinite, indistinguishable, barely perceptible, undefined. 2 indistinct writing indecipherable, illegible, unreadable, unintelligible, pale, faded. 3 indistinct noises muffled, low, muted, muttered, mumbled.

indistinguishable adjective 1 the twins/views are indistinguishable identical, alike, very similar; inf. as like as two peas in a pod. 2 his identity was indistinguishable in the dark indiscernible, imperceptible, hard to make out, indefinite, unnoticeable, obscure, camouflaged, invisible.

individual adjective 1 each individual flower/house single, separate, sole, lone, solitary, distinct, distinctive, particular, specific, peculiar, detached, isolated. 2 an individual style characteristic, distinctive, particular, peculiar, typical, personal, personalized, own, private, special, especial, singular, original, unique, exclusive, idiosyncratic. **Antonyms:** COLLECTIVE; ORDINARY.

individual noun 1 several individuals arrived late | a most unpleasant individual person, personage, human being, creature, mortal, living soul, body, character, type. 2 she's very much an individual individualist, free spirit, nonconformist, original, eccentric, bohemian, maverick, egocentric, rara avis, rare bird, rarity, loner, lone wolf.

individualist noun individual, free spirit, nonconformist, eccentric, egocentric. See INDIVIDUAL noun 2.

individualistic *adjective an individualistic way of dealing with things* freethinking, independent, nonconformist, unorthodox, unconventional, original, eccentric, bohemian, maverick, strange, odd, egocentric.

individuality *noun works of individuality* distinctiveness, distinction, originality, uniqueness, singularity, peculiarity, personality, character.

individually *adverb tutor each student individually* one at a time, one by one, singly, separately, independently, apart; personally; *lit.* severally.

indoctrinate *verb* instruct, teach, drill, ground, initiate, inculcate, impress (on), instill (in), imbue, impregnate, brainwash, propagandize, proselytize.

indolent *adjective* lazy, idle, slothful, do-nothing, sluggish, lethargic, slow, slow-moving, slack, shiftless, languid, lackadaisical, apathetic, listless, impassive, inactive, inert, torpid.
Antonyms: INDUSTRIOUS; ACTIVE.

indomitable *adjective* invincible, unconquerable, undefeatable, unbeatable, unassailable, impregnable, unyielding, unsubmissive, stalwart, stouthearted, lionhearted, staunch, resolute, firm, steadfast, determined, intransigent, inflexible, adamant, unflinching, courageous, brave, valiant, heroic, intrepid, fearless.
Antonyms: SUBMISSIVE; COWARDLY.

indubitable *adjective* beyond doubt, beyond the shadow of a doubt, indisputable, unarguable, beyond dispute/question, unquestionable, undeniable, irrefutable, incontestable, incontrovertible, certain, sure, positive, definite, absolute, conclusive.

induce *verb* **1** *induce them to go* persuade, talk into, get, prevail upon, prompt, move, inspire, instigate, influence, exert influence on, press, urge, incite, encourage, impel, actuate, motivate, inveigle, coax, wheedle. **2** *induce a reaction* bring about, bring on, cause, produce, effect, create, give rise to, generate, originate, engender, occasion, set in motion, develop, lead to.
Antonyms: DISSUADE; HINDER; DETER.

inducement *noun* **1** *offer a salary increase as an inducement* incentive, attraction, encouragement, bait, lure, reward, incitement, stimulus, influence, spur, goad, impetus, motive, provocation; *inf.* carrot, come-on. **2** *gave in to their inducement to go* persuasion, prompting, urging, incitement, encouragement, inveigling.
See INDUCE 1.

indulge *verb* **1** *indulge one's appetites* give way to, yield to, pander to, cater to, satisfy, gratify, fulfill, satiate, appease. **2** *indulge in a bout of self-pity* give oneself up to, give rein to, give free rein to, wallow in, luxuriate in, revel in. **3** *indulge the child* pamper, spoil, coddle, mollycoddle, pander to, humor, go along with, baby, pet. **indulge oneself** treat oneself, give oneself a

treat, splurge; *inf.* have a spree, paint the town red, go on the town.

indulgence *noun* **1** *the indulgence of one's appetites* satisfaction, gratification, fulfillment, satiation, appeasement. **2** *lead a life of indulgence* self-gratification, dissipation, dissoluteness, intemperance, immoderation, immoderateness, debauchery, excess, lack of restraint, unrestraint, prodigality, extravagance. **3** *traveling is his only indulgence* extravagance, luxury, treat. **4** *I was allowed the indulgence of going on board ship* privilege, courtesy, favor, treat. **5** *treat the prisoners with indulgence* tolerance, forbearance, compassion, humanity, kindness, understanding, sympathy, liberalness, liberality, forgiveness, leniency, mercy, clemency. **6** *too much indulgence was bad for the children* pampering, spoiling, coddling, mollycoddling, cosseting, humoring, partiality.

indulgent *adjective* **1** *indulgent judges* tolerant, forbearing, compassionate, humane, kind, kindly, understanding, sympathetic, liberal, forgiving, lenient, merciful, clement. **2** *indulgent parents* permissive, easygoing, compliant, fond, doting, pampering, spoiling, mollycoddling, cosseting, humoring.
Antonyms: INTOLERANT; STERN; STRICT.

industrial *adjective* manufacturing.

industrialist *noun* manufacturer, producer, captain of industry, magnate, tycoon, business/manufacturing baron, capitalist, financier.

industrious *adjective* hardworking, diligent, assiduous, sedulous, conscientious, steady, laborious, busy, busy as a bee, active, bustling, energetic, on the go, vigorous, determined, dynamic, indefatigable, tireless, persistent, pertinacious, zealous, productive.
Antonyms: IDLE; INDOLENT; LAZY.

industry *noun* **1** *involved in heavy industry* manufacturing, production, fabrication, construction. **2** *employed in the publishing industry* business, trade, commercial enterprise, field, line, craft, métier. **3** *work with industry* industriousness, diligence, assiduity, application, sedulousness, sedulity, conscientiousness, concentration, intentness, steadiness, laboriousness, busyness, activity, energy, vigor, effort, determination, dynamism, tirelessness, persistence, pertinacity, zeal, productiveness.

inebriated *adjective* intoxicated, inebriate, drunk, drunken, blind drunk, tipsy; *inf.* tight, under the influence, three sheets to the wind, plastered, stoned, loaded, blotto, pickled, out of it, smashed, sloshed, soused, well-oiled, well-lubricated, stewed to the gills, tanked (up).
Antonyms: SOBER; ABSTEMIOUS.

inedible *adjective* unedible, uneatable, not fit to eat, unconsumable, unwholesome, off, rotten, bad, putrid, poisonous.

ineffable *adjective* **1** *ineffable joy* inexpressible, unutterable, beyond words, indescribable, undefinable. **2** *the ineffable name of Jehovah* not to be uttered, unutterable, not to be spoken, unmentionable, taboo.

ineffective *adjective* **1** *ineffective attempts to hold back the water* ineffectual, vain, to no avail, unavailing, useless, worthless, unsuccessful, futile, fruitless, unproductive, profitless, abortive, inadequate, inefficient, inefficacious, powerless, impotent, idle, feeble, weak, incompetent, inept, lame, barren, sterile. **2** *ineffective people* ineffectual, unproductive, inadequate, inefficient, inefficacious, powerless, impotent, incompetent, inept, feeble, weak.

ineffectual *adjective* **1** *ineffectual efforts* ineffective, vain, unavailing, useless, worthless, futile, fruitless, unproductive, abortive, inadequate, inefficient, inefficacious, lame, inept. *See* INEFFECTIVE 1. **2** *ineffectual people* ineffective, inadequate, inefficient, inefficacious, powerless, impotent, inept. *See* INEFFECTIVE 2.

inefficient *adjective* *inefficient people/methods* ineffective, badly organized, disorganized, incompetent, inept, incapable, unprepared, ineffectual, inefficacious, unskillful, inexpert, wasteful, uneconomical, negligent, lax, slipshod, sloppy, slack.

inelegant *adjective* **1** *inelegant manners* unrefined, uncultured, uncultivated, unpolished, unsophisticated, unfinished, gauche, crude, uncouth, ill-bred, coarse, vulgar. **2** *sit in an inelegant position* awkward, clumsy, ungainly, ungraceful, graceless.

ineligible *adjective* **1** *ineligible candidates* unqualified, unfit, unequipped, unsuitable, unacceptable, undesirable, ruled out, legally disqualified; *Law* incompetent. **2** *ineligible suitors* unmarriageable, unsuitable, undesirable, unacceptable.

inept *adjective* **1** *an inept mechanic* incompetent, unadept, incapable, unskillful, unskilled, inexpert, clumsy, awkward, maladroit, undexterous, heavy-handed; *inf.* ham-handed. **2** *an inept attempt* incompetent, unadept, unskillful, inadequate, bungling, awkward, maladroit, unproductive, unsuccessful, ineffectual. **3** *an inept remark in the circumstances* out of place, badly timed, inapt, inappropriate, unsuitable, infelicitous. **4** *always doing inept things* absurd, foolish, silly, stupid, inane, nonsensical, senseless, farcical, ridiculous, ludicrous, asinine, crazy; *inf.* screwy.
Antonyms: COMPETENT; APPROPRIATE; SENSIBLE.

inequality *noun* **1** *inequality of salaries/opportunity* unequalness, disparity, imparity, imbalance, lack of balance, unevenness, disproportion, discrepancy, nonconformity, variation, variability, difference, dissimilarity, contrast. **2** *treat women with inequality* bias, prejudice, discrimination, preferentiality. **3** *the inequality of the surface* unevenness, irregularity, roughness.

inequitable *adjective* unjust, unfair, partial, prejudiced, biased, partisan, discriminatory, preferential, one-sided, intolerant, bigoted.

inequity *noun* *the inequity of the sentence/treatment* unfairness, injustice, unjustness, partisanship, partiality, bias, preferentialism, discrimination.

inert *adjective* **1** *inert bodies* inactive, unmoving, motionless, immobile, still, stock-still, stationary, static, lifeless, inanimate, unconscious, passive, out cold, comatose, dormant, dead. **2** *inert members of the company* inactive, idle, indolent, slack, lazy, slothful, dull, sluggish, lethargic, stagnant, languid, lackadaisical, listless, torpid, otiose.
Antonyms: ACTIVE; ENERGETIC.

inertia *noun* inertness, inactivity, inaction, inactiveness, motionlessness, immobility, unemployment, stagnation, stasis, passivity, idleness, indolence, laziness, sloth, slothfulness, dullness, sluggishness, lethargy, languor, listlessness, torpor.
Antonyms: ACTION; ACTIVITY; ENERGY.

inescapable *adjective* unavoidable, inevitable, unpreventable, inexorable, assured, certain, bound/sure to happen, ineludible, ineluctable.

inestimable *adjective* *of inestimable value* immeasurable, measureless, incalculable, priceless, beyond price, precious, invaluable, worth its weight in gold, worth a king's ransom, unparalleled, supreme, superlative.

inevitable *adjective* unavoidable, unpreventable, inexorable, inescapable, fixed, settled, irrevocable, fated, destined, predestined, ordained, decreed, out of one's hands, assured, certain, sure, bound/sure to happen, for sure, necessary, ineluctable.
Antonyms: avoidable; UNCERTAIN.

inexact *adjective* not accurate, not exact, imprecise, approximate, incorrect, erroneous, wrong, false, fallacious, wide of the mark.

inexcusable *adjective* unexcusable, unpardonable, unforgivable, unatonable, inexpiable, unjustifiable, unwarrantable, indefensible, blameworthy, censurable, reprehensible, outrageous.

inexhaustible *adjective* **1** *a seemingly inexhaustible supply of ammunition* unlimited, limitless, illimitable, infinite, boundless, endless, never-ending, unrestricted, bottomless, measureless, copious, abundant. **2** *inexhaustible workers* indefatigable, tireless, untiring, unwearying, weariless, unfaltering, unfailing, unflagging, unwavering, unremitting, persevering, persistent, dogged.

inexorable *adjective* **1** *the inexorable march of progress* relentless, unavoidable, inescapable, inevitable, unpreventable, irrevocable, fated, destined, certain. *See* INEVITABLE. **2** *inexorable tyrants* adamant, obdurate, unbending, unyielding, immovable, intransigent, implacable, unappeasable, unforgiving, uncompromising, inflexible, strict, severe, iron-handed, stringent, harsh, exacting, rigorous, draconian, cruel, ruthless, relentless, pitiless, merciless, remorseless.

inexpedient *adjective* impolitic, ill-advised, unadvisable, injudicious, ill-judged, unwise, imprudent, ill-considered, thoughtless, wrongheaded, foolish, detrimental, harmful.

inexpensive *adjective* low-cost, low-price, low-priced, reasonably priced, reasonable, economical, cheap, budget, reduced, sale-price, half-price, marked-down, discount, discounted, cut-rate, bargain, bargain-basement.

inexperienced *adjective* lacking experience, untrained, untutored, undrilled, unqualified, unpracticed, amateur, unskilled, uninitiated, uninformed, ignorant, unacquainted, unversed, naïve, unsophisticated, unfledged, untried, unseasoned, new, callow, immature, fresh, green, raw; *inf.* wet behind the ears.

inexpert *adjective* unskilled, unskillful, amateur, amateurish, unprofessional, untrained, unpracticed, unqualified, incompetent, maladroit, inept, clumsy, awkward, bungling, bumbling, blundering; *inf.* ham-handed.

inexplicable *adjective* unexplainable, inexplainable, unaccountable, incomprehensible, beyond comprehension/understanding, unintelligible, unfathomable, baffling, puzzling, perplexing, mystifying, insoluble, bewildering, mysterious, strange, weird, abstruse, enigmatic, inscrutable.

inexpressible *adjective* indescribable, undescribable, beyond words/description, unutterable, undefinable, unspeakable, incommunicable, ineffable.

inexpressive *adjective* expressionless, blank, vacant, empty, deadpan, dead, lifeless, poker-faced, inscrutable, emotionless, impassive, inanimate, bland, cold, stony.

inextinguishable *adjective* unquenchable, everburning, unsuppressible, irrepressible, indestructible, imperishable, undying, enduring, lasting, eternal.

inextricable *adjective* **1** *an inextricable situation* inescapable. **2** *the two family histories are inextricable* entangled, tangled, raveled, inseparable, mixed up, confused. **3** *an inextricable problem* complicated, knotty, convoluted, intricate, involved, complex, perplexing, puzzling, baffling, labyrinthine, mazelike.

infallible *adjective* **1** *an infallible remedy* unfailing, without failure, foolproof, dependable, trustworthy, reliable, sure, certain; *inf.* surefire. **2** *an infallible memory* error-free, unerring, unfailing, faultless, flawless, impeccable, unimpeachable, perfect.

infamous *adjective* **1** *an infamous robber* notorious, disreputable, ill-famed, of ill-repute, iniquitous, ignominious, dishonorable, discreditable, villainous, bad, wicked, vile, odious, nefarious. **2** *guilty of infamous conduct* abominable, outrageous, shocking, monstrous, disgraceful, dishonorable, shameful, atrocious, heinous, detestable, loathsome, hateful, wicked, vile, base, iniquitous, criminal, odious, nefarious, scandalous, egregious, flagitious. *Antonyms:* HONORABLE; REPUTABLE.

infancy *noun* **1** *healthy throughout infancy* babyhood, early years, early childhood; juvenescence. **2** *the infancy of space exploration* start, commencement, beginning, origin, rise, emergence, outset, onset, dawn, birth, cradle, conception, genesis; beginnings, early stages.

infant *noun* **1** *a cradle for the infant* baby, babe, newborn, little child, tot, little one; neonate. **2** *an infant in the publishing industry* beginner, novice, newcomer, learner, apprentice, trainee, new recruit, tyro, new boy/girl, initiate, novitiate, neophyte, ingenue, innocent, child, mere child, babe in arms; *inf.* greenhorn, rookie.

infant *adjective* *an infant industry* emergent, developing, dawning, nascent.

infantile *adjective* babyish, childish, puerile, immature, juvenile.

infantry *noun* infantrymen, foot soldiers, ranks; rank and file; *inf.* cannon fodder, GIs.

infatuated *adjective* in love, head over heels in love, hopelessly in love; enamored, besotted, captivated, bewitched, beguiled, spellbound, fascinated, enraptured, carried away, obsessed, swept off one's feet; taken with, under the spell of; *inf.* smitten, sweet on, keen on, mad about, wild about, crazy about, nuts about, stuck on, turned on by.

infatuation *noun* passing fancy, fancy, passion, obsession, fixation, craze, mania; *inf.* puppy love, crush, thing.

infect *verb* **1** *infect the wound* cause infection/disease in, make septic, contaminate, poison, ulcerate. **2** *infect the others with the germs* pass/transmit infection to, pass on to, spread to. **3** *infect the air/water* contaminate, pollute, taint, make foul, blight, spoil, mar, impair. **4** *infect others with his wickedness* influence, corrupt, pervert, debauch, debase, degrade, vitiate. **5** *infect others with his enthusiasm/laughter* influence, affect, imbue, infuse, excite, inspire, stimulate, animate.

infection *noun* **1** *an infection in the wound* septicity, septicemia, contamination, poison, ulceration; germs, bacteria. **2** *the infection of the air/water* contamination, pollution, tainting, fouling, spoiling, blighting. **3** *catch an infection of the lungs* disease, disorder, virus, contagion; *inf.* bug.

infectious *adjective* **1** *an infectious disease* infective, communicable, transmittable, transmissible, catching, spreading; contagious. **2** *infectious material* germ-laden, contaminating, polluting, septic, toxic, noxious, virulent, poisonous. **3** *her laughter/enthusiasm is infectious* catching, spreading, contagious, communicable, irresistible, compelling.

infer verb **1** *from the evidence they inferred that he was guilty* deduce, reason, conclude, gather, understand, presume, conjecture, surmise, read between the lines, theorize, hypothesize; *inf.* figure, guesstimate. **2** *his conduct inferred a guilty conscience* indicate, point to, signal, signify, demonstrate, show, bespeak, evidence. **3** *she inferred in her speech that he was a coward* imply, insinuate, hint, suggest, intimate.

inference noun **1** *dispute the inference from the evidence* deduction, conclusion, ratiocination, presumption, conjecture, surmise, reasoning, theorizing. *See* INFER 1. **2** *resent her inference that he was a coward* implication, insinuation, suggestion, intimation.

inferior adjective **1** *in an inferior position* lower, lesser, subordinate, junior, secondary, subsidiary, ancillary, second-class, second-fiddle, minor, subservient, lowly, humble, servile, menial. **2** *inferior goods* imperfect, faulty, defective, substandard, low-quality, low-grade, shoddy, cheap, reject, gimcrack. **3** *an inferior teacher* second-rate, indifferent, mediocre, incompetent, poor, bad, awful.
Antonyms: SUPERIOR; SENIOR; EXCELLENT.

inferior noun *despise his inferiors* subordinate, junior, underling, menial.

inferiority noun **1** *the inferiority of the goods* imperfection, faultiness, deficiency, shoddiness, cheapness. *See* INFERIOR adjective 2. **2** *the inferiority of the teaching* second-rateness, indifference, mediocrity, incompetence, poorness. **3** *conscious of his inferiority* inferior status/position, lowliness, subordination, subservience.

infernal adjective **1** *the infernal regions* lower, nether, hellish, Hadean, Plutonic, Plutonian, Stygian, Styxian, Tartarean, Avernal. **2** *infernal wickedness/crimes* hellish, diabolical, devilish, demonic, demoniac, fiendish, satanic, malevolent, malicious, heinous, vile, atrocious, execrable, unspeakable, outrageous. **3** *the infernal car won't start* damned, damnable, accursed, cursed, pestilential, wretched.

infertile adjective **1** *infertile soil* barren, unfruitful, unfructuous, sterile, unproductive, nonproductive, arid. **2** *infertile women* barren, sterile, infecund, childless, unprolific.

infest verb overrun, spread through, take over, overspread, pervade, permeate, penetrate, infiltrate, invade, swarm over, crawl over, beset, pester, plague.

infidel noun unbeliever, disbeliever, heathen, heretic, pagan, agnostic, atheist, irreligionist.

infidelity noun **1** *discovering the spouse's infidelity* unfaithfulness, adultery, cuckoldry; affair, liaison, intrigue, amour; *inf.* fooling/playing around, cheating, hanky-panky. **2** *the servant's infidelity to his master* breach of trust, faithlessness, unfaithfulness, treachery, perfidy, per-

fidiousness, disloyalty, falseness, traitorousness, treason, double-dealing, duplicity.
Antonyms: FIDELITY; FAITHFULNESS.

infiltrate verb **1** *water infiltrated the roof* pervade, penetrate, filter through, percolate through, seep into/through, soak into. **2** *they infiltrated the enemy's meeting* slip into, sneak into, creep into, insinuate oneself into, worm one's way into, invade, intrude on.

infinite adjective **1** *infinite space* boundless, unbounded, unlimited, limitless, without limit/end, extensive, vast. **2** *infinite numbers of insects* countless, without number, numberless, innumerable, immeasurable, incalculable, untold, uncountable, inestimable, indeterminable, vast, enormous, stupendous, prodigious. **3** *infinite depths* limitless, boundless, measureless, immeasurable, fathomless, bottomless. **4** *infinite patience* unlimited, boundless, endless, unending, no end of, absolute, never-ending, inexhaustible, interminable, total.

infinitesimal adjective minute, tiny, microscopic, minuscule, very small, teeny, wee, Lilliputian, inappreciable, insignificant, inconsiderable, trifling; *inf.* piddling.
Antonyms: HUGE; ENORMOUS; SUBSTANTIAL.

infinity noun *the infinity of space* | *stare into infinity* boundlessness, limitlessness, unlimitedness, endlessness, infinitude, infiniteness; infinite distance, space.

infirm adjective **1** *infirm people* feeble, enfeebled, weak, frail, debilitated, decrepit, disabled, in poor/declining health, failing, ailing, doddering, tottering, lame, crippled. **2** *of infirm judgment* indecisive, irresolute, wavering, vacillating, fluctuating, faltering. **3** *infirm furniture* rickety, unsteady, shaky, wobbly, unsound, flimsy, tumbledown, jerry-built, on its last legs, decayed.
Antonyms: HEALTHY; FIT; STABLE.

infirmity noun **1** *suffering from an infirmity* ailment, illness, malady, disease, disorder, sickness. **2** *moral infirmities* fault, failing, defect, flaw, weakness, imperfection, foible. **3** *the infirmity of his grandfather* feebleness, weakness, frailty, debilitation, impairment, decrepitude, disability. *See* INFIRM 1. **4** *the infirmity of his judgment* indecision, irresoluteness, irresolution, vacillation. *See* INFIRM 2. **5** *the infirmity of the furniture* ricketiness, wobbliness, unsoundness, flimsiness. *See* INFIRM 3.

inflame verb **1** *inflame the passions of the crowd* incite, excite, arouse, rouse, stir up, work up, whip up, agitate, fire, ignite, kindle, foment, impassion, provoke, stimulate, actuate. **2** *inflame the onlookers with his cruelty to the child* enrage, incense, infuriate, exasperate, anger, madden, provoke, rile. **3** *inflame the feud* aggravate, intensify, make worse, exacerbate, fan, fuel. **4** *her face inflamed with anger* redden, flush, suffuse, make glow, make hot.

inflamed adjective **1** *an inflamed arm* red, hot,

angry-looking, swollen, sore, infected, festered, septic. **2** *inflamed passions* excited, aroused, roused, stirred, kindled, impassioned. *See* INFLAME 1.

inflammation *noun* *treat the inflammation on his leg* redness, hotness, heat, swelling, soreness, sore, painfulness, tenderness, infection, festering, eruption, suppuration.

inflammatory *adjective* **1** *an inflammatory reaction to the drug* red, hot, swollen, sore, painful, tender, eruptive, allergic. **2** *an inflammatory speech* inflaming, inciting, arousing, rousing, stirring, fiery, passionate, impassioned, provocative, provoking, instigative, actuating, fomenting, rabble-rousing, demagogic, rebellious, revolutionary, insurgent, seditious, mutinous, anarchic.

inflate *verb* **1** *inflate the air mattress | inflate one's cheeks* blow up, pump up, aerate, puff up, puff out, dilate, distend, swell. **2** *his cheeks inflated* puff up, puff out, dilate, distend, swell. **3** *every time he tells the story he inflates the element of danger* increase, extend, amplify, augment, expand, intensify, exaggerate. **4** *please do not inflate his self-importance* add to, boost, augment, intensify, magnify, escalate, aggrandize. **5** *inflate prices* increase, boost, raise, escalate, step up.
Antonyms: DEFLATE; COLLAPSE; play down (*see* PLAY); DECREASE.

inflated *adjective* **1** *inflated balloons* blown-up, pumped-up, dilated. **2** *inflated prices* increased, raised, escalated, stepped up. **3** *an inflated sense of his own importance* exaggerated, magnified, aggrandized. **4** *inflated prose* high-flown, extravagant, pretentious, pompous, rhetorical, grandiloquent, bombastic, orotund.

inflection *noun* **1** *the inflection of the line* curving, curvature, bending, turning; curve, bend, turn, bow, crook, angle, arc, arch. **2** *the inflection of his voice* change of pitch/tone/timbre, flow, modulation, accentuation, emphasis, stress, cadence, rhythm. **3** *a language with inflections* conjugation, declension.

inflexible *adjective* **1** *an inflexible substance* nonflexible, rigid, stiff, unbendable, unyielding, taut, hard, firm, inelastic, unmalleable. **2** *inflexible rules* unalterable, unchangeable, immutable, unvarying, firm, fixed, hard and fast, unbendable, uncompromising, stringent, rigorous, inexorable. **3** *inflexible people/attitudes* adamant, firm, immovable, unadaptable, dyed-in-the-wool, unaccommodating, uncompliant, stubborn, obdurate, obstinate, intractable, unbending, intolerant, relentless, merciless, pitiless, uncompromising, inexorable, steely, iron-willed.

inflict *verb* administer, deal out, mete out, serve out, deliver, apply, lay on, impose, levy, exact, wreak.

infliction *noun* **1** *the infliction of punishment* administering, administration, dealing out, met-

ing out, delivering, application, imposition, levying, exaction, wreaking. **2** *recovering from his infliction* trouble, worry, suffering, affliction, hurt, torture, torment, tribulation, punishment, penalty.

influence *noun* **1** *have a good/bad influence on them* effect, impact; control, sway, ascendancy, power, mastery, agency, guidance, domination, rule, supremacy, leadership, direction, pressure. **2** *under the influence of drugs* effect, control, hold, sway, power. **3** *he has influence on the board* power, authority, sway, prestige, standing, footing; good offices, connections; *inf.* clout, pull.

influence *verb* **1** *his illness influenced his behavior* affect, have an effect on, impact on, sway, bias, incline, motivate, actuate, determine, guide, control, change, alter, transform. **2** *he tried to influence the jury* affect, sway, bias, bring pressure to bear on; *inf.* pull strings with, pull rank on. **3** *he influenced her not to go* persuade, induce, impel, incite, manipulate, prompt.

influential *adjective* **1** *an influential member of the board* powerful, important, leading, authoritative, controlling, dominant, predominant, prestigious. **2** *money was an influential issue in his decision to go* instrumental, guiding, significant, important, persuasive, telling, meaningful.
Antonyms: UNIMPORTANT; IMPOTENT; INSIGNIFICANT.

influx *noun* inrush, rush, inflow, inundation, flood, invasion, intrusion, incursion, ingress, convergence.

inform *verb* **1** *inform him of/about the facts* tell, let know, apprise, advise, notify, announce to, impart to, relate to, communicate to, acquaint, brief, instruct, enlighten, make conversant, make knowledgeable, send word to; *inf.* put in the picture, fill in, clue in/up, put wise, spill the beans to, tip off, give the low-down to, give the inside story to. **2** *optimism informs her writing* characterize, typify, pervade, permeate, suffuse, infuse, imbue, instill. **3** *her love of God informed her* inspire, animate, arouse, fire, kindle. **inform on** *inform on his accomplices* betray, denounce, incriminate, inculpate, blab on; *inf.* rat on, squeal on, tell tales about, tell on, blow the whistle on, spill the beans about, put the finger on, sell down the river, snitch on.

informal *adjective* **1** *an informal party | informal dress* nonformal, casual, unceremonious, unofficial, simple, unpretentious, everyday, relaxed, easy. **2** *informal language* colloquial, vernacular, nonliterary, simple, natural, everyday, unofficial, unpretentious; *inf.* slangy.

informality *noun* nonformality, casualness, lack of ceremony, unceremoniousness, unofficialness, simplicity, naturalness, unpretentiousness, ease, relaxedness.

information *noun* **1** *the information has been*

recorded data, facts. **2** *what information do you have?* | *has she sent any information?* knowledge, intelligence, news, notice, word, advice, counsel, instruction, enlightenment; tidings; message, report, communiqué, communication; *inf.* info, low-down, dope, poop, inside story, dirt.

informative *adjective* instructive, illuminating, enlightening, edifying, educational, revealing, telling, communicative, chatty, newsy, gossipy.

informed *adjective* knowledgeable, well-briefed, abreast of the facts, well-posted, primed, well-versed, up-to-date, au courant, *au fait*.

informer *noun* informant, betrayer, traitor, Judas; *inf.* rat, squealer, stool pigeon, tattletale, whistleblower, canary, snitch.

infraction *noun* breach, violation, transgression, contravention, infringement, intrusion, encroachment, invasion.

infrequent *adjective* few and far between, rare, occasional, sporadic, irregular, uncommon, unusual, exceptional.

infringe *verb* **1** *infringe the law* break, disobey, violate, contravene, transgress, breach, infract, disregard, take no notice of. **2** *infringe on his neighbor's land* encroach, impinge, intrude, trespass.

infringement *noun* **1** *an infringement of the rules* breaking, violation, contravention, breach, transgression, infraction, nonobservance, noncompliance. **2** *an infringement on his property* encroachment, impingement, intrusion, trespass.

infuriate *verb* enrage, incense, inflame, madden, exasperate, anger, provoke, rile, make one's blood boil, make one's hackles rise, annoy, irritate, vex, pique; *inf.* aggravate, make one see red, get one's back up, get one's goat, bug, get one.

infuriating *adjective* maddening, exasperating, provoking, annoying, irritating, vexing, vexatious, galling; *inf.* aggravating.

ingenious *adjective* *an ingenious person* | *an ingenious course of action* clever, shrewd, astute, smart, sharp, bright, brilliant, talented, masterly, resourceful, inventive, creative, original, subtle, crafty, wily, cunning, skillful, adroit, deft, capable; *inf.* on the ball.
Antonyms: STUPID; UNIMAGINATIVE.

ingenuous *adjective* *too ingenuous to lie* open, sincere, honest, frank, candid, direct, forthright, artless, guileless, simple, naïve, innocent, genuine, undeceitful, undeceptive, undissembling, undissimulating, aboveboard, trustful, truthful, unsuspicious; *inf.* on the level.
Antonyms: INSINCERE; ARTFUL.

inglorious *adjective* disgraceful, shameful, dishonorable, ignominious, discreditable, disreputable, humiliating, mortifying, unheroic, ignoble, blameworthy, culpable.

ingrained *adjective* **1** *ingrained dirt* fixed, infixed,

planted, implanted, rooted, deep-rooted, permanent, built-in. **2** *ingrained arrogance* inbred, inherent, intrinsic, hereditary, inherited, in the blood/family.

ingratiate *verb* **ingratiate oneself with** *ingratiate herself with the director* seek the favor of, curry favor with, toady to, crawl to, grovel to, fawn over, play up to, be a yes-man to, be a sycophant to; *inf.* suck up to, lick the boots of.

ingratiating *adjective* sycophantic, toadying, fawning, unctuous, obsequious, servile, overhumble, crawling, flattering, wheedling, cajoling; *inf.* bootlicking.

ingratitude *noun* ungratefulness, thanklessness, unthankfulness, lack of appreciation, unappreciativeness, nonrecognition.

ingredient *adjective* constituent, component, element, part, unit, item, feature.

ingress *noun* **1** *find the ingress to the theater* way in, entrance, entry, approach. **2** *that ticket gives you ingress to the concert* admission, admittance, access, right of entry.

inhabit *verb* live in, dwell in, reside in, occupy, lodge in, make one's home in, settle in; settle, people, populate.

inhabitant *noun* resident, resider, dweller, occupant, occupier, habitant, settler.

inhale *verb* breathe in, draw in, suck in, sniff in, gasp, gulp, inspire.
Antonyms: exhale; EXPIRE.

inharmonious *adjective* **1** *inharmonious sounds* unharmonious, unmelodious, unmusical, tuneless, discordant, dissonant, harsh, jarring, jangling, raucous, strident. **2** *holding inharmonious views* conflicting, incompatible, contradictory, irreconcilable, antagonistic, antipathetic, dissentient. **3** *an inharmonious relationship* quarrelsome, argumentative, disputatious.

inherent *adjective* **1** *an inherent tendency to high blood pressure* inborn, inbred, innate, hereditary, inherited, in the blood/family, congenital, familial. **2** *an inherent part of the boat's design* intrinsic, innate, built-in, inseparable, essential, basic, fundamental, ingrained.

---

inherent
congenital, essential, inborn, ingrained, innate, intrinsic

A quality that is **inherent** is a permanent part of a person's nature or essence (*an inherent tendency to fight back*). If it is **ingrained**, it is deeply wrought into his or her substance or character (*ingrained prejudice against women*). **Inborn** and **innate** are nearly synonymous, sharing the basic sense of existing at the time of birth, but *innate* is usually preferred in an abstract or philosophical context (*innate defects; innate ideas*), while *inborn* is reserved for human characteristics that are so deep-seated they seem to have been there from birth (*an inborn aptitude for the piano*). **Congenital** also means from the time of one's birth, but it is primarily used in medical contexts and refers to problems or defects (*congenital color-blindness; a congenital tendency toward schizophrenia*). **Intrinsic** and **essential** are broader terms that can apply to things as well as people. Something that is *essential* is part of the essence or constitution of something (*an essential ingredient; essential revisions in the text*), while an *intrinsic* quality is one that belongs naturally to a person or thing (*her intrinsic fairness; an intrinsic weakness in the design*).

---

inherit verb **1** *inherit a fortune/estate* become/fall heir to, be bequeathed, be left, be willed, come into/by. **2** *inherit the title* succeed to, accede to, assume, take over, be elevated to.
inheritance noun *value their inheritance* legacy, bequest, endowment, birthright, heritage, patrimony. **inheritance of** *his inheritance of the throne* accession to, succession to, assumption of, elevation to.
inhibit verb **1** *inhibit progress* hold back, impede, hinder, hamper, interfere with, obstruct, curb, check, restrict, restrain, constrain, bridle, rein in, balk, frustrate, arrest, prevent, stop. **2** *inhibit them from going* forbid, prohibit, ban, bar, debar, vet, interdict, proscribe.
inhibited adjective *feel inhibited in the presence of parents* shy, reticent, self-conscious, reserved, constrained, repressed, embarrassed, tongue-tied, subdued, withdrawn; *inf.* uptight. **Antonyms:** UNINHIBITED; OUTGOING; EASYGOING.
inhibition noun **1** *regret the inhibition of progress* holding back, impediment, hindrance, hampering, interference, obstruction, curb, check, restriction, restraint, constraint, bridling, balking, frustration, arrest, prevention, stopping. **2** *suffer from inhibition in the presence of parents* shyness, reticence, reserve, self-consciousness, constraint, repression, embarrassment, subduedness, withdrawnness.
inhospitable adjective **1** *an inhospitable host/welcome* unwelcoming, unsociable, unsocial, antisocial, unfriendly, uncivil, discourteous, ungracious, uncongenial, ungenerous, cool, cold, chilly, aloof, unkind, unsympathetic, hostile, ill-disposed, inimical, xenophobic. **2** *an inhospitable landscape* uninviting, unwelcoming, barren, bleak, bare, uninhabitable, sterile, desolate, lonely, empty, forbidding, hostile, inimical.
inhuman adjective **1** *an inhuman cry* nonhuman, nonmortal, animal, ghostly. **2** *inhuman people* unkind, unkindly, inconsiderate, uncompassionate, unsympathetic, unapproachable, inhumane. *See* INHUMANE.
inhumane adjective unkind, unkindly, inconsiderate, uncompassionate, unfeeling, unsympathetic, unforgiving, cold-blooded, heartless, hard-hearted, pitiless, merciless, ruthless, remorseless, brutal, cruel, harsh, savage, vicious, barbaric, barbarous, bestial, fiendish, diabolical.

381

inhumanity noun unkindness, lack of compassion/feeling/sympathy, cold-bloodedness, heartlessness, hard-heartedness, pitilessness, mercilessness, ruthlessness, remorselessness, brutality, cruelty, harshness, savagery, viciousness, barbarity, bestiality, fiendishness.
inimical adjective **1** *an inimical atmosphere* hostile, unfriendly, unkind, inhospitable, unwelcoming, unfavorable, cold, unsociable, adverse, opposed, antagonistic, contrary, antipathetic, ill-disposed. **2** *inimical to their survival* harmful, injurious, detrimental, deleterious, hurtful, damaging, dangerous, pernicious, destructive, noxious, toxic, virulent. **Antonyms:** FRIENDLY; WARM; ADVANTAGEOUS.
inimitable adjective matchless, unmatched, incomparable, unparalleled, unrivaled, unsurpassed, unsurpassable, unique, superlative, supreme, model, faultless, perfect, consummate, ideal, unexampled, nonpareil, peerless.
iniquitous adjective **1** *an iniquitous action* wicked, sinful, evil, immoral, villainous, criminal, heinous, vile, foul, base, odious, abominable, execrable, atrocious, malicious, outrageous, monstrous, shocking, scandalous, reprehensible, unjust. **2** *an iniquitous robber* wicked, evil, criminal, lawless, crooked, dishonorable, unprincipled, blackguardly, degenerate, corrupt, reprobate, immoral, dissolute.
iniquity noun **1** *his falling into iniquity* wickedness, sin, sinfulness, vice, evil, ungodliness, godlessness, wrong, wrongdoing, badness, villainy, knavery, lawlessness, crime, baseness, heinousness. **2** *appalled at his iniquities* sin, vice, offense, crime, transgression, injury, violation, atrocity, outrage. **Antonyms:** VIRTUE; RIGHT.
initial adjective *the initial stages of the enterprise* first, beginning, commencing, starting, opening, early, prime, primary, elementary, foundational, introductory, inaugural, inceptive, incipient, inchoate. **Antonyms:** FINAL; TERMINAL.
initial verb *initial the document* put one's initials on, sign, undersign, countersign; endorse.
initially adverb in/at the beginning, at first, at the start/outset, to begin/start with, originally, in the early stages.
initiate verb **1** *initiate the proceedings* begin, start off, commence, open, institute, inaugurate, get under way, set in motion, lay the foundations of, lay the first stone of, launch, actuate, instigate, trigger, originate, pioneer, sow the seeds of; start the ball rolling for. **2** *initiate the students in science* teach, instruct, coach, tutor, school, train, drill, prime, familiarize, indoctrinate, inculcate. **3** *initiate the new member into the organization* admit, introduce, induct, install, instate, incorporate, ordain, invest, enlist, enroll, sign up. **Antonyms:** END; CLOSE.

initiate noun *train the initiates in the organization* beginner, new boy/girl, newcomer, learner, trainee, apprentice, probationer, new/raw recruit, greenhorn, novice, tyro, novitiate, neophyte; *inf.* rookie.

initiation noun **1** *the initiation of the proceedings* beginning, starting, commencement, opening, institution, inauguration, launch, actuation, instigation. *See* INITIATE *verb* 1. **2** *an initiation ceremony* admission, admittance, introduction, induction, installation, ordination, investment, enlistment, enrollment, baptism.

initiative noun **1** *take the initiative* first step, first move, first blow, lead, gambit, opening move/ gambit, beginning, start, commencement. **2** *promotion for those with initiative* enterprise, inventiveness, resourcefulness, resource, originality, creativity, drive, dynamism, ambition, ambitiousness, verve, dash, leadership; *inf.* get-up-and-go, zing, push, pep, zip.

inject verb **1** *inject the child/arm* syringe, inoculate, vaccinate; *inf.* jab. **2** *inject fluid into the patient | inject heroin* introduce, intromit, insert, syringe; *inf.* shoot, shoot up, mainline. **3** *inject some enthusiasm into the class* introduce, instill, bring, infuse, imbue.

injection noun **1** *a tetanus injection* inoculation, vaccination, vaccine, shot, booster. **2** *the injection of some enthusiasm* introduction, instillment, instilling, infusion, imbuing.

injudicious adjective imprudent, unwise, inadvisable, ill-considered, ill-judged, ill-advised, impolitic, inexpedient, unrecommendable, misguided, incautious, undesirable, indiscreet, inappropriate, unsuitable, wrongheaded, wrong, harebrained, foolish, hasty, rash; *inf.* dumb.

injunction noun command, instruction, order, ruling, direction, directive, dictum, dictate, mandate, ordainment, enjoinment, admonition, precept, ultimatum.

injure verb **1** *injure his foot* hurt, harm, damage, wound, maim, cripple, lame, disable, mutilate, deform, mangle. **2** *injure his health* harm, damage, impair, weaken, enfeeble. **3** *injure his reputation by his conduct* ruin, spoil, mar, damage, blight, blemish, besmirch, tarnish, undermine. **4** *guilty of injuring his fellow citizens* do an injury to, wrong, do an injustice to, offend against, abuse, maltreat, defame, vilify, malign.

injured adjective **1** *his injured leg* hurt, wounded, broken, fractured, damaged, sore, maimed, crippled, disabled, lame. **2** *the injured party* wronged, offended, abused, maltreated, ill-treated, defamed, vilified, maligned. **3** *give him an injured look* reproachful, hurt, wounded, upset, cut to the quick, put out, unhappy, disgruntled, displeased, condemnatory, censorious.

injurious adjective *injurious to health* harmful, hurtful, damaging, deleterious, detrimental, disadvantageous, unfavorable, destructive, pernicious, ruinous, disastrous, calamitous, malignant.
Antonyms: INNOCUOUS; ADVANTAGEOUS; FAVORABLE.

injury noun **1** *dangerous machines bound to cause injury* harm, hurt, wounding, damage, impairment, affliction. **2** *his injuries taking long to heal* wound, sore, bruise, cut, gash, laceration, abrasion, lesion, contusion, trauma. **3** *do an injury to his neighbors by his conduct* injustice, wrong, ill, offense, disservice, grievance, evil.

injustice noun **1** *the injustice of the verdict* unjustness, unfairness, inequitableness, inequity, bias, prejudice, favoritism, one-sidedness, partiality, discrimination, partisanship. **2** *infamous for his injustices done to others* unfairness, unjustness, inequity, wrong, injury, offense, evil, villainy, iniquity.

inkling noun **1** *they gave no inkling of their intentions* hint, clue, intimation, suggestion, indication, whisper, suspicion, insinuation, innuendo. **2** *do not have an inkling of how best to proceed* idea, vague idea, (the) vaguest idea, notion, glimmering; (the) slightest knowledge; *inf.* (the) foggiest idea, (the) foggiest.

inky adjective *inky nights* black, pitch-black, coalblack, jet-black, sable, ebony, dark.

inlaid adjective inset; veneered, enameled, ornamented, tessellated, mosaic, studded, lined, tiled.

inland adjective *inland cities* interior, inshore, internal, up-country.

inlet noun cove, bay, arm of the sea, bight, creek, fjord, sound.

inmate noun prisoner, convict, captive, jailbird.

inmost *See* INNERMOST, INMOST.

inn noun hotel, lodge, bed and breakfast, hostelry; public house, tavern, bar, pub.

innate adjective **1** *an innate tendency* inborn, inbred, connate, congenital, hereditary, inherited, in the blood/family, inherent, intrinsic, ingrained, natural, native, indigenous. **2** *an innate part of the plan* essential, basic, fundamental, quintessential, organic, radical. **3** *an innate capacity* instinctive, intuitive, spontaneous, unlearned, untaught.

inner adjective **1** *the inner rooms* interior, inside, central, middle, further in. **2** *the inner political circle* restricted, privileged, confidential, intimate, private, exclusive, secret. **3** *the inner meaning* unapparent, veiled, obscure, esoteric, hidden, secret, unrevealed. **4** *my inner thoughts* private, secret, deep, personal, innermost, intimate, hidden. **5** *the inner human being* spiritual, emotional, mental, psychological, psychic, subconscious, unconscious, innermost.
Antonyms: OUTER; EXTERIOR; OUTSIDE.

innermost, inmost adjective **1** *the innermost section* furthest in, deepest within, central, middle. **2** *innermost beliefs* intimate, private, personal, deep, deepest, profound, secret, hidden.

innkeeper noun host, proprietor, manager, landlady, landlord, hotelier; barkeeper, barkeep.

innocence noun 1 *the innocence of the prisoners* guiltlessness, blamelessness, freedom from guilt/blame, unblameworthiness, inculpability, unimpeachability, irreproachability, clean hands. 2 *the innocence of their play* harmlessness, innocuousness, safety, lack of danger/malice, inoffensiveness. 3 *the innocence of youth* virtuousness, virtue, purity, lack of sin, sinlessness, morality, decency, righteousness, chastity, virginity, immaculateness, impeccability, spotlessness. See INNOCENT *adjective* 3. 4 *the innocence of the new army recruits* simpleness, ingenuousness, naïveté, lack of sophistication, artlessness, guilelessness, frankness, openness, credulity, inexperience, gullibility. See INNOCENT *adjective* 5.
Antonyms: GUILT; SIN; EXPERIENCE.

innocent adjective 1 *innocent prisoners* not guilty, guiltless, blameless, clear, in the clear, above suspicion, unblameworthy, inculpable, unimpeachable, irreproachable, clean-handed. 2 *innocent fun* harmless, innocuous, safe, noninjurious, unmalicious, unobjectionable, inoffensive, playful. 3 *innocent youth* virtuous, pure, sinless, moral, decent, righteous, upright, chaste, virginal, virgin, immaculate, impeccable, pristine, spotless, stainless, unblemished, unsullied, incorrupt, uncorrupted. 4 *too innocent for the world of business* simple, ingenuous, naïve, unsophisticated, artless, guileless, childlike, frank, open, unsuspicious, trustful, trusting, credulous, inexperienced, unworldly, green, gullible; *inf.* wet behind the ears. **innocent of** *innocent of guile* free from, without, lacking, void of, clear of, unacquainted with, ignorant of, unaware of, unfamiliar with, nescient of, untouched by.
Antonyms: GUILTY; SINFUL; EXPERIENCED; WORLDLY.

innocent noun *an innocent in the business world* child, babe, babe in the woods/wood, babe in arms, ingenue, novice, greenhorn.

innocuous adjective 1 *an innocuous substance* harmless, unhurtful, uninjurious, safe, danger-free, nonpoisonous. 2 *an innocuous person* harmless, inoffensive, unobjectionable, unexceptionable, unoffending, mild, peaceful, bland, commonplace, run-of-the-mill, insipid.
Antonyms: HARMFUL; DANGEROUS; INJURIOUS.

innovation noun new method/device/measure, introduction, modernism, modernization, novelty, change, alteration, variation, transformation, metamorphosis, renovation, restyling, recasting, remodeling, coining, neology, neologism.

innuendo noun insinuation, implication, suggestion, hint, overtone, allusion, inkling, imputation, aspersion.

innumerable adjective very many, numerous, countless, untold, incalculable, numberless, unnumbered, beyond number, infinite, myriad; *inf.* umpteen, masses, oodles.
Antonyms: FEW; FINITE.

inoculate verb immunize, vaccinate; *inf.* give shots/jabs.

inoculation noun immunization, vaccination, injection, shot; *inf.* jab.

inoffensive adjective 1 *an inoffensive substance* harmless, innocuous, unhurtful, safe, danger-free. 2 *an inoffensive person* harmless, innocuous, unobjectionable, unexceptionable, mild, peaceful.

inoperative adjective 1 *inoperative machines* not operative, not in operation, not working, out of order, out of service/commission/action, nonactive, broken, broken-down, defective, faulty; *inf.* down, kaput. 2 *an inoperative system* useless, ineffectual, ineffective, inefficient, inadequate, worthless, valueless, futile, unproductive, abortive.

inopportune adjective inconvenient, ill-timed, badly timed, mistimed, untimely, unseasonable, inappropriate, unsuitable, ill-chosen, inapt, infelicitous, unfavorable, unfortunate, unpropitious, inauspicious.

inordinate adjective excessive, immoderate, overabundant, extravagant, unrestrained, unrestricted, unlimited, unwarranted, uncalled-for, undue, unreasonable, disproportionate, exorbitant, extreme, outrageous, preposterous, unconscionable.
Antonyms: MODERATE; LIMITED.

inquest noun inquiry, investigation, inquisition, probe.

inquire verb *inquire about the weather* | *inquire after/about his name* ask, make inquiries (about); quiz, interrogate; *inf.* grill. **inquire into** *inquire into the cause of the fire* make inquiries into, conduct an inquiry into, question, query, investigate, research, look into, examine, explore, probe, scan, search, scrutinize, study, inspect.

inquiring adjective *an inquiring mind* questioning, investigative, curious, interested, analytical, probing, exploring, searching, scrutinizing, inquisitive.

inquiry noun 1 *police are conducting an inquiry* investigation, examination, exploration, sounding, probe, search, scrutiny, scrutinization, study, inspection, interrogation. 2 *reply to her inquiry* question, query.

inquisition noun *subject the suspects to an inquisition* interrogation, cross-examination, examination, investigation, quizzing, questioning, inquiry, inquest; *inf.* grilling, third degree.

inquisitive adjective *inquisitive neighbors* inquiring, questioning, probing, scrutinizing, curious, burning with curiosity, interested, overinterested, intrusive, meddlesome, prying, snooping, snoopy, peering, spying; *inf.* nosy.

Antonyms: INDIFFERENT; APATHETIC; UNINTERESTED.

inroad *noun* **1** *enemy inroads* invasion, raid, foray, attack, assault, onslaught, charge, offensive, sally, sortie. **2** *object to the inroads on her time* encroachment, intrusion, incursion, infringement, trespassing.

insane *adjective* **1** *driven insane by isolation* mad, severely mentally disordered, of unsound mind, deranged, demented, *non compos mentis*, out of one's mind; *inf.* unhinged, crazed, crazy, non compos. **2** *he's insane to take that job* extremely foolish, mad, mad as a hatter, raving mad, out of one's mind, unhinged, not all there, crazy; *inf.* bonkers, cracked, crackers, balmy, batty, bats, cuckoo, loony, loopy, nuts, nutty, screwy, bananas, off one's rocker/nut, out of one's head, around/round the bend, off one's trolley. **3** *an insane idea* very foolish, mad, crazy, idiotic, stupid, senseless, nonsensical, irrational, impracticable, pointless, absurd, ridiculous, ludicrous, bizarre, fatuous; *inf.* daft.

insanitary *adjective* unsanitary, unsanitized, unhygienic, impure, unclean, dirty, dirtied, filthy, contaminated, polluted, foul, feculent, infected, septic, infested, disease-ridden, germy, unhealthy, insalubrious, noxious.

insanity *noun* **1** *patients suffering from insanity* madness, severe mental disorder, mental derangement, dementia, frenzy, delirium. **2** *the insanity of the idea* folly, foolishness, madness, craziness, idiocy, stupidity, senselessness, irrationality, absurdity. *See* INSANE 3.

insatiable *adjective* insatiate, unappeasable, unquenchable, greedy, hungry, craving, voracious, ravening, gluttonous, omnivorous, avid, desirous, eager.

inscribe *verb* **1** *inscribe one's name on the book/stone* imprint, write, stamp, impress, mark, brand, engrave, etch, carve, cut. **2** *inscribe the candidates in the book* enter, register, record, write, list, enroll, enlist, engross. **3** *inscribe his novel to his son* dedicate, address.

inscription *noun* **1** *read the inscription on the gravestone* engraving, writing, etching, lettering, legend, epitaph, epigraph; words. **2** *the inscription in/on the book* dedication, address, message.

inscrutable *adjective* **1** *an inscrutable expression* enigmatic, unreadable, impenetrable, cryptic, deadpan, sphinxlike; *inf.* poker-faced. **2** *an inscrutable situation* mysterious, inexplicable, unexplainable, incomprehensible, beyond comprehension/understanding, unintelligible, puzzling, baffling, unfathomable, arcane. *Antonyms:* OPEN; EXPRESSIVE; TRANSPARENT.

insecticide *noun* insect spray, pesticide; DDT, pyrethrum.

insecure *adjective* **1** *insecure children* unconfident, lacking confidence, diffident, timid, un-certain, unsure, doubtful, hesitant, anxious, fearful, apprehensive, worried. **2** *insecure fortresses* vulnerable, open to attack, defenseless, unprotected, ill-protected, unguarded, unshielded, exposed, in danger, dangerous, perilous, hazardous. **3** *insecure bookshelves* loose, flimsy, frail, fragile, infirm, weak, unsubstantial, jerry-built, rickety, wobbly, shaky, unsteady, unstable, unsound, decrepit.

insecurity *noun* **1** *the insecurity of the children* lack of confidence/security, diffidence, timidity, uncertainty, anxiety, apprehension, worry. *See* INSECURE 1. **2** *the insecurity of the fortresses* vulnerability, defenselessness, lack of protection, peril, perilousness. *See* INSECURE 2. **3** *the insecurity of the bookshelves* looseness, flimsiness, ricketiness, instability. *See* INSECURE 3.

insensible *adjective* **1** *the hit on the head left him insensible* unconscious, insensate, senseless, insentient, anesthetized, comatose, knocked out, inert, stupefied; *inf.* out, out cold, down for the count. **2** *insensible fingers and toes* numb, benumbed, numbed, lacking feeling/sensation. **3** *a passionate person among insensible people* apathetic, dispassionate, cool, passionless, emotionless, detached, indifferent, aloof, hard, hard-hearted, tough, cruel, callous. **4** *an insensible change of temperature* imperceptible, unnoticeable, indiscernible, indistinguishable, negligible, slight, minute, minuscule. **insensible of** *insensible of their danger* unaware of, ignorant of, without knowledge of, unconscious of, unmindful of, oblivious to. **insensible to** *insensible to their suffering* indifferent to, impervious to, deaf to, unmoved by, untouched by, unaffected by, unresponsive to, inured to. *Antonyms:* CONSCIOUS; AWARE; RESPONSIVE.

insensitive *adjective* *insensitive people laughing at the funeral* heartless, unfeeling, callous, tactless, thick-skinned, uncaring, unconcerned, uncompassionate, unsympathetic. **insensitive to 1** *insensitive to pain/cold* impervious to, immune to, proof against, insusceptible to, unaffected by, nonreactive to, unreactive to. **2** *insensitive to the demands of the public* unresponsive to, impervious to, indifferent to, unaffected by, unmoved by, oblivious to, unappreciative of.

insentient *adjective* inanimate, lifeless, inert, vegetative, insensate, numb, anesthetized, comatose.

inseparable *adjective* **1** *inseparable parts* unseparable, inseverable, indivisible, undividable, indissoluble. **2** *inseparable companions* constant, devoted, close, intimate, bosom.

insert *verb* **1** *to make a call, insert a coin* put in/into, place in, press in, push in, thrust in, drive in, work in, slide in, slip in, tuck in; *inf.* pop in. **2** *insert a sentence if the paragraph is too short* put in, introduce, enter, interpolate, inset, interpose, interject, implant, infix. *Antonyms:* EXTRACT; WITHDRAW.

inject, interject, interpolate, introduce, mediate

If you want to put something in a fixed place between or among other things, you can **insert** it (*insert a new paragraph in an essay; insert photographs in the text of a book*). If it's a liquid, you'll probably want to **inject** it (*inject the flu vaccine*), although to inject can also mean to add something new or different (*inject some humor into an otherwise dreary speech*). If it's a person, you should **introduce** him or her, which suggests placing the individual in the midst of a group so as to become part of it. You can also introduce things (*introduce a new subject into the curriculum*), but if the thing you're introducing is extraneous or lacks authorization, you may have to **interpolate** it (*interpolate editorial comments*). If you have remarks, statements, or questions to introduce in an abrupt or forced manner, you'll have to **interject** them (*in the midst of his speech, she interjected what she felt were important details*). If you interject too often, however, you risk offending the speaker and may have to ask someone to **mediate**, which means to settle a dispute or bring about a compromise by taking a stand midway between extremes.

---

insert *noun an insert in the magazine* insertion, inset, supplement, circular, advertisement; *inf.* ad.

inside *noun the inside of the book* interior, inner part/side/surface; contents.

inside *adverb* **1** *go/stand inside* indoors; in/into the interior, in/into the house, in/into the building, within. **2** *inside she felt frightened* emotionally, in her thoughts/feelings, intuitively, instinctively.

inside *adjective* **1** *the inside part* interior, inner, internal, inward, on/in the inside, inmost, innermost, intramural. **2** *have inside information* confidential, classified, restricted, reserved, privileged, private, internal, privy, secret, exclusive, esoteric.

insides *plural noun the warm milk soothed his insides* stomach, abdomen, gut; internal organs, intestines, viscera, entrails, bowels, bodily/vital organs; *inf.* belly, tummy, guts, bread basket.

insidious *adjective* stealthy, subtle, surreptitious, sneaky, sneaking, cunning, crafty, designing, intriguing, Machiavellian, artful, guileful, sly, wily, tricky, slick, deceitful, deceptive, underhand, underhanded, double-dealing, duplicitous, dishonest, insincere, disingenuous, treacherous, perfidious; *inf.* crooked.
Antonyms: STRAIGHTFORWARD; ARTLESS; HONEST.

insight *noun* **1** *a person of insight* intuition, perception, awareness, discernment, understanding, penetration, acumen, perspicacity, perspicaciousness, discrimination, judgment, shrewdness, sharpness, acuteness, flair, vision. **2** *give an insight into country life* awareness, un-

derstanding, realization, revelation, observance; *inf.* eye-opener.

insignia *noun/plural noun* **1** *insignia of office* badge, decoration, medallion, ribbon, crest, emblem, symbol, sign, mark, seal, signet. **2** *politeness is meant to be the insignia of the firm* mark of distinction, trademark, label, trait, characteristic.

insignificant *adjective* **1** *insignificant details* unimportant, of minor/no importance, of little importance/import, trivial, trifling, negligible, inconsequential, of no consequence/account, of no moment/matter, inconsiderable, not worth mentioning, nugatory, meager, paltry, scanty, petty, insubstantial, unsubstantial, flimsy, irrelevant, immaterial; *inf.* dinky. **2** *insignificant members of the government* unimportant, uninfluential, powerless, small-fry.

insincere *adjective* lacking sincerity, not candid, not frank, disingenuous, dissembling, dissimulating, pretended, devious, hypocritical, deceitful, deceptive, duplicitous, dishonest, underhand, double-dealing, false, faithless, disloyal, treacherous, two-faced, lying, untruthful, mendacious, evasive, shifty, slippery.

insinuate *verb* **1** *he insinuated that she was dishonest* imply, hint, whisper, suggest, indicate, convey the impression, intimate, mention. **2** *insinuate doubts into their minds* infiltrate, implant, instill, introduce, inculcate, infuse, inject. **insinuate oneself into** *insinuate herself into his affections* worm oneself into, work one's way into, ingratiate oneself with, curry favor with; *inf.* get in with.

insinuation *noun* **1** *resent the insinuation that he was dishonest* implication, suggestion, hint, innuendo, intimation, mention, reference, allusion, aspersion, slur. **2** *the insinuation of doubts* infiltration, implanting, instilling, instillation, introduction. *See* INSINUATE 2. **3** *their insinuation into her affections* worming, ingratiation. *See* INSINUATE ONESELF INTO (INSINUATE).

insipid *adjective* **1** *an insipid person* lacking personality, colorless, anemic, drab, inanimate, spiritless, jejune, vapid, dull, uninteresting, boring, unentertaining. **2** *insipid prose* unimaginative, characterless, flat, bland, vapid, uninteresting, dull, prosaic, boring, monotonous, tedious, wearisome, dry, dry as dust, humdrum, run-of-the-mill, trite, banal, hackneyed, stale. **3** *insipid soup* tasteless, flavorless, savorless, bland, thin, watery, watered-down, unappetizing, unpalatable.
Antonyms: INTERESTING; IMAGINATIVE; TASTY.

insist *verb* **1** *if they refuse you must insist* stand firm, be firm, stand one's ground, make a stand, be resolute, be determined, be emphatic, not take no for an answer, brook no refusal. **2** *insist that they go* demand, require, command, importune, entreat, urge, exhort. **3** *she insists that she is innocent* maintain, assert, declare, hold, contend, pronounce, proclaim, aver, propound, avow, vow, swear, be emphatic, emphasize, stress, repeat, reiterate.

insistence noun **1** *her insistence that they go* requirement, command, importuning, entreaty, urging, exhortation; demands. **2** *her insistence that she is innocent* maintenance, assertion, declaration, contention, avowal, emphasis, stress. See INSIST 3. **3** *the insistence of the demands* persistence, doggedness, incessantness, urgency, coercion, exigency. See INSISTENT 2. **4** *the insistence of the crows cawing* constancy, incessantness, iteration, repetition, recurrence.

insistent adjective **1** *she is insistent that you go* emphatic, determined, resolute, tenacious, importunate, persistent, unyielding, obstinate, dogged, unrelenting, inexorable. **2** *insistent demands for payment* persistent, determined, dogged, incessant, urgent, pressing, compelling, high-pressure, pressurizing, coercive, demanding, exigent. **3** *the insistent caw of the crow* constant, incessant, iterative, repeated, repetitive, recurrent.

insolence noun impertinence, impudence, cheek, cheekiness, ill-manneredness, rudeness, disrespect, incivility, insubordination, contempt, abuse, offensiveness, contumely, audacity, nerve, boldness, brazenness, brashness, pertness, forwardness, effrontery; insults; *inf.* gall, lip, chutzpah.

insolent adjective impertinent, impudent, cheeky, rude, ill-mannered, disrespectful, insubordinate, contemptuous, insulting, abusive, offensive, audacious, bold, brazen, brash, pert, forward; *inf.* fresh.
Antonyms: POLITE; respectful; MODEST.

insoluble adjective **1** *an insoluble substance* not soluble, indissoluble, indissolvable, undissolvable. **2** *insoluble problems/puzzles/situations* insolvable, unsolvable, baffling, unfathomable, indecipherable, complicated, perplexing, intricate, involved, impenetrable, inscrutable, enigmatic, obscure, mystifying, inexplicable, incomprehensible, mysterious.

insolvency noun bankruptcy, indebtedness, liquidation, financial ruin, default, pennilessness, impoverishedness, penury, impecuniousness, beggary.

insolvent adjective bankrupt, indebted, in debt, liquidated, ruined, defaulting, in the hands of the receivers, penniless, impoverished, penurious, impecunious; *inf.* gone bust, gone to the wall, on the rocks, in the red, broke, hard up, strapped for cash.

insomnia noun sleeplessness, wakefulness, insomnolence, restlessness.

insouciant adjective carefree, nonchalant, untroubled, unworried, unconcerned, heedless, casual, easygoing, free and easy, happy-go-lucky, indifferent, frivolous, capricious.

inspect verb examine, check, go over, look over, survey, scrutinize, audit, study, pore over, view,

scan, observe, investigate, assess, appraise; *inf.* give the once-over.

inspection noun examination, check, checkup, survey, scrutiny, view, scan, observation, investigation, probe, assessment, appraisal; *inf.* once-over, going-over, look-see.

inspector noun examiner, checker, scrutinizer, scrutineer, auditor, surveyor, scanner, observer, investigator, overseer, supervisor, assessor, appraiser, critic.

inspiration noun **1** *acts as an inspiration to his work* stimulus, stimulation, motivation, encouragement, influence, muse, goad, spur, incitement, arousal, rousing, stirring. **2** *his pictures lack inspiration* creativity, originality, inventiveness, genius, insight, vision. **3** *have a sudden inspiration* bright idea, brilliant/timely thought, revelation; illumination, enlightenment.

inspire verb **1** *inspire the artist | inspire the artist's work* stimulate, motivate, encourage, influence, inspirit, animate, fire the imagination of. **2** *ambition inspired him to work* rouse, stir, spur, goad, energize, galvanize. **3** *her beauty inspired love in many men* arouse, excite, quicken, inflame, touch off, spark off, ignite, kindle, give rise to, produce, bring about, prompt, instigate.
Antonyms: DISCOURAGE; DISPIRIT; EXTINGUISH.

inspired adjective **1** *an inspired operatic performance* brilliant, outstanding, supreme, superlative, dazzling, exciting, thrilling, enthralling, wonderful, marvelous, memorable; *inf.* out of this world. **2** *an inspired guess* intuitive, instinctive.

instability noun **1** *instability of human relationships* impermanence, unendurability, temporariness, transience, inconstancy. **2** *the instability of his physical condition* unsteadiness, uncertainty, precariousness, fluidity, fluctuation. **3** *the instability of the furniture* unsteadiness, unsoundness, shakiness, ricketiness, wobbliness, frailty, flimsiness, unsubstantiality. **4** *leading lives of instability* insecurity, precariousness, unpredictability, unreliability, uncertainty; *inf.* chanciness. **5** *upset by her instability* changeableness, variability, capriciousness, volatility, flightiness, vacillation, wavering, fitfulness, oscillation.

install verb **1** *install microwave ovens* put in, insert, put in place, position, place, emplace, fix, locate, situate, station, lodge. **2** *install her as president* induct, instate, institute, inaugurate, invest, ordain, introduce, initiate, establish. **3** *install themselves in the best seats* ensconce, position, settle.
Antonyms: REMOVE; EXTRACT.

installation noun **1** *the installation of microwave ovens* putting in, insertion, positioning, placing, fixing, situating. See INSTALL 1. **2** *the installation of the president* induction, instatement, inauguration, investiture, ordination, initiation. **3** *factory installations* machinery, plant, equipment. **4** *military installations* base, camp, station, post, establishment.

installment *noun* **1** *pay for appliances by installment* part/partial payment. **2** *issue the novel in installments* part, portion, section, segment, chapter, division, episode.

instance *noun* **1** *an instance of his insolence* case, case in point, example, illustration, exemplification, occasion, occurrence. **2** *in the first instance* stage, step. **3** *they went away at his instance* behest, instigation, urging, demand, insistence, request, prompting, solicitation, entreaty, importuning, pressure.

instance *verb the teacher instanced several examples* give, cite, mention, name, specify, quote, adduce.

instant *noun* **1** *gone in an instant* moment, minute, second, split second, trice, twinkling, twinkling of an eye, flash; *inf.* jiffy, jif, sec, two shakes of a lamb's tail. **2** *at this instant I am not sure* moment, time, present time, minute, very minute, particular/specific time, moment in time, juncture, point.

instant *adjective* **1** *instant recognition* instantaneous, immediate, on-the-spot, prompt, rapid, sudden, abrupt. **2** *instant soup/coffee* pre-prepared, ready-prepared, ready-mixed, pre-cooked, fast, easy/quick to prepare, easy/quick to make. **3** *at his instant request* urgent, pressing, earnest, importunate, exigent, imperative.

instantaneous *adjective death was instantaneous* instant, immediate, on the spot, direct, prompt, expeditious, rapid, sudden, abrupt.

instantaneously *adverb* right away, straight away, immediately, at once, now, instantly, forthwith, then and there, quick as lightning, in a trice, in less than no time, in a fraction of a second, in the twinkling of an eye, before you can say Jack Robinson; *inf.* in a jiffy.

instate *verb* install, induct, inaugurate, invest, ordain, initiate.

instead *adverb I'll have chocolate ice cream instead* as an alternative/substitute/replacement, for preference. **instead of** *I'll have chocolate instead of strawberry ice cream* as an alternative to, as a substitute/replacement for, in place/lieu of, in preference to, rather than.

instigate *verb* **1** *instigate legal proceedings | instigate a rebellion* bring about, start, initiate, actuate, generate, incite, provoke, inspire, foment, kindle, stir up, whip up. **2** *instigate them to rebel* incite, encourage, egg on, urge, prompt, goad, prod, induce, impel, constrain, press, persuade, prevail upon, sway, entice.
Antonyms: HALT; DISCOURAGE.

instigation *noun the proceedings/rebellions were at his instigation* initiation, actuation, incitement, encouragement, urging, inducement, persuasion, enticement. *See* INSTIGATE.

instigator *noun* prime mover, inciter, motivator, agitator, fomenter, troublemaker, agent provocateur, ringleader, leader.

instill *verb* **1** *instill water into the substance* add

gradually, introduce, infuse, inject. **2** *instill common sense into the children* introduce, insinuate, infuse, inculcate, implant, teach, drill, arouse. **3** *instill the children with common sense* infuse, imbue, permeate, inculcate.

instinct *noun* **1** *birds migrate by instinct | she found the way here by instinct* inborn/inherent tendency, natural feeling, innate inclination, intuition, sixth sense, inner prompting. **2** *he has an instinct for poetry* talent, gift, ability, capacity, faculty, aptitude, knack, bent, trait, characteristic.

instinctive *adjective* **1** *birds' instinctive behavior pattern* inborn, inherent, innate, inbred, natural, intuitive, intuitional, involuntary, untaught, unlearned. **2** *his instinctive reaction was to hide* automatic, reflex, mechanical, spontaneous, involuntary, impulsive, intuitive, unthinking, unpremeditated.

institute *verb* **1** *institute legal proceedings* begin, start, commence, set in motion, put into operation, initiate. **2** *institute new organizations | institute reforms* found, establish, start, launch, bring into being, bring about, constitute, set up, organize, develop, create, originate, pioneer. **3** *institute the new chaplain* install, instate, induct, invest, ordain, introduce, initiate, appoint.
Antonyms: HALT; END.

institute *noun* **1** *start an educational institute* institution, organization, foundation, society, association, league, guild, consortium. **2** *build an institute for research* foundation, institution, academy, school, college, conservatory, seminary, seat of learning. **3** *legal/local institutes* law, rule, regulation, decree, tenet, principle, precedent, institution, custom, tradition, convention, practice.

institution *noun* **1** *the institution of legal proceedings* starting, commencement, initiation. **2** *the institution of new organizations* foundation, establishment, setting up, creation, origination, pioneering. *See* INSTITUTE *verb* 2. **3** *the institution of the new president* installation, instatement, induction, investiture. *See* INSTITUTE *verb* 3. **4** *start educational institutions* institute, organization, society, association. *See* INSTITUTE *noun* 1. **5** *a research institution* institute, foundation, academy, college. *See* INSTITUTE *noun* 2. **6** *in an institution for life* hospital, mental hospital, asylum, prison, reformatory. **7** *local institutions* institute, law, rule, custom, tradition, convention, practice. *See* INSTITUTE *noun* 3. **8** *the traffic cop had become an institution in the neighborhood* regular/prominent feature, familiar sight, fixture, habitué; *inf.* part of the furniture.

institutional *adjective* **1** *institutional methods* organized, established, bureaucratic, accepted, orthodox, conventional, customary, formal, systematic, methodical, orderly; *inf.* establishment. **2** *institutional food* uniform, same, unvarying, unvaried, unchanging, regimented, monotonous, bland, dull, insipid; *inf.* cafeteria. **3** *an institutional atmosphere in the building* cold, cheerless, clinical, dreary, drab, unwelcoming, uninviting, impersonal, formal, forbidding.

instruct *verb* **1** *instruct the messenger to take a reply* tell, direct, order, command, bid, charge, enjoin, demand, require. **2** *instruct the students in science* teach, educate, tutor, coach, train, school, drill, ground, prime, prepare, guide, inform, enlighten, edify, discipline. **3** *instruct them that I shall be late* inform, tell, notify, acquaint, make known to, advise, apprise. **4** *instruct one's lawyer* give the facts to, give information to, brief.

instruction *noun* **1** *get good instruction in the arts* teaching, education, tutoring, tutelage, coaching, training, schooling, drilling, grounding, priming, preparation, guidance, information, enlightenment, edification, discipline; lessons, classes, lectures. **2** *his instruction was to leave at once* direction, directive, briefing, order, command, charge, injunction, requirement, ruling, mandate.

instructions *plural noun* **1** *his instructions are to leave now* directions, orders, commands, requirements. *See* INSTRUCTION 2. **2** *read the instructions to find out* directions; key, book of rules, manual, owner's manual, guide.

instructive *adjective* instructional, informative, informational, educational, educative, enlightening, illuminating, useful, helpful, edifying, cultural, uplifting, academic, didactic, doctrinal.

instructor *noun* teacher, schoolteacher, schoolmaster, schoolmistress, educator, lecturer, professor, pedagogue, tutor, coach, trainer, adviser, counselor, guide, mentor, demonstrator.

instrument *noun* **1** *surgical instruments* implement, tool, appliance, apparatus, mechanism, utensil, gadget, contrivance, device, aid; *inf.* contraption. *See also table at* TOOL. **2** *musicians tuning their instruments* musical instrument; piano, violin, viola, cello, double bass, horn, trombone, tuba, piccolo, flute, oboe, clarinet, saxophone, drum. **3** *the ship's instruments* measuring device, gauge, meter. **4** *her information was the instrument that led to his arrest* | *the instrument of his downfall* agency, agent, prime mover, catalyst, cause, factor, channel, medium, force, mechanism, instrumentality, vehicle, organ; means. **5** *he was just the ringleader's instrument* pawn, puppet, tool, dupe, minion, flunky; *inf.* stooge.

instrumental *adjective* *she was instrumental in catching the thief* helpful, of help/assistance, useful, of use/service, contributory, active, involved, influential, significant, important.

insubordinate *adjective* rebellious, mutinous, insurgent, seditious, insurrectional, riotous, disobedient, noncompliant, defiant, refractory, recalcitrant, contumacious, undisciplined, ungovernable, uncontrollable, unmanageable, unruly, disorderly.

insubordination *noun* rebelliousness, rebellion, mutinousness, mutiny, insurgence, sedition, insurrection, riotousness, rioting, defiance, noncompliance, disobedience, refractoriness, recalcitrance, contumacy, ungovernability, unruliness.

insubstantial *adjective* **1** *insubstantial buildings/furniture* flimsy, fragile, frail, weak, feeble, jerry-built. **2** *an insubstantial argument* weak, feeble, thin, slight, tenuous, insignificant, inconsequential. **3** *insubstantial shapes* unsubstantial, unreal, illusory, illusive, delusive, hallucinatory, phantom, phantasmal, spectral, ghostlike, intangible, impalpable, incorporeal, visionary, imaginary, imagined, fanciful, chimerical, airy, vaporous.

insufferable *adjective* intolerable, unbearable, unendurable, insupportable, not to be borne, past bearing, too much to bear, impossible, too much, more than one can stand, more than flesh and blood can stand, enough to try the patience of Job, enough to test the patience of a saint, unspeakable, dreadful, excruciating, grim, outrageous.

insufficient *adjective* inadequate, deficient, in short supply, scarce, meager, scant, scanty, too small/little/few, not enough, lacking, wanting, at a premium.

insular *adjective* **1** *country people leading insular lives* isolated, detached, separate, segregated, solitary, insulated, self-sufficient. **2** *have insular ideas* narrow, narrow-minded, illiberal, prejudiced, biased, bigoted, provincial, parochial, limited, restricted.
Antonyms: LIBERAL; OPEN-MINDED; COSMOPOLITAN.

insulate *verb* **1** *insulate pipes/wires/walls* make nonconducting; heatproof, soundproof, make shockproof, cover, wrap, enwrap, encase, envelop, pad, cushion, seal. **2** *long-term hospital patients are insulated from the world* segregate, separate, isolate, detach, cut off, keep/set apart, sequester, exclude, protect, shield.

insult *verb* *insult him by calling him lazy* | *insult his honor* offend, give/cause offense to, affront, slight, hurt the feelings of, hurt, abuse, injure, wound, mortify, humiliate, disparage, discredit, depreciate, impugn, slur, revile.
Antonyms: COMPLIMENT; FLATTER.

insult *noun* *upset by their insults about his character* affront, slight, gibe, snub, barb, slur; abuse, disparagement, depreciation, impugnment, revilement, insolence, rudeness, contumely; aspersions; *inf.* dig.

insulting *adjective* *insulting behavior* offensive, affronting, slighting, abusive, injurious, wounding, mortifying, humiliating, disparaging, discrediting, depreciating, deprecatory, impugning, reviling, scurrilous, snubbing, insolent, rude, contumacious.

insuperable *adjective insuperable difficulties* insurmountable, impassable, overwhelming, invincible, unconquerable, unassailable.

insupportable *adjective* **1** *insupportable pain* insufferable, intolerable, unbearable, unendurable, more than flesh and blood can stand. *See* INSUFFERABLE. **2** *insupportable claims* unjustifiable, indefensible, untenable, unmaintainable, implausible, specious.

insurance *noun* **1** *take out travel insurance* financial protection, indemnity, indemnification, surety, security, cover, coverage, guarantee, warranty, warrant, provision. **2** *he took an umbrella as (an) insurance against the rain* safeguard, precaution, protection, provision, preventive measure.

insure *verb* **1** *insure her life/jewels* protect against death/loss/damage, indemnify, cover, underwrite, guarantee, warrant. **2** *insured against fire/theft* take out insurance, protect, guarantee.

insurgent *noun insurgents rising against the dictator* rebel, revolutionary, revolutionist, revolter, mutineer, rioter, insurrectionist, insurrectionary, seditionist, malcontent.

insurgent *adjective insurgent forces overthrowing the government* rebellious, revolutionary, revolting, mutinous, rioting, lawless, insurrectionist, insurrectionary, seditious, factious, subversive, insubordinate, disobedient.

insurmountable *adjective* insuperable, invincible, unconquerable, impassable, overwhelming, unassailable, hopeless, impossible.

insurrection *noun* rebellion, revolt, revolution, uprising, rising, riot, mutiny, sedition, coup, coup d'état, putsch; insurgency, insurgence.

intact *adjective* whole, complete, entire, perfect, all in one piece, sound, unbroken, unsevered, undamaged, unscathed, uninjured, unharmed, unmutilated, inviolate, unviolated, undefiled, unblemished, unsullied, faultless, flawless. *Antonyms:* BROKEN; damaged.

intangible *adjective* **1** *intangible things* impalpable, untouchable, not perceptible by touch, incorporeal, phantom, spectral, ghostly. **2** *an intangible air of sadness* indefinable, indescribable, vague, subtle, unclear, obscure, mysterious.

integral *adjective* **1** *an integral part of the organization* essential, necessary, indispensable, requisite, basic, fundamental, inherent, intrinsic, innate. **2** *integral parts of the machine* constituent, component, integrant. **3** *an integral design/concept* entire, complete, whole, total, full, intact, unified, integrated, undivided.

integrate *verb* **1** *integrate the various parts* unite, join, combine, amalgamate, consolidate, blend, incorporate, coalesce, fuse, merge, intermix, mingle, commingle, assimilate, homogenize, harmonize, mesh, concatenate. **2** *integrate school districts* desegregate, open up.

integrated *adjective* **1** *integrated parts* united, joined, amalgamated, consolidated, assimilated, concatenated. *See* INTEGRATE 1. **2** *integrated schools* desegregated, nonsegregated, unsegregated, racially mixed, racially balanced.

integration *noun the integration of the parts into a whole* unification, amalgamation, consolidation, incorporation, coalescing, fusing, assimilation, homogenizing, homogenization, concatenation.

integrity *noun* **1** *doubt the integrity of the council* uprightness, honesty, rectitude, righteousness, virtue, probity, morality, honor, goodness, decency, truthfulness, fairness, sincerity, candor; principles, ethics. **2** *challenge the integrity of the nation* unity, unification, wholeness, entirety, completeness, totality, cohesion. *Antonyms:* DISHONESTY; fragmentation.

intellect *noun* **1** *a person of little intellect* intelligence, reason, understanding, comprehension, mind, brain, thought, sense, judgment. **2** *leave the decisions to the intellects* intellectual, genius, thinker, mastermind; *inf.* brain, mind, egghead, Einstein.

intellectual *adjective* **1** *an intellectual exercise* mental, cerebral, academic. **2** *an intellectual family* intelligent, academic, well-educated, well-read, erudite, learned, bookish, highbrow, scholarly, studious. **3** *using only intellectual considerations* mental, cerebral, rational, logical, clinical, unemotional, nonemotional. *Antonyms:* PHYSICAL; ILLITERATE; STUPID.

intellectual *noun* **1** *one of the great intellectuals of our time* intellect, genius, thinker, mastermind. *See* INTELLECT 2. **2** *sought the company of other intellectuals* academic, academician, man/woman of letters, bluestocking, pundit, highbrow, bookworm, pedant; *inf.* egghead, walking encyclopedia.

intelligence *noun* **1** *people of great intelligence* intellect, mind, brain, brainpower, mental capacity/aptitude, reason, understanding, comprehension, acumen, wit, cleverness, brightness, brilliance, sharpness, quickness of mind, alertness, discernment, perception, perspicacity, penetration, sense, sagacity; brains; *inf.* gray matter. **2** *the intelligence came too late to save him* information, news, notification, notice, account, knowledge, advice, rumor; facts, data, reports, tidings; *inf.* low-down, poop, dope. **3** *he's in military intelligence* information collection, enemy investigation, surveillance, observation, spying.

intelligent *adjective* **1** *intelligent children* clever, bright, brilliant, sharp, quick, quick-witted, smart, apt, discerning, thinking, perceptive, perspicacious, penetrating, sensible, sagacious, well-informed, educated, enlightened, knowledgeable; *inf.* brainy. **2** *is there intelligent*

life on the planet? rational, reasoning, higher-order.
Antonyms: STUPID; SLOW.

intelligentsia *plural noun* intellectuals, academics, literati, cognoscenti, illuminati, highbrows, pedants; the enlightened. *See* INTELLECTUAL *noun* 2.

intelligible *adjective a scarcely intelligible message* understandable, comprehensible, clear, lucid, plain, explicit, unambiguous, legible, decipherable.
Antonyms: UNINTELLIGIBLE; INCOHERENT; INCOMPREHENSIBLE.

intemperate *adjective* 1 *an intemperate indulgence of the appetites* immoderate, self-indulgent, excessive, inordinate, extreme, extravagant, unreasonable, outrageous. 2 *intemperate drinkers* immoderate, excessive, drunken, drunk, intoxicated, inebriated, alcoholic. 3 *intemperate rages* uncontrolled, unrestrained, uncurbed, unbridled, ungoverned, tempestuous, violent. 4 *lead an intemperate life* immoderate, dissolute, dissipated, debauched, profligate, prodigal, loose, wild, wanton, licentious, libertine.

intend *verb* 1 *he intends to go* mean, plan, have in mind/view, propose, aim, resolve, be resolved, be determined, expect, purpose; contemplate, think of. 2 *they intended the bullet for the leader* mean, aim, destine, purpose, plan, scheme, devise.

---

intend
aim, design, mean, plan, propose, purpose

If you **intend** to do something, you may or may not be serious about getting it done (*I intend to clean out the garage some day*) but at least you have a goal in mind. Although **mean** can also imply either a firm resolve (*I mean to go, with or without her permission*) or a vague intention (*I've been meaning to write her for weeks*), it is a less formal word that usually connotes a certain lack of determination or a weak resolve. **Plan**, like *mean* and *intend*, may imply a vague goal (*I plan to tour China some day*), but it is often used to suggest that you're taking active steps (*I plan to leave as soon as I finish packing*). **Aim** indicates that you have an actual goal or purpose in mind and that you're putting some effort behind it (*I aim to be the first woman president*), without the hint of failure conveyed by *mean*. If you **propose** to do something, you declare your intention ahead of time (*I propose that we set up a meeting next week*), and if you **purpose** to do it, you are even more determined to achieve your goal (*I purpose to write a three-volume history of baseball in America*). **Design** suggests forethought in devising a plan (*design a strategy that will keep everyone happy*).

---

intense *adjective* 1 *intense heat/cold* acute, fierce, severe, extreme, harsh, strong, powerful, potent, vigorous, great, profound, deep, concen-

trated, consuming. 2 *an intense desire to learn* earnest, eager, ardent, keen, enthusiastic, zealous, excited, impassioned, passionate, fervent, fervid, burning, consuming, vehement, fanatical. 3 *an intense person* nervous, nervy, tense, fraught, overwrought, highly strung, emotional.
Antonyms: MILD; CALM.

intensify *verb* 1 *her indifference intensified his love* heighten, deepen, strengthen, increase, reinforce, magnify, enhance, fan, whet. 2 *intensify the quarrel* aggravate, exacerbate, worsen, inflame; *inf.* add fuel to the flames. 3 *intensify their efforts to find the child* increase, extend, augment, boost, escalate, step up.
Antonyms: DECREASE; DIMINISH; RELAX.

intensity *noun* 1 *the intensity of the heat* acuteness, fierceness, severity, extremeness, extremity, harshness, strength, power, powerfulness, potency, vigor, greatness, concentration. *See* INTENSE 1. 2 *the intensity of their desire* ardor, keenness, enthusiasm, zeal, excitement, passion, fervor, fervency, vehemence, fanaticism. 3 *her intensity frightens people* nervousness, tenseness, fraughtness, emotionalism, emotion.

intensive *adjective an intensive search* | *intensive revision* in-depth, concentrated, exhaustive, all-out, thorough, thoroughgoing, total, all-absorbing.

intent *adjective* 1 *an intent expression* concentrated, concentrating, fixed, steady, steadfast, absorbed, attentive, engrossed, occupied, preoccupied, rapt, enrapt, wrapped up, focused, observant, watchful, alert, earnest, committed, intense. 2 *intent on getting their own way* set on, bent on, committed to, firm about; determined, resolved to; *inf.* hell-bent on.

intent *noun it was their intent to win* intention, purpose, aim, objective, goal, end, plan. *See* INTENTION 1. **to/for all intents and purposes** virtually, in practical terms, practically, as good as.

intention *noun* 1 *it is his intention to be leader* aim, purpose, intent, goal, objective, end, end in view, target, aspiration, ambition, wish, plan, design, resolve, resolution, determination. 2 *he assaulted the old man without intention* premeditation, preconception, design, plan, calculation.

intentional *adjective an intentional crime* intended, deliberate, meant, done on purpose, willful, purposeful, purposed, planned, calculated, designed, premeditated, preconceived, predetermined, prearranged, preconcerted, considered, weighed up, studied.
Antonyms: ACCIDENTAL; INADVERTENT.

intentionally *adverb she intentionally arrived early* deliberately, on purpose, purposely, by design, willfully.

inter *verb* bury, consign to the grave, entomb, lay to rest, inhume, inearth, sepulcher.

intercede *verb intercede in the strike* | *intercede for the child with her parents* mediate, negotiate, arbitrate, intervene, interpose, step in, plead for, petition for.

intercept verb **1** *intercept the ball* stop, cut off, deflect, head off, seize, expropriate, commandeer, catch. **2** *intercept the train* check, arrest, block, obstruct, impede, cut off, deflect, head off.

intercession noun mediation, negotiation, arbitration, mediatorship, intervention, interposition, pleading, petition, entreaty, supplication; good offices.

interchange verb **1** *interchange ideas* exchange, trade, trade off, swap, barter, bandy, reciprocate. **2** *interchange the two chairs* cause to change places, switch (around), alternate, transpose.

interchange noun **1** *the interchange of ideas* exchange, trading, trade, trade-off, swap, barter, bandying, give and take, reciprocation, reciprocity, interplay, crossfire. **2** *the interchange of the two chairs* changing places, alternation, transposition, switch, switching. **3** *a car crash at the interchange* junction, intersection, crossroads.

interchangeable adjective exchangeable, transposable, equivalent, corresponding, correlative, reciprocal, comparable.

intercourse noun **1** *business intercourse* dealings; trade, traffic, commerce, communication, intercommunication, association, connection, contact, correspondence, communion, congress. **2** *sexual intercourse* sex, sexual relations, coitus, coition, copulation, carnal knowledge, intimacy, lovemaking.

interdict noun *under an interdict preventing him from visiting* prohibition, ban, injunction, restraining order, embargo, veto, proscription, preclusion, exclusion order.

interdict verb *interdict him from going* prohibit, forbid, ban, embargo, veto, proscribe, disallow, preclude, exclude, prevent.

interest noun **1** *look with interest at the new product* attentiveness, attention, undivided attention, absorption, engrossment, heed, regard, notice, scrutiny, curiosity, inquisitiveness. **2** *an object of interest* curiosity, attraction, appeal, fascination, charm, allure. **3** *a matter of interest to all of us* concern, importance, import, consequence, moment, significance, note, relevance, seriousness, weight, gravity, priority, urgency. **4** *his interests include reading and music* leisure activity, pastime, hobby, diversion, amusement, pursuit, relaxation; *inf.* thing, scene. **5** *have an interest in the business* share, stake, portion, claim, investment, involvement, participation; stock, equity. **6** *you must declare your interest in the case* involvement, partiality, partisanship, preference, prejudice, one-sidedness, favoritism, bias, discrimination. **7** *his commercial interests are in trouble* concern, business, matter, care; affairs. **8** *earn interest on investments* dividend, profit, return, percentage, gain. **9** *it is in their interests to go*

benefit, advantage, good, profit, gain. **in the interests of** for the sake/benefit of, to the advantage of, in the furtherance of.

Antonyms: BOREDOM; TEDIUM; IMPARTIALITY.

interest verb **1** *the book interests her* attract/hold/engage the attention of, attract, absorb, engross, fascinate, rivet, grip, captivate, amuse, intrigue, arouse curiosity in. **2** *the outcome of the war interests us all* affect, have an effect/bearing on, concern, involve. **3** *can I interest you in this computer?* arouse one's interest, persuade to buy, sell.

interested adjective **1** *the interested children* attentive, intent, absorbed, engrossed, curious, fascinated, riveted, gripped, captivated, intrigued. **2** *interested parties waiting in the lawyer's office* concerned, involved, implicated. **3** *no interested person can judge the contest* involved, partial, partisan, one-sided, biased, prejudiced, discriminative, discriminating.

Antonyms: APATHETIC; INDIFFERENT; DISINTERESTED.

interesting adjective absorbing, engrossing, fascinating, riveting, gripping, compelling, compulsive, spellbinding, captivating, appealing, engaging, amusing, entertaining, stimulating, thought-provoking, diverting, exciting, intriguing.

interfere verb **interfere in** *interfere in other people's business* meddle with, butt into, pry into, tamper with, intrude into, intervene in, get involved in, intercede in; *inf.* poke one's nose in, horn in on. **interfere with** *emotional problems interfering with his work* hinder, inhibit, impede, obstruct, get in the way of, check, block, hamper, handicap, cramp, trammel, frustrate, thwart, balk.

interference noun **1** *his work suffered from the interference of his emotional problems* hindrance, impediment, obstruction, handicap. **2** *resent her interference in their affairs* meddling, meddlesomeness, prying, intrusion, unwelcome intervention, intercession.

interim adjective *an interim appointment | interim measures* temporary, provisional, pro tem, stopgap, caretaker, acting, intervening, makeshift, improvised.

interim noun *in the interim we shall choose a new leader* meantime, meanwhile, intervening time, interval, interregnum.

interior adjective **1** *the interior part of the building* inner, inside, on the inside, internal, inward. **2** *the interior parts of the country* inland, non-coastal, central, up-country, remote. **3** *the country's interior affairs* home, domestic, civil, local. **4** *his interior motivation* instinctive, intuitive, impulsive, involuntary, spontaneous; *inf.* gut. **5** *his interior self* inner, spiritual, mental, psychological, emotional, private, personal, intimate, secret, hidden.

interior noun **1** *the interior of the building* inside,

inner part/side/surface, center, middle, nucleus, core, heart. **2** *the interior of the country* center, heartland, hinterland.
Antonyms: EXTERIOR; OUTSIDE.

interject *verb interject lighthearted remarks into a serious conversation* throw in, insert, introduce, interpolate, interpose, insinuate, add, mingle, intersperse.

interjection *noun* **1** *the interjection of jokes into the script* insertion, introduction, interpolation, interposition, insinuation, intermixing, intermingling, interspersion. **2** *he gave an interjection of pain* cry, exclamation, ejaculation, utterance.

interloper *noun* unwanted visitor/guest, trespasser, invader, intruder, encroacher, gatecrasher.

interlude *noun* interval, intermission, break, recess, pause, respite, rest, breathing space, halt, stop, stoppage, hiatus, delay, wait.

intermediary *noun* mediator, go-between, broker, agent, middleman, negotiator, arbitrator.

intermediate *adjective* in-between, halfway, in the middle, middle, mid, midway, medial, median, intermediary, intervening, interposed, transitional.

interment *noun* burial, burying, entombment, inhumation, sepulture, funeral; funeral rites, exequies.

interminable *adjective* **1** *an interminable road* (seemingly) endless, never-ending, without end, everlasting, ceaseless, incessant. **2** *an interminable talk* (seemingly) endless, never-ending, uninterrupted, monotonous, tedious, wearisome, boring, long-winded, wordy, loquacious, prolix, verbose, rambling.

intermingle *verb* mingle, mix, commingle, intermix, commix, blend, fuse, amalgamate, merge, combine, compound, interweave.

intermission *noun* interval, interlude, interim, entr'acte, break, recess, rest, pause, respite, lull, stop, stoppage, halt, cessation, suspension; *inf.* letup, breather, time out.

intermittent *adjective* fitful, spasmodic, irregular, sporadic, occasional, periodic, cyclic, recurrent, recurring, broken, discontinuous, on again and off again, on and off.
Antonyms: CONTINUOUS; STEADY.

intern *verb* confine, hold in custody, imprison, impound, detain.

internal *adjective* **1** *internal wall* interior, inside, inner, inward. **2** *the country's/firm's internal affairs* home, domestic, civil, interior, in-house, in-company. **3** *his internal opinion* mental, psychological, emotional, subjective, private, intimate.

international *adjective* cosmopolitan, global, universal, worldwide, intercontinental.

interpolate *verb* insert, interject, intercalate, interpose, introduce, insinuate, add, inject, put in, work in.

interpolation *noun* insert, insertion, interjection, intercalation, introduction, addition, injection.

interpose *verb* **1** *interpose a barrier between the speaker and the audience* place between, put between. **2** *interpose a few jokes in the script* insert, interject, introduce, insinuate, add. **3** *interpose in the quarrel* intervene, intercede, step in, mediate, arbitrate, interfere, intrude, obtrude, butt in, meddle; *inf.* barge in, horn in, muscle in.

interpret *verb* **1** *interpret the difficult text* explain, elucidate, expound, explicate, clarify, make clear, illuminate, shed light on, gloss, simplify, spell out. **2** *interpreted her silence as consent | it was how I interpreted his reluctance* understand, understand by, construe, take, take to mean, read. **3** *interpret the hieroglyphics* decode, decipher, crack, solve, untangle, unravel. **4** *interpret for the foreign ambassador* translate, transcribe, transliterate, paraphrase. **5** *dancers interpreting the ballet* portray, depict, present, perform, execute, enact.

interpretation *noun* **1** *the interpretation of the difficult text* explanation, elucidation, expounding, explication, clarification, exegesis. *See* INTERPRET 1. **2** *his interpretation of her silence as consent* understanding, construal, reading. **3** *the interpretation of the coded message* decoding, deciphering. *See* INTERPRET 3. **4** *the scientist's interpretation of the results* analysis, reading, diagnosis. **5** *her interpretation of the foreign ambassador's speech* translation, transcription, transliteration; paraphrase. **6** *the dancer's interpretation of the ballet* portrayal, depiction, presentation, performance, execution, rendering, rendition, enactment.

interpreter *noun* **1** *foreign language interpreter* translator, transcriber. **2** *a skillful interpreter of the dance* portrayer, performer, exponent. **3** *an interpreter of the world situation* commentator, annotator, scholiast.

interrogate *verb* question, put/pose questions to, inquire of, examine, cross-examine, cross-question, quiz, pump, grill, give the third degree to, probe, catechize; *inf.* put the screws on/to.

interrogation *noun* **1** *give way under interrogation | a long interrogation* questioning, quizzing, investigation, examination, third degree, cross-examination, cross-questioning, pumping, grilling, probing, inquisition, catechization; inquiry, catechism. **2** *complain about the policeman's interrogations* question, query, inquiry, poser.

interrogative *adjective* questioning, quizzing, quizzical, inquiring, curious, inquisitive, investigative, grilling, third-degree, inquisitorial, probing, catechistic.

interrupt *verb* **1** *interrupt his speech | she continuously interrupted* cut in (on), break in (on), barge in (on), intrude (on), disturb, heckle, interfere (with); *inf.* butt in (on), chime in (on), horn in (on), muscle in (on). **2** *interrupt the talks for a time* suspend, discontinue, break the continuity of, break, break off, hold up, delay, lay aside, leave off, postpone, stop, put a stop to, halt, bring to a halt/standstill, cease, end, cancel, sever. **3** *only a few trees interrupted the flatness of the landscape* break, break up, punctuate. **4** *the building interrupts our view* obstruct, impede, block, interfere with, cut off.

interruption *noun* **1** *resent his interruption* cutting in, interference, disturbance, intrusion, obtrusion; *inf.* butting in. *See* INTERRUPT 1. **2** *the interruption of the talks* suspension, discontinuance, breaking off, delay, postponement, stopping, halt, cessation. *See* INTERRUPT 2. **3** *there was an interruption of half an hour in the talks* intermission, interval, interlude, break, pause, recess, gap, hiatus.

intersect *verb* **1** *the highway intersects the desert* cut across/through, cut in two/half, divide, bisect. **2** *the lines intersect* cross, crisscross, meet, connect.

intersection *noun* **1** *the intersection of the lines* crossing, crisscrossing, meeting. **2** *a car crash at the intersection* road junction, junction, interchange, crossroads.

intersperse *verb* **1** *intersperse flowers among the trees* scatter, distribute, disperse, spread, strew, dot, sprinkle, pepper. **2** *intersperse drawings in the text* insert, interpose, interpolate, incorporate, intercalate. **3** *intersperse the text with illustrations* vary, diversify, variegate.

intertwine *verb* entwine, interwind, interweave, interlace, twist together, coil, twirl, convolute.

interval *noun* **1** *in the interval before the next meeting* interim, interlude, intervening time, time, period, meantime, meanwhile, wait, space. **2** *drinks served in the theater during the interval* intermission, break, half-time, pause, lull, respite, breather, breathing space, gap, hiatus, delay. **3** *the intervals between the trees* distance, space, gap, interspace. **4** *children in the playground during the interval* break, recess, playtime.

intervene *verb* **1** *in the years that intervened* come/occur between, come to pass, occur, befall, happen, arise, take place, ensue, supervene, succeed. **2** *intervene in the dispute* intercede, mediate, arbitrate, negotiate, step in, involve oneself, come into, interpose, interfere, intrude.

intervention *noun* *his intervention in the dispute* intercession, mediation, arbitration, negotiation, agency, involvement, interposing, interposition, interference, intrusion.

interview *noun* **1** *candidates nervous at the interview* conference, discussion, meeting, talk, dialogue, evaluation. **2** *the prime minister giving an interview to the press* audience, question and answer session, exchange, dialogue, colloquy, interlocution.

interview *verb* talk to, have a discussion/dialogue with, hold a meeting with, confer with, ques-tion, put questions to, sound out, examine, interrogate, cross-examine, evaluate.

interviewer *noun* **1** *the interviewer of candidates* evaluator, assessor, examiner, questioner, interrogator. **2** *the television interviewer* questioner, reporter, correspondent.

interweave *verb* **1** *interweave strands of various fabrics* weave, intertwine, twine, twist, interlace, braid, plait. **2** *their financial affairs are interwoven* intermingle, mingle, interlink, intermix, mix, blend, fuse, interlock, knit, connect, associate.

intestinal *adjective* abdominal, enteric, visceral, celiac, gastric, duodenal.

intestines *plural noun* entrails, viscera; small intestine, large intestine, bowel, colon, gut; *inf.* guts, insides, innards.

intimacy *noun* **1** *an intimacy between them* closeness, close association/relationship, familiarity, confidentiality, close friendship, comradeship, amity, affection, warmth, understanding. **2** *intimacy of lovers* sex, intercourse, sexual intercourse/relations, coition, coitus, carnal knowledge, lovemaking.

intimate *adjective* **1** *intimate friends* close, near, dear, nearest and dearest, cherished, bosom, familiar, confidential, warm, friendly, comradely, amicable; *inf.* thick, buddy-buddy. **2** *in an intimate atmosphere* informal, warm, cozy, friendly, comfortable, snug; *inf.* comfy. **3** *a diary giving intimate details* personal, private, confidential, secret, privy. **4** *his intimate views* private, innermost, inmost, inner, inward, intrinsic, deep-seated, inherent. **5** *an intimate knowledge of the law* experienced, deep, indepth, profound, detailed, thorough, exhaustive, personal, firsthand, direct, immediate. **6** *the intimate relations of lovers* sexual, carnal, fornicatory, unchaste.
 Antonyms: DISTANT; COLD; FORMAL; PUBLIC.

intimate *noun* close/best/bosom friend, constant companion, confidant, confidante, close associate, mate, crony, alter ego; *inf.* chum, pal, buddy.

intimate *verb* *intimated that he would like to be chairman* imply, suggest, let it be known, hint, insinuate, give an inkling that, indicate, signal.

intimation *noun* *the intimation that he wished the chairmanship* implication, suggestion, hint, insinuation, inkling, indication, signal, reference, allusion.

intimidate *verb* frighten, terrify, scare, alarm, terrorize, overawe, awe, cow, subdue, daunt, domineer, browbeat, bully, tyrannize, coerce, compel, bulldoze, pressure, pressurize, threaten; *inf.* push around, lean on, twist someone's arm.

intimidation *noun* **1** *the intimidation of local residents by gangs* frightening, terrorization, subduing, domineering, bullying, tyrannization, coercion, threatening; *inf.* arm-twisting. *See*

INTIMIDATE. **2** *leave his premises out of intimidation* fear, terror, alarm, awe, trepidation.

intolerable *adjective* unbearable, unendurable, beyond endurance, insufferable, insupportable, not to be borne, more than one can stand, impossible, painful, excruciating, agonizing.

intolerance *noun* **1** *blamed his intolerance on a lack of education* bigotry, illiberalism, narrow-mindedness, parochialism, provincialism, insularity, prejudice, bias, one-sidedness, partisanship; chauvinism, jingoism, racism, xenophobia, sexism, ageism, homophobia. **2** *his intolerance to/of the sun* sensitivity, hypersensitivity, allergy.

intolerant *adjective intolerant citizens objecting to newcomers* bigoted, illiberal, narrow-minded, narrow, parochial, provincial, insular, small-minded, prejudiced, biased, partial, partisan, one-sided, warped, twisted, fanatical; chauvinistic, jingoistic, racist, xenophobic, sexist, ageist, homophobic. **intolerant of** *intolerant of sun* sensitive to, hypersensitive to, allergic to.

intonation *noun* **1** *a characteristic Southern intonation* pitch, tone, timbre, cadence, lilt, inflection, accentuation, emphasis, stress. **2** *listen to the intonation of the monks* chant, chanting, incantation, invocation.

intone *verb* **1** *the choir intoned a psalm* chant/sing/recite in a monotone. **2** *intoned his speech slowly and with emphasis* utter, speak, say, articulate, voice, enunciate, pronounce, deliver.

intoxicate *verb* **1** *the cocktails intoxicated them* inebriate, make drunk, befuddle, stupefy. *See* INTOXICATED. **2** *the sunny weather intoxicated them* exhilarate, elate, thrill, invigorate, animate, enliven, excite, arouse, inflame, enrapture.

intoxicated *adjective* inebriated, inebriate, drunk, drunken, dead drunk, under the influence, tipsy, befuddled, stupefied, staggering; *inf.* drunk as a skunk, three sheets to the wind, tight, pickled, soused, under the table, sloshed, plastered, stewed, well-oiled, loaded, stoned, bombed out of one's mind, lit up, tanked up, smashed.
Antonyms: SOBER; ABSTEMIOUS.

intoxicating *adjective* **1** *intoxicating drinks* intoxicant, alcoholic, strong, spirituous, inebriant. **2** *intoxicating news* exhilarating, heady, elating, thrilling, animating, exciting.

intoxication *noun* **1** *suffering from the effects of intoxication* drunkenness, inebriation, inebriety, insobriety, alcoholism, dipsomania, tipsiness, befuddlement, stupefaction; *inf.* tightness. **2** *intoxication following the good news* exhilaration, elation, ecstasy, euphoria, thrill, invigoration, animation, excitement, rapture, delirium.

intractable *adjective* unmanageable, ungovernable, uncontrollable, uncompliant, stubborn, obstinate, obdurate, perverse, disobedient, unsubmissive, indomitable, refractory, recal-

citrant, insubordinate, rebellious, wild, unruly, rowdy.
Antonyms: MANAGEABLE; SUBMISSIVE; OBEDIENT.

intransigent *adjective* uncompromising, irreconcilable, implacable, relentless, unrelenting, inexorable, unbending, unyielding, hard-line, diehard, immovable, inveterate, rigid, tough, tenacious, stubborn, obdurate.
Antonyms: compliant; FLEXIBLE.

intrepid *adjective* fearless, unafraid, undaunted, dauntless, undismayed, unalarmed, unflinching, bold, daring, audacious, adventurous, dashing, rash, reckless, brave, courageous, valiant, valorous, stouthearted, lionhearted, gallant, manly, stalwart, plucky, game, spirited, mettlesome, doughty; *inf.* gutsy, spunky.
Antonyms: TIMID; COWARDLY.

intricate *adjective* **1** *intricate patterns* tangled, entangled, raveled, twisted, knotty, convoluted, involute, mazelike, labyrinthine, winding, serpentine, circuitous, sinuous, roundabout, fancy, elaborate, ornate, Byzantine, rococo. **2** *intricate problems* complex, complicated, difficult, involved, perplexing, puzzling, thorny, mystifying, enigmatic, obscure.
Antonyms: PLAIN; SIMPLE; STRAIGHTFORWARD.

intrigue *verb* **1** *your behavior intrigues me | intrigued by the new play* interest, absorb, arouse one's curiosity, attract, draw, pull, rivet one's attention, rivet, fascinate, charm, captivate, divert, pique, titillate. **2** *they are intriguing to overthrow the dictator* plot, conspire, scheme, connive, maneuver, machinate, devise. **3** *intriguing without her husband's knowledge* have an affair, philander, commit adultery; *inf.* carry on.

intrigue *noun* **1** *involved in an intrigue to overthrow the dictator* plot, conspiracy, collusion, conniving, cabal, scheme, ruse, stratagem, wile, dodge, artifice, maneuver, machination, trickery, double-dealing. **2** *her husband found out about the intrigue* love affair, affair, liaison, amour; adultery; *inf.* carrying on.

intriguer *noun* plotter, conspirator, conniver, collaborator, machinator, Machiavelli.

intriguing *adjective intriguing news | an intriguing play* interesting, absorbing, compelling, attractive, appealing, riveting, fascinating, captivating, diverting, titillating, tantalizing.

intrinsic *adjective* inherent, inborn, inbred, congenital, natural, native, indigenous, constitutional, built-in, ingrained, implanted, basic, fundamental, elemental, essential, true, genuine, real, authentic.
Antonyms: EXTRINSIC; EXTRANEOUS.

introduce *verb* **1** *introduce his friends to each other* present, present formally, make known, acquaint, make acquainted. **2** *introduce the speaker* present, announce, give an introduction to. **3** *introduce his talk with a short biography* preface, precede, lead into, commence, start off, begin. **4** *introduce a new method of teaching* bring in, bring into being, originate, launch, inaugurate, institute, initiate, establish, found, set in motion, organize, develop, start, begin, commence, usher in, pioneer. **5** *introduce his ideas* propose, put forward, suggest, broach, advance, bring up, set forth, submit, air, ventilate. **6** *introduce a note of solemnity to the party* insert, inject, interject, interpose, interpolate, intercalate, add, bring, infuse, instill.

introduction *noun* **1** *the introduction of friends/speakers* presentation, formal presentation. **2** *an informative introduction to the book* foreword, preface, front matter, preamble, prologue, prelude, prolegomenon, proem, exordium, lead-in; *inf.* intro, prelims. **3** *the introduction of new teaching methods* origination, launch, inauguration, institution, establishment, development, start, commencement, pioneering. *See* INTRODUCE 4. **4** *his introduction to a new way of life* baptism, initiation, inauguration, debut, first acquaintanceship. **5** *the course provides an introduction to the subject* basics, rudiments, fundamentals; groundwork. **6** *the introduction of a serious note to the party* insertion, injection, interjection, interposition, interpolation, intercalation, addition, infusion.

introductory *adjective* **1** *the speaker's introductory remarks* | *the introductory section of the book* prefatory, preliminary, precursory, lead-in, initiatory, opening, initial, starting, commencing. **2** *an introductory course* preparatory, elementary, basic, basal, rudimentary, fundamental, initiatory.
Antonyms: FINAL; closing; LAST.

introspective *adjective* inward-looking, inner-directed, introverted, self-analyzing, self-examining, subjective, contemplative, reflective, meditative, musing, pensive, brooding, preoccupied.

introverted *adjective* inward-looking, inner-directed, introspective, self-absorbed, contemplative, withdrawn, shy, reserved.

intrude *verb* **1** *not wish to intrude* interrupt, push/thrust oneself in, gatecrash, barge in, encroach, butt in, interfere, obtrude. **2** *intrude on their grief* encroach on, invade, impinge on, infringe on, trespass on, obtrude on, violate.

intruder *noun* **1** *police found an intruder in the house/grounds* burglar, housebreaker, thief, raider, invader, prowler, trespasser. **2** *the strangers were regarded as intruders at the party* unwelcome guest/visitor, gatecrasher, interloper, infiltrator.

intrusion *noun* *resent the intrusion* interruption, gatecrashing, interference, encroachment, invasion, infringement, trespass, obtrusion, violation.

intrusive *adjective* **1** *intrusive neighbors* intruding, interrupting, interfering, invasive, obtrusive, trespassing, meddlesome, inquisitive; *inf.* pushy, nosy. **2** *intrusive music* interrupting, invasive, disturbing, annoying, irritating, irksome, unwanted.

intuition *noun* **1** *knew by intuition where the child was* instinct, sixth sense, divination, presentiment, clairvoyance, second sight, extrasensory perception, ESP. **2** *I had an intuition that the child was there* feeling, feeling in one's bones, hunch, inkling, presentiment, foreboding.

intuitive *adjective* intuitional, instinctive, instinctual, innate, inborn, inherent, untaught, unlearned, involuntary, spontaneous, automatic.

intumescence *noun* swelling, distension, bloating, dilatation, tumefaction, turgescence, turgidity.

inundate *verb* **1** *the river inundating the town* flood, deluge, overflow, overrun, swamp, submerge, engulf, drown, cover, saturate, soak. **2** *inundated with correspondence* overwhelm, overpower, overburden, swamp, bog down, glut.

inundation *noun* **1** *people lost in the inundation* flood, deluge, torrent, overflow, tidal wave, flash flood, spate. **2** *not coping with the inundation of work* flood, deluge, overabundance, superabundance, plethora, excess, superfluity, surplus; *inf.* tons, heaps.

inure *verb* harden, toughen, indurate, season, temper, habituate, familiarize, accustom, naturalize, acclimatize.

invade *verb* **1** *the enemy invaded the city* march into, overrun, occupy, storm, take over, descend upon, make inroads on, attack, assail, assault, raid, plunder. **2** *invade their privacy* interrupt, intrude on, obtrude on, encroach on, infringe on, trespass on, burst in on, violate. **3** *doubts invaded his mind* assail, permeate, pervade, fill, spread over.

invader *noun* **1** *enemy invaders of the town* attacker, assailant, assaulter, raider, plunderer. **2** *invaders of their privacy* interrupter, intruder, obtruder, encroacher, infringer, trespasser, violator.

invalid[1] *adjective* *his invalid mother* ill, sick, ailing, unwell, infirm, bedridden, valetudinarian, disabled, frail, feeble, weak, debilitated; *inf.* poorly.

invalid[2] *noun* *doctors visiting invalids* ill/infirm person, valetudinarian, sufferer, patient, convalescent.

invalid[3] *adjective* **1** *the contract is now invalid* inoperative, legally void, null, null and void, void, not binding, nullified, revoked, rescinded, abolished. **2** *an invalid assumption/argument* baseless, unfounded, groundless, unjustified, unsubstantiated, unwarranted, untenable, illogical, irrational, unscientific, false, faulty, fallacious, spurious, unacceptable, inadequate, unconvincing, ineffectual, unsound, weak, useless, worthless.

invalidate *verb* **1** *invalidate the contract* render invalid, void, nullify, annul, cancel, quash, veto, negate, revoke, rescind, abolish, terminate, repeal, repudiate. **2** *invalidate the* *argument* weaken, undermine, disprove, refute, rebut, negate, discredit, debase.

invaluable *adjective* priceless, beyond price, inestimable, precious, costly, worth its weight in gold, worth a king's ransom.

invariable *adjective* unchanging, changeless, unchangeable, constant, unvarying, unvaried, invariant, unalterable, immutable, fixed, stable, set, steady, unwavering, static, uniform, regular, consistent.

invariably *adverb he invariably arrives last* always, every/each time, on every occasion, at all times, without fail/exception, regularly, consistently, repeatedly, habitually, unfailingly, infallibly, inevitably.

invasion *noun* **1** *the invasion of the city* overrunning, occupation, incursion, offensive, attack, assailing, assault, raid, foray, onslaught, plundering. **2** *the invasion of privacy* interruption, intrusion, obtrusion, encroachment, infringement, breach, infraction, trespass, violation.

invective *noun* vituperation, railing, fulmination, berating, upbraiding, castigation, reproval, admonition, denunciation, disparagement, censure, recrimination, abuse, contumely, obloquy; tirade, diatribe, philippic, harangue, tongue-lashing, reprimand, reproach, rebuke.

inveigh *verb inveigh against the decision* rail, protest, complain vehemently, fulminate, harangue; denounce, censure, condemn, criticize, disparage, denigrate, revile, abuse, vilify, impugn.

inveigle *verb* ensnare, delude, persuade, talk into, cajole, wheedle, coax, sweet-talk, beguile, tempt, decoy, lure, allure, entice, seduce, deceive.

invent *verb* **1** *invent a new machine/word* originate, create, innovate, discover, design, devise, contrive, formulate, think up, conceive, come up with, hit upon, compose, frame, coin. **2** *he invented that story* make up, fabricate, concoct, hatch, trump up, forge; *inf.* cook up.

invention *noun* **1** *the invention of the zipper | invention of new words* origination, creation, innovation, discovery, design, devising, contriving, coining, coinage. *See* INVENT 1. **2** *his most famous invention* origination, creation, innovation, discovery, design, contrivance, construction, coinage; *inf.* brainchild. **3** *an artist of great invention* inventiveness, originality, creativity, creativeness, imagination, artistry, inspiration, ingenuity, resourcefulness, genius, skill. **4** *his account of the event was pure invention* fabrication, concoction, fiction, falsification, forgery, fake, deceit, myth, fantasy, romance, illusion, sham. **5** *they refused to believe his obvious invention* fabrication, lie, untruth, falsehood, fib, piece of fiction, figment of one's imagination, yarn, story; *inf.* tall story.

inventive *adjective an inventive artist* original, creative, innovational, imaginative, artistic, inspired, ingenious, resourceful, innovative, gifted, talented, skillful, clever.
Antonyms: UNIMAGINATIVE; PEDESTRIAN.

inventor *noun* originator, creator, innovator, discoverer, author, architect, designer, deviser, developer, initiator, coiner, father, prime mover, maker, framer, producer.

inventory *noun* list, listing, checklist, catalog, record, register, tally, account, description, statement.

inverse *adjective the inverse side* opposite, converse, contrary, reverse, counter, reversed, inverted, transposed, retroverted.

inverse *noun look at the inverse of the coin* opposite side, converse side, obverse side, other side; *inf.* flip side.

inversion *noun the inversion of the boat* overturn, overturning, upturning, capsizing. *See* INVERT 1, 2.

invert *verb* **1** *invert the hourglass/sweater* turn upside down, upturn, turn inside out. **2** *the boat inverted* turn upside down, overturn, upturn, turn turtle, capsize, upset. **3** *invert the printed picture* reverse, interpose, retrovert.

invest *verb* **1** *the priest will be invested tomorrow* install, induct, inaugurate, instate, ordain, initiate, swear in, consecrate, crown, enthrone. **2** *the bride was invested in silk* clothe, attire, dress, garb, robe, gown, drape, swathe, adorn, deck. **3** *the enemy army invested the city* besiege, lay siege to, beleaguer, beset, surround, enclose.
invest in **1** *invest in the business* put/sink money into, lay out money on/for, provide capital for, fund, subsidize. **2** *invest money/energy in the venture* spend on, expend on/for, lay out for, put in/into, use up on, devote to, contribute to, donate to, give to. **3** *invest power in his heirs* vest in, confer to, bestow to, grant to, entrust to, give to, place in/upon.

investigate *verb* research, probe, explore, inquire into, make inquiries about, go/look into, search, scrutinize, study, examine, inspect, consider, sift, analyze; *inf.* check out.

investigation *noun* research, probe, exploration, inquiry, fact-finding, search, scrutinization, scrutiny, study, survey, review, examination, inspection, consideration, sifting, analysis, inquest, hearing, questioning, inquisition.

investigator *noun the investigator of the complaints* researcher, prober, explorer, inquirer, fact finder, searcher, scrutinizer, scrutineer, reviewer, examiner, inspector, analyzer, questioner, inquisitor. **private investigator** *hire a private investigator to find the criminal* (private) detective; *inf.* private eye, P.I., dick, sleuth, Sherlock, gumshoe.

investiture *noun the investiture of the priest/governor/king* investment, installation, inauguration, instatement, ordination, induction, initiation, swearing in, consecration, crowning, enthroning.

investment *noun* **1** *his business is not a safe in-*

vestment venture, speculation, risk. **2** *his investment amounts to $3,000* stake, money/capital invested; *inf.* ante. **3** *the investment of the governor* installation, inauguration, instatement, ordination. *See* INVESTITURE.

inveterate *adjective* **1** *an inveterate conservative/drinker* confirmed, habitual, inured, hardened, chronic, diehard, dyed-in-the-wool, longstanding, addicted, hard-core, incorrigible. **2** *an inveterate habit* ingrained, deep-seated, deep-rooted, deep-set, entrenched, longestablished, ineradicable, incurable.

invidious *adjective* **1** *make invidious comparisons* discriminatory, unfair, prejudicial, slighting, offensive, objectionable, deleterious, detrimental. **2** *it put her in an invidious position* unpleasant, awkward, unpopular, repugnant, hateful.
Antonyms: FAIR; DESIRABLE.

invigorate *verb* revitalize, energize, fortify, strengthen, put new strength/life/heart in, brace, refresh, rejuvenate, enliven, liven up, animate, exhilarate, pep up, perk up, stimulate, motivate, rouse, excite, wake up, galvanize, electrify.

invincible *adjective* **1** *an invincible opponent* unconquerable, undefeatable, unbeatable, unassailable, invulnerable, indestructible, impregnable, indomitable, unyielding, unflinching, dauntless. **2** *an invincible hurdle* insuperable, insurmountable, overwhelming, overpowering.
Antonyms: VULNERABLE; DEFENSELESS; WEAK.

inviolable *adjective* *inviolable rights/oaths* inalienable, untouchable, unalterable, sacrosanct, sacred, holy, hallowed.

inviolate *adjective* *a treaty still inviolate | purity still inviolate* intact, unbroken, whole, entire, complete, untouched, undamaged, unhurt, unharmed, unscathed, unmarred, unspoiled, unsullied, unstained, undefiled, unpolluted, pure, virgin.

invisible *adjective* **1** *invisible to the passersby* unseeable, out of sight, undetectable, imperceivable, indiscernible, indistinguishable, unseen, unnoticed, unobserved, hidden, concealed. **2** *invisible hairnets* inconspicuous, unnoticeable, imperceptible.

invitation *noun* **1** *reject their invitation to lunch* asking, bidding, call; *inf.* invite. **2** *accept their invitation to apply for the post* request, call, appeal, petition, solicitation, supplication, summons. **3** *the rebate was an invitation to buy the car* welcome, encouragement, provocation, overture, attraction, draw, allurement, lure, bait, enticement, temptation, tantalization; *inf.* come-on.

invite *verb* **1** *they invited him to dinner* ask, bid, summon; request someone's company/presence at. **2** *invite applications* ask for, request, call for, solicit, look for, seek, appeal for, petition, summon. **3** *invite disaster* cause, bring on, bring upon oneself, draw, make happen, in-

duce, provoke. **4** *they invite trouble by leaving the doors unlocked* welcome, encourage, foster, attract, draw, allure, entice, tempt, court, lead on.

inviting *adjective* *an inviting prospect* attractive, appealing, pleasant, agreeable, delightful, engaging, tempting, enticing, alluring, winning, beguiling, fascinating, enchanting, entrancing, bewitching, captivating, intriguing, irresistible, ravishing, seductive.
Antonyms: REPELLENT; REPULSIVE; OFFENSIVE.

invocation *noun* *an invocation for God's help* call, prayer, request, supplication, entreaty, solicitation, beseeching, imploring, importuning, petition, appeal.

invoice *noun* *receive the invoice for building alterations* bill, account, statement of charges, itemization.

invoke *verb* **1** *invoke God's help* call for, call up, pray for, request, supplicate, entreat, solicit, beseech, beg, implore, importune, call on, petition, appeal to. **2** *invoke the constitutional amendment* apply, implement, call into use, put into effect/use, resort to, use, have recourse to, initiate.

involuntary *adjective* **1** *an involuntary reaction* reflexive, reflex, automatic, mechanical, unconditioned, spontaneous, instinctive, instinctual, unconscious, unthinking, unintentional, uncontrolled. **2** *their cooperation was involuntary* unwilling, against one's will/wishes, reluctant, unconsenting, grudging, disinclined, forced, coerced, coercive, compelled, compulsory, obligatory.
Antonyms: VOLUNTARY; WILLING.

involve *verb* **1** *his new job involves total discretion* entail, imply, mean, denote, betoken, connote, require, necessitate, presuppose. **2** *try to involve everyone in the party preparations* include, count in, cover, embrace, take in, number, incorporate, encompass, comprise, contain, comprehend. **3** *the criminal tried to involve others in the crime* implicate, incriminate, inculpate, associate, connect, concern. **4** *try to introduce the students to something that involves them* interest, be of interest to, absorb, engage, engage/hold/rivet the attention of, rivet, grip, occupy, preoccupy, engross. **5** *the situation was further involved by the police activity* complicate, perplex, confuse, mix up, confound, entangle, tangle, embroil, enmesh.

involved *adjective* **1** *very involved situation/problem/politics* complicated, difficult, intricate, complex, elaborate, confused, confusing, mixed up, jumbled, tangled, entangled, convoluted, knotty, tortuous, labyrinthine, Byzantine. **2** *involved parties should declare themselves* implicated, incriminated, inculpated, associated, concerned, participating, taking part.
Antonyms: SIMPLE; DISINTERESTED.

invulnerable *adjective* *invulnerable fortresses*

impenetrable, impregnable, unassailable, unattackable, inviolable, invincible, undefeatable, secure, safe, safe and sound. **invulnerable to/against** *she seemed invulnerable to/against criticism* unwoundable by, unhurtable by, proof against, insensitive to, insusceptible to, indestructible by.
Antonym: VULNERABLE; DEFENSELESS.

inward, inwards *adverb proceed inward* inside, toward the inside, within.

inward *adjective* **1** *the inward section* interior, inside, internal, inner, innermost. **2** *his inward thoughts* private, personal, intimate, hidden, secret, confidential, privy.
Antonyms: OUTWARD; EXTERIOR; OUTSIDE.

inwardly *adverb he smiled, but inwardly he grieved* at heart, deep down/within, in one's heart, inside, privately, secretly.

iota *noun* bit, mite, speck, atom, jot, whit, particle, fraction, morsel, grain; *inf.* smidgen, smidge.

irascible *adjective* irritable, quick-tempered, short-tempered, thin-skinned, snappy, snappish, testy, touchy, edgy, surly, cross, crusty, crabbed, grouchy, crotchety, cantankerous, querulous, captious, fractious.

irate *adjective* angry, very angry, wrathful, infuriated, furious, indignant, annoyed, irritated, vexed, incensed, enraged, raging, fuming, ireful, ranting, raving, mad, in a frenzy; *inf.* foaming at the mouth.

ire *noun* anger, wrath, rage, fury, indignation, annoyance, exasperation, irritation, hot temper, resentment, choler, spleen.

iridescent *adjective* shimmering, shimmery, glittering, sparkling, dazzling, kaleidoscopic, multicolored, rainbowlike, variegated.

irk *verb* irritate, annoy, provoke, vex, pique, peeve, nettle, exasperate, ruffle, discountenance, anger, infuriate, incense, try one's patience; *inf.* get one's goat, get one's back up.

irksome *adjective* irritating, annoying, vexing, vexatious, exasperating, infuriating, tiresome, wearisome, tedious, trying, troublesome, boring, uninteresting, disagreeable.

iron *verb iron their shirts* press, smooth. **iron out** **1** *iron out the problems* straighten out, sort out, clear up, settle, solve, resolve, unravel. **2** *iron out their differences* get rid of, eliminate, eradicate, erase, harmonize, reconcile, smooth over.

ironic *adjective* **1** *an ironic remark/wit* satirical, mocking, scoffing, ridiculing, derisory, derisive, scornful, sneering, sardonic, wry, double-edged, sarcastic. **2** *ironic that he died immediately after he won the money* paradoxical, incongruous.

irons *plural noun* fetters, chains, shackles, bonds, manacles.

irony *noun* **1** *the irony of his wit* | *use irony* satire, mockery, ridicule, derision, scorn, wryness, sarcasm. **2** *it was a sad irony that he died soon after winning the money* paradox, incongruity, incongruousness.

irradiate *verb* **1** *beacons irradiating the coastline* illuminate, light up, light, brighten, cast light upon, illumine. **2** *irradiate young minds* enlighten, inform, instruct, teach, tutor, give insight to, illumine, edify, inspire. **3** *irradiate tumors/food* treat with radiation, expose to radiation, X ray.

irrational *adjective* **1** *irrational fears* illogical, unreasonable, groundless, invalid, unsound, implausible, absurd, ridiculous, silly, foolish, senseless, nonsensical, ludicrous, preposterous, crazy. **2** *an irrational person* illogical, unthinking, unintelligent, stupid, brainless, mindless, senseless, muddled, muddleheaded, confused, demented, insane, crazy, unstable.

irreconcilable *adjective* **1** *irreconcilable points of view* incompatible, at odds, at variance, opposite, contrary, incongruous, opposing, conflicting, clashing, discordant. **2** *irreconcilable enemies* implacable, unappeasable, uncompromising, inexorable, intransigent, hard-line, inflexible.

irrecoverable *adjective* unrecoverable, unregainable, unreclaimable, irretrievable, irredeemable, unsavable, unsalvageable, irreparable, lost, lost and gone, gone for ever.

irrefutable *adjective* incontrovertible, incontestable, indisputable, undeniable, unquestionable, beyond question, indubitable, beyond doubt, conclusive, decisive, definite, certain, sure, positive, definitive, fixed, final, irrefragable, apodictic.

irregular *adjective* **1** *an irregular coastline* asymmetric, unsymmetrical, without uniformity, nonuniform, uneven, broken, jagged, ragged, serrated, crooked, curving, craggy. **2** *an irregular road surface* uneven, unlevel, rough, bumpy, lumpy, knotty, pitted. **3** *an irregular pulse* uneven, unsteady, shaky, fitful, variable, erratic, spasmodic, wavering, fluctuating, aperiodic. **4** *an irregular attender of meetings* inconsistent, erratic, sporadic, variable, inconstant, desultory, haphazard, intermittent, occasional, unpunctual, unsystematic, capricious, unmethodical. **5** *irregular periods of employment* disconnected, sporadic, fragmentary, haphazard, patchy, intermittent, occasional, random, fluctuating, coming and going. **6** *his appointment was most irregular* out of order, contrary, perverse, against the rules, unofficial, unorthodox, unconventional, abnormal. **7** *an irregular result* anomalous, aberrant, deviant, abnormal, unusual, uncommon, freak, extraordinary, exceptional, odd, peculiar, strange, eccentric, bizarre, queer. **8** *lead an irregular life* immoral, dissolute, dissipated, intemperate, immoderate, lascivious, licentious, degenerate, wanton, improper, indecent, lawless, wild, unruly, disorderly. **9** *an irregular army* guerrilla, underground, resistance, mercenary.

irregularity noun **1** *the irregularity of the coastline* lack of symmetry, asymmetry, unsymmetricalness, nonuniformity, unevenness, jaggedness. *See* IRREGULAR *adjective* 1. **2** *the irregularity of the road surface* unevenness, unlevelness, roughness, bumpiness, pittedness. *See* IRREGULAR *adjective* 2. **3** *the irregularities on the surface* roughness, bump, lump, pit, hole. **4** *the irregularity of the pulse* unevenness, unsteadiness, shakiness, fitfulness, fluctuation. *See* IRREGULAR *adjective* 3. **5** *the irregularity of their attendance* inconsistency, inconstancy, desultoriness, haphazardness, intermittence, patchiness. *See* IRREGULAR *adjective* 4, 5. **6** *the irregularity of his appointment* unorthodoxy, unconventionality. *See* IRREGULAR *adjective* 6. **7** *the irregularity of the result* anomaly, anomalousness, aberrance, aberrancy, deviation, abnormality, unusualness, freakishness. *See* IRREGULAR *adjective* 7. **8** *spot the irregularities in the result* anomaly, aberration, deviation, abnormality. **9** *the irregularity of his life* immorality, dissoluteness, dissipation, intemperance, immoderation, degeneracy, lawlessness, wildness, unruliness. *See* IRREGULAR *adjective* 8.

irrelevant *adjective* inapposite, inapt, inapplicable, impertinent, nongermane, immaterial, unrelated, unconnected, inappropriate, extraneous, beside the point, not to the point, out of place, nothing to do with it, neither here nor there.

irreligious *adjective* **1** *make irreligious remarks* impious, irreverent, heretical, sacrilegious, ungodly, blasphemous, profane. **2** *trying to preach the gospel to irreligious people* atheistic, unbelieving, nonbelieving, agnostic, skeptical, infidel, heathen, pagan, unenlightened.

irreparable *adjective irreparable damage to his reputation* beyond repair, past mending, irreversible, irrevocable, irretrievable, irrecoverable, irremediable, incurable, ruinous.

irreplaceable *adjective* priceless, invaluable, inestimably precious, unique, worth its weight in gold, rare.

irrepressible *adjective* **1** *irrepressible optimism* unrestrainable, uncontainable, insuppressible, uncontrollable, unstoppable, unquenchable, unreserved, unchecked, unbridled. **2** *irrepressible children playing* bubbling over, buoyant, effervescent, ebullient, vivacious, animated, spirited, lively.

irreproachable *adjective* beyond reproach, blameless, unblameworthy, unblamable, faultless, flawless, guiltless, sinless, innocent, unimpeachable, inculpable, irreprehensible, impeccable, immaculate, unblemished, stainless, pure.

irresistible *adjective* **1** *an irresistible impulse* overwhelming, overpowering, compelling, insuppressible, irrepressible, forceful, potent, imperative, urgent. **2** *an irresistible fate* unavoidable, inevitable, inescapable, unpreventable, ineluctable, inexorable, relentless. **3** *an irresistible beauty/dessert* fascinating, alluring, enticing, seductive, captivating, enchanting, ravishing, tempting, tantalizing.

irresolute *adjective* uncertain, unsure, doubtful, dubious, undecided, indecisive, unresolved, undetermined, unsettled, vacillating, wavering, hesitant, hesitating, tentative, in two minds, oscillating.

irrespective *adjective* **irrespective of** regardless of, without regard/reference to, setting aside, discounting, ignoring, notwithstanding.

irresponsible *adjective* **1** *irresponsible people* undependable, unreliable, untrustworthy, careless, reckless, rash, flighty, giddy, scatterbrained, erratic, harebrained, featherbrained, immature; *inf.* harum-scarum. **2** *irresponsible actions* thoughtless, ill-considered, unwise, injudicious, careless, reckless, immature.

irretrievable *adjective* irrecoverable, unregainable, unsalvageable, unsavable, irreclaimable, irredeemable, irreparable, lost, hopeless.

irreverent *adjective* **1** *children irreverent to their parents* disrespectful, unrespectful, impertinent, insolent, impudent, rude, cheeky, discourteous, impolite, uncivil; *inf.* flip. **2** *irreverent remarks about God* impious, irreligious, heretical, sacrilegious, ungodly, blasphemous, profane.

irreversible *adjective irreversible damage/decisions* unalterable, irreparable, unrectifiable, irrevocable, unrepealable, final.

irrevocable *adjective irrevocable decisions/fate* unalterable, unchangeable, irreversible, unreversible, fixed, settled, fated, immutable, predetermined, predestined.

irrigation noun watering, wetting, spraying, sprinkling, moistening, soaking, flooding, inundating.

irritable *adjective* bad-tempered, ill-tempered, ill-humored, irascible, cross, snappish, snappy, edgy, testy, touchy, crabbed, peevish, petulant, cantankerous, grumpy, grouchy, crusty, dyspeptic, choleric, splenetic.
Antonyms: GOOD-HUMORED; CHEERFUL; IMPERTURBABLE.

irritate verb **1** *the barking dogs irritate the neighbors* annoy, vex, provoke, irk, nettle, peeve, get on one's nerves, exasperate, infuriate, anger, enrage, incense, make one's hackles rise, ruffle, disturb, put out, bother, pester, try one's patience; *inf.* aggravate, rub the wrong way, get one's goat, get one's back up, drive up the wall, drive one bananas. **2** *the rough cloth irritated her skin* chafe, fret, rub, pain, hurt, inflame, aggravate.

irritating *adjective irritating habits/people* annoying, vexing, provoking, irksome, exasperating, infuriating, maddening, disturbing, bothersome, troublesome, pestering; *inf.* aggravating. *See* IRRITATE 1.

irritation noun **1** *snapped at us in irritation*

irritability, annoyance, impatience, vexation, exasperation, indignation, ill-temper, crossness, anger, fury, rage, wrath, displeasure, ire; *inf.* aggravation. **2** *slow service was an irritation to the customers* | *the persistent salesman is an irritation* source of annoyance, annoyance, irritant, pest, nuisance, thorn in the/one's flesh/side; *inf.* pain in the neck/butt, pain.

island *noun* isle, islet, key, cay, atoll.

isolate *verb* set apart, segregate, cut off, separate, detach, abstract, quarantine, keep in solitude, sequester, insulate.

isolated *adjective* **1** *feeling isolated far from her friends* alone, solitary, lonely, separated, segregated, exiled, forsaken, forlorn. **2** *an isolated place* remote, out of the way, off the beaten track, outlying, secluded, hidden, unfrequented, lonely, desolate, godforsaken. **3** *an isolated example* | *an isolated case of polio* single, solitary, unique, random, unrelated, unusual, uncommon, exceptional, abnormal, atypical, untypical, anomalous, freak.

isolation *noun* **1** *the isolation of the patients was necessary* segregation, separation, detachment, abstraction, quarantine, sequestration, insulation. *See* ISOLATE. **2** *the prisoner's feeling of isolation* lack of contact, separation, segregation, exile, forlornness, aloneness, solitariness, loneliness. **3** *the isolation of the village* remoteness, seclusion, loneliness, desolation. *See* ISOLATED 2.

issue *noun* **1** *debate the issue for hours* matter, matter in question, point at issue, question, subject, topic, affair, problem, bone of contention, controversy, argument. **2** *the issue is still in doubt* result, outcome, decision, upshot, end, conclusion, consequence, termination, effect, denouement. **3** *the next issue of the magazine* edition, number, printing, print run, impression, copy, installment, version. **4** *the issue of the new stamps/paper/shares* issuing, issuance, publication, circulation, distribution, supplying, supply, dissemination, sending out, delivery. **5** *Abraham and his issue* offspring, progeny, children; heirs, scions, descendants; *inf.* brood. **6** *the issue of the stream* outflow, effusion, discharge, debouchment, emanation. **at issue** *the matters at issue* to be discussed, under discussion, for debate, in dispute, to be decided, unsettled. **take issue with** *take issue with management over pay* disagree with, dispute with, raise an objection with, make a protest to, challenge, oppose.

issue *verb* **1** *issue new stamps* | *issue a news statement* put out, give out, deal out, send out, distribute, circulate, release; disseminate, an-

nounce, proclaim, broadcast. **2** *smoke issuing from the chimney* | *liquid issuing from the pipe* emit, exude, discharge, emanate, gush, pour forth, seep, ooze. **3** *people issued from the building* emerge, come out, come forth, appear; leave. **4** *his knowledge issues from a love of books* derive, arise, stem, proceed, spring, originate, result; be a result/consequence of.
Antonyms: WITHDRAW; ENTER.

itch *verb* *her head itches* be itchy, tingle, prickle, tickle, be irritated. **itch for** *itch for a new car* long for, have a longing for, yearn for, hanker after/for, pine for/after, ache for, burn for, hunger for, thirst for, lust for, pant for, desire greatly, crave.

itch *noun* **1** *have an itch on the scalp* itchiness, tingling, prickling, tickling, irritation, burning; *Med.* formication, paresthesia. **2** *have an itch for a new car* great desire, longing, yearning, craving, hankering, ache, burning, hunger, thirst, lust; *inf.* yen.

itching *adjective* **1** *an itching scalp* itchy, tingling, prickling. *See* ITCH *noun* 1. **2** *itching to go/know* longing, yearning, craving, aching, burning, avid, agog, keen, eager, impatient, raring, dying.

itchy *adjective* itching, tingling, prickling. *See* ITCH *noun* 1.

item *noun* **1** *three items for sale* article, thing, piece of merchandise; goods. **2** *several items to be discussed* point, detail, matter, consideration, particular, feature, circumstance, aspect, component, element, ingredient. **3** *items in an account* entry, record. **4** *a news item* piece of news/information, piece, story, bulletin, article, account, report, feature, dispatch. **5** *Jim and Jane are an item now* couple, recognized couple; partners.

itemize *verb* *itemize the house contents* list, inventory, record, set out, document, register, tabulate, detail, particularize, specify, instance, enumerate, number.

iterate *verb* repeat, restate, dwell on, hammer away at, harp on about, press one's point about, emphasize, stress, underscore.

itinerant *adjective* traveling, peripatetic, journeying, wandering, roaming, roving, rambling, wayfaring, unsettled, nomadic, migratory, vagabond, vagrant, gypsy.

itinerary *noun* **1** *his itinerary takes him through France* route, planned route, travel plan, course of travel, journey. **2** *the travel agent gave her an itinerary* travel plan/schedule, schedule, timetable, program; travel arrangements. **3** *keep an itinerary of foreign journeys* diary, journal, logbook, daybook, log, record. **4** *a considerable number of itineraries are in publication* guidebook, travel guide/book, guide.

J

jab *verb jab him in the ribs | jabbing the pillow* poke, prod, dig (at/into), nudge, elbow, thrust (at/into), stab, bump, tap, punch, box; *inf.* sock.

jab *noun a jab in the ribs* poke, prod, dig, nudge, stab, punch. *See* JAB *verb*.

jabber *verb* chatter, gibber, prattle, babble, gabble, prate, blather, clack, rattle, ramble.

jack *verb* **jack up 1** *jack up the car* lift, lift up, hoist, raise, elevate, hike up, haul up. **2** *merchants jacking up prices* raise, push up, make higher, increase, boost, inflate, escalate.

jacket *noun* **1** *wearing a jacket and matching pants* sports coat, blazer, windbreaker, parka, anorak; cardigan. **2** *a jacket for a hot-water heater* casing, case, encasement, sheath, sheathing, envelope, cover, covering, wrapping, wrapper, wrap.

jackpot *noun* kitty, pool, pot, bank, first prize, main prize, prize, winnings, reward, bonanza. **hit the jackpot** win a large prize, win a lot of money, strike it rich/lucky, have a great success, be very successful; *inf.* make a killing.

jaded *adjective* **1** *a jaded appetite* satiated, sated, allayed, surfeited, glutted, cloyed, gorged, dulled, blunted. **2** *feel jaded after the week's work* tired, wearied, weary, fatigued, worn out, exhausted, spent; *inf.* played out, done, done in, bushed, pooped, fagged out.

jagged *adjective the jagged edge of the broken window* serrated, toothed, notched, indented, denticulate, pointed, spiked, barbed, uneven, rough, ridged, ragged, craggy, broken, cleft.

jail *noun sent to jail for theft* prison, lockup, jailhouse, penitentiary; *inf.* pen, clink, inside, stir, slammer, cooler, jug, can, big house.

jail *verb they jailed him for life* send to prison, imprison, send up, lock up, put away, incarcerate, confine, detain, intern, impound, immure.

jailer *noun* prison warden, warden, guard, keeper, captor; *inf.* screw.

jam[1] *verb* **1** *jam something in the door to keep it closed* wedge, sandwich, insert, force, ram, thrust, push, stick, press, cram, stuff. **2** *the ushers jammed too many people into the hall* cram, pack, crowd, squeeze, crush. **3** *the broken-down vehicles jammed the roads* obstruct, block, clog, close off, congest. **4** *the machine has jammed* become stuck, stick, stall, halt, stop.

jam[2] *noun* **1** *caught in a jam on the highway* traffic jam, holdup, obstruction, congestion, bottleneck, stoppage, gridlock. **2** *in a financial jam* predicament, plight, straits, trouble, quandary; *inf.* fix, pickle, hole, spot, tight spot, scrape.

jam[3] *noun spread jam on bread* preserve, preserves, conserve, jelly, marmalade.

jamb *noun* doorjamb, doorpost, upright, post, pillar.

jamboree *noun* gathering, celebration, get-together, rally, party, festivity, festival, fête, carnival, jubilee, revelry, merrymaking, carouse, spree; *inf.* do, shindig, blowout, bash.

jangle *verb* **1** *the chains jangled* clank, clink, clang, clash, clatter, rattle, vibrate, chime. **2** *the noise jangled his nerves* jar on, grate on, irritate, disturb.

jangle *noun the jangle of chains* clank, clink, clang, clangor, clash, clatter, rattle, cacophony, din, dissonance, reverberation, jarring.

janitor *noun* caretaker, concierge, custodian.

jar *noun store rice in a jar* glass container, container, receptacle, vessel, carafe, flagon, flask, pitcher, jug, vase, urn.

jar *verb* **1** *the knife jarred against the metal surface* grate, rasp, scratch, squeak, screech. **2** *he jarred his neck in the crash* jolt, jerk, shake, vibrate. **3** *the sound jarred his nerves | her manner jarred (on) him* grate (on), jangle, irritate, disturb, upset, discompose, irk, annoy, nettle, vex. **4** *his views jarred with hers* clash, conflict, be inharmonious, be in opposition, be at variance, be at odds.

jargon *noun* **1** *the jargon of the neighborhood kids* cant, slang, argot, idiom, usage, vernacular, dialect, patois; *inf.* lingo. **2** *technical jargon* specialized language; computerese, legalese, bureaucratese, journalese, buzzword, gobbledygook, psychobabble.

jaundiced *adjective* **1** *jaundiced skin | his jaundiced face* yellow, yellowish, yellow-tinged, yellow-skinned, sallow. **2** *a jaundiced view of life* cynical, pessimistic, skeptical, distrustful, suspicious, misanthropic, bitter, resentful, jealous, envious, narrow-minded, bigoted, prejudiced.

Antonyms: OPTIMISTIC; NAÏVE.

jaunt *noun went on a jaunt to the seaside* trip, outing, short drive, short excursion, short expedition, airing, stroll.

jaunty *adjective* **1** *in a jaunty mood* sprightly, bouncy, buoyant, lively, breezy, perky, frisky, merry, blithe, carefree, joyful. **2** *a jaunty outfit* smart, stylish, spruce, trim, dapper, fancy, flashy; *inf.* natty.

Antonyms: DEPRESSED; SERIOUS; SEDATE.

javelin *noun* spear, shaft, bolt, pike, dart.

jaw *noun* **1** *break one's jaw* jawbone, mandible, maxilla. **2** *have a jaw about old times* chat, gossip, conversation, talk, blather; *inf.* chinwag.

jaw *verb jaw about old times | the speaker jawed on* chat, chatter, gossip, talk, converse, babble, lecture, drone.

jaws *noun pl the jaws of the cave | the jaws of Hell* mouth, maw, opening, entrance, entry, ingress, orifice, aperture, abyss.

jazz *noun* **1** *listen to jazz* jazz music. **2** *her performance needs a bit of jazz* liveliness, animation, vivacity, spark, spirit, zest; *inf.* pizzazz. **3** *can't be bothered with formal invitations and all that jazz* things like that, stuff, rigmarole, paraphernalia. **jazz up** *verb jazz up her performance | jazz up the living room* brighten up, liven up, enliven, put some spirit into, put some animation into, add some color to, enhance.

jazzy *adjective jazzy car/clothes* flashy, fancy, stylish, smart, gaudy; *inf.* flash, snazzy.

jealous *adjective* **1** *jealous of her beauty* begrudging, grudging, resentful, envious, green with envy, green-eyed, covetous, desirous. **2** *a jealous lover* suspicious, distrustful, mistrustful, doubting, insecure, apprehensive of rivals, possessive. **3** *jealous of her chastity* protective, vigilant, watchful, heedful, mindful, careful, solicitous, on guard, wary.

---

jealous
covetous, envious

Envious implies wanting something that belongs to another and to which one has no particular right or claim (envious of her good fortune). **Jealous** may refer to a strong feeling of envy (it is hard not to be jealous of a man with a job like his), or it may imply an intense effort to hold on to what one possesses (*jealous of what little time she has to herself*); it is often associated with distrust, suspicion, anger, and other negative emotions (*a jealous wife*). Someone who is **covetous** has fallen prey to an inordinate or wrongful desire, usually for a person or thing that rightfully belongs to another. In other words, a young man might be *jealous* of the other men who flirt with his girlfriend, while they might be *envious* of her obvious preference for him. But the young man had better not be *covetous* of his neighbor's wife.

---

jealousy *noun* **1** *show jealousy at her rival's success* grudgingness, resentment, resentfulness, ill-will, bitterness, spite, envy, covetousness; green-eyed monster. **2** *the jealousy of her husband* suspicion, suspiciousness, distrust, mistrust, doubt, insecurity, apprehension about rivals, possessiveness. **3** *guard his honor with jealousy* vigilance, watchfulness, heedfulness, attentiveness, care.
Antonyms: GENEROSITY; TRUST.

jeans *plural noun* blue jeans, denims; *Trademark* Levis.

jeer *verb crowds jeering the politician | he jeered (at) authority* mock, ridicule, deride, taunt, gibe, scorn, contemn, flout, cry down, tease, boo, hiss; scoff at, laugh at, sneer at; *inf.* knock.
Antonyms: CHEER; APPLAUD.

jeer *noun the jeers of the crowd* mockery, ridicule, derision; banter, scoffing, teasing, sneer, taunt, gibe, boo, hiss, catcall, abuse; *inf.* knocking.

jejune *adjective* **1** *a jejune person* naïve, simple, unsophisticated, immature, inexperienced, ignorant, uninformed; *inf.* wet behind the ears. **2** *jejune behavior* childish, immature, juvenile, puerile, silly, senseless, inane. **3** *jejune prose* insipid, uninteresting, dull, vapid, arid, dry, trite, banal, boring, tedious.
Antonyms: SOPHISTICATED; MATURE; INSPIRED.

jell *verb* **1** *let the dessert jell* set, stiffen, solidify, harden, thicken, congeal, coagulate. **2** *ideas beginning to jell* take shape, take form, form, crystallize, come together.

jeopardize *verb* put in jeopardy, put at risk, risk, expose to risk, expose to danger, lay open to danger, endanger, imperil, threaten, menace, take a chance with, gamble with.

jeopardy *noun* risk, danger, endangerment, peril, hazard, precariousness, insecurity, vulnerability, threat, menace.
Antonyms: SAFETY; SECURITY.

jerk *verb* **1** *jerk him inside by the arm* pull, yank, tug, wrench, tweak, pluck. **2** *the car jerked along* jolt, lurch, bump, jump, jounce. **3** *his arm was jerking* twitch, shake, tremble, be in convulsion.

jerk *noun* **1** *pull it out with a jerk* pull, yank, tug, wrench, tweak. **2** *the car stopped with a jerk* jolt, lurch, bump, start, jar. **3** *he's a complete jerk* fool, idiot, rogue, scoundrel; *inf.* nerd, twit, dimwit, dope, creep, heel.

jerky *adjective* **1** *a jerky movement of the limbs* spasmodic, fitful, convulsive, twitchy, shaking, shaky, tremulous, uncontrolled. **2** *the jerky motion of the car* jolting, lurching, jumpy, bumpy, bouncy, jouncing, rough.
Antonyms: SMOOTH; FLUID.

jerry-built *adjective the toolshed is jerry-built* badly built, carelessly built, thrown together, gimcrack, improvised, insubstantial, flimsy, unstable, rickety, ramshackle, defective, faulty, flawed, cheap, cheapjack, shoddy.
Antonyms: STURDY; SOLID; SUBSTANTIAL.

jersey *noun* shirt, top, T-shirt, knit shirt; sweater, pullover.

jest *noun* **1** *tell jests* joke, witticism, gag, quip, bon mot; *inf.* crack, wisecrack, funny. **2** *play a jest on someone* joke, prank, hoax, practical joke, trick, jape; *inf.* lark. **3** *they did it in jest* fun, sport, play. **4** *they made a jest of him* laughingstock, butt, fool; *inf.* stooge, fall guy.

jest *verb* **1** *they joked and jested all evening* joke, tell jokes, crack jokes, quip, banter; *inf.* wisecrack. **2** *she took them seriously but they were jest-*

fool, fool around, tease, play a prank, play a practical joke, hoax, play a hoax, pull someone's leg; *inf.* kid, have someone on.

jester *noun* **1** *her uncle's a jester* joker, comic, comedian, humorist, wag, wit, quipster, prankster, hoaxer. **2** *the jesters in Shakespeare's plays* fool, court fool, clown, zany, buffoon, merry-andrew, harlequin.

jet *noun* **1** *a jet of water* stream, gush, spurt, spout, spray, rush, fountain, spring. **2** *put a jet on the hose* nozzle, spout, nose, sprinkler, sprinkler head, spray, rose, atomizer. **3** *travel in a jet | powered by a jet* jet airplane, jet plane, jetliner, jumbo jet; turbojet, jet engine, ramjet.

jet *verb* **1** *water jetted out of the hose* shoot, gush, spurt, spout, well, rush, spray, squirt, spew, stream, surge, flow, issue. **2** *jet off to Spain* fly, travel by plane, zoom.

jet *adjective* *a jet cat* jet-black, black, pitch-black, pitch, ebony, ink-black, inky, sooty, coal-black, sable, raven.

jettison *verb* **1** *jettison heavy goods from a ship* throw overboard, throw over the side, unload, eject. **2** *jettison unwanted clothes* throw out, throw away, discard, get rid of, toss out, scrap, dump.

Antonyms: KEEP; RETAIN.

jetty *noun* *tie the boat to the jetty* pier, wharf, quay, breakwater.

jewel *noun* **1** *a crown set with priceless jewels* gem, gemstone, precious stone, stone, bijou; *inf.* sparkler, rock. **2** *she wore a jewel on her dress* piece of jewelry, trinket, ornament. **3** *the jewel of his collection* choicest example, pearl, flower, pride, pride and joy, cream, crème de la crème, plum, boast. **4** *his wife is an absolute jewel* treasure, one in a million, saint, paragon; *inf.* one of a kind.

jeweler *noun* lapidary, gemologist.

jewelry *noun* jewels, gems, precious stones, treasure, regalia, trinkets, ornaments; costume jewelry. *See also table at* GEM.

Jezebel *noun* loose woman, wanton, scarlet woman, femme fatale, temptress, vamp, woman of easy virtue, whore, prostitute, harlot, hussy, trollop.

jib *verb* **jib at** **1** *jib at taking his money* balk at, recoil from, shrink from, stop short of, refuse (to). **2** *the horse jibbed at the fence* balk at, stop short at, retreat from, refuse.

jiffy *noun* moment, second, split second, minute, instant, flash, trice, twinkling of an eye; *inf.* two shakes of a lamb's tail.

jilt *verb* reject, cast aside, discard, throw over, drop, leave, forsake; *inf.* ditch, dump, give the brush-off, give the heave-ho, give the elbow.

jingle *verb* **1** *money jingling* clink, chink, jangle, rattle, clank. **2** *the bell jingled* tinkle, ding, go ding-dong, go ting-a-ling, ring, chime, tintinnabulate.

jingle *noun* **1** *the jingle of money* clink, chink. *See* JINGLE *verb* 1. **2** *the jingle of the bell* tinkle, tinkling, ding, ding-dong, ting-a-ling, ringing, tintinnabulation, chime. **3** *sing a little jingle* ditty, chorus, refrain, short song, limerick, melody, tune, catchy tune.

jingoism *noun* patriotism, excessive patriotism, blind patriotism, nationalism, chauvinism, flag-waving.

jinx *noun* curse, malediction, spell, plague, affliction; black magic, voodoo, evil eye, bad luck, evil fortune, hex.

jinx *verb* curse, cast a spell on, put a voodoo spell on, bewitch, hex.

jitter *verb* *she's jittering* be jittery, be nervous, be nervy, be uneasy, be anxious, be agitated, be on edge, be jumpy, tremble, shake, fidget. **the jitters** *noun* *it gives me the jitters* nervousness, nerves, fit of the nerves, uneasiness, anxiety, agitation, trembling, shaking, fidgeting, jumpiness; *inf.* the willies, the heebie-jeebies.

jittery *adjective* nervous, nervy, uneasy, anxious, agitated, trembling, quivering, shaking, shaky, fidgety, jumpy.

Antonyms: CALM; LAID-BACK.

job *noun* **1** *this job will take hours* work, piece of work, task, undertaking, chore, assignment, venture, enterprise, activity, business, affair. **2** *what is his job?* occupation, profession, trade, employment, vocation, calling, career, field of work, means of livelihood, métier, pursuit, position, post, situation, appointment. **3** *it is his job to open the mail* duty, task, chore, errand, responsibility, concern, function, role, charge, office, commission, capacity, contribution. **4** *we must get this job off to the distributors* work, product, batch, lot, consignment. **5** *it was a job just to get here* difficult task, problem, trouble, bother, hard time, trial, tribulation. **6** *the police arrested him for the job* crime, felony, burglary, break-in, theft.

jobless *adjective* unemployed, without paid employment, out of work, without work, workless, idle, inactive, unoccupied.

jockey *noun* rider, horse-race rider, horseman/horsewoman, equestrian.

jockey *verb* *jockey for position | jockey oneself into position | jockey him into lending money* maneuver, manipulate, engineer, elbow, insinuate, ingratiate, wheedle, coax, cajole; *inf.* finagle.

jocular *adjective* *a jocular mood | a jocular person* humorous, funny, witty, comic, comical, facetious, joking, jesting, playful, roguish, waggish, whimsical, droll, jocose, teasing, sportive, amusing, entertaining, diverting, hilarious; farcical, laughable.

Antonyms: SOLEMN; SERIOUS; EARNEST.

jocund *adjective* cheerful, cheery, merry, happy, gay, blithe, lighthearted, carefree, buoyant, jolly, jovial, in high spirits, smiling, laughing.

jog *verb* **1** *she jogs for exercise* go jogging, run slowly, dogtrot, jog trot, trot, canter, lope. **2** *they know they won't win but they are jogging* *along* trudge, plod, tramp, lumber, stump, pad. **3** *she jogged him in the ribs* nudge, prod, poke, push, elbow, tap. **4** *the sight jogged her memory* stimulate, activate, stir, arouse, prompt. **5** *his backpack jogged up and down on his back* bounce, bob, joggle, jiggle, jounce, jolt, jerk, shake.

join verb **1** *join the pieces of string/wood/metal together* fasten, attach, tie, bind, couple, connect, unite, link, splice, yoke, knit, glue, cement, fuse, weld, solder. **2** *the two clubs have joined together* join forces, amalgamate, merge, combine, unify, ally, league, federate. **3** *we joined them in their venture* join forces with, team up with, band together with, cooperate with, collaborate with, affiliate with. **4** *join the army | join a sports club | I do not want to join* enlist, sign up, enroll; become a member of, enlist in, sign up for, enroll in. **5** *join the search party* join in, participate in, take part in, partake in, contribute to, lend a hand with. **6** *his land joins ours* adjoin, conjoin, abut on, border, border on, touch, meet, verge on, reach to, extend to. **Antonyms:** DETACH; SEPARATE; LEAVE.

---

join
combine, conjoin, connect, consolidate, unite

It is possible for an individual to **join** an investment club, to **consolidate** his or her financial resources, and to **combine** a background in economics with a strong interest in retirement planning. All of these words mean to bring together or to attach two or more things. *Join* is the general term for bringing into contact or conjunction two discrete things (*join two pieces of wood; join one's friends in celebration*), while **conjoin** emphasizes both the separateness of the things that are joined and the unity that results (*her innate brilliance, conjoined with a genuine eagerness to learn, made her the ideal candidate for the job*). In contrast, to *combine* is to mix or mingle things together, often to the point where they merge with one another (*combine the ingredients for a cake*). *Consolidate* also implies a merger of distinct and separate elements, but the emphasis here is on achieving greater compactness, strength, or efficiency (*consolidate their furnishings and buy a new house together*). **Connect** implies a loose or obvious attachment of things to each other, but with each thing's identity or physical separateness preserved (*the two families were connected by blood; she connected the computer to the printer*). In a physical context, it differs from *join* in that it implies an intervening element that permits movement; in other words, the bones are *connected* by ligaments, but bricks are *joined* by mortar. When things are joined or combined so closely that they form a single thing, they are said to **unite** (*the parties were united in their support of the new law*).

joint noun **1** *reinforce the pipes at the joint* junction, juncture, intersection, nexus, knot, seam, coupling; coupler, dovetail joint. **2** *drinking in some joint* club, nightclub, bar. **3** *what a filthy joint* place, dwelling, house, establishment; *inf.* hole. **4** *smoke a joint* marijuana cigarette; *inf.* reefer.

joint adjective *a joint interest* common, shared, joined, mutual, combined, collective, cooperative, allied, united, concerted, consolidated.

jointly adverb *decide jointly* together, in combination, in conjunction, as one, mutually, in partnership, cooperatively, in cooperation, in league, in collusion; *inf.* in cahoots.

joke noun **1** *tell a joke* jest, witticism, quip, gag, yarn, pun; *inf.* wisecrack, crack, funny. **2** *play a joke on him* practical joke, prank, trick, hoax. **3** *we did it for a joke* fun, sport, play, whimsy. **4** *he is the joke of the class* laughingstock, butt, target, fair game.

joke verb **1** *they joked and jested all evening* tell jokes, crack jokes, jest, banter, quip; *inf.* wisecrack. **2** *she took them seriously but they were joking* fool, fool around, tease, pull someone's leg; *inf.* kid.

joker noun **1** *her uncle's a joker* comic, stand-up comic, comedian, humorist, funny man/woman, jester, wag, wit, quipster, prankster, practical joker, trickster; *inf.* kidder, wisecracker. **2** *who's that joker?* person, man/woman, fellow; *inf.* guy.

jolly adjective merry, gay, joyful, joyous, jovial, happy, glad, mirthful, gleeful, cheerful, cheery, carefree, buoyant, lively, bright, lighthearted, blithe, jocund, sprightly, elated, exuberant, exhilarated, jubilant, high-spirited, sportive, playful. **Antonyms:** MISERABLE; LUGUBRIOUS.

jolt verb **1** *people in the crowd jolting each other* bump against, knock against, bump into, bang into, collide with, jostle, push, shove, elbow, nudge, jar. **2** *the car jolted along* bump, bounce, jounce, start, jerk, lurch, jar. **3** *the accident jolted him* upset, disturb, perturb, shake, shake up, shock, stun, disconcert, discompose, disquiet, startle, surprise, astonish, amaze, stagger.

jolt noun **1** *one of the crowd gave him a jolt* bump, knock, bang, hit, push, shove, nudge, jar. **2** *the car moved in jolts* bump, bounce, jounce, shake, jerk, lurch, start, jar. **3** *her death came as a jolt* shock, bombshell, blow, upset, setback, surprise, bolt from the blue, thunderbolt.

jostle verb **1** *people jostling each other* bump against, knock against, bump into, bang into, collide with, jolt, push, shove, elbow. **2** *jostle her way through* push, thrust, shove, press, squeeze, elbow, force.

jot noun *not care a jot* iota, whit, little bit, bit, scrap, fraction, atom, grain, particle, morsel, mite, speck, trace, trifle, smidgen, *inf.* tinge, smidge, tad.

jot verb *jot down the details* write down, note, note down, make a note of, take down, put down, mark down, list, make a list of, register, record, chronicle.

journal *noun* **1** *keep a journal on his travels* diary, daybook, notebook, commonplace book, log, logbook, chronicle, record, register. **2** *publish medical journals* periodical, magazine, trade magazine, review, publication, professional organ. **3** *the proprietor of several national journals* newspaper, paper, daily newspaper, daily, weekly newspaper, weekly, gazette.

journalism *noun* **1** *have a job in journalism* the press, the newspaper business, the newspaper world, print media, the fourth estate; radio journalism, television journalism. **2** *their style of journalism* reporting, newspaper writing, feature writing, news coverage, broadcasting.

journalist *noun* reporter, newspaperman/newspaperwoman, newsman/newswoman, newshound, pressman/presswoman, feature writer, columnist, correspondent, contributor, commentator, reviewer, editor; broadcaster; *inf.* stringer. **journalists** the press.

journey *noun* *go on a long/short journey* trip, expedition, excursion, travels, tour, trek, voyage, cruise, safari, peregrination, roaming, roving, globe-trotting, odyssey, pilgrimage, outing, jaunt.

---

journey
excursion, expedition, jaunt,
pilgrimage, trip, voyage

While all of these nouns refer to a course of travel to a particular place, usually for a specific purpose, there is a big difference between a **jaunt** to the nearest beach and an **expedition** to the rainforest. While a **trip** may be either long or short, for business or pleasure, and taken at either a rushed or a leisurely pace (*a ski trip; a trip to Europe*), a **journey** suggests that a considerable amount of time and distance will be covered and that the travel will take place over land (*a journey into the Australian outback*). A long trip by water or through air or space is a **voyage** (*a voyage to the Galapagos Islands; a voyage to Mars*), while a short, casual trip for pleasure or recreation is a *jaunt* (*a jaunt to the local shopping mall*). **Excursion** also applies to a brief pleasure trip, usually no more than a day in length, that returns to the place where it began (*an afternoon excursion to the zoo*). Unlike the rest of these nouns, *expedition* and **pilgrimage** apply to *journeys* that are undertaken for a specific purpose. An *expedition* is usually made by an organized group or company (*a scientific expedition; an expedition to locate new sources of oil*), while a *pilgrimage* is a journey to a place that has religious or emotional significance (*the Muslims' annual pilgrimage to Mecca; a pilgrimage to the place where her father died*).

---

journey *verb* *journey to India* go, travel, go on a trip, go on an expedition, go on an excursion, tour, voyage, sail, cruise, fly, hike, trek, roam, rove, ramble, wander, meander, peregrinate, globe-trot.

jovial *adjective jovial person/comment/mood/gathering* jolly, jocular, jocose, jocund, happy, cheerful, cheery, glad, in good spirits, merry, gay, mirthful, blithe, buoyant, animated, convivial, sociable, cordial.
Antonyms: MISERABLE; MOROSE.

joy *noun* **1** *receive the gift with joy* delight, pleasure, gladness, enjoyment, gratification, happiness, rapture, glee, bliss, ecstasy, elation, rejoicing, exultation, jubilation, euphoria, ravishment, transport, felicity. **2** *their daughter is a joy* source of joy, treasure, prize, gem, jewel, pride and joy, delight. **3** *it is a joy to see you* pleasure, delight, treat, thrill. **4** *we had no joy from the bank* success, satisfaction, good fortune, luck, achievement.

joyful *adjective* **1** *joyful at the news* overjoyed, elated, beside oneself with joy, thrilled, delighted, pleased, gratified, happy, glad, blithe, gleeful, jubilant, ecstatic, exultant, euphoric, enraptured, in seventh heaven, on cloud nine; *inf.* tickled pink. **2** *we heard the joyful news* glad, happy, good, pleasing, cheering, gratifying, heartwarming. **3** *a joyful occasion/song* joyous, happy, cheerful, merry, gay, festive, celebratory.
Antonyms: DEPRESSED; MISERABLE; SAD.

joyless *adjective* **1** *a joyless existence/place* gloomy, dreary, drab, dismal, bleak, depressing, cheerless, grim, desolate, comfortless. **2** *joyless people* unhappy, sad, miserable, wretched, downcast, dejected, depressed, despondent, melancholy, mournful.

joyous *adjective* joyful, happy, cheerful, merry. *See* JOYFUL 1, 3.

jubilant *adjective* *his jubilant family welcomed him home* rejoicing, overjoyed, exultant, triumphant, elated, thrilled, euphoric, ecstatic, enraptured, rhapsodic, transported, exuberant, on top of the world, walking on air, in seventh heaven, on cloud nine; *inf.* tickled pink.
Antonyms: DOWNCAST; DESPONDENT.

jubilation *noun* exultation, triumph, elation, joy, euphoria, ecstasy, rapture, transport, exuberance.

jubilee *noun* celebration, commemoration, anniversary, holiday, feast day, festival, gala, carnival, fête, festivity, revelry.

judge *verb* **1** *judge the murder case* try, hear evidence in, sit in judgment on/of, give a verdict in, pronounce a verdict in, pass sentence in, pronounce sentence in, sentence in, decree. **2** *judge the contest* adjudicate, adjudge, umpire, referee, arbitrate, mediate. **3** *judge the entries | judge his conduct for yourself* assess, appraise, evaluate, weigh up, size up, gauge, examine, review, criticize, diagnose. **4** *judge the distance to be three miles* estimate, assess, reckon, guess, surmise; *inf.* guesstimate. **5** *I judge that he is* *not honest* | *judge him to be dishonest* consider, believe, think, form the opinion, deduce, gather, conclude.

judge *noun* **1** *the judge pronounced sentence* justice, reviewer, magistrate, his/her honor. **2** *the flower-show judge* appraiser, assessor, evaluator, critic, expert. **3** *the contest judge* adjudicator, umpire, referee, arbiter, arbitrator, mediator.

judgment *noun* **1** *he has no judgment* discernment, acumen, shrewdness, common sense, good sense, sense, perception, perspicacity, percipience, penetration, discrimination, wisdom, judiciousness, prudence, sagacity, understanding, intelligence, powers of reasoning. **2** *the judge gave his judgment* verdict, decision, adjudication, ruling, finding, opinion, conclusion, decree, sentence. **3** *in my judgment he is dishonest* opinion, view, belief, conviction, estimation, evaluation, assessment, appraisal. **4** *the Day of Judgment* | *Judgment Day* damnation, doom, fate, punishment, retribution, sentence.

judicial *adjective* **1** *judicial process/review* judiciary, juridical, judicatory, legal. **2** *a judicial mind* judgelike, impartial, unbiased, critical, analytical, discriminating, discerning, perceptive.

judicious *adjective a judicious course of action* wise, prudent, politic, sagacious, shrewd, astute, sensible, common-sense, sound, well-advised, well-considered, well-judged, considered, thoughtful, expedient, practical, discerning, discriminating, informed, intelligent, smart, clever, enlightened, logical, rational, discreet, careful, cautious, circumspect, diplomatic. **Antonyms:** INJUDICIOUS; FOOLISH; ILL-ADVISED.

jug *noun* pitcher, ewer, crock, carafe, decanter, jar, urn, vessel, receptacle, container.

juggle *verb juggle the figures* change around, alter, tamper with, falsify, fake, manipulate, maneuver, rig, massage; *inf.* fix, doctor, cook.

juice *noun* extract, sap, secretion, liquid, liquor, fluid, serum; fruit juice, meat juice.

juicy *adjective* **1** *juicy fruit* succulent, moist, lush, sappy, watery, wet, flowing. **2** *a juicy tale* racy, risqué, spicy, sensational, thrilling, fascinating, colorful, exciting, vivid. **Antonyms:** DRY; unexciting.

jumble *verb jumble up the toys* disarrange, disorganize, disorder, dishevel, muddle, confuse, tangle, shuffle, mix, mix up, mingle, put in disarray, make a shambles of, throw into chaos.

jumble *noun a jumble of toys* clutter, muddle, confusion, litter, mess, hodgepodge, mishmash, confused heap, miscellany, motley collection, mixture, medley, gallimaufry.

---

jumble
confusion, conglomeration, disarray, farrago, hodgepodge, mélange, muddle

Confusion is a very broad term, applying to any indiscriminate mixing or mingling that makes it difficult to distinguish individual elements or parts (*a confusion of languages*). The typical teenager's bedroom is usually a **jumble** of books, papers, clothing, CDs, and soda cans—the word suggests physical disorder and a mixture of dissimilar things. If the disorder exists on a figurative level, it is usually called a **hodgepodge** (*a hodgepodge of ideas, opinions, and quotations, with a few facts thrown in for good measure*). **Conglomeration** refers to a collection of dissimilar things, but with a suggestion that the collection is random or inappropriate (*a conglomeration of decorating styles*). A **mélange** can be a mixture of foods (*add peppers or zucchini to the mélange*), but it can also be used in a derogatory way (*an error-filled mélange of pseudoscience, religion, and fanciful ideas*). A **farrago** is an irrational or confused mixture of elements and is usually worse than a *conglomeration* (*a farrago of doubts, fears, hopes, and desires*), while a **muddle** is less serious and suggests confused thinking and lack of organization (*their bank records were in a complete muddle*). **Disarray** implies disarrangement and is most appropriately used when order or discipline has been lost (*his unexpected appearance threw the meeting into disarray*).

---

jumbo *adjective jumbo packet/shrimp* giant, gigantic, immense, huge, extra large, oversized.

jump *verb* **1** *jump around* spring, leap, bound, hop, bounce, skip, caper, gambol, frolic, frisk, cavort. **2** *jump over the rope* high-jump, leap over, vault, pole-vault, hurdle, clear, go over, sail over. **3** *she jumped when she heard the noise* start, flinch, jerk, recoil, twitch, quiver, shake, wince; *inf.* jump out of one's skin. **4** *jump (over) a piece of text* skip, miss, omit, leave out, cut out, pass over, overlook, disregard, ignore. **5** *jump the traffic lights* overshoot, drive through, disregard, ignore. **6** *prices jumped* rise, go up, leap up, increase, mount, escalate, surge, soar. **7** *retailers jumping prices* raise, up, increase, escalate, hike up, advance, boost, elevate, augment; *inf.* jack up. **8** *the cat jumped the mouse* pounce on, set upon, fall on, swoop down on, attack, assault; *inf.* mug. **jump at** *jump at the opportunity* grab, snatch, accept eagerly, go for enthusiastically, show enthusiasm for. **jump the gun** act prematurely, be too soon, act too soon, be previous, be ahead of time, anticipate.

jump *noun* **1** *with one jump* spring, leap, vault, bound, hop, bounce, skip. **2** *the jumps in the race* hurdle, fence, rail, hedge, obstacle, barrier, gate. **3** *a jump in the sequence* gap, break, hiatus, interruption, space, lacuna, breach, interval. **4** *she gave a jump at the sight* start, flinch, jerk, twitch, quiver, shake, wince. **5** *the car started with a jump* start, jolt, jerk, lurch, bump, jounce, jar. **6** *a jump in prices* rise, increase, upturn, upsurge, escalation, hike, boost, advance, elevation, augmentation.

jumpy adjective **1** *feeling jumpy waiting for news* nervous, edgy, on edge, jittery, agitated, fidgety, anxious, uneasy, restive, tense, alarmed, apprehensive, panicky. **2** *the jumpy movements of the car* jolting, fitful, convulsive, jerky, lurching, bumpy, jouncing, jarring.
Antonyms: CALM; LAID-BACK.

junction noun **1** *reinforcement at the junction of the pipes* joint, juncture, link, bond, connection, seam; joining, coupling, linking, welding, union. **2** *cars stop at the junction* crossroads, crossing, intersection, interchange.

juncture noun **1** *at this juncture we should vote* point, point in time, time, stage, period, critical point, crucial moment, moment of truth, turning point, crisis, crux, extremity. **2** *reinforcement at the juncture of the pipes* junction, joint, coupling, union. *See* JUNCTION 1.

jungle noun **1** *wild animals in the thick jungle* forest, tropical forest, rain forest, wilderness, wilds, the bush. **2** *a jungle of paperwork/facts* jumble, tangle, disarray, confusion, hodgepodge, heap, mass, mess, mishmash, gallimaufry. **law of the jungle** survival of the fittest, each/every man for himself, dog-eat-dog, cutthroat competition.

junior adjective **1** *the junior member* younger. **2** *the junior position* subordinate, lesser, lower, minor, secondary, inferior.

junk noun *clear up all this junk* rubbish, refuse, litter, scrap, waste, garbage, trash, debris, leavings, leftovers, remnants, castoffs, rejects, odds and ends, bric-à-brac.

junk verb *junk the unwanted things* throw out, throw away, discard, get rid of, dispose of, scrap; *inf.* dump, deep-six.

junket noun excursion, jaunt, trip, pleasure trip, tour, outing, day-trip.

jurisdiction noun **1** *under the governor's jurisdiction* authority, control, administration, command, leadership, power, dominion, sovereignty, rule, mastery, sway, say, influence. **2** *living in adjoining jurisdictions* territory, district, province, domain, principality, realm, area, zone. **3** *the jurisdiction of his authority* extent, range, scope, bounds, compass, sphere, area, field, orbit.

---

jurisdiction
authority, command, dominion, power, sovereignty, sway

The **authority** of our elected officials refers to their *power* (often conferred by rank or office) to give orders, require obedience, or make decisions. Their authority is normally limited by their **jurisdiction**, which is a legally predetermined division of a larger whole, within which someone has a right to rule or decide (*the matter was beyond his jurisdiction*). The president of the United States has more **power** than any other American official, which means that he has the ability to exert force or control over something. He does not, however, have the au-

thority to make laws on his own. As commander in chief, he does have **command** over the nation's armed forces, implying that he has the kind of authority that can enforce obedience. Back in the days when Great Britain had **dominion**, or supreme authority, over the American colonies, it was the king of England who held **sway** over this country's economic and political life—an old-fashioned word that stresses the sweeping scope of one's power. But his **sovereignty**, which emphasizes absolute or autonomous rule over something considered as a whole, was eventually challenged. The rest, as they say, is history.

---

just adjective **1** *a just judge* fair, fair-minded, equitable, evenhanded, impartial, unbiased, objective, neutral, disinterested, unprejudiced, open-minded. **2** *a just man* upright, honorable, upstanding, honest, righteous, ethical, moral, virtuous, principled, good, decent, straight, truthful, sincere. **3** *just criticism* valid, sound, well-founded, well-grounded, justified, justifiable, warrantable, defensible, reasonable. **4** *just deserts* deserved, well-deserved, merited, earned, rightful, due, proper, fitting, appropriate, apt, suitable, condign. **5** *the just heir* lawful, legitimate, legal, licit, rightful, genuine; *inf.* kosher. **6** *a just account of the events* true, truthful, accurate, correct, factual, exact, precise, close, faithful, strict.
Antonyms: UNJUST; BIASED; DISHONEST; undeserved.

just adverb **1** *I just saw him* only now, a moment ago, a second ago, a short time ago, recently, lately, not long ago. **2** *the house is just right* exactly, precisely, absolutely, completely, totally, entirely, perfectly. **3** *we just made it* only just, barely, scarcely, hardly, by a narrow margin, by a hair's breadth; *inf.* by the skin of one's teeth. **4** *she's just a child* only, merely, simply, but, nothing but, no more than. **5** *I just told him what I thought of him* really, indeed, truly, actually, certainly. **just about 1** *I've got just about every one of his books* all but, almost, nearly, practically, not quite. **2** *we lost it just about here* near, around, close to, in the vicinity of.

justice noun **1** *expect justice from the courts* justness, fairness, fair play, fair-mindedness, equitableness, equity, evenhandedness, impartiality, impartialness, lack of bias, objectivity, neutrality, disinterestedness, lack of prejudice, open-mindedness. *See* JUST adjective 1. **2** *a man of justice* justness, uprightness, integrity, honor, honesty, righteousness, ethics, morals, virtue, principle, decency, propriety. **3** *see the justice of his criticism* validity, justification, soundness, reasonableness. *See* JUST adjective 3. **4** *the justice of his heirdom* lawfulness, legitimacy, legality, licitness. **5** *demand justice* amends, recompense, redress, compensation, reparation, requital, retribution, penalty, punishment. **6** *the justice was passing sentence* judge, magistrate, sheriff.

Antonyms: INJUSTICE; BIAS.

justifiable *adjective* valid, sound, well-founded, lawful, legitimate, legal, tenable, right, defensible, supportable, sustainable, warrantable, vindicable, reasonable, within reason, sensible, acceptable, plausible.

Antonyms: UNJUSTIFIABLE; INDEFENSIBLE.

justification *noun* **1** *give as the justification of his behavior* grounds, reason, just cause, basis, explanation, rationalization, defense. *See* JUSTIFY 1. **2** *the justification of his crime* substantiation, proof, establishment, verification, legalization. *See* JUSTIFY 2. **3** *outline the justification of our fears* warranty, substantiation, reasonableness, confirmation. **4** *the justification of the accused* acquittal, absolution, exoneration, exculpation, pardon, excusing.

justify *verb* **1** *justify his behavior* give grounds for, give reasons for, show just cause for, explain, give an explanation for, rationalize, defend, stand up for, uphold, sustain. **2** *he had to justify his claim* substantiate, prove, establish, verify, certify, vindicate, legalize, legitimize. **3** *his conduct justified our worries* warrant, substantiate, bear out, show to be reasonable, prove to be right, confirm. **4** *the accused was finally justified* declare innocent, pronounce not guilty, acquit, clear, absolve, exculpate, exonerate, pardon, excuse.

justly *adverb* **1** *justly proud* justifiably, rightfully, with reason, with good reason. **2** *behave justly* fairly, equitably, impartially, without bias, objectively, without prejudice, disinterestedly. **3** *describe the incident justly* accurately, correctly, truthfully, faithfully.

jut *verb* stick out, project, protrude, poke out, bulge out, overhang, beetle.

juvenile *adjective* **1** *juvenile entrants* young, junior, minor. **2** *a juvenile attitude* childish, puerile, infantile, jejune, immature, inexperienced, callow, green, unsophisticated, naïve; *inf.* wet behind the ears.

Antonyms: ADULT; MATURE.

juxtapose *verb* place/set side by side, place parallel, put adjacent, compare.

K

kaleidoscopic *adjective* **1** *a kaleidoscopic pattern* many-colored, variegated, motley, rainbow-like, many-splendored, psychedelic. **2** *a kaleidoscopic scene* changeable, ever-changing, variable, varying, mutable, protean, ever-moving, fluid, mobile, unstable, unsteady, labile. **3** *a kaleidoscopic set of facts* complex, complicated, intricate, convoluted, confused, disordered, disarranged, jumbled, muddled, chaotic.

keel *noun* **1** *the keel of a boat* bottom, bottom side, underside. **2** *admiring the keels sailing on the sea* boat, ship, vessel, craft.

keel *verb* *the boat suddenly keeled* keel over, turn over, overturn, turn upside down, turn turtle, capsize, topple over, upset. **keel over 1** *the boat keeled over* turn over, overturn, capsize. **2** *a member of the crowd keeled over* faint, fall down in a faint, collapse, lose consciousness, pass out, black out.

keen *adjective* **1** *a keen edge to the blade* sharp, sharp-edged, sharpened, fine-edged, razor-sharp. **2** *a keen sense of smell* sharp, acute, discerning, perceptive, sensitive, discriminating. **3** *a keen mind* sharp, astute, quick-witted, sharp-witted, shrewd, perceptive, penetrating, perspicacious, clever, bright, smart, intelligent, brilliant, wise, canny, sagacious, sapient; *inf.* brainy. **4** *be the butt of her keen wit* acerbic, acid, biting, caustic, tart, pointed, mordant, trenchant, incisive, razorlike, razor-sharp, finely honed, cutting, stinging, scathing, sardonic, satirical. **5** *keen students* willing, eager, enthusiastic, avid, earnest, intent, diligent, assiduous, conscientious, zealous, fervent, fervid, impatient. **6** *keen to learn* eager, longing, yearning, impatient, itching; *inf.* rarin'. **keen on** *keen on learning/girls* fond of, devoted to, eager for, hungry for, thirsty for.

Antonyms: BLUNT; DULL; APATHETIC.

---

keen
acute, astute, penetrating, perspicacious, sharp, shrewd

A knife can be **sharp**, even **keen**, but it can't be **astute**. While *keen* and *sharp* mean having a fine point or edge, they also pertain to mental agility and perceptiveness. You might describe someone as having a *keen* mind, which suggests the ability to grapple with complex problems, or to observe details and see them as part of a larger pattern (*a keen appreciation of what victory would mean for the Democratic party*) or a *keen* wit, which suggests an incisive or stimulating sense of humor. Someone who is *sharp* has an alert and rational mind, but is not necessarily well grounded in a particular field and may in some cases be cunning or devious (*sharp enough to see how the situation might be turned to her advantage*). An **astute** mind, in contrast, is one that has a thorough and profound understanding of a given subject or field (*an astute understanding of the legal principles involved*). Like *sharp*, **shrewd** implies both practicality and cleverness, but with an undercurrent of self-interest (*a shrewd salesperson*). **Acute** is close in meaning to *keen*, but with more emphasis on sensitivity and the ability to make subtle distinctions (*an acute sense of smell*). While a keen mind might see only superficial details, a **penetrating** mind would focus on underlying causes (*a penetrating analysis of the plan's feasibility*). **Perspicacious** is the most formal of these terms, meaning both perceptive and discerning (*a perspicacious remark; perspicacious judgment*).

---

keenness *noun* **1** *the keenness of the blade* sharpness, razor-sharpness. *See* KEEN *adjective* 1. **2** *the keenness of her sense of smell* sharpness, acuteness, perceptiveness, sensitivity. *See* KEEN *adjective* 2. **3** *the keenness of his mind* sharpness, astuteness, quick-wittedness, perspicacity, sharp-wittedness, shrewdness, cleverness, brightness, intelligence, canniness. *See* KEEN *adjective* 3. **4** *the keenness of her wit* acerbity, acidity, causticity, tartness, mordancy, trenchancy, incisiveness, sardonicism, satire. *See* KEEN *adjective* 4. **5** *the keenness of the students* willingness, eagerness, enthusiasm, avidity, intentness, diligence, assiduity, zeal, fervor, devotion, impatience.

keep *verb* **1** *keep going* carry on, continue, maintain, persist, persevere. **2** *he kept the ring that she had given him* hold on to, keep hold of, retain, retain in one's possession; *inf.* hang on to. **3** *he keeps all his old newspapers* save up, accumulate, store, hoard, amass, pile up, collect, garner. **4** *keep the memory of her* preserve, conserve, keep alive, keep fresh. **5** *the druggist keeps (a supply of) insulin* sell, stock, have in stock, carry, deal in, trade in. **6** *he is responsible for keeping the estate* look after, keep in good order, tend, mind, maintain, keep up, manage, superintend. **7** *the boy keeps the sheep* tend, care for, look after, mind, guard, safeguard, protect, watch over, shield, shelter. **8** *he could not keep* *a family on his salary* provide for, support, maintain, sustain, subsidize, feed, nurture, provide board for. **9** *keep it from her* keep secret, keep hidden, hide, conceal, keep dark, withhold, hush, hush up, not breathe a word of, suppress, censor. **10** *keep one's promise/word* keep to, abide by, comply with, fulfill, carry out, effectuate, keep faith with, stand by, honor, obey, observe. **11** *keep the Sabbath* observe, hold, celebrate, commemorate, respect, ritualize, solemnize, ceremonialize. **12** *what kept you?* keep back, hold back, hold up, delay, detain, retard, hinder, obstruct, impede, hamper, constrain, check, block, hamstring, prevent. **13** *keep myself from falling* prevent, stop, restrain, check, halt. **14** *keep him from harm* keep safe, preserve, protect, guard, safeguard, shield, shelter. **keep at** *the teacher kept at us to work* keep after, badger, harp on at, nag, harass. **keep at it** *we'll finish in time if we keep at it* persist, persevere, be persistent, be pertinacious, carry on, keep going, continue, work away, see it through; *inf.* stick at/to it, stay the distance, hang on in there, slave away. **keep back 1** *what kept you back?* hold, hold up, hold back, delay, detain. *See* KEEP *verb* 12. **2** *keep back information* withhold, keep secret, keep hidden, hide, conceal, suppress. *See* KEEP *verb* 9. **keep off 1** *keep off his property* keep away from, stay away from, stay off, remain at a distance from, not go near, not approach, not stand on, not walk on, not touch, not trespass on. **2** *keep off the subject* avoid, steer clear of, not mention, not refer to, not allude to, abstain from, evade, dodge, shun, eschew. **3** *keep off chocolate/wine/cigarettes* refrain from, abstain from, give up, quit, renounce, turn aside from; *inf.* swear off. **4** *the rain kept off* stay away, not start, not begin. **keep on 1** *keep on going* go on, carry on, continue, persist, persevere. **2** *the boss decided to keep the man on* continue to employ, keep employing, retain the services of, not dismiss; *inf.* not sack. **keep to 1** *keep to his word* keep, abide by, comply with, stand by, honor. *See* KEEP *verb* 10. **2** *keep to the path/subject* not stray from, not wander from, stay with; *inf.* stick with. **keep under** *the poor were kept under by the authorities* suppress, oppress, tyrannize, tyrannize over, keep in submission, keep down, keep under one's thumb, quell, squelch. **keep up 1** *keep up the payments/progress* maintain, continue with, go on with, carry on with, keep going with. **2** *try to keep up in the race* keep pace, keep abreast, not fall behind, not lag behind. **keep up with 1** *keep up with the rest* keep pace with, keep abreast of, compete with, vie with, rival. **2** *keep up with latest developments* keep pace with, keep abreast of, keep informed about, learn about, retain an interest in. **3** *keep up with old friends* stay in touch with, keep in contact with, remain in correspondence with, be in commu-

nication with, keep alive one's friendship with, remain acquainted with.
Antonyms: give up (*see* GIVE); DISCARD; ABANDON.

keep *noun* **1** *pay for their/its keep* maintenance, support, board, room and board, subsistence, sustenance, food, nourishment, living, livelihood, upkeep. **2** *enemies storming the keep* donjon, dungeon, tower, stronghold, citadel, fortress, fort, castle. **for keeps** forever, for always, for good, once and for all.

keeper *noun* **1** *prisoners escaping their keeper* jailer, warden, guard, custodian, sentry; *inf.* screw. **2** *a museum/lighthouse keeper* curator, conservator, attendant, caretaker, steward, superintendent, overseer, administrator. **3** *his brother's keeper* guardian, escort, bodyguard, chaperon, chaperone, nursemaid, nurse.

keeping *noun* **1** *children/property in the keeping of the grandfather* keep, guardianship, protection, protectorship, trusteeship, trust, safekeeping, safeguard, care, charge, custody, possession, auspices, aegis, patronage. **2** *behavior in keeping with their beliefs* agreement, harmony, accordance, accord, concurrence, conformity, consistency, correspondence, congruity, compliance, proportion.

keepsake *noun* memento, souvenir, remembrance, reminder, token of remembrance, relic, favor.

keg *noun* *don't like keg beer* barrel, cask, vat, tun, butt, drum, hogshead, firkin, container, vessel.

kernel *noun* **1** *grown from a kernel* grain, seed, germ, stone, nut. **2** *the kernel of the problem* nub, nucleus, core, center, heart, marrow, pith, substance, essence, essential part, gist, quintessence; *inf.* nitty-gritty, nuts and bolts, brass tacks.

key *noun* **1** *key in the lock* latchkey, passkey, master key, skeleton key. **2** *the key to the problem* answer, solution, explanation, guide, clue, cue, pointer, gloss, interpretation, explication, annotation, clarification, exposition, translation. **3** *musical key* tone, pitch, timbre, tonality. **4** *a poem in a mournful key* mood, humor, vein, style, character, spirit.

keynote *noun* **1** *musical keynote* tonic, leading note. **2** *the keynote of the speech* theme, gist, salient point, substance, essence, pith, center, heart, core, nucleus, marrow.

keystone *noun* **1** *the keystone of the pillar* central stone, cornerstone, quoin. **2** *the keystone of the theory* principle, basis, foundation, linchpin.

kibosh *verb* **put the kibosh on** stop, bring to an end, put an end to, put a stop to, check, curb, nip in the bud, quell, quash, suppress, crack down on.

kick *verb* **1** *kick the ball* boot, put one's boot to, punt. **2** *the gun kicked* recoil, spring back. **3** *always kicking about something | stop your kicking* protest, resist, oppose, rebel, spurn, object, complain, grumble; *inf.* gripe, grouse, beef, bitch. **4** *kick the habit* give up, stop, abandon,

around the poor people abuse, mistreat, maltreat, push around. **2** *kick around ideas* discuss, talk over, debate, thrash out, argue the pros and cons of. **kick off** *kick off the proceedings* start, begin, commence, open, get under way, get going, start the ball rolling, initiate. **kick out** throw out, eject, expel, get rid of, force out, turn out, oust, evict, dismiss, discharge, give someone his marching orders, give someone his walking papers; *inf.* send packing, show the door to, sack, fire, give the boot to, boot out, give the ax to, throw out on one's ear, give the bum's rush to.

kick *noun* **1** *gave the ball a kick* boot, punt. **2** *she steals for kicks* thrill, excitement, stimulation, fun, pleasure, enjoyment, amusement, gratification; *inf.* buzz. **3** *the drink has quite a kick* strength, potency, tang, zip, alcoholic effect; *inf.* punch, zing. **4** *there's no kick left in the campaign* vigor, force, forcefulness, energy, vitality, vivacity, liveliness, verve, animation, enthusiasm, zest, zip; *inf.* punch, zing.

kickoff *noun* start, beginning, commencement, outset, opening, initiation.

kid *noun an adult and three kids* child, young one, young person, youngster, little one, baby, toddler, tot, infant, boy/girl, adolescent, juvenile, teenager, youth.

kid *verb* **1** *he was only kidding* tease, joke, jest, fool, fool around, pull someone's leg, be facetious. **2** *don't kid yourself* deceive, delude, fool, trick, cozen, gull, hoodwink, hoax, beguile, bamboozle.

kidnap *verb* abduct, seize, snatch, capture, hold for ransom, take as hostage.

kill *verb* **1** *he killed three people* take someone's life, slay, murder, do away with, do to death, slaughter, butcher, massacre, assassinate, liquidate, wipe out, destroy, erase, eradicate, exterminate, eliminate, dispatch, put to death, execute, hang, behead, guillotine, send to the electric chair; *inf.* bump off, do in, knock off, off, ice, fry, rub out. **2** *kill all his hopes* destroy, put an end to, ruin, extinguish, scotch, quell. **3** *kill time* pass, spend, expend, while away, fill up, occupy, use up. **4** *the walk will kill you* exhaust, overtire, tire out, fatigue, wear out, fag out, debilitate, enervate, prostrate, tax, overtax, strain. **5** *these shoes are killing me | my feet were killing me* hurt, cause pain, cause discomfort, be uncomfortable, be painful. **6** *kill the information in the file* cancel, delete, remove, erase, cut out, wipe away, eradicate, expunge, obliterate; *inf.* deep-six. **7** *kill the congressional bill* defeat, veto, vote down, reject, overrule. **8** *earplugs killing the noise* deaden, muffle, dull, dampen, smother, stifle. **9** *kill the bottle of wine* consume, drink up, drain, empty, finish; *inf.* knock back. **10** *his jokes kill me* overwhelm with laughter, amuse greatly, make someone laugh; *inf.* have someone rolling in the aisles, make someone crack up.

kill
assassinate, dispatch, execute, massacre, murder, slaughter, slay

When it comes to depriving someone or something of life, the options are seemingly endless. To **kill** is the most general term, meaning to cause the death of a person, animal, or plant, with no reference to the manner of killing, the agent, or the cause (*killed in a car accident*). Even inanimate things may be killed (*Congress killed the project when they vetoed the bill*). To **slay** is to kill deliberately and violently; it is used more often in written than in spoken English (*a novel about a presidential candidate who is slain by his opponent*). **Murder** implies a malicious and premeditated killing of one person by another (*a gruesome murder carried out by the son-in-law*), while **assassinate** implies that a politically important person has been murdered, often by someone hired to do the job (*assassinate the head of the guerilla forces*). Someone who is put to death by a legal or military process is said to be **executed** (*execute by lethal injection*), but if someone is killed primarily to get rid of him or her, the appropriate verb is **dispatch**, which also suggests speed or promptness (*after delivering the secret documents, the informer was dispatched*). While **slaughter** is usually associated with the killing of animals for food, it can also apply to a mass killing of humans (*the slaughter of innocent civilians provoked a worldwide outcry*). **Massacre** also refers to the brutal murder of large numbers of people, but it is used more specifically to indicate the wholesale destruction of a relatively defenseless group of people (*the massacre of Bethlehem's male children by King Herod*)

killer *noun* slayer, murderer, slaughterer, butcher, assassin, liquidator, destroyer, exterminator, executioner, gunman, homicide, patricide, matricide, infanticide, fratricide, sororicide, regicide; *inf.* hit man.

killing *noun* **1** *guilty of killing* slaying, murder, manslaughter, homicide, slaughter, butchery, massacre, bloodshed, carnage, liquidation, destruction, extermination, execution, patricide, matricide, infanticide. *See* KILL 1 *and* KILLER. **2** *make a killing on the stock market | she made a killing in sales* financial success, bonanza, fortune, windfall, gain, profit, piece of good luck, coup; *inf.* cleanup.

killing *adjective* **1** *a killing blow* deadly, fatal, lethal, mortal, death-dealing, murderous, homicidal. **2** *a killing walk/task* exhausting, tiring, fatiguing, debilitating, enervating, prostrating, taxing, punishing. **3** *a killing joke* hilarious, uproarious, rib-tickling, comical, amusing, laughable, absurd, ludicrous, outrageous; *inf.* screamingly funny.

killjoy noun spoilsport; inf. wet blanket, party pooper.

kilter noun condition, state, shape, fettle, trim, fitness, repair, order, working order.

kin noun no kin living in the area relatives, relations, family, connections, folks, people, kindred, kith and kin, kinfolk, kinsfolk, kinsmen/kinswomen.

kind adjective kind people/invitation kindhearted, kindly, generous, charitable, giving, benevolent, bounteous, magnanimous, bighearted, warmhearted, altruistic, philanthropic, humanitarian, humane, tender-hearted, softhearted, gentle, mild, lenient, merciful, clement, pitying, forbearing, patient, tolerant, sympathetic, compassionate, understanding, considerate, helpful, thoughtful, good, nice, decent, pleasant, benign, friendly, genial, congenial, amiable, amicable, cordial, courteous, gracious, good-natured, warm, affectionate, loving, indulgent, obliging, accommodating, neighborly.
Antonyms: UNKIND; MEAN; NASTY.

kind noun 1 different kinds of paper/creatures sort, type, variety, brand, class, category. 2 different kinds of plant genus, species, family, strain. 3 human kind race, species. 4 a difference in kind rather than degree nature, character, manner, aspect, disposition, humor, style, stamp, mold.

kindle verb 1 kindle a fire light, set alight, set on fire, set fire to, ignite, start, torch. 2 kindle interest stimulate, rouse, arouse, excite, stir, awaken, inspire, inflame, incite, induce, provoke, actuate, activate, touch off.

kindly adjective 1 a kindly old lady | a kindly expression on her face kind, kindhearted, generous, charitable, magnanimous, warmhearted, humane, gentle, sympathetic, compassionate, understanding, considerate, helpful, thoughtful, good, nice, decent, polite, friendly, genial, pleasant, amiable, amicable, cordial. 2 a kindly climate pleasant, agreeable, mild, gentle, benign, favorable, beneficial, advantageous.
Antonyms: UNKIND; MEAN; DISAGREEABLE.

kindness noun 1 the kindness of the people kindheartedness, kindliness, generosity, charitableness, charity, good will, benevolence, magnanimity, hospitality, philanthropy, warmheartedness, altruism, humanitarianism, humaneness, tender-heartedness, gentleness, mildness, leniency, clemency, patience, tolerance, sympathy, compassion, fellow feeling, understanding, considerateness, consideration, helpfulness, thoughtfulness, goodness, niceness, decency, pleasantness, friendliness, geniality, congeniality, amiability, cordiality, graciousness, warmth, affection, lovingness, love, indulgence, neighborliness. 2 do the neighbors a kindness kind act, good deed, good turn, favor, help, service, aid.

kindred noun kin, relatives, relations, family, people. See KIN.

kindred adjective 1 kindred members of the wedding party related, connected, of the same blood, of the same family, consanguineous, cognate. 2 kindred spirits enjoying the same things like, similar, resembling, corresponding, matching, congenial, allied.

king noun 1 crowned king of Sweden monarch, sovereign, ruler, crowned head, majesty, royal personage, emperor, sultan, overlord, prince. 2 king of jazz leading light, luminary, star, superstar, kingpin; inf. big wheel, mogul.

kingdom noun 1 the ruler's kingdom realm, empire, domain, country, land, nation, state, province, territory; monarchy, sovereignty. 2 the plant kingdom division, grouping, group, classification, class, category, family, genus, kind. 3 the teacher's kingdom was the classroom sphere/field of influence, area of power, dominion, province, territory.

kink noun 1 a kink in the rope twist, bend, coil, corkscrew, curl, twirl, knot, tangle, entanglement. 2 a kink in one's hair curl, wave, crimp, frizz, crinkle. 3 a kink in the neck crick, spasm, twinge, tweak, stab of pain. 4 a few kinks in the plan flaw, defect, imperfection, hitch, snag, difficulty, complication. 5 a person full of kinks quirk, whim, whimsy, caprice, vagary, eccentricity, foible, idiosyncrasy, fetish, deviation.

kinky adjective 1 a kinky rope twisted, bent, coiled, curled. See KINK 1. 2 kinky hair curly, wavy, crimped, frizzy, frizzed, crinkled. 3 kinky ideas quirky, peculiar, odd, strange, queer, bizarre, eccentric, idiosyncratic, weird, outlandish, unconventional, unorthodox, whimsical, capricious, fanciful; inf. way-out, far-out. 4 kinky sexual behavior perverted, warped, deviant, deviative, unnatural, abnormal, depraved, degenerate, lascivious, licentious, lewd, sadistic, masochistic.

kinfolk, kinsfolk noun kin, relatives, relations, family. See KIN.

kinship noun 1 kinship was thought more of than friendship blood relationship, relationship, blood ties, family ties, consanguinity, common ancestry, common lineage, kindred. 2 a kinship between the friends | kinship between their interests affinity, similarity, likeness, correspondence, concordance, alliance, association, equivalence, parallelism, symmetry.

kiosk noun booth, stand, newsstand, stall.

kismet noun destiny, fate, fortune, providence, portion, lot, one's lot in life, what is to come, what is written in the stars, the writing on the wall, God's will, predestination, preordination, predetermination, doom.

kiss verb 1 friends/lovers kissing | she kissed him | he kissed her hand salute/greet with the lips, brush the lips against, blow a kiss to, osculate; inf. peck, give a peck to, smooch, buss, neck. 2 the branches kissed the lake caress, brush lightly against, brush against, touch gently, graze, glance off.

kiss *noun* **1** *exchange kisses* salutations/greetings with the lips, hand kiss, osculation; *inf.* peck, buss, smooch. **2** *the kiss of the flowers against her cheeks* light/gentle touch, brush, graze, glance.

kit *noun* **1** *a plumber's kit | bicycle repair kit* equipment, apparatus, set of tools, tools, implements, instruments, utensils, gear, tackle, supplies, paraphernalia, accouterments, effects, stuff, trappings, appurtenances; *inf.* things, the necessary. **2** *build furniture from a kit* set of parts, set of components; do-it-yourself kit.

kitchen *noun* kitchenette, galley, cookhouse, scullery.

kittenish *adjective* playful, frolicsome, frisky, cute, coquettish, coy.

knack *noun* talent, aptitude, aptness, gift, flair, bent, forte, ability, capability, capacity, expertise, expertness, skill, skillfulness, genius, facility, propensity, dexterity, adroitness, readiness, quickness, ingenuity, proficiency, competence, handiness.
Antonyms: INABILITY; blind spot.

knave *noun* scoundrel, blackguard, villain, rogue, reprobate, miscreant, cheat, swindler, rascal, wrongdoer, evildoer, wretch, louse, cur, devil, dastard; *inf.* bounder.

knavery *noun* knavishness, villainy, baseness, roguery, unscrupulousness, cheating, swindling, duplicity, double-dealing, chicanery, deceit, deception, fraud, trickery, rascality, wrongdoing, evildoing, corruption.

knead *verb knead the dough | the masseur kneaded his body* work, manipulate, press, squeeze, massage, rub, form, shape.

kneel *verb knelt before the altar* get down on one's knees, fall to one's knees, genuflect, bow, bow down, stoop, make obeisance, kowtow.

knell *noun* **1** *hear the knell of the church bells* toll, tolling, ring, ringing, peal, chime, sound, resounding, death knell. **2** *the knell of their way of life* death knell, end, beginning of the end, presage of the end.

knell *verb* **1** *funeral bells knelling* toll, ring, peal, chime, sound, resound. **2** *the drawing of the curtains knelled the end of the day* herald, announce, proclaim, augur.

knickknack *noun* showy ornament, piece of bric-à-brac, trifle, trinket, bauble, gewgaw, gimcrack, bagatelle, bibelot, plaything.

knife *noun* blade, cutting tool, dagger, dirk; machete, sword; stiletto, scalpel; *Trademark* Swiss Army knife; cleaver; paring knife, table knife, steak knife, penknife, pocket knife, bowie knife, jackknife, switchblade.

knife *verb* stab, pierce, run through, impale, bayonet, transfix, cut, slash, lacerate, wound.

knight *noun knights went off to the Crusades* horseman, equestrian, cavalryman, gallant, protector, knight errant, Sir Lancelot, Sir Galahad, lord; dragon slayer.

knit *verb* **1** *knit wool into a sweater* loop, weave, interweave, crochet. *See also table at* WEAVE. **2** *knit one's brows* wrinkle, crease, furrow, gather, draw in, contract. **3** *the tragedy knitted the community together* join, link, bind, unite, draw (together), ally. **4** *the wound is knitting* draw together, heal, mend, become whole.

knob *noun* **1** *turn the knob on the door/machine* doorknob, handle, door handle, switch, on/off switch. **2** *iron knobs on the saddle* stud, boss, protuberance, knop. **3** *knobs on the tree* knot, knar, knur, knurl, gnarl, excrescence, protuberance. **4** *knobs on the horse's leg* bump, bulge, swelling, lump, knot, node, nodule, pustule, growth, tumor, protuberance, tumescence.

knock *verb* **1** *knock on/at the door* tap, rap, bang, pound, hammer. **2** *knock his head on the low doorframe* strike, hit, slap, smack, box, punch, cuff, buffet, thump, thwack, batter, pummel; *inf.* clip, clout, wallop. **3** *knock the play* criticize, find fault with, take apart, take to pieces, pick holes in, run down, shoot down, carp at, cavil at, deprecate, belittle, disparage, minimize, censure, condemn; *inf.* slam, lambaste, pan. **knock about/around 1** *fighters knocking each other around | knocking the furniture about* strike, hit, beat, beat up, batter, maul, punch, mistreat, maltreat, ill-treat, abuse, manhandle, hurt, cause injury to, injure, bruise, wound, damage. **2** *knock about the countryside for a while* travel, wander, roam, ramble, rove, range, saunter through/about, stroll, gallivant, traipse through/about, gad about. **knock down 1** *knock down the buildings* demolish, pull down, level, raze. **2** *knock down the trees* fell, cut down, hew. **3** *knock down his opponent* knock to the floor, floor, throw to the ground. **4** *knock down the prices/goods* lower, bring down, decrease, reduce, slash. **knock into 1** *knock into his car* knock against, bang into, bump into, collide with, run into, crash into, crash against, smash into, dash against, jolt. **2** *I knocked into her yesterday* run into, meet by chance, come across, encounter, chance upon, happen upon, stumble upon; *inf.* bump into. **knock off 1** *they knock off at 5 o'clock* stop work, finish work, finish working, finish the working day, close shop, shut down; *inf.* call it a day. **2** *knock off smoking | knock it off!* stop, finish, give up, terminate, conclude, bring to an end. **3** *knock off his rival* kill, slay, murder, assassinate, eliminate, do away with, get rid of, dispose of, finish off; *inf.* do in, bump off, off, ice, fry, rub out. **4** *knock off goods from the warehouse* steal, rob, thieve, filch, pilfer, purloin; *inf.* pinch, lift. **knock out 1** *knock him out with the blow* render unconscious, floor, prostrate; *inf.* KO, kayo, knock cold, put out cold. **2** *knock out his opponent in the first round* eliminate, defeat, beat, vanquish, overthrow. **3** *the storm knocked out the electrical supply* make inoperative, put out of order, destroy, damage.

4 *walking that far knocked her out* exhaust, wear out, tire out, tire, overtire, fatigue, weary, enervate, fag out, debilitate, make ill; *inf.* do in, poop out. **5** *they were knocked out by her performance* overwhelm, dazzle, amaze, astound, impress, affect deeply; *inf.* bowl over. **knock together** *knock together some food/shelves* put together quickly, prepare hastily, build rapidly, improvise, devise, jerry-build. **knock up** make pregnant, impregnate, inseminate.

knock *noun* **1** *a knock at the door* tap, rap, rat-tat, rat-tat-tat, bang. **2** *a knock on the head* slap, smack, blow, punch, cuff, buffet, thump, thwack; *inf.* clip, clout, wallop. **3** *the knock damaged the car* collision, crash, bang, bump, smash, thud, jolt. **4** *the knocks of the reviewers* criticism, strictures, faultfinding, carping, caviling, deprecation, disparagement, censure, condemnation; *inf.* slamming, lambasting, panning.

knockout *noun* **1** *win the boxing match by a knockout* finishing blow, *coup de grâce*; *inf.* KO, kayo. **2** *take part in a knockout (round)* elimination contest/competition. **3** *her outfit/performance was a knockout* sensation, hit, smash hit, success, triumph, winner, attraction, coup, master stroke.

knoll *noun* hillock, hill, hummock, elevation, mound, hump, knob.

knot *noun* **1** *a knot in the string/tie* loop, twist, bend, intertwinement, interlacement, ligature, joint. **2** *a knot in the wood* lump, knob, node, nodule, protuberance, knur, knurl, knar, gnarl. **3** *a knot of trees* clump, cluster. **4** *a knot of people* group, cluster, bunch, band, circle, ring, gathering, company, throng, crowd, flock, gang, assemblage, mob, pack.

knot *verb* *knot the rope to the pier* tie, loop, bind, secure, tether, lash, leash.

knotty *adjective* **1** *a knotty problem* difficult, complicated, intricate, complex, Byzantine, thorny, perplexing, baffling, mystifying, obscure, unfathomable. **2** *a knotty piece of wood* knotted, gnarled, knurled, lumpy, bumpy, nodose, nodular, rough, coarse. **3** *a knotty piece of thread* knotted, tangled, entangled, twisted, raveled.

know *verb* **1** *know what they are saying* be aware of, notice, perceive, realize, be conscious of, be cognizant of, sense, recognize; *inf.* latch on to. **2** *know the rules* have knowledge of, understand, comprehend, apprehend, be conversant with, be familiar with, be acquainted with, have memorized, have learned by heart. **3** *have known tragedy* be familiar with, be acquainted with, experience, undergo, go through. **4** *do you know her husband?* | *get to know one's neighbors* have met, be acquainted with, have dealings with, associate with, be friends with, socialize with, fraternize with, be intimate with, be close to, be on good terms

with; *inf.* be thick with. **5** *know one brand from another* distinguish, differentiate, tell, identify, make out, discern.
Antonyms: IGNORE; MISUNDERSTAND.

know-how *noun* knowledge, *savoir faire*, expertise, expertness, skill, skillfulness, proficiency, adeptness, dexterity, adroitness, aptitude, ability, capability, competence, faculty, knack, talent, gift, flair, bent, ingenuity.
Antonyms: INABILITY; IGNORANCE.

knowing *adjective* **1** *give a knowing look* astute, shrewd, perceptive, meaningful, well-informed, significant, eloquent, expressive. **2** *a knowing child* aware, astute, shrewd, perceptive, sophisticated, worldly, worldly-wise. **3** *a knowing infringement of rules* conscious, intentional, intended, deliberate, willful, purposeful, calculated, on purpose, by design.
Antonyms: INGENUOUS; INNOCENT; ACCIDENTAL.

knowingly *adverb* *would not knowingly hurt them* consciously, willingly, intentionally, deliberately, willfully, purposefully, on purpose, by design, calculatedly.

knowledge *noun* **1** *be taught by people of knowledge* learning, erudition, scholarship, letters, education, enlightenment, wisdom. **2** *his knowledge of the subject* understanding, grasp, comprehension, apprehension, cognition, adeptness, skill, expertise, proficiency, know-how, *savoir faire*. **3** *his knowledge of the area* acquaintanceship, familiarity, conversance. **4** *where do you acquire the knowledge?* information, facts, intelligence, data; news, reports, rumors.
Antonyms: IGNORANCE; ILLITERACY.

---

knowledge
erudition, information, learning, pedantry, scholarship, wisdom

How much do you know? **Knowledge** applies to any body of facts gathered by study, observation, or experience, and to the ideas inferred from these facts (*an in-depth knowledge of particle physics; first-hand knowledge about the company*). **Information** may be no more than a collection of data or facts (*information about vacation resorts*) gathered through observation, reading, or hearsay, with no guarantee of their validity (*false information that led to the arrest*). **Scholarship** emphasizes academic knowledge or accomplishment (*a special award for scholarship*), while **learning** is knowledge gained not only by study in schools and universities but by individual research and investigation (*a man of education and learning*), which puts it on a somewhat higher plane. **Erudition** is on a higher plane still, implying bookish knowledge that is beyond the average person's comprehension (*exhibit extraordinary erudition in a doctoral dissertation*). **Pedantry**, on the other hand, is a negative term for a slavish attention to obscure facts or details or an undue display of learning (*the pedantry of modern literary criti-*

cism). You can have extensive *knowledge* of a subject and even exhibit *erudition*, however, without attaining **wisdom**, the superior judgment and understanding that is based on both knowledge and experience.

---

knowledgeable *adjective knowledgeable people* well-informed, informed, educated, learned, erudite, scholarly, well-read, cultured, cultivated, enlightened. **knowledgeable about** *knowledgeable about the workings of the machine* having a knowledge of, acquainted with, familiar with, experienced in, expert in, conversant with, having an understanding of.

known *adjective a known fact* recognized, ac-

knowledged, admitted, declared, proclaimed, avowed, confessed, published, revealed.
Antonyms: UNKNOWN; SECRET.

kowtow *verb* **kowtow to** **1** *slaves kowtowing to their masters* bow to, kneel to, genuflect to, prostrate oneself to, throw oneself at the feet of, humble oneself to. **2** *he's always kowtowing to management* grovel to, fawn to, pay court to, curry favor with, bow and scrape to, toady to; *inf.* suck up to, lick the boots of.

kudos *noun* prestige, glory, acclaim, acclamation, praise, extolment, approbation, tribute, honor.
Antonym: infamy.

L

label noun **1** *put a label on the luggage/goods* identification tag, ID tag, tag, ticket, tab, sticker, marker, docket. **2** *his friends gave him the label "lefty"* epithet, name, nickname, title, sobriquet, designation, denomination, description, characterization. **3** *goods sold under the label of a famous department store* brand, brand name, trade name, trademark, proprietary name, logo.

label verb **1** *label the specimens* attach labels to, tag, tab, ticket, stamp, mark, put stickers on, docket. **2** *label him a liar* describe, designate, identify, classify, categorize, brand, call, name, term, dub.

labor noun **1** *paid well for his labor* work, employment, job, toil, exertion, effort, industry, industriousness, hard work, hard labor, travail, drudgery, sweat of one's brow, menial work; *inf.* grind, sweat. **2** *the labors of Hercules* task, job, chore, undertaking, commission, assignment, charge, venture. **3** *a lack of available labor* potential employees, employees, workers, workmen, workforce, working people, hands, laborers. **4** *in labor for many hours having the child* childbirth, birth, parturition, delivery, birth contractions, contractions, labor pains, labor pangs, travail.

---

labor
drudgery, grind, toil, travail, work

Most people have to **work** for a living, meaning that they have to exert themselves mentally or physically in return for a paycheck. But *work* is not always performed by humans (*a machine that works like a charm*). **Labor** is not only human but usually physical work (*the labor required to build a stone wall*), although it can also apply to intellectual work of unusual difficulty (*the labor involved in writing a symphony*). Anyone who has been forced to perform **drudgery** knows that it is the most unpleasant, uninspiring, and monotonous kind of labor (*a forklift that eliminates the drudgery of stacking boxes; the drudgery of compiling a phone book*). A **grind** is even more intense and unrelenting than drudgery, emphasizing work that is performed under pressure in a dehumanizing way (*the daily grind of classroom teaching*). **Toil** suggests labor that is prolonged and very tiring (*farmers who toil endlessly in the fields*), but not necessarily physical (*mothers who toil to teach their children manners*). Those who **travail** endure pain, anguish, or

suffering (*his hours of travail ended in heartbreak*).

labor verb **1** *labor for little reward* work hard, work away, toil, slave away, drudge, grub away, plod on/away, grind/sweat away, struggle, strive, drudge away, exert oneself, overwork, travail, work like a slave, work one's fingers to the bone, work like a Trojan; *inf.* kill oneself, plug away. **2** *labor the point* belabor, overemphasize, lay too much emphasis on, overdo, strain, overelaborate, dwell on, expound on, expand. **3** *labor to finish on time/labor for victory* strive, struggle, endeavor, work, make every effort, do one's best, do one's utmost. **4** *ships laboring on heavy seas* roll, pitch, heave, toss, turn. **labor under** *labor under universal disapproval | laboring under a delusion* suffer from, be a victim of, be burdened by, be overburdened by, be disadvantaged by.

labored adjective **1** *labored breathing* difficult, strained, forced, heavy, awkward. **2** *a labored style of writing* contrived, affected, studied, stiff, strained, stilted, forced, unnatural, artificial, overdone, overworked, heavy, ponderous, ornate, elaborate, overelaborate, intricate, convoluted, complex, laborious.
Antonyms: EASY; NATURAL.

laborer noun worker, workman, working man/woman, hand, manual worker, unskilled worker, blue-collar worker, drudge, menial.

laborious adjective **1** *a laborious task* hard, heavy, difficult, arduous, strenuous, fatiguing, tiring, wearying, wearisome, tedious. **2** *laborious students* painstaking, careful, meticulous, diligent, assiduous, industrious, hardworking, scrupulous, persevering, pertinacious, zealous. **3** *the laborious style of the writer* labored, strained, forced. *See* LABORED 2.
Antonyms: EASY; SIMPLE; EFFORTLESS; NATURAL.

labyrinth noun **1** *a labyrinth of hedges | the office is a labyrinth of passages* maze, warren, network, circuitous course, winding, coil, convolution, twisting and turning, meander, meandering, entanglement. **2** *the plot of the book was a labyrinth* entanglement, tangle, jungle, snarl, intricacy, confusion, perplexity, complication, puzzle, riddle, enigma, problem.

labyrinthine adjective **1** *labyrinthine paths* mazelike, meandering, winding, wandering, twisting, circuitous, tangled. **2** *labyrinthine plots* intricate, complicated, complex, involved, tortuous, convoluted, tangled, entangled, confusing, puzzling, perplexing, mystifying, bewildering, baffling.

lace noun **1** *a covering made of lace* filigree, meshwork, openwork, tatting, netting. **2** *fasten the shoes/bodice with laces* shoelace, bootlace, lacing, string, cord, thong, twine, tie.

lace verb **1** *lace the shoes/bodice* lace up, do up, fasten, secure, close, bind, tie, twine, thread, string. **2** *lace their fingers* interweave, twine, intertwine. **3** *lace her into a corset* compress, confine, constrict, squeeze. **4** *the sunset lacing the sky with color* streak, stripe, striate, band. **5** *lace the coffee with brandy* mix, blend, flavor, fortify, strengthen, stiffen; *inf.* spike. **lace into 1** *lace into the enemy* set upon, fall upon, attack, assault, assail, beat, strike, thrash, thresh, tear into; *inf.* sail into, belt. **2** *laced into me for being late* scold, chide, berate, upbraid, castigate, condemn, harangue, rant at, rave at; *inf.* lambaste.

lacerate verb **1** *lacerate her hand on barbed wire* tear, gash, slash, cut, cut open, rip, rend, mangle, mutilate, hurt, wound, injure, maim. **2** *the argument lacerated her feelings* hurt, wound, distress, harrow, torture, torment, afflict, crucify.

laceration noun **1** *the laceration of her hand* tearing, gashing, slashing. *See* LACERATE 1. **2** *the laceration on her hand* tear, gash, slash, cut, rip, rent, mutilation, wound, injury.

lachrymose adjective tearful, weeping, crying, sobbing, with tears in the eyes, close to tears, on the verge of tears, sad, mournful, woeful, lugubrious, dolorous; *inf.* weepy.

lack noun *a lack of food/talent* absence, want, need, deprivation, deficiency, privation, dearth, insufficiency, shortage, shortness, scarcity, scarceness, paucity.
Antonyms: ABUNDANCE; EXCESS; sufficiency.

---

lack
absence, dearth, privation, shortage, want

To suffer from a **lack** of food means to be partially or totally without it; to be in **want** of food also implies a lack, but with an emphasis on the essential or desirable nature of what is lacking; for example, you may experience a complete *lack* of pain following surgery, but you would be in *want* of medication if pain were suddenly to occur. **Absence**, on the other hand, refers to the complete non-existence of something or someone. A *lack* of dairy products in your diet implies that you're not getting enough; an *absence* of dairy products implies that you're not getting any at all. If the scarcity or lack of something makes it costly, or if something is in distressingly low supply, the correct word is **dearth** (*a dearth of water in the desert; a dearth of nylon stockings during World War II*). A **shortage** of something is a partial insufficiency of an established, required, or accustomed amount (*a shortage of fresh oranges after the late-season frost*), while **privation** is the negative state or absence of a corresponding

positive (*they suffered from hunger, cold, and other privations*).

---

lack verb *they lack food* be lacking, be without, have need of, need, stand in need of, require, want, feel the want of, be short of, be deficient in, miss.

lackadaisical adjective apathetic, listless, languid, languorous, lethargic, limp, sluggish, enervated, spiritless, unanimated, indifferent, halfhearted, lukewarm, uninterested, unenthusiastic, idle, lazy, indolent, inert.
Antonyms: ENTHUSIASTIC; EXCITED.

lackey noun toady, sycophant, flatterer, fawner, flunky, minion, doormat, stooge, hanger-on, parasite, camp follower, tool, puppet, instrument, pawn; *inf.* yes-man, bootlicker.

lackluster adjective **1** *lackluster prose* bland, insipid, vapid, dull, flat, dry, prosaic, run-of-the-mill, commonplace, matter-of-fact, unimaginative, uninspired, uninteresting, boring, tedious, wearisome. **2** *lackluster people* dull, uninteresting, boring, unimaginative, apathetic, spiritless, unanimated, dull-witted, vacuous.

laconic adjective **1** *a laconic reply* brief, concise, terse, succinct, short, economical, elliptical, crisp, pithy, to the point, incisive, abrupt, blunt, curt. **2** *a laconic person* of few words, untalkative, uncommunicative, reticent, reserved, taciturn, quiet, silent.
Antonyms: VERBOSE; GARRULOUS; LONG-WINDED.

lad noun boy, schoolboy, youth, juvenile, youngster, stripling, young man; *inf.* kid, little shaver.

ladder noun **1** *climb the ladder to the tree house* stepladder, set of steps; rope ladder, Jacob's ladder. **2** *the social/career ladder* hierarchy, scale, set of stages, stratification, pecking order.

laden adjective *laden with packages/worries* loaded, burdened, heavily laden, weighed down, weighted, fully charged, encumbered, hampered, oppressed, taxed.

ladle noun *a soup ladle* spoon, scoop, dipper.

ladle verb *ladle the soup/water* spoon out, scoop out, dish up/out, bail out.

lady noun **1** *give that lady your seat* woman, female; young woman, old woman. **2** *the lady and her servants* noblewoman, gentlewoman, duchess, countess, peeress, viscountess, baroness.

ladylike adjective genteel, refined, well-bred, cultivated, polished, decorous, proper, correct, respectable, well-mannered, courteous, polite, civil, gracious.

lag verb **1** *stop lagging and keep up* loiter, linger, dally, straggle, dawdle, hang back, delay, move slowly, drag one's feet; *inf.* dilly-dally. **2** *their efforts were lagging* flag, wane, ebb, fall off, diminish, decrease, ease up, let up, slacken, abate, fail, falter, grow faint. **lag behind** *lag* *behind in the race* fall behind, fall back, trail, not keep pace, bring up the rear.

laggard *noun* loiterer, lingerer, dawdler, straggler, sluggard, snail, delayer, idler, slowpoke, loafer, lounger; *inf.* lazybones.

lagoon *noun* pool, pond, lake, reservoir, tarn, bayou.

laid-back *adjective* relaxed, at ease, easy, leisurely, unhurried, casual, easygoing, free and easy, informal, nonchalant, unexcitable, imperturbable; *inf.* unflappable.
Antonyms: NERVOUS; TENSE; EDGY.

laid up *adjective* bedridden, sick/ill in bed, housebound, immobilized, incapacitated, disabled, ill, sick, ailing, on the sick list, out of action.

lair *noun* **1** *the animal's lair* den, hole, earth, covert, burrow, nest, tunnel, dugout, hollow, cave, haunt. **2** *retreat to his lair in the house* retreat, hideaway, refuge, sanctuary, sanctum, sanctum sanctorum, study, den; *inf.* hide-out.

laissez-faire *noun* free enterprise, private enterprise, individualism, free trade, nonintervention, noninterference, noninvolvement, indifference.

laissez-faire *adjective* noninterventional, noninterfering, nonrestrictive, uninvolved, indifferent, lax, loose, permissive, live-and-let-live.

lake *noun* pond, tarn, pool, reservoir, lagoon, bayou.

lambaste *verb* **1** *cruel masters lambasting the slaves* beat, thrash, flog, lash, drub, strike, thump, thwack, batter, hammer, pummel; *inf.* wallop, clout, paste, lace into. **2** *lambasted us for being late* scold, reprimand, rebuke, chide, reprove, admonish, berate, upbraid, rail at, rant at; *inf.* lace into.

lame *adjective* **1** *a lame man/leg* limping, hobbling, halting, crippled, game, disabled, incapacitated, defective. **2** *a lame excuse* weak, feeble, thin, flimsy, unconvincing, unsatisfactory, inadequate, insufficient, deficient, defective, ineffectual.

lament *verb* **1** *widows lamenting* mourn, grieve, sorrow, wail, moan, groan, weep, cry, sob, complain, keen, ululate, howl, beat one's breast. **2** *lamenting the lack of sports facilities* complain about, bemoan, bewail, deplore.

lament *noun* **1** *the laments of the bereaved* wail, wailing, lamentation, moan, moaning, groan, weeping, crying, sob, sobbing, complaint, keening, ululation, howl. **2** *play/recite a lament* dirge, requiem, elegy, monody, threnody.

lamentable *adjective* **1** *a lamentable state of affairs* deplorable, regrettable, tragic, terrible, wretched, woeful, sorrowful, distressing, grievous. **2** *a lamentable salary* miserable, pitiful, poor, meager, low, unsatisfactory, inadequate; *inf.* measly.

lamentation *noun* lament, wail, wailing, moaning, weeping, keening. *See* LAMENT *noun* 1.

lamp *noun* light, lantern; table lamp, night-light, oil lamp, gas lamp; lightbulb, headlight, headlamp, taillight.

lampoon *noun* satire, burlesque, travesty, parody, skit, caricature, pasquinade, takeoff; *inf.* send-up.

lampoon *verb* satirize, parody, caricature, ridicule, mock, make fun of, burlesque, pasquinade, take off, do a takeoff of; *inf.* send up.

lance *noun* **1** *a knight's lance* spear, pike, javelin. **2** *a doctor's lance* scalpel, knife, lancet.

lance *verb* *lance the boil* cut, cut open, slit, incise, puncture, prick, stab.

land *noun* **1** *glad to be back on land* dry land, ground, solid ground, earth, terra firma. **2** *the land is fertile there* soil, earth, loam, dirt. **3** *prefer working on the land to working in town* farmland, agricultural land, country, countryside, rural areas. **4** *houses with plenty of land around them* grounds, fields, open space, open area, expanse, stretch, tract, undeveloped land. **5** *he owns all the land here* property, grounds, acres, real estate, realty. **6** *born in a far land* country, nation, fatherland, motherland, state, realm, province, territory, district, region, area, domain.

land *verb* **1** *the plane landed* touch down, alight, make a landing, come in to land. **2** *the pilot landed the plane | the pilot landed at noon* bring down, put down, take down; make a landing, touch down. **3** *the ship landed at Boston* berth, dock, reach the shore. **4** *we landed at Boston* berth, dock, reach the shore, go ashore, disembark, debark. **5** *how did we land here?* arrive, get, reach, find oneself, end up, turn up; *inf.* wind up. **6** *land a good job* get, acquire, obtain, procure, secure, gain, net, win, carry off. **land in** *his behavior landed him in jail* bring to, lead to, cause to go to, cause to arrive in.

landlady, landlord *noun* owner, proprietor, lessor, householder; innkeeper, hotelkeeper, hotelier, host.

landmark *noun* **1** *one of the landmarks of the town* distinctive feature, prominent feature, feature, monument. **2** *a landmark in the town's history* milestone, watershed, turning point, turning, critical point, crisis, historic event. **3** *landmarks dividing the two estates* marker, demarcator, boundary line, boundary fence. **4** *landmarks indicating the distance* milepost, milestone, guidepost.

landscape *noun* countryside, scene, scenery, outlook, view, aspect, prospect, vista, panorama, perspective.

landslide *noun* **1** *killed in a landslide* avalanche, landslip, rockfall. **2** *win an election by a landslide* decisive victory, runaway victory, overwhelming majority.

lane *noun* **1** *travel through the lanes* narrow road, narrow way, passageway, passage, alley, path, pathway, footpath, track. **2** *traffic lanes* track, course, road division.

language *noun* **1** *children acquiring language*

speech, speaking, talking, words, vocabulary, utterance, verbal expression, verbalization, vocalization, communication, conversation, converse, discourse, interchange. **2** *the French language* tongue, speech, parlance, mother tongue, native tongue; *inf.* lingo. **3** *various forms of language found throughout the country/world* speech, dialect, vernacular, regionalism, provincialism, localism, rhyming slang, patois, lingua franca, barbarism, vulgarism, colloquialism, informal language, slang, idiom, idiolect, jargon, patter, cant, legalese, medicalese, journalese, newspeak, bureaucratese, pidgin English; *inf.* lingo, gobbledygook. **4** *admire the language of the speaker/writer* vocabulary, terminology, wording, phrasing, phraseology, style, diction, expression, manner of writing/speaking, rhetoric.

languid *adjective* **1** *have no patience with languid people* languishing, listless, languorous, lackadaisical, spiritless, vigorless, lacking energy, lethargic, torpid, idle, inactive, inert, indolent, lazy, sluggish, slow-moving, unenthusiastic, apathetic, indifferent. **2** *feeling languid after her illness* weak, weakly, sickly, faint, feeble, frail, limp, flagging, drooping, fatigued, enervated, debilitated. **3** *a languid response* apathetic, lukewarm, halfhearted, unenthusiastic, bored, passive.
Antonyms: ENERGETIC; VIGOROUS.

languish *verb* **1** *she languished after the tragedy* droop, flag, wilt, wither, fade, fail, weaken, decline, go into a decline, waste away; *inf.* go downhill. **2** *people languishing in institutions* waste away, rot, decay, wither away, be abandoned, be neglected, be forgotten, be disregarded. **languish for** *languish for her lover* pine for, yearn for, long for, sigh for, hunger for, desire, want, mope for, repine for, grieve for, mourn for.

languor *noun* **1** *feeling full of languor in the heat* listlessness, lethargy, torpor, idleness, inactivity, inertia, indolence, laziness, sluggishness, sleepiness, drowsiness, somnolence, dreaminess, relaxation. **2** *disturb the languor of the atmosphere* stillness, tranquillity, calm, calmness, lull, silence, windlessness.

lank *adjective* **1** *lank hair* lifeless, lusterless, limp, straggling, straight. **2** *lank youths* tall, thin, lean, lanky, skinny, spindly, gangling, gangly, scrawny, scraggy, angular, bony, gaunt, rawboned, gawky, rangy; *inf.* weedy.

lap¹ *noun* **1** *sit on mother's lap* knee, knees. **2** *live in the lap of luxury* security, secureness, safety, protection, refuge, comfort. **in one's lap** *the arrangements are in your lap* one's responsibility, one's charge, one's task, one's job, one's obligation.

lap² *noun* **1** *three laps of the stadium* circuit, circle, loop, orbit, round, compass, ambit. **2** *the last lap of the journey* round, tour, section, stage, leg.

lap³ *verb* **1** *lap blankets around her* wrap, wind,

fold, twist. **2** *lap her in blankets* wrap, swathe, cover, envelop, enfold, encase, wind, swaddle.

lap⁴ *verb* **1** *water lapping against the shore* wash, splash, beat, swish, slap, slosh. **2** *cats lapping milk* drink up, drink, lick up, sip.

lapse *noun* **1** *forgive his occasional lapse* slip, error, mistake, blunder, failing, fault, failure, omission, oversight, negligence, dereliction; *inf.* slipup. **2** *after a lapse of time* interval, gap, pause, intermission, interlude, lull, hiatus, break, passage. **3** *a lapse in standards* decline, downturn, fall, falling, falling-away, slipping, drop, deterioration, worsening, degeneration, backsliding. **4** *the lapse of her season ticket* expiry, expiration, invalidity, termination. **5** *lapse of faith* abandonment, forsaking, relinquishment, defection, renunciation, repudiation, rejection, disavowal, denial, abjuration, apostasy.

lapse *verb* **1** *standards have lapsed* decline, fall, fall off, drop, deteriorate, worsen, degenerate; *inf.* go downhill, go to pot. **2** *our friendship lapsed when we left school* cease, end, come to an end, stop, terminate. **3** *the season ticket has lapsed* become void, become invalid, expire, run out, terminate, become obsolete. **4** *lapse into silence/sleep* slide, slip, drift, sink, subside, submerge. **5** *time has lapsed* elapse, pass, go by, go on, roll on, glide by, run its course.

lapsed *adjective* **1** *lapsed season tickets* void, invalid, expired, run-out, out of date, terminated. **2** *lapsed traditions* obsolete, old, former, past, bygone, forgotten, extinct, outworn, abandoned. **3** *lapsed Christians* nonpracticing, lacking faith, backsliding, recidivist, apostate.

larceny *noun* theft, grand larceny, petty larceny, stealing, robbery, pilfering, purloining, burglary, misappropriation.

larder *noun* pantry, storage room, storeroom, store.

large *adjective* **1** *large buildings/sums* big, great, of considerable size, sizable, substantial, goodly, tall, high, huge, immense, enormous, colossal, massive, mammoth, vast, prodigious, gigantic, giant, monumental, stupendous, gargantuan, man-size, king-size, giant-size, outsize, outsized, considerable; *inf.* jumbo, whopping. **2** *a large man/woman* big, burly, heavy, bulky, thickset, powerfully built, heavyset, chunky, strapping, hulking, hefty, ample, fat, obese, corpulent. **3** *a large supply* abundant, copious, plentiful, ample, liberal, generous. **4** *take the large view | officials with large powers* wide, wideranging, large-scale, broad, extensive, farreaching, sweeping, comprehensive, exhaustive. **at large** **1** *wild animals are at large | some prisoners at large* at liberty, free, unconfined, unrestrained, roaming, on the loose, on the run, fugitive. **2** *society at large* as a whole, as a body, generally, in general, in the main. **3** *a report given at large* in detail, with full details,

exhaustively, at length. **by and large** *by and large, we are better off* on the whole, generally, in general, all things considered, taking everything into consideration, for the most part, in the main, as a rule.
Antonyms: SMALL; SLIGHT; MEAGER.

largely *adverb he is largely to blame* to a large extent, to a great degree, chiefly, for the most part, mostly, mainly, in the main, principally, in great measure.

large-scale *adjective* 1 *a large-scale police search* extensive, wide-reaching, wide-ranging, sweeping, wholesale, global. 2 *large-scale prints* enlarged, blown-up, magnified.

largesse *noun* 1 *known for her largesse* generosity, kindness, liberality, openhandedness, munificence, bounty, bountifulness, beneficence, benefaction, altruism, charity, philanthropy, almsgiving. 2 *distributing largesse* gifts, presents, contributions, donations, handouts, endowments, grants, aid, alms.

lark¹ *noun larks singing* skylark, meadowlark, songbird.

lark² *noun the innocent larks of children* prank, horseplay, trick, fooling, antic, mischief, escapade, fun, cavorting, caper, play, game, romp, frolic, sport, rollicking, gambol.

lark³ *verb children laughing and larking about* play pranks, indulge in horseplay, play tricks, fool about, make mischief, have fun, cavort, caper, play, romp, frolic, sport, rollick, gambol.

lascivious *adjective* 1 *offended by lascivious men* lewd, lecherous, lustful, licentious, promiscuous, libidinous, prurient, salacious, lubricious, concupiscent, debauched, depraved, degenerate, dissolute, dissipated. 2 *lascivious magazines/talk* lewd, blue, obscene, pornographic, smutty, gross, bawdy, risqué, suggestive, dirty, salacious; *inf.* raunchy.

lash *noun* 1 *a lash to beat the slaves* whip, horsewhip, bullwhip, scourge, flagellum, cat-o'-nine-tails. 2 *six lashes with a whip* | *with one lash of his fist* stroke, stripe, blow, hit, strike, bang, thwack, thump; *inf.* swipe, wallop, whack.

lash *verb* 1 *the centurion lashed the slaves* whip, horsewhip, scourge, birch, switch, flog, flail, flagellate, thrash, beat, strike, batter, hammer; *inf.* wallop, whack. 2 *waves lashing the ship* buffet, pound, batter, beat against, dash against, smack against, strike, knock. 3 *lash him for his behavior* berate, upbraid, castigate, scold, rebuke, chide, reprove, reproach, harangue, rant at, fulminate against, attack, censure, criticize, condemn, flay; *inf.* bawl out, lace into, lambaste. 4 *lions lashing their tails* flick, wag, wave, whip, switch. 5 *lash the boat to the side of the ship* fasten, bind, tie, tether, hitch, attach, join, rope, strap, leash, make fast, secure. **lash out at** *lash out at his critics* speak out against, burst into angry speech at, shout at, lose one's tem-

per at, attack verbally, attack physically, denounce, harangue, rant at, fulminate against, criticize, condemn, censure; *inf.* lace into.

lass *noun* girl, young woman, young lady, schoolgirl, maid, maiden, miss; *inf.* lassie.

last¹ *adjective* 1 *the last runner arrived* hindmost, rearmost, at the end, at the back, final, aftermost. 2 *his last words* final, closing, concluding, ending, finishing, terminating, ultimate, terminal. 3 *our last chance* final, only remaining, only one left. 4 *the last thing she would want* least likely, most unlikely, least suitable, least wanted, least favorite. 5 *last Thursday* latest, most recent. **last word** 1 *that is the chairman's last word on the subject* final statement, summation, ultimatum, final decision, definitive statement. 2 *have the last word in an argument* final remark, final say, closing statement, concluding remark. 3 *the last word in sports cars* most fashionable, most up-to-date, latest, newest, peak, best, epitome, quintessence, acme of perfection, cream, crème de la crème, ne plus ultra.
Antonyms: FIRST; INITIAL.

last² *adverb come last* at the end, at the rear, in the rear, behind, after.

last³ *noun stay to the last* end, ending, finish, close, conclusion, completion, finale, termination, bitter end. **at last** in the end, finally, eventually, at length, ultimately, in conclusion.

last⁴ *verb* 1 *how long will the symptoms last?* continue, go on, carry on, remain, persist, keep on. 2 *how long will the climbers last in the snow?* survive, exist, live, subsist, hold on, hold out. 3 *those shoes won't last* last long, wear well, stand up to wear, keep, endure. 4 *the heartache won't last* be permanent, be constant, last long.

last⁵ *noun shoemaker's last* mold, model, pattern, form, matrix.

last-ditch *adjective a last-ditch attempt* desperate, frantic, frenzied, wild, struggling, straining, final, last-chance, last-minute, last-gasp, all-out.

lasting *adjective a lasting peace* long-lasting, enduring, long-lived, lifelong, abiding, continuing, long-term, surviving, persisting, permanent, deep-rooted, durable, constant, eternal, undying, everlasting, perennial, perpetual, unending, never-ending, immortal, ceaseless, unceasing, interminable, imperishable, indestructible.
Antonyms: SHORT-LIVED; EPHEMERAL.

lastly *adverb lastly, I want to thank you all* finally, in conclusion, to conclude, to sum up, in drawing things to a close.

latch *noun the latch on the door* catch, fastening, hasp, hook, bar, bolt, lock.

latch *verb latch the door* fasten, secure, make fast, bar, bolt, lock.

late *adjective* 1 *she's always late* unpunctual, behind time, behind schedule, behind, behindhand, not on time, tardy, overdue, delayed, dilatory, slow. 2 *her late husband* deceased,

dead, departed, defunct, nonexistent. **3** *the late government* former, previous, preceding, past, prior. **4** *some late news* recent, fresh, new, last-minute, up-to-date, up-to-the-minute.
Antonyms: PUNCTUAL; EARLY.

late adverb **1** *he arrived late* unpunctually, behind time, behindhand, belatedly, tardily, at the last minute, at the tail end, dilatorily, slowly. **2** *we worked late yesterday* past the usual finishing/stopping/closing time, after hours. **3** *get home late from the dance* late at night, in the early hours of the morning; *inf.* in the wee small hours. **of late** lately, recently. *See* LATELY.

lately adverb of late, recently, in the past few days, in the last couple of weeks, in recent times.

latent adjective *latent talent* dormant, quiescent, inactive, passive, hidden, unrevealed, concealed, unapparent, indiscernible, imperceptible, invisible, covert, undeveloped, unrealized, potential, possible.
Antonyms: OBVIOUS; EVIDENT; CONSPICUOUS.

---

latent
abeyant, dormant, quiescent, potential
All of these words refer to what is not currently observable or showing signs of activity. A **latent** talent is one that has not yet manifested itself, while **potential** suggests a talent that exists in an undeveloped state (*a potential concert violinist*). A child may have certain *latent* qualities of which his or her parents are unaware; but teachers are usually quick to spot a *potential* artist or poet in the classroom. **Dormant** and **quiescent** are less frequently associated with people and more often associated with things. A volcano might be described as *dormant*, which applies to anything that is currently inactive but has been active in the past and is capable of becoming active again in the future. *Dormant* carries the connotation of sleeping (*plants that are dormant in the winter*), while *quiescent* means motionless (*a quiescent sea*), emphasizing inactivity without referring to past or future activity. **Abeyant**, like *dormant*, means suspended or temporarily inactive, but it is most commonly used as a noun (*personal rights and privileges kept in abeyance until the danger had passed*).

---

later adjective *the later bus* subsequent, next, following, succeeding, successive, sequential.

later adverb **1** *I can't come today, but I'll come later* later on, at a later time, at a later date, at a future time/date, at some point in the future, in the future, in time to come. **2** *he arrived, and she came later* later on, after, afterward, subsequently, by and by, in a while, after a bit.

lateral adjective sidewise, sideways, sidelong, sideward, edgewise, edgeways, indirect, oblique, slanting, askance.

latest adjective *the latest news/style* most recent, newest, up-to-date, up-to-the-minute, current, modern, fashionable, in fashion, in vogue, in; *inf.* with-it.

lather noun **1** *soap not producing much lather* suds, soapsuds, foam, froth, bubbles. **2** *horses covered in lather* sweat, perspiration. **3** *getting in a lather over the exams* nervous state, state of agitation, state of anxiety, fluster, flutter, fret, fuss, frenzy, fever, pother; *inf.* flap, sweat, tizzy, dither, twitter, state, stew.

latitude noun **1** *on the same latitude as Moscow* parallel, meridian, grid line. **2** *give his staff a great deal of latitude in decision-making | children given too much latitude* scope, scope for initiative, freedom of action, freedom from restriction, freedom, unrestrictedness, liberty, free play, carte blanche, leeway, elbowroom, license, indulgence, laxity.

latter adjective **1** *the latter is the better* last-mentioned, second-mentioned, second of the two, second. **2** *the latter part of the year/process* later, hindmost, closing, end, concluding, final. **3** *the technology of latter times* recent, latest, modern.

latter-day adjective *latter-day missionaries* modern, present-day, present-time, current, contemporary.

lattice noun latticework, fretwork, open framework, openwork, trellis, network, mesh, web, tracery, reticulation, grating, grid, grille.

laud verb **1** *laud their efforts* praise, sing the praises of, extol, hail, applaud, acclaim, commend, admire, approve of, make much of, cheer, celebrate, eulogize, panegyrize. **2** *laud the Creator* glorify, worship, magnify, exalt, pay tribute to, pay homage to, honor, adore, revere, venerate.

laudable adjective *laudable behavior/actions* praiseworthy, commendable, admirable, worthy of admiration, meritorious, deserving, creditable, worthy, estimable, of note, noteworthy, exemplary, excellent.
Antonyms: BLAMEWORTHY; CONTEMPTIBLE.

laudation noun extolment, applause, praise, acclaim, acclamation, commendation, admiration, approval, approbation, eulogy, panegyric, paean, encomium.

laudatory adjective praising, extolling, acclamatory, commendatory, admiring, approving, approbatory, complimentary, adulatory, celebratory, eulogizing, eulogistic, panegyric, panegyrical, encomiastical.

laugh verb chuckle, chortle, guffaw, giggle, titter, snigger, ha-ha, tee-hee, burst out laughing, roar/hoot with laughter, shake with laughter, be convulsed with laughter, split one's sides, be rolling in the aisles, be doubled up; *inf.* be in stitches, die laughing, crack up, break up. **laugh at 1** *laugh at the fortune-tellers* mock, ridicule, deride, scoff at, jeer at, sneer at, make fun of, poke fun at, make a fool of, make the butt of one's jokes, lampoon, satirize, taunt, tease; *inf.* send up. **2** *laugh at danger* laugh off, belittle, make light of, close one's eyes to, refuse to acknowledge, discount, rule out, ignore, dismiss, disregard, reject the possibility of, shrug off, brush aside, scoff at, pooh-pooh. **laugh off** *laugh off danger* laugh at, belittle, make light of, discount, shrug off. *See* LAUGH AT 2 (above). **laugh on the other side of one's face** *you'll be laughing on the other side of your face when the police catch up with you* show sudden disappointment, be dejected, be disheartened, be downcast, eat one's words, get a taste of one's own medicine; *inf.* get one's comeuppance.

laugh *noun* **1** *give a laugh* chuckle, chortle, guffaw, giggle, titter, snigger, roar/hoot of laughter, peal of laughter, belly laugh. **2** *her uncle's such a laugh* comedian, comic, joker, humorist, wag, wit, entertainer, clown; *inf.* card, case, caution, hoot, scream.

laughable *adjective* **1** *a laughable business proposition* ludicrous, ridiculous, absurd, derisory, derisive, risible, preposterous, outrageous. **2** *children finding the entertainment laughable* amusing, funny, humorous, hilarious, uproarious, comical, comic, entertaining, diverting, farcical, droll, mirthful, sidesplitting.
Antonyms: SERIOUS; GRAVE.

laughingstock *noun* figure of fun, dupe, butt, fool, everybody's fool, stooge, fair game, everybody's target, victim; *inf.* fall guy.

laughter *noun* **1** *hear the laughter* laughing, chuckling, chortling, guffawing, giggling, tittering, sniggering; *inf.* hooting. **2** *a source of laughter* amusement, entertainment, humor, mirth, merriment, gaiety, hilarity, glee, lightheartedness, blitheness.

launch *verb* **1** *launch the ship* set afloat, float. **2** *launch a rocket/missile* fire, discharge, propel, project, send forth, throw, cast, hurl, let fly. **3** *launch a search/project* set in motion, get going, begin, start, commence, embark upon, initiate, instigate, institute, inaugurate, establish, set up, organize, introduce, usher in, start the ball rolling. **4** *launch out into criticism* burst into, start, begin.

launder *verb* *sheets were freshly laundered* wash, wash and iron, wash and press, clean, dry-clean.

laundry *noun* **1** *put the laundry into the washing machine* wash, dirty clothes, dirty laundry, clothes to be cleaned. **2** *take the wash to a laundry* laundromat, launderette, dry cleaner's, laundry room.

laurels *plural noun* honors, awards, trophies, prizes, rewards, tributes, bays, praises, laudation, acclaim, acclamation, commendation, credit, glory, honor, distinction, fame, renown, prestige, recognition; *inf.* kudos.

lavatory *noun* toilet, rest room, bathroom, public convenience, ladies' room, men's room, powder room, washroom, privy, latrine; *inf.* can, john, head; little girls' room, little boys' room.

lavish *adjective* **1** *a lavish supply* copious, abundant, superabundant, plentiful, profuse, prolific, unlimited. **2** *too lavish in her catering* extravagant, excessive, immoderate, wasteful, squandering, profligate, prodigal, thriftless, improvident, intemperate, unrestrained, dissolute, wild. **3** *a lavish hostess* generous, liberal, bountiful, openhanded, unstinting, free, munificent, overgenerous, extravagant. **4** *a lavish display of flowers* luxuriant, lush, gorgeous, sumptuous, costly, opulent, pretentious, showy.
Antonyms: MEAGER; FRUGAL.

lavish *verb* *lavish presents/praises on his children* heap, shower, pour, deluge, give freely, give generously, give unstintingly, bestow freely, waste, squander, dissipate.

law *noun* **1** *the law of the land* system of laws, body of laws, constitution, code, legal code, charter, rules and regulations, jurisprudence. **2** *the legislature issuing laws* rule, regulation, statute, enactment, act, decree, edict, command, order, ordinance, commandment, directive, pronouncement, covenant. **3** *obey the laws of the game* rule, regulation, principle, direction, instruction, guideline. **4** *moral laws* rule, principle, precept, standard, criterion, formula, tenet, doctrine, canon. **5** *law of nature* generalization, general truth, axiom, maxim, truism. **6** *go to law* litigation, legal action, legal proceedings, lawsuit. **7** *a career in law* the legal profession, the bar. **8** *the law has arrived* police, authorities, officers of the law; *inf.* fuzz, cops, boys in blue.

law-abiding *adjective* lawful, righteous, honest, honorable, upright, upstanding, good, virtuous, orderly, peaceable, peacekeeping, peaceful, dutiful, duteous, obedient, compliant, complying.

lawbreaker *noun* criminal, felon, wrongdoer, miscreant, offender, delinquent, culprit, transgressor, violator, convict, jailbird; *inf.* crook.

lawful *adjective* **1** *lawful actions* legal, legitimate, licit, just, valid, permissible, allowable, rightful, proper, constitutional, legalized, sanctioned, authorized, warranted, approved, recognized. **2** *a lawful person* law-abiding, righteous, honorable, orderly. *See* LAW-ABIDING.
Antonyms: UNLAWFUL; ILLEGAL.

lawless *adjective* **1** *a lawless country* without law and order, anarchic, disorderly, ungoverned, unruly, insurrectionary, insurgent, revolutionary, rebellious, insubordinate, riotous, mutinous, seditious, terrorist. **2** *lawless actions* unlawful, illegal, lawbreaking, illicit, illegitimate, criminal, felonious, miscreant, transgressing, violating. **3** *lawless rage* unbridled, unrestrained, unchecked, uncontrolled, immoderate, intemperate, wild.
Antonyms: LAW-ABIDING; ORDERLY; RESTRAINED.

lawsuit *noun* suit, case, legal action, action, legal proceedings, proceedings, litigation, trial, bringing of charges, indictment.

lawyer noun attorney, legal adviser, criminal lawyer, civil lawyer, advocate, counsel, solicitor, legal practitioner.

lax adjective **1** *lax about discipline in the school* slack, slipshod, negligent, neglectful, remiss, careless, heedless, unmindful, inattentive, casual, easygoing, lenient, permissive, indulgent, overindulgent, complaisant, overtolerant. **2** *a lax description* loose, inexact, inaccurate, imprecise, unrigorous, vague, indefinite, nonspecific, broad, general. **3** *lax flesh* slack, flabby, flaccid, limp, yielding, sagging, drooping, droopy, hanging.
Antonyms: CONSCIENTIOUS; CAREFUL.

laxative noun purgative, cathartic, senna, ipecacuanha, castor oil, cod liver oil, milk of magnesia.

lay verb **1** *lay the groceries on the table* put, place, set, deposit, plant, settle, posit. **2** *lay the carpet* position, set out, arrange, dispose. **3** *lay charges* put forward, bring forward, advance, submit, present, prefer, offer, lodge. **4** *lay the blame at his door* attribute, assign, ascribe, allocate, allot, impute. **5** *I'm so sure, I will lay money on it* wager, bet, gamble, stake, give odds, hazard, risk, chance. **6** *lay plans* devise, arrange, contrive, make, prepare, work out, hatch, concoct, design, plan, plot. **7** *lay the burden on him* impose, inflict, encumber, saddle, tax, charge, burden, apply. **8** *lay eggs* deposit, produce, bear, oviposit. **lay aside 1** *lay aside the dress for the customer* put aside, put to one side, keep, save, store. **2** *lay aside one's responsibilities/thoughts* abandon, cast aside, forsake, reject, renounce, repudiate, discard, set aside, put aside, dismiss, disregard, put out of one's mind, ignore, forget, shelve. **lay bare** *lay bare one's secret thoughts* reveal, make known, disclose, divulge, show, expose, exhibit, uncover, unveil, unmask. **lay down 1** *lay down their weapons* surrender, relinquish, give up, yield, cede, turn over. **2** *it is laid down that candidates must be interviewed* set down, stipulate, formulate, prescribe, order, command, ordain, postulate, demand, proclaim, assert, maintain. **lay (one's) hands on 1** *if I ever lay (my) hands on the thief* get one's hands on, lay hold of, get (a) hold of, catch, seize. **2** *I just can't lay (my) hands on that book* find, locate, unearth, bring to light, discover, acquire, turn up. **3** *priests laying hands on members of the congregation* bless, consecrate, confirm, ordain. **lay hold of** *lay hold of the thief* get (a) hold of, get one's hands on, catch, seize, grab, snatch, clutch, grip, grasp, lay hands on. **lay in** *lay in a supply of logs* stock up on, stockpile, store, accumulate, amass, heap up, hoard, collect. **lay into 1** *lay into their attackers* set upon, assail, attack, hit out at, strike out at, let fly at; *inf.* lace/sail into, lambaste. **2** *lay into the child for being late* scold, rebuke, chide, berate, upbraid, reproach, reprove, castigate, punish, criticize, censure, condemn, rant at, rave at, harangue;

inf. lace into, lambaste. **lay it on** *he's laying it on to charm his mother-in-law* exaggerate, stretch the truth, overdo it, flatter, pay extravagant compliments, give fulsome praise, overpraise, soft-soap; *inf.* pile it on, lay it on thick, sweet-talk. **lay off 1** *lay off half of the workforce* let go, dismiss, discharge; *inf.* sack, fire. **2** *just lay off me!* stop annoying/haranguing/teasing/taunting/tormenting/harassing. **3** *lay off smoking/alcohol* quit, stop, cease, desist from, refrain from, give up, discontinue, not touch. **lay out 1** *lay out the plans* spread out, set out, arrange, display, exhibit. **2** *lay out a garden* set out, arrange, plan, design. **3** *lay out refreshments* provide, supply, furnish, give. **4** *lay out a lot of money* spend, expend, pay, disburse, contribute, give, invest; *inf.* shell out, fork out. **5** *lay out his opponent* knock out, knock unconscious, knock down, fell, floor, flatten, prostrate; *inf.* KO, kayo.

lay adjective **1** *a lay preacher* laic, laical, secular, nonclerical, nonordained. **2** *a lay member of the club* nonprofessional, amateur, nonspecialist, dilettante.

layabout noun good-for-nothing, ne'er-do-well, do-nothing, idler, loafer, lounger, shirker, slacker, drone, wastrel, fainéant, sluggard, laggard; *inf.* gold brick, lazybones, couch potato.

layman, laywoman, layperson noun *I'm not a lawyer, just an interested layman* amateur, nonprofessional, dilettante.

layoff noun *many layoffs at the factory* dismissal, discharge; *inf.* sacking, firing.

layout noun **1** *the layout of the house* arrangement, geography, plan. **2** *the magazine's layout* arrangement, design, format, formation.

layperson noun. *See* LAYMAN, LAYWOMAN, LAYPERSON.

laze verb *lazing all day in the garden* idle, do nothing, loaf, lounge, lounge about, loll around, waste time, fritter away time.

laziness noun idleness, indolence, slothfulness, sloth, inactivity, inertia, lethargy, languor, remissness, laxity.

lazy adjective idle, indolent, slothful, work-shy, inactive, inert, sluggish, lethargic, languorous, listless, torpid, slow-moving, remiss, negligent, lax.
Antonyms: ACTIVE; INDUSTRIOUS; ENERGETIC.

lead[1] verb **1** *lead him to the right spot* guide, show someone the way, conduct, lead the way, usher, escort, steer, pilot. **2** *the evidence led him to believe he was guilty* cause, induce, prompt, move, incline, dispose, predispose, persuade, sway, influence, prevail on, bring around. **3** *lead the procession* be at the head of, be at the front of, head. **4** *lead the country/discussion* command, direct, govern, rule, manage, be in charge of, regulate, preside over, head, supervise, superintend, oversee; *inf.* head up. **5** *he was leading after the first lap* be in the lead, be in front, be out in front, be ahead, be first, come first, precede. **6** *leading the field* be at the front of, be ahead of, outdistance, outrun, outstrip, leave behind, outdo, excel, exceed, surpass, outrival, outshine, eclipse, transcend. **7** *lead a happy life* have, live, pass, spend, experience, undergo. **lead off** *lead off the dance* begin, start, start off, commence, open; *inf.* kick off. **lead on** *she thinks she has won a prize, but they are just leading her on* deceive, mislead, delude, hoodwink, dupe, trick, beguile, tempt, entice, lure, tantalize, inveigle, seduce; *inf.* string along. **lead the way 1** *he led the way to the spot* guide one, conduct one, show (one) the way. **2** *the scientist led the way in space development* initiate things, take the first step, make a start, break ground, blaze a trail, lay the foundation, lay the first stone. **lead to** *his action led to disaster* cause, result in, bring on, call forth, provoke, contribute to. **lead up to** *lead up to asking them for money* prepare the way for, pave the way for, open the way for, do the groundwork for, work up to, make overtures about, make advances about, hint at, approach the subject of, introduce the subject of. *Antonyms:* FOLLOW; TRAIL.

lead[2] *noun* **1** *the runner in the lead* leading position/place, first place, advance position, van, vanguard. **2** *take the lead in the market* first position, head place, forefront, primacy, preeminence, supremacy, advantage, edge, precedence. **3** *a lead of half a lap* margin, gap, interval. **4** *act as a lead to others* example, model, pattern, standard of excellence. **5** *she's in the lead in the new play* leading role, star/starring role, title role, principal part. **6** *she's/he's the lead in the play* star, principal character, male lead, female lead, leading man, leading lady, hero, heroine. **7** *a dog's lead* leash, tether, rein, cord, rope, chain. **8** *we have no leads in the murder investigation* clue, pointer, guide, hint, tip, suggestion, indication, intimation, tip-off.

lead[3] *adjective* *in the lead position* leading, first, top, foremost, front, head, chief, principal, main, most important, premier, paramount, prime, primary. *Antonyms:* LAST; tail-end.

lead[4] *noun* **1** *sink a lead to test the depth* weight, sinker, plummet, plumb, bob. **2** *remove the lead from the gunshot wound* lead pellet, shot, ammunition.

leaden *adjective* **1** *leaden limbs* heavy, weighty, burdensome, cumbersome, inactive, inert. **2** *leaden steps* heavy, labored, lumbering, plodding, sluggish. **3** *leaden prose* heavy, unimaginative, uninspired, uninteresting, dull, boring, tedious, monotonous, insipid, vapid. **4** *leaden skies* gray, grayish, gray-colored, cloudy, gloomy, overcast, lowering, oppressive, dark, dreary, dismal, bleak.

leader *noun* **1** *the leader of the country/committee/team* ruler, head, chief, commander, director, governor, principal, captain, skipper, manager, superintendent, supervisor, overseer, foreman, kingpin; *inf.* boss, number one, head honcho. **2** *a leader of fashion* pacesetter, trendsetter, front runner. **3** *a leader in the field of genetics* front runner, innovator, pioneer, trailblazer, pathfinder, groundbreaker, originator.

leadership *noun* **1** *under the leadership of a responsible person* rule, command, headship, directorship, direction, governorship, administration, captaincy, management, supervision, control, guidance, authority, superintendency. **2** *he is competent but has no leadership qualities* authority, control, direction, guidance, initiative, influence.

leading *adjective* **1** *play the leading role* chief, main, most important, principal, foremost, supreme, paramount, dominant, superior, ruling, directing, guiding, controlling; *inf.* number-one. **2** *one of the leading writers* chief, most important, foremost, greatest, best, outstanding, preeminent, supreme, principal, top-rank, top-ranking, of the first rank, first-rate. **3** *the leading runner* front, first, in first place.

leaf *noun* **1** *a leaf from the tree/plant* frond, flag, needle, pine needle, pad, lily pad; *Tech* cotyledon. **2** *a leaf missing from the book* page, sheet, folio, flyleaf. **turn over a new leaf** *she turned over a new leaf after surviving a heart attack* reform, mend/change one's ways, become a new person, change completely, make a fresh start, get a new lease on life, make a change for the better, start with a clean slate.

leaf *verb* **1** *leafing through a book* flick, skim, browse, glance. **2** *trees leafing* bud, put out leaves, burst into leaves, turn green, foliate.

leaflet *noun* pamphlet, flyer, booklet, brochure, handbill, bill, circular.

league *noun* **1** *a league of nations* alliance, confederation, confederacy, federation, union, association, coalition, combine, consortium, affiliation, guild, corporation, conglomerate, cooperative, partnership, fellowship, syndicate, band, group. **2** *sign a league* pact, compact, covenant, treaty, concordat, contract, agreement, settlement. **3** *a football league* group, band, association. **4** *he is not in the same league as his brother* ability group, level of ability, level, class, category. **in league** *he was in league with the other crook* in alliance, allied, cooperating, collaborating, leagued, linked, hand in glove, in collusion; *inf.* in cahoots.

league *verb* **league together** *they leagued together to promote their interests* ally, join forces, unite, form an association, band together, combine, amalgamate, form a federation, confederate, collaborate.

leak *noun* **1** *see a leak in the bucket* hole, opening, crack, crevice, chink, fissure, puncture, cut, gash, slit, rent, break, rift. **2** *a water/gas leak* drip, leaking, leakage, escape, seeping, seepage, oozing, percolation, discharge. **3** *a leak of secret information to a newspaper* disclosure, divulgence, revelation, uncovering.

leak *verb* **1** *water/gas leaking* escape, drip, seep out/through, ooze out, exude, discharge, issue, gush out. **2** *leak information to the press* disclose, divulge, reveal, make known, make public, tell, impart, pass on, relate, give away, let slip; *inf.* spill the beans about, take the lid off; let the cat out of the bag.

lean *verb* **1** *the ladder leaning against the wall* | *his wife leaning on his arm* rest, be supported, be propped up, recline, repose. **2** *the pole/ship is leaning* incline, bend, slant, tilt, be at an angle, slope, bank, list, heel, careen. **lean on** *they lean on each other* depend on, be dependent on, rely on, count on, pin one's faith on, have faith in, trust, have every confidence in. **lean toward** *she leans toward anarchy* incline toward, tend toward, have a tendency toward, have a propensity for, have a proclivity for, have a preference for, be attracted to, have a liking for, gravitate toward, have an affinity with.

lean *adjective* **1** *lean people/animals* thin, slender, slim, spare, lank, skinny, scrawny, scraggy, bony, gaunt, emaciated, skin and bones, rawboned, rangy, gangling. **2** *lean meat* nonfat, low-fat, unfatty. **3** *a lean harvest* meager, scanty, sparse, poor, inadequate, insufficient. **4** *lean years for art* unproductive, unfruitful, arid, barren, bare, nonfertile.
Antonyms: FAT; ABUNDANT.

leaning *noun a leaning toward anarchy* tendency, inclination, bent, proclivity, propensity, penchant, predisposition, predilection, proneness, partiality, preference, bias, attraction, liking, fondness, taste.

leap *verb* **1** *children leaping around* jump, bound, bounce, hop, skip, romp, caper, spring, frolic, frisk, cavort, gambol, dance. **2** *leap to one's feet* jump, jump up, spring. **3** *leap the obstacle* jump, jump over, high-jump, vault over, vault, spring over, bound over, hurdle, clear, cross over, sail over. **4** *leap to help* jump, hurry, hasten, rush, hurtle. **5** *prices have leapt* increase rapidly, soar, rocket, skyrocket, shoot up, escalate, mount. **6** *leap to stardom* rocket, skyrocket, advance/mount/ascend rapidly, climb the ladder. **leap at** *leap at the chance* accept eagerly, grasp, grasp with both hands, grab, take advantage of. **leap to** *leap to conclusions* arrive at hastily, reach hurriedly, come to overhastily, form hastily.

leap *noun* **1** *clear the obstacle at the first leap* jump, vault, spring, bound, hop, skip. **2** *a leap in the number of unemployed* rapid increase, sudden rise, escalation, soaring, surge, upsurge, upswing. **by leaps and bounds** *progress by leaps and bounds* rapidly, swiftly, quickly, speedily, at an amazing rate.

learn *verb* **1** *learn French* acquire a knowledge of, gain an understanding of, acquire skill in, become competent in, grasp, master, take in,

absorb, assimilate, pick up. **2** *learn the poem* learn by heart, get by heart, memorize, commit to memory, become word-perfect in. **3** *we learned that he had gone* discover, find out, detect, become aware, gather, hear, be informed, have it brought to one's attention, understand, ascertain, discern, perceive. **learn of** *learn of his departure* find out about, hear of, get word of, be informed of, have brought to one's attention, get wind of.

learned *adjective learned professors/journals* erudite, scholarly, well-educated, knowledgeable, well-read, widely read, well-versed, bookish, well-informed, lettered, cultured, intellectual, academic, literary, studious, pedantic, sage, wise; *inf.* highbrow.
Antonyms: IGNORANT; ILLITERATE.

learner *noun* beginner, trainee, apprentice, pupil, student, novice, tyro, neophyte, initiate, greenhorn; *inf.* rookie.

learning *noun* **1** *a man of learning* erudition, scholarship, knowledge, education, letters, culture, intellect, academic attainment, book learning, information, pedantry, sageness, wisdom. **2** *an opportunity for learning* study, studying, education, schooling, instruction.

lease *verb* **1** *lease a house/car from an agency* rent, hire, charter. **2** *lease their house to visitors from Canada* rent, rent out, let, let out, hire, hire out, sublet, sublease.

lease *noun sign a lease for the house/car* rental agreement, charter, contract.

leash *noun* **1** *a dog's leash* lead, rein, tether, rope, cord, chain. **2** *keep a tight leash on his anger* rein, curb, control, check, restraint, hold.

leash *verb* **1** *leash the dog* put the leash/lead on, fasten, hitch up, tether, tie up, secure. **2** *leash one's anger* curb, control, keep under control, check, restrain, hold back, suppress.

leather *noun jackets made of leather* | *leather gloves* skin, hide, kid, doeskin, pigskin, suede; imitation leather, leatherette.

leathery *adjective* **1** *leathery skin* wrinkled, wizened, weather-beaten, rough, rugged, coriaceous. **2** *leathery meat* tough, hard, hardened, coriaceous.

leave *verb* **1** *leave hurriedly* depart, go away, go, withdraw, retire, take off, exit, take one's leave, make off, pull out, quit, be gone, decamp, disappear, say one's farewells/goodbyes; *inf.* push off, shove off, cut, split, vamoose. **2** *leave for Bermuda* set off, set sail. **3** *leave his wife* abandon, desert, forsake, discard, turn one's back on, leave in the lurch. **4** *has left his job* give up, quit, abandon, move from. **5** *leave his gloves at the hotel* leave behind, forget, mislay. **6** *leave the job to them* assign, allot, consign, hand over, give over, refer, commit, entrust. **7** *he left the estate to his nephew* bequeath, will, endow, hand down, transfer, convey; *fml.* demise, devise. **8** *the quarrel left feelings of resentment* leave behind, cause, produce, generate, result in. **leave in the lurch** *leave the firm in the lurch by walking out* let down, leave in trouble, leave helpless, leave stranded, leave high and dry, abandon, desert, forsake. **leave off** *leave off talking* stop, cease, quit, finish, halt, end, desist from, break off, give up, discontinue, refrain from. **leave out** *leave out a sentence* omit, omit by accident, fail to include, overlook. **leave out of** *please leave him out of the invitation list* exclude from, omit from, except from, eliminate from, count out of, disregard from, reject from, repudiate from. *Antonyms:* COME; ARRIVE; STAY.

leave *noun* 1 *get leave to be absent* permission, consent, authorization, sanction, warrant, dispensation, concession, indulgence. 2 *going on (a) leave for three weeks* vacation, break, time off, furlough, sabbatical, leave of absence. 3 *they took their leave* leaving, leave-taking, departure, parting, withdrawal, exit, farewell, goodbye, adieu.

leaven *noun* 1 *add leaven to the dough* leavening, ferment, raising agent, yeast, baking powder. 2 *the children were a leaven to the solemn occasion* transforming, modifying, enlivening influence, lightening effect.

leaven *verb* 1 *leaven the dough* raise, make rise, ferment, work, lighten. 2 *leaven the atmosphere of formality* permeate, infuse, pervade, penetrate, imbue, suffuse, transform, modify, lighten, enliven, stimulate.

leavings *plural noun* residue, remainder, remains, remnants, leftovers, scraps, oddments, odds and ends, fragments, junk, waste, dregs, refuse, rubbish, debris, sweepings.

lecher *noun* libertine, womanizer, lady-killer, seducer, adulterer, fornicator, pervert, debauchee, rake, roué, Don Juan, Casanova, Lothario; *inf.* dirty old man, lech, flasher.

lecherous *adjective* lustful, promiscuous, carnal, sensual, licentious, lascivious, lewd, salacious, libertine, libidinous, lubricious, concupiscent, debauched, dissolute, wanton, intemperate, dissipated, degenerate, depraved; *inf.* horny, raunchy.

lechery *noun* lust, lustfulness, promiscuity, carnality, sensualness, sensuality, licentiousness, lasciviousness, lewdness, salaciousness, salacity, libertinism, libidinousness, lubricity, concupiscence, debauchery, dissoluteness, wantonness, intemperance, dissipation, degeneracy, depravity; *inf.* horniness, raunchiness.

lecture *noun* 1 *attend a lecture on the environment* talk, speech, address, discourse, disquisition, lesson, sermon, homily, harangue. 2 *children given a lecture for being late* scolding, chiding, reprimand, rebuke, reproof, reproach, remonstration, upbraiding, berating, tirade, diatribe; *inf.* dressing-down, telling-off, talking-to.

lecture *verb* 1 *lectured on local politics* give a lecture, give a talk, talk, give a speech, make a speech, speak, give an address, discourse, expound, hold forth, give a sermon, sermonize, harangue; *inf.* spout, jaw. 2 *lecture the children for being late* scold, chide, reprimand, rebuke, reprove, reproach, remonstrate with, upbraid, berate, castigate, haul over the coals; *inf.* lambaste, give a dressing-down to, give a talking-to to, tell off.

lecturer *noun* 1 *the lecturer gave a talk on nuclear waste* speaker, public speaker, speech-maker, orator, preacher. 2 *he is a lecturer in French* university teacher, college teacher, tutor, reader, instructor, academic, academician.

ledge *noun* shelf, sill, mantel, mantelpiece, mantelshelf, projection, protrusion, overhang, ridge, step.

ledger *noun* account book, record book, register, registry, log.

lee *noun* *in the lee of the hill* shelter, protection, cover, refuge.

leech *noun* *more of a leech than a friend* clinger, hanger-on, parasite, barnacle, constant appendage, sycophant, toady, bloodsucker, extortioner, sponger; *inf.* scrounger, freeloader.

leer *verb* *leer at* ogle, look lasciviously at, look suggestively at, give sly looks to, eye, wink at, watch, stare at, sneer at, smirk at, grin at; *inf.* give someone the once-over.

leer *noun* lascivious look, lecherous glance, suggestive look, sly glance, wink, stare, sneer, smirk, grin; *inf.* the once-over.

leery *adjective* wary, chary, cautious, careful, guarded, on one's guard, suspicious, distrustful, mistrusting.

lees *plural noun* *emptied the lees from a wine glass* dregs, sediment, deposit, grounds, settlings, residue, remains; *Tech.* precipitate, sublimate.

leeway *noun* *the budget leaves little leeway for design costs* room to maneuver, room to operate, latitude, elbowroom, slack, space, margin, play.

left *adjective* 1 *the left side* left-hand, sinistral, sinister, sinistrous; port. 2 *a left politician* left-wing, leftist, socialist, radical, progressive, liberal, communist, communistic. *Antonyms:* RIGHT; REACTIONARY.

left-handed *adjective* 1 *left-handed writers* sinistral; *inf.* southpaw. 2 *a left-handed compliment* backhanded, ambiguous, equivocal, double-meaning, double-edged, dubious, indirect, enigmatic, cryptic, paradoxical, ironic, sardonic. 3 *a left-handed attempt at putting things right* awkward, clumsy, fumbling, unskillful, gauche, maladroit.

leftover *noun* *a leftover from a bygone age* survivor, residue, legacy.

leftover *adjective* *leftover food* remaining, excess, surplus, extra, uneaten, unused, unwanted.

leftovers *plural noun* *give the leftovers to the dogs* remainder, excess, surplus, leavings, uneaten food, unused supplies, scraps, odds and ends. *See* LEAVINGS.

ber, appendage, shank; *inf.* drumstick. **2** *the legs of the tripod* | *chair legs* support, upright, prop, brace, underpinning. **3** *the final leg of the journey* part, portion, segment, section, bit, stretch, stage, lap. **give someone a leg up** *give her a leg up in her career* act as someone's support, support someone, help someone up, help someone, give someone assistance, assist someone, lend someone a helping hand, come to someone's aid, aid someone, give someone a boost, boost someone, advance someone. **not have a leg to stand on** *after his accomplice confessed, he did not have a leg to stand on* have nothing to support one's story/opinion (etc.), lack support, lack validity, lack credence, be vulnerable, be defenseless. **on its last legs 1** *this furniture is on its last legs* about to break, about to collapse, dilapidated, worn out, rickety. **2** *the firm is on its last legs* about to fail, about to go bankrupt, failing, near to ruin, going to the wall; *inf.* going bust. **on one's last legs** *she's on her last legs after the long journey* exhausted, worn out, fatigued, fagged out, about to collapse, about to break down, about to die, dying, at death's door; *inf.* all in, done in, shattered. **pull someone's leg** *we were just pulling her leg* tease someone, rag someone, make fun of someone, trick someone, hoax someone, fool someone, deceive someone; *inf.* kid someone, rib someone, put on someone. **stretch one's legs** *stop the car and stretch one's legs* go for a walk, take a walk, go for a stroll, move about, promenade, get some exercise, get some air.

legacy noun 1 *willed a legacy of several million dollars* bequest, inheritance, heritage, bequeathal, endowment, gift, patrimony, heirloom; *fml.* devise. **2** *a legacy of Navajo culture* | *this is the legacy of unemployment* inheritance, heritage, tradition, hand-me-down, residue.

legal adjective 1 *legal behavior* lawful, legitimate, licit, legalized, valid, right, proper, sound, permissible, permitted, allowable, allowed, aboveboard, admissible, acceptable, authorized, sanctioned, warranted, licensed; *inf.* legit. **2** *legal processes/adviser* judicial, jurisdictive, forensic.
Antonyms: ILLEGAL; UNLAWFUL; CRIMINAL.

legality noun *dispute the legality of their actions* lawfulness, legitimacy, legitimateness, validity, rightness, rightfulness, soundness, permissibility, admissibility.

legalize verb *efforts to legalize marijuana* make legal, decriminalize, legitimize, legitimatize, legitimate, validate, ratify, permit, allow, admit, accept, authorize, sanction, warrant, license.

legate noun *a papal legate* envoy, emissary, agent, ambassador, representative, commissioner, nuncio, messenger.

legatee noun *the chief legatees mentioned in the will* beneficiary, recipient, inheritor, heir, heiress.

legation noun 1 *part of the American legation in* Britain mission, diplomatic mission, embassy, consulate, ministry, delegation, deputation, representation, envoys. **2** *the address of the American legation* embassy, consulate, diplomatic establishment, ministry.

legend noun 1 *a book of Scandinavian legends* myth, saga, epic, folk tale, folk story, traditional story, tale, story, narrative, fable, romance. **2** *Greta Garbo became a legend* famous person, celebrity, star, superstar, luminary. **3** *the legends under the photographs* | *legends on coins* caption, inscription, dedication, motto, device. **4** *the legends accompanying the tables* key, code, cipher, explanation, table of symbols.

legendary adjective 1 *legendary figures in Icelandic saga* mythical, heroic, traditional, fabled, fictitious, fictional, storybook, romantic, fanciful, fantastical, fabulous. **2** *a legendary actor* celebrated, acclaimed, illustrious, famous, famed, renowned, well-known, popular, remembered, immortal.
Antonyms: FACTUAL; HISTORICAL; UNKNOWN.

legerdemain noun 1 *magicians practicing legerdemain* sleight of hand, juggling, conjuring, prestidigitation, trickery, hocus-pocus, thaumaturgy. **2** *a politician noted for his legerdemain* trickery, cunning, artfulness, craftiness, craft, wiles, deceit, deception, dissimulation, artful argument, double-dealing, specious reasoning, sophistry.

legibility noun readability, readableness, ease of reading, decipherability, clearness, clarity, plainness, neatness.

legible adjective easily read, easy to read, readable, decipherable, clear, distinct, plain, carefully written, neat.
Antonyms: ILLEGIBLE; INDECIPHERABLE.

legion noun 1 *legions of soldiers* army, brigade, regiment, battalion, company, troop, division, unit, force. **2** *legions of people arrived for the festival* horde, host, throng, multitude, crowd, drove, mass, mob, gang, swarm, flock, herd.

legislate verb *the task of Congress to legislate* make laws, pass laws, enact laws, formulate laws, establish laws, codify laws. **legislate for** *they must legislate for more housing subsidies* pass laws for, decree, order, ordain, prescribe, authorize, make provision for.

legislation noun 1 *his office is in charge of legislation* lawmaking, law enactment, law formulation, codification, prescription. **2** *dislike the new legislation* law, body of laws, constitution, rule(s), regulation(s), act(s), bill(s), statute(s), enactment(s), charter(s), ordinance(s), measure(s), canon, code.

legislative adjective *legislative assembly/powers* lawmaking, lawgiving, judicial, jurisdictive, congressional, senatorial, parliamentary.

legislator noun lawmaker, lawgiver, congressman, congresswoman, senator, parliamentarian, politician.

legitimate *adjective* **1** *legitimate actions* legal, lawful, licit, within the law, going by the rules; *inf.* legit. **2** *the legitimate heir* lawful, rightful, genuine, authentic, real, true, proper, correct, authorized, sanctioned, warranted, acknowledged, recognized, approved; *inf.* legit, kosher. **3** *a legitimate reason for being late* valid, sound, admissible, acceptable, well-founded, justifiable, reasonable, plausible, credible, believable, reliable, logical, rational.
Antonyms: ILLEGAL; ILLEGITIMATE; INVALID.

legitimize *verb* legitimate, legalize, pronounce lawful, declare legal, decriminalize, validate, permit, warrant, authorize, sanction, license, give the stamp of approval to.

leisure *noun seek a hobby for periods of leisure* | *leisure pursuits* free time, spare time, spare moments, time to spare, idle hours, inactivity, time off, relaxation, recreation, freedom, holiday, vacation, breathing space, breathing spell, respite; *inf.* time to kill. **at one's leisure** *you can do this work at your leisure* at one's convenience, when it suits one, in one's own good time, when one can fit it in, without need for haste, without haste, unhurriedly, without hurry, when one gets around to it.
Antonyms: WORK; OCCUPATION.

leisurely *adjective at a leisurely pace* unhurried, relaxed, easy, easygoing, gentle, comfortable, restful, slow, lazy, lingering; *inf.* laid-back.
Antonyms: BRISK; HURRIED; FAST.

lend *verb* **1** *lend him a book* loan, give someone the loan of, let someone have the use of, advance. **2** *the flowers lend beauty to the room* impart, add, give, bestow, confer, provide, supply, furnish. **3** *lend his professional skill to the venture* give, contribute, donate, grant. **lend an ear to** *lend an ear to what the teacher is saying* listen to, pay attention to, take notice of, heed, pay heed to, give ear to. **lend a hand** *lend a hand with the preparations* help, help out, give a helping hand, assist, give assistance, aid, make a contribution; *inf.* pitch in. **lend itself to** *the house does not lend itself to being divided* be suitable for, be suited to, be appropriate for, be adaptable to, have the right characteristics for.
Antonyms: BORROW; DETRACT.

length *noun* **1** *what length is the cloth?* distance lengthwise, distance, extent lengthwise, extent, linear measure, span, reach. **2** *he's been here for quite a length of time* period, stretch, duration, term, span. **3** *a length of cloth* piece, portion, section, measure, segment, swatch. **4** *a speech noted for its length* longness, lengthiness, extensiveness, protractedness, elongation, prolixity, prolixness, wordiness, verbosity, verboseness, long-windedness, tediousness, tedium. **at length 1** *speak at length* for a long time, for ages, for hours, on and on, interminably, endlessly. **2** *deal at length with the problem* fully, to the fullest extent, in detail, in depth, thoroughly, exhaustively, completely. **3** *at length he agreed to accept* after a long time, after a considerable time, finally, at last, at long last, eventually, in the end, ultimately, in time. **go to any length(s)** *she would go to any lengths to save her child* do absolutely anything, go to any extreme, go to any limits, observe no limits.

lengthen *verb* **1** *lengthen a skirt* make longer, elongate, let down. **2** *the days are lengthening* grow longer, get longer, draw out, stretch. **3** *lengthen the time taken* | *lengthened his speech* make longer, prolong, increase, extend, expand, protract, stretch out, draw out.
Antonyms: SHORTEN; CURTAIL; DECREASE.

lengthy *adjective* **1** *a lengthy affair* long, very long, long-lasting, prolonged, extended, protracted, long-drawn-out. **2** *a lengthy speech* long, very long, overlong, protracted, long-drawn-out, diffuse, discursive, verbose, wordy, prolix, long-winded, tedious.
Antonyms: SHORT; BRIEF; CONCISE.

lenience, leniency *noun* **1** *the leniency of the judge* mercy, mercifulness, clemency, humanity, tolerance, compassion, indulgence, gentleness. *See* LENIENT 1. **2** *the leniency of the jail sentence* mildness, mercifulness, moderateness, lack of severity.

lenient *adjective* **1** *a lenient judge* merciful, clement, sparing, moderate, compassionate, humane, forbearing, tolerant, liberal, magnanimous, indulgent, kind, gentle, easygoing. **2** *a lenient jail sentence* mild, merciful, moderate, nonsevere.
Antonyms: MERCILESS; SEVERE; HARSH.

---

lenient
forbearing, indulgent, lax, merciful, permissive
Not all parents approach discipline in the same way. Someone who is **lenient** is willing to lower his or her standards of strictness when it comes to imposing discipline (*the principal was lenient with the students who had been caught playing hooky*). A parent who is **forbearing** struggles against giving in to negative feelings and is therefore able to abstain from hasty or ill-tempered actions, no matter what the provocation (*her father's forbearing attitude meant that she escaped with only a lecture*). **Indulgent** goes beyond forbearing and suggests catering to someone's whims (*an indulgent parent who seldom denied her child anything*). **Lax** is a negative kind of leniency involving laziness or indifference (*a lax mother who never imposed a curfew*), while **merciful** suggests a relaxing of standards on the basis of compassion (*a merciful mother who understood her daughter's anger*). To be **permissive** is also to be extremely lenient—an approach that connotes tolerance to the point of passivity (*the children's utter disregard for the rules was the result of their permissive upbringing*).

---

leper *noun* social outcast, outcast, pariah, untouchable, *persona non grata*.

leprechaun *noun* elf, sprite, fairy, gnome; *inf.* one of the little people.

lesbian *noun* homosexual, gay, homoerotic, Sapphic, tribade; *derog. inf.* butch; dyke.

lesbian *adjective* homosexual, gay, homoerotic, Sapphic, tribadic; *derog. inf.* queer.

lesion *noun* *lesions on her face after the accident* wound, injury, sore, abrasion, scratch, scrape, cut, gash, laceration, trauma.

less *adjective* *of less importance* smaller, slighter, not so much, not so great.

less *pronoun* *have less than they have* smaller amount, not so much.

less *adverb* *she reads less now* to a lesser degree, to a smaller extent, not so much.

less *preposition* *$100 less the deposit* minus, subtracting, excepting, without.

lessen *verb* **1** *the wind/pain lessened* grow less, abate, decrease, diminish, subside, moderate, slacken, die down, let up, ease off, ebb, wane. **2** *the massage lessened the pain* relieve, soothe, allay, assuage, alleviate, palliate, ease, dull, deaden, blunt, take the edge off. **3** *his behavior lessened him in their eyes* diminish, lower, reduce, minimize, degrade, discredit, devalue, belittle, humble.
Antonyms: INCREASE; MAGNIFY.

lesser *adjective* **1** *one of his lesser works* less important, minor, slighter, secondary, inferior. **2** *lesser people had to stand* subordinate, minor, inferior.

lesson *noun* **1** *have a music lesson* class, period of instruction/teaching/coaching/tutoring/schooling. **2** *children doing lessons* exercise, schoolwork, homework, assignment, school task. **3** *reading the lesson in church* Bible passage, Bible reading, scripture, text. **4** *punished as a lesson to others* example, warning, deterrent, message, moral, precept. **5** *hardship taught him valuable lessons* knowledge, wisdom, enlightenment, experience, truths.

lest *conjunction* *lest we forget* in case, in order to avoid that, for fear that.

let *verb* **1** *let them play there* allow to, permit to, give permission to, give leave to, authorize to, sanction to, grant to, warrant to, license to; give the go-ahead to, give the thumbs up to; *inf.* give the green light to. **2** *let the people through* allow to go, permit to pass. **3** *let it be known* cause, make, enable. **let down 1** *they felt he had let them down* fail to support, fail, fall short of expectation, disappoint, disillusion, forsake, abandon, desert, leave stranded, leave in the lurch, betray. **2** *let down the skirt* lengthen, make longer. **let in** *let the dog in* allow to enter, admit, open the door to, grant entrance to, give access to, give right of entry to, receive, welcome, greet. **let in on** *let them in on the deal* include in, count in on, admit, allow to share in, let participate in, take in on. **let off 1** *let off the firework* explode, detonate. **2** *letting off fumes* give off, discharge, emit, release, exude, leak. **3** *let the guilty man off* acquit, release, dis-

charge, reprieve, absolve, exonerate, pardon, forgive, exempt, spare. **let on 1** *don't let on that you know him* reveal, make known, tell, disclose, divulge, let out, let slip, give away, leak. **2** *he let on that he was deaf* pretend, feign, affect, make out, make believe, simulate, fake. **let out 1** *let the caged animals out* allow to leave, open the door for, grant exit to, let go, free, set free, release, liberate. **2** *she let out a scream* emit, utter, give vent to, produce. **3** *she let out that she knew him* reveal, make known, tell, disclose. *See* LET ON 1 (above). **let up 1** *the storm finally let up* lessen, abate, decrease, diminish, subside, moderate, slacken, die down, ease off, ebb, wane. **2** *if you don't let up, you'll have a breakdown* do less, relax one's efforts, relax, stop. **3** *please let up on the child* treat less severely, be more lenient with, be kinder to; *inf.* go easy on.

letdown *noun* *the tournament/movie/party was a letdown* disappointment, disillusionment, nonsuccess, fiasco, anticlimax; *inf.* washout.

lethal *adjective* *a lethal blow/dose | potentially lethal set of circumstances* fatal, deadly, mortal, death-dealing, murderous, poisonous, toxic, dangerous, virulent, noxious, destructive, disastrous, calamitous, ruinous.
Antonyms: HARMLESS; SAFE.

lethargic *adjective* sluggish, inactive, slow, slothful, torpid, phlegmatic, listless, languid, apathetic, passive, weary, enervated, fatigued, sleepy, narcotic.
Antonyms: ACTIVE; ENERGETIC.

lethargy *noun* sluggishness, inertia, inactivity, slowness, sloth, idleness, torpor, torpidity, lifelessness, dullness, listlessness, languor, languidness, phlegm, apathy, passivity, weariness, lassitude, fatigue, sleepiness, drowsiness, somnolence, narcosis.

letter *noun* **1** *written in bold letters | letter of the alphabet* character, alphabetical character, sign, symbol. **2** *send a letter* written message, message, written communication, communication, note, line, business letter, missive, epistle, dispatch, love letter, billet-doux, fan mail, thank-you note, reply, acknowledgment; *inf.* Dear John letter. **to the letter** *follow our instructions to the letter* with strict attention to detail, strictly, precisely, exactly, accurately, literally, word for word, verbatim. **letter of the law** *interpret agreements according to the letter of the law* exact wording, literal interpretation, form of words.

lettered *adjective* *a lettered person* learned, erudite, academic, well-educated, educated, well-read, widely read, cultured, cultivated, scholarly, literary; *inf.* highbrow.

letters *plural noun* *a man of letters* learning, scholarship, erudition, education, culture, cultivation, literature, humanities, belles lettres.

letup *noun* *no letup in the hostilities* lessening,

abatement, decrease, diminishing, diminution, subsidence, moderation, slackening, dying down, easing off, ebbing, waning.

level *adjective* 1 *a level surface* flat, smooth, even, uniform, plane, flush, horizontal. 2 *keep the temperature level* even, uniform, regular, consistent, constant, stable, steady, unchanging, unvarying, unfluctuating. 3 *the two teams are level* equal, on a level, in a position of equality, close together, neck and neck, side by side, on a par; *inf.* even-steven. 4 *hang the pictures level with each other* on the same level, on a level, at the same height, aligned, in line, balanced. 5 *have a level temper* even, even-tempered, equable, steady, stable, calm, serene, tranquil, composed, unruffled.
Antonyms: UNEVEN; BUMPY; VERTICAL; VARIABLE.

level *noun* 1 *at eye level* height, highness, altitude, elevation, distance upward. 2 *what level is he in the firm?* level of achievement, position, rank, standing, status, station, degree, grade, stage, standard. 3 *what level of expense have you in mind?* extent, amount, quantity, measure, degree, volume, size. 4 *levels of rock* layer, stratum, bed. 5 *what level do you live on?* floor, story. **on the level** *are you sure that your partner is on the level?* honest, aboveboard, straight, fair, genuine, true, sincere, open, straightforward; *inf.* upfront, kosher.

level *verb* 1 *level the surface* level out, make level, even off, even out, make flat, flatten, smooth, smooth out, plane. 2 *level the buildings* raze, raze to the ground, pull down, knock down, tear down, demolish, flatten, bulldoze, lay waste, destroy. 3 *level the trees* fell, cut down, chop down, hew down. 4 *level his opponent* knock down, knock to the ground, throw to the ground, lay out, flatten, floor, fell, knock out; *inf.* KO, kayo. 5 *his goal leveled the score* make level, equalize, make equal, even, even up. 6 *level his gun at the target* aim, point, direct, train, sight, focus, beam, zero in on, draw a bead on. **level with** *he's not leveling with you* be honest with, be aboveboard with, tell the truth to, tell all to, be frank with, be open with, hide nothing from, keep nothing back from, be straightforward with, put all one's cards on the table with; *inf.* be upfront with.

levelheaded *adjective* sensible, full of common sense, prudent, circumspect, shrewd, wise, reasonable, rational, sane, composed, calm, cool, collected, coolheaded, balanced, self-possessed, unruffled, even-tempered, imperturbable; *inf.* unflappable, together.

lever *noun* 1 *use a lever to pry the lid off* bar, crowbar, pry, prize. 2 *release the lever to operate the machine* handle, grip, pull, switch.

lever *verb* lever the lid open | *lever the load up* pry, prize, force, move, raise, lift, hoist.

leverage *noun* 1 *not enough leverage to move the load* purchase, force, strength. 2 *not have the*

leverage to win over the committee power, influence, authority, weight, ascendancy, rank; *inf.* pull, clout.

levitate *verb spiritualists claiming to be able to levitate* rise into the air, float, hover, be suspended, glide, fly.

levity *noun* 1 *showing levity at a solemn occasion* lightheartedness, carefreeness, facetiousness, light-mindedness, humor, fun, jocularity, hilarity, frivolity, flippancy, triviality, silliness, giddiness. 2 *the levity of her nature* fickleness, inconstancy, instability, unsteadiness, variability, changeability, unreliability, undependability, inconsistency, flightiness.
Antonyms: GRAVITY; CONSTANCY.

levy *noun* 1 *the levy of taxes* collection, gathering, raising, imposition, exaction, assessment. 2 *unable to pay the levy* tax, taxation, tariff, toll, excise, customs, duty, dues, imposition, impost, assessment. 3 *inspect the levy* conscripts, troops, forces, armed forces, army, militia, guard.

levy *verb* 1 *levy taxes* collect, gather, raise, impose, exact, demand, charge, tax. 2 *levy troops* conscript, call up, draft, enlist, muster, mobilize, rally, press.

lewd *adjective* 1 *lewd person/behavior* lecherous, lustful, licentious, lascivious, promiscuous, carnal, sensual, prurient, salacious, lubricious, libidinous, concupiscent, debauched, dissipated, dissolute, profligate, unchaste, wanton. 2 *lewd literature* obscene, pornographic, blue, bawdy, salacious, suggestive, ribald, indecent, vulgar, crude, smutty, dirty, coarse, gross, foul, vile; *inf.* raunchy.

lewdness *noun* 1 *the lewdness of his friends/behavior* lechery, lust, lustfulness, licentiousness, lasciviousness, promiscuity, carnality, sensuality, prurience, pruriency, salaciousness, salacity, lubricity, libidinousness, concupiscence, debauchery, dissipation, dissoluteness, profligacy, unchasteness, wantonness. 2 *the lewdness of the literature* obscenity, blueness, bawdiness, salaciousness, salacity, suggestiveness, ribaldry, indecency, vulgarity, crudeness, smut, smuttiness, dirtiness, coarseness, grossness, foulness, vileness; *inf.* raunchiness.

liability *noun* 1 *admit liability for the lost goods* responsibility, legal responsibility, accountability, answerability, blame, blameworthiness, culpability, amenableness. 2 *meet his financial liabilities* obligation, debt, indebtedness, debit, arrears, dues. 3 *the extra suitcase proved to be a liability* hindrance, encumbrance, burden, impediment, handicap, nuisance, inconvenience, drawback, drag, disadvantage, millstone around one's neck, stumbling block, cross to bear. 4 *dislike her liability to burst into tears* aptness, likelihood, inclination, tendency, disposition, predisposition, proneness.

liable *adjective not liable for customers' lost property* responsible, legally responsible, accountable, answerable, chargeable, blameworthy, at

fault, censurable. **liable to** 1 *liable to injury* exposed to, open to, subject to, susceptible to, vulnerable to, in danger of, at risk of, pregnable to. 2 *liable to burst into tears* apt to, likely to, inclined to, tending to, disposed to, predisposed to, prone to.
Antonyms: UNACCOUNTABLE; SAFE; UNLIKELY.

liaison *noun* 1 *no liaison between the departments* communication, contact, connection, interchange, link, linkage. 2 *he acts as liaison between the departments* intermediary, contact man/ woman/person, go-between. 3 *his wife found out about his liaison* affair, illicit/adulterous affair, love affair, relationship, romance, intrigue, amour, amorous/romantic entanglement, entanglement, flirtation; *inf.* hanky-panky.

liar *noun* teller of lies, teller of untruths, fibber, fibster, perjurer, falsifier, false witness, fabricator, equivocator, prevaricator, deceiver, spinner of yarns; *inf.* storyteller.

libation *noun* 1 *offer a libation to the gods* liquid offering, offering, tribute, oblation, sacrifice. 2 *in need of a libation after the long walk* drink, liquid refreshment, beverage, alcoholic drink, bracer.

libel *noun* *a writer found guilty of libel* defamation of character, defamation, denigration, vilification, disparagement, derogation, aspersions, calumny, slander, false report, traducement, obloquy, abuse, slur, smear, smear campaign.

libel *verb* *his biographer libeled him* defame, vilify, give someone a bad name, blacken someone's name, denigrate, disparage, derogate, cast aspersions on, calumniate, slander, write false reports about, traduce, abuse, revile, malign, slur, smear, fling mud at, drag someone through the mud, drag someone's name through the mud.

libelous *adjective* *published libelous remarks* defamatory, denigratory, vilifying, disparaging, derogatory, aspersive, calumnious, calumniatory, slanderous, false, misrepresentative, traducing, abusive, reviling, malicious, maligning, scurrilous, slurring, smearing, muckraking.

liberal *adjective* 1 *a liberal supply of food* abundant, copious, ample, plentiful, lavish, profuse, munificent, bountiful, rich, handsome, generous. 2 *hosts liberal with their hospitality* generous, magnanimous, openhanded, unsparing, unstinting, ungrudging, lavish, munificent, bountiful, bounteous, beneficent, bighearted, kindhearted, kind, philanthropic, charitable, altruistic, unselfish. 3 *too liberal to abide such discrimination* tolerant, unprejudiced, unbiased, unbigoted, impartial, nonpartisan, disinterested, broad-minded, enlightened, catholic, indulgent, permissive. 4 *a liberal interpretation of the law* broad, loose, flexible, nonrestrictive, free, general, nonliteral, not strict, not close, inexact, imprecise. 5 *liberal in his politics* advanced, forward-looking, pro-

gressive, reformist, radical, latitudinarian. 6 *a liberal education* wide-ranging, broad-based, general, humanistic.
Antonyms: MISERLY; NARROW-MINDED; CONSERVATIVE; REACTIONARY.

liberate *verb* *liberate prisoners* | *liberate the occupied country* set free, free, release, let out, let go, discharge, set loose, unshackle, unfetter, unchain, deliver, rescue, emancipate, manumit, unyoke.
Antonyms: CONFINE; IMPRISON.

liberation *noun* 1 *the liberation of the prisoners* freeing, release, discharge, unshackling, deliverance, emancipation, manumission. *See* LIBERATE. 2 *women seeking liberation* freedom, equality, equal rights, nondiscrimination, emancipation, enfranchisement.

liberator *noun* rescuer, savior, deliverer, freer, emancipator, manumitter.

libertine *adjective* *disapprove of their libertine ways* licentious, lustful, lecherous, lascivious, dissolute, dissipated, debauched, immoral, wanton, decadent, depraved, profligate, rakish, sensual, promiscuous, unchaste, impure, sinful, intemperate, abandoned, corrupt.

libertine *noun* lecher, seducer, debauchee, profligate, rake, roué, wanton, sensualist, reprobate, womanizer, adulterer, Don Juan, Lothario, Casanova; *inf.* lech.

liberty *noun* 1 *countries that have always had liberty* freedom, independence, autonomy, sovereignty, self-government, self-rule. 2 *prisoners gaining their liberty* freedom, liberation, release, discharge, deliverance, emancipation, manumission. 3 *have the liberty to choose* freedom, free will, volition, latitude, option, choice, noncompulsion, noncoercion. 4 *given the liberty to leave the grounds* right, prerogative, privilege, permission, sanction, authorization, license, carte blanche, dispensation, exemption. **at liberty** 1 *the thief/animal is still at liberty* free, loose, on the loose, at large, unconfined. 2 *you are at liberty to do as you wish* free, permitted, allowed, entitled. **take liberties** *made a poor impression by taking liberties with the staff* be overfamiliar, be familiar, be disrespectful, display/show/exercise impropriety/indecorum, breach etiquette, be impertinent, be insolent, be impudent, be presumptuous, be forward, be audacious.
Antonyms: DEPENDENCE; CAPTIVITY; CONSTRAINT.

---

liberty
freedom, independence, license, permission
The Fourth of July is the day on which Americans commemorate their nation's **independence**, a word that implies the ability to stand alone, without being sustained by anything else. While *independence* is usually associated with countries or nations, **freedom** and **liberty** more often apply to individuals. But unlike

freedom, which implies an absence of restraint or compulsion (*the freedom to speak openly*), *liberty* implies the power to choose among alternatives rather than merely being unrestrained (*the liberty to select their own form of government*). *Freedom* can also apply to many different types of oppressive influences (*freedom from interruption; freedom to leave the room at any time*), while *liberty* often connotes deliverance or release (*he gave the slaves their liberty*). **License** may imply the *liberty* to disobey rules or regulations imposed on others, especially when there is an advantage to be gained in doing so (*poetic license*). But more often it refers to an abuse of *liberty* or the power to do whatever one pleases (*a license to sell drugs*). **Permission** is an even broader term than *license*, suggesting the capacity to act without interference or censure, usually with some degree of approval or authority (*permission to be absent from his post*).

---

libidinous *adjective* lustful, lecherous, lascivious, lewd, carnal, sensual, salacious, prurient, concupiscent, lubricious, dissolute, debauched, degenerate, decadent, wanton, immoral, unchaste, impure, intemperate; *inf.* horny.

libido *noun has a high/low libido* sexual desire, sex drive, sexual appetite, sexiness, sexual passion, lust, lustfulness; *inf.* horniness.

license *noun* **1** *be given license to sell their wares* permission, leave, liberty, freedom, consent, authority, authorization, sanction, approval, warranty, certification, accreditation, entitlement, privilege, prerogative, right, dispensation, exemption. **2** *they have the license to do as they please* freedom, liberty, free will, latitude, choice, independence, self-determination, option. **3** *a driver's license* permit, certificate, credential, document, documentation, pass. **4** *appalled at the license at the party* licentiousness, dissoluteness, dissipation, debauchery, immorality, decadence, profligacy, immoderation, intemperateness, self-indulgence, indulgence, excess, excessiveness, lack of restraint, lack of control, irresponsibility, abandon, disorderliness, unruliness, lawlessness, anarchy.

license *verb* grant a license to, give a license to, give a permit to, authorize, give authorization to, grant the right to, give permission to, permit, allow, entitle, give the freedom to, sanction, give one's approval to, empower, warrant, certify, accredit, charter, franchise.
Antonyms: BAN; FORBID.

licentious *adjective* dissolute, lustful, lecherous, lascivious, dissipated, debauched, immoral, wanton, decadent, depraved, profligate, sensual, promiscuous, unchaste, impure, intemperate, abandoned.
Antonyms: MORAL; VIRTUOUS.

licit *adjective declared a licit action* legal, lawful, legitimate, permissible, admissible, allowable, acceptable.

lick *verb* **1** *lick the ice cream* pass the tongue over, touch with the tongue, tongue, taste, lap. **2** *flames licking the walls* touch, play over, flick over, dart over, ripple over. **3** *lick the opponents* defeat, beat, conquer, trounce, thrash, rout, vanquish, overcome, overwhelm, overpower, drub; *inf.* wipe the floor with. **4** *licked the galley slaves* beat, thrash, flog, whip, strike, hit, thwack, slap, spank; *inf.* wallop, whack, lambaste. **5** *lick the problem* get the better of, overcome, solve, find an answer to, find a solution to.

licking *noun* **1** *the team gave their opponents a good licking* defeat, beating, trouncing, thrashing, drubbing. **2** *the shipmate received a licking from the wicked captain* beating, thrashing, flogging, whipping, slapping, spanking; *inf.* walloping, tanning.

lid *noun* cover, top, cap, cork, stopper, plug. **blow the lid off** *blow the lid off the scandal* expose, reveal, bring to light, make known, make public, bring into the open.

lie[1] *noun witness found to be telling lies* untruth, falsehood, barefaced lie, fib, white lie, little white lie, fabrication, made-up story, trumped-up story, invention, piece of fiction, fiction, falsification, falsity, fairy tale/story, cock-and-bull story, dissimulation, prevarication, departure from the truth; *inf.* tall tale, whopper. **give the lie to** *the historical evidence gave the lie to his theory* disprove, contradict, negate, deny, refute, rebut, challenge, gainsay.
Antonyms: TRUTH; FACT.

lie[2] *verb the witness was lying* tell a lie, tell an untruth, tell a falsehood, perjure oneself, fib, tell a white lie, invent/make up a story, prevaricate, depart from the truth, be economical with the truth, bear false witness, lie through one's teeth; *inf.* lie like a rug.

---

lie

equivocate, fabricate, fib, prevaricate, rationalize
If your spouse asks you whether you remembered to mail the tax forms and you say Yes, even though you know they're still sitting on the passenger seat of your car, you're telling a **lie**, which is a deliberately false statement. If you launch into a lengthy explanation of the day's frustrations and setbacks, the correct word would be **prevaricate**, which is to quibble, dodge the point, or confuse the issue so as to avoid telling the truth. If you tell your spouse that you would have mailed the taxes, but then you started thinking about an important deduction you might be entitled to take and decided it would be unwise to mail them without looking into it, you're **rationalizing**, which is to come up with reasons that put your own behavior in the most favorable possible light. If you say that there was an accident in front of the post office that prevented you from find-

ing a parking space and there really wasn't, **fabricate** is the correct verb, meaning that you've invented a false story or excuse without the harsh connotations of *lie* (*she fabricated an elaborate story about how they got lost on their way home*). **Equivocate** implies saying one thing and meaning another; it usually suggests the use of words that have more than one meaning, or whose ambiguity may be misleading. For example, if your spouse says, Did you take care of the taxes today? you might equivocate by saying Yes, you took care of them—meaning that you finished completing the forms and sealing them in the envelope, but that you didn't actually get them to the post office. To **fib** is to tell a falsehood about something unimportant; it is often used as a euphemism for *lie* (*a child who fibs about eating his vegetables*).

lie³ *verb* **1** *he was lying, not sitting* recline, be recumbent, be prostrate, be supine, be prone, be stretched out, sprawl, rest, repose, relax, lounge, loll. **2** *the town lies on the other side of the hill* be, be situated, be located, be placed, be positioned, be found. **3** *two poets lie there* be buried, be interred. **4** *lie dormant* remain, continue, stay, be. **5** *his guilt lies (heavily) on him* press down, weigh down, be a great weight, be a burden, oppress. **6** *their strength lies in their faith* consist, be inherent, be present, exist, reside. **lie low** *they lay low during the police search* hide, go into hiding, hide out, conceal oneself, keep out of sight, keep a low profile, take cover, go underground; *inf.* hole up.

liege *noun* liege lord, lord, feudal lord, overlord, suzerain, master, chief, chieftain, superior.

lieutenant *noun* assistant, aide, deputy, second-in-command; right-hand man/woman, henchman, henchwoman, subordinate; *inf.* sidekick.

life *noun* **1** *as long as there is life in my body, I will dance* existence, being, animation, aliveness, viability. **2** *is there life on Mars?* | *no sign of life* living things, living beings, living creatures, human/animal/plant life, fauna, flora, human activity. **3** *many lives were lost in the war* person, human being, being, individual, mortal, soul. **4** *worked hard all her life* lifetime, days, duration of life, course of life, life span, time on earth, existence, career; *inf.* one's born days. **5** *the life of a battery* duration, active life, functioning period, period of effectiveness, period of usefulness. **6** *modern conveniences make life easier* course of life, living, activities, conduct, behavior. **7** *he should have won, but that's life* the human condition, the way of the world, the world, the times we live in, the usual state of affairs, the way it is, the way things go. **8** *he leads/has a very affluent life* way of life, way of living, manner of living, lifestyle, situation, position. **9** *he wrote a life of the poet* | *she is writing her life* biography, autobiography, life story, memoirs, history, career, diary, journal, confessions. **10** *children full of life* | *put some life in*

the party animation, vivacity, liveliness, vitality, verve, high spirits, sparkle, exuberance, buoyancy, effervescence, enthusiasm, energy, vigor, dynamism; *inf.* oomph, pizzazz, pep, zing. **11** *he was the life of the firm* life force, vital spirit, spirit, vital spark, animating spirit, moving force, lifeblood, very essence, essence, heart, core, soul, élan vital. **come to life 1** *the town comes to life at night* become active, come alive, become lively, wake up, awaken, show signs of life. **2** *toys come to life in the play* become animate, come alive, become a living creature. **for dear life** *they ran for dear life* as fast/hard (etc.) as possible, for all one is worth, in desperation, with urgency, urgently, with as much vigor as possible, like the devil. **give one's life 1** *he gave his life for his friend* die, sacrifice oneself. **2** *give one's life to teaching* dedicate oneself, devote oneself, give oneself, pledge oneself, surrender oneself.
Antonyms: DEATH; DEMISE.

life-and-death *adjective* *a life-and-death decision* vital, of vital importance, crucial, critical, urgent, momentous, important, serious.

lifeblood *noun* *manufacturing is the lifeblood of the economy* life, life force, animating spirit, moving force, driving force, vital spark, inspiration, animus, essence, heart, core, élan vital.

life-giving *adjective* vitalizing, animating, vivifying, energizing, invigorating, enlivening, stimulating.

lifeless *adjective* **1** *lifeless bodies* dead, deceased, gone, cold, defunct; motionless, limp. **2** *lifeless statues lined the corridor* inanimate, without life, inorganic, abiotic. **3** *lifeless stretches of country* barren, sterile, bare, desolate, stark, arid, unproductive, uncultivated, empty, uninhabited, unoccupied. **4** *a lifeless performance* spiritless, lacking vitality, unspirited, lackluster, apathetic, uninspired, colorless, dull, flat, stiff, wooden, tedious, uninspiring.
Antonyms: ALIVE; ANIMATE; LIVELY.

lifelike *adjective* *a lifelike portrait* true-to-life, realistic, photographic, speaking, faithful, authentic, exact, vivid, graphic, natural.

lifelong *adjective* *a lifelong commitment* for all one's life, lifetime's, lasting, constant, enduring, abiding, permanent.

lifestyle *noun* *an affluent lifestyle* way of life, way of living, manner of living, life.

lifetime *noun* **1** *many technological advances in his lifetime* life, life span, existence. *See* LIFE 4. **2** *what is the lifetime of the average battery?* life, duration, functioning period. *See* LIFE 5. **3** *wait a lifetime for a chance to travel* all one's life, a very long time; *inf.* ages, an age, forever, an eternity.

lift *verb* **1** *lift the furniture* pick up, uplift, hoist, upheave, raise, raise up, heft. **2** *lift the flag* raise high, hold up, bear aloft. **3** *your visit lifted his spirits* raise, buoy up, boost, elevate. **4** *the new*

player lifted their game improve, boost, enhance, make better, ameliorate, upgrade. **5** *the mist lifted* rise, disperse, dissipate, disappear, vanish, be dispelled. **6** *lift the ban* raise, remove, withdraw, revoke, rescind, cancel, annul, void, countermand, relax, end, stop, terminate. **7** *lift food to the famine region* airlift, transport by air, transport, move, transfer. **8** *lift one's voice* raise, make louder, louden, amplify. **9** *lift a passage from the book* plagiarize, pirate, copy, abstract. **10** *someone's lifted my purse* steal, thieve, rob, pilfer, purloin, filch, pocket, take, appropriate; *inf.* pinch, swipe.
Antonyms: DROP; LOWER.

lift *noun* **1** *give the child a lift up* hoist, heave, push, thrust, shove, help, a helping hand. **2** *the visitors gave the patient a lift* boost, pick-me-up, stimulus; *inf.* shot in the arm. **3** *the new player gave their game a lift* boost, improvement, enhancement, upgrading, amelioration. **4** *give the children a lift to school* car ride, ride, transportation.

light[1] *noun* **1** *see by the light of the sun/fire* illumination, luminescence, luminosity, shining, gleaming, brightness, brilliance, glowing, blaze, glare, incandescence, effulgence, refulgence, lambency, radiance, luster, sunlight, moonlight, starlight, lamplight, firelight, electric light, gaslight, ray of light, shaft of light, beam of light. **2** *bring the light over here* lamp, flashlight, lantern, beacon, candle, taper, torch. **3** *we like to travel in the light, not the dark* daylight, daylight hours, daytime, day, hours of sunlight. **4** *see things in a different light | things appeared in a new light* aspect, angle, slant, approach, viewpoint, point of view. **5** *light finally dawned and I solved the problem* enlightenment, illumination, understanding, comprehension, awareness, knowledge, elucidation, explanation. **6** *he was one of the lights in the theater group* leading lights, luminary, star, guiding light, expert, authority. **at light** *we shall leave at light* at first light, at dawn, at the crack of dawn, at daybreak, at sunrise, in the morning, first thing in the morning. **bring to light** *the search brought to light new evidence* reveal, disclose, expose, uncover, show up, unearth, bring to notice. **come to light** *new evidence came to light* be discovered, be uncovered, be unearthed, appear, come out, turn up, transpire. **in the light of** *in the light of his previous convictions* taking into consideration, considering, taking into account, bearing in mind, keeping in mind, mindful of, taking note of, in view of. **shed/throw (any) light on** *can you shed (any) light on this matter?* elucidate, clarify, clear up, explain, offer an/any explanation for.
Antonyms: DARK; DARKNESS; IGNORANCE.

light[2] *adjective* **1** *a light room* full of light, bright, well-lit, well-lighted, well-illuminated, sunny. **2** *wearing light clothes* light-colored, light-

toned, pale, pale-colored, subdued, pastel, pastel-colored; whitish, faded, bleached. **3** *she had light hair* light-colored, fair, blond.
Antonyms: DARK; shaded.

light[3] *verb* **1** *light the kindling* set burning, set fire to, set a match to, ignite, kindle. **2** *fireworks lit up the sky* illuminate, brighten, lighten, irradiate, flood with light, floodlight; *lit.* illumine. **3** *a smile lit up her face* irradiate, brighten, animate, make cheerful, cheer up, enliven.

light[4] *adjective* **1** *the suitcases are light* nonheavy, easy to carry, portable. **2** *small, light children* slight, thin, slender, skinny, underweight, small, tiny. **3** *wearing light clothes* lightweight, thin, flimsy, insubstantial, delicate, floaty, gossamer. **4** *a light tap on the shoulder | heard a light knock* gentle, slight, delicate, soft, weak, faint, indistinct. **5** *light tasks* moderate, easy, simple, undemanding, untaxing, unexacting, effortless, facile; *inf.* cushy. **6** *light music/reading/entertainment* nonserious, readily understood, lighthearted, entertaining, diverting, recreative, pleasing, amusing, humorous, funny, frivolous, superficial, trivial, trifling. **7** *a light attack of flu | a light jail sentence* nonsevere, mild, moderate, slight. **8** *this is no light matter* unimportant, insignificant, trivial, trifling, petty, inconsequential. **9** *a light meal* nonheavy, nonrich, nonlarge, easily digested, small, modest, scanty, skimpy, frugal. **10** *with (a) light heart* lighthearted, carefree, cheerful, cheery, happy, gay, merry, blithe, sunny, untroubled. **11** *played the piano with light fingers | was light of foot* nimble, deft, agile, supple, lithe, spry, sprightly, graceful. **12** *feeling light in the head* light-headed, giddy, dizzy, vertiginous, faint, unsteady; *inf.* woozy. **13** *light in character* frivolous, giddy, flighty, fickle, erratic, mercurial, volatile, capricious. **14** *of light morals* nonchaste, loose, promiscuous, licentious, dissolute, dissipated, wanton. **15** *light soil* nondense, porous, crumbly, friable.
Antonyms: HEAVY; WEIGHTY; SERIOUS; SEVERE.

light[5] *verb* **light into** *light into their attackers* attack, assault, set upon, fall upon, strike, beat, tear into; *inf.* lay into, let someone have it, lambaste, lace into. **light upon** *light upon a treasure | lit upon the truth* come across, chance upon, happen upon, stumble upon, hit upon, find, discover, encounter.

lighten[1] *verb* **1** *the sky lightened* become lighter, grow brighter, brighten. **2** *the flames lightened* blaze, glow, gleam, flicker, sparkle. **3** *it was lightening this morning* emit lightning, flash lightning, fulgurate. **4** *the larger windows lightened the room* make lighter, make brighter, brighten, light up, illuminate, shed light on, cast light on, irradiate. **5** *the sun had lightened the colors* whiten, bleach, pale.
Antonyms: DARKEN; ENSHROUD.

lighten[2] *verb* **1** *lighten the horse's load* make lighter, lessen, reduce, ease. **2** *lighten his burden of pain* lessen, reduce, ease, alleviate, mit-

igate, allay, relieve, assuage, ameliorate. **3** *the good news lightened his mood* brighten, cheer up, gladden, hearten, buoy up, perk up, lift, uplift, enliven, elate, inspire, revive, restore.
Antonyms: INCREASE; INTENSIFY; DEPRESS.

light-fingered *adjective tourists/storekeepers on the watch for light-fingered people* thieving, thievish, stealing, pilfering, filching, shoplifting, pickpocketing, pocket-picking, dishonest; *inf.* crooked.

light-footed *adjective* light of foot, spry, sprightly, light on one's feet, graceful, nimble, agile, lithe.

light-headed *adjective* **1** *feeling light-headed at the top of the ladder* giddy, dizzy, vertiginous, faint, unsteady, light in the head; *inf.* woozy. **2** *tired of her light-headed friends* giddy, scatterbrained, featherbrained, harebrained, flighty, dizzy, frivolous, superficial, empty-headed, vacuous, flippant, shallow, light-minded, silly, inane; *inf.* birdbrained.

lighthearted *adjective* carefree, cheerful, cheery, happy, glad, gay, merry, playful, jolly, joyful, jovial, gleeful, frolicsome, effervescent, in good spirits, blithe, sunny, untroubled; *inf.* chirpy, upbeat.
Antonyms: MISERABLE; GLOOMY.

lighthouse *noun* light tower, warning light, guiding light, beacon, pharos.

lightly *adverb* **1** *snow falling lightly* slightly, thinly, softly, gently. **2** *salt the food lightly* sparingly, sparsely, slightly. **3** *get off lightly* easily, without severe punishment, leniently. **4** *jump lightly over the fence* easily, nimbly, agilely, lithely, spryly, gracefully. **5** *dismiss the subject lightly* airily, carelessly, heedlessly, uncaringly, indifferently, thoughtlessly, flippantly, frivolously, slightingly; *inf.* breezily.

lightweight *adjective* **1** *lightweight clothes* light, thin, flimsy. *See* LIGHT[4] *adjective* 3. **2** *lightweight prose* | *he's a lightweight writer* insignificant, of no account, unimportant, of no consequence, inconsequential, insubstantial, trivial, trifling, paltry, petty, of no merit, of no value, valueless, worthless.
Antonyms: HEAVY; WEIGHTY; heavyweight; SIGNIFICANT.

likable, likeable *adjective* pleasant, nice, friendly, agreeable, amiable, genial, charming, engaging, pleasing, appealing, winning, attractive, winsome, lovable, adorable.

like *adjective* *like people are attracted to each other* | *houses of like design* similar, much the same, more or less the same, not unlike, comparable, corresponding, resembling, analogous, parallel, equivalent, of a kind, identical, matching, akin.
Antonyms: UNLIKE; DISSIMILAR; DIFFERENT.

like *preposition* **1** *he paints like Picasso* in the same way as, in the manner of, in a similar way to, after the fashion of, along the lines of. **2** *it was like him to be generous* typical of, characteristic of, in character with, in keeping with.

like *noun not see his like again* equal, match, counterpart, fellow, twin, mate, parallel, peer, compeer.

like *verb* **1** *they like each other* be fond of, have a liking/fondness for, be attracted to, be keen on, love, adore, have a soft spot for. **2** *he likes swimming* enjoy, be keen on, find/take pleasure in, love, adore, find agreeable, delight in, relish, revel in; *inf.* get a kick from. **3** *we would like you to go* | *would like a piece of cake* wish, want, desire, prefer, sooner have, rather have. **4** *how would you like it if it happened to you?* feel about, regard, think about, appreciate. **like it or lump it** *See* LUMP[3].
Antonyms: DISLIKE; HATE.

likeable *adjective. See* LIKABLE, LIKEABLE.

likelihood *noun very little likelihood of his winning* probability, good chance, chance, prospect, good prospect, reasonable prospect, possibility, distinct possibility, strong possibility.

likely *adjective* **1** *it is likely that he will go* probable, distinctly possible, to be expected, in the cards, odds-on, possible. **2** *it is likely to rain* apt, inclined, tending, disposed, liable, prone. **3** *he gave a likely enough reason* reasonable, plausible, feasible, acceptable, believable, credible, tenable, conceivable. **4** *that's a likely story!* unlikely, implausible, unacceptable, unbelievable, incredible, untenable, inconceivable. **5** *a likely place for a picnic* suitable, appropriate, fit, fitting, acceptable, proper, right, qualified, relevant, reasonable. **6** *the most likely young people in the firm* likely-to-succeed, promising, talented, gifted; *inf.* up-and-coming.
Antonyms: UNLIKELY; IMPROBABLE; INCREDIBLE.

likely *adverb* *he'll likely refuse* probably, in all probability, no doubt, doubtlessly; *inf.* like as not.

liken *verb* **liken to** *liken his work to that of Picasso* show the resemblance/similarity to, compare to, equate to/with, analogize to, draw an analogy between (something) and (something), draw a parallel between (something) and (something), parallel to, correlate to, link to, associate with.

likeness *noun* **1** *there is a distinct likeness in the faces of the two friends* alikeness, resemblance, similarity, sameness, similitude, correspondence, analogy, parallelism. **2** *appear in the likeness of Santa Claus* guise, semblance, appearance, outward form, form, shape, character. **3** *he will draw a likeness of your child* picture, drawing, sketch, painting, portrait, photograph, study, representation, image, bust, statue, statuette, sculpture, icon.

---

likeness

affinity, analogy, resemblance, similarity, similitude
Two sisters who are only a year apart in age and who are very similar to each other in terms

of appearance and personality would be said to bear a **likeness** to one another. **Similarity** applies to people or things that are merely somewhat alike (*there was a similarity between the two women, both of whom were raised in the Midwest*), while **resemblance** suggests a similarity only in appearance or in superficial or external ways (*with their short hair and blue eyes, they bore a strong resemblance to each other*). **Affinity** adds to *resemblance* a natural kinship, temperamental sympathy, common experience, or some other relationship (*she has an affinity for young children*). **Similitude** is a more literary word meaning *likeness* or *similarity* in reference to abstract things (*a similitude of the truth*). An **analogy** is a comparison of things that are basically unlike but share certain attributes or circumstances (*he drew an analogy between the human heart and a bicycle pump*).

---

likes *noun hard to remember all your likes and dislikes* preferences, favorites; likings, weaknesses, leanings.

likewise *adverb* **1** *she left early and he did likewise* in like manner, in the same way, similarly, in similar fashion, the same. **2** *we enjoyed the food and likewise the company* in addition, also, too, besides, moreover, furthermore, into the bargain, as well.

liking *noun* fondness, love, affection, desire, preference, partiality, penchant, bias, weakness, weak spot, soft spot, appreciation, taste, predilection, fancy, inclination, bent, leaning, affinity, proclivity, propensity, proneness, tendency.
Antonyms: DISLIKE; AVERSION; HATRED.

lilt *noun a lilt in her voice* rise and fall, cadence, inflection, upswing, rhythm.

limb *noun* **1** *injure a limb* arm, leg, wing, member, extremity, appendage. **2** *cut down limbs from the tree* branch, bough. **3** *a limb of a mountain* spur, projection. **4** *the society is a limb of an international organization* branch, section, member, offshoot. **out on a limb** **1** *he found himself out on a limb when he voted against the bill* isolated, stranded, segregated, set apart, separate, in a solitary position, sequestered. **2** *you will be out on a limb if you challenge the general's authority* in a precarious position, vulnerable, in a risky situation, tempting fate, in a compromising situation, taking a chance/risk; sticking one's neck out.

limber *verb* **limber up** warm up, loosen up, stretch, exercise, get ready.

limbo *noun* **in limbo** *the proposals are in limbo* abeyance, suspended, on hold, in a state of suspension, in a state of uncertainty, in a state of neglect, up in the air, hanging, hanging fire, awaiting action; *inf.* on the back burner.

limelight *noun people in the limelight | those seeking the limelight* focus of attention, public at-

tention, public notice, public eye, public recognition, publicity, glare of publicity, fame, renown, celebrity, stardom, notability, eminence, prominence, spotlight.

limit *noun* **1** *outside the 200-mile fishing limit* boundary, boundary line, bound, bounds, partition line, demarcation line, endpoint, cutoff point, termination. **2** *push his patience to the limit* extremity, utmost, greatest extent, ultimate, breaking point, endpoint, the bitter end. **3** *cross the limits of his land* boundary, border, bound, frontier, edge, perimeter, confines, periphery. **4** *impose a speed/spending limit* maximum, ceiling, limitation, restriction, curb, check, restraint. **the limit** *his latest action is the limit* the last straw, the straw that broke the camel's back, enough, more than enough; *inf.* the end, it.

limit *verb* **1** *limit their expenditure* place a limit on, restrict, curb, check, keep within bounds, hold in check, restrain, confine, control, ration, reduce. **2** *the bulky jacket limited her movement* restrict, curb, restrain, constrain, hinder, impede, hamper, check, trammel. **3** *the extent of their land is limited by high fencing* demarcate, define, delimit, delimitate, mark off, stake out, encircle, encompass, bound, circumscribe.

limitation *noun* **1** *the new rules imposed a limitation on their freedom* restriction, curb, restraint, constraint, qualification, control, check, hindrance, impediment, obstacle, obstruction, bar, barrier, block, deterrent. **2** *you must recognize your own limitations* inability, incapability, incapacity, defect, frailty, weakness. **3** *the new plan has its limitations* weak point, weakness, drawback, snag, defect.

limited *adjective* **1** *committees having only limited powers* restricted, curbed, checked, controlled, restrained, constrained. **2** *provide limited accommodation* restricted, scanty, sparse, cramped, basic, minimal, inadequate. **3** *of limited experience* restricted, little, narrow, scanty, basic, minimal, inadequate, insufficient. **4** *he's a hard worker but he's a bit limited* unintelligent, slow, slow-witted, not very bright, dull-witted, stupid, dense, unimaginative, stolid.
Antonyms: UNLIMITED; LIMITLESS; ABSOLUTE; BOUNDLESS.

limitless *adjective* **1** *a limitless expanse of forest* infinite, endless, never-ending, interminable, immense, vast, extensive, measureless. **2** *limitless optimism/enthusiasm* unlimited, boundless, unbounded, illimitable, infinite, endless, never-ending, unceasing, interminable, inexhaustible, constant, perpetual.

limp *verb* **1** *he still limps after the injury* walk with a limp, walk with a jerk, hobble, shuffle. **2** *the damaged ship limped into harbor* move slowly, crawl, drag.

limp *noun walk with a pronounced limp* lameness, hobble, jerk, uneven gait, shuffle.

limp *adjective* **1** *limp leaves/flesh* lacking firmness, floppy, drooping, droopy, soft, flaccid, flabby,

loose, slack. **2** *feeling limp after the long illness* without energy, tired, fatigued, weary, exhausted, worn-out, lethargic, enervated, feeble, frail, puny, debilitated. **3** *a limp character* weak, characterless, ineffectual, insipid, wishy-washy, vapid, jejune.
Antonyms: FIRM; STIFF; ENERGETIC; STRONG.

limpid *adjective* **1** *limpid water/eyes* clear, crystal-clear, transparent, glassy, glasslike, translucent. **2** *limpid prose* lucid, clear, plain, understandable, intelligible, comprehensible, coherent, explicit, unambiguous. **3** *limpid seas/days* calm, still, serene, tranquil, placid, peaceful, unruffled, unperturbed.

line[1] *noun* **1** *draw lines* rule, bar, score, underline, underscore, stroke, slash. **2** *lines of white through the black material* band, stripe, strip, belt, seam. **3** *lines on her face* furrow, wrinkle, crease, crow's-foot, groove, scar. **4** *admire the lines of the sculpture* | *the line of her dress/figure* outline, contour, configuration, shape, figure, delineation, silhouette, profile, cameo. **5** *the ball went over the line* | *the state line* boundary, boundary line, limit, border, borderline, frontier, demarcation line, edge, margin, perimeter, periphery. **6** *the line of the march* | *our line of flight* course, route, track, channel, path, way, road, lane, trajectory. **7** *his line of thought* direction, course, drift, tack, tendency, trend, bias, tenor. **8** *taking a tough line* | *the line of least resistance* course of action, course, procedure, technique, way, system, method, modus operandi, policy, practice, scheme, approach, avenue, position. **9** *what line is he in?* line of work, line of business, business, field, area, trade, occupation, employment, profession, work, job, calling, career, pursuit, activity, province, specialty, forte; *inf.* game. **10** *stocking a new line of cosmetics* brand, kind, sort, type, variety. **11** *a line of figures* row, column, series, sequence, succession, progression. **12** *a line of people* row, queue, procession, column, file, string, chain, array. **13** *behind enemy lines* formation, position, disposition, front, front line, firing line. **14** *he comes from a noble line* lineage, descent, ancestry, parentage, family, extraction, heritage, stock, strain, race, breed. **15** *hang the wash on the line* | *fishing line* rope, string, cord, cable, wire, thread, twine, strand, filament. **16** *drop her mother a line* note, letter, card, postcard, message, word, communication. **17** *give his usual line about having no money* spiel, story, patter, piece of fiction, fabrication. **draw the line at** *draw the line at lending him money* stop short of, bar, proscribe, set a limit at; *inf.* put one's foot down about. **in line 1** *stand in line to be served* in a row, in a column, in file, in single file, in a file, in a queue. **2** *are the two pipes in line?* in alignment, aligned, straight, plumb, true. **3** *their views are very much in line* in agreement, in accord, in harmony, in step, in conformity, in rapport. **4** *keep the junior staff in line* under control,

in order, in check, obedient, conforming with the rules. **in line for** *in line for the promotion* a candidate for, in the running for, on the short list for, being considered for, next in succession for. **lay it on the line** *lay it on the line to him that he would be fired if he were late again* speak frankly, state openly, be direct with, speak honestly, pull no punches; *inf.* give it to someone straight. **lay/put on the line** *put his job on the line* risk, put at risk, set at risk, put in danger, endanger, imperil. **toe the line** *those who do not toe the line are asked to leave* conform, obey the rules, comply with the rules, observe the rules, abide by the rules, submit, yield.

line[2] *verb* **1** *grief had lined her face* mark with lines, cover with lines, furrow, wrinkle, crease. **2** *trees lined the driveway* border, edge, fringe, bound, skirt, hem, rim. **line up 1** *line the children up* arrange in a line, arrange in lines, put in rows, arrange in columns, group, marshal. **2** *the children lined up* form a line, form lines, get into rows/columns, file, form a queue, group together, fall in. **3** *line up entertainment for the party* get together, organize, prepare, assemble, lay on, get, obtain, procure, secure, produce, come up with.

line[3] *verb* *line a skirt* | *have lined the drawers with paper* put a lining in, back, interline, face, panel, inlay, paper.

lineage *noun* line, descent, ancestry, family, extraction. *See* LINE *noun* 14.

lineament *noun* distinctive feature, feature, features, distinguishing characteristic, outline, line, contour, configuration, physiognomy, profile, face, countenance, visage.

lined *adjective* **1** *lined paper* ruled, feint. **2** *a lined face* furrowed, wrinkled, creased. **3** *lined skirt/drawers* interlined, faced. *See* LINE[3].

liner *noun* ocean liner, ship, boat, passenger vessel; airplane, aircraft, airliner; *inf.* plane.

lines *plural noun* *forget her lines* words, speech, script, part.

lineup *noun* **1** *the lineup for tonight's show/game* list of performers/players, list, roster, team, selection, array. **2** *the lineup for inspection* line, row, queue.

linger *verb* **1** *linger after the others went* stay, remain, wait around, hang around, delay, dawdle, loiter, dally, take one's time, tarry; *inf.* dilly-dally. **2** *the infection lingered* persist, continue, remain, stay, hang around, be protracted, endure. **3** *dying man is lingering* | *customs that linger (on)* (barely) stay alive, cling to life, survive, last, stay around, continue, hang on.
Antonyms: LEAVE; VANISH; DIE.

lingerie *noun* intimate apparel, underwear, underclothes, underclothing, undergarments, nightwear, nightclothes; *inf.* undies, unmentionables.

lingering *adjective* **1** *lingering doubts* remaining, surviving, persistent. **2** *a lingering illness* persistent, protracted, long-drawn-out.

lingo *noun* language, tongue, speech, jargon, terminology, phraseology, idiom, dialect, patter, vernacular, lingua franca.

linguistic *adjective* semantic, lingual, semasiological.

lining *noun a skirt/drawer lining* backing, interlining, facing, inlay.

link *noun* **1** *a link in the metal chain* ring, loop, connection, connective, coupling, joint, knot. **2** *one of the links in the organization* component, constituent, element, part, piece, member, division. **3** *a link between smoking and cancer* connection, relationship, relatedness, association, tie. **4** *strong family links* bond, tie, attachment, connection, relationship, association, affiliation, mutual interest.

link *verb* **1** *the joint linking the two pieces* join, connect, fasten together, attach, bind, unite, couple, yoke. **2** *the press linking their names together* join, connect, associate, relate, bracket.
Antonyms: DETACH; SEPARATE.

lion *noun* **1** *lions with their cubs* big cat, lioness. **2** *a lion in the battle* lionheart, lionhearted man/woman/person, hero, heroine, man/woman/person of courage, brave man/woman/person, conqueror, champion, warrior, knight. **3** *photographing the lions at the party* celebrity, person of note, dignitary, notable, VIP, public figure, luminary, star, superstar, big name, leading light, idol; *inf.* big shot, bigwig, somebody. **beard the lion in his den** defy danger, face up to danger, brave danger, confront danger, tempt fate/providence.

lionhearted *adjective* brave, courageous, valiant, gallant, intrepid, valorous, fearless, bold, daring, dauntless, stouthearted, stalwart, heroic.

lionize *verb team captain was lionized wherever he went* make much of, treat as a celebrity, glorify, exalt, magnify, acclaim, sing the praises of, praise, extol, laud, eulogize, fête, pay tribute to, put on a pedestal, hero-worship, worship, idolize, adulate, aggrandize.

lip *noun* **1** *the lip of a cup/crater* edge, rim, brim, margin, border, verge, brink. **2** *no one wants to listen to your lip* impertinence, impudence, insolence, rudeness, audacity, effrontery, cheek; *inf.* backtalk, sass. **keep a stiff upper lip** keep control of oneself, not show emotion, appear unaffected, bite one's lip; *inf.* keep one's cool. **lick one's lips** show enjoyment, show pleasure/anticipation, drool.

liquid *noun* fluid, liquor, solution, juice, sap.

liquid *adjective* **1** *liquid substances* fluid, flowing, running, runny, watery, aqueous, liquefied, melted, molten, dissolved, hydrous. **2** *liquid eyes* clear, transparent, limpid, unclouded, bright, shining, brilliant, glowing, gleaming. **3** *liquid notes* clear, pure, smooth, flowing, fluent, fluid, mellifluent, mellifluous, dulcet,

sweet, soft, melodious. **4** *liquid assets* convertible, negotiable.
Antonyms: SOLID; CLOUDY.

liquidate *verb* **1** *liquidate debts* pay, pay in full, pay off, settle, clear, discharge, square, make good, honor. **2** *liquidate a business/partnership* close down, wind up, dissolve, break up, disband, terminate, annul. **3** *liquidate assets* convert to cash, convert, cash in, sell off, sell up, realize. **4** *liquidate an enemy* kill, murder, put to death, do away with, assassinate, put an end to, eliminate, get rid of, dispatch, finish off, destroy, annihilate, obliterate; *inf.* do in, bump off, rub out, wipe out.

liquidize *verb* blend, crush, purée, pulverize, process.

liquor *noun* **1** *addicted to liquor* alcohol, alcoholic drink, spirits, strong drink, drink, intoxicant, inebriant; *inf.* booze, hard stuff, grog, the sauce, hooch, rotgut. **2** *cooking liquor* liquid, stock, broth, bouillon, juice, gravy, infusion, extract, concentrate.

list[1] *noun a list of purchases/films* catalog, inventory, record, register, roll, file, index, directory, listing, enumeration, table, tabulation, schedule, syllabus, calendar, program, series.

list[2] *verb list the purchases* make a list of, note down, write down, record, register, set down, enter, itemize, enumerate, catalog, file, tabulate, schedule, chronicle, classify, alphabetize.

list[3] *verb vessels listing* lean, lean over, tilt, tip, heel, heel over, careen, cant, incline, slant, slope.

listen *verb* **1** *listen to the speaker/speech | please listen* pay attention, be attentive, concentrate on hearing, give ear, lend an ear; hang on someone's words, keep one's ears open, prick up one's ears; *inf.* be all ears, pin back one's ears. **2** *if you had listened in the classroom, you would have passed* pay attention, take heed, heed, give heed, take notice, mind, obey, do as one is told. **listen in on** *listen in on someone's conversation* eavesdrop on, overhear, tap (into), wiretap; *inf.* bug.
Antonyms: IGNORE; DISREGARD.

listless *adjective* languid, lethargic, languishing, enervated, lackadaisical, spiritless, unenergetic, lifeless, inactive, inert, indolent, apathetic, passive, dull, heavy, sluggish, slothful, limp, languorous, torpid, supine, indifferent, uninterested, impassive.
Antonyms: ENERGETIC; LIVELY.

litany *noun* **1** *church litany* prayer, invocation, petition, supplication, devotion; *lit.* orison. **2** *a litany of complaints* recital, recitation, catalog, list, listing, enumeration.

literacy *noun* reading ability, reading proficiency, learning, book learning, education, culture, knowledge, scholarship, erudition, learnedness, enlightenment, articulateness, articulacy.

literal *adjective* **1** *a literal translation* verbatim, word-for-word, line-for-line, letter-for-letter,

exact, precise, faithful, close, strict, undeviating, true, accurate. **2** *a literal account* true, accurate, genuine, authentic, veritable, plain, simple, unexaggerated, unvarnished, unembellished, undistorted. **3** *rather a literal person* literal-minded, down-to-earth, prosaic, factual, matter-of-fact, unimaginative, colorless, commonplace, tedious, boring, dull, uninspiring.
Antonyms: LOOSE; VAGUE; INACCURATE.

literally *adverb* **1** *translated literally* word for word, verbatim, line for line, letter for letter, exactly, precisely, faithfully, closely, strictly, strictly speaking, to the letter, accurately. **2** *literally thousands of people* actually, really, truly, honestly, certainly, surely, positively, absolutely.

literary *adjective* **1** *literary works* written, published, printed, in print. **2** *a literary man* well-read, widely read, educated, well-educated, scholarly, learned, intellectual, cultured, erudite, bookish, studious, lettered; *inf.* highbrow. **3** *a literary word* formal, poetic.

literate *adjective* **1** *scarcely literate* able to read and write, educated, schooled. **2** *the most literate people of his family* educated, well-educated, well-read, scholarly, learned, intellectual, erudite, cultured, cultivated, knowledgeable, well-informed. **3** *literate prose* well-written, stylish, polished, articulate, lucid, eloquent.

literature *noun* **1** *study English literature* written works, writings, printed works, published works, letters, belles lettres. **2** *receive literature about the course* printed matter, brochure, leaflet, pamphlet, flyer, circular, information, data, facts; *inf.* info.

lithe *adjective* agile, flexible, supple, limber, loose-limbed, pliant, pliable, lissome.

litigant *noun* litigator, opponent in law, opponent, contestant, contender, disputant, plaintiff, claimant, complainant, petitioner.

litigation *noun* lawsuit, legal case, case, legal dispute, legal contest, legal action, legal proceedings, suit.

litigious *adjective* *litigious neighbors* argumentative, disputatious, quarrelsome, contentious, belligerent, aggressive, pugnacious, combative.

litter *noun* **1** *litter lying on the grass* trash, rubbish, debris, refuse, junk, odds and ends, fragments, detritus, flotsam. **2** *a litter of books everywhere* disorder, untidiness, clutter, jumble, confusion, mess, disarray, disorganization, disarrangement; *inf.* shambles. **3** *a litter of pups/piglets* | *a mother cat protecting her litter* brood, young, offspring, progeny, family, issue. **4** *invalids carried on/in litters* stretcher, cot, portable bed. **5** *strew litter in the barn* animal bedding, bedding, straw, floor covering.

litter *verb* **1** *litter the place with trash* make untidy, mess up, make a mess of, clutter up, throw into disorder, disarrange; *inf.* make a shambles of. **2** *litter papers about* scatter, strew, throw around.

little *adjective* **1** *a little person/dog/insect/car* small, short, slight, petite, tiny, wee, miniature, diminutive, minute, infinitesimal, microscopic, minuscule, dwarf, midget, pygmy, bantam; *inf.* teeny, teeny-weeny, pint-sized. **2** *he began painting when he was little* small, young, junior. **3** *after a little period* short, brief, fleeting, short-lived, momentary, transitory, ephemeral. **4** *exaggerate little difficulties* unimportant, insignificant, minor, trivial, trifling, petty, paltry, inconsequential, negligible, nugatory. **5** *gain little advantage* hardly any, small, scant, meager, skimpy, sparse, insufficient, exiguous; *inf.* piddling. **6** *nasty little minds* mean, narrow, narrow-minded, small-minded, base, cheap, shallow, petty, illiberal, provincial, parochial, insular. **7** *you sweet little thing!* sweet, nice, dear, cute, appealing.
Antonyms: BIG; LARGE; LONG; CONSIDERABLE.

little *adverb* **1** *little known as an artist* hardly, barely, scarcely, not much, only slightly, only just. **2** *snow is little seen around here* hardly ever, hardly, scarcely ever, scarcely, not much, rarely, seldom, infrequently. **little by little** gradually, slowly, bit by bit, by degrees, step by step, progressively.

little *noun* **1** *add just a little* small amount, bit, touch, trace, hint, soupçon, trifle, dash, taste, pinch, dab, spot, sprinkling, speck, modicum, grain, fragment, snippet, smidgen; *inf.* smidge. **2** *he'll go in a little* short time, little while, minute, moment, second, bit, before you can say Jack Robinson.

liturgy *noun* ritual, worship, service, ceremony, rite, observance, celebration, office, sacrament.

live *verb* **1** *when dinosaurs lived* be alive, have life, be, have being, breathe, draw breath, exist, walk the earth. **2** *patients/customs not expected to live* remain/stay alive, survive, last, endure, persist, abide, continue, stay around. **3** *live quietly* pass/spend one's life, have a life/lifestyle, conduct oneself, lead one's life, behave, comport oneself. **4** *he lives by begging* keep alive, survive, make a living, earn one's living, subsist, support oneself, maintain oneself, make ends meet, keep body and soul together. **5** *live in the city* dwell, reside, have one's home, have one's residence, lodge, be settled; *inf.* hang one's hat. **6** *he really lived when he was young* enjoy life, enjoy oneself, have fun, be happy, make the most of life, flourish, prosper, thrive. **live it up** live extravagantly, live in clover, live in the lap of luxury; *inf.* go on a spree, paint the town red, have a ball. **live on** *live on vegetables* live off, subsist on, feed on, rely for nourishment on, thrive on, eat nothing but.

live *adjective* **1** *live bodies* alive, living, having life, breathing, animate, vital, existing, existent; *inf.*

in the land of the living. **2** *a real live tiger* actual, in the flesh, not imaginary, true-to-life, genuine, authentic. **3** *a live show* nonrecorded, in real time, not taped/videotaped, unedited, with an audience. **4** *live coals* glowing, aglow, burning, alight, flaming, aflame, blazing, hot, smoldering. **5** *live electric wires* charged, connected, active, switched on. **6** *live bombs* unexploded, explodable, explosive. **7** *a live issue* current, topical, active, prevalent, important, of interest, lively, vital, pressing, burning, pertinent, controversial, debatable, unsettled. **live wire** person of energy, self-starter, self-motivator; *inf.* ball of fire, human dynamo, life of the party, go-getter, mover and shaker, hustler.
Antonyms: DEAD; INACTIVE.

livelihood *noun* **1** *earn a livelihood* living, subsistence, means of support, income, keep, maintenance, sustenance, upkeep. **2** *a poorly paid livelihood* job, work, employment, occupation, trade, profession, career.

livelong *adjective* *the livelong day* whole, entire, total, complete, full, unbroken, undivided.

lively *adjective* **1** *lively young people* full of life, active, animated, energetic, alive, vigorous, alert, spirited, high-spirited, vivacious, enthusiastic, keen, cheerful, buoyant, sparkling, bouncy, perky, sprightly, spry, frisky, agile, nimble; *inf.* chipper, peppy. **2** *maintain a lively pace* brisk, quick, rapid, swift, speedy, vigorous. **3** *a lively discussion* animated, spirited, stimulating, heated, enthusiastic, forceful, interesting, eventful. **4** *a lively scene at the beach* busy, crowded, bustling, hectic, swarming, teeming, astir, buzzing, thronging. **5** *lively writing/decoration* vivid, colorful, bright, striking, graphic, stimulating, exciting, effective, imaginative. **6** *things got lively on the battlefield* eventful, exciting, busy, dangerous; *inf.* hairy.
Antonyms: LISTLESS; LIFELESS; SLOW; APATHETIC.

liven *verb* **liven up 1** *liven the party up* enliven, put some life into, brighten up, cheer up, perk up, put some spark into, add some zest to, give a boost to, animate, vitalize, vivify; *inf.* pep up. **2** *livened up when they arrived* cheer up, brighten up, perk up; *inf.* buck up.

livery *noun* uniform, regalia, costume, dress, attire, habit, garb, clothes, clothing, suit, garments, apparel, ensemble, vestments; *inf.* getup, gear, togs.

livid *adjective* **1** *livid with his son* furious, infuriated, fuming, seething, beside oneself, incensed, enraged, exasperated, angry, indignant, wrathful, ireful; *inf.* mad, boiling. **2** *a livid patch on his forehead* discolored, bruised, black-and-blue, purplish, bluish, grayish-blue. **3** *the livid faces of the dying* ashen, deathly pale, pale, pallid, white, grayish, bloodless, ghastly.

living *adjective* **1** *living creatures* alive, live, having life, breathing, animate, vital, existing, ex-

istent; *inf.* in the land of the living. **2** *living languages* current, in use, extant, existing, existent, contemporary, operating, active, ongoing, continuing, surviving, persisting. **3** *a living likeness* exact, close, faithful, true-to-life, authentic, genuine.
Antonyms: DEAD; EXTINCT; OBSOLETE.

living *noun* **1** *earn a living* livelihood, subsistence, means of support, income, keep, maintenance, sustenance, upkeep. **2** *lose his living* job, work, employment, occupation, trade, profession, career. **3** *high living* way of life, lifestyle, manner/way/mode of living, life, conduct, behavior.

living room *noun* sitting room, drawing room, lounge, parlor, family room.

load *noun* **1** *the truck's/aircraft's load* cargo, freight, charge, burden, lading, contents, consignment, shipment; truckload, shipload, busload. **2** *the heavy load of negotiating a truce | illness added to his load* burden, onus, weight, responsibility, duty, charge, obligation, tax, strain, trouble, worry, encumbrance, affliction, oppression, handicap, trial, tribulation, cross, millstone, albatross, incubus.

load *verb* **1** *load the truck/cart* fill, fill up, lade, pack, pile, heap, stack, stuff, cram. **2** *load the staff with responsibility* burden, weigh down, weight, saddle, charge, tax, strain, encumber, hamper, handicap, overburden, overwhelm, oppress, trouble, worry. **3** *load a gun* prime, charge, fill. **4** *load the dice* weight, add weight to, bias, rig.

loaded *adjective* **1** *a loaded truck/basket* full, filled, laden, freighted, packed, stacked. **2** *a loaded gun/camera* primed, charged, filled, ready to fire/shoot, ready for use. **3** *loaded dice* weighted, biased, rigged. **4** *loaded questions* manipulative, cunning, insidious, artful, crafty, tricky, trapping. **5** *the people who live there are probably loaded* rich, wealthy, well off, well-to-do, affluent, moneyed; *inf.* well-heeled, rolling in it, flush, on easy street. **6** *got loaded at the party* drunk, intoxicated, inebriated; *inf.* plastered, stoned, smashed. *See* DRUNK *adjective*.

loaf *noun* block, cake, slab, brick, lump, hunk.

loaf *verb* *loafing at home* laze, lounge, do nothing, idle, lie around, hang about, waste time, fritter away time, take things easy, twiddle one's thumbs, sit on one's hands.

loan *noun* *a loan from the bank* lending, moneylending, advancing; advance, credit, mortgage.

loan *verb* *loan money | loaned a painting* lend, advance, give credit, give on loan, let out.

loath *adjective* *loath to go* reluctant, unwilling, disinclined, not in the mood, against, averse, opposed, resisting.
Antonyms: EAGER; ENTHUSIASTIC.

loathe *verb* hate, detest, abhor, despise, abominate, have an aversion to, not be able to bear, dislike, shrink from, recoil from, feel repugnance toward, be unable to stomach, execrate.

loathing *noun* hatred, hate, detestation, abhorrence, aversion, abomination, repugnance, disgust, revulsion, odium, antipathy, dislike, ill will, enmity, execration.

loathsome *adjective* hateful, detestable, abhorrent, odious, repugnant, disgusting, repulsive, revolting, nauseating, abominable, vile, nasty, obnoxious, horrible, offensive, disagreeable, despicable, contemptible, reprehensible, execrable; *inf.* horrid, yucky.
Antonyms: LOVABLE; DELIGHTFUL.

lob *verb lobbed the ball over the fence* throw, toss, fling, pitch, shy, hurl, loft, heave, flip; *inf.* chuck.

lobby *noun* 1 *wait for them in the lobby* porch, hall, hallway, entrance hall, entrance, vestibule, foyer, corridor, passage, passageway, anteroom, antechamber. 2 *the animal rights lobby* pressure group, interest group, lobbyists, supporters.

lobby *verb lobby the legislators* seek to influence, try to persuade, bring pressure to bear on, urge, press, pressure, solicit. **lobby for** *lobby for animal rights* press/push for, campaign for, promote, drum up support for; *inf.* pull strings for.

local *adjective* 1 *local politics* community, district, neighborhood, regional, city, town, municipal, provincial, village, parish. 2 *our local store* in the area, nearby, near, at hand, close by, neighborhood. 3 *the pain being local | administer a local anesthetic* confined, restricted, contained, limited, circumscribed, delimited, specific.
Antonyms: NATIONAL; GENERAL.

local *noun locals disliking change* local person, native, inhabitant, resident, parishioner; *derog. inf.* local yokel, homeboy.

locale *noun a suitable locale for the conference* place, site, spot, position, location, venue, area, neighborhood, locality, setting, scene.

locality *noun* 1 *the locality of the crime* vicinity, surrounding area, area, neighborhood, district, region, environs, locale; *fml.* locus. 2 *identify the locality of the car* location, position, place, whereabouts, bearings; *fml.* locus.

localize *verb succeed in localizing the infection* confine, restrict, contain, limit, circumscribe, delimit, delimitate.

locate *verb* 1 *locate the source of infection* find, find out, discover, identify, pinpoint, detect, uncover, track down, unearth, hit upon, come across, reveal, pin down, define. 2 *factories located near the sea* situate, site, position, place, put, build, establish, station, set, fix, settle.

location *noun* 1 *identify the location of the ship* position, place, situation, whereabouts, bearings, site, spot, point; *fml.* locus. 2 *a pleasant location for a house* position, place, situation, site, spot, scene, setting, venue, locale.

lock[1] *verb* 1 *lock the door* bolt, fasten, bar, secure, make secure, padlock. 2 *pieces of the puzzle locking together* interlock, engage, mesh, join,

link, unite. 3 *wheels locked* jam, become immovable, become rigid. 4 *locked in each other's arms | locked in combat* clasp, clench, entangle, entwine, embrace, hug, squeeze. **lock in** *a town locked in by hills* enclose, encircle, surround, shut in, hem in. **lock out** *lock out late arrivals* keep out, shut out, refuse entrance to, deny admittance to, exclude, bar, debar, ban, ostracize. **lock up** *lock up prisoners* shut up, shut in, confine, imprison, jail, incarcerate, put behind bars, put under lock and key, cage, coop up, fence in, pen in, wall in.
Antonyms: UNLOCK; OPEN; SEPARATE.

lock[2] *noun force the lock* bolt, catch, fastener, clasp, bar, hasp, padlock, security lock, mortise lock.

lock[3] *noun a lock of hair* strand, tuft, tress, curl, ringlet, lovelock.

locker *noun* cupboard, compartment, cabinet, cubicle; storeroom, storage room.

lockup *noun* prison, jail, cell; *inf.* cooler, slammer, jug, can, stir, clink, pokey, pen.

locomotion *noun* movement, motion, moving, action, travel, traveling, walking, perambulation, progress, progression, headway.

lodestar *noun his father's career was a lodestar to him* guiding star, guide, guiding principle, standard, model, pattern.

lodge *noun* 1 *a hunting/ski lodge* house, cottage, cabin, chalet. 2 *the Masonic lodge* branch, chapter, section, association, society, club, group, fraternity, sorority. 3 *an animal's lodge* lair, den, hole, retreat, haunt, shelter.

lodge *verb* 1 *he's lodging at the Smiths'* stay, reside, dwell, room, sojourn, stop. 2 *the Smiths can lodge all of the children* house, provide accommodation for, accommodate, put up, billet, shelter, harbor, entertain. 3 *lodge a complaint* register, submit, put forward, place, file, lay, put on record, record. 4 *the bullet lodged in his brain* become fixed, become embedded, become implanted, stick, become caught, come to rest.

lodger *noun* boarder, paying guest, guest, tenant, roomer.

lodging *noun* 1 *gave them lodging for the night* accommodation, shelter, board, housing, a roof over one's head. 2 *move to new lodgings* accommodation, rooms, place, residence, dwelling, abode, habitation; *inf.* digs.

lofty *adjective* 1 *lofty peaks* towering, soaring, tall, high, elevated, sky-high, skyscraping. 2 *lofty contempt* arrogant, haughty, proud, self-important, conceited, overweening, disdainful, supercilious, condescending, patronizing, lordly, snobbish, scornful, contemptuous, insulting, cavalier; *inf.* high-and-mighty, stuck-up, snooty, uppity. 3 *lofty thoughts/ideals* noble, exalted, grand, sublime, imposing, esoteric. 4 *lofty members of the community* eminent, leading, noted, notable, well-known, distinguished, famous, renowned, illustrious, esteemed, celebrated, noble, aristocratic. **Antonyms:** LOW; MODEST; LOWLY.

log noun **1** *logs of wood* block, piece, chunk, billet, stump, trunk, branch, bole. **2** *a ship's log* logbook, record, register, journal, diary, daybook, chart, account, tally.

log verb **1** *log details of the voyage* set down, make a note of, note/write down, jot down, register, record, book down, file, chart, tabulate, catalog. **2** *log 50 miles a day* achieve, attain, make, do, go, cover, travel, traverse.

loggerheads plural noun **at loggerheads** in conflict, at war, quarreling, fighting, wrangling, feuding, in disagreement, at odds, at variance, in opposition, estranged; *inf.* at each other's throats.

logic noun **1** *studying logic* science of reasoning, science of deduction, science of thought, dialectics, argumentation, ratiocination. **2** *her logic was flawed* line of reasoning, chain of reasoning, process of reasoning, reasoning, argument, argumentation. **3** *no logic in her actions* reason, sound judgment, judgment, wisdom, sense, good sense, common sense, rationale, relevance, coherence; *inf.* horse sense.

logical adjective **1** *a logical argument* reasoned, well-reasoned, rational, sound, cogent, coherent, well-organized, clear, consistent, relevant. **2** *the logical thing to do* rational, reasonable, sensible, intelligent, wise, judicious. **3** *the logical outcome* most likely, likeliest, plausible, obvious. **4** *not a logical person* reasoning, thinking, straight-thinking, rational, consistent. **Antonyms:** ILLOGICAL; IRRATIONAL; UNLIKELY.

logistics plural noun *the logistics of combining two schools* organization, strategy, tactics, planning, plans, management, masterminding, direction, orchestration, engineering, coordination, execution, handling.

logo noun trademark, emblem, company emblem, device, symbol, design, seal, stamp, logotype.

loiter verb **1** *loiter at street corners* hang around, hang about, linger, wait, skulk, loaf, lounge, idle, waste time; *lit.* tarry. **2** *loiter along the road* dawdle, go slowly, take one's time, go at a snail's pace, dally, stroll, saunter, delay, loll; *inf.* dilly-dally.

---

loiter
dally, dawdle, idle, lag

Someone who hangs around downtown after the stores are closed and appears to be deliberately wasting time is said to **loiter**, a verb that connotes improper or sinister motives (*the police warned the boys not to loiter*). To **dawdle** is to pass time leisurely or to pursue something halfheartedly (*dawdle in a stationery shop; dawdle over a sinkful of dishes*). Someone who **dallies** dawdles in a particularly pleasurable and

relaxed way, with connotations of amorous activity (*he dallied with his girlfriend when he should have been delivering papers*). **Idle** suggests that the person makes a habit of avoiding work or activity (*idle away the hours of a hot summer day*), while **lag** suggests falling behind or failing to maintain a desirable rate of progress (*she lagged several yards behind her classmates as they walked to the museum*).

---

loll verb **1** *lolling on the sofa* lounge, slump, flop, sprawl, relax, recline, rest, lie around, lean against, repose on. **2** *loll around the house* lounge, loaf, idle, loiter, hang about/around, vegetate, languish. **3** *with his tongue lolling* hang down, hang, hang out, hang loosely, dangle, droop, sag, flap, flop.

lone adjective **1** *a lone yachtsman* by oneself, alone, single, solitary, sole, unaccompanied, without companions, companionless, lonely. **2** *a lone parent* single, unmarried, separated, divorced, unattached, without a partner/husband/wife, partnerless, husbandless, wifeless. **3** *a lone landscape* lonely, desolate, barren, isolated, remote, deserted, uninhabited. *See* LONELY 3.

loneliness noun **1** *the loneliness of people living alone* friendlessness, lonesomeness, forlornness, isolation, sadness, despondency. *See* LONELY 1. **2** *the loneliness of his existence* aloneness, solitariness. *See* LONELY 2. **3** *the loneliness of the landscape* desolation, isolation, remoteness, seclusion, desertedness. *See* LONELY 3.

---

loneliness
alienation, desolation, disaffection, estrangement, lonesomeness, solitude

Loneliness, which refers to a lack of companionship and is often associated with unhappiness, should not be confused with **solitude**, which is the state of being alone or cut off from all human contact (*the solitude of the lighthouse keeper*). You can be in the midst of a crowd of people and still experience *loneliness*, but not *solitude*, since you are not physically alone. Similarly, if you enjoy being alone, you can have solitude without loneliness. **Lonesomeness** is more intense than *loneliness*, suggesting the downheartedness you may experience when a loved one is absent (*she experienced lonesomeness following the death of her dog*). **Desolation** is more intense still, referring to a state of being utterly alone or forsaken (*the widow's desolation*). *Desolation* can also indicate a state of ruin or barrenness (*the desolation of the volcanic islands*). **Alienation, disaffection,** and **estrangement** have less to do with being or feeling alone and more to do with emotions that change over time. *Alienation* is a word that suggests a feeling of unrelatedness, especially a feeling of distance from your social or intellectual environment (*alienation from society*). *Disaffection* suggests that you now feel indifference or even distaste toward someone of you were once fond of (*a wife's growing disaffection for her husband*), while *estrangement* is a voluntary disaffection that can result in complete separation and strong feelings of dislike or hatred (*a daughter's estrangement from her parents*).

lonely *adjective* **1** *lonely people at Christmas/feeling lonely* friendless, companionless, lonesome, forlorn, forsaken, abandoned, rejected, isolated, outcast, sad, unhappy, despondent. **2** *lead a lonely existence* lone, by oneself, alone, single, solitary, sole, companionless. **3** *a lonely landscape* desolate, barren, isolated, out-of-the-way, remote, secluded, off the beaten track, deserted, uninhabited, unfrequented, unpopulated, godforsaken, lone.
Antonyms: POPULAR; SOCIABLE; POPULOUS.

loner *noun* lone wolf, recluse, hermit, solitary, anchorite, eremite.

lonesome *adjective* lonely, friendless, forlorn, isolated, sad. *See* LONELY 1.

long *adjective* **1** *four feet long* in length, lengthways, lengthwise. **2** *a long road/way/time* lengthy, extended, extensive, stretched out, spread out. **3** *a long speech* | *ten long years* lengthy, prolonged, protracted, extended, long-drawn-out, dragged out, seemingly endless, interminable, long-winded, verbose, prolix, tedious. **before long** soon, shortly, in a short time, in a minute, in a moment, before you know it, any minute now.
Antonyms: SHORT; BRIEF.

long *verb* **long for** *long for peace* wish for, desire, want, yearn for, crave, hunger for, thirst for, itch for, covet, lust after, hope for, dream of, pine for, eat one's heart out over, have a fancy for, hanker after/after; *inf.* have a yen for.

long-drawn-out *adjective* lengthy, prolonged, protracted, interminable, tedious. *See* LONG *adjective* 3.

longing *noun* *a longing for peace* wish, desire, wanting, yearning, craving, hunger, thirst, itch, covetousness, lust, hope, dream, aspiration, pining, fancy, urge, hankering; *inf.* yen.

longing *adjective* *a longing look* wishful, desirous, yearning, craving, covetous, hopeful, wistful, avid.

long-lasting *adjective* *long-lasting friendship* long-lived, long-running, long-established, longstanding, abiding, enduring, established.

long-lived *adjective* long-lasting, enduring, durable, old.

long-standing *adjective* *long-standing invitation/arrangement* fixed, long-established, well-established, established, time-honored, time-hallowed, abiding, enduring.

long-suffering *adjective* *his long-suffering wife* patient, having the patience of Job, forbearing, tolerant, uncomplaining, stoical, resigned, easygoing, indulgent, charitable, forgiving.

long-winded *adjective* *long-winded speaker/speech* verbose, wordy, garrulous, prolix, discursive, diffuse, rambling, repetitious, lengthy,

prolonged, protracted, long-drawn-out, tedious.

look *verb* **1** *look over there!* see, take a look, glance, fix one's gaze, focus, observe, view, regard, eye, take in, watch, examine, study, inspect, scan, scrutinize, survey, check, contemplate, consider, pay attention to, run the eyes over, peep, peek, glimpse, gaze, stare, gape, ogle; *inf.* take a gander, give someone/something the once-over, rubberneck, eyeball. **2** *she looks ill* | *he looked a fool* seem, seem to be, appear, appear to be, give every appearance/indication of being, look to be, present as being, strike someone as being. **3** *the room looks east* face, front, front on. **look after** take care of, care for, attend to, tend, mind, keep an eye on, watch, sit with, nurse, take charge of, supervise, protect, guard. **look at** take a look at, observe, view, eye, watch, examine, study, inspect, scan, scrutinize, survey, check, contemplate, consider, pay attention to, run one's eyes over. *See* LOOK *verb* 1. **look back on/over** *look back on/over her life* reflect on, think about, recall, bring to mind, muse on, brood on, ponder on, reminisce about. **look down on** regard with contempt, treat with contempt, scorn, disdain, hold in disdain, sneer at, spurn, disparage, pooh-pooh, despise; *inf.* look down one's nose at, turn up one's nose at. **look for 1** *look for the lost glove* search for, hunt for, seek, look around for. **2** *look for some improvement* anticipate, expect, await, count on, reckon on, hope for, look forward to. **look forward to** anticipate, await with pleasure, wait for, be unable to wait for, count the days until, long for, hope for. **look into** investigate, explore, research, probe, search into, go into, inquire about, make inquiries about, ask questions about, ask about, delve into, dig into, examine, study, scrutinize, check, follow up on, check up on, check out. **look like** resemble, bear a resemblance to, have a look of, have the appearance of, put someone in mind of, make someone think of, take after, be the image of; *inf.* be the spitting image of, be a dead ringer for, favor. **look on** *with a crowd looking on* watch, observe, spectate, be a spectator, view, witness. **look on/upon** *look on it as a favor* | *look upon him as a brother* regard, consider, think of, deem, judge, see, take, reckon. **look out** *you'll drop it if you don't look out* watch out, beware, be on guard, be alert, be wary, be vigilant, be careful, pay attention, take heed, keep one's eyes open, keep one's eyes peeled, keep an eye out, be on the qui vive. **look out at** *the house looks out at the sea* face, overlook, front, front on, have a view of. **look over** look through, inspect, examine, check, monitor, read through, scan, run through, cast an eye over, flick through, give something/someone the once-over, check out, peruse; *inf.* eyeball. **look to 1** *look to the future* consider, give thought to, think about, turn one's thoughts to, take heed of, pay attention to. **2** *look to the family for support* turn to, resort to, have recourse to, fall back on, avail oneself of, make use of. **look up 1** *look up the information* search for, seek out, research, hunt for, track down, find, locate. **2** *look up a reference book* consult, refer to, turn to. **3** *look them up in San Diego* visit, pay a visit to, call on, go to see, look in on; *inf.* drop in on. **4** *things are looking up* get better, improve, show improvement, pick up, come along/on, make progress, make headway, shape up, perk up, ameliorate. **look up to** *look up to his brother* admire, hold in admiration, have a high opinion of, think highly of, hold in high regard, regard highly, respect, hold in esteem, esteem, revere, idolize, worship, hero-worship, put on a pedestal, lionize.

look *noun* **1** *one look at the evidence* | *gave him a worried look* sight, glance, observation, view, examination, study, inspection, scan, survey, peep, peek, glimpse, gaze, stare, gape, ogle; *inf.* eyeful, gander, look-see, once-over. **2** *an angry look* expression, face, countenance, features, mien. **3** *houses having a dilapidated/Colonial look* | *she has a depressed look about her* appearance, air, aspect, bearing, cast, demeanor, features, semblance, guise, façade, impression, effect. **4** *miniskirts are the look this year* fashion, style, latest style, vogue, trend, fad, craze, rage.

look-alike *noun* double, twin, exact likeness, image, living image, exact match, replica, clone, duplicate, doppelgänger; *inf.* spitting image, spit and image, ringer, dead ringer.

lookout *noun* **1** *on the lookout for danger* watch, guard, vigil, alertness, qui vive. **2** *lookouts located along the coast* observation post, lookout point, lookout station, lookout tower, watchtower, tower. **3** *the lookout kept watch until dawn* guard, sentry, sentinel, watchman.

loom *verb* **1** *a shape loomed out of the darkness* appear, emerge, become visible, take shape, materialize, reveal itself, appear indistinctly, take on a threatening shape. **2** *cliffs loomed above them* tower, soar, rise, rise up, mount, overhang, hang over, dominate. **3** *exams are looming* be imminent, impend, be close, be ominously close, threaten, menace.

loop *noun* **1** *loops of ribbon* coil, hoop, noose, circle, ring, oval, spiral, curl, twirl, whorl, twist, convolution. **2** *a loop in the road* bend, curve, kink, arc.

loop *verb* **1** *loop the string* coil, form a hoop with, form hoops with, make a circle with, make circles with, bend into spirals/whorls. **2** *loop the sections together* fasten, tie, join, connect. **loop around** *the road loops around the lake* encircle, form a ring around, surround, encompass.

loophole *noun* *a loophole in the law/contract*

means of evasion/avoidance, means of escape, escape, escape clause, escape route, ambiguity, omission.

loose *adjective* **1** *cows loose in the street* at large, at liberty, free, on the loose, unconfined, untied, unchained, untethered, unsecured, unshackled, unfastened, unrestricted, unbound, freed, let go, liberated, released, set loose. **2** *the handle is loose* wobbly, not secure, insecure, rickety, unsteady, movable. **3** *loose hair* untied, unpinned, unbound, hanging free, flowing, floppy. **4** *loose clothes* loose-fitting, easy-fitting, generously cut, slack, baggy, bagging, sagging, sloppy. **5** *a loose translation* inexact, imprecise, vague, indefinite, ill-defined, broad, general, nonspecific, diffuse, unrigorous, unmeticulous. **6** *loose women/morals* immoral, disreputable, dissolute, corrupt, fast, promiscuous, debauched, dissipated, degenerate, wanton, whorish, unchaste, licentious, lascivious, lustful, libertine, abandoned, profligate, reprobate, careless, thoughtless, negligent, rash, heedless, unmindful. **7** *be/hang loose* relaxed, informal, uninhibited, unreserved, frank, open, unceremonious, unconstrained. **at loose ends** *until she found a job, she was at loose ends* unsettled, restless, undecided, unemployed, with nothing to do, unoccupied, idle, twiddling one's thumbs. **break loose** escape, make one's escape, run off, run away, flee, take to one's heels, make off. **let loose 1** *let the cows loose* set free, unloose, turn loose, set loose, loose, untie, unchain, untether, unfasten, detach, unleash, let go, release, free, liberate. **2** *let loose a cry of pain* give, emit, burst out with, give forth, send forth, shout, yell, bellow. **on the loose** *cows on the loose* at liberty, free, at large, unconfined.
Antonyms: SECURE; TIGHT; LITERAL.

loose *verb* **1** *loose the dogs* let loose, set free, unloose, turn loose, set loose, untie, let go. *See* LET LOOSE (LOOSE *adj.*). **2** *loose her grip* | *persuade them to loose their control* loosen, relax, slacken, weaken, lessen, reduce, diminish, moderate, soften. **3** *loose a missile* discharge, shoot, loose off, fire off, eject, catapult.
Antonyms: CONFINE; TIGHTEN.

loose-limbed *adjective* supple, agile, limber, lithe, lissom, flexible, pliant, pliable.

loosen *verb* **1** *loosen a nut* slacken, slack, unstick. **2** *the nut loosened* become loose, work loose, work free. **3** *loosen a belt* | *loosened his pants* slacken, let out, undo, unfasten, unhook. **4** *loosen her grip* | *try to loosen government control* loose, relax, slacken, weaken, lessen, moderate. *See* LOOSE *verb* 2. **loosen up** *don't be so tense—loosen up* relax, calm down, take it easy, ease up/off; *inf.* let up, hang loose, lighten up, chill, chill out.
Antonyms: TIGHTEN; FASTEN.

loot *noun* booty, spoils, spoil, plunder, haul, stolen goods, pillage, prize; *inf.* swag, the goods, hot goods, boodle.

loot verb *looting unoccupied property* plunder, pillage, rob, burgle, steal from, ransack, sack, maraud, ravage, despoil, spoliate.

lop verb *lop hundreds of dollars from the costs* cut, cut back, slash, ax, remove, take off, trim, prune, dock, eliminate. **lop off** *lop off several branches* cut off, chop off, hack off, prune, sever, clip, clip off, dock, crop, remove, detach.

lope verb bound, stride, spring, gallop, canter, leap, jump.

lopsided adjective asymmetrical, unsymmetrical, unevenly balanced, uneven, unbalanced, off-balance, unequal, askew, squint, tilting, crooked, out of true, out of line, awry.

loquacious adjective talkative, overtalkative, garrulous, voluble, long-winded, wordy, verbose, effusive, chatty, gossipy, chattering, babbling, blathering, gibbering; *inf.* having the gift of the gab, yacking, big-mouthed, gabby.
Antonyms: RETICENT; TACITURN.

loquacity noun talkativeness, overtalkativeness, garrulousness, effusiveness, volubility, long-windedness, wordiness, verbosity, garrulity, chattiness, gossipiness, chattering, babble, blathering, gibbering; *inf.* gift of the gab, big mouth, yackety-yack, yacking, gabbiness.

lord noun **1** *swear allegiance to their lord* | *lord of all he surveys* master, lord and master, ruler, leader, chief, monarch, sovereign, king, emperor, prince, governor, commander, captain, overlord, suzerain, baron, potentate, liege. **2** *a ball attended by all the lords and ladies* noble, nobleman, peer, aristocrat, feudal lord, landowner, lord of the manor; duke, earl, viscount. **3** *believe in the Lord* God, Jesus, Jesus Christ, Christ, Christ the Lord, the Redeemer, the Savior.

lord verb **lord it** *arrogant people lording it* put on airs, be overbearing, swagger around, play the lord; *inf.* act big. **lord it over** *lord it over the new employees* order about/around, domineer, dictate to, pull rank on, tyrannize; *inf.* boss about/around.

lordly adjective **1** *a lordly disregard for others* imperious, arrogant, haughty, high-handed, overbearing, overweening, overconfident, dictatorial, authoritarian, peremptory, autocratic, tyrannical, supercilious, disdainful, condescending, patronizing; *inf.* high-and-mighty, bossy, stuck-up, snooty, uppity, hoity-toity. **2** *lordly beings/splendor* noble, aristocratic, lofty, exalted, majestic, grand, regal, princely, kingly, masterful, imperial, stately, dignified, magnificent, grandiose.

lore noun **1** *researching Cherokee lore* traditions, folklore, beliefs, superstitions, legends. **2** *bird lore* knowledge, learning, wisdom, know-how, skill.

lose verb **1** *has lost his keys* mislay, misplace, fail to keep/retain, fail to keep sight of, drop, forget. **2** *losing a lot of blood* be deprived of, suffer the loss of. **3** *trying to lose their pursuers* leave behind, outdistance, outstrip, outrun. **4** *lose the police in the crowd* escape from, evade, elude, dodge, give someone the slip, shake off, throw off, throw off the scent, duck, get rid of. **5** *lose the way* stray from, wander from, fail to keep to, fail to keep in sight. **6** *lose the opportunity* fail to grasp/take, fail to take advantage of, let pass, miss, forfeit, neglect; *inf.* pass up, lose out on. **7** *hope to win but expect to lose* | *lost the contest/battle* suffer defeat, be defeated, be the loser, be worsted, get/have the worst of it, be beaten, be conquered, be vanquished, be trounced, come off second-best, fail, come to grief, meet one's Waterloo; *inf.* lose out, come a cropper. **8** *lose time/effort* waste, squander, dissipate, spend, expend, consume, deplete, exhaust, use up. **lose out** *the poor lose out* | *he lost out on the profits* be unsuccessful, be defeated, be the loser, be disadvantaged, fail to take advantage of, fail to benefit from; *inf.* miss out on. **lose out to** *lose out to a more experienced applicant* be defeated by, be beaten by, be beaten into second place by, be replaced by.

loser noun runner-up, also-ran, the defeated, the vanquished, failure, born loser; *inf.* flop, dud, washout, lemon.

loss noun **1** *report the loss of the keys* mislaying, misplacement, dropping, forgetting. **2** *loss of blood/life/prestige/money* losing, deprivation, privation, forfeiture, bereavement, disappearance, waste, squandering, dissipation. **3** *families/firms suffering loss* deprivation, privation, detriment, disadvantage, damage, injury, impairment, harm, hurt, ruin, destruction, undoing, incapacitation, disablement. **4** *regret the civilian losses* casualty, fatality, dead, death toll, number killed/dead/wounded. **5** *firms making a loss* | *the company has made significant losses* deficit, debit, debt, lack of profit, deficiency, losing, depletion. **at a loss** *we are at a loss to understand his motives* baffled, nonplussed, mystified, stumped, stuck, puzzled, perplexed, bewildered, ignorant, lost, at one's wit's ends, confused; *inf.* clueless.

lost adjective **1** *lost children/books* missing, strayed, gone astray, mislaid, misplaced, vanished, disappeared, forgotten. **2** *lost travelers/ships* stray, astray, off-course, off-track, disorientated, having lost one's bearings, adrift, going around in circles, at sea. **3** *lost opportunities* missed, passed, forfeited, neglected, wasted, squandered, dissipated, frittered, gone by the board; *inf.* down the drain. **4** *lost tribes/traditions* extinct, dead, bygone, lost and gone, lost in time, past, vanished, forgotten, unremembered, unrecalled, consigned to oblivion. **5** *lost ships/towns/armies* destroyed, ruined, wiped out, wrecked, finished, perished, demolished, obliterated, effaced, exterminated, eradicated, annihilated, extirpated. **6** *lost souls* damned, fallen, irredeemable, irreclaimable, irretrievable, past hope, hopeless, past praying for. **7** *lost to all shame* impervious, immune, closed, unreceptive, unaffected by, unmoved by, untouched by. **8** *could tell from his face that he was lost* lost in thought, abstracted, dreamy, distrait, absentminded, somewhere else, not there, not with us. **9** *we are lost to understand the motive* at a loss, baffled, nonplussed. *See* AT A LOSS (LOSS). **lost in** *she was lost in a book* engrossed in, absorbed in, preoccupied by, taken up by, spellbound by, distracted by, entranced by, rapt.

lot *noun* **1** *draw lots* slip of paper, number, straw, counter. **2** *decided by lot* chance, luck, lottery, drawing lots, hazard, accident, serendipity, fortuity. **3** *his lot in life* fate, destiny, fortune, doom, situation, circumstances, portion, plight. **4** *the brothers' lots* share, portion, quota, ration, allowance, percentage, part, piece; *inf.* cut. **5** *sold as a lot* set, batch, collection, load, group, bundle, consignment, quantity, assortment, parcel. **6** *a lot of land | parking lots* piece of ground, plot, patch of ground, tract of land, building lot. **a lot** *smile a lot* much, a good/great deal, to a great extent, often, frequently, many times. **a lot, lots of** *a lot of people | lots of books* many, a great many, a good/great deal of, a great quantity of, quantities of, a considerable number of, numerous, a large amount of, an abundance of, plenty of, masses of, scores of; *inf.* loads of, heaps of, piles of, oodles of, stacks of, scads of, reams of, wads of, oceans of, miles of, gobs of. **draw lots** draw straws, decide on the drawing of straws. **throw/cast in one's lot** *threw in his lot with thieves* join forces, join up, form an alliance, ally, align oneself, link up, go into league, combine, join fortunes.
Antonyms: FEW; LITTLE.

lotion *noun* cream, salve, ointment, moisturizer, balm, emollient, lubricant, unguent, liniment, embrocation, pomade, hand lotion, body lotion.

lottery *noun* **1** *take part in a lottery* draw, raffle, sweepstake, game of chance, gamble, drawing of lots, lotto, bingo. **2** *life is a lottery* gamble, game of chance, risk, hazard, venture.

loud *adjective* **1** *loud music/noises* blaring, booming, noisy, deafening, resounding, reverberant, sonorous, stentorian, roaring, thunderous, tumultuous, clamorous, head-splitting, ear-splitting, ear-piercing, piercing, strident, harsh, raucous. **2** *loud behavior* noisy, rowdy, boisterous, rough, rollicking. **3** *loud young women* brash, brazen, bold, loud-mouthed, vociferous, raucous, aggressive, coarse, crude, rough, crass, vulgar, brassy; *inf.* pushy. **4** *loud demands* vociferous, clamorous, insistent, vehement, emphatic, urgent, importunate, demanding. **5** *loud colors/wallpaper* garish, gaudy, flashy, bold, flamboyant, lurid, glaring, showy, obtrusive, vulgar, tawdry, tasteless; *inf.* camp, tacky.

Antonyms: QUIET; SOFT; GENTLE; RESTRAINED.

loudly *adverb* **1** *speak/play loudly* at full/top volume, at the top of one's voice, boomingly, noisily, deafeningly, tumultuously, clamorously, piercingly, raucously. *See* LOUD 1. **2** *behave loudly* noisily, rowdily, boisterously, roughly, brashly, aggressively, coarsely, crassly.

loudmouth *noun* **1** *loudmouths showing off* braggart, brag, boaster, blusterer, swaggerer, braggadocio; *inf.* windbag, bigmouth, blowhard, gasbag. **2** *loudmouths discussing neighbors' affairs* blabbermouth, blabber, gossip, gossipmonger, scandalmonger, busybody.

loudmouthed *adjective* **1** *disturbed by loudmouthed spectators* noisy, vociferous, bragging, boasting, swaggering; *inf.* bigmouthed. **2** *upset by loudmouthed neighbors* blabbing, tactless, gossiping, indiscreet, undiplomatic.

loudspeaker *noun* speaker, speaker unit, speaker system, public address system, PA system, megaphone, microphone; *inf.* mike.

lounge *verb* **1** *lounge by the pool* laze, lie, lie around, recline, relax, take it easy, sprawl, loll, repose. **2** *lounge around/about at street corners* loaf, idle, loiter, hang, linger, skulk, waste time; *inf.* hang out.

lounge *noun* **1** *have tea in the lounge* sitting room, drawing room, living room, parlor. **2** *the lounge of a hotel* sitting room, cocktail lounge.

lour *verb See* LOWER 3.

lousy *adjective* **1** *lousy weather/workmanship/player* very bad, poor, incompetent, inadequate, unsatisfactory, inferior, careless, second-rate, terrible, miserable; *inf.* rotten, no-good. **2** *a lousy trick to play* dirty, low, mean, base, despicable, contemptible, low-down, hateful, detestable, loathsome, vile, wicked, vicious; *inf.* rotten. **lousy with** *places lousy with tourists* full of, covered in, well-supplied with, crowded with, overrun by, swarming with, teeming with, alive with, crawling with.

lout *noun* boor, oaf, dolt, churl, bumpkin, yahoo; brute, rowdy, barbarian; *inf.* slob, clodhopper, clod, lummox.

loutish *adjective* boorish, oafish, doltish, churlish, awkward, inept, blundering, maladroit, gawky; brutish, coarse; *inf.* clodhopping.

lovable *adjective* adorable, dear, sweet, cute, charming, lovely, likable, attractive, delightful, captivating, enchanting, engaging, bewitching, pleasing, appealing, winsome, winning, taking, endearing, affectionate, warmhearted, cuddly.
Antonyms: HATEFUL; LOATHSOME.

love *verb* **1** *he loves her* care for, be in love with, be fond of, feel affection for, be attracted to, be attached to, hold dear, adore, think the world of, dote on, worship, idolize, treasure, prize, cherish, be devoted to, desire, want, be infatuated with, lust after, long for, yearn for, adulate; *inf.* fancy, have a crush on, have the hots for, be soft on. **2** *she loves chocolate* like, have a liking for, have a weakness for, be partial to, have a soft spot for, be addicted to, enjoy, find enjoyment in, relish, savor, appreciate, take pleasure in, delight in; *inf.* get a kick out of, have a thing about.

Antonyms: HATE; LOATHE; DETEST.

love noun **1** *the couple's love (for/of each other)* affection, fondness, care, concern, attachment, regard, warmth, intimacy, devotion, adoration, passion, ardor, desire, lust, yearning, infatuation, adulation. **2** *her love of/for chocolate* liking, weakness, partiality, enjoyment, appreciation, relish, passion. **3** *love for/toward one's neighbor* care, caring, regard, solicitude, sympathy, warmth, friendliness, friendship, rapport, brotherhood, kindness, charity. **4** *be brave, my love* beloved, loved one, true love, love of one's life, dear, dearest, dear one, darling, sweetheart, sweet, sweet one, angel, lover, inamorato/inamorata. **5** *their love was short-lived* love affair, affair, romance, relationship, liaison. **love affair** affair, romance, relationship, meaningful relationship, liaison, amour, intrigue, affair of the heart, *affaire de coeur.* **fall in love with** become sexually attracted to, form an attachment to, develop a fondness for, become infatuated with, become smitten with; *inf.* develop a crush on. **in love with** attracted to, sexually attracted to, infatuated with, enamored of, smitten by, besotted with, devoted to, having a passion for, consumed with desire for, lusting after; *inf.* leching after, having the hots for.

lovelorn adjective lovesick, unrequited in love, spurned, jilted, miserable, unhappy, pining, moping.

lovely adjective **1** *a lovely face* beautiful, pretty, attractive, good-looking, glamorous, comely, handsome, sweet, fair, charming, adorable, enchanting, engaging, bewitching, winsome, seductive, ravishing. **2** *a lovely surprise* delightful, pleasant, nice, agreeable, pleasing, marvelous, wonderful; *inf.* terrific, fabulous, fab.

Antonyms: UGLY; HORRIBLE; DISAGREEABLE.

lovemaking noun sexual intercourse, intercourse, act of love, sexual relations, intimate relations, intimacy, copulation, coitus, coition, carnal knowledge, mating; *inf.* sex, nooky, going to bed.

lover noun **1** *send flowers to his/her lover* boyfriend, girlfriend, man friend, woman friend, mistress, ladylove, paramour, other man, other woman, beau, loved one, beloved, sweetheart, inamorato/inamorata. **2** *a lover of antiques/Italy* admirer, devotee, fan, enthusiast, aficionado; *inf.* buff, freak.

loving adjective *a loving daughter/kiss* affectionate, fond, devoted, caring, adoring, doting, solicitous, demonstrative, tender, warm, warm-hearted, friendly, kind, sympathetic, charitable, cordial, amiable, amorous, ardent, passionate.

low adjective **1** *a low table* short, small, little,

squat, stubby, stunted, truncated, dwarfish, knee-high. **2** *low land* low-lying, ground-level, sea-level, flat, sunken, depressed, subsided, nether. **3** *of low birth* | *low members of society* lowly, humble, poor, lowborn, lowbred, low-ranking, plebeian, peasant, common, ordinary, simple, plain, unpretentious, inferior, subordinate, obscure. **4** *supplies are low* sparse, meager, scarce, scanty, scant, few, little, deficient, inadequate, paltry, measly, trifling, reduced, depleted, diminished. **5** *a low hum* soft, quiet, muted, subdued, muffled, hushed, quietened, whispered, murmured, gentle, dulcet, indistinct, inaudible. **6** *feeling low* depressed, low-spirited, down, dejected, despondent, disheartened, downhearted, downcast, gloomy, glum, unhappy, sad, miserable, blue, fed up, morose, moody, heavy-hearted, forlorn; *inf.* down in the mouth, down in the dumps. **7** *in a low state of health* | *invalids getting low* weak, weakly, feeble, enfeebled, debilitated, frail, delicate, fragile, infirm, ill, ailing, unhealthy, poorly, helpless, powerless, stricken, prostrate, failing, declining, sinking, fading, dying. **8** *of low intelligence* low-grade, inferior, substandard, below par, second-rate, deficient, defective, wanting, lacking, inadequate, mediocre, unacceptable, worthless. **9** *low expectations* lowly, simple, plain, ordinary, commonplace, run-of-the-mill, modest, unambitious, unpretentious, unaspiring. **10** *have a low opinion of them* unfavorable, poor, bad, adverse, hostile, negative. **11** *a low thing to do* mean, nasty, foul, bad, wicked, evil, vile, vicious, despicable, contemptible, heinous, villainous, base, dishonorable, unprincipled, dastardly, ignoble, sordid. **12** *low creatures* mean, nasty, foul, vile, despicable, contemptible, base, villainous, hateful, loathsome, reprehensible, depraved, debased, wretched, miserable, sorry. **13** *low comedy/humor* vulgar, crude, coarse, obscene, indecent, gross, ribald, smutty, bawdy, pornographic, blue, rude, rough, unrefined, indelicate, improper, offensive. **14** *low prices/wages* cheap, inexpensive, moderate, reasonable, modest, bargain-basement.

Antonyms: HIGH; CHEERFUL; ADMIRABLE.

low verb *cattle lowing* moo, bellow.

low-down noun information, data, facts, facts and figures, intelligence, inside information; *inf.* info, dope, poop.

lower[1] adjective **1** *of lower status* lesser, lower-level, lower-grade, subordinate, junior, inferior, minor, secondary. **2** *lower bunk/lip* under, underneath, nether. **3** *lower prices* cheaper, reduced, decreased, lessened, cut, slashed, curtailed.

lower[2] verb **1** *lower the flag/weight* let down, take down, haul down, drop, let fall, let sink. **2** *lower one's voice* | *lower the volume* modulate, soften,

quieten, hush, tone down, muffle, turn down, mute. **3** *will only lower him in her eyes* degrade, debase, demean, downgrade, discredit, devalue, dishonor, disgrace, belittle, humble, humiliate, disparage. **4** *lower the temperature/ prices* reduce, bring down, decrease, lessen, cut, slash, curtail. **5** *the winds lowered* abate, die down, subside, let up, moderate, slacken, dwindle, lessen, ebb, fade away, wane, taper off, lull.
Antonyms: RAISE; INCREASE; BOOST.

lower[3] *verb See* LOUR.

lour *verb* **1** *lowering at us with disapproval* scowl, frown, look sullen, glower, glare; *inf.* give someone dirty looks. **2** *skies lowering* cloud over, look black, darken, blacken, become overcast, be gloomy, appear threatening/menacing.

low-grade *adjective* poor-quality, inferior, substandard, below standard, not up to scratch, second-rate, bargain-basement, poor, bad; *inf.* two-bit.

low-key *adjective* restrained, muted, subtle, quiet, understated, played down, toned down, relaxed, downbeat, easygoing, modulated, softened; *inf.* laid-back.

lowly *adjective* **1** *of lowly birth* | *lowly members of society* low, humble, lowborn, low-ranking, plebeian, peasant, poor, common, ordinary, inferior, subordinate. *See* LOW *adjective* 3. **2** *feeling lowly before God* humble, meek, submissive, dutiful, docile, mild, gentle, modest, unassuming. **3** *lowly ambitions* low, simple, plain, ordinary, commonplace, run-of-the-mill, modest, unambitious, unpretentious, unaspiring.
Antonyms: NOBLE; ARISTOCRATIC; ARROGANT; HIGH-FLOWN.

low-spirited *adjective* low, down, depressed, dejected, despondent, gloomy, unhappy, miserable, blue. *See* LOW *adjective* 6.

loyal *adjective* faithful, true, true-hearted, tried and true, trusted, trustworthy, trusty, true-blue, steadfast, staunch, dependable, reliable, devoted, dutiful, patriotic, constant, unchanging, unwavering, unswerving, firm, stable.
Antonyms: DISLOYAL; TREACHEROUS.

loyalty *noun* faithfulness, fidelity, fealty, allegiance, trueness, true-heartedness, trustiness, trustworthiness, steadfastness, staunchness, dependability, reliability, devotion, duty, patriotism, constancy, stability.
Antonyms: DISLOYALTY; TREACHERY.

lozenge *noun* tablet, pastille, cough drop; *Med.* troche.

lubricant *noun* lubricator, oil, grease, emollient, lard, fat, moisturizer, lotion, unguent.

lubricate *verb* **1** *lubricate the machinery* oil, grease, make slippery, moisturize. **2** *lubricate the planning process* make smooth, smooth the way for, oil the wheels for.

lucid *adjective* **1** *a lucid description* clear, clear-cut, crystal-clear, comprehensible, intelligible, understandable, plain, simple, direct, straightforward, graphic, explicit, obvious, evident, apparent, distinct, transparent, overt, cogent. **2** *he is scarcely lucid* sane, rational, in one's right mind, in possession of one's faculties, of sound mind, *compos mentis*, sensible, clearheaded; *inf.* all there, with all one's marbles. **3** *lucid pools* clear, crystal-clear, transparent, limpid, translucent, glassy, pellucid. **4** *lucid stars* bright, shining, gleaming, luminous, radiant, lustrous.
Antonyms: CONFUSED; MUDDLED; CLOUDY.

luck *noun* **1** *as luck would have it* fate, fortune, destiny, predestination, the stars, chance, fortuity, accident, hazard, serendipity. **2** *wishing you luck* good luck, good fortune, success, successfulness, prosperity, advantage, advantageousness, felicity; *inf.* lucky break. **in luck** lucky, fortunate, blessed with good luck, favored, born under a lucky star, advantaged, successful, prosperous, happy. **out of luck** unlucky, unfortunate, luckless, cursed with ill/ bad luck, unsuccessful, disadvantaged, miserable.

luckily *adverb* *luckily he survived* fortunately, by good luck, by good fortune, happily, providentially, as luck would have it, propitiously.

luckless *adjective* *luckless competitors* unlucky, unfortunate, unsuccessful, out of luck, down on one's luck, jinxed, hapless, ill-starred, ill-fated, unhappy, miserable, wretched, forlorn, starcrossed.

lucky *adjective* **1** *lucky people* fortunate, blessed with good luck, favored, born under a lucky star, charmed; successful, prosperous, happy; advantaged, born with a silver spoon in one's mouth. **2** *a lucky guess* fortunate, fortuitous, providential, advantageous, timely, opportune, expedient, auspicious, propitious.
Antonyms: UNLUCKY; UNFORTUNATE; UNFAVORABLE.

lucrative *adjective* profitable, profit-making, moneymaking, paying, high-income, well-paid, high-paying, gainful, remunerative, productive, fat, fruitful, rewarding, worthwhile.

lucre *noun* money, cash, profit, profits, gain, proceeds, winnings, pay, remuneration, earnings, income, yield, revenue; *inf.* dough, bread.

ludicrous *adjective* absurd, ridiculous, laughable, risible, derisible, comic, comical, farcical, silly, funny, humorous, droll, amusing, diverting, hilarious, crazy, zany, nonsensical, odd, outlandish, eccentric, incongruous, preposterous.
Antonyms: SENSIBLE; SERIOUS; SOLEMN.

lug *verb* **1** *lugging a heavy suitcase* carry, bear, tote, transport; *inf.* schlep. **2** *lugging a handcart behind him* haul, drag, heave, trail, tug, tow.

luggage *noun* bags, baggage, bag and baggage, cases, suitcases, trunks, things, gear, belongings, effects, goods and chattels, impedimenta, paraphernalia, accouterments.

lugubrious *adjective* mournful, doleful, melancholy, dismal, gloomy, somber, funereal, sorrowful, morose, miserable, joyless, woebegone, woeful, dirgelike, elegaic.
Antonyms: CHEERFUL; JOYFUL.

lukewarm *adjective* **1** *lukewarm water* tepid, warm, warmish, at room temperature. **2** *lukewarm about going to the party* indifferent, cool, cold, halfhearted, apathetic, unenthusiastic, uninterested, unconcerned, impassive, dispassionate, unresponsive, sluggish, phlegmatic.

lull *verb* **1** *lull the child to sleep* rock (gently), soothe, quiet, hush. **2** *lull their fears* soothe, quiet, silence, calm, hush, still, quell, assuage, allay, ease, alleviate, pacify, mitigate. **3** *the storm lulled* abate, die down, subside, let up, moderate, slacken, lessen, dwindle, decrease, diminish, ebb, fade away, wane, taper off, lower.

lull *noun* **1** *a lull in the proceedings* pause, respite, interval, break, hiatus; *inf.* letup. **2** *the lull before the storm* calm, calmness, stillness, quiet, quietness, tranquillity, silence, hush.

lullaby *noun* cradlesong, berceuse.

lumber[1] *noun* timber, wood, boards, planks, planking, beams.

lumber[2] *verb* *lumber him with her jobs* burden, load, saddle, encumber, impose upon; *inf.* land.

lumber[3] *verb* *heard him lumbering around upstairs* clump, stump, plod, trudge, stamp, shuffle, stumble, waddle.

lumbering *adjective* awkward, clumsy, heavyfooted, blundering, bumbling, inept, maladroit, ungainly, like a bull in a china shop, ungraceful, hulking, ponderous, stolid; *inf.* clodhopping.

luminary *noun* leading light, guiding light, star, superstar, megastar, leader, notable, dignitary, VIP, celebrity, big name, household name, somebody, name, important personage, lion; *inf.* bigwig, big shot, big cheese, biggie, celeb.

luminous *adjective* **1** *luminous stars/colors* lighted, lit, illuminated, shining, bright, brilliant, radiant, dazzling, glowing, effulgent, luminescent, phosphorescent, vivid, resplendent. **2** *a luminous account* lucid, clear, crystal clear, comprehensible, intelligible, plain, simple, direct, straightforward, graphic, obvious, distinct, apparent. *See* LUCID 1.

lump[1] *noun* **1** *a lump of putty/coal* chunk, wedge, hunk, piece, mass, cake, nugget, ball, dab, pat, clod, gob, wad, clump, mound. **2** *a lump on his head* bump, swelling, bruise, bulge, protuberance, protrusion, growth, carbuncle, hump, tumor, tumescence, node.

lump[2] *verb* *lump all the expenses together* put together, combine, group, unite, pool, mix together, blend, merge, mass, fuse, conglomerate, coalesce, consolidate.

lump[3] *verb* **like it or lump it** put up with it, bear it, endure it, take it, stand it, tolerate it, suffer it, brook it, live with it, take it or leave it, resign oneself to it.

lumpy *adjective* **1** *a lumpy mattress* bumpy, knobby, bulging, uneven. **2** *lumpy custard* curdled, clotted, granular, grainy.

lunacy *noun* **1** *suffering from lunacy* insanity, insaneness, madness, mental illness/derangement, dementia, dementedness, loss of reason, unsoundness of mind, mania, frenzy, psychosis; *inf.* craziness. **2** *the sheer lunacy of the decision* madness, insanity, foolishness, folly, foolhardiness, stupidity, idiocy, irrationality, illogicality, senselessness, absurdity, absurdness, silliness, inanity, ludicrousness; *inf.* craziness, daftness.
Antonyms: SANITY; SENSE; PRUDENCE.

lunatic *noun* *driving like a lunatic* maniac, madman, madwoman, imbecile, idiot, psychopath; *inf.* loony, nut, nutcase, head case, basket case, screwball, psycho.

lunatic *adjective* *a lunatic idea | it was a lunatic thing to do* mad, insane, foolish, stupid, foolhardy, idiotic, crack-brained, irrational, unreasonable, illogical, senseless, nonsensical, absurd, silly, inane, asinine, ludicrous, imprudent, preposterous; *inf.* crazy, daft.

lunch *noun* luncheon, midday meal, brunch; *dial.* dinner.

lunge *noun* **1** *make a lunge toward the open door* spring, jump, leap, bound, dash, charge, pounce, dive. **2** *take a lunge at his attacker* stab, jab, poke, thrust, swing, pass, cut, feint; *inf.* swipe.

lunge *verb* **1** *lunge toward the door* spring, jump, leap, bound, dash, charge, pounce, dive. **2** *lunged the foil into the fencing dummy* stab, jab, poke, thrust. **lunge at** *lunge at his attacker* charge, rush, jump, attack, pounce on, lash out at, take a swing at, aim a blow at; *inf.* take a swipe at.

lurch *verb* **1** *drunks lurching home* stagger, sway, reel, weave, stumble, totter. **2** *ships lurching in the storm* list, roll, pitch, toss, sway, veer, swerve.

lure *verb* *lure them into a trap | lured by greed* entice, attract, induce, inveigle, decoy, draw, lead, allure, tempt, seduce, beguile, ensnare, magnetize, cajole.

lure *noun* *use sweets as a lure to the children* enticement, attraction, inducement, decoy, draw, allurement, temptation, bait, magnet, drawing card, carrot; *inf.* come-on.

lurid *adjective* **1** *lurid colors/sunsets* overbright, brilliant, glaring, flaming, dazzling, glowing, intense, vivid, showy, gaudy, fiery, blood-red, burning. **2** *lurid descriptions of their affair* sensational, melodramatic, exaggerated, extravagant, graphic, explicit, unrestrained, shocking, startling; *inf.* full-frontal. **3** *lurid details of the murder* gruesome, gory, grisly, macabre, repugnant, revolting, disgusting, ghastly. **4** *lurid* *complexions* pale, pallid, ashen, colorless, chalk-white, white, wan, sallow, livid, ghostly, ghastly.

Antonyms: MUTED; RESTRAINED; SUBTLE.

lurk *verb* skulk, lie in wait, lie low, hide, conceal oneself, take cover, crouch, sneak, slink, prowl, steal, tiptoe.

luscious *adjective luscious fruit* delicious, juicy, sweet, succulent, mouthwatering, tasty, appetizing, delectable, palatable, toothsome; *inf.* scrumptious, yummy.

lush *adjective* **1** *lush vegetation* luxuriant, abundant, profuse, exuberant, dense, thick, riotous, overgrown, prolific, rank, teeming, junglelike, flourishing, verdant, green. **2** *lush fruits* juicy, succulent, fleshy, pulpy, ripe, soft, tender, fresh. **3** *lush penthouse* luxurious, sumptuous, grand, palatial, opulent, lavish, elaborate, extravagant; *inf.* plush, ritzy.

Antonyms: BARREN; MEAGER; DRY.

lush *noun* alcoholic, heavy/hard drinker, problem drinker, drinker, drunk, drunkard, toper, sot, dipsomaniac; *inf.* alky, boozer, tosspot.

lust *noun* **1** *physical lust* sexual desire, sexual appetite, sexual longing, sexual passion, libido, sex drive, sexuality, biological urge; lechery, lecherousness, lasciviousness, lewdness, carnality, licentiousness, salaciousness, salacity, prurience, concupiscence, wantonness; *inf.* horniness, the hots. **2** *a lust for gold/power/living* greed, greediness, desire, craving, covetousness, avidness, avidity, cupidity, longing, yearning, hunger, thirst, appetite, passion.

lust *verb* be consumed with desire for, desire, crave, covet, want, need, long for, yearn for, hunger for, thirst for, ache for; *inf.* have the hots for.

luster *noun* **1** *admire the luster of the table* sheen, gloss, shine, burnish, glow, gleam, sparkle, shimmer. **2** *the luster of the stars* brilliance, brightness, dazzle, luminousness, radiance, refulgence, lambency. **3** *bring luster to the school* honor, glory, credit, merit, prestige, renown, fame, distinction, notability.

lusterless *adjective* dull, flat, matte, unburnished, unpolished, tarnished, dingy, dim, dark, drab, gloomy, colorless, washed out, faded.

lustful *adjective* lecherous, lascivious, lewd, libidinous, licentious, salacious, prurient, concupiscent, wanton, unchaste, hot-blooded, passionate, sensual, sexy; *inf.* horny.

lustrous *adjective* shiny, shining, glossy, gleaming, glowing, bright, burnished, polished, dazzling, sparkling, glistening, twinkling, shimmering, luminous.

lusty *adjective* **1** *lusty young men* healthy, strong, vigorous, robust, hale and hearty, hearty, energetic, lively, blooming, rugged, sturdy, tough, stalwart, brawny, hefty, husky, burly,

solidly built, powerful, virile, red-blooded. **2** *a lusty cry* loud, vigorous, hearty, powerful, forceful.

luxuriant *adjective* **1** *luxuriant vegetation* lush, abundant, profuse, exuberant, dense, thick, riotous, overgrown, prolific, teeming, verdant. *See* LUSH *adjective* 1. **2** *luxuriant prose* florid, flowery, ornate, elaborate, fancy, adorned, decorated, embellished, embroidered, extravagant, flamboyant, ostentatious, showy, high-flown, baroque, rococo.

Antonyms: BARREN; MEAGER; PLAIN.

luxuriate *verb* **1** *luxuriate in a hot bath* bask in, revel in, delight in, enjoy, wallow in, savor, appreciate; *inf.* get a kick out of, get a charge from. **2** *plants luxuriating* thrive, flourish, bloom, prosper, do well, burgeon, spring up, sprout, shoot up, mushroom. **3** *luxuriating after a life of poverty* live in luxury, live in the lap of luxury, live off the fat of the land, be in clover, take it easy, relax, have the time of one's life, lead the life of Riley.

luxurious *adjective* **1** *luxurious surroundings* opulent, affluent, sumptuous, expensive, rich, costly, deluxe, lush, grand, splendid, magnificent, lavish, well-appointed, comfortable, extravagant, ornate, fancy; *inf.* plush, posh, ritzy, swanky. **2** *luxurious habits* self-indulgent, sensual, pleasure-loving, comfort-seeking, epicurean, hedonistic, sybaritic.

Antonyms: AUSTERE; SPARTAN.

luxury *noun* **1** *live in luxury* luxuriousness, opulence, affluence, sumptuousness, richness, grandeur, splendor, magnificence, lavishness, lap of luxury, bed of roses. **2** *the luxury of independence* boon, benefit, advantage, delight, bliss, comfort. **3** *one of life's luxuries* extra, nonessential, frill, extravagance, indulgence, treat, refinement.

lying *noun accused of lying* untruthfulness, fabrication, fibbing, perjury, white lies, little white lies, falseness, falsity, dishonesty, mendacity, lack of veracity, storytelling, dissimulation, dissembling, prevarication, deceit, guile, crookedness, double-dealing.

lying *adjective lying witnesses* untruthful, fabricating, false, dishonest, mendacious, dissimulating, dissembling, prevaricating, deceitful, guileful, crooked, double-dealing, two-faced.

Antonyms: TRUTHFUL; HONEST.

lynch *verb* put to death, execute, hang, kill, murder, slay; *inf.* string up.

lyric *adjective* **1** *lyric poetry* songlike, musical, melodic, melodious, expressive, deep-felt, personal, subjective, passionate, lyrical. **2** *lyric voices* light, silvery, clear, lilting, flowing, dulcet, sweet, mellifluous, mellow, lyrical.

lyrical *adjective* **1** *lyrical verse* lyric, songlike, musical, melodic, expressive, personal. *See* LYRIC 1. **2** *lyrical voices* light, silvery, clear, flowing, sweet. *See* LYRIC 2.

lyrics *plural noun the lyrics of the song* words, libretto, book, text.

M

macabre *adjective* gruesome, grisly, grim, gory, morbid, ghastly, hideous, horrific, horrible, horrifying, horrid, horrendous, terrifying, frightening, frightful, fearsome, shocking, dreadful, appalling, loathsome, repugnant, repulsive, sickening.

mace *noun* staff, club, cudgel, bludgeon.

macerate *verb* pulp, mash, squash, soften, liquefy, soak, steep.

machete *noun* knife, cutlass, cleaver.

machiavellian *adjective* devious, cunning, crafty, artful, wily, sly, scheming, designing, conniving, opportunistic, insidious, treacherous, perfidious, two-faced, double-dealing, unscrupulous, deceitful, dishonest.

machinations *plural noun* schemes, plot, intrigues, conspiracies, complots, designs, plans, devices, ploys, ruses, trick, wiles, stratagems, tactics, maneuvers, contrivances, expedients.

machine *noun* **1** *the washing machine broke down* appliance, apparatus, instrument, tool, device, contraption, gadget, mechanism, engine, motor. **2** *the competitor's machine* vehicle, car, motorcycle, airplane; *inf.* bike, motorbike, plane. **3** *machines replacing factory workers* robot, automaton, mechanical man, puppet. **4** *the party machine* organization, system, structure, agency, machinery, council, cabal, clique; *inf.* setup.

machinery *noun* **1** *factory machinery* equipment, apparatus, mechanism, gear, tackle, instruments, gadgetry. **2** *the machinery of local government* workings, organization, system, structure, agency, channel, vehicle; *inf.* setup, nuts and bolts, brass tacks, nitty-gritty.

machinist *noun* machine operator, operator, operative, worker.

machismo *noun* masculinity, manliness, virility, toughness, chauvinism, male chauvinism, sexism.

macrocosm *noun* **1** *exploration of the macrocosm* universe, cosmos, world, wide world, globe, creation, solar system. **2** *society and other macrocosms* complete system, system, total structure, structure, totality, entirety.

mad *adjective* **1** *gone mad with grief* stark (raving) mad, insane, deranged, demented, of unsound mind, crazed, lunatic, *non compos mentis*, unbalanced, unhinged, unstable, distracted, manic, frenzied, raving, distraught, frantic, hysterical, delirious, psychotic, not quite right, mad as a hatter, mad as a March hare, foaming at the mouth; *inf.* crazy, out of one's mind, off one's nut, nuts, nutty, off one's rocker, round/around the bend, balmy, batty, bonkers, crackers, cuckoo, loopy, loony, bananas, loco, dippy, screwy, with a screw loose, out of one's tree, off one's trolley, off the wall, not all there, not right/OK/okay upstairs. **2** *the vandalism made them mad* angry, furious, infuriated, irate, raging, enraged, fuming, in a towering rage, incensed, wrathful, seeing red, cross, indignant, exasperated, irritated, berserk, out of control, beside oneself; *inf.* livid, wild. **3** *a mad scheme/idea* insane, foolish, stupid, lunatic, foolhardy, idiotic, crackbrained, irrational, unreasonable, illogical, senseless, nonsensical, absurd, impractical, silly, inane, asinine, ludicrous, wild, unwise, imprudent, preposterous; *inf.* crazy, daft. **4** *mad, passionate love* wild, unrestrained, uncontrolled, abandoned, excited, frenzied, frantic, frenetic, ebullient, energetic, boisterous. **like mad 1** *run like mad* furiously, as fast as possible, as fast as one's legs can carry one, fast, hurriedly, quickly, rapidly, speedily, hastily, energetically; *inf.* like crazy, like a house on fire. **2** *love her like mad* madly, enthusiastically, unrestrainedly, wildly, passionately, intensely, ardently, fervently, to distraction, devotedly. **mad about** *mad about jazz* wildly enthusiastic about, passionate about, impassioned about, avid about, eager about, keen on, ardent about, zealous about, fervent about, fanatical about, devoted to, infatuated with, in love with; *inf.* crazy about, nuts about, hooked on, wild about, gone on.
Antonym: SANE; CALM; SENSIBLE; APATHETIC.

madcap *adjective* daredevil, impulsive, wild, reckless, rash, hotheaded, daring, adventurous, heedless, thoughtless, incautious, imprudent, indiscreet, ill-advised, hasty, foolhardy, foolish, senseless, impractical, harebrained, crackbrained; *inf.* crazy, crackpot.

madcap *noun* daredevil, hothead, adventurer/adventuress, wild man/woman.

madden *verb maddened by their behavior* | *it maddened them* anger, infuriate, send into a rage, enrage, incense, exasperate, irritate, inflame, annoy, provoke, upset, agitate, vex, irk, pique, gall, make one's hackles rise, raise one's hackles, make one's blood boil, make one see red, get one's back up; *inf.* aggravate, bug, make one livid.

maddening *adjective* infuriating, exasperating, irritating, annoying, provoking, upsetting, vexing, irksome, unsettling, disturbing, troublesome, vexatious, galling.

made-up *adjective* **1** *a made-up story* invented, fabricated, trumped-up, concocted, devised, manufactured, fictional, false, untrue, unreal, sham, specious, spurious, imaginary, mythical. **2** *trick-or-treaters with made-up faces* painted, done up, powdered, rouged. **3** *cabinets already made-up* put together, built, constructed, finished, ready, prepared, fixed.

madhouse *noun* **1** *confined to a madhouse* mental hospital, mental institution, psychiatric hospital, asylum; *inf.* nuthouse, funny farm, loony bin. **2** *the madhouse created with the wedding preparations* bedlam, babel, chaos, pandemonium, uproar, turmoil, disarray, scene of confusion, disorder, three-ring circus.

madly *adverb* **1** *behaving madly* insanely, dementedly, distractedly, frenziedly, maniacally, frantically, hysterically, deliriously, wildly; *inf.* crazily. **2** *rushing around madly* like mad, furiously, fast, hurriedly, quickly, speedily, hastily, energetically. *See* LIKE MAD 1 (MAD). **3** *love her madly* enthusiastically, wildly, intensely, fervently, to distraction. *See* LIKE MAD 2 (MAD).

madman *noun* maniac, lunatic, imbecile, psychopath; *inf.* loony, nut, nutter, nutcase, head case, basket case, screwball, psycho.

madness *noun* **1** *madness caused by grief* insanity, insaneness, dementia, mental illness/derangement, dementedness, instability of mind, unsoundness of mind, lunacy, distraction, mania, frenzy, psychosis; *inf.* craziness. **2** *with madness in her voice* anger, fury, rage, infuriation, irateness, wrath, ire, crossness, indignation, exasperation, irritation; *inf.* lividness, wildness. **3** *the madness of the decision* insanity, folly, foolishness, stupidity, lunacy, foolhardiness, idiocy, irrationality, unreasonableness, illogicality, senselessness, nonsense, nonsensicalness, absurdness, absurdity, silliness, inanity, ludicrousness, wildness, imprudence, preposterousness; *inf.* craziness, daftness. **madness about/for** *known for her madness about/for jazz* enthusiasm for, passion for, avidness for, eagerness for, keenness for, infatuation with. *See* MAD ABOUT (MAD).

maelstrom *noun* **1** *ships destroyed in a maelstrom* whirlpool, vortex, eddy, swirl, Charybdis. **2** *the maelstrom of war* turbulence, tumult, uproar, commotion, disorder, disarray, chaos, confusion, upheaval, pandemonium, bedlam.

maestro *noun* master, expert, virtuoso, genius; *inf.* ace, whiz.

magazine *noun* periodical, journal, publication, supplement, color supplement; *inf.* glossy, book.

magenta *adjective* fuchsia, reddish-purple, purplish-red, crimson, carmine.

magic *noun* **1** *believers in magic* sorcery, witchcraft, wizardry, enchantment, necromancy, the supernatural, occultism, the occult, black magic, voodoo, thaumaturgy. **2** *applauded her skills of magic* sleight of hand, legerdemain, conjuring, illusion, prestidigitation, deception, trickery, juggling; *inf.* hocus-pocus. **3** *the magic of the stage* allure, allurement, enchantment, entrancement, fascination, charm, glamour, magnetism, enticement.

magic *adjective* **1** *a magic place* magical, enchanting, entrancing, spellbinding, fascinating, captivating, charming, glamorous, magnetic, irresistible, hypnotic. **2** *the tennis game was magic* marvelous, wonderful, excellent; *inf.* brilliant, terrific, fabulous, fab.

magician *noun* **1** *frightened by the magician in the story* sorcerer, sorceress, witch, wizard, warlock, enchanter, enchantress, spell-caster, necromancer, thaumaturge. **2** *the magician at the party* illusionist, conjuror, legerdemainist, prestidigitator, juggler. **3** *he is a magician at the piano* genius, master, virtuoso, expert, marvel, wizard, maestro; *inf.* ace, whiz.

magisterial *adjective* imperious, peremptory, authoritative, masterful, lordly, domineering, dictatorial, autocratic, overbearing, overweening, high-handed, arrogant, haughty, supercilious, patronizing; *inf.* bossy.

magnanimity *noun* generosity, charitableness, charity, benevolence, beneficence, openhandedness, bigheartedness, kindness, munificence, bountifulness, largesse, altruism, philanthropy, unselfishness, selflessness, selfsacrifice, mercy, leniency.

magnanimous *adjective* generous, generous to a fault, charitable, benevolent, beneficent, openhanded, bighearted, greathearted, kind, kindly, munificent, bountiful, liberal, altruistic, philanthropic, noble, unselfish, selfless, self-sacrificing, ungrudging, unstinting, forgiving, merciful, lenient, indulgent.

Antonyms: MEAN; SELFISH; PETTY; VINDICTIVE.

magnate *noun* *a business magnate* tycoon, captain of industry, baron, industrialist, entrepreneur, financier, top executive, chief, leader, VIP, notable, nabob, grandee; *inf.* big shot, bigwig, big wheel, fat cat, mogul.

magnet *noun* **1** *a magnet attracting iron filings* lodestone, magnetite, field magnet, bar magnet, electromagnet, solenoid. **2** *the "2 for 1" sign worked as a magnet* focus, focal point, center of attraction, cynosure; lure, allurement, attraction, fascination, captivation, enticement, draw, appeal, charm, temptation, comeon.

magnetic *adjective* alluring, attractive, fascinating, captivating, entrancing, enchanting, enthralling, appealing, charming, engaging, tempting, tantalizing, seductive, inviting, irresistible, magic, bewitching, charismatic, hypnotic, mesmeric.

magnetism *noun* *the leader has great magnetism* allure, attraction, fascination, captivation, enchantment, appeal, draw, drawing power, pull, charm, temptation, seductiveness, magic, spell, charisma, hypnotism, mesmerism.

magnification noun **1** *magnification through the microscope* increase, augmentation, enlargement, extension, expansion, intensification, heightening, enhancement, aggrandizement. *See* MAGNIFY 1. **2** *the magnification of their troubles* exaggeration, overstatement, overemphasis, overplaying, dramatization, embroidery, embellishment, enhancement. *See* MAGNIFY 2.

magnificence noun splendor, splendidness, resplendence, grandeur, impressiveness, glory, majesty, nobility, pomp, pomp and circumstance, stateliness, sumptuousness, opulence, luxuriousness, luxury, lavishness, richness, brilliance, radiance, elegance, éclat; *inf.* ritziness, poshness.

magnificent adjective **1** *magnificent processions/ apartments* splendid, resplendent, grand, grandiose, impressive, imposing, striking, glorious, superb, majestic, august, noble, stately, exalted, awe-inspiring, royal, regal, kingly, princely, sumptuous, opulent, luxurious, lavish, rich, brilliant, radiant, elegant, gorgeous; *inf.* splendiferous, ritzy, posh. **2** *a magnificent performance/game* excellent, masterly, skillful, virtuoso, splendid, impressive, fine, marvelous, wonderful; *inf.* terrific, glorious, superb, brilliant, out of this world.
Antonyms: MODEST; POOR.

magnify verb **1** *bacteria visible when magnified* increase, augment, enlarge, extend, expand, amplify, intensify, heighten, deepen, broaden, widen, dilate, boost, enhance, aggrandize. **2** *magnifying their troubles* exaggerate, overstate, overdo, overemphasize, overplay, dramatize, color, embroider, embellish, enhance, inflate, make a mountain out of a molehill, draw the long bow; *inf.* make a big thing out of, blow up, blow up out of all proportion.
Antonyms: REDUCE; UNDERSTATE; play down (*see* PLAY).

magniloquence noun grandiloquence, loftiness, grandiosity, pompousness, pretentiousness, bombast, rhetoric, orotundity, fustian, boastfulness, braggadocio.

magniloquent adjective grandiloquent, high-sounding, high-flown, lofty, grandiose, pompous, pretentious, bombastic, rhetorical, declamatory, sonorous, orotund, fustian, stilted, turgid, boastful, bragging; *inf.* highfalutin.

magnitude noun **1** *estimate the magnitude of the explosion* size, extent, measure, proportions, dimensions, volume, weight, quantity, mass, bulk, amplitude, capacity. **2** *amazed at the magnitude of the epidemic* size, extent, greatness, largeness, bigness, immensity, vastness, hugeness, enormity, enormousness, expanse. **3** *underestimate the magnitude of his problem/rank* importance, significance, weight, moment, consequence, mark, notability, note, greatness, distinction, eminence, fame, renown. **of the first magnitude** of the utmost importance, of

the greatest significance, very important, of importance, of significance, of note, of moment, of consequence.
Antonyms: TRIVIALITY; smallness.

maid noun *employ a maid* maidservant, housemaid, chambermaid, servant, domestic, girl, au pair.

maiden noun *the maiden Rapunzel* girl, young woman, young lady, lass; *lit.* damsel.

maiden adjective **1** *maiden aunt* unmarried, spinster, unwed, unwedded, single, husbandless, spouseless, celibate. **2** *maiden voyage/speech* first, initial, inaugural, introductory, initiatory. **3** *maiden territory* virgin, intact, undefiled, untrodden, untapped, unused, untried, untested, fresh, new.

maidenly adjective maidenlike, virginal, chaste, pure, undefiled, virtuous, unsullied, vestal, demure, reserved, retiring, decorous, seemly, decent, gentle.

mail¹ noun **1** *collect the mail* | *reading my mail* letters, packages, parcels, correspondence, communications, airmail, registered mail; electronic mail, E-mail. **2** *criticizing the mail* postal system, postal service, post office, post.

mail² verb *mail the letter/package* send by mail/ post, send, dispatch, post, airmail.

mail³ noun *knights wearing mail* armor, coat of mail, chain mail, chain armor, plate armor.

maim verb wound, injure, hurt, cripple, disable, put out of action, lame, incapacitate, impair, mar, mutilate, disfigure, mangle.

main adjective **1** *the main office/road/issue* head, chief, principal, leading, foremost, most important, central, prime, premier, primary, supreme, predominant, preeminent, paramount, cardinal, crucial, vital, critical, pivotal, urgent. **2** *by main force* sheer, pure, utter, downright, mere, plain, brute, stark, absolute, out-and-out, direct.
Antonyms: SUBSIDIARY; MINOR.

main noun **in the main** for the most part, on the whole, mainly, mostly, by and large, all in all, effectively.

mainly adverb *the people are mainly visitors* for the most part, mostly, in the main, on the whole, largely, by and large, to a large extent, to a great degree, predominantly, chiefly, principally, substantially, overall, in general, generally, usually, commonly, as a rule.

mainspring noun *jealousy was the mainspring of the crime* motive, motivation, driving force, incentive, impulse, cause, prime mover, reason, origin, root, generator, basis.

mainstay noun *the mainstay of the family* | *she is the mainstay of the theater company* chief support, prop, linchpin, pillar, pillar of strength, bulwark, buttress, backbone, anchor, foundation, base.

maintain verb **1** *maintain friendly relations* | *must maintain efficiency* continue, keep going, keep

up, keep alive, keep in existence, carry on, preserve, conserve, prolong, perpetuate, sustain. **2** *maintain the houses/roads* keep in good condition, keep in repair, keep up, conserve, preserve, keep intact, care for, take good care of, look after. **3** *maintain a family* support, provide for, keep, finance, feed, nurture, nourish, sustain. **4** *maintain his innocence | he maintains that he is innocent* insist on, hold to, declare, assert, state, announce, affirm, aver, avow, profess, claim, allege, contend, asseverate. **5** *maintain a position* uphold, defend, fight for, stand by, take up the cudgels for, argue for, champion, support, back, advocate.
Antonyms: break off (*see* BREAK); NEGLECT; DENY.

maintenance *noun* **1** *the maintenance of friendly relations* continuation, continuance, keeping up, carrying on, preservation, conservation, prolongation, perpetuation. *See* MAINTAIN 1. **2** *pay for the maintenance of the property* upkeep, repairs, preservation, conservation, care. *See* MAINTAIN 2. **3** *the maintenance of a family is costly* supporting, keeping, upkeep, financing, feeding, nurture. *See* MAINTAIN 3.

majestic *adjective* regal, royal, kingly, queenly, princely, imperial, noble, lordly, august, exalted, awesome, elevated, lofty, stately, dignified, distinguished, magnificent, grand, splendid, resplendent, glorious, impressive, imposing, marvelous, superb, proud.

majesty *noun* **1** *the majesty of the procession* regalness, royalty, royalness, kingliness, queenliness, nobility, nobleness, augustness, exaltation, awesomeness, awe, loftiness, stateliness, dignity, magnificence, grandeur, grandness, splendor, resplendence, glory, impressiveness, superbness, pride. **2** *the majesty invested in him* sovereignty, authority, power, dominion, supremacy.

major *adjective* **1** *the major part is complete* larger, bigger, greater, main. **2** *one of our major poets* greatest, best, most important, leading, foremost, chief, main, outstanding, first-rate, notable, eminent, preeminent, supreme. **3** *a major issue | a matter of major importance* important, significant, crucial, vital, great, weighty, paramount, utmost, prime. **4** *major surgery* serious, radical, complicated.
Antonyms: MINOR; UNIMPORTANT; TRIVIAL.

majority *noun* **1** *the majority of the people/audience* larger part/number, greater part/number, most, more than half, bulk, mass, main body, preponderance, lion's share. **2** *their majority was halved* winning margin, winning difference, superiority of numbers/votes. **3** *young people reaching their majority* legal age, coming-of-age, seniority, adulthood, manhood, womanhood, maturity, age of consent.
Antonyms: minority; HANDFUL.

make *verb* **1** *make sandcastles/furniture* build, construct, assemble, put together, put up, erect, manufacture, produce, fabricate, create, form, fashion, model, mold, shape, forge. **2** *make them pay | you can't make me!* force (to), compel (to), coerce (into), press (into), drive (into), pressure (into), oblige (to), require (to), prevail upon (to), impel (to); *inf.* railroad (into), put the heat on, put the screws on, use strong-arm tactics on. **3** *make a noise/scene* cause, create, give rise to, produce, bring about, generate, engender, occasion, effect. **4** *make a bow* perform, execute, do, accomplish, carry out, effect, practice, engage in, prosecute. **5** *make him chairman* create, appoint, designate, name, nominate, select, elect, vote in, install, invest, ordain, assign. **6** *make a will/movie* compose, put together, frame, formulate, prepare, write, direct. **7** *make money | he's making a profit | can't make a good wage* gain, acquire, obtain, get, realize, secure, win, earn, net, gross, clear, bring in, take home, pocket. **8** *make tea/dinner* prepare, get ready, make arrangements for, put together, concoct, cook; *inf.* whip up, fix. **9** *make laws* draw up, frame, form, formulate, enact, lay down, establish, institute, found, originate. **10** *that makes $100* come to, add up to, total, amount to. **11** *what do you make the total to be?* estimate, calculate, compute, gauge, reckon. **12** *make a decision* come to, settle on, determine on, conclude, establish, seal. **13** *make a speech* give, deliver, utter, give voice to, enunciate, recite, pronounce. **14** *make a great leader | the sofa makes a good bed* be, act as, serve as, constitute, perform the function of, play the part of, represent, embody. **15** *make the team on her first tryout | he wanted success, and he made it* achieve, attain, get into, gain access to, gain a place in. **16** *make the bus/party* catch, arrive in time for, arrive at, reach, get to, succeed in attending.
make as if/though *make as if to run away | made as if he were mad* act as if/though, pretend, feign, give the impression, make a show of, affect, feint; *inf.* put it on. **make believe** pretend, fantasize, indulge in fantasy, daydream, build castles in the air, build castles in Spain, dream, imagine, romance, playact, act, enact. **make do** *we have very little but we make do* get by on few resources, get by, get along, scrape by, manage, cope, survive, muddle through, make the best of a bad situation. **make do with** *make do with what you have* get by with/on, make the best of, put to the best use, make the most of, improvise with. **make for 1** *make for a safe place* go toward, head for, aim for, make one's way toward, proceed toward, direct one's footsteps toward, steer a course toward, be bound for. **2** *this will make for a good relationship* contribute to, be conducive to, promote, facilitate, further, advance, forward, favor. **make off** *on seeing the police, they made off* run away/off, take to one's heels, leave, take off, beat a hasty re-

treat, flee, bolt, fly, make a getaway, make one's getaway, make a quick exit, abscond, decamp; *inf.* clear off, beat it, make tracks, split, cut and run, skedaddle, vamoose, hightail it. **make off with** *make off with his bags/money/wife* run off/away with, abscond with, steal, purloin, appropriate, kidnap, abduct; *inf.* swipe, nab, waltz off with, filch. **make out 1** *make out a figure in the distance* discern, see, distinguish, espy, behold, perceive, descry, notice, observe, recognize, pick out, detect, discover. **2** *unable to make out what she says* understand, comprehend, follow, grasp, fathom, work out, figure out, interpret. **3** *unable to make out the handwriting* decipher, work out, figure out, understand, interpret. **4** *they made out that he was violent* assert, declare, affirm, aver, allege, claim, suggest, imply, pretend. **5** *how did you make out?* get on, get along, fare, do, get by, proceed, go, progress, manage, survive. **make over** renovate, remodel, redo, restore, redecorate, brighten up, improve, upgrade; *inf.* do up. **make up 1** *their statements make up the case for the prosecution* comprise, form, compose, constitute. **2** *make up the balance* supply, furnish, provide. **3** *making up for their previous rudeness* make amends, atone, compensate, make recompense, make reparation, make redress. **4** *kiss and make up* be friends again, bury the hatchet, declare a truce, make peace, forgive and forget, shake hands, become reconciled, settle differences, mend fences. **5** *make up a prescription* prepare, mix, concoct, put together. **6** *make up an excuse* invent, fabricate, concoct, hatch, coin, trump up, dream up, think up, devise, manufacture, formulate, frame, construct; *inf.* cook up. **7** *make up a short story* compose, write, create, originate, devise. **8** *make up her face* use makeup on, apply cosmetics to, powder, rouge; *inf.* put on, do, paint, do up, apply warpaint to. **make up one's mind** come to a decision, make/reach a decision, decide, determine, resolve, settle on a plan of action, choose/determine/resolve/settle one's course of action, reach a conclusion. **make way for** *make way for the ambulance* clear the way for, make a space for, make room for, stand back for, allow to pass, allow through. **what one makes of (something/someone)** *what do you make of those people/clouds?* how one looks upon (something/someone), how one views/regards/judges/deems/evaluates/adjudges (something/someone), what one thinks of (something/someone).
Antonyms: DEMOLISH; DESTROY.

make *noun* **1** *different makes of car | buy the store's own make* brand, label, trademark, sort, type, variety, style, mark, marque. **2** *a large make of dog | a clumsy make of machine* build, form, frame, structure, construction, shape. **3** *of a different make from his brother* character, nature, temperament, temper, disposition, humor. *See* MAKEUP 3.

make-believe *noun* pretense, fantasy, daydreaming, dreaming, imagination, romancing, fabrication, playacting, charade, masquerade.

make-believe *adjective* *a make-believe world/friend* pretended, feigned, made-up, fantasy, fantasized, dream, imagined, imaginary, unreal, fictitious, mock, sham; *inf.* pretend.
Antonyms: REAL; ACTUAL.

maker *noun* *the maker of the clocks | a group of mischief-makers* manufacturer, builder, constructor, producer, creator, fabricator, author, architect, framer.

Maker *noun* God, God the Father, the Creator, the Almighty, God Almighty.

makeshift *adjective* stopgap, make-do, provisional, temporary, rough and ready, standby, substitute, improvised, jerry-built, thrown-together.

makeup *noun* **1** *putting on their makeup* cosmetics, greasepaint, foundation, powder, blusher, rouge, eye makeup, eyeliner, eye shadow, eyebrow pencil, lipstick, lip gloss; *inf.* warpaint, face paint. **2** *the makeup of the machines varies* structure, composition, constitution, formation, form, format, configuration, construction, assembly, arrangement, organization. **3** *his makeup suggests a strong family background* character, nature, temperament, temper, personality, disposition, humor, make, stamp, mold, kidney, frame of mind; *inf.* what makes someone tick.

making *noun* *the making of the cars | the art of lace-making* manufacture, manufacturing, building, construction, production, creation, fabrication, forming, molding, forging. **in the making** budding, burgeoning, coming, emergent, growing, developing, nascent.

makings *plural noun* *have the makings of a leader* potential, potentiality, promise, capacity, capability, qualities, characteristics, ingredients, materials, essentials, beginnings, basics.

maladjusted *adjective* disturbed, unstable, ill-adjusted, neurotic, alienated from society, muddled, confused; *inf.* mixed-up, screwed-up, untogether.

maladroit *adjective* awkward, clumsy, inept, bungling, bumbling, incompetent, unskillful, unhandy, ungainly, inelegant, graceless, gauche, all fingers and thumbs, like a bull in a china shop; *inf.* butterfingered, ham-handed.
Antonyms: ADROIT; GRACEFUL; ELEGANT; SKILLFUL.

malady *noun* disease, disorder, illness, sickness, ailment, affliction, complaint, infection, indisposition, infirmity.

malaise *noun* lassitude, listlessness, languor, enervation, weakness, feebleness, infirmity, illness, sickness, unease, discomfort, anxiety, angst, disquiet, melancholy, depression, despondency, dejection, weariness, ennui.

malapropism *noun* wrong word, misuse, misusage, misapplication, infelicity.

malcontent *noun young malcontents resenting the adults* grumbler, complainer, moaner, faultfinder, carper, agitator, troublemaker, rebel, mischief-maker, dissentient; *inf.* grouser, griper, nitpicker, bellyacher.

malcontent *adjective a malcontent mood in the crowd* discontented, dissatisfied, disgruntled, disaffected, restive, unhappy, grumbling, complaining, faultfinding, carping, resentful, troublemaking, rebellious, dissentious, factious; *inf.* nitpicking, bellyaching.

male *adjective male bird/plant/characteristics* masculine, manlike, manly, virile.
Antonyms: FEMALE; FEMININE.

---

male
manful, manly, mannish, masculine, virile

We speak of a **male** ancestor, a **masculine** scent, and a **manly** activity, but only of women as **mannish**. While all of these adjectives apply to what is characteristic of the male of the species (particularly the human species), *male* can refer to plants or animals as well as human beings and is used to describe whatever is biologically distinguished from the female sex (*an all-male choir; a male cat; a male holly bush*). *Masculine* refers to the qualities, characteristics, and behaviors associated with or thought to be appropriate to men and boys (*a masculine handshake*). *Manly* emphasizes the desirable qualities that a culture associates with a mature man, such as courage and independence (*the manly virtues; the manly sport of football*). *Manful* differs from *manly* primarily in its emphasis on sturdiness and resoluteness (*a manful effort to hold back tears*). **Virile** is a stronger word than *masculine* or *manly* and is applied only to mature men; it suggests the vigor, muscularity, and forcefulness—and especially the sexual potency—associated with mature manhood (*a virile man who looked like Charlton Heston in his youth*).

---

male *noun* **1** *design clothing for males* man, gentleman, boy, lad; *inf.* fellow, guy. **2** *the breeder segregated the males | the male has brighter plumage* tomcat, bull, ram, stallion, buck, stag, boar, billy goat, cock, gander, drake.

malediction *noun* curse, imprecation, execration, anathema, voodoo; damning, damnation.

malefactor *noun* criminal, lawbreaker, felon, convict, offender, wrongdoer, evildoer, villain, miscreant, delinquent, sinner, reprobate, transgressor, outlaw, trespasser; *inf.* crook.

malevolence *noun* malignance, malignity, malice, maleficence, ill nature, ill will, animosity, hostility, hatred, hate, spite, spitefulness, vindictiveness, rancor, revengefulness, viciousness.

malevolent *adjective* malign, malignant, malicious, maleficent, evil-intentioned, evil-minded, ill-natured, hostile, unfriendly, spiteful, baleful, vindictive, revengeful, rancorous, vicious, pernicious, cruel, fierce.
Antonyms: BENEVOLENT; FRIENDLY; KIND.

malformation *noun* deformity, distortion, crookedness, misshapenness, disfigurement, misproportion.

malformed *adjective* deformed, distorted, crooked, twisted, misshapen, disfigured, misproportioned.

malfunction *verb the computer is malfunctioning* develop a fault, go wrong, break down, break, fail, cease to function/work, stop working; *inf.* conk out, go kaput.

malfunction *noun* **1** *detect a malfunction in the machine* fault, defect, flaw, impairment; *inf.* glitch. **2** *complain about the malfunction of the machine* breakdown, failure, collapse; *inf.* conking out.

malice *noun* malevolence, maliciousness, malignity, malignance, evil intentions, ill will, ill feeling, animosity, animus, hostility, enmity, bad blood, hatred, hate, spite, spitefulness, vindictiveness, rancor, bitterness, grudge, venom, spleen, harm, destruction, defamation; *inf.* bitchiness, cattiness.

malicious *adjective* malevolent, malign, malignant, evil, evil-intentioned, ill-natured, hostile, spiteful, baleful, vindictive, rancorous, bitter, venomous, pernicious, harmful, hurtful, destructive, defamatory; *inf.* bitchy, catty.
Antonyms: BENEVOLENT; KINDLY; FRIENDLY.

malign *verb* slander, libel, defame, smear, run a smear campaign against, blacken someone's name/character, calumniate, vilify, speak ill of, spread lies about, accuse falsely, cast aspersions on, misrepresent, traduce, denigrate, disparage, slur, derogate; *inf.* bad-mouth, run down, drag through the mud.
Antonyms: PRAISE; EXTOL.

---

malign
calumniate, defame, libel, slander, vilify

Do you want to ruin someone's life? You can **malign** the person, which is to say or write something evil without necessarily lying (*she was maligned for her past association with radical causes*). To **calumniate** is to make false and malicious statements about someone; the word often implies that you have seriously damaged that person's good name (*after leaving his job, he spent most of his time calumniating and ridiculing his former boss*). To **defame** is to cause actual injury to someone's good name or reputation (*he defamed her by accusing her of being a spy*). If you don't mind risking a lawsuit, you can **libel** the person, which is to write or print something that defames him or her (*the tabloid libeled the celebrity and ended up paying the price*). **Slander**, which is to defame someone orally, is seldom a basis for court action but can nevertheless cause injury to someone's reputation (*after a loud and very public argument, she accused him of slandering her*). If all else fails, you can **vilify** the person, which is to engage in abusive name-calling (*even though he was found innocent by the jury, he was vilified by his neighbors*).

malignant *adjective* **1** *a malignant person | has malignant intentions* malevolent, malicious, evil, evil-intentioned, hostile, spiteful, vindictive, rancorous, venomous, pernicious, harmful, hurtful, destructive. **2** *a malignant growth* cancerous, nonbenign. **3** *a malignant disease* dangerous, virulent, uncontrollable, deadly, fatal, life-threatening, lethal.
Antonyms: BENEVOLENT; KINDLY; BENIGN.

malinger *verb* feign/fake illness, pretend to be ill, pretend to be an invalid, have a fake illness, shirk, pretend; *inf.* gold-brick.

mall *noun* shopping center/plaza/complex.

malleable *adjective* **1** *malleable substances* workable, shapable, moldable, plastic, pliant, ductile, tractile. **2** *malleable people* pliable, compliant, easily influenced, accommodating, adaptable, impressionable, manageable, susceptible, amenable, biddable, tractable, governable.

malnutrition *noun* undernourishment, poor diet, inadequate diet, unhealthy diet, lack of food, starvation, famine, anorexia.

malodorous *adjective* foul-smelling, evil-smelling, fetid, smelly, stinking, reeking, rank, noisome, mephitic; *inf.* stinking to high heaven.

malpractice *noun doctors guilty of malpractice* unprofessional conduct, unprofessionalism, dereliction, negligence, carelessness, breach of ethics, unethical behavior, misconduct, wrongdoing.

maltreat *verb* treat badly, ill-treat, ill-use, mistreat, misuse, abuse, handle/treat roughly, mishandle, manhandle, maul, bully, injure, harm, hurt, molest; *inf.* beat up, rough up, do over.

maltreatment *noun* ill treatment, ill use, mistreatment, abuse, rough handling, mishandling, manhandling, bullying, injury, harm.

mammoth *adjective* huge, enormous, giant, gigantic, vast, immense, mighty, colossal, massive, gargantuan, prodigious, monumental, stupendous, mountainous, elephantine, king-size; *inf.* whopping, humongous.

man *noun* **1** *has grown into a fine man* male, adult male, gentleman; *inf.* fellow, guy. **2** *no man is perfect* human being, human, mortal, person, individual, one, personage. **3** *the evolution of man* mankind, the human race, the human species, *Homo sapiens*, humankind, human beings, humans, people. **4** *employ a man to do the garden* workman, worker, laborer, helper, hand. **5** *the ambassador and his man* valet, manservant, gentleman's gentleman; page, footman; flunky. **6** *his sister and her man* husband, spouse, boyfriend, partner, lover, escort,

457

beau, significant other. **to a man** with no exceptions, without exception, bar none, one and all, everyone, each and every one, unanimously, as one.
Antonyms: WOMAN; FEMALE.

man *verb* **1** *man the bar/fort* supply with men/people/staff, furnish with men/people/staff, staff, crew. **2** *man the battle stations! | man the telephones* take one's position at/in, attend to, take one's place at, report to one's post at; work, operate, use, utilize, service.

manacles *plural noun* handcuffs, chains, irons, hand shackles/fetters; *inf.* cuffs, bracelets.

manage *verb* **1** *manage the team/organization* be in charge of, run, be head of, head, direct, control, preside over, lead, govern, rule, command, superintend, supervise, oversee, administer, organize, conduct, handle, guide, be at the helm of; *inf.* head up. **2** *manage to survive | will you manage?* succeed (in), contrive, engineer, bring about/off, achieve, accomplish, effect; cope, deal with the situation, get along, carry on, survive, make do, be/fare all right, weather the storm; *inf.* make out, get by. **3** *can you manage the dog/children?* cope with, deal with, handle, control, master, influence. **4** *manage a weapon* wield, use, operate, work, ply, handle, manipulate, brandish, flourish.
Antonyms: MISMANAGE; FAIL.

manageable *adjective* **1** *manageable tasks* easy, doable, practicable, possible, feasible, attainable, viable. **2** *manageable people* controllable, governable, tamable, tractable, pliant, compliant, docile, accommodating, amenable, yielding, submissive. **3** *manageable tools* handy, easy, user-friendly.
Antonyms: DIFFICULT; UNMANAGEABLE; IMPRACTICABLE; INTRACTABLE.

management *noun* **1** *the workers' dispute with management* administration, managers, employers, owners, proprietors, directors, board of directors, board, directorate, executives; *inf.* bosses, top brass. **2** *responsible for the management of the firm* administration, running, charge, care, direction, leadership, control, governing, ruling, command, superintendence, supervision, overseeing, organization, conduct, handling, guidance.

manager *noun* **1** *managers and workers* employer, director, executive, head of department, administrator, superintendent, supervisor; *inf.* boss, gaffer. **2** *the team's manager* organizer, controller, comptroller.

mandate *noun by mandate of the electorate/king* authority, bidding, direction, instruction, authorization, sanction, warrant, order, command, directive, ruling, decree, edict, dictate, charge, injunction, statute, law, ordinance, fiat, ukase.

mandatory *adjective* obligatory, compulsory,

binding, required, requisite, essential, imperative, necessary.
Antonyms: VOLUNTARY; OPTIONAL; DISCRETIONARY.

maneuver *noun* **1** *maneuver of troops* movement, deployment, operation, exercise. **2** *park the vehicle in one maneuver* skillful movement/move, movement, move, clever stroke, stroke, skillful measure/handling. **3** *get the promotion by a series of maneuvers* trick, stratagem, tactic, machination, manipulation, artifice, subterfuge, device, dodge, ploy, ruse, scheme, plan, plot, intrigue.

maneuver *verb* **1** *maneuver the car* move, work, negotiate, steer, guide, direct, manipulate. **2** *maneuvers things to suit himself* manage, manipulate, contrive, engineer, devise, plan, plot; *inf.* wangle. **3** *he is maneuvering for the leadership* scheme, intrigue, plot, use trickery/artifice, machinate, pull strings.

mange *noun* scabies, scab, itch, rash, eruption, skin infection.

manger *noun* trough, feeding trough, fodder rack.

mangle *verb* **1** *the lawn mower mangled the garden hose* mutilate, hack, cut up, lacerate, maul, tear at, rend, butcher, disfigure, deform. **2** *mangle the piece of music* spoil, ruin, mar, bungle, mess up, make a mess of; *inf.* murder.

mangy *adjective* **1** *mangy animals* scabby, scabious, scaly. **2** *mangy carpets/apartments* shabby, scruffy, moth-eaten, worn, shoddy, dirty, squalid, filthy, seedy. **3** *he's a mangy individual* contemptible, despicable, hateful, odious, nasty, mean, base, low.

manhandle *verb* **1** *accused of manhandling prisoners* handle roughly, push, pull, shove, maul, mistreat, ill-treat, abuse, injure, damage, beat, batter; *inf.* paw, knock about, beat up, rough up. **2** *having to manhandle the huge packages* move/carry/lift manually, heave, haul, push, shove, pull, tug, maneuver.

manhood *noun* **1** *reach manhood* adulthood, maturity, sexual maturity, puberty. **2** *insult his manhood* maleness, masculinity, masculineness, manliness, virility, machismo. **3** *soldiers demonstrating their manhood* manliness, bravery, courage, heroism, intrepidity, valor, boldness, mettle, spirit, fortitude. *See* MANLINESS 1.

mania *noun* **1** *treating the patient's mania* frenzy, franticness, violence, wildness, hysteria, raving, derangement, dementia. **2** *a mania for collecting old china* obsession, compulsion, fixation, fetish, fascination, preoccupation, passion, enthusiasm, desire, urge, craving, craze, fad; *inf.* thing.

maniac *noun murder committed by a maniac* madman, madwoman, mad person, deranged person, psychopath, lunatic; *inf.* loony, nutcase, nut, psycho, screwball.

manifest *verb* **1** *manifest strange symptoms* display, show, exhibit, demonstrate, present, evince, express, reveal, indicate, make plain, declare. **2** *manifest his guilt* prove, be evidence of, establish, show, evidence, substantiate, corroborate, verify, confirm, settle.
Antonyms: HIDE; MASK; DENY.

manifest *adjective a manifest disinterest in the proceedings* obvious, clear, plain, apparent, patent, noticeable, perceptible, visible, transparent, conspicuous, unmistakable, distinct, blatant, glaring.

manifestation *noun* **1** *a manifestation of solidarity* display, show, exhibition, demonstration, presentation, exposition, illustration, exemplification, indication, declaration, expression, profession. **2** *produce manifestations of their presence* evidence, proof, testimony, substantiation, sign, indication, mark, symbol, token, symptom.

manifesto *noun* proclamation, pronouncement, declaration, declaration of political policies, announcement, statement, publication, notification.

manifold *adjective* multifarious, multiple, multifold, numerous, many, several, multitudinous, various, varied, diverse, assorted, sundry, copious, abundant.

manipulate *verb* **1** *manipulate the tool/weapon* handle, wield, ply, work, operate, use, employ, utilize, exercise. **2** *manipulate his colleagues* | *has manipulated the situation* influence, control, use to one's advantage, exploit, maneuver, engineer, steer, direct, guide, pull the strings. **3** *manipulate the figures* juggle, massage, falsify, doctor, tamper with, fiddle with, tinker with; *inf.* cook.

manipulator *noun* **1** *the manipulator of the tools* handler, wielder, operator. *See* MANIPULATE 1. **2** *don't trust him—he is a manipulator* exploiter, maneuverer, conniver, intriguer, puller of strings.

mankind *noun* man, *Homo sapiens*, the human race, the human species, humankind, human beings, humans, people.

manliness *noun* **1** *show their manliness in battle* manhood, bravery, braveness, courage, courageousness, heroism, intrepidity, valor, boldness, fearlessness, stoutheartedness, dauntlessness, mettle, spirit, fortitude. **2** *cologne that claimed to evoke manliness* masculinity, virility, strength, robustness, muscularity, powerfulness, ruggedness, toughness.

manly *adjective* **1** *exhibiting manly characteristics* manful, brave, courageous, gallant, heroic, intrepid, valiant, valorous, bold, fearless, stout, stouthearted, dauntless; *inf.* macho, Ramboesque. **2** *a manly figure* masculine, all-male, virile, strong, robust, vigorous, muscular, powerful, well-built, strapping, sturdy, rugged, tough; *inf.* macho.
Antonyms: COWARDLY; UNMANLY; EFFEMINATE.

man-made *adjective* manufactured, synthetic, artificial, imitation, ersatz, plastic.

manner noun **1** *do the work in an efficient manner* way, means, method, system, approach, technique, procedure, process, methodology, routine, practice, fashion, mode, style, habit, custom. **2** *have an unfriendly manner* look, air, appearance, demeanor, aspect, mien, bearing, cast, deportment, behavior, conduct. **3** *what manner of person is he?* kind, sort, type, variety, form, nature, breed, brand, stamp, class, category.

mannered adjective affected, unnatural, artificial, stilted, theatrical, posed, stagy, pretentious, put-on; *inf.* pseudo.

mannerism noun habit, characteristic, characteristic gesture, trait, idiosyncrasy, quirk, foible, peculiarity.

mannerly adjective civil, well-mannered, well-behaved, polite, courteous, gentlemanly, ladylike, genteel, decorous, respectful, well-bred, refined, polished, civilized, cultivated, gracious, chivalrous.
Antonyms: RUDE; IMPOLITE.

manners plural noun **1** *it is bad manners to stare* social behavior, behavior, conduct, way of behaving, social habit. **2** *his parents taught him manners* correct behavior, etiquette, good form, protocol, politeness, decorum, propriety, social graces, formalities, politesse; *inf.* the done thing.

mannish adjective *she is quite mannish* masculine, manlike, unfeminine, unwomanly, unladylike, Amazonian; *inf. derog.* butch.

manse noun parsonage, rectory, parish house, deanery, vicarage.

mansion noun imposing residence, manor house, manor, hall, stately home; palace, castle.

manslaughter noun killing, slaying, murder, homicide; patricide, matricide, fratricide, infanticide, regicide.

mantle noun **1** *wearing a red mantle* cloak, cape, shawl, wrap, poncho, pelisse. **2** *a mantle of snow/darkness* covering, cover, blanket, curtain, canopy, cloud, pall, envelope, veil, cloak, shroud, screen, mask.

mantle verb *fields mantled in snow | houses mantled in darkness* cover, blanket, curtain, envelop, veil, cloak, wrap, shroud, cloud, conceal, hide, disguise, mask.

manual adjective **1** *manual work* with one's hands, laboring, physical. **2** *manual transmission* hand-operated, done by hand, by hand, nonautomatic.
Antonyms: AUTOMATIC; MECHANICAL.

manual noun *an instruction manual* handbook, set of instructions, instructions, guidebook, guide; *inf.* how-to book, bible.

manufacture verb **1** *manufacture cars* make, produce, mass-produce, build, construct, assemble, put together, create, fabricate, turn out, process, form, fashion, model, mold, shape, forge. **2** *manufacture an excuse* make up, invent, fabricate, concoct, hatch, coin, trump up,

dream up, think up, devise, formulate, frame, construct; *inf.* cook up.

manufacture noun *the manufacture of cars* making, production, mass production, construction, assembly, creation, fabrication, processing.

manufacturer noun maker, producer, builder, constructor, creator, fabricator, industrialist, captain/baron of industry.

manure noun dung, animal excrement, muck, guano, droppings, fertilizer.

many adjective *many people/books/times* numerous, innumerable, a large/great number of, countless, scores of, myriad, great quantities of, multitudinous, multiple, copious, abundant, various, sundry, diverse, several, frequent; *inf.* a lot of, umpteen, lots of, masses of, scads of, heaps of, piles of, bags of, tons of, oodles of, an army of, zillions of.

many noun *many were present | many have been thrown out* many people, many things, scores, large numbers, great quantities, a large number, a host, a horde, a crowd, a multitude, a mass, an accumulation, an abundance, a profusion, plenty; *inf.* lots, a lot, umpteen, armies, scads, heaps, piles, bags, tons, masses, oodles.
the many *have to listen to the wishes of the many* the majority, the people, the masses, the multitude, the rank and file, the crowd, the hoi polloi.
Antonym: FEW.

map noun chart, plan, plot, guide, street guide, town plan, road map, atlas, gazetteer.

map verb *map the surface of the moon* chart, plot, delineate, depict, portray. **map out** *map out the conference schedule* lay out, detail, draw up, sketch out, plan, plot out.

mar verb *marred her beauty/career/happiness* spoil, detract from, impair, damage, ruin, wreck, disfigure, blemish, scar, deface, harm, hurt, injure, deform, mutilate, maim, mangle, tarnish, taint, contaminate, pollute, sully, stain, blot, debase, vitiate; *inf.* foul up.
Antonyms: IMPROVE; ADORN.

maraud verb **1** *maraud around the countryside* foray, raid, go on forays/raids, forage, plunder, go looting, pirate, freeboot. **2** *tribes marauding the neighboring villages* raid, plunder, loot, pillage, foray, ransack, forage, ravage, harry, sack, despoil.

marauder noun raider, plunderer, pillager, looter, ravager, robber, pirate, freebooter, buccaneer, corsair, rover, bandit, brigand, rustler, highwayman.

march verb **1** *armies marching* walk, step, pace, tread, stride, footslog, tramp, hike, trudge, stalk, strut, parade, file. **2** *time marches on* move forward, advance, progress, forge ahead, make headway, go on, continue on, roll on, develop, evolve.

march noun **1** *soldiers/scouts on a march* route

march, walk, footslog, tramp, trek, hike, parade. **2** *a quick/slow march* step, pace, stride, gait. **3** *a march against the tobacco industry* demonstration, parade, procession, rally. **4** *the march of time/progress* advance, progress, progression, passage, headway, continuance, development, evolution.

margin noun **1** *the margin of the lake* edge, side, verge, border, perimeter, boundary, limits, periphery, brink, brim. **2** *the margin between the countries* border, borderland, boundary, boundary line, frontier, bounding line, demarcation line. **3** *little margin for error* leeway, latitude, scope, room, room to maneuver, space, allowance, extra, surplus. **4** *win by a narrow margin | a margin of one vote* measure of difference, degree of difference, difference, amount.

marginal adjective **1** *marginal areas* border, boundary, on the edge, peripheral. **2** *the difference is marginal* slight, small, tiny, minute, low, minor, insignificant, minimal, negligible.

marijuana noun cannabis, hashish, hemp, ganja, sinsemilla; *inf.* dope, hash, grass, pot, mary jane, tea, weed.

marinate verb marinade, soak, steep, immerse.

marine adjective **1** *marine life* sea, aquatic, saltwater, oceanic, pelagic, neritic, thalassic. **2** *marine careers* maritime, nautical, naval, seafaring, seagoing.

mariner noun sailor, seaman, seafarer, seafaring man/woman; *inf.* sea dog, (old) salt, bluejacket, tar, gob.

marital adjective *marital vows/bliss* matrimonial, marriage, wedding, conjugal, connubial, nuptial, spousal, married, wedded.

maritime adjective **1** *maritime careers* naval, marine, nautical, seafaring, seagoing. **2** *maritime areas* coastal, seaside, littoral.

mark noun **1** *marks left on the table* stain, blemish, blot, smear, trace, spot, speck, dot, blotch, smudge, splotch, bruise, scratch, scar, dent, pit, pock, chip, notch, nick, line, score, cut, incision, gash. **2** *the marks on a horse/cow* marking, blaze, spot, speckle, stripe, brand, earmark. **3** *question mark | proofreader's marks* symbol, sign, character; punctuation mark. **4** *marks showing the way* marker, guide, pointer, landmark, direction post, signpost, milestone. **5** *mark of respect* sign, symbol, indication, symptom, feature, token, badge, emblem, evidence, proof, clue, hint. **6** *recognize the artist's/corporations's mark* seal, stamp, signet, symbol, emblem, device, badge, motto, monogram, hallmark, trademark, logo, watermark, label, tag, flag. **7** *put one's mark on the document* cross, X, scribble, signature, autograph, initials, imprint. **8** *marks left by the thief* print, fingerprint, thumbprint, footprint, imprint, track, trail, trace, vestige. **9** *war left its mark on him* impression, imprint, traces, vestiges, remains, ef-

fect, impact, influence. **10** *have the mark of an honest man* characteristic, feature, trait, attribute, quality, stamp, peculiarity. **11** *the bullet/insult missed its mark* target, goal, aim, bull's-eye, objective, object, end, purpose, intent, intention. **12** *work falling below the mark* standard, required standard, norm, par, level, criterion, gauge, yardstick, rule, measure, scale. **13** *a person of mark* distinction, importance, consequence, eminence, preeminence, prominence, note, notability, fame, repute, greatness, prestige, celebrity, glory, standing, rank. **14** *nothing of mark occurred* note, noteworthiness, importance, consequence. **make one's mark** *by thirty he had made his mark in the financial world* be successful, gain success, be a success, succeed, prosper, make good, achieve recognition; *inf.* make it. **wide of the mark** **1** *his observations were wide of the mark* irrelevant, inapplicable, inapposite, inappropriate, not to the point, beside the point. **2** *his answers were wide of the mark* inaccurate, incorrect, wrong, erroneous, inexact, off-target, fallacious.

mark verb **1** *mark the table* stain, smear, smudge, scratch, scar, dent, chip, notch, score, cut, gash. *See* MARK *noun* 1. **2** *mark your property* put one's name on, name, initial, put one's seal on, label, tag, stamp, flag, hallmark, watermark, brand, earmark. **3** *mark the places on a map* name, indicate, write down, tag, label, flag. **4** *mark the students' essays* correct, assess, evaluate, appraise, grade. **5** *mark the book at $10* price, put a price tag on. **6** *the children marked his displeasure* see, notice, observe, take note of, discern, spot, recognize; *inf.* get a load of. **7** *you should mark his words* take heed of, pay heed to, heed, take notice of, pay attention to, attend to, note, mind, bear in mind, give a thought to, take into consideration. **8** *a day marked by misfortune* characterize, distinguish, identify, denote, brand, signalize. **9** *mark his birthday* celebrate, commemorate, honor, observe, recognize, acknowledge, solemnize. **10** *marked for greatness* designate, choose, select, nominate. **mark down** **1** *mark down the prices* reduce, decrease, lower, cut, take down, slash. *mark down the goods* reduce, lower the price of, make cheaper, sell at a giveaway price, put on sale. **mark off/out** *mark out the football field* mark the boundaries/limits of, measure out, demarcate, delimit. **mark up** **1** *mark up the price* raise, increase, up, hike up, escalate; *inf.* jack up. **2** *mark up the goods* increase/raise the price of.

marked adjective pronounced, decided, striking, clear, glaring, blatant, unmistakable, remarkable, prominent, signal, conspicuous, noticeable, noted, distinct, pointed, salient, recognizable, identifiable, distinguishable, obvious, apparent, evident, manifest, open, patent, written all over one.
Antonyms: IMPERCEPTIBLE; INCONSPICUOUS.

markedly adverb decidedly, strikingly, remarkably, unmistakably, conspicuously, noticeably, pointedly, distinctly, recognizably, obviously, clearly, plainly, apparently, evidently, manifestly, to a marked extent, to a great extent.

market noun 1 *shopping at the market* marketplace, mart, shopping center, bazaar. 2 *no market for such expensive goods* demand, call, want, desire, need. 3 *the market is sluggish* trade, business, commerce, buying and selling, dealing. **in the market for** wishing to buy, in need of, wanting, lacking, wishing for, desiring. **on the market** on sale, up for sale, for sale, purchasable, available, obtainable.

market verb *he markets furniture* sell, retail, offer for sale, put up for sale, vend, peddle, hawk.

marksman, markswoman noun sharpshooter, shot, good shot; *inf.* crack shot, dead shot.

maroon verb abandon, forsake, leave behind, leave, desert, strand, leave stranded, turn one's back on, leave isolated.

marriage noun 1 *their marriage lasted twenty years | join in marriage* married state, matrimony, holy matrimony, wedlock, conjugal bond, union, match. 2 *invited to their marriage* marriage ceremony, wedding, wedding ceremony, nuptials. 3 *the marriage of their skills* alliance, union, merger, unification, amalgamation, combination, affiliation, association, connection, coupling; *inf.* hookup.

married adjective 1 *married couple* wedded, wed, joined in marriage, united in wedlock; *inf.* hitched. 2 *married bliss* marital, matrimonial, connubial, conjugal, nuptial, spousal.
Antonyms: UNMARRIED; SINGLE.

marrow noun *marrow of his statement* core, kernel, nucleus, pith, heart, center, soul, spirit, essence, quintessence, gist, substance, sum and substance, meat, stuff; *inf.* nitty-gritty, nuts and bolts.

marry verb 1 *the couple married last year* be married, wed, be wed, become man and wife, become espoused; *inf.* tie the knot, walk down the aisle, take the plunge, get hitched, get yoked. 2 *he married her | she married him* wed, take to wife/husband, espouse. 3 *marry their skills* join, join together, unite, ally, merge, unify, amalgamate, combine, affiliate, associate, link, connect, fuse, weld, couple.

marsh noun marshland, bog, peatbog, swamp, swampland, morass, mire, quagmire, quag, slough, fen, bayou.

marshal verb 1 *marshal the students/troops | tried to marshal his thoughts* gather together, assemble, collect, muster, draw up, line up, align, set/put in order, arrange, deploy, dispose, rank. 2 *marshal the guests to their seats* usher, guide, escort, conduct, lead, shepherd, take.

marshy adjective boggy, swampy, muddy, miry.

martial adjective 1 *martial exploits* military, soldierly, army, naval. 2 *martial arts* militant, warlike, combative, belligerent, bellicose, aggressive, pugnacious.

martial arts plural noun judo, jujitsu, aikido, karate, kung fu, t'ai chi (chu'an), tae kwon do.

martinet noun disciplinarian, stickler for discipline, hard taskmaster.

martyr noun sufferer, victim, Christian martyr, early martyr.

martyr verb 1 *martyr them for their beliefs* make a martyr of, martyrize, put to death, burn at the stake, immolate, throw to the lions, crucify. 2 *the invading army martyred the villagers* persecute, torture, inflict agony on.

martyrdom noun persecution, ordeal, torture, torment, suffering, agony, anguish.

marvel verb *marvel at their exploits* be amazed by, be filled with amazement at, be awed by, be full of wonder at, wonder at, stare at, gape at, goggle at, not believe one's eyes/ears at.

marvel noun *his desserts are a marvel* wonder, wonderful thing, amazing thing, prodigy, sensation, spectacle, phenomenon, miracle; *inf.* something else, something to shout about, something to write home about, eye-opener.

marvelous adjective 1 *his solo climb was marvelous* amazing, astounding, astonishing, awesome, breathtaking, sensational, remarkable, spectacular, stupendous, phenomenal, wondrous, prodigious, miraculous, extraordinary. 2 *he's a marvelous singer* excellent, splendid, wonderful; *inf.* magnificent, superb, glorious, super, great, boffo, smashing, fantastic, terrific, fabulous, awesome; mean, bad, wicked.
Antonyms: ORDINARY; RUN-OF-THE-MILL; DREADFUL.

masculine adjective 1 *masculine clothes* male, manly, manlike, virile, of men, man's, men's, male-oriented. 2 *a masculine physique* manly, all-male, virile, robust, vigorous, muscular, strapping, rugged; *inf.* macho. 3 *joined the army to prove he was masculine* manly, brave, courageous, gallant, heroic, valiant, bold, fearless, stouthearted; *inf.* macho, Ramboesque. 4 *masculine woman* mannish, manlike, unfeminine, unwomanly, Amazonian; *inf. derog.* butch.
Antonyms: FEMININE; EFFEMINATE.

masculinity noun 1 *admire the masculinity of his physique* manliness, virility, robustness, vigor, muscularity, ruggedness. 2 *show their masculinity in battle* manliness, manhood, bravery, courage, courageousness, heroism, intrepidity, mettle, fortitude.

mash verb *mash the potatoes* crush, pulp, purée, smash, squash, pound, beat.

mash noun *feed the mash to the livestock* pulp, mush, paste, purée, slush, pap.

mask noun 1 *wearing masks to the party* false face, domino. 2 *wearing masks for protection* protective mask, swimming mask, snorkel mask, gas mask, safety goggles, fencing mask, ski mask, surgical mask, visor. 3 *under the mask of being a tourist* disguise, guise, concealment, cover,

cover-up, cloak, camouflage, veil, screen, front, false front, façade, blind, semblance, false colors, pretense.

mask *verb* *mask her identity/feelings* disguise, hide, conceal, cover up, obscure, cloak, camouflage, veil, screen.

mass *noun* **1** *a mass of wood/clay* concretion, lump, block, chunk, hunk, piece. **2** *gathered in a mass* | *a mass of fibers* concentration, conglomeration, aggregation, amassment, assemblage, collection. **3** *actors, in the mass, enjoy their work* total, totality, whole, entirety, aggregate. **4** *measure the body's mass* size, magnitude, bulk, dimension, capacity, greatness, bigness. **a mass of** *a mass of people* many, a large number of, an abundance of, a profusion of, numerous, countless, a myriad of, a multitude of, a group of, a crowd of, a mob of, a horde of, a throng of, a host of, a troop of; *inf.* a lot of, lots of, scads of, piles of, heaps of, tons of. **the mass of** *the mass of (the) people voted against* the majority of, the greater part of, the major part of, most (of the), the bulk of, the main body of, the preponderance of, almost all (of the), the lion's share of.

mass *adjective* *mass hysteria/suicide* | *the mass media* wholesale, universal, widespread, general, large-scale, extensive, pandemic, popular.

mass *verb* **1** *clouds massing* amass, accumulate, assemble, gather, collect, draw together, join together. **2** *generals massing their troops* assemble, gather together, marshal, muster, rally, round up, mobilize.

massacre *noun* mass slaughter, wholesale slaughter, slaughter, wholesale/indiscriminate killing, mass murder, mass homicide, mass slaying, mass execution, mass destruction, carnage, butchery, blood bath, annihilation, extermination, liquidation, decimation, pogrom, genocide, ethnic cleansing, holocaust.

massacre *verb* slaughter, butcher, slay, murder, kill, annihilate, exterminate, liquidate, decimate, eliminate, kill off, wipe out, mow down, cut down, cut to pieces.

massage *noun* *a relaxing massage* rub, rubdown, rubbing, kneading, pummeling, palpation, manipulation; reflexology, acupressure, shiatsu, aromatherapy.

massage *verb* *massage stiff limbs* rub, rub down, knead, pummel, palpate, manipulate.

masses *plural noun* *a story that appeals to the masses* common people, populace, proletariat, multitude, commonality, crowd, mob, rabble, hoi polloi; *inf.* great unwashed.

massive *adjective* huge, immense, enormous, vast, mighty, extensive, gigantic, colossal, mammoth, monumental, elephantine, mountainous, gargantuan, king-size, monstrous, prodigious, titanic, hulking, bulky, weighty, hefty, solid, substantial, big, large, great; *inf.* whopping, humongous.

Antonyms: TINY; MINUTE.

mast *noun* **1** *a ship's mast* spar, boom, yard, gaff, foremast, mainmast, topmast, mizzenmast, mizzen. **2** *the mast on top of the building* flagpole, flagstaff, pole, post, support, upright.

master *noun* **1** *master of the household/hunt* | *the dog's master* lord and master, lord, overlord, ruler, overseer, superintendent, director, manager, controller, governor, commander, captain, chief, head, headman, principal, owner, employer; *inf.* boss, top dog, big cheese, honcho. **2** *master of the ship* captain, skipper, commander. **3** *students being taught by the master* schoolmaster, headmaster, teacher, schoolteacher, tutor, instructor, pedagogue, preceptor. **4** *a master of innuendo* | *a tennis master* expert, adept, professional, authority, pundit, genius, master hand, maestro, virtuoso, prodigy, past master, grand master, wizard; *inf.* ace, pro, maven. **5** *sitting at the feet of the master* guru, teacher, spiritual leader, guide, swami.

master *adjective* **1** *master craftsmen* masterly, expert, adept, proficient, skilled, skillful, deft, dexterous, practiced, experienced; *inf.* crack. **2** *master plan* controlling, ruling, directing, commanding, dominating. **3** *master bedroom* chief, main, principal, leading, prime, predominant, foremost, great, most important.

master *verb* **1** *master one's horse/emotions* conquer, vanquish, defeat, overcome, overpower, triumph over, subdue, subjugate, govern, quell, quash, suppress, control, curb, check, bridle, tame. **2** *master the technique* learn, learn thoroughly, become proficient in, acquire skill in, grasp; *inf.* get the hang of, get clued in about.

masterful *adjective* **1** *masterful men marrying meek women* dominating, authoritative, powerful, controlling, domineering, tyrannical, despotic, dictatorial, overbearing, overweening, imperious, peremptory, high-handed, arrogant, haughty. **2** *masterful handling of the situation* masterly, expert, consummate, clever, adept, adroit, skillful, skilled, proficient, deft, dexterous, accomplished, polished, excellent, superlative, first-rate, fine, talented, gifted; *inf.* crack, ace.

Antonyms: WEAK; INEPT.

masterly *adjective* *masterly handling of the situation* masterful, expert, consummate, adept, skillful, deft, dexterous, accomplished, polished, excellent, superlative, first-rate, talented, gifted; *inf.* crack, ace.

mastermind *verb* *mastermind the project* direct, manage, plan, organize, arrange, engineer, conceive, devise, forge, originate, initiate, think up, come up with, have the bright idea of; *inf.* be the brains behind.

mastermind *noun* *the mastermind behind the plan* genius, intellect, author, architect, engineer, director, planner, organizer, deviser, originator, manager, prime mover; *inf.* brain, brains.

masterpiece *noun* magnum opus, masterwork,

chef-d'oeuvre, work of art, creation, *pièce de résistance*.

masterstroke *noun* stroke of genius, tour de force, *coup de maître*, successful maneuver, feat of triumph, triumph, victory, complete success.

mastery *noun* **1** *gain mastery over the enemy | mastery over his emotions* control, domination, command, ascendancy, supremacy, superiority, triumph, victory, the upper hand, the whip hand, rule, government, power, authority, jurisdiction, dominion, sovereignty. **2** *admire his mastery of the language* command, grasp, knowledge, familiarity with, understanding, comprehension, expertise, skill, prowess, proficiency, ability, capability; *inf.* know-how.

masticate *verb* chew, munch, champ, chomp, crunch, eat.

masturbation *noun* autoeroticism, onanism, self-gratification; *inf.* playing with oneself.

mat *noun* **1** *wipe one's feet on the mat* doormat, welcome mat, rug, carpet. **2** *a mat of hair* mass, tangle, knot, mesh.

match *noun* **1** *a tennis/boxing match* contest, competition, game, tournament, bout, event, test, trial, meet. **2** *she's no match for the champion* equal, equivalent, peer, counterpart, rival, competitor. **3** *this glove is a match for that one* mate, fellow, companion, twin, counterpart, pair, complement. **4** *the new one is an exact match for the previous one* look-alike, double, twin, duplicate, copy, replica; *inf.* spitting image, spit and image, ringer, dead ringer. **5** *make a good match* marriage, union, partnership, pairing, alliance, affiliation, combination.

match *verb* **1** *curtains that match the walls | their stories match each other* complement, blend with, harmonize with, go with, coordinate with, correspond to, accord with. **2** *these socks don't match* be a pair, be a set, be the same. **3** *her strength matches his* be equal to, be a match for, measure up to, rival, vie with, compete with, compare with, parallel, be in the same category as, keep pace with, keep up with. **4** *match him with one of her friends | match the socks* marry, pair up, mate, couple, unite, join, combine, link, ally; *inf.* hitch up, yoke.

matching *adjective* corresponding, equivalent, complementing, parallel, analogous, complementary, harmonizing, blending, toning, coordinating, the same, paired, twin, coupled, double, duplicate, identical, like.
Antonyms: UNLIKE; DIFFERENT; DISSIMILAR.

matchless *adjective* unmatched, incomparable, beyond compare, unequaled, without equal, unrivaled, unparalleled, unsurpassed, inimitable, peerless, unique, consummate, perfect, transcendent.

matchmaker *noun* marriage broker, dating agency, go-between, marriage bureau.

mate *noun* **1** *he/she is looking for a mate* husband, wife, spouse, partner, companion, helpmate,

lover; *inf.* significant other, other half, better half. **2** *where is the mate to this sock?* twin, match, companion, one of a pair, other half, equivalent. **3** *they were mates throughout the war* workmate, fellow worker, coworker, associate, colleague, companion, compeer; *inf.* shipmate, classmate, roommate, teammate.

mate *verb* **1** *animals mating* breed, copulate, couple. **2** *mate the animals* bring together, pair, couple, join.

material *noun* **1** *organic/nuclear material* matter, substance, stuff, medium, constituent elements. **2** *clothes of strong material* fabric, cloth, stuff, textile. **3** *enough material for a book* data, information, facts, facts and figures, evidence, details, notes; *inf.* info.

material *adjective* **1** *the material, rather than the spiritual, world* corporeal, physical, bodily, fleshly, tangible, substantial, concrete. **2** *material pleasures* nonspiritual, physical, bodily, fleshly, worldly, earthly, temporal. **3** *material facts* important, of consequence, consequential, momentous, weighty, vital, essential, indispensable, key, significant, meaningful. **4** *material evidence* relevant, applicable, pertinent, apposite, germane, apropos.

materialize *verb* **1** *our plans did not materialize* come into being, happen, occur, come about, come to pass, take place; *inf.* shape up. **2** *the guests did not materialize* appear, turn up, become visible, come into view, come into sight, show oneself/itself, present oneself/itself, reveal oneself/itself, come to light, emerge.

materially *adverb* *not materially affected by the plans* significantly, much, greatly, to a great extent, considerably, substantially, essentially, fundamentally, seriously, gravely.

maternal *adjective* **1** *maternal feelings* motherly, protective. *See* MOTHERLY. **2** *his maternal grandparents* on one's mother's side, on the distaff side.

maternity *noun* motherhood, motherliness, parenthood.

mathematical *adjective* **1** *mathematical problems* arithmetical, numerical, statistical, algebraic, geometrical, trigonometrical. **2** *with mathematical care* precise, exact, rigorous, unerring, correct, strict, meticulous, scrupulous, careful.

matrimonial *adjective* *matrimonial bliss/dispute* marital, marriage, wedding, conjugal, connubial, nuptial, spousal, married, wedded.

matrimony *noun* *holy matrimony*, marriage, wedlock, union.

matted *adjective* tangled, entangled, knotted, tousled, disheveled, uncombed.

matter *noun* **1** *organic/waste matter* material, substance, stuff, medium. **2** *concentrate on the matter, not the style* content, subject matter, text, argument, substance, sense, thesis. **3** *no laughing matter* affair, business, proceeding, situation, circumstance, event, happening, occurrence, incident, episode, occasion, experience. **4** *discuss important matters* subject, topic, issue, question, point, case, concern, theme. **5** *issues of little matter* importance, consequence, significance, note, import, moment, weight. **6** *what is the matter?* trouble, upset, distress, worry, problem, difficulty, complication. **as a matter of fact** actually, in actual fact, in fact, in point of fact, really, in truth, to tell the truth, truly. **no matter** it does not matter, it makes no difference, it is unimportant, never mind, don't worry about it.

matter *verb your lateness/wealth does not matter* be of importance, be of consequence, make a difference, make any difference, be relevant, carry weight, count.

matter-of-fact *adjective* factual, literal, prosaic, down-to-earth, straightforward, plain, mundane, unembellished, unvarnished, unimaginative, uncreative, unemotional, unsentimental, deadpan, flat, dull, dry, pedestrian, lifeless, humdrum.

mature *adjective* **1** *mature human beings* adult, grown-up, grown, fully grown, full-grown, of age. **2** *young people becoming very mature* sensible, responsible, wise, discriminating, shrewd, practical, sagacious. **3** *mature fruits/cheese* ripe, ripened, mellow, ready, seasoned. **4** *our plans are now mature* complete, finished, finalized, developed, prepared, ready.
Antonyms: IMMATURE; CHILDISH; GREEN.

mature *verb* **1** *when the kittens have matured* grow up, develop fully, become adult, reach adulthood, be fully grown, be full-grown, come of age. **2** *when the young people have matured* become sensible/responsible/wise/discriminating. **3** *when the fruit/cheese has matured* ripen, grow ripe, become ripe, become mellow, mellow, maturate. **4** *our plans gradually matured* be complete, be finished, be fully developed, maturate.

---

mature
age, develop, mellow, ripen

Most of us would prefer to **mature** rather than simply to **age**. *Mature* implies gaining wisdom, experience, or sophistication as well as adulthood; when applied to nonhuman living things, it indicates fullness of growth and readiness for normal functioning (*a mature crop of strawberries*). To **age**, on the other hand, is to undergo the changes that result from the passage of time, often with an emphasis on the negative or destructive changes that accompany growing old (*the tragedy aged him five years*). **Develop** is like *mature* in that it means to undergo a series of positive changes to attain perfection or effectiveness, but it can refer to a part as well as a whole organism (*the kitten's eyesight had begun to develop at three weeks*).

Ripen is a less formal word meaning to *mature*, but it usually applies to fruit (*the apples ripened in the sun*). **Mellow** suggests the tempering or moderation of harshness that comes with time or experience. With its connotations of warmth, mildness, and sweetness, it is a more positive word than *mature* or age (*to mellow as one gets older*).

---

maturity *noun* **1** *children reaching maturity* matureness, adulthood, manhood/womanhood, puberty, full growth, majority, coming-of-age. **2** *the maturity of the young people* matureness, sensibleness, sense of responsibility, responsibleness, wisdom, discrimination, shrewdness, practicality, sagacity. **3** *the maturity of the fruit/cheese* matureness, ripeness, mellowness. **4** *the maturity of our plans* matureness, completion, finalization, developed state, preparedness, readiness.

maudlin *adjective* mawkish, sentimental, oversentimental, sickeningly sentimental, tearful, lachrymose; *inf.* weepy, mushy, slushy, schmaltzy.

maul *verb* **1** *mauled by a lion* tear to pieces, claw, lacerate, mutilate, mangle. **2** *clumsy movers mauling the furniture* handle roughly, handle clumsily, manhandle, paw, molest. **3** *an angry mob mauling the terrorist* beat, batter, thrash, ill-treat; *inf.* belt, wallop, clobber, rough up, kick about. **4** *his book was mauled by the critics* censure, condemn, find fault with, give bad press to, take to pieces; *inf.* knock, slate, slam, pan, lambaste.

mausoleum *noun* tomb, sepulcher, crypt, charnel house.

maverick *noun* nonconformist, rebel, dissenter, dissident, individualist, bohemian, eccentric; *inf.* trendsetter.

mawkish *adjective* maudlin, oversentimental, sickeningly sentimental, lachrymose; *inf.* mushy, slushy, schmaltzy.

maxim *noun* aphorism, proverb, adage, saw, saying, axiom, precept, epigram, gnome.

maximum *noun* *reach its maximum* most, utmost, uttermost, extremity, upper limit, height, ceiling, top, summit, peak, pinnacle, crest, apex, vertex, apogee, acme, zenith.

maximum *adjective* *the maximum amount* highest, greatest, biggest, largest, topmost, most, utmost, supreme, maximal.
Antonyms: MINIMUM; least.

maybe *adverb* perhaps, it could be that, possibly; *lit.* peradventure.

mayhem *noun* havoc, disorder, confusion, chaos, bedlam, destruction, violence, trouble, disturbance, commotion, tumult, pandemonium.

maze *noun* **1** *a maze of hedges* labyrinth, network of paths. **2** *a maze of regulations* network, mesh, web, jungle, tangle, confusion, snarl, imbroglio.

meadow *noun* field, grassland, pasture, paddock, lea.

meager *adjective* **1** *meager supplies* paltry, sparse, scant, scanty, spare, inadequate, insufficient, insubstantial, exiguous, short, little, small, slight, slender, poor, puny, skimpy, scrimpy, miserly, niggardly, stingy, pathetic; *inf.* measly, as scarce as hens' teeth. **2** *meager bodies* thin, lean, emaciated, skinny, spare, scrawny, scraggy, bony, gaunt, starved, underfed.
Antonyms: ABUNDANT; COPIOUS; OBESE.

meagerness *noun* paltriness, sparseness, scarcity, scantiness, inadequacy, insufficiency, exiguity, shortness, slightness, skimpiness, miserliness, stinginess.

meal *noun* repast, banquet, feast, picnic, barbecue, buffet; breakfast, lunch, supper, dinner; *inf.* blowout.

mean[1] *verb* **1** *what do the words mean?* indicate, signify, betoken, express, convey, denote, designate, spell out, show, stand for, represent, symbolize, portend, connote, imply, purport, suggest, allude to, intimate, hint at, insinuate, drive at. **2** *not mean to break it* intend, have in mind, have in view, contemplate, think of, purpose, plan, have plans, set out, aim, aspire, desire, want, wish. **3** *meant to be used | not meant for the army* intend, make, design, destine, predestine, fate. **4** *this will mean war* involve, entail, lead to, result in, give rise to, bring about, cause, engender, produce. **5** *this means a lot to her* have importance, have significance, matter. **6** *dark clouds meaning rain* presage, portend, foretell, augur, promise, foreshadow.

mean[2] *adjective* **1** *a mean person/dog | a mean thing to do* nasty, disagreeable, unpleasant, unfriendly, hurtful, unkind, offensive, obnoxious, cross, ill-natured, bad-tempered, irritable, surly, cantankerous, crotchety, crabbed, crabby, grumpy; *inf.* grouchy. **2** *as mean as Scrooge* miserly, niggardly, parsimonious, tight-fisted, close-fisted, penny-pinching, penurious, greedy, avaricious, ungenerous, illiberal; *inf.* stingy, tight, cheap. **3** *a mean creature* base, dishonorable, ignoble, disreputable, vile, sordid, foul, nasty, despicable, contemptible, abominable, odious, hateful, horrible. **4** *of mean understanding/intellect* inferior, poor, limited, restricted, meager, scant. **5** *a mean hovel* shabby, poor, wretched, dismal, miserable, squalid, sordid, seedy, mangy, broken-down, rundown, dilapidated, down-at-the-heels; *inf.* scruffy, grungy. **6** *of mean birth* low, lowly, lowborn, humble, modest, common, ordinary, base, proletarian, plebeian, obscure, undistinguished, ignoble.
Antonyms: KIND; PLEASANT; HONORABLE; LUXURIOUS.

mean[3] *noun* *find a mean between frankness and rudeness* midpoint, middle, median, norm, average, middle course, middle ground, happy medium.

mean[4] *adjective* *the mean temperature* middle, me-dian, medial, average, normal, standard, medium, middling.

meander *verb* **1** *meander about in the sunshine* wander, roam, ramble, rove, stroll, amble, drift; *inf.* mosey. **2** *rivers meandering through the country* wind, zigzag, snake, curve, turn, bend.

meandering *adjective* **1** *meandering crowds* wandering, roaming, rambling. *See* MEANDER 1. **2** *meandering streams* winding, zigzag, snaking, serpentine, tortuous. **3** *meandering prose* rambling, tortuous, circuitous, indirect, roundabout, convoluted.

meaning *noun* **1** *understand the meaning of what he said* signification, sense, message, import, drift, gist, essence, substance, purport, connotation, denotation, implication, significance, thrust. **2** *what is the meaning of the word?* definition, explanation, interpretation, elucidation, explication. **3** *it was not our meaning to delay him* intention, purpose, plan, aim, goal, end, object, objective, aspiration, desire, want, wish. **4** *his life has no meaning* significance, point, value, worth, consequence, account. **5** *a glance full of meaning* significance, implication, allusion, intimation, insinuation, eloquence, expression.

meaning *adjective* meaningful, significant, pointed, eloquent. *See* MEANINGFUL 3.

meaningful *adjective* **1** *a meaningful statement/remark* significant, important, relevant, material, valid, worthwhile. **2** *a meaningful relationship* significant, important, serious, sincere, in earnest. **3** *a meaningful glance* significant, pointed, suggestive, eloquent, expressive, pregnant.
Antonyms: MEANINGLESS; UNIMPORTANT; TRIVIAL.

meaningless *adjective* **1** *meaningless babble* senseless, unintelligible, incomprehensible, incoherent. **2** *a meaningless act of violence* senseless, pointless, purposeless, motiveless, irrational, inane. **3** *lead meaningless lives* empty, futile, pointless, aimless, valueless, worthless, trivial, insignificant, inconsequential.

meanness *noun* **1** *an act of such meanness | their meanness* nastiness, disagreeableness, unpleasantness, unfriendliness, crossness, bad temper, irritability, surliness, cantankerousness. *See* MEAN[2] 1. **2** *the meanness of Scrooge* miserliness, niggardliness, parsimony, parsimoniousness, tight-fistedness, penny-pinching, penury; *inf.* stinginess, cheapness, tightness, minginess. *See* MEAN[2] 2. **3** *the meanness of the creature* baseness, vileness, sordidness, foulness, nastiness, contemptibility, abominableness, odiousness. *See* MEAN[2] 3. **4** *the meanness of his intellect* inferiority, poorness, limitations, meagerness. **5** *the meanness of the hovel* shabbiness, wretchedness, dismalness, misery, squalor, sordidness, seediness, dilapidation;

inf. grunginess. **6** *the meanness of her birth* lowness, lowliness, humbleness, commonness, baseness, obscurity, ignobility.

means *plural noun* **1** *a means of getting there* way, method, expedient, process, mode, manner, agency, medium, instrument, channel, avenue, course. **2** *a man of means* money, capital, wealth, riches, affluence, substance, fortune, property. **3** *do not have the means to buy it* money, resources, capital, finance, funds, wherewithal; *inf.* dough, bread. **by all means** of course, certainly, definitely, surely, absolutely. **by means of** *get the money by means of borrowing* through, with the help of, with the aid of. **by no means** *by no means poor* in no way, not at all, not in the least, not in the slightest, not the least bit.

meantime *adverb* **1** *meantime, I shall wait* meanwhile, in the meantime, for the time being, for now. *See* MEANWHILE 1. **2** *meantime, back at the ranch* at the same time. *See* MEANWHILE 2.

meanwhile *adverb* **1** *meanwhile, I shall wait* meantime, in the meantime, for the time being, for now, for the moment, in the intervening period, in the interim, in the interval, in the meanwhile. **2** *meanwhile, back at the ranch* at the same time, simultaneously, concurrently, coincidentally.

measurable *adjective* **1** *a measurable quantity of sand* assessable, gaugeable, estimable, appraisable, computable, quantifiable, fathomable. **2** *a measurable improvement* significant, appreciable, noticeable, visible, perceptible, obvious, striking, material.

measure *noun* **1** *find the measure of the material* measurement, size, dimension, proportions, magnitude, amplitude, mass, bulk, volume, capacity, quantity, weight, extent, expanse, area, range. **2** *use a linear measure* system, standard, units, scale. **3** *use a measure to check the size* rule, ruler, tape measure, gauge, meter, scale, yardstick. **4** *receive a measure of her father's estate* share, portion, division, allotment, part, piece, quota, lot, ration, percentage. **5** *have a measure of wit* quantity, amount, certain amount, degree. **6** *sales are the measure of the company's success* yardstick, test, standard, touchstone, criterion, benchmark. **7** *take drastic measures* action, act, course, course of action, deed, proceeding, procedure, step, means, expedient, maneuver. **8** *announce measures to control crime* statute, act, bill, law, resolution. **9** *do what you like within measure* moderation, limit, limitation, bounds, control, restraint. **10** *poetic measure* meter, cadence, rhythm. **beyond measure** immeasurably, incalculably, infinitely, limitlessly, immensely, extremely, vastly, excessively. **for good measure** as a bonus, as an extra, into the bargain, to boot, in addition, besides, as well.

measure *verb* **1** *measure the material/quantity*

calculate, compute, estimate, quantify, weigh, size, evaluate, rate, assess, appraise, gauge, measure out, determine, judge, survey. **2** *measure one's words* choose carefully, select with care, consider, think carefully about, plan, calculate. **3** *measure one's work to one's time* adapt, adjust, fit, tailor. **4** *measure his strength against his brother's* pit, set, match, test, put into competition. **measure out** mete out, measure, deal out, dole out, share, divide out, parcel out, allocate, allot, apportion, assign, distribute, administer, dispense, issue. **measure up 1** *measure up the windows for curtains* measure, take the measurements of, estimate the size of. **2** *he was sacked because he didn't measure up* come up to standard, fulfill expectations, fit/fill the bill, pass muster, be capable, be adequate, be suitable; *inf.* come up to scratch, make the grade, cut the mustard, be up to snuff. **3** *didn't measure up to the requirements* meet, come up to, equal to, match, be on a level with.

measured *adjective* **1** *measured amounts* measured out, calculated, computed, quantified. *See* MEASURE *verb* 1. **2** *measured steps* regular, steady, even, rhythmical, slow, dignified, stately, sedate, leisurely, unhurried. **3** *measured words* carefully chosen, selected with care, well-thought-out, premeditated, calculated, planned, considered, studied, deliberate, reasoned.

measurement *noun* **1** *the measurement of the quantity* calculation, computation, estimation, quantification, quantifying, weighing, sizing, evaluation, assessment, appraisal, gauging. **2** *take the first measurement at noon | the measurements of the carpet are wrong* size, dimension, proportions, magnitude, amplitude, mass, bulk, volume, capacity, extent, expanse, amount, quantity, area, length, height, depth, weight, width, range.

meat *noun* **1** *vegetarians don't eat meat* flesh, animal flesh. *See also table at* JOINT. **2** *meat and drink* food, nourishment, sustenance, provisions, rations, fare, viands, victuals, comestibles, provender, feed; *inf.* grub, eats, chow, nosh. **3** *the meat of the matter* substance, pith, marrow, heart, kernel, core, nucleus, nub, essence, essentials, gist, fundamentals, basics; *inf.* nitty-gritty, nuts and bolts.

meaty *adjective* **1** *a meaty stew/physique* meatfilled, fleshy. **2** *a meaty discussion/book* giving food for thought, substantial, pithy, meaningful, profound, deep, involved, interesting, significant.

mechanical *adjective* **1** *a mechanical device* automated, automatic, machine-driven, motor-driven, power-driven. **2** *mechanical gestures* automatic, machinelike, unthinking, unconscious, unfeeling, unemotional, cold, involuntary, instinctive, routine, habitual, perfunctory, cursory, lackluster, lifeless, unanimated, dead, casual, careless, inattentive, negligent.

mechanism noun 1 *a mechanism for folding paper* machine, apparatus, appliance, tool, device, instrument, contraption, contrivance, gadget, structure, system. 2 *the mechanism of the car* motor, workings, works, gears, components; *inf.* innards, guts. 3 *the mechanism for complaints* process, procedure, system, operation, method, technique, workings, means, medium, agency, channel.

meddle verb interfere, butt in, intrude, intervene, interlope, pry, nose; *inf.* stick one's nose in, horn in, snoop.

meddlesome adjective meddling, interfering, intrusive, prying; *inf.* snooping, nosy.

mediate verb 1 *mediate between the warring factions* act as mediator, act as (a) go-between, act as (a) middleman/intermediary, arbitrate, negotiate, conciliate, intervene, intercede, interpose, moderate, umpire, referee, act as peacemaker, reconcile differences, restore harmony, make peace, bring to terms, step in. 2 *mediate a difference of opinion* settle, arbitrate, umpire, reconcile, resolve, mend, clear up, patch up. 3 *mediate a peace settlement* bring about, effect, effectuate, make happen, negotiate.

mediation noun arbitration, negotiation, intervention, intercession, interposition, good offices, conciliation, reconciliation.

mediator noun arbitrator, arbiter, negotiator, go-between, middleman, intermediary, peacemaker, intervenor, interceder, moderator, umpire, referee, judge, conciliator, reconciler.

medicinal adjective *medicinal herbs | for medicinal purposes* medical, therapeutic, curative, healing, remedial, restorative, health-giving, analeptic.

medicine noun 1 *given medicine* medication, medicament, drug, remedy, cure, physic. 2 *study medicine* medical science, practice of medicine, healing art. **take one's medicine** accept one's punishment, take the consequences of one's actions; *inf.* get what is coming to one, take the rap, take it on the chin.

medieval adjective 1 *medieval history* of the Middle/Dark Ages, Middle-Age, Dark-Age, Gothic. 2 *his attitude is medieval* antiquated, archaic, antique, obsolete, antediluvian, primitive, outmoded, outdated, old-fashioned, passé, unenlightened; *inf.* out of the ark.

mediocre adjective 1 *her work is mediocre* indifferent, average, middle-of-the-road, middling, ordinary, commonplace, pedestrian, run-of-the-mill, tolerable, passable, adequate, uninspired, undistinguished, unexceptional; *inf.* so-so, fair-to-middling, nothing to write home about, no great shakes. 2 *mediocre goods/actors* inferior, second-rate, second-class, low-grade, poor, shabby, minor.

mediocrity noun 1 *the mediocrity of her work* mediocreness, indifference, ordinariness, commonplaceness, passableness, lack of inspiration, unexceptionalness. See MEDIOCRE 1.

2 *the mediocrity of the goods* inferiority, second-rateness, poorness, shabbiness.

meditate verb *meditating revenge* think about, consider, have in mind, intend, plan, project, design, devise, scheme, plot. **meditate on/upon** *he's meditating on/upon the past* engage in contemplation about, be in a thoughtful state about, contemplate, think about/over, muse on/about, ponder on/over, consider, concentrate on, reflect on, deliberate about/on, ruminate about/on/over, brood over, mull over, be in a brown study over; *inf.* put on one's thinking cap about.

meditation noun contemplation, thought, musing, pondering, consideration, reflection, deliberation, rumination, brooding, mulling over, reverie, brown study, concentration.

medium noun 1 *find the medium between two extremes* mean, median, midpoint, middle, center point, average, norm, standard, middle course, middle ground, compromise, happy medium. 2 *through the medium of television | want to use wood as an artistic medium* means of communication, means/mode of expression, means, agency, channel, avenue, vehicle, organ, instrument, instrumentality. 3 *organisms growing in their natural medium* habitat, element, environment, surroundings, milieu, setting, conditions, atmosphere. 4 *visit a medium to contact the dead* spiritualist, spiritist, necromancer.

medium adjective 1 *in the medium position* middle, mean, medial, median, midway, midpoint, intermediate. 2 *of medium height* average, middling.

medley noun assortment, miscellany, mixture, mélange, variety, collection, motley collection, potpourri, conglomeration, jumble, confusion, mishmash, hodgepodge, pastiche, patchwork, gallimaufry, olio, salmagundi, mixed bag, mix.

meek adjective 1 *preaching that the meek shall inherit the earth* patient, long-suffering, forbearing, resigned, gentle, peaceful, docile, modest, humble, unassuming, unpretentious. 2 *feeling meek among aggressive people* submissive, yielding, unresisting, compliant, acquiescent, deferential, weak, timid, frightened, spineless, spiritless; *inf.* weak-kneed.

Antonyms: IMPATIENT; ASSERTIVE; OVERBEARING.

meekness noun 1 *the virtue of meekness* patience, forbearance, resignation, gentleness, peacefulness, docility, modesty, humility, humbleness. 2 *overcame his meekness and won the debate* submissiveness, lack of resistance, compliance, acquiescence, deference, weakness, timidity, fearfulness, spinelessness, lack of spirit.

meet verb 1 *meet friends for lunch | met an old friend on the train* encounter, come face to face with, make contact with, run into, run across, come across, come upon, chance upon,

happen upon, light upon; *inf.* bump into. **2** *where the land and sea meet* come together, abut, adjoin, join, link up, unite, connect, touch, converge, intersect. **3** *the committee met on Saturday* gather, assemble, come together, foregather, congregate, convene, convoke, muster, rally. **4** *meet the proposal with hostility* deal with, handle, treat, cope with, approach, answer. **5** *meet the demands of the job* satisfy, fulfill, measure up to, come up to, comply with. **6** *meet one's responsibilities* carry out, perform, execute, discharge, take care of. **7** *meet the cost* pay, settle, honor, square. **8** *meet death bravely* face, encounter, undergo, experience, go through, bear, suffer, endure. **9** *meet the enemy at dawn* encounter, confront, engage, engage in battle with, join battle with, clash with, fight with.
Antonyms: AVOID; SEPARATE; DISPERSE.

meeting *noun* **1** *the meeting of the two friends/lovers* encounter, contact, assignation, rendezvous, tryst. **2** *address the meeting* gathering, assembly, conference, congregation, convention, convocation, conclave; *inf.* get-together. **3** *the meeting of land and sea* abutment, junction, conjunction, union, convergence, confluence, concourse, intersection.

melancholic, melancholy *adjective* despondent, dejected, depressed, down, downhearted, downcast, disconsolate, glum, gloomy, sunk in gloom, miserable, dismal, dispirited, low, in low spirits, in the doldrums, blue, mournful, lugubrious, woeful, woebegone, doleful, sorrowful, unhappy, heavy-hearted, low-spirited, somber, pensive, defeatist, pessimistic; *inf.* down in the dumps, down in the mouth.
Antonyms: CHEERFUL; JOYFUL; MERRY.

melancholy *noun* despondency, dejection, depression, gloom, gloominess, misery, low spirits, doldrums, blues, woe, sadness, sorrow, unhappiness, pensiveness, defeatism, pessimism, melancholia; *inf.* dumps.

mélange *noun* assortment, miscellany, mixture, medley, variety, hodgepodge. *See* MEDLEY.

melee *noun* fight, quarrel, fracas, affray, fray, rumpus, commotion, tumult, brawl, scuffle, struggle, skirmish, free-for-all, tussle; *inf.* set-to.

mellifluous *adjective* *speak in mellifluous tones* sweet, sweet-sounding, sweet-toned, dulcet, honeyed, mellow, soft, soothing, smooth, silvery, euphonious, musical.

mellow *adjective* **1** *mellow fruit* ripe, mature, well-matured, soft, juicy, tender, luscious, sweet, full-flavored, flavorsome. **2** *a mellow voice* dulcet, sweet, sweet-sounding, tuneful, euphonious, melodious, mellifluous, smooth, full, rich, well-rounded. **3** *a mellow person/mood* gentle, easygoing, pleasant, kindly, kindhearted, amicable, amiable, good-natured, affable,

gracious, genial, cheerful, relaxed. **4** *feeling mellow after two glasses of wine* tipsy; *inf.* happy, merry.
Antonyms: GREEN; unripe; HARSH; NASTY.

melodious *adjective* melodic, musical, tuneful, harmonious, lyrical, dulcet, sweet, sweet-sounding, sweet-toned, silvery, silvery-toned, euphonious.
Antonyms: DISCORDANT; HARSH; GRATING.

melodramatic *adjective* theatrical, stagy, over-dramatic, histrionic, oversensational, extravagant, overdone, overemotional; *inf.* camp, hammy.

melody *noun* **1** *composing melodies* tune, air, strain, music, refrain, theme, song. **2** *not much melody in this music* melodiousness, tunefulness, musicality, harmony, lyricism, sweetness, euphony.

melt *verb* **1** *solids melting* liquefy, dissolve, deliquesce, thaw, unfreeze, defrost, soften, fuse. **2** *the crowd melted away* disperse, vanish, vanish into thin air, fade away, disappear, dissolve, evaporate, evanesce. **3** *her story melted the jury | her story melted the jurors' hearts* soften, touch, disarm, mollify, assuage, move.

member *noun* **1** *a member of the club* associate, card-carrying member, adherent, fellow, participant. **2** *many victims had injured members* part of the body, organ, limb, appendage, extremity, arm, leg. **3** *a member of the mathematical set* element, constituent, component, part, portion.

membrane *noun* sheet, layer, film, skin, tissue, pellicle, integument.

memento *noun* souvenir, keepsake, reminder, remembrance, token, memorial, trophy, relic, vestige.

memoir *noun* *write a memoir on World War II* account, historical account, monograph, record, chronicle, essay, narrative.

memoirs *plural noun* *write one's memoirs* autobiography, life story, life, memories, recollections, personal recollections, reminiscences, experiences, journal, diary.

memorable *adjective* **1** *a memorable event/person* unforgettable, not to be forgotten, signal, momentous, significant, historic, notable, noteworthy, important, consequential, remarkable, outstanding, extraordinary, striking, impressive, distinctive, distinguished, famous, celebrated, illustrious. **2** *a memorable tune* unforgettable, catchy, striking.
Antonyms: RUN-OF-THE-MILL; COMMONPLACE; forgettable.

memorandum *noun* reminder, note, message, minute, aide-mémoire; *inf.* memo.

memorial *noun* **1** *erect a memorial to him* monument, statue, plaque, shrine, tombstone. **2** *this will serve as a memorial of him* remembrance, reminder, memento, souvenir.

memorial *adjective* *memorial service* remembrance, commemorative, commemorating, monumental.

memorize *verb* commit to memory, remember, retain, learn by heart, learn, learn word for word, learn by rote.

memory *noun* **1** *my memory of the events is faint | her memory is excellent* remembrance, recollection, powers of recall, recall, reminiscence, powers of retention, retention. **2** *build a statue in memory of him* remembrance, commemoration, honor, tribute. **3** *a computer's memory* memory bank, storage bank, store, information store.

menace *noun* **1** *an atmosphere full of menace* threat, ominousness, intimidation, warning, ill-omen, commination. **2** *he/it is a menace to the residents* threat, danger, peril, risk, hazard, jeopardy, source of apprehension/dread/fright/fear/terror. **3** *the child next door is a menace* nuisance, pest, source of annoyance, annoyance, plague, torment, troublemaker, mischief-maker.

menace *verb* **1** *older boys menacing the young ones* threaten, intimidate, issue threats to, frighten, scare, alarm, terrify, bully, browbeat, cow, terrorize. **2** *bad weather menacing* loom, impend, lower, be in the air, be in the offing.

menacing *adjective* **1** *a menacing look/silence* threatening, ominous, intimidating, frightening, terrifying, alarming, forbidding, minatory, minacious. **2** *a menacing storm* looming, lowering, impending.
Antonyms: FRIENDLY; AUSPICIOUS.

mend *verb* **1** *mend the furniture* repair, fix, put back together, patch up, restore, rehabilitate, renew, renovate, make whole, make well, cure, heal. **2** *mend socks | mend a hole in the sweater* sew, stitch, darn, patch. **3** *the patient will soon mend* get better, recover, recuperate, improve, be well, be cured, be all right. **4** *try to mend matters/the situation* put right, set straight, rectify, put in order, correct, amend, emend, improve, make better, better, ameliorate, reform.
Antonyms: BREAK; TEAR; WORSEN.

mendacious *adjective* **1** *mendacious people* lying, untruthful, dishonest, deceitful, dissembling, insincere, disingenuous, hypocritical, fraudulent, unveracious, economical with the truth. **2** *mendacious tales* lying, untrue, false, fraudulent, fictitious, falsified, fabricated, invented, made-up.

mendicant *adjective* begging, cadging; *inf.* scrounging, sponging, mooching, leeching.

mendicant *noun* beggar, tramp, vagrant, vagabond, hobo, cadger; *inf.* scrounger, sponger, moocher, bum, parasite.

menial *adjective* *menial duties/jobs* lowly, humble, low-grade, low-status, unskilled, routine, humdrum, boring, dull.
Antonyms: NOBLE; ELEVATED; ARISTOCRATIC; SKILLED.

menial *noun* servant, domestic servant, domestic, drudge, maid, laborer, slave, underling, vassal, lackey, flunky; *inf.* gofer.

menstruation *noun* period, menses, menstrual cycle, monthly flow; *inf.* the curse.

mental *adjective* **1** *mental work* intellectual, cerebral, brain, thinking. **2** *mental hospital* psychiatric. **3** *he's completely mental* mad, insane, deranged, disturbed, mentally unbalanced, mentally ill, mentally unstable, psychotic, lunatic; *inf.* crazy, out to lunch.
Antonyms: PHYSICAL; SANE.

mentality *noun* **1** *of a slightly twisted mentality* frame of mind, way of thinking, way one's mind works, mind, psychology, mental attitude, outlook, character, disposition, makeup. **2** *of low-grade mentality* intellect, intellectual capabilities, intelligence, IQ (= intelligence quotient), brainpower, brains, mind, comprehension, understanding, wit, rationality, powers of reasoning; *inf.* gray matter.

mentally *adverb* in the mind, in the brain, in the head, intellectually, psychologically.

mention *verb* **1** *he only mentioned it* allude to, refer to, touch on, speak briefly of, hint at. **2** *he mentioned your name* say, state, name, cite, quote, call attention to, adduce. **3** *don't mention this to anyone* tell, speak about/of, utter, communicate, let someone know, disclose, divulge, reveal, intimate, whisper, breathe a word of; *inf.* let on about. **don't mention it** no thanks necessary, (it was) a pleasure, any time; don't apologize, it doesn't matter, don't worry; *inf.* no problem, no sweat, no big deal, forget (about) it. **not to mention** not counting, not including, to say nothing of, as well as, besides, in addition to.

mention *noun* *made no mention of your request | a mention in the book* reference, allusion, observation, remark, statement, announcement, indication, acknowledgment, citation, recognition.

mentor *noun* guide, adviser, counselor, therapist, guru, spiritual leader, confidant, teacher, tutor, coach, instructor.

mercantile *adjective* commercial, trade, trading, marketable.

mercenary *adjective* **1** *mercenary people interested only in money* money-oriented, grasping, greedy, acquisitive, avaricious, covetous, bribable, venal; *inf.* money-grubbing. **2** *mercenary soldiers* hired, paid, bought, professional, venal.
Antonyms: ALTRUISTIC; PHILANTHROPIC; GENEROUS.

mercenary *noun* professional soldier, hired soldier, soldier of fortune; condottiere.

merchandise *noun* *damaged merchandise* goods, wares, stock, commodities, vendibles, produce.

merchandise *verb* **1** *merchandise a wide range of goods* market, sell, retail, buy and sell, distribute, deal in, trade in, traffic in, do business in, vend. **2** *merchandise the new cars* promote, advertize, publicize, push; *inf.* hype, plug.

merchant *noun* trader, dealer, trafficker, wholesaler, broker, seller, salesman, saleswoman, salesperson, vendor, retailer, store owner, storekeeper, shopkeeper, distributor.

merciful *adjective* lenient, clement, compassionate, pitying, forgiving, forbearing, sparing, humane, mild, softhearted, tender-hearted, kind, sympathetic, liberal, tolerant, generous, beneficent, benignant.
Antonyms: MERCILESS; CRUEL.

merciless *adjective* unmerciful, ruthless, relentless, inexorable, harsh, pitiless, uncompassionate, unforgiving, unsparing, unpitying, implacable, barbarous, inhumane, inhuman, hard-hearted, heartless, callous, cruel, unsympathetic, unfeeling, illiberal, intolerant, rigid, severe, stern.
Antonyms: MERCIFUL; COMPASSIONATE.

mercurial *adjective* *mecurial child/temperament* volatile, capricious, temperamental, fickle, changeable, unpredictable, variable, erratic, quicksilver, inconstant, unstable, unsteady, fluctuating, wavering, vacillating, flighty, impulsive.
Antonyms: STABLE; STEADY; CONSTANT.

mercy *noun* 1 *the mercy of the judge* leniency, clemency, compassion, compassionateness, pity, charity, forgiveness, forbearance, quarter, humanity, humaneness, mildness, softheartedness, tender-heartedness, kindness, sympathy, liberality, tolerance, generosity, beneficence. 2 *thankful for small mercies* boon, favor, piece of luck, blessing, godsend. **at the mercy of** 1 *at the mercy of the tyrant* in the power of, under/in the control of, in the clutches of. 2 *at the mercy of the storm* threatened by, prey to, open to, exposed to, defenseless against, unprotected against, vulnerable to.
Antonyms: SEVERITY; CRUELTY; INHUMANITY.

---

mercy
benevolence, charity, clemency, compassion, leniency

If you want to win friends and influence people, it's best to start with **benevolence**, a general term for goodwill and kindness (*a grandfather's benevolence*). **Charity** is even better, suggesting generous giving (*the baker gave him bread out of charity*) but also meaning tolerance and understanding of others (*she viewed his selfish behavior with charity*). **Compassion** is a feeling of sympathy or sorrow for someone else's misfortune (*he has shown compassion for the homeless*), and often includes showing **mercy**. Aside from its religious overtones, *mercy* means compassion or kindness in our treatment of others, especially those who have offended us or who deserve punishment (*mercy toward the pickpocket*). **Clemency** is mercy shown by someone whose duty or function it is to administer justice or punish offenses (*the judge*

granted clemency), while **leniency** emphasizes gentleness, softness, or lack of severity, even if it isn't quite deserved (*a father's leniency in punishing his young son*).

---

mere *adjective* *a mere child* | *the hurricane turned out to be a mere rainstorm* nothing more than, no better than, no more important than, just a, only a, pure and simple.

merge *verb* 1 *the two companies merged* join together, join forces, amalgamate, unite, combine, incorporate, coalesce, team up. 2 *merge the firms* join, amalgamate, unite, combine, incorporate, coalesce. 3 *the colors merged* blend, fuse, mingle, mix, intermix, homogenize. **merge into** *caused her personality to merge into his* run into, melt into, become assimilated into/in, become lost in, be swallowed up by, be buried in, be submerged in.
Antonyms: DIVERGE; SPLIT; SEPARATE.

merger *noun* amalgamation, combination, union, fusion, coalition, alliance, incorporation.

merit *noun* 1 *the merit of his work* excellence, goodness, quality, high quality, worth, worthiness, value. 2 *the merits of the scheme* good point, strong point, advantage, asset, plus. 3 *receive his merits* what one deserves, desert, just deserts, due, right, reward, recompense.
Antonyms: INFERIORITY; FAULT; DISADVANTAGE.

merit *verb* *merit a prize* deserve, be deserving of, earn, be worthy of, be worth, be entitled to, have a right to, have a claim to, warrant, rate, incur.

meritorious *adjective* praiseworthy, laudable, commendable, admirable, estimable, creditable, excellent, exemplary, good, worthy, deserving.
Antonyms: WORTHLESS; discreditable.

merriment *noun* cheerfulness, gaiety, high-spiritedness, high spirits, blitheness, buoyancy, carefreeness, levity, sportiveness, joy, joyfulness, joyousness, jolliness, jollity, rejoicing, jocundity, conviviality, festivity, merrymaking, revelry, mirth, mirthfulness, glee, gleefulness, laughter, hilarity, amusement, fun.

merry *adjective* 1 *merry children playing* cheerful, cheery, gay, in good spirits, high-spirited, blithe, blithesome, lighthearted, buoyant, carefree, frolicsome, sportive, joyful, joyous, rejoicing, jolly, jocund, convivial, festive, mirthful, gleeful, happy, glad, laughing. 2 *a merry tale* comical, comic, amusing, funny, humorous, facetious, hilarious. 3 *slightly merry after the party* tipsy, mellow; *inf.* happy, tiddly. **make merry** have fun, have a good time, enjoy oneself, have a party, party, celebrate, carouse, revel, rejoice; *inf.* have a ball.
Antonyms: MISERABLE; SAD; GLOOMY.

mesh *noun* 1 *wire mesh* | *purse made of fine silk mesh* network, netting, net, tracery, web, lattice, latticework, lacework, trellis, reticulation, plexus. 2 *caught in the mesh of political in-*

trigue net, tangle, entanglement, web, snare, trap.

mesh *verb* **1** *gears meshing* be engaged, connect, interlock. **2** *our ideas do not mesh* harmonize, fit together, go together, coordinate, match, be on the same wavelength, dovetail.

mesmerize *verb* **1** *hypnotists mesmerizing people* hypnotize, put into a trance, put under. **2** *he was mesmerized by her beauty* hold spellbound, spellbind, entrance, enthrall, bewitch, captivate, enchant, fascinate, grip, magnetize, hypnotize.

mess *noun* **1** *clean up the mess in the kitchen* disorder, untidiness, disarray, dirtiness, filthiness, clutter, litter; muddle, chaos, confusion, disorganization, turmoil. **2** *have to get out of this mess* plight, predicament, tight spot, tight corner, difficulty, trouble, quandary, dilemma, muddle, mix-up, confusion, imbroglio, fine kettle of fish; *inf.* jam, fix, pickle, stew. **3** *what a mess he made of the project* muddle, botch, bungle; *inf.* hash, foul-up, screw-up. **4** *cat's mess* dirt, excrement, feces, excreta.

mess *verb* *mess with the controls* fiddle, play, tinker, toy. **mess around, mess about** amuse oneself, pass the time, do nothing very much, fiddle around/about, play around/about, fool around/about. **mess up 1** *mess up the kitchen* dirty, litter, pollute, clutter up, disarrange, throw into disorder, dishevel. **2** *mess up the project* botch, bungle, muff, make a mess of, mar, spoil, ruin; *inf.* make a hash of, foul up, screw up.

message *noun* **1** *leave a message | there's a telephone message for you* communication, piece of information, news, word, tidings, note, memorandum, letter, missive, bulletin, communiqué, dispatch; *inf.* memo. **2** *the message of the sermon* meaning, import, idea, point, purport, intimation, theme, moral. **get the message** get the point, get the drift, understand, comprehend, take the hint; *inf.* understand what's what, catch on, get it, get the picture.

messenger *noun* errand boy/girl, message-bearer, message-carrier, courier, runner, envoy, emissary, agent, go-between, herald, harbinger; *inf.* gofer.

messy *adjective* untidy, disordered, dirty, filthy, grubby, slovenly, cluttered, littered, muddled, in a muddle, chaotic, confused, disorganized, in disarray, disarranged, disheveled, unkempt; *inf.* sloppy.
Antonyms: TIDY; CLEAN; ORDERLY.

metallic *adjective* **1** *metallic goods* metal, made of metal, metallike, iron, steel, stainless steel. **2** *metallic sounds* grating, harsh, jarring, jangling, dissonant, raucous. **3** *metallic colors/paint* shiny, gleaming, lustrous, polished, burnished.

metamorphosis *noun* transformation, transfiguration, change, alteration, conversion, changeover, mutation, transmutation, sea change; *inf.* transmogrification.

metaphor *noun* figure of speech, image, trope, allegory, analogy, symbol, emblem.

metaphorical *adjective* nonliteral, figurative, allegorical, symbolic, emblematic, emblematical.

mete *verb* **mete out** deal out, dole out, measure, measure out, divide out, allocate, share, parcel out, allot, apportion, assign, distribute, administer, dispense, issue.

meteoric *adjective* *meteoric rise to fame* lightning, rapid, swift, fast, quick, speedy, overnight, sudden, dazzling, brilliant, spectacular, flashing, momentary, fleeting, transient, ephemeral, evanescent, brief, short-lived.
Antonyms: SLOW; GRADUAL; LONG-DRAWN-OUT.

method *noun* **1** *use old-fashioned methods* procedure, technique, system, practice, modus operandi, process, approach, way, course of action, scheme, plan, rule, arrangement, form, style, manner, mode. **2** *method in his madness* order, orderliness, sense of order, organization, arrangement, structure, form, system, planning, plan, design, purpose, pattern, regularity.

methodical *adjective* **1** *a methodical approach* orderly, well-ordered, organized, systematic, structured, logical, well-regulated, planned, efficient, businesslike. **2** *a methodical person* organized, systematic, efficient, businesslike, meticulous, punctilious.
Antonyms: DISORGANIZED; CHAOTIC; INEFFICIENT.

meticulous *adjective* **1** *a meticulous proofreader* conscientious, careful, ultracareful, scrupulous, punctilious, painstaking, demanding, exacting, thorough, perfectionist, fastidious, particular. **2** *a meticulous report* careful, exact, precise, detailed, thorough, rigorous, painstaking.
Antonyms: CARELESS; SLOPPY; SLAPDASH.

metropolis *noun* city, capital, capital city, chief city/town; megalopolis; *inf.* hub.

mettle *noun* **1** *it showed us his true mettle* caliber, character, disposition, nature, temperament, temper, personality, makeup, stamp, kind, sort, variety, mold, kidney. **2** *soldiers of mettle* courage, courageousness, bravery, gallantry, valor, intrepidity, fearlessness, boldness, daring, grit, pluck, nerve, gameness, backbone, spirit, fortitude, indomitability; *inf.* guts, spunk.

microscopic *adjective* invisible to the naked eye, scarcely perceptible, infinitesimal, minuscule, tiny, minute.
Antonyms: MASSIVE; ENORMOUS; GIGANTIC.

midday *noun* noon, twelve noon, twelve midday, twelve o'clock, high noon, noontide, noontime, noonday; twelve hundred, twelve hundred hours.

middle *adjective* **1** *the middle point between two extremes* mid, mean, medium, medial, median, midway, halfway, central, equidistant. **2** *the* *middle ranks* intermediate, intermediary, intermedial.

middle *noun* **1** *the middle of the line/scale* mean, median, midpoint, halfway point, center, dead center. **2** *in the middle of the crowd* midst, heart, center, thick. **3** *have a thickening middle* midriff, waist, waistline.

middleman *noun* intermediary, go-between, broker, distributor.

middling *adjective* average, medium, ordinary, fair, moderate, adequate, passable, tolerable, mediocre, indifferent, run-of-the-mill, unexceptional, unremarkable; *inf.* fair-to-middling, so-so.

midget *noun* dwarf, manikin, pygmy, Tom Thumb; homunculus; *inf.* little person; *inf. derog* munchkin, gnome, shrimp.

midget *adjective* **1** *midget species of plants* dwarf, miniature, baby. **2** *midget cars/dogs* tiny, minute, miniature, very small, pocket, toy, pygmy.

midnight *noun* twelve o'clock, twelve midnight, twelve at night, dead of night, the middle of the night, the twelfth hour, the witching hour. *Antonyms:* MIDDAY; NOON.

midst *noun* middle, center, heart, bosom, core, kernel, nucleus, nub, interior, depths, thick.

midway *adverb* halfway, in the middle, at the midpoint, in the center, betwixt and between.

mien *noun* look, appearance, aspect, aura, expression, countenance, demeanor, air, manner, bearing, carriage, deportment.

miffed *adjective* annoyed, displeased, offended, aggrieved, piqued, nettled, vexed, irked, upset, hurt, put out, resentful, in a huff.

might *noun* force, power, strength, mightiness, powerfulness, forcefulness, potency, toughness, robustness, sturdiness, muscularity, vigor, energy, stamina, stoutness. **with might and main** with all one's strength, with everything one has got, as hard as one can, as hard as possible, with maximum force, full force, full blast, forcefully, powerfully, strongly, vigorously.

mighty *adjective* **1** *a mighty figure of a man | struck a mighty blow* forceful, powerful, strong, lusty, potent, tough, robust, sturdy, muscular, strapping, vigorous, energetic, stout. **2** *a mighty structure/mountain* huge, massive, vast, enormous, colossal, giant, gigantic, prodigious, monumental, mountainous, towering, titanic. *Antonyms:* PUNY; FEEBLE; TINY.

migrant *adjective* migrating, migratory, traveling, roving, roaming, wandering, drifting, nomadic, itinerant, peripatetic, vagrant, gypsy, transient, unsettled, on the move.

migrant *noun* vagrant, nomad, itinerant, traveler, gypsy, transient, rover, wanderer, drifter.

migrate *verb* **1** *migrate to another place* emigrate, move, resettle, relocate, go abroad, go overseas. **2** *itinerants migrating* travel, voyage, journey, trek, hike, rove, roam, wander, drift.

migratory *adjective* migrant, migrating, traveling, roving, wandering, nomadic, itinerant, vagrant, transient, unsettled.

mild *adjective* **1** *of a mild disposition* tender, gentle, soft, softhearted, tender-hearted, sensitive, sympathetic, warm, warmhearted, compassionate, humane, forgiving, conciliatory, forbearing, merciful, lenient, clement, placid, meek, docile, calm, tranquil, serene, peaceful, peaceable, pacific, good-natured, amiable, affable, genial, easy, easygoing, mellow. **2** *mild winds* gentle, soft, moderate, warm, balmy. **3** *mild food* bland, spiceless, nonspicy, insipid, tasteless. *Antonyms:* CRUEL; HARSH; STRONG; SPICY.

mildness *noun* **1** *the mildness of her disposition* tenderness, gentleness, softness, sensitivity, warmness, compassion, meekness, docility, calmness, tranquillity, placidity, serenity, amiability, affability, geniality, mellowness. **2** *the mildness of the winds* softness, moderation. *See* MILD 2. **3** *mildness of the food* blandness, lack of spiciness, insipidness, tastelessness.

milieu *noun* environment, surroundings, background, setting, scene, location, sphere, element.

militant *adjective* **1** *militant members of the organization* aggressive, assertive, vigorous, active, ultra-active, combative, pugnacious; *inf.* pushy. **2** *militant groups/armies* fighting, warring, combating, contending, in conflict, clashing, embattled, in arms, belligerent, bellicose. *Antonyms:* RETIRING; PACIFIC; PEACEFUL.

militant *noun* **1** *militants in the party* activist, partisan. **2** *militants meeting on the battlefield* fighter, fighting man/woman, soldier, warrior, combatant, belligerent, aggressor.

military *adjective* *military forces* army, service, soldierly, soldierlike, armed, martial.

military *noun* army, forces, armed forces, services, militia, soldiery, navy, air force, marines.

militate *verb* **militate against** *his attitude will militate against him* operate against, go against, count against, tell against, weigh against, be detrimental to, be disadvantageous to, be to the disfavor of, be counter to the interests of, conflict with the interests of.

milk *verb* **1** *milk sap from a tree | milk funds from a company* draw, draw off, express, siphon, tap, drain, extract. **2** *milk the poor people* exploit, take advantage of, impose on, bleed, suck dry.

milksop *noun* coward, weakling, namby-pamby; *inf.* mama's boy, sissy, pansy, wimp, scaredy-cat, fraidy-cat.

milky *adjective* *milky skin* white, milk-white, snow-white, whitish, creamy, pearly, nacreous, ivory, alabaster, off-white, clouded, cloudy.

mill *noun* factory, plant, foundry, works, workshop, shop; paper mill, lumber mill, steel mill, textile mill.

mill *verb* *mill coffee/grain* grind, pulverize, pound, crush, powder, crunch, granulate, com-

milling around everywhere move around/about, wander around/about, amble, meander, crowd, swarm, throng.

millstone *noun a millstone around our necks* load, burden, weight, dead weight, onus, duty, tax, obligation, responsibility, trouble, misfortune, affliction, cross to bear, cross, albatross.

mime *noun* **1** *studied mime in acting class* mummery, pantomime. **2** *entertained by a mime* mime artist, mummer, pantomimist.

mime *verb mime his intentions* use gestures to indicate, gesture, indicate by sign language.

mimic *verb* **1** *mimic his friend* impersonate, give an impersonation of, imitate, copy, ape, caricature, parody; *inf.* take off. **2** *the monkey's actions mimicked those of the man* resemble, look like, have/take on the appearance of, echo, mirror, simulate.

mimic *noun* mimicker, impersonator, impressionist, imitator, parodist, copyist, parrot, ape.

mince *verb* **1** *finely minced beef* chop/cut into tiny pieces, grind, crumble, hash. **2** *she minces along, head in the air* walk affectedly, take tiny/baby steps, strike a pose, attitudinize, pose, posture, put on airs, be affected. **3** *I won't mince (my) words* restrain, hold back, moderate, temper, soften, mitigate, refine, weaken.

mincing *adjective* affected, pretentious, overdone, overdainty, effeminate, precious; *inf.* sissy, la-di-da.

mind *noun* **1** *be all in the mind* brain, head, seat of intellect, psyche, ego, subconscious. **2** *have an active mind* brainpower, powers of thought, intellect, intellectual capabilities, mentality, intelligence, powers of reasoning, brain, brains, wits, understanding, comprehension, sense, ratiocination; *inf.* gray matter. **3** *my mind was wandering* thoughts, thinking, concentration, attention, application, absorption. **4** *bring thoughts of him to mind* memory, recollection, remembrance. **5** *be of the same mind* opinion, way of thinking, thoughts, outlook, view, viewpoint, point of view, belief, judgment, attitude, feeling, sentiment. **6** *have a mind to go home* inclination, desire, wish, urge, will, notion, fancy, intention, intent, aim, purpose, design. **7** *of unsound mind* mental balance, sanity, senses, wits, reason, reasoning, judgment. **8** *one of the great minds* genius, intellect, intellectual, thinker; *inf.* brain, egghead. **be of two minds** be undecided, be uncertain, be unsure, be hesitant, hesitate, waver, vacillate, dither, shilly-shally; be on the horns of a dilemma. **bear/keep in mind** remember, be mindful of, do not forget, take into consideration, consider, take cognizance of, take note of. **cross one's mind** occur to one, come to one, enter one's mind/head, come into one's consciousness. **put in mind** remind, call up, conjure up, suggest. **to one's mind** in one's opinion, according to one's way of thinking, to one's way

of thinking, from one's standpoint, in one's estimation, in one's judgment.
Antonyms: BODY; DISINCLINATION.

mind *verb* **1** *didn't seem to mind their rudeness/smoking* be offended by, take offense at, object to, care about, be bothered by, be upset by, be affronted by, resent, dislike, disapprove of, look askance at. **2** *mind what the teacher says* take heed of, heed, pay heed to, be heedful of, pay attention to, attend to, concentrate on, listen to, note, take notice of, mark, observe, have regard for, respect, obey, follow, comply with, adhere to. **3** *mind your own business* attend to, pay attention to, concentrate on, apply oneself to, have regard for. **4** *mind the step | mind you don't cut yourself* be careful of, be cautious of, beware of, be on one's guard for, be wary of, be watchful of, watch out for, look out for, keep one's eyes open for, take care. **5** *mind that you go* make sure, be sure, ensure that, take care. **6** *mind the house/store/baby* look after, take care of, attend to, tend, have charge of, keep an eye on, watch. **never mind** *never mind about the cost* do not bother about, pay no attention to, do not worry about, disregard, forget, do not take into consideration, do not give a second thought to.

mindful *adjective mindful of her feelings* paying attention to, heedful of, watchful of, careful of, wary of, chary of, regardful of, taking into account, cognizant of, aware of, conscious of, alert to, alive to, sensible of.
Antonyms: HEEDLESS; OBLIVIOUS.

mindless *adjective* **1** *a mindless idiot* stupid, foolish, brainless, senseless, witless, unintelligent, empty-headed, dull, slow-witted, obtuse, weak-minded, featherbrained; *inf.* birdbrained, dumb, dopey, moronic. **2** *mindless actions/violence* unthinking, thoughtless, careless, ill-advised, negligent, neglectful, brutish, barbarous, barbaric, gratuitous. **3** *mindless tasks* mechanical, automatic, routine.
Antonyms: INTELLIGENT; THOUGHTFUL; INTERESTING.

mine *noun* **1** *work in a mine* colliery, pit, excavation, well, quarry, lode, vein, deposit; coal mine, gold mine, diamond mine. **2** *the librarian/book is a mine of information* source, reservoir, quarry, repository, store, storehouse, abundant supply, wealth, mint; *inf.* gold mine. **3** *blown up by a mine* explosive, land mine, depth charge. **4** *mines built under fortifications* tunnel, trench, sap.

mine *verb* **1** *mine coal* excavate, quarry for, dig for, dig up, extract, unearth. **2** *armies mining* lay mines. **3** *mine a fortification* dig a mine/tunnel/trench/sap under, undermine, weaken.

miner *noun* coal miner, collier, pitman, gold miner.

mingle *verb* **1** *mingle the water and wine | mingle the two colors* mix, blend, combine, compound, homogenize, merge, unite, join, amalgamate, fuse. **2** *the colors mingle* intermingle, mix, intermix, coalesce, blend, fuse, merge, unite, commingle. **3** *guests mingling at the party* circulate, socialize, hobnob, fraternize, associate with others, meet people. *Antonyms:* SEPARATE; PART.

miniature *adjective* small-scale, scaled-down, mini, midget, baby, toy, pocket, dwarf, Lilliputian, reduced, diminished, small, tiny, wee, minute, minuscule, microscopic; *inf.* pint-sized. *Antonyms:* GIANT; GIGANTIC; ENORMOUS.

minimal *adjective* minimum, least, least possible, smallest, littlest, slightest, nominal, token. *Antonyms:* MAXIMUM; MOST.

minimize *verb* **1** *minimize the costs/work* keep at/ to a minimum, reduce, decrease, curtail, cut back on, prune, slash. **2** *minimize the size* reduce, decrease, diminish, abbreviate, attenuate, shrink, miniaturize. **3** *minimize his achievement* belittle, make light of, decry, discount, play down, deprecate, depreciate, underestimate, underrate. *Antonyms:* maximize; INCREASE; EXAGGERATE.

minimum *noun* *reduce to the minimum* lowest level, bottom level, bottom, depth, nadir, least, lowest, slightest.

minimum *adjective* *the minimum amount* minimal, lowest, smallest, littlest, least, least possible, slightest. *Antonyms:* MAXIMUM; MOST.

minion *noun* **1** *the general and his minions* lackey, flunky, henchman, toady, sycophant, flatterer, fawner, underling, hireling, servant, dependent, hanger-on, parasite, leech; *inf.* yes-man, bootlicker. **2** *the queen's minion* favorite, pet, darling, jewel, apple of one's eye.

minister *noun* **1** *government ministers* cabinet member, secretary, department chief. **2** *ministers saying prayers* minister of religion, clergyman, cleric, ecclesiastic, churchman, preacher, priest, parson, pastor, rector, chaplain, padre, curate, vicar. **3** *the British minister in Egypt* ambassador, diplomat, consul, plenipotentiary, envoy, emissary, legate, delegate, representative, chargé d'affaires, chargé.

minister *verb* **minister to** *minister to the patient* | *he ministered to their needs* administer to, attend to, tend, look after, take care of, see to, cater to, serve, accommodate, be solicitous of, pander to.

ministration *noun* aid, help, assistance, succor, relief, support, backing, cooperation, service.

ministry *noun* **1** *work for the ministry* government, cabinet, administration. **2** *go in for the ministry* the church, the priesthood, holy orders, the pulpit. **3** *the ministry for foreign affairs* department, office, bureau.

minor *adjective* **1** *a minor poet* little-known, unknown, lesser, insignificant, unimportant, inconsequential, inferior, lightweight, subordi-

nate. **2** *suffer minor discomfort* slight, small, insignificant, unimportant, inconsequential, trivial, negligible, trifling. *Antonyms:* MAJOR; SIGNIFICANT; CONSIDERABLE.

minstrel *noun* musician, singer, bard, troubadour; *lit.* jongleur, goliard.

mint *noun* *earn a mint* fortune, small fortune, vast sum of money, millions, king's ransom; *inf.* pile, stack, heap, packet, bundle.

mint *adjective* *in mint condition* brand-new, as new, unused, perfect, unblemished, undamaged, unmarred, untarnished, fresh, first-class; *inf.* spanking new.

mint *verb* **1** *mint coins* stamp, stamp out, punch, die, cast, strike, coin, monetize, make, manufacture, produce. **2** *mint new words* coin, invent, make up, fabricate, think up, dream up, hatch up, devise, fashion, forge, produce.

minute *noun* **1** *I'll only be a minute* | *please wait a minute* moment, short time, second, instant; *inf.* jiffy, jiff. **2** *the minute he appeared* moment, instant, point, point in time, time, juncture. **in a minute** in a short time, shortly, very soon, in a moment/second/trice/flash, in an instant, in the twinkling of an eye; *inf.* in a jiffy/jiff, in two shakes, in two shakes of a lamb's tail. **up-to-the-minute** up-to-date, ultramodern, modern, fashionable, modish, stylish, in vogue, voguish, chic, in, all the rage; *inf.* trendy, with it, now.

minute *adjective* **1** *a minute creature* tiny, minuscule, microscopic, miniature, diminutive, Lilliputian, little, small; *inf.* knee-high to a grasshopper. **2** *a minute difference* infinitesimal, negligible, trifling, trivial, paltry, petty, insignificant, inconsequential, unimportant, slight, minimal. **3** *in minute detail* detailed, exhaustive, meticulous, punctilious, painstaking, close, strict, exact, precise, accurate. *Antonyms:* GIGANTIC; HUGE.

minutely *adverb* *minutely dissected/discussed* in detail, exhaustively, meticulously, punctiliously, painstakingly, closely; *inf.* with a fine-tooth comb.

minutes *plural noun* record, log, proceedings, transactions, notes, transcript, journal, summary.

minutiae *plural noun* subtleties, niceties, finer points, particulars, minute detail, minor details, trivia, trifles, nonessentials.

miracle *noun* wonder, marvel, prodigy, phenomenon, act of thaumaturgy.

miraculous *adjective* **1** *Jesus performing miraculous feats* inexplicable, unaccountable, preternatural, superhuman, supernatural, fantastic, magical, thaumaturgic, phenomenal, prodigious, wonderful, wondrous, remarkable. **2** *it is miraculous that you have finished* amazing, astounding, remarkable, extraordinary, incredible, unbelievable; *inf.* fantastic.

mirage *noun* optical illusion, illusion, hallucination, phantasmagoria, phantasm.

mire *noun* **1** *stuck in a mire* marsh, marshland,

bog, peatbog, swamp, swampland, morass, quagmire, quag, slough, fen, bayou. **2** *mire all over their shoes* mud, slime, dirt, filth; *inf.* muck.

mire *verb* **1** *cars mired in the swamp* sink, sink down, bog down, stick in the mud. **2** *they are mired in financial problems* entangle, catch up, involve, bog down.

mirror *noun* **1** *the mirror on the wall* looking glass, glass, reflector, reflecting surface; rear-view mirror. **2** *he is a mirror of his father* reflection, twin, double, exact likeness, image, replica, copy, clone, match; *inf.* spitting image, spit and image, dead ringer.

mirror *verb* *mirroring his actions/statements* reflect, imitate, emulate, simulate, copy, follow, mimic, echo, ape, parrot, impersonate.

mirth *noun* gaiety, merriment, high spirits, cheerfulness, cheeriness, hilarity, glee, laughter, jocularity, levity, buoyancy, blitheness, lightheartedness, joviality, joyousness, fun, enjoyment, amusement, pleasure, merrymaking, festivity, revelry, sport.

mirthful *adjective* gay, high-spirited, cheerful, cheery, hilarious, gleeful, laughter-filled, jocular, buoyant, carefree, blithe, lighthearted, jovial, joyous, fun-filled, enjoyable, amusing, pleasurable, merry, jolly, festive, frolicsome, sportive, playful.
Antonyms: DEPRESSED; MISERABLE; DEJECTED.

misadventure *noun* **1** *lost it through misadventure* accident, misfortune, bad luck, ill fortune, ill/poor/hard luck, mischance. **2** *be involved in a misadventure* accident, mishap, setback, disaster, tragedy, calamity, catastrophe, contretemps, debacle.

misanthropist *noun* misanthrope, hater of mankind, recluse, hermit.

misapprehend *verb* misunderstand, be mistaken, misinterpret, misconstrue, misread, miscalculate, get the wrong idea, get it wrong, receive a false impression, be under a delusion, be barking up the wrong tree.

misapprehension *noun* misunderstanding, mistake, error, mix-up, misinterpretation, misconstruction, misreading, misjudgment, misconception, misbelief, miscalculation, wrong idea, false impression, delusion.

misappropriate *verb* **1** *misappropriate the firm's money* embezzle, steal, thieve, swindle, pocket, peculate, help oneself to; *inf.* pinch, lift. **2** *misappropriate the tools* misuse, misapply, misemploy, put to a wrong use.

misbegotten *adjective* **1** *a misbegotten scoundrel* contemptible, disreputable, dishonorable, dishonest, base, wretched. **2** *their misbegotten plans* abortive, ill-conceived, ill-advised, ill-made, badly planned, badly thought-out, harebrained.

misbehave *verb* behave badly, be bad, be naughty, be disobedient, get up to mischief, misconduct oneself, be guilty of misconduct, be bad-mannered, show bad/poor manners, be rude, fool around; *inf.* carry on, act up.

misbehavior *noun* misconduct, bad behavior, disorderly conduct, badness, naughtiness, disobedience, mischief, mischievousness, delinquency, misdeed, misdemeanor, bad/poor manners, rudeness, fooling around; *inf.* carrying on, acting up, shenanigans.

misbelief *noun* **1** *condemned by the church for his misbelief* false/erroneous/unorthodox belief, unorthodoxy, heresy. **2** *an inaccurate story based on misbelief* wrong belief, delusion, illusion, fallacy, error, mistake, misconception, misapprehension.

miscalculate *verb* *the answer is wrong—you have miscalculated* calculate wrongly, make a mistake, go wrong, err, blunder, be wide of the mark; *inf.* slip up, make a booboo.

miscarriage *noun* **1** *the woman had a miscarriage* spontaneous abortion. **2** *the miscarriage of our plans* unsuccessfulness, failure, aborting, foundering, ruination, nonfulfillment, misfiring. *See* MISCARRY 2. **3** *miscarriage of justice* failure, breakdown, mismanagement, perversion, thwarting, frustration.

miscarry *verb* **1** *the woman miscarried* have a miscarriage, abort, have a spontaneous abortion, lose the baby. **2** *our plan miscarried* go wrong, go awry, go amiss, be unsuccessful, fail, misfire, abort, be abortive, founder, come to nothing, come to grief, meet with disaster, fall through, be ruined, fall flat; *inf.* bite the dust, go up in smoke.

miscellaneous *adjective* varied, assorted, mixed, diverse, sundry, variegated, diversified, motley, multifarious, jumbled, confused, indiscriminate, heterogeneous.

miscellany *noun* assortment, mixture, mélange, variety, collection, motley collection, medley, potpourri, conglomeration, jumble, confusion, mix, mishmash, hodgepodge, pastiche, patchwork, gallimaufry, olio, salmagundi, mixed bag.

mischance *noun* **1** *we lost it by mischance* accident, misfortune, bad luck, ill fortune, ill luck, poor luck, misadventure. **2** *a life full of mischances* misfortune, mishap, misadventure, setback, failure, disaster, tragedy, calamity, catastrophe, contretemps, debacle.

mischief *noun* **1** *involved in mischief* mischievousness, naughtiness, badness, bad behavior, misbehavior, misconduct, pranks, wrongdoing, delinquency; *inf.* monkey tricks, monkey business, shenanigans, goings-on. **2** *with mischief in her eyes* impishness, roguishness, rascality, devilment. **3** *do mischief to them | did mischief to their property* harm, hurt, injury, impairment, damage, detriment, disruption, trouble.

mischievous *adjective* **1** *mischievous child* full of mischief, naughty, bad, badly behaved, misbehaving, disobedient, troublesome, vexatious; playful, frolicsome, rascally, roguish;

delinquent. **2** *a mischievous smile* playful, teasing, impish, roguish, waggish, arch. **3** *mischievous gossip* malicious, spiteful, malignant, vicious, wicked, evil. **4** *with mischievous intent* hurtful, harmful, injurious, damaging, detrimental, deleterious, destructive, pernicious. *Antonyms:* GOOD; well-behaved; HARMLESS.

misconception *noun* misapprehension, misunderstanding, mistake, error, misinterpretation, the wrong idea, a false impression, delusion. *See* MISAPPREHENSION.

misconduct *noun* **1** *scolded for their misconduct* misbehavior, bad behavior, disorderly conduct, badness, mischief, naughtiness, misdeed, misdemeanor, wrongdoing, delinquency, rudeness. *See* MISBEHAVIOR. **2** *doctors guilty of misconduct* professional misconduct, unprofessional behavior, unethical behavior, malpractice, impropriety, immorality. **3** *the misconduct of the affair* mismanagement, mishandling, misgovernment, misdirection.

misconstrue *verb* misinterpret, put a wrong interpretation on, misunderstand, misapprehend, misread, misjudge, get it wrong, get the wrong idea, receive a false impression, take the wrong way.

miscreant *noun* villain, wrongdoer, criminal, evildoer, sinner, scoundrel, wretch, reprobate, blackguard, rogue, rascal.

misdeed *noun* wrongdoing, evil deed, crime, criminal act, misdemeanor, offense, error, peccadillo, transgression, sin.

misdemeanor *noun* misdeed, wrongdoing, crime, offense, error, transgression. *See* MISDEED.

miser *noun* skinflint, penny-pincher, niggard, Scrooge; *inf.* money-grubber, cheapskate, tightwad. *Antonyms:* SPENDTHRIFT; PHILANTHROPIST.

miserable *adjective* **1** *feeling miserable* unhappy, sorrowful, dejected, depressed, downcast, downhearted, down, despondent, disconsolate, desolate, wretched, glum, gloomy, dismal, blue, melancholy, low-spirited, mournful, woeful, woebegone, sad, doleful, forlorn, crestfallen; *inf.* down in the mouth, down in the dumps. **2** *a miserable hovel* wretched, mean, poor, shabby, squalid, filthy, foul, sordid, seedy, dilapidated. **3** *miserable wretches* poverty-stricken, needy, penniless, impoverished, beggarly, destitute, indigent, down-at-the-heels, out at the elbows. **4** *miserable scoundrels* contemptible, despicable, base, mean, low, vile, sordid. **5** *miserable salaries/supplies* meager, paltry, scanty, low, poor, niggardly, pathetic. **6** *miserable weather/conditions* unpleasant, disagreeable, displeasing, uncomfortable, wet, rainy, stormy. *Antonyms:* HAPPY; CHEERFUL; LUXURIOUS; RESPECTABLE.

miserly *adjective* mean, niggardly, parsimonious, tight-fisted, close-fisted, penny-pinching, penurious, greedy, avaricious, ungenerous, illiberal; *inf.* stingy, tight, money-grubbing, cheap. *Antonyms:* GENEROUS; LAVISH; EXTRAVAGANT; SPENDTHRIFT.

misery *noun* **1** *suffer/undergo misery* distress, wretchedness, hardship, suffering, affliction, anguish, torment, torture, agony, pain, discomfort, deprivation, poverty, grief, sorrow, heartbreak, heartbrokenness, despair, depression, dejection, desolation, gloom, melancholy, woe, sadness, unhappiness. **2** *endure untold miseries* trouble, misfortune, adversity, affliction, ordeal, pain, sorrow, burden, load, blow, trial, tribulation, woe, torment, catastrophe, calamity, disaster. **3** *he's nothing but a misery* killjoy, spoilsport, pessimist, prophet of doom, complainer, moaner; *inf.* sourpuss, grouch, wet blanket. *Antonyms:* COMFORT; PLEASURE; JOY.

misfire *verb* miscarry, go wrong, go awry, go amiss, fail, fall through; *inf.* bite the dust, go up in smoke. *See* MISCARRY 2.

misfit *noun* fish out of water, square peg in a round hole, nonconformist, eccentric, maverick; *inf.* oddball, weirdo.

misfortune *noun* **1** *by misfortune we got lost* bad luck, ill fortune, ill/poor/hard luck, accident, misadventure, mischance. **2** *endure many misfortunes* trouble, setback, reverse, adversity, reverse of fortune, misadventure, mishap, stroke of bad luck, blow, failure, accident, disaster, tragedy, affliction, sorrow, misery, woe, trial, tribulation, catastrophe, calamity.

misgiving *noun* qualm, doubt, reservation, second thoughts, suspicion, distrust, anxiety, apprehension, unease, uncertainty, hesitation.

misguided *adjective* **1** *their action was misguided* mistaken, deluded, erroneous, fallacious, wrong, unwarranted, uncalled-for, misplaced, ill-advised, unwise, injudicious, imprudent, foolish. **2** *misguided people believed him* misled, misdirected, misinformed, laboring under a delusion/misapprehension, deluded, foolish, ill-advised.

mishandle *verb* **1** *mishandle the project* mismanage, misdirect, misgovern, misconduct, maladminister, bungle, botch, muff, make a mess of; *inf.* make a hash of, foul up, screw up. **2** *mishandle the prisoners* handle roughly, treat roughly, mistreat, maltreat, manhandle; *inf.* rough up. *See* MISTREAT.

mishap *noun* **1** *without further mishap* misfortune, ill fortune, ill/bad/poor/hard luck, accident, misadventure, mischance. **2** *after a series of mishaps* accident, trouble, setback, reverse, adversity, misadventure, misfortune, stroke of bad luck, blow, disaster, trial, tribulation, catastrophe, calamity.

mishmash *noun* hodgepodge, jumble, tangle, confusion, miscellany, mixture, medley, assortment, mélange, variety, collection, pot-

misinform *verb* give wrong information, mislead, misdirect, misguide, put on the wrong
track; *inf.* give a bum steer.

misinterpret *verb* put a wrong interpretation
on, misconstrue, misunderstand, misapprehend, misread.

misjudge *verb* have a wrong opinion about, be
wrong about, get the wrong idea about.

mislay *verb* lose, misplace, put in the wrong
place, lose track of, miss, be unable to find, be
unable to lay one's hands on, forget the whereabouts of, forget where one has put something.
Antonyms: FIND; LOCATE.

mislead *verb* misinform, misguide, misdirect,
delude, take in, deceive, fool, hoodwink, lead
astray, throw off the scent, send on a wild-
goose chase, pull the wool over someone's
eyes; *inf.* lead up the garden path, take for a
ride.

misleading *adjective* confusing, deceptive, deceiving, delusive, evasive, equivocal, ambiguous, fallacious, spurious, illusory, casuistic, sophistical.

mismanage *verb* misdirect, mishandle, misgovern, misconduct, maladminister, bungle,
botch, muff, make a mess of; *inf.* make a hash
of, mess up, foul up, screw up.

misogynist *noun* woman-hater, antifeminist,
male chauvinist, chauvinist; *inf.* male chauvinist pig, MCP.

misplace *verb* put in the wrong place, mislay,
lose, be unable to find, be unable to lay one's
hands on. *See* MISLAY.

misprint *noun* printing error, typographical
error, typing error, mistake, literal, corrigendum, erratum; *inf.* typo.

misquote *verb* *misquoted the president/speech/fig-
ures* misstate, misreport, misrepresent, distort,
twist, falsify, garble, muddle, get wrong.

misrepresent *verb* give a false account of, give
a false idea of, misstate, misreport, misquote,
misinterpret, falsify, distort, garble.

misrule *noun* 1 *accuse the government of misrule*
bad government, misgovernment, mismanagement, misdirection, maladministration,
negligence. 2 *misrule descended on the country*
lawlessness, disorder, chaos, anarchy.

miss[1] *verb* 1 *miss a shot* let go, bungle, botch,
muff, fail to achieve. 2 *miss the bus* fail to catch/
get, be too late for. 3 *miss the meeting* fail to attend, be too late for, absent oneself from, be
absent from, play truant from, take French
leave from; *inf.* skip. 4 *miss an opportunity* fail
to seize/grasp, let slip, let go, pass up, overlook,
disregard. 5 *I'm sorry, I missed what you said*
fail to hear/catch, fail to take in, mishear, misunderstand. 6 *they miss their father* regret the
absence/loss of, feel the loss of, feel nostalgic
for, long to see, long for, pine for, yearn for,
ache for. 7 *did not miss my wallet until I got home*
notice the absence of, find missing. 8 *try to*

miss the traffic avoid, evade, escape, dodge,
sidestep, steer clear of, give a wide berth to.
Antonyms: CATCH; GET; ATTEND.

miss[2] *noun* *one hit and three misses* failure, omission, slip, blunder, error, mistake, fiasco; *inf.*
flop.

miss[3] *noun* girl, schoolgirl, young lady, lass; *lit.*
maiden, maid, damsel.

misshapen *adjective* out of shape, deformed,
malformed, ill-proportioned, misproportioned, twisted, distorted, contorted, warped,
curved, crooked, wry, bent, hunchbacked.

missile *noun* projectile, shot, weapon, rocket,
weapon for throwing.

missing *adjective* lost, mislaid, misplaced,
nowhere to be found, absent, not present,
gone, gone astray, unaccounted for.

mission *noun* 1 *accomplish his mission* assignment, commission, task, job, errand, work,
chore, business, undertaking, operation, duty,
charge, trust, goal, aim, purpose. 2 *her mission
in life is to heal the sick* vocation, calling, pursuit, quest, undertaking. 3 *scientists asked to
join the mission* delegation, deputation, committee, commission, task force, legation.

missionary *noun* evangelist, converter, apostle,
proselytizer, preacher, minister, priest.

missive *noun* communication, message, letter,
note, memorandum, bulletin, communiqué,
report, dispatch; *inf.* memo.

misspent *adjective* dissipated, wasted, squandered, thrown away, prodigal.

mist *noun* haze, fog, smog, cloud, vapor, condensation, steam, film.

mist *verb* **mist over, mist up** become cloudy, cloud,
cloud over, become hazy, haze over, become
foggy, fog over, fog up, become blurred; steam
up.

mistake *noun* error, fault, inaccuracy, slip, blunder, miscalculation, misunderstanding, oversight, gaffe, faux pas, solecism, misapprehension, misreading; *inf.* slipup, booboo.

---

mistake
blooper, blunder, error, faux pas, goof, slip

It would be a **mistake** to argue with your boss
the day before he or she evaluates your performance, but to forget an important step in
an assigned task would be an **error**. Although
these nouns are used interchangeably in many
contexts, a *mistake* is usually caused by poor
judgment or a disregard of rules or principles
(*it was a mistake not to tell the truth at the outset*), while an *error* implies an unintentional deviation from standards of accuracy or right
conduct (*a mathematical error*). A **blunder** is a
careless, stupid, or blatant mistake involving
behavior or judgment; it suggests awkwardness or ignorance on the part of the person
who makes it (*a blunder that ruined the evening*).
A **slip** is a minor and usually accidental

mistake that is the result of haste or carelessness (*a slip of the tongue spoiled the surprise*), while a **faux pas** (which means false step in French) is an embarrassing breach of etiquette (*it was a faux pas to have meat at the table when so many of the guests were vegetarians*). **Goof** and **blooper** are humorous mistakes. A *blooper* is usually a mix-up in speech, while a *goof* is a careless error that is honestly admitted (*when confronted with the evidence, she shrugged her shoulders and said, "I made a goof!"*).

mistake *verb mistake his meaning* get wrong, misunderstand, misapprehend, misinterpret, misconstrue, misread. **be mistaken** *you are mistaken* be wrong, be in error, be at fault, be under a misapprehension, be misinformed, be misguided, be wide of the mark, be barking up the wrong tree. **mistake for** *mistake him for his brother* | *mistook her silence for arrogance* take someone for, mix someone up with, confuse someone with, misinterpret something as.

mistaken *adjective mistaken impressions/idea* wrong, erroneous, inaccurate, incorrect, false, fallacious, unsound, unfounded, misguided, misinformed, wide of the mark.
Antonyms: CORRECT; RIGHT; ACCURATE.

mistakenly *adverb* by mistake, wrongly, in error, erroneously, incorrectly, falsely, fallaciously, misguidedly.

mistreat *verb* maltreat, treat badly, ill-treat, ill-use, misuse, abuse, handle/treat roughly, mishandle, harm, hurt, molest, manhandle, maul, bully; *inf.* beat up, rough up.

mistress *noun* lover, girlfriend, partner, ladylove, paramour, kept woman, concubine, inamorata.

mistrust *verb* **1** *mistrust him* | *I mistrust his motives* feel mistrustful of, distrust, feel distrustful of, have doubts about, be suspicious of, suspect, have reservations about, have misgivings about, be wary of. **2** *mistrust his ability* have no confidence in, question, doubt, lack faith in.

mistrustful *adjective* distrustful, doubtful, dubious, suspicious, chary, wary, uncertain, cautious, hesitant, skeptical; *inf.* leery.

misty *adjective* **1** *misty weather* hazy, foggy, cloudy. **2** *a misty shape* hazy, blurred, fuzzy, dim, indistinct, vague. **3** *a misty idea of what it is* like hazy, vague, obscure, nebulous.
Antonyms: CLEAR; DISTINCT.

misunderstand *verb* misapprehend, misinterpret, misconstrue, misread, get the wrong idea, receive a false impression, be barking up the wrong tree. *See* MISAPPREHEND.

misunderstanding *noun* **1** *his misunderstanding of the statement* misapprehension, mistake, error, mix-up, misinterpretation, misconstruction, misreading, misjudgment, miscalculation, misconception, misbelief, wrong idea, delusion, false impression. **2** *the friends*

have had a misunderstanding disagreement, difference, difference of opinion, clash of views, dispute, quarrel, argument, tiff, squabble, conflict; *inf.* falling-out, spat, scrap.

misuse *verb* **1** *misuse their talents/money* put to wrong use, misapply, misemploy, abuse, squander, waste, dissipate. **2** *misuse the furniture/car* mistreat, abuse, mishandle, manhandle, harm; vandalize.

misuse *noun* **1** *the misuse of their talents/money* wrong use, misapplication, misemployment, abuse, squandering, waste, dissipation. **2** *this misuse of the verb* misusage, malapropism, barbarism, catachresis. **3** *misuse of the furniture/car* maltreatment, mistreatment, ill use, abuse, rough handling, mishandling, manhandling.

mitigate *verb* alleviate, reduce, diminish, lessen, weaken, attenuate, allay, assuage, palliate, appease, soothe, relieve, ease, soften, temper, mollify, lighten, still, quieten, quiet, tone down, moderate, modify, extenuate, calm, lull, pacify, placate, tranquilize.
Antonyms: AGGRAVATE; INCREASE; INTENSIFY.

mitigating *adjective* extenuating, exonerative, justificatory, justifying, vindicatory, vindicating, exculpatory, palliative, qualifying, modifying, tempering.

mix *verb* **1** *mix cement* | *mix the sugar and the water* admix, blend, put together, combine, mingle, compound, homogenize, alloy, merge, unite, join, amalgamate, fuse, coalesce, interweave. **2** *the two of them together just don't mix* be compatible, get along, be in harmony, be like-minded, be of the same mind; *inf.* be on the same wavelength. **3** *he never mixes at parties* socialize, mingle, associate with others, meet people. **4** *she mixes with all sorts* associate, mingle, have dealings, fraternize, hobnob. **mix up 1** *mix up a batch of drinks/granola/medicine* mix, blend, combine. **2** *mix up the dates* confuse, get confused, muddle, muddle up, get muddled up, get jumbled up, scramble, mistake. **3** *hush, or you'll mix me up* confuse, throw into confusion, muddle up, fluster, upset, disturb. **4** *he is mixed up in the crime* involve, implicate, entangle, embroil, draw into, incriminate.
Antonyms: SEPARATE; DIVIDE.

mix *noun* mixture, blend, combination, compound, alloy, merger, union, amalgamation, fusion, coalition.

mixed *adjective* **1** *a mixed collection* assorted, varied, miscellaneous, diverse, diversified, motley, heterogeneous. **2** *of mixed breed* hybrid, crossbred, interbred, mongrel. **3** *have mixed reactions* ambivalent, equivocal, unsure, uncertain.

mixed-up *adjective* *a mixed-up kid* maladjusted, ill-adjusted, disturbed, confused, muddled; *inf.* screwed-up, untogether.

mixer *noun* **1** *put it in the mixer* blender, food processor; cement mixer. **2** *she is shy, but he is* life of the party, party person.

mixture *noun* **1** *pour out the mixture* compound, blend, mix, brew, combination, concoction, alloy. **2** *a mixture of objects* assortment, variety, mélange, collection, miscellany, motley collection, medley, potpourri, conglomeration, jumble, mix, mishmash, hodgepodge, pastiche, mixed bag. **3** *the dog is a mixture* cross, crossbreed, mongrel, hybrid.

mix-up *noun* confusion, muddle, jumble, misunderstanding, mistake.

moan *noun* **1** *the moans of the injured man* groan, lament, lamentation, wail, whimper, whine. **2** *the moan of the wind* groan, sigh, sough, murmur, whisper. **3** *tired of his moans* moans and groans, complaint, complaining, whine, whining, carping; *inf.* grousing, gripe, griping, grouching, beef, beefing.

moan *verb* **1** *the injured man moans* groan, wail, whimper, whine. **2** *the wind moaning* groan, sigh, sough, murmur, whisper. **3** *always moaning about the weather* complain, whine, carp; *inf.* grouse, gripe, grouch, beef.

mob *noun* **1** *police tried to move the mob of spectators on* crowd, horde, multitude, rabble, mass, body, throng, host, pack, press, gang, drove, herd, flock, gathering, assemblage. **2** *the dictator ignored the cries of the mob* common people, masses, populace, multitude, commonality, proletariat, crowd, rabble, hoi polloi, canaille; *inf.* great unwashed. **3** *those gatecrashers left, but another mob arrived* lot, group, set, troop, company; *inf.* gang.

mob *verb* **1** *mob the star's car* | *fans mobbed the football team* crowd around, swarm around, surround, besiege, jostle. **2** *mob the theater* crowd into, cram full, fill to overflowing, fill, pack. **3** *prisoners mobbing the murderer* set upon, attack, harass, fall upon, assault.

mobile *adjective* **1** *the patient is mobile* able to move, able to move around, moving, walking, motile, ambulatory. **2** *a mobile face* expressive, animated, ever-changing, changeable. **3** *mobile library* | *set up a mobile missile launcher* movable, transportable, portable, traveling, peripatetic, locomotive. **4** *socially mobile* moving, on the move, flexible, adaptable, adjustable.

Antonyms: IMMOBILE; EXPRESSIONLESS; STATIONARY.

mobilize *verb* **1** *mobilize the troops* call up, call to arms, muster, rally, marshal, assemble, organize, make ready, prepare, ready. **2** *mobilize for action* get ready, prepare, ready oneself.

mock *verb* **1** *rebels mocking the government officials* ridicule, jeer at, sneer at, deride, treat with contempt, treat contemptuously, scorn, make fun of, poke fun at, laugh at, tease, taunt, insult, flout; *inf.* rag, kid, rib. **2** *mocked their teacher's mannerisms* imitate, mimic, parody, ape, caricature, satirize, lampoon, burlesque; *inf.* take off, send up. **3** *the wind mocked their*

attempts to proceed defy, challenge, thwart, frustrate, foil, disappoint.

mock *adjective* *mock leather/money* imitation, artificial, simulated, synthetic, ersatz, so-called, fake, sham, false, spurious, bogus, counterfeit, forged, pseudo, pretended; *inf.* pretend.

mockery *noun* **1** *a note of mockery in his voice* ridicule, jeering, sneer, derision, contempt, scorn, disdain, teasing, taunting, gibe, insult, contumely; *inf.* ribbing. **2** *the trial was a mockery* laughingstock, farce, parody, travesty, caricature, lampoon, burlesque; *inf.* takeoff, sendup, spoof. **3** *his attempt to climb the flagpole was a mockery* travesty, inanity, act of stupidity, futile act, joke, laugh.

mocking *adjective* *a mocking smile* sneering, derisive, derisory, contemptuous, scornful, disdainful, sardonic, insulting, satirical.

model *noun* **1** *a model of a train* replica, representation, mock-up, copy, dummy, imitation, facsimile, image, mannequin. **2** *this is the model of the commissioned sculpture/building* prototype, protoplast, archetype, type, mold, original, pattern, design, paradigm, sample, example, exemplar. **3** *this is the model of car I want* style, design, mode, form, mark, version, type, variety, kind, sort. **4** *she was a model as a teacher* | *a model of tact* ideal, paragon, perfect example, perfect specimen, exemplar, (the) epitome of something, (the) beau ideal, nonpareil, (the) crème de la crème. **5** *he used his wife as a model* artist's model, photographic model, sitter, poser, subject. **6** *she is a model in Paris* fashion model, mannequin.

---

model
archetype, example, ideal, paradigm, pattern, prototype

Most parents try to set a good **example** for their children, although they may end up setting a bad one. An *example*, in other words, is a precedent for imitation, either good or bad. Most parents would do better to provide a **model** for their children, which refers to a person or thing that is to be followed or imitated because of its excellence in conduct or character. *Model* also connotes a physical shape to be copied closely (*a ship's model, a model airplane*). Not all children regard their parents as an **ideal** to which they aspire, a word that suggests an imagined perfection or a standard based upon a set of desirable qualities (*the ideal gentleman; the ideal of what an artist should be*); but young people's lives often end up following the **pattern** established by their parents, meaning that their lives follow the same basic configuration or design. While **prototype** and **archetype** are often used interchangeably, they really mean quite different things. An *archetype* is a perfect and unchanging form that existing things or people can approach but never duplicate (*the* *archetype of a mother*), while a *prototype* is an early, usually unrefined version of something that later versions reflect but may depart from (*the prototype for today's gas-guzzling cars*). **Paradigm** can refer to an example that serves as a model, but today its use is primarily confined to a grammatical context, where it means a set giving all the various forms of a word, such as the conjugation of a verb.

model adjective **1** *the model building* prototypical, prototypal, archetypal, illustrative. **2** *a model teacher* ideal, perfect. *See* MODEL noun 4.
Antonyms: DEFICIENT; IMPERFECT.

moderate adjective **1** *moderate views* nonextreme, middle-of-the-road, nonradical, nonreactionary. **2** *moderate demands* nonexcessive, reasonable, within reason, within due limits, fair, just. **3** *moderate behavior* not given to excesses, restrained, controlled, temperate, sober, steady. **4** *moderate winds* temperate, calm, equable, mild. **5** *moderate work/success* average, middle-of-the-road, middling, ordinary, fair, fairish, modest, tolerable, passable, adequate, indifferent, mediocre, run-of-the-mill; *inf.* so-so, fair-to-middling. **6** *moderate amount/prices* reasonable, within reason, acceptable, average, fair, fairish, modest, lowish.
Antonyms: IMMODERATE; EXTREME; UNREASONABLE.

moderate verb **1** *the wind has moderated* die down, abate, let up, calm down, lessen, decrease, diminish, slacken. **2** *moderate the force/pain* lessen, decrease, diminish, mitigate, alleviate, allay, appease, assuage, ease, palliate, soothe, soften, calm, modulate, pacify. **3** *moderate his anger* curb, check, keep in check, keep in control, temper, regulate, restrain, subdue, repress, tame. **4** *moderating the assembly* arbitrate, mediate, referee, judge, chair, take the chair of, preside over.

moderately adverb **1** *moderately expensive* quite, rather, somewhat, fairly, reasonably, to a certain degree, to some extent, within reason, within limits. **2** *the work is moderately good* | *did moderately well in the test* fairly, tolerably, passably.

moderation noun **1** *the moderation of their behavior* | *moderation in all things* moderateness, restraint, self-restraint, control, self-control, temperateness, temperance, nonindulgence. **2** *the moderation of the force/pain* lessening, decrease, mitigation, allaying, appeasement, assuagement, soothing, calming, modulation, pacification. **3** *the moderation of the assembly* arbitration, mediation, refereeing, chairing, presiding over. **in moderation** moderately, within reason, within due limits.

modern adjective **1** *in modern times* contemporary, present-day, present-time, present, current, twentieth-century, twenty-first-century,

existing, existent. **2** *her clothes/ideas are very modern* up-to-date, up-to-the-minute, fashionable, in fashion, in, in style, in vogue, voguish, modish, the latest, new, newfangled, fresh, modernistic, ultramodern, advanced, progressive; *inf.* trendy, with-it.
Antonyms: PAST; OUT OF DATE; OLD-FASHIONED.

modernize verb **1** *modernize the methods/machinery* make modern, update, bring up to date, bring into the twentieth/twenty-first century, renovate, remodel, remake, redo, refresh, revamp, rejuvenate; *inf.* do over. **2** *the industry must modernize* get up to date, move with the times; *inf.* drag oneself into the twentieth/twenty-first century, get on the ball, get with it.

modest adjective **1** *modest about his achievements* self-effacing, self-deprecating, humble, unpretentious, unassuming, free from vanity, keeping one's light under a bushel. **2** *too modest to speak* shy, bashful, self-conscious, diffident, reserved, retiring, reticent, quiet, coy, embarrassed, blushing, timid, fearful, meek. **3** *modest behavior/clothes* decorous, decent, seemly, demure, proper, discreet, delicate, chaste, virtuous. **4** *modest demands/improvement* moderate, fair, tolerable, passable, adequate, satisfactory, acceptable, unexceptional, small, limited. **5** *a modest gift/house* unpretentious, simple, plain, humble, inexpensive, low-cost.
Antonyms: BOASTFUL; CONCEITED; IMMODEST; EXPENSIVE.

modesty noun **1** *admire his modesty* lack of vanity, humility, self-effacement, lack of pretension, unpretentiousness. **2** *her modesty prevented her speaking* shyness, bashfulness, self-consciousness, reserve, reticence, timidity, meekness. **3** *modesty of her behavior/clothes* decorum, decorousness, seemliness, demureness, propriety, chasteness. **4** *the modesty of their demands* moderation, fairness, passableness, adequacy, satisfactoriness, acceptability, smallness. **5** *the modesty of the gift/house* lack of pretension, unpretentiousness, simplicity, plainness, inexpensiveness, lack of extravagance.

modicum noun small amount, little, little bit, bit, particle, iota, jot, atom, whit, grain, speck, scrap, crumb, fragment, shred, mite, dash, drop, dab, pinch, ounce, inch, touch, tinge, trifle; *inf.* teeny bit.

modification noun **1** *the modification of the punishment* lessening, reduction, decrease, abatement, mitigation, restriction. *See* MODIFY 1. **2** *the modification of the design* altering, alteration, adjusting, adjustment, adaptation, refashioning, refining, refinement. *See* MODIFY 2. **3** *the modifications made to the plans* alteration, change, adjustment, adaptation, variation, revision, refinement, transformation.

modify verb **1** *modify the punishment* lessen, reduce, decrease, diminish, lower, abate, soften, mitigate, restrict, limit, moderate, temper, blunt, dull, tone down, qualify. **2** *modify the design* alter, make alterations to, change, adjust, make adjustments to, adapt, vary, revise, recast, reform, reshape, refashion, rework, remold, redo, revamp, reorganize, refine, transform.

modulate *verb* **1** *modulate the proportions* regulate, adjust, moderate, temper. **2** *modulate one's voice* adjust/vary/adapt/modify the tone of.

mogul *noun* notable, VIP, magnate, tycoon, baron, captain, lord; *inf.* bigwig, big shot, big cheese.

moist *adjective* **1** *moist weather* wet, wettish, damp, dampish, clammy, humid, dank, rainy, drizzly, drizzling, dewy, dripping, soggy. **2** *a moist cake* succulent, juicy, soft, spongy.

moisten *verb* make wet/wettish, wet, dampen, damp, water, soak, bedew, humidify, irrigate.

moisture *noun* water, liquid, wetness, wet, dampness, damp, humidity, dankness, wateriness, rain, dew, drizzle, perspiration, sweat.

moisturize *verb* *moisturize the skin* apply lotion/cream to, keep supple.

mold[1] *noun* **1** *set the mixture in a mold* cast, die, form, matrix, shape. **2** *the mold of history* shape, form, figure, cast, outline, line, configuration, formation, format, structure, frame, construction, build, cut, style, model, pattern, type, kind, brand, make. **3** *objects constructed on a mold* frame, framework, template. **4** *people of heroic mold* character, nature, caliber, kind, sort, ilk, stamp, type, kidney.

mold[2] *verb* **1** *mold plastic into pipes* cast, form. **2** *mold the model from clay* shape, form, fashion, model, construct, frame, make, create, design, carve, sculpt, chisel, forge. **3** *mold children's minds* influence, affect, direct, shape, form, make.

mold[3] *noun* *mold covered the woodwork* moldiness, fungus, mildew, blight, smut, must, mustiness, dry rot, rot.

moldy *adjective* mildewed, blighted, musty, fusty, decaying, rotting, rotten, bad, spoiled.

mole *noun* spot, blemish, mark, blotch, discoloration, freckle, birthmark.

molecule *noun* *not a molecule of politeness* particle, iota, jot, atom, whit, grain, speck, scrap, crumb, shred, ounce, modicum.

molest *verb* **1** *crowds molesting the celebrity* pester, annoy, nag, plague, torment, harass, badger, harry, persecute, bother, worry, trouble, needle, provoke, vex, agitate, disturb, upset, fluster, ruffle, irritate, exasperate, tease; *inf.* bug, hassle. **2** *accused of molesting children* abuse, sexually abuse, interfere with, sexually assault, rape, ravish, assault, attack, injure, hurt, harm, mistreat, maltreat, ill-treat, manhandle.

mollify *verb* *mollify his mother* | *tried to mollify her anger* calm, calm down, pacify, placate, appease, soothe, still, quiet, tranquilize.

mollycoddle *verb* pamper, coddle, cosset, spoil, overindulge, indulge, baby, featherbed, wait on hand and foot.

moment *noun* **1** *only lasted a moment* minute, short time, second, instant; *inf.* jiffy, jiff. **2** *the very moment he came* minute, instant, point, point in time, time, juncture. **in a moment** in a short time, shortly, very soon, in a minute/second/trice/flash, in an instant, in the twinkling of an eye; *inf.* in a jiff/jiffy, in two shakes, in two shakes of a lamb's tail.

momentarily *adverb* briefly, temporarily, just for a moment/second/instant/minute, for a short time.

momentary *adjective* brief, short, short-lived, fleeting, passing, transient, transitory, ephemeral, evanescent, fugitive, temporary, impermanent.

Antonyms: LENGTHY; PERMANENT.

momentous *adjective* crucial, critical, vital, decisive, pivotal, serious, grave, weighty, important, significant, consequential, of importance, of consequence, fateful, historic; *inf.* earthshaking, earth-shattering.

Antonyms: UNIMPORTANT; TRIVIAL; INSIGNIFICANT.

momentum *noun* impetus, impulse, propulsion, thrust, push, driving power/force, drive, power, energy, force.

monarch *noun* sovereign, ruler, crowned head, potentate, king, queen, emperor, empress.

monarchy *noun* **1** *abolish the monarchy* absolutism, absolute power, autocracy, monocracy, kingship, royalism, sovereignty, despotism. **2** *the country is a monarchy* kingdom, sovereign state, realm, principality, empire.

monastery *noun* religious house, religious community; friary, abbey, convent, nunnery, priory.

monastic *adjective* monastical, cloistered, cenobitic, conventual, canonical, ascetic, celibate, contemplative, meditative, sequestered, secluded, withdrawn, reclusive, recluse, eremitic, hermit-like, anchoritic.

monetary *adjective* money, cash, financial, capital, pecuniary, fiscal, budgetary.

money *noun* **1** *not enough money to buy the business* cash, hard cash, ready money, finance, capital, funds, banknotes, currency, coin, coinage, silver, copper, legal tender, specie; *inf.* wherewithal, dough, bread, loot, moolah, filthy lucre, green stuff. **2** *he is a man of money* affluence, wealth, riches, prosperity. **in the money** moneyed, well-to-do, well-off, affluent, rich, wealthy, prosperous, in clover; *inf.* rolling in it, loaded, stinking rich, well-heeled, flush, made of money, on easy street.

moneyed *adjective* well-to-do, well-off, affluent, rich, wealthy, prosperous; *inf.* in the money, rolling in it, loaded, well-heeled.

moneymaking *adjective* profitable, lucrative, gainful, paying, remunerative, successful, thriving, going.

mongrel noun *the dog is a mongrel* crossbreed, cross, half-breed, mixed breed, hybrid, cur.

mongrel adjective *a mongrel dog* crossbred, of mixed breed, hybrid.

monitor noun **1** *monitors watching shoppers/workers* detector, scanner, recorder, security system, security camera, observer, watchdog, overseer, supervisor. **2** *computer monitor* screen, receiver, display device, cathode-ray tube, CRT.

monitor verb *monitor his movements/condition* observe, scan, record, survey, follow, keep an eye on, keep track of, check, oversee, supervise.

monk noun brother, monastic, religious, friar, abbot, prior.

monkey noun **1** *monkeys in the jungle* primate, simian. **2** *the child is a little monkey* rascal, scamp, imp, rogue, mischief-maker, devil. **make a monkey of** make a fool of, make someone look a fool, make someone look foolish, make a laughingstock of, ridicule, deride, make fun of.

monkey verb **monkey around/about** fool around/about, play around/about; *inf.* mess around/about. **monkey with** fiddle with, play with, tinker with, tamper with, interfere with, meddle with, fool with, trifle with, mess with.

monkey business noun **1** *children up to monkey business* mischief, naughtiness, pranks, clowning; *inf.* carrying-on, shenanigans, goings-on. **2** *there's been some monkey business in the accounts department* dishonesty, trickery, misconduct, misdemeanor, chicanery, skullduggery; *inf.* funny business, hanky-panky.

monologue noun solioloquy, speech, address, lecture, oration, sermon.

monopolize verb **1** *monopolize the market* exercise a monopoly of, corner, control, take over, have sole rights in. **2** *monopolize the conversation* dominate, take over, not let anyone else take part in, not let anyone else get a word in edgewise. **3** *monopolize his wife* keep to oneself, take up all the attention of, not allow to associate with others.

monotonous adjective **1** *a monotonous job* unvarying, lacking/without variety, unchanging, repetitious, all the same, uniform, routine, humdrum, run-of-the-mill, commonplace, mechanical, uninteresting, unexciting, prosaic, wearisome, dull, boring, tedious, tiresome. **2** *a monotonous voice* flat, unvarying, toneless, uninflected, droning, soporific.

Antonyms: VARIED; INTERESTING; EXCITING.

monotony noun **1** *the monotony of the job* lack of variety, lack of variation, repetition, repetitiveness, sameness, uniformity, routine, routineness, humdrumness, lack of interest, lack of excitement, prosaicness, wearisomeness, dullness, boredom, tedium, tiresomeness. **2** *the monotony of her voice* flatness, tonelessness, lack of inflection, drone.

monster noun **1** *frightened by the monster in the myth* fabulous creature, mythical creature, ogre, giant, dragon, troll, bogeyman, werewolf, sea monster, behemoth. **2** *Hitler was a monster* fiend, beast, brute, barbarian, savage, villain, ogre, devil, demon. **3** *the sideshow monster was a hoax* monstrosity, miscreation, malformation, freak, freak of nature, mutant, lusus naturae. **4** *a monster of a man/building* giant, mammoth, colossus, titan, behemoth, leviathan.

monster adjective *a monster truck/tower* huge, enormous, massive, vast, immense, colossal, gigantic, monstrous, stupendous, prodigious, tremendous, giant, mammoth, gargantuan, titanic; *inf.* jumbo, whopping, humongous.

monstrosity noun **1** *a monstrosity of a building* enormity, horror, eyesore, carbuncle. **2** *the monstrosity of the attack* monstrousness, outrageousness, scandalousness, atrocity, heinousness, horror, hideousness, foulness, vileness, odiousness, viciousness, cruelty, savagery, brutishness, fiendishness, devilishness. **3** *the sideshow monstrosity was a hoax* freak, mutant. *See* MONSTER *noun* 3.

monstrous adjective **1** *Dr. Frankenstein's monstrous creatures* miscreated, malformed, unnatural, abnormal, grotesque, gruesome, repellent, freakish, mutant. **2** *monstrous trucks* huge, enormous, massive, vast, immense, colossal, gigantic, tremendous, giant. *See* MONSTER *adjective.* **3** *it was a monstrous thing to do* outrageous, shocking, disgraceful, scandalous, atrocious, heinous, evil, abominable, terrible, horrible, dreadful, hideous, foul, vile, nasty, ghastly, odious, loathsome, intolerable, contemptible, despicable, vicious, cruel, savage, brutish, bestial, barbaric, inhuman, fiendish, devilish, diabolical, satanic.

Antonyms: NORMAL; TINY; ADMIRABLE.

monument noun **1** *build a monument to the dead soldiers* memorial, statue, shrine, reliquary, sepulcher, mausoleum, cairn, pillar, column, obelisk, dolmen, megalith. **2** *place a monument on the grave* gravestone, headstone, tombstone. **3** *establish a scholarship as a monument to his talent* memorial, commemoration, remembrance, reminder, testament, witness, token.

monumental adjective **1** *a monumental effort* great, huge, enormous, immense, vast, exceptional, extraordinary, tremendous, stupendous, prodigious, staggering. **2** *a monumental error* huge, enormous, terrible, colossal, egregious, catastrophic, staggering, unforgivable, indefensible; *inf.* whopping. **3** *a monumental work of art* massive, impressive, striking, remarkable, magnificent, awe-inspiring, marvelous, majestic, stupendous, prodigious, historic, epoch-making, classic, memorable, unforgettable, enduring, permanent, immortal. **4** *monumental tributes* commemorative, celebratory, in memory, recalling to mind.

mood noun **1** *in a happy mood* humor, temper,

disposition, frame of mind, state of mind, spirit, tenor, vein. **2** *he is in a mood* bad mood, bad temper, fit of bad/ill temper, fit of irritability, fit of pique, low spirits, fit of melancholy, depression, (the) doldrums; *inf.* (the) dumps. **in the mood for/to** *in the mood for dancing* | *in the mood to dance* feeling like, inclined to, disposed toward, interested in, keen on/to, eager to, having enthusiasm for, willing to.

moody *adjective* **1** *teenagers are often moody* temperamental, changeable, unpredictable, volatile, mercurial, unstable, unsteady, erratic, fitful, impulsive, capricious. **2** *don't say anything—he's moody today* in a mood, in a bad mood, bad-tempered, ill-tempered, ill-humored, short-tempered, irritable, irascible, crabbed, crabby, cantankerous, cross, crotchety, crusty, testy, touchy, petulant, in a pique, sullen, sulky, moping, gloomy, glum, depressed, dejected, despondent, melancholic, doleful, lugubrious, introspective, in a huff, huffy; *inf.* down in the dumps, down in the mouth.
Antonyms: STABLE; AMIABLE; HAPPY.

moon *noun* satellite; *lit.* orb. **many moons ago** a long time ago, months/years ago, ages ago. **once in a blue moon** hardly ever, almost never, rarely, very seldom.

moon *verb* languish, idle, mope, daydream, be in a reverie, be in a brown study.

moor *verb* *moored the boat at the wharf* secure, fix firmly, fasten, make fast, tie up, lash, anchor, berth.

moot *adjective* *a moot point* debatable, open to debate, open to discussion, questionable, open to question, open, doubtful, disputable, arguable, contestable, controversial, unresolved, undecided.

mop *noun* **1** *clean the floor with a mop* swab, sponge; sponge mop, wet mop, dust mop, dry mop. **2** *a mop of hair* shock, mane, mass; mat, tangle.

mop *verb* **1** *mop the floor* clean, wipe, wash, swab, sponge. **2** *mop one's face* wipe, clean, dry. **mop up 1** *mop up the spilled water* soak up, absorb, sponge (up), clean up, wipe up. **2** *mop up all the profits* absorb, use up, exhaust, consume, swallow up. **3** *mop up the last bits of work* finish off, make an end of, clear up, eliminate, dispatch. **4** *mop up the enemy territory* complete the occupation of, take over, secure. **5** *mop up resisting soldiers* kill off, eliminate, dispose of, do away with.

mope *verb* **1** *moping because her friend has gone* be miserable, be sad, be despondent, pine, fret, grieve, brood, sulk. **2** *done nothing but mope about/around* idle, languish, moon.

moral *adjective* **1** *moral issues* ethical. **2** *a moral man/woman* ethical, good, virtuous, righteous, upright, upstanding, high-minded, principled, honorable, honest, just, decent, chaste, pure, blameless. **3** *moral act/behavior* good, virtuous, honorable, right, proper, fit, decent, decorous.

4 *moral support* psychological, emotional, mental.
Antonyms: IMMORAL; BAD; DISHONORABLE.

moral
ethical, honorable, righteous, sanctimonious, virtuous

You can be an **ethical** person without necessarily being a **moral** one, since *ethical* implies conformity with a code of fair and honest behavior, particularly in business or in a profession (*an ethical legislator who didn't believe in cutting deals*), while *moral* refers to generally accepted standards of goodness and rightness in character and conduct—especially sexual conduct (*the moral values she'd learned from her mother*). In the same way, you can be **honorable** without necessarily being **virtuous**, since *honorable* suggests dealing with others in a decent and ethical manner, while *virtuous* implies the possession of moral excellence in character (*many honorable businesspeople fail to live a virtuous private life*). **Righteous** is similar in meaning to **virtuous** but also implies freedom from guilt or blame (*righteous anger*); when the righteous person is also somewhat intolerant and narrow-minded, self-righteous might be a better adjective. Someone who makes a hypocritical show of being righteous is often described as **sanctimonious**—in other words, acting like a saint without having a saintly character.

moral *noun* *the moral of the story* lesson, teaching, message, homily, meaning, significance, point.

morale *noun* self-confidence, confidence, heart, spirit, hope, hopefulness, optimism, determination, zeal.

moral fiber *noun* strength of character, firmness of purpose, resolution, toughness of spirit.

morality *noun* **1** *questioned the morality of war* ethics, rights and wrongs. **2** *a man/woman of morality* ethics, goodness, virtue, righteousness, rectitude, uprightness, integrity, principles, honor, honesty, justness, decency, chasteness, chastity, purity, blamelessness. **3** *discuss morality* morals, moral code, moral standards, ethics, principles of right and wrong, standards/principles of behavior.

morals *plural noun* ethics, moral code, principles of right and wrong, principles, moral behavior/conduct, standards/principles of behavior, standards, morality, sense of morality, scruples, mores.

morass *noun* **1** *in a morass of detail* confusion, muddle, tangle, entanglement, mix-up, jumble, clutter. **2** *get stuck in a morass* marsh, marshland, bog, peatbog, swamp, quagmire, slough, fen.

moratorium *noun* suspension, postponement, stay, halt, freeze, embargo, ban, standstill, respite.

morbid *adjective* **1** *morbid thoughts/details* gruesome, grisly, macabre, hideous, dreadful, horrible, unwholesome. **2** *a morbid person* death-orientated, death-obsessed, death-fixated. **3** *don't be so morbid* gloomy, glum, dejected, melancholy, lugubrious, funereal, pessimistic. **4** *a morbid condition* diseased, infected, sickly, ailing. **5** *a morbid growth* malignant, deadly, pathological.

mordant *adjective* **1** *mordant wit/remarks* acid, caustic, trenchant, cutting, incisive, stinging, biting, acerbic, stringent, bitter, sarcastic, virulent, vitriolic, venomous, waspish. **2** *a mordant solution* acid, acidic, caustic, corrosive, vitriolic.

more *adjective* *require more space* additional, supplementary, further, added, extra, increased, spare, fresh, new.

more *adverb* *concentrate more* to a greater extent, further, longer, some more.

more *noun* *need more* additional amount/number, greater quantity/part, addition, supplement, extra, increase, incrementation.

moreover *adverb* besides, furthermore, further, more than that, what is more, in addition, also, as well, to boot.

morgue *noun* mortuary, funeral parlor, funeral home, charnel house.

moribund *adjective* **1** *moribund patients* dying, on one's deathbed, near death, near the end, breathing one's last, fading fast, failing rapidly, having one foot in the grave, on one's last legs, *in extremis*. **2** *moribund customs* dying, declining, on the decline, waning, on the way out, obsolescent, on its last legs.

morning *noun* forenoon, a.m., early part of the day, dawn, daybreak, sunrise; *lit.* morn.

moron *noun* fool, dolt, dunce, dullard, blockhead, dunderhead, ignoramus, numskull, nincompoop; *inf.* idiot, imbecile, nitwit, halfwit, dope, dimwit, dummy, schmuck.

morose *adjective* sullen, gloomy, glum, somber, sober, saturnine, lugubrious, funereal, mournful, depressed, dour, melancholy, melancholic, doleful, blue, down, low, moody, taciturn; pessimistic, sour, scowling, sulky, surly, churlish, crabbed, crabby, cross. **Antonyms:** CHEERFUL; JOYFUL; MERRY.

morsel *noun* mouthful, bite, nibble, bit, crumb, grain, particle, fragment, piece, scrap, segment, soupçon, taste.

mortal *adjective* **1** *mortal beings | the mortal world* temporal, transient, ephemeral, passing, impermanent, perishable, human, earthly, worldly, corporeal, fleshly. **2** *a mortal blow* death-dealing, deadly, fatal, lethal, killing, murderous, terminal, destructive. **3** *mortal enemies* deadly, to the death, sworn, out-and-out, irreconcilable, bitter, implacable, unrelenting, remorseless. **4** *mortal pain/fear* terrible, awful, intense, extreme, severe, grave, dire, very great,

great, unbearable, agonizing. **5** *of no mortal use* conceivable, imaginable, perceivable, possible.

mortal *noun* *mortals must die* human being, human, earthling, person, man/woman, being, body, individual.

mortality *noun* **1** *humans subject to mortality* temporality, transience, ephemerality, impermanence, perishability, humanity, earthliness, worldliness. **2** *appalled at the wartime mortality* bloodshed, death, loss of life, fatalities, killing, slaying, carnage, slaughter.

mortification *noun* **1** *their mortification at their failure* humiliation, disgrace, shame, dishonor, abasement, discomfiture, embarrassment. *See* MORTIFY 1. **2** *her mortification at their remarks* hurt, affront, offense, annoyance, displeasure, vexation, discomfiture, embarrassment. **3** *the mortification of one's passions* subduing, self-denial, control, controlling, restraint, suppression, disciplining, chastening. **4** *the mortification of flesh* gangrene, festering, necrosis, putrefaction.

mortify *verb* **1** *they were mortified by their failure* humiliate, humble, cause to eat humble pie, bring low, disgrace, shame, dishonor, abash, fill with shame, put to shame, chasten, degrade, abase, deflate, crush, discomfit, embarrass, take down a peg or two. **2** *their remarks mortified her* hurt, wound, affront, offend, annoy, displease, vex, embarrass. **3** *mortify one's passions* subdue, get under control, control, restrain, suppress, discipline, chasten. **4** *flesh mortifying* become gangrenous, fester, necrose, putrefy.

mortuary *noun* morgue, funeral parlor, funeral home, charnel house.

most *noun* *most did not vote* the majority, the greatest number, the greatest quantity/part, nearly all, almost all, the bulk, the mass. **Antonym:** minority.

mostly *adverb* **1** *they were mostly young* for the most part, on the whole, in the main, largely, mainly, chiefly, predominantly. **2** *mostly we eat at home* for the most part, usually, generally, in general, as a general rule, as a rule, ordinarily, normally, commonly.

mot *noun* bon mot, witticism, quip, pun, epigram, aphorism, maxim, saw, saying, proverb, adage, axiom.

mother *noun* female parent, materfamilias, matriarch, earth mother, foster mother, biological mother, birth mother, adoptive mother, surrogate mother; *inf.* mom, mommy, ma, mama, mater, old lady.

mother *adjective* inborn, innate, connate, native, natural.

mother *verb* **1** *mother the orphans* look after, care for, tend, raise, rear, foster, cherish, fuss over, indulge, spoil. **2** *she mothered twins | countries that have mothered geniuses* be the mother of, give birth to, bear, produce, bring forth.

motherly *adjective* maternal, protective, comforting, caring, loving, affectionate, fond, warm, tender, gentle, kind, kindly.

motion noun 1 *the motion made her sick* | *vehicles in motion* motility, mobility, locomotion, movement, moving, changing place/position, travel, traveling, going, progress, passing, passage, flow, action, activity, course. 2 *a motion with her hand* movement, gesture, gesticulation, signal, sign, wave, nod. 3 *a motion was made to adjourn* suggestion, proposition, proposal, recommendation, submission. **in motion** *trains in motion* moving, going, traveling, not at rest, on the move, under way. **set/put in motion** *set the process in motion* get going, get under way, get in operation, get working/functioning, start, begin, commence.

motion verb *motioned to me to step forward* gesture, gesticulate, signal, sign, wave, nod.

motionless adjective unmoving, still, stock-still, at a standstill, stationary, immobile, immovable, static, at rest, halted, stopped, paralyzed, transfixed, frozen, inert, lifeless.
Antonyms: MOVING; MOBILE; ACTIVE.

motivate verb 1 *it motivated him to write* move, cause, lead, persuade, prompt, actuate, drive, impel, spur, induce, provoke, incite, inspire. 2 *trying to motivate the students* give incentive to, stimulate, inspire, arouse, excite, stir, spur, goad.

motivation noun 1 *he has no motivation* ambition, drive, inspiration. 2 *you must give them some motivation to succeed* incentive, stimulus, inspiration, inducement, incitement, motive.

motive noun motivation, reason, rationale, justification, thinking, grounds, cause, basis, occasion, incentive, inducement, incitement, influence, lure, attraction, inspiration, persuasion, stimulus, spur, goad, pressure; *inf.* what makes one tick.

motley adjective 1 *motley collection of old clothes* assorted, varied, miscellaneous, mixed, diverse, diversified, variegated, heterogeneous. 2 *a motley coat* many-colored, multicolored, parti-colored, many-hued, variegated, kaleidoscopic, prismatic.
Antonyms: HOMOGENEOUS; UNIFORM.

mottled adjective blotched, blotchy, splotchy, speckled, spotted, streaked, marbled, flecked, freckled, dappled, stippled, variegated, piebald, pied, brindled.

motto noun 1 *"waste not, want not" should be your motto* maxim, aphorism, adage, saying, saw, axiom, truism, precept, epigram, proverb, byword, gnome. 2 *the club's motto* slogan, catchword, cry.

mound noun 1 *a mound of leaves* heap, pile, stack; *inf.* mountain. 2 *flat country broken by mounds* hillock, hill, knoll, rise, hummock, embankment, bank, dune.

mound verb pile, heap (up), stack (up), accumulate, amass, stockpile.

mount verb 1 *mount the stairs* ascend, go up, climb up, clamber up, make one's way up, scale. 2 *mounted the horse* get on to, get astride, get on the back of. 3 *costs mounting up* accumulate, accrue, pile up, grow, multiply. 4 *prices/fear mounting* increase, grow, escalate, intensify. 5 *mount a picture* frame, set. 6 *mount a campaign/exhibition* stage, put on, install, prepare, organize, arrange, set in motion; *inf.* get up.
Antonyms: DESCEND; ALIGHT; DECREASE.

mount noun 1 *choose a quiet mount* horse, steed. 2 *a plain mount for the gem/picture* setting, fixture, frame, support, stand, base, backing, foil.

mountain noun 1 *snowcapped mountains* peak, height, elevation, eminence, pinnacle, alp; *lit.* mount. *See also table at* RANGE. 2 *mountains of clothes* heap, pile, mound, stack, abundance; *inf.* ton.

mountainous adjective 1 *mountainous regions* hilly, high, highland, high-reaching, steep, lofty, towering, soaring, alpine, rocky. 2 *mountainous athletes* huge, enormous, immense, massive, vast, gigantic, mammoth, hulking, mighty, monumental, colossal, ponderous, prodigious.
Antonyms: FLAT; LEVEL; PUNY.

mourn verb *the widow is still mourning* grieve, sorrow, keen, lament, wail, wear black. **mourn for** *mourn for her dead husband* grieve for, sorrow over, weep for, regret/deplore the loss of, bewail, bemoan.
Antonyms: REJOICE; EXULT.

mourn
bemoan, grieve, lament, rue, sorrow

Not everyone exhibits unhappiness in the same way. **Grieve** is the strongest of these verbs, implying deep mental anguish or suffering, often endured alone and in silence (*she grieved for years over the loss of her baby*). **Mourn** is more formal and often more public; although it implies deep emotion felt over a period of time, that emotion may be more ceremonial than sincere (*the people mourned the loss of their leader*). **Lament** comes from the Latin word meaning to wail or weep, and it therefore suggests a vocal or verbal expression of loss (*The women lamented their husbands' death by shrieking and tearing their clothes*). **Bemoan** also suggests suppressed or inarticulate sounds of *grief*, often expressing regret or disapproval (*to bemoan one's fate*). **Sorrow** combines deep sadness with regret and often pertains to a less tragic loss than *grieve* or *mourn* (*to sorrow over missed opportunities*), while **rue** has even stronger connotations of regret and repentance (*she rued the day she was born*).

mournful adjective 1 *mournful music* sad, sorrowful, doleful, gloomy, somber, melancholy, lugubrious, funereal, elegiac. 2 *had such a mournful expression* | *looked so mournful* sad,

doleful, dejected, depressed, downcast, disconsolate, melancholy, gloomy, miserable, lugubrious, woeful, unhappy, heavy-hearted, somber.
Antonyms: JOYFUL; HAPPY; MERRY.

mourning noun **1** *the mourning of the bereaved* grief, grieving, sorrowing, lamentation, keening, wailing, weeping, moaning. **2** *wear mourning* black clothes, black; sackcloth and ashes.

mousy adjective **1** *a mousy person* timid, fearful, timorous, self-effacing, unobtrusive, unassertive, withdrawn, shy. **2** *mousy hair/colors* brownish-gray, grayish, gray, dun-colored, colorless, neutral, drab, dull, lackluster.

mouth noun **1** *open their mouths* lips, jaws, maw, muzzle; *inf.* trap, chops, kisser. **2** *mouth of the cave/trumpet* opening, entrance, entry, inlet, door, doorway, gateway, portal, hatch, aperture, orifice, vent, cavity, crevice, rim, lips. **3** *the mouth of the river* estuary, outlet, embouchure. **4** *he's all mouth and no action* empty talk, idle talk, babble, claptrap, boasting, bragging, braggadocio; *inf.* hot air, gas. **5** *don't take any mouth from her* impudence, cheek, insolence, impertinence, rudeness, incivility, effrontery, audacity; *inf.* lip, back talk. **down in the mouth** down, downhearted, dejected, downcast, low in spirits, depressed, dispirited, discouraged, disheartened, disconsolate, crestfallen, miserable, unhappy; *inf.* down in the dumps.

mouthful noun bite, swallow, spoonful, forkful, nibble, sip, sup, taste, drop, bit, piece, morsel, sample.

mouthpiece noun **1** *he is his company's mouthpiece* spokesman, spokeswoman, spokesperson, negotiator, intermediary, mediator, agent, representative. **2** *he publishes the mouthpiece of the union* organ, journal, periodical, publication.

movable adjective mobile, transportable, transferable, portable.

move verb **1** *men moving slowly* go, walk, march, proceed, progress, advance. **2** *move objects* carry, transport, transfer, transpose, change over, shift, switch. **3** *time moves fast* progress, advance, pass. **4** *the government must move soon* take action, act, do something, get moving. **5** *our neighbors are moving* relocate, change houses, move away, leave, go away. **6** *she was moved by the performance* affect, touch, impress, upset, disturb, disquiet, agitate; make an impression on, have an impact on, tug on someone's heartstrings. **7** *the sight moved her to tears* provoke, incite, actuate, rouse, excite, urge, incline, stimulate, motivate, influence, persuade, lead, prompt, cause, impel, induce. **8** *as the spirit moves him | she was moved to act* activate, get going, propel, drive, push, shift, motivate. **9** *nothing can move him on that | she will not move on this issue* change, budge, change someone's

mind; *inf.* do an about-face, do a U-turn. **10** *I move that the meeting be adjourned* propose, put forward, advocate, recommend, submit, urge, suggest. **11** *the goods are not moving* sell, be sold, move from the shelf, retail, be marketed.
Antonyms: STAND; STAY; DETER.

move noun **1** *birds frightened by the slightest move* movement, motion, moving, action, activity, gesture, gesticulation. **2** *arrange our move* removal, change of house/address/job, relocation, transfer. **3** *plan our next move* action, act, deed, measure, step, tack, maneuver, tactic, stratagem, ploy, ruse, trick. **4** *it's your move in the game* turn; opportunity, chance; *inf.* shot. **get a move on** hurry up, make haste, speed up, move faster, get moving; *inf.* get cracking, make it snappy, step on it, shake a leg. **make a move** take action, act, do something. **on the move 1** *cars/birds on the move* moving, in motion, going, traveling, journeying, under way, on the wing. **2** *things are on the move* progressing, making progress, advancing, moving/going forward.

movement noun **1** *the movement of the furniture* moving, carrying, transportation, transferral, shifting. **2** *make a sudden movement* moving, move, motion, action, activity, gesture, gesticulation. **3** *the movement of time* progress, progression, advance, passing, passage. **4** *the clock's movement* mechanism, machinery, works, workings, action, wheels; *inf.* innards, guts. **5** *form a peace movement* group, party, organization, faction, wing, coalition, front. **6** *mount a peace movement* campaign, crusade, drive. **7** *play the first movement* part, section, passage. **8** *a movement toward better government* trend, tendency, drift, swing, current. **9** *no movement in the stock market* rise/fall, change, variation, fluctuation. **10** *some movement has been made in the situation* progress, advance, improvement, step forward, breakthrough.

moving adjective **1** *a moving story* affecting, touching, emotive, emotional, poignant, pathetic, stirring, arousing, upsetting, disturbing. **2** *moving parts* movable, mobile, motile, unfixed. **3** *the moving force behind the scheme* driving, dynamic, impelling, motivating, stimulating, inspirational.
Antonyms: UNEMOTIONAL; IMMOBILE; INERT.

---

moving
affecting, pathetic, poignant, touching

A movie about the Holocaust might be described as **moving**, since it arouses emotions or strong feelings, particularly feelings of pathos. A movie about a young girl's devotion to her dog might more accurately be described as **touching**, which means arousing tenderness or compassion, while a movie dealing with a young girl's first experience with love would be **poignant**, since it pierces one's heart or keenly affects one's sensibilities. While *poignant* implies a bittersweet response that combines pity and longing or other contradictory emotions, **pathetic** means simply moving one to pity (*a pathetic scene in which the dog struggled to save his drowning mistress*). Almost any well-made film can be **affecting**, a more general term that suggests moving one to tears or some other display of feeling (*the affecting story of a daughter's search for her birth mother*).

---

mow *verb* cut, trim, crop, clip, scythe, shear. **mow down** *armies mowing down the townspeople* slaughter, massacre, butcher, cut to pieces, cut down, decimate.

much *adjective not much time | much trouble* a great/large amount of, a great deal of, plenty of, ample, copious, abundant; *inf.* a lot of, lots of.
Antonyms: LITTLE; SCANT.

much *adverb* **1** *I much regret it* greatly, to a great extent/degree, exceedingly, considerably, decidedly, indeed; *inf.* a lot. **2** *he's not here much* often, frequently; *inf.* a lot.

much *noun he doesn't know much* a good deal, a great deal; *inf.* a lot, lots.

muck *noun* **1** *clear the muck from the barn* dung, manure, ordure, excrement, guano, droppings, feces. **2** *clean the muck from the car* dirt, grime, filth, mud, slime, sludge, scum, mire; *inf.* gunk, grunge.

muck *verb* **muck up** botch, bungle, muff, make a mess of, mess up, mar, spoil, ruin; *inf.* make a hash of, foul up, screw up.

mud *noun* sludge, clay, silt, mire, dirt, soil.

muddle *verb* **1** *muddle the dates | he's muddled up the situation* confuse, get confused, mix up, jumble, jumble up, scramble, disarrange, disorganize, throw into disorder, get into a tangle, make a mess of, mess up. **2** *numbers muddle her* confuse, disorient, bewilder, befuddle, daze, perplex, puzzle, baffle, nonplus, confound.

muddle *noun* **1** *files in a muddle* chaos, disorder, disarray, confusion, disorganization, jumble, mix-up, mess, clutter, tangle. **2** *she's in a muddle | her mind is in a muddle* state of confusion, disorientation, bewilderment, perplexity, puzzlement, bafflement.

muddled *adjective* **1** *muddled files* chaotic, in disorder, in disarray, disorganized, jumbled, mixed-up, scrambled, tangled. **2** *muddled people* confused, disoriented, at sea, befuddled, bewildered, dazed, perplexed. See MUDDLE *verb* 2. **3** *muddled thinking/logic* confused, jumbled, incoherent, unclear, woolly, muddied.
Antonyms: ORDERLY; CLEAR; LUCID.

muddy *adjective* **1** *a muddy substance* mucky, miry, oozy, slushy, slimy. **2** *muddy ground/field* marshy, boggy, swampy. **3** *muddy shoes* mudcaked, dirty, filthy, grubby, grimy. **4** *muddy stream/liquid/colors* cloudy, murky, smoky, dingy, dull, turbid, opaque, brownish-green. **5**

muddy thinking confused, jumbled, incoherent, unclear, muddied, woolly.

muddy *verb* **1** *muddy the waters | muddied his hands* dirty, begrime, soil. **2** *muddy the issue* make unclear, cloud, confuse, mix up, jumble, scramble, get into a tangle.

muffle *verb muffle the sound* deaden, dull, dampen, stifle, smother, suppress, soften, hush, mute, silence.

muffled *adjective muffled sound* faint, indistinct, unclear, dull, muted, dampened, stifled, smothered, suppressed.

mug *noun* **1** *a mug of cocoa | beer mug* cup, tankard, stein, glass, toby jug. **2** *the sour expression gave him an ugly mug* face, countenance, visage, features; *inf.* puss, kisser, mush.

mug *verb* assault, attack, beat up, knock down, rob; *inf.* rough up, do over.

muggy *adjective* close, stuffy, sultry, oppressive, airless, humid, clammy, sticky.
Antonyms: FRESH; AIRY.

mull *verb* **mull over** think over, think about, consider, ponder, reflect on, contemplate, meditate on, deliberate about/on, muse on, ruminate over/on, weigh up, have one's mind on, examine, study, review.

multifarious *adjective* many, multiple, numerous, legion, sundry, diverse, diversified, varied, variegated, manifold, different, miscellaneous, assorted.

multiple *adjective* several, many, numerous, various, collective, manifold.

multiply *verb* **1** *people multiplying in great numbers* breed, reproduce. **2** *troubles are multiplying* increase, grow, accumulate, augment, proliferate, spread.

multitude *noun* **1** *multitude of people* crowd, assembly, throng, host, horde, mass, mob, legion, army; *inf.* a lot, lots. **2** *treated the multitude with disdain* common people, masses, populace, commonality, proletariat, mob, crowd, rabble, hoi polloi, canaille; *inf.* great unwashed.

munch *verb* chew, champ, chomp, masticate, crunch, eat.

mundane *adjective* **1** *mundane issues/prose* common, ordinary, everyday, workaday, usual, prosaic, pedestrian, routine, customary, regular, normal, typical, commonplace, banal, hackneyed, trite, stale, platitudinous. **2** *mundane, not spiritual, matters* worldly, earthly, terrestrial, secular, temporal, fleshly, carnal, sensual.
Antonyms: EXTRAORDINARY; IMAGINATIVE; SPIRITUAL.

municipal *adjective* civic, civil, city, metropolitan, urban, town, borough, community, public.

munificence *noun* **1** *the munificence of the host* bounty, bountifulness, bounteousness, liberality, generosity, charity, charitableness, magnanimity, magnanimousness, largesse. *See*

MUNIFICENT 1. **2** *the munifence of the supplies* abundance, copiousness, profusion. *See* MUNIFICENT 2.

munificent *adjective* **1** *he is a munificent provider* bountiful, bounteous, liberal, generous, free, openhanded, charitable, hospitable, bighearted, beneficent, benevolent, ungrudging, magnanimous, philanthropic. **2** *munificent supplies of food* plentiful, ample, abundant, copious, lavish, profuse, princely.
Antonyms: STINGY; MISERLY; MEAGER.

murder *noun* **1** *commit murder | guilty of murder* killing, slaying, manslaughter, homicide, slaughter, assassination, butchery, carnage, massacre. **2** *driving there at night was murder* an ordeal, a trial, a frustrating/unpleasant/difficult/dangerous experience, a misery, agony; *inf.* hell, hell on earth.

murder *verb* **1** *murder his brother* kill, slay, put to death, take the life of, shed the blood of, slaughter, assassinate, butcher, massacre; *inf.* bump off, do in, eliminate, hit, rub out, blow away. **2** *murder the song* mangle, mutilate, ruin, make a mess of, spoil, mar, destroy. **3** *they murdered our team* trounce, beat soundly, beat decisively, thrash, defeat utterly, give a drubbing to; *inf.* slaughter, hammer, make mincemeat of.

murderer *noun* killer, slayer, homicide, slaughterer, cutthroat, assassin, butcher, patricide, matricide, fratricide. *See* MURDER *noun* 1.

murderous *adjective* **1** *a murderous blow* fatal, lethal, deadly, mortal, death-dealing, homicidal, savage, barbarous, brutal, bloodthirsty, bloody. **2** *a murderous climb* arduous, difficult, strenuous, exhausting, formidable, harrowing, dangerous; *inf.* killing, hellish.

murky *adjective* **1** *murky streets/shadows* dark, dim, gloomy. **2** *murky weather* foggy, misty, cloudy, lowering, overcast, dull, gray, dismal, dreary, cheerless. **3** *murky pools* dirty, muddy, dingy, dull, cloudy, turbid, opaque. **4** *a murky past* dark, questionable, doubtful, obscure, enigmatic, nebulous, mysterious, hidden, secret.
Antonyms: BRIGHT; CLEAR; BLAMELESS.

murmur *noun* **1** *the murmur of the stream* babble, burble, whisper, rustle, buzzing, drone, sigh; *inf.* whoosh. **2** *tell him in a murmur* whisper, undertone, mutter, mumble. **3** *have heard murmurs against his presidency* mutter, grumble, moan, complaint, carping, whisper; *inf.* grouse, gripe, beef, bitch.

murmur *verb* **1** *streams murmuring* babble, burble, whisper, rustle, buzz, drone, sigh; *inf.* whoosh. **2** *murmured that she wished to leave* whisper, speak in an undertone, speak sotto voce, mutter, mumble. **murmur against** *murmur against the government* mutter against, grumble, moan, complain, carp; *inf.* grouse, gripe, beef, bitch.

Antonyms: SHOUT; YELL.

muscle *noun* **1** *strain a muscle* muscular tissue, sinew, tendon, ligament, thew. **2** *a man with muscle* muscularity, brawn; *inf.* beef. **3** *the new chairperson has no muscle* power, potency, force, forcefulness, might, strength, weight, influence; *inf.* clout, pull.

muscle *verb* **muscle in on** *trust him to muscle in on our trip* push/force one's way into, elbow one's way into, impose oneself on, invite oneself to; *inf.* butt in on.

muscular *adjective* **1** *muscular tissue/pain* sinewy, fibrous. **2** *muscular men* brawny, strapping, powerfully built, solidly built, hefty, stalwart, sturdy, rugged, burly; *inf.* beefy, husky. **3** *a muscular character/attempt* vigorous, potent, powerful, strong, energetic, active, dynamic, aggressive, determined, resolute.
Antonyms: WEAK; PUNY; FEEBLE.

muse *verb* **1** *stand and muse* think, meditate, be lost in contemplation/thought, be in a brown study, reflect, deliberate, daydream, be in a reverie. **2** *muse over the situation* think over, think about, consider, ponder, reflect on, contemplate, meditate on, deliberate about/on, mull over, ruminate over/on, weigh up, have one's mind on, examine, study, review. **3** *"I wonder," he mused* say thoughtfully/reflectively/meditatively.

mushroom *noun* *gather/cook mushrooms* fungus; field mushroom, chanterelle, morel, shiitake, wood ear; toadstool, angel of death, death cap.

mushroom *verb* *new industries mushrooming* spring up, shoot up, sprout, burgeon, burst forth, grow/develop rapidly, boom, thrive, flourish, prosper.

music *noun* melody, tune, air, rhythm, harmonization, orchestration.

musical *adjective* tuneful, melodic, melodious, harmonious, lyrical, sweet-sounding, mellifluous, dulcet, euphonious.
Antonyms: DISCORDANT; HARSH; GRATING.

musing *noun* thinking, meditation, contemplation, deliberation, pondering, reflection, rumination, daydreaming, reverie, brown study, woolgathering.

muss *verb* disarrange, misarrange, put out of place, make untidy, make a mess of, mess up, rumple, dishevel, tousle.

must[1] *noun* *the new show is a must* something not to be missed, essential, necessity, necessary thing, imperative, requirement, requisite, prerequisite.

must[2] *noun* *a smell of must* mold, mustiness, moldiness, mildew, fungus.

muster *verb* **1** *muster the soldiers* assemble, bring together, call/gather together, call up, summon, rally, mobilize, round up, marshal, collect, convoke. **2** *we must muster at dawn* assemble, gather together, come together, meet, congregate, convene. **3** *muster one's courage* call up, gather together, summon, rally, screw up.

muster *noun* *soldiers present for the muster* assembly, assemblage, rally, mobilization, call-up, roundup, convocation, meeting, congregation, convention. **pass muster** measure up, come up to scratch/snuff, be acceptable, qualify; *inf.* make the grade, fill/fit the bill.

musty *adjective* **1** *musty books/food/rooms* moldy, mildewed, mildewy, fusty, decaying, stale, stuffy, airless, damp, dank. **2** *musty ideas* antiquated, obsolete, ancient, antediluvian, out of date, outdated, old-fashioned, out-of-fashion, out-of-style, behind the times, passé, hoary, moth-eaten, worn-out, threadbare, hackneyed, trite, clichéd.
Antonyms: FRESH; MODERN.

mutable *adjective* changeable, variable, alterable, convertible, adaptable, modifiable, transformable, transmutable, inconstant, unsteady, unstable, vacillating, wavering, unsettled, inconsistent, volatile, capricious.

mutation *noun* **1** *undergo genetic mutation* change, variation, alteration, modification, transformation, metamorphosis, evolution, transmutation, transfiguration. **2** *the creature is a genetic mutation* mutant, deviant, anomaly, freak.

mute *adjective* **1** *mute with surprise* silent, speechless, wordless, unspeaking, taciturn, uncommunicative. **2** *animals born mute* dumb, voiceless, speechless, aphasic, aphonic. **3** *a mute appeal* silent, wordless, unexpressed, unspoken.
Antonyms: VOLUBLE; SPOKEN.

mute *verb* **1** *mute the sound* deaden, dull, dampen, muffle, stifle, smother, suppress, soften, quieten, soft-pedal, turn down. **2** *mute the color scheme* soften, subdue, tone down, make less intense.

muted *adjective* *muted colors* soft, softened, subdued, subtle, discreet, toned down, quiet, understated.

mutilate *verb* **1** *mutilated in the accident* cut to pieces, cut up, lacerate, hack up, butcher, mangle, cripple, maim, lame, disable, disfigure, damage, injure, impair; dismember, tear limb from limb, amputate limbs from. **2** *mutilate a text* mar, spoil, ruin, damage, butcher, mangle, distort, cut, hack, censor, bowdlerize, expurgate.

mutinous *adjective* rebellious, insurgent, insurrectionary, revolutionary, anarchistic, subversive, seditious, traitorous, insubordinate, disobedient, riotous, rioting, unruly, disorderly, restive, contumacious, refractory, out of control, uncontrollable, ungovernable, unmanageable.

mutiny *noun* rebellion, revolt, insurrection, insurgence, insurgency, uprising, rising, riot, revolution, resistance, disobedience, defiance, insubordination, protest, strike.

mutiny *verb* rebel, revolt, take part in an insurrection/insurgence/uprising, riot, rise up, resist/oppose authority, defy authority, be insubordinate, protest, strike.

mutter *verb* **1** *going along muttering* talk under one's breath, talk to oneself, whisper, speak in an undertone, speak sotto voce, mumble, murmur. **2** *mutter against the government* murmur, grumble, moan, complain, carp; *inf.* grouse, gripe, beef, bitch.

muzzle *noun* **1** *the collie's muzzle is longer than the terrier's* mouth, jaw, maw; snout, nose. **2** *put a muzzle on the dangerous dog* gag, guard, restraint, bridle.

muzzle *verb* **1** *muzzle the dog* put a muzzle on, gag, bridle. **2** *attempts to muzzle the press* silence, impose silence on, censor, suppress, stifle, inhibit, restrain, check, fetter.

myopic *adjective* **1** *too myopic to go without eyeglasses* nearsighted, shortsighted, purblind. **2** *a committee of myopic people* narrow, narrow-minded, shortsighted, insular, parochial, provincial, limited, prejudiced, intolerant, unimaginative, uncreative.

myriad *noun* *a myriad of butterflies in the sky* great number/quantity, scores, multitude, host, horde, army, legion, mass, throng, swarm, sea; *inf.* millions, thousands, oodles, zillions, a lot.

myriad *adjective* *myriad colors* innumerable, countless, incalculable, immeasurable, numerous, multitudinous, multifarious, manifold, multiple, several, many, various, sundry, diverse.

mysterious *adjective* **1** *the ways of nature are mysterious* enigmatic, inscrutable, impenetrable, incomprehensible, inexplicable, unexplainable, unfathomable, unaccountable, insoluble, obscure, arcane, abstruse, cryptic, unknown, recondite, secret, preternatural, supernatural, uncanny, mystical, peculiar, strange, weird, curious, bizarre, undisclosed, mystifying, baffling, puzzling, perplexing, bewildering, confounding. **2** *he was being very mysterious about his whereabouts* secretive, reticent, noncommittal, discreet, evasive, furtive, surreptitious.
Antonyms: OBVIOUS; STRAIGHTFORWARD; OPEN.

mystery *noun* **1** *his death remains a mystery* enigma, puzzle, secret, unsolved problem, problem, riddle, conundrum, question, question mark, closed book, unexplored ground, terra incognita. **2** *his whereabouts are clothed in mystery* secrecy, concealment, obscurity, obscuration, vagueness, nebulousness, inscrutability, inexplicability.

mystic, mystical *adjective* **1** *a mystic experience* spiritual, paranormal, transcendental, otherworldly, supernatural, preternatural, nonrational, occult, metaphysical. **2** *mystic rites* symbolic, representational, allegorical, metaphorical, emblematic, emblematical, nonliteral. **3** *mystical events* obscure, cryptic, enigmatic, abstruse, arcane, recondite, inscrutable, inexplicable, unfathomable, mysterious.

mystify *verb* confuse, bewilder, confound, perplex, baffle, nonplus, puzzle, elude, escape; *inf.* stump, beat, bamboozle.

myth *noun* **1** *read ancient myths* legend, saga, tale, story, fable, folk tale, allegory, parable, fairy tale/story, bestiary. **2** *her having a rich father was just a myth* fantasy, delusion, figment of the imagination, invention, fabrication, untruth, lie; *inf.* story, fairy tale/story, tall tale.

mythical *adjective* **1** *a mythical creature* legendary, mythological, fabled, chimerical, imaginary, imagined, fabulous, fantastical, fairy-tale, storybook, fictitious, allegorical. **2** *a mythical rich uncle* fantasy, imagined, imaginary, pretended, make-believe, unreal, fictitious, invented, fabricated, made-up, untrue; *inf.* pretend.

Antonyms: REAL; ACTUAL.

mythology *noun* body of myths, myth, myths, legend, lore, folklore, folk tales, stories.

N

nadir *noun* the lowest point, the lowest level, the bottom, rock-bottom, the depths, all-time low, as low as one can get, zero; *inf.* the pits.
Antonyms: ZENITH; ACME; CLIMAX.

nag[1] *verb* **1** *nag him about his schoolwork* scold, carp, pick on, harp on at, be on someone's back, henpeck, bully, upbraid, berate, criticize, find fault with, complain to, grumble to; *inf.* go on (and on) at. **2** *nagging their mother about buying toys* badger, pester, plague, torment, harry, goad, vex, harass, irritate; *inf.* hassle, drive up the wall.

nag[2] *noun* *was always a bit of a nag* shrew, harpy, termagant, faultfinder, carper, caviler, complainer, grumbler.

nag[3] *noun* *ride an old nag* horse, racehorse, pony, dobbin; broken-down horse, hack; *inf.* bag of bones, plug.

nagging *adjective* **1** *a nagging spouse* scolding, carping, caviling, criticizing, faultfinding, complaining, grumbling. *See* NAG[1] *verb* 1. **2** *a nagging pain* persistent, continuous, aching, painful, distressing.

nail *noun* **1** *drive a nail into the wood* pin, brad, tack, rivet, spike. **2** *cut one's nails | the animal's nails* fingernail, toenail, claw, talon, nipper, pincer.

nail *verb* **1** *nail the pieces together* pin, tack, hammer, fix, fasten, secure, join, attach. **2** *nail him at the meeting* get hold of, grab, get the attention of, make someone commit himself/herself, pin down. **3** *nailed the myth* expose, reveal, detect, uncover, unmask, bare, unearth, dig out. **4** *nail the thief* catch, seize, capture, apprehend, arrest, take into custody; *inf.* collar, nab, pinch.

naïve *adjective* **1** *they are still young and naïve* innocent, artless, childlike, simple, ingenuous, guileless, trusting, unsophisticated, unworldly, jejune, natural, unaffected, unpretentious, frank, open, candid. **2** *exploited the naïve employees* gullible, overtrusting, overtrustful, credulous, unsuspicious, unsuspecting, deceivable, dupable, callow, raw, green, immature, inexperienced; *inf.* wet behind the ears.
Antonyms: DISINGENUOUS; EXPERIENCED; WORLDLY.

naïveté *noun* **1** *the young girl's naïveté* naïveness, innocence, artlessness, simplicity, ingenuousness, guilelessness, lack of guile, unsophistication, lack of sophistication, unworldliness, naturalness, candor. **2** *took advantage of their naïveté* naïveness, gullibility, credulousness,

credulity, overtrustfulness, lack of suspicion, callowness, greenness, immaturity.

naked *adjective* **1** *naked sunbathers* stark naked, nude, in the nude, bare, stripped, exposed, unclothed, undressed, uncovered, undraped, disrobed, au naturel; *inf.* without a stitch on, in one's birthday suit, in the raw, in the altogether, in the buff, naked as the day one was born, buck naked. **2** *naked landscapes/rooms* bare, barren, stark, uncovered, denuded, stripped, treeless, grassless, unfurnished. **3** *the naked truth* undisguised, unqualified, unadorned, stark, bald, unvarnished, unveiled, unmitigated, unexaggerated, plain, simple, open, patent, evident, apparent, obvious, manifest, overt, unmistakable, blatant, glaring, flagrant. **4** *naked flames/sword* exposed, unprotected, unguarded, uncovered, unsheathed, unwrapped. **5** *feeling naked in a foreign country* defenseless, unprotected, vulnerable, exposed, helpless, weak, powerless.
Antonyms: clothed; embellished.

---

naked
bald, bare, barren, nude

Someone who isn't wearing any clothes is **naked**; this adjective is usually associated with revealing a part or all of the body (*her naked shoulder; a naked man ran from the burning building*). A *naked* person who appears in a painting or photograph is called a **nude**, a euphemistic but more socially acceptable term referring to the unclothed human body. **Bare** can describe the branches of a tree as well as human limbs; it implies the absence of the conventional or appropriate covering (*a bare wooden floor; bare legs; four bare walls*). **Bald** also suggests a lack of covering, but it refers particularly to a lack of natural covering, especially hair (*a bald head*). **Barren** implies a lack of vegetation, and it also connotes destitution and fruitlessness (*a barren wasteland that could barely support life*). A *bald* artist might paint a *nude* woman whose *bare* arms are extended against a *barren* winter landscape.

---

nakedness *noun* **1** *embarrassed at his nakedness* nudity, bareness, undress, state of undress. *See* NAKED 1. **2** *the nakedness of the landscape* bareness, barrenness, starkness. *See* NAKED 2. **3** *her feeling of nakedness in the foreign country* defenselessness, vulnerability, helplessness. *See* NAKED 5.
Antonyms: DRESS; PROTECTION.

namby-pamby *adjective* oversentimental, sentimental, mawkish, maudlin, insipid, colorless, anemic, feeble, weak, vapid, spineless, effeminate, effete, prim, prissy, mincing, simpering; *inf.* wet, wishy-washy, wimpish.

name *noun* 1 *the name of the person/family/plant/tree/book* appellation, designation, cognomen, denomination, sobriquet, title, style, label, tag, epithet, first/second name, Christian/given name, surname, family name, maiden name, nickname, pet name, stage name, pseudonym, alias, nom de guerre, nom de plume; *inf.* moniker, handle. 2 *he's a name in the theater* big name, celebrity, luminary, star, dignitary, VIP, lion; *inf.* celeb, megastar, big shot, bigwig. 3 *make his name in motion pictures* reputation, fame, renown, repute, note, distinction, eminence, prominence, prestige.

name *verb* 1 *name the child/plant* baptize, christen, give a name to, call, entitle, label, style, term, title, dub, denominate. 2 *name the criminal | name the most suitable day* identify, specify, mention, cite, give. 3 *name his successor* appoint, choose, select, pick, nominate, designate.

named *adjective* 1 *a girl named Anne* called, by the name of, under the name of, baptized, christened, entitled, styled. 2 *named individuals/articles* identified, specified, mentioned, cited, given.

nameless *adjective* 1 *nameless graves* unnamed, untitled, unlabeled, untagged, innominate. 2 *nameless poets/benefactors* unnamed, anonymous, unidentified, undesignated, unspecified. 3 *nameless fears/vices* unspeakable, unutterable, inexpressible, unmentionable, indescribable, abominable, horrible, horrific.

namely *adverb* viz, that is to say, i.e., to wit, specifically.

nap[1] *verb children napping in the afternoon* take a nap, catnap, doze, sleep lightly, rest, lie down, drowse; *inf.* drop off, nod off, snooze, catch forty winks, get some shut-eye, get/take some Z's.

nap[2] *noun take/have a nap* catnap, doze, light sleep, rest; *inf.* snooze, forty winks, (some) shut-eye.

nap[3] *noun the nap on velvet/carpets* pile, down, surface, shag, weave, grain, fiber.

narcissism *noun* self-admiration, self-love, conceit, self-conceit, vanity, egotism.

narcissistic *adjective* self-admiring, self-loving, in love with oneself, conceited, vain, egotistic.

narcotic *adjective narcotic substances* opiate, sleep-inducing, soporific, somnolent, hypnotic, anesthetic, stupefying, stupefacient, painkilling, pain-dulling, analgesic, anodyne, numbing, calming, tranquilizing, sedative.

narcotic *noun* drug, opiate, sleeping pill, anesthetic, painkiller, analgesic, anodyne, tranquilizer, sedative, soporific.

narrate *verb* tell, relate, recount, recite, unfold, give an account of, give a report of, set forth, chronicle, describe, detail, portray, sketch out, rehearse, repeat.

narration *noun* 1 *a fascinating narration* account, story, storytelling, tale, telling, relation, recital, reciting, report, chronicling, chronicle, description, portrayal, sketch, rehearsal, repetition. 2 *do the narration for the movie* voice-over, voice, spoken part.

narrative *noun* account, statement, report, chronicle, history, story, tale.

narrator *noun* 1 *spellbound by the narrator* recounter, relater, reporter, describer, chronicler, annalist, storyteller, taleteller, teller of tales, raconteur, anecdotist, author, writer. 2 *the movie's narrator* voice-over.

narrow *adjective* 1 *narrow roads/waists* not wide, not broad, narrow-gauged, slender, thin, slim, slight, spare, attenuated, tapering. 2 *narrow spaces* confined, confining, constricted, tight, cramped, close, restricted, limited, incommodious, pinched, straitened, squeezed, meager, scant, scanty, spare, scrimped, exiguous. 3 *a narrow range* limited, restricted, select, exclusive. 4 *a narrow interpretation* literal, exact, precise, close, faithful. 5 *narrow in her thinking* narrow-minded, intolerant, illiberal, prejudiced, bigoted, parochial, provincial, insular, small-minded. *See* NARROW-MINDED.
Antonyms: WIDE; BROAD; BROAD-MINDED.

narrowly *adverb* 1 *narrowly escaped with his life* barely, scarcely, just, only just, just and no more, by a hair's breadth; *inf.* by a whisker/hair. 2 *look at her opponent narrowly* closely, carefully, scrutinizingly, attentively.

narrow-minded *adjective* intolerant, illiberal, unliberal, overconservative, conservative, hidebound, dyed-in-the-wool, reactionary, close-minded, unreasonable, prejudiced, bigoted, biased, discriminatory, warped, twisted, jaundiced, parochial, provincial, insular, small-minded, petty-minded, petty, mean-spirited, prudish, straitlaced.

narrows *plural noun* strait, sound, channel, passage.

nascent *adjective* beginning, budding, embryonic, incipient, young, growing, developing, evolving, burgeoning, forming.

nastiness *noun* 1 *appalled by the nastiness of the sight/mess/taste/smell* unpleasantness, disagreeableness, vileness, foulness, loathsomeness, ugliness, offensiveness, squalor, filthiness, filth, pollution, unsavoriness, smelliness, stink; *inf.* yuckiness. *See* NASTY 1. 2 *the nastiness of the situation* dangerousness, danger, seriousness. *See* NASTY 2. 3 *the nastiness of his disposition* ill temper, ill nature, ill humor, bad-temperedness, crossness, unpleasantness, viciousness, spitefulness; *inf.* grouchiness. *See* NASTY 3. 4 *the nastiness of the weather* disagreeableness, foulness. *See* NASTY 4. 5 *the nastiness of the videos* obscenity, pornograty, lewdness. *See* NASTY 5.

nasty *adjective* **1** *a nasty sight/mess/taste/smell* unpleasant, disagreeable, distasteful, horrible, vile, foul, hateful, loathsome, revolting, disgusting, odious, obnoxious, repellent, repugnant, ugly, offensive, objectionable, noisome, squalid, dirty, filthy, impure, polluted, tainted, unpalatable, unsavory, unappetizing, evil-smelling, foul-smelling, smelly, stinking, rank, fetid, malodorous, mephitic; *inf.* yucky. **2** *a nasty illness/situation* dangerous, serious, critical, crucial, severe, alarming, threatening. **3** *a nasty person* | *nasty to his mother* ill-tempered, ill-natured, ill-humored, bad-tempered, cross, surly, unpleasant, disagreeable, vicious, spiteful, malicious, mean; *inf.* grouchy. **4** *nasty weather* unpleasant, disagreeable, foul, wet, rainy, stormy, foggy. **5** *nasty jokes/videos* obscene, pornographic, indecent, foul, vile, blue, off-color, smutty, bawdy, vulgar, ribald, risqué, lewd, lascivious, licentious.

Antonyms: DELIGHTFUL; PLEASANT; AGREEABLE.

nation *noun* country, land, state, kingdom, empire, realm, republic, confederation, union of states, commonwealth, people, race, tribe, society, community, population.

national *adjective* **1** *national, not local, issues* state, public, federal, governmental, civic, civil. **2** *national as opposed to international problems* domestic, internal, indigenous, native. **3** *a national strike/search* nationwide, countrywide, state, coast-to-coast, widespread, overall, comprehensive, general.

national *noun* *a national of this country* citizen, subject, native, resident, inhabitant.

nationalism *noun* patriotism, allegiance/loyalty/fealty to one's country, chauvinism, jingoism, xenophobia.

nationalistic *adjective* patriotic, loyal to one's country, pro one's country, chauvinistic, jingoistic, xenophobic.

nationality *noun* nation, race, ethnic group, tribe. *See also table at* PEOPLE.

nationwide *adjective* national, countrywide, state, coast-to-coast, widespread, overall, comprehensive, all-embracing, general, extensive.

native *adjective* **1** *native instinct* inborn, inherent, innate, connate, built-in, intrinsic, instinctive, intuitive, natural, natural-born, congenital, hereditary, inherited, in the blood, in the family, inbred, ingrained. **2** *native plants/produce* indigenous, original, homegrown, homemade, domestic, local. **3** *native tongue* mother, vernacular. **4** *native peoples* original, indigenous, aboriginal, autochthonous.

---

native
aboriginal, endemic, indigenous
A **native** NewYorker is probably not **indigenous**, although both words apply to persons or things that belong to or are associated with a particular place by birth or origin. *Native* means

born or produced in a specific region or country (*native plants; native dances*), but it can also apply to persons or things that were introduced from elsewhere some time ago—which is the case with most New Yorkers who consider themselves natives. *Indigenous*, on the other hand, is more restricted in meaning; it applies only to someone or something that is not only native but was not introduced from elsewhere (*the pumpkin is indigenous to America*). Generally speaking, *native* applies to individual organisms, while *indigenous* applies to races or species. Something that is **endemic** is prevalent in a particular region because of special conditions there that favor its growth or existence (*heather is endemic in the Scottish Highlands; malaria is endemic in Central America*). There are no longer any **aboriginal** New Yorkers, a word that refers to the earliest known inhabitants of a place or to ancient peoples who have no known ancestors and have inhabited a region since its earliest historical time. Australia is known for its *aboriginal* culture, which was preserved for centuries through geographical isolation.

---

native *noun* *a native of France* | *natives of other continents* inhabitant, dweller, resident, citizen, national, aborigine, autochthon.

---

native
aboriginal, endemic, indigenous
A **native** NewYorker is probably not **indigenous**, although both words apply to persons or things that belong to or are associated with a particular place by birth or origin. **Native** means born or produced in a specific region or country (*native plants, native dances*), but it can also apply to persons or things that were introduced from elsewhere some time ago-which is the case with most New Yorkers who consider themselves natives. **Indigenous**, on the other hand, is more restricted in meaning; it applies only to something or someone that is not only **native** but was not introduced from elsewhere (*the pumpkin is indigenous to America*). Generally speaking, **native** applies to individual organisms, while **indigenous** applies to races or species. Something that is **endemic** is prevalent in a particular region because of special conditions there that favor its growth or existence (*heather is endemic in the Scottish Highlands; malaria is endemic in Central America*). There are no longer any **aboriginal** New Yorkers, a word that refers to the earliest known inhabitants of a place or to ancient peoples who have no known ancestors and have inhabited a region since its earliest historical time. Australia is known for its **aboriginal** culture, which was preserved for centuries through geographical isolation.

nativity noun birth, childbirth, delivery, parturition.

natty adjective dapper, trim, spruce, well-turned-out, well-dressed, smart, stylish, fashionable, chic, elegant; inf. snazzy, trendy.

natural adjective 1 in the natural course of events usual, normal, regular, common, ordinary, everyday, typical, routine, run-of-the-mill. 2 her natural instincts native, native-born, inborn, inherent, innate, connate, built-in, intrinsic, instinctive, intuitive, natural, natural-born, congenital, hereditary, inherited, ingrained. 3 natural charm artless, ingenuous, candid, open, frank, genuine, real, authentic, simple, unsophisticated, unaffected, unpretentious, spontaneous, relaxed, unstudied. 4 natural produce organic, pure, unrefined, unpolished, unbleached, unmixed, whole, plain, real, chemical-free, additive-free.
Antonyms: ABNORMAL; UNNATURAL; ARTIFICIAL; STUDIED.

naturalist noun botanist, biologist, zoologist, ecologist, natural historian.

naturalistic adjective realistic, real-life, true-to-life, lifelike, factual, graphic, representational; inf. warts and all.

naturalize verb 1 people wishing to be naturalized endow with rights of citizenship, confer citizenship on, enfranchise. 2 plants becoming naturalized introduce, acclimatize, domesticate, acclimate. 3 new words having been naturalized adopt, accept, take in, assimilate, absorb, incorporate, homogenize.

naturally adverb 1 behave naturally artlessly, ingenuously, candidly, unaffectedly, unpretentiously, spontaneously. See NATURAL 3. 2 naturally, he is going of course, certainly, as might be expected, as you/one would expect, as was anticipated.

naturalness noun 1 the naturalness of her charm artlessness, ingenuousness, openness, genuineness, simplicity, unsophistication, lack of sophistication, lack of affectation, unpretentiousness, spontaneity. 2 the naturalness of the produce purity, pureness, wholeness, lack of chemicals, lack of additives.

nature noun 1 it is in the nature of the species character, characteristic, essence, essential qualities/attributes/features/traits, constitution, makeup, complexion, stamp, personality, identity. 2 communing with nature Mother Nature, natural forces, creation, the environment, the earth, mother earth, the world, the universe, the cosmos; landscape, scenery. 3 things of this nature kind, sort, ilk, type, variety, description, category, class, classification, species, style. 4 he has a pleasant nature temperament, temper, personality, disposition, humor, mood, outlook.

naught, nought noun nothing, nil, zero, nothingness; inf. zilch, goose egg.

naughty adjective 1 a naughty child bad, mischievous, badly behaved, misbehaving, disobedient, defiant, unruly, roguish, wayward, delinquent, undisciplined, unmanageable, ungovernable, fractious, refractory, perverse, errant; sinful, wicked, evil. 2 naughty magazines blue, risqué, smutty, dirty, off-color, indecent, improper, vulgar, bawdy, ribald, lewd, licentious.
Antonyms: GOOD; well-behaved; OBEDIENT; DECENT.

nausea noun 1 travelers overcome by nausea sickness, vomiting, retching, gagging, biliousness, queasiness, faintness, seasickness, carsickness, airsickness, motion sickness, morning sickness; inf. throwing-up. 2 horror movies causing feelings of nausea disgust, revulsion, repugnance, distaste, aversion, loathing, abhorrence, detestation, odium.

nauseate verb make sick, sicken, make one's gorge rise, turn one's stomach, revolt, disgust, repel, repulse, offend; inf. make someone want to throw up, gross out.

nauseous adjective 1 nauseous food nauseating, sickening, disgusting, revolting. 2 a nauseous sight disgusting, revolting, repulsive, repellent, repugnant, offensive, loathsome, abhorrent, odious. 3 feeling nauseous nauseated, sick, sickly, queasy, green, unwell, indisposed, seasick, carsick, airsick; inf. green around the gills, under the weather, out of sorts, below par.

nautical adjective maritime, naval, marine, seagoing, seafaring, yachting, boating, sailing.

navel noun umbilicus; inf. belly-button.

navigable adjective 1 navigable rivers negotiable, passable, traversable, clear, unobstructed. 2 navigable vessels steerable, sailable, seaworthy, watertight.

navigate verb 1 the captain/passenger navigated direct the course, plan/plot the course, give directions, map-read. 2 navigate the craft steer, pilot, maneuver, guide, direct, handle, drive, skipper. 3 navigate the Atlantic sail, sail across, cross, traverse, cruise, journey, voyage.

navigation noun 1 the navigation of the craft steering, pilotage, maneuvering, guidance, directing, handling, driving. 2 study navigation sailing, seamanship, pilotage, helmsmanship, chart-reading, map-reading.

navigator noun pilot, helmsman, seaman, mariner.

navy noun naval force(s), fleet, flotilla, armada.

near adjective 1 the store is near close, close by, nearby, alongside, at close range/quarters, accessible, within reach, close/near at hand, at hand, handy, not far off/away, a stone's throw away, neighboring, adjacent, adjoining, bordering, contiguous, proximate; inf. within spitting distance. 2 the time is near | the near future close/near at hand, approaching, coming, imminent, forthcoming, in the offing, impending, looming, proximate, immediate. 3 near relatives closely related, related, connect-

4 *a near escape* close, narrow, by a hair's breadth; *inf.* by a whisker/hair. **near miss** narrow escape; *inf.* close shave, close call.
Antonyms: FAR; DISTANT; REMOTE.

near *adverb they live near* close, nearby, close by, alongside, close/near at hand, at hand, within reach, within close range, within earshot, within sight, not far off/away, a stone's throw away; *inf.* within spitting distance.

near *preposition near the house* close to, close by, in the neighborhood of, next to, adjacent to, alongside, bordering on, contiguous to, adjoining, within reach of, a stone's throw away from; *inf.* within spitting distance of.

near *verb we are nearing our destination* get near to, draw near to, get close to, approach, come close to, come toward, move toward, lean toward.

nearly *adverb nearly gone* almost, all but, as good as, virtually, next to, close to, well-nigh, about, just about, practically, roughly, approximately, not quite; *inf.* pretty nearly/much/well.

nearness *noun* 1 *the nearness of the stores* closeness, accessibility, handiness, proximity, propinquity. *See* NEAR *adjective* 1. 2 *the nearness of the wedding day* closeness, imminence, immediacy. *See* NEAR *adjective* 2. 3 *the nearness of the relatives* closeness, intimacy, familiarity. *See* NEAR *adjective* 3.

nearsighted *adjective* shortsighted, myopic, purblind.

neat *adjective* 1 *a neat house* neat and tidy, neat as a pin, tidy, orderly, well-ordered, straight, in good order, in Bristol fashion, shipshape and Bristol fashion, in apple-pie order, spick and span. 2 *a neat person/dresser* tidy, spruce, trim, smart, dapper, well-groomed, well-turned-out, dainty, fastidious, organized, well-organized, methodical, systematic; *inf.* natty. 3 *wearing neat clothes* simple, plain, unadorned, unornamented, unpretentious, unassuming. 4 *a neat saying* elegant, well-put, apt, well-expressed, well-turned, clever, witty, pithy, felicitous. 5 *neat footwork/movements* adroit, skillful, expert, practiced, dexterous, deft, accurate, precise, nimble, agile, graceful, stylish, effortless, easy. 6 *neat drinks* straight, undiluted, unmixed, pure. 7 *a really neat car/party/person* great, terrific, wonderful, excellent, exceptional, first-class, first-rate.
Antonyms: DISORDERLY; UNTIDY; CLUMSY.

neatly *adverb* 1 *neatly dressed* tidily, smartly, simply, plainly. *See* NEAT 2, 3. 2 *neatly put* aptly, cleverly, wittily, pithily. *See* NEAT 4. 3 *neatly executed steps* adroitly, skillfully, expertly, deftly, precisely, nimbly, agilely, gracefully, effortlessly. *See* NEAT 5.

neatness *noun* 1 *the neatness of the room* tidiness, orderliness, straightness. *See* NEAT 1. 2 *the neatness of her dress* tidiness, spruceness, trimness, smartness, fastidiousness, simplicity, plainness. *See* NEAT 2, 3. 3 *the neatness of the re-*

mark elegance, cleverness, wit, pithiness, aptness, felicity. 4 *the neatness of her movements* adroitness, deftness, precision, nimbleness, grace, gracefulness, ease, effortlessness. *See* NEAT 5.

nebulous *adjective* 1 *nebulous figures in the distance* shapeless, unformed, amorphous, shadowy, dim, indistinct, indefinite, vague, unclear, obscure, misty, cloudy, hazy, fuzzy. 2 *nebulous ideas about his future career* uncertain, indefinite, indeterminate, imprecise, vague, hazy, unformed, abstract, muddled, confused, ambiguous.

necessarily *adverb* 1 *plans that are necessarily vague* of necessity, by force of circumstance, like it or not, perforce. 2 *he will not necessarily have to go* certainly, definitely, undoubtedly, inevitably, unavoidably, inescapably, automatically, incontrovertibly, inexorably.

necessary *adjective* 1 *a necessary reduction in expenditure* needed, needful, essential, required, requisite, vital, indispensable, imperative, mandatory, obligatory, compulsory, de rigueur. 2 *a necessary evil* certain, sure, inevitable, unavoidable, inescapable, inexorable, ineluctable, fated, preordained.
Antonyms: UNNECESSARY; NONESSENTIAL; DISPENSABLE.

---

necessary
essential, indispensable, requisite

Food is **essential** to human life, which means that we must have it to survive. *Essential* can also apply to something that makes up the *essence*, or necessary qualities or attributes, of a thing (*good brakes are essential to safe driving*). Clothing is **indispensable** in Northern climates, which means that it cannot be done without if the specified or implied purpose—in this case, survival—is to be achieved. **Necessary** applies to something without which a condition cannot be fulfilled (*cooperation was necessary to gather the harvest*), although it generally implies a pressing need rather than absolute indispensability. **Requisite** refers to that which is required by the circumstances (*the requisite skills for a botanist*) and generally describes a requirement that is imposed from the outside rather than an inherent need.

---

necessitate *verb* require, make necessary, demand, call for, entail, involve, exact, oblige, compel, impel, force, leave no choice but to.

necessities *plural noun food and clothing are basic necessities* needs, essentials, requisites, requirements, indispensables, fundamentals, necessaries, exigencies.

necessitous *adjective* needy, in need, in want, poor, badly off, impoverished, poverty-stricken, penniless, impecunious, penurious, destitute, indigent, disadvantaged, underprivileged, unable to make ends meet, in straitened circumstances.

necessity noun **1** *silence is a necessity* essential, requisite, requirement, prerequisite, necessary, fundamental, sine qua non, desideratum. **2** *she left out of necessity* need, needfulness, call, force/pressure of circumstance, exigency, obligation. **3** *necessity made them steal* need, neediness, want, poverty, deprivation, privation, penury, destitution, indigence. **4** *a logical necessity that night follows day* certainty, inevitability, inescapability, inexorability, ineluctability, fate, destiny.

necromancer noun spiritualist, spiritist, medium, magician, wizard, warlock, witch, sorcerer/sorceress, enchanter/enchantress, thaumaturgist.

necromancy noun spiritualism, magic, black magic, black art, wizardry, witchcraft, witchery, sorcery, enchantment, spell-casting, spell-weaving, thaumaturgy, demonology, voodooism.

necropolis noun cemetery, graveyard, churchyard, burial ground, burial place, God's acre.

née adjective born, formerly, previously, heretofore.

need verb **1** *it is not broken, but it needs work* have need of, require, necessitate, demand, call for, have occasion for; want, lack, be without. **2** *he needs her* miss, desire, yearn for, long for, pine for, crave. **3** *I did not need to go* have, be under an obligation, be obliged, be compelled, be under a compulsion.

need noun **1** *their needs are few* requirement, want, wish, demand, prerequisite, requisite, essential, desideratum. **2** *he has need of a coat* want, lack, shortage, requirement. **3** *no need to be frightened* | *there is no need to go* necessity, call, force of circumstance, exigency, obligation. **4** *people in need* neediness, want, poverty, deprivation, privation, penury, destitution, indigence. **5** *in one's hour of need* crisis, emergency, urgency, distress, trouble, extremity, exigency.

needful adjective *do what is needful* needed, requisite, required, stipulated, necessary, essential, vital, indispensable.

needle noun **1** *thread the needle* | *vaccinate with a needle* sewing needle, sharp, darner, bodkin, knitting needle; hypodermic needle. **2** *the needle on the dial/compass* arrow, pointer, indicator, magnetic needle. **3** *pricked by a needle in the woods* pine needle, thorn, pricker, bramble, briar, bristle, spine. **4** *phonograph needle* stylus.

needle verb **1** *needle them into action* goad, spur, prod, prick, sting, press, nag, persuade. **2** *deliberately needling the teacher* provoke, bait, harass, annoy, anger, irritate, vex, irk, nettle, ruffle, taunt, pester; *inf.* aggravate, rile, get to.

needless adjective unnecessary, uncalled-for,

gratuitous, undesired, unwanted, pointless, useless, dispensable, expendable, inessential. **Antonyms:** NECESSARY; USEFUL.

needlework noun needlecraft, sewing, stitching, embroidery, tapestry, crocheting.

needy adjective necessitous, poor, disadvantaged, poverty-stricken, deprived, penurious, impecunious, impoverished, penniless, destitute, indigent, on the breadline, in straitened circumstances. **Antonyms:** WEALTHY; AFFLUENT.

ne'er-do-well noun good-for-nothing, wastrel, black sheep, loafer, idler, layabout, shirker, sluggard, drone; *inf.* gold brick, lazybones, goof-off.

nefarious adjective wicked, evil, sinful, iniquitous, villainous, criminal, heinous, atrocious, vile, foul, base, abominable, odious, horrible, horrendous, dreadful, terrible, detestable, loathsome, execrable, depraved, shameful, scandalous, monstrous, outrageous, flagitious.

negate verb **1** *facts negating your theory* nullify, render null and void, annul, void, invalidate, cancel, revoke, rescind, abrogate, repeal, retract, countermand, disestablish, reject, disprove, explode, overrule. **2** *try to negate the existence of God* deny, dispute, call in/into question, gainsay, contradict, disprove, refute, discredit, disclaim, repudiate, renounce, oppose. **Antonyms:** CONFIRM; RATIFY.

negation noun **1** *the negation of the theory* nullification, voiding, cancellation, revocation, rescinding, abrogation, repeal, retraction. See NEGATE 1. **2** *the attempted negation of the existence of God* denial, contradiction, disproval, disclaiming, repudiation. See NEGATE 2. **3** *anarchy is the negation of government* opposite, reverse, antithesis, contrary, converse, want, lack, absence, deficiency. **4** *a life full of negation* nothingness, nothing, nullity, blankness, void, nonexistence, vacuity, nonentity.

negative adjective **1** *negative replies* in the negative, saying "no," rejecting, refusing, dissenting, contradictory, contradicting, contrary, opposing, opposite, opposed, denying, gainsaying. **2** *a rather negative young man* unenthusiastic, uninterested, lackadaisical, colorless, anemic, insipid, vapid, weak, spineless, purposeless. **3** *a negative reaction* pessimistic, defeatist, gloomy, gloom-laden, cynical, jaundiced, critical, faultfinding, complaining, unhelpful, unconstructive, uncooperative. **Antonyms:** POSITIVE; AFFIRMATIVE; ENTHUSIASTIC; OPTIMISTIC.

negative noun *respond with a negative* rejection, refusal, dissension, opposite, denial, contradiction. **in the negative** *reply in the negative* negatively, no, with a negative response.

neglect verb **1** *neglect their children* fail to look after, fail to provide for, abandon, forsake, leave alone. **2** *neglect his work* let slide, skimp on, shirk, be remiss about, be lax about, pay little/no attention to, not attend to, leave undone, procrastinate about. **3** *neglect to lock the door* omit, fail, forget, not remember. **4** *neglect his warning* disregard, ignore, pay no attention/heed to, overlook, disdain, scorn, slight, spurn, rebuff.

Antonyms: care for (*see* CARE); attend to (*see* ATTEND); HEED.

---

neglect
disregard, ignore, overlook, slight

One of the most common reasons why people fail to arrive at work on time is that they **neglect** to set their alarm clocks, a verb that implies a failure to carry out some expected or required action, either intentionally or through carelessness. Some people, of course, choose to **disregard** their employer's rules pertaining to tardiness, which implies a voluntary, and sometimes deliberate, inattention. Others hear the alarm go off and simply **ignore** it, which suggests not only a deliberate decision to **disregard** something but a stubborn refusal to face the facts. No doubt they hope their employers will **overlook** their frequent late arrivals, which implies a failure to see or to take action, which can be either intentional or due to haste or lack of care (*to overlook minor errors*). But they also hope no one will **slight** them for their conduct when it comes to handing out raises and promotions, which means to **disregard** or **neglect** in a disdainful way.

---

neglect *noun* **1** *parents/workers guilty of neglect* negligence, neglectfulness, lack of proper care and attention, remissness, carelessness, heedlessness, lack of concern, unconcern, slackness, laxity, laxness, failure to act, dereliction, default. **2** *his neglect of her warning* disregard, ignoring, inattention to, heedlessness, indifference to, disdain, scorn, slight, spurning, rebuff.

Antonyms: CARE; ATTENTION.

neglected *adjective* **1** *neglected children* uncared for, unkempt, mistreated, abandoned, forsaken. **2** *neglected gardens* untended, derelict, overgrown. **3** *neglected opportunities/warnings* disregarded, ignored, spurned, unappreciated, underestimated.

neglectful *adjective* negligent, remiss, lax, careless, inattentive, heedless, thoughtless, unmindful, forgetful, indifferent, uncaring.

negligence *noun* neglect, remissness, laxity, laxness, dereliction, dereliction of duty, carelessness, inattention, inattentiveness, heedlessness, thoughtlessness, lack of proper care and attention, unmindfulness, forgetfulness, inadvertence, oversight, omission, failure, disregard, default, shortcoming, indifference, slackness, sloppiness, slipshodness, procrastination.

negligent *adjective* neglectful, remiss, lax, careless, inattentive, heedless, thoughtless, unmindful, uncaring, forgetful, disregardful, in-

different, offhand, cursory, slack, sloppy, slapdash, slipshod, procrastinating, dilatory.

Antonyms: CAREFUL; ATTENTIVE; CONSCIENTIOUS.

negligible *adjective a negligible amount* trivial, trifling, insignificant, of no account, not worth bothering about, paltry, petty, tiny, minute, small, minor, inconsequential, inappreciable, imperceptible.

Antonyms: SIGNIFICANT; CONSIDERABLE.

negotiable *adjective* **1** *pay is negotiable* open to discussion, discussable, debatable, subject to bargaining, transactional. **2** *negotiable checks* transferable. **3** *negotiable roads* passable, navigable, crossable, traversable, penetrable, unblocked, unobstructed.

negotiate *verb* **1** *negotiate a deal/settlement* work out, thrash out, arrange, reach an agreement on, agree on, settle, come to terms about, conclude, pull off, bring off, contract, complete, transact, execute, fulfill, orchestrate, engineer. **2** *union and management negotiate* bargain, drive a bargain, hold talks, confer, debate, discuss, discuss terms, discuss a settlement, consult together, parley, haggle, wheel and deal, dicker. **3** *negotiate the hurdles* | *negotiating the icy roads* clear, get over, get through, pass over, make it over, cross, get past, get around, surmount.

negotiation *noun* **1** *the negotiations went on all day* bargaining, conference, debate, talk(s), discussion, consultation, parleying, haggling, wheeling and dealing, dickering. **2** *the negotiation of the settlement* working out, thrashing out, discussing the terms of, settlement, pulling off, transaction. *See* NEGOTIATE 1, 2.

negotiator *noun* arbiter, arbitrator, mediator, go-between, moderator; bargainer, parleyer, haggler, wheeler-dealer, dickerer.

neighborhood *noun* **1** *move to a different neighborhood* district, area, region, locality, part, quarter, precinct, community; *inf.* stamping ground, neck of the woods, hood. **2** *he doesn't live here but somewhere in the neighborhood* vicinity, surrounding district, environs, proximity, purlieus. **in the neighborhood of** *in the neighborhood of $500* around, about, approximately, roughly, nearly, almost, close to, just about.

neighboring *adjective neighboring town/families* adjacent, adjoining, bordering, abutting, contiguous, next, nearby, nearest, closest, near, very near, close/near at hand, not far away, in the vicinity.

neighborly *adjective* friendly, cordial, kind, helpful, obliging, generous, hospitable, companionable, sociable, amiable, affable, genial, well-disposed, civil, easy to get along with.

Antonyms: UNFRIENDLY; UNKIND.

neither *adjective neither sister* not either, not the one nor the other.

nemesis *noun* **1** *nemesis won the day* fate, destiny, retribution, vengeance. **2** *meet his* *nemesis* downfall, undoing, ruin, destruction, Waterloo.

neologism *noun* neology, new word, new term, new phrase, new expression, coinage, newly coined word, made-up word, nonce word, portmanteau word, vogue word; *inf.* buzzword.

neophyte *noun* **1** *neophytes in the religious community* novice, novitiate, convert, proselyte, catechumen. **2** *introducing the neophytes to the club* beginner, newcomer, new member, new entrant, (new) recruit, raw recruit, initiate, novice, novitiate, tyro, greenhorn, learner, trainee, apprentice, probationer, pupil, student; *inf.* rookie.

ne plus ultra *noun* the ultimate, the last word, acme, culmination, perfection, the utmost/uttermost degree.

nepotism *noun* favoritism, patronage, partisanship, partiality, preferential treatment.

nerve *noun* **1** *rock climbing requires nerve* courage, courageousness, bravery, valor, intrepidity, fearlessness, daring, coolness, coolheadedness, boldness, pluck, gameness, mettle, spirit, backbone, fortitude, endurance, firmness of purpose, resolution, stoutheartedness, determination, tenacity, steadfastness; *inf.* grit, guts, spunk, bottle. **2** *she had the nerve to ask for more* temerity, impudence, impertinence, effrontery, cheek, insolence, audacity, boldness, presumption, gall, brazenness; *inf.* brass, chutzpah.

nerve-racking *adjective* stressful, worrying, anxious, disquieting, tense, harrowing, frightening, distressing, difficult, trying, harassing; *inf.* nail-biting.

nerves *plural noun* nervousness, strain, nervous tension, tenseness, tension, stress, anxiety, worry, apprehensiveness, apprehension; *inf.* butterflies in the/one's stomach, the jitters, the willies.

nervous *adjective* **1** *a nervous person | she is of a nervous disposition* easily frightened, timid, timorous, fearful, apprehensive, anxious, edgy, highly strung, tense, strained, excitable, jumpy, hysterical. **2** *feeling nervous about the interview* on edge, edgy, tense, strained, anxious, agitated, worried, fretful, uneasy, disquieted, restless, impatient, excitable, jumpy, on tenterhooks, fidgety, ruffled, flustered, apprehensive, perturbed, fearful, frightened, scared, with one's heart in one's mouth, quaking, trembling, shaking, shaking in one's shoes, shaky; *inf.* with butterflies in one's stomach, jittery, in a state, uptight, wired.
Antonyms: BOLD; CALM; LAID-BACK.

nervous breakdown *noun* breakdown, mental breakdown, nervous collapse, personal crisis, clinical depression; *inf.* crack-up.

nervousness *noun* **1** *given to nervousness* timidity, timorousness, fearfulness, anxiety, tenseness. *See* NERVOUS 1. **2** *a feeling of nervousness about the interview* edginess, tension, nervous tension, stress, anxiety, agitation, worry, uneasiness. *See* NERVOUS 2.

nervy *adjective* pushy, presumptuous, impudent, insolent, impertinent, brash, forward, audacious, bold; *inf.* brassy, fresh.

nescient *adjective* ignorant, unaware, unconscious, unenlightened, benighted, uneducated, illiterate, unschooled, unknowledgeable.

nest *noun* **1** *birds/creatures building nests* bird's nest, aerie; wasp/wasps' nest, ant/ants' nest; lair, den, lodge, burrow. **2** *a love nest | a thieves' nest* retreat, hideaway, hiding place, shelter, refuge, den, haunt; *inf.* hideout. **3** *a nest of tables* set, stackable set, cluster, assemblage, group, series.

nest egg *noun* life savings, savings, reserve funds, reserve, money/something for a rainy day, cache.

nestle *verb* snuggle, curl up, huddle together, cuddle up, nuzzle.

net *noun* **1** *net curtains | ball hit the net* netting, tulle, fishnet, meshwork, mesh, latticework, lattice, openwork, webbing, tracery, reticulum. **2** *fishermen casting their nets | catching specimens in the net* fishing net, dragnet, drift net, seine; butterfly net, crab net. **3** *fall into the enemy's net* trap, booby trap, snare, mesh, pitfall, stratagem.

net *adjective* **1** *their net salary* take-home, after-tax, after-deductions, bottom-line, clear. **2** *the net result* final, ultimate, concluding, conclusive, closing, actual.

net *verb* *was netting $400 per week* take home, clear, earn, make, bring in, get, pocket, receive, gain, obtain, realize; *inf.* pull in.

nether *adjective* **1** *in the nether part of the store* lower, low, low-level, bottom, under, basement, underground. **2** *myths about the nether regions* infernal, hellish, underworld, Hadean, Plutonian, Stygian.
Antonyms: UPPER; higher.

nettle *verb* irritate, provoke, ruffle, try someone's patience, annoy, incense, exasperate, irk, vex, pique, bother, pester, harass, torment, plague; *inf.* aggravate, rile, peeve, rub the wrong way, get under someone's skin, get in someone's hair, get someone's goat, get to.

nettled *adjective* irritated, irritable, provoked, ruffled, annoyed, incensed, irked, vexed, piqued, harassed; *inf.* riled, peeved. *See* NETTLE.

network *noun* **1** *a pattern consisting of a network of lines* meshwork, latticework, openwork, mesh, lattice, webbing, tracery, filigree, fretwork. **2** *a network of old friends | a network of professional women* interconnection, nexus, system, complex, organization, structure, arrangement, formulation. **3** *a network of roads | electronic network* interconnection, grid, circuitry, plexus.

neurosis *noun* mental illness, mental disorder,

psychological disorder, mental disturbance, mental derangement, mental/emotional instability, psychological maladjustment, psychoneurosis, psychopathy, obsession, phobia, fixation.

neurotic *adjective* **1** *treating neurotic patients* mentally ill, mentally disturbed, mentally deranged, unstable, maladjusted, psychopathic, obsessive, phobic. **2** *his wife is completely neurotic* suffering from nerves, overanxious, obsessive, phobic, fixated, compulsive, oversensitive, hysterical, irrational.

Antonyms: STABLE; WELL-BALANCED; CALM; LAID-BACK.

neuter *adjective neuter organisms* asexual, sexless, unsexed.

neuter *verb neuter a cat/bull* castrate, geld, emasculate; spay; *inf.* fix.

neutral *adjective* **1** *referees must be neutral* impartial, unbiased, unprejudiced, open-minded, nonpartisan, without favoritism, evenhanded, disinterested, nonaligned, dispassionate, objective, detached, uninvolved, uncommitted. **2** *neutral countries during the war* noncombatant, noncombative, nonfighting, nonparticipating, nonaligned, unallied, uninvolved, noninterventionist. **3** *he was a rather neutral character* indefinite, indeterminate, unremarkable, ordinary, commonplace, average, run-of-the-mill, everyday, bland, uninteresting, colorless, insipid, dull. **4** *curtains of a neutral color* beige, ecru, gray, taupe, stone-colored, stone, pale, colorless, uncolored, achromatic, achromic.

Antonyms: BIASED; PARTISAN; COMBATANT; COLORFUL.

neutrality *noun* **1** *challenge the neutrality of the referee* impartiality, lack/absence of bias/prejudice, open-mindedness, objectivity, evenhandedness, disinterestedness, detachment. *See* NEUTRAL 1. **2** *the neutrality of the countries* noncombativeness, nonalignment, nonparticipation, noninvolvement, nonintervention, noninterventionism.

neutralize *verb* **1** *neutralize the poison* counteract, cancel, nullify, negate, annul, undo, invalidate, frustrate, be an antidote to. **2** *her warmth neutralizing their hostility* offset, counterbalance, counteract, compensate for, make up for, cancel out, negate.

never *adverb* not ever, at no time, not at any time, not once, not at all, certainly not, not in any circumstances, under no circumstances, on no account; *lit.* ne'er; *inf.* no way, not on your life, not in a million years.

Antonyms: ALWAYS; FOREVER.

never-ending *adjective* **1** *a seemingly never-ending saga* endless, unending, without end, perpetual, everlasting, interminable, without cease/ceasing, ceaseless, unceasing, incessant, nonstop, continuous, continual, uninterrupted, unbroken, unremitting, relentless, persistent; *inf.* eternal. **2** *a never-ending supply of*

books endless, infinite, limitless, boundless. **3** *their never-ending love* endless, without end, perpetual, everlasting, infinite, eternal, lasting, enduring, abiding, constant, unchanging, unwavering, unfaltering.

nevertheless *adverb* none the less, even so, however, but, still, yet, be that as it may, for all that, just the same, all the same, though, in any event/case, notwithstanding, regardless, in spite of that, despite that, nonetheless, anyway.

new *adjective* **1** *new techniques* modern, recent, advanced, state-of-the-art, present-day, contemporary, current, latest, up-to-date, up-to-the-minute, new-fashioned, modish, brand new, newly arrived, modernist, ultramodern, avant-garde, futuristic, newfangled; *inf.* way-out, far-out. **2** *in need of new ideas* modern, state-of-the-art, up-to-date, new-fashioned, novel, original, fresh, unhackneyed, imaginative, creative, experimental. **3** *a new rather than a secondhand book* brand new, unused, unworn, pristine, fresh, mint, in mint condition, virgin. **4** *new people next door | starting a new job* unfamiliar, unknown, strange, different, unaccustomed, untried. **5** *a new room on the house* additional, added, extra, supplementary, further, another. **6** *feel like a new person* refreshed, renewed, improved, restored, reinvigorated, regenerated, reborn, remodeled.

Antonyms: OLD; OBSOLETE; SECONDHAND.

newborn *adjective* just born, recently born, neonatal; *inf.* brand new.

newborn *noun* infant, baby, newborn baby, neonate; *inf.* new arrival, (little) bundle of joy.

newcomer *noun* **1** *newcomers to the town* new arrival, arrival, incomer, immigrant, settler, stranger, outsider, foreigner, alien, intruder, interloper; *inf.* johnny-come-lately. **2** *a newcomer to the game* beginner, novice, learner, trainee, probationer, new recruit, raw recruit, tyro, greenhorn, initiate, neophyte.

newfangled *adjective dislike newfangled methods/ machines* modern, ultramodern, state-of-the-art, contemporary, fashionable, gimmicky, new-fashioned.

newly *adverb* just, just recently, lately, of late.

news *noun* information, facts, data, report, story, news item, news flash, account, statement, announcement, press release, communication, communiqué, message, bulletin, dispatch, disclosure, revelation, word, talk, the latest, gossip, rumor, scandal, exposé; *inf.* info, lowdown, scuttlebutt, poop, dope.

newspaper *noun* paper, gazette, journal, tabloid, daily paper, daily, evening paper, weekly paper, weekly, scandal sheet; *inf.* rag.

next *adjective* **1** *the next patient/day* following, succeeding, successive, subsequent, later, ensuing. **2** *the next house* neighboring, adjacent, adjoining, bordering, contiguous, closest, nearest, proximate.

next adverb *next we went to the zoo* then, later, at a later time, after, afterward, thereafter, subsequently, at a subsequent time, after this/that, after that time.

nibble verb take small bites from, bite, gnaw, peck at, pick at, pick over, eat, munch, eat between meals; *inf.* snack on.

nibble noun bite, peck, munch, taste, crumb, piece, morsel, soupçon, snack, tidbit, canapé, hors d'oeuvre.

nice adjective **1** *have a nice time* good, pleasant, enjoyable, pleasurable, agreeable, delightful, amusing, satisfying, gratifying, marvelous. **2** *a nice lady/friend* pleasant, agreeable, likable, charming, delightful, amiable, friendly, kindly, genial, gracious, sympathetic, understanding, compassionate, good. **3** *nice manners/behavior* polite, courteous, civil, refined, cultivated, polished, genteel, elegant, seemly, decorous, proper, fitting, suitable, appropriate, respectable, good, virtuous. **4** *a nice distinction* fine, ultrafine, subtle, minute, precise, exact, accurate, strict, close, careful, meticulous, rigorous. **5** *a nice day* fine, dry, sunny, warm, pleasant, agreeable. **6** *she is too nice to eat with her fingers* fastidious, delicate, refined, dainty, particular, discriminating, overparticular, fussy, finicky; *inf.* persnickety. **7** *landscapers did a nice job* good, satisfactory, agreeable, acceptable, commendable, adequate, admirable.
Antonyms: UNPLEASANT; NASTY; UNREFINED; ROUGH.

nicely adverb **1** *children behaving nicely* well, politely, courteously, decorously, properly, fittingly, suitably, respectably, virtuously. *See* NICE 3. **2** *distinguish nicely between possibilities* subtly, precisely, exactly, strictly, closely, carefully, meticulously, rigorously. **3** *did nicely on the final exam* well, satisfactorily, agreeably, acceptably, commendably, adequately, admirably.

niceness noun **1** *appreciate their neighbor's niceness* pleasantness, agreeableness, friendliness, geniality. **2** *the niceness of the children's behavior* politeness, courtesy, refinement, civility, gentility, respectability. **3** *the niceness of her table manners* fastidiousness, delicacy, overrefinement, fussiness, finickiness, persnicketiness.

nicety noun **1** *the niceties of meaning* finer point, subtlety, nuance, detail. **2** *the nicety of the judgment* precision, accuracy, exactness, meticulousness, rigor.

niche noun **1** *vases placed in a niche in the wall* alcove, recess, nook, cranny, cubbyhole. **2** *his niche in life* calling, vocation, place, position, job; *inf.* slot.

nickname noun pet name, family name, familiar name, diminutive; *inf.* moniker, handle.

nifty adjective **1** *a nifty piece of footwork* agile, nim-ble, deft, adroit, skillful, neat. **2** *wearing rather nifty clothes* smart, stylish, elegant, chic; *inf.* natty.

niggardly adjective **1** *a niggardly person* mean, miserly, stingy, tight-fisted, parsimonious, penny-pinching, avaricious. **2** *a niggardly supply of food* meager, paltry, skimpy, scanty, measly, inadequate, insubstantial, miserable; *inf.* piddling.
Antonyms: GENEROUS; LAVISH; ABUNDANT.

niggle verb **1** *he was always niggling about money* fuss, nag, carp, criticize, cavil; *inf.* nitpick. **2** *many doubts were niggling him* irritate, annoy, worry, trouble, rankle.

night noun nighttime, darkness, dark, hours of darkness. **night and day** all the time, around the clock, ceaselessly, incessantly, continuously.
Antonyms: DAY; LIGHT.

nightfall noun sunset, sundown, dusk, evening, twilight; *lit.* eventide, gloaming.

nightly adjective at night, nighttime, nocturnal.

nightmare noun **1** *I have had nightmares since the accident* bad dream, incubus, phantasmagoria. **2** *the interview was a nightmare* ordeal, horror, torment, torture.

nihilism noun **1** *former believers are turning to nihilism* rejection, repudiation, renunciation, denial, abnegation; disbelief, skepticism; negativism, cynicism, pessimism. **2** *they lapsed into political nihilism* anarchy, lawlessness, disorder, chaos. **3** *he felt himself to be in a state of nihilism* nihility, nothingness, nonexistence, void.

nil noun zero, nothing, naught, none; *inf.* zilch, goose egg.

nimble adjective **1** *nimble gymnasts/movements* agile, lithe, sprightly, spry, lively, quick, quick-moving, graceful, skillful, deft. **2** *nimble of wit* quick-thinking, clever, bright, quick, quick-witted, alert.
Antonyms: STIFF; CLUMSY; DULL.

nip verb **1** *nip his arm* pinch, tweak, squeeze, grip, bite, nibble. **2** *nip (off) the withered shoots* snip, cut, lop, dock. **3** *frost nipping her cheeks* sting, bite, hurt. **nip in the bud** *her plans were nipped in the bud* stop, quash, quell, check, thwart, frustrate.

nipple noun teat, udder, mamilla, papilla.

nippy adjective icy, chilly, bitter, raw, piercing, stinging.

nirvana noun enlightenment, oblivion; paradise, heaven; bliss, joy, peace, serenity, tranquillity.

nitpicking adjective captious, hairsplitting, quibbling, faultfinding, ultracritical, critical, caviling, pedantic.

nitty-gritty noun crux, gist, substance, essence, quintessence; core, heart, center, kernel, nucleus; essentials, basics, facts; *inf.* brass tacks, nuts and bolts.

nitwit noun fool, ninny, idiot, nincompoop, dolt, dunce, ignoramus; *inf.* dope, chump, twit, dimwit, nerd, jerk.

no adverb no indeed, absolutely not, under no

circumstances, by no means, never; *inf.* not on your life, no way, nope, no siree.

Antonyms: YES; AFFIRMATIVE.

nobility *noun* **1** *born to the nobility* lords, peers, plutocracy, aristocracy, high society, elite, upper class; *inf.* upper crust. **2** *the nobility of his deed/character* magnanimity, generosity, selflessness, honor, integrity, bravery, righteousness, decency. See NOBLE 2. **3** *the nobility of his thoughts* loftiness, grandness. See NOBLE 3. **4** *he admired the nobility of the setting* impressiveness, splendor, magnificence, stateliness, grandeur.

noble *adjective* **1** *the noble people of the land* aristocratic, patrician, blue-blooded, highborn, titled, landed, born with a silver spoon in one's mouth. **2** *noble deeds/character* noble-minded, magnanimous, generous, self-sacrificing, honorable, virtuous, brave, righteous, honest, upright, true, loyal, principled, moral, decent, good. **3** *noble thoughts* lofty, grand, exalted, elevated. **4** *of noble appearance* impressive, magnificent, striking, awesome, stately, grand, dignified.

Antonyms: HUMBLE; DISHONORABLE; ignoble; BASE.

nobleman, noblewoman *noun* noble, lord, lady, peer, peeress, aristocrat, patrician.

nod *verb* **1** *nod one's head* incline, bob, bow, dip, duck. **2** *nod a greeting* signal, gesture, motion, sign, indicate. **3** *the audience began to nod* doze off, drop off, fall asleep, nap, slumber.

node *noun* protuberance, swelling, lump, growth, excrescence, knob, knot, nodule, bump, bulge.

noise *noun* sound, loud sound, din, hubbub, clamor, racket, row, uproar, tumult, commotion, rumpus, pandemonium.

noisome *adjective* disgusting, repugnant, revolting, repulsive, obnoxious; offensive, nauseating; unpleasant, disagreeable, horrible, detestable, loathsome.

noisy *adjective* **1** *noisy neighbors* rowdy, clamorous, boisterous, obstreperous. **2** *noisy music* loud, blaring, blasting, deafening, earsplitting.

Antonyms: QUIET; SOFT.

nomad *noun* itinerant, traveler, migrant, wanderer, roamer, rover; transient, vagabond, vagrant, tramp.

nominal *adjective* **1** *the nominal head* in name only, titular, formal; theoretical, self-styled; purported, supposed. **2** *a nominal sum* token, symbolic; minimal, trivial, insignificant.

nominate *verb* **1** *they nominated several candidates* name, propose, put forward, submit, present, recommend; *inf.* put up. **2** *nominated his successor* name, designate, appoint, assign, select, choose.

nonaligned *adjective* neutral, uncommitted, impartial, uninvolved, unallied.

nonbeliever *noun* atheist, agnostic, skeptic, doubter, doubting Thomas, unbeliever, disbeliever, cynic, infidel, pagan, heathen.

nonce *noun* *for the nonce* for the present, for the moment, for the present moment, for the time being, for now, for just now.

nonchalance *noun* composure, self-possession, sang-froid, equanimity, imperturbability, calm, coolness, unconcern, indifference, dispassionateness, detachment, detachedness, apathy, casualness, carefreeness, insouciance, carelessness; *inf.* cool.

nonchalant *adjective* composed, self-possessed, imperturbable, unexcitable, calm, cool, collected, cool as a cucumber, unconcerned, indifferent, unemotional, blasé, dispassionate, detached, apathetic, casual, offhand, carefree, insouciant, easygoing, careless; *inf.* laid-back.

Antonyms: ANXIOUS; CONCERNED; EXCITED.

noncombatant *adjective* noncombative, nonfighting, nonbelligerent, pacifist, civilian, neutral, nonaligned, nonparticipating.

noncommittal *adjective* cautious, guarded, circumspect, wary, careful, discreet, politic, tactful, diplomatic, prudent, playing one's cards close to one's chest, giving nothing away, sitting on the fence, unrevealing, temporizing, evasive, equivocal, vague, reserved.

Antonyms: CARELESS; INDISCREET; revealing.

non compos mentis *adjective* of unsound mind, mentally deranged, mentally unbalanced, mentally ill, insane, mad; *inf.* crazy, non compos, nuts.

nonconformist *noun* radical, dissenter, dissentient, protester, rebel, seceder, maverick, individualist, deviant, misfit, fish out of water, eccentric, iconoclast, outsider; *inf.* dropout, hippie, freak, oddball.

nondescript *adjective* indefinite, indeterminate, unclassifiable, indescribable, indistinguishable, vague, blending into the background, unremarkable, featureless, undistinguished, ordinary, commonplace, average, mediocre, unexceptional, unmemorable, uninteresting, uninspiring, dull, colorless, anemic, insipid, bland.

Antonyms: DISTINCTIVE; EXTRAORDINARY.

none *pronoun* **1** *we expected several people but none came* no one, nobody, not one, not a one, never a one, not a soul, not a single person. **2** *she expected presents but none came* nothing, nothing at all, not a thing, not a single thing, not a one, nil, zero. **3** *none of this concerns me* not any, not a part, not a bit.

Antonyms: MANY; lots.

none *adverb* *none the wiser* not at all, not a bit, in no way, to no extent.

nonentity *noun* nobody, person of no account, person of no importance, nonperson; *inf.* nothing, lightweight.

nonessential *adjective* inessential, unessential, unnecessary, needless, unneeded, unrequired, superfluous, redundant, dispensable, expendable, peripheral, unimportant, insignificant, inconsequential, irrelevant, inapplicable, inapposite, extraneous.

nonetheless *adverb* nevertheless, even so, however, still, yet, be that as it may, for all that, just the same, though, in any event, notwithstanding, regardless.

nonexistent *adjective* unreal, hypothetical, suppositional, fictional, fictitious, imagined, imaginary, fancied, fanciful, mythical, legendary, fantasy, illusory, delusive, illusionary, hallucinatory, insubstantial, inexistent, missing.

nonintervention *noun* laissez-faire, neutrality, nonparticipation, noninterference, noninvolvement, inaction, passivity.

nonobservance *noun nonobservance of the rules* ignoring, noncompliance, disobedience, unruliness, infringement, violation.

nonpareil *adjective his artistic work is nonpareil | as a writer he is nonpareil* unparalleled, unrivaled, without rival, incomparable, peerless, matchless, unmatched, without equal, unequaled, unsurpassed, unique, unbeatable, supreme.

nonpareil *noun the nonpareils of the art world* nonesuch, crème de la crème, elite, jewel, jewel in the crown, gem, paragon.

nonplus *verb* take aback, stun, dumbfound, confound, astound, astonish, amaze, surprise, disconcert, discomfit, dismay, make one halt in one's tracks, puzzle, perplex, baffle, mystify, stump, confuse, bewilder, embarrass, fluster; *inf.* faze, flummox, floor.

nonsense *noun* 1 *talk nonsense* rubbish, balderdash, drivel, gibberish, twaddle; *inf.* tripe, gobbledygook, mumbo-jumbo, poppycock, claptrap, bilge, bull. 2 *tired of their nonsense* foolishness, folly, silliness, senselessness, stupidity, ridiculousness, ludicrousness, inanity, fatuity, joking, jesting, clowning, buffoonery, drollery.
Antonyms: SENSE; WISDOM.

---

nonsense
bull, bunk, drivel, poppycock, twaddle
If you write or speak in an obscure, senseless, or unintelligible manner, you'll probably be accused of producing **nonsense**. It is the most general of these nouns and may refer to behavior as well as to what is said (*the demonstrators were told in no uncertain terms to give up this nonsense or leave the room*). **Twaddle** refers to silly, empty utterances from people who know nothing about a subject but who write or talk about it anyway (*I was sick of her twaddle about the dangers of electromagnetic fields*). **Bunk** (short for bunkum) applies to an utterance that strikes the popular fancy even though it is lacking in worth or substance (*the speech, which received enthusiastic applause, was pure bunk*). **Poppycock** applies to nonsense that is

full of complex, confused, or clichéd ideas (*the report was a strange combination of logical thinking and outright poppycock*). **Bull** is a slang term for deceitful and often boastful writing or speech (*he gave them a line of bull*). Perhaps the most insulting of these terms is **drivel**, which implies a steady flow of inane, idle, or nonsensical speech or writing similar to what might be expected from a very young child or an idiot (*his first novel was full of romantic drivel*).

nonsensical *adjective* 1 *nonsensical remarks* meaningless, incomprehensible, unintelligible, senseless, incongruous. 2 *a nonsensical scheme* foolish, absurd, silly, inane, senseless, stupid, ridiculous, ludicrous, preposterous, harebrained, irrational, idiotic, insane; *inf.* crazy, crackpot, nutty, wacky.

nonstop *adjective nonstop commentaries/rain* incessant, unceasing, ceaseless, constant, continuous, continual, without interruption, unbroken, unfaltering, steady, unremitting, relentless, persistent, endless, never-ending, unending, interminable; *inf.* eternal.

nonstop *adverb talk/rain nonstop* incessantly, unceasingly, constantly, continuously, continually, steadily, unremittingly, relentlessly, persistently, endlessly. *See* NONSTOP *adjective.*

nook *noun* 1 *a room full of nooks and crannies* corner, cranny, recess, alcove, niche, opening, cavity, crevice, gap, cubbyhole, inglenook. 2 *find a quiet nook to be alone* hideaway, retreat, refuge, shelter, den; *inf.* hide-out.

noon *noun* midday, twelve noon, twelve midday, twelve o'clock, high noon, noontime, noontide, noonday, twelve hundred, twelve hundred hours.

no one *pronoun* nobody, not a one, not anyone, not a person, not a single person, never a one, not a soul.

norm *noun* 1 *measured against the norm* standard, criterion, measure, gauge, yardstick, benchmark, touchstone, scale, rule, pattern, model, type. 2 *six hours a day is the norm* average, mean, normal rate, the usual, the rule.

normal *adjective* 1 *the normal temperature/method* usual, standard, average, common, ordinary, natural, general, commonplace, conventional, typical, regular, routine, run-of-the-mill, everyday, accustomed, habitual, prevailing, popular, accepted, acknowledged. 2 *of normal size* average, medium, middling, standard, mean. 3 *the patient is not normal* rational, well-adjusted, well-balanced, *compos mentis*, sane.
Antonyms: ABNORMAL; UNUSUAL; IRRATIONAL.

---

normal
average, natural, ordinary, regular, typical, usual
Most of us want to be regarded as **normal**, an adjective that implies conformity with established norms or standards and is the opposite of abnormal (*a normal body temperature; nor-*

Regular, like *normal*, is usually preferred to its opposite (irregular) and implies conformity to prescribed standards or established patterns (*their regular monthly meeting; a regular guy*), but *normal* carries stronger connotations of conformity within prescribed limits and sometimes allows for a wider range of differences. Few of us think of ourselves as **ordinary**, a term used to describe what is commonplace or unexceptional (*an ordinary person wearing ordinary clothes*), although many people are ordinary in some ways and extraordinary in others. **Average** also implies conformity with what is regarded as normal or ordinary (*a woman of average height*), although it tends to emphasize the middle ground and to exclude both positive and negative extremes. **Typical** applies to persons or things possessing the representative characteristics of a type or class (*a typical teenager*). Someone or something described as **natural** behaves or operates in accordance with an inherent nature or character (*his fears were natural for one so young*), while **usual** applies to that which conforms to common or ordinary use or occurrence (*we paid the usual price*).

normality *noun* **1** *return to normality* | *the normality of his surroundings* usualness, commonness, ordinariness, naturalness, commonplaceness, conventionality, regularity, routine, accustomedness, habitualness. *See* NORMAL 1. **2** *question the normality of the patient* balance, rationality, sanity.

normally *adverb* **1** *behave normally* as usual, ordinarily, naturally, conventionally, routinely, typically, regularly. **2** *normally, we eat late* usually, ordinarily, as a rule, as a general rule, generally, in general, mostly, commonly, habitually.

north *adjective* *north winds* northern, northerly, northwardly, Arctic, arctic, polar, boreal.

north *adverb* *go north* northward, northwardly.

nose *noun* **1** *have a large nose* proboscis, bill, beak, snout, muzzle, trunk; *inf.* snoot, schnoz. **2** *have a good nose* sense of smell, olfactory sense. **3** *a nose for a good story* instinct, sixth sense, intuition, insight, perception. **by a nose** *win by a nose* by a hair's breadth, by the narrowest of margins, by a narrow margin, narrowly, by the skin of one's teeth; *inf.* by a whisker/hair. **on the nose** *$200 on the nose* | *arrive at 6 p.m. on the nose* exactly, precisely, promptly, on time, on target; *inf.* on the dot, on the button.

nose *verb* **1** *dogs were nosing his arm* nudge, push, nuzzle. **2** *nose around the room* pry, search, peer, prowl, have a good look; *inf.* snoop. **3** *nose the car forward* ease, inch, move, run. **nose into** *nose into someone's business* pry into, interfere in, meddle in, inquire into; *inf.* poke one's nose into. **nose out** *dogs nosing out the thieves*

smell out, sniff out, follow the scent of, scent out, search for, detect, run to ground.

nosedive *noun* **1** *the plane/parachutist took a nosedive* dive, plunge, swoop. **2** *the nosedive taken by prices* fall, drop, plunge, decline.

nosedive *verb* **1** *the plane nosedived out of the sky* dive, plunge, swoop, drop, plummet. **2** *market prices nosedived after the news* fall, drop, plunge, plummet, go down, decline, worsen, get worse.

nosegay *noun* bouquet, posy, spray, bunch of flowers.

nosh *noun* food, fare, sustenance, meal, repast, snack, victuals, viands, comestibles, provisions, aliment; *inf.* grub, chow, eats.

nostalgia *noun* longing/yearning/pining for the past, regret, regretfulness, reminiscence, remembrance, recollection, wistfulness, homesickness.

nostalgic *adjective* wistful, sentimental, emotional about the past, maudlin, homesick.

nostrum *noun* **1** *prescribing nostrums for patients* patent medicine, medicine, medication, drug, potion, pill, quack remedy, elixir, remedy, cure, panacea, sovereign remedy, magic bullet. **2** *claiming to have a nostrum for the country's problems* remedy, cure, cure-all, panacea, solution, perfect solution, answer, magic bullet, magic formula, recipe, recipe for success.

nosy *adjective* prying, inquisitive, quizzing, probing, eavesdropping, curious, interfering, meddlesome, intrusive; *inf.* snooping, snoopy.

notability *noun* **1** *the notability of his achievements* noteworthiness, importance, significance, momentousness, memorability, impressiveness, extraordinariness. *See* NOTABLE *adjective* 1. **2** *the notability of the members* eminence, preeminence, distinction, illustriousness, greatness, prestige, fame, renown, reputation, acclaim, consequence.

notable *adjective* **1** *a notable achievement* noteworthy, remarkable, outstanding, important, significant, momentous, memorable, unforgettable, pronounced, marked, striking, impressive, uncommon, unusual, particular, special, extraordinary, conspicuous, rare, signal. **2** *notable people in the town* noted, of note, distinguished, eminent, preeminent, well-known, prominent, illustrious, great, famous, famed, renowned, celebrated, acclaimed.

Antonyms: INSIGNIFICANT; unremarkable; UNHEARD-OF; OBSCURE.

notable *noun* *the notables of the university* dignitary, celebrity, luminary, star, superstar, lion, VIP; *inf.* celeb, megastar, big shot, somebody.

notably *adverb* *notably successful* remarkably, outstandingly, significantly, markedly, strikingly, impressively, uncommonly, unusually, particularly, especially, extraordinarily, conspicuously, signally.

notation *noun* system of symbols, symbols, signs,

code, cipher, hieroglyphics, shorthand, musical notation.

notch noun **1** *make a notch in the wood* indentation, dent, nick, groove, gouge, cut, mark, incision, score, scratch, gash, slit, cleft. **2** *her singing is several notches up from the rest of the choir* degree, grade, gradation, level, step, stage, rung.

notch verb *notch the wood* indent, make an indentation in, dent, nick, gouge, cut, mark, score, scratch, gash, slit.

note noun **1** *always kept a note of her purchases* record, account, notation. **2** *write him a note* message, memorandum; letter, epistle, missive, communication, thank-you note; *inf.* memo. **3** *read the notes in the book* footnote, annotation, commentary, gloss, marginalia, explanation, explication, exposition, exegesis. **4** *worthy of note* notice, attention, attentiveness, heed, observation, consideration, thought, regard, care, mindfulness. **5** *people of note* distinction, eminence, preeminence, illustriousness, greatness, prestige, fame, renown, reputation, acclaim, consequence. **6** *a note of amusement in her voice* tone, intonation, inflection, sound, indication, hint, element.

note verb **1** *note the date in your diary* write down, put down, jot down, mark down, enter, mark, record, register. **2** *note his comments in your report* mention, make mention of, refer to, allude to, touch on, indicate, point out, make known, state. **3** *he noted their concern* take note of, take notice of, see, observe, perceive, behold, detect, take in.

notebook noun notepad, tablet, scratch pad, register, logbook, log, diary, journal, record book, personal organizer; spiral-bound notebook, three-ring notebook; *Trademark* Trapper; *inf.* memo pad.

noted adjective *a noted artist* of note, notable, distinguished, eminent, preeminent, well-known, prominent, illustrious, great, famous, famed, renowned, celebrated, acclaimed.
Antonyms: UNKNOWN; UNHEARD-OF; OBSCURE.

notes plural noun *make/take notes on the conference* | *his notes for the screenplay* jottings, record, report, commentary, chronicle, transcript, minutes, observations, impressions, synopsis, précis, sketch, outline.

noteworthy adjective *a noteworthy achievement* notable, remarkable, outstanding, important, significant, marked, striking, impressive, unusual, conspicuous, rare, signal. *See* NOTABLE adjective 1.
Antonyms: INSIGNIFICANT; ORDINARY.

nothing noun **1** *nothing to declare* not anything, nothing at all, naught, nil, not a thing, not a single thing; *inf.* zilch, zip. **2** *write nothing in the right-hand column* naught, zero, cipher, 0. **3** *the wound is a mere nothing* trifling matter, piece of trivia, matter of no importance/con-

sequence, bagatelle; *inf.* no big deal. **4** *they treat her like a nothing* nobody, person of no account, nonentity. **5** *pass into nothing* nothingness, nonexistence, nonbeing. *See* NOTHINGNESS 1. **for nothing 1** *work for nothing* free, for free, gratis, without charge, without payment, gratuitously. **2** *do all that studying for nothing* in vain, to no avail, to no purpose, futilely, needlessly. **nothing but** *nothing but a miracle can save us* only, solely, simply, purely, merely.
Antonyms: something; CELEBRITY; BEING.

nothingness noun **1** *pass into nothingness* nothing, nonexistence, nonlife, nonbeing, oblivion, void, vacuum, blankness. **2** *aware of the nothingness of his work* insignificance, unimportance, triviality, worthlessness, valuelessness, pointlessness, uselessness, meagerness.

notice noun **1** *escape my notice* attention, attentiveness, heed, note, observation, cognizance, regard, consideration, interest, thought, mindfulness, watchfulness, vigilance. **2** *see the notice on the board* information sheet, bulletin, poster, handbill, bill, circular, leaflet, pamphlet, advertisement. **3** *receive notice of their arrival* notification, apprisal, announcement, intimation, information, intelligence, news, communication, advice, instruction, order, warning. **4** *workers have received/given (their) notice* notice to quit, resignation, dismissal; *inf.* marching orders, walking papers, pink slip, the sack, the boot. **5** *plays receiving poor notices* review, write-up, critique.

notice verb see, note, take note of, observe, perceive, discern, detect, behold, descry, spot, distinguish, make out, take heed of, heed, pay attention to, take notice of, mark, regard.
Antonyms: OVERLOOK; IGNORE; DISREGARD.

noticeable adjective *no noticeable improvement* | *was it noticeable?* observable, visible, discernible, perceptible, detectable, distinguishable, distinct, evident, obvious, apparent, manifest, patent, plain, clear, conspicuous, unmistakable, pronounced, striking, blatant.
Antonyms: IMPERCEPTIBLE; UNOBTRUSIVE.

---

noticeable
conspicuous, outstanding, prominent, remarkable, striking

A scratch on someone's face might be **noticeable,** while a scar that runs from cheekbone to chin would be **conspicuous.** When it comes to describing the things that attract our attention, *noticeable* means readily noticed or unlikely to escape observation (*a noticeable facial tic; a noticeable aversion to cocktail parties*), while *conspicuous* implies that the eye (or mind) cannot miss it (*her absence was conspicuous*). Use **prominent** when you want to describe something that literally or figuratively stands out from its background (*a prominent nose; a prominent position on the committee*). It can also apply to persons or things that stand out so clearly they are generally known or recognized (*a prominent* *citizen*). Someone or something that is **outstanding** rises above or beyond others and is usually superior to them (*an outstanding student*). **Remarkable** applies to anything that is noticeable because it is extraordinary or exceptional (*remarkable blue eyes*). **Striking** is an even stronger word, used to describe something so out of the ordinary that it makes a deep and powerful impression on the observer's mind or vision (*a striking young woman over six feet tall*).

notification *noun* notice, announcement, statement, declaration, communication, message, information, advice, warning.

notify *verb* inform, tell, advise, acquaint, apprise, warn, alert, caution.

notion *noun* **1** *have strange notions about religion* idea, belief, opinion, thought, impression, view, conviction, concept, conception, conceptualization, assumption, presumption, hypothesis, theory, postulation, abstraction, apprehension, understanding. **2** *a notion to go to the sea* impulse, inclination, fancy, whim, wish, desire, caprice.

notional *adjective* hypothetical, theoretical, suppositional, speculative, conceptual, abstract, imaginary, fanciful, fancied, unreal, illusory, unsubstantiated, ideal.
Antonyms: ACTUAL; REAL.

notoriety *noun* infamy, ill/evil repute, bad reputation/name, disrepute, dishonor, scandal, opprobrium, obloquy.

notorious *adjective* **1** *a notorious murderer/liar* infamous, of ill repute, having a bad reputation/name, ill-famed, disreputable, dishonorable. **2** *a notorious murder* | *in a notorious nightclub* well-known, infamous, prominent, scandalous, opprobrious, obloquial, legendary.

notwithstanding *adverb* *notwithstanding, we must go* nevertheless, nonetheless, even so, however, still, yet, be that as it may, for all that, just the same, though, in any event, regardless.

notwithstanding *preposition* *notwithstanding the delay* despite, in spite of, regardless of.

nought *noun See* NAUGHT, NOUGHT.

nourish *verb* **1** *nourish the children* feed, nurture, provide for, care for, take care of, tend, attend to, bring up, rear. **2** *nourish growth* encourage, promote, foster, stimulate, boost, further, advance, forward, contribute to, be conducive to, assist, help, aid. **3** *nourish hopes of success* cherish, entertain, harbor, foster, hold, have.

nourishing *adjective* nutritious, nutritive, wholesome, healthy, health-giving, healthful, beneficial, good for one.
Antonyms: UNHEALTHY; unwholesome.

nourishment *noun* food, nutriment, nutrition, sustenance, subsistence, aliment, provisions, provender, meat, fare, viands, victuals, daily bread; *inf.* grub, chow, eats. nouveau riche

nouveau riche *noun* (the) newly rich, parvenu, arriviste, arrivé, upstart, social climber.

novel *adjective* new, fresh, different, original, unusual, uncommon, unfamiliar, rare, unique, singular, imaginative, unhackneyed, unconventional, creative, innovative, groundbreaking, trailblazing, modern, ultramodern, advanced, futuristic.
Antonyms: OLD; RUN-OF-THE-MILL; HACKNEYED; UNIMAGINATIVE.

novel *noun* book, story, tale, narrative, work of fiction.

novelist *noun* novel writer, author, authoress, writer, writer of fiction, fiction writer, creative writer, fictionist.

novelty *noun* **1** *the novelty of the idea/approach* newness, freshness, difference, originality, unusualness, uniqueness, rareness, imaginativeness, creativity. *See* NOVEL *adjective*. **2** *a vendor selling novelties* memento, souvenir, knickknack, trinket, bauble, trifle, gimmick, curiosity, gimcrack.

novice *noun* **1** *training the novices* beginner, newcomer, apprentice, trainee, learner, probationer, student, pupil, (new) recruit, raw recruit, tyro, initiate, novitiate, neophyte, greenhorn; *inf.* rookie. **2** *welcoming the novices to the convent* novitiate, postulant, neophyte.
Antonyms: VETERAN; EXPERT; PROFESSIONAL.

---

novice
apprentice, beginner, neophyte, probationer

All of these nouns are used to describe someone who has not yet acquired the skills and experience needed to qualify for a trade, a career, a profession, or a sphere of life. **Beginner** is the most general and informal term, used to describe someone who has begun to acquire the necessary skills but has not yet mastered them (*violin lessons for beginners*). An **apprentice** is also a beginner, usually a young person, who is serving under a more experienced master or teacher to learn the skills of a trade or profession (*he served as an apprentice to one of the great Renaissance painters*); in a broad sense, *apprentice* refers to any beginner whose efforts are unpolished. **Novice** implies that the person lacks training and experience (*a novice when it came to writing fiction*), while **neophyte** is a less negative term, suggesting that the person is eagerly learning the ways, methods, or principles of something (*he was a neophyte at this type of sailing*). A **probationer** is a beginner who is undergoing a trial period, during which he or she must prove an aptitude for a certain type of work or life (*she was a lowly probationer, with no privileges or status*).

---

novitiate *noun* *novitiates in the convent* novice, postulant, neophyte.

now *adverb* **1** *we do not have any now* just now, right now, at present, at the present time, at this time, at the moment, at this moment in time, for the time being, currently, presently.

2 *you must go now* right away, right now, immediately, at once, straight away, instantly, promptly, without delay. **now and again/then** occasionally, on occasion, sometimes, from time to time, at times, once in a while, every once in a while, at intervals, periodically.
Antonyms: THEN; LATER.

nowadays *adverb* **1** *nowadays, nearly everyone owns a car* at the present time, in these times, in this day and age, today, just now, now, at the moment, at present. **2** *I never see her nowadays* these days, any more, now, lately.

noxious *adjective* *noxious fumes/chemical* nocuous, noisome, harmful, hurtful, injurious, damaging, destructive, ruinous, pernicious, malignant, detrimental, deleterious, menacing, threatening, unwholesome, unhealthy, insalubrious, poisonous, toxic.
Antonyms: INNOCUOUS; SAFE.

nuance *noun* *nuances of color/meaning* shade, shading, gradation, subtlety, fine distinction, nicety, refinement, degree.

nucleus *noun* core, kernel, center, heart, nub, basis, pith, meat, marrow, focus, pivot.

nude *adjective* in the nude, naked, stark naked, bare, stripped, exposed, unclothed, undressed, uncovered, au naturel; *inf.* without a stitch on, in one's birthday suit, in the raw, in the altogether, in the buff, naked as the day one was born, buck naked.

nudge *verb* poke, jab, prod, dig, jog, elbow, bump, touch, push, shove.

nudge *noun* poke, jab, prod, dig, jog, dig in the ribs, elbow, bump, touch, push, shove.

nudity *noun* nakedness, bareness, bare skin, undress, state of undress.
Antonyms: DRESS; COVER.

nugget *noun* chunk, lump, piece, mass, clump, wad, hunk.

nuisance *noun* pest, bother, plague, irritant, source of annoyance, annoyance, vexation, trouble, burden, weight, problem, difficulty, worry, affliction, trial, tribulation, bore, inconvenience, disadvantage, handicap, thorn in the side/flesh; *inf.* drag.
Antonyms: HELP; BLESSING; ADVANTAGE.

null *adjective* **1** *render the ruling null* null and void, void, invalid, annulled, nullified, canceled, abolished, revoked, rescinded, repealed. **2** *the null effects of the trade embargo* ineffectual, useless, in vain, worthless, futile, powerless, unproductive, nonexistent, negative.

nullify *verb* render null and void, declare null and void, annul, void, invalidate, cancel, abolish, set aside, revoke, rescind, repeal, reverse, abrogate, discontinue, retract, withdraw, renounce, repudiate, countermand, veto, negate, terminate, dissolve, do away with, bring to an end, obliterate.
Antonyms: RATIFY; VALIDATE; CONFIRM.

numb *adjective* *numb fingers* | *feeling numb with*

grief/cold benumbed, dead, without feeling, sensationless, deadened, insensible, insensate, torpid, dull, anesthetized, drugged, dazed, stunned, stupefied, in shock, paralyzed, immobilized, frozen, chilled.
Antonyms: SENSITIVE; RESPONSIVE.

numb *verb* *cold numbing her fingers* | *grief numbing her* benumb, deaden, dull, anesthetize, drug, daze, stun, stupefy, paralyze, immobilize, freeze, chill.

number *noun* **1** *add up the numbers* figure, digit, numeral, cipher, character, symbol, unit, integer, whole number, cardinal number, ordinal number, Roman number, Arabic number. **2** *the number of accidents has increased* total, aggregate, score, tally, count, sum, summation. **3** *a large number of people* quantity, amount, group, collection, company, crowd. **4** *the latest number of the magazine* edition, issue, printing, imprint, copy.

number *verb* **1** *number the items/reasons* enumerate, count, add up, total, calculate, compute, reckon, tell, estimate, assess, take stock of. **2** *number the accounts* assign a number to, categorize by number, specify by number. **3** *number them among my friends* count, include, reckon. **4** *his days are numbered* limit, limit in number, restrict, fix.

numberless *adjective* *on numberless occasions* innumerable, countless, multitudinous, myriad, numerous, many, untold, infinite, more than one can count, immeasurable, abundant, copious.

numbing *adjective* benumbing, deadening, dulling, anesthetizing, dazing, paralyzing, freezing. *See* NUMB *verb.*

numbness *noun* lack of feeling, lack of sensation, deadness, insensibility, torpor, dullness, stupefaction, paralysis, immobility, chill.

numeral *noun* number, figure, digit, cipher, character, symbol, unit, integer.

numerous *adjective* many, very many, innumerable, myriad, multitudinous, several, quite a few, various, diverse; *inf.* a lot of, lots of.
Antonyms: FEW; SCANT.

nuncio *noun* envoy, legate, messenger, ambassador.

nuptial *adjective* matrimonial, marriage, marital, wedding, conjugal, connubial, bridal, spousal, hymeneal, married, wedded.

nuptials *plural noun* wedding, wedding ceremony, marriage ceremony, marriage.

nurse *verb* **1** *nurse the patient* take care of, care for, look after, tend, attend to, minister to, treat, doctor. **2** *a mother nursing her baby* suckle, breast-feed, feed, wet-nurse. **3** *nurse her career* nurture, encourage, promote, boost, further, advance, contribute to, assist, help. **4** *nurse feelings of resentment* harbor, have, hold, entertain, foster, cherish, nourish.
Antonyms: NEGLECT; HINDER.

nurture *verb* **1** *nurture the children* feed, nourish, provide for, care for, take care of, tend, attend to, bring up, rear. **2** *nurture the students* educate, school, train, tutor, coach. **3** *nurture growth | nurtured her career* encourage, promote, foster, stimulate, develop, cultivate, boost, further, advance, forward, contribute to, be conducive to, assist, help, aid.

Antonyms: NEGLECT; HINDER.

nurture *noun* **1** *provide nurture* food, nutrition, nutriment, sustenance, subsistence. **2** *the nurture of the children* feeding, tending, rearing. *See* NURTURE *verb* 1. **3** *the nurture of the students* education, schooling, training, discipline. **4** *the nurture of her career/hopes* encouragement, promotion, fostering, development, cultivation, boosting, furtherance, advancement.

nut *noun* **1** *squirrels eating nuts* kernel, seed, stone, peanut, hazelnut, filbert, walnut, Brazil nut, almond, pecan, cashew, macadamia nut, chestnut, acorn, beechnut. **2** *a movie nut* fan, enthusiast, aficionado, devotee, follower; *inf.* buff, freak. **3** *acting like a nut* madman, lunatic, psychopath; *inf.* maniac, nutcase, loony, weirdo, oddball, crackpot, screwball.

nutrition *noun* nourishment, nutriment, food, sustenance, subsistence, aliment, provisions, provender, victuals, daily bread.

nutritious *adjective* nourishing, nutritive, wholesome, health-giving, healthy, healthful, beneficial, good for one.

Antonyms: UNHEALTHY; unwholesome.

nuts *adjective* mad, insane, deranged, demented, irrational, *non compos mentis*, lunatic, psychopathic; *inf.* nutty, crazy, bananas, loony, loopy, batty, balmy, out of one's mind, with a screw loose, out to lunch.

nuts and bolts *plural noun* fundamentals, basics, practicalities, essentials; *inf.* nitty-gritty.

nuzzle *verb* **1** *dogs nuzzling their masters* nose, nudge, prod, push. **2** *nuzzle up to her mother* snuggle, cuddle, nestle, lie close to, curl up

nymph *noun* wood nymph, water nymph, sylph, sprite, water sprite, undine, naiad, dryad, oread.

O

oaf *noun* **1** *that oaf tripped me up* lout, blunderer, bungler, boor, bumpkin, yokel, gorilla, bull in a china shop; *inf.* clodhopper, lummox, galoot. **2** *the foolishness of an oaf* fool, dolt, blockhead, numskull, dunderhead, dunce, dullard, nincompoop, ninny, simpleton, boob; *inf.* idiot, moron, imbecile, sap, dummy, bonehead, nitwit, dimwit, halfwit, chump, clod, goon, schmuck.

oafish *adjective* **1** *new dance students feeling oafish* clumsy, awkward, loutish, gawkish, gawky, lumbering, blundering, bungling, boorish; *inf.* clodhopping. **2** *oafish behavior* dull, stupid, blockish, doltish, blockheaded, dunderheaded, slow-witted, obtuse; *inf.* dim, dense, thick, moronic, dim-witted, halfwitted, dumb, slow on the uptake, boneheaded, thickheaded.

oasis *noun* **1** *an oasis in the desert* watering hole, watering place, fertile spot. **2** *an oasis among all the noise* refuge, haven, retreat, sanctuary, sanctum, hiding place, hideaway; *inf.* hideout.

oath *noun* **1** *take an oath to tell the truth* | *on my oath* sworn statement, vow, promise, pledge, avowal, affirmation, attestation, bond, word of honor, word. **2** *spouting oaths* curse, swearword, expletive, blasphemy, profanity, imprecation, malediction, obscenity, bad/foul language, strong language, epithet, four-letter word, dirty word, bad word, naughty word; *inf.* cuss.

obdurate *adjective* **1** *obdurate children* | *he was obdurate about not going* stubborn, obstinate, headstrong, willful, adamant, firm, fixed, dogged, unyielding, unbending, inflexible, unshakable, unmalleable, intractable, pigheaded, mulish, iron-willed, hard-hearted. **2** *obdurate criminals* hardened, case-hardened, cold-blooded, tough, unresponsive, unfeeling, insensitive, impenitent, unrepenting, uncontrite, shameless.
Antonyms: AMENABLE; compliant; MALLEABLE; PENITENT.

obedience *noun* dutifulness, duteousness, duty, sense of duty, observance of the law/rules, conformity, conformability, deference, respect, compliance, acquiescence, tractability, amenability, malleability, yielding, submission, docility, meekness.

obedient *adjective* dutiful, duteous, law-abiding, rule-abiding, conforming, deferential, respectful, compliant, acquiescent, tractable, amenable, malleable, governable, under control, well-trained, yielding, submissive, docile, meek, subservient, obsequious, servile.
Antonyms: DISOBEDIENT; INTRACTABLE; UNRULY.

obeisance *noun* **1** *his obeisance to the emperor* bow, curtsy, bob, kneel, genuflection, stoop, salaam, kowtow. **2** *pay obeisance to the emperor* homage, worship, adoration, reverence, respect, veneration, honor, submission.

obelisk *noun* monolith, column, pillar, shaft, needle, monument.

obese *adjective* overweight, fat, plump, stout, ample, chubby, tubby, portly, rotund, corpulent, pudgy, paunchy, fleshy, big, heavy, on the heavy side, large, bulky, chunky, outsize, massive, gross.
Antonyms: THIN; SKINNY.

obesity *noun* fatness, corpulence, plumpness, stoutness, rotundness, rotundity, portliness, chubbiness, tubbiness, pudginess, fleshiness, bigness, largeness, bulk, grossness, weight problem, embonpoint.

obey *verb* **1** *obey the rules* abide by, comply with, adhere to, observe, conform to, respect, acquiesce in, consent to, agree to, follow. **2** *obey orders* perform, carry out, execute, put into effect, fulfill, act upon. **3** *you must obey your mother* be dutiful to, do as/what someone says, follow the orders of, carry out the orders of, heed, be regulated by, be governed by.
Antonyms: DISOBEY; IGNORE; DEFY.

obfuscate *verb* **1** *obfuscate the issue* confuse, obscure, blur, muddle, jumble, complicate, make abstruse/unclear, garble, scramble, muddy, cloud, conceal, hide, veil. **2** *the brightest of people obfuscated by the problem* puzzle, perplex, baffle, confound, bemuse, bewilder, mystify, nonplus; *inf.* stump, beat, bamboozle.

obituary *noun* death notice; *inf.* obit.

object *noun* **1** *wooden objects* thing, something, anything, body, entity, phenomenon, article, item, device, gadget; *inf.* thingamajig, thingamabob, doodad, whatsit, what's-its-name, what-d'you-call-it, thingy. **2** *the object of our discussion* subject, subject matter, substance, issue, concern. **3** *the object of their affection/abuse* focus, target, recipient, butt, victim. **4** *our object is to win* objective, aim, goal, target, end. *See* OBJECTIVE *noun.*

object *verb* **1** *they were successful but many people objected* raise objections, protest, lodge a protest, demur, beg to differ, be in opposition, remonstrate, expostulate, take exception. **2** *object to the plan* raise objections to, protest

against, lodge a protest against, argue against, oppose, be in opposition to, remonstrate against, expostulate about, take exception to, complain about.
Antonyms: APPROVE; ACCEPT.

objection noun **1** *their objection to the plan is understandable* protest, protestation, demurral, opposition, remonstration, remonstrance, expostulation, complaining about, dissatisfaction with, disapproval of. **2** *lodge/name their objections* argument, counterargument, demurral, opposition, remonstrance, remonstration, expostulation, doubt, complaint, grievance, scruple, qualm.
Antonyms: APPROVAL; ACCEPTANCE.

objectionable adjective *objectionable people/behavior/smells* offensive, obnoxious, unpleasant, disagreeable, unacceptable, nasty, disgusting, repulsive, repellent, abhorrent, repugnant, revolting, loathsome, nauseating, hateful, detestable, reprehensible, deplorable, insufferable, intolerable, despicable, contemptible, odious, vile, obscene, foul, horrible, horrid, noxious.
Antonyms: PLEASANT; AGREEABLE; ACCEPTABLE.

objective adjective *referees must be objective* unbiased, bias-free, unprejudiced, prejudice-free, impartial, neutral, uninvolved, nonpartisan, disinterested, detached, dispassionate, unswayed, evenhanded, equitable, fair, just, open-minded.
Antonyms: BIASED; PARTIAL; SUBJECTIVE.

objective noun *our objective is to win* object, aim, goal, target, end, end in view, ambition, aspiration, intent, intention, purpose, idea, point, desire, hope, design, plan, scheme, plot.

objectively adverb *look at the issue objectively* with objectivity, without bias, without prejudice, impartially, disinterestedly, with detachment, dispassionately, equitably, evenhandedly, fairly, justly, open-mindedly, with an open mind, without fear or favor.

objectivity noun absence of bias/prejudice, impartiality, disinterest, detachment, dispassion, dispassionateness, equitability, evenhandedness, fairness, open-mindedness, justness, justice.

obligate verb *we felt obligated to attend* oblige, compel, require, necessitate, impel, force, constrain, press, pressure, pressurize.

obligation noun **1** *the obligations specified by the contract* requirement, prerequisite, demand, necessity, command, order, constraint, compulsion; *inf.* must. **2** *fulfill/discharge one's obligations* duty, function, chore, task, job, assignment, commission, business, burden, charge, onus, trust, liability, responsibility, accountability, indebtedness, debt, engagement. **3** *we attended only from a sense of obligation* duty, compulsion, necessity, enforcement, duress, pressure. **4** *the obligation is still binding* contract, agreement, deed, covenant, compact,

bond, treaty, deal, pact, understanding, transaction. **under an obligation to** *under an obligation to them* obliged to, beholden to, owing someone a favor, indebted to, in someone's debt, owing someone a debt of gratitude, duty-bound to, honor-bound to, grateful to, owing someone thanks.

obligatory adjective **1** *the agreement is obligatory* binding, valid, legal, in force, effective. **2** *attendance is obligatory* compulsory, enforced, prescriptive, mandatory, necessary, essential, required, requisite, imperative, de rigueur, unavoidable, unescapable.
Antonyms: VOLUNTARY; OPTIONAL.

oblige verb **1** *ties of friendship oblige me to go* put under an obligation, leave someone no option, require, necessitate, obligate, compel, call for, force, constrain, press, pressure, pressurize, impel. **2** *will you oblige me by going?* do someone a favor, do someone a kindness, do someone a service, serve, accommodate, meet the wants/needs of, help accommodate, put oneself out for, indulge, gratify the wishes of, help, assist.

obliging adjective helpful, eager to help/please, accommodating, willing, complaisant, indulgent, friendly, kind, generous, considerate, cooperative, neighborly, agreeable, pleasant, good-natured, amiable, civil, courteous, polite.
Antonyms: DISOBLIGING; OBSTRUCTIVE; DISCOURTEOUS.

oblique adjective **1** *an oblique line* slanting, slanted, sloping, sloped, inclined, at an angle, angled, tilted, listing, diagonal, catercornered; *inf.* kitty-corner. **2** *an oblique compliment | oblique references to the crime* indirect, implied, roundabout, circuitous, circumlocutory, ambagious, evasive, backhanded.
Antonyms: STRAIGHT; DIRECT.

oblique noun *words separated by an oblique* oblique line/stroke, solidus, slanting line, slant, slash, back slash.

obliquely adverb **1** *the line runs obliquely* at an angle, slantwise, aslant, diagonally. **2** *refer obliquely to the matter* indirectly, in a roundabout way, not in so many words, not outright, circuitously, evasively.

obliterate verb **1** *obliterate all traces of the stains | had obliterated all memories of her* erase, eradicate, efface, blot out, rub out, wipe out, expunge, sponge out, delete, cross out, strike out, blue-pencil, remove, cancel. **2** *the army/village was obliterated* destroy, exterminate, annihilate, wipe out, eliminate, eradicate, extirpate, decimate, liquidate, demolish.
Antonyms: CREATE; ESTABLISH.

obliteration noun **1** *the obliteration of the stains/memories* erasing, eradication, effacement, rubbing out, blotting out, expunging, deletion, striking out, removal, cancellation. **2** *the* *obliteration of the army/village* destruction, extermination, annihilation, wiping out, elimination, eradication, extirpation, decimation, liquidation, demolition.

oblivion noun **1** *sitting in a state of oblivion as people shouted* obliviousness, heedlessness, unmindfulness, unawareness, unconsciousness, insensibility, inattentiveness, disregard, disregardfulness, forgetfulness, absentmindedness, amnesia, unconcern, abstraction, preoccupation, absorption. *See* OBLIVIOUS. **2** *the old traditions have sunk into oblivion* neglect, disuse, nonexistence, abeyance, suspension. **3** *oblivion came when he hit his head* blackness, darkness, blankness, unconsciousness, insensibility, senselessness, stupor, coma.
Antonyms: CONSCIOUSNESS; awareness; EXISTENCE.

oblivious adjective *an oblivious look on his face | they are oblivious* absentminded, abstracted, distrait, preoccupied, absorbed, faraway. **oblivious of/to** *oblivious of/to his surroundings | oblivious to danger* unheeding, heedless of, unmindful of, unaware of, unconscious of, insensible of, ignorant of, blind to, unobservant of, deaf to, inattentive to, disregardful of, neglectful of, forgetful of, careless of, unconcerned with.
Antonyms: AWARE; CONSCIOUS; ATTENTIVE.

obloquy noun **1** *bring obloquy on the family* discredit, shame, dishonor, disgrace, humiliation, loss of face, ignominy, disfavor, disrepute, ill repute, infamy, scandal, odium. **2** *undergo the obloquy of the crowd* abuse, attack, opprobrium, censure, criticism, condemnation, denunciation, reproach, castigation, reproof, upbraiding, invective, railing, tirade, defamation, denigration, vilification, slander, libel, insult, aspersions, calumny, contumely.
Antonyms: HONOR; PRAISE.

obnoxious adjective *obnoxious person/behavior/smell* offensive, objectionable, unpleasant, disagreeable, unacceptable, nasty, disgusting, repulsive, repellent, abhorrent, repugnant, revolting, loathsome, nauseating, sickening, hateful, detestable, reprehensible, deplorable, insufferable, intolerable, despicable, contemptible, odious, vile, obscene, foul, horrible, horrid, noxious.
Antonyms: DELIGHTFUL; PLEASANT; AGREEABLE.

obscene adjective **1** *obscene publications/jokes* indecent, pornographic, blue, off-color, risqué, lewd, salacious, smutty, lecherous, lascivious, licentious, prurient, lubricious, ribald, scatological, scabrous, bawdy, suggestive, vulgar, dirty, filthy, foul, coarse, gross, vile, nasty, offensive, immoral, impure, immodest, shameless, unchaste, improper, unwholesome, erotic, carnal, sexy; *inf.* raunchy. **2** *the murder was an obscene act* atrocious, heinous, vile, foul, outrageous, shocking, repugnant, repulsive, re-

volting, nauseating, sickening, wicked, evil, odious.
Antonyms: DECENT; PURE; PROPER.

obscenity noun **1** *the obscenity of the publication* indecency, lewdness, salaciousness, smuttiness, lechery, lasciviousness, licentiousness, prurience, lubricity, ribaldry, scatalogy, scabrousness, bawdiness, suggestiveness, vulgarity, dirt, dirtiness, filth, filthiness, foulness, coarseness, grossness, vileness, nastiness, immorality, impurity, immodesty, shamelessness, unchasteness, impropriety, unwholesomeness, eroticism, carnality, sexiness. **2** *the obscenity of the crime* atrocity, heinousness, vileness, foulness, repugnance, wickedness, evil. *See* OBSCENE 2. **3** *a stream of obscenities came from him* curse, oath, swearword, expletive, imprecation, blasphemy, bad/foul language, strong language, epithet, profanity, four-letter word, dirty word, bad word, naughty word; *inf.* cuss, cussword.

obscure adjective **1** *obscure references* unclear, indeterminate, opaque, abstruse, recondite, unexplained, concealed, hidden, arcane, enigmatic, deep, cryptic, mysterious, puzzling, perplexing, confusing, intricate, involved, unfathomable, incomprehensible, impenetrable, vague, indefinite, hazy, uncertain, doubtful, dubious, ambiguous, equivocal. **2** *obscure shapes looming out of the mist* indistinct, vague, shadowy, hazy, blurred, fuzzy, cloudy. **3** *obscure parts of the forest* dark, dim, black, unlit, murky, somber, gloomy, shady, shadowy. **4** *obscure villages* unknown, unheard-of, out-of-the-way, off the beaten track, remote, hidden, secluded, godforsaken. **5** *obscure poets* little-known, unknown, unheard-of, undistinguished, insignificant, inconspicuous, minor, unimportant, unrenowned, unrecognized, unhonored, unsung, inglorious.
Antonyms: CLEAR; PLAIN; DISTINCT; FAMOUS.

obscure verb **1** *obscure the main issue* confuse, blur, muddle, complicate, make abstruse, obfuscate, garble, cloud, muddy, conceal, hide, veil. **2** *clouds obscure the sun* hide, conceal, cover, veil, screen, mask, cloak, shroud, block, block out, eclipse, adumbrate. **3** *clouds obscured the sky* darken, blacken, dim, bedim.
Antonyms: CLARIFY; REVEAL; BRIGHTEN.

obscurity noun **1** *the obscurity of the reference* lack of clarity, unclearness, opaqueness, reconditeness, arcaneness, enigma, deepness, abstruseness, mystery, puzzle, confusion, intricacy, involvement, incomprehensibility, impenetrability, vagueness, uncertainty, doubtfulness, ambiguity, equivocalness. **2** *the obscurity of the village* remoteness, seclusion. *See* OBSCURE adjective 4. **3** *the obscurity of the poet* insignificance, inconspicuousness, unimportance, lack of fame/renown/honor/recognition, ingloriousness. **4** *a text full of obscurities* difficulty, problem, complication, intricacy, opacity, enigma, puzzle, perplexity, mystery, ambiguity.

obsequies *plural noun* funeral rites, funeral service, funeral, burial ceremony, burial, last offices, exequies.

obsequious *adjective* servile, subservient, submissive, slavish, menial, abject, fawning, groveling, cringing, toadying, truckling, sycophantic, ingratiating, unctuous, oily; *inf.* bootlicking, Uriah Heepish.
Antonyms: PROUD; ARROGANT.

obsequious
servile, slavish, subservient
If you want to get ahead with your boss, you might trying being **obsequious**, which suggests an attitude of inferiority that may or may not be genuine, but that is assumed in order to placate a superior in hopes of getting what one wants (*a goody two shoes whose obsequious behavior made everyone in the class cringe*). While **subservient** may connote similar behavior, it is more often applied to those who are genuinely subordinate or dependent and act accordingly (*a timid, subservient child who was terrified of making a mistake*). **Servile** is a stronger and more negative term, suggesting a cringing submissiveness (*the dog's servile obedience to her master*). **Slavish**, suggesting the status or attitude of a slave, is often used to describe strict adherence to a set of rules or a code of conduct (*a slavish adherence to the rules of etiquette*).

observable *adjective* noticeable, visible, perceptible, perceivable, detectable, discernible, recognizable, obvious, evident, apparent, manifest, patent, clear, distinct, plain, unmistakable, appreciable.

observance *noun* 1 *the observance of laws* observation of, keeping of, obeying, obedience to, adherence to, abiding by, compliance with, heeding. 2 *observance of duty/rites* carrying out, performance, execution, discharge, fulfillment, honoring. 3 *religious observances* rite, ritual, ceremony, ceremonial, celebration, festival, practice, tradition, custom, formality, form, service, office.
Antonyms: DISREGARD; NEGLECT.

observant *adjective* 1 *an observant boy spotted the thief* alert, sharp-eyed, sharp, eagle-eyed, attentive, vigilant, wide-awake, watchful, heedful, on the qui vive, on the lookout, on guard, mindful, intent, aware, conscious, with one's eyes peeled; *inf.* not missing a thing/trick, on the ball. 2 *observant members of the community/faith* dutiful, obedient, conforming, law-abiding, orthodox, practicing.
Antonyms: INATTENTIVE; DREAMY; unobservant; NEGLIGENT.

observation *noun* 1 *recall our observation of the man* seeing, noticing, watching, viewing, eyeing, witnessing. See OBSERVE 1. 2 *keep the thief/patient under observation* scrutiny, scrutinization, watch, watching, monitoring, surveil-lance, inspection, attention, consideration, study, review, examination. 3 *record your observations on the experiment* finding, result, information, datum, remark, comment, note, annotation, report, description, opinion, thought, reflection. 4 *make a sarcastic observation* remark, comment, statement, utterance, pronouncement, declaration. **observation of** *observation of the law/rules/customs* observance of, keeping of, obedience to, adherence to, compliance with, heeding of. See OBSERVANCE 1.

observe *verb* 1 *we observe him go into the bank* see, catch sight of, notice, note, perceive, discern, detect, espy, behold, watch, view, spot, witness; *inf.* get a load of. 2 *police observe the house* keep under observation, watch, keep watch on, look at, keep under surveillance, keep in sight, keep in view, spy upon, monitor, reconnoiter, scan; *inf.* keep an eye on, keep tabs on. 3 *doctors observe the patient* keep under observation, keep under scrutiny, scrutinize, watch, monitor, keep under surveillance, inspect, study, review, examine, check. 4 *"A good try," he observed* say, remark, comment, state, utter, enunciate, exclaim, announce, declare, pronounce. 5 *observe the rules* keep, obey, adhere to, abide by, heed, follow, comply with, conform to, acquiesce in, consent to, accept, respect, defer to. 6 *observe one's duty* carry out, perform, execute, discharge, fulfill. 7 *observe Christmas* celebrate, keep, recognize, commemorate, mark, remember, solemnize.
Antonyms: OVERLOOK; IGNORE; DISOBEY.

observer *noun* watcher, looker-on, onlooker, witness, eyewitness, spectator, bystander, beholder, viewer, commentator, reporter, sightseer, spotter; *inf.* rubberneck.

obsess *verb her memory obsesses him* | *memories that obsess his mind* preoccupy, haunt, monopolize, have a hold on, possess, consume, engross, have a grip on, grip, dominate, rule, control, be on one's mind, be uppermost in one's mind, prey on, plague, torment, hound, bedevil. **be obsessed by** be preoccupied with, be haunted by, be possessed by, be beset by, be consumed with, be gripped by, be dominated by, be plagued by, be bedeviled by; *inf.* have a bee in one's bonnet about, have a thing about, be hung up on.

obsession *noun* preoccupation, fixation, *idée fixe*, ruling/consuming passion, mania, enthusiasm, infatuation, compulsion, phobia, complex, fetish, craze; *inf.* bee in one's bonnet, hang-up, thing.
Antonyms: INDIFFERENCE; UNCONCERN.

obsessive *adjective an obsessive concern for hygiene* excessive, overdone, consuming, compulsive, besetting, gripping, haunting.

obsolescent *adjective* going out of use, going out of fashion, dying out, on the decline, declining, waning, on the wane, disappearing, past its prime, aging, moribund; *inf.* on the way out.

obsolete *adjective obsolete machinery/words* no longer in use, in disuse, disused, outworn, discarded, discontinued, extinct, bygone, outmoded, *démodé*, passé, antiquated, out of date, outdated, out, superannuated, old-fashioned, out of fashion, out of style, behind the times, old, dated, antique, archaic, ancient, antediluvian, time-worn, past its prime, having seen better days; *inf.* old hat.
Antonyms: CURRENT; MODERN; UP-TO-DATE.

obstacle *noun* bar, barrier, obstruction, impediment, hindrance, hurdle, barricade, blockade, stumbling block, block, blockage, curb, check, stop, stoppage, deterrent, balk, snag, difficulty, catch, drawback, hitch, interference, interruption, fly in the ointment.
Antonyms: HELP; ADVANTAGE; ENCOURAGEMENT.

obstinacy *noun* stubbornness, mulishness, pigheadedness, willfulness, perversity, refractoriness, recalcitrance, contumaciousness, firmness, steadfastness, inflexibility, immovability, intransigence, intractability, persistence, pertinacity, tenacity, doggedness, relentlessness, single-mindedness.
Antonyms: COMPLIANCE; ACQUIESCENCE.

obstinate *adjective obstinate person/resistance* stubborn, stubborn as a mule, mulish, pigheaded, headstrong, willful, self-willed, strong-minded, perverse, refractory, recalcitrant, contumacious, unmanageable, firm, steadfast, unyielding, inflexible, unbending, immovable, intransigent, intractable, uncompromising, persistent, persevering, pertinacious, tenacious, dogged, single-minded, relentless, unrelenting.
Antonyms: compliant; AMENABLE; FLEXIBLE; TRACTABLE.

obstreperous *adjective obstreperous person/behavior* unruly, disorderly, turbulent, rowdy, boisterous, rough, riotous, out of control, uncontrolled, out of hand, wild, rampaging, undisciplined, unrestrained, unbridled, ungoverned, unmanageable, noisy, loud, clamorous, raucous, rambunctious, vociferous.
Antonyms: ORDERLY; QUIET; RESTRAINED.

obstruct *verb* **1** *logs obstruct the road/river* block, barricade, bar, cut off, shut off, choke, clog (up), dam up. **2** *floods obstructing traffic* hold up, bring to a standstill, stop, halt, block, prohibit. **3** *obstructing our efforts/progress* hinder, impede, hamper, block, interfere with, interrupt, hold up, frustrate, thwart, balk, inhibit, curb, brake, bridle, hamstring, encumber, restrain, slow, retard, delay, arrest, check, stop, halt, restrict, limit.
Antonyms: CLEAR; ADVANCE; FACILITATE; HELP.

obstruction *noun* obstacle, impediment, hindrance, bar, barrier, barricade, hurdle, block,

blockage, stumbling block, blockade, curb, check, stop, stoppage, deterrent, balk, snag, difficulty, catch, drawback, restriction, hitch, fly in the ointment.
Antonyms: AID; HELP; ENCOURAGEMENT.

obstructive *adjective* **1** *obstructive measures/tactics* blocking, delaying, hindering, stalling, inhibiting, interrupting, restrictive, preventative, preventive. **2** *obstructive people* unhelpful, uncooperative, awkward.
Antonyms: HELPFUL; SUPPORTIVE; COOPERATIVE.

obtain *verb* **1** *obtain a ticket/promotion* get, get hold of, acquire, come by, procure, secure, gain, earn, take possession of, get one's hands on, seize, grab, pick up. **2** *new rules obtain* be in force, be in use, be effective, exist, stand, prevail, hold, be the case, reign, rule, hold sway.
Antonyms: LOSE; give up (*see* GIVE); RELINQUISH.

obtainable *adjective no tickets obtainable* available, to be had, procurable, at hand, ready; *inf.* on tap.

obtrusive *adjective* **1** *obtrusive colors/music* noticeable, conspicuous, obvious, unmistakable, blatant, flagrant, bold, audacious, intrusive. **2** *obtrusive behavior* forward, interfering, meddling, prying, intrusive, officious, importunate; *inf.* pushy, nosy.
Antonyms: UNOBTRUSIVE; RESTRAINED; RETIRING.

obtuse *adjective* stupid, dull, dull-witted, slow-witted, slow, uncomprehending, unintelligent, imperceptive, bovine, stolid, insensitive, thick-skinned; *inf.* dim, dense, thick, dim-witted, slow on the uptake, boneheaded, dumb, dopey.
Antonyms: BRIGHT; CLEVER.

obvious *adjective* clear, clear-cut, crystal-clear, plain, visible, noticeable, perceptible, discernible, detectable, recognizable, evident, apparent, manifest, distinct, palpable, patent, conspicuous, unconcealed, overt, pronounced, transparent, prominent, unmistakable, indisputable, undeniable, as plain as the nose on one's face, staring someone in the face; *inf.* sticking out like a sore thumb, sticking out a mile.
Antonyms: IMPERCEPTIBLE; INCONSPICUOUS; OBSCURE.

obviously *adjective* **1** *obviously pregnant* clearly, plainly, visibly, noticeably, discernibly, evidently, manifestly, distinctly, patently, unmistakably, undeniably. *See* OBVIOUS. **2** *obviously, we must go* of course, certainly, undoubtedly, clearly.

occasion *noun* **1** *we met on one or two occasions* time, juncture, point, situation, instance, case, circumstance. **2** *it was a sad occasion* event, incident, occurrence, happening, episode, affair, experience. **3** *we met at a college occasion* function, party, affair, celebration; *inf.* get-together, do. **4** *if the occasion arises* opportunity, golden opportunity, chance, opening, contingency. **5** *have occasion to believe* reason, cause, grounds, justification, call, excuse, inducement.

occasion verb occasion much grief cause, give rise to, bring about, result in, lead to, prompt, provoke, produce, create, generate, engender, originate, effect.

occasional adjective an occasional meeting/letter infrequent, intermittent, irregular, sporadic, odd, rare, casual, incidental.
Antonyms: REGULAR; HABITUAL.

occasionally adverb now and then, now and again, from time to time, sometimes, at times, every so often, once in a while, on occasion, periodically, at intervals, irregularly, sporadically, infrequently, intermittently, on and off, off and on.

occult adjective supernatural, magic, magical, mystical, mystic, preternatural, transcendental, unrevealed, secret, hidden, concealed, invisible, obscure, recondite, arcane, abstruse, esoteric, inexplicable, unfathomable, mysterious, cryptic, enigmatic.

occult noun the occult the supernatural, magic, black magic, witchcraft, sorcery, wizardry, the black arts, diabolism, devil worship, supernaturalism, mysticism.

occupancy noun occupation, tenancy, tenure, residence, residency, inhabitancy, inhabitance, inhabitation, habitation, habitancy, living, possession, possessorship, holding.

occupant noun occupier, tenant, renter, leaseholder, lessee, inhabitant, resident, dweller, householder, addressee, incumbent, inmate.

occupation noun 1 what is his occupation? job, work, profession, business, employment, employ, career, calling, métier, vocation, trade, craft, line, field, province, area. 2 occupation of the house occupancy, tenancy, tenure, residence, inhabitancy, habitation, possession, holding. See OCCUPANCY. 3 suffer the occupation of their land possession, foreign rule, invasion, seizure, takeover, conquest, capture, overthrow, subjugation, subjection.

occupational adjective employment, work, professional, business, career, vocational.

occupied adjective 1 everyone is occupied just now busy, engaged, working, at work, employed; inf. tied up, hard at it. 2 all the rooms are occupied full, engaged, taken, in use, unavailable. 3 the houses are all occupied inhabited, lived-in, tenanted, settled.
Antonyms: FREE; VACANT; EMPTY.

occupy verb 1 occupy the upstairs apartment live in, inhabit, reside in, dwell in, be the tenant of, tenant, have one's residence/abode in, make one's home in, stay in. 2 occupy her time | will occupy too much space fill, fill up, take up, use up, utilize, cover. 3 occupy a top post hold, be in, fill, have; inf. hold down. 4 occupy oneself engage, employ, absorb, engross, preoccupy, immerse, interest, involve, entertain, divert, amuse, beguile. 5 the invading army occupied their country take possession of, invade, overrun, seize, take over, capture, garrison.
Antonyms: LEAVE; ABANDON; QUIT.

occur verb 1 the accident/promotion occurred last year happen, take place, come about, come to pass, materialize, transpire, arise, crop up, turn up, befall, eventuate. 2 the disease occurs in the tropics be found, be met with, be, exist, have its being, appear, present itself, show itself, manifest itself, arise, spring up. 3 an idea occurs to me | did it not occur to you to telephone? come to mind, spring to mind, come to one, enter one's head, cross one's mind, strike one, hit one, dawn on, suggest itself.

occurrence noun 1 robbery is an everyday occurrence happening, event, incident, circumstance, affair, episode, proceeding, adventure. 2 the occurrence of the disease is nationwide existence, appearance, manifestation, materialization, springing up.

odd adjective 1 an odd person | she is becoming odd strange, eccentric, queer, peculiar, idiosyncratic, unconventional, outlandish, droll, weird, bizarre, offbeat, freakish, whimsical; inf. wacky, freaky, kinky, off-the-wall. 2 an odd happening unusual, uncommon, irregular, strange, peculiar, funny, curious, queer, abnormal, atypical, different, extraordinary, out-of-the-ordinary, exceptional, rare, remarkable, singular, deviant, aberrant, freak, freakish, bizarre, weird. 3 do odd jobs occasional, casual, temporary, part-time, seasonal, periodic, irregular, miscellaneous, various, varied. 4 at odd moments occasional, random, irregular, periodic, haphazard, chance, fortuitous, fragmentary, various, sundry. 5 an odd sock unmatched, unpaired, leftover, spare, remaining, surplus, superfluous, lone, single, solitary, sole. odd man out exception, outsider, nonconformist, misfit, maverick, individualist.
Antonyms: ORDINARY; USUAL; REGULAR.

oddity noun 1 comment on the oddity of his behavior strangeness, eccentricity, queerness, peculiarness, peculiarity, weirdness, freakishness; inf. wackiness. See ODD 1. 2 the oddity of the happening unusualness, uncommonness, peculiarness, peculiarity, abnormality, rarity, rareness, bizarreness. See ODD 2. 3 the house is an oddity | this is a grammatical oddity curiosity, rarity, anomaly, aberration, irregularity, phenomenon. 4 he is an oddity eccentric, crank, original, misfit, fish out of water, rara avis; inf. character, card, oddball, weirdo, crackpot, nut, screwball, freak, odd/queer fish. 5 the oddities of her character peculiarity, idiosyncrasy, eccentricity, mannerism, quirk, twist, kink.

oddment noun 1 oddments of material scrap, remnant, leftover, fragment, snippet, bit, piece, end, shred, sliver, stub, tail end. 2 collector of oddments miscellanea, odds and ends, sundry, knickknack, notion, novelty, souvenir, keepsake, memento.

odds *plural noun* **1** *the odds are in his favor* advantage, lead, edge, superiority, supremacy, ascendancy. **2** *the odds are that he will win* likelihood, probability, chances, balance. **3** *against heavy odds* difference, disparity, unevenness, inequality, discrepancy, variation, dissimilarity. **at odds with** **1** *at odds with each other* in conflict with, in disagreement with, on bad terms with, at daggers drawn with, at loggerheads with. **2** *at odds with his principles* out of keeping with, not in keeping with, in opposition to, at variance with. **odds and ends** bits and pieces, bits, pieces, oddments, fragments, remnants, scraps, cuttings, snippets, miscellanea, leftovers, leavings, debris.

odious *adjective* abhorrent, repugnant, disgusting, repulsive, repellent, revolting, foul, vile, unpleasant, disagreeable, loathsome, detestable, hateful, despicable, contemptible, objectionable, offensive, horrible, horrid, abominable, heinous, atrocious, execrable.
Antonyms: DELIGHTFUL; PLEASANT; AGREEABLE.

odium *noun* abhorrence, repugnance, disgust, revulsion, loathing, detestation, hatred, dislike, disapproval, antipathy, contempt.

odor *noun* **1** *the odor of cologne/baking/garbage* aroma, smell, scent, perfume, fragrance, bouquet, redolence, essence, stench, stink. **2** *an odor of ill will about the place* atmosphere, air, ambience, aura, spirit, quality, flavor, emanation.

odyssey *noun* journey, voyage, trek, quest, peregrination, crusade, pilgrimage, journeying.

off *adjective* **1** *the off side of the building* far, remote, distant, faraway. **2** *the game/deal is off* canceled, postponed, shelved. **3** *closed during the off season* slack, not busy, unbusy, idle, inactive. **4** *these answers are off* incorrect, inaccurate, wrong, in error, erroneous. **5** *called on the off chance that you were home* unlikely, doubtful, remote, improbable, implausible. **6** *the food/milk is off* bad, rotten, decomposed, moldy, high, sour, rancid, turned.
Antonyms: BUSY; ON; CORRECT.

off *adverb* **1** *taking a day off* away, absent. **2** *feeling somewhat off* ill, unwell, sick, poorly; *inf.* under the weather, below par. **off and on** on and off, sporadically, irregularly, intermittently, at intervals, periodically, once in a while, every so often, now and then, now and again, from time to time, occasionally.

offbeat *adjective* eccentric, unconventional, unorthodox, idiosyncratic, unusual, strange, bizarre, weird, freakish, outlandish, outré, Bohemian, hippie, freaky; *inf.* kinky, way-out, far-out, off-the-wall.
Antonyms: ORDINARY; CONVENTIONAL; RUN-OF-THE-MILL.

off-color *adjective* off-color jokes risqué, racy, blue, vulgar, indecent, smutty, dirty, ribald, obscene, bawdy, pornographic; *inf.* raunchy.

offend *verb* **1** *his behavior offended them* give offense to, hurt the feelings of, wound, be an affront to, affront, upset, displease, annoy, anger, incense, exasperate, vex, pique, put out, gall, irritate, provoke, ruffle, disgruntle, rankle with, outrage, insult, slight, humiliate; *inf.* rile, rattle, put someone's back up, tread/step on someone's toes. **2** *offend his ear | will offend her sense of taste | guaranteed to offend art lovers* cause offense to, be offensive to, displease, upset, be disagreeable to, put someone off, be distasteful to, repel, disgust, revolt, nauseate; *inf.* turn someone off. **3** *apologize for having offended* commit a crime, break the law, do wrong, sin, go astray, fall from grace, err, transgress.
Antonyms: PLEASE; DELIGHT.

offended *adjective* hurt, wounded, affronted, upset, displeased, annoyed, angered, incensed, exasperated, vexed, piqued, put out, irritated, ruffled, disgruntled, resentful, outraged, insulted, in a huff, huffy; *inf.* riled, miffed, rattled. *See* OFFEND 1.

offender *noun* wrongdoer, culprit, criminal, lawbreaker, miscreant, delinquent, sinner, transgressor, malefactor.

offense *noun* **1** *commit an offense* crime, illegal act, breaking of the law, breach/violation/infraction of the law, wrongdoing, wrong, misdemeanor, act of misconduct, misdeed, peccadillo, sin, transgression, act of dereliction, shortcoming, fault, lapse; *Law* malfeasance. **2** *an offense against society* affront, injury, hurt, source of harm, outrage, atrocity, insult, injustice, indignity, slight, snub. **3** *her behavior causes offense* annoyance, anger, indignation, exasperation, wrath, ire, displeasure, disapproval, dislike, animosity, resentment, pique, vexation, umbrage, antipathy, aversion, opposition, enmity. **4** *the enemy's offense* attack, assault, act of aggression, aggression, onslaught, offensive, thrust, charge, sortie, sally, invasion, incursion. **take offense at** *take offense at his remarks* be offended at/by, be affronted at/by, take umbrage at, feel upset at/by, get annoyed at, get angry at, feel piqued at/by, feel resentment at, resent, get/go into a huff about; *inf.* be miffed at/by.

offensive *adjective* **1** *an offensive remark/person* hurtful, wounding, abusive, affronting, displeasing, annoying, exasperating, vexing, galling, irritating, provocative, provoking, objectionable, outrageous, insulting, humiliating, rude, discourteous, uncivil, impolite, unmannerly, impertinent, insolent, disrespectful. **2** *an offensive smell/sight* disagreeable, unpleasant, nasty, foul, vile, objectionable, odious, abominable, detestable, loathsome, repugnant, disgusting, obnoxious, repulsive, repellent, nauseating, sickening, unpalatable, distasteful, unsavory, noisome; *inf.* horrid, yucky. **3** *the offensive army* attacking, on the attack, assaulting, invading, invasive, aggressive, com-

bative, martial, warlike, belligerent, bellicose, hostile; *inf.* on the warpath.
Antonyms: COMPLIMENTARY; PLEASANT; DEFENSIVE.

offensive
abhorrent, abominable, detestable, odious, repugnant

Looking for just the right word to express your dislike, distaste, disgust, or aversion to something? **Offensive** is a relatively mild adjective, used to describe anyone or anything that is unpleasant or disagreeable (*she found his remarks offensive; the offensive sight of garbage piled in the alley*). If you want to express strong dislike for someone or something that deserves to be disliked, use **detestable** (*a detestable man who never had a kind word for anyone*). If something is so offensive that it provokes a physical as well as a moral or intellectual response, use **odious** (*the odious treatment of women during the war in Bosnia*), and if you instinctively draw back from it, use **repugnant** (*the very thought of piercing one's nose was repugnant to her*). If your repugnance is extreme, go one step further and use **abhorrent** (*an abhorrent act that could not go unpunished*). Persons and things that are truly loathsome or terrifying can be called **abominable** (*an abominable act of desecration; the abominable snowman*), although this word is often used as an overstatement to mean "awful" (*abominable taste in clothes*).

offensive *noun many killed in the offensive* attack, assault, onslaught, drive, invasion, push, thrust, charge, sortie, sally, act of war, incursion. **be on the offensive** attack, begin to attack, attack first, be aggressive, strike the first blow, start a war/battle/quarrel; *inf.* be on the warpath.

offer *verb* **1** *offer a suggestion* put forward, propose, advance, submit, propound, suggest, recommend, make a motion of, put to the motion, move. **2** *offer to help* volunteer one's services, volunteer, offer one's service, offer assistance/help, be at someone's service, be at someone's disposal, make oneself available, show readiness/willingness to help. **3** *the job offers good career prospects* afford, provide, supply, give, furnish, make available, present, give an opportunity for. **4** *offer the house at $200,000* put up for sale, put on the market, ask for bids on/for. **5** *he has offered $150,000 for the house* put in an offer of, bid, put in a bid of, offer to buy at. **6** *offer his first harvest to the gods* | *a goat offered to the goddess* offer up, offer as a sacrifice, sacrifice. **7** *as opportunities offer* arrive, appear, happen, occur, come on the scene, present itself, show itself. **8** *offer violence/resistance* attempt, try, essay, show, give.
Antonyms: WITHDRAW; REFUSE; WITHHOLD.

offer *noun* **1** *offers of help* proposal, proposition, suggestion, submission, approach, overture. **2** *accept the highest offer* bid, bidding price. **3**

counteract their offers of resistance attempt, endeavor, essay.

offering *noun* **1** *collecting offerings from the members* contribution, donation, subscription, gift, present, alms, charity, handout. **2** *offerings to the gods* sacrifice, oblation, immolation.

offhand *adjective an offhand manner* | *her behavior was very offhand* casual, unceremonious, cavalier, careless, indifferent, perfunctory, cursory, uninterested, unconcerned, blasé, curt, abrupt, terse, brusque, discourteous, uncivil, impolite, rude; *inf.* off, couldn't-care-less, take-it-or-leave-it.
Antonyms: CAREFUL; THOROUGH.

offhand *adverb* **1** *always acts very offhand* casually, unceremoniously, cavalierly, perfunctorily, cursorily, unconcernedly, curtly, abruptly, discourteously, rudely. *See* OFFHAND *adjective.* **2** *I cannot say offhand* extempore, impromptu, ad lib, extemporaneously, without preparation, without consideration, without rehearsal, spontaneously; *inf.* off the cuff, off the top of one's head, just like that.

office *noun* **1** *his office is near his home* place of business, base, workplace, workroom, room. **2** *he has the office of treasurer* post, position, appointment, role, place, situation, station. **3** *the office of administrator is demanding* | *to hold high office* work, employment, business, duty, function, responsibility, obligation, charge, tenure. **4** *perform their domestic offices* job, work, task, chore, duty, assignment, commission, routine.

officer *noun* **1** *an officer in charge of the men* military officer, army officer, naval officer, air force officer, commissioned officer, noncommissioned officer. **2** *the officer in charge of the investigation* police officer, policeman/policewoman, officer of the law, detective, constable; *inf.* copper, cop, the law, gumshoe; *inf. derog.* pig, fuzz. **3** *the officers of the society* officeholder, office-bearer, official, committee member, board member, administrator, executive, functionary, bureaucrat. **4** *courts sending out officers* representative, agent, deputy, messenger, envoy.

offices *plural noun through the good offices of* assistance, help, aid, support, backing, patronage, aegis, auspices, intervention, intercession, mediation, advocacy, recommendation, word.

official *adjective* **1** *official permission* | *his appointment is now official* authorized, accredited, approved, validated, authenticated, certified, endorsed, sanctioned, licensed, recognized, accepted, legitimate, legal, lawful, bona fide, proper, *ex cathedra*; *inf.* kosher. **2** *an official function* formal, ceremonial, solemn, conventional, ritualistic, pompous; *inf.* stuffed-shirt.
Antonyms: UNOFFICIAL; UNAUTHORIZED; INFORMAL.

official *noun* **1** *club/party officials* officer, officeholder, office-bearer, administrator, executive. *See* OFFICER 3. **2** *officials of the court* officer, representative, agent. *See* OFFICER 4.

officiate *verb* **1** *officiate in the absence of the chairman* take charge, be in charge, preside, take the chair. **2** *officiate at the service/proceedings* be in charge of, be responsible for, chair, preside over, manage, oversee, superintend, conduct, run, operate.

officious *adjective officious bureaucrats/behavior* overzealous, overbusy, bustling, interfering, intrusive, meddlesome, meddling, prying, inquisitive, importunate, forward, obtrusive, self-important, opinionated, dictatorial, domineering; *inf.* pushy, nosy.

offing *noun* **in the offing** *a salary increase is in the offing* on the way, coming soon, coming up, close at hand, near, imminent, in prospect, on the horizon, in the cards, in the wings.

offload *verb offload the cargo/responsibility* unload, unburden, disburden, jettison, get rid of, discharge, transfer, shift; *inf.* dump.

off-putting *adjective had a rather off-putting manner* discouraging, disheartening, dispiriting, daunting, disconcerting, discomfiting, dismaying, upsetting, unsettling, unnerving, intimidating, frightening, fearsome, formidable.

offset *verb weights offsetting each other* | *this year's profits offset last year's loss* counterbalance, counterpoise, counteract, countervail, balance, balance out, cancel out, neutralize, compensate for, make up for, make good, indemnify.

offshoot *noun* **1** *plant offshoots* side shoot, shoot, sprout, branch, bough, limb, twig, sucker, tendril, runner, scion, spur. **2** *an offshoot of the Hapsburg family* descendant, scion, relation, relative, kin. **3** *an offshoot of the family firm* branch, subsidiary, adjunct, appendage. **4** *his attitude is an offshoot of his war experiences* result, outcome, aftermath, consequence, upshot, product, by-product, spin-off, ramification.

offspring *noun* child, children, family, progeny, young, youngster(s), issue, descendant(s), heir(s), successor(s), spawn; *inf.* kid(s), young 'un(s).
Antonyms: PARENT; ANCESTOR; FOREBEAR.

often *adverb* frequently, many a time, on many occasions, repeatedly, again and again, time and again, time and time again, time after time, over and over, over and over again, day in (and) day out; *lit.* oft, oft-times; *inf.* a lot.
Antonyms: SELDOM; RARELY.

ogle *verb* stare at, gaze at, eye amorously, look flirtatiously at, leer at, make eyes at, make sheep's eyes at; *inf.* give someone the once-over, undress with one's eyes.

ogre/ogress *noun* **1** *a mythical ogre* monster, giant/giantess, troll, bogeyman, bugbear, demon, devil. **2** *ruled by an ogre* frightening

person, fiend, beast, tyrant, despot, barbarian, brute, villain, sadist.

oil *noun* **1** *use oil to lubricate the surface/skin* lubricant, grease, petroleum jelly, mineral oil, baby oil, bath oil; *Trademark* Vaseline. **2** *fry in oil* cooking oil, vegetable oil; sunflower oil, corn oil, olive oil, peanut oil, canola oil, safflower oil.

oil *verb oil the surface/lock* lubricate, grease, smear with oil, make slippery/smooth, anoint.

oily *adjective* **1** *oily fish* oil-containing, oleaginous. **2** *oily food* greasy, fatty, buttery, swimming in oil/fat. **3** *oily charm/remarks* smooth, smooth-talking, honey-tongued, flattering, fulsome, glib, suave, urbane, unctuous, subservient, servile, oleaginous.

ointment *noun* medicated cream/lotion, emollient, salve, balm, liniment, embrocation, unguent, gel.

OK, okay *interjection okay, I'll go* yes, all right, right, very well, very good; *inf.* right you are, righto.

OK, okay *noun give her the OK to proceed* agreement, consent, assent, permission, authorization, endorsement, sanction, approval, seal of approval, approbation, thumbs up, go-ahead; *inf.* green light, say-so.
Antonyms: REFUSAL; DENIAL.

OK, okay *adjective an okay job* | *the movie was OK* all right, reasonable, acceptable, tolerable, passable, satisfactory, adequate, middling; *inf.* not bad, so-so, fair-to-middling.

OK, okay *verb OK the project* give one's consent to, consent to, say yes to, agree to, give one's approval to, approve, pass, authorize, sanction, give something thumbs up, give something the go-ahead, give something the/a nod, rubber-stamp; *inf.* give something the green light, give something one's say-so.
Antonyms: REFUSE; FORBID; VETO.

old *adjective* **1** *old people* older, mature, elderly, aged, advanced in years, up in years, getting on, gray-haired, grizzled, hoary, past one's prime, ancient, decrepit, senescent, senile, venerable, senior; *inf.* past it, over the hill, long in the tooth. **2** *old clothes* worn, worn-out, cast-off, shabby, torn, tattered, ragged, old-fashioned, out of date, outmoded, démodé. **3** *old farm buildings* dilapidated, broken-down, run-down, tumbledown, ramshackle, decaying, crumbling, disintegrating. **4** *old ideas* out of date, outdated, old-fashioned, outmoded, passé, archaic, obsolete, extinct, antiquated, antediluvian, superannuated; *inf.* old hat. **5** *in the old days* of old, olden, bygone, past, early, earlier, earliest, primeval, primordial, prehistoric. **6** *old customs* age-old, long-standing, long-lived, long-established, time-honored, enduring, lasting. **7** *old cars* antique, veteran, vintage. **8** *old for her years* | *he's an old hand* mature, wise, sensible, experienced, knowledgeable, well-versed, practiced, skilled, skillful, adept. **9** *an old girlfriend* ex-, former, pre-

quondam. **old age** oldness, elderliness, age, agedness, declining years, advanced years, winter/autumn of one's life, senescence, senility, dotage.
Antonyms: YOUNG; NEW; MODERN.

---

old
aged, ancient, antediluvian, antiquated, archaic, obsolete

Almost no one likes to be thought of as **old**, which means having been in existence or use for a relatively long time (*an old washing machine*). But those who are **aged**, indicating a longer life span than *old* and usually referring to persons of very advanced years, are often proud of the fact that they have outlived most of their peers. Children may exaggerate and regard their parents as **ancient**, which means dating back to the remote past, often specifically the time before the end of the Roman Empire (*ancient history*), and their attitudes as **antediluvian**, which literally means dating back to the period before the biblical Great Flood and Noah's ark (*an antediluvian transportation system*). Some people seem older than they really are, simply because their ideas are **antiquated**, which means out of vogue or no longer practiced (*antiquated ideas about dating*). Things rather than people are usually described as **archaic**, which means having the characteristics of an earlier, sometimes primitive, period (*archaic words like thou and thine*). **Obsolete** also refers to things, implying that they have gone out of use or need to be replaced by something newer (*an obsolete textbook; a machine that will be obsolete within the decade*).

---

older *adjective* the older child | she's older than I elder, more advanced in years, senior.

old-fashioned *adjective* old, former, out of fashion, outmoded, *démodé*, unfashionable, out of style, out of date, outdated, dated, behind the times, past, bygone, passé, archaic, obsolescent, obsolete, ancient, antiquated, superannuated, antediluvian, old-fogyish, old-fangled; *inf.* old hat, not with it.
Antonyms: MODERN; UP-TO-DATE; FASHIONABLE.

old-time *adjective* old-time customs/dancing old, former, past, bygone, old-fashioned, archaic, ancient.

old-timer *noun* elderly person/man/woman, senior citizen, senior, veteran; *inf. derog.* old fogy, old geezer, old codger.

old-world *adjective* 1 old-world charm old, archaic, old-fashioned, quaint, traditional, ceremonious, chivalrous, gallant, courtly. 2 *old-world cottages* old, old-fashioned, traditional, quaint, picturesque.

omen *noun* portent, sign, token, foretoken, harbinger, premonition, forewarning, warning, foreshadowing, prediction, forecast, prophecy, augury, straw in the wind, writing on the wall, auspice, presage, presentiment, feeling, vague feeling, foreboding, misgiving; *inf.* funny feeling, feeling in one's bones.

ominous *adjective* 1 *ominous clouds* | *the future was looking ominous* threatening, menacing, minatory, black, dark, gloomy, heavy, sinister, bad, unpromising, unpropitious, pessimistic, inauspicious, unfavorable, unlucky, ill-fated. 2 *ancients believing in ominous signs* oracular, augural, divinatory, prophetic, premonitory, prognostic, sibyllic.
Antonyms: PROMISING; AUSPICIOUS; PROPITIOUS.

---

ominous
fateful, forbidding, foreboding, portentous, premonitory

A sky filled with low, dark clouds might look **ominous**, but it probably wouldn't be considered **portentous**, even though the root words *omen* and *portent* are nearly synonymous. What is *ominous* is usually threatening and may imply impending disaster (*an ominous silence*), while *portentous* is more often used to describe something that provokes awe or amazement (*a portentous show of military strength*) or a very important outcome (*a portentous moment for the American people*). Like *ominous*, **foreboding** implies that something evil is coming (*foreboding words that sent shivers through us*), while **forbidding** suggests an unfriendly or threatening appearance (*a dark, forbidding castle*). **Fateful** and **premonitory** are less frightening words. What is *fateful* appears to have been inevitable or decreed by fate, with an emphasis on decisive importance (*a fateful meeting with her ex-boyfriend; a battle that would prove fateful*). Anything that serves to warn beforehand is **premonitory**, whether or not the warning concerns something negative (*a premonitory dream about her father's death; a premonitory feeling about the exam*).

---

omission *noun* 1 *the omission of his name from the list* leaving out, exclusion, exception, noninclusion, deletion, erasure, elimination, expunction. 2 *guilty of a sin of omission* neglect, neglectfulness, negligence, dereliction, forgetfulness, oversight, disregard, nonfulfillment, default, failure. 3 *note several omissions from the list* exclusion, oversight, gap, lacuna.
Antonyms: ADDITION; INCLUSION.

omit *verb* 1 *omit his name from the list* leave out, exclude, except, miss out, miss, fail to mention, pass over, drop, delete, erase, eliminate, expunge, rub out, cross out; *inf.* give something a miss. 2 *omit to close the door* | *omit closing the door* forget, neglect, fail; leave undone, overlook, skip.
Antonyms: ADD; INCLUDE.

omnipotence *noun* all-powerfulness, almightiness, supremacy, preeminence, invincibility, supreme power, absolute/unlimited power, undisputed sway, divine right.

omnipotent *adjective* all-powerful, almighty, supreme, preeminent, invincible.

omnipresent *adjective* all-present, present everywhere, ubiquitous, all-pervasive, infinite, boundless.

omniscient *adjective* all-knowing, all-wise, all-seeing, all-perceiving.

omnivorous *adjective* all-devouring, eating anything, pantophagous, indiscriminate.

on *adverb* **on and off** off and on, sporadically, irregularly, intermittently, at intervals, periodically. *See* OFF AND ON (OFF) *adverb.* **on and on** *talked/rambled on and on* at great length, incessantly, constantly, continuously, endlessly, interminably, unremittingly, relentlessly.

once *adverb* **1** *they were friends once* at one time, once upon a time, previously, formerly, in the past, in times gone by, in times past, in the old days, long ago. **2** *I saw him only once* on one occasion, one time, one single time. **3** *he did not once help* ever, at any time, on any occasion. **at once** **1** *you must leave at once* immediately, right away, right now, this moment, now, straight away, instantly, directly, forthwith, without delay; *inf.* before you can say Jack Robinson. **2** *they both arrived at once* at the same time, at one and the same time, at the same instant/moment, together, simultaneously. **once and for all** **1** *you must decide once and for all* decisively, conclusively, finally, positively, determinedly. **2** *he has gone once and for all* for always, for good, forever, permanently, finally. **once in a while** every now and again/then, now and again/then, occasionally, on the odd occasion, on occasion, at times, from time to time; *inf.* once in a blue moon.
Antonyms: NOW; OFTEN.

once *conjunction* *we will go once it stops raining* as soon as, when, after, the minute.

oncoming *adjective* *oncoming traffic* approaching, advancing, nearing, onrushing, forthcoming, imminent.

one *adjective* **1** *one person* a single, a solitary, a sole, a lone. **2** *they are now one* united, allied, joined, unified, bound, wedded, married. **one day** *one day they will come* someday.

onerous *adjective* burdensome, heavy, crushing, backbreaking, oppressive, weighty, arduous, strenuous, difficult, hard, formidable, laborious, exhausting, tiring, exigent, taxing, demanding, exacting, wearing, wearisome, fatiguing.
Antonyms: EASY; EFFORTLESS.

oneself *pronoun* the id, the self, ego; *inf.* number one, numero uno. **by oneself** **1** *stay by oneself* alone, all alone, on one's own, in a solitary state, unaccompanied, companionless, unattended. **2** *do the work by oneself* alone, all alone, on one's own, by one's own efforts, unaided,

without help, without assistance, independently.

one-sided *adjective* **1** *one-sided opinions* biased, prejudiced, partisan, partial, discriminatory, colored, inequitable, unfair, unjust, narrow-minded, bigoted. **2** *a one-sided game/discussion* uneven, unequal, unbalanced, lopsided.

one-time *adjective* *one-time journalist* ex-, former, previous, sometime, erstwhile; *lit.* quondam.

ongoing *adjective* **1** *ongoing projects* in progress, current, extant, progressing, advancing, successful, developing, evolving, growing. **2** *the work in the factory is ongoing* continuous, continual, uninterrupted, unbroken, nonstop, incessant, unending, constant.

onlooker *noun* looker-on, eyewitness, witness, observer, spectator, watcher, viewer, bystander, sightseer; *inf.* rubberneck.

only *adverb* **1** *only enough for two* just, at most, not more than, barely, scarcely. **2** *he is only saying that* just, merely, simply, purely.

only *adjective* **1** *their only son* single, one and only, solitary, sole, lone. **2** *the only place to eat* only possible, individual, unique, exclusive.

onomatopoeic *adjective* imitative, echoic.

onset *noun* **1** *the onset of the invading army* onslaught, assault, attack, charge, onrush. *See* ONSLAUGHT. **2** *the onset of trouble* start, beginning, commencement, inception, outbreak; *inf.* kickoff.
Antonyms: RETREAT; END.

onslaught *noun* assault, attack, charge, onrush, onset, storming, sortie, sally, raid, foray, push, thrust, drive, blitz.

onus *noun* burden, weight, load, responsibility, liability, obligation, duty, charge, encumbrance, cross to bear, millstone around one's neck, albatross.

ooze *verb* **1** *pus oozing from the wound* flow, discharge, exude, seep, trickle, drip, dribble, filter, filtrate, percolate, excrete, escape, leak, drain, bleed, sweat. **2** *she was positively oozing charm* exude, pour forth, send out, let loose, display, exhibit, manifest.

ooze *noun* **1** *the ooze of pus* flow, discharge, exudation, seeping, trickling, leak. *See* OOZE *verb.* **2** *the ooze at the bottom of the river* deposit, alluvium, silt, mud, slime, mire, muck.

opacity *noun* **1** *the opacity of the glass* nontransparency, nontranslucence; cloudiness, filminess, haziness. **2** *the opacity of the text* abstruseness, obscurity, unclearness, lack of clarity, enigma, unintelligibility, incomprehensibility. *See* OPAQUE 2.

opalescent *adjective* multicolored, many-hued, prismatic, rainbowlike, kaleidoscopic, iridescent, opaline, milky, pearly, nacreous.

opaque *adjective* **1** *opaque glass* nontransparent, nontranslucent, non-see-through; cloudy, filmy, blurred, hazy. **2** *a piece of opaque prose* abstruse, obscure, unclear, cryptic, enigmatic, unfathomable, unintelligible, incomprehensible, baffling, perplexing.

open *adjective* **1** *open doors* not shut, not closed, unlocked, unbolted, unlatched, unbarred, unfastened, unsecured, ajar, wide open, agape, gaping, yawning. **2** *open boxes/drains* uncovered, coverless, unlidded, topless, unsealed. **3** *open spaces/countryside* unenclosed, unfenced, exposed, unsheltered, wide, wide open, extensive, broad, spacious, sweeping, airy, uncrowded, uncluttered, undeveloped. **4** *open roads* unobstructed, unblocked, clear, passable, navigable. **5** *maps open on the table* spread out, unfolded, unfurled, unrolled, straightened out, extended, stretched out. **6** *open material/fabric* openwork, full of holes, honeycombed, lacy, filigree, airy, cellular, porous, spongy. **7** *quite open about her dislike* frank, candid, honest, forthright, direct, blunt, plainspoken, downright. **8** *the store/theater is open* open to the public, open for business, admitting customers/visitors. **9** *an open meeting/ competition* public, general, nonexclusive, accessible, nonrestrictive, unrestricted, nondiscriminatory. **10** *the job is still open* vacant, available, unfilled, unoccupied, free. **11** *open hostility* obvious, clear, noticeable, visible, apparent, evident, manifest, overt, conspicuous, patent, unconcealed, unhidden, undisguised, blatant, flagrant. **12** *three courses open to us* available, on hand, obtainable, accessible. **13** *the subject is still open* open to debate, open for discussion, yet to be decided, undecided, unresolved, unsettled, arguable, debatable, moot. **14** *keep an open mind* unbiased, prejudice-free, unprejudiced, nonpartisan, impartial, nondiscriminatory, objective, disinterested, dispassionate, detached. **15** *have an open disposition* frank, honest, artless, natural, simple, guileless, ingenuous, innocent. **16** *open hosts* openhanded, generous, liberal, bountiful, munificent. **open to** *the system is open to abuse* wide open to, allowing of, permitting, vulnerable to, exposed to, susceptible to, liable to, at the mercy of, an easy target for.
Antonyms: SHUT; closed; SECRETIVE; BIASED.

open *verb* **1** *open the door* throw open, unlock, unbolt, unlatch, unbar, unfasten. **2** *open the package* unwrap, undo, untie, unseal. **3** *open the bottle* uncork, broach, crack. **4** *the crack opened* open up, come apart, split, separate, rupture. **5** *we open tomorrow* open for business, open the/one's doors, be ready for customers/ visitors, admit customers, begin business, set up shop, put up one's shingle, start, begin, commence, start the ball rolling; *inf.* kick off. **6** *open his heart* lay bare, bare, uncover, expose, exhibit, disclose, divulge, pour out. **open out** *open out the map* spread out, unfold, unfurl, unroll, straighten out, extend, stretch out.
Antonyms: CLOSE; SHUT.

open-air *adjective* outdoor, out-of-doors, outside, alfresco.

openhanded *adjective* open, generous, liberal,

lavish, free, bountiful, bounteous, munificent; benevolent, charitable, magnanimous.

opening *noun* **1** *an opening in the fence/wall* gap, aperture, space, hole, orifice, vent, slot, break, breach, crack, split, fissure, cleft, crevice, chink, interstice, rent, rupture. **2** *an opening in the new office* vacancy, position, job, opportunity, chance. **3** *the opening of the fishing season* beginning, start, commencement, outset, inception, launch, birth, dawn; *inf.* kickoff. **4** *present at the gallery's opening* opening ceremony, official opening, launch.
Antonyms: CLOSURE; CLOSE; END; TERMINATION.

openly *adverb* **1** *she told him quite openly* frankly, candidly, honestly, forthrightly, directly, bluntly, unreservedly, straight from the shoulder, with no holds barred. **2** *conduct their affair openly* publicly, in public, in full view of people, blatantly, flagrantly, brazenly, with no attempt at concealment, overtly, unashamedly, shamelessly, unabashedly, wantonly, immodestly.

open-minded *adjective* **1** *open-minded judges* unbiased, unprejudiced, prejudice-free, nonpartisan, impartial, nondiscriminatory, objective, disinterested, dispassionate, detached, tolerant, liberal, broad-minded, undogmatic. **2** *writers should be open-minded* receptive, open to suggestions, open to new ideas, amenable.

operate *verb* **1** *the machine ceased to operate* work, function, go, run, perform, act, be in action. **2** *he can operate the machine* work, make go, run, use, utilize, employ, handle, manipulate, maneuver, ply, manage, be in charge of. **3** *operate on the patient* perform an operation, perform surgery; *inf.* put under the knife.
Antonyms: break down (*see* BREAK); FAIL.

operation *noun* **1** *the operation of the machine is crucial* working, functioning, running, performance. **2** *his operation of the machine* working, using, handling, manipulation. *See* OPERATE 2. **3** *the operation of radon testing went smoothly* activity, exercise, affair, business, undertaking, enterprise, task, job. **4** *operations on the stock exchange* transaction, business, deal, proceedings. **5** *military operations* maneuver, exercise, campaign, assault. **6** *an operation to remove the appendix* surgery, major surgery, minor surgery. **in operation** *rules/machines not yet in operation* operational, operative, in force, effective, in use, functioning, working, valid. *See* OPERATIONAL.

operational *adjective* *machines now operational* operative, workable, in operation, working, in working order, functioning, functional, going, in use, usable, in action, ready for action.
Antonyms: BROKEN; out of order.

operative *adjective* **1** *the rules are operative now* in operation, in force, effective, valid. **2** *the machines are now operative* operational, workable, working, functioning, functional, usable. *See*

OPERATIONAL. **3** *"might" is the operative word* key, relevant, significant, crucial, vital, important, essential.

Antonyms: INVALID; out of order; IRRELEVANT.

operative *noun* **1** *factory operatives* worker, workman, machinist, operator, mechanic, factory hand/employee. **2** *a foreign power's operatives* agent, secret agent, undercover agent, spy, double agent; *inf.* mole. **3** *an operative searching for clues* detective, private detective, private investigator, sleuth; *inf.* private eye, dick, gumshoe.

operator *noun* **1** *machine operators* operative, machinist, mechanic, practitioner. **2** *the operator of a car dealership* manager, businessman, businesswoman, business person, administrator, director, supervisor, superintendent. **3** *a smooth operator* maneuverer, manipulator, machinator, mover, wheeler-dealer.

opiate *noun* drug, narcotic, sedative, tranquilizer, depressant, bromide, soporific, morphine, opium, laudanum; *inf.* downer.

opinion *noun* point of view, view, viewpoint, belief, thought, thinking, way of thinking, standpoint, theory, judgment, estimation, feeling, sentiment, impression, notion, assumption, conception, conviction, persuasion, creed, dogma. **a matter of opinion** *how he should be punished is a matter of opinion* open to/for discussion, open to debate, debatable, a debatable point, open to question, a moot point, up to the individual.

---

opinion
belief, conviction, persuasion, sentiment, view

When you give your **opinion** on something, you offer a conclusion or a judgment that, although it may be open to question, seems true or probable to you at the time (*she was known for her strong opinions on women in the workplace*). A **view** is an opinion that is affected by your personal feelings or biases (*his views on life were essentially optimistic*), while a **sentiment** is a more or less settled opinion that may still be colored by emotion (*her sentiments on aging were shared by many other women approaching fifty*). A **belief** differs from an opinion or a view in that it is not necessarily the creation of the person who holds it; the emphasis here is on the mental acceptance of an idea, a proposition, or a doctrine and on the assurance of its truth (*religious beliefs; his belief in the power of the body to heal itself*). A **conviction** is a firmly-held and unshakable belief whose truth is not doubted (*she could not be swayed in her convictions*), while a **persuasion** (in this sense) is a strong belief that is unshakable because you want to believe that it's true rather than because there is evidence proving it so (*she was of the persuasion that he was innocent*).

---

opinionated *adjective* dogmatic, of fixed views,

of preconceived ideas, pontifical, doctrinaire, dictatorial, self-assertive, positive, confident, assured, cocksure, pompous, self-important, adamant, obstinate, stubborn, pigheaded, headstrong, willful, single-minded, inflexible, uncompromising, bigoted.

opponent *noun the two opponents shook hands | an opponent of the government* opposer, the opposition, rival, adversary, fellow contestant, fellow competitor, enemy, foe, antagonist, contender, dissenter, disputant.

Antonyms: ALLY; PARTNER; COLLEAGUE.

opportune *adjective wait for an opportune moment* advantageous, favorable, auspicious, propitious, good, lucky, happy, timely, well-timed, fortunate, providential, felicitous, convenient, expedient, suitable, apt, fitting, relevant, applicable, pertinent.

Antonyms: DISADVANTAGEOUS; UNFAVORABLE; INCONVENIENT.

opportunism *noun* exploitation, expediency, taking advantage, unscrupulousness, striking while the iron is hot, making hay while the sun shines, making the best of a bad situation.

opportunity *noun* lucky chance, chance, good time, golden opportunity, favorable time/occasion/moment, right set of circumstances, appropriate time/moment; *inf.* break.

oppose *verb* **1** *oppose the proposals* dislike, disapprove of, be hostile to, take a stand against, be/stand against, stand up to, stand up and be counted against, take issue with, take on, contradict, counter, argue against, counterattack, confront, resist, withstand, defy, fight, put up a fight against, combat, fly in the face of. **2** *oppose memory and imagination* compare, contrast, juxtapose, offset, balance, counterbalance, set against, pit against, parallel. **be opposed to** *be opposed to the plans | am opposed to going to war* be against, be in opposition to, dislike, be in disagreement with, disagree with, be averse to, be hostile to, be antagonistic to, be inimical to; *inf.* be anti.

Antonyms: SUPPORT; DEFEND; PROMOTE.

opposing *adjective* **1** *hold opposing opinions* opposite, differing, different, contrary, contradictory, conflicting, clashing, incompatible, at variance, irreconcilable. *See* OPPOSITE *adjective* 2. **2** *on opposing sides* opposite, rival, competitive, enemy, warring, fighting, contending, combatant.

opposite *adjective* **1** *people/houses opposite each other* facing, face-to-face with; *inf.* eyeball to eyeball with. **2** *hold opposite opinions* diametrically opposite, opposing, differing, different, unlike, contrary, reverse, contradictory, conflicting, clashing, discordant, dissident, at variance, incompatible, irreconcilable, antipathetical, poles apart. **3** *on opposite sides* opposing, rival, competitive, enemy, warring, fighting, contending, combatant.

Antonyms: SAME; IDENTICAL; LIKE.

antithetical, contradictory, contrary, reverse
All of these adjectives are usually applied to abstractions and are used to describe ideas, statements, qualities, forces, etc. that are so far apart as to seem irreconcilable. **Opposite** refers to ideas or things that are symmetrically opposed in position, direction, or character—in other words, that are set against each other in such a way that the contrast or conflict between them is highlighted (*they sat opposite each other at the table*). **Contradictory** goes a little further, implying that if one of two opposing statements, propositions, or principles is true, the other must be false. *Contradictory* elements are mutually exclusive; for example, alive and dead are contradictory terms because logically they cannot both be applied to the same thing. **Antithetical** implies that the two things being contrasted are diametrically opposed—as far apart or as different from each other as is possible (*their interests were antithetical*). **Contrary** adds connotations of conflict or antagonism (*a contrary view of the situation*), while **reverse** applies to that which moves or faces in the opposite direction (*the reverse side*).

opposite *noun* reverse, contrary, antithesis, converse, inverse, contradiction, the other extreme, the other side of the coin.

opposition *noun* **1** *express their opposition to the plans* dislike, disapproval, hostility, resistance, defiance. *See* OPPOSE 1. **2** *back the opposition* opponent, opposing side, other side, other team, rival, adversary, competition, antagonist, enemy, foe.

oppress *verb* **1** *the invading army oppressed the people* overwhelm, overpower, subjugate, enslave, suppress, crush, subdue, quash, quell, bring someone to his/her knees. **2** *the tyrant oppressed the citizens* tyrannize, crush, suppress, repress, abuse, maltreat, persecute, rule with a rod of iron, trample on, trample underfoot, ride roughshod over. **3** *oppressed by grief* weigh down, lie heavy on, weigh heavy on, burden, crush, depress, dispirit, dishearten, take the heart out of, discourage, sadden, make despondent, deject, desolate.

oppressed *adjective* **1** *the oppressed citizens* tyrannized, subjugated, enslaved, crushed, subdued, repressed, persecuted, abused, maltreated, misused, browbeaten, downtrodden, disadvantaged, underprivileged. **2** *flood victims feeling oppressed* weighed down, depressed, dispirited, despondent, dejected, desolate. *See* OPPRESS 3.

oppression *noun* **1** *the oppression of the people by the invading army* overwhelming, subjugation, subduing. *See* OPPRESS 1. **2** *the tyrant's oppression of the people* tyranny, suppression, abuse, persecution. *See* OPPRESS 2. **3** *people suffering from oppression for generations* tyranny, despotism, abuse, maltreatment, persecution,

cruelty, brutality, injustice, ruthlessness, harshness, hardship, misery, suffering, wretchedness. **4** *oppression brought on by grief* depression, despondency, dejection, desolation. *See* OPPRESS 3.

oppressive *adjective* **1** *an oppressive regime* tyrannical, despotic, draconian, iron-fisted, high-handed, repressive, domineering, harsh, crushing, cruel, brutal, ruthless, relentless, merciless, pitiless, inexorable, unjust, undemocratic. **2** *oppressive weather* muggy, close, airless, stuffy, stifling, suffocating, sultry, torrid.
Antonyms: LENIENT; HUMANE; FRESH.

oppressor *noun* tyrant, despot, autocrat, subjugator, persecutor, bully, iron hand, slave driver, taskmaster, scourge, dictator, tormentor, torturer.

opprobrium *noun* *bring opprobrium on his family* disgrace, shame, dishonor, ignominy, discredit, loss of face, disrepute, ill repute, infamy, notoriety, odium, obloquy.

opt *verb* **opt for** *opt for a red one* choose, select, pick, decide on, settle on, prefer; *inf.* go for.

optimistic *adjective* **1** *an optimistic person* disposed to look on the bright side, always expecting the best, inclined to look through rose-colored glasses, hopeful, full of hope, Pollyannaish, Panglossian. **2** *feeling optimistic about the future* | *was in an optimistic mood* positive, sanguine, hopeful, confident, bullish, cheerful, buoyant; *inf.* upbeat.
Antonyms: PESSIMISTIC; GLOOMY.

optimum *adjective* **1** *the optimum time to choose* most favorable, best, most advantageous, most appropriate, ideal, perfect. **2** *plants in optimum condition* peak, top, best, perfect, ideal, flawless, superlative, optimal; *inf.* tip-top, A-1.

option *noun* **1** *have little option* choice, freedom of choice, power to choose, right to choose. **2** *have no other option* choice, alternative, other possibility, preference.

optional *adjective* *attendance/tipping is optional* noncompulsory, not required, voluntary, up to the individual, discretionary, at one's discretion, elective.
Antonyms: COMPULSORY; OBLIGATORY; MANDATORY.

opulence *noun* **1** *the opulence of the family* affluence, wealth, richness, riches, money, fortune, prosperity. **2** *the opulence of the house/furnishings* luxury, luxuriousness, sumptuousness, lavishness; *inf.* plushiness, ritziness. **3** *the opulence of the vegetation* abundance, superabundance, copiousness, plentifulness, profuseness, prolificness, luxuriance, cornucopia.

opulent *adjective* **1** *opulent families* affluent, wealthy, rich, well-off, well-to-do, moneyed, prosperous; *inf.* well-heeled, rolling in it. **2** *opulent houses* luxurious, sumptuous, lavishly appointed; *inf.* plush, plushy, ritzy. **3** *opulent*

vegetation abundant, superabundant, copious, plentiful, profuse, prolific, luxuriant.
Antonyms: PENNILESS; POOR; SPARSE.

opus *noun* work, composition, *oeuvre*, piece, creation, production.

oracle *noun* **1** *the oracles of classical times* prophet/prophetess, seer, soothsayer, sibyl, augur, wise man/woman, sage. **2** *he regards himself as an oracle on architecture* authority, expert, mastermind, specialist, connoisseur, pundit, guru, mentor, adviser.

oracular *adjective* **1** *his statement proved oracular* prophetic, prescient, augural, divinatory, mantic. **2** *his answers are always rather oracular* ambiguous, equivocal, two-edged, obscure, enigmatic, cryptic, abstruse, arcane, puzzling, perplexing, baffling.

oral *adjective* spoken, verbal, vocal, uttered, said.

oral *noun* oral examination, interview, viva voce; *inf.* viva.

oration *noun delivered an oration* speech, lecture, address, homily, sermon, discourse, declamation, harangue, tirade; *inf.* spiel.

orator *noun* speaker, public speaker, speechmaker, lecturer, declaimer, haranguer, rhetorician, Cicero.

oratorical *adjective oratorical style* rhetorical, grandiloquent, magniloquent, high-flown, high-sounding, bombastic, grandiose, orotund, declamatory, Ciceronian.

orb *noun* sphere, globe, ball, round, circle, ring.

orbit *noun* **1** *the planet's orbit* revolution, circle, circuit, cycle, rotation, circumgyration, path, course, track, trajectory. **2** *subjects within his orbit of responsibility* sphere, sphere of influence, range, reach, scope, ambit, sweep, domain.

orbit *verb orbit the earth* revolve around, circle around, go/sail/fly around, encircle, circumnavigate.

orchestrate *verb* **1** *orchestrate the piece of music* arrange, score. **2** *orchestrate the event* organize, arrange, put together, set up, manage, stagemanage, mastermind, coordinate, integrate.

ordain *verb* **1** *ordain a new priest* appoint, confer holy orders on, frock, induct, install, invest, anoint, consecrate. **2** *his lack of success seems to have been ordained* fate, predestine, predetermine, preordain. **3** *Congress ordained that taxes be increased* decree, legislate, rule, order, command, enjoin, dictate, prescribe, pronounce. **4** *ordain new laws* decree, enact, lay down, establish, set out.

ordeal *noun* trial, test, tribulation, painful/disturbing experience, suffering, affliction, distress, agony, anguish, torture, torment, calamity, trouble, nightmare.
Antonyms: BLISS; PLEASURE.

order *noun* **1** *restore order to the room* orderliness, neatness, tidiness, trimness, harmony, apple-pie order. **2** *no sense of order in the filing system* method, organization, system, plan, uniformity, regularity, symmetry, pattern. **3** *everything is in good/working order* condition, state, shape, situation. **4** *arrange in alphabetical/numerical order* arrangement, grouping, system, systemization, organization, form, structure, disposition, classification, categorization, codification, series, sequence, progression, succession, layout, setup. **5** *give orders to fire | must obey the general's orders* command, direction, directive, instruction, behest, decree, edict, injunction, law, rule, regulation, mandate, ordinance, stipulation, dictate, say-so. **6** *lack of order in the land* law, lawfulness, law and order, discipline, control, peace, calm, quiet, quietness, peace and quiet, tranquillity. **7** *place an order for dinner/tickets* request, call, requirement, requisition, demand, booking, reservation, commission, notification, application. **8** *the lower orders of society* rank, class, caste, grade, level, degree, position, station. **9** *the social order* grouping, grading, ranking, system, class system, caste system, hierarchy, pecking order. **10** *work of a high order* kind, sort, type, variety, genre, nature. **11** *botanical/biological orders* taxonomic group, class, subclass, family, species, breed. **12** *a religious order* brotherhood, sisterhood, community. **13** *they all belong to some order* lodge, society, secret society, guild, club, association, league, union, fellowship, fraternity, confraternity, sorority, brotherhood, sisterhood, sodality. **14** *raise a point of order* procedure, correct procedure, standard procedure, ruling. **in order 1** *the library books are in order* in sequence, in series, in alphabetical order, in numerical order, in order of merit, in order of seniority, classified, categorized. **2** *the room is in order* orderly, tidy, neat, trim, shipshape, shipshape and Bristol fashion, in Bristol fashion, in apple-pie order. **3** *is it in order for her to attend?* acceptable, all right, fitting, suitable, appropriate, right, correct; *inf.* OK, okay. **out of order** *the machine is out of order* broken, broken-down, not working, unserviceable, not in working order, not functioning, nonfunctional, inoperative, in disrepair, out of commission; *inf.* down, busted, kaput, on the blink, gone haywire, on the fritz.
Antonyms: DISORDER; CHAOS; DISARRAY.

order *verb* **1** *order them to fire* give the order to, command, give the command to, instruct, direct, bid, enjoin. **2** *the judge has ordered that the courtroom be cleared* decree, ordain, rule, legislate, enjoin, prescribe, pronounce. **3** *order dinner/tickets* put in an order for, place an order for, request, call for, requisition, make one's requirements/demands known for, book, reserve, contract for, apply for, send away for. **4** *order the files better | thought it was time to order his life* put in order, set in order, organize, systematize, methodize, arrange, dispose, lay out, marshal, group, classify, catalog, codify, tabulate.

orderly adjective **1** *an orderly room* in order, neat, tidy, trim, shipshape, shipshape and Bristol fashion, in Bristol fashion, in apple-pie order. **2** *an orderly business/person* organized, well-organized, well-regulated, methodical, systematic, systematized, efficient, businesslike. **3** *an orderly class of students* well-behaved, law-abiding, nonviolent, disciplined, quiet, peaceful, controlled, restrained.
Antonyms: DISORDERLY; UNTIDY; UNRULY.

ordinarily adverb *ordinarily he is well-behaved* as a rule, generally, as a general rule, in general, in the general run of things, usually, normally, habitually, customarily, commonly.

ordinary adjective **1** *our ordinary procedure* usual, normal, standard, typical, stock, common, customary, habitual, accustomed, wonted, everyday, quotidian, regular, routine, established, settled, fixed, prevailing, humdrum. **2** *we lead very ordinary lives* | *ordinary houses* run-of-the-mill, common, conventional, standard, typical, average, commonplace, workaday, humdrum, unremarkable, unexceptional, unmemorable, pedestrian, prosaic, unpretentious, modest, plain, simple, humble. **3** *a very ordinary piece of writing* | *the dress is too ordinary* average, run-of-the-mill, pedestrian, prosaic, uninteresting, dull, uninspired, unimaginative, hackneyed, stale, undistinguished, unexceptional, unremarkable, mediocre, indifferent, second-rate.
Antonyms: UNUSUAL; EXTRAORDINARY; UNIQUE.

ordinary noun **out of the ordinary** *want something out of the ordinary* unusual, uncommon, atypical, nonstandard, exceptional, extraordinary, rare, unique, remarkable, striking, noteworthy, memorable, distinguished, impressive, outstanding, special, exciting, imaginative, creative, inspired.

organ noun **1** *he plays the organ* pipe organ, reed organ, electric organ, electronic organ, barrel organ; mouth organ, harmonica; *inf.* hurdy-gurdy. **2** *vital organs* biological structure, part, part of the body, component, constituent, element. **3** *the organ of the labor union* newspaper, paper, journal, periodical, magazine, newsletter, gazette, bulletin, publication, means of communication, mouthpiece, voice, forum.

organic adjective **1** *organic ingredients* natural, nonchemical, pesticide-free, chemical-free, additive-free. **2** *organic matter* living, live, animate, biotic, biological. **3** *the music in the play is organic, not incidental* fundamental, basic, structural, integral, inherent, innate, intrinsic, vital, essential, indispensable. **4** *society is an organic whole* structured, organized, systematic, systematized, ordered, methodical, methodized.

organism noun **1** *microscopic organisms* living entity, living thing, living structure, being, something, creature, animal, plant. **2** *the company is a complex organism* structure, system, organization, setup.

organization noun **1** *the organization of the firm/files/party* establishment, development, assembly, arrangement, regulation, coordination, systematization, methodization, categorization, administration, running, management. *See* ORGANIZE. **2** *the human body is a complex organization* structure, system, whole, unity, organism, setup. **3** *president of the organization* company, firm, concern, operation, corporation, institution, group, consortium, conglomerate, combine, syndicate, federation, confederation, association, body.

organize verb establish, set up, form, lay the foundations of, found, institute, create, originate, begin, start, develop, build, frame, construct, assemble, structure, shape, mold, put together, arrange, dispose, regulate, marshal, put in order, put straight, coordinate, systematize, methodize, standardize, collocate, group, sort, sort out, classify, categorize, catalog, codify, tabulate, be responsible for, be in charge of, take care of, administrate, run, manage, lick/knock into shape, see to.
Antonyms: DESTROY; JUMBLE; disarrange.

orgy noun **1** *a drunken orgy* drunken bout, drunken party, wild party, carousal, debauch, revel, revels, revelry, bacchanalia, saturnalia; *inf.* spree, binge, jag, bender, toot; love-in. **2** *a spending orgy* | *go on an orgy of crime* bout, overindulgence, excess, surfeit; *inf.* spree, splurge, binge.

orient, orientate verb **1** *orient himself to his new life* adapt, adjust, accommodate, familiarize, acclimatize. **2** *orient the beach chair toward the sun* direct, guide, lead, point/place/put/position something/someone in the direction of, turn. **3** *orient the course for/toward beginners* aim, direct, slant, angle, intend, design. **orient oneself** *difficult to orient oneself in the fog* get/find one's bearings, get the lay of the land, establish one's location, feel one's way.

orientation noun **1** *orientation is difficult in the dark* getting one's bearings. *See* ORIENT ONESELF (ORIENT, ORIENTATE). **2** *orientation to his new way of life* adaptation, adjustment, accommodation, familiarization, acclimatization. **3** *establish one's orientation* bearings, location, position, direction. **4** *the orientation of passengers toward the ramp* directing, direction, pointing, positioning. *See* ORIENT, ORIENTATE 2. **5** *the orientation of the course for/toward beginners* aiming, directing, designing. *See* ORIENT, ORIENTATE 3.

orifice noun opening, hole, vent, aperture, gap, space, breach, break, rent, slot, slit, cleft, cranny, fissure, crevice, rift, crack, chink.

origin noun **1** *the origin of the word* source, derivation, root, roots, provenance, etymology,

genesis, etiology. **2** *the origins of life* source, basis, base, wellspring, spring, wellhead, fountainhead, fountain, genesis, *fons et origo.* **3** *the origin of the age of electronics* birth, dawn, dawning, beginning, start, commencement, emergence, inception, launch, creation, early stages, inauguration, foundation. **4** *explore the family's origin(s)* descent, ancestry, pedigree, lineage, heritage, parentage, extraction, beginnings.
Antonyms: END; DEATH; DEMISE.

---

origin
inception, provenance, root, source
The **origin** of something is the point from which it starts or sets out, or the person or thing from which it is ultimately derived (*the origin of the custom of carving pumpkins at Halloween; the origin of a word*). It often applies to causes that were in operation before the thing itself was brought into being. **Source,** on the other hand, applies to that which provides a first and continuous supply (*the source of the river; an ongoing source of inspiration and encouragement*). **Root,** more often than *source,* applies to what is regarded as the first or final cause of something; it suggests an origin so fundamental as to be the ultimate cause from which something stems (*money is the root of all evil*). **Inception** refers specifically to the beginning of an undertaking, project, institution, or practice (*she was in charge of the organization from its inception*). **Provenance** is similarly restricted in meaning, referring to the specific place, or sometimes the race or people, from which something is derived or by whom it was invented or constructed (*in digging, they uncovered an artifact of unknown provenance*).

---

original *adjective* **1** *the original inhabitants* aboriginal, indigenous, early, earliest, first, initial, primary, primordial, primal, primeval, primitive, autochthonal, autochthonous. **2** *his work is original* innovative, innovatory, inventive, new, novel, fresh, creative, imaginative, resourceful, individual, ingenious, unusual, unconventional, unorthodox, unprecedented, groundbreaking. **3** *this painting is original* not copied, genuine, authentic, archetypal, prototypical, master.
Antonyms: LAST; unoriginal; DERIVATIVE.

original *noun* **1** *this is the original, not a copy* original work/painting, archetype, prototype, master. **2** *among architects, he is an original* standout, paragon, nonpareil, exemplar, one of a kind, nonesuch, *ne plus ultra;* individualist, eccentric, nonconformist.

originality *noun admire the originality of his work* innovativeness, innovation, inventiveness, newness, novelty, break with tradition, freshness, creativity, imaginativeness, resourceful-

ness, individuality, unusualness, unconventionality, unprecedentedness.

originally *adverb originally he was unwilling* at first, in the beginning, to begin with, at the start, at the outset, initially.

originate *verb* **1** *the spring originates in/from the mountains* arise, rise, flow, emanate, issue. **2** *the quarrel originated in/from a misunderstanding* have its origin, arise, stem, spring, result, derive, start, begin, commence. **3** *he originated the idea* give birth to, be the father/mother of, set in motion, set up, invent, dream up, conceive, discover, initiate, create, formulate, inaugurate, pioneer, introduce, establish, found, evolve, develop, generate.
Antonyms: TERMINATE; DESTROY.

originator *noun* father/mother, inventor, discoverer, initiator, architect, author, prime mover, founder, pioneer, establisher, developer. *See* ORIGINATE 3.

ornament *noun* **1** *a house full of ornaments* knickknack, trinket, bauble, gewgaw, accessory, decoration, frill, whatnot, doodad. **2** *the beautiful house/dress needs little ornament* decoration, adornment, embellishment, trimming, garnish, garnishing. **3** *the diva is the ornament of the opera company* jewel, jewel in the crown, gem, treasure, pride, flower, leading light, crème de la crème.

ornamental *adjective ornamental pool/plates* decorative, decorated, ornate, ornamented, embellished, embroidered, fancy, fanciful.

ornate *adjective* **1** *ornate furnishings* elaborate, overelaborate, decorated, embellished, ornamented, adorned, fancy, fussy, busy, ostentatious, showy, baroque, rococo; *inf.* flashy. **2** *ornate prose/speeches* elaborate, overelaborate, flowery, florid, flamboyant, labored, strained, stilted, pretentious, high-flown, high-sounding, grandiose, pompous, orotund, magniloquent, grandiloquent, oratorical, bombastic; *inf.* highfalutin.
Antonyms: PLAIN; AUSTERE; SIMPLE.

orotund *adjective* **1** *orotund voices* strong, powerful, full, rich, deep, sonorous, resonant, ringing, reverberating, booming. **2** *orotund speeches* ornate, overelaborate, labored, strained, pretentious, high-flown, grandiose, pompous, magniloquent, bombastic; *inf.* highfalutin. *See* ORNATE 2.

orthodox *adjective* **1** *hold orthodox religious beliefs* | *an orthodox Jew* conformist, doctrinal, of the faith, of the true faith, sound, conservative, correct, faithful, true, true-blue, devoted, strict, devout. **2** *orthodox behavior* conventional, accepted, approved, correct, proper, conformist, established, traditional, prevailing, customary, usual, regular, standard, *comme il faut,* de rigueur.
Antonyms: UNORTHODOX; NONCONFORMIST; UNCONVENTIONAL.

orthodoxy *noun* **1** *the orthodoxy of his religious beliefs* conformism, conformity, doctrinalism, conservatism, soundness, correctness, faithfulness, devotion, devoutness, strictness. **2** *the orthodoxy of his behavior* conventionality, conventionalism, correctness, properness, propriety, traditionalism. *See* ORTHODOX 2.

oscillate *verb* **1** *the pendulum oscillating* swing, move back and forth, move backward and forward, move to and fro. **2** *oscillate between feeling hot and cold* swing, sway, fluctuate, seesaw, waver, vacillate, vary, hesitate, yo-yo.

oscillation *noun* **1** *the oscillation of the pendulum* swing, swinging, moving backward and forward, moving to and fro. **2** *his oscillation between courses of action* fluctuation, wavering, vacillation, yo-yoing. *See* OSCILLATE 2.

ossify *verb* **1** *material ossifying with age* harden, solidify, stiffen, become rigid, fossilize, petrify. **2** *beliefs have ossified into narrow-minded dogma* become rigid, become unyielding/obdurate, become inflexible, grow unprogressive, become unreceptive, harden, solidify.

ostensible *adjective* outward, apparent, seeming, professed, alleged, claimed, purported, pretended, feigned, specious, supposed.

---

ostensible
apparent, illusory, seeming

The **apparent** reason for something is not necessarily the real reason. In this sense the word applies to what appears only on the surface, not to what is borne out by scientific investigation or an examination of the relevant facts and circumstances (*the apparent cause was only an illusion*). The **ostensible** reason for something is the reason that is expressed, declared, or avowed; but it implies that the truth is being concealed (*the ostensible purpose of the meeting was to give the two men a chance to get acquainted*). **Seeming** usually refers to the character of the thing observed rather than to a defect in the observation; it implies even more doubt than either *apparent* or *ostensible* (*her seeming innocence fooled no one*). That which is **illusory** is always deceptive; it has a character or appearance that doesn't really exist (*an illusory beauty that faded quickly in the bright light*).

---

ostensibly *adverb* apparently, allegedly, supposedly. *See* OSTENSIBLE.

ostentation *noun* showiness, show, conspicuousness, obtrusiveness, loudness, extravagance, flamboyance, gaudiness, flashiness, pretentiousness, affectation, flaunting, exhibitionism, vulgarity, bad taste; *inf.* showing off.

ostentatious *adjective* *ostentatious jewelry/manner* showy, conspicuous, obtrusive, loud, extravagant, flamboyant, gaudy, flashy, pretentious, affected, overdone, overelaborate, vulgar, kitsch. *Antonyms:* PLAIN; UNOBTRUSIVE; SUBDUED.

ostracism *noun* the cold shoulder, exclusion, barring, shunning, avoidance, boycotting, repudiation, rejection, banishment, exile. *See* OSTRACIZE.

ostracize *verb* give someone the cold shoulder, send to Coventry, exclude, shut out, bar, keep at arm's length, shun, spurn, avoid, boycott, repudiate, cast out, reject, blackball, blacklist, banish, exile, expel, excommunicate, debar, leave out in the cold. *Antonyms:* WELCOME; ACCEPT; FRATERNIZE.

other *adjective* **1** *use other means* different, unlike, variant, dissimilar, disparate, distinct, separate, alternative. **2** *need a few other examples* more, additional, further, extra, supplementary.

otherwise *adverb* **1** *hurry, otherwise we will be late* or else, or, if not. **2** *he is too young, otherwise he is fine* in other respects, in other ways, apart from that. **3** *he could not have acted otherwise* in any other way, differently.

ounce *noun* *not to have an ounce of courage* iota, whit, trace, particle, atom, speck, scrap, shred, crumb, grain, drop.

oust *verb* *ousted from his post* drive out, force out, thrust out, expel, eject, put out, evict, throw out, dispossess, dismiss, dislodge, displace, depose, unseat, topple, disinherit; *inf.* fire, sack.

out *adverb* **1** *the manager is out just now* not in, not here, not at home, gone away, away, elsewhere, absent, away from one's desk. **2** *the children have gone out* outside, outdoors, out of doors. **3** *tire them out* completely, thoroughly, entirely, wholly. **4** *the fire is out* not burning, extinguished, quenched, doused, dead. **5** *the boxer is completely out* out cold, unconscious, knocked out, senseless; *inf.* KO'd. **6** *your secret is out* revealed, disclosed, divulged, in the open, out in the open, known, exposed, common knowledge, public knowledge. **7** *the flowers are out* open, in bloom, in full bloom, blooming. **8** *long hair is out this year* unfashionable, out of fashion, dated, out of date, not in, behind the times, démodé, passé; *inf.* old hat. **9** *that idea is out* inappropriate, unsuitable, impractical, irrelevant, not worth considering. *Antonyms:* IN; INSIDE; FASHIONABLE.

out-and-out *adjective* absolute, complete, utter, downright, thorough, thoroughgoing, total, perfect, unmitigated, unqualified, consummate, inveterate, dyed-in-the-wool, true-blue.

outbreak *noun* *outbreak of disease* eruption, flare-up, upsurge, outburst, sudden appearance, start, rash.

outburst *noun* *an outburst of anger/laughter* burst, explosion, eruption, outbreak, flare-up, access, attack, fit, spasm, paroxysm.

outcast *noun* *social outcast* pariah, *persona non grata*, leper, untouchable, castaway, exile, displaced person, refugee, evictee, evacuee; *inf.* DP.

outclass *verb* surpass, be superior to, be better than, outshine, eclipse, overshadow, outdistance, outstrip, outdo, outplay, outrank, outrival, trounce, beat, defeat; *inf.* be a cut above, be head and shoulders above, run rings around, leave standing, outfox.

outcome *noun* consequence, result, end result, sequel, upshot, issue, product, conclusion, aftereffect, aftermath, wake; *inf.* payoff.

outcry *noun* clamor, howls of protest, protest, complaints, objections, fuss, outburst, commotion, uproar, tumult, hue and cry, hullaballoo, ballyhoo, racket.

outdated *adjective* out of date, out of style, out of fashion, old-fashioned, unfashionable, outmoded, dated, *démodé*, passé, behind the times, antiquated, archaic; *inf.* old hat, not with it.
Antonyms: CURRENT; MODERN; FASHIONABLE.

outdistance *verb* outstrip, outrun, outpace, leave behind, overtake, pass, shake off, lose; *inf.* leave standing.

outdo *verb* surpass, top, exceed, excel, get the better of, outstrip, outshine, eclipse, overshadow, transcend, outclass, outdistance, overcome, beat, defeat, outsmart, outmaneuver; *inf.* be a cut above, be head and shoulders above, run rings around, outfox.

outdoor *adjective* out-of-doors, outside, open-air, alfresco.
Antonyms: INSIDE; indoor.

outer *adjective* 1 *pierce the outer layer* outside, outermost, outward, exterior, external, surface, superficial. 2 *the outer areas of the estate* outlying, distant, remote, faraway, peripheral, fringe, perimeter.
Antonyms: INNER; INSIDE; INTERIOR.

outfit *noun* 1 *wearing a smart outfit* clothes, dress, ensemble, suit, costume, garb, kit, accouterments, trappings; *inf.* get-up, gear, togs. 2 *pack the fishing outfit* kit, equipment, tools, tackle, apparatus, paraphernalia. 3 *a small publishing outfit | soldiers rejoining their outfit* organization, setup, company, firm, business, (military) unit, group, team, coterie, clique.

outfit *verb* equip, fit out, rig out, supply, furnish with, provide with, stock with, provision, accouter, attire.

outfitter *noun* clothier, tailor, dressmaker, couturier, costumier, modiste, haberdasher.

outflow *noun* outflowing, outpouring, outrush, rush, discharge, issue, spurt, jet, gush, leakage, drainage, outflux, effluence, efflux.

outgoing *adjective* 1 *outgoing people* extrovert, extroverted, unreserved, demonstrative, affectionate, warm, friendly, genial, cordial, affable, hail-fellow-well-met, sociable, communicative, open, expansive, talkative, gregarious, approachable, easygoing, easy. 2 *the outgoing president* retiring, departing, leaving, withdrawing.
Antonyms: RESERVED; INTROVERTED; WITHDRAWN; INCOMING.

outing *noun* trip, excursion, jaunt, expedition, pleasure trip, tour, airing; *inf.* spin.

outlandish *adjective* strange, unfamiliar, unknown, unheard-of, odd, unusual, extraordinary, peculiar, queer, curious, singular, eccentric, quaint, bizarre, grotesque, preposterous, fantastic, outré, weird; *inf.* freaky, wacky, far-out, off-the-wall.
Antonyms: ORDINARY; COMMONPLACE; CONVENTIONAL.

outlaw *noun* fugitive, outcast, exile, pariah, bandit, desperado, brigand, criminal, robber; *inf.* villain.

outlaw *verb* *outlaw the sale of liquor* ban, bar, prohibit, forbid, embargo, make illegal, disallow, proscribe, interdict.

outlay *noun* expenditure, expenses, spending, money spent, cost, price, charge, payment, disbursement.

outlet *noun* 1 *water outlets* way out, exit, vent, outfall, valve, safety valve, duct, blowhole, channel, trench, culvert, conduit. 2 *an outlet for her emotion/creativity* means of expression, release, means of release, release mechanism, safety valve. 3 *an outlet for their farm produce* retail outlet, market, marketplace, store, shop.

outline *noun* 1 *an outline of our plans* draft, rough draft, rough, sketch, tracing, skeleton, framework, layout, diagram, plan, design, schema. 2 *give an outline of what happened* thumbnail sketch, rough idea, quick rundown, abbreviated version, summary, synopsis, résumé, précis, main points, bones, bare bones. 3 *draw an outline of the building* contour, silhouette, profile, lineaments, delineation, configuration, perimeter, circumference.

outline *verb* 1 *outline the shape* sketch, delineate, trace, silhouette. 2 *outline your ideas* sketch out, give a thumbnail sketch of, give a rough idea of, give a quick rundown on, summarize, précis.

outlook *noun* 1 *a gloomy outlook on life* view, point of view, viewpoint, perspective, attitude, frame of mind, standpoint, slant, angle, interpretation, opinion. 2 *the house has a pleasant outlook* view, vista, prospect, panorama, aspect.

outlying *adjective* outer, outermost, out-of-the-way, remote, distant, faraway, far-flung, peripheral, isolated, inaccessible, off the beaten path/track, backwoods. *See* OUT OF THE WAY.

outmoded *adjective* old-fashioned, unfashionable, out of fashion, out of style, outdated, out of date, dated, passé, *démodé*, behind the times, antiquated, archaic, obsolete; *inf.* old hat.
Antonyms: FASHIONABLE; MODERN.

out of date *adjective* 1 *out-of-date clothes* outdated, dated, old-fashioned, out of fashion, behind the times, archaic, obsolete. *See* OUTMODED. 2 *the license is out of date* expired, lapsed, elapsed, invalid, void, null and void.
Antonyms: CURRENT; MODERN; FASHIONABLE.

out of the way *adjective* *out-of-the-way places | it was out of the way* outlying, outer, outermost, remote, distant, faraway, far-flung, peripheral, isolated, lonely, inaccessible, obscure, off

Antonyms: ACCESSIBLE; NEAR; HANDY.

out of work *adjective an out-of-work actor | he is out of work* unemployed, jobless, out of a job, laid off, idle; *inf.* on the dole.

outpouring *noun* outflow, effluence, efflux, flux, outflux, debouchment, cascade, deluge, spate, stream, spurt, jet, torrent.

output *noun* production, product, amount/quantity produced, productivity, yield, harvest, achievement, accomplishment.

outrage *noun* 1 *outrages committed by the soldiers* atrocity, act of violence, evil, act of wickedness, crime, horror, enormity, brutality, barbarism, inhumane act. 2 *the pre-Christmas layoff was an outrage | the building is an outrage* offense, affront, insult, injury, abuse, indignity, scandal, desecration, violation. 3 *arouse outrage in the citizens* anger, fury, rage, indignation, wrath, annoyance, shock, resentment, horror, amazement.

outrage *verb* anger, infuriate, enrage, incense, make someone's blood boil, madden, annoy, shock, horrify, amaze, scandalize, offend, insult, affront, vex, distress.

outrageous *adjective* 1 *his outrageous behavior when drunk* intolerable, insufferable, insupportable, unendurable, unbearable, impossible, exasperating, offensive, provocative, maddening, distressing. 2 *commit outrageous acts* atrocious, heinous, abominable, wicked, vile, foul, monstrous, horrible, horrid, dreadful, terrible, horrendous, hideous, ghastly, unspeakable, gruesome. 3 *outrageous prices* immoderate, excessive, exorbitant, unreasonable, preposterous, scandalous, shocking; *inf.* steep.

Antonyms: ACCEPTABLE; MILD; MODERATE.

outré *adjective* unconventional, eccentric, odd, outlandish, strange, extraordinary, unusual, bizarre, freakish, freaky, queer, weird; *inf.* offbeat, off-the-wall, wacky, way-out, far-out.

outright *adjective* 1 *an outright fool* out-and-out, absolute, complete, utter, thorough, perfect, total, unmitigated. *See* OUT-AND-OUT. 2 *the outright winner* definite, unequivocal, unqualified, incontestable, undeniable, unmistakable.

outright *adverb* 1 *reject the proposal outright* completely, entirely, wholly, totally, categorically, absolutely. 2 *killed outright* instantly, instantaneously, immediately, at once, straight away, then and there, there and then, on the spot. 3 *tell her outright* openly, candidly, frankly, honestly, forthrightly, directly, plainly, explicitly, unreservedly.

outset *noun* start, starting point, beginning, commencement, dawn, birth, inception, opening, launch, inauguration; *inf.* kickoff.

Antonyms: CONCLUSION; END; FINISH.

outshine *verb* surpass, eclipse, put in the shade, overshadow, be superior to, be better than, outclass, outstrip, outdistance, outdo, top, tower above, dwarf, transcend, upstage; *inf.* be head and shoulders above, be a cut above, leave standing.

outside *adjective* 1 *outside layers* outer, outermost, outward, exterior, external. 2 *outside furniture/plumbing* outdoor, out-of-doors. 3 *an outside chance* unlikely, improbable, slight, slender, slim, small, faint, negligible, marginal, remote, distant, vague.

Antonyms: INSIDE; INNER; INTERIOR.

outside *adverb* go *outside* outdoors, out of doors, out of the house.

outside *noun* 1 *brown on the outside* outer side, exterior, surface, outer surface, case, skin, shell, sheath. 2 *the outside of the building* exterior, front, face, façade.

outsider *noun* alien, stranger, foreigner, outlander, immigrant, emigrant, émigré, incomer, newcomer, parvenu, arriviste, interloper, intruder, gatecrasher, outcast, misfit, odd man out.

outskirts *plural noun* vicinity, neighborhood, environs, edges, outlying districts, fringes, margin, periphery, borders, boundary, suburbs, suburbia, purlieus.

outsmart *verb* get the better of, outwit, outmaneuver, outperform, outplay, be cleverer than, steal a march on, trick, dupe, make a fool of; *inf.* outfox, put one over on, pull a fast one on, give someone the runaround, run rings around.

outspoken *adjective* candid, frank, forthright, direct, straightforward, straight-from-the-shoulder, plain, plainspoken, explicit, blunt, brusque, unequivocal, unreserved, unceremonious.

Antonyms: DIPLOMATIC; RETICENT; EVASIVE.

outstanding *adjective* 1 *an outstanding painter* preeminent, eminent, well-known, notable, noteworthy, distinguished, important, famous, famed, renowned, celebrated, great, excellent, remarkable, exceptional, superlative. 2 *the painting is outstanding* striking, impressive, eye-catching, arresting, memorable, remarkable. 3 *outstanding debts* unpaid, unsettled, owing, due. 4 *work outstanding* to be done, unfinished, remaining, pending, ongoing.

Antonyms: UNEXCEPTIONAL; MEDIOCRE; COMPLETE.

outward *adjective* 1 *outward layers* outer, outside, outermost, exterior, external, surface, superficial. 2 *no outward sign of his grief* external, superficial, visible, observable, noticeable, perceptible, discernible, apparent, evident, obvious.

Antonyms: INWARD; INNER; INTERNAL.

outwardly *adverb* 1 *outwardly visible* externally, on the outside. 2 *outwardly he seems all right* on the surface, superficially, on the face of it, to all appearances, to the eye, as far as one can see, to all intents and purposes, apparently, evidently.

outweigh *verb* be greater than, exceed, be superior to, take precedence over, have the edge on/over, preponderate.

outwit *verb* get the better of, outsmart, outmaneuver, trick, dupe; *inf.* outfox. See OUTSMART.

outworn *adjective outworn ideas/traditions* outdated, out of date, old-fashioned, out of fashion, outmoded, behind the times, ancient, archaic, antiquated, obsolescent, obsolete, disused, abandoned, cast out, rejected, discredited, tired, exhausted, stale, hackneyed, superannuated; *inf.* old hat.
Antonyms: UP-TO-DATE; FRESH; ORIGINAL.

oval *adjective* egg-shaped, ovoid, ovate, oviform, elliptical, ellipsoidal.

ovation *noun* applause, hand-clapping, handclap, clapping, cheering, cheers, acclaim, acclamation, praise, plaudits, laurels, tribute, accolade, laudation, extolment; *inf.* bouquets.

oven *noun* stove, kitchen stove, range, convection oven, microwave oven; brick oven, furnace, kiln.

over *adverb* 1 *fly over* overhead, above, on high, aloft. 2 *the relationship is over* ended, at an end, finished, concluded, terminated, no more, extinct, gone, dead, a thing of the past, ancient history. 3 *have food left over* as a reminder, as surplus, outstanding, in excess, as extra, in addition. **over and over** again and again, over and over again, repeatedly, time and again, time and time again, ad nauseam.

over *preposition* 1 *earn over $40,000* more than, above, in excess of, exceeding. 2 *he has three people over him* above, superior to, higher up than, more powerful than. **all over** *all over the world/place* throughout, all through, throughout the extent of, everywhere in, in all parts of, around. **over and above** *over and above the sum mentioned* in addition to, on top of, plus, as well as, besides, not to mention, let alone.
Antonyms: UNDER; BELOW.

overact *verb* exaggerate; *inf.* ham, camp it up, pile it on, lay it on.

overall *adjective an overall plan/improvement* comprehensive, universal, all-embracing, inclusive, all-inclusive, general, sweeping, complete, blanket, umbrella, global.

overall *adverb* overall, *things have improved* on the whole, in general, generally speaking.

overawe *verb* intimidate, daunt, disconcert, abash, dismay, frighten, alarm, scare, terrify, terrorize.

overbalance *verb* lose one's balance, lose one's footing, fall over, topple over, tip over, keel over, capsize, overturn, turn turtle.

overbearing *adjective* domineering, autocratic, tyrannical, despotic, oppressive, high-handed, lordly, officious, dogmatic, dictatorial, pompous, peremptory, arrogant, haughty,

cocksure, proud, overproud, overweening, presumptuous, supercilious, disdainful, contemptuous; *inf.* bossy, throwing one's weight about, cocky.

overblown *adjective an overblown piece of writing* overwritten, extravagant, florid, pompous, overelaborate, pretentious, high-flown, turgid, bombastic, grandiloquent, magniloquent, euphuistic, fustian, aureate.

overcast *adjective* cloudy, clouded, clouded over, overclouded, sunless, darkened, dark, murky, misty, hazy, foggy, gray, leaden, lowering, threatening, heavy, promising rain, dismal, dreary.
Antonyms: BRIGHT; CLEAR.

overcharge *verb* 1 *overcharge the customers* charge too much, cheat, swindle, fleece, shortchange; *inf.* rip off, sting, diddle, do, rook, clip. 2 *overcharge the description* overwrite, overdraw, overdo, overstate, exaggerate, hyperbolize, overcolor, overembroider, embroider, embellish; *inf.* pile it on, lay it on thick, lay it on with a trowel.

overcoat *noun* coat, topcoat, winter coat, greatcoat, raincoat, mackintosh, anorak, parka, ulster.

overcome *verb* 1 *overcome the enemy | she must overcome her resistance* conquer, defeat, vanquish, beat, be victorious over, gain a victory over, prevail over, get the better of, triumph over, best, worst, trounce, rout, gain mastery over, master, overpower, overwhelm, overthrow, subdue, subjugate, quell, quash, crush; *inf.* lick, clobber, whip, wipe (up) the floor with, blow out of the water. 2 *overcome one's disability* conquer, get the better of, triumph over, master, surmount, rise above.

overcome *adjective too overcome to react* overwhelmed, emotional, moved, affected, speechless, at a loss for words; *inf.* bowled over.

overconfident *adjective* cocksure, swaggering, blustering, self-assured, self-assertive, brash, overbearing, overweening, presumptuous, egotistic, riding/heading for a fall; *inf.* cocky.

overcritical *adjective* hypercritical, faultfinding, captious, carping, caviling, quibbling, hairsplitting, niggling, hard to please, overparticular, fussy, finicky, overexacting; *inf.* nitpicking, persnickety.

overcrowded *adjective* overfull, full to overflowing, crammed full, jammed, packed, packed as tight as sardines, congested, overloaded, overpopulated, overpeopled, overrun, thronged, swarming, teeming; *inf.* full to the gunwales, jam-packed, like the Black Hole of Calcutta.
Antonyms: DESERTED; EMPTY; VACANT.

overdo *verb* 1 *overdo the comic scenes* overact, overplay, exaggerate, do to death; *inf.* ham up, camp up, go overboard over. 2 *overdo the sympathy* do to excess, carry too far, carry to extremes, exaggerate, belabor, stretch/strain a point over, overstate, overemphasize, hyperbolize, not know when to stop, do to death; *inf.*

pile on, lay on thick, lay on with a trowel, make a production of, make a big deal out of. **3** *overdo the meat* overcook, overbake, burn, burn to a crisp. **overdo it** overwork, work too hard, strain oneself, do too much, overtax oneself, overtax one's strength, overburden oneself, overload oneself, drive oneself too hard, push oneself too far/hard, wear oneself out, burn the candle at both ends, have too many irons in the fire, have too many balls in the air, burn oneself out, bite off more than one can chew; *inf.* knock oneself out, work/run oneself into the ground.
Antonyms: UNDERSTATE; play down (*see* PLAY).

overdone *adjective* **1** *the flattery/sympathy was overdone* excessive, too much, undue, immoderate, inordinate, disproportionate, beyond the pale, extravagant, overenthusiastic, effusive, overeffusive, gushing, fulsome; *inf.* a bit much, hyped up, laid on with a trowel. **2** *overdone food* overcooked, overbaked, dried out, burned, burnt, burned/burnt to a cinder/crisp.

overdue *adjective* **1** *our arrival/visit is overdue* late, not on time, behind schedule, behindhand, delayed, belated, tardy, unpunctual. **2** *overdue bills* unpaid, owed, owing, outstanding, unsettled, in arrears.

overeat *verb* eat too much, eat like a horse, gorge oneself, stuff oneself, overindulge, overindulge oneself, surfeit, guzzle, gormandize; *inf.* binge, stuff one's face, pack it away, make a pig of oneself, pig out.

overemphasize *verb* place/put too much emphasis on, overstress, put/lay too much stress on, exaggerate, attach too much importance/weight to, make too much of, overdo, overdramatize, make something out of nothing, make a mountain out of a molehill, belabor the point; *inf.* blow up out of all proportion.
Antonyms: UNDERSTATE; play down (*see* PLAY).

overflow *verb* **1** *the water was overflowing* flow over, run over, spill over, brim over, well over, pour forth, stream forth, discharge, surge, debouch. **2** *water overflowed the land* flood, deluge, inundate, submerge, cover, swamp, engulf, drown, soak, drench, saturate. **overflowing with 1** *overflowing with people* full of, crowded with, thronged with, swarming with, teeming with, abounding in. **2** *hearts overflowing with kindness* full of, very full of, filled with, filled to the brim with, abounding in.

overflow *noun* **1** *the overflow from the cistern* excess water, overspill, spill, spillage, flood, flooding, inundation. **2** *the overflow of the meeting* surplus, additional people/things, extra people/things.

overhang *verb* stand out, stick out, extend, project, protrude, jut, jut out, beetle, bulge out, loom, cantilever.

overhaul *verb* **1** *overhaul the engine* check, check out, check over, give something a checkup, investigate, inspect, examine, service, repair, mend, recondition, renovate, revamp, fix up,

patch up. **2** *overhaul the other runners* overtake, pass, get ahead of, outdistance, outstrip, gain on, catch up with.

overhead *adverb* *clouds overhead | birds flew overhead* above, up above, high up, up in the sky, on high, aloft.

overhead *noun* expenses, expenditure, outlay, disbursement, running cost(s), operating cost(s).

overindulge *verb* **1** *overindulge and have a hangover* drink/eat too much, be immoderate, be intemperate, overdo it, drink/eat/do to excess, not know when to stop; *inf.* binge, go on a binge, paint the town red, go overboard, live it up, make a pig of oneself. **2** *overindulge the children* give in to, spoil, cosset, pamper, mollycoddle; *inf.* spoil rotten.

overjoyed *adjective* full of joy, joyful, elated, jubilant, thrilled, delighted, euphoric, ecstatic, in raptures, rapturous, enraptured, in transports, transported, delirious with happiness, on top of the world; *inf.* tickled pink, over the moon, on cloud nine, in seventh heaven.
Antonyms: DEJECTED; DEPRESSED.

overlay *verb* **1** *overlay the floor with carpet* cover, overspread, carpet, blanket. **2** *overlay the table with gold* inlay, laminate, veneer, varnish, gild, decorate, ornament.

overload *verb* overburden, weigh down, encumber, overcharge, overtax, oppress, impose (a) strain on, strain; *inf.* saddle with.

overlook *verb* **1** *he overlooked a mistake on the first page* fail to notice/observe/spot, miss, leave, neglect to notice, leave unnoticed; *inf.* slip up on. **2** *overlook tasks* leave undone, ignore, disregard, omit, neglect, forget. **3** *decide to overlook his crime* deliberately ignore, not take into consideration, disregard, take no notice of, let something pass, turn a blind eye to, wink at, blink at, excuse, pardon, forgive, condone, let someone off with; *inf.* let something ride. **4** *the house overlooks the sea* look over, look onto, front onto, open out over, have a view of, afford a view of, command a view of.
Antonyms: SPOT; NOTE; PUNISH.

overly *adverb* *not overly concerned* too, to too great an extent/degree, unduly, excessively, inordinately, immoderately.

overpower *verb* **1** *overpower the enemy* gain control over, overwhelm, overcome, get the upper hand over, gain mastery over, master, best, worst, conquer, defeat, vanquish, trounce, rout, subjugate, quell, quash, crush; *inf.* whip. **2** *his charm overpowered her* overcome, overwhelm, move, stir, affect, touch, impress, take aback; *inf.* bowl over, knock/hit for a loop, get to.

overpowering *adjective* **1** *overpowering grief* overwhelming, burdensome, weighty, unbearable, unendurable, intolerable, shattering; *inf.* mind-blowing. **2** *an overpowering smell* overstrong, suffocating, stifling, nauseating. **3** *overpowering evidence* compelling, forceful, telling, irrefutable, undeniable, unquestionable, indisputable, incontestable, incontrovertible.

Antonyms: MILD; SLIGHT.

overrate verb *overrated him | overrate his chances* overestimate, overvalue, overprize, exaggerate the worth of, think too much of, attach too much importance to, expect too much of.

Antonyms: UNDERRATE; UNDERESTIMATE.

overreach verb *overreach the enemy* get the better of, outsmart, outwit; *inf.* outfox. *See* OUTSMART. **overreach oneself** overestimate one's ability, try to do too much, go too far, try to be too clever/smart, defeat one's own ends, have one's scheme/plan(s) backfire on one, bite off more than one can chew.

overreact verb get overexcited, get upset over nothing, act irrationally, lose one's sense of proportion, make something out of nothing, make a mountain out of a molehill; *inf.* go over the top, press the panic button.

override verb **1** *his career overrides all other considerations* be more important than, take priority over, take precedence over, supersede, outweigh. **2** *override her objections* trample on, ride roughshod over, set aside, ignore, disregard, discount, pay no heed to, take no account of, close one's mind to, turn a deaf ear to.

overriding adjective *the overriding consideration* most important, predominant, principal, primary, paramount, chief, main, major, foremost, central, focal, pivotal; *inf.* number one.

Antonyms: INSIGNIFICANT; IRRELEVANT.

overrule verb *overrule their objections* rule against, disallow, override, veto, set aside, overturn, cancel, reverse, rescind, repeal, revoke, repudiate, annul, nullify, declare null and void, invalidate, void, abrogate.

overrun verb **1** *the enemy army was overrunning their country* invade, march into, penetrate, occupy, beseige, storm, attack, assail. **2** *rats overrunning the warehouses* swarm over, surge over, inundate, overwhelm, permeate, infest. **3** *weeds overrunning the garden* spread over, spread like wildfire over, grow over, cover, choke, clog; *inf.* run riot over. **4** *the lecture overran* exceed the allotted time, go/run over the allotted time, be too long.

overseer noun supervisor, superintendent, foreman, manager, master, boss; *inf.* super, honcho, boss man/lady.

overshadow verb **1** *that runner overshadows the others | the achievement of the others is overshadowed* outshine, eclipse, put in the shade, surpass, be superior to, outclass, outstrip, outdo, top, transcend, tower above, dwarf, upstage; *inf.* be head and shoulders above, be a cut above. **2** *his death overshadowed the family gathering* cast gloom over, blight, take the plea-

sure out of, bring a note of sadness to, take the edge off, mar, spoil, ruin. **3** *clouds overshadowing the sun | many trees overshadowed the garden* cloud, darken, bedim, dim, conceal, obscure, eclipse, screen, shroud, veil.

oversight noun **1** *done in oversight* carelessness, inattention, neglect, inadvertence, laxity, dereliction, omission. **2** *an oversight in the newspaper article* mistake, error, blunder, gaffe, fault, omission, slip, lapse; *inf.* slipup, goof, booboo. **3** *have oversight of the workforce* supervision, surveillance, superintendence, charge, care, administration, management, direction, control, handling.

overt adjective *overt hostility* obvious, noticeable, observable, visible, undisguised, unconcealed, apparent, plain, plainly seen, plain to see, manifest, patent, open, public, blatant, conspicuous.

Antonyms: HIDDEN; SURREPTITIOUS; COVERT.

overtake verb **1** *cars/runners overtaking each other* pass, get past, go past, go by, overhaul, leave behind, outdistance, outstrip, go faster than. **2** *misfortune overtook them* befall, happen to, come upon, hit, strike, fall upon, overwhelm, engulf, take by surprise, surprise, catch unawares, catch unprepared, catch off guard.

overthrow verb **1** *overthrow the government* cause the downfall of, remove from office, overturn, depose, oust, unseat, dethrone, disestablish. **2** *overthrow the army of occupation* conquer, vanquish, defeat, beat, rout, trounce, best, worst, subjugate, crush, quash, quell, overcome, overwhelm, overturn, overpower. **3** *squalls overthrowing boats* throw over, turn over, overturn, tip over, topple over, upset, capsize, knock over, upturn, upend, invert.

overthrow noun **1** *the overthrow of the government* downfall, deposition, ousting. *See* OVERTHROW verb 1. **2** *the overthrow of the army* defeat, vanquishing, rout, subjugation, crushing, overwhelming, overturning. *See* OVERTHROW verb 2.

overtone noun hidden meaning, secondary meaning, implication, innuendo, hint, suggestion, insinuation, association, connotation, undercurrent, nuance, flavor, coloring, vein.

overture noun **1** *miss the overture* musical introduction/opening, prelude; *inf.* curtain-raiser. **2** *the enemy making peace overtures* advances, move, opening move, conciliatory move, approach, proposal, proposition, offer, suggestion, motion.

overturn verb **1** *the boat overturned* capsize, keel over, overbalance, tip over, topple over. **2** *high winds overturning trash cans* upturn, turn over, throw over, overthrow, tip over, topple over, upset, knock over, upend, invert. **3** *overturn the previous decision* overrule, override, veto, set aside, cancel, reverse, rescind, repeal, revoke, repudiate, annul, nullify, invalidate, void, abrogate. **4** *overturn the government* overthrow, depose, oust. *See* OVERTHROW verb 1. **5** *overturn* *the army of occupation* conquer, vanquish, defeat. See OVERTHROW *verb* 2.

531

overweening ~

overweening *adjective* arrogant, haughty, proud, vain, vainglorious, conceited, self-important, egotistical, high-handed, domineering, presumptuous, lordly, peremptory, pompous, officious, blustering, self-confident, cocksure, self-assertive, opinionated, bold, forward, insolent, supercilious, disdainful, patronizing; *inf.* cocky, high and mighty, throwing one's weight around/about.
Antonyms: MODEST; DIFFIDENT; UNASSUMING.

overweight *adjective* obese, fat, plump, stout, ample, chubby, tubby, corpulent, rotund, portly, pudgy, paunchy, heavy, on the heavy side, big, hefty, large, bulky, chunky, outsize, massive, gross; *inf.* roly-poly, well-padded, well-upholstered.
Antonyms: SKINNY; SCRAWNY; anorexic.

overwhelm *verb* **1** *the generous present overwhelmed her* overcome, move, make emotional, daze, dumbfound, shake, take aback, leave speechless, stagger; *inf.* bowl over, knock for a loop, blow one's mind, flabbergast. **2** *they were overwhelmed with work/mail* inundate, flood, deluge, engulf, submerge, swamp, bury, overload, overburden, snow under. **3** *overwhelm the army of occupation* overcome, overpower, conquer, vanquish. See OVERCOME *verb* 1.

overwhelming *adjective* **1** *an overwhelming desire to laugh* uncontrollable, irrepressible, irresistible, overpowering. **2** *an overwhelming amount of mail* profuse, enormous, immense, inordinate, massive, huge, stupendous, prodigious, staggering, shattering; *inf.* mind-boggling, mind-blowing. **3** *the overwhelming majority* vast, massive, great, large.

overwork *verb* **1** *the staff are all overworking* work too hard, do too much, overdo it, work like a Trojan, work like a horse/slave, work day and night, burn the midnight oil, drive/push oneself too hard, overtax oneself, work one's fingers to the bone; *inf.* work one's tail off, work/run oneself into the ground. **2** *the factory owner overworks the employees* exploit, sweat, be a (hard) taskmaster to, overburden, oppress, be a slave driver to; *inf.* drive into the ground. **3** *overwork certain words* overuse, overemploy.

overworked *adjective* *overworked employees* stressed, under stress, stress-ridden, strained, overtaxed, overburdened, exhausted, fatigued, worn out.

overwrought *adjective* **1** *overwrought mothers* tense, agitated, nervous, on edge, edgy, keyed up, highly strung, overexcited, beside oneself, distracted, jumpy, frantic, frenzied, hysterical; *inf.* in a state, in a tizzy, uptight, wound up. **2** *overwrought decoration/designs* overornate, overelaborate, overembellished, overblown, overcharged, florid, busy, fussy, strained, contrived, overworked, baroque, rococo.
Antonyms: CALM; LAID-BACK; PLAIN.

owe *verb* be in debt to, be indebted to, be in arrears to, be under an obligation to, be obligated to, be beholden to.

owing *adjective* owed, outstanding, unpaid, payable, due, overdue, in arrears. **owing to** because of, as a result of, on account of.

own *adjective* personal, individual, particular, private.

own *noun* **hold one's own 1** *she can hold her own in any debate* maintain/keep one's position, stick up for oneself, look after one's interests. **2** *the patient is holding his own* be in a stable condition, be stable, be surviving, have a chance of survival. **on one's own 1** *live/go on one's own* alone, all alone, by oneself, unaccompanied. **2** *be on one's own* single, unmarried, unattached, footloose and fancy-free. **3** *build the business on her own* all by herself, independently, unaided, unassisted, by one's own efforts, standing on one's own two feet.

own *verb* **1** *they own three cars* possess, have in one's possession, have, keep, retain, maintain, hold, enjoy. **2** *I own that he is right* admit, allow, concede, grant, accept, acknowledge, recognize, agree. **own up** *will not own up* | *own up to the crime* confess, confess everything, admit, acknowledge (one's part/involvement), tell the truth (about one's part/involvement), make a clean breast of (one's part/involvement); *inf.* come clean.

owner *noun* **1** *the owner of the car* possessor, holder, keeper. **2** *the owner of the hotel* proprietor/proprietress/proprietrix, landlord, landlady. **3** *the dog's owner* master/mistress, keeper.

ownership *noun* possession, right of possession, proprietorship, proprietary rights, title.

ox *noun* bull, bullock, steer.

P

pace noun **1** *take one pace toward her* step, stride. **2** *walk with an ambling pace* gait, walk, tread. **3** *unable to keep up with the pace of the race* speed, swiftness, fastness, quickness, rapidity, velocity, tempo; *inf.* clip. **4** *the fast/slow pace of life there* rate of progress, tempo, momentum, measure.

pacific adjective **1** *make pacific overtures* peacemaking, placatory, placating, conciliatory, propitiatory, appeasing, mollifying, calming, mediatory, mediating, diplomatic, irenic. **2** *a pacific nation* peace-loving, peaceable, pacifist, nonviolent, nonaggressive, nonbelligerent, noncombative, mild, gentle, dovelike, dovish. **3** *pacific waters* calm, still, motionless, smooth, tranquil, peaceful, at peace, placid, unruffled, undisturbed.
Antonyms: HOSTILE; AGGRESSIVE; STORMY.

pacifist noun conscientious objector, passive resister, peace-lover, peacemaker, peacemonger, dove.

pacify verb *pacify the angry crowd* calm, calm down, placate, conciliate, propitiate, appease, mollify, soothe, tranquilize, quieten.

---

pacify
appease, conciliate, mollify, placate, propitiate
You might try to **pacify** a crying baby, to **appease** a demanding boss, to **mollify** a friend whose feelings have been hurt, and to **placate** an angry crowd. While all of these verbs have something to do with quieting people who are upset, excited, or disturbed, each involves taking a slightly different approach. *Pacify* suggests soothing or calming (*the mother made soft cooing noises in an attempt to pacify her child*). *Appease* implies that you've given in to someone's demands or made concessions in order to please (*she said she would visit his mother just to appease him*), while *mollify* stresses minimizing anger or hurt feelings by taking positive action (*her flattery failed to mollify him*). *Placate* suggests changing a hostile or angry attitude to a friendly or favorable one, usually with a more complete or long-lasting effect than *appease* (*they were able to placate their enemies by offering to support them*). You can **propitiate** a superior or someone who has the power to injure you by allaying or forestalling their anger (*they were able to propitiate the trustees by holding a dinner party in their honor*). **Conciliate** implies the use of arbitration or compromise to settle a dispute or to win someone over (*the company made every effort to conciliate its angry competitor*).

---

pack noun **1** *carry his goods in a pack* bundle, parcel, bale, truss; *inf.* bindle. **2** *carry a pack on his back* bag, backpack, rucksack, knapsack, haversack, duffel bag, kitbag. **3** *buy a pack of cigarettes* packet, container, package, carton. **4** *a pack of animals* herd, drove, flock, troop. **5** *a pack of thieves* gang, crowd, mob, group, band, company, troop, set, clique; *inf.* crew, bunch. **6** *a pack of lies* great deal, collection, parcel, assortment, mass, assemblage, bunch; *inf.* load, heap.

pack verb **1** *pack a suitcase* fill, load, bundle, stuff, cram. **2** *pack clothes in a suitcase* put, place, store, stow. **3** *pack the glass in straw* package, parcel, wrap, wrap up, box, bale, cover, protect. **4** *people packing the stadium* fill, crowd, throng, mob, cram, jam, press into, squeeze into. **5** *everyone was packing into the small car* crowd, cram, jam, squeeze, press. **6** *snow packed by the wind against the wall* compact, compress, press, tamp, ram. **pack in 1** *a show that has been packing them in for years* draw in, pull in, attract, fill the theater (etc.) with. **2** *pack in one's job* resign, leave, give up, abandon; *inf.* chuck. **pack off** *pack the children off to bed* send off, dispatch, dismiss, put away, bundle off; *inf.* send packing. **pack up 1** *pack up one's equipment for the night* put away, tidy up, clear up, store. **2** *decided to pack up for the day* finish, leave off, halt, stop, cease; *inf.* call it a day, pack it in.
Antonym: unpack.

package noun **1** *a Christmas package | a package of cookies/paper* parcel, packet, container, box, carton. **2** *agree to some provisions/items but not the (whole) package* package deal, unit, lot, combination; agreement, contract, arrangement, deal.

package verb *package the gift and send it* pack, pack up, wrap, wrap up, gift-wrap, box.

packaging noun *low-cost goods in expensive packaging* wrapping, wrappers, packing, covering, container, packet, presentation.

packed adjective *theater groups playing to packed halls* full, filled, filled to capacity, crowded, thronged, mobbed, crammed, jammed, packed like sardines, overfull, overloaded, brimful, chock-full, chockablock; *inf.* jam-packed.

packet noun pack, carton, box, container, package, bag, parcel.

pact noun sign a pact with the opposing side agreement, treaty, deal, contract, settlement, bargain, compact, covenant, bond, concordat, entente, protocol.

pad noun **1** a pad to prevent friction padding, wadding, wad, stuffing, buffer. **2** a pad to rest one's head on cushion, pillow, bolster. **3** a pad to absorb the blood gauze pad, piece/wad of cotton wool, dressing, compress. **4** write one's notes in a pad notepad, writing pad, notebook; inf. memo pad. **5** the animal's injured pad paw, foot, sole.

pad verb pad the package with tissue paper pack, stuff, line, cushion, protect.

padding noun **1** use padding to prevent the china's being damaged packing, stuffing, filling, filler, wadding, cushioning, lining, wrapping. **2** an essay with few facts and too much padding wordiness, verbiage, verbosity, verboseness, prolixity, prolixness; inf. hot air.

paddle noun use the paddles to row ashore oar, scull, sweep.

paddle verb paddle one's way to the shore row, pull, oar, scull, pole, punt.

paddock noun horses grazing in the paddock field, meadow, enclosure, yard, pen, pound, corral.

padlock noun secure the padlock on the gate lock, catch, latch, fastening, fastener.

padre noun soldiers praying with the padre minister, priest, parson, vicar, pastor, rector, reverend, chaplain, clergyman, cleric, man of God, man of the cloth.

paean noun song of praise, praise, hymn, psalm, anthem, exaltation, glorification, magnification, eulogy, encomium, panegyric, compliment, bouquet.

pagan noun missionaries trying to convert pagans unbeliever, nonbeliever, disbeliever; heathen, infidel, idolater; pantheist, atheist, polytheist.

pagan adjective missionaries challenging pagan beliefs paganistic, paganish, heathen, heathenish, heathenistic, infidel, idolatrous, pantheistic, atheistic, polytheistic.
Antonyms: RELIGIOUS; GODLY.

page[1] noun **1** a report 20 pages long sheet, side, leaf, folio, recto, verso. **2** his bravery will be recorded in the pages of history report, account, anecdote, book, volume, writing. **3** a glorious page in American history chapter, event, episode, incident, time, period, stage, phase, epoch, era, point.

page[2] noun employed by the hotel/Senate as a page messenger, page boy, messenger boy/girl, errand boy/girl; bellman, bellboy, bellhop; attendant.

page[3] verb page a hotel guest call, ask for, summon, send for.

pageant noun made grand costumes for the pageant display, spectacle, extravaganza, show, parade, scene, representation, tableau.

pageantry noun all the pageantry of a coronation pageant, display, spectacle, magnificence, pomp, splendor, grandeur, glamour, flourish, glitter, theatricality, show, showiness; inf. pizzazz.

pain noun **1** a pain in her leg soreness, hurt, ache, aching, throb, throbbing, smarting, twinge, pang, spasm, cramp, discomfort, irritation, tenderness. **2** invalids enduring pain suffering, physical suffering, agony, affliction, torture, torment. **3** the pain of losing a loved one suffering, mental suffering, emotional suffering, hurt, sorrow, grief, heartache, brokenheartedness, sadness, unhappiness, distress, misery, wretchedness, anguish, affliction, woe, agony, torment, torture. **4** that job/person is a pain nuisance, pest, bother, vexation, source of irritation, worry, source of aggravation; inf. pain in the neck, drag.

pain verb **1** her foot is still paining cause pain, be painful, hurt, be sore, ache, throb, smart, twinge, cause discomfort, be tender. **2** the memory of the event still pains her hurt, grieve, sadden, distress, make miserable/wretched, cause anguish to, afflict, torment, torture. **3** it pained her to tell him to go worry, distress, trouble, hurt, vex, embarrass.

pained adjective wear a pained expression hurt, aggrieved, reproachful, offended, insulted, vexed, piqued, upset, unhappy, distressed, wounded; inf. miffed.

painful adjective **1** a painful arm sore, hurting, aching, throbbing, smarting, cramped, tender, inflamed, irritating, agonizing, excruciating. **2** endure a painful experience disagreeable, unpleasant, nasty, distressing, disquieting, disturbing, miserable, wretched, agonizing, harrowing. **3** a painful climb arduous, laborious, strenuous, rigorous, demanding, exacting, trying, hard, tough, difficult. **4** it was painful to watch him work so slowly irksome, tedious, annoying, vexatious.
Antonyms: PAINLESS; PLEASANT; AGREEABLE.

painfully adverb **1** a leg that is painfully swollen achingly, agonizingly, excruciatingly. **2** become painfully thin distressingly, alarmingly, worryingly, excessively; inf. terribly, dreadfully. **3** it was painfully obvious that he was incompetent embarrassingly, uncomfortably, disconcertingly, markedly, woefully.

painkiller noun take painkillers for headaches analgesic, anesthetic, sedative, anodyne, palliative, lenitive; aspirin, acetaminophen, ibuprofen, codeine, morphine.

painless adjective **1** a painless medical procedure pain-free, without pain. **2** getting rid of him proved painless easy, simple, trouble-free, effortless; inf. as easy as pie, as easy as falling off a log, as easy as ABC, a piece of cake, child's play, a cinch.

pains plural noun childbirth pains contractions, pangs, labor, labor pains, birth pangs. **take (great) pains** they took (great) pains to put him at *ease* try hard, make every effort, take care, put oneself out.

painstaking *adjective* **1** *a painstaking investigation* careful, thorough, assiduous, conscientious, meticulous, punctilious, sedulous, scrupulous, searching. **2** *a painstaking student* careful, thorough, assiduous, attentive, diligent, industrious, hardworking, conscientious, meticulous, punctilious, sedulous, scrupulous, persevering, pertinacious.
Antonyms: CARELESS; NEGLIGENT; SLAPDASH.

paint *noun* **1** *buy paint for the walls* coloring, colorant, tint, dye, stain, pigment, gloss (paint), semigloss (paint), enamel, latex paint, wash, whitewash. **2** *the paint required for his picture* colorant, tint, pigment, watercolor, oil, oil paint, oil color. **3** *apply paint to her face* make-up, cosmetic, greasepaint, maquillage; *inf.* warpaint.

paint *verb* **1** *paint the walls* apply paint to, decorate, color, tint, dye, stain, whitewash. **2** *paint slogans on the walls* daub, smear, plaster, spray-paint. **3** *paint his mother | painted the scene from her window* portray, depict, delineate, draw, sketch, represent, catch a likeness of. **4** *paint a story of great happiness/misery* tell, recount, narrate, unfold, describe, depict, portray, evoke, conjure up. **paint the town red** celebrate; *inf.* go out on the town, whoop it up, have a good time, carouse, party, live it up, step out.

painting *noun* picture, illustration, portrayal, depiction, delineation, representation, likeness, drawing, sketch, portrait, landscape, seascape, still life, oil painting, watercolor; *inf.* oil.

pair *noun* **1** *the pair walked down the road* twosome, two, two people, couple, duo. **2** *a pair of pheasants* brace, couple. **3** *a pair of gloves* matched set, matching set. **4** *a coach and pair* team, yoke, span, two horses. **5** *the happy pair after their wedding* married couple, couple, man and wife, husband and wife, partners, lovers.

pair *verb* **pair off** *pair off the children for games* arrange/group in pairs, pair up, put together. **pair up** *we paired up to search for clues* get together, join up, link up, team up, unite, form a partnership.

pal *noun* *they are best pals* friend, mate, companion, crony, comrade; *inf.* chum, buddy.

palace *noun* *the king's summer palace* royal residence, castle; château, mansion, villa.

palatable *adjective* **1** *chefs providing palatable dishes* tasty, appetizing, pleasant-tasting, flavorful, flavorsome, delicious, delectable, mouthwatering, savory, luscious, toothsome; *inf.* scrumptious, yummy. **2** *unlikely to find the truth palatable* agreeable, pleasant, pleasing, pleasurable, nice, attractive, acceptable, satisfactory.
Antonyms: UNPALATABLE; TASTELESS; INSIPID; UNPLEASANT.

palate *noun* **1** *a sore palate* roof of the mouth, hard palate, soft palate. **2** *have no palate for food after witnessing the accident* appetite, desire, stomach. **3** *have a good palate | dry wines that suit her palate* sense of taste, taste, taste buds. **4** *have no palate for that style of prose* taste, liking, appreciation, enjoyment, relish, enthusiasm.

palatial *adjective* *palatial residences* luxurious, deluxe, imposing, splendid, grand, magnificent, stately, majestic, opulent, sumptuous, plush; *inf.* plushy, posh.
Antonyms: HUMBLE; MODEST; CRAMPED.

palaver *noun* **1** *always a lot of palaver when guests come to stay* fuss, fuss and bother, commotion, fluster, flurry, agitation, stir. **2** *a palaver in the boardroom* conference, discussion, meeting, talks, colloquy; *inf.* confab, powwow.

pale *adjective* **1** *a pale complexion | pale with fear* white, whitish, white-faced, colorless, anemic, wan, drained, pallid, pasty, peaky, ashen, ashy, waxen, green, as white as a sheet/ghost, deathly pale. **2** *pale colors/shades* light, light-colored, pastel, muted, low-key, restrained, faded, bleached, whitish, washed-out, etiolated. **3** *the pale light of dawn* dim, faint, weak, feeble, thin.
Antonyms: FLUSHED; DARK; BRIGHT.

---

pale
ashen, livid, pallid, wan

Someone of fair complexion who usually stays indoors and spends little time in the sun is apt to be **pale**, referring to an unusually white or colorless complexion; one can also become *pale* out of fear or illness. Someone who has lost color from being ill or under stress may be described as **pallid**, which suggests a paleness that is the result of some abnormal condition (*she appeared pallid when she left the police station*). **Wan** also connotes an unhealthy condition or sickly paleness (*her wan face smiled at him from the hospital bed*). Someone who is **ashen** has skin the pale grayish color of ashes (*ashen with fear*), while **livid** can mean either bluish to describe loss of normal coloring (*the livid face of a drowned corpse*) or reddish or flushed (*livid with rage*).

---

pale *verb* **1** *she paled at the gruesome sight* grow pale, become pale, go/turn white, blanch, lose color. **2** *other problems paled beside their financial difficulties* pale into insignificance, fade, dim, diminish, lessen, decrease in importance, lose significance.

pale *noun* **beyond the pale** *his behavior was considered beyond the pale* unacceptable, unseemly, improper, indiscreet, unsuitable, irregular, unreasonable, out-of-line.

pall *verb* *the pleasures of partying began to pall* lose its/their (etc.) interest, lose attraction, cloy, become tedious, become boring, grow tedious, grow tiresome.

pall *noun* **1** *the pall over the coffin* funeral cloth, coffin covering. **2** *a pall of smoke/darkness* dark covering, shroud, mantle, cloak. **3** *the news cast a pall over the gathering* cloud, shadow, gloom, depression, melancholy, somberness, gravity.

palliate *verb* **1** *palliate the pain* relieve, ease, soothe, alleviate, mitigate, assuage, abate, allay, dull, take the edge off, blunt. **2** *palliate an offense* extenuate, minimize, make light of, tone down, play down, downplay, make allowances for, excuse, whitewash.

pallid *adjective* **1** *pallid faces | invalids looking pallid* pale, white, whitish, white-faced, colorless, anemic, wan, drained, pasty, peaked, ashen, ashy, waxen, sickly, ghostly, ghastly, lurid, green, as white as a sheet/ghost, deathly pale, like death; *inf.* like death warmed over. **2** *a pallid performance* colorless, uninteresting, dull, boring, tedious, unimaginative, lifeless, uninspired, spiritless, bloodless, bland, vapid.
Antonyms: FLUSHED; VIVID.

pallor *noun* *the pallor of the invalid* paleness, whiteness, colorlessness, wanness, pallidness, pastiness, peakiness, ashenness, sickliness, ghastliness, luridness.

palm *verb* **palm off** *palm off a broken-down car on him* foist, fob, pass off, offload, thrust, get rid of; *inf.* unload. **grease (someone's) palm** bribe, buy off, give money to, corrupt, suborn. **have in the palm of one's hand** have control over, have power over, have at one's mercy, have in one's clutches.

palpable *adjective* **1** *a palpable swelling* tangible, feelable, touchable, solid, concrete. **2** *a palpable error* obvious, apparent, clear, plain, evident, manifest, visible, conspicuous, patent, blatant, glaring, definite, unmistakable.
Antonyms: INTANGIBLE; UNOBTRUSIVE.

palpitate *verb* **1** *with her heart palpitating* beat rapidly, pulsate, pulse, throb, flutter, quiver, vibrate, pound, thud, thump, pump. **2** *palpitating with fear* tremble, quiver, quake, quaver, shake.

paltry *adjective* **1** *a paltry sum of money* small, meager, trifling, minor, insignificant, trivial, derisory; *inf.* piddling. **2** *a paltry excuse/trick* mean, low, base, worthless, despicable, contemptible, miserable, wretched, sorry.
Antonyms: CONSIDERABLE; SUBSTANTIAL; IMPRESSIVE.

pamper *verb* *pamper oneself | pamper his/her spouse* spoil, cosset, indulge, overindulge, humor, coddle, mollycoddle, baby, wait on someone hand and foot, cater to someone's every whim, featherbed.

pamphlet *noun* leaflet, booklet, brochure, circular, flyer.

pan[1] *noun* **1** *pans simmering on the stove* saucepan, pot, frying pan, skillet, kettle, pressure cooker, casserole, wok. **2** *put a pan under the leak* container, vessel, receptacle. **3** *salt pans* depression, dip, indentation, hollow, crater, cavity.

pan[2] *verb* **1** *pan for gold* search, look, sift. **2** *critics panning the play* criticize, censure, find fault with, flay, roast, take to pieces; *inf.* slate, slam, knock. **pan out** *see how things pan out* work out, turn out, come out, fall out.

pan[3] *verb* *cameras panning the strikers' march* scan, sweep, follow, track, traverse.

panacea *noun* *a panacea for the economic ills* cure-all, cure for all ills, universal cure, universal remedy, elixir, nostrum.

panache *noun* *sing/dress with panache* dash, flourish, flamboyance, élan, style, verve, zest, brio, éclat; *inf.* pizzazz.

pancake *noun* hotcake, flapjack, griddle cake; crêpe, blintz; tortilla.

pandemic *adjective* *diseases pandemic in the African continent* widespread, universal, global, extensive, prevalent, wholesale, rife, rampant.

pandemonium *noun* *there was pandemonium when the concert was canceled* uproar, tumult, turmoil, commotion, clamor, din, hullabaloo, hubbub, hue and cry, chaos, confusion, disorder, bedlam.
Antonyms: SILENCE; TRANQUILLITY.

pander *verb* **pander to** *pander to her every whim | pander to the taste of the majority* give in to, gratify, indulge, humor, please, satisfy, cater to.

panegyric *noun* **1** *a panegyric on the hero's achievements* eulogy, paean, encomium, extolment, laudation, accolade, testimonial, tribute, exaltation, glorification. **2** *a talk full of panegyric* eulogy, praise, adulation, acclamation, extolment, laudation, exaltation, glorification.
Antonyms: CRITICISM; CENSURE.

pang *noun* **1** *hunger pang* pain, sharp pain, shooting pain, twinge, spasm, ache. **2** *feel a pang of remorse* twinge, qualm, misgiving, scruple, regret, feeling of uneasiness.

panic *noun* *feel panic at the sight of smoke* alarm, fright, fear, terror, horror, trepidation, nervousness, agitation, hysteria, perturbation, dismay, disquiet.

panic *verb* **1** *panic at the sight of smoke* be alarmed, take fright, be filled with fear, be scared, be terrified/horrified, be nervous, be agitated, be hysterical, lose one's nerve, overreact, be perturbed, be filled with dismay, go to pieces; *inf.* lose one's cool, get the jitters, get/go into a tizzy, run around like a chicken with its head cut off. **2** *the crowd was panicked into a stampede* alarm, frighten, scare, terrify, petrify, startle, agitate, unnerve.

panic-stricken, panic-struck *adjective* panicky, alarmed, frightened, scared, terrified, terror-stricken, petrified, horror-stricken, horrified, aghast, nervous, agitated, hysterical, perturbed, dismayed, disquieted; *inf.* in a tizzy.

panoply *noun* *the full panoply of a royal wedding* array, trappings, display, show, splendor.

panorama *noun* **1** *the panorama from the top of the tower* wide view, aerial view, bird's-eye view,

view, vista, spectacle. **2** *a panorama of political events* survey, overview, perspective, appraisal.

panoramic *adjective* **1** *a panoramic view from the tower* wide, extensive, sweeping, bird's-eye. **2** *a panoramic presentation of the events of the decade* wide, wide-ranging, extensive, comprehensive.

pant *verb* **1** *panting after climbing the hill* breathe heavily, puff, huff and puff, blow, gasp, wheeze. **2** *panting for water/knowledge* long, yearn, pine, ache, hunger, thirst, burn; *inf.* have a yen. **3** *with his heart panting* throb, palpitate, pulsate, pulse, pound, thump, beat rapidly.

pant *noun* *the pants from the dog* puff, gasp, wheeze.

pants *plural noun* trousers, slacks, jeans, blue jeans; *Trademark* Levis; *inf.* cords.

pap *noun* **1** *prepare pap for the baby* baby food, mush, pulp. **2** *prefer pap to serious novels* trivia, drivel, rubbish, trash, pulp.

paper *noun* **1** *go for the morning paper* newspaper, magazine, journal, gazette, tabloid, scandal sheet, daily, weekly; *inf.* rag. **2** *lose the papers to the house* legal paper, document, certificate, record, deed, instrument, assignment. **3** *write a paper on child development* essay, article, work, dissertation, treatise, thesis, monograph, study, report, analysis. **4** *put striped paper on the walls/shelves* wallpaper, wall covering, shelf paper. **on paper 1** *put your objections on paper* in writing, written down, in black and white. **2** *the plan was good only on paper* in theory, theoretically, hypothetically, in the abstract.

paper *verb* *paper the walls* wallpaper, line, hang wallpaper on, decorate. **paper over** *paper over the firm's difficulties* hide, conceal, draw a veil over, disguise, camouflage, cover up, gloss over, whitewash.

papers *plural noun* **1** *sign the adoption papers* legal paper, document, certificate. *See* PAPER *noun* 2. **2** *escape using forged papers* identification papers, identification documents, identity card, ID. **3** *go through her papers after her death* personal papers, personal documents, letters, records, files.

papery *adjective* *papery clothes/walls* paper-thin, ultrathin, flimsy, insubstantial, fragile, frail.

par *noun* *up to par* average, mean, standard, normal, norm. **below par 1** *work that is below par* below average, substandard, inferior, lacking, wanting, second-rate, poor; *inf.* not up to scratch, not up to snuff. **2** *feeling below par since having the flu* slightly unwell/unhealthy, unfit, poorly, indisposed, out of sorts; *inf.* not oneself, under the weather. **on a par with** *modern novels on a par with the classics* equal to, a match for, on a level with, on an equal footing with, of the same standard as, as good as. **par for the course** *his unruly behavior was par for the course* usual, normal, standard, typical, predictable, what one would expect. **up to par** *work no longer up to par* up to the mark, satisfactory, acceptable, good enough, adequate, passable; *inf.* up to scratch, up to snuff.

parable *noun* *the parable of/about the prodigal son* allegory, morality tale/story, story with a moral, fable, lesson.

parade *noun* **1** *watch the parade of the soldiers | Memorial Day parade* march, procession, progression, cavalcade, spectacle, pageant, array. **2** *make a parade of their wealth* display, exhibition, show, spectacle, flaunting, ostentation, demonstration; *inf.* showing-off.

parade *verb* **1** *soldiers/children parading during the celebrations* march, go in columns, file by. **2** *parade their wealth/knowledge* display, exhibit, show, demonstrate, air, make a show of, flaunt; *inf.* show off. **3** *parade up and down in her new hat* strut, swagger.

paradigm *noun* *a paradigm for others to copy* example, pattern, model, standard, gauge, criterion, archetype, prototype, paragon, exemplar.

paradise *noun* **1** *believe in paradise after death* heaven, heavenly kingdom, kingdom of heaven, abode of the saints, Elysium, the Elysian fields. **2** *Adam and Eve in paradise* the Garden of Eden, Eden. **3** *the resort island is a paradise* Eden, fairyland, Utopia, Shangri-La. **4** *it was paradise to be in love* heaven, bliss, ecstasy, supreme joy, seventh heaven.
Antonyms: HELL; TORMENT.

paradox *noun* *a paradox that there is so much poverty in such a rich country* contradiction, self-contradiction, inconsistency, incongruity, anomaly, enigma, puzzle, absurdity, oxymoron.

paradoxical *adjective* *it is paradoxical that there is so much poverty in such a rich country* contradictory, self-contradictory, inconsistent, incongruous, anomalous, enigmatic, puzzling, absurd.

paragon *noun* *a paragon of good behavior* perfect example, good example, ideal, model, pattern, exemplar, nonpareil, paradigm, standard, criterion, archetype, prototype, quintessence, epitome, apotheosis, acme, jewel, flower.

paragraph *noun* **1** *the essay should be divided into paragraphs* section, subdivision, segment. **2** *a paragraph in the local paper about the death* article, item, piece, notice, note.

parallel *adjective* **1** *parallel lines* side by side, equidistant, collateral. **2** *the judge considering a parallel case | cases parallel to each other* similar, like, resembling, analogous, comparable, equivalent, corresponding, matching, duplicate. **3** *parallel processes* concurrent, coexistent, coexisting.
Antonyms: DIFFERENT; DIVERGENT.

parallel *noun* **1** *find a parallel for the case* analog, counterpart, equivalent, correspondent, match, duplicate, equal. **2** *draw a parallel between the two cases* similarity, likeness, resemblance, analogy, correspondence, comparison, equivalence, symmetry.

parallel verb **1** *the case parallels the murder of her neighbor* be similar to, be like, resemble, bear a resemblance to, be analogous to, be an analogy with, correspond to, compare with, be comparable/equivalent to. **2** *his account of the incident parallels the policeman's* match, correspond to, agree with, be in harmony with, conform to. **3** *his rowing feat has never been paralleled* match, equal, rival, emulate.

paralysis noun **1** *paralysis of/in the legs* immobility, powerlessness, lack of feeling, numbness, palsy, incapacity, debilitation; *Med.* paresis. **2** *paralysis of the railroad* immobilization, breakdown, shutdown, stopping, stoppage, halt, standstill.

paralytic adjective *paralytic limbs* immobile, immobilized, powerless, numb, dead, palsied, incapacitated, debilitated, disabled, crippled.

paralyze verb **1** *the spider's poison paralyzed the fly* immobilize, render/make powerless, numb, deaden, dull, obtund, incapacitate, debilitate, disable, cripple. **2** *he was paralyzed in the accident* immobilize, incapacitate, debilitate, disable, cripple. **3** *paralyze the transport system* immobilize, bring to a halt, bring to a complete stop, bring to a grinding halt, bring to a standstill, freeze, put out of order/commission. **4** *paralyzed with fear* immobilize, render motionless, freeze, unnerve, terrify, shock, stun.

parameter noun *within the parameters of the budget* limit, limitation, limiting factor, restriction, constant, specification, guidelines, framework.

paramount adjective *financial considerations are paramount* most important, of greatest importance, of prime importance, of supreme importance, of greatest significance, uppermost, supreme, predominant, foremost, first and foremost, preeminent, outstanding.

paramour noun lover, illicit lover; mistress, girlfriend, kept woman, inamorata; boyfriend, inamorato; *inf.* boy toy.

paranoid adjective *paranoid about what everyone was saying about her* suspicious, mistrustful, distrustful, fearful, insecure.

parapet noun **1** *the parapet of a balcony* wall, railing, handrail, fence, barrier. **2** *soldiers sheltering behind the parapet* fortification, barricade, rampart, bulwark, bank, embankment.

paraphernalia plural noun **1** *all the artist's paraphernalia* equipment, gear, stuff, apparatus, implements, tools, materials, accouterments, trappings, appurtenances, appointments. **2** *loaded down with all her paraphernalia* baggage, bags and baggage, luggage, personal belongings, belongings, possessions, things, impedimenta; *inf.* stuff.

paraphrase verb *paraphrase the complicated instructions* reword, put in other words, rephrase, restate, rehash, interpret, gloss.

paraphrase noun *a simple paraphrase of the in-* structions rewording, rephrasing, restatement, restating, rehash, interpretation, gloss.

parasite noun *a parasite on society* | *a parasite totally dependent on others* hanger-on, sponge, sponger, cadger, leech, bloodsucker, drone; *inf.* scrounge, scrounger, freeloader.

parcel noun **1** *tie the parcel with string* package, packet, pack, bundle. **2** *a parcel of land* plot, tract, piece, lot, patch. **3** *a parcel of thieves* band, pack, gang, group, company, collection, crowd, mob, troop; *inf.* crew, bunch. **4** *a parcel of lies* pack, great deal, collection, assortment, mass, assemblage, bunch; *inf.* heap, load.

parcel verb **parcel out** *parcel out the food to the needy* distribute, divide out, share out, hand out, deal out, dole out, dispense, allocate, allot, portion out, apportion, mete out, carve up; *inf.* divvy up. **parcel up** *parcel up the goods* pack, pack up, package, wrap, wrap up, gift-wrap, tie up, do up, box, bundle up.

parched adjective **1** *parched ground/grass* dried up, dried out, dry, baked, burned, scorched, seared, desiccated, dehydrated, withered, shriveled. **2** *parched from walking in the heat* thirsty, dehydrated; *inf.* dry.
Antonyms: SODDEN; SOAKING.

pardon noun **1** *seek their pardon* forgiveness, forbearance, indulgence, condonation, clemency, lenience, leniency, mercy. **2** *the accused received a pardon* reprieve, release, acquittal, absolution, amnesty, exoneration, exculpation.

pardon verb **1** *pardon me* | *could never pardon such an offense* forgive, excuse, condone, let off. **2** *the accused man was pardoned* reprieve, release, acquit, absolve, exonerate, exculpate.
Antonyms: BLAME; PUNISH.

pardonable adjective *a pardonable error* forgivable, excusable, allowable, condonable, understandable, minor, slight, venial.

parent noun **1** *resembles his parent* mother; father; *inf.* mom, mommy, ma, mama, old woman, old lady; dad, daddy, pa, pop, old man. **2** *the parent of all his misfortune* source, root, origin, originator, wellspring, fountain, cause, author, architect.

parent verb *parent three sons* be the parent of, bring into the world, produce, procreate, look after, rear, bring up, raise.

parentage noun *of humble parentage* family, birth, origins, extraction, ancestry, lineage, descent, heritage, pedigree.

pariah noun *a social pariah* outcast, leper, *persona non grata*, untouchable, undesirable.

parish noun **1** *local administrators of the parish* county, community, district; canton. **2** *the parish choosing a new minister* parishioners, churchgoers, congregation, flock, fold.

parity noun *workers having parity of status/salary* equality, levelness, identity, sameness, unity, uniformity, evenness, equivalence, parallelism, correspondence.

park noun **1** *children playing in the park* public park, green, recreation ground, playground, play area. **2** *park surrounding the estate* parkland, grassland, lawns, grounds. **3** *few fans left in the park* stadium, arena, ballpark, ball field, baseball field, field, playing field.

park verb **1** *park the car on a yellow line* stop, pull up, leave, station. **2** *park the baby in his carriage* put, place, set, seat, leave.

parlance noun *fail to understand the parlance of the young* speech, language, talk, vocabulary, phraseology, idiom, vernacular, jargon, patter, argot, patois; *inf.* lingo.

parliament noun legislative assembly, lawmaking body, congress, senate, chamber, house, convocation, diet.

parliamentary adjective **1** *parliamentary assemblies* legislative, legislatorial, lawmaking, lawgiving, governmental, congressional, senatorial, democratic, representative. **2** *parliamentary behavior/language* orderly, proper, seemly, by the rules, according to the rule book.

parlor noun **1** *a beauty parlor* salon, shop, establishment, store. **2** *have tea in the parlor* sitting room, living room, drawing room, lounge.

parochial adjective *a parochial attitude to life* provincial, small-town, insular, restricted, inward-looking, narrow, narrow-minded, petty, small-minded, limited.
Antonyms: COSMOPOLITAN; LIBERAL.

parody noun **1** *a parody of a Gothic novel* burlesque, lampoon, satire, pastiche, caricature, mimicry, takeoff; *inf.* spoof, send-up. **2** *trial was a parody of justice* travesty, poor imitation, misrepresentation, perversion, corruption.

parody verb *parody an operatic aria* burlesque, lampoon, satirize, caricature, mimic, take off; *inf.* send up.

paroxysm noun *a paroxysm of coughing/rage* fit, attack, convulsion, spasm, seizure, outburst, outbreak, eruption.

parrot verb *parroting the teacher's words* repeat, echo, copy, imitate, mimic, ape, take off.

parry verb **1** *parry a blow* ward off, fend off, stave off, turn aside, avert, deflect, block, rebuff, repel, repulse, hold at bay. **2** *parry awkward questions* avoid, dodge, evade, elude, steer clear of, sidestep, circumvent, fight shy of; *inf.* duck.

parsimonious adjective mean, miserly, niggardly, tight-fisted, close-fisted, close, money-grubbing, Scrooge-like, scrimping, skimping, penny-pinching, penurious, ungenerous; *inf.* stingy, tight.
Antonyms: EXTRAVAGANT; GENEROUS; LAVISH.

parsimony noun meanness, miserliness, niggardliness, closeness, tight-fistedness, close-fistedness; *inf.* stinginess, tightness. *See* PARSIMONIOUS.

parson noun priest, vicar, rector, minister, reverend, pastor, clergyman, clergywoman, cleric, chaplain, ecclesiastic, churchman, churchwoman, man/woman of the cloth, man/woman of God, preacher, divine.

part noun **1** *the early part of her life* | *part of an orange* portion, division, section, segment, bit, piece, fragment, scrap, slice, fraction, chunk, wedge. **2** *spare parts* component, bit, constituent, element, module. **3** *body parts* | *parts of the body* organ, member, limb. **4** *an unknown part of the country* section, area, region, sector, quarter, territory, neighborhood. **5** *a book/ play in several parts* volume, book, section, episode. **6** *his part in the project* function, role, job, task, work, chore, responsibility, capacity, participation, duty, charge. **7** *play the part of Hamlet* role, character. **8** *learn his part* lines, words, script, lyrics. **for the most part** *for the most part, they are reliable* on the whole, in the main, by and large, all in all, generally, to all intents and purposes, mostly. **in good part** *take the teasing in good part* good-naturedly, good-humoredly, without offense, cheerfully, well. **in part** *success due in part to good luck* partly, partially, to a certain extent/degree, to some extent/degree, somewhat, in some measure. **on the part of** *an error on the part of the instructor* made by, done by, carried out by, caused by, by. **take part in** *take part in the protest* participate in, join (in), engage in, play a part in, contribute to, be associated with, associate oneself with, be involved in/with, share in, have a hand in, have something to do with, partake in. **take someone's part, take the part of** *take his mother's part in the quarrel* | *take the part of weaker candidates* take the side of, side with, support, lend/give support to, back, back up, abet, aid and abet.
Antonyms: WHOLE; ENTIRETY.

part verb **1** *the crowd parted to let the police through* divide, divide in two, separate, split, split in two, break up, sever, disjoin. **2** *the police parting the crowd* divide, separate, split up, break up, sever, cleave. **3** *couples deciding to part* separate, seek/get a separation, split up, break up, part company, go their (etc.) separate ways, divorce, get divorced, seek/get a divorce. **4** *exchange kisses before parting* take one's departure, take one's leave, leave, go, go away, say goodbye/farewell/adieu, say one's goodbyes, separate; *inf.* split, push off, hit the road. **part with** *part with her last few dollars* give up, relinquish, forgo, surrender, let go of, renounce, sacrifice, yield, cede.
Antonyms: GATHER; JOIN; MARRY; ARRIVE.

part adjective *part owner/payment* partial, half; semi-, demi-.

partake verb **partake in** *partake in the protest* take part in, participate in, join in, engage in, play a part in, contribute to, be associated with, associate oneself with, be involved in, share in, have a hand in, have something to do with. **par-**

take of 1 *partake of Christmas cheer* consume, eat, take, receive, drink, share in. 2 *their manner partook of insolence* suggest, have the qualities/attributes of, hint at, evidence, demonstrate, exhibit, show.

partial adjective 1 *a partial solution/eclipse* part, in part, limited, incomplete, imperfect, fragmentary. 2 *a partial judgment/judge* biased, prejudiced, partisan, colored, one-sided, discriminatory, preferential, interested, unjust, unfair, inequitable. **be partial to** *be partial to dark chocolate | always been partial to the beach* have a liking for, like, love, have a fondness for, be fond of, be keen on, have a weakness/taste for, have a soft spot for, be taken with, care for, have a predilection/proclivity/penchant for.
Antonyms: COMPLETE; WHOLE; UNBIASED; IMPARTIAL.

partiality noun 1 *condemn the partiality of the judge* bias, prejudice, partisanship, discrimination, preference, favoritism, unjustness, unfairness, inequity. 2 *their partiality for chocolate | always had a partiality for the beach* liking, love, fondness, keenness, taste, weakness, soft spot, inclination, predilection, proclivity, penchant.

partially adverb *partially paralyzed* partly, in part, not wholly, not fully, half, somewhat, to a certain extent/degree, to some extent/degree, in some measure, fractionally, slightly.

participant noun *participants in the protest/concert* participator, member, contributor, associate, sharer, partaker.

participate verb **participate in** *participate in the protest* take part in, join in, engage in, play a part in, contribute to, be associated with, associate oneself with, be involved in, share in, have a hand in, have something to do with, partake in.

participation noun *their participation in the protest/concert* part, contribution, association, involvement, partaking. *See* PARTICIPATE.

particle noun 1 *particles of dust* tiny bit, tiny piece, speck, spot, mote, atom, molecule. 2 *not a particle of common sense* iota, jot, whit, grain, bit, scrap, shred, morsel, mite, atom, hint, touch, trace, suggestion.

particular adjective 1 *in this particular case* specific, individual, single, distinct, precise. 2 *take particular care | a matter of particular importance* special, especial, singular, peculiar, exceptional, unusual, uncommon, notable, noteworthy, remarkable, outstanding. 3 *particular about hygiene | he is so particular about what he eats* fastidious, discriminating, selective, fussy, painstaking, meticulous, punctilious, exacting, demanding, critical, overparticular, finicky; *inf.* persnickety, choosy, picky. 4 *require a particular account of the incident* detailed, exact, precise, faithful, close, thorough, blow-by-blow, itemized, circumstantial, painstaking, meticulous, punctilious, minute.
Antonyms: GENERAL; ORDINARY; CARELESS.

particular noun **in particular** 1 *have someone in particular in mind* specific, special, distinct, precise. 2 *the desserts in particular were delicious* particularly, specifically, especially, specially.

particularize verb *particularize your reasons for leaving* specify, be specific about, detail, itemize, list, enumerate, spell out, cite.

particularly adverb 1 *a book that is particularly good* especially, specially, singularly, peculiarly, distinctly, markedly, exceptionally, unusually, uncommonly, notably, remarkably, outstandingly, surprisingly. 2 *ask for him particularly* in particular, specifically, explicitly, expressly, specially, especially.

parting noun 1 *the parting of the crowd* division, dividing, separation, separating, splitting, breaking up, severance, disjoining, detachment, partition. 2 *sad at the parting of his parents* separation, splitting up, breakup, breaking up, divorce, split, rift, rupture. 3 *partings taking place at the train station* departure, leave-taking, good-bye, farewell, adieu, valediction.

parting adjective *a parting handshake* departing, leaving, good-bye, farewell, valedictory, last, final.

partisan noun 1 *a partisan of the breakaway party* supporter, adherent, devotee, backer, champion, upholder, follower, disciple, fan, votary. 2 *partisans fighting against the ruling power* guerrilla, resistance fighter, underground fighter.

partisan adjective *a partisan attitude to the legal dispute* biased, prejudiced, colored, one-sided, discriminatory, preferential, partial, interested, unjust, unfair, inequitable.
Antonyms: IMPARTIAL; UNBIASED.

partition noun 1 *the partition of Germany* division, dividing, subdivision, separation, segregation, splitting-up, breaking-up, breakup, severance. 2 *erect a partition to divide the room* room divider, divider, dividing wall, separator, screen, barrier, wall, fence.

partition verb 1 *the Allies partitioned Germany* divide up, separate, segregate, split up, break up, sever. 2 *partition the room to make two sleeping areas* divide, divide up, subdivide, separate, separate off, screen off, wall off, fence off.

partly adverb *partly responsible for the mistake* in part, partially, not wholly, not fully, half, somewhat, to a certain extent/degree, to some extent/degree, in some measure, fractionally, slightly.

partner noun 1 *his partner in business* associate, colleague, coworker, teammate, collaborator, ally, comrade, companion, consociate. 2 *his partner in crime* accomplice, confederate, accessory, collaborator, fellow conspirator; *inf.* sidekick. 3 *bring your partner to the party* wife/husband, spouse, mate, girlfriend/boyfriend, helpmate; date, love interest.

partnership noun 1 *work in partnership with his*

brother association, cooperation, collaboration, alliance, union, fellowship, companionship, consocation. **2** *a partnership in crime* collaboration, collusion, connivance, conspiracy. **3** *the partnership formed by the brothers was bought out* company, firm, corporation, cooperative, conglomerate, combine, syndicate.

parturition *noun* childbirth, labor.

party *noun* **1** *invite guests to a party* social gathering, social function, gathering, function, reception, celebration, festivity, soirée, orgy, bacchanal; *inf.* get-together, do, bash, shindig. **2** *a hunting/search party* group, band, company, body, squad, team, crew, contingent, detachment, unit; *inf.* bunch. **3** *belong to a left-wing party* political party, alliance, affiliation, association. **4** *both parties declared that they were right* side, grouping, faction, camp, set, caucus. **5** *a certain party who shall be nameless* person, individual, human being, somebody, someone; *inf.* character. **6** *the judge speaking to both parties* litigant, plaintiff, defendant.

parvenu *noun* arrivé, arriviste, nouveau riche, social climber, intruder, upstart.

pass[1] *verb* **1** *traffic passing along the road* go, move, proceed, progress, drive, run, travel, roll, flow, course. **2** *pass her hand over her forehead* move, cross. **3** *cars passing us | other runners passing them* go past, move past, go ahead of, get ahead of, go by, overtake, outstrip, outdistance. **4** *pass the frontier/barrier* go over, go across, get across, get through, cross, traverse. **5** *pass the butter* hand over, let someone have, give, transfer. **6** *the title passes to his eldest son* be passed on, be transferred, be made over, be turned over, be signed over, go, devolve. **7** *time passed slowly* go by, proceed, progress, advance, roll by, slip by, glide by, flow by, elapse. **8** *how to pass the time* spend, occupy, fill, take up, use, employ, while away. **9** *pass all understanding* exceed, surpass, transcend. **10** *let the matter pass* go, go unheeded, go unnoticed, go unremarked, go undisputed, go uncensored. **11** *students passing their exams* get a passing grade in, get through, be successful in, succeed in, meet the requirements of, pass muster in; *inf.* come up to scratch in, come up to snuff in. **12** *the examiners passed everyone | all the material was passed* let through, declare acceptable/adequate/satisfactory, declare successful, accept, approve. **13** *pass the bill/motion* vote for, accept, approve, adopt, authorize, ratify, sanction, validate, legalize. **14** *pass judgment/sentence* pronounce, utter, express, deliver, declare. **15** *after all that has passed* happen, occur, take place, come about, befall, supervene. **16** *the storm/anger passed* blow over, run its course, ebb, die out, fade, fade away, evaporate, draw to a close, disappear, finish, end, terminate. **17** *pass urine | passing blood in the feces* discharge, excrete, eliminate, evacuate, expel, emit. **come**

to pass *it came to pass that he died* come about, happen, occur, befall, arise. **pass away** die, expire, cease (to be). *See* DIE 1, 2. **pass for** *he could pass for 30 | pass for a much younger woman* be taken for, be regarded as, be accepted as, be mistaken for. **pass off 1** *the demonstration passed off without incident* take place, happen, occur, be completed, be brought to a conclusion. **2** *the pain gradually passed off* pass, fade, fade away, disappear, vanish, die down, ebb, come to an end. **3** *pass him off as her husband* present as genuine, present with intent to deceive, give a false identity, have accepted as genuine. **pass out 1** *passing out in the heat* faint, collapse, lose consciousness, black out, keel over, swoon. **2** *pass out the exam papers* hand out, distribute, give out, deal out, dole out, allot, allocate. **pass over 1** *pass over the interruption and proceed* ignore, disregard, overlook, forget, pay no attention to, gloss over, take no notice of, close one's eyes to, turn a deaf ear to, turn a blind eye to. **2** *he was passed over for promotion* overlook, ignore, disregard, forget, neglect, not take into consideration, omit. **pass up** *pass up an opportunity for promotion* fail to take advantage of, waive, reject, refuse, decline, neglect, let slip, ignore, brush aside, forgo.

pass[2] *noun* **1** *a pass to leave the military base* warrant, permit, authorization, license, passport, visa, safe-conduct, exeat. **2** *a pass to the theater | a press pass* warrant, permit, free ticket, free admission, complimentary ticket, reduced ticket; *inf.* freebie. **3** *object to his passes* sexual advance, advance, sexual overture, sexual approach/suggestion; *inf.* proposition. **make a pass at** *make a pass at his friend's wife* make sexual advances to, make sexual overtures to, make a sexual suggestion to; *inf.* make a play for, make a proposition to, proposition.

pass[3] *noun* *a mountain pass* narrow road, gap, gorge, defile, col, canyon.

passable *adjective* **1** *work that is passable | a passable knowledge of the subject* adequate, all right, tolerable, fair, acceptable, satisfactory, mediocre, middling, ordinary, average, run-of-the-mill, moderately good, not too bad, unexceptional, indifferent; *inf.* so-so, OK, okay, nothing to write home about. **2** *roads scarcely passable in the snow* crossable, traversable, navigable, unblocked, unobstructed, open, clear.

passage *noun* **1** *the passage of time* passing, progress, advance, process, flow, course. **2** *our passage through life | their passage through foreign lands* journey, voyage, transit, trek, crossing, trip, tour. **3** *denied passage to the country* access, entry, admission, leave to travel in, permission to pass through, safe-conduct, warrant, passport, visa. **4** *his passage from boyhood to manhood | the passage from liquid to solid* change, changeover, transformation, transition, conversion, shift, switch. **5** *a passage through the mountains | underground passages* road, route, path, way, track, trail, lane, channel, course, conduit. **6** *bicycles left in the passage* passageway, corridor, hall, hallway, entrance hall, entrance, vestibule, lobby. **7** *read aloud passages from the novel* extract, excerpt, quotation, citation, section, verse. **8** *the passage of the bill by Congress* acceptance, approval, adoption, authorization, ratification, sanction, validation, enactment, legalization.

passé *adjective* out of date, outdated, dated, outmoded, outworn, old-fashioned, out of fashion, out of style, obsolete, obsolescent, archaic, antiquated, antediluvian; *inf.* old hat, fuddy-duddy.
Antonyms: MODERN; UP-TO-DATE; FASHIONABLE.

passenger *noun* rider, commuter, fare-payer, traveler, fare.

passerby *noun* *passersby helped the accident victim* bystander, onlooker, witness, spectator; *inf.* rubberneck, rubbernecker.

passing *noun* **1** *the passing of time* passage, progress, advance, process, flow, course. **2** *regret the passing of old customs* | *mourn his aunt's passing* disappearance, fading, demise, death, end, termination, expiry, loss. **3** *the passing of the bill by Congress* acceptance, approval, adoption, enactment. *See* PASSAGE 8. **in passing** *mention in passing that he was leaving* en passant, incidentally, by the by, by the way, en passant, parenthetically, in the course of conversation.

passing *adjective* **1** *a passing interest in local history* fleeting, transient, transitory, ephemeral, brief, short-lived, short, temporary, momentary. **2** *a passing glance told her everything* brief, quick, hasty, hurried, cursory, superficial, casual.
Antonyms: PERMANENT; CAREFUL.

passion *noun* **1** *do everything with great passion* intensity, fervor, fervidness, ardor, zeal, vehemence, fire, emotion, feeling, zest, enthusiasm, eagerness, excitement, animation. **2** *fly into a passion* rage, blind rage, fit of rage, fit of anger, fit of temper, temper, towering rage, outburst of anger, tantrum, fury, frenzy, paroxysm. **3** *his passion for her* love, sexual love, desire, sexual desire, lust, concupiscence, ardor, infatuation, adoration. **4** *a passion for motorcycles* | *it is their passion* enthusiasm, fascination, keen interest, obsession, fixation, craze, mania. **5** *one of the passions of his life* idol, hero/heroine, heart's desire, obsession, preoccupation.

passionate *adjective* **1** *a passionate entreaty/performance* impassioned, intense, fervent, fervid, ardent, zealous, vehement, fiery, emotional, heartfelt, zestful, enthusiastic, eager, excited, animated. **2** *a passionate lover* ardent, aroused, desirous, hot, sexy, amorous, sensual, erotic, lustful; *inf.* turned-on. **3** *a very passionate person* intense, emotional, ardent, vehement, fiery. **4** *break the vase in a passionate fit* enraged, furious, angry, hot-tempered, frenzied, violent, wild, tempestuous.
Antonyms: APATHETIC; FRIGID.

passionless *adjective* **1** *a passionless creature* cold, emotionless, frigid, passive, unfeeling, unresponsive, undemonstrative, unfeeling, withdrawn, unapproachable, aloof, detached, distant, dispassionate, remote. **2** *a passionless performance* emotionless, spiritless, lifeless, flat, zestless, insipid, lackluster, colorless, anemic, vapid.

passive *adjective* **1** *play a passive role in the marriage/business* inactive, nonactive, inert, nonparticipating, uninvolved. **2** *a passive attitude to their invaders* unresisting, nonresistant, unassertive, yielding, submissive, compliant, pliant, acquiescent, quiescent, resigned, obedient, tractable, malleable. **3** *look on with a passive expression* | *a passive person* impassive, emotionless, unmoved, unresponsive, undemonstrative, dispassionate, detached, distant, remote, aloof, indifferent.
Antonyms: ACTIVE; ASSERTIVE; EMOTIONAL.

passport *noun* **1** *show passports at the border* travel document, travel papers, papers, travel permit, visa, identity card, ID. **2** *his passport to happiness* means of access, avenue, access, entry, entrée, admission, admittance.

password *noun* *give the password to gain entry* watchword, keyword, word of identification, signal, word, open sesame, shibboleth.

past *adjective* **1** *in times past* gone by, gone, bygone, elapsed, over, over and done with, ended, former, long ago. **2** *the past few months* recent, preceding, last, latter, foregone. **3** *past achievements/chairmen* former, previous, prior, foregoing, late, erstwhile, one-time, sometime, ex-.
Antonyms: PRESENT; FUTURE.

past *noun* **in the past** *we used to go there in the past* in days gone by, in bygone days, in former times, formerly, previously, before.

past *preposition* **1** *walk past the library* in front of, by, beyond. **2** *past retirement age* beyond the limits of, beyond, in excess of.

past *adverb* *drive/hurried past* by, on, further on.

paste *noun* **1** *stick cutouts on the page/wall with paste* adhesive, glue, gum, mucilage, cement. **2** *mix to a paste* mixture, blend, compound, pulp, mush, pap. **3** *fish paste* spread, pâté, purée.

paste *verb* *paste newspaper clippings into a book* stick, fasten, glue, gum, cement.

pastel *adjective* *pastel colors* pale, soft, delicate, muted, subdued, faint, low-key.
Antonyms: DARK; BRIGHT; RICH; VIVID.

pastiche *noun* *a work that is a pastiche of various styles* medley, mélange, miscellany, blend, mixture, potpourri, mosaic, patchwork, hodgepodge, jumble, mishmash, gallimaufry, farrago.

pastille *noun* lozenge, drop, candy, jujube, troche.

pastime *noun* *take up tennis as a pastime* hobby,

leisure activity, sport, game, recreation, diversion, amusement, entertainment, distraction, relaxation.

past master *noun a past master at disguise* expert, virtuoso, wizard, genius, artist, old hand; *inf.* dab hand.

pastor *noun listen to the pastor preaching* minister, vicar, parson, priest, rector, reverend, clergyman, clergywoman, churchman, churchwoman, ecclesiastic, cleric, divine.

pastoral *adjective* **1** *a pastoral scene* rural, country, rustic, simple, idyllic, innocent, Arcadian, agricultural, bucolic, georgic. **2** *his pastoral duties* ministerial, vicarial, parsonical, priestly, rectorial, ecclesiastical, clerical.

pastry *noun* pie, strudel, tart, puff pastry, doughnut, cruller, Danish pastry; *inf.* Danish.

pasture *noun cows in the pasture* pasturage, pasture land, grassland, grass, field, grazing land, meadowland, meadow; *lit.* lea.

pat *verb* **1** *pat the child on the head | pat the dog* stroke, caress, fondle, pet. **2** *pat the mixture* tap, slap, dab. **pat oneself on the back, pat someone on the back** *pat himself on the back for bringing off the deal* congratulate, praise, commend, compliment, applaud, throw bouquets at.

pat *noun* **1** *a pat on the cheek* light blow, stroke, touch, caress. **2** *flatten the mixture with a pat* light blow, tap, slap, dab. **3** *a pat of butter* dab, lump, cake, portion. **give oneself a pat on the back, give someone a pat on the back.** *See* PAT *verb:* pat oneself on the back.

patch *noun* **1** *put a patch over the hole* piece of cloth, piece of material. **2** *a patch over the eye* cover, covering, pad, shield. **3** *a cabbage patch | patch of ground* plot, area, piece, lot, tract, parcel. **4** *encounter a bad patch* period, time, spell, stretch, interval, term.

patch *verb* **1** *patch the pants* put a patch on, cover, mend, repair, sew, sew up, stitch, stitch up. **2** *patch the roof* repair/fix hastily, do a makeshift repair on, repair/fix temporarily. **patch up 1** *patch up the roof* repair/fix hastily. **2** *patch up the quarrel* settle, resolve, set right.

patchwork *noun work that was a patchwork of different styles* pastiche, hodgepodge, mishmash, jumble, medley, mélange, miscellany, potpourri, mosaic, blend, mixture.

patchy *adjective a patchy knowledge of the subject* sketchy, uneven, varying, variable, erratic, random.
Antonyms: COMPLETE; COMPREHENSIVE; UNIFORM; CONSTANT.

patent *noun take out a patent for his invention* license, copyright, registered trademark.

patent *adjective* **1** *it was patent to everyone that she was lying | her patent dislike of him* obvious, clear, plain, evident, apparent, manifest, transparent, conspicuous, blatant, glaringly obvious, unmistakable, unconcealed. **2** *patent*

medicine patented, proprietary, licensed, branded, brand-name.
Antonyms: UNOBTRUSIVE; INCONSPICUOUS.

paternal *adjective* **1** *take a paternal interest in the boy* fatherly, fatherlike, patriarchal, protective, concerned, solicitous, kindly, benevolent. **2** *his paternal grandfather* patrilineal, patrimonial, on the father's side.

paternity *noun* **1** *dispute paternity* fatherhood. **2** *of unknown paternity* descent, extraction, lineage, parentage, family.

path *noun* **1** *a path through the forest* pathway, footpath, track, trail, walk, walkway. **2** *the moon's path around the earth* course, route, circuit, track, orbit, trajectory. **3** *unable to predict the path he will take* course of action, route, procedure, direction, approach, method, system, strategy. **4** *the path to success* way, road, avenue, route.

pathetic *adjective* **1** *children in rags were a pathetic sight* pitiful, pitiable, piteous, to be pitied, moving, touching, poignant, affecting, distressing, heartbreaking, heart-rending, sad, wretched, mournful, woeful. **2** *a pathetic attempt/performance* pitiful, lamentable, deplorable, miserable, wretched, feeble, woeful, sorry, poor, contemptible, inadequate, unsatisfactory, worthless.
Antonyms: COMICAL; CHEERFUL; ADMIRABLE; EXCELLENT.

pathological *adjective* **1** *a pathological condition* morbid, diseased. **2** *a pathological liar* irrational, compulsive, obsessive, unreasonable, illogical.

pathos *noun delivered the closing soliloquy with pathos* poignancy, pitifulness, pitiableness, piteousness, sadness, plaintiveness.

patience *noun* **1** *wait in line with patience* calmness, composure, even temper, equanimity, equilibrium, even-temperedness, serenity, tranquillity, restraint, self-restraint, imperturbability, inexcitability, tolerance, longsuffering, indulgence, forbearance, endurance, resignation, stoicism, fortitude; *inf.* unflappability, cool. **2** *a task requiring patience* perseverance, persistence, endurance, tenacity, assiduity, diligence, staying power, indefatigability, doggedness, singleness of purpose.
Antonyms: IMPATIENCE; AGITATION; EXASPERATION.

patient *adjective have to be patient about delayed flights* uncomplaining, serene, calm, composed, even-tempered, tranquil, restrained, imperturbable, inexcitable, tolerant, accommodating, long-suffering, forbearing, indulgent, resigned, stoical; *inf.* unflappable, cool.

patient *noun doctors examining patients* sick person, invalid, case, sufferer.

patio *noun* terrace, veranda, deck, piazza.

patois *noun visitors unable to understand the local patois* local speech, vernacular, dialect, local parlance; *inf.* lingo.

patrician *adjective a patrician family* aristocratic, noble, well-born, high-born, blue-blooded.

patriot *noun* nationalist, loyalist, chauvinist, flag-waver, jingoist, jingo.

patriotic *adjective* nationalist, nationalistic, loyalist, loyal, chauvinistic, flag-waving, jingoistic.

patrol *verb soldiers patrolling the border area* make the rounds of, perform sentry duty on, walk the beat of, pound the beat of, range, police, keep watch on, guard, keep guard on, keep a vigil on, monitor.

patrol *noun* 1 *make regular patrols of the border area* patrolling, round, sentry duty, beat-pounding, policing, watch, guard, vigil, monitoring. 2 *report the matter to the patrol* patrolman/patrolwoman, sentinel, sentry, garrison, guard, watchman, watch, night watchman, policeman/policewoman.

patron *noun* 1 *a patron of the theater/arts* sponsor, backer, benefactor/benefactress, promoter, friend, helper, supporter, upholder, champion, protector; *inf.* angel. 2 *regular patrons of the salon | parking for patrons only* customer, client, frequenter, shopper, buyer, purchaser; *inf.* regular.

patronage *noun* 1 *customers taking their patronage elsewhere* trade, custom, business, commerce, trafficking, shopping, buying, purchasing. 2 *their patronage of the arts* sponsorship, backing, funding, financing, promotion, help, aid, assistance, support, encouragement, championship, protection. 3 *under the patronage of the crime boss* power of appointment, right of appointment. 4 *treat his staff with patronage* patronizing, condescension, disdain, scorn, contempt, snobbery, snobbishness.

patronize *verb* 1 *patronize her subordinates* look down on, talk down to, condescend to, treat condescendingly, treat with condescension, treat like a child, treat as inferior, treat with disdain, treat scornfully/contemptuously, be snobbish to. 2 *patronize the new salon* be a customer of, be a client of, frequent, shop at, buy from, do business with, deal with, trade with. 3 *patronize the arts* be a patron of, sponsor, back, fund, finance, promote, help, aid, assist, support, encourage, champion, protect.

patronizing *adjective a patronizing attitude to younger people* condescending, supercilious, superior, haughty, lofty, lordly, disdainful, scornful, contemptuous, snobbish; *inf.* uppity, snooty.

patter[1] *verb* 1 *mice pattering across the attic floor* scurry, scuttle, trip. 2 *rain pattering on the window* pitter-patter, tap, drum, beat, pound, pelt, rat-a-tat, go pit-a-pat, pit-a-pat.

patter[2] *noun* 1 *the patter of mice on the floor above* pattering, scurrying, scuttling, tripping. 2 *the patter of rain on the window* pitter-patter, pat-tering, tap, tapping, drumming, beat, beating, pounding, pelting, rat-a-tat, pit-a-pat.

patter[3] *noun* 1 *the salesman's patter* spiel, glib talk, monologue, harangue; *inf.* sales pitch, line. 2 *can't understand the young people's patter* speech, language, jargon; *inf.* lingo. *See* PARLANCE.

pattern *noun* 1 *the pattern on the wallpaper* design, decoration, motif, marking, ornament, ornamentation, device, figure. 2 *study the rats' behavior pattern* system, order, arrangement, method, sequence. 3 *a knitting pattern* design, guide, blueprint, model, plan, template, stencil, instructions. 4 *a pattern of elegance* model, ideal, exemplar, paradigm, example, archetype, prototype, paragon, criterion, standard, gauge, norm, guide, yardstick, touchstone, benchmark. 5 *a book of textile patterns* sample, swatch, specimen.

pattern *verb pattern himself on his father* model, mold, style, form, shape.

patterned *adjective patterned carpets/china* decorated, ornamented, figured.

paucity *noun a paucity of evidence* scarcity, sparseness, sparsity, dearth, shortage, insufficiency, deficiency, lack, want, meagerness, paltriness.

Antonyms: ABUNDANCE; PLETHORA.

paunch *noun* 1 *developing quite a paunch* fat/protruding stomach/belly/abdomen, potbelly, pot; *inf.* beer belly, corporation. 2 *a belt around his paunch* stomach, belly, abdomen; *inf.* gut.

pauper *noun* poor person, penniless person, bankrupt person, bankrupt, insolvent person, beggar, mendicant, down-and-out, homeless person.

pause *noun a pause in the fighting* break, halt, cessation, stoppage, interruption, lull, respite, stay, discontinuation, gap, interlude, intermission, interval, rest, delay, hesitation; *inf.* letup, breather.

pause *verb pause for thought* stop, halt, cease, discontinue, break, take a break, desist, rest, hold back, delay, hesitate, waver; *inf.* let up, take a breather.

Antonyms: CONTINUE; PROCEED.

pave *verb pave the front path* concrete, asphalt, flag, tile, tar, macadamize. **pave the way** *pave the way for radical change* prepare, prepare the way, clear the way, make preparations, make provision, get ready, lay the foundations/groundwork, put things in order, set the scene.

pavement *noun* asphalt, concrete, blacktop, macadam; road, roadway, street; driveway.

paw *noun an animal's paw* foot, pad, forepaw, hind paw.

paw *verb* handle roughly, molest, maul.

pawn *verb pawn her necklace to pay the rent* deposit with a pawnbroker, put in pawn, give as security, pledge, mortgage; *inf.* hock, put in hock.

pawn *noun pawns in the leader's struggle for power* tool, cat's-paw, instrument, puppet, dupe; *inf.* stooge.

pay *verb* **1** *pay him for work done* give payment to, settle up with, remunerate, reimburse, recompense, reward, indemnify, requite. **2** *pay hundreds of dollars for his services* pay out, spend, expend, lay out, part with, disburse, hand over, remit, render; *inf.* dish out, shell out, fork out, cough up. **3** *pay his debts* pay off, pay in full, settle, discharge, meet, clear, square, honor, liquidate. **4** *pay the bill* settle, foot, defray, square, discharge. **5** *the business/work does not pay* make money, be profitable, make a profit, be remunerative, make a return. **6** *investments paying large sums of money* pay out, yield, return, produce, bring in; *inf.* rake in. **7** *it would pay you to listen to his advice* repay, be advantageous to, be of advantage to, be of benefit to, be beneficial to, be profitable to, be worthwhile to. **8** *pay compliments* give, bestow, extend, offer, proffer, render. **9** *pay him for what he did* pay back, punish, avenge oneself on, get revenge on. **pay back 1** *pay back the loan* repay, pay off, give back, return, reimburse. **2** *pay her back for her cruel behavior* pay, repay, punish, avenge oneself on, get revenge on, retaliate against, settle a score with, get even with. **pay for 1** *pay for their services/meal* foot the bill for, settle up for, defray the cost of; *inf.* shell out for, fork out for, cough up for. **2** *make him pay for his mistakes* be punished for, pay a penalty for, suffer for, atone for, make atonement for, pay the price for, get one's deserts for, take one's medicine for; *inf.* get one's comeuppance for. **pay off 1** *pay off his debts* pay, pay in full, settle, discharge, meet, clear, square, honor, liquidate. **2** *pay off some workers* dismiss, discharge, lay off, let go; *inf.* sack, fire. **3** *his hard work paid off* meet with success, be successful, be effective, work, get results, be profitable. **pay out** *pay out a lot of money on the mortgage* pay, spend, expend, lay out, part with, hand over, remit; *inf.* dish out, shell out, fork out, cough up. **pay up** *pay up or be sued* pay, make payment, settle up, pay in full, meet one's obligations.

pay *noun get one's pay at the end of the month* payment, salary, wages, earnings, fee, remuneration, recompense, reimbursement, reward, stipend, emoluments.

payable *adjective a bill that is payable now* due, to be paid, owed, owing, outstanding, unpaid.

payment *noun* **1** *receive payment for his services* pay, salary, wages, earnings, fee, remuneration, recompense. *See* PAY *noun.* **2** *in payment of the account* settlement, discharge, clearance, squaring, liquidation. **3** *make twelve monthly payments* installment, premium, amount, remittance.

peace *noun* **1** *the peace of the countryside* peace and quiet, peacefulness, tranquillity, restful-

ness, calm, calmness, quiet, quietness, stillness, still. **2** *a mind seeking peace* peacefulness, tranquillity, serenity, calm, calmness, composure, placidity, rest, repose, contentment. **3** *hope for peace between the countries* peacefulness, peaceableness, harmony, harmoniousness, accord, concord, amity, amicableness, goodwill, friendship, cordiality, nonaggression, nonviolence, cease-fire. **4** *the Peace of Versailles* treaty, truce, agreement, armistice, cessation of hostilities.

Antonyms: NOISE; AGITATION; CONFLICT; WAR.

peaceable *adjective* **1** *a peaceable person/temperament* unwarlike, peace-loving, nonaggressive, nonbelligerent, nonviolent, noncombative, easygoing, placid, gentle, mild, good-natured, even-tempered, amiable, amicable, pacific, pacifist, pacifistic, dovelike, dovish, irenic. **2** *a peaceable set of negotiations* peaceful, strife-free, harmonious, amicable, amiable, friendly, cordial.

Antonyms: AGGRESSIVE; BELLIGERENT; WARLIKE.

peaceful *adjective* **1** *in a peaceful setting* tranquil, restful, quiet, calm, still, undisturbed. **2** *a peaceful mind* at peace, tranquil, serene, calm, composed, placid, at rest, in repose, reposeful, undisturbed, untroubled, unworried, anxiety-free. **3** *peaceful conditions between the two countries* peaceable, at peace, on good terms, strife-free, harmonious, amicable, friendly, cordial, nonviolent, unwarlike.

Antonyms: NOISY; agitated; HOSTILE; WARRING.

peacemaker *noun call in a third party as a peacemaker* conciliator, mediator, arbitrator, pacifier, appeaser, peacemonger.

peak *noun* **1** *snow on the mountain peaks* top, summit, crest, pinnacle. **2** *climb several peaks* mountain, hill, height, alp. **3** *the peak of a cap* brim, visor, projection. **4** *at the peak of his career as a singer* height, high point, climax, culmination, zenith, acme, meridian, apogee, prime, heyday, *ne plus ultra.*

Antonyms: BOTTOM; NADIR; trough.

peak *verb* **1** *prices peaking just before Christmas* reach its/their (etc.) height, reach the highest point. **2** *the political party's popularity peaked too soon* reach its/their (etc.) height, reach the highest point, culminate, reach the high point, reach a climax, reach the zenith.

peaked *adjective* pale, wan, drained, drawn, pallid, pasty, white, whitish, anemic, ill-looking, sickly-looking.

peal *noun* **1** *hear the peal of the church bells* ring, ringing, chime, clang, resounding, reverberation, tintinnabulation. **2** *the peal of laughter* ring, ringing, roar, boom, resounding, reverberation. **3** *the peal of thunder* roar, boom, rumble, crash, clap, resounding, reverberation.

peal *verb* **1** *bells pealing* ring, ring out, chime, clang, resound, reverberate. **2** *thunder pealed around us* roar, boom, rumble, crash, resound, reverberate.

peasant *noun* **1** *peasants working the fields* small farmer, agricultural/farm worker/laborer, peon, rustic; serf. **2** *snobbishly labeling the locals as peasants* lout, boor, yokel, rube, oaf, bumpkin, provincial; *inf.* hick, hayseed, hillbilly.

peccadillo noun *treat his peccadilloes as major crimes* misdemeanor, minor offense, petty offense, indiscretion, lapse, misdeed, error, infraction; *inf.* slipup.

peck verb **1** *birds pecking the wood* bite, strike, hit, tap, rap, jab. **2** *peck her on the cheek* kiss, plant a kiss on, give someone a peck. **peck at 1** *hens pecking at the corn* pick at, pick up, eat. **2** *children pecking at their food* nibble, pick at, eat sparingly of.

peculiar adjective **1** *a peculiar smell* strange, odd, queer, funny, curious, unusual, abnormal. **2** *peculiar clothes/appearance* strange, odd, queer, funny, curious, unusual, abnormal, eccentric, unconventional, bizarre, weird, quaint, outlandish, out-of-the-way, grotesque, freakish, offbeat, droll, comical; *inf.* far-out, way-out. **3** *have a peculiar walk* characteristic, distinctive, distinct, individual, individualistic, distinguishing, special, unique, idiosyncratic, conspicuous, notable, remarkable. **4** *feel rather peculiar* unwell, poorly, ill, below par, strange, indisposed; *inf.* funny, under the weather. **peculiar to** *peculiar to that period of history* belonging to, characteristic of, typical of, representative of, indicative of, exclusive to.
Antonyms: NORMAL; ORDINARY.

peculiarity noun **1** *the peculiarity of the smell* peculiarness, strangeness, oddness, queerness, curiousness, abnormality. **2** *the peculiarity of her clothes/appearance* peculiarness, strangeness, oddness, queerness, eccentricity, unconventionality, bizarreness, weirdness, outlandishness, grotesqueness, freakishness, drollness. *See* PECULIAR 2. **3** *a geographical peculiarity of the region | a peculiarity of the breed* characteristic, feature, quality, property, trait, attribute, mark, stamp, hallmark. **4** *peculiarities of dress/behavior* abnormality, eccentricity, oddity, idiosyncrasy, quirk, foible.

pecuniary adjective *of no pecuniary advantage* financial, monetary, fiscal.

pedagogic adjective educational, teaching, academic, scholastic.

pedagogue noun **1** *learning from a pedagogue* teacher, tutor, lecturer, instructor, educator, educationalist. **2** *a pedagogue without inspiration* dogmatist, pedant.

pedant noun **1** *pedants insisting on the rules being interpreted literally* precisionist, perfectionist, formalist, dogmatist, literalist, quibbler, hairsplitter, casuist, sophist, pettifogger; *inf.* nitpicker. **2** *pedants displaying their knowledge* intellectual, academic, pedagogue, highbrow, bluestocking; *inf.* egghead.

pedantic adjective **1** *a pedantic interpretation of the rules* precise, precisionist, exact, scrupulous, overscrupulous, punctilious, meticulous, perfectionist, formalist, dogmatic, literalist, liter-

alistic, quibbling, hairsplitting, casuistic, casuistical, sophistic, sophistical, pettifogging; *inf.* nitpicking. **2** *a pedantic display of knowledge* intellectual, academic, scholastic, didactic, bookish, pedagogic, donnish, highbrow, pretentious, pompous; *inf.* egghead. **3** *a pedantic account of the incident* formal, stilted, stiff, stuffy, unimaginative, uninspired, rhetorical, bombastic, grandiloquent, high-flown, euphuistic; *inf.* highfalutin.

pedantry noun **1** *his pedantry in interpreting the rules* precision, precisionism, exactness, scrupulousness, punctiliousness, meticulousness, perfectionism, formalism, dogmatism, literalism, quibbling, hairsplitting, casuistry, sophistry, pettifogging; *inf.* nitpicking. **2** *an audience tired of the speaker's pedantry* intellectualism, scholasticism, didacticism, bookishness, pedagogism, donnishness, pretentiousness, pomposity, pompousness. **3** *the pedantry of his prose* formality, stiltedness, stiffness, stuffiness, unimaginativeness, lack of inspiration, rhetoric, bombast, grandiloquence, euphuism.

peddle verb **1** *peddle goods around town* hawk, sell, sell door-to-door, sell from door to door, tout, market, vend; *inf.* push. **2** *peddle his political views* present, offer, introduce, spread, promote, advocate, recommend.

pedestal noun *a bust of Shakespeare on a pedestal* base, support, stand, foundation, pillar, column, plinth. **put on a pedestal** *put his father on a pedestal* idealize, exalt, glorify, adulate, worship, deify.

pedestrian noun *areas for pedestrians only* person on foot, walker, stroller, hiker.
Antonym: DRIVER.

pedestrian adjective **1** *pedestrian traffic* on foot, walking. **2** *pedestrian precincts in the city* pedestrianized, for pedestrians, for pedestrians only. **3** *piece of pedestrian prose* plodding, unimaginative, uninspired, unexciting, dull, flat, prosaic, turgid, stodgy, mundane, humdrum, banal, run-of-the-mill, commonplace, ordinary, mediocre; *inf.* nothing to write home about.
Antonyms: IMAGINATIVE; INSPIRED; EXCITING.

pedigree noun **1** *proud of his aristocratic pedigree* ancestry, descent, lineage, line, extraction, heritage, parentage, birth, family, strain, stock, blood, stirps. **2** *draw up the son's/dog's pedigree* genealogy, family tree, ancestral record, line of descent.

pedigree adjective *a pedigree spaniel* pedigreed, pure-bred, thoroughbred, pure-blooded, full-blooded.

peek verb *peek into the package before Christmas* take a secret look, take a sly/stealthy look, peep, glance, cast a brief look, look hurriedly, look; *inf.* sneak a look, take a gander, have a looksee.

peek *noun take a peek into the package before Christmas* secret look, sly look, stealthy look, sneaky look, peep, glance, glimpse, brief/hurried look, look; *inf.* gander, look-see.

peel *verb* **1** *peel the skin from the fruit* pare, strip, remove, take off. **2** *peel the fruit* pare, skin, decorticate. **3** *skin peeling after getting sunburned* flake, scale off, come off in layers, desquamate. **keep one's eyes peeled** *keep one's eyes peeled for the lost kitten* keep a sharp lookout, be on the lookout, look out, watch closely, be alert, be on guard. **peel off** *peel off his wet clothes* strip off, cast off, remove, doff.

peel *noun the peel of the fruit* rind, skin, covering, zest, shell, husk, epicarp.

peep[1] *verb* **1** *peep through the keyhole* take a secret look, take a sly look, peek; *inf.* sneak a look. *See* PEEK *verb.* **2** *crocuses peeping through the snow* appear, show, come into view, become visible, emerge, spring up, pop up.

peep[2] *noun take a peep at the secret document* secret look, sly look, stealthy look, sneaky look, peek, glance. *See* PEEK *noun.*

peep[3] *verb fledglings peeping in the nest* cheep, chirp, chirrup, tweet, twitter, pipe, squeak.

peep[4] *noun* **1** *the peep of a baby bird* cheep, chirp, chirrup, tweet, twitter, piping, squeak. **2** *not a peep out of the children* sound, noise, cry, utterance, word. **3** *we expected a protest, but there was not a peep out of the opposition* complaint, grumble, moan, groan, word; *inf.* gripe, grouse.

peephole *noun look through the peephole in the door to see who is there* aperture, opening, spyhole, slit, crack, crevice, fissure.

peer *verb peer at the faded handwriting | peer through the mist* look closely, try to see, look through narrowed eyes, narrow one's eyes, screw up one's eyes, squint.

peer *noun* **1** *remained close to his peers from college* compeer, associate, colleague, friend, fellow, equal, match, like, coequal, confrère. **2** *the peers of the realm* noble, nobleman, aristocrat, lord, titled man, patrician, duke, marquess, marquis, earl, viscount, baron.

peerage *noun* nobility, aristocracy.

peerless *adjective a peerless performance* incomparable, beyond compare, matchless, unmatched, unrivaled, unsurpassed, unequaled, without equal, unparalleled, superlative, second to none, nonpareil.

peeve *verb his behavior really peeved her* irritate, annoy, anger, vex, provoke, upset, exasperate, irk, pique, nettle, get on someone's nerves, rub the wrong way; *inf.* aggravate, miff, rile, get under someone's skin, get in someone's hair.

peevish *adjective* irritable, fractious, fretful, cross, crabbed, crabby, cranky, petulant, complaining, querulous, sulky, moody, in a bad mood, grumpy, ill-tempered, ill-natured, ill-humored, surly, churlish, touchy, testy, snappish, snappy, crusty, splenetic.

peg *noun fasten the pieces of wood with a peg* pin, nail, dowel, spike, skewer, brad, screw, bolt, post. **take down a peg or two** *feel like taking the conceited young fool down a peg or two* humble, humiliate, mortify, bring down, bring low, put down, abase; *inf.* settle someone's hash.

peg *verb* **1** *peg a tent to the ground* pin, attach, fasten, fix, secure, make fast. **2** *peg prices at last year's level* fix, set, control, freeze, limit. **peg away at** *peg away at their studies* apply oneself to, work hard at, work away at, persevere at, persist in, keep at, hammer away at; *inf.* beaver away at, plug away at, stick at, stick with.

pejorative *adjective pejorative remarks* derogatory, disparaging, deprecatory, slighting.

Antonyms: COMPLIMENTARY; LAUDATORY; approbatory.

pellet *noun* **1** *a paper pellet | a pellet of bread* (compressed) ball, little ball. **2** *firing pellets from a gun* bullet, shot, lead shot, buckshot. **3** *medicinal pellets* pill, tablet, capsule, lozenge, bolus.

pell-mell *adverb* **1** *children rushing pell-mell from the school* helter-skelter, headlong, impetuously, recklessly, hurriedly, hastily. **2** *books lying pell-mell around the room* in disorder, in confusion, in a muddle, in disarray, untidily, in a mess, anyhow.

pellucid *adjective* **1** *pellucid water* transparent, translucent, clear, crystal-clear, glassy, limpid. **2** *pellucid prose* clear, lucid, coherent, articulate, intelligible, understandable, comprehensible, straightforward, simple.

pelt *verb* **1** *pelt the fortress with gunfire | pelt the strikebreakers with insults* bombard, shower, attack, assail, batter, pepper. **2** *rain came pelting upon us* pour (down), teem (down), rain cats and dogs. **3** *came pelting down the hill* race, run, sprint, dash, rush, hurry, speed, charge, career; *inf.* belt, tear, whiz.

pelt *noun a beaver's pelt* skin, hide, fleece, coat, fur.

pen[1] *noun bring pen and paper* fountain pen, ballpoint (pen), felt-tip (pen), quill (pen), marker.

pen[2] *verb pen a note* write, write down, jot down, scribble, pencil, compose, draft, commit to paper.

pen[3] *noun put animals in a pen* enclosure, fold, sheepfold, coop, chicken coop, pound, compound, corral.

pen[4] *verb* **pen in, pen up** *pen in the animals for the night* shut up, enclose, confine, fence in, coop up, corral.

penal *adjective* **1** *a penal institution* disciplinary, punitive, corrective, retributive. **2** *a penal offense* punishable, indictable, chargeable, impeachable.

penalize *verb* **1** *penalized for arriving late* punish, discipline, castigate, correct. **2** *people penalized for being poor* handicap, inflict a handicap on, disadvantage, put at a disadvantage.

Antonyms: REWARD; recompense.

penalty *noun* **1** *have to pay a penalty for his crime* punishment, punitive action, retribution, castigation, penance, fine, forfeit, sentence, mulct. **2** *one of the penalties of living in the city* handicap, disadvantage, drawback, snag, obstacle.
Antonyms: REWARD; ADVANTAGE.

penance *noun* **1** *a penance imposed by the priest* punishment, penalty. **2** *carry out a penance for one's sins* self-punishment, atonement, reparation, amends, mortification.

penchant *noun a penchant for bright colors | has a penchant for spicy food* liking, fondness, preference, taste, partiality, soft spot, inclination, bent, proclivity, predilection, love, passion, desire, fancy, whim, weakness.

pencil *noun* **1** *pencil and paper* lead/graphite pencil. **2** *a pencil of light* ray, beam, shaft, finger.

pencil *verb* **1** *pencil a note* write, write down, jot down, scribble, pen, compose, draft, commit to paper. **2** *pencil a likeness of the child* sketch, outline, draw, trace.

pendant *noun wear a pendant on a chain* locket, medallion, jewel, ornament, teardrop.

pendent *adjective a pendent light* hanging, suspended, dangling.

pending *preposition* **1** *receive bail pending trial* awaiting, waiting for, until. **2** *no action pending negotiations* during, throughout, in the course of, for the time/duration of.

pending *adjective* **1** *the lawsuit then pending* undecided, unsettled, unresolved, uncertain, awaiting action, undetermined, hanging fire, up in the air; *inf.* on the back burner. **2** *a decision is pending* imminent, impending, on the way, coming, approaching, forthcoming, near, nearing, close, close at hand, in the offing.

penetrate *verb* **1** *penetrate the skin* pierce, bore, perforate, stab, prick, gore, spike. **2** *penetrate the dense forest* go into, get in, enter, make one's way into/through, infiltrate. **3** *terror penetrated her whole being* permeate, pervade, fill, imbue, suffuse, seep through, saturate. **4** *our explanation did not penetrate* be understood, be comprehended, be taken in, be grasped, register. **5** *the explanation did not seem to penetrate his mind* get through to, be understood/comprehended by, register on, make an impression on, have an impact on. **6** *unable to penetrate the mystery* understand, comprehend, apprehend, fathom, get to the bottom of, make out, solve, resolve, work out, figure out, unravel, decipher; *inf.* crack.

penetrating *adjective* **1** *a penetrating wind* sharp, keen, biting, stinging, harsh. **2** *a penetrating voice* shrill, loud, strong, carrying, piercing, ear-piercing, earsplitting, intrusive. **3** *a penetrating mind* keen, sharp, sharp-witted, discerning, perceptive, percipient, intelligent, clever, smart, incisive, astute, shrewd, acute, discriminating. **4** *ask penetrating questions* penetrative, searching, sharp, incisive, inquisitive, analytic, in-depth.

Antonyms: MILD; SOFT; DULL.

penetration *noun* **1** *the penetration of the skin* piercing, perforation, pricking. *See* PENETRATE 1. **2** *the penetration of the forest* entry, infiltration. *See* PENETRATE 2. **3** *the penetration of her being with terror* permeation, pervasion, imbuing, suffusion. *See* PENETRATE 3. **4** *the penetration of the mystery is taking a lot of time* understanding, comprehension, apprehension, fathoming, resolution; *inf.* cracking. *See* PENETRATE 6. **5** *impressed by the penetration of their minds* keenness, sharpness, sharp-wittedness, discernment, perception, perceptiveness, insight, intelligence, cleverness, smartness, incisiveness, astuteness, shrewdness, acuteness, acuity, discrimination. **6** *admire the penetration of the questions* searchingness, sharpness, incisiveness. *See* PENETRATING 4.

penitence *noun show penitence for his sins* repentance, contrition, compunction, regret, remorse, remorsefulness, ruefulness, self-reproach, self-accusation, shame, sorrow.

penitent *adjective feel penitent about his sin | penitent children apologizing* repentant, contrite, regretful, remorseful, sorry, apologetic, conscience-stricken, rueful, ashamed, abject, sorrowful.

Antonyms: IMPENITENT; UNREPENTANT.

pen name *noun* pseudonym, nom de plume, nom de guerre, assumed name, allonym, alias.

pennant *noun pennants flying in the breeze* banner, banderole, streamer, flag, ensign, colors, bunting.

penniless *adjective* without a penny, without a penny to one's name, impecunious, penurious, impoverished, indigent, poor, as poor as a church mouse, poverty-stricken, destitute, bankrupt, in reduced circumstances, in straitened circumstances, hard up; *inf.* broke, stonebroke, flat broke, cleaned out, strapped for cash, strapped.

Antonyms: WEALTHY; AFFLUENT.

penny *noun* cent, one cent; *inf.* red cent. **a bad penny** undesirable, *persona non grata*, rascal, scoundrel, rogue, good-for-nothing; *inf.* bad egg, bad news. **a pretty penny** *will cost a pretty penny* a considerable sum (of money); *inf.* a lot (of money), lots/heaps of money, a mint, a bundle.

penny-pinching *adjective penny-pinching people refusing to give to charity* mean, miserly, parsimonious, niggardly, tight-fisted, close-fisted, penurious, scrimping, skimping, close, grasping, money-grubbing, Scrooge-like, ungenerous; *inf.* stingy, tight.

Antonyms: GENEROUS; LIBERAL; MUNIFICENT.

pension *noun* retirement pension, disability pension; superannuation, allowance, benefit, support, welfare.

pensioner *noun* retired person, retiree, senior citizen, senior.

pensive adjective *in a pensive mood* thoughtful, thinking, reflective, contemplative, musing, meditative, pondering, cogitative, ruminative, absorbed, preoccupied, serious, solemn, dreamy, dreaming, wistful, melancholy, sad.

pent-up adjective *pent-up feelings* bottled-up, repressed, suppressed, restrained, constrained, held in, kept in check, curbed, bridled.

penurious adjective **1** *unemployment had left them penurious* penniless, without a penny, impecunious, impoverished, indigent, poor, poor as a church mouse, poverty-stricken, destitute, bankrupt, in reduced circumstances, in straitened circumstances, hard up; *inf.* broke, stonebroke, flat broke, cleaned out, strapped for cash, strapped. **2** *a penurious old skinflint* mean, miserly, parsimonious, niggardly, tightfisted, scrimping, skimping, close, Scroogelike, ungenerous; *inf.* stingy, tight. *See* PENNY-PINCHING.

Antonyms: WEALTHY; GENEROUS.

penury noun *unemployment reduced them to penury* extreme poverty, pennilessness, impecuniousness, impoverishment, indigence, need, want, neediness, destitution, privation, pauperism, beggarliness, beggary, bankruptcy, insolvency, reduced circumstances, straitened circumstances.

Antonyms: WEALTH; AFFLUENCE.

people noun **1** *plural noun too many people in the hall/country* persons, individuals, human beings, humans, mortals, living souls; men, women, and children. **2** *a warlike people* race, tribe, clan, nation, country, population, populace. **3** *plural noun issue to be decided by the people* common people, ordinary people, ordinary citizens, general public, public, populace, electorate, masses, rank and file, commonalty, mob, multitude, hoi polloi, rabble; *inf.* plebs. **4** *plural noun her people live far away* family, relatives, relations, folk, kinsfolk, kin, kith and kin; *inf.* folks.

pep noun *a performance full of pep* spirit, liveliness, animation, life, sparkle, effervescence, verve, ebullience, vivacity, fire, dash, zest, exuberance, élan, vigor, vim, brio; *inf.* zip.

pepper noun **1** *season the soup with pepper* black pepper, white pepper, ground pepper, peppercorns, cayenne pepper, cayenne. **2** *stuffed peppers* capsicum, bell pepper, red pepper, green pepper, yellow pepper, sweet pepper, hot pepper, jalapeño (pepper), habañero, Scotch bonnet.

pepper verb **1** *pepper the soup/sauce* add pepper to, season, flavor, spice, spice up. **2** *pepper his speech with quotations* sprinkle, intersperse, dot, bespatter, bestrew. **3** *peppering each other with snowballs | pepper the enemy ship with mortar fire* pelt, bombard, shower, attack, assail, batter.

peppery adjective **1** *peppery food* peppered, hot, spicy, spiced, highly seasoned, pungent, fiery. **2** *a peppery old man* hot-tempered, irascible, fiery, quick-tempered, irritable, touchy, testy, crabbed, crabby, crusty, splenetic. **3** *give a peppery speech* caustic, acerbic, astringent, trenchant, cutting, sarcastic, stinging, biting, sharp.

Antonyms: MILD; BLAND; EASYGOING.

perceive verb **1** *perceive someone walking down the hill* see, catch sight of, spot, observe, glimpse, notice, make out, discern, behold, espy, detect, witness, remark. **2** *perceive the difference between right and wrong* discern, appreciate, recognize, be cognizant of, be aware of, be conscious of, know, grasp, understand, comprehend, apprehend, figure out, see, sense.

perceptible adjective *a perceptible change in her appearance | no perceptible improvement* perceivable, discernible, noticeable, detectable, distinguishable, appreciable, visible, observable, distinct, clear, plain, evident, apparent, obvious, manifest, conspicuous, patent, palpable, tangible.

Antonyms: IMPERCEPTIBLE; INCONSPICUOUS.

perception noun **1** *his perception of the magnitude of the problem* discernment, appreciation, recognition, cognizance, awareness, consciousness, knowledge, grasp, understanding, comprehension, apprehension, notion, conception, idea, sense. **2** *show great perception in his performance | his analysis shows great perception* perspicacity, discernment, perceptiveness, understanding, discrimination, insight, intuition, feeling, sensitivity.

perceptive adjective **1** *a perceptive child noticed the fire* sharp-eyed, sharp-sighted, keen-sighted, observant, alert, vigilant. **2** *one of the more perceptive theater critics* discerning, perspicacious, percipient, shrewd, understanding, discriminating, intuitive, responsive, sensitive. **3** *a perceptive analysis of the problem* discerning, perspicacious, percipient, penetrating, astute, shrewd.

Antonyms: HEEDLESS; OBTUSE; unobservant; DULL.

perch noun *birds sitting on a perch* pole, rod, branch, roost, rest.

perch verb *birds perching on a branch* sit, rest, roost, settle, alight, land.

perchance adverb **1** *if perchance he arrives on time* by chance, by any chance, fortuitously. **2** *perchance we shall find the right book* perhaps, maybe, possibly, for all one knows; *lit.* peradventure.

percipient adjective **1** *a percipient commentator* perceptive, discerning, perspicacious, astute, shrewd, understanding, discriminating, intuitive, responsive, sensitive. **2** *a percipient summing-up of the situation* perceptive, discerning, perspicacious, penetrating, astute, shrewd.

percolate verb **1** *liquid percolating through the strainer* filter, filtrate, drain, drip, ooze, seep, leach. **2** *percolate the coffee/liquid* strain, filter, filtrate, sieve, sift. **3** *coffee percolating in the pot* brew, bubble; *inf.* perk. **4** *information finally percolating through the department* go through, pass through, filter through, permeate, pervade.

percussion *noun instruments based on percussion* impact, collision, bang, clash, crash, striking, beating.

perdition *noun cursed to perdition* damnation, hellfire, hell, spiritual destruction.

peremptory *adjective* **1** *receive a peremptory request from the boss* imperious, high-handed, urgent, pressing, imperative, high-priority. **2** *behave in a peremptory manner* imperious, high-handed, overbearing, dogmatic, autocratic, dictatorial, domineering, arbitrary, tyrannical, despotic, arrogant, overweening, supercilious, lordly. **3** *a peremptory judgment* incontrovertible, irreversible, binding, absolute, final, conclusive, decisive, definitive, categorical, irrefutable.

perennial *adjective* **1** *a subject of perennial interest | perennial favorite* perpetual, everlasting, eternal, unending, never-ending, endless, undying, ceaseless, abiding, enduring, lasting, persisting, permanent, constant, unfailing, unchanging. **2** *tired of their perennial complaining* constant, continual, continuous, continuing, uninterrupted, ceaseless, persistent, recurrent, chronic, never-ending; *inf.* eternal.

perfect *adjective* **1** *a perfect set of china* complete, full, whole, entire. **2** *this piece of work is now perfect* perfected, completed, finished. **3** *a perfect fool/disaster* absolute, complete, out-and-out, thorough, thoroughgoing, downright, utter, sheer, consummate, unmitigated, unqualified. **4** *a perfect performance | a perfect piece of work* flawless, faultless, unmarred, ideal, impeccable, consummate, immaculate, exemplary, superb, superlative, supreme, excellent, wonderful. **5** *a perfect mother/student* ideal, model, without fault, faultless, flawless, consummate, exemplary, excellent, wonderful. **6** *a perfect evening* superb, exquisite, superlative, excellent, wonderful, marvelous; *inf.* out of this world, terrific, fantastic, fabulous. **7** *a perfect copy* exact, precise, accurate, faithful, correct, right, close, true, strict; *inf.* right-on. **8** *the perfect present* ideal, just right, right, appropriate, fitting, fit, suitable, apt.
Antonyms: IMPERFECT; FAULTY; DEFECTIVE.

perfect *verb perfect the technique* make perfect, render faultless/flawless, improve, better, polish, refine, elaborate, complete, consummate, put the finishing touches to.

perfection *noun* **1** *working on the perfection of their technique* perfecting, improvement, betterment, polishing, refinement, completion, consummation. **2** *try to achieve perfection in his work* perfectness, flawlessness, faultlessness, consummation, impeccability, immaculateness, exemplariness, superbness. *See* PERFECT *adjective* 4. **3** *as a singer she was perfection* a

paragon, the best, one in a million; *inf.* the tops, aces. **4** *the meal was perfection* ideal, the acme, the crown, the peak of perfection.

perfectionist *noun writers who are perfectionists* stickler for perfection, precisionist, precisian, purist, formalist.

perfectly *adverb* **1** *perfectly happy/miserable* absolutely, utterly, completely, altogether, entirely, wholly, totally, thoroughly, fully. **2** *the cake turned out perfectly | he played perfectly* to perfection, flawlessly, faultlessly, without blemish, ideally, impeccably, immaculately, superbly, exquisitely, superlatively, wonderfully.

perfidious *adjective betrayed by perfidious allies* treacherous, traitorous, treasonous, false, untrue, disloyal, faithless, unfaithful, deceitful, double-dealing, duplicitous, dishonest, two-faced.

perfidy *noun captured because of the perfidy of his allies* perfidiousness, treachery, traitorousness, falseness, infidelity, disloyalty, faithlessness, unfaithfulness, deceitfulness, deceit, double-dealing, duplicity, dishonesty, two-facedness.

perforate *verb* **1** *perforate the skin* pierce, puncture, prick, stab, gore, bore, penetrate, spike. **2** *perforate paper* put holes in, make holes in, hole, punch holes in, punch, honeycomb.

perform *verb* **1** *perform acts of charity | could perform feats of skill* do, carry out, execute, discharge, conduct, effect, bring about, bring off, accomplish, achieve, fulfill, complete. **2** *perform in Hamlet* act, play, appear. **3** *perform a new symphony* play, execute. **4** *a car performing well* function, work, operate, run, go.
Antonyms: NEGLECT; OMIT.

performance *noun* **1** *faithful in the performance of his duty* carrying out, execution, discharge, conducting, effecting, accomplishment, achievement, fulfillment. **2** *watch a musical performance* show, production, entertainment, act, presentation; *inf.* gig. **3** *his performance of Hamlet* acting, playing, representation, staging.

performer *noun* **1** *applaud the performers* actor/actress, player, entertainer, artist, artiste, thespian, trouper, musician, singer, dancer. **2** *performers of acts of charity | a performer of strange feats* doer, executor, worker, operator, architect, author.

perfume *noun* **1** *the perfume of roses | love the perfume of new-mown hay* scent, fragrance, aroma, smell, bouquet, redolence. **2** *buy some French perfume* scent, fragrance, balm, essence, eau de toilette, toilet water, eau de cologne, cologne.

perfunctory *adjective take a perfunctory look at the contract* cursory, superficial, desultory, mechanical, automatic, routine, sketchy, brief, hasty, hurried, rapid, fleeting, quick, fast, offhand, casual, indifferent, careless, inattentive, negligent.

perhaps adverb *perhaps we will meet him on the way* it may be that, maybe, possibly, it is possible that, conceivably, feasibly, for all one knows; *lit.* peradventure.

peril noun *firefighters in great peril | the peril of being lost at sea* danger, jeopardy, risk, hazard, menace, threat.
Antonyms: SAFETY; SECURITY.

perilous adjective *a perilous journey through the mountains* dangerous, fraught with danger, menacing, risky, precarious, hazardous, chancy, threatening, unsafe.
Antonyms: SAFE; SECURE.

perimeter noun **1** *the perimeter of a circle* circumference. **2** *guards patrolling the perimeter of the estate* boundary, border, frontier, limits, outer limits, confines, edge, margin, fringe, periphery.

period noun **1** *during periods of peace | over a period of several years* time, space, spell, interval, term, stretch, span. **2** *absent for a period* time, while, spell. **3** *the postwar period | the period of the French Revolution* time, days, age, era, epoch, eon. **4** *he is not going, period* finis, end, finish, conclusion, stop, halt, and that's that. **5** *irregular periods* menstruation, menstrual flow, monthly flow, menses.

periodic adjective *periodic inspections | has periodic attacks of dizziness* periodical, at fixed intervals, recurrent, recurring, repeated, cyclical, cyclic, regular, intermittent, occasional, infrequent, sporadic, every once in a while, every so often.

periodical noun *subscribe to periodicals* journal, publication, magazine, newspaper, newsletter, review, organ, almanac, yearbook, annual, quarterly, monthly, weekly, daily; *inf.* paper, rag, glossy.

peripatetic adjective **1** *peripatetic tribes* itinerant, traveling, wandering, roving, roaming, nomadic, migrant, migratory. **2** *peripatetic teachers/libraries* itinerant, traveling, mobile.

peripheral adjective **1** *peripheral zones of the city* outer, on the edge/outskirts, surrounding, neighboring. **2** *waste time discussing peripheral matters* minor, lesser, secondary, subsidiary, ancillary, unimportant, superficial, irrelevant, beside the point.
Antonyms: CENTRAL; MAJOR; IMPORTANT; VITAL.

periphery noun **1** *on the periphery of the town* outskirts, boundary, border, limits, outer limits, edge, margin, fringe, perimeter. **2** *on the periphery of the group* edge, fringe, margin.

periphrastic adjective *a periphrastic style of prose* circumlocutory, redundant, tautological, pleonastic, roundabout, indirect, rambling, wandering, ambagious.

perish verb **1** *soldiers perishing in battle* die, lose one's life, be killed, lay down one's life, meet one's death, breathe one's last, draw one's last breath; *inf.* bite the dust, kick the bucket. **2** *the* *old theories/values having perished* come to an end, die away, disappear, vanish, disintegrate, go under, be destroyed. **3** *food perishing in the heat* go bad, go sour, rot, decay, decompose.
Antonyms: LIVE; SURVIVE.

perjure verb **perjure oneself** *held in contempt of court for perjuring herself* commit perjury, lie under oath, give false evidence/testimony, bear false witness.

perjury noun **1** *found guilty of perjury | committed perjury* lying under oath, violation of oath, giving false evidence/testimony, bearing false witness, false swearing. **2** *repeated her perjury* false oath, false statement, willful/deliberate falsehood.

perk verb **perk up 1** *perking up when his friends arrived* cheer up, become cheerful, brighten up, feel happy, be gladdened, take heart; *inf.* buck up, pep up. **2** *patients perking up after treatment* brighten up, recover, recuperate, rally, revive. **3** *the vacation perked them up* cheer up, brighten up, raise someone's spirits, give someone heart, give someone a boost/lift; *inf.* pep up.

perk noun perquisite, fringe benefit. *See* PERQUISITE.

permanence noun **1** *the permanence of their separation/disability* everlastingness, perpetuity, perpetualness, permanency, eternalness, eternality, endurance. *See* PERMANENT 1. **2** *the permanence of the job/relationship* stability, lastingness, long-lastingness, fixedness, soundness, firmness.

permanent adjective **1** *the couple's separation is permanent | left with a permanent disability* everlasting, perpetual, eternal, enduring, perennial, lasting, abiding, constant, persistent, unending, endless, never-ending, immutable, unchangeable, inalterable, invariable. **2** *a permanent job/relationship* lasting, long-lasting, stable, fixed, established, sound, firm.
Antonyms: TEMPORARY; FLEETING; EPHEMERAL.

permanently adverb *permanently separated/disabled* everlastingly, perpetually, eternally, perennially, lastingly, constantly, persistently, unendingly, endlessly, immutably, inalterably, invariably, for all time, for good, for good and all, for ever and ever, for ever, evermore, for evermore, till the end of time, time without end; *inf.* till the cows come home, till hell freezes over.

permeate verb **1** *cooking smells permeating the whole house* spread through, be disseminated through, pass through, pervade, fill, diffuse through, be diffused through, extend throughout, imbue, penetrate, infiltrate, percolate through. **2** *water permeating the soil* spread through, pass through, penetrate, soak through, seep through, leak through, infiltrate, percolate through, leach through, saturate.

permissible adjective *driving with more than the permissible amount of alcohol* permitted, allowable, admissible, acceptable, tolerated, authorized, sanctioned, legal, lawful, legitimate, licit, within bounds; *inf.* legit.

permission *noun* *enter without permission | act with the permission of her mother* authorization, sanction, leave, license, dispensation, empowerment, allowance, consent, assent, acquiescence, go-ahead, thumbs up, agreement, approval, approbation, tolerance, sufferance; *inf.* green light.

permissive *adjective* *a permissive parent/upbringing* liberal, tolerant, broad-minded, open-minded, easygoing, forbearing, latitudinarian, indulgent, lenient, unrestricted, overindulgent, lax, unprescriptive.
Antonyms: INTOLERANT; STRICT.

permit *verb* **1** *parents not permitting the children to go | not permit talking in class* give permission, allow, let, authorize, give leave, sanction, grant, license, empower, enable, consent to, assent to, acquiesce in, give the go-ahead to, give the thumbs up to, agree to, approve of, tolerate, countenance, suffer, brook; *inf.* give the green light to. **2** *if time permits* allow, make possible, allow the possibility of, give an opportunity.
Antonyms: BAN; FORBID; REFUSE.

permit *noun* *a permit to sell food | a permit to enter the country* license, authorization, warrant, sanction, pass, passport, visa.

permutation *noun* *the system allows for permutation* variation, alteration, change, shift, transformation, transposition, transmutation.

pernicious *adjective* *a pernicious influence on society* destructive, ruinous, injurious, damaging, harmful, hurtful, detrimental, deleterious, deadly, lethal, fatal, wicked, evil, bad, malign, malevolent, malignant, noxious, poisonous, venomous.
Antonyms: BENEFICIAL; FAVORABLE.

peroration *noun* **1** *give a peroration at the end of a speech* closing remarks, conclusion, summation, summing-up, recapitulation; *inf.* recapping. **2** *students wearying of the lecturer's peroration* lengthy talk/lecture/speech/address, rhetorical speech, bombastic oration, harangue, declamation, diatribe.

perpendicular *adjective* **1** *the perpendicular supports* upright, vertical, on end, standing, straight. **2** *a line perpendicular to another* at right angles, at 90 degrees. **3** *perpendicular cliffs* steep, sheer, precipitous, abrupt.
Antonyms: HORIZONTAL; LEVEL.

perpetrate *verb* *perpetrate a crime | has perpetrated an indiscretion* commit, carry out, perform, execute, do, effect, effectuate, bring about, be guilty of, be to blame for, be responsible for; *inf.* pull off.

perpetual *adjective* **1** *a state of perpetual bliss | the perpetual snow of the Arctic* everlasting, eternal, never-ending, unending, endless, undying, perennial, permanent, perdurable, lasting, abiding, persisting, enduring, constant, unfailing, unchanging, unvarying, invariable. **2**

work with perpetual noise incessant, unceasing, ceaseless, unending, endless, never-stopping, nonstop, continuous, uninterrupted, unbroken, unremitting. **3** *tired of their perpetual complaints* interminable, persistent, frequent, continual, recurrent, repeated; *inf.* eternal.
Antonyms: TRANSITORY; TEMPORARY; INTERMITTENT.

perpetuate *verb* **1** *perpetuate the myth that he was a hero* keep alive, keep going, keep up, preserve, conserve, sustain, maintain, continue. **2** *perpetuate his memory with a statue* memorialize, commemorate, immortalize, eternalize.

perpetuity *noun* *in perpetuity* *membership granted in perpetuity to the founder's family* perpetually, permanently, perennially, forever, for ever, for ever and ever, for all time, until the end of time, for good, eternally, for eternity, everlastingly.

perplex *verb* **1** *her behavior perplexed him* puzzle, baffle, mystify, stump, keep someone guessing, bewilder, confound, confuse, nonplus, disconcert, dismay, dumbfound; *inf.* bamboozle. **2** *issues that perplex the situation* complicate, confuse, make involved, muddle, mix up, jumble, entangle, tangle, snarl up; *inf.* foul up.

perplexed *adjective* *explain the situation to her perplexed family | give a perplexed look* puzzled, baffled, mystified, bewildered, confused, nonplussed, disconcerted, dumbfounded; *inf.* bamboozled.

perplexing *adjective* **1** *her perplexing behavior* puzzling, baffling, mystifying, mysterious, bewildering, confusing, disconcerting, unaccountable, strange, weird. **2** *a perplexing problem* complicated, involved, intricate, complex, difficult, thorny, knotty, taxing, trying, vexing.

perplexity *noun* **1** *filled with perplexity at her behavior* puzzlement, bafflement, incomprehension, mystification, bewilderment, confusion, disconcertion, disconcertment, dismay; *inf.* bamboozlement. **2** *a problem of much perplexity* complication, involvement, intricacy, complexity, difficulty, entanglement. *See* PERPLEXING 2. **3** *the perplexities of the murder case* complication, intricacy, complexity, difficulty, mystery, puzzle, enigma, paradox.

perquisite *noun* *a perquisite of the job* fringe benefit, benefit, advantage, bonus, dividend, extra, plus; *inf.* perk, freebie.

persecute *verb* **1** *persecute people for their beliefs* oppress, tyrannize, abuse, mistreat, maltreat, ill-treat, molest, afflict, torment, torture, victimize, martyr. **2** *celebrities persecuted by the press* harass, pester, hound, badger, vex, bother, worry, annoy; *inf.* hassle.

perseverance *noun* *perseverance brought success* persistence, tenacity, pertinacity, determination, resolve, resolution, resoluteness, purposefulness, obstinacy, insistence, intransigence, patience, application, diligence, assiduity.

persevere verb **1** *persevere in his attempts to win* persist, go on, keep on, keep at, keep going, continue, carry on, struggle, work, hammer away, be tenacious, be persistent, be pertinacious, be resolute, be purposeful, be obstinate, be insistent, be intransigent, be patient, be diligent; *inf.* plug away. **2** *when you fail you must persevere* persist, go on, keep on, keep going, continue, carry on, be tenacious, be persistent, be pertinacious, be determined, be resolute, stand one's ground, stand fast, not give up; *inf.* stick to one's guns, stick to/at it.
Antonyms: give up (*see* GIVE); STOP; QUIT.

persist verb **1** *persist in his efforts to win* persevere, go on, keep on, keep going, continue, carry on; *inf.* plug away. *See* PERSEVERE 1. **2** *you must persist, not give up* persevere, keep going, carry on, be resolute, stand one's ground. *See* PERSEVERE 2. **3** *the cold weather persisted* carry on, keep on, keep up, continue, last, remain, linger, hold.
Antonyms: give up (*see* GIVE); STOP; DESIST.

persistence noun *with persistence he got a job* tenacity, determination, purposefulness, insistence, intransigence, patience, application. *See* PERSEVERANCE.

persistent adjective **1** *persistent people refusing to give up* persevering, tenacious, pertinacious, determined, resolute, purposeful, obstinate, stubborn, insistent, intransigent, obdurate, intractable, patient, diligent. **2** *persistent rain* constant, continual, continuous, continuing, interminable, incessant, unceasing, endless, unremitting, unrelenting, relentless. **3** *a persistent cough* chronic, frequent, repetitive, repetitious.
Antonyms: IRRESOLUTE; INTERMITTENT; OCCASIONAL.

persnickety adjective difficult to please, difficult, fussy, punctilious, finicky, fastidious, overparticular, particular; *inf.* nitpicking, choosy, picky.
Antonyms: EASYGOING; LAID-BACK.

person noun *not a person was left alive* individual, human being, human, creature, living soul, soul, mortal; *inf.* character.

persona noun *seen to take on the persona of his dead brother* character, personality, role, part, public face.

personable adjective *a personable young man* pleasant, agreeable, amiable, affable, likable, charming, nice, attractive, presentable, good-looking.

personage noun *events attended by political personages* person, public figure, dignitary, notable, person of note, celebrity, personality, VIP, famous name, household name, luminary, worthy; *inf.* big shot, celeb.

personal adjective **1** *his reasons for leaving are personal* individual, private, confidential, secret, one's own business. **2** *a personal style of prose* |

a personal interpretation of the music personalized, individual, idiosyncratic, characteristic, unique, peculiar. **3** *a personal letter to her boss* private, confidential, intimate. **4** *receive the personal attention of the manager* in person, individual, special. **5** *make personal remarks* insulting, slighting, derogatory, disparaging, pejorative, offensive.
Antonyms: PUBLIC; GENERAL.

personality noun **1** *of an unassuming personality* nature, disposition, character, temperament, temper, makeup, traits, psyche. **2** *an unassuming man with little personality* strength of personality, force of personality, personal identity, character, charisma, magnetism, powers of attraction, charm. **3** *several personalities attending the premiere* public figure, celebrity, VIP, famous name, household name, dignitary, notable, person of note, personage, luminary, worthy; *inf.* big shot, celeb.

personalize verb **1** *he tends to personalize issues* regard as personal, take personally, regard subjectively, be subjective about, interpret in terms of oneself. **2** *personalize his luggage* | *personalized license plate* give a personal touch to, have one's name/initials engraved on, initial, monogram, customize.

personally adverb **1** *deal with the matter personally* in person, oneself. **2** *personally speaking, I am opposed to the idea* for my (etc.) part, for my (etc.) own part, for myself (etc.), from my (etc.) own point of view, as far as I (etc.) am concerned. **take (something) personally** take as an insult, regard as a slight, take offense at, be offended by.

personification noun *he is the personification of politeness* embodiment, incarnation, epitome, quintessence, essence, symbol, representation, image, portrayal, likeness, semblance.

personify verb *personify all that was good about the country* embody, be the incarnation of, epitomize, typify, exemplify, symbolize, represent, mirror.

personnel noun *managers in charge of personnel* staff, employees, workers, workforce, labor force, manpower, human resources.

perspective noun **1** *young people have a different perspective of such matters* outlook, view, viewpoint, point of view, standpoint, vantage point, stand, stance, angle, slant, attitude, frame of mind. **2** *get a perspective of the whole valley from the tower* view, vista, bird's-eye view, prospect, scene, outlook, panorama, aspect, sweep.

perspicacious adjective *perspicacious of him to recognize her distress* discerning, perceptive, penetrating, percipient, sharp-witted, sharp, quick-witted, keen-witted, alert, clear-sighted, shrewd, acute, clever, intelligent, smart, judicious, wise, sagacious, sensitive, intuitive, understanding.
Antonyms: INATTENTIVE; DULL; STUPID.

perspicacity noun *admire his perspicacity in recognizing her distress* discernment, perception, perceptiveness, percipience, sharpness, sharp-wittedness, quick-wittedness, shrewdness, keen-wittedness, alertness, clear-sightedness, acuteness, acuity, cleverness, intelligence, smartness, judiciousness, sagacity, wisdom, sensitivity, intuition, intuitiveness, insight, understanding.

perspiration noun sweat, moisture.

perspire verb *perspire in the heat* sweat, be dripping with sweat, swelter.

persuade verb *persuade her to go | cannot be persuaded* prevail upon, win over, talk into (doing something), bring around, induce, convince, influence, sway, prompt, coerce, inveigle, cajole, wheedle; *inf.* sweet-talk, soft-soap.

Antonyms: DISSUADE; DISCOURAGE; DETER.

persuasion noun **1** *their successful persuasion of the children to go* persuading, prevailing, winning over, inducement, convincing, coercion, inveiglement, cajolery, wheedling; *inf.* sweet-talking, soft-soaping. **2** *use their powers of persuasion* persuasiveness, inducement, influence, coercion, inveiglement, cajolery, wheedling, suasion. **3** *it is his persuasion that the decision was a mistake* belief, opinion, view, point of view, conviction. **4** *Christians of different persuasions* denomination, belief, creed, credo, faith, school of thought, philosophy, sect, affiliation, camp, side, faction.

persuasive adjective *persuasive arguments* effective, effectual, convincing, cogent, plausible, compelling, forceful, eloquent, weighty, influential, telling.

Antonyms: INEFFECTIVE; WEAK.

pert adjective **1** *a pert young girl* impudent, impertinent, saucy, forward, presumptuous, audacious, bold, brash, brazen, bumptious. **2** *a pert little hat* jaunty, stylish, chic, trim, smart, spruce; *inf.* natty.

pertain verb **1** *evidence that does not pertain to the case* be connected with, relate to, be relevant to, have relevance to, concern, apply to, be pertinent to, have reference to, have a bearing upon. **2** *the house and the land pertaining to it* belong to, be a part of, be an adjunct of, go along with, be included in. **3** *the feeling of rebellion pertaining to youth* be appropriate to, be suited to, befit, fit in with, appertain to.

pertinacious adjective **1** *pertinacious people refusing to give up* persistent, persevering, tenacious, resolute, determined, purposeful, insistent, stubborn, obstinate, obdurate, strong-willed, headstrong, inflexible, intransigent, willful, mulish, pigheaded, bullheaded, intractable, refractory, perverse. **2** *make pertinacious attempts to succeed* persistent, persevering, resolute, determined, dogged, purposeful, insistent.

Antonyms: IRRESOLUTE; TENTATIVE.

pertinent adjective *make a few pertinent comments* relevant, appropriate, suitable, fitting, fit, apt, apposite, to the point, applicable, material, germane, to the purpose, apropos, ad rem.

Antonyms: IRRELEVANT; INAPPROPRIATE.

perturb verb **1** *news of the war perturbed them* disturb, make anxious, worry, alarm, trouble, upset, disquiet, discompose, disconcert, vex, bother, agitate, unsettle, fluster, ruffle, harass. **2** *perturb the smooth running of the office* throw into confusion, confuse, throw into disorder, disarrange, throw into disarray, muddle.

perturbed adjective *feel perturbed at the news | calm the perturbed people* disturbed, anxious, worried, alarmed, troubled, upset, disquieted, discomposed, disconcerted, vexed, agitated, unsettled, flustered, ruffled, harassed.

Antonyms: UNPERTURBED; CALM; TRANQUIL.

peruse verb *peruse the document* read carefully, read thoroughly, scrutinize, study, pore over, inspect, examine; scan.

pervade verb *cooking smells pervaded the entire house | terror pervaded his whole being* spread through, be disseminated through, permeate, fill, pass through, extend throughout, suffuse, diffuse through, be diffused through, imbue, infuse, penetrate, infiltrate, percolate.

pervasive adjective *pervasive cooking smells | pervasive feelings of terror* pervading, permeating, prevalent, suffusive, extensive, ubiquitous, omnipresent, rife, widespread, universal.

perverse adjective **1** *too perverse to get along with others* contrary, wayward, troublesome, unruly, difficult, awkward, unreasonable, disobedient, unmanageable, uncontrollable, rebellious, willful, headstrong, capricious, stubborn, obstinate, obdurate, pertinacious, mulish, pigheaded, bullheaded, querulous, fractious, intractable, refractory, intransigent, contumacious. **2** *take a perverse delight in annoying her* contradictory, unreasonable, irrational, illogical, senseless, abnormal, deviant, excessive, undue, immoderate, inordinate, outrageous.

Antonyms: ACCOMMODATING; REASONABLE.

perversion noun **1** *a perversion of the truth* distortion, misuse, misrepresentation, falsification, misinterpretation, misconstruction. **2** *sexual perversion* deviation, aberration, abnormality, irregularity, unnaturalness, corruption, debauchery, depravity, vice, wickedness; *inf.* kinkiness.

perversity noun **1** *disliked for his perversity* perverseness, contrariness, troublesomeness, unruliness, difficulty, awkwardness, unreasonableness, disobedience, unmanageableness, unmanageability, rebelliousness, willfulness, stubbornness, obstinacy, obduracy, pertinacity, mulishness, pigheadedness, querulousness, fractiousness, intractability, refractoriness, intransigence, contumaciousness. **2** *the perversity of his behavior* unreasonableness, irrationality, abnormality, deviation. *See* PERVERSE 2.

pervert verb **1** *pervert the course of justice* turn aside, divert, deflect, avert, subvert. **2** *pervert* *the English language* misapply, misuse, distort, garble, warp, twist, misinterpret, misconstrue. **3** *pervert young minds* lead astray, corrupt, warp, deprave, debauch, debase, degrade, vitiate.

pervert *noun* *a sexual pervert* deviant, deviate, degenerate, debauchee; *inf.* sicko, weirdo.

perverted *adjective* corrupt, corrupted, depraved, debauched, debased, vitiated, deviant, abnormal, aberrant, warped, distorted, twisted, sick, unhealthy, immoral, evil, wicked, vile; *inf.* kinky.

pessimism *noun* *his pessimism made everyone gloomy* looking on the dark side, expecting the worst, lack of hope, hopelessness, gloom, gloominess, gloom and doom, cynicism, defeatism, fatalism, distrust, doubt, suspicion, resignation, depression, dejection, despair.

pessimist *noun* *pessimists forecasting disaster* prophet of doom, cynic, defeatist, fatalist, alarmist, doubter, doubting Thomas; *inf.* doomster.

pessimistic *adjective* *a pessimistic outlook* hopeless, gloomy, gloom-ridden, cynical, defeatist, fatalistic, distrustful, alarmist, doubting, suspicious, bleak, resigned, depressed, dejected, despairing.
Antonyms: OPTIMISTIC; HOPEFUL; CHEERFUL.

pest *noun* *the neighbor/salesperson/insect is a pest* nuisance, bother, source of annoyance/irritation, vexation, irritant, thorn in one's side, problem, trouble, worry, inconvenience, trial, tribulation, the bane of one's life; *inf.* pain, pain in the neck, aggravation.

pester *verb* *photographers pestering the movie star | pestering them for money* badger, hound, irritate, annoy, bother, irk, nag, fret, worry, harass, get on someone's nerves, torment, plague, bedevil, harry; *inf.* get at, bug, hassle.

pestilence *noun* **1** *villagers dying from a/the pestilence* plague, bubonic plague, Black Death, epidemic, pandemic, disease, contagion, sickness. **2** *the pestilence of war* bane, blight, affliction, scourge, curse, torment.

pet *noun* *teacher's pet* favorite, darling, idol, apple of one's eye; *inf.* blue-eyed boy/girl, fair-haired boy/girl.

pet *adjective* **1** *a pet lamb* domesticated, domestic, tame, tamed, housebroken. **2** *a pet theory/charity* favorite, favored, cherished, prized, dear to one's heart, preferred, particular, special. **pet name** *call her daughter/husband by a pet name* affectionate name, term of endearment, endearment, nickname.

pet *verb* **1** *pet the cat* stroke, caress, fondle, pat. **2** *a couple petting romantically* make love, kiss, cuddle, embrace, caress; *inf.* neck, smooch.

peter *verb* **peter out** *the great enthusiasm petered out* fade, die away, melt away, evaporate, wane, ebb, diminish, taper off, come to nothing, die

out, fail, fall through, come to a halt, come to an end.

petition *noun* **1** *sign a petition to save the building* protest document, list of protesters, appeal, round robin. **2** *make a petition to God | made several petitions for leniency to the judge* entreaty, supplication, plea, prayer, appeal, request, application, suit.

petition *verb* *petition God | petitioned the court for mercy* entreat, beg, beseech, plead with, make a plea to, pray, appeal to, request, ask, apply to, call upon, press, adjure, present one's case to, sue.

petrify *verb* **1** *the thought of speaking in public petrified her | petrified at the strange sight* terrify, strike terror into, horrify, frighten, fill with fear, make terror-stricken, panic, alarm, scare out of one's wits, appall, paralyze, stun, stupefy, transfix. **2** *age had petrified the tree* turn to stone, fossilize, calcify, ossify.

petty *adjective* **1** *waste time discussing petty matters/details* trivial, trifling, minor, small, slight, unimportant, inessential, inconsequential, inconsiderable, negligible, paltry; *inf.* piddling, piffling. **2** *indulge in petty behavior | do it out of petty spite* narrow-minded, narrow, small-minded, mean-minded, mean, ungenerous, grudging.
Antonyms: IMPORTANT; SERIOUS; MAJOR; MAGNANIMOUS.

petulant *adjective* querulous, complaining, peevish, fretful, impatient, cross, irritable, moody, crabbed, crabby, snappish, crotchety, touchy, bad-tempered, ill-tempered, ill-humored, irascible, sulky, sullen.
Antonyms: GOOD-NATURED; EASYGOING; AFFABLE.

phantom *noun* **1** *imagine he saw phantoms in the graveyard* ghost, apparition, specter, spirit, revenant, wraith, shadow, phantasm; *inf.* spook. **2** *dreams haunted by phantoms of evil* vision, hallucination, illusion, figment of the imagination, chimera.

phase *noun* **1** *the various phases of reconstruction | an exciting phase in history* stage, part, step, chapter, point, period, time, juncture. **2** *going through a difficult phase* stage, time, period, spell. **3** *changing phases of the moon* aspect, facet, shape, form.

phase *verb* **phase in** *phase in new teaching methods* introduce gradually, incorporate by stages, begin using, ease in, start using. **phase out** *phase out the old machinery* withdraw/remove gradually, dispose of gradually, get rid of by stages, stop using, ease off, run down, wind down, wind up.

phenomenal *adjective* *enjoying phenomenal success* extraordinary, remarkable, exceptional, singular, uncommon, unheard-of, unique, unparalleled, unprecedented, amazing, astonishing, astounding, unusual, marvelous, prodigious, sensational, miraculous; *inf.* fantastic, fabulous, mind-boggling, mind-blowing.
Antonyms: ORDINARY; USUAL; RUN-OF-THE-MILL.

phenomenon noun 1 *a social phenomenon peculiar to our times* circumstance, fact, experience, occurrence, happening, event, incident, episode. 2 *the gymnast is really a phenomenon | her musical compositions are a phenomenon* marvel, prodigy, rarity, wonder, sensation, miracle, nonpareil.

philander verb *always philandering | philandering with the staff* flirt, have an affair, have a love affair, womanize, dally with, trifle/toy with the affections of, play around, fool around.

philanderer noun Casanova, Don Juan, womanizer, woman-chaser, ladies' man, flirt, Lothario, dallier, trifler; *inf.* lady-killer, wolf, stud.

philanthropic adjective *philanthropic concern/ millionaire/organization* humanitarian, humane, public-spirited, socially concerned, solicitous, unselfish, selfless, altruistic, kindhearted, benevolent, beneficent, benignant, charitable, almsgiving, generous, kind, munificent, bountiful, bounteous, liberal, openhanded, giving, helping.
Antonyms: SELFISH; STINGY; MISERLY.

philanthropist noun humanitarian, altruist, almsgiver, benefactor, patron, sponsor, giver, donor, contributor, backer, helper.

philanthropy noun humanitarianism, humanity, humaneness, public-spiritedness, social concern, unselfishness, selflessness, altruism, kindheartedness, brotherly love, benevolence, beneficence, benignity, charity, charitableness, generosity, almsgiving, kindness, munificence, bounty, bountifulness, bounteousness, liberality, openhandedness, patronage, sponsorship, giving, backing, help.

philippic noun *deliver a philippic against the state* diatribe, invective, tirade, harangue, verbal onslaught, fulmination, vituperation.

philistine noun lowbrow, ignoramus, boor, barbarian, vulgarian, yahoo, lout, clod, oaf.

philistine adjective *a philistine attitude to the arts* uncultured, uncultivated, uneducated, unenlightened, unread, lowbrow, anti-intellectual, ignorant, bourgeois, boorish, barbaric, vulgar.

philosopher noun 1 *the Greek philosopher* philosophizer, scholar, metaphysicist, metaphysician, sage, wise man, guru, pundit, seeker after truth. 2 *a philosopher rather than a doer* philosophizer, thinker, theorist, theorizer.

philosophical adjective 1 *read philosophical works* of philosophy, philosophic, metaphysical. 2 *in a philosophical mood* thoughtful, reflective, pensive, meditative, contemplative. 3 *remain philosophical in the face of failure* calm, composed, cool, collected, self-possessed, serene, tranquil, stoical, impassive, phlegmatic, unperturbed, imperturbable, dispassionate, unruffled, patient, resigned, rational, logical, realistic, practical.
Antonyms: ACTIVE; PRACTICAL; EMOTIONAL; UPSET.

philosophy noun 1 *the philosophy of Aristotle |* *studying philosophy* thought, thinking, reasoning, logic, wisdom, metaphysics, moral philosophy. *See also table at* POLITICS. 2 *his philosophy of life* beliefs, convictions, ideology, ideas, doctrine, tenets, values, principles, attitude, view, viewpoint, outlook. 3 *admire their philosophy when disaster struck* philosophicalness, calmness, calm, coolness, composure, equanimity, aplomb, self-possession, serenity, tranquillity, stoicism, impassivity, phlegm, imperturbability, dispassion, dispassionateness, patience, resignation, rationality, logic, realism, practicality; *inf.* cool.

phlegm noun 1 *coughing up phlegm* mucus, catarrh. 2 *no crisis disturbs his phlegm* calmness, calm, coolness, composure, equanimity, serenity, tranquillity, placidity, placidness, impassivity, imperturbability, dispassionateness, philosophicalness; *inf.* cool. 3 *overcame the phlegm of the students with a dynamic speaker* apathy, indifference, lack of interest, impassivity, sluggishness, lethargy, listlessness, languor, dullness, indolence, inertia, inactivity, stolidness, bovineness.

phlegmatic adjective 1 *a phlegmatic disposition* calm, cool, composed, serene, tranquil, placid, impassive, imperturbable, dispassionate, philosophical. 2 *a challenge to enthuse the phlegmatic students* apathetic, indifferent, uninterested, impassive, sluggish, lethargic, listless, languorous, dull, indolent, inert, inactive, stolid, placid, bovine.
Antonyms: EXCITABLE; QUICK-TEMPERED; ENTHUSIASTIC; ACTIVE.

phobia noun *a phobia about/toward rats* aversion, abnormal fear, irrational fear, obsessive fear, fear, dread, horror, terror, dislike, hatred, loathing, detestation, distaste, antipathy, revulsion, repulsion; *inf.* thing, hang-up.

phone noun telephone, mobile phone, car phone, cellular phone, pay phone; *inf.* horn, cell phone.

phone verb *phone her mother for a chat* telephone, call, make/place a call to, give someone a call, ring, ring up, give someone a ring; *inf.* give someone a buzz.

phony adjective 1 *taken in by phony salespeople* bogus, sham, fake, fraudulent, pseudo. 2 *phony documents* bogus, sham, counterfeit, imitation, spurious, mock, ersatz, fake, forged, feigned, simulated, make-believe, false, fraudulent. 3 *a phony French accent* bogus, sham, counterfeit, imitation, fake, feigned, assumed, simulated, affected, contrived, false, mock, pseudo.
Antonyms: AUTHENTIC; GENUINE.

phony noun 1 *the doctor is a phony* impostor, pretender, sham, fraud, fake, faker, charlatan, mountebank; *inf.* quack. 2 *the diamond is a phony* counterfeit, fake, forgery, imitation, sham.

photocopy *noun a photocopy of the document* copy, facsimile, fax; *Trademark* Xerox, Photostat.

photograph *noun* photo, snap, snapshot, picture, likeness, shot, print, slide, transparency.

photograph *verb* take a photograph/photo of, take a snapshot/snap of, snap, take a picture of, take a shot of, take a likeness of, shoot, capture on film.

photographic *adjective* **1** *a photographic record* pictorial, in photographs. **2** *a photographic description* detailed, graphic, exact, accurate, precise.

phrase *noun* **1** *in phrases and sentences* word group, group of words. **2** *a few well-chosen phrases* expression, idiomatic expression, idiom, remark, saying, utterance, witticism, tag. **3** *an elegant turn of phrase* phrasing, phraseology, way of speaking/writing, manner of speaking/writing, style of speech/writing, style, mode of speech/writing, usage, choice of words, idiom, language, diction, parlance.

phrase *verb phrase the instruction differently* put into words, put, word, express, formulate, couch, frame.

phraseology *noun* **1** *admire the writer's phraseology* way of speaking/writing, manner of speaking/writing, style of speech/writing, style, mode of speech/writing, phrasing, usage, idiom, language, diction, parlance. **2** *express it in simple phraseology* phrasing, wording, words, choice of words, language, vocabulary, terminology.

physical *adjective* **1** *physical and mental pain | physical well-being* bodily, nonmental, corporeal, corporal, somatic. **2** *novitiates rising above their physical concerns* nonspiritual, unspiritual, material, earthly, corporeal, carnal, fleshly, mortal. **3** *everything physical in the universe* material, substantial, solid, concrete, tangible, palpable, visible, real.
Antonyms: MENTAL; SPIRITUAL.

physician *noun* doctor, doctor of medicine, medical practitioner, medical man/woman, general practitioner, GP, specialist, consultant; *inf.* doc, medic, medico; *derog.* quack.

physique *noun gymnasts having muscular physiques* body, body structure, build, shape, frame, form, figure.

pick *verb* **1** *pick a new sofa from the showroom | pick him for the team* pick out, choose, select, opt for, plump for, single out, handpick, decide upon, settle upon, fix upon, sift out, prefer, favor, elect. **2** *picking apples* harvest, gather, collect, take in, pluck, pull, cull. **3** *pick a safe* break into, break open, force open, pry/prize open, crack. **pick at** *picking at their food* nibble at, peck at, toy with, play with, eat like a bird, show no appetite for, eat sparingly of. **pick off** *soldiers picked off by a sniper* shoot, shoot down, gun down, fire at, hit, take out. **pick on**

picking on a child punish repeatedly, blame regularly, constantly find fault with, criticize, badger. **pick out** **1** *picked out from a huge list of applicants* pick, choose, select, single out, handpick. *See* PICK *verb* 1. **2** *pick out his face in the crowd* make out, distinguish, tell apart, discriminate, recognize, notice. **pick up** **1** *pick up the suitcase* lift, take up, raise, hoist. **2** *business starting to pick up* improve, get better, recover, be on the road to recovery, rally, make a comeback, perk up, be on the mend, make headway, make progress, take a turn for the better. **3** *manage to pick up a first edition* find, discover, locate, come across, stumble across, happen upon, unearth, obtain, get, acquire, purchase, buy. **4** *pick up tomorrow where we left off today* take up, begin, begin again, start, start again, carry on, go on, continue. **5** *pick them up on the way* collect, go to get, call for, fetch, give someone a lift, give someone a ride. **6** *picked up by the police for questioning* take into custody, arrest, apprehend; *inf.* collar, nab, run/pull in, pinch. **7** *pick up a date at the party* strike up an acquaintance with, take up with, fall in with, strike up a casual friendship with. **8** *pick up the basic skills | pick up the local language* learn, get to know, acquire a knowledge of, master; *inf.* get the hang of. **9** *pick up malaria abroad* catch, contract, get, become infected with, become ill with, come down with. **10** *pick up some interesting news* learn, hear, get to know, glean.

pick *noun* **1** *early shoppers have the pick of the bargains* choice, selection, option, preference. **2** *the pick of the litter/crop* best, choicest, prime, cream, flower, prize, elite, créme de la créme.

picket *noun* **1** *line of pickets outside the factory* picketer, demonstrator, protester, objector, rebel, dissident. **2** *dispatch a picket to watch for the enemy* sentry, watch, guard, lookout, patrol, sentinel. **3** *drive pickets into the ground* stake, post, paling, pale, peg, upright, pike, stanchion, palisade.

picket *verb* **1** *picket the factory* form a picket at, go on a picket line at, man the picket line at, demonstrate at, launch a demonstration at, protest at, form a protest group at, blockade. **2** *picket the walls of the castle* form a sentry at, be part of the watch at, guard, patrol, form a sentinel at. **3** *picket an area for the animals* enclose, fence off, box in, stake off, secure, rail off, palisade.

pickle *noun in a financial pickle* plight, predicament, mess, trouble, problem, straits, crisis, tight corner; *inf.* jam, fix, scrape, hole, hot water, tight spot, spot, (fine) kettle of fish.

pickle *verb pickle vegetables* marinade, preserve, conserve.

pick-me-up *noun in need of a pick-me-up* tonic, restorative, energizer, bracer; boost, boost to the spirits, reviver, stimulus, invigoration; *Med.* roborant; *inf.* shot in the arm.

pickpocket *noun a wallet snatched by a pickpocket* thief, purse snatcher, petty thief.

picnic noun 1 *a picnic on the beach* outdoor meal, outdoor party, alfresco meal; cookout, barbecue. 2 *persuading her to go was no picnic* easy task, child's play; *inf.* piece of cake, walk in the park, cinch, breeze.

pictorial adjective 1 *a pictorial record of our trip* in pictures, in picture form, in photographs, photographic, in snapshots. 2 *a pictorial calendar* illustrated, with illustrations, with pictures, with sketches.

picture noun 1 *paint a picture of the house* painting, drawing, sketch, oil painting, watercolor, print, canvas, delineation, portrait, portrayal, illustration, likeness, representation, similitude, semblance. 2 *take pictures at the wedding* photograph, photo, snapshot, shot, snap, slide, print, still. 3 *his report painted a bleak picture* scene, view, image, impression, representation, vision, concept. 4 *write a graphic picture of his despair* description, portrayal, account, report, narrative, narration, story, tale, recital. 5 *the picture of health/happiness* personification, embodiment, epitome, essence, perfect example, model, exemplar, archetype. 6 *he is the picture of his father* image, living image, double, exact likeness, duplicate, replica, carbon copy, twin; *inf.* spitting image, spit and image, ringer, dead ringer. 7 *see a picture starring Abbott and Costello* movie, film, motion picture; *inf.* flick. **in the picture** *in the picture about the financial state of the firm* (fully) informed, brought up-to-date, updated; *inf.* filled in, clued in.

picture verb 1 *I can picture them still* see in one's mind, see in one's mind's eye, conjure up a picture of, conjure up an image of, imagine, call to mind, visualize, see, evoke. 2 *in the drawing they were pictured against a snowy background* paint, draw, sketch, depict, delineate, portray, illustrate, reproduce, represent.

picturesque adjective 1 *a picturesque village/setting* beautiful, pretty, lovely, attractive, scenic, charming, quaint, pleasing, delightful. 2 *a picturesque description of the events* | *use picturesque language* vivid, graphic, colorful, impressive, striking.
Antonyms: UGLY; DRAB; DULL.

piddling adjective 1 *ignore the piddling details* trivial, trifling, minor, small, unimportant, insignificant, petty, paltry, worthless, useless; *inf.* piffling. 2 *a piddling sum of money* meager, trifling, paltry, derisory, negligible, small; *inf.* measly, piffling, Mickey Mouse.

pie noun pastry, tart, quiche. **pie in the sky** false hopes, illusions, delusions, unrealizable dreams, pipedreams, daydreams, castles in the air, castles in Spain.

piebald adjective *piebald horses* pied, black and white, brown and white, dappled, brindled, spotted, mottled, speckled, flecked, variegated, pinto.

piece noun 1 *a desk delivered in several pieces* part, bit, section, segment, unit. 2 *a vase broken to pieces* | *a dress torn to pieces* bit, fragment, smithereens, shard, shred. 3 *buy a large piece of cheese/wood* bit, section, slice, chunk, lump, hunk, wedge. 4 *a piece of cloth* length, bit, remnant, scrap, snippet. 5 *a piece of his fortune* | *get a piece of the action* share, slice, portion, allotment, allocation, quota, percentage, fraction, quantity. 6 *a fine piece of Colonial furniture* example, specimen, sample, instance, illustration, occurrence. 7 *write a piece on modern theater* | *disagree with his latest piece* article, item, story, report, essay, review, paper, column. 8 *one of the finest pieces by the composer* musical work, work, composition, creation, opus. 9 *one of the artist's finest pieces* work of art, work, painting, canvas, composition, creation, opus. **all in one piece** *find the vase/car/child all in one piece* unbroken, undamaged, unhurt, uninjured, safe, sound, safe and sound. **fall/go to pieces** *people going to pieces in an emergency* panic, become agitated, lose control, lose one's head, fall apart, break down; *inf.* crack up.

piece verb *piece together the torn parts of the page* | *trying to piece together all the evidence* put together, assemble, join up, fit together, unite.

pièce de résistance noun masterpiece, masterwork, chef d'oeuvre, showpiece, jewel, jewel in the crown.

piecemeal adverb *put the story together piecemeal* piece by piece, bit by bit, gradually, in stages, in steps, little by little, by degrees, in fits and starts.

pied adjective *pied horses* piebald, black and white, dappled, brindled, spotted. *See* PIEBALD.

pier noun 1 *stand on the pier to watch the boats* wharf, dock, jetty, quay, landing stage, landing place, promenade. 2 *the piers of the bridge damaged by storms* support, upright, pillar, post, column, pile, piling, buttress.

pierce verb 1 *the spear had pierced his shoulder* penetrate, puncture, perforate, prick, stab, spike, enter, pass through, transfix. 2 *pierce the leather to make a belt* make holes in, perforate, bore, drill. 3 *a heart pierced by the suffering of others* wound, hurt, pain, cut to the quick, affect, move, sting. 4 *torches piercing the darkness* penetrate, pass through, percolate, filter through, light up. 5 *shrill sounds piercing the air* penetrate, pervade, permeate, fill.

piercing adjective 1 *a piercing glance* penetrating, sharp, keen, searching, alert, shrewd, perceptive, probing. 2 *a piercing shriek* penetrating, shrill, ear-piercing, earsplitting, high-pitched, loud. 3 *a piercing intelligence* perceptive, percipient, perspicacious, discerning, quickwitted, sharp, sharp-witted, shrewd, keen, acute, astute. 4 *a piercing pain* penetrating, sharp, stabbing, shooting, intense, severe, fierce, excruciating, agonizing, exquisite. 5 *frostbitten in the piercing cold* biting, numbing, bitter, raw, keen, freezing, frigid, arctic.

piety noun 1 *a family noted for its piety* piousness,

religiousness, religion, holiness, godliness, devoutness, devotion to God, devotion, veneration, reverence, faith, religious duty, spirituality, sanctity, religious zeal. **2** *children who were taught filial piety* obedience, duty, dutifulness, respect, respectfulness, deference, veneration.

pig noun **1** *farmers keeping pigs* hog, boar, sow, porker, grunter, swine, piglet; *inf.* piggy, oinker. **2** *pigs who left hardly any food for the others* glutton, guzzler; *inf.* hog. **3** *they live like pigs* slob, messy/filthy/dirty person. **4** *her boss is a real pig* boor, brute, swine, animal, monster; *inf.* bastard, beast, louse.

pigeon noun **1** *feeding the pigeons* squab, homing pigeon, carrier pigeon, dove. **2** *con men swindling pigeons* dupe, fool, simpleton, victim; *inf.* sucker, sap, sitting duck, sitting target, soft touch, pushover.

pigeonhole noun **1** *put the papers into the students' pigeonholes* compartment, locker, cubbyhole, niche; *inf.* cubby. **2** *apt to put people in pigeonholes* compartment, category, class, classification, slot.

pigeonhole verb **1** *pigeonhole plans for reconstruction* postpone, put off, defer, shelve; *inf.* put on ice, put on the back burner. **2** *pigeonhole her before she even started work* compartmentalize, categorize, classify, characterize, label, tag, slot.

pigheaded adjective *too pigheaded to take advice* obstinate, stubborn, stubborn as a mule, mulish, bullheaded, obdurate, tenacious, dogged, single-minded, inflexible, uncompromising, adamant, intractable, intransigent, unmalleable, headstrong, self-willed, willful, perverse, contrary, stiff-necked.

pigment noun coloring matter, coloring agent, colorant, color, tint, dye.

pile[1] noun **1** *a pile of clothes/logs/coins* heap, bundle, stack, mound, mass, accumulation, collection, assemblage, store, stockpile, hoard, load, mountain. **2** *a pile of work to do* great deal, quantity, abundance, mountain; *inf.* lot, lots, heap, ocean, stacks, oodles, tons. **3** *make a/his pile on the black market* fortune, money, wealth; *inf.* mint, stacks of money, tidy sum.

pile[2] verb **1** *pile his plate with food* heap, fill, load, stock. **2** *commuters piling on to the train* crowd, charge, tumble, stream, flock, flood, pack, squeeze, crush, jam. **pile it on** *to get our sympathy, he really piled it on* exaggerate, overstate the case, overdraw the situation, make a mountain of a molehill, build it up out of all proportion; *inf.* lay it on, lay it on with a trowel, blow it up out of all proportion. **pile up 1** *pile up the cans/apples* heap, stack. **2** *pile up logs for the winter* accumulate, amass, collect, gather, stockpile, hoard, store up, assemble, lay by/in. **3** *snow piled up by the roadsides* form piles, form heaps, heap up, amass, accumulate.

pile[3] noun *the piles supporting the bridge* pillar, column, support, post, foundation, piling, pier, buttress, upright.

pile[4] noun **1** *the pile of the carpet* soft surface, surface, nap. **2** *pile clogging the vacuum cleaner* hair, fur, down, wool, fluff.

pileup noun *a pileup on the highway* crash, multiple crash, collision, multiple collision, accident, traffic accident.

pilfer verb *pilfer money from the petty cash* steal, thieve, rob, take, filch, purloin, embezzle, misappropriate; *inf.* walk off/away with, pinch, swipe, lift.

pilgrim noun *pilgrims going to Bethlehem/Mecca* worshiper, devotee, traveler, hajji; Puritan.

pilgrimage noun *make a pilgrimage to Bethlehem/Mecca* religious expedition, holy expedition, trek, excursion, hajj.

pill noun **1** *take a pill for a headache* tablet, capsule, pellet, lozenge, bolus. **2** *she can be a real pill* nuisance, pest, bore, trial; *inf.* pain, pain in the neck, drag.

pillage verb *rival tribes invading and pillaging* plunder, rob, raid, loot, maraud, sack, ransack, ravage, lay waste, despoil, spoil, spoliate, depredate, rape.

pillage noun *the pillage of the town* pillaging, plunder, plundering, robbery, robbing, raiding, looting, marauding, sacking, ransacking, ravaging, rapine, despoiling, laying waste, spoliation, depredation.

pillar noun **1** *pillars supporting the temple* column, post, pole, support, upright, pile, piling, pilaster, stanchion, peristyle. **2** *a pillar of the community* mainstay, backbone, strength, tower of strength, support, upholder, rock.

pillory noun *put in the pillory for theft* stocks.

pillory verb *pilloried in the press for his past mistakes* brand, stigmatize, cast a slur on, denounce, show up, hold up to shame, hold up to ridicule, expose to ridicule, ridicule, heap scorn on.

pillow noun *lay one's head on the pillow* cushion, bolster, headrest.

pilot noun **1** *the pilot at the aircraft's controls* airman/airwoman, aviator, aviatrix, aeronaut, captain, commander, copilot, first/second officer; *inf.* flier. **2** *the pilot directing the ship into the harbor* navigator, guide, steersman, helmsman. **3** *act as his pilot through life* guide, leader, conductor, director.

pilot verb **1** *pilot the aircraft* fly, drive, operate, control, handle, maneuver. **2** *pilot the ship into the harbor* navigate, guide, steer. **3** *pilot the bill through Congress* guide, steer, conduct, direct, shepherd.

pilot adjective *pilot scheme* trial, test, experimental, model.

pimple noun spot, pustule, boil, swelling, papule; *inf.* blackhead, whitehead, zit.

pin verb **1** *pin the pieces of cloth together* fasten, join, attach, secure. **2** *pin the notice to the board* attach, fasten, affix, fix, stick, tack, nail. **3**

pinned under the fallen tree | *pinned against the wall* pinion, hold, press, restrain, constrain, hold fast, immobilize. **pin down 1** *bullies pinned the boy down* | *pinned down by the weight of the car* pinion, hold down, press down, restrain, constrain, hold fast, immobilize. **2** *to get his decision, you must pin him down* force, compel, make, pressure, put pressure on, pressurize, constrain, nail down. **3** *something I dislike about him but I cannot pin it down* define, put one's finger on, put into words, put words to, express in words, express, designate, name, specify, identify, home in on. **pin on** *pin the blame on him* lay on, place on, fix the responsibility for (something) on, attribute to, impute to, ascribe to.

pin noun **1** *fasten the hem with a pin* straight pin, dressmaker's/dressmaking pin, safety pin. **2** *a broken pin in the machine* peg, bolt, rivet, screw, dowel, post.

pinch verb **1** *pinch her little brother's arm* nip, tweak, squeeze, compress. **2** *shoes pinching her feet* hurt, cause pain to, pain, crush, squeeze, cramp, confine. **3** *have to pinch and scrape to live* scrimp, skimp, stint, be sparing, be frugal, be economical, economize, be niggardly/tight-fisted; *inf.* be stingy, be tight. **4** *pinch money from her mother's purse* steal, thieve, rob, take, pilfer, filch, purloin, embezzle, misappropriate; *inf.* walk away/off with, swipe, lift. **5** *burglars pinched by the police* arrest, take into custody, apprehend; *inf.* pick up, pull in, run in, nab, collar, bust.

pinch noun **1** *give her arm a pinch* nip, tweak, squeeze. **2** *a pinch of salt* small quantity, bit, touch, trace, soupçon; *inf.* smidgen, smidge, tad. **feel the pinch** *feel the pinch during a recession* be short of money, have less money, suffer hardship, suffer poverty, suffer adversity. **in a pinch** *in a pinch we could accommodate five people* if necessary, in case of necessity, if need be, in an emergency, just possibly.

pinched adjective *looking pinched and tired* drawn, haggard, gaunt, worn, peaked, pale.
Antonyms: HEALTHY; GLOWING; CHUBBY.

pine verb **pine away** *pine away with grief* decline, go into a decline, lose strength, weaken, waste away, wilt, fade, languish, droop. **pine for** *pine for her old way of life* long for, yearn for, ache for, sigh for, hunger for, thirst for, hanker for/after, crave, covet, lust after.

pinion verb **1** *pinion him to the ground* pin down, hold down, press down, restrain, constrain, hold fast, immobilize. **2** *pinion his arms to the wall* bind, tie, fasten, shackle, fetter, chain, manacle.

pink adjective **1** *pink dresses* rose, rose-colored, salmon, salmon-pink, shell-pink, pale red, flesh-colored. **2** *pink cheeks* rosy, flushed, blushing.

pink noun *the pink of condition* peak, best, height, culmination, acme, pinnacle, zenith, summit. **in the pink** *feeling in the pink* in perfect health,

in good health, very healthy, very well, hale and hearty, bursting with health, in fine fettle.

pink verb **1** *pink the leather* pierce, punch, perforate, prick, stab, bore, drill. **2** *pink the edge of the cloth* scallop, serrate, notch, crenellate.

pinnacle noun **1** *the pinnacle of her success* peak, height, culmination, high point, acme, zenith, climax, crowning point, meridian, summit, apex, vertex, apogee. **2** *snow-covered pinnacles* peak, summit, top, crest, mountain, hill. **3** *pinnacles on the temple* turret, spire, obelisk, pyramid, cone.
Antonyms: NADIR; trough.

pinpoint verb *pinpoint the cause of the trouble* identify, discover, distinguish, locate, spot, home in on, put one's finger on.

pioneer noun **1** *the pioneers of the Wild West* settler, colonist, colonizer, frontiersman/frontierswoman, explorer. **2** *the pioneers of television* | *a pioneer of cancer research* developer, innovator, groundbreaker, trailblazer, front runner, founder, founding father, architect.

pioneer verb *pioneer cancer research* | *pioneered the use of the drug* lay the groundwork for, lead the way for, prepare the way for, lay the foundations of, develop, introduce, launch, instigate, initiate, take the initiative in, institute, originate, set the ball rolling for, open up, blaze a trail for, break new ground for.

pious adjective **1** *pious church members* religious, holy, godly, spiritual, devout, devoted, dedicated, reverent, God-fearing, righteous, faithful, dutiful. **2** *patronized by pious do-gooders* sanctimonious, hypocritical, self-righteous, unctuous, pietistic, religiose; *inf.* holier-than-thou, goody-goody. **3** *pious children performing filial duties* obedient, dutiful, respectful, reverent, righteous.
Antonyms: IMPIOUS; IRRELIGIOUS.

pipe noun **1** *lay pipes under the street* tube, cylinder; conduit, main, duct, channel, conveyor, pipeline, drainpipe. **2** *smoke a pipe* brier, meerschaum, clay pipe, tobacco pipe, corncob pipe; peace pipe, calumet; hookah. **3** *playing a pipe* whistle, penny whistle, flute, recorder, fife, wind instrument. **pipes** plural noun *playing the pipes* bagpipes, panpipes.

pipe verb **1** *pipe the gas to the stove* convey, channel, transmit, bring in, siphon. **2** *listen to him piping* play on a pipe, play the pipes, tootle. **3** *birds piping* tweet, cheep, chirp, chirrup, peep, twitter, sing, warble, whistle, squeak. **4** *"why?" the little girl piped* chirp, shrill, squeal, squeak. **pipe down** *children told to pipe down* be quiet, quieten down, be silent, hush, hold one's tongue; *inf.* shut up, button up one's lip.

pipedream noun *have pipedreams of winning the lottery* fantasy, illusion, daydream, castle in the air, castle in Spain, pie in the sky, delusion.

pipeline noun *lay the pipeline under the street* pipe, conduit, main, duct, channel, conveyor. **in the**

pipeline *rising costs in the pipeline* on the way, under way, coming, imminent, about to happen, in preparation, being prepared.

piquancy *noun* **1** *the piquancy of the sauce/flavor* spice, spiciness, pepperiness, tang, pungency, sharpness, edge, tartness, zest, zip; *inf.* zing, kick, punch. **2** *the piquancy of the gossip* stimulation, intrigue, interest, fascination, allurement, raciness, saltiness, provocativeness. **3** *the piquancy of her wit* liveliness, sparkle, animation, spiritedness, sharpness, cleverness, quickness, raciness, saltiness.

piquant *adjective* **1** *a piquant sauce/flavor* spicy, highly seasoned, flavorsome, peppery, tangy, pungent, sharp, tart, zesty, biting, stinging. **2** *a piquant piece of gossip* stimulating, intriguing, interesting, fascinating, alluring, racy, salty, provocative. **3** *a piquant wit* lively, sparkling, animated, spirited, sharp, clever, quick, racy, salty.
Antonyms: BLAND; INSIPID; DULL.

pique *verb* **1** *her lack of interest piqued him* irritate, annoy, anger, displease, affront, put out, offend, irk, peeve, vex, nettle, gall, wound; *inf.* aggravate, miff, rile. **2** *pique her curiosity* arouse, rouse, awaken, excite, stimulate, kindle, stir, whet.

pique *noun* *full of pique at his behavior* irritation, annoyance, anger, displeasure, affront, offense, resentment, grudge, umbrage, vexation, gall.

piracy *noun* **1** *piracy on the high seas* buccaneering, freebooting. **2** *publishers guilty of piracy* copyright infringement, plagiarism, appropriation.

pirate *noun* **1** *pirates boarded the ship* buccaneer, rover, sea rover, sea robber, corsair, freebooter. **2** *tapes/music/poems issued by pirates* copyright infringer, plagiarist, plagiarizer.

pirate *verb* *pirate his music/poetry* infringe the copyright of, plagiarize, illegally reproduce, copy, poach; *inf.* crib, lift.

pit¹ *noun* **1** *fall down a pit* abyss, chasm, crater, hole, cavity, excavation, quarry, mine. **2** *pits in the pottery/skin* depression, hollow, dent, dint, indentation, dimple, pockmark, pock, mark.

pit² *verb* *the disease had pitted her skin* depress, dent, dint, dimple, mark, pockmark, scar. **pit against** *pit her wits against her enemy's* set against, match against, put in opposition to, oppose against.

pit³ *noun* *cherry pits* stone, pip, seed, kernel.

pitch¹ *verb* **1** *pitch a baseball | pitch the bales on to the truck* throw, cast, fling, hurl, toss, heave, launch; *inf.* chuck, lob. **2** *pitch a tent* put up, set up, erect, raise. **3** *trip and pitch forward into the lake* fall headlong, fall, tumble, topple, plunge, dive. **4** *ships pitching in the storm* lurch, roll, reel, sway, rock, flounder, keel, list. **pitch in 1** *everyone pitched in to finish the work* help, assist, lend a hand, join in, participate, play a

part, do one's bit, cooperate, collaborate. **2** *everyone pitched in to buy a present* contribute, make a contribution, make a donation, put money in; *inf.* chip in.

pitch² *noun* **1** *with one pitch* throw, cast, fling, hurl, toss, heave; *inf.* chuck, lob. **2** *excitement reached such a pitch* level, point, degree, height, extent, intensity. **3** *the pitch of the roof* angle, slope, slant, tilt, cant, dip, inclination. **4** *get the right musical pitch* tone, timbre, sound, tonality, modulation. **5** *the pitch of the ship* pitching, lurch, roll, reeling, swaying, rocking, keeling, list. **6** *taken in by the salesman's pitch* spiel, sales talk, patter; *inf.* line.

pitch³ *noun* *use pitch to make the barrels watertight* asphalt, tar, bitumen.

pitch-black *adjective* *pitch-black nights/eyes* pitch-dark, jet-black, jet, coal-black, inky, ebony, raven, sable.

pitcher *noun* *a pitcher of water* jug, ewer, jar, crock.

piteous *adjective* *hear a piteous cry/tale* pitiful, to be pitied, pitiable, pathetic, distressing, affecting. See PITIFUL 1.

pitfall *noun* *the pitfalls of running a small business* trap, snare, catch, stumbling block, hazard, peril, danger, difficulty.

pith *noun* **1** *the pith of the argument* essence, essential part, main point, point, quintessence, gist, salient point, crux, heart, heart of the matter, nub, core, meat, kernel, marrow. **2** *a speech that lacks pith* substance, weight, moment, significance, importance, import, depth, force, vigor, power, strength, cogency.

pithy *adjective* *a pithy remark | wrote a pithy piece of prose* terse, succinct, concise, condensed, compact, summary, epigrammatic, to the point, pointed, significant, meaningful, expressive, incisive, forceful.
Antonyms: VERBOSE; LONG-WINDED.

pitiful *adjective* **1** *in a pitiful condition | a pitiful sight* to be pitied, pitiable, piteous, pathetic, wretched, distressing, affecting, moving, sad, woeful, deplorable, heart-rending, heartbreaking, poignant, emotional, emotive. **2** *a pitiful excuse/coward* contemptible, despicable, poor, sorry, miserable, inadequate, worthless, base, shabby; *inf.* pathetic.

pitiless *adjective* *a pitiless tyrant* merciless, ruthless, relentless, cruel, severe, harsh, heartless, callous, brutal, inhuman, inhumane, cold-hearted, hard-hearted, unfeeling, uncaring, unsympathetic.
Antonyms: MERCIFUL; COMPASSIONATE; KINDLY.

pittance *noun* *earn a pittance* insufficient amount, tiny amount; *inf.* peanuts, chicken feed.

pity *noun* **1** *show pity for her situation* commiseration, condolence, sympathy, compassion, fellow feeling, understanding, forbearance, distress, sadness, emotion, mercy, clemency, kindness, charity. **2** *it is a pity that he left* shame, crying shame, misfortune, unfortunate thing, sad thing, sin; *inf.* crime. **take pity on** *take pity on the homeless* show compassion toward, be compassionate toward, be sympathetic/charitable toward, show sympathy for, show charity/mercy to, help.

Antonyms: INDIFFERENCE; CRUELTY; SEVERITY.

pity *verb pity the homeless* feel pity for, take pity on, feel sorry for, weep for, grieve for, commiserate with, feel sympathy for, be sympathetic toward, sympathize with, have compassion for, be compassionate toward, feel for, show understanding toward, show forbearance toward, show mercy to, be merciful toward.

pivot *noun* **1** *the machine turning on a pivot* axis, fulcrum, axle, swivel, spindle, central shaft. **2** *his job was the pivot of his life* central point, center, focal point, focus, hub, heart, *raison d'être*. **3** *he was the pivot of the company* key person, kingpin, key player, cornerstone, linchpin.

pivot *verb the machine pivots on a central shaft* turn, revolve, rotate, spin, swivel, twirl. **pivot on/upon** *his whole future pivots on their decision* turn on, revolve around, depend on, hinge on, hang on, rely on, be contingent on.

pixie *noun* elf, fairy, sprite, brownie, imp, leprechaun.

placard *noun* poster, notice, public notice, bill, sign, signboard, advertisement; *inf.* ad.

placate *verb placate the angry customer* calm, calm down, pacify, soothe, appease, conciliate, propitiate, mollify, win over.

Antonyms: AGITATE; ANGER.

place *noun* **1** *the place where the accident happened* location, spot, scene, setting, position, site, situation, venue, area, region, whereabouts, locus. **2** *a sore place on her arm* spot, area, bit, part. **3** *the names of all the places in the region* | *visit a different place each year* town, city, village, hamlet, district, locality, neighborhood, quarter, country, state, area, region. **4** *have a place in town* house, apartment, residence, home, accommodation, abode, dwelling, domicile, property; *inf.* pad. **5** *occupy a lowly place in the company* | *win first place* position, status, grade, rank, station, standing, footing, role, niche. **6** *find a place in a law firm* position, post, job, appointment, situation, office. **7** *children asked to go back to their places* seat, position, space. **8** *put the book back in its place* position, correct position, space. **9** *not your place to criticize* function, job, role, task, duty, responsibility, charge, concern, affair, prerogative. **in place** *everything must be in place before the meeting* in position, in order, set up, arranged. **in place of** *her sister went in place of her* instead of, in lieu of, in someone's place, in someone's stead, taking the place of, as a substitute for, as an alternative for, in exchange for. **out of place** **1** *with not a hair out of place* out of position, out of order, in disorder, disarranged, in disarray, disorganized, in a mess, topsy-turvy. **2** *her remarks were quite out of place* inappropriate, unsuitable, inapposite, out of keeping, unseemly, improper, unfit. **3** *feel out of place at the party* out of one's element, uncomfortable, ill-at-ease, uneasy, like a fish out of water. **put in (someone's) place** *he was trying to flirt with her but she put him in his place* take down a peg or two, humble, humiliate, mortify, make eat humble pie; *inf.* cut down to size, settle (someone's) hash. **take place** *where did the murder take place?* happen, occur, come about, transpire, crop up, befall, come to pass. **take the place of** *trying to take the place of her mother* replace, substitute for, be a substitute for, act for, stand in lieu of, cover for.

place *verb* **1** *place the books on the shelves* put, put down, position, set down, lay down, deposit, rest, stand, install, establish, settle, station, situate. **2** *place the recruits according to their test scores* order, rank, grade, group, arrange, sort, class, classify, categorize, bracket. **3** *place her trust in him* put, lay, set, invest, consign. **4** *I know his face, but I cannot place him* identify, recognize, know, remember, put one's finger on, locate. **5** *try to place graduates* find employment for, find a job for, find a home for, accommodate, find accommodation for, appoint, assign.

placid *adjective* **1** *the placid waters of the lake* still, calm, peaceful, at peace, pacific, tranquil, motionless, smooth, unruffled, undisturbed. **2** *remain placid throughout the disturbance* | *of a placid temperament* calm, cool, cool-headed, collected, composed, self-possessed, serene, tranquil, equable, even-tempered, peaceable, easygoing, unmoved, undisturbed, unperturbed, imperturbable, unexcited, unexcitable, unruffled, unemotional.

Antonyms: STORMY; EXCITED.

plagiarize *verb plagiarize part of his colleague's work* copy, pirate, poach, borrow, reproduce, appropriate; *inf.* rip off, crib, lift.

plague *noun* **1** *villagers dying from a/the plague* bubonic plague, Black Death, contagious disease, contagion, disease, pestilence, sickness, epidemic, pandemic. **2** *a plague of locusts ate the crops* huge number, multitude, host, swarm, influx, infestation. **3** *famine and other plagues* affliction, evil, scourge, curse, blight, bane, calamity, disaster, trial, tribulation, torment, visitation. **4** *rush-hour traffic is a real plague* pest, nuisance, thorn in one's side, problem, bother, source of annoyance/irritation, irritant, the bane of one's life/existence; *inf.* pain, pain in the neck, aggravation.

plague *verb* **1** *plagued with/by poor health* afflict, cause suffering to, torture, torment, bedevil, trouble. **2** *plagued by her little brother* annoy, irritate, bother, disturb, worry, pester, vex, harass, torment, tease; *inf.* hassle, bug.

plain *adjective* **1** *it was plain that he was guilty* clear, clear as crystal, crystal-clear, obvious,

evident, apparent, manifest, transparent, patent, unmistakable. **2** *plain indications of his guilt* clear, clear-cut, obvious, evident, apparent, manifest, visible, discernible, perceptible, distinct, transparent, patent, noticeable, pronounced, marked, striking, unmistakable, conspicuous. **3** *a plain statement of the facts* clear, clear-cut, simple, straightforward, uncomplicated, comprehensible, intelligible, understandable, lucid, unambiguous. **4** *live on a plain diet | have a plain lifestyle* simple, austere, stark, severe, basic, ordinary, unsophisticated, spartan. **5** *the plain furnishings | a plain style of decoration* restrained, muted, simple, austere, stark, bare, basic, unadorned, undecorated, unembellished, unornamented, unpatterned, spartan. **6** *rather a plain child* unattractive, ill-favored, ugly, unprepossessing, unlovely, homely. **7** *a plain man* simple, straightforward, ordinary, average, typical, unpretentious, unassuming, unaffected, artless, guileless, sincere, honest, plain-speaking, plainspoken, frank, candid, blunt, outspoken, forthright, direct, downright.
Antonyms: OBSCURE; FANCY; ELABORATE; ATTRACTIVE.

plain *adverb that was just plain stupid* downright, utterly, completely, totally, thoroughly, positively, incontrovertibly, unquestionably, undeniably, simply.

plain *noun* lowland, grassland, prairie, meadowland, pasture, savannah, flatland; steppe, tundra; tableland, plateau, mesa.

plainspoken *adjective pride himself on being plainspoken* plain-speaking, frank, candid, blunt, outspoken, forthright, direct, downright, unequivocal, unambiguous.
Antonyms: EVASIVE; GUARDED; AMBIGUOUS.

plaintive *adjective plaintive cries* mournful, doleful, melancholy, sad, sorrowful, unhappy, disconsolate, wretched, woeful, grief-stricken, heartbroken, brokenhearted, pathetic, pitiful, piteous.

plan *noun* **1** *draw up an escape plan | a plan to make money* plan of action, scheme, system, procedure, method, program, schedule, project, way, means, strategy, tactics, formula. **2** *our plan is to relocate* idea, scheme, proposal, project, intention, intent, aim, hope, aspiration, ambition. **3** *the architect's plan for the new building* drawing, scale drawing, blueprint, layout, sketch, diagram, chart, map, illustration, representation, delineation.

plan *verb* **1** *plan a picnic for tomorrow* arrange, organize, line up, schedule, program. **2** *plan the reconstruction of the company* devise, design, plot, formulate, frame, outline, sketch out, draft, prepare, develop, shape, build, concoct, contrive, think out. **3** *plan a garden* draw up a plan of, design, make a drawing of, draw up a layout of, sketch out, make a chart of, map out,

make a representation of. **4** *we are planning to relocate | what are you planning?* make plans, intend, aim, propose, mean, purpose, contemplate, envisage, foresee.

plane *noun* **1** *objects standing on a plane* flat surface, level surface, the flat. **2** *on a different intellectual plane* level, stratum, stage, degree, position, rank, footing. **3** *planes taking off from the airport* airplane, aircraft, airliner, jet, jumbo jet.

plane *adjective require a plane surface* flat, level, horizontal, even, flush, smooth, regular, uniform.

plane *verb* **1** *aircraft/seagulls planing through the air* glide, soar, float, drift. **2** *boats planing across the water* glide, skim, skate; *inf.* fly.

plant *noun* **1** *buy plants for the garden* flower, vegetable, herb, shrub, weed. **2** *work at the textile plant* factory, works, foundry, mill, workshop, shop, yard.

plant *verb* **1** *plant tomato seeds* put in the ground, implant, sow, scatter. **2** *plant the potted geranium* transplant, bed (out), put in the ground, implant, set (out). **3** *plant his feet firmly on the ground* place, position, set, situate. **4** *plant an idea in his head* put, place, fix, establish, lodge, imbed, insert. **5** *plant a microphone in his bedroom* place secretly, hide, conceal, secrete.

plaque *noun a commemorative plaque on the wall* plate, stone plate, metal plate, panel, slab, tablet, sign.

plaster *noun* stucco, plaster of Paris, gypsum.

plaster *verb plaster her face with makeup* cover thickly, spread, coat, smear, overlay, bedaub.

plaster down *plaster down his hair with gel* flatten, smooth down, sleek down.

plastic *adjective* **1** *as plastic as clay* moldable, shapable, ductile, fictile, pliant, pliable, supple, flexible, soft. **2** *the plastic minds of young children* impressionable, responsive, receptive, malleable, moldable, ductile, pliable, supple, flexible, compliant, tractable, manageable, controllable, docile. **3** *a plastic charm* false, artificial, synthetic, spurious, sham, bogus, assumed, superficial, specious, meretricious, pseudo; *inf.* phony.
Antonyms: RIGID; INTRACTABLE; GENUINE.

plate *noun* **1** *serve food on plates* dish, platter, dinner plate. **2** *serve up a plate of spaghetti* plateful, helping, portion, serving. **3** *a commemorative plate on the wall* plaque, tablet, sign. **4** *a book with many colored plates* illustration, picture, photograph, print, lithograph. **5** *steel plates used in shipbuilding* sheet, panel, slab.

plateau *noun* **1** *stand on the plateau to view the valley below* elevated plain, highland, upland, mesa, tableland. **2** *prices reaching a plateau after a period of inflation* quiescent period, resting/flat period, quiet time, letup, break, respite, lull.

platform *noun* **1** *deliver a speech from the platform* dais, rostrum, podium, stage, stand. **2** *nothing new in the candidate's platform* plan, plan of action, objectives, principles, tenets, program, policy, manifesto, party line.

platitude noun *a speech rife with platitudes* cliché, truism, hackneyed expression, commonplace, stock expression, trite phrase, banal phrase, banality, stereotyped phrase, bromide, inanity.

platitudinous adjective *tired of his platitudinous remarks* hackneyed, overworked, clichéd, commonplace, stock, trite, banal, stereotyped, set, stale, well-worn, tired, vapid, inane; *inf.* corny.

platonic adjective *a platonic relationship* nonromantic, nonsexual, nonphysical, friendly, spiritual, intellectual.
Antonyms: PHYSICAL; sexual.

platoon noun *the officer in charge of the platoon* squadron, squad, company, patrol, group.

platter noun serving plate, salver, plate, dish, tray.

plaudits plural noun *the plaudits of his colleagues* praise, acclaim, acclamation, applause, ovation, congratulations, compliments, cheers, bouquets, approval, approbation, commendation, accolade, pat on the back.
Antonyms: condemnation; CRITICISM.

plausible adjective *an excuse that was far from plausible* | *put forward a plausible argument* tenable, cogent, reasonable, believable, credible, convincing, persuasive, likely, probable, conceivable, imaginable.

play verb **1** *time to play* amuse oneself, entertain oneself, enjoy oneself, have fun. **2** *playing in the park* play games, frolic, frisk, gambol, romp, cavort, sport. **3** *play a musical instrument* perform on. **4** *play Ophelia in Hamlet* play the part of, act, act the part of, perform, portray, represent, execute. **5** *play a trick on* perform, carry out, execute, do, accomplish, discharge, fulfill. **6** *play football* take part in, participate in, engage in, be involved in. **7** *play the neighboring team* play against, compete against, contend against, oppose, take on, challenge, vie with, rival. **8** *told not to play with the controls* fiddle, toy, fidget, fool around; *inf.* mess around. **9** *playing with her affections* trifle, toy, dally, amuse oneself. **10** *sunlight playing on the water* | *a smile playing on her lips* move lightly, dance, flit, dart. **play around** philander, womanize, have an affair, have a love affair, fool around, cheat; *inf.* mess around. **play at being** *play at being a businesswoman* pretend to be, give the appearance of, assume/affect the role of; *inf.* make like. **play ball** *want to do business, but they refused to play ball* cooperate, collaborate, play along, go along with the plan, show willingness, be willing. **play down** *play down his part in the crime* make light of, make little of, gloss over, minimize, diminish, set little store by, underrate, underestimate, undervalue, think little of; *inf.* soft-pedal. **play for time** *try to play for time while his friend got away* stall, temporize, gain time, hang back, hang fire, procrastinate, delay, filibuster, stonewall. **play it by**

563

ear *we have no plans—we are going to play it by ear* improvise, extemporize, ad lib, take it as it comes. **play on** *friends playing on his generosity* exploit, take advantage of, profit by, capitalize on, impose on, trade on, milk, abuse, misuse; *inf.* walk all over. **play the fool** act the fool, fool around, monkey around, clown, clown around, act the clown, horse around; *inf.* mess around. **play up** *car dealers playing up the new safety features* emphasize, put/lay emphasis on, accentuate, bring/draw/call attention to, point up, underline, underscore, highlight, spotlight, give prominence to, bring to the fore, stress. **play up to** *playing up to the boss* flatter, ingratiate oneself with, try to get on the good side of, curry favor with, fawn over, toady to; *inf.* softsoap, suck up to, butter up, be all over, lick someone's boots.
Antonyms: WORK; TOIL.

play noun **1** *children at play* | *prefer play to work* amusement, entertainment, recreation, diversion, leisure, enjoyment, fun, merrymaking, revelry. **2** *appear in a play by a local dramatist* drama, stage play, stage show, radio play, television play, teleplay, comedy, tragedy, farce. **3** *the play of supernatural forces* action, activity, operation, agency, working, functioning, exercise, interaction, interplay. **4** *need more play on the fishing line* movement, freedom of movement, free motion, slack; *inf.* give. **5** *give full play to her emotions* scope, range, latitude, liberty, license, freedom, indulgence, free rein. **6** *made sarcastic remarks in play* fun, jest, joking, sport, teasing.

playboy noun pleasure seeker, man about town, socialite, rake, roué, womanizer, philanderer, ladies' man, lady-killer, lothario, Casanova, Don Juan, debauchee.

player noun **1** *one of the players in the game/tournament/competition* competitor, contestant, participant, team member, athlete, sportsman/sportswoman. **2** *one of the players in the theater company* actor/actress, performer, entertainer, artist, artiste, trouper, thespian. **3** *several of the players in the orchestra* performer, musician, instrumentalist, artist, artiste, virtuoso.

playful adjective **1** *playful kitten* | *in a playful mood* fun-loving, full of fun, high-spirited, frisky, skittish, coltish, frolicsome, sportive, mischievous, impish, puckish. **2** *a playful remark* in fun, in jest, joking, jesting, humorous, fun, facetious, waggish, tongue-in-cheek, arch, roguish.
Antonyms: SOLEMN; SERIOUS.

playground noun play area, park, playing field.

playwright noun *plays written by various playwrights* dramatist, dramaturge, dramaturgist.

plea noun **1** *make a plea to the governor to save his life* appeal, entreaty, imploration, supplication, petition, prayer, request, solicitation, suit, invocation. **2** *enter a plea of "guilty"* | *her plea was* *"not guilty"* answer, statement. **3** *evidence in support of his plea against the accused* allegation, case, suit, action, claim. **4** *ignore her pleas of a previous engagement* excuse, pretext, claim.

plead *verb plead insanity as the reason for his crime* put forward, state, assert, argue, claim, allege.

plead with *plead with the judge to show mercy* appeal to, beg, entreat, beseech, implore, petition, make supplication to, supplicate, importune, pray to, solicit, request, ask earnestly, present one's case to.

pleasant *adjective* **1** *a pleasant experience* pleasing, pleasurable, agreeable, enjoyable, entertaining, amusing, delightful, satisfying, gratifying, nice, good, fine, welcome, acceptable; *inf.* lovely. **2** *a pleasant person/manner* agreeable, friendly, amiable, affable, genial, likable, nice, good-humored, charming, engaging, winning, delightful; *inf.* lovely.

Antonyms: UNPLEASANT; DISAGREEABLE.

---

pleasant
agreeable, attractive, congenial, enjoyable, gratifying, pleasing

One might have a **pleasant** smile and a **pleasing** personality, since the former suggests something that is naturally appealing while the latter suggests a conscious attempt to please. Something that is **enjoyable** is able to give enjoyment or pleasure (*a thoroughly enjoyable evening*), while **agreeable** describes something that is in harmony with one's personal mood or wishes (*an agreeable afternoon spent relaxing in the sun*). **Gratifying** is more intense, suggesting that deeper expectations or needs have been met (*the awards ceremony was particularly gratifying for parents*). Something that is **attractive** gives pleasure because of its appearance or manner (*an attractive house in a wooded setting*), while **congenial** has more to do with compatibility (*a congenial couple*).

---

pleasantry *noun* **1** *exchange pleasantries with his neighbor* good-natured remark, polite remark. **2** *laugh at the speaker's pleasantries* joke, jest, quip, witticism, bon mot; *inf.* wisecrack.

please *verb* **1** *a gift that will please his mother* give pleasure to, be agreeable to, make pleased/happy/glad, gladden, delight, cheer up, charm, divert, entertain, amuse, tickle, satisfy, gratify, fulfill, content, suit; *inf.* tickle pink. **2** *do as one pleases* want, wish, see fit, will, like, desire, be inclined, prefer, opt.

Antonyms: DISPLEASE; dissatisfy; ANNOY; BORE.

pleased *adjective give a pleased smile* happy, glad, cheerful, delighted, thrilled, elated, contented, satisfied, gratified, fulfilled, as pleased as Punch; *inf.* on cloud nine.

pleasing *adjective* **1** *a pleasing experience* pleasant, pleasurable, agreeable, enjoyable, entertaining, amusing, delightful, satisfying, grati-

fying, nice, good, fine, welcome, acceptable; *inf.* lovely. **2** *he had/was a pleasing personality* pleasant, agreeable, friendly, amiable, affable, genial, likable, nice, good-humored, charming, engaging, winning, delightful; *inf.* lovely.

pleasure *noun* **1** *events that bring pleasure* happiness, gladness, delight, joy, enjoyment, entertainment, amusement, diversion, satisfaction, gratification, fulfillment, contentment. **2** *one of his pleasures was to play the piano* source of pleasure, delight, joy, enjoyment, diversion, recreation. **3** *the pursuit of pleasure* delight, joy, enjoyment, diversion, recreation. **4** *what is your pleasure?* wish, desire, will, inclination, preference, choice, option, purpose.

Antonyms: DISPLEASURE; SORROW; PAIN.

plebeian *adjective* **1** *of plebeian origins* lower-class, low-class, low, lowborn, working-class, proletarian, common, peasant, mean, ignoble; *inf.* blue-collar. **2** *have plebeian tastes* uncultivated, uncultured, unrefined, coarse, common, base.

Antonyms: ARISTOCRATIC; UPPER-CLASS.

plebeian *noun aristocrats looking down on the plebeians* common person, commoner, man/woman/person in the street, proletarian, peasant; *inf.* pleb.

pledge *noun* **1** *give his pledge to look after the children* promise, word, word of honor, vow, assurance, undertaking, oath, covenant, warrant. **2** *give his watch as a pledge that he would repay the loan* security, surety, guarantee, collateral, bond, earnest, deposit, pawn. **3** *give her a ring as a pledge of his love* token, symbol, sign, mark, testimony, proof, evidence.

pledge *verb* **1** *he pledged that he would support the children* promise, give one's word, vow, give one's assurance, give an undertaking, undertake, take an oath, swear, swear an oath, vouch, engage, contract. **2** *pledge one's house as security for a personal loan* mortgage, put up as collateral, guarantee, pawn.

plentiful *adjective plentiful supplies of food* abundant, copious, ample, profuse, lavish, liberal, generous, large, huge, bumper, infinite.

Antonyms: MEAGER; SPARSE; SCANTY.

plenty *noun the years of plenty* plentifulness, plenteousness, affluence, prosperity, wealth, opulence, luxury, abundance, copiousness, fruitfulness, profusion. **plenty of** *have plenty of money* enough, sufficient, a good deal of, a great deal of, masses of; *inf.* lots of, heaps of, stacks of, piles of, tons of.

plethora *noun a plethora of good advice* overabundance, superabundance, excess, superfluity, surplus, surfeit, glut.

Antonyms: DEARTH; LACK.

pliable *adjective* **1** *a pliable substance* flexible, bendable, bendy, pliant, elastic, supple, stretchable, ductile, plastic. **2** *expect the army recruits to be pliable* malleable, yielding, compliant, docile, biddable, tractable, manageable, governable, controllable, amenable, adaptable, flexible, impressionable, persuadable.

Antonyms: RIGID; INTRACTABLE; OBDURATE.

plight *noun the plight of the homeless | the plight they are in* unfortunate situation, sorry condition, predicament, trouble, difficulty, dire straits, extremity, tight corner; *inf.* hole, pickle, spot, jam.

plod *verb plod along the road* walk heavily, trudge, clump, stomp, lumber, tramp, drag oneself along. **plod away** *plod away at/with one's work* toil away, labor, slog away, drudge away, persevere, peg away, grind away; *inf.* plug away.

plot *noun* **1** *rebels planning a plot against the dictator* conspiracy, intrigue, secret plan, secret scheme, stratagem. **2** *the plot of the novel/play* action, theme, subject, story line, story, scenario, thread. **3** *grow vegetables in a plot | a burial plot* piece of ground, patch, allotment, lot, parcel.

---

plot
cabal, conspiracy, intrigue, machination

If you come up with a secret plan to do something, especially with evil or mischievous intent, it's called a **plot** (*a plot to seize control of the company*). If you get other people or groups involved in your plot, it's called a **conspiracy** (*a conspiracy to overthrow the government*). **Cabal** usually applies to a small group of political conspirators (*a cabal of right-wing extremists*), while **machination** (usually plural) suggests deceit and cunning in devising a plot intended to harm someone (*the machinations of the would-be assassins*). An **intrigue** involves more complicated scheming or maneuvering than a plot and often employs underhanded methods in an attempt to gain one's own ends (*she had a passion for intrigue, particularly where romance was involved*).

---

plot *verb* **1** *plot the escape route | plot the new construction site* map out, make a plan/drawing of, draw, draw a diagram of, draw the layout of, make a blueprint/chart of, sketch out, outline. **2** *plot the battle sites on the map* mark, chart, map. **3** *rebels plotting against the dictator* take part in a plot, scheme, conspire, participate in a conspiracy, intrigue, form an intrigue. **4** *plot the dictator's downfall* plan, hatch, scheme, construe, concoct, devise, frame, think up, dream up, conceive; *inf.* cook up.

plow *verb* **1** *plow the field* till, work, cultivate, break up, turn up. **2** *the car plowed into a snowbank* plunge, lunge, career, crash, smash, bulldoze, hurtle, drive. **3** *plow through the mud* plod, trudge, clump, push one's way, forge one's way, wade, flounder.

ploy *noun a ploy to distract the teacher* dodge, ruse, scheme, trick, stratagem, maneuver, move.

pluck *verb* **1** *pluck a rose from the bush | pluck the burning paper from the fire* pull, pull off/out, remove, extract. **2** *pluck flowers to make perfume |*

pluck blackberries for jam gather, collect, pick, harvest, take in, pull, cull. **3** *pluck the string of the guitar* finger, strum, pick, plunk, thrum, twang. **pluck at** *plucking at her mother's skirt* tug at, pull at, clutch at, snatch at, catch at, tweak; *inf.* yank (at).

pluck *noun took a lot of pluck to go into the jungle alone* courage, bravery, valor, heroism, intrepidity, fearlessness, mettle, nerve, backbone, determination, boldness, daring, spirit, audacity; *inf.* gumption, grit, guts, spunk.

plucky *adjective* courageous, brave, valiant, valorous, heroic, intrepid, fearless, mettlesome, gritty, determined, bold, daring, spirited, audacious; *inf.* gutsy, spunky.

Antonyms: COWARDLY; TIMOROUS; TIMID.

plug *noun* **1** *put a plug in the bathtub/jug* stopper, bung, cork, stopple, seal. **2** *a plug of tobacco* cake, chew, twist, quid, wad. **3** *the talk-show host gave his book a free plug* publicity, advertisement, commercial, promotion, push, mention; *inf.* ad, hype.

plug *verb* **1** *plug the hole in the tank* stop up, close off, bung, cork, dam up, block, stopper, stopple, seal off, pack, stuff. **2** *a gangster plugging his enemy* shoot, shoot down, gun down, put a bullet in, hit, take out, pick off. **3** *plug his new book on television* publicize, promote, give publicity to, advertise, play up, push, give a push to, give a mention to, write up, build up; *inf.* hype, hype up. **plug away** *plug away at the investigation | must keep plugging away* toil away, labor, slog away, plod away, drudge away, persevere, grind away.

plum *adjective get a plum job* prize, first-class, choice, best, excellent; *inf.* primo.

plumb *adverb* **1** *cliffs rising up plumb from the sea* vertically, perpendicularly, straight up, straight up and down. **2** *placed plumb in the center* exactly, precisely, right, dead; *inf.* bang, right on. **3** *plumb crazy* utterly, absolutely, completely, totally, entirely, wholly, quite, stark.

plumb *verb plumb the mysteries of computer technology* probe, search out, delve into, explore, scrutinize, investigate, inspect, examine, sound out, go into, fathom, unravel. **plumb the depths of** *plumb the depths of despair | jokes that plumb the depths of bad taste* reach the lowest possible level of, reach the lowest point, reach the nadir of.

plummet *verb* **1** *the kite/plane plummeted to the ground* fall perpendicularly, fall headlong, plunge, hurtle, nosedive, dive, drop. **2** *prices plummeted* fall steeply, plunge, tumble, nosedive, take a nosedive, drop rapidly, go down.

plump *adjective* chubby, round, rounded, of ample proportions, rotund, buxom, stout, fat, fattish, obese, corpulent, fleshy, portly, tubby, dumpy, pudgy, roly-poly; *inf.* well-upholstered, beefy.

Antonyms: THIN; SLENDER; SKINNY.

plump verb *plump down into a chair* fall, drop, flop, plunk, sink, collapse.

plunder verb **1** *enemy forces plundering the villages* rob, pillage, loot, raid, ransack, rifle, strip, fleece, ravage, lay waste, despoil, spoil, spoliate, deprecate, harry, maraud, sack, rape. **2** *plunder food* steal, thieve, rob, purloin, filch, make off with; *inf.* walk away/off with.

plunder noun **1** *the plunder of the village* plundering, robbery, robbing, pillaging, looting, raiding, ransacking, despoiling, laying waste, harrying, marauding, rapine. **2** *take their plunder back to camp* stolen goods, loot, booty, spoils, prize, pillage, ill-gotten gains; *inf.* swag.

plunge verb **1** *plunge the dagger into his back* thrust, stick, jab, push, drive. **2** *the falcon plunged into the sea* dive, nosedive, jump, plummet, drop, fall, fall headlong, swoop down, descend. **3** *plunge the house into darkness* throw, cast, pitch. **4** *plunge his burned hand into cold water* immerse, sink, dip, douse. **5** *the car plunged forward | plunge into matrimony* charge, lurch, rush, dash, hurtle, career. **6** *real-estate prices plunged during the recession* fall steeply, drop rapidly, go down, plummet, tumble, nosedive, take a nosedive.

plunge noun **1** *his plunge into the sea* dive, nosedive, jump, fall, drop, swoop, descent. **2** *the car's sudden plunge forward* charge, lurch, rush, dash. **3** *an unexpected plunge in prices* fall, drop, tumble, nosedive.

plus preposition **1** *3 plus 3 equals 6* and, added to. **2** *four people, plus their luggage* as well as, in addition to, added to, and, coupled with, with.

plus noun *use of the company car is a definite plus* bonus, extra, added advantage, additional benefit, fringe benefit, perquisite; *inf.* perk.

plush adjective *plush furnishings* luxurious, luxury, deluxe, sumptuous, lavish, gorgeous, opulent, rich, costly; *inf.* ritzy, classy.
Antonyms: PLAIN; AUSTERE; CHEAP.

plutocrat noun rich person, person of means, capitalist, tycoon, magnate, millionaire, billionaire, Midas, Croesus; *inf.* fat cat, moneybags.

ply verb **1** *plying the oars* wield, use, operate, work, utilize, employ, manipulate, handle. **2** *ply his trade as a plumber* carry on, practice, work at, engage in, pursue, follow, occupy oneself with, busy oneself with. **3** *ply them with questions* bombard, assail, besiege, beset, harass, importune; *inf.* hassle. **4** *ply them with food and drink* supply, provide, lavish, shower, load, heap. **5** *ships plying between Cape Cod and Nantucket* travel regularly, go regularly, ferry, shuttle.

poach verb **1** *poach pheasants* hunt illegally, take illegally, kill illegally, trap illegally, steal. **2** *poach on his neighbor's property* trespass, encroach, infringe, intrude. **3** *poach his friend's*

pocket noun **1** *pants pocket | pockets on the side of the suitcase* pouch, compartment, receptacle. **2** *isolated pockets of resistance to the government* small area, small region, small district, small zone.

pocket adjective *a pocket edition of the reference book* small, little, miniature, compact, concise, abridged.

pocket verb *pocketing money from the cash register* appropriate, misappropriate, steal, thieve, purloin, filch; *inf.* lift, swipe.

pod noun *pea pod* shell, husk, hull, case, shuck; pericarp.

podium noun *deliver an address from the podium* platform, stage, dais, rostrum, stand.

poem noun piece of poetry, verse composition, verse, ode, sonnet, ballad, song, lyric, lay, elegy, rhyme, limerick, haiku, jingle.

poet noun versifier, rhymer, rhymester, balladeer, lyricist, bard, minstrel; *derog.* poetaster, sonneteer, balladmonger.

poetic adjective **1** *write poetic works* of poetry, poetical, metrical, rhythmical, lyrical, elegiac. **2** *poetic language* imaginative, creative, figurative, symbolic, flowery. **3** *a poetic rendering of the symphony* aesthetic, artistic, tasteful, graceful, elegant, sensitive.

poetry noun *write poetry rather than prose* poems, verse, verses, versification, metrical composition, rhythmical composition, rhymes, rhyming.

pogrom noun massacre, wholesale/general slaughter, mass killing, mass murder, mass homicide, carnage, blood bath, genocide, ethnic cleansing, megadeath.

poignancy noun emotionalness, emotion, sentiment, feeling, pathos, sadness, sorrowfulness, tearfulness, evocativeness, pitifulness, piteousness.

poignant adjective moving, affecting, touching, emotional, sentimental, heartfelt, sad, sorrowful, tearful, evocative, pitiful, piteous, pitiable.

point noun **1** *the point of the spear/tool* sharp end, tapered end, tip, top, extremity, prong, spike, tine. **2** *ships sailing around the point* promontory, headland, head, foreland, cape, bluff. **3** *Gettysburg is a point of great interest* place, position, location, situation, site, spot, area, locality. **4** *abrupt to the point of rudeness* extent, degree, stage. **5** *reach an important point in her life* stage, position, circumstance, condition. **6** *have to go home at some point* point/moment in time, time, juncture, stage, period, moment, instant. **7** *at the point where he could not face her* critical point, decisive point, crux, moment of truth, point of no return. **8** *explain the situation point by point* detail, item, particular. **9** *get to the point | the point of the question* main point, central point, essential point, focal point, salient point, keynote, heart of the matter, essence, nub, core, pith, marrow, meat, crux.

10 *miss the point of the story* meaning, significance, signification, import, essence, gist, substance, drift, thrust, burden, theme, tenor, vein. **11** *raise various points during the discussion* subject, subject under discussion, issue, topic, question, matter, item. **12** *the various points of the argument* part, element, constituent, component, ingredient. **13** *what is the point of it?* aim, purpose, object, objective, goal, intention, reason for, use, utility. **14** *kindness is one of his strong points* characteristic, trait, attribute, quality, feature, property, predisposition, streak, peculiarity, idiosyncrasy. **15** *have more points than the other team* mark, score. **beside the point** *their religious beliefs are beside the point* irrelevant, immaterial, incidental, not to the point, not germane, not to the purpose. **in point of fact** *people think he is stupid, but in point of fact he is brilliant* in fact, as a matter of fact, actually, really, in reality, in truth, truly. **point of view 1** *listen to everyone's point of view* view, viewpoint, opinion, belief, attitude, feeling, sentiment, stand, standpoint, stance, position. **2** *look at the situation from a different point of view* viewpoint, angle, slant, perspective, standpoint, outlook. **to the point** *his remarks were very much to the point* pertinent, relevant, germane, applicable, apropos, apposite, appropriate, apt, fitting, suitable. **up to a point** *I agree with you up to a point* to some extent, to some degree, in part, partly.

point *verb* *point the gun* direct, aim, level, train. **point out** *point out the disadvantages of the proposal* call attention to, draw attention to, indicate, show, specify, designate, identify, mention, allude to. **point to** *all the evidence points to the fact that he is the murderer* indicate, show, signify, suggest, be evidence of, evidence. **point up** *point up the difference between them* emphasize, put/lay emphasis on, stress, lay stress on, accentuate, underline, underscore, give prominence to, highlight, spotlight, play up, bring to the fore.

point-blank *adverb* **1** *shot him point-blank* at close range, close up, close to. **2** *ask him point-blank for his reasons* | *refuse point-blank to go* directly, plainly, straight, straightforwardly, frankly, candidly, forthrightly, bluntly, openly, explicitly, unequivocally, unambiguously.

pointed *adjective* **1** *the pointed end of the stick* sharp, sharp-edged, edged, cuspidate, acicular. **2** *a pointed remark* cutting, trenchant, biting, incisive, penetrating, forceful, telling, significant. **3** *treat her with a pointed indifference* obvious, evident, conspicuous, striking, emphasized, unmistakable.

pointer *noun* **1** *the pointer on the speedometer* indicator, needle, hand, arrow, cursor. **2** *indicate the place on a map with a pointer* stick, rod. **3** *the older players will give you a few pointers* tip, hint, clue, piece of advice, suggestion, guideline, recommendation.

pointless *adjective* **1** *it is pointless to try to go on in this bad weather* futile, useless, in vain, unavailing, to no purpose, valueless, unproductive, senseless, absurd, foolish, nonsensical, stupid, silly. **2** *a few pointless remarks* meaningless, insignificant, vague, empty, worthless, irrelevant, senseless, fatuous, foolish, nonsensical, stupid, silly, absurd, inane.
Antonyms: USEFUL; VALUABLE; SIGNIFICANT.

poise *noun* **1** *admire her poise in difficulties* composure, equanimity, self-possession, aplomb, presence of mind, self-assurance, self-control, calmness, coolness, collectedness, serenity, dignity, imperturbability, suaveness, urbanity, elegance; *inf.* cool. **2** *admire the poise of the ballet dancers* balance, equilibrium, control, grace, gracefulness.

poise *verb* **1** *poise a jug of water on her head* balance, steady, position, support. **2** *poise oneself to jump* steady, get into position, brace, get ready, prepare. **3** *the hawk poised in midair ready to attack* hang, hang suspended, float, hover.

poised *adjective* **1** *a very poised young woman* composed, collected, self-possessed, self-assured, self-controlled, calm, cool, serene, dignified, imperturbable, unperturbed, unruffled, suave, urbane, elegant; *inf.* unflappable. **2** *soldiers poised to attack* | *poised to take over the president's job* ready, prepared, all set, standing by, waiting (and ready), waiting in the wings.
Antonyms: PERTURBED; flustered.

poison *noun* **1** *the snake's deadly poison* venom, toxin. **2** *a poison in our society* blight, bane, contagion, cancer, canker, malignancy, corruption, pollution.

poison *verb* **1** *poisoned the victim* administer poison to, give poison to, kill by poison, murder by poison. **2** *poison the environment/soil* contaminate, pollute, blight, spoil, infect, defile, adulterate. **3** *poison their minds* corrupt, warp, pervert, deprave, defile, debauch.

poisonous *adjective* **1** *poisonous snakes/plants/chemicals* venomous, toxic, mephitic, noxious, deadly, fatal, lethal. **2** *a poisonous influence on society* cancerous, malignant, corrupting, polluting, harmful, injurious, noxious, pernicious, spiteful, malicious, rancorous, malevolent, vicious, vindictive, slanderous, libelous, defamatory.
Antonyms: HARMLESS; non-toxic; BENIGN.

poke *verb* **1** *poke him in the ribs* jab, prod, dig, elbow, nudge, butt. **2** *poke a key through the hole* jab, push, thrust, shove, stick. **poke around** *poke around his possessions* rummage around, forage through, ransack, nose around, pry into. **poke fun at** *poking fun at his clumsiness* make fun of, laugh at, mock, jeer at, ridicule, deride, tease, chaff, taunt; *inf.* send up, rib, rag. **poke one's nose into** *poke your nose into my private affairs* pry into, interfere in, nose around in, intrude on, butt into, meddle with, tamper with;

inf. snoop into. **poke out** *a letter poking out from her bag* stick out, jut out, protrude, project, extend.

poke *noun* jab, prod, dig, nudge, elbow, butt, push, thrust, shove.

poky *adjective always late because he is so poky* slow, slow-moving, dawdling, unhurried, laggard.

polar *adjective* **1** *polar conditions* arctic, frozen, freezing, icy, glacial, cold. **2** *polar political ideals* opposite, opposed, diametrically opposed, contrary, antithetical, antagonistic, conflicting.

polarity *noun the growing polarity between their political views* difference, separation, opposition, contrariety, antithesis, antagonism, conflict.

pole[1] *noun* **1** *poles supporting the bridge* post, upright, pillar, stanchion, standard, support, prop, rod, shaft, mast. **2** *jump over the pole* bar, rod, stick.

pole[2] *noun our points of view are at opposite poles* extremity, extreme, limit. **be poles apart** *be poles apart in their attitudes* be completely different, be widely separated, be incompatible, be worlds apart, be at opposite extremes, be like night and day.

polemics *plural noun skilled in polemics* argument, argumentation, debate, dispute, disputation, discussion, controversy, wrangling.

police *noun send for the police | wanted by the police* police force, the law, policemen, policewomen, police officers, constabulary; *inf.* the cops, the boys in blue; *derog* the fuzz, the pigs.

police *verb* **1** *police the school buildings* patrol, make the rounds of, guard, keep guard over, keep watch on, protect. **2** *police the soccer match* keep in order, control, keep under control, regulate, enforce, administer, oversee, monitor.

policeman, policewoman *noun* police officer, officer of the law, lawman, patrolman, patrolwoman, gendarme; *inf.* cop, copper; *derog* pig.

policy *noun the government's educational policy | not company policy* plan, scheme, program, schedule, code, system, approach, procedure, guideline, theory.

polish *verb polish the table* wax, buff, rub, burnish, shine. **polish off** *polish off his meal quickly* finish, eat up, consume, devour, eat greedily, wolf down, down, bolt. **polish up (on)** *polish up (on) her French/etiquette* perfect, refine, improve, brush up.

---

polish
gloss, luster, sheen

All of these words refer to a smooth, shining, or bright surface that reflects light. If this surface is produced by rubbing or friction, the correct word is **polish** (*the car's mirrorlike polish was the result of regular waxing and buffing*). **Gloss**, on the other hand, suggests the hard smoothness associated with lacquered, varnished, or enameled surfaces (*a high-gloss paint*). **Luster** is associated with the light reflected from the surfaces of certain materials, such as silk or pearl (*a green stone with a brilliant luster*). **Sheen** describes a glistening or radiant brightness that is also associated with specific materials (*her hair had a rich, velvety sheen*).

---

polished *adjective* **1** *a polished table* waxed, buffed, burnished, shining, shiny, glossy, gleaming, lustrous, glassy, slippery. **2** *polished manners* refined, cultivated, civilized, well-bred, polite, well-mannered, genteel, courtly, urbane, suave, sophisticated. **3** *give a polished performance at the concert* expert, accomplished, masterly, skillful, proficient, adept, impeccable, flawless, faultless, perfect, consummate, exquisite, outstanding, remarkable.

Antonyms: DULL; tarnished; ROUGH; INEXPERT.

polite *adjective* **1** *too polite to interrupt/complain/belch* well-mannered, mannerly, courteous, civil, respectful, deferential, well-behaved, well-bred, genteel, polished, tactful, diplomatic. **2** *things not done in polite society* well-bred, civilized, cultured, refined, polished, genteel, urbane, sophisticated, elegant, courtly.

Antonyms: RUDE; IMPOLITE; UNMANNERLY; UNCOUTH.

politic *adjective think it politic to leave | a politic young man* wise, prudent, sensible, advisable, judicious, well-judged, sagacious, expedient, shrewd, astute, discreet, tactful, diplomatic.

political *adjective* **1** *hold a political position* governmental, ministerial, public, civic, administrative, bureaucratic. **2** *dismissed for political reasons* factional, partisan, bipartisan, power, status.

politician *noun* statesman, stateswoman, legislator, lawmaker, public servant; senator, congressman, congresswoman, representative; officeholder, bureaucrat; *inf.* politico.

politics *noun* **1** *a career in politics* government, local government, affairs of state, party politics. **2** *study politics* political science, civics, statecraft, statesmanship. **3** *plural noun what are his politics?* party politics, political alliance, political belief. **4** *plural noun resigned because of the politics within the company* power struggle, manipulation, maneuvering, jockeying for position, Machiavellianism, opportunism, realpolitik.

poll *noun* **1** *organize a poll to decide on the best candidate* vote, ballot, vote-casting, canvass, headcount, show of hands, straw vote/poll. **2** *a poll heavily in favor of the present administration* voting figures, returns, count, tally. **3** *conduct a poll to investigate people's eating habits* opinion poll, Gallup poll, survey, market research, sampling.

poll *verb* **1** *poll more votes than his opponent* register, record, return, get, gain. **2** *poll one hun-*

canvass, question, interview, survey, sample.

pollute *verb* **1** *pollute the water/soil with chemicals* | *pollute the environment* contaminate, adulterate, infect, taint, poison, befoul, foul, make dirty, make filthy. **2** *pollute the minds of the young* corrupt, poison, warp, pervert, deprave, defile, debauch. **3** *pollute the good name of the family* besmirch, sully, taint, blacken, tarnish, dishonor, debase, vitiate, desecrate.

Antonyms: PURIFY; CLEAN; DISINFECT.

---

pollute
adulterate, contaminate, defile, taint

When a factory pours harmful chemicals or wastes into the air or water, it is said to **pollute** the environment. But *pollute* may also refer to impairing the purity, integrity, or effectiveness of something (*a campaign polluted by allegations of sexual impropriety*). To **contaminate** is to spread harmful or undesirable impurities throughout something; unlike *pollute*, which suggests visible or noticeable impurities, **contaminate** is preferred where the change is unsuspected or not immediately noticeable (*milk contaminated by radioactive fallout from a nuclear plant accident*). **Adulterate** often refers to food products to which harmful, low-quality, or low-cost substances have been added in order to defraud the consumer (*cereal adulterated with sawdust*), although this word can apply to any mixture to which the inferior or harmful element is added deliberately and in the hope that no one will notice (*a report adulterated with false statistics*). To **defile** is to pollute something that should be kept pure or sacred (*a church defiled by vandals*), while **taint** implies that a trace of something toxic or corrupt has been introduced (*he contracted the disease from a tainted blood transfusion; the book is tainted by gratuitous violence*).

---

pollution *noun* **1** *chemicals involved in the pollution of our water* contaminating, contamination, adulteration, adulterating, infecting, tainting, befouling, fouling, foulness, dirtying, dirtiness, impurity, filthiness. **2** *the pollution of young minds* corruption, corrupting, poisoning, warping, depraving. *See* POLLUTE 2. **3** *the pollution of their good name* besmirching, sullying, tainting, blackening. *See* POLLUTE 3. **4** *concerned about the pollution in our society* corruption, poison, blight, contagion, cancer, canker, malignancy, bane.

pomp *noun* **1** *the pomp of the coronation* ceremony, ceremoniousness, ritual, display, pageantry, pageant, show, spectacle, splendor, grandeur, magnificence, majesty, glory, brilliance, flourish, style. **2** *more interested in pomp than substance* ostentation, exhibitionism, grandiosity, glitter, show, showiness, pomposity, vainglory, fanfaronade.

pomposity *noun* **1** *irritated by the pomposity of the official* pompousness, presumption, self-importance, presumptuousness, imperiousness, grandiosity, affectation, airs, pretentiousness, pretension, arrogance, vanity, haughtiness, pride, conceit, egotism, superciliousness, condescension, patronization; *inf.* uppishness. **2** *the pomposity of the language* pompousness, bombast, turgidity, portentousness, grandiloquence, magniloquence, euphuism, pedantry, stiltedness, fustian.

pompous *adjective* **1** *a pompous official* self-important, presumptuous, imperious, overbearing, grandiose, affected, pretentious, arrogant, vain, haughty, proud, conceited, egotistic, supercilious, condescending, patronizing; *inf.* uppity, uppish. **2** *pompous language* high-sounding, high-flown, bombastic, turgid, grandiloquent, magniloquent, euphuistic, portentous, pedantic, stilted, fustian.

Antonyms: MODEST; HUMBLE; self-effacing; UNPRETENTIOUS.

pond *noun* pool, puddle, lake, tarn, millpond, duck pond, fishpond.

ponder *verb* **1** *take time to ponder his previous behavior* think about, give thought to, consider, reflect on, mull over, contemplate, meditate on, deliberate about/on, dwell on, brood on/over, ruminate about/on/over, puzzle over, cogitate about/on, weigh up, review. **2** *sit in the dark and ponder* think, consider, reflect, meditate, contemplate, deliberate, brood, ruminate, cogitate, cerebrate.

ponderous *adjective* **1** *ponderous movements* heavy, slow, awkward, clumsy, lumbering, heavy-footed. **2** *a ponderous style* | *a piece of ponderous prose* heavy, awkward, clumsy, lumbering, heavy-footed, labored, forced, stilted, turgid, stodgy, lifeless, plodding, dull, boring, uninteresting, tedious, monotonous, dry, dreary, pedantic, verbose.

Antonyms: GRACEFUL; ELEGANT; LIVELY.

pontificate *verb* *pontificate about the rights and wrongs of the situation* hold forth, expound, declaim, preach, lay down the law, sound off, dogmatize, sermonize; *inf.* preachify.

pooh-pooh *verb* *pooh-pooh their attempts to raise money* ridicule, deride, disregard, brush aside, dismiss, make light of, belittle, hold up to scorn, treat with contempt, scoff at, sneer at.

pool[1] *noun* **1** *resting by a mountain pool* pond, water/watering hole, puddle, tide/tidal pool, lake, tarn. **2** *a pool of blood* puddle. **3** *swim six laps in the pool* swimming pool.

pool[2] *noun* **1** *a pool of parents to drive the children* | *typing pool* consortium, syndicate, collective, combine, group, team. **2** *a pool of cars for the sales reps* common supply, supply, reserve. **3** *the pool in a gambling game* stakes, bank, kitty, purse, jackpot, ante, fund.

pool[3] *verb* *pool their resources/ideas* put together, combine, amalgamate, merge, share.

poor *adjective* **1** *poor people with few belongings* |

live in poor circumstances badly off, poverty-stricken, penniless, hard up, needy, deprived, in need, needful, in want, indigent, impoverished, impecunious, destitute, penurious, beggared, in straitened circumstances, as poor as a church mouse, in the red; *inf.* broke, stone-broke, flat broke, on the rocks. **2** *live in poor surroundings* humble, lowly, mean, modest, plain. **3** *a poor diet/performance* inadequate, deficient, insufficient, unsatisfactory, below standard, below par, inferior, imperfect, bad, low-grade. **4** *a poor crop of apples* sparse, scanty, meager, scarce, skimpy, reduced, paltry, miserable, exiguous. **5** *a diet poor in nutrients* deficient, lacking, wanting, insufficient. **6** *poor furniture* | *goods of poor quality* unsatisfactory, defective, faulty, imperfect, below standard, inferior, low-grade, second-rate, third-rate, jerry-built; *inf.* junky, crummy, cheesy. **7** *poor soil* unproductive, barren, unyielding, unfruitful, uncultivable, uncultivatable, bare, arid, sterile, infecund, unfecund. **8** *you poor thing* wretched, pitiable, pitiful, unfortunate, unlucky, luckless, unhappy, hapless, ill-fated, ill-starred. **9** *a poor specimen of a man* miserable, sad, sorry, spiritless, mean, low, base, disgraceful, despicable, contemptible, abject, pathetic.
Antonyms: WEALTHY; RICH; SUPERIOR; SATISFACTORY.

poorly *adjective been too poorly to go to school* ill, unwell, sick, ailing, indisposed, below par, out of sorts; *inf.* under the weather.

poorly *adverb perform poorly in the competition* badly, inadequately, unsatisfactorily, unsuccessfully, incompetently, inexpertly.

pop *verb champagne corks popped* | *guns were popping* explode, go off, go off with a bang, go bang, bang, crack, burst, detonate. **pop in 1** *pop a coin in the slot* | *popped the ticket into her purse* insert, put in, place in, slip in, slide in, push in, stick in. **2** *pop in to see his mother* visit, go in, stop by; *inf.* drop in/by. **pop out/off** *just popping out to get a newspaper* go out quickly/briefly, leave quickly/briefly. **pop up** *snowdrops popping up all over the yard* | *a new case popped up every few weeks* appear, appear suddenly/abruptly, occur suddenly/abruptly, crop up.

pop *noun* **1** *champagne opening with a pop* | *balloons bursting with a pop* bang, crack, boom, burst, explosion, report, detonation. **2** *drink a bottle of pop* soda, soft drink; cola.

pope, Pope *noun* pontiff, Bishop of Rome, Holy Father, Vicar of Christ.

populace *noun* **1** *seeking the view of the populace* general public, public, people, population, common people, common folk, masses, commonalty, mob, multitude, rabble, rank and file, hoi polloi; *inf.* plebs. **2** *populace of the city* population, inhabitants, residents.

popular *adjective* **1** *a popular choice/teacher* |

teachers popular with the students well-liked, liked, favored, in favor, favorite, well-received, approved, admired, accepted. **2** *these items are so popular that we have run out* well-liked, liked, in favor, well-received, sought-after, in demand, desired, wanted, fashionable, in fashion, in vogue, in. **3** *popular movie stars* well-known, famous, celebrated, renowned. **4** *for the popular market* | *a range of popular cars* inexpensive, budget, low-budget, low-priced, cheap, reasonably priced, reasonable, moderately priced, modestly priced. **5** *popular literature/music/science* | *the popular press* middle-of-the-road, middlebrow, lowbrow, accessible, simple, understandable, readily understood, easy to understand, readily comprehensible; *inf.* pop. **6** *issues of popular concern* public, general, civic. **7** *popular beliefs/myths* current, prevalent, prevailing, accepted, recognized, widespread, universal, general, common, customary, usual, standard, stock, conventional.
Antonyms: UNPOPULAR; UNKNOWN; HIGHBROW.

popularity *noun* **1** *teachers gaining in popularity* | *teachers winning popularity with the students* favor, approval, approbation, admiration, acceptance. **2** *restocking the items due to their popularity* demand, fashionableness, vogue, trendiness. **3** *ideas gaining popularity* | *myths losing popularity* currency, prevalence, prevalency, recognition. **4** *the popularity of the entertainer* fame, renown, acclaim, esteem, repute.

popularize *verb* **1** *popularize classical music* simplify, make mass-market, give mass appeal to, make accessible to all. **2** *popularize the belief that the world is flat* give currency to, give credence to, universalize, generalize, spread, disseminate.

popularly *adverb it was popularly believed that the mentally ill were demonic* | *President Kennedy, popularly known as JFK* widely, generally, universally, commonly, usually, regularly, customarily, ordinarily, traditionally.

populate *verb* **1** *nomadic tribes populate the area* | *an area largely populated by nomadic tribes* inhabit, dwell in, occupy, people. **2** *newly discovered areas of the continent gradually populated by people from other countries* settle, colonize, people.

population *noun* **1** *the entire population of the town was affected by the closure of the factory* inhabitants, residents, community, people, citizenry, populace, society. **2** *the working population* | *the elderly population* people, folk, society. **3** *populations decreasing in rural areas* population count, numbers of inhabitants, census, headcount.

populous *adjective the populous urban areas of the country* densely populated, heavily populated, thickly populated, crowded.
Antonyms: EMPTY; UNINHABITED; DESERTED.

porch *noun* veranda, portico, stoa, piazza.

pore *verb* **pore over 1** *students poring over their books before the exams* | *poring over the map* study closely, read intently, peruse closely, be absorbed in, scrutinize, examine closely. **2** *poring over his problem* meditate on, brood on/over, go over, ponder, reflect on, deliberate on, mull over, muse on, think about, contemplate.

pore *noun perspiring from every pore* | *leaves absorbing moisture through their pores* opening, orifice, hole, aperture, vent, outlet; *Tech.* spiracle, stoma.

pornographic *adjective pornographic magazine/video* obscene, blue, salacious, lewd, prurient, erotic, indecent, dirty, smutty, filthy; *inf.* porn, porno.

Antonyms: DECENT; PURE.

pornography *noun* **1** *obsessed with pornography* obscenity, salaciousness, lewdness, prurience, erotica, indecency, smut, filth; *inf.* porn, porno, sexploitation. **2** *selling pornography* pornographic literature, pornographic movies/films/videos, erotica; *inf.* porn, hard porn, soft porn, porno, girlie magazines.

porous *adjective* absorbent, permeable, penetrable, pervious, spongelike, spongy, honeycombed, holey.

Antonyms: impermeable; IMPENETRABLE; IMPERVIOUS.

port *noun* seaport, harbor, harborage, haven, anchorage.

portable *adjective portable radios/computer* transportable, movable, conveyable, easily carried, lightweight, compact, handy, manageable.

portend *verb the gray sky portending a storm* | *his silence portends trouble* be a sign of, be a warning of, be an indication of, be a presage of, point to, be an omen of, herald, bode, augur, presage, forebode, foreshadow, foretell.

portent *noun* **1** *dark skies can be a portent of a storm* | *his silence was a portent of trouble* sign, indication, presage, warning, omen, harbinger, foreshadowing, augury. **2** *the lavish building was considered one of the portents of the modern world* marvel, wonder, prodigy, phenomenon, spectacle.

portentous *adjective* **1** *portentous events indicating that trouble was inevitable* ominous, warning, threatening, menacing, foreboding, foreshadowing, ill-omened. **2** *a portentous monument* marvelous, remarkable, prodigious, phenomenal, spectacular, wondrous, amazing, astounding. **3** *a portentous speech* pompous, pontifical, ponderous, solemn.

porter *noun porters carrying the luggage* carrier, bearer, baggage carrier; *inf.* redcap.

portion *noun* **1** *serve generous portions* helping, serving, piece, quantity. **2** *give a portion of his estate to each child* share, division, quota, part, bit, piece, allocation, allotment; *inf.* cut. **3** *her portion in life to serve others* lot, fate, destiny, fortune, luck.

portion *verb portion the estate among his children* share, divide, split, partition, carve up, parcel out; *inf.* divvy up. **portion out** *portion out pieces of cake* distribute, dispense, hand out, deal out,

dole out, divide out, share out, allocate, apportion, allot, parcel out, mete out; *inf.* divvy up.

portly *adjective* stout, plump, fat, corpulent, obese, tubby, of ample build, stocky.

portrait *noun* **1** *portraits of his ancestors hung on the walls* painting, picture, drawing, sketch, portrayal, representation, likeness, image, study, portraiture, canvas. **2** *have the photographer take a portrait of his daughter* photograph, photo, picture, studio portrait, study, shot, snapshot, snap, still. **3** *the writer's portrait of his childhood* description, portrayal, depiction, account, story, chronicle, thumbnail sketch, vignette, profile.

portray *verb* **1** *the artist portrayed the girl in a simple blue dress* paint a picture of, paint, draw a picture of, draw, sketch, depict, represent, delineate. **2** *portray a scene of abject poverty in his novel* describe, depict, characterize, paint a word picture of, paint in words, put into words. **3** *portray Hamlet's mother in the production* play, act the part of, play the part of, act, perform, represent, execute.

portrayal *noun* **1** *the artist's portrayal of the girl* painting, portrait, picture, drawing, sketch, representation, depiction, delineation, study. **2** *the writer's portrayal of their poverty* description, depiction, characterization, word picture, word painting. **3** *her portrayal of Hamlet's mother* acting in the role, performance, representation, interpretation.

pose *verb* **1** *ask him to pose for a portrait* sit, model, take up a position. **2** *carefully pose the subjects for his still life* arrange, position, lay out, set out, dispose, place, put, locate, situate. **3** *her posing impressed no one* strike an attitude, posture, put on an act, act, playact, attitudinize, put on airs, show off. **4** *pose a question* put forward, put, submit, advance, propound, posit. **5** *icy roads pose problems for drivers* present, set, create, cause, give rise to.

pose as *the con artist posed as a stockbroker* pretend to be, impersonate, pass oneself off as, masquerade as, profess to be, feign the identity of.

pose *noun* **1** *assume a pose for the photo session* posture, stance, position, attitude, bearing, carriage. **2** *her shyness is only a pose* act, playacting, pretense, façade, front, masquerade, posture, attitudinizing, affectation, airs.

poser *noun* **1** *the creation of the universe is a real poser* difficult question, awkward problem, vexed question, enigma, dilemma, puzzle, mystery, conundrum; *inf.* brainteaser. **2** *art students needing posers* model, sitter, subject. **3** *he is merely a poser* See POSEUR.

poseur *noun* poser, attitudinizer, posturer, playactor.

posh *adjective* *a posh hotel* luxurious, luxury, deluxe, sumptuous, opulent, lavish, rich, grand, elegant, ornate, fancy, plush; *inf.* classy, ritzy, swanky.

position noun **1** *a house in an isolated position | plants in a sunny position* situation, location, site, place, spot, area, locality, locale, scene, setting. **2** *identify the ship's position* location, bearings, whereabouts. **3** *sitting/standing in an uncomfortable position | in an upright position* posture, stance, attitude, pose, bearing. **4** *in an unfortunate financial position* situation, state, condition, circumstance, predicament, plight, pass. **5** *several people jockeying for position in the race* advantageous position, favorable position, primacy, the upper hand, the edge. **6** *declared their position on tax reform | speak from a position of knowledge* point of view, viewpoint, opinion, way of thinking, outlook, attitude, stand, standpoint, stance. **7** *apply for the vacant position of manager | his position as captain* post, job, situation, appointment, role, office, place, capacity, duty. **8** *what is his position in the class* place, level, grade, grading, rank, status, standing. **9** *people of position in society* rank, status, stature, standing, social standing, prestige, influence, reputation, importance, consequence.

position verb *position the building so that it faces south | position the soldiers in rows* place, locate, situate, put, arrange, set, settle, dispose, array.

positive adjective **1** *a set of positive rules | given positive instructions* clear, clear-cut, definite, precise, categorical, direct, explicit, express, firm. **2** *no positive proof of his guilt* real, actual, absolute, concrete, conclusive, unequivocal, incontrovertible, indisputable, undeniable, incontestable, unmistakable. **3** *they are positive that they have the solution* certain, sure, assured, confident, convinced. **4** *the results of the blood test are positive* affirmative. **5** *positive criticism* constructive, productive, helpful, practical, useful, beneficial. **6** *a positive attitude toward his work | positive thinking* confident, optimistic, assured, assertive, firm, forceful, determined, resolute, emphatic, dogmatic. **7** *positive developments have been made | positive progress* good, favorable, effective, promising, encouraging, heartening. **8** *he is a positive fool | it is a positive disgrace* utter, complete, absolute, perfect, out-and-out, outright, thoroughgoing, thorough, downright, sheer, consummate, unmitigated, rank.
Antonyms: VAGUE; UNCERTAIN; UNSURE; NEGATIVE.

positively adverb **1** *she assured us positively that he had gone | they were positively convinced* with certainty, definitely, emphatically, firmly, categorically, absolutely, without qualification, confidently, dogmatically. **2** *they were positively furious* absolutely, really, indeed, extremely, to a marked degree.

possess verb **1** *they possess two cars* own, be the owner of, have, be the possessor of, be the

proud owner/possessor of, count among one's possessions, have to one's name, hold, be blessed with, enjoy. **2** *possess a good mind* have, be endowed with, be gifted with. **3** *the invaders set out to possess all the seaports* seize, take into possession, take possession of, take over, occupy. **4** *as if demons had possessed them | what possessed her to drive so fast?* influence, control, dominate, have mastery over, bewitch, enchant, put under a spell, obsess; *inf.* get into someone.

possessed adjective **1** *like someone possessed* bewitched, enchanted, under a spell, obsessed, haunted, bedeviled, crazed, mad, demented, berserk, frenzied. **2** *a possessed young woman* self-possessed, poised, self-controlled, self-assured, self-confident, confident, calm, cool, even-tempered, composed, imperturbable; *inf.* unflappable.

possession noun **1** *her possession of the jewels* ownership, proprietorship, possessorship. **2** *their possession of the land/house* occupancy, occupation, holding, tenure, tenancy. **3** *a possession of which she was very fond* thing/article/item owned, asset. *See* POSSESSIONS.

possessions plural noun *thrown out of the house with all her possessions* belongings, things, property, luggage, baggage, bags and baggage, personal effects, goods, goods and chattels, accouterments, paraphernalia, appendages, assets, impedimenta.

possessive adjective **1** *possessive of their belongings | a possessive attitude | possessive children* acquisitive, greedy, grasping, covetous, selfish; *inf.* grabby. **2** *possessive parents* overprotective, clinging, controlling, dominating, jealous.

possibilities plural noun *the house is dilapidated, but it has possibilities | have possibilities as an actress* potential, potentiality, promise, prospects, capability.

possibility noun **1** *beyond the bounds of possibility | discuss the possibility of the plan working* feasibility, practicability, attainability, likelihood, potentiality, conceivability, probability. **2** *buying a smaller house is one possibility* likelihood, prospect, chance, hope, probability. **3** *a possibility of more violence* likelihood, prospect, chance, risk, hazard. *See* POSSIBILITIES.

possible adjective **1** *it is not humanly possible to get there on time | a dream that is not possible* feasible, able to be done, practicable, doable, attainable, achievable, realizable, within reach; *inf.* on. **2** *one of several possible outcomes* likely, potential, conceivable, imaginable, probable, credible, tenable, odds-on.
Antonyms: IMPOSSIBLE; IMPRACTICABLE; UNLIKELY.

possibly adverb **1** *he may possibly arrive tomorrow* perhaps, maybe, it may be, for all one knows, very likely; *lit.* peradventure. **2** *he will arrive if he possibly can | you cannot possibly carry all that* conceivably, by any means, by any chance, at all.

post[1] noun *put up the posts for the fence* stake, upright, pole, shaft, prop, support, column, stanchion, standard, stock, picket, pillar, pale, palisade, baluster, newel.

post[2] verb **1** *post notices on the walls* put up, stick, stick up, pin, pin up, tack, tack up, attach, affix, hang, display. **2** *details of the exams will be posted later* announce, make known, advertise, publish, publicize, circulate, broadcast.

post[3] noun *promoted to a more prestigious post* appointment, assignment, office, position, job, situation; work, employment.

post[4] verb *post guards at the front entrance* station, put, place, position, set, situate, locate.

post[5] verb *post today's sales in the ledger* enter, write in, fill in, record, register, note. **keep posted** *keep him posted on/about the patient's condition* keep informed, keep briefed, brief, advise, notify, report to; *inf.* keep in the picture, keep up-to-date, fill in.

poster noun **1** *posters advertising the carnival* placard, bill, notice, flyer, public notice, advertisement, announcement, bulletin; *inf.* ad. **2** *his bedroom walls covered with posters* (large) picture, print, reproduction.

posterity noun **1** *conserve the rain forests for posterity* future generations, succeeding generations. **2** *wish to keep his estate intact for posterity* descendants, heirs, successors, issue, offspring, progeny, children, seed.

postmortem noun postmortem examination, autopsy, necropsy.

postpone verb defer, put off, put back, delay, hold over, adjourn, shelve, table, pigeonhole; *inf.* put on ice, put on the back burner. *Antonyms:* ADVANCE; bring forward.

---

postpone
adjourn, defer, delay, suspend

All of these verbs have to do with putting things off. **Defer** is the broadest in meaning; it suggests putting something off until a later time (*defer payment; defer a discussion*). If you **postpone** an event or activity, you put it off intentionally, usually until a definite time in the future (*we postponed the party until the next weekend*). If you **adjourn** an activity, you postpone its completion until another day or place; *adjourn* is usually associated with meetings or other formal gatherings that are brought to an end and then resumed (*the judge adjourned the hearing until the following morning*). If you **delay** something, you postpone it because of obstacles (*delayed by severe thunderstorms and highway flooding*) or because you are reluctant to do it (*delay going to the dentist*). **Suspend** suggests stopping an activity for a while, usually for a reason (*forced to suspend work on the bridge until the holiday weekend was over*).

---

postponement noun deferment, deferral, delay, adjournment, moratorium, stay. *See* POSTPONE.

postscript noun **1** *add a postscript to her letter* PS, subscript, afterthought. **2** *add a postscript to the essay* subscript, afterword, addendum, appendix, codicil, appendage, supplement.

postulate verb *postulate that the population will decrease by 10 percent* assume, presuppose, suppose, presume, take for granted, posit, hypothesize, theorize.

posture noun **1** *in a reclining posture* position, pose, attitude. **2** *have an elegant posture | stand with a hunched posture* carriage, bearing, stance. **3** *the parents adopted a critical posture toward the new educational policy* attitude, position, point of view, viewpoint, opinion, way of thinking, outlook, stand, standpoint, stance, angle, slant.

posture verb pose, strike an attitude, put on an act, act, playact, attitudinize, put on airs, show off.

potency noun **1** *the potency of the drugs* powerfulness, power, strength, effectiveness, efficacy. **2** *the potency of his influence in the land* power, powerfulness, force, forcefulness, strength, vigor, might, mightiness, influence, authoritativeness, authority, dominance, energy; *lit.* puissance. **3** *admire the potency of their arguments* power, powerfulness, force, forcefulness, strength, effectiveness, cogency, conviction, persuasiveness, impressiveness.

potent adjective **1** *potent drugs* powerful, strong, effective, efficacious. **2** *he was a potent force in the land* powerful, forceful, strong, vigorous, mighty, influential, authoritative, commanding, dominant, energetic, dynamic; *lit.* puissant. **3** *a potent argument* powerful, forceful, strong, effective, cogent, compelling, convincing, persuasive, eloquent, impressive, telling. *Antonyms:* WEAK; POWERLESS; IMPOTENT.

potentate noun *the potentate of the neighboring country* ruler, monarch, king/queen, emperor/empress, sovereign, mogul.

potential adjective **1** *a potential star* budding, embryonic, developing, promising, prospective, likely, possible, probable. **2** *his potential musical ability* latent, dormant, inherent, embryonic, developing, promising. **3** *a potential disaster* likely, possible, probable.

potential noun **1** *recognize the potential of the young singer* promise, capability, capacity, ability, aptitude, talent, flair. **2** *the potential of the broken-down house* possibilities, promise, potentiality.

potion noun drink, beverage, brew, concoction, mixture, draft, elixir, philter.

potpourri noun medley, miscellany, mélange, pastiche, collage, blend, mixture, hodgepodge, mishmash, jumble, gallimaufry, farrago, olio, olla podrida.

pottery noun ceramics, earthenware, stoneware, terra-cotta.

pouch noun *carry money/tobacco in a pouch* bag, purse, wallet, container.

pounce verb *the hawk pounced when it spied its*

prey swoop down, drop down, descend. **pounce on** *the fox pounced on the mouse | the robbers pounced on the guard* swoop on, spring on, lunge at, leap at, jump at/on, bound at, make a grab for, take by surprise, take unawares, attack suddenly.

pounce *noun the fox grabbed the mouse with one pounce* swoop, spring, lunge, leap, jump, bound, grab, attack.

pound *verb* **1** *pound the solid to powder | pound the garlic to a paste* crush, beat, pulverize, smash, mash, grind, comminute, triturate. **2** *pound his opponent with his fists* beat, batter, pummel, strike, belabor, hammer, pelt, thump. **3** *pound the streets* tramp, tread heavily on, trudge, walk heavily on, stomp along, clump along. **4** *with heart pounding* beat heavily, pulsate, pulse, throb, thump, pump, palpitate, go pit-a-pat.

pound *noun stray dogs in a pound | cars in a pound* compound, enclosure, pen, confine, yard.

pour *verb* **1** *she poured cream over the fruit* let flow, decant, splash, spill. **2** *water poured from the burst pipe | blood poured from the wound* gush, rush, stream, flow, course, spout, jet, spurt. **3** *it was pouring | it poured* rain heavily/hard, come down in torrents/sheets, rain cats and dogs. **4** *people poured from the burning building | letters poured in* stream, swarm, crowd, throng, flood.

pout *verb* **1** *pout her lips provocatively/sullenly* push forward, purse. **2** *pouting because she did not get her own way* sulk, look sullen, look petulant, scowl, glower, lower, make a moue.

poverty *noun* **1** *appalled at the poverty of the homeless people* pennilessness, neediness, need, want, hardship, deprivation, indigence, impoverishment, impecuniousness, destitution, penury, privation, beggary, pauperism, straitened circumstances. **2** *the poverty of their surroundings* humbleness, lowliness, meanness, modesty, plainness. **3** *poverty of resources | the poverty of their imagination* deficiency, dearth, shortage, scarcity, paucity, insufficiency, lack, want, meagerness. **4** *the poverty of the soil/land* poorness, barrenness, unfruitfulness, bareness, aridity, aridness, sterility, infecundity. **Antonyms:** WEALTH; LUXURY; ABUNDANCE.

powder *noun* dust, fine grains, face powder, talcum powder, talc, dusting powder, baby powder, soap powder, baking powder.

powder *verb powder her face | powdered the baby* dust/sprinkle with powder, dredge/strew/scatter with powder.

powdery *adjective* **1** *powdery snow* powderlike, fine, dry, dusty, chalky, floury, friable, granulated, ground, crushed, pulverized. **2** *her powdery face and reddened lips* powder-covered, powdered.

power *noun* **1** *the power to corrupt/inspire* ability, capability, capacity, potential, potentiality. **2** *lose the power of speech* ability, capability, faculty, competence. **3** *the power behind the blow | the sheer power of his arms* powerfulness, strength, force, forcefulness, might, weight, vigor, energy, potency. **4** *have him in her power | she fell into his power* control, authority, mastery, domination, dominance, rule, command, ascendancy, supremacy, dominion, sway, sovereignty, influence. **5** *have the power to veto the rule* authority, authorization, warrant, license, right, prerogative. **6** *different kinds of power used for heating* energy, electrical power, nuclear power, solar power. **7** *the power of her oratory/argument* powerfulness, potency, strength, force, forcefulness, eloquence, effectiveness, cogency, conviction, persuasiveness. **Antonyms:** INABILITY; INCAPACITY; WEAKNESS; IMPOTENCE.

powerful *adjective* **1** *of powerful build | two powerful boxers* strong, sturdy, strapping, stout, stalwart, robust, vigorous, tough, mighty. **2** *powerful members of the committee | a country afraid of its powerful neighbors* influential, controlling, dominant, authoritative, commanding, forceful, strong, vigorous, potent, puissant. **3** *a powerful argument against leaving* forceful, strong, effective, cogent, compelling, convincing, persuasive, eloquent, impressive, telling. **4** *have powerful advertising appeal* strong, great, weighty, influential. **Antonyms:** POWERLESS; WEAK; INEFFECTIVE.

powerless *adjective* **1** *formerly influential members of the committee now totally powerless* without power, impotent. **2** *legs powerless after the accident* without power, without strength, paralyzed, disabled, incapacitated, debilitated, weak, feeble. **3** *powerless to give them any assistance* helpless, unfit, impotent, ineffectual, inadequate. **Antonyms:** POWERFUL; POTENT; STRONG.

practicability *noun question the practicability of the scheme* feasibility, possibility, viability, workability, achievability, attainability. *See* PRACTICABLE.

practicable *adjective find a practicable scheme* feasible, possible, within the bounds of possibility, within the realm of possibility, viable, workable, doable, achievable, attainable, accomplishable. **Antonyms:** IMPRACTICABLE; IMPOSSIBLE.

practical *adjective* **1** *practical experience/knowledge/background* hands-on, active, seasoned, applied, empirical, pragmatic, workaday; *inf.* nuts and bolts. **2** *practical clothing for walking | the furniture is attractive but not very practical* functional, useful, utilitarian, sensible. **3** *she is very practical* businesslike, sensible, down-to-earth, pragmatic, realistic. **4** *find a practical solution* pragmatic, matter-of-fact, down-to-earth, sensible, businesslike, realistic, utilitarian, expedient. **5** *a practical atheist | in practical control* virtual, effective, in effect, essential.

practically *adverb* **1** *practically every day* | *practically unknown* almost, nearly, very nearly, virtually, all but, in effect; *inf.* pretty nearly/well. **2** *behave practically* sensibly, with common sense, realistically, reasonably, pragmatically.

practice *noun* **1** *put the plan into practice* | *it would never work in practice* action, operation, application, effect, exercise, use. **2** *go to tennis practice* training, preparation, study, exercise, drill, workout, rehearsal. **3** *it is standard practice to close early on Sundays* procedure, method, system, usage, tradition, convention. **4** *it was his practice to visit his mother on Sundays* habit, custom, routine, wont. **5** *he engaged in the practice of law/medicine* profession, career, business, work, pursuit. **6** *buy a medical/legal practice* firm, business.

practice *verb* **1** *to practice economy/self-control* carry out, perform, do, execute, follow, pursue, observe. **2** *practice her tennis strokes* | *practicing a musical piece* work at, go through, run through, go over, rehearse, polish, refine. **3** *practice medicine/law* work at, have a career in, pursue a career in, engage in, specialize in.

practiced *adjective* *a practiced liar* experienced, seasoned, skilled, skillful, accomplished, expert, proficient, able, adept, adroit.

pragmatic *adjective* *she is very pragmatic* | *a pragmatic approach to the problem* practical, matter-of-fact, down-to-earth, sensible, businesslike, realistic, utilitarian; *inf.* nuts and bolts.
Antonyms: IMPRACTICAL; THEORETICAL; IDEALISTIC.

praise *verb* **1** *praise the musician's performance* | *praise him for his contribution* express approval of, express admiration for, applaud, acclaim, cheer, compliment someone on, congratulate someone on, pay tribute to, extol, laud, sing the praises of, eulogize about. **2** *praise God* worship, glorify, honor, exalt, adore, laud, pay tribute to, give thanks to.
Antonyms: CRITICIZE; CONDEMN.

---

praise
acclaim, commend, eulogize, extol, laud
If your dog sits when you tell him to sit, you'll want to **praise** him for his obedience. *Praise* is a general term for expressing approval, esteem, or commendation that usually suggests the judgment of a superior (*the teacher's praise for her students*). If a salesperson goes out of his way to help you, you may want to **commend** him to his superior, which is a more formal, public way of praising someone, either verbally or in writing. If you're watching a performance and want to express your approval verbally or with applause, **acclaim** is the verb you're looking for. **Laud** and **extol** suggest the highest of praise, although *laud* may imply that the praise is excessive (*the accomplishments for which she was lauded were really nothing out of the ordinary*). *Extol*, which comes from the Latin meaning to raise up, suggests that you're trying to magnify whatever or whomever you're praising (*to extol her virtues so that everyone would vote for her*). If you want to praise someone who has died recently, you will **eulogize** him or her, which means to speak or write your praise for a special occasion, such as a funeral.

---

praise *noun* **1** *express praise for his efforts* | *work worthy of praise* | *receive praise for his efforts* approval, approbation, applause, acclaim, acclamation, cheers, compliments, congratulations, commendation, tributes, accolades, plaudits, eulogy, panegyric, encomium, extolment, laudation, ovation, bouquets. **2** *praise to God* worship, glory, honor, devotion, exaltation, adoration, tribute, thanks.

praiseworthy *adjective* commendable, laudable, admirable, honorable, estimable, creditable, deserving, meritorious, worthy, excellent, exemplary, sterling, fine.
Antonyms: DISGRACEFUL; DISHONORABLE.

prance *verb* **1** *horses prancing around the field* leap, spring, jump, skip, cavort, caper, frisk, gambol. **2** *prancing about/around as if he owns the place* parade, strut, swagger.

prank *noun* *play a prank on his friend* trick, practical joke, joke, hoax, caper, stunt; *inf.* lark.

prattle *verb* chatter, jabber, babble, twitter, blather, run on, rattle on.

pray *verb* **1** *pray every night before going to bed* say one's prayers. **2** *pray the leaders to seek peace* appeal to, call upon, beseech, entreat, ask earnestly, request, implore, beg, petition, solicit, plead with, importune, supplicate, sue, invoke, crave, adjure. **pray for** *pray for mercy* appeal for, call for, ask earnestly for, request earnestly, beg for, beg, petition for, solicit, plead for, crave, clamor for. **pray to** *pray to God* offer prayers to, say prayers to, commune with.

prayer *noun* **1** *say a prayer to God* | *evening prayers* devotion, communion, litany, invocation, intercession. **2** *prayers for mercy* appeal, plea, beseeching, entreaty, petition, solicitation, supplication, suit, invocation, adjuration.

preach *verb* **1** *ministers preaching on Sunday* give a sermon, deliver a sermon, sermonize, spread the gospel, evangelize. **2** *preach the word of God* make known, proclaim, teach, spread. **3** *preach economy* advocate, recommend, advise, urge, exhort. **preach at** *tired of being preached at by her father* lecture, moralize, admonish, harangue, sermonize.

preacher *noun* **1** *a Baptist preacher* minister, reverend, parson, clergyman, clergywoman, churchman, churchwoman, ecclesiastic, cleric, missionary, revivalist, evangelist, televangelist. **2** *preachers of economy* advocate, adviser, urger, exhorter.

preaching *noun* **1** *inspired by the minister's*

preaching sermon, homily, pulpitry, evangelism. **2** *tired of her father's preaching* lecturing, moralizing, harangue, sermon, sermonizing, homily; *inf.* preachify.

preamble *noun begin his lecture without any preamble | a novel with a long preamble* opening statement, opening remarks, introduction, prefatory remarks, preface, prologue, front matter, forward matter, foreword, prelude, exordium, proem, prolegomenon; *inf.* prelims.

precarious *adjective* **1** *earn a precarious living | a precarious way of earning a living* uncertain, unsure, unpredictable, undependable, unreliable, risky, hazardous, chancy, doubtful, dubious, unsettled, insecure, unstable; *inf.* dicey. **2** *sitting in rather a precarious position at the edge of the cliff | in rather a precarious legal position* risky, hazardous, insecure, unstable, shaky, tricky, perilous, dangerous, touch-and-go; *inf.* dicey, hairy.
Antonyms: SAFE; SECURE.

precaution *noun* **1** *take a few precautions to avoid accidents* preventive measure, preventative measure, safety measure, safeguard, provision. **2** *a situation that demands precaution* foresight, foresightedness, forethought, farsightedness, anticipation, prudence, circumspection, caution, care, attentiveness, chariness, wariness.

precede *verb* **1** *his father preceded him as chairman* go before, be the predecessor of. **2** *she preceded him into the room* go before, come before, go/come ahead of, lead, usher in. **3** *the events that preceded the murder/war/victory* go before, go in advance of, antedate, antecede, lead to, lead up to, usher in, herald, pave the way for. **4** *precede her lecture with a few informal remarks* preface, prefix, introduce, begin, open, launch.
Antonyms: FOLLOW; SUCCEED.

precedence *noun a list of the officers in order of precedence* rank, seniority, superiority, preeminence, eminence, supremacy, primacy, transcendence, ascendancy. **take precedence over** *educational considerations should take precedence over financial considerations* come before, take priority over, be considered more important/urgent than, take antecedence over.

precedent *noun is there a precedent for such a punishment? | the judge's ruling has created a precedent* previous case, prior case, previous instance, prior instance, pattern, model, example, exemplar, paradigm, criterion, yardstick, standard.

preceding *adjective* **1** *as stated in the preceding paragraph* above, foregoing, previous, earlier, prior, antecedent, anterior. **2** *on the preceding day* previous, earlier, prior.

precept *noun* **1** *follow the precepts of one's religion/contract* rule, guideline, principle, working principle, code, law, tenet, canon, ordinance, statute, command, order, decree, mandate,

dictate, dictum, directive, direction, instruction. **2** *precepts that her grandmother used to quote* maxim, axiom, saying, law, adage, aphorism.

precinct *noun a police officer from the sixth precinct | must vote in your own precinct* district, ward, quarter, sector, zone, region.

precincts *plural noun* **1** *within the precincts of his estate* boundary, bounds, limits, confines. **2** *visit the old city and its precincts* surrounding area, surroundings, environs, neighborhood, vicinity, purlieus.

precious *adjective* **1** *precious metals* valuable, high-priced, costly, expensive, dear, priceless, rare, choice. **2** *precious souvenirs/memories* valued, cherished, prized, treasured, favorite, dear, beloved, adored, revered, venerated. **3** *poetry full of precious images | her manners are too precious for words* affected, artificial, chichi, overrefined, effete.
Antonyms: WORTHLESS; CHEAP.

precipice *noun* rock face, steep cliff, sheer drop, escarpment, scarp, cliff, crag, bluff.

precipitate *verb* **1** *precipitate the crisis* hasten, accelerate, expedite, speed up, push forward, bring on/about, trigger. **2** *the rider was precipitated from the startled horse | precipitated into economic disaster* hurl headlong, hurl, throw headlong, fling, thrust, heave, propel.

precipitate *adjective* **1** *his precipitate dash from the room* hurried, rapid, swift, speedy, headlong, abrupt, sudden, unexpected, breakneck, violent, precipitous. **2** *it was precipitate of him to act like that | his precipitate action* hasty, hurried, rash, heedless, reckless, impetuous, impulsive, precipitous, harebrained.

precipitous *adjective* **1** *a precipitous cliff* steep, sheer, perpendicular, abrupt, high. **2** *his precipitous exit* precipitate, hurried, abrupt. *See* PRECIPITATE *adjective* 1. **3** *his precipitous action* precipitate, hasty, impetuous. *See* PRECIPITATE *adjective* 2.

précis *noun a précis of the report* summary, synopsis, résumé, abridgment, abstract, outline, sketch, rundown, digest, epitome, compendium.

précis *verb précis the monthly report* summarize, sum up, abridge, condense, shorten, compress, abstract, outline.

precise *adjective* **1** *a precise record of events* exact, literal, actual, close, faithful, strict, express, minute, accurate, correct. **2** *at that precise moment she saw him | articles found at the precise spot where they were left* exact, very, actual, particular, specific, distinct. **3** *she is a very precise person | precise attention to detail* careful, exact, meticulous, scrupulous, conscientious, punctilious, particular, methodical, fastidious, finicky, rigid, strict, rigorous.
Antonyms: LOOSE; IMPRECISE; INACCURATE; CARELESS.

precisely *adverb* **1** *at 6 o'clock precisely* exactly, sharp, on the dot, on the button, dead on; *inf.*

right on. **2** *write out instructions very precisely* exactly, literally, strictly, minutely. *See* PRECISE 1.

precision *noun* **1** *the precision of his prose* carefulness, exactness, meticulousness, scrupulousness, conscientiousness, punctiliousness, methodicalness, rigor. **2** *the precision of the mechanism* accuracy, exactness, reliability, regularity.

preclude *verb* **1** *the rules of the club preclude drinking* | *the tenants are precluded from remodeling the house* prevent, prohibit, debar, interdict, block, bar, hinder, impede. **2** *the findings preclude any doubt as to his guilt* make impossible, rule out, eliminate.

precocious *adjective precocious children* advanced, ahead, far ahead, forward, ahead of one's peers, gifted, talented, brilliant, bright, quick, intelligent, smart, adultlike.

preconception *noun* *have a preconception that the surgeon would be a man* preconceived idea, preconceived notion, assumption, presupposition, presumption, prejudgment, prejudice, bias.

precondition *noun* *a degree in marketing is a precondition of the job* prerequisite, essential condition, requirement, necessity, essential, sine qua non; *inf.* must.

precursor *noun* **1** *the sporadic attacks proved to be the precursors of a full-scale war* forerunner, prelude, harbinger, herald, curtain-raiser. **2** *his precursor in the White House* | *a precursor of the modern computer* predecessor, forerunner, antecedent, ancestor, forebear, progenitor.

predatory *adjective* **1** *predatory birds* of preying, predacious, carnivorous, rapacious, raptorial. **2** *predatory tribes invading the country* plundering, pillaging, marauding, ravaging, looting, robbing, thieving, rapacious. **3** *her predatory relatives have left her penniless* exploitative, exploiting, imposing, greedy, acquisitive, rapacious, vulturine.

predecessor *noun* **1** *took over the job from her retiring predecessor* precursor, forerunner, antecedent. **2** *list his predecessors on a family tree* ancestor, forefather, forebear, progenitor, antecedent.
Antonyms: SUCCESSOR; DESCENDANTS.

predestine *verb* *he seemed predestined to lead a life of poverty* | *her success seemed predestined* preordain, foreordain, predetermine, fate, destine, predestinate.

predetermined *adjective* *everyone acted on a predetermined signal* prearranged, pre-agreed, predecided, preplanned, agreed, settled, fixed, set.

predicament *noun* difficult situation, problematic situation, corner, plight, tight corner, mess, emergency, crisis, dilemma, quandary, trouble; *inf.* jam, sticky situation, hole, fix, pickle, scrape, tight spot, spot.

predict *verb* *predict future events* | *predicted that something terrible would happen* forecast, foretell, prophesy, foresee, divine, prognosticate, forewarn, forebode, portend, presage, augur.

---

predict
augur, divine, forecast, foreshadow, foretell, prognosticate, prophesy

While all of these words refer to telling something before it happens, **predict** is the most commonly used and applies to the widest variety of situations. It can mean anything from hazarding a guess (*they predicted he'd never survive the year*) to making an astute inference based on facts or statistical evidence (*predict that the Republicans would win the election*). When a meteorologist tells us whether it will rain or snow tomorrow, he or she is said to **forecast** the weather, a word that means *predict* but is used particularly in the context of weather and other phenomena that cannot be predicted easily by the general public (*statistics forecast an influx of women into the labor force*). **Divine** and **foreshadow** mean to suggest the future rather than to predict it, especially by giving or evaluating subtle hints or clues. To *divine* something is to perceive it through intuition or insight (*to divine in the current economic situation the disaster that lay ahead*), while *foreshadow* can apply to anyone or anything that gives an indication of what is to come (*her abrupt departure that night foreshadowed the breakdown in their relationship*). **Foretell**, like *foreshadow*, can refer to the clue rather than the person who gives it and is often used in reference to the past (*evidence that foretold the young girl's violent end*). **Augur** means to foreshadow a favorable or unfavorable outcome for something (*the turnout on opening night augured well for the play's success*). **Prophesy** connotes either inspired or mystical knowledge of the future and suggests more authoritative wisdom than *augur* (*a baseball fan for decades, he prophesied the young batter's rise to stardom*). Although anyone who has inside information or knowledge of signs and symptoms can **prognosticate**, it is usually a doctor who does so by looking at the symptoms of a disease to predict its future outcome.

---

predictable *adjective* *a predictable reaction* foreseeable, to be expected, expected, anticipated, probable, likely, certain, sure; *inf.* in the cards.

prediction *noun* prophecy, forecast, divination, prognostication, forewarning, augury, soothsaying.

predilection *noun* *a predilection for spicy food* | *his predilection for intelligent women* liking, fondness, preference, love, partiality, taste, weakness, soft spot, fancy, inclination, leaning, bias, propensity, bent, proclivity, proneness, penchant, predisposition.

predispose *verb* **1** *his poverty-stricken childhood predisposed him to save* move, incline, dispose, persuade, influence, sway, induce, prompt. **2** *the child is predisposed to asthma* make susceptible, make subject, make prone, make vulnerable, make open.

predisposed *adjective before meeting her he was predisposed to believe her story* inclined, of a mind, willing, biased, prejudiced.

predisposition *noun* **1** *a predisposition toward rheumatism/meanness* susceptibility, proneness, tendency, inclination, vulnerability. **2** *have a predisposition toward fast cars* predilection, inclination, leaning, bias, propensity, bent, proclivity, proneness, penchant. *See* PREDILECTION.

predominance *noun* **1** *try to avoid the predominance of one group over another* dominance, control, ascendancy, leadership, mastery, supremacy, upper hand, edge, preponderance. **2** *a predominance of men on the staff | a predominance of blue in the decor* preponderance, dominance, prevalence, greater/greatest number/amount, majority, bulk.

predominant *adjective* **1** *the predominant member of the alliance* dominant, controlling, in control, ascendant, ruling, leading, principal, chief, main, supreme, more/most powerful, more/most important, superior, in the ascendancy. **2** *idleness is the predominant characteristic in that family* chief, main, principal, preponderant, most obvious, most noticeable, most prominent, prevailing, prevalent.

predominate *verb* **1** *the largest country predominates in the policymaking* be dominant, be in control, rule, hold ascendancy, hold sway, have the upper hand, carry most weight. **2** *men predominate in the profession | blue predominates in the decor* be predominant, be greater/greatest in amount/number, be prevalent, preponderate, be most prominent.

preeminence *noun* *his preeminence as a poet* excellence, distinction, prestige, prominence, eminence, importance, fame, renown, supremacy, superiority, transcendence.

preeminent *adjective* *a preeminent scientist | a scientist preeminent in his field* outstanding, leading, foremost, chief, excellent, distinguished, prominent, eminent, important, famous, renowned, supreme, superior, unrivaled, unsurpassed, transcendent.

Antonyms: UNKNOWN; UNDISTINGUISHED; OBSCURE.

preempt *verb* **1** *preempt the sale of the building by buying it themselves* forestall, prevent, invalidate. **2** *preempted the enemy's airfield* take over, appropriate, acquire, commandeer, take possession of, occupy, seize, arrogate. **3** *a news bulletin preempting the regular broadcast* supplant, displace, supersede, take the place of, replace, substitute for.

preen *verb* **1** *birds preening their feathers with their beaks* clean, smooth, arrange, plume. **2** *preen-*

ing himself in front of the mirror groom, tidy up, spruce up, smarten up, beautify, prettify, primp; doll up. **3** *preen herself on winning the prize* give a pat on the back, congratulate, be pleased with, pride, be proud of.

preface *noun* *the preface explaining how to use the book* introduction, foreword, front matter, forward matter, preamble, prologue, prelude, proem, exordium, prolegomenon; *inf.* prelims, intro.

preface *verb* *preface her speech with a short introduction* precede, prefix, introduce, begin, open, launch.

prefatory *adjective* *made a few prefatory remarks before reading his poem* preliminary, introductory, opening, precursory, initial, preparatory.

prefer *verb* **1** *of the desserts, I prefer pie* like better/best, favor, be more/most partial to, incline toward, choose, select, pick, opt for, go for, single out; *inf.* fancy. **2** *prefer to go by bus* would rather, would sooner, favor, choose, opt, elect, wish, want. **3** *prefer a proposal to the committee | prefer charges* put forward, proffer, present, offer, propose, tender, lodge, file, press. **4** *hope to be preferred in the near future* promote, upgrade, advance, move up, elevate, aggrandize.

preferable *adjective* **preferable to** *find trains preferable to planes* better than, superior to, more desirable than, more suitable than.

preferably *adverb* *looking for a house, preferably near the water | preferably, we would like to be paid in cash* for preference, by preference, from choice, by choice, much rather, rather, much sooner, sooner.

preference *noun* **1** *her preference is for a two-story house* choice, first choice, first option, liking, fancy, desire, wish, inclination, partiality, predilection, leaning, bias, bent. **2** *of the desserts, what is your preference?* choice, selection, option, pick. **3** *applicants with experience will be given preference | show preference to members of her own family* preferential treatment, favored treatment, favor, precedence, priority, advantage.

preferential *adjective* *preferential travel rates given to groups | the governor gets preferential treatment* special, better, advantageous, favored, privileged, partial, partisan.

preferment *noun* *hope for preferment in the firm* promotion, upgrading, advancement, moving up, elevation, aggrandizement.

pregnancy *noun* gestation, gravidity, parturiency.

pregnant *adjective* **1** *discover that she was pregnant* having a baby/child, expectant, with child, enceinte; *inf.* expecting, in the family way, in a delicate condition. **2** *a pregnant pause following her surprise announcement* meaningful, significant, eloquent, expressive, suggestive, loaded, charged, pointed, telling. **pregnant with** *a speech pregnant with wit | a situation pregnant with danger* full of, filled with, charged with, fraught with, abounding in, replete with, rich in.

prehistoric *adjective* **1** *prehistoric human* primeval, primordial, primitive, earliest. **2** *prehistoric attitudes about women | wear prehistoric clothes* out of date, old-fashioned, ancient, antiquated, superannuated.

prejudice *noun* **1** *have a prejudice against young people* bias, partiality, jaundiced eye, preconceived idea, preconceived notion, preconception, prejudgment, predetermination. **2** *employers showing prejudice toward older people | racial prejudice* bias, discrimination, partisanship, partiality, preference, one-sidedness, chauvinism, bigotry, narrow-mindedness, intolerance, unfairness, unjustness, racism, sexism, ageism, heterosexism. **3** *without prejudice to any future judgment | without prejudice to his claim* detriment, disadvantage, damage, injury, harm, hurt, loss.

prejudice *verb* **1** *wonder whether newspaper articles had prejudiced the attitude of the jury* bias, make partial, make partisan, color, poison, jaundice, influence, sway, predispose. **2** *his conviction may prejudice his chances* be prejudicial to, be detrimental to, be deleterious to, be disadvantageous to, damage, injure, harm, hurt, mar, spoil, impair, undermine.

prejudiced *adjective have a prejudiced attitude about women/minorities/foreigners | be prejudiced against new ideas* biased, discriminatory, partisan, partial, one-sided, jaundiced, chauvinistic, bigoted, intolerant, narrow-minded, unfair, unjust, racist, sexist, ageist.
Antonyms: UNBIASED; IMPARTIAL.

prejudicial *adjective his conviction will be prejudicial to his chances of getting a job | actions prejudicial to the country's economy* detrimental, deleterious, disadvantageous, unfavorable, damaging, injurious, harmful, hurtful, inimical.

preliminary *adjective* **1** *preliminary training | a few preliminary remarks* introductory, prefatory, prior, precursory, opening, initial, beginning, preparatory, initiatory. **2** *preliminary heats/rounds/interviews* prior, precursory, qualifying, eliminating. **3** *preliminary experiments* introductory, early, exploratory, pilot, test, trial.

preliminary *noun* **1** *dispense with the preliminaries and get on with the meeting/trial* preliminary measure, preliminary action, preparation, groundwork, first round, introduction, preamble, prelude, opening. **2** *advance to the final round after passing the preliminaries* first round, heat, trial, preliminary exam/examination.

prelims *plural noun got high marks in the prelims* preliminaries, preliminary exams, first round.

prelude *noun* **1** *the skirmishes were a prelude to full-scale war* precursor, forerunner, curtain-raiser, harbinger, herald, preliminary, introduction, start, beginning. **2** *the prelude to the narrative poem* introduction, preface, prologue, preamble, proem, exordium, prolegomenon; *inf.* intro. **3** *the prelude to the fugue* overture, introductory movement, voluntary.

premature *adjective* **1** *his premature death/birth | the premature closing of the play because of lack of support* too soon, too early, early, untimely. **2** *it was premature of him to announce his plans* too soon, hasty, precipitate, impulsive, impetuous, rash. **3** *announce premature plans* incomplete, undeveloped, immature, embryonic.

prematurely *adverb* **1** *leave prematurely* too soon, too early, before the usual time. **2** *announce his plans prematurely* too soon, too early, overhastily, precipitately.

premeditated *adjective premeditated murder* planned, preplanned, prearranged, intentional, intended, deliberate, calculated, willful.

premier *noun an international meeting of premiers* head of government, head of state, chief executive, president, prime minister, chancellor.

premier *adjective the country's premier computer firm* leading, foremost, chief, principal, head, top-ranking, top, prime, first, main.

premiere *noun the premiere of the play/movie* first night, first performance, first showing, opening, opening night, debut.

premise *noun financial advice based on the premise that the recession was over* hypothesis, thesis, assumption, presupposition, presumption, argument, postulation.

premises *plural noun the business has moved to new premises* building, property, establishment.

premium *noun* **1** *monthly premiums for life insurance* payment, installment. **2** *earned a premium of $60 on their investment* bonus, dividend. **3** *pay a premium for early delivery* additional payment, additional fee, surcharge. **4** *the boys received a premium for working late* reward, recompense, remuneration, perquisite, prize; *inf.* perk. **at a premium 1** *cannot buy a house when real estate is at a premium* high-priced, expensive, costly, upmarket. **2** *parking spaces are at a premium in the city* rare, hard to come by, in short supply, scarce, in great demand, like gold, not to be had; *inf.* not to be had for love or money. **put a premium on 1** *the teacher puts a premium on creative work* set great store by, put a high value on, regard as valuable, hold in high regard, appreciate greatly, attach great importance to. **2** *the risk of disease puts a premium on hygiene* make invaluable, make valuable, put a high value on, make essential, make important.

premonition *noun* **1** *had a premonition that something terrible was going to happen* foreboding, presage, presentiment, intuition, feeling, hunch, suspicion, sneaking suspicion, misgiving, apprehension, fear, feeling in one's bones, funny feeling. **2** *given a premonition that all was not well in the firm* forewarning, warning, sign, pre-indication, indication, omen, portent.

preoccupation noun 1 *in his preoccupation he failed to notice her* abstraction, absorption, engrossment, concentration, brown study, deep thought, musing, pensiveness, reverie, absent-mindedness, absence of mind, distraction, inattentiveness, heedlessness, oblivion, wool-gathering, daydreaming. 2 *golf is his preoccupation* chief concern, obsession, fixation, pet subject, bee in one's bonnet, *idée fixe*; *inf.* hang-up.

preoccupied adjective *she seemed rather preoccupied* lost in thought, deep in thought, immersed in thought, in a brown study, absorbed, engrossed, pensive, absentminded, distracted, abstracted, distrait, oblivious, far away, rapt.

preoccupy verb *his financial worries were preoccupying him* absorb, engross, take up one's whole attention, take up all one's time, distract, obsess.

preparation noun 1 *the preparation of their plans* making ready, arrangement, development, assembling, assembly, drawing up, production, construction, composing, composition, fashioning. 2 *finalize their preparations for battle* arrangement, provision, preparatory measure, necessary step, groundwork, spadework. 3 *the preparation of the students for the exam/contest* coaching, training, grooming, priming. 4 *a preparation used as a tranquilizer* mixture, compound, concoction, composition, tincture.

preparatory adjective *a great deal of preparatory work to be done before the store opens* preliminary, introductory, prefatory, precursory, basic, elementary, fundamental, rudimentary, preparative. **preparatory to** *much to be done preparatory to the opening of the store* in preparation for, in advance of, before, prior to, in anticipation of, leading up to.

prepare verb 1 *prepare their plans* get ready, make ready, arrange, develop, put together, assemble, draw up, produce, construct, compose, concoct, fashion, work up. 2 *prepare for the president's visit* make preparations, get ready, arrange things, make provision, get everything set, take the necessary steps, lay the groundwork, do the spadework; *inf.* gear oneself up, psych oneself up, gird up one's loins. 3 *prepare for the sports event* train, get into shape, practice, exercise, warm up. 4 *prepare for the exam* do preparation, study, do homework. 5 *prepare the students for the exam/contest* coach, train, groom, prime. 6 *prepare her/oneself for a shock* make ready, brace, steel. 7 *prepare a meal* cook, make, put together, assemble; *inf.* fix, throw together.

prepared adjective 1 *everything is prepared for the wedding* ready, in readiness, arranged, in order, set, all set, fixed, planned, primed. 2 *they are prepared to make peace* ready, disposed, predisposed, willing, inclined, of a mind, minded.

preponderance noun 1 *a preponderance of men* over women on the staff | *a preponderance of red in the room's decor* predominance, dominance, prevalence, greater number/quantity, majority, bulk. 2 *the preponderance of the group in the alliance* dominance, predominance, control, ascendancy, leadership, mastery, supremacy, upper hand, edge.

prepossessing adjective *a prepossessing child/manner* attractive, beautiful, pretty, handsome, good-looking, fetching, striking, pleasing, agreeable, appealing, likable, lovable, amiable, charming, engaging, winning, winsome, taking, enchanting, captivating, bewitching, fascinating.
Antonyms: UGLY; REPULSIVE; unprepossessing.

preposterous adjective *what a preposterous idea!* absurd, ridiculous, foolish, ludicrous, farcical, asinine, senseless, unreasonable, irrational, outrageous, shocking, astonishing, unbelievable, incredible, unthinkable; *inf.* crazy, insane.

prerequisite adjective *tolerance is prerequisite when bringing up children* necessary, needed, required, called for, essential, requisite, vital, indispensable, imperative, obligatory, mandatory.

prerequisite noun *experience is a prerequisite for the job* requirement, requisite, necessity, essential, precondition, condition, sine qua non; *inf.* must.

prerogative noun *he thinks it is his prerogative to make all the decisions* right, birthright, privilege, due, entitlement, liberty, authority, license, carte blanche.

presage verb 1 *clouds presaging a storm* be a sign of, be an indication of, be a presage of, be an omen of, be a warning of, give a warning of, portend, augur. 2 *she presaged that something terrible would happen* forecast, foretell, prophesy, predict, foresee, divine, prognosticate, forewarn.

prescribe verb 1 *the doctor prescribed antibiotics* write a prescription for, order, advise, direct. 2 *prescribe a vacation to cure her depression* advise, recommend, commend, suggest. 3 *the law prescribes strict penalties for drunk driving* | *school regulations prescribe that everyone must wear the uniform* lay down, require, direct, stipulate, specify, impose, decree, order, command, ordain, enjoin.

prescription noun 1 *the prescription of drugs is part of a doctor's job* prescribing, ordering, advising. 2 *the doctor wrote a prescription for antibiotics* instruction, order, direction. 3 *his prescription for long life was hard work* recipe, formula, direction, advice. 4 *the pharmacist made up the prescription* medicine, drug, remedy, preparation, mixture.

presence noun 1 *the presence of too much acid in the soil* existence, being. 2 *demand his presence at the meeting* attendance, company, companionship. 3 *in the presence of a great man* company, propinquity, proximity, neighborhood,

vicinity, closeness, nearness. **4** *a woman of presence* magnetism, aura, charisma, personality, attraction, self-assurance, self-possession, self-confidence, poise. **5** *impressed by her presence* dignified bearing, impressive carriage, dignified air/demeanor, dignity. **6** *she felt a presence in the attic* manifestation, apparition, supernatural being, spirit, ghost, specter, wraith.
presence of mind aplomb, levelheadedness, sang-froid, phlegm, self-assurance, self-possession, composure, calmness, calm, coolness, imperturbability, alertness, quickness, quick-wittedness; *inf.* unflappability.
Antonyms: ABSENCE; nonattendance.

present[1] *adjective* **1** *poison was present in the drink* existing, existent, extant. **2** *in the present climate* present-day, existing, current, contemporary. **3** *a doctor had to be present* in attendance, here, there, near, nearby, available, at hand, ready.
Antonyms: ABSENT; MISSING.

present[2] *noun forget the past and think about the present* today, now, here and now, the present moment, the time being. **at present** *at present he is unavailable* just now, right now, at the moment, at this time, for the moment, at the present time, currently, at this moment in time, presently. **for the present** *for the present we must economize* for the moment, for the time being, for now, in the meanwhile, in the meantime. **the present day** the present age/time, modern times, nowadays.
Antonyms: PAST; FUTURE.

present[3] *verb* **1** *present a gift to the retiring chairman* give, hand over, confer, bestow, donate, award, grant, accord. **2** *present his proposals to the committee* submit, set forth, put forward, proffer, offer, tender, advance. **3** *present his apologies/greetings* give, offer, send, tender. **4** *may I present my daughter?* introduce, make known. **5** *present their new product* show, put on show, exhibit, display, put on display, demonstrate, introduce, launch. **6** *present a new musical* put on, produce, perform, stage, mount. **7** *present a radio/television program* be the presenter of, introduce, host; *inf.* emcee. **present oneself 1** *you must present yourself for inspection tomorrow morning* be present, make an appearance, appear, attend, turn up. **2** *if the opportunity presents itself* occur, arise, happen, transpire, come about, appear.

present[4] *noun a birthday present | the money was a present* gift, donation, offering, contribution, gratuity, handout, giveaway, presentation, largesse, award, premium, bounty, boon, benefaction; *inf.* freebie.

---

present

bonus, donation, gift, gratuity, lagniappe, largesse
What's the difference between a birthday **present** and a Christmas **gift**? Both words refer to something given as an expression of friendship, affection, esteem, etc. But *gift* is a more formal term, suggesting something of monetary value that is formally bestowed on an individual, group, or institution (*a gift to the university*). *Present*, on the other hand, implies something of less value that is an expression of goodwill (*a housewarming present; a present for the teacher*). **Largesse** is a somewhat pompous term for a very generous gift that is conferred in an ostentatious or condescending way, often on many recipients (*the king's largesse; the largesse of our government*). A **gratuity** is associated with tipping and other forms of voluntary compensation for special attention or service above and beyond what is included in a charge (*known for her generous gratuities, the duchess enjoyed watching the waiters compete with each other to serve her*), while a **lagniappe** is a Southern word, used chiefly in Louisiana and southeast Texas, for either a gratuity or a small gift given to a customer along with a purchase. If you give money or anything else as a gift to a philanthropic, charitable, or religious organization, it is known as a **donation** (*donations for the poor*). But if your employer gives you money at the end of the year in addition to your regular salary, it isn't a Christmas gift; it's a Christmas **bonus**.

---

presentable *adjective make yourself presentable for the interview | go to school looking presentable* well-groomed, smartly dressed, tidily dressed, tidy, spruce, of smart appearance, fit to be seen.

presentation *noun* **1** *the presentation of his retirement gift* presenting, giving, handing over, conferral, bestowal, donation, award, granting, according. **2** *hand over a presentation to mark his retirement* gift, present, donation, offering, contribution, gratuity. *See* PRESENT[4] *noun*. **3** *the presentation of their proposals to the committee* submission, proffering, tendering, offering. **4** *the presentation of his fiancée to his family* introduction, making known, acquainting. **5** *the presentation of their new product* launch, launching, show, exhibition, display, demonstration. **6** *attend the drama club's presentation of Hamlet* production, performance, staging, mounting, showing, rendition. **7** *improve the presentation of his material* arrangement, organization, ordering, disposition, layout, scheme, system, structure.

presentiment *noun a presentiment of impending doom* foreboding, premonition, presage, intuition, feeling, hunch, suspicion, sneaking suspicion, misgiving, fear, apprehension, feeling in one's bones, funny feeling.

presently *adverb he will be here presently* soon, shortly, in a short time, in a short while, momentarily, directly, in a moment, in a minute, before long, before you can say Jack Robinson; *inf.* in a jiff/jiffy, in two shakes of a lamb's tail.

preservation noun **1** *the preservation of the rain forest* conservation, protection. *See* PRESERVE verb 1. **2** *the preservation of the town from danger* protection, defense, guarding, safeguarding, safekeeping, safety, security, salvation, sheltering, shielding. **3** *the preservation of old traditions* conservation, keeping up, keeping alive, maintenance, continuation, upholding, perpetuation. **4** *preservation of financial resources* conservation, keeping, saving, putting away. *See* PRESERVE verb 5.

preserve verb **1** *find a substance to preserve the wood* protect, safeguard, care for. **2** *preserve the town from danger* keep, protect, defend, guard, safeguard, secure, shelter, shield. **3** *preserve his work for posterity* save, keep, safeguard, maintain, perpetuate. **4** *preserve the old traditions* keep up, keep alive, keep going, maintain, continue with, uphold, prolong, perpetuate. **5** *preserve their financial resources until a rainy day* conserve, keep, save, retain, put away, put aside, store, hoard. **6** *preserve food* cure, smoke, dry, pickle, salt, marinate, kipper, freeze, freeze-dry, can; *inf.* put up, lay by.

Antonyms: DAMAGE; NEGLECT.

preserve noun **1** *an animal preserve* sanctuary, reserve, reservation, game reserve. **2** *he regards the family finances as his preserve* area, domain, field, sphere, realm; *inf.* thing.

preserves plural noun *strawberry preserves* jam, jelly, marmalade, conserve. preside

preside verb *the committee members elected him to preside* chair, be in the chair, be chairman/chairwoman/chairperson, officiate. **preside over** *preside over the company* be in charge of, be at the head/helm of, head, manage, administer, be in control of, control, be responsible for, direct, run, conduct, supervise, govern, rule, be boss of, head up, be in the driver's seat of, be/sit in the saddle of, pull the strings of, call the shots in.

president noun **1** *president of the United States* chief of state, head of state, chief executive, commander in chief. **2** *president of the society* head, chief, director, leader, captain.

press verb **1** *press the button/accelerator* press down, depress, push down, force down, bear down on. **2** *press grapes* crush, squeeze, compress, mash, reduce. **3** *press a pair of pants* iron, smooth out, put creases in, calender, mangle. **4** *press the soil/flowers* flatten, make flat, smooth out. **5** *press the child to her bosom* clasp, enfold, hold close, clutch, grasp, embrace, hug, cuddle, squeeze, crush. **6** *press her hand/arm affectionately* squeeze, give something a squeeze, pat, caress. **7** *they are pressing him to make a decision* urge, entreat, exhort, implore, put pressure on, use pressure on, pressurize, force, compel, coerce, constrain. **8** *press a claim* plead, urge, push forward, advance insistently. **9** *press around the stage to see the performers*

crowd, surge, cluster, mill, flock, gather, swarm, throng. **10** *the enemy is pressing our army* harass, besiege, attack, assail, beset, worry, torment. **be pressed for** *we are pressed for time | they are pressed for cash* be short of, have barely enough, have too little, have an insufficiency of; *inf.* be strapped for. **be pressing** *other matters are pressing* be urgent, demand attention, require attention, call for action. **press for** *they are pressing for a quick decision* call for, demand, insist on, clamor for. **press on** *we must press on to reach the summit | press on with the work* push on, make haste, hasten, hurry, proceed, continue, put one's nose to the grindstone, put one's shoulder to the wheel.

press noun **1** *freedom of the press | advertise in the press* newspapers, papers, news media, journalism, the newspaper world, the media, the fourth estate, journalists, newspapermen, newspaperwomen, reporters, gentlemen/ladies of the press. **2** *get good/bad press* press treatment, press coverage, press reporting, newspaper articles, newspaper write-ups. **3** *go to press | the presses are running* printing press. **4** *he has set up a small press* printing firm, publishing firm, publishing house. **5** *getting lost in the press* crowd, throng, multitude, mob, troop, horde, swarm, herd, flock, pack. **6** *the press of modern life* pressure, strain, stress, urgency, demands, hurry, hustle, hustle and bustle, flurry.

pressing adjective *pressing business/engagement* urgent, vital, crucial, critical, demanding, important, high-priority, exigent, pivotal.

pressure noun **1** *have to exert pressure on the door to open it | the pressure of the crowd against the barriers* force, weight, heaviness. **2** *stop the bleeding by applying pressure to the wound* compression, compressing, squeezing, crushing. **3** *police exerting pressure to get a confession* force, compulsion, coercion, constraint, duress. **4** *the pressure of the job* strain, stress, tension, burden, load, weight, trouble; *inf.* hassle. **5** *find it difficult to work under pressure* adversity, difficulty, urgency, strain, stress, tension.

pressure verb *pressure him into taking the job* put pressure on, use pressure on, press, force, compel, coerce, constrain, bulldoze, dragoon.

prestige noun *suffered a loss of prestige when he lost his job* status, kudos, standing, stature, importance, reputation, fame, renown, esteem, influence, authority, supremacy, eminence, superiority, predominance.

prestigious adjective **1** *a prestigious school* respected, esteemed, eminent, distinguished, of high standing, well-known, celebrated, illustrious, renowned, famous. **2** *a prestigious job* conferring prestige, important, prominent, impressive, high-ranking, influential, glamorous.

Antonyms: UNKNOWN; OBSCURE; MINOR; HUMBLE.

presumably adverb *presumably he will get the job*

bly, in all likelihood, all things being equal, all things considered, on the face of it, as likely as not; *inf.* as like as not.

presume *verb* **1** *I presume that your new partner is honest* | *presumed innocent until proved guilty* assume, take for granted, take it, suppose, presuppose, believe, think, imagine, judge, guess, surmise, conjecture, hypothesize, infer, deduce. **2** *do not presume to offer advice to a more experienced person* have the temerity, have the audacity, be so bold as, make so bold as, have the effrontery, go so far as, dare, venture. **presume on/upon** *presume on/upon his good nature* take advantage of, take unfair advantage of, exploit, take liberties with.

presumption *noun* **1** *his request for an invitation was pure presumption* confidence, arrogance, egotism, boldness, audacity, forwardness, insolence, impudence, bumptiousness, temerity, effrontery. **2** *our presumption is that he has run away* assumption, supposition, presupposition, belief, thought, judgment, guess, surmise, conjecture, hypothesis, premise, inference, deduction. **3** *the presumption for their hypothesis* grounds, ground, basis, reason, evidence.

presumptive *adjective* **1** *the police lack any presumptive evidence* reasonable, plausible, feasible, likely, credible, believable, that holds water. **2** *the heir presumptive* | *the presumptive heir* probable, likely, assumed, supposed, expected.

presumptuous *adjective* *it was presumptuous to offer advice to someone of her experience* | *a presumptuous person* presuming, ultraconfident, overconfident, cocksure, (overly) self-confident, self-assured, arrogant, egotistical, conceited, overbold, bold, audacious, forward, insolent, impudent, bumptious, self-assertive, overbearing, overweening, haughty; *inf.* bigheaded, swellheaded, too big for one's britches/boots, pushy.

presuppose *verb* **1** *they cannot presuppose the accuracy of his alibi* presume, assume, take for granted, suppose. **2** *approval of the plan presupposes that funding is available* require, imply, assume, presume, take for granted.

presupposition *noun* presumption, assumption, preconception, supposition, thesis, theory, premise.

pretend *verb* **1** *she is not ill—she is only pretending* put on an act, act, playact, put it on, dissemble, sham, feign, fake, fake it, dissimulate, make believe, put on a false front, posture, go through the motions. **2** *she is pretending that she knows nothing about it* make believe, affect, profess, make out, fabricate. **3** *pretend illness* sham, feign, fake, simulate, put on. **4** *pretend to the throne/title* lay claim, make a claim, aspire. **5** *pretend to be her friend* claim, profess, purport.

pretended *adjective* **1** *a pretended affection* al-leged, avowed, professed, purported, spurious, insincere, sham, bogus, fake, faked, counterfeit, affected, put-on, pseudo; *inf.* phony. **2** *a pretended friend* alleged, so-called, professed, ostensible, in name only, supposed, bogus, pseudo; *inf.* pretend.

pretender *noun* *a pretender to the throne* claimant, claimer, aspirant.

pretense *noun* **1** *she is not ill—it is just pretense* putting on an act, acting, dissembling, shamming, faking, dissimulation, make-believe, invention, imagination, posturing. See PRETEND 1. **2** *not taken in by their pretense of grief* false show, show, semblance, false appearance, appearance, false front, guise, façade, masquerade, mask, veneer, cover, charade. **3** *on the pretense that he was dying* pretext, false excuse, guise, sham, ruse, wile, trickery, lie, falsehood. See PRETEXT. **4** *I have no pretense to being expert* claim, aspiration, purporting, profession. **5** *lead humble lives without pretense* pretentiousness, display, ostentation, affectation, showiness, flaunting, posturing.
Antonyms: REALITY; FACT.

pretension *noun* **1** *make no pretensions to being an expert* | *a writer with pretensions to literary greatness* claim, aspiration, pretense, profession, purporting. **2** *dislike the pretension of her style* | *a life full of pretension* pretentiousness, affectation, ostentation, ostentatiousness, showiness, pomposity, floweriness, extravagance, flamboyance, grandiloquence, magniloquence, bombast. See PRETENTIOUS 1. **3** *the pretension of their lifestyle* affectation, ostentation, ostentatiousness, showiness, flaunting, flamboyance.

pretentious *adjective* **1** *a pretentious style of writing* affected, ostentatious, showy, overambitious, pompous, artificial, mannered, highflown, high-sounding, flowery, grandiose, elaborate, extravagant, flamboyant, grandiloquent, magniloquent, bombastic, orotund; *inf.* highfalutin. **2** *a pretentious lifestyle* affected, ostentatious, showy, flaunting, flamboyant.
Antonyms: PLAIN; SIMPLE; NATURAL; UNAFFECTED.

preternatural *adjective* *preternatural powers/experience* extraordinary, out of the ordinary, exceptional, unusual, uncommon, singular, abnormal, supernatural, paranormal.

pretext *noun* *the thief got into the old lady's house on the pretext of checking the phone lines* pretense, false excuse, excuse, ostensible reason, alleged reason, alleged plea, supposed grounds, cover, guise, sham, ruse, wile, trickery, red herring, lie, falsehood, misrepresentation.

pretty *adjective* **1** *a pretty child* attractive, lovely, good-looking, nice-looking, comely, personable, prepossessing, appealing, charming, delightful, nice, engaging, pleasing, winning, winsome, cute, as pretty as a picture. **2** *a pretty pattern* attractive, lovely, appealing,

pleasant, pleasing, charming, delightful, nice. **3** *cost a pretty penny* | *make a pretty profit* considerable, large, sizable, substantial, appreciable, fair, tolerable, goodly; *inf.* tidy.
Antonyms: PLAIN; UGLY; UNPLEASANT.

pretty *adverb* **1** *a pretty large sum of money* moderately, reasonably, fairly. **2** *feeling pretty secure* quite, rather, somewhat; *inf.* kind of.

prevail *verb* **1** *in the end, common sense prevailed* win, win out, win through, triumph, be victorious, be the victor, carry the day, prove superior, conquer, overcome, gain mastery, gain ascendancy, take the crown, rule. **2** *the economic conditions prevailing at the time* exist, be in existence, obtain, occur, be prevalent, be current, be widespread, abound, hold sway, predominate, preponderate. **prevail on/upon** *try to prevail upon him to speak at the conference* persuade, induce, talk someone into, bring someone around, convince, sway, prompt, influence, urge, exhort, pressure, bring pressure to bear on, cajole, coax; *inf.* sweet-talk.

prevailing *adjective* **1** *the prevailing attitude toward criminals* | *the prevailing fashion in hats* prevalent, current, usual, common, general, widespread, set, established, accepted, popular, fashionable, in fashion, in style, in vogue. **2** *the prevailing political party* prevalent, dominant, predominant, predominating, preponderant, most influential, ruling, governing, ascendant, principal, chief, main, supreme. **3** *the prevailing wind in the area* most frequent, most common, commonest, most usual.

prevalence *noun* **1** *the prevalence of short skirts* currency, frequency, commonness, pervasiveness, universality, popularity, fashionableness. **2** *the prevalence of sexism in the firm* | *the prevalence of malaria in the region* commonness, universality, extensiveness, ubiquity, ubiquitousness, frequency, rifeness. **3** *the prevalence of the right wing of the party* dominance, predominance, preponderance, ascendancy, mastery, supremacy.

prevalent *adjective* **1** *the prevalent opinion in the country is against the war* prevailing, current, frequent, usual, common, general, widespread, pervasive, universal, set, established, accepted, popular, fashionable, in fashion, in style, in vogue. **2** *malaria is prevalent there* common, usual, endemic, widespread, universal, extensive, frequent, ubiquitous, rampant, rife. **3** *the prevalent political party* prevailing, dominant, predominant, predominating, preponderant, ruling, governing. See PREVAILING 2.
Antonyms: UNCOMMON; RARE; UNPOPULAR.

---

prevalent
abundant, common, copious,
plentiful, prevailing, rife
Wildflowers might be **prevalent** in the mountains during the spring months, but a particular type of wildflower might be the **prevailing** one. *Prevalent*, in other words, implies widespread occurrence or acceptance in a particular place or time (*a prevalent belief during the nineteenth century*), while *prevailing* suggests that something exists in such quantity that it surpasses or leads all others in acceptance, usage, or belief (*the prevailing theory about the evolution of man*). Wildflowers might also be **abundant** in the valleys—a word that, unlike *prevalent* and *prevailing*, is largely restricted to observations about a place and may suggest oversupply (*an abundant harvest; indications of decay were abundant*). **Plentiful**, on the other hand, refers to a large or full supply without the connotations of oversupply (*a country where jobs were plentiful*). If wildflowers are **rife**, it means that they are not only *prevalent* but spreading rapidly (*speculation was rife among the soldiers*; if they're **copious**, it means they are being produced in such quantity that they constitute a rich or flowing abundance (*weep copious tears*). What often happens, with wildflowers as well as with other beautiful things, is that they become so abundant they are regarded as **common**, a word meaning usual or ordinary (*the common cold*). Like *prevalent*, *common* can apply to a time as well as a place (*an expression common during the Depression*). But neither *abundant* nor *common* connotes dominance as clearly as *prevalent* does.

---

prevaricate *verb* evade the truth, lie, hedge, fence, beat about the bush, be evasive, shilly-shally, hem and haw, dodge the issue, dodge, sidestep the issue, sidestep, equivocate, quibble, tergiversate. See LIE² *verb*.

prevarication *noun* falsehood, lie, hedging, fencing, beating about the bush, evasion, evasiveness, shilly-shallying, hemming and hawing, dodging, sidestepping, equivocation, quibbling, tergiversation. See LIE¹ *noun*.

prevent *verb* **1** *prevent the spread of the fire* | *prevent further progress* stop, put a stop to, halt, arrest, avert, nip in the bud, fend off, turn aside, stave off, ward off, block, check, hinder, impede, hamper, obstruct, balk, foil, thwart, frustrate, forestall, inhibit, hold back, restrain, prohibit, bar, deter. **2** *prevent his daughter from leaving school* stop, hinder, impede, hamper, obstruct, inhibit, hold back, restrain, prohibit, bar.
Antonyms: CAUSE; ENCOURAGE.

prevention *noun* *the prevention of the spread of the fire* | *the prevention of crime* stopping, halting, halt, arresting, staving off, warding off, checking, hindrance, hampering, obstruction, balking, foiling, frustration, restraint, prohibition, barring, deterrence. See PREVENT 1.

preventive, preventative *adjective* **1** *preventive/preventative measures against crime* precautionary, protective, deterrent. **2** *preventive medicine*

prophylactic, disease-preventing, precautionary, protective.

preventive, preventative *noun* **1** *a preventive/
preventative against crime* preventive measure,
precautionary/protective measure, safeguard,
protection, deterrent, hindrance, obstruction.
2 *a preventive/preventative against disease* pre-
ventive/preventative drug, precautionary measure, prophylactic medicine, prophylactic device, prophylactic.

previous *adjective* **1** *the previous mayor* former,
ex-, preceding, foregoing, past, sometime,
onetime, quondam, erstwhile, antecedent,
precursory. **2** *in the previous paragraph* preceding, foregoing, earlier, prior, above, precursory, antecedent, anterior. **3** *on a previous
occasion* prior, earlier, former, preceding. **previous to** *previous to this everything was fine* before, prior to, until, up to, up until, earlier than,
preceding.
Antonyms: FOLLOWING; NEXT; CONSEQUENT.

previously *adverb* *previously they lived in Kansas*
formerly, earlier on, before, until now/then,
hitherto, heretofore, once, at one time, in the
past, in years gone by.

prey *noun* **1** *lions looking for prey* quarry, game,
kill. **2** *a con man looking for prey* | *a prey for any
dishonest salesman* victim, target, dupe; *inf.* sitting duck, sitting target, fall guy, mark, easy
mark.

prey *verb* **prey on 1** *lions preying on deer* | *hawks
preying on small birds* live on, live off, eat, devour, hunt, catch, seize. **2** *con men preying on
the unsuspecting* use as a victim, victimize, exploit, take advantage of, fleece, attack, terrorize, blackmail, bleed; *inf.* con. **3** *his crime
preyed on his mind* weigh down on, weigh upon,
weigh heavily on, lie heavy on, oppress, burden, be a burden on, hang over, trouble, worry,
distress, haunt.

price *noun* **1** *what is the price of the table in the
window?* | *with prices rising* cost, asking price,
charge, fee, payment, rate, amount, figure,
value, valuation, outlay, expense, expenditure,
bill. **2** *the price of breaking the law* | *lack of pri-
vacy is the price of fame* consequence, result,
cost, penalty, sacrifice, forfeit, forfeiture, punishment. **3** *outlaws with a price on their heads*
reward, bounty, premium, recompense, compensation. **at a price** *buying black-market goods
at a price* at a high price, at an expensive price,
at a high cost, for a great deal of money, at considerable cost. **at any price** *they want that house
at any price* | *the country wants peace at any price*
whatever the price, whatever the cost, at whatever cost, no matter what the cost, no matter
the cost, cost what it may/might, expense no
object, regardless. **beyond price** *jewels/keepsakes/
virtue beyond price* priceless, of incalculable
value/worth, of inestimable value/worth, invaluable, precious, rare, irreplaceable, treasured, cherished, prized. *See* PRICELESS 1.

price *verb* *price the items at $10 each* fix the price

of, set the price of, cost, value, rate, evaluate,
assess, estimate, appraise, assay.

priceless *adjective* **1** *priceless jewels/memories/
virtue* beyond price, without price, of incalculable value/worth, of inestimable value/worth,
invaluable, precious, rare, incomparable, expensive, costly, rich, dear, irreplaceable, treasured, prized, cherished, worth its weight in
gold, worth a king's ransom. **2** *his jokes are
priceless* hilarious, extremely amusing, very
funny, comic, riotous, rib-tickling, sidesplitting; *inf.* a scream, a hoot, a laugh riot. **3** *looking priceless in that hat* absurd, ridiculous, comical, hilarious, extremely amusing, very funny;
inf. a scream, a hoot.
Antonyms: WORTHLESS; CHEAP.

prick *noun* **1** *give his finger a prick with a sharp
needle* jag, jab, stab, nick, wound. **2** *see the prick
on the surface* puncture, perforation, hole, pin-
hole, nick, wound. **3** *feel a prick on the surface
of the skin* prickle, sting, smarting, tingle, tingling, pain. **4** *the pricks of his conscience* pricking, pang, twinge, gnawing. **5** *rosebushes with
pricks* spike, thorn, barb, spine, prong, tine.

prick *verb* **1** *prick the balloon with a needle* pierce,
puncture, perforate, penetrate, make a hole in,
put a hole in, stab, nick, gash, slit, bore. **2** *she
pricked her finger on a needle* | *thorns pricked her
bare legs* jag, jab, stab, nick, wound. **3** *his eyes
began to prick in the smoke* sting, smart, tingle.
4 *his conscience began to prick him* distress, cause
distress to, trouble, worry, gnaw at, cause pain
to. **5** *ambition pricked him on to greater effort*
goad, prod, urge, spur, prompt, incite, push,
propel.

prickle *noun* **1** *the prickles on the stem of the rose*
thorn, needle, barb, spike, point, spine, spur.
2 *feel a prickle on her skin* prickling sensation,
tingle, tingling sensation, tingling, sting, stinging, smarting, itching, creeping sensation,
goose bumps/flesh/pimples, formication,
paresthesia, pins and needles.

prickle *verb* **1** *his scalp began to prickle* tingle,
sting, smart, itch, have a creeping sensation,
have goose bumps/flesh/pimples, have pins
and needles. **2** *the rough wool prickled his skin*
make something tingle, sting, make something
smart, make something itch.

prickly *adjective* **1** *a prickly branch* spiky, spiked,
thorny, barbed, bristly, spiny, pronged. **2** *a
prickly feeling in his scalp* prickling, tingling,
stinging, smarting, itching, itchy, creeping,
crawling. **3** *he is a rather prickly character* cantankerous, irascible, irritable, bad-tempered,
touchy, edgy, fractious, peevish, grumpy, snap-
pish, snappy. **4** *prickly issues* | *prickly problems*
difficult, troublesome, vexatious, tough, complicated, complex, intricate, involved, knotty,
thorny, ticklish, tricky.

pride *noun* **1** *his pride was hurt by her criticisms*
self-esteem, self-respect, ego, *amour propre*,

self-worth, self-image, self-identity, feelings, sensibilities. **2** *guilty of pride* | *puffed with pride at his achievement* conceit, vanity, arrogance, haughtiness, self-importance, self-conceit, self-love, self-glorification, egotism, presumption, hauteur, superciliousness, disdain; *inf.* bigheadedness, swellheadedness. **3** *take/have pride in his work* satisfaction, gratification, pleasure, joy, delight. **4** *the gold medalist is the pride of the swim team* pride and joy, prize, jewel, jewel in the crown, flower, gem, treasure, glory. *Antonyms:* MODESTY; HUMILITY.

pride
arrogance, conceit, egotism, self-esteem, vainglory, vanity

If you take **pride** in yourself or your accomplishments, it means that you believe in your own worth, merit, or superiority—whether or not that belief is justified (*she took pride in her accomplishments*). When your opinion of yourself is exaggerated, you're showing **conceit**, a word that combines *pride* with self-obsession. If you like to be noticed and admired for your appearance or achievements, you're revealing your **vanity**, and if you show off or boast about your accomplishments, you're likely to be accused of **vainglory**, a somewhat literary term for a self-important display of power, skill, or influence. **Arrogance** is an overbearing pride combined with disdain for others (*his arrogance led him to assume that everyone else would obey his orders*), while **egotism** implies self-centeredness or an excessive preoccupation with yourself (*blinded by egotism to the suffering of others*). While no one wants to be accused of *arrogance* or *egotism*, there's a lot to be said for **self-esteem**, which may suggest undue pride but is more often used to describe a healthy belief in oneself and respect for one's worth as a person (*she suffered from low self-esteem*).

pride *verb* **pride oneself on** *she prided herself on her punctuality* be proud of oneself for, take pride in, take satisfaction in, congratulate oneself on, flatter oneself on, give oneself a pat on the back for, revel in, glory in, exult in, boast about, brag about, crow about.

priest *noun* clergyman, minister, vicar, ecclesiastic, cleric, churchman, churchwoman, man/woman of the cloth, man/woman of God, father, padre. *See also table at* ECCLESIASTIC.

prig *noun* prude, puritan, killjoy; *inf.* goody-goody, Goody Two-shoes.

priggish *adjective* prudish, puritanical, prim, prissy, straitlaced, stuffy, starchy, sanctimonious, self-righteous, narrow-minded, censorious; *inf.* holier-than-thou, goody-goody.

prim *adjective* proper, demure, formal, precise, stuffy, starchy, straitlaced, prudish, prissy, priggish, puritanical.
Antonyms: INFORMAL; CAREFREE; LAID-BACK.

prima donna *noun* diva, leading lady, star.

primarily *adverb* *his role is primarily an administrative one* basically, essentially, in essence, fundamentally, in the first place, first and foremost, chiefly, mainly, in the main, principally, mostly, for the most part, on the whole, predominantly, predominately.

primary *adjective* **1** *the children's welfare is our primary consideration* prime, chief, main, principal, leading, predominant, most important, paramount. **2** *finding food to eat is a primary need* basic, fundamental, elemental, rudimentary, essential, prime. **3** *the primary stages of development* | *the primary stages of the disease* earliest, original, initial, beginning, first, opening, introductory. **4** *the primary stage of civilization* first, earliest, prehistoric, primitive, primeval, primal, primordial, autochthonal.
Antonyms: SECONDARY; SUBORDINATE.

prime *adjective* **1** *his prime motive was self-interest* chief, main, principal, leading, predominant, most important, major, paramount. **2** *the prime cause of the trouble* basic, fundamental, elemental, rudimentary, essential, primary. **3** *of prime quality* | *a prime site* | *prime meat* top-quality, highest, top, best, first-class, high-grade, grade A, superior, choice, select; *inf.* A-1. **4** *a prime example of what is wrong with modern society* classic, ideal, excellent, typical, standard.
Antonyms: MINOR; INFERIOR.

prime *noun* **1** *in the prime of his life* best part, peak, pinnacle, best days, height, zenith, acme, culmination, apex, heyday, full flowering. **2** *flowers in their prime* perfection, peak, full flowering, blossoming.

prime *verb* **1** *prime the machines for use* prepare, make ready, get ready, equip. **2** *prime the investigating officer* brief, give information to, inform, supply with facts; *inf.* clue in, give the low-down to, fill in. **3** *the attorney was accused of priming the witness* instruct beforehand, coach, give information to, prepare.

primeval *adjective* *primeval rocks/species* ancient, earliest, prehistoric, primitive, primordial, primal, autochthonal, pristine.

primitive *adjective* **1** *in primitive times* | *the primitive church* ancient, earliest, primeval, primordial, primal, autochthonal. **2** *primitive farming tools* crude, simple, rudimentary, undeveloped, unrefined, rough, unsophisticated, rude. **3** *primitive tribes* uncivilized, barbarian, barbaric, savage, wild. **4** *primitive art* simple, natural, unsophisticated, naïve, undeveloped, childlike. **5** *primitive artists* unsophisticated, naïve, untaught, untrained, untutored.
Antonyms: MODERN; ADVANCED; SOPHISTICATED.

primp *verb* *primp themselves for the photo* groom, tidy, smarten, spruce, preen, plume; *inf.* doll up.

prince *noun* *Monaco's ruling prince* ruler, lord, sovereign, potentate.

princely *adjective* **1** *a princely procession/array* gust, magnificent, majestic. **2** *give princely gifts | a princely sum of money* magnanimous, munificent, bounteous, bountiful, lavish, generous, openhanded, liberal.

principal *adjective* **1** *the principal members of the organization* chief, leading, preeminent, foremost, most important, most influential, dominant, controlling, ruling, in charge. **2** *the principal issues on the agenda | the principal points to be considered* chief, main, major, most important, leading, key, primary, prime, paramount. **3** *the principal cities of the world* capital, main, leading, major.
Antonyms: MINOR; SUBORDINATE; SUBSIDIARY.

principal *noun* **1** *the principals in the firm* chief, head, director, leader, manager, boss, ruler, controller; *inf.* honcho. **2** *the principals in the play* leading player, leading performer, leading man/lady, lead, star. **3** *lend him the principal to start up the business* capital, capital sum, capital funds, working capital, financial resources.

principally *adverb he is interested principally in higher education* chiefly, above all, first and foremost, mainly, in the main, primarily, for the most part, mostly, particularly, especially.

principle *noun* **1** *the basic principles of geometry | understand the principles of monetarism* truth, philosophy, idea, theory, basis, fundamental, essence, assumption. **2** *believe in the principle of equal opportunity* rule, golden rule, law, canon, tenet, code, maxim, axiom, dictum, postulate. **3** *a woman of principle | a woman without principle* morals, principles, ethics, integrity, uprightness, righteousness, probity, rectitude, sense of honor, honor, conscience, scruples. **in principle 1** *there is no reason in principle why such a machine could not be built* in theory, theoretically. **2** *they agree in principle to the plan* in essence, in general.

principles *plural noun it is against his principles to lie | have no principles* moral code, code of ethics, code, morals, ethics, beliefs, credo. *See* PRINCIPLE 3.

print *verb* **1** *print books/newspapers* set in print, send to press, run off, put to bed. **2** *they have printed thousands of copies* publish, issue. **3** *print a design on the cloth* imprint, stamp, mark. **4** *events printed forever on her memory* imprint, impress, engrave, etch, stamp, mark.

print *noun* **1** *see the story in print | the print is too small to be legible* type, letters, lettering, typeface, newsprint. **2** *buy a print of one of Monet's works* copy, reproduction, replica. **3** *buy a set of prints showing presidential homes* picture, design, engraving, lithograph. **4** *get enlarged prints* photograph, photo, snap, snapshot. **5** *chairs covered in a print* printed material/cloth, patterned material/cloth, chintz. **6** *leave prints* fingerprint, footprint, mark, impression. **in print 1** *she will believe it only if she sees it in print | likes to see his name in print* printed, in black and white, on paper. **2** *are her novels still in*

print? published, printed, available in bookstores, on the market. **out of print** *looking for a biography that is out of print* no longer published/printed, not on the market, unavailable, unobtainable.

prior *adjective a prior claim | no prior knowledge required* earlier, previous, anterior. **prior to** *prior to the conference, they had never met* before, until, up to, earlier than, preceding.
Antonyms: LATER; SUBSEQUENT.

priority *noun* **1** *the children's safety is their priority | decide on a list of priorities* first/prime concern, most important thing/act, most pressing thing/act. **2** *give priority to homeless people* precedence, preference, urgency, highest place, top place. **3** *in terms of length of service, he has priority* precedence, seniority, superiority, supremacy, paramountcy, prerogative.

priory *noun* religious house, abbey, cloister, monastery, friary, convent, nunnery.

prison *noun* jail, penitentiary, lockup, penal institution, place of detention, place of confinement, dungeon; *inf.* clink, cooler, slammer, stir, can, pen.

prisoner *noun* **1** *prisoners let out on parole* convict, jailbird; *inf.* con, lifer. **2** *the kidnappers released their prisoner | the invading army took many prisoners* prisoner of war, POW, hostage, captive, detainee, internee.

pristine *adjective* **1** *a pristine copy of the book* unmarked, unblemished, unspoiled, spotless, immaculate, clean, in mint condition, in perfect condition. **2** *pristine snow* unmarked, spotless, clean, fresh, virgin.

privacy *noun* **1** *enjoy the privacy of his study | the privacy of their walled garden* privateness, seclusion, solitude, isolation, retirement, sequestration, quietness, peace, lack of disturbance, lack of interruption, freedom from interference. **2** *accuse the press of invading her privacy* right to privacy, right to privateness, privateness, freedom from interference.

private *adjective* **1** *for her private use* personal, individual, own, particular, especial, special, exclusive. **2** *hold private talks | her private opinion* confidential, strictly confidential, not for publication, not to be made public, not to be disclosed, secret, unofficial, off-the-record, in camera, closet, privileged; *inf.* hush-hush. **3** *her private thoughts* personal, intimate, secret. **4** *a private place where the lovers meet* secluded, sequestered, quiet, secret, remote, out-of-the-way, withdrawn, retired. **5** *trespassing on private property* not open to the public, privately owned, off-limits. **6** *wish to be private* undisturbed, without disturbance, uninterrupted, without interruption, alone, solitary. **7** *a private person* reserved, retiring, self-contained, uncommunicative, noncommunicative, noncommittal, diffident, secretive. **8** *the president on a private visit* nonofficial, unofficial, nonpublic, personal. **9** *private industry/education/medicine* nonstate, private-enterprise, privatized, independent. **private investigator** *See* INVESTIGATOR.

Antonyms: PUBLIC; OPEN; GENERAL; SOCIABLE.

private *noun privates in the army* infantryman, foot soldier, enlisted man; *inf.* GI, GI Joe. **in private** *the talks were held in private* privately, secretly, in secrecy, behind closed doors, sub rosa. *See* PRIVATELY 1.

privately *adverb* **1** *the talks were held privately* in private, in camera, in secret, secretly, in secrecy, behind closed doors, in confidence, confidentially, sub rosa. **2** *privately she thought he was doing the wrong thing* personally, secretly, unofficially. **3** *they required somewhere to meet privately* out of public view, in seclusion, in solitude, alone, without being disturbed, without being interrupted.

privation *noun suffering a life of privation* deprivation, want, need, neediness, disadvantage, poverty, penury, hardship, distress, indigence, destitution.

privilege *noun* **1** *parking there is the privilege of the executives* right, birthright, prerogative, entitlement, due, sanction, advantage, benefit. **2** *enjoy diplomatic privilege* immunity, exemption, dispensation, concession, liberty, freedom. **3** *has always led a life of privilege* advantage, social advantage, advantageousness, favor, favorable circumstances, superior situation. **4** *he felt that it had been a privilege to meet her* honor, special benefit.

privileged *adjective* **1** *coming from a privileged background* advantaged, socially advantaged, favored, elite, indulgent, spoiled, protected, sheltered. **2** *that is certainly the law, but foreign diplomats are privileged* immune, exempt, excepted. **3** *punished for revealing privileged information* confidential, private, not for publication, off-the-record, secret, top-secret; *inf.* hush-hush.

privy *adjective* **privy to** *not privy to his plans* acquainted with, aware of, in on, informed of, apprised of, cognizant of; *inf.* in the know about, clued in on.

prize[1] *noun* **1** *win a prize in the lottery* winnings, jackpot, stakes, purse. **2** *win first prize in the track race* | *six prizes awarded in the flower show* trophy, medal, award, accolade, reward, premium, honor, laurels. **3** *working toward the prize of a higher salary* goal, aim, desire, hope. **4** *the prizes of war* spoils, booty, plunder, loot, pillage, pickings, trophy.

prize[2] *adjective wind destroyed his prize roses* prizewinning, award-winning, winning, champion, best, top, choice, select, first-class, first-rate, excellent; *inf.* top-notch, A-1.

prize[3] *verb prize his few remaining possessions* | *she prizes her freedom* value, set a high value on, set great store by, treasure, cherish, hold dear, ap-

preciate greatly, attach great importance to, esteem, hold in high regard.

prize[4] *verb prize the lid off* pry, lever, force, pull; *inf.* yank.

prized *adjective have his prized stamp collection stolen* valued, treasured, cherished, precious, beloved.

probability *noun* **1** *what is the probability of the government losing the election?* | *there is little probability that we will be able to go* likelihood, likeliness, prospect, expectation, chance, chances, odds, possibility. **2** *snow at Christmas is a distinct probability* probable event, likelihood, prospect, possibility, reasonable bet.

probable *adjective the probable result is a win for the home team* | *it is probable that we will arrive late* likely, most likely, odds-on, expected, to be expected, anticipated, predictable, foreseeable, in the cards, credible, quite possible, possible.

Antonyms: IMPROBABLE; UNLIKELY.

probably *adverb they will probably win* in all probability, likely, most likely, in all likelihood, as likely as not, it is to be expected that, perhaps, maybe, it may be, possibly; *inf.* as like as not.

probation *noun new trainees must do a three-month period of probation* trial, trial period, test period, tryout, experimental period. **on probation** **1** *young offenders on probation* under official supervision. **2** *trainees on probation* on trial, on a trial period.

probe *noun order a probe into the company's accounting procedures* investigation, scrutiny, scrutinization, close inquiry, inquest, exploration, examination, study, research, analysis.

probe *verb* **1** *probing the patient for lumps* | *probe the tooth with his tongue* feel, feel around, prod, poke, explore, check. **2** *probe the financial state of the company* investigate, conduct an investigation into, scrutinize, inquire into, conduct an inquiry into, carry out an inquest into, examine, subject to an examination, study, research, analyze.

problem *noun* **1** *face a seemingly impossible problem* difficulty, difficult situation, vexed question, complication, trouble, mess, predicament, plight, dilemma, quandary; *inf.* pickle, can of worms. **2** *he has business problems* | *the car's mechanical problems* difficulty, difficult situation, trouble, complication. **3** *he and his wife have had a few problems* difficulty, dispute, subject of dispute, point at issue, bone of contention. **4** *solve the arithmetical problems* | *baffled by the word problems* question, puzzle, poser, enigma, riddle, conundrum; *inf.* teaser, brainteaser. **5** *the child is a real problem* source of trouble, source of difficulty, bother, nuisance, pest, vexation; *inf.* hassle, aggravation.

problem *adjective a problem child* difficult, troublesome, delinquent, unmanageable, unruly, uncontrollable, intractable, recalcitrant, nuisance.

problematic *adjective* **1** *a problematic situation*

problematical, difficult, troublesome, complicated, puzzling, knotty, thorny, ticklish, tricky. **2** *the likely result is still problematic* doubtful, open to doubt, uncertain, unsettled, questionable, open to question, debatable, arguable.
Antonyms: SIMPLE; STRAIGHTFORWARD; CERTAIN.

procedure noun **1** *the usual office procedure | pay due attention to procedure* course of action, line of action, plan of action, policy, system, method, methodology, modus operandi, technique, means, practice, operation, strategy, way, routine, wont, custom. **2** *essential procedures for setting up the new system* action, step, process, measure, move, operation, transaction.

proceed verb **1** *proceed along Main Street | proceed upstairs slowly* make one's way, go, go on, go forward, go ahead, advance, carry on, move on, press on, progress. **2** *proceed to question him | how shall we proceed?* act, take action, take steps, take measures, go ahead, move, make a start, progress, get under way. **3** *noise proceeding from the floor below | the tragedy that proceeded from a family feud* arise, originate, spring, stem, come, derive, result, follow, ensue, emanate, issue, flow. **proceed against** *proceed against his employers for unfair dismissal* take (legal) proceedings against, begin an action against, start an action against, take to court, sue. **proceed with** *proceed with their work* go on with, continue with, continue, get on with, get ahead with.

proceeding noun *such a proceeding will have to be carefully considered* action, course of action, step, measure, move, maneuver, act, deed, operation, transaction, venture, procedure, process.

proceedings plural noun **1** *the evening's proceedings begin at 7 p.m.* activities, events, action, process, business, affairs, doings, happenings. **2** *the proceedings against him are likely to last several weeks* legal proceedings, legal action/case, case, lawsuit, litigation, trial. **3** *the proceedings of the meeting were made available to all society members* minutes, report, account, record, transactions.

proceeds plural noun *donate the proceeds of/from the book to charity* takings, profits, returns, receipts, gain, income, earnings.

process noun **1** *damaged during the manufacturing process* operation, action, activity, steps, stages. **2** *develop a new process for cleaning old stone buildings* method, system, technique, means, practice, way, procedure. **3** *the aging process* development, evolution, changes, stages, steps. **4** *in the process of time* course, advance, progress. **5** *legal processes can be very slow* proceedings, legal action, legal case, case, lawsuit, trial. **in the process** *we are in the process of cataloging our books* in the midst, in the course, in the performance, in the execution, at the stage.

procession noun **1** *a candlelit procession as part of the celebration* parade, march, column, file, train, cortege. **2** *a procession of decorated vehicles* cavalcade, motorcade. **3** *a seemingly endless procession of houseguests* stream, steady stream, string, succession, series, sequence, run.

proclaim verb **1** *proclaim the news of a royal birth | proclaim a public holiday* announce, declare, make known, give out, notify, circulate, advertise, publish, broadcast, promulgate, pronounce, blazon, trumpet, shout something from the rooftops. **2** *proclaim him king* pronounce, announce, declare someone to be. **3** *her accent proclaimed that she was French* indicate, show, reveal, testify.

proclamation noun **1** *hear the proclamation of a royal birth* announcement, declaration, notification, circulation, advertisement, publishing, broadcasting, promulgation, pronouncement, blazoning. **2** *the king's proclamation was posted in each town* announcement, declaration, pronouncement, decree, edict, order, command, rule, manifesto.

proclivity noun *a proclivity toward outbursts of rage | have peculiar sexual proclivities* tendency, inclination, leaning, propensity, bent, bias, proneness, penchant, predisposition, weakness.

procrastinate verb *procrastinate in the hope that someone else would do the work* delay, postpone action, defer action, be dilatory, use delaying tactics, stall, temporize, play for time, play the waiting game, dally, dilly-dally, drag one's feet/heels.

procreation noun *procreation of the species* sexual reproduction, generation, propagation, multiplication.

procure verb **1** *procure a copy of the book from the library* obtain, acquire, get, pick up, find, come by, get hold of, secure, get possession of, lay one's hands on, get one's hands on, gain. **2** *somehow procure the dismissal of his colleague* bring about, cause, contrive, manage, manipulate, rig; *inf.* fix. **3** *the police found that he was procuring* pimp, pander.

prod verb **1** *prod him in the ribs* poke, jab, dig, nudge, elbow, butt, push, shove, thrust. **2** *prod the child into doing some work* urge, encourage, rouse, move, motivate, stimulate, incite, spur on, impel, actuate, goad.

prod noun **1** *get a prod in the ribs from someone in the crowd* poke, jab, dig, nudge, elbow, butt, push, shove, thrust. **2** *use a prod to get the cows to go back to the farm* goad, stick, spike. **3** *giving the child a prod to get him to do some work* encouragement, prompting, prompt, motivation, stimulus, incitement, spur, goad.

prodigal adjective *a government accused of being prodigal | her prodigal catering* extravagant, spendthrift, squandering, improvident, imprudent, immoderate, profligate, excessive,

wasteful, reckless, wanton. **prodigal of/with** *prodigal with his gifts to the poor | prodigal of compliments* lavish with, liberal with, generous with, bountiful with, bounteous with, abundant in, abounding in.
Antonyms: THRIFTY; FRUGAL.

prodigious *adjective* **1** *a prodigious achievement* amazing, astonishing, astounding, staggering, stupendous, marvelous, wonderful, phenomenal, miraculous, impressive, striking, startling, extraordinary, remarkable, exceptional, unusual; *inf.* fantastic, fabulous, flabbergasting. **2** *children frightened by the prodigious creatures on the screen* enormous, huge, colossal, gigantic, giant, mammoth, immense, massive, vast, monumental, tremendous, inordinate, monstrous, grotesque, abnormal. **3** *charge a prodigious amount of money* huge, large, colossal, immense, massive, considerable, substantial, sizable; *inf.* vast, tremendous.
Antonyms: ORDINARY; UNEXCEPTIONAL; NORMAL; TINY.

prodigy *noun* **1** *the young musician is a prodigy* genius, child genius, gifted child, mastermind; *inf.* Einstein. **2** *the pyramids are among the prodigies of the world* wonder, marvel, phenomenon, sensation, miracle. **3** *the saint is a prodigy of patience* classic example, example, model, paragon, paradigm, epitome, exemplar, ideal.

produce *verb* **1** *a factory producing high-quality work* make, manufacture, create, construct, build, fabricate, put together, assemble, turn out. **2** *produce great works of art* compose, create, originate, prepare, develop, frame, fashion, turn out. **3** *produce new evidence* bring forward, set forth, present, offer, proffer, advance, show, exhibit, demonstrate, disclose, reveal. **4** *soil producing good crops | cows producing milk* yield, bear, give, bring forth, supply, provide, furnish. **5** *sows producing litters of piglets* give birth to, bring forth, bear, breed, give life to, bring into the world, procreate. **6** *his speech produced an angry reaction* cause, give rise to, evoke, bring about, set off, occasion, generate, engender, induce, initiate, start, spark off. **7** *produce plays for television* mount, stage, put on, present, direct.

produce *noun organically grown produce* crops, fruit and vegetables, fruit, vegetables, greens.

producer *noun* **1** *a country that is a major producer of cars | a producer of high-quality work* maker, manufacturer, creator, builder. *See* PRODUCE *verb* 1. **2** *producers of fine fruits and vegetables* grower, farmer. **3** *the producer of several major movies* backer, promoter, administrator, manager, impresario; *inf.* angel.

product *noun* **1** *a factory specializing in electronic products* commodity, artifact, manufactured item/article/thing. **2** *good health is the product of good nutrition | he is the product of a Victori-*

an upbringing result, outcome, effect, consequence, upshot, fruit, spin-off, legacy. **products** *marketing new products* goods, wares, merchandise.

production *noun* **1** *speed up the production of cars* producing, making, manufacture, manufacturing, creation, construction, building, fabrication, assembly. **2** *his production of great works of literature/art/music* composition, creation, origination, preparation, development, framing, fashioning. **3** *the production of new evidence* presenting, offering, proffering, advancement, exhibition, demonstration, disclosure. **4** *an increase in production* output, yield. **5** *see a production of her latest play* performance, staging, mounting. **6** *several productions staged by the company* play, film, concert, show, performance, presentation, piece. **7** *this is the writer's latest production* work, publication, book, volume, tome, novel, story, composition, piece, creation, opus. **8** *artist's latest production* work, work of art, painting, picture, piece, creation.

productive *adjective* **1** *productive soil* fertile, fruitful, fecund, rich, high-yielding. **2** *a productive worker* prolific, energetic, vigorous, efficient. **3** *not a very productive day's work* profitable, gainful, valuable, fruitful, useful, constructive, effective, worthwhile, beneficial, rewarding. **4** *an attitude scarcely productive of good labor relations* producing, causing, resulting in.
Antonyms: STERILE; BARREN; UNPRODUCTIVE.

productivity *noun* **1** *the productivity of the soil* productiveness, fertility, fecundity, fruitfulness, richness. **2** *improve the productivity of the workers/factory* productiveness, work-rate, output, yield, production, capacity, efficiency.

profane *adjective* **1** *their profane behavior in setting fire to the altar* blasphemous, sacrilegious, impious, idolatrous, irreligious, ungodly, godless, irreverent, disrespectful. **2** *shocked by their profane language* blasphemous, obscene, foul, vulgar, crude, filthy, coarse.
Antonyms: RELIGIOUS; SACRED; DECOROUS.

profanity *noun* **1** *the profanity of brawling in church* profaneness, blasphemy, sacrilege, impiety, idolatry, irreligiousness, irreverence, disrespectfulness, disrespect. **2** *issue a stream of profanities* oath, swearword, swearing, obscenity, four-letter word, curse, execration, imprecation.

profess *verb* **1** *profess satisfaction with his work* declare, announce, proclaim, assert, state, utter, affirm, avow, aver. **2** *he professed total ignorance of the situation* claim, lay claim to, allege, pretend, feign, make out, sham, fake, dissemble. **3** *profess one's faith* declare publicly, make a public declaration of, avow, confess, confirm, declare one's allegiance to, acknowledge publicly.

professed *adjective* **1** *see through her professed love for children | deserted by her professed supporters* claimed, alleged, ostensible, supposed, so-called, pretended, feigned, sham, fake, would-be. **2** *he is a professed Christian/pacifist* declared, avowed, confessed, self-confessed, self-acknowledged, confirmed.

profession noun **1** *a teacher by profession* | *seek a profession in medicine* career, calling, vocation, occupation, line of work, line of employment, position, situation, post, job, office, appointment, métier. **2** *in the medical/legal profession* sphere of work, line of work, area of work, walk of life, business. **3** *they were relieved by his professions of satisfaction* declaration, announcement, proclamation, assertion, statement, affirmation, avowal, averment. **4** *not taken in by his profession of ignorance* claim, allegation, pretense, feigning, shamming, faking, dissembling. **5** *his profession of his faith* declaration, public declaration, avowal, confession, public acknowledgment, testimony.

professional adjective **1** *he has a professional job* white-collar. **2** *a very professional worker* skilled, skillful, proficient, expert, adept, competent, efficient, experienced. **3** *a very professional piece of work* | *such a professional performance* skillful, expert, adept, masterly, excellent, fine, polished, finished. **4** *a professional tennis player* nonamateur, paid. **5** *conduct that was hardly professional* ethical, fitting. *Antonyms:* INEPT; AMATEUR; AMATEURISH.

professional noun **1** *a new office for the young professional* professional worker, white-collar worker. **2** *this tennis player is a professional now* professional player, nonamateur, paid player; *inf.* pro. **3** *the singer/tailor is a real professional* expert, skilled person, master, past master, adept, authority; *inf.* pro.

professor noun *professor of French at the university* teacher, educator, faculty member; full professor, associate professor, professor emeritus.

proffer verb *proffer assistance* | *decide to proffer one's resignation* offer, tender, present, extend, give, submit, volunteer, suggest. *Antonyms:* REFUSE; WITHDRAW.

proficiency noun *their proficiency in keyboarding* | *acquired proficiency in the art of public speaking* skill, skillfulness, adeptness, aptness, expertise, expertness, adroitness, deftness, excellence, ability, ableness, capability, competence, experience, effectiveness, accomplishment, talent.

proficient adjective *a proficient keyboarder/swimmer* | *proficient at swimming* | *proficient in French* skillful, skilled, adept, apt, expert, adroit, deft, able, capable, competent, experienced, effective, accomplished, talented, gifted. *Antonyms:* INEPT; INEXPERT; INCOMPETENT.

profile noun **1** *draw her profile* | *look better in profile* side-view, outline. **2** *the profile of the church against the sky* silhouette, outline, contour, lines, shape, form, figure. **3** *write a profile of the author* short biography, sketch, thumbnail sketch, portrait, vignette.

profit noun **1** *the profit made from the sale of the house* | *the builder's annual profit* takings, proceeds, gain, yield, return, receipts, income, earnings, winnings. **2** *you could, with profit, take her advice* | *seem to gain little profit from the experience* gain, benefit, advantage, good, value, use, avail. *Antonyms:* LOSS; DISADVANTAGE.

profit verb *it will not profit you to be openly critical of the company* benefit, be of benefit to, be of advantage to, be advantageous to, be of use/value to, be of service to, serve, do (someone) good, help, be helpful to, assist, aid, stand (someone) in good stead. **profit from** *profit from his advice* | *try to profit from the experience* derive benefit from, benefit from, reap the benefit of, gain from, derive advantage from, put to good use, learn from; *inf.* cash in on.

profitable adjective **1** *a profitable venture* profit-making, moneymaking, commercial, gainful, remunerative, paying, lucrative. **2** *a profitable company* profit-making, moneymaking, sound, solvent, in the black. **3** *find it a profitable experience* | *think the conference profitable* beneficial, advantageous, rewarding, helpful, productive, useful, worthwhile, valuable.

profligacy noun **1** *in debt because of profligacy* extravagance, improvidence, prodigality, immoderateness, recklessness, wastefulness. **2** *a relationship destroyed by profligacy* dissoluteness, dissipation, debauchery, corruption, degeneracy, depravity, immorality, promiscuity, looseness, wantonness, licentiousness, lasciviousness, lechery.

profligate adjective **1** *profligate people ending up in debt* extravagant, spendthrift, improvident, prodigal, immoderate, squandering, reckless, wasteful. **2** *a profligate cad* dissolute, dissipated, debauched, abandoned, corrupt, degenerate, depraved, reprobate, unprincipled, immoral, promiscuous, loose, wanton, licentious, lascivious, lecherous. *Antonyms:* THRIFTY; FRUGAL; MORAL.

profligate noun **1** *the profligate soon spent all of his inheritance* spendthrift, prodigal, squanderer, wastrel, waster. **2** *would never date such a profligate* debauchee, degenerate, reprobate, roué, lecher.

profound adjective **1** *a profound treatise/thinker* discerning, penetrating, thoughtful, philosophical, deep, weighty, serious, learned, erudite, wise, sagacious. **2** *unable to understand such profound doctrine* learned, erudite, serious, deep, difficult, complex, abstract, abstruse, esoteric, impenetrable. **3** *a profound love for his country* deep, intense, keen, great, extreme, sincere, heartfelt. **4** *a profound silence* deep, pronounced, total, absolute, complete, utter. **5** *profound changes taking place* far-reaching, radical, extensive, exhaustive, thoroughgoing. *Antonyms:* SHALLOW; SUPERFICIAL; SLIGHT.

profoundly adverb **1** *speak very profoundly on the poet's philosophy* discerningly, penetratingly, thoughtfully, philosophically, weightily, seriously, learnedly, eruditely, wisely, sagaciously. **2** *profoundly disturbed by the news* deeply, extremely, greatly, very, thoroughly, intensely, keenly, sincerely.

profuse adjective **1** *give profuse apologies/thanks* lavish, liberal, unstinting, generous, fulsome, extravagant, inordinate, immoderate, excessive. **2** *a profuse harvest | profuse blossom on the trees* abundant, copious, ample, plentiful, bountiful, luxuriant.
Antonyms: MEAGER; SPARSE.

---

profuse
extravagant, lavish, lush, luxuriant, prodigal
Something that is **profuse** is poured out or given freely, often to the point of exaggeration or excess (*profuse apologies*). **Extravagant** also suggests unreasonable excess, but with an emphasis on wasteful spending (*her gift was much too extravagant for the occasion*). Someone who is **prodigal** is so recklessly extravagant that his or her resources will ultimately be exhausted (*the prodigal heir to the family fortune*). Another way to end up impoverished is through **lavish** spending, a word that combines extravagance with generosity or a lack of moderation (*lavish praise; lavish furnishings*). While *lavish*, *extravagant* and *prodigal* are often used to describe human behavior, **lush** and **luxuriant** normally refer to things. What is *luxuriant* is produced in great quantity, suggesting that it is not only profuse but gorgeous (*luxuriant auburn hair*). Something described as *lush* is not only luxuriant but has reached a peak of perfection (*the lush summer grass*).

---

profusion noun *a profusion of roses on the bushes* abundance, superabundance, copiousness, quantities, scores, masses, multitude, plethora, wealth, plenitude, cornucopia; *inf.* heaps, stacks, piles, loads, mountains, tons, lots, scads, oodles.

progeny noun **1** *the parents and all their progeny* children, offspring, young ones, family, issue. **2** *the progeny of John Adams* descendants, successors, lineage, scions, seed, posterity.

program noun **1** *refer to the conference program* agenda, calendar, schedule, syllabus, list of events, order of the day. **2** *buy a program at the theater* playbill, list of performers, list of players, list of artistes. **3** *the orchestra played a varied program* list of items/pieces, series of items/pieces. **4** *watch several television programs | listen to a radio program* production, presentation, show, performance, broadcast. **5** *get the program for next semester's courses* syllabus, prospectus, schedule, list, curriculum, literature. **6** *organize a program of financial invest-*

ment schedule, scheme, plan, plan of action, project.

program verb **1** *a school trip programmed for next week* schedule, plan, line up, map out, arrange, prearrange, organize. **2** *program the VCR to record at noon* set, fix, arrange.

progress noun **1** *climbers making rapid progress toward the summit | making slow progress on the icy roads* forward movement, headway, advance, going, passage, advancement, progression. **2** *the company has made very little progress in the past few years* advance, advancement, headway, steps forward, progression, improvement, betterment, upgrading, development, growth. **in progress** *work in progress* under way, going on, ongoing, happening, occurring, taking place, proceeding, being done, being performed.

progress verb **1** *the climbers progressed up the mountain* go forward, move forward/on, make one's way, advance, go on, continue, proceed, make progress, make headway, push forward, go/forge ahead. **2** *the talks are progressing | science progresses all the time* make progress, move forward, advance, make headway, take steps forward, make strides, develop, get better, improve. **3** *the patient is progressing* make progress, get better, improve, recover, recuperate.
Antonyms: RETURN; REGRESS; DETERIORATE.

progression noun **1** *the progression from high school to college | the progression from mail clerk to managing director* progress, forward movement, upward movement, passage, advancement, advance, development. **2** *a progression of applicants/jobs* succession, sequence, series, string, stream, steady stream, parade, chain, train.

progressive adjective **1** *progressive movement* forward, onward, advancing. **2** *a progressive improvement in the crime rate | a progressive amount of violence on the streets | a progressive disease* increasing, growing, intensifying, accelerating, escalating. **3** *a progressive company | a progressive office system* modern, advanced, forward-looking, forward-thinking, go-ahead, enlightened, enterprising, up-and-coming, innovative; avant-garde. **4** *progressive ideas on education | progressive political views* radical, reforming, innovative, revolutionary, revisionist.
Antonyms: CONSERVATIVE; REACTIONARY.

prohibit verb **1** *a regulation to prohibit smoking* forbid, ban, bar, disallow, proscribe, veto, interdict, outlaw. **2** *low salaries prohibit them from buying a house* prevent, stop, rule out, preclude, make impossible, hinder, impede, hamper, obstruct, restrict, constrain.
Antonyms: ALLOW; AUTHORIZE; FACILITATE.

---

prohibit
ban, disallow, enjoin, forbid, hinder, interdict, preclude
There are a number of ways to prevent some-

thing from happening. You can **prohibit** it, which assumes that you have legal or other authority and are willing to back up your prohibition with force (*prohibit smoking*); or you can simply **forbid** it and hope that you've got the necessary clout (*forbid teenagers to stay out after midnight*). **Ban** carries a little more weight—both legal and moral—and **interdict** suggests that church or civil authorities are behind the idea. To **enjoin** (in this sense) is to prohibit by legal injunction (*the truckers were enjoined from striking*), which practically guarantees that you'll get what you want. A government or some other authority may **disallow** an act it might otherwise have permitted (*the IRS disallowed the deduction*), but anyone with a little gumption can **hinder** an activity by putting obstacles in its path (*hinder the thief's getaway by tripping him on his way out the door*). Of course, the easiest way to prohibit something is to **preclude** it, which means stopping it before it even gets started.

prohibition *noun* **1** *the prohibition of smoking in hospitals* forbidding, banning, barring, disallowing, proscription, vetoing, interdiction, outlawing. **2** *a prohibition on the sale of cigarettes to children* ban, bar, interdict, veto, embargo, injunction, proscription.

prohibitive *adjective* **1** *prohibitive measures on the employment of children* prohibitory, forbidding, banning, barring, disallowing, proscriptive, restrictive, suppressive, vetoing, interdicting, outlawing. **2** *the prohibitive cost of housing* exorbitant, extortionate, excessive, preposterous, high-priced, sky-high; *inf.* steep.

project *noun* *subsidize a project to build a library* | *initiate a recycling project* scheme, plan, program, enterprise, undertaking, venture, activity, operation, campaign.

project *verb* **1** *they are projecting a trip to Alaska* | *a projected new mall* plan, propose, map out, devise, design, outline. **2** *project missiles into space* launch, discharge, propel, hurl, throw, cast, fling, shoot. **3** *the balcony projects over the garden* jut, jut out, protrude, extend, stick out, stand out, hang over, bulge out, beetle, obtrude. **4** *project sales figures for next year* extrapolate, calculate, estimate, gauge, reckon, forecast, predict, predetermine.

projectile *noun* missile, rocket, shell, grenade, bullet.

projection *noun* **1** *a projection of rock* overhang, ledge, shelf, ridge, protuberance, protrusion, jut, bulge. **2** *their sales projection for next year* extrapolation, calculation, computation, estimate, estimation, gauge, reckoning, forecast, prediction.

proletariat *noun* workers, working class, wage earners, laboring classes, common people, ordinary people, commonalty, lower classes, lower orders, rank and file, masses, mob, rabble, hoi polloi; *inf.* plebs, great unwashed.

Antonyms: ARISTOCRACY; NOBILITY.

proliferate *verb* *the number of houses in the area has proliferated beyond belief* increase, grow rapidly, multiply, extend, expand, burgeon, accelerate, escalate, rocket, snowball, mushroom.

Antonyms: DECREASE; DWINDLE.

proliferation *noun* *the proliferation of new houses in the area* increase, growth, multiplication, spread, expansion, extension, burgeoning, acceleration, escalation, buildup, rocketing, snowballing, mushrooming.

prolific *adjective* **1** *prolific vegetation* fertile, fruitful, fecund, luxuriant, abundant, profuse, copious, rank. **2** *a prolific writer* productive.

prolix *adjective* overlong, lengthy, long-winded, long-drawn-out, prolonged, protracted, verbose, wordy, discursive, digressive, rambling, wandering, circuitous, ambagious, pleonastic.

prologue *noun* *the prologue to the play/poem/novel* introduction, foreword, preface, preamble, prelude, preliminary, exordium, proem, prolegomenon.

Antonyms: EPILOGUE; afterword.

prolong *verb* *mechanical problems with the car prolonged the journey by three hours* lengthen, make longer, elongate, extend, stretch out, draw out, drag out, protract, spin out.

prominence *noun* **1** *the prominence of her cheekbones/eyes* protruding, protrusion, protuberance, protrusiveness, jutting out, standing out. **2** *a prominence on the flat countryside* protuberance, projection, jutting, swelling, bulge. **3** *a prominence overhanging the beach* promontory, pinnacle, projection, height, crest, cliff, crag. **4** *the prominence of the tower on the skyline* conspicuousness, obviousness, obtrusiveness. *See* PROMINENT 2. **5** *newspapers giving prominence to the political scandal* importance, weight, conspicuousness, precedence, top billing. **6** *men of prominence in the community* importance, eminence, preeminence, distinction, note, prestige, stature, illustriousness, celebrity, fame, renown, acclaim.

prominent *adjective* **1** *prominent cheekbones/eyes* protruding, protuberant, protrusive, jutting, jutting out, projecting, standing out, sticking out, bulging. **2** *a prominent feature of the landscape* easily seen, conspicuous, noticeable, obvious, unmistakable, obtrusive, eye-catching, striking. **3** *a prominent member of the local community* leading, outstanding, chief, foremost, main, top, important, eminent, preeminent, distinguished, notable, noted, illustrious, celebrated, well-known, famous, renowned, acclaimed.

Antonyms: INCONSPICUOUS; OBSCURE.

promiscuity *noun* promiscuousness, dissoluteness, dissipation, licentiousness, looseness, profligacy, immorality, debauchery, wantonness.

promiscuous *adjective* sexually indiscriminating, dissolute, dissipated, fast, licentious, loose, profligate, abandoned, immoral, debauched, wanton, of easy virtue, unchaste.
Antonyms: CHASTE; MORAL; PURE.

promise *verb* 1 *promise that he will be present | promise to go | but you promised* give one's word, give one's assurance, swear, vow, take an oath, pledge, contract. 2 *skies that promise good weather | it promises well for him that he has got an interview* augur, indicate, denote, signify, be a sign of, show signs of, hint at, suggest, betoken, presage.

promise *noun* 1 *give a promise that he would be there* word, word of honor, assurance, guarantee, commitment, vow, oath, pledge, bond, contract, covenant. 2 *a promise of spring in the air* indication, hint, suggestion, sign. 3 *a young musician of promise* talent, potential, flair, ability, aptitude, capability, capacity.

promising *adjective* 1 *their first reactions to the scheme are promising | it is promising that you have a second interview* encouraging, hopeful, favorable, auspicious, propitious, optimistic, bright. 2 *a promising young writer* with potential, talented, gifted, able, apt; *inf.* up-and-coming.
Antonyms: UNFAVORABLE; UNPROMISING.

promontory *noun* headland, point, cape, head, foreland, bluff, cliff, precipice, overhang, height, projection, prominence.

promote *verb* 1 *the boss had promoted him | she has been promoted to sales manager* give promotion to, upgrade, give a higher position to, give a higher rank to, place in a higher rank, elevate, advance, move up, prefer, aggrandize. 2 *he promoted the cause of peace by his actions* advance, further, assist, aid, help, contribute to, foster, boost. 3 *the local council promotes equal rights for all* advocate, recommend, urge, support, back, endorse, champion, sponsor, espouse. 4 *companies promoting their new products* advertise, publicize, push, puff, puff up, beat the drum for; *inf.* plug, give a plug to, hype, hype up.
Antonyms: DEMOTE; OBSTRUCT; IMPEDE.

promotion *noun* 1 *get a promotion to a managerial post* upgrading, move up, elevation, advancement, preferment, aggrandizement. 2 *his promotion of peace by his actions* advancement, furtherance, furthering, assistance, aid, help, contribution to, fostering, boosting. 3 *the council's promotion of equal rights for all* advocacy, recommendation, urging, support, backing, endorsement, championship, sponsoring, espousal. 4 *the company's promotion of their new products* advertising, advertising campaign, publicity, publicizing, push, pushing, hard sell; *inf.* plug, plugging, hype, hyping.

prompt *adjective* 1 *receive a prompt reply* immediate, instant, instantaneous, swift, rapid, speedy, quick, fast, expeditious, early, punctual, in good time, timely. 2 *she is prompt to offer assistance* swift, rapid, speedy, quick, fast, ready, willing, eager.
Antonyms: SLOW; LATE; tardy; UNWILLING.

prompt *verb* 1 *what prompted them to leave?* cause, make, encourage, move, induce, urge, incite, impel, spur on, motivate, stimulate, inspire, provoke. 2 *his actions prompted an angry response* cause, give rise to, induce, call forth, occasion, elicit, evoke, provoke. 3 *he forgot his lines, so she prompted him* remind, jog someone's memory, refresh someone's memory, cue, give someone a cue, help out.
Antonyms: DISCOURAGE; DETER; RESTRAIN.

promptly *adverb* 1 *arrive promptly at 9 a.m.* punctually, on time, on the dot; *inf.* on the button, on the nose. 2 *reply to the letter promptly* at once, directly, immediately, by return, instantly, instantaneously, swiftly, rapidly, speedily, quickly, fast, expeditiously; *inf.* pronto.

promptness *noun* 1 *the promptness of his reply* immediacy, immediateness, instantaneousness, swiftness, rapidity, speediness, alacrity, quickness, fastness, expeditiousness, expedition, earliness, punctuality. 2 *the promptness of her offer to help* swiftness, rapidity, speediness, alacrity, quickness, fastness, readiness, willingness, eagerness.

promulgate *verb* 1 *promulgate the information about the project* make known, make public, publicize, announce, spread, communicate, disseminate, circulate, broadcast, publish. 2 *promulgate the new law* proclaim, announce, declare, herald, blazon, trumpet.

prone *adjective* 1 *lying prone for his rubdown* face down, face downward, in a prone position, procumbent. 2 *weary hikers lying prone at their campsite* lying down, flat, horizontal, full-length, supine, prostrate, stretched out, recumbent, procumbent. 3 *prone to lose his temper* inclined, given, likely, liable, apt, disposed, predisposed. 4 *prone to headaches* inclined, liable, subject, susceptible, disposed, predisposed.
Antonyms: UPRIGHT; VERTICAL; UNLIKELY; IMMUNE.

prong *noun* point, tip, spike, tine.

pronounce *verb* 1 *pronounce the words wrongly | have difficulty in pronouncing the letter "s"* enunciate, articulate, say, utter, sound, voice, vocalize. 2 *pronounce judgment | pronounce the patient out of danger* announce, declare, proclaim, assert, affirm, rule, decree.

pronounced *adjective* 1 *have a pronounced lisp* marked, noticeable, obvious, evident, conspicuous, striking, distinct, unmistakable. 2 *have pronounced views on the subject* decided, definite, clear, strong, positive, distinct.
Antonyms: FAINT; INCONSPICUOUS; INDEFINITE; VAGUE.

pronouncement *noun wait for the consultant's*

pronouncement on the patient's chances of survival formal statement, declaration, announcement, judgment, decree, proclamation, assertion, dictum.

pronunciation noun *have difficulty with the pronunciation of certain words* enunciation, articulation, saying, uttering, utterance, sounding, voicing, vocalization.

proof noun **1** *produce proof of your identity* evidence, certification, verification, authentication, validation, confirmation, attestation. **2** *produce proof of his guilt* evidence, demonstration, substantiation, corroboration, confirmation, attestation, testimony. **3** *send the novelist proofs of her book* galley proof, galley, page proof, trial print.

proof adjective *roofing material proof against heavy winds | how proof is the window glass?* impervious, impenetrable, resistant, repellent; waterproof, windproof, bulletproof, soundproof, childproof.

prop noun **1** *a prop holding up the side of the shed* support, upright, brace, buttress, stay, bolster, stanchion, truss, column, post, rod, pole, shaft. **2** *a prop of the local arts league* pillar, mainstay, anchor, rock, backbone, supporter, upholder, sustainer.

prop verb *prop his bike/ladder against the wall* lean, rest, set, lay, stand, balance, steady. **prop up 1** *prop up the wall of the garage* hold up, shore up, bolster up, buttress, support, brace, underpin, reinforce, strengthen. **2** *prop up a foundering business* support, give support to, bolster up, shore up, maintain, fund, finance, subsidize, underwrite.

propaganda noun *using propaganda to recruit party members* publicity material, publicity information, publicity, promotion, advertising, advertisement, selected information; newspeak, distorted truth/facts; agitprop; *inf.* hype.

propagate verb **1** *propagate plants/animals* grow, breed, multiply. **2** *animals propagating* reproduce, multiply, proliferate, breed, procreate. **3** *propagate new political ideas* spread, communicate, circulate, disseminate, transmit, distribute, broadcast, publish, publicize, proclaim, promulgate.

propel verb *propel the boat by means of oars | ambition propelling him to work long hours* move, set in motion, push forward, drive, thrust forward, force, impel.

propensity noun *a propensity to lie | a propensity for getting into trouble* tendency, inclination, leaning, bent, bias, disposition, predisposition, proneness, proclivity, penchant, susceptibility, weakness.

proper adjective **1** *the proper equipment for the sport | the proper qualifications for the job* right, suitable, fitting, appropriate, apt. **2** *the proper way to do things* right, correct, precise, accepted, acceptable, established, orthodox, conventional, formal, *comme il faut.* **3** *put the books*

in their proper place right, correct, own, individual, particular, respective, special, specific. **4** *have a very proper upbringing* seemly, decorous, respectable, decent, refined, genteel, gentlemanly/ladylike, formal, conventional, orthodox, strict, punctilious, sedate.

Antonyms: INAPPROPRIATE; WRONG; IMPROPER; UNCONVENTIONAL.

property noun **1** *the books were her personal property* possessions, belongings, things, goods, effects, chattels, assets, resources. **2** *put his money in property* real estate, buildings, land, estates, acres. **3** *herbs with healing properties | the antiseptic properties of alcohol* quality, attribute, characteristic, feature, power, peculiarity, idiosyncrasy, quirk.

prophecy noun **1** *her prophecy came true* prediction, forecast, prognostication, divination, augury. **2** *the gift of prophecy* prediction, foretelling the future, forecasting the future, fortune-telling, second sight, prognostication, divination, augury, soothsaying.

prophesy verb *the seer prophesied his death* predict, foretell, forecast, foresee, forewarn of, presage, prognosticate, divine, augur.

prophet noun seer, soothsayer, fortune-teller, diviner, clairvoyant, forecaster of the future, prognosticator, prophesier, oracle, augur, sibyl, Cassandra. **prophet of doom** pessimist, Cassandra; *inf.* doom merchant, gloom merchant.

prophetic adjective *her pessimistic remarks proved prophetic—we did indeed fail* predictive, foretelling, forecasting, presaging, prognostic, divinatory, oracular, sibylline.

prophylactic adjective *prophylactic medicine* preventive, preventative, precautionary, protective, disease-preventing.

prophylaxis noun *advocate prophylaxis in medicine* prevention, protection.

propinquity noun **1** *dislike the propinquity of the two houses/families* closeness, nearness, proximity, adjacency, contiguity. **2** *the families have a propinquity with each other* close relationship, close kinship, blood ties, family connection, proximity, consanguinity.

propitiate verb *propitiate his angry mother* appease, conciliate, placate, mollify, pacify, soothe.

propitious adjective *not a propitious time to try to sell one's house* auspicious, favorable, promising, optimistic, bright, advantageous, fortunate, lucky, happy, rosy, beneficial, opportune, suitable, timely.

Antonyms: UNFAVORABLE; INAUSPICIOUS; UNFORTUNATE.

proponent noun *a proponent of socialism* advocate, supporter, upholder, adherent, backer, promoter, endorser, champion, defender, sponsor, espouser, friend, well-wisher.

proportion noun **1** *the proportion of women to men*

on the staff ratio, distribution, relative amount/ number, relationship. **2** *give a large proportion of his income to the poor* portion, part, segment, share, quota, division, percentage, fraction, measure; *inf.* cut. **3** *the pleasing proportions of the room | facial features in perfect proportion* balance, symmetry, harmony, correspondence, congruity, agreement.

proportional *adjective have more work to do, with a proportional increase in salary* proportionate, in proportion to, corresponding, commensurate, equivalent, comparable.

proportions *plural noun a man of huge proportions* dimensions, size, measurements, mass, bulk, expanse, magnitude, extent, width, breadth.

proposal *noun* **1** *the proposal of new terms of employment* putting forward, advancing, offering, proffering, presentation, submitting. *See* PROPOSE 1. **2** *study their proposals for expansion | draw up a financial proposal* scheme, plan, project, program, motion, bid, proposition, presentation, suggestion, recommendation, tender, terms.

propose *verb* **1** *propose changes in legislation | propose that changes be made in the legislation* put forward, advance, offer, proffer, present, submit, tender, propound, suggest, recommend, advocate. **2** *they are proposing to leave now* intend, have the intention, mean, plan, have in mind, aim, purpose. **3** *propose his cousin as president of the society* put up, put forward, put up, nominate, name, suggest, recommend. **4** *propose to his girlfriend* offer marriage, ask for someone's hand in marriage, pay suit; *inf.* pop the question.

proposition *noun* **1** *an attractive business proposition* proposal, scheme, plan, project, program, motion, bid. *See* PROPOSAL 2. **2** *getting into the building unnoticed is not an easy proposition* task, job, undertaking, venture, problem. **3** *make a proposition to the woman/man at the bar* sexual advance, sexual overture, indecent proposal, improper suggestion; *inf.* come-on.

proposition *verb proposition the woman/man at the bar* make sexual advances to, make sexual overtures to, make an indecent proposal to, make an improper suggestion to, accost; *inf.* make a proposition to, make a pass at.

propound *verb propound the theory that all men are equal* put forward, advance, offer, proffer, present, submit, tender, suggest, postulate, propose, advocate.

proprieties *plural noun expected to observe the proprieties* etiquette, social conventions, social graces, social niceties, protocol, civilities, formalities, rules of conduct, accepted behavior, good manners, good form, the done thing, punctilio.

proprietor *noun* owner, possessor, title-holder, deed-holder, landowner, landlord/landlady;

host, innkeeper, hotelier, manager, restaurateur.

propriety *noun* **1** *behave with propriety* seemliness, decorum, respectability, decency, correctness, appropriateness, good manners, courtesy, politeness, civility, refinement, gentility, breeding, conventionality, orthodoxy, formality, etiquette, protocol. **2** *question the propriety of your decision* rightness, correctness, fitness, suitability, suitableness, appropriateness, aptness.

Antonyms: IMPROPRIETY; INDECORUM.

propulsion *noun fuel used for propulsion | jet propulsion* motive force, propelling force, drive, driving force, thrust, push, momentum, power.

prosaic *adjective* **1** *a prosaic style of writing | a prosaic description of her experiences abroad* unimaginative, uninspired, matter-of-fact, dull, dry, humdrum, mundane, pedestrian, lifeless, spiritless, stale, bland, vapid, banal, hackneyed, trite, insipid, monotonous, flat. **2** *lead a rather prosaic life* ordinary, everyday, usual, common, routine, humdrum, commonplace, workaday, pedestrian, mundane, dull, tedious, boring, uninspiring, monotonous.

Antonyms: IMAGINATIVE; INSPIRED; INTERESTING.

proscribe *verb* **1** *proscribe the sale of alcohol on Sundays* prohibit, forbid, ban, bar, disallow, embargo, interdict, outlaw. **2** *he was proscribed for his part in the conspiracy* outlaw, exile, expel, expatriate, deport, boycott, blackball, ostracize.

Antonyms: ALLOW; AUTHORIZE; ACCEPT.

proscription *noun* **1** *the proscription of the sale of alcohol on Sundays* prohibiting, prohibition, forbidding, banning, barring, embargo, interdicting. **2** *the proscription of her brother for his part in the conspiracy* outlawing, exile, exiling, expelling, expulsion, expatriation, deporting, deportation. *See* PROSCRIBE 2. **3** *a proscription placed on the sale of alcohol* prohibition, ban, bar, embargo, interdict.

prosecute *verb* **1** *he was prosecuted for drunk driving* bring a charge against, bring a criminal charge against, charge, prefer charges against, bring an action against, try, bring to trial, put on trial, sue, bring a suit against, interdict, arraign. **2** *prosecute an inquiry into the murder* carry on, conduct, direct, engage in, work at, proceed with, continue with. **3** *prosecute his prescribed tasks* accomplish, complete, finish, carry through, discharge, bring to an end.

proselyte *noun* convert, neophyte.

prospect *noun* **1** *there is little prospect of success* likelihood, likeliness, hope, expectation, anticipation, chance, chances, odds, probability, possibility. **2** *the prospect of being unemployed frightens him* thought, idea, contemplation, outlook. **3** *admire the prospect from the hill* view, vista, outlook, perspective, panorama, scene, spectacle. **in prospect** *there are no jobs in prospect* in store, in the offing, on the horizon, in the cards, in the wind, anticipated, expected, in view, under consideration.

prospect *verb prospect an area for diamonds* explore, search, inspect, survey, examine, check out. **prospect for** *prospect for gold* search for, look for, seek, go after.

prospective *adjective* **1** *her prospective father-in-law* future, to-be, soon-to-be, intended, expected. **2** *attract prospective customers* would-be, potential, possible, likely, hoped-for, looked-for, awaited, anticipated.

prospects *plural noun a job with few prospects* | *the prospects are good* potential, promise, possibilities, expectations, scope.

prospectus *noun the prospectus from the college* brochure, catalog, booklet, pamphlet, leaflet, literature, syllabus, program.

prosper *verb the family/business is prospering* do well, get on well, thrive, flourish, be successful, succeed, get ahead, progress, advance, get on in the world, make headway, make good, become rich, be in clover; *inf.* be on easy street, live the life of Riley.
Antonyms: FAIL; COLLAPSE; CRASH.

prosperity *noun go from poverty to prosperity* prosperousness, success, good fortune, ease, plenty, affluence, wealth, riches, the good life, luxury, life of luxury.

prosperous *adjective prosperous young men working in the city* thriving, flourishing, successful, well-off, well-to-do, affluent, wealthy, rich, moneyed, opulent, in clover; *inf.* well-heeled, in the money, on easy street.
Antonyms: POOR; PENNILESS; IMPECUNIOUS.

prostitute *noun* call girl, whore, woman of the streets, lady of the evening, streetwalker, loose woman, woman of ill repute, fallen woman, courtesan, *fille de joie*; *inf.* hooker, working girl, hustler.

prostitution *noun* whoredom, whoring, streetwalking, the oldest profession; *inf.* hustling.

prostrate *adjective* **1** *people found prostrate on the floor after the fire* prone, lying down, flat, stretched out, horizontal, full-length, procumbent. **2** *prostrate before the emperor* bowed low, humbled. **3** *prostrate with grief* overcome by/with, overwhelmed by, overpowered by, brought to one's knees by, crushed by, helpless with, paralyzed by, laid low by/with, impotent with. **4** *a country left prostrate after years of war* | *feeling prostrate after the long journey* worn out, exhausted, fatigued, tired out, dog-tired, spent, drained: *inf.* all in, done, fagged out, bushed, pooped.
Antonyms: UPRIGHT; VERTICAL; THRIVING.

prostrate *verb* **1** *the blow prostrated him* knock flat, flatten, knock down, floor, level. **2** *the heat prostrated them* | *prostrated by pain* overcome, overwhelm, overpower, bring to one's knees, crush, make helpless, paralyze, lay low, make powerless, make impotent. **3** *the long war prostrated the country* | *she was prostrated by the long*

journey wear out, exhaust, tire out, fatigue, weary, drain, sap; *inf.* fag out, poop.

protagonist *noun* **1** *the protagonist in the new play* chief character, central character, leading/main character, principal, hero/heroine, leading man/lady, title role, lead. **2** *a protagonist of feminism* leader, leading supporter, prime mover, moving spirit, standard-bearer, mainstay, spokesman, spokeswoman, spokesperson, advocate, supporter, upholder, adherent, backer, proponent, promoter, champion, exponent.

protean *adjective* ever-changing, variable, changeable, mutable, kaleidoscopic, mercurial, volatile, labile, versatile.

protect *verb* **1** *protect the child from measles/injury* | *protect the house from burglars* keep safe, save, safeguard, shield, preserve, defend, shelter, secure. **2** *soldiers protecting the castle* guard, mount/stand guard on, defend, secure, watch over, look after, take care of. **3** *protect the surface of the table with a plastic sheet* preserve, shield, cover, cover up, conceal, mask.
Antonyms: ATTACK; HARM; ASSAULT; EXPOSE.

protection *noun* **1** *provide protection against violence* safekeeping, safety, shield, preservation, defense, security. **2** *under the protection of the police* safekeeping, care, charge, keeping, defense, protectorship. **3** *wear warm clothes as a protection against the cold* | *use sunblock as protection against burning* safeguard, shield, barrier, buffer, screen, cover.

protective *adjective* **1** *wear a protective cream on her face in the sun* | *cyclists wearing protective headgear* protecting, safeguarding, shielding, covering. **2** *protective parents* careful, watchful, vigilant, paternal/maternal, fatherly/motherly; overprotective, possessive, jealous, clinging.

protector *noun* **1** *his elder brother acted as his protector* defender, champion, bodyguard, guardian, knight in shining armor, guardian angel. **2** *wear shin protectors* guard, shield, pad, cushion.

protégé/protégée *noun* student, pupil, ward, dependent, charge.

protest *verb* **1** *protesting his treatment of the staff* make a protest at/against/about, object to, raise objections to, oppose, express opposition to, take issue about/on/over, make/take a stand against, put up a fight against, take exception to, complain about, express disapproval of, express disagreement with, demur at, remonstrate about, make a fuss about, demonstrate against; *inf.* kick up a fuss about, gripe about, grouse about, beef about, bitch about. **2** *protest his innocence* declare, announce, profess, proclaim, assert, affirm, argue, attest, testify to, maintain, insist on, aver, avow. **protest against/ about** *protest against the government's spending* | *protest about their low wages* object to, oppose. *See* PROTEST *verb* 1.

Antonyms: ACCEPT; SUPPORT.

protest noun **1** *register a protest against/about his treatment of the children* objection, opposition, exception, complaint, disapproval, disagreement, dissent, demurral, remonstration, fuss, outcry, demonstration, protestation. **2** *listen to his protests that he was innocent* protestation, declaration, announcement, profession, assertion, affirmation, attestation, assurance, avowal, proclamation.

Antonyms: SUPPORT; APPROVAL.

protestation noun **1** *not to believe his protestations of innocence/loyalty* protest, declaration, announcement, assertion, affirmation. *See* PROTEST *noun 2.* **2** *his protestations against his treatment in prison* protest, objection, opposition, exception, complaint. *See* PROTEST *noun 1.*

protester noun *a crowd of protesters gathered outside the embassy* objector, opposer, opponent, complainer, demonstrator, dissenter, dissident, rebel, protest marcher, striker, agitator.

protocol noun *observe the protocol associated with royal visits | guilty of a breach of protocol* etiquette, rules of conduct, code of behavior, conventions, formalities, customs, propriety, proprieties, decorum, manners, courtesies, civilities, good form, politesse.

prototype noun *the prototype of the flying machine* original, first example, first model, pattern, paradigm, archetype.

protract verb *loves to talk at meetings and protract the discussions* prolong, extend, stretch out, draw out, lengthen, make longer, drag out, spin out, keep something going, continue.

Antonyms: CURTAIL; SHORTEN.

protracted adjective *tired of the protracted discussions* prolonged, extended, stretched out, drawn out, long-drawn-out, lengthened, lengthy, long, overlong, dragged out, spun out, interminable, never-ending, endless.

protrude verb *a piece of rock protruding from the cliff face | protruding front teeth* jut, jut out, stick out, stand out, project, extend, beetle, obtrude, bulge.

protrusion noun **1** *the protrusion of a piece of rock from the cliff face* jutting, sticking out, projection, projecting, obtrusion, obtruding. **2** *rocky protrusions on the face of the cliff* projection, swelling, bulge, protuberance, lump, bump, knob.

protuberance noun *a protuberance on the trunk of the tree* swelling, bulge, lump, bump, protrusion, projection, knob, growth, outgrowth, tumor, excrescence.

protuberant adjective *protuberant stomach/eyes* bulging, swelling, swollen, jutting, jutting out, protruding, protrusive, prominent, bulbous; humpbacked, gibbous.

Antonyms: SUNKEN; CONCAVE.

proud adjective **1** *proud parents* pleased, glad, happy, satisfied, gratified, content, apprecia-tive; *inf.* proud as a peacock. **2** *they were poor but proud* self-respecting, dignified, independent. **3** *he has become too proud to associate with his old friends* arrogant, conceited, vain, self-important, egotistical, boastful, haughty, disdainful, scornful, supercilious, snobbish, imperious, overbearing, lordly, presumptuous, overweening, high-handed; *inf.* high-and-mighty, stuck-up, uppity, snooty, highfalutin. **4** *it was a proud day when they won the cup* gratifying, satisfying, happy, memorable, notable, red-letter, glorious, marvelous. **5** *the ship was a proud sight sailing into the harbor* magnificent, splendid, grand, noble, stately, imposing, majestic, august. **proud of** *proud of their daughter* pleased with, happy about/with, satisfied with, gratified by/at, content with, appreciative of; *inf.* pleased as Punch with.

Antonyms: ASHAMED; MODEST; HUMBLE; SHAMEFUL.

prove verb **1** *prove that he was the murderer* produce/submit proof, produce/submit evidence, establish evidence, determine, demonstrate, show beyond (a/the shadow of a) doubt, substantiate, corroborate, verify, validate, authenticate, confirm. **2** *prove the new drug* analyze, check, examine, put to the test, test, try out, put to trial. **3** *the rumor proved to be correct* be found, be shown, turn out. **be proved** *she was proved the winner* emerge, come out, end up. **prove oneself** *proved themselves in battle* show one's courage/mettle, show one's ability, test oneself, be put to the test.

Antonyms: DISPROVE; INVALIDATE.

proverb noun saying, adage, maxim, saw, axiom, aphorism, gnome, dictum, apothegm.

proverbial adjective **1** *her proverbial meanness kept visitors away* legendary, notorious, infamous, famous, famed, renowned, well-known, acknowledged, accepted, traditional, time-honored. **2** *he has become the proverbial good Samaritan* axiomatic, epigrammatic, aphoristic, apothegmatic, well-known.

provide verb **1** *provide the guests with food and shelter* supply, furnish, equip, accommodate, provision, outfit. **2** *we provide meals/transportation* supply, furnish, give, offer. **3** *the novel provides insight into the war* give, bring, afford, present, offer, accord, yield, impart, lend. **4** *the contract provides that the tenants are responsible for repairs* stipulate, lay down, give as a condition, require, state, specify. **provide against** *provide against an enemy attack* make provision for, take precautions against, take steps/measures against, guard against, forearm oneself against. **provide for** **1** *provide for his family* support, maintain, keep, sustain, take care of, care for, look after. **2** *the organizers of the wedding tried to provide for every eventuality* allow for, prepare for, make preparations for, be prepared for, anticipate, arrange for, make arrangements for, get ready for, plan for, make plans for.

provided, provided that *conjunction we are going to Bermuda, provided we have enough money | the party will be outside, provided that it is not raining* providing, providing that, on (the) condition that, if, as long as, given, with the provision/proviso that, on the assumption that.

providence *noun* **1** *just have to trust in providence* God's will, divine intervention, destiny, fate, fortune. **2** *lack of providence has brought him to his present state* foresight, forethought, far-sightedness, prudence, judgment, judiciousness, shrewdness, circumspection, wisdom, sagacity, caution, care, carefulness, good management, careful budgeting, thrift, thriftiness, economy, canniness, frugality.

provident *adjective it was provident of them to take out accident insurance | provident people providing for their old age* farsighted, prudent, judicious, shrewd, circumspect, wise, sagacious, cautious, careful, thrifty, canny, economical, frugal.

providing, providing that *conjunction* provided, provided that, on condition that, if. *See* PROVIDED, PROVIDED THAT.

province *noun* **1** *the administrative center of the province* state, territory, region, area, district. **2** *that part of the business is not my province* area of responsibility, sphere of action, area of activity, field, business, line of business, line, charge, concern, duty. **3** *in the province of English literature* discipline, field, speciality, area.

provincial *adjective* **1** *provincial government/ newspapers/issues* nonnational, regional, local, municipal, state, county, district; topical. **2** *unfair in her assumption that all suburbanites are provincial* uncultured, uncultivated, unrefined, unpolished, unsophisticated, parochial, limited, small-minded, insular, naïve, uninformed, inward-looking, illiberal, narrow, narrow-minded, inflexible, bigoted, prejudiced, intolerant.
Antonyms: NATIONAL; URBAN; SOPHISTICATED.

provincial *noun insulted to be regarded as provincials* rustic, yokel, peasant; *inf.* country cousin, hick, hayseed. provision

provision *noun* **1** *the provision of conference facilities* providing, supplying, supply, furnishing, equipping, outfitting, accommodation, giving, affording. **2** *make provision for their old age | make provision for a hard winter* preparation, plan, prearrangement, arrangement, precaution, precautionary steps/measures. **3** *the housing policy makes no provision for single people* arrangement, allowance, concession. **4** *under the provisions of his will, his children inherit his estate* term, requirement, specification, stipulation. **5** *the contract document has the provision that it must be reviewed annually* proviso, condition, stipulation, clause, rider, qualification, restriction, reservation, limitation, strings.

provisional *adjective a provisional contract | get*

provisional permission provisory, temporary, interim, stopgap, transitional, to be confirmed, conditional, tentative, contingent; *inf.* pro tem.
Antonyms: PERMANENT; DEFINITE.

provisions *plural noun stock up with provisions* supplies, food supplies, stores, groceries, food, food and drink, foodstuffs, staples, rations, provender, eatables, edibles, victuals, comestibles, viands.

proviso *noun they agreed to the change with the proviso that an investigation be held* condition, stipulation, provision, clause, rider, qualification, restriction, reservation, limitation, strings.

provocation *noun* **1** *the provocation of their mother* provoking, annoying, angering, incensing, enraging, irritating, irritation, exasperating, exasperation, infuriating, infuriation, maddening, vexing, harassing, harassment, irking; *inf.* riling, aggravation. **2** *hit him under provocation* incitement, rousing, stirring, stimulation, stimulus, motivation, prompting, inducement, goading. *See* PROVOKE 2. **3** *the provocation of their anger/laughter* evocation, causing, occasioning, eliciting, inducement, inspiration, kindling, production, generation, instigation, precipitation, promotion. **4** *react to the slightest provocation* annoyance, irritation, vexation, harassment, affront, insult.

provocative *adjective* **1** *the fight was started by a provocative remark* provoking, annoying, irritating, exasperating, infuriating, maddening, vexing, galling, affronting, insulting, inflammatory, goading; *inf.* aggravating. *See* PROVOKE 1, 2. **2** *wear a provocative, low-cut dress* sexually arousing, sexually exciting, alluring, seductive, sexy, tempting, suggestive, erotic, titillating.

provoke *verb* **1** *do not provoke the hornet | his insults would provoke anyone* annoy, make angry, anger, incense, enrage, irritate, exasperate, infuriate, madden, pique, nettle, vex, harass, irk, gall, affront, insult; *inf.* rile, needle, make someone's blood boil, aggravate. **2** *provoke her into shouting at them* incite, rouse, stir, move, stimulate, motivate, excite, inflame, work/fire up, prompt, induce, spur, goad, prod, egg on. **3** *his speech provoked anger/laughter* evoke, cause, give rise to, occasion, call forth, draw forth, elicit, induce, inspire, excite, kindle, produce, generate, engender, instigate, lead to, precipitate, promote, prompt.
Antonyms: PACIFY; APPEASE; DETER.

prow *noun the prow of the ship* bow, nose, stem, fore, forepart, front, head.

prowess *noun* **1** *admire his prowess as a yachtsman | envied her prowess with a tennis racket* skill, skillfulness, expertise, expertness, facility, ability, capability, talent, genius, adroitness, adeptness, aptitude, dexterity, deftness, competence, proficiency, know-how, savoir faire. **2**

the prowess of the soldiers in battle courage, bravery, gallantry, valor, heroism, intrepidity, fearlessness, mettle, pluck, pluckiness, gameness, nerve, boldness, daring, fortitude, steadfastness, stoutness, sturdiness; *inf.* grit, guts, spunk.
Antonyms: INABILITY; ineptitude; cowardice.

prowl *verb prowling around the building* roam, range, move stealthily, slink, skulk, steal, sneak, stalk; *inf.* snoop.

proximity *noun disturbed by the proximity of the airport to the house* closeness, nearness, propinquity, adjacency, contiguity.

proxy *noun send a proxy to vote at the annual meeting* representative, deputy, substitute, agent, delegate, surrogate.

prude *noun* puritan, prig; *inf.* goody-goody, priss.

prudence *noun* **1** *question the prudence of his action* wisdom, judgment, good judgment, judiciousness, sagacity, shrewdness, common sense, sense, circumspection, farsightedness, foresight, forethought. **2** *behave with prudence rather than rashness* caution, cautiousness, care, carefulness, discretion, wariness, vigilance, heedfulness. **3** *her prudence allowed her to buy a house* providence, good management, careful budgeting, thrift, thriftiness, economy, canniness, sparingness, frugality.

prudent *adjective* **1** *a prudent decision* wise, well-judged, judicious, sagacious, sage, shrewd, sensible, circumspect, farsighted, politic. **2** *rash people being advised to be prudent* cautious, careful, discreet, wary, vigilant, heedful. **3** *prudent with her income* provident, thrifty, economical, canny, sparing, frugal.
Antonyms: UNWISE; IMPRUDENT; INCAUTIOUS; RASH.

prudish *adjective a prudish attitude/person* puritan, puritanical, priggish, prim, straitlaced, prissy, stuffy, starchy, Victorian; *inf.* goody-goody.
Antonyms: PERMISSIVE; LIBERAL; BROAD-MINDED.

prune *verb* **1** *prune the roses* trim, thin, thin out, cut back, shape. **2** *prune branches from the bushes* cut, lop, chop, clip, snip, remove. **3** *prune expenses | prune the manuscript* cut back on, cut back, pare down, make cutbacks in, cut, trim, reduce, shorten, make reductions in, retrench, curtail.

prurient *adjective prurient interests/person* lascivious, lecherous, lustful, lewd, salacious, licentious, lubricious, libidinous.

pry *verb she resents it when he pries* be inquisitive, interfere, meddle, intrude, mind other people's business, be a busybody; *inf.* stick/poke one's nose in, snoop. **pry into** **1** *pry into her private affairs* be inquisitive about, nose into, inquire into, interfere in, meddle in; *inf.* be nosy about, stick/poke one's nose into, snoop into. **2** *pry into her possessions* peer into, peek into, scrutinize, probe into, ferret around in, poke around in, nose into, nose around in, spy on; *inf.* stick/poke one's nose into, snoop into.

prying *adjective tired of their prying neighbors* inquisitive, curious, interfering, meddling, meddlesome, intrusive, probing, spying, impertinent; *inf.* nosy, snooping, snoopy.

psalm *noun* hymn, sacred song, song of praise, paean, religious song, chant, anthem.

pseudo *adjective his intellectualism is pseudo | a pseudo interest in the arts* feigned, pretended, simulated, imitation, false, artificial, ersatz, quasi-, spurious, fake, bogus, sham, mock, fraudulent, counterfeit, forged; *inf.* phony.
Antonyms: REAL; GENUINE; ACTUAL.

pseudonym *noun the pseudonym of the writer/ actor* nom de plume, pen name, stage name, professional name, assumed name, alias, allonym, false name, sobriquet, nickname, nom de guerre.

psych *verb* **psych out** *try to psych out his opponent* unsettle, upset, agitate, disturb, make nervous, put off balance, put off one's stroke, intimidate, frighten. **psych up** *have to psych himself up before the competition/interview* steel oneself, prepare, get ready, gird one's loins, get in the mood, get in the right frame of mind.

psyche *noun a disturbed psyche* soul, spirit, mind, intelligence, anima, (inner) self, essential nature, inner ego, inner man/woman, personality.

psychiatrist *noun* psychopathologist, psychotherapist, therapist, psychoanalyst, psychoanalyzer; *inf.* shrink, head-shrinker.

psychic *adjective* **1** *people thought to be psychic* clairvoyant, telepathic, telekinetic, spiritualistic. **2** *psychic powers/influences/research* supernatural, supernormal, preternatural, preternormal, psychical, extrasensory, otherworldly, paranormal, occult. **3** *psychic analysis/disorder* spiritual, mental, psychological, psychogenic.

psychological *adjective* **1** *psychological studies* mental, of the mind, cerebral, psychic, psychical. **2** *her inability to work is thought to be psychological* in the mind, all in the mind, psychosomatic, emotional, irrational, imaginary, subconscious, unconscious.

psychology *noun* **1** *studying psychology* science of the mind, science of the personality, study of the mental processes. **2** *the psychology of the typical burglar* mind, mindset, mental processes, thought processes, way of thinking, attitude, makeup; *inf.* what makes one tick.

psychopathic *adjective psychopathic killer* severely mentally ill, disturbed, insane, mad, maniac, maniacal, deranged, sociopathic, psychotic.

psychosomatic *adjective psychosomatic illnesses* stress-induced, stress-related, in the mind, all in the mind, psychological.

pub *noun* bar, tavern, barroom, taproom; *inf.* watering hole.

puberty *noun* pubescence, sexual maturity, adolescence, young adulthood, teenage years, teens.

public *adjective* **1** *public health services | public law* state, national, civic, civil, social. **2** *public sentiment is against it | increase public awareness* popular, general, common, universal, widespread. **3** *public places/parks* not private, not exclusive, accessible to all, open to the public, of free access. **4** *make his views public* known, widely known, acknowledged, overt, in circulation, published, publicized, plain, obvious. **5** *scandals about public figures* in the public eye, prominent, well-known, important, eminent, respected, influential, prestigious, famous, celebrated, illustrious.
Antonyms: PRIVATE; PERSONAL; SECRET.

public *noun* **1** *the public has/have a right to know* people, everyone, population, country, nation, community, citizens, populace, ordinary people, masses, commonalty, multitude, mob, hoi polloi, electorate, voters. **2** *actors/authors worrying about what their public think* audience, spectators, readers, followers, following, fans, admirers, patrons, clientele. **in public** *refuse to appear in public* publicly, openly, for all to see, in full view of the public.

publication *noun* **1** *the publication of the book/newspaper* publishing, production, issuing, issuance. **2** *a widely read publication* book, newspaper, magazine, periodical, journal, daily, weekly, monthly, quarterly, booklet, brochure, leaflet, pamphlet, handbill. **3** *the publication of the committee's findings* publishing, announcement, notification, reporting, declaration, communication, imparting, proclamation, disclosure, divulgence, broadcasting, publicizing, distribution, spreading, dissemination, promulgation, issuance.

publicity *noun* **1** *his marriage prompted much publicity* public attention, public interest, public notice. **2** *seeking publicity for her new book* promotion, advertising; *inf.* hype, buildup.

publicize *verb* **1** *publicize a description of the wanted man* make public, make known, bring to public notice/attention, announce, publish, broadcast, distribute, disseminate, promulgate. **2** *publicize her new book* give publicity to, promote, advertise; *inf.* hype, plug.
Antonyms: CONCEAL; WITHHOLD.

publish *verb* **1** *they publish reference books* produce, issue, print, bring out. **2** *publish the results | publish the committee's findings* make public, make known, announce, notify, report, declare, communicate, impart, proclaim, disclose, divulge, broadcast, publicize, distribute, spread, disseminate, promulgate.

pucker *verb* **1** *a dress puckered at the waist* gather, shirr, pleat, ruck, ruffle, wrinkle, crease. **2** *the unhappy child's face puckered | pucker her brows* screw up, wrinkle, crease, furrow, knit, crinkle, corrugate.

puckish *adjective* *a puckish sense of humor* mischie-vous, mischief-making, impish, implike, roguish, playful, arch, waggish.

puddle *noun* *puddles of water/blood* pool.

pudgy *adjective* small and fat/obese/corpulent, short and fat, short and stout, round, rotund, plump, roly-poly, dumpy, squat, stubby, stumpy, chubby, tubby.

puerile *adjective* *puerile behavior | has a puerile sense of humor | his writing is so puerile* childish, immature, infantile, juvenile, adolescent, foolish, silly, inane, asinine.
Antonyms: MATURE; SENSIBLE.

puff *noun* *a puff of wind* gust, blast, whiff, breath, flurry, draft.

puff *verb* *puffing while climbing the hill* breathe heavily/loudly/rapidly, pant, blow, gasp, gulp. **puff up** *the drug seemed to have puffed him up* swell, distend, inflate, dilate, bloat.

puffy *adjective* *puffy cheeks/eyes* puffed up, swollen, distended, inflated, dilated, bloated, bulging, edematous.

pugilist *noun* boxer, fighter, prizefighter; *inf.* bruiser.

pugnacious *adjective* *in a pugnacious mood* belligerent, bellicose, combative, fighting, battling, aggressive, antagonistic, quarrelsome, argumentative, disputatious, hostile, threatening, irascible, ill-tempered, bad-tempered.
Antonyms: PEACEABLE; PACIFIC; FRIENDLY.

pull *verb* **1** *the child was pulling a toy behind him* haul, drag, draw, trail, tow, tug. **2** *pull the rope to straighten it* haul, tug, jerk; *inf.* yank. **3** *pull teeth* pull out, draw out, take out, extract, remove, root out. **4** *pull a muscle/ligament* strain, sprain, wrench, stretch, tear, dislocate, damage. **pull apart 1** *children pulling apart their toys* take/pull to pieces, take/pull to bits, demolish, destroy, break. **2** *critics pulled apart her latest novel* take apart, take to pieces, criticize severely, find fault with, pick holes in, attack; *inf.* slate, pan, slam. **pull back** *the army pulled back after the defeat* withdraw, retreat, draw back, fall back. **pull down** *pull down old buildings* take down, knock down, demolish, raze to the ground, level, destroy, bulldoze, dismantle. **pull in 1** *the car pulled in to the driveway* drive in, draw in, park in. **2** *plays pulling in large audiences* pull, draw, bring in, attract, lure, catch the eye of, entice. **3** *policeman pulling known criminals in for questioning* detain, take into custody, arrest; *inf.* run in, pinch, nab, collar, nail. **4** *he pulls in $50,000 a year* earn, take home, bring in, make, clear, net, gross, pocket. **pull off 1** *pull the top off the can* remove, detach, tear off, rip off, wrench off; *inf.* yank off. **2** *pull off the export deal* bring off, carry out, accomplish, execute, succeed in. **pull oneself together** regain one's composure/calm, get a grip on oneself; *inf.* snap out of it. **pull out 1** *pull out a gun* draw out, take out, bring out, withdraw. **2** *pull out of the agreement/contest* withdraw, retreat from, leave, quit, abandon, give up, stop participating in, renege on. **pull someone's leg** *she was upset but he was only pulling her leg* tease, make fun of, poke fun at, joke with, rag, chaff, twit; *inf.* rib. **pull through** *she was very ill but pulled through* get better, recover, rally, survive, come through, recuperate. **pull up 1** *pull up the weeds* root out, uproot, dig up, grub up, extract; *inf.* yank out. **2** *buses pulling up at the stop* stop, come to a stop, halt, come to a halt, brake. **3** *the car pulled up to the curb* draw up, park at/ along/alongside, drive up.

pull *noun* **1** *give a pull at the bell rope* tug, haul, yank, jerk. **2** *the pull of the current* tug, force, forcefulness, power, exertion, effort. **3** *the pull of the sea to sailors* attraction, lure, enticement, drawing power, draw, magnetism, influence. **4** *he has enough pull with the boss to get you a job* influence, weight, leverage, muscle; *inf.* clout.

pulp *noun* **1** *the pulp of the fruit* soft part, fleshy part, flesh, marrow. **2** *reduce the mixture of vegetables to a pulp* paste, purée, mush, mash, pap, triturate. **3** *make a fortune out of writing pulp* pulp fiction, rubbish, trash, trivia, drivel, pap.

pulp *adjective pulp fiction* rubbishy, trashy, sensational, lurid.

pulsate *verb with hearts pulsating* | *loud music pulsating throughout the building* beat, throb, vibrate, pulse, palpitate, pound, thud, thump, drum.

pulse *noun the compelling pulse of the music* beat, rhythm, throb, throbbing, vibration, pulsation, pounding, thudding, thud, thumping, thump, drumming.

pulse *verb loud music pulsing throughout the building* beat, throb, vibrate, pulsate, palpitate, pound, thud, thump, drum.

pulverize *verb* **1** *pulverize the solid foods* grind, crush, pound, crumble, powder, crunch, squash, pulp, purée, liquidize, mash, comminute, triturate. **2** *pulverize his opponent in the boxing ring* defeat utterly, overwhelm, trounce, rout, flatten, crush, smash, vanquish, destroy, annihilate; *inf.* hammer.

pump *verb* **1** *pump the bicycle tires* pump up, blow up, inflate. **2** *pump blood through the body* drive, force, push, send. **3** *pump him for information* question closely, quiz, cross-examine, interrogate, give someone the third degree; *inf.* grill.

pun *noun amused by his puns* play on words, word play, double entendre, paronomasia.

punch¹ *verb punch his opponent* | *punch (down) the bread dough* strike, hit, knock, thump, thwack, box, jab, cuff, slug, smash, bash, slam, batter, pound, pummel; *inf.* sock, bop, wallop, whack, clout, plug.

punch² *noun* **1** *give his opponent a punch in the jaw* blow, hit, knock, thump, thwack, box, jab, cuff, slug, smash, bash, slam; *inf.* sock, bop,

wallop, whack, clout, plug. **2** *the speech lacked punch* strength, vigor, vigorousness, force, forcefulness, verve, drive, impact, bite, effectiveness; *inf.* oomph, pizzazz.

punch³ *verb punch the paper/ticket/metal* make a hole in, put/punch holes in, perforate, puncture, pierce, prick, drill, bore, hole.

punctilio *noun* **1** *the organizers' attentiveness to every punctilio* fine point, nicety, detail, subtlety. **2** *the punctilio appropriate to a royal visit* etiquette, conventions, formalities, code, protocol, proprieties, rules of conduct; conformity, scrupulousness, meticulousness, conscientiousness, exactitude, precision, strictness, nicety.

punctilious *adjective a punctilious attention to detail* | *a punctilious observance of the convention* careful, scrupulous, meticulous, conscientious, exact, precise, particular, strict, nice, finicky, fussy; *inf.* persnickety.
Antonyms: CARELESS; SLAPDASH.

punctual *adjective they were always punctual at meetings* | *punctual arrivals* on time, on the dot, prompt, in good time, when expected, timely, well-timed, early.
Antonyms: LATE; BEHINDHAND.

punctuality *noun require punctuality of his employees* promptness, punctualness, promptitude, timeliness, earliness.

punctuate *verb* **1** *punctuate the piece of writing* put punctuation marks in, mark with punctuation marks. **2** *his speech was punctuated with coughs* | *punctuated his speech with thumps on the table* interrupt with/by, intersperse with, pepper with, sprinkle with.

puncture *noun* **1** *the puncture of the tire* puncturing, perforation, piercing, pricking, spiking, rupturing, cutting, nicking, slitting. **2** *get/ mend a puncture in the tire* hole, perforation, prick, rupture, cut, nick, slit, leak. **3** *get/mend a puncture* flat tire; *inf.* flat.

puncture *verb* **1** *the piece of glass punctured the tire* make a hole in, perforate, pierce, bore, prick, spike, penetrate, rupture, cut, nick, slit. **2** *the news punctured his feeling of joy* | *puncture his conceit* prick, deflate, flatten, reduce.

punctured *adjective two punctured tires* flat, deflated.

pundit *noun* expert, authority, master, guru, sage, highbrow.

pungent *adjective* **1** *a pungent smell* sharp, acrid, acid, sour, biting, stinging, burning, smarting, irritating. **2** *a pungent taste* sharp, acid, sour, biting, bitter, tart, tangy, spicy, highly flavored, aromatic, piquant, peppery, hot, fiery. **3** *pungent remarks/wit* caustic, acid, biting, cutting, sharp, incisive, piercing, penetrating, scathing, pointed, acrimonious, trenchant, mordant, stringent.
Antonyms: BLAND; MILD.

punish *verb* mete out punishment to, discipline, subject to discipline, take disciplinary action against, teach someone a lesson, penalize, cas-

tigate, chastise; smack, slap, beat, cane, whip, flog, lash, scourge; mistreat, abuse, manhandle.
Antonyms: PARDON; EXONERATE.

punishing *adjective a punishing exercise routine | journey was extremely punishing* arduous, demanding, taxing, strenuous, hard, exhausting, fatiguing, wearing, tiring, grueling, uphill, backbreaking.
Antonyms: EASY; EFFORTLESS.

punishment *noun* punishing, disciplining, discipline, penalizing, penalty, retribution, castigation, castigating, chastising, chastisement; smacking, slapping, beating, caning, whipping, flogging, lashing, scourging; mistreatment, abuse, manhandling.

punitive *adjective* **1** *take punitive measures against the culprits* punishing, penalizing, disciplinary, corrective, castigating, castigatory, chastising. **2** *punitive rates of taxation* harsh, severe, stiff, taxing, cruel, savage.

puny *adjective* **1** *the bodybuilder claimed that he was once puny* weak, weakly, frail, feeble, undersized, underdeveloped, stunted, small, slight, little, dwarfish. **2** *a puny contribution* paltry, petty, trifling, trivial, insignificant, inconsequential, minor, meager; *inf.* piddling.
Antonyms: STRONG; STURDY; SUBSTANTIAL.

pupil *noun* **1** *pupils wearing school uniforms* student, schoolboy, schoolgirl, schoolchild, scholar. **2** *a pupil of Picasso* student, disciple.

puppet *noun* **1** *puppets amusing children* marionette, hand puppet, finger puppet. **2** *accused of being a puppet of management* tool, instrument, cat's-paw, pawn, dupe, mouthpiece; *inf.* stooge, yes-man.

purchase *verb* **1** *purchase a new dress/car | purchased some shares* buy, pay for, acquire, pick up, obtain, invest in, put money into. **2** *purchase victory with young lives* attain, achieve, gain, win.
Antonyms: SELL; MARKET.

purchase *noun* **1** *carry her purchases home | proud of her new purchase* buy, acquisition, investment. **2** *difficult to get any purchase on the slippery cliff face* grip, hold, foothold, footing, toehold, support, grasp, leverage, advantage.

pure *adjective* **1** *pure gold* unalloyed, unmixed, unadulterated, uncontaminated, flawless, perfect, genuine, real, true. **2** *pure air/water/food* clean, clear, fresh, unpolluted, untainted, unadulterated, uncontaminated, uninfected, wholesome, natural. **3** *pure novitiates* virgin, virginal, chaste, maidenly, virtuous, undefiled, unsullied. **4** *lead a pure life* uncorrupted, noncorrupt, moral, righteous, honorable, virtuous, honest, upright, decent, good, worthy, noble, blameless, guiltless, pious, sinless. **5** *of pure character* stainless, spotless, unsullied, unblemished, impeccable, immaculate, blameless, sinless. **6** *pure madness* sheer, utter, absolute, downright, out-and-out, complete, total, perfect, unmitigated, unqualified. **7** *pure*

science of mathematics theoretical, abstract, conceptual.
Antonyms: IMPURE; DIRTY; adulterated; IMMORAL.

purely *adverb find out purely by accident* entirely, completely, totally, wholly, solely, only, simply, just, merely.

purge *verb* **1** *purge their souls of sin* cleanse, clear, purify, make pure. **2** *purge the party of dissidents* rid, clear, empty. **3** *purge the dissidents from the party* remove, clear out, expel, eject, dismiss, oust, depose, eradicate, root out, weed out. **4** *purge him of the charge* clear, absolve, pardon, forgive, exonerate, expiate.

purge *noun* **1** *the purge of their souls* purging, cleansing, purification. **2** *the purge of the dissidents from the party* removal, expulsion, ejection, dismissal, ousting, deposal, deposition, eradication, rooting out, weeding out.

purify *verb* **1** *purify the water* make pure, clean, cleanse, decontaminate, depollute, filter, filtrate. **2** *purify the air* make pure, clean, cleanse, freshen, deodorize, decontaminate, depollute, refine. **3** *purify the hospital* make pure, clean, cleanse, decontaminate, depollute, disinfect, sterilize, sanitize, fumigate. **4** *purify their souls* purge, cleanse, clear, absolve.
Antonyms: POLLUTE; CONTAMINATE; CORRUPT.

purist *noun purists disliking the use of slang* precisionist, formalist, stickler, dogmatist, pedant, traditionalist.

puritan *noun* moral zealot/fanatic, moralist, pietist, prude; *inf.* goody-goody.

puritanical *adjective he is too puritanical | puritanical attitudes* puritan, ascetic, austere, straitlaced, narrow-minded, rigid, stiff, prudish, prim, priggish, prissy; *inf.* goody-goody.
Antonyms: PERMISSIVE; LIBERAL; BROAD-MINDED.

purity *noun* **1** *test the purity of the gold* pureness, flawlessness, perfection, genuineness. *See* PURE 1. **2** *comment on the purity of the water* pureness, cleanness, clearness, freshness, lack of pollution, untaintedness, lack of contamination, wholesomeness. **3** *the purity of the novitiates* pureness, virginity, chasteness, chastity, virtue, virtuousness. **4** *the purity that he exhibited* pureness, lack of corruption, righteousness, rectitude, morality, honor, virtuousness, honesty, integrity, uprightness, decency, goodness, worthiness, nobility, blamelessness, guiltlessness, piety, sinlessness. **5** *the purity of her character* pureness, stainlessness, spotlessness, impeccability, immaculateness, blamelessness, sinlessness.
Antonyms: IMPURITY; IMMORALITY.

purport *verb* **1** *this report purports to be an official statement* claim, allege, profess, assert, proclaim, pretend, feign, pose as. **2** *the document purports that changes are to be made* mean, signify, indicate, denote, suggest, imply, state, convey, express, show, betoken.

purport noun **1** *the purport of his message* gist, substance, drift, implication, meaning, import, tenor, thrust. **2** *his purport is to embarrass them* aim, intention, intent, object, objective, goal, plan, scheme, design, purpose.

purpose noun **1** *the purpose of his visit* reason, point, basis, motivation, cause, justification. **2** *his only purpose in life* aim, intention, object, objective, goal, end, target, ambition, aspiration, desire, wish, hope. **3** *their approach to the project lacks purpose* determination, resoluteness, resolution, resolve, firmness, steadfastness, single-mindedness, persistence, perseverance, tenacity, doggedness. **4** *to little purpose | not to much purpose* benefit, advantage, use, usefulness, value, gain, profit, avail, result, outcome, effect. **on purpose** *cheated us on purpose* purposely, intentionally, deliberately, by design, willfully, wittingly, knowingly, consciously.

purpose verb *they purposed to reach the summit that night* intend, have the intention, mean, decide, resolve, determine, plan, aim, have a mind, propose, aspire.

purposeful adjective *attack the problem in a purposeful way* determined, resolute, resolved, firm, steadfast, single-minded, persistent, persevering, tenacious, dogged, unfaltering, unwavering.

Antonyms: AIMLESS; IRRESOLUTE.

purposely adverb *damage the car purposely* on purpose, intentionally, deliberately, by design, willfully, wittingly, knowingly, consciously.

purse noun **1** *carry money in her purse* wallet, pouch; bag, handbag, pocketbook. **2** *a purse of $50,000 won by the boxer* prize, award, reward, gift, present.

purse verb *purse her lips in disapproval* press together, compress, tighten, pucker.

pursuance noun *in the pursuance of his duties* execution, discharge, performance, carrying out, doing, pursuing, prosecution, following.

pursue verb **1** *the detective pursued the thief* go after, run after, follow, chase, give chase to, hunt, stalk, track, trail, shadow; *inf.* tail. **2** *decide not to pursue the line of inquiry* follow, go on with, proceed with, keep/carry on with, continue with, continue, persist in. **3** *pursue a career in science | pursue a life in science* follow, engage in, be engaged in, be occupied in, work at, practice, prosecute, conduct, ply, apply oneself to. **4** *pursue his goal of happiness | pursue his ambition to be a doctor* strive toward, push toward, work toward, seek, search for, be intent on, aim at, have as a goal, have as an objective, aspire to. **5** *he/she pursued every eligible young woman/man* chase after, chase, run after, go after; play up to.

Antonyms: FLEE; AVOID; SHUN; ESCHEW.

pursuit noun **1** *take part in the pursuit of the thief* pursuing, chasing, chase, hunt, stalking, tracking; *inf.* tailing. *See* PURSUE 1. **2** *give up the pursuit of that line of inquiry* pursuing, following, proceeding, continuance, persistence. **3** *his pursuit of a life of crime | determined on his pursuit of a career in medicine* following, engagement, occupation, work, practicing, prosecution, conducting, plying. **4** *his pursuit of happiness | their pursuit of their ambitions* striving toward, search, aim, goal, objective, aspiration. **5** *his/her relentless pursuit of eligible young women/men* chase, chasing (after). *See* PURSUE 5.

purvey verb **1** *purvey milk to the local schools* provide, supply, furnish, sell, retail, deal in. **2** *purvey information to the public about the drought* provide, supply, furnish, make available, pass on, spread, circulate, communicate, make known, publicize, publish, broadcast, disseminate.

pus noun *pus from the wound* suppuration, discharge, secretion, ooze.

push verb **1** *push his friend into the swimming pool* shove, thrust, propel, drive, ram, jolt, butt, jostle. **2** *push one's way through the crowd* shove, thrust, force, press, squeeze, jostle, elbow, shoulder. **3** *push the button/lever* press, push down, press down, depress, exert pressure on. **4** *push him into applying for the job* encourage, prompt, press, urge, egg on, spur on, prod, goad, incite, impel, dragoon, force, coerce, constrain, browbeat, strong-arm. **5** *pushing their latest products* promote, advertise, publicize, boost; *inf.* plug, hype. **push around** *older boys pushing him around* bully, ride roughshod over, trample on, tread on, browbeat, tyrannize, intimidate, domineer. **push off** *they told him to push off* go away, leave, depart, get out; *inf.* shove off, make oneself scarce, beat it, get lost, skedaddle, hit the road.

Antonyms: PULL; DETER; DISCOURAGE.

push noun **1** *gave his friend a push into the pool* shove, thrust, ram, jolt, butt, jostle. **2** *the general launched a big push* attack, assault, advance, onslaught, onset, charge, sortie, sally. **3** *looking for salespeople with push* drive, force, ambition, enterprise, initiative, energy, vigor, vitality, spirit, verve, enthusiasm, go, vim; *inf.* get-up-and-go, gumption, pizzazz. **if push comes to shove** *if push comes to shove, we will sell the house* in an emergency, in a crisis, if things get (really) bad, in times of hardship, if one is in difficulty, in time of need, if necessary.

pushover noun **1** *the task was a pushover* easy task, something easy, child's play; *inf.* piece of cake, picnic, cinch, breeze. **2** *he doles out money because he is a pushover* fool, dupe; *inf.* sucker, soft touch, easy mark, easy touch, sap.

pushy adjective pushing, assertive, self-assertive, aggressive, forceful, forward, bold, brash, bumptious, presumptuous, cocksure, loud, obnoxious.

pusillanimous adjective cowardly, timorous,

timid, fearful, faint-hearted, lily-livered, chick-enhearted, spineless, craven; *inf.* yellow, chicken, gutless.

Antonyms: BRAVE; FEARLESS; PLUCKY.

pussyfoot *verb* **1** *pussyfoot around the house so as not to wake people* creep, tiptoe, pad, steal, sneak, prowl, slink, tread warily. **2** *stop pussyfooting and say what you think* equivocate, be evasive, evade the issue, dodge/sidestep the issue, prevaricate, hedge, fence, hem and haw, beat about the bush, sit on the fence, tergiversate.

pustule *noun* boil, blister, pimple, abscess, papule; *inf.* whitehead, blackhead, zit.

put *verb* **1** *put the books on the shelf | put him in a difficult situation* place, lay, lay down, set down, deposit, position, rest, stand, locate, situate, settle, emplace, install, posit. **2** *put into English | put it in layman's terms* translate, transcribe, turn, render, construe, transliterate, interpret, word, express, phrase, frame, formulate, couch, say, utter, voice, speak, state, pronounce, proclaim. **3** *put to good use | put them to work* set, apply, employ, use, utilize, assign, allocate, devote. **4** *put to death* commit, consign, subject, condemn, sentence, convict, doom. **5** *I would put it at five acres | put its worth at $500* assess, evaluate, value, estimate, calculate, reckon, guess, measure, establish, fix, place, set; *inf.* guesstimate. **6** *put money on a horse* place, bet, wager, gamble, stake, risk, chance, hazard. **7** *put the shot* throw, toss, fling, pitch, cast, hurl, heave, lob, let fly. **8** *put his fist through the window* thrust, drive, plunge, stick, push, force, lunge, knock, bang, smash, bash. **put across** *successfully put across the message* get across/over, convey, communicate, make clear, explain, express, spell out, make understood, clarify. **put aside 1** *put aside food/money for a rainy day* lay by, put away, set/lay aside, save, reserve, keep in reserve, keep, store, stockpile, hoard, deposit, stow away, salt away, squirrel away. **2** *put aside the newspaper* set/lay aside, put to one side, move to one side, cast aside, discard, abandon, dispense with, drop. **3** *put aside their differences* set/lay aside, forget, disregard, ignore, discount, bury, consign to oblivion. **put at/in** *put him at the bottom of the waiting list | put them in the top grade* place at/in, assign to, consign to, allocate to, rate at/in, rank at/in, grade at/in, classify at/in, categorize at/in, catalog at/in, bracket at/in. **put away 1** *put away food/money for a rainy day* put/lay aside, lay by, set/lay aside, save, keep in reserve, store, stockpile. **2** *put away the books* put back, replace, return to its place, tidy up, clear away. **3** *put away all thoughts of him* set/put/lay aside, discard, cast aside, forget, disregard, get rid of, rid oneself of, jettison, consign to oblivion. **4** *put the criminal/mental patient away* put in prison, put in a mental hospital, confine, lock up, shut away/up, commit, imprison, hospitalize, institutionalize, certify. **5** *put away quanti-*

ties of food consume, eat, eat up, swallow, gulp down, devour, down, gobble up, bolt, wolf down. **6** *put away the enemy* kill, do away with, murder, slaughter, slay, dispatch, finish off, destroy; *inf.* bump off, wipe out. **put down 1** *put down a rebellion* crush, suppress, quash, quell, stamp out, stop, repress, smash, extinguish. **2** *put their names down* write down, put in writing, note down, make a note of, jot down, take down, set down, enter, list, record, register, log. **3** *put it down to experience* mark down, set down, attribute, ascribe, impute, chalk up to, blame on. **4** *put down the sick animal* euthanize, put to sleep, put out of its misery, destroy, do away with, kill. **5** *always putting down his wife* snub, disparage, deprecate, belittle, denigrate, deflate, slight, humiliate, crush, mortify. **put forward** *put forward a theory | his name was put forward for the candidacy* submit, present, suggest, advance, tender, propose, move, introduce, offer, proffer, recommend, suggest, nominate, name. **put off 1** *put off the meeting* postpone, put back, defer, delay, adjourn, hold over, reschedule, shelve; *inf.* put on ice, put on the back burner. **2** *put off by his surly behavior | the smell put her off* discourage, dissuade, dishearten, distress, dismay, discomfit, daunt, repel, offend, disgust, revolt, sicken, nauseate. **put on 1** *put on her new suit* dress in, get dressed in, clothe oneself in, change into, slip into, don. **2** *put on the light* switch on, turn on. **3** *put on a play* stage, mount, present, produce. **4** *she is just putting on the grief* feign, fake, sham, simulate, affect. **5** *put the blame on the father/weather* place on, attribute to, impute to, impose on, fix on, attach to, assign to, allocate to, lay on, pin on. **put one over on** *he really put one over on us* trick, deceive, hoodwink, mislead, delude, fool, take in, dupe, lead on, outwit, bamboozle; *inf.* pull a fast one on, con, make a sucker of. **put out 1** *she is easily put out* annoy, anger, irritate, exasperate, infuriate, provoke, irk, vex, gall, disturb, perturb, disconcert, agitate, harass. **2** *we do not want to put you out by staying to dinner | don't put yourself out* inconvenience, put (someone) to trouble, trouble, bother, impose upon, discommode, incommode. **3** *put out the fire* extinguish, quench, douse, stamp out. **4** *put out the candle* extinguish, blow out, snuff out, douse. **5** *put out a report on the drought* bring out, issue, circulate, release, disclose, make known, make public, publish, broadcast, publicize. **put to** *put it to the committee* set before, lay before, present to, bring forward to, forward to, submit to, tender to, offer to, proffer to, put forward to, set forth to, advance to, posit to. **put up 1** *put up new houses* build, construct, erect, raise. **2** *put up his friends for the night* give accommodations to, accommodate, provide with lodging, house, give a roof to, give a bed to, entertain.

3 *put his friend up for chairman* put forward, nominate, propose, recommend. **4** *put up the money for the campaign* provide, supply, furnish, give, donate, pay, advance, pledge. **5** *put up posters* stick up, post, display, exhibit. **put up to** *put his friend up to the burglary* egg on to do/commit/(etc.), urge to do/commit/(etc.), encourage to do/commit/(etc.), persuade to do/commit/(etc.), incite to do/commit/(etc.), goad to do/commit/(etc.), spur to do/commit/(etc.). **put up with** endure, tolerate, bear, stand, abide, suffer, take, stomach, brook, accept, swallow. **put upon** *she is so obliging that she gets put upon* take advantage of, impose upon, take for granted, exploit, overwork, overburden, saddle.

putative *adjective the putative father of the baby* supposed, assumed, presumed, presumptive, acknowledged, accepted, recognized, commonly believed (to be), commonly regarded (as), alleged, reputed.

put-down *noun regard his remark as a gross putdown* snub, rebuff, slight, disparagement, sneer, humiliation.

puzzle *verb he was puzzled by her behavior* perplex, baffle, stump, beat, mystify, confuse, bewilder, nonplus, stagger, dumbfound, daze, confound; *inf.* flummox. **puzzle over** *puzzling over what she had said | puzzling over her motives* rack one's brains about, think hard about, give much thought to, mull over, muse over, ponder, brood about, wonder about. **puzzle out** *puzzle out the solution* find the answer to, work out, think out, think through, figure out, reason out, solve, resolve, decipher, find the key to, unravel; *inf.* crack.

puzzled *adjective the detectives are still puzzled* perplexed, baffled, stumped, nonplussed, beaten, mystified, confused, bewildered, confounded, staggered, dumbfounded, dazed, at a loss, at sea; *inf.* flummoxed.

puzzling *adjective a puzzling situation* difficult, hard, unclear, perplexing, knotty, baffling, enigmatic, abstruse, nonplussing, mystifying, bewildering, unfathomable, inexplicable, incomprehensible, beyond one, above one's head.
Antonyms: CLEAR; STRAIGHTFORWARD; COMPREHENSIBLE; LUCID.

pygmy *noun* **1** *insultingly called him a pygmy* small man/woman/person, midget, dwarf; *inf.* shrimp, munchkin, runt, Tom Thumb. **2** *a pygmy among intellectual giants* nonentity, nobody, lightweight; *inf.* pipsqueak.

pyromaniac *noun* arsonist, incendiary; *inf.* firebug, pyro, torch.

Q

quack noun *quacks selling fake medicines* charlatan, mountebank, impostor, fraud, fake, confidence man, pretender, humbug; *inf.* con man, phony.
quack adjective *a quack cure for colds* fake, fraudulent, counterfeit, sham; *inf.* phony.

---

quack
charlatan, dissembler, fake, impostor, mountebank
There are many different ways to describe a **fake**, a colloquial term for anyone who knowingly practices deception or misrepresentation. Someone who sells a special tonic that claims to do everything from curing the common cold to making hair grow on a bald man's head is called a **quack**, a term that refers to any fraudulent practitioner of medicine or law. **Mountebank** sometimes carries implications of quackery, but more often it refers to a self-promoting person who resorts to cheap tricks or undignified efforts to win attention (*political mountebanks*). A **charlatan** is usually a writer, speaker, preacher, professor, or some other expert who tries to conceal his or her lack of skill or knowledge by resorting to pretentious displays (*supposedly a leading authority in his field, he turned out to be nothing but a charlatan*). An individual who tries to pass himself or herself off as someone else is an **impostor** (*an impostor who bore a close physical resemblance to the king*), although this term can also refer to anyone who assumes a title or profession that is not his or her own. Although all of these deceivers are out to fool people, it is the **dissembler** who is primarily interested in concealing his or her true motives or evil purpose (*he is a dissembler who weaves a tangled web of lies*).

---

quaff verb drink, swallow, gulp down, imbibe; *inf.* guzzle, swig.
quagmire noun **1** *avoiding the muck of the quagmire* quag, bog, peat bog, marsh, swamp, morass, mire, slough, fen. **2** *in a quagmire with no place to live* difficulty, quandary, dilemma, predicament, plight, tight corner, muddle, entanglement, involvement, imbroglio, impasse, stalemate; *inf.* jam, scrape, pickle, fix, hot water, stew.
quail verb flinch, shrink, recoil, shy away, pull back, draw back, cower, cringe, shudder, shiver, tremble, shake, quake, blanch.
quaint adjective pleasantly old-fashioned, old-fashioned, old-world, (attractively) unusual,

droll, curious, whimsical, attractive, charming, sweet.
Antonyms: MODERN; NEWFANGLED.
quake verb shake, tremble, quiver, shiver, shudder, rock, vibrate, pulsate, throb.
qualification noun **1** *qualification to be a teacher* certification, training, competence, competency, accomplishment, eligibility, acceptability, suitability, preparedness, fitness, proficiency, skillfulness, adeptness, capability, aptitude; skill, ability, attribute, endowment. **2** *say what you mean without qualification* modification, limitation, restriction, reservation, stipulation, allowance, adaptation, adjustment; condition, proviso, provision, caveat.
qualified adjective **1** *a qualified doctor* certified, certificated, trained, fitted, fit, equipped, prepared, competent, accomplished, proficient, skilled, skillful, adept, practiced, experienced, expert, capable, able. **2** *a qualified approval* modified, limited, conditional, restricted, bounded, contingent, confined, circumscribed, reserved, guarded, equivocal, stipulated, adapted, adjusted.
qualify verb **1** *he qualified as a doctor* gain certification/qualifications, train, take instruction. **2** *his training qualifies him to teach* certify, license, empower, authorize, allow, permit, sanction, warrant, fit, equip, prepare, arm, make ready, ground, train, educate, coach, teach, instruct. **3** *qualify her statement* modify, limit, make conditional, restrict. **4** *qualify her criticism* modify, temper, soften, modulate, mitigate, reduce, lessen, diminish. **qualify as** *not qualify as poetry* be characterizable as, meet the requirement of, be eligible as, be designated (as).
quality noun **1** *the material is of poor quality* degree of excellence, standard, grade, level, make, sort, type, kind, variety. **2** *his quality has been recognized* excellence, superiority, merit, worth, value, caliber, talent, talentedness, eminence, preeminence, distinction. **3** *they have many good qualities* feature, trait, attribute, characteristic, aspect, property, peculiarity. **4** *differences in the quality of the two personalities* character, nature, constitution, makeup.
qualms plural noun **1** *have some qualms about going* doubt(s), misgivings, hesitation, hesitancy, reluctance, disinclination, anxiety, apprehension, disquiet, uneasiness, concern(s). **2** *have no qualms about having hurt them* pangs/twinges

of conscience, scruples, compunction, re-morse.

---

qualms
compunction, demur, misgiving, scruple

To have **qualms** is to have an uneasy feeling that you have acted or are about to act against your better judgment (*she had qualms about leaving a nine-year-old in charge of an infant*). **Misgivings** are even stronger, implying a disturbed state of mind because you're no longer confident that what you're doing is right (*his misgivings about letting his 80-year-old mother drive herself home turned out to be justified*). **Compunction** implies a momentary pang of conscience because what you are doing or are about to do is unfair, improper, or wrong (*they showed no compunction in carrying out their devious plans*). **Scruples** suggest a more highly-developed conscience or sense of honor; it implies that you have principles, and that you would be deeply disturbed if you thought you were betraying them (*her scruples would not allow her to participate in what she considered antifeminist activities*). **Demur** connotes hesitation to the point of delay, but the delay is usually caused by objections or indecision rather than a sense of conscience (*they accepted his decision without demur*).

---

quandary *noun* awkward situation, difficulty, dilemma, predicament, plight, tight corner/spot, state of uncertainty/perplexity, muddle, impasse; *inf.* jam, pickle, fix.

quantity *noun* 1 *what quantity of books/paper do you need?* number, amount, total, aggregate, sum, quota, weight. 2 *estimate the quantity* size, capacity, mass, volume, bulk, extent, length, area, time. **a quantity of** *found a quantity of books/paper* a number of, quite a number of, a good number of, several, numerous, many, a large amount of, considerable amounts of; *inf.* a lot of, lots of.

quarrel *noun the couple had a quarrel* argument, fight, disagreement, difference of opinion, dispute, disputation, squabble, altercation, wrangle, tiff, row, misunderstanding, feud, vendetta; *inf.* falling-out, spat, scrap. **quarrel with** *I have no quarrel with him* bone of contention with, complaint against/with, grievance with/against, resentment toward.
Antonyms: RECONCILIATION; AGREEMENT.

---

quarrel
**altercation, dispute, feud, row,
spat, squabble, wrangle**

Family feuds come in a variety of shapes and sizes. A husband and his wife may have a **quarrel**, which suggests a heated verbal argument, with hostility that may persist even after it is over (*it took them almost a week to patch up their quarrel*). Siblings tend to have **squabbles**, which

are childlike disputes over trivial matters, although they are by no means confined to child-hood (*frequent squabbles over who would pick up the check*). A **spat** is also a petty quarrel, but unlike *squabble*, it suggests an angry outburst followed by a quick ending without hard feelings (*another spat in an otherwise loving relationship*). A **row** is more serious, involving noisy quarreling and the potential for physical violence (*a row that woke the neighbors*). Neighbors are more likely to have an **altercation**, which is usually confined to verbal blows but may involve actual or threatened physical ones (*an altercation over the location of the fence*). A **dispute** is also a verbal argument, but one that is carried on over an extended period of time (*an ongoing dispute over who was responsible for taking out the garbage*). Two families who have been enemies for a long time are probably involved in a **feud**, which suggests a bitter quarrel that lasts for years or even generations (*the feud between the Hatfields and the McCoys*). There is no dignity at all in being involved in a **wrangle**, which is an angry, noisy, and often futile dispute in which both parties are unwilling to listen to the other's point of view.

---

quarrel *verb the couple quarreled* argue, have a fight, fight, dispute, squabble, bicker, spar, wrangle, have a misunderstanding; *inf.* have a falling-out. **quarrel with** *I cannot quarrel with his logic* find fault with, fault, criticize, object to, take exception to, complain about; *inf.* pick holes in.
Antonyms: AGREE; get on.

quarrelsome *adjective* argumentative, belligerent, disputatious, contentious, pugnacious, combative, ready for a fight, bellicose, litigious, hot-tempered, irascible, choleric, irritable.
Antonyms: PEACEABLE; dovish.

quarry *noun hunters stalking their quarry* prey, victim, prize.

quarter *noun* 1 *live in the Latin quarter of the city* district, area, region, part, side, neighborhood, locality, zone, territory, province. 2 *accept help from any quarter* direction, place, point, spot, location.

quarter *verb soldiers quartered in the town* put up, house, board, billet, accommodate, lodge, install.

quarters *plural noun* rooms, chambers, barracks; lodging(s), accommodations, billet, residence, abode, dwelling, domicile, habitation, cantonment; *inf.* digs, pad.

quash *verb* 1 *quash the jail sentence* annul, declare null and void, nullify, invalidate, void, cancel, overrule, override, overthrow, reject, set aside, reverse, revoke, rescind, repeal. 2 *quash the rebellion* crush, put down, squash, quell, subdue, suppress, repress, quench, extinguish, stamp out, put a stop to, end, terminate, defeat, destroy.
Antonyms: VALIDATE; INCITE; PROVOKE; SUPPORT.

quasi- *prefix* **1** *quasi-scientific evidence* supposedly, seemingly, apparently, nominally, pseudo. **2** *a quasi-friend* supposed, so-called, would-be, pretended, pretend, sham, fake, pseudo.

quaver *verb* *his voice quavered* quiver, vibrate, tremble, shake, waver.

queasy *adjective* sick, nauseated, nauseous, ill, indisposed, dizzy, sick to one's stomach.

queen *noun* **1** *the queen reigned for 50 years* empress, monarch, sovereign, ruler. **2** *she was the queen of Broadway* star, shining star, prima donna, idol, ideal, paragon, doyenne.

queer *adjective* **1** *queer behavior* odd, strange, unusual, extraordinary, funny, curious, peculiar, weird, outlandish, singular, eccentric, unconventional, unorthodox, atypical, abnormal, irregular, anomalous, deviant, outré, offbeat; *inf.* off-the-wall. **2** *a queer story | something queer going on* strange, peculiar, suspicious, suspect, irregular, questionable, dubious, doubtful; *inf.* fishy, shady. **3** *feel a bit queer* ill, unwell, sick, queasy, faint, dizzy, giddy, light-headed.

Antonyms: ORDINARY; CONVENTIONAL; NORMAL; WELL.

quell *verb* **1** *quell the rebellion/rebels* quash, defeat, conquer, vanquish, overpower, overcome, overwhelm, rout, crush, suppress, subdue, extinguish, stamp out, put down. **2** *quell their fears* allay, lull, put at rest, quiet, silence, calm, soothe, appease, assuage, abate, deaden, dull, pacify, tranquilize, mitigate, palliate.

Antonyms: AGITATE; EXCITE; PROVOKE.

quench *verb* **1** *quench one's thirst* satisfy, slake, sate, satiate. **2** *quench the candle* extinguish, put out, snuff out, blow out, douse. **3** *quench their desire* suppress, extinguish, stamp out, smother, stifle.

query *noun* **1** *raise a query* question, inquiry. **2** *his behavior raises a query as to his sanity* question, question mark, doubt, uncertainty, reservation, suspicion; skepticism.

query *verb* **1** *"where are we?" he queried* ask, inquire, question. **2** *he queried their fitness for the job* call into question, question, raise/entertain doubts about, doubt, have/harbor suspicions about, feel uneasy about, express reservations about, challenge, raise objections to.

quest *noun* **1** *in quest of a better life* search, seeking, pursuit, chase, hunt. **2** *their quest was the Holy Grail* goal, aim, objective, purpose, quarry, prey. **3** *knights setting out on a quest* adventure, expedition, journey, voyage, exploration, crusade.

question *noun* **1** *answer her questions* query, inquiry, interrogation. **2** *there is no question that he is ill* doubt, dubiety, dubiousness, dispute, argument, debate, controversy, reservation. **3** *there is the question of safety* issue, point at issue, problem, matter, point, subject, topic, theme. **beyond question** beyond doubt, without (a) doubt, undoubtedly, indisputably, incontestably, incontrovertibly. **in question** *the matter in question* being discussed, under discussion/consideration, at issue, on the agenda. **out of the question** impossible, inconceivable, unthinkable, unimaginable, absurd, ridiculous, preposterous.

Antonyms: ANSWER; RESPONSE; CERTAINTY.

question *verb* **1** *question the witnesses* ask questions of, interrogate, cross-examine, cross-question, quiz, catechize, interview, sound out, examine, give the third degree to; *inf.* grill, pump. **2** *question his motives* call into question, query, raise doubts about, throw doubt on, have suspicions about, express reservations about, challenge, raise objections to.

questionable *adjective* *his motive/ability is questionable* open to question/doubt, doubtful, dubious, uncertain, debatable, in dispute, arguable, controversial, controvertible.

Antonyms: CERTAIN; INDISPUTABLE.

queue *noun* *a long queue at the ticket office | a queue of parade floats* line, row, column, file, chain, string, train, succession, sequence, series, concatenation.

quibble *verb* **1** *quibble about/over a minor detail* raise petty objections, cavil, carp, pettifog, split hairs; *inf.* nitpick. **2** *he quibbles so that it is difficult to get a straight answer* be evasive, equivocate, avoid the issue, prevaricate, hedge, fudge, be ambiguous; *inf.* beat about the bush.

quick *adjective* **1** *a quick runner/worker/reader* fast, rapid, speedy, swift, fleet, express. **2** *a quick response* prompt, without delay, immediate, instantaneous, expeditious. **3** *a quick look at the map* brief, brisk, fleeting, momentary, hasty, hurried, cursory, perfunctory. **4** *the child is very quick* quick-witted, sharp-witted, alert, intelligent. *See* QUICK-WITTED. **5** *quick of temper* quick-tempered, irascible, irritable. *See* QUICK-TEMPERED.

Antonyms: SLOW; SLUGGISH; LONG; DULL.

quicken *verb* **1** *his pulse quickened* become/grow faster, speed up, accelerate. **2** *they quickened their steps/progress* speed up, accelerate, expedite, hasten, hurry, hurry up, precipitate. **3** *the documentary quickened his interest in wildlife* stimulate, stir up, arouse, rouse, incite, instigate, whet, inspire, kindle, fan, refresh, strengthen, revive, revitalize, resuscitate, revivify.

---

quicken
animate, enliven, invigorate, stimulate, vitalize

While all of these verbs mean to make alive or lively, **quicken** suggests the rousing or renewal of life, especially life that has been inert or suspended (*she felt the baby quicken during her second trimester of pregnancy*). **Animate** means to impart life, motion, or activity to something that previously lacked such a quality (*a discussion animated by the presence of so many young people*). **Stimulate** means to goad into activity from a state of inertia, inactivity, or lethargy (*the professor's constant questions stimulated her students to do more research*), while **enliven** refers to a stimulating influence that brightens or makes lively what was previously dull, depressed, or torpid (*a sudden change in the weather enlivened the group's activities*). **Invigorate** and **vitalize** both mean to fill with vigor or energy, but the former refers to physical energy (*invigorated by the climb up the mountain*), while the latter implies that energy has been imparted in a nonphysical sense (*to vitalize an otherwise dull meeting*).

quickly *adverb* **1** *run quickly* fast, rapidly, speedily, swiftly, with all speed, at speed, with all possible haste, on the double, post-haste; *inf.* like mad/crazy, hell-bent for leather, like a bat out of hell. **2** *respond quickly* promptly, without delay, immediately, instantaneously, expeditiously. **3** *read the letter quickly* rapidly, briskly, hastily, hurriedly, cursorily, perfunctorily.
Antonyms: SLOWLY; THOROUGHLY.

quick-tempered *adjective* irascible, irritable, hot-tempered, fiery, hasty, impatient, touchy, testy, snappish, quarrelsome, petulant, choleric, splenetic, volatile; *inf.* on a short fuse.
Antonyms: PLACID; CALM; PHLEGMATIC.

quick-witted *adjective* quick, intelligent, sharp-witted, nimble-witted, alert, bright, lively, smart, perceptive, discerning, shrewd; *inf.* quick on the uptake.
Antonyms: STUPID; DULL.

quid pro quo *noun* exchange, substitution, trading, trade-off, barter, compensation, recompense, requital, reprisal, retaliation.

quiescent *adjective* inert, dormant, passive, inactive, idle, still, stagnant, torpid.
Antonyms: ACTIVE; functioning.

quiet *adjective* **1** *the house was quiet* silent, hushed, noiseless, soundless, peaceful. **2** *a quiet voice* soft, low, inaudible. **3** *a quiet person* calm, serene, composed, placid, untroubled, peaceful, tranquil, gentle, mild, temperate, unexcitable, restrained, phlegmatic, imperturbable, moderate, reserved, uncommunicative, taciturn, silent. **4** *quiet colors/clothes* unobtrusive, unostentatious, restrained, muted, understated, subdued, subtle, conservative, sober, modest, demure. **5** *live in a quiet village* peaceful, sleepy, undisturbed, unfrequented, private, secluded, sequestered, retired, isolated, out of the way; *inf.* off the beaten track. **6** *the store/town/business is quiet today* inactive, not busy, sluggish. **7** *have a quiet word with him* private, confidential, secret, discreet, unofficial, off the record; *inf.* hush-hush. **8** *we kept his presence quiet* secret, unrevealed, undisclosed, uncommunicated; *inf.* hush-hush.
Antonyms: LOUD; NOISY; OBTRUSIVE; BUSY.

quiet *noun in the quiet of the evening* quietness, stillness, silence, hush, noiselessness, soundlessness, peace, peacefulness, calmness, tranquillity, serenity.

quiet *verb* **1** *quiet the noisy children* make quiet, silence, hush, shush; *inf.* shut up. **2** *the children soon quieted* become quiet, grow silent, settle down; *inf.* shut up. **3** *quiet the frightened horse* calm, calm down, soothe, tranquilize. **4** *quiet their fears* allay, soothe, calm, tranquilize, appease, lull, pacify, mollify, palliate, suppress, quell, stifle, dull, deaden.

quietly *adverb* **1** *speak quietly* softly, in a low voice, in low/hushed tones, in a whisper, in an undertone, inaudibly. **2** *creep out quietly* silently, noiselessly, soundlessly. **3** *tell him quietly that he must leave* privately, confidentially, secretly, discreetly. **4** *she is quietly confident* calmly, patiently, placidly, serenely, undemonstratively, unemotionally. **5** *dress quietly* unobtrusively, unostentatiously, with restraint, conservatively, soberly, modestly, demurely.

quilt *noun* eiderdown, comforter, bedcover, coverlet, duvet; patchwork quilt.

quintessence *noun* **1** *the novel captures the quintessence of youth* essence, essentialness, core, heart, soul, spirit, quiddity. **2** *he is the quintessence of a gentleman* embodiment, personification, exemplar, perfect example, ideal, beau ideal.

quip *noun make witty quips* witticism, wisecrack, joke, jest, bon mot, epigram, aphorism; *inf.* one-liner, crack.

quirk *noun it is one of his quirks to polish his car every day* idiosyncrasy, peculiarity, oddity, eccentricity, foible, whim, vagary, caprice, kink, mannerism, habit, characteristic, trait, feature, obsession, passion, mania, fetish, *idée fixe*; *inf.* hang-up.

quit *verb* **1** *quit smoking* give up, stop, cease, discontinue, drop, leave off, abandon, abstain from, desist from. **2** *quit his job* leave, depart from, vacate, walk out on. **3** *he has decided to quit* leave, depart, go away, take off; *inf.* call it a day, call it quits, pack it in.
Antonyms: START; BEGIN; CONTINUE.

quite *adverb* **1** *he has quite recovered* completely, fully, entirely, totally, wholly, absolutely, in all respects. **2** *he is quite talented, but not as good as his brother* fairly, relatively, moderately, reasonably, to some extent/degree, to a certain extent, rather, somewhat. **3** *it is quite delicious* truly, really, definitely, absolutely, certainly, unequivocally.

quiver *verb quiver with fear* tremble, shiver, vibrate, quaver, quake, shudder, pulsate, convulse, palpitate.

quiver *noun a quiver of fear* tremble, tremor, shiver, vibration, quaver, shudder, pulsation, convulsion, palpitation, throb, spasm, tic.

quiz *noun* **1** *study for the math quiz* test, examination; *inf.* exam. **2** *the quiz awaiting them at* *the police station* questioning, interrogation, cross-examination, cross-questioning, catechism, examination, third degree; *inf.* grilling, pumping.

quiz *verb quiz them about their movements* question, ask, interrogate, cross-examine, cross-question, catechize; *inf.* pump, grill.

quizzical *adjective a quizzical look/smile* questioning, puzzled, perplexed, baffled, mystified, mocking, teasing.

quota *noun* share, allowance, allocation, portion, ration, part, slice, measure, proportion, percentage; *inf.* cut.

quotation *noun* **1** *full of quotations from Shakespeare* citation, reference, allusion, excerpt, extract, selection, passage, line; *inf.* quote. **2** *give them a quotation for the work* estimate, estimated price, cost, charge, figure; *inf.* quote.

quote *verb* **1** *quote verses from the sonnet* repeat, iterate, recite, reproduce. **2** *he could not quote an example of what he meant* cite, give, name, instance, mention, refer to, make reference to, allude to. **3** *quote the job at $800* estimate, price, set a price for.

R

rabble noun 1 *a rabble gathered to protest the verdict* (angry) mob, horde, swarm, (disorderly) crowd, throng. 2 *inciting the rabble to revolt* common people, populace, commonality, rank and file, peasantry, hoi polloi, riff-raff; masses, lower classes, dregs of society; *inf.* great unwashed.
Antonyms: ARISTOCRACY; NOBILITY.

rabid adjective 1 *rabid dogs* rabies-infected, mad, foaming at the mouth, hydrophobic. 2 *rabid socialists/conservatives* fanatical, extreme, overzealous, overenthusiastic, fervent, unreasonable, irrational, intolerant, bigoted, narrow-minded, narrow. 3 *rabid hatred/enemies* violent, wild, frenzied, frenetic, frantic, raging, raving, maniacal, distracted, beside oneself, berserk.
Antonyms: INDIFFERENT; HALFHEARTED; MODERATE.

race[1] noun 1 *the competitors for the race* speed contest, competition, chase, pursuit, relay. 2 *the race for the presidency* contest, competition, rivalry, contention. 3 *the rushing waters of the race* channel, waterway, watercourse, sluice, spillway; current.

race[2] verb 1 *horses racing at Churchill Downs* run, take part in a race, contend, compete. 2 *race each other in the Olympics* run against, compete against, be pitted against. 3 *race to the finish line* run, sprint, dash, dart, bolt, make a dash/bolt for, speed, fly, tear, zoom, accelerate, career. 4 *we have to race to get there on time* hurry, hasten, make haste, rush; *inf.* get cracking, get a move on, step on it, shake a leg.

race[3] noun 1 *humankind divided into races* racial division, people, ethnic group. 2 *discrimination on grounds of race* racial type, blood, bloodline, stock, line, lineage, breed, strain, stirps, extraction, ancestry, parentage. 3 *sailors are a robust race* group, type, class, species.

racial adjective race-related, ethnic, ethnological.

racism noun racialism, racial discrimination, racial prejudice/bigotry, apartheid.

racist noun racialist, bigot, illiberal.

racist adjective racialist, discriminatory, prejudiced, bigoted, intolerant, illiberal.

rack noun frame, framework, stand, form, trestle, structure, holder, shelf. **on the rack** in pain, in agony, in distress, suffering; under stress/pressure/strain; *inf.* stressed out.

rack verb *racked with pain* torture, agonize, afflict, torment, persecute, plague, distress, rend, tear, harrow, crucify, convulse.

racket noun 1 *a racket coming from next door* noise, din, row, commotion, disturbance, uproar, hubbub, hullabaloo; clamor, pandemonium, tumult, shouting, yelling. 2 *he is involved in a drugs racket* criminal activity, illegal scheme/enterprise, fraud, fraudulent scheme, swindle. 3 *what racket is he in?* business, line of business, line, occupation, profession, job; *inf.* game.

raconteur noun storyteller, teller of tales, spinner of yarns, narrator, relater, romancer.

racy adjective *racy jokes* risqué, suggestive, off-color, ribald, bawdy, vulgar, coarse, crude, rude, smutty, dirty, blue, indecent, indelicate, immodest, naughty; *inf.* spicy.

radiance noun 1 *the radiance of the sun* light, shining, brightness, brilliance, luminosity, effulgence, incandescence, glow, gleam, glitter, sparkle, shimmer, glare. 2 *the radiance of the bride* joyfulness, joy, elation, rapture, blitheness, happiness, delight, pleasure, gaiety, warmth. 3 *the radiance of her beauty* resplendence, splendor, dazzlingness.

radiant adjective 1 *the radiant sun/light* irradiant, shining, bright, illuminated, brilliant, luminous, luminescent, lustrous, lucent, effulgent, refulgent, incandescent, beaming, glowing, gleaming, glittering, sparkling, shimmering, glaring. 2 *the bride was radiant* joyful, elated, in raptures, ecstatic, blissfully happy, delighted, pleased, happy, glowing; *inf.* in seventh heaven, on cloud nine. 3 *her radiant beauty* splendid, resplendent, magnificent, dazzling, glowing, vivid, intense.
Antonyms: DARK; DULL; GLOOMY.

radiate verb 1 *radiating heat/light* send out/forth, scatter, disperse, diffuse, spread, shed, give off/out, emit, emanate. 2 *radiate joy/hope* transmit, emanate, show, exhibit, demonstrate; *inf.* be the picture of. 3 *lines radiating* branch out, spread out, diverge, divaricate, issue.

radiation noun 1 *the radiation of light/X rays* emission, emanation, propagation, transmission. 2 *ultraviolet/infrared radiation* waves, rays; transmitted energy. *See also table at* WAVE.

radical adjective 1 *radical issues/errors* fundamental, basic, rudimentary, elementary, elemental, constitutional. 2 *radical change needed* thorough, complete, total, entire, absolute, utter, comprehensive, exhaustive, sweeping, far-reaching, profound, drastic, stringent, violent. 3 *radical views/actions* extremist, extreme, militant, fanatic, leftist, left-wing.

Antonyms: MINOR; SUPERFICIAL; CONSERVATIVE.

raffish *adjective* **1** *he has a raffish air* rakish, bohemian, jaunty, dashing, devil-may-care, casual, careless, disreputable, dissolute, dissipated, debauched, decadent, degenerate. **2** *raffish bars/decor* tawdry, flashy, gaudy, loud, garish, showy, vulgar, tasteless, gross, coarse, meretricious.

raffle *noun* lottery, drawing, sweepstakes.

rag *noun* (piece of) cloth, scrap, remnant, fragment; dishrag, dishcloth, dustcloth, dust rag.

rag *verb ragging him about his baby pictures* rag on, tease, poke fun at, make fun of, make a fool of, taunt; *inf.* rib.

ragamuffin *noun* urchin, guttersnipe, waif, stray, gamin.

rage *noun* **1** *be filled with rage* fury, anger, wrath, ire, high dudgeon, frenzy, madness, raving. **2** *fly into a rage* fit of rage/fury, frenzy, tantrum, paroxysm of rage/anger, rampage. **3** *the rage of the storm* violence, turbulence, tumult, fire and fury. **all the rage** *miniskirts are all the rage* ultrafashionable, ultrapopular, in demand; *inf.* trendy, the last word, the latest thing/craze.

rage *verb* **1** *the dissatisfied customer is raging* be furious, be infuriated, be angry, seethe, be beside oneself, lose one's temper, boil over, rant, rave, rant and rave, storm, fume, fulminate; *inf.* foam at the mouth, blow one's top, blow up, blow a fuse/gasket, hit the ceiling, flip one's lid, freak out. **2** *rage against the new rules* fulminate, complain vociferously, storm, inveigh, rail. **3** *the storm is raging* be violent, be at its height, be turbulent, be tempestuous.

ragged *adjective* **1** *ragged clothes* tattered, in tatters, torn, rent, in holes, holey, worn to shreds, falling to pieces, threadbare, frayed, the worse for wear. **2** *ragged children* in rags, shabby, unkempt, down and out, down-at-the-heel, poor, destitute, indigent. **3** *a ragged coastline* jagged, notched, serrated, sawtoothed, craggy, rugged, uneven, irregular. **4** *a ragged writing style* rough, crude, unpolished, unrefined, faulty, imperfect, irregular, uneven. **5** *a ragged band of soldiers* in disarray, straggling, straggly, disorganized, fragmented.

raging *adjective* **1** *dealing with a raging customer* enraged, furious, angry, infuriated, wrathful, incensed, seething, fuming, ranting, raving, mad. *See* RAGE *verb* 1. **2** *a raging storm* violent, strong, wild, stormy, turbulent, tempestuous, blustery. **3** *a raging toothache* agonizing, excruciating, painful, throbbing, aching, sore. **4** *a raging thirst* extreme, excessive, severe, very great, inordinate.

rags *plural noun dressed in rags* tatters, tattered/old clothes; torn clothing.

raid *noun* **1** *make a raid on the enemy* surprise attack, assault, onset, onslaught, invasion, incursion, foray, charge, thrust, sortie, sally. **2** *a police raid* surprise search; *inf.* bust.

raid *verb* **1** *raid the enemy lines* make a raid on, attack, assault, invade, charge, assail, storm, rush, set upon, descend upon, swoop upon. **2** *raid the enemy supplies | raid the refrigerator* plunder, pillage, loot, rifle, forage, ransack, steal from. **3** *police raiding a house* make a raid on, search thoroughly, make a search of; *inf.* bust.

raider *noun* attacker, assaulter, invader, pillager, plunderer, marauder, ransacker, sacker.

rail *verb* **rail against** *rail against the new rules* inveigh against, declaim against, rage against, protest strongly, complain bitterly about, criticize severely, censure, condemn, castigate; *inf.* lambaste.

railing *noun* rails; balustrade, fencing, barrier.

raillery *noun* banter, badinage, teasing, joking, japing, persiflage; *inf.* kidding, ragging, ribbing.

rain *noun* **1** *farmers needing rain* rainfall, precipitation, raindrops, drizzle, shower, rainstorm, cloudburst, torrent, downpour, deluge, thunderstorm. **2** *a rain of arrows* shower, hail, deluge, volley.

rain *verb* **1** *it is raining* pour, pour/come down, precipitate, shower, drizzle, rain hard, rain heavily; *inf.* rain cats and dogs, come down in buckets. **2** *arrows rained down* fall, pour out/down, drop, shower. **3** *rain gifts on them* lavish, pour, give generously, bestow.

rainy *adjective* wet, showery, drizzly, damp.

raise *verb* **1** *raise one's eyes/hat | raise the ship* lift, lift up, raise aloft, elevate, uplift, upthrust, hoist, heave up. **2** *raise the fence* set up, set upright, stand, upend, stand on end. **3** *raise his offer/prices* increase, escalate, inflate; *inf.* step up, hike, jack up. **4** *raise the volume/temperature* increase, heighten, augment, amplify, intensify; *inf.* step up. **5** *raise a statue* construct, build, erect, put up. **6** *raise money/troops* get/gather together, collect, assemble, muster, levy, accumulate, amass, scrape together. **7** *raise objections* put forward, introduce, advance, bring up, broach, suggest, moot, present. **8** *raise doubts/hopes* cause, set going, bring into being, engender, create, set afoot, kindle, arouse, awaken, excite, summon up, provoke, activate, evoke, incite, stir up, foment, whip up, instigate. **9** *raise three children* bring up, rear, nurture, educate. **10** *raise chickens* breed, rear. **11** *raise crops* grow, farm, cultivate, propagate, till, produce. **12** *raise him to captain/manager* promote, advance, upgrade, elevate, exalt. **13** *raise bread* cause to rise, leaven, puff up. **14** *raise a siege* end, bring to an end, put an end to, terminate, abandon, lift. **15** *raise the barriers* remove, get rid of, take away. **16** *raise a ghost* cause to appear, call up, call forth, summon up, conjure up.

Antonyms: LOWER²; DEMOLISH; END.

raise *noun a raise in salary* gain, (pay/wage)

increase, growth, addition, appreciation; *inf.* boost.

rake *verb* **1** *rake the leaves* scrape up, collect, gather. **2** *rake the soil* smooth, smooth out, level, even out, flatten. **3** *rake through her things* search, hunt, ransack, rummage, rifle, comb. **4** *raking the enemy ship with gunfire* sweep, enfilade, pepper. **5** *rake the side of the car* scratch, scrape, graze. **rake in** *rake in money* gather in, earn, pull in, haul in, pile up, amass, accumulate. **rake up** *rake up the past* | *rake up old memories* revive, call to mind, reminisce about, recollect.

rake *noun* roué, debauchee, dissolute man, playboy, libertine, profligate.

rakish[1] *adjective the playboy's rakish behavior* dissolute, debauched, dissipated, profligate, wanton, degenerate, depraved.

rakish[2] *adjective looking rakish in his sports car* | *wears his hat at a rakish angle* dashing, jaunty, devil-may-care, sporty, breezy, debonair, smart, dapper, spruce; *inf.* natty. rally

rally *verb* **1** *rally to support the school* come/get together, assemble, group (together), band together, convene, unite. **2** *rally the forces* call/bring together, assemble, summon, round up, muster, marshal, mobilize. **3** *they were defeated, but they rallied* regroup, reassemble, reform, reunite. **4** *she was ill, but she rallied* recover, recuperate, revive, get better/well, improve, perk up, regain one's strength, pull through, take a turn for the better, turn the corner, be on the mend, get one's second wind. **Antonyms:** DISPERSE; DETERIORATE.

rally *noun* **1** *a political rally* mass meeting, meeting, gathering, assembly, assemblage, convention, conference, congregation, convocation. **2** *a rally on the stock exchange* recovery, recuperation, improvement, revival, rehabilitation, comeback, resurgence.

ram *verb* **1** *ram the tobacco into the pipe* | *ram clothes into the suitcase* force, cram, stuff, compress, jam, squeeze, thrust, tamp. **2** *ram fence posts into the ground* drive, hammer, pound, beat, hit. **3** *his car rammed ours* strike, hit, dash against, run into, crash into, collide with, bump, slam.

ramble *verb* **1** *ramble through the countryside* take a walk, go for a walk, walk, hike, wander, stroll, saunter, amble, roam, range, rove, traipse, jaunt. **2** *the speaker rambled on* | *that writer rambles* digress, wander, speak/write discursively, go off on tangents, talk aimlessly, maunder, gibber, blather, babble, chatter, gabble, rattle on.

ramble *noun* walk, hike, wander, stroll, saunter, amble, roam, traipse, jaunt, trip, excursion, tour.

rambler *noun* walker, hiker, stroller, saunterer, wanderer, roamer, rover, drifter, traveler, wayfarer.

rambling *adjective* **1** *rambling speeches/verse* digressive, wandering, roundabout, circuitous, diffuse, periphrastic, disconnected, disjointed, maundering, long-winded, verbose, wordy, prolix. **2** *rambling suburbs* sprawling, spreading, unsystematic. **3** *rambling plants* straggling, trailing, sprawling, spreading.

ramification *noun* **1** *the action had many ramifications* consequence, aftermath, outcome, result, upshot, issue, sequel, complication, implication. **2** *the ramifications of the structure* subdivision, offshoot, branch, outgrowth, limb, scion.

ramp *noun a ramp for wheelchairs* slope, sloping surface, incline, inclined plane, gradient, acclivity, rise; access ramp.

rampage *verb bison rampaging across the plain* rush/run wildly, run riot, run amok, charge, tear.

rampage *noun* uproar, furor, mayhem, turmoil. **on the rampage** running amok, going berserk, out of control, rampaging.

rampant *adjective* **1** *rampant disease/crime* uncontrolled, out of control/hand, unrestrained, unchecked, unbridled, widespread, pandemic, epidemic, spreading like wildfire. **2** *rampant foliage* luxuriant, exuberant, rank, profuse, lavish. **3** *a coat of arms with a lion rampant* rearing, standing, upright, erect. **4** *rampant militancy* aggressive, vehement, violent, wild, fanatical.

rampart *noun the ramparts of the fortress* embankment, earthwork, parapet, fortification, fort, stronghold, bulwark, bastion, barbican.

ramshackle *adjective* tumbledown, brokendown, rundown, dilapidated, derelict, gone to rack and ruin, falling to pieces, decrepit, neglected, crumbling, rickety, shaky, unsteady, tottering, unsafe, flimsy, jerry-built.

rancid *adjective* **1** *rancid butter* sour, turned, overripe, high, gamy, rotten, bad, off, tainted, putrid. **2** *a rancid smell* rank, sour, stale, fusty, musty, foul, stinking, malodorous, evil-smelling, fetid, offensive, obnoxious, noxious, noisome. **Antonyms:** FRESH; UNSPOILED.

rancor *noun* resentment, malice, spite, ill will, hatred, malevolence, malignancy, animosity, antipathy, enmity, hostility, acrimony, venom, vindictiveness.

rancorous *adjective* resentful, malicious, spiteful, hateful, malevolent, malignant, antipathetic, hostile, acrimonious, venomous, vindictive.

random *adjective* haphazard, chance, accidental, fortuitous, serendipitous, adventitious, arbitrary, hit-or-miss, indiscriminate, sporadic, stray, spot, casual, unsystematic, unmethodical, orderless, disorganized, unarranged, unplanned, unpremeditated. **at random 1** *chose numbers at random* randomly, haphazardly, arbitrarily, leaving things to chance, without method, without conscious choice, without

prearrangement. **2** *trees planted at random* unsystematically, unmethodically, erratically, indiscriminately, sporadically, every now and then.
Antonyms: DELIBERATE; SYSTEMATIC; PREMEDITATED.

range noun **1** *range of vision | the range of his influence | range of ability* scope, compass, radius, span, scale, gamut, reach, sweep, extent, area, field, orbit, province, domain, latitude; limits, bounds, confines. **2** *a range of mountains* row, line, file, rank, string, chain, series, sequence, succession, tier. **3** *a wide range of flavors/sizes/goods/people* assortment, variety, kind, sort, type, class, rank, order, genus, species. **4** *cooking on the range* stove, cooking stove, oven. **5** *animals on the range* pasture, pasturage, grass, grassland, grazing land.

---

range
compass, gamut, latitude, reach, scope, sweep
To say that someone has a wide **range** of interests implies that these interests are not only extensive but varied. Another way of expressing the same idea would be to say that the person's interests run the **gamut** from TV quiz shows to nuclear physics, a word that suggests a graduated scale or series running from one extreme to another. **Compass** implies a range of knowledge or activity that falls within very definite limits reminiscent of a circumference (*within the compass of her abilities*), while **sweep** suggests more of an arc-shaped range of motion or activity (*the sweep of the searchlight*) or a continuous extent or stretch (*a broad sweep of lawn*). **Latitude** and **scope** both emphasize the idea of freedom, although *scope* implies great freedom within prescribed limits (*the scope of the investigation*), while *latitude* means freedom from such limits (*she was granted more latitude than usual in interviewing the disaster victims*). Even someone who has a wide *range* of interests and a broad *scope* of authority, however, will sooner or later come up against something that is beyond his or her **reach**, which suggests the furthest limit of effectiveness or influence.

---

range verb **1** *range from very hot to freezing | range from brilliant to poor* extend, stretch, reach, cover, go, run, pass, fluctuate between, vary between. **2** *range the goods on the shelves | soldiers ranged along the battlements* line up, align, draw up, put/set in order, order, place, position, arrange, dispose, array, rank. **3** *range the students according to ability* classify, class, categorize, bracket, group, grade, catalog, file, pigeonhole. **4** *sheep ranging over the hills* roam, rove, ramble, traverse, travel over, wander, meander, amble, stroll, stray, drift.

rank noun **1** *salary according to rank* grade, level, stratum, class, status, position, station, standing. **2** *persons of rank* nobility, aristocracy, high birth, eminence, distinction, influence, power, prestige, weight, importance. **3** *what is his rank*

in the organization? grade, position, gradation, point on the scale, mark, echelon, rung on the ladder. **4** *break rank* array, alignment, order, arrangement, organization. **rank and file 1** *the officers separated from the rank and file* other ranks, ordinary/private soldiers, soldiers, men, troops. **2** *government ignoring the wishes of the rank and file* ordinary people, public, general public; common people, populace, commonality, rabble.

rank verb **1** *he ranks above a captain | rank with the best* have a rank, be graded, be placed, be positioned, have a status. **2** *rank their achievements | rank him a champion* classify, class, categorize, grade.

rank adjective **1** *rank vegetation* lush, luxuriant, abundant, dense, profuse, flourishing, exuberant, vigorous, productive, spreading, overgrown, jungly. **2** *a rank smell* strong, strong-smelling, pungent, acrid, malodorous, foul-smelling, evil-smelling, stinking, rancid, putrid, fetid, unpleasant, disagreeable, offensive, revolting, sickening, obnoxious, noxious, noisome, mephitic. **3** *condemn his rank behavior/language* indecent, immodest, indecorous, coarse, gross, vulgar, shocking, outrageous, lurid, crass, scurrilous, abusive, nasty, foul, filthy, vile, obscene, smutty, risqué, profane, pornographic. **4** *a rank outsider | rank disobedience* utter, complete, total, absolute, out and out, downright, thorough, thoroughgoing, sheer, unqualified, unmitigated, arrant, flagrant, blatant, glaring, gross, egregious.

rankle verb *their insults still rankle* fester, cause resentment, cause annoyance, annoy, anger, irk, vex, peeve, irritate, rile, chafe, fret, gall, embitter; *inf.* get one's goat.

ransack verb **1** *raiders ransacking the area* plunder, pillage, raid, rob, loot, despoil, rifle, strip, fleece, sack, ravage, harry, maraud, devastate, depredate. **2** *ransack the house looking for the will* search, rummage through, rake through, scour, look all over, go through, comb, explore, turn inside out, turn over.

ransom noun **1** *pay the kidnappers a ransom* payoff, payment, price. **2** *obtain the kidnapped child's ransom* release, freedom, deliverance, liberation, rescue, redemption, restoration.

ransom verb **1** *succeed in ransoming the kidnapped child* exchange for a ransom, buy the freedom of, release, free, deliver, liberate, rescue, redeem, restore to freedom. **2** *the kidnappers have ransomed the child* exchange for a ransom, release for money, release, free, set free, deliver, liberate, set loose.

rant verb declaim, hold forth, go on and on, bluster, harangue, vociferate, shout, yell, roar, bellow, bawl, rave, rant and rave; *inf.* spout.

rant noun bombast, rhetoric, oration, declamation, discourse, harangue, tirade, diatribe, philippic, lecture, shouting, yelling, raving.

rap[1] noun **1** *a rap on the knuckles* tap, hit, blow, whack, bang, cuff, clip, clout. **2** *hear a rap at the door* knock, knocking, tap, bang, hammering, battering, rat-a-tat. **3** *take/get the rap for the accident* blame, responsibility, accountability, punishment, penalty, castigation.

rap[2] verb **1** *rap him on the knuckles* tap, hit, strike, whack, bang, cuff, clip, clout, batter; *inf.* bash. **2** *rap at the door* knock, tap, bang, hammer, batter. **3** *rap him for his mistake* criticize, censure, reproach, scold, chide, castigate.

rap[3] noun *not care/give a rap* little bit, whit, iota, jot; *inf.* damn.

rapacious adjective **1** *rapacious moneylender* grasping, acquisitive, greedy, avaricious, covetous, insatiable, predatory, usurious. **2** *rapacious invaders* plundering, pillaging, robbing, marauding, looting, piratical.

rape noun **1** *commit rape on the girl* sexual assault, ravishment, violation; date rape. **2** *the rape of the village* plundering, pillaging, ravaging, foraging, raiding, despoilment, despoliation, spoliation, marauding, sacking, ransacking, rapine. **3** *the rape of the Sabine women* abduction, carrying off, kidnapping, seizure, capture. **4** *the rape of democracy* violation, abuse, defilement, desecration.

rape verb **1** *he raped the girl* sexually assault, ravish, violate. **2** *soldiers raped the fallen village* plunder, pillage, ravage, forage, raid, despoil, spoliate, maraud, ransack, sack. **3** *the Romans raped the Sabine women* abduct, carry off, kidnap, seize, capture. **4** *terrorists raping a national institution* violate, abuse, defile, desecrate.

rapid adjective quick, fast, swift, speedy, fleet, hurried, hasty, expeditious, express, brisk, lively, prompt, precipitate.
Antonyms: SLOW; LEISURELY.

rapidity noun quickness, fastness, swiftness, speed, speediness, fleetness, hurriedness, haste, hastiness, rush, expeditiousness, alacrity, dispatch, velocity, celerity, promptness, promptitude, precipitateness.

rapidly adverb quickly, fast, swiftly, speedily, at speed, hurriedly, in a hurry, hastily, in haste, in a rush, expeditiously, briskly, promptly, precipitately, at full tilt; *inf.* before one can say Jack Robinson, like a bat out of hell, like greased lightning.

rapport noun affinity, bond, empathy, harmony, sympathy, understanding, close/special relationship, link.

rapt adjective **1** *rapt in thought* | *rapt attention* absorbed, engrossed, preoccupied, intent, concentrating, pensive, meditative. **2** *rapt by the music* | *a rapt smile* enraptured, enchanted, entranced, spellbound, bewitched, captivated, fascinated, charmed, thrilled, transported, blissful, ecstatic, ravished.
Antonyms: UNINTERESTED; INATTENTIVE.

rapture noun joy, ecstasy, elation, exaltation, exhilaration, bliss, euphoria, transport, rhapsody, ravishment, enchantment, delight, delectation, happiness, enthusiasm; *inf.* cloud nine, seventh heaven.

---

rapture
bliss, ecstasy, euphoria, transport
Happiness is one thing; **bliss** is another, suggesting a state of utter joy and contentment (*marital bliss*). **Ecstasy** is even more extreme, describing a trancelike state in which one loses consciousness of one's surroundings (*the ecstasy of young love*). Although **rapture** originally referred to being raised or lifted out of oneself by divine power, nowadays it is used in much the same sense as *ecstasy* to describe an elevated sensation of bliss (*she listened in speechless rapture to her favorite soprano*). **Transport** applies to any powerful emotion by which one is carried away (*a transport of delight*). When happiness is carried to an extreme or crosses over into mania, it is called **euphoria**. *Euphoria* may outwardly resemble *ecstasy* or *rapture*; but upon closer examination, it is usually found to be exaggerated and out of proportion (*the euphoria that came over him whenever he touched alcohol*).

---

rapturous adjective joyful, joyous, ecstatic, elated, blissful, euphoric, transported, in transports, rhapsodic, ravished, enchanted, delighted, happy; *inf.* on cloud nine, in seventh heaven.

rara avis noun rarity, rare person/thing, anomaly, aberration, freak, freak of nature, wonder, marvel, nonpareil, nonesuch, one of a kind.

rare adjective **1** *a rare specimen* unusual, uncommon, out of the ordinary, exceptional, atypical, singular, remarkable, phenomenal, strange, recherché, unique. **2** *one of his rare appearances* infrequent, few and far between, scarce, sparse, sporadic, scattered. **3** *exhibit a rare skill* outstanding, superior, first-rate, special, choice, excellent, very fine, incomparable, unparalleled, peerless, matchless; *inf.* A-1, topnotch.
Antonyms: COMMON; FREQUENT.

rarely adverb *she rarely visits* on rare occasions, seldom, infrequently, hardly/scarcely ever, hardly, scarcely, almost never, little, once in a while, only now and then, not often; *inf.* once in a blue moon.

rarity noun **1** *the rarity of the specimen* rareness, unusualness, uncommonness, singularity, strangeness, uniqueness. **2** *the rarity of the occurrences* infrequency, scarcity, sparseness, sporadicness. **3** *the rarity of his skill* superiority, excellence, incomparability. See RARE 3. **4** *that book is a rarity* rare person/thing, rara avis, anomaly, freak, wonder, marvel, one of a kind. See RARA AVIS.

rascal noun **1** *the child is a little rascal* imp, scamp, scalawag, mischief-maker, little devil. **2** *that man is a real rascal* scoundrel, villain, rogue, blackguard, ne'er-do-well, good-for-nothing, wastrel, reprobate, cad; *inf.* bounder, creep, rat, rotter.

rash *adjective* **1** *a rash young woman* reckless, impetuous, hasty, impulsive, madcap, overadventurous, adventurous, overbold, audacious, brash, daredevil, foolhardy, harum-scarum, devil-may-care, headstrong, hot-headed, incautious, careless, heedless, thoughtless, imprudent. **2** *a rash act* reckless, impetuous, hasty, impulsive, incautious, careless, unthinking, ill-advised, ill-considered, foolish, imprudent, injudicious, hare-brained, unwary, unguarded.
Antonyms: CAREFUL; CAUTIOUS; PRUDENT.

rash *noun* **1** *a rash on his face* skin eruption, outbreak, breaking out; erythema, hives, heat rash, nettle rash, diaper rash. **2** *a rash of burglaries* outbreak, spate, torrent, flood, wave, plague, epidemic, succession, series, run.

rasp *noun the rasp of knives against plates* grating, grinding, scraping, scratching.

rasp *verb* **1** *rasp the surface smooth* abrade, file, sand, sandpaper, scrape, scratch. **2** *"Go away," he rasped* screech, shrill, squawk, croak, stridulate. **3** *his behavior really rasps | it rasps my nerves* grate (upon), jar (upon), irritate, irk, set one's teeth on edge, rub one up the wrong way.

rasping *adjective* a *rasping noise/voice* grating, scratchy, jarring, discordant, creaky, harsh, rough, gravelly, croaking, croaky, gruff.

rate *noun* **1** *rate of interest* percentage, ratio, proportion, scale, degree, standard. **2** *the rate per day* pay, payment, fee, remuneration, price, cost, charge, rent, tariff; *inf.* damage. **3** *walk at a great/swift rate* pace, stride, gait, motion, speed, tempo, velocity, measure. **at any rate** in any case, anyhow, anyway, nevertheless, at all events, in any event, no matter what happens.

rate *verb* **1** *how would you rate his performance?* adjudge, judge, assess, appraise, evaluate, value, put a value on, measure, weigh up, grade, rank, classify, class, categorize. **2** *I rate him a complete fool* regard as, consider, count, deem, reckon, account, esteem. **3** *he rates respect* be worthy of, deserve, merit, be entitled to.

rather *adverb* **1** *I would rather not go* sooner, preferably, by preference, from choice, more willingly, more readily. **2** *she is tactless rather than rude* more, more truly. **3** *not a notebook, but rather a leaflet* correctly/strictly speaking, to be exact/precise. **4** *he is rather outspoken* quite, fairly, a bit, a little, slightly, somewhat, relatively, to some degree/extent; *inf.* sort of, kind of, pretty. **5** *he is not poor, rather he is very wealthy* on the contrary, instead, the truth is, actually, in reality.

ratify *verb* confirm, endorse, sign, countersign, corroborate, sanction, warrant, approve, authorize, authenticate, certify, validate, agree to, accept, consent to, uphold, bear out.

Antonyms: REJECT; REVOKE.

rating *noun* assessment, evaluation, value, appraisal, grading, grade, ranking, rank, classification, class, categorization, designation, standing, status, placing, position.

ratio *noun* proportion, comparative size/extent, correlation, correspondence, percentage, fraction, quotient.

ration *noun your ration of food/books/money for the week* allowance, quota, allotment, portion, share, measure, part, lot, amount, helping, proportion, percentage, budget.

ration *verb ration the amount per person* limit, restrict, control, conserve, budget. **ration out** *ration out the week's supplies* distribute, issue, allocate, allot, divide out, apportion, give out, share (out), deal out, hand out, pass out, dole out, measure out, mete out, parcel out.

rational *adjective* **1** *based on purely rational considerations* thinking, cognitive, mental, cerebral, reasoning, logical, analytical, conceptual. **2** *a rational decision | a rational course of action* sensible, reasonable, logical, sound, intelligent, wise, judicious, sagacious, prudent, circumspect, politic, astute, shrewd, perceptive, well-advised, well-grounded. **3** *the patient does not always seem rational* able to think/reason, in sound mind, in one's right mind, *compos mentis*, lucid, coherent, well-balanced, sane, normal; *inf.* all there.
Antonyms: IRRATIONAL; ILLOGICAL; INSANE.

rationale *noun* theory, hypothesis, thesis, exposition, logic, philosophy, reason, *raison d'être*; grounds.

rationalize *verb* **1** *rationalize his behavior* explain away, account for, make excuses/allowances for, make plausible, try to vindicate/justify. **2** *rationalize our research plans* apply logic/reasoning to, reason out, think through, elucidate, clarify, make consistent.

rations *plural noun* provisions, stores, supplies, victuals; food, provender.

rattle *verb* **1** *the windows rattled* bang, clatter, clang, clank, jangle, clink. **2** *rattle the door knocker* bang, knock, rap, clatter, clank. **3** *the car rattled along* bounce, bump, jiggle, jounce, shake, jolt, vibrate, jar. **4** *he rattled off their names* reel off, list/recite rapidly, run through. **5** *he rattled on about his job* go, chatter, babble, gabble, prattle, jabber, gibber, blather, prate; *inf.* yak. **6** *she was rattled by the experience* disconcert, disturb, fluster, upset, shake, perturb, discompose, discomfit, discountenance, frighten, scare; *inf.* faze.

raucous *adjective* strident, shrill, screeching, piercing, ear-piercing, harsh, sharp, grating, rasping, scratching, discordant, dissonant, jarring.
Antonyms: SWEET; DULCET.

ravage *verb* devastate, lay waste, leave desolate, lay/leave in ruins, ruin, wreak havoc on, destroy, level, raze, demolish, wreck, shatter, damage, pillage, plunder, despoil, harry, maraud, ransack, sack, loot.

---

ravage
despoil, devastate, pillage, plunder, sack, waste
Ravage, pillage, sack, and **plunder** are all verbs associated with the actions of a conquering army during wartime. *Ravage* implies violent destruction, usually in a series of raids or invasions over an extended period of time (*the invading forces ravaged the countryside*). *Plunder* refers to the roving of soldiers through recently conquered territory in search of money and goods (*they plundered the city and left its inhabitants destitute*), while *pillage* describes the act of stripping a conquered city or people of valuables (*churches pillaged by ruthless invaders*). *Sack* is even more extreme than pillage, implying not only the seizure of all valuables, but total destruction as well (*the army sacked every village along the coast*). **Despoil** also entails the stripping of valuables, but with less violence than *sack*; it is more common in nonmilitary contexts, where it describes a heedless or inadvertent destruction (*forests despoiled by logging companies*). **Devastate** emphasizes ruin and desolation, whether it happens to buildings, forests, or crops (*fields of corn devastated by flooding*). **Waste** comes close in meaning to *devastate*, but it suggests a less violent or more gradual destruction (*a region of the country wasted by years of drought and periodic fires*).

---

ravages *plural noun the ravages of war* devastation, desolation, ruination, ruin, havoc, destruction, demolition, depredation, wreckage, damage, pillaging, plunder, spoliation, ransacking, looting.

rave *verb* **1** *the invalid is raving* talk wildly, be delirious, babble, ramble. **2** *her parents raved at her* rant and rave, rage, deliver a tirade/harangue, storm, fulminate, explode in anger, lose one's temper, lose control, go into a frenzy, run amok; *inf.* fly off the handle, flip one's lid. **rave about/over** *rave about her performance* | *rave over his car* go into raptures over, rhapsodize over, enthuse about, praise extravagantly, praise to the skies, gush over, express delight over, acclaim, cry up; *inf.* go wild about, be mad about.

rave *adjective rave reviews* rapturous, ecstatic, enthusiastic, laudatory, praising, excellent, favorable.

ravenous *adjective* **1** *ravenous after the day's march* very hungry, starving, starved, famished. **2** *a ravenous appetite* greedy, gluttonous, voracious, insatiable, insatiate, ravening, wolfish.

ravine *noun* chasm, gorge, canyon, abyss, gulf, gully, gulch, defile, pass, gap.

raving *adjective* **1** *raving patients* delirious, out of

one's mind, irrational, frenzied, in a frenzy, deranged, hysterical, frantic, berserk, unbalanced, demented, insane, mad, crazed, wild; *inf.* crazy. **2** *a raving beauty* very great, considerable, remarkable, extraordinary, singular, striking, outstanding, stunning.

ravings *plural noun kept awake by his ravings* wild talk, babbling, rambling, gibberish.

ravish *verb* **1** *ravish the young woman* rape, sexually assault/abuse, violate. **2** *they were ravished by his performance* enchant, entrance, enthrall, captivate, bewitch, spellbind, fascinate, charm, enrapture, delight, transport, overjoy.

ravishing *adjective* beautiful, lovely, stunning, gorgeous, dazzling, radiant, enchanting, bewitching, charming.

raw *adjective* **1** *raw food* uncooked, fresh. **2** *raw sugar/silk* unrefined, crude, green, coarse, unprocessed, unprepared, untreated, unfinished, unmanufactured. **3** *raw recruits* inexperienced, untrained, unskilled, untutored, unschooled, unpracticed, untried, untested, unseasoned, undisciplined, new, callow, immature, green, ignorant, naïve, unsophisticated; *inf.* wet behind the ears. **4** *raw flesh/wounds* excoriated, skinned, grazed, abraded, scratched, chafed, open, exposed, unhealed, sore, tender. **5** *a raw day* | *raw weather* damp, wet, cold, chilly, chilling, chill, freezing, bitter, biting, nippy, nipping, piercing, penetrating. **6** *a raw literary style* unrefined, unpolished, unsophisticated, crude, rough, coarse. **7** *a raw portrayal of the miner's life* realistic, frank, candid, forthright, straightforward, blunt, outspoken, unembellished, unvarnished, naked, bare, brutal.

ray *noun* **1** *rays of light* beam, shaft, streak, stream, gleam, glint, flash, glimmer, flicker, twinkle. **2** *a ray of hope* flicker, glimmer, spark, trace, hint, indication, suggestion.

raze *verb* tear down, pull down, take down, knock down, knock to pieces, fell, level, lay low, bulldoze, flatten, demolish, ruin, wreck.

reach *verb* **1** *he reached out* | *reach out a hand* stretch, stretch out, outstretch, extend, hold out, thrust out, stick out. **2** *reach one's destination* get as far as, get to, arrive at, come to, set foot on, land at/on. **3** *reach perfection* attain, achieve, gain, accomplish, make, get to. **4** *his land reaches ours* extend to, go as far as, stretch to, neighbor, touch, border on, abut. **5** *we could not reach him that day* contact, get in touch with, get hold of, get through to, communicate with. **reach for** **1** *reach for the book* get hold of, grasp, seize, grab at, clutch at. **2** *reach that book for me* hand to, pass to, give to.

reach *noun* **1** *the rope was beyond her reach* | *within reach of safety* grasp, stretch, spread, extension, extent, span, distance. **2** *within the reach of his influence* scope, range, compass, latitude, ambit, orbit, sphere, area, field, territory, authority, jurisdiction, sway, control, command.

react *verb* **1** *react to the drug* have a reaction/

response to, respond, change/behave in response to. **2** *how did she react on hearing the news?* behave, act, conduct oneself, proceed, operate, function, cope. **3** *react against the new bill* rebel against, oppose, revolt against, rise up against.

reaction noun **1** *receive a reaction to their proposal* response, answer, reply, feedback. **2** *his harsh regime was a reaction to total disorder* counteraction, counterbalance, counterpoise, recoil, reversion, retroversion, reversal. **3** *politically, they are people of reaction* ultraconservatism, conservatism, obscurantism, the right, the right wing, the extreme right.

reactionary adjective ultraconservative, conservative, obscurantist, diehard, rightist, rightwing.
Antonyms: RADICAL; PROGRESSIVE.

read verb **1** *read the words/book* peruse, study, scan, pore over, scrutinize, run one's eye over, look at, refer to, browse through; *inf.* wade through, dip into. **2** *read his silence as consent* interpret, construe, take to mean, decipher, deduce, understand, comprehend. **3** *the thermometer is reading zero* register, record, display, show, indicate. **4** *read the future* foresee, foretell, predict, forecast, prophesy, divine. **read into** *read too much into their statement/relationship* assume from, infer from, interpolate from, read between the lines.

read noun *a quick read of the book* perusal, study, scan, scrutiny, browse, reference.

readable adjective **1** *readable exam papers* legible, easy to read, decipherable, clear, intelligible, understandable, comprehensible. **2** *readable works of fiction* enjoyable, entertaining, interesting, gripping, enthralling, stimulating.
Antonyms: ILLEGIBLE; BORING; unreadable.

readily adverb **1** *he will readily help you* willingly, without hesitation, gladly, happily, cheerfully, with pleasure, eagerly. **2** *the sofa readily converts into a bed* easily, with ease, without difficulty, effortlessly.

readiness noun **1** *the readiness of the troops for battle* preparedness, fitness. **2** *their readiness to help* willingness, inclination, aptness, eagerness, keenness, gladness; *inf.* gameness. **3** *the readiness of resources* availability, accessibility, handiness, convenience. **4** *the readiness of her answers* promptness, quickness, rapidity, swiftness, speed, speediness, punctuality, timeliness. **5** *the readiness of his wit/skill* alertness, resourcefulness, smartness, sharpness, astuteness, shrewdness, keenness, acuteness, discernment, cleverness, intelligence, brightness, aptness, adroitness, deftness, dexterity, skill, skillfulness. **in readiness** *reserves in readiness* ready, at the ready, available, on hand, accessible, handy, at one's fingertips, prepared, primed; *inf.* on tap.

reading noun **1** *his reading of the document* perusal, study, scan, scanning, scrutinization, scrutiny, browsing; recital, recitation, narra-

tion. **2** *a man of reading* book learning, learning, scholarship, knowledge, attainment, enlightenment, education, edification. **3** *his reading of the statement/situation* interpretation, construction, deciphering, deduction, understanding, comprehension, grasp, impression. **4** *several readings of the play in existence* version, edition, text, rendering. **5** *what is the reading on the gas meter?* measurement, indication.

ready adjective **1** *dinner is ready* prepared, completed, finished, organized. **2** *ready for battle | ready to go* prepared, equipped, organized, all set, in a fit state, fit. **3** *ready to help* willing, inclined, disposed, predisposed, apt, prone, given, agreeable, eager, keen, happy, glad; *inf.* game. **4** *a ready source of income* within reach, available, on hand, present, near, near at hand, accessible, handy, convenient, on call, at one's fingertips; *inf.* on tap. **5** *a ready answer* prompt, quick, rapid, swift, speedy, punctual, timely. **6** *a ready wit/skill* alert, resourceful, smart, sharp, astute, shrewd, keen, acute, perceptive, discerning, clever, intelligent, bright, apt, adroit, deft, dexterous, skillful. **7** *ready for anything* prepared, eager, enthusiastic, anxious, keen; *inf.* psyched up, geared up. **ready to** about to, on the verge/brink/edge of, in danger of, liable to, likely to.
Antonyms: INCOMPLETE; unprepared; RELUCTANT; INACCESSIBLE.

real adjective **1** *the real world | real fears/illnesses* actual, existent, occurring, factual, unimaginary, nonfictitious. **2** *real leather* authentic, genuine, bona fide, veritable, valid, legal, licit. **3** *real emotion/feelings* sincere, heartfelt, earnest, fervent, unfeigned, unpretended, unaffected, honest, truthful.
Antonyms: UNREAL; IMAGINARY; IMITATION; FALSE.

realistic adjective **1** *be realistic as to your prospects* practical, pragmatic, rational, down-to-earth, matter-of-fact, sensible, commonsensical, levelheaded, hardheaded, businesslike, hardboiled, sober, unromantic, unsentimental, unidealistic; *inf.* with both feet on the ground, no-nonsense. **2** *a realistic model of a dinosaur* lifelike, true-to-life, true, faithful, close, representational, graphic, naturalistic, authentic, genuine.
Antonyms: UNREALISTIC; IDEALISTIC; IMPRACTICAL; ROMANTIC.

reality noun **1** *come back to reality* real/actual world, actuality, physical existence, corporeality, substantiality, materiality. **2** *the reality of his work* verisimilitude, lifelikeness, authenticity, genuineness, validity. **3** *the harsh realities of life | in reality, the picture is a fake* fact, actuality, truth, all honesty.

realization noun **1** *come to the realization that he is mad* understanding, awareness, consciousness, cognizance, appreciation, recognition, perception, discernment. **2** *the realization of* *one's hopes* fulfillment, achievement, accomplishment, fruition, consummation, effecting, actualization. **3** *the realization of profits* making, clearing, obtaining. *See* REALIZE 3.

realize *verb* **1** *realize that they are rich* understand (clearly), grasp, take in, know, comprehend, apprehend, be aware, be conscious/cognizant of the fact, appreciate, recognize, perceive, discern, conceive; *inf.* get it. **2** *realize one's hopes/dreams* fulfill, achieve, accomplish, make happen, bring about, bring off, bring to fruition, consummate, effect, effectuate, perform, execute, actualize, reify. **3** *realize a profit* make, clear, acquire, gain, bring in, obtain, earn.

really *adverb* **1** *the guard dog is really a gentle pet* in reality, actually, in actuality, in fact, in truth. **2** *this is really useful* certainly, surely, truly, undoubtedly, without a doubt, indubitably, assuredly, unquestionably, indeed, absolutely, categorically. **3** *a really charming person* very, extremely, thoroughly, truly, decidedly. **4** *his career is really over* to all intents and purposes, virtually, for all practical purposes, just about, almost.

realm *noun* **1** *the realm of Denmark* kingdom, country, land, state, province, empire, domain, monarchy, principality. **2** *the realm of the imagination* | *the realm of science* world, field, sphere, area, department, region, province, orbit, zone.

reap *verb* **1** *reap the wheat* cut, harvest, gather in, bring in, take in. **2** *reap the benefits of an education* realize, receive, obtain, get, acquire, secure, procure.

rear *noun* **1** *at the rear of the garage* back, back part, hind part, back end. **2** *at the rear of the line* rear end, back end, end, tail, tail end. *Antonyms:* FRONT; VANGUARD.

rear *verb* **1** *rear three children* bring up, raise, care for, nurture, parent, educate, train, instruct. **2** *rear chickens* breed, keep, tend. **3** *rear plants* grow, cultivate. **4** *rear one's head* raise, lift up, hold up, hoist, elevate, upraise.

reason *noun* **1** *the reason for his behavior* grounds; ground, cause, basis, motive, motivation, impetus, actuation, instigation, inducement. **2** *give a reason for your absence* explanation, exposition, justification, argument, case, defense, vindication, apologia, rationalization, excuse, apology. **3** *follow reason not emotion* reasoning, intellect, intelligence, intellectuality, mind, judgment, logic, rationality, thought, understanding, apprehension, comprehension, ratiocination; brains. **4** *he has lost his reason* sanity, mind, soundness of mind; senses. **5** *keep a sense of reason in your expenditure* reasonableness, common sense, sense, good sense, practicality, practicability, shrewdness, wisdom, sagacity, moderation, propriety. **within reason** *have anything you like within reason* in

moderation, within reasonable/sensible limits, within limits/bounds.

reason *verb* **1** *unable to reason when upset* use reason, think, think straight, use one's mind, use one's brain/head, analyze, cogitate, cerebrate, intellectualize, ratiocinate; *inf.* put on one's thinking cap. **2** *he reasoned that two could live as cheaply as one* deduce, infer, conclude, work out, reckon, be of the opinion, think, surmise. **3** *reason him out of that course of action* | *reason her into it* argue, persuade, talk, urge, coax. **reason out** *reason things out* think out, think through, consider, deliberate, analyze, come to a conclusion about. **reason with** *try reasoning with him* use logic on, apply argument to, argue with, debate with, dispute with, try to persuade, plead with.

reasonable *adjective* **1** *he is a reasonable man* open to reason, moderate, fair, just, equitable, impartial, dispassionate, unbiased, disinterested, aboveboard. **2** *it seemed a reasonable idea/plan* logical, practical, rational, sensible, intelligent, wise, sound, judicious, advisable, well-thought-out, admissible, tenable, plausible. **3** *reasonable prices* moderate, inexpensive, low, modest, cheap, within one's means. **4** *his work is reasonable* tolerable, passable, acceptable, average; *inf.* OK, okay. UNREASONABLE; ILLOGICAL.

reasoned *adjective* *reasoned arguments* logical, rational, well-thought-out, clear, systematic, methodical, organized, well-expressed, well-presented.

reasoning *noun* **1** *let reasoning, not emotion, dictate your actions* reason, thinking, thought, logic, rationalization, deduction, analysis, cerebration, ratiocination. **2** *his reasoning is faulty* argument, rationale, case, hypothesis, interpretation.

reassure *verb* put one's mind at rest, put at ease, settle doubts, restore/give confidence to, encourage, hearten, buoy up, cheer up, inspirit. *Antonyms:* ALARM; UNNERVE.

rebate *noun* refund, partial refund, repayment, deduction, discount, allowance, reduction, decrease.

rebel *noun* **1** *the government acting against the rebels* revolutionary, revolutionist, insurrectionist, insurgent, revolter, mutineer, seditionist, agitator, freedom/resistance fighter, anarchist, traitor. **2** *rebels not obeying rules/fashion* dissenter, nonconformist, heretic, apostate, schismatic, recusant.

rebel *verb* *the troops are rebelling* mutiny, riot, revolt, rise up, rise up in arms, take to the streets. **rebel against** *rebel against authority* defy, disobey, refuse to obey/follow. **rebel at** *his stomach rebelled at the thought of food* recoil from, shrink from, flinch from, shy away from, pull back from, show repugnance/revulsion for/at. *Antonyms:* ACQUIESCE; CONFORM.

rebel *adjective* **1** *the rebel troops* revolutionary, insurrectionary, insurgent, mutinous, mutinying. **2** *rebel teenagers* rebellious, defiant, disobedient, resistant, dissentient, recalcitrant, unmanageable.

rebellion *noun* **1** *troops putting down a rebellion* revolt, revolution, insurrection, insurgence, insurgency, uprising, rising, mutiny, riot, civil disobedience, resistance. **2** *rebellion against rules/fashion* defiance, disobedience, resistance, dissent, nonconformity, heresy, apostasy, schism, recusancy.

rebellious *adjective* **1** *rebellious tribes/children* unruly, ungovernable, unmanageable, turbulent, disorderly, intractable, recalcitrant, incorrigible, contumacious. **2** *the rebellious protestors were imprisoned* rebelling, revolutionary, insurrectionary, insurgent, mutinous, mutinying, rioting. **3** *the rebellious students were expelled* defiant, disobedient, resistant, dissentient, nonconformist.

Antonyms: OBEDIENT; SUBSERVIENT.

rebound *verb* **1** *the ball rebounded off the wall* bounce, bounce back, spring back, recoil, ricochet, boomerang. **2** *the plan rebounded on her* misfire, backfire, have an adverse effect, come back, redound.

rebound *noun* **1** *the rebound of the ball* bounce, recoil, ricochet. **2** *the rebound of her plans* misfiring, backfiring, kickback, repercussion.

rebuff *noun* **1** *her advances/requests were met by a rebuff* rejection, refusal, spurning, repudiation, repulsion, cold shouldering, discouragement. **2** *upset by her rebuffs* snub, slight, repulse, cut, thumbs down; *inf.* brush-off, put-down, slap in the face.

rebuff *verb* *rebuff their advances* | *rebuff them* reject, refuse, decline, turn down, turn away, spurn, repudiate, repel, discourage, fend off, stave off, snub, slight, cold shoulder, cut, give the thumbs down to; *inf.* brush off, put down.

rebuke *verb* reprimand, scold, chide, admonish, reproach, reprove, remonstrate with, lecture, reprehend, censure, find fault with, berate, upbraid, castigate, take to task; *inf.* tell off, call on the carpet, lambaste, haul over the coals, chew out, bawl out.

Antonyms: PRAISE; APPLAUD.

---

rebuke
admonish, censure, reprimand, reproach, scold

All of these verbs mean to criticize or express disapproval, but which one you use depends on how upset you are. If you want to go easy on someone, you can **admonish** or **reproach**, both of which indicate mild and sometimes kindly disapproval. To *admonish* is to warn or counsel someone, usually because a duty has been forgotten or might be forgotten in the future (*admonish her about leaving the key in the lock*), while *reproach* also suggests mild criticism aimed at correcting a fault or pattern of misbehavior (*he was reproved for his lack of attention in class*). If you want to express your disapproval formally or in public, use **censure** or

reprimand. You can *censure* someone either directly or indirectly (*the judge censured the lawyer for violating courtroom procedures; a newspaper article that censured deadbeat dads*), while *reprimand* suggests a direct confrontation (*reprimanded by his parole officer for leaving town without reporting his whereabouts*). If you're irritated enough to want to express your disapproval quite harshly and at some length, you can **scold** (*to scold a child for jaywalking*). **Rebuke** is the harshest word of this group, meaning to criticize sharply or sternly, often in the midst of some action (*rebuke a carpenter for walking across an icy roof*).

---

rebuke *noun* *deliver a rebuke* reprimand, scolding, admonition, reproach, reproof, reproval, remonstration, lecture, censure, upbraiding, castigation; *inf.* tongue-lashing, lambasting, dressing-down, bawling out.

rebut *verb* *rebut the charge/evidence* refute, disprove, negate, invalidate, deny, confute, contradict, discredit, explode; *inf.* shoot full of holes.

recalcitrant *adjective* intractable, refractory, unmanageable, ungovernable, disobedient, insubordinate, defiant, contrary, wayward, willful, headstrong, perverse, contumacious, rebellious, mutinous, obstinate, obdurate.

Antonyms: AMENABLE; DOCILE; compliant.

recall *verb* **1** *recall the army reserves* summon back, call back, bring back. **2** *unable to recall his name* call to mind, remember, recollect, think of. **3** *recalling the old days* remember, recollect, reminisce about, look back on/to, think back on/to, hark back to. **4** *the sight of her recalled the old days* call/bring to mind, call up, summon up, evoke, put one in mind of. **5** *recall the verdict* revoke, retract, countermand, take back, withdraw, repeal, rescind, veto, overrule, override, invalidate, annul, nullify, cancel, recant.

recall *noun* **1** *have total recall* memory, recollection, remembrance. **2** *the recall of the verdict* | *beyond recall* revocation, retracting, countermanding, withdrawal, repeal, rescinding, vetoing, veto, invalidation, annulment, cancellation.

recant *verb* **1** *recant his former beliefs* disavow, disclaim, disown, deny, renounce, relinquish, abjure, forswear, repudiate, renege on. **2** *he was a Catholic, but he has recanted* change one's mind, apostatize, tergiversate, defect, renege. **3** *recant his evidence* recall, revoke, retract, countermand, take back, repeal, rescind, annul, cancel.

recapitulate *verb* restate, resay, repeat, reiterate, go over, run over, summarize, sum up; *inf.* recap.

recede *verb* **1** *the water receded* go back, move back, move further off, move away, retreat, withdraw, fall back, ebb, abate, subside. **2** *the* *coastline receded as we sailed away* grow less visible, become distant, become far off, fade into the distance, begin to disappear. **3** *danger receded in time* grow less, lessen, fade, diminish, decrease, dwindle, shrink, wane, fall off, taper off, peter out. **4** *his chin recedes* slope backward, slant, fall away.

receipt *noun* **1** *the receipt of the goods* | *receipt of his apology* receiving, recipience, acceptance, getting, obtaining, taking. **2** *get a receipt for the goods* sales slip/ticket, proof of purchase, slip, stub, voucher. **3** *make a list of receipts for the auditor* money/payment received, financial return, income; proceeds, profits, gains, earnings.

receive *verb* **1** *he did receive the goods* be in receipt of, accept delivery of, accept, take into one's possession. **2** *receive many benefits* get, obtain, acquire, come by, gain, take, gather, collect. **3** *he received the news at home* | *received the news with fortitude* hear, be told, find out about, learn about, gather, be informed of, be notified of, take, react to. **4** *receive bad treatment* undergo, experience, meet with, encounter, go through, sustain, be subjected to, bear, suffer. **5** *the room/container will receive 20 people/tons* hold, contain, accommodate, admit, take. **6** *receive guests* welcome, greet, entertain, be at home to.

Antonyms: GIVE; SEND; PRESENT.

recent *adjective* **1** *recent developments* new, fresh, novel, latest, late, modern, contemporary, latter-day, current, up-to-date, up-to-the-minute. **2** *his recent illness* occurring/appearing recently, not long past.

Antonyms: OLD; FORMER.

recently *adverb* *recently developed* newly, freshly, lately, not long ago, of late.

receptacle *noun* container, holder, repository.

reception *noun* **1** *the reception of the goods* receiving, acceptance. *See* RECEIVE 1. **2** *the reception of the guests* welcoming, greeting, entertaining. **3** *the celebrity/show/news receiving a warm/cool reception* acceptance, response, acknowledgment, recognition, reaction, treatment, welcome. **4** *a wedding/graduation reception* party, formal party, function, social occasion, entertainment, soirée; *inf.* do, bash.

receptive *adjective* open, open to suggestions/ideas, flexible, willing, perceptive, sensitive, alert, bright, quick, keen.

recess *noun* **1** *books arranged in a recess* alcove, niche, nook, corner, cavity, bay, oriel. **2** *in the recesses of my memory* remote/secret/dark place, interior, heart, retreat, refuge, sanctum; depths; *inf.* innards. **3** *the schoolchildren's recess* | *Congress will resume discussions after the recess* break, respite, rest, interval, intermission, time off, vacation, holiday, closure, cessation of work/business; *inf.* breather, time out.

recession *noun* **1** *the recession cost many stock-*

brokers their jobs economic decline, downturn, depression, slump; hard times. **2** *the recession of floodwaters* receding, retreat, withdrawal, ebbing, subsiding, abatement.

recipe *noun* **1** *follow the recipe for pancakes* directions, instructions; guide, cooking procedure. **2** *his suggestions are a recipe for disaster* method, technique, system, procedure, modus operandi, process, means, way, formula, prescription.

reciprocal *adjective* **1** *a reciprocal favor* return, in return, returned, requited, retaliated. **2** *reciprocal affection* mutual, shared, common, reciprocative, reciprocatory, exchanged, give-and-take, complementary, corresponding, correlative.

reciprocate *verb* **1** *reciprocate his affection* return, requite, feel/give in return, repay, give back. **2** *I will take part if she reciprocates* respond, respond in kind, return the favor/compliment, do the same. **3** *reciprocate their ideas* interchange, exchange, give and take/receive, swap, barter, trade, bandy.

recital *noun* **1** *the recital of the poem* saying, rendering, declaiming, reading, delivery. **2** *the recital of the disasters/events* enumeration, detailing, itemizing, specification; account, report, recounting, telling, relation, description, rendering, narrative, record, story, tale, chronicle. **3** *a piano recital* musical performance, performance, solo performance, concert, show.

recitation *noun* **1** *the recitation of the Gettysburg Address* recital, saying, rendering, rendition, declaiming, reading, delivery. **2** *excellently chosen recitations* verse, poem, reading, passage, piece.

recite *verb* **1** *recite a poem/passage* say, repeat, read aloud, deliver, declaim, speak, render. **2** *ask the child to recite* say a poem, read a passage. **3** *recite a list of disasters* enumerate, detail, list, itemize, reel off, rattle off, specify, particularize, describe, recount, relate, narrate, recapitulate.

reckless *adjective* rash, careless, thoughtless, incautious, heedless, unheeding, inattentive, regardless, daredevil, devil-may-care, madcap, harum-scarum, wild, precipitate, headlong, hasty, irresponsible, harebrained, foolhardy, ill-advised, imprudent, unwise, indiscreet, mindless, negligent, temerarious.

Antonyms: CAREFUL; CAUTIOUS; PRUDENT.

reckon *verb* **1** *he reckoned that she was lying* be of the opinion, think, believe, suppose, assume, surmise, conjecture, imagine, fancy, guess. **2** *she was reckoned a good painter* regard as, consider, judge, hold to be, think of as, look upon as, account, deem, rate, evaluate, gauge, count, estimate, appraise. **3** *reckon the cost* count, calculate, add up, compute, total, tally, put a figure on, give a figure to. **reckon with** *he will have her father to reckon with* cope with, deal with, contend with, handle, face.

reckoning noun 1 *according to my reckoning, the total is wrong* counting, calculation, addition, computation, working out, total, tally, summation, score. 2 *according to their reckoning, she is the best* opinion, judgment, evaluation, estimation, appraisal. 3 *deal with the reckoning of the account* settlement, paying, payment, discharging, defrayal, squaring, clearance. 4 *ask for the reckoning* bill, check, account, tally, amount due; *inf.* tab. 5 *the day of reckoning* settlement, retribution, judgment, fate, doom.

reclaim verb 1 *reclaim one's property* have returned, get back, take back, regain, retrieve, recover. 2 *reclaim the forest* retrieve, regain, reinstate, save, rescue, salvage. 3 *reclaim the criminals* redeem, reform, regenerate, save, rescue.

recline verb lie, lie down, lean, be recumbent, rest, repose, loll, lounge, sprawl, stretch out, drape oneself over.

recluse noun hermit, anchorite, ascetic, eremite, monk, nun, solitary, lone wolf, loner.

recognition noun 1 *recognition of the thief | recognition of an old friend* knowing, identification, spotting, recollection. 2 *his recognition of his defects/mistake* realization, awareness, consciousness, perception, appreciation, understanding, acknowledgment, acceptance, granting. 3 *their recognition of his claim* acknowledgment, acceptance, admittance, granting, endorsement, sanctioning, approval, validation, ratification. 4 *receive recognition as an artist* acknowledgment, appreciation, reward, honor, homage, applause.

recognize verb 1 *recognize the thief | recognize an old friend* know, know again, identify, place, spot, recall, recollect, remember, call to mind. 2 *recognize his own defects/mistake | recognized that he was wrong* realize, see, be aware/conscious of, perceive, discern, appreciate, understand, apprehend, acknowledge, accept, admit, concede, allow, grant, confess, own. 3 *recognize his claim* acknowledge, accept, admit, concede, allow, grant, endorse, sanction, put the seal of approval on, approve, validate, ratify, uphold. 4 *recognize his achievement* show appreciation of, reward, honor, pay homage to, salute, applaud.
Antonyms: FORGET; OVERLOOK; IGNORE.

recoil verb 1 *recoil from him in terror/disgust* draw back, jump back, pull back, shrink, shy away, flinch, start, wince, cower, quail. 2 *the spring recoiled* spring back, fly back, rebound, resile. 3 *the plan recoiled on the instigator* rebound, come back, redound, misfire, backfire, go wrong, have an adverse effect, boomerang. 4 *the gun recoiled* kick back, jerk back. **recoil from/at** *recoil from/at the idea* feel revulsion at, balk at, shrink from, shy away from, hesitate at, falter at.

recoil noun 1 *recoil of a gun* kickback, kick. 2 *the recoil from their plans* rebound, backlash; reaction; repercussions.

recollect verb 1 *as far as I recollect* remember, recall. 2 *I cannot recollect his name* succeed in remembering, recall, call to mind, think of, summon up, place; *inf.* put one's finger on.
Antonyms: FORGET; disremember.

recollection noun 1 *the recollection of his name* remembering, recalling, calling to mind. 2 *the photographs brought back happy recollections* memory, remembrance, reminiscence, mental image, impression. 3 *my recollection is that he was tall* memory, remembrance, power of recall.

recommend verb 1 *recommend this as a cure* advocate, commend, put in a good word for, speak favorably of, look with favor on, endorse, approve, vouch for, suggest, offer, put forward, propose, advance. 2 *I recommend caution | recommend that you go home* advise, counsel, guide, urge, exhort, enjoin. 3 *his plan has much to recommend it | his honesty recommended him to the board* make appealing/attractive/interesting, endow with appeal/attraction/interest, give an advantage to.
Antonyms: REJECT; VETO; DISAPPROVE.

recommendation noun 1 *the recommendation of the cure* advocacy, commendation, endorsement. 2 *the recommendation of caution* advising, counseling, urging. 3 *accept your recommendation as to the wine* commendation, endorsement, suggestion, tip, hint, proposal, good word, favorable mention, praise; words of approval; *inf.* plug. 4 *accept the judge's recommendation as to how to act* advice, counsel, guidance, exhortation, enjoinder. 5 *fast service is the restaurant's only recommendation* good point, advantage, favorable aspect, benefit, blessing, boon.

reconcile verb 1 *mother and daughter have been reconciled | try to reconcile the feuders* make friendly gestures/overtures, reunite, bring together, restore harmony between, make peace between, resolve differences between, bring to terms, pacify, appease, placate, propitiate, mollify. 2 *reconcile themselves to her death | become reconciled to the unfortunate situation* come to accept, accept, accommodate, get used, resign, submit, yield, make the best of, grin and bear it. 3 *reconcile their differences* settle, resolve, square, put to rights, mend, remedy, patch up, heal, cure, rectify. 4 *reconcile his philosophy and his actions* harmonize, make compatible, put in agreement, adjust, attune, make coincide, make congruent.

reconciliation noun 1 *the reconciliation of the feuders* reuniting, bringing together, pacification, placating, propitiation, mollification. 2 *the reconciliation of differences* settling, settlement, resolving, resolution, mending, remedying. 3 *bring about a reconciliation* peace, end of hostilities, harmony, concord, amity. 4 *a* *reconciliation between his philosophy and his actions* harmonizing, adjustment. *See* RECONCILE 4.

recondite *adjective recondite information/texts* obscure, esoteric, abstruse, abstract, cryptic, incomprehensible, inscrutable, arcane, deep, profound, difficult, complex, involved, mysterious, dark.
Antonyms: STRAIGHTFORWARD; OPEN.

reconnaissance *noun* preliminary survey, survey, spying, exploration, scouting, probe, investigation, scrutiny, scan, inspection, observation.

reconnoiter *verb* survey, find out the lay of the land, see how the land lies, spy out, take stock of, explore, scout, investigate, scrutinize, scan, inspect, observe; *inf.* case, check out.

reconsider *verb I have reconsidered my decision | please reconsider* think over, rethink, review, reexamine, reevaluate, reassess, think better of; think again, think twice, have second thoughts, change one's mind.

reconstruct *verb* **1** *reconstruct the house* rebuild, remake, reassemble, refashion, recreate, remodel, revamp, renovate, recondition. **2** *reconstruct the scene* recreate, reenact, piece together, build up, build up a picture/impression of. **3** *reconstruct society | reconstruct the firm* reorganize, rearrange, make over, redo, do over, overhaul, reestablish, reform.

record *noun* **1** *the records are missing* official document, register, log, logbook, file, official report/account, chronicle, diary, journal; documentation; documents, minutes, notes, annals, archives. **2** *play a record* phonograph record, long-playing record, disc, album; compact disc; single, recording, release; *inf.* platter, LP; CD. **3** *what do you know of his record?* employment/work history, employment/work performance, career to date, past performance, curriculum vitae, life history, history, background, reputation; *inf.* track record. **4** *does he have a record?* police/criminal record, history of crime; previous convictions; *inf.* rap sheet. **5** *his jump was a record* best/star performance. **6** *this is a record of his achievement* memorial, remembrance, souvenir, token, testimony, testimonial, witness, trace; documentation, evidence. **7** *climate records* information, collected information; data, reports, accounts. **off the record** *this information is off the record* confidential, in confidence, unofficial, not for publication/circulation, private, secret, sub rosa. **on record 1** *the wettest winter on record* recorded, registered, documented, officially noted. **2** *he is on record as promising improvements* recorded, officially noted, documented, publicly known.

record *verb* **1** *record the details* put on record, set down, write down, put in writing, take down, put down, enter, make a note of, document,

minute, register, chronicle, file, put on file, docket, list, log, catalog, inscribe, transcribe. **2** *record a very low temperature* register, read, indicate, show, display. **3** *record a song | record the wedding* make a record/recording of. **4** *record a music video* make, produce, cut, tape, videotape.

recorder *noun* **1** *purchase a recorder* tape recorder, video recorder, videocassette recorder; *inf.* VCR. **2** *the documents compiled by the recorder* keeper of records, record keeper, registrar, archivist, annalist, chronicler, historian. **3** *the recorder noted down the details* scribe, clerk, secretary.

recording *noun* disc, record, phonograph record, tape recording, tape, video recording, video; compact disc; *inf.* CD.

recount *verb* **1** *recount a tale* narrate, tell, relate, unfold, repeat. **2** *recount the events of the day* describe, detail, enumerate, list, specify, itemize, cite, particularize, catalog.

recoup *verb* **1** *recoup the lost property* get back, win back, regain, recover, retrieve, repossess, redeem. **2** *recoup her for her losses* reimburse, pay back, repay, recompense, compensate, indemnify.

recourse *noun their only recourse was illegal medicine* resort, way out, place/person to turn to, source of assistance, available resource, choice, option, possibility, alternative, expedient.

recover *verb* **1** *recover their stolen possessions* get back, win back, regain, recoup, retrieve, reclaim, repossess, redeem, recuperate, recapture. **2** *the invalid will recover in time* get better, get back to normal, get well, recuperate, convalesce, heal, get back on one's feet, feel oneself again, improve, mend, pick up, rally, revive, pull through, bounce back; *inf.* perk up.
Antonyms: LOSE; DETERIORATE.

---

recover
reclaim, recoup, regain, restore, retrieve
If you lose or let go of something and find it either by chance or with effort, you **recover** it (*recover the stolen artwork*). Although it is often used interchangeably with *recover*, **regain** puts more emphasis on the search or effort involved in getting back something you have been deprived of (*regain one's position as chairperson; regain one's eyesight*). **Recoup** refers to the recovery of something similar or equivalent to what has been lost, usually in the form of compensation (*he tried to recoup his gambling losses*). **Reclaim** and **restore** both involve bringing something back to its original condition or to a better or more useful state. *Reclaim* is usually associated with land (*reclaim neglected farmlands*), while *restore* is linked to buildings or objects of art (*restore an 18th-century house*). **Retrieve** implies that something has slipped beyond reach, and that a concerted effort or search is required to recover it (*her desperate*

efforts to retrieve the family dog from the flooded house).

recovery noun **1** *the recovery of their goods* recouping, regaining, retrieval, reclamation, repossession, recapture. **2** *the invalid's recovery is slow* return to normal/health, recuperation, convalescence, healing, rallying, revival. **3** *the recovery of the economy* improvement, betterment, amelioration, upturn, upswing.

recreation noun **1** *for recreation he rows* relaxation, refreshment, restoration, leisure, amusement, entertainment, distraction, diversion, pleasure, enjoyment, fun, play, sport. **2** *his favorite recreation is reading* leisure activity, pastime, hobby, diversion, distraction.
Antonyms: WORK; LABOR.

recriminate verb counteraccuse, countercharge, counterattack, make mutual accusations, retaliate, take reprisals, exact retribution.

recrimination noun counteraccusation, countercharge, counterattack, retaliation, reprisal, retribution, vengeance; mutual accusations.

recruit verb **1** *recruit soldiers | recruit new members* enlist, enroll, sign up, draft, conscript, levy, engage, obtain, acquire, procure, take on, round up, muster. **2** *recruit an army* form, raise, gather/put together, muster, assemble. **3** *recruit his finances/membership* replenish, augment, increase, enlarge, add to, build up, strengthen, reinforce, fortify, shore up; *inf.* beef up.

recruit noun **1** *army recruits* enlistee, draftee, conscript. **2** *new recruits to the society/industry* new member, new entrant, newcomer, initiate, beginner, learner, trainee, apprentice, novice, tyro, neophyte, proselyte; *inf.* rookie, greenhorn.

rectify verb put/set right, right, correct, amend, emend, remedy, repair, fix, make good, redress, reform, improve, better, ameliorate, adjust, square.
Antonyms: DAMAGE; BREAK.

rectitude noun **1** *appoint a man of rectitude* righteousness, virtue, moral virtue, morality, honor, integrity, principle, probity, uprightness, good character, decency, honesty, upstandingness, scrupulousness, incomparability. **2** *the rectitude of the judgment/results* correctness, accuracy, exactness, precision, soundness, verity.
Antonyms: DISHONOR; DISHONESTY; INACCURACY.

recuperate verb **1** *he is recuperating after an illness* recover, convalesce, get better, get back to normal, get well, regain one's strength/health, improve, mend, pick up, rally, revive, pull through, bounce back; *inf.* perk up. **2** *recuperate costs* recover, recoup, get back, regain, retrieve, reclaim.

recur verb reoccur, happen/occur again, come back, return, reappear, be repeated, repeat itself, happen repeatedly.

recurrent adjective recurring, repeated, repetitive, reiterative, periodic, cyclical, regular, habitual, continual, frequent, intermittent, chronic.
Antonyms: ISOLATED; SINGLE; UNIQUE.

recycle verb reuse, reprocess, salvage, save.

red adjective **1** *red dresses/wallpaper/flowers* reddish, crimson, scarlet, vermilion, cherry, ruby, cardinal, carmine, ruby-colored, maroon, wine, wine-colored, claret, claret-colored, russet, coral, salmon-pink, pink, cochineal, rose. **2** *she had a red face* flushed, blushing, florid, ruddy, rubicund, roseate. **3** *with red eyes* bloodshot, inflamed. **4** *red hair | horses with red coats* reddish, flaming-red, flame-colored, auburn, copper, Titian, chestnut, orange, carroty, sandy, ginger. **5** *soldiers with red hands* bloody, blood-stained, gory. **6** *red beliefs* communist, ultra-left-wing, leftist; *inf.* commie.

red noun **1** *color the walls with red* red color/pigment. **2** *wearing red* red clothes/garments. **3** *suspecting them of being reds* communist, socialist, leftist; *inf.* commie. **in the red** overdrawn, insolvent, in debt, owing money, showing a loss, bankrupt, in arrears; *inf.* on the rocks. **see red** be furious, be incensed, be infuriated, lose one's temper, become enraged, get mad, boil, seethe; *inf.* hit the roof, blow one's top.

redden noun **1** *redden her lips* make/color red. *See* RED adjective 1. **2** *she reddened in embarrassment* go red, blush, flush, color, color up, crimson.

redeem verb **1** *redeem pawned goods* reclaim, get back, regain, recover, retrieve, repossess, recoup, buy back, repurchase. **2** *redeem the vouchers* exchange, give in exchange, cash in, convert, turn in, trade in. **3** *Christ/missionaries redeeming sinners* free/save/deliver from sin, turn from sin, convert, purge/absolve of sin. **4** *his generosity redeems his bad temper* make up for, compensate for, atone for, offset, redress, outweigh. **5** *he redeemed himself by helping his neighbor* save/free from blame, vindicate, absolve, remove guilt from. **6** *redeem the slaves/hostages* free, set free, liberate, release, emancipate, ransom, rescue, save. **7** *redeem his promise/obligations* fulfill, discharge, make good, carry out, execute, keep, hold to, adhere to, abide by, obey, be faithful to, meet, satisfy.

redemption noun **1** *the redemption of possessions* reclamation, recovery, retrieval, buying back, repurchase. *See* REDEEM 1. **2** *the redemption of his faults by his generosity* compensation, atonement, redress. **3** *his redemption of himself by good works* freeing/saving from blame, vindication, absolution. **4** *the redemption of the slaves/hostages* freeing, liberation, release, emancipation, ransom, rescue, saving. **5** *the redemption of his promise/obligations* fulfillment, discharge, making good, execution, adherence, meeting, satisfying.

redolent adjective **1** *a movie redolent of another age* evocative, suggestive, reminiscent. **2** *redolent* *flower gardens* sweet-smelling, fragrant, scented, perfumed, aromatic. **3** *a redolent garbage dump* strong-smelling, odorous, smelly, foul-smelling.

redoubtable *adjective* formidable, fearsome, awe-inspiring, mighty, powerful, dreadful, terrible, awful.

redound *verb your wicked actions will redound on you one day* come back, recoil, rebound. **redound to** *his action redounded to his credit* contribute to, conduce to, be conducive to, have an effect on, affect.

redress *verb* **1** *redress a wrong* rectify, remedy, put/set right, make amends for, compensate for, make up for, make reparation/restitution for, recompense for, atone for. **2** *redress the balance of power* put right, even up, regulate, adjust, correct.

redress *noun* amends; compensation, reparation, restitution, recompense, atonement, rectification, remedying, putting right, amending.

reduce *verb* **1** *reduce the size of the garden* | *reduce the volume/speed/strength* make smaller, make less, lessen, lower, decrease, diminish, cut, curtail, contract, shorten, abbreviate, moderate, dilute, mitigate, alleviate, abate. **2** *they were reduced to tears/begging* bring to, bring to the point of, force to, drive to. **3** *they were reduced to a lower grade/rank* demote, downgrade, lower, lower in rank/status, humble. **4** *reduced yesterday's stock* lower/cut in price, lower, make cheaper, cheapen, cut, mark down, slash, discount, put on sale. **5** *she is trying to reduce* get thinner, slim, slim down, lose/shed weight, go/be on a diet, diet, lose some inches, shed some pounds, slenderize. **6** *the army reduced the enemy/city* conquer, vanquish, overpower, subdue, subjugate, overcome, overrun. **7** *they have been reduced by the recession* bankrupt, make penniless/poor, impoverish, ruin, break.

Antonyms: INCREASE; ENLARGE.

reduction *noun* **1** *the reduction in size/volume/length/speed/strength* lessening, lowering, decrease, diminution, cut, contraction, abbreviation, moderation, dilution, alleviation, abatement. **2** *their reduction to lower classes/ranks* demotion, downgrading, lowering, humbling. **3** *the reduction of goods* cheapening, discounting. *See* REDUCE 4. **4** *the reduction of the enemy/city* conquering, vanquishing, overpowering, subjugation, overrunning. **5** *what reduction did you get on the car?* discount, deduction, cut, concession, allowance. **6** *the museum has some reductions of the artist's work* smaller copy, miniature, model.

redundant *adjective* **1** *his presence was redundant* | *redundant supplies* not required, unnecessary, inessential, unwanted, de trop, surplus, supernumerary, excessive, in excess, extra; *inf.*

needed like a hole in the head. **2** *redundant passages/writings* unnecessary, inessential, padded, wordy, verbose, tautological, periphrastic, diffuse, pleonastic.

Antonyms: ESSENTIAL; VITAL.

reel *verb* **1** *drunks reeling down the street* stagger, lurch, sway, stumble, totter, wobble, falter, waver, pitch, roll. **2** *reeling from the blow* feel giddy/dizzy, feel confused, be shaken, be in shock, be upset. **3** *her mind was reeling* | *the room seemed to reel* go around (in circles), go round and round, whirl, spin, revolve, swirl, twirl, swim.

refer *verb* **refer to** **1** *refer to a dictionary* | *refer to his notes* consult, turn to, look at, look up in, seek information from, have recourse to. **2** *refer the question/person to a higher court* pass (on) to, hand on to, send on to, transfer to, remit to, direct to. **3** *he referred to her death in his speech* mention, make mention of, make reference to, allude to, touch on, speak of, cite, advert to, hint at. **4** *these figures refer to last year* apply to, be relevant to, have relevance to, concern, relate to, belong to, pertain to, have a bearing on.

referee *noun* umpire, judge, adjudicator, arbitrator, arbiter, mediator; *inf.* ref.

referee *verb* **1** *referee the game* umpire, judge, adjudicate. **2** *referee in the dispute* arbitrate, mediate, act as arbitrator/negotiator, intercede.

reference *noun* **1** *a reference to her death in his speech* mention, allusion, citation, hint. **2** *with reference to yesterday's meeting* regard, respect, relation, bearing, applicability, application, relevance, pertinence, connection, correlation. **3** *give a list of your references for the book* source, information source, citation, authority. **4** *the teacher gave her a reference* character reference, testimonial, recommendation, good word; credentials.

referendum *noun* public vote, plebiscite, popular vote, poll.

refine *verb* **1** *refine sugar/flour* purify, rarefy, clarify, clear, cleanse, strain, sift, filter, distill, process. **2** *sent to a school that would refine them* civilize, make cultivated, polish, improve, make elegant. **3** *refine the art of conversation* improve, perfect, consummate, elaborate, hone, fine-tune, complete.

refined *adjective* **1** *refined sugar/flour* purified, pure, rarefied, clarified, clear, filtered, distilled, processed. **2** *a refined lady/gentleman* cultivated, cultured, polished, civilized, civil, gracious, stylish, elegant, sophisticated, urbane, courtly, well-mannered, well-bred, gentlemanly, ladylike, genteel. **3** *refined tastes/manners* discriminating, discerning, tasteful, sophisticated, fastidious.

Antonyms: CRUDE; COARSE; UNREFINED.

refinement *noun* **1** *the refinement of sugar* purification, processing, distillation, filtration. **2** *a person of refinement* cultivation, culture, taste, discrimination, polish, finish, civility, grace, graciousness, style, elegance, finesse, sophistication, urbanity, courtliness, good breeding, politeness, gentility, politesse; good manners. **3** *the term paper needs refinement* revision, improvement, enhancement, correction, amendment. **4** *refinements of logic/language* subtlety, nicety, nuance, fine point.

reflect *verb* **1** *the surface reflects heat/light* throw back, cast back, send back, give back, scatter, diffuse. **2** *their faces reflected in the pool* mirror, image. **3** *reflect sound* send back, bounce back, echo, re-echo. **4** *his complexion reflects his state of health* indicate, express, bespeak, communicate, show, display, demonstrate, exhibit, reveal, manifest, bear out, result from. **reflect on 1** *it will reflect on the school if he does badly* discredit, put in a bad light, damage, damage the reputation of, detract from. **2** *reflect on her problems* think about, consider, give thought/consideration to, mull over, contemplate, deliberate over, ponder, meditate about, muse about, ruminate about, cogitate about, cerebrate, dwell on, brood about.

reflection *noun* **1** *the reflection of heat/sound/images* throwing back, sending back, echoing, mirroring; diffusion, radiation. **2** *look at her reflection* image, mirror image. **3** *his complexion is a reflection of the state of his health* indication, expression, display, demonstration, manifestation, result. **4** *his behavior is a reflection on the school* imputation, slur, aspersion, source of discredit, derogation. **5** *on reflection, he decided to go* thought, second thought, thinking, consideration, contemplation, deliberation, meditation, rumination, cogitation, cerebration. **6** *write down your reflections on the subject* thought, opinion, view, idea, impression, comment; findings.

reflex *adjective* *a reflex action* automatic, involuntary, spontaneous; *inf.* knee-jerk.

reform *verb* **1** *reform the system* improve, make better, better, ameliorate, amend, mend, rectify, correct, rehabilitate, change, revise, revolutionize, reorganize, reconstruct, rebuild, refashion, remodel, remake, make over, revamp, renovate. **2** *he has reformed since you knew him* mend one's ways, change for the better, turn over a new leaf, improve; *inf.* go straight, get back on the straight and narrow.
Antonyms: WORSEN; BACKSLIDE.

reform *noun the reform of the system* improvement, betterment, amelioration, amendment, rectification, correction, rehabilitation, change, revision, reorganization, reconstruction, rebuilding, refashioning, remodeling, renovation.

refractory *adjective* intractable, recalcitrant, unmanageable, ungovernable, disobedient, insubordinate, defiant, contrary, wayward, willful, headstrong, perverse, contumacious, rebellious, mutinous, obstinate, obdurate.
Antonyms: OBEDIENT; MANAGEABLE.

refrain *verb refrain from drinking* desist, abstain,

hold back, forbear, forgo, do without, avoid, eschew, cease, stop, give up, leave off, quit, renounce.

refresh *verb* **1** *refreshed by a long walk* freshen, invigorate, revitalize, revive, brace, fortify, enliven, stimulate, energize, exhilarate, reanimate, resuscitate, revivify, rejuvenate, regenerate, breathe new life into, inspirit; *inf.* perk up. **2** *refresh one's memory* stimulate, prompt, prod, jog, activate, rouse, arouse.

refreshing *adjective* **1** *a refreshing breeze* freshening, invigorating, revitalizing, reviving, bracing, stimulating, exhilarating, energizing. *See* REFRESH 1. **2** *a refreshing piece of writing* | *refreshing attitude* fresh, new, novel, original, different.

refreshments *plural noun serve refreshments after the ceremony* food, food and drink, sustenance; snacks, finger foods, drinks; *inf.* coffee-and; eats, grub, nosh, chow.

refrigerate *verb* keep cold, cool, chill, freeze.

refuge *noun* **1** *seek refuge from the elements/danger* shelter, safety, security, protection, asylum, sanctuary. **2** *regard their house as a refuge* place of safety, safe house, shelter, haven, retreat, sanctuary, harbor. **3** *borrowing money was his last refuge* resort, recourse, expedient, stopgap, tactic, stratagem, strategy.

refugee *noun* displaced/stateless person, émigré, exile, fugitive, escapee.

refund *verb refund her deposit* give back, return, repay, pay back, reimburse, make good, restore, replace.

refund *noun give the disappointed audience a refund* repayment, reimbursement, rebate.

refurbish *verb* renovate, revamp, make over, overhaul, redecorate, spruce up, recondition, refit, reequip, remodel, repair, mend; *inf.* do up, fix up.

refusal *noun* **1** *the refusal of her invitation* turning down, declining, rejecting, spurning. *See* REFUSE *verb* 1. **2** *four acceptances and one refusal to the invitation* nonacceptance, dissent, no, demurral, negation, thumbs down, rebuff; regrets; *inf.* brush-off. **3** *you can have first refusal* option, choice, consideration, opportunity.

refuse *verb* **1** *refuse an invitation/offer* turn down, decline, say no to, reject, spurn, rebuff, repudiate; *inf.* pass up. **2** *refuse to go* | *refusing the opportunity to go* decline, be unwilling; balk at, demur at, avoid, resist, protest at. **3** *refuse permission to go* withhold, not grant.
Antonyms: ACCEPT; CONSENT; GRANT.

refuse *noun* rubbish, garbage, trash, waste, debris, litter, dross; dregs, leavings, sweepings; flotsam; *inf.* junk.

regain *verb* get back, win back, recover, recoup, retrieve, reclaim, repossess, redeem, recuperate, take back, retake, recapture.

regal *adjective* royal, majestic, noble, proud, stately, magnificent, sumptuous; kingly, queenly, princely, fit for a king/queen/prince/princess.

regale *verb* **1** *regale their guests* entertain lavishly/sumptuously, ply with food and drink, wine and dine, feast, fête. **2** *regale his friends with stories of his travels* entertain, amuse, divert, delight, fascinate, captivate.

regard *verb* **1** *he seldom regards her advice* heed, pay attention to, attend to, listen to, mind, take notice of, take into consideration/account. **2** *regard the prospect with horror* look upon, view, consider, contemplate, think of, weigh up, mull over, reflect on, deliberate on. **3** *his work/aunt is well/poorly regarded* judge, adjudge, rate, value, estimate, gauge, appraise, assess, account, deem, consider, look upon, hold. **4** *the security officer regarded them closely* watch, look at, gaze at, keep an eye on, stare at, observe, view, study, scrutinize, eye, mark, behold.

regard *noun* **1** *pay no regard to his warning* heed, attention, notice, consideration, thought, mind. **2** *looked upon with regard* respect, esteem, admiration, approval, approbation, appreciation, favor, deference, affection, love. **3** *in this regard I disagree with you* respect, aspect, point, particular, detail, item, feature. **4** *she was aware of his steady regard* look, gaze, stare; observation, scrutiny.

regarding *preposition* with/in regard to, as regards, as to, with reference to, on the subject/matter of, apropos, concerning, about, respecting.

regardless *adjective* **regardless of** without regard to, disregarding, unmindful of, heedless of, without consideration of, indifferent to, negligent of.

regardless *adverb* *he decided to go, regardless* anyway, anyhow, in any case, nevertheless, nonetheless, despite everything, for all that, no matter what.
Antonyms: MINDFUL; HEEDFUL.

regards *plural noun* *send her my regards* best/good wishes, greetings, salutations, respects, compliments, remembrances.

regenerate *verb* **1** *the trip regenerated him* renew, breathe new life into, restore, invigorate, refresh, revitalize, revive, stimulate, energize, exhilarate, revivify, rejuvenate, uplift, inspirit. **2** *regenerate the political party* breathe new life into, change radically, improve, amend, reorganize, reconstruct, overhaul.

regime *noun* government, system of government, rule, reign, control, command, administration, establishment, direction, management, leadership.

regiment *verb* *nations regimented by dictators* organize/order rigidly, systematize, methodize, control strictly, discipline, keep a tight rein on, bring into line, rule with a rod of iron.

region *noun* **1** *the western region of the country* area, province, territory, division, section, sector, zone, tract, part, quarter, locality. **2** *the lumbar region of the body* part, place, section, locality, site. **3** *work in the region of metaphysics* field, sphere, orbit, ambit, realm, domain, world.

regional *adjective* **1** *regional distinctions shown on the map* geographical, topographical, zonal, territorial. **2** *organized on a regional rather than a national basis* local, localized, district, provincial, parochial.

register *noun* **1** *sign the register* | *be in the social/medical register* official list, listing, roll, roster, index, directory, catalog. **2** *historians consulting old county registers* record, chronicle, diary, journal, log; annals, archives, files. **3** *the register of her voice* range, compass, scope, scale, gamut, reach, sweep, spectrum.

register *verb* **1** *register a birth* | *register the date of arrival* record, put on record, enter, set down, chronicle, enroll, inscribe, write down, put in writing, take down, note, list, catalog. **2** *the speedometer registered 50 miles per hour* read, record, indicate, show, display. **3** *her face registered surprise* show, express, display, exhibit, evince, betray, reveal, manifest, demonstrate, reflect. **4** *his death/danger did not register* make an impression, get through, sink in, penetrate, have an effect.

regress *verb* *he had improved, but he has now regressed* retrogress, revert, relapse, lapse, backslide, fall away, go backward, degenerate, retrograde, recidivate.
Antonyms: IMPROVE; PROGRESS.

regret *verb* **1** *she regrets her action* feel sorry/contrite about, feel remorse about, wish undone, have a conscience about, repent, rue. **2** *she regrets their going* | *regretting lost opportunities* feel sorry about, lament, bemoan, be upset/disappointed about, mourn, grieve over, weep over, fret about, pine over, deplore.

regret *noun* **1** *she looks upon her actions with regret* sorrow, remorse, contrition, repentance, pangs of conscience, compunction, ruefulness, self-reproach, penitence. **2** *she regarded their going with regret* | *regret at her lost opportunities* sorrow, disappointment, lamentation, grief, mourning, pining.

regretful *adjective* sorry, apologetic, remorseful, contrite, repentant, conscience-stricken, rueful, penitent.
Antonyms: IMPENITENT; UNREPENTANT.

regrettable *adjective* deplorable, reprehensible, disgraceful, blameworthy, unfortunate, unwelcome, distressing, ill-advised.

regular *adjective* **1** *his regular route to work* usual, normal, customary, habitual, routine, typical, everyday, daily, unvarying, common, average, commonplace. **2** *regular breathing* rhythmic, periodic, steady, even, uniform, constant, unchanging. **3** *trees placed at regular intervals* even, uniform, consistent, orderly, systematic, fixed. **4** *build on a regular surface* level, smooth, flat, uniform. **5** *apply through the regular chan-*

nels official, established, fixed, stated, conventional, formal, proper, orthodox, approved, sanctioned, bona fide, standard, usual, traditional, classic, time-honored. **6** *insist on regular office procedures* methodical, systematic, well-organized, orderly, efficient, smooth-running, streamlined. **7** *he is a regular charmer/hero* real, thorough, absolute, utter, complete. **Antonyms:** IRREGULAR; UNUSUAL; ERRATIC; UNEVEN.

regulate *verb* **1** *regulate one's expenditure/lifestyle | regulate the traffic* control, direct, guide, govern, rule, manage, order, administer, handle, arrange, organize, conduct, run, supervise, oversee, superintend, monitor. **2** *regulate the clock/mechanism* adjust, balance, set, synchronize, modulate.

regulation *noun* **1** *the regulation of expenditure/lifestyles/traffic* control, direction, guidance, government, rule, management, administration, organization, conducting, handling, supervision, monitoring. **2** *the regulation of the clocks/mechanisms* adjustment, balancing, synchronization, modulation. **3** *new government/school regulations* rule, ruling, order, directive, act, law, decree, statute, edict, ordinance, pronouncement, dictum, command, procedure, requirement, prescription, precept.

regulation *adjective* *regulation dress* official, prescribed, mandatory, required, set, fixed, standard, normal, usual, customary.

rehabilitate *verb* **1** *rehabilitate the injured athlete* restore to health/normality, get back to health/normality, reintegrate, readapt, retrain. **2** *rehabilitate slum areas/houses* restore, redevelop, recondition, renovate, renew, refurbish, redecorate, mend, repair, fix up, rebuild, reconstruct. **3** *rehabilitate the criminal/alcoholic* reform, reclaim, reeducate, give new life to, redeem, regenerate, set straight, transform, give a second chance to.

rehearsal *noun* *a rehearsal of the play/concert* practice, practice session, trial performance, run-through, going-over.

rehearse *verb* **1** *rehearse the play/speech* practice, try out, run through, go over. **2** *actors rehearsing* practice, have a practice session, prepare, try out, have a trial performance, go through one's paces. **3** *rehearse the actors/children* drill, train, prepare.

reign *verb* **1** *he/she reigned for thirty years* be king/queen, be monarch/sovereign, sit on the throne, occupy the throne, wear the crown, wield the scepter. **2** *the present committee has reigned for years* be in power, govern, be in government, rule, be in command/charge/control, administer, hold sway; *inf.* be at the helm. **3** *chaos reigned* prevail, predominate, obtain, hold sway, be supreme, be rife, be rampant.

reign *noun* **1** *during the reign of the king/queen* monarchy, sovereignty. **2** *under the reign of the present government* power, government, rule, command, control, administration, charge, influence, sway, ascendancy, dominion, supremacy.

rein *noun* *act as a rein on their expenditure* check, curb, restraint, constraint, restriction, limitation, control, bridle, brake.

rein *verb* *try to rein in his impatience | rein your expenditure* check, curb, restrain, constrain, hold back, restrict, control, bridle, put the brakes on, slow down.

reinforce *verb* **1** *reinforce the bridge | reinforce his argument* strengthen, fortify, bolster up, shore up, buttress, prop up, brace, support, back up, uphold, stress, underline, emphasize. **2** *reinforce the troops* augment, increase, add to, supplement.

reinforcement *noun* **1** *the reinforcement of the bridge/argument* strengthening, fortification, bolstering, propping up, supporting, stressing, emphasizing. **2** *the reinforcement of the troops* augmentation, increasing, supplementing. **3** *act as a reinforcement of his argument* fortification, buttress, prop, brace, support, emphasis.

reinforcements *plural noun* *armies sending for reinforcements* additional troops/supplies, supplementaries, reserves; support.

reiterate *verb* repeat, repeat/go over and over, say again, belabor, dwell on, harp on, hammer away at.

reject *verb* **1** *reject an offer/invitation* refuse, turn down, decline, say no to, give the thumbs down to, spurn, rebuff, repudiate, veto, deny; *inf.* pass up. **2** *reject the bill | reject his wife* cast out, cast aside, discard, jettison, renounce, abandon, forsake, scrap, exclude, eliminate. **Antonyms:** ACCEPT; APPROVE.

reject *noun* **1** *a reject from the factory* substandard article, discard, castoff, irregular, second. **2** *one of society's rejects* failure, outcast, derelict; *inf.* dropout.

rejection *noun* **1** *the rejection of their offer/invitation* refusal, turning down, declining, spurning; *inf.* brush-off. **2** *the rejection of the bill | his rejection of his family* casting out, discarding, jettisoning, renunciation. **3** *receive a rejection* refusal, nonacceptance, no, demurral, negation, thumbs down; *inf.* brush-off.

rejoice *verb* **1** *people rejoicing on hearing the good news* be joyful, be happy, be pleased, be glad, be delighted, be elated, be overjoyed, be jubilant, be euphoric, jump for joy, exult, glory, triumph, celebrate, revel, make merry, feast. **2** *rejoice in her new baby* take delight/pleasure in, find joy in. **Antonyms:** MOURN; LAMENT.

rejoicing *noun* happiness, pleasure, gladness, delight, elation, jubilation, euphoria, exultation, glory, triumph, celebration, revelry, merrymaking, feasting.

rejoinder *noun* answer, response, reply, riposte, retort; *inf.* comeback.

relapse *verb* **1** *business improved but then relapsed* lapse, regress, retrogress, revert, backslide, fall away, go backward, slip back, degenerate, retrograde, recidivate. **2** *the patient relapsed* have/suffer a relapse, get ill/worse again, worsen, take a turn for the worse, sicken, deteriorate, sink.

relapse *noun* **1** *the business had a relapse after its improvement* lapse, regression, retrogression, reversion, backsliding, recidivism. **2** *the patient suffered a relapse* reoccurrence of illness, worsening of condition, turn for the worse, setback, deterioration.
Antonyms: IMPROVEMENT; RECOVERY.

relate *verb* **1** *relate the story of the accident* recount, tell, narrate, describe, report, impart, communicate, recite, rehearse, present, detail, delineate, chronicle, set forth. **2** *it is sometimes difficult to relate cause and effect* connect, associate, link, correlate, ally, couple, join. **relate to** *this information does not relate to the matter in hand* apply to, be relevant to, have relevance to, concern, refer to, have reference to, belong to, pertain to, bear on.

related *adjective* **1** *related issues* connected, interconnected, associated, linked, correlated, allied, affiliated, accompanying, concomitant, akin. **2** *related through marriage* connected, akin, kindred, agnate, cognate, consanguineous.
Antonyms: UNCONNECTED; SEPARATE; unrelated.

relation *noun* **1** *the relation of the story* recounting, telling, narrating, narrative, description, reporting, rehearsal, reciting. **2** *the relation between cause and effect* connection, association, linking, tie-in, correlation, alliance, bond, interdependence. **3** *have no relation to the problem in hand* applicability, application, relevance, reference, pertinence, bearing. **4** *he is my one American relation* relative, member of the family, kinsman, kinswoman, connection; kin.

relations *plural noun* **1** *business relations* connections, dealings, associations, communications; contact, interaction. **2** *romantic/sexual relations* sexual intercourse, intimacy; sexual relationship, affair, liaison; *inf.* sex. **3** *have no relations in this country* family, kin, kinsfolk, kindred; connections, folks.

relationship *noun* **1** *the relationship between cause and effect* connection, association, link, correlation, alliance, bond, tie-up, parallel, correspondence, conjunction. **2** *enter into a new relationship* friendship, love affair, affair, liaison. **3** *there is no relationship between the families* family/blood ties, kinship.

relative *adjective* **1** *consider the relative merits of the candidates* comparative, comparable, respective, correlative, parallel, corresponding. **2** *the salary scale is relative to production* proportionate, in proportion/ratio, proportional, related. **3** *facts relative to the issue* applicable, relevant,

pertaining, pertinent, germane, material, apposite, appropriate, apropos, appurtenant.

relative *noun a relative of his wife* relation, member of the family, kinsman, kinswoman, connection; kin, parent, sibling, grandparent; mother, father, brother, sister, son, daughter, stepmother, stepfather, stepchild, stepbrother, stepsister, aunt, uncle, niece, nephew, cousin, grandfather, grandmother.

relatively *adverb* **1** *for a car of this size it is relatively roomy* comparatively, in comparison, by comparison, proportionately. **2** *although ill, he is relatively cheerful* quite, rather, reasonably, somewhat.

relax *verb* **1** *relax one's grip* loosen, slacken, weaken, untighten, lessen, let up, reduce, diminish. **2** *let her muscles relax* become less tense/stiff/rigid, loosen, slacken, untighten. **3** *relax the rules* moderate, make less strict/formal, soften, ease. **4** *relax one's efforts* lessen, reduce, diminish, decrease, ease off, slacken off, let up, on, abate. **5** *tense people learning to relax* loosen up, ease up/off; *inf.* unwind, take it easy, let it all hang out, hang loose. **6** *this will relax you* loosen up, make less tense/uptight, calm, calm down, tranquilize, soothe, pacify; *inf.* unwind. **7** *he relaxes by playing the piano* be at leisure, take time off, enjoy oneself, amuse oneself, entertain oneself, rest; *inf.* let one's hair down. **8** *relax by the pool* rest, lounge, repose, take one's ease, idle, put one's feet up.
Antonyms: TIGHTEN; INCREASE; INTENSIFY; EXERCISE.

relaxation *noun* **1** *the relaxation of his grip* loosening, slackening, weakening, untightening, letting-up. **2** *the relaxation of her muscles* loosening, slackening, untightening. **3** *relaxation of rules* moderation, softening, easing. **4** *relaxation of one's efforts* lessening, reduction, easing off, abatement. **5** *tense people learning relaxation* loosening up. See RELAX 5. **6** *the relaxation of the patients* calming, tranquilization, soothing, pacification. **7** *for relaxation he plays the piano* leisure, recreation, enjoyment, amusement, entertainment, fun, pleasure, rest.

relay *verb relay the information* pass on, hand on, communicate, send, transmit, broadcast, spread, circulate.

release *verb* **1** *release the prisoners* set free, free, let go, set/turn loose, let out, liberate, deliver, emancipate, manumit. **2** *release those who had been tied up* set free, free, untie, undo, unloose, unbind, unchain, unfetter, unshackle, extricate. **3** *release her from her promise/engagement* let off, let go, excuse, absolve, acquit, exonerate, exempt. **4** *release the news | release a bulletin* make public, make known, issue, break, announce, reveal, divulge, unveil, present, disclose, publish, broadcast, put out, circulate, disseminate, distribute, spread.
Antonyms: IMPRISON; ENGAGE; SUPPRESS.

release *noun* **1** *the release of the prisoners* freeing, liberation, deliverance, emancipation, manumission. **2** *prisoners obtaining their release* freedom, liberation, deliverance, emancipation, manumission. **3** *the release of the bound victims* freeing, untying, unbinding, unchaining, extrication. See RELEASE *verb* 2. **4** *the release from her promise* excusing, absolution, acquittal, dispensation, exemption. **5** *the release of the news* issuing, breaking, announcement, divulging, publishing, publication, broadcasting, circulation. See RELEASE *verb* 4. **6** *write a press release* announcement, bulletin, publication, proclamation. **7** *the artist's latest release* recording; record, disc, compact disc; single, album; book; movie, motion picture, film; *inf.* CD; flick.

relent *verb* **1** *the judge relented and reduced the sentence* soften, become merciful/lenient, show mercy/pity, melt, capitulate, yield, give way, give in, come around, forbear, change one's mind; *inf.* do a U-turn. **2** *the pace/wind relented* let up, ease, slacken, relax, abate, drop, fall off, die down, weaken.

relentless *adjective* **1** *a relentless tyrant* unrelenting, ruthless, merciless, uncompassionate, pitiless, remorseless, unforgiving, implacable, inexorable, cruel, grim, harsh, hard, cold-hearted, fierce, strict, obdurate, unyielding, unflexible, unbending. **2** *a relentless urge/ambition* unrelenting, unremitting, undeviating, persistent, unswerving, persevering, unflagging, punishing, unfaltering, unstoppable, incessant, unceasing, nonstop, unabated, unbroken.
Antonyms: LENIENT; MERCIFUL.

relevant *adjective* applicable, pertinent, apposite, material, appurtenant, to the point/purpose, germane, admissible, appropriate, apt, fitting.

reliable *adjective* **1** *a reliable friend* dependable, trustworthy, true, tried and true, faithful, devoted, steady, steadfast, constant, unfailing, infallible, certain, sure, responsible. **2** *reliable evidence* dependable, trustworthy, authentic, well-founded, well-grounded, genuine, credible, sound. **3** *a reliable company* dependable, trustworthy, reputable, established, safe, stable.
Antonyms: UNRELIABLE; UNTRUSTWORTHY; TREACHEROUS.

reliance *noun* **1** *place no reliance on what she says* confidence, trust, faith, belief, conviction. **2** *his total reliance on his colleagues* dependence, leaning.

relic *noun* **1** *relics on view in the museum* ancient/historical object, artifact, antique, heirloom. **2** *a tradition that is a relic of another age* vestige, trace, survivor, remnant. **3** *regard the ring as a relic of a former relationship* souvenir, memento, keepsake, remembrance, reminder.

relics *plural noun* **1** *looking for Roman relics* remains, reliquiae, fragments, shards. **2** *exhume the relics* corpse, dead body; remains.

relief *noun* **1** *the relief of the pain* relieving, alle-

viating, mitigating, assuaging, allaying, soothing, easing, dulling, lessening, reduction. **2** *the medicine brought relief* alleviation, mitigation, assuagement, palliation, ease, appeasement, abatement. **3** *the relief of the people/city after the earthquake* aiding, assisting, rescuing, saving. **4** *bring relief to the starving people* aid, help, assistance, succor. **5** *bring relief from the monotony* respite, remission, interruption, break, variation, diversion, lightening, brightening; *inf.* letup. **6** *the soldier's/doctor's relief* replacement, substitute, stand-in, fill-in, alternate, understudy; *inf.* sub. **7** *details bringing the story out in sharp relief* distinctness, vividness, intensity, sharpness, focus, clarity, precision. **8** *relief from his burden* freedom, release, liberation, deliverance, exemption, extrication, discharge.

relieve *verb* **1** *relieve his pain/distress* alleviate, mitigate, assuage, allay, soothe, soften, palliate, appease, ease, dull, abate, reduce, lessen, diminish. **2** *relieve the victims/city* bring aid to, aid, help, assist, rescue, save, succor. **3** *relieve the monotony* bring respite to, interrupt, break up, vary, lighten, brighten. **4** *relieve the soldier on guard* take over from, take the place of, stand in for, substitute for. **5** *relieve them of their burdens* free, release, liberate, deliver, exempt, extricate, discharge, unburden, disburden, disencumber.
Antonyms: EXACERBATE; AGGRAVATE; WORSEN.

religious *adjective* **1** *religious festivals/discussions* church, holy, divine, theological, doctrinal, spiritual, sectarian. **2** *religious people* churchgoing, God-fearing, godly, pious, devout. **3** *pay religious attention to detail* scrupulous, conscientious, meticulous, zealous, strict, rigid, rigorous, exact, unfailing, unswerving, undeviating.
Antonyms: IRRELIGIOUS; IMPIOUS; UNGODLY.

relinquish *verb* **1** *relinquish her right to the title* give up, renounce, resign, abdicate, surrender, sign away. **2** *relinquish his position* depart from, leave, quit, vacate, pull out of, abandon, forsake. **3** *relinquish the habit* give up, discontinue, stop, cease, drop, abstain from, forbear from, forgo, desist from. **4** *relinquish her grip* release, let go, loosen, unloose.
Antonyms: KEEP; RETAIN; CONTINUE.

---

relinquish
abandon, cede, surrender, waive, yield
Of all these verbs meaning to let go or give up, **relinquish** is the most general. It can imply anything from simply releasing one's grasp (*she relinquished the wheel*) to giving up control or possession reluctantly (*after the defeat, he was forced to relinquish his command*). **Surrender** also implies giving up, but usually after a struggle or show of resistance (*the villagers were forced to surrender to the guerrillas*). **Yield** is a milder synonym for *surrender*, implying some

concession, respect, or even affection on the part of the person who is surrendering (*she yielded to her mother's wishes and stayed home*). **Waive** means to give up voluntarily a right or claim to something (*she waived her right to have a lawyer present*), while **cede** is to give up by legal transfer or according to the terms of a treaty (*the French ceded the territory that is now Louisiana*). If one *relinquishes* something finally and completely, often because of weariness or discouragement, the correct word is **abandon** (*they were told to abandon all hope of being rescued*).

relish noun 1 *eat/play with relish* enjoyment, delight, pleasure, satisfaction, gratification, appreciation, liking, zest, gusto. 2 *food with relish* flavor, taste, tang, piquancy, spiciness.
Antonyms: DISLIKE; DISTASTE.

relish verb 1 *the children relish the beach* enjoy, delight in, like, love, adore, appreciate, revel in, luxuriate in. 2 *do not relish the idea of surgery* look forward to, fancy, eagerly await/anticipate.
Antonyms: DETEST; LOATHE.

reluctance noun unwillingness, disinclination, hesitance, hesitancy, lack of enthusiasm, loathness, aversion, distaste.

reluctant adjective 1 *a reluctant hero/candidate* unwilling, disinclined, hesitant, unenthusiastic, grudging. 2 *reluctant to go* unwilling, disinclined, loath, averse, slow.
Antonyms: WILLING; EAGER; READY.

rely verb **rely on/upon** depend on/upon, count on/upon, bank on/upon, trust (in), be confident/sure of, swear by, lean on/upon, have confidence in, bet on.

remain verb 1 *only a handful remained* be left, be left over, stay behind, survive, last, abide, endure, prevail. 2 *remain at home | remain in the hospital* stay, wait, linger, tarry; *inf.* stay put. 3 *remain calm* stay, continue, persist in being.
Antonyms: GO; DEPART; LEAVE.

remainder noun remnant, residue, residuum, balance, surplus, excess, superfluity; remains, remnants, relics, vestiges, leavings, dregs.

remains plural noun 1 *the remains of a meal* remnants, leftovers, leavings, scraps; residue, debris, detritus. 2 *Roman remains* relics, reliquiae, fragments, shards. 3 *take his remains to the cemetery* corpse, dead body, body, cadaver, carcass.

remark verb *she remarked that she had been ill* mention, say, state, declare, pronounce, assert, observe. **remark on/upon** *she remarked on his appearance* comment on, pass comment on, mention.

remark noun 1 *ignore his nasty remarks* comment, statement, utterance, declaration, pronouncement, observation, reference, opinion. 2 *a performance worthy of remark* comment, attention,

mention, notice, observation, heed, acknowledgment, recognition.

remarkable adjective 1 *a remarkable achievement* out of the ordinary, extraordinary, unusual, uncommon, conspicuous, singular, signal, rare, exceptional, outstanding, striking, impressive, considerable, notable, noteworthy, memorable, preeminent, significant, important, momentous, phenomenal, wonderful. 2 *Mount Rushmore is remarkable* noteworthy, notable, conspicuous, distinctive, unusual, uncommon, peculiar, special, curious, wonderful, unique, out of the ordinary.
Antonyms: ORDINARY; COMMONPLACE; RUN-OF-THE-MILL.

remedy noun 1 *given a remedy for asthma* cure, treatment, medicine, medication, medicament, therapy, antidote, restorative, nostrum, panacea. 2 *find a remedy for the situation/problem* corrective, solution, redress, panacea.

remedy verb 1 *unable to remedy her condition* cure, heal, treat, counteract, control. 2 *remedy the situation/problem* rectify, solve, set to rights, put right, redress, fix, sort out.

remember verb 1 *I cannot remember his name* recall, call to mind, recollect, think of. 2 *remember to go | remember that it is raining* keep/bear in mind, not forget. 3 *remembering the past | he enjoys remembering* recall, recollect, reminisce; reminisce about, look/think back on, hark back to, summon up. 4 *remember the waiter* tip, reward, recompense. 5 *remember me to your parents* send greetings from, send one's regards/compliments.
Antonyms: FORGET; OVERLOOK.

remembrance noun 1 *their remembrance of times past* remembering, recalling, recollecting, recollection, reminiscing. 2 *I have a remembrance of seeing him once* memory, recollection. 3 *give her a remembrance of their meeting* keepsake, souvenir, memento, token, commemoration, memorial. 4 *send my remembrances to your parents* greetings, regards, best wishes, compliments.

remind verb 1 *remind me to go* cause one to remember, jog/refresh one's memory, prompt. 2 *it reminds me of home* cause one to remember, awake one's memories of.

reminisce verb *sit and reminisce* remember, recollect, think back, look back, dwell on the past. **reminisce about** *reminisce about the past* remember, recall, recollect, call to mind, exchange memories.

reminiscences plural noun 1 *listen to her reminiscences about the old days* memories, recollections, anecdotes; review, retrospection. 2 *publish her reminiscences* memoirs, remembrances.

reminiscent adjective *reminiscent of an Italian village* evocative, suggestive, redolent.

remiss adjective negligent, neglectful, lax, slack, slipshod, careless, forgetful, inattentive, heedless, thoughtless, unthinking, unmindful, culpable, delinquent; *inf.* sloppy.

remission noun **1** *the remission of the penalty* cancellation, revocation, repeal, rescinding. **2** *receive a remission for good behavior* reduction in sentence, reduced sentence. **3** *no remission of our efforts* relaxation, slackening, weakening, lessening, reduction, decrease, diminution, dwindling, cessation, stopping, halt. **4** *the remission of the storm/pain* easing, moderation, abatement, lessening, decrease, dwindling, wane, waning, ebb, ebbing, subsidence. **5** *the remission of payment* sending, dispatch, forwarding, transmission, posting, mailing. **6** *the remission of the matter to a committee* referral, passing on, transfer, direction. **7** *the remission of the meeting/decision* postponement, deferral, shelving, delay, suspension. **8** *given a remission for his offenses/sins* pardon, absolution, exoneration, forgiveness, indulgence.

remit verb **1** *remit a punishment/penalty* cancel, revoke, repeal, rescind, stop, halt. **2** *remit our efforts* relax, slacken, weaken, lessen, reduce, decrease, diminish, cease, stop, halt, desist from. **3** *the storm/pain remitted* ease, moderate, abate, lessen, decrease, dwindle, wane, ebb, subside. **4** *remit payment* send, dispatch, forward, transmit, post, mail. **5** *remit the matter to a committee* | *remit the case to another court* refer, pass on, hand on, send on, transfer, direct. **6** *remit the meeting/decision* postpone, defer, put off, shelve, delay, hold off, suspend, prorogue, reschedule. **7** *remit the offense/sin* pardon, forgive, excuse, overlook, pass over.

remittance noun payment, fee, allowance.

remnant noun **1** *the remnant of the army* remainder, residue, balance; remains, vestiges. **2** *a remnant of material* piece, fragment, scrap, cutoff.

remonstrate verb **1** *remonstrate with them* take issue with, argue with, dispute with, protest to, complain to, expostulate with. **2** *remonstrate against cruelty to children* argue against, protest against, object to, complain about, take a stand against, oppose.

remorse noun regret, sorrow, sorriness, contriteness, compunction, penitence, repentance, bad/guilty conscience, guilt, shame, self-reproach, ruefulness; pangs of conscience.

remorseful adjective sorry, regretful, contrite, apologetic, penitent, repentant, guilt-ridden, conscience-stricken, ashamed, chastened, rueful.

remote adjective **1** *the remote past* | *places remote from each other* distant, far, far-off, faraway, far-removed. **2** *in remote mountain villages* out-of-the-way, outlying, inaccessible, off the beaten track, isolated, secluded, lonely, godforsaken. **3** *a remote possibility* outside, unlikely, improbable, implausible, negligible, insignificant, doubtful, dubious, inconsiderable, slight, slender, slim, small, poor. **4** *she is rather remote among strangers* aloof, distant, detached, withdrawn, reserved, uncommunicative, unap-

proachable, standoffish, cool, haughty, uninvolved, indifferent, unconcerned.

Antonyms: NEAR; ACCESSIBLE; LIKELY.

removal noun **1** *the removal of dishes from the table* taking away, moving, shifting, conveying, conveyance, transfer, carrying away, transporting. **2** *his removal from office* dismissal, eviction, ejection, expulsion, ousting, dislodgment, deposition. **3** *the removal of privileges* taking away, withdrawal, deprivation, abolition. **4** *removal of errors* deletion, elimination, erasure, effacing, obliteration. **5** *the removal of weeds/opposition* uprooting, eradication, extirpation, destruction, extermination, annihilation. **6** *the removal of a limb/branch* cutting off, amputation, excision. **7** *their removal to France* move, transfer, relocation. **8** *the removal of a gang member by a rival* disposal, elimination, killing, murder, assassination, liquidation.

remove verb **1** *remove the dishes from the table* | *remove them to the sink* take away, carry away, move, shift, convey, transfer, transport. **2** *remove him from office* get rid of, dismiss, evict, eject, expel, cast out, oust, throw out, thrust out, dislodge, relegate, unseat, depose, displace; *inf.* sack, fire. **3** *remove their coats/hats* take off, doff, pull off. **4** *remove their privileges* take away, withdraw, do away with, abolish. **5** *remove the errors* delete, eliminate, erase, rub out, cross out, strike out, blue-pencil, efface, obliterate. **6** *remove the weeds/opposition* take out, pull out, uproot, eradicate, extirpate, destroy, exterminate, annihilate. **7** *remove a limb/branch* cut off, amputate, lop off, chop off, excise. **8** *remove to France* move, transfer, relocate. **9** *hire an assassin to remove him* get rid of, dispose of, do away with, eliminate, kill, murder, assassinate, liquidate; *inf.* bump off, do in.

Antonyms: PLACE; INSTALL; put on (*see* PUT).

remuneration noun payment, pay, salary, fee, emolument, stipend, honorarium, income, profit, reward, recompense, reimbursement; wages, earnings.

remunerative adjective profitable, moneymaking, paying, lucrative, gainful, financially rewarding, rich.

renaissance noun rebirth, reemergence, reappearance, resurgence, renewal, reawakening, revival, resurrection, rejuvenation, regeneration.

render verb **1** *render them helpless* make, cause to be/become, leave. **2** *pay for services rendered* | *rendered assistance* give, contribute, make available, provide, supply, furnish; do, perform. **3** *render good for evil* | *render insult for insult* give, exchange, trade, swap, return. **4** *render obedience* show, display, exhibit, evince, manifest. **5** *render an account* | *render a verdict* present, send in, submit, tender; deliver, hand down. **6** *the artist rendered her in a wistful mood* paint, portray, depict, represent. **7** *render the role of Macbeth* act, perform, play. **8** *the piano solo was well rendered* play, execute, perform, interpret. **9** *render the passage into Russian* translate, transcribe, construe, put, express. **10** *they rendered their land to the emperor* give, hand over, deliver, turn over, give up, yield, cede, surrender, relinquish. **11** *render the lands (back) to the original owners* give back, return, restore.

rendezvous *noun* **1** *have a rendezvous with her lover* appointment, date, engagement, tryst, meeting, assignation. **2** *their rendezvous is the café* meeting place, venue, tryst.

rendezvous *verb* *we shall rendezvous at dawn* meet (privately/secretly), come/gather together, gather, assemble.

renegade *noun* defector, deserter, turncoat, betrayer, traitor, dissenter, apostate, renouncer, recanter, revolutionary, rebel, mutineer.

renege *verb* go back on one's word, break one's promise, default, back out, pull out; *inf.* cop out, welsh.

renounce *verb* **1** *renounce his claim* give up, relinquish, resign, abdicate, abnegate, surrender, sign away, waive, forgo. **2** *renounce his son* repudiate, disown, cast off, discard, reject, disinherit, wash one's hands of, spurn, shun. **3** *renounce strong drink* give up, abstain from, desist from, swear off, eschew. **4** *renounce one's friendship/religion* give up, abandon, forsake, renege on, turn one's back on, abjure.

Antonyms: CLAIM; MAINTAIN; EMBRACE.

renovate *verb* modernize, recondition, refurbish, rehabilitate, overhaul, restore, revamp, remodel, repair, redecorate, refit; *inf.* do up, fix up.

renown *noun* fame, repute, acclaim, celebrity, distinction, illustriousness, eminence, preeminence, prominence, mark, note, consequence, prestige.

renowned *adjective* famous, famed, well-known, of repute, acclaimed, celebrated, distinguished, illustrious, eminent, preeminent, prominent, noted, notable, of note, of consequence, prestigious.

Antonyms: UNKNOWN; OBSCURE; UNSUNG.

rent[1] *noun* *what is the rent for the house/boat?* rental, tenant's payment, (hire) fee.

rent[2] *verb* *rent a house/boat from the owner* lease, hire, charter. **rent out** *they rent out houses/boats* let, lease, hire, hire/let out.

rent[3] *noun* *a rent in the material* tear, rip, split, gash, slash, hole, perforation, break, crack, fracture, crevice, fissure, cleft.

renunciation *noun* **1** *the renunciation of his claim* relinquishment, resignation, abdication, abnegation, surrender, waiving. **2** *the renunciation of his son* repudiation, disowning, discarding, rejecting, disinheriting, shunning, spurning. **3** *the renunciation of strong drink* giving up, abstention. **4** *the renunciation of their friendship/religion* abandonment, forsaking, reneging, abjuration.

repair[1] *verb* **1** *repair the machine* mend, fix, put right, restore, restore to working order, service, adjust, regulate, overhaul. **2** *repair the torn clothes* mend, darn, sew, patch. **3** *repair the rift in their friendship* mend, fix, patch up, heal, cure. **4** *repair the omission* make reparation for, put right, make good, rectify, correct, redress, compensate for.

Antonyms: BREAK; TEAR; HARM.

repair[2] *noun* **1** *the repair of the car* mending, fixing, restoration, servicing, overhaul. **2** *you will not notice the repair* mend, darn, patch. **3** *the furniture/car is in good repair* condition, state, form, fettle, kilter; *inf.* shape.

repair[3] *verb* **repair to** *to repair to the library* go to, withdraw to, head for, betake oneself to, take off for, leave for, depart for.

reparation *noun* *demand reparation for wrongs* redress, atonement, restitution, satisfaction, compensation, recompense, indemnity; amends, damages.

repartee *noun* witty conversation, badinage, banter, raillery, wordplay, lively exchange.

repast *noun* meal, collation, refection, snack, feast; food, nourishment; *inf.* spread, feed.

repay *verb* **1** *repay him for the money owed* pay back, refund, reimburse, recompense, remunerate, square accounts with, settle up with, indemnify. **2** *repay the money owed* pay back, give back, refund. **3** *repay him for the crime against her family* get back at, hit back, retaliate against, get even with, settle the score with. **4** *repay the wrong* avenge, revenge, make reprisal for.

repeal *verb* *repeal the act/bill* revoke, rescind, abrogate, annul, nullify, declare null and void, make void, void, invalidate, quash, set aside, cancel, countermand, retract, withdraw, recall, abjure, overrule, override, reverse.

Antonyms: INTRODUCE; RATIFY.

repeal *noun* *the repeal of the act/bill* revocation, rescinding, rescission, abrogation, annulment, nullification, voiding, invalidation, quashing, setting aside, cancellation, countermanding, retraction, withdrawal, recall, abjuration, overruling, overriding, reversal.

repeat *verb* **1** *repeat the statement/story* say again, restate, retell, iterate, recite, rehearse, recapitulate; *inf.* recap. **2** *she repeated his words* say again, restate, echo, parrot, quote, duplicate, copy, reproduce. **3** *repeat the task* do again, redo, duplicate. **repeat itself** *history repeated itself* occur again, reoccur, happen again, reappear.

repeat *noun* **1** *a repeat of his statement/story* repetition, restatement, retelling, iteration, recapitulation; *inf.* recap. **2** *a repeat of his words/actions* repetition, restatement, echoing, parroting, duplication, copy, reproduction. **3** *watch a repeat of the sitcom's first episode* rerun, replay, rebroadcast.

religion abandonment, forsaking, reneging, abjuration.

repeated *adjective* recurrent, frequent, continual, incessant, constant, endless.

repeatedly *adverb* again and again, over and over, time and time again, time after time, frequently, often, many times.

repel *verb* **1** *repel attackers/invaders* repulse, drive back, push back, thrust back, force back, beat back, hold off, ward off, fend off, stave off, parry, keep at bay, keep at arm's length, foil, check, frustrate, put to flight. **2** *repel their advances* repulse, reject, decline, turn down, rebuff. **3** *the sight of blood repels her* revolt, disgust, sicken, nauseate, make one sick, turn one's stomach, be repugnant to, make one's flesh creep, put one off, offend, shock; *inf.* turn one off, give one the creeps/heebie-jeebies.

Antonyms: WELCOME; ATTRACT; DELIGHT.

repellent *adjective* repulsive, revolting, disgusting, sickening, nauseating, distasteful, repugnant, abhorrent, offensive, obnoxious, loathsome, hateful, vile, nasty, shocking, despicable, reprehensible, contemptible, odious, abominable, horrible, horrid, foul, heinous, obscene.

repent *verb* regret, feel remorse for, rue; be penitent, be sorry, see the error of one's ways, be regretful, be contrite, feel remorse/remorseful, be conscience-stricken, reproach oneself, be ashamed, be guilt-ridden; *inf.* see the light.

repentance *noun* penitence, sorrow, sorriness, regret, contrition, contriteness, remorse, conscience, self-reproach, ruefulness, shame, guilt.

repentant *adjective* penitent, sorrowful, apologetic, regretful, contrite, remorseful, conscience-stricken, guilt-ridden, ashamed, rueful.

repercussion *noun* **1** *the repercussions of his action* effect, result, consequence, reverberation, backlash. **2** *he heard/felt the repercussion* echo, reverberation, reflection, recoil, rebound.

repetition *noun* **1** *a repetition of the statement/story* restatement, retelling, iteration, recital, rehearsal, recapitulation; *inf.* recap. **2** *her repetition of his words* repeating, restatement, echoing, parroting, quoting, copying. **3** *a repetition of his previous actions* repeat, redoing, duplication. **4** *a lot of repetition in the essay* repetitiousness, redundancy, tautology.

repetitive *adjective* *repetitive tasks/work* recurrent, unchanging, unvaried, undiversified, monotonous, tedious, boring, mechanical, automatic.

replace *verb* **1** *replace the book on the shelf* put back, return, restore. **2** *he will replace the retired teacher* take the place of, succeed, supersede, follow after, come after, supplant, substitute for, stand in for, act for, fill in for, cover for, understudy; *inf.* sub for. **3** *replace the broken vase* give in place of, give as a replacement for, give in return/exchange for.

replace
displace, supersede, supplant
When a light bulb burns out, you **replace** it, meaning that you substitute something new or functioning for what is lost, destroyed, or worn out. If something that is obsolete or ineffective is replaced by something that is superior, more up-to-date, or more authoritative, the correct verb is **supersede** (*the computer superseded the electric typewriter*). In contrast, **displace** suggests that someone or something has been ousted or dislodged forcibly, without necessarily implying that it was inferior or ineffective (*a growing number of workers were being displaced by machines*). **Supplant** is more restricted in meaning; it suggests displacement by force, fraud, or innovation (*the democratic government had been supplanted by a power-hungry tyrant*). It can also mean to uproot or wipe out (*the English immigrants gradually supplanted the island's native inhabitants*).

replacement *noun* *find a replacement for the retired teacher* successor, substitute, stand-in, fill-in, understudy, proxy, surrogate; *inf.* sub.

replenish *verb* **1** *replenish one's glass/plate* refill, top off, fill up, recharge, reload. **2** *replenish stocks of food* stock up, fill up, make up, replace, renew.

replete *adjective* **1** *guests feeling replete* full, full up, full to bursting, satiated, sated, glutted, gorged, stuffed, well-fed. **2** *replete shelves | replete with books* full, well-stocked, well-provided, brimful, brimming, chock-full, jampacked, crammed, teeming.

Antonyms: HUNGRY; EMPTY.

replica *noun* copy, carbon copy, duplicate, facsimile, model, reproduction, imitation.

reply *verb* **1** *if he writes/asks/phones, I will reply* answer, respond, make/give a response; write back, call/phone back. **2** *"not likely," she replied* answer, respond, rejoin, retort, return, riposte, come back, counter. **reply to** *reply to his question/letter* answer, give an answer to, respond to, acknowledge.

Antonyms: ASK; QUESTION.

reply *noun* answer, response, acknowledgment, rejoinder, retort, return, riposte, comeback.

report *noun* **1** *a report of the accident* account, statement, record, exposition, delineation. **2** *newspaper/television reports* article, piece, account, story, write-up, communication, communiqué, dispatch, bulletin. **3** *a company's financial report* formal statement, record, register, chronicle. **4** *a person of good report* reputation, repute, regard, character, name. **5** *the report of a gun/explosion* bang, boom, crack, crash, rumble, reverberation, noise, sound, echo.

report *verb* **1** *report the latest findings* bring word about, announce, pass on, communicate, relay, relate, tell, recount, give an account of, set forth, document, narrate, describe, delineate, detail, divulge, disclose, circulate. **2** *report the child for cheating* tell on, inform on, accuse, make a charge/complaint against; *inf.* squeal on, rat on. **3** *they will report at noon* present oneself, be present, appear, arrive, come, turn up, check in; *inf.* show up. **4** *report the proceedings of the conference* record, document, minute, write up, chronicle, write down, take down. **report on** *journalists reporting on events in Russia* write on/about, write an account of, broadcast.

reporter *noun* journalist, newsman, newswoman, pressman, correspondent, writer, broadcaster, announcer, presenter, news commentator; *inf.* newshound, hack.

repose *noun* **1** *seek repose after work* rest, relaxation, leisure, ease, inactivity, respite, time off, breathing space, sleep, slumber. **2** *a place of repose in the mountains* quiet, quietness, quietude, calm, calmness, tranquillity, peace, peacefulness, stillness, silence, hush. **3** *maintained her repose at all times* composure, calmness, calm, calm manner, poise, equanimity, self-possession.

Antonyms: WORK; ACTIVITY.

repose *verb* **1** *workers reposing at the end of the day* rest, relax, take one's ease, take a break, sleep, slumber; *inf.* take it easy. **2** *reposing on the couch* lie, lie down, recline, stretch out, sprawl.

repository *noun* store, storehouse, storeroom, reservoir, bank, safe, cache, receptacle, container.

reprehensible *adjective* blameworthy, blamable, reproachable, censurable, condemnable, reprovable, culpable, erring, errant, wrong, bad, shameful, disgraceful, discreditable, dishonorable, ignoble, objectionable, odious, opprobrious, unpardonable, indefensible, unjustifiable, inexcusable.

represent *verb* **1** *X represents the larger number* | *the tent represents home for them* stand for, correspond to, be the counterpart of, equal, be equivalent to, symbolize, mean, betoken. **2** *the Statue of Liberty represents the spirit of democracy* stand for, symbolize, personify, epitomize, typify. **3** *he represents their idea of a Frenchman* embody, incorporate, typify, exemplify, be a sample/specimen of. **4** *Cupid is usually represented as a winged boy* depict, portray, delineate, illustrate, picture, denote, paint, draw, sketch, exhibit, show, display, evoke. **5** *he represents Hamlet in the play* act as, enact, portray, appear as, perform as. **6** *he represented the children at the hearing* act for, appear for, speak for, be spokesperson for, be the representative of. **represent (oneself) as** *he represented himself as a qualified doctor* describe (oneself) as, pass (oneself) off as, pose as, pretend to be, impersonate.

representation *noun* **1** *the representation of Cupid as a winged boy* depiction, portrayal, portrait, delineation, illustration, picture, painting, drawing, sketch, image, model. **2** *have the best representation at the hearing/conference* spokesman, spokeswoman, spokesperson, representative, agent, deputy, ambassador, envoy, delegate; delegation, deputation. **3** *make representations to the court* statement, account, report, declaration, allegation, argument, protestation, remonstrance, expostulation.

representative *adjective* **1** *a representative specimen* | *a specimen representative of its genus* typical, archetypal, exemplary, characteristic, indicative, illustrative. **2** *the bald eagle is representative of the United States* emblematic, symbolic, evocative. **3** *a representative body* elected, elective, chosen, delegated, ambassadorial, authorized, accredited, official.

Antonyms: atypical; unrepresentative; EXTRAORDINARY.

representative *noun* **1** *a typical representative of its class* example, exemplification, exemplar, specimen, type, archetype, illustration, epitome, embodiment. **2** *he is the society's representative* spokesman, spokeswoman, spokesperson, agent, deputy, proxy. **3** *he is a sales representative* traveling salesman, agent; *inf.* rep. **4** *our country's representative at the conference* delegate, commissioner, ambassador, envoy. **5** *the state's representative in Congress* | *our representative on the council* congressman, congresswoman, member of Congress, senator, member of the House/Senate, assemblyman, assemblywoman, councilman, councilwoman.

repress *verb* **1** *tyrants repressing the people* subjugate, conquer, vanquish, overpower, overcome, crush, master, dominate, domineer, bully, intimidate, oppress, tyrannize. **2** *repress a rebellion* put down, quell, quash, squash, subdue, suppress, extinguish, stamp out, stop, put an end to. **3** *repress a laugh* | *repress his desire* hold/keep back, hold in, bite back, restrain, suppress, keep in check, check, inhibit, bottle up, silence, muffle, stifle, smother.

Antonyms: ENCOURAGE; SUPPORT; RELEASE; EXPRESS.

repressed *adjective* **1** *a repressed people* subjugated, oppressed, tyrannized. See REPRESS 1. **2** *a repressed laugh* restrained, suppressed, muffled, smothered. **3** *a repressed child* inhibited, withdrawn, restrained.

repression *noun* **1** *the repression of the people* subjugation, domination, oppression, tyrannization. See REPRESS 1. **2** *the repression of the rebellion* quelling, quashing, suppression. See REPRESS 2. **3** *a regime of repression* tyranny, despotism, oppression, dictatorship, authoritarianism, domination, coercion, suppression, subjugation. **4** *the repression of a laugh* holding back, biting back, restraint, suppression, smothering. See REPRESS 3.

repressive adjective *a repressive regime* repressing, tyrannical, despotic, dictatorial, authoritarian, dominating, oppressive, coercive, suppressive, harsh, severe, strict, cruel.

reprieve verb 1 *reprieve the condemned man* postpone/delay punishment of, remit/cancel punishment of, grant a stay of execution to, let off, pardon; *inf.* let off the hook. 2 *the building has been reprieved for a while* give a respite (to), save, rescue.
Antonyms: CHARGE; PUNISH.

reprieve noun *the condemned man has had a reprieve* postponement of punishment, remission/cancellation of punishment, stay of execution, pardon; *inf.* let-off.

reprimand noun *receive a reprimand from the teacher* rebuke, scolding, chiding, reproach, reproof, reproval, lecture, admonition, berating, upbraiding, castigation, tongue-lashing; *inf.* talking-to, telling-off, bawling-out, dressing-down.

reprimand verb *reprimand the students* rebuke, scold, chide, reproach, reprove, lecture, admonish, berate, upbraid, castigate, take to task, rake/haul over the coals, blame, censure, check; *inf.* give a talking-to, tell off, bawl out, give a dressing-down.

reprisal noun retaliation, revenge, vengeance, retribution, redress, requital, recrimination, an eye for an eye, tit for tat.

reproach verb *reproach the government/students for their actions* criticize, find fault with, censure, blame, admonish, condemn, reprehend, disparage, abuse, reprimand, scold, chide, reprove, berate, upbraid, castigate, take to task, rake/haul over the coals; *inf.* give a dressing-down to.

reproach noun 1 *words of reproach* criticism, faultfinding, censuring, admonition, condemnation, abuse, reprimand, scolding, reproof, reproval, upbraiding. 2 *the ugly building is a reproach to the town* discredit, disgrace, shame, source of shame, stigma, blemish, stain, slur. 3 *her behavior brought reproach to the family* discredit, disgrace, shame, dishonor, disrepute, ignominy, scorn, contempt, opprobrium, odium, obloquy.

reproachful adjective disapproving, disappointed, critical, censorious, admonitory, condemnatory, disparaging, reproving, castigatory.

reproduce verb 1 *the copier can reproduce color photographs* copy, make a copy of, duplicate, replicate, photocopy, Xerox, mimeograph, print, transcribe, clone. 2 *reproduce the effect* repeat, recreate, redo, remake, imitate, follow, emulate, echo, mirror, parallel, match, mimic, ape. 3 *the animals seem unable to reproduce* breed, procreate, bear young, produce offspring, give birth, multiply, propagate, proliferate, spawn.

reproduction noun 1 *the reproduction of color photographs* copying, duplicating, photocopying, Xeroxing, printing. *See* REPRODUCE 1. 2 *a reproduction of the painting* copy, duplicate, replica, facsimile, imitation, print. 3 *a reproduction of the photograph* copy, duplicate, facsimile, fax, photocopy, mimeograph, print; *Trademark* Xerox. 4 *animal reproduction* breeding, procreation, producing young, multiplying, propagation, proliferation.

reproof noun 1 *without a word of reproof* reproval, disapproval, disapprobation, reproach, admonition, castigation, criticism, censure, blame, condemnation. 2 *ignore their reproofs* rebuke, scolding, chiding, reproach, lecture, admonition, berating, upbraiding, castigation, criticism, faultfinding, censure.
Antonyms: APPROVAL; PRAISE.

reprove verb *reprove the students* rebuke, scold, chide, reproach, lecture, admonish, berate, upbraid, castigate, take to task, rake/haul over the coals, criticize, check, censure, blame, condemn; *inf.* give a talking-to, tell off, bawl out, give a dressing-down to.

repudiate verb 1 *repudiate one's son/faith* disown, cast off, cut off, abandon, forsake, desert, discard, reject, renounce, disavow, abjure, turn one's back on, have nothing to do with, wash one's hands of. 2 *repudiate a charge/claim* deny, contradict, gainsay, disclaim, disavow. 3 *repudiate a treaty* reject, rescind, revoke, cancel, set aside, overrule, override, disregard, ignore, flout, spurn, dishonor, disobey.
Antonyms: EMBRACE; CONFIRM; ACCEPT.

repugnance noun abhorrence, aversion, revulsion, repulsion, disgust, nausea, distaste, antipathy, dislike, loathing, hatred, reluctance, contempt, odium.

repugnant adjective abhorrent, revolting, repulsive, repellent, disgusting, sickening, nauseating, disagreeable, distasteful, offensive, objectionable, obnoxious, loathsome, hateful, despicable, reprehensible, contemptible, abominable, horrible, horrid, foul, nasty, vile, ugly, odious, heinous.
Antonyms: ATTRACTIVE; AGREEABLE; PLEASANT.

repulsive adjective abhorrent, revolting, repellent, disgusting, sickening, nauseating, disagreeable, distasteful, offensive, objectionable, obnoxious, loathsome, hateful, despicable, reprehensible, contemptible, abominable, horrible, foul, nasty, vile, ugly, odious, heinous.
Antonyms: ATTRACTIVE; AGREEABLE; PLEASANT.

reputable adjective of repute, of good repute, respectable, respected, well-thought-of, esteemed, estimable, worthy, creditable, reliable, dependable, conscientious, trustworthy, honest, honorable, aboveboard, legitimate, upright, virtuous, good, excellent.
Antonyms: DISREPUTABLE; UNTRUSTWORTHY.

reputation noun 1 *have an honest/dishonest reputation* name, estimation, character, repute, standing, position, status, station, rank. 2 *she* *has lost her reputation* good name, good character, good standing, respect, respectability, repute, esteem, fame, celebrity, renown. **3** *has lost its reputation as a good restaurant* name, standing, position, status, stature.

repute noun **1** *a house of ill repute* reputation, name, character. See REPUTATION 1. **2** *they are companies of repute* good reputation, good name, good/high standing, stature, esteem, fame, renown, celebrity, distinction.

repute verb *he is reputed to be a good player* | *reputed to be the father* think, believe, consider, hold, suppose, reckon, judge, assume, presume.

reputedly adverb *he is reputedly the father* supposedly, allegedly, apparently, seemingly.

request noun **1** *come at his request* asking, entreaty, solicitation, petitioning, application, imploration, begging, pleading, behest, supplication, demand, summons, requisition. **2** *make several requests* entreaty, appeal, petition, plea, behest, demand, call, suit.

request verb *request a favor* ask for, solicit, seek, apply for, put in for, call for, entreat, beseech, beg for, plead for, pray for, petition, implore, sue for, supplicate for, requisition, demand, desire.

require verb **1** *we require peace and quiet* need, have need of, stand in need of, lack, be short of, be deficient in, want, wish, desire, crave, miss. **2** *absolute obedience is required* demand, order, command, call for, insist on, ask for, request. **3** *they required him to go* order, instruct, command, oblige, enjoin, bid, compel. **4** *the job requires patience* call for, demand, necessitate, involve, take.

required adjective *required reading* compulsory, obligatory, mandatory, prescribed, recommended, set, essential, necessary, vital.

requirement noun **1** *list your travel requirements* need, want, lack, must, necessity, necessary/essential item, demand. **2** *what are the requirements for the job?* prerequisite, requisite, precondition, specification, qualification, sine qua non, stipulation.

requisite adjective *the requisite amount* required, prerequisite, needed, necessary, essential, indispensable, vital, called-for, demanded, obligatory, mandatory.

requisite noun **1** *list your requisites for the trip* requirement, need, want. See REQUIREMENT 1. **2** *what are the requisites for the job?* requirement, prerequisite, precondition, specification, qualification, stipulation.

requisition noun **1** *put in a requisition for supplies* application, order, claim, request, call, demand, summons. **2** *the requisition of their farm building* commandeering, appropriation, possession, occupation, seizure, confiscation.

requisition verb **1** *requisition more books* apply for, order, put in a claim for, request, call for,

demand. **2** *soldiers requisitioned the farm buildings* commandeer, appropriate, take over, take possession of, occupy, seize, confiscate.

rescind verb repeal, revoke, reverse, abrogate, retract, countermand, overturn, annul, nullify, declare null and void, void, quash, invalidate, cancel, set aside.

rescue verb save, save/deliver from danger, save the life of, come to the aid of, free, set free/loose, release, liberate, emancipate, get out, extricate, redeem, salvage, relieve.
Antonyms: ENDANGER; JEOPARDIZE; IMPRISON.

rescue noun rescuing, saving, deliverance, delivery, freeing, release, liberation, emancipation, extrication, redemption, salvage, relief.

research noun *carry out medical research* investigation, experimentation, fact-finding, testing, exploration, analysis, examination, scrutiny; experiment, assessment, study, review, inquiry, probe, inspection; tests.

research verb *research the new drug* do tests on, investigate, inquire into, look into, probe, explore, analyze, study, examine, scrutinize, review, inspect, experiment with, assess.

resemblance noun likeness, alikeness, similarity, similitude, semblance, identicalness, sameness, uniformity, correspondence, comparability, comparison, parallelism, parity, analogy, affinity, closeness, nearness, agreement, congruity, concurrence, conformity.

resemble verb *he resembles his brother* | *his work resembles hers* be like, look like, bear a resemblance to, be similar to, put one in mind of, remind one of, take after, echo, mirror, parrot, duplicate, parallel; *inf.* favor.

resent verb feel aggrieved at, take offense/umbrage at, take exception to, take amiss, be annoyed/angry at, begrudge, feel bitter about, dislike.

resentful adjective aggrieved, offended, indignant, irritated, displeased, annoyed, angry, irate, incensed, piqued, in high dudgeon, grudging, bitter, embittered, wounded; *inf.* huffed, huffy, in a huff, miffed, peeved.

resentment noun offense, indignation, irritation, displeasure, annoyance, anger, ire, pique, grudgingness, bitterness, animosity, hostility; hard feelings.

reservation noun **1** *the reservation of supplies* putting aside, conservation, saving, retention, storing. See RESERVE verb 1. **2** *the reservation of a room* booking, engaging, chartering. See RESERVE verb 2. **3** *make a reservation* advance booking, booking, engagement, prearrangement; charter/hire arrangements. **4** *have reservations concerning the plan* | *go ahead with some reservation* qualification, proviso, provision, condition, stipulation, limitation, qualm, scruple; hesitancy, doubt, demur. **5** *an American Indian reservation* reserve, preserve, enclave, sanctuary, tract, area, territory.

reserve verb **1** *reserve some food for later* put/set/lay aside, put away, keep back, keep, withhold, conserve, save, retain, store, hoard, stockpile; *inf.* hang on to. **2** *reserve a room* book, engage, arrange for, prearrange for, bespeak, charter, hire. **3** *reserve judgment* put off, postpone, defer, delay, withhold. **4** *reserve the right to refuse* keep, retain, secure; *inf.* hang on to.

reserve *noun* **1** *we have reserves of steel* store, stock, supply, reservoir, pool, cache, fund, stockpile, accumulation, backlog, hoard. **2** *agree with some reserve* reservation, qualification, proviso, condition, limitation, stipulation, qualm, scruple. **3** *her reserve puts people off* self-restraint, restraint, self-control, constraint, aloofness, detachment, distance, remoteness, formality, coolness, coldness, frigidity, reticence, unapproachability, uncommunicativeness, unresponsiveness, shyness, diffidence, secretiveness, taciturnity, silence. **4** *a nature reserve* preserve, reservation, sanctuary, park, tract, territory, area. **in reserve** available, at hand, obtainable, accessible, at one's disposal, on tap.

reserve *adjective a reserve player* in reserve, spare, extra, auxiliary, substitute, alternate.

reserved *adjective* **1** *reserved supplies* conserved, stored, stockpiled. *See* RESERVE *noun* 1. **2** *the table is reserved | reserved rooms* booked, engaged, prearranged (for), taken, spoken for, chartered, hired. **3** *she is reserved, but he is outgoing* self-restrained, aloof, detached, remote, formal, unemotional, undemonstrative, cool, cold, frigid, reticent, unapproachable, uncommunicative, unsociable, unfriendly, unresponsive, unforthcoming, shy, retiring, diffident, secret, secretive, taciturn, silent.
Antonyms: OUTGOING; COMMUNICATIVE; SOCIABLE.

reservoir *noun* **1** *picnic by the reservoir* water source/supply; lake, pool, pond. **2** *pour liquid into the reservoir* container, receptacle, holder, tank, cask, bowl, basin. **3** *reservoir of supplies/ knowledge* reserve, store, stock, supply, pool, cache, fund, stockpile.

reside *verb* **reside in** **1** *he resides in Utah* live in, dwell in, stay in, sojourn in, inhabit, occupy, be settled in. **2** *the strength residing in his personality* be inherent in, be intrinsic to, be contained/present in, rest in, lie in, dwell in, abide in, exist in. **3** *the authority residing in him* vested in, bestowed on, conferred on.

residence *noun* **1** *his residence is in London* house, home, place, dwelling, domicile, habitation; quarters. **2** *take up residence tomorrow | a residence of five years* occupation, occupancy, habitation, inhabitation, tenancy, stay, sojourn.

resident *noun* *all residents pay taxes* inhabitant, occupant, occupier, householder, dweller, resider, sojourner, tenant, local, denizen.

resident *adjective* **1** *a resident housekeeper* live-in, living-in. **2** *the resident population* inhabiting, dwelling, neighborhood, local.

residue *noun* residuum, remainder, remnant, rest, surplus, extra, excess, balance; remains, leftovers, dregs, lees.

resign *verb* **1** *he resigned yesterday* give notice, hand in one's notice, leave, quit. **2** *resign his right to the title* renounce, relinquish, give up, abdicate, surrender, cede. **3** *resign oneself to losing* reconcile. *See* RESIGNED 1. **resign from** *resigned from his post* give up, leave, quit, vacate, retire from.

resignation *noun* **1** *the resignation of his claim* renunciation, relinquishment, abdication. *See* RESIGN 3. **2** *hand over his resignation* letter of resignation, notice, notice to quit. **3** *accept the decision with resignation* resignedness, acceptance, compliance, nonresistance, submission, passivity, patience, forbearance, sufferance, toleration, endurance. **resignation from** *his resignation from his post* leaving, quitting, vacating, retirement from.

resigned *adjective* **1** *resigned to the fact that he would fail* reconciled, acquiescent, submitting, yielding, bowing, acceding. **2** *give a resigned shrug | take a resigned attitude* compliant, unresisting, nonresistant, unprotesting, passive, submissive, subdued, docile, patient, long-suffering, forbearing, tolerant, enduring, stoical.

resilient *adjective* **1** *a resilient material* elastic, springy, rubbery, flexible, pliant, supple, pliable, plastic. **2** *she was usually resilient after illnesses/injuries/disappointments* quick to recover, quick to bounce back, difficult to keep down, irrepressible, tough, strong, hardy.
Antonyms: INFLEXIBLE; RIGID.

resist *verb* **1** *material resisting the action of the rain* withstand, be proof against, repel. **2** *resist the march of progress* stop, halt, prevent, check, stem, curb, obstruct, hinder, impede, block, thwart, frustrate, inhibit, restrain. **3** *resist smoking* abstain from, refrain from, keep from, forbear from, desist from, forgo, avoid. **4** *resist the invading army* fight, battle against, stand up to, withstand, stand one's ground against, hold out against, defy, oppose, confront, struggle against, contend with.

resistance *noun* **1** *their resistance to progress* curb, obstruction, hindrance, impediment, block. *See* RESIST 2. **2** *their resistance against the invaders* fight, battle, opposition, stand, defiance, confrontation, struggle, contention.

resistant *adjective* **resistant to** *material resistant to water | diseases resistant to drugs* proof against, impervious to, unaffected by, unsusceptible to, immune to.

resolute *adjective* determined, resolved, decided, firm, fixed, set, intent, steadfast, constant, earnest, staunch, bold, courageous, serious, purposeful, deliberate, inflexible, unyielding, unwavering, unfaltering, unhesitating, unswerving, unflinching, obstinate, obdurate, strong-willed, dogged, persevering, persistent, tenacious, relentless, unshakable, dedicated.
Antonyms: IRRESOLUTE; DOUBTFUL.

resolute
constant, decisive, determined, faithful, staunch
Any of the above adjectives might apply to you if you take a stand on something and stick to it, or show your loyalty to a person, country, or cause. If you show unswerving loyalty to someone or something you are tied to (as in marriage, friendship, etc.), you would be described as **faithful** (*a faithful wife; a faithful Republican*). **Constant** also implies a firm or steady attachment to someone or something, but with less emphasis on vows, pledges, and obligations; it is the opposite of fickleness rather than of unfaithfulness (*my grandfather's constant confidant*). To be described as **staunch** carries loyalty one step further, implying an unwillingness to be dissuaded or turned aside (*a staunch friend who refused to believe the rumors that were circulating*). To be called **resolute** means that you are both staunch and steadfast, but the emphasis here is on character and a firm adherence to your own goals and purposes rather than to those of others (*resolute in insisting upon her right to be heard*). **Determined** and **decisive** are less forceful words. You can be *decisive* in almost any situation, as long as you have a choice among alternatives and don't hesitate in taking a stand (*decisive as always, she barely glanced at the menu before ordering*). *Determined*, unlike *resolute*, suggests a stubborn will rather than a conscious adherence to goals or principles (*he was determined to be home before the holidays*).

resolution *noun* **1** *admire the resolution of the competitors* resolve, determination, firmness, intentness, steadfastness, constancy, staunchness, boldness, courage, seriousness, purpose, purposefulness, obstinacy, obdurateness, obduracy, willpower, doggedness, perseverance, persistence, tenacity, staying power, dedication. *See* RESOLUTE. **2** *it is our resolution to proceed* resolve, decision, aim, intent, intention, purpose, object, plan, design, aspiration. **3** *the committee/court passed a resolution* motion, declaration, decree, verdict, judgment. **4** *the resolution of the problem/question will take time* resolving, solving, solution, answer, sorting out, working out, unraveling, disentanglement, cracking.

resolve *verb* **1** *he resolved to leave* decide, make up one's mind, determine, settle on, undertake. **2** *resolve the problem* solve, answer, sort out, work out, clear up, fathom, unravel, disentangle, crack. **3** *resolve their doubts* dispel, remove, banish, clear up. **4** *resolve the compound* break down, break up, separate, divide, disintegrate, reduce, dissolve, analyze, anatomize, dissect.

resolve *noun* **1** *their resolve is to win* resolution, decision, aim, intent, intention, purpose. *See*

RESOLUTION 2. **2** *set out with resolve* resolution, determination, firmness of purpose, staunchness, boldness, courage, purposefulness, obstinacy, perseverance, dedication. *See* RESOLUTION 1.

resort *verb* **resort to** *resort to force* fall back on, turn to, have recourse to, look to, make use of, use, utilize, avail oneself of, bring into play/service, exercise.

resort *noun* **1** *a vacation/health resort* vacation spot, retreat; spa. **2** *your only resort is to ask the police* recourse, source of help, expedient, measure, alternative, choice, possibility, hope.

resound *verb* **1** *caves resounding with the noise of waves* reverberate, resonate, echo, ring. **2** *her fame/discovery resounded throughout Europe* be talked about, be made known, spread, circulate, be proclaimed, be famed, be celebrated, be glorified.

resounding *adjective* **1** *resounding tones* reverberating, resonating, resonant, echoing, ringing, sonorous, vibrant. **2** *the party was a resounding success* very great, emphatic, striking, impressive, outstanding, notable, noteworthy.

resource *noun* **1** *use any resource to find help* expedient, resort, course, way, device; means. **2** *draw on one's coal resources* reserve, reservoir, store, stock, supply, pool, fund, stockpile, accumulation, hoard. **3** *person of resource* resourcefulness, initiative, ingenuity, inventiveness, quick-wittedness, cleverness, native wit, talent, ability, capability. **4** *rely on their country's resources* assets, reserves, materials; wealth.

resourceful *adjective* ingenious, inventive, creative, imaginative, quick-witted, clever, bright, sharp, talented, gifted, able, capable.
Antonyms: UNIMAGINATIVE; uninspired.

respect *noun* **1** *their respect for their teacher* esteem, high regard, regard, high opinion, admiration, approbation, approval, appreciation, veneration, reverence, deference, honor, praise, homage. **2** *treat the old lady with respect* deference, consideration, thoughtfulness, attentiveness, politeness, courtesy, civility. **3** *without any respect for/to rhythm* heed, regard, consideration, attention, notice. **4** *correct in all respects* aspect, facet, feature, way, sense, characteristic, particular, point, detail, matter. **5** *with respect to the matter in hand* reference, relevance, regard, relation, connection, bearing.

respect *verb* **1** *they respect their teacher* esteem, have a high opinion of, think highly of, admire, approve of, appreciate, venerate, revere, honor, praise. **2** *they respect his judgment* think highly of, have a high opinion of, value, set store by. **3** *respect other people's privacy | respect the environment* show consideration/regard for, take into consideration, take cognizance of, observe, pay heed/attention to. **4** *respect her wishes | respect the treaty* heed, observe, comply with, follow, abide by, adhere to, obey.

respectable *adjective* **1** *a respectable person/background* reputable, of good repute, upright, honest, honorable, trustworthy, aboveboard, worthy, decent, good, virtuous, admirable, well-bred, proper, decorous. **2** *a respectable effort* reasonable, fair, passable, tolerable, adequate, satisfactory; *inf.* not bad. **3** *earn a respectable salary* reasonable, fairly good, fair, considerable, ample, sizable, substantial; *inf.* not to be sneezed at.
Antonyms: DISHONORABLE; UNWORTHY; SMALL; PALTRY.

respective *adjective* individual, separate, personal, own, particular, specific, various.

respects *plural noun send/pay one's respects* greetings, regards, best wishes, compliments, remembrances.

respite *noun* **1** *a respite from work* rest, break, breathing spell, interval, intermission, recess, lull, pause, hiatus, halt; relief, relaxation; *inf.* breather, letup. **2** *a respite from the penalty* remission, reprieve, stay, stay of execution, suspension, postponement, adjournment, deferment, delay, moratorium.

respond *verb* **1** *"no," she responded* say in response, answer, reply, rejoin, retort, return, riposte, come back, counter. **2** *when the signal came, they responded by firing the cannon* react, act in response. **respond to** *respond to his question/letter* answer, reply to, say in response to, acknowledge.
Antonyms: ASK; QUESTION.

response *noun* **1** *they gave no response to the question* answer, reply, acknowledgment, rejoinder, retort, return, riposte, comeback. **2** *receive a good response to their questionnaire* reply, reaction, feedback; *inf.* comeback.

responsibility *noun* **1** *it is his responsibility to get us there* charge, duty, onus, task, role, liability, accountability, answerability. **2** *the confusion was his responsibility* blame, fault, guilt, culpability. **3** *people of responsibility* maturity, reason, sanity, sense, common sense, soundness, stability, reliability, dependability, trustworthiness, competence, conscientiousness. **4** *a post of responsibility* authority, control, power.

responsible *adjective* **1** *he is responsible for the confusion | who was responsible?* accountable, answerable, to blame, blameworthy, at fault, guilty, culpable. **2** *he is responsible to the president* answerable, accountable. **3** *the children are very responsible* mature, adult, levelheaded, rational, sane, reasonable, sensible, sound, stable, reliable, dependable, trustworthy, competent, conscientious, hardworking, industrious. **4** *a responsible position* authoritative, executive, decision-making, powerful, high, important. **responsible for** *he is responsible for the production department* in charge/control of, accountable for, liable for; *inf.* at the helm of.
Antonyms: IRRESPONSIBLE; UNTRUSTWORTHY.

responsible
accountable, answerable, liable
Responsible is an adjective that applies to anyone who is in charge of an endeavor or to whom a duty has been delegated, and who is subject to penalty or blame in case of default (*responsible for getting everyone out of the building in the event of a fire*). **Answerable** implies a legal or moral obligation for which one must answer (*the parents were held to be answerable for their children's behavior*). **Accountable** is more positive than *responsible* or *answerable*, suggesting that something has been entrusted to someone who will be called to account for how that trust has been carried out (*She was directly accountable to the department head for the funds that had been allocated to her group*). **Liable** is more restricted in scope than any of the foregoing words; it refers exclusively to the assignment of blame or the payment of monetary damages in the event of a mishap (*because he was responsible for the accident, he was held liable for damages*).

responsive *adjective* *a responsive audience* quick to react, reactive, receptive, forthcoming, sensitive, perceptive, sympathetic, susceptible, impressionable, open, alive, awake, aware, sharp.
Antonyms: impassive; APATHETIC.

rest[1] *noun* **1** *seek rest after work* repose, relaxation, leisure, ease, inactivity, respite, time off, breathing space; sleep, slumber. **2** *have a rest after work* sleep, nap, doze, slumber, siesta; *inf.* breather, snooze, forty winks, lie-down. **3** *go away for a rest* break, breathing space, interval, interlude, intermission, lull, pause, holiday, vacation; time off. **4** *a place of rest in the mountains* repose, quiet, quietness, quietude, calm, calmness, tranquillity, peace, peacefulness, stillness, silence, hush. **5** *a rest for the vase* stand, base, holder, support, prop, shelf.

rest[2] *verb* **1** *resting after work* take a rest, put one's feet up, relax, sit down, lie down, go to bed, sleep, take a nap, nap, catnap, doze, slumber; *inf.* take it easy, snooze. **2** *she rested her hands on the table* support, prop, steady, lay, place, position. **3** *the shelf rests on bricks* be supported by, be propped up by, lie on, be laid on, recline on, stand on, sit on. **4** *the result rests on the decision of the jury* depend, rely, hang, hinge, be based, be founded.

rest[3] *noun* *some will go; the rest will stay* remainder, residue, residuum, balance, remnant, surplus, excess, rump; those left, others, remains, leftovers.

rest[4] *verb* *you may rest assured* remain, stay, continue, be left. **rest with** *the arrangements rest with you* be the responsibility of, lie with, reside with.

restful *adjective* **1** *a restful effect* calming, relaxing, soothing, tranquilizing. **2** *a restful place* quiet, calm, tranquil, relaxed, peaceful, placid, still, languid, undisturbed, unhurried, sleepy.
Antonyms: STIMULATING; NOISY.

restitution *noun* reparation, redress, atonement, recompense, compensation, indemnification, indemnity, requital, retribution, remuneration, reimbursement, repayment; amends.

restive *adjective* **1** *the children were restive in church* restless, fidgety, fidgeting. **2** *the crowd grew restive* uneasy, ill at ease, edgy, on edge, tense, worked up, nervous, agitated, unquiet; *inf.* jittery, uptight. **3** *police trying to cope with restive demonstrators* unruly, unmanageable, uncontrollable, refractory, recalcitrant.
Antonyms: CALM; PEACEFUL.

restless *adjective* **1** *pass a restless night* sleepless, wakeful, tossing and turning, fitful. **2** *the crowd grew restless* uneasy, ill at ease, on edge, agitated. *See* RESTIVE 2. **3** *the restless sea* moving, in motion, on the move, changeable, changing. **4** *restless bands of people* unsettled, roaming, roving, wandering, itinerant, traveling, nomadic, peripatetic. **5** *restless children* restive, fidgety, fidgeting.
Antonyms: CALM; COMPOSED.

restoration *noun* **1** *the restoration of the building* renovation, repair, reconditioning, rehabilitation, refurbishment, rebuilding. *See* RESTORE 1. **2** *the patient's restoration* recovery, resuscitation, revitalization. **3** *the restoration of democracy* reinstitution, reestablishment, reinstatement, reinstallation.

restore *verb* **1** *restore the building* renovate, repair, fix, mend, set to rights, recondition, rehabilitate, refurbish, rebuild, reconstruct, remodel, revamp, redecorate, touch up; *inf.* do up, fix up. **2** *a rest will help to restore him* build up, resuscitate, revitalize, refresh, revive, revivify. **3** *restore the dog to its owner* return, give back, hand back, send back. **4** *restore the vase to the shelf* put back, return, replace, reinstate. **5** *restore democracy* reestablish, reinstitute, reinstate, reinstall, reinforce, reimpose.

restrain *verb* **1** *restrain the unruly children/crowd* control, keep under control, hold in check, curb, keep within bounds, subdue. **2** *restrain one's anger* control, check, suppress, repress, contain, smother, stifle, bottle up, rein in; *inf.* keep the lid on. **3** *restrain the boy from jumping* prevent, hold back, hinder, impede, obstruct, delay, inhibit. **4** *restrain the thieves* tie up, bind, chain up, fetter, pinion, confine, lock up, imprison, detain, arrest.

restrained *adjective* controlled, self-restrained, self-controlled, unemotional, undemonstrative, calm, reticent.
Antonyms: IMMODERATE; EMOTIONAL; GARISH; LOUD.

restraint *noun* **1** *he acts as a restraint on their impulsiveness* constraint, check, curb, barrier, block, hindrance, impediment, deterrent, inhibition. **2** *behave with restraint* self-restraint, self-control, self-discipline, moderation, temperateness, prudence, judiciousness. **3** *her restraint puts people off* self-restraint, self-control, self-possession, reserve, lack of emotion, coldness, formality, aloofness, detachment, reticence, uncommunicativeness. **4** *put the thieves in/under restraint* confinement, detention, imprisonment, incarceration, bondage, (a) straitjacket; bonds, chains, fetters, manacles.

restrict *verb* **1** *restrict movement* hinder, impede, hamper, retard, handicap, cramp. **2** *restrict your food consumption* limit, set/impose limits on, keep within bounds, keep under control, regulate, control, moderate. **3** *restrict the prisoners* restrain, confine, lock up, imprison, wall up, hem in.

restricted *adjective* **1** *a restricted space* cramped, confined. **2** *a restricted intake* limited, controlled, regulated, moderate. **3** *a restricted area* out of bounds, off limits; private, closed off.

restriction *noun* **1** *impose currency restrictions* constraint, limitation, control, check, curb, regulation, condition, provision, proviso, stipulation, qualification, demarcation. **2** *the restriction of the space* confinement, crampedness, constraint. **3** *restriction of movement* hindrance, impediment, handicap.

result *noun* **1** *pleased with the result of the talks* outcome, consequence, issue, upshot, sequel, effect, reaction, repercussion, event, end, conclusion, termination, aftermath, product, byproduct; fruits. **2** *the wrong result to the addition* answer, solution.

result *verb* **1** *a fight resulted from the discussion* follow, ensue, issue, develop, stem, arise, evolve, emerge, emanate, occur, happen, come about, eventuate. **2** *it resulted in a draw* end, culminate, finish, terminate.

resume *verb* **1** *resume after lunch* take up, carry on, continue, proceed, go on, recommence, restart, start/begin again. **2** *resume negotiations* take up, carry on, continue, recommence, begin again, reopen, reinstitute. **3** *resume one's seat* take up again, reoccupy, occupy again. **4** *resume ownership* take up again, take back, recover, assume again.

résumé *noun* present a résumé of the events summary, précis, synopsis, abstract, epitome, outline, sketch, abridgment, digest.

resurrect *verb* **1** *Jesus was resurrected* raise from the dead, restore to life, bring back to life. **2** *resurrect old plans/practices* revive, breathe new life into, give new life to, bring back, restore, resuscitate, revitalize, reintroduce, reinstall, reestablish; *inf.* give the kiss of life to.

resurrection *noun* **1** *the resurrection of Jesus* raising from the dead, rising/return from the dead. **2** *the resurrection of old practices* revival, rebirth, renaissance, restoration, resuscitation, rein-

troduction, reinstallation, reestablishment, **643**   resuscitate ~ return
comeback.

resuscitate *verb* **1** *resuscitate him after his collapse* give artificial respiration to, give/administer CPR to, bring around, revive, save; *inf.* give the kiss of life to. **2** *resuscitate old practices* revive, resurrect, breathe new life into, bring back, restore, reintroduce; *inf.* give the kiss of life to.

retain *verb* **1** *retain his job* | *retain the title* keep, keep possession/hold of, hold on/fast to; *inf.* hang on to. **2** *retain the old system* keep, maintain, continue, preserve, reserve. **3** *retain the facts* keep/bear in mind, memorize, remember, call to mind, recall, recollect. **4** *retain a gardener* hire, employ, engage, commission, pay. **Antonyms:** give up (*see* GIVE); DISCONTINUE; DISMISS.

retainer *noun* *pay the attorney a retainer* retaining fee, partial payment, fee, deposit, advance.

retaliate *verb* return like for like, give tit for tat, give as good as one gets, get one's own back, get back at, make reprisal(s), take/exact/wreak revenge, avenge oneself, exact retribution, reciprocate, get even with, even the score, settle a score.

retard *verb* slow down, slow up, hold back, set back, hold up, delay, hinder, hamper, obstruct, impede, decelerate, put a brake on, check, arrest, interfere with, interrupt, thwart, frustrate. **Antonyms:** ACCELERATE; EXPEDITE.

retch *verb* gag, heave, dry-heave, vomit, be sick; *inf.* throw up, puke.

reticence *noun* reserve, restraint, diffidence, uncommunicativeness, secretiveness, quietness, taciturnity, silence.

reticent *adjective* reserved, restrained, diffident, uncommunicative, unforthcoming, secretive, tight-lipped, close-mouthed, quiet, taciturn, silent; *inf.* mum. **Antonyms:** OUTGOING; TALKATIVE.

retire *verb* **1** *he retires at 65* give up work, stop working. **2** *the jury retired* withdraw, go away, go out, depart, exit, take oneself off, leave, absent oneself. **3** *they retire at midnight* go to bed, go to one's room; *inf.* turn in, call it a day, hit the hay/sack. **4** *the troops retired, defeated* withdraw, pull back, fall back, pull out, give ground/way, retreat, decamp.

retirement *noun* **1** *happy in his retirement* retired years, postwork years; *inf.* golden years. **2** *the retirement of the jury* withdrawal, exit. *See* RE-TIRE 2. **3** *they chose to live in retirement from the world* retreat, seclusion, solitude, loneliness, privacy, obscurity.

retiring *adjective* *a retiring young woman* shy, diffident, bashful, self-effacing, shrinking, unassuming, unassertive, reserved, reticent, timid, timorous, nervous, modest, demure, coy, meek, humble. **Antonyms:** BOLD; BRASH.

retract *verb* **1** *retract their horns* | *retracted his fishing line* draw in, pull in, pull back. **2** *retract one's*

statement take back, withdraw, revoke, repeal, rescind, annul, cancel, abrogate, disavow, abjure, renounce, recant, disclaim, backtrack on, renege on, do an about-turn on.

retreat *verb* **1** *the army retreated* withdraw, pull back, fall back, back off, give way/ground, decamp, depart, leave, flee, take flight, turn tail, beat a retreat, beat a hasty retreat. **2** *the tide retreated* go back, recede, ebb.

retreat *noun* **1** *the retreat of the army* withdrawal, pulling back, decamping, departure, flight, evacuation. *See* RETREAT *verb* 1. **2** *he has a retreat in the mountains* refuge, haven, shelter, den, sanctuary, sanctum sanctorum, hideaway, resort, asylum. **3** *seek retreat from the world* retirement, seclusion, solitude, privacy, sanctuary.

retrench *verb* **1** *the company must retrench* cut back, make cutbacks/savings, economize, reduce expenditure, tighten one's belt, husband one's resources; *inf.* draw in one's horns. **2** *costs must be retrenched* curtail, limit, pare, prune, reduce, decrease, diminish.

retribution *noun* punishment, justice, nemesis, what is coming to one, reckoning, reprisal, requital, retaliation, revenge, vengeance, an eye for an eye, tit for tat, measure for measure, redress, reparation, recompense, restitution; just deserts.

retrieve *verb* **1** *retrieve one's property* get back, recover, regain, win back, recoup, redeem, reclaim, repossess, recapture, salvage, rescue. **2** *dogs retrieving sticks* fetch, bring back. **3** *difficult to retrieve the situation* set right, set/put to rights, repair, mend, remedy, rectify, redress, make good.

retrograde *adjective* **1** *retrograde motion* backward, directed backward, retreating, retrogressive, reverse. **2** *retrograde policy* worsening, deteriorating, declining, on the downgrade/wane.

retrospect *noun* in retrospect on looking/thinking back, on reflection, on reconsideration, with hindsight.

return *verb* **1** *they returned at dawn* | *the symptoms returned* go back, come back, reappear, reoccur, come again, come around again. **2** *the ball/boomerang returned* rebound, recoil, boomerang. **3** *return soda bottles* | *return his love letters* give back, send back, take back, carry back, remit. **4** *return the books to the shelves* put back, replace, restore, reinstate, reinstall. **5** *return her greetings* reciprocate, repay, requite, send/give in response to. **6** *the firm returned a profit* yield, bring in, earn, make, net. **7** *"no, I won't," he returned* retort, reply, answer, respond, come back, rejoin, riposte. **8** *return the ball* hit back, send back, throw back. **9** *return a guilty verdict* bring in, deliver, announce, submit. **Antonyms:** set off (*see* SET); KEEP; RETAIN.

return noun **1** *look forward to their return* homecoming, reappearance, reoccurrence. *See* RETURN *verb* 1. **2** *the return of the ball/boomerang* rebound, recoil. **3** *the return of the books to the shelf* replacement, restoration, reinstatement, reinstallation. **4** *the store receives several returns after Christmas* thing/item returned, returned article, reject. **5** *the return on the investment* profit, yield, gain, income, revenue, interest, benefit. **6** *fill in a tax return* statement, report, account, summary, form. **7** *done in return for your help* reciprocation, repayment, response, exchange.

reveal verb **1** *the coat blew back to reveal a red dress* show, display, exhibit, expose to view. **2** *examination revealed a deep cut* bring to light, uncover, expose to view, lay bare, unearth, unveil, unmask. **3** *reveal the details of the affair* disclose, divulge, tell, let out, let on, let slip, give away, give out, leak, betray, make known/public, broadcast, publicize, publish, proclaim.
Antonyms: CONCEAL; HIDE.

revel verb *partygoers reveling all night* celebrate, make merry, have a party, party, carouse, roister; *inf.* live/whoop it up, go on a spree, have a fling, rave, paint the town red. **revel in** *revel in her victory* delight in, take pleasure in, bask in, rejoice in, relish, savor, gloat over, luxuriate in, wallow in.

revel noun *noisy revels* celebration, party, festivity, merrymaking, carousal, carouse, bacchanal; *inf.* spree, bash, jag.

revelation noun **1** *the revelation of the dress beneath* show, display, exhibition, exposure. **2** *the revelation of a deep cut* bringing to light, uncovering, unearthing. *See* REVEAL 2. **3** *the revelation of the details* disclosure, divulgence, telling, leak, betrayal, broadcasting, publicizing, communication, publishing, proclamation. **4** *amazed at his revelations* disclosure, divulgence; private/confidential information.

reveler noun celebrator, partygoer, merrymaker, pleasure-seeker, carouser.

revelry noun celebration, festivities; merrymaking, mirth, carousal.

revenge noun **1** *seek revenge* vengeance, retaliation, retribution, reprisal, requital, redress, satisfaction, eye for an eye, tit for tat, measure for measure. **2** *a heart full of revenge* vengefulness, vindictiveness, spite, spitefulness, malice, maliciousness, ill will, animosity, hostility, hate, hatred, venom, rancor, bitterness.

revenge verb *revenge an injustice* | *revenge oneself* take revenge for, avenge, make retaliation for, retaliate, exact retribution for, take reprisals for, requite, get redress/satisfaction for.

revenue noun income, return, yield, interest, gain; profits, returns, receipts, proceeds, takings, rewards.

reverberate verb resound, echo, ring, vibrate.

revere verb look up to, think highly of, admire, respect, esteem, defer to, honor, reverence, venerate, worship, pay homage to, adore, hold in awe, exalt, put on a pedestal, idolize.
Antonyms: DESPISE; SCORN.

---

revere
admire, adore, idolize, venerate, worship

We might **admire** someone who walks a tightrope between two skyscrapers, **idolize** a rock star, **adore** our mothers, and **revere** a person like Martin Luther King, Jr. Each of these verbs conveys the idea of regarding someone or something with respect and honor, but they differ considerably in terms of the feelings they connote. **Admire** suggests a feeling of delight and enthusiastic appreciation (*admire the courage of the mountain climber*), while *adore* implies the tenderness and warmth of unquestioning love (*he adored babies*). *Idolize* is an extreme form of adoration, suggesting a slavish, helpless love, (*he idolized the older quarterback*). We *revere* individuals and institutions that command our respect for their accomplishments or attributes (*he revered his old English professor*). **Venerate** and **worship** are usually found in religious contexts (*venerate saints and worship God*) but both words may be used in other contexts as well. Venerate is usually associated with dignity and advanced age (*venerate the old man who had founded the company more than 50 years ago*), while *worship* connotes an excessive and uncritical respect (*the young girls who waited outside the stage door worshiped the ground he walked on*).

---

reverence noun *regard the leader with reverence* high esteem, admiration, respect, deference, honor, veneration, worship, homage, adoration, devotion, awe, exaltation.

reverence verb *reverence the leader* revere, admire, respect, defer to, venerate, worship, adore, exalt, idolize. *See* REVERE.

reverent adjective reverential, admiring, respectful, deferential, worshiping, adoring, loving, devoted, awed, submissive, humble, meek.

reversal noun **1** *policy reversal* turn-around, turn-about, about-face, volte-face, change of heart, tergiversation; *inf.* U-turn. **2** *the reversal of roles* change, exchange, trading, trade-off, swapping. **3** *the reversal of the decision/verdict* overturn, overthrow, revocation, repeal, rescinding, annulment, invalidation. **4** *firms/families/armies suffering reversal* failure, misfortune, adversity, vicissitude; reverse, upset, setback, check, defeat. *See* REVERSE noun 3.

reverse verb **1** *reverse the collar* turn around, put back to front, turn inside out. **2** *reverse the barrel* turn upside down, upend, upturn, invert. **3** *reverse the car* move/direct backward, back, back up. **4** *reverse roles* change, change around, exchange, trade, swap. **5** *reverse the decision* alter, change, countermand, undo, set aside, upset, overturn, overthrow, revoke, repeal, void, invalidate, quash.

reverse *adjective* 1 *a reverse trend* opposite, contrary, converse, counter, inverse, contrasting, antithetical. 2 *in reverse order* reversed, backward, inverted, transposed, turned around.

reverse *noun* 1 *the reverse is the case* opposite, contrary, converse, antithesis. 2 *write on the reverse* other side, back, rear, underside, wrong side, flip side, verso. 3 *the firm/family/army has suffered reverses* reversal, upset, setback, nonsuccess, failure, misfortune, mishap, misadventure, blow, disappointment; adversity, hardship, affliction, vicissitude, defeat, rout.

review *noun* 1 *a review of the whole situation* survey, study, analysis, examination, scrutiny, assessment, appraisal. 2 *the salary structure is under review* | *undertake a salary review* reconsideration, reexamination, reassessment, reevaluation, reappraisal, revision, rethink, another look, fresh look. 3 *the general conducting a military review* inspection, parade, display, procession. 4 *his review of the play* criticism, critique, notice, assessment, evaluation, study, judgment, rating. 5 *publish a learned review* journal, periodical, magazine.

review *verb* 1 *review the situation from their point of view* survey, study, analyze, examine, scrutinize, assess, appraise. 2 *it is more than time to review salaries* reconsider, rethink, reexamine, reevaluate, reassess, reappraise, revise. 3 *review the past* remember, recall, recollect, reflect on, look back on, call to mind, summon up, evoke. 4 *review the troops* inspect, view, scrutinize. 5 *review the play/book* criticize, critique, evaluate, assess, appraise, judge, weigh up, discuss.

reviewer *noun* critic, literary/arts critic, commentator.

revile *verb* criticize, rail, abuse, berate, vilify, vituperate.

revise *verb* 1 *revise the text* emend, amend, correct, alter, change, edit, rewrite, redraft, rework, update, revamp. 2 *revise our plans/opinions* reconsider, review, reassess, alter, change.

revision *noun* 1 *the revision of the text* emendation, emending, correction, alteration, editing, updating. *See* REVISE 1. 2 *the revision of our plans/opinions* reconsideration, review, reassessment, change, alteration.

revival *noun* 1 *the revival of the collapsed man* resuscitation. *See* REVIVE 1. 2 *the revival of old traditions* resurrection, rebirth, renaissance, restoration, resuscitation, reintroduction, reinstallation, reestablishment; *inf.* comeback.

revive *verb* 1 *revive the man who collapsed* bring around, resuscitate, give artificial respiration to, give/administer CPR to, save, restore to health; *inf.* give the kiss of life to. 2 *the man soon revived* come around, recover consciousness, recover. 3 *a cup of tea revived her* refresh, restore, cheer up, comfort, enliven, revitalize. 4 *revive old traditions* breathe new life into, give

a new lease on life to, bring back, restore, resuscitate, resurrect, revitalize, reintroduce, reinstall, reestablish.

revoke *verb* repeal, rescind, abrogate, countermand, annul, nullify, declare null and void, make void, void, invalidate, quash, set aside, cancel, retract, withdraw, recall, abjure, overrule, override, reverse.
Antonyms: ENACT; RATIFY.

revolt *verb* 1 *the citizens revolted against the army* rise up, rise, take to the streets, take up arms, rebel, mutiny, show resistance (to). 2 *the filthy sight revolted me* repel, disgust, sicken, nauseate, make sick, turn one's stomach, be repugnant to, make one's skin/flesh crawl/creep, put one off, offend, shock; *inf.* turn one off, give one the creeps/heebie-jeebies.

revolting *adjective* repulsive, repellent, disgusting, sickening, nauseating, distasteful, repugnant, abhorrent, offensive, obnoxious, loathsome, hateful, foul, vile, nasty, shocking, abominable, despicable, reprehensible, contemptible, odious, heinous, obscene.
Antonyms: ATTRACTIVE; PLEASANT; AGREEABLE.

revolution *noun* 1 *the French Revolution* rebellion, revolt, insurrection, uprising, rising, insurgence, mutiny, riot, coup, coup d'état. 2 *a revolution in the fashion industry* drastic change, radical alteration, complete shift, metamorphosis, upheaval, upset, transformation, innovation, reformation, cataclysm. 3 *a revolution of the wheel* rotation, single turn, whirl, round, spin. 4 *revolution of the planets around the sun* orbital motion, orbit, spin.

revolutionary *adjective* 1 *revolutionary troops* rebellious, insurgent, insurrectionary, insurrectionist, mutinous, seditious, factious, insubordinate, subversive, extremist. 2 *revolutionary changes in education* | *revolutionary fashion* progressive, radical, innovative, new, novel, avant-garde, experimental, different, drastic.

revolutionary *noun* rebel, insurgent, insurrectionist, mutineer.

revolve *verb* 1 *the wheel revolved slowly* go around, turn around, rotate, spin, whirl. 2 *revolve around the sun* circle, orbit, gyrate, whirl. 3 *revolve the problem in her mind* turn over, think over, think about, deliberate, consider, reflect on, mull over, ponder, muse over, meditate, ruminate. **revolve around** *her life revolves around her children* be concerned/preoccupied with, focus on, concentrate on.

revulsion *noun* repulsion, disgust, nausea, distaste, aversion, repugnance, recoil, abhorrence, loathing, hate, hatred, detestation, contempt.

reward *noun* 1 *a reward for your efforts* | *a reward for finding the wallet* recompense, payment, remuneration, bonus, bounty, present, gift, tip, gratuity, prize; *inf.* cut. 2 *the criminal got his (just) reward* punishment, penalty, retribution, requital, retaliation; just deserts, deserts; *inf.* comeuppance.

reward *verb reward them for their efforts* recompense, pay, remunerate, give a bounty/present to, tip.

rewarding *adjective teaching math in the Peace Corps was a rewarding experience* satisfying, worthwhile, fulfilling, enriching, edifying, beneficial, profitable, advantageous, productive, valuable.

rhetoric *noun* **1** *the use of rhetoric to win over the crowd* oratory, eloquence, power of speech, delivery. **2** *the literary work was spoiled by rhetoric* bombast, grandiloquence, magniloquence, hyperbole, pomposity, verbosity, wordiness, long-windedness, prolixity, turgidity, extravagant language, purple prose, fustian.

rhetorical *adjective* **1** *rhetorical language/passages* extravagant, pretentious, ostentatious, pompous, high-flown, flamboyant, showy, flowery, florid, oratorical, declamatory, bombastic, grandiloquent, magniloquent, hyperbolic, verbose, long-winded, wordy, prolix, turgid, periphrastic. **2** *rhetorical skills* oratorical, linguistic, verbal, stylistic.

rhyme *noun a nursery rhyme* verse, ditty, poem, song, ode.

rhythm *noun* **1** *musical rhythm* beat, cadence, tempo, pulse, throb, lilt. **2** *poetic rhythm* flow, cadence, meter. **3** *disturb the rhythm of their lives* flow, pattern, tempo, harmony.

ribald *adjective* bawdy, risqué, blue, smutty, broad, vulgar, coarse, earthy, off-color, rude, naughty, racy, suggestive, indecent, indelicate, offensive, filthy, gross, lewd, salacious, licentious, concupiscent.

rich *adjective* **1** *rich and powerful people* wealthy, affluent, well off, well-to-do, prosperous, moneyed, propertied; *inf.* well-heeled, filthy rich, loaded, made of money, rolling in it/money, flush, worth a bundle, on easy street. **2** *rich furnishings/surroundings* opulent, expensive, costly, precious, valuable, priceless, beyond price, lavish, luxurious, lush, sumptuous, palatial, splendid, superb, resplendent, elegant, fine, exquisite, magnificent, grand, gorgeous. **3** *rich in oil/talent* well-provided, well-supplied, well-stocked, abounding, overflowing, replete, rife. **4** *rich supplies of minerals/ideas* copious, abundant, ample, plentiful, plenteous, bountiful. **5** *a rich soil* fertile, productive, fecund, fruitful, lush. **6** *rich food* creamy, fatty, heavy, spicy, highly spiced. **7** *rich wines* full-bodied, heavy. **8** *rich colors* strong, deep, intense, vivid, brilliant, warm, vibrant. **9** *rich voices/music* full, sonorous, resonant, deep, mellow, mellifluous, melodious. **10** *"that is rich, coming from you"* preposterous, outrageous, ridiculous, laughable, risible. **11** *rich jokes* amusing, comical, funny, humorous, hilarious, sidesplitting.

riches *plural noun* **1** *amass riches* money, gold, capital, property, treasure; assets, resources. **2** *a man of riches* wealth, affluence, opulence, prosperity.

richly *adverb* **1** *richly dressed/furnished* expensively, lavishly, luxuriously, sumptuously, palatially, splendidly, superbly, resplendently, magnificently. *See* RICH 2. **2** *an award/punishment richly deserved* fully, in full measure, well, thoroughly, completely, amply, utterly.

rid *verb rid the park of litter* clear, cleanse, purge, purify, free, make free, relieve, deliver, unburden. **get rid of** dispose of, do away with, throw away, remove, dispense with, eliminate, dump, unload, jettison, expel, eject, weed out.

riddle *noun* puzzle, poser, conundrum, brain-teaser, problem, enigma, mystery.

---

riddle
conundrum, enigma, mystery, paradox, puzzle
All of these terms imply something baffling or challenging. A **mystery** is anything that is incomprehensible to human reason, particularly if it invites speculation (*the mystery surrounding her sudden disappearance*). An **enigma** is a statement whose meaning is hidden under obscure or ambiguous allusions, so that we can only guess at its significance; it can also refer to a person of puzzling or contradictory character (*he remained an enigma throughout his long career*). A **riddle** is a mystery involving contradictory statements, with a hidden meaning designed to be guessed at (*the old riddle about how many college graduates it takes to change a light bulb*). **Conundrum** applies specifically to a riddle phrased as a question, the answer to which usually involves a pun or a play on words, such as What is black and white and read all over?; conundrum can also refer to any puzzling or difficult situation. A **paradox** is a statement that seems self-contradictory or absurd, but in reality expresses a possible truth (*Francis Bacon's well-known paradox, The most corrected copies are commonly the least correct*). A **puzzle** is not necessarily a verbal statement, but it presents a problem with a particularly baffling solution or tests one's ingenuity or skill in coming up with a solution (*a crossword puzzle*).

---

ride *verb* **1** *ride a horse* sit on, mount, be mounted on, bestride, manage, control. **2** *ride on a bus* | *ride in a car* travel, go, move, progress.

ride *noun a ride in a car* | *go for a ride* trip, outing, journey, jaunt; *inf.* spin.

ridicule *noun* derision, mockery, laughter, scorn, jeering, gibing, teasing, taunting, chaff, banter, badinage, raillery, satire, sarcasm, irony; *inf.* kidding, ribbing, ragging.

ridicule *verb* deride, mock, laugh at, scoff at, scorn, jeer at, gibe at, make/poke fun at, make a fool of, tease, taunt, chaff, banter; *inf.* kid, rib, rag, send up.

Antonyms: SERIOUS; SENSIBLE; REASONABLE.

rife *adjective* **1** *disease is rife* prevalent, predominant, widespread, common, general, extensive, ubiquitous, universal, global, rampant. **2** *the territory is rife with disease/vermin* abounding, overflowing, alive, swarming, teeming.

riff-raff *noun* rabble, mob, commonality, hoi polloi, scum; dregs of society, undesirables.

rifle *verb looters rifling stores during the blackout* plunder, pillage, loot, despoil, sack, ransack. **rifle through** *rifle through her belongings* ransack, rummage through, go through, rake through, search (through), turn inside out.

rift *noun* **1** *a rift in the rock* fault, split, break, breach, fissure, cleft, crevice, gap, crack, cranny, slit, chink, cavity, opening, space, hole, aperture. **2** *a rift between family members* breach, division, estrangement, schism, split, alienation, quarrel, disagreement, fight, row, altercation, conflict, feud; *inf.* falling-out.

rig *verb* **1** *rig the yacht with sails* equip, supply, furnish, provide, make ready. **2** *rig the results of the vote* falsify, fake, tamper with, doctor, engineer, manipulate, juggle, arrange, massage; *inf.* fix. **rig up** *rig up a shelter* put together, erect/assemble hastily, throw together, improvise.

right *adjective* **1** *his actions were not right* just, fair, equitable, impartial, good, upright, righteous, virtuous, proper, moral, ethical, honorable, honest, principled, lawful, legal. **2** *the right answer/procedure/way* correct, accurate, without error, unerring, exact, precise, valid; *inf.* on the mark. **3** *he is the right owner* rightful, true, genuine, authentic, lawful, legal, legitimate; *inf.* legit. **4** *the right person for the job* suitable, appropriate, fitting, fit, proper, desirable, preferable, ideal. **5** *he came at the right moment* opportune, favorable, convenient, suitable, appropriate, propitious. **6** *in his right mind* sane, sound, rational, lucid, sensible, reasonable, clear-thinking. **7** *he was ill, but he is all right now* | *the engine does not sound right* fine, healthy, in good health, well, fit, normal, sound, unimpaired, up to par; *inf.* up to snuff, up to scratch, in the pink. **8** *the right wing of politics* conservative, reactionary.
Antonyms: WRONG; UNJUST; INACCURATE.

right *adverb* **1** *go right on* straight, directly, in a straight line, as the crow flies. **2** *he will be right down* immediately, instantly, promptly, quickly, straightaway, without delay. **3** *sink right to the bottom* | *come right off its hinges* all the way, completely, entirely, totally, wholly, altogether, utterly, quite. **4** *right in the middle* exactly, precisely, just, squarely; *inf.* smack-dab. **5** *if I remember right* accurately, correctly, properly, exactly, precisely. **6** *you must behave right* | *treat them right* justly, fairly, properly, righteously, virtuously, honorably, honestly, morally, ethically. **7** *it will come out right* well, for the better/best, favorably, advantageously, to one's advantage, beneficially. **right away** at once, immediately, right now, now, straight away, this instant, instantly, promptly, directly, forthwith, without delay/hesitation; *inf.* straight off.

right *noun* **1** *know the difference between right and wrong* lawfulness, legality, goodness, righteousness, virtue, virtuousness, integrity, rectitude, propriety, morality, truth, truthfulness, honesty, honor, honorableness, justice, justness, fairness, equity, equitableness, impartiality; ethics. **2** *his position gives him the right to dismiss people* prerogative, privilege, authority, power, license, permission, warrant, sanction, entitlement. **by rights** in fairness, with justice, properly. **put to rights** right, put/set right, sort out, straighten out, rectify, fix, put in order, tidy up, repair.

right *verb* **1** *he righted himself* | *right the pole* stand/set upright. **2** *right the situation* put to rights, sort out, straighten out, rectify, fix, put in order, tidy up, repair. **3** *right a wrong* set/put right, rectify, compensate for, redress, vindicate.

righteous *adjective* **1** *righteous people* good, virtuous, upright, moral, ethical, law-abiding, honest, innocent, faultless, honorable, blameless, guiltless, pure, noble, God-fearing. **2** *righteous indignation* rightful, justifiable, well-founded, defensible, admissible, allowable, reasonable.
Antonyms: BAD; DISHONEST; SINFUL.

righteousness *noun* goodness, virtue, virtuousness, uprightness, integrity, rectitude, probity, morality, ethicalness, honesty, honor, honorableness, innocence, purity; ethics.

rigid *adjective* **1** *a rigid substance* stiff, hard, taut, inflexible, nonflexible, unbendable, unbending, unyielding, inelastic, nonpliant, unmalleable. **2** *a rigid schedule* fixed, set, firm, inflexible, unalterable, unchangeable, unvarying, invariable, hard and fast. **3** *a man of rigid principles* strict, severe, stern, stringent, rigorous, austere, spartan, harsh, inflexible, intransigent, uncompromising.
Antonyms: FLEXIBLE; LENIENT.

rigor *noun* **1** *the rigor of the regime* strictness, severity, sternness, stringency, austerity, toughness, hardness, harshness, rigidity, inflexibility, intransigence. **2** *this job must be tackled with rigor* meticulousness, punctiliousness, thoroughness, exactness, exactitude, precision, accuracy. **3** *the rigors of winter* hardship; adversity, harshness, severity.

rigorous *adjective* **1** *a rigorous regime* | *rigorous discipline* strict, severe, stern, stringent, austere, spartan, tough, hard, harsh, rigid, inflexible, intransigent, uncompromising, demanding, exacting. **2** *rigorous attention to detail* | *a rigorous search* meticulous, punctilious, painstaking, thorough, laborious, scrupulous, conscientious, nice, exact, precise, accurate. **3** *rigorous weather* harsh, severe, bad, bleak, extreme, inclement.
Antonyms: GENTLE; MILD; SLAPDASH; LAX.

rim *noun* **1** *the rim of a cup* brim, edge, lip,

circumference. **2** *the rim of a lake* edge, border, verge, margin, brink, circumference.

rind *noun* outer layer, peel, skin, husk, crust, integument, epicarp.

ring[1] *noun* **1** *wore a ring on her finger* band, circlet, hoop; gold band; wedding ring, engagement ring, diamond ring, friendship ring, pinkie ring. **2** *a ring around the moon* circle, circlet, loop, circuit, halo, disk. **3** *a circus/boxing ring* arena, enclosure, area. **4** *a ring of people stood around* circle, group, knot, gathering. **5** *a spy ring* gang, syndicate, cartel, mob, organization, confederacy, association, society, combine, alliance, league, fraternity, clique, cabal, junta.

ring[2] *verb* *a fence ringed the area* | *ring the correct answer* circle, encircle, circumscribe, encompass, loop, gird, enclose, surround, hem in, fence in, seal off.

ring[3] *noun* **1** *the ring of the bells* ringing, toll, tolling, peal, pealing, knell, chime, clang, tinkle. **2** *give her a ring* call, telephone call; *inf.* phone call, buzz.

ring[4] *verb* **1** *ring the bells* toll, sound. **2** *the halls rang with music* resound, reverberate, resonate, echo, re-echo. **ring in** *bells ringing in the new year* | *ring in a new regime* herald, signal, announce, usher in. **ring out** *the bells rang out* toll, peal, sound, chime, ding, ding-dong, clang, tinkle.

rinse *verb* *rinse the clothes by hand* | *rinse out the teapot* wash, wash out, wash lightly, clean.

riot *noun* **1** *there was a riot when he was arrested* rebellion, revolt, uprising, insurrection, insurgence, street fight, commotion, disturbance, uproar, tumult, melee, row, scuffle, fracas, fray, brawl, free-for-all. **2** *the garden was a riot of color* lavish display, splash, extravagance, flourish, show, exhibition. **run riot 1** *unsupervised children running riot* rampage, run/go wild, run amok, go berserk; *inf.* raise hell. **2** *flowers running riot in the wilderness* grow profusely, spread uncontrolled.

riot *verb* *crowds rioting in the streets* rebel, revolt, mutiny, take to the streets, run riot, rampage, go on the rampage, run wild/amok, go berserk, fight, brawl.

riotous *adjective* **1** *a riotous assembly* rebellious, mutinous, unruly, disorderly, uncontrollable, ungovernable, unmanageable, insubordinate, rowdy, wild, violent, brawling, lawless, anarchic. **2** *a riotous party* loud, noisy, boisterous, uproarious, rollicking, orgiastic. **3** *a riotous show* hilarious, uproarious, sidesplitting, too funny for words.

ripe *adjective* **1** *ripe fruit/grain/cheese* mature, fully developed, full-grown, ready to eat, ready, mellow, seasoned, tempered. **2** *our plans are now ripe* ready, all ready/set, developed, prepared, arranged, complete, finished. **3** *ripe in years* advanced, far on, old. **4** *sites ripe for development* ready, fit, suitable, right. **5** *the time is ripe* suitable, convenient, opportune, favorable, advantageous, auspicious.

Antonyms: IMMATURE; unripe; GREEN.

ripen *verb* **1** *fruit ripening on the trees* grow ripe, mature, come to maturity, mellow. **2** *ripen the fruit/cheese* make ripe, mature, bring to maturity, make mellow, season. **3** *our plans are ripening* develop, be in preparation, come to fruition.

riposte *noun* retort, rejoinder, answer, reply, response, return, sally; *inf.* comeback.

riposte *verb* retort, rejoin, answer, reply, respond, return, come back.

rise *verb* **1** *the sun rose* | *many hands rose when she asked for volunteers* arise, come/go up, move up, ascend, climb up. **2** *mountains rising above the town* rise up, tower, soar, loom, rear up. **3** *prices rose* go up, get higher, increase, soar, rocket, escalate. **4** *standards have risen* go up, get higher/better, improve, advance. **5** *her voice rose* | *noise levels rose* get higher, grow, increase, become louder, swell, intensify. **6** *the children rose on the arrival of the guest* stand up, get to one's feet, get up, jump up, leap up, spring up, become erect. **7** *he rose at dawn* arise, get up, get out of bed, wake up; *inf.* rise and shine, surface. **8** *rise from the ranks* | *rise up the social ladder* climb, make progress, advance, get on, make/work one's way, be promoted. **9** *the phoenix rose from the ashes* | *Christ rose again* come to life, come back from the dead, be resurrected. **10** *dough rising* swell, expand, enlarge. **11** *citizens rising against the troops* rebel, revolt, mutiny, stage an insurrection, take up arms, mount the barricades. **12** *the river rises in the mountains* | *the argument rose from a misunderstanding* originate, begin, start, commence, issue, spring (up), flow, emanate. **13** *her spirits rose* become more cheerful, grow buoyant, become optimistic/hopeful. **14** *the ground rises here* slope/slant upward, go uphill, climb, mount, get steeper.

Antonyms: SET; FALL; DECREASE; SIT.

rise *noun* **1** *the rise of the sun* rising, ascent. **2** *the rise in prices* increase, escalation, upsurge, upswing. **3** *a rise in standards* improvement, amelioration, advance, upturn. **4** *his rise to power* | *his rise from the ranks* climb, progress, progression, advancement, promotion, aggrandizement. **5** *a rise in the ground* | *climb the rise* incline, elevation, upward slope, acclivity, rising ground, hillock, hill.

risk *noun* **1** *there is a risk of fire* chance, possibility. **2** *take a risk* | *an element of risk in the game* chance, hazard, uncertainty, speculation, venture. **at risk** *put lives at risk* in danger, in peril, in jeopardy.

risk *verb* **1** *risk his life* put at risk, endanger, imperil, jeopardize. **2** *risk getting wet* take the risk of, chance, venture; *inf.* grin and bear it. **3** *risk $5 on the bet* gamble, hazard, chance, venture.

risky *adjective* dangerous, fraught with danger,

hazardous, perilous, unsafe, precarious, touch-and-go, tricky, uncertain; *inf.* chancy, dicey.
Antonyms: SAFE; SECURE.

risqué *adjective* off-color, indecent, indelicate, improper, suggestive, naughty, rude, coarse, earthy, crude, bawdy, smutty, dirty, spicy, racy, salacious, licentious, lewd, ribald.

rite *noun* ritual, ceremony, ceremonial, observance, service, sacrament, celebration, performance, act, practice, tradition, convention, formality, procedure, usage.

ritual *noun* 1 *the ritual of the Japanese tea ceremony* rite, ceremony, observance. *See* RITE. 2 *dislike ritual in public occasions* ceremony, tradition, convention, protocol, custom, habit, procedure, routine, stereotype.

rival *noun* 1 *he defeated his rival | they are rivals for her love* opponent, opposition, adversary, antagonist, contestant, competitor, challenger, vier, contender. 2 *in tennis she has no rival* equal, match, equivalent, fellow, peer.

rival *verb* *rival the south of France* compete with, vie with, match, equal, emulate, measure up to, compare with, bear comparison with, parallel.

rival *adjective* *rival teams* opposed, opposing, competing, in competition, contending, in conflict, conflicting.

rivalry *noun* *rivalry between brothers* opposition, competition, competitiveness, vying, contention, conflict.

road *noun* 1 *well-lit roads* street, avenue, roadway, boulevard, thoroughfare; highway, turnpike, expressway, parkway, freeway. 2 *this is the road to Dallas* way, route, direction.

roam *verb* wander (around/through), rove, ramble, meander, drift, range, travel, walk, tramp, traverse, trek, peregrinate.

roar *verb* 1 *the lion roared | the sergeant roared at the recruits* bellow, yell, bawl, shout, howl, thunder, shriek, scream, cry, bay. 2 *roar at the comedian's jokes* roar/howl with laughter, laugh heartily, guffaw; *inf.* split one's sides, roll in the aisles.

roar *noun* 1 *the lion's roar | the roar of the wind* bellow, growl, yell, bawl, shout, howl, rumble, shriek, scream, cry. 2 *his act was greeted with roars of laughter* guffaw, howl, hoot.

rob *verb* 1 *rob a bank* steal from, burgle, burglarize, hold up, break into. 2 *rob a tourist* steal from, mug; *inf.* rip off. 3 *rob them of their savings* defraud, swindle, cheat, mulct, dispossess; *inf.* diddle, bilk, do out of. 4 *rob them of peace of mind* deprive.

robber *noun* burglar, thief, mugger, stealer, pilferer, housebreaker, looter, raider, bandit, brigand, pirate, highwayman.

robbery *noun* 1 *commit robbery* burglary, theft, thievery, stealing, housebreaking, larceny, pilfering, filching, embezzlement, misappropriation, swindling, fraud. 2 *a robbery at the bank* mugging, holdup, break-in, raid; *inf.* rip-off.

robe *noun* 1 *judges' robes* vestment, habit, costume, gown. 2 *wearing a robe over pajamas* bathrobe, dressing gown, housecoat, kimono, peignoir.

robot *noun* automaton, android, machine.

robust *adjective* 1 *robust young athletes* healthy, strong, vigorous, hale and hearty, energetic, muscular, powerful, powerfully built, tough, rugged, sturdy, stalwart, strapping, brawny, burly. 2 *a robust sense of humor* earthy, crude, coarse, rough, raw, unsubtle, indecorous, unrefined. 3 *a robust attitude to life* sensible, common-sense, no-nonsense, down-to-earth, practical, realistic, pragmatic, hardheaded.
Antonyms: WEAK; FEEBLE; FRAIL.

rock *noun* 1 *rocks dislodged from the cliff* boulder, stone. 2 *that department is the rock on which the company is built* foundation, cornerstone, support, prop, mainstay. 3 *her family is her rock* bulwark, anchor, tower of strength, protection, security.

rock *verb* 1 *the cradle/boat was rocking* move to and fro, swing, sway, roll, lurch, pitch, reel, wobble, undulate, oscillate. 2 *the world was rocked by his death* stun, shock, stagger, astound, astonish, amaze, dumbfound, surprise, shake, take aback, bewilder.

rocket *verb* 1 *it rocketed into the air* shoot up, take off, soar, zoom. 2 *prices have rocketed* soar, increase rapidly, escalate; *inf.* go through the ceiling, skyrocket.

rocky[1] *adjective* 1 *a rocky shore* rock-strewn, craggy, stony, pebbly, rough.

rocky[2] *adjective* *he's a bit rocky after his illness* unsteady, unstable, shaky, tottering, teetering, wobbly, wobbling. 2 *their marriage is rather rocky* unsteady, unstable, uncertain, unsure; *inf.* iffy.

rod *noun* 1 *rods of iron* bar, stick, pole, baton, staff. 2 *spare the rod and spoil the child* cane, stick, birch, switch, wand.

rogue *noun* 1 *rogues who steal from their friends* villain, scoundrel, rascal, reprobate, swindler, fraudster, cheat, deceiver, charlatan, mountebank, sharper, wretch, cad, blackguard, ne'er-do-well, wastrel, good-for-nothing; *inf.* bounder, con man, crook, rotter. 2 *the child is a rogue* scamp, imp, rascal, little devil, mischief-maker.

role *noun* 1 *play the role of King Lear* part, character, representation, portrayal. 2 *in his role as mayor* capacity, function, position, place, situation, job, post, task.

roll *verb* 1 *the wheels rolled* go round/around, turn, turn round/around, rotate, revolve, spin, whirl, wheel. 2 *roll up a newspaper* furl, coil, fold. 3 *as time rolls by | the bus rolled along* pass, go, flow, travel. 4 *roll the lawn/pastry* flatten, level, smooth, even, press down, crush. 5 *ships rolling on the ocean* toss, rock, pitch, lurch, sway, reel. 6 *waves rolling* billow, toss, tumble.

roll noun **1** *a roll of the wheel* turn, rotation, revolution, spin, whirl. **2** *a roll of film/tape* spool, reel, bobbin, cylinder. **3** *buy rolls for lunch* bun; hard roll, crescent roll, croissant, dinner roll. **4** *on the electoral roll* register, list, file, index, roster, directory, catalog. **5** *a roll of drums* boom, reverberation, thunder, rumble. **6** *the roll of the sea* undulation, billowing, swell, tossing, pitching, rocking.

romance noun **1** *she wrote about a world of adventure and romance* fantasy, fancy, whimsy, fabrication, glamour, mystery, legend. **2** *their romance is over* love affair, affair, liaison, attachment, intrigue, courtship, amour. **3** *write romances* love story; romantic fiction, melodrama; *inf.* tearjerker. **4** *entertained us with her romances* fabrication, invention, trumped-up story, piece of fiction, fairy tale, flight of fancy, exaggeration; *inf.* tall tale/story.

romance verb *romancing the girl next door* court, woo, go out with; *inf.* go steady with, date.

romantic adjective **1** *present a romantic picture of his life* unrealistic, idealistic, visionary, Utopian, starry-eyed, optimistic, hopeful. **2** *romantic words* loving, amorous, passionate, fond, tender, sentimental; *inf.* mushy. **3** *a romantic figure in black* fascinating, mysterious, glamorous, exotic, exciting. **4** *tell a romantic tale of his adventures* fantastic, fanciful, imaginative, extravagant, exaggerated, fictitious, improbable, unlikely, implausible.
Antonyms: PRACTICAL; REALISTIC.

romantic noun romanticist, dreamer, visionary, idealist, Utopian.

room noun **1** *take up a lot of room* space, area, territory, expanse, extent, volume, elbowroom. **2** *room for improvement* scope, capacity, margin, leeway, latitude, occasion, opportunity. **3** *she has a room in that building* bedroom, apartment, office.

room verb *we roomed together in college* board, stay, dwell, reside.

rooms plural noun quarters; apartment, residence, dwelling, abode; accommodations, lodgings.

roomy adjective spacious, commodious, capacious, voluminous, ample, generous, sizable, large, broad, wide, extensive.
Antonyms: NARROW; TINY; CRAMPED.

root noun **1** *the plant's roots* radicle, radix, rhizome, tuber, tap root. **2** *the root of the problem* source, origin, fountainhead, starting point, basis, foundation, fundamental, seat, nucleus, kernel, nub, cause, reason, rationale, occasion, motivation; beginnings. **root and branch** completely, entirely, thoroughly, wholly, totally, utterly, radically.

root verb **1** *the seeds/idea rooted* take root, grow roots, become established, set. **2** *rooted to the spot | her fear was deeply rooted* fix, establish, embed, implant, entrench. **root around (in)** *root*

around (in) the drawers rummage through, rifle through, forage through, search, shuffle through, ransack. **root out 1** *root out the weeds* uproot, tear up by the roots. **2** *root out the evil* extirpate, weed out, eradicate, get rid of, remove, do away with, eliminate, abolish, destroy, erase, put an end to. **3** *root out the cause* dig out, unearth, turn up, dredge up, bring to light, discover.

rope noun *tie the logs with a rope | hang the clothes on a rope* cord, cable, line, strand, hawser.

rope verb *rope the logs together* bind, tie, fasten, lash, tether, pinion. **rope in** *rope us in to help* enlist, engage, inveigle, persuade, involve.

roster noun list, listing, rota, roll, register, schedule, agenda, calendar, directory, index, table.

rostrum noun dais, platform, stage, podium.

rosy adjective **1** *rosy cheeks* pink, pinkish, red, reddish, ruddy, rubicund, blushing, glowing, healthy looking. **2** *a rosy future* optimistic, promising, auspicious, hopeful, encouraging, bright, favorable, cheerful, happy, sunny.

rot verb **1** *the material is rotting* decompose, decay, crumble, disintegrate, corrode, perish. **2** *the food is rotting* go bad, spoil, go sour, molder, putrefy, fester. **3** *educational/moral standards are rotting* degenerate, deteriorate, decline, break down, waste away, wither away.

rot noun **1** *material suffering from rot* decomposition, decay, disintegration, corrosion, putrefaction, mold, blight. **2** *combating the rot of urban society* degeneracy, deterioration, decline, dissoluteness. **3** *talk rot* rubbish, nonsense, stuff and nonsense, bunkum, claptrap, twaddle, drivel, moonshine; *inf.* bosh, bunk, tommyrot, gobbledygook, hogwash, poppycock, bull.

rotary adjective rotating, rotational, revolving, turning, gyrating, gyratory, spinning, whirling.

rotate verb **1** *the wheels are rotating* go round/around, move round/around, turn, turn round/around, revolve, spin, whirl, swivel, reel, wheel, gyrate. **2** *the two doctors rotate | the directorship rotates* alternate, take turns, work/act in sequence, take place in rotation.

rotation noun **1** *the rotation of the wheel* revolving, spinning, whirling, gyration. See ROTATE 1. **2** *one rotation of the wheel* turn, revolution, spin, whirl, orbit. **3** *do the work in rotation* alternation, sequence, cycle.

rotten adjective **1** *rotten food | the food is/tastes/ smells rotten* bad, moldy, moldering, spoiled, tainted, sour, rancid, rank, decaying, decomposed, putrid, putrescent, festering, fetid, stinking; *inf.* off. **2** *rotten material* decomposing, decaying, crumbling, disintegrating, corroding, perishing. **3** *rotten teeth* decaying, crumbling, carious. **4** *he is a rotten creep* corrupt, dishonorable, dishonest, untrustworthy, immoral, unprincipled, unscrupulous, villainous, bad, wicked, evil, sinful, iniquitous, vicious, debauched, degenerate, dissolute, dissipated, perverted, wanton; *inf.* crooked, bent.

5 *that was a rotten thing to do* nasty, foul, mean, bad, dirty, filthy, contemptible, despicable, base, scurrilous. **6** *we had a rotten time* miserable, unpleasant, disagreeable, disappointing, regrettable, unfortunate, unlucky. **7** *it is a rotten idea* ill-considered, ill thought out, ill-advised, injudicious. **8** *what a rotten selection of goods* poor, inadequate, inferior, substandard, unsatisfactory, unacceptable; *inf.* lousy, crummy. **9** *feeling rotten with the flu* ill, sick, unwell, unhealthy, below par; *inf.* under the weather, poorly, lousy, yucky.
Antonyms: FRESH; NICE; PLEASANT; GOOD.

rotund *adjective* **1** *rotund and jolly* plump, chubby, buxom, roly-poly, tubby, well-rounded, portly, stout, corpulent, pudgy, fat, obese, heavy, fleshy. **2** *rotund speech* sonorous, full-toned, round, rich, mellow, resonant, orotund, magniloquent, grandiloquent.

rough *adjective* **1** *rough surfaces* uneven, irregular, bumpy, broken, stony, rugged, jaggy, craggy, lumpy, nodulous. **2** *dogs with a rough coat* shaggy, hairy, bushy, fuzzy, bristly, hirsute. **3** *get involved in some rough play* boisterous, rowdy, disorderly, wild, violent, savage. **4** *rough seas* turbulent, tumultuous, choppy. **5** *rough weather* inclement, stormy, squally, wild, tempestuous, wintry. **6** *he is a rough character* coarse, crude, uncouth, vulgar, unrefined, uncultured, loutish, boorish, churlish, brutish, ill-bred, ill-mannered, unmannerly, impolite, discourteous, uncivil, brusque, blunt, curt. **7** *a few rough words to say to him* curt, sharp, harsh, stern, unfeeling, insensitive. **8** *have a rough time | receive rough treatment* harsh, severe, hard, tough, difficult, unpleasant, disagreeable, nasty, cruel. **9** *had rough luck* unfortunate, undeserved. **10** *he was rough on his son* harsh, hard, stern, unrelenting, merciless, unfeeling, unfair, unjust. **11** *rough wood* crude, raw, unpolished, undressed, uncut, rough-hewn, unrefined, unprocessed. **12** *rough voices* husky, gruff, hoarse, harsh. **13** *rough sounds* discordant, inharmonious, cacophonous, harsh, grating, jarring, strident, raucous. **14** *a rough sketch* rough-and-ready, hasty, quick, sketchy, cursory, crude, incomplete, rudimentary, basic, unpolished, unrefined. **15** *a rough estimate* approximate, inexact, imprecise, vague, hazy.
Antonyms: SMOOTH; GENTLE; REFINED; PRECISE.

rough *noun a gang of roughs* ruffian, thug, bully; *inf.* tough, tough guy, roughneck, bruiser.

rough *verb* roughen, make rough. **rough out** *rough out your ideas* draft, sketch out, outline, adumbrate. **rough up** *roughed up by muggers* maltreat, mistreat, abuse, manhandle, batter, beat up, knock about; *inf.* bash.

rough-and-tumble *adjective a rough-and-tumble brawl* disorderly, scrambling, haphazard, disorganized, rowdy, wild.

round *adjective* **1** *a round shape* circular, ring-shaped, hooplike, annular, cycloid, discoid, disklike, cylindrical, spherical, spheroid, ball-shaped, globelike, globular, globate, globose, orblike, orbicular, orbiculate, bulb-shaped, balloonlike, convex, curved. **2** *a round dozen* complete, entire, whole, full, undivided, unbroken. **3** *clothes to fit a round figure* well-rounded, ample, rotund, chubby, buxom, roly-poly, tubby, portly, stout, corpulent, pudgy, fat, obese. **4** *spent, in round figures, $600* rounded off, approximate, rough; *inf.* ballpark. **5** *the round tones of the singer* sonorous, resonant, rich, full, mellow, flowing, orotund.

---

round
annular, circular, globular, spherical
What do a bicycle wheel, a basketball, and a barrel of oil have in common? All are considered to be **round**, an adjective that may be applied to anything shaped like a circle, a sphere, or a cylinder. But of these three objects, only a basketball is **spherical**, which means having a round body whose surface is equally distant from the center at all points. Something that is **globular** is shaped like a ball or a globe but is not necessarily a perfect sphere (*globular drops of oil leaking from the seam*). A wheel is **circular**, as is a Frisbee; in fact, anything with a round, flat surface in the shape of a ring or a disk may be described as *circular*—whether or not it corresponds to a perfect circle. But only the rings of a tree can be described as **annular**, a word that usually implies having a series of concentric ringlike forms or structures.

---

round *noun* **1** *shaped in a round | cut it in rounds* circle, circlet, ring, hoop, band, disk, cylinder, sphere, ball, globe, orb. **2** *a round of parties* succession, sequence, series, cycle. **3** *two rounds left in the gun* bullet, cartridge, shell. **4** *the first round of the competition* stage, level, division, lap, heat, game.

round *verb round Cape Horn* go around, move around, travel around, sail around, circumnavigate. **round off** **1** *round off the evening | round off his career* finish off, crown, cap, top off, complete, conclude, close, bring to a close/end, end, terminate. **2** *round off the edges* smooth, plane, level, sand. **round up** bring together, gather together, drive together, assemble, collect, group, muster, marshal, rally.

roundabout *adjective* **1** *a roundabout route* indirect, circuitous, meandering, winding, tortuous. **2** *a roundabout way of saying it* indirect, circuitous, discursive, oblique, circumlocutory, periphrastic.

rounds *plural noun the courier's/doctor's rounds* circuit, course, ambit, beat, routine, schedule.

rouse *verb* **1** *rouse the sleeping children* wake, wake up, call, get up. **2** *he finds it difficult to rouse* wake up, awaken, get up, get out of bed, rise. **3** *rouse the crowds to protest | rouse himself to participate* stir up, bestir, excite, incite, egg on, induce, impel, inflame, agitate, whip up, galvanize, stimulate. **4** *the supervisor was really roused* anger, annoy, infuriate, incense, exasperate, work up. **5** *rouse feelings of guilt* stir up, kindle, touch off, provoke, induce, evoke, call up, conjure up.

rousing *adjective* **1** *a rousing speech* inspiring, stimulating, exciting, stirring, inflammatory, moving, exhilarating, inspiriting, encouraging, vigorous, energetic, lively, spirited, enthusiastic, fervent. **2** *three rousing cheers* hearty, vigorous, loud, strong, great, tremendous.

rout *noun* **1** *troops put to rout* disorderly retreat, retreat, flight, headlong flight. **2** *suffer a rout at the hands of the enemy/opponents* crushing defeat, defeat, drubbing, trouncing, conquest, subjugation, overthrow, beating, thrashing; *inf.* licking, pasting.

rout *verb* **1** *they routed the enemy troops and chased them* put to rout/flight, drive off, dispel, scatter. **2** *they easily routed their enemy/opponents* defeat, drub, trounce, worst, conquer, subjugate, overthrow, crush, beat, thrash; *inf.* lick, give a pasting to.

route *noun* course, way, itinerary, road, path.

routine *noun* **1** *he hates to upset his routine* pattern, procedure, practice, custom, habit, wont, program, schedule, formula, method, system, order, way. **2** *have heard the comic's routine before* act, performance, piece, line; *inf.* spiel.

routine *adjective* **1** *carry out routine procedures* usual, normal, everyday, workaday, common, ordinary, typical, customary, habitual, wonted, scheduled, conventional, standard. **2** *he finds the work too routine* boring, tedious, tiresome, monotonous, humdrum, run-of-the-mill, hackneyed, predictable, unexciting, uninspiring.

Antonyms: UNUSUAL; EXCITING.

row[1] *noun* **1** *a row of people* line, column, queue, procession, chain, string. **2** *a row of vegetables* line, column, sequence, series. **3** *a row of seats* line, tier, rank, bank.

row[2] *noun* argument, dispute, disagreement, controversy, quarrel, squabble, tiff, fight, conflict, altercation, brawl, affray, wrangle, scuffle, free-for-all, fracas, melee; *inf.* falling-out, set-to, scrap.

rowdy *adjective* *rowdy drunks* unruly, disorderly, noisy, boisterous, loud, obstreperous, wild, rough, unrestrained, lawless.

Antonyms: PEACEFUL; QUIET; LAW-ABIDING.

rowdy *noun* *police arresting rowdies* ruffian, thug, hooligan, troublemaker, brawler; *inf.* tough, rough.

royal *adjective* **1** *a royal wave* kingly, queenly, kinglike, queenlike, princely, regal, monarchical, sovereign. **2** *royal surroundings* majestic, magnificent, impressive, glorious, splendid, imposing, grand, superb. **3** *have a royal time* excellent, fine, first-rate, first-class, marvelous, wonderful. **4** *he is a royal pain in the neck* extreme, unmitigated, absolute, relentless, outright, sheer.

rub *verb* **1** *rub her sore neck* massage, knead, embrocate. **2** *rub the cat's back* stroke, caress, fondle, pat. **3** *rub the silver lamp* polish, buff up, burnish. **rub in** *rub in the ointment* apply, put on, smear, spread, work in. **rub out/off** *rub out/off the message* erase, wipe off, efface, obliterate, expunge, remove, cancel, delete.

rub *noun* **1** *give her neck a rub* massage, kneading, embrocation. **2** *give the cat's back a rub* stroke, caress, pat. **3** *give the lamp a rub* polish, buffing, burnishing. **4** *there's the rub* difficulty, problem, trouble, drawback, snag, hitch, hindrance, obstacle, obstruction, impediment.

rubbish *noun* **1** *throw out the rubbish* garbage, trash, waste, refuse, litter, junk, debris, detritus, dross, rubble, scrap, flotsam and jetsam, sweepings, leavings, dregs, odds and ends. **2** *talking rubbish* nonsense, stuff and nonsense, drivel, gibberish, balderdash, bunkum, twaddle; *inf.* rot, tommyrot, bunk, gobbledygook, bosh, piffle, hogwash.

ruddy *adjective* *a ruddy complexion* red, reddish, pink, pinkish, rosy, rosy-cheeked, rubicund, flushed, blushing, glowing, fresh, healthy.

rude *adjective* **1** *offended by rude people* mannerless, ill-mannered, bad-mannered, impolite, discourteous, impertinent, insolent, impudent, uncivil, disrespectful, churlish, curt, brusque, blunt, offhand, short, offensive. **2** *rude tools* primitive, crude, rudimentary, rough, rough-hewn, simple. **3** *rude peasants* simple, artless, uncivilized, uneducated, untutored, ignorant, illiterate, uncultured, unrefined; rough, coarse, uncouth, oafish, loutish. **4** *rude jokes* vulgar, coarse, indelicate, smutty, dirty, naughty, risqué, blue, ribald, bawdy, licentious. **5** *a rude awakening* sudden, abrupt, sharp, violent, startling, harsh, unpleasant, disagreeable, nasty.

Antonyms: POLITE; SOPHISTICATED.

---

rude
callow, crude, ill-mannered, rough, uncivil, uncouth

Someone who lacks consideration for the feelings of others and who is deliberately insolent is **rude** (*It was rude of you not to introduce me to your friends*). **Ill-mannered** suggests that the person is ignorant of the rules of social behavior rather than deliberately rude (*an ill-mannered child*), while **uncivil** implies disregard for even the most basic rules of social behavior among civilized people (*his uncivil response resulted in his being kicked out of the classroom*). **Rough** is used to describe people who lack polish and refinement (*he was a rough but honest man*), while **crude** is a more negative term for individuals and behavior lacking culture, civility, and tact (*he made a crude gesture*). **Uncouth** describes what seems strange, awkward, or un-mannerly rather than rude (*his uncouth behavior at the wedding*). Although individuals of any age may be rude, crude, ill-mannered, or uncouth, **callow** almost always applies to those who are young or immature; it suggests naïveté and lack of sophistication (*he was surprisingly callow for a man of almost 40*).

rudimentary *adjective* **1** *rudimentary arithmetic* elementary, basic, fundamental, introductory, early. **2** *rudimentary tools* primitive, crude, rough, simple. **3** *a rudimentary organ* undeveloped, immature, incomplete, vestigial.
Antonyms: ADVANCED; SOPHISTICATED.

rudiments *plural noun* basics, fundamentals, beginnings, elements, essentials; foundation; *inf.* nuts and bolts.

rue *verb live to rue her actions* regret, be sorry about, feel apologetic/remorseful about, feel remorse for.

rueful *adjective* regretful, apologetic, sorry, remorseful, contrite, repentant, penitent, woebegone, conscience-stricken, self-reproachful, woeful, plaintive.

ruffian *noun* thug, villain, scoundrel, hoodlum, hooligan, rogue, rascal, miscreant; *inf.* rough, tough, rowdy.

ruffle *verb* **1** *ruffle feathers* disarrange, discompose, disorder, derange, rumple, dishevel, tousle, tangle, mess up; *inf.* muss up. **2** *she gets ruffled in a crisis* annoy, irritate, irk, vex, nettle, rile, anger, exasperate, fluster, agitate, harass, upset, disturb, discompose, perturb, unsettle, disconcert, worry, alarm, trouble, confuse; *inf.* rattle, shake up, hassle.

rugged *adjective* **1** *rugged terrain* rough, uneven, irregular, bumpy, rocky, stony, broken up, jagged, craggy, precipitous. **2** *rugged features* wrinkled, furrowed, lined, gnarled, irregular, weather-beaten, leathery. **3** *rugged manners* | *a rugged beauty* unrefined, unpolished, uncultured, crude, unsophisticated, graceless, inelegant. **4** *you have to be rugged to survive there* tough, hardy, robust, sturdy, strong, vigorous, stalwart, hale and hearty, muscular, brawny, solid, mighty, burly, well-built; *inf.* husky, beefy. **5** *a rugged way of life* tough, harsh, austere, spartan, exacting, taxing, demanding, difficult, hard, arduous, rigorous, strenuous, onerous.
Antonyms: SMOOTH; REFINED; FEEBLE.

ruin *noun* **1** *cities in a state of ruin* | *his plans in ruin* ruination, destruction, devastation, havoc, wreckage, demolition, disintegration, dilapidation, desolation, decay, disrepair. **2** *the ruin of the army* | *the ruin of his hopes* ruination, downfall, overthrow, defeat, undoing, conquest, elimination, termination, end. **3** *businesses facing ruin* ruination, loss, failure, bankruptcy, insolvency, financial failure, deprivation, penury, impoverishment, indigence, destitution, calamity, disaster. **4** *castle ruins* |

the ruins of our hopes remains, relics, remnants, vestiges; wreckage, wreck, remainder, debris, detritus.

ruin *verb* **1** *the rain ruined the crops/dresses* | *it ruined our plans* damage, spoil, wreak havoc on, mar, injure, wreck, botch, make a mess of, mess up, smash, shatter. **2** *the recession ruined him* bring to ruin, bankrupt, make insolvent, impoverish, pauperize. **3** *invading armies ruining cities* | *decisions ruining our hopes* destroy, devastate, lay waste, raze, demolish, crush.
Antonyms: CREATE; RESTORE; ENHANCE; ENRICH.

ruinous *adjective* **1** *a ruinous agreement* | *ruinous expenses* disastrous, devastating, calamitous, catastrophic, cataclysmic, dire, injurious, damaging, crippling, destructive. **2** *ruinous old buildings* in ruins, ruined, dilapidated, decaying, in disrepair, derelict, ramshackle, broken-down, decrepit.

rule *noun* **1** *obey the rules of the realm/society* ruling, law, bylaw, regulation, statute, ordinance, tenet, canon, order, court order, decree, commandment, directive, guideline. **2** *it is a good rule to wait for others to speak* principle, precept, standard, axiom, truth, truism, maxim, aphorism, motto. **3** *as a general rule, children are not allowed* practice, procedure, routine, custom, habit, wont, convention, standard, form. **4** *under the rule of the Tudors* | *the rule of the present government* reign, dominion, sovereignty, kingship, queenship, regime, government, administration, jurisdiction, authority, control, direction, mastery, leadership, command, ascendancy, supremacy, power, sway, influence.
as a rule generally, in general, usually, normally, ordinarily, for the most part, on the whole, mainly.

rule *verb* **1** *the king ruled for ten years* reign, sit on the throne, wear the crown, wield the scepter. **2** *the last administration ruled for only a few months* be in power, be in control, be in authority, be in command, be in charge, govern; *inf.* be at the helm. **3** *the judge ruled that he be released* order, decree, direct, pronounce, make a judgment, judge, adjudge, adjudicate, lay down, decide, determine, resolve, settle, establish. **4** *let common sense rule* prevail, obtain, hold sway, predominate, preponderate. **rule out** *rule out the possibility of arson* preclude, exclude, eliminate, reject, dismiss, disregard, ignore.
rule over *the king/president/administration rules over a wide area* preside over, govern, control, have control of, dominate, direct, administer, manage, regulate.

ruler *noun* sovereign, monarch, king, queen, emperor, empress, head of state, head, governor, president, overlord, chief, chieftain, lord, commander, leader.

ruling *noun* judgment, adjudication, finding, verdict, resolution, decree, pronouncement.
ruling *adjective* **1** *the ruling monarch* reigning,

regnant, on the throne. **2** *the ruling classes* dominant, controlling, governing, commanding, leading, in charge, upper. **3** *the ruling theory* prevalent, predominant, main, chief, principal, widespread, general, popular, universal.

ruminate *verb* *sit and ruminate* think, contemplate, deliberate, ponder, brood, meditate, muse, cogitate; *inf.* put on one's thinking cap. **ruminate on** *ruminating on her problems* think about, think over, give thought to, consider, mull over, brood about, chew over.

rummage *verb* *rummage through* *rummage through drawers/papers* search through, hunt through, forage through, rifle through, ransack, pry into.

rumor *noun* **1** *rumor has it that he has gone* gossip, hearsay, talk; *inf.* the grapevine. **2** *hear a rumor that he has gone* report, story, whisper, canard; information, word, news; tidings; *inf.* buzz.

rumor *verb* *it is rumored that they are wealthy | they are rumored to be wealthy* say, report, think, give out, put about, circulate, spread, pass around, noise abroad, disseminate, gossip, hint, suggest.

rumple *verb* **1** *rumple clothes* crumple, crease, wrinkle, crush, crinkle. **2** *rumple hair* disarrange, tousle, dishevel, ruffle, mess up; *inf.* muss up.

rumpus *noun* disturbance, row, uproar, commotion, brouhaha, fracas, brawl, free-for-all, melee, riot.

run *verb* **1** *she ran to catch the bus* race, rush, hasten, hurry, dash, sprint, bolt, dart, gallop, career along, tear along, charge along, speed along, jog along, scurry, scamper, scramble; *inf.* scoot, step on it, get a move on, hotfoot it. **2** *the prisoners ran from the camp* abscond, flee, take flight, take oneself off, make off, decamp, bolt, beat a retreat, make a run for it, clear out, make one's getaway, escape; *inf.* beat it, vamoose, skedaddle, split, cut and run, hightail it. **3** *trains run on tracks* move, go, get along, travel. **4** *the river runs by* glide, course, roll, slide. **5** *leave the engine running* go, operate, function. **6** *the lease runs for 20 years* operate, be in operation, be valid, be current, continue. **7** *the play is running until Christmas* be staged, be presented, be performed, be on, be put on. **8** *the road runs along the coast | the path runs from the lake to the village* go, continue, proceed, extend, stretch. **9** *prices/tempers are running high* get, go, reach, stretch. **10** *he has decided not to run in a race | the horse will run* compete, take part, enter, be in the race. **11** *run for president* stand, stand as candidate, be a contender, put oneself forward. **12** *water running* flow, issue, stream, pour, gush, cascade, spurt, jet, trickle, leak. **13** *walls running with water* be wet with, stream with, flow with, drip with, be flooded by. **14** *run the water* turn

on, switch on. **15** *ink ran over the surface* spread, be diffused, extend, stretch. **16** *the dye from the shirt ran all over the pants* spread, be diffused, bleed. **17** *the butter ran* melt, dissolve, liquefy, thaw. **18** *joggers running the course* travel, traverse, go over, complete, finish. **19** *run an errand* go on, do, carry out, perform, fulfill, execute. **20** *the newspaper ran a story about the accident* publish, print, feature, carry. **21** *run a business | run the office* own, operate, conduct, carry on, direct, manage, administer, be in charge/control of, control, head, lead, look after, organize, coordinate, supervise, superintend, oversee; *inf.* boss. **22** *run the children to school* drive, transport, convey. **23** *run guns* smuggle, traffic in, deal in, bootleg. **24** *run them out of town* chase, drive, propel, hunt, put to flight. **25** *ideas running through my mind* go, pass, dart, flow, slide. **26** *run your eye over the page* pass, slide, flick. **27** *tights/stockings running* unravel, tear, be snagged. **28** *her eyes are running because of the cold* stream, exude/secrete/ooze liquid. **run across** *run across an old friend* run into, come across, chance upon, stumble upon; *inf.* bump into. **run away** *the prisoners have run away* abscond, flee, make off, bolt, decamp, clear out, escape. *See* RUN *verb* 2.

run away from *he tries to run away from the problems* avoid, evade, disregard, ignore, take no notice of, pay no attention to, put to the back of one's mind, turn one's back on. **run away with** **1** *run away with his daughter* run off with, elope with, abduct, make off with. **2** *run away with the race* win easily; *inf.* win hands down, win by a mile. **run down** **1** *the driver almost ran down that woman* knock down, knock over, knock to the ground. **2** *the battery has run down | the wind-up toy is running down* stop, halt, cease to function/operate. **3** *she finally ran down the book in a secondhand shop* run to earth, unearth, track down, ferret out, hunt out, dredge up, find, discover, locate. **4** *she is always running down her neighbor* speak ill/badly of, disparage, denigrate, criticize, decry, belittle, revile, vilify; *inf.* knock. **run high** *feelings are running high* be strong, be vehement, be fervent/fervid, be passionate. **run in** *the police finally ran him in* arrest, apprehend, take into custody, jail; *inf.* pull in, collar, nab, bust. **run into** **1** *another car ran into ours* bump into, knock into, collide with, crash into, hit, strike, ram. **2** *I ran into an old friend* run across, chance upon, stumble upon; *inf.* bump into. **3** *the cost runs into thousands of dollars* reach, extend to, be as high/much as. **run low** *supplies are running low* dwindle, diminish, get less, become depleted, become exhausted. **run off** **1** *the children/dog ran off* run away, flee, make off, bolt, beat a retreat, make one's getaway, clear out, escape; *inf.* beat it, hightail it. **2** *run off several copies* copy, duplicate, Xerox. **run off with** **1** *run off with her daughter* run away with, elope, abduct, make off with. **2** *run off with the company funds* abscond with, snatch, steal, pur-

run on 1 *I hope the meeting will not run on into the afternoon* go on, continue, carry on, keep going, last. **2** *she does run on* talk a lot, talk incessantly, chatter on, ramble on. **run out** *supplies have run out* | *run out of food* be finished, give out, dry up, fail, be exhausted; exhaust. **run out on** *he has run out on his family* desert, abandon, forsake, jilt; *inf.* leave high and dry, leave in the lurch. **run over 1** *nearly ran over a rabbit with his car* run down, knock down, knock over, hit. **2** *the bathwater is running over* overflow, overbrim, spill over. **3** *run over a speech* | *run over the figures for tomorrow* run through, look over, go over, go through. **4** *could you run over yesterday's work?* run through, go over, repeat, iterate, recapitulate; *inf.* recap. **run through 1** *run through the speech/figures for tomorrow* run over, go over, look over, look through. **2** *could you run through yesterday's work?* run over, go over, repeat, recapitulate. **3** *run through money* go through, squander, fritter away, dissipate, waste; *inf.* blow. **4** *sadness runs through the book* go through, pervade, permeate, suffuse. **5** *the knight ran through his enemy with a spear* pierce, transfix, stab. **run to 1** *the cost runs to thousands* run into, reach, extend to, be as high/much as. **2** *the family runs to fat* tend to, be disposed/inclined to.
Antonyms: SAUNTER; STROLL.

run *noun* **1** *go for a run* | *break into a run* jog, sprint, dash, gallop, canter, headlong rush, scamper. **2** *the nonstop run from Providence to Boston* trip; route, way, course, itinerary. **3** *a run of fine weather* | *a run of luck/disasters* period, spell, stretch, streak, chain, string, round, cycle, sequence, series, succession. **4** *a run on silver/ice cream* demand, rush, clamor. **5** *different from the general run of applicants* kind, variety, type, sort, class, category, order. **6** *the recent run of events* tendency, trend, tide, course, direction, movement, drift, current, stream. **7** *the chickens' run* enclosure, pen, coop. **8** *a run in her tights* rip, tear, snag. **in the long run** *he will have to pay in the long run* eventually, in the end, ultimately, when all is said and done, in the final analysis. **on the run** *prisoners on the run* running away, fleeing, in flight, bolting, escaping.

runaway *noun* absconder, deserter, escapee, fugitive, truant.

runaway *adjective* **1** *a runaway horse* escaped, loose, on the loose, uncontrolled, out of control, wild. **2** *runaway children/convicts* absconding, escaping, fugitive. **3** *a runaway victory* effortless, easy; *inf.* easy as pie.

rundown *noun* *give them the rundown on/of the situation* analysis, briefing, brief, review, summary, résumé, sketch, outline; *inf.* low-down.

run-down *adjective* **1** *run-down property* dilapidated, tumbledown, ramshackle, brokendown, decaying, decayed, in ruins, ruined, gone to rack and ruin, seedy, shabby, slummy.

2 *feel run-down after an illness* debilitated, out of condition, below par, drained, exhausted, fatigued, tired, enervated, worn-out, unhealthy; *inf.* not oneself, under the weather, pooped.
Antonyms: well-kept; FIT; WELL.

runner *noun* **1** *twenty runners in the field* racer, sprinter, hurdler, jogger, athlete. **2** *runners from the plant* branch, shoot, offshoot, tendril, sucker. **3** *give the message to the runner* messenger, courier, dispatch rider, bearer, errand boy/girl.

running *noun* **1** *take part in the running* racing, race, sprinting, sprint, jogging. **2** *his running of the business* direction, administration, controlling, organization, coordination, supervision. **3** *the smooth running of the business* operation, working, functioning, performance. **4** *out of the running for the job* competition, contest, contention.

running *adjective* **1** *a running battle* continuous, unceasing, incessant, ceaseless, uninterrupted, constant, perpetual. **2** *three weeks running* in a row, in succession, in sequence, one after the other. **3** *running water* flowing, streaming, gushing. *See* RUN *verb* 12.

run-of-the-mill *adjective* ordinary, average, common, middling, mediocre, commonplace, everyday, undistinguished, unexceptional, passable, tolerable, acceptable, fair, not bad; *inf.* nothing special, so-so.
Antonyms: EXTRAORDINARY; EXCEPTIONAL.

rupture *noun* **1** *a rupture in the defenses* break, fracture, crack, split, burst, rent, tear, rift, fissure. **2** *the rupture of the defenses/artery* breaking, fracture, cracking, splitting, bursting. **3** *there has been a rupture in their relationship* | *ruptures exist within the party* rift, estrangement, schism, breakup, breach, division, alienation, variance, disagreement, quarrel, feud; *inf.* falling-out. **4** *an operation for a rupture* hernia.

rupture *verb* **1** *rupture the defenses* | *rupture an organ* break, fracture, crack, split, breach, burst, rend, tear, puncture. **2** *rupture East-West relations* sever, cut off, break off, disrupt, breach.

rural *adjective* country, countryside, pastoral, rustic, agricultural, agrarian, Arcadian.
Antonyms: URBAN; CITY; TOWN.

ruse *noun* trick, stratagem, subterfuge, artifice, device, wile, dodge, ploy, machination, maneuver, tactic, deception, hoax, blind.

rush *verb* **1** *rush to the door* hurry, make haste, hasten, run, race, dash, sprint, bolt, dart, gallop, career, tear, charge, speed, scurry, scamper; *inf.* step on it, get a move on, hotfoot it. **2** *rush the enemy* attack, assault, charge, storm, take by storm, capture, seize. **3** *rush the job through* hurry, hasten, expedite, speed up, accelerate, advance, hustle, press, push.
Antonyms: DAWDLE; DELAY.

rush *noun* **1** *make a rush on the enemy* onslaught, attack, assault, charge. **2** *a rush of water/blood* surge, flow, gush, stream, flood. **3** *no rush for the goods* hurry, haste, speed, swiftness, rapidity, dispatch. **4** *a rush for toys* demand, clamor, run (on). **5** *the Christmas rush* activity, bustle, hubbub, flurry.

rushed *adjective* *a rushed job* hurried, hasty, speedy, quick, fast, swift, rapid, expeditious, prompt.

rustic *adjective* **1** *rustic scenes* country, countryside, rural, pastoral, agricultural, agrarian, Arcadian, bucolic. **2** *rustic pleasures* unsophisticated, plain, simple, homely, homespun. **3** *rustic peasants* artless, plain, simple, homely, unassuming, guileless, naïve, ingenuous, unsophisticated, uncultured, unrefined, unpolished, homespun; coarse, rough, indelicate, uncouth, graceless, awkward, clumsy, inept, maladroit, blundering, lumbering, clodhopping, churlish, boorish.
Antonyms: URBAN; CITY; TOWN.

rustic *noun* countryman, countrywoman, countryperson, peasant, son/daughter of the soil, country cousin/bumpkin, yokel; *inf.* hillbilly, hayseed.

rustle *verb* **1** *silk rustling* | *leaves rustling in the wind* swish, whisper, whoosh. **2** *rustle cattle* steal, purloin, filch, plunder, abduct, kidnap.

rusty *adjective* **1** *rusty parts on the car* rusted, rust-covered, corroded, oxidized. **2** *rusty hair* rust-colored, reddish, reddish-brown, russet, brick-red, brick. **3** *his French is a bit rusty* deficient, impaired, diminished, weak, below par, unpracticed, out of practice, neglected, not what it was. **4** *his voice is rusty* hoarse, croaking, cracked.

rut *noun* **1** *farm roads full of ruts* furrow, groove, track, crack, hollow, hole, pothole, trough, gutter, ditch. **2** *in a rut in his job* humdrum existence, routine job, boring routine; *inf.* daily grind, treadmill, dead end.

ruthless *adjective* merciless, unmerciful, pitiless, compassionless, relentless, unrelenting, remorseless, unforgiving, unsparing, inexorable, implacable, heartless, unfeeling, hard, harsh, severe, stern, grim, cruel, vicious, brutal, barbarous, callous, savage, fierce, ferocious.
Antonyms: MERCIFUL; COMPASSIONATE; GENTLE.

S

sable *adjective* black, jet-black, jet, pitch-black, pitch, black as pitch, raven, ink-black, inky, black as ink, coal-black, black as coal, black as night.

sabotage *noun* **1** *the fire at the factory was an act of sabotage* deliberate destruction/damage/wrecking/impairment/incapacitation, subversive destruction, vandalism, subversion, treachery. **2** *the sabotage of our plans* disruption, spoiling, ruining, ruination, wrecking; *inf.* fouling up.

sabotage *verb* **1** *sabotage the factory machinery* deliberately destroy/damage/wreck, impair, incapacitate, cripple, vandalize; *inf.* foul up. **2** *sabotage our plans* disrupt, spoil, ruin, wreck; *inf.* throw a monkey wrench in the works of, put the kibosh on, foul up.

saccharine *adjective* oversweet, cloying; mawkish, maudlin, sentimental; *inf.* sappy, mushy, schmaltzy.

sack[1] *noun* bag, pack, pouch; shopping bag, tote bag, knapsack, backpack. **hit the sack** go to bed, retire, go to sleep; *inf.* turn in, hit the hay. **the sack** *delinquent workers getting the sack* a dismissal, a discharge, a termination of employment; *inf.* one's marching orders, one's walking papers, a pink slip, the boot, the old heave-ho, the ax.

sack[2] *verb* *sack workers for stealing* discharge, dismiss, terminate (someone's) employment, give the sack; *inf.* kick out, boot out.

sack[3] *verb* *enemy soldiers sacking the city* plunder, ransack, raid, loot, strip, rob, rifle, pillage, maraud, harry, forage, lay waste, wreak havoc on, destroy, ruin, devastate, ravage, vandalize, despoil, rape.

sack[4] *noun* *the sack of the city* plunder, ransacking, raid, looting, stripping, robbing, pillage, marauding, harrying, destruction, ruin, ruination, devastation, ravaging, vandalization, vandalism, despoliation, rape, rapine.

sackcloth *noun* **1** *aprons of sackcloth* sacking, hopsacking, gunny, burlap. **2** *wearing sackcloth* mourning, funeral garments, penitential garments. **in sackcloth and ashes** penitent, penitential, repentant, contrite, sorry, remorseful, regretful, conscience-stricken, guilt-ridden, ashamed, chastened, compunctious.

sacred *adjective* **1** *a sacred place* holy, blessed, blest, hallowed, consecrated, sanctified. **2** *sacred music* religious, spiritual, devotional, church, churchly, ecclesiastical. **3** *sacred beings* godly, divine, deified, supreme, venerated. **4** *in Hinduism the cow is sacred* sacrosanct, inviolable, inviolate, unimpeachable, invulnerable, protected, defended, secure, safe, unthreatened.

Antonyms: PROFANE; SECULAR; TEMPORAL.

sacrifice *noun* **1** *the job was not worth the sacrifice of her principles* giving up, renunciation, abandonment, surrender, relinquishment, yielding, ceding, forfeiture. **2** *make many sacrifices to educate their children* renunciation, relinquishment, loss, self-sacrifice. **3** *give the goat as a sacrifice to their god* offering, gifts, oblation, burnt offering. **4** *the sacrifice of the goat to their god* offering, immolations, hecatomb.

sacrifice *verb* **1** *sacrifice her principles for the job* give up, forgo, renounce, abandon, surrender, relinquish, yield, cede, forfeit. **2** *sacrifice the goat to the god* offer up, offer, immolate.

sacrilege *noun* *sacrilege to vandalize the cross* desecration, profanity, profaneness, profanation, blasphemy, impiety, irreverence, irreligion, godlessness, disrespect.

sacrilegious *adjective* profane, blasphemous, impious, irreverent, irreligious, godless, disrespectful.

sad *adjective* **1** *feeling/looking sad about his departure* unhappy, miserable, sorrowful, gloomy, melancholy, blue, mournful, woebegone, wretched, dejected, downcast, despondent, in low spirits, low-spirited, low, downhearted, depressed, doleful, glum, cheerless, dispirited, disconsolate, heartbroken, brokenhearted, sick at heart, grief-stricken, grieving; *inf.* down, down in the dumps, down in the mouth, in the pits. **2** *the sad events of the past* unhappy, unfortunate, sorrowful, miserable, sorry, depressing, upsetting, distressing, dispiriting, heartbreaking, heart-rending, pitiful, pitiable, grievous, tragic, disastrous, calamitous. **3** *the country is in a sad state* sorry, wretched, deplorable, lamentable, regrettable, unfortunate, pitiful, pitiable, pathetic, shameful, disgraceful.

Antonyms: HAPPY; CHEERFUL; FORTUNATE.

sadden *verb* cast down, deject, depress, dispirit, dampen one's spirits, cast a gloom upon, desolate, upset, distress, grieve, break one's heart, make one's heart bleed.

sadness *noun* unhappiness, misery, sorrow, gloom, melancholy, wretchedness, dejection, despondency, low spirits, depression, dolefulness, glumness, cheerlessness, disconsolateness, brokenheartedness, heartache, grief.

safe *adjective* **1** *the children are safe in bed | the jewels are safe in the bank* safe and sound, secure, protected, sheltered, guarded, defended, free from harm/danger, out of harm's way. **2** *the flood victims are safe* unharmed, all right, alive and well, well, unhurt, uninjured, unscathed, undamaged, out of danger; *inf.* OK, okay, out of the woods. **3** *the place/building is quite safe* secure, sound, risk-free, riskless, impregnable, unassailable. **4** *he is a safe person to leave the children with* reliable, dependable, responsible, trustworthy, tried and true, reputable, upright, honest, honorable. **5** *he is a safe driver | on the safe side* reliable, cautious, circumspect, prudent, unadventurous, conservative, timid, unenterprising. **6** *these crayons are quite safe for children* harmless, innocuous, nontoxic, nonpoisonous.
Antonyms: INSECURE; DANGEROUS; UNRELIABLE; HARMFUL.

safe *noun put money/jewelry in the safe* safety-deposit box, safe-deposit box, cashbox, repository, depository, locker, vault, crypt.

safeguard *noun they need to have some safeguard against fraud* protection, defense, preventive, precaution, security, surety.

safeguard *verb you must safeguard your investment* protect, look after, defend, guard, preserve, secure.
Antonyms: ENDANGER; IMPERIL.

safekeeping *noun leave the children in her safekeeping* protection, care, charge, keeping, surveillance, custody, guardianship, trusteeship, wardship.

safety *noun* **1** *worry about the safety of the children/jewels* safeness, security, secureness. *See* SAFE *adjective* 1. **2** *worry about the safety of the place/building* security, secureness, soundness, riskiness, impregnability, assailability. **3** *ships/refugees reaching safety* shelter, sanctuary, refuge.

sag *verb* **1** *the ceiling sags | the cake sags in the middle* sink, subside, curve down, slump. **2** *the hem of the skirt sags* hang unevenly, droop. **3** *his spirit sagged* fall, flag, fail, wilt, falter, weaken, languish. **4** *industrial production has sagged* fall, decline, decrease, diminish, sink, plummet, tumble; *inf.* take a nosedive.

saga *noun* epic, chronicle, legend, history, romance.

sage *adjective* **1** *give sage advice* wise, judicious, prudent, sensible, shrewd, politic. **2** *a sage old man* wise, sagacious, learned, intelligent, acute, shrewd, discerning, perspicacious; *lit.* sapient.

sage *noun* wise man/woman, learned man/woman, man/woman of letters, philosopher, thinker, savant, pundit, authority, expert, guru.

sail *verb* **1** *learn to sail* boat, cruise, yacht, ride the waves, go by water, go on a sea voyage,

voyage. **2** *we sail tonight* set sail, embark, put to sea, leave port/dock, hoist sail, raise sail, put off, shove off. **3** *he is sailing the ship* steer, captain, pilot, navigate. **4** *swans/clouds sailing by* glide, drift, float, slide, sweep, skim. **5** *sail into the air* soar, wing, fly. **sail into** *he really sailed into the driver of the other car* attack, set about, fall upon; *inf.* lay into, lambaste. **sail through** *sail through the exams* pass easily, gain success in easily; *inf.* walk.

sailor *noun* seaman, seafaring man/woman, seafarer, mariner, marine, (old) salt, sea dog, boatman, yachtsman, yachtswoman; *inf.* tar, gob.

saintly *adjective* saintlike, sainted, holy, godly, pious, God-fearing, religious, devout, blessed, virtuous, righteous, good, moral, ethical, unworldly, innocent, sinless, blameless, pure, angelic.

sake *noun* **1** *stop smoking for the baby's sake* good, well-being, welfare, behalf, benefit, advantage, interest, gain, profit, consideration, regard, concern, account, respect. **2** *for the sake of peace we agreed* cause, reason, purpose, aim, end, objective, object, goal, motive.

salacious *adjective* **1** *salacious literature* lewd, obscene, pornographic, crude, ribald, blue, smutty, filthy, dirty, indecent, indelicate. **2** *a salacious young man* lustful, lecherous, libidinous, licentious, lascivious, promiscuous, loose, wanton.

salary *noun* pay, earnings, remuneration, fee, emolument, stipend, honorarium.

sale *noun* **1** *not concerned in the actual sale of the cars* selling, vending, bargaining. **2** *she gets commission on all sales* deal, transaction. **3** *a ready sale for high-quality furniture* market, outlet, demand; buyers, purchasers, customers, consumers. **for sale** to be bought/purchased, purchasable, in stock, on the market, available, obtainable. **on sale** reduced, marked down, discounted.

salient *adjective discuss the salient points* important, main, prominent, conspicuous, striking, noticeable, obvious, remarkable, pronounced, signal, arresting.
Antonyms: UNIMPORTANT; INCONSPICUOUS.

sallow *adjective a sallow complexion* yellowish, jaundiced-looking, pallid, wan, pale, waxen, anemic, colorless, pasty, pasty-faced, unhealthy-looking, sickly looking.
Antonyms: ROSY; GLOWING.

sally *noun* **1** *enemy troops making a sally into our territory* charge, sortie, foray, thrust, offensive, drive, attack, raid, assault, onset, rush, onrush. **2** *taking a quick sally to the mountains* trip, excursion, expedition, outing, jaunt, visit, tour, airing. **3** *coming out with a series of quick sallies* witticism, bon mot, quip, joke, jest, barb; *inf.* wisecrack, crack.

salon *noun a hairdressing salon* shop, boutique, parlor.

salt *noun* **1** *salt added to the dish* sodium chloride, table salt, sea salt, rock salt. **2** *conversation in need of a little salt* spice, spiciness, flavor, piquancy, pungency, zest, bite, liveliness, vigor; *inf.* zing, zip. **3** *old salts sitting by the harbor* sailor, seaman, sea dog, mariner, seafarer; *inf.* tar, gob. **with a grain of salt** with reservations, skeptically, cynically, doubtfully, suspiciously, disbelievingly.

salty *adjective* **1** *salty water* salted, saline, briny, brackish. **2** *a salty speech* spicy, piquant, sharp, biting, witty, lively, vigorous. **3** *salty jokes* racy, riqué, lusty, improper, vulgar, crude, suggestive, gross, blue, spicy, lewd, obscene; *inf.* raunchy.

salubrious *adjective living in a salubrious place/climate* healthy, health-giving, healthful, beneficial, good for one's health, wholesome, salutary, refreshing, invigorating, bracing. *Antonyms:* UNHEALTHY; unwholesome.

salutary *adjective* **1** *learn a salutary lesson* good, beneficial, good for one, advantageous, profitable, helpful, useful, valuable, practical, timely. **2** *salutary conditions* healthy, health-giving, healthful, wholesome. *See* SALUBRIOUS.

salutation *noun* greeting, salute, address, welcome.

salute *noun raise his hat as a friendly salute* greeting, salutation, address, welcome.

salute *verb* **1** *salute one's neighbor in passing* greet, address, hail, acknowledge, pay one's respects to. **2** *salute the director's achievement* pay tribute to, pay homage to, honor, recognize, acknowledge; *inf.* take one's hat off to.

salvage *noun* **1** *the salvage of the ship* rescue, saving, recovery, reclamation, salvation. **2** *council workers collecting salvage for recycling* waste material, waste paper, scraps, remains.

salvage *verb* **1** *succeed in salvaging the ship* rescue, save, recover. **2** *salvage valuable articles from the fire | salvage her pride* rescue, save, recover, retrieve, reclaim, get back.

salvation *noun* **1** *the salvation of sinners* redemption deliverance, saving, rescue. **2** *regard his work as his salvation* lifeline, preservation, conservation. *Antonyms:* DAMNATION; DOWNFALL; DESTRUCTION.

same *adjective* **1** *the same person I saw yesterday* identical, the very same, selfsame, one and the same, the very. **2** *family members having the same mannerisms* identical, alike, duplicate, twin, indistinguishable, interchangeable, corresponding, equivalent. **3** *this same man later died* selfsame, aforesaid, aforementioned. **4** *the same old food/story* unchanging, unchanged, changeless, unvarying, unvaried, invariable, unfailing, constant, consistent, uniform. **all the same 1** *all the same, I have got to go* nevertheless, nonetheless, still, yet, be that as it may, in any event, anyhow, notwithstanding. **2** *all the same to them whether he stays or goes* immaterial, irrelevant, of no importance, not important, of no consequence, inconsequential. *Antonyms:* DIFFERENT; DISSIMILAR.

same

equal, equivalent, identical, selfsame, tantamount

All of these adjectives describe something that is not significantly different from something else. **Same** may imply, and **selfsame** always implies, that what is referred to is one thing and not two or more distinct things (*they go to the same restaurant every Friday night; this is the selfsame house in which the family once lived*). In one sense, **identical** is synonymous with *selfsame* (*the identical place where we first met*); but it can also imply exact correspondence in quality, shape, and appearance (*wearing identical raincoats*). **Equivalent** describes things that are interchangeable or that amount to the same thing in value, force, or significance (*the equivalent of a free hotel room at a luxury resort*), while **equal** implies exact correspondence in quantity, value, or size (*equal portions of food*). **Tantamount** is used to describe one of a pair of things, usually intangible, that are in effect equivalent to each other (*her tears were tantamount to a confession of guilt*).

sameness *noun complain about the sameness of the work* monotony, lack of variety, identicalness, similarity, uniformity, tedium, tediousness, routine, humdrum, predictability, repetition.

sample *noun* **1** *a sample of his handwriting* specimen, example, instance, illustration, exemplification, representative type, model, pattern. **2** *polled a sample of the population* cross section, sampling, test.

sample *verb sample the wine* try, try out, test, examine, inspect, taste, partake of.

sample *adjective* **1** *a sample section of people* representative, illustrative, typifying. **2** *a sample size of perfume bottle | a sample chapter/episode* test, trial, pilot.

sanctify *verb* **1** *sanctify the building* consecrate, make holy/sacred, bless, hallow, set apart, dedicate. **2** *sanctify sinners* free from sin, absolve, purify, cleanse, wash (someone's) sins away. **3** *a practice sanctified by tradition* sanction, ratify, confirm, warrant, legitimize, legitimatize.

sanctimonious *adjective* self-righteous, holier-than-thou, overpious, pietistic, unctuous, smug, mealy-mouthed, hypocritical, pharisaic; *inf.* goody-goody.

sanction *noun* **1** *receive the sanction of the church/authorities* authorization, warrant, accreditation, license, endorsement, permission, consent, approval, seal of approval, stamp of approval, go-ahead, approbation, acceptance, thumbs-up; backing, support; *inf.* the green light, OK. **2** *laws receiving sanction* ratification, validation, confirmation. **3** *sanctions imposed against certain crimes* penalty, punishment, penalization, penance, sentence. **4** *impose trade* *sanctions on the belligerent country* embargo, ban, boycott.

sanction *verb* **1** *unwilling to sanction the sale* authorize, warrant, accredit, license, endorse, permit, allow, consent to, approve, accept, give the thumbs up to, back, support; *inf.* give the green light to, OK. **2** *sanction the new law* ratify, validate, confirm.
Antonyms: PROHIBIT; BAN; REJECT.

sanctity *noun* **1** *the sanctity of the altar* | *the sanctity of marriage* sacredness, holiness, inviolability. **2** *the sanctity of the priest* holiness, godliness, saintliness, spirituality, religiosity, piety, devoutness, devotion, righteousness, goodness, virtue, purity.

sanctuary *noun* **1** *priests standing in the sanctuary* holy place, church, temple, shrine, altar, sanctum. **2** *find a sanctuary from his pursuers* refuge, haven, shelter, retreat, hide-out, hiding place. **3** *seek sanctuary in the church* safety, safekeeping, protection, shelter, security, immunity. **4** *a bird sanctuary* preserve, reserve, wildlife reserve, reservation.

sane *adjective* **1** *patients not absolutely sane* of sound mind, in one's right mind, *compos mentis*, rational, lucid, in possession of one's faculties; *inf.* all there. **2** *a sane decision* | *a sane course of action* sensible, reasonable, sound, balanced, levelheaded, judicious, responsible, prudent, wise, politic, advisable.
Antonyms: INSANE; MAD; FOOLISH.

sang-froid *noun* composure, coolness, calmness, self-possession, self-control, presence of mind, poise, equanimity, equilibrium, aplomb, nerve, imperturbability, unflappability.

sanguine *adjective* **1** *not sanguine of their chances of success* optimistic, confident, assured, hopeful, buoyant, cheerful, spirited. **2** *a sanguine complexion* florid, ruddy, red, rubicund.
Antonyms: PESSIMISTIC; GLOOMY.

sanitary *adjective* *sanitary conditions in the hospital/restaurant* hygienic, clean, germ-free, antiseptic, aseptic, sterile, unpolluted, salubrious, healthy.

---

sanitary

antiseptic, healthful, hygienic, salubrious, sterile
Americans thrive on cleanliness and the eradication of germs. They try to keep their homes **sanitary**, a term that goes beyond cleanliness to imply that measures have been taken to guard against infections or disease. They demand that their communities provide schools and workplaces that are **hygienic**—in other words, that adhere to the rules or standards promoting public health. But it would be almost impossible to duplicate the conditions found in a hospital, where everything that comes in contact with patients must be **sterile** or free of germs entirely. Most Americans want to make their environment **healthful**, which means conducive to the health or soundness of the body, but they are not interested in making it **antiseptic**, a word that is similar in meaning to *sterile* but implies preventing infections by destroying germs that are already present (*an antiseptic solution*). Many Americans, as they grow older, choose to move to a more **salubrious** climate, a word that means health-giving and applies primarily to an air quality that is invigorating and that avoids harsh extremes.

sanity *noun* **1** *question the patient's sanity* saneness, soundness of mind, mental health, reason, rationality, lucidness. **2** *acknowledge the sanity of the decision* sense, sensibleness, common sense, good sense, reasonableness, rationality, soundness, judiciousness, prudence, wisdom, advisability.

sap *noun* **1** *sap rising in the plants* vital fluids, life fluid, juice. **2** *full of sap and ready to go* vigor, energy, vitality, vivacity, enthusiasm, spirit; *inf.* pep, zip, oomph. **3** *a poor sap taking all the blame* fool, idiot, simpleton, nincompoop, ninny; *inf.* twit, nitwit, chump, jerk, sucker, dupe, schnook.

sap *verb* **1** *completely sapped by the heat* drain, enervate, exhaust, weaken, enfeeble, debilitate, devitalize. **2** *sap their confidence* erode, wear away, deplete, impair, drain, bleed.

sarcasm *noun* derision, scorn, mockery, ridicule, sneering, scoffing, gibing, taunting, irony, satire, lampoon, causticness, trenchancy, acerbity, acrimony, asperity, mordancy, bitterness, spitefulness.

sarcastic *adjective* derisive, derisory, scornful, mocking, sneering, jeering, scoffing, taunting, ironic, sardonic, satirical, caustic, trenchant, acerbic, acrimonious, mordant, bitter, spiteful.

sardonic *adjective* dry, wry, derisory, scornful, mocking, cynical, sneering, jeering, scoffing, contemptuous, ironic, sarcastic, caustic, trenchant, acerbic, mordant, bitter, spiteful.

Satan *noun* the Devil, the Evil One, Old Nick, Prince of Darkness, Lord of the Flies, Lucifer, Beelzebub, Moloch, Belial, Apollyon.

satanic *adjective* diabolical, fiendish, devilish, demonic, demoniac, demoniacal, hellish, infernal, accursed, wicked, evil, sinful, iniquitous, malevolent, vile, foul.

satellite *noun* **1** *launch a satellite into space* spacecraft, space capsule, space station, communications satellite, weather satellite. **2** *satellites requesting independence* protectorate, dependency, colony, dominion.

satellite *adjective* *a satellite state* dependent, tributary, subordinate, puppet, vassal.

satiate *verb* *satiated with food/pleasure* sate, fully satisfy, overfill, surfeit, stuff, glut, gorge, cloy.

satire *noun* **1** *write a satire* burlesque, parody, travesty, caricature, lampoon, skit, pasquinade; *inf.* takeoff, spoof, send-up. **2** *treat them with satire* mockery, ridicule, irony, sarcasm.

satirical *adjective* mocking, ridiculing, taunting, ironic, sarcastic, sardonic, caustic, biting, cutting, stinging, trenchant, mordant, acerbic, pungent, critical, censorious, cynical.

satirize *verb* mock, ridicule, hold up to ridicule, deride, make fun of, poke fun at, parody, lampoon, burlesque, travesty, criticize, censure; *inf.* take off, send up.

satisfaction *noun* **1** *derive satisfaction* fulfillment, gratification, pleasure, enjoyment, delight, happiness, pride, comfort, content, contentment, smugness. **2** *the satisfaction of her desires/demands* fulfillment, gratification, appeasement, assuagement, achievement. **3** *demand satisfaction for the trouble caused* damages, compensation, recompense, amends, reparation, redress, indemnity, restitution, requital, atonement, reimbursement, remuneration, payment.

Antonyms: DISSATISFACTION; DISCONTENT; LOSS.

satisfactory *adjective* adequate, all right, acceptable, fine, good enough, sufficient, competent, up to standard, up to the mark, up to par, up to scratch, passable, average; *inf.* OK, okay.

Antonyms: INADEQUATE; UNACCEPTABLE; POOR; unsatisfactory.

satisfied *adjective* **1** *satisfied desires* fulfilled, gratified, appeased, assuaged. **2** *satisfied with the results of their work* pleased, happy, content, smug; *inf.* like the cat that swallowed the canary. **3** *satisfied that he is telling the truth* convinced, persuaded, sure, positive, confident, certain.

Antonyms: DISSATISFIED; UNHAPPY; UNCERTAIN.

satisfy *verb* **1** *satisfy their appetites/thirst* satiate, sate, slake, quench. **2** *satisfy their desires/demands* fulfill, gratify, appease, assuage, meet, indulge. **3** *satisfy the heating needs* solve, resolve, answer, be the answer to, meet, serve the purpose of, be sufficient/adequate/good enough for. **4** *satisfy the qualification requirements* fulfill, meet, comply with, answer. **5** *satisfy a debt* pay, settle, discharge, square up. **6** *satisfy old scores* make reparation for, atone for, compensate for, recompense. **7** *satisfy the police that he is innocent* convince, persuade, assure, reassure, remove/dispel doubts from, put one's mind at ease/rest.

satisfying *adjective* **1** *a satisfying job* fulfilling, gratifying, pleasing, enjoyable, pleasurable. **2** *give a satisfying reason* satisfactory, reasonable, convincing, reassuring.

saturate *verb* **1** *saturate the garment* wet through, wet, soak, souse, steep, douse. **2** *the rain saturated us* wet through, soak, drench. **3** *bodies saturated with sunshine* permeate, imbue, pervade, suffuse. **4** *saturate the market* overfill, surfeit, glut, satiate, sate.

saturated *adjective* wet through, soaked, soaked to the skin, soaking, soaking wet, drenched, sodden, dripping wet, wringing wet.

sauce *noun* **1** *horseradish sauce* | *a red-wine sauce* gravy, relish, dressing, condiment. **2** *annoyed at their sauce* impudence, impertinence, insolence, rudeness, disrespect, audacity, presumption, temerity, boldness, brazenness, gall, cheek, pertness, brashness; *inf.* sauciness, brass, lip, freshness, back talk.

saucy *adjective* impudent, impertinent, insolent, rude, disrespectful, audacious, presumptuous, bold, brazen, cheeky, pert, brash; *inf.* fresh.

saunter *verb* stroll, amble, wander, meander, traipse, walk, ramble, roam, promenade; *inf.* mosey.

saunter *noun* stroll, meander, walk, turn, airing, promenade, constitutional.

savage *adjective* **1** *a savage blow* | *savage criticism* vicious, ferocious, fierce, brutal, cruel, bloody, murderous, bloodthirsty, inhuman, harsh, grim, terrible, merciless, ruthless, pitiless, sadistic, barbarous. **2** *a savage animal* fierce, ferocious, wild, untamed, undomesticated, feral. **3** *attacked by a savage gang* fierce, ferocious, wild, rough, rugged, uncivilized, barbarous, barbaric. **4** *explorers encountering savage tribes* primitive, uncivilized, uncultivated, wild.

Antonyms: MILD; TAME; CIVILIZED.

savage *noun* **1** *sailors attacked by island savages* barbarian, wild man/woman, native, primitive, heathen. **2** *calling the children savages* barbarian, boor, churl, yahoo. **3** *her attacker was a savage* brute, beast, monster, barbarian, ogre.

save *verb* **1** *save the children from death/danger* rescue, free, set free, liberate, deliver, snatch, bail out, salvage, redeem. **2** *save them from their sinful desires* protect, safeguard, guard, keep, keep safe, shield, screen, preserve, conserve. **3** *save a lot of trouble* prevent, obviate, forestall, spare, make unnecessary, rule out. **4** *save some money/supplies* put aside, set aside, put by, put away, lay by, keep, reserve, conserve, salt away, stockpile, store, hoard. **5** *time to save, not spend* economize, practice economy, be thrifty, be frugal, scrimp, budget, husband one's resources, cut costs, cut expenditure.

Antonyms: ENDANGER; CAUSE; WASTE; SPEND.

savings *plural noun* capital, assets, resources, cache, reserves, funds, nest egg.

savior *noun* rescuer, liberator, deliverer, emancipator, champion, knight in shining armor, Good Samaritan, friend in need.

Savior *noun worshipping the Savior* Christ, Jesus, Jesus Christ, the Redeemer, the Messiah, Our Lord.

savoir faire *noun* finesse, poise, aplomb, social graces, social skill, adroitness, accomplishment, style, tact, tactfulness, diplomacy, discretion, smoothness, urbanity, suaveness; *inf.* savvy.

savor *noun* **1** *the savor of fresh raspberries* taste, flavor, tang, piquancy. **2** *the savor of freshly baked bread in the air* smell, aroma, fragrance, scent, perfume, bouquet, odor. **3** *politics with a savor of fanaticism* hint, suggestion, touch, vein, tone. **4** *the savor of an adventurer's life* enjoyment, joy, excitement, interest, zest, spice, piquancy.

savor *verb* *savor the taste of the soup* | *savor the joys of freedom* taste, enjoy, enjoy to the full/fullest, enjoy to the hilt, appreciate, delight in, take pleasure in, relish, revel in, luxuriate in. **savor of** *a situation savoring of dishonesty* smack of, show signs of, exhibit traces of, suggest, be suggestive of, be indicative of, bear the hallmark of.

savory *adjective* **1** *savory smells from the kitchen* | *savory entrées* appetizing, mouthwatering, fragrant, flavorsome, flavorful, palatable, tasty, delicious, delectable, luscious, toothsome; *inf.* scrumptious. **2** *preferring savory snacks to sweets* salty, piquant, tangy, spicy.
Antonyms: UNPALATABLE; SWEET.

saw *noun* *a book of old saws* saying, proverb, maxim, aphorism, axiom, adage, epigram, dictum, gnome, apothegm, platitude, cliché.

say *verb* **1** *refuse to say his name* speak, utter, mention, voice, pronounce, put into words, give utterance to, give voice to, vocalize. **2** *"it is too expensive," he said* state, remark, announce, affirm, assert, maintain, declare, aver, allege, profess, avow; *lit.* opine; *inf.* come out with. **3** *finding it difficult to say how one feels* express, put into words, tell, phrase, articulate, communicate, make known, convey, reveal, divulge, disclose. **4** *say a short poem* recite, repeat, deliver, declaim, orate, read, perform, rehearse. **5** *what do the instructions say?* indicate, specify, designate, tell, explain, give information (about), suggest. **6** *I would say that it is four miles from here* estimate, judge, guess, hazard a guess, predict, speculate, conjecture, surmise, imagine, assume, suppose, presume. **7** *people said to be spying* state, suggest, allege, claim, put about, report, rumor. **8** *much to be said in favor of the idea* propose, advance, bring forward, offer, introduce, adduce, plead.

say *noun* **1** *everyone being entitled to a say* opinion, view, right to speak, chance to speak, turn to speak, vote, voice; *inf.* (one's) two cents, (one's) two cents worth. **2** *people having no say in the decision* share, part, influence, sway, weight, input. **that is to say** *a fortnight, that is to say fourteen days* in other words, to put it another way, to rephrase it. **to say the least** *to say the least, he is not a good worker* to put it mildly, without any exaggeration, at the very least.

saying *noun* *old sayings about the weather* proverb, maxim, aphorism, axiom, adage, saw, epigram, dictum, gnome, apothegm, platitude, cliché. **it goes without saying (that)** *it goes without saying*

that he will pay of course, naturally, it is taken for granted (that), it is understood/assumed (that), it is accepted (that), it is unquestionable (that).

---

saying
adage, aphorism, apothegm, epigram, epigraph, maxim, proverb

Once burned, twice shy is an old **saying** about learning from your mistakes. In fact, *sayings*—a term used to describe any current or habitual expression of wisdom or truth—are a dime a dozen. **Proverbs**—sayings that are well known and often repeated, usually expressing metaphorically a truth based on common sense or practical experience—are just as plentiful (*her favorite proverb was A stitch in time saves nine*). An **adage** is a time-honored and widely known proverb, such as *Where there's smoke, there's fire*. A **maxim** offers a rule of conduct or action in the form of a proverb, such as *Neither a borrower nor a lender be.* **Epigram** and **epigraph** are often confused, but their meanings are quite separate. An *epigram* is a terse, witty, or satirical statement that often relies on a paradox for its effect (*Oscar Wilde's well-known epigram that The only way to get rid of temptation is to yield to it*). An *epigraph*, on the other hand, is a brief quotation used to introduce a piece of writing (*he used a quote from T. S. Eliot as the epigraph to his new novel*). An **aphorism** requires a little more thought than an *epigram*, since it aims to be profound rather than witty (*she'd just finished reading a book of Mark Twain's aphorisms*). An **apothegm** is a pointed and often startling aphorism, such as Samuel Johnson's remark that *Patriotism is the last refuge of a scoundrel*.

---

scaffold *noun* **1** *painters standing on a scaffold* scaffolding, frame, framework, gantry. **2** *murderers going to the scaffold* gallows, gibbet.

scale[1] *noun* plate, flake, coating, coat, crust, incrustation, covering.

scale[2] *noun* *weigh it on the scale* scales, weighing machine, balance.

scale[3] *noun* **1** *on the Richter scale* | *social scale* graduated system, calibrated system, measuring system, progression, succession, sequence, series, ranking, register, ladder, hierarchy; *inf.* pecking order. **2** *a scale of a hundred miles to the inch* ratio, proportion. **3** *entertain on the grand scale* extent, scope, range, degree, reach.

scale[4] *verb* *scale the high wall* climb, ascend, go up, clamber, mount, clamber up, escalade. **scale down** *scale down the extent of the alterations* reduce, cut down, cut back on, decrease, lessen, lower, trim.

scaly *adjective* flaky, scurfy, rough, scabrous; squamous.

scamp *noun* rascal, rogue, imp, devil, monkey, wretch, scalawag, mischief-maker, troublemaker, prankster, miscreant.

scamper *verb* scurry, scuttle, dart, run, rush,

dash, race, sprint, hurry, hasten, scramble; *inf.*
scoot.

scan *verb* **1** *scan the horizon/evidence* study, examine, scrutinize, survey, inspect, take stock of, search, scour, sweep. **2** *scan the pages of the document* skim, look over, have a look at, glance over, run one's eye over, read through, leaf through, thumb through, flick through, flip through.

scandal *noun* **1** *corruption scandals destroying political careers* wrongdoing, impropriety, misconduct, offense, transgression, crime, sin. **2** *caused a scandal in the village* outrage, disgrace, embarrassment. **3** *bring scandal on the family* disgrace, shame, dishonor, disrepute, discredit, odium, opprobrium, censure, obloquy. **4** *spread scandal about the politician* scandalmongering, slander, libel, calumny, defamation, aspersion, gossip, malicious rumors, dirt, muckraking, smear campaign. **5** *his treatment of her was a scandal* disgrace, shame, pity, crying shame.

scandalize *verb* *scandalized by their unethical behavior* shock, appall, outrage, horrify, affront, disgust, offend, insult, cause raised eyebrows.

scandalous *adjective* **1** *public figures guilty of scandalous behavior* disgraceful, shameful, dishonorable, outrageous, shocking, monstrous, disreputable, improper, unseemly, discreditable, infamous, opprobrious. **2** *spread scandalous rumors* slanderous, libelous, defamatory, scurrilous, malicious, gossiping.

scant *adjective* *pay scant attention* little, minimal, limited, barely sufficient, insufficient, inadequate, deficient.

Antonyms: ABUNDANT; AMPLE; SUFFICIENT.

scanty *adjective* *scanty supplies of food* meager, scant, sparse, small, paltry, slender, negligible, skimpy, thin, poor, insufficient, inadequate, deficient, limited, restricted, exiguous.

Antonyms: ABUNDANT; AMPLE; COPIOUS.

scapegoat *noun* victim, dupe, whipping boy; *inf.* fall guy, patsy.

scar *noun* **1** *a scar left by the wound* mark, blemish, blotch, discoloration, cicatrix, disfigurement, defacement. **2** *cruelty leaves an emotional scar* damage, trauma, shock, injury, suffering, upset.

scar *verb* **1** *scarred by the wound* mark, blemish, blotch, discolor, disfigure, deface. **2** *the war scarred them emotionally* damage, traumatize, shock, injure, upset.

scarce *adjective* **1** *money being scarce* in short supply, short, meager, scant, scanty, sparse, paltry, not enough, too little, insufficient, deficient, inadequate, lacking, at a premium, exiguous. **2** *red squirrels being scarce* rare, infrequent, few and far between, seldom seen/found, sparse, uncommon, unusual.

Antonyms: PLENTIFUL; ABUNDANT; FREQUENT.

scarcely *adverb* **1** *I scarcely know them* hardly, barely, only just. **2** *I can scarcely expect them to believe that* hardly, certainly not, definitely not,

surely not, not at all, on no account, under no circumstances, by no means.

scarcity *noun* **1** *scarcity of money in the recession* dearth, shortage, undersupply, paucity, scantness, meagerness, sparseness, insufficiency, deficiency, inadequacy, lack, exiguity. **2** *the scarcity of red squirrels* rarity, rareness, infrequency, sparseness, uncommonness, unusualness.

scare *verb* frighten, make afraid, alarm, startle, make fearful, make nervous, terrify, terrorize, petrify, horrify, appall, shock, intimidate, daunt, awe, cow, panic, put the fear of God into, scare stiff, make one's blood run cold, make one's flesh crawl/creep, make one's hair stand on end; *inf.* scare the living daylights out of, scare the pants off.

scare *noun* *recovering from a scare* fright, alarm, start, fearfulness, nervousness, terror, horror, shock, panic.

scared *adjective* *scared children running away* frightened, afraid, alarmed, shaken, fearful, nervous, terrified, petrified, horrified, cowed, panic-stricken, panicky.

scarf *noun* muffler, neckerchief, kerchief, cravat, bandanna, headscarf.

scary *adjective* *a scary experience* scaring, frightening, alarming, startling, nerve-racking, terrifying, petrifying, hair-raising, horrifying, appalling, daunting.

scathing *adjective* *scathing criticism* virulent, savage, fierce, ferocious, brutal, stinging, biting, mordant, trenchant, caustic, vitriolic, withering, scornful, harsh, severe, stern.

Antonyms: MILD; GENTLE.

scatter *verb* **1** *scatter seed* | *scatter breadcrumbs for birds* disseminate, diffuse, spread, sow, sprinkle, strew, broadcast, fling, toss, throw. **2** *the crowd scattered* | *police scattered the crowd* break up, disperse, disband, separate, dissolve.

Antonyms: COLLECT; GATHER; ASSEMBLE.

---

scatter
broadcast, diffuse, dispel, disperse, disseminate, dissipate

If you **scatter** something, you throw it about in different directions, often using force (*the wind scattered leaves around the yard*). **Disperse** implies a scattering that completely breaks up a mass or assemblage and spreads the units far and wide (*the crowd dispersed as soon as the storm arrived; the ships were so widely dispersed that they couldn't see each other*). To **dispel** is to scatter or to drive away something that obscures, confuses, or bothers (*to dispel her fears*), while to **diffuse** is to lessen the intensity of something by spreading it out over a broader area (*the curtains diffused the bright sunlight pouring in the window*). **Dissipate** suggests that something has completely dissolved, disintegrated, or vanished (*early-morning mist dissipated by the sun*).

Broadcast originally meant to scatter seed, but it is also used figuratively to mean make public (*The news of the president's defeat was broadcast the next morning*). **Disseminate** also means to publish or make public, but it implies a wider audience and usually a longer duration. You can spend a lifetime *disseminating* knowledge, in other words, but you would *broadcast* the news of the birth of your first grandchild.

scatterbrained *adjective* irresponsible, forgetful, dreamy, woolgathering, with one's head in the clouds, featherbrained, harebrained, erratic, giddy.

scavenge *verb scavenging on the beach for food* search, look for, hunt, forage for, rummage for, scrounge.

scavenger *noun* forager, rummager, scrounger.

scenario *noun* **1** *discuss the scenario with the producer* plot, outline, synopsis, summary, précis, rundown, story line, structure, scheme, plan. **2** *predict a depressing scenario* sequence of events, future situation.

scene *noun* **1** *the scene of the accident* place, location, site, position, spot, setting, locale, whereabouts, arena, stage. **2** *against a scene of confusion* background, backdrop, setting, set, *mise en scène*. **3** *witnessing scandalous scenes* event, incident, happening, situation, episode, affair, moment, proceeding. **4** *look out on beautiful rural scenes* scenery, view, outlook, landscape, vista, panorama, prospect. **5** *the scene created by the bickering couple* fuss, exhibition, outburst, commotion, to-do, upset, tantrum, furor, brouhaha. **6** *football not being his scene* area of interest, field of interest, field, interest, sphere, world, milieu. **7** *appearing in every scene of the play* division.

scenery *noun* **1** *tourists admiring the scenery* view, outlook, landscape, vista, panorama, prospect. **2** *helping to move/paint the scenery* set, stage set, setting, background, backdrop, *mise en scène*.

scenic *adjective* **1** *the scenic route* picturesque, pretty, beautiful, pleasing. **2** *the scenic advantages of the area* landscape, panoramic.

scent *noun* **1** *the scent of new-mown hay* aroma, perfume, fragrance, smell, bouquet, redolence, odor. **2** *dogs losing the scent of the fox* track, trail, spoor. **3** *a scent of scandal about the affair* hint, suggestion, whiff, implication. **4** *wearing an expensive scent* perfume, fragrance, toilet water, eau de cologne.

scent *verb* **1** *dogs scenting the fox* smell, sniff, be on the track/trail of, track, trail. **2** *scenting danger/redundancy* detect, discern, recognize, become aware of, sense, get wind of, sniff out, nose out.

scented *adjective scented paper* perfumed, sweet-smelling, fragrant, aromatic.

schedule *noun* **1** *projects going according to schedule* timetable, plan, scheme, program. **2** *a busy*

schedule appointment list, list of appointments, diary, calendar, social calendar, itinerary, agenda. **3** *a schedule of services/equipment* list, catalog, syllabus, inventory.

schedule *verb schedule the meeting for tomorrow* time, timetable, arrange, organize, plan, program, book, slot (in).

scheme *noun* **1** *a scheme for recycling paper* plan, program, project, course of action, line of action, system, procedure, strategy, design, device, tactics, contrivance. **2** *an attractive color scheme* arrangement, system, organization, disposition, schema. **3** *produce the scheme for the new shopping center* outline, blueprint, design, delineation, diagram, layout, sketch, chart, map, schema. **4** *police discovering his little scheme* plot, ruse, ploy, stratagem, maneuver, machinations, subterfuge, intrigue, conspiracy; *inf.* game, racket.

scheme *verb rebels scheming to overthrow the government* plot, conspire, intrigue, maneuver, plan, lay plans.

scheming *adjective* calculating, designing, conniving, wily, crafty, cunning, sly, tricky, artful, foxy, slippery, underhand, underhanded, duplicitous, devious, Machiavellian.

Antonyms: INGENUOUS; HONEST; ABOVEBOARD.

schism *noun* division, breach, split, rift, break, rupture, separation, splintering, disunion, scission, severance, detachment, discord, disagreement.

scholar *noun* man/woman of letters, learned person, academic, intellectual, pundit, savant; *inf.* bookworm, egghead, highbrow.

scholarly *adjective* learned, erudite, academic, well-read, intellectual, scholastic, literary, studious, bookish, lettered; *inf.* egghead, highbrow.

Antonyms: ILLITERATE; IGNORANT.

scholarship *noun* **1** *works showing scholarship* learning, book learning, knowledge, education, erudition, letters. **2** *people of great scholarship* learning, book learning, letters, erudition, education, academic achievement/attainment/accomplishment. **3** *on a scholarship to the school/college* fellowship, endowment, award, grant.

scholastic *adjective her scholastic record* academic, educational, school.

school *noun* **1** *attend the local school* educational institution, nursery school, primary school, secondary school, comprehensive school, grammar school, high school, academy, seminary, public school, private school. **2** *the music school at the university* department, faculty, division. **3** *belonging to the Impressionist school of art* group, set, proponents, adherents, devotees, circle, class, sect, clique, faction, followers, following, disciples, admirers, votaries, pupils, students. **4** *teachers belonging to the old school* school of thought, outlook, persuasion, opinion, point of view, belief, faith, creed, credo, doctrine, stamp, way of life.

school verb **1** *schooled locally* educate, teach, instruct. **2** *school a horse/oneself in patience* train, coach, instruct, drill, discipline, direct, guide, prepare, prime, verse.

schooling noun **1** *refuse to continue with his schooling* education, instruction, teaching, tuition, learning, book learning. **2** *the schooling of a horse* training, coaching, instruction, drill, discipline.

schoolteacher noun instructor, educator, professor, tutor, pedagogue.

science noun **1** *the science of the universe* body of knowledge/information/facts, branch of knowledge, area of study, discipline. **2** *study science rather than the arts* physical science, physics, chemistry, biology. **3** *pursuits requiring a certain science* skill, art, expertise, expertness, proficiency, dexterity, deftness, facility.

scientific adjective **1** *scientific discoveries* chemical, biological, medical, technical. **2** *requiring a scientific approach* systematic, methodical, orderly, regulated, controlled, exact, precise, mathematical.

scintillate verb **1** *diamonds scintillating* sparkle, twinkle, flash, gleam, glitter, glint, glisten, coruscate. **2** *scintillating at the dinner party* be sparkling, be vivacious, be lively, be witty.

scintillating adjective *scintillating companions/conversation* sparkling, dazzling, vivacious, effervescent, lively, animated, ebullient, bright, brilliant, witty, exciting, stimulating, invigorating.

Antonyms: BORING; DULL; PEDESTRIAN.

scion noun **1** *a scion of a noble family* descendant, heir, offspring, issue, child. **2** *planting scions* shoot, offshoot, cutting, graft.

scoff[1] verb *scoff at* jeer at, mock at, sneer at, gibe at, taunt, laugh at, ridicule, poke fun at, make a fool of, make sport of, rag, revile, deride, belittle, pooh-pooh, scorn; *inf.* knock.

scoff[2] verb *scoff (up) all the biscuits* guzzle, gulp down, devour, finish off.

scold verb **1** *scolded them for being late* rebuke, reprimand, chide, reprove, reproach, remonstrate with, upbraid, berate, censure, lecture, castigate, rake/haul over the coals, read the riot act to, rap over the knuckles; *inf.* tell off, give a talking-to to, give a dressing-down to, bawl out. **2** *nitpickers who always scold* nag, lay down the law, rail, carp, criticize, find fault, complain; *inf.* go on.

---

scold
berate, chide, revile, upbraid, vituperate
A mother might **scold** a child who misbehaves, which means to rebuke in an angry, irritated, and often nagging way, whether or not such treatment is justified. **Chide** is a more formal term than *scold*, and it usually implies disapproval for specific failings (*she was chided by her teacher for using less instead of fewer*), while **berate** suggests a prolonged scolding, usually aimed at a pattern of behavior or way of life rather than a single misdeed and often combined with scorn or contempt for the person being criticized (*he berated his parents for being too protective and ruining his social life*). **Upbraid** also implies a lengthy expression of displeasure or criticism, but usually with more justification than scold and with an eye toward encouraging better behavior in the future (*the tennis coach upbraided her players for missing so many serves*). **Revile** and **vituperate** are reserved for very strong or even violent displays of anger. To *revile* is to use highly abusive and contemptuous language (*revile one's opponent in the press*), while **vituperate** connotes even more violence in the attack (*the angry hockey players were held apart by their teammates, but they continued to vituperate each other with the foulest possible language*).

---

scolding noun rebuke, reprimand, chiding, reproach, upbraiding, lecture, rap over the knuckles; *inf.* talking-to, bawling out.

scoop noun **1** *a scoop of ice cream* ladle, spoon, dipper. **2** *reporters getting a scoop* exclusive story, revelation, exposé.

scoop verb **1** *scoop out the hole* hollow out, gouge out. **2** *scoop out the earth from the site* hollow out, gouge out, dig, excavate. **3** *scoop up the leaves* gather up, pick up, lift.

scope noun **1** *within the scope of the inquiry* extent, range, sphere, area, field, realm, compass, orbit, reach, span, sweep, confine, limit. **2** *a job with much scope* opportunity, freedom, latitude, capacity, room to maneuver, elbowroom.

scorch verb **1** *scorched by an iron* burn, singe, char, sear, discolor. **2** *grass scorched by the sun* burn, dry up, wither, discolor, brown.

scorching adjective **1** *a scorching day* very hot, unbearably hot, sweltering, torrid; *inf.* boiling, broiling, sizzling, baking. **2** *scorching criticism* stringent, scathing, caustic, mordant, trenchant, biting, harsh, severe.

Antonyms: FREEZING; FRIGID.

score noun **1** *enter their score* number of points/goals, record of points/goals, total. **2** *a score of five to two* result, outcome. **3** *rejected on several scores* basis, grounds, reason, account, count. **4** *a score on the table/wall* notch, mark, scratch, scrape, groove, cut, nick, chip, gouge, incision, slit, gash. **5** *money to pay the score* bill, tally, reckoning, amount due, debt, obligation; *inf.* tab. **6** *a score to settle* dispute, grievance, grudge, injury, a bone to pick, a bone of contention. **know the score** be aware of the situation, be aware of the facts, know the truth of the matter, know the true state of affairs; *inf.* know what's what.

score verb **1** *score a point/goal* win, gain, achieve; *inf.* chalk up, notch up. **2** *yet to score* win a point/goal, gain a point. **3** *scoring for the two* *teams* keep count, keep a record, keep a tally. **4** *least likely to score* achieve success, win, triumph, gain an advantage, make an impression; *inf.* be a hit. **5** *score the woodwork* notch, make a notch in, mark, scratch, scrape, make a groove in, cut, nick, chip, gouge, slit, gash.

scores *plural noun* *scores of people at the concert* crowds, throngs, multitudes, droves, swarms, armies, legions.

scorn *noun* *treat the poor with scorn* contempt, contemptuousness, disdain, haughtiness, disparagement, derision, mockery, contumely.
Antonyms: ADMIRATION; PRAISE.

scorn *verb* **1** *scorn their attempts at playing* be contemptuous, hold in contempt, look down on, disdain, disparage, slight, deride, mock, scoff at, sneer at. **2** *scorn his invitation/advice* rebuff, spurn, shun, refuse, reject, turn down.

scornful *adjective* contemptuous, disdainful, haughty, supercilious, disparaging, slighting, scathing, derisive, mocking, scoffing, sneering, contumelious.

scoundrel *noun* villain, rogue, rascal, miscreant, reprobate, scapegrace, cad, good-for-nothing, ne'er-do-well, wastrel; *inf.* rotter, bounder.

scour *verb* **1** *scour the bathtub* scrub, rub, clean, cleanse, abrade, wash, wipe, polish, buff, burnish. **2** *scour the countryside | scour the newspaper* search, comb, go over, look all over, ransack, hunt through, rake through, rummage through, leave no stone unturned in.

scourge *noun* **1** *poverty was the scourge of her life* bane, curse, affliction, plague, trial, trial and tribulation, torment, torture, suffering, burden, cross to bear, thorn in one's flesh/side, nuisance, pest, punishment, penalty, visitation. **2** *punished with a scourge* whip, horsewhip, bullwhip, switch, lash, cat-o'-nine-tails, thong, flail, strap, birch.

scourge *verb* **1** *scourge the offenders* whip, horsewhip, flog, lash, strap, birch, cane, thrash, beat, leather; *inf.* belt, wallop, lambaste, tan someone's hide. **2** *scourge them with cruel words* curse, afflict, plague, torment, torture, make (one) suffer from, burden, punish.

scout *noun* **1** *scouts returning with no information* advance guard, vanguard, lookout man/woman, outrider, spy. **2** *a scout in the audience* talent scout, talent spotter, recruiter.

scout *verb* **scout for** *scout for information* search for, search out, look for, seek, hunt for, look around for, cast around for, ferret around for.
scout out *scout out the territory* reconnoiter, make a reconnaissance of, spy out, survey, make a survey of, inspect, investigate, examine, scan, study, observe; *inf.* check out, case.

scowl *verb* *old men scowling at the noisy children* frown, glower, glare, lower, look daggers, grimace.

scowl *noun* frown, glower, glare, dirty look.

scraggy *adjective* scrawny, thin, skinny, gaunt, bony, angular, rawboned.
Antonyms: FAT; PLUMP.

scramble *verb* **1** *scramble over the fence* clamber, climb, crawl. **2** *scramble to get there on time* hastily struggle, hurry, hasten, rush, race, scurry. **3** *scramble for a place in the finals* jockey, struggle, jostle, strive, contend, compete, vie. **4** *the tools were scrambled together* mix up, jumble, tangle, throw into confusion, disorganize.

scramble *noun* **1** *go for a scramble over the hills* clamber, climb, trek. **2** *a scramble to get there on time* hurry, rush, race, scurry. **3** *a scramble for concert tickets* jockeying, struggle, tussle, jostle, competition, vying.

scrap[1] *noun* **1** *a scrap of material* fragment, piece, bit, snippet, remnant, tatter. **2** *a scrap of food* piece, bit, morsel, particle, sliver, crumb, bite, mouthful. **3** *not a scrap of truth in it* bit, grain, iota, trace, whit, snatch. **4** *collect scrap* waste, junk, rubbish, scrap metal.

scrap[2] *verb* *scrap the van/plans* throw away, get rid of, discard, toss out, abandon, jettison, dispense with, shed; *inf.* ditch, junk, throw on the scrap heap.
Antonyms: KEEP; RETAIN; RESTORE.

scrap[3] *noun* fight, quarrel, argument, squabble, wrangle, tiff, row, fracas, brawl, scuffle, disagreement, clash; *inf.* set-to, run-in.

scrap[4] *verb* *children scrapping* fight, quarrel, bicker, argue, squabble, row, wrangle, brawl, disagree; *inf.* fall out, have a set-to.

scrape *verb* **1** *scrape the surface to smooth it* scour, rub, scrub, file, sandpaper. **2** *scrape food from the pans* clean, remove, erase. **3** *scraping a knife across metal* grate, rasp, grind, scratch. **4** *gates scraping in the wind* creak, grate, squeak, screech, set one's teeth on edge. **5** *fall and scrape one's knee* graze, scratch, abrade, skin, cut, lacerate, bark. **6** *scrape the side of a car* scratch, gouge, damage, deface, spoil, mark.
scrape by/along *scrape by on his earnings* barely manage to live, barely have enough to live on, keep the wolf from the door, scrape a living.
scrape through *scrape through the exams* just pass, pass and no more, pass by a narrow margin, just succeed, narrowly achieve.

scrape *noun* **1** *the scrape of a knife on metal* grating, rasping, grinding, scratching, creaking, squeaking. **2** *wash the scrape on the child's knee* graze, scratch, abrasion, cut, laceration, wound. **3** *a scrape on the woodwork* scratch, mark, defacement. **4** *getting into scrapes at school | a financial scrape* trouble, difficulty, straits, distress, mess, muddle, predicament, plight, tight spot, tight corner; *inf.* fix.

scraps *plural noun* leftovers, leavings, scrapings, remains, residue, bits and pieces, odds and ends.

scratch *verb* **1** *skin scratched by rose bushes* graze, scrape, abrade, skin, cut, lacerate, bark. **2** *scratch an itchy part* rub, scrape, tear at. **3** *scratch a knife over metal* scrape, grate, rasp, grind. **4** *scratch his name from the list* cross out, strike out, delete, erase, remove, eliminate. **5** *runners being scratched from the race* withdraw, take out, pull out, remove, eliminate. **scratch about/around** *scratch about for proof* search, hunt, cast about, rummage around, forage about, poke about.

scratch *noun* **1** *a scratch on the skin* graze, scrape, abrasion, cut, laceration, wound. **2** *a scratch on the paint* scrape, mark, line, defacement. **up to scratch** up to standard, up to par, satisfactory, acceptable, passable, sufficient, adequate, competent; *inf.* OK, okay, up to snuff.

scrawl *verb* *scrawl his name* scribble, scratch, dash off.

scrawl *noun* *unable to read his scrawl* scribble, illegible handwriting.

scrawny *adjective* scraggy, thin, skinny. *See* SCRAGGY.

scream *noun* **1** *a scream of pain* shriek, howl, shout, yell, cry, screech, yelp, squeal, wail, squawk, bawl; *inf.* holler. **2** *the entertainer is a scream* comedian, comic, joker, laugh, wit, clown; *inf.* hoot, riot, barrel of laughs, card, caution.

scream *verb* **1** *scream in pain* shriek, howl, shout, cry out, call out, yell, screech, yelp, squeal, wail, squawk, bawl; *inf.* holler. **2** *the colors screamed* clash, not go together, jar. **scream at** *the true facts screamed at us* be obvious to, be glaringly obvious to, be blatant to, be apparent to.

screech *noun* *a screech of fright* shriek, howl, shout, yell, squeal, squawk; *inf.* holler.

screech *verb* *screeching in pain* shriek, howl, shout, yell. *See* SCREECH *noun.*

screen *noun* **1** *change clothes behind a screen* partition, (room) divider. **2** *a screen on a window* mesh, net, netting, curtain, blind. **3** *act as a screen from the wind/sun* shelter, shield, protection, guard, safeguard, buffer. **4** *coal put through a screen* sieve, riddle, strainer, colander, filter, winnow.

screen *verb* **1** *screen them from the wind* shelter, shield, protect, guard, safeguard. **2** *their activities screened by darkness* conceal, hide, cover, cloak, veil, mask, camouflage, disguise. **3** *employees screened by security* check, test. **4** *screen people for cancer* check, test, examine, investigate, scan. **5** *screen coal* sieve, riddle, sift, strain, filter, winnow. **screen off** *screen off a section of the room* partition off, divide off, conceal, hide.

screw *noun* **1** *loose screws in the door* bolt, pin, fastener. **2** *tighten with two or three screws* turn, twist, twirl. **put the screws on** *put the screws on them to get the money* put pressure on, pressurize, bring force to bear on, force, coerce, compel, constrain, hold a pistol to someone's head.

screw *verb* **1** *screw the planks down* fasten, clamp, rivet, batten. **2** *screw money out of her* force, extort, extract, wrest, bleed, wring. **screw in** *screw in the bolt* tighten, turn, twist, work in. **screw up**

1 *screw up one's face in the sun* wrinkle up, pucker, crumple, contort, distort, twist. **2** *screw up a business deal* make a mess of, bungle, botch, make a botch of, ruin, spoil.

scribble *verb* *scribble a note* dash off, jot down, scrawl.

scribble *noun* *unable to read the scribble* scrawl, illegible handwriting.

scribe *noun* **1** *scribes taking dictation* amanuensis, copyist, transcriber, secretary, recorder. **2** *describes himself as a scribe* writer, author, journalist, reporter.

scrimp *verb* skimp, economize, be frugal, be thrifty, husband one's resources, tighten one's belt, draw in one's horns.

script *noun* **1** *written in a careful script* handwriting, writing, hand, pen, calligraphy. **2** *read over the script of the play* text, book, libretto, score, lines, words, manuscript.

Scripture *noun* Holy Writ, the Bible, the Holy Bible, the Gospel, the Good Book, the Word of God, the Book of Books.

scrounge *verb* *scrounge money* cadge, beg, borrow; *inf.* sponge, bum.

scrounger *noun* cadger, beggar, borrower, parasite; *inf.* sponger, freeloader.

scrub *verb* **1** *scrub the floor/bathtub* rub, scour, clean, cleanse, wash, wipe. **2** *scrub the plans* cancel, drop, discontinue, abandon, call off, give up, do away with, discard, forget about, abort.

scrub *noun* *land covered in scrub* brushwood, brush, copse, coppice, thicket.

scruffy *adjective* untidy, unkempt, disheveled, ungroomed, ill-groomed, shabby, down-at-the-heels, ragged, tattered, slovenly, messy. *Antonyms:* TIDY; NEAT; CHIC; SPRUCE.

scrumptious *adjective* delicious, tasty, mouthwatering, palatable, delectable, delightful.

scruples *plural noun* *have no scruples about stealing* qualms, twinge of conscience, compunction, hesitation, second thoughts, doubt, misgivings, uneasiness, reluctance, restraint, wavering, vacillation.

scrupulous *adjective* **1** *pay scrupulous attention to detail | a scrupulous inspection* meticulous, careful, painstaking, thorough, rigorous, strict, conscientious, punctilious, exact, precise, fastidious. **2** *scrupulous in his business dealings* honest, honorable, upright, righteous, right-minded, moral, ethical. *Antonyms:* CARELESS; SLAPDASH; DISHONEST; UNSCRUPULOUS.

scrutinize *verb* examine, study, inspect, survey, scan, look over, investigate, go over, peruse, probe, inquire into, sift, analyze, dissect.

scrutiny *noun* examination, study, inspection, survey, scan, perusal, investigation, exploration, probe, inquiry, analysis, dissection.

scuffle *noun* *involved in a barroom scuffle* struggle, fight, tussle, row, quarrel, fracas, brawl, clash, affray, rumpus, disturbance, brouhaha, commotion; *inf.* scrap, set-to.

scuffle *verb arrested for scuffling in the street* struggle, fight, exchange blows, come to blows, tussle, row, brawl, clash; *inf.* scrap.

sculpture *noun a sculpture of Jefferson* statue, statuette, bust, figure, figurine.

sculpture *verb sculpture his head in bronze* sculpt, sculp, chisel, model, fashion, shape, cast, carve, cut, hew.

scum *noun* 1 *scum forming on the surface of the beer/pond* film, layer, froth, foam; crust, algae, filth, dirt. 2 *regard his neighbors as scum* lowest of the low, dregs of society, riff-raff, rabble, canaille.

scurrilous *adjective a scurrilous attack on her character* abusive, vituperative, insulting, offensive, disparaging, defamatory, slanderous, gross, foul, scandalous.

scurry *verb scurry home in the rain* hurry, hasten, make haste, rush, race, dash, run, sprint, scamper, scramble.

scurry *noun the scurry of the crowds* hurry, haste, rush, bustle, racing, dashing, scuttling, scampering.

sea *noun* 1 *sail on the sea* ocean, brine; *lit.* deep, main; *inf.* brink, drink. 2 *rough sea/seas* waves, swell, breakers. 3 *a sea of daffodils* expanse, sheet, mass, multitude, host, profusion, abundance, plethora. **at sea** confused, perplexed, bewildered, puzzled, baffled, at a loss, mystified.

seal *noun* 1 *the presidential seal* emblem, symbol, insignia, badge, crest, token, mark, monogram. 2 *the seal around the bathtub* sealant, sealer, adhesive. 3 *receive their seal of approval* assurance, attestation, confirmation, ratification, guarantee, proof, authentication, warrant, warranty. 4 *seals swimming near the coast* seal cub.

seal *verb* 1 *seal the parcel* fasten, secure, shut, close up. 2 *seal the jars* seal up, make airtight, make watertight, close, shut, cork, stopper, stop up. 3 *seal off the area* close, shut, cordon, fence. 4 *seal the bargain* secure, clinch, settle, decide, complete. 5 *seal his appointment* confirm, guarantee, ratify, validate.

seam *noun* 1 *the seam between the lengths of material/wood* joint, join, junction. 2 *seams of coal* layer, stratum, vein, lode. 3 *seams on her brows* furrow, line, ridge, wrinkle, scar.

sear *verb* 1 *cloth seared by an iron* burn, singe, scorch, char. 2 *grass seared by the sun* burn, scorch, dry up, wither, discolor, brown. 3 *seared by an unhappy love affair* anguish, torture, torment, wound, distress, harry.

search *verb* 1 *search the house* go through, look through, hunt through, rummage through, forage through, rifle through, scour, ransack, comb, go through with a fine-tooth comb, sift through, turn upside down, turn inside out, leave no stone unturned in. 2 *search one's soul* examine, explore, investigate, inspect, survey, study, pry into. 3 *search the prisoner* examine, inspect, check; *inf.* frisk. **search for** *search for clues* look for, seek out, hunt for, look high and low for, cast around for, ferret about for, scout out; track down, uncover. **search me!** I don't know, how should I know?, why ask me?, (it) beats me, it's a mystery.

search *noun* 1 *conduct a search of the house* hunt, rummage, forage, rifling, scour, ransacking. 2 *a search for truth* exploration, pursuit, quest, probe. **in search of** *in search of happiness* looking for, on the lookout for, seeking, hunting for, in pursuit of, on the track of, questing after.

searching *adjective* 1 *a searching look* penetrating, piercing, discerning, keen, alert, sharp, observant, intent. 2 *searching questions* probing, penetrating, analytic, quizzical, inquiring, inquisitive.

season *noun in the warm season of the year* period, time, time of year, spell, term. **in season** *when strawberries are in season* available, obtainable, readily available/obtainable, common, plentiful.

season *verb* 1 *season the sauce* flavor, add flavoring to, add salt/pepper/herbs/spice(s) to, spice, pep up; *inf.* add zing to. 2 *letters seasoned with gossip* enliven, leaven, spice, pep up. 3 *season the wood* mature, mellow, prime, prepare. 4 *season one's language* temper, moderate, qualify, tone down.

seasonable *adjective* 1 *seasonable weather* usual, appropriate to the time of year. 2 *seasonable advice* opportune, timely, well-timed, appropriate, suitable, apt.

seasoned *adjective seasoned travelers* experienced, practiced, well-versed, established, habituated, long-serving, time-served, veteran, hardened, battle-scarred.
Antonyms: INEXPERIENCED; CALLOW; GREEN.

seasoning *noun add seasoning to the sauce* flavoring, salt and pepper, herbs, spices, condiments, dressing, relish.

seat *noun* 1 *enough seats for the audience/spectators* chair, bench, settee, stool. 2 *the seat of government* headquarters, location, site, whereabouts, place, base, center, hub, heart. 3 *fall on one's seat* bottom, buttocks, posterior, rump, hindquarters; *inf.* behind, backside, butt, tail, fanny; *vulg.* ass. 4 *the seat of his anxiety* grounds, cause, reason, basis, source, origin.

seat *verb* 1 *seat them next to each other* place, position, put, situate, deposit. 2 *the hall seats 500* hold, take, have room for, accommodate.

seating *noun* seats, room, places, chairs, accommodation(s).

secede *verb secede from* *secede from the organization* withdraw from, break away from, break with, separate oneself from, sever relations with, quit, split with, resign from, pull out of, drop out of, have nothing more to do with, nounce.

secluded *adjective a secluded place | the cabin was secluded* sheltered, concealed, hidden, private, unfrequented, solitary, lonely, sequestered, out-of-the-way, remote, isolated, off the beaten track/path, tucked away, cut off.
Antonyms: PUBLIC; BUSY; ACCESSIBLE.

seclusion *noun celebrities now living in seclusion* privacy, solitude, retreat, retirement, withdrawal, sequestration, isolation, concealment, hiding, secrecy.

second[1] *adjective* **1** *on the second day of the trial* next, following, subsequent, succeeding. **2** *a second helping* additional, extra, further. **3** *take a second pair of climbing boots* extra, additional, other, alternative, backup, substitute. **4** *move from the second team to the first* secondary, lower, subordinate, lesser, lower-grade, inferior. **5** *regarded as a second Einstein* other, duplicate, replicate. **second to none** *as a player he is second to none* unparalleled, without parallel, unequaled, without equal, unmatched, unique, in a class of one's own.

second[2] *noun act as second to the boxer/duelist* assistant, attendant, helper, supporter, backer, right-hand man/woman.

second[3] *verb* **1** *seconded in his research by a student* assist, help, aid, support. **2** *second the proposal* formally support, give one's support to, back, approve, give one's approval to, endorse, promote.

second[4] *noun I will be with you in a second | disappear in a second* moment, minute, instant, trice, twinkling, twinkling of an eye; *inf.* sec, jiffy, jiff, two shakes of a lamb's tail, two shakes.

secondary *adjective* **1** *ignore the secondary issues* lesser, subordinate, minor, ancillary, subsidiary, nonessential, unimportant. **2** *patients with secondary infections* derived, derivative, indirect, resulting, resultant. **3** *a secondary line of action* second, backup, reserve, relief, auxiliary, extra, alternative, subsidiary.
Antonyms: PRIMARY; PRIME; MAIN.

second-class *adjective treated as second-class citizens* second-rate, low-class, inferior, lesser, unimportant.

secondhand *adjective secondhand clothes* used, worn, nearly new, handed down; *inf.* hand-me-down.

secondhand *adverb hear the news secondhand* at second hand, indirectly; *inf.* on the grapevine.

second in command *noun* deputy, number two, substitute, subordinate, right-hand man/woman.

secondly *adverb* second, in the second place, next.

second-rate *adjective* **1** *regarded as second-rate citizens* second-class, low-class, inferior, lesser, unimportant. **2** *second-rate goods* inferior, substandard, poor-quality, low-quality, low-grade, shoddy; *inf.* tacky.

seconds *plural noun* **1** *asking the cook for seconds* second helping, further helping, more. **2** *an outlet selling seconds* rejects, imperfect goods, faulty/flawed goods, inferior goods.

secrecy *noun* **1** *the secrecy of the information* confidentiality, privateness. *See* SECRET *adjective* 1. **2** *the secrecy of their love affair* clandestineness, furtiveness, surreptitiousness, stealth, covertness. **3** *the secrecy of their meeting place* seclusion, concealment, privacy, solitariness, sequestration, remoteness.

secret *adjective* **1** *keep the matter secret* confidential, private, unrevealed, undisclosed, under wraps, unpublished, untold, unknown; *inf.* hush-hush. **2** *a secret drawer in the table* hidden, concealed, camouflaged, disguised. **3** *a secret love affair | secret political activities* hidden, clandestine, furtive, conspiratorial, undercover, surreptitious, stealthy, cloak-and-dagger, covert; *inf.* closet. **4** *a secret code/message* hidden, mysterious, cryptic, abstruse, recondite, arcane. **5** *a secret place* secluded, concealed, hidden, sheltered, private, unfrequented, solitary, lonely, sequestered, out-of-the-way, remote, tucked away. **6** *a secret person* secretive, reticent, uncommunicative. *See* SECRETIVE.
Antonyms: PUBLIC; OPEN; OBVIOUS.

---

secret
clandestine, covert, furtive, stealthy, surreptitious, underhanded

While all of these adjectives describe an attempt to do something without attracting attention or observation, **secret** is the most general term, implying that something is being concealed or kept from the knowledge of others (*a secret pact; a secret passageway*). **Covert** suggests that something is being done under cover, or concealed as if with a veil or disguise (*a covert attack; a covert threat*), while **clandestine** suggests that something illicit or immoral is being concealed (*a clandestine meeting between the two lovers*). Someone who is deliberately sneaking around and trying to do something without attracting notice is best described as **stealthy** (*the cat moved toward the bird with a slow, stealthy pace*), and **furtive** connotes even more slyness and watchfulness, as revealed not only by movements but by facial expressions (*a furtive glance; a furtive movement toward the door*). **Surreptitious** connotes guilt on the part of the individual who is acting in a stealthy or furtive manner (*a surreptitious attempt to hide the book before it was noticed*). **Underhanded** is the strongest of these words, implying fraud, deceit, or unfairness (*underhanded business dealings*).

---

secret *noun* **1** *unable to keep a secret* confidential matter, confidence, private affair. **2** *the secrets of nature* mystery, enigma, puzzle, riddle. **3** *the secret of their success* recipe, formula, key, answer, solution. **in secret 1** *talks held in secret* secretly, behind closed doors, in camera. *See* SECRETLY 1. **2** *conduct their love affair in secret* secretly, privately, discreetly. *See* SECRETLY 2.

secrete *verb* **1** *secrete a watery discharge* discharge, emit, excrete, exude, ooze, leak, give off, send out. **2** *secrete the package in a hidden drawer* hide, conceal, cover up, stow away, sequester, cache; *inf.* stash away.

Antonyms: ABSORB; REVEAL; SHOW.

secretion *noun* discharge, emission, excretion, exudate, oozing, leakage.

secretive *adjective a secretive person/nature* secret, reticent, uncommunicative, unforthcoming, reserved, taciturn, silent, quiet, tight-lipped, close-mouthed, close, playing one's cards close to one's chest, clamlike; *inf.* cagey.

Antonyms: OPEN; COMMUNICATIVE; CHATTY.

secretly *adverb* **1** *committees meeting secretly | married secretly* in secret, confidentially, privately, behind closed doors, in camera, sub rosa. **2** *conducting their love affair secretly* in secret, clandestinely, furtively, conspiratorially, surreptitiously, stealthily, on the sly, covertly; *inf.* on the q.t. **3** *secretly she admired him* privately, in one's heart, in one's innermost thoughts.

sect *noun* group, denomination, order, faction, camp, splinter group, wing, division.

sectarian *adjective sectarian groups/views* doctrinaire, partisan, factional, bigoted, prejudiced, narrow-minded, parochial, insular, hidebound, extreme, fanatic, fanatical; *inf.* clannish.

Antonyms: TOLERANT; LIBERAL; BROAD-MINDED.

sectarian *noun* bigot, partisan, fanatic, zealot, dogmatist, extremist.

section *noun* **1** *divide the wood/fruit/material into sections* part, segment, division, component, piece, portion, bit, slice, fraction, fragment. **2** *the various sections of the book* part, division, component, chapter. **3** *the reference section of the library* part, division, department, branch.

sector *noun* **1** *the manufacturing sector of the economy* part, division, area, branch, category, field. **2** *forbidden to enter the military sector* zone, quarter, district, area, region.

secular *adjective secular music/matters* lay, nonreligious, nonspiritual, nonchurch, laical, temporal, worldly, earthly.

Antonyms: HOLY; RELIGIOUS; SACRED.

secure *adjective* **1** *the children/jewels will be quite secure there* safe, free from danger, out of harm's way, invulnerable, unharmed, undamaged, protected, sheltered, shielded. **2** *the windows are quite secure* fastened, closed, shut, locked, sealed. **3** *secure steps leading to the attic* stable, fixed, steady, strong, sturdy, solid. **4** *children feeling secure | feeling secure in his job* safe, unworried, at ease, comfortable, confident, assured. **5** *look forward to a secure future* safe, re-

liable, dependable, settled, fixed, established, solid.

Antonyms: INSECURE; PRECARIOUS.

secure *verb* **1** *secure the building from attack* make safe, make sound, fortify, strengthen, protect. **2** *secure the doors and windows* fasten, close, shut, lock, bolt, chain, seal. **3** *secure the boat* tie up, moor, anchor. **4** *secure their rights* assure, ensure, insure, guarantee, underwrite, confirm, establish. **5** *finally secure all they needed* acquire, obtain, gain, get, get hold of, procure, get possession of, come by; *inf.* get one's hands on, land.

security *noun* **1** *the security of the children/jewels* safety, freedom from danger, invulnerability, protection, safekeeping, shielding. **2** *seek security from their pursuers* protection, refuge, sanctuary, asylum, safety. **3** *children losing their feelings of security* safety, lack of worry/anxiety, freedom from doubt, certainty, feeling of ease, confidence, assurance. **4** *the security of the future/job* safety, reliability, dependability. *See* SECURE *adjective* 5. **5** *tight security for the president's visit* safety measures, safeguards, guards, surveillance, defense, protection. **6** *use one's house as security for a loan* collateral, surety, guarantee, pledge.

sedate *adjective* **1** *a sedate way of life* calm, tranquil, placid, dignified, formal, decorous, proper, demure, sober, earnest, staid, stiff. **2** *remained sedate during the excitement* calm, composed, tranquil, placid, serene, unruffled, imperturbable, unflappable.

Antonyms: WILD; EXCITABLE; FAST.

sedate *verb sedate the patient* give a sedative to, put under sedation, calm down, tranquilize.

sedative *noun* tranquilizer, calmative, depressant, sleeping pill, narcotic, opiate; *inf.* downer.

sedative *adjective drugs/voices with a sedative effect* calming, tranquilizing, soothing, calmative, relaxing, assuaging, lenitive, soporific, narcotic.

sedentary *adjective sedentary workers/people* sitting, seated, deskbound, inactive.

Antonyms: ACTIVE; MOBILE.

sediment *noun* lees, dregs, grounds, deposit, residue, precipitate, settlings.

sedition *noun* **1** *speakers accused of sedition* incitement to riot/rebellion, agitation, rabble-rousing, fomentation. **2** *advocating sedition* civil disorder, rebellion, insurrection, insurgence, uprising, mutiny, rioting, subversion, treason.

seditious *adjective* **1** *a seditious speech* inciting, rabble-rousing, agitating, fomenting. **2** *a seditious element within the ranks* rebellious, insurrectionist, insurgent, mutinous, subversive, dissident, disloyal, treasonous.

seduce *verb* **1** *seducing the younger employees* lead astray, corrupt, deflower, ravish, violate. **2** *seduced into crime by the promise of wealth* attract, allure, lure, tempt, entice, beguile, ensnare.

seductive *adjective* **1** *seductive smiles/dresses* attracting, alluring, tempting, provocative, exciting, arousing, sexy. **2** *seductive music/salaries* attractive, appealing, inviting, alluring, tempting, enticing, beguiling.

see *verb* **1** *I can see the house* make out, catch sight of, glimpse, spot, notice, observe, view, perceive, discern, espy, descry, distinguish, identify, recognize. **2** *see that man over there* look at, regard, note, observe, heed, mark, behold, watch; *inf.* get a load of. **3** *saw a movie last night* watch, look at, view. **4** *see what they mean* understand, grasp, get, comprehend, follow, take in, know, realize, get the drift of, make out, fathom; *inf.* latch on to. **5** *go and see what he wants* find out, discover, learn, ascertain, determine, ask, inquire, make inquiries into/about, investigate. **6** *we will have to see* think, consider, reflect, deliberate, give thought, have a think. **7** *see that the door is locked* see to it, take care, mind, make sure, make certain, ensure, guarantee. **8** *see trouble ahead* foresee, predict, forecast, anticipate, envisage, imagine, picture, visualize. **9** *see an old friend in the street* meet, encounter, run into, stumble upon, chance upon, recognize. **10** *see the doctor* visit, pay a visit to, consult, confer with. **11** *they see each other from time to time* meet, arrange to meet, meet socially (with). **12** *he is seeing someone else now* go out with, take out, keep company with, court; *inf.* go steady with, date. **13** *see her to her car* escort, accompany, show, lead, take, usher, attend. **see about 1** *see about travel arrangements* see to, deal with, attend to, cope with, look after, take care of. *See* SEE TO (below). **2** *see about what's happening* look into, investigate, inquire about/into, make inquiries about, ask about. **see through 1** *see through his disguise* | *see through their attempts to con us* | *see through her* be undeceived by, not be taken in by, be wise to, get the measure of, fathom, penetrate; *inf.* not fall for, have someone's number. **2** *see the job through* keep at, persevere with, persist with; *inf.* stick (it) out. **3** *see a friend through misfortune* support through/during, help through/during, assist through/during, back up through/during, stand by through/during, stick by through/during. **see to** *see to the travel arrangements* see about, deal with, arrange, organize, attend to, cope with, look after, take care of, be in charge of, be responsible for.

seed *noun* **1** *growing plants from seeds* ovule, germ. **2** *issue of his seed* sperm, spermatic fluid, semen, spermatozoa. **3** *the seed of her discontent* source, origin, root, cause, reason, grounds, basis, motivation, motive. **4** *the seed of Adam* child, children, offspring, progeny, issue, descendant(s), scion(s). **go/run to seed** *the farm has gone to seed* deteriorate, decline, degenerate, decay, go to rack and ruin, become dilapidated; *inf.* go downhill, go to pot, go to the dogs.

seedy *adjective* **1** *seedy little hotels* shabby, scruffy, shoddy, run-down, dilapidated, squalid, mean, sleazy, sordid, tatty; *inf.* crummy. **2** *feeling rather seedy* unwell, ill, poorly, out of sorts, indisposed; *inf.* under the weather.

seek *verb* **1** *seek up-to-date information* search for, try to find, look for, be on the lookout for, be after, hunt for, be in quest of, be in pursuit of. **2** *seek help from a counselor* ask for, request, solicit, entreat, beg for. **3** *seek to please* try, attempt, endeavor, strive, aim, aspire.

seem *verb* *seem a pleasant place* appear, appear to be, have the appearance of being, give the impression of being, look, look like, look to be, have the look of.

seeming *adjective* *his seeming charm* apparent, ostensible, outward, external, surface, superficial, pretended, feigned, assumed, supposed. **Antonyms:** ACTUAL; REAL; GENUINE.

seemly *adjective* *seemly behavior/dress* decorous, proper, decent, becoming, fitting, suitable, appropriate, apt, apposite, meet, *comme il faut*, in good taste. **Antonyms:** UNSEEMLY; UNBECOMING; UNSUITABLE.

seep *verb* ooze, leak, exude, drip, drain, percolate.

seer *noun* prophet, soothsayer, augur, sibyl.

seesaw *verb* *emotions seesawing* fluctuate, go from one extreme to the other, swing, oscillate.

seethe *verb* **1** *liquid seething in the pan* boil, bubble, fizz, foam, froth, ferment, churn. **2** *seething at the lateness of the bus* be furious, be livid, be incensed, be in a rage, rant and rave, storm, fume, foam at the mouth, breathe fire.

segment *noun* *divide the fruit into segments* section, part, division, component, piece, portion, slice, wedge.

segregate *verb* separate, set apart, isolate, dissociate, cut off, sequester, ostracize, discriminate against.

segregation *noun* separation, setting apart, isolation, dissociation, sequestration, discrimination, apartheid, partition.

seize *verb* **1** *a drowning man seizing a lifeline* | *seize power/control* grab, grab hold of, take hold of, grasp, take a grip of, grip, clutch at. **2** *police seizing a shipment of drugs* confiscate, impound, commandeer, appropriate, take possession of, sequester, sequestrate. **3** *criminals seizing a hostage/van* snatch, abduct, take captive, kidnap, hijack. **4** *police seizing the criminals* catch, arrest, apprehend, take into custody, take prisoner; *inf.* collar, nab. **seize upon** *seize upon the meaning of the message* grasp, understand, comprehend, discern, perceive, get the drift of.

seizure *noun* **1** *the vice squad's seizure of the drugs* confiscation, commandeering, appropriation, sequestration. **2** *the seizure of the hostage/van* snatching, abduction, kidnapping, hijacking.

3 *the seizure of the criminals* arrest, apprehension; *inf.* collaring, nabbing.

seldom *adverb* rarely, hardly ever, scarcely ever, infrequently, only occasionally; *inf.* once in a blue moon.
Antonyms: OFTEN; FREQUENTLY.

select *verb* choose, pick, hand-pick, single out, opt for, decide on, settle on, prefer, favor.

select *adjective* **1** *a select range of goods* choice, hand-picked, prime, first-rate, first-class, finest, best, high-quality, top-quality, supreme, superb, excellent. **2** *a select club* exclusive, elite, limited, privileged, cliquish; *inf.* posh.
Antonyms: INFERIOR; SECOND-RATE; COMMON.

selection *noun* **1** *offer a wide selection of goods* choice, pick, option. **2** *publish a selection of his works* anthology, variety, assortment, miscellany, collection, range.

selective *adjective* *able to be selective about houses* particular, discriminating, discriminatory, discerning, fussy, careful, cautious; *inf.* choosy, picky.

self-assurance *noun* self-confidence, confidence, assertiveness, positiveness.

self-centered *adjective* egocentric, egotistic, egotistical, selfish, self-absorbed, self-seeking, wrapped up in oneself, narcissistic.

self-confidence *noun* self-assurance, confidence, self-reliance, self-dependence, self-possession, poise, aplomb, composure, sangfroid.

self-conscious *adjective* awkward, shy, diffident, bashful, blushing, timorous, nervous, timid, retiring, shrinking, ill-at-ease, embarrassed, uncomfortable.

self-control *noun* self-restraint, restraint, self-discipline, willpower, strength of will.

self-denial *noun* self-discipline, asceticism, self-abnegation, self-deprivation, abstemiousness, temperance, abstinence, self-sacrifice, selflessness, unselfishness, altruism.

self-esteem *noun* self-respect, self-regard, pride in oneself/one's abilities, faith in oneself, *amour propre*.

self-important *adjective* pompous, vain, conceited, arrogant, swell-headed, egotistical, presumptuous, overbearing, overweening, haughty, swaggering, strutting.

self-indulgence *noun* self-gratification, lack of self-restraint, unrestraint, intemperance, immoderation, excess, pleasure-seeking, pursuit of pleasure, sensualism, dissipation.

selfish *adjective* self-seeking, self-centered, egocentric, egotistic, egoistic, self-interested, self-regarding, self-absorbed; *inf.* looking out for number one.
Antonyms: UNSELFISH; ALTRUISTIC; SELFLESS.

selfless *adjective* unselfish, altruistic, generous, self-sacrificing, self-denying, magnanimous, liberal, ungrudging.

Antonyms: SELFISH; SELF-CENTERED; EGOISTIC.

self-possessed *adjective* self-assured, confident, sure of oneself, composed, cool, cool as a cucumber, calm, collected; *inf.* together.

self-respect *noun* self-esteem, self-regard, pride in oneself, pride in one's abilities, belief in one's worth, faith in oneself, *amour propre*.

self-righteous *adjective* sanctimonious, holier-than-thou, pietistic, pharisaic, unctuous, mealy-mouthed; *inf.* goody-goody.

self-sacrifice *noun* self-denial, selflessness, self-abnegation, unselfishness, altruism.

self-satisfied *adjective* pleased with oneself, well-pleased, proud of oneself, flushed with success, self-approving, complacent, smug, like the cat that swallowed the canary.

self-seeking *adjective* self-interested, opportunistic, looking out for oneself, ambitious, mercenary, out for what one can get, fortune-hunting, gold-digging; *inf.* on the make, looking out for number one.

self-styled *adjective* would-be, so-called, self-named, self-titled.

self-willed *adjective* willful, contrary, perverse, uncooperative, wayward, recalcitrant, refractory, intractable, stubborn, pigheaded, mulish, intransigent, difficult, disobedient; *inf.* cussed.

sell *verb* **1** *sell their house* put up for sale, put on sale, dispose of, vend, auction off, trade, barter. **2** *selling fruit and vegetables* trade in, deal in, be in the business of, traffic in, stock, carry, offer for sale, market, handle, peddle, hawk. **3** *goods selling well* be bought, be purchased, go, go like hot cakes, move, be in demand. **4** *selling for $5* retail, go, be found. **5** *sell the idea of self-support* get acceptance for, win approval for, get support for, get across, promote. **6** *you have been sold!* sell down the river, betray, cheat, swindle, defraud, fleece, deceive, trick, double-cross, bilk, gull; *inf.* con, stab someone in the back. **sell on** *try to sell him on the plan* persuade of, convince of, talk someone into, bring someone round to, induce to, win someone over to. **sell out 1** *bakers sold out their bread* be out of stock of, run out of, dispose of, have none left. **2** *supplies of tickets sold out* be bought up, be depleted, be exhausted. **3** *he used to have principles but he sold out for money* prostitute oneself, sell one's soul, betray one's cause/ideals, go over to the other side.
Antonyms: BUY; PURCHASE.

seller *noun* vendor, retailer, salesman, saleswoman, salesperson, shopkeeper, trader, merchant, dealer, agent, representative; *inf.* rep.

selling *noun* **1** *the selling of property* vending, trading. **2** *a career in selling* sales, salesmanship, marketing, merchandising.

semblance *noun* *only a semblance of honesty* appearance, outward appearance, show, air, guise, pretense, façade, front, veneer, mask, cloak, disguise, camouflage, pretext.

send *verb* **1** *send a letter* dispatch, forward, mail, post, remit. **2** *send a message* transmit, convey,

communicate, broadcast, televise, telecast, radio. **3** *send a stone skimming over the water* throw, fling, hurl, cast, let fly, propel, project. **4** *send one mad* drive, make, cause one to be/become. **5** *the music sent him* excite, stimulate, titillate, rouse, stir, thrill, intoxicate, enrapture, enthrall, ravish, charm, delight; *inf.* turn one on. **send for** *send for a doctor/plumber* call for, summon, request, order. **send off** *send off evil-smelling fumes* give off, discharge, emit, exude.
Antonyms: RECEIVE; GET.

senile *adjective* doddering, decrepit, failing, in one's dotage, in one's second childhood, mentally confused.

senior *adjective* **1** *senior officer* high-ranking, higher-ranking, superior. **2** *the senior of the two* older, elder.
Antonyms: JUNIOR; SUBORDINATE; INFERIOR.

sensation *noun* **1** *awake with a sensation of fear* feeling, sense, awareness, consciousness, perception, impression. **2** *their affair caused a sensation* stir, excitement, agitation, commotion, furor, scandal. **3** *the new show is a sensation* great success; *inf.* hit, smash hit, wow.

sensational *adjective* **1** *a sensational news story* spectacular, stirring, exciting, startling, staggering, dramatic, amazing, shocking, scandalous, lurid. **2** *looking sensational in the evening dress* marvelous, superb, excellent, exceptional, remarkable; *inf.* fabulous, fab, out of this world.
Antonyms: RUN-OF-THE-MILL; DULL; ORDINARY.

sense *noun* **1** *a sense of touch* feeling, sensation, faculty, sensibility. **2** *detect a sense of hostility* feeling, atmosphere, impression, aura. **3** *a sense of guilt* feeling, sensation, awareness, consciousness, perception. **4** *a sense of humor* appreciation, awareness, understanding, comprehension. **5** *have the sense to keep quiet* common sense, practicality, wisdom, sagacity, sharpness, discernment, perception, wit, intelligence, cleverness, understanding, reason, logic, brain, brains; *inf.* gumption. **6** *a word with several senses* meaning, definition, import, signification, significance, implication, nuance, drift, gist, purport, denotation. **7** *no sense in what she said/did* intelligibility, coherence, comprehensibility, logic, rationality, purpose, point.

sense *verb* *sense their hostility* feel, get the impression of, be aware of, be conscious of, observe, notice, perceive, discern, grasp, pick up, suspect, divine, intuit; *inf.* have a feeling about.

senseless *adjective* **1** *a senseless act/comment* nonsensical, stupid, foolish, silly, inane, idiotic, mindless, unintelligent, unwise, irrational, illogical, meaningless, pointless, absurd, ludicrous, fatuous, asinine, moronic, imbecilic, mad; *inf.* daft. **2** *knocked senseless by the blow* unconscious, insensible, out cold, out, cold, stunned, numb, numbed, insensate.
Antonyms: SENSIBLE; WISE; CONSCIOUS.

sensibilities *plural noun* *offend older people's sensi-*

bilities moral sense, finer feelings, susceptibilities, sense of outrage.

sensibility *noun* *a man without sensibility* sensitivity, sensitiveness, finer feelings, delicacy, taste, discrimination, discernment.

sensible *adjective* **1** *a sensible person/approach* practical, realistic, down-to-earth, wise, prudent; judicious, sagacious, sharp, shrewd, discerning, perceptive, farsighted, intelligent, clever, reasonable, rational, logical; *inf.* brainy. **2** *a sensible rise in temperature* perceptible, discernible, appreciable, noticeable, visible, observable, tangible, palpable. **sensible of** *sensible of his inadequacies* aware of, conscious of, mindful of, sensitive to, alive to, cognizant of, acquainted with.
Antonyms: FOOLISH; SILLY; UNAWARE.

---

sensible
lucid, rational, sagacious, sane
A **sensible** person brings an umbrella when rain is forecast. A **rational** one studies the weather map, observes the movement of the clouds across the sky, listens to the forecast on the radio, and then decides whether or not an umbrella is necessary. *Sensible* implies the use of common sense and an appreciation of the value of experience (*a sensible decision not to travel until his injuries had healed*), while *rational* suggests the ability to reason logically and to draw conclusions from inferences (*a rational explanation for why she failed the exam*). **Lucid** and **sane**, like *rational*, are associated with coherent thinking. *Lucid* suggests a mind free of internal pressures or distortions (*lucid intervals during which he was able to recognize his wife and children*), while *sane* indicates freedom from psychosis or mental derangement (*judged to have been sane when she committed the crime*). *Sane* also has a meaning very close to that of *sensible* (*a sane approach to disciplining problem teenagers*). A **sagacious** person is an extremely shrewd one who is both discerning and practical. He or she can look out the window and tell whether it's going to rain by studying the facial expressions of passersby as they glance nervously at the sky.

---

sensitive *adjective* **1** *sensitive skin* delicate, fine, soft, easily damaged, fragile. **2** *sensitive rather than coarse people* responsive, receptive, perceptive, discerning, discriminatory, sympathetic, understanding, empathetic. **3** *too sensitive to withstand criticism* oversensitive, easily upset, thin-skinned, touchy, temperamental. **4** *a sensitive issue* delicate, difficult, problematic, ticklish. **sensitive to** *sensitive to unfriendly atmospheres* responsive to, easily affected by, susceptible to, reactive to, sentient of.
Antonyms: INSENSITIVE; COARSE; TOUGH.

sensitivity *noun* **1** *the sensitivity of her skin* sensitiveness, delicacy, fineness, softness, fragility. **2** *the sensitivity of the artist* sensitiveness, responsiveness, receptiveness, perceptiveness, discernment, discrimination. **3** *unable to cope with her sensitivity* oversensitivity, touchiness. *See* SENSITIVE 3.

sensual *adjective* **1** *sensual rather than spiritual pleasures* physical, carnal, bodily, fleshly, animal, nonspiritual, epicurean, sybaritic. **2** *sensual curves/lips* voluptuous, sexual, sexy, erotic.
Antonyms: SPIRITUAL; ASCETIC.

sensuous *adjective sensuous music* | *the sensuous feel of satin* aesthetic, pleasing, pleasurable, gratifying.

<hr>

sensuous
epicurean, luxurious, sensual, sybaritic, voluptuous
Sensuous and **sensual** are often confused. *Sensuous* implies gratification of the senses for the sake of aesthetic pleasure, or delight in the color, sound, or form of something (*a dress made from a soft, sensuous fabric*), while **sensual** implies indulgence of the appetites or gratification of the senses as an end in itself (*he leads a life of sensual excess*). **Luxurious** implies indulgence in sensuous or sensual pleasures, especially those that induce a feeling of physical comfort or satisfaction (*a luxurious satin coverlet*), while **epicurean** refers to taking delight in the pleasures of eating and drinking (*the epicurean life of a king and his courtiers*). To be **voluptuous** is to give oneself up to the pleasures of the senses (*the symphony is voluptuous in its scoring*), but it carries a suggestion of sensual rather than sensuous enjoyment and can refer to a curvaceous and sexually attractive woman (*he was seen with a voluptuous blonde*). **Sybaritic** implies an overrefined luxuriousness, also suggesting indulgence in good food and drink and the presence of things designed to soothe and charm the senses (*he lived alone, in sybaritic splendor*).

<hr>

sentence *noun* **1** *listen to the judge delivering the sentence* judgment, verdict, pronouncement, ruling, decision, decree. **2** *serve a three-year sentence* prison sentence, jail sentence, penal sentence, prison term; *inf.* time.
sentence *verb* **1** *hear the judge sentencing the prisoners* impose a sentence on, pass judgment on, mete out punishment to, punish. **2** *sentenced to a life of pain* condemn, doom, punish, penalize.
sententious *adjective* **1** *making sententious remarks about their behavior* moralistic, moralizing, judgmental, sanctimonious, canting, pompous. **2** *a sententious style of prose* concise, succinct, terse, compact, epigrammatic, pithy, axiomatic, aphoristic.
sentiment *noun* **1** *no room for sentiment in business* emotion, emotionalism, finer feelings, tender feelings, tenderness, softness. **2** *a revolutionary sentiment obvious in her writings* feelings, attitude, belief, opinion, view, point of view. **3** *romantic novels full of sentiment* sentimentality, emotionalism, overemotionalism, mawkishness. *See* SENTIMENTALITY.

sentimental *adjective* **1** *singing sentimental love songs* emotional, overemotional, romantic, mawkish, maudlin, soppy; *inf.* mushy, slushy, soppy, schmaltzy, corny. **2** *a sentimental attachment to the town* emotional, nostalgic, affectionate, loving, tender, warm.
Antonyms: DISPASSIONATE; PRACTICAL; HARDHEADED.

<hr>

sentimental
effusive, maudlin, mawkish, mushy, romantic
If you are moved to tears by a situation that does not really warrant such a response, you're likely to be called **sentimental**, an adjective used to describe a willingness to get emotional at the slightest prompting (*a sentimental man who kept his dog's ashes in an urn on the mantel*). **Effusive** applies to excessive or insincere displays of emotion, although it may be used in an approving sense (*effusive in her gratitude for the help she had received*). **Maudlin** derives from the name Mary Magdalene, who was often shown with her eyes swollen from weeping. It implies a lack of self-restraint, particularly in the form of excessive tearfulness. **Mawkish** carries sentimentality a step further, implying emotion so excessive that it provokes loathing or disgust (*mawkish attempts to win the audience over*). Although **romantic** at one time referred to an expression of deep feeling, nowadays it is often used disapprovingly to describe emotion that has little to do with the way things actually are and that is linked to an idealized vision of the way they should be (*she had a romantic notion of what it meant to be a starving artist*). **Mushy** suggests both excessive emotion or sentimentality and a contempt for romantic love (*a mushy love story*).

<hr>

sentimentality *noun criticizing the sentimentality of the novels* emotionalism, overemotionalism, romanticism, mawkishness; *inf.* mush, slush, soppiness, corniness.
sentiments *plural noun my sentiments exactly* feeling, attitude, belief, thoughts, way of thinking, opinion, view, point of view, idea, judgment, persuasion.
sentry *noun* guard, lookout, watch, watchman, sentinel.
separate *adjective* **1** *have separate residences* individual, distinct, different, particular, autonomous, independent. **2** *the problems being quite separate* unconnected, unattached, distinct, different, disconnected, unrelated, detached, divorced, divided, discrete.
Antonyms: UNITED; SAME.
separate *verb* **1** *separate the joined pieces of wood* disconnect, detach, sever, uncouple, divide,

disjoin, sunder. **2** *old pipes separating at the joints* come apart, come away, break off, divide, disunite. **3** *the fence separating the two gardens* divide, come between, stand between, keep apart, partition. **4** *the roads separated at the foot of the hill* part, part company, go their separate ways, go different ways, diverge, split, divide. **5** *the couple separated last year* officially separate, obtain an official separation, break up, split up, part, become estranged, divorce. **6** *separate the items according to size* divide, sort, sort out, classify, categorize. **7** *separate the misbehaving child from the rest* set apart, segregate, single out, put to one side, isolate. **separate from** *a splinter group separating from the society* break away from, break with, secede from, withdraw from, sever relations with.
Antonyms: JOIN; UNITE; MARRY; MIX.

separately *adverb* **1** *all four living separately* apart, individually, independently, autonomously. **2** *the members of the group left separately* individually, one by one, one at a time, singly, severally, independently.

separation *noun* **1** *the separation of the pieces* disconnection, detachment, severance, uncoupling, division, disjunction, disunion, dissociation, segregation. **2** *upset by her parents' separation* breakup, split-up, split, parting, estrangement, parting of the ways, rift, divorce.

septic *adjective* infected, festering, poisoned, putrefying, putrefactive, putrid.

sepulcher *noun* tomb, vault, burial place, grave.

sequel *noun* *an unfortunate sequel of/to the party* follow-up, development, result, consequence, outcome, issue, upshot, end, conclusion.

sequence *noun* *sequence of events/movements/numbers* chain, course, cycle, series, progression, succession, set, arrangement, order, pattern.

sequester *verb* **1** *nuns sequestered from the world* isolate, seclude, withdraw, retire, cut off, set apart, segregate, shut off. **2** *sequester a debtor's funds* sequestrate, confiscate, take possession of, seize, appropriate, expropriate, impound, commandeer.

seraphic *adjective* **1** *seraphic beings* angelic, celestial, heavenly, holy. **2** *a seraphic smile* blissful, beatific, rapt, joyful, serene.

serendipity *noun* chance, mere chance, happy chance, luck, good fortune, fortuity, fortuitousness, accident, coincidence.

serene *adjective* calm, composed, tranquil, peaceful, placid, still, quiet, unperturbed, imperturbable, undisturbed, unruffled, unworried, unexcited, unexcitable, unflappable.

serenity *noun* calm, calmness, composure, tranquillity, peace, peacefulness, peace of mind, placidity, placidness, stillness, quietness, quiet, quietude, imperturbability.

series *noun* *a series of events/people/numbers* succession, progression, sequence, chain, course, string, train, run, cycle, set, row, arrangement, order.

serious *adjective* **1** *serious expressions* solemn, earnest, unsmiling, unlaughing, thoughtful, preoccupied, pensive, grave, somber, sober, long-faced, dour, stern, grim, poker-faced. **2** *serious problems/trouble* important, significant, consequential, of consequence, momentous, of moment, weighty, far-reaching, urgent, pressing, crucial, vital, life-and-death. **3** *serious injuries* acute, grave, bad, critical, alarming, grievous, dangerous, perilous. **4** *serious about reforming* earnest, in earnest, sincere, honest, genuine, firm, resolute, resolved, determined, fervent.
Antonyms: CHEERFUL; TRIVIAL; MINOR; FLIPPANT.

seriously *adverb* **1** *nodding seriously* solemnly, earnestly, unsmilingly, with a straight face, thoughtfully, pensively, gravely, somberly, soberly, dourly, sternly, grimly. **2** *seriously injured* severely, acutely, gravely, badly, critically, alarmingly, grievously, dangerously, perilously. **3** *seriously, you will like it here* to be serious, without joking, no joking, truthfully, I mean it.

seriousness *noun* **1** *the seriousness of their expressions* solemnity, solemness, thoughtfulness, preoccupation, pensiveness, graveness, gravity, somberness, soberness, sobriety, dourness, sternness, grimness. **2** *the seriousness of the problem* importance, significance, consequence, momentousness, moment, weightiness, weight, urgency, crucialness, vitalness. **3** *the seriousness of the injuries* severity, severeness, acuteness, gravity, graveness, badness, criticalness, grievousness, danger, dangerousness, peril, perilousness. **4** *acknowledge their seriousness about reforming* sincerity, earnestness, honesty, genuineness, firmness, resolution, resolve, determination, fervor.

sermon *noun* **1** *sermons from the pulpit* preaching, teaching, speech, homily, address, oration. **2** *she listened to a sermon on lateness by her father* lecture, moralizing, declamation, tirade, harangue, ranting, diatribe, reprimand, reproof, remonstrance, castigation; *inf.* talking-to, dressing-down.

serrated *adjective* serrate, serrulate, serrulated, serriform, sawtoothed, notched, jagged.

servant *noun* *kitchen servants* domestic, help, domestic help, helper, maid, housekeeper, butler, steward, valet; handyman, menial, drudge; slave, vassal, serf; attendant, lackey, flunky.

serve *verb* **1** *serve two masters* be in the service of, work for, be employed by, have a job with. **2** *willing to serve his fellow men* be of service for, be of use to, help, give help to, assist, give assistance to, aid, lend a hand to, do a good turn to, benefit, support, foster, minister to, succor. **3** *serve on the committee* have/hold a place, be, sit, perform duties, carry out duties, fulfill duties. **4** *will the car serve us for another year?* be useful to, be all right for, be good to/for, be adequate for, suffice, serve a purpose for, meet requirements for; *inf.* fill the bill for, do. **5** *serve three years as an apprentice/prisoner* spend, go through, carry out, fulfill, complete, discharge. **6** *serve food* dish up, give out, distribute, set out, present, provide. **7** *serve at table* wait, act as waiter/waitress, distribute food/refreshments, deal out food. **8** *serve a customer* attend to, attend to the wants of, look after, take care of, assist. **9** *it has served them well* treat, act toward, behave toward, conduct oneself toward, deal with, handle. **serve as** *sofas serving as beds* act as, do duty as, function as, fulfill the function of, do the work of, be suitable for.

service *noun* **1** *retire after fifty years' service* work, employment, period of employment, labor, duties. **2** *do him a service by telling him* good turn, assistance, help, advantage, benefit. **3** *wedding service | service of baptism* ceremony, ritual, rite, sacrament. **4** *cars due for (a) service* servicing, overhaul, check, maintenance check, repair. **5** *pay extra for service in a restaurant* serving, waiting at table, waiting, waitressing, serving food and drink. **6** *have had good service from it* treatment, behavior, conduct, handling.

service *verb* *service the washing machine* check, go over, overhaul, give a maintenance check to, repair.

serviceable *adjective* **1** *serviceable rather than fashionable shoes* functional, utilitarian, practical, nondecorative, plain, useful, durable, hardwearing, tough, strong. **2** *machinery no longer serviceable* usable, of use, functioning, operative, repairable.
Antonyms: IMPRACTICAL; INOPERATIVE.

services *plural noun* **1** *go into the services* armed services, forces, armed forces. **2** *require the services of a lawyer* work, labor, duties, assistance, ministrations.

servile *adjective* **1** *made to do servile tasks* menial, low, lowly, humble, mean, base. **2** *surrounded by servile employees* subservient, obsequious, sycophantic, fawning, toadying, groveling, submissive; *inf.* bootlicking.

serving *noun* *dish up six servings of soup* helping, portion, plateful, bowlful.

servitude *noun* slavery, enslavement, thralldom, subjugation, subjection, domination, bondage, bonds, chains, fetters, shackles, serfdom, vassalage.

session *noun* **1** *a recording session* period, time, spell, stretch; *inf.* get-together. **2** *the afternoon sessions of the summit talks* meeting, sitting, assembly, conference, discussion. **3** *studied French during the fall session* semester, school term, term.

set *verb* **1** *set the books (down) there | a house set in the woods* put, put down, place, lay, lay down, deposit, position, rest, locate, lodge, situate, station, posit; *inf.* stick, park, plunk. **2** *set the*

post in the ground | *set a jewel in the ring* fix, embed, insert, lodge, mount, arrange, install. **3** *set pen to paper* put, apply, lay, place, bring into contact with, touch. **4** *set your mind to it* apply, direct, aim, turn, address, focus, concentrate, zero in on. **5** *set one's watch* adjust, regulate, synchronize, coordinate, harmonize, collimate, calibrate, rectify, set right. **6** *set the machine to start* fix, make ready, prepare, arrange, organize. **7** *set the table* lay, make ready, prepare, arrange. **8** *set her hair* fix, style, arrange, curl, wave. **9** *the sky set with stars | a dress set with sequins* decorate, adorn, ornament, deck, bedeck, embellish, furbish, bejewel. **10** *set things in motion | set it on fire* put, cause to be, start, actuate, instigate. **11** *the gelatin/concrete will not set* solidify, stiffen, thicken, gel, jell, harden, cake, congeal, coagulate, crystallize, gelatinize. **12** *the sun setting* go down, sink, dip below the horizon, vanish, disappear, subside, decline. **13** *set them thinking* set off, start, begin, motivate (to be), cause (to be). **14** *set a new record* set up, establish, fix, create, bring into being, bring into existence, institute. **15** *set a date/time for the meeting* fix, settle (on), agree on, appoint, decide on, name, specify, stipulate, determine, designate, select, choose, arrange, schedule, confirm. **16** *set down rules* lay down, impose, establish, define, determine, stipulate, prescribe, ordain, allot. **17** *teachers setting classroom tasks* assign, allocate, allot, give, give out, distribute, dispense, mete out, deal out, dole out, prescribe. **18** *set her services at a high price* evaluate, valuate, value, assess, price, rate, estimate, reckon, calculate. **19** *faces/footsteps set toward home* direct, steer, orientate, point, incline, bend, train, aim. **set about 1** *set about clearing up* begin, start, make a start on, commence, set to, get to work, get down to, get going, tackle, undertake, address oneself to, attack, enter upon, put the wheels in motion for, set the ball rolling for, lead off, put into execution, put one's shoulder to the wheel, put one's hand to the plow for; *inf.* get cracking on, sail into. **2** *set about the intruders with a stick* attack, assault, assail; *inf.* sail into. **set apart** *behavior setting him apart from the rest* differentiate, mark off, distinguish, single out, demarcate, characterize. **set aside 1** *set aside money/food for later* lay aside, lay by, put away, put aside, set apart, save, reserve, keep in reserve, keep, put down, store, stockpile, hoard, deposit, stow away, salt away, squirrel away; *inf.* stash away. **2** *set aside the newspaper* put aside, put to one side, move to one side, cast aside, discard, abandon, dispense with, drop. **3** *set aside our differences for now* put aside, forget, disregard, ignore, discount, bury, consign to oblivion. **4** *set aside the judge's ruling* overrule, overturn, reverse, nullify, render null and void, annul, quash, dismiss, reject, cancel, repudiate, abrogate. **set back** *set back their progress* hinder, impede, ob-

check, thwart. **set down 1** *set down a list of requirements* write down, write out, put in writing, commit to writing, put down, mark down, jot down, note down, record, register, tabulate, catalog. **2** *set his incompetence down to inexperience* put down, attribute, ascribe, assign, lay at the door of, charge. **set forth 1** *set forth for the city* set out, start out, depart. *See* SET OUT 1 (below). **2** *set forth their demands* declare, state, expound, describe, detail, delineate, submit, present, bring forward, advance. **set in** *winter has set in* begin, start, commence, arrive, come, come into being. **set off 1** *set off for the city* set out, start out, set forth, depart. *See* SET OUT 1 (below). **2** *set off a bomb* detonate, explode, blow up, ignite, light. **3** *set off a flurry of selling on the stock market* cause, begin, start, commence, initiate, set in motion, prompt, touch off, incite, stimulate, encourage. **4** *a dress setting off the blue of her eyes* enhance, bring out, heighten, intensify, increase, emphasize, show off, throw into relief. **set on** attack, assault, strike, beat, beat up, fall upon, pounce on, go for, fly at; *inf.* mug, sail into. **set out 1** *they set out for the city early* set off, set forth, start out, depart, leave, take one's departure, get under way, embark, sally forth; *inf.* hit the road. **2** *I did not set out to hurt them* intend, aim, mean, aspire. **3** *set out goods on a counter* lay out, arrange, dispose, present, exhibit, display, array, expose to view. **4** *they will set out their demands* set forth, declare, state, describe. *See* SET FORTH 2 (above). **set up. 1** *they set up a statue in his memory* put up, erect, raise, elevate, construct, build, assemble. **2** *we set up a business/ scholarship* establish, institute, found, create, bring into being, start, begin, initiate, inaugurate, organize, get going, lay the foundations of. **3** *we must set up a meeting* arrange, prearrange, organize, prepare, plan, devise, fix. **set** *noun* 1 *a set of articles for sale* collection, group, assemblage, series, batch, arrangement, array, succession, progression, assortment, selection. **2** *the golfing set* circle, crowd, clique, group, gang, coterie, faction, band, company, sect; *inf.* crew. **3** *the set of his shoulder/eyes* bearing, carriage, cast, posture, position, altitude, turn, inclination. **4** *paint the set* stage set, stage setting, setting, stage scene, scene, scenery, backdrop, wings, *mise en scène*. **set** *adjective* 1 *set texts/meals* fixed, prescribed, scheduled, specified, predetermined, prearranged, determined, arranged, appointed, established, decided, agreed. **2** *her set routine* customary, regular, normal, usual, habitual, accustomed, everyday, common. **3** *give a set speech* stock, standard, habitual, routine, rehearsed, unspontaneous, hackneyed, conventional, stereotyped. **4** *people of set opinions* | *set in their ways* fixed, firm, rooted, immovable, deep-seated, ingrained, entrenched, rigid, inflexible, hidebound. **5** *all set for the journey*

ready, prepared, equipped, primed, fit. **set on** *set on getting his own way* intent on, resolved about/on, determined to be, bent on, resolute about, earnest about.
Antonyms: UNUSUAL; FLEXIBLE; OPEN-MINDED.

setback *noun their progress/plans suffered a setback* reversal, reverse, upset, check, stumbling block, hitch, holdup, hindrance, impediment, obstruction, disappointment, misfortune, blow.

setting *noun* 1 *houses in rural settings* | *animals in their natural settings* environment, surroundings, milieu, background, location, place, site. **2** *a modern setting for the play* stage setting, set, scene, stage, scenery, backdrop, *mise en scène*. **3** *an unusual setting for the jewel* mounting, frame.

settle *verb* 1 *settle in America* make one's home, set up home, take up residence, put down roots, establish oneself, go to live, move to, emigrate to. **2** *the Mormons settled (in) Utah* establish/found a colony; colonize, occupy, people, inhabit, populate. **3** *the children will not settle after the excitement* settle/calm/quiet down, be quiet, be still, relax. **4** *the sedative will settle her* calm, calm down, tranquilize, quiet, soothe, compose, pacify, lull, sedate, quell. **5** *settle the patients for the night* make comfortable, bed down, tuck in. **6** *a butterfly settling on the leaf* alight, light, land, come down, descend, repose, rest. **7** *settle a dispute* resolve, clear up, make peace in, patch up, reconcile, conclude, bring to an end. **8** *settle one's affairs* put in order, arrange, set to rights, straighten out, organize, regulate, adjust, clear up, systematize. **9** *settle one's bills/debts* pay, discharge, square, clear, liquidate. **10** *the dust settled* sink, subside, fall, gravitate. **settle for** *settle for a smaller sum* compromise on, submit to, accept, agree to, accede to, acquiesce in, assent to. **settle on** *settle on a date* decide on, agree on, determine, confirm, arrange, fix, choose, appoint, select.
Antonyms: AGITATE; DISTURB.

settlement *noun* 1 *the settlement of the area* establishing, founding, pioneering, peopling, colonization. **2** *a remote settlement* community, colony, town, village, hamlet, encampment, outpost. **3** *the settlement of the dispute* resolution, patching up, reconciliation, conclusion. **4** *reach a financial settlement with management* agreement, contract, pact, compact. **5** *the settlement of his finances* ordering, arrangement, organization, regulation, adjustment, systematization. **6** *in settlement of debts* payment, discharge, defrayal, liquidation.

settler *noun* colonist, colonizer, pioneer, frontiersman, immigrant.

set-to *noun* argument, quarrel, row, disagreement, fight, squabble, wrangle, fracas; *inf.* scrap, spat.

setup *noun* 1 *an efficient business setup* system,

organization, structure, arrangement, framework, format, composition, procedure. **2** *fell prey to their setup* trap, trick, ambush, conspiracy; *inf.* frame-up, put-up job, con job.

sever *verb* **1** *sever a limb/branch* cut off, lop off, hack off, break off, tear off. **2** *sever the log in two pieces* divide, split, cleave, rive, dissect, halve. **3** *sever relations with them* break off, discontinue, suspend, dissolve, end, bring to an end, terminate, stop, cease, conclude.
Antonyms: JOIN; MAINTAIN; BEGIN.

several *adjective* **1** *several people came* some, a number of, a few. **2** *go their several ways* separate, different, diverse, disparate, divergent, respective, individual, own, particular, specific, various, sundry.

severe *adjective* **1** *severe criticism/punishment* harsh, hard, stringent, rigorous, unsparing, relentless, merciless, ruthless, painful, sharp, caustic, biting, cutting, scathing, serious, extreme. **2** *a severe regime* harsh, hard, stern, rigorous, stringent, strict, grim, inflexible, uncompromising, inexorable, implacable, relentless, unrelenting, merciless, pitiless, ruthless, brutal, inhuman, cruel, savage, hardhearted, iron-fisted, iron-handed, autocratic, tyrannical, despotic. **3** *a severe shortage of food* extreme, very bad, serious, grave, acute, critical, dire, dangerous, perilous. **4** *severe storms/headaches* fierce, strong, violent, intense, powerful, forceful, very bad. **5** *a severe test of their stamina* demanding, taxing, exacting, tough, difficult, hard, fierce, arduous, rigorous, punishing, onerous, burdensome. **6** *a severe expression* stern, grim, cold, chilly, austere, forbidding, dour, disapproving, tight-lipped, unsmiling, somber, grave, sober, serious. **7** *a severe style of decoration* austere, stark, ultraplain, spartan, ascetic, plain, simple, modest, bare, blank, unadorned, undecorated, unembellished, restrained, functional. **8** *a severe winter* harsh, extreme, inclement, cold, freezing, frigid.
Antonyms: MILD; LENIENT; ORNATE.

---

severe
ascetic, austere, stern, strict, unmitigated

A storm, a hairdo, and a punishment may all be described as **severe**, which means harsh or uncompromising, without a hint of softness, mildness, levity, or indulgence. **Austere**, on the other hand, primarily applies to people, their habits, their way of life, and the environments they create; it implies coldness, stark simplicity, and restraint (*an austere room with only a table and chair*). **Ascetic** implies extreme self-denial and self-discipline, in some cases to the point of choosing what is painful or disagreeable (*he had an ascetic approach to life and rejected all creature comforts*). **Strict** literally means bound or stretched tight; in extended use, it

means strenuously exact (*a strict curfew; strict obedience*). **Stern** combines harshness and authority with strictness or severity (*a stern judge*). **Unmitigated** means unmodified and unsoftened in any way (*a streak of unmitigated bad luck*).

---

severely *adverb* **1** *treat the culprits severely* | *speak severely to them* harshly, stringently, unsparingly, relentlessly, painfully, sharply, with an iron hand, with a rod of iron, caustically, scathingly. **2** *injured severely* very badly, extremely badly, seriously, gravely, acutely, critically. **3** *severely dressed* austerely, starkly, spartanly, plainly, simply, without adornment, restrainedly, classically.

severity *noun* **1** *the severity of the criticism* harshness, stringency, rigorousness, relentlessness, painfulness, sharpness, causticness. **2** *the severity of the regime* harshness, hardness, sternness, rigorousness, stringency, strictness, inflexibility, relentlessness, pitilessness, ruthlessness, brutality, cruelty, savagery, tyranny, despotism. **3** *the severity of the storm/pain* fierceness, strength, violence, intensity. **4** *the severeness of her expression* sternness, graveness, gravity. *See* SEVERE 6. **5** *the severity of the decoration* austerity, starkness, spartanism, asceticism, plainness, simplicity, bareness, lack of adornment, restraint, functionalism. **6** *the severity of the winter* severeness, harshness, extremity, inclemency, coldness.

sew *verb* stitch, seam, embroider, mend, darn.

sex *noun* **1** *identify the sex of the animal* gender. **2** *attraction based on sex* sexuality, sexual attraction, sexual chemistry, sexual desire, desire, sex drive, sexual appetite, libido. **3** *lessons in sex* | *sex education* facts of life, sexual reproduction, reproduction; *inf.* the birds and the bees. **4** *have sex with him* | *a relationship without sex* intimacy, coitus, coition, coupling, copulation, carnal knowledge, making love, mating, fornication.

sexuality *noun* **1** *differences based on sexuality* sex, gender, sexual characteristics. **2** *identifying one's sexuality* sexual desire, sexual appetite, sexiness, carnality, physicalness, eroticism, lust, sensuality, voluptuousness; sexual orientation, sexual preferences.

sexy *adjective* **1** *sexy pictures* erotic, titillating, suggestive, arousing, exciting, stimulating. **2** *sexy clothes* titillating, arousing, provocative, seductive, sensuous, slinky. **3** *sexy women/men* sexually attractive, alluring, seductive, shapely.

shabby *adjective* **1** *shabby furniture/houses* dilapidated, broken-down, run-down, tumbledown, ramshackle, in disrepair, scruffy, dingy, seedy, squalid, tatty, slumlike, slummy; *inf.* tacky. **2** *shabby clothes* worn, worn-out, threadbare, ragged, frayed, tattered, faded, scruffy, tatty, the worse for wear. **3** *shabby treatment of the old lady* contemptible, despicable, dishon-

orable, disreputable, mean, base, low, dirty, odious, shameful, ignoble, unworthy, cheap, shoddy; *inf.* rotten, low-down.
Antonyms: SMART; NEAT; HONORABLE.

shackle verb 1 *shackle the prisoner* chain, fetter, put in irons, manacle, tie up, bind, tether, hobble, handcuff. 2 *no longer shackled by convention* deter, restrain, restrict, limit, impede, hinder, hamper, obstruct, encumber, check, curb, constrain, tie the hands of.

shackles plural noun 1 *prisoners in shackles* chains, fetters, bonds, irons, manacles, tethers, ropes, handcuffs; *inf.* cuffs. 2 *throw off the shackles of convention* deterrent, restraint, impediment, hindrance, obstruction, obstacle, check, curb, constraint.

shade noun 1 *sit in the shade of a tree* shadiness, shadow, shadowiness, shadows, shelter, cover. 2 *in the shade of evening* dimness, dusk, semi-darkness, twilight, gloaming, darkness, gloom, gloominess, murkiness, murk. 3 *a darker shade for the carpets* color, hue, tone, tint, tinge. 4 *act as a shade against the light* screen, shield, curtain, blind, canopy, veil, cover, covering. 5 *a word with several shades of meaning* nuance, degree, gradation, difference, variety. **a shade** *a shade better* a little, a bit, a trace, a touch, a dash, a modicum, a soupçon, slightly, marginally. **shades** *shades of Napoleon* reminder(s), intimation(s), suggestion(s), hint(s).
Antonyms: SUNLIGHT; LIGHT.

shade verb 1 *trees shading the garden* shut out the light from, block off light to, cast a shadow over, screen, darken, dim. 2 *shading the light* cover, obscure, mute, hide, conceal, veil, curtain.

shadow noun 1 *sit in the shadow of the building* shade, shadowiness, shadows, shelter, cover. 2 *in the shadow of evening* dimness, dusk, semi-darkness, twilight, gloaming, darkness, gloom. 3 *their shadows on the wall* silhouette, outline, shape. 4 *cast a shadow on their happiness* gloom, gloominess, cloud, blight, sadness, unhappiness. 5 *her younger sister was her shadow* constant companion, inseparable companion, close friend, bosom friend, intimate, alter ego; *inf.* sidekick. 6 *the policewoman acting as a shadow* watch, follower, detective; *inf.* tail. **a shadow of** 1 *not a shadow of a doubt* a bit of, a shade of, a trace of, a touch of, a dash of, a modicum of, a soupçon of, slightly, marginally. 2 *a shadow of a smile* a trace of, a hint of, a suggestion of, a suspicion of, a ghost of. 3 *a shadow of his former self* a ghost of, a specter of, a phantom of, a remnant of, a poor imitation of.

shadowy adjective 1 *shadowy parts of the garden/ house* shady, shaded, dim, dark, gloomy, murky, crepuscular, tenebrous, tenebrious. 2 *shadowy shapes on the horizon* indistinct, indeterminate, indefinite, unclear, vague, nebulous, ill-defined, indistinguishable, unsubstantial, ghostly, phantom, spectral.
Antonyms: BRIGHT; SUNNY; DISTINCT.

shady adjective 1 *shady parts of the garden* shaded, shadowy, screened, sheltered, covered, dim, dark, leafy, bowery, umbrageous, tenebrous, tenebrious. 2 *shady character* disreputable, of dubious character, suspicious, suspect, questionable, dishonest, dishonorable, untrustworthy, devious, shifty, slippery, tricky, underhand, underhanded, unscrupulous; *inf.* crooked, fishy.
Antonyms: BRIGHT; SUNNY; REPUTABLE; ABOVEBOARD.

shaft noun 1 *the shafts of the mine* passage, duct, tunnel, well, flue. 2 *shafts of light* ray, beam, gleam, streak, pencil. 3 *the shaft of a spade* pole, stick, rod, staff, shank, stem, handle, upright.

shaggy adjective hairy, hirsute, long-haired, rough, coarse, matted, tangled, unkempt, untidy.

shake verb 1 *the truck shaking on the rough roads* rock, bump, jolt, bounce, roll, sway, swing, oscillate, wobble, rattle, vibrate, jar, jerk, joggle, jounce. 2 *shaking with fear/cold* shiver, tremble, quiver, quake, shudder. 3 *shake the can of coins* jiggle, joggle, jolt, jerk, rattle, agitate, jounce. 4 *shaken by the accident/news* agitate, upset, distress, shock, alarm, disturb, perturb, fluster, unsettle, discompose, disquiet, disconcert, unnerve, ruffle, jolt, flurry, confuse, muddle; *inf.* rattle. 5 *shake her confidence* undermine, weaken, lessen, impair, harm, hurt, injure. 6 *shake a fist/stick at them* brandish, wave, flourish, swing, wield, raise. **shake off** *shake off their pursuers* escape, elude, get away from, leave behind, give the slip to, throw off, get rid of, rid oneself of, extricate oneself from. **shake up** 1 *shake up the dressing/cocktail* mix, churn up, agitate. 2 *shaken up by the accident* shake, agitate, upset, disturb, unsettle, discompose. 3 *shake up the system/firm* reorganize, rearrange, revolutionize, rouse, stir up.

---

shake
quake, quiver, shiver, shudder, tremble

Does a cool breeze make you **shiver, quiver, shudder,** or **tremble**? All of these verbs describe vibrating, wavering, or oscillating movements that, in living creatures, are often involuntary expressions of strain or discomfort. **Shake,** which refers to abrupt forward-and-backward, side-to-side, or up-and-down movements, is different from the others in that it can be done to a person or object as well as by one (*shake a can of paint; shake visibly while lifting a heavy load*). *Tremble* applies specifically to the slight and rapid shaking motion the human body makes when it is nervous, frightened, or uneasy (*his hands trembled when he picked up the phone*). To *shiver* is to make a similar movement with the entire body, but the cause is usually cold or fear (*shiver in the draft from an open door*). *Quiver* suggests a rapid and almost imperceptible vibration resulting from disturbed or irregular surface tension; it refers more often to things (*the leaves quivered in the breeze*), although people may quiver when they're under emotional tension (*her lower lip quivered and her eyes were downcast*). *Shudder* suggests a more intense shaking, usually in response to something horrible or revolting (*shudder at the thought of eating uncooked meat*). *Quake* implies a violent upheaval or shaking, similar to what occurs during an earthquake (*the boy's heart quaked at his father's approach*).

---

shake noun **1** *cargo upset by the shakes of the truck on the rough road* shaking, rocking, bump, jolt, bounce, roll, swaying, rattle, vibration, jarring, jerk. **2** *the children had the shakes* shaking, shivering, trembling, tremor, quiver, quivering, convulsion. **3** *with one shake of the can* jiggle, joggle, jolt, jerk, rattle. **4** *get quite a shake from the accident/news* upset, shock, jolt. *See* SHAKE verb 4. **5** *with a shake of his fist/stick* brandish, wave, flourish, swing.

shaky adjective **1** *with shaky limbs* shaking, trembling, tremulous, quivering, quivery, unsteady, wobbly, weak. **2** *take a few shaky steps* shaking, unsteady, faltering, wobbly, tottering, teetering, doddering, staggering. **3** *still a bit shaky after the illness* infirm, unsound, unwell, ill, below par, indisposed; *inf.* under the weather. **4** *rather shaky reasoning/grounds* questionable, dubious, tenuous, unsubstantial, flimsy, weak, nebulous, unsound, unreliable, undependable, ungrounded, unfounded. **5** *shaky bits of furniture* rickety, wobbly, flimsy, ramshackle, dilapidated, gimcrack, jerry-built.

Antonyms: STEADY; SOUND; STABLE.

shallow adjective **1** *a shallow person* frivolous, foolish, unintelligent, unthinking, trivial, insincere, superficial. **2** *shallow ideas/attitudes/remarks* frivolous, superficial, unsubstantial, trifling, trivial, petty, empty, meaningless.

Antonyms: SERIOUS; PROFOUND.

sham verb *shamming an illness* | *he is only shamming* fake, pretend, feign, counterfeit, put on, simulate, affect, imitate; dissemble, malinger, make believe.

sham noun **1** *his charm is only a sham* fake, pretense, feint, feigning, counterfeit, imposture, simulation. **2** *the doctor was a sham* impostor, fake, fraud, pretender, masquerader, dissembler, wolf in sheep's clothing, charlatan; *inf.* phony. **3** *the document is a sham* counterfeit, fake, forgery, imposture, copy, imitation, hoax.

sham adjective **1** *sham sympathy* pretended, pretend, feigned, fake, contrived, put-on, simulated, affected, artificial, insincere, ungenuine, false, bogus, spurious; *inf.* phony, pseudo. **2** *sham gold watches* fake, counterfeit, imitation, simulated, artificial, synthetic, ersatz; *inf.* phony, pseudo.

Antonyms: REAL; GENUINE; AUTHENTIC.

shamble verb shuffle, hobble, limp, falter, totter, dodder, toddle.

shambles plural noun chaos, muddle, mess, confusion, disorder, disarray, disorganization, anarchy; *inf.* disaster area.

shame noun **1** *feel shame at being imprisoned* humiliation, ignominy, mortification, loss of face, remorse, guilt, compunction, shamefacedness, embarrassment, discomfort, discomposure. **2** *bring shame on the family* disgrace, dishonor, scandal, discredit, degradation, ignominy, disrepute, infamy, odium, opprobrium, condemnation, reproach. **3** *he is a shame to the family* disgrace, discredit, blot, smirch, stain, blemish, stigma. **4** *a shame he could not be there* pity, misfortune, bad luck, ill luck, source of regret. **put to shame** *put their efforts to shame* outshine, outclass, overshadow, eclipse, surpass, excel, outstrip, outdo, outrival, put in the shade.

Antonyms: PRIDE; HONOR; CREDIT.

shamefaced adjective **1** *too shamefaced to appear after his crime* ashamed, embarrassed, guilty, conscience-stricken, remorseful, contrite, penitent, regretful, humiliated, mortified, shamed. **2** *shamefaced children hiding behind their mothers* shy, bashful, timid, timorous, shrinking, coy, sheepish.

shameful adjective **1** *shameful behavior/secrets* disgraceful, base, mean, low, vile, outrageous, shocking, dishonorable, unbecoming, unworthy, discreditable, deplorable, despicable, contemptible, reprehensible, scandalous, atrocious, heinous. **2** *shameful secrets* shaming, humiliating, mortifying, embarrassing.

Antonyms: ADMIRABLE; HONORABLE; LAUDABLE.

shameless adjective **1** *shameless about his prison sentence* unashamed, without shame, unabashed, uncontrite, unpenitent, impenitent, unregretful. **2** *shameless behavior* brazen, impudent, bold, brash, forward, audacious, immodest, unseemly, improper, unbecoming, indecorous, wanton, abandoned, indecent.

shape noun **1** *clouds of different shapes* | *pieces of plastic in all shapes and sizes* form, figure, configuration, formation, conformation, contour, outline, silhouette, profile, outward form, external appearance. **2** *in the shape of the devil* form, guise, appearance, likeness, look, semblance, image, aspect. **3** *business in poor shape* | *athletes in good shape* condition, state, health, trim, fettle, kilter. **4** *make out shapes in the distance* figure, form, outline, shadow, body, apparition. **5** *jelly/cement in a shape* mold, frame. **6** *dressmaking shapes* pattern, model.

shape verb **1** *shape the clay into a figure* form, fashion, make, create, design, mold, model, cast, frame, block, carve, sculpt, sculpture. **2** *attitudes shaped by childhood experiences* form, fashion, mold, create, produce, influence, guide, determine, define. **3** *shape a secret plan* plan, devise, prepare, develop, organize, line up. **4** *shape the dress to her figure* adjust, adapt, accommodate, alter, modify, tailor. **shape up 1** *new recruits shaping up* improve, show improvement, get better, make progress, progress, make headway, show promise. **2** *plans shaping up* take form, take shape, develop, crystallize, fall into place, come along, go forward, progress, make headway.

shapeless *adjective* **1** *shapeless hunks of clay* amorphous, formless, unformed, unshaped, unfashioned, undeveloped, embryonic. **2** *shapeless clothes* formless, ill-proportioned, inelegant, sacklike. **3** *shapeless old hats* misshapen, battered, deformed.

shapely *adjective* *shapely legs* well-formed, well-shaped, well-proportioned, elegant, curvaceous, curvy.

shard *noun* fragment, piece, particle, scrap, bit, chip, sliver, splinter, paring, shaving, remnant.

share *noun* *each receiving a fair share* division, quota, allowance, ration, allocation, allotment, portion, part, lot, measure, helping, serving; *inf.* cut, piece of the cake, piece of the action.

share *verb* **1** *share the workload* divide (up), split; *inf.* divvy (up). **2** *share the profits* divide (up), distribute, apportion, parcel out, deal out, dole out, give out; *inf.* divvy (up). **share expenses/ costs** *inf.* go halves, go halfsies, go fifty-fifty, go Dutch. **share in** *sharing in their good fortune* have a share in, have a part in, participate in, take part in, partake of, have a percentage of, have a stake in.

sharp *adjective* **1** *a sharp utensil* cutting, serrated, knifelike, edged, razor-edged, keen. **2** *a sharp piece of metal* pointed, needlelike, spear-shaped, barbed, spiky. **3** *a sharp drop to the sea* steep, sheer, abrupt, precipitous, vertical. **4** *come to a sharp stop* sudden, abrupt, rapid, unexpected. **5** *a sharp difference between the two* clear, clear-cut, distinct, marked, well-defined, crisp. **6** *a sharp pain* intense, acute, keen, piercing, cutting, extreme, severe, stabbing, shooting, stinging. **7** *a sharp taste* pungent, biting, bitter, acid, sour, tart, vinegary. **8** *a sharp smell* acrid, pungent, burning. **9** *a sharp noise* piercing, shrill, high-pitched, earsplitting, harsh, strident. **10** *exchange sharp words* harsh, curt, brusque, bitter, hard, cutting, scathing, caustic, biting, barbed, acrimonious, trenchant, sarcastic, sardonic, venomous, malicious, vitriolic, hurtful, unkind, cruel. **11** *a sharp student* sharp-witted, intelligent, bright, clever, quick. **12** *sharp intelligence/wits* keen, acute, quick, ready, smart, knowing, comprehending, shrewd, discerning, perceptive, penetrating. **13** *sharp practices | a sharp customer* unscrupulous, dishonest, cunning, wily, crafty, artful. **14** *move at a sharp pace* brisk, rapid, quick, fast, swift, vigorous, spirited, animated. **15** *a sharp dresser* smart, stylish, fashionable, chic, elegant; *inf.* dressy, snappy, natty.

Antonyms: BLUNT; GENTLE; INDISTINCT; MILD.

sharp *adjective* *arrive at 9 a.m. sharp* promptly, punctually, on time, on the dot; *inf.* on the nose.

sharp *adverb* *pull up sharp* abruptly, suddenly, all of a sudden, unexpectedly, without warning.

sharpen *verb* put an edge on, edge, whet, hone, strop, grind.

shatter *verb* **1** *shatter the windshield* smash, smash to smithereens, break, break into pieces, splinter, fracture, shiver, pulverize, crush, crack; *inf.* bust. **2** *shatter one's hopes/dreams* destroy, demolish, wreck, ruin, dash, blight, wipe out, overturn, blast, bring to naught, devastate, torpedo. **3** *shattered by their betrayal* break one's heart, devastate, crush, upset, distress, dumbfound; *inf.* knock the stuffing out of.

shave *verb* **1** *shave his beard* cut off, trim, snip off, crop. **2** *shave off pieces of wood* pare, plane, shear. **3** *shave the fence with his car* brush, graze, touch, scrape, rub.

sheath *noun* **1** *a sheath for a sword* scabbard, case, casing, cover, covering, envelope, wrapper. **2** *a contraceptive sheath* condom, contraceptive; *inf.* rubber.

shed *noun* *a garden shed* hut, outhouse, lean-to, shack.

shed *verb* **1** *trees shedding their leaves* let fall, let drop. **2** *snakes shedding their skins* cast off, slough off. **3** *shed clothes* take off, remove, strip off, doff. **4** *shed blood* pour forth, let flow, spill, discharge, exude. **5** *shed light* diffuse, send forth, radiate, disperse, scatter. **6** *companies shedding workers* discard, get rid of, dispense with, drop, declare/make redundant, dismiss; *inf.* sack, fire.

sheen *noun* shine, luster, gleam, sparkle, gloss, burnish, polish, patina.

sheepish *adjective* embarrassed, uncomfortable, ashamed, shamefaced, blushing, abashed, shy, bashful, diffident, foolish, silly.

sheer *adjective* **1** *sheer folly/magic* utter, complete, thoroughgoing, total, absolute, veritable, downright, out-and-out, unqualified, unconditional, unmitigated, unalloyed, unadulterated. **2** *a sheer cliff | a sheer drop to the sea* steep, abrupt, sharp, precipitous, vertical, perpendicular. **3** *sheer silk* diaphanous, transparent, see-through, translucent, filmy, gossamer, gauzy, ultrafine, fine, thin.

Antonyms: QUALIFIED; GRADUAL; THICK.

sheer *verb* *ships sheering* swerve, change course, slew, veer, drift, yaw. **sheer away from** *sheer away from the topic* turn away from, change the subject from, avoid, evade, dodge, deviate from.

sheet *noun* **1** *sheets and blankets* bedsheet, bed linen. **2** *a sheet of lacquered veneer on the table* layer, stratum, overlay, surface, lamina, covering, coating, coat, facing, veneer, film. **3** *sheets of glass/plastic* piece, pane, panel, plate, slab. **sheet of paper** piece of paper, leaf, page, folio.

shelf *noun* **1** *putting books/cards on shelves* ledge, bracket, mantelshelf, mantelpiece. **2** *shelves in the sea* sandbank, sandbar, reef, shoal.

shell *noun* **1** *the shell of a crab* carapace, case. **2** *the shell of a nut* casing, case, husk, pod, integument. **3** *shells in the army magazine* bullet, grenade, shot, cartridge, case. **4** *the shell of a car/ship under construction* framework, frame, structure, chassis, hull, skeleton.

shell *verb* **1** *shell peas* husk, shuck. **2** *troops shelling the city* bomb, bombard, blitz, torpedo, strafe, fire on, open fire on. **shell out** *shell out money* pay out, spend, lay out, disburse, squander; *inf.* fork out.

shelter *noun* **1** *provide shelter from danger/cold* protection, shield, cover, screen, safety, security, defense, refuge, sanctuary, asylum. **2** *a shelter for battered wives* refuge, sanctuary, retreat, haven, harbor.

shelter *verb* **1** *shelter them from the weather* protect, provide protection for, shield, cover, screen, safeguard. **2** *shelter the criminal from the police* protect, shield, screen, safeguard, provide refuge/sanctuary for, guard, harbor, conceal, hide. **take shelter** take refuge, seek protection, seek refuge/sanctuary.
Antonyms: EXPOSE; ENDANGER.

sheltered *adjective* **1** *a sheltered spot for the picnic* shady, shaded, protected, screened, shielded, secluded. **2** *lead a sheltered life* secluded, quiet, withdrawn, retired, isolated, protected, cloistered, reclusive.

shelve *verb* *shelve expansion plans* put to one side, lay aside, put off, postpone, defer, delay, suspend, table, mothball, pigeonhole, put on ice, put in cold storage, put on the back burner.

shepherd *verb* *shepherd the children to their classes* escort, conduct, usher, convoy, guide, marshal, steer.

shield *noun* *a shield against disease/attack* protection, defense, guard, safeguard, support, bulwark, screen, protector.

shield *verb* *shield one's eyes from the dust* | *shield the child from the facts* protect, screen, defend, guard, safeguard, shelter.
Antonyms: EXPOSE; ENDANGER.

shift *verb* *shift one's position on the new project* change, alter, vary, modify, reverse, do an about-face; *inf.* do a U-turn.

shift *noun* **1** *a shift in public opinion* change, alteration, variation, modification, about-face, reversal, sea change; *inf.* U-turn. **2** *an eight-hour shift* work period, stint, spell of work.

shiftless *adjective* lazy, idle, indolent, slothful, inefficient, unambitious, unenterprising, worthless, good-for-nothing, ne'er-do-well.

shifty *adjective* evasive, slippery, devious, duplicitous, deceitful, underhand, underhanded, untrustworthy, double-dealing, dishonest, wily, crafty, artful, sly, scheming, contriving.
Antonyms: HONEST; OPEN; TRUSTWORTHY.

shilly-shally *verb* be indecisive/irresolute, vacil-

late, waver, hesitate, hem and haw, oscillate, fluctuate; *inf.* blow hot and cold.

shimmer *verb* *light shimmering on the water* glisten, glint, flicker, twinkle, sparkle, gleam, glow, scintillate, dance.

shimmer *noun* *the shimmer of light on water* glistening, glint, flicker, twinkle, sparkle, gleam, glow, luster, iridescence, scintillation.

shine *verb* **1** *the sun/torch shining* emit light, give off light. **2** *with shoes/glasses shining* gleam, sparkle, glisten. **3** *lights shining in the distance* gleam, glow, glint, sparkle, twinkle, flicker, glitter, glisten, shimmer, flash, dazzle, beam, radiate, illuminate, luminesce, incandesce. **4** *with face shining* glow, beam, radiate, bloom, look healthy, look good. **5** *shine the shoes* polish, burnish, buff, wax, gloss, brush, rub up. **6** *shine at tennis* excel, be expert, be brilliant, be very good, be outstanding. **7** *shine in a crowd* stand out, be outstanding, be conspicuous, be preeminent, excel, dominate, star.

shine *noun* **1** *the shine of the street lights* light, brightness, gleam, glow, glint, sparkle, twinkle, flicker, glitter, glisten, shimmer, flash, dazzle, glare, beam, radiance, illumination, luminescence, luminosity, lambency, effulgence. **2** *put a shine on the polished table* polish, burnish, gleam, gloss, luster, sheen, patina.

shining *adjective* **1** *shining lights* gleaming, glowing, glinting, sparkling, twinkling, flickering, glittering, flashing, dazzling, incandescent, effulgent. **2** *with shining, happy faces* glowing, beaming, radiant, blooming, healthy. **3** *a shining example* | *shining stars in the theater* outstanding, preeminent, leading, illustrious, brilliant, splendid. **4** *shining tables/glasses* shiny, polished, burnished, gleaming, glossy, satiny, lustrous.

shiny *adjective* *shiny tables/glasses* shining, polished, burnished, gleaming, glossy, satiny, lustrous.
Antonyms: DULL; LUSTERLESS.

shirk *verb* *shirk work* avoid, evade, dodge, sidestep, shrink from, shun, get out of; *inf.* duck (out of).

shirker *noun* dodger, slacker, truant, malingerer, layabout, loafer, idler.

shiver *verb* *shiver with cold/fear* tremble, quiver, shake, shudder, quaver, quake, vibrate.

shiver *noun* *give a shiver of fear* tremble, quiver, shake, quaver, shudder.

shivery *adjective* *feeling shivery in the cold* | *be shivery from the fever* trembling, trembly, quivering, quivery, shaking, shaky, shuddering, quavering, quaking.

shock[1] *noun* **1** *the shock of the two cars hitting each other* impact, blow, collision, crash, clash, jolt, bump, jar, jerk. **2** *the news came as a shock* surprise, blow, upset, disturbance, state of agitation, source of distress, source of amazement/consternation, revelation, bolt from the blue, bombshell, eye-opener. **3** *suffering from shock after the accident* state of shock, trauma, traumatism, prostration, stupor, stupefaction, collapse.

shock[2] *verb shocked by the scenes of famine* appall, horrify, scandalize, outrage, repel, revolt, disgust, nauseate, sicken, offend, traumatize, distress, upset, perturb, disturb, disquiet, unsettle, discompose, agitate, astound, dumbfound, stagger, amaze, astonish, stun, flabbergast, stupefy, overwhelm, bewilder.

shock[3] *noun a shock of red hair* mass, mop, mane, thatch.

shocking *adjective shocking conditions | a shocking sight* appalling, horrifying, horrific, dreadful, awful, frightful, terrible, horrible, scandalous, outrageous, disgraceful, vile, abominable, ghastly, foul, monstrous, unspeakable, abhorrent, hideous, atrocious, repellent, revolting, odious, repulsive, repugnant, disgusting, nauseating, sickening, grisly, loathsome, offensive, distressing, upsetting, perturbing, disturbing, disquieting, unsettling, agitating, staggering, amazing, astonishing, stupefying, overwhelming, bewildering.
Antonyms: ADMIRABLE; WONDERFUL; DELIGHTFUL.

shoddy *adjective* poor-quality, inferior, second-rate, cheapjack, tawdry, rubbishy, trashy, junky, gimcrack, jerry-built; *inf.* tacky, tatty.

shoot *verb* **1** *shoot a deer* hit, wound, injure, shoot down, bring down, bag, fell, kill, slay; *inf.* pick off, pump full of lead, plug. **2** *shoot a round of bullets/arrows* fire, discharge, launch, let off, let fly, send forth, emit. **3** *runners shooting past* race, dash, sprint, bound, charge, dart, fly, hurtle, bolt, streak, flash, whisk, run, speed, hurry, hasten; *inf.* scoot. **4** *shooting animal scenes* film, photograph, take photographs of. **shoot at** *shoot at the fugitives* fire at, open fire on, aim at, snipe at, shell. **shoot up** *plants shooting up* put forth buds, bud, burgeon, sprout, germinate, appear, spring up.

shoot *noun shoots of a plant/tree* bud, offshoot, slip, scion, sucker, sprout, branch, twig, sprig, cutting, graft.

shop *noun* **1** *a dress shop* store, boutique. **2** *mechanics working in the shop* workshop; plant, factory; machine shop, auto body shop, auto repair shop.

shop *verb shop for a dress/house/car* go shopping, look to buy, be in the market for.

shore *noun* seashore, seaside, beach, coast, seaboard, waterfront, waterside, strand.

shore *verb shore up shore up the broken wall* prop up, support, hold up, underpin, strengthen, brace, buttress.

short *adjective* **1** *short people* small, little, slight, petite, tiny, wee, squat, stubby, dwarfish, diminutive, dumpy, Lilliputian; *inf.* pint-sized, pocket-sized, knee-high to a grasshopper. **2** *short bushes* low, stubby, miniature. **3** *a short piece of string* small, little, tiny, minuscule. **4** *a short report* brief, concise, succinct, to the point, compact, terse, summary, crisp, pithy, epigrammatic, abridged, abbreviated, condensed, summarized, contracted, curtailed, truncated. **5** *a short affair* brief, momentary, temporary, short-lived, impermanent, short-term, cursory, fleeting, passing, transitory, transient, ephemeral, fugacious, evanescent, meteoric. **6** *the short route* direct, straight. **7** *money/food is a bit short* deficient, lacking, wanting, insufficient, inadequate, scarce, scanty, meager, sparse, unplentiful, tight, low. **8** *he was short with her | give rather a short reply* curt, sharp, abrupt, blunt, brusque, terse, gruff, surly, testy, tart, rude, discourteous, uncivil, impolite.
Antonyms: TALL; LONG; ABUNDANT.

short *adverb stop short* abruptly, suddenly, all of a sudden, unexpectedly, without warning, out of the blue. **cut short** shorten, curtail, truncate, abbreviate, reduce, bring to an untimely end, terminate, end, stop, halt, arrest, cut off, interrupt, break up. **fall short** be deficient, be insufficient, be inadequate, disappoint, fail, not fulfill expectations; *inf.* not come up to scratch. **in short** briefly, to put it briefly, in a word, in a nutshell, in essence, to cut a long story short, to come to the point. **sell short** *always selling herself short* undervalue, underrate, underestimate, disparage, deprecate, belittle, detract from, derogate. **short of 1** *short of eggs/brains* deficient in, lacking, wanting, in need of, low on, missing. **2** *short of breaking a window, how will you get into your locked car?* other than, apart from, aside from, besides, except (for), without, excluding, leaving out, not counting, disregarding.

shortage *noun* dearth, scarcity, lack, deficiency, insufficiency, paucity, deficit, inadequacy, shortfall, want, poverty.
Antonyms: ABUNDANCE; SURFEIT; SURPLUS.

shortcoming *noun forgive his shortcomings* defect, fault, flaw, imperfection, failing, drawback, weakness, weak point, foible, frailty, infirmity.

shorten *verb* **1** *shorten the text* abbreviate, condense, abridge, cut, cut down, contract, compress, reduce, lessen, decrease, diminish, curtail, duck, trim, pare down. **2** *the days are shortening* get shorter, grow shorter, grow less.
Antonyms: LENGTHEN; EXTEND; ELONGATE.

short-lived *adjective short-lived happiness* brief, momentary, temporary, impermanent, fleeting, transitory, ephemeral. *See* SHORT *adjective* 5.

shortly *adverb* **1** *she will be with you shortly* soon, in a short while, in a little while, presently, before long, directly; *inf.* before you know it, before you can say Jack Robinson. **2** *he replied shortly* curtly, sharply, abruptly, bluntly, brusquely, tersely, gruffly, testily, tartly, rudely, discourteously, uncivilly, impolitely.

shortsighted *adjective* **1** *wear spectacles because of being shortsighted* myopic, nearsighted. **2** *a shortsighted attitude to business* lacking foresight, uncircumspect, ill-considered, unwary, imprudent, injudicious, unwise, ill-advised, thoughtless, unthinking, heedless, rash, incautious.

short-staffed *adjective* understaffed, shorthanded, undermanned, below strength.

short-tempered *adjective* quick-tempered, hot-tempered, irascible, touchy, testy, fiery, peppery, choleric; *inf.* on a short fuse.

shot *noun* 1 *hear a shot* gunfire, report (of a gun), crack, bang, blast, explosion. 2 *shot for the guns* pellet(s), bullet(s), slug(s), projectile(s), ammunition. 3 *got the ball through the hoop with one shot* throw, toss, lob, fling, hurl. 4 *a better shot than his brother* shooter, marksman, markswoman, rifleman. 5 *take a shot of the house* photograph, photo, snap, snapshot, picture; *inf.* pic. 6 *have a shot at getting there* attempt, try, effort, endeavor; *inf.* go, stab, crack, whack. 7 *it is your shot now* turn, chance, opportunity; *inf.* go. 8 *have shots before going to the tropics* injection, vaccination. 9 *a nasty/cheap shot* comment, remark, statement, utterance; *inf.* crack. **a shot in the arm** *a shot in the arm for the tourist industry* boost, fillip, lift, encouragement, stimulus. **a shot in the dark** *her answer was a shot in the dark* wild guess, random guess, guess, pure conjecture. **like a shot** *he flew out of here like a shot* without hesitation, unhesitatingly, immediately, instantly, right away, at once, like a flash. **not by a long shot** by no means, not at all, not in the least, on no account, under no circumstances.

shoulder *verb* 1 *shoulder a heavy burden/responsibility* bear, carry, support, be responsible for, take on, take upon oneself. 2 *shoulder his way to the front* push, shove, thrust, jostle, elbow, force. **give (someone) the cold shoulder** ostracize, shun, snub, ignore, rebuff, send (someone) to Coventry. **put one's shoulder to the wheel** apply oneself, exert oneself, get down to work, set to work, make an effort, strive; *inf.* buckle down, give it one's best shot. **rub shoulders with** associate with, mix with, socialize with, consort with, fraternize with, hobnob with. **shoulder to shoulder** side by side, cheek by jowl, together, united, jointly, in partnership, in cooperation, in unity, in unison, as one. **straight from the shoulder** directly, frankly, candidly, forthrightly, bluntly, plainly, explicitly, outspokenly, unequivocally, unambiguously; *inf.* pulling no punches, with no holds barred.

shout *verb* cry out, call out, yell, roar, howl, bellow, scream, bawl, call/yell at the top of one's voice, raise one's voice; *inf.* holler.

shout *noun* *a shout of pain* cry, call, yell, roar, howl, bellow, scream; *inf.* holler.

shove *verb* *shove forward* | *shove her out of the way* push, thrust, drive, force, shoulder, jostle, jolt.

shove *noun* *give him a shove* push, thrust, jostle, jolt.

shovel *verb* *shovel coal* scoop up, spade, dig, excavate.

show *verb* 1 *gray hairs beginning to show* be visible, be seen, be in view, appear, put in an appearance. 2 *show the new merchandise* exhibit, display, present, demonstrate, set forth, uncover, reveal. 3 *show his grief* indicate, express, manifest, reveal, make known, make plain, make obvious, evince, evidence, disclose, betray, divulge. 4 *show (them) the new procedures* demonstrate, point out, explain, expound, clarify, elucidate, teach, instruct in, give instructions in, tutor in, indoctrinate in. 5 *show them to their seats* escort, accompany, usher, conduct, attend, guide, lead, direct, steer. 6 *he never showed* show up, appear, put in an appearance, make an appearance, turn up, come, arrive, be present. **show off** 1 *models showing off the dresses* show to advantage, display, exhibit, demonstrate, parade, flaunt. 2 *showing off in front of the guests* put on airs, boast, brag, swagger around. **show up** 1 *sunshine showing up the dust* expose, reveal, bring to light, lay bare, make visible, make obvious, highlight, pinpoint, put the spotlight on. 2 *the red showing up well against the white* be visible, be obvious, be conspicuous, stand out, catch the eye. 3 *show him up in front of his rich friends* expose, show in a bad light, shame, put to shame, mortify, humiliate, embarrass. 4 *the guest did not show up* appear, make an appearance, put in an appearance, turn up, come, get here/there, be present; *inf.* show.
Antonyms: CONCEAL; SUPPRESS; WITHHOLD.

show *noun* 1 *a brilliant show of flowers* display, array, arrangement, exhibition, presentation, exposition, spectacle. 2 *a boat show* exhibition, demonstration, display, exposition, presentation; *inf.* expo. 3 *put on a musical show* performance, theatrical performance, production; *inf.* gig. 4 *a show of courage* appearance, outward appearance, air, guise, semblance, pretense, illusion, pose, affectation, profession, parade. 5 *doing it only for show* display, ostentation, affectation, window-dressing. 6 *run the show* organization, establishment, undertaking, enterprise, business, venture. **steal the show** be the main attraction, be the center of attraction, get all the attention, have all eyes upon one, be the cynosure.

showdown *noun* confrontation, clash, face-off, moment of truth, crisis, culmination, climax.

shower *noun* 1 *a shower of rain/snow* fall, drizzle, flurry, sprinkling. 2 *a shower of arrows* volley, raining, barrage, fusillade. 3 *a shower of gifts* abundance, profusion, plethora, flood, deluge.

shower *verb* 1 *arrows showered on them* rain, fall. 2 *shower them with gifts* deluge, inundate, overwhelm. 3 *shower gifts on them* lavish, pour, load, heap.

showing *noun* 1 *a private showing* show, exhibition, display, exposition; *inf.* expo. **2** *impressed by the company's showing* performance, track record, record, results.

show-off *noun* exhibitionist, extrovert, swaggerer, bragger, braggart, boaster, braggadocio; *inf.* blowhard.

showy *adjective showy clothes/lifestyle* ostentatious, flamboyant, elaborate, fancy, pretentious, overdone, glittering.
Antonyms: DISCREET; RESTRAINED; PLAIN.

shred *noun* **1** *shreds of material* scrap, fragment, wisp, sliver, bit, piece, remnant, snippet, tatter. **2** *not a shred of evidence* scrap, bit, iota, whit, particle, atom, modicum, trace, speck.

shred *verb shred paper/cabbage* cut up, tear up, rip up, grate.

shrew *noun acting like a shrew* virago, termagant, fury, harpy, nag.

shrewd *adjective* **1** *a shrewd businessman* astute, sharp, clever, intelligent, smart, alert, quick-witted, discerning, perspicacious, perceptive, discriminating, wise, sagacious, farseeing, canny, cunning, artful, crafty, wily, calculating; *inf.* with all one's wits about one. **2** *a shrewd plan* astute, clever, wise, judicious, farsighted, cunning, artful, crafty, wily, calculated.
Antonyms: STUPID; UNWISE; INGENUOUS.

shrewdness *noun* acumen, astuteness, sharpness, cleverness, smartness, alertness, quick-wittedness, discernment, perspicacity, perceptiveness, wisdom, sagacity, canniness, cunning, artfulness, craftiness, wiliness, calculation.

shriek *verb shriek with laughter/terror* scream, screech, squeal, yell, howl, shout, cry out, call out, whoop, wail; *inf.* holler.

shriek *noun a shriek of laughter/terror* scream, screech, squeal, yell, howl, shout, cry, call, whoop, wail; *inf.* holler.

shrill *adjective* high-pitched, high, sharp, piercing, ear-piercing, penetrating, earsplitting, screeching, shrieking.
Antonyms: LOW; SOFT; DULCET.

shrine *noun* **1** *a shrine in memory of the dead soldiers* memorial, monument, cenotaph. **2** *worship in the shrine* holy place, temple, church. **3** *the relics of the saint in a shrine* reliquary, burial chamber, tomb, sepulcher.

shrink *verb* **1** *shirts shrinking in the wash* get smaller, become/grow smaller. **2** *markets shrinking* get smaller, become/grow smaller, contract, diminish, lessen, reduce, dwindle, narrow, decline, fall off, drop off, shrivel. **3** *shrinking in fear* draw back, pull back, start back, back away, shy away, recoil, retreat, withdraw, flinch, cringe, wince.
Antonyms: STRETCH; EXPAND; CONFRONT.

shrivel *verb leaves shriveled by the sun* dry up, wither, desiccate, dehydrate, wrinkle, pucker up.

shriveled *adjective shriveled leaves/skin* dried up, withered, desiccated, dehydrated, wrinkled, puckered, wizened; *lit.* sere.

shroud *noun a shroud of mist over the hills* cover, covering, pall, cloak, blanket, cloud, veil, screen.

shroud *verb hills shrouded in mist* cover, enshroud, swathe, envelop, cloak, blanket, cloud, veil, screen, conceal, hide.

shrug *verb shrug off shrug off failure* disregard, take no notice of, not trouble about, dismiss, gloss over, play down, make light of, minimize.

shudder *verb shudder in horror* shake, shiver, tremble, quiver, quaver, quake, convulse.

shudder *noun a shudder of horror* shake, shiver, tremor, tremble, quiver, quaver, convulsion, spasm.

shuffle *verb* **1** *shuffle along the road* hobble, limp, drag one's feet, scuff one's feet. **2** *the audience shuffling their feet* scrape, scuff, drag. **3** *shuffle cards/papers* mix, intermix, shift about, rearrange, reorganize, jumble. **4** *shuffling and refusing to give a straight answer* hedge, equivocate, be evasive, prevaricate, fence, parry, beat about the bush, beg the question; *inf.* pussyfoot around.

shun *verb shun the ex-convict/publicity* avoid, evade, eschew, steer clear of, shy away from, recoil from, keep away from, keep one's distance from, cold-shoulder, give a wide berth to.

shut *verb shut the doors* close, fasten, bar, lock, secure, seal. **shut down** **1** *shut down the factory* close, close down. **2** *the factory has shut down* close, close down, cease production, come to a halt, cease operating; go on strike. **3** *shut down the machinery* switch off, stop, halt. **shut in** *shut in the dogs/prisoners* lock in, keep in, enclose, confine, restrain, imprison, hem in, fence in, corral. **shut out** **1** *shut out intruders* lock out, keep out. **2** *during negotiations, he was shut out* exclude, leave out, omit, keep out, bar, debar, ostracize, blackball, banish, exile, outlaw. **3** *shut out the light* keep out, block out, screen, cover up. **shut up** **1** *shut the sheep up in a pen* lock in, confine, imprison, coop up, box in, cage in. **2** *criminals shut up for life* imprison, jail, incarcerate, intern, immure. **3** *please shut up* keep quiet, be quiet, keep silent, fall silent; *inf.* hold one's tongue, keep one's lips sealed, pipe down, keep one's trap shut. **4** *the sound of the siren shut up the crowd* quiet, silence, hush, shush, gag; *inf.* button the lip of.
Antonyms: OPEN; UNLOCK.

shuttle *verb shuttle between the two cities* go back and forth, alternate, commute, shunt, ply.

shy *adjective* bashful, diffident, reserved, reticent, retiring, self-effacing, shrinking, withdrawn, timid, timorous, fearful, nervous, hesitant, wary, suspicious, chary, unconfident, modest, self-conscious, embarrassed, abashed.
Antonyms: BOLD; BRASH; confident.

shy *verb* **shy away from** *shy away from trouble*

shrink from, recoil from, flinch from, balk at, quail at, draw back from, back away from.

shyness *noun* bashfulness, diffidence, reserve, reservedness, reticence, timidity, timorousness, fearfulness, nervousness, hesitancy, hesitation, wariness, suspicion, chariness, lack of confidence, self-consciousness, embarrassment, modesty.

sick *adjective* **1** *unable to work when sick* unwell, ill, ailing, indisposed, poorly, below par, out of sorts, laid up; *inf.* under the weather, on the sick list. **2** *feel sick on a boat* nauseated, queasy, bilious; *inf.* green around the gills. **3** *be sick on the boat* vomit, retch, be sick to one's stomach; *inf.* throw up, puke. **4** *be sick about losing* angry, annoyed, displeased, disgruntled, distressed, disgusted; *inf.* fed up. **5** *a sick joke* morbid, macabre, ghoulish, gruesome, sadistic, perverted, cruel. **sick of** *sick of that music* tired of, weary of, bored with, surfeited with, satiated with, glutted with; *inf.* fed up with, have had (something) up to here.

Antonyms: WELL; HEALTHY.

sicken *verb* *sickened by the smell of garbage* make sick, nauseate, turn one's stomach, revolt, disgust, repel, shock, appall. **sicken of** *begin to sicken of that type of music* tire of, weary of, become bored with, have a surfeit of, be satiated with; *inf.* be fed up with, have had (something) up to here.

sickening *adjective* *the sickening smell of garbage* nauseating, nauseous, revolting, disgusting, repellent, repulsive, loathsome, distasteful, stomach-turning, shocking, appalling, offensive, vile, foul.

sickly *adjective* **1** *a sickly child* unhealthy, in poor health, chronically ill, delicate, frail, weak, feeble, puny. **2** *look sickly | a sickly complexion* pale, wan, pallid, peaky, anemic, bloodless, languid, listless; *inf.* washed-out. **3** *sickly love songs* sentimental, cloying, mawkish, maudlin, slushy, mushy, syrupy; *inf.* soppy, schmaltzy. **4** *sickly colors* pallid, insipid, wan, pale, washed-out, faded; *inf.* bilious.

sickness *noun* **1** *a terminal sickness* illness, disease, disorder, ailment, complaint, affliction, malady, infirmity, indisposition; *inf.* bug. **2** *a bout of sickness* vomiting, retching, upset stomach, stomach upset; *inf.* throwing up, puking. **3** *a feeling of sickness on the swaying boat* nausea, queasiness, biliousness.

side *noun* **1** *by the side of the lake/road* edge, border, verge, boundary, margin, rim, fringe, skirt, flank, brink, brim, periphery. **2** *on the east side of the city* part, quarter, section, sector, neighborhood. **3** *the upper side of the paper/wood* surface, face, part, facet. **4** *both sides of the question/problem* aspect, angle, facet, point of view, viewpoint, view, opinion, standpoint, position, slant. **5** *on the chairman's side in the dispute* camp, faction, caucus, party, wing, splinter

group, sect. **6** *which side do you root for?* team, squad, group. **side by side** *walk/fight side by side* close together, together, alongside each other, shoulder to shoulder, cheek by jowl, arm in arm. **take the side of** *take the side of the likely winner* side with, take the part of, support, give one's support to, favor.

Antonyms: CENTER; HEART.

side *adjective* **1** *on the side position of the battle* lateral, wing, flank. **2** *a side issue/road* minor, lesser, secondary, subordinate, subsidiary, ancillary, marginal. **3** *a side look* sidelong, oblique, indirect. *See* SIDELONG.

Antonyms: CENTRAL; MAJOR; PRIMARY.

side *verb* *side with his brother against his sister* take the side of, be on the side of, take the part of, support, give one's support to, back, give one's backing to, ally with, associate oneself with, join with, favor.

sidelong *adjective* side, sideways, oblique, indirect, covert.

sidestep *verb* *sidestep the problematic issue* avoid, skirt (around), evade, dodge, circumvent, bypass, steer clear of; *inf.* duck.

sidetrack *verb* *get sidetracked from the main issue* divert, deflect, distract, lead away from.

sideways *adverb* **1** *walk sideways* crabwise, to the side. **2** *bring the table in sideways* side first, edgeways, edgewise. **3** *look sideways at her* obliquely, indirectly, sidelong.

sideways *adjective* *a sideways glance* sidelong, side, oblique, indirect.

siege *noun* blockade, besiegement, beleaguerment, investment.

siesta *noun* nap, sleep, rest, catnap, doze; *inf.* forty winks, snooze.

sieve *noun* *use a sieve to strain the mixture* strainer, sifter, filter, colander, riddle, screen.

sieve *verb* **1** *sieve the mixture* strain, sift, filter, riddle, screen. **2** *sieve the lumps from the sauce* separate out, remove, winnow.

sift *verb* **1** *sift the flour* filter, strain, screen. **2** *sift flour onto a board* shake, sprinkle, distribute, scatter, strew. **3** *sift the lumps from the flour* separate out, remove, winnow. **sift through** **1** *sift through the evidence* examine, scrutinize, study, pore over, investigate, analyze, screen, review, probe. **2** *sift through the debris* search through, look through, rummage through, ransack.

sigh *verb* **1** *sigh with tiredness/boredom* breathe out, exhale. **2** *the wind sighing through the trees* whisper, rustle. **3** *sigh for times past* yearn, pine, long, mourn.

sight *noun* **1** *have excellent sight* eyesight, vision, eyes. **2** *within (the) sight of her father* range of vision, field of vision, view. **3** *love at first sight* view, glimpse, seeing, glance. **4** *in her father's sight, she was perfect* opinion, view, point of view, judgment, estimation, feeling, observation, perception. **5** *memorable/historic sights* spectacle, scene, display, show, exhibition, curiosity, rarity, marvel; *inf.* something to write home about. **6** *a sight in those clothes* spectacle, eye-of glimpse, get a glimpse of, see, spot, sight, descry, espy, set eyes on, have sight of. **set one's sights on** aim at/for, aspire to, strive toward, work toward, be after, seek.

sight *verb sight land* catch sight of, see, behold, spot, make out, descry, espy, perceive, observe, discern.

sign *noun* 1 *a sign of weakness/strength* indication, symptom, hint, suggestion, mark, clue, manifestation, token, evidence, proof. 2 *signs indicating the various offices in the building* signpost, notice, placard, board, marker. 3 *make a sign to follow him* gesture, signal, motion, movement, wave, gesticulation. 4 *mathematical signs | decipher the signs* symbol, mark, cipher, code, hieroglyph. 5 *look for a sign from above* omen, portent, warning, forewarning, augury, presage.

---

sign
augury, indication, manifestation, omen, signal, symptom, token

What's the difference between a **sign** and a **signal?** The former (in this sense) is a general term for anything that gives evidence of an event, a mood, a quality of character, a mental or physical state, or a trace of something (*a sign of approaching rain; a sign of good breeding; a sign that someone has entered the house*). While a sign may be involuntary or even unconscious, a *signal* is always voluntary and is usually deliberate. A ship that shows signs of distress may or may not be in trouble; but one that sends a distress *signal* is definitely in need of help. **Indication,** like *sign,* is a comprehensive term for anything that serves to indicate or point out (*he gave no indication that he was lying*). A **manifestation** is an outward or perceptible indication of something (*the letter was a manifestation of his guilt*), and a **symptom** is an indication of a diseased condition (*a symptom of pneumonia*). An object that proves the existence of something abstract is called a **token** (*she gave him a locket as a token of her love*). **Omen** and **augury** both pertain to foretelling future events, with *augury* being the general term for a prediction of the future and *omen* being a definite sign foretelling good or evil (*they regarded the stormy weather as a bad omen*).

---

sign *verb* 1 *sign one's name* write, inscribe. 2 *sign the letter* write one's name on, autograph, initial. 3 *sign the agreement* write one's name on, initial, endorse, certify, validate, authenticate. 4 *sign to her to follow* signal, indicate, beckon, gesture, motion, gesticulate, wave, nod. **sign on/up** 1 *soldier signing on for five years* enlist, join up, join the services. 2 *sign up for music classes* enroll, register, put one's name down for, enlist, become a member of. 3 *sign on new employees* employ, take on, engage, hire, recruit, take into one's employ. **sign over** *sign over the*

estate to his son* transfer, make over, hand over, turn over, assign, consign.

signal *noun* 1 *the signal to stop | a signal that someone was coming* sign, indicator, cue. 2 *a signal that winter is coming* sign, indication, token, evidence, hint. 3 *the arrival of the star was the signal for applause* incentive, impetus, stimulus, motive, cause, reason.

signal *verb* 1 *signal to her to follow* sign, give a sign, indicate, beckon, gesture, motion, gesticulate, nod. 2 *signaled his displeasure with silence* indicate, show, express, communicate. 3 *early frost signaled the start of a hard winter* be a sign of, mark, signify, designate.

signal *adjective a signal achievement* exceptional, conspicuous, notable, noteworthy, significant, memorable, outstanding, striking, remarkable, distinguished, eminent.

significance *noun* 1 *not comprehend the significance of his remark* meaning, sense, import, signification, purport, point, gist, essence, implications. 2 *the significance of the medical discovery* importance, consequence, moment, momentousness, weight, weightiness, magnitude, impressiveness, seriousness.

significant *adjective* 1 *a significant few words* meaningful, eloquent, expressive, indicative, pregnant, knowing. 2 *make significant progress* important, of importance, of consequence, momentous, of moment, weighty, material, impressive, serious, vital, critical.
Antonyms: INSIGNIFICANT; MEANINGLESS; MINOR.

signify *verb* 1 *dark clouds signifying rain* be a sign of, indicate, mean, denote, betoken, suggest, point to, portend. 2 *what do the symbols signify?* mean, denote, represent, symbolize, stand for. 3 *signify one's agreement* indicate, show, exhibit, express, communicate, intimate, announce, proclaim, declare, pronounce. 4 *his opinion does not signify* matter, be of importance, be of consequence, be important, be significant, be of significance, carry weight, count.

silence *noun* 1 *in the silence of the night* still, stillness, quiet, quietness, hush, peace, peacefulness, tranquillity, noiselessness, soundlessness. 2 *their behavior reduced him to silence* speechlessness, wordlessness, voicelessness, dumbness, muteness, taciturnity, reticence, uncommunicativeness. 3 *the need for silence about their whereabouts* secrecy, secretiveness, concealment, reticence, taciturnity, uncommunicativeness.
Antonyms: NOISE; SPEECH; COMMUNICATION.

silence *verb* 1 *silence the noisy children* quiet, hush, still, calm, pacify, subdue, quell. 2 *silence the noise of the engine* muffle, deaden, abate, extinguish. 3 *silence their complaints* put an end to, put a stop to, cut short, gag, prevent.

silent *adjective* 1 *in their silent surroundings* still, quiet, hushed, peaceful, tranquil, noiseless,

soundless. **2** *silent in the face of the opposition* speechless, unspeaking, wordless, voiceless, dumb, mute, taciturn, reticent, uncommunicative, mum, tight-lipped, tongue-tied; *inf.* struck dumb. **3** *silent criticism* unspoken, wordless, unvoiced, unsaid, unexpressed, unpronounced, tacit, implicit, understood, implied.
Antonyms: NOISY; LOQUACIOUS; SPOKEN.

silhouette *noun see her silhouette on the wall* outline, contour, profile, delineation, form, shape.

silhouette *verb silhouetted against the sky* outline, stand out, etch, delineate.

silky *adjective* silken, smooth, sleek, velvety, diaphanous.

silly *adjective* **1** *a silly person* foolish, stupid, unintelligent, idiotic, brainless, witless, unwise, imprudent, thoughtless, reckless, foolhardy, irresponsible, mad, erratic, unstable, scatterbrained, featherbrained, flighty, frivolous, giddy, fatuous, inane, immature, childish, shallow, naïve; *inf.* daft, crazy, loopy, screwy. **2** *silly actions* foolish, stupid, unintelligent, senseless, mindless, idiotic, unwise, imprudent, inadvisable, injudicious, ill-considered, misguided, unsound, impractical, pointless, meaningless, purposeless, inappropriate, illogical, irrational, unreasonable, thoughtless, reckless, foolhardy, irresponsible, erratic, harebrained, absurd, ridiculous, ludicrous, laughable, risible, farcical, preposterous, fatuous, asinine; *inf.* half-baked, daft, crazy, loopy, screwy, for the birds. **3** *knocked silly by the blow* dazed, in a daze, stunned, stupefied, groggy, benumbed.
Antonyms: SENSIBLE; CLEVER; RATIONAL.

similar *adjective* *have similar houses* like, alike, much the same, comparable, corresponding, analogous, parallel, equivalent, kindred, approximate. **similar to** *ideas similar to his* resembling, like, much the same as, comparable to, corresponding to, close to.
Antonyms: DISSIMILAR; UNLIKE; DIFFERENT.

similarity *noun a degree of similarity* resemblance, likeness, sameness, similitude, comparability, correspondence, analogy, parallel, parallelism, equivalence, approximation, closeness, affinity, kinship.

similarly *adverb* likewise, in the same way, in like matter, correspondingly, by the same token.

similitude *noun a marked degree of similitude in their views* resemblance, likeness, similarity, sameness, comparability, correspondence, closeness, analogy. *See* SIMILARITY.

simmer *verb* **1** *a stew simmering on the stove* cook gently, boil gently, bubble, stew. **2** *simmering with rage* fume, seethe, smolder, chafe, smart, be angry, be furious.

simple *adjective* **1** *a simple task | it was simple!* easy, uncomplicated, straightforward, uninvolved, effortless, manageable, elementary,

facile; *inf.* like falling off a log, a piece of cake, a cinch, no sweat. **2** *simple instructions | in simple language* clear, plain, intelligible, comprehensible, understandable, lucid, direct, straightforward, uncomplicated, uninvolved. **3** *simple clothes* plain, classic, clean-cut, unelaborate, unadorned, undecorated, without ornament/ornamentation, unembellished, unfussy, uncluttered, austere, stark, spartan, unpretentious, restrained, natural, casual, informal. **4** *simple chemical substances* noncomplex, uncompounded, uncombined, unmixed, unblended, unalloyed, pure, basic, single, elementary, fundamental. **5** *the simple truth/facts* plain, straightforward, frank, direct, candid, honest, sincere, absolute, unqualified, unvarnished, bald, stark, unadorned, unembellished. **6** *a simple country girl* unsophisticated, natural, unaffected, wholesome, innocent, artless, guileless, childlike, naïve, ingenuous, gullible, inexperienced; *inf.* green. **7** *lead a simple life* ordinary, commonplace, unpretentious, modest, homely, humble, lowly, rustic.
Antonyms: DIFFICULT; COMPLICATED; FANCY; COMPOUND.

simpleton *noun* idiot, halfwit, dolt, fool, ninny, nincompoop; *inf.* nitwit, twit, clod, dope.

simplicity *noun* **1** *the simplicity of the task* simpleness, easiness, lack/absence of complication, straightforwardness, effortlessness, elementariness, facility. **2** *the simplicity of the directions/language* simpleness, clarity, clearness, plainness, intelligibility, lucidity, lucidness, directness, straightforwardness. **3** *the simplicity of the clothes* simpleness, classic lines, clean lines, nonelaborateness, lack/absence of adornment/decoration/ornament/ornamentation/embellishment, unfussiness, plainness, lack/absence of clutter, austereness, starkness, unpretentiousness, restraint, naturalness, casualness, informality. **4** *the simplicity of the statement* simpleness, plainness, straightforwardness, frankness, directness, candidness, candor, honesty, sincerity, starkness, lack of embellishment. **5** *the simplicity of their lifestyle* ordinariness, unpretentiousness, modesty, homeliness, humbleness, lowliness.

simplify *verb* **1** *simplify the complicated instructions* make simple/simpler, make easy/easier, make plainer, clarify, decipher, disentangle, explain, paraphrase, translate, abridge, shorten, condense. **2** *simplify the procedure/method* make simple/simpler, make easy/easier, streamline, reduce to essentials.

simplistic *adjective* *a simplistic solution/attitude* oversimple, oversimplified, facile, shallow, superficial, naïve.

simply *adverb* **1** *try to express oneself simply* clearly, plainly, intelligibly, lucidly, directly, straightforwardly. **2** *dress simply* plainly, classically, unelaborately, without adornment/ decoration/ornament/ornamentation/embellishment, unfussily, without clutter, austerely, starkly, spartanly, with restraint, naturally, casually, informally. **3** *live simply* unpretentiously, modestly, humbly. **4** *break windows simply to gain attention* purely, solely, merely, only, just. **5** *simply the best painting he had ever seen* absolutely, unreservedly, positively, certainly, unconditionally, categorically, utterly, completely, altogether, totally, wholly.

simulate *verb* **1** *simulate grief* feign, pretend, fake, sham, affect, fake the appearance of. **2** *simulate flight landing conditions* reproduce, mimic, parallel, do a mock-up of.

simultaneous *adjective* *simultaneous events* concurrent, contemporaneous, concomitant, coinciding, coincident, synchronous, coexistent, parallel.

simultaneously *adverb* at the same time, concurrently, concomitantly, together, all together, in unison, in concert, in chorus.

sin *noun* **1** *commit a sin in the eyes of the church* wrong, wrongdoing, act of evil/wickedness/badness, crime, offense, misdeed, misdemeanor, transgression, error, lapse, fall from grace; *lit.* trespass. **2** *guilty of sin* wrongdoing, wrong, evil, evildoing, wickedness, badness, iniquity, crime, immorality, transgression, error, unrighteousness, ungodliness, irreligiousness, irreverence, profanity, blasphemy, impiety, sacrilege.
Antonyms: VIRTUE; GOOD.

---

sin
crime, fault, indiscretion, offense, transgression, vice

If you've ever driven through a red light or chewed with your mouth open, you've committed an **offense**, which is a broad term covering any violation of the law or of standards of propriety and taste. A **sin**, on the other hand, is an act that specifically violates a religious, ethical, or moral standard (*to marry someone of another faith was considered a sin*). **Transgression** is a weightier and more serious word for *sin*, suggesting any violation of an agreed-upon set of rules (*their behavior was clearly a transgression of the terms set forth in the treaty*). A **crime** is any act forbidden by law and punishable upon conviction (*a crime for which he was sentenced to death*). A **vice** has less to do with violating the law and more to do with habits and practices that debase a person's character (*alcohol was her only vice*). **Fault** and **indiscretion** are gentler words, although they may be used as euphemisms for *sin* or *crime*. A *fault* is an unsatisfactory feature in someone's character (*she is exuberant to a fault*), while *indiscretion* refers to an unwise or improper action (*speaking to the media was an indiscretion for which she was chastised*). In recent years, however, *indiscretion* has become a euphemism for such sins as adultery, as if to excuse such behavior by attributing it to a momentary lapse of judgment (*his indiscretions were no secret*).

sin *verb* **1** *sin against the church/family* commit a sin, do wrong, commit a crime, offend, commit an offense, transgress. **2** *punish people who sin* commit a sin, do wrong, commit a crime, commit an offense, break the law, misbehave, transgress, go astray, stray from the straight and narrow, go wrong, fall from grace.

sincere *adjective* **1** *sincere affection/beliefs* genuine, real, true, honest, unfeigned, unaffected, bona fide, honest, wholehearted, heartfelt, serious, earnest, fervent. **2** *sincere people* honest, aboveboard, trustworthy, frank, candid, straightforward, plain-dealing, no-nonsense, genuine, undeceitful, artless, guileless, ingenuous; *inf.* up-front.
Antonyms: INSINCERE; FALSE; DISHONEST.

sincerely *adverb* **1** *thank them sincerely* with all sincerity, wholeheartedly, with all one's heart, earnestly, fervently. **2** *mean it most sincerely* genuinely, really, truly, in truth, without pretense, without feigning, honestly, in good faith.

sincerity *noun* **1** *doubt the sincerity of his affections/beliefs* genuineness, truth, honesty, good faith, wholeheartedness, seriousness, earnestness, fervor. **2** *misled by their seeming sincerity* openness, honesty, trustworthiness, frankness, candor, candidness, straightforwardness, genuineness, lack of deceit, artlessness, guilelessness, ingenuousness.

sinewy *adjective* muscular, brawny, burly, powerfully built, stalwart, strapping.

sinful *adjective* **1** *sinful deeds/thoughts* wrong, evil, wicked, bad, iniquitous, criminal, immoral, corrupt, unrighteous, ungodly, irreligious, irreverent, profane, blasphemous, impious, sacrilegious. **2** *sinful people* wrongdoing, evil, evildoing, wicked, bad, criminal, erring, immoral, dissolute, corrupt, depraved.

sing *verb* **1** *children singing happily* carol, trill, warble, pipe, quaver, croon, chant, yodel. **2** *birds singing* trill, warble, chirp. **3** *sing to the police* inform, act as informer, tell tales, rat; *inf.* squeal, blow the whistle, spill the beans, fink. **sing out** call, call out, cry, cry out, shout, yell, bellow; *inf.* holler.

singe *verb* *singe the fabric/bread* scorch, burn, sear, char, blacken.

singer *noun* vocalist, soloist, songster, songstress, chorister, crooner, warbler, chanteuse, minstrel; balladeer, opera singer, diva, pop singer.

single *adjective* **1** *a single apple on the tree | send a single rose* one, one only, sole, lone, solitary, unique, isolated, by itself, exclusive. **2** *remove every single item* individual, particular, separate, distinct. **3** *preferring to remain single* unmarried, unwed, unwedded, wifeless/husbandless, spouseless, partnerless, a bachelor, unattached, free.
Antonyms: DOUBLE; MARRIED.

single *verb* **single out** *single out the best/worst hotel* separate out, set apart, put to one side, pick, choose, select, fix on, decide on.

single-handed adverb *sail the Atlantic single-handed* by oneself, alone, on one's own, solo, independently, unaided, unassisted, without help.

single-minded adjective *too single-minded to be distracted from their aim* unswerving, unwavering, undeviating, set, fixed, devoted, dedicated, committed, determined, dogged, tireless, purposeful, obsessive, monomaniacal.

singly adverb *guests arriving singly* one by one, one at a time, individually, separately, by oneself.

singular adjective **1** *a singular talent* extraordinary, exceptional, rare, unusual, unique, remarkable, outstanding, notable, noteworthy, striking, conspicuous, distinctive. **2** *singular occurrences happening in the village* strange, unusual, odd, peculiar, curious, queer, bizarre, weird, abnormal, atypical.
Antonyms: ORDINARY; COMMON; RUN-OF-THE-MILL.

sinister adjective **1** *a sinister figure* evil-looking, wicked-looking, menacing, threatening, frightening, terrifying. **2** *sinister motives* evil, wicked, bad, villainous, malevolent, criminal, base, vile, vicious, cruel, malicious, malign. **3** *sinister signs* ominous, ill-omened, inauspicious, portentous.
Antonyms: BENEVOLENT; GOOD; INNOCENT; AUSPICIOUS.

sink verb **1** *sink to one's knees | watch the sun sinking* fall, drop, descend, go down, go lower, plunge, plummet, slump. **2** *ships sinking* go under, submerge, founder, capsize. **3** *feel the ground sinking* collapse, cave in, fall in. **4** *empires/patients sinking rapidly* decline, fade, fail, deteriorate, weaken, grow weak, flag, degenerate, decay; *inf.* go downhill. **5** *would not sink to that level* stoop, lower oneself, debase oneself, be reduced. **6** *voices sinking* lower, become/get lower, drop, become softer. **7** *sink a well/shaft* dig, bore, drill, excavate. **8** *sink posts in the earth* drive, place, put down, plant, position. **9** *sink hopes of winning | sink the opposition's plans* destroy, ruin, cause the downfall of, be the ruin/ruination of, demolish, devastate; *inf.* put the kibosh on. **10** *having sunk their savings in/into the venture* invest, put, venture, risk.
Antonyms: RISE; ASCEND; IMPROVE.

sinner noun wrongdoer, evildoer, criminal, offender, miscreant, transgressor, reprobate; *lit.* trespasser.

sinuous adjective winding, curving, twisting, turning, bending, curling, coiling, undulating, serpentine.

sip verb *sip the drink* drink slowly, sup, taste, sample.

sip noun *take a sip of the drink* mouthful, swallow, drink, drop, thimbleful, sup, taste.

siren noun **1** *police sirens* alarm, alarm bell, warning bell, danger signal, tocsin. **2** *lured by the siren* seductress, temptress, femme fatale; *lit.* Circe, Lorelei; *inf.* vamp.

sit verb **1** *please sit* sit down, take a seat, settle down, be seated; *inf.* take a load off, take the load off one's feet. **2** *the books sitting on the shelf* be placed, be positioned, be situated, rest, perch. **3** *sit the package on the table* set down, place, put, deposit, rest, position, situate. **4** *committees sitting until midnight* be convened, meet, assemble, be in session. **5** *sit for her neighbors* babysit.
Antonyms: STAND; RISE; LIFT.

site noun **1** *the site of the battle* location, situation, position, place, locality, setting, scene. **2** *the building site* ground, plot, lot.

situate verb *factories situated near the river* place, position, locate, site.

situation noun **1** *houses in a rural situation* place, position, location, site, setting, milieu, environment. **2** *their financial situation* circumstances, affairs, state, state of affairs, condition, case, predicament, plight; *inf.* kettle of fish, ball game. **3** *from a lowly situation in life* status, station, standing, footing, rank, degree. **4** *apply for a situation in the new firm* post, position, place, job, employment.

size noun *the size of his feet/car* dimensions, measurements, proportions, bigness, largeness, magnitude, vastness, bulk, area, expanse, extent.

size verb *size the eggs* sort, categorize, classify.
size up *size up the opposition* appraise, assess, judge, evaluate, gauge, estimate, rate.

skeleton noun **1** *the skeleton of the building/car* framework, frame, structure, shell, chassis, support. **2** *give the skeleton of the argument* outline, sketch, bones, bare bones, draft, rough draft, plan, blueprint. **3** *the human skeleton* bones.

skeleton adjective *skeleton staff* minimum, minimal, essential.

skeptic noun **1** *supporters of his theories arguing with the skeptics* questioner, doubter, doubting Thomas, disbeliever, dissenter, scoffer, cynic. **2** *ministers of the church challenging skeptics* agnostic, unbeliever, doubter, doubting Thomas.

skeptical adjective *trying to convince skeptical opponents* doubting, doubtful, dubious, questioning, distrustful, mistrustful, suspicious, hesitant, disbelieving, misbelieving, incredulous, unconvinced, scoffing, cynical, pessimistic, defeatist.
Antonyms: CERTAIN; CREDULOUS.

skepticism noun **1** *persist in the face of skepticism* doubt, doubtfulness, dubiety, distrust, mistrust, suspicion, hesitancy, disbelief, misbelief, incredulity, scoffing, cynicism, pessimism, defeatism. **2** *religious skepticism* agnosticism, unbelief, doubt.

sketch noun **1** *draw a rough sketch of the house* drawing, preliminary drawing, outline, diagram, plan, representation, delineation. **2** *give a sketch of his plans* outline, summary, abstract, précis, résumé, skeleton, bare bones, draft, plan. **3** *performing a comic sketch* short play, skit, act, scene.

sketch *verb* *sketch the landscape on paper* draw, rough out, outline, pencil, represent, delineate, depict. **sketch out** *sketch out his plans* outline, rough out, give a summary of, summarize, give an abstract/précis/résumé of, précis, draft.

sketchy *adjective* **1** *plans still a bit sketchy* preliminary, provisional, unfinished, unrefined, unpolished, rough, crude. **2** *sketchy knowledge/information* slight, superficial, cursory, perfunctory, meager, skimpy, insufficient, inadequate, imperfect, incomplete, deficient, defective.

skill *noun* *the skill of the performer/performance* skillfulness, ability, accomplishment, adeptness, competence, efficiency, adroitness, deftness, dexterity, aptitude, expertise, expertness, art, finesse, experience, professionalism, talent, cleverness, smartness.

skilled *adjective* **1** *a skilled performer* skillful, able, good, accomplished, adept, competent, masterly, expert, talented. *See* SKILLFUL 1. **2** *a skilled performance* skillful, able, accomplished, competent, masterly, expert, first-rate. **3** *jobs for skilled workers* trained, qualified, expert, experienced, practiced.

skillful *adjective* **1** *a skillful performer* skilled, able, good, accomplished, adept, competent, efficient, adroit, deft, dexterous, masterly, expert, first-rate, experienced, trained, practiced, professional, talented, gifted, clever, smart. **2** *a skillful performance* skilled, able, accomplished, competent, masterly, deft, expert, first-rate, talented, clever.
Antonyms: INCOMPETENT; INEPT; AMATEURISH.

skim *verb* *skim through the report* read quickly, glance at, scan, run one's eye over, flip through, leaf through, thumb through.

skimp *verb* *skimp a piece of work* do hastily, do carelessly, dash off, cut corners with. **skimp on** *skimp on food/material* be sparing with, be economical with, economize on, be frugal with, be parsimonious with, be niggardly with, scrimp on, stint on, cut corners with, limit; *inf.* be stingy with.
Antonyms: SQUANDER; LAVISH.

skimpy *adjective* **1** *skimpy meals* small, meager, scanty, insubstantial, insufficient, inadequate, sketchy, paltry. **2** *skimpy dresses* short, brief, scanty, insubstantial, sketchy.

skin *noun* **1** *damage the skin* integument, epidermis, cuticle, corium, derma. **2** *fair skin* complexion, coloring. **3** *animal skin* hide, pelt, fleece, fell, integument, tegument. **4** *banana/orange skin* peel, rind, hull, husk. **5** *a skin forming on the gravy* film, coating, coat, layer, crust. **by the skin of one's teeth** *catch the train by the skin of one's teeth* only just, narrowly, barely, by a

hair's breadth; *inf.* by a whisker. **get under one's skin 1** *noisy neighbors getting under her skin* irritate, annoy, irk, vex, grate on, rub the wrong way, chafe, gall, nettle; *inf.* needle. **2** *her poetry gets under my skin* interest, absorb, engross, rivet, grip, attract, charm, enchant, mesmerize, hypnotize. **no skin off one's nose** *it's no skin off my nose if they leave* of no concern to, of no importance to, of no relevance to, of no interest to.

skin *verb* **1** *skin the fruit* peel, pare, hull, decorticate. **2** *skin one's knee* scrape, graze, abrade, cut, bark, excoriate.

skinflint *noun* miser, niggard, penny-pincher, Scrooge; *inf.* cheapskate, tightwad.

skinny *adjective* thin, lean, scrawny, emaciated, skeletal; *inf.* skin and bone.
Antonyms: FAT; PLUMP; OBESE.

skip *verb* **1** *children skipping along in the sunshine* bound, jump, leap, spring, hop, bounce, dance, caper, prance, trip, cavort, gambol, frisk, bob. **2** *skip from subject to subject* move quickly, go rapidly, pass quickly, flit, dart, zoom. **3** *skip the more boring parts of the text* omit, leave out, pass over, bypass, skim over. **4** *skip lectures* play truant from, miss, not attend, dodge; *inf.* cut, play hooky from.

skirmish *noun* battle, fight, clash, conflict, encounter, confrontation, engagement, combat, contest, tussle, scrimmage, fracas, affray, melee, quarrel, altercation, argument, dispute; *inf.* set-to, scrap.

skirmish *verb* *skirmishing with the enemy* fight, engage, combat, clash, collide, have a confrontation, come to blows, tussle, quarrel, argue, have a dispute.

skirt *verb* **1** *flowers skirting the lake* border, edge, flank. **2** *people skirting the lake* go around, walk around, circle, circumnavigate. **3** *skirt the issue* evade, avoid, dodge, steer clear of, sidestep, circumvent, bypass.

skit *noun* burlesque, parody, travesty; *inf.* spoof, takeoff, send-up.

skittish *adjective* highly strung, nervous, restive, jumpy, fidgety, excitable, restless, skittery.
Antonyms: CALM; LAID-BACK.

skulk *verb* lurk, loiter, prowl, creep, sneak, slink, steal, sidle.

sky *noun* *fly off into the sky* upper atmosphere, heaven, firmament, blue, blue yonder; *lit.* ether. **to the skies** *praise them to the skies* unreservedly, without reserve, very much, very greatly, highly, profusely, fulsomely, extravagantly, inordinately, excessively, immoderately.

slab *noun* **1** *a slab of cake/cheese* hunk, chunk, lump, slice, wedge, piece, portion. **2** *a slab of wood/stone* plank, hunk, chunk, lump, piece.

slack *adjective* **1** *slack clothes* not tight, loose, baggy, bagging, easy, hanging, flapping. **2** *slack muscles* not taut, relaxed, limp, flaccid, flabby. **3** *a slack rope* not taut, not rigid, relaxed, flexible, pliant. **4** *business a bit slack* not busy, slow, quiet, inactive, sluggish. **5** *rather slack about punctuality* lax, negligent, remiss, neglectful, careless, inattentive, offhand, slapdash, slipshod, sloppy, disorderly, disorganized.

Antonyms: TIGHT; TAUT; METICULOUS.

slack *noun* **1** *take up the slack of the rope* looseness, play; *inf.* give. **2** *no more slack left in personnel* surplus, excess, inessentials, leeway.

slack *verb* *workers slacking when the boss is away* idle, shirk, be inactive, be lazy, be indolent, be neglectful. **slack off 1** *business slacks off in the winter* get less, lessen, fall off, drop off, taper off, let up, decrease, dwindle, ebb, recede, wane. **2** *students slacking off after the exams* relax, take it/things easy, be less active.

slacker *noun* idler, shirker, loafer, dawdler, dallier, layabout, malingerer, gold brick; *inf.* clock-watcher.

slake *verb* *slake one's thirst/desire* satisfy, quench, assuage, relieve, take the edge off, gratify, satiate.

slam *verb* **1** *slam the door | the door slammed* bang, shut/close with a bang, shut/close with a crash, shut/close noisily, shut/close with force. **2** *slam the money (down) on the table* slap, bang, thump, hurl, fling, throw. **3** *a play slammed by the critics* criticize, attack, pillory, vilify, damn; *inf.* slate, pan, lambaste, run down, blast. **4** *slam the opposition* defeat utterly, rout, trounce, thrash, vanquish, conquer, crush, overwhelm, give a drubbing to; *inf.* wipe the floor with, clobber, slaughter, hammer.

slander *noun* defamation, misrepresentation, calumny, libel, aspersion, vilification, verbal abuse, muckraking, smear campaign/campaigning, backbiting, obloquy, disparagement, denigration.

slander *verb* *slander his neighbor with his lies* defame, blacken the name of, libel, cast aspersions on, malign, vilify, verbally abuse, muckrake about, smear, slur, backbite, calumniate, disparage, denigrate, decry, run down.

slanderous *adjective* defamatory, damaging, libelous, abusive, muckraking, malicious, backbiting, calumnious, disparaging, denigrating.

slang *noun* **1** *use slang rather than formal language* colloquialism, informal language. **2** *cannot understand the technicians' slang* jargon, lingo, cant, argot; *inf.* gobbledygook, technospeak, mumbo-jumbo.

slant *verb* **1** *the old floor slants | the picture on the wall slants* slope, tilt, be askew, lean, dip, shelve, list. **2** *accuse the newspaper of slanting the news* give a slant to, give a bias to, bias, angle, distort, twist.

slant *noun* **1** *the slant of the floor/picture* slope, tilt, dip, leaning, inclination, shelving, listing. **2** *giving a political slant to the news* bias, leaning,

one-sidedness, prejudice, angle, distortion, twist. **3** *require a woman's slant on the new product* angle, point of view, view, opinion, attitude.

slanting *adjective* slanted, aslant, at an angle, sloping, oblique, tilting, tilted, askew, leaning, dipping, shelving, listing, diagonal.

Antonyms: STRAIGHT; PLUMB.

slap *noun* *a slap on the back* smack, blow, hit, whack, thump, cuff, spank; *inf.* wallop. **slap in the face** *their giving the job to his assistant was a slap in the face to him* snub, insult, rebuff, putdown, repulse, humiliation, blow to one's pride.

slap *verb* **1** *slap him on the back* smack, strike, hit, whack, cuff, spank; *inf.* wallop, swipe, belt. **2** *slap the money (down) on the table* plunk, plop, slam, bang, fling, hurl, toss, throw. **3** *slap paint on* daub, plaster, spread. **slap on** *slap on a service charge* put on, add, append, tack on.

slapdash *adjective* careless, slipshod, sloppy, untidy, messy, hasty, hurried, cursory, perfunctory, disorganized, slipshod, offhand, thoughtless, heedless, negligent, neglectful, remiss.

Antonyms: CAREFUL; METICULOUS; PAINSTAKING.

slash *verb* **1** *slash the fencing dummy* cut, gash, lacerate, hack, rip, rend, slit, score, knife. **2** *slash prices* reduce/lower/decrease drastically, cut/drop/mark down greatly.

slash *noun* *the slashes in the garment* cut, gash, laceration, hack, rip, rent, slit, score, incision.

slaughter *verb* **1** *slaughter animals for food* kill, butcher. **2** *slaughter the enemy soldiers* massacre, murder, butcher, kill, put to death, put to the sword, slay, assassinate, liquidate, exterminate, annihilate. **3** *slaughter the opposition* defeat utterly, rout, trounce, thrash, vanquish, conquer, crush, overwhelm, give a drubbing to; *inf.* wipe the floor with, clobber, slam, hammer.

slaughter *noun* massacre, murder, butchery, killing, putting to death, slaying, liquidation, extermination, annihilation; bloodshed, carnage.

slave *noun* **1** *the master and his slaves* bondsman, bondswoman, bondservant, serf, vassal. **2** *slaves in the kitchen* drudge, laborer, menial worker, servant; *lit.* scullion.

slave *verb* *slaving (away) at/over the stove* toil, drudge, slog, labor, grind, work one's fingers to the bone, work day and night, work like a Trojan.

slaver *verb* slobber, drool.

slavery *noun* **1** *sold into slavery* enslavement, bondage, servitude, subjugation, thralldom, thrall, serfdom, vassalage. **2** *working there is sheer slavery* drudgery, toil, hard labor, grind.

Antonyms: FREEDOM; LIBERTY; EMANCIPATION.

slavish *adjective* **1** *slavish followers/admiration* servile, subservient, obsequious, sycophantic, deferential, groveling, fawning, cringing, menial, abject. **2** *slavish imitation* imitative, unoriginal, uninspired, unimaginative.

slay *verb* **1** *slay his enemy* kill, murder; slaughter, put to death, assassinate, do away with; *inf.* rub out. **2** *the comedian's act slayed them* amuse/entertain greatly; *inf.* have one rolling in the aisles, be a hit with, wow.

sleek *adjective* **1** *sleek hair* smooth, glossy, shiny, lustrous, silken, silky, satiny, burnished. **2** *sleek businessmen* well-fed, thriving, prosperous, well-groomed; *inf.* well-heeled.
Antonyms: DULL; ROUGH; UNKEMPT.

sleep *verb* *sleep for a few hours* be asleep, slumber, doze, nap, drowse; *lit.* rest in the arms of Morpheus; *inf.* snooze, crash, count sheep, catch some Z's, have forty winks, be in the land of Nod.

sleep *noun* *have a short sleep* slumber, doze, nap, rest, siesta, drowse; *inf.* snooze, forty winks, (bit of) shut-eye.

sleepiness *noun* drowsiness, tiredness, somnolence, somnolency, languor, languidness, lethargy, sluggishness, inactivity, heaviness, lassitude, torpor, torpidity, comatoseness.

sleepless *adjective* **1** *sleepless nights* without sleep, wakeful, restless, disturbed. **2** *sleepless people* unsleeping, wakeful, insomniac.

sleeplessness *noun* *suffer from sleeplessness* insomnia, wakefulness.

sleepwalking *noun* somnambulism, somnambulation, noctambulism, noctambulation.

sleepy *adjective* **1** *feeling sleepy | sleepy children* drowsy, tired, somnolent, languid, languorous, lethargic, sluggish, inactive, heavy, torpid, comatose. **2** *sleepy little villages* inactive, quiet, peaceful, slow-moving, slumberous.
Antonyms: awake; ALERT; ACTIVE.

slender *adjective* **1** *slender figures* slim, thin, slight, lean, narrow, svelte, willowy, sylphlike. **2** *people of slender means* slight, small, little, meager, scanty, paltry, insubstantial, inadequate, insufficient, deficient, negligible, trifling. **3** *a slender hope of success* small, slight, slim, faint, remote, feeble, flimsy, tenuous, fragile.
Antonyms: FAT; SUBSTANTIAL; CONSIDERABLE.

sleuth *noun* detective, private detective, investigator, private investigator; *inf.* private eye, dick, gumshoe.

slice *noun* **1** *a slice of cake* piece, portion, segment, sliver, wedge, chunk, hunk. **2** *a slice of the action* share, part, piece, proportion, allotment, allocation.

slice *verb* **1** *slice the cake/apple/meat* cut up, cut through, carve, divide, segment. **2** *slice a piece from the apple* cut, sever, separate.

slick *adjective* **1** *a slick presentation* smooth, smooth-running, well-organized, streamlined, efficient, polished. **2** *a slick reply* smooth, glib, fluent, plausible, specious. **3** *a slick performer/operator* smooth, efficient, skillful, deft, adroit, masterly, professional, smart, sharp, shrewd. **4** *slick businessman* suave, urbane, sophisticated, polished, smooth-speaking, glib, smarmy, unctuous.
Antonyms: CLUMSY; INEPT; UNSOPHISTICATED.

slick *verb* *slick one's hair down* smooth, flatten, plaster.

slide *verb* **1** *slide on the ice* slip, skid, slither, skate, glissade. **2** *drawers sliding in easily* slip, glide, slither. **3** *they slid from the room* pass/move quickly, slip, steal, slink. **let slide** *let the housework slide* neglect, forget, ignore, pass over, gloss over, push to the back of one's mind.

slight *adjective* **1** *a slight change* small, little, tiny, minute, inappreciable, imperceptible, subtle, modest. **2** *of slight importance* little, minor, unimportant, petty, inconsiderable, insignificant, inconsequential, negligible, irrelevant, trivial, trifling, paltry, meager, scant. **3** *a slight girl/figure* slightly built, slim, slender, small, spare, delicate, frail. **4** *a slight structure* fragile, frail, flimsy, rickety, jerry-built.
Antonyms: LARGE; SUBSTANTIAL; CONSIDERABLE.

slight *verb* *slight him by not inviting him* snub, insult, affront, rebuff, treat disrespectfully, give the cold shoulder to, keep at arm's length, disregard, ignore, neglect, take no notice of, disdain, scorn.

slight *noun* *upset by the slight* snub, insult, affront, rebuff, cold shoulder, disregard, neglect, inattention, scorn, disdain; *inf.* a slap in the face.

slighting *adjective* *a slighting remark* snubbing, insulting, disrespectful, uncomplimentary, abusive, offensive, disparaging, belittling, derogatory, disdainful, scornful.

slightly *adverb* *slightly hurt* a little, a bit, somewhat, rather, to some degree.

slim *adjective* **1** *slim girls/ankles* slender, thin, slight, lean, narrow, svelte, willowy, sylphlike. **2** *slim hopes of success* slight, small, slender, faint, remote, feeble, flimsy, tenuous, fragile.
Antonyms: FAT; THICK; SUBSTANTIAL; STRONG.

slim *verb* *trying to slim* lose weight, shed weight, lose pounds, reduce, diet, go on a diet.

slime *noun* sludge, muck, ooze, mud; *inf.* goo, gunk.

slimy *adjective* **1** *slimy surfaces* sludgy, mucky, oozy, muddy, slippery, sticky, viscous, mucous. **2** *a slimy character* despicable, contemptible, shameless, detestable, vile, low, scurvy.

sling *verb* **1** *sling it into the trash* toss, fling, throw, cast, hurl, heave, pitch, lob; *inf.* chuck. **2** *sling it from a hook* hang, suspend, dangle, swing.

sling *noun* *have one's arm in a sling* support bandage, support, bandage, strap.

slink *verb* *slinking around dark corners* steal, sneak, creep, slip, skulk, lurk.

slip[1] *verb* **1** *slip on the ice* skid, slither, lose one's footing, lose one's balance. **2** *slip from her hands* fall, slide, drop. **3** *slip from the room unnoticed* steal, slide, creep, sneak, slink. **4** *slip through the police net* break free from, escape, get away from, break away from, evade, dodge. **5** *slip the knot* untie, unfasten, undo, unbind, untangle, unsnarl. **6** *the standard of the work slipped* drop, fall off, decline, deteriorate, degenerate; *inf.* go downhill, go to the dogs. **let slip** *let slip the secret* let out, reveal, disclose, divulge, give away, leak, blurt out, come out with. **slip on** *slip on a sweater* put on, pull on, don. **slip up** make a mistake, blunder, make a blunder, miscalculate, err, go wrong; *inf.* make a booboo, screw up.

slip² *noun accused of making a slip* slipup, mistake, error, blunder, miscalculation, oversight; *inf.* boo-boo. **give the slip** *the pickpocket gave the policeman the slip* escape from, get away from, get free from, break away from, lose, evade, dodge, elude, shake off, get rid of, outwit.

slip³ *noun* **1** *written on a slip* slip of paper, piece of paper; sales slip, receipt. **2** *a slip from the plant* cutting, offshoot, scion, sprout, sprig. **slip of a** *a slip of a girl* small, slender, delicate, young.

slipper *noun* bedroom slipper, scuff, mule, moccasin.

slipperiness *noun* **1** *the slipperiness of the surface* greasiness, oiliness, sliminess, iciness; *inf.* slippiness. **2** *the slipperiness of the criminal* shiftiness, deviousness, deceit, deceitfulness, duplicitousness, craftiness, cunning, sneakiness, treachery, dishonesty, untrustworthiness.

slippery *adjective* **1** *slippery surfaces* greasy, oily, slimy, icy, glassy, smooth, soapy; *inf.* slippy. **2** *a slippery character* shifty, devious, deceitful, duplicitous, crafty, cunning, foxy, tricky, sneaky, treacherous, perfidious, two-faced, dishonest, false, unreliable, untrustworthy.

slipshod *adjective* *slipshod methods* careless, slovenly, untidy, sloppy, slapdash, disorganized, unsystematic, unmethodical.

slipup *noun* slip, mistake, error, blunder. *See* SLIP² *noun.*

slit *verb slit the material* cut, split open, slash, gash, rip, make an incision in, tear, rend, pierce, knife, lance.

slit *noun make a slit in the material* cut, split, slash, gash, rip, incision, tear, rent, fissure, opening.

slither *verb slither about on the ice* slide, slip, skid.

sliver *noun* chip, flake, splinter, shred, fragment, scrap.

slobber *verb* slaver, drool, dribble.

slogan *noun* motto, logo, catchword, jingle, rallying cry, shibboleth.

slop *verb water slopping over* spill, overflow, splash, slosh, splatter, spatter.

slope *verb gardens sloping down to the river | handwriting sloping* drop away, slant, incline, lean, tilt, dip.

slope *noun* **1** *floors on a slope* slant, inclination, angle, skew, tilt, dip, gradient. **2** *grassy slopes* hill, hillside, hillock, bank, rise, scarp, mountain.

sloping *adjective* slanting, oblique, leaning, inclining, inclined, angled, askew, tilting, dipping.

Antonyms: STRAIGHT; PLUMB.

sloppy *adjective* **1** *a sloppy mixture* watery, wet, soggy, splashy, slushy, sludgy. **2** *sloppy work* careless, slapdash, slipshod, disorganized, unmethodical, untidy, messy, slovenly, hasty, hurried, offhand. **3** *sloppy verses* sentimental, overemotional, mawkish, maudlin, gushing, gushy, effusive, banal, trite; *inf.* soppy, mushy, wet, schmaltzy.

Antonyms: CAREFUL; METICULOUS; UNEMOTIONAL.

slot *noun* **1** *money in the slot* slit, crack, hole, opening, aperture, groove, notch. **2** *broadcast a show in the noon slot* place, position, niche, space, opening, time, period.

sloth *noun* laziness, indolence, idleness, sluggishness, inertia, inactivity, lethargy, languor, slothfulness, torpor, torpidity, fainéance.

slothful *adjective* lazy, indolent, idle, sluggish, inert, inactive, lethargic, languid, languorous, torpid, fainéant.

Antonyms: INDUSTRIOUS; ACTIVE.

slouch *verb* slump, hunch, stoop, droop, bend.

slovenly *adjective* **1** *of slovenly appearance* slatternly, untidy, dirty, unclean, messy, unkempt, disheveled, bedraggled, tousled, rumpled. **2** *slovenly methods* careless, sloppy, slapdash, slipshod, disorganized, unmethodical.

Antonyms: TIDY; NEAT; CAREFUL.

slow *adjective* **1** *at a slow pace* slow-moving, unhurried, leisurely, measured, deliberate, ponderous, creeping, dawdling, loitering, lagging, laggard, sluggish, snail-like, tortoiselike. **2** *he was incorrectly labeled as slow* backward, retarded, slow-witted, dull-witted, dull, unintelligent, stupid, thick, dense; *inf.* dumb, dopey; slow on the uptake. **3** *the service being a bit slow* slow-moving, delayed, dilatory, unpunctual, tardy. **4** *a slow process* long-drawn-out, drawn-out, time-consuming, protracted, prolonged, interminable. **5** *a slow play* dull, uninteresting, tedious, boring, tiresome, wearisome, monotonous, uneventful. **6** *a slow part of the world* sleepy, unprogressive, behind-the-times, backward, stagnant; *inf.* not with it, onehorse. **7** *business being slow* not busy, slack, quiet, sluggish, slow-moving, dead. **8** *slow to anger* reluctant, hesitant, loath, unwilling, disinclined.

Antonyms: FAST; QUICK; BRISK; BRIGHT.

slow *verb* **slow down** **1** *slow down at the corner* reduce speed, decelerate, relax speed, put the brakes on. **2** *weather slowed the runners down* hold back, keep back, delay, detain, restrain. **3** *workaholics told to slow down* take it easy, ease up, relax; *inf.* let up.

slowly *adverb* **1** *walk slowly* at a slow pace, without hurrying, unhurriedly, at a leisurely pace, steadily, ploddingly, taking one's time, in one's own good time, with heavy steps, at a snail's pace. **2** *improve slowly* at a slow pace, gradually, bit by bit, by degrees.

sluggish *adjective* **1** *feeling sluggish with a hangover* inactive, inert, heavy, lifeless, apathetic, listless, lethargic, languid, languorous, torpid, phlegmatic, indolent, lazy, slothful, drowsy,

sleepy. **2** *business being sluggish* slow, slow-moving, slack, inactive, stagnant.
Antonyms: ACTIVE; ENERGETIC; BUSY.

sluggishness *noun* **1** *sluggishness caused by overeating* inactivity, inertia, heaviness, lifelessness, apathy, listlessness, lethargy, languidness, languor, lassitude, torpidity, torpor, indolence, laziness, sloth, slothfulness, drowsiness, sleepiness, somnolence. **2** *the sluggishness of business* slowness, slackness, inactivity, stagnation.

slumber *verb* sleep, be asleep, doze, nap, drowse; *lit.* rest in the arms of Morpheus; *inf.* snooze, have forty winks, be in the land of Nod.

slumber *noun* sleep, doze, nap, rest, siesta, drowse; *inf.* snooze, forty winks, (a bit of) shut-eye.

slump *noun* *a slump in sales/profits* plummeting, plunge, nosedive, collapse, fall, falling-off, drop, downturn, downswing, slide, decline, decrease, lowering, devaluation, depreciation, depression.

slump *verb* **1** *slump into a chair* collapse, sink, fall, subside. **2** *prices slumped* plummet, plunge, nosedive, fall, drop, go down, slide, decline, decrease, devalue. **3** *standards slumped* plummet, plunge, nosedive, fall, drop, decline, deteriorate, degenerate; *inf.* go downhill, go to the dogs.
Antonyms: RISE; SOAR; IMPROVE.

slur *verb* *slur his words* mumble, stumble over, stammer, drawl.

slur *noun* **1** *slurs made against/on her character* insult, slight, aspersion, imputation, slanderous statement, libelous statement, misrepresentation, smear, stain, stigma. **2** *avoid all suggestion of a slur* insult, affront, defamation, slander, libel, calumny.

slut *noun* trollop, hussy, prostitute, harlot, whore, streetwalker; *inf.* floozy, hooker.

sly *adjective* **1** *a sly character* cunning, crafty, wily, artful, foxy, tricky, conniving, scheming, devious, underhand, underhanded, shrewd, smart, astute. **2** *in a sly manner* furtive, insidious, underhand, underhanded, shifty, stealthy, sneaky, secret, surreptitious, covert, undercover, clandestine. **3** *a sly smile* roguish, impish, mischievous, playful, arch, knowing. **on the sly** *have another job on the sly* in secret, secretly, furtively, stealthily, sneakily, surreptitiously, covertly, under cover, clandestinely.
Antonyms: FRANK; HONEST; ABOVEBOARD.

smack[1] *noun* **1** *a smack on the face* slap, blow, hit, whack, thump, cuff, punch, spank, buffet, rap, bang; *inf.* wallop, clout, clip, swipe, belt, sock. **2** *the object hit the car with a smack* thud, thump, bang, wham; *inf.* wallop. **smack in the face** slap in the face, rebuff, repulse, snub.

smack[2] *verb* *smack him on the back* slap, hit, strike, whack, thump, cuff; *inf.* wallop, clout, clip, swipe, belt.

smack[3] *adverb* *run smack into the police* headlong,

right, straight, directly, bang, plumb, exactly, precisely, suddenly.

smack[4] *verb* **smack of 1** *a sauce smacking of garlic* taste of, have the flavor of. **2** *actions smacking of treachery* suggest, hint at, have overtones of, have the hallmark of, resemble, seem like, have the air of.

smack[5] *noun* **1** *dishes having a smack of garlic* taste, flavor, savor. **2** *have a smack of treachery* suggestion, hint, trace, tinge, touch, overtone, hallmark, resemblance, air.

small *adjective* **1** *a small toy* little, tiny, teeny, teeny-weeny, wee, petite, slight, minute, miniature, mini, minuscule, diminutive, undersized, puny; *inf.* pocket-size, pint-sized, teensy-weensy. **2** *a small change/mistake* slight, minor, unimportant, trifling, trivial, insignificant, inconsequential, inappreciable. **3** *from small beginnings* humble, modest, lowly, simple, unpretentious, poor, inferior. **4** *a small mind/man* narrow, narrow-minded, mean, petty.
Antonyms: BIG; LARGE; SUBSTANTIAL.

---

small
diminutive, little, miniature, minute, petite, tiny
Why do we call a house **small** and a woman **petite**? *Small* and **little** are used interchangeably to describe people or things of reduced dimensions, but *small* is preferred when describing something concrete that is of less than the usual size, quantity, value, or importance (*a small matter to discuss; a small room; a small price to pay*). *Little* more often refers to concepts (*through little fault of his own; an issue of little importance*) or to a more drastic reduction in scale (*a little shopping cart just like the one her mother used*). **Diminutive** and *petite* intensify the meaning of *small*, particularly with reference to women's figures that are very trim and compact (*with her diminutive figure, she had to shop in stores that specialized in petite sizes*). **Tiny** is used to describe what is extremely small, often to the point where it can be seen only by looking closely (*a tiny flaw in the material; a tiny insect*), while **minute** not only describes what is seen with difficulty but may also refer to a very small amount of something (*minute traces of gunpowder on his glove*). **Miniature** applies specifically to a copy, a model, or a representation of something on a very small scale (*a child's mobile consisting of miniature farm animals*).

---

small-minded *adjective* narrow-minded, bigoted, prejudiced, intolerant, hidebound, rigid, ungenerous, illiberal.

small-time *adjective* *small-time crooks* petty, minor, unimportant, insignificant, of no account, of no consequence, inconsequential.

smart *adjective* **1** *wedding guests looking smart* well-dressed, well turned out, fashionably dressed, fashionable, stylish, modish, elegant, chic, neat, spruce, trim; *inf.* natty, spiffy. **2** *smart children* clever, bright, intelligent, gifted, sharp, quick-witted, nimble-witted, shrewd, ingenious. **3** *at a smart pace* brisk, quick, fast, swift, lively, energetic, spirited, vigorous, jaunty.

Antonyms: SCRUFFY; STUPID; SLOW.

smart *verb* *eyes smarting with the smoke* sting, nip, burn, bite, pain.

smash *verb* **1** *smash the dishes* break, shatter, crash, shiver, pulverize, splinter. **2** *smash the car* crash, demolish, wreck. **3** *smash their hopes* destroy, ruin, shatter, devastate.

smash *noun* *hear the smash of dishes* breaking, shattering, crashing.

smashing *adjective* *a smashing time at the fair* marvelous, magnificent, sensational, stupendous, superb, wonderful, excellent, first-rate; *inf.* terrific, fantastic, super, great, fabulous.

smattering *noun* *a smattering of French* bit, modicum, dash, rudiments, elements.

smear *verb* **1** *children smearing paint on the walls* spread, daub, slap, plaster. **2** *smear the windows* smudge, streak, blur. **3** *smear his reputation* sully, tarnish, blacken, taint, stain, slur, defame, defile, vilify, slander, libel, calumniate.

smear *noun* **1** *a smear of paint on the walls* daub, spot, patch, splotch. **2** *smears on the windows* smudge, streak. **3** *the smears on their reputation* taint, stain, slur, blot.

smell *verb* **1** *smell something rotten/pleasant* sniff, get a sniff of, get a whiff of, nose. **2** *drains smelling* have a bad smell, stink, be stinking, reek, be malodorous; *inf.* stink to high heaven.

smell *noun* **1** *the smells of the countryside* odor, scent, whiff. **2** *the smell of new-mown hay* scent, aroma, perfume, fragrance, bouquet, redolence. **3** *what a smell from the drains!* stink, stench, reek.

---

smell
aroma, bouquet, fragrance, odor, perfume, scent, stench, stink

Everyone appreciates the **fragrance** of fresh-cut flowers, but the **stench** from the paper mill across town is usually unwelcome. Both have a distinctive **smell**, which is the most general of these words for what is perceived through the nose, but there is a big difference between a pleasant smell and a foul one. An **odor** may be either pleasant or unpleasant, but it suggests a smell that is clearly recognizable and can usually be traced to a single source (*the pungent odor of onions*). An **aroma** is a pleasing and distinctive odor that is usually penetrating or pervasive (*the aroma of fresh-ground coffee*), while **bouquet** refers to a delicate aroma, such as that of a fine wine (*after swirling the wine around in her glass, she sniffed the bouquet*). A **scent** is usually delicate and pleasing, with an emphasis on the source rather than on an

olfactory impression (*the scent of balsam associated with Christmas*). *Fragrance* and **perfume** are both associated with flowers, but *fragrance* is more delicate; a *perfume* may be so rich and strong that it is repulsive or overpowering (*the air was so dense with the perfume of lilacs that I had to go indoors*). *Stench* and **stink** are reserved for smells that are foul, strong, and pervasive, although *stink* implies a sharper sensation, while *stench* refers to a more sickening one (*the stink of sweaty gym clothes; the stench of a rotting animal*).

smelly *adjective* *smelly drains* smelling, evil-smelling, foul-smelling, stinking, malodorous, fetid, mephitic; *lit.* noisome.

smile *verb* grin, beam.

---

smile
grin, simper, smirk

The facial expression created by turning the corners of the mouth upward is commonly known as a **smile**. It can convey a wide range of emotion, from pleasure, approval, or amusement to insincerity and disinterest (*his complaint was met with a blank smile*). A **grin** is a wide smile that suggests spontaneous cheerfulness, warmth, pleasure, or amusement (*her teasing provoked an affectionate grin*). But *grin* may also describe a ferocious baring of the teeth or an angry grimace (*the grin of a skeleton*). A **simper**, on the other hand, is an expression of smugness and self-righteousness (*her simper of superiority*) as well as a silly or affected smile (*she curtsied with a girlish simper*). **Smirk** also implies an affected or self-conscious smile, but one that expresses derision or hostility (*to trick someone and then smirk as he makes a fool of himself*).

---

smirk *verb* leer, sneer, simper, grin.

smitten *adjective* **smitten with 1** *smitten with flu* suffering from, affected by, laid low with, struck down with, afflicted by. **2** *smitten with the pretty girl/the new fashion* taken with, infatuated with, enamored of, attracted by, charmed by, captivated by, enchanted by, bewitched by, beguiled by; *inf.* bowled over by, swept off one's feet by.

smog *noun* haze, fog, pollution.

smoke *verb* **1** *fires smoking* smolder, reek. **2** *smoke the salmon* cure, dry, preserve.

smoky *adjective* **1** *a smoky atmosphere* smoke-filled, reeky, hazy, foggy, smoggy, murky. **2** *smoky walls* begrimed, grimy, smoke-stained, smoke-darkened, sooty. **3** *smoky glass* dark, gray, black.

smolder *verb* **1** *fires smoldering* smoke, reek. **2** *hate smoldering in her* burn, seethe, simmer, fester. **3** *smoldering with resentment* seethe, fume, burn, boil, rage, smart.

smooth *adjective* **1** *paint smooth surfaces* even, level, flat, plane, flush, unrough, unwrinkled. **2** *smooth hair/tabletops* glossy, shiny, sleek, silky,

satiny, velvety, polished, burnished. **3** *smooth*
sea calm, still, tranquil, flat, glassy, mirrorlike.
4 *smooth progress* easy, effortless, trouble-free, simple, plain sailing. **5** *the smooth running of the machine* steady, regular, rhythmic, uninterrupted, flowing, fluid. **6** *smooth sounds* soft, soothing, mellow, dulcet, mellifluous, melodious, musical. **7** *smooth face* clean-shaven, smooth-shaven, shaven, hairless. **8** *smooth young men* smooth-tongued, suave, urbane, sophisticated, courteous, gracious, glib, persuasive, slick, oily, ingratiating, unctuous; *inf.* smarmy.
Antonyms: UNEVEN; ROUGH; IRREGULAR.

smooth *verb* **1** *smooth the surface* level, even, flatten, plane, press down, steamroll. **2** *smooth the troubled situation* ease, soothe, pacify, calm, tranquilize, alleviate, assuage, appease, palliate. **3** *smooth out/away the difficulties* get rid of, remove, eliminate. **4** *smooth his promotion* ease, make easy/easier, facilitate, clear the way for, pave the way for, open the door for, expedite, assist, aid, help, help along.

smoothness *noun* **1** *the smoothness of the road surfaces* evenness, levelness, flatness. *See* SMOOTH *adjective* 1. **2** *the smoothness of her hair* glossiness, gloss, shininess, sleekness, silkiness. **3** *the smoothness of the sea* calmness, stillness, tranquillity, flatness. **4** *the smoothness of the progress* ease, easiness, effortlessness, simplicity. **5** *the smoothness of the engine's running* steadiness, regularity, rhythm, fluidity. **6** *the smoothness of the sounds* softness, mellowness, mellifluousness, melodiousness. **7** *the smoothness of his face* clean-shavenness, smooth-shavenness, hairlessness. **8** *the smoothness of the salesman* suaveness, urbaneness, urbanity, sophistication, courteousness, glibness, slickness; *inf.* smarminess. *See* SMOOTH *adjective* 8.

smother *verb* **1** *nearly smothered by the fumes* suffocate, stifle, asphyxiate, choke. **2** *smother them with kindness* overwhelm, shower, inundate, envelop, surround. **3** *smother a fire* extinguish, dampen, damp down, put out, snuff out, stamp out. **4** *smother a laugh* stifle, muffle, repress, suppress, keep back, conceal, hide. **smother in** *smother the steak in onions* cover with, pile with, heap with.

smudge *noun* *smudges on the walls* dirty mark, mark, spot, smear, streak, stain, blotch, blot, blur, smut, splotch.

smudge *verb* **1** *walls smudged with fingerprints* mark, dirty, soil, blacken, smear, streak, daub, stain, besmirch. **2** *smudge the wet paint/lipstick* smear, streak, blur.

smug *adjective* self-satisfied, complacent, content, pleased with oneself, superior, proud of oneself, conceited.

smuggler *noun* contrabandist, runner; *inf.* bootlegger.

snack *noun* *a snack between meals* light meal, refreshments, bite, nibbles, tidbit; *inf.* bite to eat, little something.

snack *verb* *snack between meals* eat between meals, nibble, munch; *inf.* graze.

snag *noun* **1** *discover a snag in our plans* catch, drawback, hitch, stumbling block, obstacle, disadvantage, inconvenience, unseen problem, problem, complication. **2** *a snag in her tights* rip, tear, run, hole.

snag *verb* *snag one's tights* catch, rip, tear.

snap *verb* **1** *the rod/rope snapped* break, break into two, fracture, splinter, separate, come apart, crack. **2** *suddenly snap after years of stress* have a nervous breakdown, break down, collapse, lose one's mind, lose one's reason, go mad, go insane. **3** *snap one's fingers* | *burning logs popping and snapping* crack, click, crackle. **4** *dogs snapping* bite, gnash the teeth. **5** *snap into action* hurry, hasten, rush, race. **snap at** *snapping at the children* speak sharply/brusquely/curtly/abruptly/angrily at, bark at, snarl at, growl at, lash out at; *inf.* jump down the throat of, fly off the handle at. **snap out of it** *she was miserable but she snapped out of it* get over it, recover, get better, cheer up, become cheerful, perk up; *inf.* pull oneself together, get a grip on oneself, become one's old self. **snap up** *snap up the bargains* snatch at, accept eagerly, take advantage of, grab, seize, grasp, pounce upon, swoop down upon; *inf.* nab.

snap *noun* **1** *a snap of one's fingers* | *the snap of twigs beneath our feet* crack, click, crackle. **2** *with a snap of its teeth* bite, gnashing, clenching. **3** *a snap of cold weather* spell, period, time, stretch, interval. **4** *put a bit of snap into the production* liveliness, animation, sparkle, verve, vitality, vivacity, spirit, vigor, sprightliness, zest; *inf.* pizzazz, zip, zing, pep, oomph.

snappy *adjective* **1** *a snappy mood/reply* irritable, irascible, ill-tempered, cross, touchy, testy, crabbed, crotchety, grumpy, grouchy. **2** *a snappy dresser* smart, fashionable, up-to-date, stylish, chic, up-to-the-minute, modish, dapper; *inf.* natty, spiffy, trendy. **look snappy/make it snappy** hurry up, be quick, make haste, look lively; *inf.* get a move on, step on it, move it.

snare *verb* **1** *snare rabbits* trap, entrap, catch, springe, net. **2** *snare a rich spouse* ensnare, trap, catch, get hold of, seize, capture.

snare *noun* **1** *rabbits caught in a snare* trap, gin, springe, net, noose. **2** *unaware of the snares set by the opposition* trap, pitfall, trick, catch, danger, hazard, peril.

snarl[1] *verb* *dogs snarling* show one's teeth, growl. **snarl at** *snarling at everyone first thing in the morning* snap at, growl at, bark at, lash out at; *inf.* jump down the throat of, fly off the handle at.

snarl[2] *verb* **snarl up 1** *ropes getting snarled up* tangle, entangle, entwine, ravel, twist, knot. **2** *snarl up plans for reorganization* complicate, confuse, muddle; *inf.* mess up.

snatch *verb* **1** *snatch the last sandwich from the plate* seize, grab, take hold of, pluck. **2** *snatch* *the tourist's wallet* grab, steal, make off with, appropriate; *inf.* nab, swipe. **3** *snatch the millionaire's child* kidnap, abduct, grab, hold for ransom, take as hostage. **4** *snatch victory toward the end of the game* pluck, wrest, wring, seize, secure. **snatch at 1** *a drowning man snatching at the branch* grab at, make a grab for, grasp at, catch at, clutch at, grope for, reach for. **2** *snatch at the bargain/opportunity* snap up, take advantage of, accept eagerly, grab, seize, pounce upon.

snatch *noun* **1** *at one snatch* grab, pluck, grip, clutch. **2** *snatches of the song/broadcast* fragment, snippet, bit, scrap, piece, part. **3** *a snatch of sleeplessness* spell, period, time, fit, bout.

sneak *verb* **1** *sneak out of the lecture* steal, creep, slip, slide, slink, sidle. **2** *hear people sneaking around outside* creep, skulk, lurk, prowl, pad. **3** *sneak a quick look* snatch, take, catch.

sneak *noun* rascal, rogue, scoundrel, cheater, cheat.

sneaking *adjective* *a sneaking desire to be chairman* secret, private, hidden, concealed, unexpressed, unvoiced, undisclosed, undivulged, unconfessed, unavowed.

sneer *verb* *sneering rather than smiling* curl one's lip, smirk, snicker, snigger. **sneer at** *sneer at their unsuccessful attempts* scoff at, scorn, be contemptuous of, hold in contempt, disdain, mock, jeer at, gibe at, deride, taunt, insult, slight.

sneer *noun* **1** *give a sneer* smirk, snicker. **2** *endure the sneers of her enemies* jeer, jibe, taunt, insult, slight.

sneeze *verb* **not to be sneezed at** *a salary not to be sneezed at* to be taken seriously, not to be taken lightly, not to be scoffed at, not to be laughed at.

snicker *verb* snigger, sneer, smirk, titter, giggle, chortle.

snicker *noun* snigger, sneer, smirk.

sniff *verb* **1** *people with colds sniffing* snuffle, inhale, breathe in. **2** *sniff the aroma of fresh-baked bread* smell, detect the smell of, catch the scent of, get a whiff of. **sniff at** *sniffing at the less fortunate* scoff at, show contempt for, scorn, mock, disdain, turn up one's nose at, look down one's nose at, look down on.

sniff *noun* **1** *the sniffs of people with colds* snuffle, sniffle. **2** *take a sniff of the sea air* smell, scent, whiff.

snip *verb* **1** *snip the piece of cloth* cut, cut into, nick, slit, notch, incise. **2** *snip off a lock of hair* cut, clip, dock, trim, crop, prune.

snip *noun* **1** *cut it with one snip* cut, nick, slit, notch, incision. **2** *snips of cloth* scrap, cutting, bit, piece, fragment, remnant, tatter.

snippet *noun* *snippets of information* bit, piece, scrap, fragment, particle, shred, snatch.

snivel *verb* **1** *sniveling with disappointment* weep, cry, sob, whimper; *inf.* blubber. **2** *sniveling with*

a headcold sniffle, snuffle, run at the nose, have a runny/running nose.

snobbery *noun* snobbishness, social arrogance, pride, airs, condescension, haughtiness, superiority, disdain, disdainfulness, superciliousness; *inf.* snootiness, uppishness, side.

snobbish *adjective* snobby, arrogant, proud, condescending, haughty, disdainful, supercilious, patronizing; *inf.* snooty, uppity, stuck-up, hoity-toity.

snoop *verb* **snoop into** *snoop into another's affairs* pry into, spy on, interfere with, meddle with; *inf.* poke one's nose into.

snoop *noun* snooper, pryer, busybody, interferer, meddler.

snooze *verb* *snooze in front of the fire* doze, nap, catnap, drowse, sleep, slumber; *inf.* take forty winks, catch some Z's.

snooze *noun* *a snooze after lunch* doze, nap, catnap, siesta, sleep, slumber; *inf.* forty winks.

snub *verb* *snub him in public* ignore, disregard, take no notice of, shun, rebuff, repulse, spurn, slight, insult, give the cold shoulder to, cold-shoulder, affront; *inf.* cut dead, give the brush-off to, give a slap in the face to, put down.

snub *noun* *embarrassed by the snub* rebuff, repulse, slight, insult, affront; *inf.* brush-off, slap in the face, put-down.

snug *adjective* **1** *a snug little house* cozy, comfortable, warm, homelike, homely, sheltered; *inf.* comfy. **2** *a snug fit* close-fitting, tight, skintight.

snuggle *verb* nestle, cuddle, curl up, nuzzle.

soak *verb* **1** *soaked by the rain* drench, wet through, saturate, make sopping. **2** *soak the soiled dress in soapy water* steep, immerse, souse. **3** *ink soaking through the paper* permeate, penetrate, imbue.

soaking *adjective* soaking wet, soaked, soaked to the skin, wet through, drenched, sodden, saturated, sopping wet, dripping wet, wringing wet, streaming wet.

soar *verb* **1** *birds/planes soaring into the air* fly, take flight, take off, ascend, climb, rise, mount. **2** *prices soaring* rise/increase/climb rapidly, spiral.

sob *verb* *sobbing at the funeral* weep, cry, shed tears, blubber, snivel, howl, bawl; *inf.* boohoo.

sober *adjective* **1** *he was drunk but is now sober* not drunk/intoxicated, abstemious, teetotal, abstinent, temperate, moderate; *inf.* on the wagon, dry, having signed the pledge. **2** *sober speakers* serious, solemn, thoughtful, grave, earnest, calm, composed, sedate, staid, dignified, steady, levelheaded, self-controlled, strict, puritanical. **3** *discuss sober matters* serious, solemn, grave, important, crucial, weighty, ponderous. **4** *a sober account* factual, low-key, dispassionate, objective, rational, logical, well-considered, circumspect, lucid, clear. **5** *wearing sober clothes/colors* dark, dark-colored, somber, quiet, restrained, drab,

severe, austere. **sober up** 1 *sober up after the party* become sober, become clearheaded; *inf.* dry out. **2** *sober him up after all the excitement* make sober, make serious, subdue, calm down, quiet, make reflective/pensive, make one stop and think, give pause for thought.
Antonyms: DRUNK; LIGHTHEARTED; FLAMBOYANT.

sobriety *noun* **1** *the sobriety of former drunks* soberness, teetotalism, abstemiousness, abstinence, nonindulgence, temperance, moderation, moderateness. **2** *his sobriety and studiousness* soberness, seriousness, solemnness, solemnity, thoughtfulness, gravity, graveness, earnestness, calmness, composure, sedateness, staidness, dignity, dignifiedness, steadiness, levelheadedness, practicality, practicalness, self-control, self-restraint, strictness, puritanism. **3** *the sobriety of the subject* soberness, seriousness, solemnness, solemnity, gravity, graveness, importance, crucialness, weightiness, ponderousness. **4** *the sobriety of the account* soberness, factualness, dispassionateness, objectivity, rationality, logicality, circumspection, lucidity, clarity. **5** *the sobriety of the clothes/colors* soberness, darkness, somberness, quietness, restraint, drabness, severity, austerity.

so-called *adjective* **1** *so-called professional people* self-styled, professed, *soi-disant*. **2** *so-called friendship* supposed, alleged, ostensible, pretended.

sociability *noun* friendliness, affability, cordiality, neighborliness, companionability, gregariousness, convivialness, conviviality.

sociable *adjective* social, friendly, affable, cordial, neighborly, companionable, gregarious, convivial, communicative, conversable, genial, outgoing, approachable, accessible.
Antonyms: UNSOCIABLE; UNFRIENDLY; UNCOMMUNICATIVE; SOLITARY.

social *adjective* **1** *social problems* community, civil, civic, public, societal. **2** *social clubs/evenings* entertainment, recreational, amusement. **3** *not a very social person* friendly, affable, cordial, companionable, gregarious, convivial, communicative. *See* SOCIABLE.

socialize *verb lonely people not socializing with colleagues* be social, be sociable, mix, mingle, keep company, fraternize, consent, hobnob, get together, get out and about.

society *noun* **1** *enemies of society* mankind, humankind, humanity, civilization, the public, the general public, the people, the population, the world at large, the community. **2** *urban and rural societies* community, group, culture, civilization. **3** *leaders of society | marry into society* high society, polite society, the aristocracy, the gentry, the nobility, the upper classes, the elite, the smart set, the beau monde, haut monde; *inf.* the privileged classes, the upper crust, the top drawer. **4** *enjoy the society of friends* company, companionship, fellowship, friendship, camaraderie. **5** *join a society* association, club,

group, band, circle, body, fraternity, brotherhood, sisterhood, league, union, alliance, federation.

sodden *adjective* **1** *sodden clothes* soaked, soaking wet, drenched, saturated, sopping, dripping, wringing wet. **2** *sodden ground* saturated, sopping, soggy, boggy, swampy, waterlogged.

soft *adjective* **1** *soft clay/mud* mushy, squashy, doughy; *inf.* gooey. **2** *soft ground* spongy, swampy, boggy, miry, quaggy. **3** *pieces of a soft substance* pliable, pliant, supple, elastic, flexible, ductile, malleable, plastic. **4** *the soft surface of the curtains* smooth, velvety, cushiony, fleecy, downy, leathery, furry, silky, silken, satiny; *inf.* like a baby's bottom. **5** *soft winds blowing* gentle, light, mild, moderate, calm, balmy, delicate. **6** *soft lights* low, faint, dim, shaded, subdued, muted, mellow. **7** *soft colors* pale, light, pastel, subdued, muted, understated, restrained, dull. **8** *he spoke in soft tones* hushed, whispered, murmured, stifled, inaudible, low, faint, quiet, mellow, melodious, mellifluous. **9** *soft outlines* vague, blurred, fuzzy, ill-defined, indistinct, flowing, fluid. **10** *soft words* sympathetic, kind, gentle, soothing, tender, affectionate, loving, warm, sweet, sentimental, romantic; *inf.* mushy, slushy, schmaltzy. **11** *teachers too soft with the students* easygoing, tolerant, forgiving, forbearing, lenient, indulgent, permissive, liberal, lax. **12** *too soft to be a good leader* tender-hearted, docile, sensitive; spineless, feeble. **13** *soft muscles* flabby, flaccid, limp, out of condition. **14** *lead a soft life* easy, comfortable, cozy; pampered, privileged, indulged; *inf.* cushy. **15** *soft in the head* feebleminded, simple, silly; *inf.* daft, nutty.
Antonyms: FIRM; HARD; HARSH; STRICT.

soften *verb* **1** *soften the blow* ease, cushion, temper, mitigate, assuage. **2** *the winds softened* abate, moderate, lessen, diminish, calm down. **3** *they softened their harsh approach* modify, moderate, temper, tone down. **soften up** *soften him up until he agrees* work on, persuade, win over, disarm.

soggy *adjective* wet, soaking, saturated, sodden, sopping wet, boggy, swampy, waterlogged.

soil *noun* **1** *plant in light soil* earth, ground, clay, dirt. **2** *on American soil* land, country, terra firma.

soil *verb* **1** *soil her white gloves* dirty, stain, muddy, spot, smear, splash, smudge. **2** *soil his reputation* sully, stain, taint, besmirch, blot, smear.

sojourn *noun* stay, visit, stop, stopover; holiday, vacation.

solace *noun* **1** *bring solace to the bereaved* comfort, consolation, condolence, support. **2** *solace for their pain* mitigation, alleviation, assuagement, amelioration.

soldier *noun* fighter, warrior, trooper, warmonger; *inf.* cannon fodder. **soldier on** *soldier on* *through hard times* persevere, persist, keep going; *inf.* plug away, stick it out.

solecism *noun* **1** *an essay full of solecisms* mistake, error, blunder; *inf.* flub. **2** *embarrassed by her solecism at the dinner party* breach of etiquette, inappropriate behavior, impropriety, social indiscretion, faux pas.

solemn *adjective* **1** *a solemn occasion* serious, grave, important, profound; formal. **2** *a solemn procession* dignified, ceremonious, stately, majestic, imposing, impressive, grand. **3** *a solemn child* serious, somber, unsmiling; pensive, thoughtful; gloomy, glum, grim; *inf.* moody, blue. **4** *a solemn promise* earnest, sincere, honest, genuine, committed, heartfelt.

Antonyms: FRIVOLOUS; LIGHTHEARTED; INSINCERE.

solemnity *noun* **1** *the solemnity of the occasion* solemnness, graveness, gravity; dignity, formality. **2** *the solemnity of the procession* formality, ceremoniousness, dignity, stateliness, majesty. **3** *the solemnity of the child* solemnness, gravity, thoughtfulness, somberness, gloominess. **4** *the solemnity of his promise* seriousness, formality, earnestness, sincerity, fervor. **5** *attend the coronation solemnities* ceremony, proceedings, rite, ritual, formalities, celebration.

solicit *verb* **1** *solicit information/assistance* ask for, request, apply for, seek, beg, plead for, crave. **2** *solicit him for financial help* ask, beg, beseech, implore, entreat, petition, importune, supplicate. **3** *arrested for soliciting* work as a prostitute, engage in prostitution, accost people, make sexual advances; *inf.* hustle.

solicitous *adjective* **1** *solicitous inquiries about his health* | *solicitous about your health* concerned, caring, attentive, considerate, anxious, worried, nervous, uneasy, apprehensive. **2** *solicitous to be successful* eager, keen, anxious, desirous, enthusiastic, avid, zealous.

solicitude *noun* *show solicitude for his sick wife* | *solicitude for her health* concern, care, caringness, regard, attentiveness, consideration, considerateness, anxiety, worry, nervousness, uneasiness, apprehensiveness.

solid *adjective* **1** *a solid rather than liquid substance* firm, hard, thick, dense, concrete, compact, compressed, condensed. **2** *made of solid silver* complete, pure, unalloyed, unmixed, unadulterated, genuine. **3** *solid houses* sound, substantial, strong, sturdy, stout, durable, well-built, well-constructed, stable. **4** *solid arguments* sound, well-founded, well-grounded, concrete, valid, reasonable, logical, cogent, weighty, authoritative, convincing, plausible, reliable. **5** *a solid friendship* reliable, dependable, trustworthy, stable, steadfast. **6** *solid citizens* sensible, levelheaded, down-to-earth, decent, law-abiding, upright, upstanding, worthy. **7** *good solid work* sound, worthy, staid, unexciting, unimaginative, uninspired. **8** *a solid company* financially sound, sound, sol-

vent, creditworthy, in good standing, in the black, secure. **9** *a solid line of people* | *a solid hour* continuous, uninterrupted, unbroken, undivided. **10** *political support that remained solid* unanimous, united, undivided, of one mind, of the same mind, in unison, consentient.

Antonyms: LIQUID; HOLLOW; FLIMSY; UNSOUND.

solidarity *noun* *the solidarity of the workers* unity, unification, union, unanimity, singleness of purpose, like-mindedness, team spirit, camaraderie, harmony, esprit de corps.

solidify *verb* *leave the gelatin to solidify* harden, go hard, set, gel, jell, congeal, cake.

solitary *adjective* **1** *forced to lead a solitary life* lonely, lonesome, companionless, friendless, antisocial, unsocial, unsociable, withdrawn, reclusive, cloistered, introverted, hermitical. **2** *seek a solitary spot for a honeymoon* lonely, remote, out-of-the-way, isolated, secluded, hidden, concealed, private, unfrequented, unvisited, sequestered, retired, desolate. **3** *a solitary tree on the horizon* lone, single, sole, alone, by oneself/itself.

Antonyms: SOCIABLE; GREGARIOUS; BUSY.

solitary *noun* *a solitary living in the forest* loner, lone wolf, introvert, recluse, hermit, eremite, anchorite, stylite, cenobite.

solitude *noun* loneliness, remoteness, isolation, seclusion, privacy, retirement, desolation.

solution *noun* **1** *the solution to the mathematical problem* answer, result, key, resolution. **2** *the solution of the problem will take years* solving, resolving, explanation, clarification, elucidation, unraveling, unfolding. **3** *a solution of brine* suspension, emulsion, mixture, mix, blend, compound.

solve *verb* *solve the problem* find the solution to, answer, find the answer to, resolve, work out, figure out, fathom, find the key to, decipher, clear up, get to the bottom of, unravel, disentangle, unfold; *inf.* crack.

solvent *adjective* financially sound, debt-free, creditworthy; *inf.* in the black.

somber *adjective* **1** *dress in somber clothes* dark, dark-colored, dull, dull-colored, drab, dingy. **2** *in a somber mood* | *a somber expression* gloomy, depressed, sad, melancholy, dismal, doleful, mournful, joyless, cheerless, lugubrious, funereal, sepulchral.

Antonyms: BRIGHT; CHEERFUL.

somebody *noun* *her father's a somebody on the local council* VIP, person of note, notable figure, notable, public figure, dignitary, celebrity, name, luminary, personage, household name; *inf.* bigwig, big noise, big shot, big wheel, big cheese.

someday *adverb* *we will get there someday* sometime, one day, one of these days, at some time in the future, at a future time/date, one of these fine days, sooner or later, by and by, eventually, ultimately.

somehow *adverb* *get there somehow* by some

means, in some way, in one way or another, no matter how, come what may, by hook or by crook; *inf.* come hell or high water.

sometime *adverb we must visit her sometime* someday, one day, one of these days, at some time in the future, at a future time/date, by and by. *See* SOMEDAY.

sometimes *adverb we see her sometimes* occasionally, on occasion, on occasions, now and then, now and again, from time to time, once in a while, every so often, off and on.

somnolent *adjective* 1 *feeling somnolent* sleepy, drowsy, half-asleep, heavy-eyed, dozy, groggy, comatose; *inf.* dopey. 2 *a somnolent drug* soporific, sleep-inducing.

song *noun* 1 *a beautiful song* tune, air, melody; ballad, ditty, chorus, chantey, carol, anthem, hymn, psalm, chant, canticle, lay. 2 *the song of the birds* warble, chirp, trill, whistle, pipe.

sonorous *adjective* 1 *the sonorous tones of the minister* deep, rich, full, round, resonant, resounding, booming, ringing, reverberating, vibrating, pulsating. 2 *a sonorous style of prose* impressive, imposing, majestic, lofty, high-sounding, grandiloquent, declamatory, orotund, euphuistic, fustian.

soon *adverb* 1 *be there soon* shortly, in a short time, in a little while, before long, in a minute, in a moment, any minute, in the near future, in a twinkling, in the twinkling of an eye; *inf.* before you know it, before you can say Jack Robinson, pronto, in two shakes of a lamb's tale. 2 *How soon can you get here?* quickly, promptly, speedily, punctually, early.

soothe *verb* 1 *soothe the baby* quiet, calm, calm down, pacify, settle, settle down, hush, lull, tranquilize, mollify. 2 *soothe the pain* ease, assuage, alleviate, allay, moderate, mitigate, temper, palliate, soften, lessen, reduce.

Antonyms: AGITATE; DISTURB; AGGRAVATE.

soothsayer *noun* seer, augur, prophet, diviner, sibyl.

sophisticated *adjective* 1 *sophisticated people* worldly-wise, worldly, experienced, seasoned, suave, urbane, cultured, cultivated, polished, refined, elegant, stylish, cosmopolitan, blasé. 2 *sophisticated production techniques* advanced, highly developed, ultramodern, complex, complicated, elaborate, intricate.

Antonyms: UNSOPHISTICATED; NAÏVE; CRUDE.

sophistication *noun* worldliness, experience, suaveness, urbanity, urbaneness, culture, refinement, elegance, poise, finesse, savoir faire.

sophistry *noun* casuistry, quibbling, equivocation, fallaciousness, fallacy.

soporific *adjective soporific drugs* sleep-inducing, somnolent, sedative, tranquilizing, narcotic, opiate, somniferous.

soporific *noun given a soporific* sleeping potion, sleeping pill, sedative, tranquilizer, narcotic, opiate.

sorcerer *noun* magician, wizard, enchanter, warlock, necromancer, magus, thaumaturgist.

sorceress *noun* magician, witch, enchantress, necromancer, thaumaturgist.

sorcery *noun* black magic, magic, witchcraft, witchery, wizardry, necromancy, black art, enchantment, thaumaturgy.

sordid *adjective* 1 *a sordid creature* vile, foul, base, low, debased, degenerate, dishonorable, disreputable, despicable, ignominious, ignoble, abhorrent, abominable. 2 *sordid moneylenders* mean, greedy, avaricious, covetous, grasping, mercenary, miserly, niggardly, stingy. 3 *sordid hovels* filthy, dirty, foul, unclean, grimy; squalid, shabby, seedy, seamy, slummy, sleazy.

Antonyms: IMMACULATE; HONORABLE; NOBLE; GENEROUS.

sore *adjective* 1 *a sore leg* painful, in pain, aching, hurting, tender, inflamed, raw, smarting, stinging, burning, irritated, bruised, wounded, injured. 2 *feel sore about her treatment of him* distressed, upset, resentful, vexed, aggrieved, offended, hurt, pained, annoyed, angry, irritated, irked, nettled; *inf.* peeved. 3 *in sore need of some food* dire, urgent, pressing, desperate, critical, acute, extreme.

sore *noun a sore on his leg* wound, scrape, abrasion, cut, laceration, graze; boil, abscess, swelling.

sorrow *noun* 1 *the sorrow of the widow* sadness, unhappiness, grief, misery, distress, heartache, heartbreak, anguish, suffering, pain, woe, affliction, wretchedness, dejection, heaviness of heart, desolation, depression, disconsolateness, mourning. 2 *one of the great sorrows of his life* trouble, worry, woe, misfortune, affliction, trial, tribulation.

Antonyms: JOY; DELIGHT; PLEASURE.

sorrowful *adjective* 1 *sorrowful expressions* sad, unhappy, tearful, heartbroken, wretched, woebegone, miserable, dejected, desolated, depressed, disconsolate, mournful, doleful, melancholy, lugubrious. 2 *a sorrowful sight before their eyes* sorry, wretched, miserable, pitiful, piteous, pitiable, moving, affecting, pathetic, heart-rending, deplorable, lamentable.

sorry *adjective* 1 *sorry for his actions* regretful, apologetic, repentant, penitent, remorseful, contrite, ashamed, conscience-stricken, guilt-ridden, in sackcloth and ashes, compunctious. 2 *feel sorry for them* sympathetic, pitying, full of pity, compassionate, moved, commiserative, empathetic. 3 *sorry to hear about his accident* sad, unhappy, distressed, grieved, regretful, sorrowful, miserable, wretched. 4 *a sorry sight* wretched, miserable, pitiful, piteous. *See* SORROWFUL 2.

Antonyms: IMPENITENT; UNREPENTANT; SHAMELESS.

sort *noun* 1 *a new/different sort of plant/car* kind, type, variety, class, category, style, group, set, genre, genus, family, order, breed, make, brand, stamp. 2 *a good sort* person, individual, soul; *inf.* fellow, chap, guy, character, customer. **out of sorts 1** *having been out of sorts with a bad cold* unwell, unhealthy, sick, ill, indisposed, poorly, below par; *inf.* under the weather. **2** *avoid him when he is out of sorts* in a bad mood, in a bad temper, ill-tempered, irritable, cross, crabbed, touchy, testy, crotchety, grumpy, snappish. **3** *out of sorts after her broken engagement* in low spirits, dejected, depressed, downcast, gloomy, glum, melancholy, unhappy, miserable, wretched; *inf.* down, down in the mouth, down in the dumps.

sort *verb* **1** *sort the potatoes according to size* | *sort out the books in piles* classify, class, categorize, catalog, grade, rank, group, divide, arrange, order, put in order, organize, assort, systematize, methodize. **2** *teachers asked to sort out the problem/mess* clear up, tidy up, put straight, put in order, deal with. **sort out 1** *sort the books out into piles* sort, classify, class, categorize, grade, arrange, organize. **2** *sort out the weaker plants and dispose of them* separate out, put to one side, segregate, sift, pick out, select. **3** *sort out the problem* sort, clear up, put straight, put right, solve, find a solution to.

sortie *noun* *a sortie into enemy territory* sally, foray, charge, rush, onrush, raid, attack.

so-so *adjective* mediocre, average, indifferent, unexceptional, undistinguished, uninspiring, tolerable, passable; *inf.* fair to middling, no great shakes, nothing to write home about.

soul *noun* **1** *the soul as opposed to the body* spirit, psyche, inner self, true being, vital force, animating principle. **2** *the soul of discretion* personification, embodiment, incarnation, essence, epitome. **3** *not a soul in sight* person, human being, being, individual, creature. **4** *the life and soul of the party* essential part, essence, heart, core, center, vital force, driving force. **5** *performed without soul* feeling, emotion, intensity, fervor, ardor, vitality, animation, vivacity, energy, inspiration.

sound[1] *noun* **1** *not a sound was heard* noise. **2** *she made not a sound* utterance, cry. **3** *the sound of the flute* noise, music, note, chord. **4** *they do not like the sound of her plans* impression, idea, thought, concept. **5** *within sound of the church bells* hearing, distance, earshot, range.

Antonyms: SILENCE; HUSH.

sound[2] *verb* **1** *sound the trumpet/bugle* play, blow. **2** *the trumpet sounded* resound, reverberate, resonate. **3** *sound the alarm* operate, set off, ring. **4** *sound the letter "f" or "t"* pronounce, utter, voice, enunciate, articulate, vocalize. **5** *sound a word of warning* utter, express, voice, pronounce, declare, announce. **sound as though** *it sounds as though he's mad* appear/look/seem as though, give/create the impression that, strike one that, have every indication that.

sound[3] *adjective* **1** *sound lungs* healthy, in good health, in good condition, physically fit,

disease-free, hale and hearty, undamaged, uninjured, unimpaired, in good shape, in fine fettle. **2** *sound rafters in the building* solid, substantial, sturdy, well-constructed, intact, whole, undamaged, unimpaired. **3** *sound policies/arguments* solid, well-founded, well-grounded, concrete, valid, reasonable, logical, cogent, weighty, authoritative, convincing, plausible, reliable, orthodox. **4** *a sound judge of character* reliable, dependable, trustworthy, fair, good, sensible, intelligent, wise, judicious, sagacious, astute, shrewd, perceptive, foresighted. **5** *sound business* solvent, creditworthy, in good financial standing, in the black, solid, secure. **6** *a sound sleep* deep, undisturbed, unbroken, uninterrupted, untroubled, peaceful. **7** *a sound thrashing/telling-off* thorough, complete, without reserve, unqualified, out-and-out, drastic, severe.

Antonyms: UNSOUND; UNHEALTHY; FLIMSY.

sound[4] *verb* *sound the river depths* plumb, fathom, probe. **sound out** *sound out popular opinion* investigate, carry out an investigation of, conduct a survey of, research, carry out research into, explore, look into, examine, probe, canvass.

sour *adjective* **1** *sour substances* acid, acidy, acidlike, acetic, acidulous, tart, bitter, sharp, vinegary, vinegarlike, unpleasant, distasteful, pungent. **2** *sour milk/butter* turned, curdled, fermented, rancid, bad. **3** *a sour old man* embittered, nasty, unpleasant, disagreeable, bad-tempered, ill-tempered, ill-natured, sharp-tongued, irritable, crotchety, cross, crabbed, testy, touchy, snappish, peevish, grumpy; *inf.* grouchy.

Antonyms: SWEET; FRESH; AMIABLE.

sour *verb* *people soured by his treatment of them* embitter, make bitter, disenchant, alienate; *inf.* turn off.

source *noun* **1** *the source of the river* wellspring, wellhead, headspring. **2** *the source of the rumor* origin, derivation, commencement, beginning, start, rise, cause, wellspring, fountainhead, provenance, author, originator, begetter. **3** *sources listed in the essay* reference, authority, informant.

souvenir *noun* memento, keepsake, token, reminder, relic, memorabilia.

sovereign *noun* ruler, monarch, supreme ruler, king, queen, emperor, empress, czar, crowned head, potentate.

sovereign *adjective* **1** *sovereign power* supreme, absolute, unlimited, chief, paramount, principle, dominant, predominant, ruling. **2** *a sovereign state* self-ruling, self-governing, independent, autonomous. **3** *our sovereign lord* ruling, kingly, queenly, princely, royal, regal, majestic, noble. **4** *a sovereign remedy* efficient, effective, efficacious, effectual, excellent, outstanding.

sovereignty *noun* **1** *hold sovereignty over adjoining states* supremacy, dominion, power, ascen-

dancy, jurisdiction, control, sway. **2** *an island*
sovereignty kingdom, realm, country.

sow verb **1** *sow seed* scatter, disperse, strew, bestrew, disseminate, distribute, spread, broadcast. **2** *sow a field with wheat* plant. **3** *sow doubt in their minds* implant, plant, lodge, initiate, instigate, foster, promote, foment, invite.

space noun **1** *houses taking up a lot of space | not enough space for them all* room, expanse, extent, capacity, area, volume, amplitude, spaciousness, scope, elbowroom, latitude, margin, leeway. **2** *a large space between houses* interval, gap, opening, interstice, break. **3** *write your name in the space provided* blank, empty space, gap. **4** *no spaces left in the theater* empty seat, seat, place, berth, accommodation. **5** *green spaces at the edge of the city* unoccupied area, empty area, expanse, stretch, sweep. **6** *within the space of three hours* time, duration, period, span, stretch, interval. **7** *staring into space* empty space, the blue, the vacuum, the void. **8** *travel in space* outer space, the universe, the galaxy, the solar system; infinity.

space verb **1** *space the trees out around the garden* place at intervals, arrange, line up, range, order. **2** *space out the plans* interspace, set apart.

spacious adjective **1** *a spacious house* roomy, commodious, capacious, sizable, large, big, ample. **2** *spacious grounds* extensive, broad, wide, expansive, ample, large, vast.
Antonyms: CRAMPED; CLOSE.

span noun **1** *the span of the bird's wings* length, extent, reach, stretch, spread, distance. **2** *within a short span of time* time, duration, period, space, stretch, interval.

span verb **1** *a life spanning almost a century | knowledge spanning many areas* extend over, stretch across, cover, range over. **2** *bridges spanning the Hudson | planks spanning the river* bridge, cross, traverse, pass over, arch over, vault over.

spank verb smack, slap, put over one's knee; *inf.* tan someone's hide, wallop, belt, give someone a licking.

spar verb argue, bicker, squabble, wrangle, fight, quarrel, have a tiff; *inf.* have a spat.

spare adjective **1** *a spare blanket* extra, additional, reserve, supplementary, auxiliary, surplus, supernumerary. **2** *have little spare time* free, leisure, unoccupied. **3** *a spare figure | of spare build* lean, thin, slim, slender, without an ounce of fat, skinny, wiry, lank; *inf.* skin and bones. **4** *a spare helping* meager, frugal, scanty, skimpy, modest. **5** *spare with money* sparing, economical, frugal. *See* SPARING. **to spare** *a few plants to spare* left over, superfluous, surplus.
Antonyms: ESSENTIAL; OCCUPIED; FAT.

spare verb **1** *can you spare a few dollars?* afford, part with, give, provide. **2** *no staff to spare* dispense with, do without, manage without, get along without. **3** *spare the culprit* be merciful to, show mercy to, be lenient to, deal leni-

ently with, pardon, leave unpunished; *inf.* let off, go easy on. **4** *spare the tree from destruction* save, protect, guard, defend.

sparing adjective *be sparing with money/food* economical, frugal, thrifty, careful, saving, prudent, cautious, parsimonious, niggardly; *inf.* stingy, tight-fisted.
Antonyms: EXTRAVAGANT; LAVISH.

spark noun **1** *sparks of light* flicker, flash, flare, glint. **2** *not a spark of interest* bit, flicker, glimmer, trace, scrap, vestige, touch, hint, suggestion, suspicion, jot, whit, iota. **3** *require some spark in his employees* sparkle, vivacity, liveliness, animation, energy, spirit, enthusiasm, wit. *See* SPARKLE noun 2.

spark verb **spark off** *incidents sparking off wars* set off, start off, trigger off, touch off, precipitate, provoke, stir up, incite.

sparkle verb **1** *lights/diamonds sparkling* twinkle, flicker, shimmer, flash, glitter, glint, blink, wink, dance, shine, gleam, glow, coruscate. **2** *people sparkling at the party* be sparkling, be vivacious, be lively, be animated, be ebullient, be effervescent, be witty, be brilliant. **3** *wine sparkling* bubble, give off bubbles, effervesce.

sparkle noun **1** *the sparkle of lights on the river* twinkle, flicker, shimmer, flash, glitter, glint, blinking, winking, dancing, shining, gleam, glow, coruscation. **2** *require employees with some sparkle* vivacity, liveliness, life, animation, energy, vitality, spirit, enthusiasm, dash, élan, panache; *inf.* pizzazz, vim, zip, zing.

sparse adjective *a sparse population | sparse coverage of the news* scanty, meager, slight, thinly distributed.
Antonyms: ABUNDANT; PLENTIFUL.

spartan adjective *a spartan life* austere, harsh, frugal, stringent, rigorous, strict, severe, bleak, grim, ascetic, abstemious, self-denying.

spasm noun **1** *stomach spasms* contraction, convulsion, cramp, twitch. **2** *a spasm of coughing/laughter* fit, paroxysm, convulsion, attack, bout, seizure, outburst, access.

spasmodic adjective *spasmodic fits of repentance* intermittent, fitful, irregular, sporadic, erratic, periodic, recurring, recurrent.

spate noun *a spate of burglaries* rush, flood, deluge, torrent, outpouring, outbreak, cluster.

spatter verb *cars spattering mud on pedestrians* bespatter, splash, spray, shower, daub.

spawn verb *governments spawning committees* create, bring into being, give rise to, cause, originate.

speak verb **1** *speak the truth* utter, voice, express, say, pronounce, articulate, enunciate, state, tell. **2** *the lecturer spoke for two hours* give a speech, give a talk, talk, lecture, deliver an address, hold forth, discourse, orate, harangue, sermonize; *inf.* spout, spiel, speechify. **3** *speak volumes | actions speak louder than words* mean, convey, signify, impart, suggest, denote, indicate, demonstrate. **speak for** 1 *a lawyer speaking for the accused* represent, act for, act on behalf of, intercede for, act as spokesman/spokeswoman/spokesperson. 2 *speak for the motion* support, uphold, defend, stand up for, advocate. **speak of** *speak of his faults* talk about, discuss, mention, make mention of, refer to, make reference to, allude to, comment on, advert to. **speak out/up** 1 *speak out/up to be heard in the crowd* speak loudly, speak clearly, raise one's voice, make oneself heard, make oneself audible. 2 *speak out/up against the cruelty* speak boldly, speak frankly, speak openly, speak one's mind, sound off, stand up and be counted. **speak to** 1 *she spoke to him angrily* address, talk to, converse with, communicate with, have a discussion with, chat with, have a chat with, have a word with, accost; *inf.* have a confab with, chew the fat with, pass the time of day with. 2 *speak to the insubordinates* reprimand, rebuke, scold, lecture, admonish; *inf.* tell off, talk to, give a talking-to to, give a dressing-down to. 3 *speak to the motion* comment on, give information about, say something about, say a word about, touch upon, remark on.

speaker *noun an accomplished speaker* public speaker, speech-maker, lecturer, orator, declaimer, haranguer, demagogue; *inf.* spieler.

spearhead *noun the spearhead of the opposition to the plan* vanguard, van, forefront, driving force.

spearhead *verb spearhead the opposition to the plan* lead, head, be in the van/vanguard of, set in motion, initiate, launch, pioneer.

special *adjective* 1 *have a special talent | be a special person* exceptional, remarkable, unusual, rare, out-of-the-ordinary, extraordinary, singular, distinctive, notable, outstanding, unique. 2 *words with a special meaning* specific, particular, individual, distinctive, exact, precise, definite. 3 *take special care of it* especial, extra special, particular, exceptional, out-of-the-ordinary. 4 *a special occasion* significant, momentous, memorable, festive, gala, red-letter. 5 *a special tool* specific, particular, custom-built. 6 *his special interest/subject* particular, chief, main, major, primary.
Antonyms: ORDINARY; USUAL; RUN-OF-THE-MILL.

specialist *noun a specialist in electronics* expert, authority, professional, consultant, master.

specialty *noun* 1 *many specialties in the field of medicine* area of specialization, field of study. 2 *putting people at ease is her specialty* distinctive feature, forte, métier, talent, gift, pièce de résistance, claim to fame. 3 *the restaurant's specialty* specialty of the house, house special, chef's special, particular product.

species *noun a species of plant* sort, kind, type, variety, class, category, group, genus, breed, genre.

specific *adjective* 1 *give very specific instructions* well-defined, clear-cut, unambiguous, un-

equivocal, exact, precise, explicit, express, detailed. 2 *for a specific purpose* particular, specified, fixed, set, determined, distinct, definite.
Antonyms: VAGUE; GENERAL.

specification *noun* 1 *the specification of your housing requirements* stating, statement, naming, itemizing, designation, detailing, cataloging. *See* SPECIFY. 2 *a house built to their specifications* instructions, description, details, delineation, conditions, stipulations.

specify *verb specify your housing requirements* state, mention, name, stipulate, define, set out, itemize, designate, detail, list, spell out, enumerate, particularize, catalog, be specific about.

specimen *noun collect plant specimens* sample, representative, example, illustration, exemplification, instance, type, exhibit.

specious *adjective arguments found to be specious* plausible, seemingly correct, misleading, deceptive, fallacious, unsound, casuistic, sophistic.

speck *noun* 1 *specks of soot on the curtains* spot, fleck, dot, speckle, stain, mark, smudge, blemish. 2 *not a speck of food left* particle, bit, piece, atom, iota, grain, trace.

speckled *adjective speckled eggs/horses* mottled, flecked, spotted, dotted, dappled, brindled, stippled.

spectacle *noun* 1 *the spectacle of snowcapped mountains* sight, vision, scene, picture. 2 *the circus act was quite a spectacle* display, show, exhibition, pageant, parade, extravaganza. 3 *making a spectacle of himself* laughingstock, fool, curiosity.

spectacular *adjective* 1 *a spectacular display/view* striking, picturesque, impressive, magnificent, splendid, eye-catching, breathtaking, glorious, dazzling, sensational, stunning, dramatic; *inf.* out of this world. 2 *a spectacular victory* striking, impressive, remarkable, outstanding, extraordinary, sensational, dramatic, astonishing, singular.
Antonyms: ORDINARY; RUN-OF-THE-MILL; SIMPLE.

spectacular *noun a Christmas spectacular* extravaganza, display, exhibition, performance.

spectator *noun* watcher, beholder, viewer, observer, onlooker, looker-on, witness, eyewitness, bystander; *inf.* rubberneck.

specter *noun* apparition, ghost, phantom, spirit, vision, revenant; *inf.* spook.

speculate *verb speculate that he left unwillingly* conjecture, theorize, hypothesize, guess, take a guess, surmise. **speculate on** 1 *speculate on their future* muse on, reflect on, meditate about, deliberate about, cogitate about, consider, think about. 2 *speculate on the stock market* gamble on, take a risk on, venture on, take a venture on.

speculation *noun* 1 *much speculation about the creation of the universe* conjecture, theorizing, hypothesizing, supposition, guessing, surmising, musing, reflection, meditation, cogitation.

2 *unfounded speculation* conjecture, theory, hypothesis, supposition, guess, guesswork, opinion, reflection, meditation, deliberation, cogitation. **3** *his speculation on the stock market* gambling, gamble, venture, risk.

speculative *adjective* **1** *conclusions that are purely speculative* conjectural, theoretical, hypothetical, suppositional, notional, academic, tentative, unproven, vague, indefinite. **2** *speculative dealings on the stock market* gambling, risky, hazardous; *inf.* chancy, dicey.

speech *noun* **1** *the power of speech* | *express opinions in speech* communication, talk, conversation, discussion, dialogue, colloquy. **2** *slurred speech* diction, articulation, enunciation, pronunciation. **3** *give an after-dinner speech* talk, lecture, address, discourse, oration, sermon, harangue, diatribe, tirade, philippic. **4** *the speech of the Deep South* language, tongue, idiom, dialect, parlance; *inf.* lingo. **5** *given to obscene speech* utterance, remarks, comments, observations, declarations, assertions.

speechless *adjective* **1** *speechless with rage* rendered speechless, struck dumb, dumbstruck, dumbfounded, astounded, thunderstruck. **2** *speechless with modesty* tongue-tied, inarticulate, dumb, struck dumb. **3** *speechless disappointment* silent, unspoken, unexpressed, unsaid, unvoiced, tacit. *Antonyms:* LOQUACIOUS; VERBOSE.

speed *noun* *move with great speed* rapidity, swiftness, quickness, fastness, haste, hurry, hurriedness, expeditiousness, expedition, alacrity, promptness, fleetness, celerity, velocity.

speed *verb* **1** *commuters speeding homeward* hurry, hasten, make haste, rush, race, dash, sprint, scurry, scamper, charge; *inf.* tear. **2** *a driver speeding* drive too fast, break the speed limit, exceed the speed limit; *inf.* put one's pedal to the metal, step on it. **3** *speed their recovery* expedite, hasten, hurry up, accelerate, advance, further, forward, facilitate, promote, boost, aid, assist. **speed up 1** *need to speed up to win the race* make haste, hurry up, rush, increase speed, accelerate; *inf.* get moving, get a move on, step on it. **2** *speed up the process* speed, expedite, hasten, hurry, accelerate. *See* SPEED *verb* 3.

speedy *adjective* **1** *a speedy form of transport* rapid, swift, quick, fast, expeditious, fleet, high-speed. **2** *a speedy reply* rapid, swift, quick, fast, prompt, immediate, express. *Antonyms:* SLOW; LEISURELY; DILATORY.

spell¹ *verb* *the storm spelled disaster for farmers* mean, signify, amount to, add up to, signal, denote, result in, cause, bespeak, portend, augur, presage. **spell out** *spell out their reasons for leaving* specify, set out, itemize, detail, enumerate, particularize, stipulate, make clear, make plain, elucidate, clarify.

spell² *noun* **1** *recite a spell* incantation, conjuration, charm. **2** *put under a spell* trance, state of enchantment, entrancement, enthrallment,

bewitchment. **3** *fall under his spell* irresistible influence, magnetism, allure, charm, attraction, pull, draw, enticement, beguilement.

spell³ *noun* **1** *a spell of warm weather* time, period, interval, stretch, course, extent, span, patch. **2** *a spell of coughing* bout, fit, access. **3** *do a spell at the wheel* turn, stint, term, stretch, shift.

spellbinding *adjective* *a spellbinding tale* riveting, entrancing, enthralling, bewitching, fascinating, captivating, mesmerizing, mesmeric, hypnotic.

spellbound *adjective* *an audience spellbound by the actor's performance* riveted, entranced, enthralled, enraptured, transported, rapt, bewitched, fascinated, captivated, mesmerized, hypnotized; *inf.* hooked.

spend *verb* **1** *spend a great deal of money on clothes* pay out, lay out, expend, disburse; *inf.* fork out, shell out, dish out. **2** *spend hours on the task* occupy, fill, take up, use up, pass, while away. **3** *spend a lot of effort* use, use up, employ, put in, apply, devote. **4** *the storm spent its force* | *soldiers having spent all their ammunition* use up, consume, exhaust, finish off, deplete, drain. *Antonyms:* SAVE; KEEP; HOARD.

spendthrift *noun* *spendthrifts getting into debt* squanderer, prodigal, profligate, wastrel; *inf.* big spender.

spendthrift *adjective* *spendthrift habits* extravagant, thriftless, squandering, prodigal, profligate, wasteful, improvident.

spent *adjective* **1** *a spent force/talent* used up, consumed, exhausted, finished, depleted, drained, emptied; *inf.* played-out, burnt-out. **2** *feeling spent after the long walk* exhausted, worn-out, tired-out, fatigued, weary, wearied, weakened; *inf.* all in, done in, dead on one's feet, bushed, fagged out.

spew *verb* *lava spewing from the volcano* gush, pour, spurt, issue, discharge, spout, rush.

sphere *noun* **1** *ornaments in the shape of glass spheres* globe, ball, orb, globule. **2** *spheres in the sky* planet, star, moon, celestial body. **3** *a limited sphere of influence* area, field, range, scope, extent, compass, jurisdiction. **4** *in the sphere of economics* field, discipline, specialty, domain, realm, province. **5** *marry out of his sphere* social class, social level, social stratum, station, rank, status, social circumstances, walk of life.

spherical *adjective* *spherical ornaments* globe-shaped, globular, globoid, round, orblike, orbicular.

spice *noun* **1** *add spices to food* flavoring, seasoning, herb, condiment, relish. **2** *add a bit of spice to food* spiciness, flavoring, flavor, seasoning, piquancy, pungency, relish, tang, bite, zest, savor; *inf.* punch, kick. **3** *add spice to life* excitement, interest, color, piquancy, zest, gusto, pep; *inf.* zip, zing.

spicy *adjective* **1** *spicy sauces* spiced, seasoned,

flavorsome, well-seasoned, sharp, tart, hot, peppery, piquant, pungent. **2** *spicy stories about her colleagues* lively, spirited, suggestive, risqué, racy, off-color, improper, indecent, offensive; *inf.* raunchy.
Antonyms: BLAND; TASTELESS; BORING.

spike *noun spikes on top of a fence* prong, barb, stake, spine, point, projection.

spike *verb* **1** *spike one's foot on a nail* pierce, penetrate, prick, impale, injure. **2** *spike their drinks* lace, adulterate, contaminate, drug.

spill *verb* **1** *milk spilling from the jug* pour, pour out, flow, overflow, brim over, run over, slop over, well over. **2** *spill the scandalous details* reveal, disclose, divulge, leak, make known; *inf.* let out, blab.

spill *noun take a spill from a horse* fall, tumble; *inf.* header, nosedive.

spin *verb* **1** *wheels spinning* revolve, rotate, turn, turn around, circle, whirl, gyrate. **2** *spin around to face him* wheel, whirl, twirl, turn, twist, swivel, pirouette. **3** *spin the plate* revolve, rotate, turn, whirl. **4** *spin a yarn about his successes* tell, unfold, relate, narrate, recount, concoct, make up, invent, fabricate. **5** *her head was spinning* go around, whirl, reel, swim, be giddy. **spin out** *have to spin out his lecture* protract, draw out, stretch out, drag out, prolong, extend, expand, enlarge, fill out, pad out.

spin *noun* **1** *a spin of the coin* turn, revolution, rotation, whirl, gyration. **2** *a spin in the car* drive, ride, trip, run, jaunt, journey, outing, turn; *inf.* joyride.

spine *noun* **1** *injure his spine* spinal column, vertebrae, vertebral column, backbone, dorsum. **2** *a weak man lacking spine* mettle, grit, pluck, pluckiness, spirit, firmness of purpose, determination, resolution, fortitude, courage, braveness, bravery, valor, manliness. **3** *the porcupine's/shrub's spines* needle, spike, barb, quill.

spine-chilling *adjective* terrifying, horrifying, blood-curdling, hair-raising; *inf.* scary, spooky.

spineless *adjective* weak, weak-willed, feeble, spiritless, irresolute, indecisive, cowardly, timorous, timid, white-livered, unmanly, lily-livered, submissive; *inf.* chicken, yellow, yellow-bellied, gutless.
Antonyms: BOLD; BRAVE; STRONG-WILLED.

spiral *adjective spiral staircases | spiral columns of smoke* coiled, corkscrew, winding, twisting, whorled, helical, cochlear, cochleate, voluted.

spiral *noun a spiral of smoke* coil, twist, whorl, corkscrew, wreath, curlicue, helix, volute.

spiral *verb* **1** *smoke spiraling from the chimney* coil, wind, twist, swirl, wreathe. **2** *prices spiraling* soar, rocket, rise, go up, mount, increase.

spire *noun* **1** *a church spire* steeple, belfry. **2** *mountain spires* peak, pinnacle, crest, top, tip.

spirit *noun* **1** *a healthy body but a troubled spirit* soul, psyche, inner self, ego. **2** *the spirit of na-*

ture breath of life, vital spark, animating principle, life force. **3** *haunted by spirits* apparition, ghost, phantom, specter, wraith, revenant; *inf.* spook. **4** *a person of determined spirit* character, temperament, temper, disposition, humor, complexion, quality, constitution, makeup. **5** *take the criticism in the wrong spirit* attitude, way, state of mind, mood, frame of mind, point of view, reaction, feeling, humor. **6** *the spirit of the age* prevailing tendency, motivating force, animating principle, dominating characteristic, ethos, essence, quintessence, embodiment, personification, quiddity. **7** *lack the spirit to carry out the task* courage, bravery, braveness, valor, mettle, pluck, grit, pluckiness, willpower, motivation, backbone, stoutheartedness, manliness, vigor, energy, determination, firmness of purpose, resoluteness; *inf.* guts, spunk. **8** *play the song with spirit* animation, liveliness, vivacity, enthusiasm, fervor, fire, passion, energy, verve, zest, dash, élan; *inf.* pizzazz, zing, zip. **9** *the spirit of the new rule* implication, underlying message, essence, gist, tenor, drift, meaning, sense, purport. **spirit away** *spirit away the celebrity from the photographers* whisk away, carry off, steal away with, make off with, snatch, seize.
Antonym: BODY; FLESH.

spirited *adjective* **1** *put up a spirited defense* courageous, brave, valiant, valorous, heroic, mettlesome, plucky, gritty, determined, resolute. **2** *a spirited playing of the song* animated, lively, vivacious, enthusiastic, fervent, fiery, passionate, energetic.
Antonyms: TIMID; APATHETIC; LIFELESS.

spiritless *adjective* **1** *spiritless creatures putting up no defense* weak, feeble, spineless, irresolute, indecisive, cowardly, timorous, timid, submissive, unmanly, lily-livered, white-livered; *inf.* chicken, yellow, yellow-bellied, gutless. **2** *a spiritless performance* lackluster, dull, colorless, passionless, bland, insipid, vapid, indifferent, prosaic. **3** *seeming spiritless after their defeat* depressed, dejected, disconsolate, downcast, listless, languid, lethargic, sluggish, inert, lifeless.

spirits *plural noun* **1** *in low spirits | raise one's spirits* mood, humor, temperament, temper, feelings, morale, frame of mind. **2** *wine and spirits* liquor, strong liquor; *inf.* hard stuff, hooch, firewater.

spiritual *adjective* **1** *spiritual needs* nonmaterial, incorporeal, ethereal, intangible, otherworldly, unworldly. **2** *spiritual music* religious, sacred, divine, holy, nonsecular, churchly, ecclesiastic, devotional, devout.
Antonyms: MATERIAL; corporeal; SECULAR.

spit *verb* **1** *not allowed to spit in public* expectorate, hawk. **2** *spit blood* discharge, issue, eject. **3** *"get out," he spat* hiss, rasp, snort.

spit *noun* spittle, saliva, sputum.

spite *noun say it out of spite* malice, maliciousness, ill-will, malevolence, venom, malignance, hostility, evil, resentment, resentful-

ness, snideness, rancor, grudgingness, envy, hate, hatred, vengeance, vengefulness, vindictiveness. **in spite of** *happy in spite of being poor* despite, despite the fact of, notwithstanding, regardless of.
Antonyms: BENEVOLENCE; GOODWILL; CHARITY.

spite *verb do it to spite her sister* injure, harm, hurt, wound, annoy, harass, irritate, vex, offend, provoke, peeve, pique, thwart, foil, frustrate.

spiteful *adjective spiteful comments/behavior* malicious, ill-natured, malevolent, venomous, poisonous, malignant, malign, hostile, resentful, snide, rancorous, grudging, envious, vengeful, vindictive, splenetic; *inf.* bitchy, catty.

splash *verb* **1** *splash water/paint around* spatter, sprinkle, spray, shower, splatter, squirt, slosh, slop. **2** *splash clothes with mud* spatter, bespatter, spray, shower, splatter. **3** *waves splashing against the rocks* dash, beat, batter, buffet, break, wash, surge. **4** *children splashing about in water* paddle, wade, wallow, dabble. **5** *his name splashed across the newspapers* blazon, display, exhibit, plaster, publicize, broadcast, headline, flaunt, trumpet.

splash *noun* **1** *the splash of water against the rocks* splashing, dashing, beating, battering. **2** *splashes of mud on the walls* spot, splotch, daub, smudge, smear, stain. **3** *the scandal made a front-page splash* display, exhibition, splurge, sensation, impact. **4** *a splash of color* patch, burst, streak. **make a splash** *make a splash with her first novel* cause a sensation, cause a stir, attract attention, get noticed.

spleen *noun vent one's spleen on the innocent* bad temper, ill-temper, ill-nature, ill-humor, irritability, irascibility, peevishness, petulance, pique, querulousness, crossness, crabbedness, testiness, touchiness, cantankerousness, moodiness, sullenness, resentment, spite, spitefulness, bitterness, hostility, rancor, malice, maliciousness, malevolence, malignity, acrimony, animosity, bile.

splendid *adjective* **1** *splendid furnishings* magnificent, imposing, superb, grand, sumptuous, resplendent, opulent, luxurious, plush, deluxe, rich, costly, lavish, ornate, gorgeous, glorious, dazzling, brilliant, showy, elegant, handsome. **2** *a splendid reputation* distinguished, impressive, glorious, illustrious, brilliant, notable, noted, remarkable, outstanding, eminent, celebrated, renowned, noble, venerable. **3** *splendid colors* glorious, brilliant, bright, gleaming, glowing, lustrous, radiant, dazzling, refulgent. **4** *a splendid meal/vacation* excellent, fine, first-class, first-rate, marvelous, wonderful; *inf.* fantastic, terrific, great, fabulous, fab.
Antonyms: DRAB; INFERIOR; ORDINARY; UNDISTINGUISHED.

splendor *noun* **1** *the splendor of the furnishings* magnificence, grandeur, sumptuousness, opulence, luxury, luxuriousness, richness, lavishness, gloriousness, elegance. **2** *the splendor of his reputation* illustriousness, brilliance, notability, eminence, renown, venerableness. **3** *the splendor of the colors* gloriousness, brilliance, brightness, gleam, glow, luster, radiance.

splice *verb* **1** *splice the rope ends* interweave, braid, plait, intertwine, interlace, join, unite, connect, bind, fasten. **2** *splice the tapes* join, unite, connect, overlap.

splinter *noun splinters of wood* sliver, fragment, shiver, shard, chip, shaving, shred, piece, bit.

splinter *verb the glass splintered* break into pieces, break into fragments, break into smithereens, shatter, shiver, fracture, split, disintegrate, crumble.

split *verb* **1** *split the material in two* break, chop, cut, hew, lop, cleave, rend, rip, tear, slash, slit, splinter, snap, crack, rive. **2** *split the party in two* divide, separate, sever, sunder, bisect, partition. **3** *split the twins at birth* divide, separate, set apart, disunite. **4** *split the money/profits* share, divide, halve, apportion, distribute, dole out, parcel out, allot, allocate, carve up, slice up; *inf.* divvy. **5** *the road splits over the hill* divide in two, divide, fork, bifurcate. **6** *her husband split* leave, depart, take off, decamp, exit; *inf.* push off, shove off. **split up** *the couple split up* break up, separate, part, part company, become estranged, reach a/the parting of the ways, divorce, get a divorce. **split with** *split with his partner* break up with/from, separate from, part from, part company with, reach a/the parting of the ways with, dissociate oneself from.

split *noun* **1** *a split in the material* break, cut, rent, rip, tear, slash, slit, crack, fissure, breach. **2** *a split in the political party* division, rift, schism, rupture, partition, separation, breakup, alienation, estrangement.

split-up *noun after the split-up of her parents* breakup, separation, parting, estrangement, divorce.

spoil *verb* **1** *spoil the material by washing it* damage, impair, mar, blemish, disfigure, deface, injure, harm, ruin, destroy, wreck. **2** *spoil our plans* upset, mess up, disorganize, ruin, destroy, wreck. **3** *spoil her little boy* pamper, overindulge, mollycoddle, cosset, coddle, baby, spoonfeed, wait on hand and foot, kill with kindness. **4** *the food will spoil* go bad, turn, go sour, become rotten, rot, become tainted, decompose, decay.

spoils *plural noun* **1** *the spoils of high rank* benefit, advantage, gain, profit. **2** *divide up the spoils from the burglary* booty, loot, plunder, pickings, pillage; *inf.* swag, boodle.

spoilsport *noun* killjoy, damper, dog in the manger; *inf.* wet blanket, party pooper.

spoken *adjective spoken judgment* oral, verbal, uttered, voiced, expressed, by word of mouth, unwritten.

spokesman *noun* spokeswoman, spokesperson,

mouthpiece, voice, negotiator, mediator, representative.

sponge verb *sponge the walls* clean, wash, wipe, mop, rub, swab. **sponge off** live off, impose on, be a parasite on, scrounge from, beg from, borrow from; *inf.* freeload on, mooch from, bum from.

sponger noun parasite, hanger-on, scrounger, beggar, borrower; *inf.* freeloader, moocher, bum.

spongy adjective *spongy material/ground* soft, cushiony, squashy, springy, resilient, elastic, porous, absorbent.

sponsor noun *a sponsor of the new art gallery* patron, backer, promoter, subsidizer, guarantor, supporter; *inf.* angel.

sponsor verb *companies sponsoring the softball teams* be a patron of, back, put up the money for, fund, finance, promote, subsidize, act as guarantor of, support, lend one's name to.

spontaneous adjective **1** *spontaneous offers of help* voluntary, unforced, unconstrained, uncompelled, unprompted. **2** *a spontaneous vote of thanks* unplanned, unpremeditated, unrehearsed, impromptu, extempore, spur-of-the-moment, extemporaneous; *inf.* off-the-cuff. **3** *a spontaneous smile* natural, instinctive, involuntary, automatic, impulsive, impetuous.
Antonyms: FORCED; PREMEDITATED.

spoonfeed verb pamper, mollycoddle, cosset, coddle, wait on hand and foot, kill with kindness, overindulge, spoil.

sporadic adjective *sporadic showers* irregular, intermittent, scattered, random, infrequent, occasional, on and off, isolated, spasmodic.
Antonyms: FREQUENT; REGULAR; STEADY.

sport noun **1** *the world of sport* physical activity, physical exercise, physical recreation, athletics. **2** *play a variety of sports* physical activity, competitive game, pastime. **3** *flying kites for sport* amusement, entertainment, diversion, play, fun, pleasure, enjoyment. **make sport of** *making sport of the old-fashioned clothes* make fun of, laugh at, poke fun at, mock, jeer at, ridicule, taunt, gibe at, sneer at.

sport verb *sport a new tie* wear, exhibit, display, have on show, show off.

sporting adjective *a sporting gesture* sportsmanlike, fair, just, honorable, generous.

sportive adjective *students in sportive mood* playful, frolicsome, high-spirited, sprightly, jaunty, rollicking, frisky, skittish, mischievous, waggish, prankish, gamesome.

spot noun **1** *black spots on the cloth* mark, dot, speck, speckle, fleck, smudge, stain, blotch, splotch, patch. **2** *a spot on her face* pimple, pustule, papule, boil, pock, whitehead, blackhead, blemish. **3** *a dark spot on her reputation* stain, taint, blemish, defect, flaw, brand, stigma. **4** *a picnic spot* area, place, site, location, scene, setting, situation. **5** *a regular spot on the program*

place, position, niche. **6** *in a spot* difficulty, mess, trouble, plight, predicament, quandary, tight corner; *inf.* hot water, fix, jam.

spot verb **1** *spot someone following him* catch sight of, see, notice, observe, espy, discern, detect, make out, pick out, recognize, identify. **2** *the mud spotted her dress* mark, stain, dirty, soil, spatter, besmirch.

spotless adjective **1** *spotless sheets* clean, ultraclean, snowy-white, whiter-than-white. **2** *spotless houses* clean, ultraclean, spick-and-span, immaculate, shining, gleaming. **3** *of spotless character* pure, flawless, faultless, blameless, unstained, unsullied, untainted, unblemished, unimpeachable, above reproach.
Antonyms: DIRTY; FILTHY; BLAMEWORTHY; tainted.

spotlight noun *celebrities always in the spotlight* limelight, public eye, glare of publicity, publicity, public attention, public interest.

spotlight verb *a report that spotlights the financial problems* highlight, point up, draw attention to, focus on, zero in on, accentuate, underline, stress, emphasize, give prominence to, bring to the fore.

spotted adjective **1** *a spotted dog/horse* dappled, mottled, pied, piebald, speckled. **2** *a spotted dress* polka-dot, flecked.

spouse noun husband, wife, partner, mate, companion, consort, helpmate; *inf.* better half, old man/lady, missis.

spout verb **1** *oil spouting from the well* spurt, gush, spew, squirt, jet, emit, erupt, disgorge, pour, stream, flow, spray. **2** *tired of politicians spouting* declaim, orate, hold forth, ramble, rant, harangue, speechify, sermonize; *inf.* spiel.

sprawl verb **1** *people sprawling on the sofa* stretch out, lounge, lie around, repose, recline, slump, flop, loll, slouch. **2** *suburbs sprawling out into the countryside* spread, stretch, spill, ramble, straggle, trail.

spray[1] noun **1** *a spray from the sea* shower, jet, mist, drizzle, foam, froth. **2** *buy a deodorant spray* atomizer, vaporizer, aerosol, sprinkler.

spray[2] verb disperse, disseminate, sprinkle, shower.

spray[3] noun *a spray of flowers* sprig, posy, bouquet, nosegay, corsage, wreath, garland.

spread verb **1** *spread its wings | spread the map out* stretch, extend, open out, unfurl, unroll. **2** *the town is spreading out* stretch out, extend, enlarge, grow bigger, widen, broaden, grow, develop, branch out. **3** *the view spread out before them* stretch out, unfold, be on display, be exhibited, be on show, uncover, be unveiled, be revealed. **4** *spread manure on the fields* lay, put, apply, smear; *inf.* plaster. **5** *spread the bread with butter* cover, coat, layer. **6** *the disease/influence is spreading* mushroom, extend, increase, advance, proliferate, escalate. **7** *spread rumors* disseminate, circulate, transmit, make public, make known, broadcast, publicize, propagate, promulgate, bruit. **8** *spread a table* set, lay, arrange.

spread *noun* **1** *measure the spread of the bird's wings* extent, stretch, span, reach, compass, sweep. **2** *a spread of three decades* period, time, term. **3** *the spread of the disease* increase, advance, expansion, mushrooming, proliferation, escalating, diffusion. **4** *the spread of rumors* dissemination, circulation, transmission, broadcasting, publicizing, propagation. **5** *a new spread for the bed* bedspread, bedcover, cover, coverlet, counterpane, throw. **6** *a birthday spread* feast, banquet, repast; *inf.* blowout.

spree *noun* outing, fling, revel, drinking bout, orgy, debauch, bacchanal, bacchanalia; *inf.* binge, bender, jag.

sprig *noun* *a sprig of lilac* spray, branch, bough, twig, shoot.

sprightly *adjective* spry, lively, energetic, active, agile, nimble, supple, animated, vivacious, spirited, brisk, vital, lighthearted, cheerful, merry, jolly, blithe, jaunty, perky, frisky, frolicsome, playful, sportive.
Antonyms: DODDERING; SLUGGISH; LETHARGIC; INACTIVE.

spring *verb* **1** *springing to his feet* | *the cat sprang from the windowsill* jump, leap, bound, vault, hop. **2** *her family springs from a relative of James Madison* be described, descend, originate, derive, issue. **3** *disapproval springs from ignorance* originate, derive, stem, arise, emanate, proceed, start. **4** *where did you spring from?* appear, come into view, crop up; *inf.* pop up. **5** *spring his resignation on them* present unexpectedly, introduce suddenly, reveal suddenly, announce without warning. **spring back** *the branch sprang back* rebound, recoil, fly back. **spring up** *new houses springing up everywhere* appear, make a sudden appearance, come into being, come into existence, shoot up, develop quickly, mushroom, burgeon.

spring *noun* **1** *reach her in one spring* jump, leap, bound, vault, hop. **2** *injured by the spring of the branch* rebound, recoil. **3** *a mattress with little spring* springiness, bounciness, elasticity, resilience, flexibility, stretch, stretchiness, tensility. **4** *put a spring in his step* bounce, bounciness, buoyancy, liveliness, lightheartedness, merriment.

spring *adjective* *spring weather* springlike, vernal.

springy *adjective* **1** *springy mattresses* bouncy, elastic, resilient, flexible, stretchy, tensile. **2** *a springy step* bouncy, lively, lighthearted, merry.

sprinkle *verb* **1** *sprinkle water on the grass* spray, shower, splash, trickle, spatter. **2** *sprinkle salt on the icy steps* scatter, strew. **3** *sprinkle the cake with powdered sugar* dust, powder, dredge.

sprinkling *noun* **1** *a sprinkling of snow on the ground* scattering, dusting. **2** *only a sprinkling of people in the audience* handful, trickle.

sprint *verb* *sprinting for the bus* run, race, rush, dash, hotfoot it; *inf.* scoot, tear.

sprite *noun* fairy, elf, pixie, nymph, dryad, imp, goblin, leprechaun.

sprout *verb* **1** *deer sprouting antlers* send forth, put forth, grow, develop. **2** *potatoes sprouting* bud, germinate, put forth shoots. **3** *weeds sprouting up everywhere* shoot up, spring up, grow, develop, appear, mushroom, proliferate.

spruce *adjective* neat, well-groomed, well turned-out, smart, trim, dapper, elegant, chic; *inf.* natty.
Antonyms: SCRUFFY; UNTIDY; DISHEVELED.

spry *adjective* sprightly, lively, energetic, active, agile, nimble, quick.

spume *noun* foam, froth, head, lather, surf.

spunk *noun* courage, bravery, valor, pluck, pluckiness, mettle, gameness, daring, spirit, backbone; *inf.* guts.

spur *noun* **1** *the use of spurs to speed up the animals* goad, prick, prod. **2** *act as a spur to his ambition* stimulus, stimulant, incentive, inducement, encouragement, impetus. **on the spur of the moment** *make his decision on the spur of the moment* impulsively, on impulse, impetuously, impromptu, on the spot, unpremeditatedly, without thinking, without planning, suddenly, all of a sudden, unexpectedly, out of the blue.

spur *verb* **1** *spur the animal to go faster* goad, prick, prod. **2** *his early success spurred him on to try hard* stimulate, give the incentive to, induce, encourage, motivate, prompt, urge, impel.

spurious *adjective* *spurious excuses/research* counterfeit, fraudulent, fake, bogus, sham, mock, feigned, pretended, make-believe, imitation, contrived, fictitious, deceitful, specious; *inf.* phony, pseudo.
Antonyms: AUTHENTIC; GENUINE; REAL.

---

spurious
apocryphal, artificial, counterfeit, ersatz, synthetic
These adjectives pertain to what is false or not what it appears to be, although not all have negative connotations. **Artificial** implies man-made, especially in imitation of something natural (*artificial flowers; artificial turf*). A **synthetic** substance or material is one produced by a chemical process and used as a substitute for the natural substance it resembles (*boots made from synthetic rubber*). Something that is **counterfeit** is an imitation of something else—usually something rarer, finer, or more valuable—and is intended to deceive or defraud (*counterfeit bills*). **Spurious** also means false rather than true or genuine, but it carries no strong implication of being an imitation (*spurious letters falsely attributed to Winston Churchill*). **Ersatz** refers to an artificial substitute that is usually inferior (*ersatz tea made from tree bark and herbs*). The meaning of **apocryphal**, however, is much more restricted. It applies to accounts of the past that are widely circulated

but whose truth or accuracy are doubtful (*an apocryphal story about George Washington as a boy*).

---

spurn *verb* *spurn her lover/advances* reject, turn away, repulse, rebuff, repudiate, snub, slight, treat with contempt, disdain, look down one's nose at, scorn, despise, condemn; *inf.* kick in the teeth, give the air.

spurt *verb* *oil/water spurting from the well* gush, squirt, shoot, surge, well, jet, spring, pour, stream, flow, issue, emanate.

spurt *noun* **1** *a spurt of oil/water* gush, surge, jet, spray, outpouring. **2** *a sudden spurt of energy/speed* burst, outburst, fit, surge, access. **3** *put on a spurt at the end* burst of speed, turn of speed, increase of speed, burst of energy, sprint, rush.

spy *noun government documents stolen by an enemy spy* enemy agent, foreign agent, secret agent, undercover agent, secret service agent, intelligence agent, double agent, fifth columnist; *inf.* mole.

spy *verb* *spy someone on the horizon* catch sight of, spot, see, notice, observe, glimpse, make out, discern, descry, espy. **spy on** *spy on the rival firm | spy on his neighbors* keep under surveillance, watch, keep a watch on, keep an eye on, observe, keep under observation, follow, shadow, trail; *inf.* tail.

squabble *noun* quarrel, fight, row, dispute, argument, difference of opinion, tiff, wrangle, brawl; *inf.* scrap, set-to, run-in, spat.

squabble *verb* quarrel, fight, row, argue, bicker, have a dispute/tiff, have a difference of opinion, have words, wrangle, brawl; *inf.* fall out, scrap.

squad *noun* **1** *a squad of soldiers* company, platoon, troop, unit. **2** *a squad of workers* gang, band, group.

squalid *adjective* **1** *squalid hovels* dirty, filthy, dingy, grubby, grimy, mucky, slummy, slumlike, foul, vile, low, wretched, mean, nasty, seedy, sordid, sleazy, slovenly, repulsive, disgusting, neglected, dilapidated, ramshackle, broken-down, tumbledown; *inf.* grungy. **2** *squalid tales of corruption* sordid, vile, nasty, repulsive, horrible, disgraceful, shameful, abominable, odious, filthy, indecent, depraved.
Antonyms: CLEAN; SPOTLESS; PLEASANT.

squalor *noun* *the squalor of slums* squalidness, dirt, dirtiness, filth, filthiness, dinginess, grubbiness, grime, griminess, muckiness, foulness, vileness, lowness, wretchedness, meanness, nastiness, seediness, sordidness, dilapidation; *inf.* grunge.

squander *verb* *squander his savings on bad investments* waste, misspend, dissipate, fritter away, run through, lavish, splurge, be prodigal with, spend like water, pour down the drain; *inf.* blow.

square *noun* **1** *a band playing in the square* town square, village square, market square, quadrangle. **2** *regard parents as squares* fogy, old fogy, conservative, traditionalist, conventionalist, conformist; *inf.* stick-in-the-mud, fuddy-duddy.

square *adjective* **1** *a businessman square in all his dealings* fair, just, equitable, honest, straight, upright, aboveboard, ethical; *inf.* on the level. **2** *regard her parents as being square* behind the times, old-fashioned, conservative, ultraconservative, traditionalist, conventional, conformist, bourgeois, straitlaced, stuffy, unadventurous; *inf.* fuddy-duddy.

square *verb* **1** *the two accounts do not square with each other* tally, agree, be consistent, correspond, fit, conform, be in harmony, harmonize, be congruous. **2** *square the bill* settle, settle up, pay, pay in full, discharge, make good. **3** *square matters before we go* straighten out, set straight, set right, put in order, arrange.

squash *verb* **1** *squash the berries with a spoon* crush, squeeze, flatten, compress, press, smash, pulp, mash, pulverize, macerate. **2** *the audience was squashed into the hall* crowd, crush, cram, pack tight, pack like sardines, jam, squeeze, wedge. **3** *squash the rebellion* put down, quash, quell, crush, suppress, squelch, nip in the bud; *inf.* put the kibosh on.

squat *verb* *squat behind the hedge* crouch, sit on one's haunches, sit on one's heels.

squat *adjective* *a squat figure* dumpy, stubby, chunky, thickset, stocky, short.

squawk *noun* **1** *the squawk of the hens* screech, cackle, shriek, scream, yelp. **2** *squawking about the high prices* complain, protest, grumble, moan; *inf.* grouse, kick up a fuss, gripe, beef, bitch, bellyache.

squeak *noun* *the squeak of the mice* squeal, peep, pipe, yelp, whimper.

squeak *verb* **1** *mice squeaking* squeal, peep, pipe, yelp, whimper. **2** *gates squeaking in the wind* creak, scrape, grate.

squeal *noun* *the squeals of the children* shriek, yell, scream, screech, howl, shout, cry, wail.

squeal *verb* **1** *children squealing with pain/excitement* shriek, yell, scream, howl, shout, cry, shrill, wail. **2** *the burglar squealing on his associates* inform, tell tales on; *inf.* blow the whistle on, rat, snitch, put the finger on.

squeamish *adjective* **1** *feeling squeamish on the sea* queasy, nauseous, sickish, sick, queer. **2** *squeamish with regard to etiquette and morals* fastidious, particular, punctilious, finicky, fussy, scrupulous, prudish, straitlaced; *inf.* persnickety, prissy.

squeeze *verb* **1** *squeeze the sweater to remove moisture* wring, twist, press. **2** *squeeze the water from the sweater | squeeze the juice from the orange* extract, press, force, express. **3** *squeeze the oranges* compress, crush, squash, mash. **4** *squeeze his arm* grip, clutch, pinch, press, compress. **5** *the audience was squeezed into the hall* crowd, crush, cram, pack tight, pack like sardines, jam, squash, wedge. **6** *squeeze his fiancée* embrace, hug, cuddle, clasp, hold tight. **7** *squeeze money out of them* extort, wring, wrest, extract, milk; *inf.* bleed. **8** *squeeze them for money* bring pressure to bear on, pressure, pressurize, strongarm, blackmail; *inf.* put the squeeze on, lean on, bleed, put the screws on, put the bite on.

squeeze *noun* **1** *give his fiancée a squeeze* embrace, hug, cuddle, clasp, hold. **2** *give her hand a squeeze* clasp, grip, grasp, clutch. **3** *it was a bit of a squeeze in the hall* crowd, crush, jam, squash, press, congestion. **4** *a squeeze of lemon juice* drop, droplet, dash, spot, bit.

squire *noun* *country squires* landowner, landholder, country gentleman.

squire *verb* *squire her to the dance* escort, accompany, be someone's partner, be someone's companion, attend, usher, guide, conduct, lead.

squirm *verb* *squirm in their seats* | *squirm in embarrassment* wriggle, wiggle, writhe, twist, turn, shift.

squirt *verb* **1** *squirt water from a water pistol* discharge, expel, shoot, spurt. **2** *water squirting from the water pistol* eject, emit, discharge, spew out, spurt, spout, jet, stream, spray, gush, surge, pour, flow, issue. **3** *squirting people with water* splash, wet, spray, bespatter, shower, sprinkle, besprinkle.

squirt *noun* **1** *a squirt of water/cream* jet, stream, spray, flow. **2** *a nasty little squirt* insignificant person; *inf.* pipsqueak, twerp.

stab *verb* knife, pierce, puncture, run through, stick, skewer, gash, slash. **stab in the back** betray, break faith with, be a traitor to, doublecross, sell out, give a Judas kiss to; *inf.* sell down the river.

stab *noun* **1** *receive a stab in the leg* puncture, gash, slash, incision. **2** *feel a stab in the chest* pain, shooting pain, pang, twinge, ache, throb, spasm. **3** *have/take a stab at writing a novel* try, attempt, endeavor, essay, effort, venture; *inf.* go, shot, crack.

stability *noun* **1** *the stability of the structures* firmness, solidity, steadiness, secureness, strength, fastness, stoutness, sturdiness. **2** *the stability of their relationship* secureness, solidity, strength, steadiness, firmness, sureness, durability, constancy, permanence, reliability, dependability. **3** *question her stability* soundness, sense, responsibility, self-control, sanity. *See* STABLE 3.

stable *adjective* **1** *stable structures* firm, solid, steady, secure, fixed, strong, fast, stout, sturdy, moored, anchored, immovable. **2** *a stable relationship* secure, solid, strong, steady, firm, sure, steadfast, unwavering, unfaltering, unswerving, established, long-lasting, longlived, deep-rooted, well-founded, wellgrounded, abiding, durable, enduring, lasting, constant, permanent, reliable, dependable, true. **3** *a stable person* well-balanced, balanced, sound, mentally sound, steady, reasonable,

sensible, responsible, equable, self-controlled, sane.

Antonyms: rickety; INSECURE; UNSTABLE.

stack *noun* **1** *a stack of logs* heap, pile, mass, accumulation, collection, hoard, store, stock, stockpile, mound, mountain. **2** *put hay into stacks* haystack, rick, hayrick, cock, shock. **3** *a stack of money* | *stacks of money* abundance, amplitude; *inf.* great deal, lot, load, heap, ton, oodles, scads.

stack *verb* *stack logs* heap, pile, pile up, amass, accumulate, collect, hoard, store, stockpile.

stadium *noun* arena, field, amphitheater, coliseum; ballpark.

staff *noun* **1** *a shepherd's staff* rod, pole; walking stick, stick, cane, crook. **2** *the staff of office* rod, mace, scepter. **3** *reduce staff in the office* employees, workers, workforce, personnel.

staff *verb* *staff the factory with young graduates* man, people, equip, fit out, supply, furnish, provide.

stage *noun* **1** *a stage in the development* point, period, step, juncture, time, division, level. **2** *the last stage of a race/journey* lap, leg, phase, step. **3** *stand on a stage in the theater* platform, dais, rostrum, podium. **4** *the stage for many international meetings* setting, scene, site, arena, background, backdrop. **the stage** *a career connected with the stage* the theater, drama, show business, the footlights, the boards.

stage *verb* **1** *stage a production of Shakespeare* put on, produce, direct, perform, mount, present. **2** *stage a protest rally* arrange, organize, engineer, orchestrate, put together, lay on.

stagger *verb* **1** *stagger drunkenly up the road* reel, sway, teeter, totter, wobble, lurch, pitch, roll. **2** *staggered by the price of the toys* amaze, astound, dumbfound, astonish, flabbergast, shock, shake, confound, nonplus, take aback, stupefy, stun; *inf.* strike dumb. **3** *stagger the lines of bricks* alternate, vary, step.

stagnant *adjective* **1** *stagnant water* still, unflowing, motionless, standing, foul, stale, dirty, filthy, polluted, putrid, putrefied, brackish. **2** *stagnant business economy* sluggish, slow-moving, quiet, inactive, dull, static.

Antonyms: FLOWING; FRESH; ACTIVE.

stagnate *verb* **1** *water stagnating in weed-covered pools* stand, vegetate; become stagnant/still/foul/stale/dirty/filthy; fester, putrefy. **2** *businesses/economies stagnating* become stagnant, do nothing, be sluggish, lie dormant, be inert. **3** *stagnating at home all summer* vegetate, idle, be idle, laze, loaf, hang about, languish.

staid *adjective* sedate, quiet, serious, seriousminded, grave, solemn, somber, sober, proper, decorous, formal, prim, demure, stiff, starchy; *inf.* stuffy, stick-in-the-mud.

Antonyms: FRIVOLOUS; FLIGHTY; INFORMAL.

stain *verb* **1** *fabric stained with blood/rust* soil, mark, discolor, dirty, spot, blotch, blemish, smudge, smear, besmirch, begrime. **2** *stain her reputation* blacken, tarnish, sully, blemish, damage, mar, injure, defame, denigrate, dishonor, besmirch, defile, taint, blot, slur. **3** *stain the wood* varnish, dye, paint, color.

stain *noun* **1** *unable to remove the stains made by the blood* mark, spot, blotch, blemish, smudge, smear. **2** *stains on her character* blemish, damage, injury, taint, blot, slur, stigma. **3** *use a brown stain on the wood* varnish, dye, paint, colorant.

stake¹ *noun stakes for plants to grow up* post, pole, stick, upright, rod, spike.

stake² *verb* **1** *stake the rose bushes* support, prop up, hold up, brace, tether. **2** *stake a claim to part of the estate* establish, declare, state. **stake off** *stake off his garden with posts* mark off, mark out, separate off, demarcate, define, delimit, bound, circumscribe.

stake³ *noun* **1** *card players laying down $50 stakes* wager, bet, ante. **2** *have a stake in the firm* financial interest, interest, share, investment, involvement, concern.

stake⁴ *verb stake $10 on the race | stake his life on the outcome* wager, bet, place a bet of, put, gamble, pledge, chance, venture, risk, hazard.

stakes *plural noun the stakes in a horse race* prize money, purse, winnings.

stale *adjective* **1** *stale bread/cheese* unfresh, dry, dried out, hard, hardened, moldy. **2** *stale air* unfresh, stuffy, close, musty, fusty. **3** *stale beer* flat, sour, turned, spoiled. **4** *stale jokes* hackneyed, tired, worn-out, threadbare, banal, trite, stock, stereotyped, clichéd, run-of-the-mill, commonplace, platitudinous, unoriginal, unimaginative, uninspired, flat, insipid, vapid; *inf.* old hat.
Antonyms: FRESH; ORIGINAL.

stalemate *noun reach a stalemate in their talks* deadlock, impasse, standstill, stand-off.

stalk *noun the stalk of a plant* stem, branch, shoot, twig.

stalk *verb* pursue, chase, give chase to, follow, shadow, trail, track down, creep up on, hunt; *inf.* tail.

stall *noun* **1** *the vendor's stall* booth, stand, kiosk. **2** *animals in their stalls* pen, coop, sty, corral, compartment, cubicle.

stall *verb* **1** *stall until he thinks of the answer* play for time, use delaying tactics, delay, beat about the bush, hem and haw; *inf.* drag one's feet. **2** *stall his creditors* hold off, stave off, keep at bay, keep at arm's length, evade, avoid.

stalwart *adjective* **1** *stalwart young men* strong, sturdy, robust, hardy, muscular, brawny, strapping, powerfully built, burly, rugged, lusty; *inf.* husky. **2** *stalwart adventurers* brave, courageous, valiant, valorous, intrepid, fearless, manly, heroic, indomitable, bold, daring, plucky, spirited, adventurous; *inf.* gutsy.
Antonyms: PUNY; FRAIL; TIMID.

stamina *noun* endurance, staying power, indefatigability, resistance, resilience, fortitude, strength, vigor, energy, staunchness, robustness, toughness; *inf.* grit, guts.

stammer *verb stammer nervously* stutter, stumble, mumble, splutter, hesitate, falter, pause.

stammer *noun speak with a stammer* stutter, speech impediment, speech defect.

stamp *verb* **1** *stamp his name on the book* imprint, inscribe, engrave, emboss, mark, sign. **2** *her last words stamped on his mind* imprint, impress, fix. **3** *he was stamped a criminal* brand, characterize, designate, identify, categorize, style, term, label, dub, name, tag. **stamp on** *stamp on the poisonous insect* trample, step on, tread on, trample on, crush, squash. **stamp out** *stamp out the rebellion* quash, suppress, put down, quell, crush, squelch, extinguish, put an end to, eradicate, eliminate.

stamp *noun* **1** *have the stamp of genius* mark, hallmark, label, brand, tag, characteristics, quality. **2** *a man of a different stamp* kind, sort, type, variety, class, classification, form, breed, kidney, mold, cast, cut.

stampede *noun run over by the stampede of the cattle* charge, rush, flight, scattering.

stampede *verb the animals stampeded in fear | the shoppers stampeded to the sales* charge, rush, flee, take flight, dash, race, run.

stance *noun take up a liberal stance on the issue* stand, standpoint, position, line, policy, attitude, angle, slant, viewpoint, point of view, opinion.

stand *verb* **1** *ask the children to stand* be upright, be erect, rise, rise to one's feet, get to one's feet, get up. **2** *a house once stood there* be situated, be located. **3** *stand the ladder against the wall* set, place, put, position. **4** *stand and listen* stop, halt, come to a halt, come to a standstill. **5** *the orders stand* remain/be in force, remain/be valid, remain/be effective, hold, hold good. **6** *unable to stand his attitude* put up with, tolerate, bear, take, endure, abide, suffer, brook, countenance, cope with, handle; *inf.* stomach. **stand by 1** *stand by his friend* stand up for, support, be supportive of, back, uphold, be loyal to, defend, come to the defense of, stick up for, champion, take someone's part, take the side of, side with. **2** *stand by his word* adhere to, stick to, observe. **3** *soldiers asked to stand by* wait, be prepared, be ready for action. **stand for 1** *what do the initials stand for?* represent, mean, signify, denote, indicate, betoken, imply, symbolize, exemplify, illustrate. **2** *he stands for all that is good* advocate, favor, support, back, uphold, promote, argue for, speak in favor of, subscribe to. **3** *refuse to stand for her behavior* put up with, tolerate, bear, take, endure, suffer, brook, countenance; *inf.* stomach. **stand in for** *stand in for the teacher when he was ill | stand in for the leading lady* take the place of, replace, act as substitute for, do duty for, cover for, hold the fort for, act as understudy for, understudy,

act as locum for. **stand out 1** *sculptures standing out from the building* project, jut out, protrude, extend, stick out, poke out. **2** *in that dress she stood out in the crowd* be noticeable, be noticed, be conspicuous, be striking, be distinctive, be prominent, attract attention, catch the eye; *inf.* stick out a mile, stick out like a sore thumb. **stand up 1** *that argument will not stand up in court* be valid, be sound, have force, be well-founded, be well-grounded, be effective, be plausible. **2** *stand her up on a date* fail to meet, fail to keep an appointment with, fail to turn up for, let down. **stand up for 1** *stand up for his friend in trouble* stand by, support, be supportive of, defend, come to the defense of, stick up for, champion. *See* STAND BY 1 (above). **2** *stand up for what one believes* uphold, promote, argue for, speak in favor of. **stand up to** *stand up to the bully* confront, face up to, oppose openly, show resistance to, brave, defy, challenge.
Antonyms: SIT; LIE.

stand *noun* **1** *come to a stand* standstill, halt, stop, stoppage, rest. **2** *take up a stand against the new policies* firm stand, defensive position, resistance, opposition. **3** *take a liberal stand* stance, standpoint, position, line, policy, attitude. *See* STANCE. **4** *selling books in his stand* stall, booth, kiosk, cubicle. **5** *put books in stands* display case, shelf, rack, frame. **6** *give a speech from the stand in the hall* platform, stage, staging, dais, rostrum.

standard *noun* **1** *a standard by which quality is judged* yardstick, benchmark, gauge, measure, criterion, guide, guideline, norm, touchstone, model, pattern, example, exemplar, paradigm, ideal, archetype, specification, requirement, rule, principle, law, canon. **2** *works of a low standard* level, grade, quality, evaluation, worth, merit. **3** *raise the battle standard* flag, banner, pennant, streamer, ensign, colors. **4** *trees supported by standards* support, prop, post, pole, cane, upright. **5** *maintain old-fashioned standards* principle, code of behavior, code of honor, morals, ethics, ideals.

standard *adjective* **1** *standard behavior | standard shoe sizes* usual, ordinary, average, normal, common, regular, stock, set, fixed, conventional. **2** *the standard work on Shakespeare* definitive, established, classic, recognized, approved, accepted, authoritative, official.
Antonyms: ABNORMAL; UNUSUAL; UNCOMMON.

standardize *verb* *standardize procedures* make uniform, regulate, systematize, normalize, homogenize, regiment, bring into line.

stand-in *noun* *act as a stand-in for the teacher/actor/doctor* representative, deputy, substitute, second, proxy, understudy, locum, right-hand man/woman.

standing *noun* **1** *his standing in the community* status, rank, ranking, social position, position, station, footing, place, circumstances. **2** *people of standing in the community* reputation, good reputation, repute, eminence, prominence, note, noteworthiness. **3** *her husband of many years' standing* duration, length of time, existence, continuance, endurance.

standing *adjective* **1** *standing stones* upright, erect, vertical, upended, perpendicular; *Herald.* rampant. **2** *standing water* still, stagnant, static, motionless. **3** *a standing army/invitation* permanent, fixed, regular, perpetual, constant.

stand-off *noun* *the two sides have reached a stand-off* deadlock, impasse, stalemate.

standoffish *adjective* aloof, distant, cold, cool, reserved, withdrawn, remote, detached, unapproachable, unfriendly, unsociable, haughty, disdainful.

standpoint *noun* *from the standpoint of the customer* point of view, viewpoint, opinion, perspective, angle, slant, frame of reference.

standstill *noun* *factories/talks coming to a standstill* halt, stop, dead stop, stoppage, rest, pause, cessation, stand.

staple *adjective* *staple foods* chief, primary, main, principal, foremost, leading, basic, fundamental, essential, indispensable, necessary, important, vital.

star *noun* **1** *stars in the sky* heavenly body, celestial body; planet, planetoid, asteroid. **2** *born under a lucky star* astral influence, destiny, fate, fortune, lot. **3** *read his stars* horoscope, forecast, augury. **4** *one of the stars of the film* principal, leading lady, leading man, lead, name, superstar. **5** *some of the stars on the local council* celebrity, dignitary, notable, name, somebody; *inf.* VIP, bigwig, big shot, big cheese, big wheel.

star *adjective* *one of her star pupils* brilliant, great, talented, gifted, distinguished, illustrious, renowned, famous, celebrated, prominent, eminent, preeminent, principal, chief, leading, major.

stare *verb* **1** *stare into space* gaze, gape, look; *inf.* gawk. **2** *the solution was staring them in the face* be conspicuous, be obvious, be blatant, stand out, be prominent, glare.

stark *adjective* **1** *in stark contrast* sharp, sharply delineated, sharply defined, obvious, evident, clear, clear-cut. **2** *a stark landscape* desolate, bare, barren, arid, vacant, empty, forsaken, bleak, dreary, depressing, grim, harsh; *lit.* drear. **3** *stark attire* austere, severe, plain, simple, unadorned, unembellished, undecorated. **4** *stark madness* sheer, utter, absolute, downright, out-and-out, outright, total, complete, thorough, thoroughgoing, pure, unmitigated, unqualified, consummate, unmissable, patent, palpable, rank, arrant. **5** *the stark facts* bald, bare, simple, blunt, straightforward, unadorned, unembellished, harsh, grim. **6** *the stark figure of a man* naked, nude, bare, stark naked. *See* STARK NAKED (STARK *adverb*).

stark *adverb* *stark (raving) mad* completely, totally, entirely, wholly, altogether, utterly, absolutely, quite. **stark naked** naked, nude, in the nude, bare, stripped, undressed, unclad, au naturel; *inf.* in the buff, in the altogether, in the raw, in one's birthday suit.

start *verb* **1** *events starting in the morning* begin, commence, get underway, get going; *inf.* kick off. **2** *when her illness started* commence, get underway, get going, begin, appear, come into being, come into existence, arise, originate, crop up, first see the light of day. **3** *have to start now to finish the job in time* begin, commence, make a start, make a beginning, get going, go ahead, get things moving, buckle down, put one's shoulder to the wheel, put one's hand to the plow, start the ball rolling; *inf.* get moving, get down to it, get down to business/cases, get the show on the road, take the plunge, kick off, get off one's backside. **4** *start now to be there by tonight* start out, set out, set off, depart, leave, make a start; *inf.* hit the road, hit the trail, push off, get the show on the road. **5** *start the machine* set in motion, turn on, start functioning, start operating, activate. **6** *the machine started* begin working, start functioning, start operating. **7** *start the campaign* set up, establish, found, lay the foundations of, lay the cornerstone of, create, institute, initiate, launch, get going, originate, pioneer, organize. **8** *start in pain* jump, leap up, jerk, twitch, recoil, shrink, flinch, wince, shy. **9** *chipmunks starting out of the bushes* jump, leap, spring, bound, dart.
Antonyms: FINISH; END; STOP.

start *noun* **1** *present at the start of the event* beginning, commencement, opening, inception, inauguration, dawn, birth; *inf.* kickoff. **2** *at the start of her illness* beginning, commencement, onset, emergence, first appearance. **3** *the start of the trouble* origin, source, root, basis, derivation, wellspring. **4** *at the start of the campaign* establishment, foundation, institution, launch, origination. *See* START *verb* 7. **5** *get a start in the race* head start, advantage, advantageous position. **6** *finally got her start in show business* opening, opportunity, chance, helping hand, encouragement, introduction, sponsorship, patronage; *inf.* break. **7** *give a start from the pain* jump, leap, jerk, twitch, wince, spasm, convulsion.

startle *verb* *a loud noise startled the children* | *startled by the news* make one jump, disturb, agitate, perturb, unsettle, scare, frighten, alarm, surprise, astonish, shock; *inf.* give one a turn.

startling *adjective* *some starling news* | *a startling result* disturbing, unsettling, alarming, surprising, unexpected, unforeseen, astonishing, amazing, staggering, shocking, extraordinary, remarkable.

starvation *noun* extreme hunger, lack of food, death from lack of food, fasting, famine, undernourishment, malnourishment.

starving *adjective* starved, famished, ravenous,

very hungry, faint from lack of food, dying from lack of food, fasting; *inf.* able to eat a horse.

state *noun* **1** *in a state of readiness* | *in its previous state* condition, shape, situation, circumstances, state of affairs, position, predicament, plight. **2** *in a calm/nervous state* condition, mood, humor, spirits, frame of mind, attitude. **3** *she often gets into a state* state of agitation, anxiety, nerves, panic, distressed state, fluster, pother; *inf.* flap, tizzy. **4** *look at the state of this room* untidiness, mess, chaos, disorder, disarray, disorganization, confusion, clutter. **5** *a meeting of the world's states* country, nation, land, realm, kingdom, republic, territory, federation, commonwealth, body politic. *See table at* COUNTRY **6** *feel the state is too powerful* government, parliament, administration, establishment. **7** *occasions of state* pomp, ceremony, display, dignity, majesty, grandeur, glory, splendor.

state *verb* *state one's objections* express, voice, utter, say, tell, declare, set out, lay down, affirm, assert, announce, make known, reveal, disclose, divulge, pronounce, articulate, aver, proclaim, present, expound, promulgate.

stated *adjective* *at the stated times* set, settled, fixed, agreed, declared, determined, approved, authorized, ruled, ordained, accredited, official.

stately *adjective* *stately occasions* ceremonial, dignified, solemn, majestic, royal, regal, magnificent, grand, glorious, splendid, elegant, imposing, impressive, august, lofty, pompous; slow-moving, measured, deliberate.

statement *noun* *a statement of one's views* declaration, account, recitation, report, affirmation, assertion, announcement, revelation, disclosure, divulgence, pronouncement, articulation, averment, proclamation, presentation, expounding, promulgation.

static *adjective* *static prices/pressure* unmoving, unvarying, undeviating, changeless, constant, stable, steady, stationary, motionless, at a standstill, frozen.
Antonyms: MOBILE; VARIABLE.

station *noun* **1** *trains stopping at several stations* stop, stopping place. **2** *get the bus at the bus station* terminus, terminal, depot. **3** *police station* base, office, headquarters, seat. **4** *security staff at their appointed stations* post, place, position, location, site. **5** *from different stations in life* class, level, rank, grade, standing, status, caste.

stationary *adjective* **1** *stationary traffic* unmoving, motionless, at a standstill, parked. **2** *stationary price patterns* changeless, unchanging, constant, unvarying, invariable, undeviating.
Antonyms: MOVING; VARIABLE.

statue *noun* statuette, sculpture, effigy, figure, figurine, representation, likeness, image, bust, head.

statuesque *adjective* *statuesque figures/woman* dignified, stately, majestic, noble, magnificent, splendid, imposing, impressive, regal, well-proportioned, handsome, beautiful.

stature *noun* **1** *ill-developed in stature* height, tallness, size, altitude. **2** *catering to people of stature* status, importance, import, standing, consequence, eminence, preeminence, prominence, note, fame, renown.

status *noun* *of uncertain social status* standing, rank, level, grade, degree, position, importance, reputation, consequence.

staunch *adjective* *staunch supporters* loyal, faithful, dependable, reliable, steady, constant, stable, firm, steadfast, unswerving, unwavering, unhesitating, unfaltering.
Antonyms: DISLOYAL; UNFAITHFUL; UNRELIABLE.

stave *verb* **stave off** *stave off their attack* ward off, fend off, evade, avert, avoid, dodge, keep at bay, keep at arm's length, repel, repulse, rebuff.

stay *verb* **1** *stay there till we call you* remain, wait, stay put, continue, linger, pause, rest, delay, tarry. **2** *stay loyal to him* remain, continue to be, go on being. **3** *stay judgment until tomorrow* put off, postpone, suspend, adjourn, defer, hold over, hold in abeyance, delay, prorogue. **4** *stay the progress of the disease* check, curb, arrest, stop, delay, hold, prevent, hinder, impede, obstruct. **stay at** *stay at a hotel* lodge at, take a room at, be accommodated at, sojourn at, visit, reside at, take up residence, dwell at, live at.
Antonyms: LEAVE; DEPART.

stay *noun* **1** *a brief stay at a hotel* visit, sojourn, stop, stopover, holiday, vacation. **2** *a stay of judgment* postponement, suspension, adjournment, deferment, delay. **3** *a stay in his old age* prop, underprop, support, brace, bolster, buttress.

staying power *noun* endurance, stamina, resistance, resilience, fortitude, strength, vigor, energy, staunchness, robustness, toughness; *inf.* grit, guts.

steadfast *adjective* **1** *a steadfast friend* faithful, loyal, true, constant, devoted, dedicated, trustworthy, dependable, reliable, staunch. **2** *a steadfast refusal to help | steadfast in his views* steady, firm, determined, resolute, unchanging, unwavering, unfaltering, unswerving, unyielding, inflexible, uncompromising, relentless, implacable. **3** *a steadfast gaze* steady, fixed, intent, immovable, unwavering, unfaltering.
Antonyms: DISLOYAL; IRRESOLUTE.

steady *adjective* **1** *make the posts steady* firmly fixed, firm, fixed, stable, secure, immovable. **2** *a steady hand* still, unshaking, motionless, unmoving, sure. **3** *a steady gaze* steadfast, fixed, immovable, unwavering, unfaltering. **4** *a steady faith* constant, unchanging, changeless, unvarying, invariable, undeviating, continuous, continual, unceasing, ceaseless, perpetual, persistent, unremitting, unwavering, unfaltering, unfluctuating, undying, unending, endless. **5** *walk at a steady pace* uniform, even,

regular, rhythmic, consistent. **6** *a steady boyfriend* regular, habitual, usual, customary. **7** *a steady young man* well-balanced, balanced, sensible, levelheaded, rational, settled, down-to-earth, calm, equable, imperturbable, reliable, dependable, serious-minded, serious.
Antonyms: INSECURE; INCONSTANT; UNEVEN; SPORADIC.

steady *verb* **1** *steady the ladder* make steady, hold steady, stabilize, secure, balance, support. **2** *steady one's nerves* calm, calm down, settle, compose, tranquilize, control, get a grip on.

steal *verb* **1** *steal money* take, appropriate, misappropriate, pilfer, purloin, filch, walk off with, embezzle, pocket, abstract, shoplift, peculate; *inf.* pinch, swipe, lift, rip off. **2** *steal someone else's work* plagiarize, copy, pirate, appropriate, poach; *inf.* lift. **3** *steal a child* kidnap, snatch, abduct, carry off, make off with, seize, shanghai. **4** *steal a kiss | steal a few hours' sleep* snatch, obtain stealthily, get surreptitiously. **5** *steal out of the room* slip, slide, tiptoe, sneak, creep, slink, slither, flit, glide.

steal *noun* *her new dress was a steal* bargain, good buy; *inf.* giveaway.

stealing *noun* **1** *found guilty of stealing* theft, thieving, thievery, robbery, larceny, burglary, appropriation, misappropriation, pilfering, pilferage, purloining, filching, embezzlement, shoplifting, peculation; *inf.* pinching, swiping. **2** *guilty of the stealing of other people's work* plagiarizing, copying, piracy, appropriation, poaching; *inf.* lifting. **3** *the stealing of children* kidnapping, snatching, abduction, seizure, shanghaiing.

stealth *noun* *get into the house by stealth* stealthiness, secrecy, furtiveness, surreptitiousness, slyness, sneakiness, clandestineness, covertness, shadiness.

stealthy *adjective* *stealthy movements/maneuvers* secret, furtive, surreptitious, sly, sneaky, clandestine, covert, shady, underhand, underhanded, undercover.
Antonyms: ABOVEBOARD; OPEN.

steam *noun* **1** *boiling water giving off steam* vapor, fume, smoke, exhalation. **2** *run out of steam | have no steam left* energy, vigor, vitality, stamina, power, force. **let off steam** give vent to one's feelings, lose one's inhibitions, let oneself go; *inf.* let it all hang out. **under one's own steam** *get the job under one's own steam* unaided, unassisted, without help, by oneself, by one's own efforts, on one's own two feet.

steam *verb* *steaming along the road to the bus stop* rush, race, run, dash, charge, sprint, hurry, speed, hasten; *inf.* tear, zoom, zip. **get all steamed up** get agitated, get excited, get flustered, get hot and bothered, get angry, get annoyed, get furious; *inf.* lose one's cool. **steam up** *windshields steaming up* become misty/misted, become blurry/blurred, become cloudy/clouded.

steamy *adjective* **1** *a steamy atmosphere* humid, muggy, sticky, moist, damp, sweltering, boiling, like a Turkish bath, like a sauna. **2** *steamy love scenes* erotic, sexy, passionate, tempestuous, sensuous, lustful, wanton.

steel *noun* **1** *men of steel* strength, fortitude, hardiness, courage, bravery, valor, intrepidity, pluck, mettle, nerve; *inf.* grit, guts. **2** *a grip of steel* firmness, solidity, hardness. **steel oneself** *steel herself to have the operation* brace oneself, harden oneself, nerve oneself, get up courage, screw up courage.

steely *adjective* **1** *a steely color* steel-colored, gray, blue-gray, steel-gray, iron-gray. **2** *steely eyes* hard, harsh, severe, unfeeling, unsympathetic, cruel, ruthless, pitiless. **3** *steely determination* firm, determined, resolute, undaunted, unyielding, inflexible, unwavering, unfaltering.

steep *adjective* **1** *steep cliffs* sheer, abrupt, precipitous, sudden, sharp, perpendicular, vertical, declivitous, acclivitous. **2** *a steep rise in share prices* sharp, rapid, sudden, precipitate. **3** *prices at that restaurant are a bit steep* high, costly, expensive, dear, unreasonable, excessive, exorbitant; *inf.* over the top.
Antonyms: GRADUAL; GENTLE; REASONABLE.

steep *verb* **1** *steep the stained clothes in cold water* soak, saturate, immerse, submerge, wet through, drench, souse. **2** *steep the meat in wine* marinate, marinade, soak, souse. **steep in** **1** *a family steeped in misery* imbue with, permeate with, pervade with, infuse with, suffuse with, fill with. **2** *they were steeped in the classics* submerge in, immerse in, make thoroughly conversant with, make closely acquainted with.

steeple *noun* spire, tower, church tower, bell tower, campanile, turret, minaret.

steer *verb* **1** *steer the car/boat* guide, navigate, drive, pilot, be in the driver's seat of, be at the wheel of. **2** *steer the guests to the garden | steer the conversation back to the subject* guide, lead, direct, conduct, usher. **steer clear of** keep away from, keep one's distance from, keep at arm's length, give a wide berth to, avoid, evade, dodge, eschew, shun.

stem *noun* **1** *the stem of a bush* trunk, stock, peduncle. **2** *flowers/foliage on a stem* stalk, shoot, branch, twig.

stem *verb* *stem the flow of blood* check, stop, halt, hold back, contain, curb, dam, staunch. **stem from** *troubles stemming from poverty* arise from, originate from, have its origins in, be rooted in, derive from, spring from, emanate from, issue from, proceed from, be caused by, be brought about by.

stench *noun* stink, foul smell/odor, reek, mephitis; *inf.* whiff.

stentorian *adjective* stentorious, booming, roaring, thundering, thunderous, trumpeting, earsplitting, resonant, vibrant, powerful, loud, strong, full.

step *noun* **1** *reach her in one step* stride, pace. **2** *hear steps on the stairs* footstep, footfall, tread. **3** *police examining steps in the mud* footstep, footprint, print, impression, track. **4** *walk with a cheerful step* walk, gait, bearing, carriage. **5** *live just a step away* short distance, pace, stone's throw, spitting distance. **6** *the steps of a ladder* rung, tread. **7** *take a foolish step* course of action, move, act, action, deed, measure, maneuver, procedure, expedient, effort. **8** *another step toward international peace* step forward, advance, advancement, development, progression, stage, move. **9** *another step in his promotion* stage, level, grade, rank, degree. **in step** *in step with the views of the committee* in agreement, in accord, in harmony, in line, in concurrence, in conformity, in consensus, in unison. **mind/watch one's step** **1** *mind/watch your step on the broken pavement* step carefully, walk carefully, tread cautiously. **2** *mind/watch your step when doing business with him* be careful, be cautious, be wary, be circumspect, be chary, take care, take heed, be attentive, be on one's guard, look out, have one's wits about one, mind how one goes. **out of step** *out of step with modern thinking* in disagreement, at odds, out of line, at variance. **step by step** *follow the instructions step by step* by stages, by degrees, progressively, gradually, bit by bit, slowly. **take steps** *take steps to control expenditure* take action, take measures, act, take the initiative, prepare, get ready.

step *verb* *step lightly down the street* walk, tread, stride, pace, move, advance, proceed; *inf.* hoof it. **step down** *step down to make way for a younger person* resign, give up one's post/job, retire, abdicate. **step in** *the police had to step in to prevent a murder* intervene, intercede, become involved, act, take action, take measures. **step up** **1** *police stepping up their efforts* increase, boost, augment, intensify, escalate. **2** *step up the pace of production* increase, speed up, accelerate.

stereotype *noun* *the stereotype of a drill sergeant* conventional type, standardized image, hackneyed conception, cliché.

stereotype *verb* *stereotype librarians as being serious people* typecast, pigeonhole, conventionalize, standardize, label, tag, categorize.

stereotyped *adjective* *stereotyped images of a woman's role* typecast, conventional, conventionalized, standardized, hackneyed, clichéd, banal, trite, platitudinous.

sterile *adjective* **1** *sterile female* infertile, barren, infecund, unprolific. **2** *sterile soil/land* infertile, unproductive, unfruitful, unyielding, arid, dry, barren, unprolific. **3** *sterile discussions* unproductive, unfruitful, fruitless, useless, futile, vain, idle, unsuccessful, ineffectual, ineffective, worthless, abortive, unprofitable, unrewarding. **4** *sterile conditions in the hospital* sterilized, germ-free, germless, antiseptic, disinfected, aseptic, uninfected, uncontaminated, unpolluted, pure, clean.

sterility *noun* **1** *the sterility of the woman* sterileness, infertility, barrenness, infecundity, unprolificness. **2** *the sterility of the soil/land* sterileness, infertility, nonproductivity, unproductiveness, unfruitfulness, aridness, aridity. **3** *the sterility of the discussions* sterileness, unproductiveness, unfruitfulness, fruitlessness, uselessness, futility, unsuccessfulness, ineffectualness, ineffectiveness, worthlessness, abortiveness. **4** *the sterility of the hospital* sterileness, freedom from germs, asepticism, lack of infection/contamination/pollution, purity, cleanliness.

sterilize *verb* **1** *sterilize surgical instruments* disinfect, purify, fumigate. **2** *sterilize a woman* make infertile, make barren, make infecund. **3** *sterilize a man* make infertile, castrate, vasectomize. **4** *sterilize male animals* castrate, geld, neuter, emasculate; *inf.* fix. **5** *sterilize female animals* make infertile, spay; *inf.* fix.

sterling *adjective* **1** *have done sterling service* excellent, first-rate, first-class, exceptional, outstanding, splendid, superlative; *inf.* A-1. **2** *sterling friends* genuine, real, true, reliable, dependable, trustworthy, faithful, loyal.

stern *adjective* **1** *stern treatment | a stern regime* strict, harsh, hard, severe, rigorous, stringent, rigid, exacting, demanding, cruel, relentless, unsparing, inflexible, unyielding, authoritarian, tyrannical, despotic, draconian. **2** *look very stern | a stern expression* severe, forbidding, frowning, unsmiling, somber, sober, austere. **Antonyms:** LENIENT; LAX; FRIENDLY.

stern *noun* *the stern of the ship* back, rear, tail, poop.

stew *verb* **1** *stew the meat* simmer, boil, fricassee. **2** *stewing in the doctor's waiting room* be anxious, be nervous, be agitated, worry, fret, agonize, get in a panic, get worked up, get overwrought; *inf.* get in a flap, get in a tizzy.

stew *noun* **1** *make a beef stew* casserole, ragout, fricassee. **2** *get in a stew about the lost document* state of agitation, nervous state, fluster, panic, dither, pother; *inf.* flap, tizzy.

stick *noun* **1** *throw a stick for the dog | gather sticks for kindling* piece of wood, branch, twig, switch. **2** *sticks supporting plants* cane, pole, post, stake, upright. **3** *punished with a stick* cane, birch, switch, rod. **4** *beaten with a stick* cudgel, truncheon, blackjack, baton. **the sticks** *bored with living in the sticks* a remote area, rural districts, the backwoods, the hinterland, the backwater; *inf.* the middle of nowhere, the boondocks, boonies.

stick *verb* **1** *stick a fork in the potato* thrust, push, insert, jab, poke. **2** *stick his head out the window* thrust, push, poke. **3** *stick the pictures to a sheet of paper* glue, paste, tape, fasten, attach, fix, pin, tack. **4** *events that stick in the mind* remain, stay, linger, dwell, lodge, persist, continue. **5** *the car stuck in the mud* become bogged down, become embedded, become lodged, become clogged up, be fixed, become immobilized, be unable to move. **6** *machines sticking* jam, become jammed, come to a standstill, stop, halt, come to a halt, cease to work, become inoperative. **7** *stick the books over there | stick it in the drawer* put, set down, place, lay, deposit, drop, position, locate, plant; *inf.* plunk, stuff. **8** *make the accusation stick* be valid, be sound, be well-founded, be well-grounded, be convincing, be cogent, be persuasive, be relevant. **stick at** *you will have to stick at it to finish the job today* keep at, persist with, persevere with, work at; *inf.* put one's back into.

stick by *stick by his friend in his misfortune* stand by, be loyal to, remain faithful to, support, be supportive of, back, defend. **stick into** *a nail sticking into the tire | a needle sticking into his finger* pierce, penetrate, puncture, prick, spear, stab. **stick it out** *the work is hard but he can stick it out* see it through, see it through to the end, put up with it, endure it, grin and bear it, soldier on; *inf.* take it, hang in there, tough it out.

stick out **1** *sculptures sticking out from the wall* stand out, jut out, project, extend, protrude, poke out, bulge. **2** *she stuck out in the crowd* stand out, be noticeable, be obvious, be obtrusive.

sticky *adjective* **1** *sticky tape* adhesive, adherent, gummy, gluey, tacky. **2** *sticky substances* gluey, glutinous, viscous, viscid; *inf.* gooey. **3** *a sticky summer day* humid, muggy, clammy, sultry, sweltering, oppressive. **4** *a sticky situation* awkward, difficult, tricky, ticklish, delicate, thorny, touch-and-go, embarrassing; *inf.* hairy.

stiff *adjective* **1** *stiff cardboard/substance* rigid, inflexible, unyielding, inelastic, firm, hard, hardened, brittle. **2** *stiff muscles* unsupple, tight, tense, taut, aching, arthritic, rheumatic; *inf.* creaky. **3** *a stiff climb/task* difficult, hard, arduous, tough, laborious, exacting, demanding, formidable, challenging, tiring, fatiguing, exhausting, Herculean. **4** *a stiff penalty* severe, harsh, hard, stringent, rigorous, drastic, strong, heavy, draconian. **5** *put up a stiff resistance* strong, vigorous, determined, resolute, dogged, tenacious, unflagging, stubborn, obdurate. **6** *a stiff occasion* formal, ceremonial, ceremonious, dignified, proper, decorous, pompous. **7** *stiff behavior* formal, unrelaxed, prim, punctilious, chilly, cold; *inf.* starchy. **8** *a stiff drink* strong, potent, alcoholic. **9** *a stiff breeze* strong, vigorous, powerful, brisk, fresh. **Antonyms:** FLEXIBLE; SUPPLE; LENIENT; MILD.

stiffen *verb* **1** *the mixture needs time to stiffen* become stiff, thicken, set, gel, jell, solidify, harden, congeal, coagulate. **2** *need something to stiffen their resolve* strengthen, harden, fortify, brace, steel, reinforce. **3** *his muscles have stiffened* tighten, become stiff, tense, become taut, begin to ache, become arthritic/rheumatic; *inf.* become creaky.

stifle verb **1** *stifle a yawn* smother, check, restrain, keep back, hold back, hold in, withhold, choke back, muffle, suppress, curb, silence, prevent. **2** *stifle a rebellion* suppress, quash, quell, put an end to, put down, stop, extinguish, stamp out, crush, subdue, repress. **3** *it is stifling in here* suffocating, very hot, sweltering, airless, close.

stigma noun *the stigma formerly associated with illegitimacy* shame, disgrace, dishonor, slur, stain, taint.

still adjective **1** *completely still bodies | asked to be still* motionless, unmoving, without moving, immobile, unstirring, inert, lifeless, stock-still, stationary, static. **2** *the house was completely still at night* quiet, silent, hushed, soundless, sound-free, noiseless, undisturbed. **3** *a still evening* calm, mild, tranquil, peaceful, serene, restful, windless, wind-free, halcyon. **4** *a still pool/sea* calm, stagnant.
Antonyms: MOVING; NOISY; WINDY.

still noun *in the still of the night* quietness, quiet, silence, hush, soundlessness, noiselessness, calmness, calm, tranquillity, peace, peacefulness, serenity.

still adverb **1** *they are still here* at this time, yet, up to this time, even now, until now. **2** *he was badly injured, (but) still he is getting better* nevertheless, however, in spite of that, notwithstanding, for all that.

still verb **1** *try to still her fears* quiet, calm, settle, lull, pacify, soothe, allay, assuage, appease, silence, hush, subdue. **2** *the wind stilled* abate, die down, grow less, lessen, moderate, slacken, weaken.

stilted adjective **1** *a stilted manner | a stilted way of speaking* stiff, unnatural, wooden, forced, labored, constrained, unrelaxed, awkward. **2** *stilted prose* pompous, pretentious, high-flown, high-sounding, grandiloquent, pedantic, bombastic.
Antonyms: NATURAL; SPONTANEOUS; UNPRETENTIOUS.

stimulant noun **1** *act as a stimulant to the system* tonic, restorative, reviver, energizer, excitant, analeptic; *inf.* pep pill, upper, pick-me-up, bracer. **2** *act as a stimulant to further economic growth* stimulus, incentive, impetus, fillip, spur. *See* STIMULUS.

stimulate verb *stimulate economic activity* act as a stimulus/incentive/impetus/fillip/spur to, encourage, prompt, spur on, activate, stir up, excite, whip up, kindle, incite, instigate, foment, fan.

stimulating adjective **1** *a stimulating drug* tonic, restoring, restorative, reviving, energizing, analeptic; *inf.* pick-me-up. **2** *a stimulating lecture* interesting, exciting, stirring, thought-provoking, inspiring, exhilarating, rousing, intriguing, provoking, provocative.
Antonyms: SEDATIVE; UNINTERESTING; BORING.

stimulus noun *act as a stimulus to economic growth* stimulant, incentive, fillip, spur, push, drive, encouragement, inducement, incitement, goad, jog, jolt; *inf.* shot in the arm.

sting noun **1** *get a sting from a bee* prick, inflamed area, wound, injury. **2** *take the sting out of the burns* irritation, smarting, tingling, tingle, pain, hurt. **3** *the sting of unrequited love* pain, hurt, distress, anguish, agony, torture, torment. **4** *the sharp sting in his wit* sharpness, bite, edge, pungency, causticity, acrimony, malice, spite, venom. **5** *crooks planning a sting* swindle, fraud, cheating, fleecing; *inf.* rip-off.

sting verb **1** *stung by a jellyfish* prick, wound, injure, hurt. **2** *wounds stinging from the iodine | eyes stinging in the smoke* smart, tingle, burn, be irritated. **3** *stung by their son's treatment of them* hurt, wound, distress, grieve, vex, pain, anguish, torture, torment, harrow. **4** *stung by the dishonest dealer* swindle, defraud, cheat, fleece, gull, overcharge; *inf.* rip off, take for a ride.

stingy adjective mean, miserly, parsimonious, niggardly, tight-fisted, penny-pinching; *inf.* tight, cheap.
Antonyms: GENEROUS; LIBERAL; MAGNANIMOUS.

stink verb **1** *the rotten meat stinks* smell bad, give off a bad smell, reek; *inf.* smell to high heaven. **2** *his behavior stinks* be very bad, be unpleasant, be nasty, be vile, be foul, be abhorrent, be despicable, be dishonest, be corrupt.

stink noun **1** *rotten meat giving off a stink* bad smell, foul smell, stench, reek, malodor, malodorousness. **2** *there was quite a stink about the teacher's dismissal* fuss, to-do, commotion, outcry, uproar, brouhaha.

stint verb *stint on not to stint on the wine* skimp on, limit, restrict, hold back on, be sparing with, be economical with, be frugal with, be mean with, be parsimonious with, be niggardly with; *inf.* be stingy with.

stipulate verb *stipulate a delivery date as part of the agreement* specify, set down, lay down, state clearly, demand, require, insist upon, make a condition of, make a point of, make a precondition/proviso of.

stipulation noun *make several stipulations before signing the contract* specification, demand, requirement, condition, precondition, provision, proviso, prerequisite.

stir verb **1** *stir the mixture* mix, blend, beat, whip. **2** *stirred in his sleep* move, quiver, tremble, twitch. **3** *wind stirring the leaves* move, disturb, agitate, rustle. **4** *refuse to stir from the fireside* move, move an inch, budge, get up. **5** *stirring early on Christmas Day* get up, get out of bed, rise, rouse oneself, bestir oneself, move about, be up and about, be active; *inf.* be up and doing, shake a leg, look lively. **6** *stir his imagination* stimulate, excite, rouse, awaken, waken, kindle, quicken, electrify, inspire. **7** *speakers stirring the men to action* stir up, rouse, incite, provoke, inflame, goad, spur, egg on, urge, encourage, motivate, drive, impel.

stir noun *their arrival caused a stir in the town* excitement, commotion, disturbance, fuss, uproar, to-do, bustle, flurry, ferment, brouhaha.

stirring adjective *a stirring tale of adventure* exciting, dramatic, thrilling, gripping, riveting, spirited, rousing, stimulating, moving, lively, animated, heady, passionate, impassioned.
Antonyms: BORING; PEDESTRIAN.

stitch noun **1** *get a stitch after running* sharp pain, stabbing pain, stab of pain, shooting pain, pang, twinge, spasm. **2** *decorate the cloth with fancy stitches* sewing stitch.

stitch verb **1** *stitch the cloth* sew, baste. **2** *stitch the tear* sew, sew up, repair, mend, darn.

stock noun **1** *a stock of goods for sale* store, supply, range, selection, assortment, variety, collection, quantity. **2** *run out of stock before Christmas* supplies, goods, merchandise, wares, items/articles for sale, commodities. **3** *lay in a stock of wood for the winter* store, supply, stockpile, reserve, reservoir, accumulation, pile, heap, load, hoard, cache. **4** *rolling stock* equipment, apparatus, machinery, implements, appliances. **5** *employed to look after the farm stock* livestock, cattle, cows, beasts, herd, sheep, flock, pigs. **6** *the stock of the business* capital, funds, assets. **7** *have stock in the company* shares, investment, holding, money. **8** *his stock in the company is rising* standing, status, reputation, repute, position. **9** *born of good stock* descent, line of descent, lineage, ancestry, extraction, family, parentage, relatives, pedigree, genealogy, strain, breed, background. **10** *stock for soup/stews* bouillon, broth. **11** *the stock of an implement* handle, haft, grip, shaft, shank. **in stock** *a range of goods always in stock* for sale, on sale, available; *inf.* on tap. **take stock of** *take stock of the situation before proceeding* review, weigh up, appraise, make an appraisal of; *inf.* size up.

stock adjective **1** *stock sizes of clothes* standard, regular, average, readily available, widely available. **2** *stock items in a kitchen cupboard* regular, common, customary, staple, basic, fundamental, necessary, essential, indispensable. **3** *stock responses to his requests* | *stock jokes* usual, routine, run-of-the-mill, commonplace, conventional, traditional, stereotyped, clichéd, hackneyed, overused, worn-out, banal, trite.
Antonyms: IRREGULAR; UNCOMMON; ORIGINAL.

stock verb **1** *stores stocking children's clothes* sell, trade in, deal in, market, handle, supply, keep. **2** *stock the factory with modern machinery* equip, fit, outfit, furnish, accouter, supply, provide. **stock up 1** *stock up the shelves* fill, fill up, load, replenish. **2** *stock up logs for the winter* get in supplies of, obtain a store of, buy up, collect, gather, accumulate, amass, lay in, lay by, put away, deposit, store up, stockpile, hoard; *inf.* squirrel away, salt away.

stockings plural noun hosiery, hose, nylons; panty hose, tights.

stockpile verb *stockpile logs for the winter* collect, gather, accumulate, amass, pile up, store, lay in, put away, put down, deposit; *inf.* put away for a rainy day, squirrel away, salt away, stash.

stock-still adverb *stand stock-still* motionless, unmoving, without moving, immobile, immobilized, inert.

stocky adjective heavyset, thickset, dumpy, stubby, stumpy, squat, chunky, solid, sturdy, mesomorphic.
Antonyms: SLENDER; willowy.

stodgy adjective **1** *a stodgy young man* dull, uninteresting, boring, staid, sedate, stuffy. **2** *stodgy prose* dull, dull as dishwater/ditchwater, uninteresting, boring, tedious, dry, wearisome, unimaginative, uninspired, monotonous, labored, wooden, turgid. **3** *stodgy food* heavy, solid, substantial, filling, starchy, leaden, indigestible.
Antonyms: LIGHT; INTERESTING; LIVELY.

stoical adjective *remain stoical in misfortune* | *stoical attitude to misfortune* impassive, dispassionate, unimpassioned, unemotional, self-controlled, self-disciplined, philosophical, forbearing, patient, long-suffering, resigned, fatalistic, imperturbable, calm, cool, unexcitable, unflappable, phlegmatic.
Antonyms: EMOTIONAL; IMPASSIONED; MELODRAMATIC.

stoicism noun *admire his stoicism in misfortune* impassivity, dispassion, patience, self-control, self-discipline, forbearance, fortitude, endurance, resignation, acceptance, fatalism, philosophicalness, imperturbability, calmness, coolness, cool, phlegm.

stolid adjective *difficult to engage the interest of the stolid child* impassive, unemotional, apathetic, uninterested, unimaginative, indifferent, dull, stupid, bovine, lumpish, wooden, doltish, thick, dense.
Antonyms: EMOTIONAL; LIVELY; IMAGINATIVE.

stomach noun **1** *a pain in the stomach* abdomen, belly, paunch, potbelly; *inf.* tummy, gut, insides, pot, corporation, bread basket. **2** *have no stomach for rich food* appetite, taste, hunger, desire. **3** *have no stomach for the battle* appetite, inclination, desire, liking, fancy, mind, taste, fondness, relish, zest, gusto.

stomach verb **1** *unable to stomach rich food* eat, digest, swallow, find palatable. **2** *unable to stomach his arrogance* stand, put up with, bear, take, tolerate, abide, endure, suffer, swallow, submit to; *inf.* weather.

stone noun **1** *stones rolling down the mountain* pebble, rock, boulder. **2** *a ring set with three stones* precious stone, jewel, gem; *inf.* rock. **3** *erect a stone in his memory* tombstone, gravestone, headstone, memorial stone, monument. **4** *remove the stones from the fruit* kernel, pit, nut, seed, pip.

stony adjective **1** *stony ground* rocky, pebbly, gravelly, gritty, rough, hard. **2** *a stony stare* cold, chilly, frosty, icy, frigid, hard, stern,

severe, rigid, fixed, expressionless, blank, poker-faced, deadpan, sphinxlike. **3** *a stony heart | a stony attitude to the poor* unfeeling, uncaring, unsympathetic, insensitive, callous, heartless, tough, unmoved, unemotional, dispassionate, unresponsive, stern, severe, harsh, hard, cruel, cold-hearted, merciless, pitiless, ruthless, unforgiving, inflexible, unbending, unyielding, adamant, obdurate.
Antonyms: FRIENDLY; SYMPATHETIC.

stooge *noun* **1** *the comedian's stooge* butt, foil, straight man. **2** *he gets his stooges to do all the work* underling, subordinate, assistant, deputy, right-hand man/woman, girl/man Friday; *inf.* sidekick.

stoop *verb* **1** *stoop to pick something up* bend down, lean over, lean down, crouch down. **2** *stoop his head to get into the car* bend, bend down, bow, lower, duck. **3** *very tall people often stoop* slouch, slump, walk with a stoop, be round-shouldered, hunch one's shoulders, bend one's head forward. **4** *never stoops to talk to her inferiors* condescend, deign, lower oneself, humble oneself, demean oneself. **5** *refuse to stoop to crime* sink, descend, lower oneself, demean oneself, resort.

stoop *noun* **1** *with a slight stoop of her head* bending, bow, lowering, ducking. **2** *have a scholarly stoop* round-shoulderedness, hunch, droop/sag of the shoulders.

stop *verb* **1** *stop the fight* bring to a stop, halt, bring to a halt, end, bring to an end, put an end to, finish, bring to a close, terminate, bring to a standstill, wind up, discontinue, cut short, interrupt, nip in the bud. **2** *unable to stop laughing* discontinue, cease, refrain from, desist from, leave off, break off, quit, forbear from; *inf.* knock off. **3** *work has stopped for the day* come to a stop, come to a halt, end, come to an end, finish, come to a close, be over, cease, conclude, terminate, come to a standstill, pause. **4** *stop the crooks from getting away* prevent, hinder, obstruct, impede, block, check. **5** *stop their getaway flight* prevent, hinder, obstruct, impede, hamper, block, check, curb, frustrate, thwart, foil, stall, restrain, bar; *inf.* put the kibosh on. **6** *stop off/over at Newport on the way to Boston* break one's journey, stay, remain, sojourn, lodge, rest. **stop up** *stop up a leak* plug (up), seal (up), block (up), bung up, stem.
Antonyms: START; BEGIN; CONTINUE; EXPEDITE.

stop *noun* **1** *come to a stop* halt, end, finish, close, cessation, conclusion, termination, standstill, stoppage, discontinuation, discontinuance. **2** *there are ten stops on the bus route* stopping place, terminus, terminal, depot, station. **3** *aim for a stop at Miami* stopoff, stopover, stay, sojourn, overnight, rest.

stopgap *noun* temporary substitute, substitution, fill-in, makeshift, improvisation, expedient, last resort.

stopover *noun* *a stopover halfway through the journey* stop, stopoff, stay. *See* STOP *noun* 3.

stoppage *noun* **1** *the stoppage of some forms of welfare* stopping, halting, end, discontinuation, discontinuance, finish, cessation, termination. **2** *another stoppage at the factory* strike, walkout, shutdown. **3** *a stoppage in the pipe* blockage, obstruction, occlusion. **4** *a stoppage in the supply* obstruction, obstacle, impediment, check, snag. **5** *stoppages from their salaries* deduction, charge, subtraction.

stopper *noun* **1** *the stopper in a bottle* cork, lid, cap, top. **2** *put a stopper in the leak* stop, plug, bung, cork.

store *noun* **1** *a store of logs for the winter* supply, stock, stockpile, reserve, accumulation, pile, heap, load, amassment, cache, deposit, reservoir. *See* STORES. **2** *get supplies from the store* storeroom, storehouse, warehouse, repository, depository. **3** *buying shoes/food/books at the store* shop, department store, supermarket, retail outlet, emporium. **set store by** think highly of, hold in regard, hold in high regard, hold in high esteem, admire, appreciate, value, prize, esteem.

store *verb* **1** *store food in case of a shortage* stock up with, get in supplies of, stockpile, collect, gather, accumulate, amass, lay in, put away, put down, deposit, hoard; *inf.* put away for a rainy day, squirrel away, salt away, stash. **2** *store furniture* put into storage, put in store.
Antonyms: USE; DISCARD; SCRAP; JETTISON.

stores *plural noun* *get low on stores* supplies, provisions, rations, food, provender.

storm *noun* **1** *ships damaged in the storm | children soaked in the storm* gale, hurricane, cyclone, tempest, squall, cloudburst, downpour, torrent. **2** *a storm of protest* outcry, outburst, commotion, furor, brouhaha, clamor, tumult, row, disturbance, fight, trouble; *inf.* to-do, rumpus. **3** *a storm on the castle* assault, attack, offensive, onslaught, charge, raid, foray, sortie, siege. **4** *a storm of missiles* shower, spray, deluge, volley, salvo, discharge.

storm *verb* **1** *storm the castle* attack, conduct an offensive on, make an onslaught on, charge, rush, make a raid/foray/sortie on, take by storm. **2** *storm out of the room* charge, rush, headlong, flounce, stride, stamp; *inf.* stomp. **3** *storming at the incompetent recruits* rage, rant, rave, rant and rave, fume, bellow, thunder, shout; *inf.* fly off the handle, blow one's top, blow up, raise the roof, raise hell.

stormy *adjective* *stormy weather | a stormy day* blustery, blustering, windy, gusty, squally, rainy, wild, tempestuous, turbulent.
Antonyms: CALM; STILL.

story *noun* **1** *have a story published | read the children a story* short story, tale, fairy tale, fable, myth, legend, anecdote, novel, novella, romance, narrative, chronicle; *inf.* yarn. **2** *their stories of the accident did not agree* account, report, recital, record. **3** *the novel's complicated* *story* story line, plot, plot development. **4** *journalists looking for a story* news item, news report, article, feature; *inf.* scoop. **5** *told a story when she was caught* lie, white lie, untruth, falsehood, fib, piece of fiction.

stout *adjective* **1** *stout people advised to lose weight* fat, fattish, plump, portly, tubby, obese, corpulent, rotund, big, heavy, thickset, overweight, bulky, burly, brawny, fleshy; *inf.* beefy. **2** *a stout stick* strong, heavy, solid, substantial, sturdy. **3** *a stout defender of the city* stouthearted, brave, courageous, valiant, valorous, gallant, fearless, unafraid, intrepid, bold, plucky, manly, heroic, lionhearted, daring, tough, doughty; *inf.* gutsy, spunky. **4** *put up a stout resistance* firm, determined, resolute, staunch, steadfast, unyielding, unbending, unfaltering, unswerving, unwavering. **5** *launch a stout attack on the enemy* vigorous, forceful, spirited, energetic, strenuous.
Antonyms: THIN; COWARDLY; WEAK.

stouthearted *adjective stouthearted defenders of the city* stout, courageous, valiant, valorous, gallant, fearless, plucky. *See* STOUT 3.

stove *noun* oven, range.

stow *verb stow one's hand luggage in the rack* place, deposit, put, put away, pack, store, load, bundle, stuff. **stow away** *stow away on the yacht* travel secretly, hide, conceal oneself, secrete oneself.

straddle *verb* **1** *straddle the fence/horse* bestraddle, sit/stand astride. **2** *the town straddles the border* be situated on both sides of, lie on each side of. **3** *straddle an issue* be undecided about, be noncommittal about, equivocate about, vacillate about, waver about, sit on the fence about, hem and haw about.

strafe *verb* **1** *the enemy strafing the city* machinegun, bomb, shell, fire on, open fire on, shout at, bombard, rake with gunfire. **2** *getting strafed for their behavior* punish/chastise/discipline severely, reprimand/scold/upbraid harshly; *inf.* carpet.

straggle *verb* **1** *sheep straggling across the moors* wander, ramble, stray, roam, meander, rove, range, spread out. **2** *some of the runners are straggling* trail behind, fall behind, lag, string out, linger, loiter. **3** *hair straggling to her shoulders* grow untidily, be messy, be disheveled, be unkempt.

straight *adjective* **1** *in a straight line/course* direct, undeviating, unswerving, uncurving, unbent, straight as an arrow. **2** *three straight wins* successive, consecutive, in a row, running, uninterrupted, solid, nonstop. **3** *is the picture straight?* level, symmetrical, even, true, in line, aligned. **4** *get the room/things straight* in order, orderly, neat, tidy, spruce, shipshape, in place, organized, arranged, sorted out; *inf.* shipshape and Bristol fashion. **5** *a straight answer* direct, honest, faithful, sincere, frank, candid, forthright, straightforward, plainspoken, plainspeaking, plain, matter-of-fact, outspoken,

straight from the shoulder, unequivocal, unambiguous, unqualified, unmodified. **6** *incapable of straight thinking* logical, rational, sound, intelligent, unemotional, dispassionate. **7** *a straight and valued colleague* respectable, upright, upstanding, honorable, honest, sincere, decent, fair, just, righteous, right-minded, law-abiding, conventional, orthodox. **8** *straight spirits* unmixed, undiluted, unadulterated, pure, neat.
Antonyms: BENT; INDIRECT; ASKEW; EVASIVE.

straight *adverb* **1** *go straight there* directly, by a direct route, without deviating; without delay. **2** *tell them straight* straight out, directly, honestly, frankly, candidly, outspokenly, plainly, straight from the shoulder, with no holds barred, unequivocally, unambiguously; *inf.* pulling no punches. *See* STRAIGHT *adjective* 5. **3** *not thinking straight* logically, rationally, intelligently, unemotionally, dispassionately.
straight away *the work must be done straight away* right away, immediately, at once, instantly, without delay, without hesitation, straight off; *inf.* pronto, PDQ (= pretty damn quick).
straight out *tell him straight out that he is fired* straight, directly, honestly, frankly, candidly, outspokenly.

straighten *verb* **1** *straighten the carpet* make straight, adjust, arrange, put in order, make tidy, tidy up, neaten, put to rights. **2** *have her hair straightened* uncurl, untangle. **straighten out** *straighten out the mess* put in order, put right, sort out, clear up, tidy up, settle, resolve, regulate, rectify, disentangle, unsnarl. **straighten up** *she was bending down but suddenly straightened up* stand up, stand up straight, stand upright, become erect, straighten one's back.

straightforward *adjective* **1** *a straightforward answer* straight, direct, honest, frank, candid, forthright, plain-speaking, unambiguous, straight from the shoulder. *See* STRAIGHT *adjective* 5. **2** *a straightforward task* uncomplicated, easy, simple, elementary, effortless, undemanding, unexacting, routine; *inf.* easy as falling off a log, easy as pie.
Antonyms: EVASIVE; DEVIOUS; INDIRECT; COMPLICATED.

strain¹ *verb* **1** *strain a rope till it snaps* draw tight, tighten, make taut, tauten, stretch, extend, elongate, distend. **2** *strain a muscle* pull, wrench, twist, sprain, wrick, injure, hurt, damage, weaken, impair. **3** *strain one's eyes by reading too much* | *strain every nerve* tax, overtax, exert to the limit, exert something excessively, overwork, push to the limit, fatigue, tire. **4** *strain to win* make every effort, make a supreme effort, strive one's utmost, push/drive oneself to the limit, struggle, labor; *inf.* pull out all the stops, go all out, give it one's all. **5** *strain at the rope* pull, tug, heave, haul, jerk; *inf.* yank. **6** *an account that strained the truth* distort, falsify, garble, misrepresent, invert, stretch, exaggerate, embroider, overdraw. **7** *his account strained the credulity of his listeners* tax, overtax, be too much for, go beyond the limit of, exceed the range/scope of, overstep. **8** *strain the coffee* sieve, filter, percolate. **9** *strain the mixture* sieve, sift, screen, riddle, separate.

strain² *noun* **1** *the rope snapped under the strain* tightness, tautness, tension, tensity, distension. **2** *his injury is just a strain | suffer muscle strain* wrench, twist, sprain, wrick. **3** *the strain of his job* demands, exertions, burdens, pressure, stress, tension. **4** *suffer from strain* stress, pressure of work, tension, overwork, exhaustion, anxiety.

strain³ *noun* **1** *people coming from a hardy strain* stock, descent, lineage, ancestry, family, extraction, blood, breed. **2** *a new strain of flu* variety, kind, type, sort. **3** *a strain of madness in the family* trait, disposition, characteristic, tendency, susceptibility, propensity, proclivity, proneness, inclination. **4** *a strain of cruelty in an otherwise kindly man* streak, vein, element, strand, trace, indication, suggestion, suspicion. **5** *the speaker went on in the same strain for more than an hour* vein, way, tone, style, manner. **6** *the strains of a boys' choir* music, tone, melody, air, song. **7** *remember a strain of an old poem* line, snippet, fragment, scrap, bit.

strained *adjective* **1** *a strained smile/laugh* forced, artificial, unnatural, false, constrained, labored, wooden, stiff, self-conscious. **2** *a strained silence* awkward, embarrassed, uneasy, uncomfortable, tense, unrelaxed. **3** *strained relations | relations between them are strained* under a strain, tense, troubled, uneasy, hostile.
Antonyms: NATURAL; relaxed; FRIENDLY.

strainer *noun put the food through a strainer* sieve, colander, filter, sifter, screen, riddle.

strait *noun the boat crossing the strait* sound, narrows, channel, inlet, arm of the sea.

straitened *adjective live in straitened circumstances* poverty-stricken, poor, destitute, impoverished, penniless, impecunious, penurious, beggared, pauperized.

straitlaced *adjective* puritanical, prudish, prim, proper, priggish, moralistic, narrow, narrow-minded, stuffy; *inf.* fuddy-duddy.
Antonyms: PERMISSIVE; BROAD-MINDED.

straits *plural noun in dire straits* predicament, plight, difficulty, trouble, crisis, mess; *inf.* pretty kettle of fish, tight corner, hot water, jam, hole, scrape, stew.

strand¹ *noun* **1** *the strands of the wool/rope* thread, fiber, filament, length. **2** *curling strands of hair* lock, wisp, tress. **3** *the last volume drawing together the strands of the trilogy* element, component, strain, story line, theme.

strand² *noun walk on the strand* shore, seashore, beach, coast, seaside, waterfront.

stranded *adjective* **1** *she was stranded when her* purse was stolen left helpless, without help/assistance, left penniless, in dire straits, in difficulties, left in the lurch, left high and dry, abandoned, forsaken. **2** *stranded ships* grounded, beached, shipwrecked, wrecked, marooned.

strange *adjective* **1** *he had a strange expression on his face* peculiar, odd, bizarre, unusual, atypical, abnormal, surprising, weird, funny, unfamiliar. **2** *a strange land* previously unencountered, unknown, unfamiliar. **3** *a strange phenomenon* inexplicable, anomalous, unexpected, extraordinary.
Antonyms: NORMAL; ORDINARY; FAMILIAR.

stranger *noun* **1** *he was a complete stranger to her* unknown person, alien. **2** *strangers being welcomed into the community* new person, outsider, new arrival, newcomer, incomer, foreigner. **a stranger to** *a stranger to the area* unfamiliar with, unacquainted with, unaccustomed to, new to, fresh to, unused to, inexperienced in, unpracticed in, unversed in, unconversant with.

strangle *verb* **1** *he strangled his victim with a scarf* throttle, choke, strangulate, garrote. **2** *strangle artistic expression* suppress, inhibit, repress, check, restrain, hold back, curb, stifle, gag.

strap *noun straps fastening the trunk* band, belt, thong, cord, tie.

strap *verb* **1** *strap the trunk with leather thongs* fasten, secure, tie, bind, lash, truss, pinion. **2** *strap her strained ankle* bind, bandage. **3** *strap the naughty children* flog, lash, whip, scourge, beat; *inf.* belt.

stratagem *noun win only by means of a stratagem* trick, ruse, plot, cunning/crafty plan, scheme, maneuver, plan, tactic, artifice, machination, wile, subterfuge, dodge, deception.

strategic *adjective* **1** *strategic schemes* tactical, diplomatic, politic, calculated, planned, plotted, cunning, wily. **2** *strategic bases in the war* crucial, key, vital, critical, essential, important.

strategy *noun* **1** *the government's economic strategy* policy, approach, program, scheme, plan of action, master plan, schedule, blueprint, game plan. **2** *the general's strategy* art of war, martial art, military science, military tactics.

stratum *noun* **1** *the top stratum of rock* layer, tier, vein, lode. **2** *belong to the same stratum of society* class, level, grade, status, station, gradation.

stray *verb* **1** *cows straying into the neighbor's field* wander, roam, rove, go astray. **2** *strayed in later life* go astray, go wrong, do wrong, stray from the straight and narrow, err, sin, transgress, go down the primrose path. **stray from** *stray from the point* digress from, wander from, deviate from, get off the subject of, get sidetracked from, go off on a tangent from, lose the thread of.

stray *noun give strays a home* homeless animal, stray dog/cat, homeless person, waif, foundling.

stray *adjective* **1** *a stray dog* strayed, gone astray, lost, homeless, wandering, vagrant, abandoned, unclaimed. **2** *a stray customer or two |*

a stray bullet odd, random, isolated, scattered, occasional, incidental, accidental, chance, freak.

streak *noun* 1 *a streak of light in the dark sky* line, band, strip, stripe, slash, smear. 2 *a streak of cowardice in him* strain, vein, element, trace, touch, dash. 3 *a streak of lightning* bolt, flash, beam. 4 *streaks on the windows when he cleaned them* smear, smudge, mark. 5 *on a winning streak* spell, period, course, stretch, series.

streak *verb* 1 *a blue sky streaked with white* band, stripe, mark, slash, striate, fleck, daub, smear. 2 *dirty cloths streaking the glass* smear, smudge, mark. 3 *runners/cars streaking past* race, rush, speed, dash, sprint, hurtle, scurry, fly, flee, flash, whistle, zoom, zip; *inf.* tear, whiz.

stream *noun* 1 *mountain streams* river, brook, creek, rivulet, rill, freshet. 2 *a stream of blood* flow, rush, gush, surge, jet, outpouring, efflux, current, cascade. 3 *people going with the stream* flow, current, tide, course, drift.

stream *verb* 1 *water streaming from the pipe* | *tears streaming down his face* flow, run, pour, course, spill, gush, surge, flood, cascade, well. 2 *wound streaming blood* emit, issue, shed, spill. 3 *hair/flags streaming in the breeze* flow, float, swing, flap, flutter. 4 *people streaming out of the building* surge, pour, crowd.

streamer *noun* flag, pennant, banner, standard, ensign, gonfalon.

streamlined *adjective* 1 *streamlined cars* smooth, sleek, elegant. 2 *streamlined production methods* efficient, smooth-running, well-run, modernized, rationalized, slick.

street *noun* road, thoroughfare, boulevard, avenue, drive, lane.

strength *noun* 1 *men of great physical strength* | *the strength to break the door* power, might, force, brawn, muscle, muscularity, sturdiness, robustness, vigor, toughness, stamina. 2 *regain his strength* health, robustness, healthiness, vigor. 3 *adversity gave him inner strength* fortitude, courage, bravery, pluck, firmness, stamina, backbone; *inf.* grit, guts. 4 *test the strength of the castle doors* solidity, toughness, resistance, impregnability. 5 *the strength of the feeling against him* force, forcefulness, intensity, vehemence, ardor, fervency. 6 *the strength of their argument* cogency, potency, weight, effectiveness, efficacy, soundness, validity. 7 *workers who are the strength of the firm* mainstay, chief support, tower of strength, anchor, foundation stone. 8 *the firm's reliability is its main strength* advantage, asset, strong point, forte. 9 *the strength of the workforce* size, extent, magnitude, bigness, largeness, greatness. **on the strength of** *he got the job on the strength of his qualifications* on the basis of, based on, because of, on the grounds of.

Antonyms: FRAILTY; INFIRMITY; WEAKNESS; FAILING.

strengthen *verb* 1 *strengthen children's bones* make strong, make stronger, give strength to, make healthy, nourish, build up. 2 *the wind strengthened* grow strong, grow stronger, gain strength, intensify, heighten. 3 *strengthen their determination* make stronger, give strength to, fortify, give a boost to, harden, stiffen, toughen, steel. 4 *his evidence strengthened their argument* give strength to, reinforce, support, back up, bolster, authenticate, confirm, substantiate, corroborate.

strenuous *adjective* 1 *a strenuous task* arduous, laborious, taxing, demanding, difficult, hard, tough, uphill, heavy, weighty, burdensome, exhausting, tiring, fatiguing. 2 *make strenuous efforts to reach the top* energetic, active, vigorous, forceful, strong, spirited, bold, determined, resolute, tenacious, earnest, keen, zealous.

Antonyms: EASY; EFFORTLESS; HALFHEARTED.

stress *noun* 1 *the stress of his new job* | *suffer from stress* strain, pressure, tension, worry, anxiety. 2 *in times of stress* worry, anxiety, trouble, difficulty, distress, trauma. 3 *place stress on education* emphasis, priority, importance, weight, significance, value, worth, merit. 4 *place stress on the first syllable* emphasis, accent, accentuation. 5 *wire unable to bear stress* strain, tension, tensity, tightness, tautness, stretching.

stress *verb* 1 *stress the importance of education* lay stress on, emphasize, place emphasis on, give emphasis to, accentuate, underline, underscore, point up, highlight, spotlight, press home, dwell on, harp on, belabor. 2 *stress the first syllable* lay stress on, emphasize, place emphasis on, give emphasis to, place the accent on, accentuate. 3 *discover that the workers have been stressed for years* subject to stress/strain/tension, tax, overtax, pressurize, overwork, overstretch, overburden, push to the limit, push too far.

stretch *verb* 1 *the material stretches* be stretchy, be elastic, be tensile. 2 *stretch the piece of elastic/rope* extend, elongate, lengthen, expand, draw out, pull out. 3 *sweaters stretching in the wash* get larger, get bigger, enlarge, expand, pull out of shape. 4 *stretched a hand out* reach out, hold out, put forth, proffer, offer. 5 *stretch one's arms* unbend, extend, elongate. 6 *the forests stretched for miles* extend, spread, unfold, cover, range. 7 *a job that will stretch her* be a challenge to, challenge, extend, tax, push to the limit. 8 *stretch the truth* strain, overstrain, exaggerate, overdraw, push too far. **stretch out** *stretch out on the sofa* lie down, recline, sprawl (out), lounge.

Antonyms: SHORTEN; CONTRACT.

stretch *noun* 1 *stretches of forest* expanse, area, tract, extent, spread, sweep. 2 *a four-hour stretch* period, time, spell, term, space, run, stint.

strict *adjective* 1 *a strict interpretation of the rules* precise, exact, close, faithful, true, accurate,

scrupulous, meticulous, conscientious, punctilious. **2** *a strict regime/upbringing* | *strict parents* stringent, rigorous, severe, harsh, hard, stern, authoritarian, rigid, narrow, austere, illiberal, inflexible, unyielding, uncompromising. **3** *in strict confidence* absolute, utter, complete, total, perfect. **4** *strict members of the religious sect* orthodox, fundamentalist.
Antonyms: LOOSE; MODERATE; LIBERAL; LENIENT.

stricture noun **1** *pass strictures on the children's behavior* criticism, censure, blame, condemnation; *inf.* flak. **2** *be able to do what they like without strictures* restriction, limitation, control, constraint, restraint, curb, check. **3** *a stricture in the windpipe* narrowing, constriction, strangulation.

stride verb *stride along swinging their arms* step, pace, walk, stalk.

stride noun *take huge strides* long/large step, pace.

strident adjective *strident music/voices* harsh, raucous, rough, grating, discordant, rasping, jarring, shrill, loud, screeching, unmelodious, unmusical, stridulous, stridulant, stridulatory.
Antonyms: SOFT; MUSICAL; DULCET.

strife noun *a country suffering from industrial strife* conflict, friction, discord, disagreement, dissension, dispute, argument, quarreling, wrangling, bickering, controversy, contention, ill feeling, hostility, animosity.
Antonyms: PEACE; HARMONY.

strike verb **1** *strike the gong* bang, beat, hit, pound, batter. **2** *struck his opponent* hit, slap, smack, beat, batter, thrash, thump, thwack, punch, cuff, box, knock, rap, buffet, smite, cane, lash, whip; *inf.* wallop, belt, tan someone's hide, clout, whack, bash, clobber, bop, lambaste, sock, plug. **3** *the ship struck a rock* run into, knock into, bang into, bump into, smash into, collide with, be in collision with, dash against. **4** *strike the ball a good distance* hit, drive, propel; *inf.* swipe. **5** *strike a match* light, ignite. **6** *the enemy struck our army at dawn* attack, launch an attack upon, charge, make an assault on, assault, storm, set upon, fall upon. **7** *disease struck the town* | *disaster struck the family* hit, come upon, affect, afflict, smite. **8** *strike a balance* reach, achieve, arrive at, find, attain, effect. **9** *strike a bargain* agree on, come to an agreement on, settle on, sign, endorse, ratify, sanction. **10** *strike a dramatic pose* assume, adopt, take on, affect, feign. **11** *strike oil/gold* | *strike a new source of information* discover, find, come upon, light upon, chance upon, happen upon, stumble upon, unearth, uncover, turn up. **12** *an idea struck him* occur to, come to, come to the mind of, dawn on, hit. **13** *the house strikes me as unfriendly* seem to, appear to, impress, affect, have an impact on. **14** *workers striking for higher wages* go on strike, protest, walk out. **15** *strike the disputed clause from the record* delete, cross out, erase, rub out, oblit-

erate. **strike up 1** *the band struck up* begin/start/commence playing, begin/start to play. **2** *they struck up an acquaintance with her* begin, start, commence, embark on, set going, initiate.

strike noun **1** *stunned his opponent with one strike* hit, slap, smack, thump, thwack, punch, cuff, box, knock; *inf.* wallop, clout, whack, bop, plug. **2** *a lucky strike* discovery, find, unearthing, uncovering. **3** *an unexpected enemy strike* air strike, air attack, attack, assault, bombing, blitz. **4** *workers on strike* | *declare a strike* walkout, protest.

striking adjective **1** *a striking resemblance* noticeable, obvious, conspicuous, evident, visible, distinct, prominent, clear-cut, unmistakable, remarkable, extraordinary, incredible, amazing. **2** *a striking floral display* impressive, imposing, grand, splendid, magnificent, superb, marvelous, wonderful, dazzling; *inf.* great, smashing. **3** *married to a striking woman* attractive, good-looking, beautiful, glamorous, stunning, gorgeous.
Antonyms: INCONSPICUOUS; ORDINARY; unremarkable.

string noun **1** *tie the package with string* twine, cord, yarn, rope, cable, line. **2** *own a string of stores/houses* chain, series, succession. **3** *a string of people waiting to get in* line, row, queue, procession, file, column, stream, succession, sequence. **4** *a string of beads* strand, necklace.

string verb **1** *string decorations from the branches of the tree* hang, suspend, sling. **2** *string the clothesline from pole to pole* stretch, sling, run, fasten, tie, secure. **3** *string the beads* thread. **string along** *he wants to marry her, but she's just stringing him along* use, make use of, take advantage of, mislead, deceive, make a fool of, fool, lead up the garden path. **string up** hang, lynch.

stringent adjective **1** *a stringent ban on smoking* strict, firm, rigid, rigorous, severe, harsh, tough, tight, exacting, demanding, inflexible, hard and fast, uncompromising. **2** *stringent economic conditions* difficult, tight, hard, harsh, tough.
Antonyms: LENIENT; MILD; EASY.

strings plural noun *she got the job but there were strings attached* conditions, qualifications, provisions, provisos, stipulations, contingencies, limitations.

stringy adjective **1** *stringy hair* straggly, straggling. **2** *stringy young men* lanky, gangling, spindly, skinny, wiry. **3** *stringy meat* tough, fibrous, gristly, leathery.

strip verb **1** *they stripped and got into dry clothes* strip naked, undress, take one's clothes off, remove one's clothes, disrobe. **2** *strip the soaking wet child* undress, unclothe. **3** *strip the bark from the tree* peel, pare, skin, excoriate. **4** *strip paint from the doors* remove, take off, peel off, flake off. **5** *strip a machine* dismantle, break down (to pieces), take apart. **6** *the burglars stripped the house* clear out, empty out, clean out, plunder, ransack, rob. **strip of** *strip him of his rank/honors* take away from, dispossess of, deprive of, confiscate from.

strip *noun strips of paper* piece, bit, band, belt, ribbon, stripe, bar, swathe, slip, fillet.

stripe *noun a white stripe on a black background* strip, band, belt, bar.

striped *adjective wear a striped dress* banded, barred, striated, variegated.

stripling *noun* youth, adolescent, youngster, boy, lad, teenager, child, juvenile, minor, young man; *inf.* kid, young'un, shaver.

strive *verb strive to succeed* try, try hard, attempt, endeavor, make an effort, make every effort, exert oneself, do one's best, do all one can, do one's utmost, labor, toil, strain, struggle, bend over backward; *inf.* go all out, give it one's best shot. **strive against** *strove all his life against poverty/oppression* struggle with/against, fight (against), battle (against/with), combat (against), contend with, grapple with.

stroke *noun* 1 *felt the stroke of his opponent* blow, hit, slap, smack, thump, thwack, punch, cuff, box, knock, rap, buffet, smite; *inf.* wallop, clout, whack, bop. 2 *swimming/rowing strokes* movement, action, motion. 3 *a stroke of genius/diplomacy* accomplishment, achievement, feat, attainment, coup. 4 *with one stroke of the pen/brush* movement, action, mark, line. 5 *put the finishing strokes to the plan* touch, detail, bit, addition. 6 *hear five strokes of the church bell* striking, peal, ring, knell, ding-dong, boom. 7 *in the hospital since he had a stroke* thrombosis, embolism, cerebral vascular accident, CVA, seizure, shock, apoplexy.

stroke *verb stroke the cat* caress, fondle, pat, touch, rub, massage, soothe.

stroll *verb stroll (along) in the sunshine* saunter, amble, wander, meander, ramble, dawdle, promenade, go for a walk, take a walk, stretch one's legs, take the air; *inf.* mosey (along).

stroll *noun go for a stroll in the sunshine* saunter, walk, amble, wander, turn, airing, constitutional, promenade, perambulation.

strong *adjective* 1 *strong men lifting heavy weights* powerful, mighty, brawny, muscular, well-built, strapping, sturdy, burly, robust, vigorous, tough, rugged, stalwart, hardy, lusty, Herculean, strong as an ox/horse/lion. 2 *invalids becoming strong again* healthy, well, robust, vigorous, hale and hearty. 3 *strong enough to refuse the blackmailer's demands* courageous, brave, plucky, firm, resolute, strong-minded; *inf.* gutsy. 4 *intimidated by strong individuals* determined, forceful, high-powered, self-assertive, tough, formidable, aggressive, redoubtable. 5 *the vault's strong doors* solid, well-built, heavy, tough, secure, well-fortified, well-defended, well-protected, impregnable, impenetrable. 6 *strong material* heavy-duty, solid, sturdy, durable, hard-wearing, long-lasting, enduring. 7 *a strong interest in local history* keen, eager, deep, acute, dedicated, passionate, fer-

vent, zealous. 8 *arouse strong feelings against him* forceful, intense, vehement, passionate, fervent. 9 *a strong supporter of the local team* keen, eager, enthusiastic, dedicated, staunch, loyal, steadfast, passionate, fierce, fervent. 10 *a strong argument* powerful, cogent, potent, weighty, compelling, convincing, plausible, effective, efficacious, sound, valid, well-founded. 11 *a strong resemblance* marked, pronounced, distinct, definite, clear-cut, obvious, evident, unmistakable, notable, remarkable. 12 *strong colors* deep, intense, vivid, graphic. 13 *in strong light* bright, brilliant, intense, radiant, gleaming, dazzling, glaring. 14 *strong measures to reduce crime* firm, energetic, active, forceful, severe, drastic, extreme, draconian. 15 *strong coffee* concentrated, undiluted, highly flavored. 16 *strong drink* alcoholic, spirituous, intoxicating, heady. 17 *strong cheese/garlic/sauces* sharp, pungent, biting, spicy.
Antonyms: WEAK; FRAIL; TIMID; MILD.

strongbox *noun put the jewels in the strongbox* safe, safe-deposit/safety-deposit box, vault.

stronghold *noun* 1 *launch an assault on the enemy stronghold* fortress, fort, castle, keep, citadel, fastness. 2 *a conservative stronghold at the last election* bastion, center, refuge, hotbed.

strong-minded *adjective strong-minded enough to give up smoking* determined, firm, resolute, resolved, self-disciplined, uncompromising, unyielding, unbending.

strong-willed *adjective too strong-willed to take others' advice* determined, resolute, stubborn, obstinate, headstrong, self-willed, inflexible, intractable, recalcitrant, refractory.

structure *noun* 1 *wooden structures* building, edifice, construction, erection, pile, complex. 2 *the structure of the body/firm/sentence* construction, form, configuration, conformation, shape, constitution, composition, makeup, organization, system, arrangement, design, frame, framework.

structure *verb structure the curriculum to suit the students* construct, build, put together, assemble, shape, design, organize, arrange, order.

struggle *verb* 1 *struggle to obtain power* strive, try hard, endeavor, make every effort, exert oneself, do one's best, do all one can, do one's utmost, battle, labor, toil, strain, bend over backward; *inf.* go all out, give it one's best shot. 2 *boys struggling with each other* fight, grapple, wrestle, scuffle, brawl; *inf.* scrap. 3 *rivals struggling with each other for supremacy* fight, compete, contend, vie, clash, lock horns, cross swords. 4 *struggling up the hill* make one's way with difficulty, battle, battle one's way, fight one's way.

struggle *noun* 1 *his struggles to obtain power* striving, battle, endeavor, effort, exertion, labor, toiling, pains. 2 *a barroom struggle* fight, wrestling match, wrestling bout, scuffle, brawl, tussle; *inf.* scrap, set-to. **3** *opposing armies engaged in a struggle* battle, fight, combat, conflict, contest, hostilities, clash, skirmish, brush. **4** *a struggle on the committee for supremacy* battle, fight, competition, contention, vying, rivalry. **5** *a struggle just to survive* battle, fight, trial, labor, problem, trouble; *inf.* grind, hassle.

strut *verb strutting around in his new suit* swagger, prance, parade, flounce, sashay.

stub *noun* end, butt, tail end, stump, remnant.

stubborn *adjective* obstinate, headstrong, willful, strong-willed, pigheaded, mulish, dogged, persistent, adamant, inflexible, uncompromising, unbending, unyielding, unmalleable, obdurate, intractable, refractory, recalcitrant, contumacious.

Antonyms: compliant; DOCILE; MALLEABLE.

---

stubborn
dogged, intractable, obdurate, obstinate, pertinacious

If you're the kind of person who takes a stand and then refuses to back down, your friends might say you have a **stubborn** disposition, a word that implies an innate resistance to any attempt to change one's purpose, course, or opinion. People who are *stubborn* by nature exhibit this kind of behavior in most situations, but they might be **obstinate** in a particular instance (*a stubborn child, he was obstinate in his refusal to eat vegetables*). *Obstinate* implies sticking persistently to an opinion, purpose, or course of action, especially in the face of persuasion or attack. While *obstinate* is usually a negative term, **dogged** can be either positive or negative, implying both tenacious, often sullen, persistence (*dogged pursuit of a college degree, even though he knew he would end up in the family business*) and great determination (*dogged loyalty to a cause*). **Obdurate** usually connotes a stubborn resistance marked by harshness and lack of feeling (*obdurate in ignoring their pleas*), while **intractable** means stubborn in a headstrong sense and difficult for others to control or manage (*intractable pain*). No matter how stubborn you are, you probably don't want to be called **pertinacious**, which implies persistence to the point of being annoying or unreasonable (*a pertinacious panhandler*).

---

stubby *adjective clothes making her look stubby* dumpy, squat, stumpy, stocky, chunky, thickset, chubby.

stuck *adjective* **1** *posters stuck to the wall* glued, fixed, mired, fastened. **2** *stuck in the mud* immovable, immobile, fast, fixed, rooted. **3** *the problem has her stuck* baffled, beaten, stumped, at a loss, perplexed, nonplussed, at one's wits ends; *inf.* up against a brick wall. **stuck on** *stuck on the new girl* attracted to, infatuated with, keen on, enthusiastic about, fond of, in love

with, obsessed by; *inf.* mad about, wild about, hung up on. **stuck with** *stuck with his little sister for the day* left with, made responsible for, lumbered with.

stuck-up *adjective* conceited, proud, arrogant, haughty, condescending, disdainful, patronizing, snobbish; *inf.* high-and-mighty, snooty, uppity, uppish, bigheaded, swellheaded, hoity-toity.

Antonyms: MODEST; HUMBLE; UNASSUMING.

student *noun* pupil, schoolboy, schoolgirl; undergraduate; trainee, apprentice, probationer.

studied *adjective with studied indifference* deliberate, willful, conscious, calculated, purposeful, studious, contrived, affected, forced, feigned, artificial.

Antonyms: UNPREMEDITATED; NATURAL; SPONTANEOUS.

studio *noun the artist's studio* workshop, workroom, atelier.

studious *adjective* **1** *a studious pupil* scholarly, academic, intellectual, bookish, book-loving, serious, earnest. **2** *the studious checking of detail* diligent, careful, attentive, industrious, assiduous, painstaking, thorough, meticulous, punctilious, zealous, sedulous. **3** *with studious indifference* studied, deliberate, willful. *See* STUDIED.

Antonyms: CARELESS; NEGLIGENT.

study *noun* **1** *a life devoted to study* learning, scholarship, education, academic work, research, book work, reading. **2** *make a study of rural transport* investigation, inquiry, research, examination, analysis, review, survey, scrutiny. **3** *writing in his study* office, workroom, studio, library. **4** *write a study on/of Shakespeare's late plays* paper, work, essay, review. **in a brown study** lost in thought, in a reverie, thinking, reflecting, pondering, contemplating, deliberating, ruminating, daydreaming.

study *verb* **1** *study hard before the exams* apply oneself, revise, burn the midnight oil; *inf.* cram. **2** *study history* learn, read up on, read, work at; *inf.* bone up on. **3** *study the effects of sleeplessness* investigate, inquire into, research, conduct research into, look into, examine, analyze, review, survey, conduct a survey of, scrutinize. **4** *study the suspect's movements* watch, keep watch on, look at, observe, keep an eye on, keep under surveillance.

stuff *noun* **1** *make out of durable stuff* material, fabric, matter, substance. **2** *get rid of the stuff in the hall* things, objects, articles, items. **3** *travelers carrying their stuff* things, luggage, baggage, belongings, possessions, goods, goods and chattels, paraphernalia. **4** *know one's stuff* facts, information, data, subject, discipline. **stuff and nonsense** nonsense, rubbish, twaddle, balderdash, bunkum; *inf.* poppycock, rot, tommyrot, tripe, bunk, piffle, bosh.

stuff *verb* **1** *stuff a pillow* fill, pack, pad. **2** *too much furniture stuffed into the room* pack, load, cram, squeeze, crowd, stow, press, force, compress, jam, wedge. **3** *stuff the money into his wallet* thrust, shove, push, ram. **4** *stuff themselves with turkey* fill, gorge, overindulge, satiate; *inf.* make a pig of oneself. **5** *his nostrils are stuffed because of the cold* block, stop up, bung up, obstruct, choke.

stuffing *noun* **1** *stuffing for cushions* filling, filler, packing, padding, wadding. **2** *stuffing for the duck* filling, dressing, forcemeat.

stuffy *adjective* **1** *a stuffy atmosphere* airless, close, muggy, stifling, suffocating, musty, stale. **2** *a stuffy young man* dull, boring, dreary, staid, sedate, stiff, formal, pompous, starchy, prim, priggish, straitlaced, conventional, conservative, stodgy; *inf.* fuddy-duddy, square. **3** *a stuffy nose* stuffed-up, blocked.
Antonyms: AIRY; EXCITING; INFORMAL.

stultify *verb* **1** *stultify their efforts to escape* thwart, frustrate, foil, impede, obstruct, hamper, suppress, repress, nullify, negate. **2** *a mind stultified by a boring job* dull, numb, benumb, stupefy, make bored.

stumble *verb* **1** *stumble and fall* trip, lose one's balance, slip. **2** *drunks stumbling home* blunder, lumber, lurch, stagger, reel. **3** *stumble a little when giving her speech* stammer, stutter, hesitate, falter; *inf.* fluff one's lines. **stumble upon** *stumble upon an unpublished work of the novelist* chance upon, happen upon, light upon, hit upon, come across, run across, find, discover, encounter.

stump *noun* end, stub, tail end, butt, remnant, remains.

stump *verb* **1** *the last question stumped him* baffle, be too much for, put at a loss, nonplus, mystify, outwit, foil, perplex, puzzle, confound, bewilder; *inf.* flummox, stymie. **2** *stumping around in a bad temper* clomp, clump, stamp, stomp, lumber, blunder.

stun *verb* **1** *the blow stunned him* daze, stupefy, knock senseless, knock unconscious, knock out, lay out, knock stupid. **2** *stunned by the news of his death* shock, astound, dumbfound, stupefy, overwhelm, overcome, overpower, devastate, stagger, amaze, astonish, take one's breath away, confound, bewilder, confuse; *inf.* flabbergast, hit one like a ton of bricks.

stunning *adjective* **1** *a stunning range of electronic equipment* impressive, imposing, remarkable, extraordinary, staggering, incredible, amazing, astonishing, marvelous, splendid; *inf.* mind-boggling, mind-blowing. **2** *looking stunning in a new evening dress* sensational, ravishing, dazzling, wonderful, marvelous, magnificent, glorious, exquisite, impressive, splendid, beautiful, lovely; *inf.* gorgeous, out of this world, fabulous, smashing.
Antonyms: ORDINARY; RUN-OF-THE-MILL; AVERAGE.

stunt *verb* *stunt the child's growth* retard, slow, impede, hamper, hinder, check, curb, restrict, arrest, stop.

stunt *noun* *children amazed at the acrobat's stunts*

feat, exploit, trick, tour de force, act, action, deed.

stunted *adjective* *a stunted tree* dwarf, dwarfish, undersized, diminutive, tiny, small, little, baby.

stupefaction *noun* **1** *stupefaction caused by a blow to the head* daze, senselessness, state of unconsciousness, insensibility, oblivion, blackout, coma. **2** *his stupefaction at the news of his redundancy* shock, devastation, amazement, astonishment, bewilderment, confusion.

stupefy *verb* **1** *a boxer stupefied by the first blow* stun, daze, knock senseless, knock unconscious, knock out, lay out. **2** *stupefied by the news of his redundancy* stun, shock, astound, dumbfound, overwhelm, shake, devastate, stagger, amaze. *See* STUN 2.

stupendous *adjective* **1** *a stupendous achievement* amazing, astounding, astonishing, extraordinary, remarkable, wonderful, prodigious, phenomenal, staggering, breathtaking; *inf.* fantastic, mind-boggling, mind-blowing. **2** *a stupendous beast* colossal, immense, vast, gigantic, massive, huge, enormous, mighty.
Antonyms: RUN-OF-THE-MILL; ORDINARY; SLIGHT.

stupid *adjective* **1** *a stupid fellow* unintelligent, foolish, dense, brainless, mindless, doltish, dull-witted, dull, slow-witted, slow, duncelike, simpleminded, halfwitted, gullible, naïve; *inf.* thick, dim, dumb, dopey, moronic, imbecilic, cretinous. **2** *stupid error/behavior* foolish, silly, unintelligent, idiotic, brainless, mindless, crackbrained, nonsensical, irresponsible, unthinking, ill-advised, ill-considered, senseless, inept, unwise, injudicious, indiscreet, shortsighted, inane, absurd, ludicrous, ridiculous, laughable, fatuous, asinine, pointless, meaningless, futile, fruitless, mad, insane, lunatic; *inf.* crazy, cockeyed. **3** *knocked stupid by the blow* dazed, stupefied, unconscious.
Antonyms: INTELLIGENT; SENSIBLE; PRUDENT; CONSCIOUS.

---

stupid
asinine, dense, dull, dumb, obtuse, slow, unintelligent

If you want to impugn someone's intelligence, the options are almost limitless. You can call the person **stupid**, a term that implies a sluggish, slow-witted lack of intelligence. **Asinine** is a harsher word, implying asslike or foolish behavior rather than slow-wittedness (*a woman her age looked asinine in a miniskirt*). Calling someone **dumb** is risky, because it is not only an informal word (*you dumb bunny!*), but because it also means mute and is associated with the offensive expression deaf and dumb, used to describe people who cannot hear or speak. **Dense** implies an inability to understand even simple facts or instructions (*too dense to get the joke*), while **dull** suggests a sluggishness of mind unrelieved by any hint of quickness, brightness, or liveliness (*a dull stare*). **Slow** also implies a lack of quickness in comprehension or reaction and is often used as a euphemistic substitute for *stupid* (*he was a little slow intellectually*). **Obtuse** is a more formal word for slow-wittedness, but with a strong undercurrent of scorn (*it almost seemed as though he were being deliberately obtuse*). You can't go wrong with a word like **unintelligent**, which is probably the most objective term for low mental ability and the least likely to provoke an angry response (*unintelligent answers to the teacher's questions*).

stupidity *noun* 1 *the unbelievable stupidity of the fellow* lack of intelligence, unintelligence, foolishness, denseness, brainlessness, mindlessness, dull-wittedness, dullness, doltishness, slow-wittedness, slowness; *inf.* thickness, dimness, dumbness, dopiness. 2 *the stupidity of his actions* foolishness, folly, silliness, idiocy, brainlessness, senselessness, irresponsibility, injudiciousness, ineptitude, inaneness, inanity, absurdity, ludicrousness, ridiculousness, fatuousness, fatuity, asininity, pointlessness, meaningfulness, futility, fruitlessness, madness, insanity, lunacy; *inf.* craziness.

stupor *noun* in *a drunken stupor* daze, state of stupefaction/senselessness/unconsciousness, insensibility, oblivion, coma, blackout.

sturdy *adjective* 1 *sturdy young men* well-built, well-made, muscular, athletic, strong, strapping, brawny, powerfully built, powerful, solid, substantial, robust, vigorous, tough, hardy, stalwart, mighty, lusty. 2 *put up a sturdy resistance* strong, vigorous, stalwart, firm, determined, resolute, tenacious, staunch, steadfast, unyielding, unwavering, uncompromising.
Antonyms: PUNY; FRAIL; WEAK.

stutter *verb stutter nervously as she gave the speech* stammer, stumble, speak haltingly, hesitate, falter, splutter.

style *noun* 1 *an unusual style of house* kind, type, variety, sort, design, pattern, genre. 2 *try to copy the style of her favorite novelist* technique, method, methodology, approach, manner, way, mode, system. 3 *a young man with style* stylishness, smartness, elegance, polish, suaveness, urbanity, chic, flair, dash, panache, élan; *inf.* pizzazz, ritziness. 4 *used to living in style* comfort, elegance, chic, affluence, wealth, luxury. 5 *styles popular in the 1920s* fashion, trend, vogue, mode. 6 *criticize both the content and style of the novel* mode of expression, phraseology, wording, language.

style *verb* 1 *style the clothes to suit a warm climate* design, fashion, tailor, make, produce. 2 *he styled himself professor* designate, call, term, name, entitle, dub, address, denominate, label, tag.

stylish *adjective* 1 *stylish clothes* fashionable,

smart, elegant, chic, modish, à la mode, voguish, modern, up-to-date; *inf.* trendy. 2 *a stylish dresser* fashionable, smart, elegant, chic; *inf.* dressy, trendy, natty, classy, nifty, ritzy, snazzy, snappy, with it.
Antonyms: UNFASHIONABLE; DOWDY.

suave *adjective* smooth, smooth-tongued, glib, bland, sophisticated, urbane, worldly, charming, polite, civil, courteous, affable, tactful, diplomatic, civilized, polished.
Antonyms: UNSOPHISTICATED; DISCOURTEOUS; ROUGH.

subconscious *adjective subconscious images/fears* subliminal, latent, suppressed, repressed, hidden, underlying, innermost, deep, intuitive, instinctive.

subdue *verb* 1 *subdue the rebel forces* conquer, defeat, vanquish, get the better of, overpower, overcome, overwhelm, subjugate, master, gain the upper hand at, triumph over, crush, quash, quell, tame, humble, bring to his/her knees, hold in check. 2 *subdue one's desire to hit him* control, curb, restrain, check, hold back, inhibit, rein in, repress, suppress, stifle.
Antonyms: AROUSE; INCITE; PROVOKE.

subdued *adjective* 1 *subdued lighting* dim, muted, toned down, softened, soft, lowered, shaded, low-key, subtle, unobtrusive. 2 *a subdued atmosphere in the hall* quiet, hushed, noiseless, soundless, silent, still, calm. 3 *children seeming very subdued* low-spirited, downcast, dejected, depressed, down in the mouth, restrained, repressed, inactive, spiritless, lifeless, dull, passive, unexcited, unemotional, unresponsive.
Antonyms: BRIGHT; NOISY; LIVELY.

subject *noun* 1 *the subject of the talk/discussion* subject matter, topic, theme, question, substance, gist, text, thesis. 2 *subjects studied at university* branch of study, branch of knowledge, course of study, course, discipline. 3 *a suitable subject for hypnosis* case, client, patient, participant; *inf.* guinea pig. 4 *his disappearance was the subject of much speculation* occasion, basis, grounds, source. 5 *a British subject* citizen, national. 6 *the king's subjects* liege, subordinate, underling, vassal.

subject *adjective* **subject to** 1 *the house is yours, subject to the terms of the contract* conditional upon, contingent upon, dependent on. 2 *subject to colds in the winter* susceptible to, liable to, prone to, apt/likely to suffer from, in danger of, vulnerable to. 3 *subject to the laws of the land* bound by, constrained by, answerable to, accountable to.

subject *verb* **subject to** *subjected us to his anger* submit to, put through, expose to, lay open to, treat one to.

subjective *adjective present a highly subjective view of the situation* personal, personalized, individual, biased, prejudiced, bigoted, nonobjective.
Antonyms: OBJECTIVE; IMPARTIAL.

subjugate *verb subjugate a people* gain mastery over, gain ascendancy over, gain control of, bring one to his/her knees, bring under the yoke, conquer, vanquish, defeat, crush, quell, quash, overpower, overcome, subdue, tame, break, humble, tyrannize, oppress, enslave.

sublime *adjective* **1** *sublime devotion/beauty* noble, exalted, lofty, awe-inspiring, majestic, imposing, glorious, supreme, grand, great, virtuous, high-principled. **2** *a sublime meal* excellent, outstanding, first-rate, first-class, superb, perfect, ideal, wonderful, marvelous; *inf.* fantastic, fabulous. **3** *a sublime lack of concern for the truth* supreme, total, complete, utter, arrogant.

submerge *verb* **1** *watch the submarines submerging* go under water, dive, sink, plummet. **2** *submerge the dress in soapy water* immerse, dip, plunge, dunk. **3** *floodwaters submerged the streets* flood, inundate, deluge, engulf, swamp, overflow (into, onto/upon). **4** *submerged in a backlog of correspondence* overwhelm, inundate, deluge, swamp, bury, engulf. **5** *submerge his true feelings* hide, conceal, veil, cloak, repress, suppress.

Antonyms: SURFACE; come to light; REVEAL

submission *noun* **1** *he sought their submission to his demands* yielding, capitulation, agreement, acceptance, consent, accession, compliance. **2** *the submission of our army to the enemy forces* surrender, yielding, laying down one's arms. **3** *the soldiers' submission to discipline* observance, adherence, regulation, subjection. **4** *the submission of a planning proposal* presentation, presenting, proffering, tendering, proposal, proposing, introduction. **5** *the submission of his claim* sending in, entry, referral. **6** *accept his submission that his client was innocent* argument, assertion, contention, statement, averment, claim. **7** *after years of submission, they rebelled* submissiveness, yielding, compliance, malleability, acquiescence, tractability, manageability, unassertiveness, nonresistance, passivity, obedience, biddability, dutifulness, docility, meekness, patience, resignation, humility, self-effacement, deference, subservience, obsequiousness, servility, subjection, self-abasement; *inf.* bootlicking.

submissive *adjective* yielding, compliant, malleable, acquiescent, accommodating, tractable, manageable, unassertive, nonresisting, passive, obedient, biddable, dutiful, docile, meek, patient, resigned, subdued, humble, self-effacing, deferential, obsequious, servile, self-abasing; *inf.* bootlicking.

Antonyms: HEADSTRONG; OBSTINATE; INTRACTABLE.

submit *verb* **1** *submit a planning proposal* put forward, present, proffer, tender, advance, propose, suggest, introduce, move. **2** *submit a claim* put in, send in, hand in, enter, refer. **3** *submit that his client was innocent* argue, assert, contend, state, claim, aver, propound. **submit to 1** *refuse to submit to his demands* give in to, yield to, give way to, bow to, capitulate to, defer to, agree to, accept, consent to, accede to, acquiesce in, comply with, conform to. **2** *submit to the enemy forces* surrender to, give in to, yield to, lay down one's arms to, raise/show the white flag to, knuckle under to, humble oneself to, bend the knee to. **3** *submit to discipline* observe, adhere to, abide by, be governed by, be regulated by, be subject to.

subnormal *adjective* *subnormal temperatures* below normal, below average, too low, very low.

subordinate *adjective* **1** *his subordinate officers* lower-ranking, junior, lower, lesser, inferior. **2** *subordinate issues* lesser, minor, secondary, subsidiary, ancillary, auxiliary, subservient.

Antonyms: SUPERIOR; MAJOR; CENTRAL.

subordinate *noun* *be patronizing to his subordinates* junior, assistant, second, deputy, aide, underling, inferior, second fiddle; *inf.* sidekick.

sub rosa *adverb* *the discussion was sub rosa* in secret, secret, private, in confidence, confidential, behind closed doors, in camera.

subscribe *verb* **subscribe to 1** *subscribe to several learned journals* pay a subscription to, buy regularly, take regularly, contract to buy. **2** *subscribe to several charities* make a subscription to, make a donation to, donate to, give to, give money to, make a contribution to, contribute to; *inf.* chip into. **3** *subscribe to the theory of evolution* agree with, be in agreement with, accede to, consent to, accept, believe in, endorse, back, support.

subsequent *adjective* *on subsequent visits* following, ensuing, succeeding, later, future. **subsequent to** *subsequent to his illness* following, after, in the wake of.

Antonyms: PREVIOUS; PRIOR; FORMER.

subservient *adjective* servile, submissive, deferential, obsequious, sycophantic, groveling, fawning, ingratiating, toadying, unctuous; *inf.* bootlicking.

Antonyms: OVERBEARING; DOMINEERING; SUPERIOR.

subside *verb* **1** *storms subsiding* abate, let up, moderate, quiet down, calm, slacken, die down/out, peter out, taper off, recede, lessen, diminish, dwindle. **2** *water levels subsiding* go down, get lower, sink, fall back, recede.

Antonyms: INTENSIFY; RISE.

subsidiary *adjective* *discuss subsidiary issues after the main one* subordinate, secondary, ancillary, auxiliary, lesser, minor, subservient, supplementary, additional.

Antonyms: CENTRAL; PRINCIPAL; MAJOR.

subsidize *verb* *ask the local council to subsidize the project* pay a subsidy to, give a grant to, contribute to, make a contribution to, give money to, back, support, invest in, sponsor, finance, fund, underwrite, foot the bill for; *inf.* pick up the tab for.

subsidy *noun* *government subsidies for the arts*

grant, contribution, backing, support, aid, investment, sponsorship, finance, funding, subvention.

subsist verb **1** *subsist on bread and water* live, exist, eke out an existence, survive. **2** *old customs still subsist | animals thought to be extinct still subsisting* be in existence, exist, be alive, live, survive, continue, last. **subsist in** *her attractiveness subsists in her personality* lie in, reside in, have its being in, be attributable to, be ascribable to.

subsistence noun **1** *their subsistence on bread and water* existence, survival. **2** *be unaware of the subsistence of such old customs* existence, survival, continuance. **3** *contribute to the child's subsistence* keep, support, maintenance, livelihood; sustenance, provisions, food, aliment.

substance noun **1** *a hard substance* matter, material, stuff, medium, mass, fabric. **2** *ghostly figures with no substance* solidity, body, corporeality, reality, actuality, materiality, concreteness, tangibility. **3** *an argument with little substance* solidity, meaningfulness, significance, weight, power, soundness, validity, pith. **4** *a person of very little substance* character, backbone, mettle, strength of character. **5** *the substance of the novel* subject matter, subject, theme, topic, content, text, burden, essence, gist, sense, import. **6** *born poor, he became a man of substance* wealth, affluence, prosperity, money, capital, means, resources, assets, property.

substantial adjective **1** *confuse the substantial world with the world of the imagination* real, true, actual, existing, material, concrete. **2** *make a substantial contribution to the project* real, material, weighty, sizable, considerable, meaningful, significant, important, notable, major, marked, valuable, useful, worthwhile. **3** *pay substantial damages* sizable, considerable, significant, large, ample, goodly; *inf.* tidy. **4** *substantial houses* solid, sturdy, stout, strong, well-built, durable. **5** *a substantial figure of a man* large, big, solid, sturdy, stout, hefty, bulky. **6** *put forward a substantial argument* solid, meaningful, significant, weighty, powerful, sound, valid, pithy. **7** *run a substantial business | a substantial businessman* successful, profit-making, prosperous, wealthy, affluent, moneyed, well-to-do. **8** *in substantial agreement* essential, basic, fundamental.
Antonyms: INSUBSTANTIAL; SLIGHT; PALTRY; FLIMSY.

substantially adverb **1** *standards have improved substantially* considerably, significantly, greatly, to a great extent, to a marked extent, markedly. **2** *a report that is substantially accurate* largely, for the most part, by and large, in the main, in essence, essentially, materially, basically, fundamentally.

substantiate verb *substantiate their accusation against him* give substance to, prove, support, uphold, back up, bear out, validate, corroborate, verify, authenticate, confirm.

substitute noun *act as a substitute for the manager/actor/doctor* replacement, deputy, relief, proxy, reserve, surrogate, fill-in, stand-in, standby, locum, stopgap.

substitute verb **substitute for** **1** *substitute sparkling wine for champagne* use as a replacement for, replace with, use instead of, exchange for, switch with; *inf.* swap for. **2** *she substituted for him when he was ill* take the place of, replace, deputize for, act as deputy for, relieve, fill in for, act as stand-in for, cover for, take over from, act as locum for, hold the fort for.

substitute adjective acting, replacement, deputy, relief, reserve, surrogate, fill-in, stand-in, temporary, standby, locum, stopgap.

subterfuge noun **1** *think of a subterfuge to get past the doorman* trick, ruse, wile, ploy, stratagem, artifice, dodge, maneuver, pretext, expedient, intrigue, scheme, deception. **2** *use subterfuge to gain entry* trickery, intrigue, deviousness, evasion, deception, duplicity.

subtle adjective **1** *a subtle flavor* elusive, delicate, faint, understated, low-key, muted, toned down. **2** *a subtle distinction* fine, fine-drawn, nice, slight, minute, tenuous, indistinct, indefinite. **3** *a subtle intelligence* perceptive, discerning, sensitive, discriminating, penetrating, astute, keen, acute, shrewd, sagacious. **4** *subtle devices to trap the unwary* clever, ingenious, skillful, adroit, complex, intricate, strategic, cunning, crafty, wily, artful, devious.
Antonyms: OBVIOUS; OBTRUSIVE; CRUDE; ARTLESS.

subtlety noun **1** *the subtlety of the flavor* subtleness, elusiveness, delicacy, delicateness, faintness, understatedness, understatement, mutedness. **2** *the subtlety of the distinction* subtleness, fineness, niceness, nicety, slightness, minuteness, tenuousness, indistinctness, indefiniteness, lack of definition. **3** *the subtlety of his mind* perceptiveness, perception, discernment, sensitivity, discrimination, astuteness, keenness, acuteness, shrewdness, sagacity. **4** *the subtlety of the devices* cleverness, ingenuity, skillfulness, adroitness, complexity, intricacy, cunning, guile, craftiness, wiliness, artfulness, deviousness.

subtract verb *subtract 5 from 20* take away, take, deduct; *inf.* knock off.

suburb noun *a suburb of Los Angeles* outlying district, residential area, bedroom community.

suburban adjective *suburban families/attitudes* provincial, unsophisticated, parochial, insular.
Antonyms: SOPHISTICATED; COSMOPOLITAN.

subversive adjective *spread subversive rumors about the boss* undermining, discrediting, destructive, disruptive, troublemaking, inflammatory, seditious, revolutionary, treasonous.

subvert verb **1** *subvert the government* overthrow, overturn, wreak havoc on, sabotage, ruin, destroy, demolish, wreck, upset, disrupt, undermine, weaken. **2** *subverted by gifts from the* *enemy* corrupt, pervert, warp, deprave, contaminate, vitiate.

subway *noun* underground (railroad), tunnel, metro; *inf.* tube.

succeed *verb* **1** *plans that succeed* be successful, turn out well, work, work out; *inf.* pan out, do the trick. **2** *as day succeeded day* come after, follow, follow after. **3** *he succeeded him as chairman* come after, follow, replace, take the place of, supplant, supersede. **4** *he succeeded as a lawyer* achieve success, be successful, do well, make good, prosper, flourish, thrive, triumph; *inf.* make it, do all right for oneself, arrive. **succeed in** *succeed in his endeavor/ambition* be successful in, gain success in, accomplish, achieve, bring off, carry out, attain, reach, arrive at, complete, fulfill, realize, be victorious in, triumph in. **succeed to** *succeed to the throne* accede to, inherit, assume, take over, come into, be elevated to.
Antonyms: FAIL; FLOP; PRECEDE.

succeeding *adjective* *grow weaker in the succeeding days* subsequent, following, ensuing, next.
Antonyms: PRECEDING; PREVIOUS.

success *noun* **1** *gain success in his endeavor/aim* accomplishment, achievement, attainment, fulfillment, victory, triumph. **2** *plans meeting with success* successful outcome, favorable result, positive result, victory. **3** *envy his success* prosperity, affluence, wealth, life of ease, fame, eminence. **4** *the book was a success* best seller, winner; *inf.* hit, sensation. **5** *the play was a success* box-office success, winner, sell-out, triumph; *inf.* hit, box-office hit, smash hit, sensation. **6** *became a success in Hollywood* celebrity, big name, somebody, VIP, star.
Antonyms: FAILURE; FLOP; DISASTER; POVERTY.

successful *adjective* **1** *successful in his endeavor* victorious, triumphant. **2** *envying successful people* prosperous, affluent, wealthy, well-to-do, famous, eminent, at the top, top. **3** *a successful business* flourishing, thriving, booming, profitable, profit-making, moneymaking, lucrative.
Antonyms: UNSUCCESSFUL; VAIN; INEFFECTIVE; POOR.

succession *noun* **1** *a succession of events leading to disaster* sequence, series, progression, course, cycle, chain, train, run, continuation. **2** *his succession to the throne* accession, inheritance, assumption, elevation. **3** *the succession is through his eldest son* line of descent, descent, ancestral line, dynasty, lineage. **in succession** *several firms closed in (quick) succession* successively, running, one after the other, one behind the other.

successor *noun* **1** *the successor to the throne* heir, heir apparent, next-in-line. **2** *select the chairman's successor* heir, replacement, supplanter.
Antonyms: PREDECESSOR; PRECURSOR.

succinct *adjective* *a succinct report* short, brief, concise, compact, condensed, crisp, terse,

tight, to the point, pithy, summary, short and sweet, in a few well-chosen words.
Antonyms: LENGTHY; LONG-WINDED; VERBOSE.

succor *noun* *give succor to the wounded/bereaved* assistance, aid, help, comfort, relief, support.

succor *verb* *succor the wounded* give assistance to, render assistance to, assist, aid, bring aid to, help, give help to, minister to, comfort, bring comfort to, bring relief to, support.

succulent *adjective* *succulent fruit/steak* juicy, moist, luscious, mouthwatering.
Antonym: DRY.

succumb *verb* **succumb to 1** *succumb to temptation* give in to, give way to, yield to, submit to, surrender to, capitulate to, be overcome by, be overwhelmed by, fall victim to. **2** *succumb to his injuries* die from/of, pass away as a result of, be a fatality of.
Antonyms: RESIST; WITHSTAND; CONQUER.

suck *verb* **suck in 1** *suck in one's cheeks* draw in, pull in. **2** *material sucking in liquid* suck up, draw up, absorb, soak up, blot up. **suck into 1** *sucked into the whirlpool* draw into, pull into, engulf by, swallow up by, swamp by. **2** *sucked into the conspiracy against his will* draw into, lead into, inveigle into, entice into. **suck up** *materials sucking up liquid* suck in, absorb. **suck up to** *sucking up to the teacher* fawn upon, be obsequious/servile/sycophantic to; *inf.* kiss up to, bootlick.

suckle *verb* *mothers suckling their young* feed, breastfeed, nurse, give suck to.

sudden *adjective* **1** *a sudden change in the temperature* immediate, instantaneous, abrupt, unexpected, unforeseen, unanticipated, unlooked-for, without warning. **2** *his sudden rise to fame* rapid, swift, speedy, fast, quick, meteoric.
Antonyms: GRADUAL; GENTLE; prolonged.

suddenly *adverb* *suddenly it began to rain* all of a sudden, all at once, instantaneously, abruptly, unexpectedly, without warning; *inf.* out of the blue.

suds *plural noun* *soap suds* foam, lather, froth, bubbles.

sue *verb* take one to court, take legal action against, bring an action against, prefer/bring charges against, charge, bring a suit against, prosecute, bring to trial, summons, indict; *inf.* have the law on.

suffer *verb* **1** *suffered from the illness* be in pain, feel pain, be racked with pain, endure agony, hurt, ache. **2** *the divorce caused him to suffer* be distressed, be in distress, experience hardship, be upset, be miserable, be wretched, be hurt, hurt, be handicapped. **3** *suffer loss* experience, undergo, sustain, encounter, meet with, endure. **4** *his work suffered because of tardiness* be impaired, deteriorate, fall off, decline, get worse. **5** *cannot suffer his arrogance* put up with, tolerate, bear, stand, abide, endure, stomach.

suffer from *suffer from headaches* be affected by, be afflicted by, be troubled with.

suffering noun 1 *distressed by the patient's suffering* pain, agony, torment, torture, hurting. 2 *endured the suffering of poverty* distress, hardship, misery, wretchedness, hurt, pain, anguish.

suffice verb be enough, be sufficient, be adequate, do, serve, meet requirements, satisfy (demands), answer/fulfill/meet one's needs; *inf.* fill the bill, hit the spot.

sufficient adjective *sufficient stocks of food* enough, adequate, plenty of, ample; *inf.* plenty.
Antonyms: INSUFFICIENT; INADEQUATE; SPARSE.

suffocate verb 1 *was nearly suffocated by the fumes* smother, stifle, asphyxiate. 2 *she was suffocating in the heat* be breathless, be short of air, be too hot.

suffrage noun right to vote, voting rights, franchise.

suffuse verb *a blush suffusing her cheeks* | *the evening sky suffused with crimson* spread over, cover, bathe, mantle, permeate, pervade, imbue.

sugary adjective 1 *sugary tea* sugared, sweet, oversweet. 2 *sugary love songs* oversweet, syrupy, sentimental, maudlin, mawkish, sloppy, slushy, mushy; *inf.* schmaltzy.
Antonyms: SOUR; TART.

suggest verb 1 *suggest that they go by bus* | *suggest him as a replacement* propose, put forward, move, submit, recommend, advocate; *inf.* throw out. 2 *an aroma suggesting fresh-baked bread* put one in mind of, bring to mind, evoke. 3 *an appearance suggesting that he lived rough* indicate, lead (one) to believe, give the impression, give the idea. 4 *a letter suggesting that he is lying* insinuate, hint, imply, intimate.

suggestion noun 1 *put forward a suggestion that we leave* proposal, proposition, plan, motion, submission, recommendation. 2 *a suggestion of a French accent in her speech* hint, trace, touch, suspicion. 3 *object to the suggestion that he was making* insinuation, hint, implication, intimation.

suggestive adjective 1 *make suggestive remarks* provocative, titillating, sexual, sexy, indecent, indelicate, improper, off-color, smutty, dirty, ribald, bawdy, racy, blue, risqué, lewd, salacious. 2 *an aroma suggestive of freshly cut grass* redolent, indicative, evocative, reminiscent.

suit noun 1 *a woman wearing a blue suit* set of clothes, outfit, costume, ensemble. 2 *bring a suit against his employers* lawsuit, court case, action, proceedings, prosecution. 3 *take one's suit to the king* petition, appeal, request, plea, entreaty. 4 *pay suit to his friend's sister* courtship, wooing, addresses, attentions. 5 *cards in the same suit* ordinary suit, trump.

suit verb 1 *a color that suits her* become, look attractive on, enhance the appearance of, go well with, look right on. 2 *the suggested date does not suit him* be suitable for, be convenient for, be

acceptable to, meet requirements, satisfy demands, be in line with the wishes of. 3 *rich food does not suit him* be agreeable to, agree with, be good for, be healthy for. 4 *suit your speech to the occasion* make appropriate, make fitting, tailor, fashion, accommodate, adjust, adapt, modify.

suitable adjective 1 *find a suitable date* convenient, acceptable, satisfactory. 2 *wear suitable shoes* | *shoes suitable for dancing* right, appropriate, fitting, apt. 3 *not suitable behavior* appropriate, fitting, becoming, seemly, decorous, proper. 4 *a suitable candidate for the post* right, appropriate, fitting, apt, well qualified, ideal. **suitable for** *a speech suitable for the occasion* suited to, befitting, appropriate to, relevant to, pertinent to, apposite to, in keeping with, in character with, tailor-made for.
Antonyms: UNSUITABLE; UNFIT; INAPT.

suitcase noun case, travel/traveling bag, grip, valise, overnight bag.

suite noun 1 *reserve a suite at the hotel* suite of rooms, set of rooms, apartment. 2 *the suite of the king* retinue, entourage, train, escort, attendants, retainers, followers.

suitor noun 1 *unable to choose among her suitors* admirer, beau, wooer, boyfriend; *lit.* follower. 2 *the king giving audience to several suitors* petitioner, supplicant, beseecher, plaintiff, appellant.

sulk verb *sulking after losing the contest* mope, pout, be sullen, have a long face, be in a bad mood, be put out, be out of sorts, be grumpy; *inf.* be in a huff.

sulky adjective *sulky because of losing* moping, pouting, moody, sullen, piqued, disgruntled, ill-humored, grumpy.

sullen adjective *a sullen mood/expression/person* morose, unresponsive, uncommunicative, unsociable, resentful, sulky, sour, glum, gloomy, dismal, cheerless, surly, cross, angry, frowning, glowering, grumpy.
Antonyms: OUTGOING; SOCIABLE; RESPONSIVE.

sultry adjective 1 *a sultry day/atmosphere* airless, stuffy, stifling, suffocating, close, oppressive, muggy, humid, sticky, hot, sweltering. 2 *a sultry singer* sensual, sexy, voluptuous, seductive, provocative, alluring, tempting, passionate, erotic.

sum noun 1 *find the sum of the figures* sum total, grand total, tally, aggregate, answer. 2 *a large sum of money* amount, quantity. 3 *get the children to do sums* arithmetic/arithmetical problem, problem, calculation, reckoning, tally. 4 *look at the problem in its sum* entirety, totality, total, whole; *inf.* whole shebang, whole (kit and) caboodle, whole shooting match. **sum up** 1 *when the judge sums up* give a summing-up, summarize the evidence, review the evidence, summarize the argument. 2 *sum up the situation* form an opinion of, form an impression of, make one's mind up about, get the measure of, form a judgment of; *inf.* size up. 3 *sum* *up the facts* give a summary of, summarize, précis, give an abstract of, encapsulate, put in a nutshell.

summarily *adverb summarily dismissed when caught stealing* immediately, instantly, right away, straight away, at once, on the spot, directly, forthwith, promptly, speedily, swiftly, rapidly, without delay, suddenly, abruptly, peremptorily, without discussion, without formality.

summarize *verb summarize the plot of the novel in a short essay | summarize recent events* give/make a summary of, sum up, give a synopsis of, précis, give a précis of, give a résumé of, give an abstract of, abridge, condense, epitomize, outline, sketch, give the main points of, give a rundown of, review.

summary *noun a summary of the plot* synopsis, précis, résumé, abstract, abridgment, digest, epitome, outline, sketch, rundown, review, summing-up.

summary *adjective* **1** *summary dismissal/justice* immediate, instant, instantaneous, direct, prompt, speedy, swift, rapid, without delay, sudden, abrupt, hasty, peremptory, without discussion, without formality. **2** *a summary account of the long debate* abridged, abbreviated, shortened, condensed, short, brief, concise, succinct, thumbnail, cursory.
Antonyms: DILATORY; SLOW; LENGTHY.

summit *noun* **1** *the summit of the mountain* top, peak, crest, crown, apex, vertex, apogee. **2** *the summit of her stage career* peak, height, pinnacle, culmination, climax, crowning point, zenith, acme.
Antonyms: BOTTOM; BASE; NADIR.

summon *verb* **1** *summoned by the principal* send for, call for, bid, request the presence of, demand the presence of. **2** *summon a committee meeting* order, call, convene, assemble, convoke, muster, rally. **3** *summon a witness* summons, serve with a summons, cite, serve with a citation, serve with a writ, subpoena. **summon up 1** *summon up the courage to act* gather, collect, muster, rally, call into action, mobilize. **2** *summon up half-forgotten memories* call to mind, bring to mind, call up, conjure up, evoke, recall, revive. **3** *summon up evil spirits by magic* call up, conjure up, invoke, rouse up.

summons *noun* **1** *a summons to give evidence in court* citation, writ, subpoena. **2** *obey the principal's summons to attend* order, directive, command, instruction, dictum, demand.

summons *verb summons him to appear in court* serve with a summons, summon, serve with a citation/writ, subpoena.

sumptuous *adjective sumptuous furnishings* lavish, luxurious, deluxe, opulent, magnificent, gorgeous, splendid, rich, costly, expensive, dear, extravagant; *inf.* plush, ritzy.
Antonyms: HUMBLE; PLAIN; CHEAP.

sunder *verb sunder the beam* separate, divide, split, sever, cleave, rend.

sundry *adjective* **1** *sundry items* several, various, varied, miscellaneous, assorted, diverse. **2** *on sundry occasions* several, some, various, different.

sunken *adjective* **1** *a sunken terrace* at a lower level, below ground level, lowered. **2** *the sunken cheeks of the elderly man* hollow, hollowed, concave, drawn, haggard.

sunless *adjective* **1** *a sunless day* overcast, dark, gray, gloomy, murky. **2** *a sunless spot* dark, shady, shadowy, dim, gloomy, murky, bleak.

sunlight *noun sunlight does not penetrate the forest* sun, sunshine, light, daylight, light of day.

sunny *adjective* **1** *a sunny day* sunshiny, sunlit, bright, clear, fine, cloudless, unclouded, without a cloud in the sky. **2** *a sunny nature* happy, cheerful, cheery, lighthearted, bright, glad, gay, merry, joyful, buoyant, bubbly, blithe. **3** *look on the sunny side* bright, cheerful, hopeful, optimistic.
Antonyms: DULL; SHADY.

sunrise *noun* dawn, crack of dawn, daybreak, sunup, first light, morning; *lit.* aurora.

sunset *noun* sundown, nightfall, close of day, evening, twilight, dusk, gloaming.

sunshine *noun* **1** *sit and enjoy the sunshine* sun, sunlight, sun's rays. **2** *a life devoid of sunshine* happiness, laughter, cheerfulness, gladness, gaiety, merriment, joy, joyfulness, blitheness.

superb *adjective* **1** *dancers giving a superb performance* superlative, excellent, first-rate, first-class, outstanding, remarkable, dazzling, brilliant, marvelous, magnificent, wonderful, splendid, exquisite; *inf.* fantastic, fabulous, A-1. **2** *superb furnishings* magnificent, gorgeous, splendid, sumptuous, opulent, lavish, luxurious, deluxe; *inf.* plush, ritzy.
Antonyms: POOR; INFERIOR; DREADFUL.

supercilious *adjective* arrogant, haughty, conceited, proud, vain, disdainful, scornful, condescending, superior, patronizing, imperious, overbearing, lofty, lordly, snobbish, snobby; *inf.* hoity-toity, high-and-mighty, uppity, snooty, stuck-up.

superficial *adjective* **1** *superficial damage/wounds only* surface, exterior, external, outer, outside, peripheral, slight. **2** *a superficial examination* cursory, perfunctory, hasty, hurried, casual, sketchy, desultory, slapdash. **3** *a superficial similarity* outward, apparent, evident, ostensible. **4** *rather a superficial person* shallow, empty-headed, trivial, frivolous, silly. **5** *a superficial book* lightweight, insignificant, trivial.
Antonyms: DEEP; PROFOUND; THOROUGH.

---

superficial
cursory, hasty, shallow, slapdash

No one wants to be accused of being **superficial** or **shallow**, two adjectives that literally indicate a lack of depth (*a superficial wound; a shallow grave*). *Superficial* suggests too much concern with the surface or obvious aspects of something, and it is considered a derogatory term because it connotes a personality that is not genuine or sincere. *Shallow* is even more derogatory because it implies not only a refusal to explore something deeply but an inability to feel, sympathize, or understand. It is unlikely that a *shallow* person, in other words, will ever have more than superficial relationships with his or her peers. **Cursory**, which may or may not be a derogatory term, suggests a lack of thoroughness or attention to detail (*a cursory glance at the newspaper*), while **hasty** emphasizes a refusal or inability to spend the necessary time on something (*a hasty review of the facts*). If you are **slapdash** in your approach, it means that you are both careless and hasty (*a slapdash job of cleaning up*).

superfluous *adjective* 1 *sell off the superfluous furniture* spare, surplus, extra, unneeded, unrequired, excess, in excess, supernumerary. 2 *their presence was superfluous* unnecessary, needless, unneeded, inessential, uncalled-for, unwarranted, gratuitous.
Antonyms: NECESSARY; ESSENTIAL.

superhuman *adjective* 1 *require a superhuman effort* Herculean, phenomenal, prodigious, stupendous, heroic, extraordinary. 2 *superhuman intervention* divine, godlike, holy. 3 *a cry that seemed superhuman* supernatural, preternatural, preterhuman, paranormal, otherworldly.

superintend *verb* *superintend the factory* be in charge of, be in control of, preside over, direct, administer, manage, run, look after, supervise, oversee.

superintendent *noun* director, administrator, manager, supervisor, overseer, controller, boss, chief; *inf.* honcho.

superior *adjective* 1 *the superior player* better, greater, better-class, more expert, more skillful, more advanced. 2 *hold a superior position* higher, higher-ranking, higher-up. 3 *of superior quality* better, higher-grade, greater, surpassing. 4 *goods of superior leather* good-quality, high-quality, first-rate, top-quality, high-grade, of the first order, choice, select, prime, upmarket, fine. 5 *live in a superior area* high-class, upmarket, select, exclusive, snobby. 6 *act superior* | *give her a superior look* haughty, disdainful, condescending, supercilious, patronizing, lofty, lordly, snobbish, snobby; *inf.* high-and-mighty, hoity-toity, uppity, snooty, stuck-up.
Antonyms: INFERIOR; LOW.

superior *noun* *get a warning from his superior* boss, manager, chief, supervisor, foreman.
Antonyms: INFERIOR; SUBORDINATE.

superiority *noun* 1 *the superiority of their performance* better quality, supremacy. 2 *their superiority in numbers* advantage, lead, dominance.

superlative *adjective* *superlative players* | *of superlative quality* best, greatest, supreme, consummate, first-rate, first-class, of the first order, of the higher/highest order, brilliant, excellent, magnificent, outstanding, unsurpassed, unparalleled, unrivaled, peerless, matchless, transcendent; *inf.* crack, ace.
Antonyms: POOR; MEDIOCRE; UNEXCEPTIONAL.

supernatural *adjective* 1 *supernatural beings* otherworldly, unearthly, spectral, ghostly, phantom, magical, mystic, unreal. 2 *supernatural powers* paranormal, supernormal, hypernormal, psychic, miraculous, extraordinary, uncanny.

supersede *verb* 1 *workers superseded by machines* take the place of, replace, take over from, displace, supplant, oust, usurp. 2 *supersede him as chairman* replace, take the place of, take over from, succeed. 3 *the office equipment was superseded when it became obsolete* discard, cast aside, throw out, dispose of, abandon, jettison; *inf.* chuck out.
Antonyms: PRECEDE; ANTEDATE.

supervise *verb* 1 *supervise the factory* superintend, be in charge of, direct, administer, manage, run. *See* SUPERINTEND. 2 *supervise the work/ trainees* oversee, keep an eye on, watch, observe, inspect, be responsible for, guide.

supervision *noun* 1 *the supervision of the factory* administration, management, direction, control, charge, superintendence. 2 *children playing under supervision* observation, inspection, guidance.

supervisor *noun* 1 *the supervisor of the factory* director, administrator, manager, overseer, controller, boss, chief, superintendent; *inf.* honcho. 2 *the supervisors of the children/trainees* overseer, observer, inspector, guide, adviser.

supine *adjective* 1 *supine on the floor* flat on one's back, prone, prostrate, horizontal. 2 *a rather supine individual* weak, feckless, spineless, idle, inactive, indolent, lazy, slothful, languid, apathetic, indifferent; *inf.* laid-back.
Antonyms: ERECT; VERTICAL; ENERGETIC.

supper *noun* dinner, evening meal.

supplant *verb* *plotting to supplant the dictator* take the place of, take over from, replace, displace, supersede, oust, usurp, overthrow, remove, unseat.

supple *adjective* 1 *supple gymnasts* lithe, loose-limbed, limber. 2 *supple leather* pliant, pliable, flexible, bendable, stretchable, elastic.
Antonyms: STIFF; RIGID.

supplement *noun* 1 *dietary supplement* addition, supplementation, additive, extra, add-on. 2 *add a supplement to the book/document* appendix, addendum, back/end matter, tailpiece, codicil, rider. 3 *a newspaper supplement* pull-out, insert, special-feature section, magazine section.

supplement *verb* *supplement his salary with an evening job* add to, augment, increase, complement.

supplementary *adjective* **1** *a supplementary payment* supplemental, additional, extra, add-on, complementary. **2** *a supplementary section* added, appended, attached, extra.

suppliant *noun suppliants asking the judge for mercy* supplicant, petitioner, pleader, beseecher, applicant, suitor, beggar, appellant.

supplicate *verb supplicate for a pardon* plead, entreat, beseech, beg, implore, petition, appeal, solicit, ask, request, pray, invoke.

supplication *noun ignore the poor man's supplication* plea, pleading, entreaty, beseeching, begging, imploration, petition, appeal, solicitation, request, prayer, invocation.

supplies *noun army supplies running out* provisions, stores, rations, food, victuals, provender; equipment, materials, matériel.

supply *verb* **1** *supply the necessary money* provide, give, furnish, contribute, donate, grant, come up with; *inf.* fork out, shell out. **2** *supply him with food/tools* provide, furnish, equip, outfit. **3** *supply all their needs* satisfy, meet, fulfill.

supply *noun* **1** *difficult to organize the supply of wood* supplying, providing, provision, furnishing. **2** *build up a supply of logs* stock, store, reserve, reservoir, stockpile, heap, pile, mass, hoard, cache.

support *verb* **1** *beams supporting the roof* bear, carry, hold up, prop up, bolster up, brace, keep up, shore up, underpin, buttress. **2** *work to support his family* maintain, provide for, provide sustenance for, sustain, take care of, look after. **3** *support him in his hour of need* give moral support to, give strength to, be a source of strength to, comfort, help, sustain, encourage, buoy up, hearten, fortify; *inf.* buck up. **4** *bring evidence to support his argument* back up, substantiate, give force to, bear out, corroborate, confirm, verify, validate, authenticate, endorse, ratify. **5** *support several charities/enterprises* back, contribute to, give a donation to, give money to, subsidize, fund, finance. **6** *support the youngest candidate* back, champion, give help to, help, assist, aid, be on the side of, side with, vote for, stand behind, stand up for; *inf.* stick up for. **7** *support conservation measures* back, advocate, promote, further, champion, be on the side of, espouse, espouse the cause of, be in favor of, recommend, defend. **8** *cannot support his behavior* bear, put up with, tolerate, stand, abide, suffer, stomach, brook. **Antonyms:** NEGLECT; ABANDON; OPPOSE; CONTRADICT.

support *noun* **1** *the supports of the bridge* base, foundation, pillar, post, prop, underprop, underpinning, substructure, brace, buttress, abutment, bolster, stay. **2** *pay toward his family's support* keep, maintenance, sustenance, subsistence, aliment. **3** *discouraged and in need of support* moral support, friendship, strengthening, strength, encouragement, buoying up, heartening, fortification; *inf.* bucking up. **4** *give support to charities/enterprises* backing, con-

tribution, donation, money, subsidy, funding, funds, finance, capital. **5** *give his support to the youngest candidate* backing, help, assistance, aid, vote. See SUPPORT *verb* 6. **6** *in support of conservation measures* backing, advocacy, promotion, championship, espousal, recommendation. **7** *he was a great support to his mother* help, assistance, comfort, tower of strength, prop, backbone, mainstay.

supporter *noun* **1** *supporters of the charity* backer, contributor, donor, sponsor, patron, friend, well-wisher. **2** *the candidate's supporters* backer, helper, adherent, follower, ally, voter, apologist. **3** *supporters of animal welfare* backer, adherent, advocate, promoter, champion, defender, apologist. **4** *football supporter* fan, follower.

supportive *adjective need supportive friends when in trouble* helpful, encouraging, caring, sympathetic, understanding.

suppose *verb* **1** *I suppose you are right* dare say, assume, take for granted, presume, expect, imagine, believe, think, fancy, suspect, guess, surmise, reckon, conjecture, theorize, opine. **2** *suppose we arrive late* take as a hypothesis, hypothesize, postulate, posit; *inf.* let's say. **3** *creation supposes a creator* presuppose, require, imply.

supposed *adjective his supposed brother* presumed, assumed, believed, professed, so-called, alleged, putative, reputed. **supposed to** *they are not supposed to know* meant, intended, expected.

supposition *noun* **1** *his suppositions proved correct* assumption, presumption, suspicion, guess, surmise, conjecture, speculation, theory. **2** *on the supposition that he is right* assumption, hypothesis, postulation.

suppress *verb* **1** *suppress the rebellion* conquer, vanquish, put an end to, crush, quell, squash, stamp out, extinguish, put out, crack down on, clamp down on. **2** *suppress his anger/laughter* restrain, keep a rein on, hold back, control, keep under control, check, keep in check, curb. **3** *suppress the information/truth* keep secret, conceal, hide, keep hidden, keep silent about, withhold, cover up, smother, stifle, muzzle. **Antonyms:** ENCOURAGE; INCITE; PUBLICIZE.

suppression *noun* **1** *the suppression of the rebellion* conquering, crushing, extinction, crackdown, clampdown. See SUPPRESS 1. **2** *the suppression of his anger* restraint, holding back, curbing. See SUPPRESS 2. **3** *the suppression of the information/truth* concealment, withholding, cover-up, smothering, stifling, muzzling. See SUPPRESS 3.

suppurate *verb* fester, matter, maturate, gather, come to a head, discharge.

supremacy *noun* **1** *a country holding supremacy over its neighbors* ascendancy, predominance, paramountcy, dominion, sway, authority, mastery, control, power, rule, sovereignty, lordship. **2** *challenge her supremacy as top tennis player* preeminence, dominance, superiority, ascendancy, incomparability, inimitability, matchlessness, peerlessness.

supreme *adjective* **1** *the supreme commander* highest, highest-ranking, leading, chief, foremost, principal. **2** *supreme bravery | a supreme effort* extreme, greatest, utmost, uttermost, maximum, extraordinary, remarkable. **3** *the supreme sacrifice/judgment* final, last, ultimate. **reign supreme** *the athlete still reigns supreme* be superlative, be unsurpassed, be the best, be the greatest, be unrivaled, be matchless, be peerless, be preeminent, be excellent, be first-rate. *Antonyms:* SUBORDINATE; MINIMUM.

sure *adjective* **1** *we cannot be sure that he is honest* certain, definite, positive, convinced, confident, decided, assured, free from doubt, unhesitating, unwavering, unfaltering, unvacillating. **2** *sure of success* assured, certain, confident, with no doubts. **3** *a sure success/failure* assured, certain, guaranteed, inevitable, irrevocable; *inf.* in the bag. **4** *in the sure knowledge* true, certain, undoubted, absolute, categorical, well-grounded, well-founded, proven, unquestionable, indisputable, incontestable, irrefutable, incontrovertible, undeniable. **5** *a sure remedy* certain, unfailing, infallible, never-failing, reliable, dependable, trustworthy, tested, tried and true, foolproof, effective, efficacious; *inf.* sure-fire. **6** *sure friend* true, reliable, dependable, trusted, trustworthy, trusty, loyal, faithful, steadfast. **7** *with a sure hand* firm, steady, stable, secure, confident, unhesitating, unfaltering, unwavering. **be sure** *be sure to arrive on time* be certain, be careful, take care, remember. *Antonyms:* UNSURE; UNCERTAIN; DOUBTFUL.

surely *adverb* **1** *they will surely fail* for certain, certainly, definitely, assuredly, undoubtedly, without doubt, beyond the shadow of a doubt, indubitably, unquestionably, incontestably, irrefutably, incontrovertibly, undeniably, without fail, inevitably, unavoidably. **2** *walk slowly but surely* firmly, steadily, confidently, unhesitatingly.

surety *noun* **1** *use the house as surety for the loan* security, indemnity, collateral, guarantee, pledge, bond. **2** *he acted as surety for her loan* guarantor, sponsor.

surface *noun* **1** *the surface of the wood* outside, exterior, top. **2** *look beneath the surface to see his true character* outward appearance, superficial appearance, façade. **on the surface** *on the surface, the business seems profitable* at first glance, to the casual eye, outwardly, to all appearances, apparently, superficially.

surface *adjective* *a surface scratch* superficial, external, exterior, outward.

surface *verb* **1** *the submarine surfaced* come to

the surface, come up, come to the top. **2** *the old rumors have surfaced again* appear, come to light, come up, emerge, crop up. **3** *he won't surface till lunchtime* get up, get out of bed, rise, wake, awaken.

surfeit *noun* **1** *a surfeit of food and drink* excess, surplus, oversupply, superabundance, superfluity, glut. **2** *ill from a surfeit of chocolates* overindulgence, satiety, satiation. *Antonyms:* DEARTH; LACK.

surfeit *verb* *be surfeited with food/pleasure* satiate, gorge, overfeed, overfill, glut, cram, stuff, overindulge.

surge *noun* **1** *a surge of water* gush, rush, outpouring, stream, flow, sweep, efflux. **2** *a sudden surge in prices* upsurge, increase, rise, upswing, escalation. **3** *the surge of the sea* rise, swell, swelling, heaving, billowing, rolling, eddying, swirling.

surge *verb* **1** *the water surged from the broken pipe | crowds surging from the hall* gush, rush, stream, flow. **2** *the sea surged in the storm* rise, swell, heave, billow, roll, eddy, swirl.

surly *adjective* bad-tempered, ill-natured, crabbed, grumpy, crotchety, grouchy, cantankerous, irascible, testy, crusty, gruff, abrupt, brusque, churlish, uncivil, morose, sullen, sulky. *Antonyms:* GOOD-NATURED; FRIENDLY; PLEASANT.

surmise *verb* *she surmised that he was lying* guess, conjecture, suspect, deduce, assume, presume, gather, feel, be of the opinion, think, believe, imagine.

surmount *verb* **1** *many problems/obstacles to surmount* get over, overcome, conquer, triumph over, prevail over, get the better of, beat. **2** *climbers struggling to surmount the mountain* climb, ascend, scale, mount. **3** *snow surmounting the hills* top, cap, crown. **4** *mountains surmounting the houses* rise above, tower above, overtop, dominate.

surname *noun* last name, family name, patronymic.

surpass *verb* *her beauty/work surpasses that of the others* be greater than, be better than, beat, exceed, excel, transcend, outdo, outshine, outstrip, overshadow, eclipse.

surpassing *adjective* exceptional, extraordinary, remarkable, outstanding, striking, phenomenal, rare, supreme, incomparable, inimitable, unrivaled, matchless.

surplus *noun* *get rid of the surplus after the sale* excess, remainder, residue, surfeit. *Antonyms:* DEARTH; SHORTAGE; LACK.

surplus *adjective* *surplus food going to waste* excess, in excess, superfluous, leftover, unused, remaining, extra, spare.

surprise *verb* **1** *their sudden appearance surprised him* astonish, amaze, nonplus, take aback, startle, astound, stun, flabbergast, stagger, leave open-mouthed, take one's breath away; *inf.* bowl over, blow one's mind. **2** *surprise the burglars opening the safe* take by surprise, catch unawares, catch off guard, catch red-handed, catch in the act, catch napping, burst in on, spring upon, catch with his/her pants down.

surprise noun **1** *look up in surprise* astonishment, amazement, incredulity, wonder. **2** *it was a surprise when she left* shock, bolt from the blue, bombshell, revelation.

surprised adjective *a surprised look* | *the surprised children* astonished, amazed, nonplussed, startled, astounded, stunned, flabbergasted, staggered, open-mouthed, speechless, thunderstruck.

surprising adjective astonishing, amazing, startling, astounding, staggering, incredible, extraordinary, remarkable; *inf.* mind-blowing.

surrender verb **1** *surrender his right to the title* give up, relinquish, renounce, forgo, forsake, cede, abdicate, waive. **2** *surrender the keys to the car* hand over, give up, deliver (up), part with, let go of, relinquish. **3** *surrender to the enemy* give in, give oneself up, yield, submit, capitulate, lay down one's arms, raise/show the white flag, throw in the towel. **4** *surrender to his old habits* give way, yield, succumb, capitulate. **5** *surrender all hope* give up, abandon, leave behind, lose.

Antonyms: RESIST; WITHSTAND; DEFY.

surrender noun **1** *the surrender of his title* surrendering, relinquishment, renunciation, forgoing, ceding, cession, abdication, waiving. **2** *witness their surrender to the enemy* yielding, capitulation, submission. *See* SURRENDER verb 3.

surreptitious adjective *find the information by surreptitious means* stealthy, clandestine, secret, sneaky, sly, cunning, furtive, underhand, underhanded, undercover, covert.

Antonyms: OPEN; HONEST; BLATANT.

surround verb *a fence surrounds the lake* go around, encircle, enclose, encompass, ring, gird, girdle, fence in, hem in, confine.

surrounding adjective *the surrounding countryside* neighboring, nearby.

surroundings plural noun *brought up in squalid surroundings* environment, setting, milieu, element, background.

surveillance noun *under surveillance* observation, watch, scrutiny, spying, espionage.

survey verb **1** *survey the burned building* look at, take a look at, observe, view, contemplate, regard, examine, inspect. **2** *survey the evidence* look at, look over, scan, study, consider, review, examine, inspect, scrutinize, take stock of; *inf.* size up. **3** *survey a building* make a survey of, value, carry out a valuation of, estimate the value of, appraise, assess, prospect, triangulate.

survey noun **1** *undertake a survey of the evidence* study, consideration, review, overview, examination, inspection, scrutinization, scrutiny. **2** *carry out a survey of the building* valuation, appraisal. *See* SURVEY verb 3. **3** *carry out a survey into TV viewing habits* investigation, inquiry, research, study, review, probe, questionnaire.

survive verb **1** *old customs surviving in the village* live on, be extant, continue, remain, last, persist, endure, exist, be. **2** *fathers surviving their sons* outlive, outlast, live after, remain alive after. **3** *people surviving in the freezing conditions* remain alive, live, hold out, pull through, cling to life.

susceptibility noun **1** *the susceptibility of the teenagers* impressionability, credulity, credulousness, gullibility, defenselessness, vulnerability, responsiveness, sensitivity. **2** *their susceptibility to colds* liability, proneness, predisposition, propensity.

susceptible adjective **1** *con artists preying on susceptible people* impressionable, likely to be taken in, credulous, gullible, innocent, defenseless, vulnerable, receptive, easily led. **2** *susceptible to colds/disease* subject, liable, prone, inclined, predisposed, disposed.

Antonyms: SKEPTICAL; IMMUNE; RESISTANT.

suspect verb **1** *I suspect (that) you could be right* feel, have a feeling, be inclined to think, fancy, surmise, guess, conjecture, have a suspicion, speculate, have a hunch, suppose, believe, think, conclude. **2** *suspect the truth of his statement* doubt, have doubts about, harbor suspicions about, have misgivings about, be skeptical about, distrust, mistrust. **3** *police suspect her brother* regard as guilty, regard as a wrongdoer.

suspend verb **1** *suspend a light from the tree* hang, put up, swing, dangle, sling. **2** *suspend the proceedings* adjourn, interrupt, cut short, bring to an end, cease, discontinue, break off, arrest, put off, postpone, delay, defer, shelve, pigeonhole, table, put on the back burner; *inf.* put on ice. **3** *suspend him from his job/membership* debar, shut out, exclude, keep out, remove.

Antonyms: CONTINUE; RESUME.

suspense noun *in a state of suspense about the outcome* uncertainty, doubt, doubtfulness, anticipation, expectation, expectancy, excitement, tension, anxiety, nervousness, apprehension, apprehensiveness.

suspension noun **1** *the suspension of talks* adjournment, interruption, cessation, postponement, delay, deferment, shelving. **2** *his suspension from office* debarment, exclusion, removal, temporary removal.

suspicion noun **1** *his suspicion is that she will appear* feeling, surmise, guess, conjecture, speculation, hunch, supposition, belief, notion, idea, conclusion; *inf.* gut feeling. **2** *a suspicion of liqueur in the dessert* trace, touch, suggestion, hint, soupçon, tinge, shade. **suspicions** *have suspicions about his motives* doubts, misgivings, qualms, wariness, chariness, skepticism, distrust, mistrust; *inf.* funny feeling.

suspicious adjective **1** *give him suspicious looks* doubtful, unsure, wary, chary, skeptical, distrustful, mistrustful, disbelieving. **2** *police*

observing a suspicious character guilty-looking, dishonest-looking, strange-looking, queer-looking, funny-looking; *inf.* shifty, shady. **3** *suspicious circumstances* questionable, doubtful, odd, strange, irregular, queer, funny; *inf.* fishy, shady.
Antonyms: TRUSTFUL; UPRIGHT; INNOCENT.

sustain *verb* **1** *beams sustaining the weight of the roof* bear, support, carry, keep something up, prop up, shore up. **2** *sustain one's courage* keep something up, keep something going, continue, carry on, maintain, prolong, protract. **3** *sustain him in his hour of need* support, give strength to, be a source of strength to, be a tower of strength to, comfort, help, assist, encourage, buoy up, cheer up, hearten; *inf.* buck up. **4** *not enough to sustain her* keep alive, keep going, maintain, continue, preserve. **5** *enough food to sustain them* feed, nourish, keep going, nurture. **6** *sustain defeat/injury* experience, undergo, go through, suffer, endure. **7** *the court sustained his claim* uphold, validate, ratify, vindicate. **8** *evidence sustaining his allegations* confirm, verify, corroborate, substantiate, bear out, prove, authenticate, validate.

sustained *adjective a sustained interest in the business* continuing, steady, continuous, constant, prolonged, perpetual, unremitting.
Antonyms: BROKEN; INTERMITTENT; SPORADIC.

sustenance *noun* **1** *enough money to buy sustenance for his family* food, nourishment, daily bread, provisions, victuals, rations, aliment, comestibles; *lit.* provender; *inf.* grub, chow. **2** *earn just enough for sustenance* living, livelihood, means of support, maintenance, support, subsistence.

swagger *verb* **1** *swagger down the street in his new coat* strut, parade, prance. **2** *swaggering about her recent victory* boast, brag, bluster; *inf.* show off.

swagger *noun* **1** *walk with a swagger* strut, parading, prancing. **2** *tired of his swagger* boasting, bragging, bluster, swashbuckling, braggadocio, vainglory; *inf.* showing-off, swank.

swallow *verb* **1** *swallow the meat with difficulty* gulp down, eat, consume, devour, ingest; *inf.* scoff (down). **2** *swallow two drinks in quick succession* gulp down, drink, swill down; *inf.* swig, chug (down). **3** *unable to swallow her treatment of him* put up with, tolerate, endure, stand, bear, suffer, abide, stomach, brook. **4** *expect him to swallow their story* believe, accept; *inf.* fall for, buy. **5** *swallow one's pride/anger* repress, restrain, hold back, choke back, control, rein in; eat. **swallow up 1** *the waves swallowed him up* engulf, swamp, flood over, overwhelm. **2** *big companies swallowing up small ones* engulf, take over, absorb, assimilate, overrun, overwhelm, swamp.

swamp *noun* *get stuck in a swamp* marsh, bog, quagmire, mire, morass, fen, quag.

swamp *verb* **1** *heavy rains swamping the town* flood, inundate, deluge, wash out, soak, drench, saturate. **2** *swamped with applications* inundate, flood, deluge, overwhelm, engulf, snow under, overload, overburden, weigh down, besiege, beset.

swampy *adjective* marshy, boggy, soggy, soft, spongy, waterlogged, miry, quaggy.

swap *verb* **1** *children swapping toys with each other* exchange, interchange, trade, barter, switch. **2** *swap jokes/insults* exchange, trade, bandy.

swarm *noun a swarm of people* crowd, multitude, horde, host, mob, throng, stream, mass, body, army, flock, herd, pack, drove.

swarm *verb shoppers swarming to the sales* flock, crowd, throng, stream, surge. **swarming with** *a barn swarming with flies* crowded with, thronged with, overrun with, abounding in, teeming with, bristling with, alive with, crawling with, infested with.

swarthy *adjective* dark, dark-colored, dark-skinned, dark-complexioned, dusky, tanned.
Antonyms: PALE; FAIR.

swashbuckling *adjective* swaggering, dashing, daring, adventurous, bold, gallant.

swathe *verb swathed in bandages* wrap, envelop, bind, swaddle, bandage, bundle up, cover, shroud, drape.

sway *verb* **1** *trees swaying in the breeze* swing, shake, bend, lean, incline. **2** *drunks swaying on their way home* roll, stagger, wobble, rock. **3** *swaying her hips* swing, oscillate, shake. **4** *swaying between emigrating and staying* waver, hesitate, fluctuate, vacillate, oscillate. **5** *swayed by their arguments* influence, affect, persuade, prevail on, bring around, win over, induce. **6** *swayed by ambition* rule, govern, dominate, control, direct, guide.

sway *noun* **1** *colonies under the sway of the monarchy* jurisdiction, rule, government, sovereignty, dominion, control, command, power, authority, ascendancy, domination, mastery. **2** *under the sway of her parents* control, domination, power, authority, influence, guidance, direction. **hold sway** *the aged emperor still holds sway* be most powerful, hold power, rule, be in control, predominate, have ascendance, have the greatest influence.

swear *verb* **1** *swear to take care of the child | swear that he would take care of the child* promise, promise under oath, solemnly promise, pledge oneself, vow, give one's word, take an oath, swear on the Bible. **2** *he swore that he was fit to drive* vow, insist, be emphatic, pronounce, declare, assert, maintain, contend, aver. **3** *he swore when he hit his finger | swear at the other driver* curse, blaspheme, be blasphemous, utter profanities, be foul-mouthed, use bad language, take the Lord's name in vain, swear like a trooper/sailor; *inf.* cuss. **swear by 1** *swear by Almighty God* call as one's witness, appeal to, invoke. **2** *swear by her remedy for colds* have reliance on, depend on, believe in.

swearing noun *disapprove of swearing* cursing, blaspheming, profanity, imprecation, bad language.

sweat noun **1** *sweat pouring from his brow* perspiration; *Tech.* diaphoresis. **2** *in a sweat until the results came through* fluster, fret, dither, fuss, panic, state of anxiety/agitation/nervousness/worry; *inf.* state, flap, tizzy, stew, lather. **3** *it was a sweat to finish on time* labor, effort, chore, backbreaking task.

sweat verb **1** *sweating in the heat* perspire, exude perspiration, drip with perspiration/sweat, break out in a sweat. **2** *they were sweating until the results came through* fret, dither, fuss, panic, be on tenterhooks, be in a state of anxiety/agitation/nervousness, worry, agonize, lose sleep; *inf.* be on pins and needles, be in a state of anxiety/agitation/nervousness, worry, agonize, lose sleep, be in a state/flap/tizzy/stew/lather. **3** *sweat to get the work done* work hard, work like a Trojan, labor, toil, slog.

sweaty adjective *sweaty hands* sweating, perspiring, clammy, sticky.

sweep verb **1** *sweep the floor* brush, vacuum, clean. **2** *swept away by the waves* carry, pull, drag, drive. **3** *sweep from the room* glide, sail, stride, flounce. **4** *fire sweeping through the building* race, hurtle, streak, whip, spread like lightning/wildfire; *inf.* tear. **sweep aside** *sweep aside their objections* cast aside, discard, disregard, ignore, take no notice of, dismiss.

sweep noun **1** *with one sweep of her hand* gesture, movement, move, action, stroke, wave. **2** *the sweep of the road* curve, curvature, bend, arc. **3** *within the sweep of his power* span, range, scope, compass, reach. **4** *a sweep of pasture lands* stretch, expanse, extent, vastness.

sweeping adjective **1** *sweeping reforms* extensive, wide-ranging, global, broad, wide, comprehensive, all-inclusive, all-embracing, thorough, radical, far-reaching. **2** *make sweeping statements* blanket, wholesale, unqualified, indiscriminate. **3** *a sweeping victory* decisive, overwhelming, thorough, complete, total, absolute, out-and-out, thoroughgoing.

Antonyms: RESTRICTED; LIMITED; INDECISIVE.

sweet adjective **1** *sweet types of food* sweetened, sugary, sugared, honeyed, syrupy, saccharine. **2** *sweet fruit* ripe, mellow, luscious. **3** *the sweet smell of roses* sweet-smelling, fragrant, aromatic, perfumed, scented, balmy. **4** *the sweet sound of children's voices* sweet-sounding, musical, tuneful, dulcet, mellifluous, soft, harmonious, euphonious, silvery, silver-toned. **5** *the sweet sight of home* pleasant, pleasing, agreeable, delightful, welcome. **6** *have a sweet nature* good-natured, amiable, pleasant, agreeable, friendly, kindly, charming, likable, appealing, engaging, winning, winsome. **7** *sweet faces* attractive, beautiful, lovely, comely, glamorous. **8** *his sweet wife* dear, dearest, darling, beloved,

loved, cherished, precious, treasured. **sweet on** *sweet on the boy next door* fond of, taken with, in love with, enamored of, infatuated with, keen on; *inf.* gone on, mad about.

Antonyms: SOUR; HARSH; DISAGREEABLE.

sweeten verb **1** *sweeten the tea* make sweet, sugar, add sugar/honey/sweetener to. **2** *sweeten an unpleasant situation* make agreeable, soften, ease, alleviate, relieve, mitigate. **3** *sweeten her father before asking for a loan* soften, soften up, mellow, pacify, appease, mollify. **4** *sweeten the air* purify, freshen, ventilate, deodorize.

sweetheart noun **1** *his teenage sweetheart* girlfriend, boyfriend, lover, suitor, admirer, beau, paramour, inamorato, inamorata; *lit.* swain; *inf.* steady, flame. **2** *goodbye, sweetheart* dear, dearest, darling, love, beloved; *inf.* honey, sweetie, sugar, baby.

swell verb **1** *his stomach/ankle swelled up* expand, bulge, distend, become distended, inflate, become inflated, dilate, become bloated, blow up, puff up, balloon, tumefy, intumesce. **2** *the numbers have swelled* increase, grow larger, grow greater, rise, mount, escalate, accelerate, step up, snowball, mushroom. **3** *the music swelled* grow loud, grow louder, intensify, heighten.

Antonyms: SHRINK; CONTRACT; DECREASE.

swell noun **1** *the swell of the sea* billowing, undulation, surging. **2** *a swell in numbers* increase, rise, escalation, acceleration, stepping-up, snowballing, mushrooming.

swell adjective **1** *have a swell time* enjoyable, marvelous, wonderful, first-rate, excellent. **2** *a swell hotel* expensive, luxurious, deluxe, fashionable, elegant, grand; *inf.* posh, plush, ritzy.

swelling noun *treat the swelling on his head* bump, lump, bulge, blister, inflammation, protuberance, tumescence.

sweltering adjective *a sweltering day | sweltering conditions* too hot, hot, torrid, tropical, stifling, suffocating, humid, sultry, sticky, muggy, clammy, close, stuffy; *inf.* boiling, baking.

Antonyms: FREEZING; COLD; CHILLY.

swerve verb *swerve to avoid an oncoming car* change direction, go off course, veer, turn aside, skew, deviate, sheer, twist.

swift adjective **1** *a swift runner* fast, rapid, quick, speedy, fleet-footed, fleet, swift as an arrow. **2** *at a swift pace* fast, rapid, quick, brisk, lively, speedy, expeditious, express. **3** *a swift change of plan* rapid, sudden, abrupt, hasty, hurried, meteoric. **4** *a swift reply* rapid, prompt, immediate, instantaneous.

Antonyms: SLOW; LEISURELY; UNHURRIED.

swiftness noun **1** *the swiftness of the runners* fastness, rapidity, rapidness, quickness, speediness, fleetness. **2** *the swiftness of the race* fastness, rapidity, rapidness, quickness, briskness, liveliness, speed, speediness, expeditiousness. **3** *the swiftness of the change of plan* rapidity, rapidness, suddenness, abruptness, haste, hastiness, hurriedness. **4** *the swiftness of the reply* rapidity, rapidness, promptness, immediateness, immediacy, instantaneousness.

swill *verb swill bottles of beer* gulp down, drink, quaff, swallow, down, drain, guzzle; *inf.* swig, knock off. **swill out** *swill out the stables* sluice, wash down, wash out, clean out, flush out, rinse out.

swill *noun* **1** *take a swill from the beer bottle* gulp, drink, swallow; *inf.* swig. **2** *remove the swill from the pigsties* waste, slop, refuse, scourings.

swim *verb* **1** *children swimming in the pond* float, tread water. **2** *food swimming in grease* be saturated in, be drenched in, be soaked in, be steeped in, be immersed in.

swimmingly *adverb things going swimmingly* very well, smoothly, effortlessly, like clockwork, without a hitch, without difficulty, as planned; *inf.* like a dream.

swindle *verb swindle the old lady* defraud, cheat, trick, fleece, dupe, deceive, scam, rook, exploit; *inf.* con, rip off, take for a ride, pull a fast one on, bilk.

swindle *noun get the money through a swindle* fraud, trick, deception, scam, exploitation; *inf.* con job, con, rip-off.

swindler *noun done out of her money by a swindler* fraud, cheat, trickster, rogue, mountebank, exploiter; *inf.* con man, con artist, shark, bilker.

swing *verb* **1** *lights swinging from the roof* hang, be suspended, dangle, be pendent. **2** *the pendulum swings* move back and forth, sway, oscillate, wag. **3** *the road swings to the right* curve, veer, turn, lean, incline, wind, twist. **4** *swing down the road* march, stride, stroll. **5** *he swings from optimism to despair* change, fluctuate, oscillate, waver, seesaw, yo-yo. **6** *manage to swing an interview with the chairman* achieve, obtain, acquire, get, maneuver.

swing *noun* **1** *the swing of the pendulum* swaying, oscillation, wagging. **2** *music with a swing* rhythm, beat, pulse. **3** *a swing to the left at the election* move, change, variation, turn-around.

swirl *verb water swirling round and round* whirl, eddy, circulate, revolve, spin, twist, churn, swish.

switch *noun* **1** *a switch from a tree* shoot, twig, branch. **2** *hit the mutineer with a switch* cane, rod, stick, whip, thong, cat-o'-nine-tails. **3** *a sudden switch in direction* change, shift, reversal, turn-around, about-face, swerve, U-turn. **4** *the switch from one method to another* change, changeover, transfer, conversion. **5** *get a new book in a switch with his friend* exchange, trade; *inf.* swap.

switch *verb* **1** *switch directions* change, shift, reverse. **2** *switch cars* exchange, interchange, trade, barter; *inf.* swap.

swollen *adjective a swollen stomach/ankle* expanded, bulging, distended, inflated, dilated, bloated, blown-up, puffed-up, puffy, tumescent.

swoop *verb hawks swooping on their prey* pounce, dive, descend, sweep down, drop down. **swoop up** *swoop up the baby in her arms* take up, lift up, pick up, scoop up, seize, snatch, grab.

sword *noun* blade, rapier, saber, cutlass. **cross swords** fight, do battle, quarrel, have a dispute, engage in conflict, wrangle, bicker, lock horns; *inf.* have a scrap. **put to the sword** *put the traitor to the sword* put to death, execute, kill, slay, murder.

sybaritic *adjective sybaritic tastes* luxurious, self-indulgent, pleasure-seeking, sensual, voluptuous, hedonistic, epicurean, debauched, dissolute.
Antonyms: ASCETIC; ABSTEMIOUS.

sycophant *noun a great man surrounded by sycophants* toady, flatterer, Uriah Heep; *inf.* bootlicker, yes-man.

sycophantic *adjective* servile, subservient, obsequious, toadying, fawning, flattering, ingratiating, unctuous, truckling; *inf.* bootlicking.

symbol *noun* **1** *the dove is the symbol of peace* emblem, token, sign, badge, representation, figure, image, type. **2** *mathematical/chemical symbol* sign, character, mark. **3** *the symbol of the company* stamp, emblem, badge, trademark, logo, monogram.

symbolic *adjective* **1** *the dove being symbolic of peace* emblematic, representative, typical. **2** *a symbolic dance* representative, illustrative, emblematic, figurative, allegorical.

symbolize *verb the dove symbolizing peace* be a symbol of, stand for, be a sign of, represent, personify, exemplify, typify, betoken, denote, signify, mean.

symmetrical *adjective* **1** *symmetrical features* balanced, well-proportioned, proportional, in proportion, regular, even, harmonious. **2** *the two sides of the building must be symmetrical* regular, even, uniform, consistent, in agreement.
Antonyms: ASYMMETRICAL; UNEVEN; DISPROPORTIONATE.

symmetry *noun* **1** *the symmetry of her features* balance, proportions, regularity, evenness of form, harmony. **2** *the symmetry of the two sides of the building* regularity, evenness, uniformity, consistency, congruity, conformity, agreement, correspondence.

sympathetic *adjective* **1** *be sympathetic when she lost* | *give the losers a sympathetic look* compassionate, commiserating, commiserative, pitying, condoling, consoling, comforting, supportive, caring, concerned, solicitous, considerate, kindly, kind, kindhearted, warm, warmhearted, understanding, charitable, empathetic. **2** *she is a very sympathetic person/character* pleasant, agreeable, likable, congenial, friendly, sociable, companionable, neighborly, easy to get along with; *inf.* simpatico. **sympathetic to** *not very sympathetic to their cause* in sympathy with, well-disposed to, favorably disposed to, favorable to, in favor of, approving of, pro, on the side of, supporting of, encouraging of.

Antonyms: UNSYMPATHETIC; UNFEELING; INDIFFERENT; UNFRIENDLY.

sympathize *verb* **sympathize with** **1** *sympathize with the bereaved* show sympathy for, be sympathetic toward, show compassion for, be compassionate toward, commiserate with, pity, offer condolences to, console, offer consolation to, comfort, be supportive of, show understanding to, empathize with. **2** *sympathize with their cause/aims* be in sympathy with, be sympathetic toward, be in favor of, be well-disposed to, approve of, commend, back, side with, support, encourage.

Antonyms: DISREGARD; DISAPPROVE.

sympathizer *noun* **1** *the bereaved being comforted by sympathizers* commiserater, condoler, consoler, comforter, empathizer. **2** *sympathizers of their cause* advocate, supporter, backer, well-wisher, ally, partisan, fellow-traveler.

sympathy *noun* **1** *express their sympathy to the bereaved* compassion, commiseration, pity, condolence, consolation, comfort, solace, support, caring, concern, solicitude, solicitousness, consideration, kindness, kindheartedness, warmth, warmheartedness, charity, charitableness, understanding, empathy. **2** *a bond of sympathy between them* affinity, empathy, rapport, fellow feeling, harmony, accord, compatibility, closeness, friendship. **3** *show sympathy for their cause* favor, approval, approbation, good will, commendation, support, encouragement.

Antonyms: INDIFFERENCE; HOSTILITY; DISAPPROVAL.

symptom *noun* **1** *a symptom of the disease* sign, indication, signal, warning, mark, characteristic, feature. **2** *his bad behavior was a symptom of his unhappiness* expression, sign, indication, signal, mark, token, evidence, demonstration, display.

symptomatic *adjective* **symptomatic of** *pains symptomatic of heart disease* indicative of, signaling, characteristic of, suggesting, suggestive of.

synthesis *noun* **1** *the synthesis of several elements into a whole* combination, combining, union, unification, merging, amalgamation, fusion, coalescence, integration. **2** *a synthesis of two substances* combination, union, amalgam, blend, compound, fusion, coalescence.

synthetic *adjective* *synthetic leather* manufactured, man-made, fake, artificial, mock, ersatz.

Antonyms: REAL; GENUINE; NATURAL.

syrupy *adjective* **1** *syrupy desserts* oversweet, sugary, sweet, honeyed, saccharine, sticky; *inf.* gooey. **2** *syrupy love stories* sentimental, oversentimental, mawkish, maudlin, mushy, slushy, sloppy; *inf.* soppy, schmaltzy.

system *noun* **1** *the railroad/digestive system* structure, organization, order, arrangement; *inf.* setup. **2** *a new system for teaching languages* method, methodology, technique, process, procedure, approach, practice, line, attack, means, way, modus operandi. **3** *absolutely no system in his accounting methods* systematization, methodicalness, orderliness, planning, logic, tightness, routine.

systematic *adjective* *a systematic approach to the problem* structured, organized, methodical, orderly, well-ordered, planned, systematized, logical, efficient, businesslike.

Antonyms: DISORGANIZED; HAPHAZARD; CHAOTIC.

T

tab *noun hang the jacket up by the tab* loop, flap, tag.

table *noun* **1** *put the plates on the table* counter, bar, buffet, bench, stand. **2** *provide an excellent table* food, fare; meal, victuals; *inf.* spread, nosh, grub, chow. **3** *terrain characterized by tables* tableland; plateau, elevated plain, flat, mesa, steppe. **4** *a table of contents | table of geographical data* list, catalog, tabulation, inventory, digest, itemization, index. **5** *leave room in the text for tables* chart, diagram, figure, graph, plan.

table *verb table a suggestion/motion* postpone, defer, suspend, shelve; *inf.* put on ice.

tableau *noun* **1** *paint evocative tableaux of city life* picture, painting, representation, portrayal, illustration. **2** *the children's tableau was part of the show* pageant, *tableau vivant*. **3** *admire the tableau below from the mountaintop* spectacle, scene, sight.

tablet *noun* **1** *the dedication inscribed on the stone tablet* slab, panel, stone. **2** *prescribed tablets for headaches* pill, capsule, lozenge. **3** *wrote it down on his tablet* pad, notepad, memo/scratch pad, notebook.

taboo *adjective such practices are taboo | taboo language* forbidden, prohibited, banned, proscribed, vetoed, ruled out, outlawed, not permitted, not acceptable, frowned on, beyond the pale.
Antonyms: ACCEPTABLE; permitted.

taboo *noun such practices are subject to taboo* prohibition, proscription, veto, interdiction, nonacceptance; interdict, ban.

tabulate *verb* chart, systematize, systemize, arrange, order, dispose, organize, catalog, list, classify, class, codify, group, range, grade.

tacit *adjective by tacit agreement* implicit, understood, implied, taken for granted, unstated, undeclared, unspoken, unexpressed, unmentioned, unvoiced, silent, wordless.
Antonym: EXPLICIT.

taciturn *adjective* unforthcoming, uncommunicative, reticent, secretive, untalkative, tight-lipped, closemouthed, quiet, silent, mute, dumb; reserved, withdrawn, aloof, cold, detached.
Antonyms: COMMUNICATIVE; LOQUACIOUS.

tack *noun* **1** *attach the notice to the wall with a tack* nail, pin, staple, rivet. **2** *try a different tack if that one is unsuccessful* course/line of action, method, approach, process, way, policy, tactic, plan, strategy, attack.

tack *verb* **1** *tack the picture to the wall | tack the carpet to the floor* nail, pin, staple, fix, fasten, affix, put up/down. **2** *tack up the hem* stitch, baste, sew. **3** *in politics it is necessary to know when to tack* change course/direction, alter one's approach, change one's mind/attitude, have a change of heart, do an about-face; *inf.* do a U-turn. **4** *tack a postscript on the letter | tack a greenhouse to the house* add, attach, append, tag, annex.

tackle *noun fishing tackle* gear, equipment, apparatus, outfit; tools, implements, accouterments, paraphernalia, trappings; *inf.* things, stuff.

tackle *verb* **1** *tackle the task/problem* undertake, attempt, apply/address oneself to, get to grips with, set/go about, get to work at, busy oneself with, embark on, set one's hand to, take on, engage in. **2** *tackle the intruder* grapple with, seize, take hold of, confront, face up to; *inf.* have a go at. **3** *tackle him on the subject of his lateness* speak to, confront, accost, waylay, remonstrate with.

tacky[1] *adjective the paint/surface is tacky* sticky, gluey, gummy; *inf.* gooey.

tacky[2] *adjective tacky souvenirs on sale* tawdry, tasteless, kitsch, vulgar, crude, garish, gaudy, flashy.

tact *noun* diplomacy, discretion, savoir faire, sensitivity, understanding, thoughtfulness, consideration, delicacy, subtlety, finesse, skill, adroitness, dexterity, discernment, perception, judgment, prudence, judiciousness; *inf.* savvy.
Antonyms: INDISCRETION; tactlessness.

tactful *adjective* diplomatic, politic, discreet, sensitive, understanding, thoughtful, considerate, delicate, subtle, skillful, adroit, discerning, perceptive, prudent, judicious.
Antonyms: TACTLESS; INDISCREET.

tactic *noun try a different tactic to achieve success* maneuver, expedient, device, stratagem, trick, scheme, plan, ploy, course/line of action, method, approach, tack; means. *See* TACTICS.

tactical *adjective effect the takeover by tactical means* strategic, politic, planned, shrewd, skillful, adroit, clever, smart, cunning, artful.

tactics *plural noun military tactics | his clever tactics secured the takeover bid* strategy, campaign, policy; plans, battle/game plans, maneuvers.

tactless *adjective* undiplomatic, impolitic, indiscreet, insensitive, inconsiderate, indelicate, unsubtle, rough, crude, unskillful, clumsy,

awkward, inept, bungling, maladroit, gauche, **743**   **tag ~ take**
undiscerning, imprudent, injudicious.

Antonyms: TACTFUL; DIPLOMATIC; DISCREET.

tag *noun* **1** *a tag showing the price* label, ticket, sticker, docket. **2** *hang the jacket up by its tag* tab, loop, flap.

tag *verb* **1** *tag the items* label, put a ticket/sticker on, mark. **2** *tag him Lefty* name, call, nickname, title, entitle, label, dub, term, style, christen. **3** *tag a postscript to the letter* add, attach, append, affix, tack. **tag along with** *tagging along with their older brother* go with, accompany, follow, trail behind, tread on the heels of, dog.

tail *noun* **1** *the tail of the animal* brush, scut, dock; *Tech.* cauda. **2** *hurt one's tail* bottom, rump; buttocks; *inf.* butt, backside, rear. **3** *at the tail of the storm* tail-end, close, end, conclusion, termination. **4** *the pursuers are on his tail* track, trail, scent. **5** *put a tail on the crook* detective, investigator, private investigator, shadow; *inf.* sleuth, private eye, gumshoe. **turn tail** run away, flee, retreat, take to one's heels, cut and run; *inf.* skedaddle, vamoose, split, hightail it.

Antonyms: HEAD; FRONT.

tail *verb detectives tailing the crooks* follow, shadow, stalk, trail, track, dog the footsteps of, keep under surveillance.

tailor *noun* outfitter, dressmaker, couturier, clothier, costumier.

tailor *verb tailor the schedule to your needs* fit, suit, fashion, style, mold, shape, adapt, adjust, modify, convert, alter, accommodate.

taint *verb* **1** *the water/meat had become tainted* contaminate, pollute, adulterate, infect, blight, befoul, spoil. **2** *taint his reputation* tarnish, sully, blacken, stain, besmirch, smear, blot, blemish, muddy, damage, injure, harm.

taint *noun* **1** *food poisoning caused by the taint of the water* contamination, pollution, adulteration, infection, contagion. **2** *a taint on his character* stain, smear, blot, blemish, stigma. **3** *a taint of insanity in the family* trace, touch, suggestion, hint.

take *verb* **1** *take the book from her* get/lay hold of, get into one's hands, grasp, grip, clutch. **2** *take first prize* get, receive, obtain, gain, acquire, secure, procure, come by, win, earn. **3** *take several prisoners* seize, catch, capture, arrest, carry off, abduct. **4** *who took my pen/savings?* remove, appropriate, make off with, steal, filch, pilfer, purloin, pocket; *inf.* pinch, swipe. **5** *I will take a pound of apples* buy, purchase, pay for. **6** *take a single room | take a boat for the day* reserve, book, engage, rent, hire, lease. **7** *she showed me several dresses but I took the blue one* pick, choose, select, decide on, settle on, opt for. **8** *take the bus/motorway* use, make use of, utilize. **9** *take some bread and wine* consume, eat, devour, swallow; drink, imbibe. **10** *the vaccination did not take* be effective, have/take effect, be efficacious, work, operate, succeed. **11** *the journey takes three hours* use, use up, require,

call for, need, necessitate. **12** *take the box home with you* carry, fetch, bring, bear, transport, convey, cart; *inf.* tote. **13** *will you take his sister home?* escort, accompany, conduct, guide, lead, usher, convoy. **14** *take fright | take pleasure in acting* experience, be affected by, undergo. **15** *take the child's temperature* find out, discover, ascertain, determine, establish. **16** *I take it that you agreed | she took his silence to mean agreement* understand, interpret as, grasp, gather, comprehend, apprehend, assume, believe, suppose, consider, presume. **17** *take the news badly* receive, deal with, cope with. **18** *take the offer* accept, receive, adopt. **19** *take a course of study* enter upon, undertake, begin, set about. **20** *take French at school* study, learn, be taught, take up, pursue. **21** *take an oath/look* perform, execute, effect, do, make, have. **22** *take a nap* engage in, occupy oneself in. **23** *the bucket takes three gallons* hold, contain, have the capacity for, have space/room for, accommodate. **24** *I cannot take his rudeness* bear, tolerate, stand, put up with, stomach, brook. **25** *the machine takes its name from the inventor* derive, obtain, come by. **26** *the passage is taken from the Bible* extract, quote, cite, excerpt, derive. **27** *take three from five* subtract, deduct, remove. **28** *we were quite taken with the child | taken by her beauty* captivate, enchant, charm, delight, please, attract, win over, fascinate. **29** *do you think the idea will take?* catch on, become popular, gain popularity, be successful, succeed. **take after** resemble, look like, be like, favor; *inf.* be a chip off the old block, be the spitting image of. **take back 1** *take back the accusing statement* retract, withdraw, renounce, disclaim, unsay, disavow, recant. **2** *take the book back to its owner* carry back, bring back, fetch back, return. **3** *the store will not take the goods back* accept back, give a refund for, exchange, trade, swap. **4** *his wife has taken him back* accept back, welcome back, forgive. **5** *take back the land won by the enemy* get back, regain, repossess, reclaim, recapture, reconquer. **take back to** *his stories took me back to my youth* awaken/evoke one's memories of, put one in mind of, remind one of. **take down 1** *take down the details* write down, note down, make a note of, jot down, set down, record, put on record, commit to paper, document. **2** *take down the scaffolding/fence* remove, dismantle, disassemble, take apart, take to pieces, demolish, tear down, level, raze. **3** *take down the flag | took down his pants* pull down, let down, haul down, lower, drop. **4** *that should take him down a bit* humble, deflate, humiliate, mortify, take down a peg or two; *inf.* put down. **take for** *she took him for a fool* regard as, consider as, view as, look upon as. **take in 1** *take in the homeless child | take in paying guests* admit, let in, receive, welcome, accommodate, board. **2** *take* *the skirt in* make smaller/narrower, reduce in size. **3** *he didn't seem to take the news in* grasp, understand, comprehend, absorb, assimilate. **4** *said nothing but took everything in* observe, see, notice, take note of, note, perceive, regard. **5** *they were completely taken in by the con man* deceive, delude, hoodwink, mislead, trick, dupe, fool, cheat, defraud, swindle, gull; *inf.* con, bilk, pull the wool over someone's eyes. **6** *the court's jurisdiction takes in these three districts* include, encompass, embrace, contain, comprise, cover. **7** *try to take in a concert when you are there* go to, go to see, attend, visit. **take off 1** *take the lid off the jar* remove, detach, pull off. **2** *take off one's clothes* remove, discard, strip off, peel off, throw off, divest oneself of, doff. **3** *take the TV show off after just two episodes* remove, withdraw, retract. **4** *take money off the bill for poor service* deduct from, subtract from, take away from. **5** *the children took off when they saw the police* | *she took off for Australia* run away, take to one's heels, flee, decamp, disappear, leave, go, depart; *inf.* split, beat it, skedaddle, vamoose, hightail it. **6** *the plane took off* become airborne, leave the ground, lift off. **7** *the business/scheme has really taken off* succeed, do well, become popular, catch on. **8** *it is time I took myself off* take one's leave, make one's departure. **take on 1** *take on extra work* undertake, accept, tackle, turn one's hand to; *inf.* have a go at. **2** *take on extra staff* employ, engage, hire, enroll, enlist; *inf.* take on board. **3** *take him on at chess* compete against, oppose, challenge, face, pit/match oneself against, contend with, vie with, fight. **4** *suddenly his words/situation took on a new meaning* acquire, come to have, assume. **take out 1** *take out a tooth* remove, extract, pull out, yank out. **2** *take out the girl next door* go out with, escort; *inf.* date. **take over** *take over the business* | *take over the running of the household* take/assume/gain control of, take charge/command of, assume responsibility for. **take to 1** *she's taken to smoking* begin, start, commence, make a habit of, resort to. **2** *he did not take to her friend* develop a liking for, like, get on with, become friendly with. **3** *he has really taken to swimming* become good at, develop an ability/aptitude for, develop a liking for, like, enjoy, become interested in. **take up 1** *take up the carpets/pen* lift up, raise. **2** *take up surfing* become involved/interested in, engage in, begin, start, commence. **3** *practicing the piano takes up a great deal of time* use, use up, occupy, fill, consume, absorb, cover, extend over. **4** *take up the story where they left off* resume, recommence, restart, begin again, carry on, continue, pick up. **5** *take up an offer* accept, say yes to, agree to, accede to, adopt. **6** *take up a skirt/hem* shorten, make shorter; raise. **7** *take up with the wrong sort of people* become friendly/friends, go around; *inf.* hang around.

take *noun* **1** *fishermen/hunters assessing the take* catch, haul, bag. **2** *counting the take after the sale/match* takings, proceeds, returns, receipts, profits, winnings, purse, pickings, earnings; gain, income, revenue.

takeoff *noun* **1** *the takeoff of the plane* taking off, liftoff, departure, ascent, climbing, mounting, soaring, flying. **2** *amused by his takeoff of the celebrity* mimicry, impersonation, imitation, parody, mockery; *inf.* send-up, spoof.

takings *plural noun* proceeds, returns, receipts, earnings, winnings, pickings; profit, gain, income, revenue.

tale *noun* **1** *a fairy tale* story, short story, narrative, anecdote, legend, fable, myth, parable, allegory, epic, saga; *inf.* yarn. **2** *hear tales of her wild behavior* talk, rumor, gossip, hearsay; report, allegation. **3** *the child didn't see the burglar—that was a tale* lie, fib, falsehood, untruth, fabrication, piece of fiction; *inf.* story, tall story, cock-and-bull story, whopper.

talent *noun* gift, flair, aptitude, facility, knack, bent, ability, capacity, faculty, aptness, endowment, strong point, forte, genius.

talented *adjective* gifted, accomplished, able, capable, apt, deft, adept, proficient, brilliant, expert, artistic.
Antonyms: INCAPABLE; HOPELESS; INEPT.

talk *verb* **1** *talk incessantly* speak, give voice/utterance, chat, chatter, gossip, prattle, prate, gibber, jabber, babble, rattle on; *inf.* yak, gab. **2** *talk nonsense* speak, say, utter, voice, express, articulate, pronounce, enunciate, verbalize. **3** *they do not talk any more* communicate, converse, speak to each other, discuss things, confer, consult each other, have negotiations, have a tête-à-tête, parley, palaver, confabulate; *inf.* have a confab, chew the fat, jaw, rap. **4** *if you tell her your secret, she will talk* tell, reveal all, tell tales, give the game away, open one's mouth, let the cat out of the bag; *inf.* blab, squeal, spill the beans, sing. **5** *if they divorce, people will talk* gossip, spread rumors, pass comment, make remarks, criticize. **6** *the professor is talking tonight* give a talk, give/make/deliver a speech, speak, lecture, discourse. **7** *after years of silence the spy has decided to talk* speak, speak out, speak up, give voice, tell the facts, divulge information, reveal all. **talk back** *talking back to their parents* answer defiantly/impertinently, answer back, be sassy; *inf.* give lip. **talk big** brag, boast, crow, exaggerate; *inf.* blow one's own horn, shoot one's mouth off. **talk down to** *talk down to young people* speak condescendingly to, condescend to, speak haughtily to, patronize. **talk into** persuade to, cajole to, coax into, influence. **talk of** *they talked of going away* speak about, discuss, mention, make mention of, refer to, make reference to. **talk out of** dissuade from, persuade against, discourage from, deter from, stop.

talk *noun* **1** *their noisy talk kept me awake* talking, speaking, chatter, chatting, gossiping, prattling, gibbering, jabbering, babbling, gabbling; *inf.* yakking, gabbing. **2** *baby/seamen's talk* words; speech, language, dialect, jargon, cant, slang, idiom, idiolect, patois; *inf.* lingo. **3** *have a talk about their future* conversation, chat, discussion, tête-à-tête; dialogue; *inf.* confab, rap. **4** *give a talk to the society* lecture, speech, address, discourse, oration, sermon, disquisition. **5** *there is talk of a merger* gossip, rumor, hearsay. **6** *the talk in the office was of the possible merger* chat, conversation, discussion, gossip, subject, theme.

talkative *adjective* loquacious, garrulous, voluble, chatty, gossipy, long-winded, conversational, gushing, effusive; *inf.* gabby, mouthy, bigmouthed.
Antonyms: TACITURN; UNCOMMUNICATIVE.

---

talkative
garrulous, glib, loquacious, voluble
Someone who likes to talk frequently or at length might be described as **talkative** (*He was the most talkative person I'd ever met*). This word implies a readiness to engage in talk, while **loquacious** implies an inclination to talk incessantly or to keep up a constant flow of chatter (*a loquacious woman who never seemed to tire of hearing her own voice*). **Glib** and **voluble** pertain to the ease with which someone is able to converse or speak, although *voluble* may be used in either an approving or a critical sense (*a voluble speaker who was in great demand; a voluble neighbor who could not keep a secret*). *Glib* is almost always negative, referring to a superficial or slick way of speaking (*the glib manner of a used-car salesperson*). **Garrulous** also has negative overtones, implying a tedious or rambling talkativeness, usually about trivial things (*a garrulous old man who bored everyone with his stories about the old days*).

---

talker *noun* **1** *the talker bored the audience* speaker, speech-maker, lecturer, orator. **2** *the child is a good talker* speaker, communicator. **3** *they are a family of talkers* conversationalist, chatter, chatterbox, gossip.

talking-to *noun* lecture, scolding, row, reprimand, rebuke, reproof, reproach; *inf.* carpeting.

talks *plural noun talks to negotiate a peace* conference, summit, meeting, consultation, discussion, dialogue, negotiation, symposium, seminar, conclave, colloquy, palaver, parley, confabulation; *inf.* powwow.

tall *adjective* **1** *tall people* big, colossal, gigantic, lanky, rangy, gangling. **2** *three feet tall* in height, high. **3** *tall buildings* high, lofty, towering, soaring, sky-high, skyscraping. **4** *a tall story* exaggerated, unlikely, incredible, far-fetched, implausible. **tall order** demanding/exacting/difficult task, unreasonable demand/request.
Antonyms: SHORT; SMALL; LOW.

tally *noun* **1** *keep a tally of the number of visitors* count, record, running total, reckoning, enumeration, register, roll, census, poll. **2** *what was the tally at the end of the game?* score, count, result, total, sum.

tally *verb the two accounts do not tally* | *his story does not tally with hers* agree, accord, concur, coincide, conform, correspond, match, fit, harmonize.

tame *adjective* **1** *tame animals* domesticated, not wild, not fierce, gentle, docile, used to humans. **2** *the supposedly rowdy children were quite tame* subdued, docile, submissive, compliant, meek, obedient, tractable, amenable, manageable, unresisting. **3** *the horror movie turned out to be quite tame* unexciting, uninteresting, uninspired, dull, bland, flat, insipid, vapid, run-of-the-mill, mediocre, prosaic, humdrum, boring, tedious, wearisome.
Antonyms: WILD; FIERCE.

tame *verb* **1** *tame the wild cat* domesticate, break, train, gentle. **2** *tame the unruly element in the class/party* subdue, discipline, curb, control, master, overcome, suppress, repress, humble.

tamper *verb* **tamper with** **1** *tamper with the exam papers* meddle with, interfere with, monkey around with, mess about with, tinker with, fiddle with, alter/change/adjust illegally; *inf.* fool around with, poke one's nose into. **2** *tamper with the jury* influence, get at, rig, manipulate, bribe, corrupt; *inf.* fix.

tan *adjective tan shoes* yellowish-brown, brownish-yellow, light brown, pale brown, tawny.

tang *noun* **1** *the tang of orange* flavor, taste, savor. **2** *the tang of the sea* smell, odor, aroma. **3** *add some tang to the food/occasion* spice, spiciness, piquancy, relish, sharpness, zest; *inf.* ginger, punch, zip.

tangible *adjective* **1** *tangible changes to the skin* touchable, palpable, tactile, visible. **2** *tangible proof* concrete, real, actual, solid, substantial, hard, well-documented, well-defined, definite, clear, clear-cut, distinct, unmistakable, positive, discernible.
Antonyms: INTANGIBLE; ABSTRACT.

---

tangible
appreciable, corporeal, palpable, perceptible, sensible
Anything that can be grasped, either with the hand or with the mind, is **tangible** (*tangible assets; tangible objects*). **Palpable**, like *tangible*, means capable of being touched or felt (*a palpable mist*), but it is often applied to whatever evokes a tactile response from the body (*a palpable chill in the room*). **Perceptible** is used to describe something that just crosses the border between invisibility and visibility or some other sense barrier (*a perceptible change in her tone of voice; a perceptible odor of garlic*). **Sensible** (in this sense) means that which can clearly be perceived through the senses or which makes a strong impression on the mind through the

medium of sensations. In contrast to *perceptible*, something that is *sensible* is more obvious or immediately recognized (*a sensible shift in the tenor of the conversation*). **Corporeal** means bodily or material, in contrast to things that are immaterial or spiritual (*corporeal goods*). Something that is **appreciable** is large enough to be measured, valued, estimated, or considered significant. An *appreciable* change in temperature, for example, can be determined by looking at a thermometer; a *palpable* change in temperature may be slight, but still great enough to be felt; and a *perceptible* change in temperature might be so slight that it almost—but not quite—escapes notice.

---

tangle *verb* **1** *the net became tangled in the rose bush* | *the rain had tangled her hair* entangle, intertwine, intertwist, twist, snarl, ravel, knot, mat. **2** *do not tangle with the authorities* become involved, come into conflict, have a dispute, dispute, argue, quarrel, fight, wrangle, squabble, contend, cross swords, lock horns.
Antonyms: UNTANGLE; UNRAVEL.

tangled *adjective* **1** *tangled wool/hair* entangled, twisted, snarled, raveled, knotted, knotty, matted, tousled, messy; *inf.* mussed-up. **2** *tangled affairs* confused, jumbled, mixed-up, messy, chaotic, complicated, involved, convoluted, complex.

tank *noun* **1** *water tank* container, receptacle, vat, cistern. **2** *soldiers in tanks* armored car/vehicle, combat vehicle.

tantalize *verb* *tantalize them with the promise of unobtainable gold* tease, torment, torture, frustrate, disappoint, thwart, make one's mouth water, lead on, entice, titillate, allure, beguile.

tantamount *adjective* **tantamount to** *his statement was tantamount to a confession* equivalent to, equal to, as good as, synonymous with.

tantrum *noun* fit of temper/rage, fit, outburst, flare-up, blow-up, paroxysm.

tap[1] *noun* **1** *turn the tap off* spigot, faucet, stopcock, valve. **2** *put a tap on their telephone* listening device; *inf.* bug, bugging device. **on tap** *extra supplies on tap* at/on hand, available, ready, in reserve, standing by.

tap[2] *verb* **1** *tap cider from a cask* draw off, siphon off, drain, bleed. **2** *tap a cask* draw liquid from, broach, open, pierce. **3** *tap sources of information* use, make use of, put to use, utilize, draw on, exploit, milk. **4** *tap mineral resources* extract, obtain, exploit, open up, explore, probe. **5** *tap their telephone* wiretap; *inf.* bug. **6** *tap their telephone calls* wiretap, listen in to, eavesdrop on; *inf.* bug, get on record.

tap[3] *noun* **1** *give a tap at the window* knock, rap, beat. **2** *give a tap on the shoulder* touch, pat, light blow/slap.

tap[4] *verb* **1** *tap on the window* | *tap the table* knock,

rap, strike, beat, drum. **2** *tap him on the shoulder* touch, pat, strike/slap lightly.

tape *noun* **1** *the first-place runner breaking the tape* band, strip, string, ribbon. **2** *use tape to repair the crack/tear* adhesive tape, insulating tape, masking tape, strapping tape, duct tape; *Trademark* Scotch tape. **3** *play a tape* tape recording, cassette, videotape, videocassette, video, audiotape, audiocassette.

tape *verb* **1** *tape the pieces together* bind, tie, fasten, stick, seal, secure; *Trademark* Scotch tape. **2** *tape the concert/conversation* record, tape-record, video-record, video. **3** *tape off the area* seal, mark with tape.

taper *verb* *the candles taper at the top* narrow, thin, become narrow/thinner, come to a point. **taper off** *sales tend to taper off at this time of year* dwindle, diminish, lessen, decrease, reduce, subside, die off, die away, fade, peter out, wane, ebb, wind down, slacken off, thin out.

target *noun* **1** *fail to hit the target in the shooting gallery* mark, bull's-eye. **2** *the injured bird was an easy target* prey, quarry, game. **3** *our target is $50,000* | *their target is the European market* objective, goal, object, aim, end, intention, desired result. **4** *she is the target of their jokes* butt, victim, scapegoat.

tariff *noun* **1** *the tariff is on display* price list/schedule, list of charges. **2** *ask the waitress for the tariff* menu, bill of fare. **3** *pay a tariff on imports* tax, duty, toll, excise, levy, impost.

tarnish *verb* **1** *time had tarnished the brass* dull, dim, discolor, rust. **2** *silver tarnishes easily* lose its shine/luster, become dull, discolor, rust. **3** *tarnish his reputation* sully, besmirch, blacken, stain, blemish, blot, taint, befoul, drag through the mud.
Antonyms: BRIGHTEN; POLISH; ENHANCE.

tarnish *noun* **1** *remove the tarnish from the silver* discoloration, oxidation, rust. **2** *survive the tarnish on his reputation* black mark, slur, stain, blemish, blot, taint, stigma.

tart *noun* *a fruit tart* pastry, pie, quiche, strudel.

tart *adjective* **1** *a tart apple/dessert* sharp, sharp-tasting, sour, tangy, piquant, pungent, bitter, acid, acidulous, vinegary. **2** *a tart remark/wit* astringent, caustic, sharp, biting, cutting, stinging, mordant, trenchant, incisive, piercing, acrimonious, barbed, scathing, sarcastic, sardonic.
Antonyms: SWEET; KIND.

task *noun* job, duty, chore, charge, odd job, piece of work/business, assignment, commission, mission, engagement, occupation, undertaking, exercise, errand, quest. **take to task** rebuke, reprimand, reprove, reproach, upbraid, scold, berate, lecture, castigate, censure, criticize, blame; *inf.* tell off.

taste *noun* **1** *the taste of fresh raspberries* flavor, savor, relish, tang. **2** *have a taste of the pudding/sauce* bit, morsel, bite, mouthful, spoonful, sample, sip, drop, swallow, touch, soupçon. **3** *have a taste for the unknown* | *expensive tastes* liking, love, fondness, fancy, desire, preference, penchant, predilection, inclination, partiality, leaning, bent, hankering, appetite, palate, thirst, hunger. **4** *furnish the house with taste* discrimination, discernment, judgment, cultivation, culture, refinement, polish, finesse, elegance, grace, stylishness. **5** *her remark lacked taste* decorum, propriety, correctness, etiquette, politeness, tact, tactfulness, diplomacy, delicacy, nicety, discretion.

taste verb **1** *taste the sauce while cooking it* sample, test, try, nibble, sip. **2** *I cannot taste the garlic* make out, perceive, discern, distinguish, differentiate. **3** *not to taste food for days* eat, partake of, consume, devour. **4** *it tastes of onions* have a flavor of, savor of, smack of. **5** *taste success/defeat* experience, undergo, encounter, meet, come face to face with, come up against, know.

tasteful adjective **1** *a tasteful display/room* in good taste, aesthetic, artistic, harmonious, pleasing, elegant, graceful, beautiful, pretty, charming, handsome, discriminating, refined, restrained. **2** *tasteful behavior/manners* decorous, proper, seemly, correct, polite, fitting, fit, appropriate, refined, cultured, cultivated.
Antonyms: TASTELESS; TACKY; GARISH; IMPROPER.

tasteless adjective **1** *tasteless food* flavorless, unflavored, savorless, bland, insipid, watery, watered-down, weak, thin, unappetizing, uninteresting, vapid. **2** *tasteless decorations* vulgar, crude, tawdry, garish, gaudy, loud, flashy, showy, cheap, gross, meretricious. **3** *tasteless behavior* indecorous, improper, unseemly, incorrect, impolite, rude, unfitting, inappropriate, unrefined, uncultured, uncultivated. **4** *tasteless remarks* vulgar, crude, low, gross, indelicate, uncouth, crass, tactless, undiplomatic, indiscreet.
Antonyms: SPICY; APPETIZING; TASTEFUL; SEEMLY.

tasty adjective flavorsome, flavorful, full-flavored, appetizing, palatable, toothsome, delectable, delicious, luscious, mouthwatering, piquant, pungent, spicy; *inf.* scrumptious, yummy.
Antonyms: BLAND; INSIPID.

tatter noun rag, torn/ragged piece. **in tatters 1** *clothes in tatters* ragged, torn, in shreds, in bits. **2** *his career/argument in tatters* in ruins, ruined, destroyed, demolished.

tattle verb *tattling about their friend's affairs* gossip, chatter, prattle, prate, babble, rattle on; *inf.* gab.

taunt noun *ignore the taunts of the opposition* gibe, jeer, sneer, insult, barb, catcall; teasing, provocation, ridiculing, derision, mockery, sarcasm; *inf.* dig, put-down.

taunt verb *rich children taunting the poor* gibe at, jeer at, sneer at, insult, chaff, tease, torment, provoke, ridicule, deride, mock, poke fun at.

taut adjective **1** *taut ropes* tight, tightly stretched, stretched, rigid. **2** *taut muscles* tightened, flexed, tensed. **3** *a taut expression* tense,

strained, stressed, drawn; *inf.* uptight. **4** *run a taut ship* in good order/condition, orderly, in order, shipshape, tight, trim, neat, well-ordered, well-regulated, tidy, spruce, smart.
Antonyms: LOOSE; SLACK.

tautology noun repetition, repetitiveness, repetitiousness, reiteration, redundancy, pleonasm, wordiness, long-windedness, verbosity, prolixity.

tawdry adjective showy, gaudy, flashy, garish, loud, tasteless, cheap, cheapjack, shoddy, meretricious; *inf.* tacky, kitsch.
Antonyms: TASTEFUL; REFINED.

tax noun **1** *income tax* | *charge a tax on imports* levy, charge, duty, toll, excise, tariff, impost, tribute; customs. **2** *they became a tax on her health/resources* burden, load, weight, encumbrance, strain, pressure, stress, drain.

tax verb **1** *tax his salary at source* | *tax imports* levy a tax on, impose a toll on, charge duty on. **2** *work taxing his strength* make demands on, weigh heavily on, weigh down, burden, load, encumber, overload, push, push too far, stretch, strain, try, wear out, exhaust, sap, drain, enervate, fatigue, tire, weary, weaken.

taxing adjective *a taxing job* demanding, exacting, burdensome, onerous, difficult, hard, tough, heavy, tiring, exhausting, enervating, draining, sapping, stressful, wearing, trying, punishing.
Antonyms: EASY; EFFORTLESS.

teach verb **1** *teach children* give lessons to, instruct, educate, school, tutor, coach, train, drill, ground, enlighten, edify. **2** *teach French* give lessons/instruction in, instill, inculcate. **3** *teach them how to ride a bike* instruct, train, show, guide.

teacher noun schoolteacher, instructor, educator, tutor, coach, trainer, lecturer, professor, pedagogue, guide, mentor, guru.

team noun **1** *a team of workers/players* group, band, bunch, company, party, gang, crew, troupe, set, squad, side, lineup. **2** *a team of horses* pair, span, yoke.

team verb **team up** *team up with his friend to do the project* join, get/come/band together, work together, unite, cooperate, form an alliance.

tear[1] noun **1** *a tear in the material* rip, split, hole, rent, run, rupture. **2** *bandage the tear in his arm* laceration, gash, slash, scratch, cut, mutilation, injury, wound.

tear[2] verb **1** *tear the paper/cloth* rip, pull apart, pull to pieces, split, rend, sever, rive, sunder, rupture. **2** *tear the flesh* lacerate, gash, slash, pierce, stab, scratch, cut, claw, mangle, mutilate, hack, injure, wound. **3** *tear the painting from the wall* | *tear off the cover* rip, pull, wrench, yank, wrest, extract, peel, snatch, pluck, grab, seize. **4** *torn between going and staying* divide, split, rend, disrupt, break apart. **5** *torn by guilt* disrupt, distress, upset, harrow, torture, torment. **6** *children tearing down the street* run, race, sprint, gallop, rush, dash, bolt, career, dart, fly, shoot, hurry, speed, hasten; *inf.* hotfoot it, whiz, zoom, zip.

tear[3] *noun* **1** *tears ran down her cheeks* teardrop. **2** *tears of perspiration/resin* drop, droplet, globule, bead. **in tears** tearful, crying, weeping, sobbing, blubbering.

tearful *adjective* **1** *in a tearful state* in tears, crying, weeping, sobbing, blubbering, sniveling, whimpering, wailing; emotional, upset, distressed; *inf.* weepy, blubbing. **2** *a tearful parting/event* emotional, upsetting, distressing, heartbreaking, heart-rending, sad, sorrowful, piteous, pitiful, pitiable, pathetic, poignant, mournful, melancholy, lamentable, dolorous.

tease *verb* **1** *tease the cat | tease the new boy* torment, provoke, badger, bait, goad, needle, pest, bother, worry, vex, irritate, annoy, gibe, mock, ridicule, poke fun at; *inf.* aggravate. **2** *he was only teasing her* joke (with), fool (with), rag, twit; *inf.* kid, rib, have on.

technical *adjective* **1** *technical training/applications* mechanical, practical, scientific, applying science, nontheoretical. **2** *technical terms* specialist, specialized, scientific.

technique *noun* **1** *new business techniques* method, method of working, modus operandi, system, procedure, style of approach, manner, way, course of action, mode, fashion; means. **2** *admire the violinist's technique* execution, performance, skill, skillfulness, proficiency, expertise, expertness, mastery, artistry, art, craftsmanship, craft, ability, adroitness, deftness, dexterity, knack. **3** *admire his technique in dealing with management* skill, ability, capability, proficiency, capacity, aptitude, expertise, knack, talent, gift, genius; *inf.* know-how.

tedious *adjective* wearisome, wearying, tiresome, tiring, fatiguing, soporific, long-drawn-out, overlong, long-winded, prolix, dull, deadly dull, boring, uninteresting, dry, dreary, drab, unexciting, lifeless, uninspired, flat, banal, vapid, insipid, monotonous, unvaried, prosaic, humdrum, run-of-the-mill, routine. *Antonyms:* EXCITING; INTERESTING.

tedium *noun* tediousness, wearisomeness, tiresomeness, prolixity, dullness, boredom, ennui, uninterestingness, dryness, lifelessness, dreariness, drabness, flatness, banality, vapidity, insipidity, monotony, sameness.

teem *verb* **1** *fish teem in these waters* abound, be abundant, be plentiful, be copious. **2** *rivers teeming with fish | teeming with ideas* abound, swarm, crawl, bristle, seethe, brim.

teenage *adjective* adolescent, youthful, young, juvenile.

teenager *noun* young person, adolescent, youth, minor, juvenile; *inf.* teeny-bopper.

teeter *verb* **1** *teeter down the street on high heels* totter, wobble, stagger, stumble, reel, sway, roll, lurch. **2** *teeter between accepting and refusing* waver, vacillate, fluctuate, oscillate, dither, hesitate, shilly-shally, seesaw.

teetotalism *noun* abstinence, abstention, temperance, sobriety.

teetotaler *noun* abstainer, nondrinker.

telegram *noun* cable, cablegram, telex; *inf.* wire.

telepathy *noun* thought transference, clairvoyance, mind-reading, extrasensory perception, ESP, psychometry.

telephone *verb I will telephone you tomorrow* call, ring; *inf.* phone, give someone a ring/buzz, get on the blower, buzz.

telescope *noun* glass, spyglass, reflector, refractor; radio telescope/dish, infrared/X-ray telescope.

television *noun* television set; *inf.* TV, tube, boob tube, box, idiot box.

tell *verb* **1** *tell the news to everyone | tell the truth* make known, impart, communicate, announce, proclaim, broadcast, divulge, reveal, disclose, declare, state, mention, utter, voice, say, speak. **2** *tell a story* narrate, relate, recount, give an account of, report, chronicle, recite, rehearse, describe, portray, sketch, delineate. **3** *tell them tomorrow that you are going* inform, let know, make aware, apprise, notify. **4** *I tell you that he is guilty* assure, promise, guarantee, warrant. **5** *tell them to go home* instruct, bid, order, give orders, command, direct, charge, enjoin, dictate to, call upon, require. **6** *he knows her secret, but he promised not to tell* talk, tell tales, blab, give the game away, open one's mouth, let the cat out of the bag; *inf.* squeal, spill the beans, sing, rat. **7** *his friend told on him* report, inform; *inf.* squeal, rat, blow the whistle, pull the plug. **8** *his expression told how he felt* reveal, disclose, show, display, exhibit, indicate. **9** *unable to tell his reaction from his expression* deduce, make out, discern, perceive, see, identify, recognize, discover, understand, comprehend. **10** *unable to tell one from the other* distinguish, differentiate, discriminate. **11** *breeding tells* have an effect, make its presence felt, count, carry weight, have influence/force, register; *inf.* have clout.

telling *adjective* *make a telling contribution | telling evidence* marked, significant, substantial, considerable, sizable, solid, weighty, important, striking, impressive, potent, powerful, forceful, effective, effectual, cogent, influential, decisive. *Antonyms:* UNIMPORTANT; INSIGNIFICANT.

telltale *adjective* *the telltale signs of age* revealing, revelatory, suggestive, meaningful, significant, indicative; *inf.* giveaway.

temerity *noun* *have the temerity to call him a liar* effrontery, impudence, audacity, cheek, gall, presumption, presumptuousness, brazenness, rashness, recklessness, foolhardiness.

temerity
audacity, effrontery, foolhardiness, gall, impetuosity, rashness

The line that divides boldness from foolishness or stupidity is often a fine one. Someone who rushes hastily into a situation without thinking about the consequences might be accused of **rashness**, while **temerity** implies exposing oneself needlessly to danger while failing to estimate one's chances of success (*she had the temerity to criticize her teacher in front of the class*). **Audacity** describes a different kind of boldness, one that disregards moral standards or social conventions (*he had the audacity to ask her if she would mind paying for the trip*). Someone who behaves with **foolhardiness** is reckless or downright foolish (*climbing the mountain after dark was foolhardiness and everyone knew it*), while **impetuosity** describes an eager impulsiveness or behavior that is sudden, rash, and sometimes violent (*his impetuosity had landed him in trouble before*). **Gall** and **effrontery** are always derogatory terms. *Effrontery* is a more formal word for the flagrant disregard of the rules of propriety and courtesy (*she had the effrontery to call the president by his first name*), while *gall* is more colloquial and suggests outright insolence (*he was the only one who had the gall to tell the boss off*).

temper *noun* **1** *he is of an equable temper* temperament, disposition, nature, humor, mood, character, frame of mind, cast of mind, mind, attitude, stamp. *See* TEMPERAMENT 1. **2** *the temper of the times* tenor, tone, attitude, vein. **3** *he is in a temper* bad mood, ill humor, fury, rage, passion, fit of temper/pique, tantrum. **4** *a display of temper* ill humor, anger, annoyance, fury, rage, irritation, irritability, irascibility, hotheadedness, petulance, peevishness, resentment, surliness, churlishness. **5** *lose one's temper* composure, equanimity, self-control, coolness, calm, calmness, tranquillity, good humor; *inf.* cool.
temper *verb* **1** *temper the metal* toughen, anneal, harden, strengthen, fortify. **2** *temper justice with mercy* moderate, soften, tone down, modify, mitigate, alleviate, allay, palliate, mollify, assuage, lessen, weaken.
temperament *noun* **1** *of an equable/nervous temperament* disposition, nature, humor, mood, character, personality, makeup, constitution, complexion, temper, spirit, mettle, frame of mind, cast of mind, mind, attitude, outlook, stamp, quality. **2** *actors often are people of temperament* excitability, emotionalism, volatility, mercurialness, capriciousness, moodiness, oversensitivity, touchiness, hotheadedness, impatience, petulance; moods.
temperamental *adjective* **1** *temperamental differences between them | a temperamental dislike of parties* constitutional, inherent, innate, inborn, congenital, deep-rooted, ingrained. **2** *actors are often temperamental people* excitable, emotional, volatile, mercurial, oversensitive, capricious, erratic, touchy, moody, hotheaded, explosive, impatient, petulant.
Antonyms: CALM; STABLE; EASYGOING.
temperance *noun* **1** *now leading a life of temperance after his excesses* moderation, self-restraint, self-control, abstemiousness, continence, abstinence, austerity, self-denial. **2** *former alcoholics now practicing temperance* teetotalism, abstinence, abstention, sobriety, prohibition.
temperate *adjective* **1** *lead a temperate life* moderate, self-restrained, restrained, abstemious, self-controlled, self-denying, austere, continent. **2** *the temperate members of the party* teetotal, abstinent, sober. **3** *temperate winds/climates* moderate, mild, gentle, clement, balmy, pleasant, agreeable.
Antonyms: INTEMPERATE; IMMODERATE; EXTREME.
tempest *noun* **1** *ships/houses buffeted by the tempest* storm, gale, hurricane, squall, cyclone, tornado, typhoon, whirlwind. **2** *their squabble erupted into a tempest* storm, uproar, commotion, furor, disturbance, tumult, turmoil, upheaval.
tempestuous *adjective* **1** *tempestuous weather* stormy, turbulent, blustery, squally, windy, gusty, breezy. **2** *a tempestuous affair* stormy, turbulent, boisterous, violent, wild, uncontrolled, unrestrained, passionate, impassioned, emotional, intense, fierce, heated, feverish, hysterical, frenetic.
temple *noun* place/house of worship, holy place, house of God, synagogue, church, mosque, shrine, sanctuary.
tempo *noun* **1** *the lively tempo of the music* beat, rhythm, cadence, throb, pulse, pulsation. **2** *the tempo of life today* pace, rate, speed, measure.
temporal *adjective* **1** *temporal affairs* secular, nonspiritual, worldly, material, earthly, carnal. **2** *temporal measurements* of time, time-related.
Antonyms: SPIRITUAL; ETERNAL.
temporarily *adverb* **1** *temporarily out of order* for the time being, for the moment, for now, for the nonce, pro tem. **2** *he was temporarily in love with her* briefly, fleetingly, for a short time, for a little while, momentarily, transiently.
temporary *adjective* **1** *just a temporary job* short-term, impermanent, interim, provisional, pro tem, pro tempore. **2** *a temporary infatuation* brief, fleeting, passing, momentary, short-lived, here today and gone tomorrow, transient, transitory, ephemeral, fugitive, evanescent, fugacious.
Antonyms: PERMANENT; CONSTANT.

temporary
ephemeral, evanescent, fleeting, transient, transitory

Things that don't last long are called **temporary**, which emphasizes a measurable but limited duration (*a temporary appointment as chief of staff*). Something that is **fleeting** passes almost instantaneously and cannot be caught or held (*a fleeting thought; a fleeting glimpse*). **Transient** also applies to something that lasts or stays only a short time (*transient house guests*), while **transitory** refers to something that is destined to pass away or come to an end (*the transitory pleasure of eating*). **Evanescent** and **ephemeral** describe what is even more short-lived. *Ephemeral* literally means lasting for only a single day, but is often used to describe anything that is slight and perishable (*his fame was ephemeral*). *Evanescent* is a more lyrical word for whatever vanishes almost as soon as it appears. In other words, a job might be *temporary*, an emotion *fleeting*, a visitor *transient*, a woman's beauty *transitory*, and glory *ephemeral*, but the flash of a bird's wing across the sky would have to be called *evanescent*.

tempt verb **1** *tempt him to break the law by bribing him* | *she is tempted to run away* try to persuade, entice, incite, induce, egg on, urge, goad, prompt, sway, influence, persuade, cajole, coax. **2** *rows of glamorous gifts to tempt buyers* allure, lure, entice, attract, whet the appetite of, make one's mouth water, captivate, appeal to, beguile, inveigle, woo, seduce, tantalize. **3** *tempt fate* fly in the face of, risk, bait, provoke.

---

tempt
allure, beguile, entice, inveigle, lure, seduce
When we are under the influence of a powerful attraction, particularly to something that is wrong or unwise, we are **tempted**. **Entice** implies that a crafty or skillful person has attracted us by offering a reward or pleasure (*she was enticed into joining the group by a personal plea from its handsome leader*), while **inveigle** suggests that we are enticed through the use of deception or cajolery (*inveigled into supporting the plan*). If someone **lures** us, it suggests that we have been tempted or influenced for fraudulent or destructive purposes or attracted to something harmful or evil (*lured by gang members*). **Allure** may also suggest that we have been deliberately tempted against our will, but the connotations here are often sexual (*allured by her dark green eyes*). **Seduce** carries heavy sexual connotations (*seduced by an older woman*), although it can simply mean prompted to action against our will (*seduced by a clever sales pitch*). While **beguile** at one time referred exclusively to the use of deception to lead someone astray, nowadays it can also refer to the use of subtle devices to lead someone on (*a local festival designed to beguile the tourists*).

---

temptation noun **1** *subject the jury to temptation* enticement, incitement, inducement, urging, influence, persuasion, cajolery, coaxing. **2** *the*

dessert cart was a temptation allurement, lure, attraction, draw, bait, pull, enticement, inducement, invitation, decoy, snare; *inf.* come-on. **3** *the temptation of the desserts* allure, attractiveness, appeal, fascination, tantalization.

tempting adjective *a tempting array of goods* alluring, enticing, attractive, captivating, appealing, beguiling, fascinating, tantalizing, appetizing, mouthwatering.
Antonym: REPELLENT.

tenable adjective **1** *tenable theories/objections* justifiable, defensible, defendable, arguable, maintainable, supportable, plausible, credible, reasonable, rational, sound, viable. **2** *positions tenable only for a year* holdable, occupiable, available.
Antonyms: INDEFENSIBLE; UNTENABLE.

tenacious adjective **1** *the eagle held its prey in a tenacious grip* clinging, firm, fast, tight, strong, forceful, powerful, unshakable, iron. **2** *tenacious efforts/individuals* persistent, pertinacious, determined, dogged, resolute, firm, steadfast, purposeful, unshakable, unswerving, relentless, inexorable, unyielding, inflexible, stubborn, obstinate, intransigent, obdurate, strong-willed, contumacious. **3** *a tenacious memory* retentive, retaining, remembering, unforgetful. **4** *tenacious clay* sticky, gluey, adhesive, clinging.
Antonyms: LOOSE; IRRESOLUTE; HESITANT.

tenacity noun **1** *the tenacity of its grip* firmness, fastness, tightness, strength, force, forcefulness, power. **2** *admire her tenacity* persistence, pertinacity, determination, doggedness, resolution, resoluteness, resolve, firmness, steadfastness, purposefulness, purpose, strength of purpose, application, diligence, relentlessness, inexorableness, inflexibility, stubbornness, obstinacy, intransigence, obduracy, strong will. **3** *the tenacity of his memory* retentiveness. **4** *the tenacity of the clay* stickiness, glueyness, adhesiveness.

tenant noun occupier, occupant, resident, inhabitant, renter, leaseholder, lessee, holder, possessor.

tend[1] verb **1** *he tends to lose his temper* have/show a tendency, be apt/disposed/liable, be likely. **2** *the graph tends upward* move, go, head, point, gravitate.

tend[2] verb *tend the sick/cows* look after, take care of, care for, attend to, minister to, see to, cater to, nurse, wait on, watch over, watch, guard, keep an eye on, keep.

tendency noun **1** *he has a tendency to dishonesty* inclination, disposition, predisposition, proclivity, propensity, proneness, aptness, bent, leaning, penchant, susceptibility, liability. **2** *the upward tendency of the graph* movement, direction, course, drift, bias, trend.

tender adjective **1** *tender meat* not tough, easily chewed, succulent, juicy, soft. **2** *tender blossoms/shoots* easily damaged, breakable, fragile, frail, delicate, sensitive, slight, feeble. **3** *they*

are still of tender years | a tender youth young, youthful, early; immature, callow, inexperienced, green, raw. **4** *have a tender heart* compassionate, softhearted, kind, kindly, sympathetic, warm, caring, humane, gentle, solicitous, generous, benevolent, sentimental, emotional, susceptible, vulnerable. **5** *have tender feelings for her* fond, loving, affectionate, warm, emotional, amorous. **6** *awake tender memories* warm, fond, emotional, touching, moving, poignant, evocative. **7** *a tender spot on her arm* sore, painful, aching, smarting, throbbing, inflamed, irritated, red, raw, bruised. **8** *a tender subject requiring tact* delicate, sensitive, difficult, tricky, ticklish, risky.
Antonyms: TOUGH; DURABLE; CRUEL.

tender *verb* **1** *tender assistance | tender a proposal* offer, proffer, present, extend, give; volunteer, put forward, propose, suggest, advance, submit. **2** *tender for the job* put in a bid, bid, give an estimate, propose a price.

tenderness *noun* **1** *the tenderness of the meat* succulence, softness. *See* TENDER *adjective* 1. **2** *the tenderness of the blossoms/shoots* fragility, frailness, frailty, delicacy, sensitivity, sensitiveness, slightness, feebleness. **3** *the tenderness of their years* youthfulness, immaturity, callowness, inexperience, greenness. **4** *the tenderness of her heart* compassion, compassionateness, softheartedness, kindness, kindliness, sympathy, warmth, humaneness, gentleness, solicitousness, generosity, benevolence, sentimentality, emotionalism, vulnerability. **5** *the tenderness of his feelings for her* fondness, love, affection, affectionateness, warmth, emotion, amorousness. **6** *the tenderness of the topic* delicacy, delicateness, sensitivity, sensitiveness, difficulty, trickiness, ticklishness, riskiness. **7** *the tenderness of the wounded area* soreness, pain, painfulness, ache, aching, smarting, throbbing, inflammation, irritation, redness, rawness, bruising.

tenet *noun* doctrine, creed, credo, principle, belief, conviction, persuasion, view, opinion, theory, thesis, hypothesis, postulation.

tenor *noun* **1** *the tenor of his speech* drift, gist, essence, import, vein, meaning, purport, intent. **2** *follow the even tenor of his ways* settled course, prevailing trend, movement, current, flow, direction, drift.

tense *adjective* **1** *tense ropes* pulled tight, tight, taut, rigid, stretched, strained. **2** *feeling tense about the interview* strained, under a strain, under pressure, nervous, keyed up, worked up, overwrought, distraught, anxious, uneasy, worried, apprehensive, agitated, jumpy, edgy, on edge, restless, jittery, fidgety; *inf.* uptight, wound up, strung out. **3** *there were some tense moments in the negotiations/plot* nerve-racking, stressful, worrying, fraught, exciting, cliffhanging.
Antonyms: SLACK; CALM; COOL; relaxed.

tension *noun* **1** *the tension of the ropes* tightness,

tautness, rigidity, stretching, straining. **2** *the tension of waiting | full of tension* strain, stress, stressfulness, suspense, pressure, anxiety, unease, disquiet, worry, apprehensiveness, agitation, jumpiness, edginess, restlessness; nerves; *inf.* butterflies in the stomach. **3** *the tension between the two sides grew* strain, unease, ill feeling, hostility, enmity.

tentative *adjective* **1** *a tentative proposal/plan* speculative, conjectural, experimental, exploratory, trial, provisional, test, pilot, untried, unproven, unconfirmed, unsettled, indefinite. **2** *take a few tentative steps* hesitant, hesitating, faltering, wavering, uncertain, unsure, doubtful, cautious, diffident, timid.
Antonyms: DEFINITE; confident.

tenterhooks *plural noun* **on tenterhooks** in suspense, on edge, edgy, jumpy, jittery, keyed up, overwrought, anxious, apprehensive, uneasy, worried; *inf.* uptight, waiting for the ax to fall, waiting for the other shoe to drop.

tenuous *adjective* **1** *a tenuous connection between the two events* fragile, slight, flimsy, weak, insubstantial, shaky, sketchy, doubtful, dubious, nebulous, hazy, vague, unspecific, indefinite. **2** *a tenuous thread* fine, thin, slender.

tepid *adjective* **1** *tepid water* lukewarm, warmish. **2** *he is rather tepid about the idea | a tepid reaction* unenthusiastic, apathetic, halfhearted, indifferent, cool.
Antonyms: HOT; COLD; ENTHUSIASTIC.

term *noun* **1** *fail to understand the technical term* word, expression, phrase, name, title, denomination, appellation, designation. **2** *the chairman's term of office* period, time, spell, interval, stretch, span, duration, space.

term *verb* *what do they term the process?* call, name, entitle, style, dub, label, tag, designate, denominate.

terminal *adjective* **1** *a terminal illness* fatal, deadly, mortal, lethal, killing, incurable. **2** *a terminal patient* dying, on one's deathbed, near death, in the throes of death, incurable. **3** *terminal markers* boundary, bounding, limiting, confining, end, ending.
Antonyms: INITIAL; INCIPIENT.

terminal *noun* **1** *the terminals of the estate* extremity, end, boundary, bound, limit, edge. **2** *the terminal of the railroad line* terminus, last stop, depot. **3** *seated at the computer terminal* workstation, visual display unit, input/output device; *inf.* VDU.

terminate *verb* **1** *terminate the meeting as soon as you can* bring to a close/end/conclusion, close, end, conclude, finish, stop, wind up, discontinue. **2** *the meeting terminated at midnight* come to a close/end, close, end, conclude, finish, stop. **3** *they terminated his contract* end, bring to an end, stop, cease, discontinue, cancel. **4** *the match terminated in a draw* end, finish, conclude, result. **5** *his contract terminated*

last week end, come to an end, stop, cease, expire, run out, lapse. **6** *terminate a pregnancy* abort, end, put an end to, stop.
Antonyms: BEGIN; START; COMMENCE; INITIATE.

termination *noun* **1** *the termination of the meeting* closing, close, ending, end, conclusion, finish, stopping, winding-up, discontinuance; *inf.* wind-up. **2** *the termination of his contract* end, stopping, cessation, discontinuance, expiry, lapse, cancellation.

terminology *noun* *legal terminology* language, phraseology, vocabulary, nomenclature, jargon, cant, argot; terms, expressions, words; *inf.* lingo.

terminus *noun* *the bus/railroad terminus* last stop, depot, station, end of the line.

terms *plural noun* **1** *tell them in no uncertain terms* words, phrases, expressions; language, mode of expression, manner of speaking. **2** *be on good/unfriendly terms with their neighbors* relations; standing, footing, relationship. **3** *under the terms of the will/treaty* stipulations, specifications, conditions, provisions, provisos, particulars, premises, details, points, clauses. **4** *offer reduced terms in the winter* prices, rates, charges, costs, fees. **come to terms with 1** *they finally came to terms with the neighbors* reach/come to an agreement/understanding with, reach a compromise with. **2** *come to terms with her loss* become reconciled with, reach an acceptance of, learn to live with. **in terms of** *in terms of material wealth, he is poor* with regard to, as regards, regarding, with reference to, as to, in respect of.

terrible *adjective* **1** *he is a terrible bore/flirt* great, extreme, incorrigible, outrageous; *inf.* awful, dreadful, frightful, impossible. **2** *he is a terrible tennis player* bad, poor, incompetent, useless, talentless; *inf.* rotten. **3** *hostages enduring terrible experiences* dreadful, terrifying, frightening, frightful, horrifying, horrible, horrific, horrendous, terrific, harrowing, hideous, grim, unspeakable, appalling, awful, gruesome. **4** *the terrible heat/pain* extreme, severe, harsh, unbearable, intolerable, insufferable. **5** *what is that terrible smell?* nasty, foul, offensive, odious, obnoxious, vile, revolting, repulsive, abhorrent, loathsome, hateful, unpleasant, disagreeable; *inf.* dreadful, awful, horrible, horrid.
Antonyms: BRILLIANT; WONDERFUL; PLEASANT.

terribly *adverb* *terribly good/sad* very, extremely, exceedingly, decidedly, thoroughly; *inf.* awfully, dreadfully, frightfully, terrifically.

terrific *adjective* **1** *a terrific bang/speed* tremendous, great, very great, very big, huge, sizable, considerable, intense, extreme, extraordinary, excessive. **2** *she is a terrific singer* very good, excellent, superb, remarkable, magnificent, wonderful, marvelous, great, super, sensational; *inf.* fantastic, fabulous, A-1, ace, wizard, un-

real, awesome. **3** *there has been a terrific accident* dreadful, frightful, horrible, horrific, hideous, grim, appalling, awful.
Antonyms: AWFUL; DREADFUL.

terrified *adjective* terror-stricken, terror-struck, terrorized, frightened out of one's wits/skin, frightened to death, frightened, scared stiff, scared, petrified, horrified, horror-struck, alarmed, panic-stricken, intimidated, dismayed, appalled, shocked, paralyzed with fear; *inf.* spooked.

terrify *verb* terrorize, frighten to death, frighten, scare stiff, scare, petrify, horrify, make one's blood run cold, make one's flesh crawl, make one's hair stand on end, alarm, panic, intimidate, dismay, appall, shock, paralyze with fear, put the fear of God into; *inf.* spook.

territory *noun* **1** *territories governed by the same ruler* country, state, domain, county, district. **2** *an unexplored territory* region, area, terrain, tract. **3** *the financial affairs of the company are her father's territory* area, area of concern/activity, province, field, sector, department. **4** *a salesman's territory* area, section, route, beat, ambit. **5** *an animal defending its territory* area, domain, space.

terror *noun* **1** fright, fear, fear and trembling, dread, alarm, panic, intimidation, dismay, consternation, shock, horror; *inf.* heebie-jeebies. **2** *imagining all manner of terrors* bogeyman, bugbear, monster, demon, fiend, devil. **3** *that child is a little terror* hooligan, ruffian, hoodlum, villain, rogue, rascal, troublemaker; *inf.* holy terror.

terrorize *verb* **1** *terrorize the hostages* strike terror in/into, terrify, frighten to death, scare stiff, petrify, horrify. *See* TERRIFY. **2** *terrorize them into leaving their homes* coerce, browbeat, bully, intimidate, menace, threaten; *inf.* bulldoze, strong-arm.

terse *adjective* **1** *a terse description of the event* concise, succinct, compact, brief, short, to the point, crisp, pithy, elliptical, epigrammatic. **2** *she sounded terse on the phone* abrupt, curt, brusque, laconic, short, clipped, blunt.
Antonyms: LONG-WINDED; VERBOSE; POLITE.

---

terse
concise, laconic, pithy, succinct

If you don't like to mince words, you'll make every effort to be **concise** in both your writing and speaking, which means to remove all superfluous details (*a concise summary of everything that happened*). **Succinct** is very close in meaning to *concise*, although it emphasizes compression and compactness in addition to brevity (*succinct instructions for what to do in an emergency*). If you're **laconic**, you are brief to the point of being curt, brusque, or even uncommunicative (*his laconic reply left many questions unanswered*). **Terse** can also mean clipped or abrupt (*a terse command*), but it usually connotes something that is both concise and polished (*a terse style of writing that was much admired*). A **pithy** statement is not only succinct but full of substance and meaning (*a pithy argument that no one could counter*).

test noun 1 *a test to distinguish the competent from the incompetent* examination, check, assessment, evaluation, appraisal, investigation, inspection, analysis, scrutinization, scrutiny, study, probe, exploration. 2 *take the bike out for a test* trial, tryout, try, probation, assay. 3 *studying for a test* exam, examination, quiz, set of questions, questionnaire. 4 *the test of a good cake | the test by which a good cake is judged* criterion, touchstone, yardstick, standard, measure, model, pattern.

test verb 1 *test their knowledge of local history* put to the test, examine, check, assess, evaluate, appraise, investigate, scrutinize, study, probe. 2 *their behavior tested his patience* try, tax, strain, put a strain on. 3 *test the bike for oneself* try, try out, put to the test. 4 *test the water for pollution* analyze, assay, check, investigate, scrutinize, explore, probe.

testament noun 1 *left her his estate by testament* will, last wishes, last will and testament. 2 *the sculpture was a testament to his skill* attestation, testimony, evidence, proof, witness; demonstration, indication, exemplification, tribute.

testify verb 1 *asked to testify in court* give evidence, bear witness, attest, be a witness. 2 *she testified to his honesty* swear to, attest to, corroborate, substantiate, verify, vouch for, endorse, support, back up, uphold. 3 *testify that she had witnessed the accident* swear, declare, assert, affirm, state, allege, pledge, profess, avow.

testify to *tears that testified to her guilt* be evidence/proof of, confirm, corroborate, bear out, prove, show, demonstrate, establish, indicate.

Antonyms: DENY; BELIE.

testimonial noun 1 *a testimonial from his previous employer* reference, character reference, recommendation, letter of recommendation, commendation, credential, endorsement, certificate of competence. 2 *given as a testimonial to him* gift, tribute, trophy, memento, souvenir.

testimony noun 1 *challenge the testimony of the witness* evidence, attestation, sworn statement, deposition, affidavit. 2 *he stuck to his testimony that he had seen her before* statement, declaration, assertion, protestation, affirmation, profession, submission, allegation. 3 *her academic record was a testimony to her ability* proof, evidence, verification, corroboration, support; demonstration, manifestation, indication.

testy adjective touchy, irritable, irascible, petulant, cross, ill-tempered, crotchety, crabby, crabbed, snappish, querulous, peevish, grouchy, grumpy, cantankerous, crusty, peppery, fractious.

tête-à-tête noun chat, dialogue, conversation, heart-to-heart, duologue; *inf.* confab, rap.

tether noun *the goat broke free from its tether* rope, cord, chain, lead, leash, line.

tether verb *tether the goat to a stake* tie, tie up, fasten, secure, chain, rope.

text noun 1 *the index follows the text of the book* main body, contents, main matter. 2 *wrote the text of the book* words, wording, script, transcript. 3 *the speaker took foreign policy as his text* theme, subject matter, subject, matter, topic, issue, focus, point, motif. 4 *the texts chosen for the funeral service* passage, verse, quotation, extract, line, abstract, paragraph. 5 *purchasing the assigned texts for biology class* textbook, schoolbook, book, handbook, manual, reader, primer.

texture noun 1 *the texture of her skin* feel, touch, appearance, surface, grain. 2 *fabrics of varying texture* weave, structure, composition, constitution, constituency.

thank verb *thank them for their present/help* offer/extend thanks to, express/show gratitude to, show appreciation to.

thankful adjective 1 *she was thankful to reach home safely* grateful, appreciative, pleased, relieved. 2 *she was thankful to them for taking her in* grateful, indebted, obliged, under an obligation, beholden.

Antonyms: UNGRATEFUL; unappreciative.

thankless adjective 1 *thankless children* ungrateful, unthankful, unappreciative, ungracious, unmannerly. 2 *thankless tasks* unappreciated, unrewarded, unrewarding, unacknowledged, vain, in vain, fruitless, useless.

thanks plural noun *express thanks for their help* gratitude, gratefulness, appreciation, acknowledgment, recognition. **thanks to** *thanks to his late arrival we missed the bus* as a result of, because of, owing to, due to, through, by reason of.

thanks interjection thank you, many thanks, thank you kindly, much obliged, much appreciated.

thaw verb 1 *the frozen juice thawed* defrost, unfreeze, melt, soften, liquefy. 2 *at first she was very aloof, but she soon thawed* become friendly/genial/sociable, relax, loosen up, become responsive.

Antonyms: FREEZE; CHILL; SOLIDIFY.

theater noun 1 *study theater at college* drama, dramatic art, dramaturgy, the stage, show business, thespian art; *inf.* showbiz. 2 *the lecture theater* hall, room. 3 *the theater of war | the theater of civil discord* scene, field, place of action.

theatrical adjective 1 *theatrical performances/careers* dramatic, stage, dramaturgical, show business, thespian; *inf.* showbiz. 2 *theatrical gestures* dramatic, melodramatic, histrionic, emotional, exaggerated, overdone, ostentatious, showy, affected, mannered, stilted, unreal, forced, stagy; *inf.* hammy.

Antonyms: NATURAL; UNAFFECTED; LOW-KEY.

theft noun *a theft at the bookstore | arrested for theft* stealing, robbery, thieving, thievery, burglary, larceny, misappropriation, pilfering, purloining, shoplifting, embezzlement, swindling, fraud; *inf.* swiping, rip-off.

theme *noun* **1** *the theme of the speech* topic, subject, subject matter, matter, thesis, text, argument, burden, idea, keynote. **2** *play the theme from the TV series* theme song, melody, tune, air, leitmotif. **3** *the theme of the fancy dress ball* motif, leitmotif, unifying idea. **4** *students writing themes in French* essay, composition, paper, dissertation.

then *adverb* **1** *we went home then* at that point, at that time/moment, on that occasion. **2** *from then on he was ill* that point, that time/moment, that occasion. **3** *she went and then he went* next, after that, afterward, subsequently, later. **4** *they have the laundry to do, and then there's the cooking* in addition, also, besides, as well, moreover. **5** *you're tired? then you must go home* in that case, that being the case, that being so, under those circumstances. **6** *our hero then received the hand of the princess* so, therefore, thus, consequently.

theological *adjective* religious, scriptural, divine, holy, ecclesiastical, doctrinal, dogmatic.

theoretical *adjective* **1** *theoretical sciences* not practical, conceptual, abstract. **2** *a theoretical situation* hypothetical, conjectural, suppositional, speculative, notional, postulatory, assumed, presumed.
Antonyms: PRACTICAL; CONCRETE; ACTUAL; REAL.

theorize *verb* form/evolve a theory, speculate, conjecture, suppose, hypothesize.

theory *noun* **1** *one of my pet theories* hypothesis, thesis, conjecture, supposition, speculation, guess, notion, postulation, assumption, presumption, opinion, view. **2** *all very well in theory* abstract knowledge, speculative thought, hypothetical situation, the abstract. **3** *scientific theory* system, scheme, philosophy.

therapeutic *adjective* curative, curing, healing, restorative, remedial, health-giving, sanative, reparative, corrective, ameliorative, beneficial, good, advantageous, salutary.

therapy *noun* **1** *limbs responding to therapy* treatment, remedy, cure. **2** *receiving therapy for depression* psychotherapy, psychoanalysis.

thereabouts *adverb* **1** *the keys are over there or thereabouts* about there, near there, around there, around that place. **2** *we will need two hundred or thereabouts* about that, approximately that number/quantity, roughly that number/quantity.

thereafter *adverb* afterward, after that, then, next, subsequently.

therefore *adverb* and so, so, then, thus, accordingly, consequently, as a result, for that reason.

thesis *noun* **1** *his thesis is that the territory is uninhabited* theory, hypothesis, contention, argument, proposal, proposition, premise, postulation, opinion, view, idea. **2** *present a thesis for*

his doctorate dissertation, paper, treatise, disquisition, essay, composition, monograph.

thick *adjective* **1** *walls/concrete/trees that are two feet thick* across, in extent/diameter, wide, broad, deep; of great extent/diameter. **2** *thick legs* broad, wide, large, big, bulky, solid, substantial, fat; *inf.* beefy. **3** *a thick forest* dense, close-packed, concentrated, crowded, condensed, compact, impenetrable, impassable. **4** *thick cream* coagulated, heavy, firm. **5** *thick mists* dense, heavy, opaque, smoggy, soupy, murky, impenetrable. **6** *too thick to understand* stupid, dense, unintelligent, dull-witted, dull, slow-witted, slow, doltish; *inf.* dim, dim-witted, boneheaded. **7** *a thick voice* | *a voice thick with emotion* husky, hoarse, throaty, guttural, rough, indistinct, muffled. **8** *a thick accent* broad, pronounced, marked, strong, rich, obvious, distinct, decided, very great, extreme. **9** *those two are thick these days* friendly, on friendly/good terms, intimate, close, devoted, hand and/in glove, inseparable, familiar; *inf.* palsy-walsy, chummy. **lay it on thick** praise excessively, flatter, overpraise, toady; *inf.* butter up. **thick with 1** *the ground thick with ants* | *thick with dust* teeming with, swarming with, crawling with, alive with, abounding in/with, overflowing with, covered with/in. **2** *the room thick with smoke* full of, filled with; *inf.* chock-full of.
Antonyms: THIN; SPARSE; CLEVER.

thicken *verb* **1** *the gelatin/pudding would not thicken* set, gel, solidify, congeal, clot, coagulate, cake. **2** *the plot thickens* deepen, get more profound, become more involved/complicated/intricate.
Antonyms: DILUTE; thin down (*see* THIN).

thicket *noun* dense growth, tangle, copse, grove, wood.

thickness *noun* **1** *two feet in thickness* width, breadth, depth, diameter, extent. **2** *the thickness of their legs* breadth, broadness, width, wideness, largeness, bigness, bulkiness, solidness, fatness; *inf.* beefiness. **3** *the thickness of the mist* denseness, heaviness, opacity, opaqueness, soupiness, murkiness, impenetrability. **4** *his thickness is unbelievable* stupidity, denseness, dull-wittedness, dullness, slow-wittedness, doltishness; *inf.* dimness, dim-wittedness, boneheadedness. **5** *the thickness of her voice* huskiness, hoarseness, throatiness, gutturalness, roughness, graveliness, indistinctness. **6** *the thickness of his accent* broadness, pronouncedness, markedness, richness, obviousness, decidedness.

thickset *adjective* **1** *thickset linebackers* heavily/solidly built, powerfully built, well-built, heavy, burly, brawny, muscular, bulky, sturdy, stocky; *inf.* beefy. **2** *a thickset hedge/forest* dense, close-packed, crowded, compact.

thick-skinned *adjective* insensitive, unfeeling, tough, unsusceptible, impervious, invulnerable, hardened, case-hardened, callous; *inf.* hard-boiled.

Antonyms: SENSITIVE; THIN-SKINNED.

thief *noun* robber, burglar, housebreaker, larcenist, pilferer, stealer, purloiner, filcher, shoplifter, pickpocket, embezzler, bandit, swindler, fraudster; *inf.* mugger, swiper.

thieve *verb* steal, rob, pilfer, purloin, shoplift, pickpocket, filch, run off with, embezzle, swindle; *inf.* swipe, rip off, knock off, lift.

thin *adjective* **1** *thin lines* narrow, fine, attenuated. **2** *thin materials* fine, light, delicate, flimsy, diaphanous, gossamer, unsubstantial, sheer, transparent, see-through, gauzy, filmy, translucent. **3** *their models have to be thin* slim, slender, lean, slight, svelte, light, spare. **4** *thin and ill-looking* skinny, spindly, lank, lanky, scrawny, scraggy, bony, skeletal, wasted, emaciated, shrunken, anorexic, undernourished, underweight. **5** *thin hair* sparse, scanty, wispy, skimpy. **6** *the audience was rather thin* sparse, scarce, scanty, meager, paltry, scattered. **7** *a thin mixture* dilute, diluted, weak, watery, runny. **8** *a thin voice* weak, small, low, soft, faint, feeble. **9** *a thin excuse* flimsy, unsubstantial, weak, feeble, lame, poor, shallow, unconvincing, inadequate, insufficient.

Antonyms: THICK; FAT; ABUNDANT.

---

thin
gaunt, lean, skinny, slender, spare, svelte

You can't be too rich or too **thin**, but you can be too **skinny**. *Thin* describes someone whose weight is naturally low in proportion to his or her height, although it may also imply that the person is underweight (*she looked pale and thin after her operation*). *Skinny* is a more blunt and derogatory term for someone who is too thin, and it often implies underdevelopment (*a skinny little boy; a tall, skinny fashion model*). Most people would rather be called **slender**, which combines thinness with gracefulness and good proportions (*the slender legs of a Queen Anne table*), or better yet, **svelte**, a complimentary term that implies a slim, elegant figure (*after six months of dieting, she looked so svelte I hardly recognized her*). **Lean** and **spare** are used to describe people who are naturally thin, although *spare* suggests a more muscular leanness (*a tall, spare man who looked like Abraham Lincoln*). **Gaunt**, on the other hand, means so thin that the angularity of the bones can be seen beneath the skin (*looking gaunt after her latest bout with cancer*).

---

thin *verb* **thin down 1** *she has thinned down a lot* become thinner/slimmer, slim down, lose weight, reduce. **2** *thin down the mixture* dilute, water down, weaken. **thin out 1** *thin out the plants/population* reduce in number, lessen, decrease, diminish. **2** *the mist/traffic thinned out* become less dense, decrease, diminish, dwindle.

thing *noun* **1** *people matter more than things* object, article. **2** *a few things to buy* item, article. **3** *where did you get that thing?* object; *inf.* what-d'you-call-it, whatchamacallit, what's-its-name, whatsit, thingamabob, thingamajig. **4** *what a silly/difficult thing to do* action, act, deed, exploit, feat, undertaking, task, job, chore. **5** *what a silly thing to think* idea, thought, notion, concept, theory, conjecture. **6** *say silly things* statement, remark, comment, declaration, utterance, pronouncement. **7** *a terrible thing to happen* event, happening, occurrence, incident, episode. **8** *patience is a useful thing* quality, characteristic, attribute, property, trait, feature. **9** *the poor thing has no home* soul, creature, wretch. **10** *there is another thing you should know* fact, point, detail, particular, aspect. **11** *the latest thing in swimwear* style, fashion, specimen, example. **have a thing about 1** *have a thing about spiders* phobia of, fear of, dislike of, aversion to/toward, obsession with, fixation with/about; *inf.* hang-up about. **2** *have a thing about champagne* liking for/of, love for/of, fancy for, predilection for, penchant for, preference for, taste for, particularity for, inclination for, obsession with, fixation on/with/about, *idée fixe* about. **the thing 1** *the thing is to avoid annoying him* the aim, the intention, the idea, the objective, the object, the purpose. **2** *I have found just the thing for a wedding present* something ideal/appropriate/desirable, something necessary, the right thing, the very thing. **3** *the thing is that he has no money* the fact, the fact of the matter, the point, the issue, the problem.

things *plural noun* **1** *put on dry things | take night things* clothing, attire, apparel; clothes, garments; *inf.* gear, togs. **2** *I will watch your things while you get a ticket* belongings, possessions, paraphernalia; *inf.* stuff, bits and pieces. **3** *her painting things* equipment, apparatus, gear, tackle; implements, tools. **4** *things are getting worse* matters, affairs, circumstances, conditions, relations; the state of affairs, the situation.

think *verb* **1** *I think they will come* believe, suppose, expect, imagine, surmise, conjecture, guess, fancy. **2** *he is thought to be clever* consider, deem, hold, reckon, regard as, assume, presume, estimate. **3** *he is sitting thinking* ponder, meditate, deliberate, contemplate, muse, cogitate, ruminate, cerebrate, concentrate, brood, rack one's brains, be lost in thought, be in a brown study. **4** *who would have thought she would be there* expect, anticipate, imagine, surmise. **think about 1** *he is thinking about his career* contemplate, consider, deliberate about, muse on, mull over, reflect on, weigh up, review. **2** *she is thinking about her youth* think back to/on, call to mind, recall, remember, recollect. **3** *he is thinking about what it would be like to be wealthy* imagine, picture, visualize, envisage, dream about. **think better of** have second thoughts about, reconsider, change one's mind about, decide against. **think nothing of**

regard as quite usual/normal, consider routine, take in one's stride. **think one will** *I think I will go* have a mind to, consider it possible to, intend possibly to. **think over** *think over the implications* contemplate, consider, deliberate about, muse over, mull over, ponder, reflect on, weigh up, consider the pros and cons of. **think up** *think up an advertising slogan* dream up, come up with, devise, invent, create, concoct.

think *noun have a think about the situation* consideration, contemplation, deliberation, muse, reflection.

thinker *noun among the world's great thinkers* philosopher, scholar, intellectual, pundit, sage, theorist; *inf.* intellect, brain.

thinking *noun the latest thinking on welfare reform* view, opinion, outlook, judgment, assessment, appraisal, evaluation, position, theory, reasoning; conclusions, thoughts.

thinking *adjective a thinking person* rational, reasoning, logical, sensible, intelligent, philosophical, contemplative, reflective, meditative.

thin-skinned *adjective* sensitive, oversensitive, hypersensitive, supersensitive, easily offended/hurt, touchy, temperamental.
Antonyms: INSENSITIVE; UNFEELING; THICK-SKINNED.

third-rate *adjective* inferior, poor-quality, low-quality, low-grade, poor, bad, shoddy, mediocre.

thirst *noun* **1** *dying of thirst in the desert* thirstiness, dryness, parchedness, dehydration. **2** *a thirst for knowledge/novelty* desire, craving, longing, hankering, yearning, avidity, keenness, eagerness, hunger, lust, appetite, passion, covetousness; *inf.* yen.

thirst *verb* **thirst for/after** *thirsting for revenge* | *thirsted after knowledge* desire, crave, long for, hanker after, yearn for, hunger after, lust after, covet.

thirsty *adjective* **1** *thirsty people* having a thirst, parched, dehydrated; *inf.* dry. **2** *thirsty land* dry, droughty, parched, dehydrated. **3** *thirsty for knowledge* thirsting, avid, keen, eager, hungry, greedy, covetous.

thong *noun* strip, belt, strap, cord, lash, rope, tie, tether.

thorn *noun* prickle, spike, barb, spine, bristle.

thorny *adjective* **1** *thorny branches* prickly, spiky, barbed, spiny, spined, spinose, bristly, sharp, pointed. **2** *a thorny situation/issue* problematic, awkward, ticklish, difficult, tough, troublesome, bothersome, trying, taxing, irksome, vexatious, worrying, harassing, complicated, convoluted, involved.

thorough *adjective* **1** *a thorough investigation* indepth, exhaustive, complete, comprehensive, full, intensive, extensive, widespread, sweeping, all-embracing, all-inclusive, detailed. **2** *he is slow but thorough* meticulous, scrupulous, assiduous, conscientious, painstaking, punctil-

ious, methodical, careful. **3** *he is a thorough villain* thoroughgoing, out-and-out, utter, downright, sheer, absolute, unmitigated, unqualified, complete, total, perfect.
Antonyms: SUPERFICIAL; CURSORY; CARELESS.

thoroughbred *adjective* **1** *thoroughbred horses* purebred, pure, pure-blooded, full-blooded, pedigreed, pedigree. **2** *the thoroughbred students at the academy* well-bred, highborn, aristocratic, blue-blooded, elegant, graceful, refined, cultivated; *inf.* classy.

thoroughfare *noun* **1** *police directing traffic on the thoroughfare* road, roadway; main road, street; highway, freeway, turnpike, parkway, expressway, throughway; *inf.* pike. **2** *no thoroughfare* passageway, passage, way, access.

thoroughly *adverb* **1** *search the place thoroughly* | *investigate the matter thoroughly* exhaustively, from top to bottom, completely, comprehensively, fully, intensively, extensively, meticulously, scrupulously, assiduously, conscientiously, painstakingly, methodically, carefully, in detail, detailedly. **2** *she is thoroughly spoiled/correct* completely, utterly, absolutely, totally, entirely, unreservedly, positively, dead.

though *conjunction* **1** *he went though he did not want to* although, despite the fact that, in spite of the fact that, notwithstanding that. **2** *he will go though he has to walk* even though, even if, even supposing, despite the possibility that.

though *adverb* *I don't know; I'll find out though* even so, however, but, still, yet, be that as it may, for all that, nonetheless, all the same, notwithstanding.

thought *noun* **1** *incapable of thought* powers of thinking, faculty of reason, power of reasoning. **2** *lost in thought* thinking, reasoning, pondering, meditation, deliberation, cogitation, rumination, musing, mulling, reflection, introspection, contemplation, consideration, cerebration. **3** *a thought came to me as to how we should proceed* idea, notion, line of thinking, theory, opinion. **4** *I had no thought of going* intention, plan, design, purpose, aim. **5** *what are your thoughts on the matter?* judgment, conclusion, appraisal, assessment, estimation, opinion, point of view, position, stance, stand, feeling, sentiment, belief, conviction. **6** *act without thought* | *give the matter thought* consideration, attention, heed, regard, scrutiny, care, carefulness. **7** *give up all thought of winning* expectation, anticipation, hope, prospect, aspiration, dream. **8** *he has no thought for his widowed mother* thoughtfulness, consideration, care, regard, concern, solicitude, kindness, kindliness, compassion, tenderness. **9** *he could be a thought more helpful* little, touch, bit, dash, jot, tinge, trace; *inf.* tad.

thoughtful *adjective* **1** *he seems thoughtful* | *in a thoughtful mood* pensive, reflective, introspective, meditative, contemplative, ruminative, cogitative, absorbed, rapt/lost in thought, in a brown study. **2** *a thoughtful book/essay* pro-

every action he takes is thoughtful considered, circumspect, prudent, careful, cautious, heedful, wary, guarded. **4** *he is a thoughtful son* | *thoughtful acts* considerate, attentive, caring, solicitous, helpful, kind, kindly, compassionate, tender, charitable.
Antonyms: SUPERFICIAL; CARELESS; INCONSIDERATE; THOUGHTLESS.

thoughtless adjective **1** *a very thoughtless person* | *thoughtless remarks* tactless, undiplomatic, indiscreet, insensitive, inconsiderate, careless, selfish, impolite, rude. **2** *his thoughtless actions* unthinking, heedless, careless, unmindful, absentminded, injudicious, foolish, ill-advised, ill-considered, imprudent, unwise, silly, stupid, reckless, rash, precipitate, negligent, neglectful, remiss.
Antonyms: THOUGHTFUL; SENSITIVE; CONSIDERATE; CAREFUL.

thrash verb **1** *rebels thrashed by the dictator's guards* beat, whip, horsewhip, flog, lash, birch, cane, flagellate, scourge, spank, chastise, belt, wallop, lambaste; *inf.* tan. **2** *the home team thrashed the opposition* trounce, rout, vanquish, drub, give a drubbing to, defeat, beat, worst, crush; *inf.* lick, clobber, hammer, slaughter, wipe (up) the floor with. **3** *thrashing around unable to get to sleep* thresh, flail, toss and turn, jerk, twitch, squirm, writhe. **thrash out** *thrash out their differences* discuss, talk over, debate, air, argue out; resolve, settle.

thread noun **1** *embroidered with gold thread* | *needles and thread* yarn, cotton, filament, fiber. **2** *a thread of white through the dark background* strand, line, streak, strip, seam. **3** *lose the thread of the story* train of thought, story line, drift, theme, plot, subject, subject matter, motif, tenor.

thread verb **1** *thread film into a projector* | *thread beads onto a string* pass, string, ease. **2** *she threaded her way through the crowds* inch, wind, push, squeeze, shoulder, elbow.

threadbare adjective **1** *threadbare clothes/upholstery* worn, frayed, tattered, ragged, holey, shabby; *inf.* tatty. **2** *threadbare imagery/jokes/arguments* hackneyed, tired, stale, worn-out, trite, banal, platitudinous, clichéd, cliché-ridden, stock, stereotyped; *inf.* played out.

threat noun **1** *issue threats* threatening remark, warning, menace, menacing, intimidating remark; *lit.* commination. **2** *a threat of rain* | *under threat of war* warning, menace, risk, danger, omen, foreboding, portent. **3** *she is a threat to the smooth running of the company* menace, danger, risk, hazard.

threaten verb **1** *bullies threatening younger children* make threats to, menace, intimidate, browbeat, bully, pressurize; *inf.* lean on. **2** *threaten to tell* announce one's intention. **3** *rain is threatening* be imminent, impend, hang over, loom, foreshadow. **4** *a sky threatening rain* warn of, give warning of, presage, portend,

augur. **5** *pollution threatening the environment* be a threat to, menace, endanger, imperil, put at risk, put in jeopardy, jeopardize.

threatening adjective **1** *make threatening gestures* menacing, warning, intimidating, bullying, minacious, minatory. **2** *threatening signs of a storm* ominous, inauspicious, foreboding.

threesome noun trio, triumvirate, triad, trinity, troika, triunity; triplets.

threshold noun **1** *guests standing at/on the threshold* doorway, doorstep, entrance, entry. **2** *on the threshold of a new era* beginning, commencement, start, outset, inception, opening, dawn, brink, verge, debut; *inf.* kickoff. **3** *threshold of pain* lower limit, minimum.

thrift noun thriftiness, good husbandry, economy, economicalness, economizing, carefulness, frugality, frugalness, sparingness, scrimping, parsimony, penny-pinching, miserliness.

thrifty adjective economical, economizing, careful, frugal, sparing, scrimping, parsimonious, penny-pinching, miserly.
Antonyms: EXTRAVAGANT; WASTEFUL; SPENDTHRIFT.

thrill noun **1** *seeing his hero gave him a thrill* feeling of excitement/stimulation, sensation of joy, wave of pleasure, glow, tingle; *inf.* buzz, charge, kick. **2** *it was a thrill to see the baby take her first steps* thrilling experience, joy, delight, pleasure, adventure. **3** *a thrill of terror ran through him* throb, tremble, tremor, quiver, flutter, shudder, vibration.

thrill verb *seeing the Grand Canyon thrilled him* excite, stimulate, arouse, stir, electrify, move, give joy/pleasure to; *inf.* give a buzz/charge/kick to. **thrill to** *she thrilled to the music* tingle from, be excited by, feel joy from; *inf.* get a buzz/charge/kick out of; get a buzz/charge/kick from.

thrilling adjective **1** *a thrilling experience* exciting, stirring, stimulating, electrifying, rousing, moving, gripping, riveting, joyful, pleasing; *inf.* hair-raising. **2** *a thrilling sensation through the body* throbbing, trembling, tremulous, quivering, shivering, fluttering, shuddering, vibrating.
Antonyms: BORING; DULL; MONOTONOUS.

thrive verb **1** *the business/family is thriving* flourish, prosper, do/go well, boom, burgeon, succeed, advance, get ahead, make progress. **2** *plants thriving* flourish, burgeon, grow vigorously, do well, shoot up.
Antonyms: FAIL; DECLINE; WITHER.

thriving adjective **1** *a thriving business* flourishing, prosperous, prospering, booming, burgeoning, successful, advancing, progressing; *inf.* going strong. **2** *thriving plants* flourishing, burgeoning, growing, healthy, luxuriant, lush, prolific.

throat noun gullet, esophagus.

throb verb *his pulse throbbed rapidly* | *her wound*

throbbed beat, pulse, pulsate, palpitate, pound, vibrate, go pit-a-pat, thump.

throb noun *the throb of her pulse/wound* beating, beat, pulse, pulsating, palpitation, pounding, vibration, pit-a-pat, pitter-patter, thumping.

throes plural noun **1** *the throes of childbirth | death throes* agony, suffering, excruciation, pain, torture, distress; pangs. **2** *in the throes of changing jobs* turmoil, upheaval, disruption, tumult, hurly-burly, confusion, chaos, pandemonium.

throne noun **1** *a golden throne* royal seat, seat of state. **2** *succeed to the throne* sovereignty, rule, command, dominion.

throng noun *a throng of fans* crowd, horde, mob, mass, host, multitude, swarm, flock, pack, herd, drove, press, assemblage, gathering, congregation.

throng verb **1** *people thronged to see the play | they thronged forward* flock, troop, swarm. **2** *fans thronging around the star* crowd, mill, congregate, converge. **3** *fans thronging the stadium* pack, cram, jam, fill.

throttle verb **1** *the attacker throttled him* choke, strangle, strangulate, garrote. **2** *governments trying to throttle opposition* gag, muzzle, silence, stifle, suppress, control, inhibit.

through preposition **1** *go through the building* into and out of, to the other/far side of, from one side to the other of, from end to end of. **2** *he got the job through an advertisement/friend* by means/way of, through the agency of, via, using, with the help/aid/assistance of, under the aegis of, by virtue of, as a result/consequence of, on account of, owing to, because of. **3** *he worked through the night* throughout, during, until the end of. **4** *Monday through Friday* up to and including.

through adverb **1** *just walk through* from one end to another, from end to end. **2** *the baby slept through | we worked through* all the time, without a break, without an interruption, nonstop. **3** *it was a struggle but we got through* to the end/finish/termination, to the completion, to the culmination. **through and through** *he's a villain through and through* thoroughly, completely, utterly, altogether, totally, to the core, entirely, wholly, fully, unreservedly, out and out.

through adjective **1** *I am through and I am going home* finished, finished work, reached the end. **2** *the job is through now* completed, done, finished, ended, terminated; *inf.* washed up. **through with** *she says she's through with acting/boyfriends* finished with, no longer involved with, tired of, fed up with.

throughout preposition **1** *throughout the world/house* all over, all around, in every part of, everywhere in. **2** *working throughout the night* through, all through, for the duration of, until the end of.

throughout adverb **1** *the house is carpeted throughout | they painted the house throughout* all through, right through, in every part, all over, everywhere. **2** *we loved the performance; we were riveted throughout* all the time, until the end, for the duration.

throw verb **1** *throw a brick* hurl, toss, cast, sling, pitch, shy, lob, propel, launch, project, send; *inf.* heave, chuck. **2** *throw his arms in the air* move quickly/suddenly, turn quickly/suddenly. **3** *throw a shadow* cast, project, send. **4** *throw a glance/smile at him* cast, send, dart, bestow on, give. **5** *the wrestler threw his opponent* throw/hurl to the ground, fell, floor, prostrate. **6** *the horse threw his rider* unseat, dislodge. **7** *his question threw me* disconcert, discomfit, disturb, confound, astonish, surprise, dumbfound, discountenance. **8** *threw the switch* operate, turn/switch on, move. **9** *the potter throwing a vase* shape, form, mold, fashion. **10** *she threw on her clothes* pull on, put on quickly, don quickly, slip into. **throw away 1** *throw away his textbooks* throw out, discard, get rid of, dispose of, jettison, scrap, reject, dispense with; *inf.* dump, ditch. **2** *throw away a good opportunity* fail to exploit, make poor use of, waste, squander, fritter away, lose; *inf.* blow. **throw off 1** *throw off their shackles* cast off, discard, shake off, drop, jettison, free/rid oneself of, abandon. **2** *throw off one's pursuers* shake off, outdistance, outrun, evade, escape from, get away from, elude, give someone the slip, lose, leave behind. **throw out 1** *throw out old letters* throw away, discard, get rid of, dispose of, jettison, scrap. **2** *throw out the troublemakers* eject, evict, expel, show the door to, put out; *inf.* kick out. **3** *throw out a proposal* reject, give the thumbs down to, turn down, dismiss, disallow. **4** *fires throwing out heat* emit, radiate, give off, diffuse, disseminate.

throw noun *hit the target with one throw of the ball* hurl, toss, cast, sling, pitch, lob; *inf.* heave, chuck. **a throw** *jackets at $50 a throw* each, apiece, per item, for one; *inf.* a pop.

thrust verb **1** *thrust the money at the taxi driver* push, shove, ram. **2** *thrust open the door* push, shove, drive, press, prod, propel. **3** *thrust responsibility on him* force, impose, push, press, urge. **4** *fencers learning to thrust* stab, pierce, stick, jab, lunge at. **5** *thrust their way through the crowd* push, shove, press, force, shoulder, elbow, jostle.

thrust noun **1** *with one thrust of his fist* push, shove, ram, drive, press, prod. **2** *killed by the black knight's thrust* stab, jab, lunge. **3** *surprised by the enemy's sudden thrust* advance, push, drive, attack, offensive, assault, charge, onslaught, incursion, raid. **4** *upset by her nasty thrust* verbal attack/assault, criticism, censure, hostile remark. **5** *a man with thrust* drive, push, force, impetus, energy, assertiveness, aggression, ambition; *inf.* get-up-and-go. **6** *the thrust of the engine | the thrusts in the bridge* motive force, propulsive force, force, pressure. **7** *they* *failed to grasp the thrust of the speech* gist, drift, substance, essence, theme, subject, thesis.

thrusting *adjective a thrusting young salesman* forceful, pushing, forward, energetic, assertive, aggressive, insistent, ambitious; *inf.* pushy.
Antonyms: RETICENT; MEEK.

thud *noun fall with a thud* thump, clunk, crash, smack, wham, bang, wallop.

thud *verb* **1** *thudding around in heavy boots* thump, clump, clunk. **2** *branches thudding against the window* thump, clunk, crash, smack, knock, bang.

thug *noun* ruffian, tough, rough, hoodlum, bully, hooligan, villain, gangster, robber, bandit, murderer, killer, assassin; *inf.* hood, goon, mobster, hit man.

thumb *noun all thumbs* clumsy, awkward, maladroit, inept; *inf.* butterfingered, ham-handed. **thumbs down** rejection, refusal, no, negation, rebuff, disapproval. **thumbs up** acceptance, affirmation, yes, approval, encouragement; *inf.* go-ahead, OK, green light.

thumb *verb thumb through the book* leaf, flick, flip, riffle, browse, skim, scan.

thumbnail *adjective a thumbnail sketch* succinct, concise, compact, short, brief, pithy, quick, rapid.

thump *verb* **1** *he thumped her attacker* strike, hit, punch, thwack, wallop, smack, slap, batter, beat, cudgel, knock, thrash; *inf.* whack, belt, clout, lambaste. **2** *my heart/head is thumping* pound, thud, pulse, pulsate, throb, palpitate. **3** *thumping on the table* bang, batter, beat, crash, knock, rap.

thump *noun* **1** *give the attacker a thump* blow, punch, thwack, wallop, smack, slap; *inf.* whack, belt, clout, lambasting. **2** *give the table a thump* bang, knock, rap. **3** *the shoe landed with a thump* thud, clunk, crash, smack, wham, bang, wallop.

thumping *adjective* **1** *hear a thumping noise* thudding, clunking, banging. **2** *a thumping lie/majority* huge, massive, enormous, immense, vast, colossal, gigantic, mammoth, monumental, great, tremendous, impressive, extraordinary; *inf.* whopping, thundering.

thunder *noun the thunder of guns/applause* boom, booming, rumble, rumbling, outburst, roar, roaring.

thunder *verb* **1** *his voice thundered in my ear* boom, rumble, roar, blast, resound, reverberate. **2** *thundering at the crowd to be quiet* roar, bellow, bark, yell, shout. **thunder against** *workers thundering against management* fulminate against, rail against, denounce, curse, threaten.

thundering *adjective a thundering lie/majority* huge, massive, enormous, immense, vast, colossal, great, tremendous; *inf.* thumping. *See* THUMPING *adjective* 2.

thunderous *adjective thunderous voices/applause* booming, rumbling, roaring, resounding, re-

759

verberating, deafening, earsplitting, loud, noisy, tumultuous.

thunderstruck *adjective* amazed, astonished, dumbfounded, astounded, speechless, struck dumb, open-mouthed, at a loss for words, aghast, stunned, staggered, startled, taken aback, surprised, disconcerted, shocked, nonplussed, bewildered; *inf.* flabbergasted, bowled over, knocked for a loop, floored, flummoxed.

thus *adverb* **1** *hold the apparatus thus* like this, in this way, so, like so. **2** *he is the eldest son and thus inherits the estate* so, that being so, therefore, accordingly, hence, consequently, as a result, for this/that reason, on this/that account, ergo. **3** *having come thus far* so, to this extent.

thwack *verb* hit, strike, slap, smack, wallop, thump, punch, box, knock, beat, batter, pound, pummel; *inf.* whack, belt, clout, bop, slug, lambaste.

thwack *noun* hit, slap, smack, wallop, thump, punch, knock; *inf.* whack, clout, bop, slug.

thwart *verb thwart their plans | he was thwarted in his aims* frustrate, foil, balk, check, block, stop, prevent, defeat, impede, obstruct, hinder, hamper, stymie.
Antonyms: ASSIST; HELP; FACILITATE.

---

thwart
baffle, balk, foil, frustrate, inhibit

These verbs refer to the various ways in which we can outwit or overcome opposing forces. **Thwart** suggests using cleverness rather than force to bring about the defeat of an enemy or to block progress toward an objective (*thwart a rebellion; have one's goals thwarted by lack of education*). **Balk** also emphasizes setting up barriers (*a sudden reversal that balked their hopes for a speedy resolution*), but it is used more often as an intransitive verb meaning to stop at an obstacle and refuse to proceed (*he balked at appearing in front of the angry crowd*). To **baffle** is to cause defeat by bewildering or confusing (*the police were baffled by the lack of evidence*), while **foil** means to throw off course so as to discourage further effort (*her plan to arrive early was foiled by heavy traffic*). **Frustrate** implies rendering all attempts or efforts useless (*frustrated by the increasingly bad weather, they decided to work indoors*), while **inhibit** suggests forcing something into inaction (*to inhibit wage increases by raising corporate taxes*). Both *frustrate* and *inhibit* are used in a psychological context to suggest barriers that impede normal development or prevent the realization of natural desires (*he was both frustrated by her refusal to acknowledge his presence and inhibited by his own shyness*).

---

tic *noun a tic in his eye/face* twitch, spasm, jerk.

tick *noun the tick of a clock/timer* ticking, click, beat, tap, tapping, tick-tock.

tick *verb the clock/timer was ticking* click, beat, tap, sound, tick-tock. **tick off** *ticked off by their lateness* annoy, irritate, rile, aggravate; *inf.* peeve.

ticket *noun* **1** *show your ticket to enter* pass, token, stub, coupon, card. **2** *the ticket on the garment* label, tag, price tag.

tickle *verb* **1** *tickle the child under the chin* stroke, pet, touch. **2** *tickle one's fancy* interest, excite, stimulate, arouse, captivate, please, gratify, delight. **3** *we were tickled by the antics of the children* amuse, entertain, divert, cheer, gladden.

ticklish *adjective a ticklish situation* difficult, problematic, awkward, delicate, sensitive, tricky, thorny, knotty, touchy, risky, uncertain, precarious; *inf.* sticky.

tidbit *noun* **1** *keep some tidbits for the children/dogs* tasty morsel, treat, snack, delicacy; *inf.* goody. **2** *neighborhood gossips passing on tidbits* piece of gossip, bit of scandal, juicy/spicy item/story.

tide *noun the tide of events* course, movement, direction, trend, current, drift, run, tendency, tenor.

tide *verb* **tide over** *this money will tide us over until payday* help out, assist, aid, keep one going, see one through, keep one's head above water, keep the wolf from one's door.

tidings *plural noun good tidings | hear tidings of his death* news, notification, word, communication, information, intelligence, advice; reports; *inf.* info, low-down.

tidy *adjective* **1** *a tidy room/garden* neat, trim, orderly, in order, in good order, well-ordered, spruce, shipshape, well-kept, clean, spick-and-span. **2** *children looking tidy* neat, well-groomed, spruce. **3** *people who are tidy by nature* neat, orderly, organized, well-organized, methodical, systematic, businesslike. **4** *leave a tidy sum* considerable, sizable, substantial, goodly, handsome, generous, ample, largish, large, respectable, fair, decent, healthy. *Antonyms:* UNTIDY; MESSY; SCRUFFY; UNKEMPT.

tidy *verb* **1** *tidy (up) the living room | tidy your desk* clean, clean up, put to rights, put in order, straighten, make shipshape. **2** *tidy oneself (up) for the interview* spruce up, groom, smarten, neaten.

tie *verb* **1** *tie the dog to the tree | the boat was tied fast to the jetty* tie up, fasten, attach, fix, bind, secure, tether, moor, lash, join, connect, link, couple, rope, chain. **2** *tie the string/knot* knot, make a bow/knot in. **3** *the two teams tied* draw, be equal, be even, be neck and neck. **tie down** *tied down by responsibilities* restrict, confine, curb, limit, constrain, restrain, hamper, hinder, impede, cramp. **tie in** *her evidence does not tie in with that of other people* fit in, tally, concur, conform, dovetail. **tie up** **1** *tie up the dog/boat* fasten, attach, bind, secure, tether, moor, connect, rope, chain. **2** *tie up the package* wrap, wrap up, bind, truss. **3** *his capital is tied up in*-vest, commit. **4** *the meeting will tie him up all morning* occupy, engage, keep busy, engross, take up one's attention. **5** *we should tie up the meeting/arrangements/contract* finalize, conclude, bring to a conclusion, wind up, complete, finish off; *inf.* wrap up. *Antonyms:* UNTIE; LOOSEN.

tie *noun* **1** *trash bags fastened with a tie* ligature, link, fastening, fastener, clip, catch. **2** *men wearing ties* necktie, bow tie, cravat, neckerchief. **3** *family/business ties* bond, connection, relationship, kinship, affiliation, allegiance, liaison, friendship. **4** *the game ended in a tie* draw, dead heat, deadlock, stalemate.

tier *noun* **1** *tiers of seats* row, level, bank, line. **2** *the tiers of a wedding cake* layer, level. **3** *the tiers of the parking garage* level, story. **4** *the tiers of hierarchy in the firm* layer, level, echelon, rank.

tight *adjective* **1** *keep a tight grip* fast, secure, fixed, clenched, clinched. **2** *tight ropes/muscles* taut, rigid, stiff, tense, stretched, strained. **3** *a tight skirt rather than a full one* narrow, tight-fitting, close-fitting, figure-hugging. **4** *a tight mass of fibers* compact, compacted, compressed. **5** *space was a bit tight with so many people* cramped, restricted, limited, constricted. **6** *the box must be tight* impervious, impenetrable, sound, sealed, hermetic; watertight, airtight. **7** *money is a bit tight just now* scarce, scant, sparse, in short supply, limited, insufficient, inadequate. **8** *security was tight at the press conference* strict, rigorous, stringent, tough, rigid, uncompromising, exacting. **9** *in a tight situation* problematic, difficult, precarious, hazardous, dangerous, perilous, tricky, ticklish, worrying, delicate; *inf.* sticky. **10** *a piece of tight prose* concise, succinct, terse, crisp, straightforward, pithy, epigrammatic. **11** *it was a tight race* close, even, evenly matched, neck and neck. **12** *he got tight at the party* drunk, intoxicated, inebriated, tipsy; *inf.* tiddly, under the influence, plastered, smashed, wasted, wrecked, pickled, stewed, out of it, blotto, three sheets to the wind. **13** *tight with his money* tight-fisted, mean, miserly, parsimonious, stingy, niggardly. *Antonyms:* LOOSE; SLACK; GENEROUS.

tighten *verb* **1** *she tightened her grip* secure, make fast, make more secure. **2** *tighten the rope* tauten, make tight/taut, stretch, make rigid, rigidify, stiffen, tense. **3** *tighten the lid* screw on, close. **4** *tighten security* increase, make stricter, make rigorous/stringent/rigid. **5** *his throat tightened* narrow, constrict, contract. *Antonyms:* LOOSEN; slacken; RELAX.

till *preposition* **1** *he played till six o'clock | playing till they went home* until, up to, as late as, up to the time that/of. **2** *we had not seen him till then* before, prior to, previous to, earlier than.

till *noun money in the till* cash register, cashbox, cash drawer, strongbox.

till *verb till the soil/field* cultivate, work, farm, plow, dig, turn over.

tilt *verb the building tilts a bit* lean, list, slope, slant, incline, tip, cant.

tilt *noun the building/picture is at a tilt* | *with a tilt of his head* angle, slant, slope, incline, inclination, cant. **at full tilt** at full speed, at breakneck speed, headlong, very rapidly/quickly/swiftly, with great force.

timber *noun* **1** *timber for building the house* wood; lumber. **2** *the ceiling/ship's timbers* beam, spar, pole.

time *noun* **1** *in the time of the dinosaurs* age, era, epoch, period. **2** *he worked there for a time* while, spell, stretch, span, period, term. **3** *the last time I saw him* occasion, point, juncture. **4** *now is the time to act/leave* moment, point, instant, stage. **5** *the places I have been in my time* lifetime, life, life span. **6** *have a hard time* | *they were good times* condition, circumstance; situation, experience. **7** *beat time* | *in waltz time* rhythm, measure, tempo, beat, meter. **8** *he never has any time to himself* freedom, leisure, leisure time, spare time; moments, odd moments. **ahead of time** early, earlier than expected, in good time, with time to spare. **all the time 1** *they whispered all the time that he was speaking* throughout the time, for the duration of the time. **2** *he works all the time* constantly, always, at all times, perpetually, continuously, continually. **at one time 1** *at one time he worked there* at one point, once, time was when, in the past, previously, formerly, hitherto. **2** *several matches going on at one time* simultaneously, concurrently, at once, at the same time, together. **at the same time 1** *they arrived at the same time* simultaneously, together, concurrently. **2** *he is wealthy; at the same time, he lives frugally* nevertheless, nonetheless, however, but, still, yet, just the same. **at times** from time to time, every now and then, periodically, on occasion, occasionally. **behind time** late, running late, behind schedule. **behind the times** old-fashioned, out of date, dated, outmoded, obsolete, passé, antiquated; *inf.* old hat. **for the time being** for now, for the moment/present, in the meantime, meanwhile, temporarily, pro tem. **from time to time** now and then, every so often, once in a while, at times, periodically, on occasion, occasionally, sometimes. **in no time 1** *your parents will be here in no time* very soon, any moment/minute now, before one knows it; *inf.* in a jiffy. **2** *he did the job in no time* very rapidly/quickly/swiftly, speedily, at great speed, expeditiously, with dispatch. **in good time** punctually, on time; early, ahead of time, with time to spare. **in time 1** *he did not reach the station in time* early enough, punctually, in good time, at the appointed/right time, on schedule. **2** *they will forget in time* eventually, ultimately, as time goes on/by, by and by, one day, someday, sooner or later, in the long run. **many a time** often, frequently, many times, on many occasions. **on time** punctually, early enough, in good time, sharp; *inf.* on the dot. **time after time** again

and again, many times over, repeatedly, time and again, time and time again, recurrently, frequently, often, on many occasions.

time *verb* **1** *time the meeting for the afternoon* schedule, fix, set, arrange, program. **2** *time his progress* | *time the race* clock, measure, calculate, regulate, count. **3** *time the film exposure* | *time his entrance* regulate, adjust, set, synchronize.

timeless *adjective* ageless, enduring, lasting, permanent, abiding, unending, ceaseless, undying, deathless, eternal, everlasting, immortal, changeless, immutable, indestructible.
Antonyms: EPHEMERAL; FLEETING.

timely *adjective their timely intervention* opportune, well-timed, at the right time, convenient, appropriate, seasonable, felicitous.
Antonyms: ILL-TIMED; INCONVENIENT.

---

timely
opportune, propitious, seasonable
Some people seem to have a knack for doing or saying the right thing at the right time. A **timely** act or remark is one that comes at a moment when it is of genuine value or service (*a timely interruption*), while an **opportune** one comes in the nick of time, as if by accident, and exactly meets the needs of the occasion (*a storm came up at an opportune moment, squelching enthusiasm for the fight*). **Seasonable** applies to whatever is suited to the season of the year or fits in with the needs of the moment or the character of the occasion (*seasonable weather; a seasonable menu for a cold winter day*). **Propitious** means presenting favorable conditions. In other words, while a warm day in December might not be *seasonable*, it might very well be *propitious* for the sailor setting off on a round-the-world cruise.

---

timetable *noun bus timetables* | *the timetable for the conference* schedule, program, calendar, list, agenda.

timid *adjective* **1** *too timid to stand up to the bully* easily frightened, timorous, fearful, apprehensive, afraid, frightened, scared, faint-hearted, cowardly, pusillanimous; *inf.* chicken, yellow, lily-livered. **2** *too timid to speak to strangers* shy, diffident, bashful, reticent, unselfconfident, timorous, shrinking, retiring, coy, demure.
Antonyms: BOLD; BRAZEN.

timorous *adjective* **1** *too timorous to fight* timid, fearful, apprehensive. *See* TIMID 1. **2** *too timorous to introduce herself* timid, shy, diffident. *See* TIMID 2.
Antonyms: BRAVE; BOLD.

tincture *noun* **1** *tincture of iodine* solution, suspension, infusion. **2** *a tincture of pink in the material* tint, color, shade, tinge. **3** *a tincture of garlic* flavor, taste, smell, aroma, trace. **4** *a tincture of heresy in their attitude* hint, suggestion, trace, touch, dash, soupçon.

tinge verb 1 *wallpapers tinged with silver* color, tint, shade, dye, stain, suffuse, imbue. 2 *admiration slightly tinged with envy* flavor, color, suffuse, imbue.

tinge noun 1 *a tinge of silver in the wallpaper* color, tint, shade, tone, tincture, cast, dye, stain, wash. 2 *a tinge of sadness in her attitude* hint, suggestion, trace, touch, bit, dash, tincture, soupçon.

tingle verb *my fingers were tingling* prickle, prick, tickle, itch, sting, quiver, tremble.

tingle noun 1 *the tingle in her fingers* tingling, prickling, pricking, tickle, itch, quiver, trembling; *inf.* pins and needles. 2 *feel a tingle of excitement* quiver, tremor, thrill, throb.

tinker verb *tinker with the engine* | *tinker at computers* fiddle, play, toy, tamper, fool (around), mess (about).

tinkle verb *the bell tinkled* ring, chime, peal, ding, jingle.

tinkle noun *the tinkle of the wind chimes* ring, chime, peal, ding, jingle, jangle.

tinsel noun 1 *Christmas trees decorated with tinsel* metallic yarn, spangle, clinquant. 2 *dislike the tinsel of the occasion* ostentation, showiness, flashiness, pretentiousness, display, glitter, ornateness, flamboyance, gaudiness, garishness, tawdriness, meretriciousness.

tint noun 1 *several tints to choose from* shade, color, tone, tinge, cast, tincture. 2 *bold colors contrasting with tints* pastel, pale color, soft color. 3 *a hair tint* dye, rinse, colorant, coloring.

tiny adjective minute, diminutive, miniature, mini, minuscule, infinitesimal, microscopic, dwarfish, midget, pocket-sized, Lilliputian, wee, petite, small, little, insignificant, trifling, negligible, inconsequential; *inf.* teeny, teeny-weeny, itsy-bitsy, pint-sized.
Antonyms: HUGE; ENORMOUS; GIGANTIC.

tip[1] noun 1 *the tip of an iceberg* | *the mountain tip* point, peak, top, summit, apex, crown. 2 *the tip of the fingers* end, extremity. 3 *the tip of an umbrella* point, end. 4 *the chair legs have rubber tips* cap, cover.

tip[2] verb *the table tends to tip* tilt, lean, list, cant, slant. **tip over** 1 *the chair/boat tipped over* topple (over), overturn, fall over, turn topsy-turvy, capsize. 2 *he tipped over the bottle/canoe* upset, overturn, topple, upend, capsize.

tip[3] noun 1 *give the waiter a tip* gratuity, *pourboire*, baksheesh; *inf.* little something. 2 *tips on how to take out stains* hint, suggestion, recommendation, piece of advice; advice.

tip[4] verb *tip the waiter* give a tip to, reward, remunerate. **tip off** *the police had been tipped off that the fugitive was nearby* warn, forewarn, advise, inform, notify, caution, alert.

tip-off noun *the police received a tip-off about the fugitive's whereabouts* warning, forewarning, hint, clue; advice, information, notification.

tipsy adjective drunk, intoxicated, inebriated; *inf.* tiddly, tight, under the influence, merry, high.
Antonyms: SOBER; ABSTEMIOUS.

tirade noun diatribe, harangue, stream of abuse, verbal onslaught, lecture, upbraiding, denunciation, obloquy, philippic; invective, vituperation, fulmination, censure, vilification.

tire verb 1 *climbing the mountain tired him* tire out, fatigue, wear out, weary, exhaust, drain, enervate, debilitate, jade; *inf.* take it out of. 2 *he tires easily* get/grow/become tired, get fatigued, flag, droop; *inf.* poop out. 3 *their constant boasting tires me* bore, weary, irk, irritate, get on one's nerves, annoy, exasperate; *inf.* get to. **tire of** *he never tires of hearing the story* | *she tired of her lover* grow bored with, become weary of, be fed up with; *inf.* be sick of.

tired adjective 1 *feel tired after the climb* fatigued, worn out, weary, wearied, exhausted, drained, enervated, debilitated, jaded; *inf.* done, done in, all in, beat, dog-tired, bushed, pooped (out), dead on one's feet, ready to drop. 2 *tired children ready for bed* sleepy, drowsy, weary; *inf.* asleep on one's feet. 3 *tired jokes* stale, hackneyed, familiar, worn-out, outworn, well-worn, clichéd, stock, platitudinous, trite, banal; *inf.* corny. 4 *made tired by their chatter* bored, wearied, irked, irritated, annoyed, exasperated. **tired of** *he was tired of listening to the story* bored with, weary of, wearied of, fed up with; *inf.* sick of, sick to death.
Antonyms: ENERGETIC; LIVELY; FRESH.

---

tired
exhausted, fatigued, tuckered, weary

Tired is what you are after you've cleaned the house, spent two hours reading a dull report, or trained for a marathon; it means that you are drained of your strength and energy, without giving any indication of degree. **Weary**, on the other hand, is how you feel after you've had to interrupt your dinner five or six times to answer the phone. It implies not only a depletion of energy but also the vexation that accompanies having to put up with something that is, or has become, disagreeable. **Exhausted** means that you are totally drained of strength and energy, a condition that may even be irreversible (*exhausted by battling a terminal disease*). **Fatigued** is a more precise word than either *tired* or *weary*; it implies a loss of energy through strain, illness, or overwork to the point where rest or sleep is essential (*fatigued after working a 24-hour shift*). **Tuckered** is an informal word that comes close in meaning to *fatigued* or *exhausted*, but often carries the suggestion of loss of breath (*tuckered out after running up six flights of stairs*).

---

tireless adjective *tireless workers/efforts* untiring, unwearied, unflagging, indefatigable, energetic, industrious, vigorous, determined, resolute, dogged.

tiresome adjective 1 *tiresome work* wearisome,

laborious, wearing, tedious, boring, monotonous, dull, uninteresting, unexciting, humdrum, routine. **2** *she is a tiresome child* troublesome, irksome, vexatious, irritating, annoying, exasperating, trying.
Antonyms: INTERESTING; EXCITING; PLEASANT.

tiring *adjective a tiring journey/job* wearying, wearing, fatiguing, exhausting, draining, enervating, arduous, laborious, strenuous, exacting, taxing, tough.

tissue *noun a tissue of lies* web, network, fabric, nexus, mass, conglomeration, set, series, chain.

titillate *verb titillated by the romantic setting* excite, arouse, stimulate, provoke, thrill, interest, fascinate, tantalize, seduce; *inf.* turn on.
Antonyms: BORE; turn off (*see* TURN).

titillating *adjective titillating conversation* exciting, arousing, stimulating, provocative, thrilling, interesting, fascinating, tantalizing, suggestive, seductive, erotic.

title *noun* **1** *what is the title of the book/musical?* name. **2** *picture/illustration titles* credit, caption, legend, inscription, heading. **3** *what is the title of the ship's officer?* form of address, designation, appellation, name, denomination, epithet, sobriquet; *inf.* moniker, handle. **4** *disputing his title to the land* entitlement, right, claim, ownership, proprietorship, possession, holding. **5** *lose the titles to the land* deed, ownership document, proof of ownership. **6** *boxers contending for the title* championship, first place, crown; laurels.

title *verb he titled the poem "Sunburst"* entitle, name, call, designate, label, tag, style, term.

titter *noun* snicker, snigger, giggle, tee-hee, laugh, chuckle, cackle; *inf.* chortle.

titular *adjective* **1** *a titular description* naming, designative, appellative, denominative, identifying, labeling. **2** *the titular head of state* nominal, in title/name only, so-called, self-called, self-styled, *soi-disant*, token, puppet, putative.

toady *noun the boss and a couple of his toadies* sycophant, fawner, flatterer, groveler, kowtower, lackey, flunky, minion, hanger-on, parasite, leech, jackal; *inf.* yes-man, crawler, bootlicker.

toady *verb toady to he toadies to his superiors* bow and scrape to, be obsequious to, fawn on, flatter, grovel to, kowtow to, curry favor with; *inf.* butter up, fall all over, suck up to.

toast *verb* **1** *toast the bread* brown, crisp, grill. **2** *toast oneself at the fire* warm (up), heat (up). **3** *toast the winner* drink (to) the health of, drink to, pledge, salute.

toast *noun* **1** *drink/make a toast to the winner* pledge, salutation, salute, tribute; compliments, greetings. **2** *she was the toast of the town* celebrity, darling, favorite, heroine, hero.

today *noun* **1** *today is his birthday* this day, this very day. **2** *today is all that matters to the young* the present, the present time, now, the here and now, this moment, this time, this period, this age.

toddle *verb* totter, teeter, wobble, falter, dodder.
toddle off go, leave, depart.

to-do *noun* commotion, fuss, fuss and bother, bother, trouble, disturbance, uproar, tumult, brouhaha, bustle, hustle and bustle.

together *adverb* **1** *friends who work together* with each other, in conjunction, jointly, conjointly, in cooperation, as one, in unison, side by side, hand in hand, hand and/in glove, shoulder to shoulder, cheek by jowl. **2** *they arrived/shouted together* simultaneously, concurrently, at the same time, at once, all at once, in unison, with one accord, synchronously. **3** *it rained for days together* in a row, in succession, successively, consecutively, on end, one after the other, continuously, without a break, without interruption. **4** *they have got it/things together at last* organized, sorted out, straight, to rights, settled, fixed, arranged.

together *adjective she seems very together* composed, calm, cool, well-balanced, stable, well-adjusted, well-organized, efficient.

toil *verb* **1** *they toiled away on the land | toiling at their books* labor, slog, slave, push oneself, drive oneself, strive, drudge, work, work doggedly, work like a dog/slave/Trojan; *inf.* work one's fingers to the bone, sweat, grind. **2** *they toiled up the hill* labor, struggle, drag oneself; *inf.* sweat.

toil *noun years of toil wore him out* hard/heavy work, labor, slaving, drudgery, striving, industry, effort, exertion, travail, sweat of one's brow; *inf.* elbow grease, grind.

toilet *noun* lavatory, bathroom, rest room, washroom, men's room, ladies' room, powder room, convenience, urinal, latrine, privy, outhouse; *inf.* john, can.

token *noun* **1** *a white flag being a token of surrender | a token of friendship* symbol, sign, emblem, badge, representation, indication, mark, manifestation, expression, demonstration, recognition, index; evidence. **2** *keep the menu as a token of the celebration* memento, souvenir, keepsake, remembrance, reminder, memorial. **3** *slot machine tokens* disk, counter, slug, coin, substitute coin.

token *adjective* **1** *a token strike to emphasize union solidarity* symbolic, emblematic. **2** *offer token resistance* perfunctory, superficial, nominal, minimal, slight, hollow.

tolerable *adjective* **1** *the pain/noise level was scarcely tolerable* endurable, bearable, sufferable, supportable, brookable, acceptable. **2** *his work was tolerable, but far from brilliant* fairly good, fair, all right, passable, adequate, satisfactory, good enough, average, mediocre, middling, fair to middling, ordinary, run-of-the-mill, indifferent, unexceptional; *inf.* not bad, OK, so-so, nothing to write home about.
Antonyms: INTOLERABLE; UNBEARABLE; INSUFFERABLE.

tolerance noun **1** *treat the young with tolerance* toleration, open-mindedness, lack of prejudice/bias, broad-mindedness, liberalism, forbearance, patience, magnanimity, understanding, charity, lenience, lenity, indulgence, permissiveness, complaisance, laxness. **2** *his tolerance of pain | accept the situation with tolerance* toleration, endurance, sufferance, acceptance, fortitude, stamina, hardiness, resilience, toughness.

tolerant adjective *tolerant people accepting the beliefs of others | tolerant of the views of others* open-minded, unprejudiced, unbiased, unbigoted, broad-minded, liberal, catholic, forbearing, patient, long-suffering, magnanimous, sympathetic, understanding, charitable, lenient, indulgent, permissive, free and easy, easygoing, complaisant, lax.
Antonyms: INTOLERANT; NARROW-MINDED.

tolerate verb **1** *tolerate opposition | tolerate other people's views* permit, allow, admit, sanction, warrant, countenance, brook, recognize, acknowledge. **2** *unable to tolerate the pain/noise* endure, bear, suffer, take, stand, put up with, abide, accept, stomach, submit to. **3** *able to tolerate the new drug/treatment* take, receive, be treated with.

toleration noun **1** *treat the young with toleration* broad-mindedness, open-mindedness, tolerance, indulgence. See TOLERANCE 1. **2** *his toleration of the noise levels | accept it with toleration* tolerance, endurance, acceptance. See TOLERANCE 2. **3** *countries that do not practice toleration* religious tolerance, freedom of worship, religious freedom, freedom of conscience.

toll noun **1** *pay a toll to use the bridge/road* charge, fee, payment, levy, tariff. **2** *the death toll* cost, damage, loss.

toll verb **1** *bells tolling in the distance* sound, ring, peal, knell, clang. **2** *toll the bells* sound, ring. **3** *bells tolling (for) his death | tolling the outbreak of war* announce, herald, signal, warn of. **4** *clocks tolling 6 o'clock* strike, chime.

tomb noun grave, burial place/chamber, sepulcher, vault, crypt, catacomb, mausoleum.

tombstone noun headstone, gravestone, grave marker, memorial, monument.

tome noun volume, book, work, opus.

tomfoolery noun horseplay, mischief, fooling, foolery, clowning, skylarking, buffoonery, nonsense; pranks, tricks, capers, antics, larks; *inf.* shenanigans, monkey business.

tone noun **1** *the pleasant tone of the flute* sound, sound quality, color, pitch, timbre, tonality. **2** *speak in an angry tone | whisper in soft tones* tone of voice, mode of expression, expression, intonation, inflection, modulation, accentuation. **3** *the tone of his letter was optimistic* mood, air, attitude, character, manner, spirit, temper, tenor, vein, drift, gist. **4** *lower the tone of the place* style, quality, high quality. **5** *deco-*

rated *in tones of pink* tint, shade, tinge, cast, tincture.

tone verb **tone down 1** *tone down the brightness of the colors* soften, lighten, subdue, mute. **2** *tone down your aggressive approach* moderate, soften, modulate, play down, temper, subdue, dampen, restrain, soft-pedal.

tongue noun **1** *speak in a foreign tongue* language, speech, parlance, dialect, idiom, patois, vernacular; *inf.* lingo. **2** *he has a glib tongue* way of speaking, mode of expression.

tongue-tied adjective at a loss for words, wordless, speechless, bereft of speech, struck dumb, dumb, silent, mute, taciturn, inarticulate.
Antonyms: FLUENT; ARTICULATE.

tonic noun restorative, refresher, stimulant, analeptic, pick-me-up, boost, fillip; *inf.* shot in the arm, picker-upper.

too adverb **1** *the dog came, too | think, too, of her age* as well, also, in addition, besides, furthermore, moreover, to boot. **2** *she is too busy* excessively, overly, unduly, inordinately, unreasonably, extremely, very; *inf.* too-too.

tool noun **1** *the tools of his trade | kitchen tools* implement, instrument, utensil, device, apparatus, gadget, appliance, machine, contrivance, contraption, aid. **2** *he is the manager's tool* puppet, pawn, minion, lackey, flunky, henchman, toady; *inf.* stooge.

---

tool
apparatus, appliance, implement, instrument, utensil
A wrench is a **tool**, meaning that it is a device held in and manipulated by the hand and used by a mechanic, plumber, carpenter, or other laborer to work, shape, move, or transform material (*he couldn't fix the drawer without the right tools*). An **implement** is a broader term referring to any tool or mechanical device used for a particular purpose (*agricultural implements*). A washing machine is an **appliance**, which refers to a mechanical or power-driven device, especially for household use (*the newly-married couple went shopping for appliances*). A **utensil** is a hand-held implement for domestic use (*eating utensils*), while an **instrument** is used for scientific or artistic purposes (*musical instrument; surgical instrument*). **Apparatus** refers to a collection of distinct instruments, tools, or other devices that are used in connection or combination with one another for a certain purpose (*the gym was open, but the exercise apparatus had not been set up*).

---

tool verb **1** *tool leather* shape, work, cut, chase, decorate, ornament. **2** *tooling along the highway* drive, ride, motor.

top noun **1** *the top of the mountain/hill* highest point/part, summit, peak, pinnacle, crest, crown, tip, apex, vertex, apogee. **2** *he is at the top of his career* height, high point, peak, pinnacle, zenith, acme, culmination, climax, crowning point, prime, meridian. **3** *the top of* *the table/milk* upper part, upper surface, upper layer. **4** *put the top on the bottle/jar* cap, lid, stopper, cork, cover. **5** *she wore a blue top* shirt, T-shirt, blouse, jersey, sweater, sweatshirt. **6** *turnip tops* leaves, shoots; stem, stalk.

top *adjective* **1** *the top drawer/floor* topmost, uppermost, highest. **2** *top scientists* foremost, leading, principal, preeminent, greatest, finest; *inf.* top-notch. **3** *the top managers/positions in the firm* leading, chief, principal, main, highest, ruling, commanding. **4** *top goods* top-quality, top-grade, best, finest, prime, choicest, quality, excellent; *inf.* A-1, top-notch. **5** *at top speed* maximum, maximal, greatest, utmost.

top *verb* **1** *ice cream topped with chocolate sauce* cap, cover, finish, garnish. **2** *she tops the list of candidates* head, lead, be first in. **3** *donations have topped the $1,000 mark | topped our expectations | he topped his previous record* surpass, exceed, go beyond, transcend, better, best, beat, excel, outstrip, outdo, outshine, eclipse. **4** *top the mountain* reach the top of, climb, scale, ascend, mount, crest.

topcoat *noun* overcoat, greatcoat.

topic *noun* subject, subject matter, theme, issue, matter, point, question, argument, thesis, text.

topical *adjective* *write about topical issues* newsworthy, in the news, current, up-to-date, up-to-the-minute, contemporary, popular.
Antonyms: OUT OF DATE, OUTDATED.

topmost *adjective* **1** *the topmost drawer* top, uppermost, highest. **2** *the topmost authority on the subject* top, foremost, leading, principal, preeminent. **3** *the topmost people/positions in the organization* top, leading, chief, principal. *See* TOP *adjective* 3.

top-notch *adjective* first-rate, top-grade, excellent, choice, superior, superb; *inf.* A-1, ace, crack.

topple *verb* **1** *the load was unstable and toppled* fall over, tip over, keel over, overturn, capsize. **2** *his kick toppled the trash can* upset, knock over, push over, tip over, capsize. **3** *the rebels toppled the tyrant* overthrow, oust, unseat, overturn, bring down, bring low.

topsy-turvy *adverb/adjective* **1** *children turning topsy-turvy on the jungle gym* upside down, wrong side up, head over heels. **2** *turn the house topsy-turvy looking for the documents* in disorder, in confusion, in a muddle, in chaos, in disarray, in a mess, upside down.

torment *noun* **1** *endured the torment of grief/captivity/illness* agony, suffering, torture, pain, excruciation, anguish, hell, misery, distress, affliction, wretchedness. **2** *he was a torment to them* scourge, curse, plague, bane, affliction, thorn in the flesh, irritation, irritant, vexation, annoyance, worry, nuisance, bother, trouble, pest; *inf.* pain in the neck.

torment *verb* **1** *tormented by illness/bullies/conscience* cause agony/suffering/pain to, inflict anguish on, afflict, harrow, plague, torture, distress, worry, trouble. **2** *tormented the new*

teacher tease, irritate, vex, annoy, pester, harass, badger, plague, worry, be a nuisance to, bother, trouble, be a pest to.

torn *adjective* **1** *torn clothes* ragged, tattered, ripped, split, slit, cut, lacerated, rent. **2** *I am torn between the two dresses* divided, split, wavering, vacillating, irresolute, uncertain, unsure, undecided.

tornado *noun* cyclone; *inf.* twister.

torpid *adjective* sluggish, slow-moving, slow, dull, lethargic, heavy, inactive, stagnant, inert, somnolent, sleepy, languorous, languid, listless, apathetic, passive, slothful, indolent, lazy.
Antonyms: ENERGETIC; ACTIVE.

torpor *noun* torpidity, sluggishness, slowness, dullness, lethargy, heaviness, inactivity, stagnation, inertia, somnolence, sleepiness, languor, languidness, listlessness, apathy, passivity, sloth, slothfulness, indolence, laziness.

torrent *noun* **1** *torrents of floodwaters* flood, deluge, inundation, spate, cascade, rush, stream, current. **2** *get soaked in the torrent* downpour, deluge, rainstorm. **3** *a torrent of abuse* outburst, stream, volley, outpouring, barrage, battery.

torrid *adjective* **1** *the torrid conditions in the desert* hot, arid, sweltering, scorching, boiling, parching, sultry, stifling. **2** *torrid love scenes* passionate, impassioned, ardent, fervent, fervid, amorous, erotic; *inf.* steamy.
Antonyms: COLD; PASSIONLESS; UNEMOTIONAL.

tortuous *adjective* **1** *a tortuous mountain path* twisting, winding, curving, curvy, sinuous, undulating, coiling, serpentine, snaking, snaky, zigzag, convoluted, meandering, spiraling, anfractuous. **2** *a tortuous description of the incident* convoluted, roundabout, circuitous, indirect, involved, complicated, ambiguous. **3** *his tortuous policy* devious, cunning, tricky, deceitful, deceptive, guileful.
Antonyms: STRAIGHT; STRAIGHTFORWARD.

torture *noun* **1** *use torture to extract a confession* persecution, pain, ill-treatment, abuse, suffering, punishment, torment. **2** *the torture of a toothache | the torture of grief* torment, agony, anguish, distress. *See* TORMENT *noun* 1.

torture *verb* **1** *torture the hostages* persecute, inflict pain/suffering on, abuse, ill-treat, punish, torment; *inf.* work over. **2** *tortured by the pain of his wound | tortured by his conscience* torment, rack, cause agony/suffering/pain to, inflict anguish on, afflict, harrow, plague, distress, worry, trouble.

toss *verb* **1** *toss the book over here* throw, hurl, cast, sling, pitch, shy, lob, propel, launch, project; *inf.* heave, chuck. **2** *tossing and turning restlessly | tossing around unable to sleep* thrash, wriggle, writhe, squirm, roll, tumble. **3** *ships tossing around on the waves* rock, roll, sway, undulate, pitch, lurch, heave. **4** *toss one's head* throw back, throw up, jerk, jolt.

tot *noun* baby, infant, toddler, child, little one, mite.

total *noun the total of those figures is 500 | score a total of six goals* sum, sum total, aggregate, whole, entirety, totality.

total *adjective* **1** *the total number of votes | the total amount spent* complete, entire, whole, full, comprehensive, combined, aggregate, composite, integral. **2** *he is a total idiot | it was a total disaster* complete, thorough, thoroughgoing, all-out, utter, absolute, downright, out and out, outright, sheer, rank, unmitigated, unqualified.

total *verb* **1** *these figures total more than $1,000* add up to, come to, amount to. **2** *total these figures rapidly* add up, sum, count up, count, calculate, reckon. **3** *total a car* wreck, smash up, crash, destroy, demolish, write off.

totalitarian *adjective totalitarian government* one-party, monocratic, undemocratic, autocratic, authoritarian, absolute, despotic, dictatorial, tyrannical, oppressive, fascist.

Antonyms: DEMOCRATIC; autonomous.

totality *noun* **1** *the grant in its totality will not cover the expense* entirety, entireness, wholeness, fullness, completeness, inclusiveness. **2** *the totality was less than expected* total, sum, aggregate, whole, entirety; all, everything.

totally *adverb totally blind | forget totally* completely, entirely, wholly, fully, thoroughly, utterly, absolutely, quite.

totter *verb* **1** *tottering on high heels* teeter, wobble, stagger, stumble, reel, sway, roll, lurch. **2** *tables/buildings tottering in the explosion* shake, sway, rock, lurch, shudder. **3** *the regime is tottering* be unstable, be unsteady, be shaky, be on the point of collapse, falter.

touch *verb* **1** *the wires are touching* be in contact, come into contact, come together, meet, converge, be contiguous, adjoin, abut. **2** *he touched her arm* press lightly, tap, brush, graze, feel, stroke, pat, fondle, caress. **3** *do not touch the glassware* handle, hold, pick up, move, play with, toy with, fiddle with, interfere with. **4** *she did not touch her meal | never touch alcohol* eat, consume, drink, take, partake of. **5** *they were touched by the child's sad plight* affect, move, make an impression on, have an impact on, influence, upset, disturb, make sad, arouse sympathy; *inf.* get to. **6** *the recession did not touch him* have an effect on, affect, concern, involve, have a bearing on, be relevant/pertinent to. **7** *they would not touch anything illegal* be associated with, concern/involve oneself in, have dealings with, deal with, handle, be a party to. **8** *no one can touch him at tennis* come near (to), come up to, compare with, be on a par with, equal, match, be a match for, be in the same league as, parallel, rival; *inf.* hold a candle to. **9** *their speed touched 100 miles per hour | they touched rock bottom* reach, get up/down to, at-

tain, arrive at, come to. **10** *touch his father for money* ask, beg, borrow from. **touch down** *the plane touched down at midnight* land, alight, arrive. **touch off** **1** *touch off the explosive* set off, ignite, trigger, explode, detonate. **2** *the statement touched off a storm of protest* set off, start, begin, set in motion, initiate, instigate, trigger, launch. **touch on/upon** **1** *touch on the financial situation in his speech* refer to, mention, comment on, remark on, allude to, bring in, speak of, talk about, write about, deal with. **2** *his actions touched on treason* come close to, verge on, incline to, be tantamount to. **touch up** **1** *touch up the paint on the door* patch up, fix up, repair, refurbish, renovate, revamp, give a face-lift to. **2** *touch up a photograph* improve, enhance.

touch *noun* **1** *feel a touch on his arm* pressure, tap, strike, hit, blow, brush, stroke, pat, caress. **2** *sense its presence by touch* feel, feeling, sense of touch, tactile sense, tactility. **3** *the material has a velvety/steely touch* feel, texture, grain, finish, surface, coating. **4** *a touch of garlic/professionalism | a touch downhearted* small amount, bit, trace, dash, taste, spot, drop, pinch, speck, smack, suggestion, hint, soupçon, tinge, tincture, whiff, suspicion. **5** *admire the player's/artist's touch* craftsmanship, workmanship, artistry, performance, dexterity, deftness, skill, virtuosity, adroitness. **6** *the room needs a few extra touches* detail, feature, addition, accessory, fine point. **7** *I think the teacher is losing his touch* skill, skillfulness, expertise, technique, knack, adeptness, ability, talent, flair. **8** *the house needs a woman's touch* influence, effect, hand, handling, direction, management, technique, method. **9** *be/get in touch with old friends | lose touch* contact, communication, correspondence.

touch-and-go *adjective a touch-and-go situation | it was touch-and-go whether he got the job* uncertain, precarious, risky, hazardous, dangerous, critical, suspenseful, cliff-hanging, hanging by a thread.

touched *adjective* **1** *he was touched by their thoughtfulness* moved, impressed, affected, softened, warmed. **2** *he must be a bit touched to do that* unbalanced, unhinged, deranged, demented, crazed, mad, insane; *inf.* daft, balmy, batty, dotty, nutty, screwy.

touching *adjective* **1** *a touching act of kindness* moving, impressive, affecting, warming, heartwarming. **2** *a touching story of a sad childhood* affecting, moving, emotive, stirring, upsetting, disturbing, saddening, pitiful, piteous, poignant, pathetic, heartbreaking, heartrending.

touchstone *noun* criterion, yardstick, benchmark, norm, standard, gauge, guide, exemplar, model, pattern.

touchy *adjective* **1** *he is very touchy about his lack of height/results* sensitive, oversensitive, hypersensitive, easily offended, thin-skinned; testy, irascible, irritable, grouchy, grumpy, peevish, querulous, bad-tempered, captious, crabbed, cross, surly. **2** *a touchy situation* tricky, ticklish, delicate, precarious, chancy, risky, uncertain. *Antonyms:* CALM; AFFABLE; GOOD-HUMORED.

tough *adjective* **1** *a tough substance* strong, durable, resistant, resilient, sturdy, firm, solid, hard, rigid, stiff. **2** *tough meat* chewy, leathery, gristly, stringy, fibrous, sinewy. **3** *have to be tough to survive those conditions* hardy, strong, fit, sturdy, rugged, stalwart, vigorous, strapping, robust, resilient. **4** *a tough job managing the firm* difficult, hard, arduous, onerous, heavy, uphill, laborious, strenuous, exacting, taxing, stressful. **5** *teachers getting tough with the children | police getting tough with criminals* firm, strict, stern, severe, harsh, hard-hitting, adamant, inflexible. **6** *tough exam questions* difficult, hard, knotty, thorny, baffling, perplexing, ticklish. **7** *a tough way of life* hard, harsh, austere, rugged, bleak, grim, dire, rough, taxing, exacting. **8** *led astray by tough kids* rough, rowdy, unruly, disorderly, violent, wild, lawless, lawbreaking, criminal. **9** *it was tough that he had to lose* unfortunate, unlucky, hard, regrettable; *inf.* too bad. *Antonyms:* SOFT; TENDER; WEAK; EASY.

tough *noun set on by a gang of toughs* ruffian, rowdy, thug, hoodlum, hooligan, bully; *inf.* roughneck, bruiser.

toughen *verb* **1** *toughen the glass* strengthen, fortify, reinforce, harden, rigidify. **2** *toughen the laws* stiffen, tighten, make stricter, make severe; *inf.* beef up.

tour *noun* **1** *a world tour | a coach tour through France* trip, excursion, journey, expedition, jaunt, outing, peregrination. **2** *give the visitors a tour of the new building* guided tour, walk around, visit, inspection. **3** *on a golfing tour* circuit, ambit, round, course, beat. **4** *troops doing a tour in the Persian Gulf* tour of duty, duty, stint, stretch, turn.

tour *verb* **1** *touring the world | touring France* travel around/round/through, journey through, explore, vacation in. **2** *tour the new building/estate* go around, walk/drive around, visit, sightsee, inspect.

tourist *noun* visitor, sightseer, vacationer, traveler, excursionist, journeyer; *inf.* globe-trotter.

tournament *noun a tennis tournament* competition, contest, series, meeting, event, match; *inf.* tourney.

tousled *adjective tousled hair* rumpled, disheveled, uncombed, unkempt, disordered, disarranged, untidy, messy; *inf.* mussed up.

tout *verb tout their wares* hawk, peddle, sell, offer for sale.

tow *verb towing a car/sled* pull, draw, drag, haul, tug, trail, lug.

tow *noun gave the car a tow* towing, haul. **in tow** *he had his family/girlfriend in tow* in attendance, by one's side, in one's charge, under one's protection.

toward *preposition* **1** *walk toward the door/town* in the direction of, to, on the way to, en route for. **2** *his attitude toward her success* with regard to, as regards, regarding, with respect to, respecting, in relation to, concerning, about, apropos. **3** *working toward a degree* for, with the aim of, in order to obtain/achieve. **4** *the money will go toward the hospital appeal fund* as a contribution to, for, to help, to assist. **5** *toward the end of the day/journey* near, nearing, around, close to, coming to, just before, shortly before.

tower *noun* **1** *the tower at the top of the church/castle* steeple, spire, belfry, bell tower, turret, column, pillar, obelisk, minaret. **2** *soldiers manning the tower* fortress, fort, citadel, stronghold, fortification, keep, castle.

tower *verb mountains towering into the skies* soar, rise, ascend, mount, rear, reach/stand high. **tower above** *he towers above the rest of the modern poets | his writing towers above the rest* surpass, excel, outshine, outclass, overshadow, cap, top, transcend, eclipse, be head and shoulders above, put in the shade; *inf.* run circles around.

towering *adjective* **1** *towering mountain peaks | towering skyscrapers* high, tall, lofty, elevated, sky-high. **2** *in a towering rage* extreme, mighty, fierce, terrible, intense, violent, vehement, passionate, frenzied, frantic. **3** *one of the towering intellects of his age* outstanding, extraordinary, preeminent, surpassing, superior, great, incomparable, unrivaled, peerless.

town *noun* community; borough, municipality, township, urban area.

toxic *adjective* poisonous, venomous, virulent, noxious. *Antonyms:* non-toxic; HARMLESS; SAFE.

toy *noun* **1** *children's toys* plaything, game. **2** *the rich woman surrounds herself with toys* trinket, bauble, knickknack, gewgaw, trifle, triviality.

toy *adjective* **1** *a toy car | toy soldiers* model, miniature, imitation, make-believe. **2** *toy breeds of dog* small, tiny, miniature, diminutive.

toy *verb* **toy with** **1** *he is just toying with her* amuse oneself with, play around with, flirt with, dally with, sport with, trifle with. **2** *the child was toying with his food* play around with, fiddle with, fool/mess around with. **3** *he is toying with the idea of leaving* play with, think idly about, have thoughts about.

trace *noun* **1** *there was no trace left of the picnic* mark, sign, vestige, indication; evidence; remains, remnants, relics. **2** *traces of poison in the drink | no trace of emotion in his voice* bit, touch, hint, suggestion, suspicion, trifle, drop, dash, tinge, tincture, shadow, jot, iota.

---

trace
remnant, track, trail, vestige

You can follow the **track** of a deer in the snow, the **trace** of a sleigh, or the **trail** of someone who has just cut down a Christmas tree and is dragging it back to the car. A *track* is a line or a series of marks left by the passage of something or someone; it often refers specifically to a line of footprints or a path worn into the ground by the feet (*to follow the track of a grizzly bear*). **Trace** may refer to a line or a rut made by someone or something that has been present or passed by; it may also refer to a mark serving as evidence that something has happened or been there (*traces of mud throughout the house; the telephoto shots have a trace of a camera shake*). **Trail** may refer to the track created by the passage of animals or people, or to the mark or marks left by something being dragged along a surface (*they followed the trail of the injured dog*). **Vestige** and **remnant** come closer in meaning to *trace*, as they refer to what remains after something has passed away. A *vestige* is always slight when compared to what it recalls (*the last vestiges of a great civilization*), while a *remnant* is a fragment or scrap of something (*all that remained of the historic tapestry after the fire was a few scorched remnants*).

trace *verb* 1 *unable to trace the letter* find, discover, detect, unearth, uncover, track down, turn up, dig up, ferret out, hunt down. 2 *trace the bear to the forest* follow, pursue, track, trail, tail, shadow, stalk, dog. 3 *trace the river back* | *trace his ancestry back* find the origins/source/roots of. 4 *trace out the route they would take* | *trace out the policies for the year* draw, draw up, sketch, draft, outline, mark out, delineate, rough out, map, chart, record, indicate, show, depict.

track *noun* 1 *follow the tracks of the burglar/bear/motorbike* marks, impressions, prints, imprints, footprints, footmarks, footsteps; trail, spoor, scent. 2 *follow in the track of the great explorers* trail, path, pathway, way, course, route. 3 *the track of the hurricane/satellite* path, line, course, orbit, route, trajectory, flight path. 4 *follow the track through the forest* path, trail, route, way. 5 *the train left the track* rail, line; rails. 6 *run around the track* course; running track, racetrack. **keep track of** keep up with, follow, monitor, record. **lose track of** forget about, be unaware of, misplace, lose/cease contact with.

track *verb* *track the bear to the forest* follow, pursue, trail, trace, tail, shadow, stalk, dog. **track down** *track down the necessary information* hunt down, hunt out, run to earth, unearth, uncover, turn up, dig up, ferret out, nose out, bring to light, expose, discover, find out, detect.

tract[1] *noun* *tracts of forest/desert* area, region, zone, stretch, expanse, extent, plot.

tract[2] *noun* *religious tracts* pamphlet, booklet, leaflet, brochure, monograph, essay, treatise, disquisition, dissertation, thesis, lecture, homily, sermon.

tractable *adjective* malleable, controllable, manageable, governable, amenable, complaisant,

compliant, submissive, yielding, docile, dutiful, obedient.
Antonyms: DEFIANT; OBSTINATE; RECALCITRANT.

trade *noun* 1 *he is in the export trade* commerce, buying and selling, dealing, traffic, trafficking, business, marketing, merchandising; transactions. 2 *what trade is his father in?* line of work/business, line, occupation, job, career, profession, craft, vocation, calling, métier; work, employment. 3 *I will do a trade of my car with yours* swap, trade-off, exchange, switch, barter.

trade *verb* 1 *the firm is trading at a loss* do business, deal, run, operate. 2 *they trade in diamonds* | *they trade with France* buy and sell, deal, traffic, market, merchandise. 3 *he traded his stamp collection for the collection of comics* swap, exchange, switch, barter. **trade on** *he trades on his father's reputation* | *trading on her kind nature* take advantage of, make use of, exploit, capitalize on, profit from; *inf.* cash in on.

trademark *noun* 1 *a trademark for the new line of sportswear* stamp, symbol, logo, sign, emblem, badge, crest, trade name, brand name, proprietary name. 2 *creating surprise endings is the novelist's trademark* | *wearing red socks is her trademark* characteristic, speciality, feature, trait, penchant, proclivity, peculiarity, idiosyncrasy, hallmark.

trader *noun* merchant, dealer, buyer, seller, buyer and seller, marketer, merchandiser, broker.

tradition *noun* 1 *keep up the old traditions* custom, belief, practice, convention, ritual, observance, habit, institution, usage, praxis. 2 *handed on by tradition* historical convention, unwritten law, oral history, lore, folklore.

traditional *adjective* 1 *traditional Christmas fare* customary, accustomed, conventional, established, ritual, ritualistic, habitual, set, fixed, routine, usual, wonted, old, time-honored, historic, folk, familial, ancestral. 2 *keeping alive traditional customs* handed-down, folk, unwritten, oral.
Antonyms: NOVEL; UNCONVENTIONAL.

traduce *verb* *accused of traducing his neighbor* defame, slander, speak ill/evil of, misrepresent, malign, vilify, calumniate, blacken the name of, cast aspersions on.

traffic *noun* 1 *noisy traffic rushing past* vehicles, cars. 2 *the traffic in diamonds has decreased* | *drug traffic* trafficking, trade, trading, dealing, commerce, business, peddling, smuggling, bootlegging.

traffic *verb* **traffic in** *arrested for trafficking in drugs* trade in, deal in, do business in, peddle, smuggle.

tragedy *noun* disaster, calamity, catastrophe, misfortune, misadventure, affliction, adversity, sad event, serious accident, shock, blow.
Antonyms: BLESSING; COMEDY.

tragic *adjective* 1 *a tragic accident* | *a tragic end to the day* disastrous, calamitous, catastrophic, fatal, terrible, dreadful, appalling, dire, awful,

miserable, wretched, unfortunate. **2** *listen to her tragic tale* sad, unhappy, pathetic, moving, distressing, disturbing, pitiful, piteous, melancholy, doleful, mournful, dismal, gloomy. **3** *it is tragic what they have done to the river* dreadful, terrible, awful, deplorable, lamentable, regrettable.
Antonyms: FORTUNATE; HAPPY; JOYFUL.

trail noun **1** *follow the trail left by the leader* | *police on the trail of the criminal* track, scent, spoor; traces, marks, signs, footprints, footmarks. **2** *follow the trail through the forest* path, beaten path, pathway, footpath, track, road, route. **3** *the rock star had a trail of young admirers* line, queue, train, file, column, procession, following, entourage. **4** *leave a trail of disaster behind them* train, chain, series, sequence, aftermath. **5** *vapor trail* stream, tail, appendage.

trail verb **1** *the child trailed the toy behind him* tow, pull, drag, draw, haul. **2** *her long skirt trailing on the floor* drag across, sweep, dangle, hang down, droop. **3** *children trailing along* | *trailing behind their parents* trudge, plod, drag oneself, dawdle, straggle, loiter, linger, lag, fall behind. **4** *plants/creatures trailing along the ground* creep, crawl, slide, slink. **5** *they trailed him to his lair* follow, pursue, track, trace, tail, shadow, stalk, dog. **6** *the team is trailing by five points* lose, be down, be behind. **7** *their enthusiasm gradually trailed off* | *his voice trailed away* fade, fade away/out, disappear, vanish, peter out, die away, melt away.

train noun **1** *the dress had a long train* tail, appendage. **2** *leaving a train of vapor* trail, stream, track, path, wake, wash. **3** *a train of disasters followed* trail, chain, string, series, sequence, set, progression, order, concatenation. **4** *a train of people climbing the mountain* procession, line, file, column, convoy, caravan. **5** *the princess and her train* retinue, entourage, cortege, following, staff, household, court; followers, attendants. **6** *they travel by train* railway train.

train verb **1** *train the young students in reading/musical skills* instruct, teach, coach, tutor, give lessons to, school, educate, drill, prepare, ground, guide, indoctrinate, inculcate. **2** *she is training to be a teacher* study, qualify, learn, prepare. **3** *athletes having to train each night* exercise, do exercises, work out, practice, prepare. **4** *train the football team* | *train the horse for the race* coach, drill, exercise. **5** *train the gun/binoculars on the distant figure* aim, point, focus, direct, level, line up.

trainer noun *the trainer of the team* coach, instructor.

training noun **1** *getting training in the social skills* instruction, teaching, coaching, tutoring, schooling, education, drilling, preparation, grounding, guidance, indoctrination, inculcation; lessons. **2** *undergo training for the race* exercise, working out, bodybuilding, practice, preparation; exercises, physical exercises.

trait noun *one of her annoying/endearing traits* characteristic, attribute, feature, quality, property, idiosyncrasy, peculiarity, quirk.

traitor noun betrayer, backstabber, turncoat, double-crosser, double-dealer, renegade, defector, deserter, apostate, Judas, quisling, fifth columnist; *inf.* snake in the grass, two-timer.

traitorous adjective treacherous, backstabbing, double-crossing, double-dealing, disloyal, faithless, unfaithful, perfidious, false-hearted, false, untrue, renegade, seditious, apostate; *inf.* two-timing.
Antonyms: LOYAL; FAITHFUL.

trajectory noun path, track, line, course, orbit, route, flight path.

trammel noun *coping with the trammels of ill health* restraint, constraint, obstacle, bar, block, curb, check, barrier, hindrance, handicap, impediment, drawback, snag, stumbling block, shackles, fetters, bonds.

trammel verb *trammeled by responsibilities* restrict, restrain, constrain, shackle, fetter, curb, check, hinder, handicap, impede, obstruct, thwart, frustrate.

tramp verb **1** *hear him tramping upstairs* | *workmen tramping in and out of the kitchen* trudge, march, plod, stamp, stump, stomp; *inf.* traipse. **2** *spend the day tramping over the hills* trek, trudge, hike, march, slog, plod, walk, ramble, roam, range, rove; *inf.* traipse.

tramp noun **1** *tramps sleeping on freight trains* vagrant, vagabond, hobo, derelict, down-and-out, itinerant, drifter. **2** *hear the tramp of the soldiers approaching* heavy step, footstep, footfall, tread, stamp, stomping. **3** *labeled her a tramp* loose woman, slut, wanton, trollop, prostitute, whore.

trample verb **1** *trample on the grass* | *trampled in the stampede* tramp on, tread on, walk over, stamp on, squash, crush, flatten. **2** *trample on other people* | *trample on other people's feelings/rights* ride roughshod over, treat with contempt, disregard, show no consideration for, encroach on, infringe.

trance noun daze, stupor, hypnotic state, half-conscious state, dream, reverie, brown study.

tranquil adjective **1** *a tranquil life* peaceful, restful, reposeful, calm, quiet, still, serene, placid, undisturbed. **2** *a tranquil person* calm, placid, pacific, composed, cool, calm, cool and collected, serene, even-tempered, unexcitable, unflappable, unruffled, unperturbed.
Antonyms: NOISY; DISTURBED; EXCITABLE.

tranquilize verb *tranquilize the wounded animal* sedate, calm, calm down, soothe, quiet, quiet down, pacify, compose, settle someone's nerves, lull, relax.

tranquilizer noun sedative, barbiturate, opiate; *inf.* downer.

tranquillity noun **1** *love the tranquillity of the place* peace, peacefulness, restfulness, reposefulness, calm, calmness, quiet, quietness, quietude, stillness, serenity, placidity. **2** *her tranquillity is never disturbed* calm, calmness, placidity, composure, coolness, serenity, equanimity, even-temperedness, unexcitability, unflappability.

transact *verb transact business in private* carry out, conduct, do, perform, execute, enact, manage, handle, negotiate, take care of, see to, conclude, discharge, accomplish, settle.

transaction *noun* **1** *the transaction took less than an hour* business, deal, undertaking, affair, bargain, negotiation; proceedings. **2** *the transaction of business in private* conducting, performance, execution, enactment, handling, negotiation, conclusion, discharge, settlement.

transactions *plural noun publish the transactions of the historical society* records, proceedings, affairs, concerns, dealings; *inf.* doings, goings-on.

transcend *verb* **1** *transcend human belief* go beyond, exceed, overstep, rise above. **2** *her performance transcended that of her opponents* surpass, excel, be superior to, outdo, outstrip, leave behind, outrival, outrank, outshine, eclipse, overshadow.

transcendence, transcendency *noun acknowledge his transcendence* excellence, greatness, magnificence, superiority, supremacy, predominance, preeminence, ascendency, paramountcy, incomparability, matchlessness.

transcendent *adjective his transcendent talent* excellent, excelling, great, magnificent, superior, supreme, consummate, predominant, preeminent, ascendant, paramount, unsurpassed, incomparable, matchless, unrivaled, unequaled, unparalleled.

transcendental *adjective a transcendental experience* mystical, mystic, mysterious, preternatural, supernatural, otherworldly, transmundane.

transcribe *verb* **1** *transcribing his shorthand* copy out, write out, copy/write in full, type/print out. **2** *transcribe the symbols* interpret, translate, transliterate, render. **3** *transcribe the performance | now transcribed to compact disc* record, rerecord, transfer.

transcript *noun a transcript of the trial* written/recorded copy, copy, record, written/printed version, documentation.

transfer *verb* **1** *transfer the material from the house to the garage* convey, move, shift, remove, take, carry, transport. **2** *transfer the students to a different school* move, shift, remove, change, relocate. **3** *transfer his property/share to his son* turn over, sign over, hand on, hand down, pass on, transmit, convey, devolve, assign, delegate.

transfer *noun* **1** *teachers/football players asking for a transfer* move, shift, relocation, change. **2** *the property transfer has been drawn up* transfer document, conveyance; papers, deeds.

transfix *verb the onlookers were transfixed with/in*

terror root to the spot, paralyze, petrify, stop dead, hypnotize, mesmerize, rivet, spellbind, fascinate, engross, stun, astound.

transform *verb transform the girl's appearance | transform his outlook on life* change, alter, convert, metamorphose, revolutionize, transfigure, remodel, redo, reconstruct, rebuild, reorganize, rearrange, renew, translate, transmute; *inf.* transmogrify.

transformation *noun* change, radical change, alteration, conversion, metamorphosis, sea change, revolutionization, revolution, transfiguration, remodeling, reconstruction, reorganization, renewal, transmutation; *inf.* transmogrification.

transgress *verb* **1** *transgress the bounds of decency | transgress the laws of the land* go beyond, overstep, exceed, infringe, breach, break, contravene, violate, defy, disobey. **2** *they transgressed and were punished* do wrong, go astray, misbehave, break the law, err, lapse, fall from grace, stray from the straight and narrow, sin, trespass.

transgression *noun* **1** *their transgression of the bounds of taste | transgression of the law* overstepping, infringement, breach, breaking, contravention, violation, defiance, disobedience. **2** *punished for their transgressions* wrong, misdemeanor, misdeed, lawbreaking, crime, offense, lapse, fault, sin; wrongdoing, misbehavior.

transgressor *noun transgressors will be punished* wrongdoer, lawbreaker, criminal, miscreant, delinquent, villain, felon, offender, culprit, sinner, trespasser, malefactor.

transience *noun* short-livedness, transitoriness, impermanence, temporariness, brevity, briefness, shortness, evanescence, momentariness, fugitiveness, mutability.

transient *adjective* transitory, short-lived, short-term, impermanent, temporary, brief, short, ephemeral, evanescent, momentary, fleeting, flying, passing, fugitive, fugacious, mutable, here today and gone tomorrow.

Antonyms: PERMANENT; CONSTANT; PERPETUAL.

transit *noun* **1** *troop transit* movement, travel, journeying, passage, transfer, crossing. **2** *city councils budgeting for modern transit* transport, transportation, conveyance, haulage, freightage. **in transit** *goods lost in transit* en route, on the journey, on the way, on the road, during transport.

transition *noun the transition from childhood to adulthood | the transition to foreign currency* move, passage, change, transformation, conversion, changeover, metamorphosis, shift, switch, jump, leap, progression, gradation, development, evolution, transmutation.

transitional *adjective* **1** *the transitional period* transition, changing, changeover, conversion, developmental, evolutionary, intermediate, fluid, unsettled. **2** *the transitional government* transition, provisional, temporary.

transitory *adjective* transient, short-lived, short-term, impermanent, temporary, brief, short, ephemeral, evanescent, momentary, fleeting, flying, passing, fugitive, fugacious, mutable, here today and gone tomorrow.
Antonyms: PERMANENT; PERPETUAL.

translate *verb* **1** *translate the French passage into English* construe, interpret, render, convert, transcribe, transliterate. **2** *translate the legal jargon into plain English* render, paraphrase, reword, convert, decipher, decode, explain, elucidate. **3** *translate his silence as agreement* interpret, take, construe, understand, read, judge, deem. **4** *translate ideas into action* turn, change, convert, transform, alter, metamorphose, transmute; *inf.* transmogrify.

translation *noun* **1** *the translation of the French passage into English* interpretation, construing, rendering, rendition, conversion, transcription, transliteration. **2** *unable to follow the rough translation* interpretation, rendition, transcription, transliteration. **3** *the translation of the legal jargon into plain English* rendering, rendition, paraphrasing, rewording, conversion, deciphering, decoding, explanation, elucidation. **4** *the translation of ideas into action* change, conversion, transformation, alteration, metamorphosis, transmutation; *inf.* transmogrification.

transmission *noun* **1** *the transmission of mail* sending, conveyance, transport, dispatch, remission. **2** *the transmission of information/disease* transference, transferral, passing on, communication, imparting, dissemination, spreading. **3** *the transmission of late-night programs* broadcasting, relaying, sending out. **4** *a live transmission* broadcast, program.

transmit *verb* **1** *transmit the package by air* send, convey, transport, dispatch, forward, remit. **2** *transmit information/disease to others* transfer, pass on, hand on, communicate, impart, disseminate, spread, carry, diffuse. **3** *transmit late-night programs* broadcast, air, relay, send out, put on the air.

transparency *noun* **1** *the transparency of the plastic/streams* clarity, clearness, translucency, lucidity, pellucidity, limpidness, limpidity, glassiness, transpicuousness. **2** *the transparency of the material* sheerness, diaphanousness, diaphaneity, filminess, gauziness. **3** *the transparency of his lies* obviousness, patentness, unmistakableness, clearness, plainness, distinctness, apparentness, perceptibility, discernibility. **4** *appreciate her transparency* frankness, openness, candidness, directness, forthrightness, ingenuousness, artlessness. **5** *the transparency of the prose* clarity, clearness, lucidity, straightforwardness, plainness, explicitness, unambiguousness. **6** *transparencies of their vacation* slide, photograph.

transparent *adjective* **1** *transparent plastic/streams* clear, see-through, translucent, lucid, pellucid, crystal-clear, crystalline, limpid, glassy, transpicuous. **2** *made of transparent material* see-through, sheer, diaphanous, filmy, gauzy. **3** *his transparent dishonesty* obvious, patent, manifest, undisguised, unmistakable, clear, plain, visible, noticeable, recognizable, distinct, evident, apparent, perceptible, discernible. **4** *done with transparent sincerity* frank, open, candid, direct, forthright, plainspoken, straight, ingenuous, artless. **5** *a transparent account of the events* clear, lucid, straightforward, plain, explicit, unambiguous, unequivocal.
Antonyms: OPAQUE; CLOUDY.

transpire *verb* **1** *it transpired that he had been married before* become known, be revealed, be disclosed, come to light, emerge, come out. **2** *tell me what transpired at the meeting* come about, take place, happen, occur, turn up, arise, chance, befall.

transplant *verb* **1** *transplant seedlings* replant, repot, relocate. **2** *transplant organs* transfer, graft. **3** *he hated being transplanted to a different region* transfer, move, remove, shift, relocate.

transport *verb* **1** *transport the goods to the warehouse* convey, take, transfer, move, shift, bring, fetch, carry, bear, haul, lug, cart, run, ship. **2** *transport criminals to an island* banish, exile, deport, drive away, expatriate. **3** *she was transported by his piano playing* enrapture, entrance, enchant, enthrall, captivate, bewitch, fascinate, spellbind, charm, overjoy, thrill, delight, ravish, carry away.

transport *noun* **1** *road and rail transport* transportation, conveyance, transit, carriage, freight. **2** *our transport has not yet arrived* transportation, conveyance, vehicle, car, carriage. **3** *a transport of joy/rage* strong emotion.

transports *plural noun* **1** strong emotion, intense feeling, passion, fervor, vehemence. **2** *in transports over her engagement/promotion* rapture, ecstasy, elation, exaltation, exhilaration, euphoria, bliss, seventh heaven, heaven, paradise; *inf.* (on) cloud nine.

transpose *verb* *transpose the middle letters of the word* interchange, exchange, switch, swap, transfer, reverse, invert, rearrange, reorder, change, alter, convert, move.

transverse *adjective* *transverse beams* crosswise, crossways, cross, athwart.

trap *noun* **1** *rabbits caught in a trap* snare, net, mesh, ambush, pitfall, booby trap. **2** *the question was a trap to get him to confess* stratagem, setup, play, artifice, ruse, wile, trick, device, deception, subterfuge. **3** *lay a trap for the criminal* ambush, lure, decoy, bait.

trap *verb* **1** *trap the rabbits* snare, ensnare, enmesh, entrap, catch, corner. **2** *trapped into making a confession* trick, dupe, deceive, lure, inveigle, beguile, set up. **3** *they were trapped in the building* cut off, corner, confine, imprison.

trappings *plural noun* all the trappings necessary *for the pageant* | *the trappings of power* accouterments, appurtenances, appointments, trimmings, paraphernalia, fittings, things; equipage, equipment, apparatus, gear, livery, adornment, ornamentation, decoration, finery, frippery; panoply.

trash noun **1** *talk trash* rubbish, garbage, nonsense, drivel, balderdash, bunkum, twaddle; *inf.* bunk, tripe, bilge, rot, tommyrot, poppycock. **2** *empty out the trash* rubbish, waste, refuse, litter, garbage. **3** *he regards his neighbors as trash* riff-raff, scum, rabble, canaille, vermin; dregs, good-for-nothings.

trauma noun **1** *the trauma caused by the accident/ surgery* injury, wound, lesion. **2** *suffering from trauma after the attack | the trauma of divorce* shock, disturbance, disorder, distress, pain, anguish, suffering.

traumatic adjective **1** *a traumatic injury/attack* painful, agonizing, shocking, scarring, disturbing, distressing, damaging, injurious, harmful. **2** *a traumatic journey home* unpleasant, disagreeable, irksome, troublesome, vexatious, irritating, distressing.

travel verb **1** *he travels a lot in connection with his work | she plans to travel after she retires* journey, take a trip, tour, voyage, sightsee. **2** *light travels faster than sound | news travels fast* proceed, progress, advance, be transmitted, carry. **3** *travel the length of the country* journey, cross, traverse, cover, wander, ramble, roam, rove, range, wend, make one's way over. **4** *the driver/car was certainly traveling* speed, go fast/ rapidly, drive fast, go at breakneck speed; *inf.* hellbent for leather, go like a bat out of hell, tear up the miles.

travel noun *the cost of travel* traveling, journeying, touring.

traveler noun tourist, vacationer, excursionist, explorer, passenger, voyager, sightseer, globetrotter.

traveling adjective **1** *a traveling circus* itinerant, peripatetic, moving, mobile. **2** *a traveling people/tribe* itinerant, peripatetic, nomadic, migratory, migrating, wandering, roaming, roving, wayfaring, unsettled, restless, on the move/go.

travels plural noun *she wrote about her travels* journey, journeying, trip, tour, expedition, excursion, voyage, sightseeing, exploration, wandering, roaming, ramble, rambling, peregrination, *inf.* globe-trotting.

traverse verb **1** *traversing the desert* cross, go across, travel over, journey over, make one's way across, pass over, wander, roam, range. **2** *beams traversing the ceiling* go across, lie across, stretch across, extend across, cross, cut across, bridge. **3** *traverse all aspects of the subject* consider, examine, check, study, review, investigate, inspect, scrutinize, look into, look over, scan, pore over, take stock of.

travesty noun *the trial was a travesty of justice* misrepresentation, distortion, perversion, corrup-

tion, poor imitation, mockery, parody, caricature, sham, burlesque, satire, lampoon, takeoff; *inf.* send-up, spoof.

travesty verb *travesty the solemn occasion* misrepresent, distort, pervert, mock, ridicule, deride, make fun of, parody, caricature, burlesque, satirize, lampoon; *inf.* send up, spoof.

treacherous adjective **1** *betrayed by a treacherous follower* traitorous, backstabbing, double-crossing, double-dealing, disloyal, faithless, unfaithful, perfidious, duplicitous, deceitful, false-hearted, false, untrue, untrustworthy, unreliable, undependable; *inf.* two-timing. **2** *the weather conditions can be treacherous* precarious, unreliable, undependable, unstable, unsafe, risky, hazardous, dangerous, perilous, deceptive; *inf.* dicey. **3** *roads that are treacherous in winter* hazardous, dangerous, unsafe; flooded, icy, ice-covered, slippery.

Antonyms: LOYAL; FAITHFUL; RELIABLE.

treachery noun *the treachery of his best friend* traitorousness, backstabbing, double-crossing, double-dealing, disloyalty, faithlessness, unfaithfulness, perfidy, perfidiousness, treason, duplicity, deceit, deceitfulness, deception, false-heartedness, falseness, untrustworthiness; *inf.* two-timing.

tread verb **1** *tread softly so as not to wake the baby* walk, step, go, pace, march, tramp. **2** *tread the long road home* walk, hike, tramp, stride, step out, trek, march, trudge, plod. **3** *tread grapes | tread the grass (down)* trample, tramp on, step on, stamp on, squash, crush, flatten, press down. **4** *tread mud into the carpet* trample, tramp, stamp, press. **tread on** *invading troops treading on the villagers* ride roughshod over, oppress, repress, suppress, subdue, subjugate, quell, crush.

tread noun *walk with a heavy/soft tread | hear the tread of the people upstairs* step, footstep, footfall, walk, tramp.

treason noun *high treason;* betrayal, traitorousness, treachery, disloyalty, faithlessness, perfidy, disaffection, sedition, subversion, mutiny, rebellion, lese-majesty.

treasonable adjective traitorous, treacherous, disloyal, faithless, perfidious, seditious, subversive, mutinous, rebellious.

treasure noun **1** *find buried treasure | a miser gloating over his treasure* riches, valuables; wealth, fortune, hoard; jewels, gems, coins, gold, money, cash. **2** *art treasures* valuable, masterpiece. **3** *she is her father's treasure* darling, pride and joy, apple of one's eye, jewel, jewel in the crown, gem, pearl, precious, prize, paragon. **4** *advertising for a treasure* paragon, household/domestic help, housekeeper.

treasure verb **1** *she treasures their friendship* value, place great value on, prize, set great store by, think highly of, hold dear. **2** *he treasures his children* adore, cherish, love, worship, revere, venerate, dote on, prize, hold dear. **3** *treasure the souvenirs of their travels* value, prize, save, collect, accumulate, hoard, store up, lay by, stow away, squirrel away, salt away; *inf.* stash away.

treat *noun* **1** *think of a treat for her birthday* surprise, celebration, entertainment, amusement, diversion, party, feast, banquet. **2** *bringing a treat for the child* gift, present, tidbit, delicacy; *inf.* goodie. **3** *it was a treat to see her again* pleasure, delight, thrill, joy, gratification, satisfaction; fun. **4** *the drinks are his treat* gift, present, one's turn to pay.

treat *verb* **1** *treat him badly/kindly | treat his car recklessly* act toward, behave toward, deal with, handle, cope with, contend with, manage, use. **2** *treat his remarks as jokes* regard, consider, view, look upon, deal with. **3** *treat the sick patient* give treatment to, medicate, doctor, nurse, care for, attend to, minister to, cure, heal. **4** *the general treating with the enemy* have talks with, talk with, confer with, negotiate with, parley with, bargain with, make terms with, come to terms with. **5** *her book treats the question of religious doubt* deal with, discuss, go into, write/speak/talk about, discourse upon, be concerned with, touch upon, refer to, consider, study, review, analyze. **treat to 1** *treat (them) to dinner* pay for, buy for, pay/foot the bill for, finance, take out to. **2** *we were treated to a wonderful performance* entertain by, amuse by, divert by, cheer by, gratify by, delight by, regale by. **treat with** *treat the wood with creosote* apply to, put on, use on, ply with.

treatise *noun* discourse, exposition, dissertation, thesis, disquisition, study, essay, paper, monograph, tract, pamphlet, work, piece of writing.

treatment *noun* **1** *his treatment was fair/cruel* action, behavior, conduct, handling, management, use; dealings. **2** *patients/wounds responding to treatment* medical care, medication, medicament, therapy, doctoring, nursing, first aid, care, ministration; cure, remedy; drugs, therapeutics.

treaty *noun* agreement, pact, deal, compact, covenant, bargain, pledge, contract, alliance, concordat, convention, entente.

trek *verb* *trek across the rough terrain* trudge, tramp, hike, march, slog, plod, walk, ramble, roam, range, rove, travel, journey; *inf.* traipse.

trek *noun* *a trek across the desert | it is quite a trek to the park* expedition, trip, journey, hike, march, walk, odyssey.

trellis *noun* lattice, network, mesh, fret, grille, grid, grating.

tremble *verb* **1** *fingers trembling with excitement* shake, quiver, shiver, quake, twitch, wiggle. **2** *buildings trembling in the earthquake* shake, shudder, teeter, totter, wobble, rock, vibrate, oscillate, rattle. **3** *I tremble just thinking about it* fear, be afraid, be fearful, be frightened, be apprehensive, worry, be anxious.

tremendous *adjective* **1** *animals of a tremendous size | people of tremendous girth* great, huge, enormous, immense, massive, vast, colossal,

prodigious, stupendous, gigantic, gargantuan, mammoth, giant, titanic; *inf.* whopping. **2** *it made a tremendous difference* great, huge, enormous, immense, colossal, prodigious, stupendous; *inf.* whopping. **3** *there was a tremendous noise* loud, deafening, earsplitting, booming, thundering, roaring, resounding, crashing. **4** *she is a tremendous player/cook* excellent, very good, great, marvelous, remarkable, extraordinary, exceptional, wonderful, incredible; *inf.* fabulous, fantastic, terrific, super, ace, wizard. **Antonyms:** TINY; SMALL; SLIGHT; POOR.

tremor *noun* **1** *notice the tremor of her hands | a tremor of fear* tremble, trembling, shake, shaking, shiver, quiver, quaver, vibration, twitch, spasm, paroxysm. **2** *buildings damaged by a tremor* earth tremor, earthquake; *inf.* quake.

tremulous *adjective* **1** *a tremulous voice* trembling, shaking, shaky, quivering, quavering, vibrating, nervous, weak. **2** *with tremulous hands* trembling, shaking, shaky, quivery, twitching, twitchy, jittery, shuddering, jerky, spasmodic. **3** *give a tremulous look* timid, diffident, shy, timorous, fearful, frightened, scared, nervous, anxious, apprehensive, alarmed, cowardly.

trench *noun* ditch, excavation, earthwork, furrow, duct, trough, channel, conduit, cut, drain, waterway, moat, fosse.

trenchant *adjective* **1** *a trenchant wit/criticism* incisive, cutting, pointed, sharp, biting, pungent, caustic, piercing, penetrating, razor, razor-edged, mordant, scathing, acrid, acid, tart, acidulous, acerbic, astringent, sarcastic. **2** *trenchant divisions between the political parties* clear, clear-cut, distinct, defined, well-defined, sharp, crisp, unequivocal, unambiguous. **Antonyms:** DULL; KIND; ILL-DEFINED; FUZZY.

trend *noun* **1** *an upward trend in prices | votes showing a trend toward the right* tendency, drift, course, direction, bearing, current, inclination, bias, leaning, bent, swing. **2** *they like to follow the trend* fashion, vogue, style, mode, look, craze; *inf.* fad.

trend *verb* *prices trending upward | political opinions trending to the left | the river trends eastward* move, go, tend, head, drift, turn, incline, lean, shift, veer, swing.

trepidation *noun* fear, fearfulness, alarm, fright, apprehensiveness, apprehension, terror, panic, anxiety, worry, uneasiness, disquiet, unrest, agitation, trembling, nervousness, jumpiness, perturbation, discomposure, dismay, consternation; *inf.* butterflies, cold feet, jitters, cold sweat, blue funk, heebie-jeebies, willies. **Antonyms:** CALM; EQUANIMITY; COMPOSURE.

trespass *verb* do wrong, err, go astray, fall from grace, stray from the straight and narrow, sin, transgress. **trespass against** *punished for trespassing against his neighbors* do wrong to, wrong. **trespass on 1** *trespass on his land/privacy* intrude on, encroach on, infringe on, poach on, invade, obtrude on. **2** *trespass on their hospitality* take advantage of, impose upon, exploit, abuse, make use of.

trespasser *noun* **1** *trespassers will be prosecuted* intruder, interloper, unwelcome visitor, encroacher, infringer, invader, obtruder. **2** *trespassers asking for forgiveness* wrongdoer, evildoer, criminal, offender, transgressor, sinner, malefactor.

tresses *plural noun* hair; locks, curls, ringlets, braids, plaits.

trial *noun* **1** *the murder trial lasted several weeks* court case, case, hearing, inquiry, tribunal, litigation, judicial examination, legal investigation. **2** *give the applicant a trial* trial period, probation, test, test/testing period, audition. **3** *put a car through safety trials* test, testing, tryout, trial/test run, check, assay, experiment; *inf.* dry run. **4** *climb the mountain at the third trial* try, attempt, endeavor, effort, venture; *inf.* go, shot, stab, crack. **5** *she was never a trial to her mother* nuisance, pest, bother, worry, vexation, annoyance, irritant, irritation, bane, affliction, curse, burden, cross to bear, thorn in one's flesh; *inf.* pain in the neck, hassle, plague. **6** *the trials of life* trouble, worry, anxiety, vexation, load, burden, cross to bear, blow, affliction, tribulation, adversity, hardship, ordeal, pain; suffering, distress, misery, wretchedness, unhappiness, sadness, woe, grief. **7** *enter the dog in the field trials* contest, competition.

trial *adjective trial period* testing, experimental, pilot, probationary, provisional.

tribe *noun* **1** *the tribes of Israel* ethnic group, family, dynasty, clan, sept. **2** *meet a tribe of doctors at the conference* group, crowd, company, party, band, number, gang, assembly, collection; *inf.* bunch.

tribulation *noun* trouble, worry, anxiety, vexation, load, burden, cross to bear, blow, affliction, trial, adversity, hardship, ordeal, pain; suffering, distress, misery, wretchedness, unhappiness, sadness, woe, grief.

tributary *noun tributaries of the Mississippi* branch, feeder, confluent.

tribute *noun* **1** *give tributes to the heroes* gift, present, accolade, commendation, testimonial, paean, eulogy, panegyric, encomium; gratitude, applause, praise, homage, honor, exaltation, laudation, extolment, glorification; congratulations, compliments; *inf.* bouquets. **2** *the success is a tribute to their hard work* acknowledgment, recognition, testimonial, indication, manifestation; evidence, proof. **3** *foreign governments paying tributes to the emperor* homage; payment, contribution, offering, gift, donation, charge, tax, duty, levy, tariff, ransom.

Antonyms: BLAME; CRITICISM; REPROACH; condemnation.

trick *noun* **1** *he got the job by a trick* stratagem,

ploy, artifice, ruse, dodge, wile, device, maneuver, trick of the trade, deceit, deception, subterfuge, swindle, fraud; *inf.* con. **2** *a trick of the light* illusion, mirage. **3** *he has the trick of making guests feel welcome* knack, art, gift, talent, technique, ability, skill, expertise; *inf.* know-how. **4** *play tricks on the old man* | *tired of the children's tricks* hoax, practical joke, joke, prank, jape, antic, caper, frolic, lark, gambol; *inf.* leg-pull, gag, put-on. **5** *artists demonstrating their tricks* sleight of hand, legerdemain; juggling, prestidigitation. **6** *he has an annoying trick of repeating himself* idiosyncrasy, habit, mannerism, quirk, peculiarity, foible, eccentricity, characteristic, trait, practice.

trick *verb* deceive, delude, mislead, take in, cheat, hoodwink, fool, outwit, dupe, hoax, gull, cozen, defraud, swindle; *inf.* con, pull a fast one on, put one over on, shaft.

trickery *noun use trickery to get the job* guile, artifice, wiliness, deceit, deception, cheating, subterfuge, craft, craftiness, chicanery, pretense, dishonesty, fraud, swindling, imposture, double-dealing, duplicity; *inf.* conning, monkey/funny business, hanky-panky.

Antonyms: HONESTY; CANDOR.

trickle *verb* **1** *water trickled from the tap* | *blood trickled from the wound* drip, dribble, leak, ooze, seep, exude, percolate. **2** *information trickled out* | *people trickled into the meeting* come/go/pass gradually.

Antonyms: POUR; GUSH.

trickster *noun* cheat, swindler, fraud, fraudster, defrauder, confidence man, deceiver, deluder, dissembler, hoodwinker, hoaxer, phony, charlatan, rogue, scoundrel; *inf.* con man.

tricky *adjective* **1** *a tricky situation* difficult, problematic, awkward, delicate, sensitive, ticklish, thorny, knotty, touchy, risky, uncertain, precarious; *inf.* sticky. **2** *he is a tricky character* cunning, crafty, wily, artful, devious, scheming, foxy, sly, slippery, subtle, deceitful, deceptive.

Antonyms: STRAIGHTFORWARD; HONEST.

tried *adjective tried remedies* | *friends who are tried and true* tried out, tested, put to the test, proved, proven, established, sure, certain, true, dependable, reliable, trustworthy, reputable.

trifle *noun* **1** *her mind is occupied with trifles* trivia, inessentials; triviality, unimportant thing, thing of no consequence, bagatelle, nothing. **2** *buy a few trifles for Christmas* bauble, trinket, knickknack, gimcrack, gewgaw, toy, doodad, whatnot. **3** *I paid a mere trifle for it* next to nothing, hardly anything, pittance; *inf.* piddling amount. **4** *he is a trifle confused* bit, small amount, touch.

trifle *verb* **trifle with** **1** *he is just trifling with the young woman* | *trifle with her affections* amuse oneself, toy, play around with, flirt with, dally with, sport with. **2** *he is not a man to be trifled with* treat lightly, deal with casually, treat in a cavalier fashion, dismiss.

trifling *adjective* **1** *discuss trifling matters* petty, trivial, unimportant, insignificant, inconsequential, shallow, superficial, frivolous, silly, idle, foolish, empty. **2** *cost a trifling amount* trivial, small, tiny, minuscule, infinitesimal, negligible, insignificant, paltry, nominal, worthless, valueless; *inf.* piddling.

Antonyms: IMPORTANT; WEIGHTY; CONSIDERABLE.

trigger *verb* *it triggered the riot* | *her behavior triggered off his fit of rage* set off, set in motion, spark off, activate, give rise to, generate, start, cause, bring about, prompt, provoke.

trim *adjective* **1** *looking trim in her uniform* neat, tidy, neat and tidy, smart, spruce, well-groomed, well-dressed, well-turned-out, dapper, elegant; *inf.* natty. **2** *trim gardens* neat, tidy, orderly, in good order/condition, shipshape, well-maintained, well-looked-after, well-cared-for, spick-and-span. **3** *have a trim figure* | *keep trim* slim, slender, lean, svelte, streamlined, willowy, lissome, sleek, shapely, in good shape, fit, physically fit.

Antonyms: UNTIDY; MESSY; FAT.

trim *verb* **1** *trim one's hair/beard* cut, clip, snip, shear, prune, pare, even up, neaten, tidy up. **2** *trim the fat from the meat* | *trim the branches from the tree* cut, chop, hack, remove, take off. **3** *trim the annual budget* cut down, decrease, reduce, diminish, cut back on, curtail, dock, retrench. **4** *trim the Christmas tree* | *trim her evening dress* decorate, adorn, ornament, embellish, festoon. **5** *trim the dress with lace* decorate, adorn, ornament, embellish, edge, pipe, border, fringe, embroider, bespangle.

trim *noun* **1** *admire the trim on the dress* trimming, decoration, adornment, ornamentation, embellishment, edging, piping, border, fringe, frill, embroidery. **2** *give the boy/hedge/sheep a trim* haircut, cut, clip, snip, shearing, pruning, paring. **3** *the old man is still in trim* good health, good condition, good shape/form, fine fettle, shape.

trimming *noun* *admire the trimming on the dress* trim, decoration, adornment, ornamentation, edging, piping, fringe, fringing, frill, embroidery.

trimmings *plural noun* **1** *turkey with all the trimmings* accompaniments, frills, extras, accessories, accouterments, trappings, paraphernalia; garnishing, garnish. **2** *hedge/pastry trimmings* cuttings, clippings, parings, shavings.

trinket *noun* *buy a trinket as a souvenir* bauble, ornament, knickknack, trifle, gimcrack, gewgaw, piece of bric-à-brac, bibelot, doodad, whatnot.

trio *noun* threesome, triumvirate, triad, trine, trinity, triunity, triple, trilogy, triptych; triplets.

trip *noun* **1** *go on a trip to China/town* excursion, tour, expedition, voyage, jaunt, outing, run. **2** *the trip on the sidewalk* stumble, misstep, false step, slip, slide, fall, tumble, spill.

trip *verb* **1** *she tripped on the broken pavement* stumble, lose one's footing/balance, stagger, totter, slip, slide, misstep, fall, tumble. **2** *she tripped across the dance floor* skip, dance, hop, prance, bound, spring, gambol, caper, frisk, cavort, waltz. **trip up 1** *she tripped up when she tried to alter the accounts* make a mistake, blunder, go wrong, err, lapse, bungle, botch; *inf.* slip up. **2** *the defending lawyer tripped the witness up* trap, outwit, outsmart, confuse, disconcert, unsettle, discountenance; *inf.* throw.

tripe *noun* *he is talking tripe* nonsense, rubbish, drivel, twaddle, bunkum, balderdash; *inf.* claptrap, bunk, garbage, trash, hogwash, guff, rot, tommyrot, poppycock.

triple *adjective* **1** *a triple alliance* three-way, threefold, tripartite. **2** *at triple the recommended speed* three times, three times as much as, threefold, treble.

triple *noun* trio, threesome, triumvirate, triad, trine, trinity, triunity.

trite *adjective* hackneyed, banal, commonplace, ordinary, common, platitudinous, clichéd, stock, stereotyped, overused, overdone, stale, worn-out, threadbare, unimaginative, unoriginal, uninspired, dull, pedestrian, run-of-the-mill, routine, humdrum.

Antonyms: ORIGINAL; FRESH; IMAGINATIVE.

triumph *noun* **1** *his triumph over his opponent* conquest, victory, win, ascendancy, mastery, success. **2** *it was a triumph of American engineering* coup, tour de force, feat, masterstroke, achievement, attainment, accomplishment, supreme example, sensation; *inf.* hit. **3** *expressions of triumph on their faces* exultation, jubilation, jubilance, elation, rejoicing, joy, joyfulness, pride.

Antonyms: DEFEAT; FAILURE; DISASTER.

triumph *verb* **1** *the better team triumphed* win, succeed, come first, be the victor, be victorious, gain a victory, carry the day, take the honors/prize/crown. **2** *the defeated team watching the winners triumph* exult, rejoice, jubilate, celebrate, revel, glory, gloat, swagger, brag, boast. **triumph over** *triumph over his opponent/disability* beat, defeat, conquer, vanquish, best, worst, overcome, overpower, get the better of, gain ascendancy over, gain mastery of, prevail against.

triumphant *adjective* **1** *the triumphant team took a bow* winning, victorious, successful, undefeated, unbeaten, trophy-winning, prizewinning. **2** *wearing triumphant expressions* | *giving triumphant shouts* exultant, jubilant, elated, rejoicing, joyful, joyous, proud, gloating, boastful.

Antonyms: UNSUCCESSFUL; defeated; DEPRESSED.

trivia *plural noun* *ignore the trivia and address the main issue* petty details, details, minutiae, trivialities, trifles, technicalities.

trivial *adjective* **1** *raise trivial objections* unimportant, insignificant, inconsequential, flimsy,

insubstantial, petty, minor, of no account/matter, negligible, paltry, trifling, foolish, worthless; *inf.* piddling. **2** *he is a trivial young man* frivolous, small-minded, featherbrained, giddy, silly.
Antonyms: IMPORTANT; SIGNIFICANT; PROFOUND.

triviality *noun* **1** *the triviality of the objections* unimportance, insignificance, inconsequence, flimsiness, insubstantiality, pettiness, paltriness, foolishness, worthlessness. **2** *the triviality of the young man* frivolousness, small-mindedness, featherbrainedness, giddiness, silliness. **3** *do not wish to discuss trivialities* petty/mere detail, thing of no importance, trifle, technicality.

troop *noun* *a troop of people surged forward* band, group, company, assemblage, gathering, body, crowd, throng, multitude, horde, host, mob, squad, pack, drove, flock, swarm, stream; *inf.* gang, crew.

troop *verb* *the audience trooped out* flock, stream, swarm, surge, crowd, throng, mill.

troops *plural noun* *call in the troops* armed forces, army, military, services, soldiers, soldiery, fighting men/women.

trophy *noun* **1** *win the sports trophy* cup, prize, award; laurels. **2** *trophies of his time as a hunter* spoil, booty; souvenir, memento, keepsake, relic.

tropical *adjective tropical weather* hot, torrid, sweltering, boiling, sultry, steamy, humid, sticky.
Antonyms: COLD; ARCTIC.

trouble *noun* **1** *his car is causing him trouble | having trouble with the computer* worry, bother, anxiety, disquiet, unease, irritation, vexation, inconvenience, annoyance, agitation, harassment, difficulty, distress; problems. **2** *there has been a lot of trouble in her life* difficulty, misfortune, adversity, hardship, bad luck, ill luck, burden, distress, pain, suffering, affliction, torment, woe, grief, unhappiness, sadness, heartache; problems. **3** *please do not go to any trouble | our hostess went to a lot of trouble* bother, inconvenience, disturbance, fuss, effort, exertion, work, labor, attention, care, thoughtfulness; *inf.* hassle. **4** *the girl was no trouble | it was no trouble to collect the mail* nuisance, bother, inconvenience, problem, pest; *inf.* headache, pain in the neck, pain. **5** *the trouble with her is she's too old-fashioned | his trouble is he's too nice* problem, difficulty, failing, weakness, shortcoming, fault, imperfection, defect, blemish. **6** *he has stomach trouble* disorder, disease, illness, dysfunction. **7** *the bartender does not want any trouble* disturbance, disorder, unrest, fighting, strife, conflict, tumult, commotion, turbulence, lawbreaking. **in trouble** *he is in trouble financially | in trouble with the police* in difficulty, having problems, in dire straits, in a predicament; *inf.* in a tight corner, in hot water, in a jam/pickle, in a mess/spot.

trouble *verb* **1** *he is troubled by neighbors/finances* worry, bother, disturb, annoy, irritate, vex, irk, fret, pester, torment, plague, inconvenience, upset, perturb, agitate, discompose, harass, distress; *inf.* hassle. **2** *do not trouble to see me out* take the trouble/time, bother, make the effort, exert/disturb oneself, go out of one's way. **3** *he is troubled by back pain* afflict, oppress, weigh down, burden, incapacitate. **4** *I am sorry to trouble you, but may I use your phone?* bother, disturb, inconvenience, put out, impose upon, discommode, incommode.

troublemaker *noun* mischief-maker, inciter, agitator, instigator, agent provocateur, firebrand, malcontent, rabble-rouser, demagogue, stormy petrel.

troublesome *adjective* *troublesome neighbors/problems* worrying, worrisome, bothersome, tiresome, disturbing, annoying, irritating, irksome, upsetting, perturbing, harassing, distressing, difficult, problematic, demanding, taxing.
Antonyms: EASY; PLEASANT.

trough *noun* **1** *animals feeding from a trough* feeding box, feedbox, manger, rack, crib. **2** *troughs to drain away water* channel, conduit, duct, flume, gutter, drain, culvert, trench, ditch, furrow, groove, depression.

trounce *verb* **1** *they trounced the other team* defeat utterly, beat soundly, rout, drub, thrash, crush, overwhelm; *inf.* make mincemeat (out) of, walk all over, wipe the floor with, hammer, clobber, slaughter, give a pasting to. **2** *trounced for disobeying the emperor* thrash, beat, whip, flog, lash, birch, cane, spank, chastise; *inf.* belt, wallop, lambaste, tan the hide of.

troupe *noun* *a troupe of acrobats* company, band, cast.

truancy *noun* absenteeism, absence, nonattendance, French leave, shirking, malingering; *inf.* cutting, skipping.

truant *noun* absentee, dodger, malingerer, shirker, deserter.

truce *noun* cease-fire, armistice, suspension/cessation of hostilities, peace, respite, moratorium, lull; *inf.* letup.

truculent *adjective* aggressive, antagonistic, belligerent, pugnacious, bellicose, combative, contentious, hostile, obstreperous, violent, fierce, defiant, sullen, surly, bad-tempered, cross, ill-natured.
Antonyms: FRIENDLY; AMIABLE; PLACID.

trudge *verb* *trudge through the deep snow* plod, lumber, shuffle, drag one's feet, clump, slog, trek, tramp, hike.

true *adjective* **1** *what you say is true | it is true that he is dead | a true account* truthful, accurate, correct, right, valid, factual, exact, precise, faithful, genuine, reliable, veracious, honest. **2** *a true witch doctor* real, genuine, authentic, actual, bona fide, valid, legitimate; *inf.* honest-to-goodness. **3** *a true friend* loyal, faithful,

trustworthy, trusty, reliable, dependable, staunch, firm, fast, steady, constant, unswerving, unwavering, devoted, sincere, dedicated, supportive, dutiful. **4** *give a true picture of Colonial times* exact, precise, perfect, faithful, close, accurate, correct, unerring.
Antonyms: UNTRUE; FALSE; DISLOYAL; INACCURATE.

true *adverb* **1** *tell me true* truly, truthfully, honestly, sincerely, candidly, veraciously. **2** *the arrow flew true* accurately, unerringly, unswervingly, without deviating, on target; *inf.* dead on.

truly *adverb* **1** *she is truly his daughter* in truth, really, in reality, actually, in fact, genuinely, certainly, surely, definitely, decidedly, positively, absolutely, unquestionably, undoubtedly, beyond doubt/question, indubitably, beyond the shadow of a doubt. **2** *tell me truly what you think* truthfully, honestly, frankly, candidly, openly; *inf.* with no punches pulled. **3** *truly, I did not know* honestly, truthfully, genuinely, really, indeed, veritably. **4** *they are truly grateful* really, genuinely, sincerely, very, extremely, exceptionally. **5** *his valet had served him truly* loyally, faithfully, reliably, staunchly, firmly, steadily, constantly, unswervingly, devotedly, with all one's heart, sincerely, dedicatedly, dutifully. **6** *the novel does not truly depict the era* exactly, precisely, faithfully, closely, accurately, correctly, unerringly.

trump *verb* **trump up** *trump up an excuse for not going* invent, make up, fabricate, devise, concoct, hatch, contrive, fake; *inf.* cook up.

trumpet *verb* **1** *trumpet in rage* bellow, roar, bay, shout, yell, cry out, call out. **2** *trumpet the news of his appointment* proclaim, announce, herald, broadcast, promulgate, noise abroad.

truncate *verb* *truncate the time allotted | truncate the length/essay* shorten, reduce, diminish, decrease, cut short, prune, trim, lop, curtail, abbreviate.
Antonyms: LENGTHEN; EXTEND.

truncheon *noun* club, staff, stick.

trunk *noun* *put the linen in a trunk* chest, case, portmanteau, crate, storage box, box, coffer.

truss *verb* tie up, wrap up, bind up, bundle up.

truss *noun* *the truss of the bridge* support, brace, prop, strut, buttress.

trust *noun* **1** *have trust in the surgeon | take it on trust* faith, confidence, belief, conviction, credence, assurance, certainty, reliance, hope, expectation. **2** *a position of trust* responsibility, duty, obligation, commitment. **3** *the money is kept in trust for her* trusteeship, guardianship, safekeeping, protection, charge, care, custody.

trust *verb* **1** *I do not trust him | trust his judgment* put/place one's trust in, have faith/confidence in, be convinced by, pin one's hopes on. **2** *you can trust him to behave well* rely on, depend on, bank on, count on, be sure of, swear by. **3** *I trust you will come | trust everything is all right* hope, assume, presume, expect, believe, sup-

pose. **4** *he trusted his son to her* entrust, put in the hands of, turn over, assign, consign, commit, delegate.
Antonyms: DISTRUST; MISTRUST; DOUBT.

trustful *adjective* trusting, unsuspicious, unguarded, unwary, unsuspecting, unquestioning, credulous, gullible, ingenuous, naïve, innocent.
Antonyms: SUSPICIOUS; WARY.

trustworthy *adjective* *trustworthy employees* reliable, dependable, stable, staunch, loyal, faithful, trusty, responsible, sensible, levelheaded, honest, honorable, upright, ethical, righteous, principled, virtuous.
Antonyms: UNTRUSTWORTHY; UNRELIABLE; UNFAITHFUL.

trusty *adjective* *his trusty steed/valet* trustworthy, reliable, dependable, staunch, faithful, loyal, responsible.

truth *noun* **1** *no truth in what she says* truthfulness, accuracy, correctness, rightness, validity, fact, factualness, factuality, genuineness, veracity, verity, honesty. **2** *truth is stranger than fiction* reality, actuality, factuality. **3** *he is a man of truth* truthfulness, honesty, integrity, uprightness, righteousness, honor, honorableness, sincerity, candor. **4** *cite an old truth* truism, axiom, maxim, proverb, adage, aphorism, saw.

truthful *adjective* **1** *a truthful child* honest, trustworthy, veracious, candid, frank, open, forthright, straight. **2** *a truthful account* true, accurate, correct, right, valid, factual, exact, faithful, precise, genuine, reliable, veracious, honest.
Antonyms: UNTRUTHFUL; LYING; DISHONEST; INACCURATE.

try *verb* **1** *try to do well* attempt, aim, endeavor, make an effort, exert oneself, undertake, strive, assay, seek, struggle, do one's best; *inf.* have a go/shot/crack/stab. **2** *try a new brand | try something new* try out, test, put to the test, experiment with, assay, investigate, examine, appraise, evaluate, assess, experience, sample, check out. **3** *the children try her patience* tax, strain, make demands on, sap, drain, exhaust. **4** *she has been sorely tried by the children* trouble, bother, irk, vex, annoy, irritate, harass, afflict, nag, pester, plague, torment; *inf.* drive mad. **5** *try the case* hear, adjudge, adjudicate, examine.

try out *try out a new product/restaurant* try, test, put to the test, experiment with, appraise, evaluate, sample, check out.

trying *adjective* **1** *the visitors were very trying* troublesome, bothersome, tiresome, irksome, vexatious, annoying, irritating, exasperating. **2** *have a trying day* taxing, demanding, stressful, difficult, arduous, hard, tough, tiring, fatiguing, exhausting, upsetting.
Antonyms: ACCOMMODATING; EASY.

tuck *verb* **1** *tuck the shirt into the skirt* gather, push, ease, insert, stuff. **2** *tuck the material* gather, fold, ruck, ruffle, pleat. **tuck in** *tuck the child in* cover up, wrap up, put to bed, make snug/comfortable. **tuck away** *houses tucked away under the mountain* hide, conceal, secrete, stow away.

tuck *noun* *tucks in the fabric* gather, fold, ruck, ruffle, pleat.

tug *verb* **1** *tug the rope hard* | *tug her hair* pull, jerk, yank, wrench, wrest. **2** *the dog was tugging him along the road* pull, draw, drag, haul, tow, trail.

tug *noun* *give the gate a good tug* pull, jerk, yank, wrench, haul.

tuition *noun* teaching, instruction, coaching, education, schooling, training, drill, direction, guidance.

tumble *verb* **1** *the toddler tumbled suddenly* fall over, fall down, fall headlong, topple, fall head over heels, fall end over end, lose one's footing/balance, stumble, stagger, trip up. **2** *acrobats tumbling* somersault, go head over heels, flip. **3** *share prices have tumbled* plummet, plunge, slump, dive, drop, slide, fall, decrease, decline. **4** *ships tumbling about on the waves* roll, toss, pitch, heave, thrash. **5** *tumble out of bed* | *tumble into the car* fall headlong, move hurriedly, blunder, stumble. **6** *the wind had tumbled her hair* tousle, dishevel, ruffle, disarrange, disorder, mess up, rumple; *inf.* muss up.

tumble *noun* **1** *the toddler took a tumble* fall, stumble, trip, spill; *inf.* nosedive, header. **2** *the tumble of the share index* plummeting, plunge, slump, dive, drop, fall, decline, failure, collapse. **3** *acrobats demonstrating tumbles* somersault, flip, front/back flip, acrobatic feat.

tumbledown *adjective* dilapidated, ramshackle, crumbling, disintegrating, falling to pieces/bits, decrepit, ruined, in ruins, rickety, shaky, tottering, teetering.

tumid *adjective* *limbs looking tumid* swollen, enlarged, puffy, puffed up, bloated, distended, tumescent, turgid, edematose.

tumor *noun* **1** *benign tumors* lump, growth, swelling, excrescence, protuberance, tumefaction, intumescence. **2** *malignant tumor* cancerous growth, carcinoma, cancer, malignancy.

tumult *noun* **1** *we cannot hear you above the tumult* din, uproar, commotion, racket, hubbub, hullabaloo, clamor, shouting, yelling, pandemonium, babel, bedlam, noise. **2** *the meeting ended in tumult* disorder, disarray, disturbance, confusion, chaos, upheaval, uproar. **3** *police sent to deal with a tumult* riot, protest, insurrection, rebellion, breach of the peace, row, brawl, fight, quarrel, altercation, affray, fracas, melee, brouhaha; *inf.* free-for-all. **4** *emotions in tumult* turmoil, upheaval, confusion, ferment.

tumultuous *adjective* **1** *tumultuous applause* loud, noisy, clamorous, ear-shattering, deafening, ear-piercing, blaring, uproarious, unrestrained, boisterous. **2** *a tumultuous crowd* rowdy, unruly, boisterous, disorderly, disturbed, restless, agitated, excited, fierce, obstreperous, wild, violent, lawless, vociferous, noisy, rioting. **3** *tumultuous emotions* passionate, vehement, fervent, violent, raging, unrestrained, uncontrolled, frenzied, in turmoil, turbulent.

tune *noun* **1** *play a folk tune* melody, air, song, theme, strain, motif. **2** *his ideas are not in tune with modern thinking* agreement, accord, accordance, harmony, correspondence, congruence, conformity, sympathy. **3** *changed his tune* mind, attitude, view, opinion.

tune *verb* *tune the instrument* adjust, regulate, pitch, bring into harmony, attune.

tuneful *adjective* melodious, melodic, musical, rhythmical, mellifluous, sweet-sounding, dulcet, euphonious, lyrical, harmonious, pleasant, agreeable, catching, foot-tapping, easy on the ear.

Antonyms: DISCORDANT; HARSH.

tunnel *noun* **1** *miners crawling along the tunnel* underground/subterranean passage, underpass, subway. **2** *moles/rabbits making tunnels* burrow, underground passage.

tunnel *verb* **1** *prisoners tunneling under the prison* dig, excavate, burrow, mine. **2** *tunnel a way out* dig, excavate, cut, scoop out.

turbulence *noun* **1** *the turbulence of the seas* tempestuousness, storminess, roughness, choppiness, agitation. **2** *experience turbulence on the flight* irregular atmospheric motion, uneven air movement, rough air currents. **3** *the turbulence of the crowds* rowdiness, unruliness, disorderliness, restlessness, agitation, wildness, violence, noisiness. **4** *the turbulence of her emotions* agitation, instability, troubledness, turmoil.

turbulent *adjective* **1** *turbulent seas* tempestuous, stormy, raging, foaming, rough, choppy, agitated. **2** *turbulent crowds* rowdy, unruly, boisterous, disorderly, restless, agitated, obstreperous, wild, violent, lawless, noisy. **3** *affected by turbulent emotions/moods* disturbed, agitated, unsettled, unstable, troubled, distraught, in turmoil.

Antonyms: CALM; PEACEFUL; QUIET.

turf *noun* grass, patch of grass, lawn, green; sod; *lit.* sward.

turgid *adjective* **1** *turgid ankles* swollen, enlarged, puffy, puffed up, bloated, distended, tumescent, edematose. **2** *turgid prose* bombastic, high-flown, high-sounding, rhetorical, oratorical, grandiloquent, magniloquent, extravagant, pretentious, pompous, flowery, fulsome, orotund, fustian.

Antonyms: SIMPLE; PLAIN.

turmoil *noun* *the house was in turmoil just before the wedding* agitation, ferment, confusion, disorder, disarray, upheaval, chaos, pandemonium, bedlam, tumult; disturbance, bustle, flurry, commotion.

turn *verb* **1** *the wheel is turning* go around/round, rotate, revolve, circle, roll, spin, wheel, whirl, twirl, gyrate, swivel, pivot. **2** *he turned in the driveway* | *they turned for home* turn around/round, change direction/course, go back, return, reverse direction, make a U-turn. **3** *the tide is turning* change direction/course. **4** *he turned toward her* change position, veer, wheel around/round, swing around/round. **5** *turn the meat* turn over, reverse, invert, flip over, turn upside down, turn topsy-turvy. **6** *turn the hose on them* aim, direct, point, train, level, focus. **7** *his expression turned from amusement to horror* change, alter, transform, metamorphose, mutate. **8** *he turned nasty* become, come to be, get, go. **9** *the milk/butter turned* go/turn sour, sour, curdle, become rancid, go bad. **10** *the heat turned the milk/butter* turn sour, sour, curdle, make rancid, spoil, taint. **11** *my stomach is turning* be nauseated, be upset, be unsettled. **12** *the sight turned my stomach* nauseate, sicken, upset, unsettle. **13** *my head is turning* spin, feel dizzy/giddy. **14** *turn the corner* go/come around, round, pass around/round, negotiate, take. **15** *turn 40* | *turn 5 o'clock* become, reach, get to, pass. **16** *turn on/off/out the light* put, switch. **17** *turn somersaults* perform, execute, do, carry out. **18** *turn a profit* make, bring in, gain, acquire, obtain, get, procure, secure. **19** *turn a pot* shape, mold, fashion, form, cast, construct. **20** *he used to be a loyal follower, but he turned* change sides, go over, defect, desert, renege, turn renegade, break faith, apostatize, tergiversate. **turn against 1** *he suddenly turned against his old friend* become unfriendly/hostile to, take a dislike to. **2** *he turned her against her old friend* set against, make hostile to, cause to be unfriendly to/with, prejudice against, influence against. **turn away** *turn away the beggar* | *turn away those without tickets* send away, refuse admittance/entrance to, reject, rebuff, repel, cold-shoulder; *inf.* give the brush-off to. **turn back** *turn back if the weather is bad* go back, retrace one's steps, return, retreat. **turn down 1** *he turned down the applicant/proposal* reject, decline, give the thumbs down to, rebuff, repudiate, spurn, veto; *inf.* give the red light to. **2** *turn down the volume/gas* lessen, lower, reduce, decrease, diminish. **turn in 1** *turn in your homework/uniform before you leave* hand in, give in, submit, tender, hand over, deliver, return, give back, surrender. **2** *they turned in high scores* register, record, reach, achieve, attain. **3** *it is time to turn in* go to bed, retire, call it a day, go to sleep; *inf.* hit the hay/sack. **4** *her feet turn in* curve in, bend in/inward. **5** *turn him in to the police* hand over, turn over, deliver, inform on, betray; *inf.* squeal on, blow the whistle on, rat on, finger, put the finger on. **turn off 1** *turn off the electricity/heater* turn out, switch off, shut off, flick off, unplug. **2** *the driver suddenly turned off the main road* branch off, leave, quit, depart from,

deviate from. **3** *she turned off before the town* branch off, take a side road, take another road. **4** *he was turned off geography by the boring lessons* | *she was turned off by his table manners* put off, turn against; disenchant, alienate, repel, disgust, nauseate, sicken. **turn on 1** *turn on the electricity/heater* put on, switch on, flick on, plug in, operate. **2** *she turned on her husband when he criticized her friend* | *the dog turned on his master* attack, launch an attack on, fall on, set upon, become hostile to; *inf.* lay into, tear into, light into, lace into. **3** *the result turns on the number of people voting* depend on, hang on, hinge on, pivot on, rest on, be contingent on, be decided by. **4** *she is turned on by muscular men* arouse, sexually arouse, excite, titillate, stimulate, thrill, attract, please. **turn out 1** *turn her out of her house* | *the freeloader was turned out* put out, throw out, kick out, eject, evict, oust; *inf.* chuck out, bounce. **2** *turn out the delinquent workers* eject, dismiss, discharge, ax; *inf.* fire, sack, give the sack to, boot out. **3** *turn out the light/gas* turn off, put off, switch off, shut off, flick off, unplug. **4** *turn out thousands of books/toys per year* bring out, put out, produce, make, manufacture, fabricate, yield, process. **5** *a big crowd turned out to hear him* go, come, be present, attend, put in an appearance, appear, turn up, arrive, assemble, gather; *inf.* show up, show. **6** *as it turned out, we were safe* | *it turned out that she was right* happen, occur, come about, end up, prove to be the case, emerge, eventuate; *inf.* transpire, pan out. **7** *she turned out a beautiful girl* become, grow/come/get to be, develop into, end up, emerge as. **turn over 1** *the boat turned over* overturn, topple, upturn, capsize, keel over, turn turtle. **2** *they turned the boat over* overturn, upturn, upend, capsize, upset. **3** *turn over the pages* flick over, flip over, leaf over. **4** *turn over the pros and cons* consider, think about, ponder, reflect on, mull over, muse on, ruminate about. **5** *turn over the estate to his brother* hand over, transfer, consign, assign, commit. **turn to 1** *turn to drink* have recourse to, resort to, take to. **2** *turn to him for help* look to, apply to, approach, appeal to, have recourse to. **3** *turn to the next task* turn one's attention to, attend to, address/apply/devote oneself to, set about, take up, undertake. **turn up 1** *turn up the volume* increase, raise, amplify, make louder, intensify. **2** *turn up some interesting information* uncover, unearth, discover, bring to light, find, hit upon, dig up, ferret out, root out, expose. **3** *he has mislaid the book, but it will turn up* be found, be located, come to light. **4** *they did not turn up at the party* arrive, appear, put in an appearance, present oneself, be present; *inf.* show up, show. **5** *he hopes a job will turn up* present itself, occur, happen, crop up, pop up, arise, come on the scene, come to light, manifest itself; *inf.* transpire. **6** *turn up the garment* take up, raise, shorten.

turn noun **1** *give the wheel a few turns* rotation, revolution, circle, spin, whirl, twirl, gyration, swivel. **2** *take a turn to the left* change of direction/course, deviation, divergence, veer. **3** *a road full of turns* turning, bend, curve, corner, twist, winding. **4** *dislike the turn of events* trend, tendency, bias, leaning, direction, drift. **5** *a turn for the better/worse* change, alteration, variation, difference, deviation, divergence, shift. **6** *he is of an academic turn of mind* bent, tendency, inclination, bias, propensity, affinity, leaning, aptitude, talent, gift, flair, knack. **7** *it is your turn to play* time, opportunity, chance, stint, spell, move, try, attempt; *inf.* go, shot, crack. **8** *take a turn in the park* walk, stroll, saunter, amble, airing, constitutional, promenade, drive, ride, outing, excursion, jaunt; *inf.* spin. **9** *do him a good/bad turn* act, action, deed, service, gesture, favor. **10** *you gave me quite a turn* shock, start, surprise, fright, scare.

turning point noun *the turning point in their fortunes* crossroads, crisis, crisis point, critical period, crux, decisive point, moment of truth/decision.

turnout noun *there was a good turnout at the meeting* number, gathering, crowd, assembly, assemblage, audience, attendance, gate.

turnover noun **1** *the company's annual turnover is $2 million* gross revenue, volume of business, business, financial flow; sales figures. **2** *the turnover of staff is very high* change, coming and going, movement, replacement.

tussle noun struggle, wrestle, conflict, fight, battle, skirmish, scuffle, affray, brawl; *inf.* set-to, scrap.

tutor noun *tutors marking exams* teacher, instructor, coach, lecturer, educator.

tutor verb *tutor him in math* teach, instruct, coach, educate, school, train, drill, direct, guide.

TV noun *what is on TV tonight?* television; *inf.* the tube, the boob tube, the idiot box.

twaddle noun nonsense, rubbish, garbage, trash, drivel, blather, balderdash, bunkum, hogwash, gibberish, gobbledygook; *inf.* hot air, bunk, bosh, poppycock, piffle.

tweak verb *gently tweak his ear* twist, pinch, nip, twitch, squeeze, pull, jerk.

tweak noun *give his ear a tweak* twist, pinch, nip, twitch, squeeze, pull, jerk.

twig noun branch, stick, offshoot, shoot, spray, stem.

twilight noun **1** *walk home at twilight* dusk, late afternoon, early evening, gloaming. **2** *scarcely able to see her in the twilight* half-light, semidarkness, dimness. **3** *in the twilight of his career* decline, ebb, waning, closing years.

twin noun **1** *he and his brother are twins* identical twin, fraternal twin. **2** *where is the twin of that*

glove? mate, match, fellow, counterpart, complement. **3** *she is an absolute twin for the queen* double, look-alike, likeness, image, duplicate, clone; *inf.* spitting image, ringer, dead ringer.

twine noun **1** *a ball of twine* cord, string, yarn, thread. **2** *vines in a twine* coil, spiral, whorl, convolution, twist, tangle.

twine verb **1** *the plant had twined itself around the tree* entwine, coil, twist, wind, weave, wrap. **2** *twine a garland* weave, plait, braid, twist. **3** *the path twines up the mountain* twist, twist and turn, wind, curve, zigzag, meander, snake, worm.

twinge noun **1** *a twinge of rheumatism* stab of pain, spasm, pain, pang, ache, throb, tweak, tingle, cramp, stitch. **2** *a twinge of conscience* pang, uneasiness, discomfort, qualm, scruple, misgiving.

twinkle verb **1** *stars twinkling* glitter, glint, sparkle, flicker, shimmer, glimmer, gleam, dazzle, flash, wink, blink, shine, scintillate, coruscate. **2** *her eyes twinkled with amusement* sparkle, gleam, shine.

twinkle noun **1** *the twinkle of stars* twinkling, glitter, glint, sparkle, flicker, shimmer, glimmer, gleam, dazzle, flash, wink, blink, shining, scintillation, coruscation. **2** *with a twinkle of her eyes* sparkle, gleam, shining.

twinkling noun **1** *the twinkling of the stars* twinkle, glitter, glint, sparkle, flicker, shimmer. **2** *I will be there in a twinkling* instant, second, split second, moment, flash; *inf.* jiffy, shake, two shakes of a lamb's tail.

twirl verb **1** *twirl the cane* spin, whirl, twist. **2** *she twirled around/round to the music* spin, whirl, turn, pirouette, wheel, gyrate, revolve, rotate, pivot. **3** *twirl a curl of hair around/round her finger* twist, coil, wind, curl.

twirl noun **1** *give the cane a twirl* spin, whirl, twist. **2** *a series of twirls around/round the room* spin, whirl, turn, pirouette, gyration, revolution, rotation. **3** *a twirl of chocolate* twist, coil, whorl, curl.

twist verb **1** *twist the metal rod | twist it off the wall* bend, warp, misshape, deform, contort, distort; wrench, wrest. **2** *his face twisted in agony* contort, screw up. **3** *he twisted his ankle* wrench, turn, sprain. **4** *the plant had twisted itself around the tree* entwine, coil, wind, weave, wrap. **5** *twist a garland* twine, weave, plait, braid. **6** *twist a curl of hair around/round her finger* twirl, coil, wind, curl. **7** *the path twisted around/round the mountain* wind, curve, bend, twine, zigzag, meander, snake, worm. **8** *the child twisted out of his grasp* wriggle, writhe, squirm, wiggle. **9** *twist their words* distort, pervert, warp, garble, misrepresent, falsify, misquote, misreport, change, alter. **10** *she twisted her head around* swivel, screw, turn, rotate. **11** *she twisted around/round to look at him* swivel, turn, spin, pivot, rotate, revolve.

Antonyms: STRAIGHTEN; UNWIND.

twist noun **1** *with a twist of his arm* wrench, wrest, turn, contortion, pull, jerk, yank. **2** *try to repair the twist in the wire* bend, warp, kink, deformity, contortion, distortion, defect, flaw, imperfection. **3** *a painful twist of the ankle* wrench, turn, sprain. **4** *a twist of hair* coil, twirl, curl, braid. **5** *the twists in the mountain path* bend, turn, curve, winding, arc, zigzag, meander, undulation. **6** *a slight twist to his character* aberration, peculiarity, quirk, oddity, eccentricity, idiosyncrasy, foible. **7** *upset by the twist of events* development, turn, change, alteration, variation, slant.

twit *noun* fool, idiot, ass, blockhead, nincompoop, ninny, simpleton, clown; *inf.* chump, halfwit, dope.

twitch *verb* **1** *with limbs twitching* move spasmodically, jerk, jump, quiver, shiver, quaver. **2** *her eye twitched* blink, flutter, jump.

twitch *noun* **1** *his leg gave a twitch* spasm, jerk, jump, quiver, tremor, shiver, quaver. **2** *a twitch in her eye* blink, flutter, jump, tic.

twitter *verb* *birds twittering* chirrup, cheep, tweet, trill, warble, whistle, sing.

twitter *noun* *the twitter of the birds* trill, chirrup, cheep, tweet, warble, whistle, song.

two-edged *adjective* *a two-edged remark* double-edged, ambiguous, equivocal, ambivalent.

two-faced *adjective* hypocritical, insincere, deceitful, deceiving, dissembling, duplicitous, false, untrustworthy, treacherous, perfidious, double-dealing, Janus-faced.
Antonyms: SINCERE; HONEST.

tycoon *noun* magnate, baron, captain of industry, industrialist, financier, merchant prince, mogul; millionaire, multimillionaire, billionaire; *inf.* fat cat.

type *noun* **1** *a nasty type of person* | *a rare type of plant* kind, sort, variety, form, class, classification, category, group, order, set, genre, strain, species, genus; *inf.* ilk. **2** *he's a nasty type* person, individual, specimen, character. **3** *they regard her as the very type of womanhood* example, exemplar, model, pattern, essence, personification, epitome, quintessence, archetype, prototype. **4** *set in a different kind of type* print, font, face, character.

typhoon *noun* tropical storm, hurricane, squall, tempest.

typical *adjective* **1** *a typical New England winter* representative, classic, standard, stock, orthodox, conventional, true-to-type, quintessential, archetypal. **2** *what would be your typical day?* normal, average, ordinary, regular, general, customary, habitual, routine, run-of-the-mill. **3** *it is typical of him to be rude* characteristic, in character, in keeping, to be expected, usual, normal.
Antonyms: atypical; EXCEPTIONAL; UNORTHODOX; SINGULAR.

typify *verb* **1** *he typifies the self-made man* exemplify, characterize, personify, epitomize, symbolize, embody, sum up, incarnate. **2** *they have tried to typify the various sectors of society* exemplify, represent, indicate, illustrate, denote.

tyrannical *adjective* despotic, autocratic, dictatorial, absolute, arbitrary, authoritarian, high-handed, imperious, oppressive, coercive, domineering, bullying, harsh, strict, severe, cruel, brutal, unjust, unreasonable.
Antonyms: DEMOCRATIC; LIBERAL; GENTLE.

tyrannize *verb* *tyrannize over the peasants* | *tyrannize the children* rule despotically, rule with a rod of iron; oppress, suppress, repress, crush, subjugate, dominate, domineer, order around, browbeat, intimidate, bully, ride roughshod over, lord it over.

tyranny *noun* **1** *the tyranny of the country's/ school's regime* despotism, absolutism, authoritarianism, arbitrariness, high-handedness, imperiousness, oppressiveness, oppression, coercion, bullying, harshness, strictness, severity, cruelty, brutality, unjustness, unreasonableness. **2** *government by tyranny rather than democracy* despotism, autocracy, dictatorship, absolute power, authoritarianism.

tyrant *noun* despot, autocrat, dictator, absolute ruler, authoritarian, oppressor, martinet, slave driver, bully.

U

ubiquitous *adjective* everywhere, omnipresent, ever-present, in all places, all over, all over the place, pervasive, universal.

ugly *adjective* **1** *ugly people/buildings* ill-favored, hideous, plain, unattractive, unlovely, homely, unprepossessing, unsightly, displeasing; *inf.* not much to look at. **2** *an ugly sight met their eyes* hideous, horrible, horrid, frightful, terrible, disagreeable, unpleasant, foul, nasty, vile, shocking, distasteful, disgusting, revolting, repellent, repugnant, loathsome, hateful, nauseating, sickening. **3** *he is an ugly character* horrible, disagreeable, unpleasant, nasty, objectionable, offensive, obnoxious, foul, vile, base, dishonorable, dishonest, rotten. **4** *an ugly situation* threatening, menacing, ominous, sinister, dangerous, nasty, unpleasant, disagreeable. **5** *the crowd grew ugly* nasty, angry, bad-tempered, ill-natured, hostile, surly, sullen, mean, sour. **6** *gave them ugly looks* dark, threatening, menacing, hostile, spiteful, malevolent, evil.
Antonyms: BEAUTIFUL; ATTRACTIVE; PLEASANT; FRIENDLY.

ulcer *noun* ulceration, sore, open sore, abscess, gathering, boil, carbuncle, pustule.

ulterior *adjective* *an ulterior motive* hidden, concealed, unrevealed, undisclosed, undivulged, unexpressed, secret, covert, unapparent.
Antonyms: OVERT; OBVIOUS.

ultimate *adjective* **1** *the ultimate outcome | take ultimate responsibility* last, final, eventual, concluding, conclusive, terminal, end, furthest. **2** *ultimate truths* basic, fundamental, primary, elemental, radical. **3** *the ultimate gift/luxury* topmost, utmost, maximum, supreme, superlative, paramount, greatest, highest, unsurpassed, unrivaled.
Antonyms: FIRST; SECONDARY; MINIMUM.

ultimate *noun* *the ultimate in luxury* last word, utmost, height, peak, culmination, perfection, epitome, nonpareil.

ultimately *adverb* **1** *he is bound to win ultimately* in the end, in the long run, eventually, finally, sooner or later. **2** *ultimately he is an honorable person* basically, fundamentally, at heart, deep down.

ultramodern *adjective* ahead of its/one's time, futuristic, avant-garde, modernistic, advanced, progressive, forward-looking.

umbrage *noun* offense, pique, chagrin, vexation, irritation, exasperation, indignation, annoyance, anger, ire, high dudgeon, hurt, resentment, bitterness; *inf.* huff.
Antonyms: PLEASURE; GOODWILL.

umbrella *noun* *under the umbrella of the parent organization* agency, aegis, cover, protection, support, patronage, backing.

umpire *noun* *the umpire in the dispute/game* adjudicator, arbitrator, arbiter, judge, moderator, referee; *inf.* ref.

umpire *verb* *umpire in the dispute | umpire the match* adjudicate, arbitrate, judge, moderate, referee; *inf.* ref.

umpteen *adjective* countless, numerous, very many, ever so many.

unable *adjective* *unable to get about | unable to reach the standard* not able, incapable, powerless, impotent, not up/equal to, inadequate, ineffectual, incompetent, unfit, unfitted, unqualified.

unabridged *adjective* uncut, unshortened, unreduced, uncondensed, unexpurgated, full-length, complete, entire, whole, intact.

unacceptable *adjective* **1** *unacceptable terms of agreement* unsatisfactory, inadmissible, unsuitable. **2** *unacceptable behavior* insupportable, intolerable, objectionable, offensive, obnoxious, undesirable, disagreeable, distasteful, improper.

unaccompanied *adjective* *go unaccompanied | unaccompanied people* alone, on one's own, by oneself, partnerless, unescorted, solo, lone, solitary, single.

unaccomplished *adjective* **1** *unaccomplished tasks* unfinished, uncompleted, incomplete, undone, half-done, unperformed, unexecuted. **2** *unaccomplished players* inexpert, unskillful, unskilled, without finesse, blundering, talentless, amateur, dilettante.

unaccountable *adjective* **1** *an unaccountable increase in births | for some unaccountable reason* inexplicable, unexplainable, insoluble, unsolvable, incomprehensible, beyond comprehension/understanding, unfathomable, puzzling, baffling, mysterious, inscrutable, peculiar, unusual, curious, strange, queer, bizarre, extraordinary, astonishing; *inf.* weird. **2** *her colleagues have been blamed for the error, but she is unaccountable* not responsible, not answerable, not liable, free, clear, exempt, immune.

unaccustomed *adjective* *the unaccustomed luxury* unusual, unfamiliar, uncommon, unwonted, new, exceptional, out of the ordinary, extraordinary, special, remarkable, singular, rare, surprising, strange. **unaccustomed to** *unaccustomed to public speaking* unused to, not used to, new to, unpracticed at/in, unfamiliar with, inexperienced at/in, unversed in.

unaffected *adjective* **1** *unaffected children* artless, guileless, ingenuous, naïve, unsophisticated, unassuming, unpretentious, down-to-earth, without airs, natural, plain, simple. **2** *unaffected sincerity* unfeigned, unpretended, genuine, real, sincere, honest, true, candid, frank; *inf.* up-front. **unaffected by** *unaffected by the events* unchanged by, unaltered by, uninfluenced by, untouched by, unmoved by, unimpressed by, proof against, impervious to, unresponsive to, insensible to, invulnerable to.

unanimity *noun* **1** *the unanimity of the committee* agreement, accord, concord, unity, consensus, like-mindedness. **2** *the unanimity of the vote* solidity, concertedness, consensus, uniformity, consistency, congruence.
Antonyms: DISAGREEMENT; DIVISION.

unanimous *adjective* **1** *the committee was unanimous* in complete agreement/accord, of one mind, like-minded, totally in harmony, at one, with one voice, united, concordant. **2** *a unanimous vote* solid, united, concerted, uniform, consistent, congruent.

unanswerable *adjective* **1** *an unanswerable case* irrefutable, inarguable, indisputable, undeniable, incontestable, incontrovertible, conclusive, absolute, positive. **2** *unanswerable questions* insoluble, unsolvable, insolvable, unresolvable, unexplainable, inexplicable. **3** *unanswerable for the error* not answerable, not responsible, unaccountable.

unapproachable *adjective* **1** *unapproachable places* inaccessible, remote, out-of-the-way, out of reach, beyond reach, unreachable; *inf.* off the beaten path/track. **2** *the new teacher is unapproachable* aloof, standoffish, distant, remote, detached, reserved, withdrawn, uncommunicative, unresponsive, unfriendly, unsociable, cool, chilly, frigid.

unarmed *adjective* without arms/weapons, weaponless, open to attack, defenseless, unprotected, vulnerable, exposed, pregnable.

unassailable *adjective* **1** *an unassailable stronghold* impregnable, invulnerable, invincible, secure, well-defended. **2** *their unassailable right to vote* indisputable, undeniable, unquestionable, incontestable, incontrovertible, irrefutable, conclusive, absolute, positive, proven.

unassuming *adjective* modest, self-effacing, humble, meek, retiring, demure, restrained, reticent, diffident, shy, bashful, unassertive, unobtrusive, unostentatious, unpretentious, unaffected, natural, genuine, simple, artless, ingenuous.
Antonyms: BOLD; BRAZEN; PRETENTIOUS.

unattached *adjective* **1** *she is still unattached* unmarried, unwed, unwedded, unengaged, un-betrothed, wifeless, husbandless, spouseless, uncommitted, free, available, footloose and fancy free, partnerless, single, on one's own, by oneself, unescorted. **2** *a merger was discussed, but the firm is still unattached* independent, unaffiliated, unassociated, autonomous, nonaligned, self-governing, self-ruling.

unattended *adjective* **1** *an unattended garden* untended, neglected, ignored, disregarded, forgotten, forsaken, abandoned. **2** *an unattended vehicle* by itself, left alone, unguarded, unwatched. **3** *unattended young women* unaccompanied, alone, lone, on one's own, by oneself, partnerless, unescorted.

unauthorized *adjective* uncertified, unaccredited, unlicensed, unofficial, unsanctioned, unwarranted, unapproved, disallowed, prohibited, forbidden, illegal.

unavailing *adjective* vain, futile, useless, ineffective, ineffectual, unsuccessful, failed, fruitless, unproductive, pointless, to no avail/purpose, abortive, for naught.

unavoidable *adjective* inescapable, inevitable, bound to happen, inexorable, ineludible, ineluctable, certain, fated, predestined, necessary, compulsory, required, obligatory, mandatory.

unaware *adjective* **1** *unaware of what is going on | unaware that they have gone* unknowing, unconscious, ignorant, heedless, unmindful, oblivious, uninformed (about), unenlightened (about); *inf.* in the dark. **2** *politically unaware* not perceptive, undiscerning, incognizant, nondiscriminating, unresponsive.

unawares *adverb* **1** *come upon him unawares* unexpectedly, by surprise, without warning, suddenly, abruptly, unprepared, off guard; *inf.* with one's pants down. **2** *I must have dropped my keys unawares* unknowingly, unwittingly, unintentionally, unconsciously, inadvertently, without noticing, accidentally, by accident, by mistake, mistakenly.

unbalanced *adjective* **1** *unbalanced since the death of her husband* unstable, of unsound mind, mentally ill, deranged, demented, crazed, distracted, insane, mad, lunatic; *inf.* crazy, not all there, off one's head. **2** *an unbalanced report of the events* one-sided, biased, prejudiced, partisan, partial, inequitable, unjust, unfair.

unbearable *adjective* intolerable, insufferable, unsupportable, unendurable, unacceptable, more than flesh and blood can stand; *inf.* too much, enough to try the patience of a saint.

unbeatable *adjective* invincible, indomitable, unconquerable, unstoppable, unsurpassable, excelling.

unbecoming *adjective* **1** *an unbecoming hat* unflattering, unattractive, unsightly. **2** *behavior unbecoming in a young girl | unbecoming behavior* unfitting, inappropriate, unsuitable, inapt, improper, indecorous, unseemly, unladylike, ungentlemanly, indelicate, tasteless.

unbelief *noun* nonbelief, atheism, disbelief, incredulity, skepticism, doubt, agnosticism.

unbelievable *adjective* beyond belief, incredible, unconvincing, far-fetched, implausible, improbable, inconceivable, unthinkable, unimaginable, impossible, astonishing, astounding, staggering, preposterous.

unbeliever *noun* nonbeliever, atheist, disbeliever, infidel, skeptic, doubter, doubting Thomas, agnostic.

unbend *verb* 1 *unbend the twisted wire* straighten, align, flatten. 2 *she unbent enough to smile* relax, become less formal, become informal, unwind, loosen up, let oneself go; *inf.* let one's hair down, let up, let it all hang out, hang loose.

unbending *adjective* 1 *an unbending material* rigid, stiff, inflexible, unpliable, inelastic, unmalleable. 2 *an unbending person* formal, stiff, aloof, reserved; *inf.* uptight. 3 *an unbending regime* inflexible, hard-line, uncompromising, tough, harsh, strict, stern, severe, firm, resolute, determined, unrelenting, relentless, inexorable.

unbiased *adjective* impartial, unprejudiced, nonpartisan, neutral, objective, disinterested, dispassionate, detached, evenhanded, openminded, equitable, fair, fair-minded, just.

unbind *verb* 1 *unbind the hostages* release, free, set free/loose, liberate, untie, unchain, unfetter. 2 *unbind the ropes* untie, unfasten, undo, loosen, unloose.

unborn *adjective* 1 *her unborn child* expected, awaited, in utero, embryonic. 2 *unborn generations* future, to come, coming, subsequent, hereafter.

unbounded *adjective* boundless, unlimited, limitless, illimitable, infinite, unrestrained, unconstrained, uncontrolled, unchecked, unbridled, vast, immense, immeasurable.

Antonyms: LIMITED; RESTRICTED.

unbreakable *adjective* nonbreakable, shatterproof, infrangible, indestructible, toughened.

unbridled *adjective* unrestrained, unconstrained, uncontrolled, unchecked, uncurbed, ungoverned, rampant, excessive, intemperate.

unbroken *adjective* 1 *unbroken china/sets* intact, whole, undamaged, unimpaired, complete, entire. 2 *an unbroken horse* untamed, unsubdued. 3 *an unbroken series* uninterrupted, continuous, unremitting, ceaseless, unceasing, endless, incessant, constant, nonstop. 4 *unbroken sleep* uninterrupted, undisturbed, untroubled, sound. 5 *unbroken records* unbeaten, unsurpassed, unrivaled.

unburden *verb* 1 *unburden the horse* unload, disburden, unpack, disencumber. 2 *unburden one's sins/guilt* confess, confide, acknowledge, disclose, reveal, divulge, expose, lay bare, make a clean breast of; *inf.* come clean.

uncalled-for *adjective* 1 *uncalled-for advice* unsought, unasked, unsolicited, unrequested, unprompted, unwelcome, gratuitous. 2 *uncalled-for rudeness* unnecessary, needless, undeserved, unmerited, unjustified, unreasonable, inappropriate.

uncanny *adjective* 1 *uncanny happenings in the old house* strange, mysterious, odd, queer, weird, eerie, unnatural, preternatural, supernatural, unearthly, ghostly; *inf.* creepy, spooky. 2 *bear an uncanny resemblance to the president* remarkable, striking, extraordinary, exceptional, astounding, astonishing, incredible.

Antonyms: ORDINARY; RUN-OF-THE-MILL; USUAL.

unceremonious *adjective* 1 *his unceremonious departure* abrupt, sudden, hasty, hurried, undignified, rude, impolite, uncivil, discourteous, unmannerly. 2 *an unceremonious occasion* informal, without ritual, casual, simple, relaxed, easy.

uncertain *adjective* 1 *the outcome is uncertain* unknown, undetermined, unsettled, pending, in the balance, up in the air. 2 *feel uncertain about what to do* unsure, doubtful, dubious, undecided, unresolved, indecisive, irresolute, hesitant, wavering, vacillating, equivocating, vague, hazy, unclear, ambivalent, in two minds. 3 *the future is uncertain* unpredictable, unforeseeable, incalculable, speculative, unreliable, untrustworthy, undependable, risky, chancy. 4 *uncertain weather* changeable, variable, irregular, fitful, unpredictable, unreliable. 5 *in an uncertain voice* hesitant, hesitating, tentative, halting, unsure, unconfident.

uncertainty *noun* 1 *full of uncertainty about the future* unsureness, indecision, irresolution, hesitancy, vacillation, equivocation, doubt, doubtfulness, vagueness, ambivalence. 2 *the uncertainty of the future* unpredictability, unreliability, riskiness, chanciness. 3 *give voice to a few uncertainties* doubt, qualm, misgiving, quandary, dilemma. 4 *the uncertainty of the weather* changeableness, variability, irregularity, fitfulness, unpredictability, unreliability. 5 *the uncertainty in her voice | uncertainty of the baby's steps* hesitancy, tentativeness, unsureness, lack of confidence.

---

uncertainty
doubt, dubiety, skepticism

If you're not sure about something, you're probably experiencing a degree of **uncertainty**, which is a general term covering everything from a mere lack of absolute certainty (*uncertainty about the time of the dinner party*) to an almost complete lack of knowledge that makes it impossible to do more than guess at the result or outcome (*uncertainty about the country's future*). **Doubt** implies both uncertainty and an inability to make a decision because the evidence is insufficient (*considerable doubt as to her innocence*). **Dubiety** comes closer in meaning to *uncertainty* than to *doubt*, because it stresses a lack of sureness rather than an inability to reach a decision; but unlike *uncertainty*, it connotes wavering or fluctuating between one conclusion and another (*no one could fail to notice the dubiety in his voice*). If you exhibit **skepticism**, you are not so much uncertain as unwilling to believe. It usually refers to an habitual state of mind or to a customary reaction (*she always listened to his excuses with skepticism*).

unchangeable *adjective* changeless, immutable, unalterable, incommutable, invariable, firm, fixed, established, permanent, deep-rooted, enduring, abiding, lasting, indestructible, unfading, constant, perpetual, eternal.

uncharitable *adjective uncharitable in judging other's faults* harsh, severe, stern, hard, hard-hearted, censorious, uncompromising, inflexible, unforgiving, merciless, ruthless, uncompassionate, unsympathetic, ungenerous, unfeeling, unkind, unchristian.

uncharted *adjective uncharted territory* unmapped, unsurveyed, unexplored, unresearched, unplumbed, unfamiliar, unknown, strange.

uncivil *adjective* discourteous, rude, impolite, unmannerly, bad-mannered, ill-bred, ungallant, unchivalrous, ungracious, disrespectful, brusque, curt, gruff, surly, boorish, churlish, uncouth.

uncivilized *adjective* **1** *uncivilized tribes* barbarian, barbarous, barbaric, primitive, savage, wild. **2** *some of their friends are so uncivilized* uncouth, coarse, rough, boorish, vulgar, philistine, uneducated, uncultured, uncultivated, unsophisticated, unrefined, unpolished.

unclean *adjective* **1** *unclean water* dirty, filthy, polluted, fouled, impure, adulterated, tainted. **2** *unclean hands/houses* dirty, filthy, grubby, grimy, stained, besmirched, smeared, unwashed. **3** *unclean people corrupting the innocent* unchaste, impure, lustful, licentious, lewd, corrupt, sullied, degenerate, bad, wicked, evil, sinful. **4** *unclean food* forbidden, impure.

uncomfortable *adjective* **1** *uncomfortable chairs/shoes/houses* not comfortable. **2** *feel uncomfortable in their presence* uneasy, ill-at-ease, nervous, tense, edgy, self-conscious, awkward, embarrassed, discomfited, disturbed, troubled, worried, anxious, apprehensive. **3** *an uncomfortable silence* awkward, uneasy, unpleasant, disagreeable, painful, distressing, disturbing.

uncommitted *adjective* **1** *uncommitted young people* unpledged, unpromised, unengaged, unbetrothed, unmarried, free, available, unattached, single. **2** *uncommitted politically* nonaligned, nonpartisan, neutral, undecided, floating, undeclared, sitting on the fence.

uncommon *adjective* **1** *an uncommon name* unusual, rare, uncustomary, unfamiliar, strange, odd, curious, out of the ordinary, novel, singular, peculiar, queer, bizarre; *inf.* weird. **2** *those birds are uncommon here* rare, scarce, infrequent, few and far between, occasional. **3** *an uncommon resemblance/appetite* remarkable, extraordinary, exceptional, singular, outstanding, notable, noteworthy, distinctive, striking.

uncommonly *adverb uncommonly talented* unusually, remarkably, extraordinarily, exceptionally, singularly, particularly, strikingly, extremely, inordinately, incredibly, amazingly.

uncommunicative *adjective* taciturn, reserved, shy, retiring, diffident, reticent, quiet, unforthcoming, unconversational, untalkative, silent, tight-lipped, secretive, unresponsive, close, distant, remote, aloof, withdrawn, standoffish, unsociable, antisocial.

uncompromising *adjective* rigid, stiff, inflexible, unbending, unyielding, hard-line, tough, immovable, firm, determined, dogged, obstinate, obdurate, tenacious, relentless, implacable, inexorable, intransigent.

unconcern *noun* indifference, apathy, lack of interest, uninterestedness, nonchalance, insouciance, lack of involvement, passivity, dispassionateness, detachment, aloofness, remoteness.

unconcerned *adjective she is completely unconcerned despite her difficulties* unworried, untroubled, unperturbed, unruffled, unanxious, insouciant, nonchalant, carefree, blithe, without a care in the world, serene, relaxed, at ease.

unconcerned with *unconcerned with political issues* indifferent about, apathetic about, uninterested in, uninvolved with/in, dispassionate about, detached from, aloof from, remote from.

unconditional *adjective* complete, total, entire, full, plenary, outright, absolute, downright, out-and-out, utter, all-out, thoroughgoing, unequivocal, conclusive, definite, positive, indubitable, incontrovertible, categorical, unqualified, unlimited, unreserved, unrestricted.

unconnected *adjective* **1** *the two houses are unconnected* unjoined, detached, independent, separate. **2** *the two events are unconnected* unassociated, unrelated, separate. **3** *his prose style is unconnected | unconnected prose* disconnected, disjointed, rambling, diffuse, ununified, disorderly, haphazard, disorganized, incoherent, meaningless.

unconscionable *adjective* **1** *an unconscionable criminal* amoral, immoral, unethical, unprincipled, unscrupulous, dishonorable, dishonest, corrupt. **2** *an unconscionable length of time* excessive, unwarranted, uncalled-for, unreasonable, inordinate, immoderate, undue, outrageous, preposterous, inexcusable.

Antonyms: MORAL; ACCEPTABLE; MODERATE.

unconscious *adjective* **1** *fall unconscious* senseless, insensible, comatose, knocked out, stunned, dazed; *inf.* blacked out, KO'd, out like a light, laid out, out cold, out. **2** *unconscious of the noise* unaware, heedless, ignorant, in ignorance, incognizant, oblivious, insensible. **3** *deliver an unconscious insult* unintentional, unintended, accidental, unthinking, unwitting, inadvertent, unpremeditated. **4** *unconscious prejudice* instinctive, automatic, reflex, involuntary, inherent, innate, subliminal, subconscious, latent.

uncontrollable *adjective* **1** *uncontrollable children* out of control, unmanageable, ungovernable, wild, unruly, disorderly, restive, recalcitrant, refractory, intractable, incorrigible, contumacious. **2** *uncontrollable rages* ungovernable, unrestrained, wild, violent, frantic, frenzied, raging, raving, mad.

unconventional *adjective* unorthodox, irregular, informal, unusual, uncommon, uncustomary, unwonted, rare, out of the ordinary, atypical, singular, individual, individualistic, different, original, idiosyncratic, nonconformist, bohemian, eccentric, odd, strange, bizarre; *inf.* offbeat, freakish, way-out.

uncoordinated *adjective* *uncoordinated people always dropping things* clumsy, awkward, inept, maladroit, bungling, blundering, bumbling, lumbering, heavy-footed, clodhopping, graceless, ungainly; *inf.* butterfingered, all thumbs, like a bull in a china shop, klutzy.

uncouth *adjective* rough, coarse, uncivilized, uncultured, uncultivated, unrefined, unpolished, unsophisticated, provincial, crude, gross, loutish, boorish, oafish, churlish, uncivil, rude, impolite, discourteous, unmannerly, bad-mannered, ill-bred, vulgar.
Antonyms: REFINED; CULTIVATED; SOPHISTICATED.

uncover *verb* **1** *uncover the wound/food* expose, lay bare, bare, reveal, unwrap. **2** *uncover a plot against the president* discover, detect, unearth, dig up, expose, bring to light, unmask, unveil, reveal, lay bare, make known, divulge, disclose.

unctuous *adjective* **1** *unctuous followers | unctuous behavior* sycophantic, ingratiating, obsequious, fawning, servile, toadying, insincere, flattering, honey-tongued, gushing, effusive, suave, urbane, glib, smooth. **2** *unctuous substance* oily, oleaginous, greasy, soapy, saponaceous.

undaunted *adjective* undismayed, unalarmed, unafraid, unflinching, unfaltering, indomitable, resolute, unflagging, intrepid, bold, valiant, brave, courageous, heroic, doughty, plucky; *inf.* spunky.

undecided *adjective* **1** *the result is as yet undecided* uncertain, unsettled, unresolved, indefinite, unknown, unestablished, unascertained, pending, in the balance, up in the air. **2** *they are undecided as to what to do* unsure, uncertain, doubtful, dubious, unresolved, indeci-

sive, irresolute, hesitant, wavering, vacillating, equivocating, dithering, vague, hazy, unclear, ambivalent, in two minds.

undefined *adjective* **1** *an undefined reason/plan* unexplained, nonspecific, unspecified, indeterminate, unclear, vague, imprecise, inexact. **2** *undefined shapes* indefinite, indistinct, vague, hazy, nebulous, dim, obscure, blurred, shadowy, formless.
Antonyms: SPECIFIC; DEFINITE; CLEAR.

undemonstrative *adjective* unemotional, impassive, restrained, self-contained, reserved, uncommunicative, unresponsive, stiff, reticent, aloof, distant, remote, withdrawn, cool, cold, unaffectionate.

undeniable *adjective* indisputable, indubitable, unquestionable, beyond doubt/question, inarguable, incontrovertible, incontestable, irrefutable, unassailable, certain, sure, definite, positive, proven, clear, obvious, evident, manifest, patent.

under *preposition* **1** *under the tree* below, beneath, underneath, at the foot/bottom of. **2** *prices under $5 | numbers under 20* below, less than, lower than, smaller than. **3** *ranks under major* below, lower than, inferior to, subordinate to, junior to, secondary to, subservient to, reporting to, subject to, controlled by, at the mercy of, under the heel of. **4** *under repair* undergoing, receiving, in the process of. **5** *under the water* submerged by, immersed in, sunk in, engulfed by, inundated by, flooded by, drowned by. **6** *it is under his mother's name* listed under, classified under, categorized under, placed under, positioned under, included under, subsumed under. **7** *living under threat* subject to, liable to, bound by.

under *adverb* **1** *if you cannot go over the bridge, go under* below, beneath, underneath. **2** *his father kept him under* down, in an inferior position, in a subordinate position; *inf.* under someone's thumb. **3** *the swimmer went under* underwater, to the bottom, downward.

underclothes *plural noun* undergarments; underclothing, underwear, lingerie, underlinen; *inf.* underthings, undies, unmentionables.

undercover *adjective* **1** *an undercover operation | undercover behavior* secret, hidden, concealed, masked, veiled, shrouded, private, confidential, covert, clandestine, underground, surreptitious, furtive, stealthy, sly; *inf.* hush-hush. **2** *undercover agents* spying, espionage.
Antonyms: OPEN; OVERT.

undercurrent *noun* **1** *boats affected by the undercurrent* undertow, underflow. **2** *an undercurrent of discontent in the firm* undertone, overtone, hint, suggestion, implication, whisper, murmur, atmosphere, aura, tenor, flavor; vibrations; *inf.* vibes.

undercut *verb* **1** *undercut their competitors* charge less than, undersell. **2** *undercut the ore vein* cut out, cut away, gouge out, scoop out, hollow out, excavate. **3** *laws undercutting democracy* undermine, weaken, impair, damage, injure, sap, threaten, subvert, sabotage.

underdog *noun* weaker party, loser, victim, prey, scapegoat; *inf.* fall guy, stooge.

underestimate *verb* **1** *underestimate the cost* miscalculate, misjudge, set too low. **2** *underestimate the opposition* underrate, rate too low, undervalue, set little store by, not do justice to, misprize, minimize, hold cheap, belittle, disparage, look down on, deprecate, depreciate; *inf.* sell short.

undergo *verb* *undergo surgery/hardship* go through, experience, sustain, be subjected to, submit to, endure, bear, tolerate, stand, withstand, put up with, weather.

underground *adverb* **1** *animals going underground* below ground, below the surface. **2** *criminals going underground* into secrecy, into seclusion, into hiding, behind closed doors.

underground *adjective* **1** *underground shelters* subterranean, subterrestrial, below-ground, buried, sunken, hypogean. **2** *an underground organization* secret, clandestine, surreptitious, covert, undercover, concealed, hidden. **3** *underground literature* unconventional, unorthodox, experimental, avant-garde, alternative, radical, revolutionary, subversive.

underground *noun* **1** *go around London by underground* metro, subway; *inf.* tube. **2** *arresting members of the underground* resistance, opposition; partisans.

undergrowth *noun* underwood, thicket, brush, scrub, underbrush.

underhand, underhanded *adjective* deceitful, devious, crafty, cunning, scheming, sneaky, furtive, secret, clandestine, surreptitious, covert, dishonest, dishonorable, unethical, immoral, unscrupulous, fraudulent, dirty, unfair, treacherous, double-dealing, below the belt, two-timing; *inf.* crooked.
Antonyms: HONEST; HONORABLE; FAIR; ABOVEBOARD.

underline *verb* **1** *underline the word* underscore, emphasize. **2** *underline the importance of seat belts* emphasize, stress, highlight, point up, accentuate, call attention to, give prominence to.
Antonyms: play down (*see* PLAY); MINIMIZE.

underling *noun* subordinate, deputy, junior, inferior, minion, lackey, flunky, menial, retainer, hireling, servant.
Antonyms: BOSS; LEADER.

underlying *adjective* **1** *underlying issues* basic, basal, fundamental, primary, prime, root, elementary, elemental. **2** *an underlying hostility* latent, lurking, concealed, hidden, veiled, masked.
Antonyms: SUBORDINATE; OVERT.

undermine *verb* **1** *undermine their authority* weaken, impair, damage, injure, sap, threaten, subvert, sabotage; *inf.* throw a monkey wrench in/into the works of, foul up. **2** *undermine the foundations* tunnel under, dig under, burrow

under, excavate. **3** *undermine the riverbanks* wear away, erode, eat away at.

underprivileged *adjective* disadvantaged, deprived, in need, needy, in want, destitute, in distress, poor, impoverished, impecunious, badly off.

underrate *verb* underestimate, undervalue, set little store by, rate too low, not do justice to, belittle, disparage; *inf.* sell short.

undersized *adjective* undersize, underdeveloped, stunted, atrophied, dwarf, dwarfish, pygmy, runtish, short, small, little, tiny, minuscule, stubby, squat; *inf.* pint-sized, pocket-sized, knee-high to a grasshopper.

understand *verb* **1** *understand his meaning* | *understand what he says* comprehend, apprehend, grasp, see, take in, perceive, discern, make out, glean, recognize, appreciate, get to know, follow, fathom, get to the bottom of, penetrate, interpret; *inf.* get the hang/drift of, catch on, latch on to, figure out. **2** *I understand your feelings/position* appreciate, accept, commiserate with, feel compassionate toward, sympathize with, empathize with. **3** *I understand that he has left* gather, hear, be informed, learn, believe, think, conclude.
Antonyms: MISUNDERSTAND; be ignorant of (*see* IGNORANT); IGNORE.

understanding *noun* **1** *it depends on your understanding of his meaning* comprehension, apprehension, grasp, perception, discernment, appreciation, interpretation. **2** *his powers of understanding are limited* | *use your understanding* intelligence, intellect, mind, brainpower; brains, powers of reasoning; *inf.* gray matter. **3** *it is my understanding that he has gone* belief, perception, view, notion, idea, fancy, conclusion, feeling. **4** *treat the difficult problem with understanding* compassion, sympathy, empathy, insight. **5** *we have an understanding, although not a signed contract* agreement, gentleman's agreement, arrangement, bargain, pact, compact, (verbal) contract.
Antonyms: IGNORANCE; MISUNDERSTANDING; INDIFFERENCE.

understanding *adjective* *an understanding boss to give him time off* compassionate, sympathetic, sensitive, considerate, kind, thoughtful, tolerant, patient, forbearing, lenient, merciful, forgiving.

understate *verb* *understate the difficulties* downplay, play down, make light of, minimize, deemphasize; *inf.* soft-pedal.

understudy *noun* substitute, replacement, reserve, stand-in, fill-in, locum, backup, relief.

undertake *verb* *undertake the job/responsibility* take on, set about, tackle, shoulder, assume, enter upon, begin, start, commence, embark on, venture upon, attempt, try.
Antonyms: NEGLECT; FORGO, FOREGO.

undertaker *noun* funeral director, mortician.

undertone noun **1** *speak in an undertone* low tone/voice, murmur, whisper. **2** *undertones of unrest* undercurrent, hint, suggestion, intimation, inkling, insinuation, trace, tinge, touch, atmosphere, aura, tenor, flavor.
Antonyms: SHOUT; BELLOW.

undervalue verb underestimate, underrate, set little store by, rate too low, think too little of, not do justice to, belittle, disparage; *inf.* sell short.

underwater adjective submarine, subaqueous, undersea, submerged, immersed.

underwear noun underclothes, undergarments; underclothing, lingerie, underlinen; *inf.* underthings, undies, unmentionables.

underworld noun **1** *police trying to arrest members of the underworld* | *the underworld revenged his death* (crime) syndicate, criminal world, world of crime, organized crime; criminals, gangsters; Mafia, Cosa Nostra; *inf.* gangland, mob. **2** *Orpheus in the underworld* abode of the dead, nether/infernal regions, hell, Hades.

underwrite verb **1** *underwrite the official document* sign, countersign, endorse, initial. **2** *underwrite the agreement* agree to, approve, sanction, confirm, ratify, validate; *inf.* okay, OK. **3** *underwrite the new project* fund, finance, back, support, sponsor, subsidize, contribute to, insure.

undesirable adjective **1** *the undesirable side effects of the drug* unpleasant, disagreeable, nasty, unacceptable, unwanted, unwished-for. **2** *he is a most undesirable character* unpleasant, disagreeable, nasty, foul, objectionable, offensive, obnoxious, disliked, hateful, repugnant, repellent, distasteful, unsavory.

undisciplined adjective unruly, disorderly, disobedient, obstreperous, recalcitrant, refractory, uncontrolled, unrestrained, wild, willful, wayward, capricious, unsteady, untrained, unschooled; disorganized, erratic, lax.

undisguised adjective *undisguised envy* open, obvious, evident, patent, manifest, transparent, overt, unconcealed, unhidden, unmistakable.

undisputed adjective uncontested, unchallenged, unquestioned, not in question, undoubted, not in doubt, certain, accepted, acknowledged, recognized, incontestable, unquestionable, indubitable, incontrovertible, irrefutable.

undistinguished adjective ordinary, common, plain, simple, commonplace, everyday, mediocre, run-of-the-mill, pedestrian, prosaic, unexceptional, indifferent, unimpressive, unremarkable, unnoticeable, inconspicuous; *inf.* nothing special, no big deal, no great shakes, nothing to write home about.

undo verb **1** *undo buttons/laces/bonds/locks* unfasten, unhook, unbutton, untie, unlace, unbind, unfetter, unshackle, loosen, loose, disentangle, release, free, open, unlock. **2** *undo the arrange-*

ment/agreement cancel, annul, nullify, invalidate, revoke, repeal, rescind, reverse, set aside, wipe out. **3** *undo all his work/hopes* destroy, ruin, wreck, smash, shatter, annihilate, eradicate, obliterate, defeat, conquer, overthrow, overturn, topple, upset, quash, squelch, crush.

undoing noun **1** *the undoing of all his work/hopes* destruction, ruin, ruination, downfall, defeat, overthrow, collapse. **2** *his drunkenness was his undoing* fatal flaw, weakness, blight, misfortune, affliction, trouble, curse.

undone adjective *leave tasks undone* not done, unfinished, incomplete, unaccomplished, unperformed, unfulfilled, unattended to, omitted, neglected, passed over, disregarded, ignored, left, outstanding.

undoubted adjective undisputed, not in doubt, uncontested, unquestioned, not in question, certain, unquestionable, indubitable, incontrovertible, irrefutable.

undoubtedly adverb indubitably, doubtless, doubtlessly, beyond a doubt, unquestionably, beyond question, undeniably, positively, absolutely, certainly, with certainty, decidedly, definitely, assuredly, of course.

undress verb **1** *they undressed quickly* take off one's clothes, remove one's clothes, strip, disrobe. **2** *undress her daughter* unclothe, take off clothes from, remove clothes from, strip.

undue adjective unwarranted, unjustified, unreasonable, inappropriate, unsuitable, unseemly, unbecoming, improper, ill-advised, excessive, immoderate, disproportionate, inordinate, fulsome, superfluous, too much, too great, uncalled-for, unneeded, unnecessary, nonessential, unrequired.
Antonyms: DUE; APPROPRIATE; PROPER.

unduly adverb *not unduly worried* excessively, overly, overmuch, disproportionately, out of all proportion, immoderately, inordinately, unnecessarily, unreasonably, unjustifiably.

undying adjective deathless, immortal, eternal, infinite, perpetual, unending, never-ending, unceasing, ceaseless, incessant, permanent, lasting, enduring, abiding, continuing, constant, unfading, undiminished, imperishable, indestructible, undestroyed, inextinguishable.
Antonyms: TRANSIENT; EPHEMERAL.

unearth verb **1** *dogs unearthing bones* dig up, excavate, exhume, disinter, unbury. **2** *unearth new evidence* uncover, discover, find, come across, hit upon, bring to light, reveal, expose, turn up, root up, dredge up, ferret out.
Antonyms: BURY; COVER.

unearthly adjective **1** *unearthly manifestations/sounds/happenings* otherworldly, not of this world, supernatural, preternatural, ghostly, spectral, phantom, haunted, uncanny, eerie, strange; *inf.* spooky, creepy. **2** *come home at an unearthly hour* unreasonable, preposterous, abnormal, extraordinary, absurd, ridiculous; *inf.* ungodly, unholy.
Antonyms: NORMAL; ORDINARY; REASONABLE.

uneasy *adjective* **1** *feel uneasy about what was happening* ill at ease, troubled, worried, anxious, apprehensive, alarmed, disturbed, agitated, nervous, on edge, edgy, restive, restless, unsettled, discomposed, discomfited, perturbed, upset; *inf.* jittery, nervy. **2** *an uneasy peace* strained, constrained, tense, awkward, precarious, unstable, insecure. **3** *an uneasy suspicion that all was not well* worrying, alarming, dismaying, disturbing, perturbing, disquieting, unsettling, upsetting.
Antonyms: CALM; COMPOSED; TRANQUIL; STABLE.

unemotional *adjective* undemonstrative, passionless, cold, frigid, cool, reserved, restrained, self-controlled, unfeeling, unresponsive, unexcitable, unmoved, impassive, apathetic, indifferent, phlegmatic, detached.

unemployed *adjective* jobless, out of work, out of a job, workless, laid off, idle; *inf.* on the dole.

unending *adjective* endless, never-ending, interminable, perpetual, ceaseless, incessant, unceasing, nonstop, uninterrupted, continuous, continual, constant, unremitting, relentless.

unenviable *adjective an unenviable task* undesirable, unpleasant, disagreeable, nasty, painful, thankless.

unequal *adjective* **1** *unequal in size/talent/difficulty* different, differing, dissimilar, unlike, unalike, disparate, unidentical, varying, variable, not uniform, unmatched. **2** *unequal to the task* not up to, inadequate, insufficient, found wanting. **3** *the sides of the box are unequal* uneven, asymmetrical, unsymmetrical, unbalanced, lopsided, irregular, disproportionate, not matching. **4** *unequal contest* unfair, unjust, inequitable, uneven, one-sided, ill-matched.

unequaled *adjective* without equal, peerless, unmatched, unrivaled, unparalleled, without parallel, unsurpassed, incomparable, beyond compare, inimitable, perfect, supreme, paramount, second to none, nonpareil, unique.

unequivocal *adjective an unequivocal statement/demand* unambiguous, clear, clear-cut, crystal-clear, unmistakable, plain, well-defined, explicit, unqualified, categorical, outright, downright, direct, straightforward, blunt, point-blank, straight from the shoulder, positive, certain, decisive.

unethical *adjective* immoral, unprincipled, unscrupulous, dishonorable, dishonest, disreputable, dirty, unfair, underhand, underhanded, bad, wicked, evil, sinful, iniquitous, corrupt, depraved; *inf.* shady.

uneven *adjective* **1** *uneven surfaces* rough, bumpy, lumpy. **2** *his work is uneven* variable, varying, changeable, irregular, fluctuating, erratic, patchy. **3** *the sides of the box are uneven* unequal, asymmetrical, unsymmetrical, unbalanced, lopsided, irregular, disproportionate, not matching. **4** *an uneven contest* unequal, unfair, unjust, inequitable, one-sided, ill-matched.

uneventful *adjective* unexciting, uninteresting, monotonous, boring, dull, tedious, routine, unvaried, ordinary, run-of-the-mill, pedestrian, commonplace, everyday, unexceptional, unremarkable, unmemorable.

unexceptional *adjective* ordinary, usual, regular, normal, average, typical, common, everyday, run-of-the-mill, mediocre, pedestrian, unremarkable, undistinguished, unimpressive; *inf.* nothing special, nothing to write home about.

unexpected *adjective* unforeseen, unanticipated, unlooked-for, unpredicted, not bargained for, sudden, abrupt, surprising, startling, astonishing, out of the blue, chance, fortuitous.

unfair *adjective* **1** *an unfair judgment | receive unfair treatment* unjust, inequitable, partial, partisan, prejudiced, biased, one-sided, unequal, uneven, unbalanced. **2** *the punishment was unfair* undeserved, unmerited, uncalled-for, unreasonable, unjustifiable, unwarrantable, out of proportion, disproportionate, excessive, extreme, immoderate. **3** *unfair play* foul, unsporting, unsportsmanlike, dirty, below-the-belt, underhand, underhanded, unscrupulous, dishonorable; *inf.* crooked.

unfaithful *adjective* **1** *unfaithful friends* disloyal, false, false-hearted, faithless, perfidious, treacherous, traitorous, untrustworthy, unreliable, undependable, insincere. **2** *unfaithful spouses* faithless, adulterous, fickle, untrue, inconstant; *inf.* cheating, two-timing.

unfamiliar *adjective an unfamiliar face | this work is unfamiliar* unknown, new, strange, alien, unaccustomed, uncommon. **unfamiliar with** *I am unfamiliar with this method* unacquainted with, unused to, unaccustomed to, unconversant with/in, unpracticed in, inexperienced in, unskilled in, uninformed of, uninitiated in.

unfashionable *adjective* out of date, old-fashioned, outmoded, démodé, outdated, dated, behind the times, passé, archaic, obsolete, antiquated.

unfasten *verb* undo, open, loose, detach, disconnect, untie, unwrap, unbind, unlace, unhitch, untether, unlock, unbolt.

unfavorable *adjective* **1** *an unfavorable report | unfavorable reviews* adverse, critical, hostile, inimical, unfriendly, negative, discouraging, poor, bad. **2** *unfavorable circumstances* disadvantageous, adverse, unfortunate, unhappy, detrimental. **3** *come at an unfavorable moment* inconvenient, inopportune, untimely, untoward.

unfeeling *adjective unfeeling people ignoring the poor* uncaring, unsympathetic, hard-hearted, hard, harsh, heartless, apathetic, cold, callous, cruel, pitiless, inhuman.

unfit *adjective too unfit to compete in the race* out of condition, in poor condition/shape, out of kilter, flabby, unhealthy, debilitated, weak. **unfit for** **1** *unfit for the task* unsuited for/to, ill-suited for/to, unsuitable for, unqualified for, ineligible for, unequipped for, unprepared for, untrained for, incapable for, inadequate for, incompetent for, not up to, not equal to; *inf.* not cut out for. **2** *food unfit for human consumption* unsuitable for, inappropriate for, not good enough for.

unflattering *adjective* **1** *unflattering remarks* uncomplimentary, critical, blunt, candid, honest, straight from the shoulder. **2** *an unflattering hat* unbecoming, unattractive, unsightly.

unfold *verb* **1** *unfold the map* open out, spread out, stretch out, flatten, straighten out, unfurl, unroll, unravel. **2** *unfold a tale of horror* | *unfold the events of the night* narrate, relate, recount, tell, reveal, make known, disclose, divulge, present. **3** *when our plans unfold* develop, evolve, grow, mature, bear fruit.

unforeseen *adjective* unpredicted, unexpected, unanticipated, unlooked-for, not bargained for, sudden, abrupt, surprising, startling, astonishing, out of the blue.

unforgettable *adjective* memorable, impressive, striking, outstanding, extraordinary, exceptional, remarkable.

unforgivable *adjective* inexcusable, unpardonable, unwarrantable, unjustifiable, indefensible, reprehensible, deplorable, despicable, contemptible, disgraceful, shameful.

unfortunate *adjective* **1** *unfortunate circumstance* adverse, disadvantageous, unfavorable, unlucky, untoward, unpromising, hostile, inimical, disastrous, calamitous. **2** *the unfortunate girl* unlucky, out of luck, luckless, ill-starred, star-crossed, hapless, wretched, miserable, unhappy, poor. **3** *an unfortunate remark* regrettable, deplorable, ill-advised, inappropriate, unsuitable, inapt, tactless, untactful, injudicious, awkward, clumsy.

unfounded *adjective* *unfounded rumors* without basis/foundation, groundless, baseless, unsubstantiated, unproven, unsupported, uncorroborated, speculative, conjectural, spurious.

unfriendly *adjective* **1** *unfriendly neighbors/looks* unamicable, uncongenial, unsociable, inhospitable, unneighborly, unkind, unsympathetic, aloof, cold, cool, distant, disagreeable, unpleasant, surly, sour, hostile, inimical, antagonistic, aggressive, quarrelsome. **2** *an unfriendly climate/atmosphere* unfavorable, disadvantageous, unpropitious, inauspicious, hostile, inimical, alien.

ungainly *adjective* awkward, clumsy, ungraceful, graceless, inelegant, gawky, gangling, maladroit, inept, bungling, bumbling, lumbering, uncoordinated, hulking, lubberly.
Antonyms: GRACEFUL; ELEGANT.

ungodly *adjective* **1** *ungodly people/acts* godless, irreligious, impious, blasphemous, profane, immoral, sinful, wicked, iniquitous. **2** *come home at an ungodly hour* unreasonable, preposterous, outrageous, abnormal, extraordinary, absurd, ridiculous; *inf.* unholy, unearthly.

ungrateful *adjective* unthankful, unappreciative, impolite, uncivil, rude.

unguarded *adjective* **1** *an unguarded comment* careless, ill-advised, ill-considered, incautious, thoughtless, rash, foolhardy, indiscreet, imprudent, unwise, uncircumspect, undiplomatic. **2** *in an unguarded moment* off guard, unwary, inattentive, unobservant, unmindful, unheeding, heedless, distracted, absentminded. **3** *unguarded fortresses* undefended, unprotected, defenseless, vulnerable, open to attack.

unhappy *adjective* **1** *feeling unhappy* sad, miserable, sorrowful, dejected, despondent, disconsolate, brokenhearted, down, downcast, dispirited, crestfallen, depressed, melancholy, blue, gloomy, glum, mournful, woebegone, long-faced, joyless, cheerless. **2** *an unhappy girl* unfortunate, unlucky, luckless, hapless, ill-starred, ill-fated, star-crossed, wretched, miserable. **3** *unhappy circumstances* unfortunate, disadvantageous, unlucky, adverse, miserable, wretched. **4** *an unhappy choice of phrase* unfortunate, regrettable, inappropriate.

unhealthy *adjective* **1** *unhealthy children* in poor health, unwell, ill, ailing, sick, sickly, poorly, indisposed, unsound, weak, feeble, frail, delicate, debilitated, infirm. **2** *an unhealthy diet/climate* unwholesome, unnourishing, detrimental, injurious, damaging, deleterious, noxious, insalubrious. **3** *show an unhealthy interest in death* unwholesome, morbid, undesirable.

unheard-of *adjective* **1** *unheard-of authors* unknown, little-known, undiscovered, obscure, nameless, unsung. **2** *unheard-of levels of radiation* unprecedented, unexampled, exceptional, extraordinary, out of the ordinary, uncommon, unusual, unparalleled, unrivaled, unmatched, unequaled, singular, unique, unbelievable, inconceivable.
Antonyms: FAMOUS; COMMON.

unheeded *adjective* disregarded, ignored, neglected, overlooked, unobserved, unnoted.

unhinged *adjective* unbalanced, deranged, demented, out of one's mind, crazed, mad, insane; *inf.* crazy.
Antonyms: SANE; STABLE.

unholy *adjective* **1** *unholy people/acts* ungodly, godless, irreligious, impious, blasphemous, profane, immoral, sinful, wicked, iniquitous. **2** *an unholy commotion* unreasonable, preposterous, outrageous, appalling, shocking, dreadful; *inf.* ungodly.

unhoped-for *adjective* unexpected, unanticipated, unlooked-for, undreamed of, beyond one's wildest dreams, like a dream come true.

unhurried *adjective* leisurely, leisured, easy, slow, slow-moving, slow-going, slow and steady, deliberate, sedate, lingering, loitering.

unidentified *adjective* *an unidentified donor/spot* nameless, unnamed, unknown, anonymous, incognito, obscure, unmarked, undesignated, unclassified.

unification *noun* union, junction, merger, fusion, alliance, amalgamation, coalition, combination, consolidation, confederation.

uniform adjective **1** a uniform temperature constant, consistent, invariable, unvarying, unvaried, unchanging, undeviating, stable, regular, even, equal, equable. **2** all of uniform length same, alike, like, selfsame, identical, similar, equal.

Antonyms: CHANGEABLE; VARIABLE; VARIED; DIFFERENT.

uniform noun livery, regalia, habit, suit, dress, costume, garb; regimentals.

uniformity noun **1** the uniformity of the temperature is important constancy, consistency, lack of variation/change, stability, regularity, evenness, equality, equability. **2** uniformity of length of all the garments sameness, likeness, identicalness, similarity, equalness, equality. **3** tired of the uniformity of the days sameness, monotony, tedium, dullness, drabness.

unify verb unite, bring together, merge, fuse, amalgamate, coalesce, combine, blend, mix, bind, link up, consolidate.

Antonyms: SEPARATE; SPLIT; SEVER.

unimaginable adjective unthinkable, inconceivable, incredible, unbelievable, unheard-of, unthought-of, implausible, improbable, unlikely, impossible, undreamed of, fantastic, beyond one's wildest dreams; inf. mind-boggling, mind-blowing.

unimaginative adjective an unimaginative description unoriginal, uninspired, uncreative, commonplace, pedestrian, mundane, matter-of-fact, ordinary, usual, routine, humdrum, prosaic, stale, hackneyed, derived, dull, monotonous, lifeless, vapid, insipid, bland, dry.

unimportant adjective of little/no importance, insignificant, of little/no consequence, inconsequential, of no account, nonessential, immaterial, irrelevant, not worth mentioning, not worth speaking of, minor, slight, trifling, trivial, petty, paltry, insubstantial, inferior, worthless, nugatory; inf. small-fry, no great shakes, dinky.

uninhabited adjective uninhabited houses/places vacant, empty, unoccupied, untenanted, unpopulated, unpeopled, unsettled, abandoned, deserted, forsaken, unfrequented, barren, desert, desolate.

uninhibited adjective **1** her sister is completely uninhibited unreserved, unrepressed, unconstrained, unselfconscious, spontaneous, free and easy, relaxed, informal, open, candid, outspoken. **2** uninhibited behavior unrestrained, unrestricted, unrepressed, unconstrained, uncontrolled, uncurbed, unchecked, unbridled.

unintelligible adjective **1** unintelligible ramblings incomprehensible, meaningless, unfathomable, incoherent, indistinct, inarticulate, confused, muddled, jumbled. **2** unintelligible handwriting illegible, indecipherable.

unintentional adjective unintended, accidental, inadvertent, unplanned, unpremeditated, un-

calculated, chance, fortuitous, unconscious, involuntary, unwitting, unthinking.

uninterested adjective **1** uninterested in other people's problems indifferent, unconcerned, uninvolved, apathetic, blasé, unresponsive, impassive, dispassionate, aloof, detached, distant. **2** uninterested in the lecture bored, incurious.

uninteresting adjective unexciting, dull, unentertaining, boring, tiresome, wearisome, tedious, dreary, flat, monotonous, humdrum, uneventful, commonplace, dry, pedestrian, prosaic, hackneyed, stale.

uninterrupted adjective unbroken, undisturbed, continuous, continual, constant, steady, sustained, nonstop, unending, endless, ceaseless, unceasing, incessant, interminable, unremitting.

uninviting adjective unappealing, untempting, undesirable, unattractive, unappetizing, unpleasant, disagreeable, distasteful, unpalatable, repellent, revolting, repugnant, sickening, nauseating, offensive.

union noun **1** the union of three firms joining, junction, merging, merger, fusion, amalgamating, amalgamation, blend, mixture, coalition, combining, combination, consolidation, confederation. **2** the union is made up of several organizations association, alliance, league, coalition, consortium, syndicate, guild, confederation, federation, confederacy. **3** the union of the man and the woman marriage, wedding; coupling, intercourse, coition, coitus, copulation. **4** we are all in union about the plans agreement, accord, concurrence, unity, unison, unanimity, harmony, concord.

Antonyms: SEPARATION; PARTING; DIVORCE; DISAGREEMENT.

unique adjective **1** a unique specimen | the specimen is unique only, one and only, single, sole, lone, solitary, sui generis, exclusive, in a class by itself. **2** a unique opportunity/beauty unequaled, without equal, unparalleled, unexampled, unmatched, matchless, peerless, unsurpassed, unexcelled, incomparable, beyond compare, inimitable, second to none.

Antonyms: COMMON; ORDINARY; USUAL.

unison noun the committee was in unison agreement, accord, harmony, concord.

unit noun **1** the family regarded as a unit entity, whole. **2** the course is divided into units component, part, section, element, constituent, subdivision, portion, segment, module, item, member. **3** a unit of length measurement, measure, quantity.

unite verb **1** unite the two parties/firms | unite the two pieces of pipe/film join, link, connect, combine, amalgamate, fuse, weld, splice. **2** unite the two substances combine, mix, commix, admix, blend, mingle, homogenize. **3** unite this man and this woman marry, wed, join in wedlock, tie the knot between. **4** they united to fight

the common enemy join together, join forces, combine, amalgamate, band together, ally, co-operate, work/act/pull together, work side by side, pool resources.
Antonyms: SEPARATE; SPLIT; DIVORCE.

united adjective **1** *a united force/effort* combined, amalgamated, allied, cooperative, concerted, collective, pooled. **2** *united in their opinion of the plan* in agreement, agreed, in unison, of the same opinion/mind, of like mind, like-minded, at one, in accord, unanimous.

unity noun **1** *detract from the unity of the painting* oneness, singleness, wholeness, entity, integrity. **2** *their strength lies in their unity* union, unification, amalgamation, coalition, alliance, co-operation, undividedness. **3** *strive for political unity | live in unity* agreement, harmony, accord, concord, concurrence, unanimity, consensus, concert, togetherness, solidarity.
Antonyms: DIVISION; DISCORD; disunity.

universal adjective general, all-embracing, all-inclusive, comprehensive, across the board, worldwide, global, widespread, common, predominant, preponderate, omnipresent, ubiquitous, catholic.
Antonyms: PARTICULAR; RESTRICTED; LOCAL.

---

universal

catholic, common, ecumenical, general, generic
Something that is **universal** applies to every case or individual in a class or category (*a universal practice among aboriginal tribesmen; a universal truth*). **General**, on the other hand, is less precise; it implies applicability to all or most of a group or class, whether the members of that group are clearly defined or only casually associated (*a drug that has come into general use among women but has not yet won the universal acceptance of doctors*). **Generic** is often used in place of *general* when referring to every member of a genus or clearly-defined scientific category (*a generic characteristic of insects*); with reference to language, it means referring to both men and women (*a generic pronoun*). **Common** implies participation or sharing by all members of a class (*a common interest in French culture*) or frequently occurring (*a common complaint*). **Catholic** implies a wide-ranging or inclusive attitude (*known for his catholic tastes in music*), while **ecumenical** means pertaining to the whole Christian church or promoting unity among religious groups or divisions (*an ecumenical marriage ceremony*).

---

universally adverb without exception, in all instances/cases, everywhere, comprehensively, uniformly, invariably.

universe noun **1** *the wonders of the universe* cosmos, totality, whole world, Creation. **2** *the achievements of the universe* mankind, humankind, human race, humanity, people, society.

unjust adjective **1** *an unjust verdict* unfair, inequitable, prejudiced, biased, partisan, partial, one-sided. **2** *an unjust accusation* unfair, wrongful, wrong, undue, undeserved, unmerited, unwarranted, uncalled-for, unreasonable, unjustifiable.

unjustifiable adjective **1** *unjustifiable behavior* indefensible, inexcusable, unforgivable, unpardonable, uncalled-for, blameworthy, culpable, unwarrantable. **2** *unjustifiable fears/accusations* groundless, unfounded, without foundation, baseless, without basis, unsupported, unsubstantiated, unreasonable.

unkempt adjective *unkempt hair/people* untidy, disheveled, disordered, disarranged, tousled, rumpled, messy, windblown, uncombed, ungroomed, messed up, scruffy, slovenly; *inf.* sloppy, mussed up.
Antonyms: TIDY; NEAT; TRIM.

unkind adjective **1** *unkind people/remarks* unkindly, unfriendly, unamiable, uncharitable, unchristian, inhospitable, ungenerous, nasty, mean, cruel, vicious, spiteful, malicious, malevolent, harsh, pitiless, ruthless, unsympathetic, unfeeling, hard-hearted, heartless, cold-hearted. **2** *an unkind climate* inclement, harsh, intemperate.

unknown adjective **1** *the results of the test are as yet unknown* untold, unrevealed, undisclosed, undivulged, undetermined, undecided, unestablished, unsettled, unascertained, in the balance, up in the air. **2** *the donor is unknown* unidentified, unnamed, nameless, anonymous, incognito. **3** *unknown territory* unfamiliar, unexplored, uncharted, untraveled, undiscovered. **4** *unknown poets* unheard-of, little-known, obscure, undistinguished, unrenowned, unsung.

unlawful adjective against the law, illegal, illicit, illegitimate, criminal, felonious, actionable, prohibited, banned, outlawed, proscribed, unauthorized, unsanctioned, unwarranted, unlicensed.

unlike adjective unalike, dissimilar, different, distinct, disparate, contrastive, contrasted, contrary, diverse, divergent, incompatible, ill-matched, incongruous; *inf.* like day and night.

unlike preposition not like, not typical of, differently from.

unlikely adjective **1** *an unlikely chance of success* improbable, doubtful, dubious, faint, slight, remote. **2** *it is unlikely that he will win* not likely, improbable, unexpected. **3** *an unlikely excuse* improbable, implausible, questionable, unconvincing, incredible, unbelievable, inconceivable, unimaginable.

unlimited adjective **1** *unlimited freedom | unlimited room for maneuver* unrestricted, unconstrained, uncontrolled, unrestrained, unchecked, unhindered, unhampered, unimpeded, unfettered, untrammeled. **2** *unlimited power* unrestricted, absolute, total, unqualified, unconditional. **3** *unlimited supplies of money* limitless, illimitable, boundless, unbounded, immense, vast, great, extensive, immeasurable, incalculable, untold, infinite, endless.

unload *verb* *unload the burro/truck* unburden, unlade, empty, unpack.

unlock *verb* unbolt, unlatch, unbar, undo, unfasten.

unlooked-for *adjective* unforeseen, unexpected, unanticipated, not bargained for, unhoped for, undreamed of, unpredicted, sudden, abrupt, surprise, surprising, startling, astonishing, out of the blue.

unloved *adjective* unbeloved, uncared-for, uncherished, unwanted, unpopular, forsaken, rejected, jilted, disliked, hated, detested, loathed.

unlucky *adjective* **1** *an unlucky young man* luckless, out of luck, down on one's luck, unfortunate, hapless, ill-fated, ill-starred, star-crossed, wretched, miserable. **2** *an unlucky attempt* unsuccessful, failed, ill-fated. **3** *an unlucky set of circumstances* adverse, disadvantageous, unfavorable, unfortunate, untoward, unpromising, inauspicious, unpropitious, doomed, ill-fated, ill-omened.

unmanageable *adjective* **1** *an unmanageable load* unwieldy, unmaneuverable, awkward, inconvenient, cumbersome, bulky, incommodious. **2** *unmanageable children* unruly, disorderly, uncontrollable, ungovernable, out of hand, wild, difficult, refractory, recalcitrant, intractable, obstreperous, wayward, incorrigible, contumacious.

unmanly *adjective* **1** *an unmanly way of walking* effeminate, womanish; *inf.* sissy. **2** *too unmanly to fight* timid, timorous, fearful, cowardly, craven, pusillanimous; *inf.* yellow.

unmannerly *adjective* ill-mannered, mannerless, impolite, uncivil, discourteous, disrespectful, rude, ill-bred, uncouth.

unmarried *adjective* single, unwed, unwedded, spouseless, partnerless, divorced, unattached, bachelor, celibate; husbandless, wifeless.

unmistakable *adjective* *the unmistakable noise of a train* clear, plain, obvious, evident, manifest, apparent, patent, palpable, distinct, distinctive, conspicuous, well-defined, pronounced, striking, glaring, blatant, undoubted, indisputable, indubitable, beyond a doubt, unquestionable, beyond question.

unmitigated *adjective* *an unmitigated disaster* absolute, unqualified, unconditional, categorical, complete, total, thorough, thoroughgoing, downright, utter, out and out, veritable, perfect, consummate.

unmoved *adjective* **1** *unmoved furniture* in place, in position, unchanged. **2** *unmoved from their purpose* firm, steadfast, unshaken, staunch, unwavering, unswerving, undeviating, determined, resolute, decided, resolved. **3** *unmoved by the sad sight* unaffected, untouched, unstirred, unconcerned, uncaring, indifferent, impassive, unfeeling, impervious.

unnatural *adjective* **1** *his face turned an unnatural color* unusual, uncommon, extraordinary, strange, queer, odd, bizarre, preternatural. **2** *an unnatural laugh* | *unnatural behavior* affected, artificial, feigned, false, self-conscious, contrived, forced, labored, studied, strained, insincere, theatrical, stagy, mannered.

unnecessary *adjective* **1** *it is unnecessary to come early* needless, inessential. **2** *unnecessary expense/supplies* needless, unneeded, inessential, nonessential, uncalled-for, unrequired, gratuitous, useless, dispensable, expendable, redundant, superfluous.

unnerve *verb* unman, discourage, dishearten, dispirit, deject, demoralize, daunt, alarm, frighten, dismay, disconcert, discompose, perturb, upset, throw off balance, unsettle, disquiet, fluster, agitate, shake; *inf.* rattle. **Antonyms:** ENCOURAGE; HEARTEN; EMBOLDEN.

unobtrusive *adjective* **1** *an unobtrusive person* self-effacing, retiring, unassuming, modest, quiet, meek, humble, unaggressive, unassertive, low-profile. **2** *unobtrusive decorations/colors* low-key, restrained, subdued, quiet, unostentatious, unshowy, inconspicuous, unnoticeable.

unoccupied *adjective* **1** *unoccupied houses* vacant, empty, uninhabited, untenanted, tenantless. **2** *unoccupied territory* uninhabited, unpopulated, unpeopled, depopulated, deserted, forsaken, desolate, godforsaken. **3** *he is unoccupied just now* not busy, at leisure, idle, inactive, unemployed.

unofficial *adjective* **1** *an unofficial meeting* informal, casual, unauthorized, unsanctioned, unaccredited, wildcat. **2** *an unofficial rumor* unconfirmed, unauthenticated, uncorroborated, unsubstantiated.

unorthodox *adjective* **1** *unorthodox beliefs* heterodox, uncanonical, heretical, nonconformist. **2** *unorthodox methods* unconventional, unusual, uncommon, uncustomary, unwonted, out of the ordinary, nonconformist, unconforming, irregular, abnormal, divergent, aberrant, anomalous.

unpalatable *adjective* *unpalatable food/suggestions* unsavory, unappetizing, uneatable, inedible, undelectable, nasty, disgusting, repugnant, revolting, nauseating, sickening, distasteful, disagreeable, unpleasant, offensive, obnoxious, unattractive, repulsive, repellent.

unparalleled *adjective* without parallel, unequaled, without equal, matchless, unmatched, peerless, unrivaled, unprecedented, unsurpassed, unexcelled, incomparable, beyond compare, singular, unique. **Antonyms:** ORDINARY; RUN-OF-THE-MILL.

unperturbed *adjective* calm, composed, cool, collected, serene, tranquil, self-possessed, placid, unruffled, unflustered, unexcited, undismayed, untroubled, unworried; *inf.* laid-back.

unpleasant *adjective* **1** *an unpleasant taste* disagreeable, unpalatable, unsavory, unappetizing, disgusting, repugnant, revolting, nauseating, sickening. **2** *an unpleasant smell* disagreeable, offensive, obnoxious, foul, smelly, stinking. **3** *unpleasant person/personality* disagreeable, unlikable, unlovable, unattractive, nasty, ill-natured, bad-tempered, cross. **4** *an unpleasant task* disagreeable, irksome, troublesome, annoying, irritating, vexatious.

unpopular *adjective* disliked, unliked, unloved, friendless, unwanted, unwelcome, avoided, ignored, rejected, shunned, out in the cold, unattractive, undesirable, out of favor.

unprecedented *adjective* unparalleled, unequaled, unmatched, unheard-of, extraordinary, uncommon, out of the ordinary, unusual, exceptional, abnormal, singular, anomalous, atypical, remarkable, novel, original, unique; *inf.* one of a kind.

Antonyms: USUAL; NORMAL; RUN-OF-THE-MILL.

unpredictable *adjective* **1** *unpredictable results* unforeseeable, undivinable, doubtful, dubious, uncertain, unsure, in the balance, up in the air; *inf.* iffy. **2** *unpredictable people/behavior* erratic, fickle, capricious, whimsical, mercurial, volatile, unstable, undependable, unreliable.

unpremeditated *adjective* unplanned, unarranged, unprepared, unintentional, extempore, impromptu, ad lib, spontaneous, spur of the moment, on the spot, impulsive, hasty; *inf.* off the cuff.

unpretentious *adjective* **1** *an unpretentious house/lifestyle* simple, plain, modest, ordinary, humble, unostentatious, unshowy, unimposing, homely. **2** *an unpretentious person* unassuming, modest, unaffected, natural, straightforward, honest.

unprincipled *adjective* immoral, amoral, unethical, dishonorable, dishonest, unprofessional, deceitful, devious, unscrupulous, corrupt, crooked, bad, wicked, evil, villainous.

unproductive *adjective* **1** *an unproductive exercise* fruitless, futile, vain, idle, useless, worthless, valueless, ineffective, ineffectual, inefficacious, unprofitable, unremunerative, unrewarding. **2** *unproductive soil* barren, sterile.

unprofessional *adjective* **1** *unprofessional methods/conduct* unethical, unprincipled, improper, unseemly, indecorous, lax, negligent. **2** *unprofessional workers* amateur, amateurish, unskilled, inexpert, untrained, unqualified, inexperienced, incompetent.

unpromising *adjective* *unpromising prospects* unfavorable, adverse, unpropitious, inauspicious, gloomy, black, discouraging, portentous, ominous.

unqualified *adjective* **1** *unqualified teachers* uncertificated, unlicensed, untrained. **2** *unqualified to do the job* | *unqualified to comment* ineligible, unfit, incompetent, incapable, unequipped, unprepared, not equal/up, not cut out. **3** *unqualified approval* unconditional, unreserved, without reservations, categorical, unequivocal, positive, unmitigated, complete, absolute, thorough, thoroughgoing, total, utter, outright, out-and-out, perfect, consummate.

unquestionable *adjective* *his honesty is unquestionable* beyond question/doubt, indubitable, undoubted, indisputable, undeniable, irrefutable, uncontestable, incontrovertible, certain, sure, definite, positive, conclusive, self-evident, obvious.

unravel *verb* **1** *unravel knots* untangle, disentangle, straighten out, separate out, unknot, undo. **2** *unravel the problem* solve, resolve, work out, clear up, get to the bottom of, fathom; *inf.* figure out.

Antonyms: ENTANGLE; TANGLE; COMPLICATE.

unreal *adjective* *unreal characters/situation* imaginary, make-believe, fictitious, mythical, fanciful, fantastic, fabulous, hypothetical, nonexistent, illusory, chimerical, phantasmagoric, phantasmagorical.

unrealistic *adjective* **1** *an unrealistic plan* impractical, impracticable, unworkable, unreasonable, irrational, illogical, improbable, foolish, wild, absurd, quixotic; *inf.* half-baked. **2** *an unrealistic model* unreal-looking, unlifelike, nonnaturalistic.

unreasonable *adjective* **1** *unreasonable demands* excessive, immoderate, undue, inordinate, outrageous, extravagant, preposterous, unconscionable. **2** *unreasonable prices* exorbitant, extortionate, expensive; *inf.* steep. **3** *unreasonable people* irrational, illogical, opinionated, biased, prejudiced, obstinate, obdurate, willful, headstrong, temperamental, capricious. **4** *unreasonable behavior* unacceptable, preposterous, outrageous, ludicrous, absurd, irrational, illogical.

unrefined *adjective* **1** *unrefined flour* crude, raw, unpurified, unprocessed, untreated. **2** *unrefined guests/manners* uncultured, uncultivated, unsophisticated, inelegant, ungraceful, boorish, loutish, coarse, vulgar, rude, uncouth.

unrelenting *adjective* **1** *unrelenting demands/rain* relentless, unremitting, continuous, continual, constant, incessant, unceasing, nonstop, endless, unending, perpetual, unabating. **2** *unrelenting judge* relentless, merciless, pitiless, unforgiving, unsparing, ruthless, implacable, inexorable, inflexible, rigid, hard, strict, harsh, stern.

Antonyms: INTERMITTENT; LENIENT.

unreliable *adjective* **1** *unreliable friends* undependable, irresponsible, untrustworthy, erratic, fickle, inconstant. **2** *unreliable evidence* suspect, questionable, open to question/doubt, doubtful, unsound, implausible, unconvincing, fallible, specious.

unrepentant *adjective* impenitent, unrepenting, unremorseful, shameless, unregenerate, abandoned.

unreserved *adjective* **1** *unreserved seats* unbooked, unhired, unchartered. **2** *unreserved among his friends* uninhibited, extrovert, outgoing, unrestrained, demonstrative, bold, communicative, outspoken, frank, open. **3** *unreserved approval* without reservations, unqualified, unconditional, categorical, unequivocal, positive, unmitigated, absolute, complete, thorough, thoroughgoing, wholehearted, total, utter, outright, out-and-out, perfect, consummate.

unresolved *adjective* undecided, to be decided, unsettled, undetermined, pending, unsolved, unanswered, debatable, open to debate/question, doubtful, in doubt, moot, up in the air; *inf.* iffy.

unrest *noun* *industrial unrest* dissatisfaction, discontent, discontentment, unease, disquiet, dissension, dissent, discord, strife, protest, rebellion, agitation, turmoil, turbulence.
Antonyms: PEACE; CALM.

unrestricted *adjective* *access was unrestricted* unlimited, open, free, unhindered, unchecked, unbounded; *inf.* free for all, with no holds barred.

unrivaled *adjective* unparalleled, unequaled, without equal, matchless, unmatched, peerless, unsurpassed, unexcelled, incomparable, beyond compare, singular, unique.

unruly *adjective* disorderly, unmanageable, uncontrollable, rowdy, wild, irrepressible, obstreperous, refractory, recalcitrant, intractable, contumacious, disobedient, rebellious, mutinous, insubordinate, defiant, wayward, willful, headstrong.
Antonyms: ORDERLY; OBEDIENT; DOCILE.

unsaid *adjective* unspoken, unvoiced, unpronounced, unuttered, unstated, unmentioned, untold, untalked-of, tacit, suppressed, unrevealed.

unsavory *adjective* **1** *unsavory food/smell* unpalatable, unappetizing, unpleasant, disagreeable, disgusting, loathsome, repugnant, revolting, nauseating, sickening. **2** *unsavory characters* unpleasant, disagreeable, nasty, objectionable, offensive, obnoxious, repellent, repulsive, disreputable, degenerate, coarse, gross, vulgar, boorish, churlish, rude, uncouth.

unscrupulous *adjective* unprincipled, unethical, amoral, immoral, conscienceless, shameless, corrupt, dishonest, dishonorable, deceitful, devious, exploitative, wrongdoing, bad, evil, wicked; *inf.* crooked.
Antonyms: ETHICAL; HONEST.

unseat *verb* **1** *unseat the senator/king* depose, oust, remove from office, dislodge, discharge,

dethrone; *inf.* drum out. **2** *the horse unseated the rider* throw, dismount, unsaddle, unhorse.

unseemly *adjective* unbecoming, unfitting, unbefitting, indecorous, improper, unsuitable, inappropriate, undignified, unrefined, indelicate, tasteless, in poor taste, coarse, crass.

unselfish *adjective* altruistic, self-sacrificing, selfless, kind, self-denying, openhanded, generous, liberal, unsparing, ungrudging, unstinting, charitable, philanthropic.

unsettle *verb* **1** *the move unsettled the children* upset, disturb, discompose, throw off balance, confuse, perturb, discomfit, disconcert, trouble, bother, agitate, ruffle, shake; *inf.* rattle. **2** *unsettle the smooth workings of the firm* throw into confusion/disorder, disorder, disorganize, disarrange, derange.

unsettled *adjective* **1** *the children are unsettled* restless, restive, fidgety, flustered, agitated, ruffled, uneasy, anxious, edgy, on edge, tense, troubled, perturbed, shaken; *inf.* thrown, rattled. **2** *the weather is unsettled* changeable, changing, variable, inconstant, erratic, undependable, unreliable, uncertain, unpredictable. **3** *several issues are still unsettled* undecided, to be decided, unresolved, undetermined, pending, open to debate/question, doubtful, in doubt, moot, up in the air; *inf.* iffy. **4** *unsettled accounts* unpaid, payable, outstanding, owing, due, in arrears. **5** *unsettled territories* uninhabited, unpopulated, unpeopled, unoccupied.

unshakable *adjective* firm, steadfast, resolute, staunch, constant, unswerving, unwavering, unfaltering.

unsightly *adjective* ugly, unattractive, unprepossessing, hideous, horrible, repulsive, revolting, offensive, distasteful.
Antonyms: ATTRACTIVE; BEAUTIFUL.

unskilled *adjective* untrained, unqualified, inexpert, inexperienced, amateurish, unprofessional.

unsociable *adjective* unfriendly, unamiable, unaffable, uncongenial, unneighborly, inhospitable, reclusive, solitary, misanthropic, uncommunicative, unforthcoming, reticent, withdrawn, aloof, distant, remote, standoffish, cold, cool, chilly.

unsolicited *adjective* unsought, unasked-for, unrequested, undemanded, uncalled-for, unrequired, uninvited, unwelcome, gratuitous, volunteered, voluntary, spontaneous.

unsophisticated *adjective* **1** *unsophisticated country girls* unworldly, naïve, simple, innocent, inexperienced, childlike, artless, guileless, ingenuous, natural, unaffected, unpretentious, unrefined, unpolished, gauche, provincial. **2** *unsophisticated tools* crude, unrefined, basic, rudimentary, primitive, undeveloped, homespun. **3** *unsophisticated methods | unsophisticated approach to the problem* simple, straightforward, uncomplicated, uninvolved, unspecialized.

unsound *adjective* **1** *in unsound health* unhealthy, unwell, ailing, delicate, weak, frail. **2** *of unsound mind* disordered, diseased, deranged, demented, unbalanced, unhinged. **3** *unsound furniture* defective, disintegrating, broken, broken-down, rotten, rickety, flimsy, shaky, wobbly, tottery, insubstantial, unsafe, unreliable, dangerous. **4** *unsound reasoning* flawed, defective, faulty, ill-founded, weak, shaky, unreliable, illogical, unfounded, ungrounded, untenable, specious, spurious, false, fallacious, erroneous.

unspeakable *adjective* **1** *unspeakable joy* beyond words, inexpressible, unutterable, indescribable, undefinable, ineffable, unimaginable, inconceivable, unthinkable, unheard-of, overwhelming, marvelous, wonderful. **2** *an unspeakable scoundrel/crime* indescribable, indescribably bad/wicked/evil, unmentionable, appalling, shocking, horrible, frightful, terrible, dreadful, abominable, deplorable, despicable, contemptible, repellent, loathsome, odious, monstrous, heinous, execrable.

unspoiled *adjective* **1** *unspoiled countryside* preserved, intact, as good as new/before, perfect, unblemished, unimpaired, undamaged, untouched, unaffected, unchanged. **2** *unspoiled young girls* | *unspoiled despite her success* innocent, wholesome, natural, simple, artless, unaffected, pure, uncorrupted, undefiled, unblemished.

unspoken *adjective* **1** *unspoken criticism* unexpressed, unstated, undeclared, not spelled out, tacit, implicit, implied, understood, taken for granted. **2** *unspoken plea for mercy* mute, silent, wordless, unuttered.

unstable *adjective* **1** *unstable chairs* unsteady, infirm, rickety, shaky, wobbly, tottery, unsafe, unreliable, insecure, precarious. **2** *unstable people* unbalanced, unhinged, irrational, deranged, mentally ill, crazed, insane, mad. **3** *emotionally unstable* unbalanced, volatile, moody, mercurial, capricious, giddy, erratic, unpredictable. **4** *unstable prices* changeable, variable, unsettled, fluctuating, inconstant, unpredictable.

unstudied *adjective* *unstudied grace* natural, unaffected, unpretentious, without airs, artless, guileless, informal, casual, spontaneous, impromptu.
Antonyms: STUDIED; AFFECTED; PRETENTIOUS.

unsubstantial *adjective* **1** *unsubstantial furniture* insubstantial, flimsy, fragile, frail, slight, puny, inadequate, insufficient; *inf.* jerry-built. **2** *unsubstantial arguments/evidence* insubstantial, flimsy, tenuous, weak, lame, poor, unsound, faulty, ungrounded, groundless, unfounded, baseless, unsupported. **3** *unsubstantial figures* insubstantial, imaginary, unreal, impalpable,

incorporeal, illusory, chimerical, hallucinatory, phantom, ghostly.

unsubstantiated *adjective* unconfirmed, uncorroborated, unproven, not validated, unestablished, questionable, open to question, disputable.

unsuccessful *adjective* **1** *an unsuccessful attempt* without success, failed, vain, unavailing, futile, useless, worthless, abortive, nugatory, ineffective, ineffectual, inefficacious, fruitless, unproductive, unprofitable; frustrated, thwarted, foiled. **2** *an unsuccessful businessman* failed, losing, unprosperous, unlucky, luckless, out-of-luck, unfortunate, ill-starred, ill-fated.

unsuitable *adjective* inappropriate, inapt, inapposite, unfitting, unbefitting, incompatible, incongruous, out of place/keeping, ineligible, unacceptable, unbecoming, unseemly, indecorous, improper.

unsung *adjective* unacclaimed, unapplauded, uncelebrated, unhonored, unpraised, unlauded, unhailed, unacknowledged, unrecognized, unrenowned, neglected, disregarded, unknown, anonymous, nameless.
Antonyms: FAMOUS; CELEBRATED.

unsure *adjective* **1** *he was a bit unsure at first* | *unsure of himself* lacking self-confidence, unselfconfident, not confident, not self-assured, lacking assurance, insecure, hesitant, diffident. **2** *unsure what to do* undecided, irresolute, in two minds, in a dilemma/quandary, ambivalent. **3** *unsure about his motive* uncertain, unconvinced, dubious, doubtful, skeptical, distrustful, suspicious.

unsuspecting *adjective* unsuspicious, unwary, off guard, trusting, trustful, overtrustful, gullible, credulous, ingenuous, naïve, innocent, dupable, exploitable.
Antonyms: SUSPICIOUS; WARY.

unsympathetic *adjective* **1** *unsympathetic parents* unsympathizing, unkind, uncompassionate, compassionless, unpitying, pitiless, uncommiserating, uncaring, unfeeling, insensitive, unconcerned, indifferent, unresponsive, apathetic, unmoved, untouched, heartless, cold, hard-hearted, hard, harsh, callous, cruel. **2** *unsympathetic to his cause* disapproving of, opposed to, against, anti.

untangle *verb* **1** *untangle the knotted yarn* disentangle, unravel, unsnarl, straighten out. **2** *untangle the complications* straighten out, sort out, clear up.

untenable *adjective* indefensible, undefendable, insupportable, unmaintainable, unsustainable, refutable, unsound, weak, flawed, defective, faulty, implausible, specious, groundless, unfounded, baseless, unacceptable, inadmissible.

unthinkable *adjective* **1** *it is unthinkable that the territory is unexplored* inconceivable, unimaginable, unbelievable, beyond belief, impossible, beyond the bounds of possibility, implausible. **2** *it is unthinkable that he should represent* *us* not to be considered, out of the question, absurd, preposterous, outrageous.

Antonyms: IMAGINABLE; PLAUSIBLE; CONCEIVABLE.

unthinking adjective **1** *hurt by an unthinking remark* thoughtless, inconsiderate, tactless, undiplomatic, injudicious, indiscreet, insensitive, blundering, careless, rude. **2** *an unthinking kick of the ball* inadvertent, unintentional, unintended, mechanical, automatic, instinctive, involuntary.

untidy adjective **1** *untidy children* disheveled, unkempt, bedraggled, rumpled, messy, slovenly, slatternly; *inf.* mussed up, sloppy. **2** *untidy desks/rooms* disordered, disorderly, disarranged, disorganized, chaotic, confused, muddled, jumbled, topsy-turvy, at sixes and sevens; *inf.* higgledy-piggledy, every which way.

untie verb undo, loose, unbind, unfasten, unwrap, unlace, untether, unhitch, unknot.

untimely adjective **1** *an untimely visit* ill-timed, mistimed, inconvenient, inopportune, inappropriate, inapt, awkward, unsuitable, infelicitous. **2** *his untimely death* premature, early.

untiring adjective tireless, indefatigable, unfailing, unfaltering, unwavering, unflagging, unremitting, constant, incessant, unceasing, dogged, determined, resolute, steady, persistent, staunch.

untold adjective **1** *her untold story | untold secrets* unrecounted, unrelated, unnarrated, unreported, unmentioned, unstated, unspoken, unrevealed, undisclosed, undivulged, unpublished, secret. **2** *the untold horrors of the war | untold joy* unspeakable, indescribable, inexpressible, unutterable, ineffable, unimaginable, inconceivable. **3** *untold millions/damage* countless, innumerable, myriad, incalculable, immeasurable, measureless.

untoward adjective **1** *untoward developments delayed us* unfortunate, inconvenient, inopportune, untimely, awkward, annoying, troublesome, vexatious. **2** *do their best in untoward circumstances* unfortunate, unlucky, adverse, disadvantageous, inauspicious, unpropitious, hostile, inimical. **3** *see nothing untoward in his reaction* unusual, uncommon, abnormal, atypical, out of the way, out of place. **4** *find nothing untoward in his behavior at the party | the teacher's treatment of the child was untoward* unsuitable, inappropriate, unbefitting, unseemly, improper, indecorous.

Antonyms: ADVANTAGEOUS; USUAL; APPROPRIATE.

untroubled adjective unperturbed, undisturbed, unworried, unruffled, unagitated, unbothered, unconcerned, calm, cool, collected, composed, serene.

untrue adjective **1** *untrue stories/accounts* false, fallacious, fictitious, fabricated, erroneous, in error, wrong, incorrect, inaccurate, economical with the truth, inexact, flawed, unsound, distorted, misleading. **2** *untrue friends* disloyal, faithless, unfaithful, false, treacherous, perfidious, deceitful, untrustworthy, double-dealing, insincere, unreliable, inconstant. **3** *his aim was untrue* inaccurate, wide of the mark, wide, off, out of true.

untrustworthy adjective treacherous, not to be trusted, two-faced, double-dealing, duplicitous, deceitful, dishonest, dishonorable, unreliable, undependable; *inf.* slippery.

untruth noun **1** *a story full of untruth* lying, falsehood, falsity, fiction, mendacity, fabrication, inaccuracy; lies. **2** *tell an untruth* lie, falsehood, piece of fiction, fabrication, fib, white lie; *inf.* whopper.

untruthful adjective **1** *an untruthful account* false, fictitious, fabricated, fallacious, erroneous, wrong, economical with the truth, inaccurate, inexact, flawed, unsound. **2** *an untruthful person* lying, mendacious, dishonest, deceitful.

unusual adjective **1** *an unusual hairstyle/sound* uncommon, out of the ordinary, atypical, abnormal, rare, singular, odd, strange, curious, queer, bizarre, surprising, unexpected, different, unconventional, uncustomary, unwonted, unorthodox, irregular; *inf.* weird. **2** *an unusual talent* extraordinary, exceptional, singular, rare, remarkable, outstanding.

unutterable adjective **1** *unutterable joy* unspeakable, inexpressible, indescribable, beyond words/description, ineffable, unimaginable, inconceivable, overwhelming. **2** *unutterable cad* indescribable, indescribably bad, appalling, shocking, frightful, dreadful, deplorable.

unveil verb *unveil the facts | unveiled their plans* uncover, reveal, lay open/bare, expose, bring to light, disclose, divulge, make known/public.

unwarranted adjective **1** *an unwarranted entry into the palace* unauthorized, uncertified, unaccredited, unlicensed, unsanctioned, unapproved. **2** *unwarranted behavior | an unwarranted intrusion into our affairs* unjustifiable, unjustified, indefensible, inexcusable, unforgivable, unpardonable, uncalled-for, gratuitous.

unwelcome adjective **1** *unwelcome visitors* unwanted, undesired, uninvited, unpopular. **2** *unwelcome news | the unwelcome truth* unpleasant, disagreeable, unpalatable, displeasing, distasteful, undesirable.

unwell adjective ill, sick, sickly, ailing, in poor health, unhealthy, run-down, below par; *inf.* out of sorts, poorly, under the weather.

unwieldy adjective cumbersome, unmanageable, unmaneuverable, awkward, clumsy, massive, hefty, bulky, ponderous; *inf.* hulking.

Antonyms: MANAGEABLE; GRACEFUL; DAINTY.

unwilling adjective **1** *an unwilling guest | their unwilling presence* reluctant, disinclined, unenthusiastic, grudging, involuntary, forced. **2** *unwilling to go* reluctant, disinclined, averse, loath, opposed, not in the mood.

unwind verb 1 *unwind the balls of yarn | unwind the roll of bandage* undo, unravel, uncoil, unroll, untwine, untwist, disentangle. 2 *unwind by watching television* wind down, relax, calm down, slow down; *inf.* loosen up, let oneself go, take it easy, let one's hair down.

unwise adjective imprudent, injudicious, inadvisable, ill-considered, ill-judged, ill-advised, impolitic, indiscreet, shortsighted, irresponsible, foolhardy, rash, reckless, foolish, silly, unintelligent, mindless.

unwitting adjective 1 *an unwitting offender* unknowing, unconscious, unaware, ignorant. 2 *an unwitting slight* unintentional, unintended, inadvertent, unmeant, unplanned, accidental, chance.
Antonyms: CONSCIOUS; DELIBERATE.

unwonted adjective unusual, uncommon, uncustomary, out of the ordinary, exceptional, atypical, abnormal, irregular, anomalous.
Antonyms: USUAL; CUSTOMARY; HABITUAL.

unworldly adjective 1 *unworldly considerations* spiritual, spiritualistic, nonmaterial, religious. 2 *too unworldly to cope on her own* naïve, inexperienced, green, raw, uninitiated, unsophisticated, gullible, ingenuous, trusting, credulous, idealistic. 3 *unworldly beings* otherworldly, unearthly, extraterrestrial, ethereal, ghostly, spectral, phantom, preternatural, supernatural.

unworthy adjective 1 *unworthy conduct for a teacher* unsuitable, inappropriate, unbefitting, unfitting, unseemly, improper, incompatible, incongruous, inconsistent, out of character, degrading, discreditable. 2 *an unworthy cause* worthless, inferior, second-rate, undeserving, ignoble, disreputable; *inf.* lousy, crappy. 3 *an unworthy wretch* disreputable, dishonorable, base, contemptible, reprehensible. **unworthy of** *he is unworthy of her | she is unworthy of the honor conferred on her* not worthy of, not good enough for, undeserving of, ineligible for, unqualified for.

upbraid verb scold, rebuke, reproach, reprove, chide, reprimand, berate, remonstrate with, castigate, criticize, censure.

upbringing noun bringing up, rearing, raising, nurture, care, tending, training.

upgrade verb 1 *upgrade the facilities/building* improve, better, ameliorate, reform, enhance, touch up, rehabilitate, refurbish. 2 *upgrade him to a higher position* promote, advance, elevate, raise.
Antonyms: DOWNGRADE; DEMOTE.

upheaval noun disruption, disturbance, revolution, disorder, confusion, turmoil, chaos, cataclysm.

uphill adjective 1 *an uphill path* upward, ascending, climbing, mounting, rising. 2 *an uphill job* arduous, difficult, laborious, strenuous, hard, tough, burdensome, onerous, taxing, punishing, grueling, exhausting, wearisome, Herculean.

uphold verb 1 *uphold the committee's decision | uphold his right to refuse* confirm, endorse, support, back up, stand by, champion, defend. 2 *uphold the old traditions* maintain, sustain, hold to, keep.
Antonyms: OPPOSE; DISCARD.

upkeep noun 1 *pay for the upkeep of the house* maintenance, running, preservation, conservation; repairs. 2 *pay for the child's upkeep* keep, maintenance, support, subsistence, sustenance. 3 *the upkeep is deducted from his salary* outlay, running/operating costs, costs, overheads, expenses.

uplift verb 1 *uplift the load* raise, upraise, lift, hoist up, heave up, elevate. 2 *uplift his spirits* raise, improve, edify, inspire.

upper adjective 1 *the upper shelf/story* higher, further up, loftier. 2 *the upper ranks* superior, higher-ranking, elevated, greater.
Antonyms: LOWER[1]; INFERIOR.

upper-class adjective aristocratic, noble, highborn, patrician, blue-blooded; *inf.* top-drawer.

upper hand noun advantage, edge, whip hand, ascendancy, superiority, supremacy, sway, control, mastery, dominance, command.

uppermost adjective 1 *the uppermost shelf/floor* highest, furthest up, loftiest, top, topmost. 2 *the uppermost consideration | uppermost in our minds* foremost, greatest, predominant, dominant, principal, chief, main, paramount, major.

uppish adjective conceited, arrogant, overweening, self-important, self-assertive, presumptuous, supercilious, snobbish, disdainful, hoity-toity; *inf.* uppity, high and mighty, stuck-up.

upright adjective 1 *upright posts* erect, on end, vertical, perpendicular, standing up, rampant. 2 *upright members of the community* honest, honorable, upstanding, decent, respectable, worthy, reputable, good, virtuous, righteous, law-abiding, ethical, moral, high-principled, of principle, high-minded.
Antonyms: HORIZONTAL; DISHONORABLE; CROOKED.

uprising noun rising, rebellion, revolt, insurrection, insurgence, mutiny, riot, revolution, coup, coup d'état, overthrow, putsch; fighting in the streets.

---

uprising
insurgency, insurrection, mutiny, putsch, rebellion, revolution

There are a number of ways to defy the established order or overthrow a government. You can stage an **uprising**, which is a broad term referring to a small and usually unsuccessful act of popular resistance (*uprisings among angry workers all over the country*). An uprising is often the first sign of a general or widespread **rebellion**, which is an act of armed resistance against a government or authority; this term is usually applied after the fact to describe an act of resistance that has failed (*a rebellion against the landowners*). If it is successful, however, a rebellion may become a **revolution**, which often implies a war or an outbreak of violence (*the American Revolution*). Although a *revolution* usually involves the overthrow of a government or political system by the people, it can also be used to describe any drastic change in ideas, economic institutions, or moral values (*the sexual revolution*). An **insurrection** is an organized effort to seize power, especially political power, while an **insurgency** is usually aided by foreign powers. If you're on a ship, you can stage a **mutiny**, which is an insurrection against military or naval authority. But if you're relying on speed and surprise to catch the authorities off guard, you'll want to stage a **putsch**, which is a small, popular uprising or planned attempt to seize power.

uproar *noun* **1** *the place was in uproar* tumult, turmoil, turbulence, disorder, confusion, commotion, mayhem, pandemonium, bedlam; din, noise, clamor, hubbub, racket. **2** *there was an uproar when he was dismissed* outburst, row, rumpus, brouhaha, hullabaloo, affray, furor, fracas, brawl, scuffle, conflict, struggle, free-for-all; *inf.* ruckus.

uproarious *adjective* **1** *an uproarious party* noisy, loud, rowdy, disorderly, unruly, boisterous, wild, unrestrained, rollicking. **2** *an uproarious show* hilarious, hysterically/riotously funny, sidesplitting; *inf.* too funny for words, too much, rip-roaring, rib-tickling.
Antonyms: QUIET; SOLEMN.

upset *verb* **1** *upset the bucket/boat* overturn, knock over, push over, upend, tip over, topple, capsize. **2** *the news upset them* perturb, disturb, discompose, unsettle, disconcert, dismay, disquiet, trouble, worry, bother, agitate, fluster, ruffle, shake, frighten, alarm, anger, annoy, distress, hurt, grieve. **3** *upset the smooth running of the firm* disturb, throw into disorder/confusion, disorganize, disarrange, mess up, mix up, turn topsy-turvy. **4** *upset Napoleon's army* defeat, beat, conquer, vanquish, rout, overthrow, overcome, triumph over, be victorious over, get the better of, worst, thrash, trounce.

upset *noun* **1** *cause a great deal of upset* | *emotional upset* perturbation, discomposure, dismay, disquiet, trouble, worry, bother, agitation, fluster, alarm, distress, hurt. **2** *cause upset to the running of the firm* | *an upset of our plans* disturbance, disorder, confusion, disorganization, disarrangement. **3** *a stomach upset* disorder, disturbance, complaint, ailment, illness, sickness, disease, malady; *inf.* bug. **4** *the upset of the army* defeat, conquering, rout, overthrow, worsting.

upset *adjective* **1** *the upset bucket* overturned, up-

turned, upended, toppled, capsized, upside down. **2** *upset by the news* perturbed, disturbed, discomposed, unsettled, disconcerted, dismayed, disquieted, troubled, worried, bothered, anxious, agitated, flustered, ruffled, shaken, frightened, alarmed, angered, annoyed, distressed, hurt, saddened, grieved. **3** *an upset stomach* | *feeling upset in the boat* disordered, disturbed, queasy, ill, sick. **4** *our upset plans* disturbed, disordered, in disorder, confused, in confusion, disarranged, in disarray, jumbled up, messed up, chaotic, in chaos, topsy-turvy; *inf.* higgledy-piggledy.
Antonyms: CALM; COMPOSED; UNPERTURBED; ORDERLY.

upshot *noun* result, outcome, conclusion, issue, end, end result, denouement, effect, repercussion, reaction; *inf.* payoff.
Antonyms: ORIGIN; CAUSE.

upside down *adjective* **1** *the bucket was upside down* upturned, upended, wrong side up, inverted. **2** *the house is upside down* | *our plans are upside down* in disorder, in disarray, jumbled up, in a muddle, messed up, chaotic, in chaos, topsy-turvy; *inf.* at sixes and sevens, higgledy-piggledy.

upstanding *adjective* **1** *an upstanding young man* healthy, hale and hearty, strong, sturdy, robust, vigorous, hardy, stalwart, well-made, well-built. **2** *upstanding members of the community* upright, honest, honorable, decent, worthy, respectable, good, virtuous, righteous, law-abiding.

upstart *noun* parvenu, parvenue, would-be, social climber, status seeker, nouveau riche, arriviste.

up-to-date *adjective* *up-to-date clothes* modern, current, prevalent, prevailing, present-day, recent, up-to-the-minute, fashionable, in fashion, in vogue, voguish; *inf.* all the rage, trendy, with-it, now.
Antonyms: OUT OF DATE; OUTDATED; OLD-FASHIONED.

upturn *noun* **1** *an upturn in sales* upswing, increase, rise, upsurge, boost, acceleration, escalation; *inf.* step-up. **2** *an upturn in the economy* upswing, improvement, advancement, betterment, recovery, revival.

upward *adjective* *the upward slope/trend* rising, climbing, mounting, ascending, on the rise.
Antonyms: DOWNWARD; downhill.

upward, upwards *adverb* **1** *going upward* up, uphill, to the top, straight up. **2** *prices spiraling upward* toward a higher level/standing. **upwards of** *upwards of 100 miles* more than, above, over, beyond.

urban *adjective* city, cityish, citified, inner-city, town, townish, metropolitan, municipal, civic, oppidan.

urbane *adjective* suave, debonair, sophisticated, smooth, worldly, elegant, cultivated, cultured, civilized, polished, refined, gracious, charming, agreeable, affable, courtly, civil, polite, courteous, well-mannered, mannerly.

Antonyms: UNCOUTH; UNSOPHISTICATED; BOORISH.

---

urbane
cosmopolitan, genteel, sophisticated, suave
In his long career as a film star, Cary Grant was known for playing **urbane, sophisticated** roles. *Urbane* in this context suggests the social poise and polished manner of someone who is well-traveled and well-bred, while *sophisticated* means worldly-wise as opposed to naïve (*a sophisticated young girl who had spent her childhood in Paris and London*). **Cosmopolitan** describes someone who is at home anywhere in the world and is free from provincial attitudes (*a cosmopolitan man who could charm women of all ages and nationalities*), while **suave** suggests the gracious social behavior of *urbane* combined with a certain glibness or superficial politeness (*she was taken in by his expensive clothes and suave manner*). At one time **genteel** meant well-bred or refined, but nowadays it has connotations of self-consciousness or pretentiousness (*too genteel to drink wine from a juice glass*).

---

urbanity *noun* suaveness, sophistication, smoothness, worldliness, cultivation, culture, polish, refinement, graciousness, charm, affability, courtliness, civility, politeness, mannerliness.

urchin *noun* street urchin, ragamuffin, gamin, guttersnipe, waif, stray, imp, rogue, brat.

urge *verb* 1 *urge the horses on | urge the children up the hill* push, drive, propel, impel, force, hasten, hurry, speed up. 2 *urge the contestants to greater effort* spur, incite, stir up, stimulate, prod, goad, egg on, encourage, prompt; *inf.* psych up. 3 *urged him to go | "go," he urged* entreat, exhort, implore, appeal, beg, beseech, plead. 4 *urge caution* advise, counsel, advocate, recommend, suggest, support, endorse, back, champion.

Antonyms: DISSUADE; DETER; DISCOURAGE.

urge *noun a sudden urge to travel | sexual urge* desire, need, compulsion, longing, yearning, wish, fancy, impulse, itch; *inf.* yen.

urgency *noun* 1 *a matter of urgency* imperativeness, exigency, top priority, importance, necessity, seriousness, gravity, extremity, hurry, haste. 2 *the urgency in her voice* importunateness, insistence, clamorousness, earnestness, pleading, begging.

urgent *adjective* 1 *it is urgent that we operate* imperative, vital, crucial, critical, essential, exigent, top-priority, high-priority, important, necessary. 2 *urgent matters* vital, crucial, exigent, top-priority, high-priority, important, pressing, serious, grave. 3 *an urgent whisper/de-*

mand importunate, insistent, clamorous, earnest, pleading, begging.

Antonyms: UNIMPORTANT; TRIVIAL; CASUAL.

urinate *verb* pass water, micturate; *inf.* pee, wee-wee, wee, tinkle, take a leak.

usable *adjective* for use, to be used, utilizable, available, ready/fit for use, in working order, functional.

usage *noun* 1 *damaged by rough usage* use, treatment, handling, management, running, operation, manipulation, maneuvering. 2 *old usages now forgotten* custom, practice, habit, way, procedure, method, mode, form, tradition, convention. 3 *study English usage* manner of speaking/writing, mode of expression, phraseology, phrasing, idiom, idiolect.

use *verb* 1 *use tools* make use of, utilize, employ, work, operate, wield, ply, maneuver, manipulate, avail oneself of, put to use, put into service. 2 *use tact* employ, exercise, apply. 3 *him roughly* treat, handle, deal with, act/behave toward. 4 *he just uses people for his own ends* make use of, exploit, manipulate, take advantage of, impose upon, abuse; *inf.* walk all over, play for a sucker. 5 *have you used any eggs? | we have used up all the food* consume, get through, exhaust, deplete, expend, spend, waste, fritter away. **used to** accustomed to, familiar with, at home with, in the habit of, given to, prone to, wont to, habituated to, addicted to, inured to.

use *noun* 1 *for external use* usage, application, utilization, employment, operation, manipulation, maneuvering. 2 *fall to pieces from use* using, usage, wear, wear and tear. 3 *he has the use of the garden* right, privilege, prerogative. 4 *his use of other people for his own ends* exploitation, manipulation. *See* USE *verb* 4. 5 *what use is this to you?* usefulness, good, advantage, benefit, service, help, gain, profit, avail. 6 *established by long use* usage, practice, custom, habit, wont. 7 *we have no use for this machine* need, necessity, call, demand, purpose, reason.

used *adjective used car/clothing* secondhand, nearly new, cast-off; *inf.* hand-me-down.

Antonyms: NEW; PRISTINE.

useful *adjective* 1 *a useful tool* of use, functional, utilitarian, of service, practical, convenient. 2 *a useful experience* beneficial, advantageous, of help, helpful, worthwhile, profitable, rewarding, productive, valuable. 3 *he is a useful player* effective, efficacious, effectual, competent, capable, able.

Antonyms: USELESS; DISADVANTAGEOUS; INEFFECTIVE.

useless *adjective* 1 *a useless attempt | useless meetings* vain, in vain, to no avail/purpose, unavailing, unsuccessful, futile, purposeless, ineffectual, inefficacious, fruitless, unprofitable, unproductive, abortive. 2 *he is a useless player* worthless, ineffective, ineffectual, incompetent, incapable, inadequate; *inf.* no good.

Antonyms: USEFUL; BENEFICIAL; EFFECTIVE.

usher *noun* escort, guide, attendant.

usher *verb usher the people to their seats* escort, show, conduct, direct, guide, lead. **usher in** *usher in new methods* herald, pave the way for, give notice of, announce, introduce, bring in, get going, get under way, launch.

usual *adjective* 1 *his usual route* habitual, customary, accustomed, wonted, normal, regular, routine, everyday, established, set, familiar. 2 *not usual behavior* common, typical, ordinary, average, run-of-the-mill, expected, standard, stock, regular.

Antonyms: UNUSUAL; UNCOMMON; EXTRAORDINARY.

usually *adverb usually he works late* generally, as a rule, normally, by and large, in the main, mainly, mostly, for the most part, on the whole.

usurp *verb usurp the throne/position* take over, seize, expropriate, take possession of, appropriate, commandeer, lay claim to, assume.

utilitarian *adjective* practical, functional, useful, to the purpose.

utility *noun* use, usefulness, service, serviceableness, advantageousness, benefit, helpfulness, profitability, convenience, practicality, practicability, effectiveness, efficacy.

utilize *verb* use, put to use, make use of, employ, avail oneself of, have recourse to, resort to, take advantage of, turn to account.

utmost *adjective* 1 *have the utmost confidence in them* maximum, supreme, paramount, greatest, highest, most. 2 *the utmost ends of the earth* uttermost, furthest, farthest, remotest, outermost, extreme, ultimate.

utmost *noun to the utmost* maximum, most, uttermost, top, pinnacle, peak, best, finest.

utter *adjective an utter cad | feel utter happiness* absolute, complete, total, thorough, thoroughgoing, positive, downright, out-and-out, sheer, unmitigated, categorical, unqualified, unconditional, perfect, consummate.

utter *verb* 1 *utter a sound* emit, let out, give. 2 *utter threats* voice, say, speak, pronounce, express, put into words, enunciate, articulate, verbalize, vocalize.

utterance *noun* 1 *give utterance to his thoughts* voice, expression, articulation, enunciation, verbalization, vocalization. 2 *his prophetic utterances* remark, word, comment, statement, opinion.

utterly *adverb utterly delightful* absolutely, completely, totally, entirely, thoroughly, positively, extremely, categorically, perfectly, consummately, to the core.

V

vacancy noun **1** *the vacancy of the place* emptiness, voidness. **2** *a vacancy in the firm* opening, position, post, job, opportunity, slot. **3** *no vacancies in the hotel* unoccupied room, room. **4** *the vacancy of his expression* blankness, lack of expression, expressionlessness, lack of emotion/interest, emotionlessness, vacuousness. **5** *his vacancy is unbelievable* lack of thought/intelligence, brainlessness, denseness, thickness, vacuousness, vacuity, inaneness, inanity, stupidity.

vacant adjective **1** *a vacant space* empty, void, without contents. **2** *a vacant position* unoccupied, unfilled, free, empty, available. **3** *a vacant seat* empty, unoccupied, free, unengaged, not in use, unused, available; *inf.* up for grabs. **4** *a vacant house* empty, unoccupied, uninhabited, untenanted, tenantless, to let, abandoned, deserted. **5** *how to spend his vacant time* free, leisure, idle, unemployed. **6** *a vacant expression/countenance* blank, expressionless, inexpressive, deadpan, poker-faced, emotionless, uninterested, vacuous, inane. **7** *he seems to be completely vacant* without thought, unintelligent, brainless, dense, dull-witted, thick, vacuous, inane, stupid.

Antonyms: FULL; OCCUPIED; EXPRESSIVE.

vacate verb *vacate the house/post* leave, quit, depart from, evacuate, abandon, desert.

Antonyms: OCCUPY; INHABIT.

vacation noun **1** *take a vacation* break, recess, furlough, holiday, rest, respite; leave, time off. **2** *the vacation of the post* quitting, departure, evacuation. *See* VACATE.

vacillate verb shilly-shally, waver, dither, be irresolute/indecisive, hesitate, equivocate, hem and haw, keep changing one's mind, beat about the bush; *inf.* blow hot and cold.

vacuous adjective **1** *a vacuous expression* vacant, blank, expressionless, deadpan, inane. *See* VACANT 6. **2** *he seems to be completely vacuous* unintelligent, brainless, vacant, inane, stupid. *See* VACANT 7.

vacuum noun **1** *create a vacuum* emptiness, void, empty space, nothingness, vacuity. **2** *a vacuum in his life* gap, empty space, lacuna, vacuity, hollowness, need, want.

vagabond noun wanderer, itinerant, nomad, wayfarer, traveler, rover, gypsy, hobo, tramp, vagrant, derelict, beachcomber, down-and-out, bird of passage, rolling stone; *inf.* bum.

vagabond adjective *a vagabond existence* wandering, nomadic, itinerant, peripatetic, traveling, journeying, roving, roaming, vagrant, drifting, unsettled, transient, footloose.

vagary noun caprice, whim, whimsy, fancy, notion.

vagrancy noun nomadism, peripateticism, itinerancy, vagabondism, wandering, roving, roaming, drifting, homelessness.

vagrant noun tramp, hobo, beggar, itinerant, nomad, wanderer, vagabond; *inf.* bum. *See* VAGABOND noun.

vagrant adjective *a vagrant existence* tramplike, itinerant, nomadic, peripatetic, wandering, roving, vagabond, homeless. *See* VAGABOND adjective.

vague adjective **1** *a vague shape* indistinct, indeterminate, ill-defined, unclear, nebulous, amorphous, shadowy, hazy, dim, fuzzy, foggy, blurry, bleary, out of focus. **2** *a vague description* imprecise, inexact, unexplicit, nonspecific, loose, generalized, ambiguous, equivocal, hazy, woolly. **3** *have only a vague idea of what is involved* imprecise, ill-defined, hazy, nebulous. **4** *she is rather vague about her plans* uncertain, unsure, hesitant, wavering, shilly-shallying; *inf.* blowing hot and cold. **5** *her plans are rather vague* uncertain, undecided, indefinite, indeterminate, doubtful, open, speculative, conjectural; *inf.* up in the air. **6** *she is rather vague* absentminded, abstracted, dreamy, vacuous; *inf.* with one's head in the clouds.

Antonyms: DISTINCT; PRECISE; CLEAR; CERTAIN.

vaguely adverb **1** *she looks vaguely familiar* in a general way, in a way, somehow, slightly, obscurely. **2** *point vaguely in her direction* approximately, roughly, imprecisely. **3** *smiling vaguely* absentmindedly, abstractedly, vacantly, vacuously.

vain adjective **1** *vain people* conceited, self-loving, narcissistic, self-admiring, peacockish, egotistical, proud, haughty, arrogant, boastful, swaggering, imperious, overweening, cocky, affected; *lit.* vainglorious; *inf.* stuck-up, bigheaded, swellheaded. **2** *vain triumphs* futile, worthless, insignificant, pointless, meaningless, nugatory, valueless, meritless, empty, hollow, insubstantial, idle, vapid. **3** *vain attempts* unsuccessful, futile, useless, unavailing, to no avail, ineffective, inefficacious, fruitless, unproductive, abortive, unprofitable, profitless. **in vain 1** *try in vain to save him* unsuccessfully, without success, to no avail/purpose, ineffectually, with no result, fruitlessly. **2** *his efforts were in vain* unsuccessful, unavailing, to no avail/purpose, ineffectual.

Antonyms: MODEST; SUCCESSFUL.

valedictory *adjective* farewell, parting, final.

valiant *adjective* brave, courageous, valorous, heroic, stouthearted, lionhearted, gallant, manly, intrepid, fearless, undaunted, undismayed, bold, daring, audacious, staunch, stalwart, indomitable, resolute, determined.

Antonyms: COWARDLY; TIMOROUS.

valid *adjective* **1** *valid reasons/objections* sound, well-founded, well-grounded, substantial, reasonable, logical, justifiable, defensible, vindicable, authentic, bona fide, effective, cogent, powerful, convincing, credible, forceful, weighty. **2** *the ruling is still valid* lawful, legal, licit, legitimate, legally binding, binding, contractual, in force, in effect, effective.

Antonyms: INVALID; NULL; VOID; ILLEGAL.

validate *verb* **1** *validate the contract | validate his appointment* ratify, legalize, legitimize, authorize, sanction, warrant, license, approve, endorse, set one's seal to. **2** *validate a statement* verify, prove, authenticate, substantiate, confirm, corroborate, justify.

Antonyms: INVALIDATE; REVOKE; DISPROVE.

valley *noun* dale, dell, hollow, vale, glen, depression.

valor *noun* bravery, courage, heroism, stoutheartedness, gallantry, manliness, intrepidity, fearlessness, boldness, daring, staunchness, fortitude.

valuable *adjective* **1** *a valuable watch* costly, high-priced, expensive, priceless, precious. **2** *a valuable contribution/lesson* useful, helpful, beneficial, advantageous, worthwhile, worthy, important.

Antonyms: WORTHLESS; CHEAP; USELESS.

valuables *plural noun* treasures, costly articles.

value *noun* **1** *place a value on the ring* monetary value, face value, price, market price, cost. **2** *the value of a healthy diet | his advice is of great value* worth, merit, usefulness, advantage, benefit, gain, profit, good, avail, importance, significance.

value *verb* **1** *value the watch | value his worth to the firm* set a price on, price, evaluate, assess, appraise. **2** *we value his contribution greatly* rate highly, appreciate, esteem, hold in high regard, think highly of, set store by, respect, admire, prize, cherish, treasure.

valued *adjective* *a valued contribution/friendship* esteemed, highly regarded, respected, prized, cherished, treasured.

values *plural noun* *moral values* code of behavior; principles, ethics, morals, standards.

vamp *noun* seductress, siren, temptress, loose woman, adventuress.

van *noun* *in the van of new fashion* vanguard, forefront, front, front line, leading position.

Antonyms: REAR; END; TAIL.

vanguard *noun* advance guard, forefront, front, front line, front rank, leading position,

van; leaders, spearheads, trailblazers, trendsetters.

vanish *verb* **1** *she vanished in the mist* disappear, be lost to sight/view, be/become invisible, evaporate, dissipate, disperse, fade, fade away, evanesce, melt away, recede from view, withdraw, depart, leave. **2** *a way of life that has vanished | hopes of success have vanished* cease to exist/be, pass away, die out, come to an end, end, be no more, become extinct/obsolete.

Antonyms: APPEAR; MATERIALIZE.

vanity *noun* **1** *his vanity about his looks/achievements* conceit, conceitedness, self-conceit, self-admiration, self-love, narcissism, egotism, pride, haughtiness, arrogance, boastfulness, braggadocio, pretension, affectation, ostentation, show, vainglory; airs; *inf.* stuck-upness, bigheadedness, swellheadedness, showing off. **2** *the vanity of human triumphs* worthlessness, futility, futileness, insignificance, pointlessness, meaninglessness, emptiness, hollowness, insubstantiality, vapidity.

Antonyms: MODESTY; HUMILITY; WORTH.

vanquish *verb* conquer, defeat, triumph over, beat, overcome, best, worst, master, subdue, subjugate, put down, quell, quash, repress, rout, overwhelm, overrun, overthrow, crush, trounce, thrash, drub; *inf.* clobber.

vapid *adjective* insipid, flat, lifeless, colorless, bland, dull, trite, uninteresting, zestless.

Antonyms: LIVELY; COLORFUL; EXCITING.

variable *adjective* varying, variational, changeable, changeful, changing, mutable, chameleonic, protean, shifting, fluctuating, wavering, vacillating, inconstant, unsteady, unstable, fitful, capricious, fickle; *inf.* blowing hot and cold.

Antonyms: CONSTANT; UNIFORM; STEADY.

variance *noun* *an obvious variance between statements* discrepancy, disagreement, diverging. **at variance** *they are at variance about his suitability* in disagreement, in dissent, in opposition, in conflict, at odds.

variant *adjective* *variant spellings* alternative, divergent, derived, modified.

variant *noun* *a variant of the normal spelling* variation, alternative, derived form, development, modification, mutant.

variation *noun* **1** *subject to variation* change, alteration, modification, diversification. **2** *noted for its variation* variability, changeability, fluctuation, vacillation, vicissitude. **3** *a variation in sizes* varying, difference, dissimilarity. **4** *show variation from the norm* deviation, divergence, departure, difference. **5** *a variation on a theme* diversification, innovation, novelty.

varied *adjective* *a varied selection* diversified, diverse, assorted, miscellaneous, mixed, motley, heterogeneous.

Antonyms: UNIFORM; HOMOGENEOUS.

variegated *adjective* multicolored, parti-colored,

prismatic, rainbowlike, kaleidoscopic, marbled, streaked, striated, mottled, speckled, flecked.

variety noun **1** *introduce variety into your selection* variation, diversification, diversity, multifariousness, many-sidedness, change, difference. **2** *a variety of flowers were exhibited* assortment, miscellany, range, mixture, medley, motley, collection, multiplicity. **3** *a variety of rose/humor* strain, breed, kind, type, sort, class, category, classification, brand, make.

various adjective **1** *come in various shapes* varying, diverse, different, differing, dissimilar, unlike, disparate, many, assorted, mixed, miscellaneous, variegated, heterogeneous. **2** *for various reasons* numerous, many, several, varied, sundry, diverse; *lit.* divers.

varnish verb **1** *varnish the table* lacquer, japan, shellac, enamel, glaze, veneer. **2** *varnish the truth* embellish, smooth over, cover up, gloss over, mask, disguise.

varnish noun *apply a varnish to the surface* coating, lacquer, shellac, enamel, glaze, veneer.

vary verb **1** *they tend to vary in size* differ, be different, be unlike, be dissimilar. **2** *the sky varies constantly* change, be transformed, alter, metamorphose, suffer a sea change, vacillate, fluctuate. **3** *our opinions vary* be at variance, disagree, be in disagreement, differ, conflict, clash, be at odds, be in opposition, diverge. **4** *vary the speed/appearance* change, alter, modify, transform, permutate. **5** *vary from the norm* deviate, diverge, depart, differ.

vast adjective **1** *a vast shape loomed* immense, huge, enormous, massive, bulky, tremendous, colossal, prodigious, gigantic, monumental, elephantine; *inf.* hulking. **2** *vast forests* immense, extensive, broad, wide, expansive, boundless, limitless, infinite.
Antonyms: TINY; MINUTE.

vault noun **1** *look up at the vault* arched roof/ceiling, arch. **2** *hide in the vault* cellar, basement, underground chamber, tomb. **3** *valuables stored in the vault* safe, strongbox, strongroom, repository, depository. **4** *take a vault over the fence* jump, leap, spring, bound.

vault verb *vault the fence* jump, leap, jump over, leap over, spring over, bound over.

vaunt verb *always vaunting his achievements* boast about, brag about, make much of, crow about, give oneself airs about, exult in; *inf.* show off about.

veer verb change course/direction, shift direction, turn, swerve, swing, sidestep, sheer, tack, be deflected.

vegetate verb **1** *vegetating at home without a job* do nothing, idle, be inactive, laze around, lounge around, loaf around, languish, stagnate, molder; *inf.* go to seed. **2** *plants vegetating* grow, sprout, shoot up, burgeon, flourish.

vegetation noun plant life, herbage, greenery, verdure; plants, flora.

vehemence noun passion, ardor, fervor, strength, force, forcibleness, forcefulness, emphasis, vigor, intensity, violence, earnestness, keenness, enthusiasm, zeal, zealousness, spirit, spiritedness, gusto, verve.

vehement adjective passionate, ardent, impassioned, fervent, fervid, strong, forceful, forcible, powerful, emphatic, vigorous, intense, violent, earnest, keen, enthusiastic, zealous, spirited.
Antonyms: APATHETIC; INDIFFERENT.

vehicle noun **1** *park the vehicle* means of transport, transportation, conveyance; car, bus, truck. **2** *a vehicle for their propaganda* channel, medium, means, means of expression, agency, instrument, mechanism, organ, apparatus.

veil noun **1** *her face covered by a veil* face covering, mantilla, yashmak, purdah. **2** *a veil of mist covered the mountain | under a veil of secrecy* covering, cover, screen, curtain, film, mantle, cloak, mask, blanket, shroud, canopy, cloud.

veil verb **1** *try to veil his contempt | did not veil his threats* hide, conceal, cover up, camouflage, disguise, mask, screen. **2** *mist veiling the mountains* cover, envelop, mantle, cloak, blanket, shroud, canopy.

veiled adjective *thinly veiled threats* hidden, concealed, covert, disguised, camouflaged, masked, suppressed.

vein noun **1** *sever a vein* blood vessel; *Tech.* venule. **2** *a vein of ore* lode, seam, stratum. **3** *veins of blue in the white marble* streak, stripe, line, thread, marking. **4** *there was a vein of wickedness in him* streak, strain, trait, dash, hint. **5** *said in a humorous vein* humor, mood, temper, temperament, disposition, frame of mind, attitude, inclination, tendency, tenor, tone.

velocity noun speed, swiftness, fastness, quickness, rapidity, celerity.

venal adjective corrupt, corruptible, bribable, open to bribery, purchasable, buyable, mercenary, greedy, avaricious, grasping, rapacious.
Antonyms: HONORABLE; HONEST.

vendetta noun feud, blood feud, quarrel, war, conflict, rivalry, enmity.

vendor noun seller, salesperson, dealer, trader, merchant, peddler, hawker.

veneer noun **1** *a veneer of mahogany* facing, covering, coat, finishing coat, finish. **2** *a veneer of politeness* façade, front, false front, show, outward display, appearance, semblance, guise, mask, pretense, camouflage.

venerable adjective *venerable scientist/traditions* venerated, respected, revered, reverenced, worshiped, honored, esteemed, hallowed.
Antonyms: DISREPUTABLE; INFAMOUS.

veneration noun respect, reverence, worship, adoration, honor, esteem.

vengeance noun revenge, retribution, requital, retaliation, reprisal, an eye for an eye, tit for tat, measure for measure, blow for blow, quid pro quo. **with a vengeance 1** *the rain came down with a vengeance* forcefully, violently, vehemently, furiously, wildly. **2** *go at the job with a vengeance* to the utmost, to the greatest extreme, to the full, to the limit, all out, flat out.

venial *adjective a venial offense* pardonable, forgivable, excusable, allowable, tolerable, slight, minor, unimportant, insignificant, trivial.

venom *noun* **1** *suck the venom of the snake bite* poison, toxin, toxicant. **2** *speak with venom about his rival* spite, spitefulness, rancor, vindictiveness, malice, malevolence, malignity, ill will, animosity, bitterness, resentment, grudgingness, acrimony, virulence, antagonism, hostility, enmity, hatred, viciousness.

venomous *adjective* **1** *a venomous snake/bite* poisonous, toxic, lethal, deadly, fatal, noxious. **2** *a venomous remark/look* spiteful, rancorous, vindictive, malicious, malevolent, malignant, baleful, bitter, resentful, grudging, virulent, antagonistic, hostile, hate-filled, vicious.

vent *noun* **1** *an air vent* opening, outlet, aperture, hole, gap, orifice, duct, flue. **2** *give vent to his anger* outlet, free passage, expression, release.

vent *verb vent his anger on his children* give vent/expression to, express, air, utter, voice, verbalize, let out, release, pour out, emit, discharge, come out with.

ventilate *verb* **1** *ventilate a room* air, aerate, oxygenate, air-condition, freshen, cool, purify. **2** *ventilate one's views* air, give an airing to, bring into the open, discuss, debate, talk over, give expression to, express.

venture *noun* **1** *explorers engaged in a new venture* adventure, exploit, mission, risky undertaking. **2** *a business venture* enterprise, undertaking, project, speculation, fling, plunge, gamble.

venture *verb* **1** *venture to voice an opinion* dare, be so bold as, presume. **2** *venture an opinion* volunteer, advance, put forward, chance, risk. **3** *venture his life for her* risk, put at risk, endanger, hazard, put in jeopardy, jeopardize, imperil, chance, gamble. **venture out/forth** *it is now possible to venture out/forth* go, set forth, embark (on).

veracious *adjective* **1** *a veracious person* truthful, honest, sincere, frank, candid, honorable, upright, upstanding, ethical, moral, righteous, virtuous, decent, good. **2** *a veracious statement* true, truthful, accurate, exact, precise, factual, literal, realistic.
Antonyms: DISHONEST; UNTRUE.

verbal *adjective* **1** *a verbal account* oral, spoken, said, uttered, articulated. **2** *a verbal translation* word for word, verbatim, literal, close, faithful, exact, precise.

verbatim *adjective a verbatim translation* word for word, literal, exact. *See* VERBAL 2.

verbatim *adverb translate his statement verbatim* word for word, literally, to the letter, closely, faithfully, exactly, precisely.

verbose *adjective* wordy, loquacious, garrulous, long-winded, prolix, diffuse, pleonastic, circumlocutory, periphrastic, tautological.
Antonyms: SUCCINCT; TACITURN.

verbosity *noun* verboseness, wordiness, loquacity, garrulity, long-windedness, logorrhea, verbiage, prolixity, diffuseness, circumlocution, periphrasis, tautology.

verdict *noun* decision, judgment, adjudication, finding, conclusion, ruling, opinion.

verge *noun* **1** *the verges of the lake* edge, border, margin, rim, limit, boundary, end, extremity. **2** *on the verge of a breakdown/discovery* brink, threshold.

verge *verb* **verge on** *it verges on the ridiculous* approach, incline to/toward, tend toward, border on, come near.

verification *noun ask for verification of his statement* confirmation, substantiation, corroboration, attestation, validation, authentication, endorsement, accreditation, ratification; evidence, proof.

verify *verb* **1** *ask the witness to verify his statement* confirm, substantiate, prove, corroborate, attest to, testify to, validate, authenticate, endorse, accredit, ratify. **2** *our suspicions were verified* bear out, justify, give credence to, confirm, prove, substantiate.

vernacular *noun* everyday/spoken language, colloquial/native speech, conversational language, common parlance, nonstandard language, jargon, cant, patois; *inf.* lingo, patter.

versatile *adjective* **1** *a versatile member of staff* adaptable, flexible, all-around, multifaceted, resourceful, ingenious, clever. **2** *a versatile tool* adaptable, adjustable, multipurpose, handy, all-purpose.

verse *noun* **1** *write verse rather than prose* poetry; poems. **2** *a poem in several verses* stanza, strophe, canto, couplet. **3** *recited a verse about the countryside* poem, lyric, sonnet, ode, limerick, piece of doggerel, ditty, song, lay, ballad.

version *noun* **1** *tell us your version of the events* account, report, story, rendering, interpretation, construction, understanding, reading, impression, side. **2** *published in several versions* adaptation, interpretation, translation. **3** *there are several versions of the song going around* variant, variation, form, copy, reproduction.

vertical *adjective* upright, erect, on end, perpendicular.
Antonyms: HORIZONTAL; LEVEL.

vertigo *noun* dizziness, giddiness, light-headedness, loss of balance/equilibrium; *inf.* wooziness.

verve *noun* enthusiasm, vigor, force, energy, vitality, vivacity, liveliness, animation, sparkle, spirit, life, élan, dash, brio, fervor, gusto, passion, zeal, feeling, fire; *inf.* zing, zip, vim, punch, get-up-and-go, pizzazz.

very *adverb very pretty* | *done very easily*

extremely, exceedingly, to a great extent, exceptionally, uncommonly, unusually, decidedly, particularly, eminently, remarkably, really, truly; *inf.* awfully, terribly.

very *adjective* **1** *his very words* actual, exact, precise, unqualified. **2** *that is the very thing for the task* ideal, perfect, appropriate, suitable, fitting, right, just right. **3** *its very simplicity appeals to us* sheer, utter, simple, pure, plain, mere. **4** *at the very beginning* extreme, absolute.

vessel *noun* **1** *a seagoing vessel* ship, boat, yacht, craft; *lit.* barque, argosy. **2** *pour the milk into several vessels* container, receptacle.

vest *verb* **vest in** *he has the power to execute vested in him* bestow on/upon, confer on/upon, endow, entrust to/with, invest in, lodge in/with, place in/on/with, put in the hands of.

vestibule *noun* entrance hall, hall, porch, portico, foyer, lobby, anteroom.

vestige *noun* **1** *see vestiges of a pack of wolves* trace, mark, sign, indication, print, imprint, impression, track. **2** *vestiges of a lost civilization* remains, relics; evidence. **3** *not a vestige of proof* scrap, hint, suggestion, touch, tinge, suspicion, soupçon, inkling, drop, dash, jot, iota.

vestigial *adjective* **1** *vestigial signs of an extinct civilization* remaining, surviving. **2** *a vestigial tail* rudimentary, nonfunctional, undeveloped.

veteran *noun* *veterans of the acting profession* old hand, old-timer, past master, master; *inf.* pro, warhorse.
Antonyms: NOVICE; APPRENTICE.

veteran *adjective* *a veteran member of the committee* long-serving, seasoned, old, adept, expert; *inf.* battle-scarred.

veto *verb* *veto the tax cuts* | *veto the candidate for membership* reject, turn down, give the thumbs down to, prohibit, forbid, interdict, proscribe, disallow, outlaw, embargo, ban, bar, preclude, rule out; *inf.* kill, put the kibosh on.
Antonyms: APPROVE; ALLOW; ENDORSE; AUTHORIZE.

veto *noun* *the right of veto* | *have a veto over any proposal* rejection, prohibition, interdict, proscription; embargo, ban.

vex *verb* anger, annoy, irritate, incense, irk, enrage, infuriate, exasperate, pique, provoke, nettle, disturb, upset, perturb, discompose, put out, try one's patience, try, bother, trouble, worry, agitate, pester, harass, fluster, ruffle, hound, nag, torment, distress, tease, fret, gall, molest; *inf.* peeve, miff, bug, hassle, aggravate, rile, get one's goat, drive up the wall, get to.

vexation *noun* **1** *her vexation at his behavior* anger, annoyance, irritation, rage, fury, exasperation, pique, provocation, perturbation, discomposure, worry, agitation, harassment, gall. **2** *he is a vexation to them* nuisance, pest, problem, trouble, worry, bother, irritant, thorn

in one's flesh; *inf.* headache, pain, pain in the neck.

vexatious *adjective* annoying, irritating, irksome, infuriating, exasperating, provoking, upsetting, perturbing, bothersome, troublesome, worrying, worrisome, trying, distressing; *inf.* aggravating.

vexed *adjective* **1** *vexed about his behavior* | *his vexed parents* annoyed, irritated, incensed, irked, enraged, infuriated, exasperated, upset, perturbed, bothered, troubled, worried, agitated, harassed, flustered, distressed; *inf.* aggravated, peeved, miffed. **2** *the vexed question* disputed, in dispute, contested, in contention, debated, controversial, moot.

viable *adjective* *a viable plan/operation* workable, sound, feasible, practicable, applicable, usable.
Antonyms: IMPRACTICABLE; infeasible.

vibrant *adjective* **1** *vibrant pendulums* vibrating, vibratory, oscillating, swinging. **2** *vibrant music* throbbing, pulsating, resonant, reverberating, ringing, echoing. **3** *vibrant with excitement* trembling, quivering, shaking, shivering. **4** *a vibrant personality* lively, energetic, spirited, vigorous, animated, sparkling, vivacious, dynamic, electrifying. **5** *vibrant colors* vivid, bright, strong, striking.

vibrate *verb* **1** *the pendulum vibrated* oscillate, swing, move to and fro. **2** *the noise vibrated through the house* throb, pulsate, resonate, resound, reverberate, ring, echo. **3** *vibrating with excitement* pulsate, tremble, quiver, shake, quaver, shiver, shudder.

vibration *noun* **1** *the vibration of the pendulum* oscillation, swinging. **2** *the musical vibration* throb, pulsation, resonance, reverberation. **3** *the vibration of the engine* | *vibration of the bird's wings* pulsating, trembling, tremble, quivering, quiver, shake, shaking, quaver, shiver, shivering.

vicar *noun* minister, clergyman, cleric, churchman, ecclesiastic.

vicarious *adjective* *vicarious pleasure from another's joy* indirect, secondhand, surrogate, by proxy.

vice *noun* **1** *vice is rampant* sin, sinfulness, wrong, wrongdoing, wickedness, badness, immorality, iniquity, evil, evildoing, venality corruption, depravity, degeneracy. **2** *enumerate his vices* sin, wrongdoing, transgression, offense, misdeed, error, violation. **3** *chocolate/shopping is one of her vices* failing, flaw, defect, imperfection, weakness, foible, shortcoming.
Antonym: VIRTUE.

vice versa *adverb* conversely, inversely, the other way around, contrariwise.

vicinity *noun* **1** *he lives in the vicinity* surrounding district, neighborhood, locality, area, district; environs, precincts, purlieus; *inf.* this neck of the woods. **2** *the town's vicinity to Nashville* nearness, closeness, proximity, propinquity. **in the vicinity of** *in the vicinity of*

vicious *adjective* **1** *attacked by vicious dogs* fierce, ferocious, savage, dangerous, ill-natured, bad-tempered, surly, hostile. **2** *vicious gossip/remarks* malicious, malevolent, malignant, spiteful, vindictive, venomous, catty, backbiting, rancorous, caustic, mean, cruel, defamatory, slanderous; *inf.* bitchy. **3** *a vicious attack* violent, savage, brutal, fierce, ferocious, inhuman, barbarous, fiendish, sadistic, monstrous, heinous, atrocious, diabolical. **4** *fall in with a vicious band of people* corrupt, degenerate, depraved, debased, wicked, evil, sinful, bad, wrong, immoral, unprincipled, abandoned, unscrupulous, disreputable, dissolute, dissipated, debauched, profligate, libertine, vile, infamous, notorious.
Antonyms: GENTLE; KINDLY; VIRTUOUS.

vicissitude *noun the vicissitudes of a writer's life* change, alteration, transformation, inconstancy, instability, uncertainty, unpredictability, chanciness, fickleness; ups and downs.

victim *noun* **1** *victims of the attack* injured party, casualty, sufferer. **2** *they were victims of his sales patter* dupe, easy target/prey, fair game, sitting target, everybody's fool; *inf.* sitting duck, sucker, sap, fall guy, pushover. **3** *track down their victim(s)* prey, quarry, game, the hunted, target. **4** *a sacrificial victim for the gods* offering, sacrifice, scapegoat.
Antonyms: ATTACKER; ASSAILANT.

victimize *verb* **1** *bullies victimizing their classmates* persecute, bully, pick on, discriminate against, punish unfairly; *inf.* have it in for. **2** *con artists victimizing the naïve couple* exploit, prey on, take advantage of, swindle, dupe, cheat, trick, hoodwink.

victor *verb* conqueror, vanquisher, winner, champion, prizewinner, conquering hero; *inf.* champ, top dog, number one.
Antonyms: LOSER; vanquished.

victorious *adjective* conquering, vanquishing, triumphant, winning, champion, successful, prizewinning, top, first.
Antonyms: UNSUCCESSFUL; losing.

victuals *plural noun* food, food and drink; eatables, foodstuffs, viands, comestibles, food supplies, provisions, rations, stores; *inf.* eats, grub, nosh.

vie *verb vie with her for first place* compete, contend, contest.

view *noun* **1** *come into view* sight, field/range of vision, vision, eyeshot. **2** *the view from the mountain* outlook, prospect, scene, spectacle, vista, panorama; landscape, seascape. **3** *his view is that we should wait | have radical views* point of view, viewpoint, opinion, belief, judgment, way of thinking, thinking, thought, notion, idea, conviction, persuasion, attitude, feeling, sentiment, impression. **4** *a private view of the exhibition* viewing, sight, look, contemplation, observation, study, survey, inspection, scrutiny, scan. **in view of** *in view of his political opinions* considering, taking into consideration, bearing in mind, taking into account, in the light of. **on view** *pictures on view* on display, on exhibition, on show.

view *verb* **1** *view the birds through binoculars* look at, watch, observe, contemplate, regard, behold, scan, survey, inspect, gaze at, stare at, peer at. **2** *view the house* see over, be shown over, survey, examine, scrutinize, take stock of. **3** *view the prospect with dismay* look on, consider, contemplate, think about, reflect on, ponder. **4** *view himself as an upright man* see, consider, judge, deem.

viewer *noun* television watcher, watcher, spectator, onlooker, member of the audience.

viewpoint *noun* point of view, way of thinking, frame of reference, perspective, angle, slant, standpoint, position, stance, vantage point.

vigilance *noun* watchfulness, observation, surveillance, attentiveness, attention, alertness, guardedness, carefulness, caution, wariness, circumspection, heedfulness, heed.

vigilant *adjective* watchful, on the lookout, observant, sharp-eyed, eagle-eyed, attentive, alert, on the alert, on the qui vive, awake, wide awake, unsleeping, on one's guard, careful, cautious, wary, circumspect, heedful.
Antonyms: HEEDLESS; NEGLIGENT; INATTENTIVE.

---

vigilant
alert, careful, cautious, circumspect, wary, watchful

All of these adjectives connote being on the lookout for danger or opportunity. **Watchful** is the most general term, meaning closely observant (*a watchful young man who noticed everything*). If you're **vigilant**, you are watchful for a purpose (*to be vigilant in the presence of one's enemies*), and **wary** suggests being on the lookout for treachery or trickery (*wary of his neighbor's motives in offering to move the fence*). If you're **alert**, you are quick to apprehend a danger, an opportunity, or an emergency (*she was much more alert after a good night's sleep*), and if you're **careful**, you may be able to avoid danger or error altogether. **Cautious** and **circumspect** also emphasize the avoidance of danger or unpleasant situations. To be *circumspect* is to be watchful in all directions and with regard to all possible consequences (*these journalists have to be circumspect, not criticizing anyone too harshly*); to be *cautious* is to guard against contingencies (*a cautious approach to treating illness*).

---

vigor *noun* **1** *the natural vigor of country children* robustness, healthiness, strength, sturdiness, fitness, toughness. **2** *return to work with renewed vigor* energy, activity, liveliness, spryness, sprightliness, vitality, vivacity, verve, animation, dynamism, sparkle, zest, dash, élan, gusto, pep; *inf.* zip, zing, oomph, vim.

vigorous *adjective* **1** *vigorous children brought up in the country* robust, healthy, in good health, hale and hearty, strong, sturdy, fit, in good condition/shape/kilter, tough. **2** *feeling more vigorous after their vacation* energetic, lively, active, spry, sprightly, vivacious, animated, dynamic, full of life, sparkling. **3** *a vigorous attempt at winning* powerful, potent, strenuous, forceful, forcible, spirited, mettlesome, plucky, determined, resolute, aggressive, eager, keen, enthusiastic, zealous, ardent, fervent, vehement, intense, passionate. **4** *use vigorous arguments* strong, forceful, effective, cogent, valid, pointed, to the point, striking, graphic, vivid.
Antonyms: FRAIL; FEEBLE; WEAK.

vigorously *adverb* *defend himself vigorously | argue vigorously* strongly, powerfully, strenuously, forcefully, energetically, aggressively, eagerly, enthusiastically, with might and main, all out, with a vengeance, hammer and tongs; *inf.* like mad.

vile *adjective* **1** *a vile taste/smell* foul, nasty, unpleasant, disagreeable, horrid, horrible, offensive, obnoxious, odious, repulsive, repellent, revolting, repugnant, disgusting, distasteful, loathsome, hateful, nauseating, sickening. **2** *he is a vile creature | a vile thing to do* base, low, mean, wretched, foul, nasty, horrible, horrid, dreadful, disgraceful, appalling, shocking, ugly, abominable, monstrous, wicked, evil, iniquitous, sinful, vicious, corrupt, depraved, perverted, debased, reprobate, degenerate, debauched, dissolute, contemptible, despicable, reprehensible. **3** *vile weather* foul, nasty, unpleasant, disagreeable.
Antonyms: PLEASANT; AGREEABLE; ADMIRABLE.

vilify *verb* defame, run down, impugn, revile, berate, denigrate, disparage, speak ill of, cast aspersions at, criticize, decry, denounce, fulminate against, malign, slander, libel, conduct a smear campaign against, blacken the name/reputation of, calumniate, traduce; *inf.* badmouth, do a hatchet job on, pull to pieces, sling/throw mud at, drag through the mud.
Antonyms: PRAISE; COMMEND; EXALT.

villain *noun* **1** *he pretends to be honest but he is a real villain* rogue, scoundrel, blackguard, wretch, cad, reprobate, evildoer, wrongdoer, ruffian, hoodlum, hooligan, miscreant; *inf.* baddy, crook, rat, louse. **2** *the police chasing the villains* criminal, miscreant, jailbird; *inf.* crook. **3** *the child's a little villain* rascal, rogue, imp, monkey, scamp, brat; *inf.* scalawag.

villainous *adjective* **1** *a villainous attack* wicked, evil, iniquitous, sinful, nefarious, vile, foul, monstrous, shocking, outrageous, atrocious, abominable, reprehensible, hateful, detestable, horrible, heinous, diabolical, fiendish, vicious. **2** *a villainous wretch* wicked,

evil, sinful, bad, base, dishonorable, dishonest, unscrupulous, scoundrelly, unprincipled, criminal, lawless, corrupt, degenerate, reprobate, depraved, dissolute; *inf.* crooked.
Antonyms: GOOD; VIRTUOUS.

villainy *noun* wickedness, badness, evil, sin, iniquity, wrongdoing, roguery, rascality, vice, criminality, delinquency, vileness, viciousness, degeneracy, depravity, turpitude; crime, offense, misdeed.

vindicate *verb* **1** *he was vindicated when his alibi was proved* acquit, clear, absolve, free from blame, exonerate, exculpate. **2** *time vindicated his suspicions* justify, warrant, substantiate, testify to, verify, confirm, corroborate. **3** *vindicate his claim* defend, support, back, fight for, champion, uphold, maintain, sustain, stand by.
Antonyms: BLAME; CONVICT; INCRIMINATE.

vindictive *adjective* vengeful, out for revenge, revengeful, avenging, grudge-bearing, unforgiving, resentful, ill-disposed, implacable, unrelenting, unconciliative, spiteful, rancorous, venomous, malicious, malevolent, malignant.
Antonyms: FORGIVING; MERCIFUL.

---

vindictive
rancorous, spiteful, vengeful, venomous

Someone who is motivated by a desire to get even might be described as **vindictive**, a word that suggests harboring grudges for imagined wrongs (*a vindictive person who had alienated friends and neighbors alike*). **Spiteful** is a stronger term, implying a bitter or vicious vindictiveness (*a spiteful child who broke the toy she had been forced to share*). **Vengeful** implies a strong urge to actually seek vengeance (*vengeful after losing her husband in hit-and-run accident*). Someone who is **rancorous** suffers from a deep-seated and lasting bitterness, although it does not imply a desire to hurt or to be vindictive (*his rancorous nature made him difficult to befriend*). **Venomous** takes its meaning from venom referring to someone or something of a spiteful, malignant nature and suggesting a poisonous sting (*a critic's venomous attack on the author's first novel*).

---

vintage *noun* **1** *what vintage is this wine?* year, harvest, crop. **2** *the furniture is of 18th-century vintage* era, epoch, period, time. **3** *his parents are of the same vintage as mine* generation, period, time.

vintage *adjective* **1** *vintage wines* high-quality, quality, prime, choice, select, superior, best. **2** *vintage comedy* classic, ageless, enduring. **3** *this story is vintage Poe* characteristic, most typical, supreme, at his/her/its best.

violate *verb* **1** *violate a law/treaty* break, breach, infringe, contravene, infract, transgress, disobey, disregard, ignore. **2** *violate a grave* desecrate, profane, defile, blaspheme. **3** *violate their privacy* disturb, disrupt, intrude on, interfere with, encroach on, invade. **4** *violate the* *peace* disturb, disrupt, break into, upset, shatter, destroy. **5** *he was accused of violating his niece* rape, ravish, indecently assault, abuse, deflower, molest, seduce.

violence *noun* **1** *the violence of his temper* strength, forcefulness, lack of control/restraint, wildness, passion. **2** *the violence of the blow* forcefulness, powerfulness, might, savagery, ferocity, destructiveness, brutality. **3** *the violence of the storm* wildness, tempestuousness, turbulence. **4** *the violence of his dislike* strength, intensity, vehemence. **5** *the violence of the pain* sharpness, acuteness, intensity. **6** *use violence to get his way* force, brute force, roughness, ferocity, brutality, savagery; strongarm tactics.

violent *adjective* **1** *a violent temper* strong, powerful, forceful, uncontrolled, unrestrained, unbridled, uncontrollable, ungovernable, wild, passionate, raging. **2** *he is a violent person* brutal, vicious, destructive, savage, fierce, wild, intemperate, hotheaded, hot-tempered, bloodthirsty, homicidal, murderous, maniacal. **3** *a violent blow* forceful, powerful, mighty, savage, ferocious, destructive, damaging, brutal. **4** *a violent storm* wild, blustery, boisterous, raging, tempestuous, turbulent, tumultuous. **5** *a violent dislike* strong, great, intense, extreme, vehement, inordinate, excessive. **6** *a violent pain/ toothache* sharp, acute, intense, excruciating, agonizing, biting.

virgin *adjective virgin snow/territory* pure, immaculate, unblemished, spotless, stainless, unused, untouched, untainted, unspoiled, untarnished, unadulterated.

virginal *adjective* pure, chaste, virtuous, uncorrupted.

virile *adjective* manly, masculine, male, all-male, strong, vigorous, robust, powerfully built, muscular, rugged, strapping, sturdy, redblooded; *inf.* macho.
Antonyms: UNMANLY; EFFEMINATE.

virility *noun* **1** *the virility of the bodybuilders* manliness, strength, vigor, robustness, muscularity, ruggedness; *inf.* machismo. **2** *impaired virility* sexual potency, potency, sexuality. **3** *question his virility* manliness, masculinity, maleness, manhood.

virtual *adjective* **1** *traffic at a virtual standstill* more or less, near, effective, in effect, tantamount to, for all practical purposes. **2** *he is the virtual manager* in all but name, functioning as, operating as, for all practical purposes.

virtually *adverb traffic virtually at a standstill | he is virtually in charge* more or less, nearly, practically, as good as, effectively, in effect, essentially, in essence, for all practical purposes, to all intents and purposes, in all but name.

virtue *noun* **1** *admires the virtue of workers* goodness, righteousness, morality, ethicalness, uprightness, upstandingness, integrity, rectitude, honesty, honorableness, honor, incorruptibility, probity, decency, respectability, worthi-

ness, worth, trustworthiness. **2** *the virtue of youth* virginity, celibacy, purity, pureness, chastity, chasteness, innocence, modesty. **3** *generosity is one of her virtues | reliability is one of the car's virtues* good quality/point, merit, asset, credit, attribute, advantage, benefit, strength; *inf.* plus. **4** *there is no virtue in the use of such drugs* merit, advantage, benefit, usefulness, efficacy, efficaciousness, power, potency.
by virtue of *win by virtue of his talent* by reason of, by dint of, on account of, as a result of, owing to, thanks to.
Antonyms: VICE; SIN; FAILING; DISADVANTAGE.

virtuosity *noun* skill, skillfulness, mastery, expertise, prowess, excellence, craftsmanship, flair, finish, polish, panache, brilliance, éclat, wizardry.

virtuoso *noun a virtuoso on the piano* master, genius, expert, artist, maestro, wizard.

virtuoso *adjective a virtuoso performance* skillful, masterly, impressive, outstanding, dazzling, bravura.

virtuous *adjective* **1** *virtuous, hardworking people* good, righteous, moral, ethical, upright, upstanding, honest, honorable, incorruptible, decent, respectable, worthy, trustworthy. **2** *virtuous youth* virginal, celibate, pure, chaste, innocent, modest.
Antonyms: EVIL; SINFUL; PROMISCUOUS.

virulent *adjective* **1** *virulent insecticides* poisonous, toxic, venomous, deadly, lethal, fatal, noxious, harmful. **2** *a virulent form/strain of the disease* severe, extreme, violent, rapidly spreading, highly infectious/contagious, harmful, lethal. **3** *a virulent attack | virulent forms of abuse* hostile, spiteful, venomous, vicious, vindictive, malicious, malevolent, malignant, bitter, rancorous, acrimonious, abusive, aggressive, violent.

visible *adjective* **1** *hills scarcely visible in the mist* in view, perceptible, perceivable, discernible, detectable, seeable. **2** *his distress was visible to all* apparent, evident, noticeable, observable, detectable, recognizable, manifest, plain, clear, obvious, patent, palpable, unmistakable, unconcealed, undisguised, conspicuous, distinct, distinguishable.
Antonyms: INVISIBLE; HIDDEN.

vision *noun* **1** *have good vision* eyesight, sight, power of seeing; eyes. **2** *the prophet saw a vision* apparition, specter, phantom, ghost, wraith, phantasm, chimera, revelation. **3** *saw wild horses in one of his visions* dream, hallucination, chimera, optical illusion, mirage, illusion, delusion, figment of the imagination. **4** *have visions of a romantic weekend* dream, daydream, pipe dream, fantasy, image, mental picture. **5** *artists must have vision* perception, perceptiveness, insight, intuition, imagination. **6** *in need of political vision* foresight, farsightedness, prescience, breadth of view, discernment. **7** *she* *was a vision in white* dream, spectacle, picture, feast for the eyes, beautiful sight; *inf.* sight for sore eyes.

visionary *adjective* **1** *too visionary to make a success of business* idealistic, impractical, unrealistic, utopian, romantic, quixotic, dreamy, dreaming; *inf.* starry-eyed. **2** *visionary artists* perceptive, intuitive, insightful, imaginative. **3** *visionary politicians* farsighted, discerning, wise, prescient. **4** *visionary figures* unreal, imaginary, imagined, fanciful, fancied, illusory, delusory, figmental, phantasmal, phantasmagoric, spectral, ghostly, wraithlike. **5** *visionary schemes* impractical, unrealistic, unworkable, unfeasible, theoretical, hypothetical, idealistic, utopian.

visionary *noun* **1** *ancient visionaries* mystic, seer, prophet. **2** *too much of a visionary to run a business* dreamer, daydreamer, idealist, romantic, romanticist, fantasist, theorist, utopian.

visit *verb* **1** *visit his aunt* | *visit a friend in the hospital* pay a visit to, go/come to see, pay a call on, call on, look in on, stop by (to see); *inf.* pop/drop in on, look up. **2** *he is visiting his aunt this week* stay with, be the guest of. **3** *inspectors visiting the school* pay a call on, inspect, survey, examine. **4** *a city visited with the plague* attack, assail, afflict, smite, descend on, trouble, harrow, torture.

visit *noun* **1** *pay a visit to the new tenants* call, social call. **2** *their visit lasted three days* stay, sojourn, stopover.

visitation *noun* **1** *building inspectors making their annual visitation* official visit, inspection, tour of inspection, survey, review, scrutiny, examination. **2** *the peasants regarded the earthquake as a divine visitation* affliction, scourge, plague, pestilence, blight, disaster, tragedy, calamity, catastrophe, cataclysm.

visitor *noun* **1** *a visitor to the house* caller, guest. **2** *a visitor to the country* tourist, traveler, pilgrim.

visual *adjective* **1** *visual problems* seeing, optical, ocular. **2** *have visual appeal* | *the visual arts* to be seen, seeable, perceivable, discernible.

visualize *verb* conjure up, envisage, picture in the mind's eye, picture, envision, imagine, conceive.

vital *adjective* **1** *the heart performs a vital function* | *the vital organs* life-giving, life-preserving, life-sustaining, basic, fundamental, essential. **2** *matters of vital importance* essential, necessary, needed, indispensable, key, important, significant, imperative, urgent, critical, crucial, life-and-death. **3** *such a vital person* lively, animated, spirited, vivacious, vibrant, zestful, dynamic, energetic, vigorous, forceful. **4** *a vital error* deadly, lethal, fatal, fateful.
Antonyms: UNIMPORTANT; DISPENSABLE; PERIPHERAL; LISTLESS.

vitality *noun full of vitality* life, liveliness, anima-

tion, spirit, spiritedness, vivacity, vibrancy, zest, zestfulness, dynamism, energy, vigor, forcefulness.

vitriolic *adjective* *vitriolic criticism* caustic, mordant, acrimonious, bitter, acerbic, astringent, acid, acidulous, acrid, trenchant, virulent, spiteful, venomous, malicious, scathing, withering, sarcastic, sardonic; *inf.* bitchy.

vituperate *verb* revile, rail against, inveigh against, fulminate against, condemn, denounce, upbraid, berate, reprimand, castigate, chastise, rebuke, scold, chide, censure, find fault with, take to task, abuse, vilify, denigrate; *inf.* slate.

vituperation *noun* revilement, invective, condemnation, denunciation, blame, reprimand, admonition, castigation, chastisement, rebuke, scolding, faultfinding, abuse, vilification, denigration; *inf.* flak.

vivacious *adjective* lively, full of life, animated, effervescent, bubbling, ebullient, sparkling, scintillating, lighthearted, high-spirited, spirited, gay, merry, jolly, vibrant, vivid, dynamic, vital.
Antonyms: DULL; LANGUID; LISTLESS.

vivacity *noun* liveliness, animation, effervescence, ebullience, sparkle, scintillation, spiritedness, spirit, high-spiritedness, sprightliness, gaiety, merriment, jollity, vibrancy, vividness, dynamism, vitality.

vivid *adjective* **1** *vivid colors* strong, intense, colorful, rich, glowing, bright, brilliant, clear. **2** *a vivid description* graphic, clear, lively, stirring, striking, powerful, impressive, highly colored, dramatic, memorable, realistic, lifelike, true to life. **3** *a vivid personality* strong, striking, flamboyant, memorable, dynamic, lively, animated, spirited, vibrant, vital.
Antonyms: DULL; COLORLESS; NONDESCRIPT.

vocabulary *noun* **1** *have a limited vocabulary* word stock, lexicon, lexis. **2** *there is a vocabulary at the back of the book* word list, dictionary, glossary.

vocal *adjective* **1** *vocal noises* voiced, vocalized, spoken, said, uttered, expressed, articulated, oral. **2** *people vocal in their criticism* vociferous, outspoken, forthright, plainspoken, strident, free-spoken, blunt, clamorous, loud, noisy.
Antonyms: TACITURN; RETICENT.

vocation *noun* profession, calling, occupation, walk of life, career, life's work, métier, trade, craft, job, work, employment, business, line, speciality.

vociferous *adjective* **1** *vociferous complaints* loud, noisy, clamorous, vehement, insistent. **2** *vociferous people complaining* vocal, outspoken, forthright, plainspoken, strident, loud, noisy.
Antonyms: SILENT; QUIET.

---

vociferous

boisterous, clamorous, obstreperous, strident

An angry crowd might be **vociferous**, which implies loud and unrestrained shouting or crying out (*a vociferous argument*). A happy crowd might be **boisterous,** which implies noisy exuberance or high-spirited rowdiness (*a boisterous celebration of spring*). A crowd that wants something is likely to be **clamorous,** which suggests an urgent or insistent vociferousness in demanding or protesting something. If people's demands are not met, they might become **obstreperous,** which means noisy in an unruly and aggressive way, usually in defiance of authority (*an obstreperous child*). **Strident** suggests a harsh, grating loudness that is particularly distressing to the ear (*her strident voice could be heard throughout the building*).

vogue *noun* **1** *the vogue for short skirts* fashion, mode, style, trend, taste, fad, craze, rage, latest thing, last word, dernier cri; *inf.* thing. **2** *that hairstyle had a vogue in the 1920s* fashionableness, modishness, popularity, currency, prevalence, favor, acceptance.

voice *noun* **1** *lose her voice* power of speech; powers of articulation. **2** *give voice to her feelings* expression, utterance, verbalization, vocalization, airing. **3** *listen to the voice of the people* opinion, view, comment, feeling, wish, desire, vote. **4** *he is the voice of the people* spokesman, spokeswoman, spokesperson, mouthpiece, organ, agency, medium, vehicle.

voice *verb* *voice one's displeasure* put in words, express, give utterance to, utter, articulate, enunciate, mention, talk of, communicate, declare, assert, divulge, air, ventilate; *inf.* come out with.

void *adjective* **1** *a void space* empty, emptied, vacant, without contents, bare, clear, free, unfilled, unoccupied, uninhabited, untenanted, tenantless. **2** *the contract/ticket is now void* null and void, nullified, invalid, canceled, inoperative, ineffective, not binding, not in force, nonviable, useless, worthless, nugatory. **void of** *void of people* devoid of, lacking, wanting, without, destitute of.
Antonyms: FULL; OCCUPIED; VALID.

void *noun* **1** *stare into a void* empty space, emptiness, blank space, blankness, vacuum. **2** *a void left by the death of his wife* space, gap, lacuna, hole, hollow, chasm, abyss.

void *verb* **1** *void the decision* annul, nullify, disallow, invalidate, quash, cancel, repeal, revoke, rescind, reverse, abrogate. **2** *void the bowels* empty, drain, evacuate; excrete, eject, expel, emit, discharge.

---

void
abrogate, annul, invalidate, negate, nullify

To **void** a check, to **invalidate** a claim, to **abrogate** a law, and to **annul** a marriage all refer to the same basic activity, which is putting an end to something or depriving it of validity, force, or authority. But these verbs are not always interchangeable. *Annul* is the most general term, meaning to end something that exists or to

---

declare that it never really existed (*the charter was annulled before it could be challenged*). *Abrogate* implies the exercise of legal authority (*Congress abrogated the treaty between the two warring factions*), while **nullify** means to deprive something of its value or effectiveness (*nullify the enemy's attempt to establish communications*). *Void* and *invalidate* are often used interchangeably as they both mean to make null or worthless (*void a legal document by tearing it up; invalidate a check by putting the wrong date on it*). **Negate** means to prove an assertion false (*her version of the story negated everything her brother had said*) or to nullify or make something ineffective (*the study's findings were negated by its author's arrest for fraud*).

---

volatile *adjective* **1** *a volatile person* mercurial, changeable, variable, capricious, whimsical, fickle, flighty, giddy, inconstant, erratic, unstable. **2** *volatile trading conditions* changeable, variable, inconstant, erratic, unsteady, unstable, irregular, fitful. **3** *a volatile international situation* explosive, eruptive, charged, inflammatory, tense, strained. **4** *volatile substances* evaporative, vaporous, vaporescent.
Antonyms: STABLE; CONSTANT; CALM.

volition *noun* **of one's own volition** of one's own free will, of one's own choice, by one's own preference, voluntarily.

volley *noun* **1** *the police fired a volley of bullets* barrage, cannonade, battery, broadside, salvo, fusillade, shower. **2** *a volley of questions/insults* barrage, battery, stream, deluge.

volubility *noun* talkativeness, loquaciousness, loquacity, chattiness, articulacy, eloquence, fluency, glibness; *inf.* gift of the gab.

voluble *adjective* talkative, loquacious, garrulous, chatty, gossipy, chattering, articulate, eloquent, forthcoming, fluent, glib.
Antonyms: TACITURN; UNCOMMUNICATIVE.

volume *noun* **1** *publish a volume on butterflies* book, publication, tome. **2** *measure the volume* enclosed space, bulk, capacity. **3** *a volume of water escaped* quantity, amount, mass. **4** *turn down the volume* | *the volume of the music is too loud* loudness, sound, amplification.

voluminous *adjective* *wearing a voluminous cape* capacious, roomy, commodious, ample, full, big, vast, billowing.

voluntarily *adverb* of one's own free will, freely, of one's own volition/accord, willingly, by choice, by preference, spontaneously, without being asked.

voluntary *adjective* **1** *attendance is voluntary* of one's own free will, volitional, of one's own accord, optional, discretional, at one's discretion, elective, noncompulsory, nonmandatory. **2** *undertake voluntary work* unpaid, without payment, honorary, volunteer.
Antonyms: COMPULSORY; OBLIGATORY.

volunteer verb **1** *volunteer one's services* offer, tender, proffer, present, put forward, advance. **2** *he volunteered as a helper* offer one's services, present oneself, step forward.

voluptuous adjective **1** *voluptuous pleasures* hedonistic, sybaritic, epicurean, pleasure-loving, self-indulgent, sensual, carnal, licentious, lascivious. **2** *a voluptuous woman* curvy, shapely, full-figured, ample, buxom, seductive; *inf.* curvaceous.

vomit verb **1** *he suddenly vomited* be sick, retch, heave, spew; *inf.* throw up, puke, barf, toss one's cookies, lose one's lunch, upchuck, hurl. **2** *vomit blood* bring up, regurgitate, spew up, spit up. **3** *chimneys vomiting smoke* belch, eject, emit, send forth, eruct.

voracious adjective **1** *a voracious eater* gluttonous, greedy, ravenous, ravening, starving, hungry. **2** *a voracious appetite* insatiable, insatiate, unquenchable, prodigious, uncontrolled. **3** *a voracious reader* compulsive, enthusiastic, eager.

vortex noun whirlpool, maelstrom, eddy, swirl, whirlwind.

vote noun **1** *have a vote on who should be mayor* ballot, poll, election, referendum, plebiscite. **2** *get the vote* right to vote, franchise, suffrage.

vote verb **1** *vote for a new president* cast one's vote, go to the polls, mark one's ballot. **2** *vote the government in* elect, opt for, return. **3** *I vote that we go home* suggest, propose, recommend, advocate.

vouch verb **vouch for** **1** *vouch for his honesty* attest to, bear witness to, give assurance of, answer for, be responsible for, guarantee. **2** *vouch for the painting's authenticity* certify, warrant, confirm, verify, validate, substantiate.

voucher noun chit, slip, ticket, token, document.

vouchsafe verb **1** *vouchsafe them a free pardon* | *vouchsafe a reply* grant, give, accord, confer on, yield to, cede to, favor with. **2** *vouchsafe to reply* deign, condescend.

vow noun *take a vow of silence* | *wedding vows* oath, pledge, promise.

vow verb *vow to be true* swear, state under oath, pledge, promise, undertake, give one's word of honor.

voyage noun **1** *a sea voyage* crossing, cruise, passage. **2** *voyage by land and sea* journey, trip, expedition; travels.

voyage verb **1** *voyage across the Atlantic* sail, cruise. **2** *voyage through space* travel, journey, take a trip.

vulgar adjective **1** *vulgar language/jokes* rude, indecent, indecorous, indelicate, unseemly, offensive, distasteful, obnoxious, risqué, suggestive, off-color, blue, ribald, bawdy, obscene, lewd, salacious, licentious, concupiscent, smutty, dirty, filthy, pornographic, scatological; *inf.* raunchy. **2** *vulgar table manners* rude, impolite, ill-mannered, unmannerly, ill-bred, common, coarse, boorish, rough, crude. **3** *vulgar decorations* tasteless, gross, crass, unrefined, tawdry, ostentatious, showy, flashy, gaudy. **4** *the vulgar masses* common, ordinary, low, lowborn, ignorant, unsophisticated, unrefined, uneducated, illiterate, uncultured, uncultivated, uncouth, crude.
Antonyms: DECOROUS; GENTEEL; MANNERLY; TASTEFUL.

vulgarity noun **1** *the vulgarity of the language/jokes* rudeness, indelicacy, offensiveness, suggestiveness, ribaldry, obscenity, smuttiness; *inf.* raunchiness. **2** *the vulgarity of his table manners* rudeness, impoliteness, ill manners, coarseness, crudeness. **3** *the vulgarity of the decorations* tastelessness, grossness, crassness, tawdriness, ostentation, gaudiness. **4** *the vulgarity of the common masses* commonness, lowness, ignorance, unsophisticatedness, lack of refinement, uncouthness, crudeness.

vulnerable adjective **1** *vulnerable armies/children* open to attack, attackable, assailable, exposed, unprotected, unguarded, defenseless, easily hurt/wounded/damaged, powerless, helpless, weak, sensitive, thin-skinned. **2** *vulnerable to criticism/temptation* open, wide open, exposed, liable, subject.
Antonyms: INVULNERABLE; IMMUNE.

W

wad *noun* **1** *a wad of putty* | *wads of cotton* lump, mass, chunk, hunk, ball, plug, block. **2** *a wad of dollar bills* bundle, roll.

wadding *noun* stuffing, filling, packing, padding, lining.

waddle *verb* sway, wobble, totter, toddle, shuffle.

wade *verb* **1** *wade the stream* | *wade across the snow* ford, cross, traverse. **2** *children wading in the stream* paddle, splash about. **3** *wade through piles of papers* proceed with difficulty, work one's way, plow, labor, toil/plug/peg away.

waft *verb* **1** *leaves wafting down the river* | *smells wafting from the kitchen* float, glide, drift, be carried/borne/conveyed. **2** *the wind wafted the leaves toward us* carry, bear, convey, transport, transmit.

wag[1] *noun* **1** *a wag of the tail* swing, sway, vibration, quiver, shake. **2** *a wag of the finger* wiggle, wobble, wave. **3** *a wag of the head* nod, bob.

wag[2] *verb* **1** *the dog's tail wagged* swing, sway, vibrate, quiver, shake, rock, twitch. **2** *wag one's finger* waggle, wiggle, wobble, wave. **3** *wag one's head* nod, bob.

wag[3] *noun* *he's quite a wag* wit, humorist, jester, joker, jokester, comic, comedian, comedienne, wisecracker, punner.

wage *noun* *on a low wage* pay, remuneration; wages, earnings. *See* WAGES 1.

wage *verb* *wage war* carry on, conduct, execute, engage in, pursue, undertake, devote oneself to, practice.

wager *noun* *lay a wager that he will win* bet, gamble, stake, pledge, hazard.

wager *verb* *I wager that he will win* lay a wager, bet, place/make/lay a bet, lay odds, put money on, speculate.

wages *plural noun* **1** *low wages* | *collect one's wages* pay, payment, fee, remuneration, salary, emolument, stipend; earnings. **2** *the wages of sin* recompense, requital, retribution; returns, deserts.

waggish *adjective* playful, roguish, impish, mischievous, joking, jesting, jocular, jocose, facetious, witty, amusing, entertaining, droll, whimsical.

waggle *verb* *waggle one's finger/ears/bottom* wiggle, wobble, shake, sway, wag, quiver.

waif *noun* stray, foundling, orphan.

wail *noun* cry of grief/pain, lament, lamentation, weeping, sob, moan, groan, whine, complaint, howl, yowl, ululation.

wail *verb* cry, lament, weep, sob, moan, groan, whine, complain, howl, yowl, ululate.

wait *verb* **1** *wait here* stay, remain, rest, linger, tarry, abide. **2** *you will just have to wait and see* | *wait until you hear from him* be patient, hold back, stand by, bide one's time, hang fire, mark time, cool one's heels; *inf.* sit tight, hold one's horses, sweat it out. **3** *wait his arrival* await, wait for, look/watch out for, anticipate, expect, be ready for, be in readiness for. **4** *wait dinner for him* delay, postpone, put off, hold off, hold back, defer. **5** *wait for him* | *wait for his arrival* be ready, anticipate, expect. **wait on** *wait on the dinner guests* act as a waiter/waitress to, serve, attend to. **wait up** *wait up until his daughter returns* stay up, stay awake, keep vigil.

wait *noun* *have a wait of two hours for the bus* period of waiting, interval, stay, delay, holdup.

waiter, waitress *noun* steward, stewardess, server, attendant.

waive *verb* **1** *waive one's right to appeal* relinquish, renounce, give up, abandon, surrender, yield, cede. **2** *waive the rules* set aside, forgo, disregard, ignore. **3** *waive the decision until tomorrow* postpone, defer, put off, delay, shelve; *inf.* put on the back burner.
Antonyms: CLAIM; UPHOLD; PURSUE.

wake *verb* **1** *wake at dawn* awake, awaken, waken, wake up, waken up, rouse, stir, come to, get up, arise. **2** *wake the children* wake up, waken, rouse. **3** *wake him out of depression* rouse, stir up, activate, stimulate, spur, prod, galvanize, provoke. **4** *wake to the fact that he is dishonest* become aware/conscious, become alert, become mindful/heedful. **5** *wake old memories* awaken, evoke, call up, conjure up, rouse, stir, revive, resuscitate, revivify, rekindle, reignite.
Antonyms: SLEEP; SNOOZE; DOZE.

wakeful *adjective* **1** *wakeful children* unsleeping, restless, tossing and turning, insomniac. **2** *wakeful security staff* alert, on the alert, vigilant, on the lookout, on one's guard, on the qui vive, watchful, observant, attentive, heedful, wary.
Antonyms: ASLEEP; INATTENTIVE.

waken *verb* **1** *waken at dawn* wake, awaken, stir. *See* WAKE *verb* 1. **2** *waken the children* wake, rouse. *See* WAKE *verb* 2. **3** *waken old memories* wake, awaken, evoke, call up, stir, revive, rekindle. *See* WAKE *verb* 5.

walk *verb* **1** *we walked rather than take the car* go by foot, travel on foot; *inf.* go by shank's pony, hoof it. **2** *walk, don't run* stroll, saunter, amble, plod, trudge, hike, tramp, trek, march, stride, step out. **3** *walk her home* accompany, escort, convoy. **walk off/away with** **1** *walk off with the firm's money* make/run off with, carry off, snatch, steal, filch, pilfer, embezzle. **2** *walk off with the match/prize* win easily, win hands down. **walk out** **1** *he had a fight with the boss and walked out* leave suddenly, make a sudden departure, get up and go, storm out; *inf.* take off. **2** *the workers walked out at lunchtime* go on strike, call a strike, down tools, stop work. **walk out on** *walk out on his family* desert, abandon, forsake, leave, leave in the lurch, run away from, throw over, jilt; *inf.* chuck, dump.

walk noun **1** *go for a walk* stroll, saunter, amble, promenade, ramble, hike, tramp, march, constitutional, airing. **2** *he has a distinctive walk* manner of walking, gait, pace, step, stride. **3** *the walk up to the house* road, avenue, drive, promenade, path, pathway, footpath, track, lane, alley. **4** *the postman's usual walk* route, beat, round, run, circuit. **walk of life** social rank/status, sphere, area, line of work, profession, career, vocation, job, employment, trade, craft, métier.

walker noun pedestrian, hiker, rambler, wayfarer.

walkout noun strike, (work) stoppage.

walkover noun *winning the prize was a walkover* easy victory; *inf.* piece of cake, child's play, pushover.

wall noun **1** *areas of the house separated by walls* partition, room divider. **2** *the area had a wall around it* enclosure. **3** *the city walls are still standing* fortification, rampart, barricade, parapet, bulwark, stockade, breastwork.

wallet noun purse, billfold.

wallow verb **1** *a hippopotamus wallowing in mud* roll, tumble about, lie around, splash around. **2** *wallow in luxury/self-pity* luxuriate, bask, take pleasure/satisfaction, indulge oneself, delight, revel, glory.

wan adjective **1** *looking wan after illness* pale, pallid, ashen, white, white as a sheet/ghost, anemic, colorless, bloodless, waxen, pasty, peaked, tired looking, washed out, sickly. **2** *a wan light* dim, faint, weak, feeble, pale.
Antonyms: FLUSHED; RUDDY; BRIGHT.

wand noun baton, stick, rod, staff, twig, sprig.

wander verb **1** *wander over the hills* ramble, roam, meander, rove, range, prowl, saunter, stroll, amble, peregrinate, drift; *inf.* traipse. **2** *rivers wandering along* wind, meander, curve, zigzag. **3** *wander from the path/point* | *wander from the straight and narrow* stray, depart, diverge, veer, swerve, deviate. **4** *the narcotics make him wander* be incoherent, ramble, babble, talk nonsense, rave, be delirious. **wander off** lose one's way, get lost, go off course, go astray, go off on a tangent.

wander noun *have a wander in the hills/mall* ramble, saunter, stroll, amble.

wanderer noun rambler, roamer, rover, drifter, traveler, itinerant, wayfarer, nomad, bird of passage, rolling stone, gypsy; vagabond, vagrant, hobo, tramp, derelict; beggar, homeless/displaced person; *inf.* bum.

wandering adjective **1** *wandering bands of people* rambling, roaming, roving, drifting, traveling, itinerant, peripatetic, nomadic, gypsy, vagabond, vagrant, migrant, transient, homeless. **2** *wandering rivers/paths* winding, meandering, curving, bending, zigzagging.

wane verb **1** *the moon has waned* pass full moon, decrease, diminish, dwindle. **2** *his power/importance is waning* decrease, decline, diminish, dwindle, shrink, contract, taper off, subside, sink, ebb, dim, fade away, vanish, die out, draw to a close, evanesce, peter out, wind down, be on the way out, abate, fail, become weak, deteriorate, degenerate.
Antonyms: WAX; INCREASE; GROW.

wane noun *the wane of his power/importance* decline, decrease, diminution, dwindling, contraction, subsidence, ebb, vanishing, evanescence, abatement, failure, weakening, deteriorating, degenerating.

want verb **1** *wanting candy/wealth/gifts* wish, wish for, desire, demand, call for, long for, hope for, yearn for, pine for, fancy, crave, hanker after, hunger for, thirst for, lust after, covet, need; *inf.* have a yen for. **2** *he wants to emigrate* wish, desire, long, yearn. **3** *the garden wants weeding* | *the car wants gas* need, be in need of, require. **4** *poor people wanting food* have need of, lack, be without, be devoid of, be bereft of, be short of, be deficient in, have insufficient.

want noun **1** *for want of time* lack, absence, dearth, deficiency, inadequacy, insufficiency, shortness, paucity, shortage, scarcity, scarceness, scantiness. **2** *children expressing their wants* wish, desire, demand, longing, yearning, fancy, craving, hankering, hunger, thirst, lust, covetousness; *inf.* yen. **3** *give aid to people in want* need, neediness, privation, poverty, destitution, penury, indigence.
Antonyms: PRESENCE; ABUNDANCE; WEALTH.

wanting adjective **1** *find the service wanting* lacking, deficient, inadequate, imperfect, not up to standard/par, not good enough, disappointing, not acceptable, not up to expectations, flawed, faulty, defective, unsound, substandard, inferior, second-rate, patchy, sketchy. **2** *something wanting in the machine/organization* lacking, missing, absent, not there, short.
Antonyms: SUFFICIENT; ADEQUATE; ACCEPTABLE.

wanting preposition *a car wanting an engine* lacking, in need of, without, sans; *inf.* minus.

wanton adjective **1** *wanton behavior/individuals* promiscuous, fast, immoral, loose, immodest, shameless, unchaste, unvirtuous, of easy virtue, impure, abandoned, lustful, lecherous, lascivious, libidinous, licentious, libertine, dissolute, dissipated, debauched, degenerate. **2** *wanton destruction* willful, malicious, malevo-

lent, spiteful, wicked, evil, cruel, unmotivated, motiveless, arbitrary, groundless, unjustifiable, unjustified, needless, unnecessary, uncalled-for, unprovoked, gratuitous, senseless, pointless, purposefulness. **3** *a wanton wind* capricious, playful, sportive, careless, heedless, impulsive, rash, reckless, devil-may-care. **4** *weeds growing in wanton profusion* wild, unrestrained, uncontrolled, immoderate, lavish, extravagant, abundant, profuse, luxuriant.
Antonyms: MORAL; CHASTE; JUSTIFIABLE.

war *noun* **1** *a state of war between the nations* conflict, strife, hostility, enmity, antagonism, animus, ill will, bad blood. **2** *the war lasted five years* | *take part in many wars* warfare, conflict, strife, combat, fighting, struggle, armed conflict, battle, fight, confrontation, skirmish; hostilities. **3** *the war against poverty* battle, fight, campaign, crusade.
Antonyms: PEACE; HARMONY; TRUCE.

war *verb* *nations warring with nations* wage/make war, be at war, conduct a war, do combat/battle, fight, take up arms, cross swords, quarrel, wrangle.

ward *noun* **1** *a hospital ward* room, compartment, cubicle; section, division. **2** *counting the votes in the various wards* administrative district, district, division, quarter, zone. **3** *his niece is his ward* charge, protégé, protégée, dependent.

ward *verb* **ward off 1** *ward off a blow* fend off, stave off, parry, avert, deflect, turn aside. **2** *ward off intruders* drive back, repel, repulse, beat back, rout, put to flight, scatter, disperse; *inf.* send packing. **3** *ward off the attack* fend off, stave off, keep at bay, keep at arm's length, avert, rebuff, foil, frustrate, thwart, checkmate.

warden *noun* custodian, keeper, guardian, protector, guard, watchman.

wardrobe *noun* *her summer wardrobe* collection/set of clothes, trousseau.

warehouse *noun* store, storehouse, depot, depository, stockroom.

wares *plural noun* goods, products, commodities, lines; merchandise, produce, stuff, stock.

warfare *noun* armed conflict, combat, strife, fighting, battle, campaigning; hostilities.

warily *adverb* **1** *tread warily* carefully, with care, cautiously, gingerly, circumspectly, guardedly, on one's guard, on the alert, on the qui vive, watchfully, vigilantly. *See* WARY 1. **2** *treat him warily* cautiously, suspiciously, distrustfully, mistrustfully, charily; *inf.* cagily.

wariness *noun* **1** *tread with wariness* care, carefulness, caution, circumspection, alertness, attention, heedfulness, watchfulness, vigilance. **2** *treat the stranger with wariness* caution, circumspection, suspicion, distrust, mistrust.

warlike *adjective* aggressive, belligerent, bellicose, pugnacious, combative, militaristic, militant, martial.
Antonyms: PEACEFUL; PEACEABLE; PACIFIC; CONCILIATORY.

warlock *noun* sorcerer, wizard, male witch, magician.

warm *adjective* **1** *warm water* heated, tepid, lukewarm. **2** *a warm day* sunny, balmy. **3** *a warm person/personality* | *a warm heart* kindly, kind, friendly, affable, amiable, genial, cordial, sympathetic, affectionate, loving, tender, caring, charitable, sincere, genuine. **4** *receive a warm welcome* hearty, cordial, genial, friendly, hospitable, enthusiastic, eager, sincere, heartfelt, ardent, vehement, passionate, intense, fervent, effusive. **5** *the international situation is getting rather warm* heated, hostile, tense, strained, explosive, dangerous, perilous, hazardous, tricky, difficult, unpleasant, uncomfortable, disagreeable. **6** *players of the guessing game getting warm* close, near.
Antonyms: COLD; COOL; UNFRIENDLY.

warm *verb* *warm the food in the oven* warm up, make warm, heat, heat up, reheat. **warm to** *feel themselves warming to her* | *warm to the idea* feel well-disposed to, feel sympathetic to, feel a liking for, feel attracted to/toward. **warm up 1** *warm up the food* heat up. *See* WARM *verb* 1. **2** *warm the party up* liven, enliven, put some life into, cheer up, animate; *inf.* get going. **3** *warm up for the race* loosen up, limber up, condition, prepare, exercise, practice, train.

warmed up *adjective* **1** *warmed up food* reheated, heated up. **2** *warmed up ideas/prose* repeated, unoriginal, derivative, stale, hackneyed, trite, stock, banal; *inf.* old hat.

warmth *noun* **1** *feel the warmth of the fire/sun* warmness, heat, hotness. **2** *the warmth of her personality* kindness, kindliness, friendliness, affability, amiability, geniality, cordiality, sympathy, sympatheticness, affectionateness, affection, lovingness, love, tenderness, care, charitableness, charity, sincerity, genuineness. **3** *the warmth of the welcome* heartiness, cordiality, geniality, friendliness, hospitableness, hospitality, enthusiasm, eagerness, sincerity, ardor, vehemence, passion, intensity, fervor, effusiveness.
Antonyms: COOL; CHILL; APATHY.

warn *verb* **1** *write to warn them of the approaching confrontation/danger* inform, notify, give notice, give prior notice/tell, let know, acquaint, give fair warning, forewarn; *inf.* tip off, put wise. **2** *warn them to be careful* advise, exhort, urge, counsel, caution, forewarn, prewarn, put on the alert, make aware. **3** *the principal warned the unruly students* give a warning to, admonish, remonstrate with.

warning *noun* **1** *send them a warning of the approaching confrontation* information, notification, notice, word, forewarning; *inf.* tip-off. **2** *heeded the warning to be careful* caution; advice, exhortation, counseling. **3** *get a warning from the principal* admonition, remonstrance. **4** *he regarded it as a warning of things to come* omen, premonition, foretoken, token, augury, signal, sign, threat, caveat.

warrant noun **1** *they are acting under warrant of the king* authorization, consent, sanction, permission, validation, license, imprimatur, seal of approval. **2** *a warrant for his arrest | a death warrant* authorization, official document, written order; papers. **3** *a sales warrant* voucher, chit, slip, paper.

warrant verb **1** *the law warrants the procedure* authorize, consent to, sanction, permit, license, approve of. **2** *her interference was not warranted* justify, vindicate, excuse, be a defense of, explain away, account for, be a reason for, offer grounds for, support. **3** *unable to warrant the truth of the statement* guarantee, swear to, answer for, vouch for, testify to, bear witness to, support, endorse, underwrite, back up, stand by.

warrantable adjective **1** *his action was warrantable by the king* authorizable, sanctionable, approvable. **2** *his interference was scarcely warrantable* justifiable, vindicable, excusable, explainable, explicable, reasonable, supportable.

warring adjective *warring factions* conflicting, opposing, clashing, hostile, rival; *inf.* at each other's throats.

warrior noun fighter, fighting man, combatant, soldier, champion.

wary adjective **1** *be wary when you walk alone at night* careful, cautious, circumspect, chary, on one's guard, alert, on the alert/look out, on the qui vive, attentive, heedful, watchful, vigilant, observant; *inf.* wide awake, on one's toes. **2** *you should be wary of strangers* careful, cautious, chary, suspicious, distrustful, mistrustful; *inf.* leery.

Antonyms: unwary; UNSUSPECTING; INATTENTIVE; TRUSTFUL.

wash verb **1** *I must wash before breakfast* wash oneself, bathe, shower, have a bath/shower. **2** *wash one's face | wash the floor* clean, cleanse, sponge, scrub. **3** *wash one's clothes* launder, clean. **4** *wash one's hair* shampoo, clean. **5** *waves washing against the rocks* splash, dash, break, beat. **6** *his story just won't wash* be accepted, be plausible, be convincing, hold up, hold water, stand up, bear scrutiny; *inf.* stick. **7** *the current washed the boat away* carry, bear, sweep, convey, transport. **8** *wash away the riverbank* erode, abrade, wear, denude.

wash noun **1** *in need of a wash* washing, clean, cleaning, cleansing, bath, shower. **2** *I must do the wash* washing, laundry.

washed out adjective **1** *washed-out jeans* faded, blanched, bleached. **2** *washed-out colors* pale, flat, lackluster. **3** *a washed-out complexion* pale, wan, pallid, white, anemic, etiolated, colorless, drawn, haggard. **4** *feeling washed out after a hard day* exhausted, tired out, worn out, weary, fatigued, spent, drained; *inf.* all in, done in,

dead on one's feet, dead, dog-tired, played out, pooped.

Antonyms: BRIGHT; RUDDY; ENERGETIC; perky.

waspish adjective petulant, peevish, querulous, touchy, testy, irritable, irascible, cross, snappish, cantankerous, splenetic, crotchety, short-tempered, ill-tempered, bad-tempered, crabby, crabbed, grumpy.

waste verb **1** *waste resources/money | jokes wasted on the audience* squander, dissipate, fritter away, misspend, misuse, spend recklessly, throw away, go through, run through; *inf.* blow. **2** *his legs are gradually wasting away* grow weak, wither, atrophy, become emaciated. **3** *the disease had wasted his legs* weaken, enfeeble, sap the strength of, wither, debilitate, atrophy, emaciate, shrivel, shrink. **4** *the invading army wasted the land* destroy, devastate, wreak havoc on, pillage, plunder, sack, spoliate, loot, maraud, harry.

Antonyms: CONSERVE; SAVE; STRENGTHEN.

waste noun **1** *a waste of money/time* squandering, dissipation, frittering away, misspending, misuse, prodigality, unthriftiness. **2** *dispose of the waste* rubbish, refuse, garbage, trash, debris, dross; dregs, leavings. **3** *lost in the waste of Antarctica* desert, wasteland, wilderness, barrenness, emptiness, vastness.

waste adjective **1** *waste material* left over, unused, superfluous, supernumerary, unwanted, worthless, useless. **2** *the land was waste* desert, barren, uncultivated, unproductive, arid, bare, desolate, solitary, lonely, empty, void, uninhabited, unpopulated, wild, bleak, cheerless.

wasted adjective **1** *wasted resources* squandered, dissipated, exhausted, used up, misspent, misused. **2** *wasted opportunities* missed, lost, past, bungled. **3** *wasted limbs* weakened, weak, withered, atrophied, emaciated, shriveled, shrunken.

wasteful adjective *wasteful use of the supplies* prodigal, profligate, thriftless, spendthrift, extravagant, lavish.

Antonyms: THRIFTY; FRUGAL; ECONOMICAL.

wastrel noun **1** *a wastrel going through a fortune* waster, spendthrift, prodigal, squanderer, big spender. **2** *he is a complete wastrel* good-for-nothing, layabout, ne'er-do-well, idler, drone, loafer, shirker, malingerer.

watch verb **1** *watch the moon* look at, observe, view, eye, gaze at, stare at, gape at, peer at, contemplate, behold, inspect, scrutinize, survey, scan, examine. **2** *watch his movements | watch the man next door* keep watch on, keep an eye on, keep in sight, follow, spy on; *inf.* keep tabs on. **3** *watch the children* mind, take care of, look after, supervise, superintend, tend, guard, protect; babysit; *inf.* keep an eye on. **watch out 1** *watch out and don't get mugged* watch oneself, be watchful, be on the watch, look out, pay attention, take heed/care, be careful, be on the alert/lookout, keep a sharp lookout, be vigilant, be wary, be on the qui vive; *inf.* keep an eye open, keep one's eyes peeled. **2** *watch out for the delivery truck* look (out) for, wait for; *inf.* keep an eye open for. **watch over** *shepherds watch over the sheep | lawyers watching over our interests* look after, tend, take care of, guard, protect, shield, preserve.

Antonyms: IGNORE; DISREGARD; NEGLECT.

watch *noun* **1** *the time by my watch* wristwatch, pocket watch, timepiece, chronometer. **2** *on watch at night* guard, vigil, surveillance.

watchdog *noun* **1** *a watchdog guarding the premises at night* guard dog. **2** *a watchdog of consumers' interests* custodian, guardian, protector, monitor, scrutineer, inspector.

watcher *noun* spectator, onlooker, looker-on, observer, viewer, witness, spy.

watchful *adjective* *keep a watchful eye on the building* observant, alert, vigilant, attentive, heedful, sharp-eyed, eagle-eyed, wary, circumspect.

Antonyms: INATTENTIVE; CARELESS.

watchman *noun* security guard, guard, custodian, caretaker.

watchword *noun* **1** *quality is meant to be the watchword of the firm* slogan, motto, maxim, catchword, catchphrase, byword, battle/rallying cry. **2** *unable to gain entry without the correct watchword* password, magic word, sign, shibboleth.

water *noun* **1** *drink water* H$_2$0; tap water, drinking water, mineral water, bottled water. **2** *have a picnic by the water* sea, ocean, sound, bay, river, lake, pond, pool, reservoir. **hold water** *your theory won't hold water* be tenable, ring true, bear examination, work out.

water *verb* **1** *water the garden* sprinkle, moisten, dampen, wet, water down, douse, hose, spray, drench, saturate, sodden, flood. **2** *his eyes are watering* exude water, moisten, leak. **3** *water the drinks* add water to, water down, dilute, thin, weaken, adulterate. **water down** **1** *water down the drinks* water, add water to, dilute. *See* WATER *verb* 3. **2** *water down the extent of the disaster* play down, downplay, tone down, soft-pedal, understate, underemphasize.

waterfall *noun* cascade, cataract; falls.

watertight *adjective* **1** *the boat/jacket is watertight* waterproof, sound. **2** *a watertight excuse* sound, flawless, incontrovertible, indisputable, foolproof, unassailable, impregnable.

watery *adjective* **1** *a watery substance* aqueous, liquid, liquefied, fluid, hydrous. **2** *watery terrain* wet, damp, moist, sodden, soggy, saturated, waterlogged, marshy, boggy, swampy, miry. **3** *a watery soup/batter* thin, runny, weak, dilute, diluted, watered down, adulterated, tasteless, flavorless; *inf.* wishy-washy. **4** *watery colors* pale, wan, insipid; *inf.* wishy-washy. **5** *watery eyes* moist, tearful, teary, weeping, weepy, lachrymose.

Antonyms: SOLID; DRY; THICK.

wave *verb* **1** *wheat waving in the breeze* undulate, ripple, stir, flutter, flap, sway, swing, shake, quiver, oscillate. **2** *wave one's hand/flag* move up and down, move to and fro, wag, waggle, flutter. **3** *wave a sword in the air* brandish, swing, shake. **4** *wave to them to follow* gesture, gesticulate, signal, sign, beckon, indicate. **5** *her hair waves beautifully* undulate, curl, kink.

wave *noun* **1** *children playing in the waves* breaker, billow, roller, ripple, whitecap; swell, surf. **2** *a wave of visitors* stream, flow, rush, surge, flood. **3** *the waves in her hair* undulation, curl, kink. **4** *a wave of enthusiasm | a crime wave* surge, upsurge, groundswell, welling up, rush, outbreak, rash. **5** *waves in the water | light waves* ripple, vibration, oscillation, undulation.

waver *verb* **1** *his gaze did not waver | his courage began to waver* become unsteady, falter, wobble, hesitate. **2** *we wavered and someone else got in first | waver between staying and leaving* be irresolute/indecisive, hesitate, dither, equivocate, hem and haw, vacillate, beat about the bush; *inf.* shilly-shally, pussyfoot around, blow hot and cold. **3** *lights wavering* flicker, quiver, tremble.

wavy *adjective* undulating, curvy, curling, squiggly, rippled, curving, winding.

Antonyms: STRAIGHT; unswerving.

wax *verb* **1** *the moon was waxing* approach full moon, get bigger, increase in size, enlarge. **2** *his power waxed in time of war* increase, grow, develop, enlarge, magnify, extend, widen, broaden, spread, mushroom. **3** *wax lyrical about his achievements* become, grow.

Antonyms: WANE; DECREASE; FADE.

way *noun* **1** *walk along the paved way* road, roadway, street, thoroughfare, track, path, pathway, lane, avenue, drive. **2** *is this the way to their house?* route, road, course, direction. **3** *the right way to cook the meat* method, course of action, process, procedure, technique, system, plan, scheme, manner, modus operandi; means. **4** *admire the way in which she dresses* manner, style, fashion, mode. **5** *dislike his brusque way* conduct, behavior, practice, wont, manner, style, nature, personality, temperament, disposition, character; habit, custom, characteristic, trait, attribute, mannerism, peculiarity, idiosyncrasy. **6** *a long way from here to Boston* distance, length, stretch, journey. **7** *make way for the children* room, elbowroom, space. **8** *things are in a bad way* state, condition, situation; *inf.* shape. **9** *in some ways it will be useful | can I help you in any way?* feature, aspect, detail, point, particular, respect, sense. **by the way** incidentally, by the by, in passing, en passant. **give way** **1** *the bridge gave way* collapse, give, fall to pieces, crumble, cave in. **2** *he refused to help but finally gave way* yield, back down, make concessions, concede defeat, acquiesce. **on the/one's way** coming, going, proceeding, journeying, traveling.

wayfarer noun traveler, walker, hiker, rambler, wanderer, roamer, rover, nomad, gypsy, vagabond, vagrant.

wayfaring adjective traveling, journeying, walking, hiking, wandering, roaming, roving, drifting, nomadic, itinerant, peripatetic, on the move/go.

waylay verb **1** *the hijackers waylaid them* lie in wait for, ambush, hold up, attack. **2** *she waylaid the teacher to ask about her child* accost, stop and talk to, intercept, pounce on, swoop down on.

wayward adjective **1** *wayward children* willful, self-willed, headstrong, stubborn, obstinate, obdurate, perverse, contrary, uncooperative, refractory, recalcitrant, contumacious, unruly, ungovernable, unmanageable, incorrigible, intractable, difficult, fractious, disobedient, insubordinate. **2** *wayward fancies/youngster* capricious, whimsical, fickle, inconstant, changeable, changeful, variable, erratic, unpredictable, unstable, mercurial, volatile, flighty.

Antonyms: TRACTABLE; DOCILE; STABLE.

weak adjective **1** *feeling weak after illness | too weak to walk* weakly, frail, fragile, delicate, feeble, infirm, shaky, debilitated, incapacitated, ailing, indisposed, decrepit, puny, faint, enervated, tired, fatigued, exhausted, spent, worn out. **2** *too weak to stand up for his rights* cowardly, pusillanimous, timorous, timid, spineless, ineffectual, useless, inept, effete, powerless, impotent, namby-pamby, soft; *inf.* yellow, weak-kneed. **3** *weak eyes/eyesight* defective, faulty, poor, inadequate, deficient, imperfect, substandard, lacking, wanting. **4** *weak excuses* unsound, feeble, flimsy, lame, hollow, pathetic, unconvincing, untenable, implausible, unsatisfactory. **5** *a weak sound/signal* faint, low, muffled, stifled, muted, scarcely audible. **6** *a weak light* faint, dim, pale, wan. **7** *weak coffee* understrength, dilute, diluted, watery, waterish, thinned down, thin, adulterated, tasteless, flavorless, insipid; *inf.* wishy-washy.

Antonyms: STRONG; POWERFUL; FLAWLESS; CONVINCING.

---

weak
debilitated, decrepit, feeble, frail, infirm

Someone who is **weak** lacks physical, mental, or moral strength (*a weak heart; a weak excuse; too weak to resist temptation*). But there's nothing to suggest what the cause of this lack of strength might be. Someone who is **frail**, on the other hand, is weak because he or she has a slight build or delicate constitution (*a small, frail man*). Calling someone **feeble** implies that his or her weakness is pitiable (*too feeble to get out of bed*); when applied to things, *feeble* means faint or inadequate (*a feeble light*). **Infirm** suggests a loss of soundness, as from aging or illness (*poverty and illness had made him infirm*). **Debilitated** and **decrepit** also suggest that strength once present has been lost. But while someone who is young may be *debilitated* by disease, *decrepit* specifically refers to a loss of strength due to advanced age or long use (*a decrepit old woman who seldom left her house; a decrepit building that would soon be torn down*).

---

weaken verb **1** *the illness had weakened her* enfeeble, debilitate, incapacitate, sap one's strength, enervate, tire, exhaust, wear out. **2** *weaken the force of the argument* lessen, reduce, decrease, diminish, moderate, temper, sap. **3** *the force of the storm weakened* abate, lessen, decrease, dwindle, diminish, ease up, let up. **4** *weaken the argument* impair, undermine, invalidate. **5** *they first refused to help but weakened later* relent, give in, acquiesce, yield, give way, accede, come around. **6** *too much milk weakened the coffee* dilute, water down, thin, adulterate.

weakling noun coward, mouse, milksop, namby-pamby; *inf.* wimp, sissy, drip, doormat, chicken, yellowbelly, fraidy-cat, scaredy-cat.

weakness noun **1** *the weakness of the invalid* frailty, fragility, delicateness, delicacy, feebleness, infirmity, debility, incapacity, indisposition, decrepitude, puniness, enervation, fatigue. **2** *despise his weakness* cowardliness, timidity, spinelessness, ineffectuality, ineptness, powerlessness, impotence. **3** *the weakness of her eyesight* defectiveness, faultiness, inadequacy, deficiency. **4** *the weakness of the excuses* unsoundness, feebleness, flimsiness, lameness, untenability, implausibility. **5** *the weakness of the sound/signal* faintness, low intensity, mutedness. **6** *the weakness of the light* faintness, dimness. **7** *the weakness of the coffee* diluteness, wateriness, thinness, tastelessness, flavorlessness; *inf.* wishy-washiness. **8** *extravagance is one of her weaknesses* weak point, failing, foible, fault, flaw, defect, shortcoming, imperfection, blemish, Achilles' heel, chink in one's armor. **9** *she has a weakness for chocolate* soft spot, fondness, liking, love, passion, partiality, preference, penchant, predisposition, predilection, leaning, inclination, proneness, proclivity.

Antonyms: STRENGTH; POWER; FORTE.

wealth noun **1** *amass wealth* money, cash, capital, treasure, fortune, finance, property; riches, assets, possessions, resources, goods, funds; *inf.* wherewithal, dough, bread. **2** *people of wealth* richness, money, affluence, prosperity, substance; means. **3** *a wealth of beautiful pictures | a wealth of opportunities* mass, abundance, profusion, copiousness, plenitude, amplitude, bounty, cornucopia.

Antonyms: POVERTY; DEARTH.

wealthy adjective **1** *wealthy people traveling abroad* rich, well off, well-to-do, moneyed, affluent, prosperous, of means, of substance; *inf.* well-heeled, rolling in it/money, in the money, made of money, filthy/stinking rich, loaded, flush, on easy street. **2** *wealthy surroundings* rich, opulent, lavish, luxurious, sumptuous, splendid, magnificent.

Antonyms: POOR; PENNILESS; IMPOVERISHED.

---

wealthy
affluent, flush, opulent, prosperous, rich, well-to-do

If you have an abundance of money, you are **rich**. Another term for *rich* is **wealthy**, which may further imply that you are an established and prominent member of the community whose lifestyle is in keeping with your income (*a wealthy family whose influence on public opinion could not be ignored*). **Affluent** comes from the Latin word meaning to flow, and it connotes a generous income (*an affluent neighborhood*), while **opulent** suggests lavish spending or an ostentatious display of wealth (*an opulent mansion with every imaginable luxury*). One may come from an *affluent* family, in other words, and not have a particularly *opulent* lifestyle. If you're **prosperous**, you are thriving or flourishing (*a prosperous merchant; a prosperous business*). While *prosperous* suggests an economic situation that is on the rise, **flush** means having plenty of money on hand at a particular time (*she was feeling flush after receiving her first paycheck*). **Well-to-do** implies a generous income, enough to support comfortable living but not necessarily enough to be considered rich (*they were known as a well-to-do family with a strong commitment to educating their children*).

---

wear *verb* **1** *wear beautiful clothes* be dressed in, dress in, be clothed in, cloth oneself in, have on, put on, don, sport. **2** *she wore an anxious expression* have, assume, present, show, display, exhibit. **3** *wind and rain have worn the rock* erode, corrode, abrade, wash away, rub away, rub down, grind away, wear down. **4** *the carpet is starting to wear* become worn, show signs of wear, wear thin, fray, become threadbare. **5** *she is worn by the whole experience* fatigue, tire, weary, exhaust. *See* WEAR OUT 2 (below). **6** *this carpet has worn well* last, endure, hold up, survive, bear up, stand up to wear, prove durable. **wear away** *the steps have become worn away* wear, erode. *See* WEAR *verb* 3. **wear down 1** *the steps have become worn down* wear, wear away, erode. *See* WEAR *verb* 3. **2** *wear down their resistance/opposition* gradually overcome, slowly reduce/diminish, erode, undermine; *inf.* chip away at. **wear off 1** *wear the pattern off the plates* rub away, efface, fade. **2** *the novelty will soon wear off* lose effectiveness/effect, lose intensity/strength, fade, peter out, dwindle, decrease, diminish, disappear, subside, ebb, wane. **wear on** *as time wore on* pass, go by, move on, roll on. **wear out 1** *children wear out their clothes quickly* wear thin, make threadbare, fray. **2** *the job has quite worn her out* wear, fatigue, tire, weary, exhaust,

drain, strain, stress, weaken, enfeeble, prostrate, enervate; *inf.* wear to a frazzle, poop out.

wear *noun* **1** *clothes/items for everyday wear* use, service, employment. **2** *pack away her winter wear* clothing, attire, apparel, wardrobe; clothes, garments, outfits; *inf.* gear. **3** *showing signs of wear and tear* use, friction, erosion, detrition, attrition, corrosion, abrasion, deterioration, degeneration, damage.

weariness *noun suffering from weariness* fatigue, tiredness, exhaustion, enervation, lassitude, languor, listlessness, lethargy.

wearing *adjective have a wearing day | find the children wearing* fatiguing, tiring, wearying, exhausting, draining, stressful, enervating.

wearisome *adjective wearisome tasks/journeys* fatiguing, tiring, exhausting, draining, wearing, trying, irksome, boring, tedious, dull, uninteresting, monotonous, humdrum, routine.

Antonyms: REFRESHING; INTERESTING; ENJOYABLE.

weary *adjective* **1** *weary at the end of a hard day's work* fatigued, tired, exhausted, drained, worn, worn out, spent, wearied; *inf.* dead tired/beat, dead on one's feet, dog-tired, all in, done in, fagged out, pooped (out), whacked, bushed. **2** *the last weary hours/tasks | a weary journey* wearisome, fatiguing, tiring, exhausting, wearing, trying, taxing, irksome, tiresome, laborious, boring, tedious, dull. **3** *she is weary of the job | the dull job makes her weary* bored, fed up, discontented, jaded, uninterested, listless, lethargic; *inf.* sick and tired.

Antonyms: ENERGETIC; refreshed; REFRESHING; ENTHUSIASTIC.

weary *verb* **1** *the hard work wearies them* fatigue, tire, exhaust, drain, wear out; *inf.* wear to a frazzle, poop out. **2** *the repetitive job wearies him* bore, irk, make fed up, make discontented/jaded. **3** *she wearied of living abroad* grow weary, tire, get bored, have enough, grow discontented/jaded.

Antonyms: REVIVE; REFRESH; INVIGORATE.

weather *noun* meteorological/atmospheric conditions; temperature, raininess, cloudiness, dryness, humidity, windiness. **under the weather** below par, unwell, not well, out of sorts, indisposed, ailing, ill, sick; *inf.* poorly.

weather *verb* **1** *weather the wood* dry, season, expose, expose to the elements. **2** *wood weathering well | rocks weathered by storms* be exposed, undergo change, erode, wear, bleach. **3** *weather the storm/recession* come/get through, survive, withstand, live/pull through, bear up against, stand, endure, ride out, rise above, surmount, overcome, resist; *inf.* stick out.

weave *verb* **1** *weave thread into cloth | weave flowers into garlands* interlace, intertwine, interwork, intertwist, twist together, entwine, braid, plait, interknit. **2** *weave a story to account for his movements* make up, fabricate, put together, construct, invent, create, contrive. **3**

weave in and out of the crowds zigzag, wind, criss-cross.

web noun **1** *a design composed of webs* interlacing, lacework, lattice, latticework, mesh, net, netting. **2** *a web of lies/deceit* network, tissue, tangle, knot, complex.

wed verb **1** *they wed tomorrow* get married, marry, become man and wife; *inf.* get hitched, tie the knot. **2** *she weds him tomorrow* marry, take as one's wife/husband. **3** *the local minister wed them* marry, join in matrimony, make one, unite; *inf.* hitch. **4** *the two firms have been virtually wedded for years* unite, join, merge, amalgamate, fuse, link, ally. **5** *he is wedded to his work* dedicate, devote.
Antonyms: DIVORCE; SEPARATE.

wedded adjective *wedded bliss* married, marital, matrimonial, connubial, conjugal, nuptial.

wedge noun *a wedge of cheese/cake* tapered piece, chunk, lump, block.

wedge verb **1** *wedge packing material around the vase* | *wedged himself into the crowded backseat* thrust, stuff, pack, ram, force, cram, squeeze, jam. **2** *wedge the door open* secure, fasten.

weed verb **weed out** *weed out the less able candidates* separate out, get rid of, remove, dispense with, eliminate, shed, root out, eradicate, extirpate.

weekly adverb *the paper is published weekly* once a week, every week, by the week, hebdomadally.

weep verb cry, shed tears, sob, blubber, snivel, whimper, whine, moan, lament, grieve, mourn, keen, wail; *inf.* boo-hoo.
Antonyms: LAUGH; REJOICE.

weepy adjective tearful, teary, lachrymose, close to tears, whimpering, crying, sobbing, blubbering.

weigh verb **1** *weigh the potatoes* measure/gauge the weight of, put on the scales. **2** *the child weighs 50 pounds* have a weight of; *inf.* tip the scales at. **3** *weigh one plan against the other* balance, compare, evaluate. **weigh down** *he was weighed down by/with heavy luggage* load (down), overload, burden, overburden. **weigh down on** *his responsibilities weighed down on him* weigh on, bear down on, press down on, burden, be a burden to, oppress, prey on, trouble, worry, get one down. **weigh on** *his guilt weighs on his conscience* bear down, burden, oppress, prey on. **weigh up** *weigh up the situation* | *weigh up his chances of success* consider, contemplate, think over, mull over, ponder, deliberate upon, meditate on, muse on, brood over, reflect on. **weigh with** *his previous record will weigh with the committee* carry weight with, have influence with, be influential to, count with, matter to, be important/significant to. **weight**

weight noun **1** *what is the weight of the flour?* heaviness; poundage, tonnage. **2** *lack of money is a weight on his mind* burden, load, onus, mill-

stone, albatross, oppression, trouble, worry, strain, millstone around one's neck, cross to bear. **3** *how much weight is attached to his statement?* importance, significance, consequence, value, substance, force, influence; *inf.* clout. **4** *the weight of the evidence is against him* preponderance, main force, onus.

weighty adjective **1** *weighty loads* heavy, massive, burdensome, cumbersome, ponderous; *inf.* hefty. **2** *weighty responsibility* burdensome, onerous, oppressive, troublesome, worrisome, stressful, taxing, vexatious. **3** *weighty matters* important, of great import, significant, momentous, of moment, consequential, of consequence, vital, crucial, serious, grave, solemn. **4** *weighty arguments* cogent, powerful, potent, forceful, effective, effectual, persuasive, authoritative, influential.
Antonyms: LIGHT; UNIMPORTANT; TRIVIAL; WEAK.

weird adjective **1** *weird things were happening* strange, queer, uncanny, eerie, mysterious, mystifying, supernatural, preternatural, unnatural, unearthly, ghostly; *inf.* spooky, creepy. **2** *she wears weird clothes* strange, queer, odd, eccentric, bizarre, outlandish, freakish, grotesque; *inf.* offbeat, far-out, way-out.
Antonyms: NORMAL; ORDINARY; CONVENTIONAL.

welcome noun *receive a welcome from their hostess* greeting, salutation, reception, warm reception.

welcome verb **1** *welcome the guests* bid welcome to, greet, receive, embrace, receive with open arms, roll out the red carpet for, meet, usher in. **2** *welcome the news of his release* receive with gladness, be pleased by, take pleasure in, feel satisfaction at.
Antonyms: SHUN; SPURN; REJECT.

welcome adjective **1** *welcome guests* wanted, appreciated, popular, desirable. **2** *welcome news* gladly received, pleasant, pleasing, agreeable, cheering, to one's liking, to one's taste.
Antonyms: UNWELCOME; UNPOPULAR; UNPLEASANT.

welfare noun **1** *concern for the welfare of the children/firm* well-being, health, good health, soundness, happiness, comfort, security, prosperity, success, fortune, good fortune. **2** *poor families on welfare* state aid, public assistance, social security, support.

well adverb **1** *behave well* satisfactorily, in a satisfactory manner/way, correctly, rightly, properly, fittingly, suitably, nicely. **2** *get on well* agreeably, pleasantly, happily; *inf.* famously, capitally. **3** *he plays the piano well* ably, competently, proficiently, adeptly, skillfully, with skill, effectively, expertly, with expertise, admirably, excellently. **4** *treat their guests well* kindly, in a kind/kindly way, genially, affably, generously, hospitably, civilly, politely. **5** *polish it well* thoroughly, completely, efficiently, effectively, conscientiously, industriously, carefully. **6** *know the subject well* | *we don't know her well* thoroughly, fully, deeply, profoundly,

intimately, personally. **7** *look at it well* | *listen to it well* closely, attentively, carefully, conscientiously. **8** *speak well of him* highly, admiringly, with admiration, with praise, glowingly, approvingly, favorably, warmly. **9** *live well* comfortably, in comfort, prosperously. **10** *you may well be right* | *I can't very well go now* probably, possibly, likely, undoubtedly, certainly, unquestionably, justifiably, reasonably. **11** *he is well over forty* very much, considerably, to a great/marked extent/degree, markedly, substantially. **12** *it bodes well for the future* fortunately, luckily, auspiciously, propitiously. **as well** *she left and he went as well* too, also, in addition, besides, into the bargain, to boot. **as well as** *John went as well as Peter* | *buying champagne as well as wine* in addition to, besides, along with.
Antonyms: BADLY; POORLY.

well *adjective* **1** *the patient is quite well now* | *a clinic for well babies* healthy, in good health, fit, strong, robust, hale and hearty, able-bodied. **2** *all is well now* satisfactory, all right, (just) fine, good, thriving, flourishing; *inf.* OK, fine and dandy. **3** *it would be well to leave early* advisable, fitting, proper, wise, prudent, sensible.
Antonyms: ILL; POORLY; INADVISABLE.

well *noun* *a well of knowledge* source, wellspring, fount, reservoir, repository, mine.

well *verb* *blood welled from the wound* | *tears welled from her eyes* flow, stream, run, ooze, seep, trickle, pour/rush forth, issue, gush, surge, spurt, spout, jet.

well-advised *adjective* sensible, wise, prudent, judicious, circumspect, farsighted, sagacious.

well-balanced *adjective* **1** *well-balanced people/personalities* well-adjusted, sensible, reasonable, rational, levelheaded, sound, practical, discerning, logical, sane, in one's right mind. **2** *a well-balanced diet* balanced, well-proportioned, well-ordered. **3** *a well-balanced exhibition/room* balanced, symmetrical, well-proportioned, proportional, well-ordered, well-arranged, graceful, elegant.

well-being *noun* welfare, health, good health, happiness, comfort, prosperity, security.

well-bred *adjective* well brought up, mannerly, well-mannered, courteous, polite, civil, ladylike, gentlemanly, gallant, chivalrous, cultivated, refined, polished, cultured, debonair, urbane.
Antonyms: RUDE; DISCOURTEOUS; ILL-BRED.

well-built *adjective* strongly built, strong, muscular, brawny, sturdy, robust, strapping, burly, big; *inf.* hulking, husky, hefty, beefy.
Antonyms: PUNY; SLIGHT.

well-groomed *adjective* neat, neatly dressed, tidy, smart, spruce, well turned out, trim, dapper; *inf.* natty, spiffy, without a hair out of place.
Antonyms: UNTIDY; UNKEMPT; SCRUFFY.

well-known *adjective* **1** *well-known facts* | *a well-known figure around town* known, widely known, familiar, common, usual, everyday. **2** *a well-known artist* famous, famed, renowned, celebrated, noted, notable, illustrious, eminent.
Antonyms: UNKNOWN; OBSCURE; UNSUNG.

well-nigh *adverb* *well-nigh impossible* virtually, next to, practically, all but, just about, almost, nearly, more or less.

well off *adjective* **1** *his parents are poor but he is very well off* | *well-off people* wealthy, rich, well-to-do, moneyed, affluent, prosperous, of means, of substance; *inf.* well-heeled, rolling in it/money, in the money, made of money, filthy/stinking rich, loaded, flush, on easy street. **2** *he doesn't know when he is well off* fortunate, lucky, comfortable, thriving, successful, flourishing.
Antonyms: POOR; BROKE; badly off; UNFORTUNATE.

well-read *adjective* highly literate, literate, well-educated, educated, well-informed, knowledgeable, erudite.
Antonyms: ILLITERATE; IGNORANT.

well-spoken *adjective* articulate, eloquent, fluent, silver-tongued, smooth-talking; *inf.* having the gift of the gab.

well-thought-of *adjective* highly thought of, highly regarded, esteemed, respected, looked-up-to, acclaimed, revered, venerated.

well-to-do *adjective* *his parents are well-to-do* | *well-to-do parents* wealthy, rich, well off, affluent, prosperous. *See* WELL OFF.

wet *adjective* **1** *wet clothes/ground* damp, dampened, moist, moistened, wet through, soaked, drenched, saturated, sopping/dripping/wringing wet, sopping, dripping, soggy, waterlogged. **2** *a wet day* rainy, raining, pouring, showery, drizzling, damp, humid, dank, misty. **3** *a wet mixture* aqueous, watery, watered, sloppy. **wet blanket** killjoy, party pooper; *inf.* gloomy Gus.
Antonyms: DRY; ARID.

wet *noun* **1** *the wet damaged the table/land* wetness, damp, dampness, moisture, moistness, condensation, humidity, water, liquid. **2** *get in out of the wet* | *the wet affects his rheumatism* wet/rainy weather, rain, showery/damp weather, drizzle, damp; rains.

wet *verb* **1** *wet the clothes before ironing them* dampen, damp, moisten, sprinkle, spray, splash. **2** *wet the soil* water, irrigate, sprinkle, spray, douse. **3** *the rain really wet them* wet through, dampen, soak, saturate.
Antonyms: DRY; wring out.

wharf *noun* pier, quay, dock, jetty; mooring(s).

wheedle *verb* coax, cajole, beguile, charm, flatter, inveigle, win over, talk into, persuade, induce, entice, influence; *inf.* butter up.

wheel *noun* disk, hoop, circle, ring; *Tech.* annulus. **at the wheel 1** *he was at the wheel when the accident happened* driving, steering, in the driver's seat. **2** *a new man at the wheel in the firm* in charge, in command, in control; *inf.* at the helm, in the driver's seat.

wheel *verb* **1** *disks/birds wheeling around* turn, go around, circle, rotate, revolve, spin. **2** *wheel a stroller* push, shove, trundle.

wheeze *verb asthmatics wheezing* breathe audibly/noisily, gasp, whistle, hiss, rasp.

wheeze *noun give a painful wheeze* gasp, whistle, hiss.

whereabouts *noun I do not know his whereabouts | the whereabouts of his cabin* location, site, position, situation, place.

wherewithal *noun he does not have the wherewithal to travel* means, resources, funds, reserves; money, ready money, cash, capital, finance; *inf.* dough, bread, loot.

whet *verb* **1** *whet a blade* sharpen, put an edge on, edge, hone, strop, file, grind, rasp. **2** *whet the curiosity/appetite* stimulate, excite, arouse, rouse, kindle, quicken, stir, titillate, tempt.
Antonym: BLUNT.

whiff *noun* **1** *a whiff of air/smoke* puff, breath, gust, draft. **2** *catch a whiff of the perfume/garbage* smell, scent, odor, aroma, stink, reek. **3** *a whiff of scandal* hint, suggestion, trace, suspicion, soupçon.

while *noun wait for a while* time, spell, period, interval.

while *verb while away the hours* laze, idle, loaf, lounge, loiter.

whim *noun* **1** *have a sudden whim to go to the fair* notion, fancy, idea, impulse, urge, caprice, vagary, craze, passion, inclination, bent. **2** *behavior ruled by whim* whimsy, capriciousness, caprice, volatility, fickleness.

whimper *verb* whine, cry, sniffle, snivel, moan, wail, groan.

whimper *noun hear a whimper* whine, cry, moan, wail, groan.

whimsical *adjective a whimsical sense of humor | a whimsical children's story* capricious, fanciful, fantastical, playful, mischievous, waggish, quaint, unusual, curious, droll, eccentric, peculiar, queer, bizarre, weird, freakish.

whine *verb* whimper, cry; complain, grumble, moan, groan, fuss, lament; *inf.* grouse, gripe, bellyache, beef.

whine *noun listen to the dog's whines* whimper, cry, wail, groan.

whip *verb* **1** *condemned for whipping his crew* lash, flog, scourge, flagellate, birch, switch, strap, cane, thrash, beat, strike, castigate; *inf.* belt, tan, lay into, give a hiding to, beat the living daylights out of. **2** *whip cream* beat, whisk, mix. **3** *whip a handkerchief from his pocket* whisk, flash, snatch, pull, yank, jerk, produce, remove. **4** *he whipped around the corner* whisk, dart, dash, dive, dodge, shoot, tear, rush, fly, bolt, zoom. **5** *whip the opposition at football* beat, defeat, overcome, overpower, overwhelm, thrash,

trounce, crush, rout. **6** *whip them into a frenzy* rouse, stir up, incite, goad, prod, spur, prompt, agitate. **whip up** *whip up enthusiasm* rouse, stir up, provoke, excite, incite, instigate, work up.

whip *noun use a whip* lash, scourge, flagellum, horsewhip, bullwhip, cat o'nine tails, knout, birch, switch, thong, crop, riding crop, cane.

whipping *noun* **1** *gave the mutineer a whipping* lashing, flogging, scourging, flagellation, birching, caning, thrashing, beating, leathering, castigation; *inf.* belting, tanning. **2** *give the opposition a whipping* beating, thrashing, trouncing, routing.

whirl *verb* **1** *wheels/dancers whirling* turn around, circle, spin, rotate, revolve, wheel, twirl, swirl, gyrate, reel, pirouette, pivot. **2** *buses whirling past* speed, rush, race, shoot, tear, charge, whip. **3** *my head/brain is whirling* go round, spin, reel, feel dizzy/giddy.

whirl *noun* **1** *give the wheel a whirl | the whirls of the dancers* turn, spin, rotation, revolution, wheel, twirl, swirl, gyration, reel, pirouette, pivot. **2** *the social whirl* activity, bustle, flurry, to-do, hurly-burly. **3** *a whirl of parties* round, succession, series, sequence, progression, string, chain, cycle. **4** *with heads in a whirl* spin, dither, state of confusion, daze, muddle, jumble. **5** *give the new game a whirl* try, tryout, test; *inf.* go, shot, stab.

whirlpool *noun* vortex, maelstrom, eddy.

whirlwind *noun* cyclone, tornado, twister; *inf.* dust devil.

whirlwind *adjective a whirlwind romance* lightning, swift, rapid, quick, speedy, hasty, headlong, impulsive.

whisk *verb* **1** *the horse whisked its tail* wave, flick, brandish. **2** *whisk the table clean | whisk away the crumbs* brush, sweep, wipe. **3** *whisk a handkerchief out of his pocket* whip, snatch, pull, yank, jerk, produce, remove. **4** *the cat whisked around the corner* dart, dash, dive, dodge, whip, shoot, tear, rush, fly, bolt, zoom. **5** *whisk the guest away* whirl, whip, snatch. **6** *whisk eggs* whip, beat, mix.

whisk *noun* **1** *with a whisk of the tail* wave, flick, brandish. **2** *clean the table with a few whisks* brush, sweep, wipe. **3** *beat eggs with a whisk* beater.

whiskey *noun* malt whiskey, blended whiskey, Scotch (whiskey), Irish whiskey, bourbon, rye (whiskey); *inf.* hard stuff, hooch, rotgut, firewater.

whisper *verb* **1** *whisper to her friend* murmur, mutter, speak softly, speak in muted/hushed tones. **2** *whisper endearments* murmur, mutter, breathe, say/utter softly, say/utter under the breath. **3** *trees whispering in the wind* murmur, rustle, sigh, sough, swish, swoosh.
Antonyms: SHOUT; YELL.

whisper *noun* **1** *speak in a whisper* murmur, mutter, low voice, hushed tone, undertone. **2** *the whisper of trees in the wind* murmur, rustle, sigh, sough, swish, swoosh. **3** *there is a whisper that* *he has been promoted* rumor, report, insinuation, suggestion, hint; gossip, word. **4** *a whisper of perfume/hostility about the room* whiff, trace, tinge, hint, suggestion, suspicion.

whit *noun not give a whit | not a whit better* particle, bit, jot, iota, mite, little, trifle.

white *adjective* **1** *a white face* white as a ghost/sheet, chalk-white, pale, wan, pallid, ashen, anemic, colorless, bloodless, waxen, pasty, peaky, gray. **2** *white hair* gray, silver, hoary, snow-white.

white-collar *adjective white-collar workers* nonmanual, office, clerical, professional, executive, salaried.

whiten *verb clothes whitened by the sun* make white, make pale, bleach, blanch, fade, wash out, etiolate.

whitewash *noun regard the report on the accident as a whitewash* cover-up, concealment, camouflage, mask.

whitewash *verb try to whitewash his role in the accident* cover up, gloss over, conceal, camouflage, suppress, downplay, make light of, softpedal, minimize.

whittle *verb* **1** *whittle wood from the block* cut, hew, pare, shave, trim. **2** *whittle a tent peg from the wood* carve, shape, model. **whittle away 1** *inflation whittled away their savings* wear away, eat away, erode, consume, use up, undermine, destroy. **2** *the number of employees has been whittled away* reduce, lessen, decrease, diminish, cut back.

whole *adjective* **1** *three whole days | the whole book | a whole cake* entire, complete, full, total, solid, integral, unabridged, unreduced, undivided, uncut. **2** *no glasses left whole | he came home whole* intact, sound, flawless, in one piece, unimpaired, undamaged, unharmed, unhurt, uninjured, unmutilated.

Antonyms: PART; PARTIAL; INCOMPLETE; BROKEN.

whole *adverb eat/cook it whole* in one piece, in one.

whole *noun* **1** *parts making up a whole* entity, unit, ensemble, totality, entirety. **2** *the whole of the year | the whole of the country rejoiced* all, every part, every person/member/inhabitant. **on the whole 1** *on the whole, he is perfect for the job* all in all, all things considered, taking everything into consideration, by and large. **2** *on the whole, he works late* as a rule, as a general rule, generally, in general, in the main, for the most part.

wholehearted *adjective* **1** *a wholehearted fan of the group* devoted, dedicated, enthusiastic, eager, keen, zealous, earnest, serious, committed. **2** *give the movement their wholehearted support* unreserved, unqualified, unstinting, complete, committed, hearty, emphatic, real, sincere, genuine.

Antonyms: APATHETIC; HALFHEARTED; QUALIFIED.

wholesale *adjective the wholesale destruction of farmland | the wholesale distribution of free samples* indiscriminate, mass, all-inclusive, total, comprehensive, extensive, wide-ranging, sweeping, broad.

Antonyms: PARTIAL; SELECTIVE.

wholesale *adverb destroy farmland wholesale | distribute samples wholesale* indiscriminately, all at once, without exception, on a large scale, comprehensively, extensively.

wholesome *adjective* **1** *wholesome food* nutritious, nourishing, health-giving, healthful, good, good for one, strengthening. **2** *wholesome air/climate* salubrious, invigorating, bracing, stimulating, refreshing. **3** *wholesome literature/advice* moral, ethical, nonerotic, nonviolent, uplifting, edifying, helpful, beneficial, prudent.

wholly *adverb* **1** *wholly in favor of the scheme* completely, fully, entirely, totally, utterly, thoroughly, altogether, comprehensively, in every respect, perfectly, enthusiastically, with total commitment, unreservedly, heart and soul; *inf.* one hundred percent. **2** *the burden rests wholly on his shoulders* only, solely, exclusively, purely.

whoop *noun whoops of excitement/admiration* cry, call, shout, yell, scream, shriek, hoot, cheer, hurrah; *inf.* holler.

whoop *verb whoop with excitement/admiration* cry, call, shout, yell, scream, shriek, hoot, cheer; *inf.* holler.

whore *noun* prostitute, call girl, streetwalker, harlot, lady of the evening/night, *fille de joie*, woman of ill repute, wanton, loose woman, trollop, fallen woman, courtesan; *inf.* tart, hooker, hustler, slut.

wicked *adjective* **1** *a wicked man* evil, sinful, bad, black-hearted, villainous, base, vile, vicious, dishonorable, unprincipled, unrighteous, criminal, lawless, perverted, immoral, amoral, unethical, corrupt, dissolute, abandoned, dissipated, degenerate, reprobate, debauched, depraved, unholy, impious, irreligious, ungodly, godless, devilish. **2** *his wicked deeds* evil, sinful, iniquitous, wrong, bad, vile, foul, base, mean, gross, odious, obnoxious, nefarious, heinous, flagitious, infamous, dreadful, dire, grim, horrible, hideous, gruesome, monstrous, atrocious, abominable, abhorrent, loathsome, hateful, detestable, reprehensible, dishonorable, disgraceful, shameful, ignoble, ignominious, lawless, unlawful, illicit, illegal, villainous, dastardly, blackguardly, unholy, impious, impure, ungodly, godless, profane, blasphemous, irreverent, irreligious, damnable, devilish, demonic, diabolic. **3** *hurt by her wicked remarks* spiteful, malicious, malignant, nasty, offensive, hurtful, distressing, galling, vexatious. **4** *aim a wicked blow* dangerous, perilous, destructive, harmful, injurious, hurtful, painful, agonizing, ferocious, fierce, terrible, mighty. **5** *give a wicked smile | have a wicked sense of humor* mischievous, impish, roguish, arch, rascally, naughty. **6** *the weather has been wicked* bad, nasty, unpleasant, disagreeable; *inf.* dreadful, terrible, awful. **7** *he's a wicked player* excellent, expert, masterly, skillful, proficient, deft, adept, dexterous, first-rate, outstanding, superior, superlative; *inf.* top-notch. **Antonyms:** VIRTUOUS; GOOD; RIGHTEOUS.

wide *adjective* **1** *a wide river/building* broad, extensive, spacious. **2** *wide hips* broad, large, outspread, spread out, ample. **3** *wide eyes* fully open, dilated. **4** *a wide range of subjects* | *a wide knowledge* ample, broad, extensive, large, large-scale, vast, far-ranging, immense, expansive, wide-ranging, sweeping, encyclopedic, comprehensive, general, all-embracing, catholic, compendious. **5** *wide pants* full, loose, baggy, capacious, roomy, generous, commodious. **6** *his shot was wide* | *his guess was wide (of the mark)* off target, off course. **Antonyms:** NARROW; LIMITED; RESTRICTED.

wide *adverb* **1** *open your mouth wide* to the fullest/furthest extent, as far as possible, fully, completely. **2** *he shot wide* wide of the mark/target, off target, off course, astray. **wide awake 1** *still wide awake at dawn* fully awake, awake, conscious, open-eyed, not asleep. **2** *you have to be wide awake to do business with them* alert, on the alert, on the qui vive, vigilant, wary, chary, watchful, observant, attentive, heedful, aware; *inf.* on one's toes, on the ball. **wide open 1** *with eyes wide open* open wide, fully open, dilated, gaping. **2** *with arms wide open* open wide, outspread, spread open, outstretched, splayed open, fully extended. **3** *wide open to attack/criticism* exposed, vulnerable, unprotected, unguarded, defenseless, at risk, in danger. **4** *the outcome of the game was wide open* uncertain, unsure, indeterminate, unsettled, unpredictable, in the balance, up in the air; *inf.* anyone's guess.

wide-eyed *adjective* **1** *children wide-eyed at the antics of the clown* surprised, amazed, astonished, astounded. **2** *wide-eyed youngsters* naïve, impressionable, ingenuous, credulous, trusting, unsuspicious, innocent, simple, unsophisticated, inexperienced, green; *inf.* wet behind the ears.

widen *verb* **1** *widen the road* make wider, broaden. **2** *widen her knowledge* broaden, expand, extend, enlarge, increase, augment, add to, supplement. **3** *her eyes widened in surprise* open wide, dilate. **Antonyms:** NARROW; RESTRICT; LIMIT.

widespread *adjective* *widespread terror/confusion* universal, common, general, far-reaching, far-flung, prevalent, rife, extensive, sweeping, pervasive, epidemic. **Antonyms:** LOCAL; LIMITED; RARE.

width *noun* **1** *the width of the river/cloth* wideness, breadth, broadness, span, diameter, thickness, ampleness. **2** *impressed by the width of his knowl-edge* wideness, broadness, breadth, scope, range, span, extensiveness, vastness, immensity, immenseness, expansiveness, comprehensiveness, catholicity, compendiousness.

wield *verb* **1** *come out wielding a sword* brandish, flourish, wave, swing, shake, use, put to use, employ, handle, ply, manipulate. **2** *wield the power in the country* exercise, exert, be possessed of, have, have at one's disposal, hold, maintain, command, control, manage, be in charge of.

wife *noun* spouse, mate, consort, woman, helpmate, squaw, bride; *inf.* better/other half, missus, missis, old woman/lady, the little woman, the lady of the house.

wild *adjective* **1** *wild cats/horses* untamed, undomesticated, unbroken, feral, savage, fierce, ferocious. **2** *wild plants* uncultivated, natural, native, indigenous. **3** *wild peoples/tribes* uncivilized, primitive, ignorant, savage, barbaric, barbarous, brutish, ferocious, fierce. **4** *wild country/countryside* uncivilized, uncultivated, unpopulated, uninhabited, unsettled, unfrequented, empty, barren, waste, desolate, forsaken, godforsaken, isolated. **5** *a wild night* stormy, tempestuous, turbulent, blustery, howling, violent, raging, furious, rough. **6** *lead a wild life* | *wild confusion/delight* undisciplined, unrestrained, unconstrained, uncontrolled, out of control, uncurbed, unbridled, unchecked, chaotic, disorderly. **7** *a wild crowd* rowdy, unruly, disorderly, noisy, turbulent, violent, lawless, riotous, out of control, uncontrolled, unmanageable, ungovernable, unrestrained, excited, passionate, frantic. **8** *the crowd went/were wild* beside oneself, berserk, frantic, frenzied, in a frenzy, hysterical, crazed, mad, distracted, distraught, irrational, deranged, demented, raving, maniacal, rabid; *inf.* crazy. **9** *lost his temper and was wild* angry, infuriated, incensed, exasperated, in a temper, seething; *inf.* mad. **10** *wild schemes* extravagant, fantastical, impracticable, foolish, ill-advised, ill-considered, imprudent, unwise, madcap, impulsive, reckless, rash, outrageous, preposterous. **11** *wild about rock music* enthusiastic, eager, avid, agog; *inf.* crazy, mad, nuts. **12** *a wild guess* arbitrary, random, hit-or-miss, haphazard, uninformed, unknowledgeable. **13** *wild hair* uncombed, unkempt, disheveled, tousled, windblown, disarranged, untidy. **run wild 1** *weeds running wild* grow unchecked, spread like wildfire, ramble, straggle. **2** *children running wild* run free, go undisciplined/unchecked. **3** *demonstrators running wild* run riot, go on the rampage, go berserk, get out of control, cut loose. **Antonyms:** TAME; CIVILIZED; CALM; RESTRAINED.

wilderness *noun* **1** *the Arctic wilderness* desert, wasteland, waste, jungle, no-man's land; wilds. **2** *a wilderness of abandoned cars* confusion, tangle, jumble, muddle, clutter, miscellany, hodgepodge, bewilderment, maze, labyrinth.

wile noun 1 *make use of wile to get her own way* trickery, craftiness, craft, cunning, artfulness, slyness, guile, chicanery, fraud, deception, cheating. 2 *use all her wiles to get her own way* trick, dodge, ruse, subterfuge, ploy, stratagem, lure, artifice, maneuver, device, contrivance.

will[1] verb 1 *come when you will* wish, want, desire, please, see/think fit, think best, choose, prefer, opt, elect. 2 *accidents will happen* do, have a tendency to, have a habit of.

will[2] verb 1 *will him to live* impose one's will on, try to make/cause. 2 *God willed it* decree, order, ordain, command, direct, bid, intend, wish, desire. 3 *will him all her books* bequeath, leave, give, hand/pass down to, pass on to, transfer to.

will[3] noun 1 *freedom of will* volition, choice, option, decision, discretion, prerogative. 2 *he has the will to live* desire, wish, preference, inclination, fancy, mind. 3 *it is the will of God* decree, ordinance, dictate, wish, decision. 4 *he lacks the will to succeed* willpower, determination, resolution, resolve, firmness of purpose, purposefulness, single-mindedness, doggedness, commitment, moral fiber, pluck, mettle, grit, nerve. 5 *draw up his will* last will and testament, testament; last wishes. 6 *bear him ill will* feeling, disposition, attitude. **at will** *come and go at will* as one wishes/pleases, as one thinks fit, to suit oneself, at one's inclination/discretion.

willful adjective 1 *willful neglect/murder* deliberate, intentional, intended, conscious, purposeful, premeditated, planned, calculated. 2 *coping with willful children* headstrong, strong-willed, obstinate, stubborn, stubborn as a mule, mulish, pigheaded, bullheaded, obdurate, intransigent, adamant, dogged, determined, persistent, unyielding, uncompromising, intractable, refractory, recalcitrant, disobedient, contrary, perverse, wayward, self-willed.

Antonyms: ACCIDENTAL; UNINTENTIONAL; DOCILE.

willing adjective 1 *willing helpers* ready, eager, keen, enthusiastic, avid. 2 *willing to accept responsibility* prepared, ready, disposed, content, happy, so-minded, consenting, agreeable, amenable, in the mood, compliant; *inf.* game. 3 *willing help* cooperative, gladly given, cheerful, accommodating, obliging.

Antonyms: UNWILLING; RELUCTANT.

willingly adverb 1 *she went with him willingly* voluntarily, of one's own free will, of one's own accord, by choice, by volition, spontaneously, unforced. 2 *I'll willingly help you* cheerfully, happily, with pleasure, readily, without hesitation, ungrudgingly, with all one's heart.

willingness noun 1 *their willingness to learn* readiness, eagerness, keenness, enthusiasm, avidity. 2 *their willingness to accept responsibility* readiness, preparedness, consent, agreeableness, amenability.

willpower noun will, strength of will, determi-

nation, resolution, resolve, firmness of purpose, purposefulness, doggedness, commitment, single-mindedness, moral fiber, self-discipline, pluck, mettle, grit, nerve.

wilt verb 1 *plants wilting* droop, wither, shrivel, lose freshness, sag. 2 *people wilting in the heat* droop, sag, feel weak/faint, languish. 3 *their courage/determination/strength wilted* diminish, dwindle, lessen, grow less, flag, fade, melt away, ebb, wane, weaken, fail.

Antonyms: GROW; THRIVE.

wily adjective crafty, cunning, artful, sharp, astute, shrewd, scheming, intriguing, shifty, foxy, sly, guileful, deceitful, deceptive, fraudulent, cheating, underhand, underhanded; *inf.* crooked.

win verb 1 *win first prize* achieve, attain, earn, gain, receive, obtain, acquire, procure, get, secure, collect, pick up, come away with, net; *inf.* bag. 2 *win the battle/contest* be victorious in, be the victor in, achieve success in, come first in. 3 *may the best side win* be victorious, be the victor, gain the victory, overcome, achieve mastery, carry the day, finish first, come out ahead, come out on top, succeed, triumph, prevail; *inf.* win out. 4 *she won them by her beauty* | *win their hearts* charm, attract, lure, disarm. **win over/around** *win over the opposition* | *win them around to our way of thinking* talk/bring around, persuade, induce, influence, sway, prevail upon, convert.

Antonyms: LOSE; FAIL; REPEL.

win noun *their side needs a win* victory, conquest, success, triumph.

wince verb *wince in pain/embarrassment* grimace, start, flinch, blench, quail, shrink, recoil, cringe, squirm.

---

wince
cower, cringe, flinch, recoil
The same individual might **wince** when receiving a flu shot, **flinch** from a difficult task, and **cower** in fear at the approach of a tornado. All of these verbs mean to draw back in alarm, disgust, faintheartedness, or servility, but there are subtle differences among them. To *wince* is to make a slight recoiling movement, often an involuntary contraction of the facial features, in response to pain or discomfort (*to wince when a singer misses a high note*), while *flinch* may imply a similar drawing-back motion or, more abstractly, a reluctance or avoidance (*to tackle the job without flinching*). *Cower* and **cringe** both refer to stooped postures, although *cower* is usually associated with fearful trembling (*he cowered in the doorway*) while *cringe* is usually linked to servile, cowardly, or fawning behavior (*she cringed before her father's authority*). More than any of the other verbs here, **recoil** suggests a physical movement away from something (*recoil at*

the sight of a poisonous snake), although that movement may also be psychological (*recoil at the very thought of a family reunion*).

wince *noun give a wince of pain* grimace, start, flinch.

wind[1] *noun* **1** *a day almost entirely without wind* air current, current/stream of air; puff of wind, light air/wind, zephyr, breeze, gust, blast, gale. **2** *need a lot of wind to play the trombone* breath, respiration; *inf.* puff. **3** *a pompous fool full of wind* empty talk, talk, babble, blather, boasting, bluster, braggadocio; *inf.* hot air, baloney, gas. **4** *there is wind of a pay increase | wind of a scandal* rumor, gossip, hint, suggestion, inkling, intimation; news, information, report, intelligence. **in the wind** *sense that redundancies were in the wind* about to happen, in the offing, on the way, coming near, close at hand, approaching, impending, looming; *inf.* in the cards.

wind[2] *noun the path has many winds* winding, twist, turn, curve, bend, loop, coil, whorl, convolution.

wind[3] *verb* **1** *the road winds up the hill* twist, twist and turn, curve, bend, loop, zigzag, snake, spiral, meander, ramble. **2** *smoke winding up into the sky* curl, spiral, wreathe, snake. **3** *wind the yarn into a ball* twist, twine, coil, wrap, roll. **wind down 1** *the runners need to wind down after a race* unwind, relax, become less tense, ease up, calm down, cool off. **2** *we are winding the project down* bring to a close/end, make less active, ease up on. **3** *schoolwork is winding down for the summer* slacken off, ease up, taper off, dwindle, diminish, lessen, decline, come to an end/close. **wind up 1** *the events of the evening really wound her up | he gets wound up easily* make tense, strain, make nervous, work up, put on edge, agitate, fluster, disconcert, discompose. **2** *it's time to wind up the meeting/project* bring to an end/conclusion, end, conclude, terminate, finish; *inf.* wrap up. **3** *we wound up in a remote village* end up, finish, find oneself.

winded *adjective* breathless, out of breath, gasping for breath, panting.

windfall *noun* piece/stroke of good luck, unexpected gain, godsend, manna (from heaven), bonanza, jackpot.

winding *adjective a winding road* twisting, twisting and turning, curving, bending, looping, tortuous, zigzagging, snaking, spiraling, meandering, serpentine, sinuous, rambling.

winding *noun the road had many windings* wind, twist, turn, bend, loop, coil, curve, convolution, meander.

window *noun* opening, aperture.

windy *adjective* **1** *a windy day* breezy, blowy, blustery, blustering, gusty, gusting, boisterous, squally, stormy, wild, tempestuous, turbulent. **2** *a windy speech* long-winded, loquacious, wordy, verbose, rambling, meandering, prolix, diffuse, turgid, bombastic.

wing *noun* **1** *the extreme wing of the party* arm, side, branch, section, segment, group, grouping, circle, faction, clique, set, coterie, cabal. **2** *the east wing of the house* extension, annex, addition, ell.

wing *verb* **1** *birds winging through the air* fly, glide, soar. **2** *she winged to the top of her profession | winged to the finish line* soar, zoom, speed, race, hurry, hasten. **3** *the bullet winged the bird/soldier* wound, hit, clip.

wink *verb* **1** *wink an eye* blink, flutter, bat, nictate, nictitate. **2** *lights winking across the water* flash, twinkle, sparkle, glitter, gleam. **wink at** *wink at the child's mistakes* turn a blind eye to, close/shut one's eyes to, blink at, ignore, overlook, disregard, let pass, condone, tolerate.

wink *noun* **1** *the wink of an eye* blink, flutter, bat, nictiation. **2** *the winks of the lights* flash, twinkle, sparkle, glitter, gleam. **3** *I'll be with you in a wink* moment, minute, second, instant; *inf.* jiffy, jiff, two shakes of a lamb's tail.

winner *noun* champion, victor, vanquisher, conqueror, conquering hero; cup winner, prizewinner.

winning *adjective* **1** *the winning team* victorious, successful, triumphant, vanquishing, conquering. **2** *a winning smile/child* captivating, enchanting, bewitching, beguiling, disarming, taking, engaging, endearing, winsome, charming, attractive, fetching, alluring, sweet, lovely, delightful, darling, amiable, pleasing.

winnings *plural noun* proceeds, spoils, profits, take, takings, gains; booty, purse.

winnow *verb* **1** *winnow the chaff from the grain* remove, get rid of, divide, separate, part, sort out. **2** *winnow the evidence* sift, go through, examine, comb, sort out.

wintry *adjective* **1** *a wintry day | wintry showers* cold, chilly, icy, frosty, freezing, frozen, snowy, arctic, glacial, biting, piercing, nippy. **2** *a wintry smile/look* unfriendly, cool, chilly, cold, distant, remote, bleak, cheerless.

wipe *verb wipe the table* rub, brush, dust, mop, sponge, swab, clean, dry. **wipe off** *wipe the dirt off* rub off, brush off, mop up, sponge off, clean off, remove, get rid of, take off, take away, erase, efface. **wipe out** destroy, demolish, annihilate, exterminate, eradicate, eliminate, extirpate, obliterate, expunge, erase, blot out, extinguish.

wipe *noun give the table a wipe* rub, brush, dust, mop, sponge, swab, clean.

wiry *adjective* **1** *wiry children/youths* lean, spare, sinewy, tough, strong. **2** *wiry hair* strong, coarse, tough. **3** *wiry brushes* bristly, prickly, thorny, stiff, rigid.
Antonyms: FRAIL; SMOOTH.

wisdom *noun* **1** *admire the wisdom of the old man/ sayings* sageness, sagacity, cleverness, intelligence, erudition, learning, education, knowledge, enlightenment, reason, philosophy, dis-

cernment, perception, insight. **2** *admire their wisdom in leaving early* | *the wisdom of her decision* sense, common sense, prudence, judiciousness, judgment, shrewdness, astuteness, smartness, circumspection, strategy, foresight, reasonableness, rationality, logic, soundness, saneness.
Antonyms: FOLLY; STUPIDITY.

wise *adjective* **1** *she is a wise woman* | *wise sayings* sage, sagacious, clever, intelligent, erudite, learned, educated, well-read, knowledgeable, informed, enlightened, philosophic, deep-thinking, discerning, perceptive, experienced; *lit.* sapient. **2** *it was wise to leave early* | *you were wise to leave* a wise decision sensible, prudent, well-advised, judicious, politic, shrewd, astute, smart, strategic, reasonable, rational, logical, sound, sane.
Antonyms: STUPID; SILLY; FOOLISH.

wisecrack *noun* quip, witticism, rejoinder, joke, jest, pun, barb; *inf.* gag, funny, dig, zinger.

wish *verb* **1** *wish to travel abroad* want, desire, long, yearn, aspire, have an inclination. **2** *they wish you to go now* desire, demand, bid, ask, require, instruct, direct, order, command. **wish for** *wish for a long life* want, desire, long for, hope for, yearn for, pine for, have a fancy for, fancy, crave, hunger for, thirst for, lust after, covet, sigh for, set one's heart on; *inf.* hanker after, have a yen for.

wish *noun* **1** *satisfy her wish to travel* desire, liking, fondness, longing, hope, yearning, want, fancy, aspiration, inclination, urge, whim, craving, hunger, thirst, lust; *inf.* hankering, yen. **2** *you must obey their wishes* want, desire, demand, bidding, request, requirement, instruction, direction, order, command.

wishy-washy *adjective* **1** *he is a bit wishy-washy* weak, feeble, puny, ineffectual, effete, spineless, irresolute; *inf.* weak-kneed. **2** *wishy-washy colors* pallid, pale, wan, sickly. **3** *wishy-washy soup* tasteless, flavorless, insipid, watery, weak, diluted.

wistful *adjective* yearning, longing, forlorn, disconsolate, melancholy, sad, mournful, dreaming, dreamy, daydreaming, in a reverie, pensive, reflective, musing, contemplative, meditative.

wit *noun* **1** *he did not have the wit to understand* intelligence, intellect, cleverness, wisdom, sageness, sagacity, judgment, common sense, understanding, comprehension, reason, sharpness, astuteness, shrewdness, acumen, discernment, perspicacity, perception, percipience, insight, ingenuity; brains; *inf.* nous. **2** *entertained by a person of great wit* wittiness, humor, jocularity, funniness, facetiousness, drollery, waggishness, repartee, badinage, banter, raillery. **3** *one of the great wits of his time* humorist, wag, funny person, comic, jokester, banterer, farceur; *inf.* card.
Antonyms: STUPIDITY; GRAVITY.

827

wise ~ withdrawal

wit
humor, irony, repartee, sarcasm, satire
If you're good at perceiving analogies between dissimilar things and expressing them in quick, sharp, spontaneous observations or remarks, you have **wit**. **Humor**, on the other hand, is the ability to perceive what is comical, ridiculous, or ludicrous in a situation or character, and to express it in a way that makes others see or feel the same thing. It suggests more sympathy, tolerance, and kindliness than *wit* (*she maintained a sense of humor in the midst of trying circumstances*). **Irony** is the implicit humor in the contradiction between what is meant and what is expressed, or in the discrepancy between appearance and reality. An example would be to shout, in the midst of a hurricane, What a perfect day for a wedding! Although **sarcasm** may take the form of irony, it is less subtle and is often used harshly or bitterly to wound or ridicule someone. Unlike irony, however, *sarcasm* depends on tone of voice for its effect (*a fine friend you turned out to be! he said, with obvious sarcasm*). **Satire** usually implies the use of sarcasm or irony for the purpose of ridicule or criticism, often directed at institutions or political figures (*she wrote political satire for the comedy team*). If you are good at making quick, witty replies, you will be known for your **repartee**, which is the art of responding pointedly and skillfully with wit or humor in a conversational exchange (*no one could compete with her witty repartee*).

witch *noun* **1** *the witch cast a spell* sorceress, enchantress, magician, necromancer. **2** *dressed up as an ugly old witch* hag, ogress, crone, gorgon; virago, termagant, shrew, harridan.

witchcraft *noun* witchery, sorcery, black art/magic, magic, necromancy, wizardry, occultism, the occult, sortilege, thaumaturgy, wonder-working.

withdraw *verb* **1** *withdraw her son from the school* | *withdraw the poker from the fire* take back, pull back, take away, extract, remove. **2** *asked to withdraw their remarks* take back, retract, recall, unsay. **3** *Congress withdrew the bill* revoke, annul, nullify, declare void, rescind, repeal, abrogate. **4** *she withdrew into the shadows* | *withdraw from the group* draw back, go back, absent oneself, detach oneself. **5** *the troops/spectators withdrew* pull back, fall back, retire, retreat, disengage, depart, go, leave; *inf.* make oneself scarce.
Antonyms: KEEP; PROFFER; STAY; PROCEED.

withdrawal *noun* **1** *his withdrawal from the school* | *withdrawal of the poker from the fire* extraction, removal. **2** *the withdrawal of their remarks* retraction, recall, unsaying. **3** *the withdrawal of the bill* revocation, nullification, rescinding, repeal, abrogation. **4** *the with-*

drawal of the troops/spectators falling back, retreat, disengagement, departure, leaving, exit, exodus, evacuation. **5** drug withdrawal abstention, deprivation, absence.

withdrawn adjective a withdrawn person/personality retiring, reserved, uncommunicative, nonforthcoming, unsociable, taciturn, silent, quiet, introverted, detached, aloof, shrinking, self-contained, distant, private, timid, timorous, shy, bashful, diffident.
Antonyms: OUTGOING; SOCIABLE.

wither verb **1** flowers withering in the heat dry up/out, shrivel, go limp, wilt, die. **2** heat withering the flowers dry up/out, desiccate, kill off. **3** time withered their enthusiasm/hopes destroy, ruin, kill off, blight, blast. **4** gradually their enthusiasm/dreams withered wilt, decline, fade, ebb, wane, disintegrate, die, perish.

withhold verb **1** unable to withhold their laughter hold back, keep back, restrain, hold/keep in check, check, curb, repress, suppress. **2** withhold permission refuse to give/grant/allow, refuse, decline, keep back.

within preposition **1** within the walls of the city inside, in, within the confines of, enclosed by. **2** within the speed limit inside, inside the range/limits of, in the bounds of. **3** come back within half an hour before, not after, not exceeding, not more than, in the compass of.

without preposition **1** they were three days without food lacking, short of, wanting, requiring, in want/need of, deprived of, destitute of. **2** he arrived without her unaccompanied by, unescorted by, in the absence of. **3** that is the price without tax exclusive of, excluding, not including, not counting.

withstand verb withstand attack/pressure hold out against, stand up to, stand firm against, resist, fight, combat, oppose, endure, stand, tolerate, bear, put up with, take, cope with, weather, brave, defy.
Antonyms: SURRENDER; YIELD.

witness noun **1** taking statements from witnesses | a witness to the accident eyewitness, observer, spectator, onlooker, looker-on, viewer, watcher, beholder, bystander. **2** witnesses giving evidence in court testifier, attestant, deponent. **3** his ragged clothes were witness of his poverty evidence, testimony, confirmation, corroboration, proof. **bear witness** several people were asked to bear witness give evidence, testify, give testimony. **bear witness to** her canceled check bore witness to her claim that she had paid the bill testify to, attest to, be evidence of, confirm, corroborate, be proof of, prove, bear out, vouch for, betoken.

witness verb **1** they witnessed the accident see, observe, view, watch, look on at, behold, perceive, be present at, attend. **2** witness his will/signature endorse, countersign, sign. **witness to 1** his ragged clothes witnessed to his poverty bear witness to,

testify to, attest to, be evidence of, confirm, corroborate, be proof of, prove. **2** she was asked to witness to the truth of the statement testify to, give testimony about, attest to, bear witness to, give evidence about.

wits plural noun he did not have the wits to understand wit, intelligence, brains, intellect, cleverness, judgment, common sense, shrewdness, perspicacity; inf. nous.

witticism noun witty remark, clever saying, flash of wit, bon mot, quip, sally, pleasantry, riposte, joke, jest, epigram; inf. wisecrack, crack, one-liner.

witty adjective clever, original, ingenious, sparkling, scintillating, humorous, amusing, jocular, funny, facetious, droll, waggish, comic.
Antonyms: BORING; DULL.

wizard noun **1** wizards casting spells sorcerer, warlock, enchanter, witch, necromancer, magician, magus. **2** he is a wizard at the piano expert, master, adept, genius, virtuoso, maestro, star; inf. ace, whiz, wiz.

wizened adjective withered, shriveled (up), dried up, shrunken, wasted, wrinkled, lined, gnarled, worn.

wobble verb **1** the table/boat wobbled rock, sway, seesaw, teeter, shake, vibrate. **2** she wobbled down the road on high heels teeter, totter, stagger, waddle, waggle. **3** her voice wobbled with emotion shake, tremble, quiver, quaver. **4** the politicians were wobbling be undecided, be uncertain, waver, vacillate, hesitate, dither, shilly-shally.

wobble noun **1** try to prevent the wobble of the table/boat rocking, swaying, teetering, shaking. **2** walk with a wobble teeter, totter, stagger. **3** a wobble of emotion in her voice shaking, trembling, tremor, quiver, quaver.

woe noun **1** a tale of woe misery, wretchedness, misfortune, disaster, grief, anguish, affliction, suffering, pain, agony, torment, sorrow, sadness, unhappiness, distress, heartache, heartbreak, despondency, desolation, dejection, depression, gloom, melancholy. **2** she told everyone her woes trouble, misfortune, adversity, trial, tribulation, ordeal, burden, affliction, suffering, disaster, calamity, catastrophe; trials and tribulations.
Antonyms: HAPPINESS; JOY; LUCK.

woebegone adjective a woebegone face/expression miserable, sad, unhappy, sorrowful, sorrowing, disconsolate, mournful, downcast, dejected, doleful, desolate, depressed, despairing, tearful.

woeful adjective **1** telling woeful tales of poverty sad, saddening, unhappy, sorrowful, miserable, dismal, wretched, doleful, gloomy, tragic, pathetic, grievous, pitiful, plaintive, heart-rending, heartbreaking, distressing, anguished, agonizing, dreadful, terrible. **2** the army will meet a woeful fate sad, miserable, wretched, harsh, tragic, disastrous, ruinous, calamitous, catastrophic. **3** *a woeful piece of work* poor, bad, inadequate, substandard, lamentable, deplorable, disgraceful, wretched, disappointing, feeble; *inf.* rotten, appalling, terrible, lousy, shocking.

wolf *noun* *a real wolf in his younger days* lady-killer, ladies' man, philanderer, womanizer, seducer, lecher, lech, Casanova, Don Juan, lothario.

wolf *verb* *wolf his food* devour, gulp down, bolt, gobble, cram down, stuff down, gorge oneself with; *inf.* scoff, pack away.

woman *noun* **1** *women and children first* female, lady, girl, she; *derog. inf.* chick, dame. **2** *he has a new woman* girlfriend, female friend, lady love, sweetheart, partner, lover, wife, spouse.

womanish *adjective* *his womanish ways* effeminate, effete, unmanly; *inf.* sissy.

womanizer *noun* lady-killer, ladies' man, philanderer, seducer, lecher, lech, Casanova, Don Juan, lothario; *inf.* wolf.

womankind *noun* women, woman, female sex, womanhood, womenfolk.

womanly *adjective* womanlike, female, feminine, matronly, motherly.

wonder *noun* **1** *children gazing with wonder at the Christmas tree* wonderment, awe, surprise, astonishment, amazement, bewilderment, stupefaction, fascination, admiration. **2** *one of the wonders of the world* marvel, phenomenon, miracle, prodigy, curiosity, rarity, nonpareil, sight, spectacle.

wonder *verb* **1** *she wondered what to do next | he wondered where she came from* think, speculate, conjecture, ponder, meditate, reflect, deliberate, muse, ask oneself, puzzle, be curious about, be inquisitive about. **2** *I wonder you didn't walk out* be surprised, express surprise, find it surprising, be astonished/amazed. **3** *they wondered at the beauty of the church* marvel, stand amazed, stand in awe, be dumbfounded, gape, stare, goggle, look agog; *inf.* be flabbergasted, gawk, boggle.

wonderful *adjective* **1** *the church ceiling was wonderful to behold* marvelous, awe-inspiring, awesome, remarkable, extraordinary, phenomenal, prodigious, miraculous, fantastic, amazing, astonishing, astounding, surprising, incredible, unprecedented, unparalleled, unheard-of; *lit.* wondrous. **2** *a wonderful mother/pianist* superb, marvelous, magnificent, brilliant, sensational, stupendous, excellent, first-rate, outstanding, terrific, tremendous, admirable, very good; *inf.* great, super, fantastic, fabulous, tip-top, ace, A-1, wizard, bad, wicked.

Antonyms: ORDINARY; INDIFFERENT; AWFUL; DREADFUL.

wont *noun* *it is their wont to rise late* custom, habit, routine, practice, way, rule, convention.

woo *verb* **1** *woo the boss's daughter* court, pay court/suit to, seek the hand of, pursue, chase after, set one's cap at, make love to. **2** *woo fame* seek, seek to win/gain, pursue, chase after. **3** *woo the voters* seek the support/favor of. **4** *wooing consumers into buying their goods* importune, press, urge, entreat, beg, implore, supplicate, solicit, coax, wheedle.

wood *noun* **1** *made of wood* lumber, timber. **2** *wood for the fire* firewood, kindling, fuel.

wooded *adjective* woody, forested, tree-covered, tree-clad, timbered, sylvan.

wooden *adjective* **1** *wooden furniture/houses* made of wood, of wood, wood, timber. **2** *give a wooden performance* stiff, stolid, stodgy, expressionless, graceless, inelegant, ungainly, gauche, awkward, clumsy, maladroit. **3** *wearing a wooden expression | give him a wooden look* expressionless, inexpressive, blank, deadpan, empty, vacant, vacuous, glassy, impassive, lifeless, spiritless, unanimated, emotionless, unemotional, unresponsive.

woods *plural noun* *a walk in the woods* forest, woodland, wood, copse, thicket, grove; trees.

woolgathering *noun* daydreaming, dreaming, reverie, musing, abstraction, preoccupation, absentmindedness, inattention.

woolly *adjective* **1** *animals with woolly coats* fleecy, fluffy, shaggy, hairy, furry, flocculent. **2** *wearing woolly garments* woolen, made of wool, of wool, wool. **3** *a woolly TV picture* fuzzy, blurred, hazy, cloudy, foggy, indistinct, unclear, ill-defined. **4** *a woolly description | woolly thoughts* vague, hazy, indefinite, muddled, confused, disorganized.

word *noun* **1** *what's another word for "fame"?* term, expression, name. **2** *he said not a word* remark, comment, statement, utterance, expression, declaration. **3** *she gave him her word that she would repay the loan* word of honor, solemn word, promise, pledge, assurance, guarantee, undertaking, vow, oath. **4** *have a word with the teacher* chat, talk, conversation, discussion, tête-à-tête, consultation, exchange of views; *inf.* confab, chitchat, powwow. **5** *they have had word of his death* news, intimation, notice, communication, information, intelligence; tidings; message, report, account, communiqué, dispatch, bulletin; *inf.* low-down. **6** *word has it that he is a spy* rumor, talk, hearsay, gossip; *inf.* grapevine. **7** *give the word to begin* command, order, signal, go-ahead, thumbs up; *inf.* green light. **8** *the king's word is law* command, order, decree, edict, mandate, bidding, will. **9** *our word now must be success* slogan, watchword, password, catchword. **in a word** *in a word, he is mad* in short, in a nutshell, briefly, to put it briefly, succinctly, concisely. **word for word** verbatim, literal, exact, precise, accurate, close, faithful, strict, undeviating.

word *verb* *word the account differently* express, phrase, couch, put, say, utter, state.

words *plural noun* **1** *write the words of the song/opera/play* lyrics, libretto, book, text, script. **2**

she has had words with her sister angry talk, argument, disagreement, row, altercation.

wordy *adjective a wordy description* long-winded, verbose, loquacious, garrulous, voluble, prolix, protracted, discursive, diffuse, rambling, digressive, maundering, tautological, pleonastic.

work *noun* **1** *building a house involves a lot of work* effort, exertion, labor, toil, sweat, drudgery, trouble, industry; *lit.* travail; *inf.* grind, elbow grease. **2** *your work is to answer the phone* job, task, chore, undertaking, duty, charge, assignment, commission, mission. **3** *engaged in financial work | out of work | what is his work?* employment, occupation, business; job, profession, career, trade, vocation, calling, craft, line, field, métier, pursuit. **4** *he regards it as his life's work* achievement, accomplishment, deed, feat, handiwork, fulfillment, performance, production. **5** *a work of art* composition, creation, opus, piece, *oeuvre*, masterpiece. **6** *admire the work that has gone into the stained-glass window* workmanship, art, craft, skill.
Antonyms: LEISURE; PLAY; HOLIDAY; RETIREMENT.

work *verb* **1** *he works in industry* be employed, have a job, hold down a job, be engaged, earn one's living, do business, follow/ply one's trade. **2** *you will really have to work to build the house | work hard to pass the exam* exert oneself, put in effort, make efforts, labor, toil, sweat, drudge, slave, peg away; *inf.* grind, plug away, knock oneself out. **3** *work the machine* operate, control, drive, manage, direct, use, handle, manipulate, maneuver, ply, wield. **4** *this machine will not work* go, operate, function, perform, run. **5** *your idea/plan will not work* succeed, be successful, have success, go well, be effective, be effectual. **6** *work the land* cultivate, till, dig, farm. **7** *they can work miracles* bring about, achieve, accomplish, perform, carry out, execute, create, cause, contrive, effect, implement. **8** *they worked it so that the criminal got off* arrange, handle, manipulate, maneuver, contrive, bring off, carry off, pull off; *inf.* fix, fiddle, swing. **9** *work the clay* knead, shape, form, mold, fashion, model. **10** *work the peg into the hole* maneuver, manipulate, negotiate, guide, engineer, direct, edge. **11** *work one's way through the crowd* maneuver, progress, penetrate, move, make, push, elbow. **work on** *work on your mother to let you go* coax, cajole, wheedle, pester, press, nag, importune, persuade, influence, sway. **work out 1** *work out the puzzle/problem* solve, resolve, figure out. **2** *work out the answer* figure out, find out, calculate. **3** *work out a plan* develop, evolve, formulate, devise, arrange, organize, elaborate, construct, put together, plan, contrive. **4** *the plan did not work out* work, succeed, be successful, go well, go as planned/arranged/wished, be effective,

be effectual. **5** *things worked out well/badly* go, turn out, come out, develop, evolve, result; *inf.* pan out. **6** *work out to keep fit* exercise, do exercises, train, drill, practice, warm up. **work up 1** *work up to a climax* advance, progress, proceed, make headway. **2** *work up an appetite* cause, create, whet, stimulate, arouse, awaken. **3** *unable to work up any enthusiasm* stir up, arouse, rouse, awaken, excite, instigate, prompt, generate, kindle, foment. **4** *the speaker worked up the crowd* agitate, stir up, arouse, excite, animate, inflame; *inf.* get worked up, wind up.
Antonyms: REST; PLAY; FAIL.

workable *adjective* practicable, practical, viable, doable, feasible, possible.

workaday *adjective* ordinary, everyday, average, commonplace, mundane, run-of-the-mill, routine, humdrum, prosaic.

worker *noun* **1** *workers and employers* employee, hand, workman, workwoman, working man/woman/person, blue-collar worker, white-collar worker, laborer, artisan, craftsman, craftswoman, wage-earner, proletarian. **2** *workers of miracles* doer, performer, perpetrator, executor, operator. **3** *he is a real worker* hard worker, toiler, workhorse, busy bee; *inf.* workaholic.

working *adjective* **1** *working mothers* in work, employed, in a job. **2** *working models/machines* functioning, operating, going, running, in working order. **3** *a working majority/plan* effective, viable.
Antonyms: UNEMPLOYED; BROKEN.

working *noun* **1** *understand the working of the machine* functioning, operation, running process, method of working, modus operandi. **2** *the working of miracles* doing, performing, performance, perpetration, execution, operation. **3** *the workings of the clock* mechanism, machinery; works.

workman, workwoman *noun workmen/workwomen mending the roof* worker, employee, hand, laborer, artisan, tradesman, tradeswoman, operative.

workmanship *noun admire the workmanship of the tapestry/carpentry* craftsmanship, craft, artistry, art, handicraft, handwork, expertise, skill, technique, work.

workout *noun* training/practice session; physical exercise, drill, training; exercises, gymnastics, aerobics; *inf.* daily dozen.

works *plural noun* **1** *busy at the metal works* factory, plant, mill, workshop. **2** *the author's complete works* writings, productions; *oeuvre*, output. **3** *doing good works* deeds, acts, actions. **4** *the works of the clock/engine* workings, working parts, parts; mechanism, machinery, action, movement; *inf.* innards, insides, guts. **the works 1** *get the works at the beauty salon* full treatment, everything available/required; *inf.* the lot. **2** *the enemy gave the prisoners the works* harsh treatment, physical beating, torture.

workshop noun **1** *the car is still in the workshop* factory, plant, mill; garage. **2** *craftsmen at work in their workshop* workroom, studio, atelier, shop. **3** *hold a workshop in self-assertiveness* seminar, study/discussion group, class.

world noun **1** *the mountains of the world | travel around the world* earth, globe, sphere, planet. **2** *the world was shocked by the nuclear attack* whole world, world at large, mankind, man, humankind, humanity, people everywhere, people, everyone, everybody, public, general public. **3** *God created the world* universe, creation, cosmos, all existence. **4** *the earth and other worlds* planet, satellite, moon, star, heavenly body, orb. **5** *the academic world disliked the novel* society, sector, section, group, division. **6** *he works in the world of finance* area, field, department, sphere, province, domain, realm. **7** *the world of the dinosaurs/Roosevelts* age, epoch, era, period; times. **8** *it made a world of difference* vast/huge amount; *inf.* great deal, immensity. **9** *renounce the world | not interested in the world* secular interests, earthly concerns, human existence.

worldly adjective **1** *worldly considerations/pleasures* earthly, terrestrial, secular, temporal, material, materialistic, human, carnal, fleshly, corporeal, physical. **2** *traveling has made her more worldly* worldly-wise, experienced, knowing, sophisticated, cosmopolitan, urbane.
Antonyms: SPIRITUAL; NAÏVE; UNSOPHISTICATED.

worldwide adjective universal, global, international, pandemic, general, ubiquitous, extensive, widespread, far-reaching, wide-ranging.

worn adjective **1** *worn carpets/clothes* worn-out, threadbare, tattered, in tatters, ragged, frayed, shabby. **2** *worn furniture* worn-out, dilapidated, crumbling, broken-down, run-down, tumbledown, decrepit, deteriorated, on its last legs. **3** *rescue workers looking worn* haggard, drawn, strained, careworn; *inf.* all in, done in, dog-tired, dead on one's feet, played out, bushed, pooped. **4** *workers worn by long hours* worn out, exhausted, overtired, tired out, fatigued, weary, wearied, spent. **5** *worn ideas/jokes* well-worn, worn-out, obsolete, antiquated, old, hackneyed, stale; *inf.* played out. **worn-out** worn, dilapidated, exhausted.
Antonyms: NEW; MINT; ENERGETIC; FRESH.

worried adjective anxious, disturbed, perturbed, troubled, bothered, distressed, concerned, upset, distraught, uneasy, ill at ease, disquieted, fretful, agitated, nervous, edgy, on edge, tense, overwrought, worked-up, distracted, apprehensive, fearful, afraid, frightened; *inf.* uptight, on tenterhooks, antsy.
Antonyms: CAREFREE; CALM; UNCONCERNED.

worry verb **1** *she worries too much* be worried, be anxious, fret, brood. **2** *his absences worry her* cause anxiety to, make anxious, disturb, trouble, bother, distress, upset, concern, disquiet, discompose, fret, agitate, unsettle.

worry noun *their disappearance/behavior caused*

him a lot of worry anxiety, disturbance, perturbation, trouble, bother, distress, concern, care, upset, uneasiness, unease, disquiet, disquietude, fretfulness, agitation, edginess, tenseness, apprehension, fearfulness.

worsen verb **1** *his statement simply worsened the situation* make worse, aggravate, exacerbate, damage, intensify, increase, heighten. **2** *the financial situation worsened* get/grow/become worse, take a turn for the worse, deteriorate, degenerate, retrogress, decline, sink, slip, slide; *inf.* go downhill.
Antonyms: IMPROVE; ameliorate.

worship noun **1** *worship of God | acts of worship* reverence, veneration, homage, respect, honor, adoration, devotion, praise, prayer, glorification, exaltation, laudation, extolment. **2** *attend morning worship* service; religious rites/acts. **3** *the fans' worship of the star* adulation, admiration, adoration, devotion, idolization, hero-worship.

worship verb **1** *worship God* revere, venerate, pay homage to, honor, adore, praise, pray to, glorify, exalt, laud, extol. **2** *worship at the local church* attend a service, pray. **3** *he worships his wife | his fans worship him* adore, be devoted to, cherish, treasure, admire, adulate, idolize, hero-worship, lionize; *inf.* be wild about.
Antonyms: BLASPHEME; LOATHE; DESPISE.

worst verb defeat, beat, best, get the better of, gain the advantage over, trounce, rout, thrash, whip, drub, vanquish, conquer, master, overcome, overwhelm, overpower, overthrow, crush, subdue, subjugate.

worth noun **1** *the jewels are of little worth* financial value, value, price, cost. **2** *put a low worth on the house* value, valuation, price, assessment, appraisal. **3** *his advice is of little worth to you* value, use, usefulness, advantage, benefit, service, gain, profit, avail, help, assistance, aid. **4** *persons of great worth in the community* worthiness, merit, credit, value, excellence, eminence, importance.

worthless adjective **1** *the jewels are worthless* valueless, of little/no financial value, rubbishy, trashy. **2** *his advice was worthless | worthless attempts* valueless, useless, of no use, of no benefit, to no avail, futile, ineffective, ineffectual, pointless, nugatory. **3** *their worthless son ended up in prison* good-for-nothing, useless, despicable, contemptible, base, low, vile, corrupt, depraved; *inf.* no-good, no-account.
Antonyms: VALUABLE; PRECIOUS; USEFUL.

worthwhile adjective worth it, worth the effort, valuable, of value, useful, of use, beneficial, advantageous, helpful, profitable, gainful, productive, constructive, justifiable.
Antonyms: WORTHLESS; USELESS; POINTLESS.

worthy adjective **1** *worthy people not receiving recognition* virtuous, good, moral, upright, righteous, honest, decent, honorable,

respectable, reputable, trustworthy, reliable, irreproachable, blameless, unimpeachable, admirable, praiseworthy, laudable, commendable, deserving, meritorious. **2** *worthy of respect* deserving, meriting.
Antonyms: DISREPUTABLE; UNWORTHY.

worthy *noun* *local worthies* dignitary, notable, celebrity, personage, luminary, official; *inf.* VIP, big shot, bigwig, big cheese, big gun.

wound *noun* **1** *a wound in the leg that is not healing* lesion, cut, graze, scratch, gash, laceration, tear, puncture, slash, injury, sore. **2** *a wound to his pride* blow, injury, insult, slight, offense, affront; hurt, harm, damage. **3** *suffering from mental/emotional wounds* injury, hurt, pain, pang, ache, distress, grief, trauma, anguish, torment, torture.

wound *verb* **1** *the shot wounded his arm* cut, graze, scratch, gash, lacerate, tear, puncture, pierce, stab, slash, injure, hurt, damage, harm. **2** *their words wounded his pride* hurt, harm, damage, injure, insult, slight, offend, affront. **3** *his actions wounded her feelings* hurt, distress, grieve, mortify, pain, shock, traumatize.
Antonyms: HEAL; BOOST; GLADDEN.

wraith *noun* ghost, specter, shade, phantom, apparition, spirit.

wrangle *verb* *wrangle over the inheritance* have a disagreement, argue, quarrel, row, bicker, fight, clash, squabble, have words, brawl; *inf.* fall out.

wrap *verb* **1** *wrap the child in blankets* envelop, enfold, encase, enclose, cover, swathe, bundle up, swaddle. **2** *wrap the shawl around her* fold, swathe, bundle, draw, arrange. **3** *wrap the present* wrap up, package, do up, tie up, gift-wrap. **wrap up 1** *wrap up the present* wrap, gift-wrap. *See* WRAP *verb* 3. **2** *try to wrap up the meeting early* finish, end, bring to an end/close, conclude, terminate, wind up. **3** *you must wrap up well in the winter* dress warmly, wear warm clothes.
wrap *noun* shawl, stole, cloak, cape, mantle.

wrapper *noun* wrapping, cover, covering, packaging, paper; jacket, casing, case, sheath; capsule, pod, shell.

wrath *noun* anger, ire, rage, fury, annoyance, indignation, exasperation, dudgeon, high dudgeon, bad temper, ill humor, irritation, crossness, displeasure, irascibility.

wrathful *adjective* angry, irate, raging, enraged, incensed, infuriated, furious, fuming, ranting, raving, beside oneself, indignant, exasperated, bad-tempered, ill-humored, irritated, cross, displeased, irascible; *inf.* on the warpath.
Antonyms: CALM; GOOD-HUMORED.

wreath *noun* **1** *wreaths of flowers* garland, chaplet, circlet, coronet, crown, diadem, festoon, lei. **2** *wreaths of smoke* ring, loop, circle.

wreathe *verb* **1** *the display was wreathed in flowers | faces wreathed in smiles* cover, envelop, festoon, garland, adorn, decorate. **2** *the snake* wreathed itself around the tree trunk twist, wind, coil, twine, entwine, curl, spiral, wrap. **3** *smoke wreathing from the chimneys* coil, wind, spiral, curl.

wreck *noun* **1** *the divers failed to salvage the wreck* shipwreck, sunken ship/vessel, derelict. **2** *the wreck of the car/house/dreams* wreckage, debris, rubble, detritus; ruins, remains, remnants, fragments, pieces, relics. **3** *upset by the wreck of their car/house/dream* wrecking, wreckage, destruction, devastation, ruination, ruin, demolition, smashing, shattering, disruption, disintegration, undoing.

wreck *verb* **1** *wreck the car* smash, demolish, ruin, damage; *inf.* write off. **2** *wreck their plans/hopes* destroy, devastate, ruin, demolish, smash, shatter, disrupt, undo, spoil, mar, play havoc with. **3** *the new crew wrecked the ship* shipwreck, sink, capsize, run aground. **4** *the liner wrecked on its first voyage* founder, run aground, sink.
Antonyms: BUILD; CREATE; SAVE; REPAIR.

wreckage *noun* **1** *clear away the wreckage of the car/house/accident* wreck, debris; ruins, remains, remnants, fragments. *See* WRECK *noun* 2. **2** *upset by the wreckage of their car/house/dream* wreck, wrecking, destruction, ruination, ruin, demolition, smashing. *See* WRECK *noun* 3.

wrench *noun* **1** *remove the root with one wrench* twist, pull, tug, yank, wrest, jerk, jolt. **2** *the wrist injury is just a wrench* sprain, twist, strain. **3** *the wrench of a broken heart* pain, ache, pang, anguish, distress, trauma.

wrench *verb* **1** *wrench the root from the ground* twist, pull, tug, yank, wrest, jerk, tear, rip, force. **2** *wrench one's ankle/wrist* sprain, twist, strain.

wrest *verb* *wrest the gun from him* twist, wrench, pull, snatch, take away, remove.

wrestle *verb* *wrestling in the ring* grapple, contend. **wrestle with 1** *wrestle with one's conscience* struggle with, grapple with, fight with, contend with, battle with, combat with. **2** *wrestle with the problem* struggle with, contend with, come to grips with, face up to, pit oneself against; *inf.* plug away at.

wretch *noun* **1** *pity the wretches living on the streets* poor creature/soul/thing, miserable creature, unfortunate, poor devil. **2** *that's the wretch who stole her purse* scoundrel, villain, ruffian, rogue, rascal, blackguard, reprobate, criminal, delinquent, miscreant; *inf.* creep, jerk, louse, rat, swine, skunk.

wretched *adjective* **1** *feeling wretched at leaving home* miserable, unhappy, sad, brokenhearted, sorrowful, sorry, distressed, disconsolate, downcast, down, downhearted, dejected, crestfallen, cheerless, depressed, melancholy, gloomy, mournful, doleful, forlorn, woebegone, abject. **2** *feeling wretched during the sea voyage* ill, unwell, sick, sickly, ailing, below par; *inf.* under the weather, out of sorts. **3** *lead a wretched existence* miserable, unhappy, poor,

hard, harsh, grim, difficult, unfortunate, sorry, pitiful, tragic. **4** *wretched people living in poverty* miserable, poor, unhappy, unfortunate, unlucky, hapless, pitiable. **5** *the wretched drug dealer is back in prison* contemptible, despicable, base, low, vile. **6** *the food was wretched* poor, bad, substandard, low-quality, inferior, pathetic, worthless.
Antonyms: HAPPY; WELL; FORTUNATE.

wriggle *verb* **1** *children wriggling in their seats* twist, squirm, writhe, jiggle, jerk. **2** *wriggle along the ground* twist and turn, zigzag, wiggle, snake, crawl, slink. **3** *wriggle out of the task* avoid, evade, dodge, duck, extricate oneself.

wriggle *noun the wriggles of the children* squirming, writhing, jiggling, jerk.

wriggly *adjective a wriggly line* wiggly, wiggling, twisting, zigzag, zigzagging.

wring *verb* **1** *wring the clothes* twist, squeeze. **2** *wring the information from him* extract, force, coerce, exact, extort, wrest, wrench, screw.

wrinkle *noun wrinkles in her face | wrinkles in the material* crease, fold, pucker, gather, furrow, ridge, line, corrugation, crinkle, crumple, rumple; crow's-foot.

wrinkle *verb time had wrinkled her face | sitting wrinkled the dress* crease, pucker, gather, furrow, line, corrugate, crinkle, crumple, rumple.

writ *noun* court order, summons, decree.

write *verb* **1** *write their names* write down, put in writing, put in black and white, commit to paper, jot down, note, set down, take down, record, register, list, inscribe, scribble, scrawl. **2** *write an essay/letter* compose, draft, create, pen, dash off. **3** *don't forget to write* write a letter, correspond, communicate; *inf.* drop a line/note. **write down** put in writing, jot down, note, set down, take down, record, register, list. **write off 1** *write off the debt* forget about, disregard, give up for lost, cancel, annul, nullify, wipe out, cross out, score out. **2** *don't write off your opponent* disregard, regard as finished, dismiss.

writer *noun* author, wordsmith, penman, hack; novelist, essayist, biographer, journalist, columnist, scriptwriter; scribe; *inf.* scribbler, pen/pencil pusher.

writhe *verb* twist about, twist and turn, roll about, squirm, wriggle, fidget, jerk, thrash, flail, toss, struggle.

writing *noun* **1** *the writing is illegible* handwriting, hand, penmanship, script, print, calligraphy, chirography, scribble, scrawl. **2** *have his writing published* work, opus, book, volume, publication, composition.

wrong *adjective* **1** *the wrong answer | he is wrong in his calculation* incorrect, inaccurate, in error, erroneous, mistaken, inexact, imprecise, unsound, faulty, false, wide of the mark, off target; *inf.* off beam, barking up the wrong tree. **2** *chose the wrong moment to speak* unsuitable,

inappropriate, inapt, inapposite, undesirable, infelicitous. **3** *the wrong way to behave on such an occasion* unsuitable, inappropriate, undesirable, unacceptable, unfitting, improper, unseemly, indecorous, unconventional. **4** *it is wrong to steal* unlawful, illegal, illicit, lawless, criminal, delinquent, felonious, dishonest, dishonorable, corrupt, unethical, immoral, bad, wicked, evil, sinful, iniquitous, blameworthy, culpable; *inf.* crooked. **5** *something wrong with his phone/heart* amiss, awry, out of order, not right, faulty, defective. **6** *iron the dress on the wrong side* inside, reverse, opposite, inverse.
Antonyms: RIGHT; CORRECT; APPROPRIATE; LEGAL.

wrong *adverb* **1** *guess wrong* wrongly, incorrectly, inaccurately, erroneously, mistakenly, inexactly, imprecisely, falsely. **2** *things went wrong* badly, amiss, awry, astray. **get wrong** *get the message wrong* misunderstand, misinterpret, misapprehend, misconstrue. **go wrong 1** *you cannot go wrong if you follow the instructions* make a mistake, go astray, err; *inf.* slip up, make a booboo. **2** *things went wrong from the start* go badly, go amiss, go awry. **3** *their plans/marriage went wrong* fail, fall through, come to nothing, misfire, miscarry; *inf.* come to grief, flop. **4** *when did he go wrong?* go astray, err, commit a crime/sin, stray from the straight and narrow, fall from grace; *inf.* go to the dogs.

wrong *noun* **1** *not know right from wrong* badness, immorality, sin, sinfulness, wickedness, evil, iniquity, unlawfulness, crime, dishonesty, dishonor, injustice, transgression, abuse; *inf.* crookedness. **2** *commit a wrong | do us a wrong* bad deed/act/action, misdeed, offense, injury, crime, infringement, infraction, injustice, grievance, outrage, atrocity. **in the wrong** *you were in the wrong to accuse him* in error, mistaken, at fault, to blame, blameworthy, culpable, guilty, off course, off target, wide of the mark; *inf.* off the beam.
Antonyms: RIGHT; VIRTUE; HONOR.

wrong *verb* **1** *he wronged his wife* abuse, mistreat, maltreat, ill-treat, ill-use, harm, hurt, do injury to. **2** *you wrong him by calling him a thief* misrepresent, malign, dishonor, impugn, vilify, defame, slander, libel, denigrate, insult; *inf.* badmouth.

wrongdoer *noun* lawbreaker, criminal, delinquent, culprit, offender, felon, villain, miscreant, evildoer, sinner, transgressor, malefactor.

wrongful *adjective wrongful dismissal/arrest* unfair, unjust, improper, unjustified, unwarranted, unlawful, illegal, illegitimate, illicit.

wry *adjective* **1** *make a wry face* twisted, distorted, contorted, crooked, lopsided, askew. **2** *a wry wit/remark* ironic, sardonic, mocking, sarcastic, dry, droll, witty, humorous.

Xerox *verb Xerox the document* photocopy, copy, duplicate, reproduce; *Trademark* Photostat.

Xerox *noun get a Xerox of the document* photocopy, copy, duplicate; *Trademark* Photostat.

X ray *noun* X-ray image, radiogram, radiograph.

Y

yank *verb yank the weeds out* pull, tug, jerk, wrench.

yank *noun remove the tooth with one yank* pull, jerk, wrench.

yap *verb* **1** *dogs yapping* yelp, bark. **2** *people yapping* yack, chatter, gossip, jabber, prattle, gibber, babble, gabble.

yardstick *noun* measure, standard, gauge, scale, guide, guideline, touchstone, criterion, benchmark, model, pattern.

yarn *noun* **1** *use a fine yarn* thread, fiber, strand. **2** *tell a good yarn* story, tale, anecdote, fable; *inf.* tall tale/story, cock and bull story.

yawning *adjective a yawning gap* wide, wide open, gaping, cavernous, chasmic.

year *noun have a good year* | *the academic year* twelve-month period/session; calendar year, fiscal year. **year in, year out** regularly, without a break, unfailingly.

yearly *adjective a yearly event* annual, once a year, every year.

yearly *adverb published yearly* annually, once a year, per annum.

yearn *verb yearn for a child* | *yearn to go abroad* long, pine, have a longing, crave, desire, want, wish, hanker, have a fancy, hunger, thirst; *inf.* have a yen.

yearning *noun* longing, craving, desire, want, wish, hankering, fancy, hunger, thirst, lust, ache, burning; *inf.* yen.

yell *verb* shout, cry out, howl, scream, shriek, screech, squeal, roar, bawl, whoop; *inf.* holler.

yell *noun* shout, cry, howl, scream, shriek, screech, squeal, roar, bawl, whoop; *inf.* holler.

yen *noun* hankering, desire, want, wish, fancy, longing, craving, hunger, thirst, lust.

yes *adverb yes, I'll come* all right, of course, by all means, sure, certainly, in the affirmative; *inf.* yeah, yep, uh-huh, OK.

yet *adverb* **1** *he has not appeared yet* as yet, so/thus far, up till/to now, until now. **2** *there is yet more to come* still, in addition, additionally, besides, also, too, as well, further, into the bargain, to boot. **3** *I was not expecting him yet* now, just/right now, by now, already, so soon.

yield *verb* **1** *fields yielding a good crop* produce, bear, give, give forth, supply, provide. **2** *investments yielding a good return* give, return, bring in, fetch, earn, net, produce, supply, provide, generate, furnish. **3** *yield one's place in the team to another* | *yield the crown to the conqueror* give up, surrender, relinquish, part with, deliver up, turn over, give over, remit, cede, re-

nounce, resign, abdicate, forgo. **4** *the army yielded after a long battle* admit/concede defeat, surrender, capitulate, submit, lay down one's arms, give in, give up the struggle, succumb, raise/show the white flag; *inf.* throw in the towel, cave in. **5** *the material yields on pressure* give, bend, stretch, be flexible/pliant. **yield to** *yield to their demands* submit to, bow down to, comply with, accede to, agree to, consent to, go along with, grant, permit, allow, sanction, warrant.

Antonyms: RESIST; WITHSTAND; DEFY.

yoke *noun* **1** *the yoke of the oxen* harness, collar, coupling. **2** *under the yoke of the tyrant* oppression, tyranny, enslavement, slavery, servitude, bondage, thrall. **3** *the yoke of marriage* tie, link, bond.

yoke *verb* **1** *yoke the oxen* harness, hitch up, couple, join up. **2** *yoked in marriage* join, unite, link, bond, tie.

yokel *noun* rustic, countryman, countrywoman, peasant, country bumpkin, provincial; *inf.* country cousin; hayseed, hillbilly.

young *adjective* **1** *young people* youthful, juvenile, junior, adolescent, in the springtime of life, in one's salad days. **2** *young industries* new, recent, undeveloped, fledgling, in the making.

Antonyms: OLD; ELDERLY; MATURE.

young *noun bear young* offspring, progeny, family, issue; little ones, babies; litter, brood.

youngster *noun* young adult/person, youth, juvenile, teenager, adolescent, young hopeful; lad, boy, young man/woman, lass, girl; *inf.* kid, shaver, young 'un.

youth *noun* **1** *in their youth they were beautiful* young days, early years, teens; early life, adolescence; boyhood, girlhood. **2** *the coach was a good friend to the youths* boy, girl, young man/woman/lady, lad, youngster, juvenile, teenager, adolescent; *inf.* kid. **3** *the youth of today* young people, young, younger generation; *inf.* kids.

Antonyms: AGE; old age.

youthful *adjective* **1** *youthful dancers* young, juvenile. **2** *looking very youthful* fresh-faced, young-looking. **3** *he is a youthful sixty-five* young, active, vigorous, spry, sprightly.

Antonyms: OLD; ELDERLY; DODDERING.

---

youthful
adolescent, callow, immature, juvenile, puerile
Everyone wants to look **youthful**, an adjective that means possessing, or appearing to

possess, the qualities associated with youth (*a youthful enthusiasm for the job*). But no one wants to be called **immature**, which means childish or emotionally underdeveloped and usually pertains to behavior and attitudes rather than to physical appearance (*still immature despite the fact that he was almost thirty*). **Juvenile** suggests immaturity of mind or body and is applied especially to things that are designed for boys and girls in their early teens (*juvenile books*), while **adolescent** applies to the period between puberty and maturity and suggests the physical awkwardness and emotional instability associated with the teenage years (*an adolescent response to criticism*). Young men in particular are often described as **callow**, which means immature in terms of experience (*a callow youth who had never lived away from his family*). Of all these words, **puerile** is probably the most insulting, because it is so often used to describe adults who display the immature behavior of a child (*a puerile piece of writing; a puerile revolt against his aging parents*).

Z

zany *adjective a zany sense of humor | a zany personality* eccentric, peculiar, odd, ridiculous, absurd, comic, clownish, madcap, funny, amusing; *inf.* weird, wacky, daft, screwy, kooky.
Antonyms: ORDINARY; RUN-OF-THE-MILL; CONVENTIONAL.

zap *verb* **1** *zap the fly with a swatter* kill, slay, murder, put to death, liquidate, destroy; *inf.* do in, knock off. **2** *zap the ball over the net* hit, strike, slap; *inf.* whack. **3** *zap the opposing team* defeat, beat, conquer, vanquish, trounce, rout, overcome, overpower, overthrow, crush.

zeal *noun* **1** *his zeal for life/hockey* ardor, fervor, fervency, passion, fire, devotion, vehemence, intensity, enthusiasm, eagerness, keenness, earnestness, vigor, energy, verve, gusto, zest, fanaticism; *inf.* zing. **2** *put off by their religious/ political zeal* zealotry, fanaticism, extremism. *See* ZEALOTRY.
Antonyms: APATHY; INDIFFERENCE.

zealot *noun a religious/political zealot* enthusiast, fanatic, extremist, radical, militant, bigot; *inf.* fiend.

---

zealot
bigot, enthusiast, extremist, fanatic

An **enthusiast** displays an intense and eager interest in something (*a sky-diving enthusiast*). A **fanatic** is not only intense and eager but possibly irrational in his or her enthusiasm; *fanatic* suggests extreme devotion and a willingness to go to any length to maintain or carry out one's beliefs (*a fly-fishing fanatic who hired a helicopter to reach his favorite stream*). A **zealot** exhibits not only extreme devotion but vehement activity in support of a cause or goal (*a feminist zealot who spent most of her time campaigning for women's rights*). An **extremist** is a supporter of extreme doctrines or practices, particularly in a political context (*a paramilitary extremist who anticipated the overthrow of the government*). But it is the **bigot** who causes the most trouble, exhibiting obstinate and often blind devotion to his or her beliefs and opinions. In contrast to *fanatic* and *zealot*, the term *bigot* implies intolerance and contempt for those who do not agree (*a bigot who could not accept his daughter's decision to marry outside her religion*).

---

zealotry *noun religious/political zealotry* zeal, fanaticism, extremism, single-mindedness, radicalism, militancy, dogmatism, bigotry.

zealous *adjective zealous athletes/fans* ardent, fervent, fervid, passionate, impassioned, devoted, intense, enthusiastic, eager, keen, earnest, vigorous, energetic, zestful, fanatical.
Antonyms: APATHETIC; INDIFFERENT.

zenith *noun zenith of his achievement/powers* highest/high point, crowning point, height, top, acme, peak, pinnacle, climax, prime, meridian, apex, apogee, vertex.
Antonyms: NADIR; BOTTOM.

zero *noun* **1** *a series of zeros* naught, nothing, cipher. **2** *win absolutely zero* nothing, naught, nil; *inf.* zilch, zippo. **3** *economic growth is at zero* lowest point, nadir, rock bottom.

zero *verb* **zero in on** *his talk zeroed in on the economy* focus on, center on, concentrate on, home in on, pinpoint.

zero hour *noun* appointed hour/time, crucial/ vital/crisis moment, moment of truth.

zest *noun* **1** *approach the project with zest* relish, gusto, enthusiasm, eagerness, zeal, vigor, liveliness, energy, enjoyment, joy, delectation, appetite; *inf.* zing, oomph. **2** *add zest to the dish/ occasion* piquancy, spice, pungency, flavor, relish, tang, savor, interest; *inf.* kick.
Antonyms: APATHY; INDIFFERENCE; DISTASTE.

zing *noun* zest, enthusiasm, eagerness, gusto, zeal, life, liveliness, spirit, animation, vitality, vivacity, sparkle, vigor, pep, energy, vim, élan, dash, brio; *inf.* go, oomph, zip, pizzazz.

zip *noun a bit of zip to your playing* zest, enthusiasm, eagerness, gusto, life, liveliness, spirit, animation, sparkle, pep, élan, brio; *inf.* oomph, zing. *See* ZING.

zip *verb he zipped off before I could speak* rush, dash, pelt, race, tear, shoot, fly, scurry, speed, hurry, hasten; *inf.* whiz, zoom.

zone *noun* area, sector, section, belt, district, region, province.

zoom *verb* **1** *planes/flies zooming around* fly, buzz. **2** *they zoomed off before he could question them* rush, dash, pelt, race, tear, shoot, fly, scurry, speed, hurry, hasten; *inf.* whiz, zip.

Writer's Toolkit

Writer's Toolkit

Punctuation Guide

Punctuation is an essential element of good writing because it makes the author's meaning clear to the reader. Although precise punctuation styles may vary somewhat among published sources, there are a number of fundamental principles worthy of consideration. Discussed below are the punctuation marks used in English:

comma
semicolon
colon
period
question mark
exclamation point
apostrophe
quotation marks
parentheses
dash
hyphen

Comma

The comma is the most frequently used mark of punctuation in the English language. It signals to the reader a pause, which generally clarifies the author's meaning, and establishes a sensible order to the elements of written language. Among the most typical functions of the comma are the following:

1. It can separate the clauses of a compound sentence when there are two independent clauses joined by a conjunction, especially when the clauses are not very short:

    It never occurred to me to look in the attic, and I'm sure it didn't occur to Rachel either.

    The Nelsons wanted to see the Grand Canyon at sunrise, but they overslept that morning.

2. It can separate the clauses of a compound sentence when there is a series of independent clauses, the last two of which are joined by a conjunction:

    The bus ride to the campsite was very uncomfortable, the cabins were not ready for us when we got there, the cook had forgotten to start dinner, and the rain was torrential.

3. It is used to precede or set off, and therefore indicate, a nonrestrictive dependent clause (a clause that could be omitted without changing the meaning of the main clause):

    I read her autobiography, which was published last July.

    They showed up at midnight, after most of the guests had gone home.

    The coffee, which is freshly brewed, is in the kitchen.

4. It can follow an introductory phrase:

    Having enjoyed the movie so much, he agreed to see it again.

    Born and raised in Paris, she had never lost her French accent.

    In the beginning, they had very little money to invest.

5. It can set off words used in direct address:

    Listen, people, you have no choice in the matter.

    Yes, Mrs. Greene, I will be happy to feed your cat.

6. The comma can separate two or more coordinate adjectives (adjectives that could otherwise be joined with *and*) that modify one noun:

   The cruise turned out to be the most entertaining, fun, and relaxing vacation I've ever had.

   The horse was tall, lean, and sleek.

   Note that cumulative adjectives (those not able to be joined with *and*) are not separated by a comma:

   She wore bright yellow rubber boots.

7. Use a comma to separate three or more items in a series or list:

   Charlie, Melissa, Stan, and Mark will be this year's soloists in the spring concert.

   We need furniture, toys, clothes, books, tools, housewares, and other useful merchandise for the benefit auction.

   Note that the comma between the last two items in a series is sometimes omitted in less precise style:

   The most popular foods served in the cafeteria are pizza, hamburgers and nachos.

8. Use a comma to separate and set off the elements in an address or other geographical designation:

   My new house is at 1657 Nighthawk Circle, South Kingsbury, Michigan.

   We arrived in Pamplona, Spain, on Thursday.

9. Use a comma to set off direct quotations (note the placement or absence of commas with other punctuation):

   "Kim forgot her gloves," he said, "but we have a pair she can borrow."

   There was a long silence before Jack blurted out, "This must be the world's ugliest painting."

   "What are you talking about?" she asked in a puzzled manner.

   "Happy New Year!" everyone shouted.

10. A comma is used to set off titles after a person's name:

    Katherine Bentley, M.D.

    Steven Wells, Esq., is the addressee.

Semicolon

The semicolon has two basic functions:

1. It can separate two main clauses, particularly when these clauses are of equal importance:

   The crowds gathered outside the museum hours before the doors were opened; this was one exhibit no one wanted to miss.

   She always complained when her relatives stayed for the weekend; even so, she usually was a little sad when they left.

2. It can be used as a comma is used to separate such elements as clauses or items in a series or list, particularly when one or more of the elements already includes a comma:

   The path took us through the deep, dark woods; across a small meadow; into a cold, wet cave; and up a hillside overlooking the lake.

   Listed for sale in the ad were two bicycles; a battery-powered, leaf-mulching lawn mower; and a maple bookcase.

Colon

The colon has five basic functions:

1. It can introduce something, especially a list of items:

   In the basket were three pieces of mail: a postcard, a catalog, and a wedding invitation.

   Students should have the following items: backpack, loose-leaf notebook, pens and pencils, pencil sharpener, and ruler.

2. It can separate two clauses in a sentence when the second clause is being used to explain or illustrate the first clause:

   We finally understood why she would never go sailing with us: she had a deep fear of the water.

   Most of the dogs in our neighborhood are quite large: two of them are St. Bernards.

   3. It can introduce a statement or a quotation:

   His parents say the most important rule is this: Always tell the truth.

   We repeated the final words of his poem: "And such is the plight of fools like me."

4. It can be used to follow the greeting in a formal or business letter:

   Dear Ms. Daniels:

   Dear Sir or Madam:

5. In the U.S., use a colon to separate minutes from hours, and seconds from minutes, in showing time of day and measured length of time:

   Please be at the restaurant before 6:45.

   Her best running time so far has been 00:12:35.

Period

The period has two basic functions:

1. It is used to mark the end of a sentence:

   It was reported that there is a shortage of nurses at the hospital. Several of the patients have expressed concern about this problem.

2. It is often used at the end of an abbreviation:

   On Fri., Sept. 12, Dr. Brophy noted that the patient's weight was 168 lbs. and that his height was 6 ft. 2 in. (Note that another period is not added to the end of the sentence when the last word is an abbreviation.)

Question Mark and Exclamation Point

The only sentences that do not end in a period are those that end in either a question mark or an exclamation point.

Question marks are used to mark the end of a sentence that asks a direct question (generally, a question that expects an answer):

Is there any reason for us to bring more than a few dollars?

Who is your science teacher?

Exclamation points are used to mark the end of a sentence that expresses a strong feeling, typically surprise, joy, or anger:

I want you to leave and never come back!

What a beautiful view this is!

Apostrophe

The apostrophe has two basic functions:

1. It is used to show where a letter or letters are missing in a contraction:

   The directions are cont'd [continued] on the next page.

   We've [we have] decided that if she can't [cannot] go, then we aren't [are not] going either.

2. It can be used to show possession:

   a. The possessive of a singular noun or an irregular plural noun is created by adding an apostrophe and an s:

   the pilot's uniform

   Mrs. Mendoza's house

   a tomato's bright red color

   the oxen's yoke

   b. The possessive of a regular plural noun is created by adding just an apostrophe:

   the pilots' uniforms [referring to more than one pilot]

   the Mendozas' house [referring to the Mendoza family]

   the tomatoes' bright red color [referring to more than one tomato]

Quotation Marks

Quotation marks have two basic functions:

1. They are used to set off direct quotations (an exact rendering of someone's spoken or written words):

   "I think the new library is wonderful," she remarked to David.

   We were somewhat lost, so we asked, "Are we anywhere near the art gallery?"

   In his letter he had written, "The nights here are quiet and starry. It seems like a hundred years since I've been wakened by the noise of city traffic and squabbling neighbors."

   Note that indirect quotes (which often are preceded by that, if, or whether) are not set off by quotation marks:

   He told me that he went to school in Boston.

   We asked if we could still get tickets to the game.

2. They can be used to set off words or phrases that have specific technical usage, or to set off meanings of words, or to indicate words that are being used in a special way in a sentence:

   The part of the flower that bears the pollen is the "stamen."

   When I said "plain," I meant "flat land," not "ordinary."

   Oddly enough, in the theater, the statement "break a leg" is meant as an expression of good luck.

   What you call "hoagies," we call "grinders" or "submarine sandwiches."

   He will never be a responsible adult until he outgrows his "Peter Pan" behavior.

Note that sometimes single quotation marks (the 'stamen.'), rather than double quotation marks as above (the "stamen."), may be used to set off words or phrases. What is most important is to be consistent in such usage.

Parentheses

Parentheses are used, in pairs, to enclose information that gives extra detail or explanation to the regular text. Parentheses are used in two basic ways:

1. They can separate a word or words in a sentence from the rest of the sentence:

   On our way to school, we walk past the Turner Farm (the oldest dairy farm in town) and watch the cows being fed.

   The stores were filled with holiday shoppers (even more so than last year). (Note that the period goes outside the parentheses, because the words in the parentheses are only part of the sentence.)

2. They can form a separate complete sentence:

   Please bring a dessert to the dinner party. (It can be something very simple.) I look forward to seeing you there. (Note that the period goes inside the parentheses, because the words in the parentheses are a complete and independent sentence.)

Dash

A dash is used most commonly to replace the usage of parentheses within sentences. If the information being set off is in the middle of the sentence, a pair of dashes is used; if it is at the end of the sentence, just one dash is used:

   On our way to school, we walk past the Turner Farm—the oldest dairy farm in town—and watch the cows being fed.

   The stores were filled with holiday shoppers—even more so than last year.

Hyphen

A hyphen has three basic functions:

1. It can join two or more words to make a compound, especially when so doing makes the meaning more clear to the reader:

   We met to discuss long-range planning.

   There were six four-month-old piglets at the fair.

   That old stove was quite a coal-burner.

2. It can replace the word "to" when a span or range of data is given. This kind of hyphen is sometimes also called a dash:

   John Adams was president of the United States 1797-1801.

   Today we will look for proper nouns in the L-N section of the dictionary.

   The ideal weight for that breed of dog would be 75-85 pounds.

3. It can indicate a word break at the end of a line. The break must always be between syllables:

   It is important for any writer to know that there are numerous punctuation principles that are considered standard and proper, but there is also flexibility regarding acceptable punctuation. Having learned the basic "rules" of good punctuation, the writer will be able to adopt a specific and consistent style of punctuation that best suits the material he or she is writing.

Usage Guide

Even the best writers are sometimes troubled by questions of correct usage. A guide to some of the most common questions is provided below, with discussion of the following topics:

singular or plural

1. When subject and complement are different in number (i.e., one is singular, the other plural), the verb normally agrees with the subject, e.g.,

   (Plural subject)
   Their wages were a mere pittance.

   Liqueur chocolates are our specialty.

(The Biblical *The wages of sin is death* reflects an obsolete idiom in which wages took a singular verb.)

   (Singular subject)
   What we need is customers.

   Our specialty is liqueur chocolates.

2. A plural word or phrase used as a name, title, or quotation counts as singular, e.g.,

   Sons and Lovers *has always been one of Lawrence's most popular novels.*

3. A singular phrase (such as a prepositional phrase following the subject) that happens to end with a plural word should nevertheless be followed by a singular verb, e.g.,

   Everyone except the French wants (not *want*) *Britain to join.*

   One in six has (not *have*) *this problem.*

See also -*ics, s plural or singular.*

-s plural or singular

Some nouns, though they have the plural ending -s, are nevertheless usually treated as singular, taking singular verbs and pronouns referring back to them.

1. *News*

2. Diseases:

measles	*rickets*
mumps	*shingles*

Measles and *rickets* can also be treated as ordinary plural nouns.

3. Games:

billiards	*craps*
dominoes	*quoits*
checkers	*darts*

4. Countries:

the Bahamas	*the Netherlands*
the Philippines	*the United States*

These are treated as singular when considered as a unit, which they commonly are in a political context, or when the complement is singular, e.g.,

> *The Philippines* is *a predominantly agricultural country.*

> *The United States* has *withdrawn its ambassador.*

The Bahamas and *the Philippines* are also the geographical names of the groups of islands that the two nations comprise, and in this use can be treated as plurals, e.g.,

> *The Bahamas were settled by British subjects.*

See also *-ics.*

comparison of adjectives and adverbs

The two ways of forming the comparative and superlative of adjectives and adverbs are:

(*a*) Addition of suffixes *-er* and *-est*. Monosyllabic adjectives and adverbs almost always require these suffixes, e.g., *big* (*bigger, biggest*), *soon* (*sooner, soonest*), and normally so do many adjectives of two syllables, e.g., *narrow* (*narrower, narrowest*), *silly* (*sillier, silliest*).

(*b*) Use of adverbs *more* and *most*. These are used with adjectives of three syllables or more (e.g., *difficult, memorable*), participles (e.g., *bored, boring*), many adjectives of two syllables (e.g., *afraid, awful, childish, harmless, static*), and adverbs ending in *-ly* (e.g., *highly, slowly*).

Adjectives with two syllables sometimes use suffixes and sometimes use adverbs. There are many that never take the suffixes, e.g.,

antique	*bizarre*
breathless	*constant*
futile	*steadfast*

There is also a large class that is acceptable with either, e.g.,

clever	*pleasant*
handsome	*tranquil*
solemn	*cruel*
common	*polite*

The choice is largely a matter of preference.

nouns ending in -*ics*

Nouns ending in -*ics* denoting subjects or disciplines are sometimes treated as singular and sometimes as plural. Examples are:

apologetics	*mechanics*
genetics	*politics*
optics	*economics*
classics (as a study)	*metaphysics*
linguistics	*statistics*
phonetics	*electronics*
mathematics	*obstetrics*
physics	*tactics*
dynamics	*ethics*

When used strictly as the name of a discipline they are treated as singular:

Psychometrics is *unable to investigate the nature of intelligence.*

So also when the complement is singular:

Mathematics is *his strong point.*

When used more loosely, to denote a manifestation of qualities, often accompanied by a possessive, they are treated as plural:

His politics were *a mixture of fear, greed, and envy.*

I don't understand the mathematics of it, which are *complicated.*

The acoustics in this hall are *dreadful.*

So also when they denote a set of activities or pattern of behavior, as commonly with words like:

acrobatics	*athletics*
dramatics	*gymnastics*
heroics	*hysterics*

E.g., *The mental gymnastics required to believe this* are *beyond me.*

group possessive

The group possessive is the construction by which the ending -'s of the possessive case can be added to the last word of a noun phrase, which is regarded as a single unit, e.g.,

The king of Spain's daughter

John and Mary's baby

Somebody else's umbrella

A quarter of an hour's drive

Expressions like these are natural and acceptable.

may or *might*

There is sometimes confusion about whether to use *may* or *might* with the perfect tense when referring to a past event, e.g., *He may have done* or *He might have done*.

1. If uncertainty about the action or state denoted by the perfect remains, i.e., at the time of speaking or writing the truth of the event is still unknown, then either *may* or *might* is acceptable:

   As they all wore so many different clothes of identically the same kind . . . there may *have been several more or several less.*

   For all we knew our complaint went unanswered, although of course they might *have tried to call us while we were out of town.*

2. If there is no longer uncertainty about the event, or the matter was never put to the test, and therefore the event did not in fact occur, use *might*:

   If that had come ten days ago my whole life might *have been different.*

   You should not have let him come home alone; he might *have gotten lost.*

It is a common error to use *may* instead of *might* in these circumstances:

   If they had not invaded, then eventually we may *have agreed to give them aid.*

   I am grateful for his intervention, without which they may *have remained in the refugee camp indefinitely.*

   Schoenberg may *never have gone atonal but for the breakup of his marriage.*

In each of these sentences *might* should be substituted for *may*.

I or *me*, *we* or *us*, etc.

There is often confusion about which case of a personal pronoun to use when the pronoun stands alone or follows the verb *to be*.

1. When the personal pronoun stands alone, as when it forms the answer to a question, strictly formal usage requires it to have the case it would have if the verb were supplied:

   Who called him?—I (in full, *I called him* or *I did*).

   Which of you did he approach?—Me (in full, *he approached me*).

Informal usage permits the objective case in both kinds of sentence, but this is not acceptable in formal style. However, the subjective case often sounds stilted. One can avoid the problem by providing a verb, e.g.,

   Who likes cooking?—I do.

   Who can cook?—I can.

   Who is here?—I am.

2. When a personal pronoun follows *it is, it was, it may be, it could have been*, etc., formal usage requires the subjective case:

   Nobody could suspect that it was *she.*

   We are given no clues as to what it must have felt like to be he.

Informal usage favors the objective case (not acceptable in formal style):

   I thought it might have been him *at the door.*

   Don't tell me it's them *again!*

When *who* or *whom* follows, the subjective case is obligatory in formal usage and quite usual informally:

> *It was* I *who painted that sign.*

The informal use of the objective case often sounds incorrect:

> *It was* her *who would get into trouble.*

In constructions that have the form *I am* + noun or noun phrase + *who*, the verb following *who* agrees with the noun (the antecedent of *who*) in number (singular or plural):

> *I am the sort of person who* likes *peace and quiet.*

> *You are the fourth of my colleagues who's told me that* ('s = *has*, agreeing with *the fourth*).

we (with phrase following)

Expressions consisting of *we* or *us* followed by a qualifying word or phrase, e.g., *we Americans, us Americans,* are often misused with the wrong case of the first person plural pronoun. In fact the rules are exactly the same as for *we* or *us* standing alone.

If the expression is the subject, *we* should be used:

> (Correct)
> *Not always laughing as heartily as* we Americans *are supposed to do.*

> (Incorrect)
> *We all make mistakes, even* us judges (substitute *we judges*).

If the expression is the object or the complement of a preposition, *us* should be used:

> (Correct)
> *To* us Americans, *personal liberty is a vital principle.*

> (Incorrect)
> *The president said some nice things about* we reporters *in the press corps* (substitute *us reporters*).

I who, you who, etc.

The verb following a personal pronoun (*I, you, he,* etc.) + *who* should be the same as what would be used with the pronoun as a subject:

> *I, who* have *no savings to speak of, had to pay for the work.*

> *They made me, who* have *no savings at all, pay for the work* (not *who has*).

When *it is* (*it was,* etc.) precedes *I who,* etc., the same rule applies: the verb agrees with the personal pronoun:

> *It's I who* have *done it.*

> *It could have been we who* were *mistaken.*

you and I or *you and me*

When a personal pronoun is linked by *and* or *or* to a noun or another pronoun, there is often confusion about which case to put the pronoun in. In fact the rule is exactly as it would be for the pronoun standing alone.

1. If the two words linked by *and* or *or* constitute the subject, the pronoun should be in the subjective case, e.g.,

> *Only* she *and her mother cared for the old house.*

That's what we would do, that is, John and I would.

Who could go?—Either you or he.

The use of the objective case is quite common in informal speech, but it is nonstandard, e.g.,

Perhaps only her *and Mrs. Natwick had stuck to the christened name.*

That's how we look at it, me *and Martha.*

Either Mary had to leave or me.

2. If the two words linked by *and* or *or* constitute the object of the verb, or the complement of a preposition, the objective case should be used:

The afternoon would suit her *and John better.*

It was time for Kenneth and me *to go down to the living room.*

The use of the subjective case is very common informally. It probably arises from an exaggerated fear of the error indicated under 1 above. It remains, however, nonstandard, e.g.,

It was this that set Charles and I *talking of old times.*

Why is it that people like you and I *are so unpopular?*

Between you and I . . .

This last expression is very commonly heard. *Between you and me* should always be substituted.

collective nouns

Collective nouns are singular words that denote many individuals, e.g., *audience, government, orchestra, the clergy, the public.*

It is normal for collective nouns, being singular, to be followed by singular verbs and pronouns (*is, has, consists,* and *it* in the examples below):

The government is *determined to beat inflation, as* it *has* promised.

Their family is *huge:* it consists *of five boys and three girls.*

The bourgeoisie is *despised for not being proletarian.*

The singular verb and pronouns are preferable unless the collective is clearly and unmistakably used to refer to separate individuals rather than to a united body, e.g.,

The cabinet has *made* its *decision.*

but

The cabinet are *sitting at* their *places around the table with the president.*

The singular should always be used if the collective noun is qualified by a singular word like *this, that, every,* etc.:

This family is *divided.*

Every team has its *chance to win.*

none (pronoun)

The pronoun *none* can be followed either by singular verb and singular pronouns, or by plural ones. Either is acceptable, although the plural tends to be more common.

Singular: *None of them* was *allowed to forget for a moment.*

Plural: *None of the orchestras ever* play *there.*

None of the authors expected their *books to become best-sellers.*

as

In the following sentences, formal usage requires the subjective case (*I, he, she, we, they*) on the assumption that the pronoun would be the subject if a verb were supplied:

You are just as intelligent as he (in full, *as he is*).

He . . . might not have heard the song so often as I (in full, *as I had*).

Informal usage permits *You are just as intelligent as* him.

Formal English uses the objective case (*me, him, her, us, them*) only when the pronoun would be the object if a verb were supplied:

I thought you preferred John to Mary, but I see that you like her just as much as him (which means *. . . just as much as you like him*).

Easily Confused Words

The following words are often used wrongly or carelessly, or confused with other similar words.

adverse/averse

Adverse means "unfavorable, opposed," and is usually applied to situations and events, not people, e.g., *The new drug has adverse side effects.* **Averse** is related in origin and also has the sense of "opposition," but its use is best restricted to describing a person's attitude, e.g., *I would not be averse to the prospect of traveling with you.*

affect/effect

Both these words are both verbs and nouns, but only **effect** is common as a noun, usually meaning "a result, consequence, impression, etc.," e.g., *My father's strictness had no effect on my desire to learn.* As verbs they are used differently. **Affect** means "to produce an effect upon," e.g., *Smoking during pregnancy can affect a baby's development.* **Effect** means "to bring about," e.g., *Alterations were effected with some sympathy for the existing fabric.*

aggravate

This word is commonly used in informal contexts to mean "to annoy or exasperate," rather than "to make worse or more serious"; this is considered incorrect by many people. An example of correct usage is *The psychological stress aggravates the horse's physical stress.*

alibi

The chief meaning of this word is "evidence that when something took place one was elsewhere," e.g., *He has no alibi for Wednesday afternoon.* It is also sometimes used informally to mean "an excuse, pretext, or justification"; this is considered incorrect by many people.

all right/alright

Although found widely, **alright** remains nonstandard, even where standard spelling is somewhat cumbersome, e.g., *I wanted to make sure it was all all right.*

all together/altogether

These variants are used in different contexts. **All together** means "all at once" or "all in one place or in one group," e.g., *They came all together; We managed to get three bedrooms all together* (i.e., near each other). **Altogether** means "in total," e.g., *The hotel has twenty rooms altogether.*

alternate/alternative

In British English **alternate** means "every other," e.g., *There will be a dance on alternate Saturdays,* whereas **alternative** means "available as another choice," e.g., *an alternative route.* In American usage, however, **alternate** can be used to mean "available as another choice".

altogether see all together.

amend/emend

Amend, meaning "to make improvements or corrections in," is often confused with **emend,** a more technical word used in the context of textual correction. Examples of each are: *The Constitution was amended to limit presidential terms of office; The poems have been collected, arranged, and emended.*

anticipate

Anticipate in the sense "expect, foresee" is well-established in informal use (e.g., *He anticipated a restless night*), but is regarded as incorrect by some people. The formal sense, "deal with or use before the proper time," is illustrated by the sentence *The specialist would find that the thesis he had been planning had already been anticipated.*

anyone/any one

Anyone is written as two words only to emphasize a numerical sense, e.g., *Any one of us can do it.* Otherwise it is written as one word (e.g., *Anyone who wants to can come*).

averse see adverse.

baluster/banister

A **baluster** is usually part of a balustrade, or decorative railing, whereas a **banister** supports the handrail of a staircase. **Banister** can also mean the handrail with its supports.

born/borne

Born is used with reference to birth (e.g., *was born in Detroit*). **Borne**, meaning "carried," is used in the expression *borne by* followed by the name of the mother (e.g., *was borne by Mary*), as well as in other senses (e.g., *a litter borne by four slaves*).

censor/censure

Both these words are both verbs and nouns, but **censor** is used to mean "to cut unacceptable parts out of a book, movie, etc." or "a person who does this," while **censure** means "to criticize harshly" or "harsh criticism."

chronic

This word is often used to mean "habitual, inveterate," e.g., *a chronic liar.* This used is considered to be incorrect by some people. The precise meaning of this word is "persisting for a long time" and it is used chiefly of illnesses or other problems, e.g., *Over one million people in the US have chronic bronchitis.*

complacent/complaisant

Complacent means "smugly self-satisfied," e.g., *After four consecutive championships the team became complacent,* while **complaisant**, a much rarer word, means "deferential, willing to please," e.g., in *When released from the kennel, the dogs are very peaceful and complaisant.*

compose/comprise

Both these words can be used to mean "to constitute or make up" but **compose** is preferred in this sense, e.g., *Citizens act as witnesses in the courts and finally may compose the jury.* **Comprise** is correctly used to mean " to be composed of, consist of," e.g., *Each crew comprises a commander, a gunner, and a driver.*

continual/continuous

Continual is used of something that happens very frequently, e.g., *There were continual interruptions,"* whereas **continuous** is used of something that happens without pause, e.g., *There was a dull, continuous background noise.*

crucial

Crucial is used in formal contexts to mean "decisive, critical,", e.g., *The first five years of a child's life are crucial.* Its use to mean "very important," as in *It is crucial not to forget your passport,* should be restricted to informal contexts.

decimate

Historically, the meaning of the word **decimate** is "kill one in every ten of (a group of people)." This sense has been superseded by the later, more general sense "kill or destroy (a large proportion of)," as in *the plague has decimated the population.*

definite/definitive

Definitive in the sense "(of an answer, verdict, etc.) decisive, unconditional, final" is sometimes confused with **definite**. However, **definite** does not have the connotations of authority: *a definite no* is simply a firm refusal, whereas *a definitive no* is an authoritative judgment or decision that something is not the case.

deprecate/depreciate

Deprecate means "to express disapproval of, to deplore," e.g., *The establishment magazines began by deprecating the film's attitude towards terrorism,* while **depreciate** (apart from its financial senses) means "to disparage or belittle," e.g., *He was depreciating his own skills out of a strong sense of humility.*

dilemma

This word should be used with regard to situations in which a difficult choice has to be made between undesirable alternatives, as in *You see his dilemma? Whatever he did next, his wife would find out, divorce him, and get custody of the child.* Its use to mean simply "a difficult situation" is considered incorrect by some people.

disinterested/uninterested

Disinterested is sometimes used in informal contexts to mean "not interested or uninterested," but this is widely regarded as incorrect. The proper meaning is "impartial," e.g., *I for one am making a disinterested search for information.* The use of the noun **disinterest** to mean "a lack of interest" is also objected to, but it is rarely used in any other sense.

effect see affect.

emend see amend.

enormity

This word is commonly used to mean "great size," e.g., *wilting under the enormity of the work,* but this is regarded as incorrect by some people. The original and preferred meaning is "extreme wickedness," as in *the enormity of the crime.*

exceptionable/exceptional

Exceptionable means "open to objection," e.g., *There was nothing exceptionable in her behavior,* and is usually found in negative contexts. It is sometimes confused with the much commoner word **exceptional** meaning "unusual, outstanding."

feasible

The correct meaning of this word is "practicable" or "possible," e.g., *Walking at night was not feasible without the aid of a flashlight.* It should not be used to mean "likely" or "probable."

flammable see inflammable.

flaunt/flout

These words are often confused because both suggest an element of arrogance or showing off. However, **flaunt** means "to display ostentatiously," e.g., *He liked to flaunt his wealth,* while **flout** means "to express contempt for or disobey (laws, convention, etc.)," e.g., *The fine is too low for those who flout the law continuously.*

-fuls/-s full

The combining form **-ful** is used to form nouns meaning "the amount needed to fill," e.g., *cupful, spoonful.* The plural form of such words is -s, (*cupfuls, spoonfuls,* etc.). *Three cups full* would denote the individual cups rather than a quantity regarded in terms of a cup used as a measure, and would be used in contexts such as *They brought us three cups full of water.*

fulsome

This word means "excessive, cloying, or insincere," but is often imprecisely used to mean "generous," as in the phrase *fulsome praise.*

hoi polloi

This phrase is usually preceded by *the,* e.g., *The hoi polloi grew weary and sat on the floor.* Strictly speaking, the *the* is unnecessary because *hoi* means "the" (in Greek).

hopefully

Some purists object to the use of this word as a sentence modifier, with the meaning "it is to be hoped," e.g., *Hopefully, all the details will be in this evening's newspapers.* However, this usage is not only very common but is long-established in English and in keeping with similar uses of other sentence-modifying adverbs such as *regrettably* and *frankly.*

impedance/impediment

Impedance is a specialized electrical term, while **impediment** is an everyday term meaning "a hindrance or obstruction,", e.g., *He would have to write by hand but that was no impediment.*

imply see infer.

inchoate

This word means "just begun or rudimentary, undeveloped," e.g., *All was as yet in an inchoate state,* but it is often used incorrectly to mean "chaotic" or "incoherent." The *ch* is pronounced hard, like *k.*

incredible/incredulous

The adjective **incredible** means "unbelievable" or "not convincing" and can be applied to a situation, statement, policy, or threat to a person, e.g., *I find this testimony incredible.* **Incredulous** means "disinclined to believe; skeptical" and is usually applied to a person's attitude, e.g., *You shouldn't wonder that I'm incredulous after all your lies.*

infer/imply

Infer should be used to mean "to deduce or conclude," as in *We can infer from these studies that . . . .* Its use to mean "to imply or suggest" is widely considered incorrect.

inflammable/flammable/nonflammable

Both **inflammable** and **flammable** mean "easily set on fire or excited." The opposite is **nonflammable.** Where there is a danger of **inflammable** being understood to mean the opposite, i.e., "not easily set on fire," **flammable** should be used to avoid confusion.

ingenious/ingenuous

These words are sometimes confused. **Ingenious** means "clever, skillful, or resourceful," e.g., *an ingenious device,* while **ingenuous** means "artless" or "frank," e.g., *charmed by the ingenuous honesty of the child.*

intense/intensive

Intense is sometimes wrongly used instead of **intensive** to describe a course of study that covers a large amount of material in a short space of time.

interment/internment

Interment means "the burial of a corpse," while **internment** means "the confining of a prisoner, etc."

irregardless see regardless.

inveigh/inveigle

Inveigh (usually **inveigh against**) means "to speak or write about (something) with great hostility," while **inveigle** means "to persuade (someone) to do something by means of deception or flattery."

jibe/jive

Jibe has several meanings; one is "to be in accord; to agree." A common error is to use **jive** for this sense, but **jive** as a verb really means "to taunt or sneer at," "to talk nonsense," or "to dance, especially to swing, jazz, or rock and roll music."

latter

This word means "the second-mentioned of two." Its use to mean "the last-mentioned of three or more" is common, but considered incorrect by some people since **latter** means "later" rather than "latest." *Last* or *last-mentioned* is to be preferred where three or more things are involved.

laudable/laudatory

These words are sometimes confused. **Laudable** is the more common and means "commendable" or "praiseworthy," e.g., *The foundation pursued a laudable charitable program that involved the foundation and maintenance of schools and hospitals.* **Laudatory** means "expressing praise," e.g., *The proposed legislation enjoyed a good reception—including a laudatory front page endorsement from the city's only daily newspaper.*

lay/lie

In standard English **lay** is a transitive verb and **lie** intransitive. The intransitive use of **lay,** as in *It gave him the opportunity of laying on the grass at lunchtime,* is best avoided. Similarly, the transitive use of **lie,** as in *Lie it on the table* is also avoided by careful speakers and writers. In the first example *laying* should be *lying* and in the second *lie* should be *lay.* These two verbs are often confused owing to their close similarity in form, including the fact that the past tense of *lie* is *lay*. A mnemonic using the traditional child's prayer *Now I lay me down to sleep . . .* serves as a reminder that *lay* is transitive (with direct object *me*).

leading question
This phrase means "a question that prompts the answer wanted" and was originally a legal term. In weakened use it tends to mean "an awkward, pointed, or loaded question," or even "principal question," but these usages are considered incorrect by some people.

liable
This word is commonly used with *to* to mean "likely to do something undesirable," e.g., *Without his glasses he's liable to smash into a tree.* This usage is considered incorrect by some people. Correct usage is exemplified by the sentence *You could be liable for a heavy fine if you are at fault.*

lie see **lay.**

like
The use of **like** as a conjunction meaning "as" or "as if," e.g., *I don't have a wealthy set of in-laws like you do; They sit up like they're begging for food,* is considered incorrect by some people.

locate
In formal English it is not acceptable to use **locate** to mean merely "find," e.g., *It drives him out of his mind when he can't locate something.* **Locate** is used more precisely to mean "discover the exact place or position of," e.g., *One club member was proposing to use an echo sounder to help locate fish in the lake.*

luxuriant/luxurious
These words are sometimes confused. **Luxuriant** means "lush, profuse, or prolific," e.g., *forests of dark luxuriant foliage; luxuriant black eyelashes.* **Luxurious**, a much commoner word, means "supplied with luxuries, extremely comfortable," e.g., *a luxurious hotel.*

masterful/masterly
These words overlap in meaning and are sometimes confused. Apart from meaning "domineering," **masterful** also means "masterly" or "very skillful." However, **masterful** is generally used in this sense to describe a person, e.g., *He's just got a marginal talent that he's masterful at exploiting,* while **masterly** usually describes an achievement or action, e.g., *This was a masterly use of the backhand volley.*

mutual
This word is sometimes used with no sense of reciprocity, simply to mean "common to two or more people," as in *a mutual friend; a mutual interest.* Such use is considered incorrect by some people, for whom **common** is preferable.

nonflammable see **inflammable.**

off/off of
The use of **off of** to mean **off**, e.g., *He took the cup off of the table,* is nonstandard and to be avoided.

perquisite/prerequisite
These words are sometimes confused. **Perquisite** usually means "an extra benefit or privilege," e.g., *There were no perquisites that came with the job, apart from one or two special privileges.* **Prerequisite** means "something required as a precondition," e.g., *A general education in the sciences is a prerequisite of professional medical training.*

plus
The use of **plus** as a conjunction meaning "and furthermore," e.g., *plus we will be pleased to give you personal financial advice,* is considered incorrect by many people.

prerequisite see **perquisite.**

prescribe/proscribe
These words are sometimes confused, but they are nearly opposite in meaning. **Prescribe** means "to advise the use of" or "impose authoritatively," whereas **proscribe** means "to reject, denounce, or ban." Examples of each are as follows:

The teachers would prescribe topics to be dealt with.

The superintendent proscribed tabloid newspapers from all school libraries.

A dictatorial regime which both prescribes and proscribes literature.

prevaricate/procrastinate

Prevaricate means "to act or speak evasively," e.g., *When the teacher asked what I was reading, I knew I would have to prevaricate or risk a detention*. It is sometimes confused with **procrastinate**, which means "to postpone or put off an action," e.g., *He hesitates and procrastinates until the time for action is over.*

proscribe see prescribe.

protagonist

The correct meaning of this word is "chief or leading person," e.g., *The choreographer must create movements that display each protagonist's particular behavior and reactions*. However, it is also used, usually with *of* or *for*, to mean "an advocate or champion of a cause, etc.," e.g., *. . . the flawed economics of the nuclear protagonist's case.*

refute

Strictly speaking, **refute** means "to prove (a person or statement) to be wrong," e.g., *No amount of empirical research can either confirm or refute it*. However, it is also sometimes used to mean "to deny or repudiate." This usage is considered incorrect by some people.

regardless/irregardless

The latter word, with its illogical negative prefix, is widely heard, perhaps arising under the influence of such perfectly correct forms as *irrespective*. It is avoided by careful users of English.

scenario

The proper meaning of this word is "an outline of a plot" or "a postulated sequence of events." It should not be used in standard English to mean "situation," e.g., *a nightmare scenario.*

Scotch/Scots/Scottish

In Scotland the terms **Scots** and **Scottish** are preferred to **Scotch** and they mean the same (e.g., *a Scots/Scottish accent, miner, farmer*, etc.) **Scotch** is used in various compound nouns such as *Scotch broth, egg, fir, mist, terrier*, and *whiskey*. Similarly, **Scotsman** and **Scotswoman** are preferred to **Scotchman** and **Scotchwoman**.

seasonable/seasonal

Seasonable means "usual or suitable for the season" or "opportune," e.g., *Although seasonable, the weather was not suitable for picnics*. **Seasonal** means "of, depending on, or varying with the season," e.g., *Seasonal changes posed problems for mills situated on larger rivers.*

'til/till see until.

tortuous/torturous

These words sound similar but have different meanings. **Tortuous** means "full of twists and turns" or "devious; circuitous," e.g., *Both paths have proved tortuous and are strewn with awkward boulders*. **Torturous** is an adjective that is derived from *torture* and means "involving torture; excruciating," e.g., *I found the concert a torturous experience because of the loudness of the music.*

triumphal/triumphant

These words are sometimes confused. The more common, **triumphant**, means "victorious" or "exultant," e.g., *She had chaired a difficult meeting through to its triumphant conclusion*, or *Rosie returned triumphant with the file that had been missing*. **Triumphal** means "used in or celebrating a triumph," e.g., *The last element to be added was the magnificent triumphal arch*, or *The victorious troops marched in a triumphal tickertape parade.*

turbid/turgid

Turbid is used of a liquid or color to mean "muddy; not clear," or of literary style, etc., to mean "confused," e.g., *the turbid utterances and twisted language of Carlyle*. **Turgid** means "swollen, inflated, or enlarged," but is also often used to describe literary style that is pompous or bombastic, e.g., *Communications from corporate headquarters were largely turgid memos filled with bureaucratic lingo.*

until/till/'til

Until is more formal than **till**, and is more usual at the beginning of a sentence, e.g., *Until the 1920s it was quite unusual for women to wear short hair.* **'Til** is considered incorrect in standard English and should be avoided.

venal/venial

These words are sometimes confused. **Venal** means "corrupt, able to be bribed, or involving bribery," e.g., *Their high court is venal and can take decades to decide a case.* **Venial** is used among Christians to describe a certain type of sin and means "pardonable, excusable, not mortal," e.g., *The Reformation renounced purgatory as an intermediate stage in which those who had committed venial sins might earn their way into heaven.*

worth while/worthwhile

Worth while (two words) is used only predicatively, e.g., *Nobody had thought it worth while to call the police,* and means "worth the time or effort spent." **Worthwhile** (one word) also has this meaning but can be used both predicatively and attributively, e.g., *Only in unusual circumstances would investment be worthwhile* (predicative), or *He was a worthwhile subject for the 'cure'* (attributive). In addition, **worthwhile** has the sense "of value or importance," e.g., *It's great to be doing such a worthwhile job.*

Diacritical Marks

(to distinguish sounds or values of letters)

´   acute (as in the French word *née*)
`   grave (as in the French word *père*)
~   tilde (as in the Spanish word *piñata*)
^   circumflex (as in the word *rôle*)
¯   macron (as used in pronunciation: *āge, īce.*)
˘   breve (as used in pronunciation: *tăp, rĭp*)
¨   dieresis (as in the word *naïve*)
¸   cedilla (as in the word *façade*)

Proofreader's Marks

Mark	Meaning	Mark	Meaning
℘	delete	⸘ ⸌	quotation marks
℮	delete and close up	{ }	parentheses
℘#	delete and leave space	ℇ ℈	square brackets
∧	insert	=	hyphen
#	space	⊦M	em-dash
⊙	period	⊦N	en-dash
⋏	comma	¶	new paragraph
⋏	semicolon	dictionʃary	break line or word
⋮ or ⊙	colon	⅌	set as superscript
⌄	apostrophe	⅄	set as subscript

Mark	Meaning
diction(ry/a)y	transpose
(tr)	transpose (note in margin)
(⒊)	spell out
(SP)	spell out (note in margin)
dictionary	capitalize
(cap)	set as capitals (note in margin)
Ðictionary	make lower case
(lc)	set in lower case (note in margin)
dictionary	make boldface
(bf)	set in boldface (note in margin)
dictionary	make italic
(ital)	set in italic (note in margin)
dictionary	small caps
(sc)	set in small caps (note in margin)
(lf)	lightface (note in margin)
(rom)	set in roman (note in margin)